HALSBURY'S
Laws of England

FIFTH EDITION
2011

Volume 4

This is volume 4 of the Fifth Edition of Halsbury's Laws of England, containing the following titles: AUCTION, BAILMENT AND PLEDGE, BOUNDARIES, BRITISH NATIONALITY and BROADCASTING.

The title AUCTION replaces the Fourth Edition title AUCTION, contained in volume 2(3) (Reissue). The title BAILMENT AND PLEDGE replaces the Fourth Edition titles BAILMENT, contained in volume 3(1) (2005 Reissue), and PLEDGES AND PAWNS, contained in volume 36(1) (2007 Reissue). The title BOUNDARIES replaces the Fourth Edition title BOUNDARIES, contained in volume 4(1) (2002 Reissue). The title BRITISH NATIONALITY replaces part of the Fourth Edition title BRITISH NATIONALITY, IMMIGRATION AND ASYLUM, contained in volume 4(2) (2002 Reissue). The title BROADCASTING completes the replacement of the Fourth Edition title TELECOMMUNICATIONS AND BROADCASTING, contained in volume 45(1) (2005 Reissue).

Volumes 4(2) (2002 Reissue) and 36(1) (2007 Reissue) should be retained until remaining material is replaced. Volumes 2(3) (Reissue), 3(1) (2005 Reissue), 4(1) (2002 Reissue) and 45(1) (2005 Reissue) have been completely replaced and may now be archived.

For a full list of volumes comprised in a current set of Halsbury's Laws of England please see overleaf.

Fifth Edition volumes:

1 (2008), 2 (2008), 4 (2011), 6 (2011), 7 (2008), 8 (2010), 11 (2009), 12 (2009), 13 (2009), 14 (2009), 15 (2009), 18 (2009), 21 (2011), 24 (2010), 25 (2010), 26 (2010), 27 (2010), 28 (2010), 39 (2009), 40 (2009), 41 (2009), 45 (2010), 46 (2010), 48 (2008), 49 (2008), 50 (2008), 52 (2009), 53 (2009), 54 (2008), 61 (2010), 65 (2008), 66 (2009), 67 (2008), 68 (2008), 69 (2009), 72 (2009), 73 (2009), 77 (2010), 78 (2010), 79 (2008), 81 (2010), 82 (2010), 83 (2010), 89 (2011), 90 (2011), 92 (2010), 93 (2008), 94 (2008), 97 (2010), 100 (2009), 101 (2009), 102 (2010), 103 (2010)

Fourth Edition volumes (bold figures represent reissues):

1(1) (2001 Reissue), **1**(2) (2007 Reissue), **2**(2), **3**(2) (2002 Reissue), **4**(2) (2002 Reissue), **5**(3) (2008 Reissue), **5**(4) (2008 Reissue), **7**(3) (2004 Reissue), **7**(4) (2004 Reissue), **8**(1) (2003 Reissue), **8**(2), **8**(3), **9**(1), **9**(2) (2006 Reissue), **12**(1), **12**(2) (2007 Reissue), **12**(3) (2007 Reissue), **13** (2007 Reissue), **14**, **15**(1) (2006 Reissue), **15**(2) (2006 Reissue), **15**(3) (2007 Reissue), **15**(4) (2007 Reissue), **16**(2), **17**(2), **18**(2), **19**(1) (2007 Reissue), **19**(2) (2007 Reissue), **19**(3) (2007 Reissue), **21** (2004 Reissue), **22** (2006 Reissue), **23**(1), **23**(2), **24**, **25** (2003 Reissue), **26** (2004 Reissue), **27**(1) (2006 Reissue), **27**(2) (2006 Reissue), **27**(3) (2006 Reissue), **28**, **29**(2), **30**(1), **30**(2), **31** (2003 Reissue), **34**, **35**, **36**(1) (2007 Reissue), **36**(2), **39**(1A), **39**(1B), **39**(2), **41** (2005 Reissue), **42**, **44**(1), **44**(2), **48** (2007 Reissue), **49**(1) (2005 Reissue), **50** (2005 Reissue), **51**, **52**

Additional Materials:

Criminal Law, Evidence and Procedure (*Investigatory Powers*) containing vol **11**(1) (2006 Reissue) paras 390, 394, 395, 407–415, 420–438, 451, 452, 506–526, vol **11**(2) (2006 Reissue) paras 804–818, 851, 852, 856–902, 908–911, 924–940, 945–1041, vol **11**(3) (2006 Reissue) paras 1086–1088, 1090–1093; *Local Government Finance* containing vol **29**(1) (Reissue) paras 514–618, 624–634; *Restitution* containing vol **40**(1) (2007 Reissue) paras 1–200; *Road Traffic* (*Tramways*) containing vol **40**(3) (2007 Reissue) paras 1532–1634; *Tort* (*Conversion and Wrongful Interference with Goods*) containing vol **45**(2) (Reissue) paras 542–686

Fourth and Fifth Edition volumes:

2010 Consolidated Index (A–E), 2010 Consolidated Index (F–O), 2010 Consolidated Index (P–Z), 2011 Consolidated Table of Statutes, 2011 Consolidated Table of Statutory Instruments, etc, 2011 Consolidated Table of Cases (A–L), 2011 Consolidated Table of Cases (M–Z, ECJ Cases)

Updating and ancillary materials:

2011 Annual Cumulative Supplement; Monthly Current Service; Annual Abridgments 1974–2009

March 2011

HALSBURY'S
Laws of England

FIFTH EDITION

LORD MACKAY OF CLASHFERN
Lord High Chancellor of Great Britain
1987–97

Volume 4

2011

 LexisNexis®

Members of the LexisNexis Group worldwide

United Kingdom	LexisNexis, a Division of Reed Elsevier (UK) Ltd, Halsbury House, 35 Chancery Lane, LONDON, WC2A 1EL, and London House, 20–22 East London Street, EDINBURGH, EH7 4BQ
Australia	LexisNexis Butterworths, Chatswood, New South Wales
Austria	LexisNexis Verlag ARD Orac GmbH & Co KG, Vienna
Benelux	LexisNexis Benelux, Amsterdam
Canada	LexisNexis Canada, Markham, Ontario
China	LexisNexis China, Beijing and Shanghai
France	LexisNexis SA, Paris
Germany	LexisNexis GmbH, Dusseldorf
Hong Kong	LexisNexis Hong Kong, Hong Kong
India	LexisNexis India, New Delhi
Italy	Giuffrè Editore, Milan
Japan	LexisNexis Japan, Tokyo
Malaysia	Malayan Law Journal Sdn Bhd, Kuala Lumpur
New Zealand	LexisNexis NZ Ltd, Wellington
Poland	Wydawnictwo Prawnicze LexisNexis Sp, Warsaw
Singapore	LexisNexis Singapore, Singapore
South Africa	LexisNexis Butterworths, Durban
USA	LexisNexis, Dayton, Ohio

FIRST EDITION	*Published in 31 volumes between 1907 and 1917*
SECOND EDITION	*Published in 37 volumes between 1931 and 1942*
THIRD EDITION	*Published in 43 volumes between 1952 and 1964*
FOURTH EDITION	*Published in 56 volumes between 1973 and 1987, with reissues between 1988 and 2008*
FIFTH EDITION	*Commenced in 2008*

A CIP Catalogue record for this book is available from the British Library.

ISBN 13 (complete set, standard binding): 9781405734394

ISBN 13: 9781405744652

ISBN 978-1-4057-4465-2

9 781405 744652

Typeset by Letterpart Ltd, Reigate, Surrey
Printed and bound in Great Britain by CPI William Clowes Beccles NR34 7TL
Visit LexisNexis at www.lexisnexis.co.uk

Editor in Chief

THE RIGHT HONOURABLE

LORD MACKAY OF CLASHFERN

LORD HIGH CHANCELLOR OF GREAT BRITAIN

1987–97

Editor of this Volume

DAVID HAY, MA, LLM,
of the Inner Temple, Barrister

Senior Editor

GAVIN DILLOW, MA

Commissioning Editor

CLAIRE RAMSBOTTOM, LLB, MSC

Indexer

ALEXANDRA CORRIN, LLB,
of Gray's Inn, Barrister

Managing Editors

CLARE BLANCHARD, BA

HELEN HALVEY, LLB

Publisher

SIMON HETHERINGTON, LLB

AUCTION

Consultant Editor

FRANKLIN MEISEL, LLB,

of the Middle Temple, Barrister;
Senior Lecturer in Law, Aston Business School, University of Aston

BAILMENT AND PLEDGE

Consultant Editor

NORMAN PALMER, CBE, MA, BCL, Hon Dr Juris,

of Gray's Inn, Barrister;
one of Her Majesty's Counsel (Honoris Causa);
Emeritus Professor of the Law of Art and Cultural Property,
University College London; Visiting Professor of Law, King's College London;
Chairman, Treasure Valuation Committee

BOUNDARIES

Consultant Editor

STEPHEN JOURDAN, MA,

of Gray's Inn, Barrister;
one of Her Majesty's Counsel;
Recorder (Civil);
Deputy Adjudicator to HM Land Registry

BRITISH NATIONALITY

Consultant Editor

LAURIE FRANSMAN, LLB,

of the Middle Temple, Barrister;
one of Her Majesty's Counsel

BROADCASTING

Consultant Editor

DR ANDREW SCOTT, LLB, MPhil, PhD,

Senior Lecturer, Department of Law,
London School of Economics and Political Science

The law stated in this volume is in general that in force on 1 February 2011, although subsequent changes have been included wherever possible.

Any future updating material will be found in the Current Service and annual Cumulative Supplement to Halsbury's Laws of England.

TABLE OF CONTENTS

Volume 4

AUCTION

BAILMENT AND PLEDGE

BOUNDARIES

HOW TO USE HALSBURY'S LAWS OF ENGLAND

Volumes

Each text volume of Halsbury's Laws of England contains the law on the titles contained in it as at a date stated at the front of the volume (the operative date).

Information contained in Halsbury's Laws of England may be accessed in several ways.

First, by using the tables of contents.

Each volume contains both a general Table of Contents, and a specific Table of Contents for each title contained in it. From these tables you will be directed to the relevant part of the work.

Readers should note that the current arrangement of titles can be found in the Current Service.

Secondly, by using tables of statutes, statutory instruments, cases or other materials.

If you know the name of the Act, statutory instrument or case with which your research is concerned, you should consult the Consolidated Tables of statutes, cases and so on (published as separate volumes) which will direct you to the relevant volume and paragraph. The Consolidated Tables will indicate if the volume referred to is a Fifth Edition volume.

(Each individual text volume also includes tables of those materials used as authority in that volume.)

Thirdly, by using the indexes.

If you are uncertain of the general subject area of your research, you should go to the Consolidated Index (published as separate volumes) for reference to the relevant volume(s) and paragraph(s). The Consolidated Index will indicate if the volume referred to is a Fifth Edition volume.

(Each individual text volume also includes an index to the material contained therein.)

Additional Materials

The reorganisation of the title scheme of Halsbury's Laws for the Fifth Edition means that from time to time Fourth Edition volumes will be *partially* replaced by Fifth Edition volumes.

In certain instances an Additional Materials softbound book will be issued, in which will be reproduced material which has not yet been replaced by a Fifth Edition title. This will enable users to remove specific Fourth Edition volumes from the shelf and save valuable space pending the replacement of that material in the Fifth Edition. These softbound books are supplied to volumes subscribers free of charge. They continue to form part of the set of Halsbury's Laws Fourth Edition Reissue, and will be updated by the Annual Cumulative Supplement and monthly Noter-Up in the usual way.

Updating publications

The text volumes of Halsbury's Laws should be used in conjunction with the annual Cumulative Supplement and the monthly Noter-Up.

The annual Cumulative Supplement

The Supplement gives details of all changes between the operative date of the text volume and the operative date of the Supplement. It is arranged in the same volume, title and paragraph order as the text volumes. Developments affecting particular points of law are noted to the relevant paragraph(s) of the text volumes. As from the commencement of the Fifth Edition, the Supplement will clearly distinguish between Fourth and Fifth Edition titles.

For narrative treatment of material noted in the Cumulative Supplement, go to the Annual Abridgment volume for the relevant year.

Destination Tables

In certain titles in the annual *Cumulative Supplement*, reference is made to Destination Tables showing the destination of consolidated legislation. Those Destination Tables are to be found either at the end of the titles within the annual *Cumulative Supplement*, or in a separate *Destination Tables* booklet provided from time to time with the *Cumulative Supplement*.

The Noter-Up

The Noter-Up is contained in the Current Service Noter-Up booklet, issued monthly and noting changes since the publication of the annual Cumulative Supplement. Also arranged in the same volume, title and paragraph order as the text volumes, the Noter-Up follows the style of the Cumulative Supplement. As from the commencement of the Fifth Edition, the Noter-Up will clearly distinguish between Fourth and Fifth Edition titles.

For narrative treatment of material noted in the Noter-Up, go to the relevant Monthly Review.

REFERENCES AND ABBREVIATIONS

ACT	Australian Capital Territory
A-G	Attorney General
Admin	Administrative Court
Admlty	Admiralty Court
Adv-Gen	Advocate General
affd	affirmed
affg	affirming
Alta	Alberta
App	Appendix
art	article
Aust	Australia
B	Baron
BC	British Columbia
C	Command Paper (of a series published before 1900)
c	chapter number of an Act
CA	Court of Appeal
CAC	Central Arbitration Committee
CA in Ch	Court of Appeal in Chancery
CB	Chief Baron
CCA	Court of Criminal Appeal
CCR	County Court Rules 1981 (SI 1981/1687) as subsequently amended
CCR	Court for Crown Cases Reserved
C-MAC	Courts-Martial Appeal Court
CO	Crown Office
COD	Crown Office Digest
CPR	Civil Procedure Rules 1998 (SI 1998/3132) as subsequently amended (see the Civil Court Practice)
Can	Canada
Cd	Command Paper (of the series published 1900–18)
Cf	compare
Ch	Chancery Division
ch	chapter
cl	clause

Cm	Command Paper (of the series published 1986 to date)
Cmd	Command Paper (of the series published 1919–56)
Cmnd	Command Paper (of the series published 1956–86)
Comm	Commercial Court
Comr	Commissioner
Court Forms (2nd Edn)	Atkin's Encyclopaedia of Court Forms in Civil Proceedings, 2nd Edn. See note 2 post.
Court Funds Rules 1987	Court Funds Rules 1987 (SI 1987/821) as subsequently amended
CrimPR	Criminal Procedure Rules 2010 (SI 2010/60) as subsequently amended
DC..............................	Divisional Court
DPP	Director of Public Prosecutions
EAT	Employment Appeal Tribunal
EC	European Community
ECJ..............................	Court of Justice of the European Community
EComHR..............................	European Commission of Human Rights
ECSC..............................	European Coal and Steel Community
ECtHR Rules of Court..........	Rules of Court of the European Court of Human Rights
EEC..............................	European Economic Community
EFTA	European Free Trade Association
EWCA Civ	Official neutral citation for judgments of the Court of Appeal (Civil Division)
EWCA Crim..............................	Official neutral citation for judgments of the Court of Appeal (Criminal Division)
EWHC..............................	Official neutral citation for judgments of the High Court
Edn..............................	Edition
Euratom	European Atomic Energy Community
Ex Ch..............................	Court of Exchequer Chamber
ex p	ex parte
Fam	Family Division
Fed	Federal
Forms & Precedents (5th Edn)..............................	Encyclopaedia of Forms and Precedents other than Court Forms, 5th Edn. See note 2 post.
GLC	Greater London Council
HC	High Court
HC	House of Commons
HK	Hong Kong
HL..............................	House of Lords

IAT	Immigration Appeal Tribunal
ILM	International Legal Materials
INLR	Immigration and Nationality Law Reports
IRC	Inland Revenue Commissioners
Ind	India
Int Rels	International Relations
Ir	Ireland
J	Justice
JA	Judge of Appeal
Kan	Kansas
LA	Lord Advocate
LC	Lord Chancellor
LCC	London County Council
LCJ	Lord Chief Justice
LJ	Lord Justice of Appeal
LoN	League of Nations
MR	Master of the Rolls
Man	Manitoba
n	note
NB	New Brunswick
NI	Northern Ireland
NS	Nova Scotia
NSW	New South Wales
NY	New York
NZ	New Zealand
OHIM	Office for Harmonisation in the Internal Market
OJ	The Official Journal of the European Community published by the Office for Official Publications of the European Community
Ont	Ontario
P	President
PC	Judicial Committee of the Privy Council
PEI	Prince Edward Island
Pat	Patents Court
q	question
QB	Queen's Bench Division
QBD	Queen's Bench Division of the High Court
Qld	Queensland
Que	Quebec
r	rule
RDC	Rural District Council
RPC	Restrictive Practices Court

RSC	Rules of the Supreme Court 1965 (SI 1965/1776) as subsequently amended
reg	regulation
Res	Resolution
revsd	reversed
Rly	Railway
s	section
SA	South Africa
S Aust	South Australia
SC	Supreme Court
SI	Statutory Instruments published by authority
SR & O	Statutory Rules and Orders published by authority
SR & O Rev 1904	Revised Edition comprising all Public and General Statutory Rules and Orders in force on 31 December 1903
SR & O Rev 1948	Revised Edition comprising all Public and General Statutory Rules and Orders and Statutory Instruments in force on 31 December 1948
SRNI	Statutory Rules of Northern Ireland
STI	Simon's Tax Intelligence (1973–1995); Simon's Weekly Tax Intelligence (1996-current)
Sask	Saskatchewan
Sch	Schedule
Sess	Session
Sing	Singapore
TCC	Technology and Construction Court
TS	Treaty Series
Tanz	Tanzania
Tas	Tasmania
UDC	Urban District Council
UKHL	Official neutral citation for judgments of the House of Lords
UKPC	Official neutral citation for judgments of the Privy Council
UN	United Nations
V-C	Vice-Chancellor
Vict	Victoria
W Aust	Western Australia
Zimb	Zimbabwe

NOTE 1. A general list of the abbreviations of law reports and other sources used in this work can be found at the beginning of the Consolidated Table of Cases.

NOTE 2. Where references are made to other publications, the volume number precedes and the page number follows the name of the publication; eg the reference '12 Forms & Precedents (5th Edn) 44' refers to volume 12 of the Encyclopaedia of Forms and Precedents, page 44.

NOTE 3. An English statute is cited by short title or, where there is no short title, by regnal year and chapter number together with the name by which it is commonly known or a description of its subject matter and date. In the case of a foreign statute, the mode of citation generally follows the style of citation in use in the country concerned with the addition, where necessary, of the name of the country in parentheses.

NOTE 4. A statutory instrument is cited by short title, if any, followed by the year and number, or, if unnumbered, the date.

TABLE OF STATUTES

TABLE OF STATUTORY INSTRUMENTS

TABLE OF CIVIL PROCEDURE

Civil Procedure Rules 1998, SI 1998/3132 (CPR)

Practice Directions supplementing CPR

TABLE OF EUROPEAN UNION LEGISLATION

TABLE OF CONVENTIONS ETC

TABLE OF
NON-STATUTORY MATERIAL

TABLE OF CASES

PARA

PARA

Decisions of the European Court of Justice are listed below numerically. These decisions
are also included in the preceding alphabetical list.

AUCTION

1. INTRODUCTION

1.   Definition of 'auction'. An auction is a manner of selling or letting property by bids, usually to the highest bidder by public[1] competition[2]. The prices which the public is asked to pay are the highest which those who bid can be tempted to offer by the skill and tact of the auctioneer under the excitement of open competition[3]. Although the word 'auction' is derived from the Latin *auctio* (an increase), a 'Dutch auction' is one where property is offered at a certain price and then successively at lower prices until one is accepted[4].

1   The term 'public' may be contrasted with 'private' auctions. There is no authoritative definition of public or private auction, but 'public' probably denotes that the general public has a right of attendance and participation as opposed to private auctions where specific persons only are invited to attend and participate. The distinction may be significant, for example, in relation to sales of land: see PARA 15.

2   There is no comprehensive statutory definition of an auction. The Mock Auctions Act 1961 (repealed) referred to the necessity for competitive bidding: see PARA 51. As to auction sales generally see PARAS 40–67.

3   See *Frewen v Hays* (1912) 106 LT 516 at 518, PC, per Lord Macnaghten; and *Bexwell v Christie* (1776) 1 Cowp 395 at 397 per Lord Mansfield. However, there exist auctions where the lot goes to the highest bidder but the element of open competition is lacking in that bidders are unaware of rival bids. Postal auctions provide an example. These are conducted in a manner similar to that of selling by tenders. As to postal auctions see PARA 56. See also as to internet auctions PARA 57.

4   See *Demerara Turf Club Ltd v Wight* [1918] AC 605, PC.

2.   Definition of 'auctioneer'. An auctioneer[1] is an agent[2] who sells goods or other property by auction[3].

1   The use of the term 'auctioneer' in an apprenticeship deed or other instrument formerly imported that the person so described was duly licensed: see *Creaser v Hurley* (1915) 32 TLR 149. As to the abolition of auctioneers' licences see PARA 4.

2   As to agency of auctioneers see PARA 7.

3   *Wheatley v Smithers* [1906] 2 KB 321, DC (revsd on appeal on the facts: see *Wheatley v Smithers* [1907] 2 KB 684, CA). An auctioneer is not, however, an agent when he sells his own goods or property: see PARA 7. As to auctioneers see PARAS 3–39.

2. THE AUCTIONEER

(1) QUALIFICATIONS; APPOINTMENT

3.   Qualifications for practice.   No special qualification is required by one who carries on the business of an auctioneer[1]. Any person is at liberty to do so, provided that he complies with the companies legislation, where it applies[2]. An auctioneer is under no obligation to become a member of a professional association, but if he does so, he is bound by the rules of conduct laid down by the association of which he is a member[3].

1   As to the meaning of 'auctioneer' see PARA 2.
2   As to companies legislation see COMPANIES. Note that there are provisions which require the majority of the persons constituting a partnership for the purpose of carrying on the business of auctioneering to be members of a professional body: see PARA 6.

3   *Faraday v Auctioneers' and Estate Agents' Institute of United Kingdom* [1936] 1 All ER 496, CA.

4.   Licensing requirements.   An auctioneer[1] does not require any general auctioneers' licence for the purposes of carrying on his business[2], and a person hawking goods from place to place for sale by auction[3] no longer requires a hawker's licence[4]. However, several London boroughs have introduced codes of practice and licence conditions relating to auctions conducted within their localities, which regulate such matters as display of name, conduct of bidding, post-sale advertising and declarations as to ownership of goods[5].

An auctioneer requires an excise licence for the sale of excisable commodities[6].

An auctioneer may sell by auction, expose for sale by auction or have in his possession for sale by auction a firearm[7] or ammunition[8] without being registered as a firearms dealer[9], if he has obtained from the chief officer of police[10] for the area[11] in which the auction is held a permit[12] and complies with the terms of the permit[13]. The auctioneer or his servant may possess firearms or ammunition in the ordinary course of his business as an auctioneer without holding a firearms certificate[14]. The offence of carrying, without lawful authority or reasonable excuse, a loaded shot gun, an air weapon (whether loaded or not), any other firearm (whether loaded or not) together with suitable ammunition, or an imitation firearm, in a public place may be committed if, at the material time, the public has or is permitted to have access, whether on payment or otherwise, to the premises or place[15].

An auctioneer who advances money on bills of sale[16] with a view to obtaining business, and not with the primary object of lending money, does not require a licence[17].

The exportation of certain classes of goods may be subject to control under powers derived from the Export Control Act 2002[18]. Most antiques and collectable items produced more than 50 years before exportation[19] may only be exported under the authority of a licence in writing granted by the Secretary of State, and in accordance with all the conditions attached to the licence, or an EU licence[20]. Sales at auction which fail to comply with any condition attaching to the relevant licence will render the auctioneer, as agent of the seller, liable to criminal penalties[21].

Except in relation to certain wild birds specified in the Wildlife and Countryside Act 1981[22], the sale or offering or exposing for sale of any live wild bird, or an egg or any part of such, or any dead wild bird or any part of, or anything derived from it, by a person is an offence unless he is licensed to do so[23].

1   As to the meaning of 'auctioneer' see PARA 2.
2   The excise duty on auctioneers' licences was abolished and the provisions of the Auctioneers Act 1845 requiring auctioneers' licences were repealed by the Finance Act 1949 s 14, Sch 11 Pt I.
3   As to the meaning of 'auction' see PARA 1.
4   The requirement of a hawker's licence under the Hawkers Act 1888 was repealed by the Local Government Act 1966 ss 35, 43, Sch 3 Pt I, Sch 6 Pt I. As to hawkers see further MARKETS, FAIRS AND STREET TRADING vol 29(2) (Reissue) PARA 1117 et seq.
5   The conditions are made pursuant to the Greater London Council (General Powers) Act 1984 s 28(3).
6   See the Customs and Excise Management Act 1979 s 101 (amended by the Finance Act 1986 s 8(6), Sch 5 para 1; and the Finance Act 1994 s 9, Sch 4 para 5). As to excisable commodities see CUSTOMS AND EXCISE vol 12(2) (2007 Reissue) PARA 389 et seq; and as to excise licenses see CUSTOMS AND EXCISE vol 12(3) (2007 Reissue) PARA 622 et seq.
7   'Firearm' means a lethal barrelled weapon of any description from which any shot, bullet or other missile can be discharged and includes: (1) any prohibited weapon, whether it is such a lethal weapon or not; (2) any component part of such a lethal or prohibited weapon; and (3) any accessory to any such weapon designed or adapted to diminish the noise or flash caused by firing the weapon: see the Firearms Act 1968 s 57(1); and CRIMINAL LAW vol 26 (2010) PARA 578.
8   'Ammunition' means ammunition for any firearm and includes grenades, bombs and other like missiles, whether capable of use with a firearm or not, and also includes prohibited ammunition: Firearms Act 1968 s 57(2).
9   'Firearms dealer' means a person who, by way of trade or business: (1) manufactures, sells, transfers, repairs, tests or proves firearms or ammunition to which the Firearms Act 1968 s 1 (see CRIMINAL LAW vol 26 (2010) PARAS 578–581) applies or shot guns; or (2) sells or transfers air weapons: s 57(4) (amended by the Violent Crime Reduction Act 2006 s 31(3)). 'Registered', in relation to a firearms dealer, means registered either: (a) in Great Britain, under the Firearms Act 1968 s 33 (police register) (see CRIMINAL LAW vol 26 (2010) PARA 642); or (b) in Northern Ireland, under the corresponding legislation: s 57(4). As to the meaning of 'shot gun' see CRIMINAL LAW vol 26 (2010) PARA 579; and as to the meaning of 'air weapon' see CRIMINAL LAW vol 26 (2010) PARA 580.
10 As to the chief officer of police see POLICE vol 36(1) (2007 Reissue) PARA 178 et seq.
11 'Area' means a police area: Firearms Act 1968 s 57(4).
12 Ie a permit in the form prescribed by the Secretary of State: Firearms Act 1968 ss 9(2), 57(4). For the form of permit see the Firearms Rules 1998, SI 1998/1941, r 9(2)(a), Sch 4 Pt III (auctioneer's firearm permit), r 9(2)(b), Sch 4 Pt IV (auctioneer's shot gun permit). 'Secretary of State' means one of Her Majesty's Principal Secretaries of State: Interpretation Act 1978 s 5, Sch 1.
       It is an offence for a person knowingly or recklessly to make a statement false in any material particular for the purpose of procuring, either for himself or for another person, the grant of a permit under the Firearms Act 1968 s 9(2) (see the text and notes 7–11, 13): s 9(3) (amended by the Firearms (Amendment) Act 1997 s 52, Sch 2 para 2(2)).
13 Firearms Act 1968 s 9(2). If the auctioneer does not have such a permit, or if he does not comply with the terms of his permit, he commits an offence: see s 3(1) (amended by the Violent Crime Reduction Act 2006 s 65, Sch 5); and CRIMINAL LAW vol 26 (2010) PARA 584. As to the auction of firearms see also PARA 66.
14 Firearms Act 1968 s 9(1). For offences in relation to s 9(1) see the Firearms (Amendment) Act 1988 s 14; and CRIMINAL LAW vol 26 (2010) PARA 600. As to the meaning of 'certificate' see CRIMINAL LAW vol 26 (2010) PARA 585.
15 See the Firearms Act 1968 ss 19, 57(4) (s 19 amended by the Anti-social Behaviour Act 2003 s 37(1)).
16 As to bills of sale see generally FINANCIAL SERVICES AND INSTITUTIONS vol 50 (2008) PARA 1620 et seq.
17 *Furber v Fieldings Ltd* (1907) 23 TLR 362. As to licences to carry on consumer credit, consumer hire or ancillary credit businesses see the Consumer Credit Act 1974 Pt III (ss 21–41ZB); and CONSUMER CREDIT vol 21 (2011) PARA 22 et seq.
18 See the Export Control Act 2002 s 1; and TRADE AND INDUSTRY vol 97 (2010) PARA 811 et seq.

19 Ie objects of cultural interest: see the Export of Objects of Cultural Interest (Control) Order 2003, SI 2003/2759, art 1, Sch 1.
20 See the Export of Objects of Cultural Interest (Control) Order 2003, SI 2003/2759, art 2; and TRADE AND INDUSTRY vol 97 (2010) PARA 816.
21 See the Export of Objects of Cultural Interest (Control) Order 2003, SI 2003/2759, art 5. As to the penalties see TRADE AND INDUSTRY vol 97 (2010) PARA 816.
22 Ie the Wildlife and Countryside Act 1981 s 6, Sch 3 (birds which may be sold): see ANIMALS vol 2 (2008) PARA 1007.
23 See the Wildlife and Countryside Act 1981 s 6(1), (2) (s 6(2) amended by the Countryside and Rights of Way Act 2000 ss 81(1), 102, Sch 12 paras 3, 10(6), Sch 16 Pt IV), the Wildlife and Countryside Act 1981 s 16(4); and ANIMALS vol 2 (2008) PARAS 1006, 1007, 1019. As to the auction of wild animals see also PARA 65.

5. Form of contract between seller and auctioneer. There are no special rules affecting the form of contract[1] between the seller and the auctioneer[2], and, subject to the ordinary exceptions common to all forms of agency, the contract may be either oral or in writing[3].

1 As to forms of contract generally see CONTRACT vol 9(1) (Reissue) PARA 620 et seq.
2 As to the meaning of 'auctioneer' see PARA 2.
3 See *Coles v Trecothick* (1804) 9 Ves 234; and AGENCY vol 1 (2008) PARAS 14, 19.

6. Auctioneers in partnership. As in the case of partnerships in general, a partnership for the purpose of carrying on the business of auctioneering is not subject to any restriction as to the number of persons who may constitute the partnership[1]. Nor is a limited partnership for the purpose of carrying on the business of auctioneering subject to any such restrictions[2].

It has been held that a firm of auctioneers is not a trading partnership[3], and therefore a member of the firm has no implied authority to bind his partners by giving a bill of exchange[4] in the firm name[5].

1 As to partnerships see generally PARTNERSHIP.
2 See the Limited Partnership Act 1907 s 4(2) (amended by the Banking Act 1979 s 51(2), Sch 7; and by SI 2002/3203). As to limited partnerships see PARTNERSHIP vol 79 (2008) PARA 218 et seq.
3 As to the meaning of 'trading partnership' see PARTNERSHIP vol 79 (2008) PARA 6.
4 As to bills of exchange see FINANCIAL SERVICES AND INSTITUTIONS vol 49 (2008) PARA 1400 et seq.
5 *Wheatley v Smithers* [1906] 2 KB 321, DC (revsd on appeal on the facts, but the court declined to express any view as to whether an auctioneer was a trader: see *Wheatley v Smithers* [1907] 2 KB 684, CA).

(2) AUCTIONEER'S AUTHORITY

7. Agency of auctioneer. An auctioneer[1] is primarily the agent of the seller[2]. He can, however, sell his own property and a buyer can take no objection to the sale on that ground[3]. Hitherto, the auctioneer was also treated as the buyer's agent[4] for the limited purpose of signing on his behalf such notes or memoranda of sale as were formerly required, but this is no longer the case[5].

Whereas an estate agent has (usually) only a revocable mandate to bring about a stipulated result[6] the auctioneer is a 'skilled agent to whom complete control of operations is given by the owner of the goods'[7]. He is employed, therefore, as an independent contractor rather than as an employee[8].

1 As to the meaning of 'auctioneer' see PARA 2.
2 As to agency of auctioneers see further AGENCY vol 1 (2008) PARA 13.
3 *Flint v Woodin* (1852) 22 LJ Ch 92.

4 See *Chaney v Maclow* [1929] 1 Ch 461, CA; *Sims v Landray* [1894] 2 Ch 318; *Bell v Balls* [1897] 1 Ch 663, 66 LJ Ch 397; *Van Praagh v Everidge* [1902] 2 Ch 266, 71 LJ Ch 598 (revsd on the ground that there was no sufficient memorandum: *Van Praagh v Everidge* [1903] 1 Ch 434, 72 LJ Ch 260, CA); *Phillips v Butler* [1945] Ch 358, [1945] 2 All ER 258.

5 The requirement for written formalities was contained in the Law of Property Act 1925 s 40, which has since been repealed. It is replaced by the Law of Property (Miscellaneous Provisions) Act 1989 s 2 requiring written contracts, but not in relation to public auctions of land: see SALE OF LAND vol 42 (Reissue) PARA 29.

6 *Luxor (Eastbourne) Ltd v Cooper* [1941] AC 108, [1941] 1 All ER 33, HL.

7 *Walker v Crabb* (1916) 61 Sol Jo 219 at 220 per Atkin J.

8 *Walker v Crabb* (1916) 61 Sol Jo 219. As to the meaning of 'employee' see EMPLOYMENT vol 39 (2009) PARA 2. As to the distinction between a contract of service and a contract for service see EMPLOYMENT vol 39 (2009) PARA 1.

8.   Extent of authority.   Apart from express instructions enlarging or limiting it, the implied authority of the auctioneer[1] is a general authority to sell by auction[2] and deal in the way usual and customary amongst auctioneers[3]. The authority does not extend so as to make the seller liable for injury caused by the auctioneer's negligence to a person attending the sale unless the seller has instructed the auctioneer to do any unlawful act or thing whereby the injury was caused[4].

An auctioneer has no implied authority to conclude a sale by private contract[5], even if the sale proves abortive and he is offered more than the reserve price[6]. If however, the seller accepts a buyer introduced by the auctioneer, and himself concludes a sale to that buyer by private treaty, the auctioneer may have a right to claim remuneration[7].

In some cases, where property has not reached its reserve and has been bought in, and immediately afterwards the auctioneer has sold the property at the reserve price to a person present at the bidding, the sale has been held good as, in effect, a sale by auction[8]. The true ratio decidendi of these cases, however, would seem to be that the instructions to sell were primarily to raise a minimum price pursuant to a court order or terms of compromise of a dispute, with sale by auction merely being stipulated as a convenient method of sale. Moreover, these cases involved claims by principals to enforce contracts against reluctant buyers. Such claims could have succeeded simply on the basis of ratification. It would therefore be unsafe to regard these cases as authority for the proposition that a power to sell otherwise than by auction would be implied. In one case where a seller was held bound by a private treaty sale effected by the auctioneer after the reserve was not reached at auction, the overriding object of the sale was held to be to achieve a minimum price howsoever obtained, the auction being merely the preferred method[9].

1 As to the meaning of 'auctioneer' see PARA 2.

2 *Howard v Braithwaite* (1812) 1 Ves & B 202 at 210; *Hawkins v Rogers* [1951] IR 48 per Dixon J. See also *Toulmin v Millar* (1887) 3 TLR 836, HL, per Lord Watson. As to the meaning of 'auction' see PARA 1.

3 *Collen v Gardner* (1856) 21 Beav 540. Guidance notes for good practice have been issued by the Royal Institution of Chartered Surveyors and by the Society of Fine Art Auctioneers.

4 *Walker v Crabb* (1916) 61 Sol Jo 219, 33 TLR 119 (where the auctioneer was liable in respect of injuries caused by an unruly mare, and the seller was held not to be liable, notwithstanding that the sale was carried out on his premises, because both the sale and the chattel were entirely within the control of the auctioneer).

5 *Marsh v Jelf* (1862) 3 F & F 234.

6 *Daniel v Adams* (1764) Amb 495; *Re Loft* (1844) 2 LTOS 397.

7 *Green v Bartlett* (1863) 14 CBNS 681 (where the authority to sell otherwise than by auction was express). As to remuneration see PARA 24.

8 *Else v Barnard, ex p Courtauld* (1860) 28 Beav 228; *Bousfield v Hodges* (1863) 33 Beav 90.
9 *Garnier v Bruntlett* (1974) 236 Estates Gazette 867 (sale to realise security).

9. Sale below reserve price. If a reserve price is fixed[1] by the seller and the sale or lot is expressed to be subject to a reserve, the auctioneer[2] has no authority to sell below it[3]. If he purports to do so no contract is concluded between the seller and buyer as all bids amount only to conditional offers and any acceptance is similarly conditional on the reserve being reached or exceeded[4]. Moreover the auctioneer cannot be liable to the disappointed buyer for breach of any warranty of authority to sell to the highest bidder below reserve in the face of an express 'subject to reserve sale'[5].

Where the sale is notified to be subject to the seller's right to fix a reserve, the auctioneer is similarly unable to sell below any reserve actually set and the buyer is put on notice as to whether one has been fixed[6].

It may be that an auctioneer announces a sale to be without reserve where, in fact, the seller has fixed one. In such a case a valid contract may be enforceable by a buyer who has bid below the reserve[7].

Conversely if no reserve is fixed and the auctioneer rightly advertises the sale as 'without reserve', liability will attach to the auctioneer if, subsequently, the seller withdraws the lot, buys it in or fixes a reserve so that it is not sold to the highest bidder, and although no sale will in these circumstances be achieved the auctioneer will be liable on a collateral contract that the sale be without reserve[8]. It is suggested that in such a case the auctioneer would be able to look to the seller-principal for indemnification[9]. The position would be otherwise if it is the auctioneer who unilaterally withdraws the lot after bidding has commenced[10].

1 It should be expressly set. The courts may not imply the setting of reserves: *Nelson v Hicks* (1899) QR 15 SC 465 (no implication that sales were subject to reserves by reason only of the fact that the goods were sent to the auctioneer accompanied by invoices).
2 As to the meaning of 'auctioneer' see PARA 2.
3 *McManus v Fortescue* [1907] 2 KB 1, CA.
4 *McManus v Fortescue* [1907] 2 KB 1, CA. As to offer and acceptance see CONTRACT vol 9(1) (Reissue) PARA 631.
5 *McManus v Fortescue* [1907] 2 KB 1, CA.
6 *Fay v Miller, Wilkins & Co* [1941] Ch 360, [1941] 2 All ER 18, CA (where the auctioneers were liable, however, for breach of warranty of authority having gone on to effect a memorandum as then required by the Law of Property Act 1925 s 40 (now repealed: see PARA 7 note 5) thus rendering the contract no longer conditional).
7 See *Rainbow v Howkins* [1904] 2 KB 322, DC, where it was held that the auctioneer had apparent authority to sell without reserve in the absence of any express notice to the contrary. This was expressly doubted in *McManus v Fortescue* [1907] 2 KB 1, CA, where, however, the existence of a reserve was expressly notified. The finding of apparent authority defeated the claim for breach of warranty of authority. The buyers also failed to enforce the contract of sale, notwithstanding that the auctioneer was held to be authorised to effect it, since no memorandum as then required by the Sale of Goods Act 1893 s 4 (now repealed) was signed.
8 *Warlow v Harrison* (1859) 1 E & E 309, Ex Ch. The contract is made by the auctioneer making a unilateral offer to this effect which is accepted by the highest bona fide bidder by virtue of his bid: see *Warlow v Harrison* (1859) 1 E & E 309, Ex Ch at 316–317 per Martin B (obiter). This analysis was approved and employed in *Tully v Irish Land Commission* (1961) 97 ILT 174; and in *Barry v Heathcote Ball & Co (Commercial Auctions) Ltd* [2001] 1 All ER 944, sub nom *Barry v Davies (t/a Heathcote Ball & Co)* [2000] 1 WLR 1962, CA. Cf *Fenwick v Macdonald, Fraser & Co Ltd* (1904) 6 F 850, Ct of Sess.
9 *Warlow v Harrison* (1859) 1 E & E 309.
10 See *Barry v Heathcote Ball & Co (Commercial Auctions) Ltd* [2001] 1 All ER 944, sub nom *Barry v Davies (t/a Heathcote Ball & Co)* [2000] 1 WLR 1962, CA.

10. Authority to receive payment. An auctioneer[1] has implied authority to receive the deposit on sales both of land and of goods[2], but no implied authority by virtue of his agency[3] alone to receive the purchase money[4]. Thus a buyer who pays the purchase money to an auctioneer who lacks express authority to receive it is not discharged from liability to the seller. Where in a sale of goods, as is generally the case, the conditions contemplate that the auctioneer is to complete the sale, the position is different and he is then usually authorised to receive the purchase money[5]. This does not mean necessarily that he is under a duty to collect the price[6].

The auctioneer has authority to receive payment of the deposit by cash. He may accept a cheque[7], provided he exercises reasonable caution, but cannot be compelled to do so[8]. This authority is confined to cheques presently payable, and does not extend to receiving payment of the deposit by bill of exchange[9] or post-dated cheque[10]. He cannot give credit[11], or allow a set-off due from the seller to the buyer[12]. Otherwise the auctioneer has no right, in the absence of express instructions, to take payment of the purchase money otherwise than in cash[13]. An auctioneer should today ensure that his consignment agreement does expressly permit the taking of payment otherwise than in cash where large sums may be involved. Receipt of a sum of 15,000 euros or more in cash renders an auctioneer a high value dealer for the purposes of the Money Laundering Regulations 2007[14] and those regulations will apply to him[15].

Where the auctioneer has received payment by cheque or bill of exchange without or in excess of any express or implied authority, the seller is not bound by the payment, the buyer still remains liable[16] and the auctioneer may be sued by the seller for any damages sustained by him[17]. Where the auctioneer does receive the deposit he should do so as agent for the seller rather than as stakeholder[18] in order to protect his lien[19]. Normally, however, he will hold it as stakeholder.

1   As to the meaning of 'auctioneer' see PARA 2.
2   *Mynn v Joliffe* (1834) 1 Mood & R 326; *Williams v Millington* (1788) 1 Hy Bl 81; *Capel v Thornton* (1828) 3 C & P 352; *Butwick v Grant* [1924] 2 KB 483, DC.
3   As to agency of auctioneers see PARA 7.
4   *Drakeford v Piercy* (1866) 7 B & S 515; *Butwick v Grant* [1924] 2 KB 483, DC.
5   *Sykes v Giles* (1839) 5 M & W 645.
6   See *Fordham v Christie, Manson & Woods Ltd* (1977) 121 Sol Jo 529, 244 Estates Gazette 213. See also PARA 23.
7   *Farrer v Lacy, Hartland & Co* (1885) 31 ChD 42, CA.
8   *Johnston v Boyes* [1899] 2 Ch 73.
9   As to bills of exchange see generally FINANCIAL SERVICES AND INSTITUTIONS vol 49 (2008) PARA 1400 et seq.
10 *Williams v Evans* (1866) LR 1 QB 352; *Papé v Westacott* [1894] 1 QB 272, CA.
11 *Williams v Evans* (1866) LR 1 QB 352; *Papé v Westacott* [1894] 1 QB 272, CA.
12 *Brown v Staton* (1816) 2 Chit 353.
13 *Earl Ferrers v Robins* (1835) 2 Cr M & R 152; *Sykes v Giles* (1839) 5 M & W 645.
14 Ie the Money Laundering Regulations 2007, SI 2007/2157: see FINANCIAL SERVICES AND INSTITUTIONS vol 48 (2008) PARA 539 et seq.
15 As to the application of the regulations to high value dealers see the Money Laundering Regulations 2007, SI 2007/2157, reg 3(1)(g); and FINANCIAL SERVICES AND INSTITUTIONS vol 48 (2008) PARA 540.
16 *Sykes v Giles* (1839) 5 M & W 645. See *Hodgens v Keon* [1894] 2 IR 657; and *Boothman v Byrne* (1923) 57 ILT 36.
17 *Earl Ferrers v Robins* (1835) 2 Cr M & R 152.
18 As to auctioneers as stakeholders see PARA 58.
19 As to auctioneers' lien see PARA 25.

11.   Authority to warrant.   It used to be the case that an auctioneer[1] had no authority, except by express instructions, to give a warranty at the auction[2], and that an unauthorised warranty would not bind the seller[3]. However, it is now the case that an agent[4] may have usual or apparent authority to make warranties binding on his principal[5]. Where the auctioneer does make unauthorised representations, he may be personally liable to the buyer for breach of warranty of authority[6]. He will also have to indemnify his seller if he makes representations rendering the latter liable to the buyer, for example in misrepresentation[7].

If a seller makes it clear that his descriptions are to be applied to the lots, the auctioneer will be liable to him for any loss caused by his failure to do so[8].

1 As to the meaning of 'auctioneer' see PARA 2.
2 As to the meaning of 'auction' see PARA 1.
3 *Payne v Lord Leconfield* (1882) 51 LJQB 642.
4 As to agency of auctioneers see PARA 7.
5 See *Mendelssohn v Normand Ltd* [1970] 1 QB 177 at 183–184, [1969] 2 All ER 1215 at 1218, CA, per Lord Denning MR (an oral promise or a representation of fact made by one party which induces the other to contract can be relied on provided apparent authority to make such a statement exists). This proposition was considered in the context of auctions with regard to a representation relating to the property made by the auctioneer before sale, and it was held that the seller was not liable for misrepresentation as he had expressly drawn the attention of the public to the limits placed upon the auctioneer's authority to make binding representations: see *Overbrooke Estates Ltd v Glencombe Properties Ltd* [1974] 3 All ER 511, [1974] 1 WLR 1335 (approved in *Collins v Howell-Jones* [1981] 2 EGLR 108, (1980) 259 Estates Gazette 331, CA; and applied in *Moore v Khan-Ghouri* [1991] 2 EGLR 9, [1991] 32 EG 63, CA). This suggests that in the absence of such a notification the representation could have been binding on the seller. Clearly, where the seller does authorise the representation, he will be bound by it: *Museprime Properties Ltd v Adhill Properties Ltd* (1990) 61 P & CR 111, [1990] 2 EGLR 196.
6 See PARA 30.
7 See PARA 32.
8 *Brown v Draper & Co* (1975) 233 Estates Gazette 929, CA.

12. Delegation of authority. An agent has no power, without the authority of his principal, to delegate his agency to another[1]. It follows that an auctioneer[2] employed to sell must, in general, effect the sale himself[3]. Thus, he cannot delegate to his clerk[4], unless the principal has clearly assented. Different considerations would arise where the principal instructs a firm of auctioneers rather than an individual, but it would seem that even then only a person practising as an auctioneer would be impliedly authorised[5].

The context in which the question of delegation has most commonly arisen is that of signature by a clerk of the memoranda formerly required in sales both of land and of goods[6]. Such signature might be made on behalf of either seller or buyer. Whilst the authorities themselves are not particularly strong, there exist categorical dicta that the auctioneer had no usual or implied authority to delegate the signing of a memorandum to his clerk so as to bind the seller[7]. It appears to be free from doubt that there is no implied power to delegate signature to the clerk so as to bind the buyer[8].

All matters incidental to the sale which it might be useful to delegate should be expressly agreed between the parties. It is within the clerk's authority to receive the deposit[9].

1 'Delegatus non potest delegare': see AGENCY vol 1 (2008) PARA 48 et seq.
2 As to the meaning of 'auctioneer' see PARA 2. As to agency of auctioneers see PARA 7.
3 *Coles v Trecothick* (1804) 9 Ves 234; *Henderson v Barnewall* (1827) 1 Y & J 387.
4 *Coles v Trecothick* (1804) 9 Ves 234; *Henderson v Barnewall* (1827) 1 Y & J 387; *Bird v Boulter* (1833) 4 B & Ad 443.
5 *Wilson & Sons v Pike* [1949] 1 KB 176, [1948] 2 All ER 267, CA. See PARA 15.
6 See PARA 7 note 5.

7   *Gosbell v Archer* (1835) 2 Ad & El 500 (although here the clerk clearly signed only as a witness); *Peirce v Corf* (1874) LR 9 QB 210 (clerk signing sales ledger not shown to bidders). However, contrast *Dyas v Stafford* (1881) 7 LR IR 590.
8   *Bell v Balls* [1897] 1 Ch 663. As to the nature and exercise of authority to sign contracts see PARA 15.
9   *Gosbell v Archer* (1835) 2 Ad & El 500.

13.   Termination of authority.   The agency of the auctioneer[1] is normally an agency for sale by auction[2] only[3], and therefore, when the property has been knocked down, the auctioneer's authority is at an end except for the purpose of carrying out the contract made at the auction. He cannot introduce into it any stipulations as to title[4]. Normally the auctioneer has no authority to accept rescission of the contract in the absence of an express term in the consignment agreement[5].

1   As to the meaning of 'auctioneer' see PARA 2. As to agency of auctioneers see PARA 7.
2   As to the meaning of 'auction' see PARA 1.
3   *Seton v Slade* (1802) 7 Ves 265 at 276 per Lord Eldon LC. See also *Blackburn v Scholes* (1810) 2 Camp 341.
4   *Seton v Slade* (1802) 7 Ves 265.
5   *Nelson v Aldridge* (1818) 2 Stark 435. Contrast *Stevens v Legh* (1853) 22 LTOS 84, where the seller failed in his claim for breach of contract against the auctioneer who had returned the purchase price after fraud had been discovered. It is fairly common for auctioneers' conditions to provide expressly for a right to accept rescission, for example, where a forgery is discovered. Where an auctioneer gives the buyer a right to return a forgery as in *Marie Zelinger de Balkany v Christie, Manson & Woods Ltd* (1997) 16 Tr LR 163, he should ensure that he has such a right expressed in his consignment contract with his seller-client. As to rescission of contract see CONTRACT vol 9(1) (Reissue) PARA 1014.

14.   Revocation of authority.   Up to the time of the conclusion of the sale, and until the property is finally knocked down, the auctioneer's[1] authority is revocable either expressly or in any of the events which ordinarily determine agencies[2], unless the contract is such as to give the auctioneer an authority coupled with an interest[3].

The authority can be withdrawn even though the auctioneer has incurred expenses[4] and advertised the property for sale[5], as the advertisement is the act of the auctioneer and he has no ostensible authority to make representations as to the existence or extent of his own authority. The auctioneer will be liable in trespass if, after the determination of his authority, he insists on entering the seller's premises for the purpose of effecting a sale[6].

If the authority has in fact been revoked, the auctioneer can give the highest bidder no right to the property, even though the bidder is unaware of the revocation[7]. It remains to be decided whether, unlike an estate agent, an auctioneer can, in the absence of express contractual provision, recover damages on the revocation of his authority for preventing him from earning his commission[8]. It may be said that an auctioneer contracts to put the property to auction[9], and is therefore obliged, in contradistinction to an estate agent, to endeavour to sell the property in that fashion.

1   As to the meaning of 'auctioneer' see PARA 2.
2   *Warlow v Harrison* (1859) 1 E & E 309, Ex Ch. However, if the property is sold 'without reserve', revocation after bidding had commenced would render the auctioneer, and, in these circumstances, his principal liable on the collateral contract to sell to the highest bona fide bidder: see PARA 9. As to the agency of auctioneers see PARA 7. As to the termination of agency see AGENCY vol 1 (2008) PARA 170 et seq.
3   For example, if an auctioneer is entrusted with goods for sale to repay previous advances, the authority is irrevocable: see *Charlesworth v Mills* [1892] AC 231, HL. The authority is not,

however, irrevocable if the auctioneer pays money on the understanding that he is to sell the goods and recoup himself from the proceeds of sale: *Chinnock v Sainsbury* (1860) 30 LJ Ch 409. As to irrevocable authority see AGENCY vol 1 (2008) PARA 171 et seq.

4   *Taplin v Florence* (1851) 10 CB 744. The auctioneer does not, however, lose his right to be indemnified against the expenses he has incurred: see PARA 26.
5   *Warlow v Harrison* (1859) 1 E & E 309, Ex Ch; *Taplin v Florence* (1851) 10 CB 744.
6   *Taplin v Florence* (1851) 10 CB 744.
7   *Manser v Back* (1848) 6 Hare 443.
8   See *Luxor (Eastbourne) Ltd v Cooper* [1941] AC 108, [1941] 1 All ER 33, HL; and *Warlow v Harrison* (1859) 1 E & E 309, Ex Ch, per Martin B. It is common for auctioneers' conditions of trading specifically to provide for payment in the event of withdrawal of lots.
9   As to the meaning of 'auction' see PARA 1.

15.   Nature and exercise of authority to sign contract.   As has been stated[1], it is no longer the case that a contract for the sale or other disposition of an interest in land made at public auction[2] must be evidenced in writing and the requirement of writing in the case of sales of land[3] does not apply[4]. Thus the well-established implied authority to sign a memorandum evidencing the sale on behalf of the seller and buyer is no longer of relevance. In order to achieve evidential certainty of the terms of the contract of sale, which can now be made orally[5], it can be made a term of that contract that the parties sign a contract containing the terms. Alternatively, the terms under which the bidding is conducted may prevent a contract arising at the fall of the hammer and provide that one only comes into existence when such signed documentation is effected. If, in this latter situation, it is sought to permit the auctioneer to act as agent[6] in signing, that authority must be expressly given.

1   See PARA 7 note 5.
2   As to the meaning of 'auction' see PARA 1.
3   See the Law of Property (Miscellaneous Provisions) Act 1989 s 2; and SALE OF LAND vol 42 (Reissue) PARA 29.
4   Law of Property (Miscellaneous Provisions) Act 1989 s 2(5)(b).
5   As to oral contracts see CONTRACT vol 9(1) (Reissue) PARA 620.
6   As to agency of auctioneers see PARA 7.

(3) AUCTIONEER'S DUTIES TO SELLER

(i) General Duties

16.   Exercise of skill and knowledge.   Being a person who professes to carry on a business requiring skill and knowledge, an auctioneer[1] must display such skill and knowledge in acting for his seller as is reasonably to be expected from competent auctioneers, and must follow the course of business ordinarily recognised by custom[2] or prescribed by statute[3]. In the exercise of skill and knowledge by an auctioneer, the standard of care will vary depending upon whether he is regarded as a specialist or a general practitioner[4]. If the former, he will not be liable if, albeit that there is a body of professional opinion which considers that the actions were wrong, there also exists an equally competent body of professional opinion which supports the manner in which the auctioneer carried out his duty[5]. An auctioneer who is a 'general practitioner' will be regarded as negligent only if it is found that no auctioneer of ordinary skill and care would have acted as he did[6].

An auctioneer will be liable in damages for a breach of any duty, nominal where no material injury results[7], or substantial and of an amount to compensate the seller for any actual loss sustained through the negligence of the auctioneer[8] or of persons employed by him[9]. It is not negligent for an auctioneer, in the exercise of his judgment, not to insist upon a payment of a deposit by a buyer[10]. However, it has been held to be negligent to allow the buyer to take away the goods before he has paid the price[11].

1 As to the meaning of 'auctioneer' see PARA 2.
2 *Denew v Daverell* (1813) 3 Camp 451; *Jones v Nanney* (1824) 13 Price 76. Guidance notes for good practice have been issued by the Royal Institution of Chartered Surveyors and by the Society of Fine Art Auctioneers.
3 See the Supply of Goods and Services Act 1982 s 13 (implied term about care and skill); and SALE OF GOODS AND SUPPLY OF SERVICES vol 41 (2005 Reissue) PARA 97. The implied term under s 13 may be contractually negatived or varied under s 16: see SALE OF GOODS AND SUPPLY OF SERVICES vol 41 (2005 Reissue) PARA 102.
   See also *Coppen v Moore (No 2)* [1898] 2 QB 306; *Christie, Manson and Woods v Cooper* [1900] 2 QB 522.
4 *Luxmoore-May v Messenger May Baverstock (a firm)* [1990] 1 All ER 1067, [1990] 1 WLR 1009, CA (applying *Maynard v West Midlands Regional Health Authority* [1985] 1 All ER 635, [1984] 1 WLR 634, HL).
5 See *Alchemy (International) Ltd v Tattersalls (Ltd)* [1985] 2 EGLR 17, 276 Estates Gazette 675.
6 *Luxmoore-May v Messenger May Baverstock (a firm)* [1990] 1 All ER 1067, [1990] 1 WLR 1009, CA. As to negligence see generally NEGLIGENCE.
7 *Hibbert v Bayley* (1860) 2 F & F 48.
8 *Parker v Farebrother* (1853) 21 LTOS 128.
9 As to vicarious liability see TORT vol 97 (2010) PARA 680 et seq. As to damages see generally DAMAGES.
10 *Cyril Andrade Ltd v Sotheby & Co* (1931) 47 TLR 244 (deposit was only payable by the buyer 'if required to do so'). Cf *Hibbert v Bayley* (1860) 2 F & F 48, where there was a condition that the highest bidder should immediately pay a deposit, and it was held to be negligent to allow him to leave without doing so.
11 *Brown v Staton* (1816) 2 Chit 353. See PARA 18.

17. Duty to describe the property accurately and to its best advantage. The auctioneer[1] will generally be under an obligation in tort, and may be specifically required by contract, to describe the seller's property with such care as is necessary in order to ensure that a proper price is obtained[2]. This may involve a duty to research and value a lot[3].

Unless the contract between the auctioneer and the seller permits the auctioneer to apply his own descriptions to the property he must apply any descriptions expressly or impliedly instructed, and if he fails to do so will be liable in damages for the difference between the price achieved and that which the property would have realised if it had been described as instructed[4]. Where a consignment agreement gave the auctioneer 'sole and complete discretion' as to descriptions to be given in the catalogue and other literature the court implied a term as to 'Wednesbury reasonableness'[5] into the contract so as to render the auctioneer liable for any arbitrary, capricious, perverse or irrational exercise of the discretion[6].

If the auctioneer describes the property without authority or in breach of his duty to the seller so that the latter becomes liable to the buyer (for example, under the Misrepresentation Act 1967[7] or under the Sale of Goods Act 1979[8]), the auctioneer will be liable to indemnify the seller for causing that loss; it is otherwise if the misdescriptions are authorised[9].

There are statutory criminal sanctions in certain circumstances where an auctioneer sells misdescribed goods or land[10].

1 As to the meaning of 'auctioneer' see PARA 2.
2 *Cuckmere Brick Co Ltd v Mutual Finance Ltd* [1971] Ch 949, [1971] 2 All ER 633, CA.

3   *Luxmoore-May v Messenger May Baverstock (a firm)* [1990] 1 All ER 1067, [1990] 1 WLR 1009, CA.

4   *Brown v Draper & Co* (1975) 119 Sol Jo 300, 233 Estates Gazette 929, CA.

5   As to 'Wednesbury reasonableness' see ADMINISTRATIVE LAW vol 1(1) (2001 Reissue) PARA 59.

6   *Elidor Investments SA & ANR v Christie, Manson Woods Ltd* [2009] EWHC 3600 (QB).

7   A misrepresentation can take the form of a misleading photograph: see *Atlantic Estates plc v Ezekiel* [1991] 2 EGLR 202, [1991] 35 EG 118, CA (depiction was of a thriving wine bar, but in fact the liquor licence had been revoked); *St Marylebone Property Co Ltd v Payne* [1994] 2 EGLR 25, [1994] 45 EG 156 (photograph of auctioned land containing endorsements inaccurately showing lateral extent and characteristics of the property). A misrepresentation can also take the form of a misstatement of law: see *Pankhania v Hackney London Borough Council* [2002] All ER (D) 22 (Aug); [2004] EWHC 323 (Ch), [2004] 1 EGLR 135, [2004] All ER (D) 205 (Jan) (property described as subject to a contractual licence when it was subject to a lease protected under the Landlord and Tenant Act 1954 Pt II (ss 23–46)).

8   Under the Sale of Goods Act 1979, where there is a contract for the sale of goods by description, there is an implied term that the goods will correspond with the description: see s 13(1) (amended by the Sale and Supply of Goods Act 1994 s 7, Sch 2 para 5(4)(a)); and SALE OF GOODS AND SUPPLY OF SERVICES vol 41 (2005 Reissue) PARA 72 et seq. A sale of goods is not prevented from being a sale by description by reason only that, being exposed for sale or hire, they are selected by the buyer: Sale of Goods Act 1979 s 13(3). As to the sale of goods by description see SALE OF GOODS AND SUPPLY OF SERVICES vol 41 (2005 Reissue) PARA 72 et seq.

9   *Museprime Properties Ltd v Adhill Properties Ltd* (1990) 61 P & CR 111, [1990] 2 EGLR 196. See *Boyter v Thomson* [1995] 2 AC 628, [1995] 3 All ER 135, HL (an undisclosed principal was liable to a buyer for breach of an implied term under the Sale of Goods Act 1979 s 14(1)–(4) (see SALE OF GOODS AND SUPPLY OF SERVICES vol 41 (2005 Reissue) PARA 82)).

10   See PARAS 60–61.

18. Duties in respect of goods. Since the auctioneer[1] is a bailee for reward, he must exercise ordinary care and diligence in keeping the goods entrusted to him[2]. He has a possession coupled with an interest in goods which he is employed to sell, and not a bare custody[3], and is liable for any loss or damage which may occur through his default or negligence[4]. If he has contracted to store goods as a bailee he is in breach of contract if he arranges for someone else to take possession of them, as the contract is one of which his personal care is of the essence[5]. If he has undertaken to insure goods which he is employed to sell he must give notice to his principal if, for any reason, he is unable to effect the insurance[6].

In the absence of authority from the seller, it is the duty of the auctioneer not to part with possession of the goods until the buyer has paid the price. If the auctioneer does so and the buyer fails to pay, the auctioneer will be liable to the seller for the amount[7].

Except where his right of lien[8] exists, an auctioneer must redeliver goods to the seller on demand, either before sale if the authority to sell is revoked, or after sale if the goods are unsold. Like other bailees, he is estopped[9] from setting up the title of a third person against the bailor, unless the bailment is determined by what is equivalent to an eviction by title paramount, and the auctioneer defends upon the right and title and by the authority of such third person[10]. Even with such authority he cannot set up the title of the third person if he was aware of the adverse claim at the time when he accepted his employment[11].

1   As to the meaning of 'auctioneer' see PARA 2.

2   *Maltby v Christie* (1795) 1 Esp 340. The auctioneer may contract out of his liability as bailee and otherwise: *Spriggs v Sotheby Parke Bernet & Co Ltd* [1986] 1 Lloyd's Rep 487, [1986] 1 EGLR 13, CA (a pre-Unfair Contract Terms Act 1977 case where the exclusion clause was upheld). As to care and diligence of bailees see BAILMENT AND PLEDGE.

3   *Williams v Millington* (1788) 1 Hy Bl 81 at 85; *Woolfe v Horne* (1877) 2 QBD 355.

4   *Lilley v Doubleday* (1881) 7 QBD 510; *McMahon v Field* (1881) 7 QBD 591, CA.

5   *Edwards v Newland & Co (E Burchett Ltd, third party)* [1950] 2 KB 534, [1950] 1 All ER
    1072, CA (applying *British Waggon Co and Parkgate Waggon Co v Lea & Co* (1880) 5 QBD
    149, DC).
6   *Callander v Oelrichs* (1838) 5 Bing NC 58.
7   *Brown v Staton* (1816) 2 Chit 353. See PARA 16.
8   As to auctioneers' lien see PARA 25.
9   As to estoppel see ESTOPPEL vol 16(2) (Reissue) PARA 1083 et seq.
10 *Biddle v Bond* (1865) 6 B & S 225; *Thorne v Tilbury* (1858) 3 H & N 534. See also BAILMENT
    AND PLEDGE. Whereas the limitations on the right to plead the jus tertii were abolished by the
    Torts (Interference with Goods) Act 1977 s 8 (see TORT vol 45(2) (Reissue) PARA 644), it is
    questionable whether the auctioneer is thereby enabled to resist claims by sellers to return the
    property or their proceeds of sale. A claim for wrongful interference is one to which the
    provisions of the Torts (Interference with Goods) Act 1977 apply: see s 1 (amended by the by the
    Consumer Protection Act 1987 s 48, Sch 4; and by SI 1987/2049). A seller seeking the return of
    his property or its proceeds could invariably claim under the terms of the contract of agency,
    and that appears to be outside the Torts (Interference with Goods) Act 1977. As to the scope of
    the Torts (Interference with Goods) Act 1977 see TORT vol 45(2) (Reissue) PARA 545.
11 *Re Sadler, ex p Davies* (1881) 19 ChD 86, CA.

(ii) Fiduciary Duties

19.   Fiduciary duties owed to the seller.   There are duties owed to the seller
which arise out of the fiduciary relationship inherent in the agency[1]: duties which
are imposed so that there cannot be a position such that the auctioneer's[2] duty to
the seller and his own interests conflict. These are: (1) bidding on behalf of the
buyer[3]; (2) purchasing the seller's property[4]; (3) obtaining a secret profit[5]; and
(4) the duty to account[6].

1   As to agency of auctioneers see PARA 7.
2   As to the meaning of 'auctioneer' see PARA 2.
3   See PARA 20.
4   See PARA 21.
5   See PARA 22.
6   See PARA 23.

20.   Bidding on behalf of the buyer.   Accepting commission bids on behalf of
the buyer creates an obvious potential conflict of interest[1] since the auctioneer[2] is
then acting for two parties whose interests are antithetical. Most auctioneers do
accept commissions to bid for potential buyers and this will be unobjectionable
only if the consent, actual or tacit, of the seller is obtained[3]. This is usually done
by making it clear in the consignment conditions that the auctioneer is willing to
accept commissions for prospective buyers.

1   *Fullwood v Hurley* [1928] 1 KB 498, CA: 'If and so long as the agent is the agent of one party
    he cannot engage to become the agent of another ...'. Cf *Bexwell v Christie* (1776) 1 Cowp 395,
    where obiter the contrary was suggested. See *Fordham v Christie, Manson & Woods Ltd* (1977)
    121 Sol Jo 529, 244 Estates Gazette 213 at 215 per May J.
2   As to the meaning of 'auctioneer' see PARA 2.
3   *Fullwood v Hurley* [1928] 1 KB 498, CA.

21.   Purchase by auctioneer.   A purchase by the auctioneer[1] himself without
the seller's consent is voidable, and will be set aside at the instance of the seller,
even after a long lapse of time, unless there is evidence that the seller consented
to the purchase after disclosure of all material facts known to the auctioneer[2]. It
is not enough to put the seller on inquiry, the auctioneer must make a full
disclosure of all material facts[3]. If he purchases without such disclosure he
becomes a trustee of the property for his principal and is strictly accountable as

such[4]. The burden of proof that there was full disclosure and that the seller acquiesced in the sale lies on the auctioneer[5].

Even after such full disclosure, the auctioneer will not, however, be entitled to commission on the sale unless the principal has expressly agreed to pay commission in the changed circumstances[6]. The presumption is that the auctioneer has ceased to be an agent[7] and has become a contracting principal. The same applies if he has only a part interest in the purchase, for example, if he is one of a syndicate or if he is a shareholder in a purchasing company[8]. The embargo on the auctioneer buying his principal's property ceases once the auctioneer's agency is terminated[9].

1 As to the meaning of 'auctioneer' see PARA 2.
2 *Oliver v Court* (1820) 8 Price 127; *Salomons v Pender* (1865) 3 H & C 639. See *Ex p Lacey* (1802) 6 Ves 625; *Sanderson v Walker* (1807) 13 Ves 601; and *Downes v Grazebrook* (1817) 3 Mer 200. As to voidable contracts see CONTRACT vol 9(1) (Reissue) PARA 607.
3 *Dunne v English* (1874) LR 18 Eq 524; *Boston Deep Sea Fishing and Ice Co v Ansell* (1888) 39 ChD 339, CA; *Oliver v Court* (1820) 8 Price 127; *Baskett v Cafe* (1851) 4 De G & Sm 388; *Lees v Nuttall* (1834) 2 My & K 819; *Whitcomb v Minchin* (1820) 5 Madd 91.
4 *Lees v Nuttall* (1834) 2 My & K 819.
5 *Wentworth v Lloyd* (1863) 32 Beav 467.
6 *Hocker v Waller* (1924) 29 Com Cas 296; *Great Luxembourg Rly Co v Magnay (No 2)* (1858) 25 Beav 586; *McPherson v Watt* (1877) 3 App Cas 254, HL; *Salomons v Pender* (1865) 3 H & C 639; *Lees v Nuttall* (1834) 2 My & K 819.
7 As to agency of auctioneers see PARA 7.
8 *Wentworth v Lloyd* (1863) 32 Beav 467; *Salomons v Pender* (1865) 3 H & C 639.
9 *Young v Hill, Ford and Newton* (1883) 2 NZLR 62; cf *Oliver v Court* (1820) 8 Price 127 (agency continued after auctioneer left the rostrum).

22.   Obtaining a secret profit.   It is an inexorable rule drawn from the law of trusts that an auctioneer[1] must not use his position to gain a profit from the transaction from a third party[2]. Any such profit must be passed to the seller unless he consents to the profit being made[3].

1 As to the meaning of 'auctioneer' see PARA 2.
2 *Hippisley v Knee Bros* [1905] 1 KB 1. As to the rule that trustees must not profit from their trust see EQUITY vol 16(2) (Reissue) PARA 858; TRUSTS vol 48 (2007 Reissue) PARA 926 et seq.
3 *Hippisley v Knee Bros* [1905] 1 KB 1. It is thought that this will only apply if, as is nowadays unusual, the auctioneer invoices the seller separately for such items. See AGENCY vol 1 (2008) PARA 91.

23.   Duty to account.   Whilst there is no general duty to obtain the purchase money[1], an auctioneer[2] must account for any money received by him on the seller's behalf, and be ready to pay it over to him[3]. If he fails to keep proper accounts or fails to pay or transfer money or property to his principal he will be liable to a claim for an account[4]. The auctioneer is in a fiduciary position in respect of such money[5], and an order to pay can be made against him as trustee, which, if disobeyed, renders him liable to committal for contempt[6].

In general, payment should be made to the seller, and not to his solicitors except by his express directions[7]. The relevance of the fact that the duty arises out of the fiduciary relationship between the auctioneer and his seller client is that the seller can trace the property in the hands of his agent in priority to the latter's ordinary trade and other creditors[8].

1 *Fordham v Christie, Manson & Woods Ltd* (1977) 121 Sol Jo 529, 244 Estates Gazette 213. See PARA 10.
2 As to the meaning of 'auctioneer' see PARA 2.
3 As to accountability of trustees for profit see TRUSTS vol 48 (2007 Reissue) PARA 928.
4 Ie under CPR Pt 25: see CIVIL PROCEDURE vol 11 (2009) PARA 315 et seq.

5 *Re Cotton, ex p Cooke* (1913) 108 LT 310, CA.
6 *Crowther v Elgood* (1887) 34 ChD 691, CA. See, however, *Henry v Hammond* [1913] 2 KB 515, where *Crowther v Elgood* (1887) 34 ChD 691, CA, does not appear to have been cited. As to civil contempt of court see CONTEMPT OF COURT vol 9(1) (Reissue) PARA 458 et seq.
7 *Brown v Farebrother* (1888) 58 LJ Ch 3. As to payments in sales under court direction see SALE OF LAND vol 42 (Reissue) PARA 133 ET SEQ.
8 *Re Cotton, ex p Cooke* (1913) 108 LT 310, CA. Contrast where the auctioneer sells as principal: *Murphy v Jonathon Howlett (a firm)* (1960) 176 Estates Gazette 311. As to following and tracing trust property see TRUSTS vol 48 (2007 Reissue) PARA 1134.

(4) AUCTIONEER'S RIGHTS AGAINST SELLER

24. Remuneration. The remuneration payable to an auctioneer[1] by a private seller may be fixed by express agreement as to both its amount and the events on which it is to be paid[2].

In order to found a legal claim for commission or other remuneration there must be a contractual relationship[3]. The contract on which the relationship is based may be implied from the circumstances or may arise from custom or usage[4]. Where a valid claim to remuneration arises but the amount has not been agreed, the auctioneer will be entitled to a fair and reasonable amount[5].

Where a letter is written to the principal setting out the terms on which remuneration is payable and the principal does not dissent from them, he may be taken to have assented to them[6]. A failure to dissent, however, will not by itself create a contract in contradistinction to incorporating terms into an existing mandate[7].

In most instances where the services of the auctioneer have been fully performed a customary rate of payment will be treated as the measure of a reasonable amount[8].

The scale of payments to auctioneers is fixed by law in the case of a sale under a distress[9], sales under the Insolvency Act 1986[10], sales by the sheriff under a writ of fieri facias[11] and in the case of a sale of land under the directions of the High Court[12].

Before commission is payable, the auctioneer has to show that the events upon the happening of which he has acquired a vested right to commission have happened[13]. What these events are will vary from case to case[14].

The auctioneer may be entitled to commission on a sale to a buyer introduced by the auctioneer even where no sale by auction[15] has been actually effected, if the terms of the contract so stipulate[16]. The auctioneer may be entitled to commission on a sale before the date of the auction where the buyer is found by his client, the seller, but not if the sale is effected by some third party with the right to sell[17].

An auctioneer who is also a trustee cannot make a profit out of the execution of the trust, unless authorised by the terms of the trust to do so, and therefore, in the absence of such authorisation, cannot in general claim remuneration for the sale of trust property of which either he or his partner is trustee[18].

The right to claim commission may be lost by the auctioneer's negligence[19] or misconduct[20].

There is no room for any implied term that the seller will not revoke his auctioneer's authority to sell and thus prevent the commission being earned[21], but if the seller has unjustifiably prevented its being earned by breaking his contract with the buyer the court may imply such a term[22]. If the justifiable revocation prevents the auctioneer from bringing about the event upon which commission is payable, none is recoverable, but a reasonable sum may be. It has been held that a quantum meruit claim can be maintained[23], but this contradicts earlier authority equating the position of estate agents and auctioneers[24], which is to be preferred. There seems to be nothing, however, to prevent the auctioneer from making express contractual provision for situations where he is prevented from earning his commission.

The rationale against the auctioneer being paid commission or a reasonable sum, in the absence of express provision where he has not brought about the event on which it is to be payable does not apply to expenses paid out, and these are recoverable[25].

If two auctioneers claim commission in respect of the sale of the same property, the seller cannot interplead unless the claims are adverse, that is, unless they are claims to the same money[26].

1 As to the meaning of 'auctioneer' see PARA 2.

2 *Re Page (No 3)* (1863) 32 Beav 487; *Beningfield v Kynaston* (1887) 3 TLR 279, CA; *Peacock v Freeman* (1888) 4 TLR 541, CA. For general rules and construction of contracts as to the payment of commission agency see AGENCY vol 1 (2008) PARA 101 et seq.

3 *Toulmin v Millar* as reported in (1887) 58 LT 96, HL, per Lord Watson.

4 As to implied contracts see CONTRACT vol 9(1) (Reissue) PARA 618.

5 *Manson v Baillie* (1855) 2 Macq 80, HL; *Miller v Beal* (1879) 27 WR 403.

6 *John E Trinder & Partners v Haggis* [1951] WN 416, CA, Denning LJ dissenting.

7 *Way and Waller Ltd v Ryde* [1944] 1 All ER 9, CA.

8 Auctioneers today tend to charge a percentage of the sale price, often on a sliding scale.

9 See the Law of Distress Amendment Act 1888 s 8(2) (repealed, as from a day to be appointed, by the Tribunals, Courts and Enforcement Act 2007 ss 86, 146, Sch 14 para 19, Sch 23 Pt 4; at the date at which this volume states the law, no such day had been appointed); the Distress for Rent Rules 1988, SI 1988/2050, rr 10, 11, App 1 (r 11 amended by SI 1999/2360; Distress for Rent Rules 1988, SI 1988/2050, App 1 amended by SI 2003/1858 and SI 2003/2141); and DISTRESS vol 13 (2007 Reissue) PARA 1058. When the repeal of the Law of Distress Amendment Act 1888 s 8(2) takes effect, the procedure for the sale of controlled goods taken under an enforcement power will be governed by the Tribunals, Courts and Enforcement Act 2007 s 62(1), Sch 12 para 41; such sale will generally be required to be by public auction unless the court orders otherwise: see CIVIL PROCEDURE vol 12 (2009) PARA 1399. No provision is made in the Tribunals, Courts and Enforcement Act 2007 as to the scale of payments for the auctioneer, but regulations under the Act may make further provision about the conduct of sales: see Sch 12 para 42. As to the procedure for taking control of goods under Sch 12 generally see CIVIL PROCEDURE vol 12 (2009) PARA 1389 et seq.

10 See the Insolvency Act 1986; the Insolvency Rules 1986, SI 1986/1925; and BANKRUPTCY AND INDIVIDUAL INSOLVENCY.

11 See the Sheriffs Act 1887 s 20(2) (amended by the Statute Law Revision Act 1908); and the Order Fixing the Fees to be taken by Sheriffs or Sheriff's Officers Concerned in the Execution of Writs of Fieri Facias 1920, SR & O 1920/1250 (amended by the Courts and Legal Services Act 1990 s 74(1)(b), (3); by SI 1956/502; SI 1956/2081; SI 1962/2417; SI 1971/808; SI 1982/89; and SI 1988/1384; and by virtue of the Decimal Currency Act 1969 s 10(1)). As from a day to be appointed, the Sheriffs Act 1887 s 20(2) does not apply to the execution of process under a power to use the procedure in the Tribunals, Courts and Enforcement Act 2007 Sch 12 (taking control of goods): Sheriffs Act 1887 s 20(2A) (prospectively added by the Tribunals, Courts and Enforcement Act 2007 s 62(3), Sch 13 para 20). At the date at which this volume states the law, no such day had been appointed. As to the procedure for taking control of goods under the Tribunals, Courts and Enforcement Act 2007 Sch 12 see CIVIL PROCEDURE vol 12 (2009) PARA 1389 et seq.

12 See CPR 40.16; *Practice Direction PD 40D—1. Court's Powers in Relation to Land*; and CIVIL PROCEDURE vol 12 (2009) PARAS 1215–1216. Where the court has ordered the sale of land under CPR 40.16, auctioneers' and estate agents' charges may, unless the court orders otherwise, include commission, fees for valuation of the land, charges for advertising the land and other expenses and disbursements, but not charges for surveys: *Practice Direction PD 40D—1. Court's Powers in Relation to Land* para 5.1(1). The court's authorisation is required for charges relating to surveys: para 5.1(2). If the total amount of the auctioneer's and estate agent's charges authorised under para 5.1(1) does not exceed 2.5% of the sale price, and does not exceed the rate of commission that that agent would normally charge on a sole agency basis,

the charges may, unless the court orders otherwise, be met by deduction of the amount of the charges from the proceeds of sale without the need for any further authorisation from the court: para 5.2. However, (1) if a charge made by an auctioneer or estate agent (whether in respect of fees or expenses or both) is not authorised under para 5.1(1); (2) if the total amount of the charges so authorised exceeds the limits set out in para 5.2; (3) if the land is sold in lots or by valuation; or (4) if the sale is of investment property, business property or farm property, an application must be made to the court for approval of the fees and expenses to be allowed: para 5.3. An application under para 5.3 may be made by any party or, if he is not a party, by the person having conduct of the sale, and may be made either before or after the sale has taken place: para 5.4.

13 *Luxor (Eastbourne) Ltd v Cooper* [1941] AC 108, [1941] 1 All ER 33, HL (an estate agency case). Contra if he has a sole agency: *Gross Fine and Krieger Chalfen v Gaynor* (1974) 233 Estates Gazette 1015.

14 See *Peacock v Freeman* (1888) 4 TLR 541, CA (no commission payable where land knocked down to a buyer but rescinded by the seller in accordance with the conditions of sale, commission being payable if the property was 'sold'); and *Skinner v Andrews and Hall* (1910) 26 TLR 340, CA (commission payable in similar circumstances, the contract providing for commission to be payable on a 'sale ... under the hammer').

15 As to the meaning of 'auction' see PARA 1.

16 *Green v Bartlett* (1863) 14 CBNS 681. See also *Bayley v Chadwick* (1878) 39 LT 429, HL; and *Clark v Smythies* (1860) 2 F & F 83. The question whether the sale is the result of the auctioneer's intervention is in each case a question of fact: see *Lumley v Nicholson* (1886) 34 WR 716.

17 *John Meacock & Co v Abrahams (Loescher, third party)* [1956] 3 All ER 660, [1956] 1 WLR 1463, CA (mortgagors, the seller client being the mortgagee).

18 *Matthison v Clarke* (1854) 3 Drew 3 (where the auctioneer was merely a mortgagee with a power of sale). See *Salomons v Pender* (1865) 3 H & C 639; *Broad v Selfe* (1863) 2 New Rep 541; and *Kirkman v Booth* (1848) 11 Beav 273. As to the inability of trustees to charge for services see TRUSTS vol 48 (2007 Reissue) PARA 930. It is unlikely that an auctioneer will be able to bring himself within the provisions relating to the remuneration of professional trustees contained in the Trustee Act 2000: see TRUSTS vol 48 (2007 Reissue) PARAS 931–932.

19 *Denew v Daverell* (1813) 3 Camp 451; *Duncan v Blundell* (1820) 3 Stark 6; *Jones v Nanney* (1824) 13 Price 76.

20 *White v Chapman* (1815) 1 Stark 113. As to loss of remuneration through misconduct see further AGENCY vol 1 (2008) PARA 110.

21 *Luxor (Eastbourne) Ltd v Cooper* [1941] AC 108, [1941] 1 All ER 33, HL.

22 *Alpha Trading Ltd v Dunnshaw-Patten Ltd* [1981] QB 290, [1981] 1 All ER 482, CA.

23 *Frank Swain (a firm) v Whitfield Corpn Ltd* (1962) 183 Estates Gazette 479, CA.

24 *John Meacock & Co v Abrahams (Loescher, third party)* [1956] 3 All ER 660, [1956] 1 WLR 1463, CA.

25 *Chinnock v Sainsbury* (1860) 30 LJ Ch 409 per Romilly MR but only as reported in (1860) 3 LT at 259. See similar dicta in *John Meacock & Co v Abrahams (Loescher, third party)* [1956] 3 All ER 660 at 663, [1956] 1 WLR 1463 at 1467, CA, per Lord Denning LJ.

26 *Greatorex v Shackle* [1895] 2 QB 249 at 252 per Wright J. As to interpleader see CIVIL PROCEDURE vol 12 (2009) PARA 1585 et seq.

25.   Lien. By the custom of their business, auctioneers[1] have a lien[2] on goods entrusted to them for sale and on the deposit and purchase money for their charges and remuneration[3]. They also have a lien on documents of title to land. The lien not only entitles the auctioneer to retain the goods against claims by the principal seller, but also allows him to resist claims to the goods made by the buyer in support of his rights against the seller, and he will not in that situation be susceptible to a claim in tort for wrongful interference with goods[4].

This lien attaches to goods whether they are sold at the auctioneer's premises or at those of the seller[5]. It is a charge on the proceeds of sale in priority to any assignment by the seller, and the auctioneer cannot be compelled to marshal the proceeds of several sales in order to give effect to the rights of an assignee of the purchase money of certain of the sales[6]. The lien will be lost if the auctioneer waives it[7], and he may be estopped from establishing it by having earlier denied the seller's title[8].

1   As to the meaning of 'auctioneer' see PARA 2.
2   As to agents' liens see AGENCY vol 1 (2008) PARA 114 et seq. As to lien generally see LIEN.
3   *Williams v Millington* (1788) 1 Hy Bl 81. However, see *Skinner v Trustee of the Property of Reed (Bankrupt)* [1967] Ch 1194, [1967] 2 All ER 1286 (no lien on deposit received by auctioneer as stakeholder where outstanding incumbrances exceed the amount of the purchase price or the balance of it, as the property never became that of the seller); and PARA 58.
4   *Lane v Tewson* (1841) 12 Ad & El 116n. See also *Marcq v Christie Manson & Woods Ltd (t/a Christie's)* [2003] EWCA Civ 731, [2004] QB 286, [2003] 3 All ER 561. As to wrongful interference with goods see TORT vol 45(2) (Reissue) PARA 542 et seq.
5   *Williams v Millington* (1788) 1 Hy Bl 81; *Robinson v Rutter* (1855) 4 E & B 954.
6   *Webb v Smith* (1885) 30 ChD 192, CA.
7   *Scarfe v Morgan* (1838) 4 M & W 270.
8   *Dirks v Richards* (1842) 4 Man & G 574. It is thought that merely accepting alternative security will not amount to abandonment of the lien.

26.   Indemnity.   The seller is bound to indemnify the auctioneer[1] for any damages sustained by the auctioneer in the ordinary course of his employment as the natural consequence of the contract of agency[2] and, in the absence of any agreement to the contrary, for any expenses incurred[3]. Where an auctioneer is sued and claims an indemnity, he may make an additional claim against his principal[4].

The seller's duty to indemnify the auctioneer extends to a case where property for sale has been received by an auctioneer in good faith from a principal who was not the true owner and the auctioneer has been held liable for conversion[5]. However, the indemnity does not extend to cases where the auctioneer has been sued and damages have been recovered from him for some act which is not a wrongful act done in pursuance of his employment, unless the auctioneer defends with the principal's express or implied authority[6]. The judgment against the auctioneer creates no estoppel against the principal unless he had such authority[7]. The auctioneer will not be entitled to an indemnity where he incurs a liability by virtue of a mistake of the law[8] or where he has been negligent[9].

1   *Williams v Lister & Co (Llewellyn Bros, third parties)* (1913) 109 LT 699, CA; *Adamson v Jarvis* (1827) 4 Bing 66. As to the meaning of 'auctioneer' see PARA 2. As to an agent's right of indemnity generally see AGENCY vol 1 (2008) PARAS 111–113.
2   As to agency of auctioneers see PARA 7.
3   Among the expenses properly incurred is money paid to protect the goods from distress as long as they remain the seller's property, but money paid after the sale and when the property in them has passed to the buyer is not chargeable against the seller: *Sweeting v Turner* (1871) LR 7 QB 310; *Chinnock v Sainsbury* (1860) 30 LJ Ch 409; *Brittain v Lloyd* (1845) 14 M & W 762.
4   Ie under CPR Pt 20: see CIVIL PROCEDURE vol 11 (2009) PARA 618 et seq.
5   *Spurrier v Elderton* (1803) 5 Esp 1; *Adamson v Jarvis* (1827) 4 Bing 66. On a sale on behalf of the sheriff an auctioneer is not entitled to indemnity against the sheriff: *Farebrother v Ansley* (1808) 1 Camp 343.
6   *Halbronn v International Horse Agency and Exchange Ltd* [1903] 1 KB 270; *Frixione v Tagliaferro & Sons* (1856) 10 Moo PCC 175 at 200 (doubted in *Williams v Lister & Co (Llewellyn Bros, third parties)* (1913) 109 LT 699, CA). See *Tomlinson v Scottish Amalgamated Silks Ltd (Liquidators)* 1935 SC 1, HL.
7   *Halbronn v International Horse Agency and Exchange Ltd* [1903] 1 KB 270; *Frixione v Tagliaferro & Sons* (1856) 10 Moo PCC 175.
8   *Capp v Topham* (1805) 6 East 392 (failure to avoid auction duty being payable on abortive sale).
9   *Jones v Nanney* (1824) 13 Price 76.

(5) AUCTIONEER'S LIABILITIES TO BUYER

27. Liability on contract of sale. Where an auctioneer[1] sells for an undisclosed principal, he is personally liable on the contract[2]. Where an auctioneer discloses the fact that he is selling as an agent[3], but does not name his principal, he is personally liable on the contract unless a contrary intention appears, the presumption being that the buyer is only willing to contract with the unknown man if the auctioneer makes himself personally liable. This presumption does not, however, arise in the case of the sale of a specific chattel which the buyer knows is not the auctioneer's property[4].

The extent of his liability and the nature of his obligations, for example, as to warranty of title or delivery of the property sold, must in each case depend on the contract of sale and the circumstances of the case[5]. He does not, however, make himself a party to the contract of sale as does an agent acting for an undisclosed principal when he acts merely for an unidentified one[6], and it seems that the extent of the liability is one for non-delivery[7]. The duty to deliver is the other side of the coin that gives the auctioneer the right to sue for the price[8].

Contracts for the sale or other disposition of an interest in land made at public auction[9] are now both valid and enforceable on the fall of the hammer without writing or evidence in writing[10]. It is possible to provide that such a contract is merely a contact to enter into a written agreement of sale. In such circumstances the auctioneer might be empowered to sign the second, written contract of sale on behalf of the seller[11] and it is possible for the auctioneer to sign in such a way that he attracts personal liability on the contract[12].

1   As to the meaning of 'auctioneer' see PARA 2.
2   *Hanson v Roberdeau* (1792) Peake 120; *Franklyn v Lamond* (1847) 4 CB 637; *Evans v Evans* (1835) 3 Ad & El 132. See *Page v Sully* (1918) 63 Sol Jo 55. Whilst this may be regarded as axiomatic since the buyer is unaware of the fact of the agency, there have been dicta to the contrary on the basis that an auctioneer can only sell another's property: see eg *Mainprice v Westley* (1865) 6 B & S 420 at 429 per Blackburn J. That view is clearly erroneous, for an auctioneer can sell his own property: *Flint v Woodin* (1852) 9 Hare 618.
3   As to agency of auctioneers see PARA 7.
4   *Benton v Campbell, Parker & Co* [1925] 2 KB 410 at 414–415 per Salter J. There are dicta in *Mainprice v Westley* (1865) 6 B & S 420 suggesting that the auctioneer may escape liability by contracting merely as agent without disclosing his principal's name.
5   *Wood v Baxter* (1883) 49 LT 45; *Payne v Elsden* (1900) 17 TLR 161; *Salter v Woollams* (1841) 2 Man & G 650.
6   *Wood v Baxter* (1883) 49 LT 45.
7   *Wood v Baxter* (1883) 49 LT 45. See *Hanson v Roberdeau* (1792) Peake 120 and *Franklyn v Lamond* (1847) 4 CB 637 (where failure to deliver was, in each case, the complaint). *Benton v Campbell, Parker & Co* [1925] 2 KB 410 establishes that the auctioneer does not give any warranty as to title, save that he knows of no defect in that of the seller. See *Rainbow v Howkins* [1904] 2 KB 322 at 325, DC, preferring *Woolfe v Horne* (1877) 2 QBD 355 to *Mainprice v Westley* (1865) 6 B & S 420 ('We are of opinion, on the authority of *Woolfe v Horne*, which is a more recent decision than *Mainprice v Westley*, ... that an action for wrongful refusal to deliver a chattel sold at public auction may in some circumstances successfully be brought against the auctioneer, although the principal's name is disclosed to the buyer at the time of the sale').
8   *Benton v Campbell, Parker & Co* [1925] 2 KB 410. As to when auctioneers may sue in their own name see PARA 33.
9   As to the meaning of 'auction' see PARA 1.
10 See PARA 7 note 5.
11 As now permitted by the Law of Property (Miscellaneous Provisions) Act 1989 s 2(3): see SALE OF LAND vol 42 (Reissue) PARA 29 et seq. The power previously was only to sign the evidentiary memorandum under the Law of Property Act 1925 s 40 (now repealed).

12 See *Fisher v Marsh* (1865) 6 B & S 411. The statutory power enabling contracts for the sale of land to be signed by agents is novel and it remains to be seen what the ambit of such a liability, if any, might be.

28. Independent contractual liability. In some circumstances an auctioneer[1] will be held to have incurred independent direct contractual liability to the buyer. Where the conditions of sale provide that the auctioneer will repurchase goods, for example where a work of art turns out to be a forgery, this will give rise to contractual rights against the auctioneer[2].

1   As to the meaning of 'auctioneer' see PARA 2.
2   *Marie Zelinger de Balkany v Christie, Manson & Woods Ltd* (1995) 16 Tr LR 163.

29. Auctioneer joined as defendant. If the auctioneer[1] is made a defendant to a claim by the buyer for specific performance or rescission, he will in general be dismissed from the claim on paying the balance of the deposit into court after deducting his charges, but he will not be so dismissed if relief is claimed against him personally on some ground, such as his misconduct at the auction[2].

1   As to the meaning of 'auctioneer' see PARA 2.
2   *Heatley v Newton* (1881) 19 ChD 326, CA (where the allegations involved fraud so that payment into court of the deposit did not discharge the auctioneer). See *Annesley v Muggridge* (1816) 1 Madd 593; *Yates v Farebrother* (1819) 4 Madd 239 (both cases involving suits by sellers for the deposit, but the principles apply equally to claims by the buyer). In *Earl of Egmont v Smith* (1877) 6 ChD 469 it was suggested that if the deposit was small, the defendant should be joined only if he does not pay the sum into court.

30. Breach of warranty of authority and fraud. Where an auctioneer[1] sells property without or in excess of his authority, he is, like other agents, liable to the buyer for breach of warranty of authority[2]. Where the auctioneer sells goods of which his principal is not the true owner, a liability in conversion[3] will arise, and if the buyer finds himself sued by the true owner he may in turn seek to recover from the auctioneer. The auctioneer will only be liable for breach of warranty as to his seller's title if he has expressly warranted it[4].

The buyer is entitled to sue the auctioneer personally for any fraud to which the auctioneer is privy[5].

1   As to the meaning of 'auctioneer' see PARA 2.
2   *Anderson v John Croall & Sons Ltd* (1904) 6 F 153, Ct of Sess. See *Fay v Miller, Wilkins & Co* [1941] Ch 360, [1941] 2 All ER 18, CA, where the auctioneers were liable to the buyer for breach of warranty of authority in knocking the property down below the reserve because they took the further step of signing the then required memorandum in writing on his behalf. This was said to waive the conditional nature of the bid and its acceptance. Now that the memorandum is no longer required (see PARA 7 note 5) and both land and chattel sales are effected at the fall of the hammer, the position would seem to be the same in both types of sale, namely that purporting to sell under a reserve when the buyer is on notice either of the existence of one or of the right of the seller to fix one, will not give rise to liability on the part of the auctioneer for breach of warranty of authority. As to warranty of an agents' authority see AGENCY vol 1 (2008) PARAS 160–161.
3   As to auctioneers' liability for conversion see PARA 34.
4   See PARA 34.
5   *Heatley v Newton* (1881) 19 ChD 326, CA. See also PARA 50 text and notes 6, 7.

31. Liability as bailee. Normally specific goods are sold at auction[1]. In such sales property in the goods will, unless a contrary intention appears, pass to the buyer on the fall of the hammer[2]. Thereafter, the goods will belong to the buyer. If, as is sometimes provided by the auction conditions, the buyer is entitled to a certain time to collect the goods, in the interim the auctioneer[3] will hold them as bailee for him[4]. He will then be under a duty to take reasonable care of them[5]. If the property and risk in the goods do not pass to the buyer until, say, he has paid for and collected them, there will be no such liability on the part of the auctioneer to the buyer, but he will remain bailee for the seller, whose goods they still are.

1 As to the meaning of 'auction' see PARA 1.

2 See the Sale of Goods Act 1979 s 18 r 1; and *Dennant v Skinner and Collom* [1948] 2 KB 164, [1948] 2 All ER 29.

3 As to the meaning of 'auctioneer' see PARA 2.

4 As to bailment generally see BAILMENT AND PLEDGE.

5 The auctioneer's duty is not that of a bailee for reward: see BAILMENT AND PLEDGE.

32. Liability for misrepresentations. Whilst the auctioneer[1] will not incur personal civil liability to the buyer for misrepresentations under the Misrepresentation Act 1967[2], there seems no reason in principle why he should not, in appropriate circumstances, be liable in tort to the buyer for deceit[3], negligent misstatement[4] or contractually on a collateral warranty where he induces the formation of the contract of sale by making a false representation[5].

1 As to the meaning of 'auctioneer' see PARA 2.

2 *Resolute Maritime Inc v Nippon Kaiji Kyokai, The Skopas* [1983] 2 All ER 1, [1983] 1 WLR 857; applied in *Morin v Bonhams & Brooks Ltd* [2003] EWHC 467 (Comm), [2003] 2 All ER (Comm) 36, [2003] All ER (D) 267 (Mar). As to the Misrepresentation Act 1967 see MISREPRESENTATION AND FRAUD.

3 See *Derry v Peek* (1889) 14 App Cas 337, 58 LJ Ch 864, HL; and MISREPRESENTATION AND FRAUD vol 31 (2003 Reissue) PARA 789 et seq; TORT vol 97 (2010) PARA 519.

4 See *Hedley Byrne & Co Ltd v Heller & Partners Ltd* [1964] AC 465, [1963] 2 All ER 575, HL; and MISREPRESENTATION AND FRAUD vol 31 (2003 Reissue) PARA 798; NEGLIGENCE vol 78 (2010) PARA 14. See also the discussion in *Morin v Bonhams & Brooks Ltd* [2003] EWHC 467 (Comm), [2003] 2 All ER (Comm) 36, [2003] All ER (D) 267 (Mar); affd [2003] EWCA Civ 1802, [2004] 1 All ER (Comm) 880, [2004] 1 Lloyd's Rep 702, [2003] All ER (D) 334 (Dec) (misstatement of kilometrage of car made in catalogue by foreign subsidiary of London auctioneer); and *Thomson v Christie Manson & Woods Ltd* [2005] EWCA Civ 555, [2005] All ER (D) 176 (May) (catalogue entry for antique vases not negligent).

In *McCullagh v Lane Fox & Partners Ltd* (1995) 49 Con LR 124, [1996] 1 EGLR 35, CA, it was held that an estate agent who misrepresented the acreage of a property was not liable to the buyer; the agent's immunity stemmed partly from a finding that it was not reasonable for the buyer to rely on the agent rather than his own surveyor and partly from an effective disclaimer of liability which, in the circumstances, was held to be reasonable under the Unfair Contract Terms Act 1977 (see CONTRACT vol 9(1) (Reissue) PARA 790 et seq). However, the same reasoning may not apply to an auctioneer selling property where sales are not subject to contract and where it may not be reasonable to put the buyer to his own inquiries. Where a disclaimer is found to be reasonable under the Unfair Contract Terms Act 1977, it may still be non binding as unfair under the Unfair Terms in Consumer Contracts Regulations 1999, SI 1999/2083 (see CONTRACT). See also *Duncan Investments Ltd v Underwoods (a firm)* [1998] EGCS 98, [1998] 6 PNLR 754, CA (where a similar disclaimer as the one in *McCullagh v Lane Fox & Partners* (1995) 49 Con LR 124, [1996] 1 EGLR 35, CA, was held ineffective; the agent went beyond the advice normally given on behalf of a seller in connection with the sale).

5 See *Andrews v Hopkinson* [1957] 1 QB 229, [1956] 3 All ER 422; and CONTRACT vol 9(1) (Reissue) PARA 767. In *Ahmed v Landstone Leisure Ltd* [2009] EWHC 125 (Ch), [2009] BPIR 227, [2009] All ER (D) 69 (Feb), a combination of the auction catalogue, the site layout, the 'For Sale' signs, and the statements made by the auctioneer until he had read out an addendum at the auction, to the effect that any reference to a site area of 2.25 acres should be ignored, all demonstrated that down to that point, the auctioneer had been representing that what was being sold was the whole site, which was about 2.25 acres in extent, and not part of it; in those circumstances, there was a seriously arguable case that the sale contract and accompanying cheque had been induced by misrepresentation ('It is said on behalf of the Respondent that an auctioneer usually has no implied or ostensible authority to make representations. I very much

doubt whether that principle can apply where the auctioneer is merely identifying the property he is offering for sale. That after all is the very job he is employed to do': per Judge Purle QC at [26].)

(6) AUCTIONEER'S RIGHTS AGAINST BUYER

33. When auctioneer may sue in own name. An auctioneer[1] may, by reason of his lien[2] on or special property in goods, maintain a claim in his own name for the price of goods sold and delivered by him[3]. This is so even where he sells and delivers as agent[4] for a disclosed principal[5], but this right does not extend, in the absence of special contract, to suing for the purchase money of land if he sells as agent for a disclosed principal[6], or for rent for the use and occupation of land let by him by auction[7].

There are dicta which suggest that the right to sue, apart from those cases where the auctioneer sues on a quite separate contract, is dependent on the continued existence of the lien[8]. However, it is suggested that the better view is that it arises out of the lien but does not depend on continued possession; where, as is often the case, the auctioneer wishes to sue just because he has parted with the possession, which is the basis of the lien, he sues on an implied contract arising out of the delivery without payment[9].

Where the auctioneer is suing on his own account and not merely for the principal, as where he has already accounted for the sale price to him, he will be unaffected by any set-off which the buyer may have against the seller[10]. If the auctioneer can be taken to have assented to such a settlement or had notice not to account to the seller, he may be disentitled to recover from the buyer[11]. He will also be unable to recover if it has been agreed that the price should be satisfied otherwise than by payment[12].

Once, however, the auctioneer has been paid his fees and charges he cannot recover in circumstances where there is a set-off, since he is then merely suing for his principal[13]. Where the goods sold are not the property of the seller, and are claimed by the true owner before payment by the buyer, the auctioneer cannot maintain a claim for the price even though the buyer has taken away the goods under an express promise to pay[14].

1   As to the meaning of 'auctioneer' see PARA 2.

2   As to auctioneers' lien see PARA 25.

3   *Williams v Millington* (1788) 1 Hy Bl 81. See *Benton v Campbell, Parker & Co Ltd* [1925] 2 KB 410 at 416 per Salter J ('The auctioneer sues for the price by virtue of his special property and his lien, and also, in most cases, by virtue of his contract with the buyer, that the price shall be paid into his hands, and not by virtue of the contract of sale'). See also *Wilson & Sons v Pike* [1949] 1 KB 176 at 182, [1948] 2 All ER 267 at 269, CA, per Tucker LJ. This right to sue in his own name does not impose a duty obtain the purchase money: *Fordham v Christie, Manson & Woods Ltd* (1977) 121 Sol Jo 529, 244 Estates Gazette 213. Note that the auctioneer's right extends to the whole price, not merely that necessary to cover his own charges: *Chelmsford Auctions Ltd v Poole* [1973] QB 542, [1973] 1 All ER 810, CA.

4   As to agency of auctioneers see PARA 7.

5   *Williams v Millington* (1788) 1 Hy Bl 81. See *Freeman v Farrow* (1886) 2 TLR 547, where an auctioneer was held entitled to sue even where the sale was effected by the owner himself on the auctioneer's premises, the contract having specifically provided therefor. However, in sales outside the ring in cattle auctions the analysis is different: see *Murphy v Howlett* (1960) 176 Estates Gazette 311. See also *Mackenzie v Cormack* 1950 SC 183, Ct of Sess, where it was held that an auctioneer, although acting on behalf of a disclosed principal, could sue the buyer for the payment of the price of the goods sold to him irrespective of whether the sale was conducted in the auction room or on the seller's premises.

    In *Cleave v Moore* (1857) 28 LTOS 255, and *Hodgens v Keon* [1894] 2 IR 657, an auctioneer who had taken an IOU in respect of a deposit on the sale of land was allowed to sue the buyer, but the ratio decidendi was that by so doing the auctioneer had in fact advanced the money to the buyer. See also *Robinson, Fisher and Harding v Behar* [1927] 1 KB 513. In this situation the auctioneer's rights to sue are unaffected by factors vitiating the contract of sale: *Hindle v Brown* (1907) 98 LT 44; affd (1908) 98 LT 791, CA. Where a buyer fails to pay the deposit as required by the conditions of sale, the auctioneer may put up the property for sale again and the buyer will be denied specific performance: *Morrow v Carty* [1957] NI 174.

6   *Cherry v Anderson* (1876) IR 10 CL 204.

7   *Evans v Evans* (1835) 3 Ad & El 132; *Fisher v Marsh* (1865) 6 B & S 411. As to the meaning of 'auction' see PARA 1.

8   *Coppin v Walker* (1816) 7 Taunt 237. See note 9.

9   *Coppin v Craig* (1816) 7 Taunt 243. *Coppin v Walker* (1816) 7 Taunt 237 can be explained on the basis that the auctioneer's actions negatived any such implication of a contract.

10   *Robinson v Rutter* (1855) 4 E & B 954; *Manley & Sons Ltd v Berkett* [1912] 2 KB 329.

11   *Grice v Kenrick* (1870) LR 5 QB 340.

12   *Bartlett v Purnell* (1836) 4 Ad & El 792.

13   *Holmes v Tutton* (1855) 5 E & B 65; *Manley & Sons Ltd v Berkett* [1912] 2 KB 329.

14   *Dickenson v Naul* (1833) 4 B & Ad 638.

(7) AUCTIONEER IN RELATION TO THIRD PERSONS

(i) Liabilities

34.   Liability for conversion. A claim for conversion lies against an auctioneer[1] who, with or without knowledge of the true ownership of goods, has dealt with the property in and possession of those goods without the true owner's consent or authority[2], unless the case is governed by the Factors Act 1889[3]. The auctioneer's liability is strict and he is liable to the true owner even if he is completely ignorant of the want of title or the right to sell of the seller-principal[4].

A mere advertisement for sale without an actual sale does not constitute a conversion; nor does the return of unsold goods to the seller[5]. Greater difficulty, however, surrounds situations where the auctioneer does not effect the sale itself but plays some role in bringing the seller and buyer together. If the auctioneer is in possession of the goods but the seller and buyer effect a private treaty sale, it has been suggested that no act of conversion has been committed by the auctioneer[6]. However, it has been held that where auctioneers had an elaborate provisional bid procedure designed to bring about a private treaty sale of a lot that had not been sold at auction[7], they were liable in conversion and could not be said to be mere conduits[8].

Normally the sale of goods not owned by the seller-principal effected by the auctioneer will not vest title in the buyer[9]. Even where it does by virtue of the recognised exceptions to the general principle[10], this does not assist the auctioneer as the sale was not only intended to, but also had the effect of, depriving the owner of property.

It has been suggested that when goods are delivered to an auctioneer by a mercantile agent acting in the course of his ordinary business who is in possession of the goods with the true owner's consent, the auctioneer is not liable for dealing with the goods, provided the dealing is in good faith and without notice of the true owner's claim[11]. However, that requires the delivery to the auctioneer to be treated as a 'disposition' and that this is so has been denied[12].

If the auctioneer has notice of the adverse claim of the true owner, he is thereafter liable for the value, not only of goods sold by him, but also of those unsold by him and returned to his principal[13].

When the auctioneer's liability is established, the measure of damages is the true value of the goods, normally at the time when the judgment is given[14], and not merely the sum realised at the auction[15].

The auctioneer may also be liable for failing to deliver the goods up to the true owner who claims them, but he is entitled to make reasonable inquiries[16]. In appropriate cases he may interplead[17].

There can, however, be no liability if the principal had title at the time of sale. This may involve a question of foreign law[18]. On the other hand, an auctioneer may find himself exposed to a conversion claim by virtue of the application of a foreign limitation period more generous to the claimant than corresponding English periods[19].

1   As to the meaning of 'auctioneer' see PARA 2.
2   *Barker v Furlong* [1891] 2 Ch 172; *Consolidated Co v Curtis & Son* [1892] 1 QB 495; *Brown v Hickinbotham* (1881) 50 LJQB 426, CA; *Featherstonhaugh v Johnson* (1818) 8 Taunt 237; *Adamson v Jarvis* (1827) 4 Bing 66; *Cochrane v Rymill* (1879) 40 LT 744, CA; *Hardacre v Stewart* (1804) 5 Esp 103. See *Kuwait Airways Corpn v Iraqi Airways Co* [2001] 1 All ER (Comm) 557, [2001] 3 WLR 1117, CA; affd [2002] UKHL 19, [2002] 2 AC 883, [2002] 3 All ER 209. As to conversion see TORT vol 45(2) (Reissue) PARA 548 et seq.
3   See *Shenstone & Co v Hilton* [1894] 2 QB 452; *Waddington & Sons v Neale & Sons* (1907) 96 LT 786. As to dispositions under the Factors Act 1889 see AGENCY vol 1 (2008) PARA 148.
4   *Union Transport Finance Ltd v British Car Auctions Ltd* [1978] 2 All ER 385, 246 Estates Gazette 131, CA.
5   *Marcq v Christie Manson & Woods Ltd (t/a Christie's)* [2003] EWCA Civ 731, [2004] QB 286, [2003] 3 All ER 561.
6   *Cochrane v Rymill* (1879) 40 LT 744, CA (obiter, where the auctioneer was in fact held liable, as he had dealt with the property by giving the seller an advance on the proceeds of sale and had a lien on the goods). See other cases where auctioneers were held not liable in conversion as they acted as a mere conduit: *National Mercantile Bank v Rymill* (1881) 44 LT 767, CA (sale by private treaty before auction, auctioneer taking his commission and giving delivery order to buyer); *Turner v Hockey* (1887) 56 LJQB 301 (mere communication of offer: see explanation given in *Consolidated Co v Curtis & Son* [1892] 1 QB 495 at 502–503 per Collins J); *Barker v Furlong* [1891] 2 Ch 172 (mere setting of price (obiter)). See the text and notes 7–8.
7   As to the meaning of 'auction' see PARA 1.
8   *RH Willis & Son (a firm) v British Car Auctions Ltd* [1978] 2 All ER 392, [1978] 1 WLR 438, CA (casting doubt on *National Mercantile Bank v Rymill* (1881) 44 LT 767, CA; and *Turner v Hockey* (1887) 56 LJQB 301). See note 6.
9   'Nemo dat quod non habet': see the Sale of Goods Act 1979 s 21(1); and SALE OF GOODS AND SUPPLY OF SERVICES vol 41 (2005 Reissue) PARA 150 et seq.
10 See the Sale of Goods Act 1979 ss 21–23, 25; and SALE OF LAND vol 42 (Reissue) PARA 150 et seq. The recognised exceptions used to include the rule of market overt, which was abolished by the Sale of Goods (Amendment) Act 1994 s 1 as from 3 January 1995. The rule provided that where goods, other than goods belonging to the Crown, were sold in market overt according to the usage of the market, the buyer acquired a good title to the goods, provided that he bought them in good faith and without any notice of any defect or want of title on the part of the seller. A buyer after 3 January 1995 is not able to claim title by reason of a purchase in market overt, but a seller who claims to be the true owner by virtue of his purchase in market overt before 3 January 1995 will continue to be able to plead that exception, and an auctioneer acting for one who can rely on the exception is not guilty of conversion. As to the abolition of market overt see further MARKETS, FAIRS AND STREET TRADING vol 29(2) (Reissue) PARA 1026.
11 See *Shenstone & Co v Hilton* [1894] 2 QB 452. See also AGENCY.
12 *Waddington & Sons v Neale & Sons* (1907) 96 LT 786.
13 *Davis v Artingstall* (1880) 49 LJ Ch 609.
14 *Sachs v Miklos* [1948] 2 KB 23, [1948] 1 All ER 67, CA.
15 *Davis v Artingstall* (1880) 49 LJ Ch 609 per Fry J.
16 *Lee v Bayes and Robinson* (1856) 18 CB 599; *Turner v Ford* (1846) 15 M &W 212.
17 As to interpleader by auctioneers see PARA 39.
18 *Winkworth v Christie, Manson & Woods Ltd* [1980] Ch 496, [1980] 1 All ER 1121.
19 See *Gotha City v Sotheby's (No 2)* (1998) Times, 8 October.

35. Other duties to third parties. An auctioneer[1] owes a general duty of care to third parties who attend auctions[2] and especially duties to ensure their safety whilst at the auction premises over which the auctioneer has control. This could include the seller's premises[3]. He also may in appropriate circumstances be liable in nuisance[4]. However, the provision of online auction services does not by itself give rise to any joint liability on the part of the auctioneer for trade mark infringements committed by users of its services[5].

An auctioneer acting in the course of a business of dealing in works of art is jointly and severally liable with the seller for the payment of resale royalty on works of art in which copyright subsists, on any sale of such a work which is a resale subsequent to the first transfer of ownership by the author ('droit de suite')[6]. Auctioneers' conditions of sale commonly provide that buyers are liable for payment of the royalty.

1 As to the meaning of 'auctioneer' see PARA 2.
2 See NEGLIGENCE. As to the meaning of 'auction' see PARA 1.
3 *Walker v Crabb* (1916) 33 TLR 119; *Kenworthy v Stephenson & Son, Thorp and Whittaker* [1997] CLY para 3766 (auctioneers admitted liability where a visitor to a horse auction was injured by a horse being tried out by a potential buyer).
4 *Benjamin v Storr* (1874) LR 9 CP 400. As to nuisance see generally NUISANCE vol 78 (2010) PARA 101.
5 See *L'Oréal SA v eBay International AG* [2009] EWHC 1094 (Ch), [2009] RPC 693, [2010] IP & T 95, [2009] All ER (D) 169 (Jun).
6 See the Artist's Resale Right Regulations 2006, SI 2006/346; and COPYRIGHT, DESIGN RIGHT AND RELATED RIGHTS vol 9(2) (2006 Reissue) PARA 774 et seq.

36. Executorship de son tort. If an auctioneer[1] intermeddles with the estate of a deceased person without the authority of a properly constituted executor, he may render himself liable as an executor de son tort[2].

1 As to the meaning of 'auctioneer' see PARA 2.
2 See *Nulty v Fagan* (1888) 22 LR Ir 604. As to executors de son tort see WILLS AND INTESTACY vol 103 (2010) PARAS 1263.

(ii) Rights

37. Right to possession of goods. By virtue of his lien[1] and special property an auctioneer[2] can maintain a claim for trespass[3] or conversion[4] against persons wrongfully interfering with or converting goods[5]. He has, however, no such property in, or right of claim in respect of, unsevered fixtures because these are land and an auctioneer employed to sell such fixtures has only a right to detach and remove them and not, before such severance, possession of them[6].

1 As to agents' liens see AGENCY vol 1 (2008) PARA 114 et seq.
2 As to the meaning of 'auctioneer' see PARA 2.
3 As to trespass to goods see TORT vol 45(2) (Reissue) PARAS 659–660.
4 As to conversion see TORT vol 45(2) (Reissue) PARA 548 et seq. As to the distinction between trespass and conversion see TORT vol 45(2) (Reissue) PARA 661.
5 *Williams v Millington* (1788) 1 Hy Bl 81 at 85 per Heath J; *Robinson v Rutter* (1855) 4 E & B 954 at 956. See also PARA 18.
6 *Davis v Danks* (1849) 3 Exch 435.

38. Privilege from distress. Goods delivered to an auctioneer[1] for sale are privileged from distress[2] whilst on the auctioneer's premises, as being chattels delivered to a person exercising a public trade to be dealt with in the way of his trade or employ[3]. The privilege attaches to the goods either at the auctioneer's ordinary place of business or on premises temporarily hired for the auction[4], and even though the auctioneer's occupation of the premises is not lawful[5]. It also extends to goods in the yard of a house[6]. It does not, however, cover goods which are on the owner's premises, and such goods remain liable to distraint although they are the subject matter of a sale by auction[7]. The law is now largely governed by statute[8].

1 As to the meaning of 'auctioneer' see PARA 2.
2 As to trade privileges from distress see DISTRESS vol 13 (2007 Reissue) PARA 932 et seq.
3 See *Adams v Grane and Osborne* (1833) 1 Cr & M 380 (privilege is granted for the benefit of trade).
4 As to the meaning of 'auction' see PARA 1.
5 *Brown v Arundell* (1850) 10 CB 54.
6 *Williams v Holmes* (1853) 8 Exch 861.
7 *Lyons v Elliott* (1876) 1 QBD 210.
8 See the Law of Distress Amendment Act 1908, which gives the owner of the goods suffering distress, not being interested in the premises where distraint is carried out, the right to serve notice of his interest in the goods; and DISTRESS vol 13 (2007 Reissue) PARA 951 et seq. The Act is repealed by the Tribunals, Courts and Enforcement Act 2007 ss 86, 146, Sch 14 para 20 Sch 23 Pt 4 as from a day to be appointed. From that date, distress will be replaced by the procedure of enforcement by taking control of goods under the Tribunals, Courts and Enforcement Act 2007 s 62(1), Sch 12, but provision is made for goods to be made exempt from the procedure by regulations: see Sch 12 paras 3(1), 4(1), 11(2). At the date at which this volume states the law, no such day had been appointed. As to enforcement by taking control see CIVIL PROCEDURE vol 12 (2009) PARA 1389 et seq. As to goods which maybe taken see CIVIL PROCEDURE vol 12 (2009) PARA 1392.

39. Interpleader by auctioneer. Where adverse claims are made to goods or money in the hands of an auctioneer[1], the auctioneer may interplead[2], subject to the ordinary rules governing interpleader[3]. In order to interplead the auctioneer must be subject to a claim or expect to be sued in respect of the goods[4]. If that is not the case but a third party disputes the seller's right to sell, the auctioneer will be advised not to put the lot up for sale without securing an express indemnity from the seller.

1 As to the meaning of 'auctioneer' see PARA 2.
2 See CPR Sch 1 RSC Ord 17 r 1(1)(a). As to interpleader see CIVIL PROCEDURE vol 12 (2009) PARA 1585 et seq.
3 For the application to auctioneers of the ordinary rules as to the identity of the property claimed see *Wright v Freeman* (1879) 48 LJQB 276; *Hoggart v Cutts* (1841) 1 Cr & Ph 197. As to collusion see *Thompson v Wright* (1884) 13 QBD 632; *Ingham v Walker* (1887) 3 TLR 448, CA.
4 See CPR Sch 1 RSC Ord 17 r 1(1)(a).

3. THE AUCTION SALE

(1) CONDUCT OF THE AUCTION

40. Time and place of sale. There are no special restrictions affecting the time and place when and where a sale by auction[1] may be held[2], and an auctioneer[3] has the same right of admission to a public market to exercise his calling as have traders entering to sell their own goods[4].

A sale by auction should not be held at any place in contravention of any person's legal rights, for example, in a house in respect of which restrictive covenants against sales by auction exist[5], or under such circumstances as to constitute an infringement of market rights[6]. An injunction will not be granted to restrain the sale by auction on leasehold premises of furniture belonging to the house[7].

In livestock sales there are special statutory controls relating to the premises[8].

1 As to the meaning of 'auction' see PARA 1.
2 *Keith v Reid* (1870) LR 2 Sc & Div 39, HL. The restriction on sales on Sundays imposed by the Sunday Observance Act 1677 s 1, was repealed as obsolete by the Statute Law (Repeals) Act 1969 s 1, Schedule Pt IV. As to Sunday trading see TRADE AND INDUSTRY vol 97 (2010) PARA 908 et seq. See also *Phillips v Parnaby* [1934] 2 KB 299, DC; *Dolton, Bournes & Dolton Ltd v Osmond* [1955] 2 All ER 258, [1955] 1 WLR 621, CA.
3 As to the meaning of 'auctioneer' see PARA 2.
4 *London Corpn v Lyons Son & Co (Fruit Brokers) Ltd* [1936] Ch 78, CA. See *Nicholls v Tavistock UDC* [1923] 2 Ch 18. As to the right to attend markets see MARKETS, FAIRS AND STREET TRADING vol 29(2) (Reissue) PARA 1024.
5 *Toleman v Portbury* (1872) LR 7 QB 344.
6 *Elwes v Payne* (1879) 12 ChD 468. See *Abergavenny Improvement Comrs v Straker* (1889) 42 ChD 83; and *Hailsham Cattle Market Co v Tolman* [1915] 2 Ch 1, CA. As to market rights see MARKETS, FAIRS AND STREET TRADING vol 29(2) (Reissue) PARA 1021 et seq.
7 *Reeves v Cattell* (1876) 24 WR 485. Cf *Moses v Taylor* (1862) 11 WR 81.
8 See PARA 46.

41. Advertisement of auction. The advertisement of an auction[1] is merely an intimation of an intention to sell, and therefore, in the absence of fraud, intending buyers who attend an auction have no right of claim if the property is not put up for sale[2]. Even when the property is put up, it may be withdrawn before the fall of the hammer[3].

When, however, the advertisement amounts to a representation of fact that the auctioneer is authorised to sell, and this representation is fraudulent, persons incurring expense on the faith of it can sue the auctioneer in tort[4].

1 As to the meaning of 'auction' see PARA 1.
2 *Harris v Nickerson* (1873) LR 8 QB 286.
3 *Fenwick v Macdonald, Fraser & Co* (1904) 6 F 850, Ct of Sess. As to withdrawal of property see PARA 55.
4 *Richardson v Silvester* (1873) LR 9 QB 34.

42. Particulars and conditions of sale. It is customary for an auctioneer[1] to settle the particulars and conditions of sale[2] on sales of goods, but not on sales of real property[3]. When he undertakes to settle the conditions, he must do so with the skill and knowledge which may reasonably be expected of one who practises as an auctioneer[4], and if he sells without imposing conditions which are usual and prudent for the seller's protection, he may, even in the case of a sale of real property, be held liable for negligence at the suit of the seller[5].

It is necessary in order that the conditions of sale may be incorporated into the contract of sale that they be communicated to bidders, and this can be done by notice, for example by exhibition in the auction room[6] or by reproduction in the auction catalogue. Such communication must take place before the conclusion of the contract[7].

Most conditions affect the seller, auctioneer and the buyer, that is the highest bidder. Some, however, affect bidders generally[8]. If such conditions are to bind bidders generally they must do so by virtue of the court finding a collateral contract between the auctioneer and the bidders[9].

Conditions of an exclusionary nature or those modifying or limiting the liability of the auctioneer or seller are subject to statutory control[10] whereby they may be rendered void[11] or subject to a test of reasonableness[12].

A number of conditions are implied by the Sale of Goods Act 1979[13]. In relation to auctions, those of widest application are the implied conditions of correspondence with description and satisfactory quality. Auction sales are sales by description and are therefore affected by the statutory provisions[14]. Descriptions, especially statements about provenance in fine art sales, are invariably subject to some form of express caveat or exclusion of liability in auction conditions. To be valid, these must satisfy the tests of reasonableness and fairness[15]. As regards satisfactory quality, the implied term only applies to sellers who sell in the course of a business[16]. Where, as is frequently the case, the auctioneer sells on behalf of a principal who is not selling in the course of a business the implied condition will still apply unless either the auctioneer takes steps to bring to the notice of the buyer the fact that the seller is a private seller or the buyer knows that fact[17].

1   As to the meaning of 'auctioneer' see PARA 2.

2   In *Couchman v Hill* [1947] KB 554 at 559, [1947] 1 All ER 103 at 105, CA, Scott LJ expressed the view that a printed condition that the seller will take no responsibility for errors of description of things or animals specifically offered for sale on inspection is reasonable for visible defects, but not for qualities which are invisible, and he recommended the point for consideration by the auctioneers' associations. Cf *Druce & Co Ltd v Leveson* (1952) 102 L Jo 721 (where the buyer was held to have assented to a printed condition to which attention was drawn by the auctioneer). Conditions of sale are now generally subject to the Unfair Contract Terms Act 1977 (see CONTRACT vol 9(1) (Reissue) PARA 790 et seq) and the Unfair Terms in Consumer Contracts Regulations 1999, SI 1999/2083 (see CONTRACT). See the text and note 10. As to the sale of goods by auction see CONSUMER PROTECTION vol 21 (2011) PARA 564 et seq; and as to the sale of land by auction see SALE OF LAND vol 42 (Reissue) PARAS 84–85.

3   *Pike v Wilson* (1854) 1 Jur NS 59.

4   See PARA 16.

5   *Denew v Daverell* (1813) 3 Camp 451.

6   *Mesnard v Aldridge* (1801) 3 Esp 271; *Bywater v Richardson* (1834) 1 Ad & El 508. Cf *Torrance v Bolton* (1872) 8 Ch App 118 (property described in printed particulars; subsequent oral description not enough to show buyer not misled). See *Scriven Bros & Co v Hindley & Co* [1913] 3 KB 564. As to the construction of a particular condition see *Robinson, Fisher and Harding v Behar* [1927] 1 KB 513 (where a condition that lots uncleared 'shall' be resold was held to be purely permissive).

7   *Dennant v Skinner and Collom* [1948] 2 KB 164, [1948] 2 All ER 29. As to the incorporation of written terms see CONTRACT vol 9(1) (Reissue) PARA 688 et seq.

8   Eg conditions relating to the conduct of the auction: control of bidding, withdrawal of bids, etc.

9   As found in *Shandel v Jacobs* 1949 (1) SA 320.

10 See the Unfair Contract Terms Act 1977 (see CONTRACT vol 9(1) (Reissue) PARA 790 et seq); and the Unfair Terms in Consumer Contracts Regulations 1999, SI 1999/2083 (see CONTRACT). The statutory provisions apply both to the conditions of sale affecting buyers and to the consignment conditions regulating the relationship between the auctioneer and his seller client.

11 See the Unfair Contract Terms Act 1977 s 6(1) (s 6(1), (2) amended by the Sale of Goods Act 1979 s 63, Sch 2 para 19); and CONTRACT vol 9(1) (Reissue) PARA 826; SALE OF GOODS AND SUPPLY OF SERVICES vol 41 (2005 Reissue) PARA 103; CONSUMER PROTECTION vol 21 (2011) PARA 431.

12 See the Unfair Contract Terms Act 1977 s 6(2), (3) (s 6(2) as amended: see note 11). As to the test of reasonableness see SALE OF GOODS AND SUPPLY OF SERVICES vol 41 (2005 Reissue) PARA 104; CONSUMER PROTECTION vol 21 (2011) PARA 432.

As originally enacted, the Unfair Contract Terms Act 1977 provided that a sale by auction was not, in any circumstances, treated as a consumer sale for the purposes of the provisions relating to the exclusion of terms implied by the Sale of Goods Act 1979: see the Unfair Contract Terms Act 1977 s 12(2); and CONTRACT vol 9(1) (Reissue) PARA 832; CONSUMER PROTECTION vol 21 (2011) PARA 431. As from 31 March 2003, the Unfair Contract Terms Act 1977 was amended so as to provide that a sale by auction is not to be regarded as a consumer sale if the buyer: (1) is an individual and the goods are second hand goods sold at public auction at which individuals have the opportunity of attending the sale in person; (2) is not an individual and the goods are sold by auction or by competitive tender: see s 12(2) (substituted by SI 2002/3045). There is, however, no similar provision with regard to the Unfair Terms in Consumer Contracts Regulations 1999, SI 1999/2083: see CONTRACT.

13 See the Sale of Goods Act 1979 s 12 (implied terms about title), s 13 (sale by description), s 14 (implied terms about quality and fitness), s 15 (sale by sample); and SALE OF GOODS AND SUPPLY OF SERVICES vol 41 (2005 Reissue) PARAS 69 et seq; CONSUMER PROTECTION vol 21 (2011) PARA 426.

14 See the Sale of Goods Act 1979 s 13 (amended by the Sale and Supply of Goods Act 1994 s 7, Sch 2 para 5(4)); and SALE OF GOODS AND SUPPLY OF SERVICES vol 41 (2005 Reissue) PARAS 72–74.

15 See the Unfair Contract Terms Act 1977 s 11, Sch 2; and the Unfair Terms in Consumer Contracts Regulations 1999, SI 1999/2083, regs 5, 6.

16 See the Sale of Goods Act 1979 s 14(2) (substituted by the Sale and Supply of Goods Act 1994 s 1(1)); and SALE OF GOODS AND SUPPLY OF SERVICES vol 41 (2005 Reissue) PARA 77 et seq.

17 See the Sale of Goods Act 1979 s 14(5); and SALE OF GOODS AND SUPPLY OF SERVICES vol 41 (2005 Reissue) PARA 82. An undisclosed principal may additionally be exposed to liability to a buyer for breach of such an implied term: see *Boyter v Thomson* [1995] 2 AC 628, [1995] 3 All ER 135, HL.

43. Sale in lots. Where property is put up for sale[1] by auction[2] in lots, each lot is prima facie deemed to be the subject of a separate contract of sale[3]. For the purposes of stamp duty[4], the sale of each lot is normally treated as a separate contract[5].

1 'Sale' includes a bargain and sale as well as a sale and delivery: Sale of Goods Act 1979 s 61(1).
2 As to the meaning of 'auction' see PARA 1.
3 Sale of Goods Act 1979 s 57(1). 'Contract of sale' includes an agreement to sell as well as a sale: s 61(1). As to contracts of sale see further SALE OF GOODS AND SUPPLY OF SERVICES vol 41 (2005 Reissue) PARA 27 et seq. As to the law of contract generally see CONTRACT.
4 As to stamp duty see STAMP DUTIES AND STAMP DUTY RESERVE TAX.
5 *Roots v Lord Dormer* (1832) 4 B & Ad 77; *Watling v Horwood* (1847) 12 Jur 48; *A-G v Cohen* [1937] 1 KB 478, [1937] 1 All ER 27, CA.

44. Property subject to fixed agricultural charge. An auctioneer[1] selling by auction[2] property subject to a fixed agricultural charge[3] is not concerned to see that the statutory obligations governing the right to sell the property[4] have been complied with notwithstanding that he may be aware of the existence of the charge[5].

1 As to the meaning of 'auctioneer' see PARA 2.
2 As to the meaning of 'auction' see PARA 1.
3 As to fixed agricultural charges see the Agricultural Credits Act 1928 s 5(3); and AGRICULTURAL PRODUCTION AND MARKETING vol 1 (2008) PARA 1328 et seq.
4 See the Agricultural Credits Act 1928 s 6(1), (2); and AGRICULTURAL PRODUCTION AND MARKETING vol 1 (2008) PARA 1329.

5   See the Agricultural Credits Act 1928 s 6(3); and AGRICULTURAL PRODUCTION AND MARKETING
    vol 1 (2008) PARA 1329.

45.   Sale of residential investment property by public auction.   Special rights of
first refusal are granted to certain tenants[1] such that a landlord[2] may not dispose
of any estate or interest[3] in qualifying premises[4] unless he has served a notice[5] on
the tenants conferring a right of first refusal[6]. This regime was originally geared
to private treaty sales, but subsequent legislation has provided an alternative
procedure where the landlord wishes, as is commonly the case, to dispose of his
residential investments by public auction[7].

There are, in particular, special notice requirements where the landlord
proposes to make the disposal by means of a sale at a public auction[8]. A landlord
commits an offence if, without reasonable excuse, he makes a relevant disposal
affecting any qualifying premises without having first complied with the notice
requirements[9], or in contravention of any prohibition or restriction imposed[10] by
the Landlord and Tenant Act 1987[11]. Where a landlord has failed to serve notice
or has failed to comply with the statutory requirements[12], the tenants have
various rights[13] against the buyer[14].

These provisions thus modify the general rule that a sale by auction is
complete when the auctioneer announces its completion by the fall of the
hammer.

1   Any reference in the Landlord and Tenant Act 1987 Pt I (ss 1–20) to a tenant of a particular
    description is to be construed, in relation to any time when the interest under his tenancy has
    ceased to be vested in him, as a reference to the person who is for the time being the successor in
    title to that interest: s 20(3). As to qualifying tenants see LANDLORD AND TENANT vol 27(3)
    (2006 Reissue) PARA 1748.
2   As to landlords to whose premises the right of first refusal applies see LANDLORD AND TENANT
    vol 27(3) (2006 Reissue) PARA 1747.
3   See LANDLORD AND TENANT vol 27(3) (2006 Reissue) PARA 1750.
4   Ie any premises to which at the time of the disposal the Landlord and Tenant Act 1987 Pt I
    applies: see LANDLORD AND TENANT vol 27(3) (2006 Reissue) PARA 1746.
5   Ie in accordance with the Landlord and Tenant Act 1987 s 5B: see the text to note 8; and
    LANDLORD AND TENANT vol 27(3) (2006 Reissue) PARA 1754.
6   As to the statutory requirements see the Landlord and Tenant Act 1987 ss 6–10; and as to
    tenants' right of first refusal see further LANDLORD AND TENANT vol 27(3) (2006 Reissue) PARA
    1744 et seq.
7   See the Landlord and Tenant Act 1987, as amended by the Housing Act 1996; and the text and
    notes 8–14. See further LANDLORD AND TENANT.
8   See the Landlord and Tenant Act 1987 s 5B (added by the Housing Act 1996 s 92(1), Sch 6 Pt I);
    and LANDLORD AND TENANT vol 27(3) (2006 Reissue) PARA 1754. As to the meaning of
    'auction' see PARA 1.
9   Ie under the Landlord and Tenant Act 1987 s 5B: see the text to note 8; and LANDLORD AND
    TENANT vol 27(3) (2006 Reissue) PARA 1754.
10 Ie by the Landlord and Tenant Act 1987 ss 6–10: see LANDLORD AND TENANT vol 27(3) (2006
    Reissue) PARA 1758 et seq.
11 See the Landlord and Tenant Act 1987 s 10A(1) (s 10A added by the Housing Act 1996 s 91(1));
    and LANDLORD AND TENANT vol 27(3) (2006 Reissue) PARA 1782. A person guilty of an offence
    under the Landlord and Tenant Act 1987 s 10A is liable on summary conviction to a fine not
    exceeding level 5 on the standard scale: s 10A(2) (as so added). As to failure to comply with
    tenants' right of first refusal see further s 10A(3)–(5) (as so added); and LANDLORD AND
    TENANT vol 27(3) (2006 Reissue) PARA 1782. As to the standard scale see SENTENCING AND
    DISPOSITION OF OFFENDERS vol 92 (2010) PARA 142.
12 See note 6.
13 Ie the right to information as to the terms of disposal (see the Landlord and Tenant Act 1987
    s 11A); the right of qualifying tenants to take benefit of the contract (s 12A); the right of
    qualifying tenants to compel sale by the purchaser (s 12B); and the right of qualifying tenants to
    compel grant of new tenancy by superior landlord (s 12C): see LANDLORD AND TENANT
    vol 27(3) (2006 Reissue) PARA 1770 et seq.

14 See the Landlord and Tenant Act 1987 s 11(1) (substituted by the Housing Act 1996 s 92(1), Sch 6 Pt II).

46.   Sale of cattle in mart.   An auctioneer[1] must not, unless exempted by order[2] of the Secretary of State[3], sell cattle[4] at any mart where cattle are habitually or periodically sold, unless such facilities for weighing cattle are provided at the mart as are required in the case of sale of cattle at a market or fair to which the Markets and Fairs (Weighing of Cattle) Acts 1887 and 1891 apply[5]. Default in complying with these requirements renders the auctioneer or his employer, if he is employed by any person, liable on summary conviction to a fine[6].

An auctioneer must not offer for sale in any market, fair or mart in or near which a weighing machine is provided[7] any cattle[8] fit for immediate slaughter unless they have been weighed on the machine and their weight as so ascertained is disclosed to intending buyers at the time of the offer for sale, either by announcement made by the auctioneer or in some other manner calculated to bring it to their notice[9]. Any auctioneer who offers for sale any cattle in contravention of these statutory provisions is liable on summary conviction to a fine[10]. The Secretary of State[11] may by order[12] declare that these statutory provisions do not apply to any market, fair or mart[13].

1   As to the meaning of 'auctioneer' see PARA 2.
2   Such orders, being local in nature, are not noted in this work.
3   The Markets and Fairs (Weighing of Cattle) Act 1887 refers to the Board of Agriculture, whose functions under s 4(1) (see the text and notes 1–2, 4–5) were transferred to the Ministry of Agriculture, Fisheries and Food by the Ministry of Agriculture and Fisheries Act 1919, and the Transfer of Functions (Ministry of Food) Order 1955, SI 1955/554. The functions of the Minister of Agriculture, Fisheries and Food were transferred to the Secretary of State by the Ministry of Agriculture, Fisheries and Food (Dissolution) Order 2002, SI 2002/794. As to the Secretary of State see PARA 4 note 12.
4   For these purposes, 'cattle' includes rams, ewes, wethers, lambs and swine: Markets and Fairs (Weighing of Cattle) Act 1887 s 3. As to the sale of cattle generally see ANIMALS vol 2 (2008) PARA 725 et seq; MARKETS, FAIRS AND STREET TRADING vol 29(2) (Reissue) PARA 1103 et seq.
5   See the Markets and Fairs (Weighing of Cattle) Act 1891 s 4(1). The power to exempt an auctioneer from the requirements of s 4(1) may be exercised where the circumstances are such as to render the enforcement of those requirements inexpedient: see the Markets and Fairs (Weighing of Cattle) Act 1926 s 2 (amended by the Statute Law (Repeals) Act 1975). Functions under the Markets and Fairs (Weighing of Cattle) Acts 1887 and 1926 may be delegated to the Meat and Livestock Commission: see the Agriculture Act 1967 s 4(1); and AGRICULTURAL PRODUCTION AND MARKETING vol 1 (2008) PARA 1061. Functions of local authorities under the Agriculture Act 1967 are 'relevant functions' for the purposes of the Regulatory Enforcement and Sanctions Act 2008 Pt 1 (ss 1–21) (see s 4, Sch 3; and LOCAL GOVERNMENT vol 69 (2009) PARA 733); thus the Local Better Regulation Office may give guidance to local authorities as to the exercise of those functions (see s 7; and LOCAL GOVERNMENT vol 69 (2009) PARA 734). As to the weighing of cattle at markets see MARKETS, FAIRS AND STREET TRADING vol 29(2) (Reissue) PARA 1103 et seq.
6   Markets and Fairs (Weighing of Cattle) 1891 s 4(3). The reference in the text to a fine is a reference to a fine not exceeding level 2 on the standard scale, or in case of a continuing offence a fine not exceeding £10 for every day during which the offence continues: s 4(3) (amended by virtue of the Criminal Law Act 1977 s 31(6); and by virtue of the Criminal Justice Act 1982 ss 37, 46). As to the standard scale see SENTENCING AND DISPOSITION OF OFFENDERS vol 92 (2010) PARA 142.
7   Ie provided in order to comply with the Markets and Fairs (Weighing of Cattle) Acts 1887 and 1891. A weighing machine provided under the Markets and Fairs (Weighing of Cattle) Acts 1887 and 1891 includes one provided under the Food Act 1984 s 57: see s 57(2).
8   For these purposes, 'cattle' means bulls, cows, oxen and heifers: Markets and Fairs (Weighing of Cattle) Act 1926 s 1(3).
9   Markets and Fairs (Weighing of Cattle) Act 1926 s 1(1).

10 Markets and Fairs (Weighing of Cattle) Act 1926 s 1(2). The reference in the text to a fine is a reference to a fine not exceeding level 1 on the standard scale for each head of cattle so offered for sale: s 1(2) (amended by virtue of the Criminal Law Act 1977 s 31(6); and by virtue of the Criminal Justice Act 1982 ss 37, 46).

11 See note 3.

12 Such orders, being local in nature, are not noted in this work.

13 Markets and Fairs (Weighing of Cattle) Act 1926 s 1(4).

47. Display of auctioneer's name and address. Before beginning an auction[1] the auctioneer[2] must place or cause to be placed a ticket or board bearing his true and full first name and surname and his residence painted, printed or written thereon in large letters publicly visible and legible, and must place or cause to be placed a copy of the Auctions (Bidding Agreements) Acts 1927 and 1969 in some conspicuous part of the auction room and must keep them there during the whole time the auction is being held[3]. The penalty for a contravention of these statutory provisions on conviction is a fine[4].

1 In addition to the statutory provisions regulating sales which are dealt with in this title, see the following other titles: SALE OF LAND vol 42 (Reissue) PARAS 133–136, for sales under CPR Pt 40 by order of the High Court; BANKRUPTCY AND INDIVIDUAL INSOLVENCY, for sales on behalf of a trustee in bankruptcy; CIVIL PROCEDURE vol 12 (2009) PARA 1266, for sales by an enforcement officer; DISTRESS vol 13 (2007 Reissue) PARA 1044 et seq, for sales under distress; COMPANIES vol 15 (2009) PARA 1437 et seq, for sales in the winding up of companies; CROWN PROPERTY, for sales of Crown land; WILLS AND INTESTACY vol 103 (2010) PARA 1030, for sales by personal representatives; LICENSING AND GAMBLING vol 67 (2008) PARA 214, for sales of goods deposited with innkeepers; MORTGAGE vol 77 (2010) PARA 440 et seq, for sales by mortgagees; TRUSTS vol 48 (2007 Reissue) PARA 1041 et seq, for sales of trust property. As to the meaning of 'auction' see PARA 1.

2 As to the meaning of 'auctioneer' see PARA 2.

3 See the Auctioneers Act 1845 s 7; the Auctions (Bidding Agreements) Act 1927 s 3; and the Auctions (Bidding Agreements) Act 1969 s 4.

4 See the Auctioneers Act 1845 s 7.

48. Notification of reserve and of seller's right to bid. A sale[1] of goods by auction[2] may be notified to be subject to a reserve or upset price[3], and a right to bid may also be reserved expressly by or on behalf of the seller[4]. Where a sale by auction is not notified to be subject to a right to bid by or on behalf of the seller, it is not lawful for the seller to bid himself or to employ any person to bid at the sale[5], or for the auctioneer[6] knowingly to take any bid from the seller or any such person[7]. Such a sale may be treated as fraudulent by the buyer[8].

The particulars or conditions of sale by auction of any land[9] must state whether such land will be sold without reserve[10], or subject to a reserve price or whether a right to bid is reserved[11]. Where it is stated that land is to be sold without reserve, then it is not lawful for the seller to employ any person to bid at such sale, or for the auctioneer[12] to take knowingly any bidding from any such person[13]. Where any sale by auction of land is declared either in the particulars or conditions to be subject to a right for the seller to bid, it is lawful for the seller or any one person on his behalf to bid at such auction in such manner as he may think proper[14]. However, the conditions announced as governing the seller's reserve to bid must be strictly complied with[15].

1 As to the meaning of 'sale' see PARA 43 note 1.

2 As to the meaning of 'auction' see PARA 1.

3 It seems to have been formerly a rule in equity that where a sale of land was not notified to be without reserve one bidder might, even without express stipulation, be employed to prevent a sale at an undervalue: *Green v Baverstock* (1863) 14 CBNS 204 at 208 per Willes J; but see *Mortimer v Bell* (1865) 1 Ch App 10, CA, per Lord Cranworth LC.

4   See the Sale of Goods Act 1979 s 57(3). Where, in respect of a sale by auction, a right to bid is expressly reserved (but not otherwise) the seller or any one person on his behalf may bid at the auction: s 57(6). 'Seller' means a person who sells or agrees to sell goods: s 61(1).

5   See *Parnell v Tyler* (1833) 2 LJ Ch 195 (where it was held that even the employment by a third person of the seller's solicitor's clerk invalidated the sale).

6   As to the meaning of 'auctioneer' see PARA 2.

7   Sale of Goods Act 1979 s 57(4). This statutory provision enacts the common law rule. The buyer has alternative remedies to sue for the tort or to avoid the contract. See generally *Crowder v Austin* (1826) 3 Bing 368 (highest bidder to be buyer; seller whose servant pushed up bidding cannot recover price); *R v Marsh* (1831) 1 Cr & J 406 (bona fide bid for himself by seller's agent); *Thornett v Haines* (1846) 15 M & W 367 (sale without reserve; puffer employed without notice by seller; buyer may recover deposit from auctioneer); *Green v Baverstock* (1863) 14 CBNS 204 (highest bidder to be buyer; claim by auctioneer for non-clearance of goods). As to improper or fraudulent acts likely to prevent the goods put up from realising their fair value, such as damping the sale or 'knock out', see PARA 52.

8   Sale of Goods Act 1979 s 57(5).

9   'Land' means any interest in any messuages, lands, tenements, or hereditaments, of whatever tenure: Sale of Land by Auction Act 1867 s 3.

10 Any words may be used to render it clear, when such is the case, that the sale is without reserve: *Hills & Grant Ltd v Hodson* [1934] Ch 53. See also *Gilliat v Gilliat* (1869) LR 9 Eq 60 (although the dictum of Lord Romilly MR is not, it is suggested, reflective of the words used in the Sale of Land by Auction Act 1867).

11 Sale of Land by Auction Act 1867 s 5 (amended by the Statute Law Revision Act 1893). Notification of a reserve price is not in itself a reservation of the right to bid: *Gilliat v Gilliat* (1869) LR 9 Eq 60.

12 For these purposes, 'auctioneer' means any person selling by public auction any land, whether in lots or otherwise: Sale of Land by Auction Act 1867 s 3.

13 Sale of Land by Auction Act 1867 s 5 (as amended: see note 11).

14 See the Sale of Land by Auction Act 1867 s 6; and *Thornett v Haines* (1846) 15 M & W 367.

15 *Parfitt v Jepson* (1877) 46 LJQB 529 (where the seller reserved a right to bid once, and the sale was set aside because he bid three times).

49. Conditions of sale and oral modifications. Oral statements made by the auctioneer[1] may or may not form part of the contract of sale[2]. Oral statements made to the buyer by the auctioneer before the sale may amount to conditions or warranties[3] which override the written conditions of sale[4].

There used to be a distinction drawn between sales of goods and those of land as regards the effect of oral modifications of the conditions[5]. The difficulty in the case of land sales was that parol evidence could not be introduced to vary a written contract[6]. Now that there is no requirement of writing to render a contract for the sale of land by auction valid or enforceable[7], that distinction may no longer be maintained. Oral statements may be used, where the contract is reduced to writing, to show that the written version was not what was actually agreed or that the contract is void for mistake[8].

Oral corrections of misdescriptions in the particulars at the time of the sale may defeat the buyer's right to enforce specific performance with compensation[9].

1   As to the meaning of 'auctioneer' see PARA 2.

2   *Druce & Co Ltd v Leveson* (1952) 102 L Jo 721 (buyer taken to have assented to conditions of sale forming part of contract where she heard auctioneer make oral reference to conditions of sale prior to the sale). Statements by the auctioneer may, however, amount to an offence under the Consumer Protection from Unfair Trading Regulations 2008, SI 2008/1277, or, in land sales, under the Property Misdescriptions Act 1991: see PARA 60; and CONSUMER PROTECTION vol 21 (2011) PARA 551 et seq. As to what statements are and are not part of the contract see CONTRACT; SALE OF GOODS AND SUPPLY OF SERVICES; SALE OF LAND.

3   The distinction between a condition, which gives a right to reject the thing sold and treat the contract as ended by the breach of the condition, and a warranty, which gives a right of claim for damages for breach, is considered in CONTRACT vol 9(1) (Reissue) PARA 993 et seq. A party entitled to the benefit of a condition may, in effect, turn it into a warranty by electing to claim damages: see *Wallis, Son and Wells v Pratt and Haynes* [1911] AC 394, HL.

4   *Couchman v Hill* [1947] KB 554, [1947] 1 All ER 103, CA (confirmatory description (heifer unserved) made by auctioneer and seller before sale overrode stultifying condition in printed terms). See *Harling v Eddy* [1951] 2 KB 739, [1951] 2 All ER 212, CA (seller's oral guarantee of soundness of heifer amounted to a condition of the contract). As to warranty on sale of animals see ANIMALS vol 2 (2008) PARA 725 et seq.

5   With goods, if there was no requirement of written evidence and no written contract, oral statements could modify the conditions of sale: *Eden v Blake* (1845) 13 M & W 614.

6   *Gunnis v Erhart* (1789) 1 Hy Bl 289; *Shelton v Livius* (1832) 2 Cr & J 411; *Ogilvie v Foljambe* (1817) 3 Mer 53; *Higginson v Clowes* (1805) 15 Ves 516; *Clowes v Higginson* (1813) 1 Ves & B 524; *Winch v Winchester* (1812) 1 Ves & B 375; *Anson v Towgood* (1820) 1 Jac & W 637. As to the parol evidence rule see CONTRACT vol 9(1) (Reissue) PARA 622.

7   See PARA 7 note 5.

8   *Swaisland v Dearsley* (1861) 30 LJ Ch 652; *Winch v Winchester* (1812) 1 Ves & B 375; *Manser v Back* (1848) 6 Hare 443; *Re Hare and O'More's Contract* [1901] 1 Ch 93.

9   *Farebrother v Gibson* (1875) 1 De G & J 602. As to the remedy of specific performance see SPECIFIC PERFORMANCE.

50. Bidding. The method of bidding and the amount of the bids are usually regulated by the conditions of sale[1]. A sale[2] by auction[3] is complete when the auctioneer announces its completion by the fall of the hammer, or in other customary manner, and until the announcement is made any bidder may retract his bid[4].

Fictitious bids made by a third person without the privity of the seller or the auctioneer do not invalidate the sale, nor do they affect the seller's right to specific performance[5].

If an auctioneer pretends to accept bids which have not been made, a claim will lie against him for the deposit and interest upon it[6]. He might also be sued in fraud, and where fraud is alleged in a claim brought by the buyer against the auctioneer and the seller for rescission of the contract, the auctioneer cannot claim to be dismissed from the claim upon paying the deposit into court[7]. It remains to be decided whether the auctioneer 'taking bids out of the air' (a practice by no means unknown) is guilty of fraud by false representation[8].

If two or more persons take part in an auction[9] and by means of sham bidders and bidding, induce persons to buy at excessive prices, they are guilty of a criminal conspiracy[10].

1   Where the conditions provide that, in case any dispute arises respecting a bid, the auctioneer may determine the bid or the property may, at the seller's option, either be put up again at the last undisputed bid or be withdrawn, there is a sufficient dispute for those conditions to apply if a bid is overlooked, even if the property is knocked down to the only bid seen by the auctioneer: see *Richards v Phillips* [1969] 1 Ch 39, [1968] 2 All ER 859, CA. See also *Frank R Thorold (Pty) Ltd v Estate Late Beit* 1996 (4) SA 705. As to the meaning of 'auctioneer' see PARA 2.

2   As to the meaning of 'sale' see PARA 43 note 1.

3   As to the meaning of 'auction' see PARA 1.

4   Sale of Goods Act 1979 s 57(2); and see *Payne v Cave* (1789) 3 Term Rep 148. In an unconditional sale of specific goods the property in the goods passes on the fall of the hammer: see the Sale of Goods Act 1979 s 18 r 1; and *Dennant v Skinner and Collom* [1948] 2 KB 164, [1948] 2 All ER 29.

5   *Union Bank of London v Munster* (1887) 37 ChD 51. As to the remedy of specific performance see SPECIFIC PERFORMANCE.

6   *Heatley v Newton* (1881) 19 ChD 326, CA.

7   *Heatley v Newton* (1881) 19 ChD 326, CA.

8   Ie under the Fraud Act 2006 s 2 (which replaces the offence of obtaining property by deception under the Theft Act 1968 s 15 (repealed)): see CRIMINAL LAW vol 25 (2010) PARA 305. All the main constituents of the offence appear to be committed but there may be problems relating to causation, especially where genuine bids intervene.

9   Formerly known as a mock auction: see PARA 51.

10   *R v Lewis* (1869) 11 Cox CC 404. As to common law conspiracy see CRIMINAL LAW vol 25 (2010) PARA 79 et seq.

51.   Mock auctions.   The Mock Auctions Act 1961, under which it was an offence to promote or conduct, or to assist in the conduct of, a mock auction at which one or more lots consisting of or including one or more certain specified articles[1] were offered for sale, was repealed on 26 May 2008[2]. The Consumer Protection from Unfair Trading Regulations 2008[3], which came into force on that day[4], do not specifically deal with mock auctions, but the regulations prohibit unfair commercial practices[5] generally, and practices such as formerly constituted conducting a mock auction would now be prohibited under the regulations[6].

Engaging in unfair commercial practices is an offence[7].

1   The articles covered by the Mock Auctions Act 1961 were any plate, plated articles, linen, china, glass, books, pictures, prints, furniture, jewellery, articles of household or personal use or ornament or any musical or scientific instrument or apparatus: see s 3(2) (repealed).

2   See the Consumer Protection from Unfair Trading Regulations 2008, SI 2008/1277, reg 30(3), Sch 4 Pt 1. Under the Mock Auctions Act 1961, a sale of goods by way of competitive bidding was taken to be a mock auction if, but only if, during the course of the sale: (1) any such lot was sold to a person bidding for it, and either it was sold to him at a price lower than the amount of his highest bid for that lot, or part of the price at which it was sold to him was repaid or credited to him or was stated to be so repaid or credited; or (2) the right to bid for any such lot was restricted, or was stated to be restricted, to persons who had bought or agreed to buy one or more articles; or (3) any articles were given away or offered as gifts: see s 1(3) (repealed). 'Sale of goods by way of competitive bidding' meant any sale of goods at which the persons present, or some of them, were invited to buy articles by way of competitive bidding, and 'competitive bidding' included any mode of sale whereby prospective buyers might be enabled to compete for the purchase of articles, whether by way of increasing bids or by the offer of articles to be bid for at successively decreasing prices or otherwise: s 3(1) (repealed); and see *Lomas v Rydeheard* (1975) 119 Sol Jo 233, DC; *Clements v Rydeheard* [1978] 3 All ER 658, DC; *Allen v Simmons* [1978] 3 All ER 662, [1978] 1 WLR 879, DC; *R v Pollard* (1983) 148 JP 679, CA.

3   Ie the Consumer Protection from Unfair Trading Regulations 2008, SI 2008/1277.

4   See the Consumer Protection from Unfair Trading Regulations 2008, SI 2008/1277, reg 1.

5   For these purposes, 'commercial practice' means any act, omission, course of conduct, representation or commercial communication (including advertising and marketing) by a trader, which is directly connected with the promotion, sale or supply of a product to or from consumers, whether occurring before, during or after a commercial transaction (if any) in relation to a product: Consumer Protection from Unfair Trading Regulations 2008, SI 2008/1277, reg 2(1). 'Trader' means any person who in relation to a commercial practice is acting for purposes relating to his business, and anyone acting in the name of or on behalf of a trader; and 'consumer' means any individual who in relation to a commercial practice is acting for purposes which are outside his business: reg 2(1).

6   See the Consumer Protection from Unfair Trading Regulations 2008, SI 2008/1277, reg 3(1). A commercial practice is unfair if it (1) contravenes the requirements of professional diligence and it materially distorts or is likely to materially distort the economic behaviour of the average consumer with regard to the product (reg 3(2), (3)); or (2) is a misleading action, a misleading omission, aggressive, or a specified unfair commercial practice (regs 3(2), (4), 5–7, Sch 1). 'Average consumer' is specifically defined: see reg 2(1), (2)–(6); and SALE OF GOODS AND SUPPLY OF SERVICES.

7   See the Consumer Protection from Unfair Trading Regulations 2008, SI 2008/1277, regs 8–12; and SALE OF GOODS AND SUPPLY OF SERVICES. A person guilty of any such offence is liable, on summary conviction, to a fine not exceeding the statutory maximum or, on conviction on indictment, to a fine or imprisonment for a term not exceeding two years or both: reg 13. As to the statutory maximum see SENTENCING AND DISPOSITION OF OFFENDERS vol 92 (2010) PARA 140.

52.   Damping the sale and bidding agreements.   Improper or fraudulent acts, which are likely to prevent the property put up from realising its fair value and to 'damp' the sale, will invalidate any purchase by persons guilty of or privy to such acts, so that the buyer will be disentitled to specific performance and the auctioneer[1] will be justified in withdrawing the property[2]. Furthermore, if a person maliciously makes false statements with the consequence that no sale results, the unsuccessful seller can sue for malicious falsehood[3].

At common law, an agreement between two or more persons not to bid against each other at an auction, even if amounting to what is popularly known as a 'knock-out', is not illegal, nor does it invalidate the sale[4].

Where two or more persons agree not to bid against each other at an auction on the understanding that the successful buyer will convey part of the property purchased to the other or others, equity gives relief if the buyer fails to implement his promise[5].

If any dealer[6] agrees to give, or gives, or offers any gift or consideration to any other person as an inducement or reward for abstaining, or for having abstained, from bidding at a sale by auction either generally or for any particular lot, or if any person agrees to accept, or accepts, or attempts to obtain from any dealer any such gift or consideration, he is guilty of an offence[7].

However, where a dealer has previously to an auction entered into an agreement in writing with one or more persons to purchase goods at the auction bona fide on a joint account and has before the goods were purchased at the auction deposited a copy of the agreement with the auctioneer, such an agreement is not treated as an agreement made in contravention of these statutory provisions[8]. A copy of the Auctions (Bidding Agreements) Act 1927 is one of the particulars required to be conspicuously displayed in the auction room[9].

1   As to the meaning of 'auctioneer' see PARA 2.
2   *Twining v Morrice* (1788) 2 Bro CC 326; *Mason v Armitage* (1806) 13 Ves 25; *Fuller v Abrahams* (1821) 6 Moore CP 316.
3   *Mayer v Pluck* (1971) 223 Estates Gazette 33, 219. As to malicious falsehood see LIBEL AND SLANDER vol 28 (Reissue) PARA 274.
4   *Rawlings v General Trading Co* [1921] 1 KB 635, CA; *Cohen v Roche* [1927] 1 KB 169 (followed in *Harrop v Thompson* [1975] 2 All ER 94, [1975] 1 WLR 545).
5   *Pallant v Morgan* [1953] Ch 43, [1952] 2 All ER 951 (applying *Chattock v Muller* (1878) 8 ChD 177) (the successful buyer buys for himself and the person who refrains from bidding jointly). The '*Pallant v Morgan* equity' principles were considered in *Banner Homes Group plc v Luff Development Ltd* [2000] Ch 372 and *Baynes Clarke v Corless* [2010] EWCA Civ 338, [2010] All ER (D) 01 (Apr).
6   'Dealer' means a person who in the normal course of his business attends sales by auction for the purpose of purchasing goods with a view to reselling them: Auctions (Bidding Agreements) Act 1927 s 1(2). It is submitted that the Auctions (Bidding Agreements) Act 1927 does not apply to sales of land by auction. As to the meaning of 'auction' see PARA 1.
7   Auctions (Bidding Agreements) Act 1927 s 1(1). The penalty on summary conviction is a fine not exceeding the prescribed sum or a term of imprisonment not exceeding six months or both, or on conviction on indictment a fine or a term of imprisonment not exceeding two years or both: see s 1(1); and the Auctions (Bidding Agreements) Act 1969 s 1(1) (amended by virtue of the Magistrates' Courts Act 1980 s 32(2)). As to the consequences of conviction of an offence under the Auctions (Bidding Agreements) Act 1927 see PARA 53. As to the prescribed sum see SENTENCING AND DISPOSITION OF OFFENDERS vol 92 (2010) PARA 141.
    In England and Wales a prosecution for an offence under the Auctions (Bidding Agreements) Act 1927 s 1 must not be instituted without the consent of the Attorney General: s 1(3). As to the Attorney General see CONSTITUTIONAL LAW AND HUMAN RIGHTS vol 8(2) (Reissue) PARA 529 et seq.
    It was held before the passing of the Auctions (Bidding Agreements) Act 1969 (which introduced trial on indictment) that the offence, being the creation of statute and not an offence at common law, was triable only as provided by the Auctions (Bidding Agreements) Act 1927 and not on indictment, and that a count in an indictment which alleged a conspiracy to contravene the Auctions (Bidding Agreements) Act 1927 and, on the facts, amounted substantially to the statutory offence, was bad: *R v Barnett* [1951] 2 KB 425, [1951] 1 All ER 917, CCA. Since the offence is now triable on indictment it would seem that a charge of conspiracy to contravene the Auctions (Bidding Agreements) Act 1927 will now lie.

8 Auctions (Bidding Agreements) Act 1927 s 1(1) proviso.
9 See the Auctions (Bidding Agreements) Act 1927 s 3. As to the display of the Auctions (Bidding Agreements) Act 1927 see PARA 47.

53. Persons convicted under Auctions (Bidding Agreements) Act 1927 not to attend auctions. On a conviction under the Auctions (Bidding Agreements) Act 1927[1], the court may order that the person so convicted or that person and any representative of him must not (without permission of the court) for a period from the date of such conviction, in the case of a summary conviction, of not more than one year, or in the case of a conviction on indictment, of not more than three years, enter upon any premises where goods intended for sale by auction[2] are on display or to attend or participate in any way in any sale by auction[3]. In any proceedings against a person in respect of a contravention of such an order consisting in the entry upon premises where goods intended for sale by auction were on display, it is a defence for him to prove that he did not know, and had no reason to suspect, that goods so intended were on display on the premises[4]. In any proceedings against a person in respect of a contravention of an order consisting in his having done something as the representative of another, it is a defence for him to prove that he did not know, and had no reason to suspect, that that other was the subject of an order[5]. A person is not guilty of an offence of contravening an order by reason only of his selling property by auction or causing it to be so sold[6]. A copy of the Auctions (Bidding Agreements) Act 1969 is one of the particulars to be conspicuously displayed in the auction room[7].

1 Ie a conviction under the Auctions (Bidding Agreements) Act 1927 s 1(1): see PARA 52.
2 As to the meaning of 'auction' see PARA 1.
3 Auctions (Bidding Agreements) Act 1969 s 2(1). In the event of a contravention of an order under s 2(1), the person who contravenes it (and, if he is the representative of another, that other also) is guilty of an offence and liable on summary conviction, to a fine not exceeding the prescribed sum; and on conviction on indictment, to imprisonment for a term not exceeding two years or to a fine or to both: s 2(2) (amended by virtue of the Magistrates' Courts Act 1980 s 32(2)). As to the prescribed sum see SENTENCING AND DISPOSITION OF OFFENDERS vol 92 (2010) PARA 141.
4 Auctions (Bidding Agreements) Act 1969 s 2(3).
5 Auctions (Bidding Agreements) Act 1969 s 2(3).
6 Auctions (Bidding Agreements) Act 1969 s 2(4).
7 See the Auctions (Bidding Agreements) Act 1969 s 4. As to the display of the Auctions (Bidding Agreements) Act 1969 see PARA 47.

54. Seller's right to avoid contract. Where goods are purchased at an auction[1] by a person who has entered into an agreement with another or others that the other or the others (or some of them) will abstain from bidding for the goods (not being an agreement to purchase the goods bona fide on a joint account) and he or the other party, or one of the other parties, to the agreement is a dealer[2], the seller may avoid the contract under which the goods are purchased[3]. Where a contract is avoided by virtue of this provision, then, if the buyer has obtained possession of the goods and restitution is not made, the persons who were parties to the agreement that one or some of them should abstain from bidding for the goods the subject of the contract are jointly and severally liable to make good to the seller the loss (if any) he sustained by reason of the operation of the agreement[4].

1 As to the meaning of 'auction' see PARA 1.
2 As to the meaning of 'dealer' see PARA 52 note 6; definition applied by virtue of the Auctions (Bidding Agreements) Act 1969 s 3(5).

3   Auctions (Bidding Agreements) Act 1969 s 3(1).
4   Auctions (Bidding Agreements) Act 1969 s 3(2).

55.   Withdrawal of property.   Before the completion of the sale the seller may withdraw the property from the auction[1], provided that the sale is subject to a reserve which has not been reached[2]. Where the sale is not subject to a reserve price and the property has been withdrawn during the auction, the seller or the auctioneer[3], if the latter has not disclosed his principal, is liable to an action for damages by the highest bidder on an implied undertaking that the sale shall be without reserve[4].

1   As to the meaning of 'auction' see PARA 1.
2   *McManus v Fortescue* [1907] 2 KB 1, CA.
3   As to the meaning of 'auctioneer' see PARA 2.
4   See PARA 9.

(2)   POSTAL AND INTERNET AUCTIONS

56.   Postal auctions.   Auctions[1] have traditionally involved public participation by persons gathered together in a physical space[2]. However, postal auctions are common in some trades, such as philately and the sale of memorabilia. Bids are made by returning a bidding form before a deadline, and may be sent not only by post[3], but also in some cases by fax[4] or e-mail. As bidders are unaware of the level of other bids being made, bids increase in increments, with the winning bid being one increment above the second highest bid[5]. The seller or the buyer or both may be charged a premium[6]. Catalogues or lists may be issued[7], and lots may be subject to reserves[8] or estimates[9].

1   As to the meaning of 'auction' see PARA 1.
2   As to place of auction see PARA 40.
3   As to offer and acceptance see CONTRACT vol 9(1) (Reissue) PARA 631 et seq. As to contracts made at a distance and the operation of the postal rule see CONTRACT vol 9(1) (Reissue) PARA 676 et seq.
4   As to contracts made by instantaneous communications see CONTRACT vol 9(1) (Reissue) PARA 683.
5   As to bidding see PARA 50.
6   As to remuneration of auctioneers see PARA 24.
7   As to the duty owed to the seller to describe property accurately see PARA 17. As to liability for misrepresentation see PARA 32.
        Where an auctioneer applies a false or misleading description to goods or land he is guilty of an offence: see PARAS 60–61.
8   As to sales below reserve prices see PARA 9.
9   As to estimates see PARA 61.

57.   Internet auctions.   The use of the internet to facilitate auctions[1] has become increasingly popular and can take several forms. In some instances live auctions use the internet to advertise the stock online, while the auction is held elsewhere; in other cases ('virtual' auctions), the auction itself is held online; and there is a hybrid type, in which the internet is used to enable bidding to be made online at a physical auction.

The first type is akin to the traditional auction with an online catalogue. A potential bidder, having seen an item of interest in an online catalogue, will normally inspect the item and attend the sale in person or make other arrangements to bid (such as a commission bid[2] or telephone bid), and the normal auction procedure and law apply to the sale itself[3]. The physical auction with internet bidding is a development from the practice of accepting telephone bids, which may slow down the auction but expands the field of bidders significantly. This method is being used increasingly, and will necessitate increasing reliance on the catalogue particulars in the absence of physical inspection.

Virtual auctions have become very popular recently, as indicated by the success of eBay. Such auctions can take place in real time with participants taking part over the internet, or ascending bids may be 'posted' for lots over the internet with the hammer falling on the expiry of a specified time limit (usually between three and ten days) and the highest bid, above any set reserve, received by the expiry of that time securing the lot. The online auctioneer[4] facilitates the sale and a contract is made between buyer and seller. It has been held in Australia that such auctions are auctions properly so called[5]. Where the website acts as an auctioneer, the rules relating to traditional auctions will apply. Some websites such as eBay claim to act not as an auctioneer but only as a platform to bring sellers and buyers together and not to involve themselves in the contract of sale, but as eBay charges a fee to sellers and collects commission on sales, and provides advice and other services, it is arguable that it is acting as an auctioneer. Problems arising from internet-only auctions include fraudulent practices such as distortion of the bidding process[6], failure of the seller to deliver goods sold and failure of the buyer to pay, although eBay has implemented measures, such as feedback on buyers and sellers and payment using PayPal, to address the problems[7].

1   As to the normal meaning of 'auction' see PARA 1.

2   As to commission bids see PARA 20.

3   See PARA 3 et seq. If distance makes personal attendance impracticable, the bidder will often ask for a condition report.

4   As to the meaning of 'auctioneer' see PARA 2.

5   See *Peter Smythe v Vincent Thomas* [2007] NSWSC 844. This would take such auctions, in common with traditional auctions, outwith the provisions of the Consumer Protection (Distance Selling) Regulations 2000, SI 2000/2334. A buyer under a purely online auction sale would, however, potentially be a consumer for the purposes of the Unfair Contract Terms Act 1977 (see PARA 42 note 12) since an individual buyer does not have the opportunity to attend the sale in person.

6   Eg by 'shill bidding', under which a seller bids in his own auction to boost the price of his goods. The first eBay seller to be prosecuted for this practice was found guilty of an offence under the Consumer Protection from Unfair Trading Regulations 2008, SI 2008/1277: see *The Independent*, 5 July 2010.

7   Its technology can also, it avers, detect shill bidding and other illegal activities. Where an online sale is not an auction, the Consumer Protection (Distance Selling) Regulations 2000, SI 2000/2334, which are specifically excluded from application to auctions, may apply: see reg 5; and CONSUMER PROTECTION vol 21 (2011) PARA 420 et seq.

     Recent decisions of the courts in Germany and France have imposed obligations on eBay in respect of sales of counterfeit goods; but in *L'Oréal SA v eBay International* [2009] EWHC 1094 (Ch), [2009] RPC 693, [2010] IP & T 95, [2009] All ER (D) 169 (Jun) it was held that eBay Europe's current provision of online auction services does not by itself give rise to any joint liability on its part for trade mark infringements committed by users of its services. See also *Quads 4 Kids v Campbell* [2006] EWHC 2482 (Ch), [2006] All ER (D) 162 (Oct) (eBay's procedure to safeguard the rights of intellectual property owners, allowing purported owners of such rights to report alleged infringement to it using an online form, with the subsequent withdrawal of items from auction listings by eBay, could amount to a threat by the purported owners to bring infringement proceedings).

(3) THE DEPOSIT

58. Auctioneer as stakeholder. In the absence of special agreement[1], the auctioneer[2] receives the deposit as stakeholder for the seller and the buyer[3], and it is his duty to hold it until the completion or rescission of the contract, and to pay it to the party ultimately entitled[4].

If the auctioneer pays the money prematurely to either seller or buyer, and it turns out that the person paid was not entitled to it, the auctioneer is liable to make good the money to the party to the contract eventually held to be entitled[5].

Where the buyer is entitled to the return of the deposit, the auctioneer can set up the buyer's right to the money in answer to any claim to it made by the seller[6].

An auctioneer may exercise his lien[7] for his charges and disbursements against the deposit where the sale goes off by reason of the buyer's default, or against the seller, where the sale is completed and the deposit becomes part of the purchase price[8]. If, however, the incumbrances are greater than the purchase price or, where the seller has become bankrupt, the balance of it, the auctioneer can be in no better position than the seller, and cannot enforce his lien against the deposit[9]. Where the seller charges the proceeds of sale to the buyer subsequently to the sale the lien will take priority[10].

The auctioneer should be ready to account for the deposit[11], but he is not liable to invest the deposit so as to be accountable for interest on it for the period during which he rightfully holds it as stakeholder, nor until demand for repayment has been made by some person entitled to receive it[12]. If the auctioneer as stakeholder does invest the deposit there are dicta suggesting that he is entitled to keep the interest[13].

1   In land sales the contract normally will have an express provision that the auctioneer is to hold the deposit as stakeholder: see the Standard Conditions of Sale (4th Edn, 2003). As to the Standard Conditions of Sale see SALE OF LAND vol 42 (Reissue) PARA 1 et seq.

2   As to the meaning of 'auctioneer' see PARA 2.

3   *Harington v Hoggart* (1830) 1 B & Ad 577. See *Edwards v Hodding* (1814) 5 Taunt 815, where it was held that a solicitor who was also the auctioneer received the purchase money as auctioneer and not as solicitor and agent for the seller. As to the receipt of a cheque by the auctioneer in payment of the deposit see PARAS 10, 59.

4   *Gray v Gutteridge* (1828) 1 Man & Ry KB 614; *Yates v Farebrother* (1819) 4 Madd 239; *Edwards v Hodding* (1814) 5 Taunt 815; *Burrough v Skinner* (1770) 5 Burr 2639; *Furtado v Lumley* (1890) 54 JP 407; *Spurrier v Elderton* (1803) 5 Esp 1; *Spittle v Lavender* (1821) 2 Brod & Bing 452; *Berry v Young* (1788) 2 Esp 640n; *Stevens v Legh* (1853) 22 LTOS 84. The auctioneer may pay over to the seller even when the latter is insolvent: *White v Bartlett* (1832) 9 Bing 378.

5   *Burrough v Skinner* (1770) 5 Burr 2639; *Furtado v Lumley* (1890) 54 JP 407; *Edwards v Hodding* (1814) 5 Taunt 815.

6   *Stevens v Legh* (1853) 22 LTOS 84; *Murray v Mann* (1848) 2 Exch 538. See also PARA 13.

7   As to auctioneers' lien see PARA 25.

8   *Skinner v Trustee of the Property of Reed (a Bankrupt)* [1967] Ch 1194 at 1200, [1967] 2 All ER 1286 at 1289 per Cross J.

9   *Skinner v Trustee of the Property of Reed (a Bankrupt)* [1967] Ch 1194 at 1200, [1967] 2 All ER 1286 at 1289 per Cross J.

10 *Webb v Smith* (1885) 30 ChD 192, CA.

11 *Brown v Staton* (1816) 2 Chit 353; *Crosskey v Mills* (1834) 1 Cr M & R 298.

12 *Lee v Munn* (1817) 8 Taunt 45; *Harington v Hoggart* (1830) 1 B & Ad 577; *Gaby v Driver* (1828) 2 Y & J 549.

13 *Potters (a firm) v Loppert* [1973] Ch 399 at 414–415, [1973] 1 All ER 658 at 669 per Pennycuick V-C. Cf *Burt v Claude Cousins & Co Ltd* [1971] 2 QB 426, [1971] 2 All ER 611, CA. The view in *Potters (a firm) v Loppert* [1973] Ch 399, [1973] 1 All ER 658 maintains the distinction between the position of one who takes as stakeholder and one who is an agent.

59. Loss of deposit. Where the deposit is lost either by infraction of the auctioneer[1] or otherwise (for example, his insolvency) it would seem that the loss falls on the seller rather than the buyer[2]. Whilst, in principle this seems to treat the auctioneer as though he were the seller's agent, the rationale seems to be that it is the seller who selects the auctioneer to be the stakeholder and must take the risk of loss occasioned by his lack of honesty or financial stability.

1 As to the meaning of 'auctioneer' see PARA 2.

2 The authorities are mainly fairly ancient and are not entirely compelling. See *Fenton v Browne* (1807) 14 Ves 144 (but there the auctioneer clearly held the deposit as agent of the seller, and where, as will be the case in the absence of specific provision, he holds it as stakeholder the position should be that risk should fall on whichever party ultimately becomes entitled to it); *Smith v Jackson and Lloyd* (1816) 1 Madd 618 (seller treated as having the benefit of the stake because it was part payment and he could require investment of it: the first rationale is not convincing, where, as here, completion did not take place and the second justification is, it is submitted, wrong); *Rowe v May* (1854) 18 Beav 613 (but there the auctioneer seems to have been treated as agent of the seller rather than the stakeholder). As to auctioneers as stakeholders see PARA 58.

(4) SALES GIVING RISE TO CRIMINAL SANCTIONS

60. Misdescribed goods. An auctioneer[1] who misdescribes goods or fails to disclose material information about goods may be guilty of an offence under the Consumer Protection from Unfair Trading Regulations 2008[2], which replace a number of important statutes including, in particular, the Trade Descriptions Act 1968. The regulations prohibit unfair commercial practices[3], including misleading actions and misleading omissions[4].

A commercial practice is a misleading action if it satisfies the conditions in either head (1) or head (2) below[5], namely:

(1)   if:

    (a)   it contains false information and is therefore untruthful in relation to any of certain specified matters[6] or if it or its overall presentation in any way deceives or is likely to deceive the average consumer[7] in relation to any of the specified matters, even if the information is factually correct; and

    (b)   it causes or is likely to cause the average consumer to take a transactional decision he would not have taken otherwise[8];

(2)   if:

    (a)   it concerns any marketing of a product (including comparative advertising) which creates confusion with any products, trade marks, trade names or other distinguishing marks of a competitor; or

    (b)   it concerns any failure by a trader to comply with a commitment contained in a code of conduct which the trader has undertaken to comply with, if the trader indicates in a commercial practice that he is bound by that code of conduct and the commitment is firm and capable of being verified and is not aspirational,

and it causes or is likely to cause the average consumer to take a transactional decision he would not have taken otherwise, taking account of its factual context and of all its features and circumstances[9].

A commercial practice is a misleading omission if, in its factual context, taking account of certain specified matters[10]:

(i)   the commercial practice omits material information[11];

(ii)   the commercial practice hides material information;

(iii)   the commercial practice provides material information in a manner which is unclear, unintelligible, ambiguous or untimely; or

(iv)   the commercial practice fails to identify its commercial intent, unless this is already apparent from the context,

and as a result it causes or is likely to cause the average consumer to take a transactional decision he would not have taken otherwise[12].

A trader is guilty of an offence if he engages in a commercial practice which is a misleading action as specified above otherwise than by reason of the commercial practice satisfying the condition in head (2)(b)[13], or if he engages in a commercial practice which is a misleading omission[14]. A defence of due diligence[15], a defence of innocent publication of an advertisement[16], and a defence that the offence was due to the default of another person[17], are provided.

1   As to the meaning of 'auctioneer' see PARA 2.

2   Ie under the Consumer Protection from Unfair Trading Regulations 2008, SI 2008/1277, reg 9 or 10: see the text and notes 13–14. As to the 2008 regulations generally see SALE OF GOODS AND SUPPLY OF SERVICES.

3   As to the meaning of 'commercial practice' see PARA 51 note 5.

4   See the Consumer Protection from Unfair Trading Regulations 2008, SI 2008/1277, reg 3; PARA 51 note 6; and SALE OF GOODS AND SUPPLY OF SERVICES.

5   Consumer Protection from Unfair Trading Regulations 2008, SI 2008/1277, reg 5(1).

6   The matters referred to in the text are: (1) the existence or nature of the product; (2) the main characteristics of the product (as defined below); (3) the extent of the trader's commitments; (4) the motives for the commercial practice; (5) the nature of the sales process; (6) any statement or symbol relating to direct or indirect sponsorship or approval of the trader or the product; (7) the price or the manner in which the price is calculated; (8) the existence of a specific price advantage; (9) the need for a service, part, replacement or repair; (10) the nature, attributes and rights of the trader (as defined below); (11) the consumer's rights or the risks he may face: Consumer Protection from Unfair Trading Regulations 2008, SI 2008/1277, reg 5(4).

    In head (2), the 'main characteristics of the product' include: (a) availability of the product; (b) benefits of the product; (c) risks of the product; (d) execution of the product; (e) composition of the product; (f) accessories of the product; (g) after-sale customer assistance concerning the product; (h) the handling of complaints about the product; (i) the method and date of manufacture of the product; (j) the method and date of provision of the product; (k) delivery of the product; (l) fitness for purpose of the product; (m) usage of the product; (n) quantity of the product; (o) specification of the product; (p) geographical or commercial origin of the product; (q) results to be expected from use of the product; and (r) results and material features of tests or checks carried out on the product: reg 5(5). In head (10), the 'nature, attributes and rights' as far as concern the trader include the trader's: (i) identity; (ii) assets; (iii) qualifications; (iv) status; (v) approval; (vi) affiliations or connections; (vii) ownership of industrial, commercial or intellectual property rights; and (viii) awards and distinctions: reg 5(6). In head (11), 'consumer's rights' include rights the consumer may have under the Sale of Goods Act 1979 Pt 5A (ss 48A–48F) or the Supply of Goods and Services Act 1982 Pt IB (ss 11M–11S) (see SALE OF GOODS AND SUPPLY OF SERVICES): Consumer Protection from Unfair Trading Regulations 2008, SI 2008/1277, reg 5(7).

7   'Average consumer' is specifically defined: see reg 2(1), (2)–(6); and SALE OF GOODS AND SUPPLY OF SERVICES.

8   Consumer Protection from Unfair Trading Regulations 2008, SI 2008/1277, reg 5(2).

9   Consumer Protection from Unfair Trading Regulations 2008, SI 2008/1277, reg 5(3).

10 The matters referred to in the text are: (1) all the features and circumstances of the commercial practice; (2) the limitations of the medium used to communicate the commercial practice (including limitations of space or time); and (3) where the medium used to communicate the commercial practice imposes limitations of space or time, any measures taken by the trader to

make the information available to consumers by other means: Consumer Protection from Unfair Trading Regulations 2008, SI 2008/1277, reg 6(2).

11 For these purposes, 'material information' means: (1) the information which the average consumer needs, according to the context, to take an informed transactional decision; and (2) any information requirement which applies in relation to a commercial communication as a result of an EU obligation: Consumer Protection from Unfair Trading Regulations 2008, SI 2008/1277, reg 6(3). Where a commercial practice is an invitation to purchase, the following information will be material if not already apparent from the context in addition to any other information which is material information under reg 6(3): (a) the main characteristics of the product, to the extent appropriate to the medium by which the invitation to purchase is communicated and the product; (b) the identity of the trader, such as his trading name, and the identity of any other trader on whose behalf the trader is acting; (c) the geographical address of the trader and the geographical address of any other trader on whose behalf the trader is acting; (d) either: (i) the price, including any taxes; or (ii) where the nature of the product is such that the price cannot reasonably be calculated in advance, the manner in which the price is calculated; (e) where appropriate, either: (i) all additional freight, delivery or postal charges; or (ii) where such charges cannot reasonably be calculated in advance, the fact that such charges may be payable; (f) the following matters where they depart from the requirements of professional diligence: (i) arrangements for payment; (ii) arrangements for delivery; (iii) arrangements for performance; (iv) complaint handling policy; (g) for products and transactions involving a right of withdrawal or cancellation, the existence of such a right: reg 6(4).

12 Consumer Protection from Unfair Trading Regulations 2008, SI 2008/1277, reg 6(1).

13 Consumer Protection from Unfair Trading Regulations 2008, SI 2008/1277, reg 9.

14 Consumer Protection from Unfair Trading Regulations 2008, SI 2008/1277, reg 10. A person guilty of an offence under the Consumer Protection from Unfair Trading Regulations 2008, SI 2008/1277, reg 9 or 10 is liable, on summary conviction, to a fine not exceeding the statutory maximum or, on conviction on indictment, to a fine or imprisonment for a term not exceeding two years or both: reg 13. As to the statutory maximum see SENTENCING AND DISPOSITION OF OFFENDERS vol 92 (2010) PARA 140. As to offences committed by bodies of persons see reg 15; and SALE OF GOODS AND SUPPLY OF SERVICES.

15 See the Consumer Protection from Unfair Trading Regulations 2008, SI 2008/1277, reg 17; and SALE OF GOODS AND SUPPLY OF SERVICES. In any proceedings against a person for an offence under reg 9 or 10 it is a defence for that person to prove: (1) that the commission of the offence was due to (a) a mistake; (b) reliance on information supplied to him by another person; (c) the act or default of another person; (d) an accident; or (e) another cause beyond his control; and (2) that he took all reasonable precautions and exercised all due diligence to avoid the commission of such an offence by himself or any person under his control: reg 17(1). However, a person is not entitled to rely on the defence by reason of the matters referred to in head (1)(b) or (c) without leave of the court unless: (i) he has served on the prosecutor a notice in writing giving such information identifying or assisting in the identification of that other person as was in his possession; and (ii) the notice is served on the prosecutor at least seven clear days before the date of the hearing: reg 17(2).

16 See the Consumer Protection from Unfair Trading Regulations 2008, SI 2008/1277, reg 18; and SALE OF GOODS AND SUPPLY OF SERVICES. In any proceedings against a person for an offence under reg 9 or 10 committed by the publication of an advertisement it is a defence for a person to prove that: (1) he is a person whose business it is to publish or to arrange for the publication of advertisements; (2) he received the advertisement for publication in the ordinary course of business; and (3) he did not know and had no reason to suspect that its publication would amount to an offence under the regulation to which the proceedings relate: reg 18(1). For these purposes, 'advertisement' includes a catalogue, a circular and a price list: reg 18(2).

17 See the Consumer Protection from Unfair Trading Regulations 2008, SI 2008/1277, reg 16; and SALE OF GOODS AND SUPPLY OF SERVICES. Where a person 'X' commits such an offence under reg 9 or 10 or would have committed an offence but for a defence under reg 17 or 18, and the commission of the offence, or of what would have been an offence but for X being able to rely on a defence under reg 17 or 18, is due to the act or default of some other person 'Y', then Y is guilty of the offence, subject to regs 17 and 18, whether or not Y is a trader and whether or not Y's act or default is a commercial practice: reg 16(1), (2). Y may be charged with and convicted of the offence by virtue of reg 16(2) whether or not proceedings are taken against X: reg 16(3). So, for example, if an auctioneer applies a false or misleading description of goods from information supplied by his seller-client, the latter may be charged even where he is not a trader.

61. Misdescribed land. The Property Misdescriptions Act 1991 provides similar protection in respect to misdescribed land[1] as the provisions in respect of misdescribed goods[2]. Where a false[3] or misleading statement[4] about a prescribed matter[5] is made by an auctioneer[6] in the course of an estate agency business[7], the person by whom the business is carried on is guilty of an offence[8]. Where the making of the statement is due to the act or default of an employee, the employee is guilty of an offence, and the employee may be proceeded against and punished whether or not proceedings are also taken against his employer[9]. In proceedings against a person for such an offence it is a defence for him to show that he took all reasonable steps and exercised all due diligence to avoid committing the offence[10].

An estimate of the likely price of a lot which is below the reserve may amount to a misleading statement about the price[11].

1 As to false or misleading statements in relation to property see further CONSUMER PROTECTION vol 21 (2011) PARA 551.

2 As to the provisions in respect of misdescribed goods see PARA 60.

3 For these purposes, 'false' means false to a material degree: Property Misdescriptions Act 1991 s 1(5)(a).

4 For these purposes, a statement is misleading if (though not false) what a reasonable person may be expected to infer from it, or from any omission from it, is false: Property Misdescriptions Act 1991 s 1(5)(b). For these purposes, a statement may be made by pictures or any other method of signifying meaning as well as by words and, if made by words, may be made orally or in writing: s 1(5)(c).

5 For these purposes, a prescribed matter is any matter relating to land which is specified in an order made by the Secretary of State: Property Misdescriptions Act 1991 s 1(5)(d). As to the Secretary of State see PARA 4 note 12. An order under s 1 may make different provision for different cases, and include such supplemental, consequential and transitional provisions as the Secretary of State considers appropriate: s 1(7). The power to make such an order is exercisable by statutory instrument which is subject to annulment in pursuance of a resolution of either House of Parliament: s 1(7). In exercise of the power under s 1 the Property Misdescriptions (Specified Matters) Order 1992, SI 1992/2834, has been made: see CONSUMER PROTECTION vol 21 (2011) PARA 552.

6 As to the meaning of 'auctioneer' see PARA 2.

7 For these purposes, a statement is made in the course of an estate agency business if (but only if) the making of the statement is a thing done as mentioned in the Estate Agents Act 1979 s 1(1) (see AGENCY vol 1 (2008) PARA 240; CONSUMER PROTECTION vol 21 (2011) PARA 550) and the Estate Agents Act 1979 either applies to it or would apply to it but for s 1(2)(a) (exception for things done in course of profession by practising solicitor or employee) (see AGENCY vol 1 (2008) PARA 241): Property Misdescriptions Act 1991 s 1(5)(e). For the purposes, any reference in s 1 or the Estate Agents Act 1979 s 1 to disposing of or acquiring an interest in land is to be construed in accordance with s 2 (see AGENCY vol 1 (2008) PARA 240): Property Misdescriptions Act 1991 s 1(6).

8 See the Property Misdescriptions Act 1991 s 1(1). A person guilty of an offence under s 1 is liable, on summary conviction, to a fine not exceeding the statutory maximum and, on conviction on indictment, to a fine: s 1(3). As to the statutory maximum see SENTENCING AND DISPOSITION OF OFFENDERS vol 92 (2010) PARA 140.

    No contract is void or unenforceable, and no right of action in civil proceedings in respect of any loss arises, by reason only of the commission of an offence under the Property Misdescriptions Act 1991 s 1: see s 1(4).

9 Property Misdescriptions Act 1991 s 1(2). See note 8.

10 Property Misdescriptions Act 1991 s 2(1). As to the defence of due diligence see further s 2(2)–(4); and CONSUMER PROTECTION vol 21 (2011) PARA 553.

11 See the Property Misdescriptions (Specified Matters) Order 1992, SI 1992/2834, art 2, Schedule para 16. This does not apply to new dwellings or to commercial property: Schedule para 16 proviso. New dwellings were covered by the Consumer Protection Act 1987 s 20 (misleading price indications; now repealed) and would now fall within the Consumer Protection from Unfair Trading Regulations 2008, SI 2008/1277: see SALE OF GOODS AND SUPPLY OF SERVICES.

62.   Unhallmarked gold, silver or platinum.   An auctioneer[1] is guilty of an offence, which is one of strict liability[2], if in the course of his trade or business he applies to an unhallmarked item a description indicating that it is wholly or partly made of gold, silver or platinum, or if he supplies or offers to supply an unhallmarked article to which such a description is applied[3]. Goods are unhallmarked if they do not bear the approved hallmarks and the sponsor's mark, or if they have been the subject of improper alteration[4]. Problems may be encountered particularly with imported items, especially those manufactured in countries where there exists self-regulatory hallmarking, the items being marked by the manufacturer rather than some official assay office.

1   As to the meaning of 'auctioneer' see PARA 2.
2   *Chilvers v Rayner* [1984] 1 All ER 843, [1984] 1 WLR 328, DC.
3   See the Hallmarking Act 1973 s 1(1). See generally TRADE MARKS AND TRADE NAMES vol 48 (2007 Reissue) PARA 467 et seq.
4   See the Hallmarking Act 1973 s 2(4).

63.   Unsafe and dangerous goods.   The Consumer Protection Act 1987 makes it an offence to sell or possess for the purposes of sale a wide range of goods which are unsafe or do not conform to certain standards[1]. It is also specifically an offence to sell pharmaceuticals[2]. Auctioneers undertaking 'household clearances' need to be particularly on guard.

1   See the Consumer Protection Act 1987 Pt II (ss 11–19); and CONSUMER PROTECTION vol 21 (2011) PARA 675 et seq. Whereas the Consumer Protection Act 1961 (repealed) contained a specific exception for those, such as auctioneers, selling as agents, the later Acts do not. As to the meaning of 'auctioneer' see PARA 2.
      There are numerous consumer protection measures made by the European Union: see CONSUMER PROTECTION vol 21 (2011) PARA 403. See eg European Parliament and Council Directive 2001/95 (OJ L11 15.1.2004, p 4) on general product safety, which is implemented in the United Kingdom by the General Product Safety Regulations 2005, SI 2005/1803. These regulations apply to second-hand products (although not to those sold as antiques: see regs 9(2), 30): see SALE OF GOODS AND SUPPLY OF SERVICES.
2   See the Medicines Act 1968 ss 7, 45(1); and MEDICINAL PRODUCTS AND DRUGS.

64.   Unroadworthy vehicles.   It is an offence for an auctioneer[1] to sell or supply, or to offer to sell or supply, or to expose for sale unroadworthy vehicles[2]. An auctioneer may not be convicted of an offence in respect of the supply of a motor vehicle or trailer if he proves that it was supplied or altered, as the case may be, for export from Great Britain[3], or that he had reasonable cause to believe that the vehicle or trailer would not be used on a road in Great Britain or would not be so used until it had been put into a condition in which it might lawfully be so used[4]. If such a vehicle is sold, the contract made at auction is not invalidated by any infringement of the statutory provisions[5].

1   As to the meaning of 'auctioneer' see PARA 2.
2   See the Road Traffic Act 1988 s 75 (amended by the Road Traffic Act 1991 ss 16(2), (3), (4), (5), 83, Sch 8); and CONSUMER PROTECTION vol 21 (2011) PARA 631; ROAD TRAFFIC vol 89 (2011) PARA 497. A person guilty of an offence under the Road Traffic Act 1988 s 75 is liable on summary conviction to a fine not exceeding level 5 on the standard scale: Road Traffic Offenders Act 1988 ss 9, 33(1), Sch 2 Pt I. As to the standard scale see SENTENCING AND DISPOSITION OF OFFENDERS vol 92 (2010) PARA 142.
3   See the Road Traffic Act 1988 s 75(6)(a).
4   See the Road Traffic Act 1988 s 75(6)(b).
5   See the Road Traffic Act 1988 s 75(7).

65.   Wild birds, wild animals and endangered species.   Except in relation to certain wild birds specified in the Wildlife and Countryside Act 1981[1], the sale or offering or exposing for sale of any live wild bird, or an egg or any part of such, or any dead wild bird or any part of, or anything derived from it, is an offence unless authorised under a licence by the appropriate authority[2]. The position is the same with regard to certain live or dead wild animals[3]. Endangered species are dealt with, as to restrictions upon importation and exportation, by the Endangered Species (Import and Export) Act 1976, which subjects their sale to a licensing system[4].

1 Ie the Wildlife and Countryside Act 1981 s 6, Sch 3 (birds which may be sold): see ANIMALS vol 2 (2008) PARA 1007.

2 See the Wildlife and Countryside Act 1981 ss 6(1), (2), 16(4) (s 6(2) amended by the Countryside and Rights of Way Act 2000 ss 81(1), 102, Sch 12 paras 3, 10(6), Sch 16 Pt IV); and ANIMALS vol 2 (2008) PARAS 1006, 1007, 1019. The 'appropriate authority' for these purposes is the Secretary of State or, in relation to Wales, the Welsh Ministers acting concurrently with the Secretary of State: Wildlife and Countryside Act 1981 s 16(9)(b) (amended by the Marine and Coastal Access Act 2009 s 10(1), (3)); National Assembly for Wales (Transfer of Functions) Order 1999, SI 1999/672, art 2, Sch 1; Government of Wales Act 2006 s 162, Sch 11 para 30.
   So far as relating to the restricted English inshore region, 'the appropriate authority' means the Marine Management Organisation: Wildlife and Countryside Act 1981 s 16(8A) (prospectively added by the Marine and Coastal Access Act 2009 s 10(2)). As to the restricted English inshore region see the Wildlife and Countryside Act 1981 s 16(12) (prospectively added by the Marine and Coastal Access Act 2009 s 10(4)). At the date at which this volume states the law, no days had been appointed for bringing these amendments into effect. As to the Secretary of State see PARA 4 note 12.
   A person guilty of an offence under the Wildlife and Countryside Act 1981 s 6(1), (2) or s 9(5) (see the text to note 3) is liable on summary conviction to imprisonment for a term not exceeding six months or to a fine not exceeding level 5 on the standard scale, or to both: s 21(1) (substituted by the Countryside and Rights of Way Act 2000 Sch 12 para 10(1), (2), (6)). As to the standard scale see SENTENCING AND DISPOSITION OF OFFENDERS vol 92 (2010) PARA 142. Where an offence was committed in respect of more than one bird, nest, egg, other animal, plant or other thing, the maximum fine which may be imposed is determined as if the person convicted had been convicted of a separate offence in respect of each bird, nest, egg, animal, plant or thing: see the Wildlife and Countryside Act 1981 s 21(5) (amended by the Countryside and Rights of Way Act 2000 Sch 12 para 10(1), (5), Sch 16 Pt IV).

3 See the Wildlife and Countryside Act 1981 s 9(5), Sch 5; and ANIMALS vol 2 (2008) PARA 1015. See note 2.

4 See the Endangered Species (Import and Export) Act 1976; and ANIMALS vol 2 (2008) PARA 966 et seq.

66. Firearms and other offensive weapons. It is an offence if by way of trade or business an auctioneer[1] sells, exposes for sale or transfer, or has in his possession for sale, any firearm[2] or ammunition[3] to which the Firearms Act 1968 applies[4], or a shot gun[5] or an air weapon[6], without being registered as a firearms dealer[7] or obtaining a permit[8] from the chief officer of police[9] for the area[10] in which the auction[11] is held and complying with the terms of the permit[12]. It is an offence for a person to sell or transfer to any other person in the United Kingdom, other than a registered firearms dealer, any firearm or ammunition to which the Firearms Act 1968 applies[13], or a shot gun, unless that other produces a firearm certificate[14] authorising him to purchase or acquire it or, as the case may be, his shot gun certificate, or shows that he is by virtue of the Firearms Act 1968 entitled to purchase or acquire it without holding a certificate[15]. A criminal offence is not committed under the Firearms Act 1968 in the sale of antique firearms sold, transferred, purchased, acquired or possessed as a curiosity or ornament[16]. Firearms are regarded as antique if they are 100 years old but they may be so regarded even if they are of less age[17].

Other offensive weapons[18] are treated separately[19]. It is an offence to sell or expose for sale such weapons, punishable on summary conviction by a term of imprisonment[20] or a fine[21], or both[22]. There is a general exclusion for antiques, which are simply defined as weapons over 100 years old[23].

1   As to the meaning of 'auctioneer' see PARA 2.
2   As to the meaning of 'firearm' see PARA 4 note 7. As to the law relating to firearms generally see CRIMINAL LAW vol 26 (2010) PARA 578 et seq.
3   As to the meaning of 'ammunition' see PARA 4 note 8.
4   Ie the Firearms Act 1968 s 1: see CRIMINAL LAW vol 26 (2010) PARAS 578–581.
5   As to the meaning of 'shot gun' see CRIMINAL LAW vol 26 (2010) PARA 579.
6   As to the meaning of 'air weapon' see CRIMINAL LAW vol 26 (2010) PARA 580.
7   See the Firearms Act 1968 s 3(1) (amended by the Violent Crime Reduction Act 2006 ss 31(1), 65, Sch 5); and CRIMINAL LAW vol 26 (2010) PARA 584. As to the meaning of 'firearms dealer' see PARA 4 note 9; and as to the meaning of 'registered' see PARA 4 note 9.
8   Ie a permit in the form prescribed by the Secretary of State: Firearms Act 1968 ss 9(2), 57(4). For the form of permit see the Firearms Rules 1998, SI 1998/1941, r 9(2)(a), Sch 4 Pt III (auctioneer's firearm and ammunition permit), r 9(2)(b), Sch 4 Pt IV (auctioneer's shot gun permit). As to the Secretary of State see PARA 4 note 12.
9   As to the chief officer of police see POLICE vol 36(1) (2007 Reissue) PARA 178 et seq.
10 As to the meaning of 'area' see PARA 4 note 11.
11 As to the meaning of 'auction' see PARA 1.
12 See the Firearms Act 1968 s 9(2); and PARA 4.
13 Ie the Firearms Act 1968 s 1: see CRIMINAL LAW vol 26 (2010) PARAS 578–581.
14 As to the meaning of 'certificate' see CRIMINAL LAW vol 26 (2010) PARA 585.
15 Firearms Act 1968 s 3(2). However, it is not an offence under s 3(2) for a person: (1) to part with the possession of any firearm or ammunition, otherwise than in pursuance of a contract of sale or hire by way of gift or loan, to a person who shows that he is by virtue of the Firearms Act 1968 entitled to have possession of the firearm or ammunition without holding a certificate; or (2) to return to another person a shot gun which he has lawfully undertaken to repair, test or prove for the other: s 8(2).
16 See the Firearms Act 1968 s 58(2). It is not a defence that one has an honest belief that the firearm is an antique if in fact or law it is not: *R v Howells* [1977] QB 614, [1977] 3 All ER 417, CA; *R v Hussain* [1981] 2 All ER 287, [1981] 1 WLR 416, CA.
17 *Richards v Curwen* [1977] 3 All ER 426, [1977] 1 WLR 747; *Bennett v Brown* (1980) 71 Cr App Rep 109, DC. See, however, the comments of Watkins J in *Bennett v Brown* (1980) 71 Cr App Rep 109, DC ('… no reasonable bench of justices could conclude, regardless of whether or not a firearm could be used in a war at any time, that a firearm which has been manufactured during this century is an antique').
18 See the Criminal Justice Act 1988 (Offensive Weapons) Order 1988, SI 1988/2019, art 2, Schedule para 1 (amended by SI 2002/1668; SI 2004/1271; and SI 2008/973).
19 See the Criminal Justice Act 1988 s 141; and CRIMINAL LAW vol 26 (2010) PARA 657.
20 Ie a term of imprisonment not exceeding six months: see the Criminal Justice Act 1988 s 141(1).
21 Ie a fine not exceeding level 5 on the standard scale: see the Criminal Justice Act 1988 s 141(1). As to the standard scale see SENTENCING AND DISPOSITION OF OFFENDERS vol 92 (2010) PARA 142.
22 See the Criminal Justice Act 1988 s 141(1).
23 See the Criminal Justice Act 1988 (Offensive Weapons) Order 1988, SI 1988/2019, Schedule para 2.

67–100. Sales of residential investment land.

It is an offence to dispose of residential investment land in breach of the statutory provisions providing tenants with rights of first refusal[1].

1   See the Landlord and Tenant Act 1987 s 10A(1) (added by the Housing Act 1996 s 91(1)). See PARA 45. A person guilty of an offence under Landlord and Tenant Act 1987 s 10A is liable on summary conviction to a fine not exceeding level 5 on the standard scale: s 10A(2) (as so added). As to the standard scale see SENTENCING AND DISPOSITION OF OFFENDERS vol 92 (2010) PARA 142.

BAILMENT AND PLEDGE

1. INTRODUCTION

(1) MEANING AND CLASSIFICATION

101. Meaning of 'bailment'. Under modern law[1], a bailment arises whenever one person (the bailee) is voluntarily in possession of goods belonging to another person (the bailor)[2]. The legal relationship of bailor and bailee can exist independently of any contract, and is created by the voluntary taking into custody of goods which are the property of another, as in cases of sub-bailment or of bailment by finding[3]. The element common to all types of bailment is the imposition of an obligation, because the taking of possession in the circumstances involves an assumption of responsibility for the safe keeping of the goods[4]. A claim against a bailee can be regarded as a claim on its own, sui generis, arising out of the possession had by the bailee of the goods[5].

A bailment is distinguishable from a sale[6], which is effected wherever chattels are delivered on a contract for a money consideration called the price, and not for the return of the identical chattels in their original or an altered form[7]. It must also be distinguished from the relationship of *mutuum*, which involves the delivery of fungible goods by an existing owner accompanied by an obligation on the part of the deliveree to deliver equivalent but different goods back to the deliveror[8]. The relationship of bailor and bailee is also to be distinguished from the relationship of licensor and licensee which, in the absence of special contractual provisions, carries no active obligation on the part of the licensor towards the licensee in relation to the chattel subject to the licence[9].

To constitute a bailment (which derives its name from the old French word *bailler*, to deliver or put into the hands of), the actual or constructive possession of a specific chattel must be vacated by its owner or possessor (the bailor), or his agent duly authorised for that purpose, in favour of another person (the bailee)[10] in order that the latter may keep the same or perform some act in connection with it, for which such actual or constructive possession of the chattel is necessary, thereafter returning the identical subject matter in its original or an altered form[11].

Thus a bailment may arise by attornment involving a constructive delivery of possession, as where, for example, a warehouseman holding goods as agent for an owner agreed to hold them for another person pursuant to the owner's instructions[12]. There can be a bailment by an owner without his ever having taken possession of the chattel concerned, so long as the title to it or the right to possess it has passed to him[13].

1   The modern definition of bailment is more spacious than that accepted in earlier times. According to the traditional definition, bailment is a delivery of personal chattels on trust, usually on a contract, express or implied, that the trust shall be duly executed, and the chattels redelivered in either their original or an altered form, as soon as the time or use for, or condition on, which they were bailed shall have elapsed or been performed. See Bac Abr Bailment; and see also 2 Bl Com 452; Jones on Bailments (4th Edn, 1833) pp 1, 117; Story on Bailments (9th Edn, 1878) s 2; 2 Kent's Com Pt V, s 559; 1 Bell's Com lib 2, Pt 3, c 2, s 4, art 2. This definition was approved and adopted in *Re S Davis & Co Ltd* [1945] Ch 402. But modern authority rejects the universal equation between bailment and contract (while recognising of course that many bailments are contractual): see the text and notes 1–13; Palmer on Bailment (3rd Edn, 2009) para 1-025. Modern authority has also clarified the relationship between bailment and trust, emphasising that since bailment can give rise to legal remedies a person must have a legal and not merely an equitable interest in the chattel in order to qualify as a bailor: *MCC Proceeds Inc v Lehman Bros International (Europe)* [1998] 4 All ER 675, [1998] 2 BCLC 659, CA (which appears to accept that a right of possession arising from an equitable interest might suffice to

qualify the holder to sue in conversion and thereby suggests that the holder of such a right might also stand as a bailor of the possessor); *Shell UK Ltd v Total UK Ltd* [2010] EWCA Civ 180, [2010] 3 All ER 793, [2010] 3 WLR 1192. The use of the word 'trust' in the definition cited earlier in this note does not therefore signify that bailments are a form of trust in the literal sense, but rather that, in the ordinary case, the goods are entrusted to the bailee.

It has been held that 'The important question is not the literal meaning of bailment but the circle of relationships within which its characteristic duties will apply. For most practical purposes, any person who comes knowingly into the possession of another's goods is, prima facie, a bailee': Palmer on Bailment (3rd Edn, 2009) para 23-001, cited with approval in *East West Corpn v DKBS AF 1912 A/S, Utaniko Ltd v P & O Nedlloyd BV* [2003] EWCA Civ 83 at [26], [2003] QB 1509 at [26], [2003] 2 All ER 700 at [26] per Mance LJ. As to conversion generally see TORT vol 45(2) (Reissue) PARA 548 et seq.

2   *KH Enterprise v Pioneer Container, The Pioneer Container* [1994] 2 AC 324, [1994] 2 All ER 250, [1994] 1 Lloyd's Rep 593, PC; *East West Corpn v DKBS AF 1912 A/S, Utaniko Ltd v P & O Nedlloyd BV* [2003] EWCA Civ 83, [2003] QB 1509, [2003] 2 All ER 700; *Sandeman Coprimar SA v Transitos y Integrales SL* [2003] EWCA Civ 113, [2003] QB 1270, [2003] 3 All ER 108, [2003] 2 Lloyd's Rep 172; *P & O Trans European Ltd v Wincanton Ltd* [2001] EWCA Civ 227, [2001] All ER (D) 174 (Feb); *Compania Portorafti Commerciale SA v Ultramar Panama Inc, The Captain Gregos (No 2)* [1990] 2 Lloyd's Rep 395 at 405, CA, per Bingham LJ: cf *Marcq v Christie Manson & Woods Ltd (t/a Christie's)* [2003] EWCA Civ 731, [2004] QB 286, [2003] 3 All ER 561. As to where a person is not aware that he is in possession of goods belonging to another see PARA 104.

3   See *Morris v CW Martin & Sons Ltd* [1966] 1 QB 716 at 731–732, [1965] 2 All ER 725 at 734–735, CA, per Diplock LJ; *Fairline Shipping Corpn Ltd v Adamson* [1975] QB 180 at 189, [1974] 2 All ER 967 at 975 per Kerr J; *Parastatidis v Kotaridis* [1978] VR 449 at 454–455 per Harris J; *Punch v Savoy's Jewellers Ltd* (1986) 26 DLR (4th) 546 at 551, Ont CA per Cory JA; *Compania Portorafti Commerciale SA v Ultramar Panama Inc, The Captain Gregos (No 2)* [1990] 2 Lloyd's Rep 395 at 405, CA, per Bingham LJ. See also *East West Corpn v DKBS AF 1912 A/S, Utaniko Ltd v P & O Nedlloyd BV* [2003] EWCA Civ 83, [2003] QB 1509, [2003] 2 All ER 700; *Sandeman Coprimar SA v Transitos y Integrales SL* [2003] EWCA Civ 113, [2003] QB 1270, [2003] 3 All ER 108, [2003] 2 Lloyd's Rep 172. As to bailment by finding see PARA 116; as to sub-bailment see PARA 110.

4   *KH Enterprise v Pioneer Container, The Pioneer Container* [1994] 2 AC 324, [1994] 2 All ER 250, [1994] 1 Lloyd's Rep 593, PC; *Gilchrist Watt and Sanderson Pty Ltd v York Products Pty Ltd* [1970] 3 All ER 825 at 831, [1970] 1 WLR 1262 at 1268, PC. See also *Global Dress Co Ltd v WH Boase & Co Ltd* [1966] 2 Lloyd's Rep 72 at 76, CA; *Learoyd Bros & Co and Huddersfield Fine Worsteds Ltd v Pope & Sons (Dock Carriers) Ltd* [1966] 2 Lloyd's Rep 142 at 147–148; *Moukataff v British Overseas Airways Corpn* [1967] 1 Lloyd's Rep 396 at 416; *Lee Cooper Ltd v CH Jeakins & Sons Ltd* [1967] 2 QB 1, [1965] 1 All ER 280; *Chesworth v Farrar* [1967] 1 QB 407 at 415–416, [1966] 2 All ER 107 at 112; and PARA 110.

5   See *Building and Civil Engineering Holidays Scheme Management Ltd v Post Office* [1966] 1 QB 247 at 261, [1965] 1 All ER 163 at 167, CA, per Lord Denning MR; *Singer Co (UK) Ltd v Tees and Hartlepool Port Authority* [1988] 2 Lloyd's Rep 164 at 167–168 per Steyn J; *Sutcliffe v Chief Constable of West Yorkshire* [1996] RTR 86, (1995) 159 JP 770, CA; and see *Sandeman Coprimar SA v Transitos y Integrales SL* [2003] EWCA Civ 113, [2003] QB 1270, [2003] 3 All ER 108, [2003] 2 Lloyd's Rep 172; *Yearworth v North Bristol NHS Trust* [2009] EWCA Civ 37, [2010] QB 1, [2009] 2 All ER 986.

6   See SALE OF GOODS AND SUPPLY OF SERVICES vol 41 (2005 Reissue) PARA 1. Where goods are delivered to a buyer under a contract of sale which contains a reservation of title clause, the relationship may concurrently amount to one of bailment: *Clough Mill Ltd v Martin* [1984] 3 All ER 982 at 987, [1985] 1 WLR 111 at 116, CA, per Goff LJ; cf *Borden (UK) Ltd v Scottish Timber Products Ltd* [1981] Ch 25, [1979] 3 All ER 961, CA. As to transactions between brewers and mineral water manufacturers and their customers which amount to bailments and not sales of bottles see *Cantrell and Cochrane Ltd v Neeson* [1926] NI 107, CA; *Barlow & Co v Hanslip* [1926] NI 113n (an English decision). See also *William Leitch & Co Ltd v Leydon, AG Barr & Co Ltd v Macgeoghegan* [1931] AC 90, HL. See generally on the relationship between bailment and sale Palmer on Bailment (3rd Edn, 2009) paras 3-031–3-078, 8-018–8-036, 9-013–9-014; as to the distinction between gift and bailment see Palmer on Bailment (3rd Edn, 2009) paras 3-013–3-027.

7   *South Australian Insurance Co v Randell* (1869) LR 3 PC 101 at 108, 113, approving 2 Kent's Com (11th Edn) s 589; *Mercer v Craven Grain Storage Ltd* (17 March 1994, unreported), HL; *P & O Trans European Ltd v Wincanton Ltd* [2001] EWCA Civ 227, [2001] All ER (D) 174 (Feb).

8 See *P & O Trans European Ltd v Wincanton Ltd* [2001] EWCA Civ 227, [2001] All ER (D) 174 (Feb), CA; and PARA 140.

9 *Ashby v Tolhurst* [1937] 2 KB 242 at 249, [1937] 2 All ER 837 at 840, CA, per Greene MR (held no delivery of possession; only a licence to leave car on parking ground); *Tinsley v Dudley* [1951] 2 KB 18 at 26, [1951] 1 All ER 252 at 256–257, CA, per Evershed MR (parking of vehicles by invitation or permission on private ground: no transfer of possession or custody); and see also *BRS (Contracts) Ltd v Colney Motor Engineering Co Ltd* (1958) Times, 27 November, CA; *BG Transport Service Ltd v Marston Motor Co Ltd* [1970] 1 Lloyd's Rep 371 (both vehicle parking cases: no bailment); *Fred Chappell Ltd v National Car Parks Ltd* (1987) Times, 22 May (retention of keys by vehicle owner, and no barrier at car park: no bailment); *Lotus Cars Ltd v Southampton Cargo Handling plc, The Rigoletto* [2000] 2 All ER (Comm) 705, [2000] 2 Lloyd's Rep 532, CA; *PF Walsh Plant Ltd v Wilton Contracts (London) Ltd* (17 March 2000, unreported), CA. A caravan site owner is not ordinarily a bailee of the caravans, but if he undertakes winter storage he may become a bailee then: *Halbauer v Brighton Corpn* [1954] 2 All ER 707, [1954] 1 WLR 1161, CA, applied in *Hinks v Fleet* [1987] BTLC 289, CA; but see *Wilmers and Gladwin Pty Co v WAL Building Supplies Pty Ltd* (1955) 55 SR NSW 442, NSW SC (plaintiff rented storage bay in building; for access he had to communicate with defendant, who had the only key but who never handled the plaintiff's goods: held no bailment).

10 For delivery, there must be a transfer of the exclusive right of possession: see *Midland Silicones Ltd v Scruttons Ltd* [1959] 2 QB 171 at 189, [1959] 2 All ER 289 at 296; on appeal [1961] 1 QB 106 at 119, [1960] 2 All ER 737 at 740, CA; affd sub nom *Scruttons Ltd v Midland Silicones Ltd* [1962] AC 446 at 470, [1962] 1 All ER 1 at 8, HL (no bailment); *Lotus Cars Ltd v Southampton Cargo Handling plc, The Rigoletto* [2000] 2 All ER (Comm) 705, [2000] 2 Lloyd's Rep 532, CA; *Spectra International plc v Hayesoak Ltd* [1997] 1 Lloyd's Rep 153, Central London County Court (ie at first instance: see also [1998] 1 Lloyd's Rep 162, CA); *East West Corpn v DKBS AF 1912 A/S* [2003] EWCA Civ 83 at [47], [2003] QB 1509 at [47], [2003] 2 All ER 700 at [47], per Mance LJ for the Court (concurrent rights of possession). As to constructive delivery where a seller continues to hold goods as bailee for the buyer see *Michael Gerson (Leasing) Ltd v Wilkinson* [2001] QB 514, [2001] 1 All ER 148, CA: cf *Forsythe International (UK) Ltd v Silver Shipping Co Ltd and Petroglobe International Ltd, The Saetta* [1994] 1 All ER 851, [1994] 1 WLR 1334, [1993] 2 Lloyd's Rep 268. Placing a coat in an unattended anteroom at a hotel or restaurant may in particular circumstances constitute a transfer of possession: *Samuel v Westminster Wine Co Ltd* (1959) Times, 16 May. See also *Shorters Parking Station Ltd v Johnson* [1963] NZLR 135, NZ SC; *Mendelssohn v Normand Ltd* [1970] 1 QB 177, [1969] 2 All ER 1215, CA (both vehicle parking cases in which cars were left in garage attendant's custody: held to be bailment in each case). For a comparison of the relationship of bailor and bailee with that of master and servant see *Fowler v Lock* (1872) LR 7 CP 272 (on appeal (1874) LR 9 CP 751n, Ex Ch); *Venables v Smith* (1877) 2 QBD 279; *Gates v R Bill & Son* [1902] 2 KB 38, CA; and cf *Hewitt v Bonvin* [1940] 1 KB 188, CA; Palmer on Bailment (3rd Edn, 2009) Chapter 7. See further EMPLOYMENT vol 39 (2009) PARA 6. Cases may occur in which there is a transfer of possession intended by both parties to be a bailment, though obtained by the transferee by deceit; and then perhaps there is a contract of bailment (though voidable by the bailor), for there is a real consent by him (though induced by fraud) and the taking would not be trespassory and would not therefore amount to theft. If, however, one party means only to give a bailment and the other party accepts the chattel, meaning not to hold it on a bailment but to appropriate it contrary to the known intention of the bailor, there is no concurrence of intention and no contract; there is only an outward appearance of consent on the bailor's part to the physical delivery of the chattel, and the possession therefore does not pass by contract but by wrong. In such a case the taking of the chattel by the pretended bailee is trespassory and will support an indictment for theft: see *Lake v Simmons* [1927] AC 487, HL, distinguished in *John Rigby (Haulage) Ltd v Reliance Marine Insurance Co Ltd* [1956] 2 QB 468, [1956] 3 All ER 1, CA; and generally as to mistake in contract under modern law *Shogun Finance Ltd v Hudson* [2003] UKHL 62, [2004] 1 AC 919, [2004] 1 All ER 215. See also the Theft Act 1968 ss 1–6, 15; and CRIMINAL LAW vol 25 (2010) PARA 278 et seq.

11 *South Australian Insurance Co v Randell* (1869) LR 3 PC 101. Cf *Borden (UK) Ltd v Scottish Timber Products Ltd* [1981] Ch 25, [1979] 3 All ER 961, CA; *Clough Mill Ltd v Martin* [1984] 3 All ER 982 at 987, [1985] 1 WLR 111 at 116, CA, per Goff LJ (bailment may arise although bailee empowered to intermix goods or dispose of them to third parties). But cf *P & O Trans European Ltd v Wincanton Ltd* [2001] EWCA Civ 227, [2001] All ER (D) 174 (Feb).

12 See *Dublin City Distillery Ltd v Doherty* [1914] AC 823 at 847, HL, per Lord Atkinson; and see PARA 229. Cf *Re Goldcorp Exchange Ltd (in receivership)* [1995] 1 AC 74, [1994] 2 All ER

806, PC; *East West Corpn v DKBS AF 1912 A/S, Utaniko Ltd v P & O Nedlloyd BV* [2003] EWCA Civ 83, [2003] QB 1509, [2003] 2 All ER 700.

13 *Belvoir Finance Co Ltd v Stapleton* [1971] 1 QB 210 at 217, [1970] 3 All ER 664 at 667, CA (plaintiff finance company obtained title to car under executed illegal contract of sale and, without taking delivery of it, hired it out to a company which converted it: hiring company held to be bailees); *Transcontainer Express Ltd v Custodian Security Ltd* [1988] 1 Lloyd's Rep 128 at 135, CA, per Slade LJ (where the point was not decided); *Edwards v Newland & Co (E Burchett Ltd, third party)* [1950] 2 KB 534, [1950] 1 All ER 1072, CA; *Johnson Matthey Ltd v Constantine Terminals Ltd and International Express Co Ltd* [1976] 2 Lloyd's Rep 215; and see *East West Corpn v DKBS AF 1912 A/S* [2003] EWCA Civ 83 at [47], [2003] QB 1509 at [47], [2003] 2 All ER 700 at [47], per Mance LJ for the Court.

102. Possession. It is generally accepted that the possession by one person of a tangible chattel belonging to another person is essential in order for bailment to arise[1]. Being in possession of the goods of another, however, does not necessarily render someone a bailee; there must be a voluntary possession[2]. The question of possession may arise in several ways in relation to bailment.

First, there are numerous cases where the requirement of a transfer of possession is in issue. It has been suggested that to create bailment by way of hire[3], possession of the hired chattel is not necessary where a servant is supplied by the lessor to operate and maintain the chattel[4]; but in general the weight of authority is that in such cases there is no bailment unless possession vests in the hirer[5]. Possession as a licensee will not suffice to create bailment. Where a person leaves or deposits a chattel on another person's land[6] with the permission of the landowner in circumstances which do not confer possession of the chattel on the landowner, the owner of the chattel is said to be a mere licensee of the space occupied by the chattel and his apparent delivery does not give rise to a bailment. The distinction between licences and bailments has been the subject of much authority and depends on a multiplicity of factors: bailment requiring a transfer of possession and the voluntary acceptance of the common law duty of safekeeping, a licence by contrast amounting to no more that a grant of permission to the user of a chattel to leave it on the licensor's land on the understanding that neither possession is transferred nor responsibility for guarding the chattel accepted[7]. Much will depend on the facts, but certain categories of cases may be of assistance in identifying the existence of a bailment rather than a licence: the transfer of the means of access to or control over the chattel[8]; procedures for recovery of possession, such as the existence of a system by which persons retrieving vehicles are scrutinised before being allowed to leave[9]; the amount of fees or charges and the time at which they are paid[10]; the presence of parking attendants[11]; the parties' previous relationship and the commercial standing of the occupier[12]; the high value of the goods deposited[13]. On the other hand, the granting of the exclusive right to use a particular identified part of premises for storage or safekeeping will generally indicate a licence rather than a bailment, as where a lodger in a boarding house leaves articles in his room while absent from the premises[14], a householder stores furniture in a locked room[15] or a customer keeps items in a rented safe-deposit at a bank (at least where the safe-deposit box is one to which the customer has the only key)[16]. In most cases the factors have to be balanced in order to reach a determination whether there is a bailment or a licence.

There are cases where the owner's whole interest is transferred to the deliveree and not merely his possession. In some cases courts have had to decide whether a grant of possession of goods is accompanied by a transfer of property, creating a gift or loan rather than bailment. The nature of the transaction must, in the absence of a deed of gift or declaration of trust, be proved by evidence of intention and delivery[17]. Hire-purchase and conditional sale agreements take effect as bailment followed immediately by sale of the chattel, possession and subsequently ownership of the same chattel being transferred[18]. The nature of the transaction where goods are purchased in a container and a small deposit is paid which is refundable on the return of the container, is not entirely clear: it may be a gratuitous bailment of the container, in the nature of a loan, or a sale of the container to the customer subject to a promise that it would be repurchased on return, or a hire of the container to the customer[19]. However, a clear reservation of ownership at the time of delivery will prevent the passing of title to the purchaser and render him a bailee of the container[20].

Conversely, ceasing to have possession of another's chattel does not necessarily mean that the possessor does not owe the obligations of a bailee, for example if he ceases to be in possession as a result of his own default[21] or if he sub-bails the chattel to a third person who is to carry out work on it[22]. It has been implied in some cases that the duties of a bailee may be owed even although the alleged bailee has never taken possession, as when he negligently fails to take possession of goods which he was ordered to do and the goods are stolen[23], or when a person with a personal duty to take possession wrongfully delegates the task to another[24].

Possession does not require there to be physical custody, as long as the bailee has both the means and the mental element of some immediate control[25]. On the other hand, physical custody does not always create bailment, as for example with the examination of goods in a shop or an auction house or the examination of a passenger's goods by a customs officer[26]. For bailment to arise, it may be necessary that there has been not only a transfer of access to or dominion over a chattel, but for this to have conferred on the recipient the physical control or some other insignia of possession over the chattel to the exclusion of at least the bailor. The requirements of possession may be less strict, however, where it is sought to establish continued possession of a chattel of which the original possession is undisputed[27].

1   See *Ayers v South Australian Banking Co* (1871) LR 3 PC 548; and PARA 101. In some cases of pawn or pledge the courts have accepted the pledging of a document representing a chose in action, thus apparently extending this type of bailment to include possession of intangible things: see *Carter v Wake* (1877) 4 ChD 605 (bearer bonds); cf *Bristol and West of England Bank v Midland Rly Co* [1891] 2 QB 653, CA; and see PARA 190.

2   See *Kamidian v Holt* [2008] EWHC 1483 (Comm), [2009] Lloyd's Rep IR 242, [2008] All ER (D) 394 (Jun) (mere handling or fleeting physical custody; no bailment). The voluntary assumption of possession will ordinarily be taken as entailing a voluntary assumption or undertaking of responsibility for the safe keeping of the goods.

3   As to bailment by hire of chattels see PARA 175 et seq.

4   See *Fowler v Lock* (1872) LR 7 CP 272 at 282 per Byles J (obiter).

5   See eg *Southland Harbour Board v Vella* [1974] 1 NZLR 526, NZ CA; *Silverman v Imperial London Hotels Ltd* (1927) 137 LT 57.

6   Or even attached to another's chattel: see *Seaspan International Ltd v The Kostis Prois* (1973) 33 DLR (3d) 1.

7   Palmer on Bailment (3rd Edn, 2009) para 5-001; *Heffron v Imperial Parking Co Ltd* (1974) 46 DLR (3d) 642 at 647, Ont CA, per Estey JA. See also *Ashby v Tolhurst* [1937] 2 KB 242, [1937] 2 All ER 837, CA (no delivery of possession; only a licence to leave car on parking ground); *Tinsley v Dudley* [1951] 2 KB 18, [1951] 1 All ER 252, CA (parking of vehicles by invitation or permission on private ground: no transfer of possession or custody). See *Lotus Cars Ltd v Southampton Cargo Handling plc, The Rigoletto* [2000] 2 All ER (Comm) 705, [2000] 2 Lloyd's Rep 532, CA; and see generally Palmer on Bailment (3rd Edn, 2009) Chapter 5.

8 Eg parking a car on a parking lot and at the request of the attendant handing over the car ignition key strongly indicates bailment: *Shorter's Parking Station Ltd v Johnson* [1963] NZLR 135.

9 See eg *Sydney City Council v West* (1964) 82 WN (Pt 1) (NSW) 139, NSW SC; affd (1965) 114 CLR 481, [1966] ALR 538, Aust HC (ticket to be presented before taking delivery; bailment); and *Davis v Pearce Parking Station Pty Ltd* (1954) 91 CLR 642, Aus HC.

10 The amount may, if large, indicate bailment: *BG Transport Service Ltd v Marston Motor Co Ltd* [1970] 1 Lloyd's Rep 371 at 378; *James Buchanan & Co Ltd v Hay's Transport Services Ltd and Duncan Barbour & Son Ltd* [1972] 2 Lloyd's Rep 535 at 542. Payment made at the time of withdrawal rather than at the time of deposit may indicate a bailment: see eg *Shipbuilders Ltd v Benson* [1992] 3 NZLR 549; cf *Becvar v Jarvis Norfolk Hotel Ltd* [1999] CLY 833, county court.

11 See eg *Lotus Cars Ltd v Southampton Cargo Handling plc, The Rigoletto* [2000] 2 All ER (Comm) 705, [2000] 2 Lloyd's Rep 532, CA.

12 See eg *James Buchanan & Co Ltd v Hay's Transport Services Ltd and Duncan Barbour & Son Ltd* [1972] 2 Lloyd's Rep 535.

13 *James Buchanan & Co Ltd v Hay's Transport Services Ltd and Duncan Barbour & Son Ltd* [1972] 2 Lloyd's Rep 535; cf *Maritime Coastal Containers Ltd v Shelburne Marine Ltd* (1982) 52 NSR (2d) 51.

14 *Edwards v West Herts Group Hospital Management Committee* [1957] 1 All ER 541, [1957] 1 WLR 415, CA.

15 *Peers v Samson* (1824) 4 Dow & Ry 636.

16 See eg *People v Mercantile Safe Depisit Co* 143 NY Supp 849 (1914); *Comr of Taxation (Cth) v ANZ Banking Group Ltd* (1979) 53 ALJR 336, Aust HC.

17 Palmer on Bailment (3rd Edn, 2009) paras 3-011–3-027. As to gifts inter vivos see GIFTS vol 52 (2009) PARA 201 et seq.

18 As to hire-purchase agreements see CONSUMER CREDIT vol 21 (2011) PARA 66; and as to conditional sale agreements see CONSUMER CREDIT vol 21 (2011) PARA 64; *Re Bond Worth Ltd* [1980] Ch 228, [1979] 3 All ER 919.

19 Eg liquids in bottles. See *Geddling v Marsh* [1920] 1 KB 668.

20 See *Manders v Williams* (1849) 4 Exch 339; *Penfolds Wines Pty Ltd v Elliott* (1946) 74 CLR 204, Aust HC.

21 See eg *Goodman v Boycott* (1862) 2 B & S 1; *Houghland v RR Low (Luxury Coaches) Ltd* [1962] 1 QB 694, [1962] 2 All ER 159, CA; cf *A-G v Observer Ltd, A-G v Times Newspapers Ltd* [1990] 1 AC 109 at 286, sub nom *A-G v Guardian Newspapers Ltd (No 2)* [1988] 3 All ER 545 at 661–662, HL, per Lord Goff of Chieveley.

22 See PARA 110.

23 See *Quiggin v Duff* (1836) 1 M & W 174; cf *O'Neill v McCormack & Co* (1913) 15 WALR 33; *T Kishen & Co v Birkart South East Asia Pte Ltd* [1997] 1 SLR 105.

24 See *Edwards v Newland & Co (E Burchett Ltd, third party)* [1950] 2 KB 534, [1950] 1 All ER 1072, CA.

25 See eg *R v Purdy* [1975] QB 288, [1974] 3 All ER 465, CA (police officer who left arrest warrant in police car 50 or 60 yards away while making an arrest was held to have had the warrant in his possession).

26 See *Zien v The Queen* (1984) 15 DLR (4th) 283; affd on this point (1986) 26 DLR (4th) 121 at 125.

27 See eg *Young v Hichens* (1844) 6 QB 606; *Balmoral Supermarket Ltd v Bank of New Zealand Ltd* [1974] 2 Lloyd's Rep 164, [1974] 2 NZLR 155.

103. Subject matter. The law of bailment applies to all tangible chattels[1] excluding real property[2] and fixtures annexed thereto[3], and live human beings[4] (although modern authority may allow for the bailment of human tissue or remains[5]), but including animals either dead or alive[6].

1 The fact that the item in question can be defined as a 'chattel' is central to the concept of bailment: see *Rosenthal v Alderton* [1946] 1 All ER 583 at 584 per Evershed J; and Palmer on Bailment (3rd Edn, 2009) para 8-038. Modern law may, however, be evolving to allow the bailment of intangible: see Palmer on Bailment (3rd Edn, 2009) Chapter 30.

2 However, an equitable mortgage created by the deposit of title deeds can be accompanied by a legal lien on the deeds: see *Ex p Whitbread* (1812) 19 Ves 209 at 210 per Lord Eldon LC; the Law of Property (Miscellaneous Provisions) Act 1989 s 2; and LIEN vol 68 (2008) PARA 812.

3   See note 1. Fixtures severed and returned to chattel form may be bailed: see Palmer on Bailment
    (3rd Edn, 2009) para 8-038.
4   See Palmer on Bailment (3rd Edn, 2009) para 1-006.
5   See *Yearworth v North Bristol NHS Trust* [2009] EWCA Civ 37, [2010] QB 1, [2009] 2 All ER
    986.
6   See e g *Villecourt v Pricewaterhouse Coopers* [2003] SKQB 275; *SHL Corpn v Harvey* (1981)
    34 NBR 249; and Palmer on Bailment (3rd Edn, 2009) Chapter 31.

104.   Knowledge.   While it is possible to be in possession of goods without
knowledge of their presence, their nature, their location or even their existence[1],
possession without knowledge of what is possessed does not generally render the
possessor a bailee. However, although a possessor who is unaware that he is in
possession of goods belonging to another is not a bailee, he may owe to the
owner a duty to take reasonable care to identify the owner's interest before
destroying or otherwise dealing in the goods[2]. Three situations have been
identified where 'undisclosed or surreptitious bailment' may arise[3]: (1) where a
person, while being wholly unaware of the presence of the goods within his
possession, in fact has possession of them[4]; (2) where a person is aware that he is
a bailee of certain goods (such as containers) but is unaware of some particular
item of their contents[5]; (3) where a person is aware of the specific possession of
goods within his possession but erroneously believes that they are his own[6].
There may be a fourth situation, namely where a bailee of goods from a
non-owner is unaware of the ownership of the true proprietor and therefore of
the fact that he may be liable as a sub-bailee or a substitutional bailee[7]. In most
of the decisions on 'unconscious' bailment the question has been whether there
was a duty of care on the part of the possessor to safeguard the goods against
theft, and the possessor's liability has been made conditional on his actual or
constructive knowledge or notice of, and thus his implied consent to the
possession of, the goods. Other obligations may include a duty to avoid
inadvertently occasioned damage, a duty to abstain from deliberate conduct
which may constitute conversion of the goods, a duty to refrain from intentional
damage or destruction, and a duty to institute reasonable inquiries as to the
position, identity and interests of the owner where a reasonable person in the
position of the passenger should have appreciated that the owner would wish to
be consulted about any proposed action towards the goods[8]. A possessor who
has not consented to possession but is actually or should reasonably be aware of
the presence in his possession of goods belonging to another will be treated (at
least initially)[9] as an involuntary bailee and is not liable except for deliberate
(and perhaps reckless) damage to the goods[10].

1   See e g *Merry v Green* (1841) 7 M & W 623; and for further authority Palmer on Bailment (3rd
    Edn, 2009) Chapter 6.
2   *AVX Ltd v EGM Solders Ltd* (1982) Times, 7 July ('unconscious' bailees held liable for
    destroying or otherwise dealing in goods which they erroneously believed to be their property);
    and see *Robot Arenas Ltd v Waterfield* [2010] EWHC 115 (QB), [2010] All ER (D) 67 (Feb). Cf
    Marcq v Christie Manson & Woods Ltd (t/a Christie's) [2003] EWCA Civ 731, [2004] QB 286,
    [2003] 3 All ER 561, where the claimant sought to impose a similar duty of care on an
    auctioneer who had returned to the person who had delivered it to the auctioneer for sale a
    stolen painting that had been previously registered on a professional register of stolen art; the
    court (distinguishing *AVX Ltd v EGM Solders Ltd* (1982) Times, 7 July) refused to discover any
    duty of care on the defendant possessor to check who was entitled to the painting before
    returning it. See generally Palmer on Bailment (3rd Edn, 2009) Chapter 6; Hudson (2005) 10
    Art Antiquity and Law 201.
3   See *AVX Ltd v EGM Solders Ltd* (1982) Times, 7 July per Staughton J.
4   See e g *Berglund v Roosevelt University* 310 NE (3d) 773 (1974).

5   See eg *Moukataff v British Overseas Airways Corpn* [1967] 1 Lloyd's Rep 396; *Mendelssohn v Normand Ltd* [1970] 1 QB 177, [1969] 2 All ER 1215, CA; *Heffron v Imperial Parking Co Ltd* (1974) 46 DLR (3d) 642 at 647, Ont CA.

6   In such cases, the unconscious bailee must, before dealing with the goods, use what is in all the circumstances the case a sufficient standard of care to ascertain that they truly are his goods: *AVX Ltd v EGM Solders Ltd* (1982) Times, 7 July per Staughton J. Cf *Consentino v Dominion Express Co* (1906) 4 WLR 498, Manitoba CA. See also *Marcq v Christie Manson & Woods Ltd (t/a Christie's)* [2003] EWCA Civ 731, [2004] QB 286, [2003] 3 All ER 561.

7   See Palmer on Bailment (3rd Edn, 2009) para 6-005. As to sub-bailment see PARA 110.

8   *Robot Arenas Ltd v Waterfield* [2010] EWHC 115 (QB), [2010] All ER (D) 67 (Feb).

9   A possessor in this position who continues to hold possession of the goods when he could relieve himself of possession may in due course become a voluntary possessor and thus owe the conventional obligations of a bailee: cf *Marcq v Christie Manson & Woods Ltd (t/a Christie's)* [2003] EWCA Civ 731, [2004] QB 286, [2003] 3 All ER 561.

10 *Howard v Harris* (1884) Cab & El 253; *Neuwith v Over Darwen Industrial Co-operative Society* (1894) 63 LJQB 290. But a misdirection (however well-intentioned) made to a third party without reasonable precautions to establish the deliveree's credentials and bona fides may ground a liability in conversion: *Elvin and Powell Ltd v Plummer, Roddis Ltd* (1933) 78 Sol Jo 48, 50 TLR 158.

105.   Gaining the status of bailor.   A bailor's interest (or 'reversion') need not consist of full residual ownership in the chattel, but might take the form of a right of possession superior to that of the possessor, which right of possession might be immediate or deferred according to circumstance[1]. It appears that the necessary right of possession might be purely contractual in origin[2], and it is possible that two people might enjoy concurrent rights of immediate possession over a chattel in particular circumstances[3].

1   *East West Corpn v DKBS AF 1912 A/S, Utaniko Ltd v P & O Nedlloyd BV* [2003] EWCA Civ 83, [2003] QB 1509, [2003] 2 All ER 700; *Mayflower Foods Ltd v Barnard Bros Ltd* (9 August 1996, unreported), Judge Hegarty QC; *Transcontainer Express Ltd v Custodian Security Ltd* [1988] 1 Lloyd's Rep 128, CA; *The Hamburg Star* [1994] 1 Lloyd's Rep 399, QB; *Indian Herbs (UK) Ltd v Hadley & Ottoway Ltd* [1999] EWCA Civ 627; and see further Palmer 'Possessory Title' in *Interests in Goods* (2nd Edn, 1998) ch 3: cf *MCC Proceeds Inc v Lehman Bros International (Europe)* [1998] 4 All ER 675, [1998] 2 BCLC 659, CA; *China-Pacific SA v Food Corpn of India* [1982] AC 939, [1981] 3 All ER 688, HL.

2   *MCC Proceeds Inc v Lehman Bros International (Europe)* [1998] 4 All ER 675, [1998] 2 BCLC 659, CA, per Mummery, Pill and (semble) Hobhouse LJJ, citing Buckley LJ in *International Factors Ltd v Rodriguez* [1979] QB 351, [1979] 1 All ER 17, CA; *Government of the Islamic Republic of Iran v Barakat Galleries Ltd* [2007] EWCA Civ 1374 at [30], [2009] QB 22 at [20], [2008] 1 All ER 1177 at [30], per Lord Philips of Worth Matravers CJ for the Court.

3   *East West Corpn v DKBS AF 1912 A/S, Utaniko Ltd v P & O Nedlloyd BV* [2003] EWCA Civ 83 at [34]–[39], [2003] QB 1509 at [34]–[39], [2003] 2 All ER 700 at [34]–[39], per Mance LJ.

106.   Classification.   The legal concept of bailment as creating a relationship which gives rise to legal duties owed on each side is derived from Roman law[1]. In a seminal eighteenth century case that has profoundly influenced later thinking, bailment was divided into six classes[2], which were later rearranged into five classes[3], as follows:

(1)   the gratuitous deposit[4] of a chattel with the bailee, who is simply to keep it for the bailor;

(2)   the delivery[5] of a chattel to the bailee, who is to do something without reward for the bailee to or with the chattel;

(3)   the gratuitous loan[6] of a chattel by the bailor to the bailee for the bailee to use;

(4)   the pawn or pledge[7] of a chattel by the bailor to the bailee, who is to hold it as a security for a loan[8] or debt or the fulfilment of an obligation; and

(5)   the hire[9] of a chattel or services by the bailor to the bailee for reward.

Bailments may also be classified as being either gratuitous or for reward: thus the first three classes above mentioned, being without recompense to the other party, are designated gratuitous bailments; the others are bailments for reward, or (where contractual in origin) bailments for valuable consideration. Of the three kinds of gratuitous bailments, it will be noticed that the first two are wholly for the benefit of the bailor, and the third wholly for the benefit of the bailee. This classification is the one adopted in this title, which deals only with the general law of bailment and not with particular forms of bailment, for which reference should be made to other titles[10].

Modern authority now recognises many variations on these basic models of bailment[11], and many examples that do not fit precisely into any particular category[12]. One form of bailment to which much importance has become attached in modern times is the contract of hire-purchase, which has in it not only the element of bailment, but also the element of sale[13]. This type of contract is considered separately in this work[14].

1   See *Morris v CW Martin & Sons Ltd* [1966] 1 QB 716 at 731, [1965] 2 All ER 725 at 734, CA, per Diplock LJ. See also *East West Corpn v DKBS AF 1912 A/S, Utaniko Ltd v P & O Nedlloyd BV* [2003] EWCA Civ 83, [2003] QB 1509, [2003] 2 All ER 700. The works of such foreign jurists as Pothier and Domat have in the past been cited, together with the law as found in the Digest and Institutes of Justinian: Just Inst lib 3, tit 14, 24.
2   See *Coggs v Bernard* (1703) 2 Ld Raym 909 per Holt CJ.
3   See Jones on Bailment (1st Edn, 1781) pp 35–36. Story considered that bailment might be rearranged in three classes: (1) in which the trust is exclusively for the bailor's or a third person's benefit; (2) in which the trust is exclusively for the bailee's benefit; and (3) in which the trust is for the benefit of both parties or of both or one of them and a third party: Story on Bailments (9th Edn, 1878) s 3. Story in his treatise nevertheless adhered to Jones's classification; so did Chancellor Kent: 2 Kent's Com Pt V, s 559. For further discussion of the various classifications of bailment see Palmer on Bailment (3rd Edn, 2009) Chapter 3.
4   Ie *depositum*. See further PARAS 111–125. Sometimes a bailment that is colloquially regarded as a loan may in fact be for reciprocal advantage: see e g *Kamidian v Holt* [2008] EWHC 1483 (Comm), [2009] Lloyd's Rep IR 242, [2008] All ER (D) 394 (Jun) (bailment of historic artefact to exhibition venue).
5   Ie *mandatum*. See further PARAS 126–134.
6   Ie *commodatum*. See further PARAS 135–143.
7   Ie *pignus*, sometimes called *vadium*: see PARA 188.
8   Where interest is payable on the loan in respect of which the chattel is held as security by the bailee, he can aptly be described as a bailee for mutual advantage: see *Canadian Imperial Bank of Commerce v Doucette* (1968) 70 DLR (2d) 657 (PEI SC in banco) (bank in possession of machinery by seizure under statutory lien and claim).
9   Ie *locatio conductio*. This is sometimes divided into four sub-classes: (1) the hiring of a chattel for use (*locatio rei*) (see PARAS 175–187); (2) the hiring of work or labour on or with regard to a chattel (*locatio operis faciendi*) (see PARAS 156–173); (3) the hiring of custody, i e of services in and about the keeping of the chattel (*locatio custodiae*) (see PARAS 145–155); and (4) the hire of the carriage of chattels (*locatio operis mercium vehendarum*) (see CARRIAGE AND CARRIERS vol 7 (2008) PARA 1).
10   See e g AGENCY; AUCTION; CARRIAGE AND CARRIERS; FINANCIAL SERVICES AND INSTITUTIONS vol 49 (2008) PARA 791 et seq; LICENSING AND GAMBLING vol 67 (2008) PARA 197 et seq; LIEN.
11   See Palmer on Bailment (3rd Edn, 2009) para 3-009.
12   See e g *Gamer's Motor Centre (Newcastle) Pty Ltd v Natwest Wholesale Australia Pty Ltd* (1987) 163 CLR 236, Aust HC.
13   See PARA 177. As to sale see SALE OF GOODS AND SUPPLY OF SERVICES vol 41 (2005 Reissue) PARA 1 et seq.
14   See CONSUMER CREDIT vol 21 (2011) PARA 93 et seq.

107.   Degree of care and diligence.   Of the various rights and duties of bailors and bailees, that most discussed is the degree of care and diligence required of the bailee in each kind of bailment. That degree has, from the time of the Roman

Empire until fairly recent times, been held to vary according to the benefits derived from the bailment by the bailor and the bailee respectively[1]. Thus an ordinary degree of care and skill was traditionally required where both benefited from the transaction[2]; slighter diligence, perhaps, where the benefit was wholly that of the bailor[3]; and greater diligence where the benefit accrued only to the bailee[4]. More recently, however, it has been recognised that the common law duty of every bailee is to take reasonable care of his bailor's goods, and not to convert them[5]. The standard of care required is therefore the standard demanded by the circumstances of each particular case[6]. To try to put a bailment into a watertight compartment, such as gratuitous bailment or bailment for reward, can be misleading[7]; in certain cases there may be general duties that apply across the spectrum of bailments at large[8]. It must be remembered, however, that bailment is frequently a contract, and the parties may always vary the incidents by the terms of the contract[9]. Their failure to take this opportunity can result in their being denied the benefit of a duty that might otherwise have been consensually imposed[10].

1 　*Giblin v McMullen* (1868) LR 2 PC 317.
2 　Ie a bailment for mutual advantage: see PARA 106 note 3.
3 　Eg as in the first two classes mentioned in PARA 106.
4 　Eg as in the third class mentioned in PARA 106.
5 　*Morris v CW Martin & Sons Ltd* [1966] 1 QB 716 at 726, 732, 738, [1965] 2 All ER 725 at 731, 735, 738, CA. See also *Marcus v Official Solicitor* [1997] EWCA Civ 886 (differing standard of care owed by gratuitous bailee and involuntary bailee; standard less severe in latter case); *East West Corpn v DKBS AF 1912 A/S, Utaniko Ltd v P & O Nedlloyd BV* [2003] EWCA Civ 83, [2003] QB 1509, [2003] 2 All ER 700 (a bailee has a general duty not to convert goods and to protect them from theft, loss or damage, and he has a responsibility for the acts of others whose services he engaged to fulfil his duty); and *Photolibrary Group Ltd v Burda Senator Verlag GmbH* [2008] EWHC 1343 (QB), [2008] 2 All ER (Comm) 881, [2008] All ER (D) 219 (Jun). The movement towards a single all-purpose standard is chronicled in Palmer on Bailment (3rd Edn, 2009) paras 9-002, 10-005–10-025, 11-005–11-113, 12-023–12-024.
6 　*Houghland v RR Low (Luxury Coaches) Ltd* [1962] 1 QB 694 at 698, [1962] 2 All ER 159 at 161, CA. See also *Sutcliffe v Chief Constable of West Yorkshire* [1996] RTR 86, (1995) 159 JP 770, CA (discussing the duty of care owed by the police to the owner of a seized vehicle while the vehicle is in their possession); *East West Corpn v DKBS AF 1912 A/S, Utaniko Ltd v P & O Nedlloyd BV* [2003] EWCA Civ 83, [2003] QB 1509, [2003] 2 All ER 700 (the nature of a bailee's duties varies according to the circumstances in which and the purposes for which the goods were delivered to the bailee); *G Bosman (Transport) Ltd v LKW Walter International Transportorganisation AG* [2002] EWCA Civ 850, [2002] All ER (D) 13 (May) (bailee has a personal obligation to look after goods; present bailee not unrewarded as holding possession as part of remunerated commercial operations). See also *Swann v Seal* (19 March 1999, unreported), CA; *P & O Trans European Ltd v Wincanton Ltd* [2001] EWCA Civ 227, [2001] All ER (D) 174 (Feb). The standard has moved from gross negligence to the requirement to exercise reasonable care: see *Yearworth v North Bristol NHS Trust* [2009] EWCA Civ 37, [2010] QB 1, [2009] 2 All ER 986. As to gross negligence see e g *Martin v LCC* [1947] KB 628, [1947] 1 All ER 783; *Mayor of Fitzroy v National Bank of Australasia Ltd* (1890) 16 VLR 342 at 360–361; *Giblin v McMullen* (1868) LR 2 PC 317. As to the ordinary and reasonable standard of care see e g *Brown v National Bank of Australasia Ltd* (1890) 16 VLR 475. Cf also *JP Morgan Chase Bank v Springwell Navigation Corpn* [2008] EWHC 1793 (Comm) at [194]–[205] per Gloster J. If you confide a casket of jewels to the custody of a yokel, you cannot expect him to take the same care of it that a banker would: see Jones on Bailment (4th Edn, 1833) p 100; Palmer on Bailment (3rd Edn, 2009) Chapters 10, 11. See also PARAS 111 note 9, 121, 146. As to conversion, bailment and the police see TORT vol 45(2) (Reissue) PARA 609.
7 　*Houghland v RR Low (Luxury Coaches) Ltd* [1962] 1 QB 694 at 698, [1962] 2 All ER 159 at 161, CA.
8 　Eg the duty to collect goods within a reasonable time: see *JJD SA (a company) v Avon Tyres Ltd* (1999) Times, 25 January (see also PARAS 116, 173). See also the analysis in *Yearworth v North Bristol NHS Trust* [2009] EWCA Civ 37, [2010] QB 1, [2009] 2 All ER 986.

9   See eg *P & O Trans European Ltd v Wincanton Ltd* [2001] EWCA Civ 227, [2001] All ER (D) 174 (Feb). There is a strong likelihood that a bailment transacted in commercial circumstances will be contractual: *Photolibrary Group Ltd v Burda Senator Verlag GmbH* [2008] EWHC 1343 (QB) at [68], [2008] 2 All ER (Comm) 881 at [68], [2005] All ER (D) 219 (Jun) at [68] per Jack J.

10   See eg *P & O Trans European Ltd v Wincanton Ltd* [2001] EWCA Civ 227, [2001] All ER (D) 174 (Feb).

(2) JOINT BAILORS AND JOINT BAILEES

108. Joint bailors. Where chattels belonging to co-owners are delivered to a bailee to hold on behalf of all, it is implied, unless expressly stipulated to the contrary, that he shall deliver up possession only upon the demand of all the co-owners[1]. He is, therefore, justified in refusing to redeliver the chattels on the demand of one or some of them only, and a claim will not lie against him for such a refusal[2]. But if, in such a case, he delivers up the chattels to one of the co-owners upon his sole request, no claim will lie against him for so doing unless all the bailors join for that purpose; and as the person to whom they were actually redelivered cannot join with his co-owners in maintaining a claim for a breach occasioned by his own act, no claim will lie against the bailee[3]. As, however, the bailee would occupy a position equivalent to that of a trustee of the chattels for all the co-owners, he would be held liable in equity to those who were injured by his breach of trust[4]. Two co-owners, having made a joint demand, may bring separate claims[5].

1   *Broadbent v Ledward* (1839) 11 Ad & El 209.

2   *Atwood v Ernest* (1853) 13 CB 881; *May v Harvey* (1811) 13 East 197; *Nathan v Buckland* (1818) 2 Moore CP 153. But it is otherwise if one co-owner has a special property in the entire chattel (*Nyberg v Handelaar* [1892] 2 QB 202, CA; cf *Khan v Grocutt* [2002] EWCA Civ 1945, [2003] RTR 314, [2003] Lloyd's Rep IR 464), or if, though belonging to co-owners, the chattel is delivered to the bailee by one only to hold on his behalf (*May v Harvey* (1811) 13 East 197), in which case the bailee would be estopped from denying the bailor's title: see PARA 229. *Broadbent v Ledward* (1839) 11 Ad & El 209, turned upon a question of pleading only, and the observation of Lord Denman CJ at 212, that if any inconvenient consequence arises to the defendant from detaining the property of joint owners, it might have been avoided by giving it up to any of them, is a dictum only. If it means that, in general, a bailee, entrusted by co-owners with property to hold on behalf of all, may lawfully deliver it to one, without the authority or even against the wish of the others, it cannot, it is submitted, be regarded as law. See also *MCC Proceeds Inc v Lehman Bros International (Europe)* [1998] 4 All ER 675, [1998] 2 BCLC 659, CA, where it was held that a person had title to sue in conversion if he had either actual possession or an immediate legal right to possession at the time of conversion, but not if he had merely an equitable interest in the goods. It appears from the court's approval in this case of a statement by Buckley LJ in *International Factors Ltd v Rodriguez* [1979] QB 351 at 359–360, [1979] 1 All ER 17 at 22, CA, that this right of immediate possession can arise from contract and exist without any underlying proprietary right. See also to similar effect *Government of the Islamic Republic of Iran v Barakat Galleries Ltd* [2007] EWCA Civ 1374, [2009] QB 22, [2008] 1 All ER 1177; and see further TORT vol 45(2) (Reissue) PARA 560.

3   *Brandon v Scott* (1857) 7 E & B 234.

4   *Brandon v Scott* (1857) 7 E & B 234 at 237 per Lord Campbell CJ. See also *Harper v Godsell* (1870) LR 5 QB 422.

5   *Bleaden v Hancock* (1829) 4 C & P 152.

109. Joint bailees. Where a chattel is bailed to two or more bailees, each is responsible for the acts and defaults of his co-bailees done or made within the scope of their authority[1]. Probably, however, a joint bailee is not responsible if the act or default is not negligence in the performance of the bailment, but something wholly outside it[2].

1   *Davey v Chamberlain* (1802) 4 Esp 229; *Coupé Co v Maddick* [1891] 2 QB 413 at 415 per
    Cave J; Story on Bailments (9th Edn, 1878) s 116. See also *Colbeck v Diamanta (UK) Ltd*
    [2002] EWHC 616 (QB), [2002] All ER (D) 336 (Feb).
2   Story on Bailments (9th Edn, 1878) s 116. This would seem to follow upon principle from the
    analogous cases of a bailee's responsibility for his servants. See PARAS 148, 186, 239; and see
    Morris v CW Martin & Sons Ltd [1966] 1 QB 716, [1965] 2 All ER 725, CA.

(3) SUB-BAILMENT AND OTHER EXTENDED OR AMBULATORY BAILMENTS

110.   Sub-bailment.   A sub-bailee is a person to whom the actual possession of
goods is transferred by someone who is not himself the owner of goods, but who
has a present right to possession of them as bailee of the owner[1]. When the
sub-bailee accepts possession of the goods he thereby assumes the obligations of
a bailee towards the original bailor (who is normally termed the head bailor)[2].
The nature of these obligations will, as in the case of an ordinary bailment, vary
according to the circumstances in which and the purposes for which the goods
are delivered[3]. Thus if the sub-bailment is for reward, the sub-bailee will owe to
the head bailor all the duties of a bailee for reward[4]. The bailor has a right to
make a claim against the sub-bailee for breach of any of his duties either if the
bailor has the right to immediate possession of the goods or if they are
permanently injured or lost[5]. The sub-bailee also owes, concurrently, the same
duties to the original bailee[6], whose obligations to the bailor are not extinguished
by the sub-bailment[7]. The relationship between the head bailor and the
sub-bailee exists independently of any contract between them, or of any
attornment[8].

   The bailor is bound by any exclusion or limitation clause[9] contained in the
sub-bailment, irrespective of any contract between him and the sub-bailee, if he
has expressly or impliedly consented to the making of the sub-bailment on such
terms[10]. Older authority, now disapproved[11], held that the bailor could also be
bound by any exclusion or limitation clause contained in the sub-bailment, to the
imposition of which he had not expressly or impliedly consented, if the exclusion
or limitation clause represented an essential part of the sub-bailee's consideration
for entering into the sub-bailment, at least where the duty that the head bailor
sought to enforce against the sub-bailee would not have arisen but for the fact of
the sub-bailment[12]. However, it now appears that while the owner's consent is
irrelevant to a possessor's position as his bailee (so that a person who voluntarily
takes possession of another's goods holds them as bailee of that person even if he
takes possession without that person's consent) a sub-bailee can invoke the terms
of the sub-bailment under which he received the goods from an intermediate
bailee as qualifying his responsibility only if the owner actually (or perhaps
ostensibly) consented to such terms[13].

1   *China-Pacific SA v Food Corpn of India, The Winson* [1982] AC 939 at 959, [1981] 3 All ER
    688 at 693, HL, per Lord Diplock; and see *Marcq v Christie Manson & Woods Ltd (t/a
    Christie's)* [2003] EWCA Civ 731 at [44]–[55], [2004] QB 286 at [44]–[55], [2003] 3 All ER
    561 at [44]–[55], per Tuckey LJ. Under a sub-bailment, the original bailee remains responsible
    for the goods as a bailee and retains a right to the possession of the goods when the
    sub-bailment expires: cf *Transcontainer Express Ltd v Custodian Security Ltd* [1988] 1 Lloyd's
    Rep 128, CA, where the intermediate carriers failed to adduce evidence of any right to resume
    possession of the goods from the sub-carriers. Contrast the substitutional bailment, under which
    the original bailee withdraws from the bailment relationship once he has conferred possession
    upon the incoming bailee, and the incoming bailee takes his place as the direct bailee of the
    bailor. This variety of bailment is illustrated by the position of ship-owners once the cargo is
    off-loaded on to salvage vessels provided by a salvor to carry the cargo to a place of safety:

China-Pacific SA v Food Corpn of India, The Winson [1982] AC 939, [1981] 3 All ER 688, HL; and see *Kamidian v Holt* [2008] EWHC 1483 (Comm), [2009] Lloyd's Rep IR 242, [2008] All ER (D) 394 (Jun). There is a third variety of extended bailment, sometimes known as the quasi-bailment, under which the intermediate party does not personally obtain possession of the goods before engaging the ultimate bailee to take possession: see *Metaalhandel JA Magnus BV v Ardfields Transport Ltd and Eastfell Ltd (t/a Jones Transport)* [1988] 1 Lloyd's Rep 197; *KH Enterprise v Pioneer Container, The Pioneer Container* [1994] 2 AC 324, [1994] 2 All ER 250, [1994] 1 Lloyd's Rep 593, PC; *P & O Trans European Ltd v Wincanton Ltd* [2001] EWCA Civ 227, [2001] All ER (D) 174 (Feb), CA. See also Palmer on Bailment (3rd Edn, 2009) Chapter 23; [1983] Current Legal Problems 93.

2   *Morris v CW Martin & Sons Ltd* [1966] 1 QB 716, [1965] 2 All ER 725, CA; *Gilchrist Watt and Sanderson Pty Ltd v York Products Pty Ltd* [1970] 3 All ER 825, [1970] 1 WLR 1262, PC; *China-Pacific SA v Food Corpn of India, The Winson* [1982] AC 939 at 957–959, [1981] 3 All ER 688 at 692–693, HL, per Lord Diplock ('A person who holds possession of goods as sub-bailee of an original direct bailee also owes some duty of care towards the owner'). In most cases, it would appear that the sub-bailee's lack of knowledge as to the identity of the original bailor does not affect his obligations towards him: *Balsamo v Medici* [1984] 2 All ER 304 at 310–311, [1984] 1 WLR 951 at 959 per Walton J. The fact that the sub-bailee acts as an independent contractor as agent for the bailee does not prevent a sub-bailment from arising: see *Lotus Cars Ltd v Southampton Cargo Handling plc, The Rigoletto* [2000] 2 All ER (Comm) 705, [2000] 2 Lloyd's Rep 532, CA; and see *Transcontainer Express Ltd v Custodian Security Ltd* [1988] 1 Lloyd's Rep 128, CA. It has been held on particular facts that the relationship between bailor and sub-bailee could not be described as based on agreement: see *Dresser UK Ltd v Falcongate Freight Management Ltd* [1992] QB 502 at 511, [1992] 2 All ER 450 at 457, CA, per Bingham LJ. But the relationship of the ultimate bailee and the original bailor may be contractual in particular circumstances (*Sandeman Coprimar SA v Transitos y Integrales SL* [2003] EWCA Civ 113, [2003] QB 1270, [2003] 3 All ER 108, [2003] 2 Lloyd's Rep 172) or it may be affected by some direct agreement, understanding or other communication falling short of contract between those parties: *European Gas Turbines v MSAS Cargo International Inc* unreported, 26 May 2000, QB. Moreover, the doctrine of sub-bailment on terms may (independently of contract) enable the enforcement of positive obligations between the parties to the sub-bailment, and not merely immunities from liability: *Sandeman Coprimar SA v Transitos y Integrales SL* [2003] EWCA Civ 113, [2003] QB 1270, [2003] 3 All ER 108, [2003] 2 Lloyd's Rep 172. See also *Matrix Europe Ltd v Uniserve Holdings Ltd* [2009] EWHC 919 (Comm), [2009] All ER (D) 126 (May) (accidental sub-bailment).

3   *Morris v CW Martin & Sons Ltd* [1966] 1 QB 716 at 731, [1965] 2 All ER 725 at 734, CA, per Diplock LJ.

4   *Morris v CW Martin & Sons Ltd* [1966] 1 QB 716 at 729, [1965] 2 All ER 725 at 733, CA, per Lord Denning MR. As to the nature of such duties see PARA 146. They might include the normal bailee's common law estoppel on pleading jus tertii and denying the bailor's title: *The Hamburg Star* [1994] 1 Lloyd's Rep 399 (point arguable); and see as to the bailee's estoppel generally PARA 229. See also *James Buchanan & Co Ltd v Hay's Transport Services Ltd and Duncan Barbour & Son Ltd* [1972] 2 Lloyd's Rep 535 (gratuitous sub-bailee).

5   See *Kahler v Midland Bank Ltd* [1950] AC 24, [1949] 2 All ER 621, HL; *Morris v CW Martin & Sons Ltd* [1966] 1 QB 716 at 728–729, [1965] 2 All ER 725 at 733, CA, per Lord Denning MR; *Moukataff v British Overseas Airways Corpn* [1967] 1 Lloyd's Rep 396 at 415 per Browne J; *East West Corpn v DKBS AF 1912 A/S, Utaniko Ltd v P & O Nedlloyd BV* [2003] EWCA Civ 83, [2003] QB 1509, [2003] 2 All ER 700, per Mance J; *HSBC Rail (UK) Ltd v Network Rail Infrastructure Ltd (formerly Railtrack plc)* [2005] EWCA Civ 1437, [2006] 1 All ER 343, [2006] 1 WLR 643, per Longmore J.

6   See Pollock and Wright on Possession p 169. See also *The Winkfield* [1902] P 42, CA, cited in *Morris v CW Martin & Sons Ltd* [1966] 1 QB 716 at 728–729, [1965] 2 All ER 725 at 732–733, CA, per Lord Denning MR.

7   *Gilchrist Watt and Sanderson Pty Ltd v York Products Pty Ltd* [1970] 3 All ER 825 at 829, [1970] 1 WLR 1262 at 1267, PC; Palmer on Bailment (3rd Edn, 2009) paras 23-013–23-026. See further *Metaalhandel JA Magnus BV v Ardfields Transport Ltd and Eastfell Ltd (t/a Jones Transport)* [1988] 1 Lloyd's Rep 197 (intermediate party under quasi-bailment held liable for defaults of ultimate bailee). The position will be otherwise under a substitutional bailment, where the original bailee withdraws from the relationship and the incoming bailee takes his place as the direct bailee of the original owner: see note 1.

8   *KH Enterprise v Pioneer Container, The Pioneer Container* [1994] 2 AC 324, [1994] 2 All ER 250, [1994] 1 Lloyd's Rep 593, PC; *East West Corpn v DKBS AF 1912 A/S, Utaniko Ltd v P & O Nedlloyd BV* [2003] EWCA Civ 83, [2003] QB 1509, [2003] 2 All ER 700; *Sandeman*

Coprimar SA v Transitos y Transportes Integrales SL [2003] EWCA Civ 113, [2003] QB 1270, [2003] 3 All ER 108, [2003] 2 Lloyd's Rep 172; *Gilchrist Watt and Sanderson Pty Ltd v York Products Ltd* [1970] 3 All ER 825, [1970] 1 WLR 1262, PC; *Dresser UK Ltd v Falcongate Freight Management Ltd* [1992] QB 502 at 511, [1992] 2 All ER 450 at 457, CA, per Bingham LJ. Cf *Compania Portorafti Commerciale SA v Ultramar Panama Inc, The Captain Gregos (No 2)* [1990] 2 Lloyd's Rep 395 at 404–406, CA, per Bingham LJ.

9   The principle no longer appears to be confined to terms which purport to exclude or restrict the liability of the sub-bailee: *Sandeman Coprimar SA v Transitos y Integrales SL* [2003] EWCA Civ 113, [2003] QB 1270, [2003] 3 All ER 108, [2003] 2 Lloyd's Rep 172; *KH Enterprise v Pioneer Container, The Pioneer Container* [1994] 2 AC 324, [1994] 2 All ER 250, [1994] 1 Lloyd's Rep 593, PC; and cf *The Forum Craftsman* [1985] 1 Lloyd's Rep 291, CA. Although the party seeking to rely on an exemption clause usually must show that the loss or damage to the other party is within the scope of the clause (see the text to notes 10–12), the burden of proof rests on the party seeking to establish the liability: see PARA 147.

10   *KH Enterprise v Pioneer Container, The Pioneer Container* [1994] 2 AC 324, [1994] 2 All ER 250, [1994] 1 Lloyd's Rep 593, PC; *East West Corpn v DKBS AF 1912 A/S, Utaniko Ltd v P & O Nedlloyd BV* [2003] EWCA Civ 83, [2003] QB 1509, [2003] 2 All ER 700; *Singer Co (UK) Ltd v Tees and Hartlepool Port Authority* [1988] 2 Lloyd's Rep 164, following *Morris v CW Martin & Sons Ltd* [1966] 1 QB 716 at 729–730, [1965] 2 All ER 725 at 733, CA, per Lord Denning MR (obiter); *Hispanica de Petroleos SA v Vencedora Oceanica Navegacion SA, The Kapetan Markos NL (No 2)* [1987] 2 Lloyd's Rep 321 at 336, CA, per Nicholls LJ, and at 340 per Dillon LJ. The owner against whom this defence is invoked must have bailed the goods to the original bailee before the original bailee bailed them to the defendant; unless the defendant subsequently attorns to the new owner (as to which see PARA 231), the defendant cannot invoke the defence against someone who becomes the owner of the goods after the goods have been bailed to the defendant: *Compania Portorafti Commerciale SA v Ultramar Panama Inc, The Captain Gregos (No 2)* [1990] 2 Lloyd's Rep 395, CA. In *Singer Co (UK) Ltd v Tees and Hartlepool Port Authority* [1988] 2 Lloyd's Rep 164 at 168, Steyn J left open the question whether a mere ostensible authority in the original bailee to sub-bail the goods on certain exculpatory terms would suffice to enable the sub-bailee to invoke those terms in a claim against him by the sub-bailee. But cf note 12.

11   *KH Enterprise v Pioneer Container, The Pioneer Container* [1994] 2 AC 324, [1994] 2 All ER 250, [1994] 1 Lloyd's Rep 593, PC.

12   *Johnson Matthey & Co Ltd v Constantine Terminals Ltd* [1976] 2 Lloyd's Rep 215. The validity of this principle had been left open in *Singer Co (UK) Ltd v Tees and Hartlepool Port Authority* [1988] 2 Lloyd's Rep 164 at 168 per Steyn J, and the principle itself appears to have been approved in *Compania Portorafti Commerciale SA v Ultramar Panama Inc, The Captain Gregos (No 2)* [1990] 2 Lloyd's Rep 395, CA. See further *Swiss Bank Corpn v Brinks-MAT Ltd* [1986] 2 Lloyd's Rep 79 at 98 per Bingham J. But see now Palmer on Bailment (3rd Edn, 2009) paras 23-033–23-034, 38-161–38-174; and the text to note 13. Note the principle that a third party to a contract cannot be subjected to the burden of an exemption clause although under the Contracts (Rights of Third Parties) Act 1999 s 1(4) if a third party wishes to enforce a term conferring a benefit on him he can only do so subject to and in accordance with any other terms of the contract (which may impose burdens and conditions upon the enjoyment of any benefit): see CONTRACT vol 9(1) (Reissue) PARA 822.

13   *KH Enterprise v Pioneer Container, The Pioneer Container* [1994] 2 AC 324, [1994] 2 All ER 250 at 262, PC, disapproving *Johnson Matthey & Co Ltd v Constantine Terminals Ltd* [1976] 2 Lloyd's Rep 215 (see note 12). These principles were applied in *Sonicare International Ltd v East Anglia Freight Terminal Ltd* [1997] 2 Lloyd's Rep 48, Cty Ct; and *Spectra International plc v Hayesoak Ltd* [1998] 1 Lloyd's Rep 162, CA. See also *Lukoil-Kaliningradmorneft plc v Tata Ltd* [1999] All ER (D) 413, CA; *Lotus Cars Ltd v Southampton Cargo Handling plc, The Rigoletto* [2000] 2 All ER (Comm) 705, [2000] 2 Lloyd's Rep 532, CA; *Homburg Houtimport BV v Agrosin Private Ltd, The Starsin* [2003] UKHL 12, [2004] 1 AC 715, [2003] 2 All ER 785; *East West Corpn v DKBS AF 1912 A/S, Utaniko Ltd v P & O Nedlloyd BV* [2003] EWCA Civ 83, [2003] QB 1509, [2003] 2 All ER 700; *Sandeman Coprimar SA v Transitos y Transportes Integrales SL* [2003] EWCA Civ 113, [2003] QB 1270, [2003] 3 All ER 108, [2003] 2 Lloyd's Rep 172. However, see *The Mahkutai* [1996] AC 650, [1996] 3 All ER 502, [1996] 2 Lloyd's Rep 1, PC, where *KH Enterprise v Pioneer Container, The Pioneer Container* [1994] 2 AC 324, [1994] 2 All ER 250 at 262, PC, was distinguished; see also *Marcq v Christie Manson & Woods Ltd (t/a Christie's)* [2003] EWCA Civ 731, [2004] QB 286, [2003] 3 All ER 561 (delivery of stolen painting by alleged non-owner to auction house; semble, no sub-bailment between auction house and original owner in that, inter alia, the auction house did not consent to holding possession on behalf of the original owner as bailee of that person).

2. GRATUITOUS BAILMENT

(1) DEPOSIT

(i) Meaning and Categories of Deposit

A. DEPOSIT GENERALLY

111. Meaning of 'deposit'. Bailment by deposit[1] may be defined as a bailment of a chattel, to be kept for the bailor gratuitously[2], and returned upon demand[3]. This definition is sufficient for most purposes, and is complete, if it is understood that a return to the bailor covers delivery over to his nominee, for in some cases the primary object of the bailment may be that the bailee delivers over the chattel upon demand to a third party, and not to the actual bailor himself. This kind of bailment must always relate to a specific chattel[4].

As the bailee is to receive no reward for his services, there can never be an executory contract of deposit, for there can be no claim upon an unsupported agreement[5], and until there is actual delivery and acceptance of the subject matter of the trust, there is no obligation on the bailee's part to carry out his promise[6]. In similar vein, the bailment by way of deposit is not a contract even after the bailee has taken possession[7]. As soon, however, as the bailee actually accepts[8] the chattel, he becomes in some degree responsible for it[9] whilst it remains in his possession or under his control: he must exercise reasonable care and skill towards it, he must discharge any promissory undertaking that he has give in relation to the chattel[10], and he is also bound, upon demand[11], to redeliver it to the true owner or his nominee, unless he has good excuse in law for not doing so[12].

1 Ie *depositum*: see PARA 106.
2 A bailment may be a bailment for reward even though the consideration does not flow from the bailor. Thus if a member of a tenant's family deposits baggage with the landlord in the baggage room of the building containing the tenant's flat, the bailment is not gratuitous: *Andrews v Home Flats Ltd* [1945] 2 All ER 698, CA; cf *Chapman (or Oliver) v Saddler & Co* [1929] AC 584 at 596, HL (business operation in which bailor and bailee both relied for safety on the care of the bailor); *G Bosman (Transport) Ltd v LKW Walter International Transportorganisation AG* [2002] EWCA Civ 850, [2002] All ER (D) 13 (May) (bailment not gratuitous as goods had been received and kept at claimant's yard as part of contractual obligations to transport them onwards); and see PARA 145. See also *Khan v Grocutt* [2002] EWCA Civ 1945, [2003] RTR 314, [2003] Lloyd's Rep IR 464, where the gratuitous bailment was care of vital insurance documents.
3 2 Bl Com 453. See also PARA 230.
4 Pothier's Contrat de Dépôt s 2.
5 Ie the maxim *ex nudo pacto non oritur actio* applies. See *Parastitidis v Kotaridis* [1978] VR 449 at 455 per Harris J (obiter).
6 Pothier's Contrat de Dépôt s 7.
7 See Palmer on Bailment (3rd Edn, 2009) Chapter 10; *Yearworth v North Bristol NHS Trust* [2009] EWCA Civ 37, [2010] QB 1, [2009] 2 All ER 986; *Photolibrary Group Ltd v Burda Senator Verlag GmbH* [2008] EWHC 1343 (QB), [2008] 2 All ER (Comm) 881, [2008] All ER (D) 219 (Jun).
8 See *Blount v War Office* [1953] 1 All ER 1071, [1953] 1 WLR 736 (acceptance of goods although locked in strong room of requisitioned building).
9 See *Houghland v RR Low (Luxury Coaches) Ltd* [1962] 1 QB 694, [1962] 2 All ER 159, CA; and PARA 107; and *Yearworth v North Bristol NHS Trust* [2009] EWCA Civ 37, [2010] QB 1, [2009] 2 All ER 986 (bailment of sperm by men to hospital unit: unit had chosen to take possession of the sperm; its assumption of responsibility for careful storage had been express

and unequivocal; it had acquired exclusive possession of the sperm; it had held itself out to the men as able to deploy special skill in preserving the sperm; it had extended and broken a particular promise to the men).

10 *Mitchell v Ealing London Borough Council* [1979] QB 1, [1978] 2 All ER 779; *Toor v Bassi* [1999] EGCS 9, CA.

11 Quaere whether, in particular circumstances, the bailor might be bound by a promise not to call for redelivery before a particular time: see Palmer on Bailment (3rd Edn, 2009) para 14-006 (such a promise supported by consideration) and see further PARA 125. For the circumstances under which demand and refusal are or are not necessary to found a claim see PARA 232.

12 *Coggs v Bernard* (1703) 2 Ld Raym 909; *Phipps v New Claridge's Hotel Ltd* (1905) 22 TLR 49 (plaintiff handed over dog to one of defendant's servants, and as the dog could not be found when wanted, the defendant was liable); *Ultzen v Nicols* [1894] 1 QB 92 (where a diner at a restaurant handed his coat to a waiter, and it was gone when sought for). See also *Kahler v Midland Bank Ltd* [1950] AC 24, [1949] 2 All ER 621, HL (delivery by bailee to true owner would have been illegal by the proper law of the contract of bailment between bailor and bailee). The same rule appears to apply to all kinds of bailment. If the chattels bailed are not forthcoming, or are damaged, the onus is in the first place upon the bailee to show circumstances negativing negligence on his part: *Port Swettenham Authority v TW Wu & Co (M) Sdn Bhd* [1979] AC 580, [1978] 3 All ER 337, PC; *British Road Services Ltd v Arthur V Crutchley & Co Ltd (Factory Guards Ltd, third party)* [1968] 1 All ER 811, [1968] 1 Lloyd's Rep 271, CA; *Joseph Travers & Sons Ltd v Cooper* [1915] 1 KB 73, CA; *Houghland v RR Low (Luxury Coaches) Ltd* [1962] 1 QB 694, [1962] 2 All ER 159, CA; cf *Thomas v High* [1960] SR NSW 401, NSW FC. See also *Wiehe v Dennis Bros* (1913) 29 TLR 250 (pony left in possession of vendor); *Williams v Curzon Syndicate Ltd* (1919) 35 TLR 475, CA (goods deposited at club and stolen by porter who had been engaged without sufficient inquiry into his antecedents); *Copland v Brogan* 1916 SC 277, Ct of Sess (gratuitous carriage of bag containing money); cf *Brook's Wharf and Bull Wharf Ltd v Goodman Bros* [1937] 1 KB 534 at 538–539, [1936] 3 All ER 696 at 701–702, CA; *Gutter v Tait* (1947) 177 LT 1, CA (bailee robbed partly owing to his own lack of care); *Ballet v Mingay* [1943] KB 281, [1943] 1 All ER 143, CA (failure of bailee who had parted with goods to prove that his parting with them was within purview of contract); and see PARA 149 note 3. The bailee need not establish the precise cause of the loss: *Bullen v Swan Electric Engraving Co* (1907) 23 TLR 258, CA; *Phipps v New Claridge's Hotel Ltd* (1905) 22 TLR 49; and see also *Brook's Wharf and Bull Wharf Ltd v Goodman Bros* [1937] 1 KB 534, [1936] 3 All ER 696; and PARA 149 notes 4–5. Cf *Woods v Duncan* [1946] AC 401, [1946] 1 All ER 420n, HL; and see PARAS 121, 132, 136. As to the onus of proof in the case of bailment for reward see PARA 149.

B. DEPOSIT THAT DOES NOT DERIVE FROM ORIGINAL EXPRESS AGREEMENT

(A) Quasi-depositum Types of Bailment

112. Deposit without agreement. While the orthodox or literal transaction by way of depositum is a consensual bailment (deriving from express agreement between bailor and bailee)[1] there exist certain analogous forms of relationship based on one person's unrewarded possession of another's goods which, while not directly the product of agreement, may produce obligations akin to those of an orthodox bailment by way of depositum and might in some cases have traditionally been viewed as deriving from an implied agreement as to possession[2].

1 See PARA 111.
2 See eg PARA 113 (necessary deposit), PARA 114 (deposit under mistake), PARA 115 (accidental deposit), PARAS 116–119 (finding of chattels) and PARA 120 (involuntary deposit).

(B) Necessary, Mistaken or Accidental Deposit

113. Necessary deposit. A necessary deposit is one which is made under peculiar stress of circumstances, such as fire, flood, shipwreck, civil riot, or other unforeseen disaster. If, under such conditions, an owner of a chattel entrusts it to the care of a bystander or neighbour, and that person accepts it, it has been suggested that the confidence of the owner in the recipient, and the acceptance by him, constitute an obligation which can be satisfied only by a very strict measure of care on the part of the bailee; but it seems that his duties are merely those of any ordinary depositary[1]. Consequently the owner would probably recover damages only in the event of the depositary's being guilty of negligence or bad faith whilst the chattel was in his custody[2].

Where in the event of some sudden threat or emergency a person takes it upon himself to look after the property of another for the purpose of keeping it safe, that assumption of possession will give rise to a bailment and the bailee would appear to owe a duty of care to the owner in relation to the bailed property[3].

1 Jones on Bailments (4th Edn, 1833) p 48; Story on Bailments (9th Edn, 1878) s 83.
2 Story on Bailments (9th Edn, 1878) s 83.
3 See *R v Ngan* [2008] 2 NZLR 48, NZ SC (police gathering of scattered banknotes along road-side held to be bailees 'of necessity'). The standard of responsibility expected might be that of a gratuitous bailee, and the onus is on the bailee to show that the care required by law has been taken. An unauthorised assumption of possession may also constitute a conversion: see e g *Tear v Freebody* (1858) 4 CBNS 228.

114. Deposit under mistake. If a man who is mentally incapable of appreciating what he is doing, or who is under a mistake as to the identity of the person with whom he is dealing, entrusts another with a chattel, the recipient becomes a bailee[1]. This is consistent with the general principle that a bailment arises whenever one person is voluntarily in possession of goods that belong to another, and that it is the consent of the putative bailor that is critical to bailment, the consent of the putative bailor being generally[2] immaterial to the relationship[3]. Similarly, where one party had not intended to deliver goods to another but the latter had intended to accept delivery of the goods, the latter was held to be a bailee and liable as such[4].

1 *R v Reeves* (1859) 5 Jur NS 716, where a man who was lying on the ground, partially tipsy, permitted an acquaintance to take his watch out of his pocket on the supposition that the acquaintance was actuated by a friendly motive; it was held that the evidence was sufficient to convict the person of the statutory offence of larceny as a bailee (i e now the offence of theft: see the Theft Act 1968 ss 1–6; and CRIMINAL LAW vol 25 (2010) PARA 278 et seq).
2 Cf the relationship of sub-bailment: see PARA 110.
3 *KH Enterprise v Pioneer Container, The Pioneer Container* [1994] 2 AC 324, [1994] 2 All ER 250, [1994] 1 Lloyd's Rep 593, PC.
4 See *Matrix Europe Ltd v Uniserve Holdings Ltd* [2009] EWHC 919 (Comm), [2009] All ER (D) 126 (May) (bailment for reward).

115. Accidental deposit. An accidental deposit is made where a chattel, through circumstances over which neither the owner nor the recipient has any immediate control, is deposited on the land or premises of another. Examples are timber carried by the tide in a navigable river and left at low water on the towing path[1], fruit dropped on a neighbour's garden, or a tree which has fallen on the field of an adjacent proprietor. In such cases, so long as the involuntary depositary does no overt act to the chattel thus deposited on his land, he incurs no responsibility to the true owner in respect of it. But if he interferes with it an implied bailment is created, with all its obligations and responsibilities; and if he not only interferes with it, but uses it for his own purposes, this user amounts to a conversion, especially if the misuse is intentional[2].

1 *Nicholson v Chapman* (1793) 2 Hy Bl 254 at 257 per Eyre CJ (a person who voluntarily retrieves timber deposited on a river bank has no lien for his expenses in retrieving it, and is

liable in conversion if he does not deliver it up to the owner on demand). But it is doubtful whether the finder would succeed in a claim for his expenses on a quantum meruit: see PARA 116; cf *Lampleigh v Brathwait* (1615) Hob 105; and see also CONTRACT. Cf *Binstead v Buck* (1776) 2 Wm Bl 1117.

2 *Mulgrave v Ogden* (1591) Cro Eliz 219; *Isaack v Clark* (1615) 2 Bulst 306. See also *Mills v Brooker* [1919] 1 KB 555 (fruit from lopped branch of overhanging tree). As to conversion generally see TORT vol 45(2) (Reissue) PARA 548 et seq and as to involuntary and unwitting bailees see TORT vol 45(2) (Reissue) PARAS 606–607.

(C) Finding of Chattels

116. Bailment by finding. Where a lost chattel is found in a public place[1], the finder[2] is under no obligation to take charge of it at all[3]. However, an occupier of land may owe an obligation to search for chattels which are lost upon his land, and to take them into custody[4]. If, moreover, the finder actually takes a lost chattel into his custody, he constitutes himself a depositary, and assumes the obligations of a depositary to the true owner[5], including the obligations to take reasonable steps to locate the owner and acquaint him with the finding and the present whereabouts of the chattel[6], to exercise due care for the safety of the chattel[7] until its return to the owner and to return it to him on demand[8]. Further, the finder cannot claim a lien on the chattel for any expense to which he may have been put in keeping or preserving it[9]. Unless the true owner has intentionally abandoned the chattel[10], his title to it is not lost and he may recover the chattel, provided that his right to bring a claim has not become barred by lapse of time, from any one in whose hands it may be found[11]. The possession of the finder, however, is rightful and continues rightful until the owner demands the return of the chattel, and by taking the chattel into his custody he does no wrong to the true owner, unless he dishonestly appropriates it at any time with the intention of permanently depriving the owner of it, in which case the taking may be a trespass[12] and the finder is guilty of theft[13].

1 For provisions for the disposal of articles left in public conveyances, etc see AIR LAW; RAILWAYS, INLAND WATERWAYS AND CROSS-COUNTRY PIPELINES; ROAD TRAFFIC. Cf the Police (Property) Act 1897; and POLICE vol 36(1) (2007 Reissue) PARAS 520–522. For provisions as to the disposal of abandoned vehicles see the Road Traffic Regulation Act 1984 s 101; and ROAD TRAFFIC vol 89 (2011) PARA 642. No provision, however, is made for the common case of property being found in the street and taken to the police; presumably the finder in taking it to the police is fully discharging his duty and will not be liable to the owner whatever the police may do: see *Hollins v Fowler* (1875) LR 7 HL 757 at 766 per Blackburn J. Cf YB 27 Hen 8, fo 13, pl 35: 'If a man comes into possession by a bailment, then he is answerable by virtue of the bailment and if he bails the goods over or they are taken from his possession, still he is answerable to the bailor by virtue of the bailment. But otherwise if a man comes by goods by finding, for he is only answerable by reason of his possession and if, without wrongful act, he is out of possession before he who has the right has brought his action he is not answerable'. See also *Marcq v Christie Manson & Woods Ltd (t/a Christie's)* [2003] EWCA Civ 731, [2004] QB 286, [2003] 3 All ER 561, where an auction house that received a stolen Dutch master painting (registered with a professional register of stolen art) from someone other than the person from whom it was stolen, and redelivered the work to the deliveror when it was unsold, was held not liable in conversion provided that it had acted in good faith and without notice or knowledge of any adverse claim to the work; the auction house was also held to owe no duty as a bailee, as a person akin to a finder, or as an involuntary or 'unconscious' bailee to verify the deliveror's title before redelivering to him. As to chattels found on private property see PARA 119. As to conversion generally see TORT vol 45(2) (Reissue) PARA 548 et seq; as to conversion by involuntary and unwitting bailees see TORT vol 45(2) (Reissue) PARAS 606–607; and as to conversion and the police see TORT vol 45(2) (Reissue) PARA 609.

2 To call the finder a bailee would not be etymologically accurate in all cases, because the word 'bailee' is derived from the French *bailler*, to deliver or hand over, and there is no delivery or handing over to the finder: see *Gilchrist Watt and Sanderson Pty Ltd v York Products Pty Ltd* [1970] 3 All ER 825 at 831, [1970] 1 WLR 1262 at 1268, PC. In the English courts the word

'bailment' has, however, acquired a meaning wide enough to include cases of 'bailment by finding' and cases of sub-bailment (as to which see PARA 110) where there is no contractual relationship between bailor and bailee or sub-bailee respectively: see *Gilchrist Watt and Sanderson Pty Ltd v York Products Pty Ltd* [1970] 3 All ER 825 at 832, [1970] 1 WLR 1262 at 1270, PC; *Morris v CW Martin & Sons Ltd* [1966] 1 QB 716 at 732, [1965] 2 All ER 725 at 734, CA, per Diplock LJ; *Southland Hospital Board v Perkins Estate* [1986] 1 NZLR 373 at 375 per Cook J (obiter); *Compania Portorafti Commerciale SA v Ultramar Panama Inc, The Captain Gregos (No 2)* [1990] 2 Lloyd's Rep 395 at 405, CA, per Bingham LJ. See also *East West Corpn v DKBS AF 1912 A/S, Utaniko Ltd v P & O Nedlloyd BV* [2003] EWCA Civ 83, [2003] QB 1509, [2003] 2 All ER 700.

3   *Kowal v Ellis* (1977) 76 DLR (3d) 546 at 547, Man CA per O'Sullivan JA.
4   *Parker v British Airways Board* [1982] QB 1004 at 1018, [1982] 1 All ER 834 at 843, CA, per Donaldson LJ (obiter).
5   *Isaack v Clark* (1615) 2 Bulst 306 at 312 per Coke CJ; *Newman v Bourne and Hollingworth* (1915) 31 TLR 209 (master held liable for servant's lack of care); *Parker v British Airways Board* [1982] QB 1004 at 1018, [1982] 1 All ER 834 at 843, CA, per Donaldson LJ (obiter); *R v Ngan* [2008] 2 NZLR 48, NZ SC. Cf Story on Bailments (9th Edn, 1878) ss 85–87, criticising the view expressed in Bac Abr Bailment D. See also *Marcq v Christie Manson & Woods Ltd (t/a Christie's)* [2003] EWCA Civ 731, [2004] QB 286, [2003] 3 All ER 561.
6   *Parker v British Airways Board* [1982] QB 1004 at 1018, [1982] 1 All ER 834 at 843, CA, per Donaldson LJ (obiter).
7   As in ordinary bailment the obligation arises because in the circumstances the taking of possession involves an assumption of responsibility for the chattel's safe keeping: see *Gilchrist Watt and Sanderson Pty Ltd v York Products Pty Ltd* [1970] 3 All ER 825, [1970] 1 WLR 1262, PC; and PARA 101 note 4. Cf *R v Ngan* [2008] 2 NZLR 48, NZ SC.
8   See PARA 232.
9   *Binstead v Buck* (1776) 2 Wm Bl 1117. It seems that he has no claim for compensation in any form: see PARA 115 note 1; *Kowal v Ellis* (1977) 76 DLR (3d) 546 at 547–548, Man CA per O'Sullivan JA. But cf *China-Pacific SA v Food Corpn of India* [1982] AC 939, [1981] 3 All ER 688, HL.
10 *Robot Arenas Ltd v Waterfield* [2010] EWHC 115 (QB), [2010] All ER (D) 67 (Feb). 'If one is possessed of a jewel, and casts it into the sea or a public highway, this is such an express dereliction, that a property will be vested in the first fortunate finder that will seize it to his own use. But … if he loses or drops it by accident, it cannot be collected from thence that he designed to quit the possession, and therefore in such case the property still remains in the loser, who may claim it again of the finder': 2 Bl Com 9.
11 *Clayton v Le Roy* [1911] 2 KB 1031 at 1048, CA, per Fletcher Moulton LJ. The observations in this and other cases, such as *Miller v Dell* [1891] 1 QB 468, CA, must be read subject to the Limitation Act 1980 ss 3, 32: see PARA 235; and LIMITATION PERIODS vol 68 (2008) PARAS 940, 942, 948, 983 et seq, 1220 et seq. There used also to be an exception to this if the chattel was sold in market overt; however, the doctrine of sales in market overt (which was contained in the Sale of Goods Act 1979 s 22(1)) was abolished by the Sale of Goods (Amendment) Act 1994 s 1: see MARKETS, FAIRS AND STREET TRADING vol 29(2) (Reissue) PARA 1026; SALE OF GOODS AND SUPPLY OF SERVICES vol 41 (2005 Reissue) PARA 23. See also PARA 236 note 14.
12 *Merry v Green* (1841) 7 M & W 623, where a person purchased, at a public auction, a bureau, in a secret drawer of which he later found money, which he appropriated to his own use. At the time of the sale neither the buyer nor the seller knew that the bureau contained anything, and Parke B said, at 631, that, though there was a delivery of the bureau, and a lawful property in it thereby vested in the finder, there was no delivery so as to give a lawful possession of the money. It was therefore a simple case of finding, and the property in the money remained in the seller. See also PARA 117. See Palmer on Bailment (3rd Edn, 2009) para 6-001.
13 See the Theft Act 1968 ss 1–6; and CRIMINAL LAW vol 25 (2010) PARA 278 et seq. Where a finder comes into possession of a chattel as a result of his trespassing upon another's land, the finder may acquire no rights in the chattel as against the occupier, even where the occupier had no possession of the chattel immediately prior to the trespass: *Parker v British Airways Board* [1982] QB 1004 at 1009, [1982] 1 All ER 834 at 837, CA, per Donaldson LJ (obiter).

117. Finding by bailee or purchaser. If a bailee entrusted with a chattel for a specific purpose, such as its repair or alteration, finds concealed in it some property, that property belongs to the owner of the chattel and not to the bailee, and if the bailee commits some act in regard to property not warranted by the purpose for which the chattel was delivered to him, that unwarranted act amounts to a conversion at least and may amount to theft[1].

So, if a person purchases a chattel, such as a bureau, and subsequently finds concealed in it some article the existence of which was unknown to both buyer and seller at the time of the purchase, the property in that article will, apart from special circumstances such as the proved intention of the parties to sell and buy the chattel and its contents, known and unknown, remain in the seller[2] and will not pass to the buyer, who will become a mere depositary of the article, and may be guilty of theft if he appropriates it to himself although, as regards criminal liability, an important factor in determining the question is the honest belief of the purchaser as to what was to be conveyed to him at the time of the purchase[3].

1   *Cartwright v Green* (1803) 8 Ves 405 at 409 per Lord Eldon; and see Palmer on Bailment (3rd Edn, 2009) para 6-001 fn 1. See also the Theft Act 1968 ss 2, 3; and CRIMINAL LAW vol 25 (2010) PARA 278 et seq. As to conversion generally see TORT vol 45(2) (Reissue) PARA 548 et seq.
2   This statement was approved in *Thomas v Greenslade* (1954) Times, 6 November. See also PARA 116 note 12. See Palmer in Meisel (ed) *Property and Protection, Essays in Honour of Brian Harvey* (2000) ch 1, especially p 13 note 80.
3   See the Theft Act 1968 s 2.

118.   Finder's rights against third parties.   Subject to the special position of chattels found on private property[1], as against everyone save the true owner or the finder's master or principal[2], the property in a chattel found vests in the finder on his taking possession of it[3], and thereafter, as a party voluntarily in possession[4] of that chattel, he has many of the rights and obligations which belong to a bailee, including a duty of care towards the owner. Consistently with this position, he can generally maintain a claim against any person (except the true owner, or his agent) who might dispossess him of it, either by taking it out of his possession or by converting it to his own use after receiving it from him, and recover the full value of the article if he sues in trover[5]. The wrongdoer cannot defend himself by showing that the real title was in some third person[6] unless he invokes the statutory machinery whereby a defendant in a claim for wrongful interference with goods can show that someone other than the claimant has a better title to the goods[7]. If the value cannot be established without the production of the article, and the wrongdoer fails to produce it, it may be presumed against him that the article was of the finest quality of its kind and its value may be assessed on that basis[8] in accordance with the principle that all things are presumed against a wrongdoer[9].

1   Where the party first in possession may be the occupier, see PARA 119.
2   A person who, as a servant, finds a thing in the course of his employment finds it for his master or principal: *South Staffordshire Water Co v Sharman* [1896] 2 QB 44, DC, as explained in *Hannah v Peel* [1945] KB 509 at 519, [1945] 2 All ER 288 at 293; *Parker v British Airways Board* [1982] QB 1004 at 1017, [1982] 1 All ER 834 at 843, CA, per Donaldson LJ (obiter). See also *Byrne v Hoare* [1965] Qd R 135.
3   However, chattels found in the sea, whether jetsam (sunk under water), flotsam (afloat on the surface of the water) or ligan (sunk under water but tied to a buoy), or chattels cast ashore by shipwreck, belong to the Crown if the true owner fails to appear, unless the right to them has been granted to a subject: 1 Bl Com 290–292. The same principle applies to the finding of whales or sturgeon (which are royal fish), whether in the sea or cast ashore: 1 Bl Com 290. See further CROWN PROPERTY vol 12(1) (Reissue) PARAS 271–272. For another qualification to the principle (ie that property in a chattel found vests in the finder on his taking possession of it) see *Waverley Borough Council v Fletcher* [1996] QB 334, [1995] 4 All ER 756, CA (a plaintiff local authority owning a public park was held to have a superior right to a valuable brooch over the defendant, who using a metal detector had discovered the brooch; the local authority being entitled to possess goods found on its property against all but the rightful owner, the court

adding that metal detecting was not a recreation of the sort permitted under the terms under which the authority held the land on behalf of the general public). See also PARA 119.

4   See PARA 237.

5   *Jeffries v Great Western Rly Co* (1856) 5 E & B 802 at 807 per Crompton J; *Armory v Delamirie* (1722) 1 Stra 505; and see notes thereon in 1 Smith LC (13th Edn) 393. As to the right to sue in trover, which is the form of claim for conversion, see TORT vol 45(2) (Reissue) PARA 542 et seq. It is possible that a finder who assumes possession of the chattel by virtue of an act of trespass against an occupier on whose land the goods were situated at the time of the trespass obtains no title against that occupier, irrespective of whether the occupier had a prior possession: *Parker v British Airways Board* [1982] QB 1004 at 1009–1010, 1017, [1982] 1 All ER 834 at 837, 843, CA, per Donaldson LJ (obiter). However, even an unlawfully acquired possession can confer sufficient title to enable the possessor to sue a third party interloper, that is someone other than the true owner or a landowner from whose land the chattel was taken by trespass: *Parker v British Airways Board* [1982] QB 1004, [1982] 1 All ER 834, CA.

6   *Jeffries v Great Western Rly Co* (1856) 5 E & B 802 at 805 per Lord Campbell CJ. But see PARAS 232, 236–237.

7   See the Torts (Interference with Goods) Act 1977 s 8; PARAS 229, 231, 237; and TORT vol 45(2) (Reissue) PARA 560 et seq. For procedural rules concerning parties in claims for wrongful interference with goods, and the power of the court to order, in certain circumstances, that certain persons be deprived of the right to bring a claim against the defendant, see CPR 19.5A; and CIVIL PROCEDURE vol 11 (2009) PARAS 212, 588.

8   *Mortimer v Cradock* (1843) 12 LJCP 166 at 167 per Tindal CJ; *Armory v Delamirie* (1722) 1 Stra 505.

9   Ie *omnia praesumuntur contra spoliatorem*: this embodies the grounds of the decision in *Armory v Delamirie* (1722) 1 Stra 505. See also *Indian Oil Corpn Ltd v Greenstone Shipping SA, The Ypatianna* [1988] QB 345, [1987] 3 All ER 893. But c f *Zabihi v Janzemini* [2009] EWCA Civ 851, [2009] All ER (D) 357 (Jul) noted by Palmer (2009) 14 Art, Antiquity and Law 375; and PARA 233 note 39. As to cases where the maxim shifts the onus of proof see *Williamson v Rover Cycle Co* [1901] 2 IR 189 at 202; affd [1901] 2 IR 615, Ir CA. See also *Malhotra v Dhawan* [1997] 8 Med LR 319, CA; *Colbeck v Diamanta (UK) Ltd* [2002] EWHC 616 (QB), [2002] All ER (D) 336 (Feb).

119.   Chattels found on private property. So far as relates to chattels (other than treasure[1], waifs[2] and estrays[3]) found on private property, the possession of land carries with it, in general, possession of everything which is attached to or under that land and, in the absence of a better title elsewhere, the right to possess it[4]. Consequently, if a chattel is found on land by some person other than the owner of the land, that owner, though previously unaware of its existence, and not the finder is, except as against the owner of the chattel, entitled to it[5].

The difficulty arises where the chattel is lying unattached on the surface of the land. If the property on which it is found is an inn, the innkeeper may be entitled to it, for he is said to enjoy a special property in the goods of his guests[6]. If the landowner's servant or agent finds it in the course of his employment or agency, the landowner is entitled to it; the landowner may also be entitled when the finder has committed a trespass[7]. But a landowner does not necessarily possess a thing which is lying unattached on the surface of his land even though the thing is not possessed by someone else[8]. To establish possession in such circumstances, the landowner must demonstrate a manifest intention to exercise exclusive control over anything which might be on the premises[9].

1   Ie formerly 'treasure trove', which was gold or silver of unknown ownership found concealed in a private place. As to the meaning of 'treasure' see NATIONAL CULTURAL HERITAGE vol 77 (2010) PARA 1086. As to treasure generally see the Treasure Act 1996; and NATIONAL CULTURAL HERITAGE vol 77 (2010) PARA 1084 et seq. See also CROWN PROPERTY vol 12(1) (Reissue) PARA 373.

2   Ie goods stolen and thrown away by the thief in his flight: see CONSTITUTIONAL LAW AND HUMAN RIGHTS vol 8(2) (Reissue) PARA 369; CROWN PROPERTY vol 12(1) (Reissue) PARA 371.

3   Ie animals of unknown ownership found wandering in a manor or lordship: see
     CONSTITUTIONAL LAW AND HUMAN RIGHTS vol 8(2) (Reissue) PARA 369; CROWN PROPERTY
     vol 12(1) (Reissue) PARA 372.
4   *Parker v British Airways Board* [1982] QB 1004, [1982] 1 All ER 834, CA; *South Staffordshire
     Water Co v Sharman* [1896] 2 QB 44 at 46, DC, quoting with approval Pollock and Wright's
     Possession in the Common Law p 41. See also *Hannah v Peel* [1945] KB 509 at 520, [1945]
     2 All ER 288 at 293–294; *Re Cohen, National Provincial Bank Ltd v Katz* [1953] Ch 88, [1953]
     1 All ER 378.
5   *South Staffordshire Water Co v Sharman* [1896] 2 QB 44, DC. Where the property on which the
     chattels are found is in the occupation of a lessee, they belong to the lessor, not the lessee, if they
     were there when the lease was granted, unless the terms of the lease are wide enough to cover
     them: *Elwes v Brigg Gas Co* (1886) 33 ChD 562, Ex Ch. But if they were not then on the
     property they would seem to belong to the lessee on the principle laid down in *South
     Staffordshire Water Co v Sharman* [1896] 2 QB 44, DC. See also *London Corpn v Appleyard*
     [1963] 2 All ER 834, [1963] 1 WLR 982 (lessee entitled as against finder, but lessor entitled as
     against lessee under special provision in lease). See also *Waverley Borough Council v Fletcher*
     [1996] QB 334, [1995] 4 All ER 756, CA (owner of public park held to have superior right to
     valuable brooch found there over the finder); and PARA 118 note 3.
6   *Bridges v Hawkesworth* (1851) 21 LJQB 75 at 76 per Patteson J. As to innkeepers see
     LICENSING AND GAMBLING vol 67 (2008) PARA 183 et seq.
7   *Hannah v Peel* [1945] KB 509 at 519–520, [1945] 2 All ER 288 at 293–294; and see *Parker v
     British Airways Board* [1982] QB 1004, [1982] 1 All ER 834, CA; and PARAS 116, 118. Cf
     Hibbert v McKiernan [1948] 2 KB 142, [1948] 1 All ER 860, DC (where a man trespassed on
     the property of a golf club and took a ball which he found on the links and was held guilty of
     larceny).
8   *Parker v British Airways Board* [1982] QB 1004 at 1009, [1982] 1 All ER 834 at 837, CA, per
     Donaldson LJ (obiter); *Hannah v Peel* [1945] KB 509 at 520, [1945] 2 All ER 288 at 294;
     Kowal v Ellis (1977) 76 DLR (3d) 546, Man CA.
9   *Parker v British Airways Board* [1982] QB 1004, [1982] 1 All ER 834, CA; *Kowal v Ellis*
     (1977) 76 DLR (3d) 546, Man CA. Thus where an airline passenger found a bracelet on the
     floor of an executive lounge at Heathrow Airport, the passenger and not the British Airways
     Board was held entitled to possession (see *Parker v British Airways Board* [1982] QB 1004,
     [1982] 1 All ER 834, CA); where a customer found on the floor of a shop a packet of banknotes
     accidentally dropped by a stranger who could not be traced, the finder, not the shopkeeper, was
     held entitled to possession (see *Bridges v Hawkesworth* (1851) 21 LJQB 75, which has been
     much discussed by distinguished commentators, some of whom have supported it for reasons
     which differ from each other and from the reasons given by the court which decided it, while
     one at least has suggested that it was wrongly decided (see *Hannah v Peel* [1945] KB 509 at
     515–517, [1945] 2 All ER 288 at 291–292); but the decision in *Bridges v Hawkesworth* (1851)
     21 LJQB 75 was upheld and explained in *Parker v British Airways Board* [1982] QB 1004,
     [1982] 1 All ER 834, CA); and where a soldier found a brooch in a house which had been
     requisitioned from the owner, who had never occupied the house himself, the finder, not the
     owner of the house, was held entitled to possession of the brooch (see *Hannah v Peel* [1945] KB
     509, [1945] 2 All ER 288). See further PERSONAL PROPERTY vol 35 (Reissue) PARAS 1211, 1220.

(D) Unrewarded and Involuntary Possession

120. Involuntary deposit. Where a chattel is sent, without request or
arrangement, by one person to another who does not hold himself out as willing
to receive it, the person to whom it is sent is deemed to be an involuntary bailee
and will ordinarily owe no responsibility to the sender to exercise reasonable
care for its safe custody or protection[1], but must not deliberately convert it to his
own use and must take reasonable care when purporting to redeliver the chattel
to the owner or his authorised representative (which would otherwise render him
liable in conversion)[2]. It has, however, been suggested that an involuntary bailee
may owe a duty of care, the standard varying according to what is reasonable in
the particular circumstances[3]. In most cases, the standard would be low because
of the involuntary nature of the transaction, but in some a higher standard
would apply[4]. In appropriate circumstances a bailment may decline in character
from originally voluntary to ultimately involuntary[5].

Where unsolicited[6] goods are sent[7] to a person ('the recipient') with a view to his acquiring[8] them, the recipient has no reasonable cause to believe that they were sent with a view to their being acquired for the purposes of a business and the recipient has neither agreed to acquire nor agreed to return them, the recipient may, as between himself and the sender[9], use, deal with or dispose of the goods as if they were an unconditional gift to him and the rights of the sender to the goods are extinguished[10].

Conversely, it has been suggested that where a man without previous request from the owner offers to take charge of a chattel, such an offer constitutes an inducement to the bailor to part with the possession of the chattel, and binds the bailee to exercise special care in its custody[11], but English law does not appear to recognise this refinement[12].

1   *Howard v Harris* (1884) 1 Cab & El 253 (plaintiff author, being asked by the defendant, the lessee of a theatre, to send him a synopsis of his play, sent the whole manuscript, which the defendant lost; it was held that no duty of any kind was cast on the defendant by sending him something he had not asked for: see per Williams J at 254). This decision accords with that in *Lethbridge v Phillips* (1819) 2 Stark 544 (where a picture was, without the defendant's knowledge or request, sent to the defendant's house, and was there injured). Cf *Neuwith v Over Darwen Industrial Co-operative Society* (1894) 63 LJQB 290; *Scotland v Solomon* [2002] EWHC 1886 (Ch), 146 Sol Jo LB 218, [2002] All ER (D) 71 (Sep); and see *City Television v Conference and Training Office Ltd* [2001] EWCA Civ 1770 (a fraudster hired four plasma screens and ancillary equipment from the claimants to be delivered to the defendants' premises apparently for an international conference, the fraudster cancelled the conference at the last moment telling the defendants by telephone that deliverymen would be coming to collect the equipment and when they arrived the defendants telephoned the fraudster (but not the claimants) to confirm that the equipment could go: the equipment was never seen again; it was held that the fraudster could not be said even ostensibly to be the bailor and any duty of care had to be owed by the defendants to the claimants, and clearly such duty had been breached); and *Griffin v George Hammond plc* (16 March 1999, unreported), CA (an involuntary bailee must act reasonably and if he does all that could reasonably be expected of him he is not liable). A slight assumption of control, however, may make the person a depositary: see *Newman v Bourne and Hollingsworth* (1915) 31 TLR 209. Even so, if without negligence and acting reasonably as involuntary bailee he does something to the goods, for example, delivers them to a person falsely representing himself to be the owner, which results in the loss of the property, he will not be liable: *Elvin and Powell Ltd v Plummer, Roddis Ltd* (1933) 78 Sol Jo 48, 50 TLR 158: see also *Motis Exports Ltd v Dampskibsselskabet AF 1912* [2000] 1 All ER (Comm) 91, [2000] 1 Lloyd's Rep 211, CA (see also Rix J at [1999] 1 All ER (Comm) 571, [1999] 1 Lloyd's Rep 837, QB). In *Marcq v Christie Manson & Woods Ltd (t/a Christie's)* [2003] EWCA Civ 731, [2004] QB 286, [2003] 3 All ER 561 the principle in *Elvin and Powell Ltd v Plummer, Roddis Ltd* was distinguished.

2   This seems to follow on principle: see *Elvin and Powell Ltd v Plummer, Roddis Ltd* (1933) 78 Sol Jo 48, 50 TLR 158; and *Robot Arenas Ltd v Waterfield* [2010] EWHC 115 (QB), [2010] All ER (D) 67 (Feb); and compare the cases cited in PARA 115 note 2. See also the analogous principles governing the buyer's acceptance of goods not in accordance with the contract, as to which see *Grimoldby v Wells* (1875) LR 10 CP 391; *Harnor v Groves* (1855) 15 CB 667; *Chapman v Morton* (1843) 11 M & W 534, now embodied in the Sale of Goods Act 1979 s 35 (see SALE OF GOODS AND SUPPLY OF SERVICES vol 41 (2005 Reissue) PARA 196 et seq).

3   See *JJD SA v Avon Tyres Ltd* (23 February 2000, unreported), CA, in which Lord Bingham of Cornhill CJ tentatively favoured a duty to abstain from gross negligence; to similar effect *Marcus v Official Solicitor* [1997] EWCA Civ 886; and *Duet Marketing Corpn v Spetifore* (1986) 32 BLR 148 at 157 per Southin J. The relevant circumstances would include the nature and value of the goods, the conditions in which they have been deposited, the facilities at the defendant's disposal, the readiness with which he could have returned them and (where known to the defendant) the conduct of the owner.

4   Cf *Nelson v Mackintosh* (1816) 1 Stark 237; *Consentino v Dominion Express Co* (1906) 4 WLR 498, Manitoba CA, per Perdue JA (dissenting).

5   *Marcus v Official Solicitor* [1997] EWCA Civ 886.

6   'Unsolicited' means, in relation to goods sent or services supplied to any person, that they are sent or supplied without any prior request made by or on behalf of the recipient: Consumer Protection (Distance Selling) Regulations 2000, SI 2000/2334, reg 24(6).

7 'Send' includes deliver: Consumer Protection (Distance Selling) Regulations 2000, SI 2000/2334, reg 24(6).
8 'Acquire' includes hire: Consumer Protection (Distance Selling) Regulations 2000, SI 2000/2334, reg 24(6).
9 'Sender', in relation to any goods, includes: (1) any person on whose behalf or with whose consent the goods are sent; (2) any other person claiming through or under the sender or any person mentioned in head (1); and (3) any person who delivers the goods: Consumer Protection (Distance Selling) Regulations 2000, SI 2000/2334, reg 24(6).
10 Consumer Protection (Distance Selling) Regulations 2000, SI 2000/2334, reg 24(1)–(3). Regulation 24 applies only to goods sent and services supplied after 31 October 2000: regs 1(1), 24(10). See generally CONSUMER PROTECTION vol 21 (2011) PARA 445 et seq.
11 Jones on Bailments (4th Edn, 1833) pp 47, 121, following Pothier and the Roman lawyers.
12 Story on Bailments (9th Edn, 1878) s 82.

(ii) Bailee's Obligations

121. Measure of diligence. In order that a claim may be maintained in the case of a gratuitous deposit, the depositary must have been guilty of fraud[1], breach of orders, or such want of reasonable care as to constitute negligence[2]. In negligence the standard of care required of a gratuitous bailee is that demanded by the circumstances of the particular case[3]: thus the measure of diligence demanded of a gratuitous depository is as a rule that degree of diligence which men of common prudence generally exercise about their own affairs[4], but if the bailee is notoriously dissipated, negligent or imprudent, and the bailor was aware of the fact, a presumption might perhaps be raised that the bailor expected of him only such amount of care as the bailee was in the habit of bestowing on his own chattels of a similar nature[5]. The fact that the bailee keeps chattels deposited with him in the same manner as he keeps his own may be, but is not necessarily, sufficient to exempt a gratuitous bailee from liability[6].

The amount of diligence which is required may also be affected by the particular locality in which the bailment is effected. Thus in agricultural districts it may be usual to leave barns, in which horses and other cattle are kept, unlocked at night; but in cities a corresponding practice would be deemed a great want of caution[7].

In each case it has to be decided whether, having regard to any exempting conditions[8] and all the circumstances of the particular case[9], including the nature, portability, value and character of the chattel, there has been a breach of duty on the bailee's part to justify a finding of negligence[10]. The fact that the chattel was lost or injured whilst in the bailee's possession raises prima facie a presumption against him[11], but he may rebut it by proving that he was not to blame for the loss or injury, even if he is unable to show how it happened[12].

Except by special agreement, a gratuitous depository is not liable to his bailor for the misfeasances of third parties whereby the chattel bailed is damaged or stolen, unless it can be shown that he was guilty of negligence of a sufficiently culpable kind in its control or custody, or of fraud[13].

The bailee must return the chattel bailed to the bailor on demand[14].

1 *Moore v Mourgue* (1776) 2 Cowp 479 at 480 per Lord Mansfield CJ.
2 The term 'gross negligence' adds nothing and has been disapproved: see *Houghland v RR Low (Luxury Coaches) Ltd* [1962] 1 QB 694 at 697–698, [1962] 2 All ER 159 at 160–161, CA; and PARA 107. See also *Khan v Grocutt* [2002] EWCA Civ 1945, [2003] RTR 314, [2003] Lloyd's Rep IR 464 (where the defendant was a gratuitous bailee of important insurance documents which he failed to take reasonable steps to preserve and reproduce when needed). But c f *JJD SA v Avon Tyres Ltd* (23 February 2000, unreported), CA (cited in PARA 120 note 3); *Marcus v Official Solicitor* [1997] EWCA Civ 886 (gross negligence).

3   *Houghland v RR Low (Luxury Coaches) Ltd* [1962] 1 QB 694 at 698, [1962] 2 All ER 159 at
     161, CA, per Ormerod LJ. The views expressed in older cases that the standard of care was to
     be adjudged according to rules peculiar to bailment are not now consistent with the modern law
     of negligence and these cases must now be read in the light of *Houghland v RR Low (Luxury
     Coaches) Ltd* [1962] 1 QB 694, [1962] 2 All ER 159, CA, and later authority: see note 4. See
     also *Yearworth v North Bristol NHS Trust* [2009] EWCA Civ 37 at [48], [2010] QB 1, [2009]
     2 All ER 986. If a gratuitous bailee holds himself out to the bailor as able to deploy some special
     skill in relation to the chattel, his duty is to take such care of it as is reasonably to be expected
     of a person with such skill: *Wilson v Brett* (1843) 11 M & W 113; *Yearworth v North Bristol
     NHS Trust* [2009] EWCA Civ 37 at [48], [2010] QB 1, [2009] 2 All ER 986. As to the degree of
     care and diligence required in different kinds of bailment see PARA 107.
4   *China-Pacific SA v Food Corpn of India, The Winson* [1982] AC 939 at 960, [1981] 3 All ER
     688 at 694, HL, per Lord Diplock; *Port Swettenham Authority v TW Wu & Co (M) Sdn Bhd*
     [1979] AC 580 at 589, [1978] 3 All ER 337 at 339, PC. See also *Giblin v McMullen* (1868) LR
     2 PC 317; *Bullen v Swan Electric Engraving Co* (1907) 23 TLR 258, CA; *Blount v War Office*
     [1953] 1 All ER 1071, [1953] 1 WLR 736; and PARA 123. In several modern authorities, the
     duty is simply stated as one of reasonable care in all the circumstances: *Garlick v W & H
     Rycroft Ltd* [1982] CA Transcript 277; *Mitchell v Ealing London Borough Council* [1979] QB
     1 at 6, [1978] 2 All ER 779 at 781 per O'Connor J; and see *James Buchanan & Co Ltd v Hay's
     Transport Services Ltd and Duncan Barbour & Son Ltd* [1972] 2 Lloyd's Rep 535; *Hedley
     Byrne & Co Ltd v Heller & Partners Ltd* [1964] AC 465 at 526, [1963] 2 All ER 575 at
     608, HL, per Lord Devlin.
5   *The William* (1806) 6 Ch Rob 316. See also *Coggs v Bernard* (1703) 2 Ld Raym 909 at 914 per
     Holt CJ.
6   *Coggs v Bernard* (1703) 2 Ld Raym 909 at 914 per Holt CJ; *Giblin v McMullen* (1868) LR
     2 PC 317 at 339 per Lord Chelmsford. Cf *Doorman v Jenkins* (1834) 2 Ad & El 256, where the
     defendant coffee-house keeper accepted from the plaintiff the deposit of a sum with which to
     take up a bill which would be presented there for payment, and placed it with money of his own
     to a larger amount in a cash-box which he kept in the taproom, whence it was stolen on a day
     on which the room was open to the public while the rest of the house was closed;
     Lord Denman CJ at 258 said that it did not follow from the defendant's having lost his own
     money at the same time as the plaintiff's that he had taken such care of the plaintiff's money as
     a reasonable man would ordinarily take of his own. This was approved in *Giblin v McMullen*
     (1868) LR 2 PC 317 at 339. See also *Morris v CW Martin & Sons Ltd* [1966] 1 QB 716 at 725,
     [1965] 2 All ER 725 at 731, CA, per Lord Denning MR; *Nelson v Macintosh* (1816) 1 Stark
     237; *Dartnall v Howard and Gibbs* (1825) 4 B & C 345; *Garlick v W & H Rycroft Ltd* [1982]
     CA Transcript 277.
7   Story on Bailments (9th Edn, 1878) s 13.
8   See PARAS 122, 147.
9   *Houghland v RR Low (Luxury Coaches) Ltd* [1962] 1 QB 694, [1962] 2 All ER 159, CA. See
     also *Garlick v W & H Rycroft Ltd* [1982] CA Transcript 277.
10   *Giblin v McMullen* (1868) LR 2 PC 317. See also *Ryder v Wombwell* (1868) LR 4 Exch 32 at
     38–39.
11   *Houghland v RR Low (Luxury Coaches) Ltd* [1962] 1 QB 694, [1962] 2 All ER 159, CA.
12   The onus is always on the bailee, whether a bailee for reward or a gratuitous bailee, to prove
     that the loss of goods bailed to him was not caused by his negligence: *Port Swettenham
     Authority v TW Wu & Co (M) Sdn Bhd* [1979] AC 580, [1978] 3 All ER 337, PC; *Mitchell v
     Ealing London Borough Council* [1979] QB 1, [1978] 2 All ER 779. See also *Wiehe v Dennis Bros*
     (1913) 29 TLR 250; *Ludgate v Lovett* [1969] 2 All ER 1275 at 1277, [1969] 1 WLR 1016 at
     1019, CA, per Harman LJ; *Graham v Voigt* (1989) 95 FLR 146 (Aus FC); *Walsh v Holst
     & Co Ltd* [1958] 3 All ER 33 at 37, [1958] 1 WLR 800 at 805, CA, per Hodson LJ. See also
     Toor v Bassi [1999] EGCS 9, CA (gratuitous bailee unable to rebut presumption of failing to
     deal reasonably with an unequivocal demand made by the owner for the return of the goods).
     See also PARAS 111 note 11, 149. As to the burden of proof with regard to deviation by a
     gratuitous bailee, see *Mitchell v Ealing London Borough Council*; cf *JJD SA (a company) v
     Avon Tyres Ltd* (1999) Times, 25 January, per Evans-Lombe J; *Toor v Bassi* [1999] EGCS
     9, CA; and see generally PARA 111.
13   *Coggs v Bernard* (1703) 2 Ld Raym 909 at 913; *Nelson v Macintosh* (1816) 1 Stark 237 at 238;
     Giblin v McMullen (1868) LR 2 PC 317; Jones on Bailments (4th Edn, 1833) pp 46–47.
14   See *Cranch v White* (1835) 1 Bing NC 414 at 420; *Wetherman v London and Liverpool Bank of
     Commerce Ltd* (1914) 31 TLR 20; *United States of America and Republic of France v Dollfus
     Mieg et Cie SA and Bank of England* [1952] AC 582 at 611, [1952] 1 All ER 572 at 585, HL;
     and PARA 232. It appears, however, that the demand must allow a reasonable time for

compliance. As to whether the bailor is bound by a promise, made at or before the time of delivery to the bailee, not to call for the return of the goods before a particular time, see Palmer on Bailment (3rd Edn, 2009) para 10-045 (such promises potentially enforceable by reason of reciprocal consideration); cf Paton *Bailment in the Common Law* (1952) p 101. As to whether the bailor owes an obligation to collect the goods within a particular time, see Palmer on Bailment (3rd Edn, 2009) para 10-052.

122. Liability limited or enlarged by special agreement. A gratuitous bailee may, by special agreement, limit or exclude his liability for any loss of, or damage to, the chattel[1]. His liability then depends upon the terms of the agreement[2], subject to any statutory controls imposed upon the disclaimer[3]. It is immaterial for this purpose whether the special agreement is oral or in writing[4].

Although the relationship of depositor and depositary is not, because of the lack of consideration moving from the depositor, contractual[5], it appears that the depositary can also enlarge his liability to the depositor by special agreement[6]. Consequently, if the bailee, in assuming possession of the chattel, expressly undertakes to keep it safely, he enlarges the measure of his responsibility, and by virtue of his special agreement may even make himself an insurer of it[7]. Similarly, a gratuitous bailee who undertakes to return the goods only to a particular person, or only upon particular conditions, will be answerable for the breach of that special undertaking[8]. Again, it appears immaterial for this purpose whether the special agreement is oral or in writing[9]. Yet such a bailee's responsibility is limited in some respects, for though his undertaking to keep the chattel safely binds him to exercise reasonable care to keep it safely against all parties and to answer for accidents or theft[10], he will not be liable in the case of casualties happening by an act of God, or by the Queen's enemies[11].

Where a gratuitous bailee by way of deposit undertakes to redeliver the goods to the bailor at a particular time or place, and fails to discharge that undertaking, the bailee becomes an insurer of the goods and is strictly liable for any subsequent loss or damage[12]. However, the making of a second appointment with the bailor may cause the bailee's responsibility for the goods to revert to a duty of reasonable care[13]. This will not, however, relieve the bailee from his strict responsibility for misadventures occurring to the goods before the making of that second appointment[14]. Further, where the goods are damaged or lost at some time after the bailee's failure to meet the original appointment, and the bailee has since made a second appointment, the burden rests on the bailee to show that the misadventure occurred after the making of the second appointment and thus after his responsibility has reverted to that of an ordinary bailee[15].

1   *Brown v National Bank of Australasia* (1890) 16 VLR 475; Palmer on Bailment (3rd Edn, 2009) para 10-040.

2   *Trefftz v Canelli* (1872) LR 4 PC 277 at 281; *Kettle v Bromsall* (1738) Willes 118 at 121; *Orchard v Connaught Club* (1930) 46 TLR 214. See also *Kay v Shuman* (1954) Times, 22 June; and PARA 147 note 1. It may be argued that this special agreement constitutes a contract, the depositor's consideration being his relieving the depositary from the normal duty of reasonable care owed by an unrewarded bailee; sed quaere.

3   The exclusion or restriction of liability for negligence is now subject to the provisions of the Unfair Contract Terms Act 1977: see CONTRACT vol 9(1) (Reissue) PARA 820 et seq. See also PARAS 110, 147.

4   *Coggs v Bernard* (1703) 2 Ld Raym 909 at 915.

5   *Morris v CW Martin & Sons Ltd* [1966] 1 QB 716 at 731–732, [1965] 2 All ER 725 at 734–735, CA, per Diplock LJ (obiter); *Thomas v High* (1960) SRNSW 401, NSW SC; *Parastatidis v Kotaridis* [1978] VR 449 at 454–455 per Harris J (obiter); but cf *New Zealand Shipping Co Ltd v AM Satterthwaite & Co Ltd* [1975] AC 154 at 167, [1974] 1 All ER 1015 at 1019, PC. See also *East West Corpn v DKBS AF 1912 A/S, Utaniko Ltd v P & O Nedlloyd BV*

[2003] EWCA Civ 83, [2003] QB 1509, [2003] 2 All ER 700; *Sandeman Coprimar SA v Transitos y Integrales SL* [2003] EWCA Civ 113, [2003] QB 1270, [2003] 3 All ER 108, [2003] 2 Lloyd's Rep 172.

6   *Yearworth v North Bristol NHS Trust* [2009] EWCA Civ 37, [2010] QB 1, [2009] 2 All ER 986; *Kettle v Bromsall* (1738) Willes 118.

7   *Kettle v Bromsall* (1738) Willes 118; *Yearworth v North Bristol NHS Trust* [2009] EWCA Civ 37 at [48], [2010] QB 1 at [48], [2009] 2 All ER 986 at [48].

8   *Trefftz v Canelli* (1872) LR 4 PC 277 at 281; but cf *Parastatidis v Kotaridis* [1978] VR 449.

9   *Coggs v Bernard* (1703) 2 Ld Raym 909 at 915.

10   *Kettle v Bromsall* (1738) Willes 118.

11   *Coggs v Bernard* (1703) 2 Ld Raym 909 at 918.

12   *Mitchell v Ealing London Borough Council* [1979] QB 1, [1978] 2 All ER 779.

13   *Mitchell v Ealing London Borough Council* [1979] QB 1 at 9, [1978] 2 All ER 779 at 784 per O'Connor J.

14   See note 13.

15   See note 13. Cf *JJD SA (a company) v Avon Tyres Ltd* (1999) Times, 25 January; *Toor v Bassi* [1999] EGCS 9, CA.

123.   Deposits with bankers or traders.   Where a customer leaves valuables with his bankers[1] for safe custody, or allows a printer or any other trader to retain his plates or chattels upon which the trader may have worked, it is by no means certain that the bailment is gratuitous[2] as opposed to one for reward to the bailee[3]. Even if no specific charge for keeping is made, it may well be that the custodian indirectly obtains some consideration for the service, either in being allowed to continue to keep the customer's account[4], or in the prospect of future work[5]. On balance, it seems that such depositaries should be characterised as bailees for reward[6].

1   In *Giblin v McMullen* (1868) LR 2 PC 317, bankers with whom the plaintiff's testator had deposited for safe custody a box (of which he kept the key) containing debentures were found to be gratuitous bailees, whereas in *Re United Service Co, Johnston's Claim* (1871) 6 Ch App 212, bankers were held to be bailees for reward. See also FINANCIAL SERVICES AND INSTITUTIONS vol 49 (2008) PARAS 860, 875.

2   Ie *depositum*: see PARA 106.

3   Ie *locatio custodiae*: see PARA 106.

4   *Port Swettenham Authority v TW Wu & Co (M) Sdn Bhd* [1979] AC 580 at 589, [1978] 3 All ER 337 at 340, PC (obiter). See also *Kahler v Midland Bank Ltd* [1948] 1 All ER 811 at 819–820, CA, per Scott LJ; on appeal, without reference to this point, [1950] AC 24, [1949] 2 All ER 621, HL.

5   *Bullen v Swan Electric Engraving Co* (1906) 22 TLR 275 at 277 per Walton J; affd (1907) 23 TLR 258, CA. See also PRESS, PRINTING AND PUBLISHING vol 36(2) (Reissue) PARA 408.

6   Palmer on Bailment (3rd Edn, 2009) Chapter 9. Cf *Bullen v Swan Electric Engraving Co* (1906) 22 TLR 275 at 277 per Walton J (affd (1907) 23 TLR 258, CA); and see *Mitchell v Davis* (1920) 37 TLR 68.

124.   Use of chattel precluded.   The bailee is precluded from using the bailed chattel for his own personal advantage in any manner whatsoever without the bailor's consent, express or implied, unless such use is necessary for its preservation[1]. Apart from such necessary use, if the bailee applies the chattel to any purpose other than that of bare custody (including an unauthorised detention of the goods beyond the time at which he has promised or is otherwise obliged to return them) he becomes responsible for any loss or damage resulting from his unlawful departure from the terms of the bailment[2], except where the cause of the loss or damage is independent of his acts and is inherent in the chattel itself[3]. The bailee's act in doing something inconsistent with the terms of the contract terminates his status as a bailee, and causes the possessory title to revert to the bailor, entitling him to maintain a claim of trover[4].

This rules applies a fortiori when the bailee's unwarranted action results in either the destruction or permanent alteration in character of the thing bailed[5].

If the chattel deposited is contained in a sealed or locked receptacle, the depositary has no right to open it, and it is a breach of the confidential relation on which this contract is based if he does so unnecessarily[6]; and it may be negligence to omit to take steps to see that the receptacle is not opened[7].

1   Bac Abr Bailment A. See also *Re Tidd, Tidd v Overell* [1893] 3 Ch 154, where money was handed over to be taken care of, but with the intention that the bailee might use it; and North J held, at 156, that it was received, not as a loan, but as a trust for safe custody.
2   *Mitchell v Ealing London Borough Council* [1979] QB 1, [1978] 2 All ER 779; *Toor v Bassi* [1999] EGCS 9, CA; Pothier's Contrat de Dépôt ss 34, 35; Palmer on Bailment (3rd Edn, 2009) Chapter 10.
3   *Lilley v Doubleday* (1881) 7 QBD 510 at 511 per Grove J (a case of bailment for reward). See further *Mitchell v Ealing London Borough Council* [1979] QB 1, [1978] 2 All ER 779, applying *Shaw & Co v Symmons & Sons Ltd* [1917] 1 KB 799 (failure to return bailed goods at the appointed time).
4   *Fenn v Bittleston* (1851) 7 Exch 152; *Plasycoed Collieries Co Ltd v Partridge, Jones & Co Ltd* [1912] 2 KB 345 at 351 per Hamilton J; *R v Price* (1913) 9 Cr App Rep 15, CCA. The statement in the text was approved, as applying generally to bailments, in *North Central Wagon and Finance Co Ltd v Graham* [1950] 2 KB 7 at 15, [1950] 1 All ER 780 at 784, CA, per Cohen LJ; and see *Alexander v Railway Executive* [1951] 2 KB 882 at 887, [1951] 2 All ER 442 at 445 per Devlin J; *Reliance Car Facilities Ltd v Roding Motors* [1952] 2 QB 844 at 851, [1952] 1 All ER 1355 at 1358, CA, per Hodson LJ; *Union Transport Finance Ltd v British Car Auctions Ltd* [1978] 2 All ER 385, CA. As to trover or conversion (included in wrongful interference with goods) see TORT vol 45(2) (Reissue) PARA 542 et seq.
5   *Wilkinson v Verity* (1871) LR 6 CP 206.
6   Pothier's Contrat de Dépôt s 38. See also *R v Robson* (1861) Le & Ca 93.
7   See *Blount v War Office* [1953] 1 All ER 1071, [1953] 1 WLR 736.

125.   Consequence of breach of duty.   If a bailee deals with the chattels entrusted to him in a way not authorised by the bailor, he takes upon himself the risk of so doing.

If, therefore, the bailee without necessity, and without the bailor's permission, fails to keep the chattel entrusted to him in the place where he has undertaken to keep it, that is to say, in the absence of express agreement, in the place where he himself usually keeps his own chattels of a similar description, he becomes by reason of his breach of duty an insurer of the chattel, and is liable to the bailor for any loss or damage caused[1], unless he can show that the loss or damage did not arise out of his breach of duty, but must have taken place as inevitably at the one place as at the other[2]. Similarly, a bailee by way of deposit who undertakes to redeliver the goods to the bailor at a particular time, and fails to do so, becomes thereafter an insurer of the goods[3]. The bailee's promise would appear to be enforceable irrespective of the absence of contract. If the bailee without necessity, and without the bailor's express or implied permission, sells the chattel, a claim for conversion will lie against him[4].

A bailee is not free to divest himself of responsibility and substitute that of another without the bailor's consent[5].

1   Pothier's Contrat de Dépôt s 38; Palmer on Bailment (3rd Edn, 2009) para 10-020; cf *Mytton v Cock* (1738) 2 Stra 1099; *Ronnenberg v Falkland Islands Co* (1864) 17 CBNS 1; *Mitchell v Ealing London Borough Council* [1979] QB 1, [1978] 2 All ER 779 (delay in redelivery).
2   *Lilley v Doubleday* (1881) 7 QBD 510 at 511 per Grove J; *Davis v Garrett* (1830) 6 Bing 716 at 724 per Tindal CJ (cases of bailment for reward). Cf *Coldman v Hill* [1919] 1 KB 443, CA; and see PARAS 131, 138.
3   *Mitchell v Ealing London Borough Council* [1979] QB 1, [1978] 2 All ER 779 (local authority, in possession of former tenant's goods as gratuitous bailee, made appointment for redelivery but failed to keep it; local authority held strictly liable for subsequent theft, notwithstanding

reasonable care in custody of the goods); and *Toor v Bassi* [1999] EGCS 9, CA (gratuitous bailee owed duty through agent to take reasonable care of car left on premises; not to make an arrangement for its return through indifference or idleness amounted to negligence and defendant was insurer of the car as from the time that, with reasonable diligence, an arrangement could have been made for returning it). See also *Shaw & Co v Symmons & Sons Ltd* [1917] 1 KB 799, a case of bailment for reward, on which O'Connor J relied in *Mitchell v Ealing London Borough Council* [1979] QB 1, [1978] 2 All ER 779. See further *Toor v Bassi* [1999] EGCS 9, CA; and PARA 124.

4   *Sachs v Miklos* [1948] 2 KB 23 at 36, [1948] 1 All ER 67 at 68, CA; *Munro v Willmott* [1949] 1 KB 295, [1948] 2 All ER 983. A bailee who no longer wishes to retain the goods but is unaware of the bailor's current whereabouts might gain the bailor's deemed consent to a disposal by writing to him at his last known address requesting that he remove his goods and then (in the absence of a satisfactory response) writing again to warn him that the goods are to be disposed of: *Sachs v Miklos* [1948] 2 KB 23 at 40, [1948] 1 All ER 67 at 69, CA, per Lord Goddard CJ; *Infolines Public Networks Ltd v Nottingham City Council* [2009] EWCA Civ 708 at [11], [2009] All ER (D) 12 (Sep) at [11], per Keene LJ. But there is no doubt about the efficacy of this method, partly because under the law of contract silence does not ordinarily connote acceptance (see CONTRACT vol 9(1) (Reissue) PARA 655). As to agency of necessity see generally AGENCY vol 1 (2008) PARA 24. As to conversion generally see TORT vol 45(2) (Reissue) PARA 548 et seq.

5   See *Blount v War Office* [1953] 1 All ER 1071, [1953] 1 WLR 736.

(2) MANDATE

126. Meaning of 'mandate'. Mandate[1] is another species of bailment gratuitously undertaken by the bailee. It may be defined as a bailment of a specific chattel[2] in regard to which the bailee engages to do some act without reward[3]. It has much in common with deposit[4], but whereas in the case of deposit the principal object of the contract is to provide for the safe custody of the thing, and any service or labour, such as feeding an animal or preserving a perishable article, is merely accessory, in the case of mandate the safe custody of the chattel deposited is ancillary to an undertaking by the bailee to do some act to it, or to perform some service in connection with it[5]. In this sense, therefore, it may be said that the great distinction between mandate and deposit is that the former lies in feasance and the latter in custody[6].

In this form of bailment, the bailer's confidence in the capacity, skill and honour of the bailee duly to perform the task or employment undertaken by him, and not merely or chiefly the bailee's promise to safeguard the chattel while in his charge, has been held to constitute the consideration moving the bailor to deliver it into his custody[7]. Under modern law, however, it now seems preferable to recognise that the transaction of mandate (in common with that of deposit)[8] does not give rise to a contract[9].

An executory transaction of mandate creates no legal obligation, for a person undertaking to perform a voluntary act is not liable if he merely refuses or neglects to perform it[10], and the agreement remains executory at any rate until delivery of the chattel is accepted[11].

1   Ie *mandatum*: see PARA 106.
2   Money may be regarded as a chattel in this context, whether entrusted to the mandatary in the form of cash or obtained by him by means of a cheque or other negotiable instrument, or as the proceeds of the sale of property which he was authorised to sell on the mandator's behalf. Even where the identical coins need not be used, the mandator may be entitled to treat the equivalent of the sum entrusted to the mandatary as his property, and not merely as a debt due to him, if it is not used or laid out in accordance with the contract. Similarly, the mandator may claim as his own or obtain a charge upon any property purchased with the money in whole or in part, even if it is not the property which ought to have been purchased, and he may follow it if it is lent or given away by the mandatary: see *Taylor v Plumer* (1815) 3 M & S 562; *Re Strachan,*

ex p Cooke (1876) 4 ChD 123, CA; *Re Hallett's Estate, Knatchbull v Hallett* (1880) 13 ChD 696, CA; *Banque Belge Pour L'Etranger v Hambrouck* [1921] 1 KB 321, CA. See also *Lipkin Gorman v Karpnale Ltd* [1991] 2 AC 548, [1992] 4 All ER 512, HL; *Trustee of the Property of FC Jones & Sons (a firm) v Jones* [1997] Ch 159, [1996] 4 All ER 721, CA; *Foskett v McKeown* [2001] 1 AC 102, [2000] 3 All ER 97, HL. Similarly, the mandatory may claim as his own or obtain a charge upon any property purchased with the money in whole or in part, even if it is not the property which ought to have been purchased. He may follow it if it is lent or given away by the mandatary and may also receive any resulting profits. See *Trustee of the Property of FC Jones & Sons (a firm) v Jones* [1997] Ch 159, [1996] 4 All ER 721, CA.

3   Story on Bailments (9th Edn, 1878) s 137; Palmer on Bailment (3rd Edn, 2009) para 11-001. See also Heineccius, Pandects par 3, lib 17, s 230.
4   See PARAS 111–125.
5   *Coggs v Bernard* (1703) 2 Ld Raym 909 at 918.
6   Jones on Bailments (4th Edn, 1833) p 53. This distinction is criticised by Story on Bailments (9th Edn, 1878) s 140; see further Palmer on Bailment (3rd Edn, 2009) para 11-002.
7   *Coggs v Bernard* (1703) 2 Ld Raym 909 at 919; *Banbury v Bank of Montreal* [1918] AC 626 at 657, PC; and see Story on Bailments (9th Edn, 1878) s 140; Pothier's Contrat de Mandat c 1.
8   See PARA 111.
9   See Palmer on Bailment (3rd Edn, 2009) para 11-001; and see *Yearworth v North Bristol NHS Trust* [2009] EWCA Civ 37, [2010] QB 1, [2009] 2 All ER 986.
10 *Skelton v London and North Western Rly Co* (1867) LR 2 CP 631 at 636 per Willes J; *Elsee v Gatward* (1793) 5 Term Rep 143 at 148 per Lord Kenyon CJ; *Balfe v West* (1853) 13 CB 466; and see *Coggs v Bernard* (1703) 2 Ld Raym 909 at 919. See also NEGLIGENCE.
11 See further PARA 128; and PARA 122 as to the effect of superadded promises given by a depositary on or before receiving possession of the goods.

127.   Extent of bailee's obligations.   The bailee, or mandatary, when he has entered upon the execution of the task which he has undertaken, is bound, in common with all others who render a gratuitous service[1], apart from special contract, to act prudently and honourably and to exercise reasonable care and diligence[2]. This imposes upon him the duty to use such care and diligence a reasonable person would ordinarily use in the performance of the task in question and such skill as he possesses[3]. In addition, if, because the bailee holds himself out as possessing a professional or other special skill, the bailor entrusts him with the performance of a task which requires the exercise of such skill, he must use it[4].

The public profession of an art is a representation that the person professing it possesses the necessary skill and ability. When, therefore, a skilled worker or artist is employed, he warrants impliedly that he is possessed of sufficient skill to perform the task that he undertakes, even if the undertaking be without reward[5].

1   *Wilkinson v Coverdale* (1793) 1 Esp 74; *Dartnall v Howard and Gibbs* (1825) 4 B & C 345; *Gladwell v Steggall* (1839) 5 Bing NC 733; *Harris v Perry & Co* [1903] 2 KB 219, CA; *Karavias v Callinicos* [1917] WN 323, CA; *Pratt v Patrick* [1924] 1 KB 488.
2   *Houghland v RR Low (Luxury Coaches) Ltd* [1962] 1 QB 694, [1962] 2 All ER 159, CA; *Remme v Wall* (1978) 29 NSR (2d) 39; and see *Copland v Brogan* 1916 SC 277, Ct of Sess. Earlier expressions of the mandatary's duty in terms of gross negligence would now appear discredited: Palmer on Bailment (3rd Edn, 2009) paras 11-009–11-011.
3   *Beauchamp v Powley* (1831) 1 Mood & R 38; *Beal v South Devon Rly Co* (1864) 3 H & C 337 at 342 per Crompton J; *Shiells and Thorne v Blackburne* (1789) 1 Hy Bl 159.
4   *Shiells and Thorne v Blackburne* (1789) 1 Hy Bl 159 at 162 per Heath J. See *Bourne v Diggles* (1814) 2 Chit 311; *O'Hanlon v Murray* (1860) 12 ICLR 161; *Wilson v Brett* (1843) 11 M & W 113, where a skilled horseman gratuitously riding a horse to show it to a purchaser on its owner's behalf was held liable for injuring it by riding it on improper ground.
5   *Harmer v Cornelius* (1858) 5 CBNS 236; *Shiells and Thorne v Blackburne* (1789) 1 Hy Bl 158. Cf PARA 162; and see *Barclays Bank plc v Fairclough Building Ltd* [1995] QB 214 at 222–223, [1995] 1 All ER 289 at 295–296, CA, per Beldam LJ.

128.   Bailee's liability.   The bailee's failure to discharge his obligations[1] renders him liable to be sued in tort for negligence, or in an independent claim for breach of bailment, if that failure causes damage to the bailor. In addition, as in the case of a depositary, he is responsible to the bailor for the loss of or any damage to the chattel entrusted to him arising out of any breach of duty on his part in respect of its safe custody[2].

Moreover, the acceptance of the bailment of the chattel by the bailee may constitute a sufficient entering upon the task or service undertaken to make him liable to the bailor if he neglects to carry out his promise, and damage is thereby directly caused to the bailor, even if the neglect amounts only to nonfeasance[3]. There is uncertainty as to the juridical basis of this obligation. Older authorities held that where the bailor's only obligation was to hand over the chattel, his doing so constituted performance of his part of the agreement and was the consideration for the bailee's promise to carry out the particular act or perform the service concerned[4]. Under modern law, however, a contractual analysis seems inappropriate. Nor can it be maintained that the bailee's failure to perform constitutes (otherwise than in the most exceptional cases) the tort of negligence[5]. On balance, the duty to perform is preferably regarded as an incident peculiar to the bailment relationship[6].

It is possible that, owing to the gratuitous nature of the undertaking, the bailee may relieve himself of responsibility by returning the chattel to the bailor at any such time as will enable the undertaking to be performed otherwise[7].

1 See PARA 127.
2 See PARA 121.
3 *Wilkinson v Coverdale* (1793) 1 Esp 74; *Streeter v Horlock* (1822) 1 Bing 34; *Oriental Bank Corpn v R* (1867) 6 NSWSCR 122 at 125 per Faucett J; *Pilcher v Leyland Motors Ltd* [1932] NZLR 449 at 464–467 per Ostler J; *Roufos v Brewster and Brewster* (1971) 2 SASR 218 at 223–224 per Bray CJ; but c f *Heaton v Richards* (1881) 2 NSWLR 73; *Parastatidis v Kotaridis* [1978] VR 449 at 454–455 per Harris J. See further Story on Bailments (9th Edn, 1878) s 171(a)–(c). If, for instance, a bailee undertakes gratuitously to present a bill of exchange for payment and gives all the necessary notices of dishonour on behalf of the holder and receives the bill for him, and then does nothing, and the acceptor is made bankrupt and the holder loses all his remedies against the drawer and indorsers owing to the non-presentment of the bill on the due date, it would appear that the bailee would be liable. See also *Chapman v Morley* (1891) 7 TLR 257.
4 Story on Bailments (9th Edn, 1878) s 171(a)–(c). See *Shillibeer v Glyn* (1836) 2 M & W 143; and c f *Whitehead v Greetham* (1825) 2 Bing 464, Ex Ch.
5 *General Accident Fire and Life Assurance Corpn Ltd v Tanter, The Zephyr* [1985] 2 Lloyd's Rep 529 at 538–539, CA, per Mustill LJ; *Argy Trading Development Co Ltd v Lapid Developments Ltd* [1977] 3 All ER 785, [1977] 1 WLR 444.
6 Palmer on Bailment (3rd Edn, 2009) para 11-005; *Yearworth v North Bristol NHS Trust* [2009] EWCA Civ 37, [2010] QB 1, [2009] 2 All ER 986.
7 Story on Bailments (9th Edn, 1878) s 164.

129. When bailee is excused from liability. If a contract of mandate is contained in a written instrument which is expressed in ambiguous terms, and the bailee is in fact misled and adopts one interpretation when the bailor intended him to follow the other, then the bailor will be bound, and the bailee will be exonerated[1].

In the case of impossible undertakings the bailee is not liable, unless the bailee when giving the undertaking can be treated as having undertaken to perform in any event. This conclusion is most likely to follow where the bailee knows of the impossibility of the task when undertaking to perform it, but in principle liability for non-performance may follow even without such awareness. The impossibility must, in any case, be absolute and not relative in order to constitute a defence; mere difficulty in execution or the violation of trade custom is not sufficient ground for excusing non-performance when once the task is entered upon[2].

An agreement of mandate for the performance of an immoral or illegal act cannot be enforced, as no court will enforce an illegal contract or transaction or allow itself to be made the instrument of enforcing obligations alleged to arise out of a contract or transaction which is illegal. It is immaterial whether or not the defendant has pleaded the illegality[3].

1 Story on Agency (9th Edn) s 74. See *Ireland v Livingston* (1872) LR 5 HL 395; cf *European Asian Bank AG v Punjab and Sind Bank (No 2)* [1983] 2 All ER 508, [1983] 1 WLR 642, CA. As to interpretation of contracts see CONTRACT vol 9(1) (Reissue) PARA 772 et seq.
2 *Tufnell v Constable* (1838) 7 Ad & El 798. As to the discharge of contracts on the ground of impossibility or frustration see CONTRACT vol 9(1) (Reissue) PARA 888 et seq.
3 *Scott v Brown, Doering, McNab & Co, Slaughter and May v Brown, Doering, McNab & Co* [1892] 2 QB 724 at 728, CA, per Lindley LJ, citing *Holman v Johnson* (1775) 1 Cowp 341. See further CONTRACT.

130. Bailee's duty to account. A bailee who, under a mandate, receives money or chattels on account of his principal is bound to account for them[1]. If the mandatary without the bailor's authority deposits them in his own name, with other chattels of his own of the same kind, in the hands of a third party, he is liable to his principal for any loss or damage to them during the existence of the deposit; and this is so even if his principal was aware of his course of procedure, if he did not assent to it[2].

When the return of the bailed chattel constitutes part of the bailee's obligation, he must restore not only the chattel itself, but also all increments, profits and earnings immediately derived from it[3].

The bailee is also liable to account to the bailor for any secret profits which he may have received in respect of the conduct or management of the business which he has undertaken gratuitously to perform[4].

1 *Massey v Banner* (1820) 4 Madd 413.
2 *Massey v Banner* (1820) 4 Madd 413. But the bailor might be deemed on an objective analysis of the circumstances to have consented, or might be estopped from asserting that he did not consent.
3 Pothier's Contrat de Mandat ss 58–60. Thus if animals are to be restored, their young also belong to the bailor, and if a vehicle has been delivered to be let for hire, the bailee must account for the hire earned, as well as for the vehicle: Story on Bailments (9th Edn, 1878) s 194. See *Strand Electric and Engineering Co Ltd v Brisford Entertainments Ltd* [1952] 2 QB 246, [1952] 1 All ER 796, CA; and PARAS 152, 187, 233. Compare the case of *mutuum*, which is discussed in PARA 140. See also *P & O Trans European Ltd v Wincanton Ltd* [2001] EWCA Civ 227, [2001] All ER (D) 174 (Feb).
4 See *Kimber v Barber* (1872) 8 Ch App 56, CA; and AGENCY vol 1 (2008) PARA 92 et seq.

131. Misuse of bailed chattel. When under a mandate a bailee does some act to the bailed chattel unauthorised by the agreement made between himself and the bailor, he becomes responsible for any subsequent loss or damage which may be caused to the chattel by his unwarranted act[1].

1 *Nelson v Macintosh* (1816) 1 Stark 237; *Miles v Cattle* (1830) 4 Moo & P 630; Palmer on Bailment (3rd Edn, 2009) para 11-024. Cf PARAS 125, 138.

132. Duty to return chattel. As a general rule, a bailee under a mandate is bound to redeliver to his principal the chattel entrusted to him upon the fulfilment of the purpose for which he received it; but if it has been destroyed or damaged without any default on his part, he will (in the absence of special agreement or some positive rule of law) be exempt from any claim for damage or non-delivery[1].

1 Story on Bailments (9th Edn, 1878) s 25.

133.   Delegation by bailee.   As a general rule there is no power of delegation in the contract of mandate; the legal presumption is that the undertaking is personal to the bailee and may not be handed over by him to another[1]. Consistently with this, and in conformity with the equivalent principle governing depositaries, the mandatary will be strictly liable for loss or damage occurring after an unauthorised delegation (or detention)[2]. But where in the ordinary course of business the custody would naturally devolve upon, or the acts be performed by, some servant or agent of the bailee, delegation is permissible[3]. In such a case the bailee is not liable if, without any negligence on his delegate's part, any loss or damage happens to the chattel during the period of delegation[4].

1   *Bringloe v Morrice* (1676) 1 Mod Rep 210; Palmer on Bailment (3rd Edn, 2009) para 11-024. Cf *Edwards v Newland & Co (E Burchett Ltd, third party)* [1950] 2 KB 534, [1950] 1 All ER 1072, CA; and see PARA 146.
2   Palmer on Bailment (3rd Edn, 2009) para 11-024; and see PARA 125.
3   *Lord Camoys v Scurr* (1840) 9 C & P 383 at 386 per Coleridge J, where the bailee, having received a mare to try, was held entitled to put a competent person on the mare to try her. See also AGENCY vol 1 (2008) PARA 48 et seq.
4   *Lord Camoys v Scurr* (1840) 9 C & P 383.

134.   Reimbursement of bailee.   As a general rule, a bailee under a mandate is entitled to his actual disbursements and out-of-pocket expenses in connection with the service he gives, as otherwise a gratuitous act would become a burden[1]. It seems, however, that this entitlement (being the product of an implied agreement) may be displaced by an expression of contrary intention or by other particular circumstances relating to the mandate[2]. A mandatary who, in discharge of his duty of care, takes measures to protect the bailed goods from exceptional hazards may be entitled to recover the cost of their preservation[3].

1   Story on Bailments (9th Edn, 1878) s 154; Pothier's Contrat de Mandat ss 68–78. Cf PARA 137.
2   Palmer on Bailment (3rd Edn, 2009) para 11-030.
3   *China-Pacific SA v Food Corpn of India, The Winson* [1982] AC 939, [1981] 3 All ER 688, HL; *ENE Kos v Petroleo Brasileiro SA (Petrobas)* [2010] EWCA Civ 772, [2010] 2 Lloyd's Rep 409, [2010] All ER (D) 49 (Jul); and see AGENCY.

(3)   GRATUITOUS LOAN FOR USE

135.   Nature of gratuitous loan for use.   In deposit[1] and mandate[2] the bailor has (at least nominally) all the advantages of the bailment. In gratuitous loan for use[3] the reverse is the case. This is a bailment where a chattel is lent by its owner to the bailee for the express purpose of conferring a benefit upon the bailee, without any corresponding advantage to its owner[4].

By English law this agreement is confined to goods, chattels or personal property, and does not, as under the Roman civil law, extend to real estate[5]. The loan of the use of real estate or chattels real is no more than a licence beneficially to occupy a tenement or other hereditament belonging to the licensor for a particular or indeterminate period[6]. Consequently there can be no bailment of a structure affixed to real property.

1   Ie *depositum*: see PARAS 106, 111–125.
2   Ie *mandatum*: see PARAS 106, 126–134.
3   Ie *commodatum*: see PARA 106.
4   Cf *P & O Trans European Ltd v Wincanton Ltd* [2001] EWCA Civ 227, [2001] All ER (D) 174 (Feb), where on an alleged continuing bailment of pallets the transaction was held not to be one of *commodatum* or loan. Bailments expressly designated as 'loans' may in fact be beneficial to both parties: the purported loan of a work of art to a museum or gallery for display at an

exhibition, for example, may be beneficial to the bailor as well as the bailee: see *Kamidian v Holt* [2008] EWHC 1483 (Comm), [2009] Lloyd's Rep IR 242, [2008] All ER (D) 394 (Jun).
5 Story on Bailments (9th Edn, 1878) s 223.
6 *Williams v Jones* (1865) 3 H & C 602, Ex Ch.

136. Borrower's obligations. The lender must be taken to lend for the purpose of a beneficial use by the borrower. The borrower, therefore, is not responsible for reasonable wear and tear[1]. Older authority holds that, as the borrower alone receives benefit from the agreement, he is liable for the slightest degree of negligence; and he is bound to exercise the utmost degree of care in regard to the bailed chattel[2] and anything accessory to it[3]. Under modern law, however, the borrower's responsibility is likely to be regarded as one of reasonable care and diligence in all the circumstances of the case[4].

What is proper diligence, and what constitutes actionable neglect, on the part of a borrower in his custody of the chattel lent depends upon the circumstances of each particular case, the nature of the chattel lent, the location in which the loan is to be discharged and the character and occupation of the borrower[5].

As a general rule the borrower is not liable if, without any default on his part, the performance of his agreement becomes an absolute impossibility; nor is he liable for loss or injury arising from a third person's wrongful act which could not be reasonably foreseen or prevented, or from the results of external and irresistible violence[6].

The borrower's liability, however, is qualified where a special agreement is substituted for the obligation imposed by the common law, and possibly also, though this has been denied, where there has been an offer of the chattel by the lender to the borrower[7].

The borrower is liable if he detains the chattel from its owner after demand, or after the agreed time for its return has expired. In that event, he becomes liable as an insurer[8].

1 *Blakemore v Bristol and Exeter Rly Co* (1858) 8 E & B 1035 at 1051 per Coleridge J; *Pomfret v Ricroft* (1669) 1 Wms Saund 321 at 323. See also *Moorhouse v Angus & Robertson (No 2) Pty Ltd* [1981] 1 NSWLR 700 at 708 per Samuels JA, NSW CA.
2 *Coggs v Bernard* (1703) 2 Ld Raym 909 at 915 per Holt CJ. See also *Vaughan v Menlove* (1837) 3 Bing NC 468 at 475 per Tindal CJ; Jones on Bailments (4th Edn, 1833) pp 64–65. This view of the measure of the borrower's responsibility is also taken by Pothier, who says that it is not sufficient for the borrower to exert the same ordinary care which fathers of families are accustomed to use about their own affairs, but that he ought to exert all possible care, such as the most careful persons apply to their own affairs, and that he is liable, not only for a slight fault, but also for the slightest fault: Pothier's Prêt à Usage s 48.
   This superlative degree of carefulness (the *exactissima diligentia* of the Roman law) has, however, been doubted by some jurists, one of whom states that the person to whom the thing is lent is not obliged to answer for any uncontrollable force, or for the loss or damage of the thing which happens by any fortuitous case, provided the accident does not intervene through his fault or neglect, for it is necessary that he should take the same care of the thing as every prudent man would take of his own goods, since this contract is entered into for his sake: Ayliffe's New Pandect of Roman Civil Law book 4, tit 16, p 517.
3 Jones on Bailments (4th Edn, 1833) p 66.
4 *Swann v Seal* (19 March 1999, unreported), CA; but note that the question was left open as not arising for decision in *P & O Trans European Ltd v Wincanton Ltd* [2001] EWCA Civ 227, [2001] All ER (D) 174 (Feb); and see further *Walker v Watson* [1974] 2 NZLR 175; *Fairley & Stevens (1966) Ltd v Goldsworthy* (1973) 34 DLR (3d) 554 at 562, 568 per Dubinsky J (obiter); Palmer on Bailment (3rd Edn, 2009) para 12-023.
5 Wherever a hirer is responsible (see PARA 183), a fortiori a borrower is also responsible; and he may be responsible where a hirer is not, seeing that greater diligence is required of him.
6 Pothier's Prêt à Usage ss 38–55, 56. See also note 2. Consequently, if the borrower's house is destroyed by fire and, owing to his exertions in saving his own chattels, he is unable to save the chattel he has borrowed, it is extremely doubtful whether he must compensate the owner for its

destruction merely because he preferred his own property to that which had been lent to him for his benefit: Pothier's Prêt à Usage s 56. Pothier, basing himself upon the Roman law, takes the view that he must compensate the owner, and Sir William Jones accedes to this doctrine (Jones on Bailments (4th Edn, 1833) p 69), but it is very doubtful if it is law in England. Cf Story on Bailments (9th Edn, 1878) s 345 et seq. A borrower, however, is usually liable to the lender for any loss or damage, if he borrowed the chattel from its owner merely for the purpose of saving his own chattels from risk of damage or destruction. He may, however, be exempt if he can prove that he had previously disclosed to its owner that his object in borrowing it was to enable him to avoid hazarding his own property: Jones on Bailments (4th Edn, 1833) p 70.

7　Pothier's Prêt à Usage s 52. Cf PARA 120 text and notes 4–5.

8　Jones on Bailments (4th Edn, 1833) p 70. Cf *Mitchell v Ealing London Borough Council* [1979] QB 1, [1978] 2 All ER 779 (deposit); *Shaw & Co v Symmons & Sons* [1917] 1 KB 799 (bailment for reward). As to improper use see PARA 139.

137.　Borrower's expenses. If in his use of what is lent the borrower is put to any ordinary expense, such as filling a car with petrol, he must, in the absence of any agreement to the contrary, bear the expense himself, for it is he who derives advantage from the use[1].

Extraordinary expenses incurred by the borrower in the preservation of the chattel lent, whether arising from inherent defect, or viciousness peculiar to the chattel itself, or from circumstances altogether beyond his control, such as the tortious acts of third parties, may be recoverable from the lender if, in incurring those expenses, the borrower was performing his duty of care. It is doubtful, however, whether the borrower has a lien on the chattel for the amount of such charges if paid by him[2].

1　*Handford v Palmer* (1820) 2 Brod & Bing 359; 1 Domat book 1, tit 5, s 3, art 4.

2　The French jurists say that the lender must pay such expenses: Pothier's Prêt à Usage ss 81–83; 1 Domat book 1, tit 5, s 3, art 4; cf Story on Bailments (9th Edn, 1878) ss 273, 274; and PARA 134. See also *China-Pacific SA v Food Corpn of India, The Winson* [1982] AC 939, [1981] 3 All ER 688, HL; *ENE Kos v Petroleo Brasileiro SA (Petrobas)* [2010] EWCA Civ 772, [2010] 2 Lloyd's Rep 409, [2010] All ER (D) 49 (Jul).

138.　Lender's obligations. If the lender is aware of any defect in the chattel which is not apparent to a reasonable person in the borrower's position, and which renders it unfit for the purpose for which it is lent, and the lender fails to communicate the fact to the borrower, who in consequence is injured, the borrower can recover damages against the lender for the injuries so caused[1]. So also, if the chattel lent has been put on one side and not used for years, and is then lent without any intimation to the borrower of this fact and, in consequence of its being out of repair, injury is caused to the borrower, he can recover in a claim against the lender[2]. In order to fix the lender with liability, the use must be of a kind contemplated by him at the time of lending, or subsequently authorised by him[3].

It is uncertain whether the lender is liable for defects in the chattel of which he was unaware, but of which he should reasonably have been aware, when he delivered the chattel to the borrower. Older authority holds that the lender is not liable for injuries occasioned by such defects[4]. Under modern law, however, it would appear that the lender owes a duty of reasonable care to warn the borrower of any defect in the chattel of which the lender should reasonably have been aware[5].

The lender is not liable to third parties for damage caused by the negligent use of the chattel by the bailee[6].

1　*Blakemore v Bristol and Exeter Rly Co* (1858) 8 E & B 1035 at 1051 per Coleridge J; *Coughlin v Gillison* [1899] 1 QB 145 at 147, CA, per AL Smith LJ; *MacCarthy v Young* (1861) 6 H & N

329. The bailor may indeed be liable to a third party who is injured by reason of the bailee's user of the defective chattel: see *Blacker v Lake and Elliot Ltd* (1912) 106 LT 533, DC; and NEGLIGENCE. Cf *Pivovaroff v Chernabaef* (1978) 21 SASR 1 (warning given by bailor).

2   *Coughlin v Gillison* [1899] 1 QB 145 at 148, CA, per Rigby LJ.

3   *Blakemore v Bristol and Exeter Rly Co* (1858) 8 E & B 1035; *Say v Cementation Construction Ltd* (18 October 1995, unreported), CA.

4   *MacCarthy v Young* (1861) 6 H & N 329; *Coughlin v Gillison* [1899] 1 QB 145, CA. Cf *Longmeid v Holliday* (1851) 6 Exch 761 at 767–768 per Parke B. The same rule applies to gifts: *Gautret v Egerton* (1867) LR 2 CP 371 at 375 per Willes J. The operations of lending and giving are known to the law, and the rule relating to them must be strictly confined to the special relations thereby created: see *McAlister (or Donoghue) v Stevenson* [1932] AC 562 at 591, HL, per Lord Atkin (where in the phrase 'letting or giving', 'letting' is obviously a slip for 'lending'). Different considerations, therefore, apply to the case of a master providing things to be used by his servants for his business: see *Baker v James* [1921] 2 KB 674. For a somewhat exceptional extension of this principle see *Chapman (or Oliver) v Saddler & Co* [1929] AC 584, HL, distinguishing *Caledonian Rly Co v Mulholland* [1898] AC 216, HL. It is, however, artificial to regard the relationship of gratuitous bailment as obtaining in the situation of the common interchange of tools and machinery between employers and workpeople; the user there is not gratuitous because each has an interest in the mutual prosecution of the common work, and in this situation the ordinary law of negligence applies, the issues being whether the danger was reasonably foreseeable if no precautions were taken, and whether the defendant was under a duty to take reasonable precautions to guard against the risk: see *Griffiths v Arch Engineering Co (Newport) Ltd* [1968] 3 All ER 217 at 220 per Chapman J; *Say v Cementation Construction Ltd* (18 October 1995, unreported), CA. See also TORT vol 97 (2010) PARA 675; NEGLIGENCE. As to the liability of an employer whose employee suffers personal injuries because of a defect in equipment provided by the employer, where the defect is attributable wholly or partly to the fault of a third party, see the Employers' Liability (Defective Equipment) Act 1969 s 1; and EMPLOYMENT vol 39 (2009) PARA 33; HEALTH AND SAFETY AT WORK vol 52 (2009) PARA 412.

5   See *Griffiths v Arch Engineering Co (Newport) Ltd* [1968] 3 All ER 217; *Wheeler v Copas* [1981] 3 All ER 405; *Campbell v O'Donnell* [1967] IR 226, Ir SC; *Pivovaroff v Chernabaeff* (1978) 21 SASR 1 (in none of which did the question fall to be decided); Palmer on Bailment (3rd Edn, 2009) paras 12-002–12-008. See also *Flack v Hudson* [2001] QB 698, [2001] 2 WLR 982, CA.

6   *Hewitt v Bonvin* [1940] 1 KB 188, CA. The bailor will be excused from liability only if the bailee is a person of ordinary discretion. To place a chattel in the hands of a child or other person incapable of appreciating its dangerous propensities, whether by way of gift, loan or otherwise, is an act of negligence and raises different questions: see *Dixon v Bell* (1816) 5 M & S 198; *Say v Cementation Construction Ltd* (18 October 1995, unreported), CA; and NEGLIGENCE vol 78 (2010) PARA 50.

139.   Use of chattel lent. The borrower must use the chattel only for the particular purpose for which it was lent to him, and if he uses it for any materially different purpose he becomes liable as an insurer[1].

Generally speaking, the permission accorded by the owner of a chattel to a borrower to use it is purely personal, and cannot, except by the owner's express consent, be extended to a third party[2]. The reason for this limitation is that the chattel is lent by the owner to a person with whose capacity and honesty he is presumably familiar. Therefore, should the borrower license a third party to use it, the bailment is thereby determined, and the borrower becomes responsible for any later misadventure that may occasion loss, damage or destruction to the chattel[3].

When, however, the actual use by a third party is necessary for the reasonable enjoyment of the chattel lent, the mere fact of its being lent for use implies a limited power of delegation in the borrower[4]. Thus the loan of a traction engine, a threshing machine, or some other piece of machinery, must, in the majority of cases, of necessity imply both superintendence and use by some person other than the actual and responsible borrower[5].

1   Bac Abr Bailment C; Pothier's Prêt à Usage s 21. See also *Coggs v Bernard* (1703) 2 Ld Raym 909 at 915 per Holt CJ ('if a man should lend another a horse to go westward or for a month, if the bailee go northward or keep the horse above a month, if any accident happen to the horse in the northern journey, or after the expiration of the month, the bailee will be chargeable'). Cf *Wilson v Shepherd* 1913 SC 300, Ct of Sess (defender, at the request of the bailee of aerated water bottles belonging to the pursuer, put paraffin into them). Cf PARA 131. Note that the French rule is the same (Code Civil art 1881).

2   Palmer on Bailment (3rd Edn, 2009) paras 12-027–12-029; Story on Bailments (9th Edn, 1878) s 234.

3   *Bringloe v Morrice* (1676) 1 Mod Rep 210; cf *Ballett v Mingay* [1943] KB 281, [1943] 1 All ER 143, CA; and see *Gwilliam v Twist* [1895] 2 QB 84, CA.

4   Story on Bailments (9th Edn, 1878) s 234 (if A lends his horse to B to make a certain ride, B alone may ride him, but that if he lends his horses and carriage to B for a month the use of them by B's family may be fairly presumed to be contemplated by A).

5   See *Lord Camoys v Scurr* (1840) 9 C & P 383, where the defendant was held entitled to put up a groom to ride a mare lent to the defendant for trial.

(4) GRATUITOUS QUASI-BAILMENT

140. Nature of gratuitous quasi-bailment. Gratuitous quasi-bailment, or *mutuum*, is the loan of something which is not to be returned in specie, but which is to be replaced by something similar and equivalent[1]. The contract of *mutuum* differs from that of gratuitous loan for use, or *commodatum*[2], in that in the latter a bare possession of the chattel lent, as distinguished from the property in it, vests in the borrower, the general property in it still remaining in the lender; whereas in *mutuum* that property in the chattel passes from the lender to the borrower.

Mutuum is confined to chattels which are intended to be consumed and which are capable of being estimated by number, weight, or measure, such as money, corn, or wine[3]. A familiar example is the borrowing of a packet of sugar from a neighbour.

The essence of the transaction in the case of such loans is not that the borrower should return to the lender the identical chattels lent, for such specific return would ordinarily render the loan valueless, but that upon demand or at a fixed date the lender should receive from the borrower an equivalent quantity of goods of similar quality. Thus if money is advanced, its value in money must be returned, and if corn, wine or sugar is lent, then similar corn, wine or sugar of an equivalent amount must be returned; and enhancement in the commercial value of the commodity lent will not justify the borrower in tendering a less quantity than he actually received[4].

It is not, however, a transaction of *mutuum* if a bargain is made by which an equivalent value of wine is to be returned for oil, or meat for corn. Such an exchange constitutes a contract of barter, and therefore comes within a different category of transaction altogether[5].

1   Just Inst lib 3, tit 14; *Parastatidis v Kotaridis* [1978] VR 449 at 456 per Harris J, where the text was approved. Cf *Coleman v Harvey* [1989] 1 NZLR 723 at 725, NZ CA, per Cooke P. See also *P & O Trans European Ltd v Wincanton Ltd* [2001] EWCA Civ 227, [2001] All ER (D) 174 (Feb) (circulation of pallets for mutual benefit in connection with transportation of goods; transaction held not one of mutuum).

2   See PARA 135.

3   1 Domat book 1, tit 6, s 1; Story on Bailments (9th Edn, 1878) ss 283, 284.

4   1 Domat book 1, tit 6, s 1, art 9.

5   1 Domat book 1, tit 6, s 1, art 10; Jones on Bailments (4th Edn, 1833) pp 64, 102. As to barter see SALE OF GOODS AND SUPPLY OF SERVICES vol 41 (2005 Reissue) PARA 1.

141.   Duty to return chattel.   As a necessary consequence of the absolute transfer of the property in, as well as the custody of, the chattel lent, the borrower is not, by reason of its accidental loss or destruction, released from his obligation to return to the owner its equivalent in kind upon demand, for it is the borrower's property, and the rule is that the risk passes with the property in the chattel[1].

An actual demand is, however, a condition precedent to a claim for the non-delivery of the equivalent; just as where a man deposits money in the hands of another, to be kept for his use, the possession of the bailee is deemed the possession of the owner until an application and refusal, or other denial of the right. For the purposes of the Limitation Act 1980, time runs against the bailor from the date of such demand only[2].

1   Ie *ejus est periculum, cujus est dominium:* Story on Bailments (9th Edn, 1878) s 283; St Germain's Doctor and Student (ed Murchall) (1815) 2nd dial chap xxxviii.
2   *Re Tidd, Tidd v Overell* [1893] 3 Ch 154 at 156 per North J, approving 2 Pothier's Law of Obligations (ed Evans) 126; and see *South Australian Insurance Co v Randell* (1869) LR 3 PC 101; cf *Schwarzschild v Harrods Ltd* [2008] EWHC 521 (QB), [2008] All ER (D) 299 (Mar); and LIMITATION PERIODS. See also PARA 235.

142.   Pro-mutuum.   Whenever a person, acting under misapprehension as to an existing fact or state of facts, delivers to another a chattel which cannot be restored in specie, there arises the quasi-contract of *pro-mutuum*, which imposes upon the recipient the obligation to restore its equivalent. *Pro-mutuum* differs from *mutuum*[1] in that this obligation is imposed by law, whereas in *mutuum* it arises out of the voluntary agreement between the lender and the borrower; it resembles *mutuum* in that the subject matter to which it relates must always consist of money or fungibles, that is, chattels which, owing to their being consumed in the using, cannot be restored in specie.

The liability arises only out of an actual delivery of such chattels by one person to another, and the repayment of the obligation in chattels answering to the generic description of those advanced will always satisfy it. Thus if one man owes another 20 bushels of wheat, and by a mistake as to the amount of his indebtedness, pays to his creditor 30 bushels in satisfaction of the supposed liability, the recipient is a bailee to his former debtor of the bushels overpaid, and, as such, is bound to account to him for the surplus[2]. A similar liability arises if a man discharges a debt twice over, or pays the debt of another under a mistaken assumption of fact as to his liability[3]; the general rule in such cases is that where money is paid to another under a mistake of fact, a claim will lie to recover it[4]. As, however, the original cause of the obligation is the payer's mistake, the recipient is, as a rule, bound only to repay to him the actual amount overpaid, without interest[5]. A demand is a condition precedent to a claim[6].

1   See PARA 140; and see further RESTITUTION.
2   Though it will be for the deliveree to determine which 10 bushels shall be rendered back to the deliveror.
3   Pothier's Contrat de Prêt de Consommation ss 132–134. See also *Cox v Prentice* (1815) 3 M & S 344; *Newall v Tomlinson* (1871) LR 6 CP 405; *Milnes v Duncan* (1827) 6 B & C 671.
4   *Kelly v Solari* (1841) 9 M & W 54 at 58 per Parke B. See MISTAKE; RESTITUTION. Mistaken over-payment will generally nowadays fall to be redressed under the law of unjust enrichment.
5   Pothier's Contrat de Prêt de Consommation s 138.
6   *Kelly v Solari* (1841) 9 M & W 54; and see RESTITUTION. See PARA 232.

143.   Intermixture of chattels.   Where the chattels of two persons are intermixed by agreement[1], so that the several portions can no longer be distinguished, the proprietors have (subject of course to any agreement to the contrary) an interest in common in proportion to the respective shares[2].

If a bailee, without his bailor's consent, intermixes his own chattels with those belonging to his bailor, and the intermixed goods are of substantially the same nature and quality and cannot in practice be separated, the mixture will be generally held in common in such proportion as each party contributed to the combination[3]. This general rule applies where the intermixture results from an act of God or the act of an unauthorised third party[4] as well as from the inadvertence or wilful conduct of a bailee[5]. However, any cost attendant upon the separation into shares must be borne by the bailee[6]. Moreover, a proprietor who, by wilfully intermixing his chattels with those of another, has destroyed the evidence by which the innocent proprietor could show how much he has lost must suffer from the resulting uncertainty[7]. In such a case, there is a presumption of utmost value in favour of the innocent proprietor[8], and he will be awarded the largest proportion of the whole that is consistent with the evidence[9]. If there is a complete absence of evidence as to the quantity of the innocent proprietor's goods which has been contributed to the mixture, the whole belongs to him[10].

If there is a diversity in quality in the intermixed substances the whole should be divided and a greater allowance made to the owner whose substance is better or finer than that of the other[11].

1　See Just Inst lib 2, tit 1, s 28; and as to mixtures generally see Palmer on Bailment (3rd Edn, 2009) Chapter 8.

2　2 Bl Com 405; *Sandeman & Sons v Tyzack and Branfoot Steamship Co Ltd* [1913] AC 680 at 694–695, HL, per Lord Moulton; *Coleman v Harvey* [1989] 1 NZLR 723, NZ CA (where the text was approved). As to following trust money see EQUITY vol 16(2) (Reissue) PARA 861 et seq.

3　*Indian Oil Corpn Ltd v Greenstone Shipping SA (Panama), The Ypatianna* [1988] QB 345, [1987] 3 All ER 893; *Mercer v Craven Grain Storage Ltd* [1994] CLC 328, HL; *P & O Trans European Ltd v Wincanton Ltd* [2001] EWCA Civ 227, [2001] All ER (D) 174 (Feb); *Glencore International AG v Metro Trading International Inc* [2002] EWCA Civ 138; and cf *Re Stapylton Fletcher Ltd* [1995] 1 All ER 192, [1994] 1 WLR 1181, [1994] BCC 532, Ch (Companies Court); *Re Goldcorp Exchange Ltd (in receivership)* [1995] 1 AC 74, [1994] 2 All ER 806, PC. As to sale of goods from bulk see the Sale of Goods (Amendment) Act 1995; and SALE OF GOODS AND SUPPLY OF SERVICES vol 41 (2005 Reissue) PARA 134 et seq.

4　See *Spence v Union Marine Insurance Co Ltd* (1868) LR 3 CP 427, where the doctrine was applied to goods belonging to different owners on board ship, which had become indistinguishable owing to the obliteration of identification marks; *Gill and Duffus (Liverpool) Ltd v Scruttons Ltd* [1953] 2 All ER 977, [1953] 1 WLR 1407, where bags of chestnuts in the hold of a ship, which were consigned to different merchants, burst on the voyage. As to the limits of the applicability of this doctrine to such cases, see *Sandeman & Sons v Tyzack and Branfoot Steamship Co Ltd* [1913] AC 680, HL. The dictum of Lord Russell of Killowen in *Smurthwaite v Hannay* [1894] AC 494 at 505, HL, must be read in the light of the latter case. See further SHIPPING AND MARITIME LAW. See also Mackeldey's Modern Civil Law (special part), Book 1, s 270.

5　*Indian Oil Corpn Ltd v Greenstone Shipping SA (Panama), The Ypatianna* [1988] QB 345, [1987] 3 All ER 893; and see *Coleman v Harvey* [1989] 1 NZLR 723, NZ CA, especially at 726–727 per Cooke P. Formerly, it was thought that a bailee who wilfully intermixed his goods with those of another proprietor could not claim ownership of any part of the combined corpus, which belonged in its entirety to the innocent proprietor: see *Lupton v White* (1808) 15 Ves 432 at 440 per Lord Eldon; 2 Bl Com 405; *Colwill v Reeves* (1811) 2 Camp 575 at 576 per Lord Ellenborough (if a man puts corn into my bag, in which there is before some corn, the whole is mine, because it is impossible to distinguish what was mine from what was his; but it is impossible that articles of furniture can be blended together so as to create the same difficulty). But see *Sandeman & Sons v Tyzack and Branfoot Steamship Co Ltd* [1913] AC 680 at 695, HL, per Lord Moulton.

6　*Buckley v Gross* (1863) 3 B & S 566 at 575 per Blackburn J; *Jones v Moore* (1841) 4 Y & C Ex 351.

7 *Indian Oil Corpn Ltd v Greenstone Shipping SA (Panama), The Ypatianna* [1988] QB 345, [1987] 3 All ER 893, applying *Armory v Delamirie* (1722) 1 Stra 505. See also *Colbeck v Diamanta (UK) Ltd* [2002] EWHC 616 (QB), [2002] All ER (D) 336 (Feb); Palmer on Bailment (3rd Edn, 2009) paras 37-011–37-012.

8 Provided that there is sufficient evidence to determine the general parameters of that value: see *Zabihi v Janzemini* [2009] EWCA Civ 851, [2009] All ER (D) 357 (Jul).

9 *Indian Oil Corpn Ltd v Greenstone Shipping SA (Panama), The Ypatianna* [1988] QB 345, [1987] 3 All ER 893; *Armory v Delamirie* (1722) 1 Stra 505; *Colbeck v Diamanta (UK) Ltd* [2002] EWHC 616 (QB), [2002] All ER (D) 336 (Feb).

10 *Indian Oil Corpn Ltd v Greenstone Shipping SA (Panama), The Ypatianna* [1988] QB 345 at 370–371, [1987] 3 All ER 893 at 907–908 per Staughton J. Cf *Zabihi v Janzemini* [2009] EWCA Civ 851, [2009] All ER (D) 357 (Jul); Palmer on Bailment (3rd Edn, 2009) paras 37-012–37-019.

11 Ayliffe's New Pandect of Roman Civil Law Book 3, tit 3, p 292.

3. BAILMENT FOR VALUABLE CONSIDERATION

(1) INTRODUCTION

144. The four types of bailment for valuable consideration. There are four types of bailment for valuable consideration: (1) hire of custody, in which possession of a chattel is transferred temporarily with the object of transferring custody[1]; (2) hire of chattels, in which the hirer obtains the right to use the chattel hired in return for the payment to the owner of the price of the hiring[2]; (3) hire of work and labour, in which one of the two contracting parties undertakes to do something to a chattel, for example, to carry it or repair it, in consideration of a reward to be given to him[3]; and (4) pledge, in which a chattel is delivered to a bailee to be held by him as security for a debt or other engagement[4].

1 See PARAS 145–155.
2 See PARAS 175–187.
3 See PARAS 156–173.
4 See PARAS 188–228.

(2) HIRE OF CUSTODY

(i) Nature of the Contract

145. Hire of custody distinguished from deposit. The hire of custody[1] is a form of bailment comparable in some respects to that of deposit[2]. The two forms of bailment, however, differ materially in that whilst in deposit there is no reciprocity of advantage, all the benefit being conferred on the bailor, in the contract of hire of custody there is a mutual advantage to both the owner of the chattel and the person who undertakes to keep it safely for reward[3].

The contract of custody for reward, which is consensual[4] and need not be evidenced by writing, requires for its inception the concurrence of the following conditions: (1) the subject matter must be a chattel; (2) the possession of the chattel must be capable of transfer from one party to the other and must actually be transferred[5]; (3) the custody of the chattel must be the object of the transfer of possession; and (4) the transfer of the custody must be temporary and not permanent[6].

Given these conditions, the custodian's obligation for hire commences as soon as by any overt act he evidences an intention of exercising responsibility over the chattel entrusted to him, for instance, by applying a crane to raise goods into a warehouse[7].

1 Ie *locatio custodiae*: see PARA 106 note 9.
2 Ie *depositum*: see PARAS 106, 111–125. The liability of an innkeeper (ie the proprietor of a hotel within the meaning of the Hotel Proprietors Act 1956) differs from that of an ordinary bailee and is governed by s 2: see LICENSING AND GAMBLING vol 67 (2008) PARA 198 et seq.
3 Story on Bailments (9th Edn, 1878) s 442. The reward need not be money; it may be money's worth, and there need not be a specific reward for the custody if there is a reward for services which in fact cover the custody: see *Martin v LCC* [1947] KB 628, [1947] 1 All ER 783 (hospital taking charge of patient's property); *Andrews v Home Flats Ltd* [1945] 2 All ER 698, CA (landlords of block of flats providing a room for baggage). See also *G Bosman (Transport) Ltd v LKW Walter International Transportorganisation AG* [2002] EWCA Civ 850, [2002] All ER (D) 13 (May).
4 *Buxton v Baughan* (1834) 6 C & P 674; *G Bosman (Transport) Ltd v LKW Walter International Transportorganisation AG* [2002] EWCA Civ 850, [2002] All ER (D) 13 (May).

5   *Ashby v Tolhurst* [1937] 2 KB 242, [1937] 2 All ER 837, CA (car placed in car park on payment
     of a fee for which a receipt, called a 'car park ticket', was given; it was held that there was no
     contract of bailment, but mere licence); *Tinsley v Dudley* [1951] 2 KB 18, [1951] 1 All ER
     252, CA (customer's motorcycle stolen from yard of public house, which was not an inn; the
     licensee was held not liable as the motorcycle had not been delivered into his possession and he
     was unaware that it had been brought onto his premises; there was therefore no bailment). See
     also the other cases cited in PARA 101 note 9.
6   Pothier's Contrat de Louage s 6 (mutatis mutandis).
7   *Thomas v Day* (1803) 4 Esp 262. See also *Chapman v Great Western Rly Co* (1880) 5 QBD
     278; *Cailiff v Danvers* (1792) Peake 114; *Mitchell v Lancashire and Yorkshire Rly Co* (1875)
     LR 10 QB 256. See also *Re Webb* (1818) 8 Taunt 443; *Bourne v Gatliffe* (1841) 3 Man & G
     643; *Cairns v Robins* (1841) 8 M & W 258; *Heugh v London and North Western Rly Co*
     (1870) LR 5 Exch 51; *Great Western Rly Co v Crouch* (1858) 3 H & N 183, Ex Ch; and
     CARRIAGE AND CARRIERS vol 7 (2008) PARAS 22–23.

(ii) Bailee's Obligations

146.   Care and diligence.   A custodian for reward[1] must exercise reasonable
care for the safety of the article entrusted to him[2]. The standard of care and
diligence imposed on the custodian is that demanded by the circumstances of the
particular case[3]. The precautions required of him may therefore be more exacting
than those required of a gratuitous depositary[4].

On demand he must return the chattel to the bailor or deliver it in accordance
with his instructions[5]; if he fails to do so, or if he misdelivers, the owner may
recover damages from him. Where the owner has the immediate right to
possession of the chattel, and either the bailee or a third party wrongdoer has
committed an act of conversion or unauthorised damage to the chattel, the
owner may bring a claim direct against the wrongdoer[6].

The custodian is therefore bound to take reasonable care to see that the place
in which the chattel is kept[7], and the tackle used in connection with it[8], are fit
and proper for the purpose, to see that the chattel is in proper custody[9], to
protect it against unexpected danger should that arise[10], to recover, or enable the
owner to recover, it if it is stolen[11], and to safeguard the bailor's interest against
adverse claims[12]. If the chattel is injured through his negligence, the bailee will
not be excused on the ground that it has been subsequently destroyed by
inevitable mischance[13].

In the absence of any special contract binding the bailee to some higher
responsibility, or of any deviation on his part from the principal terms of the
bailment, the bailee is not an insurer[14] and therefore, in the absence of negligence
on his part, he is not liable for the loss of or damage to the chattel due to some
accident[15], fire[16], the acts of third parties, or the unauthorised acts of his servants
acting outside the scope of their employment[17]. But if he entrusts the duty to take
care of the chattel to a servant or agent, he is answerable for the manner in
which that servant or agent carries out his duty[18].

The custodian must deal with the chattel in the manner authorised by the
bailor[19]; he may not without authority hand it over to a third party for storage[20].
If he deals with it in a manner not authorised, he takes upon himself the risk of
so doing, and may be precluded from relying upon stipulations inserted in the
contract in his favour[21]. He will also be liable for any ensuing loss or damage,
except such as arises from causes which he shows to be independent of his acts
or inherent in the chattel itself[22].

The obligation to take due care exists independently of contract. A claim
based on breach of the obligation can be founded on bailment or on tort[23].

1   Among such custodians are included auctioneers, agisters of cattle, warehousemen, forwarding merchants and wharfingers: Story on Bailments (9th Edn, 1878) s 442. See also *Scarborough v Cosgrove* [1905] 2 KB 805, CA; *Paterson v Norris* (1914) 30 TLR 393 (boarding-house keepers); *Olley v Marlborough Court Ltd* [1949] 1 KB 532, [1949] 1 All ER 127, CA (proprietor of hotel which is not an inn); *Martin v LCC* [1947] KB 628, [1947] 1 All ER 783 (hospital managers). As to dock and harbour authorities see SHIPPING AND MARITIME LAW.

2   *Port Swettenham Authority v TW Wu & Co (M) Sdn Bhd* [1979] AC 580, [1978] 3 All ER 337, PC; *Coldman v Hill* [1919] 1 KB 443, CA; *British Road Services Ltd v Arthur V Crutchley & Co Ltd (Factory Guards Ltd, third party)* [1968] 1 All ER 811, [1968] 1 Lloyd's Rep 271, CA; *Lockspeiser Aircraft Ltd v Brooklands Aircraft Co Ltd* (1990) Times, 7 March; *G Bosman (Transport) Ltd v LKW Walter International Transportorganisation AG* [2002] EWCA Civ 850, [2002] All ER (D) 13 (May).

3   *Houghland v RR Low (Luxury Coaches) Ltd* [1962] 1 QB 694 at 698, [1962] 2 All ER 159 at 161, CA. See also PARA 107. The bailor's knowledge of the conditions in which the bailee proposes to keep the goods (or in which he keeps goods of a similar nature) does not ordinarily affect the bailee's obligation to keep the goods with reasonable care and skill: *Brabant & Co v King* [1895] AC 632, PC; *Edwards v Newland & Co (E Burchett Ltd, third party)* [1950] 2 KB 534, [1950] 1 All ER 1072, CA; *Thames Tideway Properties Ltd v Serfaty & Partners* [1999] 2 Lloyd's Rep 110, Central London County Court, at paras 34–35 per Brian Knight QC. The position can differ, however, where the bailee can show that, by reason of such knowledge or other matters, the bailor consented to a lower standard of safekeeping than would otherwise have been imposed in the circumstances: see, e g *Idnani v Elisha* [1979] RTR 488, CA; *Saunders (Mayfair) Furs Ltd v Chas Wm Davies Ltd* [1966] 1 Lloyd's Rep 78; cf *Thames Tideway Properties Ltd v Serfaty & Partners* [1999] 2 Lloyd's Rep 110, Central London County Court, at paras 34–35 per Brian Knight QC. Also see generally Palmer on Bailment (3rd Edn, 2009) paras 14-010–14-051.

4   *Port Swettenham Authority v TW Wu & Co (M) Sdn Bhd* [1979] AC 580 at 589, [1978] 3 All ER 337 at 339, PC; *Garlick v W & H Rycroft Ltd* [1982] CA Transcript 277. See PARA 121; and see *Samuel v Westminster Wine Co Ltd* (1959) Times, 16 May. See also *Coggs v Bernard* (1703) 2 Ld Raym 909 at 914, 916 per Holt CJ; *Morris v CW Martin & Sons Ltd* [1966] 1 QB 716 at 725–726, [1965] 2 All ER 725 at 731, CA, per Lord Denning MR; *James Buchanan & Co Ltd v Hay's Transport Services Ltd and Duncan Barbour & Son Ltd* [1972] 2 Lloyd's Rep 535. See Jones on Bailments (4th Edn, 1833) pp 86–87; *Dean v Keate* (1811) 3 Camp 4; and see the note to that case at 3 Camp 5. See also *Frans Maas (UK) Ltd v Samsung Electronics (UK) Ltd* [2004] EWHC 1502 (Comm), [2005] 2 All ER (Comm) 783, [2004] 2 Lloyd's Rep 251.

5   *Hooper v London and North Western Rly Co* (1880) 50 LJQB 103 at 105, DC; *Alexander v Railway Executive* [1951] 2 KB 882 at 884–885, [1951] 2 All ER 442 at 444. A delivery order is a mere authority to a buyer to receive possession of goods; by itself it spells no promise of delivery: *Alicia Hosiery Ltd v Brown Shipley & Co Ltd* [1970] 1 QB 195 at 198, [1969] 2 All ER 504 at 510. As to the meaning of 'delivery' see SALE OF GOODS AND SUPPLY OF SERVICES vol 41 (2005 Reissue) PARA 163.

6   *Manders v Williams* (1849) 4 Exch 339 at 314; *Kahler v Midland Bank Ltd* [1950] AC 24, [1949] 2 All ER 621, HL. See further PARA 236. As to conversion generally see TORT vol 45(2) (Reissue) PARA 548 et seq and as to conversion by bailees see TORT vol 45(2) (Reissue) PARA 605.

7   *Searle v Laverick* (1874) LR 9 QB 122; *Brabant & Co v King* [1895] AC 632, PC; *Turner v Stallibrass* [1898] 1 QB 56, CA; *Martin v LCC* [1947] KB 628, [1947] 1 All ER 783; *British Road Services Ltd v Arthur V Crutchley & Co Ltd (Factory Guards Ltd, third party)* [1968] 1 All ER 811, [1968] 1 Lloyd's Rep 271, CA. Cf *Marfell v South Wales Rly Co* (1860) 8 CBNS 525 at 537 per Byles J. See *Saunders (Mayfair) Furs Ltd v Chas Wm Davies Ltd* [1966] 1 Lloyd's Rep 78.

8   *Thomas v Day* (1803) 4 Esp 262.

9   *Quiggin v Duff* (1836) 1 M & W 174 at 180 per Lord Abinger CB. Cf *Re United Service Co, Johnston's Claim* (1871) 6 Ch App 212. It is not sufficient for the bailee merely to institute a safe security system if he fails on a given occasion to operate that system with reasonable diligence and care: *Spriggs v Sotheby Parke Bernet & Co Ltd* [1986] 1 Lloyd's Rep 487, CA; *Port Swettenham Authority v TW Wu & Co (M) Sdn Bhd* [1979] AC 580, [1978] 3 All ER 337, PC; *Global Dress Co Ltd v WH Boase & Co Ltd* [1966] 2 Lloyd's Rep 72, CA; Palmer on Bailment (3rd Edn, 2009) Chapter 14.

10   *Brabant & Co v King* [1895] AC 632, PC, at 640. See also *Liverpool Grain Storage and Transit Co Ltd v Charlton and Bagshaw* (1918) 146 LT Jo 20, HL. However, if the bailee provides a reasonably fit place for storing the chattels he is not responsible if that place proves

defective under exceptional and unlooked-for stress: *Searle v Laverick* (1874) LR 9 QB 122; *Broadwater v Blot* (1817) Holt NP 547; *Edwards v Newland & Co (E Burchett Ltd, third party)* [1950] 2 KB 534 at 540, [1950] 1 All ER 1072 at 1080, CA, per Somervell LJ (premises damaged by enemy action).

11 The duty to seek to recover the stolen chattel exists even though the theft occurred without default on the part of the bailee: *Coldman v Hill* [1919] 1 KB 443, CA.

12 *Ranson v Platt* [1911] 2 KB 291, CA. See PARA 229.

13 *Story on Bailments* (9th Edn, 1878) s 450(a).

14 *Coggs v Bernard* (1703) 2 Ld Raym 909 at 918 per Holt CJ ('He is only to do the best he can. And if he be robbed it is a good account. If he receives money and keeps it locked up with reasonable care he shall not be answerable for it though it be stolen'). See also *Liver Alkali Co v Johnson* (1874) LR 9 Exch 338, Ex Ch; *Consolidated Tea and Lands Co v Oliver's Wharf* [1910] 2 KB 395.

15 *Searle v Laverick* (1874) LR 9 QB 122 (building collapsing).

16 *Garside v Trent and Mersey Navigation Proprietors* (1792) 4 Term Rep 581; *Chapman v Great Western Rly Co* (1880) 5 QBD 278; *Turner v Civil Service Supply Association* [1926] 1 KB 50; *Fagan v Green and Edwards Ltd* [1926] 1 KB 102; *Watkins v Cottell* [1916] 1 KB 10; *F & C Clarke Ltd and Pickwick Foods Ltd v Redburn Wharves Ltd* [1974] 1 Lloyd's Rep 52.

17 *Finucane v Small* (1795) 1 Esp 315 (theft); *Mintz v Silverton* (1920) 36 TLR 399 (theft by servant, there being no negligence in selecting the servant); contrast *Williams v Curzon Syndicate Ltd* (1919) 35 TLR 475, CA; and *Nahhas v Pier House (Cheyne Walk) Management Ltd* (1984) 270 Estates Gazette 328; *Sanderson v Collins* [1904] 1 KB 628, CA (servant took out carriage for his own purpose, without his master's knowledge); *Central Motors (Glasgow) Ltd v Cessnock Garage and Motor Co* 1925 SC 796, Ct of Sess (night watchman of garage took out car for his own purpose, the master having delegated to him the duty of keeping the car safely); *Aitchison v Page Motors Ltd* (1935) 154 LT 128 (manager of garage, with authority to do so, collected customer's car from manufacturer's works, and used it for his own purposes).

18 *Port Swettenham Authority v TW Wu & Co (M) Sdn Bhd* [1979] AC 580, [1978] 3 All ER 337, PC; *Morris v CW Martin & Sons Ltd* [1966] 1 QB 716 at 728, 736, 741, [1965] 2 All ER 725 at 732, 737, 740, CA (sub-bailee liable for his servant's theft); *East West Corpn v DKBS AF 1912 A/S, Utaniko Ltd v P & O Nedlloyd BV* [2003] EWCA Civ 83, [2003] QB 1509, [2003] 2 All ER 700 (loss of goods through acts of port agents); *Frans Maas (UK) Ltd v Samsung Electronics (UK) Ltd* [2004] EWHC 1502 (Comm), [2005] 2 All ER (Comm) 783, [2004] 2 Lloyd's Rep 251 (employees to whom security of bailee's premises are entrusted may qualify as employees to whom the bailor has entrusted part of his duty of care relating to goods held at those premises); *Brink's Global Services Inc v Igrox Ltd* [2009] EWHC 1871 (Comm), [2009] All ER (D) 261 (Jul) (affd [2010] EWCA Civ 1207, [2010] All ER (D) 260 (Oct)). See also *Adams (Durham) Ltd and Day v Trust Houses Ltd* [1960] 1 Lloyd's Rep 380 at 386 (unauthorised driving of car by servant); *British Road Services Ltd v Arthur V Crutchley & Co Ltd (Factory Guards Ltd, third party)* [1968] 1 All ER 811 at 820, 824, CA (negligence of independent contractor). This responsibility appears to be part of the general law: *Lister v Hesley Hall Ltd* [2001] UKHL 22, [2002] 1 AC 215, [2001] 2 All ER 769; *Brink's Global Services Inc v Igrox Ltd* [2010] EWCA Civ 1207, [2010] All ER (D) 260 (Oct); Palmer on Bailment (3rd Edn, 2009) para 14-007 et seq.

19 *Streeter v Horlock* (1822) 1 Bing 34 at 36; *Lilley v Doubleday* (1881) 7 QBD 510 at 511 per Grove J.

20 *Edwards v Newland & Co (E Burchett Ltd, third party)* [1950] 2 KB 534, [1950] 1 All ER 1072, CA. See also *East West Corpn v DKBS AF 1912 A/S, Utaniko Ltd v P & O Nedlloyd BV* [2003] EWCA Civ 83, [2003] QB 1509, [2003] 2 All ER 700.

21 *Gibaud v Great Eastern Rly Co* [1921] 2 KB 426 at 431, CA, per Lord Sterndale MR, and at 435 per Scrutton LJ; *London and North Western Rly Co v Neilson* [1922] 2 AC 263 at 273–274, HL, per Lord Atkinson; *Buerger v Cunard Steamship Co* [1925] 2 KB 646 at 663, CA, per Atkin LJ (affd sub nom *Cunard Steamship Co v Buerger* [1927] AC 1, HL); *Alexander v Railway Executive* [1951] 2 KB 882, [1951] 2 All ER 442 (allowing an unauthorised person to have access to goods deposited in a railway parcels office); *Garnham, Harris and Elton Ltd v Alfred W Ellis (Transport) Ltd* [1967] 2 All ER 940, [1967] 1 WLR 940 (unauthorised sub-bailment). See Palmer on Bailment (3rd Edn, 2009) paras 14-060–14-061, 14-104; and see generally as to exclusion clauses and similar exculpatory terms CONTRACT.

22 *Davis v Garrett* (1830) 6 Bing 716 at 724 per Tindal CJ; *James Morrison & Co Ltd v Shaw, Savill and Albion Co Ltd* [1916] 2 KB 783 at 795–796, CA, per Swinfen Eady LJ, and at 800 per Phillimore LJ; *Lilley v Doubleday* (1881) 7 QBD 510 (where the defendant contracted to warehouse certain goods for the plaintiff at a particular place but, contrary to the terms of his

agreement, he warehoused part of them at another place where, without any negligence on his part, they were destroyed); *Edwards v Newland & Co (E Burchett Ltd, third party)* [1950] 2 KB 534, [1950] 1 All ER 1072, CA (where the defendants, who had undertaken to store furniture, sub-contracted for the storage with a third party without the bailor's knowledge). Cf *Shaw & Co v Symmons & Sons* [1917] 1 KB 799 (goods destroyed by fire when detained in breach of contract); and see PARAS 125, 130, 139.

23 *Jackson v Mayfair Window Cleaning Co Ltd* [1952] 1 All ER 215 at 218. See also *Chesworth v Farrar* [1967] 1 QB 407, [1966] 2 All ER 107. See further the Torts (Interference with Goods) Act 1977 s 2(2); and TORT vol 45(2) (Reissue) PARA 543 et seq. See also PARA 235; and CIVIL PROCEDURE.

147. Limitation of bailee's liability. The bailee may limit or relieve himself from his common law liability[1] by special conditions in the contract[2]; but in cases of ambiguity these will be strictly construed[3]. They will be held not to exempt him from responsibility for losses due to his negligence unless the words used are clear and adequate for the purpose[4].

The burden is on the bailee to prove[5] that the loss or damage to the chattel occurred without any neglect, default or misconduct on his part or on the part of any servant to whom he may have entrusted any part of his duty of care[6], or that it occurred by negligence of a kind from liability for which he is exempted[7]. The more destructive or restrictive of rights an exempting condition is, the clearer must be the indication, by some sufficiently prominent or explicit notice, that the bailor is to be bound by it[8].

The construction of exemption clauses in cases of misdelivery may give rise to special difficulty[9]. Very carefully chosen words are required to protect a bailee from liability for misdelivery[10]. Unauthorised delivery ordinarily goes to the root of the relationship of bailor and bailee and may not be excused under the terms of a general exemption clause[11]. The question depends ultimately, however, upon the language of the clause. If it is clear and specific enough to apply to the particular breach (however severe) the bailee will be protected. There is no rule of law which prevents an exclusion or limitation clause from being given effect, irrespective of its language, simply by virtue of the severity of the breach or its consequences[12].

Where conditions are relied on the custodian must show that the bailor knew or should reasonably have known of them and can thus be taken to have assented to them; the mere fact that they are the custodian's usual terms will not be sufficient[13]. Moreover, a bailee may deprive himself of the right to rely on a contractual exemption by going outside the purview of the contract[14] or by innocent misrepresentation[15].

1   The exclusion and restriction of liability for negligence and breach of contract is now subject to the provisions of the Unfair Contract Terms Act 1977 (see CONTRACT vol 9(1) (Reissue) PARA 790 et seq); and to the Unfair Terms in Consumer Contracts Regulations 1999, SI 1999/2083, and other EU regulations (see CONSUMER PROTECTION vol 21 (2011) PARAS 433–444).

2   *Van Toll v South Eastern Rly Co* (1862) 12 CBNS 75 at 84 per Erle CJ; *Harris v Great Western Rly Co* (1876) 1 QBD 515 (approved in *Gibaud v Great Eastern Rly Co* [1921] 2 KB 426, CA); *Joseph Travers & Sons Ltd v Cooper* [1915] 1 KB 73, CA; *Barton v Ruislip Dog Sanatorium Ltd* (1917) 33 TLR 458; *Reynolds v Boston Deep Sea Fishing and Ice Co Ltd* (1922) 38 TLR 429, CA; *Rutter v Palmer* [1922] 2 KB 87, CA; *Orchard v Connaught Club Ltd* (1930) 46 TLR 214; *HMF Humphrey Ltd v Baxter, Hoare & Co Ltd* (1933) 149 LT 603 (buyer of goods stored in warehouse bound by conditions of contract made between warehouseman and seller); *British Traders and Shippers Ltd v Ubique Transport and Motor Engineering Co (London) Ltd and Port of London Authority* [1952] 2 Lloyd's Rep 236 (where the bailees were held not to be relieved from liability); *Hollier v Rambler Motors (AMC) Ltd* [1972] 2 QB 71, [1972] 1 All ER 399, CA; *Spriggs v Sotheby Parke Bernet & Co Ltd* [1986] 1 Lloyd's Rep 487, CA. Cf *Calico Printers' Association Ltd v Barclays Bank* (1931) 145 LT 51, CA. See also note 11; and see *L Harris (Harella) Ltd v Continental Express Ltd and Burn Transit Ltd* [1961]

1 Lloyd's Rep 251. As to whether a sub-bailee can rely on an exempting condition made between the bailor and the bailee see *Morris v CW Martin & Sons Ltd* [1966] 1 QB 716 at 729, 731, 741, [1965] 2 All ER 725 at 733, 734, 740, CA; *Singer Co (UK) Ltd v Tees and Hartlepool Port Authority* [1988] 2 Lloyd's Rep 164; *KH Enterprise v Pioneer Container, The Pioneer Container* [1994] 2 AC 324, [1994] 2 All ER 250, [1994] 1 Lloyd's Rep 593, PC; and PARA 110. As to the incorporation and construction of conditions see *Richardson, Spence & Co and Lord Gough Steamship Co v Rowntree* [1894] AC 217, HL; *Parker v South Eastern Rly Co, Gabell v South Eastern Rly Co* (1877) 2 CPD 416; *Lyons & Co v Houghton* [1915] 1 KB 489 at 502, DC, per Atkin J; *Jarl Trä AB v Convoys Ltd* [2003] EWHC 1488 (Comm), [2003] 2 Lloyd's Rep 459, [2008] All ER (D) 328 (Jun).

3 This is on the general principle that a person wishing to exempt himself from his legal liabilities must do so in express and unambiguous terms: see *Price & Co v Union Lighterage Co* [1903] 1 KB 750 (affd [1904] 1 KB 412, CA); *Rutter v Palmer* [1922] 2 KB 87 at 94, CA; *Producer Meats (North Island) Ltd v Thomas Borthwick & Sons (Australia) Ltd* [1964] 1 NZLR 700, [1965] 1 Lloyd's Rep 130, NZ CA, where the words used were held to be inadequate to exempt the respondents from negligence. The courts should not manufacture ambiguity, and should endeavour to give effect to commercial contracts in accordance with their ordinary, common-sense meaning: *Photo Production Ltd v Securicor Transport Ltd* [1980] AC 827 at 851, [1980] 1 All ER 556 at 568, HL, per Lord Diplock.

4 *Canada Steamship Lines Ltd v R* [1952] AC 192 at 207–208, [1952] 1 All ER 305 at 309, PC; *Olley v Marlborough Court Ltd* [1949] 1 KB 532, [1949] 1 All ER 127, CA; *Alderslade v Hendon Laundry Ltd* [1945] KB 189, [1945] 1 All ER 244, CA; *Gillespie Bros & Co Ltd v Roy Bowles Transport Ltd* [1973] QB 400, [1973] 1 All ER 193, CA; *Lamport & Holt Lines Ltd v Coubro and Scrutton (M & I) Ltd and Coubro and Scrutton (Riggers and Shipwrights) Ltd, The Raphael* [1982] 2 Lloyd's Rep 42, CA; *EE Caledonia Ltd v Orbit Valve plc* [1995] 1 All ER 174, [1994] 1 WLR 1515, [1994] 2 Lloyd's Rep 239; *Morris v Breaveglen Ltd* (9 May 1997, unreported); *Toomey v Eagle Star Insurance Co Ltd (No 2)* [1995] 2 Lloyd's Rep 88, [1995] 4 Re LR 314, QBD; *Granville Oil & Chemicals Ltd v Davies Turner & Co Ltd* [2003] EWCA Civ 570, [2003] 1 All ER (Comm) 819, [2003] 2 Lloyd's Rep 356; and see CONTRACT. Cf *Chapelton v Barry UDC* [1940] 1 KB 532, [1940] 1 All ER 356, CA. See also the text to note 7.

5 Ie provided that the case against him has not been pleaded solely in negligence: see *J Spurling Ltd v Bradshaw* [1956] 2 All ER 121 at 125, [1956] 1 WLR 461 at 466, CA, per Denning LJ. See PARA 149.

6 *Morris v CW Martin & Sons Ltd* [1966] 1 QB 716 at 726, [1965] 2 All ER 725 at 731, CA, per Lord Denning MR; *Port Swettenham Authority v TW Wu & Co (M) Sdn Bhd* [1979] AC 580, [1978] 3 All ER 337, PC; *Frans Maas (UK) Ltd v Samsung Electronics (UK) Ltd* [2004] EWHC 1502 (Comm), [2005] 2 All ER (Comm) 783, [2004] 2 Lloyd's Rep 251; *Brink's Global Services Inc v Igrox Ltd* [2009] EWHC 1871 (Comm), [2009] All ER (D) 261 (Jul) (affd [2010] EWCA Civ 1207, [2010] All ER (D) 260 (Oct)). For examples of the discharge or non-discharge of the burden on particular facts, see *Coopers Payen Ltd v Southampton Container Terminal Ltd* [2003] EWCA Civ 1223, [2004] 1 Lloyd's Rep 331, [2003] All ER (D) 220 (Jul); *Arlington Productions Ltd v Pinewood Studios Ltd* [2004] EWHC 32 (QB), [2004] All ER (D) 168 (Jan).

7 *Woolmer v Delmer Price Ltd* [1955] 1 QB 291, [1955] 1 All ER 377 (unexplained loss); approved in *Levison v Patent Steam Carpet Cleaning Co Ltd* [1978] QB 69, [1977] 3 All ER 498, CA. See also *Aktieselskabet de Danske Sukkerfabrikker v Bajamar Compania Naviera SA, The Torenia* [1983] 2 Lloyd's Rep 210; *Euro Cellular (Distribution) plc v Danzas Ltd* [2004] EWHC 11 (Comm), [2004] All ER (D) 42 (Jan).

8 *Thornton v Shoe Lane Parking Ltd* [1971] 2 QB 163, [1971] 1 All ER 686, CA. See also *Mendelssohn v Normand Ltd* [1970] 1 QB 177, [1969] 2 All ER 1215, CA; *Metaalhandel JA Magnus BV v Ardfields Transport Ltd and Eastfell Ltd (t/a Jones Transport)* [1988] 1 Lloyd's Rep 197; *Jarl Trä AB v Convoys Ltd* [2003] EWHC 1488 (Comm), [2003] 2 Lloyd's Rep 459, [2003] All ER (D) 328 (Jun).

9 *Sydney City Council v West* (1965) 114 CLR 481, [1966] ALR 538, Aust HC (where it was held by a majority of three to two that the bailee was not exempted from negligent misdelivery; three judges considered that exemption could have been achieved by adequate wording, and the two judges in the minority considered that it had been; two of the judges in the majority held that unauthorised delivery, being not a mere act of negligence in relation to some act authorised by the bailment contract, precluded the bailee from relying on the exemption clause). See *Hollins v J Davy Ltd* [1963] 1 QB 844, [1963] 1 All ER 370. See also PARA 110.

10 *Ashby v Tolhurst* [1937] 2 KB 242 at 258, [1937] 2 All ER 837 at 847, CA, per Scott LJ. See *Hollins v J Davy Ltd* [1963] 1 QB 844, [1963] 1 All ER 370, where the words were held to be sufficient to exempt the bailee from liability for innocent misdelivery. See also *KH Enterprise v*

Pioneer Container, The Pioneer Container [1994] 2 AC 324, [1994] 2 All ER 250, [1994] 1 Lloyd's Rep 593, PC; *Lotus Cars Ltd v Southampton Cargo Handling plc, The Rigoletto* [2000] 2 All ER (Comm) 705, [2000] 2 Lloyd's Rep 532, CA; *Motis Exports Ltd v Dampskibsselskabet AF 1912* [2000] 1 All ER (Comm) 91, [2000] 1 Lloyd's Rep 211, CA. See further PARA 110.

11 *Sze Hai Tong Bank Ltd v Rambler Cycle Co Ltd* [1959] AC 576 at 587–588, [1959] 3 All ER 182 at 185, PC; *Motis Exports Ltd v Dampskibsselskabet AF 1912 A/S* [2000] 1 All ER (Comm) 91, [2000] 1 Lloyd's Rep 211, CA. See also PARA 110.

12 *Photo Production Ltd v Securicor Transport Ltd* [1980] AC 827, [1980] 1 All ER 556, HL; *Ailsa Craig Fishing Co Ltd v Malvern Fishing Co Ltd* [1983] 1 All ER 101, [1983] 1 WLR 964, HL; *George Mitchell (Chesterhall) Ltd v Finney Lock Seeds Ltd* [1983] 2 AC 803, [1983] 2 All ER 737, HL; *Frans Maas (UK) Ltd v Samsung Electronics (UK) Ltd* [2004] EWHC 1502 (Comm), [2005] 2 All ER (Comm) 783, [2004] 2 Lloyd's Rep 251 (exclusion of liability for employee wilful default allowed). See also the Unfair Contract Terms Act 1977 s 9(1); the Unfair Terms in Consumer Contracts Regulations 1999, SI 1999/2083; and CONTRACT vol 9(1) (Reissue) PARAS 805, 829. See further PARA 110.

13 *Walker v Jackson* (1842) 10 M & W 161 at 170; *Long v District Messenger and Theatre Ticket Co* (1916) 32 TLR 596. See also *Victoria Fur Traders Ltd v Roadline (UK) Ltd and British Airways Board* [1981] 1 Lloyd's Rep 570, DC (standard terms of bailee not known to owners and not incorporated into contract with owners' agent); *Metaalhandel JA Magnus BV v Ardfields Transport Ltd and Eastfell Ltd (t/a Jones Transport)* [1988] 1 Lloyd's Rep 197.

14 *Martin v N Negin Ltd* (1945) 172 LT 275, CA.

15 *Curtis v Chemical Cleaning and Dyeing Co* [1951] 1 KB 805, [1951] 1 All ER 631, CA. As to the burden of proof see *Levison v Patent Steam Carpet Cleaning Co Ltd* [1978] QB 69, [1977] 3 All ER 498, CA; *Euro Cellular (Distribution) plc v Danzas Ltd* [2004] EWHC 11 (Comm), [2004] All ER (D) 42 (Jan).

148. Acts of employees. The custodian bailee is responsible to the owner of the chattel entrusted to him both for the negligence of his agents or employees[1], and for their acts of fraud or other wrongful acts[2], provided that those acts were committed in the course of their employment[3]. Although such a custodian usually incurs no responsibility where an act of fraud or negligence is committed by a servant or agent not in the course of his employment or outside the scope of his authority[4], the custodian may be liable if he was negligent in engaging the servant whose act occasioned the loss[5].

1 *Randelson v Murray* (1838) 8 Ad & El 109. This includes the negligence of the bailor's servants if placed under the bailee's control: *AH Bull & Co v West African Shipping Agency and Lighterage Co* [1927] AC 686, PC; *GW Leggott & Son v CH Normanton & Son* (1928) 98 LJKB 145; *L Harris (Harella) Ltd v Continental Express Ltd and Burn Transit Ltd* [1961] 1 Lloyd's Rep 251; contrast *Société Maritime Française v Shanghai Dock and Engineering Co Ltd* [1921] 2 AC 417n, PC. See also *G Bosman (Transport) Ltd v LKW Walter International Transportorganisation AG* [2002] EWCA Civ 850, [2002] All ER (D) 13 (May); *East West Corpn v DKBS AF 1912 A/S, Utaniko Ltd v P & O Nedlloyd BV* [2003] EWCA Civ 83, [2003] QB 1509, [2003] 2 All ER 700.

2 *Barwick v English Joint Stock Bank* (1867) LR 2 Exch 259 at 265; *Mackay v Commercial Bank of New Brunswick* (1874) LR 5 PC 394; *Dyer v Munday* [1895] 1 QB 742, CA; *Lloyd v Grace, Smith & Co* [1912] AC 716, HL; *Central Motors (Glasgow) Ltd v Cessnock Garage and Motor Co* 1925 SC 796, Ct of Sess; *Aitchison v Page Motors Ltd* (1935) 154 LT 128; *Adams (Durham) Ltd and Day v Trust Houses Ltd* [1960] 1 Lloyd's Rep 380; *W Carsen & Co Ltd v Eastern Canada Stevedoring Co* [1962] 2 Lloyd's Rep 209, Ont CA. Cf PARA 184.

3 *Port Swettenham Authority v TW Wu & Co (M) Sdn Bhd* [1979] AC 580, [1978] 3 All ER 337, PC; *Morris v CW Martin & Sons Ltd* [1966] 1 QB 716, [1965] 2 All ER 725, CA; and see *United Africa Co Ltd v Saka Owoade* [1955] AC 130, [1957] 3 All ER 216, PC; *Rustenburg Platinum Mines Ltd v South African Airways* [1979] 1 Lloyd's Rep 19, CA (obiter); *East West Corpn v DKBS AF 1912 A/S, Utaniko Ltd v P & O Nedlloyd BV* [2003] EWCA Civ 83, [2003] QB 1509, [2003] 2 All ER 700; *Lister v Hesley Hall Ltd* [2001] UKHL 22, [2002] 1 AC 215, [2001] 2 All ER 769; *Brink's Global Services Inc v Igrox Ltd* [2009] EWHC 1871 (Comm), [2009] All ER (D) 261 (Jul) (affd [2010] EWCA Civ 1207, [2010] All ER (D) 260 (Oct)). It is commonly stated that the employee must be one to whom the bailee has entrusted the goods: *Port Swettenham Authority v TW Wu & Co (M) Sdn Bhd* [1979] AC 580, [1978] 3 All ER 337,

PC; *Morris v CW Martin & Sons Ltd* [1966] 1 QB 716, [1965] 2 All ER 725, CA; *Swiss Bank Corpn v Brinks-MAT Ltd* [1986] 2 Lloyd's Rep 79. See also the cases cited in note 2 and see *Lister v Hesley Hall Ltd* [2001] UKHL 22, [2002] 1 AC 215, [2001] 2 All ER 769 (entrustment of duty of care the determinative factor); cf *Photo Production Ltd v Securicor Transport Ltd* [1980] AC 827, [1980] 1 All ER 556, HL.

4   Cf *Swiss Bank Corpn v Brinks-MAT Ltd* [1986] 2 Lloyd's Rep 79; and see *Irving v Post Office* [1987] IRLR 289, CA; *Heasmans v Clarity Cleaning Co Ltd* [1987] ICR 949, [1987] IRLR 286, CA. See also PARA 146 note 17. It is to be observed that, in *Central Motors (Glasgow) Ltd v Cessnock Garage and Motor Co* 1925 SC 796, Ct of Sess the Lord President reserved for consideration the general question whether the misconduct of the custodian's servant can ever be a defence to the custodian in view of *Lloyd v Grace, Smith & Co* [1912] AC 716, HL. See further *Armagas Ltd v Mundogas SA, The Ocean Frost* [1986] AC 717, [1986] 2 All ER 385, HL. See also AGENCY vol 1 (2008) PARA 121 et seq; EMPLOYMENT.

5   *Williams v Curzon Syndicate Ltd* (1919) 35 TLR 475, CA. See also *Adams (Durham) Ltd and Day v Trust Houses Ltd* [1960] 1 Lloyd's Rep 380; *Nahhas v Pier House (Cheyne Walk) Management Ltd* (1984) 270 Estates Gazette 328.

149.   Onus of proof. When a chattel entrusted to a custodian is lost, injured or destroyed, the onus of proof[1] is on the custodian to show that the injury did not happen in consequence of any neglect on his part, or on the part of his servants acting within the course of their employment[2], to use such care and diligence as a prudent or careful man would exercise in relation to the property[3]. If he succeeds in showing this, he is not bound to show how or when the loss or damage occurred[4]. If a custodian declines either to produce the chattel entrusted to him when required to do so by the owner, or to explain how it has disappeared, the refusal amounts prima facie to evidence of breach of duty on his part, and throws on him the onus of showing that he exercised due care in the custody of the chattel and in the selection of the servants employed by him in the warehousing[5].

1   See also PARA 147 text and notes 5–7. The onus may shift: see *Brazier v Whelan* (1960) Times, 21 July (custody of racehorse which died from disease).

2   The onus extends to requiring the custodian to prove that the chattel was not stolen or otherwise maltreated by any servant of his to whom he had entrusted the chattel, or to whom he had delegated the whole or any part of his duty of care: see PARA 186.

3   *Mackenzie v Cox* (1840) 9 C & P 632; *Reeve v Palmer* (1858) 5 CBNS 84, Ex Ch; *Phipps v New Claridge's Hotel Ltd* (1905) 22 TLR 49; *Brook's Wharf and Bull Wharf Ltd v Goodman Bros* [1937] 1 KB 534 at 538–539, [1936] 3 All ER 696 at 701–702, CA; *Gutter v Tait* (1947) 177 LT 1, CA; *Edwards v Newland & Co (E Burchett Ltd, third party)* [1950] 2 KB 534, [1950] 1 All ER 1072, CA; *British Traders and Shippers Ltd v Ubique Transport and Motor Engineering Co (London) Ltd and Port of London Authority* [1952] 2 Lloyd's Rep 236; *WLR Traders (London) Ltd v British and Northern Shipping Agency Ltd and I Leftley Ltd* [1955] 1 Lloyd's Rep 554; *British Road Services Ltd v Arthur V Crutchley & Co Ltd (Factory Guards Ltd, third party)* [1968] 1 All ER 811, [1968] 1 Lloyd's Rep 271, CA; *Transmotors v Robertson, Buckley & Co* [1970] 1 Lloyd's Rep 224 (failure to discharge onus); *Morris v CW Martin & Sons Ltd* [1966] 1 QB 716, [1965] 2 All ER 725, CA; *Port Swettenham Authority v TW Wu & Co (M) Sdn Bhd* [1979] AC 580, [1978] 3 All ER 337, PC; *Lockspeiser Aircraft Ltd v Brooklands Aircraft Co Ltd* (1990) Times, 7 March; *Fankhauser v Mark Dykes Pty Ltd* [1960] VR 376, Vict FC; *Hobbs v Petersham Transport Co Pty Ltd* (1971) 45 ALJR 356, Aust HC; *G Bosman (Transport) Ltd v LKW Walter International Transportorganisation AG* [2002] EWCA Civ 850, [2002] All ER (D) 13 (May); *East West Corpn v DKBS AF 1912 A/S, Utaniko Ltd v P & O Nedlloyd BV* [2003] EWCA Civ 83, [2003] QB 1509, [2003] 2 All ER 700; and see PARA 111 note 12. As to misdelivery see *Becker v Lavender Ltd* (1946) 62 TLR 504; and cf *Alexander v Railway Executive* [1951] 2 KB 882, [1951] 2 All ER 442. If the bailee or his servants are guilty of negligence, and it is doubtful whether the negligence caused the loss or injury, the onus is on him to prove that it did not: *Joseph Travers & Sons Ltd v Cooper* [1915] 1 KB 73, CA; *Coldman v Hill* [1919] 1 KB 443, CA. Similarly, if he relies on an exemption, he must prove that the facts bring him within it: *Levison v Patent Steam Carpet Cleaning Co Ltd* [1978] QB 69, [1977] 3 All ER 498, CA; *Euro Cellular (Distribution) plc v Danzas Ltd* [2004] EWHC 11 (Comm), [2004] All ER (D) 42 (Jan); *London and North Western*

Rly Co v JP Ashton & Co [1920] AC 84, HL; cf PARA 121. If the time of the loss is material to the question whether the bailee is liable, the bailee must prove when the loss occurred: *Re S Davis & Co Ltd* [1945] Ch 402 (liability of liquidator); *Mitchell v Ealing London Borough Council* [1979] QB 1, [1978] 2 All ER 779 (gratuitous bailment).

4   *Bullen v Swan Electric Engraving Co* (1907) 23 TLR 258, CA; *Brook's Wharf and Bull Wharf Ltd v Goodman Bros* [1937] 1 KB 534 at 539, [1936] 3 All ER 696 at 702, CA; Palmer on Bailment (3rd Edn, 2009) para 14-012; approved in *Coopers Payen Ltd v Southampton Container Terminal Ltd* [2003] EWCA Civ 1223 at [28], [2004] 1 Lloyd's Rep 331 at [28], [2003] All ER (D) 220 (Jul) at [28] per Clarke LJ (proof of true cause may be helpful, though not essential, to bailee's defence). See also PARAS 111, 121.

5   See generally *Arlington Productions Ltd v Pinewood Studios Ltd* [2004] EWHC 32 (QB), [2004] All ER (D) 168 (Jan); *Coopers Payen Ltd v Southampton Container Terminal Ltd* [2003] EWCA Civ 1223, [2004] 1 Lloyd's Rep 331, [2003] All ER (D) 220 (Jul) at [28]; and see further *Platt v Hibbard* (1827) 7 Cowen 497 at 500 per Walworth J (US case). Contrast *HC Smith Ltd v Great Western Rly Co* [1922] 1 AC 178, HL (refusal to account for loss did not amount to proof of 'wilful misconduct' of defendants' servants within an exception to a clause exempting the defendants from liability).

150. Insurance.

150. **Insurance.** A custodian is not ordinarily responsible to the owner of the chattel entrusted to him in case of its destruction by fire[1], unless he has deviated from the terms of the bailment or broken his duty of care, or undertaken some special contractual responsibility covering the particular event. If, however, he insures the chattel he has such an insurable interest in it that, as against the insurers, he is entitled to recover its full value[2]. A custodian who recovers insurance money occupies the position of a trustee to the owner of the chattel covered by the insurance for its value, less his agreed or reasonable charges for warehousing; and after demand by the owner and refusal by the custodian to account for the proceeds, a claim will lie against him at the suit of the owner for money had and received[3].

A custodian will be bound by an express undertaking to insure the goods and will be liable for loss suffered by the bailor in consequence of the custodian's failure to do so[4]. In the absence of such an express undertaking, however, it would appear that (otherwise, perhaps, than in exceptional cases[5]) none will be implied[6].

1   *Sidaways v Todd* (1818) 2 Stark 400 at 401 per Abbott J; *Maving v Todd* (1815) 4 Camp 225. See also the cases cited in PARA 146 note 16.

2   *Waters and Steel v Monarch Fire and Life Assurance Co* (1856) 5 E & B 870. See also *Hepburn v A Tomlinson (Hauliers) Ltd* [1966] AC 451, [1966] 1 All ER 418, HL; and *Re Routledge, ex p Bateman* (1856) 8 De GM & G 263. See further *Albacruz (Cargo Holders) v Albazero (Owners), The Albazero* [1977] AC 774 at 846, [1976] 3 All ER 129 at 136–137, HL, per Lord Diplock; *Feasey v Sun Life Assurance Company of Canada*; *Steamship Mutual Underwriting Association (Bermuda) Ltd v Feasey* [2003] EWCA Civ 885, [2003] 2 All ER (Comm) 587, [2003] Lloyd's Rep IR 637; Palmer on Bailment (3rd Edn, 2009) para 39-002; and DAMAGES vol 12(1) (Reissue) PARA 1102. The chattels destroyed must be covered by the terms of the policy: *North British and Mercantile Insurance Co v Moffatt* (1871) LR 7 CP 25. See further INSURANCE vol 25 (2003 Reissue) PARA 698 et seq.

3   *Sidaways v Todd* (1818) 2 Stark 400. See also *Hepburn v A Tomlinson (Hauliers) Ltd* [1966] AC 451, [1966] 1 All ER 418, HL; *Re E Dibbens & Sons Ltd (in liquidation)* [1990] BCLC 577; *DG Finance Ltd v Scott and Eagle Star Insurance Co Ltd* (15 June 1995, unreported), CA; and DAMAGES vol 12(1) (Reissue) PARA 1102.

4   *Lockspeiser Aircraft Ltd v Brooklands Aircraft Co Ltd* (1990) Times, 7 March.

5   *Eastman Chemical International AG v NMT Trading Ltd and Eagle Transport Ltd* [1972] 2 Lloyd's Rep 25 (carriage).

6   *Koromvokis v Gregsons Auctioneers Pty Ltd* (20 November 1986, unreported), CA; Palmer on Bailment (3rd Edn, 2009) paras 14-013–14-018.

151. Work to be done on chattels.

151. **Work to be done on chattels.** The obligations of the custodian in the ordinary course of business are frequently varied and enhanced by the addition

of a contract on his part to perform some act in connection with the chattels[1]. This additional undertaking raises a series of obligations between the owner of the chattel and the bailee which are collateral to the bare obligation of safe custody. In such cases a further undertaking on the bailee's part will be implied to exercise the appropriate capability, care and fidelity in the conduct of the particular employment for which the chattel was entrusted to him, for when a person undertakes for reward to perform any work he must be considered as bound to use a degree of diligence adequate to the performance of it[2].

1   See eg *Bevan v Waters* (1828) 3 C & P 520 (training horses); *Forth v Simpson* (1849) 13 QB 680 (training horses); *Curling v Wood* (1847) 16 M & W 628, Ex Ch (mooring a ship); *Reynolds v Boston Deep Sea Fishing and Ice Co Ltd* (1922) 38 TLR 429, CA (negligence in placing ship on slipway for repairs). See further SHIPPING AND MARITIME LAW.
2   Jones on Bailments (4th Edn, 1833) pp 98–99; and see PARA 161 et seq.

152. Measure of damages. In a claim against a custodian founded on the custodian's breach of the duty of care, the measure of damages recoverable is generally the actual value of the chattel where it is lost or destroyed, and its diminution in value where it is damaged[1]. However, the claimant may also, in particular cases, be entitled to recover the cost of reinstatement and any consequential damage flowing from the negligence which is not too remote in law, which may include damages for loss of use of the chattel[2], or profits lost from the destruction of it[3]. Damages for inconvenience or loss of enjoyment may also be awarded in certain circumstances[4]. In cases of deliberate wrongdoing towards the chattel, aggravated and exemplary damages may also be awarded[5].

There is no general implied undertaking on the part of a mere custodian to be answerable for consequential damages, and the simple deposit of chattels with him in the ordinary course of business raises no notice by implication that such damages are likely to be incurred[6].

1   See generally Palmer on Bailment (3rd Edn, 2009) Chapter 37. The bailee's general liability is of course subject to any contractual terms which may govern the dealings between the parties.
2   *Davis v Oswell* (1837) 7 C & P 804; *Mediana (Owners) v Comet (Owners, Master and Crew), The Mediana* [1900] AC 113, HL; *Brandeis Goldschmidt & Co Ltd v Western Transport Ltd* [1981] QB 864, [1982] 1 All ER 28, CA. As to damages where there is a fall in market value of the goods between the date of conversion and the date of their return see *Trailways Transport Ltd v Thomas* [1996] 2 NZLR 443, NZHC. As to damages where there is a loss flowing naturally and directly from the wrongful usurpation and conversion see *Kuwait Airways Corpn v Iraqi Airways Co* [2002] UKHL 19, [2002] 2 AC 883, [2002] 3 All ER 209. As to conversion generally see TORT vol 45(2) (Reissue) PARA 548 et seq.
3   *Bodley v Reynolds* (1846) 8 QB 779; *France v Gaudet* (1871) LR 6 QB 199, Ex Ch; *The Arpad* [1934] P 189, CA. See also *Strand Electric and Engineering Co Ltd v Brisford Entertainments Ltd* [1952] 2 QB 246, [1952] 1 All ER 796, CA; *Trailways Transport Ltd v Thomas* [1996] 2 NZLR 443, NZ HC; *Kuwait Airways Corpn v Iraqi Airways Co* [2002] UKHL 19, [2002] 2 AC 883, [2002] 3 All ER 209.
4   See PARA 233.
5   See PARA 233.
6   *Henderson v North Eastern Rly Co* (1861) 9 WR 519, 4 LT 216; *Building & Civil Engineering Holidays and Scheme Management Ltd v Post Office* [1966] 1 QB 247, [1965] 1 All ER 163, CA. As to the requirement that may arise in particular cases of the bailee's implied undertaking to answer for a particular form of loss or damage see *Transfield Shipping Inc v Mercator Shipping Inc, The Achilleas* [2008] UKHL 48, [2009] 1 AC 61, [2008] 4 All ER 159; *Sylvia Shipping Co Ltd v Progress Bulk Carriers Ltd, The Sylvia* [2010] EWHC 542 (Comm), [2010] 2 Lloyd's Rep 81, [2010] All ER (D) 184 (Mar); *Siemens Building Technologies FE Ltd v Supershield Ltd* [2010] EWCA Civ 7, [2010] 2 All ER (Comm) 1185, [2010] 1 Lloyd's Rep 349. As to financial redress recoverable by a bailor against a bailee see further *Strand Electric and Engineering Co Ltd v Brisford Entertainments Ltd* [1952] 2 QB 246 at 253–254, [1952] 1 All ER 796 at 800–801, CA, per Denning LJ (reasonable hiring charge; and see Palmer on

Bailment (3rd Edn, 2009) paras 33-006–33-011); *Lockspeiser Aircraft Ltd v Brooklands Aircraft Co Ltd* (1990) Times, 7 March; and PARA 233. Compare the liability of a common carrier, who may be liable for loss of market or other consequential damage: see *Simpson v London and North Western Rly Co* (1876) 1 QBD 274; and CARRIAGE AND CARRIERS vol 7 (2008) PARAS 775, 777, 779.

153. Liability to distress. Generally, the owner of goods who has given them to another for custody is protected from those goods being distrained for payment of rent in respect of the premises where the goods are stored[1].

At common law, chattels delivered to a person exercising a public trade to be carried, wrought, worked up or managed in the way of the trade are privileged from distress for rent due from the person in whose custody they are[2]. Under the Law of Distress Amendment Act 1908, protection is given to the goods of strangers who have no interest in the land[3]. The Act allows such a bailor to recover the goods from the distraining landlord, or to recover their value[4].

Statute governs the levying of distress upon livestock agisted on an agricultural holding[5]; and machinery and breeding stock upon such a holding which are not the property of the tenant are privileged from distress[6].

1 See the Law of Distress Amendment Act 1908; and DISTRESS vol 13 (2007 Reissue) PARA 951 et seq.
2 See DISTRESS vol 13 (2007 Reissue) PARA 932. Examples of trades whose custodianship of goods has allowed privilege from distress to be claimed under this rule are warehousemen and wharfingers (*Miles v Furber* (1873) LR 8 QB 77; *Thompson v Mashiter* (1823) 1 Bing 283); factors or agents for sale (*Gilman v Elton* (1821) 3 Brod & Bing 75; *Findon v McLaren* (1845) 6 QB 891); auctioneers, if on their own premises (*Williams v Holmes* (1853) 8 Exch 861) but otherwise not (*Lyons v Elliott* (1876) 1 QBD 210); and tradesmen who have to work on the goods (*Simpson v Hartopp* (1744) Willes 512; *Muspratt v Gregory* (1838) 3 M & W 677). Agisters and livery stable-keepers were probably on the same footing as warehousemen (*Parsons v Gingell* (1847) 4 CB 545, deciding against the privilege, being disapproved in *Miles v Furber* (1873) LR 8 QB 77).
3 Ie subject to certain exceptions: see the Law of Distress Amendment Act 1908 s 4 (amended by the Consumer Credit Act 1974 s 192(3)(b), Sch 5 Pt I; the Agricultural Holdings Act 1986 s 100, Sch 14 para 4; the Agricultural Tenancies Act 1995 s 40, Schedule para 2; the Access to Justice Act 1999 s 106, Sch 15 Pt V Table (3); and the Civil Partnership Act 2004 s 261(1), Sch 27 para 3). The Law of Distress Amendment Act 1908 is repealed, as from a day to be appointed, by the Tribunals, Courts and Enforcement Act 2007 ss 86, 146, Sch 14 para 20, Sch 23 Pt 4. From that date, distress will be replaced by the procedure of enforcement by taking control of goods under the Tribunals, Courts and Enforcement Act 2007 s 62(1), Sch 12, but provision is made for goods to be made exempt from the procedure by regulations: see Sch 12 paras 3(1), 4(1), 11(2). At the date at which this volume states the law, no such day had been appointed. As to enforcement by taking control see CIVIL PROCEDURE vol 12 (2009) PARA 1389 et seq. As to goods which may be taken see CIVIL PROCEDURE vol 12 (2009) PARA 1392.
4 See the Law of Distress Amendment Act 1908 s 1 (amended by the Perjury Act 1911 s 17, Schedule); and the Law of Distress Amendment Act 1908 s 2 (amended by the Access to Justice Act 1999 s 78(2), Sch 11 para 11). See note 3.
5 As to the meaning of 'agricultural holding' see the Agricultural Holdings Act 1986 s 1; and AGRICULTURAL LAND vol 1 (2008) PARA 323. As to agistment see ANIMALS vol 2 (2008) PARAS 721–723.
6 Agricultural Holdings Act 1986 s 18 (repealed, as from a day to be appointed, by the Tribunals, Courts and Enforcement Act 2007 Sch 14 paras 41, 42, Sch 23 Pt 4). At the date at which this volume states the law, no such day had been appointed. The Law of Distress Amendment Act 1908 does not apply to livestock within the Agricultural Holdings Act 1986 s 18: Law of Distress Amendment Act 1908 s 4(1) (as amended: see note 3). See further AGRICULTURAL LAND vol 1 (2008) PARA 347.

(iii) Bailee's Lien

154. When bailee's lien is available. As a general rule a custodian for reward has, in the absence of some special agreement[1], no lien[2] for his charges upon the chattel entrusted to him for safe custody alone[3], though, unless the terms of the contract exclude it[4], he acquires a lien if, with the owner's consent, he expends labour and skill upon it for its improvement[5]. Nevertheless, by implication of law, wharfingers[6], packers[7], and possibly warehousemen[8], have a general lien[9] for their charges upon the chattels of their bailors, but in the case of wharfingers this implication may be rebutted in any particular district by local usage[10]. This general lien takes precedence of claims by the Crown[11], and the costs of defending it may be added to the security[12].

A general lien is presumed in the case of factors, bankers and stockbrokers, in the absence of a special contract[13], which is always construed strictly against the claimant[14]; consequently such bailees may retain chattels or securities deposited with them, not only as security for the particular loan in respect of which they were so deposited, but also for a general balance of accounts[15]. A similar rule prevails, as part of the law merchant, in certain other trades, although in all such cases the custom establishing the existence of a general lien must be proved strictly[16].

In the absence of a particular trade custom[17], a specific lien on a particular chattel cannot be enlarged so as to include a general balance of account[18]. If in such a case, after the bailor demands the particular chattel and tenders the specific amount due on it, the bailee refuses to redeliver, not only is his lien gone[19], but he is also liable to the true owner in a claim of trover for the tort of conversion[20]. The mere demand by the bailee of a sum exceeding that which is really due to him does not usually dispense with the necessity of tender by the bailor of the amount actually due, especially if the bailee particularises his demand and claims to hold the chattel for the correct sum to which he is entitled, as well as for the excessive one[21].

A bailee who keeps a chattel to enforce his lien on it cannot ordinarily charge for keeping it[22].

At common law a railway authority has been held to have a lien on all chattels deposited with it for safe custody[23] for the amount of its reasonable charges. This lien applies not only against the person who actually deposited the chattel, but also against its true owner, or a third party, even though they may not have had privity with the original contracting parties[24].

A lien is exercisable against a bailor owner of a chattel in respect of work done to it by an artificer at the bailee's instance provided that the intermediate bailee had the authority of the bailor owner (whether express or implied) to create a lien in the particular events; it is possible that an ostensible or apparent authority will alternatively suffice for this purpose[25]. Implied authority might be discoverable where the work is reasonably incidental to the bailee's reasonable use of the chattel, and the owner has not expressly excluded the bailee's authority to have the work done[26].

1 For an example of a special agreement see *Jowitt & Sons v Union Cold Storage Co* [1913] 3 KB 1. Contrast *United States Steel Products Co v Great Western Rly Co* [1916] 1 AC 189, HL.

2 See *Rushforth v Hadfield* (1806) 7 East 224 (common carrier). See also *Majeau Carrying Co Pty Ltd v Coastal Rutile Ltd* (1973) 1 ALR 1, Aust HC; and PARA 170.

3 *Judson v Etheridge* (1833) 1 Cr & M 743; *Jackson v Cummins* (1839) 5 M & W 342; *Smith v Dearlove* (1848) 6 CB 132. See generally Palmer on Bailment (3rd Edn, 2009) paras 14-096–14-103. Cf *Orchard v Rackstraw* (1850) 9 CB 698 (no lien by livery stable-keeper for money paid to veterinary surgeon at owner's request for attendance on horse).

4 *Forth v Simpson* (1849) 13 QB 680; *Hatton v Car Maintenance Co Ltd* [1915] 1 Ch 621. See also *Borden (UK) Ltd v Scottish Timber Products Ltd* [1981] Ch 25, [1979] 3 All ER 961, CA (title retention clause; held to be ineffective).

5   *Bevan v Waters* (1828) 3 C & P 520; *Scarfe v Morgan* (1838) 4 M & W 270. No lien attaches if the work is merely to maintain the chattel in its former condition: *Hatton v Car Maintenance Co Ltd* [1915] 1 Ch 621; *Re Southern Livestock Producers Ltd* [1963] 3 All ER 801, [1964] 1 WLR 24. As to workman's lien see PARA 170.

6   *Bock v Gorrissen* (1860) 2 De GF & J 434 at 443 per Lord Campbell LC; *Spears v Hartly* (1800) 3 Esp 81.

7   *Re Witt, ex p Shubrook* (1876) 2 ChD 489, CA. Cf *K Chellaram & Sons (London) Ltd v Butlers Warehousing and Distribution Ltd* [1978] 2 Lloyd's Rep 412, CA (consolidators of goods; no lien); *Jarl Trä AB v Convoys Ltd* [2003] EWHC 1488 (Comm), [2003] 2 Lloyd's Rep 459, [2003] All ER (D) 328 (Jun) (handlers, storers and wharfingers of goods; limited lien).

8   *R v Humphery* (1825) M'Cle & Yo 173; but see *Leuckhart v Cooper* (1836) 3 Bing NC 99. See also *Re Catford, ex p Carr v Ford* (1894) 71 LT 584; *Hill & Sons v London Central Markets Cold Storage Co Ltd* (1910) 102 LT 715.

9   As to the distinction between a general lien and a particular lien see LIEN vol 68 (2008) PARAS 817–818.

10   *Holderness v Collinson* (1827) 7 B & C 212. As to usages generally see CUSTOM AND USAGE vol 12(1) (Reissue) PARA 650 et seq.

11   *R v Humphery* (1825) M'Cle & Yo 173 (a decision which seems, however, to have turned on its special facts); *K Chellaram & Sons (London) Ltd v Butlers Warehousing and Distribution Ltd* [1978] 2 Lloyd's Rep 412 at 415, CA, per Megaw LJ.

12   *Moet v Pickering* (1878) 8 ChD 372 at 376, CA, per Cotton LJ.

13   *Bock v Gorrissen* (1860) 2 De GF & J 434. See AGENCY vol 1 (2008) PARA 114; FINANCIAL SERVICES AND INSTITUTIONS vol 49 (2008) PARA 860.

14   *Kinnear v Midland Rly Co* (1868) 19 LT 387.

15   *Re London and Globe Finance Corpn* [1902] 2 Ch 416; *Jones v Peppercorne* (1858) John 430.

16   *Re Spotten & Co, ex p Provincial Bank* (1877) 11 IR Eq 412. For cases where liquidation or bankruptcy avoids a general lien by contract see *Re Bushell, ex p Great Western Rly Co* (1882) 22 ChD 470, CA; *Wiltshire Iron Co v Great Western Rly Co* (1871) LR 6 QB 776; cf *George Barker (Transport) Ltd v Eynon* [1974] 1 All ER 900, [1974] 1 WLR 462, CA; and see generally LIEN. As to the law merchant see CUSTOM AND USAGE vol 12(1) (Reissue) PARA 662 et seq.

17   *Re Spotten & Co, ex p Provincial Bank* (1877) 11 IR Eq 412; *Bock v Gorrissen* (1860) 2 De GF & J 434; *Leuckhart v Cooper* (1836) 3 Bing NC 99.

18   *Jones v Tarleton* (1842) 9 M & W 675.

19   *Dirks v Richards* (1842) 4 Man & G 574; but see *Scarfe v Morgan* (1838) 4 M & W 270.

20   *The Norway* (1864) 3 Moo PCCNS 245 at 265. As to trover or conversion (included in wrongful interference with goods) see TORT vol 45(2) (Reissue) PARA 542 et seq.

21   *Scarfe v Morgan* (1838) 4 M & W 270. See also *Albemarle Supply Co Ltd v Hind & Co* [1928] 1 KB 307 at 318–319, CA, per Scrutton LJ.

22   *Somes v British Empire Shipping Co* (1860) 8 HL Cas 338; and see *Delantera Amadora SA v Bristol Channel Shiprepairers Ltd and Swansea Dry Dock Co, The Katingaki* [1976] 2 Lloyd's Rep 372; *Rashtriya Chemicals and Fertilisers Ltd v Huddart Parker Industries Ltd, The Boral Gas* [1988] 1 Lloyd's Rep 342; *Morris v Beaconsfield Motors Ltd* [2001] EWCA Civ 1322, [2001] All ER (D) 335 (Jul); *Jarl Trä AB v Convoys Ltd* [2003] EWHC 1488 (Comm), [2003] 2 Lloyd's Rep 459, [2010] All ER (D) 328 (Jun). Aliter, perhaps where the bailee's retention of the chattel is predominantly for the benefit of the bailor: *China-Pacific SA v Food Corpn of India, The Winson* [1982] AC 939 at 962–963, [1981] 3 All ER 688 at 696, HL, per Lord Diplock, and at 964 and 697 per Lord Simon of Glaisdale. Cf *ENE Kos v Petroleo Brasileiro SA (Petrobas)* [2010] EWCA Civ 772, [2010] 2 Lloyd's Rep 409, [2010] All ER (D) 49 (Jul). Alternatively, of course, the contract might provide to that effect: cf *Morris v Beaconsfield Motors Ltd* [2001] EWCA Civ 1322, [2007] All ER (D) 335 (Jul) per Rimer J.

23   *Van Toll v South Eastern Rly Co* (1862) 12 CBNS 75; *Pratt v South Eastern Rly Co* [1897] 1 QB 718, DC; *Roche v Cork, Blackrock and Passage Rly Co* (1889) 24 LR Ir 250; *Henderson v North Eastern Rly Co* (1861) 9 WR 519, 4 LT 216.

24   *Singer Manufacturing Co v London and South Western Rly Co* [1894] 1 QB 833 at 836, DC, per Mathew J, and at 837 per Collins J. In that case Collins J also based the lien upon the bailee's implied authority. In *Pennington v Reliance Motor Works Ltd* [1923] 1 KB 127 at 129, McCardie J expressed the view that the true ratio in *Singer Manufacturing Co v London and South Western Rly Co* [1894] 1 QB 833, DC, was implied authority; but in *Cassils & Co and Sassoon & Co v Holden Wood Bleaching Co Ltd* (1914) 84 LJKB 834 at 840–841, CA, Buckley LJ was of opinion that a common law lien apart from contract exists in favour of a carrier or innkeeper and that *Singer Manufacturing Co v London and South Western Rly Co* [1894] 1 QB 833, DC, was rightly decided on this ground as well as on the ground of implied authority. Cf *Robins & Co v Gray* [1895] 2 QB 501, CA (innkeeper); *K Chellaram & Sons*

(London) Ltd v Butlers Warehousing and Distribution Ltd [1978] 2 Lloyd's Rep 412, CA; *Jarl Trä AB v Convoys Ltd* [2003] EWHC 1488 (Comm), [2003] 2 Lloyd's Rep 459, [2003] All ER (D) 328 (Jun).

25 *Tappenden v Artus* [1964] 2 QB 185, [1963] 3 All ER 213, CA. See also LIEN vol 68 (2008) PARA 824; Palmer on Bailment (3rd Edn, 2009) paras 36-029–36-038.

26 *Tappenden v Artus* [1964] 2 QB 185, [1963] 3 All ER 213, CA (repairs to car to make it roadworthy).

155. Loss of lien. The bailee's lien[1] is lost if the bailee loses possession of the chattel[2], or if he does anything amounting to a waiver[3], or if the identity of the chattel is lost by intermixture or confusion with other chattels of a similar nature belonging to a different owner[4]. The bailee's assertion of a right to retain the chattel otherwise than by way of lien may operate as a waiver of the lien[5].

As a general rule, a right of lien confers no right to sell the chattel[6] unless that right is expressly conferred by statute[7], and sale without right causes loss of the lien[8].

1 See PARA 154.

2 *Hutton v Bragg* (1816) 7 Taunt 14; *Pennington v Reliance Motor Works Ltd* [1923] 1 KB 127. Cf *Sweet v Pym* (1800) 1 East 4; *Dicas v Stockley* (1836) 7 C & P 587; *Barratt v Gough-Thomas* [1951] Ch 242, [1950] 2 All ER 1048, CA (solicitor); contrast *North Western Bank Ltd v John Poynter, Son and Macdonalds* [1895] AC 56, HL; *Albemarle Supply Co Ltd v Hind & Co* [1928] 1 KB 307, CA. See further LIEN.

3 *Mulliner v Florence* (1878) 3 QBD 484, CA, where the bailee sold the goods and thereby lost his lien; *Hill & Sons v London Central Markets Cold Storage Co Ltd* (1910) 102 LT 715; *Jarl Trä AB v Convoys Ltd* [2003] EWHC 1488 (Comm), [2003] 2 Lloyd's Rep 459, [2008] All ER (D) 328 (Jun).

4 *Grant v Humphery* (1862) 3 F & F 162.

5 *White v Gainer* (1824) 2 Bing 23 at 24 per Best CJ; *Weeks v Goode* (1859) 6 CBNS 367; *Boardman v Sill* (1808) 1 Camp 410n; *Dirks v Richards* (1842) 4 Man & G 574.

6 *Pothonier and Hodgson v Dawson* (1816) Holt NP 383 at 385 per Gibbs CJ; *Smart v Sandars* (1848) 5 CB 895; *Thames Iron Works Co v Patent Derrick Co* (1860) 1 John & H 93; *Bolwell Fibreglass Pty Ltd v Foley* [1984] VR 97, Vict SC.

7 Eg the statutory right of a bailee to dispose of uncollected goods: see PARA 173.

8 Cf *Mulliner v Florence* (1878) 3 QBD 484, CA, where an innkeeper was held not have a right to sell his guest's horses over which he had a lien. The law on this point was altered by the Innkeepers Act 1878: see LICENSING AND GAMBLING vol 67 (2008) PARA 214. Some liens can be enforced by sale by means of a claim for such relief: Story's Commentaries on Equity Jurisprudence (3rd English Edn) s 1217. For the statutory power of a bailee to sell uncollected goods see PARA 173. The provisions of the Reserve and Auxiliary Forces (Protection of Civil Interests) Act 1951, which restrict the exercise of certain remedies in relation to persons called up or volunteering for service in the armed forces, do not affect any right or power of a person to sell goods in his custody as a bailee if it is a right or power arising by reason of default in the payment of a debt: s 2(2) proviso (iv).

(3) HIRE OF WORK AND LABOUR

(i) Nature of the Contract

156. Nature of contract. Hire of work and labour[1] is a class of bailment that derives from an agreement under which one of the two contracting parties undertakes to do something to a chattel, for example, to carry it or repair it, in consideration of a reward to be given to him[2]. It is essential to constitute a valid contract of this description that there should be some work to be performed in connection with a specified chattel, and that a reward should be agreed to be given in return for the labour[3].

The distinction between this contract and that of sale lies in the fact that the work and labour results in nothing which can properly be deemed the subject of a sale, inasmuch as the chattel upon which the work is performed, or the materials out of which the chattel delivered to the hirer is made, are already the property of the hirer, and do not, as in the case of sale, become his property by virtue of the contract[4]. The contract is none the less one of work and labour where, though the principal materials belong to the hirer, the workman furnishes accessories or ornaments, as in the case of a tailor who is employed to make up the hirer's cloth, and who supplies his own buttons and thread[5]. If proceedings are brought to recover payment for work done and materials supplied for the purposes of the work, the value of the materials should be expressly claimed[6].

Certain terms are implied by statute[7] into contracts for the supply of a service[8]. In the Supply of Goods and Services Act 1982, a 'contract for the supply of a service' means a contract under which a person ('the supplier') agrees to carry out a service[9]. A contract is a contract for the supply of a service whether or not goods are also transferred or to be transferred, or bailed or to be bailed by way of hire, under the contract, and whatever is the nature of the consideration for which the service is to be carried out[10].

1   Ie *locatio operis faciendi*: see PARA 106 note 9.
2   Jones on Bailments (4th Edn, 1833) pp 90–91; Palmer on Bailment (3rd Edn, 2009) Chapter 15. As to carriers see CARRIAGE AND CARRIERS.
3   It does not appear that the consideration need be monetary in order to constitute a contract for the hire of work and labour: cf Pothier's Contrat de Louage ss 397–402; *Keys v Harwood* (1846) 2 CB 905.
4   Cf *Lee v Griffin* (1861) 1 B & S 272 at 277 per Blackburn J; and see PARA 101. A contract, however, is not necessarily one of sale even where the workman supplies the materials, if the substance of the contract is that skill and labour have to be exercised and the materials are merely auxiliary: see *Grafton v Armitage* (1845) 2 CB 336 (explaining *Atkinson v Bell* (1828) 8 B & C 277); *Clay v Yates* (1856) 1 H & N 73; *Robinson v Graves* [1935] 1 KB 579, CA. Contrast *J Marcel (Furriers) Ltd v Tapper* [1953] 1 All ER 15, [1953] 1 WLR 49; and see further SALE OF GOODS AND SUPPLY OF SERVICES vol 41 (2005 Reissue) PARA 3.
5   Story on Bailments (9th Edn, 1878) s 423. Cf the cases cited in note 4. Where materials are used in engineering or building operations to construct or erect engines or buildings, the contract will normally be one for work and labour: *Clark v Bulmer* (1843) 11 M & W 243; *Tripp v Armitage* (1839) 4 M & W 687; *Chanter v Dickinson* (1843) 5 Mann & G 253.
6   *Heath v Freeland* (1836) 1 M & W 543, Ex Ch; cf *Cotterell v Apsey* (1815) 6 Taunt 322 (contract to build house, supplying labour and materials; value of materials not recoverable as goods sold, though original contract superseded as result of deviation).
7   Ie the Supply of Goods and Services Act 1982 Pt II (ss 12–16).
8   See the Supply of Goods and Services Act 1982 s 13 (see PARA 162), s 14 (see PARA 161), s 15 (see PARA 157). The Secretary of State may by order made by statutory instrument, subject to annulment in pursuance of a resolution of either House of Parliament, provide that one or more of ss 13–15 is or are not to apply to services of a description specified in the order; and such an order may make different provision for different circumstances: s 12(4), (5). As to the orders that have been made see the Supply of Services (Exclusion of Implied Terms) Order 1982, SI 1982/1771; the Supply of Services (Exclusion of Implied Terms) Order 1983, SI 1983/902; the Supply of Services (Exclusion of Implied Terms) Order 1985, SI 1985/1; and PARA 162. Functions of a local authority under the Supply of Goods and Services Act 1982 are 'relevant functions' for the purposes of the Regulatory Enforcement and Sanctions Act 2008 Pt 1 (ss 1–21): see PARA 178 note 3.
9   Supply of Goods and Services Act 1982 s 12(1). A contract of service or apprenticeship is not a contract for the supply of a service: s 12(2).
10 Supply of Goods and Services Act 1982 s 12(3). Where a right, duty or liability would arise under a contract for the supply of a service by virtue of Pt II, it may, subject to s 16(2) and the Unfair Contract Terms Act 1977 (particularly s 3: see CONTRACT vol 9(1) (Reissue) PARA 823), be negatived or varied by express agreement, or by the course of dealing between the parties, or by such usage as binds both parties to the contract: Supply of Goods and Services Act 1982 s 16(1). An express term does not negative a term implied by Pt II unless inconsistent with it: s 16(2). Nothing in Pt II prejudices: (1) any rule of law which imposes on the supplier a duty stricter than that imposed by s 13 (see PARA 162); or (2) subject to head (1), any rule of law

whereby a term not inconsistent with Pt II is to be implied into a contract for the supply of a service: s 16(3). Part II has effect subject to any other enactment which defines or restricts the rights, duties or liabilities arising in connection with a service of any description: s 16(4).

(ii) Owner's Obligations

157. Obligation to remunerate and pay for materials. The hirer of labour must, at the time or times and in the manner appointed, pay the workman the agreed price. Where, under a contract for the supply of a service, the consideration for the service is not determined by the contract, left to be determined in a manner agreed by the contract or determined by the course of dealing between the parties, there is an implied term that the party contracting with the supplier will pay a reasonable charge[1]. What is a reasonable charge is a question of fact[2].

The acceptance of services does not, however, in all cases necessarily imply that such services are to be remunerated. In general, remuneration cannot be successfully claimed for services voluntarily performed without request[3]. In general, whether or not work and labour is to be remunerated depends upon the contract under which the work was done[4], but the engagement of a man whose trade it is to do the work in question prima facie implies a contract by the employer to pay him a fair and reasonable price for his work[5]. A person called in to do work of a class which he holds himself out as qualified to do, which will be useful only if effective, and which he is left to do in his own way, can recover nothing if it proves ineffective and the employer gets no benefit from it[6]. A workman's right to make a claim for the agreed remuneration for work completed does not arise until the work is done and the employer has had a reasonable opportunity of ascertaining whether it has been properly done[7].

Where one person is engaged by another to do work, the workman can prima facie look for his remuneration only to the actual party commissioning the work[8], unless it is known to both parties that the work is for the benefit of a third party for whom the commissioning party is acting merely as agent[9].

The hirer must also (subject to the particular terms of the contract) pay for all materials employed by the workman in the manufacture, alteration or repair of the chattel which is the subject of the contract, provided they are necessary for the completion of the work, and were either specifically or impliedly ordered[10].

1   Supply of Goods and Services Act 1982 s 15(1). As to the meaning of 'contract for the supply of a service' see PARA 156. The statutory definition corresponds with the obligation implied at common law: see *Jewry v Busk* (1814) 5 Taunt 302; *Brown v Nairne* (1839) 9 C & P 204; cf *Cannon v Miles* [1974] 2 Lloyd's Rep 129, CA. If it can be established that a particular rate of remuneration is customary for a particular employment, that rate is accepted as just and reasonable: *Brown v Nairne* (1839) 9 C & P 204 at 205; and see eg *Price v Hong Kong Tea Co* (1861) 2 F & F 466; *A-G v Drapers' Co* (1869) LR 9 Eq 69; *Debenham v King's College, Cambridge* (1884) Cab & El 438; *Faraday v Tamworth Union* (1916) 86 LJ Ch 436. See also AGENCY vol 1 (2008) PARA 101; AUCTION; BUILDING CONTRACTS, ARCHITECTS, ENGINEERS, VALUERS AND SURVEYORS. If there is no trade usage, the court may take into account any bargaining between the parties: *Scarisbrick v Parkinson* (1869) 20 LT 175; *Way v Latilla* [1937] 3 All ER 759, HL. See also *Barclays Bank plc v Fairclough Building Ltd* [1995] QB 214, [1995] 1 All ER 289, CA. As to evidence of usage see CUSTOM AND USAGE. Functions of a local authority under the Supply of Goods and Services Act 1982 are 'relevant functions' for the purposes of the Regulatory Enforcement and Sanctions Act 2008 Pt 1 (ss 1–21): see PARA 178 note 3.

2   Supply of Goods and Services Act 1982 s 15(2).

3   Cf *Taylor v Laird* (1856) 25 LJ Ex 329 at 332 per Pollock CB: 'Suppose I clean your property without your knowledge, have I then a claim on you for payment? One cleans another's shoes;

what can the other do but put them on? Is that evidence of a contract to pay for the cleaning?'. See RESTITUTION vol 40(1) (2007 Reissue) PARA 128.

4 For examples of the principle see *Reeve v Reeve* (1858) 1 F & F 280; *Taylor v Brewer* (1813) 1 M & S 290; *Moffatt v Laurie* (1855) 15 CB 583; *Ex p Metcalfe* (1856) 6 E & B 287; *Hingeston v Kelly* (1849) 18 LJ Ex 360; and AGENCY vol 1 (2008) PARA 101; BUILDING CONTRACTS; EMPLOYMENT.

5 See AGENCY vol 1 (2008) PARA 101; EMPLOYMENT vol 39 (2009) PARA 22 et seq.

6 *Farnsworth v Garrard* (1807) 1 Camp 38 at 39 per Lord Ellenborough: 'If there has been no beneficial service there shall be no pay, but if some benefit has been derived, though not to the extent expected, this shall go to the amount of the plaintiff's demand; ... the claim shall be co-extensive with the benefit'. Cf *Duncan v Blundell* (1820) 3 Stark 6 at 7 per Bayley J; *Pearce v Tucker* (1862) 3 F & F 136. See also PARA 162.

7 *Hughes v Lenny* (1839) 5 M & W 183. As to remuneration by way of quantum meruit see PARA 158; and RESTITUTION.

8 *Meriel v Wymondsold* (1661) Hard 205. See also the cases cited in PARA 164 note 5.

9 *Chidley v Norris* (1862) 3 F & F 228. But the immediate employer is liable if he leads the person employed to believe that he, and not the third party, will pay for the work: *Chidley v Norris* (1862) 3 F & F 228. See also AGENCY vol 1 (2008) PARA 157.

10 Story on Bailments (9th Edn, 1878) s 425; *Wilmot v Smith* (1828) 3 C & P 453.

158. Payment where work not completed. The issue of whether payment may be demanded prior to completion of the work will depend as a matter of construction upon whether the contract consists of an entire obligation (sometimes called a 'lump sum contract') or divisible obligations[1].

Where a man is employed to do work under a divisible contract, there is an express or implied agreement that payments will be made in proportion to the work performed[2], unless a trade custom to the contrary can be proved[3]. Where the work is not completed, whether through the fault of the workman[4] or otherwise[5], in the absence of an express or implied agreement to complete it, the hirer may nevertheless have to pay for the work actually done and for the materials provided[6].

A man who undertakes to do specified work in connection with a chattel for an agreed sum to be paid on completion (a lump sum contract), but who fails substantially to complete the work, is not entitled to recover the price agreed upon, nor even the actual value of the work he has done on a quantum meruit basis[7], unless the failure to complete it is due to the hirer's default or the parties can be held to have entered into a new contract, or the failure to perform is due to impossibility or frustration[8].

However, where a man engages to do work for a lump sum payable on completion and the work is substantially performed, the hirer cannot, as a rule, repudiate liability on the ground that the work is in some respects not in accordance with the specification if the breach does not go to the root of the contract; in such a case he is liable to pay the agreed price, less a deduction based on the cost of making good the defects or omissions proved[9]. Even if in such a case the parties have made entire performance a condition precedent to payment, a hirer who takes the benefit of the work done waives the condition and must pay the agreed price subject to appropriate deductions[10].

If the employer refuses to perform or renders himself incapable of performing his part of the contract or by his own acts prevents the full performance of the contract by the workman, the workman may rescind the contract and sue upon a quantum meruit[11]; or he may sue for damages for breach of contract[12]. Where a person sues upon a quantum meruit he must be prepared to show what the work was worth[13].

If a new contract is made to pay for the work actually done, the workman is entitled to recover the price agreed upon less a deduction, the measure of the deduction being generally the sum which it would take to alter or complete the work so as to make it correspond with the specification[14].

Where a contract has become impossible of performance or has been frustrated, the parties' rights and liabilities under it are governed by statute[15].

Where the hirer is under no obligation to pay for the work done, he incurs no additional obligation by reason of the fact that the workman has incorporated his own materials with those of the hirer[16].

1 See CONTRACT vol 9(1) (Reissue) PARA 942. Notice, however, that in most sizeable modern contracts the contractual terms will provide for payment by instalments, thus generally rendering this distinction irrelevant.

2 *Roberts v Havelock* (1832) 3 B & Ad 404; *The Tergeste* [1903] P 26; cf *J Rosenthal & Sons Ltd v Esmail* [1965] 2 All ER 860, [1965] 1 WLR 1117, HL.

3 *Gillett v Mawman* (1808) 1 Taunt 137. See CUSTOM AND USAGE.

4 *Roberts v Havelock* (1832) 3 B & Ad 404.

5 *Menetone v Athawes* (1764) 3 Burr 1592.

6 *Appleby v Myers* (1867) LR 2 CP 651 at 660 per Blackburn J.

7 *Sinclair v Bowles* (1829) 9 B & C 92. Cf *Sumpter v Hedges* [1898] 1 QB 673, CA (building contract), followed in *Wheeler v Stratton* (1911) 105 LT 786, DC, and *Small & Sons Ltd v Middlesex Real Estates Ltd* [1921] WN 245. See also *Munro v Butt* (1858) 8 E & B 738; *Ellis v Hamlen* (1810) 3 Taunt 52; *Gillett v Mawman* (1808) 1 Taunt 137; *Adlard v Booth* (1835) 7 C & P 108 (explained in *Appleby v Myers* (1867) LR 2 CP 651 at 652 per Blackburn J); *Cutter v Powell* (1795) 6 Term Rep 320; *Bates v Hudson* (1825) 6 Dow & Ry KB 3; *Hulle v Heightman* (1802) 2 East 145; *Vigers v Cook* [1919] 2 KB 475, CA; *Crosthwaite v Gardner* (1852) 18 QB 640; *Bolton v Mahadeva* [1972] 2 All ER 1322, [1972] 1 WLR 1009, CA. See generally BUILDING CONTRACTS, ARCHITECTS, ENGINEERS, VALUERS AND SURVEYORS; CONTRACT; EMPLOYMENT.

8 *Hoenig v Isaacs* [1952] 2 All ER 176 at 181–182, CA, per Denning LJ; *Appleby v Myers* (1867) LR 2 CP 651 at 661 per Blackburn J.

9 *Hoenig v Isaacs* [1952] 2 All ER 176, CA, applying *Mondel v Steel* (1841) 8 M & W 858 and *H Dakin & Co Ltd v Lee* [1916] 1 KB 566, CA. See also *Bolton v Mahadeva* [1972] 2 All ER 1322, [1972] 1 WLR 1009, CA. As to the effect of negligence or lack of skill on the workman's part see further PARA 162.

10 *Hoenig v Isaacs* [1952] 2 All ER 176 at 181, CA, per Denning LJ.

11 See e g *Planchè v Colburn* (1831) 8 Bing 14; *Kewley v Stokes* (1846) 2 Car & Kir 435; *Prickett v Badger* (1856) 1 CBNS 296; *Burn v Miller* (1813) 4 Taunt 745; *Craven-Ellis v Canons Ltd* [1936] 2 KB 403 at 410–411, [1936] 2 All ER 1066 at 1072–1073, CA, per Greer LJ. See further AGENCY vol 1 (2008) PARA 108; BUILDING CONTRACTS, ARCHITECTS, ENGINEERS, VALUERS AND SURVEYORS; CONTRACT.

12 See AGENCY vol 1 (2008) PARA 108; BUILDING CONTRACTS, ARCHITECTS, ENGINEERS, VALUERS AND SURVEYORS; CONTRACT.

13 *Basten v Butler* (1806) 7 East 479.

14 *Thornton v Place* (1832) 1 Mood & R 218 at 219 per Parke J; *Ranger v Great Western Rly Co* (1854) 5 HL Cas 72.

15 See the Law Reform (Frustrated Contracts) Act 1943; and CONTRACT vol 9(1) (Reissue) PARAS 903, 912 et seq.

16 *Sinclair v Bowles* (1829) 9 B & C 92.

159. Extras. If a workman without any order or request does more work than was originally stipulated for in the contract, and the hirer did not acquiesce in the change, although the extra work is essential to the proper performance of the contract, the hirer, in the absence of bad faith or concealment[1], is not bound to pay more than the sum originally agreed upon by him[2]. So if a workman, employed to do specified work on a chattel for an agreed sum, instead of doing the specified work does different, even if better, work, he can recover from the hirer neither the agreed sum under the special contract, nor the value of the work done on a quantum meruit basis, unless the hirer has sanctioned or acquiesced in the change. The mere fact that the hirer has received the chattel on which the work has been done and has sold it at an enhanced price does not amount to acquiescence[3].

But extra work which, during the course of the work, has been ordered or assented to by the hirer, must be paid for on a quantum meruit basis. In such a case, the contract is binding so far as it can be traced, and the quantum meruit applies to the remainder[4].

1　Story on Bailments (9th Edn, 1878) s 425.
2　*Brown v Lord Rollo* (1832) 10 Sh 667, Ct of Sess; *Wilmot v Smith* (1828) 3 C & P 453. See generally BUILDING CONTRACTS, ARCHITECTS, ENGINEERS, VALUERS AND SURVEYORS; CONTRACT.
3　*Forman & Co Pty Ltd v The Liddesdale* [1900] AC 190, PC. Cf *Munro v Butt* (1858) 8 E & B 738; and PARA 157 note 3.
4　*Napier v Lang* (1834) 12 Sh 523, Ct of Sess; *Shipton v Casson* (1826) 5 B & C 378.

160.　Hirer must not obstruct workman. The hirer must afford the workman every reasonable facility for entering upon and completing the contract which he has undertaken to perform[1]. If, after the contract has been entered upon, the hirer wilfully obstructs the workman and thereby retards him in his employment, or intervenes without just cause so as to prevent its completion, he is liable to the workman for the loss actually caused by his interference[2]. A similar duty and liability in case of default is imposed upon the hirer, if it is one of the terms of the bargain that he will supply the workman with the necessary materials for the employment undertaken[3].

1　*Wells v Army and Navy Co-operative Society Ltd* (1902) 86 LT 764; *Prickett v Badger* (1856) 1 CBNS 296; *Green v Lucas* (1875) 33 LT 584, CA; *Russell v Viscount Sa da Bandeira* (1862) 13 CBNS 149; *Courtnay v Waterford and Central Ireland Rly* Co (1878) 4 LR Ir 11.
2　*Mackay v Dick* (1881) 6 App Cas 251, HL. See also *Lilley v Barnsley* (1844) 2 Mood & R 548. The workman can claim damages for breach of contract, or under a quantum meruit claim to recover a reasonable remuneration for his partial performance: *Planchè v Colburn* (1831) 8 Bing 14. Cf *White & Carter (Councils) Ltd v McGregor* [1962] AC 413, [1961] 3 All ER 1178, HL; *Hounslow London Borough Council v Twickenham Garden Developments Ltd* [1971] Ch 233, [1970] 3 All ER 326; *Bolwell Fibreglass Pty Ltd v Foley* [1984] VR 97; and see CONTRACT.
3　Pothier's Contrat de Louage s 410.

(iii)　Workman's Obligations

161.　Obligation to do the work. The first obligation of the workman is to perform his undertaking[1]. If the workman agrees to perform work which will put the hirer's goods in a certain condition, and the hirer relies on the workman's skill and judgment, the workman owes an absolute obligation to put the goods into that condition and his failure to do so constitutes a total failure of consideration[2]. The workman will be relieved of the duty to perform, however, if the performance is rendered impossible by the hirer's act[3] or by circumstances beyond the workman's control, as where the chattel upon which the work is to be performed is accidentally destroyed by fire[4]. However, the fact that the work was, by its nature, impossible to perform will not relieve the workman from liability for failure to perform where the hirer has relied on his skill and judgment[5]. The workman is responsible if the impossibility should have been foreseen by him, and if the hirer has acted in good faith in relying on his ability to perform the work[6]. Where no time for performance is fixed, the undertaking must be performed within a reasonable time[7]. Where, under a contract for the supply of a service[8] by a supplier acting in the course of a business[9], the time for the service to be carried out is not fixed by the contract, left to be fixed in a manner agreed by the contract or determined by the course of dealing between the parties, there is an implied term that the supplier will carry out the service within a reasonable time[10]. What is a reasonable time is a question of fact[11]. If by his own act the workman incapacitates himself from performing his contract, he forthwith becomes liable for the breach[12].

1   *Alderslade v Hendon Laundry Ltd* [1945] KB 189 at 193, [1945] 1 All ER 244 at 246, CA, per Lord Greene MR. See also Palmer on Bailment (3rd Edn, 2009) para 15-037 et seq; Story on Bailments (9th Edn, 1878) s 428.
2   *GK Serigraphics v Dispro Ltd* [1980] CA Transcript 916.
3   See e g *Holme v Guppy* (1838) 3 M & W 387; and see generally CONTRACT.
4   *Menetone v Athawes* (1764) 3 Burr 1592. See also *Appleby v Myers* (1867) LR 2 CP 651. As to the discharge of contracts on the ground of impossibility of performance or frustration, and for statutory provisions as to the effect of frustration, see CONTRACT vol 9(1) (Reissue) PARA 888 et seq.
5   *Duncan v Blundell* (1820) 3 Stark 6 at 7 per Bayley J; *Pearce v Tucker* (1862) 3 F & F 136.
6   *Combe v Simmonds* (1853) 1 WR 289; *Pearce v Tucker* (1862) 3 F & F 136.
7   See e g *Wigginton v Dodd* (1862) 2 F & F 844; and see CONTRACT vol 9(1) (Reissue) PARA 929.
8   As to the meaning of 'contract for the supply of a service' see PARA 156.
9   As to the meaning of 'business' see PARA 180 note 4.
10 Supply of Goods and Services Act 1982 s 14(1). Functions of a local authority under the Supply of Goods and Services Act 1982 are 'relevant functions' for the purposes of the Regulatory Enforcement and Sanctions Act 2008 Pt 1 (ss 1–21): see PARA 178 note 3.
11 Supply of Goods and Services Act 1982 s 14(2). As to the exclusion of implied terms see s 16; the Unfair Contract Terms Act 1977; PARA 156; and CONTRACT vol 9(1) (Reissue) PARA 820 et seq.
12 See e g *Planchè v Colburn* (1831) 8 Bing 14; and see generally CONTRACT.

162.   Obligation to exercise skill. In a contract for the supply of a service[1] where the supplier is acting in the course of a business[2], there is an implied term that the supplier will carry out the service with reasonable care and skill[3]. This provision is in conformity with the general rule of common law that all workmen undertake to use the skills appropriate to their particular crafts[4]. The acceptance by a person of work of a class which he holds himself out as qualified to do amounts to a warranty on his part that he possesses the requisite skill and ability to do that work[5]. Where there is neither a general nor a particular representation of skill and ability, a workman incurs no responsibility in respect of his want of either. If, for instance, a man should employ a general labourer to clean or mend his watch, the employer would probably be held to have incurred all risks himself[6]. Moreover, the public profession of an art or craft amounts only to a representation that the artificer or craftsman is reasonably competent to carry out any work of the class he professes to do, and does not make him an insurer; he contracts only to display sufficient skill and knowledge of his calling to perform all ordinary duties connected with it[7].

When through negligence or lack of skill the workman fails to perform in a workmanlike manner the work he has undertaken, he may forfeit in whole or part his claim to remuneration[8], and, in addition, he may become liable to the hirer for the loss sustained in consequence of his breach of duty[9]; but acceptance by the hirer of the labour after a slight and unimportant breach of the contract may amount to a waiver of the breach[10].

Where the contract is a contract for work and materials, and the hirer makes known the purpose for which the materials are intended and that he relies on the workman's skill and judgment, there is implied at common law a warranty that the materials are fit for the purpose. The workman is accordingly liable for damage resulting from unfitness of the materials, even though they may have been supplied by a third party[11]. In a contract for work and materials there is also, at common law, irrespective of the hirer's reliance on the workman's skill and judgment, an implied warranty that the materials are of good or merchantable quality[12]. These warranties have now been substantially superseded by statute[13].

1   As to the meaning of 'contract for the supply of a service' see PARA 156.

2   As to the meaning of 'business' see PARA 180 note 4.

3   Supply of Goods and Services Act 1982 s 13; Palmer on Bailment (3rd Edn, 2009) para 15-037 et seq. As to implied terms in contracts see CONTRACT vol 9(1) (Reissue) PARA 778 et seq. As to the exclusion of implied terms see the Supply of Goods and Services Act 1982 s 16; the Unfair Contract Terms Act 1977; PARA 156; and CONTRACT. Functions of a local authority under the Supply of Goods and Services Act 1982 are 'relevant functions' for the purposes of the Regulatory Enforcement and Sanctions Act 2008 Pt 1 (ss 1–21): see PARA 178 note 3.

     In exercise of his power under the Supply of Goods and Services Act 1982 s 12(4) (see PARA 156), the Secretary of State has provided by order that s 13 is not to apply to the following services: (1) the services of an advocate in court or before any tribunal, inquiry or arbitrator and in carrying out preliminary work directly affecting the conduct of the hearing (Supply of Services (Exclusion of Implied Terms) Order 1982, SI 1982/1771, art 2(1)); (2) the services rendered to a company by a director of the company in his capacity as such (art 2(2)); (3) the services rendered to a building society by a director in his capacity as such (Supply of Services (Exclusion of Implied Terms) Order 1983, SI 1983/902, art 2(1)(a)); (4) the services rendered to an industrial or provident society by any member of the committee of management or other directing body in his capacity as such (art 2(1)(b)); (5) the services rendered by an arbitrator, including an umpire, in his capacity as such (Supply of Services (Exclusion of Implied Terms) Order 1985, SI 1985/1, art 2).

     As to the duty of care owed by tour operators under the Supply of Goods and Services Act 1982 s 13 see *Wilson v Best Travel Ltd* [1993] 1 All ER 353, DC.

4   Ie *spondet peritiam artis*. See *Smith v Eric S Bush, Harris v Wyre Forest District Council* [1990] 1 AC 831 at 843, [1989] 2 All ER 514 at 519–520, HL, per Lord Templeman.

5   *Duncan v Blundell* (1820) 3 Stark 6; *Harmer v Cornelius* (1858) 5 CBNS 236 at 246 per Willes J; 1 Bell's Com lib 3, part 1, c 3, s 2, tit Skill; *Coggs v Bernard* (1703) 2 Ld Raym 909; *Barclays Bank plc v Fairclough Building Ltd* [1995] QB 214, [1995] 1 All ER 289, CA. Compare PARA 127 notes 1–3 (gratuitous bailment). See also the cases cited in PARA 161 note 6; and see NEGLIGENCE vol 78 (2010) PARAS 23, 47 et seq.

6   Jones on Bailments (4th Edn, 1833) p 100; *Harmer v Cornelius* (1858) 5 CBNS 236 at 246 per Willes J.

7   *Smith v Eric S Bush, Harris v Wyre Forest District Council* [1990] 1 AC 831 at 843, [1989] 2 All ER 514 at 519–520, HL, per Lord Templeman; *Lanphier v Phipos* (1838) 8 C & P 475 at 479 per Tindal CJ.

8   Cf *Cousins v Paddon* (1835) 2 Cr M & R 547; *Bracey v Carter* (1840) 12 Ad & El 373; *Shaw v Arden* (1832) 9 Bing 287; *Moneypenny v Hartland* (1824) 1 C & P 352; *Pardow v Webb* (1842) Car & M 531; and see further PARA 158. See also AGENCY vol 1 (2008) PARA 101 et seq; BUILDING CONTRACTS, ARCHITECTS, ENGINEERS, VALUERS AND SURVEYORS.

9   *Combe v Simmonds* (1853) 1 WR 289; Story on Bailments (9th Edn, 1878) s 431; cf *Seare v Prentice* (1807) 8 East 348; and see NEGLIGENCE.

10   *Lucas v Godwin* (1837) 3 Bing NC 737; *Hoenig v Isaacs* [1952] 2 All ER 176, CA.

11   *GH Myers & Co v Brent Cross Service Co* [1934] 1 KB 46, DC; *Stewart v Reavell's Garage* [1952] 2 QB 545, [1952] 1 All ER 1191 (applying principles laid down in relation to the sale of goods); cf *Cammell Laird & Co Ltd v Manganese Bronze and Brass Co Ltd* [1934] AC 402, HL; *Samuels v Davis* [1943] KB 526, [1943] 2 All ER 3, CA; *Dodd and Dodd v Wilson and McWilliam* [1946] 2 All ER 691 (implied condition of fitness of toxoid used by veterinary surgeons); *Watson v Buckley, Osborne, Garrett & Co Ltd and Wyrovoys Products Ltd* [1940] 1 All ER 174; *Holmes v Ashford* [1950] 2 All ER 76, CA; *Ingham v Emes* [1955] 2 QB 366, [1955] 2 All ER 740, CA; *Young and Marten Ltd v McManus Childs Ltd* [1969] 1 AC 454, [1968] 2 All ER 1169, HL (roof tiling); *Gloucestershire County Council v Richardson* [1969] 1 AC 480, [1968] 2 All ER 1181, HL (concrete columns for construction project). As to implied conditions of fitness on the sale of goods see SALE OF GOODS AND SUPPLY OF SERVICES vol 41 (2005 Reissue) PARAS 77–82.

12   See the cases cited in note 11.

13   See PARA 165 et seq.

163. Obligation to exercise care. As the workman is entitled to a reward, either by express agreement or by implication, he is obliged not only to perform his work with reasonable care and skill, but also to take ordinary care of the chattel entrusted to him[1], and to restore it to the hirer at the expiration of the period for which it was entrusted to him. If, therefore, he detains it beyond the proper period, he is guilty of a breach of duty, the measure of damages for which is prima facie the sum which would have been earned in the ordinary course of employment of the chattel during the period of its detention[2]; and the workman is liable as an insurer if it becomes lost or destroyed[3]. Where, however, it is lost or injured whilst properly in the workman's custody, he will be responsible for the full amount of the damage sustained, unless he can show[4] that the loss or injury is not attributable to any want of reasonable care on his part[5].

The workman is liable for any loss of the chattel arising from the unauthorised act of his servant, providing that the servant was acting within the scope of his employment[6].

1 Jones on Bailments (4th Edn, 1833) p 91; *Leck v Maestaer* (1807) 1 Camp 138; *Clarke v Earnshaw* (1818) Gow 30; *Becker v Lavender Ltd* (1946) 62 TLR 504 (misdelivery); *Sinclair v Juner* 1952 SC 35, Ct of Sess; *Spriggs v Sotheby Parke Bernet & Co Ltd* [1986] 1 Lloyd's Rep 487, CA.

2 *Re Trent and Humber Co, ex p Cambrian Steam Packet Co* (1868) 4 Ch App 112 at 117 per Lord Cairns LC.

3 *Shaw & Co v Symmons & Sons* [1917] 1 KB 799.

4 See PARAS 149, 184 note 1.

5 *Leck v Maestaer* (1807) 1 Camp 138; *Clarke v Earnshaw* (1818) Gow 30. Cf *Gillett v Mawman* (1808) 1 Taunt 137; *Wilson v Powis* (1826) 11 Moore CP 543; *Jobson v Palmer* [1893] 1 Ch 71; *Bullen v Swan Electric Engraving Co* (1907) 23 TLR 258, CA; *Morison, Pollexfen and Blair v Walton* (1909), cited [1915] 1 KB at 90, HL; *Joseph Travers & Sons Ltd v Cooper* [1915] 1 KB 73, CA; *Cowan v Blackwill Motor Caravan Conversions Ltd* [1978] RTR 421, CA; *Idnani v Elisha* [1979] RTR 488, CA (motor repairers); *Spriggs v Sotheby Parke Bernet & Co Ltd* [1986] 1 Lloyd's Rep 487, CA (auctioneer in possession of diamond); *Lockspeiser Aircraft Ltd v Brooklands Aircraft Co Ltd* (1990) Times, 7 March (aircraft); *Coopers Payen Ltd v Southampton Container Terminal Ltd* [2003] EWCA Civ 1223, [2004] 1 Lloyd's Rep 331, [2003] All ER (D) 220 (Jul) (movement of equipment). Cf *Sinclair v Juner* 1952 SC 35, Ct of Sess. The liability continues after the work is done until the original relationship is expressly altered (*Mitchell v Davis* (1920) 37 TLR 68); or until the bailor has, by committing a repudiatory breach of his implied obligation to collect the goods within a reasonable time, forfeited the right to sue for breach of the bailee's duty of reasonable care (*Pedrick v Morning Star Motors Ltd* (14 February 1979, unreported), CA; *Ridyard v Roberts* (16 May 1980, unreported), CA; *JJD SA (a company) v Avon Tyres Ltd* (1999) Times, 25 January).

6 *Morris v CW Martin & Sons Ltd* [1966] 1 QB 716, [1965] 2 All ER 725, CA; and see the cases cited in PARAS 146, 148.

164. Delegation. In general, the workman's obligation to perform the work is personal to him. The hirer is presumed to have engaged the workman on the strength of his personal skill and reputation. The workman cannot, therefore, delegate the work to a third party and is prohibited from conferring possession on a third party for that purpose[1]. This general rule applies irrespective of whether the contract expressly obliges the workman to perform in person or not and irrespective of whether the hirer has proved that he relied on the workman's personal skill and reputation in entrusting the work to him[2]. A workman who delegates in breach of the general rule does so at his peril[3]. He becomes strictly liable for the safety of the goods as an insurer[4]. Further, the third party to whom the work is delegated in breach of the general rule cannot bring a claim in contract to recover the cost of his services from the hirer, because there is no privity of contract between the hirer and himself[5].

The general rule may be displaced by the express terms of the contract, or by a course of dealing between the parties[6], or by the particular circumstances of the case. In some cases the nature of the work will be such that permission to delegate or sub-contract can be inferred[7]. In others, the workman may be entitled to delegate non-specialist aspects of the work, such as the return carriage of the goods to the hirer when the work is completed[8]. But the workman remains liable for any default which his delegate or sub-contractor commits during the period of his possession of the goods[9].

If the party who has commissioned the work has, after receiving notice that the contract has been transferred to a third party, allowed the assignee to proceed with the work, there may be a novation of the contract, and the assignee is in that event entitled to sue the employer for the value of the work done by him[10]. Whether there is a novation depends upon the circumstances of the case.

The right of a workman to receive payment for his work, as distinct from the liability to perform the work, may be assigned in the same manner as any other debt[11].

1   *Davies v Collins* [1945] 1 All ER 247, CA; *Martin v N Negin Ltd* (1945) 172 LT 275, CA (dry-cleaning; but in both cases the court relied on the express terms of the contract); *Edwards v Newland & Co (E Burchett Ltd, third party)* [1950] 2 KB 534, [1950] 1 All ER 1072, CA (warehousing); *Garnham, Harris & Elton Ltd v Alfred W Ellis (Transport) Ltd* [1967] 2 All ER 940, [1967] 1 WLR 940 (carriage; but goods exceptionally valuable and sub-carriers negligently selected); *Hobbs v Petersham Transport Co Pty Ltd, Petersham Transport Co Pty Ltd v ASEA Electric (Australia) Pty Ltd* (1971) 45 ALJR 356 at 362 per Windeyer J, Aust HC (carriage); *Cassils & Co and Sassoon & Co v Holden Wood Bleaching Co Ltd* (1914) 84 LJKB 834 at 839–840, CA, per Buckley LJ, at 843–844 per Phillimore LJ, and at 845–846 per Pickford LJ (bleaching); *Morgan v Maurer & Son* (1964) 30 Ir Jur Rep 31 (repair of watch); *East West Corpn v DKBS AF 1912 A/S, Utaniko Ltd v P & O Nedlloyd BV* [2003] EWCA Civ 83, [2003] QB 1509, [2003] 2 All ER 700 (warehousing and port agents); *Southway Group Ltd v Wolff and Wolff* (1991) 28 Con LR 109, 57 BLR 33, CA (developing fitted kitchens). Cf the Supply of Goods and Services Act 1982 s 13; and see PARA 162; and AGENCY vol 1 (2008) PARA 48 et seq; CONSUMER PROTECTION vol 21 (2011) PARA 429; CONTRACT vol 9(1) (Reissue) PARA 873; SALE OF GOODS AND SUPPLY OF SERVICES vol 41 (2005 Reissue) PARA 97.

2   *Edwards v Newland & Co (E Burchett Ltd, third party)* [1950] 2 KB 534, [1950] 1 All ER 1072, CA.

3   See the cases cited in note 1; and PARA 146.

4   For qualifications on the workman's liability as an insurer see PARAS 162–163.

5   *Schmaling v Thomlinson* (1815) 6 Taunt 147; and see *Cull v Backhouse* (1793) 6 Taunt 148n, note (a). See generally AGENCY vol 1 (2008) PARA 54 et seq.

6   *Krieger v Bell* [1943] SASR 153 at 172 per Mayo J, S Aust SC (repair of truck).

7   *Edwards v Newland & Co (E Burchett Ltd, third party)* [1950] 2 KB 534 at 539, [1950] 1 All ER 1072 at 1076, CA, per Somervell LJ, and at 542 and 1081 per Denning LJ; *Robson v Drummond* (1831) 2 B & Ad 303; *British Waggon Co and Parkgate Waggon Co v Lea & Co* (1880) 5 QBD 149.

8   *Punch v Savoy Jewellers Ltd* (1986) 26 DLR (4th) 546, Ont CA (repair of brooch; method of return carriage failed to take account of value of brooch; bailee liable).

9   *Genn v Winkel* (1912) 28 TLR 483, CA; *Palmer on Bailment* (3rd Edn, 2009) paras 15-032–15-035. See also *British Road Services Ltd v Arthur V Crutchley & Co Ltd (Factory Guards Ltd, third party)* [1968] 1 All ER 811, [1968] 1 Lloyd's Rep 271, CA (warehouseman entitled to delegate security of warehouse to carefully selected firm of security guards, but remained answerable for defaults of latter); *G Bosman (Transport) Ltd v LKW Walter International Transportorganisation AG* [2002] EWCA Civ 850, [2002] All ER (D) 13 (May) (yard owner responsible for the goods delivered to the yard to look after irrespective of the identity of the person to whom it delegated the discharge of its duties). See also *East West Corpn v DKBS AF 1912 A/S, Utaniko Ltd v P & O Nedlloyd BV* [2003] EWCA Civ 83, [2003] QB 1509, [2003] 2 All ER 700.

10   *Aspinall v London and North Western Rly Co* (1853) 11 Hare 325; *Oldfield v Lowe* (1829) 9 B & C 73. As to the assignor's rights against the assignee see *Humphreys v Jones* (1850) 5 Exch 952.

11 *Russell & Co Ltd v Austin Fryers* (1909) 25 TLR 414. As to the assignment of rights under contracts see generally CHOSES IN ACTION vol 13 (2009) PARAS 6, 13 et seq; CONTRACT vol 9(1) (Reissue) PARA 754 et seq.

165. Liability for materials supplied by workman. Certain terms are implied by statute into contracts for the transfer of goods[1]. In the Supply of Goods and Services Act 1982, a 'contract for the transfer of goods' means a contract under which one person transfers or agrees to transfer to another the property in goods, other than an excepted contract[2]. An excepted contract means any of the following: (1) a contract for the sale of goods[3]; (2) a hire-purchase agreement[4]; (3) a transfer or agreement to transfer which is made by deed and for which there is no consideration other than the presumed consideration imported by the deed[5]; (4) a contract intended to operate by way of mortgage, pledge, charge or other security[6].

For the purposes of the Act, a contract is a contract for the transfer of goods whether or not services are also provided or to be provided under the contract, and (subject to the provisions relating to excepted contracts[7]) whatever is the nature of the consideration for the transfer or agreement to transfer[8].

A contract for work and materials[9] is a contract for the transfer of goods unless otherwise excepted. Thus where a bailee for work and labour agrees, in addition to performing work upon the bailor's goods, to supply materials which are to be added to or intermixed with the bailor's goods, this is a contract for the transfer of goods unless it is an excepted contract within one of the categories described above.

Where a right, duty or liability would arise under a contract for the transfer of goods by implication of law, it may be negatived or varied by express agreement[10], or by the course of dealing between the parties, or by such usage as binds both parties to the contract[11]. An express condition or warranty does not negative a condition or warranty implied by statute[12] into a contract for the transfer of goods, unless inconsistent with it[13].

1 See the Supply of Goods and Services Act 1982 ss 1–5A; and SALE OF GOODS AND SUPPLY OF SERVICES vol 41 (2005 Reissue) PARAS 32, 70 et seq.
2 Supply of Goods and Services Act 1982 s 1(1) (s 1(1), (3) amended by the Sale and Supply of Goods Act 1994 s 7, Sch 2 para 6(2)). Functions of a local authority under the Supply of Goods and Services Act 1982 are 'relevant functions' for the purposes of the Regulatory Enforcement and Sanctions Act 2008 Pt 1 (ss 1–21): see PARA 178 note 3.
3 Supply of Goods and Services Act 1982 s 1(2)(a). As to the meaning of 'goods' see PARA 175. 'Transferee', in relation to a contract for the transfer of goods, means (depending on the context) a person to whom the property in the goods is transferred under the contract, or a person to whom the property is to be so transferred, or a person to whom the rights under the contract of either of those persons have passed: s 18(1). 'Transferor', in relation to a contract for the transfer of goods, means (depending on the context) a person who transfers the property in goods under the contract, or a person who agrees to do so, or a person to whom the duties under the contract of either of those persons have passed: s 18(1).
4 Supply of Goods and Services Act 1982 s 1(2)(b). As to the meaning of 'hire-purchase agreement' see PARA 175 note 11.
5 Supply of Goods and Services Act 1982 s 1(2)(d).
6 Supply of Goods and Services Act 1982 s 1(2)(e).
7 See the Supply of Goods and Services Act 1982 s 1(2) (amended in relation to England and Wales by SI 2005/871 and in relation to Northern Ireland by SI 2005/1452); and the text and notes 3–6.
8 Supply of Goods and Services Act 1982 s 1(3) (as amended: see note 2).
9 See PARA 156.
10 Ie subject to the Supply of Goods and Services Act 1982 s 11(2) (see the text and note 13) and the Unfair Contract Terms Act 1977 (see CONTRACT vol 9(1) (Reissue) PARA 820 et seq).
11 Supply of Goods and Services Act 1982 s 11(1).

12 See the text and note 1.
13 Supply of Goods and Services Act 1982 s 11(2). Nothing in ss 1–5A prejudices the operation of any other enactment or rule of law whereby any condition or warranty (other than one in relation to quality or fitness) is to be implied in a contract for the transfer of goods: s 11(3).

166. Right to transfer goods. In a contract for the transfer of goods[1], except as otherwise provided[2], there is: (1) an implied condition on the part of the transferor[3] that in the case of a transfer of the property in the goods he has a right to transfer the property and in the case of an agreement to transfer the property in the goods that he will have such a right at the time when the property is to be transferred[4]; (2) an implied warranty that the goods are free, and will remain free until the time when the property is to be transferred, from any charge or encumbrance not disclosed or known to the transferee[5] when the contract is made[6]; (3) an implied warranty that the transferee will enjoy quiet possession of the goods, except so far as it may be disturbed by the owner or other person entitled to the benefit of any charge or encumbrance disclosed or known to the transferee when the contract is made[7].

In a contract for the transfer of goods, in the case of which there appears from the contract, or there is to be inferred from its circumstances, an intention that the transferor should transfer only such title as he or a third person may have[8], there is: (a) an implied warranty that all charges or encumbrances known to the transferor and not known to the transferee have been disclosed to the transferee before the contract is made[9]; (b) an implied warranty that the transferee's quiet possession of the goods will not be disturbed by any of the following: (i) the transferor[10]; (ii) in a case where the parties intend that the transferor should transfer only such title as a third person may have, that person[11]; or (iii) anyone claiming through or under the transferor or through or under that third person, otherwise than under a charge or encumbrance disclosed or known to the transferee before the contract is made[12].

Provision is made for the exclusion or restriction of liability for breach of these implied terms[13].

1   As to the meaning of 'contract for the transfer of goods' see PARA 165.
2   Ie by the Supply of Goods and Services Act 1982 s 2(3)–(5): see the text and notes 8–12.
3   As to the meaning of 'transferor' see PARA 165 note 3.
4   Supply of Goods and Services Act 1982 s 2(1). See SALE OF GOODS AND SUPPLY OF SERVICES vol 41 (2005 Reissue) PARA 70. Functions of a local authority under the Supply of Goods and Services Act 1982 are 'relevant functions' for the purposes of the Regulatory Enforcement and Sanctions Act 2008 Pt 1 (ss 1–21): see PARA 178 note 3.
5   As to the meaning of 'transferee' see PARA 165 note 3.
6   Supply of Goods and Services Act 1982 s 2(2)(a). See SALE OF GOODS AND SUPPLY OF SERVICES vol 41 (2005 Reissue) PARA 70.
7   Supply of Goods and Services Act 1982 s 2(2)(b). See SALE OF GOODS AND SUPPLY OF SERVICES vol 41 (2005 Reissue) PARA 70.
8   Supply of Goods and Services Act 1982 s 2(3).
9   Supply of Goods and Services Act 1982 s 2(4).
10   Supply of Goods and Services Act 1982 s 2(5)(a).
11   Supply of Goods and Services Act 1982 s 2(5)(b).
12   Supply of Goods and Services Act 1982 s 2(5)(c).
13   See the Supply of Goods and Services Act 1982 s 11(1), (2); the Unfair Contract Terms Act 1977; PARA 165 text and notes 10–13; and CONTRACT vol 9(1) (Reissue) PARA 820 et seq.

167. Correspondence with description. Where, under a contract for the transfer of goods[1], the transferor[2] transfers or agrees to transfer the property by description[3], there is an implied condition that the goods will correspond with the description[4]. If the transferor transfers or agrees to transfer the property by sample as well as by description it is not sufficient that the bulk of the goods corresponds with the sample if the goods do not also correspond with the description[5].

Provision is made for exclusion of these implied terms[6] and also for modification of remedies for breach of statutory condition in non-consumer cases[7].

1 As to the meaning of 'contract for the transfer of goods' see PARA 165.

2 As to the meaning of 'transferor' see PARA 165 note 3.

3 Supply of Goods and Services Act 1982 s 3(1). A contract is not prevented from being a contract by description by reason only that, being exposed for supply, the goods are selected by the transferee: s 3(4). As to the meaning of 'transferee' see PARA 165 note 3. Functions of a local authority under the Supply of Goods and Services Act 1982 are 'relevant functions' for the purposes of the Regulatory Enforcement and Sanctions Act 2008 Pt 1 (ss 1–21): see PARA 178 note 3.

4 Supply of Goods and Services Act 1982 s 3(2).

5 Supply of Goods and Services Act 1982 s 3(3).

6 See the Supply of Goods and Services Act 1982 s 11; the Unfair Contract Terms Act 1977; PARA 165; and CONTRACT vol 9(1) (Reissue) PARA 820 et seq.

7 Where in the case of a contract for the transfer of goods the transferee would have the right to treat the contract as repudiated by reason of a breach on the part of the transferor of a term implied by the Supply of Goods and Services Act 1982 ss 3, 4 (see PARA 168) or s 5(2)(a) or (c) (see PARA 169), but the breach is so slight that it would be unreasonable for him to do so, then, if the transferee does not deal as consumer, the breach is not to be treated as a breach of condition but may be treated as a breach of warranty: s 5A(1) (s 5A added by the Sale and Supply of Goods Act 1994 s 7, Sch 2 para 6(5)). The Supply of Goods and Services Act 1982 s 5A applies unless a contrary intention appears in, or is to be implied from, the contract: s 5A(2) (as so added). It is for the transferor to show that a breach is so slight as to fall within s 5A(1): s 5A(3) (as so added). As to the meaning of 'dealing as consumer' see PARA 179 note 7. See further SALE OF GOODS AND SUPPLY OF SERVICES vol 41 (2005 Reissue) PARA 75.

168. Satisfactory quality. Except as otherwise provided by the Supply of Goods and Services Act 1982[1], and subject to the provisions of any other enactment, there is no implied condition or warranty about the quality or fitness for any particular purpose of goods supplied under a contract for the transfer of goods[2].

Where, under such a contract, the transferor[3] transfers the property in goods in the course of a business[4], there is an implied condition that the goods supplied under the contract are of satisfactory quality[5]. This implied condition, however, does not extend to any matter making the quality of goods unsatisfactory: (1) which is specifically drawn to the transferee's attention before the contract is made; (2) where the transferee examines the goods before the contract is made, which that examination ought to reveal; or (3) where the property in the goods is transferred by reference to a sample[6], which would have been apparent on a reasonable examination of the sample[7].

If, under a contract for the transfer of goods, the transferor transfers the property in goods in the course of a business and the transferee, expressly or by implication, makes known to the transferor, or, where the consideration or part of the consideration for the transfer is a sum payable by instalments and the goods were previously sold by a credit-broker[8] to the transferor, to that credit-broker, any particular purpose for which the goods are being acquired[9], then there is an implied condition that the goods supplied under the contract are reasonably fit for that purpose, whether or not that is a purpose for which such goods are commonly supplied[10]. This provision does not apply, however, where the circumstances show that the transferee does not rely, or that it is unreasonable for him to rely, on the skill or judgment of the transferor or credit-broker[11].

An implied condition or warranty about quality or fitness for a particular purpose may be annexed by usage to a contract for the transfer of goods[12].

The provisions described above apply to a transfer by a person who in the course of a business is acting as agent for another as they apply to a transfer by a principal in the course of a business, except where that other is not transferring in the course of a business and either the transferee knows that fact or reasonable steps are taken to bring it to the transferee's notice before the contract concerned is made[13].

Provision is made for the exclusion of these terms[14] and also for modification of remedies for breach of statutory condition in non-consumer cases[15].

1   Ie by the Supply of Goods and Services Act 1982 s 4 (see the text and notes 2–13) and s 5 (see PARA 169).
2   Supply of Goods and Services Act 1982 s 4(1). As to the meaning of 'contract for the transfer of goods' see PARA 165. See also PARA 162. Functions of a local authority under the Supply of Goods and Services Act 1982 are 'relevant functions' for the purposes of the Regulatory Enforcement and Sanctions Act 2008 Pt 1 (ss 1–21): see PARA 178 note 3.
3   As to the meaning of 'transferor' see PARA 165 note 3.
4   As to the meaning of 'business' see PARA 180 note 4.
5   Supply of Goods and Services Act 1982 s 4(2) (substituted by the Sale and Supply of Goods Act 1994 s 7, Sch 2 para 6(3)). For these purposes and for the purposes of the Supply of Goods and Services Act 1982 s 5 (see PARA 169), goods are of satisfactory quality if they meet the standard that a reasonable person would regard as satisfactory, taking account of any description of the goods, the price (if relevant) and all the other circumstances: s 4(2A) (added by the Sale and Supply of Goods Act 1994 Sch 2 para 6(3)). If the transferee deals as consumer, the relevant circumstances mentioned in the Supply of Goods and Services Act 1982 s 4(2A) include any public statements on the specific characteristics of the goods made about them by the transferor, the producer or his representative, particularly in advertising or on labelling: s 4(2B) (s 4(2B)–(2D) added by SI 2002/3045). A public statement is not by virtue of the Supply of Goods and Services Act 1982 s 4(2B) a relevant circumstance for the purposes of s 4(2A) in the case of a contract for the transfer of goods, if the transferor shows that: (1) at the time the contract was made, he was not, and could not reasonably have been, aware of the statement; (2) before the contract was made, the statement had been withdrawn in public or, to the extent that it contained anything which was incorrect or misleading, it had been corrected in public; or (3) the decision to acquire the goods could not have been influenced by the statement: s 4(2C) (as so added). The provisions of s 4(2B), (2C) do not prevent any public statement from being a relevant circumstance for the purposes of s 4(2A) (whether or not the transferee deals as consumer) if the statement would have been such a circumstance apart from those provisions: s 4(2D) (as so added). As to the meaning of 'transferee' see PARA 165 note 3. As to the meaning of 'consumer' see PARA 180 note 5.
6   As to samples see PARA 169.
7   Supply of Goods and Services Act 1982 s 4(3) (substituted by the Sale and Supply of Goods Act 1994 Sch 2 para 6(3)).
8   As to the meaning of 'credit-broker' see PARA 180 note 9.
9   Supply of Goods and Services Act 1982 s 4(4).
10   Supply of Goods and Services Act 1982 s 4(5).
11   Supply of Goods and Services Act 1982 s 4(6).
12   Supply of Goods and Services Act 1982 s 4(7). See also SALE OF GOODS AND SUPPLY OF SERVICES vol 41 (2005 Reissue) PARA 83.
13   Supply of Goods and Services Act 1982 s 4(8).
14   See the Supply of Goods and Services Act 1982 s 11; the Unfair Contract Terms Act 1977 s 7; PARA 165; and CONTRACT vol 9(1) (Reissue) PARA 820 et seq.
15   See the Supply of Goods and Services Act 1982 s 5A; PARA 167 note 7; and SALE OF GOODS AND SUPPLY OF SERVICES vol 41 (2005 Reissue) PARA 85.

169. Sample. Where, under a contract for the transfer of goods[1], the transferor[2] transfers or agrees to transfer the property in the goods by reference to a sample[3], there is: (1) an implied condition that the bulk will correspond with the sample in quality[4]; (2) an implied condition that the transferee[5] will have a reasonable opportunity of comparing the bulk with the sample[6]; and (3) an implied condition that the goods will be free from any defect, making their quality unsatisfactory, which would not be apparent on reasonable examination of the sample[7].

Provision is made for the exclusion of these terms[8] and also for modification of remedies for breach of statutory condition in non-consumer cases[9].

1   As to the meaning of 'contract for the transfer of goods' see PARA 165.
2   As to the meaning of 'transferor' see PARA 165 note 3.
3   Supply of Goods and Services Act 1982 s 5(1). For this purpose, a transferor transfers or agrees to transfer goods by reference to a sample where there is an express or implied term to that effect in the contract concerned: s 5(4). Functions of a local authority under the Supply of Goods and Services Act 1982 are 'relevant functions' for the purposes of the Regulatory Enforcement and Sanctions Act 2008 Pt 1 (ss 1–21): see PARA 178 note 3.
4   Supply of Goods and Services Act 1982 s 5(2)(a).
5   As to the meaning of 'transferee' see PARA 165 note 3.
6   Supply of Goods and Services Act 1982 s 5(2)(b).
7   Supply of Goods and Services Act 1982 s 5(2)(c) (amended by the Sale and Supply of Goods Act 1994 s 7, Sch 2 para 6(4)(b), Sch 3). See also the Supply of Goods and Services Act 1982 s 4(2A); and PARA 168 note 5. Cf PARA 180 note 5; and see SALE OF GOODS AND SUPPLY OF SERVICES vol 41 (2005 Reissue) PARA 95.
8   See the Supply of Goods and Services Act 1982 s 11; the Unfair Contract Terms Act 1977 s 7; PARA 165 text and notes 10–13; and CONTRACT vol 9(1) (Reissue) PARA 820 et seq.
9   See the Supply of Goods and Services Act 1982 s 5A; PARA 167 note 7; and SALE OF GOODS AND SUPPLY OF SERVICES vol 41 (2005 Reissue) PARA 95.

(iv) Lien

170.   Workman's lien.   Everyone to whom a chattel is delivered in order that he may, for reward, do work upon it, and who does work upon the chattel which improves it[1], has at common law a lien on the chattel for the amount of the remuneration due to him for the work done, and therefore is not bound to restore it until his remuneration is paid[2], unless that lien is excluded by express agreement or is otherwise inconsistent with the express or implied terms of the contract[3]. But if a chattel is bailed to a workman for the sole purpose of his working with it, and not upon it, no lien attaches[4].

This lien applies, apart from agreement, only to the sum actually due to the workman for materials and labour expended by him in connection with the repair or alteration of the chattel, and does not extend to charges for warehousing[5]. Nor will the fact that the owner of the chattel is aware that an additional charge will be made for each day during which his property is detained in the valid exercise of the lien suffice to render him liable for such charges. Thus the owner of a ship who knew that he must pay for dock room while the vessel was being repaired was held to have made no implied promise to pay any additional charge for the period during which his vessel was detained as security for the shipwright's charges, although he had received notice that such charges would be made[6].

Should the owner sell the chattel bailed, the workman's lien prima facie attaches only for the amount of the debt due to him at the time when he has notice of the sale, and not for any after-accruing debt[7].

1   See *Hatton v Car Maintenance Co Ltd* [1915] 1 Ch 621 (where an agreement by defendants for three years to maintain plaintiff's car, supplying all petrol and other things necessary for the running of the car and a driver, was held to give no lien). See also *Re Southern Livestock*

     Producers Ltd [1963] 3 All ER 801, [1964] 1 WLR 24; *Fraser v Equatorial Shipping Co Ltd and Equatorial Lines Ltd, The Ijaola* [1979] 1 Lloyd's Rep 103, DC.

2   *Re Matthews, ex p Ockenden* (1754) 1 Atk 235; *Franklin v Hosier* (1821) 4 B & Ald 341; *Hollis v Claridge* (1813) 4 Taunt 807; *Scarfe v Morgan* (1838) 4 M & W 270; *Blake v Nicholson* (1814) 3 M & S 167; *Chase v Westmore* (1816) 5 M & S 180; Story on Bailments (9th Edn, 1878) s 440; Palmer on Bailment (3rd Edn, 2009) paras 15-072–15-094. See also PARA 154 text to note 26. See further LIEN vol 68 (2008) PARA 841 et seq.

3   *Raitt v Mitchell* (1815) 4 Camp 146; *Chase v Westmore* (1816) 5 M & S 180 at 186 per Lord Ellenborough CJ; *Scarfe v Morgan* (1838) 4 M & W 270 at 283 per Parke B; *Forth v Simpson* (1849) 13 QB 680; *Wilson v Lombank Ltd* [1963] 1 All ER 740, [1963] 1 WLR 1294; and contrast *Re Westlake, ex p Willoughby* (1881) 16 ChD 604.

4   *Steadman v Hockley* (1846) 15 M & W 553 at 556 per Pollock CB; *Bleaden v Hancock* (1829) 4 C & P 152; *Welsh Development Agency (Holdings) Ltd v Modern Injection Mouldings Ltd* (6 March 1986, unreported).

5   *Somes v British Empire Shipping Co* (1860) 8 HL Cas 338; *Morris v Beaconsfield Motors Ltd* [2001] EWCA Civ 1322, [2001] All ER (D) 335 (Jul); *Bruce v Everson* (1883) Cab & El 18; *Hartley v Hitchcock* (1816) 1 Stark 408; and see PARA 154. The position may be otherwise where the workman retains possession of the goods predominantly for the benefit of the hirer: see *China-Pacific SA v Food Corpn of India, The Winson* [1982] AC 939 at 962–963, [1981] 3 All ER 688 at 696, HL, per Lord Diplock, and at 964 and 697 per Lord Simon of Glaisdale (where the point was left open).

6   *Somes v British Empire Shipping Co* (1860) 8 HL Cas 338; and see PARA 154.

7   *Barry v Longmore* (1840) 4 Per & Dav 344.

171. Lien of third parties. When a bailee of goods delivers them to a third party to do work upon them, and the circumstances[1] are such as to support the implication that he had the owner's authority to do so, as when he expressly agrees with his bailor to keep the chattel bailed from injury, and this term in the agreement necessarily implies its repair by a third party, or a trade custom in that behalf can be proved, the third party who does the work on the bailee's order has an effective lien on the chattel against the owner, although there may have been no privity of contract between the owner and himself[2]. It seems that a lien will also attach against the owner in favour of a third party to whom the bailee has delivered goods, even in the absence of authority from the owner to the bailee to do so, if the third party was under a common law obligation to receive the goods, as for example where he is a carrier or an innkeeper[3]. Where, however, the third party is not under such an obligation, he will have no lien in the absence of an implied (or, possibly, an ostensible[4]) authority on the bailee's part to deliver the goods to him[5].

1   Such circumstances commonly arise where a car is let under a hire-purchase agreement. The hirer has a right to pass it to a third party for repair: see *Bowmaker Ltd v Wycombe Motors Ltd* [1946] KB 505 at 509, [1946] 2 All ER 113 at 115; and PARA 154 text to note 26. See also *Tappenden v Artus* [1964] 2 QB 185, [1963] 3 All ER 213, CA (implied authority for repairs necessary to make car roadworthy). See generally Palmer on Bailment (3rd Edn, 2009) paras 36-029–36-038.

2   *Keene v Thomas* [1905] 1 KB 136; *Green v All Motors Ltd* [1917] 1 KB 625, CA; *Albemarle Supply Co Ltd v Hind & Co* [1928] 1 KB 307, CA, where it was held that the lien attached although it was stipulated that the bailee should have no right to create a lien in respect of the repairs to the chattel by a third party, the third party having no notice of this limitation on the bailee's authority; *Cassils & Co and Sassoon & Co v Holden Wood Bleaching Co Ltd* (1914) 84 LJKB 834, CA, where the third party failed to prove the authority of the owner. See also *K Chellaram & Sons (London) Ltd v Butlers Warehousing and Distribution Ltd* [1978] 2 Lloyd's Rep 412, CA (bailee container shipping line delivered goods to third party for purposes of packing into containers); *Jarl Trä AB v Convoys Ltd* [2003] EWHC 1488 (Comm), [2003] 2 Lloyd's Rep 459, [2003] All ER (D) 328 (Jun).

3   *Singer Manufacturing Co v London and South Western Rly Co* [1894] 1 QB 833 at 837, DC, per Collins J, who based the lien, inter alia, upon a railway company's obligation to give reasonable facilities for the receipt and safe custody of baggage. But see *Pennington v Reliance Motor Works Ltd* [1923] 1 KB 127 at 129 per McCardie J; and see PARA 154.

4   *Tappenden v Artus* [1964] 2 QB 185 at 195–196, [1963] 3 All ER 213 at 216, CA, per
     Diplock LJ (obiter); Palmer on Bailment (3rd Edn, 2009) para 36-034.
5   *Hiscox v Greenwood* (1802) 4 Esp 174; *Buxton v Baughan* (1834) 6 C & P 674; *Cassils & Co
     and Sassoon & Co v Holden Wood Bleaching Co Ltd* (1914) 84 LJKB 834, CA; *Pennington v
     Reliance Motor Works Ltd* [1923] 1 KB 127; *Bowmaker Ltd v Wycombe Motors Ltd* [1946] KB
     505, [1946] 2 All ER 113 (bailee's authority under hire-purchase agreement terminated by
     termination of the agreement).

172.   Loss of lien.   The lien is lost by a relinquishment of possession on the
part of the workman[1], or by any act or agreement amounting to waiver[2].

1   *Jacobs v Latour* (1828) 5 Bing 130; *Hartley v Hitchcock* (1816) 1 Stark 408; *Legg v Evans*
     (1840) 6 M & W 36 at 42 per Parke B; *Sweet v Pym* (1800) 1 East 4; *Pennington v Reliance
     Motor Works Ltd* [1923] 1 KB 127; *Hatton v Car Maintenance Co Ltd* [1915] 1 Ch 621.
     Contrast *Albemarle Supply Co Ltd v Hind & Co* [1928] 1 KB 307, CA.
2   *White v Gainer* (1824) 2 Bing 23; *Morris v Beaconsfield Motors Ltd* [2001] EWCA Civ 1322,
     [2001] All ER (D) 335 (Jul). As to the position where the bailor countermands the work before
     its completion see *Lilley v Barnsley* (1844) 1 Car & Kir 344; *Green v All Motors Ltd* [1917]
     1 KB 625 at 633–634, CA, per Scrutton LJ; *Cremer v General Carriers Ltd* [1974] 1 All ER 1,
     [1974] 1 WLR 341; c f *Bolwell Fibreglass Pty Ltd v Foley* [1984] VR 97, Vict SC. See Palmer on
     Bailment (3rd Edn, 2009) paras 15-080–15-081.

(v) Disposal of Uncollected Goods

173.   Power to sell uncollected goods.   There is provision[1] for sale by the
bailee of goods in his possession or under his control where: (1) the bailor is in
breach of an obligation to take delivery of them[2] or, if the terms of the bailment
so provide, to give directions for their delivery; or (2) the bailee could impose
such an obligation[3] by giving notice to the bailor but is unable to trace or
communicate with him; or (3) the bailee can reasonably expect to be relieved of
any duty to safeguard the goods on giving notice to the bailor, but is unable to
trace or communicate with him[4]. The bailee's power can be exercised only if he
has either given notice to the bailor of his intention to sell the goods[5] or he has
failed to trace or communicate with him with a view to giving such notice after
having taken reasonable steps for the purpose[6], and if he is reasonably satisfied
that the bailor owns the goods[7]. The bailee is liable to account to the bailor for
any proceeds of sale less any costs incurred[8]. Such a sale gives a good title to the
purchaser as against the bailor[9] but where the bailor is not in fact the owner,
does not give good title against the owner or a person claiming under him[10].

Where a bailee of goods to which these provisions apply satisfies the court
that he is entitled to sell the goods, or would be had he given notice[11], the court
may: (a) authorise the sale subject to any conditions; (b) authorise the bailee to
deduct from the proceeds any costs of sale and any amount due to him from the
bailor; and (c) direct the payment of the net proceeds into court to be held for the
bailor[12].

1   The provisions of the Torts (Interference with Goods) Act 1977 s 12 do not apply where the
     goods were bailed before the commencement of that Act: s 12(9); *Anderson and Anderson v
     Earlanger* [1980] CLY 133. As to the commencement of the Torts (Interference with Goods)
     Act 1977 see the orders made under s 17(2); and TORT vol 45(2) (Reissue) PARA 546.
2   For examples of cases where such an obligation was held to have been broken see *Pedrick v
     Morning Star Motors Ltd* (14 February 1979, unreported), CA; *Ridyard v Roberts* (16 May
     1980, unreported), CA; *JJD SA (a company) v Avon Tyres Ltd* (1999) Times, 25 January. Cf
     Mitchell v Davis (1920) 37 TLR 68.
3   The bailee under any sort of bailment can impose an obligation on the bailor to collect goods by
     issuing written notice where those goods have been accepted for repair or other treatment, or for
     valuation or appraisal, or where they have been put in the bailee's custody and his obligation as
     custodian is over: Torts (Interference with Goods) Act 1977 s 12(2), Sch 1 Pt I paras 1–5. The

notice must: (1) specify the bailee's name and address, and particulars of the goods and the address at which they are held; (2) state that the goods are ready or will be ready at the termination of the contract; and (3) specify the amount, if any, due to the bailee in respect of the goods before the giving of the notice: Sch 1 Pt I para 1(3). The notice must be issued after the repair, valuation or appraisal has been carried out, or after the ending of the obligation to act as custodian (or at the same time as any notice terminating the obligation as custodian): see Sch 1 Pt I paras 2–4. As to the form and delivery of the notice see Sch 1 Pt I para 1(2), (4).

4   Torts (Interference with Goods) Act 1977 s 12(1). The provisions of s 12 and Sch 1 have effect subject to the terms of the bailment: s 12(8). For the purposes of ss 12, 13 and Sch 1, 'bailor' and 'bailee' include their respective successors in title: s 12(7)(a). References to what is payable, paid or due to the bailee in respect of the goods include references to what would be payable by the bailor to the bailee as a condition of delivery of the goods at the relevant time: s 12(7)(b).

5   Torts (Interference with Goods) Act 1977 s 12(3)(a). Notice of intention to sell must be in writing, and must be sent by registered letter or recorded delivery service (Sch 1 Pt II para 6(4)); and the notice must specify the name and address of the bailee, give sufficient particulars of the goods and the address or place where they are held, specify the date on or after which the bailee proposes to sell the goods, and specify the amount if any due to the bailee in respect of the goods before the giving of the notice (Sch 1 Pt II para 6(1)). The interval between the giving of notice and proposed sale must be long enough to allow the bailor a reasonable opportunity of taking delivery of the goods and, if any amount is due to the bailee in respect of the goods, the interval must be at least three months: Sch 1 Pt II para 6(2), (3).

The bailee may not give notice or exercise his right to sell the goods pursuant to such a notice if he has notice that the bailor is questioning or refusing to pay all or some of the sum the bailee claims is due in respect of the goods because of a dispute concerning those goods: see Sch 1 Pt II para 7.

6   Torts (Interference with Goods) Act 1977 s 12(3)(b).
7   Torts (Interference with Goods) Act 1977 s 12(3).
8   Torts (Interference with Goods) Act 1977 s 12(5). The account must be taken on the footing that the bailee has adopted the best method of sale reasonably available in the circumstances: s 12(5)(a). Where s 12(3)(a) applies (see the text and note 5), any sum payable to the bailee in respect of goods, which accrued before notice of intention to sell was given, is deductible from the proceeds of sale: s 12(5)(b).
9   Torts (Interference with Goods) Act 1977 s 12(6).
10 Torts (Interference with Goods) Act 1977 s 12(4). A bailee who does not activate the procedures under s 12 when at liberty to do so, and who later disposes of the goods, may incur a greater liability for damages than would otherwise have been the case: *Irving v Keen* (3 March 1995, unreported), CA.
11 Ie notice under the Torts (Interference with Goods) Act 1977 Sch 1: see the text and notes 1–5.
12 Torts (Interference with Goods) Act 1977 s 13(1). A decision of the court is conclusive, subject to any right of appeal, of the bailee's entitlement to sell the goods, as against the bailor, and gives the purchaser good title against the bailor: s 13(2). The county court has jurisdiction save that in Northern Ireland a county court only has jurisdiction if the value of the goods does not exceed the county court limit mentioned in the County Courts (Northern Ireland) Order 1980, SI 1980/397, art 10(1): Torts (Interference with Goods) Act 1977 s 13(3) (amended by SI 1991/724). See COURTS AND TRIBUNALS.

(vi) Carriage for Reward

174.   Duty of care arising from carriage for reward. A private carrier who undertakes the carriage of goods for reward becomes a bailee of them and has the ordinary responsibility of a bailee for goods entrusted to him, that is, to take reasonable care of the goods while they are in his possession and to refrain from converting them or from damaging them by any other intentional act[1]. In a contract for the supply of a service where the supplier is acting in the course of a business there is also an implied term that the supplier will carry out the service with reasonable care and skill[2]. The appropriate measure of care in a given case will depend on all circumstances pertaining to the nature and condition of the goods themselves, assurances or undertakings made by either party and the normal practice of a reasonably competent carrier in the situation in question[3].

1　See e g *Hunt & Winterbotham (West of England) Ltd v BRS (Parcels) Ltd* [1962] 1 QB 617, [1962] 1 All ER 111, CA; *J Spurling Ltd v Bradshaw* [1956] 2 All ER 121, [1956] 1 WLR 461, CA; *Morris v CW Martin & Sons Ltd* [1966] 1 QB 716, [1965] 2 All ER 725, CA; *American Express Co v British Airways Board* [1983] 1 All ER 557, [1983] 1 WLR 701; and CARRIAGE AND CARRIERS vol 7 (2008) PARA 59 and the other cases noted thereto.

2　See the Supply of Goods and Services Act 1982 s 13; and SALE OF GOODS AND SUPPLY OF SERVICES vol 41 (2005 Reissue) PARA 97. For an application of this provision to carriers see *Metaalhandel JA Magnus BV v Ardfields Transport Ltd and Eastfell Ltd (t/a Jones Transport)* [1988] 1 Lloyd's Rep 197. As to exclusion of implied terms see the Unfair Contract Terms Act 1977; the Supply of Goods and Services Act 1982 s 16; CONTRACT vol 9(1) (Reissue) PARA 820 et seq; and SALE OF GOODS AND SUPPLY OF SERVICES vol 41 (2005 Reissue) PARA 100 et seq.

3　See further CARRIAGE AND CARRIERS vol 7 (2008) PARA 59.

(4) HIRE OF CHATTELS

(i) Nature of the Contract

175. Hire of chattels. Hire[1] is a class of bailment. It is a contract by which the hirer obtains the right to use the chattel hired in return for the payment to the owner of the price of the hiring[2]. The general property in the chattel is not changed, but remains in the owner[3], although upon delivery the hirer becomes legally possessed of the chattel hired[4], so that if it is lent for a time certain, even the true owner is debarred during that time from resuming possession against the hirer's will and, should he do so, becomes liable in damages for the wrongful seizure[5].

The contract must not be based on an immoral or illegal consideration, nor must it conduce to immorality or illegality[6].

Statutory control is exercised over certain types of hiring[7], and it is an offence, for example, to let on hire, or offer to let on hire, a motor cyclist's protective helmet which is not of a prescribed or authorised type[8], and to hire, offer for hire or expose or have in one's possession for hire a flick knife or gravity knife[9].

Certain terms are implied by statute into contracts for the hire of goods[10]. In the Supply of Goods and Services Act 1982, a 'contract for the hire of goods' means a contract, other than a hire-purchase agreement[11], under which one person bails or agrees to bail goods to another by way of hire[12]. 'Goods' includes all personal chattels, other than things in action and money, and in particular includes emblements, industrial growing crops, and things attached to or forming part of the land which are agreed to be severed before the transfer, bailment or hire concerned or under the contract concerned[13]. For these purposes, a contract is a contract for the hire of goods whether or not services are provided or to be provided under the contract, and whatever is the nature of the consideration for the bailment or agreement to bail by way of hire[14].

Where a right, duty or liability would arise under a contract for the hire of goods by implication of law, it may generally[15] be negatived or varied by express agreement, or by the course of dealing between the parties, or by such usage as binds both parties to the contract[16]. An express condition or warranty does not, however, negative a condition or warranty implied by the statute unless inconsistent with it[17].

Nothing in the Supply of Goods and Services Act 1982 prejudices the operation of any other enactment or rule of law whereby any condition or warranty, other than one relating to quality or fitness, is to be implied into a contract for the hire of goods[18].

1　Ie *locatio conductio rei*: see PARA 106 text and note 9.

2   Jones on Bailments (4th Edn, 1833) p 86; Pothier's Contrat de Louage s 1; 1 Domat book 1, tit 4, s 1, art 1. Cf *General Motors Acceptance Corpn (UK) Ltd v IRC* [1987] STC 122, CA (cars supplied by finance company to dealers on sale or return; held not let on hire for the purposes of the Finance Act 1976 Sch 5 para 29(2)(c) (now repealed)). See also *Lloyds UDT Finance Ltd v Chartered Finance Trust Holdings plc (Britax International GmbH, Pt 20 defendant)* [2002] EWCA Civ 806, [2002] STC 956, [2002] All ER (D) 527 (May) (where a company was involved in the business of leasing motor vehicles to the public and there was consideration of the concept of hiring for the purposes of provisions (now repealed) of the Capital Allowances Act 1990); *TRM Copy Centres (UK) Ltd v Lanwall Services Ltd* [2009] UKHL 35, [2009] 4 All ER 33, [2009] 1 WLR 1375 (photocopiers; no hiring at common law and no consumer hire agreement under the Consumer Credit Act 1974 s 15 (see CONSUMER CREDIT vol 21 (2011) PARA 53)).

3   As to the nature of the hirer's interest see *Australian Guarantee Corpn Ltd v Ross* [1983] 2 VR 319 at 329–330 per Marks J, Vic Sup Ct, FC; Palmer on Bailment (3rd Edn, 2009) Chapter 21; Story on Bailments (9th Edn, 1878) s 370a. Where the contract of hire is specifically enforceable the hirer may have an equitable interest in the chattel: *Bristol Airport plc v Powdrill* [1990] Ch 744 at 759, [1990] 2 All ER 493 at 502, CA, per Browne-Wilkinson V-C (obiter: lease of aircraft). As to special provisions where a motor vehicle has been bailed under a hire-purchase agreement or has been agreed to be sold under a conditional sale agreement, and before the property has become vested in the debtor, he makes a disposition to another person see the Hire-Purchase Act 1964 s 27(1) (substituted by the Consumer Credit Act 1974 s 192(3)(a), Sch 4 para 22); *Hitchens v General Guarantee Corpn Ltd* [2001] All ER (D) 246 (Feb), CA, applying *Carlyle Finance Ltd v Pallas Industrial Finance* [1999] 1 All ER (Comm) 659, [1999] RTR 281, CA; and CONSUMER CREDIT vol 21 (2011) PARA 134. See also *Shogun Finance Ltd v Hudson* [2003] UKHL 62, [2004] 1 AC 919, [2004] 1 All ER 215.

4   As to the right to terminate a written contract for breach of an oral promise made at the time it was entered into see *Quickmaid Rental Services Ltd v Reece (t/a Forge Service Station)* (1970) 114 Sol Jo 372, CA. See also *Hitchens v General Guarantee Corpn Ltd* [2001] All ER (D) 246 (Feb), CA; and note 3.

5   Supply of Goods and Services Act 1982 s 7. See PARA 178. See also Bac Abr Bailment C; *Lee v Atkinson and Brooks* (1609) Yelv 172; *Turner v Hardcastle* (1862) 11 CBNS 683. The measure of damages is the hirer's interest in the chattel: cf *Brierly v Kendall* (1852) 17 QB 937; *Chinery v Viall* (1860) 5 H & N 288; *Johnson (Assignee of Cumming) v Stear* (1863) 15 CBNS 330; *Halliday v Holgate* (1868) LR 3 Exch 299 at 301. In such a case the bailor may also be guilty of theft: *Rose v Matt* [1951] 1 KB 810, [1951] 1 All ER 361, DC.

6   The maxim *ex turpi causa non oritur actio* applies to this as to any other contract: *Pearce v Brooks* (1866) LR 1 Exch 213 at 217 per Pollock CB. See generally CONTRACT.

7   See PARA 176.

8   Road Traffic Act 1988 s 17(2), (5). The offence is punishable on summary conviction by a fine not exceeding level 3 on the standard scale: Road Traffic Offenders Act 1988 s 9, Sch 2 Pt I. See ROAD TRAFFIC vol 40(1) (2007 Reissue) PARA 640. As to the standard scale see SENTENCING AND DISPOSITION OF OFFENDERS vol 92 (2010) PARA 142. Functions of a local authority under the Road Traffic Act 1988 s 17 are 'relevant functions' for the purposes of the Regulatory Enforcement and Sanctions Act 2008 Pt 1 (ss 1–21) (see s 4, Sch 3; and LOCAL GOVERNMENT vol 69 (2009) PARA 733); thus the Local Better Regulation Office may give guidance to local authorities as to the exercise of those functions (see s 7; and LOCAL GOVERNMENT vol 69 (2009) PARA 734). They are 'regulators' specified for the purposes of imposing civil sanctions in respect of offences under the Road Traffic Act 1988: see the Regulatory Enforcement and Sanctions Act 2008 s 37, Sch 6; and ADMINISTRATIVE LAW.

9   Restriction of Offensive Weapons Act 1959 s 1(1) (amended by the Restriction of Offensive Weapons Act 1961 s 1; and the Criminal Justice Act 1988 s 46(2), (3)). The penalty on summary conviction is a fine not exceeding level 5 on the standard scale or imprisonment for a term not exceeding six months, or both: Restriction of Offensive Weapons Act 1959 s 1(1) (as so amended).

10   See the Supply of Goods and Services Act 1982 ss 7–10; and PARA 178 et seq. As to the modification of remedies for breach of statutory condition in non-consumer cases see s 10A; and PARAS 179–181. Note also the definition of a consumer hire agreement in the Consumer Credit Act 1974 s 15: see CONSUMER CREDIT vol 21 (2011) PARA 53. As to the effect of the Consumer Credit Act 1974 on contracts of hire see CONSUMER CREDIT vol 21 (2011) PARA 93 et seq, 66. The bailment required by s 15 is bailment by way of hire, i e a bailment under which the person who receives possession agrees to pay for the use of the chattel in cash or in kind during the period of his possession of it. A bailment that is gratuitous is outwith the scope of the Act: *TRM Copy Centres (UK) Ltd v Lanwall Services Ltd* [2009] UKHL 35, [2009] 4 All ER 33, [2009]

1 WLR 1375 (claimants were paying the retailer commission on each copy made on the photocopier as consideration for the benefit the claimants obtained by having their machine and its promotional material located in a place where it was easily visible and accessible by the retailer's customers; held photocopier not being hired by retailer as bailee).

11 'Hire-purchase agreement' has the same meaning as in the Consumer Credit Act 1974 (see s 189(1); and CONSUMER CREDIT vol 21 (2011) PARA 66): Supply of Goods and Services Act 1982 s 18(1).

12 Supply of Goods and Services Act 1982 s 6(1) (s 6(1), (3) amended by the Sale and Supply of Goods Act 1994 s 7, Sch 2 para 6(6); in relation to England and Wales by SI 2005/871; and in relation to Northern Ireland by SI 2005/1452).

13 Supply of Goods and Services Act 1982 s 18(1) (definition amended by the Sale and Supply of Goods Act 1994 ss 6, 7, Sch 1 para 2(b), Sch 3).

14 Supply of Goods and Services Act 1982 s 6(3) (as amended: see note 12).

15 Ie subject to the Supply of Goods and Services Act 1982 s 11(2) (see the text and note 17) and the Unfair Contract Terms Act 1977 (see CONTRACT vol 9(1) (Reissue) PARA 820 et seq). Functions of a local authority under the Supply of Goods and Services Act 1982 and the Unfair Contract Terms Act 1977 are 'relevant functions' for the purposes of the Regulatory Enforcement and Sanctions Act 2008 Pt 1 (ss 1–21) (see s 4, Sch 3; and LOCAL GOVERNMENT vol 69 (2009) PARA 733); thus the Local Better Regulation Office may give guidance to local authorities as to the exercise of those functions (see s 7; and LOCAL GOVERNMENT vol 69 (2009) PARA 734).

16 Supply of Goods and Services Act 1982 s 11(1).

17 Supply of Goods and Services Act 1982 s 11(2).

18 Supply of Goods and Services Act 1982 s 11(3).

176. Control of hiring. The Secretary of State[1] may by order provide for imposing, in respect of the disposal, acquisition or possession of articles of any description under agreements for letting on hire, such prohibitions or restrictions as appear to him to be required for restricting excessive credit[2].

The Secretary of State may make regulations for the purpose of ensuring compliance with the general safety requirement[3]. The regulations may prohibit the hiring or offering to hire or agreeing to hire any goods, or possessing any goods for hire, and contravention of the regulations is an offence[4]. In addition to the requirements under the Consumer Protection Act 1987, the General Product Safety Regulations 2005[5] impose requirements in regard to the safety of products intended for consumers or likely to be used by consumers if such products are placed on the market by producers or supplied by distributors.

Special provision is made in relation to a television dealer[6] who lets a television set on hire, arranges for a set to be so let by another dealer, or holds himself out as willing to engage in those activities[7].

1 The Emergency Laws (Re-enactments and Repeals) Act 1964 refers to the Board of Trade or the Secretary of State: see further TRADE AND INDUSTRY vol 97 (2010) PARA 802.

2 Emergency Laws (Re-enactments and Repeals) Act 1964 s 1(1) (amended by the Consumer Credit Act 1974 s 192(3)(a), Sch 4 Pt I para 23(1); and by virtue of SI 1970/1537). The Control of Hiring and Hire-Purchase and Credit Sale Agreements (Revocation) Order 1982, SI 1982/1034, was made under the Emergency Laws (Re-enactments and Repeals) Act 1964 s 1 revoking the Hire-Purchase and Credit Sale Agreements (Control) Order 1976, SI 1976/1135, and the Control of Hiring Order 1977, SI 1977/770, thereby bringing to an end the previously existing control of hiring, hire-purchase and credit sales agreements under that provision. As to the effect of the Consumer Credit Act 1974 on contracts of hire see CONSUMER CREDIT vol 21 (2011) PARA 93 et seq, 66; see also PARA 175.

3 See the Consumer Protection Act 1987 s 11; and CONSUMER PROTECTION vol 21 (2011) PARA 676. The Secretary of State may also issue prohibition notices and notices to warn: see s 13; and CONSUMER PROTECTION vol 21 (2011) PARA 681 et seq. As to the regulations made or having effect see CONSUMER PROTECTION vol 21 (2011) PARA 696 et seq. Functions of a local authority under the Consumer Protection Act 1987 are 'relevant functions' for the purposes of the Regulatory Enforcement and Sanctions Act 2008 Pt 1 (ss 1–21) (see s 4, Sch 3; and LOCAL

GOVERNMENT vol 69 (2009) PARA 733); thus the Local Better Regulation Office may give guidance to local authorities as to the exercise of those functions (see s 7; and LOCAL GOVERNMENT vol 69 (2009) PARA 734).

4　See the Consumer Protection Act 1987 ss 12, 46(1); and CONSUMER PROTECTION vol 21 (2011) PARA 678. Local authorities are 'regulators' specified for the purposes of imposing civil sanctions in respect of offences under the Consumer Protection Act 1987 s 12: see the Regulatory Enforcement and Sanctions Act 2008 s 37, Sch 6; and ADMINISTRATIVE LAW.

5　Ie the General Product Safety Regulations 2005, SI 2005/1803: see CONSUMER PROTECTION vol 21 (2011) PARA 652 et seq. Together with the Consumer Protection Act 1987, the General Product Safety Regulations 2005, SI 2005/1803, comprise a code both for the protection of the public against unsafe products and for the protection of the interests of manufacturers and suppliers.

6　As to the meaning of 'television dealer' see BROADCASTING PARA 952.

7　See the Wireless Telegraphy Act 1967 s 2(1) (amended by the Broadcasting Act 1990 s 180, Sch 18 Pt II paras 1, 3; by SI 1996/1864; and by virtue of SI 1974/691). Note that the Wireless Telegraphy Act 1967 s 2(1) is subject to exceptions: see s 2(1A), (2) (s 2(1A) added, and s 2(2) amended, by SI 1996/1864). See further BROADCASTING PARA 952 et seq.

177.　Nature of hire-purchase.　The contract of hire-purchase or, more accurately, the contract of hire with an option of purchase, is one under which the owner of a chattel lets it out on hire and undertakes to sell it to, or that it shall become the property of, the hirer, conditionally on his making a certain number of payments[1]. It is a modern development in commercial life, and some rules with regard to bailments which were laid down before hire-purchase contracts were contemplated cannot logically be applied to them. Hire-purchase contains not only the element of bailment but also the element of sale[2]. It is therefore treated elsewhere in this work[3].

1　*Helby v Matthews* [1895] AC 471, HL; *Re Davis & Co, ex p Rawlings* (1888) 22 QBD 193, CA. As to special provisions where a motor vehicle has been bailed under a hire-purchase agreement or has been agreed to be sold under a conditional sale agreement and, before the property has become vested in the debtor, he makes a disposition to another person see the Hire-Purchase Act 1964 s 27(1); *Hitchens v General Guarantee Corpn Ltd* [2001] All ER (D) 246 (Feb), CA, applying *Carlyle Finance Ltd v Pallas Industrial Finance* [1999] 1 All ER (Comm) 659, [1999] RTR 281, CA; and CONSUMER CREDIT vol 21 (2011) PARA 134. See also *Shogun Finance Ltd v Hudson* [2003] UKHL 62, [2004] 1 AC 919, [2004] 1 All ER 215.

2　*Karflex Ltd v Poole* [1933] 2 KB 251 at 263–264 per Goddard J. See also *Chubb Cash Ltd v John Crilley & Son (a firm)* [1983] 2 All ER 294, [1983] 1 WLR 599, CA; *Chartered Trust v King* [2001] All ER (D) 310 (Feb), Ch.

3　See CONSUMER CREDIT vol 21 (2011) PARAS 1 et seq, 66 et seq, 93.

(ii) Owner's Obligations

178.　Right to hire goods and quiet enjoyment.　In a contract for the hire of goods[1] there is an implied condition on the part of the bailor[2] that in the case of a bailment he has the right to transfer possession of the goods by way of hire, and in the case of an agreement to bail that he will have such a right at the time of the bailment[3]. In such a contract there is also an implied warranty that the bailee[4] will enjoy quiet possession of the goods for the period of the bailment except so far as the possession may be disturbed by the owner or other person entitled to the benefit of any charge or encumbrance disclosed or known to the bailee before the contract is made[5]. These provisions do not affect the right of the bailor to repossess the goods under an express or implied term of the contract[6].

1　As to the meaning of 'contract for the hire of goods' see PARA 175.

2   'Bailor', in relation to a contract for the hire of goods, means (depending on the context) a
    person who bails the goods under the contract, or a person who agrees to do so, or a person to
    whom the duties under the contract of either of those persons have passed: Supply of Goods and
    Services Act 1982 s 18(1).
3   Supply of Goods and Services Act 1982 s 7(1). See SALE OF GOODS AND SUPPLY OF SERVICES
    vol 41 (2005 Reissue) PARA 71. Functions of a local authority under the Supply of Goods and
    Services Act 1982 are 'relevant functions' for the purposes of the Regulatory Enforcement and
    Sanctions Act 2008 Pt 1 (ss 1–21) (see s 4, Sch 3; and LOCAL GOVERNMENT vol 69 (2009) PARA
    733); thus the Local Better Regulation Office may give guidance to local authorities as to the
    exercise of those functions (see s 7; and LOCAL GOVERNMENT vol 69 (2009) PARA 734).
4   'Bailee', in relation to a contract for the hire of goods, means (depending on the context) a
    person to whom the goods are bailed under the contract, or a person to whom they are to be so
    bailed, or a person to whom the rights under the contract of either of those persons have passed:
    Supply of Goods and Services Act 1982 s 18(1).
5   Supply of Goods and Services Act 1982 s 7(2). See also *Lee v Atkinson and Brooks* (1609) Yelv
    172; *Warman v Southern Counties Car Finance Corpn Ltd* [1949] 2 KB 576, [1949] 1 All ER
    711. Cf *European and Australian Royal Mail Co Ltd v Royal Mail Steam Packet Co* (1861) 30
    LJCP 247. As to exclusion of these terms see the Supply of Goods and Services Act 1982 s 11;
    the Unfair Contract Terms Act 1977 s 7; PARA 175; and CONTRACT vol 9(1) (Reissue) PARA 820
    et seq.
6   Supply of Goods and Services Act 1982 s 7(3). As to whether the hirer may be entitled to
    equitable relief from forfeiture see *On Demand Information plc (in administrative receivership)
    v Michael Gerson (Finance) plc* [2000] 4 All ER 734, [2000] 2 All ER (Comm) 513, [2001]
    1 WLR 155, CA; and EQUITY vol 16(2) (Reissue) PARA 801 et seq. As to whether a threat to
    repossess goods from a lessee might constitute duress, see *Alf Vaughan & Co Ltd (in
    administrative receivership) v Royscot Trust plc* [1999] 1 All ER (Comm) 856, Ch (no duress
    where repossession lawful under terms of agreement and general law; pressure not illegitimate;
    position not affected by hirer's potential ability to invoke equitable relief against forfeiture).

179.   Correspondence with description.   Where, under a contract for the hire
of goods[1], the bailor[2] bails or agrees to bail the goods by description[3], there is an
implied condition that the goods will correspond with the description[4]. If under
the contract the bailor bails or agrees to bail goods by reference to a sample as
well as a description it is not sufficient that the bulk of the goods corresponds
with the sample if the goods do not also correspond with the description[5].

Provision is made for exclusion of these terms[6] and for modification of
remedies for breach of statutory condition in non-consumer cases[7].

1   As to the meaning of 'contract for the hire of goods' see PARA 175.
2   As to the meaning of 'bailor' see PARA 178 note 2.
3   Supply of Goods and Services Act 1982 s 8(1). A contract is not prevented from being a contract
    by description by reason only that, being exposed for supply, the goods are selected by the
    bailee: s 8(4). As to the meaning of 'bailee' see PARA 178 note 4. Functions of a local authority
    under the Supply of Goods and Services Act 1982 are 'relevant functions' for the purposes of the
    Regulatory Enforcement and Sanctions Act 2008 Pt 1 (ss 1–21): see PARA 178 note 3.
4   Supply of Goods and Services Act 1982 s 8(2).
5   Supply of Goods and Services Act 1982 s 8(3).
6   See the Supply of Goods and Services Act 1982 s 11; the Unfair Contract Terms Act 1977; PARA
    175; and CONTRACT vol 9(1) (Reissue) PARA 820 et seq.
7   Where in the case of a contract for the hire of goods the bailee would have the right to treat the
    contract as repudiated by reason of a breach on the part of the bailor of a term implied by the
    Supply of Goods and Services Act 1982 ss 8, 9 (see PARA 180) or s 10(2)(a) or (b) (see PARA 181)
    but the breach is so slight that it would be unreasonable for him to do so, then, if the bailor does
    not deal as consumer, the breach is not to be treated as a breach of condition but may be treated
    as a breach of warranty: s 10A(1) (s 10A added by the Sale and Supply of Goods Act 1994 s 7,
    Sch 2 para 6(9)). The Supply of Goods and Services Act 1982 s 10A applies unless a contrary
    intention appears in, or is to be implied from, the contract: s 10A(2) (as so added). It is for the
    bailor to show that a breach is so slight as indicated in s 10A(1): s 10A(3) (as so added).
    'Dealing as consumer' is to be construed in accordance with the Unfair Contracts Act 1997 Pt I
    (ss 1–14) (see CONTRACT vol 9(1) (Reissue) PARA 820 et seq): see the Supply of Goods and

Services Act 1982 s 18(4) (added by the Sale and Supply of Goods Act 1994 s 7, Sch 2 para 6(10)). As to conditions and warranties see also SALE OF GOODS AND SUPPLY OF SERVICES vol 41 (2005 Reissue) PARA 62 et seq.

180. Satisfactory quality. Except as otherwise provided[1] and subject to the provisions of any other enactment, there is no implied condition or warranty about the quality or fitness for any particular purpose of goods bailed under a contract for the hire of goods[2].

Where, under such a contract, the bailor[3] bails goods in the course of a business[4], there is an implied condition that the goods supplied under the contract are of satisfactory quality[5]. This implied condition, however, does not extend to any matter making the quality of goods unsatisfactory: (1) which is specifically drawn to the bailee's attention before the contract is made; (2) where the bailee examines the goods before the contract is made, which that examination ought to reveal; or (3) where the goods are bailed by reference to a sample[6], which would have been apparent on a reasonable examination of the sample[7].

Where, under a contract for the hire of goods, the bailor bails goods in the course of a business[8] and the bailee, expressly or by implication, makes known to the bailor in the course of negotiations conducted by him in relation to the making of the contract, or to a credit-broker[9] in the course of negotiations conducted by that broker in relation to goods sold by him to the bailor before forming the subject matter of the contract, any particular purpose for which the goods are being bailed[10], there is an implied condition that the goods supplied under the contract are reasonably fit for that purpose, whether or not that is a purpose for which such goods are commonly supplied[11]. This provision does not apply, however, where the circumstances show that the bailee does not rely, or that it is unreasonable for him to rely, on the skill or judgment of the bailor or person by whom the antecedent negotiations are conducted[12].

An implied condition or warranty about quality or fitness for a particular purpose may be annexed by usage to a contract for the hire of goods[13].

The provisions described above apply to a bailment by a person who in the course of a business is acting as agent for another as they apply to a bailment by a principal in the course of a business, except where that other is not bailing in the course of a business and either the bailee knows that fact or reasonable steps are taken to bring it to the bailee's notice before the contract concerned is made[14].

Provision is made for the exclusion of these terms[15] and for modification of remedies for breach of statutory condition in non-consumer cases[16].

1   Ie by the Supply of Goods and Services Act 1982 s 9 (see the text and notes 2–14), s 10 (see PARA 181).
2   Supply of Goods and Services Act 1982 s 9(1). As to the meaning of 'contract for the hire of goods' see PARA 175. Functions of a local authority under the Supply of Goods and Services Act 1982 are 'relevant functions' for the purposes of the Regulatory Enforcement and Sanctions Act 2008 Pt 1 (ss 1–21): see PARA 178 note 3.
3   As to the meaning of 'bailor' see PARA 178 note 2.
4   'Business' includes a profession and the activities of any government department or local or public authority: Supply of Goods and Services Act 1982 s 18(1).
5   Supply of Goods and Services Act 1982 s 9(2) (substituted by the Sale and Supply of Goods Act 1994 s 7, Sch 2 para 6(7)). For these purposes and for the purposes of the Supply of Goods and Services Act 1982 s 10 (see PARA 181), goods are of satisfactory quality if they meet the standard that a reasonable person would regard as satisfactory, taking account of any description of the goods, the consideration for the bailment (if relevant) and all other relevant circumstances: s 9(2A) (added by the Sale and Supply of Goods Act 1994 Sch 2 para 6(7)). If the

bailee deals as consumer, the relevant circumstances mentioned in the Supply of Goods and Services Act 1982 s 9(2A) include any public statements on the specific characteristics of the goods made about them by the bailor, the producer or his representative, particularly in advertising or on labelling: s 9(2B) (s 9(2B)–(2D) added SI 2002/3045). A public statement is not by virtue of the Supply of Goods and Services Act 1982 s 9(2B) a relevant circumstance for the purposes of s 9(2A) in the case of a contract for the hire of goods, if the bailor shows that: (1) at the time the contract was made, he was not, and could not reasonably have been, aware of the statement; (2) before the contract was made, the statement had been withdrawn in public or, to the extent that it contained anything which was incorrect or misleading, it had been corrected in public; or (3) the decision to acquire the goods could not have been influenced by the statement: s 9(2C) (as so added). The provisions of s 9(2B), (2C) do not prevent any public statement from being a relevant circumstance for the purposes of s 9(2A) (whether or not the bailee deals as consumer) if the statement would have been such a circumstance apart from those provisions: s 9(2D) (as so added). As to the meaning of 'bailee' see PARA 178 note 4. 'Consumer' means any natural person who, in the contracts covered by the Sale and Supply of Goods to Consumers Regulations 2002, SI 2002/3045, is acting for purposes which are outside his trade, business or profession: reg 2.

6   As to samples see PARA 181.
7   Supply of Goods and Services Act 1982 s 9(3) (substituted by the Sale and Supply of Goods Act 1994 Sch 2 para 6(7)).
8   See note 4.
9   'Credit-broker' means a person acting in the course of a business of credit-brokerage carried on by him: Supply of Goods and Services Act 1982 s 18(1). 'Credit-brokerage' means the effecting of introductions: (1) of individuals desiring to obtain credit to persons carrying on any business so far as it relates to the provision of credit; or (2) of individuals desiring to obtain goods on hire to persons carrying on a business which comprises or relates to the bailment of goods under a contract for the hire of goods; or (3) of individuals desiring to obtain credit, or to obtain goods on hire, to other credit-brokers: s 18(1).
10 Supply of Goods and Services Act 1982 s 9(4).
11 Supply of Goods and Services Act 1982 s 9(5). Proof that the chattel suffered a defect under s 9(5) might disable the lessor from relying on an express indemnity in the hire agreement: see *Blackpool Ladder Centre Ltd v BWB Partnership* [2000] All ER (D) 1802 (Nov), CA. At common law, it has been held that, in the case of a hiring of a specific motor vehicle, the lessor's obligation to provide a vehicle which is reasonably fit for its purpose is not a continuing obligation but need be satisfied only at the commencement of the hiring: *UCB Leasing Ltd v Holtom* [1987] RTR 362, CA (but Balcombe LJ suggested (at 375) that the position may be otherwise in relation to the hiring of a single item of unspecific domestic equipment such as a gas stove). See also SALE OF GOODS AND SUPPLY OF SERVICES vol 41 (2005 Reissue) PARA 89.
12 Supply of Goods and Services Act 1982 s 9(6).
13 Supply of Goods and Services Act 1982 s 9(7). See also SALE OF GOODS AND SUPPLY OF SERVICES vol 41 (2005 Reissue) PARA 88.
14 Supply of Goods and Services Act 1982 s 9(8).
15 See the Supply of Goods and Services Act 1982 s 11; the Unfair Contract Terms Act 1977 s 7; PARA 175; and CONTRACT vol 9(1) (Reissue) PARA 820 et seq.
16 See the Supply of Goods and Services Act 1982 s 10A; PARA 179 note 7; and SALE OF GOODS AND SUPPLY OF SERVICES vol 41 (2005 Reissue) PARAS 76, 89–90, 96.

181.   Sample. Where, under a contract for the hire of goods[1], the bailor[2] bails or agrees to bail the goods by reference to a sample[3] there is an implied condition: (1) that the bulk will correspond with the sample in quality[4]; and (2) that the bailee[5] will have a reasonable opportunity of comparing the bulk with the sample[6]; and (3) that the goods will be free from any defect, making their quality unsatisfactory, which would not be apparent on reasonable examination of the sample[7].

Provision is made for the exclusion of these terms[8] and for modification of remedies for breach of statutory condition in non-consumer cases[9].

1   As to the meaning of 'contract for the hire of goods' see PARA 175.
2   As to the meaning of 'bailor' see PARA 178 note 2.
3   For this purpose, a bailor bails or agrees to bail goods by reference to a sample where there is an express or implied term to that effect in the contract concerned: Supply of Goods and Services

Act 1982 s 10(4). Functions of a local authority under the Supply of Goods and Services Act 1982 are 'relevant functions' for the purposes of the Regulatory Enforcement and Sanctions Act 2008 Pt 1 (ss 1–21): see PARA 178 note 3.

4   Supply of Goods and Services Act 1982 s 10(2)(a).
5   As to the meaning of 'bailee' see PARA 178 note 4.
6   Supply of Goods and Services Act 1982 s 10(2)(b).
7   Supply of Goods and Services Act 1982 s 10(2)(c) (amended by the Sale and Supply of Goods Act 1994 s 7, Sch 2 para 6(8)(a)). 'Unsatisfactory' is to be construed in accordance with the Supply of Goods and Services Act 1982 s 9: see s 9(2A); and PARA 180. See also SALE OF GOODS AND SUPPLY OF SERVICES vol 41 (2005 Reissue) PARAS 88–92.
8   See the Supply of Goods and Services Act 1982 s 11; the Unfair Contract Terms Act 1977 s 7; PARA 175; and CONTRACT vol 9(1) (Reissue) PARA 820 et seq.
9   See the Supply of Goods and Services Act 1982 s 10A; PARA 179 note 7; and SALE OF GOODS AND SUPPLY OF SERVICES vol 41 (2005 Reissue) PARAS 76, 89–90, 96.

182. Repair of chattel. Where the owner has agreed with the hirer to keep the chattel lent in proper repair[1], the owner is entitled to resume possession of it for the limited purpose of executing repairs[2]. It is said that the hirer, if actually inconvenienced thereby, is entitled to an allowance or reduction from the rent for the period during which he has been deprived of the use of the chattel[3], but this probably depends on the nature of the thing itself and the inferences to be drawn from the terms of the contract and the surrounding circumstances.

An owner's liability to repair may be discharged by a party to whom he assigns the chattel[4].

1   This may be implied from the nature of the contract: *Sutton v Temple* (1843) 12 M & W 52 at 60, where Lord Abinger said that if a carriage be let for hire, and it break down on the journey, the letter of it is liable, and not the party who hired it. But in general the owner owes no duty in the absence of express contract to service and maintain the chattel during the period of the hiring: *Hadley v Droitwich Construction Co Ltd (Joseph Pugsley & Sons Ltd, third party)* [1967] 3 All ER 911, [1968] 1 WLR 37, CA. The cost of feeding a hired horse falls on the hirer unless it is otherwise agreed (Story on Bailments (9th Edn, 1878) s 393), and so does the cost of filling a hired car with petrol.
2   Story on Bailments (9th Edn, 1878) s 385.
3   Pothier's Contrat de Louage s 77; 1 Domat book 1, tit 4, s 3, art 7.
4   *British Waggon Co v Lea & Co* (1880) 5 QBD 149, DC (distinguishing *Robson v Drummond* (1831) 2 B & Ad 303); approved in *Southway Group Ltd v Wolff and Wolff* (1991) 28 Con LR 109, 57 BLR 33, CA. The position might be otherwise where the hirer contracted in reliance on the lessor's personal qualifications: cf PARA 183 text and note 12. As to the assignment of contracts see further CONTRACT.

(iii) Hirer's Obligations

183. Payment of rent. The hirer must pay at the agreed time the rent[1] agreed upon for the use of the chattel hired. His failure to do so is a breach of contract which entitles the owner to sue for damages and may, in an appropriate case, entitle the owner to bring the bailment to an end and retake possession of the chattel. A persistent failure to pay rent, which evinces an intention no longer to be bound by the contract, will generally be construed as a repudiation of the bailment entitling the owner to retake possession of the chattel and to claim loss of bargain damages[2]. But a failure to pay a single instalment on the due date will not normally amount to a repudiation by the hirer and will not entitle the owner to recover the chattel, unless the contract expressly states that failure to pay a single instalment on the due date will entitle the owner to terminate the contract and recover the chattel[3]. A contractual provision which provides that a failure to pay an instalment on the due date will entitle the owner to retake possession of the chattel will terminate the primary obligations of the parties remaining unperformed but it does not affect the hirer's secondary obligation to pay damages and therefore the measure of damages recoverable is limited to the recovery of the instalments due and unpaid at the date of termination[4]. Where, however, the contract provides that punctual payment of rent is of the essence of the contract then the damages recoverable are not confined to the arrears of rent as at the date of termination but extend to the loss of future instalments (discounted so as to give their present value), the costs of repossession and interest on these sums less the increased value to the owner of the right to earlier repossession of the chattel than would have been the case if the lease had run its course[5]. Stipulation for payment of a greater sum may fall foul of the penalty clause rule[6], unless the sum payable is simply the acceleration of an existing liability or a present debt[7] or the sum is payable on an event which is not a breach of contract[8], in which cases the penalty clause rule is inapplicable. A clause which is held to be a penalty clause is not struck out of the contract but the clause will not be enforced beyond the actual loss of the party seeking to rely upon it[9], and the clause cannot be relied upon as evidence of an intention that the owner be entitled to loss of bargain damages in the event of a breach[10]. If the owner sells the chattel before the end of the period of hire, this operates as a rescission of the contract and so the owner cannot recover the rent in accordance with the contract but is relegated to an ordinary claim for damages[11].

If the owner of a chattel hired for a fixed term assigns his interest in the chattel to a third party, the hirer, upon notice in writing of the assignment, becomes liable to pay future instalments of rent to the third party[12], unless it can be inferred that the hirer contracted by reference to the owner's personal qualifications, in which case the contract cannot be enforced against the hirer after the owner has assigned his interest in the chattel[13].

1   Where a photocopy business installed photocopiers in shops and sub-post offices under an agreement with the retailer, and the retailer and the retailer's customers paid an agreed fee for each copy made which was accounted for to the photocopy business less commission, this was not rent for the photocopiers: see *TRM Copy Centres (UK) Ltd v Lanwall Services Ltd* [2009] UKHL 35, [2009] 4 All ER 33, [2009] 1 WLR 1375.

2   *Interoffice Telephones Ltd v Robert Freeman Co Ltd* [1958] 1 QB 190, [1957] 3 All ER 479, CA; *Yeoman Credit Ltd v Waragowski* [1961] 3 All ER 145, [1961] 1 WLR 1124, CA; *Overstone Ltd v Shipway* [1962] 1 All ER 52, [1962] 1 WLR 117, CA; *Yeoman Credit Ltd v McLean* [1962] 1 WLR 131n, 105 Sol Jo 990; *Phillips v Brewin Dolphin Bell Lawrie Ltd* [1999] 2 All ER 844, [1999] 1 WLR 2052, CA; *Dalkia Utilities Services plc v Celtech International Ltd* [2006] EWHC 63 (Comm), [2006] 2 P & CR 173, [2006] 1 Lloyd's Rep 599.

3   *Bowmakers Ltd v Barnet Instruments Ltd* [1945] KB 65, [1944] 2 All ER 579, CA.

4   *Financings Ltd v Baldock* [1963] 2 QB 104, [1963] 1 All ER 443, CA; *Brady v St Margaret's Trust Ltd* [1963] 2 QB 494, [1963] 2 All ER 275, CA; *Charterhouse Credit Co Ltd v Tolly* [1963] 2 QB 683, [1963] 2 All ER 432, CA; *Anglo-Auto Finance Co Ltd v James* [1963] 3 All ER 566, [1963] 1 WLR 1042, CA; *United Dominions Trust (Commercial) Ltd v Ennis* [1968] 1 QB 54, [1967] 2 All ER 345, CA; *Eshun v Moorgate Mercantile Co Ltd* [1971] 2 All ER 402, [1971] 1 WLR 722, CA.

5   *Lombard North Central plc v Butterworth* [1987] QB 527, [1987] 1 All ER 267, CA; cf *UCB Leasing Ltd v Holtom* [1987] RTR 362, CA.

6   *Dunlop Pneumatic Tyre Co Ltd v New Garage and Motor Co Ltd* [1915] AC 79, HL; *O'Dea v Allstates Leasing System (WA) Pty Ltd* (1983) 57 ALJR 172, Aust HC. See generally CONTRACT.

7   *Protector Endowment Loan and Annuity Co v Grice* (1880) 5 QBD 592, CA; *Wallingford v Mutual Society and Official Liquidator* (1880) 5 App Cas 685, HL; *O'Dea v Allstates Leasing System (WA) Pty Ltd* (1983) 57 ALJR 172, Aust HC; *Oresundsvarvet Aktiebolag v Lemos, The Angelic Star* [1988] 1 Lloyd's Rep 122, CA.

8   *Alder v Moore* [1961] 2 QB 57, [1961] 1 All ER 1, CA; *Export Credits Guarantee Department v Universal Oil Products Co* [1983] 2 All ER 205, [1983] 1 WLR 399, HL; *Associated*

Distributors Ltd v Hall [1938] 2 KB 83, [1938] 1 All ER 511, CA; *Re Apex Supply Co Ltd* [1942] Ch 108, [1941] 3 All ER 473; *Bridge v Campbell Discount Co Ltd* [1962] AC 600, [1962] 1 All ER 385, HL.

9   *Jobson v Johnson* [1989] 1 All ER 621, [1989] 1 WLR 1026, CA.

10 *AMEV-UDC Finance Ltd v Austin* (1986) 60 ALJR 741, Aust HC.

11 *Wright v Melville* (1828) 3 C & P 542.

12 *British Waggon Co and Parkgate Waggon Co v Lea & Co* (1880) 5 QBD 149, DC.

13 *Robson v Drummond* (1831) 2 B & Ad 303 (explained in *British Waggon Co and Parkgate Waggon Co v Lea & Co* (1880) 5 QBD 149, DC); cf *Jackson v Swarbrick* [1870] WN 133. As to the assignment of contracts generally see further CONTRACT. As to whether such an assignment constitutes a bill of sale see *Re Davis & Co, ex p Rawlings* (1888) 22 QBD 193, CA; and FINANCIAL SERVICES AND INSTITUTIONS vol 50 (2008) PARA 1672.

184.   Care of chattel.   In general, the hirer owes only an obligation to take reasonable care of the chattel hired, and is not liable for loss or injury happening to it, unless caused by his own want of due care, or that of his servants[1]. His liability may be extended or diminished by the terms of a special contract, which will be construed with reference to the age and condition of the particular chattel at the time of the hiring[2] and the circumstances of the injury[3].

Apart from special contract, the hirer is not responsible for fair wear and tear[4]; nor is he under any obligation to do any repairs or incur expenses[5] except such as are naturally incidental to the due performance of his obligation to take reasonable care[6]. If he should exceed his duty and execute repairs for which he is not responsible, it is doubtful whether he has any right to claim to be reimbursed by the owner, even though the repairs are necessary and the expenditure reasonable, and therefore it is advisable for him not to execute them without first consulting the owner[7].

A term of the contract between the parties that the hirer shall keep the chattel from injury amounts, by implication, to an authority from the owner to the hirer to do all acts necessary for preserving the thing hired, and, as against the owner, a third party can acquire a lien on the chattel for the cost of repairing it at the hirer's request[8].

The hirer must not use the chattel hired for any purpose other than that for which it was hired; thus a horse hired as a hack and not for hunting or driving must be used as a hack only, and the hirer will be responsible in case of damage arising from its use for any other purpose[9].

1   *British Crane Hire Corpn Ltd v Ipswich Plant Hire Ltd* [1975] QB 303, [1974] 1 All ER 1059, CA (negligent to order mobile crane to manoeuvre over marshy ground without protection of navimats); *Sanderson v Collins* [1904] 1 KB 628, CA; *Bray v Mayne* (1818) Gow 1; *Handford v Palmer* (1820) 2 Brod & Bing 359; *Dean v Keate* (1811) 3 Camp 4, where the hirer of a horse prescribed for it himself when it fell sick instead of calling in a veterinary surgeon; *Ludgate v Lovett* [1969] 2 All ER 1275, [1969] 1 WLR 1016, CA; cf *Blackpool Ladder Centre Ltd v BWB Partnership* [2000] All ER (D) 1802 (Nov), CA. The fact that the chattel is injured whilst in the hirer's possession raises a prima facie presumption against him: see *Dollar v Greenfield* (1905) Times, 19 May, HL, per Lord Halsbury LC; *Fawcett v Smethurst* (1914) 84 LJKB 473; and the cases cited in PARA 149 note 3, the principle of which would seem to apply here. For an earlier decision to the contrary see *Cooper v Barton* (1810) 3 Camp 5n.

2   *Vendair (London) Ltd v Giro Aviation Co Ltd* [1961] 1 Lloyd's Rep 283 (hirers undertaking to return aircraft in 'condition equivalent to when supplied'; hirers liable for fair wear and tear and not merely for deterioration caused by breach of duty of reasonable care); *Schroder v Ward* (1863) 13 CBNS 410; *Brice & Sons v Christiani and Nielsen* (1928) 44 TLR 335; *Moons Motors Ltd v Kiuan Wou* [1952] 2 Lloyd's Rep 80, CA (contract for hire of car making hirer responsible for repairing damage by accident and stating that a policy of insurance was in force in relation to the use of the car, although no policy was in fact in force covering damage by accident; it was held that the owner was not entitled to recover from the hirer in respect of damage caused by collision).

3 *British Crane Hire Corpn Ltd v Ipswich Plant Hire Ltd* [1975] QB 303, [1974] 1 All ER 1059, CA (trade usage; printed conditions incorporated into oral contract). See further *Ritchie's Car Hire Ltd v Bailey* (1958) 108 L Jo 348 (car hirer not liable for accident unless due to his act or default; to avoid a cat he hit a tree; it was held to be an inevitable accident).

4 See *Pomfret v Ricroft* (1669) 1 Wms Saund 321; *Blakemore v Bristol and Exeter Rly Co* (1858) 8 E & B 1035. These are cases of gratuitous loan, but the principle seems to apply here. See further *Moorhouse v Angus & Robertson (No 2) Pty Ltd* [1981] 1 NSWLR 700 at 708 per Samuels JA (obiter), NSW CA.

5 *Sutton v Temple* (1843) 12 M & W 52 at 60 per Lord Abinger CB; *Hyman v Nye* (1881) 6 QBD 685. For a case of special contract excluding such repairs see *Reading v Menham* (1832) 1 Mood & R 234. See further *Sunrock Aircraft Corpn Ltd v Scandinavian Airlines System Denmark-Norway-Sweden* [2007] EWCA Civ 882, [2007] 2 Lloyd's Rep 612, [2007] All ER (D) 153 (Aug); cf *Wicks Farming Pty Ltd v Waraluck Mining Pty Ltd* [1996] 1 Qd R 99, Qld CA (burden of proof in respect of wear and tear).

6 Eg feeding a hired horse: see Story on Bailments (9th Edn, 1878) s 393. The same would presumably apply to putting oil into a hired car.

7 Story on Bailments (9th Edn, 1878) s 392. As to the lien exercisable by a repairer against a bailor see PARA 154 text to note 26.

8 *Keene v Thomas* [1905] 1 KB 136. See PARA 171.

9 *Burnard v Haggis* (1863) 14 CBNS 45.

185. Return of chattel. The hirer must return the hired chattel at the expiration of the agreed term[1]. This obligation applies notwithstanding the fact that the task of returning the chattel has become more difficult or costly as a result of some unexpected event occurring independently of the hirer's negligence[2]. But if the performance of his contract to return the chattel becomes impossible because it has perished, this impossibility excuses the hirer provided it did not arise from the fault of the hirer or from some risk which he had taken upon himself[3]. The hirer's common law duty to return the chattel can, of course, be diminished or enlarged by special contract[4].

1 *British Crane Hire Corpn Ltd v Ipswich Plant Hire Ltd* [1975] QB 303, [1974] 1 All ER 1059, CA (which turned on the wording of a special contract); *Mills v Graham* (1804) 1 Bos & PNR 140 at 145 per Mansfield CJ. See also *Ballett v Mingay* [1943] KB 281, [1943] 1 All ER 143, CA, where a minor bailee parted with possession of the goods to a third party who lost them, and the minor was held liable in detinue in the absence of any proof by him that, in parting with the goods, he had not stepped outside the bailment altogether. The last two cases, and *Burnard v Haggis* (1863) 14 CBNS 45 (see PARA 184 text and note 9), were cases of minor hirers, who cannot be sued upon the contract of bailment unless the thing hired is a necessary, but may be sued upon independent torts committed in relation to the bailed chattel. As to the liability of minors and children generally see CHILDREN AND YOUNG PERSONS.

2 *British Crane Hire Corpn Ltd v Ipswich Plant Hire Ltd* [1975] QB 303 at 311–312, [1974] 1 All ER 1059 at 1063, CA, per Lord Denning MR, and at 313 and 1064 per Sir Eric Sachs.

3 *British Crane Hire Corpn Ltd v Ipswich Plant Hire Ltd* [1975] QB 303, [1974] 1 All ER 1059, CA; *Taylor v Caldwell* (1863) 3 B & S 826 at 838 per Blackburn J. It would seem that the bailee cannot escape his obligation to return the goods merely by proving that they were destroyed and asserting that the obligation has thus been frustrated; rather he must go further and establish positively that the destruction occurred independently of his default and fell outside his control. In *Jackson (Edinburgh) Ltd v Constructors John Brown Ltd* 1965 SLT 37, Ct of Sess, the hired chattel was damaged by fire, and in order to exculpate themselves the hirers had only to prove that the fire was accidental, i e that it was not caused by their deliberate act or negligence. See further *Port Swettenham Authority v TW Wu & Co (M) Sdn Bhd* [1979] AC 580 at 590, [1978] 3 All ER 337 at 340, PC (' ... The onus is always upon the bailee ... to prove that the loss of any goods bailed to him was not caused by any fault of his or of any of his servants or agents to whom he entrusted the goods for safekeeping'); *Aktieselskabet de Danske Sukkerfabrikker v Bajamar Compania Naviera SA, The Torenia* [1983] 2 Lloyd's Rep 210 at 216 per Hobhouse J ('... it does not suffice for the bailee to prove that the goods have been lost or destroyed while in his possession; he must go further and prove that he is protected from liability by some common law or contractual defence'). Neither of the last two authorities mentioned involved a bailment by way of hire; rather, they involved bailments for custody and carriage respectively. But it would seem that a similar principle is applicable to contracts of hire.

Cf *Joseph Constantine Steamship Line Ltd v Imperial Smelting Corpn Ltd, The Kingswood* [1942] AC 154, [1941] 2 All ER 165, HL; *J Lauritzen AS v Wijsmuller BV, The Super Servant Two* [1990] 1 Lloyd's Rep 1, CA. As to the effect of impossibility of performance on contracts see CONTRACT vol 9(1) (Reissue) PARA 888 et seq.

4 *British Crane Hire Corpn Ltd v Ipswich Plant Hire Ltd* [1975] QB 303, [1974] 1 All ER 1059, CA.

186. Liability for servant's misconduct. The negligence of the hirer's servant is, if committed within the scope of the servant's employment, the negligence of the master[1]. The master is therefore liable for any want of care towards the hired chattel shown by the servant in the course of his employment[2]. Such liability may arise even though the servant acts in a manner which the master has forbidden, or would not have authorised had he known of the act[3].

The master is also liable where the servant commits a deliberate wrong to the chattel, such as damage or theft, if the master has entrusted the chattel to the servant and has entrusted any part of his duty of care to him[4]. In that case, the servant commits the wrong in the course of his employment[5]. But where the master has not entrusted the chattel to the servant and has not delegated any part of his duty of care to the servant, the wrong is not committed in the course of the servant's employment and the master is not liable[6].

1 *Smith v Stages* [1989] AC 928, [1989] 1 All ER 833, HL (not a case of bailment); and see generally AGENCY vol 1 (2008) PARA 121 et seq; TORT vol 97 (2010) PARA 680 et seq.
2 *British Crane Hire Corpn Ltd v Ipswich Plant Hire Ltd* [1975] QB 303, [1974] 1 All ER 1059, CA (instruction to take mobile crane over marshy ground without navimats). See also *Dollar v Greenfield* (1905) Times, 19 May (horse bolting from stable). Cf *Arbon v Fussell* (1862) 3 F & F 152 (negligent entrustment of management of chattel to incompetent servant).
3 *Smith v Stages* [1989] AC 928, [1989] 1 All ER 833, HL; *Limpus v London General Omnibus Co* (1862) 1 H & C 526; and see TORT vol 97 (2010) PARA 690 et seq.
4 *Morris v CW Martin & Sons Ltd* [1966] 1 QB 716, [1965] 2 All ER 725, CA (sub-bailment for work and labour); *Sanderson v Collins* [1904] 1 KB 628, CA, distinguishing *Coupé Co v Maddick* [1891] 2 QB 413. See PARA 148. See also Palmer on Bailment (3rd Edn, 2009) para 21-069. The onus of negativing such conduct is, in common with the general onus of negativing negligence by the servant, on the hirer: *Port Swettenham Authority v TW Wu & Co (M) Sdn Bhd* [1979] AC 580, [1978] 3 All ER 337, PC (custody); *Transmotors Ltd v Robertson, Buckley & Co Ltd* [1970] 1 Lloyd's Rep 224 (carriage); Palmer on Bailment (3rd Edn, 2009) para 21-059.
5 *Morris v CW Martin & Sons Ltd* [1966] 1 QB 716 at 738–739, [1965] 2 All ER 725 at 739, CA, per Salmon LJ. See also generally *Lister v Hesley Hall Ltd* [2001] UKHL 22, [2002] 1 AC 215, [2001] 2 All ER 769.
6 Cf *Leesh River Tea Co Ltd v British India Steam Navigation Co Ltd, The Chyebassa* [1967] 2 QB 250, [1966] 3 All ER 593, CA.

187. Measure of damage. A bailor is entitled to recover damages from the bailee if the chattel is damaged or destroyed by the negligence[1] or breach of contract of the bailee[2]. In the event of damage to a chattel, the bailor is entitled to recover the cost of repair plus a sum representing the permanent diminution in value of the chattel[3]. The bailor may also claim damages for loss of use of the property during any necessary period of repair or recovery[4]. In certain circumstances it may be possible to claim loss of profits where there has been damage to a profit-earning chattel[5].

If a chattel is destroyed, then the bailor can recover the value of the goods at the time of their destruction, together with any consequential damages which are not too remote in law[6]. In particular cases the cost of reinstatement (exceeding any diminution in value) may be recoverable[7].

1 Which may sound in tort or in bailment: *Sutcliffe v Chief Constable of West Yorkshire* [1996] RTR 86.

2   Ie subject to any exclusion clauses in the contract of bailment. See generally DAMAGES vol 12(1)
    (Reissue) PARA 1088 et seq.
3   See *Hughes v Quentin* (1838) 8 C & P 703, where the bailee's injury of an animal led to liability
    for the farrier's bill for keep and treatment, and the difference between the animal's original and
    subsequent value.
4   This is often quantified in terms of the cost of hiring an alternative: see *Davis v Oswell* (1837)
    7 C & P 804, where the plaintiff was obliged to hire other horses; *Mediana (Owners) v Comet
    (Owners, Master and Crew), The Mediana* [1900] AC 113 at 117, HL; *Brandeis Goldschmidt
    & Co Ltd v Western Transport Ltd* [1981] QB 864, [1982] 1 All ER 28, CA; *Hillesden
    Securities Ltd v Ryjak Ltd* [1983] 2 All ER 184, [1983] 1 WLR 959. Cf *Saleslease Ltd v Davis*
    [2000] 1 All ER (Comm) 883, [1999] 1 WLR 1664, CA (lessor's damages against third party
    who took possession from hirer, his tenant).
5   This has been said to depend on the knowledge of the bailee of the profit-making capacity of the
    chattel: see *Bodley v Reynolds* (1846) 8 QB 779; and cf *France v Gaudet* (1871) LR 6 QB 199,
    Ex Ch; *The Arpad* [1934] P 189, CA; *Strand Electric and Engineering Co Ltd v Brisford
    Entertainments Ltd* [1952] 2 QB 246, [1952] 1 All ER 796, CA. See PARA 233; and DAMAGES
    vol 12(1) (Reissue) PARAS 863–864, 1096.
6   See DAMAGES vol 12(1) (Reissue) PARA 862 et seq; TORT vol 45(2) (Reissue) PARA 542 seq.
7   See DAMAGES vol 12(1) (Reissue) PARA 862 et seq; TORT vol 45(2) (Reissue) PARA 542 seq.

(5) PLEDGES AND PAWNS

(i) Nature of Pledges and Pawns

188.   Classes of pawns. The remaining class of bailment for valuable
consideration is pledge[1], whereby a chattel is delivered to a bailee to be held by
him as security for a debt or other engagement[2].

There are two classes of pawn[3], namely: (1) those governed by statute[4]; and
(2) all other cases. The statutory control is embodied in the Consumer Credit
Act 1974[5]. In other cases, the contract of pawn is governed by the general law.
The general law applies also to pawns governed by statute, unless expressly
excluded by statute[6].

1   Ie *pignus*, or *vadium*: see PARA 106.
2   *Coggs v Bernard* (1703) 2 Ld Raym 909 at 913 per Holt CJ; Jones on Bailments (4th Edn, 1833)
    p 36; Story on Bailments (9th Edn, 1878) s 286. See also *Marcq v Christie Manson &
    Woods Ltd (t/a Christie's)* [2003] EWCA Civ 731, [2004] QB 286, [2003] 3 All ER 561 (where
    the issue was whether an auction house was holding a painting (of the prior theft of which it had
    no notice) as pledgee or party akin to a pledgee).
3   As to the meaning of 'pawn' see PARA 189.
4   As to statutory control see PARA 228; and CONSUMER CREDIT vol 21 (2011) PARA 52.
5   For the relevant provisions of the Consumer Credit Act 1974 see PARA 228; and see generally
    CONSUMER CREDIT vol 21 (2011) PARA 1 et seq.
6   *Jones v Marshall* (1889) 24 QBD 269, DC.

(ii) Pledge or Pawn at Common Law

A. INTRODUCTION

189.   Meanings of 'pawn', 'pawnor', 'pawnee' and 'pawnbroker'. A 'pawn' or
'pledge'[1] is a bailment of personal property as a security for some debt or
engagement[2].

A 'pawnor' is one who, being liable to an engagement, gives to the person to
whom he is liable a thing to be held as a security for the payment of his debt or
the fulfilment of his liability[3]. A 'pawnee' is one who receives a pawn or pledge[4].

A 'pawnbroker' is one whose business is to lend money[5], usually in small sums, upon pawn or pledge[6]. Since the repeal of the Pawnbrokers Act 1872, there is no longer a statutory definition of 'pawnbroker'[7].

1   At common law, 'pawn' and 'pledge' were used interchangeably to denote both the bailment and the thing bailed, although there was the distinction in practice that 'pawn' was not used in respect of the pledging of bills of lading. The Consumer Credit Act 1974 has drawn a new distinction between the thing put to pawn and the rights of the pawnee in that thing, the former being distinguished by 'pawn' and the latter by 'pledge': see CONSUMER CREDIT vol 21 (2011) PARA 217. As to consumer credit legislation in relation to pawns and pledges see PARA 228; and CONSUMER CREDIT vol 21 (2011) PARA 217 et seq.
2   Story on Bailments (9th Edn) (1878) s 286. It is described by Holt CJ, in *Coggs v Bernard* (1703) 2 Ld Raym 909 at 913, as the fourth sort of bailment 'when goods or chattels are delivered to another as a pawn to be a security to him for money borrowed of him by the bailor'. The different definitions are collected in *Donald v Suckling* (1866) LR 1 QB 585 at 594: see PARAS 106, 188. As to the meaning of 'pledge' under the Factors Act 1889 see AGENCY vol 1 (2008) PARA 148.
3   3 Bouvier's Law Dictionary 2539. As to the meaning of 'pawnor' in relation to pawns subject to the Consumer Credit Act 1974 see s 189(1); and CONSUMER CREDIT vol 21 (2011) PARA 217.
4   3 Bouvier's Law Dictionary 2539. As to the meaning of 'pawnee' for the purposes of the Consumer Credit Act 1974 see s 189(1); and CONSUMER CREDIT vol 21 (2011) PARA 217.
5   As to the business of lending money subject to the Consumer Credit Act 1974 generally see PARA 228; and CONSUMER CREDIT vol 21 (2011) PARA 1 et seq.
6   3 Bouvier's Law Dictionary 2539.
7   As to the repeal of the Pawnbrokers Acts 1872 and 1960 see PARA 228; and CONSUMER CREDIT vol 21 (2011) PARA 11.

190.   General characteristics of the contract of pawn.   The contract of pawn or pledge is one of the five classes of bailment[1]. It is distinguishable from a transaction of mortgage in two main ways[2]. In the first place, it is essential to the contract of pawn that the property pledged should be actually or constructively[3] delivered to the pawnee[4], whereas on a mortgage the property passes by assignment, and possession by the mortgagee is not essential in every case[5]. Secondly, whereas on a legal mortgage[6] of personal property the mortgagee acquires by assignment an absolute interest in the property subject to a right of redemption, in pawn the pawnee has only a special property or a special interest[7] in the pledge, while the general property in it remains in the pawnor[8] and wholly reverts to him on discharge of the debt or engagement[9].

Pawn has been described as a security where, by contract, a deposit of goods is made a security for a debt and the right to the property vests in the pawnee so far as is necessary to secure the debt; in this sense, it is intermediate between a simple lien and a mortgage which wholly passes the property in the thing conveyed[10].

Pawn does not amount to an equitable mortgage[11], or to a bill of sale[12].

The identity of pledge as a form of bailment carries other general implications. The pawnee is a fiduciary and holds the surplus proceeds of any sale of the chattel on trust for the pawnor and is bound to pay such surplus to the pawnor without the need for the pawnor to make a demand for payment[13]. The pawnee must take reasonable care of the goods[14] and may be answerable to a guarantor of the debt, as well as the pawnor, if through lack of care the security is lost or impaired[15].

1   See PARA 106. There is no requirement that the agreement be made or evidenced in writing save for the statutory requirements as to credit agreements and pawn-receipts in the case of agreements to which the Consumer Credit Act 1974 applies (see PARA 228; and CONSUMER CREDIT vol 21 (2011) PARAS 179 et seq, 219–220). As to the meanings of 'pawn' and 'pledge' see PARA 189.

2   As to mortgage generally see MORTGAGE vol 77 (2010) PARA 101 et seq.
3   See e g *Official Assignee of Madras v Mercantile Bank of India Ltd* [1935] AC 53, PC.
4   As to the meaning of 'pawnee' see PARA 189.
5   *Ryall v Rowles* (1750) 1 Atk 165 at 166; *Re Morritt, ex p Official Receiver* (1886) 18 QBD 222 at 232, CA, per Cotton LJ, and at 234 per Fry LJ.
6   Pawn does not amount to an equitable mortgage of an interest in personal property: see the text and note 11.
7   *Donald v Suckling* (1866) LR 1 QB 585; *Burdick v Sewell* (1883) 10 QBD 363 at 367 (affd *Sewell v Burdick* (1884) 10 App Cas 74, HL). As to the special property or special interest see further PARA 209. See also *Halliday v Holgate* (1868) LR 3 Exch 299 at 302, Ex Ch. Although the pawnee may sell he has no right to acquire the property in the goods himself by means of foreclosure: see *Carter v Wake* (1877) 4 ChD 605 at 606.
8   As to the meaning of 'pawnor' see PARA 189.
9   *Ryall v Rowles* (1750) 1 Atk 165; *Jones v Smith* (1794) 2 Ves 372; *Re Morritt, ex p Official Receiver* (1886) 18 QBD 222, CA; *Fraser v Byas* (1895) 11 TLR 481; *George Attenborough & Son v Solomon* [1913] AC 76 at 84, HL, per Viscount Haldane LC.
10 *Halliday v Holgate* (1868) LR 3 Exch 299 at 302, Ex Ch, per Willes J. As to the difference between pawn and lien see PARA 191.
11 *Carter v Wake* (1877) 4 ChD 605; *Re Richardson, Shillito v Hobson* (1885) 30 ChD 396 at 403, CA, per Fry LJ. For the law relating to an equitable mortgage or charge of an interest in personal property see MORTGAGE vol 77 (2010) PARA 139 et seq.
12 *Re Hardwick, ex p Hubbard* (1886) 17 QBD 690, CA; *Waight v Waight and Walker* [1952] P 282, [1952] 2 All ER 290. As to the avoidance of bills of sale by way of security unless in the statutory form or unless certain other conditions are fulfilled see FINANCIAL SERVICES AND INSTITUTIONS vol 50 (2008) PARA 1818 et seq. The bills of sale legislation affects documents, but not oral transactions: see FINANCIAL SERVICES AND INSTITUTIONS vol 50 (2008) PARA 1839.
13 See *Mathew v TM Sutton Ltd* [1994] 4 All ER 793, [1994] 1 WLR 1455. See also the Consumer Credit Act 1974 s 121(3); and CONSUMER CREDIT vol 21 (2011) PARA 226.
14 *Giles v Carter* (1965) 109 Sol Jo 452.
15 *Bank of Credit and Commerce International SA v Aboody* [1990] 1 QB 923, [1992] 4 All ER 955, CA.

191. Difference between pawn and lien. The rights of the pawnee[1] in the thing pawned are distinguishable from a common law lien[2] in that whereas the holder of a lien has no inherent power of sale, that right accrues automatically to the pledgee in the event of the pledgor's default. A further distinction has traditionally been discerned in the fact that the pledgee acquires a special property or special interest[3] in the property pawned, whereas a person exercising a lien has only a right to detain the subject matter of the lien until he is paid[4]. Consistently with this distinction, it has been held that a lien holder cannot transfer his interest to a third person[5], although authority favouring the assignability of that interest[6] and indeed the generally proprietory nature of the interest[7] can be cited. Furthermore, while pledge is necessarily consensual, lien although capable of being consensual is basically a common law self-help remedy arising independently of agreement[8].

On the other hand, pledge is similar to a legal lien in that actual or constructive delivery occurs and possession passes to the pledge, and a lien is at least is some senses a proprietary interest capable of being enforced against an assignee of the pledgor's reversion[9]; in this respect lien does not differ as radically from pledge as is sometimes understood[10].

1   As to the meaning of 'pawnee' see PARA 189.
2   As to pawn distinguished from lien see LIEN vol 68 (2008) PARA 815.
3   As to the special property or special interest see PARA 209. In respect of regulated consumer credit agreements, the Consumer Credit Act 1974 specifically recognises that the interests of both the pawnee and the pawnor may be passed by assignment or operation of law: see s 189(1); and PARA 189.
4   *Yungmann v Briesemann* (1892) 67 LT 642, CA; and see *Gladstone v Birley* (1817) 2 Mer 401. As to the nature of lien see LIEN vol 68 (2008) PARA 820.

5 *Donald v Suckling* (1866) LR 1 QB 585 at 612 per Blackburn J.
6 *Bull v Faulkner* (1848) 2 De G & Sm 772; *Vered v Inscorp Holdings Ltd* (1993) 31 NSWLR 290, NSW SC.
7 *Legg v Evans* (1840) 6 M & W 36 at 41, per Parke B; *Rogers v Kennay* (1846) 9 QB 592 at 595–596, per Patterson J.
8 See *Tappenden v Artus* [1964] 2 QB 185 at 195, [1963] 3 All ER 213 at 216, CA, per Diplock LJ ('The common law remedy of a possessory lien, like other primitive remedies such as abatement of nuisance, self-defence or ejection of trespassers to land, is one of self-help. It is a remedy in rem exercisable on the goods, and its exercise requires no intervention by the courts'). See also LIEN vol 68 (2008) PARA 815.
9 *The Freightline One* [1986] 1 Lloyd's Rep 266 at 270 per Sheen J obiter; *Rich v Aldred* (1704) 6 Mod 216, per Lord Holt; *Franklin v Neate* (1844) 13 M & W 481 at 486, per Rolfe B.
10 See *Marcq v Christie Manson & Woods Ltd (t/a Christie's)* [2003] EWCA Civ 731, [2004] QB 286, [2003] 3 All ER 561, which has been questioned (see Palmer on Bailment (3rd Edn, 2009) para 22-007).

192. Things capable of being pawned. The subject matter of the contract of pawn[1] usually consists of goods and chattels capable of actual or constructive delivery[2], but other forms of personal property, including negotiable instruments, may be the subject of the contract where they can be identified[3].

1 As to the meaning of 'pawn' see PARA 189.
2 *Coggs v Bernard* (1703) 2 Ld Raym 909. As to what constitutes delivery see PARA 200.
3 The following cases serve as illustrations: *Taylor v Chester* (1869) LR 4 QB 309 (half a £50 note); *Lockwood v Ewer (or Lady Child v Chanstilet)* (1742) 9 Mod Rep 275 (East India stock); *Donald v Suckling* (1866) LR 1 QB 585 (debentures); *Langton v Waite* (1868) LR 6 Eq 165 (railway stock); *Halliday v Holgate* (1868) LR 3 Exch 299, Ex Ch (scrip certificates). As to an injunction to restrain an unlawful pledge of negotiable instruments see CIVIL PROCEDURE vol 11 (2009) PARA 478. The Consumer Credit Act 1974 ss 114–122 do not apply to a pledge of documents of title or of bearer bonds or to a non-commercial agreement or to exempt agreements: see PARA 228. Where compensation is paid under the Compensation (Defence) Act 1939 in respect of property which is subject to a pledge, the sum paid is deemed to be comprised in the pledge: Compensation (Defence) Act 1939 s 14(1) (numbered as such by the Statute Law (Repeals) Act 1989). This provision is not confined to cases where the owner is the pledgor; but see *Earl of Radnor v Folkestone Pier and Lift Co* [1950] 2 All ER 690, where such a restriction was assumed.

193. Unlawful contracts of pawn. By statute, contracts of pawn[1] relating to the following kinds of property have been made unlawful[2]: (1) military, air force and naval equipment[3]; (2) any document issued by or on behalf of the Secretary of State[4] in connection with any benefit, pension or allowance[5]; and (3) firearms or ammunition[6].

1 As to the meaning of 'pawn' see PARA 189.
2 As to offences by persons carrying on consumer credit businesses see PARA 228; and CONSUMER CREDIT vol 21 (2011) PARAS 219, 227.
3 See the Army Act 1955 ss 46, 195, 196, 211; the Air Force Act 1955 ss 46, 195, 196, 210; and the Naval Discipline Act 1957 ss 31, 98, 99 (all repealed by the Armed Forces Act 2006, but have been saved until 8 November 2010 by the Armed Forces, Army, Air Force and Naval Discipline Acts (Continuation) Order 2009, SI 2009/1752). The Armed Forces Act 2006 does not contain provisions to this effect; but see ss 24, 25 (damage to or loss of public or service property; misapplication of such property). As to the avoidance of purported assignments of or charges on military pay, pensions, benefits, bounties, grants or allowances see s 356; and ARMED FORCES vol 2(2) (Reissue) PARAS 218, 271. The Armed Forces, Army, Air Force and Naval Discipline Acts (Continuation) Order 2009, SI 2009/1752, also provides for the continuation of the Armed Forces Act 2006 until 8 November 2010. For restrictions in respect of pensions see CHOSES IN ACTION vol 13 (2009) PARA 94 et seq.
4 Ie the Secretary of State for Work and Pensions: see SOCIAL SECURITY AND PENSIONS vol 44(2) (Reissue) PARA 1.
5 See the Social Security Administration Act 1992 s 182(1)(a); and SOCIAL SECURITY AND PENSIONS vol 44(2) (Reissue) PARA 404.

6 The Firearms Act 1968 makes it an offence for a pawnbroker to take in pawn any firearm or ammunition to which s 1 applies (see CRIMINAL LAW vol 26 (2010) PARAS 579–582) or a shot gun: see s 3(6); and CRIMINAL LAW vol 26 (2010) PARA 595. A pawnbroker acting in contravention of s 3(6) is liable on summary conviction to imprisonment for a term not exceeding three months or to a fine not exceeding level 3 on the standard scale or to both: s 51(1), Sch 6 Pt I (Sch 6 Pt I amended by, or by virtue of, the Criminal Justice Act 1972 s 28(1)–(4); the Magistrates' Courts Act 1980 s 32(2); the Criminal Justice Act 1982 ss 38, 46; the Criminal Justice Act 1988 s 44; the Firearms (Amendment) Act 1988 ss 13(5), 23(7); the Criminal Justice and Public Order Act 1994 s 157(3), (5)(a), Sch 8 Pt III; the Firearms (Amendment) Act 1994 ss 1(2), 2(3); the Firearms (Amendment) Act 1997 ss 43(3), 52, Sch 2 paras 1, 4(2), 14, Sch 3; the Anti-social Behaviour Act 2003 ss 37(2), 38(1), (5), 92, Sch 3; the Criminal Justice Act 2003 ss 280(2), (3), 288, Sch 26 para 20; the Violent Crime Reduction Act 2006 ss 30(1), (4), (5), 33(1), (6), 34(1), (4), (5), 40(2), (3), 41, 65, Sch 5; by SI 1992/2823; and by the Crime and Security Act 2010 s 46(1), (4)). The Firearms Act 1968 does not define 'pawnbroker', and since the repeal of the Pawnbrokers Acts 1872 to 1960 there is no longer any statutory definition of 'pawnbroker'; but for a definition see PARA 189. As to the standard scale see SENTENCING AND DISPOSITION OF OFFENDERS vol 92 (2010) PARA 142. Functions of a local authority under the Firearms Act 1968 are 'relevant functions' for the purposes of the Regulatory Enforcement and Sanctions Act 2008 Pt 1 (ss 1–21) (see s 4, Sch 3; and LOCAL GOVERNMENT vol 69 (2009) PARA 733); thus the Local Better Regulation Office may give guidance to local authorities as to the exercise of those functions (see s 7; and LOCAL GOVERNMENT vol 69 (2009) PARA 734).

  It is also an offence to take in pawn small arms where their barrels are marked with any forged or counterfeit stamp, or with any part of any such stamp: see the Gun Barrel Proof Act 1868 s 121(1) para (5) (amended by the Gun Barrel Proof Act 1978 s 8(1), Sch 3 para 10(1), (2)); and the Gun Barrel Proof Act 1868 s 122(2) (s 122 amended by the Gun Barrel Proof Act 1978 s 8(2), Sch 3 para 11, Sch 4). Furthermore, every person who takes in pawn small arms where their barrels are not duly proved and marked commits an offence: see the Gun Barrel Proof Act 1868 s 122(5) (as so amended).

194. Discrimination by pawnee. A person concerned with the provision of services[1] to the public or a section of the public must not discriminate[2] against a person requiring the service by not providing the person with the service[3].

1 For these purposes, a reference to the provision of a service includes a reference to the provision of goods or facilities: see Equality Act 2010 s 31(2); and DISCRIMINATION.
2 As to the meaning of 'discrimination' see the Equality Act 2010 ss 13–19; and DISCRIMINATION.
3 See the Equality Act 2010 s 29; and DISCRIMINATION.

195. Pawns by persons under a disability. The Infants Relief Act 1874 provided that a contract, whether by specialty or by simple contract[1], entered into by a minor for the repayment of money lent or to be lent was absolutely void[2]. However, the Minors' Contracts Act 1987 disapplied the Infants Relief Act 1874[3], so that contracts made by a minor after 9 June 1987[4] again become subject to the rules of common law governing contracts with children[5]. The Infants Relief Act 1874 seemed to have made it impossible for a minor to make a valid contract of pawn[6], and if any such contract was made the pawnee could neither recover the principal nor sue for interest, unless perhaps the loan was to provide necessaries[7].

  A contract of pawn made by a drunken person follows the ordinary law of contract[8]. The capacity of a person suffering from mental disorder to enter into a binding contract is discussed elsewhere in this work[9].

1 See CONTRACT vol 9(1) (Reissue) PARA 615 et seq.
2 See the Infants Relief Act 1874 s 1 (repealed); and CHILDREN AND YOUNG PERSONS vol 5(3) (2008 Reissue) PARA 14.
3 See the Minors' Contracts Act 1987 s 1(a).
4 Ie the date on which the Minors' Contracts Act 1987 s 1 came into force: s 5(2).
5 As to the common law rules governing contracts with children see CHILDREN AND YOUNG PERSONS vol 5(3) (2008 Reissue) PARA 12 et seq.

6   As to the meanings of 'pawn' and 'pawnee' see PARA 189.
7   There is no direct authority on this point, but see CHILDREN AND YOUNG PERSONS vol 5(3) (2008 Reissue) PARAS 18–19. In respect of regulated agreements under the Consumer Credit Act 1974, a person who takes any article in pawn from an individual whom he knows to be, or who appears to be and is, a minor commits an offence: see PARA 228; and CONSUMER CREDIT vol 21 (2011) PARA 219.
8   See CONTRACT vol 9(1) (Reissue) PARA 717.
9   See MENTAL HEALTH vol 30(2) (Reissue) PARA 600 et seq.

B. THE CONTRACT OF PLEDGE OR PAWN

196. Who may pawn at common law. At common law the capacity of a person to enter into a contract of pawn is governed by the same rules as are applicable to contracts in general[1].

1   See CONTRACT vol 9(1) (Reissue) PARA 630. As to pawns by persons under disability see PARA 195. As to the meaning of 'pawn' see PARA 189. As to the capacity of an executor to pledge his testator's assets see *George Attenborough & Son v Solomon* [1913] AC 76, HL; and TRUSTS vol 48 (2007 Reissue) PARA 602.

197. Mercantile agents or factors. The capacity of mercantile agents[1] or factors to enter into a contract of pawn is regulated by statute[2]. At common law, a mercantile agent cannot bind his principal to a contract of pawn without the principal's authority[3].

Where, with the owner's consent, a mercantile agent is in possession[4] of goods[5] or of the documents of title[6] to goods, any pledge[7] of the goods made by him when acting in the ordinary course of business of a mercantile agent is as valid as if he were expressly authorised by the owner of the goods to make the pledge, provided that the pledgee acts in good faith and has no notice at the time of the pledge that the agent has no authority to make it[8].

The statutory authority of a mercantile agent to pledge exists notwithstanding the usage of a particular trade that such an agent has no authority to pledge goods entrusted to him for sale[9], and the same principle applies to a mercantile agent who is entrusted with goods for sale on the terms of sale or return[10].

1   As to the meaning of 'mercantile agent', and as to agreements with his clerk or other authorised person, see AGENCY vol 1 (2008) PARAS 12, 148.
2   See the Factors Act 1889; and AGENCY vol 1 (2008) PARA 148. As to the meaning of 'pawn' see PARA 189.
3   *Fuentes v Montis* (1868) LR 3 CP 268 at 277 per Willes J (on appeal LR 4 CP 93, Ex Ch); *Cole v North Western Bank* (1875) LR 10 CP 354 at 363, Ex Ch, per Blackburn J; *City Bank v Barrow* (1880) 5 App Cas 664, HL; *Farquharson Bros & Co v King & Co* [1902] AC 325, HL. See also AGENCY vol 1 (2008) PARAS 12, 43, 141 et seq. The mercantile agent who pledges without the owner's authority will be liable to the owner for conversion, as might the pledgee. Receipt of goods by way of pledge is conversion if the delivery is conversion: see the Torts (Interference with Goods) Act 1977 s 11(2); and PARA 225.
4   As to the effect of obtaining possession by fraud and of revocation of consent see AGENCY vol 1 (2008) PARA 148.
5   'Goods' includes wares and merchandise (see the Factors Act 1889 s 1(3)) and household furniture (see *Lee v Butler* [1893] 2 QB 318 at 321, CA).
6   As to the meaning of 'documents of title' see AGENCY vol 1 (2008) PARA 148. As to documents of title given by a mercantile agent see AGENCY vol 1 (2008) PARA 149.
7   As to the meaning of 'pledge' for the purposes of the Factors Act 1889 see AGENCY vol 1 (2008) PARA 148. Goods entrusted by a mercantile agent to an auctioneer for sale are not thereby dealt with by way of pledge even when the auctioneer before sale makes advances upon them to him: *Waddington & Sons v Neale & Sons* (1907) 96 LT 786; and see *Biggs v Evans* [1894] 1 QB 88. As to auction generally see AUCTION.
8   Factors Act 1889 s 2(1). See also *Lloyds Bank Ltd v Bank of America National Trust and Savings Association* [1938] 2 KB 147, [1938] 2 All ER 63, CA; *City Fur Manufacturing Co Ltd*

v Fureenbond (Brokers) London Ltd [1937] 1 All ER 799; *Beverley Acceptances v Oakley* [1982] RTR 417; and AGENCY vol 1 (2008) PARAS 148–149.

9   *Oppenheimer v Attenborough & Son* [1908] 1 KB 221, CA. See also *Janesich v George Attenborough & Son* (1910) 26 TLR 278. By asking a friend to pledge goods entrusted to him for sale, a mercantile agent is not pledging goods in the ordinary course of his business as a mercantile agent: *De Gorter v Attenborough & Son* (1904) 21 TLR 19.

10   *Weiner v Harris* [1910] 1 KB 285, CA.

198.   Pledges by sellers and buyers of goods.   Where a seller of goods is in possession of them after the sale and delivers them under a pledge, the pledge has effect, if the goods are received in good faith and without notice of the sale, as if the owner of the goods had expressly authorised their delivery[1]. Protection is similarly afforded where a buyer, having bought or agreed to buy goods, obtains possession of them with the seller's consent and delivers them under a pledge[2]. This protection extends to pledges effected by a mercantile agent[3] acting for the seller or buyer of goods who has continued in possession of the goods, or who has bought or agreed to buy them[4].

1   See the Factors Act 1889 s 8; and the Sale of Goods Act 1979 s 24. See further AGENCY vol 1 (2008) PARAS 145, 165; SALE OF GOODS AND SUPPLY OF SERVICES vol 41 (2005 Reissue) PARA 157. As to the meaning of 'pledge' see PARA 189. These provisions extend to documents of title to goods as well as to the goods themselves, and to other dispositions as well as to pledges. The provisions of the Sale of Goods Act 1979 relating to contracts of sale do not apply to any transactions in the form of a contract of sale which is intended to operate by way of pledge: see s 62(4); and SALE OF GOODS AND SUPPLY OF SERVICES vol 41 (2005 Reissue) PARA 8. A mere written agreement to pledge unaccompanied by actual or constructive delivery may not be exempt from the requirement of the Sale of Goods Act 1979 if such a transaction is to have effect as a result of the documents only: see *Dublin City Distillery (Great Brunswick Street, Dublin) Ltd v Doherty* [1914] AC 823 at 848, HL. Functions of a local authority under the Sale of Goods Act 1979 are 'relevant functions' for the purposes of the Regulatory Enforcement and Sanctions Act 2008 Pt 1 (ss 1–21) (see s 4, Sch 3; and LOCAL GOVERNMENT vol 69 (2009) PARA 733); thus the Local Better Regulation Office may give guidance to local authorities as to the exercise of those functions (see s 7; and LOCAL GOVERNMENT vol 69 (2009) PARA 734).

2   See the Factors Act 1889 s 9; and the Sale of Goods Act 1979 s 25(1). A buyer under a conditional sale agreement is not a buyer or someone who has agreed to buy for the purposes of both the Factors Act 1889 s 9 and the Sale of Goods Act 1979 s 25(1): see the Factors Act 1889 s 9(i) (added by the Consumer Credit Act 1974 s 192(3)(a), Sch 4 para 2); and the Sale of Goods Act 1979 s 25(2)(a). See further SALE OF GOODS AND SUPPLY OF SERVICES vol 41 (2005 Reissue) PARA 158. For the relevant provisions as to ordinary hire purchase agreements see CONSUMER CREDIT vol 21 (2011) PARA 93 et seq. As to the effect of dispositions by a buyer on the rights of an unpaid seller, and as to the rights of a pledgee as against an unpaid seller see SALE OF GOODS AND SUPPLY OF SERVICES vol 41 (2005 Reissue) PARA 236 et seq.

3   As to the meaning of 'mercantile agent' see AGENCY vol 1 (2008) PARA 12.

4   See the Factors Act 1889 ss 8, 9; and the Sale of Goods Act 1979 ss 24, 25. Where the pledge falls outside these provisions, both pledgor and pledgee may be liable in conversion to the owner: receipt of goods by way of pledge is conversion if the delivery is conversion (see the Torts (Interference with Goods) Act 1977 s 11(2); and PARA 225).

199.   Proof of property.   Subject to the provisions relating to mercantile agents[1], mere possession by a pawnor[2] is not sufficient proof of property in the thing pawned against the real owner[3].

If the pawnor has no authority to make the pledge, the pawnee cannot hold the goods pledged against the real owner[4], unless the owner has so acted as to clothe the pawnor with apparent authority to make the pledge[5]. An authority to an agent to sell does not extend by implication to a pledge so as to give the pawnee a good title as against the real owner[6].

1   See PARAS 197–198.

2   As to the meanings of 'pawnor' and 'pawnee' see PARA 189.

3   *Hoare v Parker* (1788) 2 Term Rep 376; *Kingsford v Merry* (1856) 1 H & N 503 at 516, Ex Ch. As to the rights of the true owner where the goods pawned have been pawned without his authority see PARA 222 et seq.

4   *Williams v Barton* (1825) 3 Bing 139, Ex Ch. See also *Advanced Industrial Technology Corpn Ltd v Bond Street Jewellers Ltd* [2006] EWCA Civ 923, [2006] All ER (D) 21 (Jul).

5   *Cole v North Western Bank* (1875) LR 10 CP 354 at 363, Ex Ch, per Blackburn J; *Henderson & Co v Williams* [1895] 1 QB 521, CA; *Fry and Mason v Smellie and Taylor* [1912] 3 KB 282, CA; *Fuller v Glyn, Mills, Currie & Co* [1914] 2 KB 168. See further AGENCY vol 1 (2008) PARA 145; ESTOPPEL vol 16(2) (Reissue) PARA 1058 et seq.

6   *City Bank v Barrow* (1880) 5 App Cas 664 at 669–670, HL.

200. Delivery of chattel pawned. A contract to pawn a chattel, even though money is advanced on the faith of it, is not sufficient in itself to pass any special property or interest in the chattel to the pawnee[1]. Delivery of the chattel pawned in consideration of the debt or advance is a necessary element in the making of a contract of pawn[2]. This delivery may be actual, in the sense of physical delivery of the chattel, or constructive in the sense that, although the chattel is legally delivered, it does not actually pass from the hands of the pawnor to those of the pawnee[3].

Constructive delivery may be effected even where the chattel remains in the possession of the pawnor for a special purpose[4]. It may be effected by some symbolic act such as the delivery of a key of a warehouse in which goods are stored[5] or of the key of a room in which a collection is stored[6]. Where the chattel is in the custody of a third person, such as a warehouseman, who holds for the owner so that in law his possession is that of the owner, constructive delivery may be effected by an order from the owner to the third person to hold the chattel for the pawnee, which must be perfected by an acknowledgment by the third person that he holds the chattel for the pawnee[7]. The delivery to and receipt by a transferee of a document of title to goods, other than a bill of lading[8], does not at common law[9] amount to delivery and receipt of the goods[10].

1   *Dublin City Distillery Ltd v Doherty* [1914] AC 823 at 843, HL, where earlier decisions on constructive delivery are reviewed by Lord Atkinson. As to special property or interest see PARA 209. As to the meanings of 'pawn', 'pawnee' and 'pawnor' see PARA 189.

2   *Martin v Reid* (1862) 11 CBNS 730 at 734 per Erle CJ; *Ayers v South Australian Banking Co* (1871) LR 3 PC 548 at 554.

3   *Martin v Reid* (1862) 11 CBNS 730; *Meyerstein v Barber* (1866) LR 2 CP 38 at 52. For a summary of the common law see *Official Assignee of Madras v Mercantile Bank of India Ltd* [1935] AC 53 at 58, PC.

4   *Reeves v Capper* (1838) 5 Bing NC 136.

5   *Young v Lambert* (1870) LR 3 PC 142.

6   *Hilton v Tucker* (1888) 39 ChD 669; and see *Wrightson v McArthur and Hutchisons (1919) Ltd* [1921] 2 KB 807, where goods were held in rooms on the pledgor's premises, and the key delivered to the pledgee with an irrevocable licence to remove the goods as desired. See also PERSONAL PROPERTY vol 35 (Reissue) PARA 1254.

7   *Official Assignee of Madras v Mercantile Bank of India Ltd* [1935] AC 53, PC; and see *Alicia Hosiery Ltd v Brown Shipley & Co Ltd* [1970] 1 QB 195, [1969] 2 All ER 504.

8   A transfer of a bill of lading operates to pass the property in the goods specified in it in accordance with the intention of the parties: see *Sewell v Burdick* (1884) 10 App Cas 74, HL; *Bristol and West of England Bank v Midland Rly Co* [1891] 2 QB 653, CA; and CARRIAGE AND CARRIERS vol 7 (2008) PARA 315.

9   For the exception made by the Factors Act 1889 see s 3; and AGENCY vol 1 (2008) PARA 148.

10   *Farina v Home* (1846) 16 M & W 119; *Dublin City Distillery Ltd v Doherty* [1914] AC 823 at 848, HL; *Official Assignee of Madras v Mercantile Bank of India Ltd* [1935] AC 53 at 58, PC. In *Grigg v National Guardian Assurance Co* [1891] 3 Ch 206, the delivery order was given by the pawnor direct to the warehouseman.

201.   When advance and delivery are not simultaneous.   The delivery of a chattel must be in pursuance of the contract, but the advance and delivery need not be contemporaneous. Thus a pledge[1] may be perfected by delivery after the advance has been made[2]; and where goods are delivered for appraisal with a view to making an advance on the security of the goods, there is a good delivery for the purpose of making a pledge whenever that pledge should be created[3]. When the advance is made before possession is given, the intended pawnee[4] has only a right of action on the contract and no interest in the thing pawned[5].

1 As to the meaning of 'pledge' see PARA 189.
2 *Hilton v Tucker* (1888) 39 ChD 669.
3 *Blundell-Leigh v Attenborough* [1921] 3 KB 235, CA.
4 As to the meaning of 'pawnee' see PARA 189.
5 *Howes v Ball* (1827) 7 B & C 481; *Donald v Suckling* (1866) LR 1 QB 585 at 613. Quaere however whether an immediate right of possession conferred by contract on the prospective pledgee might not at least afford a sufficient interest to enable the prospective pledgee to sue in conversion both the prospective pledgor who fails to deliver the chattel to the prospective pledgee and any third party who interferes with the chattel contrary to the prospective pledgee's right of possession: cf *Government of the Islamic Republic of Iran v Barakat Galleries Ltd* [2007] EWCA Civ 1374, [2009] QB 22, [2008] 1 All ER 1177.

202.   Extinction of contract of pawn.   The contract of pawn[1] is extinguished by the satisfaction of the debt or engagement and the redelivery of the property pledged to the pawnor, since there is an implied undertaking on the pawnee's part to redeliver the property to the pawnor on payment by the pawnor of the sum advanced with interest[2]. The essence of this extinction of the contract lies in the pawnee being divested wholly of his special property or interest and possession in the property pledged[3]. However, the pawnee has the right to hand back to the pawnor the property pledged for a special purpose without affecting his security and without extinguishing the contract[4].

1 As to the meanings of 'pawn', 'pawnee' and 'pawnor' see PARA 189.
2 *Singer Manufacturing Co v Clark* (1879) 5 Ex D 37. For an unusual case see *Alicia Hosiery Ltd v Brown Shipley & Co Ltd* [1970] 1 QB 195, [1969] 2 All ER 504, where it was held that a delivery by a pledgee in constructive possession of goods to a purchaser of the goods of a delivery note in favour of the purchaser does not involve an undertaking by the pledgee that the goods will be delivered pursuant to the order. Delivery of such an order relieves the pledgee from his constructive possession of the goods, and he is not, without more, liable for their subsequent detention by the actual holder of the goods.
3 See *Babcock v Lawson* (1880) 5 QBD 284, CA. As to the pawnor's remedies on the pawnee's failure to redeliver see PARA 208. As to special property or interest see PARA 209.
4 *North Western Bank Ltd v Poynter, Son and Macdonalds* [1895] AC 56, HL, where the pawnee returned a bill of lading to the pawnor, making the pawnor his agent to sell the goods comprised in it (distinguishing *Tod & Son v Merchant Banking Co of London* (1883) 10 R 1009, Ct of Sess); *Lloyds Bank Ltd v Bank of America National Trust and Savings Association* [1938] 2 KB 147, [1938] 2 All ER 63, CA. The general practice of banks in releasing documents pledged with them to facilitate the realisation of assets without prejudice to their rights as pledgees was approved in *Re David Allester Ltd* [1922] 2 Ch 211: see FINANCIAL SERVICES AND INSTITUTIONS vol 49 (2008) PARA 986. However, the bank may be unable to recover the documents if a third person has acquired a valid title to them under the Factors Act 1889: *Lloyds Bank Ltd v Bank of America National Trust and Savings Association* [1938] 2 KB 147, [1938] 2 All ER 63, CA.

C. WARRANTIES AND RIGHTS OF PAWNOR

203.   Implied warranty of title.   At common law there is an implied undertaking on the part of the pawnor[1] that the property pawned is his own, or that he has the authority of the owner to pawn it, and that it may be safely delivered back to him[2].

1   As to the meanings of 'pawn' and 'pawnor' see PARA 189.
2   *Singer Manufacturing Co v Clark* (1879) 5 Ex D 37 at 42 per curiam; *Cheesman v Exall* (1851) 6 Exch 341. See also *Advanced Industrial Technology Corpn Ltd v Bond Street Jewellers Ltd* [2006] EWCA Civ 923, [2006] All ER (D) 21 (Jul), in which it was held that a false representation created by non-disclosure by the pawnor that he did not have the authority of the owner of the goods to pawn them could be sued upon by the pawnee quite independently of the warranty envisaged in *Singer Manufacturing Co v Clark* (1879) 5 Ex D 37. As to dishonest pawning see PARA 223; and as to pawned goods obtained by misrepresentation see PARA 224.

204.   Warranties as to quality. Generally a pawnor[1] does not warrant the quality of the property pawned[2]. However, if he makes a false and fraudulent representation as to quality for the purpose of obtaining property by it from the pawnee, the pawnor may be guilty of an offence[3].

1   As to the meanings of 'pawn', 'pawnor' and 'pawnee' see PARA 189.
2   A contract intended to operate by way of pledge is not a contract for the transfer of goods for the purposes of the Supply of Goods and Services Act 1982 in its application to England and Wales: see s 1(2)(e); and SALE OF GOODS AND SUPPLY OF SERVICES vol 41 (2005 Reissue) PARA 32.
3   See *R v Roebuck* (1856) Dears & B 24, CCR; *R v Ardley* (1871) LR 1 CCR 301; *R v Francis* (1874) LR 2 CCR 128. Under the Fraud Act 2006 the offence is that of fraud by false representation, but there must be an intention to make a gain for himself or another, or to cause loss to the pawnee or to expose him to a risk of loss: see ss 1, 2(1); and CRIMINAL LAW vol 25 (2010) PARA 305.

205.   Sale by pawnor before redemption. Before redemption a pawnor[1] may sell the thing pledged; and after such a sale the purchaser has the same interest in the thing as the pawnor had[2].

1   As to the meaning of 'pawnor' see PARA 189.
2   *Franklin v Neate* (1844) 13 M & W 481.

206.   The right to redeem. A pawnor[1] has an absolute common law right to redeem the thing pawned upon tender of the amount advanced, since the general property in it remains in him[2]. In the absence of any agreement as to time for payment he may redeem at any time during his life[3], and upon the pawnee's death this right continues against the pawnee's personal representatives[4]. The right to redeem necessarily depends upon tender of the debt by the pawnor to the pawnee[5], and it is lost if the pawnee has lawfully sold the subject of the pawn[6]. The right to redeem a pawn is not barred by any statute of limitation during the pawnor's lifetime[7].

1   As to the meanings of 'pawn', 'pawnee' and 'pawnor' see PARA 189.
2   As to the provisions relating to the redemption of pledges under the Consumer Credit Act 1974 see PARA 228; and CONSUMER CREDIT vol 21 (2011) PARAS 221–222. The principle of consolidation of securities (as to which see MORTGAGE vol 77 (2010) PARA 498 et seq) does not apply to a contract of pawn: *Vanderzee v Willis* (1789) 3 Bro CC 21 (not available as against personal representatives of deceased pawnor), disapproving *Demandray v Metcalf* (1715) Prec Ch 419.
3   *Sir John Ratcliff v Davis* (1610) Yelv 178, where it was held that the right to redeem was personal to the pawnor and that it was extinguished on his death and did not pass to his executor. The rule was expressly disapproved of in New York in *Cortelyon v Lansing* (1805) 2 Caines Cas Err 200; and it seems inconsistent with the statutory rule that in the case of the death of a person on or after 25 July 1934 all causes of action vested in him survive for the benefit of his estate: see the Law Reform (Miscellaneous Provisions) Act 1934 s 1(1); and WILLS AND INTESTACY vol 103 (2010) PARA 1279. For agreements to which the Consumer Credit Act 1974 applies, the statutory definition of 'pawnor' would include personal representatives: see PARA 189.
4   *Sir John Ratcliff v Davis* (1610) Yelv 178; Bac Abr, Bailment (B).
5   *Coggs v Bernard* (1703) 2 Ld Raym 909 at 917.

6   See PARAS 214–215.
7   *Kemp v Westbrook* (1749) 1 Ves Sen 278. A time may be fixed for redemption upon the
    expiration of which, in the absence of redemption, the pawnee has a power of sale: see further
    PARAS 214–215; and LIMITATION PERIODS vol 68 (2008) PARA 1129. As to the time for
    redemption and power of sale see the Consumer Credit Act 1974 ss 116, 120–121; and
    CONSUMER CREDIT vol 21 (2011) PARAS 221–222, 225.

207.   Partners' right to redeem.   When goods are pawned[1] by several partners
jointly, the right to redeem lies in them jointly and not severally. Any partner
acting for the firm may redeem but all must join if an action is brought to
recover the thing pawned[2].

1   As to the meaning of 'pawn' see PARA 189.
2   *Harper v Godsell* (1870) LR 5 QB 422. As to the rights of partners generally see PARTNERSHIP.

208.   Action for recovery by pawnor.   A pawnor[1] cannot maintain an action
for conversion[2] against a pawnee for the pledge unless the pawnor has a right to
its immediate possession[3]; consequently until tender or payment of the debt the
pawnor cannot generally maintain an action for conversion of the pledge[4]. A
pawnor may sue a pawnee who refuses to restore the pledge after tender of the
debt[5]; but, if the ownership of the pledge is in doubt, the refusal, if made
reasonably and to obtain a reasonable time for the purposes of investigation, will
not ground such an action[6]. In similar circumstances the assignee of a pawnor
may bring an action for conversion[7], and may recover damages for
non-delivery[8].

If before the pledge is redeemed the pawnee deals unlawfully with the pledge[9],
as by sale, transfer or repledge, the contract of pawn is not thereby determined
unless there is clear provision to that effect in the contract of pledge. Moreover,
unless the contract is determined the pawnor may not recover in conversion
inasmuch as he has no right to immediate possession unless and until he
redeems[10]. However, if the pawnee's unlawful dealing with the pledge (for
example, purporting to dispose of a greater interest than the pawnee has in the
pledge) renders it more difficult for the pawnor to redeem the pledge, then, if any
real damage has been caused to the pawnor, the pawnee has committed a legal
wrong against him[11].

1   As to the meanings of 'pawn', 'pledge', 'pawnee' and 'pawnor' see PARA 189.
2   Conversion is the dealing with goods in a manner inconsistent with the right of the party who
    has either possession or the immediate right of possession, coupled with an intention to deny
    that person's right to them, or to assert a right inconsistent with it. The relief available where
    goods are detained includes an order for delivery or an order for damages, or a choice between
    the two: see the Torts (Interference with Goods) Act 1977 s 3(2); and see also *General and
    Finance Facilities Ltd v Cooks Cars (Romford) Ltd* [1963] 2 All ER 314, [1963] 1 WLR
    644, CA. See further TORT vol 45(2) (Reissue) PARA 542 et seq. The measure of damages is
    generally the market value of the goods concerned: see eg *J and E Hall Ltd v Barclay* [1937]
    3 All ER 620 at 623, CA, per Greer LJ; and DAMAGES vol 12(1) (Reissue) PARA 861. As to the
    measure of damages where the claimant has a limited interest only see PARA 225 note 4.
3   *Halliday v Holgate* (1868) LR 3 Exch 299; *Donald v Suckling* (1866) LR 1 QB 585. See also
    Wilson v Robertsons (London) Ltd [2006] EWCA Civ 1088, 150 Sol Jo LB 1019, [2006] All ER
    (D) 410 (Jul); *Wilson v First County Trust Ltd* [2003] UKHL 40, [2004] 1 AC 816, [2003] 2 All
    ER (Comm) 491, [2003] 4 All ER 97. As to the pawnee's right to possession see PARA 210.
4   As to the pawnor's right to redeem see PARA 206.
5   *Anon* (1693) 2 Salk 522; *Coggs v Bernard* (1703) 2 Ld Raym 909 at 917; *Donald v Suckling*
    (1866) LR 1 QB 585 at 610; *Yungmann v Briesemann* (1892) 67 LT 642, CA; and see *Pigot v
    Cubley* (1864) 15 CBNS 701.
6   *Vaughan v Watt* (1840) 6 M & W 492; and see *Clayton v Le Roy* [1911] 2 KB 1031 at
    1051, CA. As to a pawnee's refusal to deliver the pawn under the Consumer Credit Act 1974
    where the ownership is in doubt see s 117(2); and CONSUMER CREDIT vol 21 (2011) PARA 222.

7   *Franklin v Neate* (1844) 13 M & W 481.

8   *Bristol and West of England Bank v Midland Rly Co* [1891] 2 QB 653, CA.

9   A pawnee can without the previous consent of the pawnor repledge the goods (and so transmit his interest to a third party) for an amount not exceeding the original debt, unless that power is expressly excluded by the parties: *Mores v Conham* (1610) Owen 123 at 124.

10   *Donald v Suckling* (1866) LR 1 QB 585 at 610, 616, 618 (repledge for sum greater than that owed by pawnor), explaining *Johnson (Assignee of Cumming) v Stear* (1863) 15 CBNS 330; *Halliday v Holgate* (1868) LR 3 Exch 299, Ex Ch. The unlawful action of the pawnee may be sufficient to put the contract at an end where the pawnor has a special personal confidence in the pawnee and therefore stipulates that the pledge be kept by him alone: see *Donald v Suckling* (1866) LR 1 QB 585 at 615 per Blackburn J. In *Pigot v Cubley* (1864) 15 CBNS 701, it was held that the pawnor could sue on an unlawful sale by the pawnee, but in that case the amount of the debt was tendered after the sale, and the decision may perhaps be supported on the ground that there was an agreement not to sell until a certain time. As to the exercise of a power of sale see PARA 215.

11   *Halliday v Holgate* (1868) LR 3 Exch 299 at 302, Ex Ch; and see *Donald v Suckling* (1866) LR 1 QB 585 at 611–612 (tort), and at 618 (breach of contract).

D. RIGHTS, DUTIES AND REMEDIES OF PAWNEE

209. Special property of the pawnee. A pawnee[1] has a special property or special interest[2] in the pledge, whereas the general property in it continues in the owner[3]. That special property or interest exists so that the pawnee can compel payment of the debt[4], or can sell the goods when the right to do so arises[5]. This special property or interest may (though the point is uncertain) differ from the mere right of detention enjoyed by the holder of a lien[6], in that a pawnee may assign or pledge his special property or interest[7] in the goods or may, as agent of the pawnor, in due course, sell the goods, whereas the unauthorised sale of the subject matter of a lien does not transfer the right of the holder of the lien[8]. The special property or interest of the pawnee does not in any event arise until possession is given to the pawnee[9]. If during the contract there is any increase in the value of the security, the pawnee is entitled to that increase as part of his security[10].

1   As to the meanings of 'pawn', 'pledge', 'pawnee' and 'pawnor' see PARA 189.

2   In *The Odessa* [1916] 1 AC 145 at 158–159, PC, the Judicial Committee criticised the use of the term 'special property' on the ground that, when the pawnee's right to sell (see PARAS 214–215) is examined, the so-called 'special property' which that right is said to create is in truth no property at all. The use of the expression 'special interest' was preferred.

3   *Sir John Ratcliff v Davis* (1610) Yelv 178; *Harper v Godsell* (1870) LR 5 QB 422; and see PARAS 190, 199. A pawnee has an insurable interest in the goods, and both pawnee and pawnor may have a proprietary interest in the proceeds of any claim enforced by the other: Paton's *Bailment in the Common Law* (1952); and see INSURANCE vol 25 (2003 Reissue) PARA 698.

4   *Coggs v Bernard* (1703) 2 Ld Raym 909. As to the right of action for debt see PARA 216.

5   *Re Hardwick, ex p Hubbard* (1886) 17 QBD 690 at 698, CA, per Bowen LJ. As to the power of sale see PARA 214.

6   As to lien generally see LIEN.

7   *Donald v Suckling* (1866) LR 1 QB 585 at 614 per Blackburn J; and see PARA 211.

8   *Donald v Suckling* (1866) LR 1 QB 585 at 612 per Blackburn J; and see *Treuttel v Barandon* (1817) 8 Taunt 100. Note, however, authority acknowledging the ability of a lien-holder to assign his limited interest under the lien to someone to whom he assigns his obligations: *Bull v Faulkner* (1848) 2 G & M 772; *Vered v Inscorp Holdings Ltd* (1993) 31 NSWLR 290, De G & Sm, NSW SC. Cf, however, *The Odessa* [1916] 1 AC 145 at 159, PC, where the Judicial Committee declared that the pawnee's special interest creates no right in property in favour of the pawnee, and that it gives him no more than a right such as a lienholder possesses, but with this added incident, that he can sell the property of his own motion and without any assistance from the court.

9   *Howes v Ball* (1827) 7 B & C 481. As to what amounts to delivery see PARA 200.

10   Story on Bailments (9th Edn) (1878) s 292.

210. Pawnee's right to possession. Where goods are pawned[1], the pawnee has the right to their possession and, until the money for which the pledge is a security is tendered or paid, is the only person who can sue in conversion[2]. A claim by the pawnee to be the absolute owner of the goods pawned does not excuse the pawnor from the necessity of tendering the amount due, and does not revest in him the right to the immediate possession of the goods without payment or tender of the amount due[3].

1   As to the meanings of 'pawn', 'pledge', 'pawnee' and 'pawnor' see PARA 189.
2   *Gledstane v Hewitt* (1831) 1 Cr & J 565; *Owen v Knight* (1837) 4 Bing NC 54; *Martin v Reid* (1862) 11 CBNS 730; *Broadbent v Varley* (1862) 12 CBNS 214; *Mecklenburgh v Gloyn* (1865) 13 WR 291. As to the right of action in conversion see PARA 208 note 2; and as to the pawnee's right of action see PARA 217.
3   *Yungmann v Briesemann* (1892) 67 LT 642, CA; and see PARA 208. However, the bailee of goods who has a lien on them and who sets up a claim for a sum other than that which is due, or sets up a claim inconsistent with the right of the owner, loses his lien and his detention becomes unlawful, and the owner of the goods can sue without tendering or paying the amount due: *Dirks v Richards* (1842) Car & M 626; *Yungmann v Briesemann* (1892) 67 LT 642, CA. See also PARA 191; and LIEN vol 68 (2008) PARA 851.

211. Assignment of pawnee's rights. A pawnee's[1] special property or special interest in the pledge[2] may be assigned to a third person by way of assignment of the pawnee's interest or of a sub-pledge by him[3]. Such a transfer is not inconsistent with the contract of pawn so long as it purports to transfer no more than the pawnee's interest against the pawnor, the pawnee in the meantime being responsible for due care being taken for the safe custody of the property[4]. At the same time the pawnor may in such a case recover damages if the property is damaged in the hands of the third person, or if he is prejudiced by any delay in the delivery of the property to him after tender of his debt[5].

1   As to the meanings of 'pawn', 'pledge', 'pawnee' and 'pawnor' see PARA 189.
2   As to the special property or special interest see PARA 209.
3   *Donald v Suckling* (1866) LR 1 QB 585; *Halliday v Holgate* (1868) LR 3 Exch 299, Ex Ch. See also *Mores v Conham* (1610) Owen 123; and MORTGAGE vol 77 (2010) PARA 257.
4   *Donald v Suckling* (1866) LR 1 QB 585 at 615–616 per Blackburn J; and see *Nicholson v Hooper* (1838) 4 My & Cr 179. As to the pawnee's duty of care see PARA 212.
5   *Donald v Suckling* (1866) LR 1 QB 585 at 618 per Cockburn CJ.

212. Pawnee's duty of care. The common law requires nothing extraordinary of a pawnee[1], but only that he use ordinary care in the safekeeping and redelivering of the pledge[2]. Thus, if he loses the goods pawned without default on his part he may still recover the debt, and the loss falls on the owner. However, if the pawnee keeps the goods pawned after tender of the debt and they are stolen, he is liable, for after tender he keeps them at his own risk[3]. The pawnee may also be liable in damages where he sells pawned goods without the right to do so[4].

1   As to the meanings of 'pawn', 'pledge' and 'pawnee' see PARA 189.
2   *Coggs v Bernard* (1703) 2 Ld Raym 909 at 917; *Syred v Carruthers* (1858) EB & E 469 (accidental fire); but cf *Foley v O'Hara* (1920) 54 ILT 167. As to the principles of liability for negligence generally see NEGLIGENCE. As to the general principles applicable to bailments see PARA 121.
3   *Anon* (1693) 2 Salk 522.
4   *Wilson v Robertsons (London) Ltd* [2006] EWCA Civ 1088, 150 Sol Jo LB 1019, [2006] All ER (D) 410 (Jul).

213. Pawnee's right to use the pledge. A pawnee[1] may not use the pledge if it would be the worse for such use, but if this is not so he may make a reasonable use of it at his own risk[2]. If he is put to expense in his custody, he may take a reasonable profit from the property to recompense him[3]. If, to preserve the pledge, reasonable use is necessary, the pawnee must exercise that use, and if the use of the property is beneficial to it, it seems that the pawnee can use it[4]. The pawnee is responsible for the conduct of his employee to whom he entrusts the pledge and is liable for any loss or damage as a result of his or his employee's misuse of the goods in the course of the employee's employment[5].

1   As to the meanings of 'pawnee' and 'pledge' see PARA 189.
2   *Coggs v Bernard* (1703) 2 Ld Raym 909 at 916–917 per Holt CJ; *Anon* (1693) 2 Salk 522 (e g clothes would be the worse for use; not so jewels, which would be used at the pawnee's risk; a horse may be ridden or a cow milked). See also *Cooke v Haddon* (1862) 3 F & F 229, where the consumption by the pawnee of part of some wine pledged to him was held to forfeit his rights in it. As to the usual rules for a bailment see PARA 124.
3   *Coggs v Bernard* (1703) 2 Ld Raym 909 at 917 per Holt CJ.
4   Story on Bailments (9th Edn) (1878) ss 329–330; and see Paton's Bailment in the Common Law 369–370.
5   Palmer on Bailment (3rd Edn, 2009) Chapter 22.

214. Power of sale. The contract of pawn[1] carries with it an implication that the security may be made available to satisfy the obligation[2]. Under this implication a pawnee has a power of sale on default of payment if the time for payment has been fixed[3]. If there is no stipulated time for payment, the pawnee may demand payment, and in default of payment may sell, on notice to the pawnor of his intention to do so[4]. The pawnor retains his right to redeem at any moment up to sale[5], that is at any moment up to the time of the exercise by the pawnee of his power of sale by entering into a valid contract of sale[6].

1   As to the meanings of 'pawn', 'pledge', 'pawnee' and 'pawnor' see PARA 189.
2   *Pothonier and Hodgson v Dawson* (1816) Holt NP 383; *Re Hardwick, ex p Hubbard* (1886) 17 QBD 690, CA; *Re Morritt, ex p Official Receiver* (1886) 18 QBD 222 at 232, CA, per Cotton LJ. As to the statutory power of sale under the Consumer Credit Act 1974 see PARA 228; and CONSUMER CREDIT vol 21 (2011) PARA 225.
3   *Re Morritt, ex p Official Receiver* (1886) 18 QBD 222 at 235, CA, per Fry LJ. The right of a pawnbroker to deal with a pledge is not affected by the Reserve and Auxiliary Forces (Protection of Civil Interests) Act 1951: see s 2(2) proviso (iii); and ARMED FORCES vol 2(2) (Reissue) PARA 81. As to the exercise of the power of sale see PARA 215.
4   *Martin v Reid* (1862) 11 CBNS 730; *Pigot v Cubley* (1864) 15 CBNS 701; *France v Clark* (1883) 22 ChD 830 (citing with approval Story on Bailments (9th Edn) (1878) s 308; and distinguishing *Re Tahiti Cotton Co, ex p Sargent* (1874) LR 17 Eq 273; *Burdick v Sewell* (1883) 10 QBD 363 at 367).
5   *France v Clark* (1883) 22 ChD 830 (affd (1884) 26 ChD 257, CA); *Re Morritt, ex p Official Receiver* (1886) 18 QBD 222 at 232, CA, per Cotton LJ. As to the right to redeem see PARA 206; and as to the pawnor's remedy against the pawnee in case of an illegal sale see PARA 208. In the case of pledges regulated by statute, the pawnor's right to redeem at any moment up to sale is specifically reserved: see the Consumer Credit Act 1974 s 116(3); and CONSUMER CREDIT vol 21 (2011) PARA 221.
6   *The Ningchow* [1916] P 221 at 224 per Sir Samuel Evans P.

215. Exercise of the power of sale. If a pawnee[1] sells the pledge he does so by virtue and to the extent of the pawnor's ownership, and not with a new title of his own[2]. The right of sale is exercisable by virtue of an implied authority from the pawnor and for the benefit of both parties[3]. The pawnee must appropriate the proceeds of the sale to the pawnor's debt, for the money resulting from the sale is the pawnor's money to be so applied. The pawnee must account to the pawnor for any surplus after paying the debt[4] and is liable in equity and as a fiduciary to pay interest on those monies[5]. He must take care that the sale is a provident sale, and if the goods pawned are in bulk he must not sell more than is reasonably sufficient to pay off the debt, for he holds possession only for the purpose of securing himself the advance which he has made[6].

If sale by the pawnee of the pledge does not realise the amount of his debt, the pawnee can sue for the deficit[7].

1 As to the meanings of 'pawn', 'pledge', 'pawnee' and 'pawnor' see PARA 189.

2 At common law, a sale by a pawnbroker pawnee did not carry with it any warranty as to the title of goods sold: *Morley v Attenborough* (1849) 3 Exch 500 (cited with approval in *Sims v Marryat* (1851) 17 QB 281 at 290). This is now abrogated by the Sale of Goods Act 1979 s 12, which implies terms as to title into all contracts of sale: see SALE OF GOODS AND SUPPLY OF SERVICES vol 41 (2005 Reissue) PARA 69.

3 *The Odessa* [1916] 1 AC 145 at 159, PC. As to the statutory provisions under the Consumer Credit Act 1974 relating to realisation of pawns see PARA 228; and CONSUMER CREDIT vol 21 (2011) PARAS 225–226.

4 See the Consumer Credit Act 1974 s 121(3); and CONSUMER CREDIT vol 21 (2011) PARA 226.

5 *Mathew v TM Sutton Ltd* [1994] 4 All ER 793, [1994] 1 WLR 1455. As to the principle governing the rate of interest see *Burdick v Garrick* (1870) 5 Ch App 233 at 241 per Lord Hatherley (applied in *Wallersteiner v Moir* [1974] 3 All ER 217, [1974] 1 WLR 991; *Wallersteiner v Moir (No 2)* [1975] QB 373, [1975] 1 All ER 849).

6 As to the pawnee's specific obligations pursuant to the Consumer Credit Act 1974 regarding the value to be realised see PARA 228; and CONSUMER CREDIT vol 21 (2011) PARA 226.

7 This arises in consequence of the loan contract made between the pawnor and the pawnee, the pledge being no more than security for the repayment of such loan. See the Consumer Credit Act 1974 s 121(4); and PARA 216.

216. Pawnee's right of action for debt. A pawnee[1] has a right of action for his debt notwithstanding the possession by him of the pledge[2] subject to the rights of the pawnor[3]. Where the pledge is of a perishable nature and no time for redemption has been fixed, the right of action remains, notwithstanding that the pledge perishes, and the pawnor has no remedy[4]. If by his own default the pawnee is unable to return the security against payment of the debt the pawnor has a good defence to the action[5].

1 As to the meanings of 'pawnee', 'pawnor' and 'pledge' see PARA 189.

2 *Anon* (1701) 12 Mod Rep 564 per Holt CJ; *South-Sea Co v Duncomb* (1731) 2 Stra 919; *Lawton v Newland* (1817) 2 Stark 72.

3 As to the pawnor's rights see PARA 206 et seq.

4 *Sir John Ratcliff v Davis* (1610) Yelv 178.

5 *Ellis & Co's Trustee v Dixon-Johnson* [1925] AC 489 at 493, HL, per Lord Sumner, where, however, the order in the special circumstances of the case was to set off the money value of the shares pledged against the debt. As to the position where the goods pledged have been lost without the default of the pawnee see PARA 212.

217. Pawnee's right of action for possession. Where a pawnee[1] is wrongfully deprived of possession of the pledge he may maintain an action, and the measure of damages is the full value of the thing taken and not merely the amount for which it stands security[2]. He may maintain such an action without joining the pawnor as a party[3].

1 As to the meanings of 'pawnee', 'pawnor' and 'pledge' see PARA 189.

2 *Swire v Leach* (1865) 18 CBNS 479; and see *Chabbra Corpn Pte Ltd v Owners of the Jag Shakti, The Jag Shakti* [1986] AC 337, [1986] 1 All ER 480, [1986] 1 Lloyd's Rep 1, PC. See also DAMAGES vol 12(1) (Reissue) PARAS 860, 867. The pawnee is under a duty to account to the pawnor for the excess of any damages recovered over the amount secured: *Swire v Leach* (1865) 18 CBNS 479. Compare this measure with the limitations referred to in PARA 225 note 4. As to the nature of the pawnee's interest see PARA 209; and as to his sole right to sue see PARA 210.

3 *Saville v Tankred* (1748) 1 Ves Sen 101. As to the tort of conversion generally see PARA 208 note 2.

218. No right of foreclosure. A pawnee[1] has no right of foreclosure since he never had the absolute ownership at law, and his equitable rights cannot exceed his special property or special interest[2], the contract of pawn differing in this respect from that of mortgage[3].

1 As to the meanings of 'pawnee' and 'pawn' see PARA 189.

2 *Carter v Wake* (1877) 4 ChD 605 at 606 per Jessel MR; *Fraser v Byas* (1895) 11 TLR 481. As to the special property or special interest see PARA 209.

3 See *Lockwood v Ewer (or Lady Child v Chanstilet)* (1742) 9 Mod Rep 275; and PARA 190. As to mortgage generally see MORTGAGE vol 77 (2010) PARA 101 et seq.

E. INTERVENING RIGHTS OF THIRD PERSONS

219. Execution against goods pawned. Where judgment has been obtained against a pawnor[1] of goods and execution has issued on it, the sheriff may not seize the goods pawned unless he satisfies the pawnee's claim[2].

If execution issues against a pawnee the sheriff may seize goods in pawn in the pawnee's possession, but may sell only those in respect of which the period for redemption has expired[3]. With respect to the rest he has a right to possess the qualified or special interest of the pawnee[4], to sell when the time for redemption has expired, or to receive any money paid for the redemption of the chattel[5].

1 As to the meanings of 'pawn', 'pawnee' and 'pawnor' see PARA 189.

2 *Legg v Evans* (1840) 6 M & W 36; *Rogers v Kennay* (1846) 9 QB 592; and see CIVIL PROCEDURE vol 12 (2009) PARAS 1322, 1346. As to sheriffs and their powers see SHERIFFS.

3 *Re Rollason, Rollason v Rollason, Halse's Claim* (1887) 34 ChD 495. As to the period of redemption of agreements within the Consumer Credit Act 1974 see PARA 228; and CONSUMER CREDIT vol 21 (2011) PARA 221. See also CIVIL PROCEDURE vol 12 (2009) PARAS 1322, 1346.

4 As to the special interest of the pawnee see PARA 209.

5 *Re Rollason, Rollason v Rollason, Halse's Claim* (1887) 34 ChD 495.

220. Distress. Goods pawned with a pawnbroker are not liable to distress; but the privilege does not, apparently, extend to goods pawned with a person who is not a pawnbroker[1].

1 *Swire v Leach* (1865) 18 CBNS 479. It should be noted that in this case the pawnee was a pawnbroker by trade, and his position was compared to that of a wharfinger or warehouse-keeper. As to goods which may, or may not, be distrained, and as to the measure of damages in cases of wrongful distress, see DISTRESS. Since the repeal of the Pawnbrokers Acts 1897 to 1960 there is no longer a statutory definition of 'pawnbroker'. As from a day to be appointed, distress will be replaced by the procedure of enforcement by taking control of goods under the Tribunals, Courts and Enforcement Act 2007 s 62(1), Sch 12, but provision is made for goods to be made exempt from the procedure by regulations: see Sch 12 paras 3(1), 4(1), 11(2). At the date at which this volume states the law, no such day had been appointed. As to enforcement by taking control see CIVIL PROCEDURE vol 12 (2009) PARA 1389 et seq. As to goods which may be taken see CIVIL PROCEDURE vol 12 (2009) PARA 1392.

221. Bankruptcy of a pawnor or pawnee. The bankruptcy of a pawnor or a pawnee[1] vests the bankrupt's estate in the trustee of a bankrupt's estate immediately upon his appointment taking effect, or in the case of the official receiver, on his becoming trustee[2]. Where any property which is, or is to be, comprised in the bankrupt's estate vests in the trustee it so vests without any conveyance, assignment or transfer[3].

Where a person is adjudged bankrupt, any disposition of property made by that person during the period beginning with the day of the presentation of the petition for the bankruptcy order and ending with the vesting of the bankrupt's estate in a trustee is void except to the extent that it is or was made with the consent of the court, or was subsequently ratified by the court[4].

After the making of a bankruptcy order no person who is a creditor of the bankrupt in respect of a debt provable in the bankruptcy has a remedy against the property or person of the bankrupt in respect of the debt, nor may any such person, before the discharge of the bankrupt, commence any action or other legal proceedings against the bankrupt except with the leave of the court and on such terms as the court may impose[5]. This does not affect the right of a secured creditor[6] of the bankrupt to enforce his security[7]. On the bankruptcy of the pawnor, the pawnee is a secured creditor in the bankruptcy with respect to goods pawned before the date of the bankruptcy order[8].

Where any goods of an undischarged bankrupt are held by any person by way of pledge, pawn or other security, the official receiver may, after giving notice in writing of his intention to do so, inspect the goods[9]. Where such notice is given to any person, that person is not entitled, without leave of the court, to realise his security unless he has given the trustee of the bankrupt's estate a reasonable opportunity of inspecting the goods and of exercising the bankrupt's right of redemption[10].

Where the pawnor becomes insolvent, a pawnee has priority over the holder of a floating charge where the pledge was granted before the charge had crystallised[11].

1   As to the meanings of 'pawn', 'pledge', 'pawnee' and 'pawnor' see PARA 189.
2   See the Insolvency Act 1986 s 306(1); and BANKRUPTCY AND INDIVIDUAL INSOLVENCY vol 3(2) (2002 Reissue) PARA 381. The doctrine of marshalling (see EQUITY vol 16(2) (Reissue) PARA 758) has been applied by analogy where brokers pledge a client's securities with their own to a bank to secure an overdraft: see *Re Burge, Woodall & Co, ex p Skyrme* [1912] 1 KB 393.
3   See the Insolvency Act 1986 s 306(2); and BANKRUPTCY AND INDIVIDUAL INSOLVENCY vol 3(2) (2002 Reissue) PARA 381.
4   See the Insolvency Act 1986 s 284(1), (3); and BANKRUPTCY AND INDIVIDUAL INSOLVENCY vol 3(2) (2002 Reissue) PARA 205.
5   See the Insolvency Act 1986 s 285(3); and BANKRUPTCY AND INDIVIDUAL INSOLVENCY vol 3(2) (2002 Reissue) PARA 206.
6   A debt is secured to the extent that the person to whom the debt is owed holds any security for the debt (whether a mortgage, charge, lien or other security) over any property of the person by whom the debt is owed: see the Insolvency Act 1986 s 383(2)–(4); and BANKRUPTCY AND INDIVIDUAL INSOLVENCY vol 3(2) (2002 Reissue) PARA 548.
7   See the Insolvency Act 1986 s 285(4); and BANKRUPTCY AND INDIVIDUAL INSOLVENCY vol 3(2) (2002 Reissue) PARA 206.
8   As to secured creditors generally see BANKRUPTCY AND INDIVIDUAL INSOLVENCY vol 3(2) (2002 Reissue) PARA 548 et seq.
9   See the Insolvency Act 1986 s 285(5); and BANKRUPTCY AND INDIVIDUAL INSOLVENCY vol 3(2) (2002 Reissue) PARA 206.
10 See the Insolvency Act 1986 s 285(5); and BANKRUPTCY AND INDIVIDUAL INSOLVENCY vol 3(2) (2002 Reissue) PARA 206.
11 As to floating charges generally see COMPANIES vol 15 (2009) PARA 1269 et seq.

222. Rights of the true owner. The general rule is that, in order to make a pawn[1] valid against the owner of the goods pawned, it must be shown that the pawnor has authority to pawn[2]. To this general rule there are exceptions where the person in possession has a title defeasible on account of fraud[3]; where the owner of the goods by his conduct is estopped from denying the apparent authority of the pawnor[4]; where the transaction is protected by the provisions relating to mercantile agents and sellers and purchasers of goods in possession of the goods or documents of title to them[5]; and where title to or property in the goods has passed to the pawnee pursuant to statute[6].

1   As to the meanings of 'pawn', 'pawnee' and 'pawnor' see PARA 189.
2   *Cole v North Western Bank* (1875) LR 10 CP 354 at 362–363, Ex Ch, per Blackburn J. As to actions by the true owner see PARA 225.
3   See PARAS 223–224.
4   See PARA 199.
5   See PARAS 197–199.
6   See PARA 228; and CONSUMER CREDIT vol 21 (2011) PARA 224.

223. Stolen goods. Where goods have been stolen or obtained by fraud[1] the property in the goods remains in the owner[2]. If the stolen goods are pawned[3], the owner may maintain an action for their recovery[4].

1   As to theft see CRIMINAL LAW vol 25 (2010) PARA 278 et seq; and as to fraud see CRIMINAL LAW vol 25 (2010) PARA 305 et seq.
2   The position will differ where the possessor has a voidable title that is defeasible by reason of a prior misrepresentation by fraud which induced the owner to part with possession: see PARA 224. As to the position regarding the implied passing of title by virtue of the Sale of Goods Act 1979 see s 23; and SALE OF GOODS AND SUPPLY OF SERVICES vol 41 (2005 Reissue) PARA 154.
3   As to the meaning of 'pawn' see PARA 189.
4   *Leicester & Co v Cherryman* [1907] 2 KB 101, DC; and see *Singer Manufacturing Co v Clark* (1879) 5 Ex D 37.

224. Goods obtained by misrepresentation. Where goods have been obtained under a contract by which the owner voluntarily parts with the possession of the goods and either intends to pass the property or intends to confer a power to pass the property in the goods, the fact that the contract was induced by means of misrepresentation[1] renders the contract voidable only and not void[2]. If before the contract is avoided the goods are pawned[3], the pawnee who takes the goods in good faith without notice of the misrepresentation obtains a good title to them[4]. Older authority holds that the burden of proof that the pawnee took the goods with notice or otherwise than in good faith lies on the owner[5].

1   The cases cited in notes 2–5 were all decided in the context of fraudulent misrepresentation, but the same principles would seem to be applicable in the case of an innocent misrepresentation: see MISREPRESENTATION AND FRAUD vol 31 (2003 Reissue) PARA 762.
2   The contract may be a contract for the outright sale of the goods to the person who obtains them (see *Phillips v Brooks Ltd* [1919] 2 KB 243); or it may be a contract for 'sale or return' or 'sale on appro' (see *Kirkham v Attenborough* [1897] 1 QB 201, CA; *London Jewellers Ltd v Attenborough* [1934] 2 KB 206, CA); or it may be a contract between the owner and an agent for sale (see *Folkes v King* [1923] 1 KB 282, CA). See further SALE OF GOODS AND SUPPLY OF SERVICES vol 41 (2005 Reissue) PARA 155. As to the voidability of contracts induced by misrepresentation see MISREPRESENTATION AND FRAUD vol 31 (2003 Reissue) PARA 783. As to voidable contracts see CONTRACT vol 9(1) (Reissue) PARA 607.
3   As to the meanings of 'pawn' and 'pawnee' see PARA 189.
4   *Higgons v Burton* (1857) 26 LJ Ex 342; *Attenborough v St Katharine's Dock Co* (1878) 3 CPD 450, CA; *Phillips v Brooks Ltd* [1919] 2 KB 243. See also the Sale of Goods Act 1979 s 23; and SALE OF GOODS AND SUPPLY OF SERVICES vol 41 (2005 Reissue) PARA 154.
5   *Whitehorn Bros v Davison* [1911] 1 KB 463, CA. See also *Jameson v Union Bank of Scotland* (1913) 109 LT 850. But cf *Marcq v Christie Manson & Woods Ltd (t/a Christie's)* [2002] EWHC 2148 (QB) at [52], [2002] 4 All ER 1005 at 52, per Jack J (affd without direct reference to this point [2003] EWCA Civ 731, [2004] QB 286, [2003] 3 All ER 561).

225. Actions by the true owner. Where goods have been wrongly pawned[1], the true owner may maintain an action for conversion against the pawnor, and is generally entitled to recover by way of damages the value of the goods converted[2]. He may also maintain an action against the pawnee, since receipt of goods by way of a pledge is conversion if the delivery of the goods is conversion[3]. In such a case the measure of damages is the value of the goods converted, but as an alternative to an order for damages the court may order delivery up of the goods concerned[4].

1   As to the meanings of 'pawn', 'pledge', 'pawnee' and 'pawnor' see PARA 189.
2   *Parker v Godin* (1728) 2 Stra 813. As to conversion, and for the normal measure of damages, see PARA 208 note 2.
3   See the Torts (Interference with Goods) Act 1977 s 11(2). This provision abrogated the former rule at common law to the contrary (see *Miller v Dell* [1891] 1 QB 468, CA) and brings pawns and pledges into line with the normal rule in sale of goods cases (see e g *Hollins v Fowler* (1875) LR 7 HL 757). For a discussion of the scope of the Torts (Interference with Goods) Act 1977 s 11(2) see *Marcq v Christie Manson & Woods Ltd (t/a Christie's)* [2003] EWCA Civ 731 at [42], [2004] QB 286 at [42], [2003] 3 All ER 561 at [42], per Tuckey LJ, criticised by Palmer on Bailment (3rd Edn, 2009) paras 22-010–22-011. See further TORT vol 45(2) (Reissue) PARAS 555, 572.
4   As to remedies generally see PARA 208 note 2. Where goods have been pawned by a bailee (eg a hirer under a hire purchase agreement) and the pawnee acquired his special interest in the pawn before the determination of the bailment, the measure of damages is not the full value of the goods, but the value of the claimant's interest in them: *Belsize Motor Supply Co v Cox* [1914] 1 KB 244; and see PARA 233.

226.   Property in the possession of the police.   Any magistrates' court may direct the delivery of property of any kind which has come into the possession of the police in connection with investigation of a suspected offence to the person who appears to the court to be the owner of it, on the application of the person claiming it or of the police[1].

1   See the Police (Property) Act 1897 s 1(1) (amended by the Theft Act 1968 s 33(3), Sch 3 Pt III; the Criminal Justice Act 1972 s 58; the Consumer Credit Act 1974 s 192(3)(b), Sch 5 Pt 1; the Statute Law (Repeals) Act 1989; and the Police (Property) Act 1997 s 4(1)); and POLICE vol 36(1) (2007 Reissue) PARA 520. The Police (Property) Act 1897 does not apply to Northern Ireland: see the Police (Northern Ireland) Act 1998 s 74(3), Sch 6.

227.   Interpleader.   Where adverse claims to pawned property are made against a pawnee[1], he may perhaps have a right to interplead, notwithstanding his interest in the debt for which the property has been pledged[2].

1   As to the meanings of 'pawn', 'pledge' and 'pawnee' see PARA 189.
2   There is no reported case on this point, but see CPR Sch 1 RSC Ord 17; and CIVIL PROCEDURE vol 12 (2009) PARA 1585 et seq. See also *De Rothschild Frères v Morrison, Kekewich & Co, Banque de Paris et des Pays Bas v Morrison, Banque de France v Morrison* (1890) 24 QBD 750, CA (wharfinger interpleading even though having a claim for payment of charges); *Best v Hayes* (1863) 1 H & C 718 (auctioneer claiming commission); *Attenborough v St Katharine's Dock Co* (1878) 3 CPD 450, CA.

(iii)   Consumer Credit Legislation in relation to Pawns

228.   Statutory regulation of pledges and pawns under the Consumer Credit Act 1974.   Pawnbroking was formerly regulated by the Pawnbrokers Acts 1872 and 1960. The Consumer Credit Act 1974 repealed those Acts[1] and provided a new code for pawnbroking[2]. Articles taken in pawn[3] under a regulated consumer credit agreement[4] are subject to the relevant provisions of the Consumer Credit Act 1974[5] unless exempt. In practice, most contracts of pawn fall within the statutory control[6]. However, the provisions do not apply to a pledge of documents of title or of bearer bonds[7], or a non-commercial agreement[8].

Apart from making various special provisions relating to pledges[9], the Consumer Credit Act 1974 makes provisions concerning the seeking of business[10], the formalities of entry into credit agreements[11], various matters arising during the currency of agreements[12], cancellation[13], determination[14], and the re-opening of unfair relationships[15]. The Act also deals with other types of securities[16].

A licence issued by the Office of Fair Trading is required in order to carry on a consumer credit business, a consumer hire business or an ancillary credit business[17], and it is an offence to engage in any activity for which a licence is required without one[18]. Generally, a pawnee engaging in consumer credit business will require a licence under these provisions[19].

In relation to contracts of pawn which are subject to the Consumer Credit Act 1974, pawn records must be kept[20]. The Act further makes provision for pawn-receipts[21], the various offences that may arise under a contract of pawn[22], the redemption period and procedure for redemption[23], the failure to redeem[24], and the realisation of pawns[25].

1   See the Consumer Credit Act 1974 s 192(3)(b), Sch 5; and CONSUMER CREDIT vol 21 (2011) PARA 11.
2   See the Consumer Credit Act 1974 ss 114–121; and CONSUMER CREDIT vol 21 (2011) PARA 217 et seq. Functions of a local authority under the Consumer Credit Act 1974 are 'relevant functions' for the purposes of the Regulatory Enforcement and Sanctions Act 2008 Pt 1 (ss 1–21) (see s 4, Sch 3; and LOCAL GOVERNMENT vol 69 (2009) PARA 733); thus the Local Better Regulation Office may give guidance to local authorities as to the exercise of those functions (see s 7; and LOCAL GOVERNMENT vol 69 (2009) PARA 734). They are 'regulators' specified for the purposes of imposing civil sanctions in respect of offences under the Consumer Credit Act 1974: see the Regulatory Enforcement and Sanctions Act 2008 s 37, Sch 6; and ADMINISTRATIVE LAW.
3   As to the meaning of 'pawn' for the purposes of the Consumer Credit Act 1974 see s 189(1); and CONSUMER CREDIT vol 21 (2011) PARA 217. As to the meanings of 'pledge', 'pawnor' and 'pawnee' see also s 189(1); and CONSUMER CREDIT vol 21 (2011) PARA 217.
4   As to regulated agreements see the Consumer Credit Act 1974 ss 8(3), 189(1); and CONSUMER CREDIT vol 21 (2011) PARA 51. As to consumer credit agreements see ss 8(1), (3), 189(1); and CONSUMER CREDIT vol 21 (2011) PARA 52. Under the Consumer Credit Act 1974, the distinctions between pawnbrokers, moneylenders and other providers of credit are no longer relevant, the old pawn agreement being now one species of the credit transaction and coming within the definition of a regulated agreement.
5   See note 2.
6   The financial limit of the statutory control was originally for credit not exceeding £25,000: see the Consumer Credit Act 1974 s 8(2) (now repealed); and CONSUMER CREDIT vol 21 (2011) PARA 52. This limit has been abolished, so that all agreements are subject to regulation unless specifically exempted: see the Consumer Credit Act 2006 s 2(1)(b).
7   See the Consumer Credit Act 1974 s 114(3)(a) (amended by the Banking Act 1979, s 38(2)); and CONSUMER CREDIT vol 21 (2011) PARA 217.
8   See the Consumer Credit Act 1974 s 114(3)(b); and CONSUMER CREDIT vol 21 (2011) PARA 217.
9   See note 2.
10 See the Consumer Credit Act 1974 Pt IV (ss 43–54); and CONSUMER CREDIT vol 21 (2011) PARA 140 et seq.
11 See the Consumer Credit Act 1974 Pt V (ss 55–74); and CONSUMER CREDIT vol 21 (2011) PARA 167 et seq.
12 See the Consumer Credit Act 1974 Pt VI (ss 75–86); and CONSUMER CREDIT vol 21 (2011) PARA 242 et seq.
13 See the Consumer Credit Act 1974 ss 67–73; and CONSUMER CREDIT vol 21 (2011) PARA 195 et seq.
14 See the Consumer Credit Act 1974 ss 86A–103; and CONSUMER CREDIT vol 21 (2011) PARA 264 et seq.
15 See the Consumer Credit Act 1974 ss 140A–140D; and CONSUMER CREDIT vol 21 (2011) PARA 287 et seq.
16 See the Consumer Credit Act 1974 Pt VIII (ss 105–126); and CONSUMER CREDIT vol 21 (2011) PARA 209 et seq.
17 See the Consumer Credit Act 1974 s 21 (amended by the Consumer Credit Act 2006 s 33(1)); and CONSUMER CREDIT vol 21 (2011) PARA 26. As to the meanings of 'consumer credit

business', 'consumer hire business' and 'business' see s 189(1), (2); and CONSUMER CREDIT vol 21 (2011) PARA 52. As to the meaning of 'ancillary credit business' see ss 145(1), 189(1); and CONSUMER CREDIT vol 21 (2011) PARA 290.

18 See the Consumer Credit Act 1974 s 39(1); and CONSUMER CREDIT vol 21 (2011) PARA 26. As to licensing generally see CONSUMER CREDIT vol 21 (2011) PARA 22 et seq.

19 See the Consumer Credit Act 1974 s 21(1); and CONSUMER CREDIT vol 21 (2011) PARA 26.

20 See the Consumer Credit Act 1974 s 26 (substituted by SI 2001/3649); the Consumer Credit (Conduct of Business) (Pawn Records) Regulations 1983, SI 1983/1565; and CONSUMER CREDIT vol 21 (2011) PARA 218.

21 See the Consumer Credit Act 1974 ss 114, 118; and CONSUMER CREDIT vol 21 (2011) PARAS 219, 223.

22 See the Consumer Credit Act 1974 ss 114(2), 115, 119(1); and CONSUMER CREDIT vol 21 (2011) PARAS 219, 227.

23 See the Consumer Credit Act 1974 ss 116, 117; and CONSUMER CREDIT vol 21 (2011) PARAS 221–222.

24 See the Consumer Credit Act 1974 s 120; and CONSUMER CREDIT vol 21 (2011) PARA 224.

25 See the Consumer Credit Act 1974 s 121; and CONSUMER CREDIT vol 21 (2011) PARA 225.

4. CONSIDERATIONS COMMON TO ALL CLASSES OF BAILMENT

(1) ESTOPPEL OF BAILEE

229. Estoppel. At common law[1], a bailee is estopped from setting up against his bailor's demand for a redelivery of the chattel bailed the right or title of a third person to the property in it[2].

This estoppel ceases, however, when the bailment on which it is founded is determined by what is equivalent to an eviction by title paramount[3]; and the bailee is thereby discharged from all liability to the bailor, unless there is a special contract, or the bailee is in some way to blame for the eviction[4]. It is not enough that the bailee has become aware of the title of a third person, or that an adverse claim has been made upon him[5]. Unless he has been actually evicted he can set up the title of a third person only where he does so on behalf and on the express authority of that third person[6]. Requests for information may not be administered by a bailee to his bailor for the purpose of showing that the bailor has parted with his title in the chattel to a third person, unless the bailee justifies his detention of it by setting up the title of such third person with his consent[7].

This estoppel appears to have been substantially abrogated by statute. The defendant in a claim for wrongful interference with goods[8] is entitled to show, in accordance with rules of court[9], that a third person has a better right than the claimant as respects all or any part of the interest claimed by the claimant, or in right of which he sues[10]. The bailee's estoppel may be preserved, however, where the bailor sues otherwise than in tort[11].

1   The common law rule is substantially abrogated by statute: see the Torts (Interference with Goods) Act 1977 s 8; and the text and notes 8–10. See also PARA 231 text and notes 11–15.

2   *Biddle v Bond* (1865) 6 B & S 225; *Betteley v Reed* (1843) 4 QB 511; *Re Sadler, ex p Davies* (1881) 19 ChD 86, CA; *Leese v Martin* (1873) LR 17 Eq 224; *China-Pacific SA v Food Corpn of India, The Winson* [1982] AC 939 at 959, [1981] 3 All ER 688 at 694, HL, per Lord Diplock; *Redler Grain Silos Ltd v BICC Ltd* [1982] 1 Lloyd's Rep 435 at 438, CA, per Kerr LJ, and at 440 per Stephenson LJ. See further ESTOPPEL. The rule might in theory apply as between a sub-bailee and a head bailor, as well as between the sub-bailee and his head bailee, though a double estoppel may raise difficult issues and the question is not settled: *The Hamburg Star* [1994] 1 Lloyd's Rep 399, QB (point arguable). This rule does not apply to hire-purchase: *Karflex Ltd v Poole* [1933] 2 KB 251; and see CONSUMER CREDIT vol 21 (2011) PARA 29 et seq. There may be specialist application or adaptation of the general principles to cater for sub-bailment (as to which see PARA 110), substitutional bailment (as to which see PARA 110), quasi-bailment (as to which see PARA 140 et seq) and finder-bailment (as to which see PARA 116 et seq). See generally Palmer on Bailment (3rd Edn, 2009) paras 4-054–4-055, 23-028, 26-008, 26-018, 43-039.

3   *Biddle v Bond* (1865) 6 B & S 225 at 234 per Blackburn J.

4   *Ross v Edwards & Co* (1895) 73 LT 100, PC.

5   *Betteley v Reed* (1843) 4 QB 511 at 517 per Lord Denman CJ; *Leese v Martin* (1873) LR 17 Eq 224.

6   *Rogers, Sons & Co v Lambert & Co* [1891] 1 QB 318 at 325, CA, per Lord Esher MR. See also *Thorne v Tilbury* (1858) 3 H & N 534 at 539 per Bramwell B, and at 540 per Watson B, expressing the opinion that the bailee may show that the bailor's title has expired since the bailment. This opinion is adopted by Lopes LJ in *Rogers, Sons & Co v Lambert & Co* [1891] 1 QB 318 at 328, CA. Cf *Webb v Ireland and A-G* [1988] IR 353, Ir SC (bailee acquiring title from third party). Where a plaintiff failed to recover property from a bailee because she did not establish a gift to herself from a predecessor in title, the bailee was precluded, in proceedings by the personal representatives of the predecessor in title, from asserting against them that the property belonged to the former plaintiff: *Re Savoy Estate Ltd, Remnant v Savoy Estate Ltd* [1949] Ch 622, [1949] 2 All ER 286, CA.

7   *Rogers, Sons & Co v Lambert & Co* [1891] 1 QB 318, CA. Cf *Webb v Ireland and A-G* [1988] IR 353 Ir SC.

8   Ie trespass to goods, conversion (or trover), negligence so far as it results in damage to goods or an interest in goods, and any other tort so far as it results in damage to goods or an interest in goods: see the Torts (Interference with Goods) Act 1977 s 8(1). As to the scope of the Torts (Interference with Goods) Act 1977 see TORT vol 45(2) (Reissue) PARA 545.

9   See TORT vol 45(2) (Reissue) PARAS 644, 678.

10 Torts (Interference with Goods) Act 1977 s 8(1). This provision also states that any rule of law to the contrary (sometimes called jus tertii) is abolished. See also PARAS 231, 237; and TORT vol 45(2) (Reissue) PARAS 644, 678. For procedural rules concerning parties in claims for wrongful interference with goods, and the power of the court to order, in certain circumstances, that certain persons be deprived of the right to bring a claim against the defendant, see CPR 19.5A; and CIVIL PROCEDURE vol 11 (2009) PARAS 212, 588.

11 See TORT vol 45(2) (Reissue) PARAS 644, 678.

230.   Interpleader. If a third person claims the chattel and threatens the bailee with proceedings, and the bailor nevertheless insists on his title, the bailee may interplead[1].

A bailee who forbears to interplead makes himself a party to a possibly wrongful detention by retaining the chattel for the bailor, and he must then stand or fall by the bailor's title[2]. Conversely, if he allows the third person to obtain the chattel, he may be liable to the bailor[3].

1   As to interpleader see CPR Sch 1 RSC Ord 17; CPR Sch 2 CCR Ord 33; and CIVIL PROCEDURE vol 12 (2009) PARA 1585 et seq. Where there are competing claims made to goods held by a bailee, a bailee may interplead or he may invoke the procedure set out in the Torts (Interference with Goods) Act 1977 s 8: see PARA 237; and TORT vol 45(2) (Reissue) PARA 644. See *Redler Grain Silos Ltd v BICC Ltd* [1982] 1 Lloyd's Rep 435 at 438, CA, per Kerr LJ, and at 440 per Stephenson LJ. For procedural rules concerning parties in claims for wrongful interference with goods, and the power of the court to order, in certain circumstances, that certain persons be deprived of the right to bring a claim against the defendant, see CPR 19.5A; and CIVIL PROCEDURE vol 11 (2009) PARAS 212, 588. There may be specialist application or adaptation of the general principles to cater for sub-bailment (as to which see PARA 110), substitutional bailment (as to which see PARA 110), quasi-bailment (as to which see PARA 140 et seq) and finder-bailment (as to which see PARA 116 et seq).

2   *Wilson v Anderton* (1830) 1 B & Ad 450 at 456 per Lord Tenterden CJ.

3   *Ranson v Platt* [1911] 2 KB 291, CA.

231.   Attornment. At common law, where a bailee in possession of goods attorns to a person other than his original bailor, he becomes the bailee of that person[1]. It would appear that he holds the goods as the attornee's bailee on the same terms as those on which he held them for the original bailor[2]. Subject to those terms, the attornee can recover damages from the bailee for any tort which the bailee commits against the chattel after his attornment[3].

At common law[4], the bailee who attorns is estopped from denying the attornee's title[5]. He cannot impugn the attornee's title by pleading that a superior title resides in a third party[6]. The rule applies even though the chattel comes into the bailee's possession after he has agreed to attorn; although an attornment made by a person out of possession has no immediate effect, it applies when he obtains possession[7].

As a general rule, to perfect an attornment, the goods must be specific, or there must be a specific appropriation so as to make them specific[8]. But on a sale of goods, where the seller has acknowledged the buyer's right to dispose of goods remaining in the seller's possession, the seller cannot subsequently defeat the right of a third person claiming under the buyer on the ground that, by reason of the want of any specific appropriation, no property has passed to the buyer and thus to that person[9]. Similarly, where the bailee of a seller attorns to a buyer in respect of a specified portion of an undivided parcel, he is estopped from denying the buyer's claim to the portion, notwithstanding that it has not been specifically appropriated from the parcel[10].

The common law rule that a bailee is estopped from pleading the jus tertii has been substantially abrogated by statute[11]. The defendant in a claim for wrongful interference with goods[12] is entitled to show, in accordance with rules of court[13], that a third person has a better right than the claimant as respects all or any part of the interest claimed by the claimant, or in right of which he sues[14]. The bailee's estoppel may survive, however, where the attornee elects to sue otherwise than in tort[15].

1   *Hawes v Watson* (1824) 2 B & C 540; *Gosling v Birnie* (1831) 7 Bing 399; *Henderson & Co v Williams* [1895] 1 QB 521 at 529, CA, per Lord Halsbury; Palmer on Bailment (3rd Edn, 2009) Chapter 25.

2   *Leigh & Sillavan v Aliakmon Shipping Co Ltd, The Aliakmon* [1986] AC 785 at 812, [1986] 2 All ER 145 at 151, HL, per Lord Brandon of Oakbrook (obiter); *Compania Portorafti Commerciale SA v Ultramar Panama Inc, The Captain Gregos (No 2)* [1990] 2 Lloyd's Rep 395 at 404–405, CA, per Bingham LJ (obiter); *HMF Humphrey Ltd v Baxter, Hoare & Co Ltd* (1933) 149 LT 603; *Britain and Overseas Trading (Bristles) Ltd v Brooks Wharf and Bull Wharf Ltd* [1967] 2 Lloyd's Rep 51 at 60 per Widgery J (obiter); *Cremer v General Carriers SA* [1974] 1 All ER 1, [1974] 1 WLR 341. See also *MCC Proceeds Inc v Lehman Bros International (Europe)* [1998] 4 All ER 675, [1998] 2 BCLC 659, CA; *East West Corpn v DKBS AF 1912 A/S, Utaniko Ltd v P & O Nedlloyd BV* [2003] EWCA Civ 83, [2003] QB 1509, [2003] 2 All ER 700; *Homburg Houtimport BV v Agrosin Private Ltd, The Starsin* [2003] UKHL 12, [2004] 1 AC 715, [2003] 2 All ER 785; *Mitsui & Co Ltd v Novorossiysk Shipping Co, The Gudermes* [1993] 1 Lloyd's Rep 311 at 324 per Staughton LJ.

3   *Henderson & Co v Williams* [1895] 1 QB 521 at 530, CA, per Lord Halsbury (in a case of conversion, damages are prima facie to be estimated at the market value of the goods at the date of conversion). As to conversion generally see TORT vol 45(2) (Reissue) PARA 548 et seq.

4   The common law rule has been substantially abrogated by statute: see the Torts (Interference with Goods) Act 1977 s 8(1); and the text and notes 11–15.

5   See the cases cited in note 1.

6   As to the right to plead jus tertii see PARAS 229, 237; and TORT vol 45(2) (Reissue) PARA 644.

7   *Holl v Griffin* (1833) 10 Bing 246 at 248 per Tindal CJ; *Maynegrain Pty Ltd v Compafina Bank* [1982] 2 NSWLR 141 at 146 per Hope JA, NSW CA; revsd on another ground (1984) 58 ALJR 389, PC. Cf *Homburg Houtimport BV v Agrosin Private Ltd, The Starsin* [2003] UKHL 12, [2004] 1 AC 715, [2003] 2 All ER 785.

8   *Unwin v Adams* (1858) 1 F & F 312; *Tanner v Scovell* (1845) 14 M & W 28; *Laurie and Morewood v John Dudin & Sons* [1926] 1 KB 223, CA.

9   *Woodley v Coventry* (1863) 2 H & C 164; cf *Ant Jurgens Margarinefabrieken v Louis Dreyfus & Co* [1914] 3 KB 40.

10   *Maynegrain Pty Ltd v Compafina Bank* [1982] 2 NSWLR 141, NSW CA; revsd on another ground (1984) 58 ALJR 389, PC. Cf *Re London Wine Co (Shippers) Ltd* [1986] PCC 121; *Re Stapylton Fletcher Ltd* [1995] 1 All ER 192, [1994] 1 WLR 1181, [1994] BCC 532, Ch (Companies Court); *Re Goldcorp Exchange Ltd (in receivership)* [1995] 1 AC 74, [1994] 2 All ER 806, PC; and cf, as to sales of goods from bulk, the Sale of Goods (Amendment) Act 1995; and SALE OF GOODS AND SUPPLY OF SERVICES vol 41 (2005 Reissue) PARA 134 et seq.

11   See the Torts (Interference with Goods) Act 1977 s 8(1); PARAS 229, 237; and TORT vol 45(2) (Reissue) PARAS 644, 678.

12   Ie trespass to goods, conversion (or trover), negligence so far as it results in damage to goods or to an interest in goods, and any other tort so far as it results in damage to goods or to an interest in goods: see the Torts (Interference with Goods) Act 1977 s 1; and TORT vol 45(2) (Reissue) PARA 545.

13   As to the power to make rules see the Torts (Interference with Goods) Act 1977 s 8(2); and TORT vol 45(2) (Reissue) PARA 644. This power is without prejudice to any other power of making rules of court: see s 8(3); and TORT vol 45(2) (Reissue) PARA 644. For procedural rules concerning parties in claims for wrongful interference with goods, and the power of the court to order, in certain circumstances, that certain persons be deprived of the right to bring a claim against the defendant, see CPR 19.5A; and CIVIL PROCEDURE vol 11 (2009) PARAS 212, 588.

14   See the Torts (Interference with Goods) Act 1977 s 8(1); PARA 237; and TORT vol 45(2) (Reissue) PARAS 644, 678.

15 See the Torts (Interference with Goods) Act 1977 s 8(1); PARA 237; and TORT vol 45(2) (Reissue) PARAS 644, 678.

(2) CLAIMS AND DAMAGES

232. Demand for the goods. In a claim for conversion based on the defendant's wrongful detention of goods, it is ordinarily necessary to show that a demand has been made for the goods[1]. On the occasions when such a demand must be made, the claim will lie after the bailee has wrongfully refused or failed to comply with the demand[2]. The bailee cannot justify or excuse his failure to comply with the demand merely by proving that the chattel is no longer in his control or custody, or in that of anyone over whom he can exercise control, if he parted with it without just cause[3] or negligently lost it or allowed it to be destroyed[4]; but he is excused if he can show that his failure to return the chattel arises from its loss or destruction, before the demand for its return, without any default on his part[5]. If the chattel is lost or destroyed while it is wrongfully detained by him after the demand for its return, he is liable as an insurer[6].

Where, before any demand has been made, the bailee has done an act amounting to conversion of the chattel, a demand is not necessary in order to entitle the bailor to sue him[7].

1 See TORT vol 45(2) (Reissue) PARA 556 et seq; and see *Baldwin v Cole* (1704) 6 Mod Rep 212; *M'Combie v Davies* (1805) 6 East 538; *Alexander v Southey* (1821) 5 B & Ald 247 at 250 per Best J; *Jones v Dowle* (1841) 9 M & W 19; *Burroughes v Bayne* (1860) 5 H & N 296; *Pillot v Wilkinson* (1863) 2 H & C 72 (affd (1864) 3 H & C 345, Ex Ch). See also *Belsize Motor Supply Co v Cox* [1914] 1 KB 244; *Viscount Churchill v Whetnall, Lord Aberconway v Whetnall* (1918) 87 LJCh 524; *Alicia Hosiery Ltd v Brown Shipley & Co Ltd* [1970] 1 QB 195, [1969] 2 All ER 504; *Howard E Perry & Co Ltd v British Railways Board* [1980] 2 All ER 579, [1980] 1 WLR 1375; *Finlayson v Taylor* (1983) 133 NLJ 720. See generally Palmer on Bailment (3rd Edn, 2009) paras 1-075–1-085. The claimant may be relieved of the necessity for demand where the defendant made it obvious that any demand would be refused.

2 *Clayton v Le Roy* [1911] 2 KB 1031 at 1052, CA, per Farwell LJ; *Miller v Dell* [1891] 1 QB 468, CA, where the action was detinue or conversion and the cause of action was held to accrue from the date of demand for documents of title fraudulently taken from the plaintiff and deposited with the defendant's predecessor in title.

3 See PARA 147.

4 See the Torts (Interference with Goods) Act 1977 s 2(2); *Jones v Dowle* (1841) 9 M & W 19 at 20 per Parke B; *Reeve v Palmer* (1858) 5 CBNS 84; *Genn v Winkel* (1912) 107 LT 434 at 437, CA, per Fletcher Moulton LJ; *Lockspeiser Aircraft Ltd v Brooklands Aircraft Co Ltd* (1990) Times, 7 March. It appears that in a case where the bailee has wrongfully vacated his possession of the goods, time runs against the bailor's right of action from the date when the bailee parted with possession: see PARA 235. See also PARAS 147, 149.

5 *Taylor v Caldwell* (1863) 3 B & S 826 at 838 per Blackburn J. As to the onus of proof see PARAS 111 note 12, 149. See also PARA 185. See further *Jackson (Edinburgh) Ltd v Constructors John Brown Ltd* 1965 SLT 37, Ct of Sess.

6 *Shaw & Co v Symmons & Sons* [1917] 1 KB 799 (contractual bailment for reciprocal benefit); *Mitchell v Ealing London Borough Council* [1979] QB 1, [1978] 2 All ER 779; *Toor v Bassi* [1999] EGCS 9, CA (gratuitous bailment).

7 See e g *Grainger v Hill* (1838) 4 Bing NC 212; and see PARA 124. As to conversion generally see TORT vol 45(2) (Reissue) PARA 548 et seq and as to conversion by bailees see TORT vol 45(2) (Reissue) PARA 605.

233. Remedies and measure of damages. There is a choice of remedies in bailment as it is a transaction sui generis[1] and a claim against a defaulting bailee may (according to circumstance) lie in contract, tort or bailment[2]. The measure of damages is that appropriate to the cause of action. A restitutionary claim, grounded on either the bailor's or the bailee's unjust enrichment at the expense of the other, may also be available[3].

Negligence and conversion are the principal torts committed by a defaulting bailee[4]. Whenever they constitute the particular causes of action upon which the bailor sues, damages are awarded according to the specific rules governing those torts. In each case, damages are normally compensatory[5], the object being to restore the bailor to the position which he occupied before the tort was committed[6]. There is a broad degree of flexibility in assessing the damages payable[7]. In conversion, damages are usually (though there is no hard and fast rule) measured by the value of the chattel converted at the time of the conversion[8], together with any consequential damage flowing from the conversion which is not too remote to be recoverable by law[9]. Recoverable consequential damages may include aggravated damages[10], exemplary damages[11], and damages for psychiatric injury, inconvenience or loss of enjoyment[12], in addition to consequential monetary losses[13]. The time at which value is taken is generally the time most appropriate to achieve justice between the parties[14]; this may (according to circumstance) be the value at the date of judgment, or the value at the date of conversion, or the value at some intermediate date[15].

Where a bailment arises by contract, the bailor may sue in contract to recover damages for loss of his expectation interest[16]. Subject to ordinary principles of remoteness[17] (and other constraints)[18], such damages will normally seek to put the bailor in the position which he would have occupied, had the breach not occurred[19]. This is the measure commonly applied in claims for breach of contracts of carriage, hire, storage or repair; and the same measure is likely to apply in claims for breach of a bailee's duty to insure the chattel[20]. The bailor may alternatively claim for his reliance loss, that is, for costs or liabilities which he has incurred in reliance on the bailee's due performance of the contract, and which are now wasted by reason of the breach[21]. The normal principles of remoteness and other limiting factors govern such a claim[22]. Generally the bailor has an unfettered choice between the two forms of loss, and may even combine elements of each, provided this does not involve double claiming[23]. However, reliance losses cannot be recovered where the bailee shows that their award would allow the bailor to escape from a bad bargain[24]. Where a bailment is founded on contract, damages are likely to correspond to the measure awarded for breach of contract[25], even though the claim is for breach of bailment. Other than in a case of deviation[26] normal principles of remoteness are likely to apply[27].

Where a bailment is consensual but not contractual, and the bailor sues in bailment for breach of some express or implied promise by the bailee, a measure akin to that in contract may be awarded, subject to the bailee's contemplation[28], and, where appropriate, to his having undertaken responsibility for the particular loss in issue[29].

In many claims (under both contractual and non-contractual bailment) the measure of damages in bailment will correspond with that in tort for negligence or conversion[30]. The sum required to restore the bailor to the position which he occupied before the wrong was committed, and the sum required to put him in the position he would have occupied had bailment been performed, may in each case be the value of the chattel, together with incidental costs[31]. In certain circumstances, a bailee who, in breach of bailment, detains the bailed chattel and uses or otherwise derives benefit from it must pay to the bailor a reasonable hire charge for the period of detention and use[32].

A consignor of goods who is party to the contract of carriage[33], but suffers no substantial loss from the carrier's breach as the property in the goods has passed from him before the breach occurred, cannot ordinarily recover substantial damages, because recovery would offend the general rule that damages are compensatory[34].

A right to substantial damages for the loss of, or damage to, goods can be proved by showing possession or ownership of the goods at the time of the wrong regardless of whether the goods are at the risk of the owner or possessor; here it is the loss to the proprietary or possessory interest that is compensated rather than some other or different economic loss[35].

In a claim for the tort of negligence founded on the loss of, or damage to, goods, the claimant must show either the legal property in the goods[36], or a possessory title to them, at the time of loss or damage[37]. Legal property confers a right to substantial damages, and a similar right exists where a bailor has a possessory right falling short of legal ownership in goods, and these goods are lost or damaged while in the bailee's possession[38].

It has been said that where, by reason of a bailee's actual or presumed fault, a bailor cannot prove the value of goods lost or destroyed, the highest possible value is presumed against the bailee[39].

Damages and related matters in regard to proceedings against third parties in respect of the destruction of, or damage to, the chattels bailed are discussed elsewhere in this title[40].

1   *Building and Civil Engineering Holidays Scheme Management Ltd v Post Office* [1966] 1 QB 247 at 261–262, [1965] 1 All ER 163 at 167–168, CA, per Lord Denning MR; *Sutcliffe v Chief Constable of West Yorkshire* [1996] RTR 86; *East West Corpn v DKBS AF 1912 A/S, Utaniko Ltd v P & O Nedlloyd BV* [2003] EWCA Civ 83, [2003] QB 1509, [2003] 2 All ER 700; *Yearworth v North Bristol NHS Trust* [2009] EWCA Civ 37, [2010] QB 1, [2009] 2 All ER 986. See also Palmer on Bailment (3rd Edn, 2009) paras 1-097–1-099.

2   *Sutcliffe v Chief Constable of West Yorkshire* [1996] RTR 86 at 90, CA, per Otton J. See also PARA 107 note 6. As to damages in tort see DAMAGES vol 12(1) (Reissue) PARA 851 et seq. As to damages in contract see DAMAGES vol 12(1) (Reissue) PARA 941 et seq. As to damages in bailment see further DAMAGES vol 12(1) (Reissue) PARA 1088 et seq; Palmer on Bailment (3rd Edn, 2009) Chapter 37.

3   As to restitutionary claims by bailees, grounded on the unjust enrichment of bailors, see eg *China-Pacific SA v Food Corpn of India, The Winson* [1982] AC 939, [1981] 3 All ER 688, HL; *Brook's Wharf and Bull Wharf Ltd v Goodman Bros* [1937] 1 KB 534, [1936] 3 All ER 696, CA; and DAMAGES vol 12(1) (Reissue) PARA 1088. As to restitutionary claims by bailors, grounded on gains which have accrued to a bailee in breach by reason of the breach and which exceed the loss inflicted on the bailor, see DAMAGES vol 12(1) (Reissue) PARA 1099.

4   *Morris v CW Martin & Sons Ltd* [1966] 1 QB 716 at 738, [1965] 2 All ER 725 at 739, CA, per Salmon LJ. As to negligence generally see NEGLIGENCE. As to conversion generally see TORT vol 45(2) (Reissue) PARA 548 et seq.

5   *Building and Civil Engineering Holidays Scheme Management Ltd v Post Office* [1966] 1 QB 247 at 261–262. See also PARA 152; and DAMAGES vol 12(1) (Reissue) PARA 1091. The bailor recovers no more than his loss, which may, according to circumstance, be measured prospectively or retrospectively. In general, a bailor is entitled to recover the sum which will either put him in the position he should have occupied on performance or return him to the position he occupied before breach. As to compensation generally see DAMAGES vol 12(1) (Reissue) PARA 815 et seq.

6   *BBMB Finance (Hong Kong) Ltd v Eda Holdings Ltd* [1991] 2 All ER 129, [1990] 1 WLR 409.

7   *IBL Ltd v Coussens* [1991] 2 All ER 133, CA (conversion; full value awardable for 'irretrievable' conversion).

8   *Mercer v Jones* (1813) 3 Camp 477; *Reid v Fairbanks* (1853) 13 CB 692; *France v Gaudet* (1871) LR 6 QB 199 at 204, Ex Ch; *Solloway v McLaughlin* [1938] AC 247, [1937] 4 All ER 328, PC; *BBMB Finance (Hong Kong) Ltd v Eda Holdings Ltd* [1991] 2 All ER 129, [1990]

1 WLR 409, PC; *Chubb Cash Ltd v John Crilley & Son (a firm)* [1983] 2 All ER 294, [1983] 1 WLR 599, CA, where it was held that the price reached at a subsequent sale of the converted chattel at a public auction was prima facie good evidence of its value at the date of the auction and, on the facts, good evidence of its value at the time of the earlier conversion. The claimant may be entitled to additional damages if the goods have risen in market value between the conversion and judgment, subject to the usual rules of mitigation: *Greening v Wilkinson* (1825) 1 C & P 625; *Johnson v Hook* (1883) 31 WR 812; *Sachs v Miklos* [1948] 2 KB 23, [1948] 1 All ER 67, CA; *Aitken v Gardiner and Watson* [1956] OR 589, 4 DLR (2d) 119 (Can), Ont HC. As to damages being the fall in market value of the goods between the date of conversion and the date of their return see *Trailways Transport Ltd v Thomas* [1996] 2 NZLR 443, NZ HC. See also *IBL Ltd v Coussens* [1991] 2 All ER 133, CA. See generally TORT vol 45(2) (Reissue) PARA 615 et seq. As to what constitutes market value see TORT vol 45(2) (Reissue) PARA 627. See also the text and notes 14–15.

9   *General and Finance Facilities Ltd v Cooks Cars (Romford) Ltd* [1963] 2 All ER 314, [1963] 1 WLR 644, CA. See also *Douglas Valley Finance Co Ltd v S Hughes (Hirers) Ltd* [1969] 1 QB 738, [1966] 3 All ER 214; *Sandeman Coprimar SA v Transitos y Transportes Integrales* SL [2003] EWCA Civ 113, [2003] QB 1270, [2003] 3 All ER 108, [2003] 2 Lloyd's Rep 172. As to damages flowing naturally and directly from the wrongful usurpation and conversion see *Kuwait Airways Corpn v Iraqi Airways Co* [2002] UKHL 19, [2002] 2 AC 883, [2002] 3 All ER 209. See further TORT vol 45(2) (Reissue) PARA 630.

10 *Mafo v Adams* [1970] 1 QB 548 at 558, [1969] 3 All ER 1404 at 1410, CA, per Widgery LJ. See DAMAGES vol 12(1) (Reissue) PARA 1111 et seq.

11 *Borders (UK) Ltd v Metropolitan Police Comr* [2005] EWCA Civ 197, 149 Sol Jo LB 301, [2005] All ER (D) 60 (Mar) (exemplary damages may be awarded even where restitutionary relief is alternatively available); *Cook v Saroukos* (1989) 97 FLR 33, Aust FC; *Egan v State Transport Authority* (1982) 31 SASR 481, S Aust SC (action in detinue by contractor for wrongful seizure of plant). As to the circumstances in which exemplary damages are available see *Rookes v Barnard* [1964] AC 1129, [1964] 1 All ER 367, HL; *Cassell & Co Ltd v Broome* [1972] AC 1027, [1972] 1 All ER 801, HL. See DAMAGES vol 12(1) (Reissue) PARA 1115 et seq.

12 *Yearworth v North Bristol NHS Trust* [2009] EWCA Civ 37, [2010] QB 1, [2009] 2 All ER 986; *Graham v Voigt* (1989) 95 FLR 146, Aus FC; *Harris v Lombard New Zealand Ltd* [1974] 2 NZLR 161 at 169–170; *Millar v Candy* (1981) 58 FLR 145, Aust; and DAMAGES vol 12(1) (Reissue) PARA 957.

13 *Saleslease Ltd v Davis* [2000] 1 All ER (Comm) 883, [1999] 1 WLR 1664, CA (claim for damages based on bailor's loss of opportunity to re-bail profit-earning chattel to alternative lessee; loss held irrecoverable as could not have been reasonably anticipated by lessee in breach). See also TORT vol 45(2) (Reissue) PARA 630. As to the recovery of a reasonable hiring charge against the unlawful detainer under principles recognised in *Strand Electric and Engineering Co Ltd v Brisford Entertainments Ltd* [1952] 2 QB 246, [1952] 1 All ER 796, CA, see generally note 32; PARA 187; DAMAGES vol 12(1) (Reissue) PARAS 1096–1099; Palmer on Bailment (3rd Edn, 2009) paras 33-006–33-015, 37-029.

14 *IBL Ltd v Coussens* [1991] 2 All ER 133, CA.

15 *IBL Ltd v Coussens* [1991] 2 All ER 133, CA.

16 As to bailment by contract see PARA 145 et seq. As to the expectation interest see DAMAGES vol 12(1) (Reissue) PARA 977 et seq.

17 As to remoteness of damage see DAMAGES vol 12(1) (Reissue) PARAS 1015–1034.

18 As to limiting factors see DAMAGES vol 12(1) (Reissue) PARA 1015 et seq.

19 See DAMAGES vol 12(1) (Reissue) PARA 977 et seq.

20 *Lockspeiser Aircraft Ltd v Brooklands Aircraft Co Ltd* (1990) Times, 7 March, QB. As to whether a bailee owes an obligation to insure the goods, see PARA 150.

21 *CCC Films (London) Ltd v Impact Quadrant Films* [1985] QB 16, [1984] 3 All ER 298. As to reliance loss see DAMAGES vol 12(1) (Reissue) PARA 987 et seq.

22 See DAMAGES vol 12(1) (Reissue) PARA 1015 et seq.

23 As to double recovery see DAMAGES vol 12(1) (Reissue) PARA 948.

24 See DAMAGES vol 12(1) (Reissue) PARA 989.

25 As to damages in contract see DAMAGES vol 12(1) (Reissue) PARA 941 et seq.

26 As to deviation from the terms of the bailment see DAMAGES vol 12(1) (Reissue) PARA 1095.

27 Eg *McMahon v Field* (1881) 7 QBD 591, 50 LJQB 552, CA: see DAMAGES vol 12(1) (Reissue) PARA 1092. As to the normal principles of remoteness in a claim for breach of contract see DAMAGES vol 12(1) (Reissue) PARA 1015 et seq.

28 *Building and Civil Engineering Holidays Scheme Management Ltd v Post Office* [1966] 1 QB 247, [1965] 1 All ER 163, CA; *Yearworth v North Bristol NHS Trust* [2009] EWCA Civ 37, [2010] QB 1, [2009] 2 All ER 986. See also DAMAGES vol 12(1) (Reissue) PARA 1093.

29 *Transfield Shipping Inc v Mercator Shipping Inc, The Achilleas* [2008] UKHL 48, [2009] 1 AC 61, [2008] 4 All ER 159; *Sylvia Shipping Co Ltd v Progress Bulk Carriers Ltd, The Sylvia* [2010] EWHC 542 (Comm), [2010] 2 Lloyd's Rep 81, [2010] All ER (D) 184 (Mar); *Siemens Building Technologies FE Ltd v Supershield Ltd* [2010] EWCA Civ 7, [2010] 2 All ER (Comm) 1185, [2010] Lloyd's Rep 349; Palmer on Bailment (3rd Edn, 2009) para 37-019.

30 See DAMAGES vol 12(1) (Reissue) PARA 1094. As to damages in tort generally see DAMAGES vol 12(1) (Reissue) PARAS 851 et seq.

31 As to damages in relation to chattels see DAMAGES vol 12(1) (Reissue) PARA 860 et seq. If the goods have been restored to their owner after a conversion the owner may be required to give credit for their value and his damages must accordingly be reduced by that amount: *Brandeis Goldschmidt & Co Ltd v Western Transport Ltd* [1981] QB 864 at 873, [1982] 1 All ER 28 at 34, CA, per Brandon LJ. See also *IBL Ltd v Coussens* [1991] 2 All ER 133, CA. The measure for damages is generally subject to an allowance for any increase in the value of the goods due to expenditure or work on them by the defendant: see the Torts (Interference with Goods) Act 1977 s 6; and TORT vol 45(2) (Reissue) PARA 623. See also the text to note 39.

32 See *Strand Electric and Engineering Co Ltd v Brisford Entertainments Ltd* [1952] 2 QB 246, [1952] 1 All ER 796, CA; *Hillesden Securities Ltd v Ryjak Ltd* [1983] 2 All ER 184, [1983] 1 WLR 959; *Gray's Truck Centre Ltd v Olaf L Johnson Ltd* (25 January 1990, unreported), CA; *Saleh Farid v Theodorou and Blacklake Securities* (30 January 1992, unreported), CA; *Gaba Formwork Contractors Pty Ltd v Turner Corpn Ltd* (1993) 32 NSWLR 175, NSW SC; and DAMAGES vol 12(1) (Reissue) PARAS 1096–1099. See also PARA 187.

33 See CARRIAGE AND CARRIERS vol 7 (2008) PARA 752 et seq. See also *Albacruz (Cargo Owners) v Albazero (Owners), The Albazero* [1977] AC 774, [1976] 3 All ER 129, HL; and DAMAGES vol 12(1) (Reissue) PARA 1105.

34 See *Albacruz (Cargo Owners) v Albazero (Owners), The Albazero* [1977] AC 774, [1976] 3 All ER 129, HL; and DAMAGES vol 12(1) (Reissue) PARA 1105, where the principal exception to the proposition is discussed. Also see generally *Panatown Ltd v Alfred McAlpine Construction Ltd* [2001] 1 AC 518, [2000] 4 All ER 97, HL.

35 See *Obestain Inc v National Mineral Development Corpn Ltd, The Sanix Ace* [1987] 1 Lloyd's Rep 465; and DAMAGES vol 12(1) (Reissue) PARA 1106. In a claim based on damage to a reversionary interest in goods, where the claimant lacked any immediate right of possession at the time of the wrong, the claimant must show some enduring impairment of the goods or of his reversionary interest in them: see *East West Corpn v DKBS AF 1912 A/S, Utaniko Ltd v P & O Nedlloyd BV* [2003] EWCA Civ 83, [2003] QB 1509, [2003] 2 All ER 700; *HSBC Rail (UK) Ltd v Network Rail Infrastructure Ltd (formerly Railtrack plc)* [2005] EWCA Civ 1437, [2006] 1 All ER 343, [2006] 1 WLR 643; and TORT vol 97 (2010) PARA 606.

36 Mere equitable property is insufficient unless accompanied by a possessory title: *MCC Proceeds Inc v Lehman Bros International (Europe)* [1998] 4 All ER 675, [1998] 2 BCLC 659, CA, explaining *International Factors Ltd v Rodriguez* [1979] QB 351, [1979] 1 All ER 17, CA. See also CARRIAGE AND CARRIERS vol 7 (2008) PARA 757; TORT vol 97 (2010) PARA 606.

37 *Leigh & Sillavan Ltd v Aliakmon Shipping Co Ltd, The Aliakmon* [1986] AC 785 at 808, [1986] 2 All ER 145 at 148, HL, per Lord Brandon of Oakbrook. See further DAMAGES vol 12(1) (Reissue) PARA 1107.

38 See *Obestain Inc v National Mineral Development Corpn Ltd, The Sanix Ace* [1987] 1 Lloyd's Rep 465; and DAMAGES vol 12(1) (Reissue) PARA 1107.

39 See *Armory v Delamirie* (1722) 1 Stra 505; *Indian Oil Corpn v Greenstone Shipping SA (Panama), The Ypatianna* [1988] QB 345, [1987] 3 All ER 893; and DAMAGES vol 12(1) (Reissue) PARA 1108. Cf *Zabihi v Janzemini* [2009] EWCA Civ 851, [2009] All ER (D) 357 (Jul) (in the absence of evidence to the contrary, it would seem more logical to assume that the goods were of fair average quality rather than the best or worst of their kind; here both parties refused to give evidence of value of stolen jewels). See also PARAS 118, 143. As to changes in value and market value see notes 8, 31.

40 See PARAS 236–239.

234. Judgments and methods of enforcement. In addition to an order for the payment of damages[1], the forms of judgment available in an action involving bailment include an order for the return of the goods and a declaratory judgment.

A High Court judgment or order for the delivery of any goods which does not give a person against whom the judgment is given or order made the alternative of paying the assessed value of the goods may be enforced by one or more of the following means[2]: (1) writ of delivery to recover the goods without alternative provision for recovery of their assessed value (a 'writ of specific delivery')[3]; (2) in certain cases[4], an order of committal[5] or a writ of sequestration[6]. A judgment or order for the delivery of any goods or payment of their assessed value may be enforced by one or more of the following means: (a) writ of delivery to recover the goods or their assessed value; (b) by order of the court, writ of specific delivery; (c) in certain cases[7], writ of sequestration[8]. In county courts, except where an Act or rule of court provides otherwise, a judgment or order for the delivery of any goods is enforceable by warrant of delivery or warrant of specific delivery as appropriate[9].

A judgment for damages may be recovered by any of the following methods[10]: (i) a writ of fieri facias[11] or warrant of execution[12]; (ii) a third party debt order[13]; (iii) a charging order[14], stop order[15] or stop notice[16]; (iv) in a county court, an attachment of earnings order[17]; (v) the appointment of a receiver[18]. As from a day to be appointed, the procedure of taking control of goods and selling them to recover a sum of money[19] will be available where an enactment, writ or warrant confers power to use that procedure[20].

A declaratory judgment does not require enforcement: it is complete in itself, since the relief is the declaration[21].

1   As to damages see PARA 233.
2   See CIVIL PROCEDURE vol 12 (2009) PARA 1248. As to enforcement generally see CIVIL PROCEDURE vol 12 (2009) PARA 1223 et seq.
3   See CPR Sch 1 RSC Ord 45 r 4(1)(a); and CIVIL PROCEDURE vol 12 (2009) PARA 1268.
4   Ie where (1) a person required by a judgment or order to do an act within a time specified in the judgment or order refuses or neglects to do it within that time or, as the case may be, within that time as extended or abridged under a court order or by the written agreement of the parties; or (2) a person disobeys a judgment or order requiring him to abstain from doing an act: see CPR Sch 1 RSC Ord 45 r 5; and CIVIL PROCEDURE vol 12 (2009) PARA 1249.
5   See CPR Sch 1 RSC Ord 45 r 4(1)(b); and CIVIL PROCEDURE vol 12 (2009) PARA 1249.
6   See CPR Sch 1 RSC Ord 45 r 4(1)(c); and CIVIL PROCEDURE vol 12 (2009) PARA 1269.
7   See note 4.
8   See CPR Sch 1 RSC Ord 45 r 4(2); and CIVIL PROCEDURE vol 12 (2009) PARA 1248.
9   See CPR Sch 2 CCR Ord 26 r 16; and CIVIL PROCEDURE vol 12 (2009) PARAS 1248, 1291.
10 See *Practice Direction PD 70—Enforcement of Judgments and Orders* para 1.1; and CIVIL PROCEDURE vol 12 (2009) PARA 1245.
11 See CIVIL PROCEDURE vol 12 (2009) PARAS 1266, 1273 et seq. As from a day to be appointed, writs of fieri facias (except writs of fieri facias de bonis ecclesiasticis) are to be renamed writs of control: see the Tribunals, Courts and Enforcement Act 2007 s 62(4)(a) (not yet in force). At the date at which this volume states the law, no such day had been appointed.
12 See CIVIL PROCEDURE vol 12 (2009) PARA 1283 et seq.
13 See CIVIL PROCEDURE vol 12 (2009) PARA 1411 et seq.
14 See CIVIL PROCEDURE vol 12 (2009) PARA 1467 et seq.
15 See CIVIL PROCEDURE vol 12 (2009) PARA 1486 et seq.
16 See CIVIL PROCEDURE vol 12 (2009) PARA 1492 et seq.
17 See CIVIL PROCEDURE vol 12 (2009) PARA 1431 et seq.
18 See CIVIL PROCEDURE vol 12 (2009) PARA 1497 et seq.
19 Ie the procedure in the Tribunals, Courts and Enforcement Act 2007 Sch 12.
20 See the Tribunals, Courts and Enforcement Act 2007 Pt 3 Ch 1 (ss 62–70) and Sch 12; and CIVIL PROCEDURE vol 12 (2009) PARA 1386 et seq. The statutory rules replace the common law rules about the exercise of the powers which will become powers to use the procedure in Sch 12: see s 65(1). At the date at which this volume states the law, no day had been appointed for bringing the statutory provisions into force.
21 See CIVIL PROCEDURE vol 12 (2009) PARA 1223.

235.   Limitation of actions.   A claim in tort under the Torts (Interference with Goods) Act 1977 must be brought within six years of the cause of action accruing[1]. A claim in negligence is also subject to the six year limitation period from the accrual of the claim, except in the case of personal injuries where, in general, a three year time limit from the accrual of the cause of action, or the date of knowledge (if later), applies[2].

In the case of a conversion, the limitation period begins to run from the date of the conversion, and, subject to fraud by the defendant[3], this is so even where the owner does not become aware of the conversion until later[4]. In a case of conversion by wrongful detention alone, time runs from the refusal of a lawful demand for the return of the goods in question[5] or their equivalent.

In the case of successive conversions or detentions, time normally runs from the accrual of the cause of action in respect of the original conversion or detention[6].

Special provisions apply to the limitation of actions for damages brought under Part I of the Consumer Protection Act 1987[7].

1   Limitation Act 1980 s 2. A claim may also, where appropriate, be brought in contract where there is also a six year limitation period (s 5), but the accrual of a claim in contract is rarely later than the accrual of the cause of action in tort. See generally LIMITATION PERIODS. As to special periods of limitation see LIMITATION PERIODS vol 68 (2008) PARA 998 et seq; as to general periods of limitation see LIMITATION PERIODS vol 68 (2008) PARAS 952–954; as to title deeds see LIMITATION PERIODS vol 68 (2008) PARA 992; and as to property converted by a trustee see LIMITATION PERIODS vol 68 (2008) PARA 1142. As to pleading c f CIVIL PROCEDURE; LIMITATION PERIODS vol 68 (2008) PARA 943 et seq.

2   See the Limitation Act 1980 ss 11–13; and LIMITATION PERIODS. As to the date of knowledge see s 14 (amended by the Consumer Protection Act 1987 s 6, Sch 1 Pt I para 3). As to the discretion to extend the time limit see the Limitation Act 1980 s 33 (amended by the Consumer Protection Act 1987 Sch 1 Pt I para 6).

3   See the Limitation Act 1980 s 32 (amended by the Consumer Protection Act 1987 Sch 1 Pt I para 5; and the Latent Damage Act 1986 s 2(2)); and c f LIMITATION PERIODS vol 68 (2008) PARA 1220 et seq.

4   *Granger v George* (1826) 5 B & C 149; *RB Policies at Lloyd's v Butler* [1950] 1 KB 76, [1949] 2 All ER 226. However, the limitation period may not run where the goods have been stolen from the claimant: see the Limitation Act 1980 s 4 (amended by the Fraud Act 2006 s 14(1), Sch 1 para 18); and LIMITATION PERIODS vol 68 (2008) PARA 990. As to conversion generally see TORT vol 45(2) (Reissue) PARA 548 et seq.

5   *Philpott v Kelley* (1835) 3 Ad & El 106; *Miller v Dell* [1891] 1 QB 468, CA. It appears that a demand and refusal is still required under the Torts (Interference with Goods) Act 1977 s 2(2) because the provision assumes that the bailee's default would formerly have given rise to an action in detinue, and such an action had to be prefaced by a demand.

6   See the Limitation Act 1980 s 3(1); and c f LIMITATION PERIODS vol 68 (2008) PARA 988. There is a special time limit for goods which are converted by theft: see s 4 (as amended: see note 4); and LIMITATION PERIODS vol 68 (2008) PARA 990. As to the extent that bailment could be regarded as an independent cause of action rather than being framed as a claim in contract or tort for the purposes of limitation periods see *KH Enterprise v Pioneer Container, The Pioneer Container* [1994] 2 AC 324 at 340–342, [1994] 2 All ER 250 at 260–262, [1994] 1 Lloyd's Rep 593 at 600–602, PC; *Sutcliffe v Chief Constable of West Yorkshire* [1996] RTR 86 at 90, CA; *Sandeman Coprimar SA v Transitos y Integrales SL* [2003] EWCA Civ 113 at [59], [2003] QB 1270 at [59], [2003] 3 All ER 108 at [59], [2003] 2 Lloyd's Rep 172 at [59]; *Building and Civil Engineering Holidays Scheme Management Ltd v Post Office* [1966] 1 QB 247 per Lord Denning at 260–261. See also PARA 110; Palmer on Bailment (3rd Edn, 2009) Chapter 40.

7   See the Limitation Act 1980 s 11A; and CONSUMER PROTECTION vol 21 (2011) PARA 651; LIMITATION PERIODS vol 68 (2008) PARA 1003. As to the Consumer Protection Act 1987 Pt I (ss 1–9) see CONSUMER PROTECTION vol 21 (2011) PARA 642 et seq.

(3) RIGHTS AND OBLIGATIONS AS REGARDS THIRD PERSONS

236.   Bailor's right to sue.   Where there has been a sub-bailment[1] the owner has concurrent rights with the bailee against the sub-bailee; and if the owner has consented to the sub-bailment he will be bound by the terms of the sub-bailment contract[2].

Where the owner of a chattel has, under a contract of bailment, deprived himself of his right to its use or possession for a time, as in the case of hiring for reward or of pledge, he cannot during that time bring a claim for the conversion[3] of the chattel[4] unless the act of conversion adversely affects his reversionary interest or his absolute property in it, such as by destroying the chattel or permanently injuring it[5]. Similarly, although a bailee in possession, or with the immediate right to possession, can sue in negligence for the full value of goods, being obliged to account for that value to his bailor to the extent that he has suffered no loss, it does not follow that the bailor/owner has a similar right to sue for the full value, being accountable to the bailee to the extent that the loss is that of the bailee[6].

Where the bailee is merely a bailee during pleasure, as is the case in any gratuitous bailment[7], or under any contract of carriage where the terms of carriage do not specifically deal with this question[8], the bailor may, by reason of his immediate right of possession, sue for the conversion of the chattel a third party who wrongfully takes it out of the bailee's possession, for an end has been put to the bailment[9].

A bailor who can at any moment demand the return of the object bailed has been said to have possession throughout the continuance of the bailment, for he has the right to immediate possession and by reason of this right can exercise those possessory remedies which are available to the possessor[10]. But the preferable modern view appears to be that the bailee has possession even under bailment at will[11].

Further, where the bailee, by a wrongful dealing with the chattel, has determined the bailment, all third persons, however innocent, who purport in any way to deal with the property in the chattel[12] are guilty of conversion and liable to the bailor[13], unless protected by the Factors Act 1889[14].

1   See PARA 110.

2   *KH Enterprise v Pioneer Container, The Pioneer Container* [1994] 2 AC 324, [1994] 2 All ER 250, [1994] 1 Lloyd's Rep 593, PC; *Singer Co (UK) Ltd v Tees and Hartlepool Port Authority* [1988] 2 Lloyd's Rep 164; *East West Corpn v DKBS AF 1912 A/S, Utaniko Ltd v P & O Nedlloyd BV* [2003] EWCA Civ 83, [2003] QB 1509, [2003] 2 All ER 700; and see PARA 110.

3   *Gordon v Harper* (1796) 7 Term Rep 9. Still less can he maintain a claim of trespass. As to conversion generally see TORT vol 45(2) (Reissue) PARA 548 et seq.

4   *Bradley v Copley* (1845) 1 CB 685 at 697 per Tindal CJ. For the same reason the purchaser of goods retained by the vendor in exercise of his lien cannot maintain trover. As to trover or conversion (included in wrongful interference with goods) see TORT vol 45(2) (Reissue) PARA 542 et seq.

5   *Mears v London and South Western Rly Co* (1862) 11 CBNS 850; *Hall v Pickard* (1812) 3 Camp 187; *Meux v Great Eastern Rly Co* [1895] 2 QB 387, CA; *MCC Proceeds Inc v Lehman Bros International (Europe)* [1998] 4 All ER 675, [1998] 2 BCLC 659, CA; *East West Corpn v DKBS AF 1912 A/S, Utaniko Ltd v P & O Nedlloyd BV* [2003] EWCA Civ 83, [2003] QB 1509, [2003] 2 All ER 700; *HSBC Rail (UK) Ltd v Network Rail Infrastructure Ltd (formerly Railtrack plc)* [2005] EWCA Civ 1437, [2006] 1 All ER 343, [2006] 1 WLR 643. The third person cannot defend himself by pleading that the injury was due to the joint negligence of himself and the bailee: *Wellwood v King Ltd* [1921] 2 IR 274, CA. The owner, however, must

prove damage to his interest: *Tancred v Allgood* (1859) 4 H & N 438. See also *Kuwait Airways Corpn v Iraqi Airways* Co [2002] UKHL 19, [2002] 2 AC 883, [2002] 3 All ER 209.

6   *HSBC Rail (UK) Ltd v Network Rail Infrastructure Ltd (formerly Railtrack plc)* [2005] EWCA Civ 1437, [2006] 1 All ER 343, [2006] 1 WLR 643.

7   *Nicolls v Bastard* (1835) 2 Cr M & R 659; *Manders v Williams* (1849) 4 Exch 339. The owner may, perhaps, even maintain trespass.

8   *Gordon v Harper* (1796) 7 Term Rep 9 at 12 per Grove J. But the terms of the contract of carriage will often provide otherwise and will, if so, deprive the bailment of its character as a bailment at will: *Transcontainer Express Ltd v Custodian Security Ltd* [1988] 1 Lloyd's Rep 128 at 134–135, CA, per Slade LJ.

9   'No proposition can be more clear than that either the bailor or the bailee of a chattel may maintain an action in respect of it against a wrongdoer, the latter by virtue of his possession, the former by reason of his property': *Manders v Williams* (1849) 4 Exch 339 at 344 per Parke B. A claim by one, however, is a bar to a claim by the other: *Nicolls v Bastard* (1835) 2 Cr M & R 659 at 660 per Parke B. See also *O'Sullivan v Williams* [1992] 3 All ER 385, [1992] RTR 402, [1992] NLJR 717, CA. As to the bailor's right to sue see also DAMAGES vol 12(1) (Reissue) PARAS 1103–1104.

10 See *United States of America and Republic of France v Dollfus Mieg et Cie SA and Bank of England* [1952] AC 582 at 605, [1952] 1 All ER 572 at 581, HL, per Earl Jowitt, and at 611 and 585 per Lord Porter. The person having the right to immediate possession is not infrequently referred to in English law as being the possessor.

11 Cf *Transcontainer Express Ltd v Custodian Security Ltd* [1988] 1 Lloyd's Rep 128, CA. See also *MCC Proceeds Inc v Lehman Bros International (Europe)* [1998] 4 All ER 675, [1998] 2 BCLC 659, CA.

12 *Barker v Furlong* [1891] 2 Ch 172. See also *Wilson v Lombank Ltd* [1963] 1 All ER 740, [1963] 1 WLR 1294. But certain classes of possessor, who receive the possession of goods from someone who has no right to their possession and later return the goods to that person, may avoid liability in conversion to the true owner, if (inter alia) they can show that they acted in good faith and had no notice of any adverse claim: *Hollins v Fowler* (1875) LR 7 HL 757 at 766 per Blackburn J; *Marcq v Christie Manson & Woods Ltd (t/a Christie's)* [2003] EWCA Civ 731, [2004] QB 286, [2003] 3 All ER 561.

13 *Cooper v Willomatt* (1845) 1 CB 672; *Bryant v Wardell* (1848) 2 Exch 479; *Fenn v Bittleston* (1851) 7 Exch 152 at 159; *Loeschman v Machin* (1818) 2 Stark 311; *Consolidated Co v Curtis & Son* [1892] 1 QB 495; *North Central Wagon and Finance Co Ltd v Graham* [1950] 2 KB 7, [1950] 1 All ER 780, CA; *Marcq v Christie Manson & Woods Ltd (t/a Christie's)* [2003] EWCA Civ 731, [2004] QB 286, [2003] 3 All ER 561. See also *Union Transport Finance Ltd v British Car Auctions Ltd* [1978] 2 All ER 385, applying *North Central Wagon and Finance Co Ltd v Graham* [1950] 2 KB 7, [1950] 1 All ER 780, CA. See also *Chubb Cash Ltd v John Crilley & Son (a firm)* [1983] 2 All ER 294, [1983] 1 WLR 599, CA; *MCC Proceeds Inc v Lehman Bros International (Europe)* [1998] 4 All ER 675, [1998] 2 BCLC 659, CA. It is not certain whether a premature sale or sub-pledge by a pledgee determines the bailment within the meaning of the rule: see *Johnson (Assignee of Cumming) v Stear* (1863) 15 CBNS 330; *Donald v Suckling* (1866) LR 1 QB 585; *Halliday v Holgate* (1868) LR 3 Exch 299; and PARAS 208, 211. But if the holder of a lien wrongfully parts with the goods the bailment is determined: *Scott v Newington* (1833) 1 Mood & R 252; *Donald v Suckling* (1866) LR 1 QB 585 at 604 per Mellor J; *Mulliner v Florence* (1878) 3 QBD 484, CA.

14 See the Factors Act 1889 s 2; and AGENCY vol 1 (2008) PARA 148. A further protection used to be sales in market overt but this doctrine (which was contained in the Sale of Goods Act 1979 s 22(1)) was abolished by the Sale of Goods (Amendment) Act 1994 s 1: see MARKETS, FAIRS AND STREET TRADING vol 29(2) (Reissue) PARA 1026; SALE OF GOODS AND SUPPLY OF SERVICES vol 41 (2005 Reissue) PARA 23. See also PARA 116 note 11.

237. Bailee's right to sue. In accordance with the general principle of law that possession gives title as against a stranger[1], the bailee of a chattel under any species of bailment may at common law sue for the tort of trespass or conversion or maintain a claim for damages for the destruction of, or injury to, the chattel against the wrongdoer in all cases in which an absolute owner of a chattel may do so, and may recover in each case the same damages as he could if he were the absolute owner[2]. Thus in proceedings by a bailee against a third party in respect of the destruction of, or damage to, the chattel bailed[3], the bailee may at common law recover the full value of the chattel in respect of its destruction or the full cost of repairing any damage to it, and in addition any further damage which he may personally sustain by reason of his being deprived of its use while it is being repaired[4].

The fact that the bailee is under no responsibility to the bailor for the loss of or damage to the goods resulting from the act of the tortfeasor does not at common law avoid his right of action against him; for the common law rule that the wrongdoer cannot set up against the person in possession the jus tertii, unless he is claiming under it, is absolute, and the relation between the bailor and the bailee is immaterial[5].

The common law rule that a wrongdoer cannot plead the jus tertii in defence to a claim by a bailee has been substantially abrogated by statute[6]. The defendant in a claim for wrongful interference with goods[7] is entitled to show, in accordance with rules of court[8], that a third person has a better right than the claimant as regards all or any part of the interest claimed by the claimant, or in right of which he sues[9]. This provision therefore displaces the bailee's former entitlement to recover full damages from a third party wrongdoer, except where the wrongdoer elects not to plead the jus tertii, or there is an exception to the operation of the provision[10], or (perhaps) where the bailee sues otherwise than in tort[11].

A bailee who is not merely a bailee during pleasure may sue the bailor for the tort of conversion if the bailor wrongfully deprives him of the chattel[12].

1   This principle has been substantially abrogated by statute: see the Torts (Interference with Goods) Act 1977 s 8; and the text and notes 6–11. For procedural rules concerning parties in claims for wrongful interference with goods, and the power of the court to order, in certain circumstances, that certain persons be deprived of the right to bring a claim against the defendant, see CPR 19.5A; and CIVIL PROCEDURE vol 11 (2009) PARAS 212, 588.

2   *Burton v Hughes* (1824) 2 Bing 173 at 175 per Best CJ; *Rooth v Wilson* (1817) 1 B & Ald 59; *Croft v Alison* (1821) 4 B & Ald 590; *Raynor v Childs* (1862) 2 F & F 775; *Sutton v Buck* (1810) 2 Taunt 302; *The Winkfield* [1902] P 42, CA (where the cases are reviewed); *The Okehampton* [1913] P 173, CA; *East West Corpn v DKBS AF 1912 A/S, Utaniko Ltd v P & O Nedlloyd BV* [2003] EWCA Civ 83, [2003] QB 1509, [2003] 2 All ER 700; *O'Sullivan v Williams* [1992] 3 All ER 385, [1992] RTR 402, [1992] NLJR 717, CA; *Chartered Trust plc v King* [2001] All ER (D) 310 (Feb), Ch. See also PARA 118. As to the measure of damages see PARAS 152, 233. As to the bailee's right to sue see also DAMAGES vol 12(1) (Reissue) PARAS 1100–1102.

3   For the bailor's right to bring such proceedings see PARA 236; and DAMAGES vol 12(1) (Reissue) PARAS 1103–1104.

4   For exceptions, see Palmer on Bailment (3rd Edn, 2009) paras 4-096–4-098 (and also see paras 4-079, 4-134–4-135) approved in *Chartered Trust plc v King* [2001] All ER (D) 310 (Feb), Ch. As to the measure of damages where the chattel is being used other than for profit see *The Greta Holme* [1897] AC 596, HL; *Mersey Docks and Harbour Board v Marpessa (Owners)* [1907] AC 241, HL. See also *Sandeman Coprimar SA v Transitos y Transportes Integrales SL* [2003] EWCA Civ 113, [2003] QB 1270, [2003] 3 All ER 108, [2003] 2 Lloyd's Rep 172, CA; and PARA 233. In Admiralty cases the bailee can recover interest from the date of damage: *The Rosalind* (1920) 90 LJP 126. The court has a general power to award interest on damages: see the Senior Courts Act 1981 s 35A; and DAMAGES vol 12(1) (Reissue) PARA 848. The Senior Courts Act 1981 was previously known as the Supreme Court Act 1981 and was renamed by the Constitutional Reform Act 2005 s 59(5), Sch 11 Pt 1 as from 1 October 2009: see the Constitutional Reform Act 2005 (Commencement No 11) Order 2009, SI 2009/1604; and COURTS AND TRIBUNALS.

5   *The Winkfield* [1902] P 42, CA, overruling *Claridge v South Staffordshire Tramway Co* [1892] 1 QB 422; *Worthington v Tipperary County Council* [1920] 2 IR 233, CA. See PARA 238 note 2. However, see *O'Sullivan v Willams* [1992] 3 All ER 385, [1992] RTR 402, CA (bailor's claim for damages was settled, which put an end to any further claim by the bailee as the bailor's damages in respect of the goods included whatever use the bailor chose to permit the bailee to make of them).

6   See the Torts (Interference with Goods) Act 1977 s 8(1); and TORT vol 45(2) (Reissue) PARA 644.

7 Ie trespass to goods, conversion (or trover), negligence so far as it results in damage to goods or to an interest in goods, and any other tort so far as it results in damage to goods or to an interest in goods: see the Torts (Interference with Goods) Act 1977 s 1(1); and TORT vol 45(2) (Reissue) PARA 545.

8 As to the power to make rules see the Torts (Interference with Goods) Act 1977 s 8(2); and TORT vol 45(2) (Reissue) PARA 644. This power is without prejudice to any other power of making rules of court: s 8(3).

9 See the Torts (Interference with Goods) Act 1977 s 8(1). This provision also states that any rule of law to the contrary (sometimes called jus tertii) is abolished.

10 See TORT vol 45(2) (Reissue) PARA 644.

11 Cf TORT vol 45(2) (Reissue) PARA 644.

12 *Roberts v Wyatt* (1810) 2 Taunt 268; cf *Craig v Shedden* (1859) 1 F & F 553; *Sands v Shedden* (1851) 1 F & F 556; *MCC Proceeds Inc v Lehman Bros International (Europe)* [1998] 4 All ER 675, [1998] 2 BCLC 659, CA; *Chartered Trust plc v King* [2001] All ER (D) 310 (Feb), Ch; and see PARA 175 note 5.

238. Bailee's duty to account to bailor. As between himself and the bailor, the bailee must account to the bailor for everything that he may recover from a third person beyond his own interest[1], and must therefore pay over to him any sum which he has recovered as representing the value of the chattel, its permanent deterioration, or the cost of repairing it if he has not himself repaired it. If the bailee sues, therefore, he ought in general to claim and be awarded the full damages, for then no further claim can be brought by the bailor[2].

1 *Eastern Construction Co Ltd v National Trust Co Ltd and Schmidt* [1914] AC 197 at 210, PC; *The Joannis Vatis* [1922] P 92, CA; *Chartered Trust plc v King* [2001] All ER (D) 310 (Feb), Ch; and see PARAS 231, 237 note 5; and TORT vol 45(2) (Reissue) PARAS 631, 644. See also Palmer on Bailment (3rd Edn, 2009) paras 4-117–4-120.

2 *Eastern Construction Co Ltd v National Trust Co Ltd and Schmidt* [1914] AC 197, PC; *Worthington v Tipperary County Council* [1920] 2 IR 233, CA, per O'Connor MR; and see PARA 236 note 9; Palmer on Bailment (3rd Edn, 2009) Chapter 4. If, however, the bailor has, before action, transferred to the wrongdoer the ownership of the goods, the bailee cannot recover more than the value of his own interest, and the wrongdoer in relying on such a transfer is not setting up a jus tertii but a jus sui: *Eastern Construction Co Ltd v National Trust Co Ltd and Schmidt* [1914] AC 197, PC.

239. Liability of bailee and bailor to third persons. At common law, the bailee alone is responsible to third parties for any injury which they may sustain by reason of his negligence or other wrongful act in the control or management of the chattel, for he is not the agent of the bailor in this connection[1].

On the other hand, if the owner of a chattel, though he places it at the disposal of someone else, retains control over it by himself or his servants, so that there is no bailment, he remains responsible to third parties for any injury or damage caused by negligence in its management[2] or by the dangerous qualities of the chattel itself; but in this latter case his liability is not dependent upon his retaining a measure of control and extends to any person he knows or ought to have contemplated might use it[3].

Whether there is a bailment or not is a question which must depend upon the particular circumstances of the case[4].

In other respects the question of liability to third parties is determined by general principles. The bailee is liable for the acts of his servants acting within the scope of their employment, but not for their unauthorised acts when acting outside the scope of their employment[5].

1 *Smith v Bailey* [1891] 2 QB 403, CA; *Gibson v O'Keeney* [1928] NI 66, CA; *Britt v Galmoye and Nevill* (1928) 44 TLR 294; *Hewitt v Bonvin* [1940] 1 KB 188, CA; *Everett's Blinds Ltd v Thomas Ballinger Ltd* [1965] NZLR 266, NZ CA. Cf *Wellwood v King Ltd* [1921] 2 IR 274, CA; and EMPLOYMENT. As to the bailor's liability under the Consumer Protection Act 1987

Pt II (ss 11–19) see CONSUMER PROTECTION vol 21 (2011) PARA 675 et seq. Under the London Hackney Carriages Act 1843, the proprietor of a cab is liable for the negligence of the driver, even though the driver is not his servant but only a bailee: see *Venables v Smith* (1877) 2 QBD 279; *Smith v General Motor Cab Ltd* [1911] AC 188, HL (and the cases cited at 192 by Lord Atkinson); and ROAD TRAFFIC vol 40(3) (2007 Reissue) PARAS 1477 et seq, 1491.

2   *Reichardt v Shard* (1914) 31 TLR 24, CA; *Samson v Aitchison* [1912] AC 844, PC; *Pratt v Patrick* [1924] 1 KB 488; *Ormrod v Crosville Motor Services Ltd (Murphie, third party)* [1953] 1 All ER 711, [1953] 1 WLR 409; and see TORT vol 97 (2010) PARA 703.

3   *White v Steadman* [1913] 3 KB 340 at 347; *Griffiths v Arch Engineering Co (Newport) Ltd* [1968] 3 All ER 217. The bailor may have a defence to a claim by the third party in respect of the defective condition of the chattel if he has given the bailee a sufficient warning about that condition: *Pivovaroff v Chernabaeff* (1978) 21 SASR 1, S Aust SC, FC; and see *Lexmead (Basingstoke) Ltd v Lewis* [1982] AC 225, sub nom *Lambert v Lewis* [1981] 1 All ER 1185, HL; *Hurley v Dyke* [1979] RTR 265, HL. Cf *Hadley v Droitwich Construction Co Ltd* [1967] 3 All ER 911, [1968] 1 WLR 37, CA.

4   To prove a bailment, the owner must show that he had let out the chattel to a hirer and that the hirer or his agent had control over it to the exclusion of all interference with the working or management either by the owner or his agents: *Smith v Bailey* [1891] 2 QB 403, CA; *Nicholson v Harrison* (1856) 27 LTOS 56. See also PARA 101; Palmer on Bailment (3rd Edn, 2009) Chapter 36.

5   See eg the cases cited in PARA 148 notes 1–4. As to liability for a servant's acts see AGENCY vol 1 (2008) PARA 121 et seq; TORT vol 97 (2010) PARA 680 et seq. As to liability where a servant is hired by one employer from another see *Mersey Docks and Harbour Board v Coggins and Griffiths (Liverpool) Ltd* [1947] AC 1, [1946] 2 All ER 345, HL; and TORT vol 97 (2010) PARAS 711–714.

(4) WAR DAMAGE

240–300. Modification of liability in respect of war loss or damage. Certain obligations of a bailor or bailee, whether imposed by the provisions (express or implied) of a contract or by any enactment, rule of law or custom, are deemed not to extend to loss or damage by war[1]. The obligations in respect of which this exception applies are obligations to insure against loss of or damage to the goods; to repair damage to the goods; to replace the goods in the event of loss; to restore the goods or deliver them up in good repair, notwithstanding such loss or damage; to continue to pay for the hire of the goods; and to pay damages or compensation for any loss of or damage to the goods[2].

A bailee is not, however, relieved from any liability for loss of or damage to goods occurring while they are being kept or transported in a manner or at a place which is contrary to the terms of any contract relating to their custody or transport[3] unless he satisfies the court that he had reasonable grounds for believing that the goods were less likely to be lost or damaged while being so kept or transported than while being kept or transported in accordance with the terms of the contract[4]. Nor is a bailee or bailor relieved of any contractual liability which is expressly related to war by the terms of the contract[5], other than, in the case of a bailee, a liability imposed by: (1) a hire-purchase agreement or a conditional sale agreement within the meaning of the Consumer Credit Act 1974 being (in either case) a consumer credit agreement defined by that Act; or (2) a consumer hire agreement as defined by that Act[6].

1   Liability for War Damage (Miscellaneous Provisions) Act 1939 s 1(1). For this purpose, 'loss by war' and 'damage by war' mean respectively loss (including destruction) and damage caused by or in repelling enemy action, or by measures taken to avoid the spreading of the consequences of damage caused by or in repelling enemy action: s 8(2). The onus is on the party seeking to avoid liability to establish that the loss or damage was loss or damage by war: *Re S Davis & Co Ltd* [1945] Ch 402 at 407 (goods stored in premises which were damaged by enemy action); cf *Edwards v Newland & Co (E Burchett Ltd, third party)* [1950] 2 KB 534, [1950] 1 All ER

1072, CA (goods entrusted by bailee to third party without bailor's knowledge; third party's premises damaged by bomb; goods subsequently lost; bailee was held to be in breach of contract and liable for loss). As to war damage see WAR AND ARMED CONFLICT vol 49(1) (2005 Reissue) PARAS 533–534.

2 Liability for War Damage (Miscellaneous Provisions) Act 1939 s 1(1).

3 As to the general liability of a bailee who deals with the goods entrusted to him in an unauthorised manner see PARAS 125, 131, 139, 146.

4 Liability for War Damage (Miscellaneous Provisions) Act 1939 s 1(2).

5 Liability for War Damage (Miscellaneous Provisions) Act 1939 s 1(3).

6 Liability for War Damage (Miscellaneous Provisions) Act 1939 s 1(3) proviso (amended by the Consumer Credit Act 1974 s 192(3)(a), Sch 4 Pt I para 9). See CONSUMER CREDIT vol 21 (2011) PARAS 93 et seq, 116 et seq.

BOUNDARIES

1. DELIMITATION OF BOUNDARIES

(1) NATURE OF BOUNDARIES

301. Definition of a boundary. A boundary is an imaginary line[1] which marks the confines or line of division of two contiguous parcels of land[2]. The term is also used to denote the physical objects[3] by reference to which the line of division is described as well as the line of division itself. In this sense boundaries may be classified as natural or artificial, according to whether or not such physical objects are man-made[4].

Boundaries are fixed: (1) by proved acts of the respective owners[5]; or (2) by statutes or by orders of the authorities having jurisdiction[6]; or (3) in the absence of such acts, statutes or orders, by legal presumption[7].

1   *A-G v Chambers, A-G v Rees* (1859) 4 De G & J 55 at 65; *Wishart v Wyllie* (1853) 1 Macq 389, HL.

2   An ancient market may exist without metes and bounds: *Stepney Corpn v Gingell, Son and Foskett Ltd* [1909] AC 245, HL.

3   Eg walls, fences or hedges. As to protection of hedgerows see OPEN SPACES AND COUNTRYSIDE vol 78 (2010) PARA 700 et seq; and as to high hedges see NUISANCE vol 78 (2010) PARA 131 et seq.

4   See *Mackenzie v Bankes* (1878) 3 App Cas 1324 at 1339, HL. Natural or artificial objects that may form or locate boundaries include: waters (*Scratton v Brown* (1825) 4 B & C 485; *Bickett v Morris* (1866) LR 1 Sc & Div 47; *Holford v Bailey* (1849) 13 QB 426); the seashore (*A-G v Chambers* (1854) 4 De GM & G 206; *Baxendale v Instow Parish Council* [1982] Ch 14, [1981] 2 All ER 620); faults intersecting mines where the property consists of a mine (*Davis v Shepherd* (1866) 1 Ch App 410); fences (Woolrych *The Law of Party Walls and Fences* p 281); party walls (*Matts v Hawkins* (1813) 5 Taunt 20; *Cubitt v Porter* (1828) 8 B & C 257). See also PARAS 319–329.

5   See PARA 303 et seq.

6   See PARA 315 et seq. In the Building Regulations 1972, SI 1972/317 (revoked) and the Building Regulations 1976, SI 1976/1676 (revoked), 'boundary' was specially defined so that in relation to a building the term meant the boundary of the land belonging to the building and such land was deemed to include any abutting part of any street, canal or river, but only up to the centre line thereof. More recent legislation, however, has imposed less detailed control and has not contained such a definition: see the Building Regulations 1991, SI 1991/2768 (revoked); the Building Regulations 2000, SI 2000/2531 (revoked); the Building Regulations 2010, SI 2010/2214; and BUILDING.

7   See PARA 319 et seq.

302. Boundaries, horizontal and vertical. Ordinarily, land is divided either horizontally[1] or vertically, but the division may be made in any other way[2]. Where the division is vertical, the imaginary line of division extends up to the sky, so that the surface carries with it the superincumbent column of air[3], and down to the centre of the earth[4], unless the minerals or other strata have been severed[5], on the principle *cujus est solum, ejus est usque ad coelum et ad inferos*[6].

In the case of a lease or conveyance of a building or flat forming part of a building, the external walls enclosing the property demised will be included[7] and a part of any internal partition wall[8] unless there is provision to the contrary[9]. Where a lease of a top floor flat expressly includes the roof and roofspace, the demise will include the airspace above the roof[10] and may also include the roofspace horizontally adjacent to such a flat unless expressly excluded[11]. Where a flat is demised by reference to a floor of a building, the demise will normally include all the vertical space up to the bottom of the floor above[12].

1 Eg flats and maisonettes, or where the surface and minerals are separately owned. As to the severance of minerals see eg *Rowbotham v Wilson* (1860) 8 HL Cas 348; and MINES, MINERALS AND QUARRIES vol 31 (2003 Reissue) PARA 20 et seq.

2 See the Law of Property Act 1925 s 205(1)(ix); the Trustee Act 1925 s 12(2) (amended by the Trusts of Land and Appointment of Trustees Act 1996 s 25(1), Sch 3 para 3(2)); and REAL PROPERTY vol 39(2) (Reissue) PARAS 76–77.

3 *Corbett v Hill* (1870) LR 9 Eq 671; *Wandsworth Board of Works v United Telephone Co* (1884) 13 QBD 904, CA, per Bowen LJ; *Truckell v Stock* [1957] 1 All ER 74, [1957] 1 WLR 161, CA; *Kelsen v Imperial Tobacco Co (of Great Britain and Ireland) Ltd* [1957] 2 QB 334, [1957] 2 All ER 343; *Ward v Gold* (1969) 211 Estates Gazette 155; *Straudley Investments Ltd v Barpress Ltd* [1987] 1 EGLR 69, CA (landlord could not construct fire escapes on and above roof of property demised). For further consideration of the proposition and of the Civil Aviation Act 1982 s 76, which restricts action in trespass in respect of the flight of aircraft over land, see *Baron Bernstein of Leigh v Skyviews and General Ltd* [1978] QB 479, [1977] 2 All ER 902 (use of airspace for aerial photography).

4 *Duke of Devonshire v Pattinson* (1887) 20 QBD 263 at 273, CA, per Fry LJ; *Corbett v Hill* (1870) LR 9 Eq 671.

5 See note 1.

6 Ie he who possesses land possesses also that which is above it and below it. See *Star Energy Weald Basin Ltd v Bocardo SA* [2010] UKSC 35 at [8]–[28], [2010] 3 All ER 975 at [8]–[28]. This principle, however, will not exclude from the premises the foundations and eaves of the building extending beyond the surface boundary line: *Truckell v Stock* [1957] 1 All ER 74, [1957] 1 WLR 161, CA; cf *Laybourn v Gridley* [1892] 2 Ch 53 (part of a loft room protruding into the property conveyed above ground level was included in the conveyance). It will operate to include a cellar beneath the property even where the only access at the time of the conveyance is from adjoining retained property: *Grigsby v Melville* [1973] 3 All ER 455, [1974] 1 WLR 80, CA. See also *Solomon v Vintners' Co* (1859) 4 H & N 585 at 600 per Pollock CB; *Mitchell v Mosley* [1914] 1 Ch 438 at 450, CA; *Railways Comr v Valuer-General* [1974] AC 328, [1973] 3 All ER 268, PC. Certain minerals are excluded from private ownership (eg petroleum: see the Petroleum Act 1998 s 2; and FUEL AND ENERGY vol 19(3) (2007 Reissue) PARA 1634). See also MINES, MINERALS AND QUARRIES vol 31 (2003 Reissue) PARA 20.

7 *Carlisle Café Co and Todd v Muse Bros & Co* (1897) 67 LJCh 53; *Hope Bros Ltd v Cowan* [1913] 2 Ch 312; *Goldfoot v Welch* [1914] 1 Ch 213; *Sturge v Hackett* [1962] 3 All ER 166, [1962] 1 WLR 1257, CA. See PARA 311.

8 *Hope Bros Ltd v Cowan* [1913] 2 Ch 312 at 316 ('the demise of a room must necessarily include, unless it be excepted, some part of the wall which bounds it'); *Phelps v City of London Corpn* [1916] 2 Ch 255 at 263.

9 Eg *Cockburn v Smith* [1924] 2 KB 119, CA (lease of 'all that suite of rooms' where the flat was the top floor of a building did not include the roof of the building so the roof and guttering remained in the landlord's possession and control). See also *Douglas-Scott v Scorgie* [1984] 1 All ER 1086, [1984] 1 WLR 716, CA; *Tennant Radiant Heat Ltd v Warrington Development Corpn* [1988] 1 EGLR 41, CA (lease of one small unit in large single storey block included the portion of the roof above because of references in the tenant's covenants).

10 *Davies v Yadegar* (1990) 22 HLR 232, [1990] 1 EGLR 71, CA (alteration by tenant involving altering profile of roof was not a trespass). Cf *Tideway Investments and Property Holdings Ltd v Wellwood* [1952] Ch 791, [1952] 2 All ER 514, CA (proposed erection of flue pipes at side of flat protruding into the landlord's airspace and attached to balconies retained by the landlord was a trespass). See also *Haines v Florensa* (1990) 59 P & CR 200, [1990] 1 EGLR 73, CA (lease expressly included roof in the demise).

11 *Hatfield v Moss* [1988] 2 EGLR 58, CA (demise of a top floor flat which included the main roof was also held to include the adjacent roof space notwithstanding a plan, attached for the purposes of identification only, which appeared to exclude it). See also PARAS 304, 310.

12 *Sturge v Hackett* [1962] 3 All ER 166, [1962] 1 WLR 1257, CA; *Graystone Property Investments Ltd v Margulies* (1983) 47 P & CR 472, CA (demise therefore included roof voids above the false ceiling and below the flat above). Cf *Munt v Beasley* [2006] EWCA Civ 370, [2006] All ER (D) 29 (Apr), where the tenant of a top floor flat had converted the overhead loft space to living accommodation and it was held that, whilst common sense supported the contention that the loft was included in the demise it was not supported by the language of the lease. The lease did not include the loft. It referred to the flat 'on the first floor' and the loft was not on the first floor where M's flat was situated, it was above it. It was true that the plans of the flats drawn by the landlord referred to the 'upstairs flat' and to 'the upper and lower flat' rather than to the 'first floor flat', but the loft was not shown or mentioned on them, nor was the roof. It was doubtful whether the omission of the loft was deliberate. It was more probable

that the omission was the result of a mistake or oversight in documenting the agreement of the parties. See also *Ravengate Estates Ltd v Horizon Housing Group Ltd* [2007] EWCA Civ 1368, [2008] 01 EG 135 (CS), [2007] All ER (D) 294 (Dec), where the airspace above a balcony and above the roof was included in the demise. 'That conclusion is reached on the basis of the true construction of the lease. It is therefore not necessary to consider the various authorities placed before us as to the extent to which air space is and is not carried with a grant of land, though for my part had it been necessary to do so I would have found in favour of the application of the presumption that a grant normally carries the airspace': per Mann LJ.

(2) BOUNDARIES FIXED BY THE ACT OF THE PARTIES

(i) By Agreement

303. Boundary agreements. Boundaries may be fixed by an agreement[1] made between two or more adjacent owners where their boundaries are not clearly defined or have become lost or confused. In general, such an agreement need not be in writing[2] and, a fortiori, need not be by deed; for, if it was fairly made, it will be presumed that it did not involve any alienation of land but that the boundaries settled were the true and ancient limits[3]. Even where a conveyance apparently conveys a disputed strip of land to one adjoining owner, the erection of a fence or wall by that owner leaving the disputed strip accessible only to the other adjoining owner may be evidence of an express or implied agreement that the boundary is to be represented by that fence or wall[4]. Moreover, the settlement of boundaries is a mutual consideration sufficient to support a contract not made by deed, even where the land is situated out of the jurisdiction[5].

Where, prior to the contract for the sale of land, the boundary was marked out on the land itself and agreed to by the parties, the court may have regard to this as part of the 'surrounding circumstances' in construing vague parcels in the subsequent conveyance[6]. However, where a conveyance clearly shows the line of the boundary, the existence of a wall parallel to the boundary is not sufficient to form a basis for a boundary agreement and extrinsic evidence as to where the parties intended the boundary to be is not admissible[7].

1 As to questions of misdescription of boundaries in agreements for the sale of land see *King v Wilson* (1843) 6 Beav 124; and SALE OF LAND vol 42 (Reissue) PARA 250. As to the remedy of rectification for misdescription of boundaries in conveyances or transfers see *Berkeley Leisure Group Ltd v Williamson* [1996] EGCS 18, CA; and PARA 310. As to the making of an agreement see *Fairacre Investments Ltd v Earlrose Golf and Leisure Ltd* [2006] EWHC 678 (Ch), [2006] All ER (D) 286 (Feb) (the authority of the claimant's predecessor in title's representative did not extend to making boundary agreements with neighbouring landowners without reference to and approval by the beneficial owners of the land; accordingly, any agreement could not have been binding on the claimant's predecessor in title, or on the claimant).

2 *Burns v Morton* [1999] 3 All ER 646, [2000] 1 WLR 347, CA (where it was held that there had been an implied oral agreement between the adjoining owners that a new wall should demarcate the boundary between the properties); *Joyce v Rigolli* [2004] EWCA Civ 79, [2004] 1 P & CR D55, 148 Sol Jo LB 234 (where an agreement's principal purpose is to identify a border, even if the agreement results in a small exchange of land there is no requirement for it to be evidenced in writing); *Stephenson v Johnson* [2000] EGCS 92; Court of Appeal (boundary agreements could be highly informal and the court should not be slow to find that one existed given that agreement was better than litigation. It is not necessary for a court to have to find an offer and an acceptance. The course of the parties' conduct should be looked at and if, on the balance of probabilities, an agreement is established, that is sufficient). For a Scottish case where the mutual boundary was adjusted by verbal agreement between the owners see *Hetherington v Galt* (1905) 7 F 706, Ct of Sess.

3 *Penn v Lord Baltimore* (1750) 1 Ves Sen 444; *Taylor v Parry* (1840) 1 Man & G 604; *Neilson v Poole* (1969) 20 P & CR 909. Such an agreement, therefore, does not constitute either: (1) a

contract for the sale or other disposition of an interest in land required, prior to 27 September 1989, to be evidenced in writing under the Law of Property Act 1925 s 40 (repealed) or, since that date, to be made in writing under the Law of Property (Miscellaneous Provisions) Act 1989 s 2 (see DEEDS AND OTHER INSTRUMENTS vol 13 (2007 Reissue) PARA 145; SALE OF LAND vol 42 (Reissue) PARA 29); or (2) a conveyance of land, since the Law of Property Act 1925 s 52 requires a conveyance of a legal estate to be made by deed (see DEEDS AND OTHER INSTRUMENTS vol 13 (2007 Reissue) PARA 14). Nor is such an agreement registrable as an estate contract (ie as a Class C land charge under the Land Charges Act 1972 s 2(4)(iv): see LAND CHARGES vol 26 (2004 Reissue) PARAS 628, 632): *Neilson v Poole* (1969) 20 P & CR 909. In *Melhuish v Fishburn* [2008] EWCA Civ 1382, [2009] All ER (D) 23 (Jan), the Court of Appeal held that the judge was right to find that the agreement to demarcate a boundary was not a contract for the sale or other disposition of an interest in land for the purposes of the Law of Property (Miscellaneous Provisions) Act 1989 s 2; *Joyce v Rigolli* [2004] EWCA Civ 79, [2004] 1 P & CR D55, 148 Sol Jo LB 234 applied. That conclusion was not affected by the fact that the agreement contemplated that F would have to pay if he benefited from it. A boundary agreement must specifically relate to the location of the boundary, and not merely to the maintenance of physical features: *Welding v Charalamous* [2009] EWCA Civ 1578 (14 December 2009, unreported).

4   See *Stephenson v Johnson* [2000] EGCS 92, CA (the boundary was unclear, but the fence that was erected by one party was approved by the other party's surveyor; it was held that a boundary agreement could be inferred from the parties' conduct); *Burns v Morton* [1999] 3 All ER 646, [2000] 1 WLR 347, CA (the erection of a wall by the defendant on his own land a few inches away from and in substitution for a fence on the boundary between the properties enabled the court to hold that, since the conveyances declared that any dividing wall was to be a party wall, there was an implied oral agreement that the new wall should demarcate the boundary between the two properties even though the agreement to a small degree altered the boundary from where it had previously been).

5   *Penn v Lord Baltimore* (1750) 1 Ves Sen 444. Cf *British South Africa Co v De Beers Consolidated Mines Ltd* [1910] 2 Ch 502, CA; revsd on a question of construction, sub nom *De Beers Consolidated Mines Ltd v British South Africa Co* [1912] AC 52, HL.

6   *Willson v Greene (Moss, third party)* [1971] 1 All ER 1098, [1971] 1 WLR 635, applying *Webb v Nightingale* (1957) 169 EG 330, CA. These authorities establish that a boundary on a plan which is expressed to be for the purposes of identification only can be overridden in favour of a boundary pegged out on the land by an agreement between the parties beforehand; but this approach did not operate to exclude a plaintiff's right of way over an unmarked grass verge later conveyed to a defendant who fenced it off: *Scott v Martin* [1987] 2 All ER 813 at 818, [1987] 1 WLR 841 at 848, CA, per Nourse LJ. As to the admissibility of evidence of 'surrounding circumstances' see PARA 332.

7   *Woolls v Powling* (1999) Times, 9 March, [1999] All ER (D) 125, CA. See also PARA 332.

(ii) By Assurance

304.   Definition in conveyance.   Boundaries may, and generally should, be fixed by the deed or deeds conveying one or both of the properties concerned[1]. Nevertheless, conveyances of land commonly leave the exact line of existing boundaries undetermined[2]. It is only in comparatively rare cases that the exact line assumes any real significance, and the steps necessary to achieve precision can be time-consuming and expensive, for boundaries cannot be fixed unilaterally unless the adjoining land is also in the ownership of the vendor[3]. Where, however, partition of a property is undertaken, the conveyances or transfers, in order to identify the property to which they relate, should incorporate a plan which is on a scale sufficiently large to represent the property and its boundaries in precise detail[4] and should describe the property conveyed with such particularity and precision that there is no room for doubt about the boundaries of each parcel conveyed[5].

The property may be described in any way sufficient to identify it[6], for example by its name or street number, by its abuttals or relation to known adjacent physical features (for instance a road or river), by its dimensions, by a description of its nature, or by reference to its present or former mode of occupation; and in general may be described either by verbal description alone or by verbal description supplemented by a plan[7]. It is unsafe, in the preparation of a conveyance, to rely exclusively on a plan the lines on which are to be taken as the true description of the boundaries of the property conveyed just as if they were contained in the body of the deed[8], for even a well-drawn plan is accurate only within the limits of the scale adopted[9].

1 The definition contained in a conveyance prevails in the demarcation of a boundary: *Burns v Morton* [1999] 3 All ER 646, [2000] 1 WLR 347, CA (provision in conveyance that any division walls or fences were to be party walls and that future walls were to straddle the boundary; it was held that a new wall, built by the defendant a few inches inside the fence that previously demarcated the boundary, became the boundary by implied agreement between the adjoining owners). See also PARA 303.

   There is a statutory presumption as between vendor and purchaser of the accuracy of recitals, statements and descriptions in deeds more than 20 years old: see the Law of Property Act 1925 s 45(6); and SALE OF LAND vol 42 (Reissue) PARAS 150, 285.

2 See *Alan Wibberley Building Ltd v Insley* [1999] 2 All ER 897, [1999] 1 WLR 894, HL, where the background to and the reasons for the general boundaries approach in both registered and unregistered conveyancing is discussed. As to boundaries of registered land see PARA 309.

3 For this reason the general conditions of sale of land most commonly used absolve the vendor from having to prove the exact line of the boundaries: see the Standard Conditions of Sale (4th Edn, 2003) para 4.4; and SALE OF LAND vol 42 (Reissue) PARA 109. As to the Standard Conditions of Sale see SALE OF LAND vol 42 (Reissue) PARA 1. For the effect of similar conditions see *Curling v Austin* (1862) 2 Drew & Sm 129. See *Seeckts v Derwent* [2004] EWCA Civ 393, 148 Sol Jo LB 417, [2004] All ER (D) 554 (Mar), where Carnwath LJ at [22] quoted the first three sentences of the text to this paragraph with approval.

4 *Kingston v Phillips* [1976] CA Transcript 279, CA, per Buckley LJ; applied in *Scarfe v Adams* [1981] 1 All ER 843, CA.

5 *Scarfe v Adams* [1981] 1 All ER 843 at 845, CA, per Cumming-Bruce LJ (where a plan on a scale of 1:2500 was described as 'worse than useless'). See also *Mayer v Hurr* (1983) 49 P & CR 56, CA.

6 *Carlisle Café Co and Todd v Muse Bros & Co* (1897) 67 LJCh 53; *Hope Bros Ltd v Cowan* [1913] 2 Ch 312; *Goldfoot v Welch* [1914] 1 Ch 213.

7 A plan for identification only of an existing property which has been a complete unit for some time with the perimeters fenced off would take second place to the description of such a property in the parcels by its postal address: *Targett and Targett v Ferguson and Diver* (1996) 72 P & CR 106 at 115, CA, per Sir John Balcombe.

   In the case of compulsory acquisition of land where the Acquisition of Land Act 1981 applies, the compulsory purchase order must describe by reference to a map the land to which it applies: see the Compulsory Purchase of Land (Prescribed Forms) (Ministers) Regulations 2004, SI 2004/2595, reg 3, Schedule; the Compulsory Purchase of Land (Prescribed Forms) (National Assembly for Wales) Regulations 2004, SI 2004/2732, reg 3, Schedule; and COMPULSORY ACQUISITION OF LAND vol 18 (2009) PARA 558 et seq. See further *Protheroe v Tottenham and Forest Gate Rly Co* [1891] 3 Ch 278, CA.

   In the case of registered land, an instrument dealing with part of the land comprised in a title is required to be accompanied by a plan showing the land dealt with, unless such part is clearly defined on the title plan of the registered title, in which case it may be defined by reference to that title plan: see the Land Registration Rules 2003, SI 2003/1417, r 213; and LAND REGISTRATION.

8 *Lyle v Richards* (1866) LR 1 HL 222; *Llewellyn v Earl of Jersey* (1843) 11 M & W 183. As to the right of a purchaser to have a plan to supplement the verbal description in his conveyance see *Re Sharman and Meade's Contract* [1936] Ch 755, [1936] 2 All ER 1547; and SALE OF LAND vol 42 (Reissue) PARA 148. Where the boundary is the centre of a road or river it is better to say so, or to mark it so on the plan, but, at least in the case of roads, it is not the practice of the Land Registry to do this: see *Russell v Barnet London Borough Council* (1984) 83 LGR 152, [1984] 2 EGLR 44; and PARAS 309, 323. As to the Land Registry see LAND REGISTRATION vol 26 (2004 Reissue) PARA 1064.

9 Thus in *Taylor v Parry* (1840) 1 Man & G 604 the plan was on such a small scale that a boundary could not be accurately traced and as the land was sufficiently described in the body of the deed, the plan was not allowed to control the description. See also *Scarfe v Adams* [1981] 1 All ER 843, CA; and notes 4–5.

305. The relative importance of the verbal description of the parcels and plan. In a conveyance, it is common for a verbal description of the parcels of land to be followed by words incorporating a plan to be referred to 'for the purposes of identification only'. The principal effect of these words, at least where the description is clear, is to confine the use of the plan to ascertaining where the land is situated and to prevent the plan controlling the verbal description of the parcels[1]. The effect is similar to that in registered conveyancing, that is, indicating the general boundaries only[2]. Thus where the conveyance shows that a particular acreage is to be conveyed, but the adoption of a boundary from the plan would leave only a reduced acreage, the boundary on the plan must yield to the acreage indicated by the conveyance[3]. However, when a court is required to decide what property passed under a conveyance, it will have regard to the conveyance as a whole, including any plan which forms part of it and the plan may be looked at to assist in the understanding of the description of the parcels[4]. Accordingly, the qualifying words 'for the purpose of identification only' do not prevent the use of the plan to determine a true boundary where this is the sole means which the conveyance affords to indicate where the boundary is intended to be drawn, provided such reference is in order to elucidate problems which are left undecided and does not contradict or control the verbal description in the parcels[5].

Phrases such as 'more particularly delineated' or 'more particularly described' or 'more precisely delineated' used in reference to a plan are words which tend to show that in the case of conflict or uncertainty the plan is to prevail over any verbal description[6].

Where both forms of expression are used together, as in the phrase 'for the purposes of identification only more particularly delineated', they tend to be mutually stultifying[7]. Such language is confusing and inconclusive, and it does not give the plan any predominance over the parcels; in such a case the court must establish the true construction of the conveyance[8].

Where there are no controlling words, but the parcels are described by reference to a plan, the natural inference is that it was the intention of the parties that the plan should show the boundaries of the land which the conveyancing document was purporting to pass[9]. However, the document must be construed in the light of the actual state of the *locus in quo* at the time and what a reasonable layman would think he was purchasing[10].

1   See *Hopgood v Brown* [1955] 1 All ER 550, [1955] 1 WLR 213, CA, per Jenkins LJ; *Neilson v Poole* (1969) 20 P & CR 909; *Wigginton & Milner Ltd v Winster Engineering Ltd* [1978] 3 All ER 436, [1978] 1 WLR 1462, CA, per Buckley LJ; *Hatfield v Moss* [1988] 2 EGLR 58, CA; *Strachey v Ramage* [2008] EWCA Civ 384, [2008] 2 P & CR 154, [2008] All ER (D) 267 (Apr). A plan so referred to does not comply with the Land Registration Rules 2003, SI 2003/1417, r 213 (as to which see LAND REGISTRATION vol 26 (2004 Reissue) PARA 1083.

In *Hubert C Leach Ltd v Hayward* [1994] NPC 77, the parcels included disputed land; the plan 'for purposes of identification' did not. It was held that the words overrode the plan; a plan attached to a conveyance for the purpose of identification, even if the word 'only' was omitted, did not prevail over words used in a conveyance which identified the parcels to be conveyed. See also *Druce v Druce* [2003] EWCA Civ 535, [2004] 1 P & CR 424, [2003] All ER (D) 122 (Feb): if a plan is attached to a conveyance for the purpose of identification only, the verbal description in the conveyance prevails over any other indication in the plan. On the other hand, if the property is described by reference to the plan, the plan prevails. If both phrases are used, it is a question of interpretation of the conveyance whether the plan prevails over the verbal description in the conveyance itself. In most cases, the likely construction is that the verbal description is to prevail.

2   *Alan Wibberley Building Ltd v Insley* [1999] 2 All ER 897, [1999] 1 WLR 894, HL, per Lord Hoffmann. See further PARA 309.

3   *Wigginton & Milner Ltd v Winster Engineering Ltd* [1978] 3 All ER 436 at 447, [1978] 1 WLR
    1462 at 1475, CA, per Bridge LJ; and see *Moreton C Cullimore (Gravels) Ltd v Routledge*
    (1977) 121 Sol Jo 202, CA. So where a measurement had been inserted into a conveyance by
    common mistake and the plan showed what had been intended, it was necessary to seek a decree
    of rectification of the conveyance: *Berkeley Leisure Group Ltd v Williamson* [1996] EGCS
    18, CA. Where there was a conflict between dimensions in figures on a plan by which a property
    transferred was described and dimensions arrived at by scaling off the plan, the conflict was to
    be resolved by reference to such inferences as might be drawn from topographical features that
    existed when the transfer was executed: *Cook v JD Wetherspoon plc* [2006] EWCA Civ 330,
    [2006] 2 P & CR 326, [2006] All ER (D) 461 (Mar) (on the basis of those features the judge had
    correctly concluded that a boundary based upon the red edging on the plan would coincide with
    features on the ground which could sensibly be regarded as boundary features). In *Saxon v
    Moore* [2005] EWHC 27 (Ch), the wording of the parcels clause took precedence over the plan.
4   *Wigginton & Milner Ltd v Winster Engineering Ltd* [1978] 3 All ER 436 at 445, [1978] 1 WLR
    1462 at 1473, CA, per Buckley LJ.
5   *Wigginton & Milner Ltd v Winster Engineering Ltd* [1978] 3 All ER 436 at 447, [1978] 1 WLR
    1462 at 1475, CA, per Bridge LJ (reference to a plan, described as being for the purposes of
    identification only and clearly linked to a description in a schedule which was by reference to
    Ordnance Survey numbers, was the only way to discover what the parties intended to be the
    boundary); applied in *Scott v Martin* [1987] 2 All ER 813, [1987] 1 WLR 841, CA. See also
    Targett and Targett v Ferguson and Diver (1996) 72 P & CR 106, CA (parcels clause of
    conveyance of a building plot not explicit enough to identify the boundary and, in the light of
    the fencing covenants and the 'T' marks, the boundary was declared to be that shown on the
    plan); *Woolls v Powling* (1999) Times, 9 March, [1999] All ER (D) 125, CA (plan clearly
    identified and delineated the relevant boundary).
6   *Eastwood v Ashton* [1915] AC 900, HL; *Fisher v Winch* [1939] 1 KB 666, [1939] 2 All ER
    144, CA; *Wallington v Townsend* [1939] Ch 588, [1939] 2 All ER 225; *Kensington Pension
    Developments Ltd v Royal Garden Hotel (Oddenino's) Ltd* [1990] 2 EGLR 117.
7   *Neilson v Poole* (1969) 20 P & CR 909 at 916 per Megarry J (delineation so described was held
    to be only for the purpose of showing the identity of the property and so negatived any use of
    the plan to show precise boundaries); *Wigginton & Milner Ltd v Winster Engineering Ltd*
    [1978] 3 All ER 436 at 444, [1978] 1 WLR 1462 at 1472, CA; and see *Moreton C Cullimore
    (Gravels) Ltd v Routledge* (1977) 121 Sol Jo 202, CA. See also *Woolls v Powling* (1999) Times,
    9 March, [1999] All ER (D) 125, CA.
8   *Neilson v Poole* (1969) 20 P & CR 909 at 916 per Megarry J; *Alan Wibberley Building Ltd v
    Insley* [1999] 2 All ER 897, [1999] 1 WLR 894, HL (where it was held that it was unlikely that
    a vendor would retain a useless strip of land beyond a hedge and including a ditch so the intent
    was more likely to have been that the plan was for purposes of identification only); *Druce v
    Druce* [2002] All ER (D) 234 (Apr); affd [2003] EWCA Civ 535, [2004] 1 P & CR 424, [2003]
    All ER (D) 122 (Feb).
9   *AJ Dunning & Sons (Shopfitters) Ltd v Sykes & Son (Poole) Ltd* [1987] Ch 287 at 289, [1987]
    1 All ER 700 at 706, CA (by a majority, it was held that the coloured edging on a plan attached
    to a transfer prevailed over a reference to a registered title number).
10 *Toplis v Green* [1992] EGCS 20, CA; *Alan Wibberley Building Ltd v Insley* [1999] 2 All ER 897
    at 902, [1999] 1 WLR 894 at 899, HL, per Lord Hoffmann. In *Howton v Hawkins* (1966) 199
    Estates Gazette 229, 110 Sol Jo 547, [1966] EGD 547, where there was a transfer of 'the land
    shown and edged with red on the plan and known as 45, Corsehill Street being part of the land
    being comprised in the above mentioned title', Cross J held that the description of the properties
    as 'the land known as' took priority over the plan. In *Clarke v O'Keefe* (1997) 80 P & CR 126,
    there was a transfer of 'the land shown and edged with red on the plan bound up within and
    known as Land adjoining Pyle Manor Chale'. The plan was an Ordnance Survey plan and
    useless for determining boundaries, so it was held that extrinsic evidence should be admitted.
    The parties had staked out the boundary line and that is where the boundary lay. Peter
    Gibson LJ said: 'It was said as long ago as 1969 by no less an authority than Megarry J, in
    Neilson v Poole (1969) 210 Estates Gazette 113, (1969) 20 P & CR 909 at p 912, that the then
    modern tendency was towards admitting evidence in boundary disputes and assessing the weight
    of that evidence rather than excluding it. That tendency has, in my experience, not diminished in
    the intervening years ... I do not derive much assistance from the absence in the transfer of
    words such as 'for identification purposes only'.

306.   The admission of extrinsic evidence.   In order to determine a boundary
by reference to the provisions of a conveyance, extrinsic evidence is admissible of

all material facts existing at the time of execution of the deed, so that the court may have the same knowledge as the parties to the deed then had[1]. The question is: what would the reasonable layman think he was in fact buying?[2]. It has been said that such extrinsic evidence is not admissible as an aid to interpreting a conveyance, unless the relevant provisions of the deed are uncertain, contradictory or ambiguous[3]; but, more recently, that statement has been doubted, and it has been said that extrinsic evidence of the background to the conveyance is always admissible as part and parcel of the process of contextual construction[4]. That is certainly the case if the terms of the transfer do not clearly define the land or interest transferred[5]. Once it is admissible, there is no reason to limit the extrinsic evidence to what is found in earlier documents of title without regard to what is found on the site[6]. If the conveyance is unclear or ambiguous, evidence of the subsequent conduct of the parties to the original conveyance is admissible, subject to it being of probative value in determining what the parties intended[7].

1 *Lord Waterpark v Fennell* (1859) 7 HL Cas 650; *Ward v Gold* (1969) 211 Estates Gazette 155; *Willson v Greene (Moss, third party)* [1971] 1 All ER 1098, [1971] 1 WLR 635; and as to the admissibility of extrinsic evidence see PARA 332. As to extrinsic evidence for the interpretation of deeds see DEEDS AND OTHER INSTRUMENTS vol 13 (2007 Reissue) PARA 198 et seq.

2 *Toplis v Green* [1992] EGCS 20, applied in *Seeckts v Derwent* [2004] EWCA Civ 393 at [21], 148 Sol Jo LB 417 at [21], [2004] All ER (D) 554 (Mar) at [21].

3 *Grigsby v Melville* [1973] 3 All ER 455, [1974] 1 WLR 80, CA; *Scarfe v Adams* [1981] 1 All ER 843, CA; *Berkeley Leisure Group Ltd v Williamson* [1996] EGCS 18, CA; *Woolls v Powling* (1999) Times, 9 March, [1999] All ER (D) 125, CA. If such a transfer does not truly express the bargain between the vendor and the purchaser the only remedy available is by way of rectification of the transfer. See also *Horn v Phillips* [2003] EWCA Civ 1877, [2003] All ER (D) 348 (Dec), where Jacob LJ followed *Scarfe v Adams* [1981] 1 All ER 843, CA, and also said, at [13]: 'The court of course can admit, and must admit, extrinsic evidence if it finds ambiguity or meaninglessness or the like, but the court should not be astute to go out of its way to find ambiguity or uncertainty where there is none. These documents are intended to affect not only the parties to them, but subsequent purchasers and surrounding land owners. Prima facie they are to be relied upon unless there is something fairly obviously wrong with them'.

4 *Pennock v Hodgson* [2010] EWCA Civ 873 at [12], 154 (30) Sol Jo LB 33 at [12], [2010] All ER (D) 287 (Jul) at [12] per Mummery LJ ('Looking at evidence of the actual and known physical condition of the relevant land at the date of the conveyance and having the attached plan in your hand on the spot when you do this are permitted as an exercise in construing the conveyance against the background of its surrounding circumstances. They include knowledge of the objective facts reasonably available to the parties at the relevant date. Although, in a sense, that approach takes the court outside the terms of the conveyance, it is part and parcel of the process of contextual construction. The rejection of extrinsic evidence which contradicts the clear terms of a conveyance is consistent with this approach'). See also *Neilson v Poole* (1969) 20 P & CR 909; *Scarfe v Adams* [1981] 1 All ER 843 at 848, CA, per Cumming-Bruce LJ, and at 851 per Griffiths LJ; *Mayer v Hurr* (1983) 49 P & CR 56, CA; *Alan Wibberley Building Ltd v Insley* [1999] 2 All ER 897 at 899, [1999] 1 WLR 894 at 896, HL, per Lord Hoffmann ('if it becomes necessary to establish the exact boundary, the deeds will almost invariably have to be supplemented by such inferences as may be drawn from topographical features which existed, or may be supposed to have existed, when the conveyances were executed'); *Partridge v Lawrence* [2003] EWCA Civ 1121 at [29], [2004] 1 P & CR 176 at [29], [2003] All ER (D) 133 (Jul) at [29] per Peter Gibson LJ ('one construes a document against the background knowledge which would have been available to the parties').

5 See *Scarfe v Adams* [1981] 1 All ER 843 at 851, CA, per Griffiths LJ; *Partridge v Lawrence* [2003] EWCA Civ 1121 at [28]–[29], [2004] 1 P & CR 176 at [28]–[29], [2003] All ER (D) 133 (Jul) at [28]–[29] per Peter Gibson LJ.

6 *Mayer v Hurr* (1983) 49 P & CR 56, CA.

7 *Van Diemen's Land Co v Table Cape Marine Board* [1906] AC 92 at 98, PC; *Watcham v A-G of the East Africa Protectorate* [1919] AC 533 at 540, [1918–1919] All ER Rep 455 at 459, PC; *Neilson v Poole* (1969) 20 P & CR 909; *St Edmundsbury and Ipswich Diocesan Board of Finance v Clark (No 2)* [1973] 3 All ER 902, [1973] 1 WLR 1572 (affd [1975] 1 All ER 772, [1975] 1 WLR 468, CA); *Ali v Lane* [2006] EWCA Civ 1532, [2007] 1 P & CR 26, [2006] All

ER (D) 271 (Nov) (in construing a conveyance relating to disputed land where the information contained in the conveyance was unclear or ambiguous, the judge had been entitled to have regard to extrinsic evidence, including evidence of subsequent conduct, subject to it being of probative value in determining what the parties had intended); *Haycocks v Neville* [2007] EWCA Civ 78, [2007] 1 EGLR 78 (held, judge had been entitled to reject the findings of both parties' experts, and adopt an intermediate position on where the boundary line was situated; in doing so, the judge had not substituted her own expertise, but had made a determination which flowed from the totality of the evidence; she was entitled to have regard to evidence of matters occurring since the boundary was fixed, including what the parties had done); *Bradford v James* [2008] EWCA Civ 837, [2008] BLR 538, [2009] All ER (D) 248 (Jul) (a plan annexed to a conveyance was unclear and extrinsic evidence was admissible to clarify and construe the conveyance and ascertain the intentions of the parties to see if a cobbled area was included in a conveyance; plans for conversion of barn in existence at the date of 1976 conveyance were extrinsic evidence and showed the front door opening onto the cobbled area in dispute; evidence of later events, including the subsequent conduct of the parties, was more consistent with the exclusion of the cobbled area from the conveyance of the farm than with its inclusion); *Piper v Wakeford* [2008] EWCA Civ 1378, [2009] 1 P & CR D38, [2008] All ER (D) 197 (Dec) (the root 1908 conveyance referred to a plan that showed an area set out in numbered plots; words in the parcels clause were self-contradictory and the plan was of very poor quality; held, the judge had been entitled to rely on the subsequent conduct of one or other of the parties to the 1908 conveyance (applying *Ali v Lane* [2006] EWCA Civ 1532, [2007] 1 P & CR 26, [2006] All ER (D) 271 (Nov), *Haycocks v Neville* [2007] EWCA Civ 28, [2007] 1 EGLR 78 and *Bradford v James* [2008] EWCA Civ 837, [2008] BLR 538, [2009] All ER (D) 248 (Jul)); the evidence of a surveyor as to the difficulty of reconciling the measurement of the area stated in the 1908 conveyance entitled the judge not to be guided by the stated area as part of the description of the land conveyed).

This is an exception to the general rule that an agreement cannot be construed in the light of the subsequent actions of the parties: *L Schuler AG v Wickman Machine Tool Sales Ltd* [1974] AC 235, [1973] 2 All ER 39, HL.

307. Effect of Law of Property Act 1925 on boundaries. Since 31 December 1881, under the Law of Property Act 1925[1] a conveyance of land is deemed to include, and operates to convey with the land, all buildings, erections, fixtures, commons, hedges, ditches, fences, ways, waters, watercourses, liberties, privileges, easements, rights, and advantages whatsoever, appertaining or reputed to appertain to the land, or any part thereof, or, at the time of conveyance, demised, occupied, or enjoyed with or reputed or known as part or parcel of or appurtenant to the land or any part of it[2]. A conveyance of land, having houses or other buildings on it, is deemed to include and operates to convey with the land, houses or other buildings, all outhouses, erections, fixtures, cellars, areas, courts, courtyards, cisterns, sewers, gutters, drains, ways, passages, lights, watercourses, liberties, privileges, easements, rights and advantages whatsoever, appertaining or reputed to appertain to the land, houses or other buildings conveyed, or any of them, or any part thereof, or at the time of conveyance, demised, occupied or enjoyed with, or reputed or known as part or parcel of or appurtenant to, the land, houses or other buildings, conveyed, or any of them, or any part thereof[3]. Whether the statutory provision can operate to enlarge the boundaries of premises which pass under a conveyance is uncertain. In one case, it was treated as having that effect in relation to part of a shed which stood on an adjoining property[4]. However, in later cases, it was doubted judicially whether the statutory provision can have the effect of increasing the physical extent of the land actually transferred beyond that which is, as a matter of construction, transferred by the conveyance[5]; and it has been held that, on a transfer of land in a registered title, the statutory provision does not operate to transfer the transferor's possessory title in an adjacent but separate registered title[6].

1   See the Law of Property Act 1925 s 62 (replacing the Conveyancing Act 1881 s 6); and DEEDS
     AND OTHER INSTRUMENTS vol 13 (2007 Reissue) PARA 236; and EASEMENTS AND PROFITS A
     PRENDRE vol 16(2) (Reissue) PARA 57.

2   Law of Property Act 1925 s 62(1), (6).

3   Law of Property Act 1925 s 62(2), (6).

4   *Fairweather v St Marylebone Property Co Ltd* [1962] 1 QB 498, CA; on appeal [1963] AC
     510, HL (part of a shed lay on one parcel of land, and the remainder on another; the lessee of
     one parcel held possession of the whole shed for 31 years, then granted a sublease of the parcel
     demised to him; the county court judge held that this sublease operated, under the Law of
     Property Act 1925 s 62 (see DEEDS AND OTHER INSTRUMENTS vol 13 (2007 Reissue) PARA 236,
     to demise the whole shed to the sublessee, including that part of the shed on the adjoining
     parcel; it was not argued in the Court of Appeal or the House of Lords that this was wrong and
     Holroyd Pearce LJ in the Court of Appeal said it was correct ('the judge rightly decided that by
     virtue of section 62 of the Law of Property Act, 1925, this lease included by implication the use
     of the shed which Millwood was enjoying at the time of the demise')).

5   See *Commission for the New Towns v Gallagher Ltd* [2002] EWHC 2668 (Ch), [2003]
     2 P & CR 24, [2002] All ER (D) 235 (Dec) obiter per Neuberger J ('is section 62 apt to include
     other physical land, not referred to in the conveyance, with the land expressly to be conveyed?
     In my view, while, in very exceptional circumstances, it might be possible (a point which I leave
     open), it would not be a permissible result in a normal case ... In my view, 'enjoyed with' refers
     to incorporeal hereditaments, such as easements, and not to physical property. So, too, with the
     word, 'appurtenant"); and *Tower Hamlets London Borough Council v Barrett* [2005] EWCA
     Civ 923, [2006] 1 P & CR 132, [2005] All ER (D) 257 (Jul) obiter per Neuberger LJ ('I am in
     some doubt as to whether section 62 can have the effect of increasing the physical extent of the
     land actually transferred beyond that which is, as a matter of construction, transferred by the
     transfer in question ... as it is unnecessary to decide the point, I think it safer to leave it open').

6   *Site Developments (Ferndown) Ltd v Cuthbury Ltd* [2010] EWHC 10 (Ch) at [167]–[171],
     [2010] All ER (D) 127 (Jan) preferring the Australian decision in *Kirk v Sutherland* [1949] VLR
     33 to the Canadian decision in *Fleet v Silverstein* [1963] 1 OR 153.

308.   Use of Ordnance Survey maps.   Ordnance Survey maps, which are
increasingly used as the basis of conveyance plans[1], do not purport to fix private
boundaries[2]. Where there are boundary features, such as hedges or fences,
between parcels of land, it is the practice of the Ordnance Survey to draw the
boundary line down the middle of these features regardless of whether the true
boundary lies to one side or the other[3]. If a conveyance of part of an estate is by
reference to a plan, not said to be for the purposes of identification only, which
has been copied from the Ordnance Survey map, then the land will be bounded
by the centre of the hedge or other boundary feature shown on the plan for that
is where the parties to the conveyance intended it to be[4]. Where, however, there
are two plots of land which have never been in common ownership, the fact that
a conveyance of one plot identifies the land for the purposes of identification
only by reference to an Ordnance Survey map which shows the boundary to be
in the middle of the hedge does not displace the line of the boundary already
established by the hedge and ditch presumption[5].

1   Ordnance Survey maps are the basis of all registered descriptions of registered land: see PARA
     309. Ordnance maps are Crown copyright and may not be reproduced without permission: see
     COPYRIGHT, DESIGN RIGHT AND RELATED RIGHTS vol 9(2) (2006 Reissue) PARAS 144–149. As to
     the Ordnance Survey see NATIONAL CULTURAL HERITAGE vol 77 (2010) PARA 1110 et seq.
          Generally, the Ordnance Survey map shows features over 0.3 m high by firm black lines and
     those less than 0.3 m high by dotted black lines. Within private gardens the only features the
     Ordnance Survey map shows are permanent buildings over 12 square metres in area, roads and
     tracks over 100 m long and other continuous features such as streams and features that mark
     the line of an administrative boundary. Where there are two features close together on the
     ground, and the gap cannot be shown on the scale at which the map is drawn, only one feature
     will be shown on the Ordnance Survey map. The accuracy of an Ordnance Survey map depends
     on its scale; details are given in Land Registry Practice Guide 40 (October 2005) Appendix 1
     (available at www.landregistry.gov.uk). The elongated 'S' mark known as a 'field tie' or an 'areas

brace symbol' was used to join areas of land together to give a single field parcel number. This area was measured to give the combined total area measurement.

2   *Alan Wibberley Building Ltd v Insley* [1999] 2 All ER 897 at 904, [1999] 1 WLR 894 at 901, HL, per Lord Hope of Craighead. The Ordnance Survey Act 1841, authorising the completion of a general survey of Great Britain, does not extend to ascertaining private boundaries, and private titles remain unaffected by it: see s 12; and NATIONAL CULTURAL HERITAGE vol 77 (2010) PARA 1117. See *Willsher v Scott* [2007] EWCA Civ 195, [2007] All ER (D) 279 (Mar) (Ordnance Survey maps do not purport to fix or record the legal boundary between adjoining plots of land and they offer an uncertain guide as to the precise boundary line). As to Ordnance Survey maps as evidence see PARA 337; and NATIONAL CULTURAL HERITAGE vol 77 (2010) PARA 1111. As to the admissibility in evidence of maps and plans generally see PARA 342.

3   *Fisher v Winch* [1939] 1 KB 666, [1939] 2 All ER 144, CA; *Davey v Harrow Corpn* [1958] 1 QB 60, [1957] 2 All ER 305, CA, per Lord Goddard CJ.

4   *Fisher v Winch* [1939] 1 KB 666, [1939] 2 All ER 144, CA; *Alan Wibberley Building Ltd v Insley* [1999] 2 All ER 897, [1999] 1 WLR 894, HL. As to the normal presumption of ownership in the case of hedges and ditches, etc see PARA 319 et seq.

5   *Alan Wibberley Building Ltd v Insley* [1999] 2 All ER 897, [1999] 1 WLR 894, HL. As to the hedge and ditch presumption see note 4; and PARA 321.

309.   Registered land. The plans used by the Land Registry for the registration of titles (known as title plans) are based on the Ordnance Survey maps[1] and ordinarily are deemed to show only what are described as the general boundaries[2]. In such cases the exact line of the boundary is left undetermined; for instance, it may be unclear whether it includes a hedge or wall and ditch; or whether it runs along the centre of a wall or fence or its outer or inner face, or how far it runs within or beyond it; or whether or not the land registered includes the whole or any part of any adjoining road or stream[3]. The precise boundary must, if the question arises, be established by topographical and other evidence[4]; and the established legal presumptions[5] may apply to registered land with evidence being given as to the position prior to registration of the title[6]. Altering the boundary line on the title plan is not treated as 'rectification' for the purposes of the Land Registration Act 2002[7]; it merely produces another general boundary in a more accurate position than the current general boundary and does not affect the possession of the registered proprietor[8].

1   See the Land Registration Act 2002 s 1(2); and the Land Registration Rules 2003, SI 2003/1417, r 5(a) (amended by SI 2008/1919). The Land Registry may therefore be expected to follow the practice of the Ordnance Survey as to boundary features, as to which see PARA 308. As to the Land Registry see LAND REGISTRATION vol 26 (2004 Reissue) PARA 1064; and as to the Ordnance Survey see NATIONAL CULTURAL HERITAGE vol 77 (2010) PARA 1110 et seq. See Land Registry Practice Guide 40 (October 2005), available at www.landregistry.gov.uk, which provides helpful information about the plans and records held and maintained by Land Registry, and explains the pre-registration requirements for lodging plans in different types of applications.

2   See Land Registration Act 2002 s 60(1); and LAND REGISTRATION vol 26 (2004 Reissue) PARA 869. A general boundary does not determine the exact line of the boundary: s 60(2). See also *Alan Wibberley Building Ltd v Insley* [1999] 2 All ER 897, [1999] 1 WLR 894, HL; *Lee v Barrey* [1957] Ch 251, [1957] 1 All ER 191, CA (plan on a land certificate, which was a copy from the filed plan, differed from that attached to the transfer and the plan on the transfer prevailed); *Hesketh v Willis Cruisers Ltd* (1968) 19 P & CR 573, CA; *Pardoe v Pennington* (1996) 75 P & CR 264, CA. As to the procedure whereby land may exceptionally be registered with fixed boundaries see the Land Registration Act 2002 s 60(3), (4); the Land Registration Rules 2003, SI 2003/1417, Pt 10 (rr 117–123); PARA 316; and LAND REGISTRATION vol 26 (2004 Reissue) PARAS 871–874.

3   As to the legal presumptions applicable to boundary features where there is no express or clear provision see PARAS 319–329.

4   *Alan Wibberley Building Ltd v Insley* [1999] 2 All ER 897 at 900, [1999] 1 WLR 894 at 897, HL, per Lord Hoffmann.

5   See PARAS 319–329.

6   *Hall v Dorling* (1996) 74 P & CR 400, CA. See also *Russell v Barnet London Borough Council* (1984) 83 LGR 152, (1984) 2 EGLR 44 per Tudor Evans J (presumption that the soil of a highway belonged to the owner of land adjoining the highway not rebutted by plans annexed to the entries in the Land Registry title).

7   Ie the Land Registration Act 2002 s 65, Sch 4: see LAND REGISTRATION vol 26 (2004 Reissue) PARA 976 et seq.

8   *Derbyshire County Council v Fallon* [2007] EWHC 1326 (Ch), [2007] 45 EG 164, [2007] All ER (D) 78 (Jun); *Strachey v Ramage* [2008] EWCA Civ 384, [2008] 2 P & CR 154, [2008] All ER (D) 267 (Apr).

310. Effect of inaccuracy. In a conveyance of land, the land should be described with the utmost accuracy that is practicable as, in the case of real ambiguity, the grant will be construed against the grantor[1], except where the grantor is the Crown[2]. Inaccuracy in a statement of dimensions or in a plan, however, does not vitiate a sufficiently certain description of the land conveyed except where the dimensions are an essential part of the description or definition, and not merely a cumulative description[3].

Where a mistake has been made, then, depending on the circumstances, rectification or rescission may be available[4].

It may be a defence to a claim instituted by the vendor to enforce a contract that the land is wrongly described, and that, as a result, the vendor has title to less than that which the contract describes[5], but if the misdescription was innocent and is not substantial[6], the vendor is entitled under an open contract[7] to an order for specific performance with, if appropriate, an abatement of the price[8].

A misrepresentation, even if innocent, involving a misdescription of the property, whether as a term of the contract or in the course of negotiations, which induced the purchaser to enter into the contract will be a bar to specific performance and entitle the purchaser to rescind[9].

Where a conveyance of land intended to form a building plot stated the dimensions of three sides but not the fourth, repeating in substantially identical terms the description in earlier conveyances, and a plan, referred to for the purposes of facilitating identification only, showed the fourth boundary as a straight line, the court inferred that the true boundary of the fourth side was a straight line, and the fact that there had been an encroachment on the land, before the conveyance in question but since the description was originally formulated, was not allowed to affect the construction of the deed[10].

1   *Mellor v Walmesley* [1905] 2 Ch 164, CA; *Cornish v Accident Insurance Co Ltd* (1889) 23 QBD 453 at 456. As to the admissibility of extrinsic evidence in cases of ambiguously described boundaries see PARA 332. A purchaser of part of land having a common title may, in the case of unregistered land, require notice to be preserved, by indorsement on or annexation to some document retained by the vendor and forming part of the common title, of covenants in the conveyance to him affecting other land comprised in the common title: see the Law of Property Act 1925 s 200; and SALE OF LAND vol 42 (Reissue) PARA 298.

2   See *A-G v Ewelme Hospital* (1853) 17 Beav 366 at 386; *Feather v The Queen* (1865) 6 B & S 257 at 283–284, 29 JP 709 at 709; *Earl of Lonsdale v A-G* [1982] 1 WLR 887 at 901 per Slade J ('... if the wording of a grant by the Crown is clear and unequivocal, the grantee is entitled to rely on it as much as if the grantor had been any other subject of the Crown; if, on the other hand, the wording is obscure or equivocal, the court must lean towards the construction more favourable to the Crown, unless satisfied that another interpretation of the relevant words in their context is the true one');and DEEDS AND OTHER INSTRUMENTS vol 13 (2007 Reissue) PARA 179. As to Crown land generally see CROWN PROPERTY.

3   *Mellor v Walmesley* [1905] 2 Ch 164 at 174, CA; *AJ Dunning & Sons (Shopfitters) Ltd v Sykes & Son (Poole) Ltd* [1987] Ch 287, [1987] 1 All ER 700, CA; and see *Llewellyn v Earl of Jersey* (1843) 11 M & W 183. As to ambiguity in the description see PARA 331; and DEEDS AND OTHER INSTRUMENTS vol 13 (2007 Reissue) PARAS 208–209.

4   See MISTAKE vol 77 (2010) PARAS 52–68. Rescission is normally only available where there is misrepresentation: see MISREPRESENTATION AND FRAUD vol 31 (2003 Reissue) PARAS 701, 812 et seq. As to rescission of contracts generally see CONTRACT vol 9(1) (Reissue) PARA 986 et seq. Where the mistake has arisen from an innocent misrepresentation, damages may be awarded in lieu of rescission: see the Misrepresentation Act 1967 s 2(2); and MISREPRESENTATION AND FRAUD vol 31 (2003 Reissue) PARA 834. Whether or not a representation is innocent, damages may be awarded in a proper case if they have been expressly claimed, eg as an alternative to rescission: see MISREPRESENTATION AND FRAUD vol 31 (2003 Reissue) PARA 781. As to damages generally see DAMAGES vol 12(1) (Reissue) PARA 801 et seq.

5   See *Flight v Booth* (1834) 1 Bing NC 370; *Mortlock v Buller* (1804) 10 Ves 292; *Scott v Hanson* (1829) 1 Russ & M 128; *Price v Macaulay* (1852) 2 De GM & G 339; *Clayton v Leech* (1889) 41 ChD 103, CA. See also SALE OF LAND; SPECIFIC PERFORMANCE.

6   *Walker v Boyle* [1982] 1 All ER 634 at 644, [1982] 1 WLR 495 at 506 per Dillon J, who was of the opinion that only a trifling misrepresentation, where the truth would have no effect on the purchaser, would entitle a purchaser to specific performance.

7   The Standard Conditions of Sale (4th Edn, 2003) deal specifically with misleading or inaccurate plans or statements: see condition 7.1 (and see also the Standard Commercial Property Conditions of Sale (2nd Edn, 2004) condition 9.1); and SALE OF LAND vol 42 (Reissue) PARA 110. As to the Standard Conditions of Sale see SALE OF LAND vol 42 (Reissue) PARA 1.

8   *Jacobs v Revell* [1900] 2 Ch 858; *Watson v Burton* [1956] 3 All ER 929, [1957] 1 WLR 19; *St Pier v Shirley* (1961) 179 Estates Gazette 837. See further SPECIFIC PERFORMANCE.

9   *Walker v Boyle* [1982] 1 All ER 634 at 644, [1982] 1 WLR 495 at 506 per Dillon J (failure to disclose a boundary dispute entitled a purchaser to rescind). See also *Charles Hunt Ltd v Palmer* [1931] 2 Ch 287. This is subject to the terms of the contract, which may attempt to limit the circumstances in which rescission for misrepresentation is permitted. See note 7; and MISREPRESENTATION AND FRAUD; SALE OF LAND; SPECIFIC PERFORMANCE.

10 *Hopgood v Brown* [1955] 1 All ER 550, [1955] 1 WLR 213, CA. Cf *Willson v Greene (Moss, third party)* [1971] 1 All ER 1098, [1971] 1 WLR 635. See also *Targett and Targett v Ferguson and Diver* (1996) 72 P & CR 106, CA. See further PARAS 304, 314, 332.

311.   How far boundary included in property bounded.   Whether a boundary is, or is not, included in the property which it is described as bounding depends upon the particular circumstances of each case. Thus in the case of adjoining properties bounded by a hedge and ditch, there is no inaccuracy in describing either property as so bounded, though the boundary may be wholly included in one and excluded from the other[1]. However, where the nature of the object named as a boundary (for example, a house or land) is such that an independent title to it would in the natural course of events be made, the boundary object is excluded from the subject matter of the grant[2].

A demise of part of a building bounded by an external wall includes both sides of the wall enclosing the part demised[3], and a demise bounded by a partition wall includes half or some part of the partition wall[4], unless such construction is expressly or impliedly excluded by the terms of the lease, but does not necessarily include the roof of the building[5]. In modern leases of part of a building it is standard practice for the extent of the property to be defined with considerable exactitude.

'T-marks' on a plan may be taken as indicating ownership of boundary features; an inward-facing T marking indicates ownership of a boundary, but not what the boundary is nor where it is located. The natural implication is that they are intended to represent existing boundary features. In at least one case the court has preferred T-marks to measured dimensions as the determinative features of boundaries[6].

1   *Re Belfast Dock Act 1854, ex p Earl of Ranfurly* (1867) IR 1 Eq 128 at 140. As to the presumptions of ownership in the case of hedges, ditches, roads and rivers see PARAS 319–329. As to the practice of the Ordnance Survey and Land Registry in relation to such features see

PARAS 308–309. As to the Ordnance Survey see NATIONAL CULTURAL HERITAGE vol 77 (2010) PARA 1110 et seq; and as to the Land Registry see LAND REGISTRATION vol 26 (2004 Reissue) PARA 1064.

2 *Lord v Sydney City Comrs* (1859) 12 Moo PCC 473; and see *City of Boston v Richardson* 13 Allen (Mass) 146 (1866) at 154.

3 *Carlisle Café Co and Todd v Muse Bros & Co* (1897) 67 LJCh 53; *Hope Bros Ltd v Cowan* [1913] 2 Ch 312; *Goldfoot v Welch* [1914] 1 Ch 213; *Sturge v Hackett* [1962] 3 All ER 166, [1962] 1 WLR 1257, CA. As to vertical and horizontal boundaries of flats and properties forming parts of buildings see PARA 302.

4 *Hope Bros Ltd v Cowan* [1913] 2 Ch 312; *Phelps v City of London Corpn* [1916] 2 Ch 255.

5 See *Delgable Ltd v Perinpanathan* [2005] EWCA Civ 1724, [2006] 2 P & CR 289, [2006] 1 EGLR 78, CA (although the external walls were included in the sublease, it did not follow that the roof was included; the references contained in the sublease provisions, relating to decorations and rebuilding following an insurance risk, to 'buildings and structures' did not, in the context of a sublease of part of a building, require that each of those two words was intended to have a distinct meaning, nor did the use of the word 'building' show that the roof formed part of what was demised; in the circumstances, the roof was not demised by the sublease).

6 See *Seeckts v Derwent* [2004] EWCA Civ 393, 148 Sol Jo LB 417, [2004] All ER (D) 554 (Mar) per Carnwath LJ.

(iii) By Undisturbed Possession

312. Effect of the Limitation Act 1980. The right to boundaries fixed by agreement or assurance may be lost, and a new boundary may be acquired under the Limitation Act 1980[1] after undisturbed possession by another of the land falling between the old and the new boundaries for a period of 12 years[2] or, in particular circumstances, for a longer period[3]. With effect from 13 October 2003, however, time does not run under the Limitation Act 1980 against any person, other than a chargee, in relation to an estate in land or rentcharge the title to which is registered[4].

In order that the Act may operate, the person claiming a possessory title must show ordinary possession[5] of the land for the requisite period without consent of the owner[6]. In the absence of discontinuance of possession, there will be a dispossession of the paper owner in any case where a squatter assumes possession in the ordinary sense of the word[7]. A claimant, who must have been in adverse possession for the requisite period[8], must show both factual possession of the land and the requisite intention to possess the land[9].

Factual possession requires an appropriate degree of physical control[10]. The intention to possess the land falling between the old and the new boundaries must be an intention made clear and plain to the world by the acts of the claimant[11] for the claimant must not only have the subjective intention to possess the land but also show by outward conduct that it was his intention[12]. Possession on the part of the claimant does not have to be inconsistent with that of the person entitled to the paper title in the land[13]; though a true owner will not be found to have discontinued possession if he intends to use the land for a particular purpose at a future date, he will be dispossessed by a claimant who performs sufficient acts[14] and has sufficient intention to constitute adverse possession[15]. So mere non-user on the part of the owner is not sufficient evidence of discontinuance of possession without acts establishing possession on the part of the person claiming the land[16]; and if the acts alleged are too trivial to amount to the taking of actual possession or if the necessary intention has not been shown, the true owner is not dispossessed[17].

A claim may be made by adverse possession to a boundary wall, even if the claim is to half of a party wall longitudinally divided[18]. If the claim relates to part only of a length of a wall, then there must be a clear and definite division between that part of the wall claimed and that part which the claimant does not claim[19]. Where a house is erected against a wall which belongs to and is situated on the land of the adjoining owner, using that wall to form one side of the house, the passage of time alone will not give the owner of the house a statutory title to the wall[20], though probably he would acquire an easement of support for his roof[21].

Where on a boundary wall an inscription stating that the wall belongs to the adjoining owner is allowed to remain, acquisition of the wall by adverse possession is virtually excluded, and no question of a statutory title, or of adverse possession, or of cesser of possession, can properly arise[22].

1 As to the Limitation Act 1980 see LIMITATION PERIODS. A submission that the principles of adverse possession are the sole or main way to resolve disputes relating to the lines of boundaries and that a court should not strive to find a boundary agreement varying that which has been agreed in a conveyance was not accepted in *Stephenson v Johnson* [2000] EGCS 92, CA. See also PARA 303.

2 See the Limitation Act 1980 ss 15, 17, Sch 1; and LIMITATION PERIODS vol 68 (2008) PARAS 1025, 1095. See also *Buckinghamshire County Council v Moran* [1990] Ch 623, [1989] 2 All ER 225, CA; *Marshall v Taylor* [1895] 1 Ch 641, CA; *Norton v London and North Western Rly Co* (1879) 13 ChD 268, CA. In a case concerned with adverse possession of subterranean minerals, it was said that, where title is founded on adverse possession, the title will normally be limited to the area of which actual possession has been enjoyed (*Glyn v Howell* [1909] 1 Ch 666 at 678); but acts of possession on parts of a defined tract of land on the surface have in a number of cases been treated as evidence of possession of the whole, provided that there is such a common character of locality as to raise a reasonable inference that, if one part belongs to the person in possession, so do the other parts (see eg *Roberts v Swangrove* [2007] EWHC 513 (Ch) at [54]–[57], [2007] 2 P & CR 17 at [54]–[57], [2007] All ER (D) 233 (Mar) at [54]–[57]). Adverse possession may cease: (1) by the occupier vacating the premises; (2) by the occupier giving a written acknowledgment of the true owner's title (see the Limitation Act 1980 ss 29, 30; and LIMITATION PERIODS vol 68 (2008) PARAS 1182–1184); (3) by the true owner's grant of a tenancy or licence to the occupier (even a unilateral licence: see *BP Properties Ltd v Buckler* (1987) 55 P & CR 337, [1987] 2 EGLR 168, CA); or (4) by the true owner physically re-entering upon the land: *Markfield Investments Ltd v Evans* [2001] 2 All ER 238 at [12], [2001] 1 WLR 1321 at [12]. An application to the Land Registry to warn off a caution registered by an adverse possessor is not an action to recover land for the purposes of the Limitation Act 1980 s 15 and so does not prevent time continuing to run: *JA Pye (Oxford) Ltd v Graham* [2000] Ch 676, [2000] 3 WLR 242; affd (but without reference to this point) [2002] UKHL 30, [2003] 1 AC 419, [2002] 3 All ER 865. See further LIMITATION PERIODS vol 68 (2008) PARA 1025.

3 Eg the period may be longer if the land is held on trust or is settled land and there are future beneficial interests (see the Limitation Act 1980 s 18, Sch 1 para 4 (s 18 amended by the Trusts of Land and Appointment of Trustees Act 1996 s 25(2), Sch 4)); or if the owner is under a disability (see the Limitation Act 1980 s 28 (amended by the Administration of Justice Act 1985 ss 57(3), 69(5), Sch 9 para 14; the Defamation Act 1996 s 5(3), (6); and the Consumer Protection Act 1987 s 6, Sch 1 Pt I para 4)); or if the land is held on lease (see *Fairweather v St Marylebone Property Co Ltd* [1963] AC 510, [1962] 2 All ER 288, HL; *Central London Commercial Estates Ltd v Kato Kagaku Co Ltd* [1998] 4 All ER 948).

4 See PARA 313.

5 Ie in the sense of entitling a person to maintain an action for trespass: *Powell v McFarlane* (1977) 38 P & CR 452 at 469 per Slade J, applied in *JA Pye (Oxford) Ltd v Graham* [2002] UKHL 30 at [32], [2003] 1 AC 419 at [32], [2002] 3 All ER 865 at [32] per Lord Browne-Wilkinson.

6 *JA Pye (Oxford) Ltd v Graham* [2002] UKHL 30 at [36], [2003] 1 AC 419 at [36], [2002] 3 All ER 865 at [36] per Lord Browne-Wilkinson. See also *Buckinghamshire County Council v Moran* [1990] Ch 623, [1989] 2 All ER 225, CA.

7 For the distinction between dispossession and discontinuance of possession see *Rains v Buxton* (1880) 14 ChD 537 at 539–540. See also *Kynoch Ltd v Rowlands* [1912] 1 Ch 527, CA; *Treloar v Nute* [1977] 1 All ER 230, [1976] 1 WLR 1295, CA, per Sir John Pennycuick; *Hounslow London Borough Council v Minchinton* (1997) 74 P & CR 221, CA (the continuing presence of

a hedgerow, shrubs and trees planted on a strip of land later fenced off by the paper owner is not sufficient to maintain possession of the land against the adjoining owner who takes adverse possession).

8   See the Limitation Act 1980 Sch 1 para 8(1) (which gives statutory authority to the rules previously laid down by the courts); and LIMITATION PERIODS vol 68 (2008) PARAS 1034, 1078. The statutory definition of adverse possession means land in possession of a person in whose favour time can run, and is directed not to the nature of the possession but to the capacity of the squatter: *JA Pye (Oxford) Ltd v Graham* [2002] UKHL 30 at [35], [2002] 3 All ER 865 at [35], [2003] 1 AC 419 at [35]. See also *Buckinghamshire County Council v Moran* [1990] Ch 623, [1989] 2 All ER 225, CA; *Philpot v Bath* (1904) 20 TLR 589 (affd (1905) 21 TLR 634, CA); *Marshall v Robertson* (1905) 50 Sol Jo 75; *Bligh v Martin* [1968] 1 All ER 1157, [1968] 1 WLR 804; *Sze To Chun Keung v Kung Kwok Wai David* [1997] 1 WLR 1232, PC.

9   *Powell v McFarlane* (1977) 38 P & CR 452 at 470 per Slade J, applied in *JA Pye (Oxford) Ltd v Graham* [2002] UKHL 30 at [40], [2003] 1 AC 419 at [40], [2002] 3 All ER 865 at [40] per Lord Browne-Wilkinson. See also *Buckinghamshire County Council v Moran* [1990] Ch 623, [1989] 2 All ER 225, CA. See notes 13–14.

10   *Powell v McFarlane* (1977) 38 P & CR 452 at 470–471 per Slade J, applied in *JA Pye (Oxford) Ltd v Graham* [2002] UKHL 30 at [41], [2003] 1 AC 419 at [41], [2002] 3 All ER 865 at [41] per Lord Browne-Wilkinson. See also note 13.

11   *Powell v McFarlane* (1977) 38 P & CR 452 at 472 per Slade J; *Wilson v Martin's Executors* [1993] 1 EGLR 178, CA; *Prudential Assurance Co Ltd v Waterloo Real Estate Inc* [1999] 2 EGLR 85, CA.

12   *Prudential Assurance Co Ltd v Waterloo Real Estate Inc* [1999] 2 EGLR 85 at 87, CA, per Peter Gibson LJ. See also *JA Pye (Oxford) Ltd v Graham* [2002] UKHL 30 at [76], [2003] 1 AC 419 at [76], [2002] 3 All ER 865 at [76] per Lord Hutton (where the evidence establishes that the person claiming title has used it in the way in which an owner would, then in a normal case he will not have to adduce additional evidence to establish the intention to possess).

13   See the Limitation Act 1980 Sch 1 para 8(4); and LIMITATION PERIODS vol 68 (2008) PARA 1078. This provision abrogates the decision in *Wallis's Cayton Bay Holiday Camp Ltd v Shell-Mex and BP Ltd* [1975] QB 94, [1974] 3 All ER 575, CA (where an adverse possessor, whose use was not inconsistent with the present or future owner's enjoyment of the land, was said to have an implied licence from the true owner). Further, the alleged 'special rule' at common law that where land is acquired or retained by the owner for specific future purposes then acts of trespass which are not inconsistent with such purpose do not amount to dispossession, based on a dictum of Bramwell LJ in *Leigh v Jack* (1879) 5 ExD 264 at 273, CA, was held not to have survived the enactment of the Limitation Act 1980 Sch 1 para 8(4) and to have been erroneous prior to that Act: *Buckinghamshire County Council v Moran* [1990] Ch 623, [1989] 2 All ER 225, CA (approving the dissenting judgment of Stamp LJ in *Wallis's Cayton Bay Holiday Camp Ltd v Shell-Mex and BP Ltd* [1975] QB 94 at 109–110, [1974] 3 All ER 575 at 585, CA, and the judgment of Slade J in *Powell v McFarlane* (1977) 38 P & CR 452). See also *JA Pye (Oxford) Ltd v Graham* [2002] UKHL 30, [2003] 1 AC 419, [2002] 3 All ER 865.

14   Factual possession signifies an appropriate degree of physical control, a single and exclusive possession measured by an objective standard: *Powell v McFarlane* (1977) 38 P & CR 452 at 470–471 per Slade J (pasturing a cow and exercising shooting rights were equivocal). Enclosure of the land is the strongest possible evidence of adverse possession: *Buckinghamshire County Council v Moran* [1990] Ch 623, [1989] 2 All ER 225, CA (cultivating a plot as a part of a garden and putting a padlock on a gate in a fence erected by the true owner). The ploughing and cultivation of agricultural land has been held to suffice: *Seddon v Smith* (1877) 36 LT 168, CA; *JA Pye (Oxford) Ltd v Graham* [2002] UKHL 30, [2003] 1 AC 419, [2002] 3 All ER 865. Note, however, *West Bank Estates Ltd v Arthur* [1967] 1 AC 665, [1966] 3 WLR 750, PC (cutting of timber and grass did not amount to adverse possession); *Wilson v Martin's Executors* [1993] 1 EGLR 178, CA (repairing a fence and cutting trees and taking fallen timber were insufficient acts to constitute adverse possession of a piece of woodland). Receipt of rent will constitute adverse possession even if the true owner is in possession: *Bligh v Martin* [1968] 1 All ER 1157, [1968] 1 WLR 804. Parking of cars may be evidence of possession: *Williams v Usherwood* (1981) 45 P & CR 235, CA; but note *Pavledes v Ryesbridge Properties Ltd* (1989) 58 P & CR 459. See also *Treloar v Nute* [1977] 1 All ER 230, [1976] 1 WLR 1295, CA (levelling the land); *Bladder v Phillips* [1991] EGCS 109, CA.

15   The necessary intention is an intention to possess to the exclusion of all others and not an intent to own the land: *JA Pye (Oxford) Ltd v Graham* [2002] UKHL 30 at [42]–[43], [2003] 1 AC 419 at [42]–[43], [2002] 3 All ER 865 at [42]–[43] per Lord Browne-Wilkinson. See also *Buckinghamshire County Council v Moran* [1990] Ch 623 at 644, [1989] 2 All ER 225 at 238, CA (not following dicta to the contrary in *Littledale v Liverpool College* [1900] 1 Ch 19 at

      23, CA, per Lindley MR and in *George Wimpey & Co Ltd v Sohn* [1967] Ch 487 at 510, [1966] 1 All ER 232 at 240, CA, per Russell LJ). The fact that the adverse possessor's belief of ownership is founded on a mistaken premise does not help the paper owner: *Bligh v Martin* [1968] 1 All ER 1157, [1968] 1 WLR 804; *Williams v Usherwood* (1981) 45 P & CR 235, CA.

16   *Smith v Lloyd* (1854) 9 Exch 562 at 572, approving the judgment of Blackburne CJ in *McDonnell v McKinty* (1847) 10 ILR 514 at 526; *Tecbild Ltd v Chamberlain* (1969) 20 P & CR 633, CA; *Powell v McFarlane* (1977) 38 P & CR 452. See also *Williams v Usherwood* (1981) 45 P & CR 235, CA.

17   *Williams Bros Direct Supply Stores Ltd v Raftery* [1958] 1 QB 159, [1957] 3 All ER 593, CA, as explained in *Buckinghamshire County Council v Moran* [1990] Ch 623, [1989] 2 All ER 225, CA. Acts which are equivocal as to the intention to exclude the true owner will not suffice: *Tecbild Ltd v Chamberlain* (1969) 20 P & CR 633 at 642, CA, per Sachs LJ; *George Wimpey & Co Ltd v Sohn* [1967] Ch 487, [1966] 1 All ER 232, CA; *Wilson v Martin's Executors* [1993] 1 EGLR 178, CA.

18   *Prudential Assurance Co Ltd v Waterloo Real Estate Inc* [1999] 2 EGLR 85, CA (in this case the claimant satisfied the court that it was in exclusive possession of the whole of the length of the wall claimed and that the paper owner had been dispossessed or had discontinued possession; the intention to possess was shown by works to the wall including repairs, cutting through the wall and attaching things to it); and see also *Palfrey v Wilson* [2007] EWCA Civ 94, [2007] All ER (D) 179 (Feb).

19   *Prudential Assurance Co Ltd v Waterloo Real Estate Inc* [1999] 2 EGLR 85 at 88, CA, per Peter Gibson LJ.

20   *Phillipson v Gibbon* (1871) 6 Ch App 428; *Waddington v Naylor* (1889) 60 LT 480. See also *Murly v M'Dermott* (1838) 8 Ad & El 138.

21   *Waddington v Naylor* (1889) 60 LT 480. See further EASEMENTS AND PROFITS A PRENDRE.

22   *Phillipson v Gibbon* (1871) 6 Ch App 428.

313. Limitation in relation to registered land. Under the Land Registration Act 2002, no period of limitation[1] is to run against any person, other than a chargee, in relation to an estate in land the title to which is registered[2], and accordingly, where a period of limitation does not run against a person, his title is not extinguished[3].

A person may apply to the registrar to be registered as the proprietor of a registered estate in land if he has been in adverse possession of the estate for the period of ten years ending on the date of the application[4]. Notice of such an application must be given by the registrar to certain persons, including the proprietor of the estate to which the application relates, the proprietor of any registered charge on the estate and, where the estate is leasehold, the proprietor of any superior registered estate[5]. The applicant is entitled to be registered as the new proprietor of the estate[6], unless a person given notice of the application by the registrar requires the application to be dealt with under the provisions[7] requiring any of the three statutory conditions to be met[8]. Under those provisions, the applicant is only entitled to be registered if any one of three conditions is met[9]. The first condition is that it would be unconscionable because of an equity by estoppel for the registered proprietor to seek to dispossess the applicant, and the circumstances are such that the applicant ought to be registered as the proprietor[10]. The second condition is that the applicant is for some other reason entitled to be registered as the proprietor of the estate[11]. The third condition, which relates specifically to boundaries, is that: (1) the land to which the application relates is adjacent to land belonging to the applicant; (2) the exact line of the boundary between the two has not been determined[12]; (3) for at least ten years of the period of adverse possession ending on the date of the application, the applicant (or any predecessor in title) reasonably believed that the land to which the application relates belonged to him; and (4) the estate to which the application relates was registered more than one year prior to the date of the application[13].

1   Ie under the Limitation Act 1980 s 15: see LIMITATION PERIODS vol 68 (2008) PARA 1016.
2   See the Land Registration Act 2002 s 96(1).
3   See the Land Registration Act 2002 s 96(3). As to adverse possession see LIMITATION PERIODS vol 68 (2008) PARA 1078 et seq; REAL PROPERTY vol 39(2) (Reissue) PARA 258.
4   See the Land Registration Act 2002 s 97, Sch 6 para 1; and LAND REGISTRATION vol 26 (2004 Reissue) PARA 1025 et seq. As to the meaning of 'adverse possession' for these purposes see Sch 6 paras 11, 12; and LAND REGISTRATION vol 26 (2004 Reissue) PARA 1026. As to rectification of the register see LAND REGISTRATION vol 26 (2004 Reissue) PARAS 981–982. The Land Registration Act 2002 Sch 6 applies to the registration of an adverse possessor of a registered rentcharge in the modified form set out in the Land Registration Rules 2003, SI 2003/1417, Sch 8: r 191; and see LAND REGISTRATION vol 26 (2004 Reissue) PARA 1036 et seq.
        Where a registered estate in land was held in trust for a person by virtue of the Land Registration Act 1925 s 75(1) (repealed) immediately before the coming into force of the Land Registration Act 2002 s 97 (for these purposes 13 October 2003), he is entitled to be registered as the proprietor of the estate: s 134, Sch 12 para 18(1); Land Registration Act 2002 (Commencement No 4) Order 2003, 2003/1725, art 2(1). A person has a defence to any action for the possession of land (in addition to any other defence he may have) if he is entitled under the Land Registration Act 2002 Sch 12 para 18 to be registered as the proprietor of an estate in the land: Sch 12 para 18(2). Where in an action for possession of land a court determines that a person is entitled to a defence under Sch 12 para 18, the court must order the registrar to register him as the proprietor of the estate in relation to which he is entitled under Sch 12 para 18 to be registered: Sch 12 para 18(3). Entitlement under Sch 12 para 18 is to be disregarded for the purposes of s 131(1) (proprietor in possession: see LAND REGISTRATION vol 26 (2004 Reissue) PARA 877): Sch 12 para 18(4).
        Rules may make transitional provision for cases where a rentcharge was held in trust under the Land Registration Act 1925 s 75(1) (repealed) immediately before the coming into force of the Land Registration Act 2002 s 97: Sch 12 para 18(5). Where a rentcharge was so held in trust immediately before the coming into force of s 97, the beneficiary of the trust may apply (1) to be registered as proprietor of the rentcharge; or (2) for the registration of the rentcharge to be cancelled: Land Registration Rules 2003, SI 2003/1417, r 224.
5   See the Land Registration Act 2002 Sch 6 para 2; and LAND REGISTRATION vol 26 (2004 Reissue) PARA 1028.
6   See the Land Registration Act 2002 Sch 6 para 4; and LAND REGISTRATION vol 26 (2004 Reissue) PARA 1029.
7   Ie under the Land Registration Act 2002 Sch 6 para 5: see the text and notes 9–13.
8   See the Land Registration Act 2002 Sch 6 para 3; and LAND REGISTRATION vol 26 (2004 Reissue) PARA 1029.
9   See the Land Registration Act 2002 Sch 6 para 5(1).
10 See the Land Registration Act 2002 Sch 6 para 5(2).
11 See the Land Registration Act 2002 Sch 6 para 5(3).
12 Ie under rules made by virtue of the Land Registration Act 2002 s 60(3): see PARA 316.
13 See the Land Registration Act 2002 Sch 6 para 5(4). See further LAND REGISTRATION vol 26 (2004 Reissue) PARA 1029.

(iv) By Estoppel

314.   Estoppel. If a party takes possession of a piece of land under an expectation, created or encouraged by and with the consent of the true owner, that he is to have an interest in the land and upon the faith of such promise or expectation and without objection by the true owner lays out money on the land or alters his position to his detriment, the court will compel the true owner to give effect to such promise or representation[1]. Knowledge of the correct position by the true owner or the party alleged to be estopped is not an essential prerequisite for the estoppel to operate but merely one of the relevant factors in the overall inquiry[2]. Acting in a transaction on an agreed assumption between two adjoining owners as to the position of a boundary will result in each being estopped against the other from questioning that assumption[3]. If the previous owner of land would have been estopped by his conduct from maintaining an action for infringement of his boundaries by an adjoining owner, his successor in title is in no better position[4].

1   *Ramsden v Dyson* (1866) LR 1 HL 129 at 170 per Lord Kingsdown; *Willmott v Barber* (1880) 15 ChD 96; *Plimmer v Wellington Corpn* (1884) 9 App Cas 699, PC; *Hopgood v Brown* [1955] 1 All ER 550, [1955] 1 WLR 213, CA; *Inwards v Baker* [1965] 2 QB 29, [1965] 1 All ER 446, CA; *Ward v Kirkland* [1967] Ch 194, [1966] 1 All ER 609; *ER Ives Investment Ltd v High* [1967] 2 QB 379, [1967] 1 All ER 504, CA; *Crabb v Arun District Council* [1976] Ch 179, [1975] 3 All ER 865, CA; *Pascoe v Turner* [1979] 2 All ER 945, [1979] 1 WLR 431, CA; *Taylors Fashions Ltd v Liverpool Victoria Trustees Co Ltd* [1982] QB 133n, [1981] 1 All ER 897; *Shaw v Applegate* [1978] 1 All ER 123, [1977] 1 WLR 970, CA; *Gillett v Holt* [2001] Ch 210, [2000] 2 All ER 289, CA. See also ESTOPPEL.
2   *Taylors Fashions Ltd v Liverpool Victoria Trustees Co Ltd* [1982] QB 133n at 152, [1981] 1 All ER 897 at 916 per Oliver J.
3   Spencer Bower *Estoppel by Representation* (4th Edn, 2004) p 180; *Amalgamated Investment and Property Co Ltd v Texas Commerce International Bank Ltd* [1982] QB 84, [1981] 1 All ER 923; and see ESTOPPEL. The courts may prefer to find an inferred agreement as to the boundary line rather than an estoppel: see eg *Stephenson v Johnson* [2000] EGCS 92, CA. As to settling boundaries by agreement see PARA 303.
4   *Hopgood v Brown* [1955] 1 All ER 550, [1955] 1 WLR 213, CA.

(3) BOUNDARIES FIXED BY STATUTORY OR JUDICIAL AUTHORITY

315. Common land. There remains a power to make orders fixing boundaries in connection with land not liable to be inclosed[1]. These powers may be regarded as obsolete[2].

In the past it has been difficult to determine the boundaries of any particular stretch of common land, since many stretches of common land are contiguous, inter-commonage may blur the boundaries, and there are legal restrictions on placing fences or other physical boundaries round common land[3]. However, the Commons Registration Act 1965 made elaborate provisions for the registration of common land, the rights of common over it and of its owners[4]. Now, once land is registered as common land, the register is authoritative as to, inter alia, the boundaries of the common[5].

1   Ie under the Inclosure Acts 1845 to 1882: see COMMONS vol 13 (2009) PARA 419. See in particular the Inclosure Act 1845 s 148; and COMMONS vol 13 (2009) PARA 419.
2   See the *Report of the Royal Commission on Common Land 1955–1958* (Cmnd 462) (1958) Ch III para 82, App II para 56, App III para 43; and COMMONS vol 13 (2009) PARA 419. See also the Statute Law (Repeals) Act 1998 s 1(1), Sch 1 Pt VI, which repealed many provisions of the Inclosure Acts 1845 to 1882.
3   See *Smith v Earl Brownlow* (1870) LR 9 Eq 241. As to statutory restrictions on the inclosure of commons see the Law of Property Act 1925 s 194 (repealed in relation to England; and in Wales as from a day to be appointed); and COMMONS vol 13 (2009) PARA 419. At the date at which this volume states the law, no day had been appointed for the repeal in relation to Wales to take effect.
4   See the Commons Registration Act 1965 s 1; and COMMONS vol 13 (2009) PARA 508. The provisions of the Commons Registration Act 1965 relating to registration are repealed by the Commons Act 2006 s 53, Sch 6 Pt 1 and are to be replaced by those of Pt 1 (ss 1–25) of the 2006 Act; at the date at which this volume states the law the repeal has taken effect, and the majority of provisions of Pt 1 are in force, only in relation to the pilot areas in England, and the Commons Registration Act 1965 remains in force in the remainder of England and in Wales: see COMMONS vol 13 (2009) PARA 506. As to the pilot areas in England see COMMONS vol 13 (2009) PARA 467.
5   See the Commons Registration Act 1965 s 10 (repealed by the Commons Act 2006 s 53, Sch 6 Pt 1; repeal in force in relation to England in respect of the pilot areas); the Commons Registration (General) Regulations 1966, SI 1966/1471, regs 16(5), 31, 36 (reg 16(5) amended

by SI 1990/311); the Commons Registration (Objections and Maps) Regulations 1968, SI 1968/989, reg 9 (amended by SI 1990/311); and COMMONS vol 13 (2009) PARA 508 et seq. See also note 4. As to amendment of the registers where land becomes common land see the Commons Registration Act 1965 s 13; the Commons Registration (New Land) Regulations 1969, SI 1969/1843; and COMMONS vol 13 (2009) PARA 516. As to amendment of the registers where land ceases to be common land see the Commons Registration Act 1965 s 13; the Commons Registration (General) Regulations 1966, SI 1966/1471, reg 27; and COMMONS vol 13 (2009) PARA 493. As to the removal of land from the registers of common land see the Commons Registration Act 1965 ss 13, 14; the Common Land (Rectification of Registers) Regulations 1990, SI 1990/311; and COMMONS vol 13 (2009) PARAS 516, 519. As to the deregistration of land see the Commons Act 2006 ss 16, 17 (in force in relation to England; s 17(3), (10) in force in relation to Wales); the Commons (Deregistration and Exchange Orders) (Interim Arrangements) (England) Regulations 2007, SI 2007/2585; the Deregistration and Exchange of Common Land and Greens (Procedure) (England) Regulations 2007, SI 2007/2589; and COMMONS vol 13 (2009) PARAS 545–548.

316.   Boundaries of registered land.   Normally, the title plan of land registered under the Land Registration Act 2002 is deemed to indicate only the general boundaries of the land[1]. However, a proprietor of a registered estate may apply to the registrar for the exact line of the boundary of that registered estate to be determined, accompanying the application with a plan, or a plan and a verbal description, identifying the exact line of the boundary claimed and showing sufficient surrounding physical features to allow the general position of the boundary to be drawn on the Ordnance Survey map, and evidence to establish the exact line of the boundary[2]. The registrar, if satisfied as to the prescribed matters[3], must give notice of the application and of the effect of failure to object to the owners of the land adjoining the boundary to be determined (except the applicant) and unless any recipient of the notice objects to the application within the time fixed, the registrar must complete the application[4]. Where the registrar completes an application, he must make appropriate amendments to the individual registers and title plans[5].

Where: (1) there is a transfer of part of a registered estate in land, or the grant of a term of years absolute which is a registrable disposition of part of a registered estate in land; (2) there is a common boundary; and (3) there is sufficient information in the disposition to enable the registrar to determine the exact line of the common boundary, the registrar may determine the exact line of the common boundary without an application and, if he does, he must amend the individual registers and title plans accordingly[6].

1   See PARA 309. There is no longer a requirement for there to be a Land Registry general map: see the Land Registration (No 2) Rules 1999, SI 1999/2097, r 3 (lapsed) (revoking the Land Registration Rules 1925, SR & O 1925/1093, r 273).

2   See the Land Registration Act 2002 ss 1(2), 60(3), (4); the Land Registration Rules 2003, SI 2003/1417, r 118; and LAND REGISTRATION vol 26 (2004 Reissue) PARA 871. 'Boundary' includes part only of a boundary: Land Registration Rules 2003, SI 2003/1417, r 117. Land Registry Practice Guide 40 (October 2005), available at www.landregistry.gov.uk, provides practical guidance on the Registry's approach to boundaries.

3   See the Land Registration Rules 2003, SI 2003/1417, r 119(1)(a)–(c); and LAND REGISTRATION vol 26 (2004 Reissue) PARA 873. Where the registrar is not so satisfied, he must cancel the application: r 119(7).

4   See the Land Registration Rules 2003, SI 2003/1417, r 119 (amended by SI 2008/1919); and LAND REGISTRATION vol 26 (2004 Reissue) PARA 873. However, where the evidence supplied in accordance with the Land Registration Rules 2003, SI 2003/1417, r 118(2)(b) includes an agreement in writing as to the line of the boundary with an owner of the land adjoining the property or a court order determining the line of the boundary, the registrar need not give notice of the application to that owner: r 119(2) (substituted by SI 2008/1919).

5   See the Land Registration Rules 2003, SI 2003/1417, r 120; and LAND REGISTRATION vol 26 (2004 Reissue) PARA 872.

6 See the Land Registration Rules 2003, SI 2003/1417, r 122; and LAND REGISTRATION vol 26 (2004 Reissue) PARA 874.

317. Commissions. Courts exercising jurisdiction in equity have power to order an inquiry, whether by way of a formal commission or by proceedings in chambers[1], to ascertain boundaries when they have become confused, but a mere confusion of boundaries is not per se sufficient ground (except by consent) to support a claim for a commission[2], which would only be granted where some equity was shown arising out of the inequitable conduct of one of the parties[3]. As a rule the commission will direct that, in the event of the boundaries being so confused and obliterated that the commissioners are unable to distinguish them, they are to set out new lands of equal value with those the boundaries of which have been confused[4].

1 See *Searle v Cooke* (1889) 43 ChD 519 at 527 per Kay J (affd (1890) 43 ChD 519 at 529, CA); and EQUITY.
2 See *Marquis of Bute v Glamorganshire Canal Co* (1845) 1 Ph 681 at 684.
3 *Speer v Crawter* (1817) 2 Mer 410; *Miller v Warmington* (1820) 1 Jac & W 484; and see EQUITY. There is no recent instance of a commission being granted.
4 *Ambler's Case* (1770) cited 4 Ves 184; *Willis v Parkinson* (1817) 2 Mer 507.

318. Common law actions. Boundaries may also be determined by the court in actions for the recovery of land[1], or for trespass[2], nuisance[3], breach of the covenants for title implied in a conveyance[4], a declaration or injunction[5] or indeed any action in which the title of one of the parties is in issue[6]. In none of these cases does the judgment operate in rem, determining the true boundary conclusively as against all the world, for these actions are all in personam, and the judgment is binding only as between the parties[7]. In an action for the recovery of land the claimant must prove that he is entitled to recover the land as against the person in possession of it[8] and he must recover on the strength of his own title, not on the weakness of the defendant's title[9]. A party to an action in which title is in issue is entitled to disclosure of any deeds or documents in the possession of the other party[10], or of a stranger[11], which contain any evidence as to the title.

1 See eg *Williams Bros Direct Supply Stores Ltd v Raftery* [1958] 1 QB 159, [1957] 3 All ER 593, CA; *Hopgood v Brown* [1955] 1 All ER 550, [1955] 1 WLR 213, CA. As to actions for the recovery of land see REAL PROPERTY vol 39(2) (Reissue) PARA 259 et seq.
2 See eg *Norton v London and North Western Rly Co* (1879) 13 ChD 268, CA; *Littledale v Liverpool College* [1900] 1 Ch 19, CA; *Truckell v Stock* [1957] 1 All ER 74, [1957] 1 WLR 161, CA; *Kelsen v Imperial Tobacco Co (of Great Britain and Ireland) Ltd* [1957] 2 QB 334, [1957] 2 All ER 343; *Grigsby v Melville* [1973] 3 All ER 455, [1974] 1 WLR 80, CA. See also *Hawkes v Howe* [2002] EWCA Civ 1136, [2002] All ER (D) 446 (Jul). As to trespass to land see TORT vol 97 (2010) PARA 562 et seq.
3 See eg *Davey v Harrow Corpn* [1958] 1 QB 60, [1957] 2 All ER 305, CA. As to nuisance see NUISANCE vol 78 (2010) PARAS 104, 109 et seq.
4 See eg *Eastwood v Ashton* [1915] AC 900, HL.
5 See eg *Mackenzie v Bankes* (1878) 3 App Cas 1324, HL; *Marshall v Taylor* [1895] 1 Ch 641, CA; *Scarfe v Adams* [1981] 1 All ER 843, CA; *Scott v Martin* [1987] 2 All ER 813, [1987] 1 WLR 841, CA; *Mahmood v Yui Tong Man* (1996) 74 P & CR 320, CA. The power to make a binding declaration of right is a discretionary one (*Russian Commercial and Industrial Bank v British Bank for Foreign Trade Ltd* [1921] 2 AC 438, HL), and a declaration will not be made against a person who has asserted no right nor formulated any specific claim (*Re Clay, Clay v Booth* [1919] 1 Ch 66, CA) or whose claim was too indirect (*Thorne RDC v Bunting* [1972] Ch 470, [1972] 1 All ER 439). As to the jurisdiction of the county court to make a declaration or injunction relating to land see the County Courts Act 1984 s 38; and CIVIL PROCEDURE vol 11 (2009) PARA 345; COURTS AND TRIBUNALS vol 24 (2010) PARA 768.

6 See eg *George Wimpey & Co Ltd v Sohn* [1967] Ch 487, [1966] 1 All ER 232, CA (vendor and purchaser summons); *Watson v Burton* [1956] 3 All ER 929, [1957] 1 WLR 19 (specific performance); *Epps v Esso Petroleum Co Ltd* [1973] 2 All ER 465, [1973] 1 WLR 1071 (application for rectification of land register).

7 Eg *A-G v Beynon* [1970] Ch 1 at 15, [1969] 2 All ER 263 at 270 per Goff J. As to the distinction between actions in rem and actions in personam see *Castrique v Imrie* (1870) LR 4 HL 414.

8 If the claimant has been wrongly dispossessed he may succeed against the wrongdoer notwithstanding that the true title may be shown to be in a third person: *Asher v Whitlock* (1865) LR 1 QB 1; *Fowley Marine (Emsworth) Ltd v Gafford* [1968] 2 QB 618, [1968] 1 All ER 979, CA.

9 *Goodtitle d Parker v Baldwin* (1809) 11 East 488; *Danford v McAnulty* (1883) 8 App Cas 456, HL; *Alan Wibberley Building Ltd v Insley* [1999] 2 All ER 897 at 901, [1999] 1 WLR 894 at 898, HL, per Lord Hoffmann. As to the position where the claimant is not in possession see *Palmer v Palmer* [1892] 1 QB 319; and REAL PROPERTY.

10 *Burrell v Nicholson* (1833) 1 My & K 680 at 681 per Lord Brougham; *A-G v Emerson* (1882) 10 QBD 191, CA; *Neilson v Poole* (1969) 20 P & CR 909. A party may be entitled to see the parcels of deeds without being entitled to see the operative part: *Lind v Isle of Wight Ferry Co* (1860) 2 LT 503. As to disclosure see CIVIL PROCEDURE vol 11 (2009) PARA 538 et seq.

11 See the Civil Evidence Act 1968 s 16(1)(b); and CIVIL PROCEDURE vol 11 (2009) PARA 970.

(4) BOUNDARIES FIXED BY LEGAL PRESUMPTIONS

319. Rebuttable presumptions. An artificial boundary structure belongs to the owner of the land on which it exists, but very often it is difficult to determine precisely where the boundary lies and hence to whom the feature belongs. If, on their true construction[1] with such extrinsic evidence as is admissible[2], the title deeds do not clearly fix the position of the boundary of land in relation to certain boundary features, resort may be had to well-established legal presumptions which apply in relation to those features and which assist the inferences which may be drawn from them[3]. All the presumptions recognised and obtaining in the case of boundaries are rebuttable, and not irrebuttable or conclusive presumptions[4]; that is to say, evidence to rebut the presumptions is always admissible, but, until it is produced, the presumptions necessarily apply[5].

1 The presumptions are only applicable if the deeds are unclear and admissible evidence does not answer any ambiguities: see *Stone v Clarke* (1840) 1 Met 378; *Fisher v Winch* [1939] 1 KB 666 at 669, [1939] 2 All ER 144 at 145, CA, per Sir Wilfrid Greene MR, and at 674 and 148 per Goddard LJ.

2 See PARA 332.

3 *Alan Wibberley Building Ltd v Insley* [1999] 2 All ER 897 at 900, [1999] 1 WLR 894 at 897, HL, per Lord Hoffmann.

4 Ie *praesumptiones juris* and not *praesumptiones juris et de jure*: see Denning LJ 'Presumptions and Burdens' (1945) 61 LQR 379; *Huyton-with-Roby UDC v Hunter* [1955] 2 All ER 398 at 400, [1955] 1 WLR 603 at 609, CA, per Denning LJ; *Joseph Constantine Steamship Line Ltd v Imperial Smelting Corpn Ltd* [1942] AC 154 at 193, [1941] 2 All ER 165 at 191, HL, per Lord Wright. See also CIVIL PROCEDURE vol 11 (2009) PARA 1096 et seq.

5 See *Alan Wibberley Building Ltd v Insley* [1999] 2 All ER 897, [1999] 1 WLR 894, HL (where there is no evidence as to the precise boundary line, the presumptions are the best guide to the line of the boundary); *Hall v Dorling* (1996) 74 P & CR 400, CA. See PARAS 304, 321. As to the application of these presumptions to registered titles see PARA 309.

320. Fences. In the case of wooden fences, it is likely to be inferred that, in the absence of freeboard[1], the owner of land will use his land to the fullest extent so that the fence will be deemed to belong to the person on whose side the rails and posts are placed, the palings being placed on his neighbour's side[2], but where there is a dispute it would be necessary to show acts of ownership; that is, an owner may establish acts of ownership by himself to show that the fence is his or acts of ownership by his neighbour to show that the fence is the latter's responsibility[3]. Alternatively, the owners may have agreed to share responsibility[4]. However, where a fenced close adjoins a piece of waste land, there is a presumption that the fence belongs to the owner of the close[5].

1 As to freeboard see PARAS 321 note 8, 350.

2 If the fence was erected the reverse way, the palings would not enclose the small strips of land between the posts.

3 As to evidence by acts of ownership see PARA 334.

4 As to party fences see PARA 364 et seq.

5 *White v Taylor (No 2)* [1969] 1 Ch 160 at 200, [1968] 1 All ER 1015 at 1037 per Buckley J. See also *Hawkes v Howe* [2002] EWCA Civ 1136, [2002] All ER (D) 446 (Jul), where this paragraph was cited with approval.

321. Hedges and ditches. No man making a ditch may cut into his neighbour's soil, but usually he makes it at the very extremity of his own land, forming a bank on his own side with the soil which he excavates from the ditch, on the top of which bank a hedge is usually planted[1]. Therefore, where two fields, or a field and the garden of a dwelling, are separated by a hedge or bank and an artificial ditch, the presumption or inference drawn from the hedge and ditch feature is that the boundary prima facie runs along the side of the ditch further from the hedge or bank[2]. This is based on the assumptions that: (1) the ditch was dug after the boundary was drawn; and (2) the ditch was dug and the hedge then planted[3]. The presumption is therefore only applicable when it is known that the ditch is artificial[4]. If the ditch was made while the lands either side were in common ownership, the presumption will be inapplicable because the ditch was there before the boundary was drawn[5]. Further, the presumption does not apply where the title deeds show what the boundary is[6], so a conveyance which describes or delimits the land transferred by reference to an Ordnance Survey map or plan on which the boundaries are marked as a centre line of the hedge will rebut the presumption[7].

An impression once prevailed in some districts that the owner of a bank and ditch is entitled to four feet of width for the base of the bank and four feet of width for the ditch, but, apart from any local custom, there is no rule to this effect[8].

Acts of ownership such as trimming and pollarding a hedge and cleaning a ditch, even though continued for many years by an adjoining owner, do not rebut the presumption that the ditch and hedge belong to the owner of the land nearer to the hedge, particularly if the acts were done without the knowledge of the presumptive owner[9]. Title to a ditch beside a hedge, or such a ditch that has been filled in, may be claimed under the Limitation Act 1980 in accordance with standard principles[10].

Where two pieces of land are divided by two ditches one on each side of a hedge or bank, or by two hedges or banks one on each side of a ditch, or by an old hedge or bank without any ditches at all, or by a ditch alone with no bank or hedge, then there is no presumption as to the ownership of the hedges, ditches, or banks, but it must be proved by acts of ownership exercised over them[11].

If the adjoining owners on each side concurrently exercise acts of ownership, and it is not known what quantity of land each of the owners originally contributed towards the formation of the ditch or bank, that may be evidence that the hedge, ditch or bank is a party fence[12]. If the true boundary is known, however, it will not be altered merely by concurrent acts of ownership[13].

1   *Vowles v Miller* (1810) 3 Taunt 137 at 138 per Lawrence J; *Alan Wibberley Building Ltd v Insley* [1999] 2 All ER 897 at 900, [1999] 1 WLR 894 at 897, HL, per Lord Hoffmann.

2   *Noye v Reed* (1827) 1 Man & Ry KB 63 at 65 per Bayley J; *Guy v West* (1808) cited in 2 Selwyn's NP (13th Edn) 1244; *Hall v Dorling* (1996) 74 P & CR 400, CA.

3   *Alan Wibberley Building Ltd v Insley* [1999] 2 All ER 897 at 900, [1999] 1 WLR 894 at 897, HL, per Lord Hoffmann. So if the ditch was in existence before the boundary was drawn, or the hedge existed before the ditch was dug, there is no room for the presumption to operate.

4   *Marshall v Taylor* [1895] 1 Ch 641 at 647, CA. This limitation was treated as correct in *Collis v Amphlett* [1918] 1 Ch 232 at 253, CA, per Warrington LJ, and at 260 per Scrutton LJ (revsd on the facts [1920] AC 271, HL).

5   *Alan Wibberley Building Ltd v Insley* [1999] 2 All ER 897 at 903, [1999] 1 WLR 894 at 900, HL, per Lord Hoffmann, explaining *Fisher v Winch* [1939] 1 KB 666, [1939] 2 All ER 144, CA (although this was not the basis of the decision).

6   *Fisher v Winch* [1939] 1 KB 666, [1939] 2 All ER 144, CA (where, per Goddard LJ at 673–674 and 148, it was stressed that the principle is a rebuttable presumption and not a custom); *Davey v Harrow Corpn* [1958] 1 QB 60, [1957] 2 All ER 305, CA; *Falkingham v Farley* (1991) Times, 11 March, CA (presumption rebutted by strong evidence of a carefully prepared plan executed for the purpose of an auction of the land in 1914).

7   *Rouse v Gravelworks Ltd* [1940] 1 KB 489, [1940] 1 All ER 26, CA; *Davey v Harrow Corpn* [1958] 1 QB 60, [1957] 2 All ER 305, CA. Such a conveyance cannot, however, operate to pass title to a strip of land such as the ditch where no title previously existed: *Alan Wibberley Building Ltd v Insley* [1999] 2 All ER 897 at 904, [1999] 1 WLR 894 at 902, HL, per Lord Hope of Craighead. As to the use of Ordnance Survey maps see PARA 308.

8   *Vowles v Miller* (1810) 3 Taunt 137; *Fisher v Winch* [1939] 1 KB 666 at 673, [1939] 2 All ER 144 at 148, CA, per MacKinnon LJ, applying *Collis v Amphlett* [1918] 1 Ch 232 at 259, CA, per Scrutton LJ (whose dissenting judgment was upheld when the decision was reversed in the House of Lords (see [1920] AC 271, HL)). In some places a right of 'freeboard' or 'deerleap' extending several feet beyond the hedge is claimed by local custom, possibly as a way of limiting encroachment by the ditch onto the adjoining land: see further PARA 350. As to local customs see generally CUSTOM AND USAGE. Where, on a map attached to an award made under a local Act for the regulation of a common, the boundary of the common was delineated by a line drawn along the line of 'growers' in a hedge dividing the common from the land of an adjacent owner, the hedge belonging to such owner, there was no presumption that the owner was entitled to a ditch-width on the outside of the line of growers: *Collis v Amphlett* [1920] AC 271, HL.

9   *Henniker v Howard* (1904) 90 LT 157, DC; *Earl of Craven v Pridmore* (1902) 18 TLR 282, CA. See also *Searby v Tottenham Rly Co* (1868) LR 5 Eq 409. Cf *Marshall v Taylor* [1895] 1 Ch 641, CA (trimming a hedge alongside a ditch which had been filled in would not have prevented a claim that title had been acquired by limitation over the site of the ditch). However, it seems that putting foundations of a dwelling into part of the ditch and laying a concrete path over a part of the ditch that has been filled in may be sufficient for a claim based on adverse possession of that part: see *Hall v Dorling* (1996) 74 P & CR 400, CA. See also the text and note 10.

10 See *Marshall v Taylor* [1895] 1 Ch 641, CA; *Hall v Dorling* (1996) 74 P & CR 400, CA. As to claims based on adverse possession under the Limitation Act 1980 see PARA 312.

11 *Guy v West* (1808) cited in 2 Selwyn's NP (13th Edn) 1244. Cf *Re Belfast Dock Act 1854, ex p Earl of Ranfurly* (1867) IR 1 Eq 128. But if the presumption does apply, acts of ownership done without the knowledge of the owner will not rebut the presumption: see note 9.

12 Prior to 1 January 1926 (the date of the commencement of the Law of Property Act 1925), it would have been evidence that the hedge, ditch or bank was held in tenancy in common. It is doubtful whether a hedge and ditch is a structure that can fall within the provisions relating to party walls and fences: see PARA 364 et seq.

13 Woolrych *The Law of Party Walls and Fences* p 283. Cf *Matts v Hawkins* (1813) 5 Taunt 20.

322. Hedges and ditches beside highways.

The principles relating to hedges and ditches generally[1] also apply in the rare case of hedges and ditches running along the side of a public highway where the soil of the highway is not owned by the owners of the adjoining land[2]. The hedge and ditch are presumed to be owned by the owner of the adjoining land, for he could only lawfully have dug the ditch in his own land[3]. The presumption, however, would yield to contrary evidence, for example evidence that the ditch was constructed by the owners of the road, in which case the ditch would remain part of the road[4]. Moreover, a ditch running alongside a highway between the road and fence may be dedicated as part of the highway[5], but the presumption is that a ditch, which is not prima facie adapted for exercise by the public of their right to pass and repass, is not part of the highway[6].

Where a highway of a definite width has been laid out under inclosure legislation[7], there is no presumption that an adjoining ditch and hedge form part of the highway, if the highway by itself is of the definite width[8].

1   See PARA 321.
2   As to the more usual presumption in the case of highways see PARA 323. As to highways generally see HIGHWAYS, STREETS AND BRIDGES.
3   *Doe d Pring v Pearsey* (1827) 7 B & C 304. See also *Chippendale v Pontefract RDC* (1907) 71 JP 231 (county court); *Hanscombe v Bedfordshire County Council* [1938] Ch 944, [1938] 3 All ER 647. See also HIGHWAYS, STREETS AND BRIDGES vol 21 (2004 Reissue) PARA 205. As to the circumstances in which an obligation exists to fence see PARA 351.
4   *Searby v Tottenham Rly Co* (1868) LR 5 Eq 409.
5   *Chorley Corpn v Nightingale* [1907] 2 KB 637, CA. See also HIGHWAYS, STREETS AND BRIDGES vol 21 (2004 Reissue) PARA 205.
6   *Hanscombe v Bedfordshire County Council* [1938] Ch 944, [1938] 3 All ER 647. See also HIGHWAYS, STREETS AND BRIDGES vol 21 (2004 Reissue) PARA 205.
7   As to inclosure see COMMONS vol 13 (2009) PARA 418 et seq.
8   *Simcox v Yardley RDC* (1905) 69 JP 66. See also HIGHWAYS, STREETS AND BRIDGES vol 21 (2004 Reissue) PARA 205.

323.   Highway boundaries.   Where land is bounded by a highway, or a private right of way, there are three interrelated presumptions which may apply.

The first presumption is that the boundary is, as a general rule, a line drawn along the middle of the highway[1] or private right of way[2]. This arises because the owners of land adjoining[3] the highway or way are presumed, in the absence of any evidence to the contrary, to own the subsoil as far as the middle of the road[4] and the airspace above the soil subject only to the right of passage over the surface[5] and the rights of the highway authority[6]. The presumption obtains also where the land was formerly of copyhold tenure[7] and the better view is that it also applies in the case of leaseholders[8].

The second presumption is that subsoil up to the centre of the highway will pass in a conveyance or transfer without express mention[9]; the mere fact that a conveyance describes land as being bounded by a highway[10] or that measurements or a plan by reference to which land is conveyed exclude any part of the highway will not rebut the presumption[11], for it would be absurd to suppose that the grantor retained the soil of the highway, which in nearly every case would be wholly valueless[12]. However, the presumption may readily yield to indications of a contrary intention[13], as in the case of the conveyance of a plot on a building estate[14].

These presumptions apply under the general boundaries rule in the case of registered land[15], but it is not the practice of the Land Registry to show the half-width of the highway as being within the title so the boundary line shown on a Land Registry plan does not rebut the presumption[16].

The third presumption (sometimes referred to as the 'hedge to hedge' presumption) is that, where a highway is bounded on both sides by fences or hedges, the highway is not confined to any metalled portion but is presumed to extend up to both such hedges or fences provided that it is clear that they were placed to separate the adjoining land from the highway[17]. The presumption depends on the fence or hedge being erected by reference to the highway in order to separate private land from land over which public rights of way are exercised, and this fact must be established before the presumption applies[18]. Where a highway passes through unenclosed land the boundary of the highway is the edge of the metalled portion unless there is evidence of use of any additional land as part of the highway[19].

If the highway is separated from the adjoining land by a wayside strip[20] then the presumption is that the highway rights extend over such wayside strip but the subsoil belongs to the adjoining owner[21].

1 *Goodtitle d Chester v Alker and Elmes* (1757) 1 Burr 133; *Anon* (1773) Lofft 358; *Stevens v Whistler* (1809) 11 East 51; *Cooke v Green* (1823) 11 Price 736; *Coverdale v Charlton* (1878) 4 QBD 104; *St Edmundsbury and Ipswich Diocesan Board of Finance v Clark (No 2)* [1973] 3 All ER 902, [1973] 1 WLR 1572 (affd [1975] 1 All ER 772, [1975] 1 WLR 468, CA); *Bridges v Harrow London Borough Council* (1981) 260 Estates Gazette 284; *Russell v Barnet London Borough Council* (1984) 83 LGR 152, [1984] 2 EGLR 44. The presumption is applicable to properties in the town as well as the country (*Re White's Charities, Charity Comrs v London Corpn* [1898] 1 Ch 659), to cases where one owner's adjoining land is primarily covered with water (*Frost v Richardson* (1910) 103 LT 416, CA), and to cases where no grant or conveyance has to be construed (*City of London Land Tax Comrs v Central London Rly Co* [1913] AC 364, HL). The presumption would also seem to apply, in the absence of evidence to rebut it, where properties are divided by a public footpath or bridleway. It primarily applies where the conveyancing history of the land and the road is unknown: *Giles v County Building Constructors (Hertford) Ltd* (1971) 22 P & CR 978. Where modern roads have been constructed on land compulsorily acquired or purchased, the presumption does not apply. As to the acquisition of land for highway purposes see the Highways Act 1980 ss 238–262; and HIGHWAYS, STREETS AND BRIDGES vol 21 (2004 Reissue) PARA 77 et seq. As to highways generally see HIGHWAYS, STREETS AND BRIDGES.

2 *Holmes v Bellingham* (1859) 29 LJCP 132; *Smith v Howden* (1863) 14 CBNS 398; *Pardoe v Pennington* (1996) 75 P & CR 264, CA. As to private ways generally see EASEMENTS AND PROFITS A PRENDRE.

3 Land adjoins a highway for this purpose although separated from it by a public right of way not being part of the street: *Ware UDC v Gaunt* [1960] 3 All ER 778, [1960] 1 WLR 1364, DC. As to the analogous issue of when a property is 'fronting' the street for the purposes of the Highway Act 1980 ss 203, 205 (private street works: see HIGHWAYS, STREETS AND BRIDGES vol 21 (2004 Reissue) PARA 146 et seq) see *Warwickshire County Council v Adkins* (1967) 66 LGR 486, DC; and HIGHWAYS, STREETS AND BRIDGES vol 21 (2004 Reissue) PARA 154.

4 Ie *usque ad medium filum viae*. The presumption is based on convenience, to prevent disputes as to precise boundaries and on the supposition that each owner contributed a portion of land when the highway was formed: *Holmes v Bellingham* (1859) 29 LJCP 132. For an appraisal of the rationale of the rule see *St Edmundsbury and Ipswich Diocesan Board of Finance v Clark (No 2)* [1973] 3 All ER 902 at 914, [1973] 1 WLR 1572 at 1583–1584 per Megarry J.

5 *Harrison v Duke of Rutland* [1893] 1 QB 142, CA; *City of London Land Tax Comrs v Central London Rly Co* [1913] AC 364, HL; *Lang v House* (1961) 178 Estates Gazette 801. But the owner cannot use the subsoil so as to interfere with the use of the highway: *Goodson v Richardson* (1874) 9 Ch App 221.

6 The surface of the road or highway vests in the highway authority together with so much of the soil as is necessary for the authority to perform its statutory duties: *Hertfordshire County Council v Lea Sand Ltd* (1933) 98 JP 109 at 112. This is a legal interest in fee simple of the 'top spit' determinable on the land ceasing to be a highway: *Tithe Redemption Commission v Runcorn UDC* [1954] Ch 383 at 407, [1954] 1 All ER 653 at 661, CA, per Denning LJ. As to the vesting of highways maintainable at public expense see also the Highways Act 1980 s 263; and HIGHWAYS, STREETS AND BRIDGES vol 21 (2004 Reissue) PARA 225. Thus, apart from statute, the highway authority could not prevent the construction of cellars under the highway or the erection of telephone wires or buildings above the highway which did not interfere with passage: *Wandsworth Board of Works v United Telephone Co* (1884) 13 QBD 904; *New Towns Commission v Hemel Hempstead Corpn* [1962] 3 All ER 183 sub nom *Hemel Hempstead Developments Corpn v Hemel Hempstead Borough Council* [1962] 1 WLR 1158. Statutory provisions restricting building and other works in, under or over the highway have substantially altered the law: see the Highways Act 1980 ss 169–180; and HIGHWAYS, STREETS AND BRIDGES.

7 *Doe d Pring v Pearsey* (1827) 7 B & C 304; *Tilbury v Silva* (1890) 45 ChD 98, CA. As to the abolition of copyhold tenure see CUSTOM AND USAGE vol 12(1) (Reissue) PARA 643; REAL PROPERTY vol 39(2) (Reissue) PARA 31.

8   *Haynes v King* [1893] 3 Ch 439; *Dwyer v Rich* (1871) IR 6 CL 144, Ex Ch; *Tilbury v Silva* (1890) 45 ChD 98. However, in relation to leaseholders the applicability of the presumption was expressly reserved in *Landrock v Metropolitan District Rly Co* (1886) 3 TLR 162, CA, per Lord Esher MR and in *Mappin Bros v Liberty & Co Ltd* [1903] 1 Ch 118 per Joyce J. *Tilbury v Silva* (1890) 45 ChD 98, CA was accepted as a correct statement of the law in *Southern Centre of Theosophy Inc v State of South Australia* [1982] AC 706 at 715, [1982] 1 All ER 283 at 287, PC. Cf *Davies v Yadegar* (1990) 22 HLR 232, [1990] 1 EGLR 71, CA (lease includes airspace above a demised roof). See also PARA 302.

9   *London and North Western Rly Co v Westminster Corpn* [1902] 1 Ch 269 (affd [1905] AC 426, HL); *City of London Land Tax Comrs v Central London Rly Co* [1913] AC 364, HL. This presumption will not apply in cases where there is an intention to exclude the road: *Mappin Bros v Liberty & Co Ltd* [1903] 1 Ch 118 (lease by commissioners abutting Regent Street which they had laid out; the presumption was rebutted when regard was had to the statutory powers and the terms of the lease).

10   *Beckett v Corpn of Leeds* (1872) 7 Ch App 421. As to how far boundary features generally are included in the property described see PARA 311.

11   *Berridge v Ward* (1861) 10 CBNS 400, approved in *Pardoe v Pennington* (1996) 75 P & CR 264, CA; *Pryor v Petre* [1894] 2 Ch 11, CA. See also *City of London Land Tax Comrs v Central London Rly Co* [1913] AC 364 at 379, HL, per Lord Shaw of Dunfermline ('The presumption [of ownership *ad medium filum*] operates not only in cases where the boundary is expressed to be by the highway or street, but also in the cases where the properties are delineated by plan or colour or measurement'), quoted with approval in *Southern Centre of Theosophy Inc v State of South Australia* [1982] AC 706 at 718, [1982] 1 All ER 283 at 289, PC. Cf *Mellor v Walmesley* [1905] 2 Ch 164, CA (a case concerning the foreshore: see PARA 325); *Micklethwait v Newlay Bridge Co* (1886) 33 ChD 133, CA (a case concerning a river: see PARA 327).

12   *Lord v Sydney City Comrs* (1859) 12 Moo PCC 473. There may, however, be something in the context to rebut the presumption, such as a covenant on the part of the grantor to make up the road, and of course the presumption does not apply where the grantor did not own the half-width of road.

13   *Pryor v Petre* [1894] 2 Ch 11 at 19, CA, per Lindley LJ; *Pardoe v Pennington* (1996) 75 P & CR 264, CA (an assent of part of an estate did not include the soil under a bridleway since the presumption was rebutted by the attendant circumstances).

14   *Giles v County Building Constructors (Hertford) Ltd* (1971) 22 P & CR 978 (property more particularly delineated on a plan held to exclude any part of the roadway of the building estate); *Plumstead Board of Works v British Land Co* (1874) LR 10 QB 16 (revsd on other grounds (1874) LR 10 QB 203); *Leigh v Jack* (1879) 5 ExD 264, CA.

15   See PARA 309.

16   *Russell v Barnet London Borough Council* (1984) 83 LGR 152, [1984] 2 EGLR 44 (plans used for the registration of title are of little evidential value). As to the Land Registry see LAND REGISTRATION vol 26 (2004 Reissue) PARA 1064.

17   *A-G v Beynon* [1970] Ch 1, [1969] 2 All ER 263; *Hinds and Diplock v Breconshire County Council* [1938] 4 All ER 24; *Offin v Rochford RDC* [1906] 1 Ch 342; *Naydler v Hampshire County Council* (1973) 226 Estates Gazette 1761; cf *Minting v Ramage* [1991] EGCS 12, CA (fence to fence presumption was rebutted where the highway ran across a common and it was shown that the fence abutting the common pre-dated the highway). As to the extent of the public right of passage where the highway runs between fences see HIGHWAYS, STREETS AND BRIDGES vol 21 (2004 Reissue) PARA 202.

18   *A-G v Beynon* [1970] Ch 1 at 12–13, [1969] 2 All ER 263 at 268 per Goff J; *Hale v Norfolk County Council* [2001] Ch 717, [2001] 2 WLR 1481, CA (evidence showed there was no intention to fence against the highway and so no presumption of dedication of the land between the fence and the highway).

19   *Easton v Richmond Highway Board* (1871) LR 7 QB 69. See also HIGHWAYS, STREETS AND BRIDGES vol 21 (2004 Reissue) PARA 201. By virtue of the Highways Act 1980 s 160A, Sch 12A, provision is made for determining both the minimum and the maximum width of a footpath, bridleway or highway where the width is not proved: see HIGHWAYS, STREETS AND BRIDGES vol 21 (2004 Reissue) PARA 489.

20   See HIGHWAYS, STREETS AND BRIDGES vol 21 (2004 Reissue) PARA 219.

21   *Steel v Prickett* (1819) 2 Stark 463; *Offin v Rochford RDC* [1906] 1 Ch 342.

324.   Railways.   The presumption that a grant of land described as bounded by a highway passes one-half of the soil of the highway does not obtain in the case of conveyances of land described as bounded by a railway[1], and therefore a grant of land so described will not pass a right to the minerals under the railway[2]. However, the minerals may be vested in the adjoining owner by virtue of the conveyance when the railway undertaking acquired the land[3].

1   This is because the land acquired for the railway would have been acquired as a separate plot. As to railways generally see RAILWAYS, INLAND WATERWAYS AND CROSS-COUNTRY PIPELINES.

2   *Thompson v Hickman* [1907] 1 Ch 550. See MINES, MINERALS AND QUARRIES vol 31 (2003 Reissue) PARAS 24, 308. As to the duty to fence railways see PARA 353.

3   Conveyances under the Railways Clauses Consolidation Act 1845 s 77 do not pass mines and minerals unless they are expressly included: see MINES, MINERALS AND QUARRIES vol 31 (2003 Reissue) PARA 308.

325. Seashore or foreshore. The boundary line between the seashore[1] and the adjoining land is, in the absence of usage or evidence to the contrary[2], the line of the median high tide between the ordinary spring and neap tides[3].

The boundary of land abutting upon the seashore may vary from time to time, and in the case of a conveyance of land described as bounded by the seashore, then, as the medium high and low water marks shift, so does the boundary of the land shift also; for there may be a movable freehold[4]. This rule applies whether or not the grant of the land adjoining the seashore is accompanied by a map showing the boundary or contains a parcels clause stating the area of the land and whether or not the original boundary can be identified[5], but a fixed boundary may result if clear words and an intention so to do are shown in the conveyance[6].

The boundary of the seashore or foreshore with the high seas is probably the median low tide between the ordinary spring and neap tides[7].

1   The seashore (or foreshore, which has the same meaning: *Mellor v Walmesley* [1905] 2 Ch 164, CA) consists of the land lying between the high and low water marks: *A-G v Chambers* (1854) 4 De GM & G 206; *A-G v Chambers, A-G v Rees* (1859) 4 De G & J 55. The same rule probably applies where a property is described as being bounded by the 'sea beach': *Government of the State of Penang v Beng Hong Oon* [1972] AC 425, [1971] 3 All ER 1163, PC; *Southern Centre of Theosophy Inc v State of South Australia* [1982] AC 706 at 718, [1982] 1 All ER 283 at 289, PC. As to the rule that prima facie the seashore belongs to the Crown see further CROWN PROPERTY vol 12(1) (Reissue) PARA 242 et seq. As to the seaward limits of territorial jurisdiction see INTERNATIONAL RELATIONS LAW vol 61 (2010) PARA 121 et seq; WATER AND WATERWAYS vol 100 (2009) PARA 31 et seq.

2   See e g *Esquimault and Nanaimo Rly Co v Treat* (1919) 121 LT 657, PC ('coast line' held to mean the boundary at high water mark).

3   *A-G v Chambers* (1854) 4 De GM & G 206. Cf *Lowe v Govett* (1832) 3 B & Ad 863.

4   *Scratton v Brown* (1825) 4 B & C 485; *Smart & Co v Suva Town Board* [1893] AC 301, PC; *Government of the State of Penang v Beng Hong Oon* [1972] AC 425, [1971] 3 All ER 1163, PC; *Southern Centre of Theosophy Inc v State of South Australia* [1982] AC 706, [1982] 1 All ER 283, PC. Cf *Secretary of State for India in Council v Foucar & Co* (1933) 61 LR Ind App 18, PC. As to the effect of accretion and diluvion see PARA 329; and WATER AND WATERWAYS vol 100 (2009) PARA 39 et seq.

5   *Southern Centre of Theosophy Inc v State of South Australia* [1982] AC 706 at 716, [1982] 1 All ER 283 at 287–288, PC; *A-G v M'Carthy* [1911] 2 IR 260 (boundary could still be altered even where the former line of ordinary high water could be ascertained by markers).

6   *Baxendale v Instow Parish Council* [1982] Ch 14, [1981] 2 All ER 620 (conveyance by Crown, with plan of some precision, of land then part of the foreshore and between high and low water marks was held to be a conveyance of a fixed area of land and of the movable freehold of the foreshore which had retreated). See also *Southern Centre of Theosophy Inc v State of South Australia* [1982] AC 706 at 718, [1982] 1 All ER 283 at 289, PC.

7   See *R v Howlett* (1967) Times, 4 February (convictions quashed on other grounds (1968) 112 Sol Jo 150, CA); *Baxendale v Instow Parish Council* [1982] Ch 14, [1981] 2 All ER 620. As to the limits of the seashore see generally WATER AND WATERWAYS vol 100 (2009) PARA 34.

326. Lakes. Since the bed of even large inland lakes does not vest in the Crown[1], the ownership of the bed of a lake is determined in accordance with normal rules of title. A lake entirely within the boundaries of one piece of land will pass with it without express reference and if the lake is in different ownership, it is submitted that the boundary will be the normal edge of the lake unless the relevant conveyance sets precise boundaries[2].

Where there is a lake bounded by a number of separate proprietors on its edge, the titles may be such as to show that one has the exclusive title to the lake, or, even where the titles do not show it, there may be evidence of possession for such a long time as to show either that there has been exclusive possession by one proprietor, or that there are boundary lines set by the title deeds, or that there has been 'promiscuous possession'[3]. In the absence of any clear title or evidence as to possession[4], the position is doubtful; there does not appear to be any presumption as to the boundary[5].

The doctrine of accretion to boundaries applies to inland lakes[6].

1   *Bristow v Cormican* (1878) 3 App Cas 641, HL. See also *Johnston v O'Neill* [1911] AC 552, HL.

2   There is no direct authority, but see *Southern Centre of Theosophy Inc v State of South Australia* [1982] AC 706, [1982] 1 All ER 283, PC.

3   *Mackenzie v Bankes* (1878) 3 App Cas 1324 at 1340, HL, per Lord Blackburn discussing the Scots law.

4   See *Fowley Marine (Emsworth) Ltd v Gafford* [1968] 2 QB 618, [1968] 1 All ER 979, CA.

5   In *Marshall v Ulleswater Steam Navigation Co Ltd* (1863) 3 B & S 732, the question whether the soil of lakes prima facie belongs to riparian owners *ad medium filum aquae* was left undecided, though it was said to be clear that the soil of land covered with water might, together with the water and fishing rights therein, be specially appropriated to a third person, whether he had land or not on the borders thereof or adjacent thereto. See also *Bristow v Cormican* (1878) 3 App Cas 641 at 666, HL, per Lord Blackburn; *Bloomfield v Johnston* (1868) IR 8 CL 68 at 95, 97. As to the application of the *usque ad medium filum aquae* rule under Scots law see *Mackenzie v Bankes* (1878) 3 App Cas 1324 at 1338, HL, per Lord Selborne, where it was suggested that there should be a medium line down the centre of the lake in the case of two properties and radial lines in the case of several riparian owners. See further WATER AND WATERWAYS vol 100 (2009) PARA 31.

6   *Southern Centre of Theosophy Inc v State of South Australia* [1982] AC 706, [1982] 1 All ER 283, PC, overruling *Trafford v Thrower* (1929) 45 TLR 502. As to the doctrine of accretion see PARA 329; and WATER AND WATERWAYS vol 100 (2009) PARA 77.

327.   Tidal and non-tidal rivers.   Where land is said to be bounded by a river, a distinction must be made between tidal rivers and non-tidal rivers.

In those parts of rivers where the tide flows and reflows, the soil between the medium high water mark and medium low water mark prima facie belongs to the Crown[1], and therefore the boundary between the bed of a tidal river and the adjoining land is, as a general rule, the line of medium high water mark[2]. A tidal river is one where the water is subject to the ebb and flow of the tide[3] whether the movement is lateral or vertical[4]. The right of the Crown ceases at that point in the river where the tide ceases to ebb and flow[5].

In the case of non-tidal rivers or streams[6], whether navigable or not, the boundary is in general the line of mid-stream, because, in the absence of any evidence to the contrary[7], the bed[8] of such rivers and streams is presumed to belong to the riparian owners as far as the middle of the stream[9]. Similarly, a conveyance of a property bounded by a stream normally includes the bed of the stream to the median line[10]. Where the ordinary presumption is rebutted, and the bed of the river is the property of some person other than the riparian owners, the boundary is the water line when the river is in its normal state, without reference to the extraordinary freshets of the winter or spring or the extreme droughts of the summer or autumn[11].

The ownership of a several fishery in a river, navigable or non-navigable, public or private, raises a presumption that the freehold in the bed of the river is vested in the owner of the fishery[12].

1   Hale's de Jure Maris (Hargrave's Law Tracts 12, 25); *Sir Henry Constable's Case* (1601) 5 Co Rep 106a; *Lyon v Fishmongers' Co* (1875) 10 Ch App 679; *R v Smith* (1780) 2 Doug KB 441; *Lord Advocate for Scotland v Hamilton* (1852) 1 Macq 46, HL; *Gann v Whitstable Free Fishers* (1865) 11 HL Cas 192; *Lord Fitzhardinge v Purcell* [1908] 2 Ch 139. As to ownership of the soil in tidal inland waters see further WATER AND WATERWAYS vol 100 (2009) PARAS 71–73. As to the right of navigation in tidal waters see WATER AND WATERWAYS vol 100 (2009) PARAS 46, 72; WATER AND WATERWAYS vol 101 (2009) PARA 689 et seq.

2   *A-G v Chambers* (1854) 4 De GM & G 206; *Bridgwater Trustees v Bootle-cum-Linacre* (1866) LR 2 QB 4 (parish boundary); *Mellor v Walmesley* [1905] 2 Ch 164 at 179–180, CA.

3   *Reece v Miller* (1882) 8 QBD 626, DC; *Ingram v Percival* [1969] 1 QB 548, [1968] 3 All ER 657, DC. See also *Yorkshire Derwent Trust Ltd v Brotherton* (1988) 59 P & CR 60 at 77–78 per Vinelott J; affd sub nom *A-G (ex rel Yorkshire Derwent Trust Ltd) v Brotherton* [1992] 1 AC 425, [1992] 1 All ER 230, HL.

4   *Ingram v Percival* [1969] 1 QB 548 at 555, [1968] 3 All ER 657 at 659, DC, per Lord Parker of Waddington CJ.

5   See e g *Micklethwait v Vincent* (1892) 67 LT 225, CA.

6   A stream, river or brook implies water in motion as distinguished from stagnant water: *M'Nab v Robertson* [1897] AC 129, HL.

7   Eg evidence that the grantor at the time of the grant in question did not own to the centre. In *Ecroyd v Coulthard* [1898] 2 Ch 358, CA, the ordinary presumption was rebutted in the case of an award under a private Inclosure Act when the river bed did not form part of the lands which were authorised to be allotted.

8   A bed of a stream has been defined as the soil under the water between the banks: *Gooldon v Thames Conservators* (1955) unreported, HL, noted at 19 Conv (NS) 172.

9   Hale's de Jure Maris (Hargrave's Law Tracts 5); *Wishart v Wyllie* (1853) 1 Macq 389, HL; *Wright v Howard* (1823) 1 Sim & St 190. Cf *R v Landulph Inhabitants* (1834) 1 Mood & R 393; *Edleston v Crossley & Sons Ltd* (1868) 18 LT 15; *Micklethwait v Newlay Bridge Co* (1886) 33 ChD 133, CA; *Blount v Layard* [1891] 2 Ch 681n, CA; *Herbert v Pegrum* [2005] EWCA Civ 120, [2005] All ER (D) 307 (Jan) (there is a presumption that where a stream separates properties, the boundary between the properties lies along the middle of the stream). As to ownership of the soil in non-tidal inland waters see further WATER AND WATERWAYS vol 100 (2009) PARA 74 et seq. As to the right of navigation in non-tidal waters see WATER AND WATERWAYS vol 101 (2009) PARA 701 et seq.

10 *Micklethwait v Newlay Bridge Co* (1886) 33 ChD 133, CA; *Dwyer v Rich* (1870) IR 4 CL 424; *Thames Conservators v Kent* [1918] 2 KB 272, CA (where land was bounded by two ways, in this case a towpath and a river, the presumption extended to cover the river as well as the towpath so that the whole of the soil of the towpath was vested in the adjoining owner); *Hesketh v Willis Cruises Ltd* (1968) 19 P & CR 573, CA. The presumption applies on the grant of a lease: *Tilbury v Silva* (1890) 45 ChD 98; *Southern Centre of Theosophy Inc v State of South Australia* [1982] AC 706, [1982] 1 All ER 283, PC; *Maddern v Atkins* [1992] EGCS 82.

11 *Hindson v Ashby* [1896] 2 Ch 1 at 25, CA, per AL Smith LJ, quoting *State of Alabama v State of Georgia* 64 US 505 (1859) at 515; *Foster v Wright* (1878) 4 CPD 438 at 448. See also *Jones v Williams* (1837) 2 M & W 326 (one riparian owner successfully claimed the whole bed of a stream by showing acts of ownership over it).

12 *Holford v Bailey* (1849) 13 QB 426 at 444; *A-G v Emerson* [1891] AC 649 at 654, HL; *Hanbury v Jenkins* [1901] 2 Ch 401; *Duke of Beaufort v John Aird & Co* (1904) 20 TLR 602. As to the ownership of a several fishery see AGRICULTURE AND FISHERIES vol 1(2) (2007 Reissue) PARA 805 et seq.

328.   Islands.   There are no special presumptions applicable to existing islands[1]. If an island arises in a tidal river, it will belong to the Crown; if it arises in a non-tidal river, it will belong to the near side owner if entirely on one side of the median line or to the adjoining riparian owners in proportion as the centre line of the stream bisects it[2].

1   As to the presumptions generally applicable see PARAS 325–327. There is some uncertainty as to the application of the mid-stream boundary presumption to existing islands in rivers: see *Great*

Torrington Commons Conservators v Moore Stevens [1904] 1 Ch 347 (*medium filum aquae* drawn through stream between bank and island, plaintiffs showing no evidence of title to island); *Menzies v Marquess of Breadalbane* (1901) 4 F 55, Ct of Sess (*medium filum* drawn between two banks and through two islands).

2 *Wedderburn v Paterson* (1864) 2 M 902; *Earl Zetland v Glover Incorporation of Perth* (1870) LR 2 Sc & Div 70, HL. See also WATER AND WATERWAYS vol 100 (2009) PARAS 73, 79.

329. Effect of accretion or diluvion. By the doctrine of accretion, which applies to all land with a water boundary[1], the title of the owner of the adjoining land extends to that land as added to or detracted from by accretion or diluvion[2]. The doctrine applies whether or not the original grant of the land is accompanied by a map showing the boundary[3], or contains a parcels clause stating the specific measurement or area of the land[4], and whether or not the original boundary can be identified[5]. Consequently, if by gradual and imperceptible accretions in the ordinary course of nature, land is added to the riverside, such land belongs to the riparian owners, and the boundary line correspondingly advances[6]. The doctrine of accretion also applies to changes caused by human action[7] and to natural causes other than fluvial action[8]. The doctrine operates against the Crown[9]. The land added by accretion is subject to the same leasehold or other interests and customs as affected the land to which the accretion took place[10].

The doctrine only applies where the accretion is by gradual and imperceptible means[11] and therefore is not applicable where a tidal[12] or non-tidal[13] river separating two properties suddenly changes its course.

The application of the doctrine of accretion may be excluded in any particular case but the intention to do so must be plainly shown[14].

In the case of registered land, the fact that a registered estate in land is shown in the register as having a particular boundary does not affect the operation of accretion or diluvion[15]. An agreement about the operation of accretion or diluvion in relation to a registered estate in land has effect only if registered in accordance with the relevant rules[16].

1 *Southern Centre of Theosophy Inc v State of South Australia* [1982] AC 706, [1982] 1 All ER 283, PC, where the doctrine of accretion is stated as applying to land bounded by rivers, lakes and the sea. The Privy Council disagreed with the decision in *Trafford v Thrower* (1929) 45 TLR 502, where the judge held that accretion did not apply to an inland lake (the Norfolk Broads). As to the doctrine of accretion see further WATER AND WATERWAYS vol 100 (2009) PARAS 39 et seq, 77.

2 *Southern Centre of Theosophy Inc v State of South Australia* [1982] AC 706 at 716, [1982] 1 All ER 283 at 287, PC. For a case where land was lost to the Crown by application of the principle see *Re Hull and Selby Rly Co* (1839) 5 M & W 327.

3 *Government of the State of Penang v Beng Hong Oon* [1972] AC 425, [1971] 3 All ER 1163, PC.

4 *A-G of Southern Nigeria v John Holt & Co (Liverpool) Ltd* [1915] AC 599 at 612, PC.

5 *A-G v M'Carthy* [1911] 2 IR 260; *Brighton and Hove General Gas Co v Hove Bungalows Ltd* [1924] 1 Ch 372 at 391–393 per Romer J; *Secretary of State for India in Council v Foucar & Co* (1933) 61 LR Ind App 18, PC.

6 *Lopez v Muddun Mohun Thakoor* (1870) 13 Moo Ind App 467, PC.

7 *Brighton and Hove General Gas Co v Hove Bungalows Ltd* [1924] 1 Ch 372; *A-G v Chambers, A-G v Rees* (1859) 4 De G & J 55 at 68–69 ('a rule which applies to a result and not to the manner of its production'). See also *Clarke v Edmonton City* [1929] 4 DLR 1010, Can SC.

8 *Southern Centre of Theosophy Inc v State of South Australia* [1982] AC 706, [1982] 1 All ER 283, PC (accretion caused by wind-blown sand).

9 *Re Hull and Selby Rly Co* (1839) 5 M & W 327; *Southern Centre of Theosophy Inc v State of South Australia* [1982] AC 706, [1982] 1 All ER 283, PC.

10 *Tilbury v Silva* (1890) 45 ChD 98; *Mercer v Denne* [1904] 2 Ch 534 (land added by accretion was held subject to the same custom for fishermen to dry their nets).

11 Bracton's de Legibus Bk 2 Ch 2, 68; *R v Lord Yarborough* (1828) 2 Bli NS 147 (gain of an average of five and a half yards per annum over 26 or 27 years properly held by a jury to be imperceptible); *A-G v M'Carthy* [1911] 2 IR 260 at 277; *Southern Centre of Theosophy Inc v State of South Australia* [1982] AC 706, [1982] 1 All ER 283, PC (observable movement of sand dunes said not to constitute observable movement of a land boundary out to sea so the judge was entitled to conclude movement was imperceptible). The reason for the requirement that the accretion be gradual or imperceptible was said in the latter case to be elusive (at 721 and 291) but it is clear that the distinction is drawn between progressions that justly belong to the riparian owner and large changes or avulsions that should more properly be allocated to his neighbour. If there are gradual and imperceptible accretions to the bank of a river then not only does the additional land accrete to the riparian owner but the boundary in the centre of the stream is automatically adjusted: *Foster v Wright* (1878) 4 CPD 438.

12 *Carlisle Corpn v Graham* (1869) LR 4 Exch 361 at 368. In such a case, the soil under the new tidal river channel remains the property of the original owner, so that if the river reverts to its original course, the soil of the new channel becomes again the exclusive property of that owner: see WATER AND WATERWAYS vol 100 (2009) PARA 71.

13 *Ford v Lacy* (1861) 7 H & N 151; *Thakurain Ritraj Koer v Thakurain Sarfaraz Koer* (1905) 21 TLR 637.

14 See eg *Baxendale v Instow Parish Council* [1982] Ch 14, [1981] 2 All ER 620 (note that in *Southern Centre of Theosophy Inc v State of South Australia* [1982] AC 706, [1982] 1 All ER 283, PC, no opinion was expressed on the correctness or otherwise of this decision). See also *Nesbitt v Mablethorpe UDC* [1918] 2 KB 1, CA.

15 See the Land Registration Act 2002 s 61(1); and LAND REGISTRATION vol 26 (2004 Reissue) PARA 870.

16 See the Land Registration Act 2002 s 61(2); the Land Registration Rules 2003, SI 2003/1417, r 123; and LAND REGISTRATION vol 26 (2004 Reissue) PARA 870.

2. EVIDENCE OF BOUNDARIES

(1) EVIDENCE FROM THE TITLE

330. Primary evidence in the documents of title. Evidence of boundaries differs in kind and in degree. The title deeds of the parties concerned constitute the primary evidence and must be considered first[1]; and the boundaries as indicated in the title deeds prevail if they are clear and unambiguous[2]. The construction of a deed is a matter for the court, but extrinsic evidence may be admissible to assist the court[3]. In the absence of clear evidence in the title deeds, the court may be guided by the applicable presumptions, if any[4]; evidence may be brought to rebut those presumptions[5] but, in the absence of evidence to displace them, those presumptions will apply[6].

As a general rule, where a deed refers to known physical and natural objects by means of which the boundaries of land conveyed are described, and also contains a statement of area, the former controls the latter in case of discrepancy[7]; and if reference is made to some physical object not in existence at the time, and the parties subsequently erect some object intending it to conform to the deed, the boundary indicated by that object is binding upon them, even though it may not actually conform to the line of boundary or to the acreage contained in the deed[8].

1   As to the disclosure of documents see PARA 318 note 10; and CIVIL PROCEDURE vol 11 (2009) PARA 538 et seq.
2   See PARA 304.
3   As to the admissibility of extrinsic evidence see PARA 332. As to the interpretation of deeds generally see DEEDS AND OTHER INSTRUMENTS vol 13 (2007 Reissue) PARA 164 et seq.
4   See PARAS 319–329.
5   *Duke of Beaufort v Swansea Corpn* (1849) 3 Exch 413; *Hale v Norfolk County Council* [2001] Ch 717, [2001] 2 WLR 1481, CA.
6   *Alan Wibberley Building Ltd v Insley* [1999] 2 All ER 897, [1999] 1 WLR 894, HL.
7   *Llewellyn v Earl of Jersey* (1843) 11 M & W 183; *Manning v Fitzgerald* (1859) 29 LJEx 24; *Lyle v Richards* (1866) LR 1 HL 222. See also PARA 304. As to the effect of inaccuracy see PARA 310.
8   See *Taylor v Parry* (1840) 1 Man & G 604. Cf *Hopgood v Brown* [1955] 1 All ER 550, [1955] 1 WLR 213, CA.

331. Conflicting descriptions in the deeds. Generally, all words and parts of a deed conveying property are relevant to the ascertainment of the property's boundaries but where a deed contains a sufficient and ascertained description of the property and also a false description[1], the false description is rejected as surplusage under the maxim *falsa demonstratio non nocet cum de corpore constat*[2]. However, where the principal words of the description lack the certainty necessary for the rejection of the subordinate description as a *falsa demonstratio* and the subordinate description can be read as limiting the principal description, the deed will be construed accordingly[3]. Thus if premises are described in general terms and a particular description is added, the latter controls the former[4].

If the description of the land intended to be conveyed is couched in such ambiguous terms that it is doubtful what were intended to be the boundaries of the land, and the language of the description equally admits of two different constructions, the one of which would make the quantity conveyed agree with the quantity mentioned in the deed, while the other would make the quantity altogether different, the former construction must prevail[5].

1   Eg an inaccurate description of abuttals (*Francis v Hayward* (1882) 22 ChD 177, CA; *Mellor v Walmesley* [1905] 2 Ch 164, CA) or of occupancy (*Wilkinson v Malin* (1832) 2 Cr & J 636); or an inaccurate boundary used on a plan (*Maxted v Plymouth Corpn* (1957) 169 Estates Gazette 427, [1957] CLY 243, CA). The description which is rejected as false need not follow the true description; the whole description must be looked at fairly to see what are the leading words of description and what is the subordinate matter: *Hardwick v Hardwick* (1873) LR 16 Eq 168 at 175 per Lord Selborne LC. See also *Llewellyn v Earl of Jersey* (1843) 11 M & W 183; *Manning v Fitzgerald* (1859) 29 LJEx 24. As to inaccurate descriptions see also DEEDS AND OTHER INSTRUMENTS vol 13 (2007 Reissue) PARA 226 et seq.

2   Ie a false description does not vitiate when the subject matter is clear: see *Jack v McIntyre* (1845) 12 Cl & Fin 151, HL (where boundaries defined were held not to be limited by a specific reference to part of land situated within them); *Anstee v Nelms* (1856) 1 H & N 225 (where the description of the situation was wrong as regards the county, but right as regards the parish and otherwise); *White v Birch* (1867) 36 LJCh 174 (where a wrong description of land as 'in my own occupation' was rejected as *falsa demonstratio*); *Eastwood v Ashton* [1915] AC 900 at 912, HL; but cf *Re Seal, Seal v Taylor* [1894] 1 Ch 316, CA (where the words 'as the same are now occupied by me' in a will were construed as limiting the parcels). See further DEEDS AND OTHER INSTRUMENTS vol 13 (2007 Reissue) PARAS 227–228; and as to the interpretation of deeds generally see DEEDS AND OTHER INSTRUMENTS vol 13 (2007 Reissue) PARA 164 et seq.

3   See *Slingsby v Grainger* (1859) 7 HL Cas 273 at 283 per Lord Chelmsford LC; *Boyle v Mulholland* (1860) 10 ICLR 150.

4   *Doe d Smith v Galloway* (1833) 5 B & Ad 43; *Travers v Blundell* (1877) 6 ChD 436, CA; *Herrick v Sixby* (1867) LR 1 PC 436; *Re Seal, Seal v Taylor* [1894] 1 Ch 316, CA; *Re Brocket, Dawes v Miller* [1908] 1 Ch 185.

5   *Herrick v Sixby* (1867) LR 1 PC 436. The former rule that if a deed contained two conflicting descriptions that which came first in the deed prevailed (see *Dowtie's Case* (1584) 3 Co Rep 9b) does not appear to be the present law (see *Cowen v Truefitt Ltd* [1899] 2 Ch 309, CA; *Eastwood v Ashton* [1915] AC 900, HL), save perhaps in the rare case where the two descriptions are both of sufficient and equal certainty (see eg *Roe v Lidwell* (1859) 11 ICLR 320). See further DEEDS AND OTHER INSTRUMENTS vol 13 (2007 Reissue) PARA 228.

332.   Admissibility of extrinsic evidence.   Extrinsic evidence is admissible of all objective material facts existing at the time of execution of the deed which were reasonably available to the parties at the relevant date, as part and parcel of the process of contextual construction[1]. Extrinsic evidence is not admissible to contradict, vary or add to the terms of a deed[2] but only to put before the court the same knowledge of the subject matter of the deed as was in the possession of the parties to it at the time of its execution[3]. It may also be admitted where the description of the boundaries of a property is too general, contradictory, uncertain or ambiguous[4], and the ambiguity is latent[5]. Thus where the parcels are approximate and a plan is referred to for identification only, the court can look at, and accept, a boundary where it has been physically marked on the ground and agreed by the parties[6]; where a transfer, read as a whole, cannot be reconciled with the line on a small scale plan, the court may admit in evidence auction particulars which clarify where the boundary is meant to be drawn[7]; and where a plan attached to a transfer is entirely unclear, the court may look at all the relevant documentation including replies to preliminary inquiries[8]. Extrinsic evidence has also been admitted in the case of a demise of land by admeasurement 'with the houses now erected or being erected thereon', to show that the foundations of the houses were actually laid at the date of the demise and extended beyond the limits of the boundaries shown on the plan, with the result that the admeasurements and plan were rejected as *falsa demonstratio*[9]. Where the extent of a grant of land is stated in an ambiguous manner in a conveyance or transfer, it is legitimate to interpret the deed by the extent of the user or possession which subsequently proceeded upon it[10], but no amount of user will prevail against the plain meaning of words[11]. Where boundaries depend upon the construction of an ancient grant (that is, a grant dating from beyond the time of living memory) evidence of modern usage may assist[12].

Where an owner divides his land into parts and conveys each part to a different person, the court, in seeking to determine the boundaries defined by one of the conveyances, may admit the other conveyances in evidence to assist in resolving an ambiguity[13].

Where an agreement refers specifically to a plan, oral evidence is admissible to identify the plan referred to, but where there is no clear evidence to show what particular plan was agreed upon and there is no sufficient verbal description of the boundaries, the agreement is void for uncertainty[14]. However, where a plan forms part of a conveyance, for example where it is drawn on or bound up inside the conveyance, the fact that the plan is not referred to in the conveyance does not necessarily oblige the court to disregard the plan[15].

Extrinsic evidence is not admissible to contradict or vary clear descriptions of boundaries. Thus if a deed contains a full description of the land, evidence that a strip of land not included in the description was always occupied by the owner of the land undoubtedly conveyed by the deed is not admissible to contradict the deed[16]. Similarly, if the court is satisfied that the description and plan taken together clearly delimit the boundary, extrinsic evidence to show that the parties agreed the boundary to be other than that shown on the plan is not admissible[17]. Where two leases of adjoining properties were renewed by reference to the same plans as were incorporated in the original leases the parties were held to be bound by the terms of the renewed leases, despite an agreement made prior to the renewal by both tenants and their landlord that a strip of land forming part of the land demised by one of the original leases should be transferred to the other tenant[18].

Where there is no ambiguity in the descriptions contained in a deed, evidence to show that it was intended to convey more than appears in the description does not become admissible merely because a further description is added with which the subject matter clearly intended to be conveyed does not agree[19].

1 See PARA 304.

2 *Smith v Doe d Earl of Jersey* (1821) 2 Brod & Bing 473 at 541, HL, per Park J; *Grigsby v Melville* [1973] 3 All ER 455, [1974] 1 WLR 80, CA; *Scarfe v Adams* [1981] 1 All ER 843, CA. If a deed does not show the true boundary as intended between vendor and purchaser but its terms are clear, then the only remedy is by way of rectification of the transfer: *Scarfe v Adams* [1981] 1 All ER 843 at 851, CA. See also *Berkeley Leisure Group Ltd v Williamson* [1996] EGCS 18, CA; *Horn v Phillips* [2003] EWCA Civ 1877, [2003] All ER (D) 348 (Dec). As to rectification see MISTAKE vol 77 (2010) PARA 57 et seq.

3 *Murly v M'Dermott* (1838) 8 Ad & El 138; *Baird v Fortune* (1861) 4 Macq 127; *Van Diemen's Land Co v Table Cape Marine Board* [1906] AC 92 at 98, PC; *Shannon Ltd v Venner Ltd* [1965] Ch 682, [1965] 1 All ER 590, CA; *Ward v Gold* (1969) 211 Estates Gazette 155; *Willson v Greene (Moss, third party)* [1971] 1 All ER 1098, [1971] 1 WLR 635; *Toplis v Green* [1992] EGCS 20, CA; *Targett and Targett v Ferguson and Diver* (1996) 72 P & CR 106, CA; cf *Doe d Preedy v Holtom* (1835) 4 Ad & El 76. As to the admissibility of extrinsic evidence generally see DEEDS AND OTHER INSTRUMENTS vol 13 (2007 Reissue) PARA 185 et seq; and as to the interpretation of deeds generally see DEEDS AND OTHER INSTRUMENTS vol 13 (2007 Reissue) PARA 164 et seq.

4 *Doe d Gore v Langton* (1831) 2 B & Ad 680 at 691–692 (where property was conveyed with the 'hereditaments thereunto belonging' and extrinsic evidence was admitted to show the boundaries of such hereditaments); *Lord Waterpark v Fennell* (1859) 7 HL Cas 650 (where property was conveyed by name and parol evidence was admitted to connect property with that name); *Lister v Pickford* (1865) 34 Beav 576; *Neilson v Poole* (1969) 20 P & CR 909 (conveyance with plan annexed was uncertain so extrinsic evidence was admitted); *Willson v Greene (Moss, third party)* [1971] 1 All ER 1098, [1971] 1 WLR 635; *Scarfe v Adams* [1981] 1 All ER 843, CA; *Mayer v Hurr* (1983) 49 P & CR 56, CA (the plan on a conveyance was on

too small a scale to show the precise boundary and the colouring on the plan did not accord with the features on the site thus creating an ambiguity); *Haynes v Brassington* [1988] EGCS 100, CA. Cf *Grigsby v Melville* [1973] 3 All ER 455, [1974] 1 WLR 80, CA (as a matter of construction the deed was clear, certain and unambiguous so there was no room for evidence about the inconvenient consequences of the result); *Woolls v Powling* (1999) Times, 9 March, [1999] All ER (D) 125, CA (a plan for the purposes of identification only clearly showed the line of the boundary; extrinsic evidence was inadmissible); and see the text and note 17. See also notes 6–8.

5 *Lyle v Richards* (1866) LR 1 HL 222 at 239 per Lord Westbury; *Goodtitle d Radford v Southern* (1813) 1 M & S 299 at 301.

6 *Willson v Greene (Moss, third party)* [1971] 1 All ER 1098, [1971] 1 WLR 635; *Neilson v Poole* (1969) 20 P & CR 909. Cf *Woolls v Powling* (1999) Times, 9 March, [1999] All ER (D) 125, CA (a plan stated to be 'for purposes of identification only' can be used to determine where a boundary lies, and if a conveyance is then clear as to the position of the boundary line, extrinsic evidence is not admissible).

7 *Scarfe v Adams* [1981] 1 All ER 843, CA.

8 See *Toplis v Green* [1992] EGCS 20, CA.

9 *Manning v Fitzgerald* (1859) 29 LJEx 24. See PARA 331.

10 See PARA 306.

11 *North Eastern Rly Co v Lord Hastings* [1900] AC 260 at 263, HL, per Lord Halsbury LC; *Van Diemen's Land Co v Table Cape Marine Board* [1906] AC 92 at 97, PC.

12 This is in accordance with the wider general rule and the presumption omnia praesumuntur rite esse acta; such evidence can relate to questions such as whether an ancient grant of a manor included the sea coast down to low water mark (*Calmady v Rowe* (1844) 6 CB 861; *Duke of Beaufort v Swansea Corpn* (1849) 3 Exch 413; *A-G v Jones* (1862) 2 H & C 347; *Le Strange v Rowe* (1866) 4 F & F 1048; *A-G for Ireland v Vandeleur* [1907] AC 369, HL), whether the words 'river L' in an ancient patent comprised the riverbed so far or not so far as the sea (*Marquis of Donegall v Lord Templemore* (1858) 9 ICLR 374; *Re Belfast Dock Act 1854, ex p Earl of Ranfurly* (1867) IR 1 Eq 128), and whether a castle was within the boundary of a county hundred (*Duke of Newcastle v Broxtowe Hundred* (1832) 4 B & Ad 273). As to the construction of ancient grants see further CUSTOM AND USAGE.

13 *Neilson v Poole* (1969) 20 P & CR 909; *Druce v Druce* [2002] All ER (D) 234 (Apr); affd [2003] EWCA Civ 535, [2004] 1 P & CR 424, [2003] All ER (D) 122 (Feb).

14 *Hodges v Horsfall* (1829) 1 Russ & M 116.

15 *Leachman v L and K Richardson Ltd* [1969] 3 All ER 20, [1969] 1 WLR 1129, distinguishing *Wyse v Leahy* (1875) IR 9 CL 384. In the case of dealings with only part of the land comprised in a registered title, the instrument must have attached to it a plan signed by the disponor or applicant unless such part is clearly defined on the title plan of the registered title, in which case it may be defined by reference to that title plan: see the Land Registration Rules 2003, SI 2003/1417, r 213; and LAND REGISTRATION.

16 *Barton v Dawes* (1850) 10 CB 261; *Boyle v Mulholland* (1860) 10 ICLR 150; *Webber v Stanley* (1864) 16 CBNS 698 at 752; *Smith v Ridgway* (1866) LR 1 Exch 331; *Pedley v Dodds* (1866) LR 2 Eq 819 (where a devise of a farm 'in the parish of R' was held not to include lands in other parishes previously occupied with the same farm); *Curtis v Chamberlain* (1969) 212 Estates Gazette 277, CA.

17 *Woolls v Powling* (1999) Times, 9 March, [1999] All ER (D) 125, CA.

18 *Curtis v Chamberlain* (1969) 212 Estates Gazette 277, CA.

19 *Goodtitle d Radford v Southern* (1813) 1 M & S 299 at 301; *Dublin and Kingstown Rly Co v Bradford* (1857) 7 ICLR 624; *Doe d Smith v Galloway* (1833) 5 B & Ad 43; *Llewellyn v Earl of Jersey* (1843) 11 M & W 183; *Roe v Lidwell* (1859) 11 ICLR 320; *Doe d Renow v Ashley* (1847) 10 QB 663. See also PARA 331.

(2) PARTICULAR KINDS OF EVIDENCE

(i) Acts of the Parties

333. Agreement for sale. Like other extrinsic evidence, an agreement for the sale of property is admissible in interpreting, but not for the purpose of contradicting, the subsequent conveyance[1]. A contract which includes a draft transfer showing the land to be transferred binds the vendor to convey the property so delineated[2].

Particulars of sale at an auction at which property was sold have been admitted as evidence of boundaries[3] where the conveyance was ambiguous[4], and to rebut the presumption that the ownership of a several fishery in a river carries with it the ownership of the bed of the river[5]. Answers to preliminary inquiries have also been admitted as evidence of boundaries[6].

1   *Willson v Greene (Moss, third party)* [1971] 1 All ER 1098, [1971] 1 WLR 635 (evidence of pre-contract negotiations in respect of a boundary admitted where the parcels in a conveyance were vague and the plan expressed to be for identification purposes only); *Briggs v McCusker* [1996] 2 EGLR 197 at 198; and see PARA 332; and DEEDS AND OTHER INSTRUMENTS. The suggestion in *Williams v Morgan* (1850) 15 QB 782 that an agreement is not evidence for the purpose of proving the boundaries of the property subsequently conveyed by deed, because the agreement is merged in the deed, must now be regarded as wrong. As to the admissibility of an agreement for the purposes of rectification of a deed see MISTAKE vol 77 (2010) PARA 57 et seq.
2   *Seabreeze Properties Ltd v Haw* [1990] EGCS 114 (specific performance ordered of a contract where the draft transfer included a plan with the land 'edged red'; an action to rectify failed).
3   Eg to rebut the presumption relating to hedges and ditches: *Falkingham v Farley* (1991) Times, 11 March, CA.
4   *Scarfe v Adams* [1981] 1 All ER 843, CA. See also PARA 332.
5   *Ecroyd v Coulthard* [1897] 2 Ch 554; affd [1898] 2 Ch 358, CA. As to the principles on which extrinsic evidence is admissible in such circumstances see PARAS 319, 332. As to the presumption see PARA 327.
6   *Toplis v Green* [1992] EGCS 20, CA.

334. Acts of ownership. Evidence of acts of ownership is admissible on an issue as to the title or boundaries to property[1]. Under this rule, evidence has been admitted of such acts as fishing a river or pond[2], felling a tree[3], preventing persons from trespassing[4], maintaining a ditch[5], and perambulation of a manor by the lord, even in the absence of anyone on behalf of the rival claimant[6].

Ancient documents coming from the proper custody[7] and purporting on the face of them to show exercise of ownership, such as leases[8], licences in the nature of leases[9], or documents showing that a person in possession is vindicating that possession against someone else[10], are also admissible under this rule. In the case of a lease the payment of rent is an additional fact equally admissible[11], but proof of such payment is not essential to the lease being admitted[12].

However, such acts of ownership as clipping, trimming and pollarding a hedge or cleaning a ditch, though admissible in evidence, are not conclusive as to the title to the hedge or ditch where the presumption of law is to the contrary[13]. Though acts done upon one part of land within a clearly defined boundary may be evidence of the ownership of the whole land within such boundary[14], where there is a disputed strip of land on a boundary, acts of ownership by either party on land outside the disputed strip are no evidence of title to the land within it[15].

1   *Curzon v Lomax* (1803) 5 Esp 60 (where it was said that to prove a right to the soil, acts of ownership exercised by one party were conclusive evidence against a supposed title from presumptive evidence of boundaries which had never been ascertained by possession); *Stanley v White* (1811) 14 East 332 (evidence of acts of ownership in one part of a belt of trees could be evidence of the same right throughout the whole). See *Jones v Williams* (1837) 2 M & W 326, where the question was whether the middle or one side of a stream was the boundary between two properties, and evidence of acts of ownership was admitted to prove the second proposition; and cf PARA 327. See also *University College, Oxford v Oxford Corpn* (1904) 20 TLR 637. As to acts of ownership see also CIVIL PROCEDURE vol 11 (2009) PARA 1071.
2   *A-G v Emerson* [1891] AC 649, HL; *Duke of Beaufort v John Aird & Co* (1904) 20 TLR 602; *Carlisle Corpn v Graham* (1869) LR 4 Exch 361; *Ecroyd v Coulthard* [1897] 2 Ch 554 (affd [1898] 2 Ch 358, CA). As to the presumption of ownership in such cases see PARAS 326–327.

3 *Doe d Stansbury v Arkwright* (1833) 2 Ad & El 182n; *Lord St Leonards v Ashburner* (1870) 21
   LT 595.
4 *Brew v Haren* (1874) IR 9 CL 29 (affd (1877) IR 11 CL 198); *Neill v Duke of Devonshire*
   (1882) 8 App Cas 135, HL.
5 *Hall v Dorling* (1996) 74 P & CR 400, CA.
6 *Woolway v Rowe* (1834) 1 Ad & El 114. Perambulation was, in former times, one of the ways
   of ascertaining and preserving not only public boundaries, such as those of parishes, towns,
   counties and forests, but also quasi-private boundaries, eg of seigniories, lordships and manors.
   A perambulation of a hundred was not usual; but there was no reason why a hundred, as well as
   a parish or manor, should not thus have its bounds ascertained: *Lord Chesterfield v Harris*
   [1908] 2 Ch 397 at 407, CA, per Cozens-Hardy MR. See Vin Abr Perambulation. As to parish
   boundary perambulations see *Weeks v Sparke* (1813) 1 M & S 679 at 687, 689; *Taylor v Devey*
   (1837) 7 Ad & El 409. As to perambulations see CUSTOM AND USAGE vol 12(1) (Reissue) PARA
   640. As to the boundaries of ecclesiastical parishes see ECCLESIASTICAL LAW vol 14 PARA 534 et
   seq; and as to the boundaries of parishes as units of local government see LOCAL GOVERNMENT
   vol 69 (2009) PARAS 27 et seq, 70 et seq. It is not clear whether the perambulation of a private
   estate was ever made.
7 As to the presumption of the authenticity of a document more than 20 years old produced from
   proper custody see *Doe d Oldham v Wolley* (1828) 8 B & C 22; and CIVIL PROCEDURE vol 11
   (2009) PARA 869. See also PARA 338.
8 *Malcolmson v O'Dea* (1863) 10 HL Cas 593; *Bristow v Cormican* (1878) 3 App Cas 641 at
   653, HL (boundaries of a private fishery); *Duke of Beaufort v John Aird & Co* (1904) 20 TLR
   602; *Prudential Assurance Co Ltd v Waterloo Real Estate Inc* [1999] 2 EGLR 85, CA.
9 *Rogers v Allen* (1808) 1 Camp 309; *Malcolmson v O'Dea* (1863) 10 HL Cas 593.
10 *Blandy-Jenkins v Earl of Dunraven* [1899] 2 Ch 121 at 125, CA. As to the value of acts of
   ownership in support of ancient documents see also *Hastings Corpn v Ivall* (1874) LR 19 Eq
   558; *Bristow v Cormican* (1878) 3 App Cas 641, HL; *Lord Advocate v Lord Blantyre* (1879) 4
   App Cas 770 at 791, HL (where the title to the foreshore was evidenced partly by grant and
   partly from acts of ownership); *Neill v Duke of Devonshire* (1882) 8 App Cas 135, HL (where
   possession of a fishery was evidenced by the production of, inter alia, a report of certain ancient
   proceedings in court in a possessory action).
11 *Bristow v Cormican* (1878) 3 App Cas 641, HL.
12 *Malcolmson v O'Dea* (1863) 10 HL Cas 593.
13 *Henniker v Howard* (1904) 90 LT 157, DC; *Earl of Craven v Pridmore* (1902) 18 TLR
   282, CA. See also *Simcox v Yardley RDC* (1905) 69 JP 66; *Minting v Ramage* [1991] EGCS
   12, CA. As to the presumptions of law see PARAS 321–322.
14 *Neill v Duke of Devonshire* (1882) 8 App Cas 135, HL; *Hanbury v Jenkins* [1901] 2 Ch 401 at
   417. The erection and maintenance of piles on a portion of a foreshore is an act of ownership
   only as regards the particular portion of the foreshore upon which the piles stand: *Duke of
   Beaufort v John Aird & Co* (1904) 20 TLR 602 at 603.
15 *Clark v Elphinstone* (1880) 6 App Cas 164, PC (latent ambiguity in description of boundary).
   Cf *Doe d Barrett v Kemp* (1831) 7 Bing 332; *Tutill v West Ham Board of Health* (1873) LR 8
   CP 447; *Leeke v Portsmouth Corpn* (1912) 107 LT 260.

(ii) Hearsay Evidence

335. The principle of admissibility. The Civil Evidence Act 1995 provides
that in civil proceedings[1] evidence must not be excluded on the ground that it is
hearsay[2]. This principle means that many of the former difficulties in bringing
evidence of historic boundaries where the deeds are not clear have been
resolved[3].

A party wishing to adduce hearsay evidence in a boundary dispute must give
to the other party such notice of that fact and, on request, such particulars
relating to the evidence as is reasonable and practicable in the circumstances for
the purpose of enabling any matters arising from its being hearsay to be dealt
with[4]. It is for the court to estimate the weight to be given to the hearsay
evidence, having regard to any circumstances from which any inference can
reasonably be drawn as to the reliability or otherwise of the evidence[5].

1   For these purposes, 'civil proceedings' means civil proceedings, before any tribunal, in relation
     to which the strict rules of evidence apply, whether as a matter of law or by agreement of the
     parties: see the Civil Evidence Act 1995 s 11; and CIVIL PROCEDURE vol 11 (2009) PARA 808.
2   See the Civil Evidence Act 1995 s 1(1); and CIVIL PROCEDURE vol 11 (2009) PARA 808. 'Hearsay'
     means a statement made otherwise than by a person while giving oral evidence in the
     proceedings which is tendered as evidence of the matters stated: see s 1(2)(a); and CIVIL
     PROCEDURE vol 11 (2009) PARA 808.
3   See further CIVIL PROCEDURE.
4   See the Civil Evidence Act 1995 s 2(1); and CIVIL PROCEDURE vol 11 (2009) PARA 811.
5   See the Civil Evidence Act 1995 s 4(1); and CIVIL PROCEDURE vol 11 (2009) PARA 815. As to the
     matters to which the court is to have particular regard in weighing the evidence see s 4(2); and
     CIVIL PROCEDURE vol 11 (2009) PARA 815.

336.   Evidence formerly admissible at common law.   The common law
exceptions to the rule against the admissibility of hearsay evidence in civil
proceedings were effectively preserved by the Civil Evidence Act 1968[1]. Though
the common law rule relating to the admissibility of admissions adverse to a
party has been superseded[2], the Civil Evidence Act 1995 provides that other
common law rules relating to admissibility are to continue to have effect[3] and are
not altered but only identified and preserved by the statutory provisions[4].

1   See the Civil Evidence Act 1968 s 9(1), (2) (repealed).
2   See the Civil Evidence Act 1995 s 7(1); and CIVIL PROCEDURE vol 11 (2009) PARAS 819, 825.
3   See the Civil Evidence Act 1995 s 7(2), (3); and CIVIL PROCEDURE vol 11 (2009) PARAS 820–823.
4   See the Civil Evidence Act 1995 s 7(4); and CIVIL PROCEDURE vol 11 (2009) PARA 820. As to the
     preserved common law rules as they relate to boundaries see PARAS 337–340.
        In many cases, such as statements from public documents, the evidence will also be
     admissible under the provisions and procedures of the Civil Evidence Act 1995 itself (see e g s 9;
     and PARA 339), but the advantage of admission under the preserved common law rules is that
     the notice and weighting provisions (ie ss 2, 4: see PARA 335) do not apply.

337.   Published works.   Under the preserved common law rule[1], published
works dealing with matters of a public nature (for example, histories, scientific
works, dictionaries and maps) are admissible in civil proceedings[2] as evidence of
facts of a public nature stated in them[3]. Thus standard atlases and maps may be
used to prove facts of public knowledge[4].
    An Ordnance Survey map to which no reference is made in the title deeds[5] is
not admissible[6] to show the boundary of a parish[7] or the boundary between the
lands of adjoining owners[8], because when power was conferred to complete the
Ordnance Survey of Great Britain it was expressly provided that this power was
not to extend to the ascertaining or alteration of local or private boundaries and
that titles to land were not to be affected[9]. However, an Ordnance Survey map
may be received in evidence[10] to show the position of the median line of a river[11]
or of some physical object existing at the time the map was made[12], such as the
existence or otherwise of a track across land[13].
    A county history giving the boundaries of a county was not admissible under
the common law rule as evidence of the boundaries of a manor even though they
were admittedly coterminous in part with the boundaries of the county[14].
    A book of general history may be given in evidence to ascertain ancient facts
of a public nature[15] but not particular customs or private rights[16].

1   As to the preservation of the common law rule see note 3; and PARA 336.
2   As to the meaning of 'civil proceedings' see PARA 335 note 1.
3   See the Civil Evidence Act 1995 s 7(2)(a); and CIVIL PROCEDURE vol 11 (2009) PARA 820.
     Section 7(2)(a) provides that the common law rule effectively preserved by the Civil Evidence
     Act 1968 s 9(1), (2)(b) (repealed) is to continue to have effect after the repeal of that Act. See
     also PARA 336; and CIVIL PROCEDURE.

4 In *R v Orton* (1874) Stephen's Digest of the Law of Evidence (12th Edn) p 56, maps of Australia were given in evidence to show the situation of places where the defendant said he had lived. In *Birrell v Dryer* (1884) 9 App Cas 345 at 352, HL, per Lord Blackburn, the court accepted an Admiralty chart as evidence. As to maps and plans as evidence see further PARA 342.

5 See *Wakeman v West* (1836) 7 C & P 479 (old leases produced from bishop's registry read in evidence but an old map produced from the same custody but not referred to therein was not admissible under the common law rule). See, however, PARA 335. See also *Plaxton v Dare* (1829) 10 B & C 17 (ancient leases admissible as evidence of a parish boundary).

6 Ie under the preserved common law rule: see the text and notes 1–3. Nor is it admissible under the preserved common law rules relating to public documents (see PARA 338) or evidence of reputation (see PARA 340). See, however, PARA 335.

7 *Bidder v Bridges* (1885) 54 LT 529.

8 *Tisdall v Parnell* (1863) 14 ICLR 1 at 27–28; *Coleman v Kirkaldy* [1882] WN 103. See *Swift v M'Tiernan* (1848) 11 I Eq R 602; *Mercer v Denne* [1905] 2 Ch 538, CA.

9 See the Ordnance Survey Act 1841 s 12; PARA 308; and NATIONAL CULTURAL HERITAGE vol 77 (2010) PARA 1117. As to Ordnance Survey maps as evidence see further NATIONAL CULTURAL HERITAGE vol 77 (2010) PARA 1111.

10 Ie under the Civil Evidence Act 1995 s 7(2)(a): see the text and note 3.

11 *Great Torrington Commons Conservators v Moore Stevens* [1904] 1 Ch 347.

12 *A-G and Croydon RDC v Moorsom-Roberts* (1908) 72 JP 123; *Caton v Hamilton* (1889) 53 JP 504.

13 *A-G v Antrobus* [1905] 2 Ch 188 at 203; *A-G v Meyrick and Jones* (1915) 79 JP 515; *Minting v Ramage* [1991] EGCS 12, CA (1838 tithe map admitted to determine whether a highway then existed across a common).

14 *Evans v Getting* (1834) 6 C & P 586; *White and Jackson v Beard* (1839) 2 Curt 480 at 487, 492.

15 *Read v Bishop of Lincoln* [1892] AC 644, PC. See also *White and Jackson v Beard* (1839) 2 Curt 480 at 492 (boundaries of a parish).

16 *Evans v Getting* (1834) 6 C & P 586 at 587n. See also CIVIL PROCEDURE vol 11 (2009) PARA 941.

338. Public documents. Public documents[1] (for example, public registers and returns made under public authority with respect to matters of public interest) are admissible in civil proceedings[2] as evidence of facts stated in them[3]. The extent to which statements in public documents are admissible to prove any particular facts stated depends on the nature of the document and the objects for which it was drawn up.

The Domesday Book is a record of a public inquisition or survey, and therefore admissible as evidence of boundaries[4].

A Crown survey, if made under proper authority, as, for example, pursuant to an Act of Parliament, with the intent that it should be open to public inspection, and produced from the records of the court or other proper custody, is also admissible as a public document in questions of boundary[5], even where the commission under which it was made is lost, provided that there is evidence that the survey was made under due authority[6].

Surveys which are not made under proper authority[7] or with the intent that they should be open to public inspection[8] are treated merely as private memorials and are not admissible in evidence as public documents[9]. This rule applies to surveys made on behalf of the Crown when it is beneficially interested[10].

Tithe commutation maps are public documents[11] and are admissible in evidence provided that: (1) the question to be determined is one relating to public or general rights as opposed to private rights[12]; and (2) the matter of fact sought to be determined is one within the duty of the commissioners or valuers who prepared them[13]. Inclosure awards[14] are similarly admissible[15] and may be particularly valuable on the issue of the boundaries of highways laid out under or by virtue of such awards.

Entries in the court rolls of manorial courts are also public documents[16] and the contents may be admissible as such as evidence of any fact stated therein, though such evidence was not always usable by the lord in proof of the boundaries of his manor[17].

Documents not less than 20 years old, produced from proper custody, are presumed to be validly executed or published[18].

1   As to the meaning of 'public document' see *Sturla v Freccia* (1880) 5 App Cas 623 at 643, HL, per Lord Blackburn ('a public document ... is made for the purpose of the public making use of it and being able to refer to it'). See also *Thrasyvoulos Ioannou v Papa Christoforos Demetriou* [1952] AC 84 at 94, [1952] 1 All ER 179 at 185–186, PC; *R v Sealby* [1965] 1 All ER 701.

2   As to the meaning of 'civil proceedings' see PARA 335 note 1.

3   See the Civil Evidence Act 1995 s 7(2)(b); and CIVIL PROCEDURE vol 11 (2009) PARA 821. Section 7(2)(b) provides that the common law rule effectively preserved by the Civil Evidence Act 1968 s 9(1), (2)(c) (repealed) is to continue to have effect after the repeal of that Act. See also PARA 336; and CIVIL PROCEDURE. For details of the rule relating to public documents see *Irish Society v Bishop of Derry* (1846) 12 Cl & Fin 641, HL; *Sturla v Freccia* (1880) 5 App Cas 623, HL; and CIVIL PROCEDURE vol 11 (2009) PARA 902 et seq.

4   The Domesday Book was compiled by royal commissioners shortly after the Norman conquest. It contains a general survey of most of the counties in England, and specifies the name and local position of every place, its possessor at the time of King Edward the Confessor and at the time of the survey, together with particulars, quantities and descriptions of the land. Its value as evidence is obviously limited by the difficulty usually experienced of applying the ancient descriptions to modern circumstances. In *Alcock v Cooke* (1829) 5 Bing 340 and *Duke of Beaufort v John Aird & Co* (1904) 20 TLR 602, extracts from the Domesday Book were given in evidence.

5   *Evans v Merthyr Tydfil UDC* [1899] 1 Ch 241, CA (where the survey was made in discharge of a public duty imposed by statute). See *Doe d William IV v Roberts* (1844) 13 M & W 520 (ancient survey of extent of Crown lands); *New Romney Corpn v New Romney Sewers Comrs* [1892] 1 QB 840, CA (map made under the authority of a royal commission).

6   *Rowe v Brenton* (1828) 8 B & C 737 at 747. See *Smith v Earl Brownlow* (1870) LR 9 Eq 241 at 252. See also the Civil Evidence Act 1995 s 8; and CIVIL PROCEDURE vol 11 (2009) PARA 816.

7   *Evans v Taylor* (1838) 7 Ad & El 617 (where a survey of the boundaries of a manor purporting to be made under the statute Extenta Manerii (temp incert), which gave no power to define boundaries of manors, was held not to be admissible as evidence of a boundary, either as a public document or on the ground of reputation); *Mercer v Denne* [1905] 2 Ch 538, CA (where a map in the possession of the Admiralty, not being an Admiralty chart, was held not to be admissible).

8   *Thrasyvoulos Ioannou v Papa Christoforos Demetriou* [1952] AC 84, [1952] 1 All ER 179, PC.

9   Vin Abr Evidence A b 15, s 12; *Daniel v Wilkin* (1852) 7 Exch 429; *White v Taylor* [1969] 1 Ch 150, [1967] 3 All ER 349. They may be admissible by applying the general principle (see PARA 335) or on other common law grounds, eg as evidence of reputation (see *Freeman v Read* (1863) 4 B & S 174, where a parliamentary survey made in the time of the Commonwealth was admitted as good evidence; and PARA 340) or records (see *Mellor v Walmesley* [1905] 2 Ch 164, CA; and PARA 339).

10 *Phillips v Hudson* (1867) 2 Ch App 243 (survey made by Augmentation Office for the purposes of the Crown as a private owner); *Mercer v Denne* [1905] 2 Ch 538, CA. Cf *Evans v Merthyr Tydfil UDC* [1899] 1 Ch 241, CA, where a surveyor's report made under 34 Geo 3 c 75 (1794) s 8 (repealed) (an Act for the Better Management of the Land Revenue of the Crown) was held to be a public document and admissible in evidence.

11 *Giffard v Williams* (1869) as reported in 38 LJCh 597 at 604; revsd on other grounds (1870) 5 Ch App 546. The actual admission of the tithe map as evidence of private title in that case appears to have been wrong: see *Wilberforce v Hearfield* (1877) 5 ChD 709. Tithe maps are either first class, that is, identified by the Tithe Commissioner's seal, or second class, which indicates that there was some failure to satisfy all the stringent requirements. Both have been admitted in evidence: *Smith v Lister* (1895) 64 LJQB 154; *A-G v Antrobus* [1905] 2 Ch 188 at 193–194.

12 *Knight v David* [1971] 3 All ER 1066, [1971] 1 WLR 1671; *Wilberforce v Hearfield* (1877) 5 ChD 709; *Frost v Richardson* (1910) 103 LT 22 (affd 103 LT 416, CA). In *Smith v Lister* (1895) 64 LJQB 154, such a map was received in evidence as to the waste of a manor. Cf *Hammond v Bradstreet* (1854) 10 Exch 390 at 395. The provision in the Tithe Act 1836 s 64 (now spent) for such maps and confirmed apportionments to be satisfactory, ie conclusive, evidence was limited

to their being satisfactory or conclusive for the purposes of that Act and was not intended to make them evidence of boundaries between private estates (*Wilberforce v Hearfield* (1877) 5 ChD 709) or even of public rights of way (*Copestake v West Sussex County Council* [1911] 2 Ch 331 at 341; *Stoney v Eastbourne RDC* [1927] 1 Ch 367 at 395–397, 407–408, CA, explaining *A-G v Antrobus* [1905] 2 Ch 188 at 193–194); *Kent County Council v Loughlin* (1975) 119 Sol Jo 528, CA (tithe map was treated as of great value and importance in determining whether a lane was a private street or a highway).

13 *Knight v David* [1971] 3 All ER 1066, [1971] 1 WLR 1671 (ascertainment of proprietorship held to be within the duty of the commissioners who prepared a tithe commutation map and the map held to be admissible at common law as a statement relating to public rights).

14 Ie made under the Inclosure Act 1801, the Inclosure Act 1845 or by virtue of a private or local Act: see COMMONS vol 13 (2009) PARA 418 et seq.

15 *A-G v Antrobus* [1905] 2 Ch 188 at 193; *Roberts v Webster* (1967) 66 LGR 298; *Fisons Horticulture Ltd v Bunting* (1976) 240 Estates Gazette 625.

16 See the Law of Property Act 1922 s 144A; the Manorial Documents Rules 1959, SI 1959/1399; and CUSTOM AND USAGE vol 12(1) (Reissue) PARA 701.

17 *Irwin v Simpson* (1758) 7 Bro Parl Cas 306; *Standen v Chrismas* (1847) 10 QB 135. Such documents may be admissible by applying the general principle (see PARA 335) or as acts or assertions of ownership (see PARA 334) or as evidence of reputation (see PARA 340): *Roe d Beebee v Parker* (1792) 5 Term Rep 26; *Evans v Rees* (1839) 10 Ad & El 151; *Richards v Bassett* (1830) 10 B & C 657; *Coote v Ford* (1900) 17 TLR 58.

18 See the Evidence Act 1938 s 4; and CIVIL PROCEDURE vol 11 (2009) PARA 869.

339. Records. Many documents which may assist in determining boundaries may be admissible by virtue of the Civil Evidence Act 1995, which provides that a document[1] which is shown to form part of the records[2] of a business[3] or public authority[4] may be received in evidence without further proof[5]. For a document to be taken to form part of the records of a business or public authority, a certificate to that effect signed by an officer[6] of the business or authority to which the records belong must be produced to the court[7].

Under the preserved common law rule[8], certain records (for example, the records of certain courts, treaties, Crown grants, pardons and commissions) are admissible in civil proceedings[9] as evidence of facts stated in them[10]. Thus extracts from former land tax or poor rate assessments, which are evidence of seisin, are admissible in boundary questions[11].

1 For these purposes, 'document' means anything in which information of any kind is recorded: Civil Evidence Act 1995 s 13.

2 For these purposes, 'records' means records in whatever form: Civil Evidence Act 1995 s 9(4). For the purposes of the Civil Evidence Act 1968 s 4 (repealed), it was held that records are those which a historian would regard as primary sources, that is, documents which either give effect to a transaction itself or which contain a contemporaneous register of information supplied by those with a direct knowledge of the facts: *H v Schering Chemicals Ltd* [1983] 1 All ER 849 at 852, [1983] 1 WLR 143 at 146 per Bingham J (summaries of research were not records). See also *Re Koscot Interplanetary (UK) Ltd, Re Koscot AG* [1972] 3 All ER 829 (a compilation of the results of legal proceedings is probably not a record); *Savings and Investment Bank Ltd v Gasco Investments (Netherlands) BV* [1984] 1 All ER 296, [1984] 1 WLR 271 (a statutory report containing a selection of evidence and expressing opinion in comments and conclusions was not a record); *R v Governor of Pentonville Prison, ex p Osman* [1989] 3 All ER 701, [1990] 1 WLR 277 (all documents giving effect to a transaction were part of the record of it); *Re D (A Minor) (Wardship: Evidence)* [1986] 2 FLR 189 (notes taken by a solicitor to assist in the preparation of pleadings were not a record).

3 For these purposes, 'business' includes any activity regularly carried on over a period of time, whether for profit or not, by any body (whether corporate or not) or by an individual: Civil Evidence Act 1995 s 9(4).

4 For these purposes, 'public authority' includes any public or statutory undertaking, any government department and any person holding office under Her Majesty: Civil Evidence Act 1995 s 9(4).

5 See the Civil Evidence Act 1995 s 9(1); and CIVIL PROCEDURE vol 11 (2009) PARA 817. The court must estimate the weight to be given to such records in accordance with s 4: see PARA 335.

The court may, having regard to the circumstances of the case, direct that all or any of the provisions of s 9 do not apply in relation to a particular document or record: s 9(5). This power is likely to be relevant where the court has doubts about the reliability of the record.

6   For these purposes, 'officer' includes any person occupying a responsible position in relation to the relevant activities of the business or public authority or in relation to its records: Civil Evidence Act 1995 s 9(4).
7   See the Civil Evidence Act 1995 s 9(2); and CIVIL PROCEDURE vol 11 (2009) PARA 817.
8   As to the preservation of the common law rule see note 10; and PARA 336.
9   As to the meaning of 'civil proceedings' see PARA 335 note 1.
10 See the Civil Evidence Act 1995 s 7(2)(c); and CIVIL PROCEDURE vol 11 (2009) PARA 822. Section 7(2)(c) provides that the common law rule effectively preserved by the Civil Evidence Act 1968 s 9(1), (2)(d) (repealed) is to continue to have effect after the repeal of that Act. See also PARA 336; and CIVIL PROCEDURE.

11 *Doe d Smith v Cartwright* (1824) 1 C & P 218; *Plaxton v Dare* (1829) 10 B & C 17 (old rates made by parish officers on the occupiers of the land in question); *Doe d Stansbury v Arkwright* (1833) 2 Ad & El 182n; *Doe d Strode v Seaton* (1834) 2 Ad & El 171; *Anstee v Nelms* (1856) 1 H & N 225 at 232–233. See also *Swift v M'Tiernan* (1848) 11 I Eq R 602.

340.   Reputation.   Evidence of reputation[1], that is to say, of the common or general attribution to a person or thing of a particular feature, may be oral or documentary, so that deeds, leases and other private documents may be admitted as declaratory of their contents; and the evidence need not necessarily be supported by usage[2].

Under the preserved common law rule[3], evidence of reputation or family tradition is admissible in civil proceedings[4] for the purpose of proving or disproving the existence of any public[5] or general right or of identifying any person or thing[6]. Cases where the common law rule has been held to apply include those where the question related to the boundaries of a town[7], parish[8] or manor[9] or to the boundaries between counties, parishes, hamlets or manors[10], or between a reputed manor and land belonging to a private individual[11] or between old and new land in a manor[12].

General reputation may be admissible in proof of identification[13]. Thus the general repute existing in a testator's family or neighbourhood has been received to identify the subject matter of a demise[14].

At common law[15], evidence of reputation is inadmissible both as to particular facts as opposed to general rights[16] and in cases of a private nature[17], for example as to the boundaries between two private properties, except where the private boundaries coincide with public ones[18].

Where evidence of reputation is admissible, a private map made by a person having means of knowledge who has since died is admissible as such evidence, provided that the map is found in the proper custody and proof of the death of the maker of the map is furnished[19].

1   'Reputation is in general weak evidence and, when it is admitted, it is the duty of the judge to impress on the minds of the jury how little conclusive it ought to be': *Weeks v Sparke* (1813) 1 M & S 679 at 687 per Lord Ellenborough CJ; but the rationale of receiving such evidence is that it may be the only evidence of the line of ancient boundaries. As to evidence of reputation see further *R v Bedfordshire Inhabitants* (1855) 4 E & B 535 at 541 per Lord Campbell CJ; *Morewood v Wood* (1791) 14 East 327 at 330; and CIVIL PROCEDURE vol 11 (2009) PARA 827 et seq.
2   *Crease v Barrett* (1835) 1 Cr M & R 919. See also CIVIL PROCEDURE.
3   As to the preservation of the common law rule see note 6; and PARA 336.
4   As to the meaning of 'civil proceedings' see PARA 335 note 1.

5   The word 'public' in this context was explained in *Mercer v Denne* [1905] 2 Ch 538 at 560, CA, per Vaughan Williams LJ. See also *Evans v Merthyr Tydfil UDC* [1899] 1 Ch 241, CA; *Knight v David* [1971] 3 All ER 1066, [1971] 1 WLR 1671.

6 See the Civil Evidence Act 1995 s 7(3)(b)(ii); and CIVIL PROCEDURE vol 11 (2009) PARA 827. Section 7(3) provides that the common law rules effectively preserved by the Civil Evidence Act 1968 s 9(3), (4) (repealed) are to continue to have effect after the repeal of that Act. See also PARA 336; and CIVIL PROCEDURE.

7 *Ireland v Powell* (1802) cited 7 Ad & El at 555 (where the question was whether a turnpike was within the boundary of a town); *R v Bliss* (1837) 7 Ad & El 550.

8 *R v Mytton* (1860) 2 E & E 557. See also *Coombs v Coether and Wheeler* (1829) Mood & M 398; *Cooke v Banks* (1826) 2 C & P 478; *Plaxton v Dare* (1829) 10 B & C 17.

9 *Doe d Jones v Richards* (1798) Peake Add Cas 180; *Talbot v Lewis* (1834) 6 C & P 603; *Doe d Padwick v Skinner* (1848) 3 Exch 84.

10 *Nicholls v Parker* (1805) 14 East 331n (boundaries of common; whether in parish and manor of A or parish and manor of B); *Thomas v Jenkins* (1837) 6 Ad & El 525; *Brisco v Lomax* (1838) 8 Ad & El 198 at 213 (boundaries of hamlet and private estate identical); *Evans v Rees* (1839) 10 Ad & El 151 (boundaries between parishes and counties).

11 *Doe d Molesworth v Sleeman* (1846) 9 QB 298, where declarations made by a person who had since died were admitted as to boundaries. As to declarations made by persons who have since died see PARA 341. See also *Curzon v Lomax* (1803) 5 Esp 60, where it was said that the right to the soil was evidenced by acts of ownership exercised on it, not by presumptive evidence of property arising from supposed boundaries the rights to which had never been ascertained by possession. As to acts of ownership see PARA 334.

12 *Barnes v Mawson* (1813) 1 M & S 77 at 81 per Lord Ellenborough CJ.

13 See the Civil Evidence Act 1995 s 7(3)(b)(ii); and CIVIL PROCEDURE vol 11 (2009) PARA 827.

14 *Anstee v Nelms* (1856) 1 H & N 225.

15 As to the admissibility of hearsay evidence under the Civil Evidence Act 1995 s 1 see PARA 335; and CIVIL PROCEDURE vol 11 (2009) PARA 808.

16 *Outram v Morewood* (1793) 5 Term Rep 121 at 123 per Lord Kenyon CJ ('although a general right may be proved by traditional evidence, yet a particular fact cannot'). Thus evidence is inadmissible to prove that a person, who has since died, planted a tree near a road and stated at the time of planting that his object was to show where the boundary of the road was when he was a boy (*R v Bliss* (1837) 7 Ad & El 550; and see *R v Berger* [1894] 1 QB 823, DC), or that a stone was erected as a boundary mark at a particular place (*R v Bliss* (1837) 7 Ad & El 550), or that perambulations had taken a particular line (*Taylor v Devey* (1837) 7 Ad & El 409). See also *Mercer v Denne* [1905] 2 Ch 538, CA. As to perambulations and other acts of ownership see PARA 334.

17 See the Civil Evidence Act 1995 s 7(3)(b)(ii); and CIVIL PROCEDURE vol 11 (2009) PARA 827. See also *R v Bedfordshire Inhabitants* (1855) 4 E & B 535 at 542.

18 *Thomas v Jenkins* (1837) 6 Ad & El 525; *Brisco v Lomax* (1838) 8 Ad & El 198 at 213. See also *R v Bliss* (1837) 7 Ad & El 550 at 554 (boundary of a road).

19 *Bishop of Meath v Marquess of Winchester* (1836) 3 Bing NC 183 at 200; *R v Milton Inhabitants* (1843) 1 Car & Kir 58. See also *Pipe v Fulcher* (1858) 1 E & E 111; *Pollard v Scott* (1790) Peake 18 (cases where private maps were held inadmissible) and *Vyner v Wirral RDC* (1909) 73 JP 242. As to the admissibility in evidence of maps generally see PARA 342.

341. Declarations by persons who have since died. Declarations made by persons who have since died are admissible evidence in two specific situations[1]: (1) where the declaration was made in the course of a duty or professional business if consisting of matters or facts within the deceased's personal knowledge and made at the time of the fact recorded[2]; and (2) where the declaration concerns public or general rights and interests, provided that it was made before any dispute or controversy arose[3].

1 As to the admissibility of hearsay evidence generally see the Civil Evidence Act 1995 s 1; PARA 335; and CIVIL PROCEDURE vol 11 (2009) PARA 808.

2 *Price v Earl of Torrington* (1703) 1 Salk 285; *Mellor v Walmesley* [1905] 2 Ch 164, CA (professional land surveyor's field book notes taken during a drainage survey were admissible); *Mercer v Denne* [1905] 2 Ch 538, CA (records of an old survey inadmissible as there was nothing to show that they were made contemporaneously with the doing of something which it was the duty of the official to record); *White v Taylor* [1969] 1 Ch 150, [1967] 3 All ER 349 (draft report by a valuer made under the Tithe Act 1836 inadmissible because he had no direct knowledge of the matters recorded).

3   *Brisco v Lomax* (1838) 8 Ad & El 198 at 213 (boundaries of hamlet and private estate); *Evans v Rees* (1839) 10 Ad & El 151 (boundaries between parishes and counties). The rights must affect a class or group of people: *R v Bedfordshire Inhabitants* (1855) 4 E & B 535 at 541. See also *Evans v Merthyr Tydfil UDC* [1899] 1 Ch 241, CA (evidence admissible as to whether a piece of land was a common); *White v Taylor* [1969] 1 Ch 150, [1967] 3 All ER 349 (draft under the Tithe Act 1836 related to individual and not general rights).

(iii) Other Documentary Evidence

342.   Maps and plans. The general rule at common law as regards maps and surveys was that they were not receivable in evidence in the strict sense of the word either for or against the parties making them[1]. However, under the Civil Evidence Act 1995 many maps and plans may be admissible in evidence, particularly if they qualify as records held by public authorities[2]. They may also be admissible under the preserved common law rules[3], as published works dealing with matters of a public nature[4], as public documents[5], or as evidence of reputation[6]. As between two adjoining proprietors a private map is admissible in a dispute as to boundaries if, at the time the map was made, the two adjoining properties belonged to the person from whom both parties derive their respective titles[7].

A map annexed to a deed is part of the deed, and as a rule must be used as evidence of the parcels[8]. Where the connection is clear, the map need not be actually annexed to the deed to which it refers[9]; nor in all circumstances need it be referred to in the deed itself[10].

An inaccurate map does not affect or vitiate clear descriptions of parcels[11] but under certain circumstances a map or survey may override a verbal description of parcels[12].

On the extinguishment of manorial incidents under the Law of Property Act 1922[13], any plan made or approved by the Minister of Agriculture and Fisheries[14] and any definition of boundaries by him was conclusive as between the lord of the manor and the tenant[15], but it would not, it seems, be conclusive as to the boundaries before the date of determination[16].

Although a map attached to an award under an Inclosure Act[17] is evidence as to whether a road is a highway or not, it is not evidence of the boundaries of the highway where the strip of land bordering the highway is not dealt with in the award[18].

1   *Anon* (1718) 1 Stra 95; *Wilkinson v Allott* (1777) 3 Bro Parl Cas 684 (boundaries of glebe lands); *Pollard v Scott* (1790) Peake 18 (map taken by parish overseers no evidence as to boundary of a highway, and plan made by the lord of manor not usable as against tenants of the manor); *Wakeman v West* (1836) 7 C & P 479; *Phillips v Hudson* (1867) 2 Ch App 243 at 247 (where it was held that the tenant of a manor could not use against the lord a plan made by the lord). As to maps and surveys see also PARAS 337–338; and as to Ordnance Survey maps see PARAS 308, 337.
2   See the Civil Evidence Act 1995 s 9; PARA 339; and CIVIL PROCEDURE vol 11 (2009) PARA 817.
3   As to the preservation of the common law rules see PARA 336.
4   See the Civil Evidence Act 1995 s 7(2)(a); PARA 337; and CIVIL PROCEDURE vol 11 (2009) PARA 820.
5   See the Civil Evidence Act 1995 s 7(2)(b); PARA 338; and CIVIL PROCEDURE vol 11 (2009) PARA 821.
6   See the Civil Evidence Act 1995 s 7(3)(b)(ii); PARA 340; and CIVIL PROCEDURE vol 11 (2009) PARA 827.
7   *Doe d Hughes v Lakin* (1836) 7 C & P 481; *Neilson v Poole* (1969) 20 P & CR 909.
8   *Wakeman v West* (1836) 7 C & P 479; *Lyle v Richards* (1866) LR 1 HL 222; cf *Fraser v Anderson* 1951 SLT 51, Sh Ct. As to the use of plans for the description of parcels see *Re Sansom and Narbeth's Contract* [1910] 1 Ch 741; *Re Sparrow and James' Contract* (1902)

[1910] 2 Ch 60; *Re Sharman and Meade's Contract* [1936] Ch 755, [1936] 2 All ER 1547. See also DEEDS AND OTHER INSTRUMENTS; SALE OF LAND.

9   *Yates v Harris* (1702) 1 Stra 95n (old map found with muniments of title which agreed with the boundaries adjusted on an old purchase). As to the admissibility of extrinsic evidence to link the two see PARA 332.

10 *Leachman v L and K Richardson Ltd* [1969] 3 All ER 20, [1969] 1 WLR 1129. Cf, as to registered land, the Land Registration Rules 2003, SI 2003/1417, r 213: see PARA 332; and LAND REGISTRATION.

11 *Mellor v Walmesley* [1905] 2 Ch 164, CA; *Willis v Watney* (1881) 51 LJCh 181.

12 *Barnard v De Charleroy* (1899) 81 LT 497, PC; *Eastwood v Ashton* [1915] AC 900, HL; *Wallington v Townsend* [1939] Ch 588, [1939] 2 All ER 225. As to conflicting descriptions see PARA 331.

13 See CUSTOM AND USAGE vol 12(1) (Reissue) PARAS 641 et seq, 695 et seq; REAL PROPERTY vol 39(2) (Reissue) PARAS 31–35.

14 As to subsequent changes in the minister's style and title, and transfers of functions, see CONSTITUTIONAL LAW AND HUMAN RIGHTS vol 8(2) (Reissue) PARA 435.

15 See the Manorial Incidents (Extinguishment) Rules 1925, SR & O 1925/810, r 34(5) (spent).

16 *R v St Mary, Bury St Edmunds, Inhabitants* (1821) 4 B & Ald 462; cf *R v Milton Inhabitants* (1843) 1 Car & Kir 58.

17 As to inclosure and the Inclosure Acts see COMMONS vol 13 (2009) PARA 418 et seq.

18 *R v Berger* [1894] 1 QB 823, DC. A map accompanying an award of conservators of a common, relating to the 'improvement' of the common, and not also to the 'adjustment of rights' was not conclusive as to boundaries: *Collis v Amphlett* [1918] 1 Ch 232, CA; revsd on the facts [1920] AC 271, HL. As to highways see PARA 323; and HIGHWAYS, STREETS AND BRIDGES.

343.   Ecclesiastical terriers. Ecclesiastical terriers, which are schedules of the temporal possessions of parochial churches and chapels kept by the minister and churchwardens of the church or chapel concerned[1], are receivable in evidence[2] provided they have come from the proper custody[3].

A terrier of glebe lands is evidence against, but not for, the parson, unless signed by the parson and by churchwardens not nominated by the parson. Its value as evidence is increased if it was signed also by some substantial parishioners[4].

1   As to church property generally see ECCLESIASTICAL LAW.

2   See the Civil Evidence Act 1995 s 7(2)(b), (c); PARAS 338–339; and CIVIL PROCEDURE vol 11 (2009) PARAS 821–822. See also *Coombs v Coether and Wheeler* (1829) Mood & M 398; *A-G v Stephens* (1855) 6 De GM & G 111.

3   See *Atkins v Hatton* (1794) 2 Anst 386; *Coombs v Coether and Wheeler* (1829) Mood & M 398; *Croughton v Blake* (1843) 12 M & W 205 at 208 (where it was said that the custody need not be the most proper custody); *Earl v Lewis* (1801) 4 Esp 1. As to proper custody see generally CIVIL PROCEDURE.

4   Buller's Nisi Prius 248. Cf *Carr v Mostyn* (1850) 5 Exch 69, where returns made by parsons in answer to inquisitions made by the bishop regarding the boundaries, etc, of a parochial chapelry were admitted as evidence.

344.   Verdict or award. A verdict of a jury in a former action relating to a boundary is admissible as evidence of reputation in a subsequent action between different parties[1], provided the boundary in dispute was of public or general interest and not of mere private interest[2]. Ancient orders of sessions containing statements respecting boundaries[3] and presentments of manorial courts setting out boundaries[4] are also admissible as evidence of reputation[5], or, in certain cases, as public documents[6], or as records compiled by a person[7], or as acts or assertions of ownership[8]; but decrees purporting to be made by courts not known to the law are not so admissible[9].

An award of an arbitrator is not admissible as evidence of reputation[10], but in a subsequent suit between the same parties or those claiming through them such an award is admissible, not as hearsay, but as evidence properly so called[11].

1 As to the admissibility of judgments and orders in subsequent actions between the same parties see *Green v New River Co* (1792) 4 Term Rep 589; *Legatt v Tollervey* (1811) 14 East 302. See also CIVIL PROCEDURE.

2 *Evans v Rees* (1839) 10 Ad & El 151; *Reed v Jackson* (1801) 1 East 355; *Talbot v Lewis* (1834) 6 C & P 603; *Brisco v Lomax* (1838) 8 Ad & El 198 at 210 (where Littledale J said that a verdict was not reputation, but was as good evidence as reputation); *Neill v Duke of Devonshire* (1882) 8 App Cas 135, HL. See also the Civil Evidence Act 1995 s 7(3); PARA 340; and CIVIL PROCEDURE. As to the value of verdicts see *Lee v Johnstone* (1869) LR 1 Sc & Div 426.

3 *Duke of Newcastle v Broxtowe Hundred* (1832) 4 B & Ad 273.

4 *Evans v Rees* (1839) 10 Ad & El 151. As to manorial books generally see PARA 338. As to manorial courts see CUSTOM AND USAGE vol 12(1) (Reissue) PARA 699 et seq.

5 See PARA 340.

6 See PARA 338.

7 See PARA 339.

8 See PARA 334.

9 *Rogers v Wood* (1831) 2 B & Ad 245 (informal legal tribunal comprising Lord Treasurer, Lord Chancellor and the law officers).

10 *Evans v Rees* (1839) 10 Ad & El 151.

11 *Breton v Knight* (1837) cited in 1 Roscoe's Evidence in Civil Actions (20th Edn) p 223.

3. TREES AND FENCES

(1) TREES ON BOUNDARIES

345. Ownership of boundary trees. The ownership of a tree on a boundary is a question of fact in each case but such a tree will prima facie belong to the owner of the land on which it was planted[1]. Where ownership is disputed, the topping and lopping of a tree is evidence of acts of ownership[2]. It has been held that a tree planted right on a boundary which then extends its trunk and roots over the boundary was owned in common by the two landowners[3]; but the better view is that such a tree remains in the ownership of the land on which it was planted even when the trunk, roots and branches extend into the adjoining property[4].

1 *Masters v Pollie* (1620) 2 Roll Rep 141 (plaintiff had cut down a tree and had sawn it into boards, and in an action of trespass for breaking into the plaintiff's close and taking away his boards the defendant contended that, as the roots extended into his soil and had been nourished by it, he was entitled to a share of the tree; but it was held that, as the body of the tree was in the plaintiff's land, the whole of the tree belonged to the plaintiff though it was admitted that, had the plaintiff planted the tree in the soil of the defendant, it would have been otherwise).

2 *Davey v Harrow Corpn* [1958] 1 QB 60 at 70, [1957] 2 All ER 305 at 308, CA, per Lord Goddard CJ.

3 *Waterman v Soper* (1698) 1 Ld Raym 737. A legal tenancy in common is not now possible; joint ownership would seem to be inappropriate and a trust unnecessarily complicated. It seems that the Law of Property Act 1925 s 38, which makes provision in relation to party walls or other structures (see PARA 365), does not apply to trees.

4 See e g *Elliott v Islington London Borough Council* [1991] 1 EGLR 167, CA.

346. Right to lop overhanging trees. Where the branches of a tree belonging to one landowner or occupier overhang the land of an adjoining owner or occupier, the latter may at any time cut off those parts which overhang[1] without notice to the former[2], provided that in so doing he does not trespass on the adjoining land. However, an adjoining owner is not entitled to lop his neighbour's tree as a precautionary measure before it overgrows his land merely because he knows that in the course of time the boughs will probably overhang his land[3]. The right to lop is a right to abate a nuisance constituted by overhanging branches and does not carry with it a right to appropriate severed branches or fruit growing on overhanging branches[4]. Where the overhanging tree is subject to a tree preservation order[5], the order does not apply to the lopping of a tree to abate a nuisance[6].

Encroaching roots are treated as falling within the same principle as overhanging branches, so that there is a right to cut encroaching roots[7]. Where the roots of a tree situate in the highway cause damage to the property of an adjoining owner then, providing the damage is reasonably foreseeable, the highway authority may be liable in nuisance[8].

1 *Earl of Lonsdale v Nelson* (1823) 2 B & C 302 at 311 per Best J.

2 *Lemmon v Webb* [1895] AC 1, HL. See also *Pickering v Rudd* (1815) 4 Camp 219. In *Joseph Dayani v Bromley London Borough Council* [2001] BLR 503, a tenant who lopped a tree to abate a nuisance on his own neighbouring land was held not liable in negligence to his landlord either as tenant of the property or as owner of the neighbouring property.

3 *Norris v Baker* (1616) 1 Roll Rep 393. He may, however, be entitled to an injunction if substantial damage is a virtual certainty and also imminent: *Lemos v Kennedy Leigh Development Co Ltd* (1961) 105 Sol Jo 178, CA (where an injunction in respect of encroaching roots was refused); *McCombe v Read* [1955] 2 QB 429, [1955] 2 All ER 458. As to remedies

when damage has already occurred see PARA 347. As to rights to lop trees threatening to overhang highways see PARA 349. As to injunctions see CIVIL PROCEDURE vol 11 (2009) PARA 331 et seq.

4   *Mills v Brooker* [1919] 1 KB 555. As to the right to claim damages if the remedy of abatement is not exercised and damage subsequently occurs see PARA 347. It is not clear whether a claim for damages will lie (eg to recover the cost of employing a contractor to lop the branches) if the remedy of abatement is exercised. The judgments in *Kendrick v Bartram* (1677) 2 Mod Rep 253 and *Smith v Giddy* [1904] 2 KB 448 suggest that an action could be maintained for damages incurred prior to abatement. See also the dissenting judgment of Scrutton LJ in *Job Edwards Ltd v Birmingham Navigations* [1924] 1 KB 341 at 356, CA. Contra 3 Bl Com (21st Edn) pp 219–220; *Lagan Navigation Co v Lambeg Bleaching, Dyeing and Finishing Co Ltd* [1927] AC 226 at 244, HL, per Lord Atkinson, who was of the opinion that the exercise of a right of abatement 'destroys any right of action in respect of the nuisance'. As to abatement of a nuisance see NUISANCE vol 78 (2010) PARA 214 et seq.

5   As to tree preservation orders see the Town and Country Planning Act 1990 s 198; and PLANNING vol 83 (2010) PARA 1035 et seq.

6   See the Town and Country Planning Act 1990 s 198(6); and PLANNING vol 83 (2010) PARA 1038. This provision is repealed by the Planning Act 2008 ss 192(1), (2)(b), 238, Sch 13 as from a day to be appointed. At the date at which this volume states the law, no such day had been appointed. If an overhanging branch is considered a nuisance per se (*Lemmon v Webb* [1895] AC 1, HL) then it would appear that an overhanging branch on a tree subject to a preservation order can be lopped under the common law. It has been argued that to gain the statutory exemption now contained in the Town and Country Planning Act 1990 s 198(6) there must be proof of actual damage: see Bailey *A Tree is a Tree* (1978) 75 LS Gaz 1000.

7   See eg *Lemmon v Webb* [1894] 3 Ch 1 at 34, CA, per Kay LJ; *Smith v Giddy* [1904] 2 KB 448; *Butler v Standard Telephones and Cables Ltd* [1940] 1 KB 399, [1940] 1 All ER 121 (applying *Middleton v Humphries* (1913) 47 ILT 160); *McCombe v Read* [1955] 2 QB 429, [1955] 2 All ER 458; *Davey v Harrow Corpn* [1958] 1 QB 60, [1957] 2 All ER 305, CA; *Solloway v Hampshire County Council* (1981) 79 LGR 449, CA; *Bridges v Harrow London Borough Council* (1981) 260 Estates Gazette 284; *Russell v Barnet London Borough Council* (1984) 83 LGR 152, [1984] 2 EGLR 44; *Hurst v Hampshire County Council* (1998) 96 LGR 27, [1997] 2 EGLR 164, CA. The adjoining owner acquires no property in the encroaching roots or in the trees: *Masters v Pollie* (1620) 2 Roll Rep 141 (see PARA 345 note 1). See also *Hetherington v Galt* (1905) 7 F 706, Ct of Sess.

8   *Delaware Mansions Ltd v Westminster City Council* [2001] UKHL 55, [2002] 1 AC 321, [2001] 4 All ER 737 (tree roots causing damage to a neighbouring building; held to be a continuing nuisance of which the defendant knew or ought to have known and the affected owner could recover the cost of reasonably necessary remedial work provided that a reasonable opportunity for abatement had been given); *Hurst v Hampshire County Council* (1998) 96 LGR 27, [1997] 2 EGLR 164, CA (the adoption of a highway vests in the highway authority sufficient property in the trees to ground an action for nuisance, whether the tree was planted and growing before the dedication of the highway, or planted and growing after the dedication, or planted under statutory powers). See also PARA 349. As to highways and highway authorities see generally HIGHWAYS, STREETS AND BRIDGES.

347.   Liability for damage caused by trees.   Although an adjoining owner has the right to trim hedges and lop the branches of trees belonging to another which overhang his land, the burden of so doing, or of watching to see when such action is required, ought not to be put on him by the acts of the owner of the land on which the trees are growing. Thus an action in nuisance for an injunction and damages will lie against an owner or occupier who allows the branches of his trees to overhang his boundary and cause injury to his neighbour's property[1], or who allows the roots of his trees to burrow under the boundary and cause damage[2], provided that the owner of the tree has, or ought to have had, knowledge of the existence of the problem and the danger thereby created[3]. Where the tree is a nuisance to the adjoining owner, then an injunction may in appropriate circumstances be obtained against the owner for the removal of the tree[4]. If the overhanging trees or encroaching roots are not in fact causing damage, it seems that the only right of the person whose land is affected is to cut back the overhanging or encroaching portions[5].

On the same principle, a person who permits the branches of poisonous trees growing near his boundary to extend over the land of an adjoining owner will be liable in nuisance, if the branches are eaten by the adjoining owner's cattle, for any consequent injury to the cattle[6]; but since a lessee takes the property as he finds it, a tenant who takes land with the branches of yew trees overhanging it from the landlord's adjoining land so as to be within reach of cattle cannot recover from the landlord damages for injury to cattle through eating the branches[7]. Nor will any action lie if the branches do not extend over the boundary but the adjoining owner's cattle trespass by reaching over the boundary and so eat the foliage of poisonous trees growing there[8].

No right to have trees overhanging the land of another, or with their roots encroaching, can be acquired by prescription or under the Limitation Act 1980, since the trees grow from year to year[9].

Local authorities have powers to deal with complaints about high hedges which are having an adverse effect on a neighbour's enjoyment of his property[10].

1   *Smith v Giddy* [1904] 2 KB 448. As to actions in nuisance see NUISANCE vol 78 (2010) PARA 173 et seq. As to injunctions see CIVIL PROCEDURE vol 11 (2009) PARA 331 et seq. As to damages see DAMAGES vol 12(1) (Reissue) PARA 801 et seq.

2   *Delaware Mansions Ltd v Westminster City Council* [2001] UKHL 55, [2002] 1 AC 321, [2001] 4 All ER 737. See also *McCombe v Read* [1955] 2 QB 429, [1955] 2 All ER 458; *Davey v Harrow Corpn* [1958] 1 QB 60, [1957] 2 All ER 305, CA; *Morgan v Khyatt* [1964] 1 WLR 475, PC; *Masters v Brent London Borough Council* [1978] QB 841, [1978] 2 All ER 664.

3   *Delaware Mansions Ltd v Westminster City Council* [2001] UKHL 55, [2002] 1 AC 321, [2001] 4 All ER 737; *Leakey v National Trust for Places of Historic Interest or Natural Beauty* [1980] QB 485 at 522, [1980] 1 All ER 17 at 33, CA, per Megaw LJ; *Solloway v Hampshire County Council* (1981) 79 LGR 449, CA (risk of subsidence by encroaching roots not reasonably foreseeable when caused by a pocket of clay soil); *Russell v Barnet London Borough Council* (1984) 83 LGR 152, [1984] 2 EGLR 44 (risk was foreseeable and action should have been taken when tree was situated next to a house built on London clay). See also *Bridges v Harrow London Borough Council* (1981) 260 Estates Gazette 284; *Hurst v Hampshire County Council* (1998) 96 LGR 27, [1997] 2 EGLR 164, CA.

4   *Elliott v Islington London Borough Council* [1991] 1 EGLR 167, CA (mature horse chestnut belonging to the local authority had grown to invade the plaintiff's property and deflect his wall; injunction to remove, in absence of a tree preservation order, upheld notwithstanding the tree's amenity value). Cf *Atkinson v Castan* (1991) Times, 17 April, CA.

5   *Smith v Giddy* [1904] 2 KB 448 at 451 per Kennedy J. The fact that the claimant possesses this remedy is no answer to an action for damages if any damage has in fact been sustained: *Smith v Giddy* [1904] 2 KB 448 at 451 per Wills J; and see *Mills v Brooker* [1919] 1 KB 555. The same principle was applied to a fence leaning a few inches at the top in *Mann v Saulnier* (1959) 19 DLR (2d) 130 (NB App Div). Allowing a tree to grow over the land of another is not in itself an actionable trespass: *Lemmon v Webb* [1894] 3 Ch 1 at 11–12, CA, per Lindley LJ (affd [1895] AC 1, HL); *Davey v Harrow Corpn* [1958] 1 QB 60 at 70, [1957] 2 All ER 305 at 308, CA, per Lord Goddard CJ; cf *Kelsen v Imperial Tobacco Co (of Great Britain and Ireland) Ltd* [1957] 2 QB 334, [1957] 2 All ER 343 (projecting advertising sign was trespass, not nuisance).

6   *Crowhurst v Amersham Burial Board* (1878) 4 ExD 5 at 10, as explained in *Davey v Harrow Corpn* [1958] 1 QB 60, [1957] 2 All ER 305, CA. As to liability for similar injuries based on liability for dangerous fences or breach of an obligation to fence see PARAS 358, 360.

7   *Cheater v Cater* [1918] 1 KB 247, CA; *Erskine v Adeane, Bennett's Claim* (1873) 8 Ch App 756. Whether the tenant would have a claim if the branches, at the beginning of the tenancy, either were not overhanging at all or were overhanging but out of reach was left undecided in *Cheater v Cater* [1918] 1 KB 247, CA. Both of these cases are based on a distinction between disputes between adjoining owners and disputes between landlord and tenant (see *Cheater v Cater* [1918] 1 KB 247 at 254, CA). See also *Shirvell v Hackwood Estates Co Ltd* [1938] 2 KB 577, [1938] 2 All ER 1, CA, a case argued and decided in negligence and not nuisance, which applied *Cheater v Cater* [1918] 1 KB 247, CA, in relation to an unsuccessful action for personal injury caused to a servant of a tenant by the fall of an overhanging branch of a dead tree. In the light

of the decisions in *Leakey v National Trust for Places of Historic Interest or Natural Beauty* [1980] QB 485, [1980] 1 All ER 17, CA (overruling *Giles v Walker* (1890) 24 QBD 656 (see note 8)) and *Holbeck Hall Hotel Ltd v Scarborough Borough Council* [2000] QB 836, [2000] 2 All ER 705, CA, a claim in nuisance might now succeed on the facts of these cases.

8 *Ponting v Noakes* [1894] 2 QB 281. Cf *Wilson v Newberry* (1871) LR 7 QB 31 (no action where clippings from poisonous trees were taken on to neighbour's land by a third party). An action will lie if poisonous leaves from trees growing on the land of one owner are blown onto the adjoining land and cause injury to cattle eating them: see *Davey v Harrow Corpn* [1958] 1 QB 60 at 71–72, [1957] 2 All ER 305 at 310, CA, per Lord Goddard CJ. *Giles v Walker* (1890) 24 QBD 656, which held that an owner of land was not liable for damage caused by thistledown blown onto his neighbour's land, was overruled in *Leakey v National Trust for Places of Historic Interest or Natural Beauty* [1980] QB 485, [1980] 1 All ER 17, CA.

9 *Lemmon v Webb* [1895] AC 1, HL; *Davey v Harrow Corpn* [1958] 1 QB 60 at 70, [1957] 2 All ER 305 at 309, CA, per Lord Goddard CJ. As to the Limitation Act 1980 see LIMITATION PERIODS.

10 See the Anti-social Behaviour Act 2003 Pt 8 (ss 65–84); and NUISANCE vol 78 (2010) PARA 131 et seq. Such functions are 'relevant functions' for the purposes of the Regulatory Enforcement and Sanctions Act 2008 Pt 1 (ss 1–21) (see s 4, Sch 3; and LOCAL GOVERNMENT vol 69 (2009) PARA 733); thus the Local Better Regulation Office may give guidance to local authorities as to the exercise of those functions (see s 7; and LOCAL GOVERNMENT vol 69 (2009) PARA 734).

348. Entry on neighbour's land. There is some authority for the proposition that if a man is unable to lop his trees without the boughs falling upon the land of his neighbour, he may justify the felling upon his neighbour's land[1], and that if a tree grows so that the fruit falls upon the land of another, the owner of the tree may enter upon the other's land for the purpose of taking possession of the fruit[2].

1 *Dike and Dunston's Case* (1586) Godb 52.

2 *Mitten v Faudrye* (1626) Poph 161 at 163. It has been observed that: 'If trees grow in my hedge, hanging over another man's land, and the fruit of them falls into the other's land, I may justify my entry to gather up the fruit, if I may make no longer stay there than is convenient, nor break his hedge' (Vin Abr Trespass L a); and it is stated that the same rule applies when trees are blown over by the wind (Vin Abr Trespass H a 2). Cf *Anthony v Haney* (1832) 8 Bing 186. However, the existence of such a right seems to have been doubted in *Mills v Brooker* [1919] 1 KB 555 at 558 per Bray J.

349. Trees adjoining or planted in highways. Local authorities and the Secretary of State[1] are invested with statutory powers to order the lopping or pruning of trees or hedges overhanging a highway or any other road or footpath to which the public has access so as to endanger or obstruct the passage of vehicles or pedestrians[2]. Local authorities and the Secretary of State are also empowered to order the felling of trees or hedges which are dead, diseased, damaged or insecurely rooted and therefore likely to cause danger by falling onto a highway or other road or footpath to which the public has access[3].

Subject to specified exemptions, no tree or shrub may be planted in a highway or within 15 feet from the centre of a made-up carriageway[4], but the highway authority may license the occupier or the owner of any premises adjoining the highway to plant or to retain trees in such part of the highway as may be specified in the licence[5]. A highway authority may plant trees in a highway maintainable at public expense by it[6] but no such tree may be planted or allowed to remain so as to be a nuisance or injurious to the owner or occupier of premises adjacent to the highway[7].

A tree in the highway or upon the highway verge may remain the property of the landowner adjoining the highway[8] so that such an owner may be liable to a user of the highway if the tree or a branch thereof constitutes a nuisance[9], but liability will only arise when the owner becomes aware of its being a nuisance[10].

Notwithstanding the strict ownership of a tree in a highway, the relevant highway authority has a right and duty to remove a tree which constitutes a nuisance[11].

Moreover, a highway authority may be liable to an adjoining owner for damage caused by encroaching roots, even if that owner is the strict owner of the tree[12], since a highway authority has a sufficient interest in, and control of, such trees under statutory powers[13]. A local authority which is not the highway authority but is the owner of the soil in which the tree stands may be liable for nuisance caused by encroaching tree roots[14]. In all cases, there must be a reasonably foreseeable risk that the encroaching roots would cause damage[15].

1   The Highways Act 1980 refers to the Minister of Transport, but his functions were transferred to the Secretary of State: see HIGHWAYS, STREETS AND BRIDGES vol 21 (2004 Reissue) PARA 49. See also CONSTITUTIONAL LAW AND HUMAN RIGHTS vol 8(2) (Reissue) PARA 509. Certain functions of the Secretary of State, so far as exercisable in relation to Wales, have been transferred to the National Assembly for Wales and subsequently to the Welsh Ministers: see the National Assembly for Wales (Transfer of Functions) Order 1999, SI 1999/672, art 2, Sch 1; the Government of Wales Act 2006 s 162, Sch 11 para 30; and CONSTITUTIONAL LAW AND HUMAN RIGHTS. As to the office of Secretary of State see PARA 387 note 7.

2   See the Highways Act 1980 s 154(1); and HIGHWAYS, STREETS AND BRIDGES vol 21 (2004 Reissue) PARA 379. This power extends to hedges and trees which obstruct or interfere with the view of drivers of vehicles or the light from a public light, or which overhang a highway so as to endanger or obstruct the passage of horse-riders: see s 154(1); and HIGHWAYS, STREETS AND BRIDGES vol 21 (2004 Reissue) PARA 379. As to the power to require trees or hedges to be cut or lopped to remove damage caused by the exclusion of the sun or wind from the highway see s 136; and HIGHWAYS, STREETS AND BRIDGES vol 21 (2004 Reissue) PARA 347. As to the power to order the lopping of trees and hedges interfering with airfields see the Land Powers (Defence) Act 1958 s 10. The functions of highway authorities under the Highways Act 1980 are 'relevant functions' for the purposes of the Regulatory Enforcement and Sanctions Act 2008 Pt 1 (ss 1–21) (see s 4, Sch 3; and LOCAL GOVERNMENT vol 69 (2009) PARA 733); thus the Local Better Regulation Office may give guidance to local authorities as to the exercise of those functions (see s 7; and LOCAL GOVERNMENT vol 69 (2009) PARA 734). They are 'regulators' specified for the purposes of imposing civil sanctions in respect of offences under the Highways Act 1980: see the Regulatory Enforcement and Sanctions Act 2008 s 37, Sch 6; and ADMINISTRATIVE LAW.

3   See the Highways Act 1980 s 154(2); and HIGHWAYS, STREETS AND BRIDGES vol 21 (2004 Reissue) PARA 379. As to tree preservation orders see PARA 346 notes 5–6; and PLANNING vol 83 (2010) PARA 1035 et seq.

4   See the Highways Act 1980 s 141; and HIGHWAYS, STREETS AND BRIDGES vol 21 (2004 Reissue) PARA 352.

5   See the Highways Act 1980 s 142; and HIGHWAYS, STREETS AND BRIDGES vol 21 (2004 Reissue) PARA 555. As to highway authorities see HIGHWAYS, STREETS AND BRIDGES vol 21 (2004 Reissue) PARA 49 et seq.

6   See the Highways Act 1980 s 96(1); and HIGHWAYS, STREETS AND BRIDGES vol 21 (2004 Reissue) PARA 554. The power to maintain trees, and to prune trees, applies to all categories of trees planted in a highway, whether planted before or after the dedication of the highway or planted by the highway authority under its statutory powers: *Hurst v Hampshire County Council* [1997] 2 EGLR 164 at 166, CA, per Stuart-Smith LJ.

7   See the Highways Act 1980 s 96(6); and HIGHWAYS, STREETS AND BRIDGES vol 21 (2004 Reissue) PARA 554. This provision, unlike s 96(1) (see the text and note 6), applies only to trees planted by the highway authority under its statutory powers: *Hurst v Hampshire County Council* [1997] 2 EGLR 164 at 166, CA, per Stuart-Smith LJ. If damage is caused to property by exercise of the powers under the Highways Act 1980 s 96, then compensation may be recovered from the authority by which the powers were exercised: see s 96(7); and HIGHWAYS, STREETS AND BRIDGES vol 21 (2004 Reissue) PARA 554. It appears that s 96(7) applies to all categories of trees: *Hurst v Hampshire County Council* (1984) 83 LGR 152, [1997] 2 EGLR 164 at 166, CA, per Stuart-Smith LJ.

8   *Stillwell v New Windsor Corpn* [1932] 2 Ch 155; *British Road Services Ltd v Slater* [1964] 1 All ER 816, [1964] 1 WLR 498; *Russell v Barnet London Borough Council* [1984] 2 EGLR 44.

9   *British Road Services Ltd v Slater* [1964] 1 All ER 816, [1964] 1 WLR 498, applying *Sedleigh-Denfield v O'Callaghan* [1940] AC 880, [1940] 3 All ER 349, HL. As to the liability of the occupier of land adjoining a highway for injury caused by a tree falling on the highway see *Caminer v Northern and London Investment Trust Ltd* [1951] AC 88, [1950] 2 All ER 486, HL (owner of a tree which caused injury as it fell not liable in either nuisance or negligence where the tree was apparently sound and an inspection would not have revealed any damage); *Cunliffe v Bankes* [1945] 1 All ER 459; *Brown v Harrison* (1947) 177 LT 281; *Quinn v Scott* [1965] 2 All ER 588, [1965] 1 WLR 1004. See also HIGHWAYS, STREETS AND BRIDGES; NUISANCE vol 78 (2010) PARA 155 et seq.

10   *British Road Services Ltd v Slater* [1964] 1 All ER 816 at 820, [1964] 1 WLR 498 at 504 per Lord Parker of Waddington CJ. The fact that the highway authority has powers and duties in relation to the tree does not necessarily exonerate the adjoining owner: *British Road Services Ltd v Slater* [1964] 1 All ER 816 at 819, [1964] 1 WLR 498 at 502 per Lord Parker of Waddington CJ.

11   See *Stillwell v New Windsor Corpn* [1932] 2 Ch 155; *British Road Services Ltd v Slater* [1964] 1 All ER 816, [1964] 1 WLR 498; and HIGHWAYS, STREETS AND BRIDGES vol 21 (2004 Reissue) PARA 227. See also the Highways Act 1980 s 96; the text and notes 6–7; and HIGHWAYS, STREETS AND BRIDGES vol 21 (2004 Reissue) PARA 554.

12   The presumption that the soil of the highway to the median line (*usque ad medium filum viae*) belongs to the owners of the adjoining land may apply: *Goodtitle d Chester v Alker and Elmes* (1757) 1 Burr 133 at 143 per Lord Mansfield. See further HIGHWAYS, STREETS AND BRIDGES vol 21 (2004 Reissue) PARA 217. The presumption is not rebutted by the Land Registry practice of excluding adjoining highways from title plans: *Russell v Barnet London Borough Council* (1984) 83 LGR 152, [1984] 2 EGLR 44. As to the Land Registry see LAND REGISTRATION vol 26 (2004 Reissue) PARA 1064.

13   *Delaware Mansions Ltd v Westminster City Council* [2001] UKHL 55, [2002] 1 AC 321, [2001] 4 All ER 737; *Hurst v Hampshire County Council* [1997] 2 EGLR 164, CA; *Solloway v Hampshire County Council* (1981) 79 LGR 449, CA. See also *Russell v Barnet London Borough Council* (1984) 83 LGR 152, [1984] 2 EGLR 44 (disapproved in part in *Hurst v Hampshire County Council* [1997] 2 EGLR 164 at 166, CA, per Stuart-Smith LJ). Although only a person with an interest in land may maintain an action for nuisance (*Hunter v Canary Wharf Ltd* [1997] AC 655, [1997] 2 All ER 426, HL), the fact that the damage that caused the nuisance occurred prior to the claimant's purchase is irrelevant (*Delaware Mansions Ltd v Westminster City Council* [2001] UKHL 55, [2002] 1 AC 321, [2001] 4 All ER 737).

14   *Bridges v Harrow London Borough Council* (1981) 260 Estates Gazette 284.

15   *Delaware Mansions Ltd v Westminster City Council* [2001] UKHL 55, [2002] 1 AC 321, [2001] 4 All ER 737 (liability for continuing nuisance caused by tree roots since the defendant council knew, or ought to have known, of the problem); *Solloway v Hampshire County Council* (1981) 79 LGR 449, CA (where there was a small pocket of clay soil which was insufficient to appear on the geological map, the risk was not foreseeable), applying *Davey v Harrow Corpn* [1958] 1 QB 60, [1957] 2 All ER 305, CA, but subject to the proviso in *Leakey v National Trust for Places of Historic Interest or Natural Beauty* [1980] QB 485 at 522, [1980] 1 All ER 17 at 33, CA, per Megaw LJ; *Russell v Barnet London Borough Council* (1984) 83 LGR 152, [1984] 2 EGLR 44. See also NUISANCE vol 78 (2010) PARAS 182, 229 et seq.

(2) RIGHTS, DUTIES AND LIABILITIES OF OWNERS OF FENCES

(i) Introduction

350. Definitions of fences. Although fences are frequently used to mark the situation of boundaries, none the less they are primarily guards against intrusion, or barriers to prevent persons or animals straying out, and therefore in this sense the term includes not only hedges, banks, and walls, but also ditches[1]. But an external or party wall forming part of a building and alongside or on the boundary of land is not usually regarded as a fence[2].

For the purposes of the Animals Act 1971, 'fencing' includes the construction of any obstacle designed to prevent animals from straying[3].

A fence has been held not to be a 'building or erection' within the meaning of a local Act prohibiting the making of a building or erection within ten feet of the head of a wharf[4].

The term 'freeboard' or 'freebord' land is commonly applied to a strip of land, varying in width according to local custom, outside and adjoining the fence of a manor, park, forest, or other estate, which belongs to or of which a right of user is claimed by the owner of the land within the fence[5].

1 Woolrych *The Law of Party Walls and Fences* p 281 ('A fence may consist of almost any kind of enclosure or division but a hedge, ditch, bank or wall will be most commonly found to answer that term').
2 As to buildings on boundaries see PARA 311. As to party walls see PARA 364 et seq.
3 See the Animals Act 1971 s 11; and ANIMALS vol 2 (2008) PARA 754.
4 *A-G and Great Yarmouth Port and Haven Comrs v Harrison* (1920) 89 LJCh 607, CA.
5 See 46 Sol Jo (1901) 118; Mon Angl Pt II, fol 241; Selden Society, Pleas of the Forest. See also PARA 321 note 8. Richmond Park, for instance, has a freeboard of sixteen and a half feet outside the boundary wall.

(ii) Extent of Duty to Fence

351. Extent of duty to fence. At common law, in the absence of a specific duty arising from agreement[1], prescription or implied grant[2], or custom[3], there is no general obligation upon a landowner to fence his land either against or for the benefit of his neighbour[4] or the public[5]. There is, however, a common law duty to erect or repair a fence where persons using the highway might otherwise be endangered[6], and in certain circumstances where the absence of a fence would constitute a nuisance[7], and there may also be liability at common law or by virtue of statute[8] for damage arising in circumstances where the existence of a proper fence would have prevented the damage[9].

The general rule applies as between adjoining tenants of the same landlord, notwithstanding that their leases contain covenants with the landlord to keep their fences in repair[10].

A landlord who leases a part of his land and retains the rest in his hands is under no obligation, apart from express agreement[11] or implied grant[12], to keep the fences bounding the retained land in repair so as to prevent the lessee's cattle from straying onto his land[13].

Where a duty to fence does arise[14], the duty can normally only exist as between adjacent properties[15]. Such a duty will not generally carry with it the right to enter on the neighbouring land to do repairs unless an express right of entry exists[16] or such a right could be implied[17]. However, there are statutory rights to enter in relation to party walls[18].

1 *Hilton v Ankesson* (1872) 27 LT 519; *Jones v Price* [1965] 2 QB 618, [1965] 2 All ER 625, CA. Cf *Green v Eales* (1841) 2 QB 225. See also *Boyle v Tamlyn* (1827) 6 B & C 329. As to duties arising by agreement see PARA 354.
2 *Lawrence v Jenkins* (1873) LR 8 QB 274; *Barber v Whiteley* (1865) 34 LJQB 212; *Jones v Price* [1965] 2 QB 618, [1965] 2 All ER 625, CA. As to duties arising by prescription or implied grant see PARA 355.
3 *Egerton v Harding* [1975] QB 62 at 71, [1974] 3 All ER 689 at 694, CA, per Scarman LJ. As to duties arising by custom see PARA 356.
4 *Star v Rookesby* (1710) 1 Salk 335; *Churchill v Evans* (1809) 1 Taunt 529; *Hilton v Ankesson* (1872) 27 LT 519; *Co-operative Wholesale Society Ltd v British Railways Board* (1995) Times, 20 December, CA.
5 *Cornwell v Metropolitan Sewers Comrs* (1855) 10 Exch 771 at 773 per Pollock CB; *Blyth v Topham* (1608) Cro Jac 158; *British Railways Board v Herrington* [1972] AC 877, [1972] 1 All ER 749, HL. As to restrictions on the right to erect fences see the Law of Property

Act 1925 s 194 (repealed in relation to England); and COMMONS vol 13 (2009) PARA 567. As to fencing restrictions in relation to common land see PARA 315; and as to planning restrictions see PARA 363.

6	See, however, *Hoskin v Rogers* (1985) Times, 25 January, CA (accident on a highway resulting from cattle straying due to inadequate fencing; though the owner of the cattle was liable, the owner of the land was not liable in negligence where the land was let on a 'without attention' grass purchase agreement at a time when the fencing was adequate and there was no evidence that the owner was aware that it had become inadequate).

7	See PARA 352.

8	Eg the Animals Act 1971 ss 4, 5 (see PARA 361), and the Occupiers' Liability Act 1957 and the Occupiers' Liability Act 1984 (see NEGLIGENCE vol 78 (2010) PARA 29 et seq).

9	See PARA 361.

10	*Holgate v Bleazard* [1917] 1 KB 443; but quaere if this rule may not have been abrogated, at least in part, by the Animals Act 1971 s 5(6) (see PARA 361). Cf the Defective Premises Act 1972 s 4, which provides that a landlord who has maintenance or repairing obligations owes, to all persons who might be reasonably expected to be affected by the state of the premises, a duty to take such care as is reasonable in all the circumstances to see that they are reasonably safe from personal injury or damage to property caused by a relevant defect: see LANDLORD AND TENANT vol 27(1) (2006 Reissue) PARA 475.

11	As to the prescribed terms deemed to be incorporated into a contract of tenancy of an agricultural holding see the Agricultural Holdings Act 1986 s 7(1); the Agriculture (Maintenance, Repair and Insurance of Fixed Equipment) Regulations 1973, SI 1973/1473; and AGRICULTURAL LAND vol 1 (2008) PARAS 332–333. As to the repair of walls and fences see reg 3, Schedule paras 1(1), 5; and AGRICULTURAL LAND vol 1 (2008) PARA 333.

12	See *Crow v Wood* [1971] 1 QB 77, [1970] 3 All ER 425, CA; and PARA 355.

13	*Erskine v Adeane, Bennett's Claim* (1873) 8 Ch App 756.

14	See PARAS 352–356.

15	*Anon* (1496) Keil 30; *King v Rose* (1673) Freem KB 347; *Dovaston v Payne* (1795) 2 Hy Bl 527; *Sutcliffe v Holmes* [1947] KB 147 at 154, [1946] 2 All ER 599 at 602, CA, per Somervell LJ.

16	There is no general common law right of entry onto the land of another to repair or maintain structures abutting the boundary (see e g *John Trenberth Ltd v National Westminster Bank Ltd* (1979) 39 P & CR 104) though such a right can exist as an easement and arise by implied grant or prescription (see *Ward v Kirkland* [1967] Ch 194, [1966] 1 All ER 609; and EASEMENTS AND PROFITS A PRENDRE). Since the enactment of the Party Wall etc Act 1996, statutory rights of access are now available: see the text and note 18; and PARA 386. See also the Access to Neighbouring Land 1992; and NUISANCE vol 78 (2010) PARAS 116, 185. See also EASEMENTS AND PROFITS A PRENDRE.

17	An implied right may exist where the duty to fence is owed to the neighbour and the only method of fulfilling that duty is to enter onto that neighbour's land: see Aldridge *Boundaries, Walls and Fences* (10th Edn, 2009) p 67.

18	See note 16; and PARA 386.

352. Common law duties to fence. At common law an owner of land across or by the side of which a highway runs is, as a general rule, under no duty to fence off his land from the highway to prevent injury to those straying from the road, for persons so straying from a highway do so, generally, at their peril[1]. However, where there is an artificial structure or object[2] or an excavation[3] on land which if it were left unfenced would amount to a public nuisance[4] by reason of its adjoining a highway[5] or being sufficiently near to it to be dangerous to persons lawfully using the highway[6], a common law duty is cast on the person occupying the land[7] to fence the work[8]. This is so whether the work existed before or was made after the occupier first took possession and whether or not, if he is a tenant, he is liable to his landlord[9]. If the occupier neglects this duty, it may be enforced by a mandatory order to abate the nuisance[10], and the occupier is liable for any injury caused to persons lawfully passing along the highway, or to their property, even though the obligation of fencing the highway as such is by statute expressly imposed on someone else[11], except where the work has existed from time immemorial[12] or, at all events, was made before the dedication of the highway[13].

A similar duty may, perhaps, exist where the work, though not near a highway, is near a private way which the public is invited to use[14].

There is no duty on the occupier of land to fence a danger arising from some natural feature, such as a river, as distinguished from a danger artificially created[15]; nor is the owner of land adjoining a highway bound to do anything to remove a danger which has been created by something done on the highway by the highway authority[16]. There is no common law duty on a highway authority to fence against such dangers unless it has long been accustomed to do so[17].

It has also been held that persons opening pits or quarries in land of which they do not own the surface have a common law duty to fence so as to prevent injury to cattle belonging to the owner of the surface[18].

1 *Hardcastle v South Yorkshire Rly and River Dun Co* (1859) 4 H & N 67; *Binks v South Yorkshire Rly and River Dun Co* (1862) 3 B & S 244; *Jordin v Crump* (1841) 8 M & W 782 at 788 per Alderson B; *Potter v Perry* (1859) 23 JP 644; *Hawken v Shearer* (1887) 56 LJQB 284; *Hounsell v Smyth* (1860) 7 CBNS 731; *Prentice v Assets Co Ltd* (1890) 17 R 484, Ct of Sess. Cf *Devlin v Jeffray's Trustees* (1902) 5 F 130, Ct of Sess; *Jenkins v Great Western Rly Co* [1912] 1 KB 525, CA. As to the fencing of highways by adjoining owners see HIGHWAYS, STREETS AND BRIDGES vol 21 (2004 Reissue) PARA 332. As to the power of highway authorities to erect and maintain fences see HIGHWAYS, STREETS AND BRIDGES vol 21 (2004 Reissue) PARA 552. As to statutory duties to fence see PARA 353. As to the liability of a landowner whose animals stray on to the highway see PARA 361; and ANIMALS vol 2 (2008) PARA 754.
2 Eg a brazier bearing a ladle of molten lead (*Crane v South Suburban Gas Co* [1916] 1 KB 33, DC), or a low archway (*Bedman v Tottenham Local Board of Health* (1887) 4 TLR 22), or a live electric wire (*British Railways Board v Herrington* [1972] AC 877 at 914, [1972] 1 All ER 749 at 771, HL, per Lord Wilberforce).
3 Eg a basement access area (*Coupland v Hardingham* (1813) 3 Camp 398; *Barnes v Ward* (1850) 9 CB 392; *Barker v Herbert* [1911] 2 KB 633, CA), a canal (*Manley v St Helens Canal and Rly Co* (1858) 2 H & N 840), a pond (*Ross v Keith* (1888) 16 R 86, Ct of Sess), or a gap in area railings caused by a car accident (*Stevenson v Edinburgh Magistrates* 1934 SC 226, Ct of Sess).
4 *Barnes v Ward* (1850) 9 CB 392; *Cornwell v Metropolitan Sewers Comrs* (1855) 10 Exch 771 at 774 per Martin B. As to nuisances generally see NUISANCE vol 78 (2010) PARA 101 et seq.
5 *Barnes v Ward* (1850) 9 CB 392; *Hounsell v Smyth* (1860) 7 CBNS 731.
6 *Hardcastle v South Yorkshire Rly and River Dun Co* (1859) 4 H & N 67 at 75 per Pollock CB; *Hadley v Taylor* (1865) LR 1 CP 53; *Prentice v Assets Co Ltd* (1890) 17 R 484, Ct of Sess. If an excavation is not near enough to the highway to be dangerous at ordinary times, there is no duty to fence it merely because the weather is foggy: *Caseley v Bristol Corpn* [1944] 1 All ER 14, CA.
7 *Hadley v Taylor* (1865) LR 1 CP 53; cf *Cheetham v Hampson* (1791) 4 Term Rep 318; *Bishop v Bedford Charity Trustees* (1859) 1 E & E 714. But the owner, though not in occupation, is liable also where, as between himself and the occupier, he has undertaken the duty of fencing: *Payne v Rogers* (1794) 2 Hy Bl 350; *Wilchick v Marks and Silverstone* [1934] 2 KB 56. Cf *Bush v Steinman* (1799) 1 Bos & P 404. See also the Defective Premises Act 1972 s 4 (see PARA 351 note 10; and LANDLORD AND TENANT vol 27(1) (2006 Reissue) PARA 475) and the Occupiers' Liability Act 1984 s 1 (see PARA 353; and NEGLIGENCE vol 78 (2010) PARA 40).
8 *A-G v Roe* [1915] 1 Ch 235. As to the consequences of neglect of the duty see PARA 360. As to duties of care in relation to property see NEGLIGENCE.
9 *A-G v Roe* [1915] 1 Ch 235.
10 *A-G v Roe* [1915] 1 Ch 235. As to abatement of a nuisance see NUISANCE vol 78 (2010) PARAS 217, 221; and as to actions for public nuisance see NUISANCE vol 78 (2010) PARA 187 et seq.
11 *Wettor v Dunk* (1864) 4 F & F 298.
12 *Cornwell v Metropolitan Sewers Comrs* (1855) 10 Exch 771 (ditch); *Wilson v Halifax Corpn* (1868) LR 3 Exch 114 at 118 per Kelly CB.
13 *Fisher v Prowse, Cooper v Walker* (1862) 2 B & S 770; *Robbins v Jones* (1863) 15 CBNS 221.
14 *Binks v South Yorkshire Rly and River Dun Co* (1862) 3 B & S 244 at 254 per Blackburn J; *Corby v Hill* (1858) 4 CBNS 556 at 561 per Byles J. But see *Melville v Renfrewshire County Council* 1920 SC 61, Ct of Sess. See also the Occupiers' Liability Act 1957; the Occupiers' Liability Act 1984; and NEGLIGENCE vol 78 (2010) PARA 29 et seq.

15 *Morrison v London Midland and Scottish Rly Co* 1929 SC 1, Ct of Sess.

16 *Horridge v Makinson* (1915) 84 LJKB 1294 (pavement raised by highway authority but opening left to preserve access to coal chute); *Nicholson v Southern Rly Co and Sutton and Cheam UDC* [1935] 1 KB 558 (change of level); *Myers v Harrow Corpn* [1962] 2 QB 442, [1962] 1 All ER 876, DC.

17 *R v Whitney* (1835) 7 C & P 208 at 211; *Whyler v Bingham RDC* [1901] 1 KB 45 at 48, 50. As to statutory powers and duties see PARA 353; and HIGHWAYS, STREETS AND BRIDGES vol 21 (2004 Reissue) PARA 552.

18 *Williams v Groucott* (1863) 4 B & S 149; *Hawken v Shearer* (1887) 56 LJQB 284; *Sybray v White* (1836) 1 M & W 435 at 440 per Parke B (distinguished in *Hickey v Tipperary County Council* [1931] IR 621, where the plaintiff was the owner and occupier of the quarry as well as of the land in which it stood and the defendants, who had merely a licence to take stone, were held not liable to fence). The liability to fence is a continuing liability on the successors in title of the person working the quarry: *M'Morrow v Layden* [1919] 2 IR 398. As to the statutory duty to fence pits and quarries see PARA 353. As to the duty of care owed by occupiers of land for the safety of lawful visitors and other persons see the Occupiers' Liability Act 1957; the Occupiers' Liability Act 1984; and NEGLIGENCE vol 78 (2010) PARA 29 et seq.

353. Statutory obligations to fence. There are numerous statutes which impose duties to fence on the owners or occupiers of particular classes of property.

The owner[1] of an abandoned mine, or a mine which has not been worked for a period of 12 months[2], must secure that the surface entrance to every shaft or outlet of that mine is provided with an efficient device to prevent any person from accidentally falling down the shaft or from accidentally entering the outlet, and must also secure that every such device is properly maintained[3]. Failure to comply with this obligation results in the mine being a statutory nuisance[4]. Similarly a quarry (whether being worked or not) which is not provided with an efficient and properly maintained barrier to prevent anyone falling into the quarry and which by reason of its accessibility[5] from a highway or a place of public resort[6] constitutes a danger to members of the public is a statutory nuisance[7]. Where there is a danger to the public from an excavation on land accessible to the public from a highway or place of public resort, by reason of the excavation being unenclosed or inadequately enclosed, then a local authority can require works, which may include fencing, to remove the danger in question[8]. In default, or in cases where the council does not know the owner or occupier of the land, the council may carry out the necessary work itself[9].

Under the Highways Act 1980[10], a duty is imposed upon the owner of land adjoining a street[11] to fence adequately anything on the land which is a source of danger to persons using the street, as, for example, a building in the course of demolition[12]. Where the only source of danger is the difference in levels between the street and the adjoining land caused by the highway authority raising the level of the street, there cannot be said to be a danger in or on the adjoining land so as to impose a duty on the landowner to fence[13]. A highway authority may erect fences or posts for the purpose of preventing access to a highway maintainable at public expense by it; but not so as to interfere with a gate required for agricultural access nor to obstruct a public right of way or means of access for which planning permission has been granted or for which such permission was not required[14].

It is the duty of the Parsonages Board or the Diocesan Board of Finance to repair and maintain the fences of parsonages[15].

Statutory fencing obligations may continue to exist under the Inclosure Acts[16]. In general, allotments under these Acts had to be fenced at the expense of the allottees[17], but any such obligations are not enforceable against successors in title of the allottees[18].

A railway undertaking acquiring land compulsorily is under a duty to fence off the land used for the railway from the adjoining land, and to maintain the fences at all times thereafter for the protection of the land not taken for railway use[19], but when the undertaking first acquires the land the obligation to fence may be released by the vendor in return for the payment of compensation[20]. When the obligation is not so released when the land is acquired, the obligation to maintain fences is an indefinite one and devolves on any successors to the original undertaking and is not affected merely by the cessation of the use of the line and removal of the track[21].

Although the Occupiers' Liability Act 1957 and the Occupiers' Liability Act 1984 do not impose any specific liability to fence, an occupier will often only be able to discharge the common duty of care owed to lawful visitors[22] or the duty of care owed to a person who is not a visitor[23] by fencing dangers on the land. Similarly, it may be necessary to fence in order to avoid liability under the provisions of the Animals Act 1971[24] or the Defective Premises Act 1972[25].

Obligations to fence may also be imposed in particular circumstances by local Acts[26]. Where there is a statutory obligation to fence and no other sufficient remedy is provided for breach of the obligation, a mandatory order may be granted for the purpose[27].

1 Ie as defined by the Mines and Quarries Act 1954 s 181: see MINES, MINERALS AND QUARRIES vol 31 (2003 Reissue) PARA 512.
2 There is an exception in the case of mines (other than of coal, stratified ironstone, shale or fireclay) which have not been worked since 9 August 1872 (see the Mines and Quarries Act 1954 s 151(1) proviso); but even here there may be a statutory nuisance (s 151(2)(b)). See further MINES, MINERALS AND QUARRIES vol 31 (2003 Reissue) PARA 530. As to statutory nuisances see the Environmental Protection Act 1990 s 79; and NUISANCE vol 78 (2010) PARA 156. See also NUISANCE vol 78 (2010) PARA 115. Functions of local authorities under the Mines and Quarries Act 1954 and the Environmental Protection Act 1990 are 'relevant functions' for the purposes of the Regulatory Enforcement and Sanctions Act 2008 Pt 1 (ss 1–21) (see s 4, Sch 3; and LOCAL GOVERNMENT vol 69 (2009) PARA 733); thus the Local Better Regulation Office may give guidance to local authorities as to the exercise of those functions (see s 7; and LOCAL GOVERNMENT vol 69 (2009) PARA 734). Local authorities are 'regulators' specified for the purposes of imposing civil sanctions in respect of offences under the Environmental Protection Act 1990 s Pt III (ss 79–84): see the Regulatory Enforcement and Sanctions Act 2008 s 37, Sch 6; and ADMINISTRATIVE LAW.
3 See the Mines and Quarries Act 1954 s 151(1); and MINES, MINERALS AND QUARRIES vol 31 (2003 Reissue) PARA 530.
4 See the Mines and Quarries Act 1954 s 151(2)(a); and MINES, MINERALS AND QUARRIES vol 31 (2003 Reissue) PARA 530; NUISANCE vol 78 (2010) PARA 156.
5 'Accessibility' means capability of access without reasonable let or hindrance: cf *Henaghan v Rederiet Forangirene* [1936] 2 All ER 1426.
6 This includes places where the public resort in fact, even though not of right: cf *Kitson v Ashe* [1899] 1 QB 425, DC.
7 See the Mines and Quarries Act 1954 s 151(2)(c); and MINES, MINERALS AND QUARRIES vol 31 (2003 Reissue) PARA 530; NUISANCE vol 78 (2010) PARA 156. As to the fencing of surface entrances to the shafts of working mines see the Mines (Shafts and Winding) Regulations 1993, SI 1993/302, reg 9. As to tips associated with mines and quarries and the duty to make such tips secure see the Mines and Quarries (Tips) Act 1969; and MINES, MINERALS AND QUARRIES vol 31 (2003 Reissue) PARA 540 et seq.
8 See the Local Government (Miscellaneous Provisions) Act 1976 s 25(1), (2); and LOCAL GOVERNMENT vol 69 (2009) PARA 581. Functions of local authorities under the Local Government (Miscellaneous Provisions) Act 1976 are 'relevant functions' for the purposes of the Regulatory Enforcement and Sanctions Act 2008 Pt 1: see note 2.

9   See the Local Government (Miscellaneous Provisions) Act 1976 s 25(1), (5); and LOCAL GOVERNMENT vol 69 (2009) PARA 581.

10 Ie under the Highways Act 1980 s 165: see HIGHWAYS, STREETS AND BRIDGES vol 21 (2004 Reissue) PARA 371. As to animals straying on the highway see ANIMALS vol 2 (2008) PARA 754; HIGHWAYS, STREETS AND BRIDGES vol 21 (2004 Reissue) PARA 350. As to the power of a highway authority to provide pillars, wall, rails or fences in a highway or private street for the purpose of safeguarding users of the highway or street see ss 66(2), 67(1); and HIGHWAYS, STREETS AND BRIDGES vol 21 (2004 Reissue) PARAS 545–546.

11 'Street' includes any highway, road, lane, footway, square, court, alley or passage whether a thoroughfare or not: see the Highways Act 1980 s 329(1) (substituted by the New Roads and Street Works Act 1991 s 168(1), Sch 8 Pt I para 15); the New Roads and Street Works Act 1991 s 48(1); and HIGHWAYS, STREETS AND BRIDGES vol 21 (2004 Reissue) PARA 9.

12 It seems that this provision has no application where the existing fence ought to be repaired by the highway authority: see *Rotherham Corpn v Fullerton* (1884) 50 LT 364.

13 *Myers v Harrow Corpn* [1962] 2 QB 442, [1962] 1 All ER 876, DC.

14 See the Highways Act 1980 s 80(1), (3); and HIGHWAYS, STREETS AND BRIDGES vol 21 (2004 Reissue) PARA 233. In an area of the countryside where walls of a particular construction are a feature, references in s 80 include references to walls of that construction: see the Wildlife and Countryside Act 1981 s 72(12).

15 Provision is made for the execution of repairs by the Repair of Benefice Buildings Measure 1972, and fences are brought within its scope by ss 2(1), 4, 5, 9: see ECCLESIASTICAL LAW. As to dwelling houses deemed to be parsonage houses for the purpose of this Measure see the Endowments and Glebe Measure 1976 s 33; and ECCLESIASTICAL LAW.

16 As to the Inclosure Acts see COMMONS vol 13 (2009) PARA 418 et seq.

17 See eg the Inclosure Act 1845 s 83; and COMMONS vol 13 (2009) PARA 420.

18 See *Marlton v Turner* [1998] 3 EGLR 185 (county court).

19 See the Railways Clauses Consolidation Act 1845 s 68; *Cooper v Railway Executive (Southern Region)* [1953] 1 All ER 477, [1953] 1 WLR 223; and RAILWAYS, INLAND WATERWAYS AND CROSS-COUNTRY PIPELINES vol 39(1A) (Reissue) PARAS 326, 337–338. The extent of this duty to fence is limited to marking off the railway property and there is no general duty to erect or maintain fences sufficient to exclude adult or child trespassers: *Proffitt v British Railways Board* [1985] CLY 2302, CA.

20 See the Railways Clauses Consolidation Act 1845 s 68 proviso; and RAILWAYS, INLAND WATERWAYS AND CROSS-COUNTRY PIPELINES vol 39(1A) (Reissue) PARAS 326, 329, 338.

21 *R Walker & Sons (a firm) v British Railways Board (Lancashire County Council, third party)* [1984] 2 All ER 249, [1984] 1 WLR 805. As to the extent of the statutory obligation see RAILWAYS, INLAND WATERWAYS AND CROSS-COUNTRY PIPELINES vol 39(1A) (Reissue) PARA 338.

22 See the Occupiers' Liability Act 1957 s 2; and NEGLIGENCE vol 78 (2010) PARA 29 et seq. Cf *Munro v Porthkerry Park Holiday Estates* [1984] LS Gaz R 1368 (owner of a licensed premises not liable when an intoxicated customer climbed over a fence and fell to his death down a cliff).

23 See the Occupiers' Liability Act 1984 s 1; and NEGLIGENCE vol 78 (2010) PARA 40. Even if there is a duty to fence, the landowner incurs no liability for an accident if there is a finding of fact that the presence of a fence would not have prevented access to the land by the claimant: *Scott v Associated British Ports* [2000] All ER (D) 1937, CA.

24 See PARA 361; and ANIMALS vol 2 (2008) PARA 754.

25 See PARA 358; and LANDLORD AND TENANT vol 27(1) (2006 Reissue) PARA 475. As to the Defective Premises Act 1972 see also BUILDING CONTRACTS, ARCHITECTS, ENGINEERS, VALUERS AND SURVEYORS vol 4(3) (Reissue) PARA 77 et seq.

26 See eg *Rotherham Corpn v Fullerton* (1884) 50 LT 364.

27 See *R v Luton Roads Trustees* (1841) 1 QB 860. As to mandatory orders see JUDICIAL REVIEW vol 61 (2010) PARA 703 et seq.

354.   Duty arising by agreement.   The erection and repair of fences may be made the subject of an agreement[1]. Where part of an estate is being sold, it is important that the contract should state expressly who is to erect or maintain the boundary fence between the part sold and the part retained and that this provision be carried into the conveyance, for in the absence of such a provision neither party will be under any obligation to fence[2]. A covenant to fence or to maintain fences is a positive covenant, and therefore the burden of such a covenant entered into on the sale of land cannot run with the land so as to bind the assigns of the covenantor[3].

In leases, too, covenants for the erection and maintenance of fences are common[4]. A covenant to repair all the external parts of the demised premises renders the covenantor liable to repair a boundary wall adjoining other buildings[5]. In the absence of an express covenant, the tenant of premises let for a term of years, but not from year to year, is liable to repair fences as part of his liability for permissive waste[6], and for this purpose he is allowed, as between himself and his landlord, reasonable estovers[7]. The obligation under such a covenant is owed only to the other party, so a third party, for example a neighbour, is not entitled to sue in respect of a breach[8].

Though a covenant to fence does not bind successors in title to the covenantor unless contained in a lease, it may be that a duty to fence partakes of sufficient characteristics of an easement to lie in grant[9].

An agreement to fence may also, it seems, be implied. Thus in the case of an ancient inclosure it is a fair and reasonable presumption that the lord imposed as part of the terms on which the exclusive possession was to be granted to the incloser a stipulation that for the future he would take upon himself the duty of fencing as against the cattle of the commoners[10]; and an inclosure of the waste lands under an Inclosure Act does not put an end to the liability[11].

1   *Hilton v Ankesson* (1872) 27 LT 519; *Firth v Bowling Iron Co* (1878) 3 CPD 254; *Doe d Mence v Hadley* (1849) 14 LTOS 102; *Nussey v Provincial Bill Posting Co and Eddison* [1909] 1 Ch 734, CA. The development of 'open-plan' estates has meant the imposition of covenants restricting the erection of fences: see e g *Shepherd Homes Ltd v Sandham* [1971] Ch 340, [1970] 3 All ER 402; *Shepherd Homes Ltd v Sandham (No 2)* [1971] 2 All ER 1267, [1971] 1 WLR 1062; *Harlow Development Corpn v Meyers* (1979) 249 Estates Gazette 1283 (county court).

2   *Holbach v Warner* (1623) Cro Jac 665; *Barber v Whiteley* (1865) 34 LJQB 212. But see *Doyly v Drake* (1605) Moore KB 775, where four judges were equally divided in opinion on the question whether the vendor or the purchaser was under an obligation to fence. As to the consequences of failure to fence see PARAS 360–361.

3   *Rhone v Stephens* [1994] 2 AC 310, [1994] 2 All ER 65, HL. See also *Haywood v Brunswick Permanent Benefit Building Society* (1881) 8 QBD 403, CA; *Austerberry v Oldham Corpn* (1885) 29 ChD 750, CA; *Jones v Price* [1965] 2 QB 618 at 633, [1965] 2 All ER 625 at 630, CA, per Willmer LJ; but c f *Halsall v Brizell* [1957] Ch 169, [1957] 1 All ER 371; *Shiloh Spinners Ltd v Harding* [1973] AC 691, [1973] 1 All ER 90, HL; and note 9. The common law rule also applies to a perpetual obligation under an inclosure award to keep a hedgerow in repair: *Marlton v Turner* [1998] 3 EGLR 185 (county court). A positive covenant in a lease entered into prior to 1996 is, however, in general enforceable as between the assigns of the lessor and lessee, if it touches or concerns the thing assigned: see *Spencer's Case* (1583) 5 Co Rep 16a. See also the Law of Property Act 1925 ss 78, 79, 141, 142; and LANDLORD AND TENANT vol 27(1) (2006 Reissue) PARA 554 et seq. As to enforcement of covenants relating to tenancies entered into on or after 1 January 1996 see the Landlord and Tenant (Covenants) Act 1995; and LANDLORD AND TENANT vol 27(1) (2006 Reissue) PARA 578 et seq. As to covenants running with the land see EQUITY.

4   As to implied agreements relating to fencing in the case of agricultural tenancies see PARA 351 note 11; and AGRICULTURAL LAND.

5   *Green v Eales* (1841) 2 QB 225. If there is a covenant to repair the demised premises, it is a question of construction as to whether any boundary wall is included in the demised premises: *Blundell v Newlands Investment Trust* (1958) 172 Estates Gazette 855. It would appear that a boundary fence or wall would not be included in the covenant implied by the Landlord and Tenant Act 1985 s 11 (see LANDLORD AND TENANT vol 27(1) (2006 Reissue) PARAS 416–420) into short residential lettings to keep in repair the structure and exterior of a dwelling house: c f *Brown v Liverpool Corpn* [1969] 3 All ER 1345, CA; *Hopwood v Cannock Chase District Council* [1975] 1 All ER 796, [1975] 1 WLR 373, CA.

6   *Cheetham v Hampson* (1791) 4 Term Rep 318; *Torriano v Young* (1833) 6 C & P 8. As to permissive waste see LANDLORD AND TENANT vol 27(1) (2006 Reissue) PARA 431 et seq.

7   Co Litt 41 b. Only felling of oak, ash and elm over 20 years old or other wood by local custom for immediate fencing requirements is permitted. As to estovers and the tenant's right to timber see LANDLORD AND TENANT vol 27(1) (2006 Reissue) PARA 187.

8   *Holgate v Bleazard* [1917] 1 KB 443. However, under the Animals Act 1971 s 5(6), a person
    whose livestock have strayed onto land in the ownership or occupation of another may plead as
    a defence to a claim under s 4 the breach of a fencing obligation owed by a third party having an
    interest in the claimant's land: see PARA 361; and ANIMALS vol 2 (2008) PARA 755.
9   *Jones v Price* [1965] 2 QB 618 at 639, [1965] 2 All ER 625 at 634, CA, per Diplock LJ ('The
    rationalisation ... is that [the duty to fence] can arise by prescription at common law, from
    which it must follow that, in theory, it is capable of being created by covenant or grant' though
    the form of such grant was, it was said, difficult to envisage); *Crow v Wood* [1971] 1 QB 77 at
    84, [1970] 3 All ER 425 at 429, CA, per Lord Denning MR and at 86 and 430 per Edmund
    Davies LJ ('that a duty to fence can arise by express or implied grant seems clear'); *Egerton v
    Harding* [1975] QB 62 at 71, [1974] 3 All ER 689 at 694, CA, per Scarman LJ ('A duty to
    fence ... could arise by grant or custom'). For a contrary opinion see *Jones v Price* [1965] 2 QB
    618 at 647, [1965] 2 All ER 625 at 639, CA, per Winn LJ ('Only a duty ... existing
    immemorially could possibly prevail'). There appears to be no case where it has been sought to
    establish an easement to fence by means of an express grant.
10 *Egerton v Harding* [1975] QB 62, [1974] 3 All ER 689, CA. In that case, a duty to fence against
    a common was upheld; it was shown that there was an immemorial usage of fencing against the
    common as a matter of obligation and it was sufficient that this use could have arisen from a
    lawful origin which might have been an implied grant when the waste lands of the manor were
    inclosed or granted by way of copyhold, or by custom. As to duties arising by custom see PARA
    356.
11 *Godfrey v Godfrey* (1470) YB 10 Edw 4 18; *Barber v Whiteley* (1865) 34 LJQB 212; *Egerton v
    Harding* [1975] QB 62 at 71, [1974] 3 All ER 689 at 694, CA, per Scarman LJ. Cf *Haigh v West*
    [1893] 2 QB 19, CA; *Sutcliffe v Holmes* [1947] KB 147, [1946] 2 All ER 599, CA.

355.   Duty arising by prescription or implied grant. A landowner[1] may be
bound by prescription to maintain a sufficient[2] fence between his land and that
of his neighbour[3]. In that case he is liable for all damage (for example, injuries
sustained by straying animals) resulting from the defective state of the fence,
subject only to the defence that the fence was damaged by act of God or vis
major[4]. The servient owner is liable notwithstanding that he had no notice of the
want of repair[5]. This right, which has been described as a 'spurious easement'[6], is
not within the terms of the Prescription Act 1832[7], and, therefore, a prescriptive
right to have a fence kept in repair must be made out according to one of the
alternative methods[8].

To establish a prescriptive right according to the old common law[9] requires
proof of exercise of the right from time immemorial, that is 1189[10]. Thus proof
that the right did not exist, or could not have existed, at any moment of time
since 1189 will defeat the claim. In practice, in the absence of such proof, long
exercise of the right to call upon the servient owner as of right to repair his fence
at his own expense may be sufficient to establish the easement[11]. The mere fact
that the adjoining owner has for many years carried out repairs for the purpose
of maintaining a fence between his land and that of his neighbour is no evidence
of any legal obligation to repair, for such repairs may have been made solely for
his own benefit[12].

Alternatively, a prescriptive right may be established under the doctrine of the
lost modern grant[13].

A customary or prescriptive right to have a fence kept in order will pass as a
right in the nature of an easement by implied grant on a conveyance, by virtue of
the Law of Property Act 1925[14].

1   Where a tenant is in occupation, the remedy in the case of non-repair lies against the tenant and
    not the landlord: *Cheetham v Hampson* (1791) 4 Term Rep 318; *Lawrence v Jenkins* (1873) LR
    8 QB 274.
2   It seems that the obligation is to have such a fence as is used in the locality for keeping out the
    animals usually found there: *Coaker v Willcocks* [1911] 2 KB 124, CA.
3   *Jones v Price* [1965] 2 QB 618, [1965] 2 All ER 625, CA; *Faldo v Ridge* (1605) Yelv 74;
    Holbach v Warner (1623) Cro Jac 665; *Star v Rookesby* (1710) 1 Salk 335; *Nowel v Smith*

(1599) Cro Eliz 709; *Anon* (1674) 1 Vent 264; *Cheetham v Hampson* (1791) 4 Term Rep 318; *Boyle v Tamlyn* (1827) 6 B & C 329; *Lawrence v Jenkins* (1873) LR 8 QB 274; *Cordingley v Great Western Rly Co* (1948) 98 L Jo 35.

4   See the cases cited in note 3. There is no requirement that prior notice of disrepair be given.

5   *Lawrence v Jenkins* (1873) LR 8 QB 274.

6   See Gale on Easements (4th Edn, 1868) p 460; (15th Edn, 1986) p 39 note 59, cited in *Jones v Price* [1965] 2 QB 618 at 635, [1965] 2 All ER 625 at 628–629, CA, per Willmer LJ, at 639 and 634 per Diplock LJ, and at 644 and 636 per Winn LJ and in *Egerton v Harding* [1975] QB 62 at 68, [1974] 3 All ER 689 at 691, CA, per Scarman LJ. In *Jones v Price* [1965] 2 QB 618 at 631, [1965] 2 All ER 625 at 628, CA, Willmer LJ referred to it as a quasi-easement.

7   As to prescription under the Prescription Act 1832 see EASEMENTS AND PROFITS A PRENDRE vol 16(2) (Reissue) PARA 99 et seq.

8   As to the methods of claiming prescriptive rights see EASEMENTS AND PROFITS A PRENDRE vol 16(2) (Reissue) PARA 75.

9   *Hilton v Ankesson* (1872) 27 LT 519; *Lawrence v Jenkins* (1873) LR 8 QB 274.

10 See further EASEMENTS AND PROFITS A PRENDRE vol 16(2) (Reissue) PARA 81 et seq.

11 *Jones v Price* [1965] 2 QB 618, [1965] 2 All ER 625, CA; *Hilton v Ankesson* (1872) 27 LT 519; *Boyle v Tamlyn* (1827) 6 B & C 329; *Lawrence v Jenkins* (1873) LR 8 QB 274; cf *Barber v Whiteley* (1865) 34 LJQB 212. As to an obligation to repair a sea wall see *London and North Western Rly Co v Fobbing Levels Sewers Comrs* (1896) 66 LJQB 127.

12 *Jones v Price* [1965] 2 QB 618, [1965] 2 All ER 625, CA.

13 *Barber v Whiteley* (1865) 34 LJQB 212; *Sutcliffe v Holmes* [1947] KB 147, [1946] 2 All ER 599, CA. The question whether the doctrine of lost modern grant applied was in effect reserved in *Jones v Price* [1965] 2 QB 618 at 640, [1965] 2 All ER 625 at 634, CA, per Diplock LJ, but assumed in *Egerton v Harding* [1975] QB 62 at 68, [1974] 3 All ER 689 at 691, CA, per Scarman LJ. See also *Tehidy Minerals Ltd v Norman* [1971] 2 QB 528, [1971] 2 All ER 475, CA; *Crow v Wood* [1971] 1 QB 77, [1970] 3 All ER 425, CA. See further EASEMENTS AND PROFITS A PRENDRE vol 16(2) (Reissue) PARA 91 et seq.

14 See the Law of Property Act 1925 s 62; and *Crow v Wood* [1971] 1 QB 77, [1970] 3 All ER 425, CA; cf *Ward v Kirkland* [1967] Ch 194, [1966] 1 All ER 609. See also EASEMENTS AND PROFITS A PRENDRE.

356.   Duty arising by custom.   Although it was once thought that an obligation to fence could not arise by custom[1], it has more recently been held that a duty to fence against another's land can arise in this way[2]. Where there is an immemorial usage of fencing against a common as a matter of obligation, the duty to fence is proved provided such a duty could have a lawful origin; custom may be one such origin[3].

1   *Polus v Henstock (Bolus v Hinstocke)* (1670) 1 Vent 97, 2 Keb 686; *Jones v Price* [1965] 2 QB 618 at 639, [1965] 2 All ER 625 at 633–634, CA, per Diplock LJ.

2   *Egerton v Harding* [1975] QB 62, [1974] 3 All ER 689, CA.

3   See note 2.

357.   Extinguishment of liability.   A man is not bound to fence against his own land[1], and therefore, where a man is bound to fence against adjoining land, his obligation to maintain the fences comes to an end when he purchases that land[2]. Further, if a duty to fence against adjoining land has been once extinguished by the unity of possession and ownership, it will not be revived by the lands afterwards passing into the hands of different persons[3]. In order, however, that a prescriptive right may be extinguished by unity of ownership, the two estates must be equal in duration, in quality, and in all other circumstances of right[4].

The liability of an owner to fence against adjoining land may also be extinguished by statutory authority, but only if he acts in strict accordance with the statute[5].

1   See PARA 351.

2   *Sackville v Milward* (1444) YB 22 Hen 6 fo 7 pl 12; *Boyle v Tamlyn* (1827) 6 B & C 329.

3   *Polus v Henstock (Bolus v Hinstocke)* (1670) 1 Vent 97, 2 Keb 686.

4   *R v Hermitage Inhabitants* (1692) Carth 239. See EASEMENTS AND PROFITS A PRENDRE.
5   *Winter v Charter* (1829) 3 Y & J 308 (liability not extinguished when owner consented to
    highway authority breaking down part of fence prematurely).

(iii) Liability for Dangerous Fences

358.   Liability for dangerous fences.   A person whose fence is in such a state,
whether by reason of its mode of construction or its disrepair, as to constitute a
danger to occupiers of adjoining land or persons lawfully using the highway, is
liable for any damage which may thereby result to such persons[1]. The adjoining
owner may recover damages even if he has abated the nuisance by taking down
the dangerous wall or fence with the consent of its owner[2].

Where a landlord has undertaken an obligation in a lease to a tenant for the
maintenance or repair of a fence, or has reserved a right of entry to repair, then a
duty is owed to all persons who might reasonably be expected to be affected by
defects in the state of the fence to take such care as is reasonable in all the
circumstances to see that they are reasonably safe from personal injury or from
damage to their property caused by a defect in the fence[3].

The owner of a cattle market who takes a toll for his own benefit is
responsible if the fences of the cattle pens are in a dangerous condition, for
example, spiked and of insufficient height, and the cattle are injured in
consequence[4].

Local authorities and the Secretary of State are empowered to require the
removal of any barbed wire which constitutes a nuisance to the highway[5].

If a retaining wall is to be constructed so that any cross-section of it will be
within four yards of a street and any part of it will be more than four feet six
inches higher than street level, plans, sections and specifications for it must first
be approved by the local authority[6]. If any such retaining wall is in such
condition as to be liable to endanger persons using the street, the local authority
may require the owner or occupier to carry out work to obviate the danger[7].

1   See eg *Firth v Bowling Iron Co* (1878) 3 CPD 254 (owner liable when pieces of rusty fence fell
    into adjoining pasture and were eaten by cattle, causing their death; ground of liability not clear
    but probably nuisance); *Stewart v Wright* (1893) 9 TLR 480, DC (barbed wire fence adjoining a
    highway; nuisance); *Fenna v Clare & Co* [1895] 1 QB 199, DC (low wall topped with sharp
    spikes adjoining a highway; nuisance); *Harrold v Watney* [1898] 2 QB 320, CA (rotten fence
    adjoining highway; nuisance); *Haley v London Electricity Board* [1965] AC 778, [1964]
    3 All ER 185, HL (blind man tripped over punner-hammer used as fence to excavation in
    pavement; negligence). Cf *Mann v Saulnier* (1959) 19 DLR (2d) 130 (NB App Div) (fence
    leaning over adjoining land by a few inches at its top held not to be trespass or nuisance in the
    absence of special damage). A fence erected adjoining a highway which has become so
    dilapidated as to constitute a nuisance may be a public nuisance under the Building Act 1984
    ss 77, 78: see BUILDING vol 4(2) (2002 Reissue) PARA 398. See also the Highways Act 1980 s 79
    (prevention of obstruction to the view at corners: see HIGHWAYS, STREETS AND BRIDGES vol 21
    (2004 Reissue) PARA 502); s 154 (overhanging hedges and trees: see HIGHWAYS, STREETS AND
    BRIDGES vol 21 (2004 Reissue) PARA 379); s 164 (barbed wire fences: see the text and note 5;
    and HIGHWAYS, STREETS AND BRIDGES vol 21 (2004 Reissue) PARA 373); s 167 (retaining walls
    near streets: see the text and notes 6–7; and HIGHWAYS, STREETS AND BRIDGES vol 21 (2004
    Reissue) PARA 282). See generally NEGLIGENCE; NUISANCE vol 78 (2010) PARA 173 et seq.
2   *Co-operative Wholesale Society Ltd v British Railways Board* (1995) Times, 20 December, CA
    (adjoining owner could recover the cost of demolition of the dangerous wall but not the cost of
    rebuilding it in the absence of any duty to fence).
3   See the Defective Premises Act 1972 s 4(1), (4); and LANDLORD AND TENANT vol 27(1) (2006
    Reissue) PARA 475.
4   *Lax v Darlington Corpn* (1879) 5 ExD 28, CA. As to markets and fairs generally see MARKETS,
    FAIRS AND STREET TRADING. As to injuries to cattle see also PARAS 347, 360.

5   See the Highways Act 1980 s 164; and HIGHWAYS, STREETS AND BRIDGES vol 21 (2004 Reissue) PARA 373. Mere apprehension of injury from barbed wire does not give an adjoining occupier a right to damages: *Meara v Daly* (1914) 48 ILT 223. As to the Secretary of State see PARA 349 note 1. Functions of local authorities under the Highways Act 1980 are 'relevant functions' for the purposes of the Regulatory Enforcement and Sanctions Act 2008 Pt 1 (ss 1–21) (see s 4, Sch 3; and LOCAL GOVERNMENT vol 69 (2009) PARA 733); thus the Local Better Regulation Office may give guidance to local authorities as to the exercise of those functions (see s 7; and LOCAL GOVERNMENT vol 69 (2009) PARA 734). Local authorities are 'regulators' specified for the purposes of imposing civil sanctions in respect of offences under the Highways Act 1980: see the Regulatory Enforcement and Sanctions Act 2008 s 37, Sch 6; and ADMINISTRATIVE LAW.

6   See the Highways Act 1980 s 167(1), (2); and HIGHWAYS, STREETS AND BRIDGES vol 21 (2004 Reissue) PARA 282.

7   See the Highways Act 1980 s 167(5); and HIGHWAYS, STREETS AND BRIDGES vol 21 (2004 Reissue) PARA 282.

(iv) Liability for Failure to Fence

359. Damages for breach of covenant. Where there has been a breach of a covenant to build a wall, the measure of damages awarded to a claimant covenantee is the cost to the claimant of erecting on his own land a boundary wall of the contract specification, provided that the intention to execute the work is genuine and reasonable[1]. The cost is assessed at the date of judgment unless the claimant should have taken action, or done the work, at an earlier date[2]. The cost of construction is not the absolute measure of damages; so if the claimant declines specific performance and elects a remedy in damages, and there is no likelihood that the wall will be ever built, then the measure of damages is the actual loss to the claimant, namely the diminution in the value of the adjoining land[3].

1   *Radford v De Froberville* [1978] 1 All ER 33, [1977] 1 WLR 1262 (as the covenant specified a wall, the defendant could not argue that damages should be limited to the cost of the cheapest possible fence). The court, in such a case, may insist on an undertaking from the claimant to build the wall with the money awarded: *Radford v De Froberville* [1978] 1 All ER 33 at 54, [1977] 1 WLR 1262 at 1283 per Oliver J; *Wigsell v School for Indigent Blind* (1880) 43 LT 218 at 222. As to the measure of damages for breach of contract see DAMAGES vol 12(1) (Reissue) PARA 941 et seq.

2   *Radford v De Froberville* [1978] 1 All ER 33, [1977] 1 WLR 1262; *Johnson v Agnew* [1980] AC 367 at 401, [1979] 1 All ER 883 at 896, HL, per Lord Wilberforce; *Dodd Properties (Kent) Ltd v Canterbury City Council* [1980] 1 All ER 928, [1980] 1 WLR 433.

3   *Wigsell v School for Indigent Blind* (1882) 8 QBD 357, DC; *Tito v Waddell (No 2)* [1977] Ch 106 at 334, [1977] 3 All ER 129 at 318 per Megarry V-C; *Radford v De Froberville* [1978] 1 All ER 33 at 46–55, [1977] 1 WLR 1262 at 1274–1285 per Oliver J. As to the circumstances in which specific performance will be granted of a covenant to build see *Wolverhampton Corpn v Emmons* [1901] 1 KB 515, CA; *Carpenters Estates Ltd v Davies* [1940] Ch 160, [1940] 1 All ER 13; and SPECIFIC PERFORMANCE.

360. Consequences of neglect to fence where there is a duty to fence. Where there is a specific duty to fence, breach of that duty may give rise to a claim for damages[1] or possibly for specific performance[2] or an injunction[3] at the suit of the person to whom that duty is owed[4]. Liability for the breach may also extend to consequential damage. Thus a person under an obligation to fence for the benefit of the adjoining owner who fails to do so may be liable if the animals of the adjoining owner[5], lawfully on the adjoining land[6], stray onto his land and are there injured[7]. However, what constitutes a fence is a matter of construction of the fencing obligation[8]. Conversely, a person under an obligation to fence who is in breach of that obligation cannot avail himself of the statutory right of action[9] when livestock belonging to any other person stray onto his land and damage it, if it is shown that the livestock would not have strayed onto his land but for his breach of the fencing obligation[10]. Where animals do stray in such circumstances, it has been held that the landowner is not justified in simply driving them off his own land: he must return them to the close from which they escaped by his default[11].

1   See PARA 359; and DAMAGES vol 12(1) (Reissue) PARA 801 et seq.
2   See PARA 359; and SPECIFIC PERFORMANCE.
3   See PARA 352; and CIVIL PROCEDURE vol 11 (2009) PARA 331 et seq.
4   *Ricketts v East and West India Docks etc Rly Co* (1852) 12 CB 160; *Dawson v Midland Rly Co* (1872) LR 8 Exch 8, where it was held that the obligation on railway companies under the Railways Clauses Consolidation Act 1845 s 68 (see PARA 353; and RAILWAYS, INLAND WATERWAYS AND CROSS-COUNTRY PIPELINES vol 39(1A) (Reissue) PARAS 326, 337–338) is only to fence as against the owners and occupiers of adjoining land and persons claiming under them.
5   The principle extends to animals of which the adjoining owner is only a gratuitous bailee: *Rooth v Wilson* (1817) 1 B & Ald 59. Cf *Broadwater v Blot* (1817) Holt NP 547. See further BAILMENT AND PLEDGE.
6   See the notes to *Pomfret v Ricroft* (1669) 1 Wms Saund 321 at 322. Thus a licensee with a right to graze land could recover as occupier of that land: *Dawson v Midland Rly Co* (1872) LR 8 Exch 8.
7   *Powell v Salisbury* (1828) 2 Y & J 391; *Anon* (1674) 1 Vent 264; *M'Morrow v Layden* [1919] 2 IR 398; *Rooth v Wilson* (1817) 1 B & Ald 59.
8   *Ellis v Arnison* (1822) 1 B & C 70. Cf *Coaker v Willcocks* [1911] 2 KB 124, CA (no liability to fence against Scottish sheep on Dartmoor as compared with local sheep); *Cooper v Railway Executive (Southern Region)* [1953] 1 All ER 477, [1953] 1 WLR 223 (no liability when fence was strong enough for all normal purposes).
9   See the Animals Act 1971 s 4; and ANIMALS vol 2 (2008) PARA 755. See also PARA 361.
10 See the Animals Act 1971 s 5(1), (6); and ANIMALS vol 2 (2008) PARA 755. See also PARA 361.
11 *Carruthers v Hollis* (1838) 8 Ad & El 113.

361.   Consequences of neglect to fence where there is no duty to fence. Even where there is no specific duty to fence[1], an owner or occupier of land may be liable in negligence[2] for damage or injury sustained by others because there is no fence[3] or it is inadequate or defective[4].

It may therefore be necessary to fence to fulfil adequately the duty of care owed to lawful visitors under the Occupiers' Liability Act 1957 or the duty owed to persons other than visitors under the Occupiers' Liability Act 1984[5].

Under the Animals Act 1971 it may be necessary to fence to keep in livestock, as the owner of livestock is generally liable for any damage the animals may cause[6], and it is no defence that the person who suffered the damage could have prevented it by fencing unless he, or any other person having an interest in the land, had a duty to fence[7] and the livestock would not have strayed but for a breach of that duty[8]. There is also a duty to take care to prevent damage from animals straying on the highway so that, having regard to the nature of the animals, fencing may be required to fulfil this duty; but the Act does provide that where a person places animals on certain unfenced land and has the right to do so, he is not to be regarded as being in breach of his duty of care merely by reason of having placed them there[9].

1   As to the consequences of neglect to fence where there is a duty to fence see PARA 360.
2   See NEGLIGENCE.
3   *Hurst v Taylor* (1885) 14 QBD 918, DC (person injured by straying off a public footpath at a point of diversion where no fence had been erected by the defendant who had effected the diversion under statutory powers).
4   See eg *Hilder v Associated Portland Cement Manufacturers Ltd* [1961] 3 All ER 709, [1961] 1 WLR 1434. See also *Rylands v Fletcher* (1868) LR 3 HL 330; and NUISANCE vol 78 (2010) PARA 148 et seq.
5   As to the duty of care see NEGLIGENCE vol 78 (2010) PARA 29 et seq.

6   See the Animals Act 1971 s 4(1); and ANIMALS vol 2 (2008) PARA 755.
7   It is not clear whether, to negative liability, the duty to fence has to be one owed to the possessor
    of the livestock or whether a duty to a third party, eg a landlord or an adjoining owner, would
    suffice. In the latter event, this provision would appear to reverse the principles applied in
    Holgate v Bleazard [1917] 1 KB 443 and in *Sackville v Milward* (1444) YB 22 Hen 6 fo 7 pl 12.
    It appears, however, that the Animals Act 1971 has not abrogated the rule that where a person
    puts his livestock into his own field and they escape into the field of an adjoining owner and
    thence into the field of a third party, in an action by the third party (which would now be under
    the Animals Act 1971 s 4) the owner of the livestock cannot set up as a defence that the
    adjoining owner was in breach of a duty to fence owed to him (see *Anon* (1470) YB 10 Edw 4
    fo 7 pl 19; *Sutcliffe v Holmes* [1947] KB 147 at 154–156, [1946] 2 All ER 599 at 602–603, CA,
    per Somervell LJ). In such a case the owner of the livestock may have a right of recourse against
    the adjoining owner: *Holbach v Warner* (1623) Cro Jac 665; *Right v Baynard* (1674) Freem KB
    379 at 380 per Twisden J.
8   See the Animals Act 1971 s 5(1), (6); and ANIMALS vol 2 (2008) PARA 755.
9   See the Animals Act 1971 s 8; and ANIMALS vol 2 (2008) PARA 754.

(v) Enforcing Covenants not to Fence

362. Enforcing covenants not to fence. A restrictive covenant not to fence is
enforceable in accordance with standard principles[1]. A mandatory injunction
will normally be given without the need to show that the claimant has suffered
loss[2], although there is a discretion to refuse to grant such an injunction[3].

1   See CIVIL PROCEDURE vol 11 (2009) PARA 331 et seq; EQUITY. See also DAMAGES vol 12(1)
    (Reissue) PARA 1126.
2   *Shepherd Homes Ltd v Sandham* [1971] Ch 340, [1970] 3 All ER 402. See also *Shepherd
    Homes Ltd v Sandham (No 2)* [1971] 2 All ER 1267, [1971] 1 WLR 1062; *Harlow
    Development Corpn v Meyers* (1979) 249 Estates Gazette 1283 (county court).
3   *Shepherd Homes Ltd v Sandham* [1971] Ch 340, [1970] 3 All ER 402 (mandatory injunction on
    a motion to remove a fence refused partly because of delay and partly because of the high degree
    of assurance required that at trial it would appear that the injunction was rightly granted). The
    concept, however, of using judicial discretion to produce a fair result has been doubted in
    Charrington v Simons & Co Ltd [1971] 2 All ER 588 at 592, [1971] 1 WLR 598 at 603, CA,
    per Russell LJ.

(vi) Fences and Planning Law

363. Permitted development. In general, subject to the fulfilment of certain
conditions, development consisting of the erection or construction of gates,
fences, walls or other means of enclosure not exceeding one metre in height
where abutting on a highway used by vehicular traffic or two metres in height in
any other case, and their maintenance, improvement or alteration, is permitted
by development orders made under the Town and Country Planning Act 1990
and may be undertaken without specific permission[1].

1   See the Town and Country Planning Act 1990 s 59; the Town and Country Planning (General
    Permitted Development) Order 1995, SI 1995/418, art 3, Sch 2 Pt 2 Class A; and PLANNING
    vol 81 (2010) PARAS 313, 387 et seq. The fence or wall must operate as a means of enclosure but
    the fact that it has some other purpose (eg retaining soil) does not deprive it of the statutory
    privilege: *Prengate Properties Ltd v Secretary of State for the Environment* (1973) 71 LGR 373,
    25 P & CR 311.

4. PARTY WALLS

(1) INTRODUCTION

364. In general. The law relating to party walls is now an amalgam of common law rules[1] and the statutory regime of the Party Wall etc Act 1996[2]. This statutory regime governing the rights of adjoining owners[3] has superseded rights of support based on common law or prescription[4], provided that the provisions of the Act are complied with[5]. Where the procedures of the Act are invoked, the common law rights and obligations do not apply[6], and a person who wishes to do any work in relation to a party wall as defined by the Act will have only the rights given by the Act and no other rights[7]. The common law rules and remedies will now only apply in those situations not covered by the Act or where the procedures of the Act are not followed[8].

The Party Wall etc Act 1996, in substance, extends the regime previously applicable only to London under the London Building Acts (Amendment) Act 1939[9] to the whole of England and Wales[10]. The wording of the Party Wall etc Act 1996 is not identical to that formerly contained in the London Building Acts (Amendment) Act 1939, but the provisions are very similar. Decisions on that Act and its statutory antecedents[11] will therefore be relevant to the interpretation of the Party Wall etc Act 1996 except where the new wording compels an alternative meaning.

1   As to common law rights and duties in relation to party walls see PARA 370 et seq.
2   The Party Wall etc Act 1996 was brought into force, subject to savings, on 1 July 1997: see s 22(1), (2), (3); and the Party Wall etc Act 1996 (Commencement) Order 1997, SI 1997/670. The Party Wall etc Act 1996 extends to England and Wales only (see s 22(4)), but its provisions do not apply to land which is situated in inner London and in which there is an interest belonging to the Honourable Society of the Inner Temple, the Honourable Society of the Middle Temple, the Honourable Society of Lincoln's Inn, or the Honourable Society of Gray's Inn (see s 18(1)). For these purposes, 'inner London' means Greater London other than the outer London boroughs: s 18(2). As to the outer London boroughs see LONDON GOVERNMENT vol 29(2) (Reissue) PARA 30. The provisions of the Party Wall etc Act 1996 apply to land in which there is an interest belonging to Her Majesty in right of the Crown, an interest belonging to a government department, or an interest held in trust for Her Majesty for the purposes of any such department: s 19(1). They also apply to land which is vested in, but not occupied by, Her Majesty in right of the Duchy of Lancaster, and to land which is vested in, but not occupied by, the possessor for the time being of the Duchy of Cornwall: s 19(2). As to land in which the Crown has an interest see CROWN PROPERTY.
     As to statutory rights, duties and procedures in relation to party walls see PARA 377 et seq. Any sum payable in pursuance of the Party Wall etc Act 1996 (otherwise than by way of fine) is recoverable summarily as a civil debt: s 17.
3   As to the meaning of 'adjoining owner' see PARA 380 note 5.
4   As to rights of support see *Dalton v Angus & Co* (1881) 6 App Cas 740, HL; and EASEMENTS AND PROFITS A PRENDRE vol 16(2) (Reissue) PARA 180 et seq. As to prescription see EASEMENTS AND PROFITS A PRENDRE vol 16(2) (Reissue) PARA 74 et seq.
5   See *Louis v Sadiq* (1997) 74 P & CR 325, [1997] 1 EGLR 136, CA, which was decided in relation to the London Building Acts (Amendment) Act 1939 (defendant committed an actionable nuisance and had failed to invoke the statutory procedures; a subsequent statutory notice could not enable him to take advantage of the statutory defence). Cf *Selby v Whitbread & Co* [1917] 1 KB 736, which was decided in relation to the London Building Act 1894 (where it was held that the Act was in substitution for the common law and formed a governing and exhaustive code when its procedures were validly invoked).
6   *Louis v Sadiq* (1997) 74 P & CR 325, [1997] 1 EGLR 136, CA; *Upjohn v Seymour Estates Ltd* [1938] 1 All ER 614, 54 TLR 465. The cases cited above were decided in relation to earlier similar legislation.
7   See *Standard Bank of British South America v Stokes* (1878) 9 ChD 68 at 73–74; *Lewis and Solome v Charing Cross, Euston and Hampstead Rly Co* [1906] 1 Ch 508 at 516–517. See

further PARA 370. He cannot choose to rely on the very limited rights available at common law and so avoid the statutory procedures: see *Standard Bank of British South America v Stokes* (1878) 9 ChD 68 (the construction of a basement necessitated the cutting away and strengthening of the foundations to a party wall held in common, an action permitted at common law, but it was held that the statutory procedures applied and notice had to be served). The cases cited above were all decided in relation to earlier similar legislation.

8 See *Upjohn v Seymour Estates Ltd* as reported in (1938) 54 TLR 465 (work commenced before any award under the London Building Act 1930 so common law remedies applied); *Burlington Property Co Ltd v Odeon Theatres Ltd* [1939] 1 KB 633, [1938] 3 All ER 469, CA; *Gyle-Thompson v Wall Street (Properties) Ltd* [1974] 1 All ER 295, [1974] 1 WLR 123 (award in excess of jurisdiction and after procedural irregularities enabled adjoining owner to seek remedy at common law); *London and Manchester Assurance Co Ltd v O and H Construction Ltd* [1989] 2 EGLR 185 (mandatory orders to remove a structure erected on the site of a demolished party wall without employing the procedures of the London Building Acts).

9 Ie under the London Building Acts (Amendment) Act 1939 Pt VI (ss 44–59), which has been repealed: see the Party Wall etc Act 1996 s 21; and the Party Wall etc Act 1996 (Repeal of Local Enactments) Order 1997, SI 1997/671. As to the London Building Acts (Amendment) Act 1939 see further BUILDING vol 4(2) (2002 Reissue) PARA 302.

10 See note 2. The purpose of the Party Wall etc Act 1996 was stated in Parliament to be to extend the tried and tested provisions of the London Building Acts to the whole of England and Wales: see 568 HL Official Report (5th series), 31 January 1996, col 1536.

11 The London Building Acts (Amendment) Act 1939 Pt VI (now repealed) consolidated provisions from earlier London Building Acts. As to the London Building Acts see BUILDING vol 4(2) (2002 Reissue) PARAS 301–302.

(2) THE CREATION OF PARTY WALLS AT COMMON LAW

365. Meaning of 'party wall' at common law. The term 'party wall' may be used in a number of different senses[1]. At common law, the term may now be used in relation to: (1) a wall which belongs entirely to one of the adjoining owners, but is subject to an easement or right in the other to have it maintained as a dividing wall between the two adjoining properties[2]; (2) a wall divided vertically into two strips, one belonging to each of the adjoining owners[3]; (3) a wall divided vertically into halves, each half being subject to a cross easement in favour of the owner of the other half[4].

Prior to 1926, there was a fourth category of party wall at common law, namely a wall of which two adjoining owners were tenants in common[5]; but a tenancy in common of land can no longer exist as a legal estate[6]. In cases where a wall was held in common before 1926, and in cases of a disposition or other arrangement made after 1925 under which a tenancy in common would be created, if such a holding were permissible, the wall is severed vertically as between the respective owners; and the owner of each part has such rights to support and user[7] over the rest of the wall or structure as may be requisite for conferring rights corresponding to those which would have subsisted if a valid tenancy in common had been in existence or had been created[8]. The effect of the Law of Property Act 1925 is therefore to substitute for this obsolete meaning of 'party wall' a holding in which the wall is severed vertically as in head (3) above, although the owners have rights corresponding to those under the former law[9]. Such party walls can therefore now be treated as party walls falling within head (3) above.

A wall may be in part of its length and height a party wall and as regards the rest an external wall[10].

1 Four categories of party wall were enumerated in *Watson v Gray* (1880) 14 ChD 192 at 194 per Fry J. One is now obsolete: see the text and notes 5–6.
   See also *Weston v Arnold* (1873) 8 Ch App 1084 at 1089 per James LJ ('a party wall is a thing which belongs to two persons as part owners, or divides two buildings one from another').

    As to the meaning of 'party wall' for the purposes of the Party Wall etc Act 1996 see PARA 377.

2   *Watson v Gray* (1880) 14 ChD 192 at 195 per Fry J. As to the extent of this right see PARA 371. As to easements generally see EASEMENTS AND PROFITS A PRENDRE.

3   *Matts v Hawkins* (1813) 5 Taunt 20.

4   *Jones v Pritchard* [1908] 1 Ch 630; *Bradburn v Lindsay* [1983] 2 All ER 408. See also the Law of Property Act 1925 s 38(1); and the text and note 8.

5   *Wiltshire v Sidford* (1827) 1 Man & Ry KB 404; *Cubitt v Porter* (1828) 8 B & C 257. See also *Mason v Fulham Corpn* [1910] 1 KB 631 at 637, DC. The four categories of party wall were enumerated in *Watson v Gray* (1880) 14 ChD 192 at 194 per Fry J: see note 1.

6   See the Law of Property Act 1925 ss 1(6), 34(2) (s 34(2) amended by the Trusts of Land and Appointment of Trustees Act 1996 s 5, Sch 2 para 3(2)); and REAL PROPERTY vol 39(2) (Reissue) PARA 207.

7   See *Rees v Skerrett* [2001] EWCA Civ 760, [2001] 1 WLR 1541; *Upjohn v Seymour Estates Ltd* [1938] 1 All ER 614, 54 TLR 465 (right to support of a party wall included right to protection from exposure to the elements that withdrawal of such support entailed). In *Phipps v Pears* [1965] 1 QB 76, [1964] 2 All ER 35, CA, the existence of an easement of shelter or protection from the weather was denied. However, this case did not relate to a party wall but to an external wall built to abut the external wall of an adjoining property; and it was distinguished in *Rees v Skerrett* [2001] EWCA Civ 760, [2001] 1 WLR 1541. See also *Bradburn v Lindsay* [1983] 2 All ER 408.

8   See the Law of Property Act 1925 ss 38(1), 39(5), Sch 1 Pt V para 1; and REAL PROPERTY vol 39(2) (Reissue) PARA 62.

9   As to the incidents of such a holding see PARA 374.

10 *Weston v Arnold* (1873) 8 Ch App 1084; *Drury v Army and Navy Auxiliary Co-operative Supply Ltd* [1896] 2 QB 271, DC; *Newton v Huggins & Co Ltd* (1906) 50 Sol Jo 617; and see *Colebeck v Girdlers Co* (1876) 1 QBD 234; *Knight v Pursell* (1879) 11 ChD 412; *London, Gloucestershire and North Hants Dairy Co v Morley and Lanceley* [1911] 2 KB 257, DC; *Dean v Walker* (1996) 73 P & CR 366, CA. See also *Johnston v Mayfair Property Co* [1893] WN 73.

366. Creation of party walls in single ownership. A party wall at common law[1] in single ownership will rarely be created expressly since an owner is not restricted unless and until the adjoining owner acquires rights over it. Until such rights are proved the wall will not rank as a party wall at common law and will only be a party wall to the extent agreed or used and no further[2]. Such rights can be created by agreement or by prescription[3]. If a boundary wall belonging to one owner is used for support by the adjoining owner for the necessary period and there is a resulting prescriptive easement of support, then the wall will be a party wall of this type[4].

    A party wall of this type will not qualify as a party wall for the purposes of the Party Wall etc Act 1996[5] unless it separates buildings belonging to different owners[6], nor will it be a party fence wall[7].

1   As to the meaning of 'party wall' at common law see PARA 365.

2   *Weston v Arnold* (1873) 8 Ch App 1084; *Drury v Army and Navy Auxiliary Co-operative Supply Ltd* [1896] 2 QB 271, DC; *Newton v Huggins & Co Ltd* (1906) 50 Sol Jo 617; *London, Gloucestershire and North Hants Dairy Co v Morley and Lanceley* [1911] 2 KB 257, DC.

3   As to prescription see EASEMENTS AND PROFITS A PRENDRE vol 16(2) (Reissue) PARA 74 et seq.

4   A party wall of this type, where the wall belongs entirely to one owner, subject to an easement of support in favour of the other, may have occurred in *Sheffield Improved Industrial and Provident Society v Jarvis* [1871] WN 208. As to easements generally see EASEMENTS AND PROFITS A PRENDRE.

5   As to the statutory meaning of 'party wall' see PARA 377. It may become a party wall for the purposes of the Party Wall etc Act 1996 if it is the external wall of a building and the adjoining owner constructs a building against it but perhaps only if the parties so agree or if by the passage of time the adjoining owner can claim adverse possession of the surface of the wall. As to adverse possession see LIMITATION PERIODS vol 68 (2008) PARA 1078 et seq.

6   See PARA 377 head (2).

7   As to the meaning of 'party fence wall' see PARA 377.

367. Creation of party walls divided vertically. Where a wall is built on the boundary of two adjoining pieces of land, so that the centre of the wall coincides with the boundary line, the property in the wall follows the property in the land upon which it stands and the wall prima facie is a party wall at common law in the second sense[1]. It is a question of fact whether a party wall is fairly built half on each side of the boundary, and any minute inaccuracy of measurement will be disregarded[2]. In such a case, even if the wall was constructed at the joint expense of the neighbouring owners, it is not subject to joint ownership[3].

For the purposes of the Party Wall etc Act 1996, this type of wall is at least a party fence wall[4] but if the wall also separates buildings belonging to different owners, it will be a party wall[5].

1 As to party walls in the second sense see PARA 365 head (2). See also *Matts v Hawkins* (1813) 5 Taunt 20; *Hutchinson v Mains* (1832) Alc & N 155. Cf *Waddington v Naylor* (1889) 60 LT 480; *Mayfair Property Co v Johnston* [1894] 1 Ch 508. However, an easement of support for one half of the wall by the other may be acquired by prescription or by grant, express, implied or presumed: see *Dalton v Angus & Co* (1881) 6 App Cas 740, HL; and EASEMENTS AND PROFITS A PRENDRE. It is thought that this type of party wall will be rare since reciprocal easements will often be implied or presumed. As to the creation of party walls subject to reciprocal easements see PARA 368.

2 *Reading v Barnard* (1827) Mood & M 71.

3 *Matts v Hawkins* (1813) 5 Taunt 20. Separate ownership of the two halves, with express cross-easements of support, was suggested in a note to *Wiltshire v Sidford* (1827) 1 Man & Ry KB 404, as a means of avoiding this type of party wall.

4 As to the meaning of 'party fence wall' see PARA 377.

5 As to the statutory meaning of 'party wall' see PARA 377.

368. Creation of party walls subject to reciprocal easements. Where the circumstances in which the wall was built and the amount of land contributed by each adjoining owner were unknown, it was presumed under the common law that the wall belonged to the owners of the adjoining properties as tenants in common[1]. The common user by adjoining owners of a party wall separating their properties is prima facie evidence that the wall and the land on which it stands would under the former law have belonged equally to them as tenants in common[2]. Moreover, before 1926, a conveyance of one house, by the owner of two houses separated by a wall, was held to pass an undivided half of the wall and, therefore, to create a tenancy in common of the wall[3]. A declaration in a conveyance that a wall should be and remain a party wall was also held to create a tenancy in common of the wall[4]. Thus, under the former law, tenancy in common was the most usual method of holding a party wall[5].

The common law presumption still applies, but takes effect subject to the effect of the Law of Property Act 1925, which substitutes a vertical division of the wall with reciprocal easements[6]. Many party walls will now be held in this way[7] and such walls will usually constitute either party walls[8] or party fence walls[9] for the purposes of the Party Wall etc Act 1996.

Where houses have been erected in contiguity by the same owner and therefore necessarily require mutual support, there is, either by a presumed grant or by a presumed reservation, a right to such mutual support, so that the owner who sells one of the houses grants as against himself such a right, and on his own part also reserves the right, whether the houses are parted with at one time or at separate times[10]. The dividing walls accordingly become party walls at common law within either the first or third sense[11] and, in any event, they will be party walls for the purposes of the Party Wall etc Act 1996[12].

The grant of a divided half of an outside wall of a house, with the intention of making the wall a party wall between that house and an adjoining house to be built by the grantee, will be deemed to create in favour of the grantor and the grantee such easements as may be necessary to carry out what was the common intention of the parties with regard to the use of the wall, the nature of the easements varying with the particular circumstances of each case[13].

1   *Wiltshire v Sidford* (1827) 1 Man & Ry KB 404; *Cubitt v Porter* (1828) 8 B & C 257.

2   *Cubitt v Porter* (1828) 8 B & C 257; *Wiltshire v Sidford* (1827) 1 Man & Ry KB 404 at 408; *Jones v Read* (1876) IR 10 CL 315; *Standard Bank of British South America v Stokes* (1878) 9 ChD 68 at 71.

3   *Wiltshire v Sidford* (1827) 1 Man & Ry KB 404.

4   *Watson v Gray* (1880) 14 ChD 192.

5   *Watson v Gray* (1880) 14 ChD 192.

6   See the Law of Property Act 1925 s 38(1); and PARA 365. As to easements generally see EASEMENTS AND PROFITS A PRENDRE.

7   It was assumed that the party wall was held in this way in *Rees v Skerrett* [2001] EWCA Civ 760 at [5], [15], [2001] 1 WLR 1541 at [5], [15] per Lloyd J. As to the effect of such holdings see PARA 374.

8   As to the statutory meaning of 'party wall' see PARA 377.

9   As to the meaning of 'party fence wall' see PARA 377.

10 *Richards v Rose* (1853) 9 Exch 218. Cf *Wheeldon v Burrows* (1879) 12 ChD 31, CA, disapproving *Pyer v Carter* (1857) 1 H & N 916. Contrast *Scales v Vandeleur* (1913) 48 ILT 36; affd (1914) 48 ILT 38, CA (landlord not liable for damage to tenant's premises caused by dilapidated condition of adjoining premises belonging to, but not in the occupation of, the landlord).

11 As to party walls in the first and third sense see PARA 365 heads (1), (3).

12 See PARA 377.

13 *Jones v Pritchard* [1908] 1 Ch 630 at 635. See also *Richards v Rose* (1853) 9 Exch 218; *Lyttelton Times Co Ltd v Warners Ltd* [1907] AC 476, PC.

369.   Effect of a party wall declaration.   A declaration in a deed that a wall is a party wall normally creates a party wall at common law in the third sense[1]. Whether or not such a declaration creates an express obligation or covenant to repair, contrary to the general rule[2], will depend upon the true construction of the declaration. Any such express repairing obligation, imposing positive burdens, will not bind successors in title[3] and the common law principle of mutual benefit and burden[4] is unlikely to apply to party walls[5].

An express declaration that a wall is a party wall brings it within the provisions of the Party Wall etc Act 1996[6], and the common law rights and obligations will then be supplanted[7].

1   See the Law of Property Act 1925 s 38(1); and *Watson v Gray* (1880) 14 ChD 192. As to party walls in the third sense see PARA 365 head (3).

2   See *Leigh v Dickeson* (1884) 15 QBD 60, CA; and PARA 376.

3   See *Halsall v Brizell* [1957] Ch 169, [1957] 1 All ER 371.

4   See DEEDS AND OTHER INSTRUMENTS vol 13 (2007 Reissue) PARA 64.

5   See *Rhone v Stephens* [1994] 2 AC 310, [1994] 2 All ER 65, HL (where it was held that reciprocal benefits and burdens of support did not make an independent obligation to repair an overhanging roof enforceable). See also EASEMENTS AND PROFITS A PRENDRE.

6   Ie unless, exceptionally, a party wall in single ownership was expressly created: see PARA 366. As to the statutory meaning of 'party wall' see PARA 377. As to the rights and duties arising by virtue of the Party Wall etc Act 1996 see PARA 377 et seq.

7   See PARA 364.

(3) RIGHTS AND DUTIES IN RELATION TO PARTY WALLS AT COMMON LAW

370. In general. The common law rules relating to party walls and rights of support now only apply in those situations not covered by the Party Wall etc Act 1996 or where the procedures of the Act are not followed[1]. Under the common law rules, the rights and duties inter se of adjoining owners in respect of party walls depend upon the category into which the party wall falls[2] and upon the circumstances of the case.

1   See PARA 364. As to statutory rights, duties and procedures in relation to party walls see PARA 377 et seq.

2   As to the categories see *Watson v Gray* (1880) 14 ChD 192 at 194 per Fry J; and PARA 365.

371. Party walls in single ownership. A party wall in the first sense[1] is a wall which belongs entirely to one of the owners of adjoining lands but is subject to an easement or right in the other to have it maintained as a dividing wall between the two properties[2]. This description of the easement or right[3] is somewhat misleading, as it does not mean that the owner of the wall is required to take any positive steps, for example to keep the wall in repair. Apart from any special local custom or express contract, the owner of the wall is subject to no liability if, by reason of natural decay or other circumstances beyond his control, the wall falls down or otherwise passes into such a condition that the easement or right over it becomes difficult or impossible to exercise; he is liable only for positive acts producing these consequences[4]. Nevertheless, the adjoining owner is entitled to repair the wall so far as is reasonably necessary for the enjoyment of his easement, and to enter on his neighbour's land for that purpose[5], but he is not entitled to reimbursement of any part of his expense[6].

The mere fact that a wall on the land of one owner acts to divide the property from land vested in another does not make it a party wall or give the adjoining owner rights over it, but even if the adjoining owner has no rights over the wall, he may nevertheless abate any nuisance caused by lack of repair and recover the cost of dismantling the wall, although the cost of rebuilding the wall is not recoverable[7].

A wall is only a party wall to the extent that there is a right to use it as such[8]. Subject to the easement of the adjoining owner, the owner of the wall may deal with it as he pleases[9] and, provided he uses it for the contemplated objects and without negligence or want of due care, he is not responsible for any nuisance or inconvenience thereby occasioned[10].

As far as the owner of the wall is concerned, he will, in the absence of agreement, have a right of natural support only[11]. The taking away of the soil giving natural support is not itself wrongful but becomes actionable when actual damage is sustained[12] and the servient owner who authorises the acts is liable for work done by an independent contractor[13]. An easement of support for the wall itself can be acquired by prescription[14]. Once acquired, such an easement is not extinguished unless the mode of use of the support is altered or increased so as to impose a substantial additional restriction upon the adjoining servient owner[15].

1   As to party walls in the first sense see PARA 365 head (1).

2   This is the only type of party wall at common law which may not be a party wall or party fence wall for the purposes of the Party Wall etc Act 1996; however, if the wall, notwithstanding being in single ownership, separates buildings belonging to different owners, then it will be a party

wall for the purposes of the Act: see PARA 377. As to the statutory meaning of 'party wall' and as to the meaning of 'party fence wall' see PARA 377. As to easements generally see EASEMENTS AND PROFITS A PRENDRE.

3   The description derives from *Watson v Gray* (1880) 14 ChD 192 at 194.

4   See *Jones v Pritchard* [1908] 1 Ch 630 at 637, discussing *Taylor v Whitehead* (1781) 2 Doug KB 745; *Pomfret v Ricroft* (1669) 1 Wms Saund 321; *Sack v Jones* [1925] Ch 235 at 242.

5   *Jones v Pritchard* [1908] 1 Ch 630 at 638; *Bond v Norman, Bond v Nottingham Corpn* [1939] Ch 847, [1939] 3 All ER 669 (affd [1940] Ch 429, [1940] 2 All ER 12, CA). If the party wall separates buildings belonging to two different owners, the procedures of the Party Wall etc Act 1996 (see PARA 377 et seq) would now have to be followed: see PARA 364.

6   *Stockport and Hyde Division of Macclesfield Hundred Highway Board v Grant* (1882) 51 LJQB 357; *Leigh v Dickeson* (1884) 15 QBD 60, CA. Cf *Co-operative Wholesale Society Ltd v British Railways Board* (1995) Times, 20 December, CA (cost of demolition recovered).

7   *Co-operative Wholesale Society Ltd v British Railways Board* (1995) Times, 20 December, CA.

8   *Weston v Arnold* (1873) 8 Ch App 1084; *Drury v Army and Navy Auxiliary Co-operative Supply Ltd* [1896] 2 QB 271, DC; *Newton v Huggins & Co Ltd* (1906) 50 Sol Jo 617; *London, Gloucestershire and North Hants Dairy Co v Morley and Lanceley* [1911] 2 KB 257, DC.

9   Ie except where the provisions of the Party Wall etc Act 1996 provide for restrictions on the freedom of a building owner: see PARAS 364, 377 et seq.

10   *Jones v Pritchard* [1908] 1 Ch 630 at 636. The consequence at common law was that if a house was demolished by one owner, thereby removing a wall on a boundary which was wholly owned by such owner, the adjoining owner who had no right of support had no claim; the pulling-down owner only had to be careful to interfere as little as possible with the adjoining structures but was not required to shore them up or take active steps for their protection: *Southwark and Vauxhall Water Co v Wandsworth District Board of Works* [1898] 2 Ch 603 at 612, CA. If, as may be more usual, there was an easement of support, the result could be different: *Bradburn v Lindsay* [1983] 2 All ER 408. See also *Brace v South East Regional Housing Association Ltd* (1984) 270 Estates Gazette 1286; *Rees v Skerrett* [2001] EWCA Civ 760, [2001] 1 WLR 1541. Now, however, any wall on a boundary which separates buildings belonging to different owners will be subject to the provisions of the Party Wall etc Act 1996: see PARAS 364, 377 et seq.

11   *Dalton v Angus & Co* (1881) 6 App Cas 740, HL. See also *Holbeck Hall Hotel Ltd v Scarborough Borough Council* [2000] QB 836, [2000] 2 All ER 705, CA (a landowner owes a measured duty of care to a neighbour in respect of hazards which threaten the natural support of the buildings of the neighbouring landowner).

12   *Backhouse v Bonomi* (1861) 9 HL Cas 503. No action will lie for the cost of work to avert future damage: *Midland Bank plc v Bardgrove Property Services Ltd* [1991] 2 EGLR 283. See also *Benzie v Happy Eater Ltd* [1990] EGCS 76.

13   *Bower v Peate* (1876) 1 QBD 321.

14   See eg *Ray v Fairway Motors (Barnstaple) Ltd* (1968) 20 P & CR 261, CA. As to easements acquired by prescription see EASEMENTS AND PROFITS A PRENDRE.

15   *Luttrel's Case* (1601) 4 Co Rep 86a; *Ray v Fairway Motors (Barnstaple) Ltd* (1968) 20 P & CR 261, CA. See EASEMENTS AND PROFITS A PRENDRE.

372.   Party walls divided vertically.   In the rare case of a party wall in the second sense[1] (that is, a wall divided vertically into two halves, each separately owned, neither owner having any easement[2] over the other's half of the wall), neither owner is entitled at common law to support from the other. The right at common law for either owner to pull down that portion of the wall standing on his own land, even if sufficient support may not be left for the portion of the wall which belongs to his neighbour[3], provided that the work is done reasonably and without negligence[4], is now superseded by the statutory code in the Party Wall etc Act 1996[5]. Nevertheless, an adjoining owner may recover damages from his neighbour if his property is damaged as a result of his neighbour's negligence or nuisance, for example from the collapse of a building on his neighbour's land known to be in a dilapidated or ruinous state, or from the negligent conduct of building operations on his neighbour's land[6]. The common law rule that if there is no negligence a person who excavates close to his boundary, and in so doing shakes the foundations of his neighbour's wall so that the wall falls down, is not liable for such injury in the absence of proof that he is under some duty to support the wall[7] is also now superseded by the statutory code[8].

An easement of support for one half of the wall by the other may be acquired by prescription, or by grant, express, implied or presumed[9].

In the absence of an easement of support for the wall, the owner of the wall will only have an easement of support for the land in its natural state[10]; to succeed in an action for interference with such an easement, the owner of the wall must prove that, in the absence of the wall, the excavations of the adjoining owner would have resulted in a substantial collapse of the natural soil so as to found a cause of action by itself. If such movement of soil can be shown, then consequent damage to the wall or buildings can be recovered as consequent to the infringement of the natural right[11].

1   As to party walls in the second sense see PARA 365 head (2).
2   As to easements generally see EASEMENTS AND PROFITS A PRENDRE.
3   *Wigford v Gill* (1591) Cro Eliz 269; *Wiltshire v Sidford* (1827) 1 Man & Ry KB 404; *Peyton v London Corpn* (1829) 9 B & C 725; *Colebeck v Girdlers Co* (1876) 1 QBD 234 (lessee who had covenanted to keep property in repair could not perform the covenant as a result of the inadequate support of a party wall owned by the lessor; no implied covenant of support for the lessee's property); *Mayfair Property Co v Johnston* [1894] 1 Ch 508. This inconvenient result of this type of party wall was the reason for presuming, where possible, a tenancy in common: see *Cubitt v Porter* (1828) 8 B & C 257. Where there would formerly have been a tenancy in common, the wall is now held in divided halves, each being subject to certain rights in favour of the other: see PARAS 365, 374.
4   *Kempston v Butler* (1861) 12 ICLR 516. Under the Building Act 1984, the local authority may require the demolisher to make weatherproof any wall laid bare: see ss 80, 81(1), 82(1)(b); and BUILDING vol 4(2) (2002 Reissue) PARAS 400–401. See also *Chadwick v Trower* (1839) 6 Bing NC 1; *Kempston v Butler* (1861) 12 ICLR 516; *Peyton v London Corpn* (1829) 9 B & C 725. As to the effect of a demolition order under what is now the Housing Act 1985 s 265 see *Bond v Norman, Bond v Nottingham Corpn* [1939] Ch 847, [1939] 3 All ER 669 (affd [1940] Ch 429, [1940] 2 All ER 12, CA); and HOUSING vol 22 (2006 Reissue) PARA 415. Local authorities are 'regulators' specified for the purposes of imposing civil sanctions in respect of offences under the Building Act 1984: see the Regulatory Enforcement and Sanctions Act 2008 s 37, Sch 6; and ADMINISTRATIVE LAW.
5   See PARAS 364, 377 et seq.
6   *Walters v Pfeil* (1829) Mood & M 362; *Dodd v Holme* (1834) 1 Ad & El 493; *Chauntler v Robinson* (1849) 4 Exch 163; *Todd v Flight* (1860) 9 CBNS 377 (distinguished in *Brew Bros Ltd v Snax (Ross) Ltd* [1970] 1 QB 612, [1970] 1 All ER 587, CA); *St Anne's Well Brewery Co v Roberts* (1928) 140 LT 1, CA. See also *Bradburn v Lindsay* [1983] 2 All ER 408; *Brace v South East Regional Housing Association Ltd* (1984) 270 Estates Gazette 1286; *Rees v Skerrett* [2001] EWCA Civ 760, [2001] 1 WLR 1541; *Video London Sound Studios Ltd v Asticus GMS Ltd* [2001] All ER (D) 168 (Mar) (demolition contractors working on party wall dislodged debris which damaged equipment in claimant's building; equipment not fixture and so not within London Building Acts (Amendment) Act 1939 s 46 (repealed); defendants not liable in negligence because damage not reasonably foreseeable to competent contractor but liable in nuisance because damage of some kind was foreseeable). See further PARA 375; and NEGLIGENCE vol 78 (2010) PARA 39; NUISANCE vol 78 (2010) PARA 116 et seq.
7   *Gayford v Nicholls* (1854) 9 Exch 702; *Wyatt v Harrison* (1832) 3 B & Ad 871; *Murchie v Black* (1865) 19 CBNS 190; *Smith v Thackerah* (1866) LR 1 CP 564. See also the comments on the latter case in *A-G v Conduit Colliery Co* [1895] 1 QB 301 at 308.
8   See PARAS 364, 384.
9   Such an easement converts the wall into a party wall in the third sense: see PARA 365 head (3). As to the creation of easements see EASEMENTS AND PROFITS A PRENDRE vol 16(2) (Reissue) PARA 46 et seq. As to rights of support see *Dalton v Angus & Co* (1881) 6 App Cas 740, HL; and EASEMENTS AND PROFITS A PRENDRE vol 16(2) (Reissue) PARA 180 et seq. As to subsidence caused by mining see MINES, MINERALS AND QUARRIES vol 31 (2003 Reissue) PARA 184 et seq.
10 *Dalton v Angus & Co* (1881) 6 App Cas 740, HL.
11 *Ray v Fairway Motors (Barnstaple) Ltd* (1968) 20 P & CR 261 at 268, CA, per Willmer LJ, and at 271 per Russell LJ. Only movement of soil below the level of the wall foot is relevant for this purpose.

373. Party walls subject to reciprocal easements. In the common case of a party wall in the third sense[1], that is to say, a wall divided vertically into halves subject to cross-easements, the whole wall is subject to such reciprocal rights as may be necessary to carry out the common intention of the parties as to the user of the wall, the nature of the rights varying in each case but usually involving a right of support[2]. Such easements are not affected directly by the Party Wall etc Act 1996, since nothing in that Act authorises any interference with an easement of light or other easements in or relating to a party wall[3]. Either party may use the wall for the contemplated purposes, and provided this is done without negligence there will be no liability for any nuisance or inconvenience which arises[4].

Where the cross-easements include an easement of support and one owner acts in a way so as to interfere with or remove that support[5], then, in the absence of provision of equally efficient alternative support, the owner who has lost the support may protect it from interference by an action for nuisance[6] or for disturbance of the easement of support[7]. The cross-easements are binding on a local authority which demolishes the servient property under a demolition order[8], so that it must provide equivalent alternative support[9]. There is no right of support between buildings which do not adjoin each other; thus the demolition of the next-but-one house in a terrace gives no cause of action for deprivation of support[10].

As in the case of a wall belonging entirely to one owner but subject to an easement of support[11] (which is really the position here if each divided half of the wall is considered individually), the right to have the wall maintained does not mean that either party is normally required to take any positive steps, for example to keep the wall in repair[12]. However, the removal of a building adjoining one half of a party wall in such a way that the wall is exposed to the elements does impose a duty to take reasonable steps to provide weatherproofing for the dividing wall[13]. The common law position was that each party was entitled, at his own expense[14], to repair the other's half of the wall, as well as his own, so far as reasonably necessary for the enjoyment of his easements[15], but this limited entitlement is now superseded by the more extensive statutory rights available[16]. The existence of a right in one owner to enter to repair the party wall and abate any nuisance[17] does not relieve the other defaulting owner from liability for nuisance[18].

1 As to party walls in the third sense see PARA 365 head (3).
2 See *Jones v Pritchard* [1908] 1 Ch 630. As to easements generally see EASEMENTS AND PROFITS A PRENDRE. As to rights of support see *Dalton v Angus & Co* (1881) 6 App Cas 740, HL; and EASEMENTS AND PROFITS A PRENDRE vol 16(2) (Reissue) PARA 180 et seq.
3 Party Wall etc Act 1996 s 9(a). However, works authorised by virtue of the machinery of the Act may well mean a temporary interference is inevitable.
4 *Jones v Read* (1876) IR 10 CL 315; *Jones v Pritchard* [1908] 1 Ch 630 at 636.
5 Interference or removal of support after properly invoking the procedures of the Party Wall etc Act 1996 is not actionable but the adjoining owner will instead have the benefit and protection of the provisions of that Act: cf *Selby v Whitbread & Co* [1917] 1 KB 736; and see PARAS 364, 377 et seq. The case cited above was decided in relation to earlier similar legislation (see PARA 364).
6 *Bradburn v Lindsay* [1983] 2 All ER 408 (demolition of one of pair of semi-detached houses); *Brace v South East Regional Housing Association Ltd* (1984) 270 Estates Gazette 1286 (subsidence caused by drying out of clay soil after demolition of adjoining terraced property). As to actions for nuisance see PARA 375; and NUISANCE vol 78 (2010) PARAS 175 et seq, 187 et seq.
7 *Rees v Skerrett* [2001] EWCA Civ 760, [2001] 1 WLR 1541 (damages, awarded for breach of an easement of support after the demolition of an adjoining property and exposure of a previously internal party wall, included a sum for damage caused by the wind).

8 Ie an order under the Housing Act 1985 s 265 (or a clearance order under earlier legislation): see HOUSING vol 22 (2006 Reissue) PARA 415.

9 *Bond v Norman, Bond v Nottingham Corpn* [1939] Ch 847, [1939] 3 All ER 669; affd [1940] Ch 429, [1940] 2 All ER 12, CA.

10 *Solomon v Vintners' Co* (1859) 4 H & N 585.

11 See PARA 371.

12 *Bond v Nottingham Corpn* [1940] Ch 429 at 438–439, [1940] 2 All ER 12 at 18, CA, per Sir Wilfrid Greene MR; *Jones v Pritchard* [1908] 1 Ch 630; *Sack v Jones* [1925] Ch 235.

13 *Rees v Skerrett* [2001] EWCA Civ 760, [2001] 1 WLR 1541, applying *Leakey v National Trust for Places of Historic Interest or Natural Beauty* [1980] QB 485, [1980] 1 All ER 17, CA; *Bradburn v Lindsay* [1983] 2 All ER 408. See also note 7; and PARA 375.

14 *Stockport and Hyde Division of Macclesfield Hundred Highway Board v Grant* (1882) 51 LJQB 357; *Leigh v Dickeson* (1884) 15 QBD 60, CA.

15 *Jones v Pritchard* [1908] 1 Ch 630 at 638.

16 See PARAS 364, 377 et seq.

17 As to abatement of a nuisance see NUISANCE vol 78 (2010) PARA 214 et seq.

18 *Leakey v National Trust for Places of Historic Interest or Natural Beauty* [1980] QB 485, [1980] 1 All ER 17, CA; *Bradburn v Lindsay* [1983] 2 All ER 408. See also PARA 375; and NUISANCE vol 78 (2010) PARA 181 et seq.

374. Party walls subject to the Law of Property Act 1925. Where a party wall was held in common prior to 1926 each of the tenants in common was entitled to the use of, that is support from, the wall, with mutual rights to prevent its destruction. However, a tenancy in common of land can no longer exist as a legal estate[1]. The Law of Property Act 1925[2] now gives to the owner of each part such rights to support and user[3] over the rest of the structure as may be requisite for conferring rights corresponding to those which would have subsisted if there were a valid tenancy in common[4]. However, the Act in one respect at least reduced the owner's rights, for in an action for damages against a third party the owner of one half of a party wall can only recover for the damage to that half of the wall which is vested in him[5].

A person interested in a party structure affected by the Law of Property Act 1925 may apply to the court for a declaration of the rights and interests of those interested, and the court may make such order as it thinks fit[6].

The common law rights in such party walls, although still preserved by the Law of Property Act 1925, will be superseded by the statutory regime of the Party Wall etc Act 1996 where that Act applies[7]. The rule that one tenant in common could not maintain trespass against the other for an injury done to the wall, unless there had been a complete ouster, or some destruction of the common property[8] may continue to have some limited relevance but the principles relating to demolition and underpinning are not now available[9].

1 See the Law of Property Act 1925 ss 1(6), 34(2); PARA 365; and REAL PROPERTY vol 39(2) (Reissue) PARA 207.

2 See the Law of Property Act 1925 ss 38(1), 39(5), Sch 1 Pt V para 1; PARA 365; and REAL PROPERTY vol 39(2) (Reissue) PARA 62.

3 See *Upjohn v Seymour Estates Ltd* [1938] 1 All ER 614 (right to support of a party wall included right to protection from exposure to the elements that withdrawal of such support entailed). In *Phipps v Pears* [1965] 1 QB 76, [1964] 2 All ER 35, CA, the existence of an easement of shelter or protection from the weather was denied, although this case did not relate to a party wall but to an external wall built to abut the external wall of an adjoining property. See also *Bradburn v Lindsay* [1983] 2 All ER 408. As to easements generally see EASEMENTS AND PROFITS A PRENDRE. As to rights of support see *Dalton v Angus & Co* (1881) 6 App Cas 740, HL; and EASEMENTS AND PROFITS A PRENDRE vol 16(2) (Reissue) PARA 180 et seq.

4 The effect of this appears to be the assimilation of this obsolete category of party wall with the third type of party wall at common law: see PARA 365 head (3).

5   *Apostal v Simons* [1936] 1 All ER 207, CA. As regards the other half of the wall, which is the property of the adjoining owner, any remedy for interference with rights of support must be against that adjoining owner. As to actions for damages see PARA 375; and DAMAGES vol 12(1) (Reissue) PARA 801 et seq.

6   See the Law of Property Act 1925 ss 38(2), 39(5), Sch 1 Pt V para 3; and REAL PROPERTY vol 39(2) (Reissue) PARA 63.

7   See PARAS 364, 377 et seq.

8   See *Murly v M'Dermott* (1838) 8 Ad & El 138; *Voyce v Voyce* (1820) Gow 201 (hedge grubbed up); *Murray v Hall* (1849) 7 CB 441 (actual expulsion); *Jones v Read* (1876) IR 10 CL 315 (taking down wall without intention of rebuilding); *Standard Bank of British South America v Stokes* (1878) 9 ChD 68; *Watson v Gray* (1880) 14 ChD 192; *Stedman v Smith* (1857) 8 E & B 1. See also *Noye v Reed* (1827) 1 Man & Ry KB 63; *Jacobs v Seward* (1872) LR 5 HL 464. See also *Firmstone v Wheeley* (1844) 2 Dow & L 203 (where it was held that if a wall was knocked down, the owner might maintain an action for trespass; but he could not, by omitting to rebuild it, hold the defendant responsible for any consequential damage).

9   Under the common law, it was held that the demolition of the whole wall for the purpose of erecting a better one as soon as possible was not such a destruction as would enable one tenant in common to maintain an action for trespass against the other: *Cubitt v Porter* (1828) 8 B & C 257; *Jones v Read* (1876) IR 10 CL 315; *Colebeck v Girdlers Co* (1876) 1 QBD 234 at 243. Contrast *Stedman v Smith* (1857) 8 E & B 1 (one tenant in common after pulling down a building on his side of the wall increased the height of the wall and built a house with the roof occupying the entire width of the top, and also inserted a stone with an inscription stating that the wall was his; held sufficient ouster) with *Watson v Gray* (1880) 14 ChD 192 (one tenant in common excluded the other from using the party wall by placing an obstruction on the wall; the only remedy of the other was to remove the obstruction). The demolishing owner had to exercise reasonable skill and care, and carry out the work without delay: *Pfluger v Hocken* (1858) 1 F & F 142; *Hughes v Percival* (1883) 8 App Cas 443, HL; *Jolliffe v Woodhouse* (1894) 10 TLR 553, CA; *Cribb v Kynoch Ltd* [1907] 2 KB 548 at 559, DC. See also *Newton v Huggins & Co Ltd* (1906) 50 Sol Jo 617. Neither owner could underpin the wall unless it could be done without injury to the other's property: *Bradbee v Christ's Hospital* (1842) 4 Man & G 714 at 761; *Standard Bank of British South America v Stokes* (1878) 9 ChD 68. See also *Mayfair Property Co v Johnston* [1894] 1 Ch 508.

     However, these common law rights are no longer available and the building owner has the rights given by the Party Wall etc Act 1996 and no others: cf *Standard Bank of British South America v Stokes* (1878) 9 ChD 68 at 73–74; *Lewis and Solome v Charing Cross, Euston and Hampstead Rly Co* [1906] 1 Ch 508 at 516–517; and see PARAS 364, 377 et seq. The last two cases cited above were decided in relation to earlier similar legislation (see PARA 364).

375. Disrepair giving rise to an actionable nuisance.

Most, but not all[1], party walls exist with an easement of support[2]; but such an easement does not normally impose at common law a direct positive obligation to repair[3]. However, if neglect or failure to act gives rise to an actionable nuisance[4], then an obligation to repair may arise indirectly as a consequence. In the absence of such repair or maintenance work, an adjoining owner who suffers from the disrepair may recover damages to cover the cost of remedial works to the party wall to abate the nuisance[5]. Such damages can also include the cost of finishing a party wall now exposed to the elements to a reasonable standard of weatherproofing and appearance[6].

Where the provisions of the Party Wall etc Act 1996 apply, they supersede common law remedies in relation to rights of support[7].

1   Eg party walls at common law in the second sense: see PARA 365 head (2).

2   As to easements generally see EASEMENTS AND PROFITS A PRENDRE. Nothing in the Party Wall etc Act 1996 authorises any interference with any easement in or relating to a party wall: see s 9(a); and PARA 373.

3   *Jones v Pritchard* [1908] 1 Ch 630; *Sack v Jones* [1925] Ch 235. See also PARA 373. The Party Wall etc Act 1996 provides extensive rights to repair (although not an obligation to repair): see PARA 382.

4   See further NUISANCE vol 78 (2010) PARA 117.

5 *Bradburn v Lindsay* [1983] 2 All ER 408 (neglect and dilapidation of one of a pair of semi-detached houses resulted in dry rot in the party wall and demolition by the local authority of the derelict house, which was in a ruinous condition, thus leaving the party wall largely unsupported; damages, both to cover cost of eradicating the dry rot and erection of supporting buttresses, were recovered on the basis that the defaulting owner owed a duty to take reasonable steps to abate the nuisance, which could have been reasonably foreseen); *Brace v South East Regional Housing Association Ltd* (1984) 270 Estates Gazette 1286 (demolition of end of terrace property, converting a party wall into a flank wall, caused shrinkage and subsidence; notwithstanding a party wall agreement, damages for the nuisance caused by the interference with the right of support were recovered); *Rees v Skerrett* [2001] EWCA Civ 760, [2001] 1 WLR 1541 (demolition of end of terrace property, converting a party wall into a flank wall, resulted in damage from wind suction; the protection afforded by the right of support extended to the effect of such weathering and damages were recovered not only for withdrawal of support but also for breach of the duty to weatherproof the wall after demolition). Damages are not recoverable for the cost of works to prevent anticipated damage: *Midland Bank plc v Bardgrove Property Services Ltd* [1992] 2 EGLR 168, CA. See generally NUISANCE vol 78 (2010) PARA 101 et seq. As to abatement of a nuisance see NUISANCE vol 78 (2010) PARA 214 et seq. As to damages generally see DAMAGES vol 12(1) (Reissue) PARA 801 et seq.

6 *Bradburn v Lindsay* [1983] 2 All ER 408 at 414, applying *Leakey v National Trust for Places of Historic Interest or Natural Beauty* [1980] QB 485, [1980] 1 All ER 17, CA; *Rees v Skerrett* [2001] EWCA Civ 760, [2001] 1 WLR 1541. This is notwithstanding the decision in *Phipps v Pears* [1965] 1 QB 76, [1964] 2 All ER 35, CA, in a case where there was no easement of support or a party wall, that there is no separate easement of protection from the weather. Indeed, the withdrawal of support where an easement of support exists may impose a duty to take reasonable steps to weatherproof a dividing wall once it is exposed to the elements as a result of the demolition: *Rees v Skerrett* [2001] EWCA Civ 760, [2001] 1 WLR 1541 at [31] per Lloyd J, applying *Holbeck Hall Hotel Ltd v Scarborough Borough Council* [2000] QB 836, [2000] 2 All ER 705, CA.

7 See PARAS 364, 377 et seq. See also *Selby v Whitbread & Co* [1917] 1 KB 736 (where it was held that the statutory right of protection superseded the common law rights of support and an action for damages for the withdrawal of support at common law could not be maintained). This case was decided in relation to earlier similar legislation (see PARA 364).

376.   Recovery of the expense of repairing or building the wall at common law.   In the absence of an actionable nuisance[1], there was at common law no general right of contribution between adjoining owners to the expense of building, maintaining or repairing a party wall[2]. A right of contribution could only arise under express contract[3], or a contract implied from common user[4] or other circumstances[5], or a local custom[6].

Where the provisions of the Party Wall etc Act 1996 regulating the apportionment of the burden of such expenses[7] apply, they supersede any such limited common law rights of contribution[8].

1 See PARA 375; and NUISANCE vol 78 (2010) PARA 117.
2 *Leigh v Dickeson* (1884) 15 QBD 60, CA (one co-owner could not compel the other co-owner to contribute). As to the meaning of 'party wall' at common law see PARA 365.
3 *Stuart v Smith* (1816) 2 Marsh 435. As such a contract creates a positive obligation, it is not binding on the successors in title of the obligee: *Austerberry v Oldham Corpn* (1885) 29 ChD 750, CA; and see PARA 354.
4 *Christie v Mitchison* (1877) 36 LT 621.
5 *Irving v Turnbull* [1900] 2 QB 129, DC. See also *Thacker v Wilson* (1835) 3 Ad & El 142.
6 *Robinson v Thompson* (1890) 89 LT Jo 137, DC.
7 See PARA 390.
8 See PARA 364.

(4) RIGHTS AND DUTIES UNDER THE PARTY WALL ETC ACT 1996

377.   Statutory definition of 'party wall' etc.   For the purposes of the Party Wall etc Act 1996, 'party wall' means:

(1)   a wall which forms part of a building[1] and stands on lands of different
       owners to a greater extent than the projection of any artificially formed
       support on which the wall rests[2]; and

(2)   so much of a wall not being a wall referred to in head (1) above as
       separates buildings belonging to different owners[3].

A wall which is not part of a building but which stands on lands of different
owners and which is used or constructed to be used for separating adjoining
lands is defined for the purposes of the Act as a 'party fence wall', but this does
not include a wall constructed on the land of one owner the artificially formed
support of which projects into the land of another owner[4].

For the purposes of the Act, 'party structure' means a party wall and also a
floor partition or other structure separating buildings or parts of buildings
approached solely by separate staircases or separate entrances[5].

1   'Building' is not defined in the Party Wall etc Act 1996; however, it seems that it may be given a
    wide meaning: see *Frederick Betts Ltd v Pickfords Ltd* [1906] 2 Ch 87 (where it was held that a
    covered yard or cart shed was a building and the wall was consequently a party wall within the
    London Building Act 1894). This case was decided in relation to earlier similar legislation (see
    PARA 364).
2   Party Wall etc Act 1996 s 20. Thus if only the foundations of the wall project across the line of
    junction or boundary, then the wall is not a party wall for the purposes of the Act unless it
    separates buildings belonging to two different owners (see head (2) in the text). As to the
    meaning of 'owner' see PARA 379 note 2.
3   Party Wall etc Act 1996 s 20. See also *Knight v Pursell* (1879) 11 ChD 412 at 414 per Fry J
    (where it was suggested that a party wall is defined by reference to mode of use rather than
    rights of ownership). It has been held that if an adjoining owner connects without authority into
    an external boundary wall constructed entirely on the land of his neighbour, then an injunction
    will lie to order a disconnection from the building so that it ceases to be a party wall: *Frederick
    Betts Ltd v Pickfords Ltd* [1906] 2 Ch 87. The cases cited above were decided in relation to
    earlier similar legislation (see PARA 364).
4   Party Wall etc Act 1996 s 20. A party fence wall is a party wall at common law in either the
    second or third sense: see PARA 365 head (2) or head (3).
5   Party Wall etc Act 1996 s 20. The effect of this definition is to extend the application of the Act
    from the vertical boundaries to horizontal boundaries between flats.

378.   External walls and fence walls adjoining boundaries.   A wall in single
ownership that does not divide buildings is not a party wall[1] or party fence wall[2]
for the purposes of the Party Wall etc Act 1996[3]. Such walls may be boundary
walls in the sense that they stand alongside the boundary of a property and
delimit it. They will be either external walls or fence walls[4]. The building of such
walls can carry the right to place below the level of the land of the adjoining
owner necessary footings and foundations[5].

1   As to the statutory meaning of 'party wall' see PARA 377.
2   As to the meaning of 'party fence wall' see PARA 377.
3   Such a wall may, however, be a party wall at common law within the first sense if subject to an
    easement in favour of the adjoining owner: see PARA 365 head (1).
4   These terms are used in the Party Wall etc Act 1996 (see eg s 1(4); and PARA 380 head (2)),
    although they are not expressly defined.
       'External wall' appears to mean the outside wall of a building. For the purposes of the
    London Building Act 1930, 'external wall' is defined as the outer wall or vertical enclosure of
    any building not being a party wall: see s 5. See also *Pembery v Lamdin* [1940] 2 All ER 434
    (decided in relation to a landlord's covenant to keep external walls in tenantable repair), in
    which it was held that an external wall is one that forms part of the enclosure of a premises.
       'Fence wall' appears to mean a wall designed to fence off property, i e a wall that would be a
    party fence wall if it had been constructed to stand on lands of different owners (see PARA 377).
5   See PARA 381.

379. Introduction of statutory procedures. The Party Wall etc Act 1996 provides procedures[1] for situations where lands of different owners[2] adjoin and are not built on at the line of junction[3], or are built on at the line of junction only to the extent of a boundary wall[4] (not being a party fence wall[5] or the external wall[6] of a building)[7], and either owner is about to build on any part of the line of junction[8].

1 Ie by virtue of the Party Wall etc Act 1996 s 1: see PARAS 380–381. As to the Party Wall etc Act 1996 generally see PARA 364.
2 'Owner' includes: (1) a person in receipt of, or entitled to receive, the whole or part of the rents or profits of land; (2) a person in possession of land, otherwise than as a mortgagee or as a tenant from year to year or for a lesser term or as a tenant at will; and (3) a purchaser of an interest in land under a contract for purchase or under an agreement for a lease, otherwise than under an agreement for a tenancy from year to year or for a lesser term: Party Wall etc Act 1996 s 20. It has been held that 'owner' does not include a statutory tenant: see *Frances Holland School v Wassef* [2001] 2 EGLR 88 (county court) (a case decided in relation to earlier similar legislation: see PARA 364).
3 Party Wall etc Act 1996 s 1(1)(a). 'Line of junction' is not defined in the Party Wall etc Act 1996, but is used throughout the Act to refer to the non-physical boundary line between adjoining properties.
4 'Boundary wall' is not defined in the Party Wall etc Act 1996, but appears to mean a wall marking a boundary whether or not it stands on, or adjoins, the boundary.
5 As to the meaning of 'party fence wall' see PARA 377.
6 As to the meaning of 'external wall' see PARA 378 note 4.
7 Party Wall etc Act 1996 s 1(1)(b).
8 Party Wall etc Act 1996 s 1(1).

380. Statutory procedure where one owner wishes to build a party wall or party fence wall. A building owner[1] who desires to build a party wall[2] or party fence wall[3] on the line of junction[4] must, at least one month before he intends the building work to start, serve on any adjoining owner[5] a notice which indicates his desire to build and describes the intended wall[6].

After having been served with a notice of desire to build, an adjoining owner may serve on the building owner a notice indicating his consent to the building of a party wall or party fence wall[7]. If such a consent notice is served, then the wall must be built half on the land of each of the two owners or in such other position as may be agreed between them[8]. The expense of building the wall is shared between the two owners, in such proportion as has regard to the use made or to be made of the wall by each of them and to the cost of labour and materials prevailing at the time when that use is made by each owner respectively[9].

If the adjoining owner does not consent[10] to the building of a party wall or party fence wall, the building owner may only build the wall:

(1)   at his own expense[11]; and
(2)   as an external wall[12] or a fence wall[13], as the case may be, placed wholly on his own land[14].

Where the building owner builds such a wall wholly on his own land he has the right to place below the level of the land of the adjoining owner such projecting footings and foundations[15] as are necessary for the construction of the wall[16]. The building owner must compensate any adjoining owner and any adjoining occupier[17] for any damage to his property occasioned by the building of the wall[18] and by the placing of any such necessary footings or foundations[19].

The Party Wall etc Act 1996 provides for the determination of any dispute that arises under these provisions between the building owner and any adjoining owner or occupier[20].

1   'Building owner' means an owner of land who is desirous of exercising rights under the Party Wall etc Act 1996: s 20. See *Lehmann v Herman* [1993] 1 EGLR 172 (where a husband and wife were joint tenants and both together constituted the 'building owner'; therefore a notice served on behalf of only one of two or more joint tenants is not served by the building owner and is invalid). This case was decided in relation to earlier similar legislation (see PARA 364).

2   As to the statutory meaning of 'party wall' see PARA 377.

3   As to the meaning of 'party fence wall' see PARA 377.

4   As to the meaning of 'line of junction' see PARA 379 note 3.

5   'Adjoining owner' means any owner of land, buildings, storeys or rooms adjoining those of the building owner: Party Wall etc Act 1996 s 20. If there is more than one adjoining owner of the same land, such as a freeholder and long leaseholder, or freeholder and tenant for a term exceeding a year, both must be served: see *Fillingham v Wood* [1891] 1 Ch 51. It has been held that service upon only one of two or more joint tenants is sufficient: see *Crosby v Alhambra Co Ltd* [1907] 1 Ch 295. The cases cited above were decided in relation to earlier similar legislation (see PARA 364).

6   Party Wall etc Act 1996 s 1(2). As to when s 1 applies see PARA 379.

7   Party Wall etc Act 1996 s 1(3). There is no time limit under s 1(3) on serving a consent notice, but cf the time limit under s 1(4) (see note 10).

     Since a consent notice will have the consequence of requiring the adjoining owner to share the costs of building (see the text and note 9), consent is only likely to be forthcoming if a party wall is advantageous to the adjoining owner.

8   Party Wall etc Act 1996 s 1(3)(a).

9   Party Wall etc Act 1996 ss 1(3)(b), 11(3).

10   For these purposes, 'consent' means consent by a notice served within the period of 14 days beginning with the day on which the notice described in the Party Wall etc Act 1996 s 1(2) (see the text and note 6) is served: s 1(4). An adjoining owner who does not consent to the building of a party wall or party fence wall need take no action.

11   Party Wall etc Act 1996 s 1(4)(a), (7).

12   As to the meaning of 'external wall' see PARA 378 note 4.

13   As to the meaning of 'fence wall' see PARA 378 note 4.

14   Party Wall etc Act 1996 s 1(4)(b).

15   'Foundation', in relation to a wall, means the solid ground or artificially formed support resting on solid ground on which the wall rests: Party Wall etc Act 1996 s 20. 'Special foundations' means foundations in which an assemblage of beams or rods is employed for the purpose of distributing any load: s 20.

16   Party Wall etc Act 1996 s 1(6). The right is exercisable at any time in the period which begins one month after the day on which the notice was served on the adjoining owner, and ends 12 months after that day: s 1(6)(a), (b).

17   'Adjoining occupier' means any occupier of land, buildings, storeys or rooms adjoining those of the building owner: Party Wall etc Act 1996 s 20.

18   Party Wall etc Act 1996 s 1(7)(a).

19   Party Wall etc Act 1996 s 1(7)(b).

20   Any such dispute is to be determined in accordance with the Party Wall etc Act 1996 s 10 (see PARAS 387–389): see s 1(8).

381. Statutory procedure where one owner wishes to build a wall adjacent to the boundary. A building owner[1] who desires to build on the line of junction[2] a wall placed wholly on his own land must, at least one month before he intends the building work to start, serve on any adjoining owner[3] a notice which indicates his desire to build and describes the intended wall[4]. Where the building owner builds such a wall wholly on his own land he has the right to place below the level of the land of the adjoining owner such projecting footings and foundations[5] as are necessary for the construction of the wall[6]. The building owner must build the wall at his own expense[7] and must compensate any adjoining owner and any adjoining occupier[8] for any damage to his property occasioned by the building of the wall[9] and by the placing of any such necessary footings or foundations[10].

The Party Wall etc Act 1996 provides for the determination of any dispute that arises under these provisions between the building owner and any adjoining owner or occupier[11].

1   As to the meaning of 'building owner' see PARA 380 note 1.
2   As to the meaning of 'line of junction' see PARA 379 note 3.
3   As to the meaning of 'adjoining owner' see PARA 380 note 5.
4   Party Wall etc Act 1996 s 1(5). As to when s 1 applies see PARA 379. Such a boundary wall is not a party wall or a party fence wall for the purposes of the Act nor a party wall at common law. As to the statutory meaning of 'party wall' see PARA 377. As to the meaning of 'party fence wall' see PARA 377. As to the meaning of 'party wall' at common law see PARA 365. The reason for invoking the procedures of the Act will be to obtain the right to project foundations and footings (see the text and notes 5–6) and to obtain the ancillary rights of entry which may be necessary to build the wall. As to rights of entry see PARA 386. As to restrictions on excavation and construction adjacent to a boundary see PARA 384.
    No notice need be served if the footings and foundations are to be on the land of the building owner, but this may effectively result in an abandonment of a narrow strip of land to the adjoining owner (see eg *Burns v Morton* [1999] 3 All ER 646, [2000] 1 WLR 247, CA). See also PARA 303.
5   As to the meaning of 'foundation' see PARA 380 note 15.
6   Party Wall etc Act 1996 s 1(6). The right is exercisable at any time in the period which begins one month after the day on which the notice was served on the adjoining owner, and ends 12 months after that day: s 1(6)(a), (b).
7   Party Wall etc Act 1996 s 1(7).
8   As to the meaning of 'adjoining occupier' see PARA 380 note 17.
9   Party Wall etc Act 1996 s 1(7)(a).
10 Party Wall etc Act 1996 s 1(7)(b).
11 Any such dispute is to be determined in accordance with the Party Wall etc Act 1996 s 10 (see PARAS 387–389): see s 1(8).

382.   Rights to repair or do works affecting a party wall.   Where lands of different owners[1] adjoin and at the line of junction[2] those lands are built on or a boundary wall, being a party fence wall[3] or the external wall[4] of a building, has been erected, a building owner[5] has the following rights[6]:

(1)   to underpin[7], thicken or raise a party structure[8], a party fence wall, or an external wall which belongs to the building owner and is built against a party structure or party fence wall[9];

(2)   to make good, repair, or demolish and rebuild, a party structure or party fence wall in a case where such work is necessary on account of defect[10] or want of repair of the structure or wall[11];

(3)   to demolish a partition which separates buildings belonging to different owners but does not conform with statutory requirements and to build instead a party wall which does so conform[12];

(4)   in the case of buildings connected by arches or structures over public ways or over passages belonging to other persons, to demolish the whole or part of such buildings, arches or structures which do not conform with statutory requirements and to rebuild them so that they do so conform[13];

(5)   to demolish a party structure which is of insufficient strength or height for the purposes of any intended building of the building owner and to rebuild it of sufficient strength or height for those purposes (including rebuilding to a lesser height or thickness where the rebuilt structure is of sufficient strength and height for the purposes of any adjoining owner)[14];

(6)   to cut into a party structure for any purpose (which may be or include the purpose of inserting a damp proof course)[15];

(7)   to cut away from a party wall, party fence wall, external wall or boundary wall any footing or any projecting chimney breast, jamb or flue, or other projection on or over the land of the building owner in order to erect, raise or underpin any such wall or for any other purpose[16];

(8)   to cut away or demolish parts of any wall or building of an adjoining owner overhanging the land of the building owner or overhanging a party wall, to the extent that it is necessary to cut away or demolish the parts to enable a vertical wall to be erected or raised against the wall or building of the adjoining owner[17];

(9)   to cut into the wall of an adjoining owner's building in order to insert a flashing or other weather-proofing of a wall erected against that wall[18];

(10)   to execute any other necessary works incidental to the connection of a party structure with the premises adjoining it[19];

(11)   to raise a party fence wall, or to raise such a wall for use as a party wall, and to demolish a party fence wall and rebuild it as a party fence wall or as a party wall[20];

(12)   to reduce, or to demolish and rebuild, a party wall or party fence wall to: (a) a height of not less than two metres where the wall is not used by an adjoining owner to any greater extent than a boundary wall; or (b) a height currently enclosed upon by the building of an adjoining owner[21];

(13)   to expose a party wall or party structure hitherto enclosed subject to providing adequate weathering[22].

1   As to the meaning of 'owner' see PARA 379 note 2.
2   As to the meaning of 'line of junction' see PARA 379 note 3.
3   As to the meaning of 'party fence wall' see PARA 377.
4   As to the meaning of 'external wall' see PARA 378 note 4.
5   As to the meaning of 'building owner' see PARA 380 note 1.
6   Party Wall etc Act 1996 s 2(1). The rights are exercisable either with consent or by serving a party structure notice and observing the statutory procedure: see PARA 383. These rights replace any which existed at common law: see *Standard Bank of British South America v Stokes* (1878) 9 ChD 68 at 73–74; *Lewis and Solome v Charing Cross, Euston and Hampstead Rly Co* [1906] 1 Ch 508 at 516–517; and see PARA 364. The cases cited above were decided in relation to earlier similar legislation (see PARA 364).
7   The term 'underpinning' in the Party Wall etc Act 1996 s 2(2)(a) includes any works that are necessary in order to effect the underpinning, including excavation to reach the proposed location of the underpinning: *Manu v Euroview Estates Ltd* [2008] 1 EGLR 165 at [94] (county court).
8   As to the meaning of 'party structure' see PARA 377.
9   Party Wall etc Act 1996 s 2(2)(a). Where such work is not necessary on account of defect or want of repair of the structure or wall concerned, the right is exercisable: (1) subject to making good all damage occasioned by the work to the adjoining premises or to their internal furnishings and decorations; and (2) where the work is to a party structure or external wall, subject to carrying any relevant flues and chimney stacks up to such a height and in such materials as may be agreed between the building owner and the adjoining owner concerned or, in the event of dispute, determined in accordance with s 10 (see PARAS 387–389): s 2(3)(a), (b). For these purposes, 'relevant flues and chimney stacks' are those which belong to an adjoining owner and either form part of or rest on or against the party structure or external wall: s 2(3). As to the meaning of 'adjoining owner' see PARA 380 note 5.

      Where work is carried out in exercise of the right mentioned in s 2(2)(a) (see head (1) in the text), and the work is necessary on account of defect or want of repair of the structure or wall concerned, the expenses must be defrayed by the building owner and the adjoining owner in such proportion as has regard to: (a) the use which the owners respectively make or may make of the structure or wall concerned; and (b) responsibility for the defect or want of repair concerned, if more than one owner makes use of the structure or wall concerned: s 11(4). The concept of 'responsibility' in s 11(4)(b) does not equate with legal liability; the test is whether, as a matter of common-sense impression, one party has been more the cause of the relevant defect, damage or disrepair than the other: *Manu v Euroview Estates Ltd* [2008] 1 EGLR 165 at [138]–[139] (county court).

10 In considering whether a party structure is defective, the proper course is to consider how far it is effective for the purpose for which it is used, or intended to be used; the right conferred is confined to making good the party structure so that it becomes effective in those respects in which it is defective: see *Barry v Minturn* [1913] AC 584 at 589, HL (dampness in a wall is not a defect unless its existence renders the wall less effective for the purposes for which it is used or intended to be used). This case was decided in relation to earlier similar legislation (see PARA 364).

11 Party Wall etc Act 1996 s 2(2)(b). Where work is carried out in exercise of the right mentioned in s 2(2)(b), the expenses must be defrayed by the building owner and the adjoining owner in such proportion as has regard to: (1) the use which the owners respectively make or may make of the structure or wall concerned; and (2) responsibility for the defect or want of repair concerned, if more than one owner makes use of the structure or wall concerned: s 11(5).

12 Party Wall etc Act 1996 s 2(2)(c). As to the statutory meaning of 'party wall' see PARA 377.

13 Party Wall etc Act 1996 s 2(2)(d). A building or structure which was erected before 18 July 1996 (ie the day on which the Party Wall etc Act 1996 was passed) is deemed to conform with statutory requirements if it conforms with the statutes regulating buildings or structures on the date on which it was erected: s 2(8).

14 Party Wall etc Act 1996 s 2(2)(e). The Party Wall etc Act 1996 provides an express power to rebuild to a lesser height in order to nullify the decision in *Gyle-Thompson v Wall Street Properties Ltd* [1974] 1 All ER 295, [1974] 1 WLR 123 (surveyor's award set aside as the London Buildings Acts gave a building owner no power to rebuild to a reduced height).

This right is exercisable subject to: (1) making good all damage occasioned by the work to the adjoining premises or to their internal furnishings and decorations; and (2) carrying any relevant flues and chimney stacks up to such a height and in such materials as may be agreed between the building owner and the adjoining owner concerned or, in the event of dispute, determined in accordance with the Party Wall etc Act 1996 s 10 (see PARAS 387–389): s 2(4)(a), (b). For these purposes, 'relevant flues and chimney stacks' are those which belong to an adjoining owner and either form part of or rest on or against the party structure: s 2(4).

Where the adjoining premises are laid open in exercise of the right mentioned in s 2(2)(e) (see head (5) in the text), a fair allowance in respect of disturbance and inconvenience must be paid by the building owner to the adjoining owner or occupier: s 11(6). See also PARA 385. As to the meaning of 'adjoining occupier' see PARA 380 note 17.

15 Party Wall etc Act 1996 s 2(2)(f). Any right falling within s 2(2)(f) is exercisable subject to making good all damage occasioned by the work to the adjoining premises or to their internal furnishings and decorations: s 2(5).

16 Party Wall etc Act 1996 s 2(2)(g). Any right falling within s 2(g) is exercisable subject to making good all damage occasioned by the work to the adjoining premises or to their internal furnishings and decorations: s 2(5).

17 Party Wall etc Act 1996 s 2(2)(h). Any right falling within s 2(2)(h) is exercisable subject to making good all damage occasioned by the work to the adjoining premises or to their internal furnishings and decorations: s 2(5).

18 Party Wall etc Act 1996 s 2(2)(j). This right is exercisable subject to making good all damage occasioned by the work to the wall of the adjoining owner's building: s 2(6).

19 Party Wall etc Act 1996 s 2(2)(k).

20 Party Wall etc Act 1996 s 2(2)(l).

21 Party Wall etc Act 1996 s 2(2)(m). This right is exercisable subject to: (1) reconstructing any parapet or replacing an existing parapet with another one; or (2) constructing a parapet where one is needed but did not exist before: s 2(7).

Where a building owner proposes to reduce the height of a party wall or party fence wall under s 2(2)(m) (see head (12) in the text), the adjoining owner may serve a counter notice under s 4 (see PARA 383) requiring the building owner to maintain the existing height of the wall: s 11(7). In such case, the adjoining owner must pay to the building owner a due proportion of the cost of the wall so far as it exceeds two metres in height, or the height currently enclosed upon by the building of the adjoining owner: s 11(7).

22 Party Wall etc Act 1996 s 2(2)(n).

383. Exercise of rights of repair. The statutory rights to repair or do other works to a party wall[1] may be exercised with the consent in writing of the adjoining owners and the adjoining occupiers[2]. In other cases, before exercising any such right, a building owner[3] must serve on any adjoining owner a notice (a 'party structure notice')[4] stating the name and address of the building owner[5], the nature and particulars of the proposed work[6] and the date on which the proposed work will begin[7]. In cases where the building owner proposes to construct special foundations[8], the notice must include plans, sections and details of construction of the special foundations together with reasonable particulars of the loads to be carried thereby[9]. A party structure notice must be served at least two months before the date on which the proposed work will begin[10]. It will cease to have effect if the work to which it relates: (1) has not begun within the period of 12 months beginning with the day on which the notice is served[11]; and (2) is not prosecuted with due diligence[12].

If an adjoining owner agrees with the works proposed in the party structure notice, he may serve a notice on the building owner indicating his consent within a period of 14 days beginning with the day on which the party structure notice was served[13]. If no such notice is served, then the adjoining owner is deemed to have dissented from the notice and a dispute is deemed to have arisen between the parties[14].

An adjoining owner may, having been served with a party structure notice, serve on the building owner a notice (a 'counter notice') setting out certain requirements in respect of the proposed works[15]. In respect of a party fence wall or party structure[16], a counter notice may require that the building owner build in or on the wall or structure to which the notice relates such chimney copings, breasts, jambs or flues, or such piers or recesses or other like works, as may reasonably be required for the convenience of the adjoining owner[17]. In respect of special foundations to which the adjoining owner consents[18], a counter notice may require that the special foundations be placed at a specified greater depth than that proposed by the building owner, or be constructed of sufficient strength to bear the load to be carried by columns of any intended building of the adjoining owner, or both[19]. In either case, a counter notice must specify the works required by the notice to be executed and must be accompanied by plans, sections and particulars of such works[20]. It must be served within the period of one month beginning with the day on which the party structure notice is served[21].

A building owner on whom a counter notice has been served must comply with the requirements of the counter notice unless the execution of the works required by the counter notice would: (a) be injurious to him; (b) cause unnecessary inconvenience to him; or (c) cause unnecessary delay in the execution of the works pursuant to the party structure notice[22]. A building owner may serve a consent notice[23], and is then able to proceed with the works in the party structure notice as modified by the requirements of the counter notice. If the building owner does not serve a notice indicating his consent to the requirements contained in the counter notice within the period of 14 days beginning with the day on which the counter notice was served, he is deemed to have dissented from the notice and a dispute is deemed to have arisen between the parties[24].

The exercise of the statutory rights does not authorise any interference with an easement of light or other easements in or relating to a party wall[25].

1 Ie under the Party Wall etc Act 1996 s 2: see PARA 382. As to the statutory meaning of 'party wall' see PARA 377.
2 See the Party Wall etc Act 1996 s 3(3)(a). As to the meaning of 'adjoining owner' see PARA 380 note 5; and as to the meaning of 'adjoining occupier' see PARA 380 note 17.

3   As to the meaning of 'building owner' see PARA 380 note 1. A valid notice cannot be given by
    someone who is not a building owner even if the person giving the notice expects shortly to
    enter into occupation and so qualify as a building owner: see *Spiers & Son Ltd v Troup* (1915)
    84 LJKB 1986 at 1991. This case was decided in relation to earlier similar legislation (see PARA
    364).

4   Party Wall etc Act 1996 s 3(1). Nothing in s 3 requires a building owner to serve any party
    structure notice before complying with any notice served under any statutory provisions relating
    to dangerous or neglected structures: s 3(3)(b). However, this exception extends only to the
    work specified in the relevant statutory notice: see *Spiers & Son Ltd v Troup* (1915) 84 LJKB
    1986 (where the building owner was required to take down a dangerous party wall he could
    recover the due proportion of the expenses incurred in pulling down the wall but, in the absence
    of a party structure notice, not of rebuilding it). The notice ought to be so clear and intelligible
    that the adjoining owner may be able to see what counter-notice he should give to the building
    owner: see *Hobbs Hart & Co v Grover* [1899] 1 Ch 11 at 15, CA, per Lindley MR. So a notice
    will be bad if the details given in the notice are vague or hypothetical: see *Spiers & Son Ltd v
    Troup* (1915) 84 LJKB 1986 at 1991 per Scrutton J. The cases cited above were decided in
    relation to earlier similar legislation (see PARA 364). Where notice has not been served under the
    Party Wall etc Act 1996 s 3, the effect of the statutory scheme is not to exclude a common law
    remedy: see *Roadrunner Properties Ltd v Dean* [2003] EWCA Civ 1816, [2004] 1 EGLR 73,
    [2004] 11 EG 140 (cracking appeared a few weeks after neighbour had cut a channel into party
    wall using a hammer drill; held, the coincidence indicated that the drilling had caused the
    cracking and the driller could not take advantage of his failure to serve a party wall notice).

5   Party Wall etc Act 1996 s 3(1)(a).

6   Party Wall etc Act 1996 s 3(1)(b).

7   Party Wall etc Act 1996 s 3(1)(c).

8   As to the meaning of 'special foundations' see PARA 380 note 15.

9   Party Wall etc Act 1996 s 3(1)(b).

10 Party Wall etc Act 1996 s 3(2)(a).

11 It seems that this time limit does not apply where the statutory dispute procedure is being
    operated: see *Leadbetter v Marylebone Corpn* [1905] 1 KB 661, CA. This case was decided in
    relation to earlier similar legislation (see PARA 364).

12 Party Wall etc Act 1996 s 3(2)(b).

13 See the Party Wall etc Act 1996 s 5. The time for giving a notice is often extended by agreement:
    cf *Chartered Society of Physiotherapy v Simmonds Church Smiles* [1995] 1 EGLR 155 (counter
    notice). This case was decided in relation to earlier similar legislation (see PARA 364).

14 Party Wall etc Act 1996 s 5. As to the resolution of disputes see PARAS 387–389.

15 Party Wall etc Act 1996 s 4(1). A counter notice will be appropriate when the adjoining owner
    consents to the proposed works but wishes to secure modifications or changes to the proposals.
    The adjoining owner has to pay for the works required by the counter notice: see s 11(9); and
    PARA 390. However, where an adjoining owner wishes to do works himself, such as raising or
    building upon the party wall, he becomes a building owner and must give a party structure
    notice: see *Leadbetter v Marylebone Corpn* [1904] 2 KB 893, CA. This case was decided in
    relation to earlier similar legislation (see PARA 364).

16 As to the meanings of 'party fence wall' and 'party structure' see PARA 377.

17 Party Wall etc Act 1996 s 4(1)(a).

18 Ie under the Party Wall etc Act 1996 s 7(4): see PARA 385.

19 Party Wall etc Act 1996 s 4(1)(b).

20 Party Wall etc Act 1996 s 4(2)(a).

21 Party Wall etc Act 1996 s 4(2)(b).

22 Party Wall etc Act 1996 s 4(3).

23 See the Party Wall etc Act 1996 s 5.

24 Party Wall etc Act 1996 s 5.

25 Party Wall etc Act 1996 s 9(a). See also *Crofts v Haldane* (1867) LR 2 QB 194 (where it was
    held that a party structure could not be raised so as to interfere with ancient rights of light). This
    case was decided in relation to earlier similar legislation (see PARA 364).

384. Restrictions on excavation and construction adjacent to boundaries. A
building owner[1] is subject to statutory restrictions and requirements[2] when he
proposes to excavate[3], or excavate for and erect a building or structure on his
own land, within specified distances of a building or structure[4] of an adjoining

owner[5]. For this purpose, all owners of buildings or structures within these distances are deemed to be adjoining owners[6].

The restrictions apply where:

(1)   a building owner proposes to excavate, or excavate for and erect a building or structure, within a distance of three metres measured horizontally from any part of a building or structure of an adjoining owner, and any part of the proposed excavation, building or structure will within those three metres extend to a lower level than the level of the bottom of the foundations[7] of the building or structure of the adjoining owner[8];

(2)   a building owner proposes to excavate, or excavate for and erect a building or structure, within a distance of six metres measured horizontally from any part of a building or structure of an adjoining owner, and any part of the proposed excavation, building or structure will within those six metres meet a plane drawn downwards in the direction of the excavation, building or structure of the building owner at an angle of 45 degrees to the horizontal from the line formed by the intersection of the plane of the level of the bottom of the foundations of the building or structure of the adjoining owner with the plane of the external face of the external wall of the building or structure of the adjoining owner[9].

In any case where the restrictions apply, the building owner must, at least one month before beginning to excavate, or excavate for and erect a building or structure, serve on the adjoining owner a notice indicating his proposals and stating whether he proposes to underpin or otherwise strengthen or safeguard the foundations of the building or structure of the adjoining owner[10]. An owner on whom such a notice has been served may serve a notice indicating his consent to it[11]. If he does not serve a consent notice within 14 days beginning with the day on which the building owner's notice was served, he is deemed to have dissented from that notice and a dispute is deemed to have arisen between the parties[12]. The building owner's notice ceases to have effect if the work to which the notice relates: (a) has not begun within the period of 12 months beginning with the day on which the notice was served[13]; and (b) is not prosecuted with due diligence[14].

The building owner may, and if required by the adjoining owner must, at his own expense underpin or otherwise strengthen or safeguard the foundations of the building or structure of the adjoining owner so far as may be necessary[15].

On completion of any work executed in pursuance of the provisions described above, the building owner must, if so requested by the adjoining owner, supply him with particulars including plans and sections of the work[16].

Nothing in the provisions described above relieves the building owner from any liability to which he would otherwise be subject for injury to any adjoining owner or any adjoining occupier[17] by reason of work executed by him[18].

1   As to the meaning of 'building owner' see PARA 380 note 1.

2   Ie by virtue of the Party Wall etc Act 1996 s 6.

3   The terms 'excavate' and 'excavation' are not defined in the Party Wall etc Act 1996 but would appear to include all operations which involve the removal of earth, soil or rocks from the ground.

4   Although 'structure' is not defined in the Party Wall etc Act 1996, an adjoining structure would appear to include a boundary wall in the sole ownership of the adjoining owner but not a party wall between the two properties since it would not be a structure of an adjoining owner. It seems that an underground pipe, cable or sewer is not a structure.

5   The precise position of the boundary or line of junction is not relevant to this issue. As to the meaning of 'line of junction' see PARA 379 note 3. As to the meaning of 'adjoining owner' see PARA 380 note 5; and see also the text and note 6.

6   See the Party Wall etc Act 1996 ss 6(4), 20. The building or structure need not, therefore, be situated on land that has a common boundary with the land of the building owner.

7   As to the meaning of 'foundation' see PARA 380 note 15.

8   Party Wall etc Act 1996 s 6(1).

9   Party Wall etc Act 1996 s 6(2).

10 Party Wall etc Act 1996 s 6(5). The notice must be accompanied by plans and sections showing: (1) the site and depth of any excavation the building owner proposes to make; and (2) if he proposes to erect a building or structure, its site: s 6(6). The notice must be served in accordance with s 15: see PARA 391. A notice under s 6 must give the adjoining owner the necessary information as to the site and depth of any excavation in order to assess any risk to the stability of its building and to decide whether to invoke its right under s 6(3) (see the text to note 15) to require the underpinning. A notice that gives no indication of depth will be inadequate even if it would be easy, as a practical matter, to supply its deficiencies by, for example, contacting the engineer who prepared the drawing in question: *Manu v Euroview Estates Ltd* [2008] 1 EGLR 165 at [105], [108]–[109] (county court). However, a party wall surveyor can waive a defect in a notice by accepting to act as if the notice were valid. Failure to object at the earliest practicable moment could and would reasonably be interpreted by the other party as an election to proceed under the notice in any event: *Manu v Euroview Estates Ltd* [2008] 1 EGLR 165 at [113] (county court).

11 See the Party Wall etc Act 1996 s 6(7). The consent notice may be used to require the building owner to make any necessary underpinning or otherwise safeguard the foundations: see the text and note 15.

12 Party Wall etc Act 1996 s 6(7). As to the resolution of disputes see PARAS 387–389.

13 It seems that this time limit does not apply where the statutory dispute procedure is being operated: see *Leadbetter v Marylebone Corpn* [1905] 1 KB 661, CA. This case was decided in relation to earlier similar legislation (see PARA 364).

14 Party Wall etc Act 1996 s 6(8). 'Diligence' has been said to import a need to work continuously, industriously and efficiently towards achievement of the obligation: *West Faulkner Associates (a firm) v Newham London Borough Council* (1994) 42 Con LR 144, CA (decided in the context of a JCT construction contract).

15 Party Wall etc Act 1996 s 6(3). The duty to underpin or otherwise strengthen or safeguard foundations would appear to include all parts of the adjoining building or structure where it is necessary to do so and not just those parts of it within the statutory distances.

16 Party Wall etc Act 1996 s 6(9).

17 As to the meaning of 'adjoining occupier' see PARA 380 note 17.

18 Party Wall etc Act 1996 s 6(10).

385. Obligations of a building owner exercising the statutory rights. A building owner[1] must not exercise any right conferred on him by the Party Wall etc Act 1996 in such a manner or at such time as to cause unnecessary inconvenience[2] to any adjoining owner[3] or to any adjoining occupier[4]. Any works executed in pursuance of the Act must comply with statutory requirements[5]. They must be executed in accordance with such plans, sections and particulars as may be agreed between the owners or, in the event of dispute, determined in accordance with the statutory dispute resolution procedure[6].

Where a building owner in exercising any right conferred on him by the Party Wall etc Act 1996 lays open[7] any part of the adjoining land or building he must at his own expense make and maintain so long as may be necessary a proper hoarding, shoring or fans or temporary construction for the protection of the adjoining land or building and the security of any adjoining occupier[8].

Nothing in the Party Wall etc Act 1996 authorises the building owner to place special foundations[9] on land of an adjoining owner without his previous consent in writing[10].

The building owner must compensate any adjoining owner and any adjoining occupier for any loss or damage[11] which may result to any of them by reason of any work executed in pursuance of the Party Wall etc Act 1996[12]. Where the adjoining premises are laid open in exercise of the right to demolish a party structure[13], a fair allowance must be paid by the building owner to the adjoining owner or occupier in respect of disturbance or inconvenience[14].

Where the building owner is required to make good damage under the Party Wall etc Act 1996[15], the adjoining owner may require that the expenses of such making good be determined in accordance with the statutory dispute resolution procedure[16] and paid to him in lieu of the carrying out of work to make the damage good[17].

1   As to the meaning of 'building owner' see PARA 380 note 1.
2   The onus of justifying such inconvenience rests with the building owner: see *Barry v Minturn* [1913] AC 584 at 592, HL (a building owner could not insist on a vertical damp proof course on the adjoining owner's side of the party wall where the wall was only a garden wall on the adjoining owner's side). This case was decided in relation to earlier similar legislation (see PARA 364).
3   As to the meaning of 'adjoining owner' see PARA 380 note 5.
4   Party Wall etc Act 1996 s 7(1). As to the meaning of 'adjoining occupier' see PARA 380 note 17. The benefit of this obligation is extended to adjoining occupiers even though they have no right to take part in the process of resolving disputes under s 10: see PARA 387.
5   Party Wall etc Act 1996 s 7(5)(a). This is an obligation to comply with the statutory requirements applicable to the work proposed: see eg the Building Act 1984; the Building Regulations 2010, SI 2010/2214; and BUILDING. See also the Health and Safety at Work etc Act 1974; and HEALTH AND SAFETY AT WORK.
6   Party Wall etc Act 1996 s 7(5)(b). No deviation may be made from those plans, sections and particulars except such as may be agreed between the owners (or surveyors acting on their behalf) or, in the event of dispute, determined in accordance with statutory dispute resolution procedure: s 7(5). As to the resolution of disputes see PARAS 387–389. As to the meaning of 'surveyor' see PARA 387 note 4.
7   As well as the requirement of protection, the laying open of adjoining premises may give rise to a liability to pay a fair allowance in respect of disturbance or inconvenience: see the text and note 14.
8   Party Wall etc Act 1996 s 7(3). This obligation will arise even if the adjoining owner has consented to the work or even if the work commences after an award which makes specific provision for protection.
9   As to the meaning of 'special foundations' see PARA 380 note 15.
10 Party Wall etc Act 1996 s 7(4).
11 Loss or damage would appear to cover both damage incurred while the works are being carried out and any long term damage or loss sustained as a consequence of the effect of the works on the adjoining property. It seems that it may now extend to loss or damage to trade carried on from the adjoining property, which was not covered under the London Building Acts (see *Adams v Marylebone Borough Council* [1907] 2 KB 822, CA).
12 Party Wall etc Act 1996 s 7(2). See note 14. The court may take into account the coincidence between the carrying out of work and the damage to the adjoining property when drawing inferences as to causation: *Roadrunner Properties Ltd v Dean* [2003] EWCA Civ 1816, [2004] 1 EGLR 73, [2004] 11 EG 140.
13 Ie the right granted by the Party Wall etc Act 1996 s 2(2)(e): see PARA 382 head (5).
14 See the Party Wall etc Act 1996 s 11(6); and PARA 382 note 14. This provision has its origins in the London Building Act 1894 (see PARA 364), but the wider compensation obligation contained in the Party Wall etc Act 1996 s 7(2) (see the text and note 12) has no counterpart in the earlier legislation. The duty to pay a fair allowance under s 11(6) for disturbance and inconvenience where an inadequate party structure is demolished does not now add significantly to the new more general duty to compensate under s 7(2).
15 The duty to make good may arise when many of the statutory rights are exercised: see the Party Wall etc Act 1996 s 2; and PARA 382.
16 See PARAS 387–389.
17 See the Party Wall etc Act 1996 s 11(8); and PARA 390.

386.   Rights of entry. Rights of entry are given to a building owner[1] and surveyors[2] appointed under the Party Wall etc Act 1996 which are exercisable after due notice has been given[3]. No land or premises may be entered by any person unless the building owner serves a notice of intention to enter on the owner and the occupier of the land or premises[4]. In case of emergency, such notice of intention to enter must be given as may be reasonably practicable[5]. In any other case, the notice of intention to enter must be served in a period of not less than 14 days ending with the day of the proposed entry[6].

After service of a notice of intention to enter, a building owner, his servants, agents and workmen may during usual working hours enter and remain on any land or premises for the purpose of executing any work in pursuance of the Party Wall etc Act 1996 and may remove any furniture or fittings or take any other action necessary for that purpose[7]. If the premises are closed, the building owner, his agents and workmen may, if accompanied by a constable or other police officer, break open any fences or doors in order to enter the premises[8]. A surveyor appointed or selected to settle a dispute[9] may during usual working hours enter and remain on any land or premises for the purpose of carrying out the object for which he is appointed or selected[10].

If an occupier of land or premises refuses to permit a person to do anything which he is entitled to do with regard to the land or premises[11] and the occupier knows or has reasonable cause to believe that the person is so entitled, the occupier is guilty of an offence[12]. If a person hinders or obstructs another person in attempting to do anything which he is entitled to do with regard to land or premises[13], and knows or has reasonable cause to believe that that other person is so entitled, then he is guilty of an offence[14]. A person guilty of either of these offences is liable on summary conviction to a fine of an amount not exceeding level 3 on the standard scale[15].

1   As to the meaning of 'building owner' see PARA 380 note 1.
2   As to the meaning of 'surveyor' see PARA 387 note 4.
3   Ie by virtue of the Party Wall etc Act 1996 s 8.
4   See the Party Wall etc Act 1996 s 8(3), (6). Where access is required for a surveyor, the notice must be served by the building owner who is a party to the dispute that has arisen: see s 8(6). The notice must be served in accordance with s 15: see PARA 391.
5   See the Party Wall etc Act 1996 s 8(3)(a), (6)(a).
6   See the Party Wall etc Act 1996 s 8(3)(b), (4), (6)(b).
7   Party Wall etc Act 1996 s 8(1).
8   Party Wall etc Act 1996 s 8(2).
9   Ie under the Party Wall etc Act 1996 s 10: see PARA 387.
10 Party Wall etc Act 1996 s 8(5). The surveyor does not have statutory power to break open any fences or doors.
11 Ie under the Party Wall etc Act 1996 s 8(1) or s 8(5): see the text and notes 7, 10.
12 Party Wall etc Act 1996 s 16(1).
13 Ie under the Party Wall etc Act 1996 s 8(1) or s 8(5): see the text and notes 7, 10.
14 Party Wall etc Act 1996 s 16(2).
15 Party Wall etc Act 1996 s 16(3). As to the standard scale see SENTENCING AND DISPOSITION OF OFFENDERS vol 92 (2010) PARA 142.

387.   Dispute resolution procedure.   Where a dispute arises[1] or is deemed to have arisen[2] between a building owner and an adjoining owner in respect of any matter connected with any work to which the Party Wall etc Act 1996 relates, the dispute is resolved by operating the statutory procedure as described below[3], leading to an award by a surveyor or surveyors[4]. Either both parties must concur in the appointment of one surveyor (known as an 'agreed surveyor')[5], or each party must appoint a surveyor[6] and the two surveyors so appointed must forthwith select a third surveyor[7] (all of whom together are known as the 'three surveyors')[8]. All appointments and selections must be in writing and cannot be rescinded by either party[9].

If either party to the dispute refuses to appoint a surveyor, or neglects to appoint a surveyor for a period of ten days beginning with the day on which the other party serves a request on him, the other party may make the appointment on his behalf[10].

The proceedings for settling a dispute must begin de novo if an agreed surveyor: (1) refuses to act; (2) neglects to act for a period of ten days beginning with the day on which either party serves a request on him; (3) dies before the dispute is settled; or (4) becomes or deems himself incapable of acting[11]. If, before the dispute is settled, a surveyor appointed[12] by a party to the dispute dies, or becomes or deems himself incapable of acting, the party who appointed him may appoint another surveyor in his place with the same power and authority[13]. If an appointed surveyor[14] refuses to act effectively, the surveyor of the other party may proceed to act ex parte and anything so done by him is as effectual as if he had been an agreed surveyor[15]. If an appointed surveyor[16] neglects to act effectively for a period of ten days beginning with the day on which either party or the surveyor of the other party serves a request on him, the surveyor of the other party may proceed to act ex parte in respect of the subject matter of the request and anything so done by him is as effectual as if he had been an agreed surveyor[17]. If a third surveyor selected by the appointed surveyors[18]: (a) refuses to act; (b) neglects to act for a period of ten days beginning with the day on which either party or the surveyor appointed by either party serves a request on him; or (c) dies, or becomes or deems himself incapable of acting, before the dispute is settled, then the other two of the three surveyors must forthwith select another surveyor in his place with the same power and authority[19].

1   Disputes to be determined under the Party Wall etc Act 1996 s 10 include disputes over: building on the line of junction (see s 1(8); and PARAS 380–381); work which involves carrying flues or chimney stacks to an increased height (see s 2(3)(b), (4)(b); and PARA 382); any deviation from previously agreed plans (see s 7(5)(b); and PARA 385); responsibility for expenses (see s 11(2); and PARA 390); and security for expenses (see s 12(1), (2); and PARA 390). Any other dispute between the building owner and any adjoining owner is also to be determined under the statutory procedure: cf *Selby v Whitbread & Co* [1917] 1 KB 736 at 744–745 (where it was held that the statutory procedure covered differences that were questions of fact, questions of law and mixed questions of fact and law). This case was decided in relation to earlier similar legislation (see PARA 364). As to the meaning of 'building owner' see PARA 380 note 1; and as to the meaning of 'adjoining owner' see PARA 380 note 5.

2   Under the Party Wall etc Act 1996, a dispute is deemed to have arisen in several situations, including: where a party structure notice or a counter notice has been given and the recipient has not indicated his consent (see s 5; and PARA 383); where an adjoining owner does not consent to a notice proposing adjacent excavation or construction (see s 6(7); and PARA 384); and where an adjoining owner serves notice of objection to an account from the building owner (see s 13(2); and PARA 390). As to the meanings of 'party structure notice' and 'counter notice' see PARA 383.

3   Ie the procedure set out in the Party Wall etc Act 1996 s 10.

4   'Surveyor' means any person not being a party to the matter appointed or selected under the Party Wall etc Act 1996 s 10 to determine disputes in accordance with the procedures set out in the Party Wall etc Act 1996: s 20. There is no specific statutory requirement for the person appointed or selected to have any professional qualification or expertise as a surveyor.

    As to the award determining disputed matters see PARA 388.

5   Party Wall etc Act 1996 s 10(1)(a).

6   Party Wall etc Act 1996 s 10(1)(b). An appointment of a surveyor under s 10(1)(b) can be made before the service of a party wall notice in respect of the proposals to which that notice relates; the appointment will take effect under the Act as and when a dispute is deemed to have arisen: *Manu v Euroview Estates Ltd* [2008] 1 EGLR 165 at [85] (county court).

7   If either surveyor appointed under the Party Wall etc Act 1996 s 10(1)(b) by a party to the dispute refuses to select a third surveyor (ie under s 10(1) or under s 10(9) (see the text and note 19)) or neglects to do so for a period of ten days beginning with the day on which the other surveyor serves a request on him, then the appointing officer or, in cases where the relevant appointing officer or his employer is a party to the dispute, the Secretary of State may on the application of either surveyor select a third surveyor who has the same power and authority as if he had been selected under s 10(1) or s 10(9): s 10(8). 'Appointing officer' means a person appointed under the Party Wall etc Act 1996 by the local authority to make appointments under s 10(8): s 20.

   In any enactment, 'Secretary of State' means one of Her Majesty's principal Secretaries of State: see the Interpretation Act 1978 s 5, Sch 1. The office of Secretary of State is a unified office, and in law each Secretary of State is capable of performing the functions of all or any of them: see CONSTITUTIONAL LAW AND HUMAN RIGHTS vol 8(2) (Reissue) PARA 355. Functions of the Secretary of State under the Party Wall etc Act 1996, so far as exercisable in relation to Wales, have been transferred to the National Assembly for Wales and subsequently to the Welsh Ministers: see the National Assembly for Wales (Transfer of Functions) Order 1999, SI 1999/672, art 2, Sch 1; and the Government of Wales Act 2006 s 162, Sch 11 para 30. As to the establishment, constitution and functions of the National Assembly for Wales and the Welsh Ministers see CONSTITUTIONAL LAW AND HUMAN RIGHTS.

8   Party Wall etc Act 1996 s 10(1)(b).
9   Party Wall etc Act 1996 s 10(2). The appointment or selection of a surveyor is consequently irrevocable.
10 Party Wall etc Act 1996 s 10(4). The power is expressly limited to failure or neglect to appoint under s 10(1)(b) and does not extend to a failure or neglect to appoint afresh under s 10(5) (see the text and note 13) after a surveyor duly appointed dies or is incapable of acting.
11 Party Wall etc Act 1996 s 10(3).
12 Ie under the Party Wall etc Act 1996 s 10(1)(b): see the text and note 6.
13 Party Wall etc Act 1996 s 10(5).
14 Ie a surveyor appointed under the Party Wall etc Act 1996 s 10(1)(b) by a party to the dispute (see the text and note 6), or appointed under s 10(4) (see the text and note 10) or s 10(5) (see the text and note 13).
15 Party Wall etc Act 1996 s 10(6). Refusal to act effectively in this context would appear to refer to a refusal to take any effective step towards resolving the dispute. Since such a refusal permits the other party's surveyor to make an award on his own, it may be limited to a refusal designed to frustrate the statutory process. See *Frances Holland School v Wassef* [2001] 2 EGLR 88 (county court) (where it was held that the formalities must be strictly complied with when a surveyor wishes to proceed to make an award ex parte). This case was decided in relation to earlier similar legislation (see PARA 364).
16 Ie a surveyor appointed under the Party Wall etc Act 1996 s 10(1)(b) by a party to the dispute (see the text and note 6), or appointed under s 10(4) (see the text and note 10) or s 10(5) (see the text and note 13).
17 Party Wall etc Act 1996 s 10(7).
18 Ie under the Party Wall etc Act 1996 s 10(1)(b): see the text and note 8.
19 Party Wall etc Act 1996 s 10(9).

388.   Award determining disputed matters. The agreed surveyor[1] or, as the case may be, the three surveyors[2] or any two of them[3] must settle by award[4] any matter: (1) which is connected with any work to which the Party Wall etc Act 1996 relates[5]; and (2) which is in dispute between the building owner[6] and the adjoining owner[7]. Either of the parties or either of the surveyors appointed by the parties may call upon the third surveyor[8] to determine the disputed matters and he must then make the necessary award[9].

An award may determine: (a) the right to execute any work; (b) the time and manner of executing any work; and (c) any other matter arising out of or incidental to the dispute including the costs of making the award[10]. An award may impose on the building owner both an immediate obligation to execute the specified works and a continuing obligation to maintain the party wall[11]. An award may not make any interference with an easement of light or other easements in or relating to a party wall[12], nor may it prejudicially affect any right of any person to preserve or restore any right or other thing in or connected with a party wall in case of the party wall being pulled down or rebuilt[13]. An award may not purport to decide future disputes that have not yet arisen[14]. An award which is beyond the powers given by the Party Wall etc Act 1996 will be void, either in whole[15] or in part[16]. An award made by surveyors under the Party Wall etc Act 1996 is not an arbitration for the purposes of the Arbitration Act 1996[17].

The reasonable costs incurred in: (i) making or obtaining an award; (ii) reasonable inspections of work to which the award relates; and (iii) any other matter arising out of the dispute, must be paid by such of the parties as the surveyor or surveyors making the award determine[18].

Where the surveyors appointed by the parties make an award, the surveyors must serve it forthwith on the parties[19]. Where an award is made by the third surveyor[20] he must, after payment of the costs of the award, serve it forthwith on the parties or their appointed surveyors[21]; and if it is served on their appointed surveyors, they must serve it forthwith on the parties[22].

1 As to the meaning of 'agreed surveyor' see PARA 387. As to the meaning of 'surveyor' see PARA 387 note 4.
2 As to the meaning of 'three surveyors' see PARA 387.
3 If the two surveyors appointed by the parties can agree, they do not need to involve the third surveyor. If they cannot agree, then the third surveyor must be brought into the process.
4 See *Selby v Whitbread & Co* [1917] 1 KB 736 at 743 (where it was held that the jurisdiction of the surveyors is continuous and exclusive, permitting a number of awards). See also *Chartered Society of Physiotherapy v Simmonds Church Smiles* [1995] 1 EGLR 155 (where there was an award by the two surveyors appointed by the parties and a subsequent award by the third surveyor after a difference arose about consequential damage). The cases cited above were decided in relation to earlier similar legislation (see PARA 364).
5 Party Wall etc Act 1996 s 10(10)(a).
6 As to the meaning of 'building owner' see PARA 380 note 1.
7 Party Wall etc Act 1996 s 10(10)(b). As to the meaning of 'adjoining owner' see PARA 380 note 5. If more than one adjoining owner is in dispute with the building owner, the dispute procedure must be activated separately for each such adjoining owner: see eg *Marchant v Capital & Counties plc* [1983] 2 EGLR 156, CA (where the adjoining freeholder, the occupying adjoining leaseholder and the building owner appointed surveyors). This case was decided in relation to earlier similar legislation (see PARA 364). Until such time as the Party Wall etc Act 1996 is invoked and either the building owner has obtained consent or acquires a statutory authority under the s 10 procedure, the building owner cannot rely upon a statutory defence under procedures with which he has failed to comply. If the building owner subsequently obtains authority for building works which were started without authority, that authority abates the common law rights from the time of the subsequent consent or when the Act procedure was successfully invoked. An award can, therefore, cover works carried out before the Act was invoked: *Rodrigues v Sokal* [2008] EWHC 2005 (TCC), [2008] TCLR 11, [2008] All ER (D) 149 (Oct).
8 Ie the surveyor selected under the Party Wall etc Act 1996 s 10(1)(b): see PARA 387.
9 Party Wall etc Act 1996 s 10(11). In such circumstances, the resolution of the dispute and power to make the award pass solely to the third surveyor.
10 Party Wall etc Act 1996 s 10(12). See *Woodhouse v Consolidated Property Corpn Ltd* [1993] 1 EGLR 174 at 177, CA, per Glidewell LJ (since the surveyors are not authorised to determine other disputes arising between the parties, an award determining the cause of a collapse of a party wall was one made without jurisdiction); *Burlington Property Co Ltd v Odeon Theatres Ltd* [1939] 1 KB 633, [1938] 3 All ER 469, CA (award could not permit the building owner to substitute wider openings in the party wall for existing windows). The past history of a party wall is not a relevant consideration to the issue that the surveyors have to decide: see *Barry v Minturn* [1913] AC 584, HL (where it was held that the fact that a predecessor in title of the building owner had utilised a garden party wall as an outside wall of a home extension was not relevant in resolving the problem of dampness in the wall). The cases cited above were decided in relation to earlier similar legislation (see PARA 364). The right of an owner under a party wall award to have the adjoining owner carry out works and to enter and carry them out in default is not an interest in land capable of being protected by a caution: *Observatory Hill Ltd v Camtel Investments SA* [1997] 1 EGLR 140, [1997] 18 EG 126.

Any period appointed by the award for executing any work does not, unless otherwise agreed between the building owner and the adjoining owner, begin to run until after the expiration of the period prescribed by the Party Wall etc Act 1996 for service of the notice in respect of which the dispute arises or is deemed to have arisen: s 10(12) proviso. The minimum time limit for notices relating to building on the line of junction or adjacent excavation or construction is one month (see ss 1(2), 6(5); and PARAS 380, 384), and for repairs and other work authorised by s 2 it is two months (see s 3(2); and PARA 383). As to the service of notices see PARA 391.

11 See *Marchant v Capital & Counties plc* [1983] 2 EGLR 156, CA (where it was held that a continuing obligation to maintain the party wall in a weatherproof condition was within the powers of the surveyors but it was said that it was better for a party wall award to prescribe for particular works to have a certain long term result rather than to impose a continuing obligation). This case was decided in relation to earlier similar legislation (see PARA 364).

12 Party Wall etc Act 1996 s 9(a). See also *Crofts v Haldane* (1867) 2 LR QB 194. This case was decided in relation to earlier similar legislation (see PARA 364). As to easements generally see EASEMENTS AND PROFITS A PRENDRE.

13 Party Wall etc Act 1996 s 9(b).

14 See *Leadbetter v Marylebone Corpn* [1904] 2 KB 893, CA (where it was held that an award which purported to give the adjoining owner the right to raise the wall at a future date was to that extent invalid). This case was decided in relation to earlier similar legislation (see PARA 364).

15 See *Woodhouse v Consolidated Property Corpn Ltd* [1993] 66 P & CR 234, [1993] 1 EGLR 174, CA; *Gyle-Thompson v Wall Street (Properties) Ltd* [1974] 1 All ER 295, [1974] 1 WLR 123 (award invalid procedurally as the proper notices had not been served and substantively as the award purported to grant a right which was not available under the Act). The cases cited above were decided in relation to earlier similar legislation (see PARA 364).

16 See *Selby v Whitbread & Co* [1917] 1 KB 736 at 748, CA (an award void in part may be good as to the remainder provided the part which is bad can be separated with reasonable clearness); *Leadbetter v Marylebone Corpn* [1904] 2 KB 893, CA; *Re an Arbitration between Stone and Hastie* [1903] 2 KB 463, CA; *Burlington Property Co Ltd v Odeon Theatres Ltd* [1939] 1 KB 633, [1938] 3 All ER 469, CA. The cases cited above were decided in relation to earlier similar legislation (see PARA 364).

17 See *Chartered Society of Physiotherapy v Simmonds Church Smiles* [1995] 1 EGLR 155. Earlier cases, however, often use the language of arbitration (see *Burlington Property Co Ltd v Odeon Theatres Ltd* [1939] 1 KB 633, [1938] 3 All ER 469, CA) or even assume the procedure of the Arbitration Acts (see ARBITRATION vol 2 (2008) PARA 1209 et seq) can apply (see *Re an Arbitration between Stone and Hastie* [1903] 2 KB 463, CA). See also *Barry v Minturn* [1913] AC 584, HL, where the surveyors were described as constituting a tribunal. The cases cited above were decided in relation to earlier similar legislation (see PARA 364).

18 Party Wall etc Act 1996 s 10(13). A surveyor cannot order a party to pay costs in connection with litigation that was contemplated but not in fact instigated; the power is restricted to costs connected with the statutory dispute resolution mechanism: *Blake v Reeves* [2009] EWCA Civ 611, [2010] 1 WLR 1, [2009] All ER (D) 253 (Jun).

19 Party Wall etc Act 1996 s 10(14).

20 Ie after he assumed sole jurisdiction after being called upon to do so under the Party Wall etc Act 1996 s 10(11): see the text and note 9.

21 Party Wall etc Act 1996 s 10(15)(a).

22 Party Wall etc Act 1996 s 10(15)(b).

389. Appeal against an award. Either of the parties to the dispute may, within the period of 14 days[1] beginning with the day on which an award[2] is served on him, appeal to the county court against the award[3]. The county court may rescind the award or modify it in such manner as the court thinks fit[4], and may make such order as to costs as the court thinks fit[5].

Apart from this right to appeal[6], the award is conclusive[7] and may not be questioned in any court[8].

1 It seems that this is a strict time limit: see *Riley Gowler v National Heart Hospital* [1969] 3 All ER 1401, CA. This case was decided in relation to earlier similar legislation (see PARA 364).

2 As to the making of an award see PARA 388.

3   Party Wall etc Act 1996 s 10(17). An appeal under s 10(17) is a statutory appeal governed by
    CPR Pt 52 (see CIVIL PROCEDURE vol 12 (2009) PARA 1658 et seq): *Zissis v Lukomski* [2006]
    EWCA Civ 341, [2006] 1 WLR 2778, [2006] All ER (D) 63 (Apr).
4   Party Wall etc Act 1996 s 10(17)(a). See *Chartered Society of Physiotherapy v Simmonds
    Church Smiles* [1995] 1 EGLR 155 (the court has wide powers on an appeal, if required, to
    rescind or to modify an award in such manner as it thinks fit, to substitute its own finding or
    conclusion for any finding or conclusion of the surveyors and for that purpose to receive any
    evidence (whether of fact or opinion) relevant to an issue raised by the appeal, including
    evidence which was not or could not have been available to the surveyors when the award was
    made). This case was decided in relation to earlier similar legislation (see PARA 364).
5   Party Wall etc Act 1996 s 10(17)(b).
6   Exercise of the right to appeal will mean the award is not conclusive unless and until confirmed
    on appeal. See *Chartered Society of Physiotherapy v Simmonds Church Smiles* [1995] 1 EGLR
    155 (where the Arbitration Acts were excluded). This case was decided in relation to earlier
    similar legislation (see PARA 364).
7   An award will only be conclusive if it is valid. An invalid award (see PARA 388) may be
    challenged even if the time for an appeal has passed: see *Re an Arbitration between Stone and
    Hastie* [1903] 2 KB 463, CA (validity could be raised when steps were taken to enforce an
    award which directed the making of a payment by the building owner to the adjoining occupier,
    which was held to be beyond the jurisdiction of the surveyors); *Gyle-Thompson v Wall Street
    (Properties) Ltd* [1974] 1 All ER 295, [1974] 1 WLR 123 (adjoining owner successfully
    obtained an injunction preventing the building owner from acting on an invalid award). The
    cases cited above were decided in relation to earlier similar legislation (see PARA 364).
8   Party Wall etc Act 1996 s 10(16).

390.   Expenses of work.   The expenses of work under the Party Wall etc
Act 1996 are to be defrayed by the building owner[1], except where the Act
otherwise provides[2]. Any dispute as to responsibility for expenses must be settled
in accordance with the statutory dispute resolution procedure[3].

Where works are carried out, and some of the works are carried out at the
request of the adjoining owner[4] or in pursuance of a requirement made by him,
then the adjoining owner must defray the expenses of carrying out the works
requested or required by him[5]. Where use is subsequently made by the adjoining
owner of work carried out solely at the expense of the building owner, the
adjoining owner must pay a due proportion of the expenses incurred by the
building owner in carrying out that work[6].

Where consent in writing has been given to the construction of special
foundations[7] on land of an adjoining owner, and the adjoining owner erects any
building or structure and its cost is found to be increased by reason of the
existence of those foundations, the owner of the building to which the
foundations belong must, on receiving an account with any necessary invoices
and other supporting documents within the period of two months beginning
with the day of the completion of the work by the adjoining owner, repay to the
adjoining owner so much of the cost as is due to the existence of the
foundations[8].

Where the building owner is required to make good damage under the Party
Wall etc Act 1996, the adjoining owner has a right to require that the expenses of
such making good be determined in accordance with the statutory dispute
resolution procedure and paid to him in lieu of the carrying out of work to make
the damage good[9].

An adjoining owner may serve a notice requiring the building owner, before
he begins any work in the exercise of rights conferred by the Party Wall etc
Act 1996, to give such security as may be agreed between the owners or in the
event of dispute determined in accordance with the statutory dispute resolution
procedure[10]. Where: (1) an adjoining owner serves such a notice on the building
owner; or (2) in the exercise of rights conferred by the Act an adjoining owner

requires the building owner to carry out any work the expenses of which are to be defrayed in whole or in part by the adjoining owner, the building owner may before beginning the work to which the notice or requirement relates serve a notice on the adjoining owner requiring him to give such security as may be agreed between the owners or in the event of dispute determined in accordance with the statutory dispute resolution procedure[11]. If, within the period of one month beginning with the day on which the building owner serves such a notice or, in the event of dispute, the date of the determination by the surveyor or surveyors[12], the adjoining owner does not comply with the notice or the determination, then the adjoining owner's notice or requirement[13] to which the building owner's notice relates ceases to have effect[14].

Within the period of two months[15] beginning with the day of the completion of any work executed by a building owner of which the expenses are to be wholly or partially defrayed by an adjoining owner[16] the building owner must serve on the adjoining owner an account in writing[17]. This account must show particulars and expenses of the work[18], and any deductions to which the adjoining owner or any other person is entitled in respect of old materials or otherwise[19]. In preparing the account the work must be estimated and valued at fair average rates and prices according to the nature of the work, the locality and the cost of labour and materials prevailing at the time when the work is executed[20]. Within the period of one month beginning with the day of service of the account, the adjoining owner may serve on the building owner a notice stating any objection he may have to the account and a dispute is then deemed to have arisen between the parties[21]. If within that one month period, the adjoining owner does not serve such a notice he is deemed to have no objection to the account[22].

All expenses to be defrayed by an adjoining owner in accordance with an account served as described above must be paid by the adjoining owner[23]. Until the adjoining owner pays these expenses to the building owner, the property in any works executed under the Party Wall etc Act 1996 to which the expenses relate is vested solely in the building owner[24].

The right to receive payment[25] after a sale or transfer by the building owner of his property vests in the transferee[26] but not apparently in any occupying tenant[27].

1 Party Wall etc Act 1996 s 11(1). As to the meaning of 'building owner' see PARA 380 note 1.

2 Exceptions occur, for example, where a new party wall is constructed by agreement (see the Party Wall etc Act 1996 ss 1(3)(b), 11(3); and PARA 380); where underpinning, etc is necessitated by a defect or want of repair and both owners make use of the wall (see ss 2(2)(a), 11(4); and PARA 382); where work is carried out to repair or rebuild a party structure or party fence wall is necessitated by a defect or want of repair (see ss 2(2)(b), 11(5); and PARA 382); and where the building owner wishes to reduce the height of a wall and the adjoining owner serves a counter notice requiring the existing height to be maintained (see ss 2(2)(m), 11(7); and PARA 382).

3 Party Wall etc Act 1996 s 11(2). As to the resolution of disputes see PARAS 387–389.

4 As to the meaning of 'adjoining owner' see PARA 380 note 5.

5 Party Wall etc Act 1996 s 11(9). This would appear to include both informal requests and requirements made by written counter notice. The adjoining owner does not have to pay for underpinning which he has required by virtue of s 6(3): see PARA 384.

6 Party Wall etc Act 1996 s 11(11). For this purpose, the building owner is taken to have incurred expenses calculated by reference to what the cost of the work would be if it were carried out at the time when the subsequent use is made: s 11(11). Cf *Re an Arbitration between Stone and Hastie* [1903] 2 KB 463, CA (an adjoining owner who later made use of a raised party wall did not have to pay a contribution to a lessee of the building owner when it was the building owner who had incurred the expense of raising the wall). This case was decided in relation to earlier similar legislation (see PARA 364).

7   As to the meaning of 'special foundations' see PARA 380 note 15.
8   Party Wall etc Act 1996 s 11(10). As to the implications of this provision for the enforcement of obligations against successors in title see the text and notes 25–27.
9   Party Wall etc Act 1996 s 11(8). See also PARA 385.
10 Party Wall etc Act 1996 s 12(1). This provision extends to cases where work is being carried out only on the building owner's land: see *Kaye v Lawrence* [2010] EWHC 2678 (TCC), [2010] All ER (D) 264 (Oct).
11 Party Wall etc Act 1996 s 12(2).
12 As to the determination of disputes see PARAS 387–389. As to the meaning of 'surveyor' see PARA 387 note 4.
13 Ie the notice mentioned in head (1) in the text or the requirement mentioned in head (2) in the text.
14 Party Wall etc Act 1996 s 12(3).
15 See *Spiers & Son Ltd v Troup* (1915) 84 LJKB 1986 (where it was held that the time limit was not merely directory but that time was of the essence and a claim for contribution could not be made if the account was served late). This case was decided in relation to earlier similar legislation (see PARA 364).
16 Ie in accordance with the Party Wall etc Act 1996 s 11: see the text and notes 1–9. See also PARAS 382–383, 385.
17 Party Wall etc Act 1996 s 13(1).
18 Party Wall etc Act 1996 s 13(1)(a).
19 Party Wall etc Act 1996 s 13(1)(b).
20 Party Wall etc Act 1996 s 13(1).
21 Party Wall etc Act 1996 s 13(2).
22 Party Wall etc Act 1996 s 13(3).
23 Party Wall etc Act 1996 s 14(1).
24 Party Wall etc Act 1996 s 14(2). Since this provision is a security for payment of the amount due under the account which has been served, it would appear to be a form of charge over land which ceases on payment of the account: see *Mason v Fulham Corpn* [1910] 1 KB 631. This case was decided in relation to earlier similar legislation (see PARA 364).
25 Such a right may arise, for example, under the Party Wall etc Act 1996 s 1(3)(b) (allocation of expenses of building a new party wall on the line of junction to be defrayed from time to time in proportion to use: see PARA 380), s 11(10) (contribution to be made by a building owner where special foundations later increases the cost of development by an adjoining owner: see the text and note 8), and s 11(11) (adjoining owner later making use of works paid for by a building owner: see the text and note 6).
26 See *Mason v Fulham Corpn* [1910] 1 KB 631. The service of a notice under the Party Wall etc Act 1996 or the existence of an award are, if material to the transaction, facts which should be disclosed to an intending purchaser: see *Carlish v Salt* [1906] 1 Ch 335. The cases cited above were decided in relation to earlier similar legislation (see PARA 364).
27 See *Re an Arbitration between Stone and Hastie* [1903] 2 KB 463, CA. This case was decided in relation to earlier similar legislation (see PARA 364).

391–400.   Service of notices. A notice or other document required or authorised to be served[1] under the Party Wall etc Act 1996 may be served on a person either by delivering it to him in person or by sending it by post to him at his usual or last-known residence or place of business in the United Kingdom[2]. In the case of a body corporate, a notice or other document may be served by delivering it to the secretary or clerk of the body corporate at its registered or principal office or sending it by post to the secretary or clerk of that body corporate at that office[3].

In the case of a notice or other document required or authorised to be served on a person as owner of premises, it may alternatively be served by addressing it to 'the owner' of the premises (naming them), and delivering it to a person on the premises or, if no person to whom it can be delivered is found there, fixing it to a conspicuous part of the premises[4].

A notice served on behalf of only one of two or more joint tenants is not served by the building owner and is invalid[5].

1   The Party Wall etc Act 1996 does not prescribe any form of notice but the context makes clear that the notices must be in writing. The validity of any notice will be decided in the light of the principles established in *Mannai Investment Co Ltd v Eagle Star Life Assurance Co Ltd* [1997] AC 749, [1997] 3 All ER 352, HL (notice determining a lease), where it was held that a notice could be effective despite a minor error, provided that it would unambiguously inform a reasonable recipient how and when it was to operate). Failure to serve a notice should not allow the owner to obtain a forensic advantage: see *Roadrunner Properties Ltd v Dean* [2003] EWCA Civ 1816, [2004] 11 EG 140.
2   Party Wall etc Act 1996 s 15(1)(a), (b).
3   Party Wall etc Act 1996 s 15(1)(c).
4   Party Wall etc Act 1996 s 15(2).
5   See *Lehmann v Herman* [1993] 1 EGLR 172 (where a husband and wife were joint tenants both together constituted the building owner). It may, however, be sufficient to serve one of two or more joint adjoining owners: see *Crosby v Alhambra Co Ltd* [1907] 1 Ch 295. The cases cited above were decided in relation to earlier similar legislation (see PARA 364). As to the meaning of 'building owner' see PARA 380 note 1; and as to the meaning of 'adjoining owner' see PARA 380 note 5.

BRITISH NATIONALITY

1. INTRODUCTION

(1) CENTRAL ADMINISTRATION

401. The Home Office and its executive agencies. Issues relating to nationality[1] generally fall within the remit of the Secretary of State for the Home Department[2], whose department is commonly known as the Home Office[3]. The UK Border Agency, an agency of the Home Office which was formed in April 2008, deals inter alia with citizenship and permission to stay in the United Kingdom[4]. The Identity and Passport Service, another executive agency of the Home Office, is responsible for issuing UK passports and for the registration of births, marriages and deaths in England and Wales[5].

The Foreign and Commonwealth Office[6] has some functions relating to immigration, working with the UK Border Agency to manage migration to the United Kingdom[7].

1 As to British nationality see PARA 403 et seq.
2 As to the Secretary of State see PARA 402.
3 As to the Home Office generally see CONSTITUTIONAL LAW AND HUMAN RIGHTS vol 8(2) (Reissue) PARA 466 et seq.
4 As to the UK Border Agency see its website at www.ukba.homeoffice.gov.uk.
5 As to the Identity and Passport Service see its website at www.ips.gov.uk. The IPS was formerly also responsible for issuing identity cards for British citizens, until the abolition of such identity cards by the Identity Documents Act 2010. As to passports see further PARA 483.
6 As to the Foreign and Commonwealth Office see CONSTITUTIONAL LAW AND HUMAN RIGHTS vol 8(2) (Reissue) PARA 459 et seq.
7 See the Foreign and Commonwealth Office website at www.fco.gov.uk.

402. The Secretary of State. Acts of Parliament relating to British nationality confer various powers and duties on the Secretary of State[1]. The office of Secretary of State is a unified office, and in law each Secretary of State is capable of performing the functions of all or any of them[2]. In practice, functions relating to British nationality mostly belong to the Secretary of State for the Home Department, who is commonly known as the Home Secretary[3].

The Secretary of State may arrange for any of his functions (except his powers to make regulations or rules[4]) relating to:

(1) registration and naturalisation[5];
(2) renunciation, resumption and deprivation of British citizenship[6] or British overseas territories citizenship[7];
(3) renunciation and deprivation of British national (overseas) status[8],

to be exercised, in the Channel Islands or the Isle of Man, by the Lieutenant-Governor in cases concerning British citizens or citizenship and, in any British overseas territory[9], by the Governor in cases concerning British overseas territories citizens or citizenship and in cases concerning British nationals (overseas) or British national (overseas) status[10]. The arrangements may provide for any such function to be exercisable only with the approval of the Secretary of State[11].

Any discretion vested by or under the British Nationality Act 1981 in the Secretary of State, a Governor or a Lieutenant-Governor must be exercised without regard to the race, colour or religion of any person who may be affected by its exercise[12].

1 In any enactment, 'Secretary of State' means one of Her Majesty's principal Secretaries of State: see the Interpretation Act 1978 s 5, Sch 1.

2　See CONSTITUTIONAL LAW AND HUMAN RIGHTS vol 8(2) (Reissue) PARA 355.
3　As to the Home Secretary see CONSTITUTIONAL LAW AND HUMAN RIGHTS vol 8(2) (Reissue) PARA 466 et seq. See also PARA 401.
4　See the British Nationality Act 1981 s 43(3). As to the general power to make regulations see PARA 404.
5　See the British Nationality Act 1981 s 43(2)(a).
6　As to British citizens and citizenship see PARAS 406, 421–444.
7　See the British Nationality Act 1981 s 43(2)(b) (amended by virtue of the British Overseas Territories Act 2002 s 2(2)(a)). As to British overseas territories citizens and citizenship (formerly known as British dependent territories citizens and citizenship) see PARAS 406, 445–458.
8　See the British Nationality Act 1981 s 43(2)(c) (added by SI 1986/948). As to British national (overseas) status see PARAS 406, 465–467.
9　As to British overseas territories (formerly known as dependent territories) see PARA 445 note 1.
10　See the British Nationality Act 1981 ss 43(1), 50(1) (s 43(1) amended by the British Overseas Territories Act 2002 s 7, Sch 2; and by SI 1986/948; and by virtue of the British Overseas Territories Act 2002 ss 1(1)(b), 2(2)(a), (b)).
11　British Nationality Act 1981 s 43(4).
12　British Nationality Act 1981 s 44(1). See further PARA 424 note 7.

(2) LEGISLATION

403. British nationality legislation. British nationality law is now mainly contained in the British Nationality Act 1981[1], supplemented by various other Acts[2] and by subordinate legislation[3]. The British Nationality Act 1981 created a new nationality structure, with effect from 1 January 1983[4], and repealed previous nationality legislation which was contained in the British Nationality Acts 1948 to 1965[5]. However, the national status on and after 1 January 1983 of a person born before that date frequently depends upon the status he had, or would in hypothetical circumstances have had, under the British Nationality Acts 1948 to 1965[6]. In addition, the British Nationality Act 1948 itself, with effect from 1 January 1949[7], created a new concept of citizenship[8], the applicability of which to those already in existence on that date depended upon their status under the law in force prior to that date[9]. Thus, though now repealed[10], the British Nationality Acts 1948 to 1965 continue to be of relevance during the lifetime of anybody born up to and including 31 December 1982; and, in the case of a person born before 1 January 1949, not one but two repealed statutory codes may be relevant[11].

Part 1 of the Nationality, Immigration and Asylum Act 2002[12] made further provision relating to nationality, including provision for: (1) additional requirements for naturalisation[13]; (2) a citizenship ceremony, oath and pledge[14]; (3) new powers relating to deprivation of citizenship[15]; (4) a duty to give reasons for decisions[16]; (5) the abolition of discrimination based on illegitimacy[17]; and (6) the power to register as British citizens certain classes of persons perceived as having been unfairly treated by earlier nationality law[18].

More recently, the Immigration, Asylum and Nationality Act 2006 has made amendments relating to the procedure for British nationality applications and deprivation of citizenship[19], and Part 2 of the Borders, Citizenship and Immigration Act 2009[20] has made further amendments as to the acquisition of British citizenship.

The Identity Cards Act 2006 provided among other things for the issue of ID cards to British citizens and for verifying information provided in connection with applications for the issue of a passport. That Act was repealed by the Identity Documents Act 2010, but the provisions as to verification were re-enacted in the latter statute[21].

1   The British Nationality Act 1981 (with the exception of s 49 (now repealed) and s 53, which came into force on the passing of the Act, ie 30 October 1981) came into force on 1 January 1983: see s 53(1), (2), (3); and the British Nationality Act 1981 (Commencement) Order 1982, SI 1982/933. See also the British Nationality (Falkland Islands) Act 1983 s 5(2). The British Nationality Act 1981 s 49 contained provisions relating to registration and naturalisation under the British Nationality Acts 1948 to 1965 between the passing and the commencement of the British Nationality Act 1981, and was repealed together with those Acts on 1 January 1983 (see note 5): s 52(8), Sch 9.
     The British Nationality Act 1981 extends to Northern Ireland: s 53(4). The general statutory definition of the United Kingdom includes Great Britain together with Northern Ireland: see the Interpretation Act 1978 s 5, Sch 1. 'Great Britain' means England, Scotland and Wales: Union with Scotland Act 1706, preamble art I; Interpretation Act 1978 s 22(1), Sch 2 para 5(a). For the purposes of the British Nationality Act 1981, 'United Kingdom' means Great Britain, Northern Ireland, the Channel Islands and the Isle of Man: s 50(1). See further CONSTITUTIONAL LAW AND HUMAN RIGHTS vol 8(2) (Reissue) PARA 3.
2   Other relevant Acts include eg the British Nationality (Falklands Islands) Act 1983; the British Overseas Territories Act 2002; the Nationality, Immigration and Asylum Act 2002; and the Borders, Citizenship and Immigration Act 2009. Several of the relevant Acts relate to Hong Kong: see eg the Hong Kong Act 1985; the British Nationality (Hong Kong) Act 1990; the Hong Kong (War Wives and Widows) Act 1996; and the British Nationality (Hong Kong) Act 1997.
3   Subordinate legislation which affects substantive rights and status includes eg the British Protectorates, Protected States and Protected Persons Order 1982, SI 1982/1070 (amended by SI 1983/1699 and SI 2009/1892); the British Dependent Territories Citizenship (Designated Service) Order 1982, SI 1982/1710 (amended by SI 2008/1240); the Hong Kong (British Nationality) Order 1986, SI 1986/948 (amended by SI 1993/1795); the British Nationality (Hong Kong) (Selection Scheme) Order 1990, SI 1990/2292 (amended by SI 1993/1789); and the British Citizenship (Designated Service) Order 2006, SI 2006/1390 (amended by SI 2007/744, SI 2009/2054 and SI 2009/2958). As to subordinate legislation dealing with procedural and administrative matters see PARA 404.
4   See note 1.
5   See the British Nationality Act 1981 s 52(8), Sch 9. The British Nationality Acts 1948 to 1965 included the British Nationality Act 1948; the British Nationality Act 1958; the British Nationality Act 1964; the British Nationality (No 2) Act 1964; and the British Nationality Act 1965. The provisions of these Acts are repealed in their entirety except for the British Nationality Act 1948 s 3 (limitation of criminal liability of Commonwealth and Irish citizens; status of Irish citizens and British protected persons) and ss 32(3), 33(1), 34(1) (interpretation): see PARAS 410, 488.
6   The position is similar in relation to the Immigration Act 1971: ie that Act is substantially amended by the British Nationality Act 1981 s 39, Sch 4, but certain provisions of the British Nationality Act 1981 (see eg s 11 (acquisition of British citizenship at commencement: see PARA 422)) depend upon the Immigration Act 1971 prior to those amendments.
7   Ie the date of commencement of the British Nationality Act 1948: see s 34(2) (repealed).
8   Ie citizenship of the United Kingdom and colonies: see the British Nationality Act 1948 Pt II (ss 4–22) (repealed); and PARAS 414–419.
9   See the British Nationality and Status of Aliens Acts 1914 to 1943, comprising the British Nationality and Status of Aliens Act 1914; the British Nationality and Status of Aliens Act 1918; the British Nationality and Status of Aliens Act 1922; the British Nationality and Status of Aliens Act 1933; and the British Nationality and Status of Aliens Act 1943. The provisions of these Acts were repealed as from 1 January 1949 (see the British Nationality Act 1948 s 34(3), Sch 4 Pt II (repealed)) except for the British Nationality and Status of Aliens Act 1914 ss 17, 18 (status of aliens) and ss 27, 28 (interpretation): see PARA 411. That Act was renamed the Status of Aliens Act 1914: see s 28(2) (amended by the British Nationality Act 1948 s 34(3), Sch 4 Pt II).
10   See the text and note 5.
11   Note also that present status often depends upon previous status of parents and grandparents: see eg *R v Secretary of State for Foreign and Commonwealth Affairs, ex p Ross-Clunis* [1991] 2 AC 439, sub nom *Ross-Clunis v Secretary of State for Foreign and Commonwealth Affairs* [1991] 3 All ER 353, HL.

12 Ie the Nationality, Immigration and Asylum Act 2002 ss 1–15, mainly operating to amend the British Nationality Act 1981 and other legislation.
13 See the Nationality, Immigration and Asylum Act 2002 ss 1, 2.
14 See the Nationality, Immigration and Asylum Act 2002 s 3, Sch 1.
15 See the Nationality, Immigration and Asylum Act 2002 ss 4, 5.
16 See the Nationality, Immigration and Asylum Act 2002 s 7.
17 See the Nationality, Immigration and Asylum Act 2002 s 9.
18 See the Nationality, Immigration and Asylum Act 2002 ss 12, 13.
19 See the Immigration, Asylum and Nationality Act 2006 ss 49, 50(4), 56.
20 Ie the Borders, Citizenship and Immigration Act 2009 ss 39–49.
21 See the Identity Documents Act 2010 s 10; and PARA 483 note 6.

404. General power to make regulations and Orders in Council. The Secretary of State[1] may by regulations make provision generally for carrying into effect the purposes of the British Nationality Act 1981[2]. In particular, provision may be made:

(1) for prescribing anything which under the Act is to be prescribed[3];
(2) for prescribing the manner in which, and the persons to and by whom, applications for registration or naturalisation may or must be made[4];
(3) for determining whether a person has sufficient knowledge of a language for the purpose of an application for naturalisation[5];
(4) for determining whether a person has sufficient knowledge about life in the United Kingdom for the purpose of an application for naturalisation[6];
(5) for the registration of anything required or authorised by or under the Act to be registered[7];
(6) for the time within which an obligation to make a citizenship oath and pledge at a citizenship ceremony must be satisfied[8];
(7) for the time within which an obligation to make a citizenship oath or pledge must be satisfied[9];
(8) for the content and conduct of a citizenship ceremony[10];
(9) for the administration and making of a citizenship oath or pledge[11];
(10) for the registration and certification of the making of a citizenship oath or pledge[12];
(11) for the completion and grant of a certificate of registration or naturalisation[13];
(12) for the giving of any notice required or authorised to be given to any person under the Act[14];
(13) for the cancellation of the registration of, and the cancellation and amendment of certificates of naturalisation[15] relating to, persons deprived of citizenship[16] or of British national (overseas) status[17], and for requiring such certificates to be delivered up for those purposes[18];
(14) for the births and deaths of persons of any class or description born or dying in a Commonwealth country[19] to be registered there by the High Commissioner for Her Majesty's government in the United Kingdom[20] or by members of his official staff[21];
(15) for the births and deaths of persons of any class or description born or dying in a foreign country[22] to be registered there by consular officers or other officers in the service of Her Majesty's government in the United Kingdom[23];
(16) for enabling the births and deaths of British citizens, British overseas territories citizens, British nationals (overseas), British overseas citizens, British subjects and British protected persons[24] born or dying in any

country in which Her Majesty's government in the United Kingdom has for the time being no diplomatic or consular representatives to be registered[25]:

(a)   by persons serving in the diplomatic, consular or other foreign service of any country which, by arrangement with Her Majesty's government in the United Kingdom, has undertaken to represent that government's interest in that country[26]; or

(b)   by a person authorised in that behalf by the Secretary of State[27];

(17)   as to the consequences of failure to comply with provision made under any of heads (1) to (16)[28].

Regulations[29] may make different provision for different circumstances[30]. The power to make regulations is exercisable by statutory instrument[31].

Her Majesty may by Order in Council provide for certain legislation[32] to apply, with such adaptations and modifications as appear necessary, to births and deaths registered: (i) in accordance with regulations[33]; or (ii) at a consulate of Her Majesty in accordance with regulations[34] or in accordance with instructions of the Secretary of State[35]; or (iii) by a High Commissioner for Her Majesty's government in the United Kingdom or members of his official staff in accordance with instructions of the Secretary of State[36].

Any regulations or Orders in Council made under the powers described above[37] are subject to annulment in pursuance of a resolution of either House of Parliament[38].

In addition, power is given to the Secretary of State to require, by order, a specified fee to be charged in respect of certain matters relating to nationality[39].

1   As to the Secretary of State see PARA 402.
2   British Nationality Act 1981 s 41(1). As to the regulations that have been made see the British Nationality (Falkland Islands) Regulations 1983, SI 1983/479 (now lapsed); the British Nationality (Hong Kong) Regulations 1986, SI 1986/2175 (amended by SI 2003/540 and SI 2007/3137); the British Nationality (General) Regulations 2003, SI 2003/548 (amended by SI 2003/3158, SI 2004/1726, SI 2005/2114, SI 2005/2785, SI 2007/3137 and SI 2009/3363); and the British Nationality (British Overseas Territories) Regulations 2007, SI 2007/3139. See also note 21.
3   British Nationality Act 1981 s 41(1)(a).
4   British Nationality Act 1981 s 41(1)(b). As to applications for registration or naturalisation see PARA 484.
5   British Nationality Act 1981 s 41(1)(ba) (added by the Nationality, Immigration and Asylum Act 2002 s 1(3)). Regulations under the British Nationality Act 1981 s 41(1)(ba) or (bb) (see the text and note 6) may, in particular: (1) make provision by reference to possession of a specified qualification; (2) make provision by reference to possession of a qualification of a specified kind; (3) make provision by reference to attendance on a specified course; (4) make provision by reference to attendance on a course of a specified kind; (5) make provision by reference to a specified level of achievement; (6) enable a person designated by the Secretary of State to determine sufficiency of knowledge in specified circumstances; (7) enable the Secretary of State to accept a qualification of a specified kind as evidence of sufficient knowledge of a language: s 41(1A) (added by the Nationality, Immigration and Asylum Act 2002 s 1(4)).
6   British Nationality Act 1981 s 41(1)(bb) (added by the Nationality, Immigration and Asylum Act 2002 s 1(3)).
7   British Nationality Act 1981 s 41(1)(c).
8   British Nationality Act 1981 s 41(1)(d) (s 41(1)(d) substituted and s 41(1)(da)–(de) added by the Nationality, Immigration and Asylum Act 2002 s 3, Sch 1 paras 3, 4). Regulations under the British Nationality Act 1981 s 41(1) may provide for the extension of any time-limit for the making of oaths and pledges of citizenship: s 41(3)(a) (amended by the Nationality, Immigration and Asylum Act 2002 Sch 1 paras 3, 6). As to oaths and pledges of citizenship see PARA 484.
9   British Nationality Act 1981 s 41(1)(da) (as added: see note 8).
10 British Nationality Act 1981 s 41(1)(db) (as added: see note 8).
11 British Nationality Act 1981 s 41(1)(dc) (as added: see note 8).
12 British Nationality Act 1981 s 41(1)(dd) (as added: see note 8).

13 British Nationality Act 1981 s 41(1)(de) (as added: see note 8). Regulations under s 41(1)(d)–(de) may, in particular: (1) enable the Secretary of State to designate or authorise a person to exercise a function (which may include a discretion) in connection with a citizenship ceremony or a citizenship oath or pledge; (2) require, or enable the Secretary of State to require, a local authority to provide specified facilities and to make specified arrangements in connection with citizenship ceremonies; (3) impose, or enable the Secretary of State to impose, a function (which may include a discretion) on a local authority or on a registrar: s 41(3A) (added by the Nationality, Immigration and Asylum Act 2002 Sch 1 paras 3, 7). 'Local authority' means (a) in relation to England and Wales, a county council, a county borough council, a metropolitan district council, a London Borough Council and the Common Council of the City of London; and (b) in relation to Scotland, a council constituted under the Local Government etc (Scotland) Act 1994 s 2, and 'registrar' means (i) in relation to England and Wales, a superintendent registrar of births, deaths and marriages (or, in accordance with the Registration Service Act 1953 s 8, a deputy superintendent registrar); and (ii) in relation to Scotland, a district registrar within the meaning of the Registration of Births, Deaths and Marriages (Scotland) Act 1965 s 7(12): British Nationality Act 1981 s 41(3B) (added by the Nationality, Immigration and Asylum Act 2002 Sch 1 paras 3, 7).

14 British Nationality Act 1981 s 41(1)(e).

15 As to certificates of naturalisation see PARA 484.

16 As to citizenship see PARAS 406, 421 et seq.

17 As to British national (overseas) status see PARAS 406, 465–467.

18 British Nationality Act 1981 s 41(1)(f) (amended by SI 1986/948).

19 Ie a country mentioned in the British Nationality Act 1981 Sch 3: see PARA 409 note 16.

20 As to the meaning of 'United Kingdom' see PARA 403 note 1.

21 British Nationality Act 1981 s 41(1)(g). As to the regulations that have been made under s 41(1)(g), (h), (i) (see heads (14)–(16) in the text) see the Registration of Overseas Births and Deaths Regulations 1982, SI 1982/1123 (amended by SI 1982/1647, SI 1985/1574 and SI 1997/1466).

22 'Foreign country' means a country other than the United Kingdom, a British overseas territory, a country mentioned in the British Nationality Act 1981 Sch 3 (see PARA 409 note 16), and the Republic of Ireland: s 50(1) (definition amended by virtue of the British Overseas Territories Act 2002 s 1(1)(b)). As to British overseas territories (formerly known as dependent territories) see PARA 445 note 1.

23 British Nationality Act 1981 s 41(1)(h). See also note 21.

24 As to British citizens and citizenship see PARAS 406, 421–444; as to British overseas territories citizens and citizenship (formerly known as British dependent territories citizens and citizenship) see PARAS 406, 445–458; as to British nationals (overseas) see PARAS 406, 465–467; as to British overseas citizens see PARAS 406, 459–463; as to British subjects see PARAS 407, 469–474; and as to British protected persons see PARAS 408, 476–480.

25 British Nationality Act 1981 s 41(1)(i) (amended by the British Overseas Territories Act 2002 s 2(2)(b); and by SI 1986/948). See also note 21.

26 British Nationality Act 1981 s 41(1)(i)(i). See also note 21.

27 British Nationality Act 1981 s 41(1)(i)(ii). See also note 21.

28 British Nationality Act 1981 s 41(1)(j) (added by the Immigration, Asylum and Nationality Act 2006 s 50(4)). Regulations may also prospectively be made: (1) for amending the British Nationality Act 1981 Sch 1 para 4B(3)(a) or (b) or (4)(a) or (b) (qualifying period for naturalisation as a British citizen under s 6: see PARAS 439 note 8, 441 note 8) to substitute a different number for the number for the time being specified there; (2) for determining whether a person has, for the purposes of an application for naturalisation under s 6, participated in activities prescribed for the purposes of Sch 1 para 4B(5)(a); and (3) for determining whether a person is to be treated for the purposes of such an application as having so participated: s 41(1)(bc)–(be) (added, as from a day to be appointed, by the Borders, Citizenship and Immigration Act 2009 s 41(2)). Regulations under the British Nationality Act 1981 s 41(1)(bc) may make provision so that: (a) the number specified in Sch 1 para 4B(3)(a) is the same as the number specified in Sch 1 para 4B(4)(a); (b) the number specified in Sch 1 para 4B(3)(b) is the same as the number specified in Sch 1 para 4B(4)(b): s 41(1B) (added, as from a day to be appointed, by the Borders, Citizenship and Immigration Act 2009 s 41(3)). Regulations under the British Nationality Act 1981 s 41(1)(bd) or (be): (i) may make provision that applies in relation to time before the commencement of the Borders, Citizenship and Immigration Act 2009 s 41; (ii) may enable the Secretary of State to make arrangements for such persons as the Secretary of State thinks appropriate to determine whether, in accordance with those regulations, a person has, or (as the case may be) is to be treated as having, participated in an

activity: s 41(1C) (added, as from a day to be appointed, by the Borders, Citizenship and Immigration Act 2009 s 41(3)). At the date at which this volume states the law, no day had been appointed for these purposes.

29   Ie under the British Nationality Act 1981 s 41(1).

30   British Nationality Act 1981 s 41(3) (amended by the Immigration, Asylum and Nationality Act 2006 ss 52(7), 61, Sch 2 para 1(b)(i), Sch 3).

31   British Nationality Act 1981 s 41(6).

32   Ie any Act or Northern Ireland legislation to which the British Nationality Act 1981 s 41(4) applies: see s 41(4). Section 41(4) applies to: (1) the Births and Deaths Registration Act 1953, the Registration Service Act 1953 and the Registration of Births, Deaths and Marriages (Scotland) Act 1965; and (2) so much of any Northern Ireland legislation for the time being in force as relates to the registration of births and deaths: British Nationality Act 1981 s 41(5). As to legislation relating to the registration of births, deaths and marriages see REGISTRATION CONCERNING THE INDIVIDUAL vol 39(2) (Reissue) PARA 501 et seq.

33   British Nationality Act 1981 s 41(4)(a). See also note 36. The regulations referred to in the text are regulations made in pursuance of s 41(1)(g)–(i) (see heads (14)–(16) in the text) or of the British Nationality Act 1948 s 29(1)(f), (g) (repealed).

34   The regulations referred to in the text are regulations made under the British Nationality and Status of Aliens Acts 1914 to 1943.

35   British Nationality Act 1981 s 41(4)(b). See also note 36.

36   British Nationality Act 1981 s 41(4)(c). An order under s 41(4) may exclude, in relation to births and deaths so registered, any of the provisions of s 45 (evidence: see PARA 486): s 41(4). As to the order that has been made see the Registration (Entries of Overseas Births and Deaths) Order 1982, SI 1982/1526.

37   Prospectively, this applies to regulations other than regulations referred to in the British Nationality Act 1981 s 42(8). Any regulations (whether alone or with other provision): (1) under s 41(1)(a) for prescribing activities for the purposes of Sch 1 para 4B(5)(a); or (2) under s 41(1)(bc), (bd) or (be), may not be made unless a draft has been laid before and approved by a resolution of each House of Parliament: s 41(8) (added, as from a day to be appointed, by the Borders, Citizenship and Immigration Act 2009 s 41(5)). At the date at which this volume states the law, no such day had been appointed.

38   British Nationality Act 1981 s 41(7) (amended, as from a day to be appointed, by the Borders, Citizenship and Immigration Act 2009 s 41(4)). At the date at which this volume states the law, no such day had been appointed.

39   See the Immigration, Asylum and Nationality Act 2006 ss 51, 52; and PARA 485.

(3) CONCEPTS OF BRITISH NATIONALITY

405.   United Kingdom nationals.   While the term 'British nationality' is used to refer to the various forms of British status governed by the law of the United Kingdom[1], the term 'British national' is not a term of United Kingdom law[2]. However, the term 'national of the United Kingdom' has a meaning in United Kingdom law by virtue of European Union law, which uses the concept 'nationals of a member state'. In European Union law, it is for each member state to define who are its nationals[3]. For the purposes of European Union law, 'national' in relation to the United Kingdom refers to: (1) British citizens[4]; (2) British subjects who have the right of abode in the United Kingdom and are therefore outside the scope of United Kingdom immigration control[5]; and (3) British overseas territories citizens[6] who acquire their citizenship from a connection with Gibraltar[7].

1   The terms 'nationality' and 'citizenship' tend to be used synonymously in United Kingdom law, but confusion on this point was introduced by the Borders, Citizenship and Immigration Act 2009 and the Green Paper (February 2008) that preceded it; 'probationary citizenship' is an immigration status not a form of nationality. As to citizenship see PARAS 406, 421 et seq. The term 'British nationality' was sometimes used to refer to the status of citizen of the United Kingdom and colonies and of British subject under previous nationality law: see eg the British Nationality Act 1948 s 32(7) (repealed); and *R v Secretary of State for Foreign and Commonwealth Affairs, ex p Ross-Clunis* [1991] 2 AC 439, sub nom *Ross-Clunis v Secretary of*

State for Foreign and Commonwealth Affairs [1991] 3 All ER 353, HL. As to citizenship of the United Kingdom and colonies see PARAS 414–419. As to British subjects see PARAS 407, 469–474. As to the meaning of 'United Kingdom' see PARA 403 note 1.

2 For a discussion of the term 'British national' see *R v Secretary of State for the Home Department, ex p Thakrar* [1974] QB 684 at 709–710, sub nom *Thakrar v Secretary of State for the Home Department* [1974] 2 All ER 261 at 272–273, CA, per Lawton LJ (applicant claimed to be a British protected person; held that 'British nationals' have no underlying or inherent right to admission to the United Kingdom, even if they have nowhere else to go, and they are subject to relevant United Kingdom legislation). See also *AL (Malaysia BOCs) Malaysia* [2009] UKAIT 00026. See further PARA 476 note 9. As to the scope of the common law right of abode see *DPP v Bhagwan* [1972] AC 60, [1970] 3 All ER 97, HL. As to the right of abode see also PARAS 412, 420.

3 See Case C-192/99 R *(on the application of Kaur) v Secretary of State for the Home Department* [2001] All ER (EC) 250, sub nom *R v Secretary of State for the Home Department, ex p Manjit Kaur* [2001] ECR I-1237, ECJ.

4 This does not include a British citizen from the Channel Islands and Isle of Man: see the Treaty of Accession (Brussels, 22 January 1972; TS 16 (1979); Cmnd 7461), Third Protocol. See also note 7.

5 As to British subjects see PARAS 407, 469–474.

6 As to British overseas territories citizens and citizenship (formerly known as British dependent territories citizens and citizenship) see PARAS 406, 445–458.

7 New Declaration by the Government of the United Kingdom of Great Britain and Northern Ireland on the definition of the term 'Nationals' (Rome, 31 December 1982; TS 67 (1983); Cmnd 9062). See also Case C-192/99 R *(on the application of Kaur) v Secretary of State for the Home Department* [2001] All ER (EC) 250, sub nom *R v Secretary of State for the Home Department, ex p Manjit Kaur* [2001] ECR I-1237, ECJ (confirming the meaning of United Kingdom national).

Note that when British citizenship was extended to British overseas territories citizens (see the British Overseas Territories Act 2002 s 3; and PARA 423), the term 'national' was not redefined to exclude British citizens from the British overseas territories. As to British overseas territories (formerly known as dependent territories) see PARA 445 note 1.

406. British citizens, British overseas territories citizens, British overseas citizens and British national (overseas) status. From 1 January 1949 to 31 December 1982[1], United Kingdom nationality law provided for a single citizenship[2], namely citizenship of the United Kingdom and colonies[3]. From 1 January 1973[4], holders of this single citizenship were distinguished according to whether or not they had the right of abode in the United Kingdom[5].

The British Nationality Act 1981, which came into force on 1 January 1983[6], abolished this single status and created three categories of citizenship: (1) British citizenship[7]; (2) British overseas territories citizenship[8]; (3) British overseas citizenship[9]. British national (overseas) status was created with effect from 1 July 1987[10].

Only British citizenship carries with it the right of abode in the United Kingdom[11]. Holders of the other categories of citizenship and those with British national (overseas) status are subject to United Kingdom immigration control[12].

1 Ie between the date of commencement of the British Nationality Act 1948 (see PARA 403 note 7) and that of the British Nationality Act 1981 (see note 6; and PARA 403 note 1).

2 See the British Nationality Acts 1948 to 1965. As to the British Nationality Acts 1948 to 1965 see PARA 403 note 5. As to the repeal and the continued relevance of the British Nationality Acts 1948 to 1965 see PARA 403.

The terms 'citizenship' and 'nationality' tend to be used synonymously in United Kingdom law; but see PARA 405 note 1. As to United Kingdom nationals see PARA 405. As to Commonwealth citizens see PARA 409.

3 As to citizenship of the United Kingdom and colonies see the British Nationality Act 1948 Pt II (ss 4–22) (repealed); and PARAS 414–419.

4 Ie the date on which provisions of the Immigration Act 1971 came into force: see PARA 420 note 2.

5   Certain Commonwealth citizens also had the right of abode: see PARA 420 heads (4)–(5). As to the right of abode prior to 1 January 1983 see PARA 420. As to the right of abode generally see PARA 412; and BRITISH NATIONALITY, IMMIGRATION AND ASYLUM vol 4(2) (2002 Reissue) PARA 85. As to the meaning of 'United Kingdom' see PARA 403 note 1.

6   Ie the date of commencement of the British Nationality Act 1981: see PARA 403 note 1.

7   See the British Nationality Act 1981 Pt I (ss 1–14); the British Nationality (Falkland Islands) Act 1983; the British Nationality (Hong Kong) Act 1990; and PARAS 421–444.

8   See the British Nationality Act 1981 Pt II (ss 15–25); and PARAS 445–458. The dependent territories are now referred to as overseas territories and consequently British dependent territories citizens and British dependent territories citizenship are now styled British overseas territories citizens and British overseas territories citizenship respectively: see the White Paper *Partnership for Progress and Prosperity—Britain and the Overseas Territories* (Cm 4264) (1999); and the British Overseas Territories Act 2002 ss 1, 2. Since 21 May 2002, most persons who were British overseas territories citizens immediately before that date have enjoyed British citizenship: see s 3; and PARA 423.

9   See the British Nationality Act 1981 Pt III (ss 26–29); and PARAS 459–463.

10   See the Hong Kong Act 1985 s 2, Schedule para 2; the Hong Kong (British Nationality) Order 1986, SI 1986/948, art 4; and PARAS 465–467.

11   See note 5; PARA 412; and BRITISH NATIONALITY, IMMIGRATION AND ASYLUM vol 4(2) (2002 Reissue) PARAS 84–85.

12   See the Immigration Act 1971 s 1; and BRITISH NATIONALITY, IMMIGRATION AND ASYLUM vol 4(2) (2002 Reissue) PARA 83 et seq.

407. British subjects. Prior to 1 January 1949[1], the status of British subject was the single common nationality of those owing allegiance to the British Crown[2].

From 1949 to 1982 inclusive, the class of British subjects[3] included all citizens of the United Kingdom and colonies[4], all citizens of the Commonwealth countries mentioned in the British Nationality Act 1948[5], and certain Irish citizens[6]. Some British subjects held that status only, without citizenship[7]. In this period, British subject status was derivative in the sense that it was only acquired, generally speaking, by the acquisition of citizenship of the United Kingdom and colonies or of a Commonwealth country.

From 1 January 1983[8], the status of British subject ceased to be a common status enjoyed in addition to citizenship and became a miscellaneous, residual and disappearing category[9].

1   Ie the date of commencement of the British Nationality Act 1948: see PARA 403 note 7.

2   The term was introduced by the Union with Scotland Act 1706. The status of subject was originally governed by common law, but increasingly modified and codified by statute: see 1350 (25 Edw 3 Stat 2); 1708 (7 Anne c 5); 1711 (10 Anne c 5); 1730 (4 Geo 2 c 21); 1772 (13 Geo 3 c 21); 1844 (7 & 8 Vict c 66); 1870 (33 & 34 Vict c 14); and the British Nationality and Status of Aliens Acts 1914 to 1943. As to the British Nationality and Status of Aliens Acts 1914 to 1943 see PARA 403 note 9.

3   From 1 January 1949 to 31 December 1982 the terms 'British subject' and 'Commonwealth citizen' had the same meaning: see the British Nationality Act 1948 s 1(2) (repealed). As to Commonwealth citizens see PARA 409.

4   See the British Nationality Act 1948 s 1(1) (repealed). As to citizens of the United Kingdom and colonies see PARAS 414–419. As to the repeal and the continued relevance of the British Nationality Acts 1948 to 1965 see PARA 403.

5   See the British Nationality Act 1948 s 1(1) (repealed). The reference in the text to Commonwealth countries is a reference to any country mentioned in s 1(3) (see PARA 409 note 4), which was amended from time to time by various Acts and Orders in Council and is now repealed.

6   See the British Nationality Act 1948 s 2 (repealed). See also note 9. As to Irish British subjects see PARA 470.

7   As to British subjects without citizenship see the British Nationality Act 1948 ss 13(1), 16, 32(7), Sch 3 (all repealed); the British Nationality Act 1965 (repealed); and PARAS 416, 471. See also note 9.

8   Ie the date of commencement of the British Nationality Act 1981: see PARA 403 note 1.

9   In any enactment or instrument passed or made after 1 January 1983, 'British subject' means a person who has the status of a British subject under the British Nationality Act 1981: s 51(2). In relation to any time after 1 January 1983, any reference in any enactment or instrument passed or made before that date to a person who is a British subject (or a British subject without citizenship) by virtue of the British Nationality Act 1948 s 2, s 13 or s 16 (all repealed) or by virtue of the British Nationality Act 1965 (repealed) (see the text and notes 6–7) is to be construed as a reference to a person who is a British subject under the British Nationality Act 1981: s 51(3)(c). As to British subject status under the British Nationality Act 1981 see further PARAS 469–474.

408. British protected persons. The status of British protected person[1] arose as a result of the government of the United Kingdom exercising some form of administration or control over territories which were not colonies or otherwise part of the Crown's dominions[2]. Although there are no longer any such territories, some persons have retained British protected person status; nobody is now eligible to acquire it save certain persons with a British protected person parent who would otherwise be stateless[3].

British protected persons are not aliens[4]; they have no right of abode in the United Kingdom[5] but are subject to United Kingdom immigration control[6]; and it seems that constitutionally, as protected aliens in origin, they may not even hold British nationality[7].

1   As to British protected persons see further PARAS 476–480.
2   See *R v Secretary of State for the Home Department, ex p Thakrar* [1974] QB 684 at 709–710, sub nom *Thakrar v Secretary of State for the Home Department* [1974] 2 All ER 261 at 272–273, CA, per Lawton LJ; and PARA 476.
3   See PARA 476.
4   See PARA 476. As to aliens see PARA 411.
5   As to the right of abode see PARA 412. See also PARA 420.
6   See PARA 476. As to immigration control see BRITISH NATIONALITY, IMMIGRATION AND ASYLUM vol 4(2) (2002 Reissue) PARA 83 et seq.
7   See *R v Secretary of State for the Home Department, ex p Thakrar* [1974] QB 684, sub nom *Thakrar v Secretary of State for the Home Department* [1974] 2 All ER 261, CA; *R v Chief Immigration Officer, Gatwick Airport, ex p Harjendar Singh* [1987] Imm AR 346; and PARA 476.
    British protected persons lose that status upon acquisition of a citizenship under the British Nationality Act 1981 or another nationality (see the British Protectorates, Protected States and Protected Persons Order 1982, SI 1982/1070, art 10; and PARA 476 et seq), although they could, coincidentally, be citizens of the United Kingdom and colonies (see PARA 476). As to citizens of the United Kingdom and colonies see PARAS 414–419.

409. Commonwealth citizens. From 1 January 1949 to 31 December 1982[1] the term 'Commonwealth citizen' had the same meaning as 'British subject'[2], and included a person who was a citizen of the United Kingdom and colonies[3] or of a country mentioned in the relevant provision of the British Nationality Act 1948[4], or who qualified in some other way as a British subject[5]. The British Nationality Act 1981 introduced a new list of countries whose citizens are Commonwealth citizens[6], and the terms 'Commonwealth citizen' and 'British subject' are no longer synonymous[7]. Since the commencement of the British Nationality Act 1981[8], the following, and no others, have the status of Commonwealth citizen[9]: every person who is[10] a British citizen[11], a British overseas territories citizen[12], a British national (overseas)[13], a British overseas citizen[14] or a British subject, or who is a citizen of any country[15] which is mentioned in the relevant provision of the British Nationality Act 1981[16].

Commonwealth citizens may vote[17] and sit in Parliament[18].

1   Ie between the date of commencement of the British Nationality Act 1948 (see PARA 403 note 7) and that of the British Nationality Act 1981 (see PARA 403 note 1).

2   British Nationality Act 1948 s 1(2) (repealed). As to British subjects see PARAS 407, 469–474.

3   See the British Nationality Act 1948 s 1(1) (repealed); and PARA 407. As to citizens of the United Kingdom and colonies see PARAS 414–419.

4   See the British Nationality Act 1948 s 1(1) (repealed); and PARA 407. The reference in the text is a reference to any country mentioned in s 1(3), which was amended from time to time by various Acts and Orders in Council and is now repealed.

The countries mentioned in s 1(3) as originally enacted (the 'original Commonwealth countries') were: Canada; Australia; New Zealand; South Africa; Newfoundland; India; Pakistan; Southern Rhodesia and Ceylon. The countries mentioned in s 1(3) immediately before its repeal were: Canada; Australia; New Zealand; India; Ceylon; Ghana; Malaysia; the Republic of Cyprus; Nigeria; Sierra Leone; Tanzania; Jamaica; Trinidad and Tobago; Uganda; Kenya; Malawi; Zambia; Malta; the Gambia; Guyana; Botswana; Lesotho; Singapore; Barbados; Mauritius; Swaziland; Tonga; Fiji; the Bahamas; Grenada; Bangladesh; Seychelles; Solomon Islands; Tuvalu; Dominica; Kiribati; Saint Vincent and the Grenadines; Papua New Guinea; Western Samoa; Nauru; the New Hebrides; Zimbabwe. Newfoundland became part of Canada in 1949: see the Newfoundland (Consequential Provisions) Act 1950. South Africa left the Commonwealth in 1961, effective in United Kingdom law on 31 May 1962 (although it rejoined in 1994: see note 16): see the South Africa Act 1962. Pakistan left the Commonwealth in 1972, effective in United Kingdom law on 1 September 1973 (although it rejoined in 1989: see note 16): see the Pakistan Act 1973. Southern Rhodesia was treated as an independent Commonwealth country for the purposes of British nationality law but remained constitutionally a colony; between 1958 (for purposes of British nationality law, although it joined in 1953) and 1964 it was part of the Federation of Rhodesia and Nyasaland (see the British Nationality Act 1958; and the Rhodesia and Nyasaland Act 1963); it remained within the Crown's dominions in United Kingdom law until independence within the Commonwealth as Zimbabwe in 1980 (see the Southern Rhodesia Act 1965; the Southern Rhodesia Act 1979; the Zimbabwe Act 1979; and the Zimbabwe (Independence and Membership of the Commonwealth) (Consequential Provisions) Order 1980, SI 1980/701). Ceylon became Sri Lanka in 1972 (see the Sri Lanka Republic Act 1972) and the New Hebrides attained independence within the Commonwealth under the name Vanuatu in 1980 (see the New Hebrides Act 1980). As to the Commonwealth generally see COMMONWEALTH.

In any enactment or instrument passed or made before the commencement of the British Nationality Act 1981 (ie 1 January 1983: see PARA 403 note 1), for any reference to the British Nationality Act 1948 s 1(3) there is to be substituted a reference to the British Nationality Act 1981 Sch 3 (see note 16), unless the context makes it inappropriate: s 52(1).

5   See PARA 407.

6   See note 16.

7   The British Nationality Act 1981 provides that the expressions 'British subject' and 'Commonwealth citizen', where they appear in any enactment or instrument passed or made before its commencement (ie 1 January 1983: see PARA 403 note 1), have the same meaning: s 51(1). In connection with a moment in time prior to 1 January 1983, those expressions both refer to: (1) a person who under the British Nationality Act 1948 was at that time a citizen of the United Kingdom and colonies; (2) a person who, under any enactment then in force in a country mentioned in s 1(3) (see note 4) as then in force, was at that time a citizen of that country; and (3) any other person who had at that time the status of a British subject under the British Nationality Act 1948 or any other enactment then in force: British Nationality Act 1981 s 51(1)(a). See further PARA 407. In connection with any time on or after 1 January 1983, those expressions both generally refer to a person who has the status of Commonwealth citizen under the British Nationality Act 1981 (see the text and notes 8–16): s 51(1)(b). See, however, s 51(3)(c); and PARA 407 note 9.

However, in any enactment or instrument passed or made after 1 January 1983, the expressions have different meanings: see s 51(2). In such enactments or instruments, 'Commonwealth citizen' means a person who has the status of a Commonwealth citizen under the British Nationality Act 1981 (see the text and notes 8–16): s 51(2). As to the meaning of 'British subject' in such enactments or instruments see PARA 407 note 9.

For the purposes of the British Nationality Act 1981 itself, 'Commonwealth citizen' means a person who has the status of a Commonwealth citizen under that Act: s 50(1).

8   Ie 1 January 1983: see PARA 403 note 1.

9   See the British Nationality Act 1981 s 37(1) (amended by the British Nationality (Falkland Islands) Act 1983 s 4(3); the British Overseas Territories Act 2002 ss 2(2)(b), 5, Sch 1 para 4; and SI 1986/948).

10 Ie under the British Nationality Act 1981, the British Nationality (Falkland Islands) Act 1983, the British Overseas Territories Act 2002, or the Hong Kong (British Nationality) Order 1986, SI 1986/948.

11 As to British citizens and citizenship see PARAS 406, 421–444.

12 As to British overseas territories citizens and citizenship (formerly known as British dependent territories citizens and citizenship) see PARAS 406, 445–458.

13 As to British national (overseas) status see PARAS 406, 465–467.

14 As to British overseas citizens see PARAS 406, 459–463.

15 Ie under any enactment for the time being in force in that country: see the British Nationality Act 1981 s 37(1)(b).

16 See the British Nationality Act 1981 s 37(1) (as amended: see note 9). The reference in the text is a reference to any country mentioned in Sch 3. Her Majesty may by Order in Council amend Sch 3 by the alteration of any entry, the removal of any entry, or the insertion of any additional entry: s 37(2). Any such Order in Council is subject to annulment in pursuance of a resolution of either House of Parliament: s 37(3).

The countries mentioned in Sch 3 are: Antigua and Barbuda; Australia; the Bahamas; Bangladesh; Barbados; Belize; Botswana; Brunei; Cameroon; Canada; Republic of Cyprus; Dominica; Fiji; the Gambia; Ghana; Grenada; Guyana; India; Jamaica; Kenya; Kiribati; Lesotho; Malawi; Malaysia; Maldives; Malta; Mauritius; Mozambique; Namibia; Nauru; New Zealand; Nigeria; Pakistan; Papua New Guinea; Rwanda; St Christopher and Nevis; St Lucia; St Vincent and the Grenadines; Seychelles; Sierra Leone; Singapore; Solomon Islands; South Africa; Sri Lanka; Swaziland; Tanzania; Tonga; Trinidad and Tobago; Tuvalu; Uganda; Vanuatu; Western Samoa; Zambia; Zimbabwe: Sch 3 (amended by the Brunei and Maldives Act 1985 s 1, Schedule para 8; the St Christopher and Nevis Modification of Enactments Order 1983, SI 1983/882; the British Nationality (Brunei) Order 1983, SI 1983/1699; the British Nationality (Pakistan) Order 1989, SI 1989/1331; the British Nationality (Namibia) Order 1990, SI 1990/1502; the British Nationality (South Africa) Order 1994, SI 1994/1634; the British Nationality (Cameroon and Mozambique) Order 1998, SI 1998/3161; and the British Nationality (Rwanda) Order 2010, SI 2010/246). Cyprus became a republic in 1960, but the Sovereign Base Areas of Akrotiri and Dhekelia remain a British overseas territory: see the Cyprus Act 1960 s 2(1); the British Nationality Act 1981 s 50(1), Sch 6; and PARA 445 note 1. South Africa (which withdrew in 1961: see note 4) rejoined the Commonwealth in 1994; Pakistan (which left in 1972: see note 4) rejoined in 1989; and Fiji rejoined the Commonwealth in 1997 after leaving in 1987. Membership of the Commonwealth may be suspended. At the date at which this volume states the law, Zimbabwe had withdrawn from the Commonwealth, but it has not been removed from the British Nationality Act 1981 Sch 3. Rwanda, although not having had any prior juridical connection with any member of the Commonwealth, became a member on 28 November 2009. References in the British Nationality Act 1981 to any country mentioned in Sch 3 include references to the dependencies of that country: s 50(12). As to the Commonwealth generally see COMMONWEALTH.

17 See the Representation of the People Act 1983 ss 1(1)(c), 2(1)(c) (both substituted by the Representation of the People Act 2000 s 1(1)); and ELECTIONS AND REFERENDUMS vol 15(3) (2007 Reissue) PARAS 110, 112.

18 The Act of Settlement (1700 or 1701) s 3 disqualifies certain persons from membership of either House of Parliament, but the disqualification does not apply in relation to Commonwealth citizens: see the British Nationality Act 1981 s 52(6), Sch 7 (Sch 7 repealed in part by the Electoral Administration Act 2006 ss 18(7), 74(2), Sch 2); and see the Constitutional Reform and Governance Act 2010 s 47. See also PARLIAMENT vol 78 (2010) PARA 899. As to the citation of the Act of Settlement see CONSTITUTIONAL LAW AND HUMAN RIGHTS vol 8(2) (Reissue) PARA 35.

410.   Irish citizens. Citizens of the Republic of Ireland[1] are not Commonwealth citizens[2] and are not aliens[3]. Certain Irish citizens retain the status of British subject[4].

Any law in force on 31 December 1948 in any part of the United Kingdom and colonies[5] continues to have effect in relation to citizens of the Republic of Ireland, until provision to the contrary is made by the authority having power to alter that law[6].

Irish citizens may vote[7] and sit in Parliament[8].

1   The Ireland Act 1949 recognised and declared that the Republic of Ireland, formerly known as Eire, ceased as from 18 April 1949 to be part of His Majesty's dominions: see s 1 (amended by the Northern Ireland Constitution Act 1973 s 41(1), Sch 6 Pt I). The Republic of Ireland is not, however, a foreign country: see the Ireland Act 1949 s 2(1); the British Nationality Act 1981 s 50(1); and PARA 404 note 22.

2   As to Commonwealth citizens see PARA 409.

3   As to aliens see PARA 411.

4   As to Irish British subjects see PARA 470; and as to British subjects generally see PARAS 407, 469–474.

5   Ie any law in force at the date of commencement of the British Nationality Act 1948, whether by virtue of a rule of law or an Act of Parliament or any other enactment or instrument whatsoever, and any law which by virtue of any Act of Parliament passed before that date comes into force on or after that date: see s 3(2). Section 3(2) also refers to any law in force at that date in any protectorate or United Kingdom trust territory (see PARA 415 note 6), but no protectorates or United Kingdom trust territories now remain.

6   See the British Nationality Act 1948 s 3(2); and the Ireland Act 1949 ss 3, 4 (s 3 amended by the British Nationality Act 1981 s 52(6), Sch 7). As to limitation of liability in respect of crimes outside the United Kingdom and colonies see PARA 488.

7   See the Representation of the People Act 1983 ss 1(1)(c), 2(1)(c) (both substituted by the Representation of the People Act 2000 s 1(1)); and ELECTIONS AND REFERENDUMS vol 15(3) (2007 Reissue) PARAS 110, 112.

8   The Act of Settlement (1700 or 1701) s 3 disqualifies certain persons from membership of either House of Parliament, but the disqualification does not apply in relation to citizens of the Republic of Ireland: see the British Nationality Act 1981 s 52(6), Sch 7 (Sch 7 repealed in part by the Electoral Administration Act 2006 ss 18(7), 74(2), Sch 2); and see the Constitutional Reform and Governance Act 2010 s 47. See also PARLIAMENT vol 78 (2010) PARA 899. As to the citation of the Act of Settlement see CONSTITUTIONAL LAW AND HUMAN RIGHTS vol 8(2) (Reissue) PARA 35.

411. Aliens. An alien is a person who is neither a Commonwealth citizen[1] nor a British protected person[2] nor a citizen of the Republic of Ireland[3]. Aliens therefore include both persons having the nationality or citizenship of some other sovereign state recognised by the United Kingdom[4], and stateless persons. A person is stateless if no state exists according to the municipal law of which he is its national[5].

Aliens may not vote[6], nor may they sit in Parliament[7]. An alien may generally acquire, hold, inherit, succeed to and dispose of real and personal property[8]. An alien is triable in the ordinary way[9]. It is a criminal offence for an alien to attempt or do any act calculated or likely to cause sedition or disaffection amongst the forces of Her Majesty or Her Majesty's allies, or amongst the civilian population[10], or to promote or attempt to promote industrial unrest in any industry in which he has not been bona fide engaged for at least the two immediately preceding years in the United Kingdom[11]. In certain circumstances an alien may be employed in the Civil Service[12].

Aliens do not have, and cannot as aliens acquire, the right of abode in the United Kingdom[13] and they are subject to immigration control[14]. EEA nationals are in a special position by virtue of the provisions of European Union law[15].

1   As to Commonwealth citizens see PARA 409.

2   As to British protected persons see PARAS 408, 476–480.

3   British Nationality Act 1981 s 50(1). This definition also applies in relation to any time after the date of commencement of the British Nationality Act 1981 (ie 1 January 1983: see PARA 403 note 1) for the purposes of any statutory provision, whether passed or made before or after that date, and for the purposes of any other instrument whatever made after that date: see s 51(4). See also the British Nationality Act 1948 ss 3(3), 32(1) (s 32(1) now repealed).

4   Whether a person is a national or citizen of any such country is, in general, a matter for the law of that country, though probably the United Kingdom would not recognise the claim of another country to confer citizenship upon a person who had no connection with it, or to deprive a person of its citizenship in a manner abhorrent to human rights; further, changes during time of

war in nationality of enemy aliens according to the law of the enemy country (whether newly promulgated or pre-existing) will not be recognised until the end of hostilities; and a high standard of proof may be required from a person who appears to be an enemy alien but claims not to be: *Stoeck v Public Trustee* [1921] 2 Ch 67; *Oppenheimer v Cattermole* [1976] AC 249, [1975] 1 All ER 538, HL (and see the cases cited therein); Convention on Certain Questions relating to the Conflict of Nationality Laws (The Hague, 12 April 1930; TS 33 (1937); Cmd 5553) arts 1, 2. See also *Bibi v Secretary of State for the Home Department* [1987] Imm AR 340, CA. As to a person claiming nationality of a territory not recognised by Her Majesty's government as a state see *Hak Rok Djang and Tai il Djou v Secretary of State for the Home Department* [1985] Imm AR 125, IAT. As to the meaning of 'United Kingdom' see PARA 403 note 1.

5   *Stoeck v Public Trustee* [1921] 2 Ch 67 at 78; Convention relating to the Status of Stateless Persons (New York, 28 September 1954; TS 41 (1960); Cmnd 1098) art 1.1. If the court is satisfied that a person is a national of another state according to its law, it will so hold, even though the authorities of that state deny the nationality; this may result in statelessness: *Bibi v Secretary of State for the Home Department* [1987] Imm AR 340, CA. Every stateless person has duties to the country in which he finds himself, in particular that he conform to its laws and regulations as well as to measures taken for the maintenance of public order; save where the Convention relating to the Status of Stateless Persons contains more favourable provisions, stateless persons are to be accorded the same treatment as is accorded to aliens generally; a stateless person lawfully present should not be expelled save on grounds of national security or public order: arts 2, 7.1, 31. As to the limited effect of the Convention in domestic law see *R v Immigration Appeal Tribunal, ex p Patel* [1987] Imm AR 164. See also the United Nations Convention on the Reduction of Statelessness (New York, 30 August 1961; TS 158 (1975); Cmnd 6364). Note that a stateless person who is unable to return to the country of his former habitual residence falls within the definition of a refugee: *R v Chief Immigration Officer, Gatwick Airport, ex p Harjendar Singh* [1987] Imm AR 346; Convention relating to the Status of Refugees (Geneva, 28 July 1951; TS 39 (1954); Cmd 9171) and Protocol (New York, 31 January 1967; TS 15 (1969); Cmnd 3906) art 1A(2). See, however, *Revenko v Secretary of State for the Home Department* [2001] QB 601, [2000] Imm AR 610, CA (a well-founded fear of persecution is a prerequisite of refugee status; mere statelessness or inability to return to the country of former habitual residence is insufficient). As to the meaning of 'refugee' see BRITISH NATIONALITY, IMMIGRATION AND ASYLUM vol 4(2) (2002 Reissue) PARA 239.

6   As to the right to vote see ELECTIONS AND REFERENDUMS vol 15(3) (2007 Reissue) PARA 110 et seq.

7   See the Act of Settlement (1700 or 1701) s 3; and PARLIAMENT vol 78 (2010) PARA 899. As to the citation of the Act of Settlement see CONSTITUTIONAL LAW AND HUMAN RIGHTS vol 8(2) (Reissue) PARA 35.

8   See the Status of Aliens Act 1914 s 17 (amended by the British Nationality Act 1948 s 34(3), Sch 4 Pt II). The Status of Aliens Act 1914 was formerly called the British Nationality and Status of Aliens Act 1914: see PARA 403 note 9.

     The Status of Aliens Act 1914 s 17 does not operate so as to: (1) confer any right on an alien to hold real property situated out of the United Kingdom; or (2) qualify an alien for any office or for any municipal, parliamentary, or other franchise; or (3) qualify an alien to be the owner of a British ship; or (4) entitle an alien to any right or privilege as a British subject, except such rights and privileges in respect of property as s 17 expressly gives him; or (5) affect any estate or interest in real or personal property to which any person has or may become entitled in pursuance of any disposition made before 12 May 1870, or in pursuance of any devolution by law on the death of any person dying before that day: s 17 proviso.

     As to the restriction on the employment of aliens on British ships registered in the United Kingdom see the Aliens Restriction (Amendment) Act 1919 s 5 (amended by the Former Enemy Aliens (Disabilities Removal) Act 1925 s 1, Sch 2). As from a day to be appointed the Aliens Restriction (Amendment) Act 1919 s 5 is repealed by the Merchant Shipping Act 1995 s 314, Sch 12. At the date at which this volume states the law no such day had been appointed.

9   See the Status of Aliens Act 1914 s 18 (amended by the British Nationality Act 1948 Sch 4 Pt II). An alien owes local allegiance and is entitled to claim protection when within the realm (including overseas possessions); the allegiance continues as long as the protection is afforded or claimed, and apparently even if it is temporarily unavailable: *Calvin's Case* (1608) 7 Co Rep 1a; *De Jager v A-G of Natal* [1907] AC 326, PC; *Markwald v A-G* [1920] 1 Ch 348, CA; *Joyce v DPP* [1946] AC 347, [1946] 1 All ER 186, HL; *Re P (GE) (An Infant)* [1965] Ch 568, [1964] 3 All ER 977, CA (a court in the United Kingdom had wardship jurisdiction over an alien infant of stateless parents whose father took him to Israel). Though an alien is unlikely to be called for jury service as he will not be on the electoral register, if he is called he may not sit on a jury if

challenged by any party to the proceedings: see the Aliens Restriction (Amendment) Act 1919 s 8. As from a day to be appointed s 8 is repealed by the Criminal Justice Act 1972 ss 64(2), 66(7), Sch 6 Pt I. At the date at which this volume states the law no such day had been appointed.

10 See the Aliens Restriction (Amendment) Act 1919 s 3(1). The penalty is a maximum of ten years' imprisonment on conviction on indictment, or three months' imprisonment on summary conviction: see s 3(1) (amended by virtue of the Criminal Justice Act 1948 s 1(1)).

11 See the Aliens Restriction (Amendment) Act 1919 s 3(2). The penalty is imprisonment for a maximum of three months on summary conviction: see s 3(2). As from a day to be appointed, the penalty of imprisonment is replaced by a fine not exceeding level 3 on the standard scale: s 3(2) (prospectively amended by the Criminal Justice Act 2003 s 304, Sch 32 Pt 2 para 153). At the date at which this volume states the law no such day had been appointed. As to the standard scale see SENTENCING AND DISPOSITION OF OFFENDERS vol 92 (2010) PARA 142.

12 See the Aliens' Employment Act 1955 s 1 (amended by SI 1991/1221; and SI 2007/617). See also the Aliens Restriction (Amendment) Act 1919 s 6; and the Act of Settlement (1700 or 1701) s 3. As to the employment in the Civil Service of Northern Ireland of nationals of EEA states, Switzerland and Turkey see the European Communities (Employment in the Civil Service) Order 1991, SI 1991/1221, arts 3–7 (art 3 amended and arts 4–7 added by SI 2007/617).

13 As to the right of abode see PARA 412. See also PARA 420. The right of abode can only be acquired by acquiring British citizenship: see PARAS 406, 421–444. As there are no restrictions in United Kingdom law on holding multiple nationalities, a person can be a foreign national and a British citizen simultaneously.

14 As to immigration control see BRITISH NATIONALITY, IMMIGRATION AND ASYLUM vol 4(2) (2002 Reissue) PARA 83 et seq. The Immigration Act 1971 is not to be taken to supersede or impair any Crown prerogative power exercisable in relation to aliens: see s 33(5); and BRITISH NATIONALITY, IMMIGRATION AND ASYLUM vol 4(2) (2002 Reissue) PARA 84. As to prerogative powers generally see CONSTITUTIONAL LAW AND HUMAN RIGHTS vol 8(2) (Reissue) PARA 367 et seq; CROWN AND ROYAL FAMILY vol 12(1) (Reissue) PARA 46 et seq.

15 Although they do not have the right of abode, EEA nationals who are workers or who otherwise have the right of free movement, and their families, do not require leave to enter the United Kingdom: see PARA 412; and BRITISH NATIONALITY, IMMIGRATION AND ASYLUM vol 4(2) (2002 Reissue) PARAS 225–237. As to EEA nationals see BRITISH NATIONALITY, IMMIGRATION AND ASYLUM vol 4(2) (2002 Reissue) PARA 225 et seq. Each member state defines its own nationals.

412. The right of abode. A person has the right of abode in the United Kingdom[1] if:

    (1)   he is a British citizen[2]; or

    (2)   he is a Commonwealth citizen[3] who was a Commonwealth citizen having the right of abode immediately before the commencement of the British Nationality Act 1981[4], and who has not ceased to be a Commonwealth citizen in the meanwhile[5].

Those having the right of abode in the United Kingdom are free to live in, and to come and go into and from, the United Kingdom without let or hindrance[6] except such as may be required[7] to enable their right to be established[8] or as may be otherwise lawfully imposed upon any person[9]. Those not having that right may live, work and settle in the United Kingdom by permission and subject to regulation and control of their entry into, stay in and departure from the United Kingdom[10]. Certain EEA nationals and their families may have the right to live in, and to come and go into and from the United Kingdom, but this right arises by virtue of European Union law provisions for the free movement of workers and others within the European Union, and they do not have the right of abode in the United Kingdom under domestic law[11].

The right of abode is enacted as part of immigration rather than nationality law[12]; but it is an important adjunct of British citizenship since, with the diminishing exception of the Commonwealth citizens mentioned in head (2) above, only British citizens have the right of abode[13]. British overseas territories citizens, British overseas citizens, and British nationals (overseas) do not have the right of abode in the United Kingdom[14]. Their right to live in, enter, or leave any other place, including any British overseas territory[15] by virtue of which they hold their British nationality, depends upon the law in force in that place or territory[16] and is not part of the domestic law of the United Kingdom.

The Secretary of State may by regulations make provision for the issue to a person of a certificate that he has the right of abode in the United Kingdom[17]. The regulations may, in particular: (a) specify to whom an application must be made; (b) specify the place, which may be outside the United Kingdom, to which an application must be sent; (c) provide that an application must be accompanied by specified information; (d) provide that an application must be accompanied by specified documents; (e) specify the consequences of failure to comply with a requirement under any of heads (a) to (d); (f) provide for a certificate to cease to have effect after a period of time specified in or determined in accordance with the regulations; and (g) make provision about the revocation of a certificate[18].

1 Ie under the Immigration Act 1971 s 2 (see the text and notes 2–5); and PARA 420 note 1. Under s 2 (as originally enacted), certain citizens of the United Kingdom and colonies had the right of abode (see PARA 420); only citizens of the United Kingdom and colonies who previously had the right of abode became British citizens, and so continued to enjoy that right, on 1 January 1983 (see the British Nationality Act 1981 s 11; and PARA 422). As to citizenship of the United Kingdom and colonies see PARAS 414–419. As to British citizens and citizenship see PARAS 406, 421–444. Those who did not have the right of abode became British overseas territories citizens (then known as British dependent territories citizens) (see PARAS 406, 445–458) or British overseas citizens (see PARAS 406, 459–463): see ss 23, 26; and PARAS 446, 460. As to the meaning of 'United Kingdom' see PARA 403 note 1. As to the right of abode see further BRITISH NATIONALITY, IMMIGRATION AND ASYLUM vol 4(2) (2002 Reissue) PARA 85.

2 Immigration Act 1971 s 2(1)(a) (s 2 substituted by the British Nationality Act 1981 s 39(2)). See also PARA 420.

3 As to Commonwealth citizens see PARA 409.

4 Ie 1 January 1983: see PARA 403 note 1. As to the right of abode before that date see note 1; and PARA 420. As to Commonwealth citizens having the right of abode before that date see PARA 420 heads (4), (5).

5 Immigration Act 1971 s 2(1)(b) (as substituted: see note 2). See also PARA 420. In general, the Immigration Act 1971 (except ss 2, 5(2)) applies to such Commonwealth citizens as if they were British citizens: see s 2(2) (amended by the Immigration Act 1988 s 3(3)); and PARA 420.

The Secretary of State may by order remove from a specified person a right of abode in the United Kingdom which he has under the Immigration Act 1971 s 2(1)(b): s 2A(1) (s 2A added by the Immigration, Asylum and Nationality Act 2006 s 57(1)). Such an order may be made only if the Secretary of State thinks it would be conducive to the public good for the person to be excluded or removed from the United Kingdom: Immigration Act 1971 s 2A(2) (as so added). Such an order may be revoked by order of the Secretary of State: s 2A(3) (as so added). While an order has effect in relation to a person, s 2(2) (see above) will not apply to him and any certificate of entitlement granted to him will have no effect: s 2A(4) (as so added).

As to restrictions on the right of abode of polygamous wives see the Immigration Act 1988 s 2; and BRITISH NATIONALITY, IMMIGRATION AND ASYLUM vol 4(2) (2002 Reissue) PARA 85 note 11.

6 This does not, however, give a British citizen the right to bring in a spouse who does not have the right of abode, without complying with the requirements of immigration law: *R v Secretary of State for the Home Department, ex p Rofathullah* [1989] QB 219, sub nom *R v Secretary of State for the Home Department, ex p Ullah* [1988] 3 All ER 1, CA; cf *R v Secretary of State for the Home Department, ex p Phansopkar* [1976] QB 606, [1975] 3 All ER 497, CA (where a marriage before 1 January 1983 gave the wife the right of abode). See, however, the text and note 11; and PARA 411 note 15.

7 Ie under and in accordance with the Immigration Act 1971.

8 A person seeking to enter the United Kingdom and claiming to have the right of abode must prove that he has that right by means of an appropriate passport or a certificate of entitlement: see the Immigration Act 1971 s 3(9); PARA 483; and BRITISH NATIONALITY, IMMIGRATION AND ASYLUM vol 4(2) (2002 Reissue) PARA 85. 'Certificate of entitlement' means a certificate under the Nationality, Immigration and Asylum Act 2002 s 10 that a person has the right of abode in

the United Kingdom: Immigration Act 1971 s 33(1) (definition substituted by the Nationality, Immigration and Asylum Act 2002 s 10(5)(b)). See the text and notes 16–17.

9   See the Immigration Act 1971 s 1(1); and BRITISH NATIONALITY, IMMIGRATION AND ASYLUM vol 4(2) (2002 Reissue) PARA 84.

10   See the Immigration Act 1971 s 1(2); and BRITISH NATIONALITY, IMMIGRATION AND ASYLUM vol 4(2) (2002 Reissue) PARA 86.

11   See BRITISH NATIONALITY, IMMIGRATION AND ASYLUM vol 4(2) (2002 Reissue) PARAS 225–237. As to EEA nationals see BRITISH NATIONALITY, IMMIGRATION AND ASYLUM vol 4(2) (2002 Reissue) PARA 225 et seq. Each member state defines its own nationals. See also PARA 411 note 15.

     The residence right of EEA nationals and their families should not be seen as an additional and freestanding form of right of abode (although in many cases the practical effect will be the same); its basis is an extension throughout the European Economic Area of a right already held in one member state. This residence right is subject to satisfaction of the conditions upon which the right depends in European Union law: see BRITISH NATIONALITY, IMMIGRATION AND ASYLUM vol 4(2) (2002 Reissue) PARA 225 et seq.

12   As to immigration law see BRITISH NATIONALITY, IMMIGRATION AND ASYLUM vol 4(2) (2002 Reissue) PARA 83 et seq.

13   A person can be, for example, a dual British citizen and British overseas territories citizen and as such will have the right of abode in the United Kingdom. Only a (non-Irish) British subject and a British protected person cannot simultaneously hold another form of British nationality: see the British Nationality Act 1981 s 35; and the British Protectorates, Protected States and Protected Persons Order 1982, SI 1982/1070, art 10.

14   As to British overseas territories citizens and citizenship (formerly known as British dependent territories citizens and citizenship) see PARAS 406, 445–458. As to British overseas citizens see PARAS 406, 459–463. As to British national (overseas) status see PARAS 406, 465–467. Such persons, and British subjects and British protected persons, have no right to enter the United Kingdom, even if expelled from their place of residence with nowhere else to go; they are subject to United Kingdom immigration law: *R v Secretary of State for the Home Department, ex p Thakrar* [1974] QB 684, sub nom *Thakrar v Secretary of State for the Home Department* [1974] 2 All ER 261, CA. As to the right of entry see also *East African Asians v United Kingdom* (1973) 3 EHRR 76, EComHR. As to the scope of the common law right of abode see *DPP v Bhagwan* [1972] AC 60, [1970] 3 All ER 97, HL.

15   As to British overseas territories (formerly known as dependent territories) see PARA 445 note 1.

16   *Thornton v Police* [1962] AC 339, [1962] 3 All ER 88n, PC (citizenship of the United Kingdom and colonies did not confer the right to live in a colony (Fiji), and an exclusionary immigration rule of that colony was not repugnant to the British Nationality Act 1948). The same is, no doubt, true of each of the types of citizenship into which citizenship of the United Kingdom and colonies has been split.

17   Nationality, Immigration and Asylum Act 2002 s 10(1).

18   Nationality, Immigration and Asylum Act 2002 s 10(2) (amended by the Immigration, Asylum and Nationality Act 2006 ss 50(5), 52(7), 61, Sch 2 para 4, Sch 3). The regulations may: (1) make provision which applies generally or only in specified cases or circumstances; (2) make different provision for different purposes; (3) include consequential, incidental or transitional provision: Nationality, Immigration and Asylum Act 2002 s 10(3). The regulations: (a) must be made by statutory instrument, and (b) are subject to annulment in pursuance of a resolution of either House of Parliament: s 10(4). As to regulations made under s 10 see the Immigration (Certificate of Entitlement to Right of Abode in the United Kingdom) Regulations 2006, SI 2006/3145 (amended by SI 2009/1892).

413.   Nationality and the Convention for the Protection of Human Rights and Fundamental Freedoms (1950).

The Convention for the Protection of Human Rights and Fundamental Freedoms (1950)[1] itself contains no right to a nationality[2] and no rights or freedoms based on nationality, but the Fourth Protocol[3] guarantees certain nationality-based rights approximating to the United Kingdom concept of the right of abode[4]. The Fourth Protocol has been signed but not ratified by the United Kingdom. However, it is possible for the provisions of the Convention for the Protection of Human Rights and Fundamental Freedoms (1950) that have been ratified to protect individuals in circumstances that are associated with the Fourth Protocol[5].

1 Ie the Convention for the Protection of Human Rights and Fundamental Freedoms (Rome, 4 November 1950; TS 71 (1953); Cmd 8969): see CONSTITUTIONAL LAW AND HUMAN RIGHTS.

2 The right to a nationality has been most recently guaranteed in the European Convention on Nationality (Strasbourg, 6 November 1997; ETS 166 (2000)) art 4a. Unlike previous treaties relating to nationality, the European Convention on Nationality is a comprehensive nationality code which is expected to be widely ratified across Europe. The Convention entered into force on 1 March 2000, but at the date at which this volume states the law it had not been signed by the United Kingdom.

3 Ie the Convention for the Protection of Human Rights and Fundamental Freedoms (1950), Fourth Protocol (Strasbourg, 16 September 1963; ETS 46; Cmnd 2309).

4 See the Convention for the Protection of Human Rights and Fundamental Freedoms (1950) Fourth Protocol art 3.

5 See eg *East African Asians v United Kingdom* (1973) 3 EHRR 76, EComHR, where the European Commission of Human Rights found that there could be a breach of the Convention for the Protection of Human Rights and Fundamental Freedoms (1950) art 3 in the absence of ratification of the Fourth Protocol. As to the European Commission of Human Rights, which has now been replaced by the European Court of Human Rights, see CONSTITUTIONAL LAW AND HUMAN RIGHTS vol 8(2) (Reissue) PARA 172.

2. PREVIOUS NATIONALITY LAW

414. In general. A full account of previous nationality and immigration law, now repealed, is beyond the scope of this work; but two aspects of that law as it was prior to 1 January 1983[1] are crucial for the understanding of the law now in force: citizenship of the United Kingdom and colonies[2], and the right of abode[3]. Citizenship of the United Kingdom and colonies no longer exists, having been replaced by new categories of citizenship[4]; the right of abode still exists but the provisions determining who holds it have been repealed and replaced[5]. In order to determine the current national status of a former citizen of the United Kingdom and colonies (and sometimes his or her children), it is necessary to determine how that citizenship was acquired, and whether the person had the right of abode in the United Kingdom. The right of abode is dealt with in immigration rather than nationality legislation[6], but it must be treated in any account of British nationality law because: (1) although the right to live in the country of one's nationality is normally inherent in that nationality[7], yet in the case of British nationality the position is more complex[8]; (2) the right of abode under previous immigration law was an important qualification for acquisition of British citizenship when it came into existence[9]; and (3) with the exception of a diminishing class of Commonwealth citizens, only British citizens now have the right of abode[10].

1 Ie the date of commencement of the British Nationality Act 1981: see PARA 403 note 1.
2 See PARAS 415–419. For a full account see Fransman *British Nationality Law* (2nd Edn, 1998; 3rd Edn, 2011).
3 See PARA 420.
4 As to citizenship since 1 January 1983 see PARAS 406, 421 et seq.
5 As to the right of abode since 1 January 1983 see PARA 412.
6 As to immigration law see BRITISH NATIONALITY, IMMIGRATION AND ASYLUM vol 4(2) (2002 Reissue) PARA 83 et seq.
7 See eg the Convention for the Protection of Human Rights and Fundamental Freedoms (Rome, 4 November 1950; TS 71 (1953); Cmd 8969), Fourth Protocol (Strasbourg, 16 September 1963; ETS 46; Cmnd 2309) art 3, which has been signed but not ratified by the United Kingdom. See further PARA 413.
8 Some people without British nationality have this right, while many people with British nationality do not: see PARAS 412, 420.
9 See PARAS 420, 422. British citizenship is one of the categories of citizenship introduced on 1 January 1983 by the British Nationality Act 1981: see PARAS 406, 421–444.
10 See PARA 412. As to Commonwealth citizens see PARA 409.

415. Citizenship of the United Kingdom and colonies; acquisition on 1 January 1949 under transitional arrangements. Upon the coming into force of the British Nationality Act 1948 on 1 January 1949[1] the following British subjects became citizens of the United Kingdom and colonies:

(1) one who was born or naturalised in the United Kingdom and colonies[2] or became a British subject by annexation of territory[3];

(2) one whose father[4] was born or naturalised in the United Kingdom or the colonies or became a British subject by annexation of territory[5];

(3) one who was born in a protectorate, protected state or United Kingdom trust territory[6];

(4) one who did not qualify under heads (1) to (3) above and was not an Irish citizen[7] or an actual or potential citizen of a Commonwealth country[8];

(5) one who was the wife or former wife of a man who acquired citizenship under heads (1) to (4) above or would have done so but for his death[9].

Certain persons were deemed to have been British subjects on 31 December 1948[10].

A person was potentially a citizen of one of the original Commonwealth countries[11] which had as yet no citizenship law[12] if he, or his nearest ancestor in the male line who acquired British nationality otherwise than by reason of his parentage[13], acquired British nationality either by birth within the territory of that country, or by naturalisation granted by the government of that country, or by the annexation of any territory then forming part of that country; in addition, a woman married or formerly married to any such person was a potential citizen of the country of which her husband was, or would but for his death have been, a potential citizen[14].

1 See PARA 403 note 7.

2 Ie the territories comprising the United Kingdom and colonies on 1 January 1949. A person was naturalised (before 1 January 1949) in the United Kingdom and colonies if a certificate of naturalisation was granted to him by the Secretary of State or (under the British Nationality and Status of Aliens Act 1914 (now known as the Status of Aliens Act 1914: see PARA 403 note 9)) by the government of any British possession other than a country listed in the British Nationality Act 1948 s 1(3) (now repealed) (see note 11; and PARA 409 note 4) as a Commonwealth country, or if he was deemed (by the British Nationality and Status of Aliens Act 1914 s 27(2) (now repealed)) to be a person to whom a certificate of naturalisation was granted, if the certificate in which his name was included was granted by the Secretary of State or by the government of any such British possession, or if he was deemed to be a naturalised British subject by reason of his residence with his father or mother: British Nationality Act 1948 s 32(1) (now repealed). A certificate of naturalisation is required; neither a seaman's Certificate of Nationality and Identity (issued 1937) nor a National Registration Identity Card (issued 1940) was sufficient: *Uddin v Secretary of State for the Home Department* [1990] Imm AR 104, CA. See also *A-G v HRH Prince Ernest Augustus of Hanover* [1957] AC 436, [1957] 1 All ER 49, HL (effect of 4 Anne c 16 (1705) naturalising the descendants of the Electress Sophia of Hanover). In addition, any person who, by the law in force immediately before 1 January 1949 in any colony or protectorate, enjoyed the privileges of naturalisation within that colony or protectorate only, was deemed to have become immediately before 1 January 1949 a British subject naturalised in the United Kingdom and colonies: British Nationality Act 1948 s 32(6) (now repealed). As to the repeal and the continued relevance of the British Nationality Act 1948 see PARA 403. As to the Secretary of State see PARA 402.

3 British Nationality Act 1948 s 12(1) (now repealed). In *R v Ketter* [1940] 1 KB 787, [1939] 1 All ER 729, CCA (in relation to Palestine), mandated territory was not annexed and its inhabitants did not become British subjects. But see *Lesa v A-G of New Zealand* [1983] 2 AC 20, [1982] 3 WLR 898, PC (in relation to Western Samoa).

4 A man is the 'father', for these purposes, only of his legitimate children: British Nationality Act 1948 s 32(2) (now repealed).

5 British Nationality Act 1948 s 12(2) (now repealed). Such a person was a citizen by descent only: s 12(8) (now repealed). As to the significance of citizenship by descent see PARA 417.

6 Ie a territory which had that status on 1 January 1949: see the British Nationality Act 1948 ss 12(3), 30, 32(1) (all now repealed); and the British Protectorates, Protected States and Protected Persons Order in Council 1949, SI 1949/140 (now revoked). 'United Kingdom trust territory' meant a territory administered by the government of the United Kingdom under the trusteeship system of the United Nations: British Nationality Act 1948 s 32(1) (now repealed). See also PARA 476 notes 1, 13.

7 Ie save in the case of certain Irish citizens born before 6 December 1922: see the Ireland Act 1949 s 5(2) (now repealed).

8 Ie a country listed in the British Nationality Act 1948 s 1(3) as originally enacted (see note 11; and PARA 409 note 4): see ss 12(4), 32(7) (both now repealed); *R v Secretary of State for Foreign and Commonwealth Affairs, ex p Ross-Clunis* [1991] 2 AC 439, sub nom *Ross-Clunis v Secretary of State for Foreign and Commonwealth Affairs* [1991] 3 All ER 353, HL. Such a person was a citizen by descent only: British Nationality Act 1948 s 12(8) (now repealed). As to acquisition by potential citizens of Commonwealth countries see PARA 416.

9 British Nationality Act 1948 s 12(5) (now repealed).

10 See the British Nationality Act 1948 s 14 (now repealed) (women who ceased to be British subjects by reason of marriage), s 15 (now repealed) (persons who ceased to be British subjects

by failure to make a declaration of retention of British nationality), s 17 (now repealed) (persons whose birth occurred before 1 January 1949 but was not registered until afterwards), s 32(6) (now repealed) (persons with local naturalisation in a colony or protectorate). See also ss 16, 23, 24 (all now repealed) (relating to minors). As to Irish British subjects born before 6 December 1922 who remained British subjects see the Ireland Act 1949 s 5; and PARA 470.

11 Ie Canada, Australia, New Zealand, South Africa, Newfoundland, India, Pakistan, Southern Rhodesia, Ceylon: see the British Nationality Act 1948 s 1(3) (as originally enacted); and PARA 409 note 4.

12 See PARA 416.

13 For this purpose, 'ancestor' included father, and 'acquired British nationality' referred to acquisition of the status of British subject under the law in force prior to 1 January 1949. Thus a person born in Athens in 1948, whose father became a British subject by birth in 1905 in the Colony of the Cape of Good Hope (later part of South Africa) but became a citizen of the United Kingdom and colonies only because his own father had been born in the United Kingdom, did not himself become a citizen of the United Kingdom and colonies (in 1949) or, therefore, a British citizen (in 1983), because the father acquired British nationality by being born a British subject, not by his acquisition of citizenship in 1949. In other words, the child's father was indeed the nearest ancestor in the male line to acquire British nationality otherwise than by parentage, and so the child became a potential citizen of South Africa on 1 January 1949 and not a citizen of the United Kingdom and colonies under the British Nationality Act 1948 s 12(4) (now repealed) (see head (4) in the text): *R v Secretary of State for Foreign and Commonwealth Affairs, ex p Ross-Clunis* [1991] 2 AC 439, sub nom *Ross-Clunis v Secretary of State for Foreign and Commonwealth Affairs* [1991] 3 All ER 353, HL; revsg *R v Secretary of State for Foreign and Commonwealth Affairs, ex p Ross-Clunis* [1991] Imm AR 316, CA.

14 British Nationality Act 1948 s 32(7) (now repealed).

416. Citizenship of the United Kingdom and colonies; acquisition by potential citizens of Commonwealth countries. A person who was a British subject on 31 December 1948 and was on 1 January 1949 potentially a citizen of any of the then existing Commonwealth countries[1], but not actually a citizen of any of those countries or a citizen of the United Kingdom and colonies or of the Republic of Ireland[2], remained from that date a British subject without citizenship until (or unless[3]) he became a citizen of the United Kingdom and colonies, a citizen of an independent Commonwealth country, a citizen of the Republic of Ireland[4], a citizen of Pakistan (as of 1 September 1973[5]), or an alien[6].

Upon the coming into force of a citizenship law in any of the original Commonwealth countries which did not already have one on 1 January 1949, potential citizens of that country who were still British subjects without citizenship automatically became citizens of the United Kingdom and colonies, unless they then became citizens of that (or any other) country[7]. 'Citizenship law' meant an enactment of the legislature of the relevant country declared by order of the Secretary of State[8] at the request of that country to be an enactment making provision for citizenship thereof; orders were made[9] in respect of all the relevant countries except India and Pakistan[10]. Accordingly this provision for automatic citizenship of the United Kingdom and colonies was never triggered in the case of potential citizens of India or Pakistan[11]. Former citizens of the Federation of Rhodesia and Nyasaland who did not become citizens of Southern Rhodesia on 1 January 1964 (when the Federation was dissolved) became citizens of the United Kingdom and colonies[12]. This was a unique provision because it provided for automatic acquisition of citizenship of the United Kingdom and colonies by persons who had actually acquired citizenship of a particular Commonwealth country (before losing it again).

1 See PARA 409 note 4.
2 See, however, PARA 415 note 7.

3   As to those who have remained to this day British subjects without citizenship, now British subjects simpliciter, see PARA 471.

4   See, however, PARA 415 note 7.

5   See PARA 409 note 4.

6   British Nationality Act 1948 s 13(1) (now repealed). For these purposes, an 'alien' was someone who was not a British subject, a British protected person or a citizen of the Republic of Ireland: s 32(1) (now repealed). As to the repeal and the continued relevance of the British Nationality Act 1948 see PARA 403.

7   British Nationality Act 1948 s 13(2) (now repealed); *Uddin v Secretary of State for the Home Department* [1990] Imm AR 104, CA. Such persons were deemed to be citizens by descent only: British Nationality Act 1948 s 13(3) (now repealed). As to the significance of citizenship by descent see PARA 417.

8   As to the Secretary of State see PARA 402.

9   See the Citizenship Law (Canada) Order 1948, SI 1948/2779 (which extended to Newfoundland: see the Newfoundland (Consequential Provisions) Act 1950); the Citizenship Law (Australia) Order 1949, SI 1949/170; the Citizenship Law (New Zealand) Order 1949, SI 1949/7; the Citizenship Law (Union of South Africa) Order 1949, SI 1949/2448; the Citizenship Law (Southern Rhodesia) Order 1950, SI 1950/61; and the Citizenship Law (Ceylon) Order 1948, SI 1948/2780.

10   Although those countries have laws providing for citizenship, no orders were made so they do not fall within the definition: see *Gowa v A-G* (1984) 129 Sol Jo 131, CA; affd [1985] 1 WLR 1003, HL.

11   See also PARA 471.

12   See the Rhodesia and Nyasaland Act 1963; and the Federation of Rhodesia and Nyasaland (Dissolution) Order in Council 1963, SI 1963/2085, s 74(2).

417. Citizenship of the United Kingdom and colonies; acquisition on or after 1 January 1949 under the Act's permanent provisions. From 1949 to 1982 inclusive, citizenship was acquired as follows:

(1)   by birth in the United Kingdom and colonies, except by those whose father was entitled to diplomatic immunity and was not a citizen of the United Kingdom and colonies, and anyone whose father was an enemy alien[1] and who was born in a place under enemy occupation[2];

(2)   by adoption in the United Kingdom by a citizen (in the case of a joint adoption, a male citizen) of the United Kingdom and colonies[3];

(3)   by descent[4] from a father who was a citizen of the United Kingdom and colonies at the time of the child's birth[5], save that if the father was a citizen by descent only[6], the child would not be a citizen unless: (a) he or his father was born in a protectorate, protected state, mandated territory or trust territory[7] or any place in a foreign country[8] where the Crown had jurisdiction over British subjects; or (b) the birth occurred in a foreign country and was registered at a United Kingdom consulate within a year[9]; or (c) the father was in Crown service[10] at the time of the birth; or (d) the child was born in a Commonwealth country but did not become a citizen of that country under its citizenship law[11];

(4)   by registration by the Secretary of State or, in a colony, protectorate or United Kingdom trust territory, by the Governor[12], or, in a Commonwealth country, by the High Commissioner[13];

(5)   by naturalisation (the normal method for aliens and British protected persons) by the Secretary of State or, in a colony, protectorate or United Kingdom trust territory, by the Governor[14];

(6)   by incorporation of territory[15].

1   As to the meaning of 'alien' see PARA 416 note 6. The British Nationality Act 1948 did not define 'enemy alien'.

2   See the British Nationality Act 1948 s 4 (amended by the Diplomatic Privileges Act 1964 s 5(2); and now repealed). As to the repeal and the continued relevance of the British Nationality

Act 1948 see PARA 403. From 16 September 1964 if the person would be stateless as a result of the proviso, he became a citizen of the United Kingdom and colonies if his mother was one; and a new-born infant found abandoned within the United Kingdom and colonies was presumed to have been born there unless the contrary was shown: British Nationality (No 2) Act 1964 s 2 (now repealed).

3 See the Adoption of Children Act 1949 s 8, the Adoption Act 1950 s 16, the Adoption Act 1958 s 19(1) and the Adoption Act 1964 s 1(3) (all now repealed). Overseas adoption within the meaning of the Adoption Act 1968 s 4 (now repealed) and its replacement, the Adoption Act 1976 s 72(2) (now repealed), did not (and does not) confer citizenship: see *Secretary of State for the Home Department v Lofthouse* [1981] Imm AR 166, IAT; *R v Secretary of State for the Home Department, ex p Brassey* [1989] Imm AR 258; *Tahid v Secretary of State for the Home Department* [1991] Imm AR 157, CA. As to adoption generally see CHILDREN AND YOUNG PERSONS vol 5(3) (2008 Reissue) PARA 323 et seq.

4 Citizenship of the United Kingdom and colonies was not inconsistent with the simultaneous possession of British protected person status (see PARAS 408, 476–480): *Motala v A-G* [1992] 1 AC 281, [1991] 4 All ER 682, HL (citizenship of the United Kingdom and colonies acquired by descent and British protected person status acquired by birth in Northern Rhodesia).

5 Registration as a citizen of the United Kingdom and colonies did not confer citizenship by descent upon an existing child: *Uddin v Secretary of State for the Home Department* [1990] Imm AR 104, CA. A man was the 'father' only of his legitimate children: British Nationality Act 1948 s 32(2) (now repealed).

6 This was a term of art (as it still is: see PARAS 425, 456), covering not only persons who became citizens by descent under the British Nationality Act 1948 s 5 (now repealed) (or British subjects by descent under previous law) but also persons whose citizenship, acquired by virtue of other provisions, was deemed to be by descent only for the purpose of s 5 (now repealed): see eg ss 12(8), 13, Sch 3 para 3 (all now repealed); the British Nationality (No 2) Act 1964 s 1(4) (now repealed); and PARAS 415–416.

7 As to protectorates and protected states see PARA 415 note 6. A trust territory (as opposed to a United Kingdom trust territory, i e one administered by the United Kingdom government: see PARA 415 note 6) was a territory administered by the government of any part of His Majesty's dominions under the trusteeship system of the United Nations; and a mandated territory was a territory administered by the government of any part of His Majesty's dominions in accordance with a mandate from the League of Nations: British Nationality Act 1948 s 32(1) (now repealed).

8 See the British Nationality Act 1948 ss 30, 32(1) (both now repealed). A foreign country was a country other than the United Kingdom, a colony, a Commonwealth country listed in s 1(3) (now repealed) (see PARA 409 note 4), the Republic of Ireland, or a protectorate, protected state, mandated territory or trust territory: s 32(1) (now repealed). See also the Foreign Jurisdiction Acts 1890 and 1913.

9 It could be registered later, with the actual or deemed permission of the Secretary of State; and he was not to withhold permission if the person would otherwise have been stateless: British Nationality (No 2) Act 1964 s 3 (now repealed). As to the Secretary of State see PARA 402.

10 Ie under His Majesty's government in the United Kingdom or in Northern Ireland, or under the government of any colony, protectorate, protected state, United Kingdom mandated territory or trust territory, whether or not the service was in any part of the dominions: British Nationality Act 1948 s 32(1) (now repealed). A Secretary of State's certificate that a person was in such Crown service was conclusive evidence of the fact: s 27(4) (now repealed).

11 See the British Nationality Act 1948 s 5 (now repealed).

12 British Nationality Act 1948 s 8(1) (s 8 amended by the Immigration Act 1971 s 2, Sch 1; now repealed).

13 British Nationality Act 1948 s 8(2) (as amended (see note 12); now repealed); s 12(7) (now repealed). Some of those who acquired citizenship by registration were deemed to be citizens by descent only: see note 6.

The conditions of entitlement to and eligibility for registration between 1 January 1949 and 31 December 1982 were complex and changing: see ss 5A, 6, 7, 9, 12(6) (all now repealed); the British Nationality Act 1958 s 3 (now repealed); the British Nationality Act 1964 s 1 (now repealed); the British Nationality (No 2) Act 1964 ss 1, 3, Schedule (all now repealed); the British Nationality Act 1965 ss 1, 4 (both now repealed); and the Immigration Act 1971 s 2(5), Sch 1 (both now repealed). It is the fact and place of registration (and for the purposes of citizenship by descent, the provision under which the registration was effected: see PARAS 425, 456), not the conditions of eligibility, which affect current national status. In the absence of documentary evidence such as a certified copy of the entry or a certificate of citizenship or a passport (which is evidence not proof), it is necessary to establish whether registration was effected from the register itself. See also *Gowa v A-G* [1985] 1 WLR 1003, HL (an application for registration was not granted in 1951 in the mistaken belief that the applicants were already citizens; it was held that an application could be considered and granted notwithstanding changes in the law and the fact that the applicants had ceased to fulfil the conditions of eligibility). As to the possible effect of estoppel see PARA 482.

14   See the British Nationality Act 1948 ss 10, 18, Sch 2 (all now repealed); and the Commonwealth Immigrants Act 1962 s 12(2) (now repealed).

     Again, it is the fact and place of naturalisation rather than the conditions of eligibility which are relevant. Naturalisation was effected by the grant of a certificate of naturalisation, rather than by entry in a register: British Nationality Act 1948 s 10 (now repealed).

15   See the British Nationality Act 1948 s 11 (now repealed), which provided that persons specified in a consequential Order in Council would acquire citizenship. No orders were ever made under this provision. However, the uninhabited island of Rockall was incorporated into the United Kingdom on 10 February 1972 by the Island of Rockall Act 1972.

418.   Citizenship of the United Kingdom and colonies; automatic loss. Although provision was made for a person to acquire citizenship of the United Kingdom and colonies[1] by birth or registration or naturalisation in a colony, or by virtue of his father's birth in a colony, during the years 1949 to 1982 the vast majority of colonies achieved independence and most of them became independent Commonwealth countries[2], with citizenship laws of their own[3]. Provision was made for loss of citizenship of the United Kingdom and colonies by specified persons who became, or were eligible to become, citizens of the newly independent country, subject to various provisos for retention. Though many such provisions had a common format, providing for automatic loss of citizenship of the United Kingdom and colonies in specified circumstances, they differed in detail between countries; accordingly, in order to ascertain whether a one-time citizen of the United Kingdom and colonies, connected with a former colony, still had that status immediately before 1 January 1983, so as to acquire one of the forms of British nationality introduced on that date, it is necessary to consult the legislation affecting that colony[4].

1   See PARA 417. As to citizenships already in existence on 1 January 1949 see PARA 415.

2   Such countries were added to the list in the British Nationality Act 1948 s 1(3) (now repealed) (see PARA 409 note 4). As to the repeal and the continued relevance of the British Nationality Act 1948 see PARA 403.

3   Citizenship was normally provided for in the independence constitution enacted by the United Kingdom legislature, often supplemented or replaced by legislation of the country's own legislature: see note 4; and COMMONWEALTH.

4   It may be necessary to investigate not only the former colony with which the subject of investigation appears to be connected, but also any other colony with which the parents, or even grandparents, of such person had connections. See Fransman *British Nationality Law* (2nd Edn, 1998; 3rd Edn, 2011). See also *Bulmer v A-G* [1955] Ch 558, [1955] 2 All ER 718; *Mohamed v Secretary of State for the Home Department* [1979–80] Imm AR 103, IAT (Kenya); *R v Secretary of State for the Home Department, ex p Mahaboob Bibi* [1985] Imm AR 134 (Burma and Mauritius); *Patel v Secretary of State for the Home Department* [1988] Imm AR 521, IAT (Zambia). For a case in which minors held the dual status of citizen of the United Kingdom and colonies and British protected person but automatically lost both upon independence of their country of birth (Zambia) see *Motala v A-G* [1992] 1 AC 281, [1991] 4 All ER 682, HL.

     The precise conditions of automatic loss of citizenship of the United Kingdom and colonies are contained in the United Kingdom enactment providing for independence together with the citizenship law of the new independent country (of which some, but not all, were made by the United Kingdom). See further:

(1)   the Aden, Perim and Kuria Muria Islands Act 1967 (repealed); the British Nationality (Kuria Muria Islands) Order 1967, SI 1967/1778 (lapsed); and the British Nationality (People's Republic of Southern Yemen) Order 1968/1310 (lapsed);

(2)   the Bahamas Independence Act 1973; and the Bahamas Independence Order 1973, SI 1973/1080;

(3)   the Barbados Independence Act 1966; and the Barbados Independence Order 1966, SI 1966/1455;

(4)   the Belize Act 1981; and the Belize Independence Order 1981, SI 1981/1107 (spent);

(5)   the Botswana Independence Act 1966; and the Botswana Independence Order 1966, SI 1966/1171 (spent);

(6)   the Cyprus Act 1960; the Republic of Cyprus Order in Council 1960, SI 1960/1368 (spent); and the British Nationality (Cyprus) Order 1960, SI 1960/2215;

(7)   the Fiji Independence Act 1970; and the Fiji Independence Order 1970, dated 30 September 1970 (made under the royal prerogative);

(8)   the Gambia Independence Act 1964; and the Gambia Independence Order 1965, SI 1965/135 (amended by SI 1970/1114);

(9)   the Ghana Independence Act 1957; the British Nationality Act 1958 (repealed); and the Ghana (Constitution) Order in Council 1957, SI 1957/277 (spent);

(10)   the Guyana Independence Act 1966; and the Guyana Independence Order 1966, SI 1966/575 (lapsed);

(11)   the Jamaica Independence Act 1962; and the Jamaica (Constitution) Order in Council 1962, SI 1962/1550;

(12)   the Kenya Independence Act 1963; and the Kenya Independence Order in Council 1963, SI 1963/1968 (spent);

(13)   the Kiribati Act 1979; and the Kiribati Independence Order 1979, SI 1979/719;

(14)   the Lesotho Independence Act 1966; and the Lesotho Independence Order 1966, SI 1966/1172 (spent);

(15)   the Malawi Independence Act 1964; and the Malawi Independence Order 1964, SI 1964/916 (spent);

(16)   the Malaysia Act 1963;

(17)   the Malta Independence Act 1964; and the Malta Independence Order 1964, SI 1964/1398 (spent);

(18)   the Mauritius Independence Act 1968; and the Mauritius Independence Order 1968 (dated 4 March 1968);

(19)   the Nigeria Independence Act 1960; and the Nigeria (Constitution) Order in Council 1960, SI 1960/1652 (spent);

(20)   the Rhodesia and Nyasaland Act 1963; the British Nationality Act 1958 (repealed); the Federation of Rhodesia and Nyasaland (Constitution) Order in Council 1953, SI 1953/1199 (revoked and spent); and the Federation of Rhodesia and Nyasaland (Dissolution) Order in Council 1963, SI 1963/2085 (amended by SI 1970/892);

(21)   the Seychelles Act 1976; and the Seychelles Independence Order 1976, SI 1976/894;

(22)   the Sierra Leone Independence Act 1961; and the Sierra Leone (Constitution) Order in Council 1961, SI 1961/741 (spent);

(23)   the Solomon Islands Act 1978; and the Solomon Islands Independence Order 1978, SI 1978/783 (spent);

(24)   the Swaziland Independence Act 1968; and the Swaziland Independence Order 1968, SI 1968/1377 (spent);

(25)   the Tanganyika Independence Act 1961; and the Tanganyika (Constitution) Order in Council 1961, SI 1961/2274 (spent);

(26)   the Trinidad and Tobago Independence Act 1962; and the Trinidad and Tobago (Constitution) Order in Council 1962, SI 1962/1875 (spent);

(27)   the Tuvalu Act 1978; and the Tuvalu Independence Order 1978 (dated 25 July 1978) (spent);

(28)   the Uganda Independence Act 1962; and the Uganda (Independence) Order in Council 1962, SI 1962/2175 (spent);

(29)   the West Indies Act 1967; the Antigua and Barbuda Constitution Order 1981, SI 1981/1106 (lapsed); the Antigua and Barbuda Modification of Enactments Order 1981, SI 1981/1105 (lapsed); the Dominica Constitution Order 1978, SI 1978/1027 (amended by SI 1978/1521) (now lapsed); the Dominica Modification of Enactments Order 1978, SI 1978/1030 (amended by SI 1978/1622) (now lapsed); the Grenada Constitution Order 1973, SI 1973/2155 (lapsed); the Grenada Modification of Enactments Order 1973, SI 1973/2156 (lapsed); the St Lucia Constitution Order 1978, SI 1978/1901 (lapsed); the St Lucia Modification of Enactments Order 1978, SI 1978/1899 (lapsed); the St Vincent Constitution Order 1979, SI 1979/916 (lapsed); and the St Vincent Modification of Enactments Order 1979, SI 1979/917 (lapsed);

(30)   the Zambia Independence Act 1964; and the Zambia Independence Order 1964, SI 1964/1652 (spent);

(31)   the Zanzibar Act 1963.

419. Citizenship of the United Kingdom and colonies; deprivation, renunciation and resumption. Registered and naturalised citizens of the United Kingdom and colonies could be deprived of their citizenship[1] on the ground that it was obtained by fraud, false representation or material concealment[2], and naturalised citizens could also be deprived of citizenship on the ground of disloyalty or disaffection, or trading or communicating with the enemy in time of war[3], or 12 months' imprisonment (or more) in any country within five years of naturalisation[4]. The Secretary of State[5] was required to give notice in writing of the ground on which he proposed to make a deprivation order[6], and could not deprive a person of citizenship unless satisfied that it was not conducive to the public good that he should continue to be a citizen of the United Kingdom and colonies[7]. However, citizenship by naturalisation or registration acquired by fraud of a serious and causative nature may be of no effect[8].

A citizen of the United Kingdom and colonies was entitled to renounce that citizenship[9] (to assist those who were or wished to be citizens of a country which did not permit dual nationality), provided[10] he had some other citizenship or nationality or acquired one within six months[11].

A person who had renounced citizenship of the United Kingdom and colonies in order to become or remain a citizen of a Commonwealth country[12] was entitled[13] to be registered as a citizen of the United Kingdom and colonies provided he had a specified qualifying connection with the United Kingdom or with a protectorate or protected state[14] or, if a woman, she had been married to a person who had, or would if living have had, such a connection[15].

1 As to deprivation of British subject status see the British Nationality Act 1965 s 3 (now repealed). As to the repeal and the continued relevance of the British Nationality Acts 1948 to 1965 see PARA 403.
2 British Nationality Act 1948 s 20(2) (now repealed). Registration of a minor under s 7(1) (now repealed) under a false name and parentage, on application of someone other than his parent or guardian, was invalid: *R v Secretary of State for the Home Department, ex p Parvaz Akhtar* [1981] QB 46, [1980] 2 All ER 735, CA. It is not clear whether the same was true of registration of an adult on his own application under the British Nationality Act 1948 s 6(1) (now repealed) under his true name but false parentage; but it probably was not, provided that on the true facts he qualified for registration: *Hamida Begum v Visa Officer, Islamabad* [1981] Imm AR 126, IAT.
3 British Nationality Act 1948 s 20(3)(a), (b) (now repealed).
4 British Nationality Act 1948 s 20(3)(c) (now repealed). From 16 September 1964 a person could not be deprived of citizenship if he would as a result be stateless: British Nationality (No 2) Act 1964 s 4(1) (now repealed). Provisions relating to deprivation in the case of long residence abroad or deprivation of Commonwealth or Irish citizenship (ie the British Nationality Act 1948 ss 20(4), 21) were repealed in 1964.
5 As to the Secretary of State see PARA 402.
6 British Nationality Act 1948 s 20(6) (now repealed). In some cases the person was entitled to an inquiry.
7 British Nationality Act 1948 s 20(5) (now repealed). Cf PARAS 444, 458, 467.
8 See PARA 444.
9 Ie by declaration, registration of which terminated the citizenship: British Nationality Act 1948 s 19 (now repealed). The Secretary of State could withhold registration of a declaration made by a foreign national (ie one with dual nationality) in time of war.
10 Ie as from 25 May 1964.
11 British Nationality Act 1964 s 2 (now repealed). Cf PARAS 443, 457, 463, 467, 474, 480.
12 See PARA 409; and COMMONWEALTH.
13 Ie as from 25 May 1964.
14 As to protectorates and protected states see PARA 415 note 6.
15 British Nationality Act 1964 s 1 (now repealed). Now only British citizenship (see PARAS 406, 421–444) and British overseas territories citizenship (formerly known as British dependent territories citizenship) (see PARAS 406, 445–458) may be resumed in a similar manner: see PARAS 443, 457.

420.   The right of abode prior to 1 January 1983.   The right of abode in the United Kingdom[1] was introduced into United Kingdom law on 1 January 1973[2], and under current law is a benefit of British citizenship[3]. In order to ascertain current national status, however, it is frequently necessary to consider the qualifications for the right of abode under previous law[4]. Prior to 1 January 1983[5] the following enjoyed the right of abode in the United Kingdom[6]:

(1)   a citizen of the United Kingdom and colonies who had that citizenship by birth, adoption, naturalisation or registration in the United Kingdom, the Channel Islands or the Isle of Man[7], but not including a woman whose registration[8] (irrespective of the date of it) was based on her marriage on or after 28 October 1971[9] to a citizen of the United Kingdom and colonies[10];

(2)   a citizen of the United Kingdom and colonies born to or legally adopted[11] by a parent who had that citizenship at the time of the birth or adoption, if the parent either: (a) then had that citizenship by his birth, adoption, naturalisation or registration in the United Kingdom, the Channel Islands or the Isle of Man[12]; or (b) had been born to or legally adopted by a parent who at the time of that birth or adoption had that citizenship by his birth, adoption, naturalisation or registration in the United Kingdom, the Channel Islands or the Isle of Man[13]; but the reference to registration (of the parent or grandparent) did not include registration (irrespective of the date of it) of a woman on the basis of her marriage on or after 28 October 1971 to a citizen of the United Kingdom and colonies[14];

(3)   a citizen of the United Kingdom and colonies who had at any time been settled in the United Kingdom[15], the Channel Islands or the Isle of Man and had at that time and while such a citizen been ordinarily resident[16] there for the previous five years or longer[17];

(4)   a Commonwealth citizen[18] born to or legally adopted by a parent who at the time of the birth or adoption had citizenship of the United Kingdom and colonies by his birth in the United Kingdom, the Channel Islands or the Isle of Man[19];

(5)   a woman who was a Commonwealth citizen and the wife of a man who fell within heads (1) to (4) above, or who but for his death before 1 January 1949 would have fallen within head (1) or head (2) above[20].

In relation to the parent of a child born after the parent's death, references to the time of the child's birth are to be read as references to the time of the parent's death[21].

'Parent' includes the mother[22] of an illegitimate child[23].

References to birth in the United Kingdom include birth on a ship or aircraft registered in the United Kingdom, or on an unregistered ship or aircraft of the government of the United Kingdom, and similarly with references to birth in the Channel Islands or the Isle of Man[24].

References to registration in the United Kingdom include registration in an independent Commonwealth country by the United Kingdom High Commissioner[25], but in the case of registration of minors only if the registration was effected before 28 October 1971[26]. However, registration or naturalisation granted by the Governor of a colony, protectorate or United Kingdom trust territory does not constitute registration or naturalisation in the United Kingdom[27].

References to citizenship of the United Kingdom and colonies are, in relation to a time before the year 1949, to be construed as references to British nationality and, in relation to British nationality and to a time before 31 March 1922, 'the United Kingdom' means Great Britain and Ireland[28].

1 This was formerly also called 'patriality', those with the right being known as patrials; but these terms are now obsolete: see the Immigration Act 1971 s 2(6) (as in force prior to 1 January 1983); and the British Nationality Act 1981 s 39(2), (6), Sch 4. As to the right of abode under the law as now in force see PARA 412. As to the meaning of 'United Kingdom' see PARA 403 note 1. See also the text and note 28.

2 See the Immigration Act 1971 s 1(1); and PARA 412. See also BRITISH NATIONALITY, IMMIGRATION AND ASYLUM vol 4(2) (2002 Reissue) PARAS 84–85. The Immigration Act 1971 replaced restrictions on the rights of certain British subjects and citizens of the United Kingdom and colonies to enter the United Kingdom which were introduced by the Commonwealth Immigrants Act 1962 (repealed) and enlarged by the Commonwealth Immigrants Act 1968 (repealed).

3 See the Immigration Act 1971 s 2; and PARA 412. See also PARA 420. As to British citizens and citizenship see PARAS 406, 421–444.

4 Ie under the Immigration Act 1971 s 2 (as in force prior to 1 January 1983). As to the significance of the right of abode under previous law see eg PARA 422.

5 Ie the date on which the provisions of the Immigration Act 1971 s 2 were substituted by the British Nationality Act 1981: see PARA 403 note 1.

6 The right of abode is not capable of being conferred by administrative discretion or acquired by estoppel, but is something a person either is or is not entitled to under statute: *Christodoulidou v Secretary of State for the Home Department* [1985] Imm AR 179, IAT; *Secretary of State for the Home Department v Gold* [1985] Imm AR 66, IAT. As to estoppel see PARA 482.

7 Immigration Act 1971 ss 2(1)(a), 33(1) (s 2(1)(a) as in force prior to 1 January 1983).

8 Ie under the British Nationality Act 1948 s 6(2) (now repealed). As to the repeal and the continued relevance of the British Nationality Act 1948 see PARA 403.

9 Ie the date on which the Immigration Act 1971 was passed.

10 Immigration Act 1971 s 2(2) (as in force prior to 1 January 1983).

11 For these purposes, 'legally adopted' means adopted in pursuance of an order made by any court in the United Kingdom, the Channel Islands or the Isle of Man or by any adoption specified as an overseas adoption by order of the Secretary of State under the Adoption Act 1976 s 72(2) (now repealed) or its predecessor, the Adoption Act 1968 s 4 (repealed): Immigration Act 1971 s 33(1) (as in force prior to 1 January 1983); and see *Tahid v Secretary of State for the Home Department* [1991] Imm AR 157, CA. Cf the current definition: see the Immigration Act 1971 s 33(1) (amended by the Adoption (Intercountry Aspects) Act 1999 s 15(1), Sch 2 para 2(b); and the Adoption and Children Act 2002 s 139(1), Sch 3 para 15(b)); and BRITISH NATIONALITY, IMMIGRATION AND ASYLUM vol 4(2) (2002 Reissue) PARA 161 note 2.

An overseas adoption may not confer citizenship: *Secretary of State for the Home Department v Lofthouse* [1981] Imm AR 166, IAT. See further CONFLICT OF LAWS.

12 Citizenship by birth in a colony is insufficient: *Pereira v Entry Clearance Officer, Bridgetown* [1979–80] Imm AR 79, IAT.

13 Immigration Act 1971 ss 2(1)(b), 33(1) (s 2(1)(b) as in force prior to 1 January 1983). See also *Hussein v Secretary of State for the Home Department* [1975] Imm AR 69.

14 Immigration Act 1971 s 2(2) (as in force prior to 1 January 1983).

15 For these purposes, a person was settled in the United Kingdom if he was ordinarily resident there without being subject under the immigration laws to any restriction on the period for which he could remain: Immigration Act 1971 s 2(3)(d) (as in force prior to 1 January 1983). Cf the similar wording of s 33(2A) (see BRITISH NATIONALITY, IMMIGRATION AND ASYLUM vol 4(2) (2002 Reissue) PARA 134). See also *Thomas Tak Sang Kwok v Secretary of State for the Home Department* [1984] Imm AR 226, IAT. Ordinary residence is not to be equated with domicile and accordingly a person could be settled without having the intention to remain permanently: *Raj Begum* (6 August 1985, unreported), IAT; applying *Shah v Barnet London Borough Council* [1983] 2 AC 309, [1983] 1 All ER 226, HL.

16 A person was not to be treated as ordinarily resident in the United Kingdom at a time when he was there in breach of the immigration laws: Immigration Act 1971 s 33(1), (2). A person who, albeit inadvertently, failed to apply for an extension of stay before his leave to remain expired was in the United Kingdom in breach of the immigration laws, however short the gap between expiry and application: *R v Secretary of State for the Home Department, ex p Margueritte* [1983] QB 180, [1982] 3 All ER 909, CA; *Shah v Barnet London Borough Council* [1983] 2 AC

309, [1983] 1 All ER 226, HL; *Immigration Appeal Tribunal v Chelliah* [1985] Imm AR 192, CA; *Dungarwalla v Secretary of State for the Home Department* [1989] Imm AR 476, IAT. This applied also to overstaying or unlawful entry before the coming into force of the Immigration Act 1971: *Azam v Secretary of State for the Home Department* [1974] AC 18, [1973] 2 All ER 765, HL; *Lui v Secretary of State for the Home Department* [1986] Imm AR 287; *Cheong* (20 February 1986, unreported) (4390), IAT; *Poon* (1 July 1991, unreported) (7904), IAT (rejecting the submission that under the Commonwealth Immigrants Acts 1962 and 1968 (both repealed) the grant of an extension of leave by the Secretary of State retrospectively validated earlier periods of overstaying). As to the meaning of 'ordinary residence' see also *Levene v IRC* [1928] AC 217, HL; *IRC v Lysaght* [1928] AC 234, HL; *University College, London v Newman* (1986) Times, 8 January, CA (nomad ordinarily resident within an area; see also *R v Immigration Appeal Tribunal, ex p Siggins* [1985] Imm AR 14; *Re Brauch* [1978] Ch 316, [1978] 1 All ER 1004, CA); *Britto v Secretary of State for the Home Department* [1984] Imm AR 93, IAT (ordinary residence in two places at once); *Osman* (13 June 1984, unreported) (3257), IAT; *Patel v Secretary of State for the Home Department* [1984] Imm AR 147, IAT; *R v Immigration Appeal Tribunal, ex p Ng* [1986] Imm AR 23.

17 Immigration Act 1971 s 2(1)(c) (as in force immediately before 1 January 1983). The five-year period had to be continuous, so an aggregate of five years' lawful residence broken by periods of overstay was not within the provision (*R v Immigration Appeal Tribunal, ex p Hamood* (7 February 1983, unreported), DC; *Secretary of State for the Home Department v Lai* (12 January 1984, unreported) (3087), IAT); and the period had to have been complete by 1 January 1983, so a period broken by overstaying could not be completed after that date (*Immigration Appeal Tribunal v Chelliah* [1985] Imm AR 192, CA). See also the cases cited in note 16.

Note that while children born abroad before 1 January 1983 to a father who acquired citizenship by registration or naturalisation in the United Kingdom would have the right of abode (see head (2) in the text), children born abroad before 1 January 1983 to a father who, being already a citizen, acquired the right of abode by five years' residence would not have the right of abode; but children born abroad after 1 January 1983 to such a person will have the right of abode, because he will have become a British citizen and they will be born British citizens by descent (see PARAS 422, 424, 425).

18 As to Commonwealth citizens see PARA 409.

19 Immigration Act 1971 s 2(1)(d) (as in force prior to 1 January 1983).

20 Immigration Act 1971 s 2(2) (as in force prior to 1 January 1983); *R v Secretary of State for the Home Department, ex p Phansopkar* [1976] QB 606, [1975] 3 All ER 497, CA. A woman marrying after 1 January 1983 does not acquire this right and is subject to immigration control: *Brahmbhatt v Chief Immigration Officer, Heathrow Airport* [1984] Imm AR 202, CA.

21 Immigration Act 1971 s 2(3) (as in force prior to 1 January 1983).

22 But not the father: *C v Entry Clearance Officer, Hong Kong* [1976] Imm AR 165, IAT; *Re M (an infant)* [1955] 2 QB 479, [1955] 2 All ER 911, CA.

23 Immigration Act 1971 s 2(3)(a) (as in force prior to 1 January 1983).

24 Immigration Act 1971 s 2(3)(b) (as in force prior to 1 January 1983).

25 Ie under the British Nationality Act 1948 s 6 (now repealed) or s 7 (now repealed), under arrangements made by virtue of s 8(2) (now repealed).

26 Ie the date when the Immigration Act 1971 was passed: s 2(4) (as in force prior to 1 January 1983).

27 *Keshwani v Secretary of State for the Home Department* [1975] Imm AR 38, IAT; *R v Immigration Appeal Tribunal, ex p de Sousa* [1977] Imm AR 6; *Mohamed v Secretary of State for the Home Department* [1979–80] Imm AR 103, IAT.

28 Immigration Act 1971 s 2(3)(c) (as in force prior to 1 January 1983).

3. BRITISH CITIZENSHIP

421. In general. British citizenship is the primary category of British nationality, and is the only category carrying the right of abode in the United Kingdom[1]. British citizenship may be acquired in various ways[2]. It may be conferred by statute, and many people automatically acquired British citizenship on 1 January 1983 upon the commencement of the British Nationality Act 1981[3]. British citizenship may also be acquired by birth, adoption or descent[4] or by registration[5] or naturalisation[6].

1   As to the right of abode see PARA 412. Even if they are nationals of other countries, Commonwealth citizens may be capable of having the right of abode in the United Kingdom if they acquired that right prior to 1983: see PARA 412. As to Commonwealth citizens see PARA 409.
      Certain EEA nationals and their families may have the right to live in, and to come and go into and from the United Kingdom, but this right arises by virtue of European Union law provisions for the free movement of workers and others within the European Union, and they do not have the right of abode in the United Kingdom under domestic law: see BRITISH NATIONALITY, IMMIGRATION AND ASYLUM vol 4(2) (2002 Reissue) PARAS 225–237. As to EEA nationals see BRITISH NATIONALITY, IMMIGRATION AND ASYLUM vol 4(2) (2002 Reissue) PARA 225 et seq. Each member state defines its own nationals.
2   In addition to the methods mentioned in the text, the principle of estoppel and legitimate expectation must be considered: see PARA 482.
3   See PARA 422. See also the British Overseas Territories Act 2002 s 3, under which British citizenship was conferred on most persons who were British overseas territories citizens immediately before 21 May 2002; and PARA 423. As to British overseas territories citizens and citizenship (formerly known as British dependent territories citizens and citizenship) see PARAS 406, 445–458.
4   See PARA 424. As to citizenship by descent see PARA 425.
5   See PARAS 426–437. As to resumption, which is a form of acquisition by registration, see PARA 443. See also the transitional registration provisions contained in the British Nationality Act 1981 Sch 8.
6   See PARAS 438–442. See also the transitional naturalisation provisions contained in the British Nationality Act 1981 Sch 8.

422. Automatic acquisition on 1 January 1983 under transitional arrangements. With one proviso, all those who on 31 December 1982 were citizens of the United Kingdom and colonies[1] and had the right of abode in the United Kingdom[2] under the Immigration Act 1971 as then in force[3] automatically became British citizens on 1 January 1983[4]. The proviso is that a person who was registered as a citizen of the United Kingdom and colonies on the ground that he was stateless and that his mother was a citizen of the United Kingdom and colonies at his birth[5] did not become a British citizen unless one of the two following conditions was satisfied, namely that: (1) his mother became a British citizen automatically on 1 January 1983[6] or would have done so but for her death; or (2) he had the right of abode in the United Kingdom on 31 December 1982 on the ground of previous settlement and five years' prior ordinary residence in the United Kingdom[7].

A person automatically became a British citizen on 1 January 1983 if immediately before that date he was a citizen of the United Kingdom and colonies by virtue of having been registered as such in a Commonwealth country[8] by the United Kingdom High Commissioner[9] on the ground that: (a) he[10] was a British subject on 31 December 1948[11] who would automatically have become a citizen of the United Kingdom and colonies on 1 January 1949[12] but for his citizenship or potential citizenship of a Commonwealth country; (b) he was descended in the male line from a person who was born or naturalised within the United Kingdom[13]; (c) he intended to make his ordinary place of residence within the United Kingdom and colonies; and (d) he had a close connection with the United Kingdom[14].

A person automatically became a British citizen with effect from 1 January 1983[15] if: (i) that person became a British overseas territories citizen[16] on that date[17]; and (ii) immediately before that date: (A) that person was a citizen of the United Kingdom and colonies by birth, naturalisation or registration in the Falkland Islands; or (B) one of that person's parents or grandparents was such a citizen or would have been but for his death; or (C) that person, being a woman, was the wife or former wife of a man who became a British citizen on 1 January 1983 by virtue of head (A) or head (B) above or would have done so but for his death[18].

1   As to citizenship of the United Kingdom and colonies see PARAS 414–419.
2   As to the meaning of 'United Kingdom' see PARA 403 note 1.
3   See PARA 420. A person had the right of abode in the United Kingdom on the basis of marriage to a citizen of the United Kingdom and colonies by registration only if the registration was completed before 1 January 1983: *R v Secretary of State for the Home Department, ex p Amina Bibi* [1995] Imm AR 185; affd sub nom *Amina Bibi v Secretary of State for the Home Department* [1996] Imm AR 175, CA.
4   British Nationality Act 1981 s 11(1). The date referred to in the text is the date on which the British Nationality Act 1981 came into force: see PARA 403 note 1. In order to determine whether a person falls within s 11(1), it may be necessary to trace ancestry to determine whether a person automatically became a citizen of the United Kingdom and colonies on 1 January 1949 under the British Nationality Act 1948: see eg *R v Secretary of State for Foreign and Commonwealth Affairs, ex p Ross-Clunis* [1991] 2 AC 439, sub nom *Ross-Clunis v Secretary of State for Foreign and Commonwealth Affairs* [1991] 3 All ER 353, HL. See further PARA 415. As to the repeal and the continued relevance of the British Nationality Acts 1948 to 1965 see PARA 403. It may not always be clear whether a person became a British citizen on 1 January 1983, eg where the right of abode depends on establishing settlement and five years' ordinary residence at any time before 1 January 1983 under the Immigration Act 1971 s 2(1)(c) as then in force: see eg *Britto v Secretary of State for the Home Department* [1984] Imm AR 93, IAT; *Patel v Secretary of State for the Home Department* [1984] Imm AR 147, IAT. For the circumstances in which such a person is a British citizen by descent see the British Nationality Act 1981 s 14(1)(b); and PARA 425.
5   Ie under the British Nationality (No 2) Act 1964 s 1 (now repealed).
6   Ie under the British Nationality Act 1981 s 11(1), as a former citizen of the United Kingdom and colonies with the right of abode: see the text and notes 1–4.
7   See the British Nationality Act 1981 s 11(2). The right referred to in the text is a right by virtue of the Immigration Act 1971 s 2(1)(c) as then in force (ie excluding the right of abode acquired under other provisions): see PARA 420 head (3).
    A person who qualified under the British Nationality Act 1981 s 11(2) is a British citizen by descent: see PARA 425. Those excluded from British citizenship under s 11(2) became either British overseas territories citizens (then known as British dependent territories citizens) (see PARAS 406, 445–458) or British overseas citizens (see PARAS 406, 459–463).
8   Ie a country listed at the time of the registration as a Commonwealth country in the British Nationality Act 1948 s 1(3) (see PARA 409 note 4), which was amended from time to time by various Acts and Orders in Council and is now repealed.
9   Ie under the British Nationality Act 1948 s 12(6) (now repealed). The Secretary of State made arrangements for the exercise in any country mentioned in s 1(3) (now repealed) (see note 8) of any of his functions under s 12(6) (now repealed) by the High Commissioner: see s 12(7) (now repealed). As to the Secretary of State see PARA 402.
10 Or, if he was a minor at the date of registration, the parent who applied for registration.
11 Ie immediately prior to the commencement of the British Nationality Act 1948: see s 34(2) (now repealed).
12 Ie under the British Nationality Act 1948 s 12(4) (now repealed): see PARA 415.
13 Ie from a person possessing one of the qualifications specified in the British Nationality Act 1948 s 12(1)(a), (b) (now repealed). For the purposes of the British Nationality Act 1981, a person is taken to have been naturalised in the United Kingdom if, but only if: (1) he was granted a certificate of naturalisation under any of the former nationality Acts by the Secretary

of State or, in the Channel Islands or Isle of Man, the Lieutenant-Governor; or (2) he was deemed to be naturalised by virtue of the British Nationality and Status of Aliens Act 1914 s 27(2) (now repealed) on the basis of a certificate of naturalisation granted to his parents by the Secretary of State which included his name; or (3) he was deemed by virtue of the Naturalization Act 1870 s 10(5) (now repealed) to be naturalised because while he was a minor his parents were naturalised and he resided in the United Kingdom with them: see the British Nationality Act 1981 s 50(6)(a). 'The former nationality Acts' means the British Nationality Acts 1948 to 1965, the British Nationality and Status of Aliens Acts 1914 to 1943, and any Act repealed by the British Nationality and Status of Aliens Acts 1914 to 1943 or by the Naturalization Act 1870: British Nationality Act 1981 s 50(1). As to the British Nationality Acts 1948 to 1965 see PARA 403 note 5; and as to the British Nationality and Status of Aliens Acts 1914 to 1943 see PARA 403 note 9. See also *Re Carlton* [1945] Ch 280, [1945] 1 All ER 559; and PARA 415 note 2. The British Nationality and Status of Aliens Act 1914 is now known as the Status of Aliens Act 1914: see PARA 403 note 9.

14   British Nationality Act 1981 s 11(3). A person who qualified under the British Nationality Act 1981 s 11(3) is a British citizen by descent: see PARA 425.

Since a citizen of the United Kingdom and colonies whose father or grandfather was born or naturalised in the United Kingdom would have the right of abode in the United Kingdom and so qualify for automatic British citizenship under s 11(1) (see the text and notes 1–4), s 11(3) only applies to persons who were registered under the British Nationality Act 1948 s 12(6) (now repealed) (see note 9) on the ground of the birth or naturalisation in the United Kingdom of a more remote male ancestor.

15   Ie under the British Nationality (Falkland Islands) Act 1983, which received Royal Assent on 28 March 1983 but is deemed to have come into force on 1 January 1983: see ss 4(1), 5(2).

16   See PARAS 406, 445–458.

17   Ie under the British Nationality Act 1981 s 23: see PARA 446. Section 23 has now been amended so as to take into account the effect of the renaming of British dependent territories citizenship as British overseas territories citizenship.

18   British Nationality (Falkland Islands) Act 1983 s 1(1) (amended by virtue of the British Overseas Territories Act 2002 s 2(3)). Those who satisfy the conditions in head (B) or head (C) in the text are British citizens by descent, unless they also qualify under some other provision making them British citizens otherwise than by descent: see the British Nationality (Falkland Islands) Act 1983 s 3; and PARA 425.

423. Automatic acquisition on 21 May 2002 under transitional arrangements. In general, any person who was a British overseas territories citizen[1] immediately before 21 May 2002[2] became a British citizen on that date[3]. This does not apply, however, to a person who is a British overseas territories citizen by virtue only of a connection with the Sovereign Base Areas of Akrotiri and Dhekelia[4].

A person who:

(1)   was born on or after 26 April 1969 and before 1 January 1983[5];

(2)   was born to a woman who at the time was a citizen of the United Kingdom and colonies[6] by virtue of her birth in the British Indian Ocean Territory[7];

(3)   immediately before 21 May 2002[8], was neither a British citizen nor a British overseas territories citizen[9],

became a British citizen on 21 May 2002[10].

1   As to British overseas territories citizens and citizenship (formerly known as British dependent territories citizens and citizenship) see PARAS 406, 445–458.

2   Ie the date of the commencement of the British Overseas Territories Act 2002 s 3: see s 8(2); and the British Overseas Territories Act 2002 (Commencement) Order 2002, SI 2002/1252, art 2(a).

3   British Overseas Territories Act 2002 s 3(1). A person who is a British citizen by virtue of s 3 is a British citizen by descent for the purposes of the British Nationality Act 1981 if, and only if: (1) he was a British overseas territories citizen by descent immediately before 21 May 2002; and (2) where at that time he was a British citizen as well as a British overseas territories citizen, he was a British citizen by descent: British Overseas Territories Act 2002 s 3(3). As to citizenship by descent see PARA 425.

4   British Overseas Territories Act 2002 s 3(2).

5   British Overseas Territories Act 2002 s 6(1)(a).
6   As to citizenship of the United Kingdom and colonies see PARAS 414–419.
7   British Overseas Territories Act 2002 s 6(1)(b).
8   Ie the date of the commencement of the British Overseas Territories Act 2002 s 6: see s 8(2); and the British Overseas Territories Act 2002 (Commencement) Order 2002, SI 2002/1252, art 2(b).
9   British Overseas Territories Act 2002 s 6(1)(c).
10 British Overseas Territories Act 2002 s 6(1). A person who is a British citizen by virtue of s 6(1) is a British citizen by descent for the purposes of the British Nationality Act 1981: British Overseas Territories Act 2002 s 6(2).

424. Acquisition by birth, adoption, descent and abandonment. A person born in the United Kingdom[1] on or after 1 January 1983[2] or in a qualifying territory[3] on or after 21 May 2002[4] is a British citizen if[5] at the time of the birth[6] his father or mother[7] is a British citizen[8], or settled in the United Kingdom or that territory[9]. There is a rebuttable presumption that a new-born infant who is found abandoned in the United Kingdom or who is found on or after 21 May 2002 in a qualifying territory fulfils these qualifications[10].

A person born in the United Kingdom or a qualifying territory on or after 13 January 2010[11] is a British citizen if at the time of the birth his father or mother is a member of the armed forces[12].

Where: (1) on or after 1 January 1983 any court in the United Kingdom or, on or after 21 May 2002, any court in a qualifying territory makes an order authorising the adoption of a minor[13] who is not a British citizen; or (2) a minor who is not a British citizen is adopted under a Convention adoption[14], then, if the following requirements are met, that minor is a British citizen as from the date on which the order is made or the Convention adoption is effected, as the case may be[15]. The requirements are that on the date on which the order is made or the Convention adoption is effected (as the case may be): (a) the adopter or, in the case of a joint adoption, one of the adopters is a British citizen; and (b) in a case within head (2), the adopter or, in the case of a joint adoption, both of the adopters are habitually resident in the United Kingdom or in a designated territory[16]. Where an order or a Convention adoption in consequence of which any person became a British citizen ceases to have effect, whether on annulment or otherwise, the cesser is not to affect the status of that person as a British citizen[17].

A person born outside the United Kingdom on or after 1 January 1983 and before 21 May 2002 is a British citizen if at the time of the birth his father or mother[18] is a British citizen: (i) otherwise than by descent[19]; or (ii) serving outside the United Kingdom, as a result of recruitment inside the United Kingdom, in Crown service under the government of the United Kingdom or service designated[20] by the Secretary of State[21] as closely associated with the activities outside the United Kingdom of Her Majesty's government in the United Kingdom[22]; or (iii) serving outside the United Kingdom in service under an EU institution, as a result of recruitment within a country which at the time of the recruitment was a member of the European Union[23]. In relation to persons born on or after 21 May 2002, these provisions apply to those born outside the United Kingdom and the qualifying territories[24]. Such a person is a British citizen if at the time of the birth his father or mother[25] is a British citizen: (A) otherwise than by descent[26]; or (B) serving outside the United Kingdom and the qualifying territories, as a result of recruitment inside the United Kingdom or the qualifying territories, in Crown service under the government of the United Kingdom or of a qualifying territory or service designated[27] by the Secretary of State as closely associated with the activities outside the United Kingdom and the qualifying territories of Her Majesty's government in the United Kingdom or in a qualifying territory[28]; or (C) serving outside the United Kingdom and the qualifying territories in service under an EU institution, as a result of recruitment within a country which at the time of the recruitment was a member of the European Union[29].

A person born in a British overseas territory on or after 1 January 1983 who would otherwise be born stateless is a British citizen if at the time of his birth his father or mother is a British citizen[30].

1   As to the meaning of 'United Kingdom' see PARA 403 note 1.
        A person born outside the United Kingdom aboard a ship or aircraft is deemed to have been born in the United Kingdom if at the time of the birth the ship or aircraft was registered in the United Kingdom or was an unregistered ship or aircraft of the government of the United Kingdom and: (1) at the time of the birth his father or mother was a British citizen (see note 6); or (2) he would otherwise have been born stateless: see the British Nationality Act 1981 s 50(7)(a). Subject to s 50(7)(a), a person born outside the United Kingdom aboard a ship or aircraft is to be regarded as born outside the United Kingdom, whoever was the owner of the ship or aircraft at the time, and irrespective of whether or where it was then registered: s 50(7)(b). 'Ship' includes a hovercraft: s 50(1).
        For the purposes of the British Nationality Act 1981, a person born outside a qualifying territory (see note 3) aboard a ship or aircraft is deemed to have been born in such a territory if at the time of the birth the ship or aircraft was registered in that territory or was an unregistered ship or aircraft of the government of that territory and: (a) at the time of the birth his father or mother was a British citizen or a British overseas territories citizen; or (b) he would otherwise have been born stateless: s 50(7A)(a) (s 50(7A) added by the British Overseas Territories Act 2002 s 5, Sch 1 para 5). Subject to the British Nationality Act 1981 s 50(7A)(a), a person born outside a qualifying territory aboard a ship or aircraft is to be regarded as born outside such a territory, whoever was the owner of the ship or aircraft at the time, and irrespective of whether or where it was then registered: s 50(7A)(b) (as so added). As to British overseas territories citizens and citizenship (formerly known as British dependent territories citizens and citizenship) see PARAS 406, 445–458.
        For the purposes of the British Nationality Act 1981, a person born outside a British overseas territory, other than a qualifying territory, aboard a ship or aircraft is deemed to have been born in such a territory if at the time of the birth the ship or aircraft was registered in that territory or was an unregistered ship or aircraft of the government of that territory and: (i) at the time of the birth his father or mother was a British overseas territories citizen; or (ii) he would otherwise have been born stateless: s 50(7B)(a) (s 50(7B) added by the British Overseas Territories Act 2002 Sch 1 para 5). Subject to the British Nationality Act 1981 s 50(7B)(a), a person born outside a British overseas territory, other than a qualifying territory, aboard a ship or aircraft is to be regarded as born outside such a territory, whoever was the owner of the ship or aircraft at the time, and irrespective of whether or where it was then registered: s 50(7B)(b) (as so added). As to British overseas territories (formerly known as dependent territories) see PARA 445 note 1.
2   Ie the date on which the British Nationality Act 1981 came into force: see PARA 403 note 1.
3   'Qualifying territory' means a British overseas territory other than the Sovereign Base Areas of Akrotiri and Dhekelia: British Nationality Act 1981 s 50(1) (definition added by the British Overseas Territories Act 2002 Sch 1 para 5).
4   Ie the 'appointed day': the date on which the provisions of the British Overseas Territories Act 2002 Sch 1 (which contains provisions amending the British Nationality Act 1981) came into force: see the British Nationality Act 1981 s 50(1) (definition added by the British Overseas Territories Act 2002 Sch 1 para 5); the British Overseas Territories Act 2002 s 8(2); and the British Overseas Territories Act 2002 (Commencement) Order 2002, SI 2002/1252, art 2(a).
5   This qualification was a major change of policy. Previously every person born in the United Kingdom acquired British nationality unless, by reason of diplomatic immunity or of birth to an enemy alien father in a place then occupied by the enemy (see PARA 417 head (1)), he was not born within allegiance to the Crown.
6   In relation to a person born after the death of his father or mother, any reference in the British Nationality Act 1981 to the status or description of the father or mother of a person at the time of that person's birth is to be construed as a reference to the status or description of the parent in question at the time of that parent's death; and where that death occurred before, and the birth occurs after, the commencement of the British Nationality Act 1981 (ie 1 January 1983:

see PARA 403 note 1), the status or description which would have been applicable to the father or mother had he or she died after that date is deemed to be the status or description applicable to him or her at the time of his or her death: s 48.

7   Originally, for the purposes of the British Nationality Act 1981, the relationship of mother and child was taken to exist between a woman and any child (legitimate or illegitimate) born to her, but (subject to s 47 (now repealed)) the relationship of father and child was taken to exist only between a man and any legitimate child born to him; and the expressions 'mother', 'father', 'parent', 'child' and 'descended' were to be construed accordingly: s 50(9) (as originally enacted). A person born out of wedlock and legitimated by the subsequent marriage of his parents was to be treated for the purposes of the British Nationality Act 1981, as from the date of the marriage, as if he had been born legitimate: s 47(1) (now repealed). A person was deemed for the purposes of s 47 to have been legitimated by the subsequent marriage of his parents if by the law of the place in which his father was domiciled at the time of the marriage the marriage operated immediately or subsequently to legitimate him, and not otherwise: s 47(2) (now repealed).

   In relation to a child born on or after 1 July 2006 (see the Nationality, Immigration and Asylum Act 2002 s 162(5); and the Nationality, Immigration and Asylum Act 2002 (Commencement No 11) Order 2006, SI 2006/1498, art 2), for the purposes of the British Nationality Act 1981:

   (1)   a child's mother is the woman who gives birth to the child (s 50(9) (substituted by the Nationality, Immigration and Asylum Act 2002 s 9(1)));

   (2)   a child's father is: (a) the husband, at the time of the child's birth, of the woman who gives birth to the child; or (b) where a person is treated as the father of the child under the Human Fertilisation and Embryology Act 1990 s 28 or the Human Fertilisation and Embryology Act 2008 s 35 or 36, that person; or (c) where a person is treated as a parent of the child under the Human Fertilisation and Embryology Act 2008 s 42 or s 43, that person; or (d) where none of heads (a)–(c) applies, a person who satisfies prescribed requirements as to proof of paternity (British Nationality Act 1981 s 50(9A) (added by the Nationality, Immigration and Asylum Act 2002 s 9(1); and amended by the Human Fertilisation and Embryology Act 2008 s 56, Sch 6 Pt 1 para 22)). The expressions 'parent', 'child' and 'descended' are to be construed in accordance with the British Nationality Act 1981 s 50(9), (9A): s 50(9C) (s 50(9B), (9C) added Nationality, Immigration and Asylum Act 2002 s 9(1)).

   In head (2)(d) 'prescribed' means prescribed by regulations of the Secretary of State; and the regulations (i) may confer a function (which may be a discretionary function) on the Secretary of State or another person; (ii) may make provision which applies generally or only in specified circumstances; (iii) may make different provision for different circumstances; (iv) must be made by statutory instrument; and (v) are subject to annulment in pursuance of a resolution of either House of Parliament: s 50(9B) (as so added). For the purposes of head (2)(d): (A) the person must be named as the father of the child in a birth certificate issued within one year of the date of the child's birth; or (B) the person must satisfy the Secretary of State that he is the father of the child: British Nationality (Proof of Paternity) Regulations 2006, SI 2006/1496, reg 2. The Secretary of State may determine whether a person is the father of a child for the purpose of head (B), and for this purpose the Secretary of State may have regard to any evidence which he considers to be relevant, including, but not limited to, DNA test reports and court orders: reg 3.

   Although the British Nationality Act 1981 s 44(1) (see PARA 402) prohibits discrimination on grounds of race, colour or religion, s 50(9) as originally enacted expressly discriminated against illegitimate children. The Family Law Reform Act 1987 made general provision for the abolition of discrimination against illegitimate children, but amendment of the British Nationality Act 1981 s 50(9) followed only some years later. In *R (on the application of Montana) v Secretary of State for the Home Department* [2001] 1 WLR 552, [2001] 1 FCR 358, CA, a refusal to register an illegitimate child as a British citizen under the British Nationality Act 1981 s 3(1) (see PARA 427) was held not to be a breach of the Convention for the Protection of Human Rights and Fundamental Freedoms (Rome, 4 November 1950; TS 71 (1953); Cmd 8969) art 8, or of art 8 taken together with art 14. The facts of that case are unlikely to arise again as, even before the amendment to the British Nationality Act 1981 s 50(9) Home Office policy was to register children under the British Nationality Act 1981 s 3(1) where but for their illegitimacy they would be British citizens.

8   British Nationality Act 1981 s 1(1)(a) (s 1(1) amended by the British Overseas Territories Act 2002 Sch 1 para 1).

9   British Nationality Act 1981 s 1(1)(b) (as amended: see note 8). A person is settled in the United Kingdom or in a British overseas territory if he is ordinarily resident there without being subject under the immigration laws to any restriction on the period for which he may remain: ss 1(8),

50(2) (s 50(2) amended by virtue of the British Overseas Territories Act 2002 s 1(1)(b)). However, a person is not to be regarded: (1) as having been settled in the United Kingdom if he is entitled to an exemption under the Immigration Act 1971 s 8(2) (exemption orders: see BRITISH NATIONALITY, IMMIGRATION AND ASYLUM vol 4(2) (2002 Reissue) PARA 88 et seq) (unless the exemption order provides otherwise), s 8(3) (members of diplomatic missions and their families: see BRITISH NATIONALITY, IMMIGRATION AND ASYLUM vol 4(2) (2002 Reissue) PARA 88) or s 8(4)(b) or s 8(4)(c) (foreign servicemen: see BRITISH NATIONALITY, IMMIGRATION AND ASYLUM vol 4(2) (2002 Reissue) PARA 89), or to any corresponding exemption under former immigration laws (British Nationality Act 1981 s 50(3)(a)); or (2) as having been settled in a British overseas territory at any time when he was under the immigration laws entitled to any exemption corresponding to any such exemption as is mentioned in head (1) (s 50(3)(b) (amended by virtue of the British Overseas Territories Act 2002 s 1(1)(b))). See *R v Secretary of State for the Home Department, ex p Chaumun* [1999] INLR 479.

For the purposes of the British Nationality Act 1981 s 1(1), a person to whom a child is born in the United Kingdom on or after 1 January 1983 is to be regarded as being settled in the United Kingdom at the time of the birth if: (a) he would fall to be so regarded but for being at that time entitled to an exemption under the Immigration Act 1971 s 8(3) (see BRITISH NATIONALITY, IMMIGRATION AND ASYLUM vol 4(2) (2002 Reissue) PARA 88) or by virtue of the Immigration (Exemption from Control) Order 1972, SI 1972/1613 (see BRITISH NATIONALITY, IMMIGRATION AND ASYLUM vol 4(2) (2002 Reissue) PARAS 88, 90–91, 162); and (b) immediately before he became entitled to that exemption he was settled in the United Kingdom; and (c) he was ordinarily resident in the United Kingdom from the time when he became entitled to the exemption to the time of the birth, unless at the time of the birth either parent is a person entitled to immunity from jurisdiction under the Diplomatic Privileges Act 1964 (see INTERNATIONAL RELATIONS LAW vol 61 (2010) PARA 265 et seq): see the British Nationality Act 1981 s 50(4); and the Immigration (Exemption from Control) Order 1972, SI 1972/1613, art 6 (added by SI 1982/1649).

A person is not to be treated as ordinarily resident in the United Kingdom or in a British overseas territory at a time when he is there in breach of the immigration laws: British Nationality Act 1981 s 50(5) (amended by virtue of the British Overseas Territories Act 2002 s 1(1)(b)). 'Immigration laws' means, in relation to the United Kingdom, the Immigration Act 1971 and any law for purposes similar to that Act which is for the time being or has at any time been in force in any part of the United Kingdom and, in relation to a British overseas territory, any law for purposes similar to the Immigration Act 1971 which is for the time being or has at any time been in force in that territory: British Nationality Act 1981 s 50(1) (definition amended by virtue of the British Overseas Territories Act 2002 s 1(1)(b)). For the purposes of the British Nationality Act 1981 s 50(5) (and for the purposes of s 4(2), (4) (see PARA 428) and Sch 1 (see PARA 438)) a person is in the United Kingdom in breach of the immigration laws if, and only if, he: (i) is in the United Kingdom; (ii) does not have the right of abode in the United Kingdom within the meaning of the Immigration Act 1971 s 2 (see PARA 412); (iii) does not have leave to enter or remain in the United Kingdom (whether or not he previously had leave); (iv) does not have a qualifying CTA entitlement; (v) is not entitled to reside in the United Kingdom by virtue of any provision made under European Communities Act 1972 s 2(2) (whether or not he was previously entitled); (vi) is not entitled to enter and remain in the United Kingdom by virtue of the Immigration Act 1971 s 8(1) (see BRITISH NATIONALITY, IMMIGRATION AND ASYLUM vol 4(2) (2002 Reissue) PARA 87) (whether or not he was previously entitled); and (vii) does not have the benefit of an exemption under the Immigration Act 1971 s 8(2)–(4) (see BRITISH NATIONALITY, IMMIGRATION AND ASYLUM vol 4(2) (2002 Reissue) PARA 88 et seq) (whether or not he previously had the benefit of an exemption): British Nationality Act 1981 s 50A(1), (4) (s 50A added by the Borders, Citizenship and Immigration Act 2009 s 48(1) with effect from 13 January 2010 to replace corresponding provision in the Nationality, Immigration and Asylum Act 2002 s 11). For the purposes of head (iv), a person has a qualifying CTA entitlement if he (A) is a citizen of the Republic of Ireland; (B) last arrived in the United Kingdom on a local journey (within the meaning of the Immigration Act 1971) from the Republic of Ireland; and (C) on that arrival, was a citizen of the Republic of Ireland and was entitled to enter without leave by virtue of the Immigration Act 1971 s 1(3): British Nationality Act 1981 s 50A(5) (as so added). The Immigration Act 1971 s 11(1) (see BRITISH NATIONALITY, IMMIGRATION AND ASYLUM vol 4(2) (2002 Reissue) PARA 93) applies for the purposes of the British Nationality Act 1981 s 50A as it applies for the purposes of the 1971 Act: British Nationality Act 1981 s 50A(6) (as so added). Section 50A applies only for the purpose of determining on or after the relevant day (ie 13 January 2010) (aa) whether a person born on or after the relevant day is a British citizen under s 1(1); (bb) whether, on an application under s 1(3) or 4(2) (see PARAS 426, 428) made on or after the relevant day, a person is entitled to be registered as a British citizen; or (cc) whether, on an application under s 6(1) or (2) (see PARAS 438–442) made on or after the relevant day, the applicant fulfils the requirements of Sch 1 for naturalisation as a British citizen under s 6(1) or (2): s 50A(2), (8) (as so added); Borders, Citizenship and Immigration Act 2009 (Commencement No 1) Order 2009, SI 2009/2731, art 4(g). The British Nationality Act 1981 s 50A is without prejudice to the generality of a reference to being in a place outside the United Kingdom in breach of immigration laws, and a reference in a provision other than one specified in s 50A(1) to being in the United Kingdom in breach of immigration laws: British Nationality Act 1981 s 50A(7) (as so added). Transitional provision is made for persons born, and specified applications made, before 13 January 2010: see the British Nationality Act 1981 s 50A(3); and the Borders, Citizenship and Immigration Act 2009 s 48(2)–(5). See also PARA 420 notes 15–16; and BRITISH NATIONALITY, IMMIGRATION AND ASYLUM vol 4(2) (2002 Reissue) PARA 134.

10 See the British Nationality Act 1981 s 1(2) (amended by the British Overseas Territories Act 2002 Sch 1 para 1).

11 See the British Nationality Act 1981 s 1(9) (added by the Borders, Citizenship and Immigration Act 2009 s 42(1), (6)); and the Borders, Citizenship and Immigration Act 2009 (Commencement No 1) Order 2009, SI 2009/2731, art 4(a).

12 British Nationality Act 1981 s 1(1A) (added by the Borders, Citizenship and Immigration Act 2009 s 42(2)). Subject to the British Nationality Act 1981 s 50(1B), references in that Act to being a member of the armed forces are references to being: (1) a member of the regular forces within the meaning of the Armed Forces Act 2006; or (2) a member of the reserve forces within the meaning of that Act subject to service law by virtue of s 367(2) (a), (b) or (c) (see ARMED FORCES vol 2(2) (Reissue) PARAS 306–313): British Nationality Act 1981 s 50(1A) (s 50(1A), (1B) added by the Borders, Citizenship and Immigration Act 2009 s 49(1)). A person is not to be regarded as a member of the armed forces by virtue of the British Nationality Act 1981 s 50(1A) if the person is treated as a member of a regular or reserve force by virtue of: (a) the Armed Forces Act 2006 s 369 (see ARMED FORCES vol 2(2) (Reissue) PARAS 306–313); or (b) the Visiting Forces (British Commonwealth) Act 1933 s 4(3) (see ARMED FORCES vol 2(2) (Reissue) PARA 255): British Nationality Act 1981 s 50(1B) (as so added).

13 'Minor' means a person who has not attained the age of 18 years: British Nationality Act 1981 s 50(1).

14 'Convention adoption' means an adoption effected under the law of a country or territory in which the Convention on the Protection of Children and Co-operation in respect of Intercountry Adoption (The Hague, 29 May 1993) is in force, and certified in pursuance of art 23(1): British Nationality Act 1981 s 50(1), (14) (definition in s 50(1) and s 50(14) added by the Adoption and Children Act 2002 s 137(3), (6)(a), (7)).

15 British Nationality Act 1981 s 1(5) (substituted by the Adoption (Intercountry Aspects) Act 1999 s 7(1); and amended by the British Overseas Territories Act 2002 Sch 1 para 1; and the Adoption and Children Act 2002 s 137(4)(a)).

16 British Nationality Act 1981 s 1(5A) (added by the Adoption (Intercountry Aspects) Act 1999 s 7(1); and amended by the Adoption and Children Act 2002 s 137(4)(b)). As to intercountry adoptions see CHILDREN AND YOUNG PERSONS vol 5(3) (2008 Reissue) PARA 483 et seq.
As to the bearing of the acquisition of citizenship carrying with it the right of abode on the decision whether to make an adoption order see *Re H* [1982] Fam 121, [1982] 3 All ER 84; *Re W* [1986] Fam 54, [1985] 3 All ER 449, CA; *Re B* [1999] 2 AC 136, [1999] 2 All ER 576, HL. Note that whereas under previous law the right of abode (though not citizenship of the United Kingdom and colonies: see PARAS 414–419) could be acquired by an overseas adoption as well as by a domestic adoption (see PARA 420 note 11), that right can now only be acquired by acquisition of British citizenship.

17 See the British Nationality Act 1981 s 1(6) (amended by the Adoption (Intercountry Aspects) Act 1999 s 7(2)). See *Re K (A Minor) (Adoption: Nationality)* [1995] Fam 38, [1994] 3 All ER 553, CA, where it was held that the wording of the British Nationality Act 1981 s 1(6) as then in force did not affect the right of the Secretary of State to appeal against an adoption order (which would confer British nationality) made eight days short of the child's majority in respect of a child with no right of abode in United Kingdom.

18 British Nationality Act 1981 s 2(1).

19 See the British Nationality Act 1981 s 2(1)(a). For the purposes of the British Nationality Act 1981, a person who is a British citizen by virtue of s 2(1)(a) is a British citizen by descent: see s 14(1)(a); and PARA 425. See also the British Nationality (Falkland Islands) Act 1983 s 3; the British Nationality (Hong Kong) Act 1990 s 2(1); and PARAS 432–433. For circumstances in which a person inherits British citizenship from a parent who has it by descent see further the British Nationality Act 1981 Sch 2 para 2; and the text and note 30. Acquisition of British citizenship from a father is no longer subject to legitimacy: see note 7.

20 Ie designated by order made by statutory instrument subject to annulment in pursuance of a resolution of either House of Parliament. As to the order that has been made see the British Citizenship (Designated Service) Order 2006, SI 2006/1390 (amended by SI 2007/744, SI 2009/2958 and SI 2009/2958).

21 As to the Secretary of State see PARA 402.

22 See the British Nationality Act 1981 s 2(1)(b), (2)–(4). For the purposes of the British Nationality Act 1981, a person who is a British citizen by virtue of s 2(1)(b) is not a British citizen by descent: see s 14(1); and PARA 425. A certificate given by or on behalf of the Secretary of State that a person was at any time in Crown service under the government of the United Kingdom or that a person's recruitment for such service took place in the United Kingdom is conclusive evidence of that fact: see s 45(4); and PARA 486.

23 See the British Nationality Act 1981 s 2(1)(c); and the European Union (Amendment) Act 2008 s 3(6). For the purposes of the British Nationality Act 1981, a person who is a British citizen by virtue of s 2(1)(c) is not a British citizen by descent: see s 14(1); and PARA 425.

24 British Nationality Act 1981 s 2(1) (s 2(1), (2), (3) amended by the British Overseas Territories Act 2002 Sch 1 para 2).

25 British Nationality Act 1981 s 2(1) (as amended: see note 24).

26 See the British Nationality Act 1981 s 2(1)(a). See also note 19.

27 See note 20.

28 See the British Nationality Act 1981 s 2(1)(b), (2)–(4) (s 2(1)(b), (2), (3) as amended: see note 24). See also note 22.

29 See the British Nationality Act 1981 s 2(1)(c) (as amended: see note 24); and the European Union (Amendment) Act 2008 s 3(6). See also note 23.

30 See the British Nationality Act 1981 s 36, Sch 2 para 2 (Sch 2 para 2 amended by virtue of the British Overseas Territories Act 2002 s 1(1)(b)). For the purposes of the British Nationality Act 1981, a person who is a British citizen by virtue of Sch 2 para 2 is a British citizen by descent: see s 14(1)(h); and PARA 425. This provision only applies where the parent is a British citizen by descent; otherwise the child would be a British citizen by descent anyway: see the text and note 19.

425. Legal definition of 'by descent'. Normally, British citizenship can only be transmitted to one generation; a person who is a British citizen by descent does not as a general rule automatically pass that citizenship to his or her children[1]. For this purpose British citizenship 'by descent' is a term of art[2], with an exhaustive statutory definition[3]. By statute, the following British citizens are British citizens by descent:

(1)   a person born outside the United Kingdom[4] on or after 1 January 1983[5] who is a British citizen by virtue only of his father or mother being at the time of the birth[6] a British citizen otherwise than by descent[7];

(2)   a person born outside the United Kingdom on or after 1 January 1983 who is registered as a British citizen[8], being the child of a British citizen by descent one of whose parents was a British citizen otherwise than by descent[9];

(3)   a person born outside the United Kingdom on or after 1 January 1983 who is registered as a British citizen under the transitional provisions[10] for children born between 1 January 1983 and 31 December 1987 to certain male former citizens of the United Kingdom and colonies by descent[11];

(4)   a person born outside the United Kingdom before 1 January 1983 who was a citizen of the United Kingdom and colonies by descent[12], and became a British citizen on 1 January 1983[13]; but such a person is a British citizen otherwise than by descent if his father was at the time of his birth serving outside the United Kingdom in a specified type of public service[14];

(5)   a person born outside the United Kingdom before 1 January 1983 who became a British citizen on 1 January 1983[15] and immediately before that date was deemed under any provision of the British Nationality

Acts 1948 to 1965[16] to be a citizen of the United Kingdom and colonies by descent only, or would have been so deemed if male[17]; but such a person is a British citizen otherwise than by descent if his father was at the time of his birth serving outside the United Kingdom in a specified type of public service[18];

(6)   a person born outside the United Kingdom before 1 January 1983 who became a British citizen on 1 January 1983[19] and immediately before that date had the right of abode[20] in the United Kingdom:

    (a)   by virtue only of connection with the United Kingdom through a parent or grandparent who had citizenship of the United Kingdom and colonies by birth, adoption, naturalisation or registration in the United Kingdom, the Channel Islands or the Isle of Man[21]; or

    (b)   by virtue only of such a connection and settlement in the United Kingdom with five years' ordinary residence there[22];

but such a person is a British citizen otherwise than by descent if his father was at the time of his birth serving outside the United Kingdom in a specified type of public service[23];

(7)   a woman born outside the United Kingdom before 1 January 1983 who became a British citizen on 1 January 1983[24] and immediately before that date had the right of abode[25] in the United Kingdom by virtue only of marriage to a man who immediately before that date had the right of abode:

    (a)   by virtue only of connection with the United Kingdom through a parent or grandparent who had citizenship of the United Kingdom and colonies by birth, adoption, naturalisation or registration in the United Kingdom, the Channel Islands or the Isle of Man[26]; or

    (b)   by virtue only of such a connection and settlement in the United Kingdom with five years' ordinary residence there[27];

but she is a British citizen otherwise than by descent if her father was at the time of her birth serving outside the United Kingdom in a specified type of public service[28];

(8)   a woman born outside the United Kingdom before 1 January 1983 who became a British citizen on 1 January 1983[29] and immediately before that date was a citizen of the United Kingdom and colonies by registration[30] on the basis of marriage to a man who became a British citizen by descent on 1 January 1983 or would have done so but for his earlier death or renunciation[31] of citizenship[32]; but she is a British citizen otherwise than by descent if her father was at the time of her birth serving outside the United Kingdom in a specified type of public service[33];

(9)   a person registered as a British citizen under the provision for discretionary registration of minors[34] whose father or mother was at the time of his birth a British citizen or (if the birth was before 1 January 1983) a citizen of the United Kingdom and colonies who became a British citizen on 1 January 1983[35] or would have done so but for his or her death[36];

(10)   a person registered as a British citizen[37] whose entitlement derived from his being a British overseas territories citizen[38] treated as a national of the United Kingdom for the purposes of the European Union treaties[39];

(11) a woman born outside the United Kingdom before 1 January 1983 who was registered as a British citizen[40] on the basis of marriage to a man who on 1 January 1983 became a British citizen[41] by descent or would have done so but for his earlier death or renunciation[42] of citizenship of the United Kingdom and colonies[43]; but she is a British citizen otherwise than by descent if her father was at the time of her birth serving outside the United Kingdom in a specified type of public service[44];

(12) a person who registered as a British citizen[45] following previous renunciation of citizenship of the United Kingdom and colonies[46] who, had he not renounced it, would have become a British citizen by descent on 1 January 1983[47];

(13) a person who, having formerly been a British citizen by descent, renounced and subsequently resumed his British citizenship by registration[48];

(14) a person born in a British overseas territory[49] on or after 1 January 1983 who is a British citizen by virtue of provisions contained in the British Nationality Act 1981[50] for reducing statelessness[51];

(15) a person who became a British citizen[52] with effect from 1 January 1983 only because he was a British overseas territories citizen with a parent or grandparent born, naturalised or registered in the Falkland Islands as a citizen of the United Kingdom and colonies[53];

(16) a woman who became a British citizen[54] with effect from 1 January 1983 only by virtue of previous marriage to a man who was, or had a parent or grandparent who was, born, naturalised or registered in the Falkland Islands as a citizen of the United Kingdom and colonies[55];

(17) a person registered as a British citizen under the British Nationality (Hong Kong) Act 1990[56] as the spouse or child of a person registered as a British citizen pursuant to the Citizenship Selection Scheme under that Act[57];

(18) a person, previously a British overseas territories citizen, who became a British citizen[58] with effect from 21 May 2002 by virtue of the British Overseas Territories Act 2002 and who: (a) immediately before that date was a British overseas territories citizen by descent; and (b) where at that time he was a British citizen as well as a British overseas territories citizen, was then a British citizen by descent[59];

(19) a person born on or after 26 April 1969 and before 1 January 1983 whose mother was at the time a citizen of the United Kingdom and colonies by virtue of her birth in the British Indian Ocean Territory and who, having previously been neither a British citizen nor a British overseas territories citizen, became a British citizen[60] with effect from 21 May 2002 by virtue of the British Overseas Territories Act 2002[61].

1   Ie unless the parent is in government or European Union service abroad: see the British Nationality Act 1981 s 2(1)–(3); and PARA 424.

2   Thus some who acquire citizenship through a parent are not classified as British citizens by descent (eg children of persons in Crown service abroad: see note 1; and PARA 424), while some who acquire citizenship otherwise than through a parent are so classified (eg certain women acquiring citizenship or right of abode by marriage: see heads (7) and (8) in the text).

3   A British citizen by descent cannot overcome the statutory classification by naturalising to become a British citizen otherwise than by descent: *R (on the application of Ullah) v Secretary of State for the Home Department* [2001] EWCA Civ 659, [2002] QB 525, [2001] Imm AR 439.

4   As to the meaning of 'United Kingdom' see PARA 403 note 1.

5   Ie the date on which the British Nationality Act 1981 came into force: see PARA 403 note 1.

6   See PARA 424 notes 6–7.

7 See the British Nationality Act 1981 s 14(1)(a). See also s 2(1)(a); and PARA 424. The citizenship acquired by a child born outside the United Kingdom to a British citizen in government or European Union service outside the United Kingdom is British citizenship otherwise than by descent, even if the parent is a citizen by descent: see ss 2(1)(b), (c), 14(1)(a); and PARA 424.

8 Ie under the British Nationality Act 1981 s 3(2): see PARA 427.

9 See the British Nationality Act 1981 s 14(1)(a).

10 Ie under the British Nationality Act 1981 s 9 (now repealed): see PARA 437.

11 See the British Nationality Act 1981 s 14(1)(a). As to citizenship of the United Kingdom and colonies see PARAS 414–419.

12 Ie by virtue of the British Nationality Act 1948 s 5 (now repealed), which conferred citizenship on a person whose father (but not mother) was a citizen otherwise than by descent: see PARA 417.

13 See the British Nationality Act 1981 s 14(1)(b)(i). As to those who became British citizens on 1 January 1983 see PARA 422.

14 See the British Nationality Act 1981 s 14(2). The specified types of public service are: (1) Crown service under the government of the United Kingdom, for which he was recruited in the United Kingdom; (2) service designated under s 2(3) (see PARA 424) as being closely associated with the activities outside the United Kingdom of Her Majesty's government in the United Kingdom, for which he was recruited in the United Kingdom; and (3) service under an EU institution, for which he was recruited in a country which at the time of the recruitment was an EU member state: see s 14(2), (3); European Union (Amendment) Act 2008 s 3(6). This excepting provision is necessary because under the British Nationality Act 1948 s 5 (now repealed) (see note 12; and PARA 417) children born before 1 January 1983 of citizens by descent in Crown service were citizens by descent, whereas the British Nationality Act 1981 is so worded that such children born after 1 January 1983 are not citizens by descent: see ss 2(1), 14(1)(a); note 7; and PARA 424. A certificate given by or on behalf of the Secretary of State that a person was at any time in Crown service under the government of the United Kingdom or that a person's recruitment for such service took place in the United Kingdom is conclusive evidence of that fact: see s 45(4); and PARA 486.

15 See note 13; and PARA 422.

16 As to the British Nationality Acts 1948 to 1965 see PARA 403 note 5.

17 See the British Nationality Act 1981 s 14(1)(b)(ii). Prior to the British Nationality Act 1981 women could not transmit citizenship to their children, so there was no need to deem their citizenship to be by descent only, since the purpose of such deeming was to prevent transmission. As to deemed descent see eg the British Nationality Act 1948 ss 12(8), 13, Sch 3 para 3 (all now repealed); the British Nationality (No 2) Act 1964 s 1(4) (now repealed); and PARA 417 note 6.

18 See note 14.

19 See note 13; and PARA 422.

20 As to the right of abode prior to 1 January 1983 see PARA 420.

21 As to such a connection see the Immigration Act 1971 s 2(1)(b) (as then in force).

22 See the British Nationality Act 1981 s 14(1)(b)(iii). As to the requirement of settlement with five years' ordinary residence see the Immigration Act 1971 s 2(1)(c) (as then in force).

23 See note 14.

24 See note 13; and PARA 422.

25 The woman would have had the right of abode under the Immigration Act 1971 s 2(2) (as then in force): see PARA 420.

26 See note 21.

27 See the British Nationality Act 1981 s 14(1)(b)(iii). See also note 22.

28 See note 14.

29 See note 13; and PARA 422.

30 Ie under the British Nationality Act 1948 s 6(2) (now repealed).

31 See PARA 419.

32 See the British Nationality Act 1981 s 14(1)(b)(iv).

33 See note 14.

34 Ie the British Nationality Act 1981 s 3(1): see PARA 427. As to the meaning of 'minor' see PARA 424 note 13.

35 See note 13; and PARA 422.

36 See the British Nationality Act 1981 s 14(1)(c).

37 Ie by virtue of the British Nationality Act 1981 s 4B, s 4C or s 5: see PARAS 428, 429, 431.

38 As to British overseas territories citizens and citizenship (formerly known as British dependent territories citizens and citizenship) see PARAS 406, 445–458.

39 See the British Nationality Act 1981 s 14(1)(d) (amended by the Nationality, Immigration and Asylum Act 2002 s 12(2), 13(2)).

40 Ie under the British Nationality Act 1981 s 8: see PARA 437. Section 8 temporarily extended the former right of a woman to registration under the British Nationality Act 1948 s 6(2) (repealed) on the basis of marriage to a citizen of the United Kingdom and colonies: see head (8) in the text; and PARA 437.

41 See note 13; and PARA 422.

42 See PARA 419.

43 See the British Nationality Act 1981 s 14(1)(e).

44 See note 14.

45 Ie under the British Nationality Act 1981 s 10, which provides for registration following renunciation of previous citizenship of certain persons with an appropriate qualifying connection with the United Kingdom: see PARA 443.

46 See PARA 419.

47 See the British Nationality Act 1981 s 14(1)(f). See also note 13; and PARA 422. This ensures that the person who renounces and resumes citizenship will not be in a better position than if he had never renounced it.

48 See the British Nationality Act 1981 s 14(1)(g). As to resuming citizenship by registration see s 13; and PARA 443. Cf note 45.

49 As to British overseas territories (formerly known as dependent territories) see PARA 445 note 1.

50 Ie the British Nationality Act 1981 Sch 2 para 2: see PARA 424. As to other provisions for reducing statelessness see PARA 436.

51 See the British Nationality Act 1981 s 14(1)(h) (amended by virtue of the British Overseas Territories Act 2002 s 1(1)(b)).

52 Ie under the British Nationality (Falkland Islands) Act 1983.

53 See the British Nationality (Falkland Islands) Act 1983 s 3(1); and see PARA 422 heads (i), (ii)(B). A person who became a British citizen with effect from 1 January 1983 by virtue of the application to him of any of the provisions of the British Nationality Act 1981 as well as by virtue of the application to him of any provision of the British Nationality (Falkland Islands) Act 1983 is a British citizen by descent if, and only if, he: (1) would have been a British citizen by descent if the British Nationality (Falkland Islands) Act 1983 had not been passed; and (2) would not be a British citizen but for s 1(1)(b)(ii) (see PARA 422 heads (i), (ii)(B)) or s 1(1)(b)(iii) (see head (16) in the text; note 55; and PARA 422 heads (i), (ii)(C)): see s 3(2).

54 Ie under the British Nationality (Falkland Islands) Act 1983.

55 See the British Nationality (Falkland Islands) Act 1983 s 3(1); and see PARA 422 heads (i), (ii)(C). See also note 53.

56 Ie by virtue of the British Nationality (Hong Kong) Act 1990 s 1(4), Sch 2: see PARA 433.

57 See the British Nationality (Hong Kong) Act 1990 s 2(1); and PARA 433. As to registration as a British citizen pursuant to the Citizenship Selection Scheme see s 1(1), Sch 1; and PARA 433.

58 Ie by virtue of the British Overseas Territories Act 2002 s 3: see PARA 423.

59 See the British Overseas Territories Act 2002 s 3(3); and PARA 423.

60 Ie by virtue of the British Overseas Territories Act 2002 s 3(1): see PARA 423.

61 See the British Overseas Territories Act 2002 s 6(2); and PARA 423.

426. Acquisition by registration: birth in the United Kingdom. A person born in the United Kingdom[1] on or after 1 January 1983[2] who does not automatically acquire British citizenship by birth[3] is entitled[4] to be registered as a British citizen if:

(1)   while he is a minor[5], an application for his registration as a British citizen is made on the ground that his father or mother[6] has become a British citizen or has become settled in the United Kingdom[7]; or

(2)   an application for his registration as a British citizen is made at any time after he attains the age of ten years[8], on the ground that during each of the first ten years of his life he has not been absent from the United Kingdom for more than 90 days[9].

A person born in the United Kingdom on or after 13 January 2010[10] who does not automatically acquire British citizenship by birth[11] is entitled to be registered as a British citizen if, while he is a minor:

(a)   his father or mother becomes a member of the armed forces[12]; and

(b)   an application is made for his registration as a British citizen[13].

1　See PARA 424 note 1. As to the meaning of 'United Kingdom' see PARA 403 note 1.
2　Ie the date of commencement of the British Nationality Act 1981: see PARA 403 note 1.
3　Ie by virtue of the British Nationality Act 1981 s 1(1), (1A) or (2): see PARA 424.
4　This is subject to overriding considerations of public policy, where the qualifying conditions are fulfilled by criminal activity: *R v Secretary of State for the Home Department, ex p Puttick* [1981] QB 767, [1981] 1 All ER 776, DC (married status on which entitlement depended valid but obtained by perjury and forgery). In addition, an application for registration of an adult or young person as a British citizen under the British Nationality Act 1981 s 1(3), (3A), (4) must not be granted unless the Secretary of State is satisfied that the adult or young person is of good character: s 41A(1) (s 41A added by the Borders, Citizenship and Immigration Act 2009 s 47(1) to replace corresponding provision in the Immigration, Asylum and Nationality Act 2006 s 58). 'Adult or young person' means a person who has attained the age of ten at the time when the application is made: British Nationality Act 1981 s 41A(5) (as so added).
5　As to the meaning of 'minor' see PARA 424 note 13.
6　As to the meanings of 'father' and 'mother' see PARA 424 note 7.
7　See the British Nationality Act 1981 s 1(3) (amended by the Borders, Citizenship and Immigration Act 2009 s 42(1), (3)). See PARA 424 note 9. As to applications see PARA 484.
8　For the purposes of the British Nationality Act 1981, a person attains any particular age at the beginning of the relevant anniversary of the date of his birth: s 50(11)(b).
9　See the British Nationality Act 1981 s 1(4) (amended by virtue of the British Overseas Territories Act 2002 s 1(1)(b)). For the purposes of the British Nationality Act 1981, any reference to a day on which a person was absent from the United Kingdom or from a British overseas territory or from the British overseas territories is a reference to a day for the whole of which he was so absent: s 50(10)(b) (amended by virtue of the British Overseas Territories Act 2002 s 1(1)(b)). If in the special circumstances of any particular case the Secretary of State thinks fit, he may waive longer periods of absence: see the British Nationality Act 1981 s 1(7). As to the exercise of discretion see s 44; and PARA 402. As to the Secretary of State see PARA 402.
10　See PARA 424 note 11.
11　Ie by virtue of the British Nationality Act 1981 s 1(1), (1A) or (2): see PARA 424.
12　As to the meaning of 'member of the armed forces' see PARA 424 note 12.
13　British Nationality Act 1981 s 1(3A), (9) (added by the Borders, Citizenship and Immigration Act 2009 s 42(1), (4), (6)). See also note 4.

427.　Acquisition by registration: minors.　The Secretary of State[1] may, if he thinks fit[2], grant any application[3] for registration of a minor as a British citizen[4].

A person born outside the United Kingdom[5] before 21 May 2002[6] is entitled[7], on an application made while he is a minor, to be registered as a British citizen if: (1) one of his parents was a British citizen by descent[8] at the time of the birth[9]; and (2) the father or mother of that parent was a British citizen otherwise than by descent at the time of the birth of that parent, or became a British citizen otherwise than by descent on 1 January 1983[10] or would have done so but for his or her death; and (3) (save in the case of a person born stateless[11]) that parent had been in the United Kingdom at the beginning of any three year period ending not later than the date of the birth and had not been absent from the United Kingdom for more than 270 days during that period[12]. In relation to persons born on or after 21 May 2002, these provisions apply to those born outside the United Kingdom and the qualifying territories[13], and head (3) above requires presence in the United Kingdom or a qualifying territory[14].

A person born outside the United Kingdom before 21 May 2002 is entitled[15], on an application made while he is a minor, to be registered as a British citizen if: (a) at the time of that person's birth his father or mother was a British citizen by descent; and (b) that person and his father and mother were in the United Kingdom at the beginning of the period of three years ending with the date of the application and none of them has been absent from the United Kingdom for more than 270 days during that period; and (c) his father and mother consent to the registration in the prescribed manner[16]. In relation to persons born on or after 21 May 2002, these provisions apply to those born outside the United

Kingdom and the qualifying territories, and head (b) above requires presence in the United Kingdom or a qualifying territory[17].

1 As to the Secretary of State see PARA 402.
2 As to the exercise of discretion see the British Nationality Act 1981 s 44; and PARA 402.
3 As to applications see PARA 484.
4 See the British Nationality Act 1981 s 3(1). See also *R (on the application of Montana) v Secretary of State for the Home Department* [2001] 1 WLR 552, [2001] 1 FCR 358, [2001] 1 WLR 552, CA (where a refusal of an application made by a British father under the British Nationality Act 1981 s 3(1) for registration of an illegitimate child born abroad was held not to be in breach of human rights); and PARA 424 note 7. As to the meaning of 'minor' see PARA 424 note 13.
      An application for registration of an adult or young person as a British citizen under the British Nationality Act 1981 s 3(1), (2) or (5) must not be granted unless the Secretary of State is satisfied that the adult or young person is of good character: s 41A(1) (s 41A added by the Borders, Citizenship and Immigration Act 2009 s 47(1) to replace corresponding provision in the Immigration, Asylum and Nationality Act 2006 s 58). As to the meaning of 'adult or young person' see PARA 426 note 4.
      Provided that the application is made during minority, the Secretary of State may determine it, and effect registration, after the age of majority has been reached, although an oath of allegiance may then be necessary: *Gowa v A-G* [1985] 1 WLR 1003, HL. As to oaths of allegiance see PARA 484.
      A person registered under the British Nationality Act 1981 s 3(1) is a British citizen by descent if at the time of his birth his father or mother was a British citizen, or was at that time a citizen of the United Kingdom and colonies and became a British citizen on 1 January 1983 or would have done so but for his or her death: see s 14(1)(c); and PARA 425. As to citizenship of the United Kingdom and colonies see PARAS 414–419.
5 See PARA 424 note 1. As to the meaning of 'United Kingdom' see PARA 403 note 1.
6 Ie the date on which the provisions of the British Overseas Territories Act 2002 Sch 1 (which contains provisions amending the British Nationality Act 1981) came into force: see the British Overseas Territories Act 2002 s 8; and the British Overseas Territories Act 2002 (Commencement) Order 2002, SI 2002/1252, art 2(a).
7 See note 4 and PARA 426 note 4.
8 As to British citizenship by descent see PARA 425.
9 See PARA 424 notes 6–7.
10 Ie the date of commencement of the British Nationality Act 1981: see PARA 403 note 1.
11 A person born stateless need only satisfy heads (1) and (2) in the text. As to registration of stateless persons see also PARA 436.
12 See the British Nationality Act 1981 s 3(2), (3) (s 3(2) amended by the Borders, Citizenship and Immigration Act 2009 s 43(1), (2)). As to references to days of absence from the United Kingdom see PARA 426 note 9. A person registered under the British Nationality Act 1981 s 3(2) is a British citizen by descent: see s 14(1)(a); and PARA 425.
13 As to the meaning of 'qualifying territory' see PARA 424 note 3.
14 See the British Nationality Act 1981 s 3(2), (3) (amended by the British Overseas Territories Act 2002 Sch 1 para 3). See also note 12.
15 See note 4 and PARA 426 note 4.
16 See the British Nationality Act 1981 s 3(5). As to references to days of absence from the United Kingdom see PARA 426 note 9. Where a parent, in pursuance of s 3(5)(c), consents to the registration of a person as a British citizen under s 3(5), the consent must be expressed in writing and signed by the parent: see the British Nationality (General) Regulations 2003, SI 2003/548, reg 14 (substituted by SI 2009/3363). As to the power to make regulations see PARA 404.
      If the person's father or mother died, or their marriage or civil partnership was terminated, on or before the date of the application, or his father and mother were legally separated on that date, the references to his father and mother in head (b) in the text are to be read either as references to his father or as references to his mother; and if his father or mother died on or before that date, the reference to his father and mother in head (c) in the text is to be read as a reference to either of them: British Nationality Act 1981 s 3(6) (amended by the Nationality, Immigration and Asylum Act 2002 s 9(2); and the Civil Partnership Act 2004 s 261(1), Sch 27 para 71).
      A person registered under the British Nationality Act 1981 s 3(5) is not a British citizen by descent: see s 14; and PARA 425.
17 See the British Nationality Act 1981 s 3(5) (amended by the British Overseas Territories Act 2002 Sch 1 para 3). See also note 16.

428. Acquisition by registration: holders of other types of British nationality.
The holders of other types of British nationality[1] may be able to acquire British citizenship by registration. Thus a British overseas territories citizen[2], a British overseas citizen[3], a British national (overseas)[4], a British subject[5] or a British protected person[6], is entitled[7], on application[8], to be registered as a British citizen if he satisfies each of the following four requirements[9]: (1) he was in the United Kingdom[10] at the beginning of the period of five years ending with the date of application and was not absent during that period for more than 450 days[11]; (2) in the 12 months preceding the application he was not absent from the United Kingdom for more than 90 days[12]; (3) during the 12 months preceding the application he was not subject under the immigration laws[13] to any restriction on the period for which he might remain in the United Kingdom[14]; (4) he was not at any time during the period of five years ending with the date of application in the United Kingdom in breach of the immigration laws[15].

The Secretary of State may, if he thinks fit, register as a British citizen any British overseas territories citizen, British national (overseas), British overseas citizen, British subject or British protected person who has at any time served: (a) in Crown service under the government of a British overseas territory; or (b) in paid or unpaid service as a member of any body established by law in a British overseas territory members of which are appointed by or on behalf of the Crown[16].

In the case of a British overseas territories citizen, since 21 May 2002 the Secretary of State has had a discretion to register him as a British citizen, whether or not the above requirements have been satisfied[17]. However, since 21 May 2002, most British overseas territories citizens also have British citizenship in any event[18].

A person who has the status of British overseas citizen, British subject under the British Nationality Act 1981, British protected person or British national (overseas), is entitled to be registered as a British citizen if: (i) he applies for registration under these provisions; (ii) the Secretary of State is satisfied that the person does not have, apart from the status mentioned above, any citizenship or nationality; and (iii) the Secretary of State is satisfied that the person has not after the relevant day[19] renounced, voluntarily relinquished or lost through action or inaction any citizenship or nationality[20].

1   A person holding a citizenship or status mentioned in this paragraph does not necessarily have formal British nationality: see further PARA 405 et seq.
2   As to British overseas territories citizens and citizenship (formerly known as British dependent territories citizens and citizenship) see PARAS 406, 445–458. Note that since 21 May 2002 most persons who were British overseas territories citizens immediately before that date have enjoyed British citizenship (in addition to, not in place of, their British overseas territories citizenship), without the need for registration: see the text and note 18.
3   As to British overseas citizens see PARAS 406, 459–463.
4   As to British national (overseas) status see PARAS 406, 465–467.
5   As to British subjects see PARAS 407, 469–474.
6   As to British protected persons see PARAS 408, 476–480.
7   See PARA 426 note 4.
8   As to applications see PARA 484.
9   See the British Nationality Act 1981 s 4(1), (2) (s 4(1) amended by virtue of the British Overseas Territories Act 2002 s 2(2)(b); and by SI 1986/948).
    An application for registration of an adult or young person as a British citizen under the British Nationality Act 1981 s 4(2) or (5) must not be granted unless the Secretary of State is satisfied that the adult or young person is of good character: s 41A(1) (s 41A added by the Borders, Citizenship and Immigration Act 2009 s 47(1) to replace corresponding provision in the Immigration, Asylum and Nationality Act 2006 s 58). As to the meaning of 'adult or young person' see PARA 426 note 4. As to the Secretary of State see PARA 402.

There are similar requirements for naturalisation, but for naturalisation other conditions must also be met: see PARA 438. There is a right to be registered under the British Nationality Act 1981 s 4 provided the requirements are fulfilled, but naturalisation is entirely discretionary. As to the additional discretion to register a British overseas territories citizen as a British citizen under s 4A see the text and note 17.

10 As to the meaning of 'United Kingdom' see PARA 403 note 1.

11 See the British Nationality Act 1981 s 4(2)(a). As to references to days of absence from the United Kingdom see PARA 426 note 9. A person settled in the United Kingdom on 31 December 1982 need not have been in the United Kingdom at the beginning of the five year period mentioned in s 4(2)(a): see s 4(3). The Secretary of State may, if he thinks fit, treat the person to whom the application relates as fulfilling the requirement specified in s 4(2)(a), although the number of days on which he was absent from the United Kingdom exceeds the number mentioned: see s 4(4)(a). As to the exercise of discretion see the British Nationality Act 1981 s 44; and PARA 402.

12 See the British Nationality Act 1981 s 4(2)(b). As to references to days of absence from the United Kingdom see PARA 426 note 9. The Secretary of State may, if he thinks fit, treat the person to whom the application relates as fulfilling the requirement specified in s 4(2)(b), although the number of days on which he was absent from the United Kingdom exceeds the number mentioned: see s 4(4)(a).

13 As to the meaning of 'immigration laws' see PARA 424 note 9.

14 See the British Nationality Act 1981 s 4(2)(c). The Secretary of State may, if he thinks fit, disregard any such restriction as is mentioned in s 4(2)(c) provided the person to whom the application relates was not subject to the restriction on the date of the application: see s 4(4)(b).

15 See the British Nationality Act 1981 s 4(2)(d). The Secretary of State may, if he thinks fit, treat the person to whom the application relates as fulfilling the requirement specified in s 4(2)(d), although he was in the United Kingdom in breach of the immigration laws in the period mentioned: see s 4(4)(c). As to being in the United Kingdom in breach of the immigration laws see PARA 424 note 9.

16 See the British Nationality Act 1981 s 4(5), (6) (s 4(6) amended by the British Overseas Territories Act 2002 s 1(1)(b)); and note 9. As to British overseas territories (formerly known as dependent territories) see PARA 445 note 1.

17 See the British Nationality Act 1981 s 4A(1) (s 4A added by the British Overseas Territories Act 2002 s 4). This does not apply in the case of a British overseas territories citizen who: (1) is such a citizen by virtue only of a connection with the Sovereign Base Areas of Akrotiri and Dhekelia; or (2) has ceased to be a British citizen as a result of a declaration of renunciation: British Nationality Act 1981 s 4A(2) (as so added). As to renunciation see PARA 443.

18 See the British Overseas Territories Act 2002 s 3; and PARA 423.

19 For the purposes of head (iii) in the text, 'relevant day' means (1) in the case of a person to whom the British Nationality Act 1981 s 4B applies by virtue of his being a British national (overseas) only, 19 March 2009; and (2) in any other case, 4 July 2002: s 4B(3) (s 4B added by the Nationality, Immigration and Asylum Act 2002 s 12(1); British Nationality Act 1981 s 4B(3) added by the Borders, Citizenship and Immigration Act 2009 s 44(1), (4)).

20 British Nationality Act 1981 s 4B(1), (2) (as added (see note 19); amended by the Borders, Citizenship and Immigration Act 2009 ss 44(2), (3), 56, Schedule Pt 2).

429. Acquisition by registration: certain persons born before 1983. A person is entitled to be registered as a British citizen if he applies for registration under these provisions and he satisfies each of the following conditions[1]. The first condition is that the applicant was born before 1 January 1983[2]. The second condition is that the applicant would at some time before 1 January 1983 have become a citizen of the United Kingdom and colonies[3] under specified provisions[4] of the British Nationality Act 1948[5]. The third condition is that immediately before 1 January 1983 the applicant would have had the right of abode in the United Kingdom[6] had he become a citizen of the United Kingdom and colonies as described in above[7].

The purpose of this provision is to offer British citizenship to certain persons born before 1983 who would have become British citizens automatically on 1 January 1983 if the law prior to that date had not barred women from transmitting British nationality to their children.

1　See the British Nationality Act 1981 s 4C(1) (s 4C added by the Nationality, Immigration and Asylum Act 2002 s 13(1)). An application for registration of an adult or young person as a British citizen under the British Nationality Act 1981 s 4C must not be granted unless the Secretary of State is satisfied that the adult or young person is of good character: s 41A(1) (s 41A added by the Borders, Citizenship and Immigration Act 2009 s 47(1) to replace corresponding provision in the Immigration, Asylum and Nationality Act 2006 s 58). As to the meaning of 'adult or young person' see PARA 426 note 4. As to the Secretary of State see PARA 402.

　　The Secretary of State cannot rely on public policy to deprive a person of registration as a British citizen under the British Nationality Act 1981 s 4C where he has done nothing wrong and meets the necessary conditions to be registered; all that is needed under s 4C is that the conditions set out in s 4C are met: *R (on the application of Hicks) v Secretary of State for the Home Department* [2005] EWHC 2818 (Admin), (2005) Times, 28 December, [2005] All ER (D) 179 (Dec).

2　British Nationality Act 1981 s 4C(2) (as added: see note 1). The date referred to in the text is the date of commencement of the British Nationality Act 1981: see PARA 403 note 1.

3　As to citizenship of the United Kingdom and colonies see the British Nationality Act 1948 Pt II (ss 4–22) (repealed); and PARAS 414–419.

4　Ie: (1) under the British Nationality Act 1948 s 5 or Sch 3 para 3 (now repealed) if assumption A had applied; or (2) under s 12(3), (4) or (5) (now repealed) if assumption B had applied and as a result of its application the applicant would have been a British subject immediately before 1 January 1949; or (3) under s 12(2) (now repealed) if one or both of the following had applied: (a) assumption A had applied; (b) assumption B had applied and as a result of its application the applicant would have been a British subject immediately before 1 January 1949: British Nationality Act 1981 s 4C(3)(a)–(c) (s 4C as added (see note 1); s 4C(3) substituted by the Borders, Citizenship and Immigration Act 2009 s 45(1), (3)).

　　Assumption A is that: (i) the British Nationality Act 1948 s 5 or s 12(2) or Sch 3 para 3 (as the case may be) (all now repealed) provided for citizenship by descent from a mother in the same terms as it provided for citizenship by descent from a father; and (ii) references in that provision to a father were references to the applicant's mother: British Nationality Act 1981 s 4C(3A) (s 4C as added (see note 1); s 4C(3A)–(3D), (5) added by the Borders, Citizenship and Immigration Act 2009 s 45(3)). Assumption B is that: (A) a provision of the law at some time before 1 January 1949 which provided for a nationality status to be acquired by descent from a father provided in the same terms for its acquisition by descent from a mother; and (B) references in that provision to a father were references to the applicant's mother: British Nationality Act 1981 s 4C(3B) (as so added). For the purposes of s 4C(3B), a nationality status is acquired by a person ('P') by descent where its acquisition (aa) depends, amongst other things, on the nationality status of one or both of P's parents; and (bb) does not depend upon an application being made for P's registration as a person who has the status in question: s 4C(3C) (as so added). As to citizenship by descent see PARA 425.

　　For the purposes of the interpretation of the British Nationality Act 1948 s 5 (now repealed) in its application in the case of assumption A to a case of descent from a mother, the reference in s 5(1) proviso to 'a citizen of the United Kingdom and colonies by descent only' includes a reference to a female person who became a citizen of the United Kingdom and colonies by virtue of s 12(2), (4) or (6) only, s 13(2), Sch 3 para 3 (all now repealed), or the British Nationality (No 2) Act 1964 s 1(1)(a) or (c) (now repealed): British Nationality Act 1981 s 4C(5) (s 4C as added (see note 1); s 4C(5) added by the Borders, Citizenship and Immigration Act 2009 s 45(4)).

5　British Nationality Act 1981 s 4C(3) (s 4C as added (see note 1); s 4C(3) as substituted (see note 4)). For the purposes of s 4C(3), it is not to be assumed that any registration or other requirements of the provisions mentioned in that subsection or in s 4C(3B) (see note 4) were met: s 4C(3D) (as added: see note 4).

6　Ie by virtue of the Immigration Act 1971 s 2: see PARA 412; and BRITISH NATIONALITY, IMMIGRATION AND ASYLUM vol 4(2) (2002 Reissue) PARA 85.

7　British Nationality Act 1981 s 4C(4) (as added: see note 1).

430. Acquisition by registration: children of members of the armed forces. A person ('P') born outside the United Kingdom[1] and the qualifying territories[2] on or after 13 January 2010[3] is entitled to be registered as a British citizen if: (1) an application is made for P's registration under these provisions; and (2) each of the following conditions is satisfied[4]. The first condition is that, at the time of P's birth, P's father or mother[5] was: (a) a member of the armed forces[6]; and (b) serving outside the United Kingdom and the qualifying territories[7]. The second condition is that, if P is a minor[8] on the date of the application, the consent of P's father and mother to P's registration as a British citizen has been signified in the prescribed manner[9]. But if P's father or mother has died on or before the date of the application, the reference above to P's father and mother is to be read as a reference to either of them[10]. The Secretary of State may, in the special circumstances of a particular case, waive the need for the second condition to be satisfied[11].

1 As to the meaning of 'United Kingdom' see PARA 403 note 1.
2 As to the meaning of 'qualifying territory' see PARA 424 note 3.
3 Ie the day appointed for the commencement of the Borders, Citizenship and Immigration Act 2009 s 46: see the British Nationality Act 1981 s 4D(6) (s 4D added by the Borders, Citizenship and Immigration Act 2009 s 46); and the Borders, Citizenship and Immigration Act 2009 (Commencement No 1) Order 2009, SI 2009/2731, art 4(e).
4 See the British Nationality Act 1981 s 4D(1) (as added: see note 3). An application for registration of an adult or young person as a British citizen under s 4D must not be granted unless the Secretary of State is satisfied that the adult or young person is of good character: s 41A(1) (s 41A added by the Borders, Citizenship and Immigration Act 2009 s 47(1)). As to the meaning of 'adult or young person' see PARA 426 note 4. As to the Secretary of State see PARA 402.
5 As to the meanings of 'father' and 'mother' see PARA 424 note 7.
6 As to the meaning of 'member of the armed forces' see PARA 424 note 12.
7 British Nationality Act 1981 s 4D(2) (as added: see note 3).
8 As to the meaning of 'minor' see PARA 424 note 13.
9 British Nationality Act 1981 s 4D(3) (as added: see note 3). Where a parent, in pursuance of s 4D(3), consents to the registration of a person as a British citizen under s 4D, the consent must be expressed in writing and signed by the parent: see the British Nationality (General) Regulations 2003, SI 2003/548, reg 14 (substituted by SI 2009/3363).
10 British Nationality Act 1981 s 4D(4) (as added: see note 3).
11 British Nationality Act 1981 s 4D(5) (as added: see note 3).

431. Acquisition by registration: British nationals for the purposes of EU law.
The British Nationality Act 1981 provides that a British overseas territories citizen[1] who falls to be treated as a national of the United Kingdom[2] for the purposes of the European Union Treaties[3] is entitled[4], on application[5], to be registered as a British citizen[6]. The only British overseas territories citizens who fulfil this description are those who acquired that citizenship from a connection with Gibraltar[7].

However, since 21 May 2002, most persons who were British overseas territories citizens immediately before that date have enjoyed automatic British citizenship[8].

1 As to British overseas territories citizens and citizenship (formerly known as British dependent territories citizens and citizenship) see PARAS 406, 445–458.
2 As to the meaning of 'United Kingdom' see PARA 403 note 1.
3 See PARA 405.
4 See PARA 426 note 4.
5 As to applications see PARA 484.
6 British Nationality Act 1981 s 5 (amended by the British Overseas Territories Act 2002 s 2(2)(b)); European Union (Amendment) Act 2008 s 3(6). The British Nationality Act 1981 s 5 thus provides for an entitlement to register as a British citizen by those who are EU citizens by virtue of the United Kingdom's definition of 'United Kingdom national' for the purposes of EU law (see PARA 405) and who are not otherwise British citizens already. An application for registration of an adult or young person as a British citizen under s 5 must not be granted unless the Secretary of State is satisfied that the adult or young person is of good character: s 41A(1) (s 41A added by the Borders, Citizenship and Immigration Act 2009 s 47(1)). As to the meaning

of 'adult or young person' see PARA 426 note 4. As to the Secretary of State see PARA 402. A person registered under the British Nationality Act 1981 s 5 is a British citizen by descent: see s 14(1)(d); and PARA 425.

7   See PARA 405. As to Gibraltar see COMMONWEALTH vol 13 (2009) PARA 859. See also note 8.
8   See the British Overseas Territories Act 2002 s 3; and PARA 423. Prior to this, Gibraltarians who were British overseas territories citizens and United Kingdom nationals for the purposes of EU law had greater rights to live and work in other member states of the European Union than they had with respect to the United Kingdom, since British overseas territories citizenship did not carry the right of abode in the United Kingdom, and a person cannot exercise EU rights of freedom of movement in the member state of which he is a national: see PARAS 411–412; BRITISH NATIONALITY, IMMIGRATION AND ASYLUM vol 4(2) (2002 Reissue) PARA 225 et seq. However, the British Nationality Act 1981 s 5 is not otiose by virtue of the extension by the British Overseas Territories Act 2002 of British citizenship to British overseas territories citizens, because people registering or naturalising in Gibraltar on or after 21 May 2002 are British overseas territories citizens but not automatically British citizens. They will be 'British nationals' for EU purposes (see PARA 405) and therefore eligible under the British Nationality Act 1981 s 5 to register by entitlement as British citizens.

432. Acquisition by registration: Falkland Islands. British nationality legislation contains special provisions in relation to the Falkland Islands[1], but the provision for discretionary registration as British citizens of British nationals connected with the Falkland Islands[2] was repealed with effect from 21 May 2002[3]. However, the Colony of the Falkland Islands is a British overseas territory[4], and since 21 May 2002 most persons who are British overseas territories citizens[5] also have British citizenship[6].

1   See eg the provision made as regards automatic acquisition of British citizenship with effect from 1 January 1983; and PARA 422.
2   Ie the British Nationality (Falkland Islands) Act 1983 s 2 (repealed). See also the British Nationality (Falkland Islands) Regulations 1983, SI 1983/479 (lapsed).
3   See the British Overseas Territories Act 2002 s 7, Sch 2; and the British Overseas Territories Act 2002 (Commencement) Order 2002, SI 2002/1252, art 2(c).
4   See the British Nationality Act 1981 s 50(1), Sch 6; and PARA 445 note 1. As to British overseas territories (formerly known as dependent territories) see PARA 445 note 1. As to the Falkland Islands see COMMONWEALTH vol 13 (2009) PARA 858.
5   As to British overseas territories citizens and citizenship (formerly known as British dependent territories citizens and citizenship) see PARAS 406, 445–458.
6   See the British Overseas Territories Act 2002 s 3; and PARA 423. Moreover, this provision has been subsumed by the British Nationality Act 1981 s 4C: see PARA 429.

433. Acquisition by registration under the Citizenship Selection Scheme: Hong Kong. On 1 July 1997 Hong Kong ceased to be a British overseas territory[1]. Provision was made so that some of the people of Hong Kong could be registered before that date as British citizens while remaining resident in Hong Kong[2]. The Secretary of State[3] was required to register as British citizens, before 30 June 1997, up to 50,000 persons of good character recommended to him for that purpose by the Governor of Hong Kong under a scheme referred to as the Citizenship Selection Scheme[4]. Those eligible for inclusion in the scheme were persons settled in Hong Kong who were British overseas territories citizens[5] by virtue of a connection with Hong Kong[6], or British nationals (overseas)[7], British overseas citizens[8], British subjects[9], or British protected persons[10]; a person was also eligible if he applied before 26 July 1990[11] for registration or naturalisation as a British overseas territories citizen by virtue of a connection with Hong Kong, provided that the application would have been successful in the absence of his registration under these provisions as a British citizen[12]. The Secretary of State could direct the Governor to make not more than a specified proportion of his recommendations in a specified period or periods[13]. Spouses and minor children of persons registered under these provisions could also be registered as British citizens on the Governor's recommendation[14].

1   See the Hong Kong Act 1985 s 1(1); the Hong Kong (British Nationality) Order 1986, SI 1986/948, art 5 (amended by virtue of the British Overseas Territories Act 2002 s 1(2)); and COMMONWEALTH vol 13 (2009) PARA 727. As to its status as a dependent territory before 1 July 1997 see the British Nationality Act 1981 s 50(1), Sch 6 (as then in force). As to the consequences of its changed status see further PARAS 458, 462, 465 et seq. As to British overseas territories (formerly known as dependent territories) see PARA 445 note 1.

2   See the British Nationality (Hong Kong) Act 1990. Most provisions of that Act came into force on 7 November 1990 (see the British Nationality (Hong Kong) Act 1990 (Commencement) Order 1990, SI 1990/2210); for the exception see note 5. Provision had earlier been made for the continuation of a form of British nationality, namely, British national (overseas) status: see PARAS 465–467.

3   As to the Secretary of State see PARA 402.

4   See the British Nationality (Hong Kong) Act 1990 ss 1(1), (2), 6(2), Sch 1 paras 1–3. The terms of the scheme were set out in an Order in Council: see Sch 1 para 1; and the British Nationality (Hong Kong) (Selection Scheme) Order 1990, SI 1990/2292 (amended by SI 1993/1789). No such order could be made unless a draft of it had been laid before and approved by a resolution of each House of Parliament: see the British Nationality (Hong Kong) Act 1990 Sch 1 para 1.

The Citizenship Selection Scheme provided for applications to be made by eligible persons in one of four classes (ie the general occupational class, the disciplined services class, the sensitive service class and the entrepreneurs class), for each of which there was a quota: see the British Nationality (Hong Kong) (Selection Scheme) Order 1990, SI 1990/2292, Schedule (amended by SI 1993/1789). Within the general occupational class and the disciplined services class, applicants were selected according to a points system: see the British Nationality (Hong Kong) (Selection Scheme) Order 1990, SI 1990/2292, Schedule (as so amended).

The Governor could make regulations with respect to the manner in which applications were to be made: see the British Nationality (Hong Kong) Act 1990 s 3(1), (2). The Governor had to appoint a committee to advise him and could authorise public officers to exercise certain functions in respect of applications, although only the Governor could make a recommendation for registration: see s 3(3). Neither the Secretary of State nor the Governor, nor any public officer authorised under s 3(3) to carry out any function, was required to give any reason for any decision made by him in the exercise of a discretion vested in him by or under the British Nationality (Hong Kong) Act 1990, and such a decision was not subject to appeal or liable to be questioned in any court (see ss 1(5), 3(4) (s 1(5) now repealed)); but the discretion had to be exercised without regard to the race, colour or religion of any person affected by it (see the British Nationality Act 1981 s 44(1); and PARA 402 (applied by the British Nationality (Hong Kong) Act 1990 s 2(3))).

Further provision was made for the notification of decisions and for the taking of oaths of allegiance: see the British Nationality (Hong Kong) (Registration of Citizens) Regulations 1990, SI 1990/2211 (spent; amended by virtue of the British Overseas Territories Act 2002 s 1(2)). As to the taking of oaths of allegiance generally see PARA 484.

A person registered as a British citizen by virtue of the British Nationality (Hong Kong) Act 1990 s 1(1) became a British citizen otherwise than by descent: see s 2(1).

5   As to British overseas territories citizens and citizenship (formerly known as British dependent territories citizens and citizenship) see PARAS 406, 445–458. The British Nationality (Hong Kong) Act 1990 s 2(2) (amended by virtue of the British Overseas Territories Act 2002 s 2(3)), which has not been brought into force, provided for a person to lose his British overseas territories citizenship if he became a British citizen under the Act.

6   References in the British Nationality (Hong Kong) Act 1990 Sch 1 para 4 to a connection with Hong Kong are to be construed in accordance with the Hong Kong (British Nationality) Order 1986, SI 1986/948, art 2: British Nationality (Hong Kong) Act 1990 Sch 1 para 4(3). The Hong Kong (British Nationality) Order 1986, SI 1986/948, art 2 (amended by virtue of the British Overseas Territories Act 2002 s 2(3)) provides that a person is to be taken to have a connection with Hong Kong if:

(1)   he, his father or his mother was born, naturalised or registered in Hong Kong or found abandoned there as a new-born infant; save that a person born in Hong Kong on or after 1 January 1983 is not to be taken to have a connection with Hong Kong by virtue of birth there unless, at the time of his birth, one of his parents was either settled in Hong Kong or was a British overseas territories citizen by virtue of his having a connection with Hong Kong (Hong Kong (British Nationality) Order 1986, SI 1986/948, art 2(1)(a), (3)); or

(2)   he, his father or his mother was adopted (whether or not in Hong Kong) and the adopter or, in the case of a joint adoption, one of the adopters was at the time of the adoption a British overseas territories citizen by virtue of his having a connection with Hong Kong (art 2(1)(b)); or

(3)   he, his father or his mother was registered outside Hong Kong on an application based (wholly or partly) on any of the following: (a) residence in Hong Kong; (b) descent from a person born in Hong Kong; (c) descent from a person naturalised, registered or settled in Hong Kong (whether before or after the birth of the person registered); (d) descent from a person adopted in the circumstances specified in head (2); (e) marriage to a person who was a British overseas territories citizen by virtue of having a connection with Hong Kong, or would have been but for his death or renunciation of citizenship; (f) Crown service under the government of Hong Kong; (g) where citizenship was renounced and subsequently resumed, birth, naturalisation or registration in Hong Kong (art 2(1)(c)); or

(4)   at the time of his birth his father or mother was settled in Hong Kong (art 2(1)(d)); or

(5)   his father or mother was born to a parent who at the time of the birth was a citizen of the United Kingdom and colonies by virtue of a connection with Hong Kong (art 2(1)(e)); or

(6)   being a woman, she was married before 1 January 1983 to man who was a British overseas territories citizen by virtue of his having a connection with Hong Kong, or who would have been but for his death (art 2(1)(f)).

For the purposes of art 2(1), 'registered' means registered as a British overseas territories citizen or, before 1 January 1983, as a citizen of the United Kingdom and colonies: art 2(2). As to citizens of the United Kingdom and colonies see PARAS 414–419. As to legitimated and posthumous children see the British Nationality Act 1981 ss 47 (now repealed), 48, 50(9) (as originally enacted) (see PARA 424 notes 6–7); applied by the Hong Kong (British Nationality) Order 1986, SI 1986/948, arts 1(4), 7(7)(c).

7   As to British national (overseas) status see PARAS 406, 465–467.

8   As to British overseas citizens see PARAS 406, 459–463.

9   As to British subjects see PARAS 407, 469–474.

10 As to British protected persons see PARAS 408, 476–480.

11 Ie the date on which the British Nationality (Hong Kong) Act 1990 was passed.

12 British Nationality (Hong Kong) Act 1990 Sch 1 para 4(1) (amended by virtue of the British Overseas Territories Act 2002 s 2(3)). Nothing in the British Nationality (Hong Kong) Act 1990 entitled a recommended person to be registered as a British citizen if the Secretary of State had reason to believe that he ceased to satisfy the requirements of Sch 1 para 4 after the recommendation was made: s 6(3).

13 See the British Nationality (Hong Kong) Act 1990 s 1(3).

14 See the British Nationality (Hong Kong) Act 1990 s 1(4), Sch 2 paras 1, 2. The Governor could not make such a recommendation except in pursuance of an application made to him by or on behalf of the spouse or child in question: see Sch 2 para 2.

    Where a person married after his registration as a British citizen under these provisions, he had to be settled in Hong Kong at the time of the marriage in order for his spouse to qualify: see Sch 2 para 3. References in Sch 2 to a minor child of a person registered under s 1(1) are references to a person who was his child on the date of registration and who was a minor on the date of the application under Sch 2 para 2 (see Sch 2 para 4(1)); and references to a child include a child adopted under an adoption order made in Hong Kong, and for this purpose an illegitimate child is the child of his mother but not his father (see Sch 2 para 4(2)). As to legitimated and posthumous children see the British Nationality Act 1981 ss 47 (now repealed), 48, 50(9) (as originally enacted) (see PARA 424 notes 6–7); applied by the British Nationality (Hong Kong) Act 1990 s 2(3). For these purposes, it was immaterial whether the spouse or child in question was settled in Hong Kong or had any citizenship or nationality otherwise than under the British Nationality Act 1981: British Nationality (Hong Kong) Act 1990 Sch 2 para 5.

    A person registered as a British citizen by virtue of Sch 2 became a British citizen by descent: see s 2(1). As to citizenship by descent see PARA 425.

434. Acquisition by war wives and widows by registration: Hong Kong. The Secretary of State[1] may, on an application made for the purpose, register as a British citizen any woman who, before 18 July 1996[2], was the recipient or intended recipient of a UK settlement letter[3] if: (1) she has her residence, or principal residence, in Hong Kong; (2) where she is no longer married to the man in recognition of whose service the assurance was given, she has not remarried; and (3) the Secretary of State is satisfied that she is of good character[4].

1   As to the Secretary of State see PARA 402.
2   Ie the date on which the Hong Kong (War Wives and Widows) Act 1996 was passed.
3   'UK settlement letter' means a letter written by the Secretary of State which: (1) confirmed the assurance given to the intended recipient that, in recognition of her husband's service, or her late or former husband's service, in defence of Hong Kong during the 1939–45 war, she could come to the United Kingdom for settlement at any time; and (2) was sent by the Secretary of State to the Hong Kong Immigration Department for onward transmission to the intended recipient (whether or not she in fact received it): Hong Kong (War Wives and Widows) Act 1996 s 1(2). As to the meaning of 'United Kingdom' see PARA 403 note 1.
4   Hong Kong (War Wives and Widows) Act 1996 s 1(1) (amended by the Borders, Citizenship and Immigration Act 2009 ss 47(2), 56, Schedule Pt 2). There are very few women to whom these provisions can apply. A woman who is registered as a British citizen by virtue of the Hong Kong (War Wives and Widows) Act 1996 is a British citizen otherwise than by descent: see s 2(1).

435.   Acquisition by ethnic minorities by registration: Hong Kong. The Secretary of State[1], on an application made for the purpose, must register as a British citizen any person who is ordinarily resident in Hong Kong at the time of the application and who satisfies the requirements of head (1) or head (2) below[2]. The requirements are that, immediately before 4 February 1997[3]:

(1)   the person: (a) was ordinarily resident in Hong Kong; (b) was a British overseas territories citizen[4] by virtue only of a connection with Hong Kong[5]; and (c) would have been a stateless person if he had not been such a citizen, or such a citizen and a British national (overseas)[6]; or

(2)   the person: (a) was ordinarily resident in Hong Kong; (b) was a British overseas citizen[7], a British subject[8] or a British protected person[9]; and (c) would have been a stateless person if he had not been such a citizen, subject or person[10].

However, a person who, on or after 4 February 1997, renounces or renounced, or otherwise gives up or gave up of his own volition, the status of a national or citizen of a country or territory outside the United Kingdom, cannot be registered[11].

1   As to the Secretary of State see PARA 402.
2   British Nationality (Hong Kong) Act 1997 s 1(1). A person could not be registered under these provisions before 1 July 1997: see s 1(7).
     An adult or young person may not be registered under s 1(1) unless the Secretary of State is satisfied that the adult or young person is of good character: s 1(5A) (s 1(5A), (5B) added by the Borders, Citizenship and Immigration Act 2009 s 47(3)). 'Adult or young person' means a person who has attained the age of ten years at the time when the application for registration is made: British Nationality (Hong Kong) Act 1997 s 1(5B) (as so added).
     The legislation provides for Hong Kong's ethnic minorities, namely those who but for holding a citizenship (other than British citizenship) or status under United Kingdom nationality law would be stateless, by giving them access to a substantive nationality (ie British citizenship). Persons who are ethnically Chinese already have a substantive nationality (under the nationality law of the People's Republic of China).
     A person who is registered as a British citizen under s 1(1), and who satisfies the requirements of s 1(2) (see head (1) in the text), is treated for the purposes of the British Nationality Act 1981 as a British citizen by descent or a British citizen otherwise than by descent, depending on whether his previous status was held by descent or otherwise than by descent: see s 2(1). A person who is registered as a British citizen under s 1(1), and who satisfies the requirements of s 1(3) (see head (2) in the text) is treated for the purposes of the British Nationality Act 1981 as a British citizen by descent: see s 2(2).
3   As to the application of these provisions to a person born at any time on or after 4 February 1997, or acquiring the status referred to in heads (1)(b) and (2)(b) in the text at any time on or after that date, see s 1(4), (5).

4   As to British overseas territories citizens and citizenship (formerly known as British dependent territories citizens and citizenship) see PARAS 406, 445–458.

5   A person has a connection with Hong Kong for the purposes of the British Nationality (Hong Kong) Act 1997 s 1(2) if:

    (1)   he, his father or his mother was born, naturalised or registered in Hong Kong or found abandoned there as a new-born infant (s 1(2), Schedule para 1(1)(a));

    (2)   he, his father or his mother was adopted (whether or not in Hong Kong) and the adopter (or, in the case of a joint adoption, one of the adopters) was at the time of the adoption a British overseas territories citizen by virtue of a connection with Hong Kong (Schedule para 1(1)(b) (amended by virtue of the British Overseas Territories Act 2002 s 2(3)));

    (3)   he, his father or his mother ('the registered person') was registered outside Hong Kong on an application based (wholly or partly) on any of the following: (a) residence in Hong Kong; (b) descent from a person born in Hong Kong; (c) descent from a person naturalised, registered or settled in Hong Kong (whether before or after the birth of the registered person); (d) descent from a person adopted (whether or not in Hong Kong) in the circumstances specified in head (2); (e) marriage to a person who is a British overseas territories citizen by virtue of a connection with Hong Kong or would, but for his death or renunciation of citizenship, have been such a citizen by virtue of such a connection; (f) Crown service under the government of Hong Kong; (g) where the registered person had previously renounced citizenship of the United Kingdom and colonies or British overseas territories citizenship, birth, naturalisation or registration in Hong Kong (British Nationality (Hong Kong) Act 1997 Schedule para 1(1)(c) (amended by virtue of the British Overseas Territories Act 2002 s 2(3)));

    (4)   at the time of his birth his father or mother was settled in Hong Kong (British Nationality (Hong Kong) Act 1997 Schedule para 1(1)(d));

    (5)   his father or mother was born to a parent who at the time of the birth was a citizen of the United Kingdom and colonies by virtue of a connection with Hong Kong (Schedule para 1(1)(e)); or

    (6)   being a woman, she was married before 1 January 1983 to a man who was a British overseas territories citizen by virtue of a connection with Hong Kong or would, but for his death or renunciation of citizenship, be such a citizen by virtue of such a connection (Schedule para 1(1)(f) (amended by virtue of the British Overseas Territories Act 2002 s 2(3))).

For the purposes of the British Nationality (Hong Kong) Act 1997 Schedule para 1(1), 'registered' means registered:

    (i)   as a British overseas territories citizen; or

    (ii)   before 1 January 1983, as a citizen of the United Kingdom and colonies,

and 'registration' is to be construed accordingly: Schedule para 1(2) (amended by virtue of the British Overseas Territories Act 2002 s 2(3)). As to citizenship of the United Kingdom and colonies see PARAS 414–419.

    However, a person born in Hong Kong on or after 1 January 1983 cannot be taken to have a connection with Hong Kong under head (1) by virtue of his birth there unless, at the time of his birth, one of his parents was settled in Hong Kong or was a British overseas territories citizen by virtue of a connection with Hong Kong: see the British Nationality (Hong Kong) Act 1997 Schedule para 2 (amended by virtue of the British Overseas Territories Act 2002 s 2(3)).

6   British Nationality (Hong Kong) Act 1997 s 1(2) (amended by virtue of the British Overseas Territories Act 2002 s 2(3)). As to British national (overseas) status see PARAS 406, 465–467.

7   As to British overseas citizens see PARAS 406, 459–463.

8   As to British subjects see PARAS 407, 469–474.

9   As to British protected persons see PARAS 408, 476–480.

10   British Nationality (Hong Kong) Act 1997 s 1(3).

11   British Nationality (Hong Kong) Act 1997 s 1(6). As to the meaning of 'United Kingdom' see PARA 403 note 1.

436. Acquisition by registration: statelessness. A person born in the United Kingdom or a British overseas territory[1] on or after 1 January 1983[2], who is and always has been stateless[3], is entitled to be registered as a British citizen if: (1) an application for his registration is made when he is under 22 years old[4]; (2) he was in the United Kingdom or a British overseas territory at the beginning of the period of five years ending with the date of application; (3) during that period he has not been absent from both the United Kingdom and the British overseas territories for more than 450 days; and (4) during that period he has spent more days (or part days) in the United Kingdom than in the British overseas territories[5].

A person born outside the United Kingdom and the British overseas territories on or after 1 January 1983, who is and always has been stateless, is entitled on application to registration as a British citizen if: (a) at the time of his birth his father or mother[6] was a British citizen; (b) he himself was in the United Kingdom or a British overseas territory at the beginning of the period of three years ending with the date of application; and (c) during that period he has not been absent from both the United Kingdom and the British overseas territories for more than 270 days[7].

Provision is made for the registration of certain stateless persons born before 1 January 1983[8].

1   See PARA 424 note 1. As to the meaning of 'United Kingdom' see PARA 403 note 1. As to British overseas territories (formerly known as dependent territories) see PARA 445 note 1.

2   Ie the date of commencement of the British Nationality Act 1981: see PARA 403 note 1.

3   A person born in a British overseas territory to a British citizen parent is automatically a British citizen if he would otherwise be stateless; and a person born in the United Kingdom to a British overseas territories citizen parent is automatically a British overseas territories citizen if he would otherwise be stateless: see PARAS 424, 448. As to British overseas territories citizens and citizenship (formerly known as British dependent territories citizens and citizenship) see PARAS 406, 445–458.

4   As to applications see PARA 484. As to when, for the purposes of the British Nationality Act 1981, a person attains any particular age, see PARA 426 note 8.

5   British Nationality Act 1981 s 36, Sch 2 para 3(1), (2)(a) (Sch 2 para 3 amended by virtue of the British Overseas Territories Act 2002 s 1(1)(b); and the Nationality, Immigration and Asylum Act 2002 ss 8, 161, Sch 9). As to references to days of absence from the United Kingdom or a British overseas territory or the British overseas territories see PARA 426 note 9. If he spent more days or part days in the British overseas territories than in the United Kingdom he will be registered as a British overseas territories citizen: see the British Nationality Act 1981 Sch 2 para 3(2)(b); and PARA 451.

    If in the special circumstances of any particular case the Secretary of State thinks fit, he may treat the person as fulfilling the requirements of head (3) in the text although the number of days on which he was absent from both the United Kingdom and the British overseas territories exceeds the number mentioned: see Sch 2 para 6 (amended by virtue of the British Overseas Territories Act 2002 s 1(1)(b)). As to the Secretary of State see PARA 402. As to the exercise of discretion see the British Nationality Act 1981 s 44; and PARA 402.

6   See PARA 424 notes 6–7.

7   See the British Nationality Act 1981 Sch 2 para 4 (amended by virtue of the British Overseas Territories Act 2002 ss 1(1)(b), 2(2)(b)). As to references to days of absence from the United Kingdom or a British overseas territory or the British overseas territories see PARA 426 note 9. As to the registration of stateless persons see also PARAS 451, 461, 473. If in the special circumstances of any particular case the Secretary of State thinks fit, he may treat the person as fulfilling the requirements of head (c) in the text although the number of days on which he was absent from both the United Kingdom and the British overseas territories exceeds the number mentioned: see Sch 2 para 6 (as amended: see note 5).

8   See the British Nationality Act 1981 Sch 2 para 5.

437. Acquisition by registration: special cases. A number of statutory provisions extended certain entitlements to registration under the previous nationality law for limited periods to enable those satisfying the conditions to register as British citizens, but the periods during which applications for such registration could be made have now expired[1]. Those provisions dealt with: (1) registration of certain Commonwealth or Irish citizens who had been ordinarily resident in the United Kingdom for a minimum of five years (and in some cases Crown service, or other relevant service, was treated as ordinary residence in the

United Kingdom)[2]; (2) registration of a woman on the basis of marriage[3]; (3) registration of a person born in a foreign country[4] before 1 January 1988 whose father was (or but for his death would have been) a British citizen by descent[5].

1   See the British Nationality Act 1981 ss 7–9 (now repealed). For analogous provisions relating to British overseas territories citizenship see PARA 452. Broadly, those who satisfied the conditions in a manner connected with the United Kingdom were able to register as British citizens, while those who satisfied the conditions in a manner connected with a British overseas territory were able to register as British overseas territories citizens. As to British overseas territories citizens and citizenship (formerly known as British dependent territories citizens and citizenship) see PARAS 406, 445–458; and as to British overseas territories (formerly known as dependent territories) see PARA 445 note 1. As to the meaning of 'United Kingdom' see PARA 403 note 1.
2   See the British Nationality Act 1981 s 7 (now repealed).
3   See the British Nationality Act 1981 s 8 (now repealed). Some persons so registered are British citizens by descent: see s 14(1)(e); and PARA 425.
4   As to the meaning of 'foreign country' see PARA 404 note 22.
5   See the British Nationality Act 1981 s 9 (now repealed). This right to British citizenship by registration is restricted to persons born within five years of the commencement of the British Nationality Act 1981 (ie from 1 January 1983: see PARA 403 note 1): see s 9(1) (now repealed). As to the requirements see s 9(2) (now repealed).
    A person registered by virtue of s 9 is a British citizen by descent: see s 14(1)(a); and PARA 425.

438.   Acquisition by naturalisation, based on five years' residence.   Prior to 1983, naturalisation was the method by which adult aliens and adult British protected persons, and no others, acquired citizenship[1]; and those who had the status of British subject or Commonwealth citizen acquired citizenship by registration[2]. Acquisition by minors was, and still is, by registration. Since the expiry of the periods during which previous registration provisions were extended in special cases[3], adult Commonwealth citizens who do not hold another form of British nationality[4] now normally have to apply for naturalisation in order to acquire citizenship. British citizenship and British overseas territories citizenship[5] are the only forms of British nationality which can be acquired by naturalisation[6].

The following provisions apply until a day to be appointed[7]. A person must fulfil prescribed requirements[8] in order to be eligible for naturalisation as a British citizen but, even when these requirements are fulfilled, the grant of a certificate of naturalisation is at the discretion of the Secretary of State[9]. The requirements for naturalisation are different in some respects for an applicant who is married to, or in a civil partnership with, a British citizen[10], or who is in Crown service overseas or married to a British citizen in such service[11]. The standard requirements of general application are that:

(1)   the applicant is of full age and capacity[12], and is of good character[13];
(2)   the applicant was in the United Kingdom[14] at the beginning of the period of five years ending with the date of the application[15];
(3)   the applicant was not absent from the United Kingdom for more than 450 days during that five year period[16];
(4)   the applicant was not absent from the United Kingdom for more than 90 days during the 12 months preceding the application[17];
(5)   the applicant was not at any time during the 12 months preceding the application subject under the immigration laws[18] to any restriction on the period for which he might remain in the United Kingdom[19];
(6)   the applicant was not, at any time in the period of five years preceding the application, in the United Kingdom in breach of the immigration laws[20];

(7)   the applicant has a sufficient knowledge of the English, Welsh or Scottish Gaelic language[21];

(8)   the applicant has sufficient knowledge about life in the United Kingdom[22];

(9)   the applicant intends, if granted naturalisation as a British citizen, either to make his home or principal home in the United Kingdom, or to enter or continue in Crown service under the government of the United Kingdom, or service under an international organisation of which the United Kingdom or its government is a member, or service in the employment of a company or association established in the United Kingdom[23].

For the purposes of the residence requirements, a person is to be treated as having been absent from the United Kingdom during any of the following periods, even though he is physically present there[24]:

(a)   any period when he was entitled, or was part of the family and household of a person entitled, to exemption from immigration control by reason of diplomatic immunity[25] or as a member of the forces[26];

(b)   any period when he was: (i) detained in pursuance of a sentence passed on him by a court in the United Kingdom or elsewhere for any offence[27], or under a hospital order[28] made in connection with his conviction of an offence[29], or under any power of detention conferred by the immigration laws[30]; or (ii) unlawfully at large or absent without leave from any such detention[31] and in consequence liable to be arrested or taken into custody[32].

1   See the British Nationality Act 1948 s 10 (repealed). Before 1 January 1949 British protected persons were aliens. As to British protected persons see PARAS 408, 476–480. As to aliens see PARA 411.

2   As to British subjects see PARA 407; and as to Commonwealth citizens see PARA 409.

3   See the British Nationality Act 1981 ss 7–9 (repealed); and PARA 437.

4   As to the acquisition of British citizenship by holders of other types of British nationality see PARA 428.

5   As to British overseas territories citizens and citizenship (formerly known as British dependent territories citizens and citizenship) see PARAS 406, 445–458.

6   A British citizen by descent cannot naturalise so as to become a British citizen otherwise than by descent: see *R (on the application of Ullah) v Secretary of State for the Home Department* [2001] EWCA Civ 659, [2002] QB 525, [2001] Imm AR 439. As to citizenship by descent see PARAS 425, 456.

7   The provisions of the British Nationality Act 1981 s 6, Sch 1 are prospectively amended as from a day to be appointed; at the date at which this volume states the law no such day had been appointed. As to the new requirements see PARA 439.

8   See the British Nationality Act 1981 s 6, Sch 1; and the text and notes 10–32. Where a fact leading to naturalisation is subsequently found to be incorrect, this does not automatically nullify the naturalisation: *R v Secretary of State for the Home Department, ex p Ejaz* [1994] QB 496, [1994] 2 All ER 436, CA. It seems that the Secretary of State is entitled on grounds of public policy to decline to accept that a condition is satisfied where this has been achieved by means of criminal activity: *R v Secretary of State for the Home Department, ex p Puttick* [1981] QB 767, [1981] 1 All ER 776, DC (married status on which entitlement depended valid but obtained by perjury and forgery). As to the Secretary of State see PARA 402. As to applications see PARA 484. As to withdrawal of citizenship acquired by naturalisation when obtained by fraud, false representation or concealment of a material fact see PARA 444.

9   See the British Nationality Act 1981 s 6. As to the exercise of discretion see the British Nationality Act 1981 s 44(1); and PARA 402. It was held in *R v Secretary of State for the Home Department, ex p Fayed* [1997] 1 All ER 228, [1998] 1 WLR 763, CA, that the British Nationality Act 1981 s 44(2) (now repealed), which provided that there was no requirement to give reasons, did not relieve the Secretary of State of his obligation to be fair or deprive the court of its power to ensure that the needs of fairness were met (natural justice required the applicant in that case to be given notice of the Secretary of State's concerns, prior to a decision, so as to

have an opportunity to answer them). Following the repeal of the British Nationality Act 1981 s 44(2) by the Nationality, Immigration and Asylum Act 2002 ss 7(1), 161, Sch 9, reasons must now be given for a decision. See further PARA 402. For an insight into the exercise of the naturalisation discretion see *Review of the Circumstances Surrounding an Application for Naturalisation by Mr S P Hinduja in 1998* (HC Paper (2000–01) no 287). In particular, see the policies disclosed in the 'Nationality Instructions' on the website of the UK Border Agency.

10 See PARA 440. The provisions were amended with effect from 5 December 2005 so as to include civil partnerships: see the Civil Partnership Act 2004 s 261(1), Sch 27 para 72; the Civil Partnership Act 2004 (Commencement No 2) Order 2005, SI 2005/3175; and PARA 440.

11 See PARA 442.

12 A person is of full age if he has attained the age of 18 years, and is of full capacity if he is not of unsound mind: British Nationality Act 1981 s 50(11)(a). Where a provision of the British Nationality Act 1981 requires an applicant to be of full capacity, the Secretary of State may waive the requirement in respect of a specified applicant if he thinks it in the applicant's best interests: s 44A (added by the Immigration, Asylum and Nationality Act 2006 s 49).

13 See the British Nationality Act 1981 s 6(1), Sch 1 para 1(1)(b). The Secretary of State is entitled to adopt a high standard in assessing whether an applicant is of good character: see *Al Fayed v Secretary of State for the Home Department* [2001] Imm AR 134, CA.

14 As to the meaning of 'United Kingdom' see PARA 403 note 1.

15 British Nationality Act 1981 Sch 1 para 1(1)(a), (2)(a). As to when a person is deemed to be absent from the United Kingdom see the text and notes 24–32. If in the special circumstances of any particular case the Secretary of State thinks fit, he may treat the applicant as having been in the United Kingdom for the whole or any part of any period during which he would otherwise be deemed to have been absent: Sch 1 para 2(b) (Sch 1 para 2 renumbered as para 2(1), as from a day to be appointed, by the Borders, Citizenship and Immigration Act 2009 s 39(4)). At the date at which this volume states the law, no such day had been appointed. As to the exercise of discretion see the British Nationality Act 1981 s 44(1); and PARA 402.

16 British Nationality Act 1981 Sch 1 para 1(1)(a), (2)(a). As to references to days of absence from the United Kingdom see PARA 426 note 9. As to when a person is deemed to be absent from the United Kingdom see the text and notes 24–32. If in the special circumstances of any particular case the Secretary of State thinks fit, he may treat the applicant: (1) as fulfilling the requirement specified in the British Nationality Act 1981 Sch 1 para 1(2)(a), although the number of days on which he was absent from the United Kingdom exceeds the number mentioned; (2) as having been in the United Kingdom for the whole or any part of any period during which he would otherwise be deemed to have been absent: Sch 1 para 2(a), (b) (prospectively renumbered: see note 15).

17 British Nationality Act 1981 Sch 1 para 1(1)(a), (2)(b). As to references to days of absence from the United Kingdom see PARA 426 note 9. As to when a person is deemed to be absent from the United Kingdom see the text and notes 24–32. If in the special circumstances of any particular case the Secretary of State thinks fit, he may treat the applicant: (1) as fulfilling the requirement specified in Sch 1 para 1(2)(b), although the number of days on which he was absent from the United Kingdom exceeds the number mentioned; (2) as having been in the United Kingdom for the whole or any part of any period during which he would otherwise be deemed to have been absent: Sch 1 para 2(a), (b) (prospectively renumbered: see note 15).

18 As to the meaning of 'immigration laws' see PARA 424 note 9.

19 British Nationality Act 1981 Sch 1 para 1(1)(a), (2)(c). If in the special circumstances of any particular case the Secretary of State thinks fit, he may disregard any such restriction as is mentioned in Sch 1 para 1(2)(c), not being a restriction to which the applicant was subject on the date of the application: Sch 1 para 2(c) (prospectively renumbered: see note 15). Persons in the United Kingdom with the right of abode under the Immigration Act 1971 s 2 (see PARA 412), or with an entitlement to move within the common travel area, or with indefinite leave, as well as certain persons exempt from immigration control and certain EEA nationals and members of their families (see the Immigration (European Economic Area) Regulations 2006, SI 2006/1003, reg 15; and BRITISH NATIONALITY, IMMIGRATION AND ASYLUM vol 4(2) (2002 Reissue) PARA 237) are not subject to any restriction on the period for which they may remain.

20 British Nationality Act 1981 Sch 1 para 1(1)(a), (2)(d). If in the special circumstances of any particular case the Secretary of State thinks fit, he may treat the applicant as fulfilling the requirement specified in Sch 1 para 1(2)(d) although he was in the United Kingdom in breach of the immigration laws during the period mentioned: Sch 1 para 2(d) (prospectively renumbered: see note 15). As to being in the United Kingdom in breach of the immigration laws see PARA 424 note 9.

21 British Nationality Act 1981 Sch 1 para 1(1)(c). If in the special circumstances of any particular case the Secretary of State thinks fit, he may waive the need to fulfil either or both of the

requirements specified in Sch 1 para 1(1)(c) and Sch 1 para 1(1)(ca) (see the text and note 22) if he considers that because of the applicant's age or physical or mental condition it would be unreasonable to expect him to fulfil that requirement or those requirements: Sch 1 para 2(e) (amended by the Nationality, Immigration and Asylum Act 2002 s 1(2); and prospectively renumbered (see note 15)).

22 British Nationality Act 1981 Sch 1 para 1(1)(ca) (added by the Nationality, Immigration and Asylum Act 2002 s 1(1)). See note 21.

23 British Nationality Act 1981 Sch 1 para 1(1)(d). For these purposes, a company incorporated abroad but registered as an overseas company with a place of business in the United Kingdom is a company 'established' in the United Kingdom: *R v Secretary of State for the Home Department, ex p Mehta* [1992] Imm AR 512.

24 British Nationality Act 1981 Sch 1 para 9(1) (amended, as from a day to be appointed, by the Borders, Citizenship and Immigration Act 2009 s 49(2)). This is subject to the British Nationality Act 1981 Sch 1 para 2(b): see notes 15–17.

25 The exemption referred to in the text is an exemption arising under the Immigration Act 1971 s 8(3): see BRITISH NATIONALITY, IMMIGRATION AND ASYLUM vol 4(2) (2002 Reissue) PARA 88.

26 See the British Nationality Act 1981 Sch 1 para 9(1)(a). The exemption referred to in the text is an exemption arising under the Immigration Act 1971 s 8(4): see BRITISH NATIONALITY, IMMIGRATION AND ASYLUM vol 4(2) (2002 Reissue) PARA 89.

27 See the British Nationality Act 1981 Sch 1 para 9(1)(b)(i).

28 Ie a hospital order made under the Mental Health Act 1983 Pt III (ss 35–55 or the Criminal Procedure (Scotland) Act 1975 s 175 or s 376 or the Mental Health (Northern Ireland) Order 1986, SI 1986/595 (NI 4), Pt III (arts 42–61). See further MENTAL HEALTH vol 30(2) (Reissue) PARA 486 et seq.

29 See the British Nationality Act 1981 Sch 1 para 9(1)(b)(ii) (amended by the Mental Health Act 1983 s 148, Sch 4 para 60; and by SI 1986/596).

30 See the British Nationality Act 1981 Sch 1 para 9(1)(b)(iii). As to powers of detention conferred by the immigration laws see BRITISH NATIONALITY, IMMIGRATION AND ASYLUM vol 4(2) (2002 Reissue) PARAS 156, 166.

31 Ie when he was liable to detention as mentioned in the British Nationality Act 1981 Sch 1 para 9(1)(b)(i) or Sch 1 para 9(1)(b)(ii) (see the text and notes 27–29) or when his actual detention under any such power as is mentioned in Sch 1 para 9(1)(b)(iii) (see the text and note 30) was required or specifically authorised.

32 See the British Nationality Act 1981 Sch 1 para 9(1)(c), (d).

439.   Acquisition by naturalisation, based on qualifying period. New requirements which a person must fulfil in order to be eligible for naturalisation as a British citizen are prescribed as from a day to be appointed[1]. As before, even when these requirements are fulfilled, the grant of a certificate of naturalisation is at the discretion of the Secretary of State[2]. The requirements for naturalisation remain different in some respects for an applicant who is married to or the civil partner of a British citizen[3], or who is in Crown service overseas or married to a British citizen in such service, or who is or has been a member of the armed forces[4]. The standard requirements of general application are that:

(1)   the applicant is of full age and capacity[5], and is of good character[6];

(2)   the applicant ('A') was in the United Kingdom[7] at the beginning of the qualifying period[8];

(3)   the number of days on which A was absent from the United Kingdom in each year of the qualifying period does not exceed 90[9];

(4)   A had a qualifying immigration status[10] for the whole of the qualifying period[11];

(5)   on the date of the application A has probationary citizenship leave, permanent residence leave, a qualifying CTA entitlement, a Commonwealth right of abode or a permanent EEA entitlement[12];

(6)   where on the date of the application A has probationary citizenship

leave granted for the purpose of taking employment[13] in the United Kingdom, A has been in continuous employment since the date of the grant of that leave[14]; and

(7)   A was not at any time in the qualifying period in the United Kingdom in breach of the immigration laws[15];

(8)   the applicant has a sufficient knowledge of the English, Welsh or Scottish Gaelic language[16];

(9)   the applicant has sufficient knowledge about life in the United Kingdom[17];

(10)   the applicant intends, if granted naturalisation as a British citizen, either to make his home or principal home in the United Kingdom, or to enter or continue in Crown service under the government of the United Kingdom, or service under an international organisation of which the United Kingdom or its government is a member, or service in the employment of a company or association established in the United Kingdom[18].

The periods during which, for the purposes of the residence requirements, a person is to be treated as having been absent from the United Kingdom, even though he is physically present there, remain the same[19]:

(a)   any period when he was entitled, or was part of the family and household of a person entitled, to exemption from immigration control by reason of diplomatic immunity[20] or as a member of the forces[21];

(b)   any period when he was: (i) detained in pursuance of a sentence passed on him by a court in the United Kingdom or elsewhere for any offence[22], or under a hospital order[23] made in connection with his conviction of an offence[24], or under any power of detention conferred by the immigration laws[25]; or (ii) unlawfully at large or absent without leave from any such detention[26] and in consequence liable to be arrested or taken into custody[27].

1   Ie by the British Nationality Act 1981 s 6, Sch 1 (amended, as from a day to be appointed, by the Borders, Citizenship and Immigration Act 2009 ss 39–41, 56, Schedule Pt 2). At the date at which this volume states the law, no such day had been appointed under the Borders, Citizenship and Immigration Act 2009 s 58(2). As to the existing requirements for naturalisation see PARA 438.

2   See the British Nationality Act 1981 s 6; and PARA 438 note 9.

3   See PARA 441. It has been stated that the category of person for the purposes of the British Nationality Act 1981 s 6(2) (currently spouses and civil partners of British citizens: see PARA 440) is to be expanded to include other relationships with British citizens and also with permanent residents: see further PARA 441.

4   See PARA 442.

5   As to when a person is of full age and of full capacity, and as to waiver of the requirement, see PARA 438 note 12.

6   See the British Nationality Act 1981 s 6(1), Sch 1 para 1(1)(b). The Secretary of State is entitled to adopt a high standard in assessing whether an applicant is of good character: see *Al Fayed v Secretary of State for the Home Department* [2001] Imm AR 134, CA.

7   As to the meaning of 'United Kingdom' see PARA 403 note 1.

8   British Nationality Act 1981 Sch 1 para 1(1)(a), (2)(a) (Sch 1 para 1(1)(a) prospectively amended by the Borders, Citizenship and Immigration Act 2009 ss 39(1), 56, Schedule Pt 2; British Nationality Act 1981 Sch 1 para 1(2) prospectively substituted by the Borders, Citizenship and Immigration Act 2009 s 39(2) (see note 1)). The qualifying period for the purposes of the British Nationality Act 1981 Sch 1 para 1 is a period of years which ends with the date of the application in question: Sch 1 para 4B(1) (Sch 1 para 4B prospectively added by the Borders, Citizenship and Immigration Act 2009 s 41(1) (see note 1)). The length of the period is determined in accordance with the following provisions: British Nationality Act 1981 Sch 1 para 4B(2) (as so prospectively added). In the case of an applicant who does not meet the activity condition, the number of years in the period is eight: Sch 1 para 4B(3) (as so

prospectively added). In the case of an applicant who meets the activity condition, the number of years in the period is six: Sch 1 para 4B(4) (as so prospectively added). The applicant meets the activity condition if the Secretary of State is satisfied that the applicant: (1) has participated otherwise than for payment in prescribed activities; or (2) is to be treated as having so participated: Sch 1 para 4B(5) (as so prospectively added).

If in the special circumstances of any particular case the Secretary of State thinks fit, he may treat the applicant as having been in the United Kingdom for the whole or any part of any period during which he would otherwise be deemed to have been absent: Sch 1 para 2(1)(b) (Sch 1 para 2 prospectively renumbered as Sch 1 para 2(1) by the Borders, Citizenship and Immigration Act 2009 s 39(4) (see note 1)).

9 British Nationality Act 1981 Sch 1 para 1(1)(a), (2)(b) (as prospectively amended and substituted: see notes 1, 8). As to when a person is deemed to be absent from the United Kingdom see PARA 438 text and notes 23–31. If in the special circumstances of any particular case the Secretary of State thinks fit, he may treat the applicant as fulfilling the requirement specified in Sch 1 para 1(2)(b) although the number of days on which the applicant was absent from the United Kingdom in a year of the qualifying period exceeds 90: Sch 1 para 2(1)(a) (prospectively substituted by the Borders, Citizenship and Immigration Act 2009 s 39(4) (see note 1)). As to the exercise of discretion see the British Nationality Act 1981 s 44(1); and PARA 402.

10 A person has a qualifying immigration status for the purposes of the British Nationality Act 1981 Sch 1 para 1(2) if the person has: (1) qualifying temporary residence leave; (2) probationary citizenship leave; (3) permanent residence leave; (4) a qualifying CTA entitlement; (5) a Commonwealth right of abode; or (6) a temporary or permanent EEA entitlement: Sch 1 para 2A(1) (prospectively added by the Borders, Citizenship and Immigration Act 2009 s 39(11) (see note 1)). A person who is required for those purposes to have a qualifying immigration status for the whole of the qualifying period need not have the same qualifying immigration status for the whole of that period: British Nationality Act 1981 Sch 1 para 2A(2) (as so prospectively added). For the purposes of Sch 1, a person has qualifying temporary residence leave if: (a) the person has limited leave to enter or remain in the United Kingdom; and (b) the leave is granted for a purpose by reference to which a grant of probationary citizenship leave may be made: Sch 1 para 11(1), (2) (Sch 1 para 11 prospectively added by the Borders, Citizenship and Immigration Act 2009 s 49(3) (see note 1)). A person has probationary citizenship leave if the person has limited leave to enter or remain in the United Kingdom and the leave is of a description identified in rules under the Immigration Act 1971 s 3 (see BRITISH NATIONALITY, IMMIGRATION AND ASYLUM vol 4(2) (2002 Reissue) PARA 86) as 'probationary citizenship leave'; and the reference in the British Nationality Act 1981 Sch 1 para 11(2) to a grant of probationary citizenship leave is to be construed accordingly: Sch 1 para 11(3) (as so prospectively added). A person has permanent residence leave if the person has indefinite leave to enter or remain in the United Kingdom: Sch 1 para 11(4) (as so prospectively added). A person has a qualifying CTA entitlement if the person: (i) is a citizen of the Republic of Ireland; (ii) last arrived in the United Kingdom on a local journey (within the meaning of the Immigration Act 1971) from the Republic of Ireland; and (iii) on that arrival, was a citizen of the Republic of Ireland and was entitled to enter without leave by virtue of the Immigration Act 1971 s 1(3) (entry from the common travel area: see BRITISH NATIONALITY, IMMIGRATION AND ASYLUM vol 4(2) (2002 Reissue) PARA 94): British Nationality Act 1981 Sch 1 para 11(5) (as so prospectively added). A person has a Commonwealth right of abode if the person has the right of abode in the United Kingdom by virtue of the Immigration Act 1971 s 2(1)(b) (see PARA 412): British Nationality Act 1981 Sch 1 para 11(6) (as so prospectively added). A person has a permanent EEA entitlement if the person is entitled to reside in the United Kingdom permanently by virtue of any provision made under the European Communities Act 1972 s 2(2) (see PARA 412): British Nationality Act 1981 Sch 1 para 11(7) (as so prospectively added). A person has a temporary EEA entitlement if the person does not have a permanent EEA entitlement but is entitled to reside in the United Kingdom by virtue of any provision made under the European Communities Act 1972 s 2(2): British Nationality Act 1981 Sch 1 para 11(8) (as so prospectively added). A reference in Sch 1 para 11 to having leave to enter or remain in the United Kingdom is to be construed in accordance with the Immigration Act 1971: British Nationality Act 1981 Sch 1 para 11(9) (as so prospectively added).

11 British Nationality Act 1981 Sch 1 para 1(1)(a), (2)(c) (as prospectively amended and substituted: see notes 1, 8). If in the special circumstances of any particular case the Secretary of State thinks fit, he may treat the applicant as fulfilling the requirement specified in Sch 1 para 1(2)(c) where the applicant has had a qualifying immigration status for only part of the qualifying period: Sch 1 para 2(1)(ba) (prospectively added by the Borders, Citizenship and Immigration Act 2009 s 39(5) (see note 1)).

12 British Nationality Act 1981 Sch 1 para 1(1)(a), (2)(d) (as prospectively amended and substituted: see notes 1, 8). If in the special circumstances of any particular case the Secretary of State thinks fit, he may treat the applicant as fulfilling the requirement specified in Sch 1 para 1(2)(d) where the applicant has had probationary citizenship leave but it expired in the qualifying period: Sch 1 para 2(1)(bb) (prospectively added by the Borders, Citizenship and Immigration Act 2009 s 39(5) (see note 1)).

13 In the British Nationality Act 1981 Sch 1 para 1(2)(e) (see head (6) in the text) and para 2(1)(ca) (see note 14), 'employment' includes self-employment: Sch 1 para 2(5) (prospectively added by the Borders, Citizenship and Immigration Act 2009 s 39(10) (see note 1)).

14 British Nationality Act 1981 Sch 1 para 1(1)(a), (2)(e) (as prospectively amended and substituted: see notes 1, 8). If in the special circumstances of any particular case the Secretary of State thinks fit, he may treat the applicant as fulfilling the requirement specified in Sch 1 para 1(2)(e) although the applicant has not been in continuous employment since the date of the grant mentioned there: Sch 1 para 2(1)(ca) (prospectively added by the Borders, Citizenship and Immigration Act 2009 s 39(7) (see note 1)).

15 British Nationality Act 1981 Sch 1 para 1(1)(a), (2)(f) (as prospectively amended and substituted: see notes 1, 8). As to being in the United Kingdom in breach of the immigration laws see PARA 424 note 9. If in the special circumstances of any particular case the Secretary of State thinks fit, he may treat the applicant as fulfilling the requirement specified in Sch 1 para 1(2)(f) although he was in the United Kingdom in breach of the immigration laws in the qualifying period: Sch 1 para 2(1)(d) (prospectively amended by the Borders, Citizenship and Immigration Act 2009 s 39(8) (see note 1)).

16 British Nationality Act 1981 Sch 1 para 1(1)(c). If in the special circumstances of any particular case the Secretary of State thinks fit, he may waive the need to fulfil either or both of the requirements specified in Sch 1 para 1(1)(c) and Sch 1 para 1(1)(ca) (see the text and note 17) if he considers that because of the applicant's age or physical or mental condition it would be unreasonable to expect him to fulfil that requirement or those requirements: Sch 1 para 2(1)(e) (amended by the Nationality, Immigration and Asylum Act 2002 s 1(2); and prospectively renumbered (see notes 1, 8)).

17 British Nationality Act 1981 Sch 1 para 1(1)(ca) (added by the Nationality, Immigration and Asylum Act 2002 s 1(1)). See note 16.

18 British Nationality Act 1981 Sch 1 para 1(1)(d). As to the meaning of 'established' for these purposes see PARA 438 note 23.

19 See the British Nationality Act 1981 Sch 1 para 9(1); and PARA 438 text and notes 23–31. This is subject to Sch 1 para 2(1)(b) (see note 8): Sch 9 para 9(1) (prospectively amended by the Borders, Citizenship and Immigration Act 2009 s 49(2) (see note 1)).

20 The exemption referred to in the text is an exemption arising under the Immigration Act 1971 s 8(3): see BRITISH NATIONALITY, IMMIGRATION AND ASYLUM vol 4(2) (2002 Reissue) PARA 88.

21 See the British Nationality Act 1981 Sch 1 para 9(1)(a). The exemption referred to in the text is an exemption arising under the Immigration Act 1971 s 8(4): see BRITISH NATIONALITY, IMMIGRATION AND ASYLUM vol 4(2) (2002 Reissue) PARA 89.

22 See the British Nationality Act 1981 Sch 1 para 9(1)(b)(i).

23 Ie a hospital order made under the Mental Health Act 1983 Pt III (ss 35–55) or the Criminal Procedure (Scotland) Act 1975 s 175 or s 376 or the Mental Health (Northern Ireland) Order 1986, SI 1986/595 (NI 4), Pt III (arts 42–61). See further MENTAL HEALTH vol 30(2) (Reissue) PARA 486 et seq.

24 See the British Nationality Act 1981 Sch 1 para 9(1)(b)(ii) (amended by the Mental Health Act 1983 s 148, Sch 4 para 60; and by SI 1986/596).

25 See the British Nationality Act 1981 Sch 1 para 9(1)(b)(iii). As to powers of detention conferred by the immigration laws see BRITISH NATIONALITY, IMMIGRATION AND ASYLUM vol 4(2) (2002 Reissue) PARAS 156, 166.

26 Ie when he was liable to detention as mentioned in the British Nationality Act 1981 Sch 1 para 9(1)(b)(i) or Sch 1 para 9(1)(b)(ii) (see the text and notes 23–24) or when his actual detention under any such power as is mentioned in Sch 1 para 9(1)(b)(iii) (see the text and note 25) was required or specifically authorised.

27 See the British Nationality Act 1981 Sch 1 para 9(1)(c), (d).

440. Acquisition by naturalisation: spouses and civil partners of British citizens. The following provisions apply until a day to be appointed[1]. An applicant who, on the date of the application[2], is married to a British citizen[3] or is the civil partner of a British citizen is eligible for naturalisation as a British citizen, and may be granted a certificate of naturalisation by the Secretary of State[4] if the following requirements[5] are fulfilled:

(1) the applicant is of full age and capacity[6], and is of good character[7];

(2) the applicant has a sufficient knowledge of the English, Welsh or Scottish Gaelic language[8];

(3) the applicant has sufficient knowledge about life in the United Kingdom[9];

(4) the applicant was in the United Kingdom[10] at the beginning of the period of three years ending with the date of the application[11];

(5) the applicant was not absent from the United Kingdom for more than 270 days during that three year period[12];

(6) the applicant was not absent from the United Kingdom for more than 90 days in the 12 months preceding the application[13];

(7) on the date of the application the applicant was not subject under the immigration laws[14] to any restriction on the period for which he might remain in the United Kingdom[15];

(8) the applicant was not, at any time in the period of three years preceding the application, in the United Kingdom in breach of the immigration laws[16].

1 The provisions of the British Nationality Act 1981 s 6, Sch 1 are prospectively amended as from a day to be appointed; at the date at which this volume states the law no such day had been appointed. As to the new requirements see PARA 441.

2 As to applications see PARA 484.

3 As to applicants married to British citizens who are in Crown service overseas see PARA 442. Before 1 January 1983, the wife but not the husband of a citizen of the United Kingdom and colonies was entitled to be registered as a citizen under the British Nationality Act 1948 s 6(2) (now repealed), a right which in limited form was extended as a right to register as a British citizen until 31 December 1987 (see PARA 437). As to citizenship of the United Kingdom and colonies see PARAS 414–419. The current provisions give equal access to citizenship for both wives and husbands and civil partners of citizens, imposing (shortened) residence conditions on both. The requirements are substantially amended by the Borders, Citizenship and Immigration Act 2009 as from a day to be appointed: see PARA 441.

4 See the British Nationality Act 1981 s 6(2) (amended by the Civil Partnership Act 2004 s 261(1), Sch 27 para 72). As to the Secretary of State see PARA 402. As to the exercise of discretion see the British Nationality Act 1981 s 44(1); and PARA 402.

5 See the British Nationality Act 1981 Sch 1 paras 3, 4.

6 British Nationality Act 1981 s 6(2). As to the meanings of 'full age' and 'full capacity', and as to the discretion to waive the requirement in respect of a specified applicant, see PARA 438 note 12. A woman's previous entitlement to registration under the British Nationality Act 1948 s 6(2) (now repealed) did not require her to be of full age or capacity.

7 British Nationality Act 1981 Sch 1 paras 1(1)(b), 3(e) (Sch 1 para 3(e) amended by the Nationality, Immigration and Asylum Act 2002 s 2(1)(a)). The Secretary of State is entitled to adopt a high standard in assessing whether an applicant is of good character: see *Al Fayed v Secretary of State for the Home Department* [2001] Imm AR 134, sub nom *R v Secretary of State for the Home Department, ex p Al Fayed* (2000) Times, 7 September, CA.

8 British Nationality Act 1981 Sch 1 paras 1(1)(c), 3(e) (Sch 1 para 3(e) as amended: see note 7). If in the special circumstances of any particular case the Secretary of State thinks fit, he may waive the need to fulfil either or both of the requirements specified in Sch 1 para 1(1)(c) and Sch 1 para 1(1)(ca) (see the text and note 9) if he considers that because of the applicant's age or physical or mental condition it would be unreasonable to expect him to fulfil that requirement or those requirements: Sch 1 paras 2(e), 4 (Sch 1 para 2(e) amended by the Nationality, Immigration and Asylum Act 2002 s 1(2)).

9 British Nationality Act 1981 Sch 1 paras 1(1)(ca), 3(e) (Sch 1 para 1(1)(ca) added by the Nationality, Immigration and Asylum Act 2002 s 1(1); British Nationality Act 1981 Sch 1 para 3(e) as amended (see note 7)). See also note 8.

10 As to the meaning of 'United Kingdom' see PARA 403 note 1.

11 British Nationality Act 1981 Sch 1 para 3(a). As to when a person is deemed to be absent from the United Kingdom see PARA 438. If in the special circumstances of any particular case the

Secretary of State thinks fit, he may treat the applicant as having been in the United Kingdom for the whole or any part of any period during which he would otherwise be deemed to have been absent: Sch 1 paras 2(b), 4. The Secretary of State may waive the need to fulfil all or any of the requirements specified in Sch 1 para 3(a) if on the date of the application the person to whom the applicant is married, or of whom the applicant is the civil partner, is serving in service to which s 2(1)(b) (see PARA 424) applies, that person's recruitment for that service having taken place in the United Kingdom: see Sch 1 paras 2(f), 4 (amended by the Civil Partnership Act 2004 Sch 27 para 78); and PARA 442.

12 British Nationality Act 1981 Sch 1 para 3(a). As to references to days of absence from the United Kingdom see PARA 426 note 9. As to when a person is deemed to be absent from the United Kingdom see PARA 438. If in the special circumstances of any particular case the Secretary of State thinks fit, he may treat the applicant: (1) as fulfilling the requirement specified in the British Nationality Act 1981 Sch 1 para 3(a), although the number of days on which he was absent from the United Kingdom exceeds the number mentioned; (2) as having been in the United Kingdom for the whole or any part of any period during which he would otherwise be deemed to have been absent: Sch 1 paras 2(a), (b), 4. The Secretary of State may waive the need to fulfil all or any of the requirements specified in Sch 1 para 3(a) if on the date of the application the person to whom the applicant is married, or of whom the applicant is the civil partner, is serving in service to which s 2(1)(b) (see PARA 424) applies, that person's recruitment for that service having taken place in the United Kingdom: see Sch 1 paras 2(f), 4 (as amended: see note 11); and PARA 442.

13 British Nationality Act 1981 Sch 1 para 3(b). As to references to days of absence from the United Kingdom see PARA 426 note 9. As to when a person is deemed to be absent from the United Kingdom see PARA 438. If in the special circumstances of any particular case the Secretary of State thinks fit, he may treat the applicant: (1) as fulfilling the requirement specified in Sch 1 para 3(b), although the number of days on which he was absent from the United Kingdom exceeds the number mentioned; (2) as having been in the United Kingdom for the whole or any part of any period during which he would otherwise be deemed to have been absent: Sch 1 paras 2(a), (b), 4. The Secretary of State may waive the need to fulfil all or any of the requirements specified in Sch 1 para 3(b) if on the date of the application the person to whom the applicant is married, or of whom the applicant is the civil partner, is serving in service to which s 2(1)(b) (see PARA 424) applies, that person's recruitment for that service having taken place in the United Kingdom: see Sch 1 paras 2(f), 4 (as amended: see note 11); and PARA 442.

14 As to the meaning of 'immigration laws' see PARA 424 note 9.

15 British Nationality Act 1981 Sch 1 para 3(c). See further PARA 442 note 20. Certain EEA nationals, nationals of Switzerland, and members of their families are not subject to any restriction on the period for which they may remain: see the Immigration (European Economic Area) Regulations 2006, SI 2006/1003, reg 15, taken together with reg 30, Sch 2 para 2; and BRITISH NATIONALITY, IMMIGRATION AND ASYLUM vol 4(2) (2002 Reissue) PARA 237.

16 British Nationality Act 1981 Sch 1 para 3(d). If in the special circumstances of any particular case the Secretary of State thinks fit, he may treat the applicant as fulfilling the requirement specified in Sch 1 para 3(d) although he was in the United Kingdom in breach of the immigration laws during the period mentioned: Sch 1 paras 2(d), 4. As to being in the United Kingdom in breach of the immigration laws see PARA 424 note 9.

441.   Acquisition by naturalisation: persons with relevant family association. New requirements which a person must fulfil in order to be eligible for naturalisation, replacing naturalisation as the spouse or civil partner of a British citizen, are prescribed as from a day to be appointed[1]. As from such day, an applicant who, on the date of the application[2], has a relevant family association[3] is eligible for naturalisation as a British citizen, and may be granted a certificate of naturalisation by the Secretary of State[4] if the following requirements[5] are fulfilled. Those requirements are, in the case of any person ('A') who applies for naturalisation as a British citizen[6]:

(1)   the following residence and status requirements[7];

      (a)   that A was in the United Kingdom at the beginning of the qualifying period[8];

      (b)   that the number of days on which A was absent from the United Kingdom in each year of the qualifying period does not exceed 90[9];

      (c)   that: (i) A had a relevant family association for the whole of the qualifying period; and (ii) A had a qualifying immigration status[10] for the whole of that period[11];

      (d)   that on the date of the application: (i) A has probationary citizenship leave[12], or permanent residence leave[13], based on A's having the relevant family association mentioned above; or (ii) A has a qualifying CTA entitlement[14] or a Commonwealth right of abode[15]; and

      (e)   that A was not at any time in the qualifying period in the United Kingdom in breach of the immigration laws[16];

  (2)   the intention requirement specified below[17]:

      (a)   that A's intentions are such that, in the event of a certificate of naturalisation as a British citizen being granted to A, A's home or (if A has more than one) A's principal home will be in the United Kingdom[18];

      (b)   that A intends, in the event of such a certificate being granted to A, to enter into, or continue in, service of a specified description[19]; or

      (c)   that, in the event of such a certificate being granted to A: (i) the person with whom A has the relevant family association referred to above ('B') intends to enter into, or continue in, service of a specified description[20]; and (ii) A intends to reside with B for the period during which B is in the service in question[21];

  (3)   that A is of good character[22];

  (4)   that A has a sufficient knowledge of the English, Welsh or Scottish Gaelic language[23]; and

  (5)   that A has sufficient knowledge about life in the United Kingdom[24].

1   Ie by the British Nationality Act 1981 s 6, Sch 1 (amended, as from a day to be appointed, by the Borders, Citizenship and Immigration Act 2009 ss 39–41, 56, Schedule Pt 2). At the date at which this volume states the law, no such day had been appointed under the Borders, Citizenship and Immigration Act 2009 s 58(2). As to the existing requirements see PARA 440, and as to naturalisation generally see PARA 438.

2   As to applications see PARA 484.

3   For the purposes of the British Nationality Act 1981 s 6 and Sch 1, a person ('A') has a relevant family association if A has a connection of a prescribed description to a person of a prescribed description: s 6(3) (s 6(3), (4) prospectively added by the Borders, Citizenship and Immigration Act 2009 s 40(2) (see note 1)). If in the special circumstances of any particular case the Secretary of State thinks fit, the Secretary of State may for the purposes of the British Nationality Act 1981 s 6(3) treat A as having a relevant family association on the date of the application although the relevant family association ceased to exist before that date: s 6(4) (as so prospectively added). As to the Secretary of State see PARA 402. As to the exercise of discretion see the British Nationality Act 1981 s 44(1); and PARA 402.

      At the date at which this volume states the law no such descriptions had been prescribed. On 19 March 2009 Lord Brett stated that the category of person for the purposes of the British Nationality Act 1981 s 6(2) (currently spouses and civil partners of British citizens: see PARA 440) is to be expanded to include other relationships with British citizens and also with permanent residents.

4   See the British Nationality Act 1981 s 6(2) (amended by the Civil Partnership Act 2004 s 261(1), Sch 27 para 72; and prospectively by the Borders, Citizenship and Immigration Act 2009 s 40(1) (see note 1)).

5   See the British Nationality Act 1981 Sch 1 paras 3, 4 (prospectively substituted: see note 1). As to applicants married to British citizens who are in Crown service overseas see PARA 442.

6   British Nationality Act 1981 Sch 1 para 3(1) (Sch 1 para 3 prospectively substituted by the Borders, Citizenship and Immigration Act 2009 s 40(3) (see note 1)).

7   British Nationality Act 1981 Sch 1 para 3(1)(a), (2) (as prospectively substituted: see notes 1, 6).

8   British Nationality Act 1981 Sch 1 para 3(2)(a) (as prospectively substituted: see notes 1, 6). The qualifying period for the purposes of Sch 1 para 3 is a period of years which ends with the date of the application in question: Sch 1 para 4B(1) (Sch 1 para 4B prospectively added by the Borders, Citizenship and Immigration Act 2009 s 41(1) (see note 1)). The length of the period is determined in accordance with the following provisions: British Nationality Act 1981 Sch 1 para 4B(2) (as so prospectively added). In the case of an applicant who does not meet the activity condition, the number of years in the period is five: Sch 1 para 4B(3) (as so prospectively added). In the case of an applicant who meets the activity condition, the number of years in the period is three: Sch 1 para 4B(4) (as so prospectively added). The applicant meets the activity condition if the Secretary of State is satisfied that the applicant: (1) has participated otherwise than for payment in prescribed activities; or (2) is to be treated as having so participated: Sch 1 para 4B(5) (as so prospectively added).

9   British Nationality Act 1981 Sch 1 para 3(2)(b) (as prospectively substituted: see notes 1, 6). If in the special circumstances of any particular case the Secretary of State thinks fit, the Secretary of State may (1) treat A as fulfilling the requirement specified in Sch 1 para 3(2)(b), although the number of days on which A was absent from the United Kingdom in a year of the qualifying period exceeds 90 (Sch 1 para 4(a) (Sch 1 para 4 prospectively substituted by the Borders, Citizenship and Immigration Act 2009 s 40(4) (see note 1))); (2) treat A as having been in the United Kingdom for the whole or any part of any period during which A would otherwise fall to be treated under the British Nationality Act 1981 Sch 1 para 9(1) as having been absent (Sch 1 para 4(b) (as so prospectively substituted)).

10   Subject to the British Nationality Act 1981 Sch 1 para 3(5) (see note 11), a person has a qualifying immigration status for the purposes of Sch 1 para 3 if the person has: (1) qualifying temporary residence leave based on a relevant family association; (2) probationary citizenship leave based on a relevant family association; (3) permanent residence leave based on a relevant family association; (4) a qualifying CTA entitlement; or (5) a Commonwealth right of abode: Sch 1 para 4A(1) (Sch 1 para 4A prospectively added by the Borders, Citizenship and Immigration Act 2009 s 40(5) (see note 1)). As to the meaning of 'qualifying temporary residence leave' see PARA 439 note 10. For the purposes of the British Nationality Act 1981 Sch 1 paras 3, 4A, the leave mentioned in head (1), (2) or (3) is based on a relevant family association if it was granted on the basis of the person having a relevant family association: Sch 1 para 4A(2) (as so prospectively added). A person who is required for the purposes of Sch 1 para 3 to have, for the whole of the qualifying period, a qualifying immigration status and a relevant family association need not, for the whole of that period: (a) have the same qualifying immigration status; or (b) (subject to Sch 1 para 3(5)) have the same relevant family association: Sch 1 para 4A(3) (as so prospectively added). Where, by virtue of Sch 1 para 4A(3)(a), a person relies upon having more than one qualifying immigration status falling within head (1), (2) or (3): (i) subject to Sch 1 para 3(5), it is not necessary that the leave to which each status relates is based on the same relevant family association; and (ii) in a case where Sch 1 para 3(5) applies, the relationship by reference to which the persons referred to in Sch 1 para 3(5) are partners need not be of the same description in respect of each grant of leave: Sch 1 para 4A(4) (as so prospectively added).

11   British Nationality Act 1981 Sch 1 para 3(2)(c) (as prospectively substituted: see notes 1, 6). This is subject to Sch 1 para 3(5): Sch 1 para 3(2)(c) (as so prospectively substituted). Where the relevant family association referred to in s 6(2) is (in accordance with regulations under s 41(1)(a) (see PARA 404)) that A is the partner of a person who is a British citizen or who has permanent residence leave, the requirement specified in head (c)(i) in the text is fulfilled only if A was that person's partner for the whole of the qualifying period and, for the purposes of head (c)(ii) in the text, A can rely upon having a qualifying immigration status falling within Sch 1 para 4A(1)(a), (b) or (c) (see note 10 heads (1), (2), (3)) only if that partnership is the relevant family association upon which the leave to which the status relates is based: Sch 1 para 3(5) (as so prospectively substituted). For the purposes of Sch 1 para 3(5), A is a person's partner if that person is A's spouse or civil partner or is in a relationship with A that is of a description that the regulations referred to in that Sch 1 para 3(5) specify, and the marriage, civil partnership or other relationship satisfies the conditions (if any) that those regulations specify: Sch 1 para 3(6) (as so prospectively substituted). For the purposes of Sch 1 para 3(5), the relationship by reference to which A and the other person are partners need not be of the same description for the whole of the qualifying period: Sch 1 para 3(7) (as so prospectively substituted).
    If in the special circumstances of any particular case the Secretary of State thinks fit, the Secretary of State may: (1) treat A as fulfilling the requirement specified in Sch 1 para 3(2)(c)(i) (including where it can be fulfilled only as set out in Sch 1 para 3(5)) where a relevant family association of A's has ceased to exist (Sch 1 para 4(c) (as prospectively substituted: see notes 1, 9)); (2) treat A as fulfilling the requirement specified in Sch 1 para 3(2)(c)(ii) (including where it

can be fulfilled only as set out in Sch 1 para 3(5)) where A has had a qualifying immigration status for only part of the qualifying period (Sch 1 para 4(d) (as so prospectively substituted)).

12 As to the meaning of 'probationary citizenship leave' see PARA 439 note 10.

13 As to the meaning of 'permanent residence leave' see PARA 439 note 10.

14 As to the meaning of 'qualifying CTA entitlement' see PARA 439 note 10.

15 British Nationality Act 1981 Sch 1 para 3(2)(d) (as prospectively substituted: see notes 1, 6). As to the meaning of 'Commonwealth right of abode' see PARA 439 note 10. If in the special circumstances of any particular case the Secretary of State thinks fit, the Secretary of State may treat A as fulfilling the requirement specified in Sch 1 para 3(2)(d) where A has had probationary citizenship leave but it expired in the qualifying period: Sch 1 para 4(e) (as prospectively substituted: see notes 1, 9).

16 British Nationality Act 1981 Sch 1 para 3(2)(e) (as prospectively substituted: see notes 1, 6). If in the special circumstances of any particular case the Secretary of State thinks fit, the Secretary of State may treat A as fulfilling the requirement specified in Sch 1 para 3(2)(e) although A was in the United Kingdom in breach of the immigration laws in the qualifying period: Sch 1 para 4(f) (as prospectively substituted: see notes 1, 9).

17 British Nationality Act 1981 Sch 1 para 3(1)(b), (3) (as prospectively substituted: see notes 1, 6).

18 British Nationality Act 1981 Sch 1 para 3(3)(a) (as prospectively substituted: see notes 1, 6).

19 British Nationality Act 1981 Sch 1 para 3(3)(b) (as prospectively substituted: see notes 1, 6). The descriptions of service referred to are: (1) Crown service under the government of the United Kingdom; (2) service under an international organisation of which the United Kingdom, or Her Majesty's government in the United Kingdom, is a member; or (3) service in the employment of a company or association established in the United Kingdom: Sch 1 para 3(4) (as so prospectively substituted).

20 See note 19.

21 British Nationality Act 1981 Sch 1 para 3(3)(c) (as prospectively substituted: see notes 1, 6).

22 British Nationality Act 1981 Sch 1 para 3(1)(c) (as prospectively substituted: see notes 1, 6).

23 British Nationality Act 1981 Sch 1 para 3(1)(d) (as prospectively substituted: see notes 1, 6). If in the special circumstances of any particular case the Secretary of State thinks fit, the Secretary of State may waive the need to fulfil either or both of the requirements specified in Sch 1 para 3(1)(d) and (e) (see the text and note 24) if the Secretary of State considers that because of A's age or physical or mental condition it would be unreasonable to expect A to fulfil that requirement or those requirements: Sch 1 para 4(g) (as prospectively substituted: see notes 1, 9).

24 British Nationality Act 1981 Sch 1 para 3(1)(e) (as prospectively substituted: see notes 1, 6). See note 23.

442. Acquisition by naturalisation: Crown service outside the United Kingdom or service in the armed forces. Until a day to be appointed[1], an applicant who, on the date of the application[2], is serving outside the United Kingdom[3] in Crown service under the government of the United Kingdom may be granted a certificate of naturalisation by the Secretary of State[4] without a residence requirement if the following requirements are fulfilled[5]:

(1) the applicant is of full age and capacity[6], and is of good character[7];

(2) the applicant has a sufficient knowledge of the English, Welsh or Scottish Gaelic language[8];

(3) the applicant has sufficient knowledge about life in the United Kingdom[9]; and

(4) the applicant intends, if granted naturalisation as a British citizen, to make his home or principal home in the United Kingdom, or to continue in Crown service under the government of the United Kingdom, or to enter or continue in service under an international organisation of which the United Kingdom or its government is a member, or to enter or continue in service in the employment of a company or association established in the United Kingdom[10].

As from a day to be appointed[11], if in the special circumstances of a particular case that is an armed forces case[12] or an exceptional Crown service case[13] the

Secretary of State thinks fit, the Secretary of State may waive[14] the need to fulfil all or any of the residence requirements[15] provided that the requirements in heads (1) to (4) are fulfilled[16].

Until a day to be appointed[17], an applicant whose spouse or civil partner is a British citizen serving outside the United Kingdom, as a result of recruitment in the United Kingdom, in Crown service or in service designated as closely associated with government activities[18], must satisfy the naturalisation conditions for spouses or civil partners of British citizens[19], save that (in addition to the discretion to waive or relax certain requirements in all such cases) the Secretary of State has a discretion to waive the need to fulfil some of the residence requirements[20]. As from a day to be appointed[21], not only all the residence requirements, but also the requirements of family association, qualifying immigrant status and leave to remain or right of abode, may be waived[22] in the case of spouses or civil partners of British citizens serving outside the United Kingdom[23].

A certificate given by or on behalf of the Secretary of State that a person was at any time in Crown service under the government of the United Kingdom or that a person's recruitment for such service took place in the United Kingdom is conclusive evidence of that fact[24].

1 As from a day to be appointed, the British Nationality Act 1981 Sch 1 para 1(1)(a) is prospectively amended, Sch 1 para 1(3) is prospectively repealed, and Sch 1 para 2(2)–(4) is prospectively added by the Borders, Citizenship and Immigration Act 2009 ss 39, 56, Schedule Pt 2. At the date at which this volume states the law no such day had been appointed.

2 As to applications see PARA 484.

3 As to the meaning of 'United Kingdom' see PARA 403 note 1.

4 As to the Secretary of State see PARA 402. As to the exercise of discretion see the British Nationality Act 1981 s 44(1); and PARA 402.

5 See the British Nationality Act 1981 s 6(1), Sch 1 para 1(1)(a), (3); and see note 1.

6 See the British Nationality Act 1981 s 6(1). As to the meanings of 'full age' and 'full capacity', and as to the discretion to waive the requirement in respect of a specified applicant, see PARA 438 note 12.

7 British Nationality Act 1981 Sch 1 para 1(1)(b). The Secretary of State is entitled to adopt a high standard in assessing whether an applicant is of good character: see *Al Fayed v Secretary of State for the Home Department* [2001] Imm AR 134, sub nom *R v Secretary of State for the Home Department, ex p Al Fayed* (2000) Times, 7 September, CA.

8 British Nationality Act 1981 Sch 1 para 1(1)(c). If in the special circumstances of any particular case the Secretary of State thinks fit, he may waive the need to fulfil either or both of the requirements specified in Sch 1 para 1(1)(c) and Sch 1 para 1(1)(ca) (see the text and note 9) if he considers that because of the applicant's age or physical or mental condition it would be unreasonable to expect him to fulfil that requirement or those requirements: Sch 1 para 2(e) (amended by the Nationality, Immigration and Asylum Act 2002 s 1(2)).

9 British Nationality Act 1981 Sch 1 para 1(1)(ca) (added by the Nationality, Immigration and Asylum Act 2002 s 1(1)). See note 8.

10 British Nationality Act 1981 Sch 1 para 1(1)(d). For these purposes, a company incorporated abroad but registered as an overseas company with a place of business in the United Kingdom is a company 'established' in the United Kingdom: *R v Secretary of State for the Home Department, ex p Mehta* [1992] Imm AR 512.

11 See note 1.

12 An armed forces case is a case where, on the date of the application, the applicant is or has been a member of the armed forces: British Nationality Act 1981 Sch 1 para 2(3) (prospectively added: see note 1). As to the meaning of 'member of the armed forces' see PARA 424 note 12.

13 An exceptional Crown service case is a case where: (1) the applicant is, on the date of the application, serving outside the United Kingdom in Crown service under the government of the United Kingdom; and (2) the Secretary of State considers the applicant's performance in the service to be exceptional: British Nationality Act 1981 Sch 1 para 2(4) (as so prospectively added).

14 Ie for the purposes of the British Nationality Act 1981 Sch 1 para 1.

15 Ie the requirements specified in the British Nationality Act 1981 Sch 1 para 1(2): see PARA 438 heads (2)–(6).

16 See the British Nationality Act 1981 s 6(1), Sch 1 para 1(1), 2(2); and see note 1.

17 The British Nationality Act 1981 s 6(2) is prospectively amended, s 6(3), (4) prospectively added, and Sch 1 paras 3, 4 prospectively substituted, by the Borders, Citizenship and Immigration Act 2009 s 40 as from a day to be appointed. At the date at which this volume states the law no such day had been appointed.

18 Ie the spouse or civil partner must be serving in service to which the British Nationality Act 1981 s 2(1)(b) applies: see PARA 424.

19 See PARA 440.

20 See the British Nationality Act 1981 s 6(2), Sch 1 paras 2(f), 3, 4(d) (amended by the Civil Partnership Act 2004 s 261(1), Sch 27 paras 72, 78). The residence requirements which may be waived are all or any of the requirements set out in the British Nationality Act 1981 Sch 1 para 3(a), (b): see PARA 440 heads (4)–(6).

   While presence in breach of the immigration laws is waivable in all cases (see Sch 1 paras 2(d), 3(d), 4), there is no provision for waiver of the requirement that on the date of the application the applicant must not be subject under the immigration laws to any restriction on the period for which he may remain in the United Kingdom (see Sch 1 para 3(c)), even in the case of a person living with a British citizen spouse or civil partner who is serving abroad. A person who is not in the United Kingdom may not have leave to enter or remain in the United Kingdom, since as a general rule leave lapses on departure (see the Immigration Act 1971 s 3(4); the Immigration (Leave to Enter and Remain) Order 2000, SI 2000/1161, art 13; and BRITISH NATIONALITY, IMMIGRATION AND ASYLUM vol 4(2) (2002 Reissue) PARA 86). There is no positive requirement that the applicant have indefinite leave, only a negative requirement that the applicant should not be subject to any restriction on the period for which he may remain; a person who is not in the United Kingdom may not be subject to a restriction on the period for which he may remain in the United Kingdom, since such restriction can only be attached to leave to enter or remain and he may have none. Accordingly, there may be no need to waive the British Nationality Act 1981 Sch 1 para 3(c) in the case of a person living with a British citizen spouse or civil partner who is serving abroad; it may simply have no effect. Although the discretion to waive the residential requirements appears from Sch 1 para 2(f) (as applied to Sch 1 para 3 by Sch 1 para 4(d)) to be limited to the requirements in Sch 1 para 3(a) and (b), taken together with the other discretions and the above arguments (no time restrictions when outside the United Kingdom without leave), effectively the residential requirements become waivable (or avoidable) in their entirety.

21 See note 17.

22 Ie taking the discretions in the British Nationality Act 1981 Sch 1 para 4 cumulatively, and not just the discretion in Sch 1 para 4(h) in isolation.

23 See the British Nationality Act 1981 s 6(2), Sch 1 paras 3, 4(h) (prospectively substituted: see note 17); and PARA 441. If in the special circumstances of any particular case the Secretary of State thinks fit, the Secretary of State may waive the need to fulfil all or any of the requirements specified in Sch 1 para 3(2)(a), (b), (c) or (d) (see PARA 441 head (1)(a)–(d)) (including where Sch 1 para 3(2)(c) can be fulfilled only as set out in Sch 1 para 3(5): see PARA 441 note 11) if: (1) on the date of the application, the person with whom A has the relevant family association referred to in s 6(2) (see PARA 441 text and note 3) is serving in service to which s 2(1)(b) (see PARA 424) applies; and (2) that person's recruitment for that service took place in the United Kingdom: Sch 1 para 4(h) (as so prospectively substituted). As to other requirements which may be waived generally under Sch 1 para 4(a)–(g) see PARA 441 notes 9, 11, 15, 16, 23.

24 See the British Nationality Act 1981 s 45(4); and PARA 486.

443. Renunciation and resumption. A British citizen of full age and capacity[1] may renounce his citizenship by declaration, upon registration of which he ceases to be a British citizen[2]. However, the person must have or be about to acquire some other citizenship or nationality[3]. The Secretary of State[4] must be satisfied on this point; and even if the declaration is registered, should the renouncer not acquire some such other citizenship within six months, the registration will be of no effect and he will remain a British citizen[5]. The Secretary of State may withhold registration of a declaration of renunciation in wartime[6].

A person who has renounced British citizenship is entitled, once only, to be registered as a British citizen if he is of full capacity, and had to renounce his

British citizenship in order to retain or acquire some other citizenship or nationality[7]. In addition, the Secretary of State has a discretion[8] to register any person of full capacity who renounced British citizenship, whatever the reason for the renunciation[9].

Previous nationality law provided for renunciation and resumption of citizenship of the United Kingdom and colonies[10]. That citizenship cannot now be resumed as it no longer exists; but there is provision for a person who renounced it to be registered as a British citizen. A person who renounced citizenship of the United Kingdom and colonies is entitled, once only, to be registered as a British citizen if on 31 December 1982[11] he would have been entitled to registration as a citizen of the United Kingdom and colonies under the British Nationality Act 1964[12] on the basis of a qualifying connection with the United Kingdom or of marriage to a person with such a qualifying connection[13]. In addition, the Secretary of State has a discretion to register as a British citizen any person who renounced citizenship of the United Kingdom and colonies, provided that that person has a qualifying connection with the United Kingdom or has been married to, or has been the civil partner of, a person who has or would if living have such a connection[14]. A person is to be taken to have the appropriate qualifying connection with the United Kingdom if he, his father or his father's father: (1) was born in the United Kingdom; or (2) is or was a person naturalised in the United Kingdom; or (3) was registered as a citizen of the United Kingdom and colonies in the United Kingdom or in a Commonwealth country[15].

1 As to the meanings of 'full age' and 'full capacity', and as to the discretion to waive the requirement in respect of a specified applicant, see PARA 438 note 12. For the purpose of renunciation only, a person who has been married, or has formed a civil partnership, is deemed to be of full age: British Nationality Act 1981 s 12(5) (amended by the Civil Partnership Act 2004 s 261(1), Sch 27 para 74).

2 See the British Nationality Act 1981 s 12(1), (2). As to declarations of renunciation see the British Nationality (General) Regulations 2003, SI 2003/548, regs 8, 9, Sch 5 (Sch 5 amended by SI 2005/2114; and SI 2007/3137). As to the power to make regulations see PARA 404.

3 See the British Nationality Act 1981 s 12(3).

4 As to the Secretary of State see PARA 402.

5 See the British Nationality Act 1981 s 12(3).

6 See British Nationality Act 1981 s 12(4).

7 See British Nationality Act 1981 s 13(1), (2). An application for registration of an adult or young person as a British citizen under s 13(1), (3) (see the text and notes 8–9), or under s 10(1), (2) (see the text and notes 13–14), must not be granted unless the Secretary of State is satisfied that the adult or young person is of good character: s 41A(1) (added by the Borders, Citizenship and Immigration Act 2009 s 47(1) to replace corresponding provision in the Immigration, Asylum and Nationality Act 2006 s 58). As to the meaning of 'adult or young person' see PARA 426 note 4.

8 As to the exercise of discretion see the British Nationality Act 1981 s 44(1); and PARA 402.

9 See the British Nationality Act 1981 s 13(3). See also note 7.

10 See PARA 419. As to citizenship of the United Kingdom and colonies see PARAS 414–419.

11 Ie immediately before the commencement of the British Nationality Act 1981: see PARA 403 note 1.

12 Ie under the British Nationality Act 1964 s 1(1) (now repealed), which made provision for registration of persons who renounced citizenship in order to acquire or retain citizenship of a Commonwealth country.

13 See the British Nationality Act 1981 s 10(1), (3) (s 10(1) amended by the Nationality, Immigration and Asylum Act 2002 ss 5(a), 161, Sch 9). See also note 7. As to the meaning of 'United Kingdom' see PARA 403 note 1. The qualifying connection is that specified in the British Nationality Act 1981 s 10(4) (see the text and note 15), and not that specified in the British Nationality Act 1964: *R v Secretary of State for the Home Department, ex p Patel and Wahid* [1991] Imm AR 25, DC.

14 See the British Nationality Act 1981 s 10(2) (amended by the Nationality, Immigration and Asylum Act 2002 ss 5(a), 161, Sch 9; and the Civil Partnership Act 2004 s 261(1), Sch 27 para 73). See also note 7.

15 British Nationality Act 1981 s 10(4). The reference in the text to a Commonwealth country is a reference to a country which was at the time of registration a Commonwealth country listed in the British Nationality Act 1948 s 1(3) (repealed). See further PARA 409 note 4.

  If the qualifying connection is with a British overseas territory (formerly known as a dependent territory) (see PARA 445 note 1), the resumed citizenship will be British overseas territories citizenship (formerly known as British dependent territories citizenship) (see PARAS 406, 445–458): see the British Nationality Act 1981 s 22; and PARA 457.

444. Deprivation of citizenship. The Secretary of State[1] may by order deprive a person of a citizenship status[2] if the Secretary of State is satisfied that deprivation is conducive to the public good[3]. However, the Secretary of State may not make such an order if he is satisfied that the order would make a person stateless[4].

The Secretary of State may by order deprive a person of a citizenship status which results from his registration[5] or naturalisation[6] if the Secretary of State is satisfied that the registration or naturalisation was obtained by means of fraud, false representation or concealment of a material fact[7]. Where a person acquired a citizenship status by the operation of a law which applied to him because of his registration or naturalisation under an enactment having effect before 1 January 1983[8], the Secretary of State may by order deprive the person of the citizenship status if the Secretary of State is satisfied that the registration or naturalisation was obtained by means of fraud, false representation or concealment of a material fact[9].

Before making an order under these provisions in respect of a person the Secretary of State must give the person written notice specifying: (1) that the Secretary of State has decided to make an order; (2) the reasons for the order; and (3) the person's right of appeal[10].

A person who is given notice[11] of a decision to make an order in respect of him depriving him of citizenship status may appeal against the decision to the First-tier Tribunal[12]. However, this does not apply to a decision if the Secretary of State certifies that it was taken wholly or partly in reliance on information which in his opinion should not be made public: (a) in the interests of national security; (b) in the interests of the relationship between the United Kingdom and another country; or (c) otherwise in the public interest[13]. In such cases an appeal lies to the Special Immigration Appeals Commission[14].

Fraud of a sufficiently serious and causative nature may render the registration or naturalisation acquired by the fraud of no effect[15]. The person will never have been a citizen, and therefore there is nothing of which he can be deprived; one consequence of this is that the overriding safeguard, preventing deprivation if it would make the person stateless, is of no effect in such cases. Nor is there a right to an appeal; but a person whose citizenship is alleged to be a nullity on this ground may bring the matter before the courts[16].

1 As to the Secretary of State see PARA 402.

2 A reference to a person's 'citizenship status' is a reference to his status as: (1) a British citizen; (2) a British overseas territories citizen; (3) a British overseas citizen; (4) a British national (overseas); (5) a British protected person; or (6) a British subject: British Nationality Act 1981 s 40(1) (s 40 substituted by the Nationality, Immigration and Asylum Act 2002 s 4(1)). As to British citizens and citizenship see PARAS 406, 421–444; as to British overseas territories citizens see PARAS 406, 445–458; as to British overseas citizens see PARAS 406, 459–463; as to British nationals (overseas) see PARAS 406, 465–467; as to British protected persons see PARAS 408, 476–480; and as to British subjects see PARAS 407, 469–474.

3 British Nationality Act 1981 s 40(2) (s 40 as substituted (see note 2); s 40(2) further substituted by the Immigration, Asylum and Nationality Act 2006 s 56(1)). As to the exercise of discretion see s 44(1); and PARA 402. As to the removal of a person's name from the register after an order has been made depriving him of British citizenship see the British Nationality (General) Regulations 2003, SI 2003/548, reg 11. As to the cancellation of a certificate of naturalisation see reg 12. As to the power to make regulations see PARA 404.

4 British Nationality Act 1981 s 40(4) (as substituted: see note 2).

5 See PARAS 426–437.

6 See PARAS 438–442.

7 British Nationality Act 1981 s 40(3) (as substituted: see note 2). See also Case C-135/08 *Rottmann v Freistaat Bayern* [2010] All ER (EC) 635, [2010] All ER (D) 53 (Mar), ECJ (it is not contrary to European Union law for a member state to withdraw from a citizen of the European Union the nationality of that state acquired by naturalisation when that nationality has been obtained by deception, provided that the decision to withdraw observes the principle of proportionality).

8 Ie the date of commencement of the British Nationality Act 1981: see PARA 403 note 1.

9 British Nationality Act 1981 s 40(6) (as substituted: see note 2).

10 British Nationality Act 1981 s 40(5) (as substituted: see note 2). The right of appeal referred to in the text is that under s 40A(1) (see the text and notes 11–12) or under the Special Immigration Appeals Commission Act 1997 s 2B (see BRITISH NATIONALITY, IMMIGRATION AND ASYLUM). As to the notice see the British Nationality (General) Regulations 2003, SI 2003/548, reg 10.

11 Ie under the British Nationality Act 1981 s 40(5).

12 British Nationality Act 1981 s 40A(1) (s 40A added by the Nationality, Immigration and Asylum Act 2002 s 4(1); s 40(1) amended by the Asylum and Immigration (Treatment of Claimants, etc) Act 2004 s 26(7), Sch 2 Pt 1 para 4(a); and by SI 2010/21). On 15 February 2010, Immigration and Asylum Chambers were established in both tiers of the unified tribunals framework, replacing the former Asylum and Immigration Tribunal.

The following provisions of the Nationality, Immigration and Asylum Act 2002 apply in relation to an appeal under the British Nationality Act 1981 s 40A as they apply in relation to an appeal under the Nationality, Immigration and Asylum Act 2002 s 82, 83 or 83A: (1) s 87 (successful appeal: direction); (2) ss 103A–103E (review and appeal); (3) s 106 (rules); (4) s 107 (practice directions); and (5) s 108 (forged document: proceedings in private): British Nationality Act 1981 s 40A(3) (s 40A as so added; s 40A(3) substituted by the Asylum and Immigration (Treatment of Claimants, etc) Act 2004 Sch 2 Pt 1 para 4(b); and amended by the Immigration, Asylum and Nationality Act 2006 ss 56(2), 61, Sch 3; and the Immigration, Asylum and Nationality Act 2006 ss 14, 56(2), Sch 1 para 13). For the purpose of the Nationality, Immigration and Asylum Act 2002 s 87, a direction may, in particular, provide for an order under the British Nationality Act 1981 s 40 to be treated as having had no effect: s 40A(3)(a) (as so added and substituted).

13 British Nationality Act 1981 s 40A(2) (as added: see note 12).

14 As to the Special Immigration Appeals Commission see BRITISH NATIONALITY, IMMIGRATION AND ASYLUM.

15 *R v Secretary of State for the Home Department, ex p Sultan Mahmood* [1981] QB 58n, [1980] 3 WLR 312n, CA; *R v Secretary of State for the Home Department, ex p Parvaz Akhtar* [1981] QB 46, [1980] 2 All ER 735, CA; *R v Secretary of State for the Home Department, ex p Puttick* [1981] QB 767, [1981] 1 All ER 776, DC; *Khawaja v Secretary of State for the Home Department* [1984] AC 74, [1983] 1 All ER 765, HL. However, see *R v Secretary of State for the Home Department, ex p Ejaz* [1994] QB 496, [1994] 2 All ER 436, CA (the applicant, holding a certificate of naturalisation, is a British citizen even if that certificate had been obtained through fraud unless and until she is deprived of that status by the Secretary of State under the British Nationality Act 1981 s 40).

16 Such a matter is normally brought before the courts by application for judicial review, seeking a declaration and, if appropriate, a quashing order. See JUDICIAL REVIEW vol 61 (2010) PARA 601 et seq.

4. BRITISH OVERSEAS TERRITORIES CITIZENSHIP

445. In general. British overseas territories[1] and British overseas territories citizens were formerly known as dependent territories and British dependent territories citizens[2]. From 1 January 1983[3] British overseas territories citizens, whose British nationality comes from their connection with a British overseas territory[4], were distinguished from British citizens[5], whose nationality comes from a connection with the United Kingdom[6] itself. British overseas territories citizenship may be acquired by statute[7], by birth, adoption or descent[8] or by registration[9] or naturalisation[10].

The British Nationality Act 1981 makes provision enabling certain British overseas territories citizens to acquire British citizenship by registration[11]. However, since 21 May 2002[12] most persons who were British overseas territories citizens immediately before that date have additionally enjoyed British citizenship[13].

British overseas territories citizenship per se does not carry with it the right of abode in the United Kingdom[14]. The right of abode in a British overseas territory is a matter for the internal law of that territory.

1　'British overseas territory' means a territory mentioned in the British Nationality Act 1981 Sch 6: s 50(1) (definition added by the British Overseas Territories Act 2002 s 1(1)(a)). The territories which are British overseas territories are: Anguilla; Bermuda; British Antarctic Territory; British Indian Ocean Territory; Cayman Islands; Falkland Islands; Gibraltar; Montserrat; Pitcairn, Henderson, Ducie and Oeno Islands; St Helena, Ascension and Tristan da Cunha; South Georgia and the South Sandwich Islands; the Sovereign Base Areas of Akrotiri and Dhekelia (ie the areas mentioned in the Cyprus Act 1960 s 2(1): see COMMONWEALTH vol 13 (2009) PARAS 748, 864); Turks and Caicos Islands; Virgin Islands: British Nationality Act 1981 Sch 6 (amended by the British Overseas Territories Act 2002 s 1(1)(c); SI 1983/882, SI 1986/948, SI 2001/3497 and SI 2009/2744). See further COMMONWEALTH vol 13 (2009) PARA 801 et seq.

2　See PARA 406 note 8.

3　Ie the date of commencement of the British Nationality Act 1981: see PARA 403 note 1.

4　A person may not be registered as a British overseas territories citizen under a provision of the British Nationality Act 1981 by virtue of a connection with Hong Kong: Nationality, Immigration and Asylum Act 2002 s 14.

5　As to British citizens and citizenship see PARAS 406, 421–444.

6　As to the meaning of 'United Kingdom' see PARA 403 note 1.

7　See PARAS 446–447.

8　See PARA 448.

9　See PARAS 449–452. As to resumption, which is a form of acquisition by registration, see PARA 457.

10　See PARAS 453–455.

11　See PARA 428.

12　Ie the date of the commencement of the British Overseas Territories Act 2002 s 3: see s 8; and the British Overseas Territories Act 2002 (Commencement) Order 2002, SI 2002/1252, art 2(a).

13　See the British Overseas Territories Act 2002 s 3; and PARA 423.

14　As to the right of abode see PARA 412.

446. Automatic acquisition on 1 January 1983 under transitional arrangements. A person who on 31 December 1982[1] was a citizen of the United Kingdom and colonies[2], and who satisfied one of a number of conditions connecting him with a British overseas territory[3], became a British overseas territories citizen[4] on 1 January 1983[5]. The conditions were as follows, namely that:

(1)　he acquired his citizenship of the United Kingdom and colonies by birth, naturalisation[6] or registration in a British overseas territory[7];

(2)　at the time of his birth one of his parents[8] was a citizen of the United

Kingdom and colonies by birth, naturalisation or registration in a British overseas territory or was himself born to a parent who at the time of that birth was a citizen by birth, naturalisation or registration in such a territory[9];

(3)   being a woman, she was at any time before 1 January 1983 the wife of a man who on that date became a British overseas territories citizen under head (1) or head (2) above, or who would have done but for his death[10];

(4)   he became a citizen of the United Kingdom and colonies by registration, otherwise than in a British overseas territory, as a minor child[11] or as a stateless person[12], and his father or mother (in the case of a minor) or his mother (in the case of a stateless person) was a citizen of the United Kingdom and colonies at the time of the registration or would have been but for his or her death and became a British overseas territories citizen on 1 January 1983 or would have done but for his or her death[13];

(5)   he became a citizen of the United Kingdom and colonies by registration[14], otherwise than in a British overseas territory, by virtue (inter alia) of a male ancestor who satisfied specified conditions[15] and who was born or naturalised in a British overseas territory or became a British subject by annexation of any territory included in a British overseas territory[16];

(6)   he had resumed citizenship of the United Kingdom and colonies by registration[17], otherwise than in a British overseas territory, by virtue of an appropriate qualifying connection[18] with a British overseas territory or, in the case of a woman, by virtue of having been married to a man who had such a connection at the time of registration (or would have done but for his death)[19].

A person was not disqualified from becoming a British overseas territories citizen under the provisions described above merely because he also became a British citizen on 1 January 1983[20].

1   Ie immediately before the commencement of the British Nationality Act 1981: see note 5.
2   As to citizens of the United Kingdom and colonies see PARAS 414–419.
3   As to British overseas territories (formerly known as dependent territories) see PARA 445 note 1.
4   British overseas territories citizens were formerly known as British dependent territories citizens: see PARAS 406, 445.
5   See the British Nationality Act 1981 s 23; and the text and notes 6–19. The date referred to in the text is the date of commencement of the British Nationality Act 1981: see PARA 403 note 1.
6   A person is taken to have been naturalised in a British overseas territory if, but only if: (1) a certificate of naturalisation was granted to him under any of the former nationality Acts by the Governor of that territory or by a person, or office-holder, specified in a direction given in relation to that territory under the West Indies Act 1967 Sch 3 para 4 (now repealed); or (2) his name was included in a certificate of naturalisation granted by the Governor of that territory and he was deemed to be a person to whom the certificate of naturalisation was granted by virtue of the British Nationality and Status of Aliens Act 1914 s 27(2) (now repealed); or (3) he is a person who by the law in force in that territory enjoyed the privileges of naturalisation within that territory only: British Nationality Act 1981 s 50(6)(b) (amended by virtue of the British Overseas Territories Act 2002 s 1(1)(b)). As to the meaning of 'former nationality Acts' see PARA 422 note 13. The British Nationality and Status of Aliens Act 1914 is now known as the Status of Aliens Act 1914: see PARA 403 note 9.
7   See the British Nationality Act 1981 s 23(1)(a) (s 23(1) amended by virtue of the British Overseas Territories Act 2002 ss 1(1)(b), 2(2)(b)).
8   See PARA 424 notes 6–7.
9   See the British Nationality Act 1981 s 23(1)(b) (as amended: see note 7). For the purposes of s 23(1)(b), references to citizenship of the United Kingdom and colonies, in relation to a time before 1949 (ie before the British Nationality Act 1948 came into force: see PARA 403 note 7),

are to be construed as references to British nationality (note that prior to 1 January 1949 the single common nationality was the status of British subject: see PARA 407): British Nationality Act 1981 s 23(6).

10 See the British Nationality Act 1981 s 23(1)(c) (as amended: see note 7).

11 Ie under the British Nationality Act 1948 s 7 (now repealed): see PARA 417 note 13. Under this provision the Secretary of State had a discretion to register the minor child of any citizen of the United Kingdom and colonies upon application of the parent or guardian, and in special circumstances to register any minor: see s 7 (now repealed). See further PARA 482 note 4. As to the Secretary of State see PARA 402.

12 Ie under the British Nationality (No 2) Act 1964 s 1 (now repealed): see PARA 417. Under this provision a person who had always been stateless was entitled to registration if: (1) his mother was a citizen of the United Kingdom and colonies at the time of his birth; or (2) the place where he was born was at the time of his application for registration part of the United Kingdom and colonies; or (3) he satisfied conditions as to parentage, or as to residence and parentage: see s 1, Schedule (now repealed). Those satisfying the condition in head (1) or head (3) were citizens by descent only: s 1(4) (now repealed). As to citizenship by descent see PARA 456.

13 See the British Nationality Act 1981 s 23(2) (amended by virtue of the British Overseas Territories Act 2002 ss 1(1)(b), 2(2)(b)).

14 Ie under the British Nationality Act 1948 s 12(6) (now repealed): see PARA 417 note 13. Under this provision a person who would have become a citizen of the United Kingdom and colonies on 1 January 1949 but for his citizenship or potential citizenship of a Commonwealth country (see PARAS 415–416), could be registered (together with his minor children) if: (1) he was descended in the male line from an ancestor who was born or naturalised in the United Kingdom and colonies or became a British subject by annexation of territory; (2) he intended to make his ordinary place of residence within the United Kingdom and colonies; and (3) the Secretary of State thought it fitting that he should become a citizen by reason of his close connection with the United Kingdom and colonies: see s 12(6) (now repealed).

15 As to the conditions see the British Nationality Act 1948 s 12(1) (now repealed); and PARA 415 head (1). See also note 14 head (1).

16 See the British Nationality Act 1981 s 23(3) (amended by virtue of the British Overseas Territories Act 2002 ss 1(1)(b), 2(2)(b)).

17 Ie under the British Nationality Act 1964 s 1 (now repealed): see PARA 419. Those who could resume citizenship under this provision were those who renounced citizenship in order to acquire or retain citizenship of a Commonwealth country which did not permit dual citizenship, and who (or, in the case of a woman, whose husband) had a qualifying connection with the United Kingdom and colonies: see s 1 (now repealed); and PARA 419.

18 For these purposes, a person had an appropriate qualifying connection if he, his father or his father's father was born, naturalised or registered as a citizen of the United Kingdom and colonies in a British overseas territory, or became a British subject by annexation of any territory included in a British overseas territory: see the British Nationality Act 1981 s 23(5) (amended by virtue of the British Overseas Territories Act 2002 s 1(1)(b)). For these purposes, the qualifying connections specified in the British Nationality Act 1964 are now irrelevant: see *R v Secretary of State for the Home Department, ex p Patel and Wahid* [1991] Imm AR 25, DC.

19 See the British Nationality Act 1981 s 23(4) (amended by virtue of the British Overseas Territories Act 2002 ss 1(1)(b), 2(2)(b)).

20 Eg certain Falkland Islanders who became British overseas territories citizens under the British Nationality Act 1981 s 23 became at the same time British citizens under the British Nationality (Falkland Islands) Act 1983 s 1: see PARA 422.

447. Automatic acquisition on 21 May 2002 under transitional arrangements. A person who:

(1) was born on or after 26 April 1969 and before 1 January 1983[1];

(2) was born to a woman who at the time was a citizen of the United Kingdom and colonies[2] by virtue of her birth in the British Indian Ocean Territory[3]; and

(3) immediately before 21 May 2002[4] was not a British overseas territories citizen[5],

became a British overseas territories citizen on 21 May 2002[6].

1 See the British Overseas Territories Act 2002 s 6(1)(a), (3)(a).
2 As to citizenship of the United Kingdom and colonies see PARAS 414–419.

3   See the British Overseas Territories Act 2002 s 6(1)(b), (3)(a).
4   Ie the date of the commencement of the British Overseas Territories Act 2002 s 6: see s 8; and the British Overseas Territories Act 2002 (Commencement) Order 2002, SI 2002/1252, art 2(b).
5   See the British Overseas Territories Act 2002 s 6(3)(b). British overseas territories citizens were formerly known as British dependent territories citizens: see PARAS 406, 445.
6   British Overseas Territories Act 2002 s 6(3). A person who is a British overseas territories citizen by virtue of s 6(3) is a British overseas territories citizen by descent for the purposes of the British Nationality Act 1981: British Overseas Territories Act 2002 s 6(4). As to citizenship by descent see PARA 456.

448. Acquisition by birth, adoption or descent. A person born in a British overseas territory[1] on or after 1 January 1983[2] is a British overseas territories citizen[3] if at the time of the birth his father or mother[4] is a British overseas territories citizen or is settled in a British overseas territory[5]. There is a rebuttable presumption that a new-born infant found abandoned in a British overseas territory fulfils these qualifications[6].

A person born in the United Kingdom[7] on or after 1 January 1983 who would otherwise be stateless is a British overseas territories citizen if at the time of the birth his father or mother is a British overseas territories citizen[8].

Where on or after 1 January 1983 an order authorising the adoption of a minor[9] is made by a court in a British overseas territory, he is a British overseas territories citizen (if he is not already) from the date of the order provided the adopter (or, in the case of a joint adoption, one of the adopters) is a British overseas territories citizen on that date[10]. Where: (1) a minor who is not a British overseas territories citizen is adopted under a Convention adoption[11]; (2) on the date on which the adoption is effected: (a) the adopter or, in the case of a joint adoption, one of the adopters is a British overseas territories citizen; and (b) the adopter or, in the case of a joint adoption, both of the adopters are habitually resident in a designated territory; and (3) the Convention adoption is effected under the law of a country or territory outside the designated territory, the minor is a British overseas territories citizen as from that date[12]. In either case, the minor remains a British overseas territories citizen even if the order ceases to have effect[13].

A person born outside the British overseas territories on or after 1 January 1983 is a British overseas territories citizen if at the time of the birth his father or mother is a British overseas territories citizen: (i) otherwise than by descent[14]; or (ii) serving outside the British overseas territories, as a result of recruitment in a British overseas territory, in Crown service under the government of a British overseas territory or in service designated[15] by the Secretary of State as closely associated with the activities outside the British overseas territories of the government of any British overseas territory[16].

1   See PARA 424 note 1. As to British overseas territories (formerly known as dependent territories) see PARA 445 note 1.
2   Ie the date of commencement of the British Nationality Act 1981: see PARA 403 note 1.
3   British overseas territories citizens were formerly known as British dependent territories citizens: see PARAS 406, 445. Since 21 May 2002, most persons who were British overseas territories citizens immediately before that date have enjoyed British citizenship: see the British Overseas Territories Act 2002 s 3; and PARA 423.
4   See PARA 424 notes 6–7.
5   British Nationality Act 1981 s 15(1) (amended by virtue of the British Overseas Territories Act 2002 ss 1(1)(b), 2(2)(b)). This is so even if the father's or mother's connection is with a British overseas territory other than that where the person is born. As to when a person is settled in a British overseas territory see PARA 424 note 9.
6   See the British Nationality Act 1981 s 15(2) (amended by virtue of the British Overseas Territories Act 2002 ss 1(1)(b), 2(2)(b)).

7   As to the meaning of 'United Kingdom' see PARA 403 note 1.
8   See the British Nationality Act 1981 s 36, Sch 2 para 1 (amended by virtue of the British Overseas Territories Act 2002 s 2(2)(b); and by the Nationality, Immigration and Asylum Act 2002 ss 9(5)(a), 161, Sch 9).
9   As to the meaning of 'minor' see PARA 424 note 13.
10 See the British Nationality Act 1981 s 15(5) (amended by virtue of the British Overseas Territories Act 2002 ss 1(1)(b), 2(2)(b)).
11 As to the meaning of 'Convention adoption' see PARA 424 note 14.
12 British Nationality Act 1981 s 15(5A) (added by the Adoption and Children Act 2002, s 137(3), (5)(a)).
13 See the British Nationality Act 1981 s 15(6) (amended by virtue of the British Overseas Territories Act 2002 s 2(2)(b); and by the Adoption and Children Act 2002 s 137(3), (5)(b)).
14 As to citizenship by descent see PARA 456.
15 Ie by order made by statutory instrument subject to annulment in pursuance of a resolution of either House of Parliament: see the British Nationality Act 1981 s 16(3), (4) (s 16(3) amended by virtue of the British Overseas Territories Act 2002 s 1(1)(b)); and the British Dependent Territories Citizenship (Designated Service) Order 1982, SI 1982/1710 (amended by virtue of the British Overseas Territories Act 2002 ss 1(2), 2(3); and by SI 2008/1240).
16 See the British Nationality Act 1981 s 16(1), (2) (amended by virtue of the British Overseas Territories Act 2002 ss 1(1)(b), 2(2)(b)). A person who acquires citizenship under the British Nationality Act 1981 s 16(1)(a) (see head (i) in the text) is a British overseas territories citizen by descent but a person who acquires citizenship as a result of s 16(1)(b) (see head (ii) in the text) is not: see s 25(1)(a); and PARA 456.

449. Acquisition by registration: birth in a British overseas territory. A person born in a British overseas territory[1] on or after 1 January 1983[2] who is not a British overseas territories citizen[3] by birth[4] is entitled to be registered as a British overseas territories citizen if: (1) an application[5] is made while he is a minor[6] on the ground that his father or mother has become a British overseas territories citizen or has settled in a British overseas territory[7]; or (2) an application is made at any time after he attains the age of ten years[8] on the ground that during each of the first ten years of his life he has not been absent from the British overseas territory in which he was born for more than 90 days[9]. A person may not be registered as a British overseas territories citizen under a provision of the British Nationality Act 1981 by virtue of a connection with Hong Kong[10].

1   As to British overseas territories (formerly known as dependent territories) see PARA 445 note 1.
2   Ie the date of commencement of the British Nationality Act 1981: see PARA 403 note 1.
3   British overseas territories citizens were formerly known as British dependent territories citizens: see PARAS 406, 445. Since 21 May 2002, most persons who were British overseas territories citizens immediately before that date have enjoyed British citizenship: see the British Overseas Territories Act 2002 s 3; and PARA 423.
4   Ie under the British Nationality Act 1981 s 15(1), (2): see PARA 448.
5   As to applications see PARA 484.
6   As to the meaning of 'minor' see PARA 424 note 13.
7   See the British Nationality Act 1981 s 15(3) (amended by virtue of the British Overseas Territories Act 2002 ss 1(1)(b), 2(2)(b)). As to when a person is settled in a British overseas territory see PARA 424 note 9. An application for registration of an adult or young person as a British overseas territories citizen under the British Nationality Act 1981 s 15(3) or (4) (see the text and note 9) must not be granted unless the Secretary of State is satisfied that the adult or young person is of good character: s 41A(2) (s 41A added by the Borders, Citizenship and Immigration Act 2009 s 47(1) to replace corresponding provision in Immigration, Asylum and Nationality Act 2006 s 58). As to the meaning of 'adult or young person' see PARA 426 note 4.
8   As to when, for the purposes of the British Nationality Act 1981, a person attains any particular age, see PARA 426 note 8.
9   British Nationality Act 1981 s 15(4) (amended by virtue of the British Overseas Territories Act 2002 ss 1(1)(b), 2(2)(b)). As to references to days of absence from a British overseas territory see PARA 426 note 9. See also note 7. If in the special circumstances of any particular case the Secretary of State thinks fit, he may treat the person to whom the application relates as

fulfilling the requirements specified in the British Nationality Act 1981 s 15(4) although the number of days on which he was absent from the British overseas territory in which he was born exceeds the number mentioned: see s 15(7) (amended by virtue of the British Overseas Territories Act 2002 s 1(1)(b)). As to the Secretary of State see PARA 402. As to the exercise of discretion see the British Nationality Act 1981 s 44(1); and PARA 402.

10   Nationality, Immigration and Asylum Act 2002 s 14.

450. Acquisition by registration: minors. The Secretary of State[1] may, if he thinks fit[2], grant any application[3] for registration of a minor[4] as a British overseas territories citizen[5].

A person born outside the British overseas territories[6] is entitled[7], on an application made within 12 months[8] from his birth, to be registered as a British overseas territories citizen if: (1) one of his parents was a British overseas territories citizen by descent[9] at the time of the birth[10]; (2) the father or mother of that parent was a British overseas territories citizen otherwise than by descent at the time of the birth of that parent, or became a British overseas territories citizen otherwise than by descent on 1 January 1983[11] or would have done so but for his or her death; and (3) that parent had been in a British overseas territory at the beginning of any three year period ending not later than the date of the birth and had not been absent from that territory for more than 270 days during that period[12].

A person born outside the British overseas territories is entitled, on an application made while he is a minor, to be registered as a British overseas territories citizen if: (a) at the time of his birth his father or mother was a British overseas territories citizen by descent; (b) that person and his father and mother were in one and the same overseas territory (no matter which) at the beginning of the period of three years ending with the date of the application and none of them has been absent from that territory for more than 270 days during that period; and (c) his father and mother consent to the registration in the prescribed manner[13].

1   As to the Secretary of State see PARA 402.
2   As to the exercise of discretion see the British Nationality Act 1981 s 44; and PARA 402.
3   As to applications see PARA 484.
4   As to the meaning of 'minor' see PARA 424 note 13.
5   See the British Nationality Act 1981 s 17(1) (amended by virtue of the British Overseas Territories Act 2002 s 2(2)(b)). An application for registration of an adult or young person as a British overseas territories citizen under the British Nationality Act 1981 s 17(1), (5) (see the text and note 13) must not be granted unless the Secretary of State is satisfied that the adult or young person is of good character: s 41A(2) (s 41A added by the Borders, Citizenship and Immigration Act 2009 s 47(1) to replace corresponding provision in Immigration, Asylum and Nationality Act 2006 s 58). As to the meaning of 'adult or young person' see PARA 426 note 4. British overseas territories citizens were formerly known as British dependent territories citizens: see PARAS 406, 445. Since 21 May 2002, most persons who were British overseas territories citizens immediately before that date have additionally enjoyed British citizenship: see the British Overseas Territories Act 2002 s 3; and PARA 423. A person may not be registered as a British overseas territories citizen under a provision of the British Nationality Act 1981 by virtue of a connection with Hong Kong: Nationality, Immigration and Asylum Act 2002 s 14.
      A person registered under the British Nationality Act 1981 s 17(1) is a British overseas territories citizen by descent if at the time of his birth his father or mother was a British overseas territories citizen, or was at that time a citizen of the United Kingdom and colonies and became a British overseas territories citizen on 1 January 1983 or would have done so but for his or her death: s 25(1)(c) (amended by virtue of the British Overseas Territories Act 2002 s 2(2)(b)); and see PARA 456. As to citizenship of the United Kingdom and colonies see PARAS 414–419.
6   As to British overseas territories (formerly known as dependent territories) see PARA 445 note 1.

7   Ie subject to overriding considerations of public policy, where the qualifying conditions are fulfilled by criminal activity: *R v Secretary of State for the Home Department, ex p Puttick* [1981] QB 767, [1981] 1 All ER 776, DC (married status on which entitlement depended was valid but obtained by perjury and forgery).

8   If in the special circumstances of any particular case he thinks fit, the Secretary of State may treat the reference to 12 months as a reference to six years: British Nationality Act 1981 s 17(4).

9   As to citizenship by descent see PARA 456.

10 See PARA 424 notes 6–7.

11 Ie the date of commencement of the British Nationality Act 1981: see PARA 403 note 1.

12 See the British Nationality Act 1981 s 17(2), (3) (amended by virtue of the British Overseas Territories Act 2002 ss 1(1)(b), 2(2)(b)). As to references to days of absence from a British overseas territory see PARA 426 note 9. A person born stateless need only satisfy heads (1) and (2) in the text. As to registration of stateless persons see also PARA 451. A person registered under the British Nationality Act 1981 s 17(2) is a British overseas territories citizen by descent: see s 25(1)(a); and PARA 456.

13 See the British Nationality Act 1981 s 17(5) (amended by virtue of the British Overseas Territories Act 2002 ss 1(1)(b), 2(2)(b)). As to references to days of absence from a British overseas territory see PARA 426 note 9. As to the manner of signifying parental consent to registration see the British Nationality (Dependent Territories) Regulations 2007, SI 2007/3139, reg 11. As to the power to make regulations see PARA 404.

   If the person's father or mother died, or their marriage or civil partnership was terminated, on or before the date of the application, or his father and mother were legally separated on that date, the references to his father and mother in head (b) in the text are to be read either as references to his father or as references to his mother; and if his father or mother died on or before that date, the reference to his father and mother in head (c) in the text is to be read as a reference to either of them: British Nationality Act 1981 s 17(6) (amended by virtue of the British Overseas Territories Act 2002 s 2(2)(b); and by the Nationality, Immigration and Asylum Act 2002 ss 9(3), 161, Sch 9; and the Civil Partnership Act 2004 s 261(1), Sch 27 para 75).

451.   Acquisition by registration: statelessness. A person born in the United Kingdom or a British overseas territory[1] on or after 1 January 1983[2], who is and always has been stateless[3], is entitled to be registered as a British overseas territories citizen if: (1) an application for his registration is made when he is under 22 years old[4]; (2) he was in the United Kingdom or a British overseas territory at the beginning of the period of five years ending with the date of application; (3) during that period he has not been absent from both the United Kingdom and the British overseas territories for more than 450 days; and (4) during that period he has spent more days (or part days) in the British overseas territories than in the United Kingdom[5].

A person born outside the United Kingdom and the British overseas territories on or after 1 January 1983, who is and always has been stateless, is entitled on application to registration as a British overseas territories citizen if: (a) at the time of his birth his father or mother[6] was a British overseas territories citizen; (b) he himself was in the United Kingdom or a British overseas territory at the beginning of the period of three years ending with the date of application; and (c) during that period he has not been absent from both the United Kingdom and the British overseas territories for more than 270 days[7].

Provision is made for the registration of certain stateless persons born before 1 January 1983[8].

1   See PARA 424 note 1. As to the meaning of 'United Kingdom' see PARA 403 note 1. As to British overseas territories (formerly known as dependent territories) see PARA 445 note 1.

2   Ie the date of commencement of the British Nationality Act 1981: see PARA 403 note 1.

3   A person born in a British overseas territory to a British citizen parent is automatically a British citizen if he would otherwise be stateless; and a person born in the United Kingdom to a British overseas territories citizen parent is automatically a British overseas territories citizen if he would otherwise be stateless: see PARAS 424, 448. As to British citizens and citizenship see PARAS 406, 421–444.

British overseas territories citizens were formerly known as British dependent territories citizens: see PARAS 406, 445. Since 21 May 2002, most persons who were British overseas territories citizens immediately before that date have enjoyed British citizenship: see the British Overseas Territories Act 2002 s 3; and PARA 423.

4   As to applications see PARA 484. As to when, for the purposes of the British Nationality Act 1981, a person attains any particular age, see PARA 426 note 8.

5   British Nationality Act 1981 s 36, Sch 2 para 3(1), (2)(b) (Sch 2 para 3 amended by virtue of the British Overseas Territories Act 2002 s 1(1)(b); and by the Nationality, Immigration and Asylum Act 2002 ss 8, 161, Sch 9). As to references to days of absence from the United Kingdom or the British overseas territories see PARA 426 note 9. If he spent more days or part days in the United Kingdom than in the British overseas territories he will be registered as a British citizen: see the British Nationality Act 1981 Sch 2 para 3(2)(a); and PARA 436.

If in the special circumstances of any particular case the Secretary of State thinks fit, he may treat the person as fulfilling the requirements of head (3) in the text although the number of days on which he was absent from both the United Kingdom and the British overseas territories exceeds the number mentioned: see Sch 2 para 6 (amended by virtue of the British Overseas Territories Act 2002 s 1(1)(b)). As to the Secretary of State see PARA 402. As to the exercise of discretion see the British Nationality Act 1981 s 44; and PARA 402.

6   See PARA 424 notes 6–7.

7   See the British Nationality Act 1981 Sch 2 para 4 (amended by virtue of the British Overseas Territories Act 2002 ss 1(1)(b), 2(2)(b)). As to references to days of absence from the United Kingdom or the British overseas territories see PARA 426 note 9. As to the registration of stateless persons see also PARAS 436, 461, 473. If in the special circumstances of any particular case the Secretary of State thinks fit, he may treat the person as fulfilling the requirements of head (c) in the text although the number of days on which he was absent from both the United Kingdom and the British overseas territories exceeds the number mentioned: see Sch 2 para 6 (as amended: see note 5).

8   See the British Nationality Act 1981 Sch 2 para 5.

452.   Acquisition by registration: special cases. A number of statutory provisions extended certain entitlements to registration under the previous nationality law for limited periods to enable those satisfying the conditions to register as British overseas territories citizens[1], but the periods during which applications for such registration could be made have now expired[2].

Those provisions dealt with: (1) registration of certain Commonwealth or Irish citizens who had been ordinarily resident in a British overseas territory for a minimum of five years (and in some cases Crown service, or other relevant service, was treated as ordinary residence in the United Kingdom)[3]; (2) registration of a woman on the basis of marriage[4]; (3) registration of a person born in a foreign country[5] before 1 January 1988 whose father was (or but for his death would have been) a British overseas territories citizen by descent[6].

1   British overseas territories citizens and citizenship were formerly known as British dependent territories citizens and citizenship: see PARAS 406, 445. Since 21 May 2002, most persons who were British overseas territories citizens immediately before that date have additionally enjoyed British citizenship: see the British Overseas Territories Act 2002 s 3; and PARA 423.

2   See the British Nationality Act 1981 ss 19–21 (now repealed). For analogous provisions relating to British citizenship see PARA 437. Broadly, those who satisfied the conditions in a manner connected with the United Kingdom were able to register as British citizens, while those who satisfied the conditions in a manner connected with a British overseas territory were able to register as British overseas territories citizens. As to British citizens and citizenship see PARAS 406, 421–444. As to the meaning of 'United Kingdom' see PARA 403 note 1. As to British overseas territories (formerly known as dependent territories) see PARA 445 note 1.

3   See the British Nationality Act 1981 s 19 (now repealed).

4   See the British Nationality Act 1981 s 20 (now repealed). Some persons so registered became British overseas territories citizens by descent: see s 25(1)(f); and PARA 456.

5   As to the meaning of 'foreign country' see PARA 404 note 22.

6   See the British Nationality Act 1981 s 21 (now repealed). A person so registered became a British overseas territories citizen by descent: see s 25(1)(a); and PARA 456.

453. Acquisition by naturalisation: general. British overseas territories citizenship[1] is the only form of British nationality, apart from British citizenship[2], which can be acquired by naturalisation. In order to be eligible for naturalisation as a British overseas territories citizen, a person must fulfil prescribed requirements[3] but, even when these requirements are fulfilled, the grant of a certificate of naturalisation is at the discretion of the Secretary of State[4]. The requirements for naturalisation are different in some respects for an applicant who is married to, or is the civil partner of, a British overseas territories citizen[5], or who is serving outside the relevant territory[6] in Crown service under the government of that territory or married to a British overseas territories citizen in such service[7]. The standard requirements of general application are that:

(1) the applicant is of full age and capacity[8], and is of good character[9];

(2) the applicant was in the relevant territory at the beginning of the period of five years ending with the date of the application[10];

(3) the applicant was not absent from the relevant territory for more than 450 days during that five year period[11];

(4) the applicant was not absent from the relevant territory for more than 90 days during the 12 months preceding the application[12];

(5) the applicant was not at any time during the 12 months preceding the application subject under the immigration laws[13] to any restriction on the period for which he might remain in the relevant territory[14];

(6) the applicant was not, at any time in the period of five years preceding the application, in the relevant territory in breach of the immigration laws[15];

(7) the applicant has a sufficient knowledge of the English language or any other language recognised for official purposes in the relevant territory[16];

(8) the applicant intends, if granted naturalisation, either to make his home or principal home in the relevant territory, or to enter or continue in Crown service under the government of that territory, or service under an international organisation of which that territory or its government is a member, or service in the employment of a company or association established in that territory[17].

For the purposes of the residence requirements, a person is to be treated as having been absent from any particular British overseas territory during any of the following periods, even though he is physically present there[18]:

(a) any period when he was entitled, or was part of the family and household of a person entitled, to exemption from immigration control by reason of diplomatic immunity[19] or as a member of the forces[20];

(b) any period when he was: (i) detained in pursuance of a sentence passed on him by a court in that territory or elsewhere for any offence[21], or under a direction[22] corresponding to a hospital order[23] and made in connection with his conviction of an offence[24], or under any power of detention conferred by the immigration laws of that territory[25]; or (ii) unlawfully at large or absent without leave from any such detention[26] and in consequence liable to be arrested or taken into custody[27].

1 British overseas territories citizens and citizenship were formerly known as British dependent territories citizens and citizenship: see PARAS 406, 445. Since 21 May 2002, most persons who were British overseas territories citizens immediately before that date have additionally enjoyed British citizenship: see the British Overseas Territories Act 2002 s 3; and PARA 423.

2 As to the acquisition of British citizenship by naturalisation see PARAS 438–442. Since 1983 the provisions for naturalisation as a British overseas territories citizen have mirrored those for

naturalisation as a British citizen, but the Borders, Citizenship and Immigration Act 2009 departs from this, as it applies to British citizenship only. As to the amendments made by the Borders, Citizenship and Immigration Act 2009 see PARAS 438–442, in particular PARAS 439, 441.

3 See the British Nationality Act 1981 s 18, Sch 1; and the text and notes 8–27. It seems that the Secretary of State is entitled on grounds of public policy to decline to accept that a condition is satisfied where this has been achieved by means of criminal activity: *R v Secretary of State for the Home Department, ex p Puttick* [1981] QB 767, [1981] 1 All ER 776, DC (married status on which entitlement depended was valid but obtained by perjury and forgery). As to the Secretary of State see PARA 402. As to applications see PARA 484.

4 See the British Nationality Act 1981 s 18 (amended by virtue of the British Overseas Territories Act 2002 ss 1(1)(b), 2(2)(b)). As to the exercise of discretion see the British Nationality Act 1981 s 44(1); and PARA 402. See also PARA 438 note 9.

5 See PARA 454.

6 Every application under the British Nationality Act 1981 s 18 must specify the British overseas territory which is to be treated as the relevant territory for the purposes of that application: see s 18(3) (amended by virtue of the British Overseas Territories Act 2002 s 1(1)(b)). Although British overseas territories citizenship is a common status for all British overseas territories, all the conditions for naturalisation must be satisfied in respect of the same territory; one cannot, for example, satisfy the residence condition by residence in different territories, or satisfy the past residence condition in one territory while intending to make one's permanent home in a different territory. As to British overseas territories (formerly known as dependent territories) see PARA 445 note 1.

7 See PARA 455.

8 British Nationality Act 1981 s 18(1). As to the meanings of 'full age' and 'full capacity', and as to the discretion to waive the requirement in respect of a specified applicant, see PARA 438 note 12.

9 See the British Nationality Act 1981 s 18(1), Sch 1 para 5(1)(b) (s 18(1), Sch 1 para 5(1) amended by virtue of the British Overseas Territories Act 2002 s 2(2)(b)).

10 British Nationality Act 1981 Sch 1 para 5(1)(a), (2)(a) (Sch 1 para 5(1) as amended: see note 9). As to when a person is deemed to be absent see the text and notes 18–27. If in the special circumstances of any particular case the Secretary of State thinks fit, he may treat the applicant as having been in the relevant territory for the whole or any part of any period during which he would otherwise be deemed to have been absent: Sch 1 para 6(b).

11 British Nationality Act 1981 Sch 1 para 5(1)(a), (2)(a) (Sch 1 para 5(1) as amended: see note 9). As to references to days of absence from a British overseas territory see PARA 426 note 9. As to when a person is deemed to be absent see the text and notes 18–27. If in the special circumstances of any particular case the Secretary of State thinks fit, he may treat the applicant: (1) as fulfilling the requirement specified in the British Nationality Act 1981 Sch 1 para 5(2)(a), although the number of days on which he was absent from the relevant territory exceeds the number mentioned; (2) as having been in the relevant territory for the whole or any part of any period during which he would otherwise be deemed to have been absent: Sch 1 para 6(a), (b).

12 British Nationality Act 1981 Sch 1 para 5(1)(a), (2)(b) (Sch 1 para 5(1) as amended: see note 9). As to references to days of absence from a British overseas territory see PARA 426 note 9. As to when a person is deemed to be absent see the text and notes 18–27. If in the special circumstances of any particular case the Secretary of State thinks fit, he may treat the applicant: (1) as fulfilling the requirement specified in Sch 1 para 5(2)(b), although the number of days on which he was absent from the relevant territory exceeds the number mentioned; (2) as having been in the relevant territory for the whole or any part of any period during which he would otherwise be deemed to have been absent: Sch 1 para 6(a), (b).

13 As to the meaning of 'immigration laws' see PARA 424 note 9.

14 British Nationality Act 1981 Sch 1 para 5(1)(a), (2)(c) (Sch 1 para 5(1) as amended: see note 9). If in the special circumstances of any particular case the Secretary of State thinks fit, he may disregard any such restriction as is mentioned in Sch 1 para 5(2)(c), not being a restriction to which the applicant was subject on the date of the application: Sch 1 para 6(c).

15 British Nationality Act 1981 Sch 1 para 5(1)(a), (2)(d) (Sch 1 para 5(1) as amended: see note 9). If in the special circumstances of any particular case the Secretary of State thinks fit, he may treat the applicant as fulfilling the requirement specified in Sch 1 para 5(2)(d) although he was in the relevant territory in breach of the immigration laws during the period mentioned: Sch 1 para 6(d). As to being in the relevant territory in breach of the immigration laws see PARA 424 note 9.

16 British Nationality Act 1981 Sch 1 para 5(1)(c) (Sch 1 para 5(1) as amended: see note 9). 'Relevant territory' has the meaning given by s 18(3) (see note 6): Sch 1 para 10. If in the special

circumstances of any particular case the Secretary of State thinks fit, he may waive the need to fulfil the requirement specified in Sch 1 para 5(1)(c) if he considers that because of the applicant's age or physical or mental condition it would be unreasonable to expect him to fulfil it: Sch 1 para 6(e).

17　British Nationality Act 1981 Sch 1 para 5(1)(d) (Sch 1 para 5(1) as amended: see note 9).

18　British Nationality Act 1981 Sch 1 para 9(2) (amended by virtue of the British Overseas Territories Act 2002 s 1(1)(b)). This is subject to the British Nationality Act 1981 Sch 1 para 6(b): see notes 10–12.

19　The exemption referred to in the text is an exemption arising under the Immigration Act 1971 s 8(3): see BRITISH NATIONALITY, IMMIGRATION AND ASYLUM vol 4(2) (2002 Reissue) PARA 88.

20　See the British Nationality Act 1981 Sch 1 para 9(2)(a). The exemption referred to in the text is an exemption arising under the Immigration Act 1971 s 8(4): see BRITISH NATIONALITY, IMMIGRATION AND ASYLUM vol 4(2) (2002 Reissue) PARA 89.

21　See the British Nationality Act 1981 Sch 1 para 9(2)(b)(i).

22　Ie a direction (however described) made under any law for purposes similar to the Mental Health Act 1983 Pt III (ss 35–55) (see MENTAL HEALTH vol 30(2) (Reissue) PARA 486 et seq) which was for the time being in force in the relevant territory.

23　Ie a hospital order made under the Mental Health Act 1983 Pt III: see MENTAL HEALTH vol 30(2) (Reissue) PARA 486 et seq.

24　See the British Nationality Act 1981 Sch 1 para 9(2)(b)(ii) (Sch 1 para 9(2) amended by the Mental Health Act 1983 s 148, Sch 4 para 60).

25　See the British Nationality Act 1981 Sch 1 para 9(2)(b)(iii).

26　Ie when he was liable to detention as mentioned in the British Nationality Act 1981 Sch 1 para 9(2)(b)(i) or Sch 1 para 9(2)(b)(ii) (see the text and notes 21–24) or when his actual detention under any such power as is mentioned in Sch 1 para 9(2)(b)(iii) (see the text and note 25) was required or specifically authorised.

27　See the British Nationality Act 1981 Sch 1 para 9(2)(c), (d).

454. Acquisition by naturalisation: spouses and civil partners of British overseas territories citizens. An applicant who, on the date of the application[1], is married to a British overseas territories citizen[2] or is the civil partner of such a citizen, is eligible for naturalisation as a British overseas territories citizen, and may be granted a certificate of naturalisation by the Secretary of State[3] if the following requirements[4] are fulfilled[5]:

(1)　the applicant is of full age and capacity[6], and is of good character[7];

(2)　the applicant has a sufficient knowledge of the English language or any other language recognised for official purposes in the relevant territory[8];

(3)　the applicant was in the relevant territory[9] at the beginning of the period of three years ending with the date of the application[10];

(4)　the applicant was not absent from the relevant territory for more than 270 days during that three year period[11];

(5)　the applicant was not absent from the relevant territory for more than 90 days in the 12 months preceding the application[12];

(6)　on the date of the application the applicant was not subject under the immigration laws[13] to any restriction on the period for which he might remain in the relevant territory[14];

(7)　the applicant was not, at any time in the period of three years preceding the application, in the relevant territory in breach of the immigration laws[15].

1　As to applications see PARA 484.

2　British overseas territories citizens were formerly known as British dependent territories citizens: see PARAS 406, 445. Since 21 May 2002, most persons who were British overseas territories citizens immediately before that date have additionally enjoyed British citizenship: see the British Overseas Territories Act 2002 s 3; and PARA 423.

As to applicants married to or in civil partnership with British overseas territories citizens who are in Crown service outside the relevant British overseas territory see PARA 455. As to British overseas territories (formerly known as dependent territories) see PARA 445 note 1. As to the relevant territory see PARA 453 note 6.

3   As to the Secretary of State see PARA 402. As to the exercise of discretion see the British Nationality Act 1981 s 44(1); and PARA 402.

4   Ie the requirements of the British Nationality Act 1981 Sch 1 paras 7, 8.

5   British Nationality Act 1981 s 18(2) (amended by virtue of the British Overseas Territories Act 2002 s 2(2)(b); and by the Civil Partnership Act 2004 s 261(1), Sch 27 para 76).

6   British Nationality Act 1981 s 18(2). As to the meanings of 'full age' and 'full capacity', and as to the discretion to waive the requirement in respect of a specified applicant, see PARA 438 note 12.

7   British Nationality Act 1981 Sch 1 para 7(e) (amended by the Nationality, Immigration and Asylum Act 2002 s 2(2)(a)), applying the British Nationality Act 1981 Sch 1 para 5(1)(b).

8   British Nationality Act 1981 Sch 1 para 7(e) (as amended: see note 7), applying the British Nationality Act 1981 Sch 1 para 5(1)(c). If in the special circumstances of any particular case the Secretary of State thinks fit, he may waive the need to fulfil the requirement specified in Sch 1 para 5(1)(c) if he considers that because of the applicant's age or physical or mental condition it would be unreasonable to expect him to fulfil it: Sch 1 paras 6(e), 8.

9   See PARA 453 note 6.

10 British Nationality Act 1981 Sch 1 para 7(a). As to when a person is deemed to be absent from the relevant territory see PARA 453. If in the special circumstances of any particular case the Secretary of State thinks fit, he may treat the applicant as having been in the relevant territory for the whole or any part of any period during which he would otherwise be deemed to have been absent: Sch 1 paras 6(b), 8(a), (b). The Secretary of State may waive the need to fulfil all or any of the requirements specified in Sch 1 para 7(a) if on the date of the application the person to whom the applicant is married, or of whom the applicant is the civil partner, is serving in service to which s 16(1)(b) (see PARA 448 head (ii)) applies, that person's recruitment for that service having taken place in a British overseas territory: see Sch 1 paras 6(f), 8(d) (amended by the British Overseas Territories Act 2002 s 1(1)(b); and the Civil Partnership Act 2004 Sch 27 para 78); and PARA 455.

11 British Nationality Act 1981 Sch 1 para 7(a). As to references to days of absence from a British overseas territory see PARA 426 note 9. As to when a person is deemed to be absent from the relevant territory see PARA 453. If in the special circumstances of any particular case the Secretary of State thinks fit, he may treat the applicant: (1) as fulfilling the requirement specified in the British Nationality Act 1981 Sch 1 para 7(a), although the number of days on which he was absent from the relevant territory exceeds the number mentioned; (2) as having been in the relevant territory for the whole or any part of any period during which he would otherwise be deemed to have been absent: Sch 1 paras 6(a), (b), 8(b). The Secretary of State may waive the need to fulfil all or any of the requirements specified in Sch 1 para 7(a) if on the date of the application the person to whom the applicant is married, or of whom the applicant is the civil partner, is serving in service to which s 16(1)(b) (see PARA 448 head (ii)) applies, that person's recruitment for that service having taken place in a British overseas territory: see Sch 1 paras 6(f), 8(d) (as amended: see note 10); and PARA 455.

12 British Nationality Act 1981 Sch 1 para 7(b). As to references to days of absence from a British overseas territory see PARA 426 note 9. As to when a person is deemed to be absent from the relevant territory see PARA 453. If in the special circumstances of any particular case the Secretary of State thinks fit, he may treat the applicant: (1) as fulfilling the requirement specified in Sch 1 para 7(b), although the number of days on which he was absent from the relevant territory exceeds the number mentioned; (2) as having been in the relevant territory for the whole or any part of any period during which he would otherwise be deemed to have been absent: Sch 1 paras 6(a), (b), 8(b). The Secretary of State may waive the need to fulfil all or any of the requirements specified in Sch 1 para 7(b) if on the date of the application the person to whom the applicant is married, or of whom the applicant is the civil partner, is serving in service to which s 16(1)(b) (see PARA 448 head (ii)) applies, that person's recruitment for that service having taken place in a British overseas territory: see Sch 1 paras 6(f), 8(d) (as amended: see note 10); and PARA 455.

13 As to the meaning of 'immigration laws' see PARA 424 note 9.

14 British Nationality Act 1981 Sch 1 para 7(c). See further PARA 442 note 20.

15 British Nationality Act 1981 Sch 1 para 7(d). If in the special circumstances of any particular case the Secretary of State thinks fit, he may treat the applicant as fulfilling the requirement specified in Sch 1 para 7(d) although he was in the relevant territory in breach of the immigration laws during the period mentioned: Sch 1 paras 6(d), 8(b).

455. Acquisition by naturalisation: Crown service overseas. An applicant who, on the date of the application[1], is serving outside the territory specified in the application as the relevant British overseas territory[2] in Crown service under the government of that territory[3] may be granted a certificate of naturalisation by the Secretary of State[4] if the following requirements are fulfilled[5]:

(1) the applicant is of full age and capacity[6], and is of good character[7];

(2) the applicant has a sufficient knowledge of the English language or any other language recognised for official purposes in the relevant territory[8];

(3) the applicant intends, if granted naturalisation, to make his home or principal home in the relevant territory, or to continue in Crown service under the government of that territory, or to enter or continue in service under an international organisation of which that territory or its government is a member, or to enter or continue in service in the employment of a company or association established in that territory[9].

An applicant whose spouse or civil partner is a British overseas territories citizen[10] serving outside the British overseas territories, as a result of recruitment in a British overseas territory, in Crown service under the government of a British overseas territory, or in service designated as closely associated with government activities[11], must satisfy the naturalisation conditions for spouses or civil partners of British overseas territories citizens[12], save that (in addition to the discretion to waive or relax certain requirements in all such cases) the Secretary of State has a discretion to waive the need to fulfil some of the residence requirements[13].

1 As to applications see PARA 484.
2 As to British overseas territories (formerly known as dependent territories) see PARA 445 note 1. As to the relevant territory see PARA 453 note 6.
3 See the British Nationality Act 1981 s 18(1), Sch 1 para 5(1)(a), (3) (s 18(1), Sch 1 para 5(1) amended by virtue of the British Overseas Territories Act 2002 s 2(2)(b)).
4 As to the Secretary of State see PARA 402. As to the exercise of discretion see the British Nationality Act 1981 s 44(1); and PARA 402.
5 See the British Nationality Act 1981 s 18(1), Sch 1 para 5 (as amended: see note 3).
6 British Nationality Act 1981 s 18(1). As to the meanings of 'full age' and 'full capacity', and as to the discretion to waive the requirement in respect of a specified applicant, see PARA 438 note 12.
7 See the British Nationality Act 1981 Sch 1 para 5(1)(b).
8 British Nationality Act 1981 Sch 1 para 5(1)(c). If in the special circumstances of any particular case the Secretary of State thinks fit, he may waive the need to fulfil the requirement specified in Sch 1 para 5(1)(c) if he considers that because of the applicant's age or physical or mental condition it would be unreasonable to expect him to fulfil it: Sch 1 para 6(e).
9 British Nationality Act 1981 Sch 1 para 5(1)(d) (as amended: see note 3).
10 British overseas territories citizens were formerly known as British dependent territories citizens: see PARAS 406, 445. Since 21 May 2002, most persons who were British overseas territories citizens immediately before that date have additionally enjoyed British citizenship: see the British Overseas Territories Act 2002 s 3; and PARA 423.
11 Ie the spouse or civil partner must be serving in service to which the British Nationality Act 1981 s 16(1)(b) applies: see PARA 448 head (ii).
12 See PARA 454.
13 See the British Nationality Act 1981 s 18(2), Sch 1 paras 6(f), 7, 8(d) (s 18(2) amended by virtue of the British Overseas Territories Act 2002 s 2(2)(b); and by the Civil Partnership Act 2004 s 261(1), Sch 27 para 76; British Nationality Act 1981 Sch 1 para 7 amended by virtue of the British Overseas Territories Act 2002 s 2(2)(b); and by the Nationality, Immigration and Asylum Act 2002 s 2(2)(a); and the British Nationality Act 1981 Sch 1 para 8 amended by virtue of the British Overseas Territories Act 2002 s 1(1)(b); and by the Nationality, Immigration and Asylum Act 2002 ss 2(2)(b), 161, Sch 9; and the Civil Partnership Act 2004 Sch 27 para 78). The residence requirements which may be waived are all or any of the requirements set out in the British Nationality Act 1981 Sch 1 para 7(a), (b): see PARA 454 heads (3)–(5). See further PARA 442 note 20.

456. Statutory meaning of 'British overseas territories citizenship by descent'.
As with British citizenship[1], a person who is a British overseas territories citizen[2] by descent does not as a general rule automatically pass that citizenship to his or her children[3]; and British overseas territories citizenship 'by descent' is a term of art, with an exhaustive statutory definition[4]. By statute, the following British overseas territories citizens are British overseas territories citizens by descent:

(1) a person born outside the British overseas territories[5] on or after 1 January 1983[6] who is a British overseas territories citizen by virtue only of his father or mother being at the time of the birth[7] a British overseas territories citizen otherwise than by descent[8];

(2) a person born outside the British overseas territories on or after 1 January 1983 who is registered as a British overseas territories citizen[9], being the child of a British overseas territories citizen by descent one of whose parents was a British overseas territories citizen otherwise than by descent[10];

(3) a person born outside the British overseas territories on or after 1 January 1983 who was registered as a British overseas territories citizen under the transitional provisions[11] for children born between 1 January 1983 and 31 December 1987 to certain male former citizens of the United Kingdom and colonies by descent[12];

(4) a person born outside the British overseas territories before 1 January 1983 who was a citizen of the United Kingdom and colonies by descent[13], and became a British overseas territories citizen on 1 January 1983[14]; but such a person is a British overseas territories citizen otherwise than by descent if his father was at the time of the birth serving outside the British overseas territories in a specified type of public service for which he was recruited in a British overseas territory[15];

(5) a person born outside the British overseas territories before 1 January 1983 who became a British overseas territories citizen on 1 January 1983[16] and immediately before that date was deemed under any provision of the British Nationality Acts 1948 to 1965[17] to be a citizen of the United Kingdom and colonies by descent only, or would have been so deemed if male[18]; but such a person is a British overseas territories citizen otherwise than by descent if his father was at the time of the birth serving outside the British overseas territories in a specified type of public service for which he was recruited in a British overseas territory[19];

(6) a person registered as a British overseas territories citizen under the provision for discretionary registration of minors[20] whose father or mother was at the time of his birth a British overseas territories citizen or (if the birth was before 1 January 1983) a citizen of the United Kingdom and colonies who became a British overseas territories citizen on 1 January 1983[21] or would have done so but for his or her death[22];

(7) a person born outside the British overseas territories before 1 January 1983 who became a British overseas territories citizen on that date[23] by virtue of being a former citizen of the United Kingdom and colonies one of whose parents was such a citizen at the time of the birth, that parent having that citizenship by birth, naturalisation or registration in a British overseas territory or himself born to a parent who at the time of the birth so had that citizenship[24]; but such a person is a British overseas

territories citizen otherwise than by descent if his father was at the time of the birth serving outside the British overseas territories in a specified type of public service for which he was recruited in a British overseas territory[25];

(8)　a woman who became a British overseas territories citizen on 1 January 1983[26] by virtue of marriage to a man who became a British overseas territories citizen by descent on 1 January 1983 under head (4), head (5) or head (7) above[27], or would have done so but for his death[28]; but she is a British overseas territories citizen otherwise than by descent if her father was at the time of her birth serving outside the British overseas territories in a specified type of public service for which he was recruited in a British overseas territory[29];

(9)　a woman born outside the British overseas territories before 1 January 1983 who became a British overseas territories citizen by registration[30] by virtue of marriage to a man who became a British overseas territories citizen by descent on 1 January 1983[31], or would have done so but for his death or renunciation of citizenship of the United Kingdom and colonies[32]; but she is a British overseas territories citizen otherwise than by descent if her father was at the time of her birth serving outside the British overseas territories in a specified type of public service for which he was recruited in a British overseas territory[33];

(10)　a person registered as a British overseas territories citizen[34] following previous renunciation of citizenship of the United Kingdom and colonies[35] who would, had he not renounced it, have become a British overseas territories citizen by descent on 1 January 1983[36] under head (4), head (5), head (7) or head (8) above[37];

(11)　a person who, having formerly been a British overseas territories citizen by descent, renounced and subsequently resumed his British overseas territories citizenship[38] by registration[39];

(12)　a person born in the United Kingdom[40] after 1 January 1983 who is a British overseas territories citizen by virtue of provisions contained in the British Nationality Act 1981[41] for reducing statelessness[42];

(13)　a person born on or after 26 April 1969 and before 1 January 1983 whose mother was at the time a citizen of the United Kingdom and colonies by virtue of her birth in the British Indian Ocean Territory and who, not having previously been a British overseas territories citizen, became such a citizen[43] with effect from 21 May 2002 by virtue of the British Overseas Territories Act 2002[44].

1　As to British citizens and citizenship see PARAS 406, 421–444. As to British citizenship by descent see PARA 425.

2　British overseas territories citizens and citizenship were formerly known as British dependent territories citizens and citizenship: see PARAS 406, 445. Since 21 May 2002, most persons who were British overseas territories citizens immediately before that date have additionally enjoyed British citizenship: see the British Overseas Territories Act 2002 s 3; and PARA 423.

3　Ie unless the parent is in government service abroad: see the British Nationality Act 1981 s 16(1)–(3); and PARA 448.

4　See the text and notes 5–44. See also PARA 425 note 2.

5　As to British overseas territories (formerly known as dependent territories) see PARA 445 note 1.

6　Ie the date of commencement of the British Nationality Act 1981: see PARA 403 note 1.

7　See PARA 424 notes 6–7.

8　See the British Nationality Act 1981 s 25(1)(a) (s 25(1) amended by virtue of the British Overseas Territories Act 2002 ss 1(1)(b), 2(2)(b)). See also the British Nationality Act 1981 s 16(1)(a); and PARA 448. A child born outside the British overseas territories to a British overseas territories citizen in government service outside the British overseas territories is a

British overseas territories citizen otherwise than by descent, even if the parent is a citizen by descent: see ss 16(1)(b), 25(1)(a) (as so amended); and PARA 448 note 16.

9 Ie under the British Nationality Act 1981 s 17(2): see PARA 450.

10 See the British Nationality Act 1981 s 25(1)(a) (as amended: see note 8).

11 Ie under the British Nationality Act 1981 s 21: see PARA 452.

12 See the British Nationality Act 1981 s 25(1)(a) (as amended: see note 8). As to citizenship of the United Kingdom and colonies see PARAS 414–419.

13 Ie by virtue of the British Nationality Act 1948 s 5 (now repealed), which conferred citizenship on a person whose father (but not mother) was a citizen otherwise than by descent: see PARA 417.

14 See the British Nationality Act 1981 s 25(1)(b)(i) (as amended: see note 8). As to those who became British overseas territories citizens on 1 January 1983 see PARA 446.

15 See the British Nationality Act 1981 s 25(2) (amended by virtue of the British Overseas Territories Act 2002 ss 1(1)(b), 2(2)(b)). The specified types of public service are: (1) Crown service under the government of a British overseas territory; (2) service designated under the British Nationality Act 1981 s 16 (see PARA 448) as being closely associated with the activities outside the British overseas territories of the government of any British overseas territory, for which he was recruited in a British overseas territory: see s 25(2) (as so amended), s 25(3) (amended by virtue of the British Overseas Territories Act 2002 s 1(1)(b)). This excepting provision is necessary because under the British Nationality Act 1948 s 5 (now repealed) (see note 13; and PARA 417) children born outside the United Kingdom and colonies before 1 January 1983 of citizens by descent in Crown service were citizens by descent, whereas under the British Nationality Act 1981 such children born after 1 January 1983 are not citizens by descent: see ss 16(1), 25(1)(a); note 8; and PARA 448 note 16.

16 See note 14; and PARA 446.

17 As to the British Nationality Acts 1948 to 1965 see PARA 403 note 5.

18 See the British Nationality Act 1981 s 25(1)(b)(ii) (as amended: see note 8). Prior to the British Nationality Act 1981 women could not transmit citizenship to their children, so there was no need to deem their citizenship to be by descent only, since the purpose of such deeming was to prevent transmission. As to deemed descent see eg the British Nationality Act 1948 ss 12(8), 13, Sch 3 para 3 (all now repealed); the British Nationality (No 2) Act 1964 s 1(4) (now repealed); and PARA 417 note 6.

19 See note 15.

20 Ie the British Nationality Act 1981 s 17(1): see PARA 450.

21 See note 14; and PARA 446.

22 See the British Nationality Act 1981 s 25(1)(c) (as amended: see note 8).

23 Ie by virtue of the British Nationality Act 1981 s 23(1)(b): see PARA 446 head (2). See also PARA 446 note 9.

24 British Nationality Act 1981 s 25(1)(d) (as amended: see note 8).

25 See note 15.

26 Ie under the British Nationality Act 1981 s 23(1)(c): see PARA 446.

27 Ie under the British Nationality Act 1981 s 25(1)(b) or s 25(1)(d).

28 See British Nationality Act 1981 s 25(1)(e) (as amended: see note 8).

29 See note 15.

30 Ie under the British Nationality Act 1981 s 20: see PARA 452.

31 Ie under the British Nationality Act 1981 s 25. See also note 14; and PARA 446.

32 See the British Nationality Act 1981 s 25(1)(f) (as amended: see note 8). As to renunciation of citizenship of the United Kingdom and colonies see PARA 419.

33 See note 15.

34 Ie under the British Nationality Act 1981 s 22, which provides for registration following renunciation of previous citizenship of certain persons with an appropriate qualifying connection with a British overseas territory: see PARA 457.

35 See PARA 419.

36 See note 31.

37 See the British Nationality Act 1981 s 25(1)(g) (as amended: see note 8). The text refers to becoming a British overseas territories citizen by descent under s 25(1)(b), s 25(1)(d) or s 25(1)(e). The provisions of s 25(1)(g) ensure that the person who renounces and resumes citizenship will not be in a better position than if he had never renounced it.

38 Ie under the British Nationality Act 1981 s 13 (as applied by s 24): see PARA 457.

39 See the British Nationality Act 1981 s 25(1)(h) (as amended: see note 8). The provisions of s 25(1)(h) ensure that the person who renounces and resumes citizenship will not be in a better position than if he had never renounced it.

40 As to the meaning of 'United Kingdom' see PARA 403 note 1.

41 Ie the British Nationality Act 1981 Sch 2 para 1: see PARA 448. As to other provisions for reducing statelessness see PARA 451.

42 See the British Nationality Act 1981 s 25(1)(i) (as amended: see note 8).

43 Ie by virtue of the British Overseas Territories Act 2002 s 6(3): see PARA 447.

44 See the British Overseas Territories Act 2002 s 6(4); and PARA 447.

457. Renunciation and resumption. A British overseas territories citizen[1] of full age and capacity[2] may renounce his citizenship by declaration, upon registration of which he ceases to be a British overseas territories citizen[3]. However, the person must have or be about to acquire some other citizenship or nationality[4]. The Secretary of State[5] must be satisfied on this point; and even if the declaration is registered, should the renouncer not acquire some such other citizenship within six months, the registration will be of no effect and he will remain a British overseas territories citizen[6].

A person who has renounced British overseas territories citizenship[7] is entitled, once only, to be registered as a British overseas territories citizen if he is of full capacity, and had to renounce his British overseas territories citizenship in order to retain or acquire some other citizenship or nationality[8]. In addition, the Secretary of State has a discretion[9] to register any person of full capacity who renounced British overseas territories citizenship, whatever the reason for the renunciation[10].

A person who under previous nationality law renounced citizenship of the United Kingdom and colonies[11], and who wishes to resume British nationality, may in certain circumstances do so by registration as a British overseas territories citizen. A person who renounced citizenship of the United Kingdom and colonies is entitled, once only, to be registered as a British overseas territories citizen if on 31 December 1982[12] he would have been entitled to registration as a citizen of the United Kingdom and colonies under the British Nationality Act 1964[13] on the basis of a qualifying connection with a British overseas territory[14] or of marriage to a person with such a qualifying connection[15]. In addition, the Secretary of State has a discretion to register as a British overseas territories citizen any person who renounced citizenship of the United Kingdom and colonies, provided that he has a qualifying connection with a British overseas territory or that he has been married to, or has been the civil partner of, a person who has or would if living have such a connection[16]. A person is to be taken to have the appropriate qualifying connection with a British overseas territory if he, his father or his father's father: (1) was born in that territory; or (2) is or was a person naturalised in that territory[17]; or (3) was registered as a citizen of the United Kingdom and colonies in that territory; or (4) became a British subject by reason of the annexation of any territory included in that territory[18].

1 The provisions of the British Nationality Act 1981 s 12 (see PARA 443) are applied to British overseas territories citizens and citizenship by s 24 (amended by virtue of the British Overseas Territories Act 2002 s 2(2)(a), (b)). British overseas territories citizens were formerly known as British dependent territories citizens: see PARAS 406, 445. Since 21 May 2002, most persons who were British overseas territories citizens immediately before that date have additionally enjoyed British citizenship: see the British Overseas Territories Act 2002 s 3; and PARA 423.

2 As to the meanings of 'full age' and 'full capacity', and as to the discretion to waive the requirement in respect of a specified applicant, see PARA 438 note 12. For the purpose of renunciation only, a person who has been married, or has formed a civil partnership, is deemed to be of full age: British Nationality Act 1981 s 12(5) (amended by the Civil Partnership Act 2004 s 261(1), Sch 27 para 74); applied by the British Nationality Act 1981 s 24 (as amended: see note 1).

3   See the British Nationality Act 1981 s 12(1), (2); applied by s 24 (as amended: see note 1). As to declarations of renunciation see the British Nationality (British Overseas Territories) Regulations 2007, SI 2007/3139, regs 8, 9, Sch 4. As to the power to make regulations see PARA 404.

4   See the British Nationality Act 1981 s 12(3); applied by s 24 (as amended: see note 1).

5   As to the Secretary of State see PARA 402.

6   See the British Nationality Act 1981 s 12(3); applied by s 24 (as amended: see note 1).

7   The provisions of the British Nationality Act 1981 s 13 (see PARA 443) are applied to British overseas territories citizens and citizenship by s 24 (as amended: see note 1).

8   See the British Nationality Act 1981 s 13(1), (2); applied by s 24 (as amended: see note 1). An application for registration of an adult or young person as a British overseas territories citizen under s 24 must not be granted unless the Secretary of State is satisfied that the adult or young person is of good character: s 41A(2) (s 41A added by the Borders, Citizenship and Immigration Act 2009 s 47(1) to replace corresponding provision in Immigration, Asylum and Nationality Act 2006 s 58). As to the meaning of 'adult or young person' see PARA 426 note 4.

9   As to the exercise of discretion see the British Nationality Act 1981 s 44(1); and PARA 402.

10   See the British Nationality Act 1981 s 13(3); applied by s 24 (as amended: see note 1). See also note 8.

11   As to citizenship of the United Kingdom and colonies see PARAS 414–419. As to renunciation of citizenship of the United Kingdom and colonies see PARA 419.

12   Ie immediately before the commencement of the British Nationality Act 1981: see PARA 403 note 1.

13   Ie under the British Nationality Act 1964 s 1(1) (now repealed), which made provision for registration of persons who renounced citizenship in order to acquire or retain citizenship of a Commonwealth country.

14   As to British overseas territories (formerly known as dependent territories) see PARA 445 note 1.

15   See the British Nationality Act 1981 s 22(1), (3) (s 22(1) amended by virtue of the British Overseas Territories Act 2002 ss 1(1)(b), 2(2)(b); and by the Nationality, Immigration and Asylum Act 2002 ss 5(b), 161, Sch 9). The qualifying connection is that specified in the British Nationality Act 1981 s 22(4) (see the text and note 18), and not that specified in the British Nationality Act 1964: *R v Secretary of State for the Home Department, ex p Patel and Wahid* [1991] Imm AR 25, DC. An application for registration of an adult or young person as a British overseas territories citizen under the British Nationality Act 1981 ss 22(1), (2) must not be granted unless the Secretary of State is satisfied that the adult or young person is of good character: s 41A(2) (as added: see note 8). As to the meaning of 'adult or young person' see PARA 426 note 4.

16   See the British Nationality Act 1981 s 22(2) (amended by virtue of the British Overseas Territories Act 2002 ss 1(1)(b), 2(2)(b); and by the Nationality, Immigration and Asylum Act 2002 ss 5(b), 161, Sch 9; and the Civil Partnership Act 2004 Sch 27 para 77). See note 15.

17   As to when a person is taken to have been naturalised in a British overseas territory see PARA 446 note 6.

18   British Nationality Act 1981 s 22(4) (amended by virtue of the British Overseas Territories Act 2002 s 1(1)(b)). As to British subjects see PARAS 407, 469–474. If the person has an appropriate qualifying connection with the United Kingdom he may be entitled, or eligible, to be registered as a British citizen: see the British Nationality Act 1981 s 10; and PARA 443.

458. Deprivation and loss. A British overseas territories citizen[1] may be deprived of his citizenship status if the Secretary of State[2] is satisfied that deprivation is conducive to the public good or, if the status results from registration[3] or naturalisation[4], if the Secretary of State is satisfied that the registration or naturalisation was obtained by means of fraud, false representation or concealment of a material fact[5]. Registration or naturalisation as a British overseas territories citizen obtained by serious and causative fraud may be of no effect[6].

Provision is made for British overseas territories citizenship to be lost automatically when a British overseas territory, by virtue of a connection with which that citizenship is held, attains independence. For example, on 1 July 1997 any person who, immediately before that date, was a British overseas territories citizen by virtue (wholly or partly) of a connection with Hong Kong[7], and would not have been such a citizen but for that connection, ceased to hold British overseas territories citizenship[8]; and similar provision was made in respect of the independence of St Christopher and Nevis on 19 September 1983[9].

1　British overseas territories citizens were formerly known as British dependent territories citizens: see PARAS 406, 445. Since 21 May 2002, most persons who were British overseas territories citizens immediately before that date have additionally enjoyed British citizenship: see the British Overseas Territories Act 2002 s 3; and PARA 423.

2　As to the Secretary of State see PARA 402.

3　See PARAS 449–452, 457.

4　See PARAS 453–455.

5　See the British Nationality Act 1981 s 40(1)(b), (2)–(6) (s 40 substituted by the Nationality, Immigration and Asylum Act 2002 s 4(1); British Nationality Act 1981 s 40(2) further substituted by the Immigration, Asylum and Nationality Act 2006 s 56(1)); and PARA 444. As to appeals against deprivation see the British Nationality Act 1981 s 40A; and PARA 444.

6　Cf PARA 444.

7　As to who has a connection with Hong Kong for these purposes see the Hong Kong (British Nationality) Order 1986, SI 1986/948, art 2; and PARA 433 note 6.

8　See the Hong Kong Act 1985 s 2(2), Schedule para 2(1)(a); the Hong Kong (British Nationality) Order 1986, SI 1986/948, art 3; and PARA 462. A person who would, as a result, otherwise be stateless, became a British overseas citizen: see art 6(1); and PARA 462. As to British overseas citizens see PARAS 406, 459–463. A person may not be registered as a British overseas territories citizen under a provision of the British Nationality Act 1981 by virtue of a connection with Hong Kong: Nationality, Immigration and Asylum Act 2002 s 14.

　　The British Nationality (Hong Kong) Act 1990 made provision for the acquisition of British citizenship by some of the people of Hong Kong: see PARA 433. As to British citizens and citizenship see PARAS 406, 421–444. Section 2(2) provided for a person to lose his British overseas territories citizenship if he became a British citizen under the British Nationality (Hong Kong) Act 1990, but this provision has not been brought into force: see PARA 433 note 5.

9　See the St Christopher and Nevis Modification of Enactments Order 1983, SI 1983/882, art 2(2).

5. BRITISH OVERSEAS CITIZENSHIP

459. In general. To replace the single status of citizenship of the United Kingdom and colonies[1], the restructured nationality law which took effect on 1 January 1983[2] provided two major permanent categories of citizenship[3], each with territorial associations: (1) British citizenship[4], linked with the territory of the United Kingdom[5] itself (and Gibraltar and, retrospectively, the Falkland Islands); and (2) British overseas territories citizenship[6], linked with all the British overseas territories[7]. However, not all former citizens of the United Kingdom and colonies could be accommodated within these two categories, because some were not, or were no longer, sufficiently closely connected to any of those places. Accordingly, the structure provided a third citizenship category: British overseas citizenship[8]. Unlike the other two, this is not an independent, perpetuated national status, but is a residuary category, designed to provide a form of British national status for those who would otherwise have lost it altogether on the abolition of citizenship of the United Kingdom and colonies, and for preventing statelessness[9] among persons who, by reason of family or territorial connections, have some ground for looking to British nationality for relief from that condition. By reason of the very restricted criteria for acquisition of British overseas citizenship, in particular the fact that it cannot be acquired by birth or descent (save in limited circumstances to prevent statelessness), or by naturalisation, it will in the course of time disappear[10]. It does not carry the right of abode in the United Kingdom or elsewhere[11].

1   As to citizenship of the United Kingdom and colonies see PARAS 414–419.
2   Ie the date of commencement of the British Nationality Act 1981: see PARA 403 note 1. As to British nationality legislation see PARA 403.
3   See PARA 406.
4   As to British citizens and citizenship see PARAS 406, 421–444.
5   As to the meaning of 'United Kingdom' see PARA 403 note 1.

6   As to British overseas territories citizens and citizenship (formerly known as British dependent territories citizens and citizenship) see PARAS 406, 445–458.
7   As to British overseas territories (formerly known as dependent territories) see PARA 445 note 1.

8   A fourth category with residuary and non-permanent characteristics similar to those of British overseas citizenship was introduced in 1986, namely British national (overseas) status: see PARAS 465–467.

9   This is an international obligation under the United Nations Convention on the Reduction of Statelessness (New York, 30 August 1961; TS 158 (1975); Cmnd 6364).
10   See PARAS 460–462. Apart from discretionary registration of minors, British overseas citizenship can now only be acquired by people who would otherwise be stateless.
11   As to the right of abode see PARA 412.

460. Automatic acquisition under transitional arrangements. British overseas citizenship may be acquired automatically[1] either by operation of law or by birth.

Any person who immediately before 1 January 1983[2] was a citizen of the United Kingdom and colonies[3], and who did not on that day become either a British citizen[4] or a British overseas territories citizen[5], became on that day a British overseas citizen[6].

British overseas citizenship can be acquired at birth only by persons who would otherwise be born stateless[7]. Such a person will be a British overseas citizen by birth if he is born on or after 1 January 1983 in the United Kingdom or in a British overseas territory[8], and at the time of his birth his father or mother[9] is a British overseas citizen[10].

Provision was also made for acquisition of British overseas citizenship automatically on 1 July 1997, and thereafter by birth, to prevent statelessness resulting from the return of Hong Kong to the People's Republic of China[11].

1　Ie without application. As to applications see PARA 484.
2　Ie the date of commencement of the British Nationality Act 1981: see PARA 403 note 1.
3　As to citizenship of the United Kingdom and colonies see PARAS 414–419.
4　As to British citizens and citizenship see PARAS 406, 421–444. As to the automatic acquisition of British citizenship on 1 January 1983 see PARA 422.
5　As to British overseas territories citizens and citizenship (formerly known as British dependent territories citizens and citizenship) see PARAS 406, 445–458. As to the automatic acquisition of British overseas territories citizenship on 1 January 1983 see PARA 446.
6　British Nationality Act 1981 s 26 (amended by virtue of the British Overseas Territories Act 2002 s 2(2)(b)). A person who is apparently a British overseas citizen may turn out not to be so: e g because he in fact became a British citizen on 1 January 1983, having previously acquired the right of abode by settlement and five years' ordinary residence (see PARA 420 head (3)) (*Britto v Secretary of State for the Home Department* [1984] Imm AR 93, IAT) or because he had lost citizenship of the United Kingdom and colonies (*Bibi v Secretary of State for the Home Department* [1987] Imm AR 340, CA (where a woman living in India, born in Burma in 1927 to a father born in Mauritius in 1908, did not lose citizenship of the United Kingdom and colonies under the Burma Independence Act 1947, but did lose it under the Mauritius Independence Act 1968 because she then became a citizen of Mauritius, even though the Mauritian authorities refused to recognise her as a citizen)).
7　The provisions of the British Nationality Act 1981 are designed to comply with the United Nations Convention on the Reduction of Statelessness (New York, 30 August 1961; TS 158 (1975); Cmnd 6364).
8　As to the meaning of 'United Kingdom' see PARA 403 note 1. As to British overseas territories (formerly known as dependent territories) see PARA 445 note 1.
9　See PARA 424 notes 6–7.
10　See the British Nationality Act 1981 s 36, Sch 2 paras 1, 2 (amended by virtue of the British Overseas Territories Act 2002 ss 1(1)(b), 2(2)(b) respectively; and by the Nationality, Immigration and Asylum Act 2002 ss 9(5)(a), 161, Sch 9).
11　See PARA 462.

461. Acquisition by registration. The Secretary of State[1] may, if he thinks fit, grant any application[2] for registration of a minor[3] as a British overseas citizen[4]. Otherwise, acquisition by registration as a British overseas citizen is now possible only for stateless persons[5].

A person born outside the United Kingdom[6] and the British overseas territories[7] on or after 1 January 1983[8], who is and always has been stateless, is entitled on application to registration as a British overseas citizen if: (1) at the time of his birth his father or mother[9] was a British overseas citizen; (2) he himself was in the United Kingdom or a British overseas territory at the beginning of the period of three years ending with the date of application; and (3) during that period he has not been absent from both the United Kingdom and the British overseas territories for more than 270 days[10].

Provision is made for the registration of certain stateless persons born before 1 January 1983[11].

In addition to the provisions described above, special provision is made in relation to Hong Kong in order to prevent statelessness[12].

1　As to the Secretary of State see PARA 402.
2　As to applications see PARA 484.
3　As to the meaning of 'minor' see PARA 424 note 13.
4　British Nationality Act 1981 s 27(1). This power is exercised very sparingly as British overseas citizenship is intended to be a transitional category. As to the exercise of discretion see s 44(1); and PARA 402. An application for registration of an adult or young person as a British overseas citizen under s 27(1) must not be granted unless the Secretary of State is satisfied that the adult or young person is of good character: s 41A(3) (s 41A added by the Borders, Citizenship and

Immigration Act 2009 s 47(1) to replace corresponding provision in Immigration, Asylum and Nationality Act 2006 s 58). As to the meaning of 'adult or young person' see PARA 426 note 4.

5   The right of certain women (wives of citizens of the United Kingdom and colonies) and children (born in foreign countries between 1 January 1983 and 31 December 1987 whose fathers were citizens of the United Kingdom and colonies by descent) to be registered as citizens of the United Kingdom and colonies under previous legislation was extended as a right to registration as British overseas citizens in limited form and for limited periods which have now expired: see the British Nationality Act 1981 ss 27(2), 28 (both now repealed).

6   As to the meaning of 'United Kingdom' see PARA 403 note 1.

7   As to British overseas territories (formerly known as dependent territories) see PARA 445 note 1.

8   Ie the date of commencement of the British Nationality Act 1981: see PARA 403 note 1.

9   See PARA 424 notes 6–7.

10   See the British Nationality Act 1981 s 36, Sch 2 para 4 (amended by virtue of the British Overseas Territories Act 2002 ss 1(1)(b), 2(2)(b)). As to references to days of absence from the United Kingdom or the British overseas territories see PARA 426 note 9. As to the registration of stateless persons see also PARAS 436, 451, 473. If in the special circumstances of any particular case the Secretary of State thinks fit, he may treat the person as fulfilling the requirements of head (3) in the text although the number of days on which he was absent from both the United Kingdom and the British overseas territories exceeds the number mentioned: see the British Nationality Act 1981 Sch 2 para 6 (amended by virtue of the British Overseas Territories Act 2002 s 1(1)(b)).

11   See the British Nationality Act 1981 Sch 2 para 5.

12   See PARA 462.

462.   Hong Kong statelessness. With effect from 1 July 1997 British sovereignty over Hong Kong ceased[1]; Hong Kong ceased to be a British overseas territory[2] and the territory reverted to China[3]. On that date, all those who had British overseas territories citizenship[4] by virtue (wholly or partly) of a connection with Hong Kong[5], and who but for that connection would not have had such citizenship, lost it[6]. Before that date, some had already acquired British citizenship under the Citizenship Selection Scheme[7], and others acquired British national (overseas) status created for this eventuality[8], but neither acquisition was automatic and British national (overseas) status cannot be transmitted to children. In keeping with its residuary character, British overseas citizenship was made available to prevent remaining Hong Kong British overseas territories citizens becoming stateless on 1 July 1997, and their children and grandchildren being born stateless thereafter[9].

A person who on 1 July 1997 lost British overseas territories citizenship because he had it only by virtue of a connection with Hong Kong, and who would otherwise have been stateless as a result, became on that date a British overseas citizen[10]. A person born on or after 1 July 1997, who would otherwise have been born stateless, is a British overseas citizen if at the time of his birth his father or mother[11] is a British national (overseas) or a British overseas citizen who acquired that status on 1 July 1997 as a result of losing British overseas territories citizenship[12]. The child of such a British overseas citizen[13], born stateless outside the British overseas territories on or after 1 July 1997, is entitled to registration as a British overseas citizen if an application is made within 12 months of the birth[14], and the father or mother of the parent in question was, immediately before 1 July 1997, a British overseas territories citizen otherwise than by descent[15] by virtue of having a connection with Hong Kong, or would have been but for his or her death[16].

Certain British overseas citizens and others from Hong Kong who, but for their British status, would be stateless, have since 1 July 1997 been eligible for registration by entitlement as British citizens under the British Nationality (Hong Kong) Act 1997[17].

1   See the Hong Kong Act 1985 s 1; and COMMONWEALTH 13 (2009) PARA 727.

2   As to British overseas territories (formerly known as dependent territories) see PARA 445 note 1.

3   Now the People's Republic of China, though the People's Republic did not, of course, exist when Hong Kong came under British sovereignty in the nineteenth century.

. 4   As to British overseas territories citizens and citizenship (formerly known as British dependent territories citizens and citizenship) see PARAS 406, 445–458.

5   As to who has a connection with Hong Kong for these purposes see the Hong Kong (British Nationality) Order 1986, SI 1986/948, art 2; and PARA 433 note 6.

6   See the Hong Kong Act 1985 s 2(2), Schedule para 2(1)(a) (amended by virtue of the British Overseas Territories Act 2002 s 2(3)); and the Hong Kong (British Nationality) Order 1986, SI 1986/948, art 3 (amended by virtue of the British Overseas Territories Act 2002 s 2(3)). See also PARA 458.

7   See the British Nationality (Hong Kong) Act 1990; the British Nationality (Hong Kong) (Selection Scheme) Order 1990, SI 1990/2292; and PARA 433.

8   As to British national (overseas) status see PARAS 406, 465–467.

9   See the text and notes 10–16. Note that under Chinese nationality law all Hong Kong Chinese are Chinese nationals, and are therefore not stateless.

10 See the Hong Kong Act 1985 Schedule para 2(1)(a), (3) (Schedule para 2(1)(a) as amended: see note 6); and the Hong Kong (British Nationality) Order 1986, SI 1986/948, arts 3, 6(1) (amended by virtue of the British Overseas Territories Act 2002 s 2(3)).

11 As to legitimated and posthumous children see the British Nationality Act 1981 ss 47, 48, 50(9) (s 47 now repealed); and PARA 424 notes 6–7 (applied by the Hong Kong (British Nationality) Order 1986, SI 1986/948, arts 1(4), 7(7)(c)).

12 See the Hong Kong Act 1985 Schedule para 2(3); and the Hong Kong (British Nationality) Order 1986, SI 1986/948, art 6(2).

13 Ie a person who acquired British overseas citizenship by virtue of the Hong Kong (British Nationality) Order 1986, SI 1986/948, art 6(2) (see the text and note 12) and who held that citizenship at the time of the child's birth.

14 This may be extended to six years, if in the special circumstances of any particular case the Secretary of State thinks fit: see the Hong Kong (British Nationality) Order 1986, SI 1986/948, art 6(5). As to the Secretary of State see PARA 402. As to the exercise of discretion see the British Nationality Act 1981 s 44; and PARA 402.

15 As to citizenship by descent see PARA 456.

16 See the Hong Kong Act 1985 Schedule para 2(3); and the Hong Kong (British Nationality) Order 1986, SI 1986/948, art 6(3), (4) (amended by virtue of the British Overseas Territories Act 2002 ss 1(2), 2(3) respectively).

17 See PARA 435.

463.   Renunciation; absence of provisions for resumption, automatic loss or deprivation. A British overseas citizen[1] of full age and capacity[2] may renounce his citizenship by declaration, upon registration of which he ceases to be a British overseas citizen[3]. However, the person must have or be about to acquire some other citizenship or nationality[4]. The Secretary of State[5] must be satisfied on this point; and even if the declaration is registered, should the renouncer not acquire some such other citizenship within six months, the registration will be of no effect and he will remain a British overseas citizen[6].

There is no provision for resumption of British overseas citizenship once renounced, or for its acquisition by a person who renounced citizenship of the United Kingdom and colonies[7]. Nor are there any provisions for automatic loss, or deprivation, of British overseas citizenship.

1   The provisions of the British Nationality Act 1981 s 12 (see PARA 443) are applied to British overseas citizens and citizenship by s 29.

2   As to the meanings of 'full age' and 'full capacity', and as to the discretion to waive the requirement in respect of a specified applicant, see PARA 438 note 12. For the purpose of renunciation only, a person who has been married, or has formed a civil partnership, is deemed to be of full age: British Nationality Act 1981 s 12(5) (amended by the Civil Partnership Act 2004 s 261(1), Sch 27 para 74); applied by the British Nationality Act 1981 s 29.

3 See the British Nationality Act 1981 s 12(1), (2); applied by s 29. As to declarations of renunciation see the British Nationality (General) Regulations 2003, SI 2003/548, regs 8, 9, Sch 5 (Sch 5 amended by SI 2005/2114; and SI 2007/3137). As to the power to make regulations see PARA 404.
4 See the British Nationality Act 1981 s 12(3); applied by s 29.
5 As to the Secretary of State see PARA 402.
6 See the British Nationality Act 1981 s 12(3); applied by s 29.
7 As to citizenship of the United Kingdom and colonies see PARAS 414–419.

464. Access to British citizenship. There are several means by which a British overseas citizen may be able to acquire British citizenship[1] by registration. Firstly, a British overseas citizen is entitled[2], on application[3], to be registered as a British citizen if he satisfies the statutory requirements as to residence in the United Kingdom[4]. Secondly, the Secretary of State[5] may, if he thinks fit, register as a British citizen any British overseas citizen who has at any time served in specified Crown service in a British overseas territory[6]. Thirdly, a person who has the status of British overseas citizen is entitled to be registered as a British citizen if he applies for registration[7] and the Secretary of State is satisfied that the person does not have any citizenship or nationality, apart from such status, and that the person has not after the relevant day[8] renounced, voluntarily relinquished or lost through action or inaction any citizenship or nationality[9]. There is also a broad discretion to register any minor as a British citizen[10].

1 As to British citizens and citizenship see PARAS 406, 421–444.
2 As to factors overriding entitlement see PARA 426 note 4.
3 As to applications see PARA 484.
4 See the British Nationality Act 1981 s 4(1)–(4); and PARA 428. As to the meaning of 'United Kingdom' see PARA 403 note 1. As to the requirement of good character in the case of an application for registration of an adult or young person as a British citizen under s 4(2) or (5) see s 41A(1); and PARA 428 note 9. As to the meaning of 'adult or young person' see PARA 426 note 4.
5 As to the Secretary of State see PARA 402.
6 See the British Nationality Act 1981 s 4(5), (6); and PARA 428. As to British overseas territories (formerly known as dependent territories) see PARA 445 note 1.
7 Ie under the British Nationality Act 1981 s 4B.
8 As to the meaning of 'relevant day' see PARA 428 note 19.
9 See the British Nationality Act 1981 s 4B(1), (2); and PARA 428.
10 Ie under the British Nationality Act 1981 s 3(1): see PARA 427.

6. BRITISH NATIONAL (OVERSEAS) STATUS

465.   In general. The status of British national (overseas) was created specifically to provide a form of British nationality for the people of Hong Kong before they automatically ceased to be British overseas territories citizens[1] on 1 July 1997[2], when sovereignty over Hong Kong passed from the United Kingdom to the People's Republic of China[3]. It is even more limited and temporary than British overseas citizenship[4]. It came into existence on 1 July 1987[5], and since the end of 1997 it cannot be acquired by any person or by any means at all[6]; it will accordingly not outlive those who acquired it between those dates. It does not carry the right of abode in the United Kingdom[7], and it is arguably a status with a related passport facility rather than a true citizenship or nationality[8], although it has been referred to as 'a new form of British nationality'[9].

1   As to British overseas territories citizens and citizenship (formerly known as British dependent territories citizens and citizenship) see PARAS 406, 445–458.
2   As to the loss of citizenship see the Hong Kong Act 1985 s 2(2), Schedule (amended by virtue of the British Overseas Territories Act 2002 s 2(3)); the Hong Kong (British Nationality) Order 1986, SI 1986/948, art 3 (amended by virtue of the British Overseas Territories Act 2002 s 2(3)); and PARAS 458, 462.
3   See the Hong Kong Act 1985 s 1; PARA 462; and COMMONWEALTH vol 13 (2009) PARA 727.
4   See PARA 459.
5   See the Hong Kong Act 1985 Schedule para 2 (amended by virtue of the British Overseas Territories Act 2002 s 2(3)); and the Hong Kong (British Nationality) Order 1986, SI 1986/948, art 4(1).
6   See PARA 466.
7   As to the right of abode see PARA 412. As to the meaning of 'United Kingdom' see PARA 403 note 1.
8   It is unlikely that the same could be said of British overseas citizenship (see PARAS 459–463) and of British subject status (see PARAS 469–474), since both are continuations (in somewhat different form) of a previously existing national status, and continue to be capable of acquisition, albeit only to avoid statelessness.
9   See eg the Hong Kong (British Nationality) Order 1986, SI 1986/948, art 4(1); and the Hong Kong Act 1985 Schedule para 2(1)(b).

466.   Acquisition. Any person who was a British overseas territories citizen[1] by virtue (wholly or partly) of a connection with Hong Kong[2], and who but for that connection would not have been such a citizen, was entitled before 1 July 1997 to be registered as a British national (overseas) and to hold or be included in a passport appropriate to that status[3]. In the case of persons born during the six months from 1 January to 30 June 1997 inclusive, the period for acquisition of the status and passport was extended until the end of 1997[4].

1   As to British overseas territories citizens and citizenship (formerly known as British dependent territories citizens and citizenship) see PARAS 406, 445–458.
2   As to who has a connection with Hong Kong for these purposes see the Hong Kong (British Nationality) Order 1986, SI 1986/948, art 2; and PARA 433 note 6.
3   Hong Kong (British Nationality) Order 1986, SI 1986/948, art 4(2) (amended by virtue of the British Overseas Territories Act 2002 s 2(3); and by SI 1993/1795). Applications had to be made in accordance with the British Nationality (Hong Kong) Regulations 1986, SI 1986/2175, regs 3–5, Sch 1. A timetable for the receipt of applications was introduced: see the Hong Kong (British Nationality) Order 1986, SI 1986/948, art 4(2), (6), Sch 2 (art 4(2) amended, and art 4(6), Sch 2 added, by SI 1993/1795; the Hong Kong (British Nationality) Order 1986, SI 1986/948, Sch 2 amended by virtue of the British Overseas Territories Act 2002 s 2(3)). An application made after a given deadline could be accepted if the applicant showed that there were special circumstances which justified his being registered as a British national (overseas): Hong Kong (British Nationality) Order 1986, SI 1986/948, art 4(4) (added by SI 1993/1795). Where any person was registered or naturalised after, or less than three months before, the

relevant deadline as a British overseas territories citizen by virtue (wholly or partly) of his having a connection with Hong Kong and he made an application within three months after the date of his registration or naturalisation, the Secretary of State had to register him as a British national (overseas): see the Hong Kong (British Nationality) Order 1986, SI 1986/948, art 4(5) (added by SI 1993/1795; and amended by virtue of the British Overseas Territories Act 2002 s 2(3)).

4   Hong Kong (British Nationality) Order 1986, SI 1986/948, art 4(2). It appears that a child born in the first half of 1997, in respect of whom an application was not made until the second half, acquired British overseas citizenship automatically on 1 July 1997 if he would otherwise have been stateless (see PARA 462) and accordingly holds each status.

467. Loss, deprivation and renunciation. A British national (overseas) who ceased at any time before 1 July 1997 to be a British overseas territories citizen[1] ceased at the same time to be a British national (overseas)[2].

A British national (overseas)[3] of full age and capacity[4] may renounce his citizenship by declaration, upon registration of which he ceases to be a British overseas citizen[5]. However, the person must have or be about to acquire some other citizenship or nationality[6]. The Secretary of State[7] must be satisfied on this point; and even if the declaration is registered, should the renouncer not acquire some such other citizenship within six months, the registration will be of no effect and he will remain a British national (overseas)[8]. There is no provision for resumption of British national (overseas) status once renounced.

A person may be deprived of British national (overseas) status if the Secretary of State[9] is satisfied that deprivation is conducive to the public good or on the ground of fraud, false representation or concealment of material fact[10]. Registration as a British national (overseas) obtained by serious and causative fraud may be of no effect[11].

1   As to British overseas territories citizens and citizenship (formerly known as British dependent territories citizens and citizenship) see PARAS 406, 445–458.

2   Hong Kong (British Nationality) Order 1986, SI 1986/948, art 4(3) (amended by virtue of the British Overseas Territories Act 2002 s 2(3)). British national (overseas) status was not, of course, affected by the automatic loss of British overseas territories citizenship on 1 July 1997 under art 3: see PARAS 458, 462, 465.

3   The provisions of the British Nationality Act 1981 s 12 (see PARA 443) are applied to British overseas citizens and citizenship by the Hong Kong (British Nationality) Order 1986, SI 1986/948, art 7(10).

4   As to the meanings of 'full age' and 'full capacity', and as to the discretion to waive the requirement in respect of a specified applicant, see PARA 438 note 12. For the purpose of renunciation only, a person who has been married, or has formed a civil partnership, is deemed to be of full age: British Nationality Act 1981 s 12(5) (amended by the Civil Partnership Act 2004 s 261(1), Sch 27 para 74); applied by the Hong Kong (British Nationality) Order 1986, SI 1986/948, art 7(10).

5   See the British Nationality Act 1981 s 12(1), (2); applied by the Hong Kong (British Nationality) Order 1986, SI 1986/948, art 7(10). As to declarations of renunciation see the British Nationality (Hong Kong) Regulations 1986, SI 1986/2175, regs 6, 7, Sch 2 (reg 7 amended by virtue of the British Overseas Territories Act 2002 s 1(2); the British Nationality (Hong Kong) Regulations 1986, SI 1986/2175, Sch 2 amended by SI 2007/3137).

6   See the British Nationality Act 1981 s 12(3) (applied by the Hong Kong (British Nationality) Order 1986, SI 1986/948, art 7(10)).

7   As to the Secretary of State see PARA 402.

8   See the British Nationality Act 1981 s 12(3) (applied by the Hong Kong (British Nationality) Order 1986, SI 1986/948, art 7(10)).

9   As to the Secretary of State see PARA 402.

10   See the British Nationality Act 1981 s 40(1)(d), (2)–(6) (s 40 substituted by the Nationality, Immigration and Asylum Act 2002 s 4(1); British Nationality Act 1981 s 40(2) further substituted by the Immigration, Asylum and Nationality Act 2006 s 56(1)); and PARA 444. As to appeals against deprivation see the British Nationality Act 1981 s 40A; and PARA 444.

11   Cf PARA 444.

468. Access to British citizenship. There are several means by which a British national (overseas) may be able to acquire British citizenship[1] by registration. Firstly, a British national (overseas) is entitled[2], on application[3], to be registered as a British citizen if he satisfies the statutory requirements as to residence in the United Kingdom[4]. Secondly, the Secretary of State[5] may, if he thinks fit, register as a British citizen any British national (overseas) who has at any time served in specified Crown service in a British overseas territory[6]. Thirdly, a person who has the status of British national (overseas) is entitled to be registered as a British citizen if he applies for registration[7] and the Secretary of State is satisfied that the person does not have any citizenship or nationality, apart from such status, and that the person has not after the relevant day[8] renounced, voluntarily relinquished or lost through action or inaction any citizenship or nationality[9]. There is also a broad discretion to register any minor as a British citizen[10].

1   As to British citizens and citizenship see PARAS 406, 421–444.
2   As to factors overriding entitlement see PARA 426 note 4.
3   As to applications see PARA 484.
4   See the British Nationality Act 1981 s 4(1)–(4); and PARA 428. As to the meaning of 'United Kingdom' see PARA 403 note 1. As to the requirement of good character in the case of an application for registration of an adult or young person as a British citizen under s 4(2) or (5) see s 41A(1); and PARA 428 note 9. As to the meaning of 'adult or young person' see PARA 426 note 4.
5   As to the Secretary of State see PARA 402.
6   See the British Nationality Act 1981 s 4(5), (6); note 4; and PARA 428. As to British overseas territories (formerly known as dependent territories) see PARA 445 note 1.
7   Ie under the British Nationality Act 1981 s 4B.
8   As to the meaning of 'relevant day' see PARA 428 note 19.
9   See the British Nationality Act 1981 s 4B(1), (2); and PARA 428.
10 Ie under the British Nationality Act 1981 s 3(1): see PARA 427.

7. BRITISH SUBJECT STATUS

469. In general. Until 1 January 1949[1] the single common form of British nationality was the status of British subject[2]. Upon the introduction with effect from that date of the distinction between citizenship of the United Kingdom and colonies[3] and citizenship of independent Commonwealth countries[4], the status of British subject remained the underlying common nationality of all such citizens[5], as well as of certain Irish citizens[6], and for some it remained their only national status[7]. From 1 January 1983[8], however, the vast majority of holders of British nationality ceased to be British subjects[9], although they remained Commonwealth citizens[10]. Save in the case of certain Irish citizens[11], the status of British subject is now incompatible with any other form of nationality[12]. Retention of the status of British subject depends upon the grounds upon which the status was held under previous legislation[13]. The status can now only be newly acquired by certain persons who would otherwise be stateless and, in the discretion of the Secretary of State, minors[14]. It will in the course of time disappear altogether[15].

1   Ie the date of commencement of the British Nationality Act 1948: see PARA 403 note 7.
2   See PARA 407.
3   As to citizenship of the United Kingdom and colonies see PARAS 414–419.
4   As to Commonwealth citizens see PARA 409.
5   See the British Nationality Act 1948 s 1(1) (now repealed); and PARA 407. The British Nationality Act 1948 continues to be of relevance in deciding whether a person has retained British subject status. As to the repeal and the continued relevance of the British Nationality Act 1948 see PARA 403.
6   See the British Nationality Act 1948 s 2 (now repealed); and PARA 470.
7   See the British Nationality Act 1948 s 13(1), Sch 3 (both now repealed); and PARA 471.
8   Ie the date of commencement of the British Nationality Act 1981: see PARA 403 note 1.
9   See PARAS 406–407. Under the British Nationality Act 1981 most holders of British nationality became British citizens (see PARAS 421–444), British overseas territories citizens (formerly known as British dependent territories citizens) (see PARAS 445–458) or British overseas citizens (see PARAS 459–463). The status of British national (overseas) (see PARAS 465–467) was not introduced until 1 July 1987.

10   The terms 'British subject' and 'Commonwealth citizen' in any enactment or instrument passed or made before 1 January 1983 are, in relation to any time prior to 1983, interchangeable but, in relation to any time since 1 January 1983, the terms have not been interchangeable and must be taken to refer, respectively, only to those who are British subjects under the British Nationality Act 1981 or Commonwealth citizens under the British Nationality Act 1981: see s 51(1), (2), (3)(c); and PARAS 407, 409. See also s 30, 31; and PARAS 470–471. Since 1 January 1983 nobody can have the status of Commonwealth citizen or British subject otherwise than under the British Nationality Act 1981: s 37(4).
11   See PARA 470.
12   See the British Nationality Act 1981 s 35; and PARA 474.
13   See PARAS 470–471.
14   See PARAS 472–473. As to the exercise of discretion see the British Nationality Act 1981 s 44(1); and PARA 402.
15   Cf British overseas citizens (see PARA 459) and British nationals (overseas) (see PARA 465).

470. Retention and deemed retention: Irish British subjects. The retention of the status of British subject by certain Irish citizens is an extension of a provision which came into force on 1 January 1949[1] and was repealed with effect from 1 January 1983[2]; it applies only to those who immediately before 1 January 1949 were both citizens of Eire[3] and British subjects, and accordingly will become defunct when there are no longer any such persons in existence.

From 1949 to 1982 inclusive, any person who immediately before 1 January 1949 was both a citizen of Eire and a British subject was entitled to give notice to the Secretary of State[4] claiming, on specified grounds[5], to remain a British subject[6]. If he did so, he was deemed never to have lost[7] his status as a British subject[8]. Such notice could be given, with the same result, on behalf of a child under 16 by his parent or guardian[9].

Anyone who remained a British subject as the result of the giving of such notice before 1 January 1983 remains a British subject after that date[10], and is deemed to have remained a British subject continuously since 1 January 1949[11]. Any citizen of the Republic of Ireland who could have remained a British subject by the giving of such notice but did not do so before 1 January 1983 may give notice in writing to the Secretary of State claiming to remain a British subject on either or both of the following grounds, namely: (1) that he is or has been in Crown service under the government of the United Kingdom[12]; or (2) that he has associations by way of descent, residence or otherwise with the United Kingdom or with any British overseas territory[13]. Upon doing so he becomes a British subject[14], and is deemed to have remained a British subject since 1 January 1949[15].

Unlike other British subjects, citizens of the Republic of Ireland who remain British subjects under the provisions described above do not lose that status upon acquisition of another citizenship or nationality[16].

1   Ie the date of commencement of the British Nationality Act 1948: see PARA 403 note 7.
2   Ie the date of commencement of the British Nationality Act 1981: see PARA 403 note 1.
3   Eire became known as the Republic of Ireland on 18 April 1949: see the Ireland Act 1949 s 1; and PARA 410 note 1.
4   As to the Secretary of State see PARA 402.
5   What the grounds were is now of less importance than whether notice was given; however, the grounds specified were: (1) that he was in Crown service under the United Kingdom government; (2) that he held a British passport issued by the government of the United Kingdom or of any colony, protectorate, United Kingdom mandated territory or United Kingdom trust territory; or (3) that he had associations by way of descent, residence or otherwise with the United Kingdom or with any colony or protectorate or any United Kingdom mandated or trust territory (see PARAS 415 note 6, 417 note 7): British Nationality Act 1948 s 2(1)(a)–(c) (now repealed). As to the repeal and the continued relevance of the British Nationality Act 1948 see PARA 403.
6   See the British Nationality Act 1948 s 2(1) (now repealed).
7   Ie despite any gap between the coming into force of the British Nationality Act 1948 and the giving of such notice. The effect of giving notice was not that he re-acquired that status but that he was deemed to have retained it without interruption.
8   See the British Nationality Act 1948 s 2(1) (now repealed).
9   See the British Nationality Act 1948 s 2(2) (now repealed).
10 See the British Nationality Act 1981 s 31(1), (2).
11 See the British Nationality Act 1981 s 31(4).
12 As to the meaning of 'United Kingdom' see PARA 403 note 1.
13 See the British Nationality Act 1981 s 31(3) (amended by virtue of the British Overseas Territories Act 2002 s 1(1)(b)). As to British overseas territories (formerly known as dependent territories) see PARA 445 note 1.
14 See the British Nationality Act 1981 s 31(3) (as amended: see note 13).
15 See British Nationality Act 1981 s 31(4). The provision for giving notice on behalf of a child under 16 is not repeated, since only those in existence before 1 January 1949 are eligible.
16 See the British Nationality Act 1981 s 35; and PARA 474. Before 1 January 1983 only a small minority of British subjects had no other citizenship or nationality; the vast majority did (being citizens either of the United Kingdom and colonies or of a Commonwealth country). These Irish citizen British subjects are now the only persons in that position.

471. Retention: British subjects without citizenship. The intention of the British Nationality Act 1948 was that all existing British subjects should thereafter have, in addition, a citizenship status: either of the United Kingdom and colonies[1], or of a Commonwealth country[2]. However, not all the original

Commonwealth countries[3] had citizenship laws in force on 1 January 1949[4]. A person who was, or who was deemed to be[5], a British subject on 31 December 1948, and who on 1 January 1949 was potentially a citizen of one of the original Commonwealth countries[6] but not actually such a citizen, became on that date a British subject without citizenship, and retained that status until a citizenship law came into force in that country[7] or he became a citizen of the United Kingdom and colonies, a citizen of any Commonwealth country, a citizen of the Republic of Ireland, or an alien[8]. However, for the purposes of British nationality law no citizenship law came into force in India or Pakistan[9], so that potential citizens of those countries remained British subjects without citizenship unless they acquired some other nationality. Any such person who was still a British subject without citizenship immediately before 1 January 1983[10] became on that date a British subject[11]; but the status of British subject is lost if the person acquires any other citizenship or nationality whatever[12].

A person who, before 1 January 1949, ceased to be a British subject[13] because, while he was a minor, his parent ceased to be a British subject, and who would otherwise have become a British subject without citizenship as described above[14], was entitled to make a declaration of his intention to resume British nationality[15], and upon registration of the declaration by the Secretary of State he became a British subject without citizenship[16]. Any person who, as a result of such a declaration, was a British subject without citizenship immediately before 1 January 1983, became on that date a British subject[17]; but the status of British subject is lost if the person acquires any other citizenship or nationality whatever[18].

From 5 October 1965[19] to 31 December 1982[20], an alien woman was entitled, on application, to be registered[21] as a British subject if she had been married to a man who, at the date of the application, was, or would but for his death have been, a British subject without citizenship under the provisions described above[22], or a citizen of the Republic of Ireland who had remained a British subject as a result of giving notice[23]. The status of British subject so acquired was lost if she became a citizen of the United Kingdom and colonies, a citizen of any Commonwealth country[24], or a citizen of the Republic of Ireland[25], or if she was deprived of it on the ground of fraud, false representation or concealment of any material fact[26]. Any woman who was still a British subject immediately before 1 January 1983 by reason of such registration became on that date a British subject[27]. The right to register was extended until 31 December 1987[28]. A woman who is a British subject by virtue of registration[29] under the provisions described above will lose that status if she acquires any other citizenship or nationality whatever[30].

1   As to citizenship of the United Kingdom and colonies see PARAS 414–419.

2   Some people were both, but the general scheme was alternative: see *R v Secretary of State for Foreign and Commonwealth Affairs, ex p Ross-Clunis* [1991] 2 AC 439, sub nom *Ross-Clunis v Secretary of State for Foreign and Commonwealth Affairs* [1991] 3 All ER 353, HL. As to Commonwealth citizens see PARA 409.

3   Ie those listed in the British Nationality Act 1948 s 1(3) as originally enacted: see PARA 409 note 4.

4   Ie the date of commencement of the British Nationality Act 1948: see PARA 403 note 7. As to the repeal and the continued relevance of the British Nationality Acts 1948 to 1965 see PARA 403.

5   See PARA 415 text and note 10.

6   As to those who were potentially citizens of a Commonwealth country see PARA 415.

7   When a citizenship law came into force in that country he became a citizen of the United
    Kingdom and colonies unless he became, or had previously become, a citizen of that
    Commonwealth country or of any other country: see the British Nationality Act 1948 ss 12(4),
    13 (now repealed); and PARA 416.
8   See the British Nationality Act 1948 s 13 (now repealed). As to aliens see PARA 411.
9   India and Pakistan had their own citizenship laws, of course, but only laws designated by the
    Secretary of State fulfilled the definition of 'citizenship law' for the purposes of British
    nationality, and no such designation was ever made in the case of these countries: see the British
    Nationality Act 1948 s 32(8) (now repealed); *Gowa v A-G* [1985] 1 WLR 1003, HL; and PARA
    416. As to the Secretary of State see PARA 402.
10 Ie the date of commencement of the British Nationality Act 1981: see PARA 403 note 1.
11 See the British Nationality Act 1981 s 30(a). Note that the words 'without citizenship' have been
    dropped.
12 See the British Nationality Act 1981 s 35; and PARA 474.
13 Ie under the British Nationality and Status of Aliens Act 1914 s 12(1) (now repealed). The
    British Nationality Act 1948, which repealed this provision, also renamed the British
    Nationality and Status of Aliens Act 1914 as the Status of Aliens Act 1914: see PARA 403 note 9.
14 See the British Nationality Act 1948 s 13 (now repealed); and the text to note 8. In determining
    whether a woman who had married an alien would have become a British subject without
    citizenship, her marriage was to be disregarded: see s 16 (now repealed).
15 The declaration could be made at any time before 1 January 1950, or (if later) within one year
    of his twenty-first birthday, or such longer period as the Secretary of State might allow: see the
    British Nationality Act 1948 s 16 (now repealed). However, a declaration could not be made on
    or after 1 January 1983 (ie the date on which the repeal of s 16 took effect).
16 See the British Nationality Act 1948 s 16 (now repealed).
17 See the British Nationality Act 1981 s 30(a). Note that the words 'without citizenship' have been
    dropped.
18 See the British Nationality Act 1981 s 35; and PARA 474.
19 Ie the date of the commencement of the British Nationality Act 1965: see s 5(4) (now repealed:
    see note 20). See also note 4.
20 After this date the British Nationality Act 1965 was repealed: see the British Nationality
    Act 1981 s 52(8), Sch 9.
21 Ie under the British Nationality Act 1965 s 1 (now repealed: see note 20). If she had previously
    renounced or been deprived of citizenship of the United Kingdom and colonies, or been deprived
    of British subject status, such registration was discretionary.
22 Ie the British Nationality Act 1948 ss 13, 16 (both now repealed): see the text to notes 8, 16.
23 Ie under the British Nationality Act 1948 s 2(1) (now repealed): see PARA 470.
24 See PARA 409 note 4. If her registration was based on her husband's potential citizenship of
    Pakistan, she lost the status of British subject under these provisions on becoming a citizen of
    Pakistan: see the British Nationality Act 1965 s 2(2A) (added by the Pakistan Act 1973 s 1(2),
    Sch 1; now repealed).
25 British Nationality Act 1965 s 2 (now repealed).
26 Ie under the British Nationality Act 1965 s 3 (now repealed), which applied the provisions of the
    British Nationality Act 1948 s 20 (now repealed) (see PARA 419) relating to notice and the right
    to an inquiry to such a person.
27 See the British Nationality Act 1981 s 30(b).
28 See the British Nationality Act 1981 s 33 (now repealed). Her husband had to be a British
    subject on the date of application, and she had to have been married to him throughout the
    period from 1 January 1983 to the date of application: see s 33 (now repealed).
29 Ie whether registered before or after 1 January 1983.
30 See the British Nationality Act 1981 s 35; and PARA 474.

472.   Acquisition by birth: statelessness.   Only persons who would otherwise
have no other citizenship or nationality can become British subjects by birth. A
person born in the United Kingdom[1] or a British overseas territory[2] on or after
1 January 1983[3], who would otherwise be born stateless, is a British subject if at
the time of his birth his father or mother[4] was a British subject[5], unless he is born
a British citizen[6], a British overseas territories citizen[7] or a British overseas
citizen[8] because one of his parents has that status[9]. He will lose the status of
British subject if he acquires any other citizenship or nationality whatever[10].

1   As to the meaning of 'United Kingdom' see PARA 403 note 1.
2   As to British overseas territories (formerly known as dependent territories) see PARA 445 note 1.
3   Ie the date of commencement of the British Nationality Act 1981: see PARA 403 note 1.
4   See PARA 424 notes 6–7.
5   See the British Nationality Act 1981 s 36, Sch 2 paras 1(1), (2), 2(1), (2) (Sch 2 para 1 amended by virtue of the British Overseas Territories Act 2002 s 2(2)(b); and by the Nationality, Immigration and Asylum Act 2002 ss 9(5)(a), 161, Sch 9; and the British Nationality Act 1981 Sch 2 para 2(1) amended by virtue of the British Overseas Territories Act 2002 s 1(1)(b)).
6   As to British citizens and citizenship see PARAS 406, 421–444.
7   As to British overseas territories citizens and citizenship (formerly known as British dependent territories citizens and citizenship) see PARAS 406, 445–458.
8   As to British overseas citizens see PARAS 406, 459–463.
9   See the British Nationality Act 1981 Sch 2 paras 1(3), 2(3). As to the circumstances in which a person who would otherwise be born stateless acquires British citizenship by birth see PARA 424; as to the circumstances in which a person who would otherwise be born stateless acquires British overseas territories citizenship by birth see PARA 448; and as to the circumstances in which a person who would otherwise be born stateless acquires British overseas citizenship by birth see PARA 460.
10   See the British Nationality Act 1981 s 35; and PARA 474. This does not apply to those who are British subjects by virtue of s 31 (see PARA 470): see s 35.

473. Acquisition by registration. A person born outside the United Kingdom[1] and the British overseas territories[2] on or after 1 January 1983[3], who is and always has been stateless, is entitled on application[4] to registration as a British subject if: (1) at the time of his birth his father or mother[5] was a British subject, but neither of them was a British citizen, a British overseas territories citizen or a British overseas citizen[6]; (2) he himself was in the United Kingdom or a British overseas territory at the beginning of the period of three years ending with the date of application; and (3) during that period he has not been absent from both the United Kingdom and the British overseas territories for more than 270 days[7]. A person so registered will lose the status of British subject if he acquires any other citizenship or nationality whatever[8].

The Secretary of State may, if he thinks fit, grant any application for registration of a minor as a British subject[9]. A person so registered will lose the status of British subject if he acquires any other citizenship or nationality whatever[10].

1   As to the meaning of 'United Kingdom' see PARA 403 note 1.
2   As to British overseas territories (formerly known as dependent territories) see PARA 445 note 1.
3   Ie the date of commencement of the British Nationality Act 1981: see PARA 403 note 1.
4   As to applications see PARA 484.
5   See PARA 424 notes 6–7.
6   If one of his parents was a British citizen, a British overseas territories citizen or a British overseas citizen, the applicant is entitled to registration as that kind of citizen: see PARAS 436, 451, 461. As to British citizens and citizenship see PARAS 406, 421–444; as to British overseas territories citizens and citizenship (formerly known as British dependent territories citizens and citizenship) see PARAS 406, 445–458; and as to British overseas citizens see PARAS 406, 459–463.
7   See the British Nationality Act 1981 s 36, Sch 2 para 4 (amended by virtue of the British Overseas Territories Act 2002 ss 1(1)(b), 2(2)(b)). As to references to days of absence from the United Kingdom or the British overseas territories see PARA 426 note 9. As to the registration of stateless persons see also PARAS 436, 451, 461. If in the special circumstances of any particular case the Secretary of State thinks fit, he may treat the person as fulfilling the requirements of head (3) in the text although the number of days on which he was absent from both the United Kingdom and the British overseas territories exceeds the number mentioned: see the British Nationality Act 1981 Sch 2 para 6 (amended by virtue of the British Overseas Territories Act 2002 s 1(1)(b)). As to the Secretary of State see PARA 402. As to the exercise of discretion see the British Nationality Act 1981 s 44(1); and PARA 402.
8   See the British Nationality Act 1981 s 35; and PARA 474.
9   See the British Nationality Act 1981 s 32. As to the meaning of 'minor' see PARA 424 note 13. An application for registration of an adult or young person as a British overseas citizen under

s 32 must not be granted unless the Secretary of State is satisfied that the adult or young person is of good character: s 41A(4) (s 41A added by the Borders, Citizenship and Immigration Act 2009 s 47(1) to replace corresponding provision in Immigration, Asylum and Nationality Act 2006 s 58). As to the meaning of 'adult or young person' see PARA 426 note 4.

10 See the British Nationality Act 1981 s 35.

474. Renunciation and loss. A British subject[1] of full age and capacity[2] may renounce his status by declaration, upon registration of which he ceases to be a British subject[3]. However, the person must have or be about to acquire some other citizenship or nationality[4]. The Secretary of State[5] must be satisfied on this point; and even if the declaration is registered, should the renouncer not acquire some such other citizenship within six months, the registration will be of no effect and he will remain a British subject[6]. There is no provision for resumption of the status of British subject, once renounced.

Any person who is a British subject under the British Nationality Act 1981, except one who has retained (or is deemed to have retained) that status by virtue of the special provisions for Irish citizens[7], will cease automatically to be a British subject if, in whatever circumstances and whether under the British Nationality Act 1981 or otherwise, he acquires any other citizenship or nationality whatever[8].

1 The provisions of the British Nationality Act 1981 s 12 (see PARA 443) are applied to British subjects by s 34.

2 As to the meanings of 'full age' and 'full capacity', and as to the discretion to waive the requirement in respect of a specified applicant, see PARA 438 note 12. For the purpose of renunciation only, a person who has been married, or has formed a civil partnership, is deemed to be of full age: British Nationality Act 1981 s 12(5) (amended by the Civil Partnership Act 2004 s 261(1), Sch 27 para 74); applied by the British Nationality Act 1981 s 34.

3 See the British Nationality Act 1981 s 12(1), (2) (applied by s 34). As to declarations of renunciation see the British Nationality (General) Regulations 2003, SI 2003/548, regs 8, 9, Sch 5 (Sch 5 amended by SI 2005/2114; and SI 2007/3137). As to the power to make regulations see PARA 404.

4 See the British Nationality Act 1981 s 12(3) (applied by s 34). Note that, unless he is an Irish British subject (see PARA 470), acquisition of any other citizenship or nationality will automatically have destroyed British subject status without the need for renunciation: see the text and note 8.

5 As to the Secretary of State see PARA 402.

6 See the British Nationality Act 1981 s 12(3) (applied by s 34).

7 See PARA 470.

8 British Nationality Act 1981 s 35. As to automatic loss under the earlier law see the British Nationality Act 1948 ss 13(1), 16(2) (both now repealed); and the British Nationality Act 1965 s 2(2) (now repealed).

475. Access to British citizenship. There are several means by which a British subject may be able to acquire British citizenship[1] by registration. Firstly, a British subject is entitled[2], on application[3], to be registered as a British citizen if he satisfies the statutory requirements as to residence in the United Kingdom[4]. Secondly, the Secretary of State[5] may, if he thinks fit, register as a British citizen any British subject who has at any time served in specified Crown service in a British overseas territory[6]. Thirdly, a person who has the status of British subject is entitled to be registered as a British citizen if he applies for registration[7] and the Secretary of State is satisfied that the person does not have any citizenship or nationality, apart from such status, and that the person has not after the relevant day[8] renounced, voluntarily relinquished or lost through action or inaction any citizenship or nationality[9]. There is also a broad discretion to register any minor as a British citizen[10].

1 As to British citizens and citizenship see PARAS 406, 421–444.
2 As to factors overriding entitlement see PARA 426 note 4.
3 As to applications see PARA 484.
4 See the British Nationality Act 1981 s 4(1)–(4); and PARA 428. As to the meaning of 'United Kingdom' see PARA 403 note 1. As to the requirement of good character in the case of an application for registration of an adult or young person as a British citizen under s 4(2) or (5) see s 41A(1); and PARA 428 note 9. As to the meaning of 'adult or young person' see PARA 426 note 4.
5 As to the Secretary of State see PARA 402.
6 See the British Nationality Act 1981 s 4(5), (6); and PARA 428. As to British overseas territories (formerly known as dependent territories) see PARA 445 note 1.
7 Ie under the British Nationality Act 1981 s 4B.
8 As to the meaning of 'relevant day' see PARA 428 note 19.
9 See the British Nationality Act 1981 s 4B(1), (2); and PARA 428. Section 4B effectively renders the s 4 provisions defunct, except in the case of Irish British subjects.
10 Ie under the British Nationality Act 1981 s 3(1): see PARA 427.

8. BRITISH PROTECTED PERSON STATUS

476. In general. The status of British protected person[1] arose as a result of the government of the United Kingdom[2] exercising some form of administration or control over territories which were not colonies or otherwise part of the Crown's dominions[3], either of its own motion in the case of protectorates and protected states, or under the auspices of the United Nations or the League of Nations in the case of United Kingdom trust territories or mandated territories[4]. Although there are no longer any such territories, some persons who acquired British protected person status have retained it; but nobody is now eligible to acquire it save certain persons with a British protected person parent who would otherwise be stateless[5]. The status of British protected persons is anomalous: they are not aliens[6]; they have no right of abode in the United Kingdom[7] and are subject to United Kingdom immigration control[8]; and it appears that they may not even hold British nationality, at least for some purposes[9]. British protected persons may be employed in any civil capacity under the Crown[10]. The status is now held, or acquired, either by virtue of the Solomon Islands Act 1978[11], or by virtue of an Order in Council[12] made in relation to any territory which was at any time before 1 January 1983 a protectorate or protected state for the purposes of the British Nationality Act 1948, or a United Kingdom trust territory within the meaning of that Act[13]. The status of British protected person is lost upon the subsequent acquisition of another nationality, including British citizenship, British overseas territories citizenship and British overseas citizenship[14], although the status was held to be consistent with citizenship of the United Kingdom and colonies[15] so that both could be held simultaneously under the British Nationality Act 1948[16].

1   British protected persons are now statutorily defined as those who have that status by virtue of the Solomon Islands Act 1978 (see PARA 477) or who are members of any class of person declared to be British protected persons by an Order in Council for the time being in force under the British Nationality Act 1981 s 38: s 50(1). Section 38 provides that Her Majesty may by Order in Council made in relation to any territory which was at any time before 1 January 1983 a protectorate or protected state for the purposes of the British Nationality Act 1948 or a United Kingdom trust territory within the meaning of that Act (see note 13; and PARA 415 note 6) declare any class of person who are connected with that territory and are not citizens of any Commonwealth country (see PARA 409 note 16) which consists of or includes that territory to be British protected persons for the purposes of the British Nationality Act 1981: s 38(1). Any order so made is subject to annulment in pursuance of a resolution of either House of Parliament: s 38(2). As to the order that has been made see the British Protectorates, Protected States and Protected Persons Order 1982, SI 1982/1070 (amended by SI 1983/1699 and SI 2009/1892); and PARAS 478–480.

      The order provides that, in relation to any time before 1 January 1983, a British protected person means a person who had that status by virtue of any provision of the British Protectorates, Protected States and Protected Persons Order 1949, SI 1949/140, the British Protectorates, Protected States and Protected Persons Order 1965, SI 1965/1864, the British Protectorates, Protected States and Protected Persons Order 1969, SI 1969/1832, the British Protectorates, Protected States and Protected Persons Order 1974, SI 1974/1895, or the British Protectorates, Protected States and Protected Persons Order 1978, SI 1978/1026, or by virtue of the Botswana Independence Act 1966 s 3(2), the Gambia Independence Act 1964 s 2(2), the Kenya Independence Act 1963 s 2(1), the Nigeria Independence Act 1960 s 2(1), the Zambia Independence Act 1964 s 3(2), the Ghana Independence Act 1957 s 2, the Malawi Independence Act 1964 s 2(2), the Sierra Leone Independence Act 1961 s 2(1), the Uganda Independence Act 1962 s 2(1), or the Tanganyika Independence Act 1961 s 2(1) (all repealed): see the British Protectorates, Protected States and Protected Persons Order 1982, SI 1982/1070, art 2(1), Schedule. See also the text and note 13.

2   As to the meaning of 'United Kingdom' see PARA 403 note 1.

3   See *R v Secretary of State for the Home Department, ex p Thakrar* [1974] QB 684 at 709–710, sub nom *Thakrar v Secretary of State for the Home Department* [1974] 2 All ER 261 at 272–273, CA, per Lawton LJ.

4   As to protectorates, protected states and United Kingdom trust territories see PARA 415 note 6; and as to mandated territories see PARA 417 note 7. The League of Nations was dissolved in 1946.

5   See PARA 479.

6   See the British Nationality Act 1981 ss 50(1), 51(4); and PARA 411. See also the British Nationality Act 1948 ss 3(3), 32(1) (s 32(1) now repealed).

7   As to the right of abode see PARA 412. See also PARA 420.

8   As to immigration control see BRITISH NATIONALITY, IMMIGRATION AND ASYLUM vol 4(2) (2002 Reissue) PARA 83 et seq. It seems that British protected persons do not have the right to enter the United Kingdom, even if expelled from their country of residence with nowhere else to go: see *East African Asians v United Kingdom* (1973) 3 EHRR 76, EComHR.

9   *R v Secretary of State for the Home Department, ex p Thakrar* [1974] QB 684, [1974] 2 All ER 261, CA; *R v Chief Immigration Officer, Gatwick Airport, ex p Harjendar Singh* [1987] Imm AR 346 per Nolan J who, upon being convinced that a British protected person had no right to enter the United Kingdom even when he had nowhere else to go, held that he must be a person 'not having a nationality', and accordingly a refugee, for the purposes of the Convention relating to the Status of Refugees (Geneva, 28 July 1951; TS 39 (1954); Cmd 9171) and Protocol (New York, 31 January 1967; TS 15 (1969); Cmnd 3906) (which was not referred to in *R v Secretary of State for the Home Department, ex p Thakrar* [1974] QB 684, [2000] Imm AR 610, [1974] 2 All ER 261, CA). See, however, *Revenko v Secretary of State for the Home Department* [2001] QB 601, CA (a well-founded fear of persecution is a prerequisite of refugee status; mere statelessness or inability to return to the country of former habitual residence is insufficient). As to the meaning of 'refugee' see BRITISH NATIONALITY, IMMIGRATION AND ASYLUM vol 4(2) (2002 Reissue) PARA 239.

    To the limited extent that the term 'British nationality' has been used in British nationality law, it was sometimes used as a synonym for pre-1949 British subject status: see PARA 405. British protected persons were excluded from that class, but they are not aliens (see the text and note 6) and have been issued with British passports (which describe the holder's 'nationality' as 'British Protected Person'). Notwithstanding *R v Chief Immigration Officer Gatwick Airport, ex p Harjendar Sing* [1987] Imm AR 346, it still may be arguable that British protected person status is a form of nationality and, if so, that it can only be a form of British nationality.

10 See the Aliens Employment Act 1955 s 1 (amended by SI 1991/1221; and SI 2007/617).

11 See note 1; and PARA 477.

12 See note 1; and PARA 479.

13 See the British Nationality Act 1981 ss 38, 50(1). These varied from time to time, and included: the Aden Protectorate (later known as the Protectorate of South Arabia), the Bechuanaland Protectorate, the British Solomon Islands Protectorate, the Gambia Protectorate, the Kenya Protectorate, the Nigeria Protectorate, Northern Rhodesia (a protectorate), the Northern Territories of the Gold Coast (a protectorate), the Nyasaland Protectorate, the Sierra Leone Protectorate, the Somaliland Protectorate, Swaziland (which has been both a protectorate and a protected state), the Uganda Protectorate, the Zanzibar Protectorate, Kamaran (a protectorate), the Malay States (ie Johore, Pahang, Negri Sembilan, Selangor, Perak, Kedah, Perlis, Kelantan and Trengganu) (protected states), Brunei (a protected state), Tonga (a protected state), the Maldive Islands (a protected state), the Persian Gulf States (ie Kuwait, Bahrain, Qatar, and the Trucial Sheikhdoms of Oman, namely Abu Dhabi, Ajman, Dubai, Kalba, Ras al Khaimah, Sharjah and Umm al Quaiwain) (protected states), the New Hebrides (a protected state), Canton Island (a protected state), the Cameroons Trust Territory, Tanganyika (a trust territory) and Togoland Trust Territory: see the British Protectorates, Protected States and Protected Persons Order 1949, SI 1949/140 (amended by SI 1952/457, SI 1952/1417, SI 1953/1773, SI 1958/259, SI 1958/590, SI 1960/1366, SI 1961/2325 and SI 1962/1333; and now revoked); the British Protectorates, Protected States and Protected Persons Order 1965, SI 1965/1864 (amended by SI 1967/247 and SI 1967/1271; and now revoked); the British Protectorates, Protected States and Protected Persons Order 1969, SI 1969/1832; the British Protectorates, Protected States and Protected Persons Order 1974, SI 1974/1895 (revoked); the British Protectorates, Protected States and Protected Persons Order 1978, SI 1978/1026 (spent); and the British Protectorates, Protected States and Protected Persons Order 1982, SI 1982/1070 (amended by SI 1983/1699 and SI 2009/1892). See also note 1. It should not be assumed that the territory of the protectorate, protected state or trust territory was identical with the territory which now bears the relevant name (eg there was both a Kenya Colony and a Kenya Protectorate; and likewise for Sierra Leone).

14 See the British Protectorates, Protected States and Protected Persons Order 1982, SI 1982/1070, art 10; and PARAS 478–480. As to British citizens and citizenship see PARAS 406, 421–444; as to British overseas territories citizens and citizenship (formerly known as British dependent territories citizens and citizenship) see PARAS 406, 445–458; and as to British overseas citizens and citizenship see PARAS 406, 459–463.

15 As to citizenship of the United Kingdom and colonies see PARAS 414–419.

16 *Motala v A-G* [1992] 1 AC 281, [1991] 4 All ER 682, HL (a case involving the Northern Rhodesia (Zambia) Protectorate where it was further held that the citizenship of the United Kingdom and colonies was also lost by the acquisition of Zambian nationality).

477. The Solomon Islands. On 7 July 1978 the former Solomon Islands protectorate became an independent Commonwealth country[1]. Those who before that day were British protected persons by virtue of a connection with the protectorate[2] continued to be British protected persons unless on that day they became citizens of the Solomon Islands[3], or were then citizens of the United Kingdom and colonies[4]. If a child was born during the period 7 July 1978 to 6 July 1980, inclusive, to a man[5] born in the Solomon Islands who had remained a British protected person, the child was a British protected person if he did not acquire citizenship of the United Kingdom and colonies or any other nationality at birth[6]. In either case, the status of British protected person was lost on acquisition of citizenship of the Solomon Islands or the United Kingdom and colonies[7] or on possession (on or after 7 July 1980) of any other nationality[8].

On 7 July 1980 citizens of the United Kingdom and colonies with a connection with the Solomon Islands[9], and children fathered by such persons who were born between 7 July 1978 and 6 July 1980, inclusive, with citizenship of the United Kingdom and colonies by descent only[10], lost their citizenship of the United Kingdom and colonies and became British protected persons unless they then had any other nationality[11]. They lost that status on acquisition of citizenship of the Solomon Islands or the United Kingdom and colonies, or if they acquired any other nationality[12].

From 16 August 1978 to 31 December 1982[13], the wife of a Solomon Islands British protected person[14] could on application be registered as a British protected person, provided she was not a citizen of the Solomon Islands; she lost that status on becoming a citizen of the Solomon Islands or the United Kingdom and colonies, or on or after 7 July 1980 upon acquiring another nationality, but only if her husband also lost it[15]. Solomon Islanders could also take advantage of the then existing provisions for registration of stateless persons as British protected persons[16].

1 See the Solomon Islands Act 1978 ss 1, 2(1) (s 2(1) repealed). In the normal way of independence legislation, the Act laid down the circumstances in which persons would cease to be citizens of the United Kingdom and colonies as a result of independence: see PARA 418. As to citizenship of the United Kingdom and colonies see PARAS 414–419.

2 A person had a connection with the Solomon Islands protectorate if he or his father: (1) was born in the Solomon Islands; or (2) while resident in the Solomon Islands, became a citizen of the United Kingdom and colonies by naturalisation or registration: see the Solomon Islands Act 1978 s 3(1). A woman had such a connection if she acquired citizenship of the United Kingdom and colonies on the ground of marriage to such a person: see s 3(2). However, nobody had such a connection if: (a) he, his father or his father's father was born in the United Kingdom or a colony or associated state (as at 7 July 1978), or became a British subject by annexation of any territory of a colony or associated state (as at 7 July 1978), or was naturalised or registered as a citizen of the United Kingdom and colonies in the United Kingdom or a colony or associated state (as at 7 July 1978), or was registered by a High Commissioner under the British Nationality Act 1948 s 8(2) (now repealed) or s 12(7) (now repealed) (although women registered under s 6(2) (now repealed) on the ground of marriage were not excluded); or (b) his father or father's father would, if living immediately before 1 January 1949, have become a person naturalised in the United Kingdom and colonies under the British Nationality Act 1948

    s 32(6) (now repealed) by virtue of having enjoyed the privileges of naturalisation in a colony or associated state (as at 7 July 1978): see the Solomon Islands Act 1978 s 3(3)–(5).

3   See the Solomon Islands Independence Constitution, Solomon Islands Independence Order 1978, SI 1978/783, Schedule, Ch III (spent). There was also a local Citizenship Ordinance 1978 (No 7).

4   See the Solomon Islands Act 1978 s 4(1).

5   A man is the father only of his legitimate children, but a child legitimated by subsequent marriage of his parents is treated as if he had been born legitimate: see the Solomon Islands Act 1978 s 6(2), (3) (substituted and amended respectively by the British Nationality Act 1981 s 52(6), Sch 7). See also PARA 424 notes 6–7.

6   See the Solomon Islands Act 1978 s 4(2). A person had or acquired another nationality if he was or became a citizen of an independent Commonwealth country, or of a foreign country (ie a country other than the United Kingdom, a colony, an independent Commonwealth country, a protectorate, protected state, mandated territory or trust territory) or of the Republic of Ireland: see the Solomon Islands Act 1978 s 6(1), (2) (as originally enacted); and the British Nationality Act 1948 s 32(1) (now repealed).

7   From 1 January 1983, this also applies on the acquisition of British citizenship, British overseas territories citizenship, British overseas citizenship, or British national (overseas) status: see the British Nationality Act 1981 s 51(3)(a) (amended by the British Nationality (Falkland Islands) Act 1983 s 4(3); the British Overseas Territories Act 2002 ss 1(1)(b), 5, Sch 1 para 6; and SI 1986/948). As to British citizens and citizenship see PARAS 406, 421–444; as to British overseas territories citizens and citizenship (formerly known as British dependent territories citizens and citizenship) see PARAS 406, 445–458; as to British overseas citizens and citizenship see PARAS 406, 459–463; and as to British national (overseas) status see PARAS 406, 465–467.

    British protected person status was not inconsistent with citizenship of the United Kingdom and colonies, at least in the case of a person who qualified for both at birth; such a person could be both a British protected person and a citizen of the United Kingdom and colonies simultaneously until the acquisition of citizenship of the Solomon Islands or another nationality, at which point both would be lost: *Motala v A-G* [1992] 1 AC 281, [1991] 4 All ER 682, HL; and see PARA 476 text and note 16.

8   See the Solomon Islands Act 1978 s 4(3). A British protected person who was the wife of a British protected person did not lose that status, either on 7 July 1978 or thereafter, by reason of other national status unless her husband did so: see s 5(2). As to the operation of an analogous automatic loss provision under the British Protectorates, Protected States and Protected Persons Order 1969, SI 1969/1832 (now revoked), and the Uganda Independence Act 1962, see *R v Secretary of State for the Home Department, ex p Thakrar* [1974] QB 684, sub nom *Thakrar v Secretary of State for the Home Department* [1974] 2 All ER 261, CA.

9   See note 2.

10   See PARA 417 note 6.

11   See the Solomon Islands Act 1978 s 2(2)–(4).

12   See the Solomon Islands Act 1978 s 4(4).

13   Ie between the dates on which the British Protectorates, Protected States and Protected Persons Order 1978, SI 1978/1026, came into force and after which it was superseded by the British Protectorates, Protected States and Protected Persons Order 1982, SI 1982/1070.

14   Ie a man who at the date of the wife's application was a British protected person under the Solomon Islands Act 1978.

15   See the British Protectorates, Protected States and Protected Persons Order 1978, SI 1978/1026, art 7 (lapsed).

16   See the British Protectorates, Protected States and Protected Persons Order 1978, SI 1978/1026, arts 7(3), 10 (lapsed). As to provisions for stateless persons see now the British Protectorates, Protected States and Protected Persons Order 1982, SI 1982/1070, art 7; and PARA 479.

478. Retention of British protected person status. A person[1] who on 31 December 1982[2] was a British protected person[3] continues thereafter to be a British protected person[4]; save that a person who is a British protected person by virtue of connection[5] with a former protectorate[6], a former trust territory[7] or a former Arabian protectorate[8], or by registration as the wife of a Solomon Islands British protected person[9] or as the stateless child of a British protected person[10], loses British protected person status if he acquires British citizenship[11], British overseas territories citizenship[12], British overseas citizenship[13] or another nationality[14].

1 Ie other than a Solomon Islander. As to Solomon Islanders see PARA 477.

2 Ie immediately before the commencement of the British Protectorates, Protected States and Protected Persons Order 1982, SI 1982/1070, which came into operation on 1 January 1983: see art 1.

3 Ie by virtue of the British Protectorates, Protected States and Protected Persons Order 1978, SI 1978/1026 (now lapsed), which continued the British protected person status of those who had it under previous orders (see PARA 476 note 1).

4 See the British Protectorates, Protected States and Protected Persons Order 1982, SI 1982/1070, art 6.

5 From 16 August 1978, when the British Protectorates, Protected States and Protected Persons Order 1978, SI 1978/1026 (now lapsed) came into force, it was no longer possible to acquire British protected person status by virtue of such a connection, save in the case of a connection with Brunei or in the case of wives of Solomon Islanders (as to whom see PARA 477). Citizens or nationals of Brunei ceased to be British protected persons on 1 January 1984: see the British Nationality (Brunei) Order 1983, SI 1983/1699, arts 1, 2.

6 Ie the Bechuanaland, Gambia, Kenya, Nigeria, Nyasaland, Sierra Leone and Uganda Protectorates, Northern Rhodesia and the Northern Territories of the Gold Coast: British Protectorates, Protected States and Protected Persons Order 1982, SI 1982/1070, art 2(1), Schedule Pt I.

7 Ie Tanganyika, the Cameroons under United Kingdom trusteeship and Togoland under United Kingdom trusteeship: British Protectorates, Protected States and Protected Persons Order 1978, SI 1978/1026, art 2(1), Schedule Pt II.

8 Ie Kamaran and the Protectorate of South Arabia (previously Aden): British Protectorates, Protected States and Protected Persons Order 1978, SI 1978/1026, art 2(1).

9 Ie under the British Protectorates, Protected States and Protected Persons Order 1978, SI 1978/1026, art 7 (lapsed): see PARA 477.

10 Ie under the British Protectorates, Protected States and Protected Persons Order 1978, SI 1978/1026, art 10 (lapsed) or the British Protectorates, Protected States and Protected Persons Order 1982, SI 1982/1070, art 7: see PARAS 477, 479.

11 As to British citizens and citizenship see PARAS 406, 421–444.

12 As to British overseas territories citizens and citizenship (formerly known as British dependent territories citizens and citizenship) see PARAS 406, 445–458.

13 As to British overseas citizens and citizenship see PARAS 406, 459–463.

14 British Protectorates, Protected States and Protected Persons Order 1982, SI 1982/1070, art 10 (amended by virtue of the British Overseas Territories Act 2002 s 2(3)). For the purposes of the British Protectorates, Protected States and Protected Persons Order 1982, SI 1982/1070, a person has or acquires another nationality if he becomes a citizen of a Commonwealth country (see PARA 409 note 16) or of a foreign country (see PARA 404 note 22) or of the Republic of Ireland: art 2(3). As to the operation of an analogous automatic loss provision under the British Protectorates, Protected States and Protected Persons Order 1969, SI 1969/1832 (now revoked), and the Uganda Independence Act 1962, see *R v Secretary of State for the Home Department, ex p Thakrar* [1974] QB 684, sub nom *Thakrar v Secretary of State for the Home Department* [1974] 2 All ER 261, CA.

British protected person status was not inconsistent with citizenship of the United Kingdom and colonies, at least in the case of a person who qualified for both at birth; such a person could be both a British protected person and a citizen of the United Kingdom and colonies simultaneously until the acquisition of citizenship of another country, at which point both would be lost: *Motala v A-G* [1992] 1 AC 281, [1991] 4 All ER 682, HL; and see PARA 476 text and note 16. As to citizenship of the United Kingdom and colonies see PARAS 414–419.

479. Acquisition of British protected person status. A person born in the United Kingdom[1] or a British overseas territory[2] on or after 1 January 1983[3], who would otherwise be born stateless, is a British protected person if his father or mother or a woman who is treated as his parent[4] was a British protected person at the time he was born[5]. A person born[6] outside the United Kingdom and the British overseas territories is entitled, on application[7], to be registered as a British protected person if: (1) he is and always has been stateless; and (2) his father, his mother or a woman treated as his mother[8] was a British protected person at the time he was born[9]; and (3) he was in the United Kingdom or any British overseas territory or territories at the beginning of the three year period ending with the date of application and has not during that period been absent from both the United Kingdom and the British overseas territory or territories for more than 270 days[10]. A person so registered[11] ceases to be a British protected person upon acquiring British citizenship[12], British overseas territories citizenship[13], British overseas citizenship[14] or another nationality[15].

1 As to the meaning of 'United Kingdom' see PARA 403 note 1.
2 As to British overseas territories (formerly known as dependent territories) see PARA 445 note 1.
3 Ie the date of the commencement of the British Protectorates, Protected States and Protected Persons Order 1982, SI 1982/1070: see PARA 478 note 2. British protected person status is governed by this Order rather than by the British Nationality Act 1981, and in this respect is similar to British national (overseas) status and different from the other forms of British nationality status.
4 Ie by virtue of the Human Fertilisation and Embryology Act 2008 s 42 or s 43 (see CHILDREN AND YOUNG PERSONS). The provisions of the British Protectorates, Protected States and Protected Persons Order 1982, SI 1982/1070, art 7 apply to an illegitimate child if the relevant parent is the mother: see art 7(4). A person legitimated by the subsequent marriage or civil partnership of his parents, according to the law of the father's or second female parent's domicile at the time of the marriage or civil partnership, is treated for the purpose of determining whether he is a British protected person as if he had been born legitimate: see art 3(1), (2) (art 3 substituted by SI 2009/1892). A person is deemed for these purposes to have been legitimated by the subsequent marriage or civil partnership of his parents if, by the law of the place in which the father or second female parent was domiciled at the time of the marriage or civil partnership, the marriage or civil partnership operated immediately or subsequently to legitimise them, and not otherwise: British Protectorates, Protected States and Protected Persons Order 1982, SI 1982/1070, art 3(2) (as so substituted). 'Second female parent' means the woman who is a parent of the child by virtue of (1) the Human Fertilisation and Embryology Act 2008 s 42 (which relates to treatment provided to a woman who is at the time of treatment a party to a civil partnership or, in certain circumstances a void civil partnership); or (2) s 43 (which relates to treatment provided to a woman who agrees that second woman is to be parent) where the woman: (a) is the civil partner of the child's mother at the time of the child's birth; or (b) was the civil partner of the child's mother at any time during the period beginning with the time mentioned in s 43(b) and ending with the child's birth: British Protectorates, Protected States and Protected Persons Order 1982, SI 1982/1070, art 3(3) (as so substituted). In the case of a posthumous child, the reference to the status of the father, mother or parent under the Human Fertilisation and Embryology Act 2008 s 42 or s 43 at the time of the birth is, in relation to a person born after the death of his father, mother or parent by virtue of s 42 or 43, to be construed as a reference to the status of the parent in question at the time of that parent's death; if the parent died before 1 January 1983 and the child was born after that date, the parent is taken to have the status he would have had if he had died after that date: see the British Protectorates, Protected States and Protected Persons Order 1982, SI 1982/1070, art 4 (amended by SI 2009/1892). See also PARA 424 notes 6–7. As to the law of domicile see CONFLICT OF LAWS.
5 See the British Protectorates, Protected States and Protected Persons Order 1982, SI 1982/1070, art 7(1) (amended by virtue of the British Overseas Territories Act 2002 s 1(2); and by SI 2009/1892). This corresponds to the British Nationality Act 1981 Sch 2 paras 1, 2, conferring other forms of British nationality in equivalent circumstances.
    For these purposes, a person born aboard a registered ship, hovercraft or aircraft is deemed to have been born in the place where the ship, hovercraft or aircraft was registered, and a person born aboard an unregistered ship, hovercraft or aircraft of the government of any country is deemed to have been born in that country, provided that he is only deemed to have been born in the United Kingdom or a British overseas territory if he was born stateless: see the British Protectorates, Protected States and Protected Persons Order 1982, SI 1982/1070, art 8(1), (3) (art 8(1) amended by virtue of the British Overseas Territories Act 2002 s 1(2)). There is a rebuttable presumption that a new-born infant found abandoned was born in the territory in which he was so found: see the British Protectorates, Protected States and Protected Persons Order 1982, SI 1982/1070, art 8(2).
6 Ie whether before or after 1 January 1983.
7 In the case of a person who is under the age of 18 or who is of unsound mind, the application may be made by his parent or guardian or any person who has assumed responsibility for his welfare: see the British Protectorates, Protected States and Protected Persons Order 1982, SI 1982/1070, arts 2(2), 7(3). As to applications generally see PARA 484.

8 Ie by virtue of the Human Fertilisation and Embryology Act 2008 s 42 or s 43.

9 See note 4.

10 See the British Protectorates, Protected States and Protected Persons Order 1982, SI 1982/1070, art 7(2) (amended by virtue of the British Overseas Territories Act 2002 s 1(2); and by SI 2009/1892). If, in the special circumstances of any particular case, the Secretary of State thinks fit, he may treat the requirement in head (3) in the text as having been fulfilled although the number of days on which the person was absent from both the United Kingdom and the British overseas territories exceeded the number mentioned: see the British Protectorates, Protected States and Protected Persons Order 1982, SI 1982/1070, art 7(5) (amended by virtue of the British Overseas Territories Act 2002 s 1(2)). This corresponds to the British Nationality Act 1981 Sch 2 para 4, conferring other forms of British nationality in equivalent circumstances. As to the Secretary of State see PARA 402. As to the exercise of discretion see s 44; and PARA 402.

A person registered under the British Protectorates, Protected States and Protected Persons Order 1982, SI 1982/1070, art 7 is a British protected person by registration as from the date on which he is registered: art 9.

11 It seems that this does not apply to a person who is a British protected person by birth under the British Protectorates, Protected States and Protected Persons Order 1982, SI 1982/1070, art 7(1) (see the text and note 5).

12 As to British citizens and citizenship see PARAS 406, 421–444.

13 As to British overseas territories citizens and citizenship (formerly known as British dependent territories citizens and citizenship) see PARAS 406, 445–458.

14 As to British overseas citizens and citizenship see PARAS 406, 459–463.

15 See the British Protectorates, Protected States and Protected Persons Order 1982, SI 1982/1070, art 10 (amended by virtue of the British Overseas Territories Act 2002 s 2(3)). British protected person status was not, however, inconsistent with the simultaneous possession of citizenship of the United Kingdom and colonies: *Motala v A-G* [1992] 1 AC 281, [1991] 4 All ER 682, HL; and see PARA 476 text and note 16. See also PARA 478 note 14. As to citizenship of the United Kingdom and colonies see PARAS 414–419.

480. Renunciation of British protected person status.

A person of full age and capacity[1] who is a British protected person[2], and either has or satisfies the Secretary of State[3] that he will after renunciation acquire British citizenship[4], British overseas territories citizenship[5], British overseas citizenship[6], or another nationality[7], may renounce his British protected person status by declaration[8], upon registration of which he ceases to be a British protected person[9]. However, if he does not acquire such a citizenship or another nationality within six months, he is and is deemed to have remained a British protected person notwithstanding the registration[10]. There is no provision for the resumption of British protected person status once renounced.

1 For these purposes, a person is of full age if he has attained the age of 18 years and is of full capacity if he is not of unsound mind: British Protectorates, Protected States and Protected Persons Order 1982, SI 1982/1070, art 2(2).

2 Ie by virtue of the British Protectorates, Protected States and Protected Persons Order 1982, SI 1982/1070: see PARAS 478–479. There is no provision for renunciation by those who are British protected persons by virtue of the Solomon Islands Act 1978: see PARA 477.

3 As to the Secretary of State see PARA 402.

4 As to British citizens and citizenship see PARAS 406, 421–444.

5 As to British overseas territories citizens and citizenship (formerly known as British dependent territories citizens and citizenship) see PARAS 406, 445–458.

6 As to British overseas citizens and citizenship see PARAS 406, 459–463.

7 See also PARA 478 note 14.

8 See the British Protectorates, Protected States and Protected Persons Order 1982, SI 1982/1070, art 11(1) (amended by SI 1983/1699; and by virtue of the British Overseas Territories Act 2002 s 2(3)).

9 See the British Protectorates, Protected States and Protected Persons Order 1982, SI 1982/1070, art 11(2). The Secretary of State may withhold registration of a declaration made during wartime: see art 11(3).

10 See the British Protectorates, Protected States and Protected Persons Order 1982, SI 1982/1070, art 11(2). As to the automatic loss of British protected person status on acquisition of British or other nationality see the Solomon Islands Act 1978 s 4; the British Protectorates, Protected

States and Protected Persons Order 1982, SI 1982/1070, art 10; and PARAS 476–479. See also *R v Secretary of State for the Home Department, ex p Thakrar* [1974] QB 684, sub nom *Thakrar v Secretary of State for the Home Department* [1974] 2 All ER 261, CA (analogous automatic loss provision); *Motala v A-G* [1992] 1 AC 281, [1991] 4 All ER 682, HL (British protected person status not inconsistent with simultaneous possession of citizenship of the United Kingdom and colonies).

481. Access to British citizenship. There are several means by which a British protected person may be able to acquire British citizenship[1] by registration. Firstly, a British protected person is entitled[2], on application[3], to be registered as a British citizen if he satisfies the statutory requirements as to residence in the United Kingdom[4]. Secondly, the Secretary of State[5] may, if he thinks fit, register as a British citizen any British protected person who has at any time served in specified Crown service in a British overseas territory[6]. Thirdly, a person who has the status of British protected person is entitled to be registered as a British citizen if he applies for registration[7] and the Secretary of State is satisfied that the person does not have any citizenship or nationality, apart from such status, and that the person has not after the relevant day[8] renounced, voluntarily relinquished or lost through action or inaction any citizenship or nationality[9]. There is also a broad discretion to register any minor as a British citizen[10].

1 As to British citizens and citizenship see PARAS 406, 421–444.
2 As to factors overriding entitlement see PARA 426 note 4.
3 As to applications see PARA 484.
4 See the British Nationality Act 1981 s 4(1)–(4); and PARA 428. As to the meaning of 'United Kingdom' see PARA 403 note 1. As to the requirement of good character in the case of an application for registration of an adult or young person as a British citizen under s 4(2) or (5) see s 41A(1); and PARA 428 note 9. As to the meaning of 'adult or young person' see PARA 426 note 4.
5 As to the Secretary of State see PARA 402.
6 See the British Nationality Act 1981 s 4(5), (6); and PARA 428. As to British overseas territories (formerly known as dependent territories) see PARA 445 note 1.
7 Ie under the British Nationality Act 1981 s 4B.
8 As to the meaning of 'relevant day' see PARA 428 note 19.
9 See the British Nationality Act 1981 s 4B(1), (2); and PARA 428. Section 4B effectively renders the s 4 provisions defunct (as British protected persons by definition have no other nationality and so qualify under s 4B without the need for residence in the United Kingdom or Crown service).
10 Ie under the British Nationality Act 1981 s 3(1): see PARA 427.

9. MISCELLANEOUS MATTERS

482. Estoppel, legitimate expectation and unfairness. It is a general principle of law that an excess of statutory power cannot be validated by the operation of an estoppel[1]. Thus, a public authority can deny the validity of its own earlier conduct[2]. However, it appears that an assurance or representation of fact as to a person's citizenship status made by a public official, whose duties include such matters, to the person affected[3], and relied upon by that person to his detriment, can in certain circumstances preclude the Crown from denying such citizenship, even if the assurance or representation was given otherwise than in a manner or form prescribed by law[4].

If, in the exercise of its discretion, the Crown resiles from an earlier assurance as to the practice which it would follow, or the grant or recognition of citizenship status, such a decision may be open to challenge on the grounds that it is a breach of a legitimate expectation that the assurance would be honoured[5], or is otherwise unfair[6].

1   No public authority can, by making an assurance or representation, either extend the scope of its statutory powers or debar itself and its successors from exercising a statutory discretion or performing a statutory duty in the future: see ADMINISTRATIVE LAW vol 1(1) (2001 Reissue) PARA 23; ESTOPPEL vol 16(2) Reissue) PARAS 960, 1053. As to estoppel generally see ESTOPPEL. As to the private law concept of estoppel and the public law concept of a legitimate expectation created by a public authority see eg *R v East Sussex County Council, ex p Reprotech (Pebsham) Ltd* [2002] UKHL 8, [2002] 4 All ER 58, [2003] 1 WLR 348. See also note 5.

2   See eg *Minister of Agriculture and Fisheries v Matthews* [1950] 1 KB 148, [1949] 2 All ER 724; *Rhyl UDC v Rhyl Amusements Ltd* [1959] 1 All ER 257, [1959] 1 WLR 465.

3   Or, in the case of a child, to his parent or guardian. See also note 4.

4   *Gowa v A-G* (1984) 129 Sol Jo 131, CA; affd on different grounds [1985] 1 WLR 1003, HL. See also ADMINISTRATIVE LAW vol 1(1) (2001 Reissue) PARA 23.

    Both the scope and the existence of such a principle are problematic. In *Gowa v A-G* (1984) 129 Sol Jo 131, CA, an application was made to the Governor of Tanganyika in 1951 for registration of seven minor children as citizens of the United Kingdom and colonies (under the discretionary power of the British Nationality Act 1948 s 7(1) (now repealed)). A responsible official stated, in a letter, that they were already citizens of the United Kingdom and colonies; accordingly no further action was taken on the applications. The statement was erroneous; but by the time the Crown asserted the true position, they were no longer eligible for registration (being no longer minors). The Court of Appeal held by a majority that the Crown was estopped by the letter from denying that they were citizens of the United Kingdom and colonies. However, the decision is of limited impact. The Crown conceded that but for the mistake the children would have been registered. If the effect of the estoppel was to treat the children as having been granted citizenship when they ought to have been, the Court of Appeal was not sanctioning any extension or amendment of statutory powers or violating the principles set out in the text and note 1. The position would be otherwise if the effect of the estoppel was to treat the misstatement in the letter as true, since there was no statutory or other lawful support for the statement; it seems that *Gowa v A-G* (1984) 129 Sol Jo 131, CA, would not extend to cases of misstatement of a status which depends upon satisfaction of mandatory criteria: see *Christodoulidou v Secretary of State for the Home Department* [1985] Imm AR 179 at 182–183, IAT. The House of Lords in *Gowa v A-G* [1985] 1 WLR 1003, HL, affirmed the Court of Appeal's decision on a different basis (holding that the undetermined application remained pending and there was still power to grant the registration despite intervening changes of fact and law); the 'difficult' estoppel point was expressly left open: *Gowa v A-G* [1985] 1 WLR 1003 at 1005, HL, per Lord Roskill, and at 1010 per Lord Griffiths. In the light of this House of Lords' judgment, Mann J declined to express a view on whether the concept of estoppel existed in public law: see *R v Immigration Appeal Tribunal, ex p Kandemir* [1986] Imm AR 136 at 143 (on the facts in this case there was no detriment). Both the Home Office and the Immigration Appeal Tribunal have since accepted that, in the light of *Gowa v A-G* [1985] 1 WLR 1003, HL, the doctrine of estoppel could in principle apply to the grant and recognition of citizenship status where an assurance was given in the exercise of a discretionary power: see *Vun Liew v Secretary of State for the Home Department* [1989] Imm AR 62, IAT (on the facts in this case the scope of the assurance was too narrow to sustain the claim); *R v Secretary of State for the Home Department, ex p Ram* [1979] 1 All ER 687, [1979] 1 WLR 148, DC (mistaken grant of indefinite leave to remain). However, it appears that another government department is not able to bind the Home Secretary so as to fetter his discretion: *R v Immigration Appeal Tribunal, ex p Ahluwalia* [1979–80] Imm AR 1 at 7–8.

5   As to legitimate expectations see JUDICIAL REVIEW vol 61 (2010) PARA 649. The estoppel argument and the legitimate expectation argument have been said to be 'substantially the same': *Oloniluyi v Secretary of State for the Home Department* [1989] Imm AR 135 at 146, CA, per Dillon LJ. Cf *R v East Sussex County Council, ex p Reprotech (Pebsham) Ltd* [2002] UKHL 8, [2002] 4 All ER 58, [2003] 1 WLR 348 (there is an analogy between private law estoppel and the public law concept of a legitimate expectation created by a public authority, but it is no more than an analogy). See also *Vun Liew v Secretary of State for the Home Department* [1989] Imm AR 62, IAT (legitimate expectation argument rejected for the same reasons as the estoppel argument); *R v Secretary of State for the Home Department, ex p Ram* [1979] 1 All ER 687, [1979] 1 WLR 148, DC (grant of indefinite leave to remain not vitiated by immigration officer's mistake where no deception).

6   See *R (on the application of Rechachi) v Secretary of State for the Home Department* [2006] EWHC 3513 (Admin), [2006] All ER (D) 341 (Dec) (revised policy for successful asylum applications, providing for exceptional cases, lawful); and JUDICIAL REVIEW vol 61 (2010) PARA 648. As to procedural fairness see JUDICIAL REVIEW vol 61 (2010) PARA 625 et seq.

483.   Passports and proof of national status. A passport may be granted by the Crown at any time to enable a British subject to travel[1] to and enter foreign countries[2]. In form a passport is a request in the Queen's name to afford the holder free passage and any necessary assistance. It also serves as a certificate of identity and citizenship for the purpose of entry into the United Kingdom[3]. Passports are issued under the royal prerogative[4] in the discretion of the Secretary of State[5], who has power to require relevant information[6]; and passports are the property of the Crown, not of the passport-holder[7]. A passport may also be revoked or impounded in the discretion of the Crown[8]. British passports are issued by the Identity and Passport Service ('IPS')[9] or by diplomatic representatives abroad[10].

A British passport does not confer citizenship[11]; it is merely evidence of it, and of the right to claim the Crown's protection[12]. However, a British citizen[13] is required to prove his status if any question about it arises for the purposes of immigration law[14], and on arrival in the United Kingdom[15] this must generally be done by production of a United Kingdom passport describing him as a British citizen[16]. A person seeking to enter the United Kingdom and claiming to have the right of abode there may also prove that he has that right by production of a certificate of entitlement certifying that he has the right of abode[17]. There is an appeal against refusal of a certificate of entitlement[18] but not against refusal of a passport; however, refusal of a passport is subject to judicial review[19].

In accordance with international obligations[20], travel documents may be issued to lawfully resident refugees[21] and stateless persons[22].

1   The possession of a valid passport may be made a condition of a contract of carriage by the carrier.

2   A British citizen's right at common law to leave and return to the United Kingdom is not dependent on the possession of a British passport: Report of the Committee Privy Councillors appointed to inquire into the Recruitment of Mercenaries 1976 (Cmnd 6569) para 17. However, the possession of a passport is now almost always required by the authorities to enable a person to enter a country. A passport would not be available to enable its holder to travel in an enemy country in time of war.

3   Eg in respect of examination by an immigration officer: see the Immigration Act 1971 s 4, Sch 2 para 4(2)(a); and BRITISH NATIONALITY, IMMIGRATION AND ASYLUM vol 4(2) (Reissue) PARA 114.

4   As to the royal prerogative see CONSTITUTIONAL LAW AND HUMAN RIGHTS vol 8(2) (Reissue) PARA 367 et seq; CROWN AND ROYAL FAMILY vol 12(1) (Reissue) PARA 46 et seq.

5   See *R v Secretary of State for Foreign and Commonwealth Affairs, ex p Everett* [1989] QB 811, [1989] 1 All ER 655, CA; *Secretary of State for the Home Department v Lakdawalla* [1972] Imm AR 26, IAT. In the United Kingdom passports are the responsibility of the Secretary of State for the Home Department, but the Secretary of State for Foreign and Commonwealth Affairs remains responsible for passport applications made abroad: see PARA 401. As to the Secretary of State see PARA 402. British passports issued in the common format agreed between member states of the European Union do not confer or evidence any different national status from the previous British passport format, and are still issued by the United Kingdom authorities rather than by any special European Union authority.

6   The Secretary of State may require certain persons to provide him with information by a date specified in the requirement if it appears to him that they may have information that could be used: (1) for verifying information provided to the Secretary of State for the purposes of, or in connection with, an application for the issue of a passport; or (2) for determining whether to withdraw an individual's passport: see the Identity Documents Act 2010 s 10(1), (2). For these purposes, 'information' includes documents (including stamps and labels) and records; and the 'issue' of a document includes its renewal, replacement or re-issue (with or without modifications): s 10(12). The persons on whom a requirement to provide information may be imposed are: (a) a Minister of the Crown; (b) a government department; (c) a Northern Ireland department; (d) the Welsh Ministers; (e) the Registrar General for England and Wales; (f) the Registrar General of Births, Deaths and Marriages for Scotland; (g) the Registrar General of Births and Deaths in Northern Ireland; (h) a qualifying credit reference agency; and (i) any other person specified for the purposes of s 10 by an order made by the Secretary of State: s 10(3).

   A credit reference agency is 'qualifying' if, at the time a requirement is imposed, the agency is acting for the purposes of a contract for the provision to the Secretary of State of information that could be used as mentioned in head (1) or (2) above: s 10(4). A requirement imposed under s 10 on a qualifying credit reference agency is enforceable in civil proceedings for an injunction or any other appropriate remedy or relief: Identity Documents Act 2010 s 10(5).

   The persons who may be specified under s 10(3)(i) (see head (i) above) include any person who carries out a function that is conferred by or under an enactment (whenever passed or made) and falls to be carried out on behalf of the Crown: s 10(6). An order under s 10(3)(i) may provide that where a requirement is imposed under s 10 on the person specified in the order, the duty to comply with the requirement is enforceable as mentioned in s 10(5): s 10(7). At the date at which this volume states the law, no order had been made under s 10(3)(i).

   In a case within head (1) above, where a passport is issued, information provided in accordance with s 10 must be destroyed no later than 28 days after the passport is issued (s 10(8)); and in a case within head (2) above, where a passport is not withdrawn, information provided in accordance with s 10 must be destroyed no later than 28 days after the determination is made not to withdraw the passport (s 10(9)). However, these provisions do not apply in a case where it appears to the Secretary of State to be desirable to retain the information for the purpose of: (i) preventing or detecting crime; or (ii) apprehending or prosecuting offenders: s 10(10).

   The Secretary of State may make payments to a person providing information in accordance with s 10 in respect of the provision of the information: s 10(11).

   As to the offence of possessing or making false identity documents see ss 4–9; and REGISTRATION CONCERNING THE INDIVIDUAL.

7   A passport issued on behalf of the Crown remains the property of the Crown. If the holder becomes bankrupt, the passport is the property of the Crown and not of the bankrupt: *Suwalsky v Trustee and Official Receiver* [1928] B & CR 142, 4 BILC 780.

8   Most frequently passports are refused, withheld or revoked because of the risk that the holder will leave the country in order to evade justice: 764 HC Official Report (5th series), 13 May 1968, col 183. The issue of a passport is only refused in exceptional circumstances: 102 HC Official Report (6th series), 21 October 1986, written answers, col 802. As to cases in which a passport has been denied on political grounds see 764 HC Official Report (5th series), 14 May 1968, col 1041. As to the right of the police to retain the passport of a person suspected of a criminal offence see *Ghani v Jones* [1970] 1 QB 693, [1969] 3 All ER 1700, CA.

9   The Identity and Passport Service is responsible for issuing UK passports and for the registration of births, marriages and deaths in England and Wales. It is an executive agency of the Home Office. Further information may be obtained from its website, www.ips.gov.uk.

10   All adults (aged 16 and over) applying for a passport for the first time must attend an interview with IPS in person to confirm their identity. Application for a passport may be made to and fees paid through the Passport Office, London; the Passport Offices in Durham, Glasgow, Liverpool, Newport or Peterborough; or the Passport Agency in Belfast. The necessary form for this purpose may be obtained from a passport office, certain post offices, by telephone application or

online from IPS. See further www.direct.gov.uk/passports. Provision is made for the charging of fees for passports and documents of identity. Fees for passport applications are charged under the Consular Fees Order 2009, SI 2009/700 (amended by SI 2009/1745), made under the Consular Fees Act 1980 s 1(1). See the Consular Fees Order 2009, SI 2009/700, art 3, Sch 1 Pt III (passport applications made to the Foreign and Commonwealth Office), Sch 1 Pt IB (passport applications made in the United Kingdom) (Sch 1 substituted by SI 2009/1745).

11 Thus if a passport is issued showing a person to have a status he does not in fact hold, it may be withdrawn and cannot be relied on to assert that status, since the conditions of entitlement to the status are a matter of law which the person does not fulfil: *Christodoulidou v Secretary of State for the Home Department* [1985] Imm AR 179, IAT; *Secretary of State for the Home Department v Gold* [1985] Imm AR 66, IAT (citizens of the United Kingdom and colonies issued with passports erroneously showing them to have the right of abode, which would have constituted them British citizens on 1 January 1983: see PARAS 420, 422). See, however, PARA 482.

12 Whether such protection will be afforded is a matter for the Crown's discretion; it is not a right: *China Navigation Co Ltd v A-G* [1932] 2 KB 197, CA. In the case of a person who, as an alien, does not in fact have that right, acquisition of a passport by misrepresentation that he has British nationality extends his claim to protection, and hence his local allegiance, when he leaves the United Kingdom, as long as he holds the passport, even though, presumably, were the misrepresentation discovered the claim to protection would be regarded as unfounded: *Joyce v DPP* [1946] AC 347, [1946] 1 All ER 186, HL. If such an alien were to adhere to the Queen's enemies, he would be guilty of treason.

13 As to British citizens and citizenship see PARAS 406, 421–444.

14 See the Immigration Act 1971 s 3(8) (amended by the British Nationality Act 1981 s 39(6), Sch 4 paras 2, 4); and BRITISH NATIONALITY, IMMIGRATION AND ASYLUM vol 4(2) (2002 Reissue) PARA 84. As to the burden of proof see *Re Bamgbose* [1990] Imm AR 135, CA. It has been held that the production of a genuine United Kingdom passport, issued to the person who is seeking to enter the country and describing him as a British citizen, discharges the burden of proof of citizenship, and the burden on the Secretary of State to prove that it was obtained by fraud is high: see *R v Secretary of State for the Home Department, ex p Obi* [1997] 1 WLR 1498, [1997] Imm AR 420.

15 As to the meaning of 'United Kingdom' see PARA 403 note 1.

16 The requirement to present a British passport to British authorities in order to be allowed to return home is a relative novelty; passports being formerly thought of as 'intended to be presented to the Governments of foreign nations and to be used for that individual's protection as a British subject in foreign countries': *R v Brailsford* [1905] 2 KB 730, 4 BILC 769. Only a full British passport (or a certificate of entitlement) will suffice: *Minta v Secretary of State for the Home Department* [1992] Imm AR 380, CA (where the Court of Appeal confirmed that it is inappropriate for the court on a judicial review application to assess the factual validity of a claim to citizenship). As to the requirements for admission see BRITISH NATIONALITY, IMMIGRATION AND ASYLUM vol 4(2) (2002 Reissue) PARA 93 et seq. However, where a person on arrival produces an ostensibly valid passport or certificate of entitlement, the burden lies on the Secretary of State to prove that the person is not entitled to it: *Aboagye v Immigration Officer, Newhaven* (16 September 1991, unreported) (8144), IAT (burden not discharged). See also note 12.

Formerly production of a passport describing a person as a citizen of the United Kingdom and colonies with the right of abode would suffice, but this status ceased to exist on 1 January 1983 and passports issued before that date will now have expired. As to citizenship of the United Kingdom and colonies see PARAS 414–419.

17 See the Immigration Act 1971 s 3(9) (substituted by the Immigration, Asylum and Nationality Act 2006 s 30; and amended by the Identity Documents Act 2010 s 12, Schedule para 1). See also PARA 412 note 8. As to the right of abode see PARA 412. As to certificates of entitlement see further PARA 412. Note that a certificate of patriality issued under the Immigration Act 1971 and in force immediately before 1 January 1983 (ie the date of commencement of the British Nationality Act 1981: see PARA 403 note 1) has effect after that date as if it were a certificate of entitlement, unless the holder ceases to have right of abode in the United Kingdom on that date: see the British Nationality Act 1981 s 39(8) (amended by the Immigration Act 1988 s 3(3)).

A person who is a British citizen by operation of law might prefer to obtain a certificate of entitlement if, eg, he has another nationality which would be jeopardised by a claim to United Kingdom government protection which a passport would involve. The Immigration (Certificate of Entitlement to Right of Abode in the United Kingdom) Regulations 2006, SI 2006/3145, provide that a certificate of entitlement will only be issued to a person with the right of abode in the United Kingdom who does not hold a passport or ID card describing him as a British citizen:

see reg 6. The intention is to require a person to choose between British citizen document and a non-British document endorsed with a certificate of entitlement. As to the meaning of 'hold' see *SL Malaysia* [2010] UKUT 164 (IAC).

Commonwealth citizens without British citizenship who had the right of abode before 1 January 1983 and have retained it (see PARA 412) can prove it only by production of a certificate of entitlement, not being entitled to a United Kingdom passport. As to Commonwealth citizens see PARA 409.

18 The appeal lies to an adjudicator with a further appeal, with leave, to the immigration appeal tribunal. As to appeals see BRITISH NATIONALITY, IMMIGRATION AND ASYLUM vol 4(2) (2002 Reissue) PARA 173 et seq.

19 See *R v Secretary of State for Foreign and Commonwealth Affairs, ex p Everett* [1989] QB 811, [1989] 1 All ER 655, CA; *Council of Civil Service Unions v Minister for the Civil Service* [1985] AC 374, [1984] 3 All ER 935, HL. As to judicial review generally see JUDICIAL REVIEW vol 61 (2010) PARA 601 et seq.

20 See the Convention relating to the Status of Refugees (Geneva, 28 July 1951; TS 39 (1954); Cmd 9171) and Protocol (New York, 31 January 1967; TS 15 (1969); Cmnd 3906); Convention relating to the Status of Stateless Persons (New York, 28 September 1954; TS 41 (1960); Cmnd 1098) arts 27, 28, Schedules.

21 As to the meaning of 'refugee' see BRITISH NATIONALITY, IMMIGRATION AND ASYLUM vol 4(2) (2002 Reissue) PARA 239. As to refugees and asylum see BRITISH NATIONALITY, IMMIGRATION AND ASYLUM vol 4(2) (2002 Reissue) PARA 238 et seq.

22 These documents are issued by the Home Office to those who have been recognised as refugees or stateless under the Conventions mentioned in note 20. The obligation in international law gives no right in domestic law; but see eg *R v Chief Immigration Officer, Gatwick Airport, ex p Harjendar Singh* [1987] Imm AR 346 at 357. In a suitable case refusal of a travel document might well be amenable to judicial review. In addition to these travel documents, as a matter of discretion, certificates of identity may be issued to persons resident here who have been unreasonably refused passport facilities by their own countries (or, in some cases, who cannot reasonably be expected to apply for them) and who need to travel.

484.   Applications for naturalisation and registration; oaths of allegiance. Any application for registration as a British citizen[1], British overseas territories citizen[2], British overseas citizen[3] or British subject[4], or for a certificate of naturalisation as a British citizen[5] or a British overseas territories citizen[6], must be made to the appropriate authority[7] and must satisfy certain requirements[8]. All applications must: (1) be made in writing; (2) state the name, address and date and place of birth of the applicant; and (3) contain a declaration that the particulars stated are true[9]. Further details are required, depending on the type of application[10]. An application may be made on behalf of someone not of full age or capacity by his father or mother or any person who has assumed responsibility for his welfare[11].

A person of full age[12] may not be registered under the British Nationality Act 1981 as a British citizen or a British overseas territories citizen unless he has made the relevant citizenship oath and pledge[13] at a citizenship ceremony[14]. A person of full age may not be registered under the British Nationality Act 1981 as a British overseas citizen or a British subject unless he has made the relevant citizenship oath[15]. A certificate of naturalisation as a British citizen or a British overseas territories citizen may not be granted under the British Nationality Act 1981 to a person of full age unless he has made the relevant citizenship oath and pledge at a citizenship ceremony[16]. Where the Secretary of State thinks it appropriate because of the special circumstances of a case he may disapply any of the above requirements or modify the effect of any of them[17].

A person who is registered under the British Nationality Act 1981 as a citizen of any description or as a British subject is to be treated as having become a citizen or subject: (a) immediately on making the required citizenship oath and pledge[18]; or (b) where the requirement for an oath and pledge is disapplied, immediately on registration[19]. A person granted a certificate of naturalisation under the British Nationality Act 1981 as a citizen of any description is to be treated as having become a citizen: (i) immediately on making the required citizenship oath and pledge[20]; or (ii) where the requirement for an oath and pledge is disapplied, immediately on the grant of the certificate[21].

1 As to British citizens and citizenship see PARAS 406, 421–444. As to the acquisition of British citizenship by registration see PARAS 426–437.

2 As to British overseas territories citizens and citizenship (formerly British dependent territories citizens and citizenship) see PARAS 406, 445–458. As to the acquisition of British overseas territories citizenship by registration see PARAS 449–452.

3 As to British overseas citizens see PARAS 406, 459–463. As to the acquisition of British overseas citizenship by registration see PARA 461.

4 As to British subjects see PARAS 407, 469–474. As to the acquisition of the status of British subject by registration see PARA 473.

5 As to naturalisation as a British citizen see PARAS 438–442.

6 As to naturalisation as a British overseas territories citizen see PARAS 453–455.

7 As to the authority to whom an application is to be made see the British Nationality (General) Regulations 2003, SI 2003/548, reg 4; and the British Nationality (British Overseas Territories) Regulations 2007, SI 2007/3139, reg 4. As to the power to make regulations see PARA 404.

8 See the British Nationality (General) Regulations 2003, SI 2003/548, reg 3; and the British Nationality (British Overseas Territories) Regulations 2007, SI 2007/3139, reg 3. The requirements for establishing sufficient knowledge of the English language and life in the United Kingdom for the purpose of an application for naturalisation as a British citizen are specified in the British Nationality (General) Regulations 2003, SI 2003/548, reg 5A (added by SI 2004/1726; and substituted by SI 2005/2785). For the purposes of the British Nationality Act 1981, an application is to be taken to have been made at the time of its receipt by a person authorised to receive it on behalf of the person to whom it is made; and references to the date of such an application are references to the date of its receipt by a person so authorised: s 50(8).

The requirements may include a requirement to observe a deadline; eg certain applications made by virtue of a connection with Hong Kong had to be made on or before 31 March 1996: see s 42(6) (as originally added by SI 1993/1795; and amended by virtue of the British Overseas Territories Act 2002 s 2(2)(b); now substituted: see note 14). See further PARA 433.

9 See the British Nationality (General) Regulations 2003, SI 2003/548, reg 3, Sch 1 Pt I; and the British Nationality (British Overseas Territories) Regulations 2007, SI 2007/3139, reg 3, Sch 1 Pt I.

10 See the British Nationality (General) Regulations 2003, SI 2003/548, reg 3, Sch 2 (amended by SI 2005/2114, SI 2005/2785, SI 2007/3137 and SI 2009/3363); and the British Nationality (British Overseas Territories) Regulations 2007, SI 2007/3139, reg 3, Sch 2.

11 See the British Nationality (General) Regulations 2003, SI 2003/548, reg 5; and the British Nationality (British Overseas Territories) Regulations 2007, SI 2007/3139, reg 5. See also the British Nationality (General) Regulations 2003, SI 2003/548, Sch 1 Pt II; and the British Nationality (British Overseas Territories) Regulations 2007, SI 2007/3139, Sch 1 Pt II.

12 As to the meanings of 'full age' and 'full capacity', and as to the discretion to waive the requirement in respect of a specified applicant, see PARA 438 note 12.

13 Ie as specified in the British Nationality Act 1981 Sch 5.

14 British Nationality Act 1981 s 42(1), (3) (s 42 substituted by the Nationality, Immigration and Asylum Act 2002 s 3, Sch 1 para 1). For the form of the citizenship oath and pledge see Sch 5 paras 1, 2 (Sch 5 substituted by the Nationality, Immigration and Asylum Act 2002 Sch 1 para 2). For the form of words in Welsh which may be used as an alternative to the form of citizenship oath and pledge set out in the British Nationality Act 1981 Sch 5 para 1, see the Citizenship Oath and Pledge (Welsh Language) Order 2007, SI 2007/1484, art 3. The oath must be taken within three months of the giving of a notice that the registration is to be effected or that the certificate of naturalisation is to be granted, or within such longer time as the Secretary of State may allow: see the British Nationality (General) Regulations 2003, SI 2003/548, reg 6(2)–(5) (reg 6 substituted by SI 2003/3158); and the British Nationality (British Overseas Territories) Regulations 2007, SI 2007/3139, reg 6(1), (3), (4). As to the administration of the oath see the British Nationality (General) Regulations 2003, SI 2003/548, reg 6(1), Sch 3 (amended by SI 2003/3158); and the British Nationality (British Overseas Territories) Regulations 2007, SI 2007/3139, reg 6(2), Sch 3. As to arrangements for, and the conduct of, citizenship ceremonies see the British Nationality (General) Regulations 2003, SI 2003/548, reg 6A (added by SI 2003/3158).

An oath of allegiance was never required for registration as a British national (overseas), since only British overseas territories citizens were eligible for such registration. As to British national (overseas) status see PARAS 406, 465–467.

15 British Nationality Act 1981 s 42(5) (as substituted: see note 14). For the form of the citizenship oath see Sch 5 paras 3, 4 respectively (as substituted: see note 14). The Oaths Act 1978 ss 5, 6 (affirmation) apply to a citizenship oath; and a reference in the British Nationality Act 1981 to a citizenship oath includes a reference to a citizenship affirmation: s 42(7) (as so substituted). For the forms of words in Welsh which may be used as an alternative to the forms of affirmation set out in the Oaths Act 1978 s 6, see the Citizenship Oath and Pledge (Welsh Language) Order 2007, SI 2007/1484, art 4. See CIVIL PROCEDURE vol 11 (2009) PARA 1023.

16 British Nationality Act 1981 s 42(2), (4) (as substituted: see note 14). For the form of the citizenship oath and pledge see Sch 5 paras 1, 2 (as substituted: see note 14).

17 British Nationality Act 1981 s 42(6) (as substituted: see note 14).

18 Ie in accordance with the British Nationality Act 1981 s 42. In the application of s 42B(1) to registration as a British overseas citizen or as a British subject the reference to the citizenship oath and pledge is to be taken as a reference to the citizenship oath: s s 42B(3) (s 42B added by the Nationality, Immigration and Asylum Act 2002 Sch 1 para 1).

19 British Nationality Act 1981 s 42B(1) (as added: see note 18).

20 Ie in accordance with the British Nationality Act 1981 s 42.

21 British Nationality Act 1981 s 42B(2) (as added: see note 18). As to the form of a certificate of naturalisation see the British Nationality (General) Regulations 2003, SI 2003/548, reg 7 (substituted by SI 2007/3137); and the British Nationality (British Overseas Territories) Regulations 2007, SI 2007/3139, reg 7.

485.   Fees. The Secretary of State[1] may by order require an application or claim in connection with immigration or nationality[2] (whether or not under an enactment) to be accompanied by a specified fee[3]. The Secretary of State may by order provide for a fee to be charged by him, by an immigration officer or by another specified person in respect of: (1) the provision on request of a service (whether or not under an enactment) in connection with immigration or nationality; (2) a process (whether or not under an enactment) in connection with immigration or nationality; (3) the provision on request of advice in connection with immigration or nationality; or (4) the provision on request of information in connection with immigration or nationality[4]. Where an order provides for a fee to be charged, regulations made by the Secretary of State: (a) must specify the amount of the fee; (b) may provide for exceptions; (c) may confer a discretion to reduce, waive or refund all or part of a fee; (d) may make provision about the consequences of failure to pay a fee; (e) may make provision about enforcement; and (f) may make provision about the time or period of time at or during which a fee may or must be paid[5].

A fee imposed under these provisions may relate to a thing whether or not it is done wholly or partly outside the United Kingdom; they are without prejudice to the Consular Fees Act 1980 and to any other power to charge a fee[6].

1 As to the Secretary of State see PARA 402.

2 A reference in the Immigration, Asylum and Nationality Act 2006 s 51 to anything in connection with immigration or nationality includes a reference to anything in connection with an enactment (including an enactment of a jurisdiction outside the United Kingdom) that relates wholly or partly to immigration or nationality: s 52(6).

3 Immigration, Asylum and Nationality Act 2006 s 51(1). In exercise of the power conferred by s 51(1), (2), the Secretary of State has made the Immigration and Nationality (Fees) (No 2) Order 2007, SI 2007/807 (amended by SI 2008/166; SI 2009/420). This order is to be replaced by the Immigration and Nationality (Fees) Order 2011, SI 2011/445, on the coming into force of regulations made under the Immigration, Asylum and Nationality Act 2006 s 51(3) (see the text and note 5) in connection with setting the level of the fees and charges covered in the Immigration and Nationality (Fees) Order 2011, SI 2011/445: see art 9.

Fees paid by virtue of the Immigration, Asylum and Nationality Act 2006 s 51 must: (1) be paid into the Consolidated Fund; or (2) be applied in such other way as the relevant order may specify: s 51(4). As to the Consolidated Fund see CONSTITUTIONAL LAW AND HUMAN RIGHTS vol 8(2) (Reissue) PARA 711 et seq; PARLIAMENT vol 78 (2010) PARA 1028.

4   Immigration, Asylum and Nationality Act 2006 s 51(2).

5   Immigration, Asylum and Nationality Act 2006 s 51(3). An order or regulations under s 51: (1) may make provision generally or only in respect of specified cases or circumstances; (2) may make different provision for different cases or circumstances; (3) may include incidental, consequential or transitional provision; and (4) must be made by statutory instrument: s 52(3). See the Immigration and Nationality (Fees) (No 2) Regulations 2010, SI 2010/2807; and the Immigration and Nationality (Cost Recovery Fees) (No 2) Regulations 2010, SI 2010/2226.

6   Immigration, Asylum and Nationality Act 2006 s 52(1). Section 51 is without prejudice to the application of the Finance (No 2) Act 1987 s 102 (government fees and charges); and an order made under that section in respect of a power repealed by the Immigration, Asylum and Nationality Act 2006 Sch 2 is to have effect as if it related to the powers under s 51 in so far as they relate to the same matters as the repealed power: s 52(2). An order under s 51: (a) may be made only with the consent of the Treasury; and (b) may be made only if a draft has been laid before and approved by resolution of each House of Parliament: s 52(4). Regulations under s 51: (i) may be made only with the consent of the Treasury; and (ii) are subject to annulment in pursuance of a resolution of either House of Parliament: s 52(5).

486.   Evidence. Every document purporting to be a notice, certificate, order or declaration, or an entry in a register, or a subscription of an oath of allegiance, given, granted or made under the British Nationality Act 1981 or any of the former nationality Acts[1] is to be received in evidence and, unless the contrary is proved, is to be deemed to have been given, granted or made by or on behalf of the person by whom or on whose behalf it purports to have been given, granted or made[2]. Prima facie evidence of any such document may be given by the production of a document purporting to be certified as a true copy of it by such person and in such manner as may be prescribed[3]. Any entry in a register made under the British Nationality Act 1981 or any of the former nationality Acts is to be received as evidence (and in Scotland as sufficient evidence) of the matters stated in the entry[4]. A certificate given by or on behalf of the Secretary of State that a person was at any time in Crown service under the government of the United Kingdom[5] or that a person's recruitment for such service took place in the United Kingdom is, for the purposes of the British Nationality Act 1981, conclusive evidence of that fact[6].

1   As to the meaning of 'former nationality Acts' see PARA 422 note 13.

2   British Nationality Act 1981 s 45(1). Section 45 applies for the purposes of the British Nationality (Falkland Islands) Act 1983 as it applies for the purposes of the British Nationality Act 1981: British Nationality (Falkland Islands) Act 1983 s 4(1), (2)(d). The British Nationality Act 1981 s 45 has effect as if any reference in it to the British Nationality Act 1981 included a reference to the Hong Kong (British Nationality) Order 1986, SI 1986/948: see art 7(7)(a).

3   British Nationality Act 1981 s 45(2). A document may be certified to be a true copy of a document by means of a statement in writing to that effect signed by a person authorised by the Secretary of State, the Lieutenant-Governor, the High Commissioner or the Governor in that behalf: see the British Nationality (General) Regulations 2003, SI 2003/548, reg 13; and the British Nationality (British Overseas Territories) Regulations 2007, SI 2007/3139, reg 10. See also the British Nationality (Hong Kong) Regulations 1986, SI 1986/2175, reg 11. As to the power to make regulations see PARA 404. As to the Secretary of State see PARA 402.

4   British Nationality Act 1981 s 45(3).

5   As to the meaning of 'United Kingdom' see PARA 403 note 1.

6   British Nationality Act 1981 s 45(4).

487.   Offences. Any person who for the purpose of procuring anything to be done or not to be done under the British Nationality Act 1981 makes any statement which he knows to be false[1] in a material particular, or recklessly makes any statement which is false in a material particular, commits an offence[2].

Any person who, without reasonable excuse, fails to comply with any requirement imposed on him by regulations with respect to the delivering up of certificates of naturalisation[3], commits an offence[4].

A conspiracy to obtain a passport by false or fraudulent representations tending to produce a public mischief has been held to constitute an indictable offence[5].

1   As to the effect of fraud, false representation or concealment of material fact on registration or naturalisation see PARAS 444, 458, 467.

2   See the British Nationality Act 1981 s 46(1). The penalty on summary conviction is imprisonment for a term not exceeding three months or a fine not exceeding level 5 on the standard scale, or both: see s 46(1) (amended by virtue of the Criminal Justice Act 1982 ss 37, 46). As to the standard scale see SENTENCING AND DISPOSITION OF OFFENDERS vol 92 (2010) PARA 142. As from a day to be appointed, the maximum term of imprisonment to which an offender is liable is 51 weeks: see the British Nationality Act 1981 s 46(1) (prospectively amended by the Criminal Justice Act 2003 s 280(2), (3), Sch 26 para 29). At the date at which this volume states the law, no such day had been appointed. If he is not a British citizen, the offender is also liable to deportation: see the Immigration Act 1971 s 3(6) (amended by the British Nationality Act 1981 s 39(6), Sch 4 paras 2, 4); and BRITISH NATIONALITY, IMMIGRATION AND ASYLUM vol 4(2) (2002 Reissue) PARA 160 et seq.

    As to the time within which proceedings in the case of an offence under the British Nationality Act 1981 s 46(1) must be brought see s 46(3), (4). For the purposes of trial, the offence is deemed to have been committed either at the place at which it actually was committed or at any place at which the person accused may be: s 46(5).

    Section 46 applies for the purposes of the British Nationality (Falkland Islands) Act 1983 as it applies for the purposes of the British Nationality Act 1981: British Nationality (Falkland Islands) Act 1983 s 4(1), (2)(e). The British Nationality Act 1981 s 46(1) has effect as if any reference in it to the British Nationality Act 1981 included a reference to the Hong Kong (British Nationality) Order 1986, SI 1986/948: see art 7(7)(b). As to the application of the British Nationality Act 1981 s 46(1) and s 46(2) (see the text and note 4) to Jersey see s 46(6).

3   As to regulations relating to the delivering up of certificates of naturalisation see the British Nationality (General) Regulations 2003, SI 2003/548, reg 12; and PARA 444. See also PARA 458. Citizenship by registration is effected by the entry in the register, cancellation of which is within the authorities' control (though documentary evidence of it in the hands of the registered person would no longer be valid); but citizenship by naturalisation is effected by the grant to the citizen of a certificate of naturalisation, and it is accordingly the certificate itself which requires cancellation.

4   See the British Nationality Act 1981 s 46(2). See also note 2. The penalty on summary conviction is a fine not exceeding level 4 on the standard scale: s 46(2) (amended by virtue of the Criminal Justice Act 1982 ss 37, 46). If he is not a British citizen, the offender is also liable to deportation: see the Immigration Act 1971 s 3(6) (as amended: see note 2); and BRITISH NATIONALITY, IMMIGRATION AND ASYLUM vol 4(2) (2002 Reissue) PARA 160 et seq.

    For the purposes of trial, the offence is deemed to have been committed either at the place at which it actually was committed or at any place at which the person accused may be: s 46(5).

5   *R v Brailsford* [1905] 2 KB 730, 4 BILC 769. However, obtaining a passport by means of false declarations might be an offence apart from conspiracy: see *R v Brailsford* [1905] 2 KB 730 at 737 per Lord Alverstone CJ. As to the issue of passports see PARA 483. As to forgery of a passport see CRIMINAL LAW vol 25 (2010) PARA 339 et seq.

488–500.   Limitation of criminal liability.   A British subject[1] or citizen of the Republic of Ireland[2] is not guilty of an offence against the laws of any part of the United Kingdom and colonies[3] by reason of anything done or omitted in any Commonwealth country[4] or in the Republic of Ireland or in any foreign country[5], unless: (1) the act or omission would be an offence if he were an alien[6]; and (2) in the case of an act or omission in any Commonwealth country or in the Republic of Ireland, it would be an offence if the country in which the act is done or the omission made were a foreign country[7].

1   As to British subjects see PARAS 407, 469–474.
2   See PARA 410.

3   As to the meaning of 'United Kingdom' see PARA 403 note 1. For the purposes of the British Nationality Act 1948, references to the colonies include references to the Channel Islands and the Isle of Man: s 33(1).

4   See PARA 409 notes 4, 16.

5   As to the meaning of 'foreign country' see PARA 404 note 22.

6   As to aliens see PARA 411.

7   See the British Nationality Act 1948 s 3(1); and the Ireland Act 1949 ss 1(1), (3), 3 (s 3 amended by the British Nationality Act 1981 s 52(6), Sch 7). See also the Foreign Jurisdiction Acts 1890 and 1913. The British Nationality Act 1948 s 3(1) does not apply to the contravention of any provision of the Merchant Shipping Act 1995 (see SHIPPING AND MARITIME LAW): see the British Nationality Act 1948 s 3(1) proviso (amended by the Merchant Shipping Act 1995 s 314(2), Sch 13). The Antarctic Treaty Act 1967 (see ANIMALS vol 2 (2008) PARA 990) provides that the British Nationality Act 1948 s 3(1) does not have effect in relation to any offence under that Act: see the Antarctic Treaty Act 1967 s 10(8). As from a day to be appointed s 10(8) is repealed by the Antarctic Act 1994 s 33, Schedule. At the date at which this volume states the law no such day had been appointed. The limitation of liability by the British Nationality Act 1948 s 3(1) is expressly preserved in relation to the extra-territorial effect given to the Air Navigation Order 2005, SI 2005/1970 (see AIR LAW): see art 149.

    The limitation in the British Nationality Act 1948 s 3(1) also extended to the laws of any protectorate or United Kingdom trust territory (see PARA 415 note 6), but no protectorates or United Kingdom trust territories now remain.

BROADCASTING

1. INTRODUCTION

(1) DEVELOPMENT OF BROADCASTING

501. Development of broadcasting. The concept of 'broadcasting' developed over the course of the twentieth century, from its origins in analogue radio and television broadcasting to the delivery of audio-visual media content across a range of 'platforms'. The success of the experimental broadcasts by wireless telegraphy made by the Marconi company[1] saw the advent of the broadcasting era, first with analogue radio and subsequently with analogue television broadcasting. In the United Kingdom, the British Broadcasting Company (which represented the interests of a number of radio manufacturers) was licensed by the Postmaster General[2] in 1923[3], and enjoyed a monopoly over public broadcasting until it was replaced in 1927 by the British Broadcasting Corporation ('BBC')[4]. Experimental television broadcasting transmissions were made by the BBC from 1929. In 1935, the corporation was licensed by the Postmaster General to provide a public television service. This was first broadcast in 1936, with a second channel, BBC2, being launched in 1964. A second national, analogue television broadcasting service was established from 1954 with the creation of the Independent Television Authority and the progressive allocation of regional franchises[5]. Independent radio was legitimised from 1972[6], having operated unlicensed for some years[7]. Further analogue television broadcasting services were introduced, with Channel 4 (provided originally by the Independent Broadcasting Authority) launching in 1982 and Channel 5 in 1997[8].

1   As to the development of wireless telegraphy and the Marconi company see PARA 509.
2   As to the former office of Postmaster General, and as to the distribution of his functions, see POST OFFICE vol 36(2) (Reissue) PARAS 1–3.
3   See the licence granted on 18 January 1923 for the establishment of eight radiotelephone stations and the transmission from them of broadcast matter for general reception and the agreement with respect to the broadcasting of news and general information (Cmd 1822). See also the supplementary agreement of 1 October 1923 (Cmd 1976).
4   Agreement dated 9 November 1926 (Cmd 2755). See also the licence and agreement between the Postmaster General and the Governors Designate of the British Broadcasting Corporation (Cmd 2756). As to the British Broadcasting Corporation see PARAS 603–626.
5   See the Television Act 1954 s 1 (repealed).
6   The Sound Broadcasting Act 1972 s 1(1) (repealed) renamed the Independent Television Authority as the Independent Broadcasting Authority ('IBA'). Under the Sound Broadcasting Act 1972 s 2 (repealed), the IBA assumed the function of providing local sound broadcasting services.
7   As to the licensing of radio see PARAS 723–783.
8   As to Channel 4 see PARAS 627–643; and as to Channel 5 see PARAS 677–681.

502. The current broadcasting landscape. The latter part of the twentieth century saw the proliferation of audio-visual media platforms, which first facilitated the development of multi-channel broadcasting. With the advent of digital technologies, broadcasting is moving from being an exclusively scheduled 'push' medium to being a 'pull' medium, with consumers selecting desired content from menus of available programming. In addition, new technological possibilities, including High Definition ('HD') and 3-D television, have been developed and introduced by a number of broadcasters. The roll-out of different technologies has occurred at varying times and in varying sequences in different countries. In the United Kingdom, cable television (that is, the delivery of audio-visual media content over telecommunications networks) was first introduced in 1984[1], but remained relatively undeveloped until the 1990s. Following consolidation in the sector, the sole provider of cable television in the United Kingdom is Virgin Media. Direct-to-home satellite broadcasting was first receivable in the United Kingdom (unlicensed) in 1978. Subscription-service Sky Television was launched in 1989, and merged with British Satellite Broadcasting to form BSkyB in 1990[2].

Analogue broadcasting is being replaced by digital terrestrial broadcasting, which reduces spectrum use[3]. The digital terrestrial television service remains in large measure free-to-air, with the main component (branded as 'Freeview') being launched in 2002[4]. In more recent times, viable services delivering audio-visual media content across broadband internet (Internet Protocol Television ('IPTV')) and 3G mobile phone telecommunications networks have also emerged[5].

1   This followed the establishment of the Cable Authority under the Cable and Broadcasting Act 1984 s 1 (repealed). As to cable and satellite broadcasting see PARAS 716–722.
2   At the date at which this volume states the law, News Corporation had a substantial holding in BSkyB and was seeking sole ownership.
3   Digital terrestrial broadcasting in the United Kingdom is operated across six multiplexes, of which some were allocated to the pre-existing analogue channel providers and the remainder made available by the regulator on a competitive basis. The process of 'digital switchover' (ie the ending of analogue transmission in favour of digital terrestrial transmission) was initiated in the United Kingdom in 2007 and is due to be completed in 2012. As to digital terrestrial broadcasting see PARA 690 et seq. As to digital switchover see PARAS 620, 702.
4   Freeview is now jointly run by the BBC, ITV, Channel 4, Sky and Arqiva.
5   As to the internet and telecommunications networks see PARA 600; and TELECOMMUNICATIONS.

(2) LEGISLATION RELATING TO BROADCASTING

503.   Overview of relevant law.   The law regarding broadcasting is concerned with both the content delivered across audio-visual media platforms, and the structure of the markets in which media organisations operate. Some of this law is general in nature, while some relates specifically to broadcasting.

Copyright and related aspects of intellectual property law will determine which media organisations are positioned to exploit and generate revenue from disparate forms of media content[1]. Libel law[2], law relating to misuse of private information[3], data protection law[4], and the law of confidentiality[5] can constrain the freedom of broadcasters to air content that may impinge upon private interests. Publication of certain forms of content may be restricted for reasons of public interest; for example, the law of contempt of court precludes any broadcast that creates a substantial risk that the course of justice in the proceedings in question will be seriously impeded or prejudiced[6], while the range of restrictions on the reporting of court proceedings applies to broadcasters as to other media organisations.

As regards the regulation of industry structure, competition law applies to broadcasting as to other industry sectors so as to avoid mergers that have resulted or may be expected to result in a substantial lessening of competition, to prohibit anti-competitive agreements between firms, and to prohibit any abuse of a dominant position[7]. Similarly, provisions of the Treaty on the Functioning of the European Union[8] are applicable so as to prohibit the granting by a member state to a broadcaster (or in some circumstances by a public broadcaster to others) of any aid that affects trade between member states should such aid distort or threaten to distort competition by favouring certain undertakings.

1   As to copyright see COPYRIGHT, DESIGN RIGHT AND RELATED RIGHTS. Aside from copyright, trademark law, the law of passing off (unfair competition), and confidence can be relevant, for

    example, in the legal control of television programme formats. See CONFIDENCE AND DATA PROTECTION; TRADE MARKS AND TRADE NAMES.

2   If false and defamatory, broadcast content may give rise to a claim in libel and not slander: see the Defamation Act 1952 s 16(1); the Broadcasting Act 1990 s 166; and PARA 945. See also LIBEL AND SLANDER.

3   See CONFIDENCE AND DATA PROTECTION.

4   See CONFIDENCE AND DATA PROTECTION.

5   See CONFIDENCE AND DATA PROTECTION.

6   See the Contempt of Court Act 1981 s 2(2); and CONTEMPT OF COURT vol 9(1) (Reissue) PARA 413.

7   See the Enterprise Act 2002 ss 35, 36; the Competition Act 1998 ss 2, 18; and COMPETITION vol 18 (2009) PARAS 115, 125–128, 184. As to media mergers see also PARAS 839–849.

8   See the Treaty on the Functioning of the European Union (Rome, 25 March 1957; TS 1 (1973); Cmnd 5179) arts 107–109. The Treaty was formerly known as the Treaty Establishing the European Community; it has been renamed and its provisions renumbered: see PARA 506 note 27.

504. Legislation relating to broadcasting. The main specific statutes governing broadcasting are the Broadcasting Act 1990[1], the Broadcasting Act 1996[2] and the Communications Act 2003[3].

Among the matters governed by the Broadcasting Act 1990 are the regulation by OFCOM[4] of independent television services generally[5], television broadcasting on Channels 3, 4 and 5[6], additional services provided on television broadcasting frequencies[7], television broadcasting by the Welsh Authority[8], independent radio services[9], sound broadcasting services[10], and additional services provided on sound broadcasting frequencies[11]. The Act also makes provision relating to the transfer of undertakings[12], foreign satellite services[13], the transfer to the BBC of functions connected with television licences[14], Gaelic television programmes[15], a national television archive[16], and the power to give broadcasting bodies etc directions relating to international obligations[17].

The matters governed by the Broadcasting Act 1996 include digital terrestrial television broadcasting[18] and digital terrestrial sound broadcasting[19]. The Act also contains provisions relating to sporting and other events of national interest[20], broadcasting standards[21], and the transfer of property, rights and liabilities relating to the BBC transmission network[22].

The Communications Act 2003 deals with, among other matters, the functions of OFCOM in relation to the BBC[23], the regulation of independent television services[24], the regulation of independent radio services[25], the public service remit for television[26], must-offer obligations affecting public service television[27], other specific obligations relating to television broadcasting[28], media ownership and control of television and radio services[29], the licensing of television reception[30] and on-demand television programmes[31].

1   The Broadcasting Act 1990 extends to the whole of the United Kingdom, with the exception of s 162, Sch 15 (England and Wales only), s 163 (Scotland only), s 164 (England and Wales and Scotland) and s 165 (Northern Ireland only): s 204(3), (4). As to the meaning of 'United Kingdom' see PARA 510 note 13.

    Certain provisions of the Broadcasting Act 1990 have been extended to the Channel Islands and the Isle of Man: see the Broadcasting Act 1990 (Jersey) Order 1991, SI 1991/193; the Broadcasting Act 1990 (Jersey) (No 2) Order 1991, SI 1991/1710 (amended by SI 1994/1064, SI 1999/1314, SI 1999/1315, SI 2003/3196 and SI 2003/3203); the Broadcasting Act 1990 (Guernsey) Order 1991, SI 1991/191; the Broadcasting Act 1990 (Guernsey) (No 2) Order 1991, SI 1991/1709 (amended by SI 1994/1064, SI 1999/1314, and SI 2003/3192); the Broadcasting Act 1990 (Isle of Man) Order 1991, SI 1991/192; and the Broadcasting Act 1990 (Isle of Man) (No 2) Order 1991, SI 1991/998 (amended by SI 2003/3193).

2   The Broadcasting Act 1996 extends to Northern Ireland: s 150(2). Certain provisions of the Act have been extended to the Channel Islands and the Isle of Man: see the Broadcasting Act 1996

(British Broadcasting Corporation–Transmission Network) (Jersey) Order 1997, SI 1997/1757; the Broadcasting (Jersey) Order 2003, SI 2003/3203 (amended by SI 2004/308); the Broadcasting Act 1996 (British Broadcasting Corporation–Transmission Network) (Guernsey) Order 1997, SI 1997/1755; the Broadcasting (Guernsey) Order 2003, SI 2003/3192; the Broadcasting Act 1996 (British Broadcasting Corporation–Transmission Network) (Isle of Man) Order 1997, SI 1997/1756; and the Broadcasting (Isle of Man) Order 2003, SI 2003/3193 (amended by SI 2004/309).

3 As to the Communications Act 2003 see TELECOMMUNICATIONS vol 97 (2010) PARA 1.
4 As to OFCOM see PARA 507. As to the general duties of OFCOM in relation to broadcasting see PARA 507.
5 See the Broadcasting Act 1990 ss 3–5, 13, Sch 2; and PARAS 662, 665, 674, 821–827, 593.
6 See the Broadcasting Act 1990 Pt I Ch II (ss 14–42), Ch IIA (ss 42A, 42B), s 66; and PARAS 667–676, 681, 689, 813, 864–866, 885.
7 See the Broadcasting Act 1990 Pt I Ch V (ss 48–55); and PARAS 703–710.
8 See the Broadcasting Act 1990 Pt I Ch VI (ss 56–64); and PARAS 644–661.
9 See the Broadcasting Act 1990 Pt III Ch I (ss 85–97B), Sch 2; and PARAS 702, 724–726, 829–836.
10 See the Broadcasting Act 1990 Pt III Ch II (ss 98–111B); and PARAS 730–748.
11 See the Broadcasting Act 1990 Pt III Ch IV (ss 114–120); and PARAS 772–778.
12 See the Broadcasting Act 1990 Pt IV (ss 127–141); and PARAS 507, 550–563.
13 See the Broadcasting Act 1990 ss 177–178; and PARA 597.
14 See the Broadcasting Act 1990 s 180; and PARA 952. As to the meaning of 'BBC' see PARA 603 note 1; and as to the BBC see PARAS 603–626.
15 See the Broadcasting Act 1990 ss 183–184; and PARAS 800–808.
16 See the Broadcasting Act 1990 s 185; and PARA 810.
17 See the Broadcasting Act 1990 s 188; and PARA 506.
18 See the Broadcasting Act 1996 Pt I (ss 1–39), Sch 1; and PARAS 502, 690–696, 698–701, 711–713.
19 See the Broadcasting Act 1996 Pt II (ss 40–72), Sch 1 Pt II; and PARAS 727–728, 754–758, 760–768, 770–771, 779–782, 837.
20 See the Broadcasting Act 1996 Pt IV (ss 97–105); and PARAS 915–922.
21 See the Broadcasting Act 1996 Pt V (ss 107–130); and PARAS 906–914.
22 See the Broadcasting Act 1996 Pt VI (ss 131–135), Schs 5, 6; and PARAS 551–563.
23 See the Communications Act 2003 s 198; and PARA 854.
24 See the Communications Act 2003 Pt 3 Ch 2 (ss 211–244); and PARAS 641, 665–666, 686–688, 697, 715–718, 857, 861–863, 943.
25 See the Communications Act 2003 Pt 3 Ch 3 (ss 245–262); and PARAS 723, 729, 749–753.
26 See the Communications Act 2003 ss 264–271A; and PARAS 640, 642–643, 662–663, 677–678, 682–683, 788–791.
27 See the Communications Act 2003 ss 272–275; and PARAS 720–722, 796.
28 See the Communications Act 2003 ss 276–347; and PARAS 661, 664, 684–685, 792–794, 797, 851–852, 875–878, 880, 882–884, 890–891, 897–899, 901–902.
29 See the Communications Act 2003 Pt 3 Ch 5 (ss 348–357), Sch 14; and PARAS 814–821, 823, 831, 838.
30 See the Communications Act 2003 Pt 4 (ss 363–368); and PARAS 948–951.
31 See the Communications Act 2003 Pt 4A (ss 368A–368R); and PARAS 784–787, 867–871, 881, 903–905.

505. Digital Britain. The most recent legislation to affect broadcasting is the Digital Economy Act 2010, which was part of an initiative of the government, known as 'Digital Britain', which aimed to secure for the United Kingdom a place at the front of digital and telecommunications innovation and quality. The Act came into force partly on 8 April 2010 and partly on 8 June 2010[1], while certain provisions[2] are to be brought into force by order[3]. It makes, inter alia, a number of amendments relating to broadcasting. It extends the role of OFCOM to include reporting on and media content[4]; it requires Channel Four to provide public service content on a range of media[5]; it gives more flexibility over the licensing of Channel 3 and Channel 5 services and allows OFCOM to appoint providers of regional and local news[6]; it modifies the licensing regime to facilitate switchover to digital radio[7]; and it provides OFCOM with additional powers in relation to electromagnetic spectrum access[8].

1 See the Digital Economy Act 2010 s 47(1), (2).
2 Ie the Digital Economy Act 2010 ss 19–21, 29, 40(2), (3), (5) and (6), 41(1), (2) (partly), 43, 45 (partly), Sch 1 paras 2–4, 6–9, 10(2), Sch 2 (partly).
3 See the Digital Economy Act 2010 s 47(3), (4).
4 See the Digital Economy Act 2010 s 2; and PARA 789.
5 See the Digital Economy Act 2010 ss 22, 23; and PARAS 639, 640.
6 See the Digital Economy Act 2010 ss 24–26; and PARAS 665, 666.
7 See the Digital Economy Act 2010 ss 30, 33; and PARAS 702, 743.
8 See the Digital Economy Act 2010 ss 38, 39; and PARAS 520–521, 528.

506. European and international obligations. There are a number of European and international obligations of a general nature which relate to the law of broadcasting.

The European Parliament and Council Directive on the coordination of certain provisions laid down by law, regulation or administrative action in member states concerning the provision of audiovisual media services (the Audiovisual Media Services Directive)[1], aims to avoid distortions of competition, improve legal certainty, help complete the internal market and facilitate the emergence of a single information area, and to that end to secure that at least a basic tier of coordinated rules apply to all audiovisual media services, both television broadcasting (that is, linear audiovisual media services) and on-demand audiovisual media services (that is, non-linear audiovisual media services)[2]. It recognises that regulatory policy in the audiovisual media services sector must safeguard certain public interests, such as cultural diversity, the right to information, media pluralism, the protection of minors and consumer protection, and enhance public awareness and media literacy, now and in the future[3].

It provides general rules for all audiovisual media services[4] and some provisions applicable only to on-demand audiovisual media services[5]. It makes provision concerning exclusive rights and short news reports in television broadcasting[6]; the promotion of distribution and production of European television programmes[7]; television advertising and teleshopping[8]; the protection of minors in television broadcasting[9]; the right of reply in television broadcasting[10]; a contact committee[11]; and cooperation between regulatory bodies of the member states[12]. The Directive expressly respects the principles of the Unesco Convention on the Protection and Promotion of the Diversity of Cultural Expressions[13].

The purpose of the European Convention on Transfrontier Television[14] is the facilitation of the transfrontier transmission and the retransmission of television programme services[15]. The Convention covers: (1) programming matters[16], including the responsibilities of the broadcaster[17] and the right of reply[18]; (2) advertising[19]; (3) sponsorship[20]; (4) mutual assistance[21]; (5) a standing committee[22]; (6) alleged violations of the Convention[23]; and (7) the settlement of disputes[24], including conciliation[25] and arbitration[26].

The Treaty on the Functioning of the European Union[27] is expressed to be without prejudice to the competence of member states to provide for the funding of public service broadcasting in so far as such funding is granted to broadcasting organisations for the fulfilment of the public service remit as conferred, defined and organised by each member state, and in so far as such funding does not affect trading conditions and competition in the European

Union to an extent which would be contrary to the common interest (although the realisation of the remit of that public service must be taken into account)[28].

In addition, the EU legislation on telecommunications[29] may have an impact on broadcasting, given the use of cable networks for the purposes of delivering television programmes[30].

Certain broadcasting bodies must carry out any functions which the Secretary of State[31] may by order direct them to carry out for the purpose of enabling the government to give effect to any international obligations of the United Kingdom[32]. Those bodies are the BBC[33] and the Welsh Authority[34].

1　Ie European Parliament and Council Directive (EU) 2010/13 (OJ L95, 15.4.2010, p 1). This Directive repealed European Parliament and Council Directive (EC) 89/552 (OJ L298, 17.10.89, p 23) (amended by EC Council Directive 97/36 (OJ L202, 30.7.97, p 60) and European Parliament and Council Directive (EC) 2007/65 (OJ L332, 18.12.2007, p 27)), which required compliance with its terms by 3 October 1991 (see European Parliament and Council Directive (EC) 89/552 (OJ L298, 17.10.89, p 23) art 25 (now repealed)), and the amending Directives by 31 December 1998 and 19 December 2009 respectively (see EC Council Directive 97/36 (OJ L202, 30.7.97, p 60) art 2) and European Parliament and Council Directive (EC) 2007/65 (OJ L332, 18.12.2007, p 27) art 3(1)). As to compliance with Directive 2007/65 see the Audiovisual Media Services Regulations 2009, SI 2009/2979. See also EC Commission Decision 2007/730 (OJ L295, 14.11.2007, p 12) on the compatibility with EU law of measures taken by the United Kingdom pursuant to Directive 89/552 art 3a(1) (co-ordination of certain provisions concerning the pursuit of television broadcasting activities) (see now European Parliament and Council Directive (EU) 2010/13 (OJ L95, 15.4.2010, p 1) art 14(1)).

2　See European Parliament and Council Directive (EU) 2010/13 (OJ L95, 15.4.2010, p 1) recital (11).

3　See European Parliament and Council Directive (EU) 2010/13 (OJ L95, 15.4.2010, p 1) recital (12).

4　See European Parliament and Council Directive (EU) 2010/13 (OJ L95, 15.4.2010, p 1) Ch II, Ch III (arts 2–11).

5　See European Parliament and Council Directive (EU) 2010/13 (OJ L95, 15.4.2010, p 1) Ch IV (arts 12–13).

6　See European Parliament and Council Directive (EU) 2010/13 (OJ L95, 15.4.2010, p 1) Ch V (arts 14–15).

7　See European Parliament and Council Directive (EU) 2010/13 (OJ L95, 15.4.2010, p 1) Ch VI (arts 16–18). A service constitutes television broadcasting for the purposes of the Directive if it consists of the initial transmission of television programmes intended for reception by the public, namely, an indeterminate number of potential television viewers, to whom the same images are transmitted simultaneously: Case C-89/04 *Mediakabel BV v Commissariaat voor de Media* [2005] All ER (D) 17 (Jun), ECJ. The Directive does not preclude member states from requiring television operators to earmark part of their revenue for the funding of specific films: Case C-222/07 *Union de Televisiones Comerciales Asociadas (UTECA) v Administracin General del Estado* [2009] 3 CMLR 34, [2009] All ER (D) 66 (Mar), ECJ.

8　See European Parliament and Council Directive (EU) 2010/13 (OJ L95, 15.4.2010, p 1) Ch VII (arts 19–26). As to the method of calculating the number of permissible interruptions of televised films for advertising authorised by the Directive see Case C-6/98 *Arbeitsgemeinschaft Deutscher Rundfunkanstalten (ARD) v PRO Sieben Media AG* [2000] All ER (EC) 3, [1999] ECR I-7599, ECJ. As to what constitutes a film made for television and what connections between films are necessary for the films to constitute a series for the purposes of European Parliament and Council Directive 89/552 (OJ L298, 17.10.89, p 23) art 11 (repealed: see now European Parliament and Council Directive (EU) 2010/13 (OJ L95, 15.4.2010, p 1) art 20) see Case C-245/01 *RTL Television GmbH v Niedersächsische Landesmedienanstalt für privaten Rundfunk* [2004] All ER (EC) 129, [2003] ECR I-12489, ECJ. Images on advertising hoardings visible in the background of pictures broadcast during sporting events are not television advertising for purposes of the Directive: Case C-262/02 *EC Commission v France* [2005] All ER (EC) 157, [2004] ECR I-6569, ECJ; Case C-429/02 *Bacardi France SAS v Télévision Française 1 SA (TF1)* [2005] All ER (EC) 157, [2004] ECR I-6613, ECJ.

9　See European Parliament and Council Directive (EU) 2010/13 (OJ L95, 15.4.2010, p 1) Ch VIII (art 27).

10　See European Parliament and Council Directive (EU) 2010/13 (OJ L95, 15.4.2010, p 1) Ch IX (art 28).

11 See European Parliament and Council Directive (EU) 2010/13 (OJ L95, 15.4.2010, p 1) Ch X (art 29).

12 See European Parliament and Council Directive (EU) 2010/13 (OJ L95, 15.4.2010, p 1) Ch XI (art 30).

13 Paris, 20 October 2005. See European Parliament and Council Directive (EU) 2010/13 (OJ L95, 15.4.2010, p 1) recital (7).

14 Ie the European Convention on Transfrontier Television (Strasbourg, 5 May 1989; ETS 132), which came into force in the United Kingdom on 1 May 1993: see the Council of Europe Chart of Signatories, Ratifications and Accessions. The Convention is amended by the Protocol amending the European Convention on Transfrontier Television (Strasbourg, 1 October 1998; European Treaty Series 171), accepted by the United Kingdom as from 1 March 2002.

15 European Convention on Transfrontier Television (Strasbourg, 5 May 1989; ETS 132) art 1.

16 European Convention on Transfrontier Television (Strasbourg, 5 May 1989; ETS 132) Ch II (arts 7–10).

17 European Convention on Transfrontier Television (Strasbourg, 5 May 1989; ETS 132) art 7.

18 European Convention on Transfrontier Television (Strasbourg, 5 May 1989; ETS 132) art 8.

19 European Convention on Transfrontier Television (Strasbourg, 5 May 1989; ETS 132) Ch III (arts 11–16).

20 European Convention on Transfrontier Television (Strasbourg, 5 May 1989; ETS 132) Ch IV (arts 17–18).

21 European Convention on Transfrontier Television (Strasbourg, 5 May 1989; ETS 132) Ch V (art 19).

22 European Convention on Transfrontier Television (Strasbourg, 5 May 1989; ETS 132) Ch VI (arts 20–22).

23 European Convention on Transfrontier Television (Strasbourg, 5 May 1989; ETS 132) Ch VIII (art 24).

24 European Convention on Transfrontier Television (Strasbourg, 5 May 1989; ETS 132) Ch IX (arts 25–26).

25 European Convention on Transfrontier Television (Strasbourg, 5 May 1989; ETS 132) art 25.

26 European Convention on Transfrontier Television (Strasbourg, 5 May 1989; ETS 132) art 26.

27 Ie the Treaty on the Functioning of the European Union (Rome, 25 March 1957; TS 1 (1973); Cmnd 5179). The Treaty was formerly known as the Treaty Establishing the European Community; it has been renamed by the Treaty of Lisbon Amending the Treaty Establishing the European Union and the Treaty Establishing the European Community (Lisbon, 13 December 2007; ECS 13 (2007); Cm 7294) and its provisions renumbered by virtue of the Treaty of Amsterdam (OJ C340, 10.11.97, p 1) and by the Treaty of Lisbon.

28 Treaty on the Functioning of the European Union Protocol 32 (added by the Treaty of Amsterdam). As to public service broadcasting see PARAS 621, 655, 788–790, 875–877. See Case C-17/00 *De Coster v Collège des Bourgmestre et Échevins de Watermael-Boitsfort* [2002] All ER (EC) 154, [2001] ECR I-9446, ECJ (national system of taxation of satellite dishes contrary to freedom to provide services under Treaty on the Functioning of the European Union art 49 (now art 56)).

29 See TELECOMMUNICATIONS vol 97 (2010) PARA 82.

30 See eg Case C-336/07 *Kabel Deutschland Vertrieb und Service GMbH & Co KG v Niedersächsische Landesmedienanstalt für Privaten Rundfunk* [2008] ECR I-10889, [2009] 2 CMLR 117, ECJ (European Parliament and Council Directive (EC) 2002/22 (OJ L108, 24.4.2002, p 51) on universal service and users' rights relating to electronic communications networks and services art 31 does not preclude national legislation which requires a cable operator to provide access to its analogue cable network to television channels and services that are already being broadcast terrestrially, thereby resulting in the utilisation of more than half of the channels available on that network, and which provides, in the event of a shortage of channels available, for an order of priority of applicants resulting in full utilisation of the channels available on that network, provided that those obligations do not give rise to unreasonable economic consequences, which is a matter for the national courts to establish).

31 As to the Secretary of State see PARA 507 note 32.

32 Broadcasting Act 1990 s 188(1). Such an order is subject to annulment in pursuance of a resolution of either House of Parliament: s 188(3). At the date at which this volume states the law no order had been made and none has effect as if so made. However, certain European obligations (see PARA 503) may provide the subject matter for such orders in the future.

Any power of the Secretary of State to make regulations or an order under the Broadcasting Act 1990 is exercisable by statutory instrument: s 200(1). Any regulations or order made by the Secretary of State under the Broadcasting Act 1990 may make: (1) different provision for different cases; and (2) such supplemental, incidental, consequential or transitional provision or savings as the Secretary of State considers appropriate: s 200(2).

33 As to the meaning of 'BBC' see PARA 603 note 1; and as to the BBC see PARAS 603–626.

34 See the Broadcasting Act 1990 s 188(2) (amended by the Communications Act 2003 s 406(7), Sch 19). As to the meaning of 'the Welsh Authority' see PARA 644 note 3; and as to television broadcasting by the Welsh Authority see PARAS 644–661.

(3) REGULATION OF BROADCASTING

507. Development of broadcasting regulation. The problems of spectrum scarcity associated with analogue terrestrial broadcasting entailed that broadcasting was a regulated activity in the United Kingdom virtually from its inception.

The BBC, which provided the only legitimate broadcasting service in the United Kingdom from the mid-1920s until the mid-1950s for television and the early 1970s for radio, has always been constrained by the terms of its Royal Charter and overseen by a Board of Governors[1]. In 2007 the BBC Board of Governors was replaced by a new regulatory body, the BBC Trust, and an Executive Board headed by the BBC Director General[2].

The Independent Television Authority ('ITA') was established to supervise the commercial television broadcasting service, Independent Television ('ITV')[3]; it was responsible for transmission stations used by the ITV network and also determined the franchise areas and awarded the franchises to regional commercial broadcasters[4]. In 1972, the ITA assumed a further responsibility for local commercial sound broadcasting services, and was renamed the Independent Broadcasting Authority ('IBA') in consequence[5].

The Cable Authority was established under the Cable and Broadcasting Act 1984, and held responsibility for cable programming services[6] and direct broadcasting by satellite[7].

Both the IBA and the Cable Authority were dissolved under the Broadcasting Act 1990[8], and replaced by the Independent Television Commission ('ITC')[9] and the Radio Authority[10]. The ITC licensed and supervised programme services[11] but did not itself provide them. Unlike the IBA, the ITC was not concerned with sound broadcasting services except when provided by way of a local delivery service[12]. The Radio Authority was established to regulate independent radio broadcasting.

The Communications Act 2003 contained a power to dissolve the ITC and the Radio Authority[13], and on 29 December 2003 their respective functions were in large measure transferred to the Office of Communications[14] ('OFCOM')[15]. OFCOM was established by the Office of Communications Act 2002 as from 1 July 2002 to take over the functions of former regulators and to have such other functions as may be conferred on it by or under any enactment (including the Communications Act 2003)[16]. In relation to broadcasting, the functions of OFCOM include the grant of wireless telegraphy licences[17], the regulation of independent television services[18], functions in relation to the BBC[19], overseeing and reporting on the public service remit for television[20], the making of an annual review and report on television and radio[21], the regulation of television broadcasting on Channels 3, 4 and 5[22], the regulation of the services provided by the Welsh Authority[23], the regulation of digital terrestrial television broadcasting[24], the regulation of the provision of additional services in relation to television broadcasting[25], the regulation of independent radio services[26] and sound broadcasting[27], the overseeing of broadcasting standards[28] and the promotion of employment opportunities in broadcasting[29]. OFCOM has power to make rules and regulations under the Communications Act 2003[30] and the Wireless Telegraphy Act 2006[31].

The Secretary of State[32] holds various powers and responsibilities relating to broadcasting under the Communications Act 2003 and the Wireless Telegraphy Act 2006. These include the guarantee of borrowing by OFCOM[33], consultation with OFCOM, giving approvals and directions, and overseeing the functions of OFCOM[34]. The Secretary of State has power to make regulations under the Communications Act 2003[35] and the Wireless Telegraphy Act 2006[36].

1   As to the BBC see PARAS 603–626.
2   See PARAS 604–610, 612.
3   See the Television Act 1954 s 1 (repealed).
4   The first six franchises (the weekday and weekend franchises for London, the Midlands and the North of England) were allocated in 1954, and the last in 1961 as sufficient technological capacity was developed across the United Kingdom. The ITA continued in existence under the Television Act 1964 s 1 (repealed).
5   See the Sound Broadcasting Act 1972 ss 1, 2 (repealed). The IBA was continued in existence by the Independent Broadcasting Authority Act 1973 s 1 (repealed) and by the Broadcasting Act 1981 s 1 (repealed). As to the transfer of the undertakings of the Independent Broadcasting Authority, and for transitional arrangements, see the Broadcasting Act 1990 Pt IV (ss 127–141); and PARA 550.
6   Cable and Broadcasting Act 1984 ss 2–9, 22–36 (repealed).
7   Cable and Broadcasting Act 1984 ss 37–41 (repealed).
8   See the Broadcasting Act 1990 ss 127–141.
9   Broadcasting Act 1990 s 1 (repealed). The purpose of the establishment of the ITC in place of the two existing bodies was that all independent sector television services should be brought within the ambit of a single agency which can look across the board: *Broadcasting in the '90s: Competition, Choice and Quality* (Cm 517) (November 1988) para 6.5.
     All property, rights and liabilities to which the Cable Authority was entitled or subject immediately before the transfer date (1 January 1991) became the property, rights and liabilities of the ITC: Broadcasting Act 1990 s 128(1). The Cable Authority continued in existence in a reduced form and with limited functions after the transfer date until 10 September 1998, at which point it was dissolved by order of the Secretary of State: see the Broadcasting Act 1990 s 128(2)–(4) (repealed); and the Dissolution of the Cable Authority Order 1998, SI 1998/2237 (lapsed). The Secretary of State was not permitted to make a dissolution order unless he was satisfied, after consultation with the relevant bodies, that nothing further remained to be done by the Cable Authority under or by virtue of the Broadcasting Act 1990 Sch 10: see s 128(5) (repealed).
     The IBA was dissolved on 2 October 2003: see the Dissolution of the Independent Broadcasting Authority Order 2003, SI 2003/2554. The Secretary of State was not permitted to make a dissolution order unless he was satisfied, after consultation with the relevant bodies, that nothing further remained to be done by the IBA under or by virtue of the Broadcasting Act 1990 Sch 9: see s 127(6).
10   Broadcasting Act 1990 s 83 (repealed).
11   'Programme service' means any of the following services (whether or not it is, or it requires to be, licensed) (Broadcasting Act 1990 s 201(1) (amended by the Communications Act 2003 s 406(7), Sch 19)), namely:
     (1)   any service which is a programme service within the meaning of the Communications Act 2003 (see TELECOMMUNICATIONS vol 97 (2010) PARA 16) (Broadcasting Act 1990 s 201(1)(aa) (added by the Communications Act 2003 s 360(1)(a)));
     (2)   any other service which consists in the sending, by means of an electronic communications network (within the meaning of the Communications Act 2003: see TELECOMMUNICATIONS vol 97 (2010) PARA 60), of sounds or visual images or both, either: (a) for reception at two or more places in the United Kingdom (whether they are so sent for simultaneous reception or at different times in response to requests made by different users of the service); or (b) for reception at a place in the United Kingdom for the purpose of being presented there to members of the public or to any group of persons (Broadcasting Act 1990 s 201(1)(c) (amended by the Communications Act 2003 s 360(1)(b))).

Head (2) does not apply to so much of a service consisting only of sound programmes as: (i) is a two-way service (within the meaning of the Communications Act 2003 s 248(4): see PARA 749 note 9); (ii) satisfies the conditions in s 248(5) (see PARA 749 text and notes 10–11); or (iii) is provided for the purpose only of being received by persons who have qualified as users of the service by reason of being persons who fall within s 248(7)(a) or (b) (see PARA 749 text and notes 12–13): Broadcasting Act 1990 s 201(2A) (added by the Communications Act 2003 s 360(2)). Head (2) also does not apply to so much of a service not consisting only of sound programmes as: (A) is a two-way service (within the meaning of the Communications Act 2003 s 232: see PARA 716 note 6); (B) satisfies the conditions in s 233(5) (see PARA 688 text and notes 6–7); or (C) is provided for the purpose only of being received by persons who have qualified as users of the service by reason of being persons who fall within s 233(7)(a) or (b) (see PARA 688 text and notes 8–9): Broadcasting Act 1990 s 201(2B) (added by the Communications Act 2003 s 360(2)).

12 Broadcasting Act 1990 s 72(2)(d), (e) (repealed).

13 Communications Act 2003 s 31(4). At the date at which this volume states the law, no order had been made under s 31(4).

14 Transitional provision is made in relation to any period between the repeal of the Broadcasting Act 1990 s 1, Sch 1 on 29 December 2003 and the day on which the ITC ceases to exist by virtue of an order under the Communications Act 2003 s 31(4) (see the text and note 10): see the Office of Communications Act 2002 (Commencement No 3) and Communications Act 2003 (Commencement No 2) Order 2003, SI 2003/3142, art 6(1). Transitional provision is also made in relation to any period between the repeal of the Broadcasting Act 1990 s 83, Sch 8 on 29 December 2003 and the day on which the Radio Authority ceases to exist by virtue of an order under the Communications Act 2003 s 31(4) (see the text and note 4): see the Office of Communications Act 2002 (Commencement No 3) and Communications Act 2003 (Commencement No 2) Order 2003, SI 2003/3142, art 6(2). See TELECOMMUNICATIONS vol 97 (2010) PARAS 12, 43.

15 As to the use of the abbreviation see eg the Broadcasting Act 1990 s 202(1) (definition added by the Communications Act 2003 s 360(3), Sch 15 Pt 1 para 68(1), (2)); the Broadcasting Act 1996 s 147(1) (definition added by the Communications Act 2003 Sch 15 Pt 2 para 141); the Communications Act 2003 s 405(1); the Wireless Telegraphy Act 2006 s 115(1).

16 See TELECOMMUNICATIONS vol 97 (2010) PARA 2 et seq. OFCOM is a designated regulator for the purposes of the Regulatory Enforcement and Sanctions Act 2008 Pt 1 (ss 1–21): see s 37(1), Sch 5; and ADMINISTRATIVE LAW.

17 See PARA 514 et seq.

18 See PARA 662 et seq.

19 See PARA 854 et seq.

20 See PARA 788 et seq.

21 See PARA 853.

22 See PARA 667 et seq.

23 See PARA 644 et seq.

24 See PARA 690 et seq.

25 See PARA 703 et seq.

26 See PARA 723 et seq.

27 See PARA 730 et seq.

28 See PARA 872 et seq.

29 See PARA 799.

30 See TELECOMMUNICATIONS vol 97 (2010) PARA 45.

31 See PARA 511.

32 In any enactment, 'Secretary of State' means one of Her Majesty's principal Secretaries of State: see the Interpretation Act 1978 s 5, Sch 1. This title relates to matters within the responsibilities of both the Secretary of State for Business, Innovation and Skills and the Secretary of State for Culture, Media and Sport. As to the office of Secretary of State see CONSTITUTIONAL LAW AND HUMAN RIGHTS vol 8(2) (Reissue) PARA 355.

33 See TELECOMMUNICATIONS vol 97 (2010) PARA 37.

34 See TELECOMMUNICATIONS vol 97 (2010) PARA 14 et seq.

35 See TELECOMMUNICATIONS vol 97 (2010) PARA 77.

36 See PARA 511.

2. REGULATION OF AUDIO-VISUAL MEDIA PLATFORMS

(1) INTRODUCTION

508. Available platforms and modes of delivery. Broadcasting regulation is concerned with both the audio-visual media content and the structure of the delivery platform markets. The need to regulate content has traditionally been predicated on the need to protect audiences. The need to regulate market structure was originally predicated upon the fact of spectrum scarcity, when broadcasting relied on analogue transmission of radio signals, but there is now a multiplicity of platforms across which audio-visual media content can be delivered, including terrestrial broadcasting (analogue and digital) by means of wireless telegraphy, delivery of audio-visual content by way of 3G mobile phone networks, direct-to-home satellite broadcasting, delivery across cable networks, and delivery across broadband internet (Internet Protocol Television ('IPTV' or 'television-over-the-Internet'))[1]. The radio spectrum remains a scarce resource, and broadcasting platforms that utilise the radio spectrum require a wireless telegraphy licence[2]. Not all of these platforms, however, utilise the radio spectrum, and they are therefore not subject to the licensing regime but regulation is achieved by means of sectoral regulation, competition law, and so on. Broadcasting platforms that utilise communications networks to deliver content now benefit from a general authorisation subject to general conditions of entitlement[3].

1 Some services deploy combinations of these technologies.
2 See PARA 509 et seq.

3 See the Communications Act 2003 Pt 2 (ss 32–184), which provided for the implementation of the EU telecommunications package: European Parliament and Council Directive (EC) 2002/21 (OJ L108, 24.4.2002, p 33) on a common regulatory framework for electronic communications networks and services; European Parliament and Council Directive (EC) 2002/19 (OJ L108, 24.4.2002, p 7) on access to, and interconnection of, electronic communications networks and associated facilities; European Parliament and Council Directive (EC) 2002/20 (OJ L108, 24.4.2002, p 21) on the authorisation of electronic communications networks and services; and European Parliament and Council Directive (EC) 2002/22 (OJ L108, 24.4.2002, p 51) on universal service and users' rights relating to electronic communications networks and services. See PARA 600; and TELECOMMUNICATIONS vol 97 (2010) PARAS 82, 92 et seq.

(2) LICENSING OF RADIOCOMMUNICATIONS

(i) Introduction

509. Development of wireless telegraphy and use in broadcasting. Marconi's invention of wireless telegraphy was patented in 1896. The technology is differentiated from electrical telegraphy in that the messages are transmitted by electromagnetic means rather than via a physical cable connection. In 1897, the Marconi Wireless Telegraph Company Limited was formed and commenced the commercial exploitation of this new method of communication.

In 1904, the United Kingdom Parliament intervened to prohibit the establishment of any wireless telegraph station or the installation or working of any apparatus for wireless telegraphy except under licence from the Postmaster General[1]. The licensing regime is now underpinned by the Wireless Telegraphy Act 2006[2]. It takes account of the fact that the radio spectrum is a finite resource for which demand greatly exceeds supply in many frequency bands and in many geographic areas[3]. A licence is an authority granted by OFCOM[4] authorising a named person (or persons) to install or use radio equipment in a clearly defined way.

In recognition of the fact that radio spectrum does not align with national borders, international co-operation has long been a feature of spectrum management policy. The Commonwealth Telecommunications Board was established under the Commonwealth Telegraphs Act 1949, and was later replaced by the Commonwealth Telecommunications Bureau[5]. An agency of the United Nations, the International Telecommunication Union, now co-ordinates global exploitation of the radio spectrum, promotes international co-operation in assigning satellite orbits, and establishes worldwide standards to foster interconnection of communications systems[6].

A number of broadcasting services utilise the radio spectrum: analogue and digital terrestrial broadcasting; satellite broadcasting, 3G mobile phone networks and, in limited respects, cable television. All such uses of United Kingdom radio spectrum must be licensed or recognised, unless exempted, under wireless telegraphy legislation[7]. Notably, however, few of the main broadcasters themselves hold such licences; they prefer to contract with third parties for the provision of transmission services.

1 Wireless Telegraphy Act 1904 s 1(1) (repealed). As to the licensing and the regulation of wireless telegraphy generally see PARA 510 et seq. As to the former office of Postmaster General, and as to the distribution of his functions, see POST OFFICE vol 36(2) (Reissue) PARAS 1–3.
2 See PARA 510 et seq.
3 See PARA 510 et seq.
4 As to OFCOM see PARA 507. As to the functions of OFCOM in relation to the radio spectrum see PARAS 537–548: and as to spectrum trading see PARA 549. As to directions to OFCOM by the Secretary of State in respect of its spectrum functions see TELECOMMUNICATIONS vol 97 (2010) PARA 18.
5 The Bureau was established by the Commonwealth Telecommunications Act 1968 and later known as the Commonwealth Telecommunications Organisation.
6 See TELECOMMUNICATIONS vol 97 (2010) PARA 65.
7 As to bidding for grants of recognised spectrum access see PARA 522.

(ii) Wireless Telegraphy Licensing

A. INTRODUCTION

510. Legislation relating to wireless telegraphy. The Wireless Telegraphy Act 2006 is the principal statute concerned with wireless telegraphy[1]. It repealed or amended the legislation formerly applicable, notably the Wireless Telegraphy Act 1949[2]. The Wireless Telegraphy Act 2006 regulates the radio spectrum generally[3], specifying the radio spectrum functions of OFCOM[4], providing for wireless telegraphy licences[5], grants of recognised spectrum access[6], management of the radio spectrum[7] and enforcement[8]. It regulates and provides for the approval of wireless telegraphy apparatus[9], and prohibits broadcasting from sea or air[10]. A number of its provisions[11] apply: (1) to all stations[12] and apparatus in or over, or for the time being in or over, the United Kingdom[13] or UK territorial sea[14]; and (2) subject to any limitations that the Secretary of State[15] may by regulations determine, to all stations and apparatus on board any ship or aircraft that is registered in the United Kingdom but is not for the time being in or over the United Kingdom or UK territorial sea[16]; and (3) subject to any limitations which the Secretary of State may by regulations determine, to all apparatus which is not in or over the United Kingdom or UK territorial sea but was released from within the United Kingdom or UK territorial sea or from a ship or aircraft that is registered in the United Kingdom[17]. The Act also contains provisions as to fixed penalties[18], entry, search and seizure[19], disposal and forfeiture[20], enforcement and civil proceedings[21], disclosure of information[22], and as to documents, electronic documents and the timing and location of things done electronically[23].

EU legislation affecting wireless telegraphy includes Directives relating to mobile satellite services[24], which are required to be implemented in the United Kingdom[25].

1   For the purposes of the Wireless Telegraphy Act 2006, 'wireless telegraphy' means the emitting or receiving, over paths that are not provided by any material substance constructed or arranged for the purpose, of electromagnetic energy of a frequency not exceeding 3,000 gigahertz that: (1) serves for conveying messages, sound or visual images (whether or not the messages, sound or images are actually received by anyone), or for operating or controlling machinery or apparatus; or (2) is used in connection with determining position, bearing or distance, or for gaining information as to the presence, absence, position or motion of an object or of a class of objects: ss 115(1), 116(1), (2). This definition also applies for the purposes of the Communications Act 2003: see s 405(1) (definition substituted by the Wireless Telegraphy Act 2006 s 123, Sch 7 paras 25, 34(1), (3)). 'Person' includes a body of persons corporate or unincorporate: Interpretation Act 1978 s 5, Sch 1.

     The Secretary of State may by order modify the above definition of 'wireless telegraphy' by substituting a different frequency for the frequency that is for the time being specified in the Wireless Telegraphy Act 2006 s 116(2): s 116(3). No order is to be made containing provision authorised by s 116(3) unless a draft of the order has been laid before Parliament and approved by a resolution of each House: s 116(4). As to the Secretary of State see PARA 507 note 32. At the date at which this volume states the law, no order had been made under s 116(3).

     References to the emission of electromagnetic energy, or to emission (as opposed to reception), include references to the deliberate reflection (whether continuous or intermittent) of electromagnetic energy by means of apparatus designed or specially adapted for the purpose: s 115(1), (2).

     In the Wireless Telegraphy Act 2006 (except P 5 (ss 77–95) (prohibition of broadcasting from sea or air)) a reference to the sending or conveying of a message includes a reference to the making of a signal or the sending or conveying of a warning or information, and a reference to the reception of a message is to be construed accordingly: s 115(7).

2   See the Wireless Telegraphy Act 2006 s 125, Sch 9. Other statutes repealed include the whole of the Marine etc Broadcasting (Offences) Act 1967 and parts of the Wireless Telegraphy Act 1967, the Telecommunications Act 1984 and the Communications Act 2003.

3   See the Wireless Telegraphy Act 2006 Pt 2 (ss 8–26); and PARA 514 et seq.

4   See the Wireless Telegraphy Act 2006 Pt 1 (ss 1–7); and PARAS 537–543. As to OFCOM see PARA 507.

5   See the Wireless Telegraphy Act 2006 Pt 2 Ch 1 (ss 8–17); and PARA 514 et seq.

6   See the Wireless Telegraphy Act 2006 Pt 2 Ch 2 (ss 18–26); and PARAS 522, 544, 545, 600.

7   See the Wireless Telegraphy Act 2006 Pt 2 Ch 3 (ss 27–34); and PARAS 544, 546–548.

8   See the Wireless Telegraphy Act 2006 Pt 2 Ch 4 (ss 35–44), Ch 5 (ss 45–53); and PARAS 514, 519, 525–530, 572–577.

9   See the Wireless Telegraphy Act 2006 Pt 3 (ss 54–68), Pt 4 (ss 69–76); and PARA 568 et seq. In the Wireless Telegraphy Act 2006 'wireless telegraphy apparatus' means apparatus for the emitting or receiving, over paths that are not provided by any material substance constructed or arranged for the purpose, of energy to which s 116(2) (see note 1) applies: ss 115(1), 117(1). 'Apparatus for wireless telegraphy' or 'wireless telegraphy apparatus' does not include records or cassettes which are actually used at the relevant time: *Rudd v Secretary of State for Trade and Industry* [1987] 2 All ER 553, [1987] 1 WLR 786, HL.

10   See the Wireless Telegraphy Act 2006 Pt 5 (ss 77–95); and PARAS 588–590.

11   Ie the Wireless Telegraphy Act 2006 ss 8–11, 35–38, 45–49, 55–58 and 68 (see PARA 514 et seq), and regulations under s 54 (see PARA 568): see s 119(2).

12   In the Wireless Telegraphy Act 2006, 'wireless telegraphy station': (1) means a station for the emitting or receiving, over paths that are not provided by any material substance constructed or arranged for the purpose, of energy to which s 116(2) (see note 1) applies; and (2) includes the wireless telegraphy apparatus of a ship or aircraft: ss 115(1), 117(2). A reference in the 2006 Act to apparatus on board a ship includes a reference to apparatus on a kite or captive balloon

flown from a ship: s 115(8). 'Ship' includes every description of vessel used in navigation (s 115(1)) and includes hovercraft (Hovercraft (Application of Enactments) Order 1972, SI 1972/971).

13 'United Kingdom' means Great Britain and Northern Ireland: Interpretation Act 1978 s 5, Sch 1. 'Great Britain' means England, Wales and Scotland: Union with Scotland Act 1706, preamble art I; Interpretation Act 1978 s 22(1), Sch 2 para 5(a). Neither the Channel Islands nor the Isle of Man is within the United Kingdom. See further CONSTITUTIONAL LAW AND HUMAN RIGHTS vol 8(2) (Reissue) PARA 3. The Wireless Telegraphy Act 2006 extends to Northern Ireland (s 118(1)), and may be extended to the Isle of Man and (with the exception of ss 62–67) to the Channel Islands: see s 118(3), (4); the Wireless Telegraphy (Jersey) Order 2006, SI 2006/3324; the Wireless Telegraphy (Guernsey) Order 2006, SI 2006/3325; and the Wireless Telegraphy (Isle of Man) Order 2007, SI 2007/278.

The following provisions of the Wireless Telegraphy Act 2006 extend to the Isle of Man with modifications: Pt 1 (general provisions about radio spectrum); Pt 2 (regulation of radio spectrum), except ss 30, 49, 51; in Pt 3 (regulation of apparatus), ss 54–61, 68; Pt 4 (approval of apparatus etc); Pt 5 (prohibition of broadcasting from sea or air); in Pt 6 (general), ss 97–103, 105–112, 115–119, 121–126; Schs 1–3, 5, 7, 8: Wireless Telegraphy (Isle of Man) Order 2007, SI 2007/278, art 2, Sch 1.

The following provisions of the Wireless Telegraphy Act 2006 extend to Jersey with modifications: in Pt 1 (general provisions about radio spectrum), ss 1, 3–7; Pt 2 (regulation of radio spectrum), except ss 30, 51; in Pt 3 (regulation of apparatus), ss 54–61, 68; Pt 5 (prohibition of broadcasting from sea or air); in Pt 6 (general), ss 97–103, 105–108, 110–119, 121, 122, 124, 125 and 126; Schs 1–3, 5, 7–9: Wireless Telegraphy (Jersey) Order 2006, SI 2006/3324, art 2, Sch 1.

The following provisions of the Wireless Telegraphy Act 2006 extend to Guernsey with modifications: in Pt 1 (general provisions about radio spectrum), ss 1, 3–7; Pt 2 (regulation of radio spectrum), except s 51; in Pt 3 (regulation of apparatus), ss 54–61, 68; Pt 4 (approval of apparatus etc); Pt 5 (prohibition of broadcasting from sea or air); in Pt 6 (general), ss 97–103, 105–108, 110–119, 121–126; Schs 1–3, 5, 7–9: Wireless Telegraphy (Guernsey) Order 2006, SI 2006/3325, art 2, Sch 1.

14 Wireless Telegraphy Act 2006 s 119(1)(a). 'UK territorial sea' means the territorial sea adjacent to the United Kingdom: s 115(1). Her Majesty may by Order in Council provide: (1) for an area of UK territorial sea to be treated, for the purposes of any provision of the Wireless Telegraphy Act 2006, as if it were situated in such part of the United Kingdom as may be specified in the Order; and (2) for jurisdiction with respect to questions arising in relation to UK territorial sea under any such provision to be conferred on courts in a part of the United Kingdom so specified: s 120(1). An Order in Council under the Petroleum Act 1998 s 11 (application of civil law to offshore installations etc: see FUEL AND ENERGY vol 19(3) (2007 Reissue) PARA 1679) or the Energy Act 2004 s 87 (application of civil law to renewable energy installations etc: see FUEL AND ENERGY vol 19(2) (2007 Reissue) PARA 1312) may make provision for treating: (a) an installation with respect to which provision is made under that section and which is outside UK territorial sea but in waters to which that section applies; and (b) waters within 500 metres of the installation, as if, for the purposes of any provision of the Wireless Telegraphy Act 2006, they were situated in such part of the United Kingdom as is specified in the Order: s 120(2). 'Installation' includes any floating structure or device maintained on a station by whatever means, and installations in transit: s 120(6). The jurisdiction conferred on a court by an Order in Council under s 120 is in addition to any jurisdiction exercisable apart from s 120 by that or any other court: s 120(3). Section 121(3) (see PARA 511) applies to the power to make an Order in Council under s 120 as it applies to any power of the Secretary of State to make an order under the Wireless Telegraphy Act 2006, but as if references in s 121(3) to the Secretary of State were references to Her Majesty in Council: s 120(4). A statutory instrument containing an Order in Council under s 120 is subject to annulment in pursuance of a resolution of either House of Parliament: s 120(5). As to territorial waters generally see WATER AND WATERWAYS vol 100 (2009) PARA 31.

15 The functions of the Secretary of State under the Wireless Telegraphy Act 1949 s 1 (now the Wireless Telegraphy Act 2006 ss 8, 9, 11, Sch 1 para 5) in so far as they relate to programme making may be exercised by, or by employees of, such person (if any) as may be authorised in that behalf by the Secretary of State: Contracting out (Functions relating to Wireless Telegraphy) Order 1996, SI 1996/2290, art 3. For these purpose, 'programme making' includes the making of a programme for broadcast, the making of a film, presentation, advertisement or audio or video tape, and the staging or performance of an entertainment, sporting or other public event: art 2. 'Broadcast' and 'programme' are to be construed in accordance with the Broadcasting Act 1990 s 202(1) (see PARAS 668 note 2, 667 note 7 respectively): Contracting out (Functions

relating to Wireless Telegraphy) Order 1996, SI 1996/2290, art 2. Under the Wireless Telegraphy Act 2006, these are functions of OFCOM.

16 Wireless Telegraphy Act 2006 s 119(1)(b). Her Majesty may by Order in Council direct that a reference in s 119(1) to a ship or aircraft registered in the United Kingdom is to be construed as including a reference to a ship or aircraft: (1) registered in the Isle of Man, in any of the Channel Islands or in a colony; or (2) registered under the law of any other country or territory outside the United Kingdom that is for the time being administered by Her Majesty's Government in the United Kingdom: s 119(3). For the purposes of the Interpretation Act 1978 Sch 2 para 4(3) (meaning of 'colony' in existing enactments: see STATUTES vol 44(1) (Reissue) PARA 1383), the Wireless Telegraphy Act 2006 s 119(3) is to be treated as if contained in an Act passed before the commencement of that Act: Wireless Telegraphy Act 2006 s 119(4).

The Secretary of State may also make regulations for regulating the use, on board a foreign-registered ship or aircraft while it is within the limits of the United Kingdom and UK territorial sea, of wireless telegraphy apparatus on board the ship or aircraft: s 50(1). A foreign-registered ship or aircraft is one that: (a) is not registered in the United Kingdom; and (b) is registered in a country other than the United Kingdom, the Isle of Man or any of the Channel Islands: s 50(6). The regulations may make different provision for ships or aircraft registered in different countries: s 50(4). The regulations may provide: (i) for the punishment of persons contravening the regulations by a fine; (ii) for the forfeiture of any wireless telegraphy apparatus in respect of which an offence under the regulations is committed: s 50(2). The maximum fine for each offence under the regulations is an amount not exceeding level 5 on the standard scale or a lesser amount: s 50(3). As to the standard scale see SENTENCING AND DISPOSITION OF OFFENDERS vol 92 (2010) PARA 142.

17 Wireless Telegraphy Act 2006 s 119(1)(c). See also note 8. If an offence is committed under any of ss 11, 35–38, 46–48, 58 and 68, then where the offence is committed in relation to a station or apparatus on board or released from a ship or aircraft, the captain or person for the time being in charge of the ship or aircraft is guilty of the offence (as well as anyone who is guilty of it apart from this provision): s 105(1), (2). This does not apply, however, where the offence consists in the use by a passenger on board the ship or aircraft of receiving apparatus that is not part of the wireless telegraphy apparatus, if any, of the ship or aircraft: s 105(3).

18 See the Wireless Telegraphy Act 2006 s 96; and PARA 530.

19 See the Wireless Telegraphy Act 2006 ss 97–100; and PARAS 580–581.

20 See the Wireless Telegraphy Act 2006 ss 101–104; and PARAS 581–582.

21 See the Wireless Telegraphy Act 2006 ss 105–110; note 17; PARA 578; and TELECOMMUNICATIONS vol 97 (2010) PARA 211.

22 See the Wireless Telegraphy Act 2006 s 111; and PARA 512.

23 See the Wireless Telegraphy Act 2006 ss 112–114; and PARA 513.

24 Ie European Parliament and Council Decision (EC) 626/2008 on the selection and authorisation of systems providing mobile satellite services (MSS) (OJ L172, 2.7.2008, p 15) and Commission Decision (EC) 2009/449 on the selection of operators of pan-European systems providing mobile satellite services (MSS) (OJ L149, 12.6.2009, p 65).

25 See the Provision of Mobile Satellite Services (European Union) Regulations 2010, SI 2010/672; and PARAS 564–567, 583.

511.   Orders and regulations under the Wireless Telegraphy Act 2006. Every power conferred by the Wireless Telegraphy Act 2006 on the Secretary of State[1] to make orders or regulations is exercisable by statutory instrument[2]. With certain exceptions[3], a statutory instrument containing an order or regulations made in exercise of such a power, is subject to annulment in pursuance of a resolution of either House of Parliament[4]. Every power of the Secretary of State to make an order or regulations under the Wireless Telegraphy Act 2006 includes power: (1) to make different provision for different cases (including different provision in respect of different areas); (2) to make provision subject to such exemptions and exceptions as the Secretary of State thinks fit; and (3) to make such incidental, supplemental, consequential and transitional provision as the Secretary of State thinks fit[5].

Every power of OFCOM[6] to make regulations or an order under the Wireless Telegraphy Act 2006 is exercisable by statutory instrument, and the Statutory Instruments Act 1946[7] is to apply in relation to those powers as if OFCOM were a Minister of the Crown[8]. Where an instrument made under such a power falls to be laid before Parliament, OFCOM must, immediately after it is made, send it to the Secretary of State for laying by him[9]. Before making any regulations or order under such a power, OFCOM must: (a) give a notice of its proposal to do so to such persons representative of the persons appearing to OFCOM to be likely to be affected by the implementation of the proposal as OFCOM thinks fit; (b) publish notice of its proposal in such manner as it considers appropriate for bringing it to the attention of the persons who, in its opinion, are likely to be affected by it and are not given notice by virtue of head (a); and (c) consider any representations that are made to OFCOM, before the time specified in the notice[10]. A notice for these purposes must: (i) state that OFCOM proposes to make the regulations or order in question; (ii) set out the general effect of the regulations or order; (iii) specify an address from which a copy of the proposed regulations or order may be obtained; and (iv) specify a time before which any representations with respect to the proposal must be made to OFCOM[11]. Every power of OFCOM to make regulations or an order under the Wireless Telegraphy Act 2006 includes power: (A) to make different provision for different cases (including different provision in respect of different areas); (B) to make provision subject to such exemptions and exceptions as OFCOM thinks fit; and (C) to make such incidental, supplemental, consequential and transitional provision as OFCOM thinks fit[12].

1   As to the Secretary of State see PARA 507 note 32.
2   Wireless Telegraphy Act 2006 s 121(1).
3   Ie other than an order under s 5 (see PARA 542), regulations under s 49(4)(g) (see PARA 576), an order under s 111 (see PARA 512), an order under s 116 (see PARA 510) or an order under Sch 8 para 26 or 27 (transitory modifications relating to the Justice (Northern Ireland) Act 2002 and the Communications Act 2003 s 180, Sch 6).
4   Wireless Telegraphy Act 2006 s 121(2). See STATUTES vol 44(1) (Reissue) PARA 1516.
5   Wireless Telegraphy Act 2006 s 121(3).
6   As to OFCOM see PARA 507.
7   As to the Statutory Instruments Act 1946 see STATUTES vol 44(1) (Reissue) PARA 1501 et seq.
8   Wireless Telegraphy Act 2006 s 122(1), (2).
9   Wireless Telegraphy Act 2006 s 122(3).
10 Wireless Telegraphy Act 2006 s 122(4).
11 Wireless Telegraphy Act 2006 s 122(5). The time specified for the purposes of s 122(5)(d) must be no earlier than the end of the period of one month beginning with the day after the latest day on which the notice is given or published for the purposes of s 122(4): s 122(6).
12 Wireless Telegraphy Act 2006 s 122(7).

512. Disclosure of information under the Wireless Telegraphy Act 2006.
Information[1] with respect to a particular business which has been obtained in exercise of a power conferred by the Wireless Telegraphy Act 2006 is not, so long as that business continues to be carried on, to be disclosed without the consent of the person for the time being carrying on that business[2]. This has effect subject to the following provisions[3].

The prohibition on disclosure does not apply to any disclosure of information which is made[4]:

(1)   for the purpose of facilitating the carrying out by OFCOM[5] of any of its functions[6];

(2)   for the purpose of facilitating the carrying out by any relevant person[7] of any relevant function[8];

(3)   for the purpose of facilitating the carrying out by the Comptroller and Auditor General of any of his functions[9];

(4)   for any of the purposes specified in relation to criminal proceedings and investigations[10] under the Anti-terrorism, Crime and Security Act 2001[11];

(5)   for the purpose of any civil proceedings brought under or because of the Wireless Telegraphy Act 2006 or any of the certain specified[12] enactments or instruments[13]; or

(6)   for the purpose of securing compliance with an international obligation of the United Kingdom[14].

Nothing in these provisions: (a) limits the matters that may be published under specified provisions of the Communications Act 2003[15]; (b) limits the matters that may be included in, or made public as part of, a report made by OFCOM because of a provision of the Office of Communications Act 2002 or the Communications Act 2003; (c) prevents the disclosure of anything for the purposes of a report of legal proceedings[16] in which it has been publicly disclosed; (d) applies to information that has been published or made public as mentioned in heads (a) to (c)[17].

A person commits an offence if he discloses information in contravention of these provisions[18].

1   'Information' includes accounts, estimates and projections and any document: Wireless Telegraphy Act 2006 s 115(1).
2   Wireless Telegraphy Act 2006 s 111(1).
3   Wireless Telegraphy Act 2006 s 111(2).
4   Wireless Telegraphy Act 2006 s 111(3).
5   As to OFCOM see PARA 507.
6   Wireless Telegraphy Act 2006 s 111(3)(a).
7   The following are relevant persons: (1) a Minister of the Crown and the Treasury; (2) the Scottish Executive; (3) a Northern Ireland department; (4) the Office of Fair Trading; (5) the Competition Commission; (6) the Consumer Panel; (7) the Welsh Authority; (8) a local weights and measures authority in Great Britain; (9) any other person specified for these purposes in an order made by the Secretary of State: Wireless Telegraphy Act 2006 s 111(4). 'The Consumer Panel' means the panel established under the Communications Act 2003 s 16; and 'the Welsh Authority' means the authority whose name is, by virtue of the Broadcasting Act 1990 s 56(1), Sianel Pedwar Cymru: Wireless Telegraphy Act 2006 s 111(12). As to the Consumer Panel see TELECOMMUNICATIONS vol 97 (2010) PARAS 28–29; and as to the Welsh Authority see PARA 645 et seq. As to the Secretary of State see PARA 507 note 32; and as to the making of orders by the Secretary of State see PARA 511. No order is to be made containing provision authorised by s 111(4) or (5) unless a draft of the order has been laid before Parliament and approved by a resolution of each House: s 111(11).
8   Wireless Telegraphy Act 2006 s 111(3)(b). The following are relevant functions: (1) any function conferred by or under the Wireless Telegraphy Act 2006; (2) any function conferred by or under any enactment or instrument mentioned in s 111(6) (see note 12); (3) any other function specified for these purposes in an order made by the Secretary of State: s 111(5); and see note 7. As to the meaning of 'enactment' see PARA 793 note 5; definition applied by s 111(12).
9   Wireless Telegraphy Act 2006 s 111(3)(c). As to the Comptroller and Auditor General see CONSTITUTIONAL LAW AND HUMAN RIGHTS vol 8(2) (Reissue) PARAS 724–726.
10 Ie under the Anti-terrorism, Crime and Security Act 2001 s 17(2)(a)–(d): see CRIMINAL LAW vol 25 (2010) PARA 384.
11 Wireless Telegraphy Act 2006 s 111(3)(d). The Anti-terrorism, Crime and Security Act 2001 s 18 (restriction on disclosure of information for overseas purposes: see CRIMINAL LAW vol 25 (2010) PARA 384) has effect in relation to a disclosure because the Wireless Telegraphy Act 2006 s 111(3)(d) as it has effect in relation to a disclosure in exercise of a power to which the Anti-terrorism, Crime and Security Act 2001 s 17 applies: Wireless Telegraphy Act 2006 s 111(8).
12 Ie: (1) the Wireless Telegraphy Act 1967; (2) the Trade Descriptions Act 1968; (3) the Fair Trading Act 1973; (4) the Consumer Credit Act 1974; (5) the Competition Act 1980; (6) the Telecommunications Act 1984; (7) the Consumer Protection Act 1987; (8) the Broadcasting Act 1990; (9) the Broadcasting Act 1996; (10) the Competition Act 1998; (11) the Enterprise Act 2002; (12) the Communications Act 2003; (13) the Consumer Protection (Northern Ireland)

Order 1987, SI 1987/2049 (NI 20); (14) the Business Protection from Misleading Marketing Regulations 2008, SI 2008/1276; (15) the Consumer Protection from Unfair Trading Regulations 2008, SI 2008/1277: Wireless Telegraphy Act 2006 s 111(6) (amended by SI 2008/1277).

13 Wireless Telegraphy Act 2006 s 111(3)(e).

14 Wireless Telegraphy Act 2006 s 111(3)(f). 'International obligation of the United Kingdom' includes any EU obligation and any obligation which will or may arise under any international agreement or arrangements to which the United Kingdom is party: s 115(1); European Union (Amendment) Act 2008 s 3(6). As to the meaning of 'United Kingdom' see PARA 510 note 13.

15 Ie the Communications Act 2003 s 15, 26 or 390: see TELECOMMUNICATIONS vol 97 (2010) PARAS 27, 34, 86.

16 'Legal proceedings' means civil or criminal proceedings in or before any court, or proceedings before any tribunal established by or under any enactment: Wireless Telegraphy Act 2006 s 111(12).

17 Wireless Telegraphy Act 2006 s 111(7).

18 Wireless Telegraphy Act 2006 s 111(9). A person who commits an offence under s 111(9) is liable: (1) on summary conviction, to a fine not exceeding the statutory maximum; (2) on conviction on indictment, to imprisonment for a term not exceeding two years or to a fine or to both: s 111(10). As to the statutory maximum see SENTENCING AND DISPOSITION OF OFFENDERS vol 92 (2010) PARA 140.

513. Notifications and electronic working. Where provision made (in whatever terms) by or under the Wireless Telegraphy Act 2006 authorises or requires a notification[1] to be given to any person or a document[2] of any other description (including a copy of a document) to be sent to any person, the notification or document may be given or sent to the person in question: (1) by delivering it to him; (2) by leaving it at his proper address[3]; or (3) by sending it by post to him at that address[4].

The notification or document may be given or sent to a body corporate by being given or sent to the secretary or clerk of that body[5]. The notification or document may be given or sent to a firm by being given or sent to a partner in the firm or a person having the control or management of the partnership business[6]. The notification or document may be given or sent to an unincorporated body or association by being given or sent to a member of the governing body of the body or association[7].

Where: (a) the giving or sending of a notification or other document by its delivery to a particular person ('the recipient') is authorised under the Wireless Telegraphy Act 2006[8]; and (b) the notification or other document is transmitted to the recipient by means of an electronic communications network[9] or by other means but in a form that nevertheless requires the use of apparatus by the recipient to render it intelligible[10], the transmission has effect for the purposes of that Act as a delivery of the notification or other document to the recipient, but only if the requirements imposed by or under the following provisions are complied with[11].

Where the recipient is OFCOM[12]: (i) it must have indicated its willingness to receive the notification or other document in a manner mentioned in head (b); (ii) the transmission must be made in such manner and satisfy such other conditions as it may require; and (iii) the notification or other document must take such form as OFCOM may require[13]. Where the person making the transmission is OFCOM, it may[14] determine the manner in which the transmission is made and the form in which the notification or other document is transmitted[15].

Where the recipient is a person other than OFCOM, the recipient, or the person on whose behalf the recipient receives the notification or other document, must have indicated[16] to the person making the transmission the recipient's willingness to receive notifications or documents transmitted in the form and manner used[17].

The Secretary of State[18] may by order make provision specifying, for the purposes of the Wireless Telegraphy Act 2006, the manner of determining: (A) the times at which things done under that Act by means of electronic communications networks are done; and (B) the places at which such things are so done, and at which things transmitted by means of such networks are received[19]. Such provision may include provision as to the country or territory in which an electronic address is to be treated as located[20]. An order made by the Secretary of State may also make provision about the manner of proving in any legal proceedings that something done by means of an electronic communications network satisfies the requirements of the Wireless Telegraphy Act 2006 for the doing of that thing and the matters mentioned in heads (A) and (B)[21]. An order may provide for such presumptions to apply (whether conclusive or not) as the Secretary of State considers appropriate[22].

1   'Notification' includes notice: Wireless Telegraphy Act 2006 ss 112(8), 113(9).
2   'Document' includes anything in writing: Wireless Telegraphy Act 2006 ss 112(8), 113(9).
3   For the purposes of the Wireless Telegraphy Act 2006 s 112 and the Interpretation Act 1978 s 7 (service of documents by post) in its application to the Wireless Telegraphy Act 2006 s 112, the proper address of a person is: (1) in the case of a body corporate, the address of the registered or principal office of the body; (2) in the case of a firm, unincorporated body or association, the address of the principal office of the partnership, body or association; (3) in the case of a person to whom the notification or other document is given or sent in reliance on any of subsections (3) to (5), the proper address of the body corporate, firm or (as the case may be) other body or association in question; and (4) in any other case, the last known address of the person in question: s 112(6). In the case of a company registered outside the United Kingdom, a firm carrying on business outside the United Kingdom or an unincorporated body or association with offices outside the United Kingdom, the references in s 112(6) to its principal office include references to its principal office within the United Kingdom (if any): s 112(7).
4   Wireless Telegraphy Act 2006 s 112(1), (2). References to giving or sending a notification or other document to a person include references to transmitting it to him and to serving it on him: ss 112(8), 113(9). Section 112 has effect subject to s 113 (see the text and notes 8–17): s 112(9).
5   Wireless Telegraphy Act 2006 s 112(3).
6   Wireless Telegraphy Act 2006 s 112(4).
7   Wireless Telegraphy Act 2006 s 112(5).
8   Ie under the Wireless Telegraphy Act 2006 s 112.
9   As to the meaning of 'electronic communications network' see TELECOMMUNICATIONS vol 97 (2010) PARA 60; definition applied by the Wireless Telegraphy Act 2006 s 115(1).
10 For the purposes of the Wireless Telegraphy Act 2006 s 113(1), something is not to be regarded as in an intelligible form if it cannot be readily understood without being decrypted or having some comparable process applied to it: s 113(2).
11 Wireless Telegraphy Act 2006 s 113(1), (3).
12 As to OFCOM see PARA 507.
13 Wireless Telegraphy Act 2006 s 113(4).
14 Ie subject to the Wireless Telegraphy Act 2006 s 113(6).
15 Wireless Telegraphy Act 2006 s 113(5). An indication, requirement or determination given, imposed or made by OFCOM for the purposes of s 113 is to be given, imposed or made by being published in such manner as it considers appropriate for bringing it to the attention of the persons who, in its opinion, are likely to be affected by it: s 113(8).
16 An indication to any person for the purposes of the Wireless Telegraphy Act 2006 s 113(6): (1) must be given to that person in such manner as he may require; (2) may be a general indication or one that is limited to notifications or documents of a particular description; (3) must state the address to be used and must be accompanied by such other information as that person requires for the making of the transmission; and (4) may be modified or withdrawn at any time by a notice given to that person in such manner as he may require: s 113(7).
17 Wireless Telegraphy Act 2006 s 113(6).
18 As to the Secretary of State see PARA 507 note 32.

19 Wireless Telegraphy Act 2006 s 114(1). As to the making of orders by the Secretary of State see PARA 511.
20 Wireless Telegraphy Act 2006 s 114(2).
21 Wireless Telegraphy Act 2006 s 114(3).
22 Wireless Telegraphy Act 2006 s 114(4).

B. GRANT OF LICENCES

514. Necessity for wireless telegraphy licence. It is unlawful to establish or use[1] a wireless telegraphy station[2], or to install or use wireless telegraphy apparatus[3], except under and in accordance with a licence (a 'wireless telegraphy licence')[4] granted by OFCOM[5].

OFCOM may by regulations exempt from this requirement the establishment, installation or use of wireless telegraphy stations or wireless telegraphy apparatus of such classes or descriptions as may be specified in the regulations, either absolutely or subject to such terms, provisions and limitations as may be so specified[6].

If OFCOM is satisfied, as respects the use of stations or apparatus of a particular description, that the use of stations or apparatus of that description is not likely to involve undue interference[8] with wireless telegraphy it must make regulations[7] exempting the establishment, installation and use of a station or apparatus of that description from the licensing requirement[9].

The establishment or use of a station for wireless telegraphy, and the installation or use of any apparatus for wireless telegraphy, by a member of a visiting force or any person working in support of such a force or by a member of a headquarters, if done in the course of his duty as such is excepted from these provisions[10] to such extent as is provided for in any agreement in force between the United Kingdom government and: (1) the government or the service authorities of the country to which the visiting force belongs; or (2) the headquarters[11].

1 'Use' only means actually using and does not include having available for use: *Rudd v Secretary of State for Trade and Industry* [1987] 2 All ER 553, [1987] 1 WLR 786, HL.
2 As to the meaning of 'wireless telegraphy station' see PARA 510 note 12 and as to the meaning of 'wireless telegraphy' see PARA 510 note 1. See also *Floe Telecom Ltd (in liquidation) v Office of Communications* [2009] EWCA Civ 47, [2009] Bus LR 1116, [2009] All ER (D) 88 (Feb) (meaning of 'radio equipment' in licence).
3 As to the meaning of 'wireless telegraphy apparatus' see PARA 510 note 9.
4 'Wireless telegraphy licence' means a licence granted under the Wireless Telegraphy Act 2006 s 8: s 115(1). As to the grant of licences see PARA 515.
5 Wireless Telegraphy Act 2006 s 8(1). As to OFCOM see PARA 507. This does not apply to: (1) the use of a television receiver (within the meaning of the Communications Act 2003 Pt 4 (ss 363–368) (see PARA 948 note 1)) for receiving a television programme; or (2) the installation of a television receiver for use solely for that purpose: Wireless Telegraphy Act 2006 s 8(2). There is also an exemption for the use of wireless telegraphy apparatus which complies with certain terms, provisions and limitations, where the apparatus is on board a ship which is registered in the United Kingdom, the Isle of Man or any of the Channel Islands: see the Wireless Telegraphy (Mobile Communication Services on Board Ships) (Exemption) Regulations 2011, SI 2011/316 (coming into force on 10 March 2011).
   A person commits an offence if he contravenes the Wireless Telegraphy Act 2006 s 8: s 35(1). A person who commits an offence under s 35 consisting in the establishment or use of a wireless telegraphy station, or the installation or use of wireless telegraphy apparatus, for the purpose of making a broadcast is liable: (a) on summary conviction, to imprisonment for a term not exceeding 12 months or to a fine not exceeding the statutory maximum or to both; (b) on conviction on indictment, to imprisonment for a term not exceeding two years or to a fine or to both: s 35(2). A person who commits an offence under s 35 consisting in the installation or use of receiving apparatus is liable on summary conviction to a fine not exceeding level 3 on the

standard scale: s 35(4). A person who commits an offence under s 35 other than one falling within s 35(2) or (4) is liable on summary conviction to imprisonment for a term not exceeding 51 weeks or to a fine not exceeding level 5 on the standard scale or to both: s 35(5). In s 35, 'broadcast' has the same meaning as in Pt 5 (ss 77–95): s 35(7); see PARA 588 note 4. As to the statutory maximum see SENTENCING AND DISPOSITION OF OFFENDERS vol 92 (2010) PARA 140. As to the standard scale see SENTENCING AND DISPOSITION OF OFFENDERS vol 92 (2010) PARA 142. As to powers of entry, search and seizure see PARAS 580–582. As to offences in relation to wireless telegraphy see further PARAS 572–579.

For the defendant to be convicted of an offence under s 8(1) the prosecution must show that he knew that he was using the apparatus in question, but does not have to show that he did so with a guilty mind: *R v Blake* [1997] 1 All ER 963, [1997] 1 WLR 1167, CA.

6   Wireless Telegraphy Act 2006 s 8(3). See the following regulations made under Wireless Telegraphy Act 1949 s 1 (repealed): the Wireless Telegraphy (Reciprocal Exemption of European Radio Amateurs) Regulations 1988, SI 1988/2090 (establishment, installation and use of certain amateur stations by radio amateurs who hold a European Conference of Postal and Telecommunications Administrations ('CEPT') amateur radio licence); the Wireless Telegraphy Apparatus (Receivers) (Exemption) Regulations 1989, SI 1989/123 (amended by SI 1991/436) (stations and apparatus which are only capable of receiving transmissions); the Wireless Telegraphy Apparatus (Citizens' Band European Users) (Exemption) Regulations 1989, SI 1989/943 (establishment, installation and use of certain Citizens' Band stations); the Wireless Telegraphy (Testing and Development Under Suppressed Radiation Conditions) (Exemption) Regulations 1989, SI 1989/1842 (establishment, installation and use of any station or apparatus for the testing or development of that, or any other, station or apparatus under suppressed radiation conditions); the Wireless Telegraphy (Exemptions) Regulations 2003, SI 2003/74 (amended by SI 2003/2155; SI 2005/3481; SI 2006/2994; SI 2008/236; SI 2008/2426; SI 2010/2512) (network user stations, cordless telephone apparatus, land mobile-satellite service stations, and certain short range devices including metal detectors and model control equipment); the Wireless Telegraphy (Automotive Short Range Radar) (Exemption) (No 2) Regulations 2005, SI 2005/1585 (amended by SI 2008/237; and SI 2010/1484); the Wireless Telegraphy (Radio Frequency Identification Equipment) (Exemption) Regulations 2005, SI 2005/3471 (amended by SI 2007/1282); and the following regulations made under the Wireless Telegraphy Act 2006 s 8(3): the Wireless Telegraphy (Mobile Communication Services on Aircraft) (Exemption) Regulations 2008, SI 2008/2427; the Wireless Telegraphy (Vehicle Based Intelligent Transport Systems) (Exemption) Regulations 2009, SI 2009/65; the Wireless Telegraphy (Ultra-Wideband Equipment) (Exemption) Regulations 2009, SI 2009/2517 (amended by SI 2010/2761); and the Wireless Telegraphy (Exemption and Amendment) Regulations 2010, SI 2010/2512.

7   Ie under the Wireless Telegraphy Act 2006 s 8(3).

8   As to the meaning of 'interference' see PARA 541 note 2; and as to 'undue interference' see PARA 568 note 6.

9   Wireless Telegraphy Act 2006 s 8(4), (5).

10   Ie the Wireless Telegraphy Act 2006 Pt 2 Ch 1 (ss 8–17).

11   Visiting Forces and International Headquarters (Application of Law) Order 1999, SI 1999/1736, art 7(1), (5); Wireless Telegraphy Act 2006 s 124, Sch 8 para 4(1). As to the meaning of 'United Kingdom' see PARA 510 note 13.

515.   Grant of wireless telegraphy licences.   Wireless telegraphy licences[1] are granted by OFCOM[2]. Licences may be issued subject to such terms, provisions and limitations as OFCOM thinks fit[3], including in particular: (1) in the case of a licence to establish a station for wireless telegraphy[4], limitations as to the position and nature of the station, the purposes for which, the circumstances in which and the persons[5] by whom the station may be used and the apparatus[6] that may be installed or used there[7]; and (2) in the case of any other licence, limitations as to the apparatus that may be installed or used and the places where, the purposes for which, the circumstances in which, and the persons by whom the apparatus may be used[8]. Such terms, provisions and limitations may also include, in particular: (a) terms, provisions and limitations as to strength or type of signal, as to times of use and as to the sharing of frequencies; (b) terms, provisions or limitations imposing prohibitions on the transmission or broadcasting of particular matters by the holder of the licence; (c) terms or provisions requiring the transmission or broadcasting of particular matters by that person; (d) terms, provisions or limitations requiring a satellite uplinker[9] to suspend or cease uplinking, by means of satellite uplink apparatus, a service named by OFCOM in a notice given to the satellite uplinker[10]; and (e) terms or provisions requiring a satellite uplinker to provide OFCOM with such information[11] necessary for the purpose of determining whether the relevant statutory provisions[12] apply in relation to a service uplinked by the satellite uplinker or for any purpose connected with the giving of a notice as OFCOM may request by a notice in writing[13].

A wireless telegraphy licence may be granted: (i) in relation to a particular station or particular apparatus; or (ii) in relation to any station or apparatus falling within a description specified in the licence, and such a description may be expressed by reference to such factors (including factors confined to the manner in which it is established, installed or used) as OFCOM thinks fit[14].

Compliance with the requirement[15] to refrain from sending messages when warned that a distress signal from shipping is about to be broadcast and, if required, to transmit such a message[16] is deemed to be a condition of every wireless telegraphy licence[17].

OFCOM may not revoke a licence without good cause, and even then must offer a refund if the holder has done nothing wrong[18].

1 As to the meaning of 'wireless telegraphy licence' see PARA 514 note 4. From 8 December 2006, it is no longer necessary to hold a wireless telegraphy licence in order to operate citizens' band radio equipment, providing that the equipment is operated in accordance with the Wireless Telegraphy (Exemptions) Regulations 2003, SI 2003/74, Sch 10 (added by SI 2006/2994). It is unnecessary for residents of certain European countries to hold a United Kingdom wireless telegraphy licence: see the Wireless Telegraphy Apparatus (Citizen's Band European Users) (Exemption) Regulations 1989, SI 1989/943. As to the granting of television licences by the BBC see the Communications Act 2003 Pt 4 (ss 363–368); and PARA 948 et seq. As to the BBC see PARAS 603–626.

2 See the Wireless Telegraphy Act 2006 s 9(1). See also PARA 516. As to OFCOM see PARA 507.

3 Wireless Telegraphy Act 2006 s 9(1). In imposing terms, provisions or limitations on a wireless telegraphy licence, OFCOM may impose only those that it is satisfied are: (1) objectively justifiable in relation to the networks and services to which they relate; (2) not such as to discriminate unduly against particular persons or against a particular description of persons; (3) proportionate to what they are intended to achieve; and (4) in relation to what they are intended to achieve, transparent: s 9(7). The terms, provisions and limitations of a wireless telegraphy licence granted to a person must not duplicate obligations already imposed on him by general conditions set under the Communications Act 2003 s 45 (power of OFCOM to set conditions in relation to electronic communications networks and services: see TELECOMMUNICATIONS vol 97 (2010) PARA 98): Wireless Telegraphy Act 2006 s 9(6).

4 As to the meaning of 'wireless telegraphy station' see PARA 510 note 12.

5 As to the meaning of 'person' see PARA 510 note 1.

6 As to the meaning of 'wireless telegraphy apparatus' see PARA 510 note 9.

7 Wireless Telegraphy Act 2006 s 9(2).

8 Wireless Telegraphy Act 2006 s 9(3).

9 'Satellite uplinker' means a person who operates satellite uplink apparatus, but where a person is employed or engaged to operate satellite uplink apparatus under the direction or control of another person, references to a satellite uplinker are references only to that other person; and 'satellite uplink apparatus' means wireless telegraphy apparatus, the purpose of which is to emit, to one or more satellites, energy to which the Wireless Telegraphy Act 2006 s 116(2) (see PARA 510 note 1) applies: s 115(1) (definitions added by SI 2009/2979).

10 Ie under the Wireless Telegraphy Act 2006 s 9A: see PARA 594.

11 As to the meaning of 'information' see PARA 512 note 1.

12 Ie the Wireless Telegraphy Act 2006 s 9A: see PARA 594.

13 Wireless Telegraphy Act 2006 s 9(4) (amended by SI 2009/2979). The Wireless Telegraphy Act 2006 s 9 has effect subject to regulations made under s 14 (see PARA 521): s 9(8).

14 Wireless Telegraphy Act 2006 s 9(5).
15 For this requirement see the Merchant Shipping Act 1995 s 91(5); and SHIPPING AND MARITIME LAW vol 94 (2008) PARA 642.
16 Merchant Shipping Act 1995 s 91(6).
17 Wireless Telegraphy Act 2006 s 10, Sch 1 para 4.
18 *Congreve v Home Office* [1976] QB 629, [1976] 1 All ER 697, CA, where it was held that the Secretary of State had no power, on the holder's refusal to pay a supplementary charge, to revoke a licence taken out in anticipation of a proposed increase in the licence fee. As to revocation of licences see PARA 518.

516.   Procedure for grant of wireless telegraphy licences. An application for a grant of a wireless telegraphy licence[1] is to be determined in accordance with procedures prescribed in regulations made by OFCOM[2]. Such procedures must include provision for time limits for dealing with the granting of licences, requirements that must be met for the grant of a licence, and particulars of the terms, provisions and limitations to which a licence may be made subject[3]. The time limits fixed in relation to any application must require a decision on the application to be made, notified to the applicant and published:

(1)   in the case of an application for a licence relating to a frequency allocated in accordance with the United Kingdom Plan for Frequency Authorisation[4], not more than six weeks[5] after the day of the receipt of the application; and

(2)   in any other case, as soon as possible after the receipt of the application[6].

Where OFCOM proposes to refuse a licence it must give to the applicant the reasons for the proposed refusal and specify a period of not less than one month within which representations about the proposed refusal may be made[7]. The grounds on which a licence may be refused by OFCOM include a failure by the applicant to provide information[8] which OFCOM reasonably requires in order to satisfy itself that the applicant is able to comply with terms, provisions or limitations to which the licence may be made subject[9].

1   As to the meaning of 'wireless telegraphy licence' see PARA 514 note 4.
2   Wireless Telegraphy Act 2006 s 10, Sch 1 para 1(1). See the Wireless Telegraphy (Licensing Procedures) Regulations 2010, SI 2010/1823. As to OFCOM see PARA 507.
3   Wireless Telegraphy Act 2006 Sch 1 para 1(2). Under the Wireless Telegraphy (Licensing Procedures) Regulations 2010, SI 2010/1823, a decision on an application for the grant of a licence must be made, notified to the applicant and published: (1) in the case of any licence relating to radio frequencies allocated for use in the United Kingdom Plan for Frequency Authorisation, not more than six weeks after the day of the receipt of the application; and (2) in any other case as soon as possible after the day of the receipt of the application: reg 4. Requirements that must be met for the grant of a licence are specified as follows. Licences must be granted by OFCOM, either in relation to particular equipment or in relation to any equipment falling within the description specified in the licence and expressed by reference to such factors (including factors confined to the manner in which it is established, installed or used), as are described in the licence: reg 5(1). An applicant for the grant of a licence (whether in respect of a station or apparatus) must complete the licence application form which is appropriate for the class of licence being applied for and must provide: (a) the name and address of the applicant; (b) where the duration for which the licence is required is less than 12 months, the duration; and (c) where additional information is specified as being required for the class of licence concerned, that information: reg 5(2). An applicant for the grant of a licence in respect of a station must also provide: (i) the frequencies on which the applicant wishes to operate the station; (ii) the location of any proposed fixed station; (iii) the position of any remote control point for a fixed station; (iv) the purpose or type of service for which the proposed station is intended; (v) the type of station proposed for use; (vi) the intended geographical range of operation; (vii) the type, position, direction, signal strength, output power and signal beam width of each antenna forming part of the proposed station; (viii) the modulation characteristics and data bit rate of transmissions by the proposed station and any transmissions which are for

the purpose of station recognition; (ix) the call sign desired by the applicant; (x) information required for station site clearance in accordance with OFCOM's Radio Site clearance process; (xi) in the case of an application in respect of a mobile station, an indication of whether or not the station is to be established on board an aircraft, a ship or a train; and (xii) if the application is in relation to more than one fixed station, the length and direction of proposed transmission signal paths between stations: reg 5(3). Additional information is required for the grant of aeronautical licences (see Schedule Pt 1 (paras 1–2)), maritime licences (see Schedule Pt 2 (paras 3–4)), licences for programme making and special events (see Schedule Pt 3 (para 5)), licences for satellite services (see Schedule Pt 4 (paras 6–7)), and science and technology licences (see Schedule Pt 5 (para 8)).

Particulars of the terms, provisions and limitations of licences are specified as follows. Licences are granted subject to: (A) a limitation as to the type of equipment which is authorised; (B) a limitation as to the circumstances of use; (C) a term providing for the licence to commence on the date of its grant and continue in force until revoked by OFCOM or surrendered by the licensee; (D) terms as to the circumstances in which OFCOM may revoke or vary the licence; (E) terms providing for the manner and payment of fees; (F) a term as to access and inspection by OFCOM of equipment; (G) terms as to the modification or restriction in use of equipment and the circumstances in which OFCOM may require any such equipment to be temporarily closed down; and (H) terms, provisions and limitations as to strength and type of signal: reg 6(1). Licences are also granted subject to the other terms, provisions and limitations in the case of any particular licence which are contained in the publication Wireless Telegraphy Act Licences (Terms, Provisions and Limitations) 2010 published by OFCOM: Wireless Telegraphy (Licensing Procedures) Regulations 2010, SI 2010/1823, reg 6(2).

Copies of the publications referred to in regs 4(a), 5(3)(j) and 6(2) are available from OFCOM at Riverside House, 2a Southwark Bridge Road, London SE1 9HA and on the OFCOM website at http://www.ofcom.org.uk.

4   As to the United Kingdom Plan for Frequency Authorisation see PARA 538.

5   The period of six weeks specified may be extended by OFCOM where it appears to it necessary to do so:
    (1)   for the purpose of enabling the requirements of any international agreement relating to frequencies or to orbital positions or to satellite co-ordination to be complied with; or
    (2)   in a case where a determination falls to be made as to which of a number of applicants is the more or most suitable to be licensed, for the purpose of securing that the procedure for the making of that determination is fair, reasonable, open and transparent,
but in the latter case the period may not be extended by more than eight months: Wireless Telegraphy Act 2006 Sch 1 para 2(2), (3).

6   Wireless Telegraphy Act 2006 Sch 1 para 2(1).

7   Wireless Telegraphy Act 2006 Sch 1 para 4.

8   As to the meaning of 'information' see PARA 512 note 1.

9   Wireless Telegraphy Act 2006 Sch 1 para 3.

517.   Duration, revocation and variation of wireless telegraphy licences. A wireless telegraphy licence[1] continues in force, unless previously revoked by OFCOM[2], for such period as may be specified in the licence[3].

OFCOM may revoke a wireless telegraphy licence or vary its terms, provisions or limitations: (1) by a notice in writing given to the holder of the licence; or (2) by a general notice applicable to licences of the class to which the licence belongs, published in such way as may be specified in the licence[4].

The terms that OFCOM may include in a wireless telegraphy licence include terms restricting the exercise by it of its power[5] to revoke or vary the licence[6]. Such terms include, in particular, terms providing that the licence may not be revoked or varied except with the consent of the holder of the licence or in such other circumstances and on such grounds as may be specified in the licence[7]. Despite any term or provision included in a wireless telegraphy licence in accordance with these provisions, OFCOM may at any time by giving the holder of the licence a notice in writing revoke the licence or vary its terms, provisions or limitations, if it appears to OFCOM to be necessary or expedient to do so in the interests of national security or for the purpose of securing compliance with an international obligation of the United Kingdom[8].

Where a wireless telegraphy licence (not being one that relates solely to receiving apparatus[9]) has expired or has been revoked, it is the duty of the person to whom the licence was granted and any other person in whose possession or under whose control the licence may be to cause it to be surrendered to OFCOM if required by OFCOM to do so[10]. A person[11] commits an offence if he has a duty to cause a wireless telegraphy licence to be surrendered to OFCOM and without reasonable excuse he fails or refuses to do so[12].

1   As to the meaning of 'wireless telegraphy licence' see PARA 514 note 4.
2   As to OFCOM see PARA 507.
3   Wireless Telegraphy Act 2006 s 10, Sch 1 para 5.
4   Wireless Telegraphy Act 2006 Sch 1 para 6.
5   Ie under the Wireless Telegraphy Act 2006 Sch 1 para 6: see the text and note 4.
6   Wireless Telegraphy Act 2006 Sch 1 para 8(1).
7   Wireless Telegraphy Act 2006 Sch 1 para 8(2). The circumstances or grounds may relate to matters relevant for the purposes of any other enactment (and may, in particular, be dependent on the exercise of a statutory discretion under any other enactment): Sch 1 para 8(3). A licence containing terms included because of Sch 1 para 8(1) may also provide that regulations made under s 45 (see PARA 519): (1) do not apply in relation to a station or apparatus to which the licence relates; or (2) apply in relation to such a station or such apparatus to such extent only, or subject to such modifications, as may be specified in the licence: Sch 1 para 8(4).
8   Wireless Telegraphy Act 2006 Sch 1 para 8(5). As to the meaning of 'United Kingdom' see PARA 510 note 13.
9   'Receiving apparatus' means wireless telegraphy apparatus that is not designed or adapted for emission (as opposed to reception): Wireless Telegraphy Act 2006 s 115(1). As to the meaning of 'emission' see PARA 510 note 1.
10   Wireless Telegraphy Act 2006 s 11(1), (2).
11   As to the meaning of 'person' see PARA 510 note 1.
12   Wireless Telegraphy Act 2006 s 11(3). A person who commits an offence under s 11 is liable on summary conviction to a fine not exceeding level 3 on the standard scale: s 11(4). As to the standard scale see SENTENCING AND DISPOSITION OF OFFENDERS vol 92 (2010) PARA 142.

518.   Variation or revocation of wireless telegraphy licences.   Where OFCOM[1] proposes to revoke or vary a wireless telegraphy licence[2], it must give the person holding the licence a notification stating the reasons for the proposed revocation or variation and specifying the period during which the person notified has an opportunity: (1) to make representations about the proposal; and (2) if the proposal is the result of a contravention of a term, provision or limitation of the licence, to comply with that term, provision or limitation[3]. The period for doing those things must be the period of one month beginning with the day after the one on which the notification was given[4]. However, OFCOM may, if it thinks fit, allow a longer period for doing those things by specifying a longer period in the notification or by subsequently, on one or more occasions, extending the specified period[5]. The person notified has a shorter period for doing those things if a shorter period is agreed between OFCOM and the person notified[6]. The person notified also has a shorter period if: (a) OFCOM has reasonable grounds for believing that the case is urgent[7] or a case of serious and repeated contravention[8]; (b) it has determined that, in the circumstances, a shorter period would be appropriate; and (c) the shorter period has been specified in the notification[9]. Where OFCOM has given a notification[10] that it proposes to revoke or vary a wireless telegraphy licence, it must, within the period of one month beginning with the end of the period for the making of representations about the proposal contained in that notification: (i) decide whether or not to revoke or vary the licence in accordance with its proposal, or in accordance with that proposal but with modifications; and (ii) give the person holding the licence a notification of its decision[11].

None of the above provisions applies to a proposal to revoke or vary a licence if the proposal is made at the request or with the consent of the holder of the licence[12].

1 As to OFCOM see PARA 507.
2 As to the meaning of 'wireless telegraphy licence' see PARA 514 note 4. As to the power to revoke or vary a licence see PARA 517.
3 Wireless Telegraphy Act 2006 Sch 1 para 7(1), (2). As to notification see PARA 513.
4 Wireless Telegraphy Act 2006 Sch 1 para 7(3).
5 Wireless Telegraphy Act 2006 Sch 1 para 7(4).
6 Wireless Telegraphy Act 2006 Sch 1 para 7(5).
7 A case is urgent if the failure to revoke or vary the licence will result in, or create an immediate risk of: (1) a serious threat to the safety of the public, to public health or to national security; or (2) serious economic or operational problems for persons, other than the person in contravention, who: (a) use wireless telegraphy stations or wireless telegraphy apparatus; or (b) are communications providers or make associated facilities available: Wireless Telegraphy Act 2006 Sch 1 para 7(7). As to the meaning of 'wireless telegraphy station' and 'wireless telegraphy apparatus' see PARA 510 notes 12, 9 respectively. 'Communications provider' has the same meaning as in the Communications Act 2003 (see TELECOMMUNICATIONS vol 97 (2010) PARA 17); and 'associated facility' has the meaning given by the Communications Act 2003 s 32 (see TELECOMMUNICATIONS vol 97 (2010) PARA 17): Wireless Telegraphy Act 2006 s 115(1).
8 A contravention of a term, provision or limitation of a licence is a repeated contravention, in relation to a proposal to revoke or vary a licence, if it falls within the Wireless Telegraphy Act 2006 Sch 1 para 7(9): Sch 1 para 7(8). A contravention falls within Sch 1 para 7(9) if: (1) a previous notification under Sch 1 para 7(1) has been given in respect of the same contravention or in respect of another contravention of a term, provision or limitation of the same licence; and (2) the subsequent notification under Sch 1 para 7(1) is given no more than 12 months after the day of the making by OFCOM of a determination for the purposes of Sch 1 para 7(10) (see the text and notes 10–11) that the contravention to which the previous notification related did occur: Sch 1 para 7(9). The reference in Sch 1 para 7(9) to a contravention of a term, provision or limitation of the same licence includes a reference to a contravention of a term, provision or limitation contained in a previous licence of which the licence in question is a direct or indirect renewal: Sch 1 para 7(13).
9 Wireless Telegraphy Act 2006 Sch 1 para 7(6).
10 Ie under the Wireless Telegraphy Act 2006 Sch 1 para 7(1): see the text and note 3.
11 Wireless Telegraphy Act 2006 Sch 1 para 7(10). The notification: (1) must be given no more than one week after the making of the decision to which it relates; and (2) must, in accordance with that decision, either revoke or vary the licence or withdraw the proposal for a revocation or variation: Sch 1 para 7(11).
12 Wireless Telegraphy Act 2006 Sch 1 para 7(12).

519. Regulations relating to licensing. OFCOM[1] may make regulations prescribing the things that are to be done, or not done, in connection with the use of a wireless telegraphy station[2] or wireless telegraphy apparatus[3]. Such regulations may, in particular, require the use of a wireless telegraphy station or wireless telegraphy apparatus to cease on the demand of such persons as may be prescribed by or under the regulations[4].

OFCOM may make regulations imposing on a person to whom a wireless telegraphy licence[5] relating to a wireless telegraphy station or wireless telegraphy apparatus is granted or who is in possession or control of such a station or such apparatus, the following obligations[6]: (1) obligations as to permitting and facilitating the inspection of the station or apparatus[7]; (2) obligations as to the condition in which the station or apparatus is to be kept; (3) in the case of a station or apparatus for the establishment, installation or use of which a wireless telegraphy licence is necessary, obligations as to the production of the licence, or of such other evidence of the licensing of the station or apparatus as may be prescribed by the regulations[8].

OFCOM may make regulations requiring the holder of a wireless telegraphy licence in respect of which sums are or may become due after the grant of the licence, or after its renewal, to keep and produce such accounts and records as may be specified in the regulations[9]. OFCOM may make regulations requiring the holder of a wireless telegraphy licence authorising the establishment or use of a wireless telegraphy station to exhibit at the station such notices as may be specified in the regulations[10].

A person commits an offence if: (a) he contravenes regulations made under these provisions; or (b) he causes or permits a wireless telegraphy station or wireless telegraphy apparatus to be used in contravention of such regulations[11].

1   As to OFCOM see PARA 507.
2   As to the meaning of 'wireless telegraphy station' see PARA 510 note 12.
3   Wireless Telegraphy Act 2006 s 45(1). As to the meaning of 'wireless telegraphy apparatus' see PARA 510 note 9. Regulations under s 45 have effect subject to regulations under s 14 (see PARA 521): s 45(7). The approval of the Secretary of State is required for the making by OFCOM of regulations under s 45: s 45(9). A statutory instrument containing regulations made by OFCOM under s 45 is subject to annulment in pursuance of a resolution of either House of Parliament: s 45(10). As to the Secretary of State see PARA 507 note 32.
4   Wireless Telegraphy Act 2006 s 45(2). See the Wireless Telegraphy Apparatus (Citizens' Band European Users) (Exemption) Regulations 1989, SI 1989/943; the Wireless Telegraphy (Testing and Development Under Suppressed Radiation Conditions) (Exemption) Regulations 1989, SI 1989/1842; and the Wireless Telegraphy (Exemption) Regulations 2003, SI 2003/74 (amended by SI 2003/2155; SI 2010/2512).
5   As to the meaning of 'wireless telegraphy licence' see PARA 514 note 4.
6   Wireless Telegraphy Act 2006 s 45(3).
7   Nothing in regulations under the Wireless Telegraphy Act 2006 s 45 requires a person to concede any form of right of entry into a private dwelling-house for the purpose of permitting or facilitating the inspection of receiving apparatus: s 45(8). As to the meaning of 'receiving apparatus' see PARA 517 note 9.
8   Wireless Telegraphy Act 2006 s 45(4). See the Wireless Telegraphy Apparatus (Citizens' Band European Users) (Exemption) Regulations 1989, SI 1989/943; the Wireless Telegraphy (Testing and Development Under Suppressed Radiation Conditions) (Exemption) Regulations 1989, SI 1989/1842; and the Wireless Telegraphy (Exemption) Regulations 2003, SI 2003/74 (amended by SI 2003/2155; SI 2010/2512).
9   Wireless Telegraphy Act 2006 s 45(5).
10 Wireless Telegraphy Act 2006 s 45(6).
11 Wireless Telegraphy Act 2006 s 46(1). A person who commits an offence under s 46 consisting in a contravention, in relation to receiving apparatus, of regulations made under s 45 is liable on summary conviction to a fine not exceeding level 3 on the standard scale: s 46(2). A person who commits an offence under s 46 other than one falling within s 46(2) is liable on summary conviction to a fine not exceeding level 5 on the standard scale: s 46(3). As to the standard scale see SENTENCING AND DISPOSITION OF OFFENDERS vol 92 (2010) PARA 142.

520.   Charges for wireless telegraphy licences. A person[1] to whom a wireless telegraphy licence[2] is granted[3] must pay to OFCOM[4], on the grant of the licence and, if regulations made by OFCOM so provide, subsequently at such times during its term and at such times in respect of its variation or revocation as may be prescribed by the regulations: (1) such sums as OFCOM may prescribe by regulations; or (2) if regulations made by OFCOM so provide, such sums (whether on the grant of the licence or subsequently) as OFCOM may determine in the particular case[5].

Regulations made under this power may: (a) confer exemptions from provisions of the regulations in particular cases; and (b) provide for sums paid to be refunded, in whole or in part, in such cases as may be specified in the regulations or in such cases as OFCOM thinks fit[6].

On the grant of a licence in respect of which sums will or may subsequently become payable under such regulations, OFCOM may require such security to be given, by way of deposit or otherwise, for the payment of those sums as it thinks fit[7].

Where OFCOM exercises a power to prescribe[8] sums payable in respect of wireless telegraphy licences, other than a power to prescribe sums payable where a licence is varied or revoked at the request or with the consent of the holder of the licence, OFCOM may, if it thinks fit in the light (in particular) of the matters to which it must have regard in exercising its radio spectrum functions[9], prescribe sums greater than those necessary to recover costs incurred by it in connection with its radio spectrum functions[10].

1   As to the meaning of 'person' see PARA 510 note 1.
2   As to the meaning of 'wireless telegraphy licence' see PARA 514 note 4. As to the grant of licences see PARA 515.
3   References in the Wireless Telegraphy Act 2006 ss 12–16 to the grant of a wireless telegraphy licence include references to the grant of a licence by way of renewal of a previous licence: s 17.
4   As to OFCOM see PARA 507.
5   Wireless Telegraphy Act 2006 s 12(1), (2). Regulations under s 12 do not apply in relation to a licence granted in accordance with regulations under s 14 (see PARA 521), but this is subject to s 12(6): s 12(5) (amended by the Digital Economy Act 2010 s 38(1), (2)). Regulations under or for the purposes of the Wireless Telegraphy Act 2006 s 12(1)(b) (see head (1) in the text), so far as it relates to payments during the term of a licence, may be made so as to apply in relation to a licence granted in accordance with regulations under s 14, but only in the following cases: (1) where provision included in the licence with the consent of the holder of the licence provides for the regulations to apply; (2) where the licence includes terms restricting the exercise by OFCOM of its power to revoke the licence before the end of a period and that period has expired; (3) where the licence would, but for a variation, have ceased to have effect at the end of a period and that period has expired; (4) where the licence is a surrendered-spectrum licence: s 12(6) (s 12(6)–(9) added by the Digital Economy Act 2010 s 38(3)). Provision may not be made by virtue of the Wireless Telegraphy Act 2006 s 12(6)(c) or (d) (heads (3), (4)) without the consent of the Secretary of State: s 12(7) (as so added). A wireless telegraphy licence is a 'surrendered-spectrum licence' if: (a) it is granted under arrangements involving (before the grant or later) the variation, revocation or expiry of another wireless telegraphy licence; (b) the arrangements are with a view to enabling the holder of that other licence to comply with a limit applying to frequencies in respect of which a person may hold licences; and (c) it authorises the use after that variation, revocation or expiry of a frequency whose use until then was or is authorised by that other licence: s 12(8) (as so added). In relation to a surrendered-spectrum licence there may be more than one such other licence ('predecessor licence') and a licence may be a predecessor licence to more than one surrendered-spectrum licence: s 12(9) (as so added). As to the Secretary of State see PARA 507 note 32.

    In its application to the powers of OFCOM to make regulations under ss 12–14, s 122 (see PARA 511) is subject to s 16: see s 16(1). The requirements as to giving notice (s 122(4)–(6)) do not apply in any case in which it appears to OFCOM that by reason of the urgency of the matter it is inexpedient to publish a notice in accordance with s 122(4)(b): s 16(2).

    See the Wireless Telegraphy (Licence Charges) Regulations 2005, SI 2005/1378 (amended by SI 2006/2894, SI 2007/2326, SI 2008/139, SI 2008/2106 and SI 2009/66).

6   Wireless Telegraphy Act 2006 s 12(3).
7   Wireless Telegraphy Act 2006 s 12(4).
8   'Prescribe' means prescribe by regulations or determine in accordance with regulations: Wireless Telegraphy Act 2006 s 13(3).
9   Ie under the Wireless Telegraphy Act 2006 s 3: see PARA 539. 'Radio spectrum functions', in relation to OFCOM, means its functions under the enactments relating to the management of the radio spectrum; and 'the enactments relating to the management of the radio spectrum' has the meaning given by the Communications Act 2003 s 405 (see TELECOMMUNICATIONS vol 97 (2010) PARA 17): Wireless Telegraphy Act 2006 s 115(1).
10 Wireless Telegraphy Act 2006 s 13(1), (2).

**521.	Bidding for wireless telegraphy licences.** Having regard to the desirability of promoting the optimal use of the electromagnetic spectrum, OFCOM[1] may by regulations provide that, in such cases as may be specified in the regulations, applications for wireless telegraphy licences[2] must be made in accordance with a procedure that involves the making by the applicant of a bid specifying an amount that he is willing to pay to OFCOM in respect of the licence[3]. The regulations may make provision with respect to the grant of the licences to which they apply and the terms, provisions and limitations subject to which such licences are granted[4]. The regulations may, in particular:

(1)	require the applicant's bid to specify the amount he is willing to pay[5];

(2)	require that amount to be expressed: (a) as a cash sum; (b) as a sum determined by reference to a variable (such as income attributable wholly or in part to the holding of the licence); (c) as a combination of the two; or (d) (at the applicant's choice) in any one of the ways falling within heads (a) to (c) that is authorised by the regulations[6];

(3)	require that amount to be expressed in terms of: (a) the making of a single payment; (b) the making of periodic payments; (c) a combination of the two; or (d) (at the applicant's choice) any one of the ways falling within heads (a) to (c) that is authorised by the regulations[7];

(4)	specify requirements (for example, technical or financial requirements, requirements relating to fitness to hold the licence and requirements intended to restrict the holding of two or more wireless telegraphy licences by any one person) which must be met by applicants for a licence[8];

(5)	require an applicant to pay a deposit to OFCOM[9];

(6)	specify circumstances in which a deposit is, or is not, to be refundable[10];

(7)	specify matters to be taken into account by OFCOM (in addition to the bids made in accordance with the procedure provided for in the regulations) in deciding whether, or to whom, to grant a licence[11];

(8)	specify the other terms, provisions and limitations subject to which a licence to which the regulations apply is to be granted[12];

(9)	make any provision relating to charges for licences[13].

Regulations do not require OFCOM to grant a wireless telegraphy licence on the completion of the procedure provided for in the regulations, except in such circumstances as may be provided for in the regulations[14].

A wireless telegraphy licence granted in accordance with the regulations must specify:

(i)	the sum or sums which in consequence of the bids made are, in accordance with the regulations, to be payable in respect of the licence; or

(ii)	the method for determining that sum or those sums,

and that sum or those sums must be paid to OFCOM by the person to whom the licence is granted in accordance with the terms of the licence[15]. In determining the sum or sums payable in respect of a wireless telegraphy licence, regard may be had to bids made for other wireless telegraphy licences and for grants of recognised spectrum access[16].

The regulations may provide that where a person applies for a licence in accordance with a procedure provided for in the regulations but subsequently refuses the licence applied for, that person must make such payments to OFCOM as may be determined in accordance with the regulations by reference to bids made for the licence[17].

1 As to OFCOM see PARA 507.

2 As to the meaning of 'wireless telegraphy licence' see PARA 514 note 4.

3 Wireless Telegraphy Act 2006 s 14(1). In its application to the powers of OFCOM to make regulations under ss 12–14, s 122 (see PARA 511) is subject to s 16: see s 16(1). The requirements as to giving notice (s 122(4)–(6)) do not apply in any case in which it appears to OFCOM that by reason of the urgency of the matter it is inexpedient to publish a notice in accordance with s 122(4)(b): s 16(2). Nor do those provisions apply in the case of any regulations under s 14 modifying previous regulations under s 14 in a case not falling within s 16(2), if it appears to OFCOM: (1) that the modifications would not adversely affect the interests of any person or otherwise put him in a worse position or, as regards someone else, put him at a disadvantage; and (2) in so far as the modifications affect a procedure that has already begun, that no person would have acted differently had the modifications come into force before the procedure began: s 16(3).

As to the regulations made under the Wireless Telegraphy Act 1998 s 3 (repealed) see the Wireless Telegraphy (Third Generation Licences) Regulations 1999, SI 1999/3162; the Wireless Telegraphy (Broadband Fixed Wireless Access Licences) Regulations 2000, SI 2000/2039; the Wireless Telegraphy (Broadband Fixed Wireless Access Licences) Regulations 2001, SI 2001/3193; the Wireless Telegraphy (Public Fixed Wireless Access Licences) Regulations 2002, SI 2002/1911; the Wireless Telegraphy (Licence Award) Regulations 2006, SI 2006/338; and the Wireless Telegraphy (Licence Award) (No 2) Regulations 2006, SI 2006/1806. Regulations made under the Wireless Telegraphy Act 2006 are the Wireless Telegraphy (Licence Award) Regulations 2007, SI 2007/378 (amended by SI 2007/847); the Wireless Telegraphy (Licence Award) (No 2) Regulations 2007, SI 2007/3380; and the Wireless Telegraphy (Licence Award) Regulations 2008, SI 2008/686.

As to the power of the Secretary of State under the equivalent provisions of the Wireless Telegraphy Act 1998 s 3 (repealed) see *Mercury Personal Communications Ltd v Secretary of State for the Department of Trade and Industry* [1999] All ER (D) 1105, sub nom *R v Secretary of State for Trade and Industry, ex p Mercury Personal Communications Ltd* (1999) Times, 20 October, CA.

4 Wireless Telegraphy Act 2006 s 14(2). As to references to the grant of a licence see PARA 520 note 3.

5 Wireless Telegraphy Act 2006 s 14(3)(a).

6 Wireless Telegraphy Act 2006 s 14(3)(b).

7 Wireless Telegraphy Act 2006 s 14(3)(c).

8 Wireless Telegraphy Act 2006 s 14(3)(d).

9 Wireless Telegraphy Act 2006 s 14(3)(e).

10 Wireless Telegraphy Act 2006 s 14(3)(f).

11 Wireless Telegraphy Act 2006 s 14(3)(g).

12 Wireless Telegraphy Act 2006 s 14(3)(h).

13 Wireless Telegraphy Act 2006 s 14(3)(i).

14 Wireless Telegraphy Act 2006 s 14(4).

15 Wireless Telegraphy Act 2006 s 14(5). This is subject to s 14(5A): s 14(5) (amended by the Digital Economy Act 2010 s 38(4), (5)). The regulations may, with the consent of the Secretary of State, make provision permitting or requiring a surrendered-spectrum licence to which the regulations apply to include: (1) provision requiring all or part of a sum that would otherwise be payable to OFCOM under the Wireless Telegraphy Act 2006 s 14(5) to be paid to a person who was or is the holder of a predecessor licence; (2) provision requiring a sum in addition to that payable to OFCOM under s 14(5) to be paid to such a person; (3) provision specifying any such sum or part or the method for determining it: s 14(5A) (added by the Digital Economy Act 2010 s 38(6)). As to the meanings of 'surrendered-spectrum licence' and 'predecessor licence' see PARA 520 note 5; definitions applied by the Wireless Telegraphy Act 2006 s 14(9) (added by the Digital Economy Act 2010 s 38(7)). As to the Secretary of State see PARA 507 note 32. The Wireless Telegraphy Act 2006 s 12(4) (power to require security: see PARA 520) applies in relation to sums that will or may become payable under regulations under s 12 after the grant of a wireless telegraphy licence as it applies in relation to sums that will or may become payable under regulations under s 12: s 14(8).

16 Wireless Telegraphy Act 2006 s 14(6). 'Grant of recognised spectrum access' means a grant made under s 18 (see PARA 544): s 115(1). As to bidding for grants of recognised spectrum access see PARA 522.

17 Wireless Telegraphy Act 2006 s 14(7).

522. Bidding for grants of recognised spectrum access. Having regard to the desirability of promoting the optimal use of the electromagnetic spectrum, OFCOM[1] may by regulations provide that, in such cases as may be specified in the regulations, applications for grants of recognised spectrum access[2] must be made in accordance with a procedure that involves the making by the applicant of a bid specifying an amount that he is willing to pay to OFCOM in respect of the grant[3]. The regulations may make provision with respect to the grants to which they apply and the restrictions and conditions subject to which such grants are made[4].

The regulations may, in particular:

(1)   require the applicant's bid to specify the amount he is willing to pay[5];

(2)   require that amount to be expressed: (a) as a cash sum; (b) as a sum determined by reference to a variable (such as income attributable wholly or in part to the use of wireless telegraphy[6] to which the grant relates); (c) as a combination of the two; or (d) (at the applicant's choice) in any one of the ways falling within heads (a) to (c) that is authorised by the regulations[7];

(3)   require that amount to be expressed in terms of: (a) the making of a single payment; (b) the making of periodic payments; (c) a combination of the two; or (d) (at the applicant's choice) in any one of the ways falling within heads (a) to (c) that is authorised by the regulations[8];

(4)   specify requirements (for example, technical or financial requirements, requirements relating to the use of wireless telegraphy to which the grant relates and requirements intended to restrict the holding of two or more grants of recognised spectrum access by any one person) which must be met by applicants for a grant[9];

(5)   require an applicant to pay a deposit to OFCOM[10];

(6)   specify circumstances in which such a deposit is, or is not, to be refundable[11];

(7)   specify matters to be taken into account by OFCOM (in addition to the bids made in accordance with the procedure provided for in the regulations) in deciding whether, or to whom, to make a grant of recognised spectrum access[12];

(8)   specify the other restrictions and conditions subject to which a grant to which the regulations apply is to be made[13]; and

(9)   make any provision referred to in the provisions[14] relating to the power to make regulations about charges[15].

Regulations made under these provisions do not require OFCOM to make a grant of recognised spectrum access on the completion of the procedure provided for in the regulations, except in such circumstances as may be provided for in the regulations[16].

A grant of recognised spectrum access made in accordance with the regulations must specify:

(i)   the sum or sums which in consequence of the bids made are, in accordance with the regulations, to be payable in respect of the grant; or

(ii)   the method for determining that sum or those sums;

and that sum or those sums must be paid to OFCOM by the person to whom the grant is made in accordance with the terms of the grant[17]. In determining the sum or sums payable in respect of a grant, regard may be had to bids made for other grants of recognised spectrum access and for wireless telegraphy licences[18].

The regulations may provide that where a person applies for a grant of recognised spectrum access in accordance with a procedure provided for in the regulations but subsequently refuses the grant applied for, that person must make such payments to OFCOM as may be determined in accordance with the regulations by reference to bids made for the grant[19].

1 As to OFCOM see PARA 507. As to the duty of OFCOM to secure the optimal use of the spectrum see the Communications Act 2003 s 3; and TELECOMMUNICATIONS vol 97 (2010) PARA 16.

2 As to the meaning of 'grant of recognised spectrum access' see PARA 521 note 16, and as to such grants see PARA 544.

3 Wireless Telegraphy Act 2006 s 23(1). As to the making of regulations by OFCOM see s 122; and PARA 511. In its application to the powers of OFCOM to make regulations under ss 21–23, s 122 is subject to the following provisions of s 25: s 25(1). Section 122(4)–(6) does not apply in any case in which it appears to OFCOM that by reason of the urgency of the matter it is inexpedient to publish a notice in accordance with s 122(4)(b): s 25(2). Section 122(4)–(6) does not apply in the case of any regulations under s 23 modifying previous regulations under s 23 in a case not falling within s 25(2), if it appears to OFCOM: (1) that the modifications would not adversely affect the interests of any person or otherwise put him in a worse position or, as regards someone else, put him at a disadvantage; and (2) in so far as the modifications affect a procedure that has already begun, that no person would have acted differently had the modifications come into force before the procedure began: s 25(3).

4 Wireless Telegraphy Act 2006 s 23(2).

5 Wireless Telegraphy Act 2006 s 23(3)(a).

6 As to the meaning of 'wireless telegraphy' see PARA 510 note 1.

7 Wireless Telegraphy Act 2006 s 23(3)(b).

8 Wireless Telegraphy Act 2006 s 23(3)(c).

9 Wireless Telegraphy Act 2006 s 23(3)(d).

10 Wireless Telegraphy Act 2006 s 23(3)(e).

11 Wireless Telegraphy Act 2006 s 23(3)(f).

12 Wireless Telegraphy Act 2006 s 23(3)(g).

13 Wireless Telegraphy Act 2006 s 23(3)(h).

14 Ie the Wireless Telegraphy Act 2006 s 21(3): see PARA 545 note 5.

15 Wireless Telegraphy Act 2006 s 23(3)(i).

16 Wireless Telegraphy Act 2006 s 23(4).

17 Wireless Telegraphy Act 2006 s 23(5). Section 21(4) (power to require security: see PARA 545) applies in relation to sums that will or may become payable under regulations under s 23 after the making of a grant of recognised spectrum access as it applies in relation to sums that will or may become payable under regulations under s 21: s 23(8).

18 Wireless Telegraphy Act 2006 s 23(6). As to the meaning of 'wireless telegraphy licence' see PARA 514 note 4. as to bidding for such licences see PARA 521.

19 Wireless Telegraphy Act 2006 s 23(7).

523. Recovery of sums payable to OFCOM. In the case of a sum which is to be paid to OFCOM[1]:

(1)   under any of the provisions relating to the granting of licences for wireless telegraphy[2] or to the grant of recognised spectrum access[3];

(2)   in pursuance of any provision of any regulations under those provisions; or

(3)   because of any terms contained as a result of those provisions in a wireless telegraphy licence or any conditions contained as a result of those provisions in a grant of recognised spectrum access[4],

the sum must be paid to OFCOM as soon as it becomes due in accordance with that provision or those terms or conditions and, if it is not paid, it is to be recoverable by OFCOM accordingly[5].

1 As to OFCOM see PARA 507.

2   Ie under the Wireless Telegraphy Act 2006 ss 12–14: see PARAS 520–521. As to the meaning of 'wireless telegraphy' see PARA 510 note 1. As to references to the grant of a licence see PARA 520 note 3.

3   Ie under the Wireless Telegraphy Act 2006 ss 21–23: see PARAS 522, 545. As to the meaning of 'grant of recognised spectrum access' see PARA 521 note 16, and as to such grants see PARA 544.

4   Wireless Telegraphy Act 2006 ss 15(1), 24(1).

5   Wireless Telegraphy Act 2006 ss 15(2), 24(2).

524. Information as to apparatus in vehicles. The power of the Secretary of State[1] to specify the declaration to be made and the particulars to be furnished by a person applying for a vehicle licence[2] includes power to require that the declaration and particulars extend to any matters relevant for the enforcement of the provisions relating to wireless telegraphy licensing[3] in respect of any wireless telegraphy apparatus[4] installed in the vehicle[5]. Accordingly, the Secretary of State is not required to issue a vehicle licence under the Vehicle Excise and Registration Act 1994 where the applicant fails to comply with such a requirement[6].

A person commits an offence if in providing information[7] that he is required to provide because of this power: (1) he makes a statement that he knows to be false in a material particular; or (2) he recklessly makes a statement that is false in a material particular[8].

1   Ie under the Vehicle Excise and Registration Act 1994 s 7(1): see CUSTOMS AND EXCISE vol 12(3) (2007 Reissue) PARA 761. As to the Secretary of State see PARA 507 note 32.

2   Ie within the meaning of the Vehicle Excise and Registration Act 1994: see CUSTOMS AND EXCISE.

3   Ie for the enforcement of the Wireless Telegraphy Act 2006 s 8: see PARA 514. As to the meaning of 'wireless telegraphy' see PARA 510 note 1.

4   As to the meaning of 'wireless telegraphy apparatus' see PARA 510 note 9.

5   Wireless Telegraphy Act 2006 s 51(1), (2).

6   Wireless Telegraphy Act 2006 s 51(3).

7   As to the meaning of 'information' see PARA 512 note 1.

8   Wireless Telegraphy Act 2006 s 51(4). A person who commits an offence under s 51(4) is liable on summary conviction to a fine not exceeding level 3 on the standard scale: s 51(5). As to the standard scale see SENTENCING AND DISPOSITION OF OFFENDERS vol 92 (2010) PARA 142. Where s 51(4) applies, it applies instead of the Vehicle Excise and Registration Act 1994 s 45 (false or misleading declarations and information): Wireless Telegraphy Act 2006 s 51(6).

C. CRIMINAL PROCEEDINGS ETC

525. Contraventions of conditions for use of wireless telegraphy. Where OFCOM[1] determines that there are reasonable grounds for believing that a person[2] is contravening or has contravened: (1) a term, provision or limitation of a wireless telegraphy licence[3]; or (2) a term, provision or limitation of an exemption from a licensing requirement[4], it may give that person a notification[5]. A notification under these provisions: (a) sets out the determination made by OFCOM; (b) specifies the term, provision or limitation, and the contravention, in respect of which that determination has been made; and (c) specifies the period during which the person notified has an opportunity of doing the things specified below[6]. Those things are: (i) making representations about the matters notified; and (ii) complying with any notified term, provision or limitation of which he remains in contravention[7]. The period for doing those things must be the period of one month beginning with the day after the one on which the notification was given[8].

1   As to OFCOM see PARA 507.

2   As to the meaning of 'person' see PARA 510 note 1.

3 As to the meaning of 'wireless telegraphy licence' see PARA 514 note 4.
4 Ie under the Wireless Telegraphy Act 2006 s 8(3): see PARA 514.
5 Ie a notification under the Wireless Telegraphy Act 2006 s 39: s 39(1). As to notification see PARA 513.
6 Wireless Telegraphy Act 2006 s 39(2).
7 Wireless Telegraphy Act 2006 s 39(3).
8 Wireless Telegraphy Act 2006 s 39(4). This is subject to s 39(5)–(8): s 39(4) (amended by SI 2009/2979). OFCOM may, if it thinks fit, allow a longer period for doing those things either by specifying a longer period in the notification or by subsequently, on one or more occasions, extending the specified period: Wireless Telegraphy Act 2006 s 39(5). The person notified has a shorter period for doing those things if a shorter period is agreed between OFCOM and the person notified: s 39(6). The person notified also has a shorter period if: (1) OFCOM has reasonable grounds for believing that the case is a case of repeated contravention; (2) it has determined that, in those circumstances, a shorter period would be appropriate; and (3) the shorter period has been specified in the notification: s 39(7). The person notified also has a shorter period if: (a) OFCOM has reasonable grounds for believing that that person is contravening, or has contravened, a notice given under s 9A (see PARA 594) or a term or provision as mentioned in s 9(4)(e) (see PARA 515; head (e)); (b) OFCOM has determined, taking into account all relevant circumstances, that a shorter period would be appropriate; and (c) the shorter period has been specified in the notification: s 39(8) (added by SI 2009/2979). As to the meaning of 'repeated contravention' for these purposes see PARA 526.

526. Meaning of 'repeated contravention'. For the purposes of the provisions of the Wireless Telegraphy Act 2006 relating to contravention of terms, provisions or limitations of a wireless telegraphy licence or exemption[1], a contravention is a repeated contravention, in relation to a notification[2] with respect to that contravention, if, in the case of a contravention of a term, provision or limitation of a wireless telegraphy licence[3], it falls within head (1) or (2) below[4] or, in the case of a contravention of a term, provision or limitation of an exemption[5], it falls within head (3) or (4)[6] below[7].

(1) A contravention of a term, provision or limitation of a wireless telegraphy licence falls within this head if: (a) a previous notification[8] has been given in respect of the same contravention or in respect of another contravention of a term, provision or limitation of the same licence; (b) the person who was given that notification subsequently took steps for remedying[9] the notified contravention; and (c) the subsequent notification is given no more than 12 months after the day of the giving of the previous notification[10].

(2) A contravention of a term, provision or limitation of a wireless telegraphy licence falls this head if: (a) the person concerned has been convicted of an offence[11] in respect of the contravention to which the notification relates or in respect of another contravention of a term, provision or limitation of the same licence; and (b) the subsequent notification is given before the end of the period of 12 months[12] from the contravention in respect of which that person was convicted of that offence[13].

(3) A contravention of a term, provision or limitation of an exemption falls within this head if: (a) a previous notification[14] has been given in respect of the same contravention or in respect of another contravention of the same term, provision or limitation; (b) the person who was given that notification subsequently took steps for remedying the notified contravention; and (c) the subsequent notification is given no more than 12 months after the day of the giving of the previous notification[15].

(4) A contravention of a term, provision or limitation of an exemption falls within this head if: (a) the person concerned has been convicted of an

offence[16] in respect of the contravention to which the notification relates or in respect of another contravention of the same term, provision or limitation; and (b) the subsequent notification is given before the end of the period of 12 months[17] from the contravention in respect of which that person was convicted of that offence[18].

1 Ie the Wireless Telegraphy Act 2006 s 39: see PARA 525. As to the meaning of 'wireless telegraphy licence' see PARA 514 note 4.
2 Ie a notification under the Wireless Telegraphy Act 2006 s 39: see PARA 525.
3 References to a contravention of a term, provision or limitation of a wireless telegraphy licence include references to a contravention of a term, provision or limitation contained in a previous licence of which the licence in question is a direct or indirect renewal: Wireless Telegraphy Act 2006 s 40(9).
4 Ie within the Wireless Telegraphy Act 2006 s 40(2) or (3).
5 Ie under the Wireless Telegraphy Act 2006 s 8(3): see PARA 514.
6 Ie within the Wireless Telegraphy Act 2006 s 40(4) or (5).
7 Wireless Telegraphy Act 2006 s 40(1).
8 Ie a notification under the Wireless Telegraphy Act 2006 s 39: see PARA 525.
9 References to remedying a contravention include references to: (1) doing any thing the failure to do which, or the failure to do which within a particular period or before a particular time, constituted the whole or a part of the contravention; (2) paying an amount to a person by way of compensation for loss or damage suffered by that person in consequence of the contravention; (3) paying an amount to a person by way of compensation in respect of annoyance, inconvenience or anxiety to which he has been put in consequence of the contravention; (4) otherwise acting in a manner that constitutes an acknowledgement that the notified contravention did occur: Wireless Telegraphy Act 2006 s 40(8).
10 Wireless Telegraphy Act 2006 s 40(2).
11 Ie under the Wireless Telegraphy Act 2006 s 35: see PARA 514.
12 In calculating the periods of 12 months mentioned in the Wireless Telegraphy Act 2006 s 40(3)(b) and (5)(b), the period between the institution of the criminal proceedings which led to the conviction and the conclusion of those proceedings is to be left out of account: s 40(6). For the purposes of s 40(6) criminal proceedings are taken to be concluded when no further appeal against conviction may be brought without the permission of the court and: (1) in a case where there is no fixed period within which that permission can be sought, permission has been refused or has not been sought; or (2) in a case where there is a fixed period within which that permission can be sought, that permission has been refused or that period has expired without permission having been sought: s 40(7).
13 Wireless Telegraphy Act 2006 s 40(3).
14 Ie a notification under the Wireless Telegraphy Act 2006 s 39: see PARA 525.
15 Wireless Telegraphy Act 2006 s 40(4).
16 Ie under the Wireless Telegraphy Act 2006 s 35: see PARA 514.
17 See note 12.
18 Wireless Telegraphy Act 2006 s 40(5).

527.   Procedure for prosecutions of wireless telegraphy offences. The following provisions[1] apply to proceedings against a person[2] ('the defendant') for an offence[3] consisting in the contravention of: (1) the terms, provisions or limitations of a wireless telegraphy licence[4]; or (2) the terms, provisions or limitations of an exemption[5] from a licensing requirement[6]. Such proceedings are not to be brought unless, before they are brought, OFCOM[7] has: (a) given the defendant a notification[8] in respect of the contravention to which the proceedings relate; and (b) considered any representations about the matters notified which were made by the defendant within the period allowed[9] for representations[10].

Proceedings to which these provisions apply are not to be brought against a person in respect of a contravention if: (i) it is a contravention to which a notification given to that person[11] relates; and (ii) that person has, during the period allowed[12], complied with the notified term, provision or limitation[13].

1 Ie the Wireless Telegraphy Act 2006 s 41.
2 As to the meaning of 'person' see PARA 510 note 1. As to offences by bodies corporate see the Wireless Telegraphy Act 2006 s 110; and TELECOMMUNICATIONS vol 97 (2010) PARA 211.
3 Ie under the Wireless Telegraphy Act 2006 s 35: see PARA 514.
4 As to the meaning of 'wireless telegraphy licence' see PARA 514 note 4.
5 Ie under the Wireless Telegraphy Act 2006 s 8(3): see PARA 514.
6 Wireless Telegraphy Act 2006 s 41(1).
7 As to OFCOM see PARA 507.
8 Ie under the Wireless Telegraphy Act 2006 s 39: see PARA 525.
9 Ie the period allowed under the Wireless Telegraphy Act 2006 s 39: see PARA 525.
10 Wireless Telegraphy Act 2006 s 41(2). Section 41(2) does not apply where OFCOM has certified that it would be inappropriate to follow the procedure in s 39 because of an immediate risk of: (1) a serious threat to the safety of the public, to public health or to national security; or (2) serious economic or operational problems for persons (other than the defendant) who: (a) use wireless telegraphy stations or wireless telegraphy apparatus; or (b) are communications providers or make associated facilities available: s 41(4). As to the meaning of 'wireless telegraphy station' see PARA 510 note 12; as to the meaning of 'wireless telegraphy apparatus' see PARA 510 note 9. As to the meanings of 'communications provider' and 'associated facility' see PARA 518 note 7.

Where proceedings to which s 41 applies are as a result of s 41(4) brought without a notification having been given to the defendant and the defendant is convicted in those proceedings of the offence under s 35, the court, in determining how to deal with that person, must have regard, in particular, to the matters specified in s 41(6): s 41(5). The matters are: (i) whether the defendant has ceased to be in contravention of the terms, provisions or limitations in question and (if so) when; and (ii) any steps taken by the defendant (whether before or after the commencement of the proceedings) for securing compliance with the obligations imposed on him by virtue of those terms, provisions or limitations: s 41(6).
11 Ie under the Wireless Telegraphy Act 2006 s 39: see PARA 525.
12 Ie allowed by the Wireless Telegraphy Act 2006 s 39.
13 Wireless Telegraphy Act 2006 s 41(3). Where OFCOM gives a notification under s 39 in respect of a contravention and that notification is given before the end of six months after the day of the contravention, the time for the bringing of proceedings for a summary offence in respect of that contravention is extended until the end of six months from the end of the period allowed, in the case of that notification, for doing the things mentioned in s 39(3) (see PARA 525 heads (i), (ii)): s 41(7). This has effect notwithstanding anything in the Magistrates' Courts Act 1980 s 127 (see MAGISTRATES vol 29(2) (Reissue) PARA 589) or the Magistrates' Courts (Northern Ireland) Order 1981, SI 1981/1675 (NI 26), art 19 (limitation on time for bringing summary proceedings): Wireless Telegraphy Act 2006 s 41(8).

528. Special procedure for contraventions by multiplex licence holders. OFCOM[1] may impose a penalty on a person[2] if:

(1) that person is or has been in contravention in any respect of the terms, provisions or limitations[3] of a general multiplex licence[4];

(2) the contravention relates to terms, provisions or limitations about service content[5];

(3) OFCOM has notified that person that it appears to it that those terms, provisions or limitations have been contravened in that respect[6]; and

(4) that contravention is not one in respect of which proceedings for an offence[7] have been brought against that person[8].

Where OFCOM imposes a penalty on a person under these provisions, it must: (a) notify that person of that decision and of OFCOM's reasons for that decision; and (b) in that notification, fix a reasonable period after it is given as the period within which the penalty is to be paid[9].

A penalty imposed under these provisions: (i) must be paid to OFCOM; and (ii) if not paid within the period fixed by it, is recoverable by OFCOM accordingly[10]. The amount of a penalty imposed under these provisions[11] is to be such amount, not exceeding the greater of the following, as OFCOM thinks fit[12], but the amount of the penalty may not exceed the greater of: (A) £250,000; and (B) 5 per cent of the relevant amount of gross revenue[13].

No proceedings for an offence under the enforcement provisions relating to management of the radio spectrum[14] may be commenced against a person in respect of a contravention in respect of which a penalty has been imposed by OFCOM under the above provisions[15].

1   As to OFCOM see PARA 507.

2   Wireless Telegraphy Act 2006 s 42(1). As to the meaning of 'person' see PARA 510 note 1.

3   For the purposes of the Wireless Telegraphy Act 2006 s 42, a licence is a general multiplex licence, in relation to the time of a contravention, if: (1) it is a wireless telegraphy licence containing terms, provisions or limitations as a result of which the services for the purposes of which the use of the licensed station or apparatus is authorised are confined to, or are allowed to include, one or more multiplex services; and (2) at that time, there is no licence under the Broadcasting Act 1996 Pt I (ss 1–39) or Pt II (ss 40–72) in force in respect of a multiplex service to be broadcast using that station or apparatus: s 42(5). For the purposes of s 42(5), 'multiplex service' means: (a) a service for broadcasting for general reception consisting in the packaging together of two or more services that are provided for inclusion together in that service by a combination of the relevant information in digital form; or (b) a service provided with a view to its being a service falling within head (a) but in the case of which only one service is for the time being comprised in digital form in what is provided: s 42(6). As to the meaning of 'wireless telegraphy licence' see PARA 514 note 4. As to the meaning of 'information' see PARA 512 note 1.

4   Wireless Telegraphy Act 2006 s 42(1)(a).

5   Wireless Telegraphy Act 2006 s 42(1)(b). Ie terms, provisions or limitations falling within s 9(4)(b) or (c): see PARA 515.

6   Wireless Telegraphy Act 2006 s 42(1)(c).

7   Ie under the Wireless Telegraphy Act 2006 Pt 2 Ch 4 (ss 35–44).

8   Wireless Telegraphy Act 2006 s 42(1)(d).

9   Wireless Telegraphy Act 2006 s 42(2). As to notification see PARA 513.

10   Wireless Telegraphy Act 2006 s 42(3).

11   Ie the Wireless Telegraphy Act 2006 s 42.

12   Wireless Telegraphy Act 2006 s 43(1).

13   Wireless Telegraphy Act 2006 s 43(2). 'The relevant amount of gross revenue' means the amount specified in s 44: s 43(3). The Secretary of State may by order amend s 43 so as to substitute a different amount for the amount for the time being specified in head (A) in the text: s 43(4). No order is to be made containing provision authorised by s 43(4) unless a draft of the order has been laid before Parliament and approved by a resolution of each House: s 43(5). At the date at which this volume states the law, no such order had been made. As to the power of the Secretary of State to make orders under the Wireless Telegraphy Act 2006 see s 121; and PARA 511. As to the Secretary of State see PARA 507.

The relevant amount of gross revenue for the purposes of s 43 or s 43A (see PARA 529), in relation to a penalty imposed on a person, is: (1) where the last accounting period of that person which falls before the contravention was a period of 12 months, the relevant part of his gross revenue for that period; and (2) in any other case, the amount which, by making any appropriate apportionments or other adjustments of the relevant part of his gross revenue for the accounting period or periods mentioned in s 44(2), is computed to be the amount representing the annual rate for the relevant part of his gross revenue: s 44(1) (amended by the by the Digital Economy Act 2010 s 39(2)). 'Gross revenue', in relation to a person, means the gross revenue of an undertaking carried on by that person; and 'accounting period', in relation to a person, means a period in respect of which accounts of the undertaking carried on by him are prepared or, if one such period is comprised in another, whichever of those periods is or is closest to a 12 month period: Wireless Telegraphy Act 2006 s 44(11).

The accounting period or periods referred to in s 44(1) are: (a) every accounting period of his to end within the period of 12 months immediately preceding the contravention; and (b) if there is no such accounting period, the accounting period of his which is current at the time of the contravention: s 44(2). A reference to the relevant part of a person's gross revenue, in relation to a contravention of the terms, provisions or limitations of a licence, is a reference to so much of his gross revenue as is attributable to the provision of the service to which that licence relates: s 44(3). Sections 32 and 33 (see PARA 533) are to apply for the purpose of ascertaining the amount of a person's gross revenue for any period for the purposes of ss 43, 43A and 44 as they apply for the purpose of obtaining information for statistical purposes about matters relating to the establishment, installation or use by that person of a wireless telegraphy station or wireless telegraphy apparatus: s 44(10) (amended by the by the Digital Economy Act 2010 s 39(2)).

For the purposes of the Wireless Telegraphy Act 2006 s 44: (i) the gross revenue of a person for a period; and (ii) the extent to which a part of a person's gross revenue is attributable to the provision of any service, are to be ascertained in accordance with such principles as may be set out in a statement made by OFCOM: s 44(4). Such a statement may provide for the amount of a person's gross revenue for an accounting period that is current when the amount falls to be calculated to be taken to be the amount estimated by OFCOM, in accordance with the principles set out in the statement, to be the amount that will be his gross revenue for that period: s 44(5). OFCOM may revise a statement made under s 44(4) from time to time: s 44(6). A statement made or revised under s 44 may set out different principles for different cases: s 44(7). Before making or revising a statement under s 44, OFCOM must consult the Secretary of State and the Treasury: s 44(8). OFCOM must (A) publish the statement made under s 44(4) and every revision of it; and (B) send a copy of the statement and of every such revision to the Secretary of State, and the Secretary of State must lay copies of the statement and of every such revision before each House of Parliament: s 44(9).

14 Ie the Wireless Telegraphy Act 2006 Pt 2 Ch 4.
15 Wireless Telegraphy Act 2006 s 42(4).

529. Special procedure for contraventions of certain provisions. OFCOM[1] may impose a penalty on a person[2] if:

(1) that person is or has been in contravention in any respect of a provision, term or limitation of a wireless telegraphy licence[3];

(2) OFCOM has notified that person that it appears to it that the provision, term or limitation has been contravened in that respect[4];

(3) these provisions apply to that contravention by virtue of provision included in the licence[5]; and

(4) that contravention is not one in respect of which proceedings for an offence[6] have been brought against that person[7].

Where OFCOM imposes a penalty on a person under these provisions, it must: (a) notify that person of that decision and of its reasons for that decision; and (b) in that notification, fix a reasonable period after it is given as the period within which the penalty is to be paid[8]. Such a penalty: (i) must be paid to OFCOM; and (ii) if not paid within the period fixed by it, is to be recoverable by it accordingly[9]. The amount of such a penalty is to be such amount not exceeding 10 per cent of the relevant amount of gross revenue[10] as OFCOM thinks: (A) appropriate; and (B) proportionate to the contravention in respect of which it is imposed[11].

No proceedings for an offence under the enforcement provisions relating to management of the radio spectrum[12] may be commenced against a person in respect of a contravention in respect of which a penalty has been imposed by OFCOM under the above provisions[13].

1 As to OFCOM see PARA 507.
2 Wireless Telegraphy Act 2006 s 43A(1) (s 43A added by the Digital Economy Act 2010 s 39(1)). As to the meaning of 'person' see PARA 510 note 1.
3 Wireless Telegraphy Act 2006 s 43A(1)(a) (as added: see note 2). As to the meaning of 'wireless telegraphy licence' see PARA 514 note 4.
4 Wireless Telegraphy Act 2006 s 43A(1)(b) (as added: see note 2).
5 Wireless Telegraphy Act 2006 s 43A(1)(c) (as added: see note 2). A licence may provide in accordance with s 43A(1)(c) that s 43A applies to the contravention of a provision, term or limitation only if it appears to OFCOM that a direction under s 5 (see PARA 542) requires the provision, term or limitation to be included in the licence: s 43A(2) (as so added).
6 Ie under the Wireless Telegraphy Act 2006 Pt 2 Ch 4 (ss 35–44).
7 Wireless Telegraphy Act 2006 s 43A(1)(d) (as added: see note 2).
8 Wireless Telegraphy Act 2006 s 43A(3) (as added: see note 2). As to notification see PARA 513.
9 Wireless Telegraphy Act 2006 s 43A(4) (as added: see note 2).

10 As to the relevant amount of gross revenue see the Wireless Telegraphy Act 2006 s 43; and PARA
    528 note 13.
11 Wireless Telegraphy Act 2006 s 43A(6) (as added: see note 2).
12 Ie the Wireless Telegraphy Act 2006 Pt 2 Ch 4.
13 Wireless Telegraphy Act 2006 s 43A(5) (as added: see note 2).

530. Fixed penalties for certain wireless telegraphy offences. The following provisions apply to an offence under the Wireless Telegraphy Act 2006[1] which is a summary offence[2]; such an offence is referred to as a 'relevant offence'[3].

The fixed penalty for a relevant offence is such amount as may be prescribed in relation to that offence by regulations made by the Secretary of State[4]. The amount prescribed by regulations is not to be more than 25 per cent of the maximum fine on summary conviction for the offence in question[5].

If OFCOM[6] has reason to believe that a person has committed a relevant offence, it may send a fixed penalty notice[7] to that person[8]. If an authorised person[9] has, on any occasion, reason to believe that a person is committing a relevant offence, or has on that occasion committed a relevant offence, he may hand that person a fixed penalty notice[10]. A fixed penalty notice must:

(1)   state the alleged offence;
(2)   give such particulars of the circumstances alleged to constitute that offence as are necessary for giving reasonable information about it;
(3)   state the fixed penalty for that offence;
(4)   specify the relevant officer to whom the fixed penalty may be paid and the address at which it may be paid;
(5)   state that proceedings against the person to whom it is issued cannot be commenced in respect of the offence until the end of the suspended enforcement period;
(6)   state that such proceedings cannot be commenced if the penalty is paid within the suspended enforcement period;
(7)   inform the person to whom it is issued of his right to ask to be tried for the alleged offence; and
(8)   explain how that right may be exercised and the effect of exercising it[11].

The suspended enforcement period for these purposes is the period of one month beginning with the day after that on which the fixed penalty notice was issued or such longer period as may be specified in the notice[12].

If it appears to a person who has issued a fixed penalty notice that it was wrongly issued, he may withdraw the notice by a further notice to the person to whom it was issued and, if he does so, the relevant officer[13] must repay any amount paid in respect of the penalty[14]. A person who issues or withdraws a fixed penalty notice must send a copy of the notice or of the notice of withdrawal to the relevant officer specified in the notice being issued or withdrawn[15].

If a fixed penalty notice is issued to a person ('the alleged offender')[16], proceedings for the offence to which the notice relates cannot be brought against the alleged offender until the person who issued the notice has been notified by the relevant officer specified in the notice that payment of the fixed penalty has not been made within the suspended enforcement period[17]. If the alleged offender asks to be tried for the alleged offence, however, the suspension does not apply and proceedings may be brought against him[18]. A request to be tried[19] must be made by a notice given by the alleged offender in the manner specified in the fixed penalty notice and before the end of the suspended enforcement period[20].

If the alleged offender decides to pay the fixed penalty, he must pay it to the relevant officer specified in the notice[21]. Payment of the penalty may be made by properly addressing[22], pre-paying and posting a letter containing the amount of the penalty (in cash or otherwise)[23]; this does not prevent the payment of a penalty by other means[24]. If a person claims to have made payment by that method and shows that his letter was posted, then unless the contrary is proved, payment is to be regarded as made at the time at which the letter would be delivered in the ordinary course of post[25]. If the fixed penalty specified in a fixed penalty notice is paid within the period specified in that notice, no proceedings for the offence to which that notice relates may be brought against the alleged offender[26].

In proceedings for a relevant offence[27], a certificate by OFCOM: (a) that a copy of a statement by a person authorised by OFCOM was included in, or given with, a fixed penalty notice; (b) that the notice was a notice with respect to the relevant offence; and (c) that that notice was issued to the accused on a date specified in the certificate, is evidence that a copy of the statement was served on the alleged offender by delivery to him on that date[28].

In any proceedings, a certificate: (i) that payment of a fixed penalty was, or was not, received by the relevant officer specified in the fixed penalty notice by a date specified in the certificate; or (ii) that a letter containing an amount sent by post in payment of a fixed penalty was marked as posted on a date specified in the certificate, is evidence of the facts stated if the certificate purports to be signed by that officer[29].

The Secretary of State may by regulations make provision as to any matter incidental to the operation of these provisions, and in particular for prescribing any information or further information to be provided in a notice, notification, certificate or receipt, and for prescribing the duties of relevant officers and the information to be supplied to and by them[30].

1   Other than the Wireless Telegraphy Act 2006 Pt 4 (ss 69–76) (approval of apparatus), as to which see PARAS 534–536.
2   Wireless Telegraphy Act 2006 s 96, Sch 4 para 1(1).
3   Wireless Telegraphy Act 2006 Sch 4 para 1(2).
4   Wireless Telegraphy Act 2006 Sch 4 para 2(1).
5   Wireless Telegraphy Act 2006 Sch 4 para 2(2).
6   As to OFCOM see PARA 507.
7   'Fixed penalty notice' means a notice offering the opportunity of the discharge of any liability to conviction of the offence to which the notice relates by payment of a fixed penalty in accordance with the Wireless Telegraphy Act 2006 Sch 4: Sch 4 para 2(3).
8   Wireless Telegraphy Act 2006 Sch 4 para 3(1).
9   'Authorised person' means a person authorised by OFCOM, for the purposes of the Wireless Telegraphy Act 2006 Sch 4 para 3(3), to issue fixed penalty notices on OFCOM's behalf: Sch 4 para 3(4).
10 Wireless Telegraphy Act 2006 Sch 4 para 3(3). References in Sch 4 to the person by whom a fixed penalty notice is issued, in relation to a notice handed to a person in accordance with Sch 4 para 3(3), are references to OFCOM: Sch 4 para 3(5).
11 Wireless Telegraphy Act 2006 Sch 4 para 4(1).
12 Wireless Telegraphy Act 2006 Sch 4 para 4(2).
13 'Relevant officer', in relation to England and Wales, means the designated officer for the magistrates' court: Wireless Telegraphy Act 2006 Sch 4 para 13. As to the designated officer for the magistrates' court see MAGISTRATES.
14 Wireless Telegraphy Act 2006 Sch 4 para 5.
15 Wireless Telegraphy Act 2006 Sch 4 para 6.
16 Wireless Telegraphy Act 2006 Sch 4 para 7(1).
17 Wireless Telegraphy Act 2006 Sch 4 para 7(2).
18 Wireless Telegraphy Act 2006 Sch 4 para 7(3).

19 A 'request to be tried' is a request made in accordance with the Wireless Telegraphy Act 2006 Sch 4 para 7(3): see Sch 6 para 7(5).
20 Wireless Telegraphy Act 2006 Sch 4 para 7(4).
21 Wireless Telegraphy Act 2006 Sch 4 para 8(1).
22 A letter is properly addressed for the purposes of the Wireless Telegraphy Act 2006 Sch 4 para 8(2) if it is addressed in accordance with the requirements specified in the fixed penalty notice: Sch 4 para 8(6).
23 Wireless Telegraphy Act 2006 Sch 4 para 8(2).
24 Wireless Telegraphy Act 2006 Sch 4 para 8(5).
25 Wireless Telegraphy Act 2006 Sch 4 para 8(3), (4).
26 Wireless Telegraphy Act 2006 Sch 4 para 9.
27 Wireless Telegraphy Act 2006 Sch 4 para 10(1).
28 Wireless Telegraphy Act 2006 Sch 4 para 10(2). The statement is to be treated as properly served for the purposes of the Criminal Justice Act 1967 s 9 (proof by written statement: see CRIMINAL PROCEDURE vol 28 (2010) PARA 657) even though the manner of service is not authorised by s 9(8): Wireless Telegraphy Act 2006 Sch 4 para 10(3). In any proceedings in which service of a statement is proved by a certificate by OFCOM, for the purposes of the requirement that a copy of a statement to be tendered in evidence must be served before hearing on other parties to the proceedings by or on behalf of the party proposing to tender it (see the Criminal Justice Act 1967 s 9(2)(c); and CRIMINAL PROCEDURE vol 28 (2010) PARA 657), service of the statement is to be taken to have been effected by or on behalf of the prosecutor: Wireless Telegraphy Act 2006 Sch 4 para 10(4), (5). If the alleged offender makes a request to be tried, the period of time for objection to the statement being tendered in evidence (ie under the Criminal Justice Act 1967 s 9(2)(d): see CRIMINAL PROCEDURE vol 28 (2010) PARA 657) is to be seven days beginning with the day after the one on which the request to be tried was made: Wireless Telegraphy Act 2006 Sch 4 para 10(4), (6).
29 Wireless Telegraphy Act 2006 Sch 4 para 11.
30 Wireless Telegraphy Act 2006 Sch 4 para 12. As to the meaning of 'information' see PARA 512 note 1.

D. WIRELESS PERSONNEL

531. Qualification of wireless personnel. The Secretary of State[1] may hold examinations to determine the competence of the persons examined to fill positions in connection with the operation of wireless telegraphy stations[2] or wireless telegraphy apparatus[3], and he may issue certificates of competence to persons successful in such examinations[4].

The Secretary of State may issue written authorities to such persons as he thinks fit authorising them to fill such positions in connection with the operation of wireless telegraphy stations or wireless telegraphy apparatus as may be specified in the authority[5]. The positions that may be so specified are positions for the holding of which the possession of such an authority is a necessity or a qualification under a wireless telegraphy licence[6] granted under the Wireless Telegraphy Act 2006 or a licence granted under a corresponding law of a country or territory under the sovereignty of Her Majesty[7].

The Secretary of State may charge such fees, if any, as he may determine: (1) to persons applying to take part in an examination under these provisions; (2) to applicants for, or for copies of, a certificate or authority issued under these provisions[8].

Where any such authority has ceased to be in force or has been suspended[9], it is the duty of the person to whom the authority was issued and any other person in whose possession or under whose control the authority may be, to cause it to be surrendered to the Secretary of State if required by the Secretary of State to do so[10]. A person commits an offence if he has a duty to cause an authority to be surrendered to the Secretary of State and without reasonable excuse he fails or refuses to do so[11].

1 As to the Secretary of State see PARA 507.
2 As to the meaning of 'wireless telegraphy station' see PARA 510 note 12; and as to the meaning of 'wireless telegraphy' see PARA 510 note 1.
3 As to the meaning of 'wireless telegraphy apparatus' see PARA 510 note 9.
4 Wireless Telegraphy Act 2006 s 52(1). The certificates of competence are to be of such types as the Secretary of State may from time to time determine: s 52(2).
5 Wireless Telegraphy Act 2006 s 52(3).
6 As to the meaning of 'wireless telegraphy licence' see PARA 514 note 4.
7 Wireless Telegraphy Act 2006 s 53(4). As to Her Majesty's dominions see COMMONWEALTH vol 13 (2009) PARA 707.
8 Wireless Telegraphy Act 2006 s 52(7).
9 As to the suspension of authorities see PARA 532.
10 Wireless Telegraphy Act 2006 s 53(1).
11 Wireless Telegraphy Act 2006 s 53(2). An offender is liable on summary conviction to a fine not exceeding level 3 on the standard scale: s 53(3). As to the standard scale see SENTENCING AND DISPOSITION OF OFFENDERS vol 92 (2010) PARA 142.

532. Suspension of authority. If it appears to the Secretary of State[1] that there are sufficient grounds to do so, he may at any time suspend an authority[2] to fill a position in connection with the operation of wireless telegraphy stations[3] or wireless telegraphy apparatus[4] with a view to the revocation of the authority[5].

On suspending an authority, the Secretary of State must give the person to whom it was issued a notice informing him of the suspension, the grounds for it and his rights in connection with the suspension, informing him that if he does not avail himself of those rights the Secretary of State may revoke the authority[6]. The person to whom the authority was issued may, within such period and in such manner as may be specified in the notice, request that the question whether the authority should be revoked, or its suspension continued or terminated, be referred to an advisory committee[7]. Where such a request is made, the Secretary of State must, unless he terminates the suspension, refer the question to an advisory committee[8].

Where a question is referred to an advisory committee, the committee must inquire into the matter, consider representations by the person to whom the authority was issued, and then make a report to the Secretary of State, stating the facts as found by the committee and the action that, in its opinion, ought to be taken as respects the revocation of the authority or the continuation or termination of its suspension[9]. The Secretary of State must consider the report[10]. After the Secretary of State has considered the report of the advisory committee or, if no request for a reference to an advisory committee has been made within the period and in the manner specified, on the expiry of that period, the Secretary of State must (as he thinks fit): (1) revoke the authority; (2) terminate the suspension of the authority; or (3) continue the suspension for such period as he thinks fit[11].

Where the Secretary of State revokes the authority or continues its suspension, the Secretary of State must, if requested to do so by the person to whom the authority was issued, inform him of the opinion expressed by the advisory committee as to the action that ought to be taken as respects the revocation of the authority or the continuation or termination of its suspension[12].

1 As to the Secretary of State see PARA 507.
2 Ie an authority under the Wireless Telegraphy Act 2006 s 52(3): see PARA 531.
3 As to the meaning of 'wireless telegraphy station' see PARA 510 note 12.
4 As to the meaning of 'wireless telegraphy apparatus' see PARA 510 note 9.
5 Wireless Telegraphy Act 2006 s 52(5).
6 Wireless Telegraphy Act 2006 s 52(6), Sch 3 para 1(1). Where it appears to the Secretary of State that it is not reasonably practicable to give the notice to the person to whom the authority was

issued, the Secretary of State must take such steps, by advertisement or otherwise, to bring the notice to the person's knowledge as appear to the Secretary of State to be reasonable in the circumstances: Sch 3 para 1(2), (3).

7   Wireless Telegraphy Act 2006 Sch 3 para 2(1), (2). The advisory committee consists of three persons appointed by the Secretary of State: Sch 3 para 2(4). The three persons appointed are to be an independent chairman selected by him, a person nominated by such body or bodies representing employers of wireless operators as seem to the Secretary of State to be appropriate for the purpose, and a person nominated by such association or associations representing wireless operators as seem to the Secretary of State to be appropriate for the purpose: Sch 3 para 2(5). The Secretary of State is to pay: (1) the expenses incurred by an advisory committee under Sch 3, to the extent determined by him; and (2) such sums as he may determine in respect of the expenses of the members of the committee: Sch 3 para 4.

8   Wireless Telegraphy Act 2006 Sch 3 para 2(3).
9   Wireless Telegraphy Act 2006 Sch 3 para 2(6), (7).
10   Wireless Telegraphy Act 2006 Sch 3 para 2(8).
11   Wireless Telegraphy Act 2006 Sch 3 para 3(1), (2).
12   Wireless Telegraphy Act 2006 Sch 3 para 3(3), (4).

E. APPROVALS AND INFORMATION

533.   Information requirements in relation to wireless telegraphy licences.

OFCOM[1] may require a person who is using or has established, installed or used a wireless telegraphy station[2] or wireless telegraphy apparatus[3] to provide OFCOM with all such information relating to the establishment, installation or use of the station or apparatus and any related matters, as OFCOM may require for statistical purposes[4].

OFCOM may not require such provision of information except: (1) by a demand for information that sets out OFCOM's reasons for requiring the information and the statistical purposes for which it is required; and (2) where the making of a demand for that information is proportionate to the use to which the information is to be put in the carrying out of OFCOM's functions[5]. A demand for information must be contained in a notice given to the person from whom the information is required[6]. A person required to give information must provide it in such manner and within such reasonable period as may be specified by OFCOM[7].

A person commits an offence if he fails to provide information in accordance with a requirement of OFCOM under these provisions[8]. In proceedings against a person for such an offence it is a defence for the person to show: (a) that it was not reasonably practicable for him to comply with the requirement within the period specified by OFCOM; but (b) that he has taken all reasonable steps to provide the required information after the end of that period[9]. A person commits an offence if: (i) in pursuance of a requirement, he provides information that is false in any material particular; and (ii) at the time he provides it, he knows it to be false or is reckless as to whether or not it is false[10].

OFCOM must prepare and publish a statement of its general policy with respect to the exercise of its powers under these provisions and the uses to which it is proposing to put information obtained under them[11]. OFCOM may from time to time revise that statement as it thinks fit[12]. Where OFCOM makes such a statement (or revises it), it must publish the statement (or the revised statement) in such manner as it considers appropriate for bringing it to the attention of persons who, in its opinion, are likely to be affected by it[13]. OFCOM must, in exercising its powers to require information, have regard to the statement for the time being in force[14].

1   As to OFCOM see PARA 507.

2 As to the meaning of 'wireless telegraphy station' see PARA 510 note 12.
3 As to the meaning of 'wireless telegraphy apparatus' see PARA 510 note 9.
4 Wireless Telegraphy Act 2006 s 32(1). This has effect subject to the following provisions of s 32:
   s 32(2). As to the meaning of 'information' see PARA 512 note 1.
5 Wireless Telegraphy Act 2006 s 32(3).
6 Wireless Telegraphy Act 2006 s 32(4).
7 Wireless Telegraphy Act 2006 s 32(5).
8 Wireless Telegraphy Act 2006 s 33(1). A person who commits an offence under s 33(1) is liable
   on summary conviction to a fine not exceeding level 3 on the standard scale: s 33(3). As to the
   standard scale see SENTENCING AND DISPOSITION OF OFFENDERS vol 92 (2010) PARA 142.
9 Wireless Telegraphy Act 2006 s 33(2).
10 Wireless Telegraphy Act 2006 s 33(4). A person who commits an offence under s 33(4) is liable
   on summary conviction to a fine not exceeding level 5 on the standard scale: s 33(5).
11 Wireless Telegraphy Act 2006 s 34(1).
12 Wireless Telegraphy Act 2006 s 34(2).
13 Wireless Telegraphy Act 2006 s 34(3).
14 Wireless Telegraphy Act 2006 s 34(4).

534. Approvals. Where an instrument of a specified kind[1] contains provision framed by reference to relevant apparatus[2] for the time being approved under the Wireless Telegraphy Act 2006[3] for the purposes of that instrument, the relevant authority may approve relevant apparatus for the purposes of such an instrument[4]. The relevant authority may require a person applying for an approval to comply with such requirements as the relevant authority may think appropriate; and those requirements may include a requirement to satisfy some other person with respect to a particular matter[5].

An approval may apply: (1) to particular apparatus or to apparatus of a description specified in the approval; (2) for the purposes of a particular instrument or for the purposes of instruments that are of a description specified in the approval[6]. An approval may specify conditions that must be complied with if the approval is to apply to apparatus specified in the approval (or to apparatus of a description so specified) for purposes specified in the approval[7]. The relevant authority may at any time vary or withdraw an approval[8].

The relevant authority may by order provide for the charging of fees in respect of the exercise of any function by or on behalf of the relevant authority connected with approvals[9].

1 Ie a wireless telegraphy licence granted under the Wireless Telegraphy Act 2006 s 8 (see PARA
   514 et seq); regulations made under s 8(3) (see PARA 514); regulations made under s 54 as to the
   use and sale of apparatus (see PARA 568); an order under s 62, restricting dealings in and the
   custody of certain apparatus (see PARA 571); and any authority given under s 62(5): s 69(2). See
   the Wireless Telegraphy (Exemption) Regulations 2003, SI 2003/74 (amended by SI 2003/2155;
   SI 2005/3481; SI 2006/2994; SI 2008/236; SI 2008/2426; SI 2010/2512).
2 'Relevant apparatus' in the Wireless Telegraphy Act 2006 Pt 4 (ss 69–76) means wireless
   telegraphy apparatus or apparatus designed or adapted for use in connection with wireless
   telegraphy apparatus: s 76. As to the meaning of 'wireless telegraphy apparatus' see PARA 510
   note 9.
3 Ie under the Wireless Telegraphy Act 2006 s 69.
4 Wireless Telegraphy Act 2006 s 69(1), (3). 'Relevant authority' means, in such cases as may be
   specified in an order made by the Secretary of State, the Secretary of State, and, in any other
   case, OFCOM: s 71(1). Where an application for the purposes of s 69 is made to the Secretary
   of State or OFCOM and it appears to the person to whom it is made that it should have been
   made to the other, that person is to refer the application to the other, and the application is to be
   proceeded with as if made to the person to whom it is referred: s 71(2). As to the Secretary of
   State see PARA 507 note 32. As to OFCOM see PARA 507.
      A person appointed by the relevant authority may exercise a function conferred on the
   relevant authority by s 69 to such extent and subject to such conditions as may be specified in
   the appointment: s 70(1).
5 Wireless Telegraphy Act 2006 s 69(4).

6   Wireless Telegraphy Act 2006 s 69(5).
7   Wireless Telegraphy Act 2006 s 69(6). A condition so specified may impose on the person to whom the approval is given a requirement to satisfy a person from time to time with respect to a particular matter: s 69(7).
8   Wireless Telegraphy Act 2006 s 69(8).
9   Wireless Telegraphy Act 2006 s 70(2). The Finance Act 1990 s 128 (power to provide for repayment of fees etc) applies in relation to the power under the Wireless Telegraphy Act 2006 s 70(2) to make an order as it applies in relation to any power to make such an order conferred before that Act was passed: s 70(3). An appointment under s 70(1) (see note 4) may authorise the person appointed to retain any fees received by him in pursuance of an order under s 70(2): s 70(3). Nothing in s 70(2) precludes a person (not being the relevant authority or a person acting on behalf of the relevant authority) by whom a matter falls to be determined for the purposes of a requirement imposed in pursuance of s 69(4) or (7) from charging a fee in respect of the carrying out of a test or other assessment made by him: s 70(4). Any sums received by the Secretary of State under s 70 must be paid into the Consolidated Fund: s 70(5). As to the Consolidated Fund see CONSTITUTIONAL LAW AND HUMAN RIGHTS vol 8(2) (Reissue) PARA 711 et seq; PARLIAMENT vol 78 (2010) PARAS 1028–1031. See the Wireless Telegraphy Apparatus Approval and Examination Fees Order 1997, SI 1997/3050; and the Wireless Telegraphy (Citizens' Band and Amateur Apparatus) (Various Provisions) Order 1998, SI 1998/2531 (amended by SI 2000/1013).

535.   Marking of wireless telegraphy apparatus.   Where it appears to OFCOM[1] to be expedient that relevant apparatus[2] of a particular description should be marked with or accompanied by particular information or instruction relating to the apparatus or its installation or use, it may by order: (1) impose requirements for securing that relevant apparatus of that description is so marked or accompanied; and (2) regulate or prohibit the supply of any such relevant apparatus in cases where the requirements are not complied with[3].

In the case of apparatus supplied[4] in circumstances where the required information or instruction would not be conveyed until after delivery, an order may require the whole or part of the information or instruction to be also displayed near the apparatus[5].

A person commits an offence if in the course of a trade or business he supplies, or offers to supply[6], apparatus in contravention of an order under these provisions[7].

1   As to OFCOM see PARA 507.
2   As to the meaning of 'relevant apparatus' see PARA 534 note 2.
3   Wireless Telegraphy Act 2006 s 72(1), (2). The requirements imposed by the order may extend to the form and manner in which the information or instruction is given: s 72(3). The approval of the Secretary of State is required for the making by OFCOM of an order under s 72: s 72(5). A statutory instrument containing an order made by OFCOM under s 72 is subject to annulment in pursuance of a resolution of either House of Parliament: s 72(6). See the Wireless Telegraphy (Citizens' Band and Amateur Apparatus) (Various Provisions) Order 1998, SI 1998/2531 (amended by SI 2000/1013); and the Wireless Telegraphy (Cordless Telephone Apparatus) (Restriction and Marking) Order 1999, SI 1999/2934 (amended by SI 2000/1014 and SI 2003/2155). As to the Secretary of State see PARA 507.
4   The Consumer Protection Act 1987 s 46 has effect for the purpose of construing references in the Wireless Telegraphy Act 2006 to the supply of any thing as it has effect for the purpose of construing references in that Act to the supply of goods: Wireless Telegraphy Act 2006 s 115(1), (6). See CONSUMER PROTECTION vol 21 (2011) PARA 647.
5   Wireless Telegraphy Act 2006 s 72(4).
6   A person is to be treated as offering to supply apparatus if: (1) he exposes apparatus for supply; or (2) he has apparatus in his possession for supply: Wireless Telegraphy Act 2006 s 74(2).
7   Wireless Telegraphy Act 2006 s 74(1). A person who commits an offence under s 74(1) is liable on summary conviction to a fine not exceeding level 5 on the standard scale: s 74(4). As to the standard scale see SENTENCING AND DISPOSITION OF OFFENDERS vol 92 (2010) PARA 142. Proceedings for an offence under s 74 may be commenced at any time within the period of 12 months beginning with the day after the commission of the offence: s 74(5).

Where the commission by one person ('A') of an offence under s 74(1) or (3) (see PARA 536) is due to the act or default of another ('B'), B also commits the offence; and B may be charged with and convicted of the offence by virtue of this subsection whether or not proceedings are taken against A: s 75(1). In proceedings for an offence under s 74(1) or (3) it is a defence for the defendant to prove that he took all reasonable steps and exercised all due diligence to avoid committing the offence: s 75(3). A person may not rely on a defence under s 75(2) which involves an allegation that the commission of the offence was due to the act or default of another person unless: (1) at least seven clear days before the hearing he has given to the prosecutor a notice in writing giving such information identifying or assisting in the identification of the other person as was then in his possession; or (2) the court grants him leave: s 75(4).

536. Information to be given in advertisements. Where it appears to OFCOM[1] to be expedient that a particular description of advertisements[2] for relevant apparatus[3] should contain or refer to particular information relating to the apparatus or its installation or use, OFCOM may by order impose requirements as to the inclusion in advertisements of that description of that information or an indication of the means by which that information may be obtained[4]. A person who publishes an advertisement for apparatus to be supplied[5] in the course of a trade or business commits an offence if the advertisement fails to comply with a requirement imposed by an order under these provisions[6].

1 As to OFCOM see PARA 507.
2 'Advertisement' includes a catalogue, a circular and a price list: Wireless Telegraphy Act 2006 s 76.
3 As to the meaning of 'relevant apparatus' see PARA 534 note 2.
4 Wireless Telegraphy Act 2006 s 73(1), (2). An order under s 73 may specify the form and manner in which the information or indication required by the order is to be included in a particular description of advertisements: s 73(3). The approval of the Secretary of State is required for the making by OFCOM of an order under s 73: s 73(4). A statutory instrument containing an order made by OFCOM under s 73 is subject to annulment in pursuance of a resolution of either House of Parliament: s 73(5). As to the Secretary of State see PARA 507.
5 As to the meaning of 'supply' see PARA 535 note 4.
6 Wireless Telegraphy Act 2006 s 74(3). A person who commits an offence under s 74(3) is liable on summary conviction to a fine not exceeding level 5 on the standard scale: s 74(4). Proceedings for an offence under s 74 may be commenced at any time within the period of 12 months beginning with the day after the commission of the offence: s 74(5). As to the standard scale see SENTENCING AND DISPOSITION OF OFFENDERS vol 92 (2010) PARA 142. In proceedings for an offence under s 74(3) it is a defence for the defendant to prove that: (1) at the time of the alleged offence he was a person whose business it was to publish or arrange for the publication of advertisements; (2) he received the advertisement for publication in the ordinary course of business; and (3) he did not know and had no reason to suspect that publication of the advertisement would amount to an offence under s 74(3): s 75(4). For other defences, and as to the liability of a person whose act or default caused the commission of the offence, see s 75(1)–(3); and PARA 535 note 7.

F. SPECTRUM USE

537. General functions of OFCOM in relation to radio spectrum. It is a function of OFCOM[1]: (1) to give such advice in relation to the use of the electromagnetic spectrum for wireless telegraphy[2]; (2) to provide such other services[3]; and (3) to maintain such records, as it considers appropriate for the purpose of facilitating or managing the use of the spectrum for wireless telegraphy[4]. It is a function of OFCOM, in relation to the use of the electromagnetic spectrum for wireless telegraphy: (a) to give such further advice; (b) to provide such other services; and (c) to maintain such other records, as the Secretary of State[5] may require for the purpose of securing compliance with the international obligations of the United Kingdom[6]. The advice, other services and records that OFCOM may give, provide or maintain under these provisions[7] include advice, other services and records with respect to the use of the electromagnetic spectrum at places outside the United Kingdom[8].

The powers of OFCOM to carry out research, or to arrange for others to carry out research[9], are to be exercisable, in particular, for ascertaining, for the purpose of carrying out OFCOM's functions under these provisions, information about: (i) the demands for use of the electromagnetic spectrum for wireless telegraphy in the United Kingdom; (ii) the effects, in the United Kingdom, of any such use of the spectrum; (iii) likely future developments in relation to those matters; and (iv) any other connected matters that OFCOM thinks relevant[10].

OFCOM may make a grant to any person if, in its opinion, the making of the grant is likely to promote: (A) the efficient use in the United Kingdom of the electromagnetic spectrum for wireless telegraphy; or (B) the efficient management of that use[11].

Where OFCOM is required to give advice or provide another service to a person under these provisions, it may make the giving of the advice or the provision of the other service conditional on the payment to it of such sums as it may determine in advance or as may be agreed between it and that person[12].

1   As to OFCOM see PARA 507.
2   In the Wireless Telegraphy Act 2006 s 1, references to providing a service to a person include references to a service consisting in: (1) the entry of that person's particulars in a register or other record kept by OFCOM for the purpose of carrying out its functions under s 1; or (2) the taking of steps for the purposes of determining whether to grant an application for an entry in a register or record so kept: s 1(9).
3   As to the meaning of 'wireless telegraphy' see PARA 510 note 1.
4   Wireless Telegraphy Act 2006 s 1(1).
5   As to the Secretary of State see PARA 507.
6   Wireless Telegraphy Act 2006 s 1(2). As to the meaning of 'international obligation of the United Kingdom' see PARA 512 note 14. As to the meaning of 'United Kingdom' see PARA 510 note 13.
7   Ie the Wireless Telegraphy Act 2006 s 1.
8   Wireless Telegraphy Act 2006 s 1(3).
9   Ie under the Communications Act 2003 Pt 1 (ss 1–31): see TELECOMMUNICATIONS vol 97 (2010) PARA 26 et seq.
10 Wireless Telegraphy Act 2006 s 1(4).
11 Wireless Telegraphy Act 2006 s 1(5). A grant: (1) may be made to a person holding a wireless telegraphy licence or a grant of recognised spectrum access or to any other person; and (2) is to be made on such terms and conditions as OFCOM considers appropriate; and the terms and conditions may include terms requiring the repayment of the grant in specified circumstances: s 1(6). As to the meaning of 'wireless telegraphy licence' see PARA 514 note 4; and as to the meaning of 'grant of recognised spectrum access' see PARA 521 note 16.
     The consent of the Treasury is required: (a) for the making of a grant under s 1(5); and (b) for the terms and conditions on which such a grant is made: s 1(7). As to the Treasury see CONSTITUTIONAL LAW AND HUMAN RIGHTS vol 8(2) (Reissue) PARAS 512–517.
12 Wireless Telegraphy Act 2006 s 1(8).

538.   United Kingdom Plan for Frequency Authorisation.   OFCOM[1] must, from time to time as it thinks fit, publish a plan ('the United Kingdom Plan for Frequency Authorisation')[2]. The plan must set out: (1) in relation to the United Kingdom[3], the frequencies[4] that: (a) have been allocated for particular wireless telegraphy[5] purposes; and (b) are available for assignment; and (2) the purposes for which the different frequencies have been allocated[6].

1   As to OFCOM see PARA 507.
2   Wireless Telegraphy Act 2006 s 2(1).
3   As to the meaning of 'United Kingdom' see PARA 510 note 13.

4　'Frequency' includes frequency band: Wireless Telegraphy Act 2006 s 115(1).
5　As to the meaning of 'wireless telegraphy' see PARA 510 note 1.
6　Wireless Telegraphy Act 2006 s 2(2).

539.　Duties of OFCOM when carrying out spectrum functions. In carrying out its radio spectrum functions[1], OFCOM[2] must have regard, in particular, to: (1) the extent to which the electromagnetic spectrum is available for use, or further use, for wireless telegraphy[3]; (2) the demand for use of the spectrum for wireless telegraphy; and (3) the demand that is likely to arise in future for the use of the spectrum for wireless telegraphy[4]. In carrying out those functions, OFCOM must also have regard, in particular, to the desirability of promoting: (a) the efficient management and use of the part of the electromagnetic spectrum available for wireless telegraphy; (b) the economic and other benefits that may arise from the use of wireless telegraphy; (c) the development of innovative services; and (d) competition in the provision of electronic communications services[5].

1　As to the meaning of 'radio spectrum functions' see PARA 520 note 9.
2　As to OFCOM see PARA 507.
3　As to the meaning of 'wireless telegraphy' see PARA 510 note 1.
4　Wireless Telegraphy Act 2006 s 3(1).
5　Wireless Telegraphy Act 2006 s 3(2). As to the meaning of 'electronic communications service' see the Communications Act 2003 s 32, applied by the Wireless Telegraphy Act 2006 s 115(1); and TELECOMMUNICATIONS vol 97 (2010) PARA 60. In the application of s 3 to OFCOM's radio spectrum functions, other than its functions under ss 13 and 22 (see TELECOMMUNICATIONS vol 97 (2010) PARAS 25, 32), OFCOM may disregard such of the matters mentioned in s 3(1) and (2) as appear to it: (1) to be matters to which it is not required to have regard apart from s 3; and (2) to have no application to the case in question: s 3(3), (4). Where it appears to OFCOM that a duty under s 3 conflicts with one or more of its duties under the Communications Act 2003 ss 3–6 (see TELECOMMUNICATIONS vol 97 (2010) PARAS 16–19)), priority must be given to its duties under those sections: s 3(5). Where it appears to OFCOM that a duty under s 3 conflicts with another in a particular case, it must secure that the conflict is resolved in the manner it thinks best in the circumstances: s 3(6).

540.　Power of OFCOM to retain costs of carrying out spectrum functions. As from a day to be appointed[1], OFCOM[2] has power to make a statement of the principles under which it may retain any or all of the amounts paid to it in pursuance of obligations imposed by the Wireless Telegraphy Act 2006[3] in relation to the licensing of wireless telegraphy or the grant of recognised spectrum access[4]. Where such a statement of principles authorises the retention of an amount, OFCOM is not required[5] to pay it into the appropriate Consolidated Fund[6]. Principles contained in a statement made by OFCOM must be such as appear to it to be likely to secure, on the basis of such estimates of the likely costs as it is practicable to make[7]:

(1)　that, on a year by year basis, the aggregate amount of the amounts retained by OFCOM does not exceed the amount required by OFCOM for meeting the annual cost to OFCOM of carrying out specified[8] functions[9];

(2)　that the amounts retained by OFCOM are objectively justifiable and proportionate to the costs in respect of which they are retained[10]; and

(3)　that the relationship between meeting the cost of carrying out those functions and the amounts retained is transparent[11].

A statement may include provision which, for the purposes of the principles contained in the statement and of the preparation of accounts for each financial year[12], requires an amount actually received in one year: (a) to be treated as referable to costs incurred in that year and in one or more subsequent years; and (b) to be brought into account, in each of those years, in accordance with an apportionment for which provision is made in the statement[13]. A deficit or surplus shown (after applying this principle for all previous years) by an account prepared for each financial year is to be carried forward and taken into account in determining what is required by OFCOM in relation to the following year for meeting the costs of carrying out the specified[14] functions[15].

A statement of principles, if it is expressed to apply for a limited period, does not apply to any amounts paid to OFCOM after the end of that period, and in any event, does not apply to amounts paid to OFCOM after a withdrawal of the statement takes effect[16]. OFCOM may revise a statement made under these provisions[17]. The consent of the Treasury is required for the making, revision or withdrawal of a statement[18]. Where OFCOM makes or revises a statement, it must publish so much of the statement or revised statement as appears to it necessary for demonstrating that the statement or revision complies with heads (1) to (3) above[19].

1   Ie by an order made by the Secretary of State under the Communications Act 2003 s 411(2) bringing into force s 401. At the date at which this volume states the law, no such order had been made. As to the Secretary of State see PARA 507 note 32.
2   As to OFCOM see PARA 507.
3   Ie the Wireless Telegraphy Act 2006 Pt 2 Ch 1 or 2 (ss 8–17, 18–26): see PARA 514 et seq.
4   Communications Act 2003 s 401(1) (amended by the Wireless Telegraphy Act 2006 s 123, Sch 7 paras 25, 33(1), (2)).
5   Ie in accordance with the Communications Act 2003 s 400: see TELECOMMUNICATIONS vol 97 (2010) PARA 47.
6   Communications Act 2003 s 401(2). As to the Consolidated Fund see CONSTITUTIONAL LAW AND HUMAN RIGHTS vol 8(2) (Reissue) PARA 711 et seq; PARLIAMENT vol 78 (2010) PARAS 1028–1031.
7   Communications Act 2003 s 401(3).
8   The specified functions are: (1) OFCOM's functions under the enactments relating to the management of the radio spectrum except those specified in the Communications Act 2003 s 401(5); and (2) the function of taking any steps that OFCOM considers it necessary to take in preparation for the carrying out of any of the functions mentioned in head (1) or for the purpose of facilitating the carrying out of those functions or otherwise in connection with carrying them out: s 401(4). As to the meaning of 'radio spectrum functions' see PARA 520 note 9. The excepted functions of OFCOM are: (a) its functions under s 22(2) (see TELECOMMUNICATIONS vol 97 (2010) PARA 32); (b) its functions under the Wireless Telegraphy Act 2006 s 1(1), (2) so far as carried out in relation to the use of the electromagnetic spectrum at places outside the United Kingdom, and its functions under s 1(5) (see PARA 537); (c) its functions under s 4 (see PARA 541); (d) its functions under s 7 (see PARA 543); (e) its functions under s 30 (see PARA 549); (f) its functions under ss 42–44 (see PARA 528); (g) any functions conferred on it under ss 47–49 (see PARAS 572, 576); and (h) any function not falling within heads (a)–(g) in so far as the costs of carrying it out are met from payments made to OFCOM by virtue of the Communications Act 2003 s 28 or the Wireless Telegraphy Act 2006 s 1(8) (see PARA 537; and TELECOMMUNICATIONS vol 97 (2010) PARA 36): s 401(5) (amended by the Wireless Telegraphy Act 2006 Sch 7 para 33(3), (4)).
9   Communications Act 2003 s 401(3)(a).
10 Communications Act 2003 s 401(3)(b).
11 Communications Act 2003 s 401(3)(c).
12 Ie under the Communications Act 2003 s 400(4): see TELECOMMUNICATIONS vol 97 (2010) PARA 47.
13 Communications Act 2003 s 401(6).
14 Ie specified in the Communications Act 2003 s 401(4) (see note 8).
15 Communications Act 2003 s 401(7).
16 Communications Act 2003 s 401(8).
17 Communications Act 2003 s 401(9).
18 Communications Act 2003 s 401(10). As to the Treasury see CONSTITUTIONAL LAW AND HUMAN RIGHTS vol 8(2) (Reissue) PARAS 512–517.
19 Communications Act 2003 s 401(11).

541. Advisory service in relation to interference. It is a function of OFCOM[1] to provide a service consisting in the giving of advice and assistance to persons complaining of interference[2] with wireless telegraphy[3].

1	As to OFCOM see PARA 507.
2	For the purposes of the Wireless Telegraphy Act 2006, wireless telegraphy is interfered with if the fulfilment of the purposes of the telegraphy is prejudiced (either generally or in part and, in particular, as respects all, or as respects any, of the recipients or intended recipients of a message, sound or visual image intended to be conveyed by the telegraphy) by an emission or reflection of electromagnetic energy: s 115(1), (3). As to the meaning of 'wireless telegraphy' see PARA 510 note 1.
3	Wireless Telegraphy Act 2006 s 4.

542. Directions with respect to the radio spectrum. The Secretary of State[1] may by order give general or specific directions to OFCOM[2] about the carrying out by OFCOM of its radio spectrum functions[3]. Such an order may require OFCOM to secure that such frequencies of the electromagnetic spectrum as may be specified in the order are kept available or become available for such uses or descriptions of uses, or for such users or descriptions of users, as may be so specified[4]. An order may require OFCOM to exercise its powers under specified provisions[5]: (1) in such cases; (2) in such manner; (3) subject to such restrictions and constraints; and (4) with a view to achieving such purposes, as may be specified in, or determined by the Secretary of State in accordance with, the order[6].

Provision is made in relation to the procedure for directions under the above provisions[7].

1	As to the Secretary of State see PARA 507 note 32.
2	As to OFCOM see PARA 507.
3	Wireless Telegraphy Act 2006 s 5(1). As to the meaning of 'radio spectrum functions' see PARA 520 note 9. As to the order that has been made see the Wireless Telegraphy Act 2006 (Directions to OFCOM) Order 2010, SI 2010/3024. As to the power of the Secretary of State to make orders under the Wireless Telegraphy Act 2006 see s 121; and PARA 511.
4	Wireless Telegraphy Act 2006 s 5(2).
5	Ie the Wireless Telegraphy Act 2006 s 8(3) (exemptions from requirement of wireless telegraphy licence: see PARA 514), ss 12–14, 21–23 (charges for wireless telegraphy licences and grants of recognised spectrum access: see PARAS 520–522).
6	Wireless Telegraphy Act 2006 s 5(3). Section 5 does not restrict the Secretary of State's power under the Communications Act 2003 s 5 (directions in respect of networks and spectrum functions: see TELECOMMUNICATIONS vol 97 (2010) PARA 18): Wireless Telegraphy Act 2006 s 5(5).
7	See the Wireless Telegraphy Act 2006 s 6. An order under s 5 must state the purpose for which a direction is given, unless it falls within s 5(2) or (3): s 6(1). Before making an order under s 5, the Secretary of State must consult OFCOM and such other persons as he thinks fit (s 6(2)), but this does not apply where the Secretary of State considers that the urgency of the case makes it inexpedient to consult before making the order (s 6(3)). No order is to be made under s 5 unless a draft of the order has been laid before Parliament and approved by a resolution of each House: s 6(4). This does not apply, however, where: (1) before or in the course of the consultation required by s 6(2); or (2) after the consultation and before or after a draft of the order has been laid before Parliament, the Secretary of State considers that the urgency of the case is or has become such that he should make the order straight away: s 6(5). Where under s 6(5) the Secretary of State makes an order under s 5 without a draft of the order having been approved, the order ceases to have effect at the end of the period of 40 days beginning with the day on which it was made unless, before the end of that period, it has been approved by a resolution of each House of Parliament: s 6(6). For the purposes of s 6(6): (a) the order's ceasing to have effect is without prejudice to anything previously done, or to the making of a new order; and (b) in reckoning the period of 40 days no account is to be taken of any period during which Parliament is dissolved or prorogued or during which both Houses are adjourned for more than four days: s 6(7).

543.   Special duty in relation to television multiplexes.   The following provisions[1] apply where OFCOM[2], in exercise of its radio spectrum functions[3], has reserved frequencies for the broadcasting of television programmes[4]. OFCOM must, in carrying out those functions, exercise its powers so as to secure, so far as practicable, that the following requirement[5] is satisfied[6], namely, that sufficient capacity is made available on the reserved frequencies for ensuring, in the case of every licensed television multiplex service[7], that the qualifying services[8] are broadcast by means of that multiplex service[9].

1   Ie the Wireless Telegraphy Act 2006 s 7.
2   As to OFCOM see PARA 507.
3   As to the meaning of 'radio spectrum functions' see PARA 520 note 9.
4   Wireless Telegraphy Act 2006 s 7(1).
5   Ie the requirement of the Wireless Telegraphy Act 2006 s 7(3) (see the text and notes 7–9).
6   Wireless Telegraphy Act 2006 s 7(2).
7   For the purposes of the Wireless Telegraphy Act 2006 s 7(3), 'licensed television multiplex service' means a television multiplex service the provision of which is authorised by a licence under the Broadcasting Act 1996 Pt I (ss 1–39): Wireless Telegraphy Act 2006 s 7(4). For these purposes, 'television multiplex service' has the same meaning as in the Communications Act 2003 Pt 3 (ss 198–362) (see PARA 697): Wireless Telegraphy Act 2006 s 7(5).
8   For the purposes of the Wireless Telegraphy Act 2006 s 7, 'qualifying service' has the same meaning as in the Communications Act 2003 Pt 3 (see PARAS 686 note 22, 690): s 7(5).
9   Wireless Telegraphy Act 2006 s 7(3).

544.   Recognised spectrum access.   The following provisions[1] apply where: (1) a person[2] is proposing to use or to continue to use a wireless telegraphy station[3] or wireless telegraphy apparatus[4]; (2) the circumstances of the use are circumstances specified for the purposes of these provisions in regulations made by OFCOM[5]; (3) that use does not require a wireless telegraphy licence[6] but will involve the emission of electromagnetic energy[7] with a view to the reception of anything at places in the United Kingdom[8] or in UK territorial sea[9] (and for these purposes it is immaterial whether the emissions are from a place within the United Kingdom or from a place outside the United Kingdom)[10].

On an application by that person, OFCOM may make a grant of recognised spectrum access in respect of any use by him of anything for wireless telegraphy that is specified in the grant[11]. A grant of recognised spectrum access made to a person must set out, by reference to such factors as OFCOM thinks fit (including, so far as it thinks fit, frequencies, times and places of reception and strength and type of signal), the respects in which the use of anything by that person for wireless telegraphy is recognised by the grant[12]. A grant of recognised spectrum access to a person is made by giving him a notification containing the grant[13]. A grant of recognised spectrum access may be made subject to such restrictions and conditions as OFCOM thinks fit, including, in particular, restrictions or conditions as to strength or type of signal, as to times of use and as to the sharing of frequencies[14]. The restrictions and conditions of a grant of recognised spectrum access made to a person must not duplicate obligations already imposed on him by general conditions[15]. Where a grant of recognised spectrum access is made subject to restrictions and conditions, the restrictions and conditions must be set out in the notification by which the grant is made[16].

The following provisions[17] apply to the functions of OFCOM set out below[18]:

(a)   its functions[19] with respect to the granting of wireless telegraphy licences[20];

(b)   its functions[21] with respect to the making of grants of recognised spectrum access[22]; and

(c)   any of its other radio spectrum functions[23] in the carrying out of which it is appropriate for it to have regard to: (i) whether wireless telegraphy licences are in force; or (ii) the terms, provisions or limitations of wireless telegraphy licences that are in force[24].

In carrying out those functions, OFCOM must take into account: (A) the existence of any grant of recognised spectrum access that is in force; and (B) the provisions imposing the restrictions and conditions subject to which such a grant has effect, to the same extent as it would take into account a wireless telegraphy licence with terms, provisions or limitations making equivalent provision[25].

OFCOM may by regulations make provision for the conversion, on the application of the licence holder, of a wireless telegraphy licence into a grant of recognised spectrum access, and for the conversion, on the application of the holder of the grant, of a grant of recognised spectrum access into a wireless telegraphy licence[26].

1   Ie the Wireless Telegraphy Act 2006 s 18.
2   As to the meaning of 'person' see PARA 510 note 1.
3   As to the meaning of 'wireless telegraphy station' see PARA 510 note 12.
4   As to the meaning of 'wireless telegraphy apparatus' see PARA 510 note 9.
5   As to OFCOM see PARA 507. As to such regulations see the Wireless Telegraphy (Recognised Spectrum Access) Regulations 2007, SI 2007/393; and the Wireless Telegraphy (Crown Recognised Spectrum Access) Regulations 2009, SI 2009/16 (amended by SI 2011/438).
6   As to the meaning of 'wireless telegraphy licence' see PARA 514 note 4.
7   As to the meaning of 'emission of electromagnetic energy' see PARA 510 note 1.
8   As to the meaning of 'United Kingdom' see PARA 510 note 13.
9   As to the meaning of 'UK territorial sea' see PARA 510 note 14.
10 Wireless Telegraphy Act 2006 s 18(1), (2).
11 Wireless Telegraphy Act 2006 s 18(3). As to bidding for grants of recognised spectrum access see PARA 522. As to charges for recognised spectrum access see PARA 545. For further provision as to the making, revocation and modification of grants of recognised spectrum access see s 19, Sch 2.
12 Wireless Telegraphy Act 2006 s 18(4).
13 Wireless Telegraphy Act 2006 s 18(5). As to notification see PARA 513.
14 Wireless Telegraphy Act 2006 s 18(6).
15 Wireless Telegraphy Act 2006 s 18(7). The text refers to general conditions set under the Communications Act 2003 s 45 (power of OFCOM to set conditions in relation to electronic communications networks and services): see TELECOMMUNICATIONS vol 97 (2010) PARA 98.
16 Wireless Telegraphy Act 2006 s 18(8).
17 Ie the Wireless Telegraphy Act 2006 s 20.
18 Wireless Telegraphy Act 2006 s 20(1).
19 Ie under the Wireless Telegraphy Act 2006 ss 8, 9 (licensing of the use of the radio spectrum: see PARA 514 et seq).
20 Wireless Telegraphy Act 2006 s 20(1)(a).
21 Ie under the Wireless Telegraphy Act 2006 s 18: see the text and notes 1–16.
22 Wireless Telegraphy Act 2006 s 20(1)(b).
23 As to the meaning of 'radio spectrum functions' see PARA 520 note 9.
24 Wireless Telegraphy Act 2006 s 20(1)(c).
25 Wireless Telegraphy Act 2006 s 20(2).
26 Wireless Telegraphy Act 2006 s 27. As to the making of regulations by OFCOM see s 122; and PARA 511. See also PARA 522 note 3.

545. Charges for recognised spectrum access. A person[1] to whom a grant of recognised spectrum access is made[2] must pay to OFCOM[3]: (1) on the making of the grant; and (2) if regulations made by OFCOM so provide, subsequently at such times during its term and such times in respect of its modification or revocation as may be prescribed by the regulations, the sums described below[4]. The sums are: (a) such sums as OFCOM may prescribe by regulations; or (b) if regulations made by OFCOM so provide, such sums (whether on the making of the grant or subsequently) as OFCOM may determine in the particular case[5]. On the making of a grant of recognised spectrum access in respect of which sums will or may subsequently become payable under such regulations, OFCOM may require such security to be given, by way of deposit or otherwise, for the payment of those sums as it thinks fit[6].

Where OFCOM exercises a power[7] to prescribe[8] sums payable in respect of grants of recognised spectrum access, other than a power to prescribe sums payable where a grant is modified or revoked at the request or with the consent of the holder of the grant, OFCOM may, if it thinks fit in the light (in particular) of the matters to which it must have regard[9] when carrying out its radio spectrum functions[10], prescribe sums greater than those necessary to recover costs incurred by it in connection with its radio spectrum functions[11].

1   As to the meaning of 'person' see PARA 510 note 1.
2   As to the meaning of 'grant of recognised spectrum access' see PARA 521 note 16 and as to grants of recognised spectrum access see PARA 544. As to bidding for grants of recognised spectrum access see PARA 522. References in the Wireless Telegraphy Act 2006 ss 21–25 to the making of a grant of recognised spectrum access include references to the making of a grant by way of renewal of a previous grant: s 26.
3   As to OFCOM see PARA 507.
4   Wireless Telegraphy Act 2006 s 21(1).
5   Wireless Telegraphy Act 2006 s 21(2). Regulations under s 21 may: (1) confer exemptions from provisions of the regulations in particular cases; and (2) provide for sums paid to be refunded, in whole or in part, in such cases as may be specified in the regulations or in such cases as OFCOM thinks fit: s 21(3). Regulations under s 21 do not apply in relation to a grant of recognised spectrum access made in accordance with regulations under s 23 (bidding for grants: see PARA 522): s 21(5). As to regulations made under s 21 see the Wireless Telegraphy (Recognised Spectrum Access Charges) Regulations 2007, SI 2007/392. As to the making of regulations by OFCOM see s 122; and PARA 511. See also PARA 522 note 3.
6   Wireless Telegraphy Act 2006 s 21(4).
7   Ie under the Wireless Telegraphy Act 2006 s 21.
8   For these purposes, 'prescribe' means prescribe by regulations or determine in accordance with regulations: Wireless Telegraphy Act 2006 s 22(3).
9   Ie under the Wireless Telegraphy Act 2006 s 3: see PARA 539.
10 As to the meaning of 'radio spectrum functions' see PARA 520 note 9.
11 Wireless Telegraphy Act 2006 s 22(1), (2).

546.   Crown use of the radio spectrum. The Secretary of State[1] may, out of money provided by Parliament, make payments to OFCOM[2] of such amounts as he considers appropriate in respect of: (1) the establishment and use, by or on behalf of the Crown, of a wireless telegraphy station[3]; (2) the installation and use, by or on behalf of the Crown, of wireless telegraphy apparatus[4]; (3) any grant of recognised spectrum access[5] made to the Crown[6]. The payments made under these provisions are to be made at such times and, so far as made in relation to use, in relation to such periods, as the Secretary of State considers appropriate[7].

1   As to the Secretary of State see PARA 507 note 32.
2   As to OFCOM see PARA 507.
3   As to the meaning of 'wireless telegraphy station' see PARA 510 note 12.
4   As to the meaning of 'wireless telegraphy apparatus' see PARA 510 note 9.
5   As to the meaning of 'grant of recognised spectrum access' see PARA 521 note 16.
6   Wireless Telegraphy Act 2006 s 28(1). As to the grant of recognised spectrum access see PARA 544.
7   Wireless Telegraphy Act 2006 s 28(2).

547.   Limitations on authorised spectrum use. If it considers it appropriate to impose limitations on the use of particular frequencies for the purpose of securing the efficient use of the electromagnetic spectrum, OFCOM[1] must make an order imposing the limitations[2]. Such an order may do one or both of the following: (1) specify frequencies for the use of which OFCOM will grant or make only a limited number of wireless telegraphy licences[3] and grants of recognised spectrum access[4]; or (2) specify uses for which, on specified frequencies, OFCOM will grant or make only a limited number of wireless telegraphy licences and grants of recognised spectrum access[5]. Where OFCOM makes an order under these provisions, it must set out the criteria which OFCOM will apply in determining in accordance with the order: (a) the limit on the number of wireless telegraphy licences and grants of recognised spectrum access to be granted or made for the specified frequencies or uses; (b) the persons to whom licences will be granted or grants of recognised spectrum access made[6].

OFCOM must exercise its powers[7] with respect to wireless telegraphy licences and its powers[8] with respect to grants of recognised spectrum access, in accordance with the orders for the time being in force under these provisions[9].

OFCOM must keep under review any order for the time being in force under these provisions[10]. OFCOM must make an order revoking or amending the provisions of an order if, on reviewing it, it considers it necessary to do so for the purpose of securing the efficient use of the electromagnetic spectrum[11].

An order under these provisions may make provision by reference to determinations which: (i) are made from time to time by OFCOM in accordance with the provisions of such an order; and (ii) are published by OFCOM from time to time in such manner as may be provided for in such an order[12].

1 As to OFCOM see PARA 507.

2 Wireless Telegraphy Act 2006 s 29(1). As to the making of orders by OFCOM see s 122; and PARA 511. See the Wireless Telegraphy (Limitation of Number of Licences) Order 2003, SI 2003/1902 (amended by SI 2006/2786), made under the former legislation; and the Wireless Telegraphy (Limitation of Number of Concurrent Spectrum Access Licences) Order 2006, SI 2006/341; the Wireless Telegraphy (Limitation of Number of Spectrum Access Licences) Order 2006, SI 2006/1809; the Wireless Telegraphy (Limitation of Number of Spectrum Access Licences) Order 2007, SI 2007/379; the Wireless Telegraphy (Limitation of Number of Grants of Recognised Spectrum Access) Order 2007, SI 2007/394; the Wireless Telegraphy (Limitation of Number of Spectrum Access Licences) (No 2) Order 2007, SI 2007/3381; the Wireless Telegraphy (Limitation of Number of Spectrum Access Licences) Order 2008, SI 2008/687; the Wireless Telegraphy (Limitation of Number of Spectrum Access Licences) (No 2) Order 2008, SI 2008/3197; the Wireless Telegraphy (Limitation of Number of Grants of Crown Recognised Spectrum Access) Order 2009, SI 2009/15; and the Wireless Telegraphy (Limitation of Number of Grants of Crown Recognised Spectrum Access) Order 2011, SI 2011/441. As to the making of regulations by OFCOM see s 122; and PARA 511.

3 As to the meaning of 'wireless telegraphy licence' see PARA 514 note 4.

4 As to the meaning of 'grant of recognised spectrum access' see PARA 521 note 16 and as to the grant of recognised spectrum access see PARA 544.

5 Wireless Telegraphy Act 2006 s 29(2).

6 Wireless Telegraphy Act 2006 s 29(3). OFCOM must satisfy itself that any criteria set out as a result of s 29(3) are: (1) objectively justifiable in relation to the frequencies or uses to which they relate; (2) not such as to discriminate unduly against particular persons or against a particular description of persons; (3) proportionate to what they are intended to achieve; and (4) in relation to what they are intended to achieve, transparent: s 29(4).

7 Ie under the Wireless Telegraphy Act 2006 Pt 2 Ch 1 (ss 8–17): see PARA 514 et seq.

8 Ie under the Wireless Telegraphy Act 2006 Pt 2 Ch 2 (ss 18–26): see PARAS 544, 545.

9 Wireless Telegraphy Act 2006 s 29(5).

10 Wireless Telegraphy Act 2006 s 29(6).

11 Wireless Telegraphy Act 2006 s 29(7).

12 Wireless Telegraphy Act 2006 s 29(8).

548. Wireless telegraphy register. OFCOM[1] may by regulations make provision for the establishment and maintenance of a register of relevant information[2]. OFCOM may include relevant information in the register if, and only if, it is relevant information of a description prescribed by regulations under these provisions[3]. Subject to such conditions (including conditions as to payment) as may be prescribed by regulations, a register of relevant information is to be open to inspection by the public[4].

1 As to OFCOM see PARA 507.
2 See the Wireless Telegraphy Act 2006 s 31(1); and the Wireless Telegraphy (Register) Regulations 2004, SI 2004/3155, reg 3. The regulations came into force on 23 December 2004 (see reg 1), and do not extend to the Channel Islands or the Isle of Man (see reg 2). Information is relevant information for the purposes of the Wireless Telegraphy Act 2006 s 31(1) if it relates to: (1) the grant, renewal, transfer, variation or revocation of wireless telegraphy licences; or (2) the making, renewal, transfer, modification or revocation of grants of recognised spectrum access: s 31(3). As to the meaning of 'wireless telegraphy licence' see PARA 514 note 4. As to the grant of recognised spectrum access see PARA 544. As to the making of regulations by OFCOM see s 122; and PARA 511.
3 Wireless Telegraphy Act 2006 s 31(2). As to the description of relevant information that has been prescribed for the purposes of s 31(2) see the Wireless Telegraphy (Register) Regulations 2004, SI 2004/3155, reg 4, Schedule (amended by SI 2006/340; SI 2006/1808; SI 2007/381; SI 2007/3389; SI 2008/689; SI 2008/2104; SI 2008/3193; SI 2009/14; SI 2011/439).
4 Wireless Telegraphy Act 2006 s 31(4). At the date at which this volume states the law, no such conditions had been prescribed.

(iii) General Issue of Spectrum Trading

549. Spectrum trading. OFCOM[1] may by regulations authorise the transfer to another person[2] by the holder of a wireless telegraphy licence[3] or the holder of a grant of recognised spectrum access[4], of rights and obligations arising as a result of such a licence or grant[5]. The transfers that may be so authorised are[6]:

(1) transfers of all or any of the rights and obligations under a licence or grant such that the rights and obligations of the person making the transfer become rights and obligations of the transferee to the exclusion of the person making the transfer[7];

(2) transfers of all or any of those rights and obligations such that the transferred rights and obligations become rights and obligations of the transferee while continuing, concurrently, to be rights and obligations of the person making the transfer[8]; and

(3) transfers falling within either of heads (1) and (2) under which the rights and obligations that are acquired by the transferee take effect:

    (a) if they are rights and obligations under a wireless telegraphy licence, as rights and obligations under a grant of recognised spectrum access; and

    (b) if they are rights and obligations under a grant of recognised spectrum access, as rights and obligations under a wireless telegraphy licence[9].

Regulations authorising the transfer of rights and obligations under a wireless telegraphy licence or a grant of recognised spectrum access may[10]:

(i) authorise a partial transfer to be made by reference to such factors and apportionments and to have effect in relation to such matters and periods, as may be described in, or determined in accordance with, the regulations[11];

(ii) by reference to such factors (including the terms and conditions of the licence or grant in question) as may be specified in or determined in accordance with the regulations, restrict the circumstances in which, the extent to which and the manner in which a transfer may be made[12];

(iii) require the approval or consent of OFCOM for the making of a transfer[13];

(iv) provide for a transfer to be effected by the surrender of a wireless telegraphy licence or grant of recognised spectrum access and the grant or making of a new one in respect of the transfer[14];

(v) confer power on OFCOM to direct that a transfer must not be made, or is to be made only after compliance with such conditions as OFCOM may impose in accordance with the regulations[15];

(vi) authorise OFCOM to require the payment to it of such sums as may be determined by or in accordance with the regulations in respect of determinations made by OFCOM for the purposes of the regulations or in respect of an approval or consent given for those purposes[16];

(vii) make provision for the giving of security (whether by the giving of deposits or otherwise) in respect of sums payable in pursuance of any regulations under these provisions[17];

(viii) make provision as to the circumstances in which security given under such regulations is to be returned or may be retained[18];

(ix) impose requirements as to the procedure to be followed for the making of a transfer and, in particular, as to the notification about a transfer that must be given to OFCOM, or must be published, both in advance of its being made and afterwards[19];

(x) impose requirements as to the records to be kept in connection with any transfer, and as to the persons to whom such records are to be made available[20];

(xi) set out the matters to be taken into account in the making of determinations under regulations under these provisions[21].

The transfer of rights and obligations under a wireless telegraphy licence or grant of recognised spectrum access is void except to the extent that it is made either in accordance with regulations under these provisions or in accordance with a provision[22] which: (A) is contained in a wireless telegraphy licence granted before 29 December 2003[23] or in the first or any subsequent renewal on or after that date of a licence so granted; and (B) allows the holder of the licence to confer the benefit of the licence on another in respect of any station or apparatus to which the licence relates[24]. A transfer is also void if it is made in contravention of a direction given by OFCOM in exercise of a power conferred by regulations under these provisions[25].

1 As to OFCOM see PARA 507.
2 As to the meaning of 'person' see PARA 510 note 1.
3 As to the meaning of 'wireless telegraphy licence' see PARA 514 note 4.
4 As to the meaning of 'grant of recognised spectrum access' see PARA 521 note 16 and as to the grant of recognised spectrum access see PARA 544.
5 Wireless Telegraphy Act 2006 s 30(1). As to the making of regulations by OFCOM see s 122; and PARA 511. As to the regulations see the Wireless Telegraphy (Spectrum Trading) Regulations 2004, SI 2004/3154 (amended by SI 2006/339, SI 2006/1807, SI 2007/380, SI 2007/3387, SI 2008/688, SI 2008/2105 and SI 2008/3192) (made under the former legislation); and the Wireless Telegraphy (Recognised Spectrum Access and Licence) (Spectrum Trading) Regulations 2009, SI 2009/17 (amended by SI 2001/440).
6 Wireless Telegraphy Act 2006 s 30(2).
7 Wireless Telegraphy Act 2006 s 30(2)(a).
8 Wireless Telegraphy Act 2006 s 30(2)(b).

9   Wireless Telegraphy Act 2006 s 30(2)(c).
10 Wireless Telegraphy Act 2006 s 30(3).
11 Wireless Telegraphy Act 2006 s 30(3)(a).
12 Wireless Telegraphy Act 2006 s 30(3)(b).
13 Wireless Telegraphy Act 2006 s 30(3)(c).
14 Wireless Telegraphy Act 2006 s 30(3)(d).
15 Wireless Telegraphy Act 2006 s 30(3)(e).
16 Wireless Telegraphy Act 2006 s 30(3)(f).
17 Wireless Telegraphy Act 2006 s 30(3)(g).
18 Wireless Telegraphy Act 2006 s 30(3)(h).
19 Wireless Telegraphy Act 2006 s 30(3)(i). As to notification see PARA 513.
20 Wireless Telegraphy Act 2006 s 30(3)(j).
21 Wireless Telegraphy Act 2006 s 30(3)(k).
22 Ie falling within the Wireless Telegraphy Act 2006 s 30(5).
23 Ie the commencement of the Communications Act 2003 s 168 (now repealed): see the Office of Communications Act 2002 (Commencement No 3) and Communications Act 2003 (Commencement No 2) Order 2003, SI 2003/3142.
24 Wireless Telegraphy Act 2006 s 30(5).
25 Wireless Telegraphy Act 2006 s 30(6).

(iv) Sale of IBA and BBC Transmission Assets

A. TRANSFER OF IBA ASSETS

550. Transfer of IBA assets to nominated company. The Secretary of State[1] by order appointed 1 January 1991[2] as the transfer date for the coming into force of a scheme[3] providing for the division of the property, rights and liabilities of the Independent Broadcasting Authority ('IBA')[4] between[5]:

(1)   the Independent Television Commission ('ITC')[6];
(2)   the Radio Authority[7]; and
(3)   a company nominated for these purposes by the Secretary of State[8].

The IBA continued in existence in a reduced form and with limited functions after the transfer date until such time as it was dissolved by order made by the Secretary of State[9]. Transitional provision was made in relation to the IBA's broadcasting services[10].

Where property, rights and liabilities of the IBA vested in the nominated company in accordance with the transfer scheme[11], provision was made for securities[12] of the nominated company to be issued to the Secretary of State or his nominee[13].

Provision was made for the Secretary of State to fix a target investment limit in relation to the aggregate of the shares for the time being held in the nominated company by any Minister of the Crown[14] or any nominee of his ('the government shareholding')[15].

Provision was made for the Secretary of State to make a direction that specified sums should be carried by the nominated company to a reserve ('the statutory reserve'), to be applied by the nominated company in paying up unissued shares of the company to be allotted to members of the company as fully paid bonus shares[16].

Provision was made: (1) for the Secretary of State, with the consent of the Treasury[17], to make loans to the nominated company out of money provided by Parliament, as long as the company was wholly owned by the Crown; and (2) for the repayment of any such loan and the payment of interest on it[18].

Provision was made that, as long as the nominated company was wholly owned by the Crown, the aggregate amount outstanding in respect of the principal of any relevant borrowing[19] of the company was not to exceed a sum determined by the Secretary of State with the consent of the Treasury[20].

1   As to the Secretary of State see PARA 507.
2   See the Broadcasting (Transfer Date and Nominated Company) Order 1990, SI 1990/2540, art 2.
3   As to the provisions of the scheme see the Broadcasting Act 1990 s 127, Sch 9.
4   The IBA was constituted under the Broadcasting Act 1981 s 1, Sch 1 (repealed).
5   Broadcasting Act 1990 s 127(1). The IBA was empowered to dispose of certain transmitting equipment with the approval of the Secretary of State: see s 132.
6   Broadcasting Act 1990 s 127(1)(a). As to the ITC see PARA 507.
7   Broadcasting Act 1990 s 127(1)(b). As to the Radio Authority see PARA 507.
8   See the Broadcasting Act 1990 s 127(1)(c), (2). The company nominated was National Transcommunications Limited: see the Broadcasting (Transfer Date and Nominated Company) Order 1990, SI 1990/2540, art 3. National Transcommunications Ltd, or ntl, subsequently focused on cable assets (and now operates as Virgin Media) and in 2004 sold on its terrestrial broadcasting operations to Macquarie Communications Infrastructure Group, which adopted the name Arqiva. In September 2008, Arquiva bought and merged with National Grid Wireless (originally the United Kingdom subsidiary of Crown Castle, which had been formed from the domestic transmitter network of the BBC, which was privatised in 1997); it is now owned by a consortium of shareholder groups.
9   See the Broadcasting Act 1990 s 127(3)–(5), Sch 9. As to the dissolution of the IBA see PARA 507.
10 See the Broadcasting Act 1990 ss 129–133, Sch 11.
11 Ie the scheme made under the Broadcasting Act 1990 s 127, Sch 9: see s 135(1).
12 'Securities', in relation to a company, includes shares, debentures, bonds and other securities of the company, whether or not constituting a charge on the assets of the company: Broadcasting Act 1990 s 141(1).
13 See the Broadcasting Act 1990 ss 135, 136 (s 135 amended by SI 2009/1941).
14 References in the Broadcasting Act 1990 s 137 to a Minister of the Crown include references to the Treasury: see s 137(7). As to the Treasury see CONSTITUTIONAL LAW AND HUMAN RIGHTS vol 8(2) (Reissue) PARAS 512–517.
15 See the Broadcasting Act 1990 s 137. See the Broadcasting (Investment Limit in Nominated Company) Order 1992, SI 1992/281, art 2, which sets the target investment limit of the government shareholding at nil.
16 See the Broadcasting Act 1990 s 138 (amended by SI 2008/948).
17 As to the Treasury see CONSTITUTIONAL LAW AND HUMAN RIGHTS vol 8(2) (Reissue) PARAS 512–517.
18 See the Broadcasting Act 1990 s 139. As to the limit on the aggregate amount outstanding in respect of the principal of loans see s 139(2), (3).
19 'Relevant borrowing', in relation to the nominated company, means: (1) loans made to that company or to any subsidiary of that company, other than: (a) loans so made by any such subsidiary or (as the case may be) by that company; and (b) loans made to that company by the Secretary of State under the Broadcasting Act 1990 s 139; and (2) loans which are to be treated as having been made to that company, including loans which are to be treated as having been so made by virtue of the issue of debentures in pursuance of s 135: s 140(2). As to the meaning of 'subsidiary' see the Companies Act 2006 s 1159 (see COMPANIES vol 14 (2009) PARA 25); definition applied by the Broadcasting Act 1990 s 141(1) (amended by SI 2009/1941). As to the Secretary of State see PARA 507 note 32.
20 Broadcasting Act 1990 s 140(1). As to the Treasury see CONSTITUTIONAL LAW AND HUMAN RIGHTS vol 8(2) (Reissue) PARAS 512–517.

B. TRANSFER OF BBC ASSETS

551.   Power of the BBC to make transfer schemes relating to its transmission network. The BBC[1] may make a scheme or schemes providing for the transfer to any person[2] or persons of such property, rights and liabilities of the BBC as are specified in, or determined in accordance with the scheme, being property, rights and liabilities which, immediately before the day on which the scheme comes into force, subsist for the purposes of or in connection with or are otherwise attributable to the BBC transmission network[3]. The transmission assets of the BBC were transferred in 1997[4].

1   As to the meaning of 'BBC' see PARA 603 note 1; and as to the BBC see PARAS 603–626.
2   As to the meaning of 'person' see PARA 510 note 1.
3   Broadcasting Act 1996 s 131(1). 'The BBC transmission network' means so much of the undertaking of the BBC as is concerned with the provision of broadcasting transmission services or services related to those services: s 131(2). As to taxation provisions with respect to transfer schemes see s 135(4), Sch 7 (amended by the Capital Allowances Act 2001 ss 578, 580, Sch 2 para 97, Sch 4; the Finance Act 2008 s 8(2), Sch 2 para 70(d); the Corporation Tax Act 2009 s 1322, Sch 1 Pt 2 paras 445, 446; the Corporation Tax Act 2010 s 1177, Sch 1 Pt 2 para 294; and by SI 2003/2867, and SI 2009/1941); the BBC Home Service Transfer Scheme (Capital Allowances) Order 1997, SI 1997/491; and the BBC World Service Transfer Scheme (Capital Allowances) Order 1997, SI 1997/1354.
4   The transmission assets of the BBC were transferred to Castle Transmission Services, owned by Crown Castle International. Crown Castle UK was bought by National Grid Transco plc (now National Grid plc) on 31 August 2004 and renamed National Grid Wireless on 11 October 2005; it is now owned by Arqiva (as to which see PARA 550 note 8).

552.   Contents and effect of transfer schemes.   A transfer scheme[1] may define the property, rights and liabilities to be transferred to a particular person[2] by specifying or describing the property, rights and liabilities in question[3], by referring to all (or all but so much as may be excepted) of the property, rights and liabilities comprised in a specified part of the BBC's undertaking[4], or partly in one way and partly in the other[5]. A transfer scheme must appoint the day on which it is to come into force[6].

The Broadcasting Act 1996 has effect, in relation to any provision of a transfer scheme for the transfer of any property, rights or liabilities, so as to transfer the property, rights or liabilities, at the beginning of the day appointed for the coming into force of the scheme, and without further assurance, from the BBC to the person to whom they are allocated under the scheme and to vest them in that person; and the provisions of that scheme in relation to that transfer have effect from that time accordingly[7]. The Act also has effect, in relation to any provision of a transfer scheme for the creation of any interest or right[8], so as to create the specified interests and rights, at the beginning of the day appointed for the coming into force of the scheme and without further assurance[9].

1   'Transfer scheme' means a scheme made under the Broadcasting Act 1996 s 131(1) (see PARA 551): s 131(3).
2   Broadcasting Act 1996 s 131(4), Sch 5 para 1(1). As to the meaning of 'person' see PARA 510 note 1.
        The provisions of Sch 5 para 1(1)–(4) have effect subject to so much of a transfer scheme as provides for the transfer of any of the property, rights or liabilities to be transferred in accordance with the scheme, or the creation of any of the rights or interests to be created in accordance with the scheme, to be effected by or under any agreement or instrument entered into or executed in pursuance of an obligation imposed by virtue of Sch 5 para 2(1)(g) (see PARA 553): Sch 5 para 1(5).
3   Broadcasting Act 1996 Sch 5 para 1(1)(a).
4   Broadcasting Act 1996 Sch 5 para 1(1)(b). As to the meaning of 'BBC' see PARA 603 note 1; and as to the BBC see PARAS 603–626.
5   Broadcasting Act 1996 Sch 5 para 1(1)(c).
6   Broadcasting Act 1996 Sch 5 para 1(2).
7   Broadcasting Act 1996 Sch 5 para 1(3).
8   Ie by virtue of the Broadcasting Act 1996 Sch 5 para 2 (see PARA 553): see Sch 5 para 1(4).
9   Broadcasting Act 1996 Sch 5 para 1(4).

553.   Division of the BBC's undertaking by scheme.   For the purposes of making any such division as the BBC[1] considers appropriate of any of its property, rights and liabilities between two or more persons[2] (including any division between the BBC and any one or more other persons), a transfer scheme[3] may contain provision[4]:

(1)   for the creation in favour of the BBC of an interest or right in or in relation to property transferred in accordance with that scheme to any person[5];

(2)   for the creation, in favour of a person to whom any transfer is made, of an interest or right in or in relation to property so transferred to another[6];

(3)   for giving effect to a transfer to any person by the creation, in favour of that person, of an interest or right in or in relation to property retained by the BBC[7];

(4)   for rights and liabilities to be transferred so as to be enforceable by or against more than one transferee[8] or by or against both one or more transferees and the BBC[9];

(5)   for rights and liabilities enforceable by or against more than one person in accordance with any provision falling within head (4) above to be enforceable in different or modified respects by or against each or any of them[10];

(6)   for the creation of new rights and liabilities as between different transferees and as between any transferee and the BBC[11]; and

(7)   without prejudice to head (6) above, for imposing on any transferee or the BBC an obligation to enter into such written agreements with any other person on whom any corresponding obligation is, could be or has been imposed by virtue of this provision (whether in the same or a different scheme)[12], or to execute such instruments in favour of any such person[13].

A transfer scheme may contain such supplemental and incidental provision with respect to the interests, rights and liabilities of third parties[14] in relation to anything to which the scheme relates as the BBC considers to be necessary or expedient for the purposes of any such division as is mentioned above, or in connection with anything contained in the scheme[15]. The provision that may be contained in a transfer scheme must include provision for interests, rights or liabilities to which any third party is entitled or subject in relation to anything to which the scheme relates to be modified in such respects or in such manner as may be specified or determined under the scheme[16].

An obligation imposed on any person under head (7) above is enforceable by the bringing, by any person with or in favour of whom the agreement or instrument is to be entered into or executed, of civil proceedings for an injunction or for other appropriate relief[17].

1   As to the meaning of 'BBC' see PARA 603 note 1; and as to the BBC see PARAS 603–626.
2   As to the meaning of 'person' see PARA 510 note 1.
3   As to the meaning of 'transfer scheme' see PARA 552 note 1; and as to the power to make transfer schemes see PARA 551.
4   Broadcasting Act 1996 s 131(4), Sch 5 para 2(1).
5   Broadcasting Act 1996 Sch 5 para 2(1)(a).
6   Broadcasting Act 1996 Sch 5 para 2(1)(b).
7   Broadcasting Act 1996 Sch 5 para 2(1)(c).
8   References, in relation to a transfer scheme, to a transferee include references to any person in whose favour any interest or right is created in accordance with the scheme: Broadcasting Act 1996 Sch 5 para 2(5)(a).
9   Broadcasting Act 1996 Sch 5 para 2(1)(d).
10   Broadcasting Act 1996 Sch 5 para 2(1)(e).

11 Broadcasting Act 1996 Sch 5 para 2(1)(f).
12 Broadcasting Act 1996 Sch 5 para 2(1)(g)(i).
13 Broadcasting Act 1996 Sch 5 para 2(1)(g)(ii).
14 The reference, in relation to a transfer scheme, to a third party is a reference to a person other than the BBC, or any person who (apart from any provision made by virtue of the Broadcasting Act 1996 Sch 5 para 2(1)(e) (see the text and note 10) or Sch 5 para 2(2) (see the text and note 15)) is a transferee: Sch 5 para 2(5)(b).
15 Broadcasting Act 1996 Sch 5 para 2(2). The provisions of Sch 5 para 2(2), (3) are without prejudice to the generality of Sch 5 para 4(1) (see PARA 555): Sch 5 para 2(6).
16 Broadcasting Act 1996 Sch 5 para 2(3). See also note 15.
17 Broadcasting Act 1996 Sch 5 para 2(4).

554.   Property to which a scheme may relate.   The property, rights and liabilities that are capable of being transferred in accordance with a transfer scheme[1] include[2]:

(1)   property, rights and liabilities that would not otherwise be capable of being transferred or assigned by the BBC[3];

(2)   rights and liabilities of the BBC under any agreement or arrangement for the payment of pensions, allowances and gratuities[4];

(3)   property acquired at a time after the making of the scheme and before it comes into force, and rights and liabilities which arise or may arise in respect of anything occurring after the making of the scheme[5];

(4)   property situated anywhere in the United Kingdom[6] or elsewhere and rights and liabilities under the law of any part of the United Kingdom or of any country or territory outside the United Kingdom[7]; and

(5)   rights and liabilities under enactments[8].

The transfers authorised by head (1) above, and the interests and rights that may be created in accordance with a transfer scheme, include transfers, interests and rights which are to take effect as if there were no such requirement to obtain any person's consent or concurrence[9], no such liability in respect of a contravention of any other requirement[10], and no such interference with any interest or right[11], as there would be, in the case of any transaction apart from the Broadcasting Act 1996, by reason of provisions having effect (whether under any enactment or agreement or otherwise) in relation to the terms on which the BBC is entitled or subject to any property, right or liability[12].

Where apart from this provision any person would have an entitlement, in consequence of anything done or likely to be done by or under the Broadcasting Act 1996, to terminate, modify, acquire or claim an interest or right which is vested in the BBC at the passing of the Act[13] or acquired by the BBC after that time, or to treat any such interest or right as modified or terminated, then[14]:

(a)   for the purposes of the transfer of the interest or right in accordance with a transfer scheme, that entitlement is not enforceable in relation to that interest or right until after its transfer in accordance with such a scheme[15]; and

(b)   that entitlement is enforceable[16] in relation to the interest or right after its transfer only in so far as the scheme contains provision for it to be transferred subject to the provisions conferring that entitlement[17].

1 As to the meaning of 'transfer scheme' see PARA 552 note 1; as to the power to make transfer schemes see PARA 551.
2 Broadcasting Act 1996 s 131(4), Sch 5 para 3(1). Subject to Sch 5 para 3(5), (6) (see notes 12, 17), nothing in Sch 5 para 3(1) or Sch 5 para 3(2) (see note 12) enables:
    (1)   any agreement or instrument entered into or executed in pursuance of an obligation imposed by virtue of Sch 5 para 2(1)(g) (see PARA 553); or
    (2)   anything done under any such agreement,

to give effect to any transfer, or to create any interest or right, which could not apart from Sch 5 para 3 have been made by or under that agreement or instrument: Sch 5 para 3(4).

3 Broadcasting Act 1996 Sch 5 para 3(1)(a). As to the meaning of 'BBC' see PARA 603 note 1; and as to the BBC see PARAS 603–626.

4 Broadcasting Act 1996 Sch 5 para 3(1)(b).

5 Broadcasting Act 1996 Sch 5 para 3(1)(c).

6 As to the meaning of 'United Kingdom' see PARA 510 note 13.

7 Broadcasting Act 1996 Sch 5 para 3(1)(d).

8 Broadcasting Act 1996 Sch 5 para 3(1)(e).

9 Broadcasting Act 1996 Sch 5 para 3(2)(a). As to the meaning of 'person' see PARA 510 note 1.

10 Broadcasting Act 1996 Sch 5 para 3(2)(b).

11 Broadcasting Act 1996 Sch 5 para 3(2)(c).

12 Broadcasting Act 1996 Sch 5 para 3(2). See also note 2. A transfer scheme may provide for:

   (1) the transfers to which effect is to be given by or under any agreement or instrument entered into or executed in accordance with the scheme; or

   (2) the interests or rights that are to be created by or under any such agreement or instrument,

   to include, to such extent as may be specified in the scheme, any such transfer, interest or right as is mentioned in Sch 5 para 3(2): Sch 5 para 3(5).

13 The Broadcasting Act 1996 received the Royal Assent on 24 July 1996.

14 Broadcasting Act 1996 Sch 5 para 3(3).

15 Broadcasting Act 1996 Sch 5 para 3(3)(a).

16 Ie without prejudice to the Broadcasting Act 1996 Sch 5 para 3(1)–(3)(a) or to Sch 5 para 4(2)(a) (see PARA 555): see Sch 5 para 3(3)(b).

17 Broadcasting Act 1996 Sch 5 para 3(3)(b). A transfer scheme may provide that Sch 5 para 3(3) is to apply in relation to the provisions of any agreement or instrument which is to be entered into or executed in accordance with the scheme, and in relation to any proposal for such an agreement or for the execution of such an instrument, as if the reference in Sch 5 para 3(3)(b) to provision contained in the scheme included a reference to provision contained, in accordance with the scheme, in the agreement or instrument: Sch 5 para 3(6).

555. Supplemental provisions of schemes. A transfer scheme[1] may contain supplemental, incidental, consequential and transitional provision for the purposes of, or in connection with, any transfer[2] of property, rights or liabilities for which the scheme provides or in connection with any other provisions contained in the scheme; and any such provision may include different provision for different cases or different purposes[3]. A transfer scheme may, in relation to transfers in accordance with the scheme, make provision, either generally or for such purposes as may be specified in the scheme[4]:

(1) for the transferee to be treated as the same person in law as the BBC[5];

(2) for agreements made, transactions effected or other things done by or in relation to the BBC to be treated, so far as may be necessary for the purposes of or in connection with the transfers, as made, effected or done by or in relation to the transferee[6];

(3) for references in any agreement (whether or not in writing) or in any deed, bond, instrument or other document to, or to any member or officer of, the BBC to have effect, so far as may be necessary for the purposes of or in connection with any of the transfers, with such modifications as are specified in the scheme[7];

(4) for proceedings commenced by or against the BBC to be continued by or against the transferee[8]; and

(5) for any such disputes as to the effect of the scheme as arise between different transferees, or between any transferee on the one hand and the BBC on the other, to be referred to such arbitration as may be specified in or determined under the scheme[9].

Where any person is entitled, in consequence of any transfer made in accordance with a transfer scheme or in pursuance of any of the above provisions, to possession of a document[10] relating in part to the title to, or to the management of, any land or other property in England and Wales[11], the scheme may contain provision for treating that person as having given another person an acknowledgment in writing of the right of that other person to production of the document and to delivery of copies of the document[12].

A certificate issued by the Secretary of State[13] to the effect that any property, right or liability of the BBC vested at a particular time in accordance with a transfer scheme in a person specified in the certificate is conclusive evidence of the matters stated in the certificate[14].

1   As to the meaning of 'transfer scheme' see PARA 552 note 1; and as to the power to make transfer schemes see PARA 551.
2   References to a transfer include references to the creation in any person's favour of any interest or right, and references to a transferee are to be construed accordingly: Broadcasting Act 1996 s 131(4), Sch 5 para 4(5)(a). As to the meaning of 'person' see PARA 510 note 1.
3   Broadcasting Act 1996 Sch 5 para 4(1).
4   Broadcasting Act 1996 Sch 5 para 4(2). The provisions of Sch 5 para 4(2), (3) (see the text and note 11) are without prejudice to the generality of Sch 5 para 4(1) (see the text and note 3): Sch 5 para 4(6).
5   Broadcasting Act 1996 Sch 5 para 4(2)(a). As to the meaning of 'BBC' see PARA 603 note 1; and as to the BBC see PARAS 603–626.
6   Broadcasting Act 1996 Sch 5 para 4(2)(b).
7   Broadcasting Act 1996 Sch 5 para 4(2)(c). As to the members and officers of the BBC see PARA 604 et seq.
8   Broadcasting Act 1996 Sch 5 para 4(2)(d).
9   Broadcasting Act 1996 Sch 5 para 4(2)(e).
10   References to a person who is entitled, in consequence of any transfer, to possession of a document include references to the BBC in a case where the BBC is entitled to retain possession of any document following any transfer: Broadcasting Act 1996 Sch 5 para 4(5)(b).
11   Broadcasting Act 1996 Sch 5 para 4(3). See also note 4.
12   Broadcasting Act 1996 Sch 5 para 4(3)(a). The Law of Property Act 1925 s 64 (production and safe custody of documents: see SALE OF LAND vol 42 (Reissue) PARA 132) has effect accordingly, and on the basis that the acknowledgment did not contain any such expression of contrary intention as is mentioned in that provision: Broadcasting Act 1996 Sch 5 para 4(3)(b).
13   As to the Secretary of State see PARA 507 note 32.
14   Broadcasting Act 1996 Sch 5 para 5.

556. Duties in relation to foreign property, rights and liabilities. It is the duty of the BBC[1] and of any person[2] to whom any foreign property, right or liability[3] is transferred to take all such steps as may be requisite to secure that the vesting in the transferee, in accordance with the transfer scheme[4], of the foreign property, right or liability is effective under the relevant foreign law[5]. Until the vesting in the transferee in accordance with the scheme of any foreign property, right or liability is effective under the relevant foreign law, it is the duty of the BBC to hold that property or right for the benefit of, or to discharge that liability on behalf of, the transferee[6]. Nothing in these provisions is to be taken as prejudicing the effect under the law of any part of the United Kingdom of the vesting in the transferee in accordance with the scheme of any foreign property, right or liability[7]. The BBC has all such powers as may be requisite for the performance of these duties, but it is the duty of a person to whom a transfer is made in accordance with a transfer scheme to act on behalf of the BBC (so far as possible) in performing the duties so imposed on it[8].

Where any foreign property, rights or liabilities are acquired or incurred by the BBC in respect of any other property, rights or liabilities[9], and by virtue of these provisions the BBC holds the other property or rights for the benefit of another person or discharges the liability on behalf of another person[10], the property, rights or liabilities acquired or incurred are immediately to become property, rights or liabilities of that other person, and these provisions have effect accordingly in relation to the property, rights or liabilities acquired or incurred[11].

Any expenses incurred by the BBC under these provisions must be met by the person to whom the transfer in question is made[12]. Any obligation imposed is enforceable as if contained in a contract between the BBC and the person to whom the transfer in question is made[13].

1 As to the meaning of 'BBC' see PARA 603 note 1; and as to the BBC see PARAS 603–626.
2 As to the meaning of 'person' see PARA 510 note 1.
3 References to any foreign property, right or liability are references to any property, right or liability as respects which any issue arising in any proceedings would have to be determined (in accordance with the rules of private international law) by reference to the law of a country or territory outside the United Kingdom: Broadcasting Act 1996 s 131(4), Sch 5 para 6(6). See further CONFLICT OF LAWS. As to the meaning of 'United Kingdom' see PARA 510 note 13.
4 As to the meaning of 'transfer scheme' see PARA 552 note 1; and as to the power to make transfer schemes see PARA 551.
5 Broadcasting Act 1996 Sch 5 para 6(1).
6 Broadcasting Act 1996 Sch 5 para 6(2).
7 Broadcasting Act 1996 Sch 5 para 6(3).
8 Broadcasting Act 1996 Sch 5 para 6(4).
9 Broadcasting Act 1996 Sch 5 para 6(5)(a).
10 Broadcasting Act 1996 Sch 5 para 6(5)(b).
11 Broadcasting Act 1996 Sch 5 para 6(5).
12 Broadcasting Act 1996 Sch 5 para 6(7).
13 Broadcasting Act 1996 Sch 5 para 6(8).

557. Modification of scheme by agreement. The following provisions apply where any person[1] to whom anything has been transferred in accordance with a transfer scheme[2] agrees in writing with the BBC[3] or another person to whom anything has been transferred in accordance with that or any other transfer scheme that, for the purpose of modifying the effect of the scheme or, as the case may be, of modifying the effect of either or both of the schemes, there should be a transfer from one to the other as from a date appointed by the agreement[4] of any of the property, rights or liabilities transferred in accordance with the scheme or either of them[5], and of any or all of the property, rights or liabilities acquired or incurred since the transfer in respect of the transferred property, rights or liabilities[6].

If the agreement is entered into within the period of 12 months after the time when a transfer in accordance with a transfer scheme of property, rights or liabilities to any of its parties comes into force[7], and the Secretary of State[8] has given his approval to the transfer for which the agreement provides and to its terms and conditions[9], then the transfer for which the agreement provides takes effect on the date appointed by the agreement in the like manner as a transfer for which provision is made by a transfer scheme[10].

Subject to the approval of the Secretary of State, the provisions that may be contained in a modification agreement[11] include any such provision in relation to any transfer for which it provides as may be contained, in relation to any transfer for which a transfer scheme provides, in that scheme[12]. However, nothing in any modification agreement may provide for any interests or rights to be created, as opposed to transferred, except as between persons who are parties to the agreement[13]. Before refusing his approval[14], or giving his approval in a case where the BBC is not a party to the proposed agreement[15], the Secretary of State must consult the BBC[16].

1   As to the meaning of 'person' see PARA 510 note 1.
2   References to a transfer in accordance with a transfer scheme include references to the creation of any interest, right or liability in accordance with such a scheme: Broadcasting Act 1996 s 131(4), Sch 5 para 7(6). As to the meaning of 'transfer scheme' see PARA 552 note 1; and as to the power to make transfer schemes see PARA 551.
3   As to the meaning of 'BBC' see PARA 603 note 1; and as to the BBC see PARAS 603–626.
4   Broadcasting Act 1996 Sch 5 para 7(1).
5   Broadcasting Act 1996 Sch 5 para 7(1)(a).
6   Broadcasting Act 1996 Sch 5 para 7(1)(b).
7   Broadcasting Act 1996 Sch 5 para 7(2)(a).
8   As to the Secretary of State see PARA 507 note 32.
9   Broadcasting Act 1996 Sch 5 para 7(2)(b).
10   Broadcasting Act 1996 Sch 5 para 7(2).
11   'Modification agreement' means any agreement providing for a transfer which is to take effect in accordance with the Broadcasting Act 1996 Sch 5 para 7(2): Sch 5 para 7(7).
12   Broadcasting Act 1996 Sch 5 para 7(3).
13   Broadcasting Act 1996 Sch 5 para 7(4).
14   Broadcasting Act 1996 Sch 5 para 7(5)(a).
15   Broadcasting Act 1996 Sch 5 para 7(5)(b).
16   Broadcasting Act 1996 Sch 5 para 7(5).

558. Compensation. Where, in consequence of any provisions included in a transfer scheme[1] for the purposes of any division of the BBC's undertaking[2], the interests, rights or liabilities of a third party[3] are modified as mentioned below, the third party is entitled to such compensation as may be just[4] in respect of any diminution attributable to that modification in the value of any of his interests or rights[5], or any increase attributable to that modification in the burden of his liabilities[6].

The modifications are modifications by virtue of which[7]:

(1)   an interest of the third party in any property is transformed into, or replaced by[8] an interest in only part of that property[9], or separate interests in different parts of that property[10];

(2)   a right of the third party against the BBC is transformed into, or replaced by, two or more rights which do not include a right which, on its own, is equivalent (disregarding the person against whom it is enforceable) to the right against the BBC[11]; or

(3)   a liability of the third party to the BBC is transformed into, or replaced by, two or more separate liabilities at least one of which is a liability enforceable by a person other than the BBC[12].

Where:

(a)   a third party would, apart from any provisions of a transfer scheme or certain other specified provisions[13], have become entitled to, or to exercise, any interest or right arising or exercisable in respect of the transfer or creation in accordance with such a scheme of any property, rights or liabilities[14]; and

(b)   the provisions of that scheme or of the specified provisions have the effect of preventing that person's entitlement to, or to exercise, that interest or right from arising on any occasion in respect of anything mentioned in head (a) above[15]; and

(c)   provision is not made by a transfer scheme for securing that an entitlement to, or to exercise, that interest or right or an equivalent interest or right, is preserved or created so as to arise in respect of the first occasion when corresponding circumstances next occur after the coming into force of the transfers for which the scheme provides[16], the third party is entitled to such compensation as may be just in respect of the extinguishment of the interest or right[17].

A liability to pay such compensation falls on the persons not being themselves third parties who, as the case may be:

(i)   have interests in the whole or any part of the property affected by the modification in question[18];

(ii)   are subject to the rights of the person to be compensated which are affected by the modification in question[19];

(iii)   are entitled to enforce the liabilities of the person to be compensated which are affected by that modification[20]; or

(iv)   benefit from the extinguishment of such entitlement[21],

and that liability must be apportioned between those persons in such manner as may be appropriate having regard to the extent of their respective rights or liabilities or the extent of the benefit they respectively obtain from the extinguishment[22].

Any dispute as to whether, or as to the person by whom, any such compensation is to be paid, and any dispute as to the amount of any compensation to be paid by any person, must be referred to and determined, where the claimant requires the matter to be determined in England, Wales or in Northern Ireland, by an arbitrator appointed by the Lord Chancellor[23], or, where the claimant requires the matter to be determined in Scotland, by an arbiter appointed by the Lord President of the Court of Session[24].

It is the duty of the BBC where it appears to it in the case of any transfer scheme or modification agreement that there are persons whose property, rights or liabilities are affected in a manner that may give rise to an entitlement to such compensation, to give notice to every such person[25]. Such a notice must be given as soon as reasonably practicable after the scheme or agreement is made[26]. It must set out the general effect of the scheme or, as the case may be, of the agreement and must describe the respects in which it appears to the BBC that the property, rights or liabilities of the person to whom it is given are affected[27]. Where it is not reasonably practicable for a notice to any person to be given to that person, the BBC must instead take such steps for publishing the contents of the notice as it may consider appropriate for the purpose of bringing the matters to which the notice relates to the attention of that person[28].

1   As to the meaning of 'transfer scheme' see PARA 552 note 1; and as to the power to make transfer schemes see PARA 551. The Broadcasting Act 1996 s 131(4), Sch 5 para 8 has effect in relation to the provisions of any agreement or instrument entered into or executed in pursuance of an obligation imposed by virtue of Sch 5 para 2(1)(g) (see PARA 553), and to any modification agreement, as it has effect in relation to the provisions of a transfer scheme: Sch 5 para 8(7).

2   Ie any such division as is mentioned in the Broadcasting Act 1996 Sch 5 para 2(1) (see PARA 553): see Sch 5 para 8(1). As to the meaning of 'BBC' see PARA 603 note 1; and as to the BBC see PARAS 603–626.

3   'Third party', in relation to provisions capable of giving rise to compensation under the Broadcasting Act 1996 Sch 5 para 8, means any person other than: (1) the BBC or any of its wholly-owned subsidiaries (as defined by the Companies Act 2006 s 1159 (see COMPANIES vol 14 (2009) PARA 25)); (2) the Secretary of State; or (3) any person whose consent to those provisions has been given for the purposes of the Broadcasting Act 1996 s 132(2) (see PARA 560) or who has agreed to those provisions by virtue of being a party to a modification agreement: Sch 5 para 8(8) (amended by SI 2009/1941). As to the Secretary of State see PARA 507 note 32. As to the meaning of 'person' see PARA 510 note 1. As to the meaning of 'modification agreement' see PARA 557 note 11.

4   Broadcasting Act 1996 Sch 5 para 8(1).

5   Broadcasting Act 1996 Sch 5 para 8(1)(a).

6   Broadcasting Act 1996 Sch 5 para 8(1)(b).

7 Broadcasting Act 1996 Sch 5 para 8(2).
8 Broadcasting Act 1996 Sch 5 para 8(2)(a).
9 Broadcasting Act 1996 Sch 5 para 8(2)(a)(i).
10 Broadcasting Act 1996 Sch 5 para 8(2)(a)(ii).
11 Broadcasting Act 1996 Sch 5 para 8(2)(b).
12 Broadcasting Act 1996 Sch 5 para 8(2)(c).
13 Ie the Broadcasting Act 1996 Sch 5 para 3(3): see PARA 554.
14 Broadcasting Act 1996 Sch 5 para 8(3)(a).
15 Broadcasting Act 1996 Sch 5 para 8(3)(b).
16 Broadcasting Act 1996 Sch 5 para 8(3)(c).
17 Broadcasting Act 1996 Sch 5 para 8(3).
18 Broadcasting Act 1996 Sch 5 para 8(4)(a).
19 Broadcasting Act 1996 Sch 5 para 8(4)(b).
20 Broadcasting Act 1996 Sch 5 para 8(4)(c).
21 Broadcasting Act 1996 Sch 5 para 8(4)(d).
22 Broadcasting Act 1996 Sch 5 para 8(4). Where any liability falls by virtue of Sch 5 para 8(4) on
    the BBC, Sch 5 para 8(4) has effect subject to so much of any transfer scheme (including the one
    which gives rise to the liability) as makes provision for the transfer of that liability to any other
    person: Sch 5 para 8(5).
23 Broadcasting Act 1996 Sch 5 para 8(6)(a). As to the Lord Chancellor see CONSTITUTIONAL LAW
    AND HUMAN RIGHTS vol 8(2) (Reissue) PARA 477 et seq.
24 Broadcasting Act 1996 Sch 5 para 8(6)(b).
25 Broadcasting Act 1996 Sch 5 para 9(1).
26 Broadcasting Act 1996 Sch 5 para 9(2).
27 Broadcasting Act 1996 Sch 5 para 9(3).
28 Broadcasting Act 1996 Sch 5 para 9(4).

559. Consideration for transfer. A transfer[1] in accordance with a transfer
scheme may be made for consideration or for no consideration and, if it is made
for consideration, the consideration may, in particular, take the form of the issue
of shares or securities[2].

1 'Transfer', except for the purposes of the Broadcasting Act 1996 s 135, Sch 7 paras 13–18,
   includes:
   (1)   any transfer effected by or under an agreement or instrument entered into or executed
          in pursuance of an obligation imposed by a provision contained in a transfer scheme by
          virtue of s 131(4), Sch 5 para 2(1)(g) (see PARA 553);
   (2)   the creation of interests, rights or liabilities by or under any such agreement or
          instrument; and
   (3)   the creation of interests, rights or liabilities by virtue of any provision contained in a
          transfer scheme by virtue of Sch 5 para 2 (see PARA 553),
   and references to a transfer in accordance with a transfer scheme (or any description of transfer
   scheme) are to be construed accordingly: Sch 7 para 1(1); definition applied by Sch 5 para 10(2).
   As to the meaning of 'transfer scheme' see PARA 552 note 1; and as to the power to make
   transfer schemes see PARA 551.
2 Broadcasting Act 1996 Sch 5 para 10(1).

560. Powers of Secretary of State in relation to transfer schemes. A transfer
scheme[1] does not take effect unless it is approved by the Secretary of State[2], and
where such a scheme is submitted to the Secretary of State for his approval, he
may modify the scheme before approving it[3]. The Secretary of State may not
approve a transfer scheme containing any provision in accordance with which
any person[4] other than a wholly-owned subsidiary[5] of the BBC[6] becomes entitled
or subject to any property, rights and liabilities unless it appears to the Secretary
of State that the person has consented to the provisions of the scheme so far as
they relate to him[7]. However, this does not require the consent of any person to
so much of a transfer scheme[8] as relates to property, rights or liabilities to which

that person is already entitled or subject[9], and appears to the Secretary of State to be made for purposes that are no more than supplemental or incidental to the other provisions of the scheme[10].

Before declining to approve a transfer scheme[11], or modifying such a scheme[12], the Secretary of State must consult the BBC and every person who is a transferee under the scheme[13]. It is the duty of the BBC and every person who is a transferee under a transfer scheme to provide the Secretary of State with all such information and other assistance as he may reasonably require for the purposes of, or in connection with, the exercise of any power conferred on him[14].

1   As to the meaning of 'transfer scheme' see PARA 552 note 1; and as to the power to make transfer schemes see PARA 551.
2   As to the Secretary of State see PARA 507 note 32.
3   Broadcasting Act 1996 s 132(1).
4   As to the meaning of 'person' see PARA 510 note 1.
5   For these purposes, 'wholly-owned subsidiary' has the meaning given by the Companies Act 2006 s 1159 (see COMPANIES vol 14 (2009) PARA 25): Broadcasting Act 1996 s 132(6) (amended by SI 2009/1941).
6   As to the meaning of 'BBC' see PARA 603 note 1; and as to the BBC see PARAS 603–626.
7   Broadcasting Act 1996 s 132(2).
8   Broadcasting Act 1996 s 132(3).
9   Broadcasting Act 1996 s 132(3)(a).
10 Broadcasting Act 1996 s 132(3)(b).
11 Broadcasting Act 1996 s 132(4)(a).
12 Broadcasting Act 1996 s 132(4)(b).
13 Broadcasting Act 1996 s 132(4).
14 Broadcasting Act 1996 s 132(5).

561.   Agreements with respect to transfer schemes. The BBC[1] may enter into any such agreement with another person[2] as it thinks fit for the purpose of accepting or imposing contractual obligations with respect to, or to anything connected with, the manner in which its powers to make transfer schemes[3] are to be exercised[4]. Any agreement may, in particular, provide for the making of payments, or the issue of shares or securities, to the BBC (by way of consideration or otherwise) in respect of anything created or transferred in accordance with a transfer scheme[5]. The consent of the Secretary of State[6] is required for the making by the BBC of such an agreement[7].

1   As to the meaning of 'BBC' see PARA 603 note 1; and as to the BBC see PARAS 603–626.
2   As to the meaning of 'person' see PARA 510 note 1.
3   Ie by virtue of the Broadcasting Act 1996 s 131 (see PARA 551): see s 133(1). As to the meaning of 'transfer scheme' see PARA 552 note 1; and as to the power to make transfer schemes see PARA 551.
4   Broadcasting Act 1996 s 133(1).
5   Broadcasting Act 1996 s 133(2).
6   As to the Secretary of State see PARA 507 note 32.
7   Broadcasting Act 1996 s 133(3).

562.   Statutory accounts. The following provisions have effect for the purposes of any statutory accounts[1] of a successor company[2]. The vesting in the company effected by any preparatory scheme[3] is to be taken to have been effected immediately after the end of the last financial year of the BBC to end before the coming into force of the scheme[4], and to have been a vesting of such property, rights and liabilities as are determined by or under the scheme[5]. The value of any asset and the amount of any liability which is taken by virtue of these provisions to have been vested in the company is to be taken to have been[6]:

(1) in the case where the value or amount is determined by or under the preparatory scheme, that value or amount[7]; and (2) in any other case, the value or amount assigned to the asset or liability for the specified purposes[8] in respect of its last financial year to end before the day on which the preparatory scheme comes into force[9].

1   'Statutory accounts', in relation to a company, means any accounts of that company prepared for the purposes of any provision of the Companies Act 2006 (including group accounts) (see generally COMPANIES vol 15 (2009) PARA 775 et seq): Broadcasting Act 1996 s 134, Sch 6 para 2(5) (amended by SI 2008/948).
2   Broadcasting Act 1996 Sch 6 para 2(1). 'Successor company' means a company to which property, rights or liabilities are transferred in accordance with a preparatory scheme at a time when the company is a wholly-owned subsidiary of the BBC: Sch 6 para 1(1). For these purposes, 'transfer' includes:
    (1)   any transfer effected by or under an agreement or instrument entered into or executed in pursuance of an obligation imposed by a provision contained in a preparatory scheme by virtue of Sch 5 para 2(1)(g) (see PARA 553);
    (2)   the creation of interests, rights or liabilities by or under any such agreement or instrument; and
    (3)   the creation of interests, rights or liabilities by virtue of any provision contained in a preparatory scheme by virtue of Sch 5 para 2 (see PARA 553),
    and references to a transfer in accordance with a preparatory scheme are to be construed accordingly: Sch 6 para 1(1). 'Preparatory scheme' means a transfer scheme whose main purpose is to provide for a transfer of property, rights or liabilities from the BBC to a wholly-owned subsidiary of the BBC: Sch 6 para 1(1). 'Wholly-owned subsidiary' has the meaning given by the Companies Act 2006 s 1159 (see COMPANIES vol 14 (2009) PARA 25): Broadcasting Act 1996 Sch 6 para 1(1) (amended by SI 2009/1941). As to the meaning of 'BBC' see PARA 603 note 1; and as to the BBC see PARAS 603–626. As to the meaning of 'transfer scheme' see PARA 552 note 1; and as to the power to make transfer schemes see PARA 551.
3   Broadcasting Act 1996 Sch 6 para 2(2). Any reference in Sch 6 to vesting in accordance with a preparatory scheme or vesting effected by a preparatory scheme is to be construed as a reference to vesting as a result of a transfer in accordance with a preparatory scheme: Sch 6 para 1(2).
4   Broadcasting Act 1996 Sch 6 para 2(2)(a).
5   Broadcasting Act 1996 Sch 6 para 2(2)(b).
6   Broadcasting Act 1996 Sch 6 para 2(3).
7   Broadcasting Act 1996 Sch 6 para 2(3)(a).
8   Ie for the purposes of the account or accounts prepared by the BBC for the purposes of Article 18(2) of the Charter: see the Broadcasting Act 1996 Sch 6 para 2(3)(b). 'The Charter' means the Royal Charter of 1 May 1996 for the continuance of the British Broadcasting Corporation (see now the *Royal Charter for the Continuance of the British Broadcasting Corporation* (Cm 6925) (2006); and as to accounts see art 45: see PARAS 604 et seq, 626): Broadcasting Act 1996 Sch 6 para 1(1).
9   Broadcasting Act 1996 Sch 6 para 2(3)(b). If an account or accounts are prepared by the BBC for the purposes of art 18(2) (now art 45(1)) of the Charter in respect of the residual part of a financial year, that residual part must be treated as a financial year of the BBC for the purposes of the Broadcasting Act 1996 Sch 6 para 2(3): Sch 6 para 2(4).

563.   Distributable reserves and dividends.   Where statutory accounts[1] of a successor company[2] prepared as at any time would show the company as having net assets[3] in excess of the aggregate of its called-up share capital[4] and the amount, apart from any property, rights and liabilities transferred[5] to it in accordance with any preparatory scheme[6], of its undistributable reserves[7], then, for certain purposes of the statutory provision relating to profits available for distribution[8] and of the preparation as at that time of any statutory accounts of the company, that excess is to be treated, except so far as the Secretary of State[9] may otherwise direct, as representing an excess of the company's accumulated realised profits over its accumulated realised losses[10]. For the purposes of the statutory provision relating to restrictions on the distribution of assets[11], so much of any excess of a company's net assets as falls, in accordance with such a direction, to be treated otherwise than as representing an excess of the company's accumulated realised profits over its accumulated realised losses is to be treated (subject to any modification of that direction by a subsequent direction) as comprised in the company's undistributable reserves[12].

Such a direction may provide, in relation to any amount to which it applies, that, on the realisation (whether before or after the company in question ceases to be a wholly-owned subsidiary[13] of the BBC[14]) of such profits and losses as may be specified or described in the direction, so much of that amount as may be determined in accordance with the direction is to cease to be treated as comprised in the company's undistributable reserves[15] and is to fall to be treated as comprised in the company's accumulated realised profits[16].

The Secretary of State may not give such a direction in relation to a successor company at any time after the company has ceased to be a wholly-owned subsidiary of the BBC[17]. The consent of the Treasury[18] is required for the giving of such a direction[19].

Where a distribution is proposed to be declared during any accounting reference period[20] of a successor company which includes a transfer date[21] or before any accounts are laid or filed in respect of such a period, the statutory provisions relating to the relevant accounts for determining whether a distribution may be made by a company[22] have effect with certain modifications[23].

Certain provisions of the Trustee Investments Act 1961[24] apply to dividends payable in relation to successor companies[25].

1 References, in relation to a company, to statutory accounts are references to accounts of that company prepared in respect of any period in accordance with the requirements of the Companies Act 2006 (see COMPANIES vol 15 (2009) PARA 775 et seq), or with those requirements applied with such modifications as are necessary where that period is not an accounting reference period: Broadcasting Act 1996 s 134, Sch 6 para 3(6) (amended by SI 2008/948).
2 As to the meaning of 'successor company' see PARA 562 note 2.
3 'Net assets' has the meaning given by the Companies Act 2005 s 831(2) (see COMPANIES vol 15 (2009) PARA 1393): Broadcasting Act 1996 Sch 6 para 3(6) (as amended: see note 1).
4 Broadcasting Act 1996 Sch 6 para 3(1)(a). 'Called-up share capital' has the same meaning as in the Companies Act 1985 (see COMPANIES vol 15 (2009) PARA 1045): Broadcasting Act 1996 Sch 6 para 3(6) (as amended: see note 1).
5 As to the meaning of 'transfer' see PARA 562 note 2; and as to the power to make transfer schemes see PARA 551.
6 As to the meaning of 'preparatory scheme' see PARA 562 note 2.
7 Broadcasting Act 1996 Sch 6 para 3(1)(b). 'Undistributable reserves' has the meaning given by the Companies Act 1985 s 831(4) (see COMPANIES vol 15 (2009) PARA 1393): Broadcasting Act 1996 Sch 6 para 3(6) (as amended: see note 1).
8 Ie the Companies Act 2006 s 830 (see COMPANIES vol 15 (2009) PARA 1390): see the Broadcasting Act 1996 Sch 6 para 3(1) (amended by SI 2008/948).
9 As to the Secretary of State see PARA 507 note 32.
10 Broadcasting Act 1996 Sch 6 para 3(1).
11 Ie the Companies Act 2006 s 831 (see COMPANIES vol 15 (2009) PARA 1393): see the Broadcasting Act 1996 Sch 6 para 3(2) (amended by SI 2008/948).
12 Broadcasting Act 1996 Sch 6 para 3(2).
13 As to the meaning of 'wholly-owned subsidiary' see PARA 562 note 2.
14 As to the meaning of 'BBC' see PARA 603 note 1; and as to the BBC see PARAS 603–626.
15 Ie as mentioned in the Broadcasting Act 1996 Sch 6 para 3(2): see Sch 6 para 3(3).
16 Broadcasting Act 1996 Sch 6 para 3(3).
17 Broadcasting Act 1996 Sch 6 para 3(4).
18 As to the Treasury see CONSTITUTIONAL LAW AND HUMAN RIGHTS vol 8(2) (Reissue) PARAS 512–517.
19 Broadcasting Act 1996 Sch 6 para 3(5).

20 'Accounting reference period' has the meaning given by the Companies Act 2006 s 391 (see COMPANIES vol 15 (2009) PARA 712): Broadcasting Act 1996 Sch 6 para 4(5) (amended by SI 2008/948).

21 For these purposes, 'a transfer date', in relation to a successor company, means the date of the coming into force of any preparatory scheme in accordance with which property, rights or liabilities are transferred to that company: Broadcasting Act 1996 Sch 6 para 4(5).

22 Ie the Companies Act 2006 ss 836–840 (see COMPANIES vol 15 (2009) PARA 1395 et seq): see the Broadcasting Act 1996 Sch 6 para 4(1) (amended by SI 2008/948).

23 The Companies Act 2006 ss 836–840 (see COMPANIES vol 15 (2009) PARA 1395 et seq) have effect as if references in s 836 to the company's accounts or to accounts relevant under that provision, and references in s 839 to initial accounts, included references to such accounts as, on the assumptions stated below (see heads (1)–(5)), would have been prepared under s 394 (see COMPANIES vol 15 (2009) PARA 716) in respect of the relevant year: Broadcasting Act 1996 Sch 6 para 4(1) (as amended: see note 22). 'The relevant year', in relation to any transfer date, means the last complete financial year ending before that date: Sch 6 para 4(5). 'Complete financial year' means a financial year ending with 31 March: Sch 6 para 4(5).

The assumptions mentioned above are:

(1) that the relevant year had been a financial year of the successor company (Sch 6 para 4(2)(a));

(2) that the vesting in accordance with the preparatory scheme had been a vesting of all the property, rights and liabilities transferred to the company in accordance with that scheme and had been effected immediately after the beginning of that year (Sch 6 para 4(2)(b));

(3) that the value of any asset and the amount of any liability of the BBC vested in the successor company in accordance with the preparatory scheme had been the value or (as the case may be) amount determined by or under the scheme or (if there is no such determination) the value or amount assigned to the asset or liability for the purposes of the account or accounts prepared by the BBC for the purposes of Article 18(2) (now Article 45(1)) of the Charter in respect of its financial year immediately preceding the relevant year (Broadcasting Act 1996 Sch 6 para 4(2)(c));

(4) that any securities of the successor company issued or allotted before the declaration of the distribution had been issued or allotted before the end of the relevant year (Sch 6 para 4(2)(d)); and

(5) such other assumptions (if any) as may appear to the directors of the successor company to be necessary or expedient for these purposes (Sch 6 para 4(2)(e)).

As to the meaning of 'the Charter' see PARA 562 note 8.

If an account or accounts are prepared by the BBC for the purposes of Article 18(2) of the Charter in respect of the residual part of a financial year, that residual part is to be treated as a financial year of the BBC for the purposes of the Broadcasting Act 1996 Sch 6 para 4(2)(c): Sch 6 para 4(3).

The relevant accounts are not to be regarded as statutory accounts for the purposes of Sch 6 para 2 (see PARA 562): Sch 6 para 4(4).

24 Ie the Trustee Investments Act 1961 s 1, Sch 1 Pt IV para 3(b) (Sch 1 repealed, except in so far as it is applied by or under any other enactment, by virtue of the Trustee Act 2000 s 40(1), (3), Sch 2 Pt I para 1(1), Sch 4 Pt I) (which provides that shares and debentures of a company do not count as wider-range and narrower-range investments respectively unless the company has paid dividends in each of the five years immediately preceding that in which the investment is made: see TRUSTS vol 48 (2007 Reissue) PARA 1020 et seq): see the Broadcasting Act 1996 Sch 6 para 5(1).

25 For the purpose of applying the Trustee Investments Act 1961 Sch 1 Pt IV para 3(b) (repealed with savings: see note 24) (see TRUSTS vol 48 (2007 Reissue) PARA 1107) in relation to investment in shares or debentures of a successor company during the calendar year in which the transfer date falls ('the first investment year') or during any year following that year, the successor company is deemed to have paid a dividend as there mentioned: (1) in every year preceding the first investment year which is included in the relevant five years; and (2) in the first investment year, if that year is included in the relevant five years and the successor company does not in fact pay such a dividend in that year: Broadcasting Act 1996 Sch 6 para 5(1). For these purposes, 'the transfer date', in relation to a successor company, means the first date on which any preparatory scheme in accordance with which property, rights or liabilities are transferred to that company comes into force: Sch 6 para 5(2). 'The relevant five years' means the five years immediately preceding the year in which the investment in question is made or proposed to be made: Sch 6 para 5(2).

(3) AUTHORISATION OF FREQUENCY USE

564. Authorisation of frequency use for the provision of mobile satellite services. OFCOM[1] must grant an authorisation[2] to each of the selected applicants[3] for use in the United Kingdom[4] of the frequencies specified for that selected applicant[5] subject to the following conditions[6]. OFCOM must ensure that the authorisations are subject to the specified common conditions[7], namely: (1) the selected applicants must use the frequencies which those applicants are authorised to use for the provision of mobile satellite services[8]; (2) each selected applicant must meet specified milestones[9] by 14 May 2011; (3) each selected applicant must honour all commitments given by that applicant in its application or during the comparative selection procedure[10]; (4) each selected applicant must provide OFCOM with an annual report detailing the status of development of their proposed mobile satellite system[11]. An authorisation may include objectively justified, non-discriminatory, proportionate and transparent conditions or obligations to ensure communications between emergency services and authorities during major disasters[12].

An authorisation is to be granted for 18 years with effect from 14 May 2009[13]. An authorisation is not transferable[14]. OFCOM may not charge the selected applicants for the granting of an authorisation[15].

OFCOM must monitor compliance by the selected applicants of the conditions of their authorisations[16]. Where:

(a)   there has been a contravention by either of the selected applicants of one or more of the conditions specified in their authorisation; or

(b)   OFCOM has taken action[17] against either of the selected applicants in respect of such a contravention,

OFCOM must provide the European Commission with information about the contravention or action within 12 months of such contravention or action[18].

OFCOM may require the selected applicants to provide it with all such information as OFCOM considers necessary for the purpose of carrying out its functions under these provisions, including the verification of compliance by the selected applicants with the conditions of their authorisations[19]. A selected applicant required to provide information must provide it in such a manner and within such reasonable period as may be specified by OFCOM[20].

1   As to OFCOM see the Authorisation of Frequency Use for the Provision of Mobile Satellite Services (European Union) Regulations 2010, SI 2010/672, reg 1(2); and PARA 507.

2   Ie under the Authorisation of Frequency Use for the Provision of Mobile Satellite Services (European Union) Regulations 2010, SI 2010/672. 'An authorisation' means an authorisation granted under reg 3, subject to the conditions contained in reg 4: reg 1(2).

3   'The selected applicants' means Inmarsat Ventures Ltd and Solaris Mobile Ltd, which are identified as the eligible applicants under Commission Decision (EC) 2009/449 on the selection of operators of pan-European systems providing mobile satellite services (MSS) (OJ L149, 12.6.2009, p 65) art 2: Authorisation of Frequency Use for the Provision of Mobile Satellite Services (European Union) Regulations 2010, SI 2010/672, reg 1(2).

4   As to the meaning of 'United Kingdom' see PARA 510 note 13.

5   Ie in Commission Decision 2009/449 (EC) (OJ L149, 12.6.2009, p 65) art 3. Those frequencies are: (1) for Inmarsat Ventures Ltd: from 1980 to 1995MHz for earth to space communications and from 2170 to 2185MHz for space to earth communications; and (2) for Solaris Mobile Ltd: from 1995 to 2010MHz for earth to space communications and from 2185 to 2200MHz for space to earth communications: Authorisation of Frequency Use for the Provision of Mobile Satellite Services (European Union) Regulations 2010, SI 2010/672, reg 3(2). As to the offence of unauthorised use of the specified frequencies see PARA 583.

6   Authorisation of Frequency Use for the Provision of Mobile Satellite Services (European Union) Regulations 2010, SI 2010/672, reg 3(1). The Regulations (which came into force on 31 March

2010: reg 1(1)) implement in the United Kingdom European Parliament and Council Decision (EC) 626/2008 on the selection and authorisation of systems providing mobile satellite services (MSS) (OJ L172, 2.7.2008, p 15) and Commission Decision (EC) 2009/449 on the selection of operators of pan-European systems providing mobile satellite services (MSS) (OJ L149, 12.6.2009, p 65).

7   Ie specified in European Parliament and Council Decision (EC) 626/2008 on the selection and authorisation of systems providing mobile satellite services (MSS) (OJ L172, 2.7.2008, p 15) art 7(2).

8   'Mobile satellite services' means radio communication services provided by an electronic communications network and associated facilities capable of providing radio communication services between a mobile earth station in the United Kingdom and one or more space stations, or between mobile earth stations in the United Kingdom by means of one or more space stations: Authorisation of Frequency Use for the Provision of Mobile Satellite Services (European Union) Regulations 2010, SI 2010/672, reg 1(2). As to the meanings of 'electronic communications network' and 'associated facilities' see TELECOMMUNICATIONS vol 97 (2010) PARA 60; definitions applied by the Provision of Mobile Satellite Services (European Union) Regulations 2010, SI 2010/672, reg 1(2).

9   Ie milestones 6–9 set out in European Parliament and Council Decision (EC) 626/2008 on the selection and authorisation of systems providing mobile satellite services (MSS) (OJ L172, 2.7.2008, p 15) Annex.

10 Ie the procedure referred to in European Parliament and Council Decision (EC) 626/2008 on the selection and authorisation of systems providing mobile satellite services (MSS) (OJ L172, 2.7.2008, p 15) arts 4, 6.

11 Authorisation of Frequency Use for the Provision of Mobile Satellite Services (European Union) Regulations 2010, SI 2010/672, reg 4(1).

12 Authorisation of Frequency Use for the Provision of Mobile Satellite Services (European Union) Regulations 2010, SI 2010/672, reg 4(3).

13 Authorisation of Frequency Use for the Provision of Mobile Satellite Services (European Union) Regulations 2010, SI 2010/672, reg 4(2).

14 Authorisation of Frequency Use for the Provision of Mobile Satellite Services (European Union) Regulations 2010, SI 2010/672, reg 4(4).

15 Authorisation of Frequency Use for the Provision of Mobile Satellite Services (European Union) Regulations 2010, SI 2010/672, reg 4(5).

16 Authorisation of Frequency Use for the Provision of Mobile Satellite Services (European Union) Regulations 2010, SI 2010/672, reg 5(1).

17 Ie under the Authorisation of Frequency Use for the Provision of Mobile Satellite Services (European Union) Regulations 2010, SI 2010/672. See PARA 565.

18 Authorisation of Frequency Use for the Provision of Mobile Satellite Services (European Union) Regulations 2010, SI 2010/672, reg 5(2).

19 Authorisation of Frequency Use for the Provision of Mobile Satellite Services (European Union) Regulations 2010, SI 2010/672, reg 5(3).

20 Authorisation of Frequency Use for the Provision of Mobile Satellite Services (European Union) Regulations 2010, SI 2010/672, reg 5(4).

565.   Contravention of conditions of authorisations. Where OFCOM[1] determines that there are reasonable grounds for believing that a selected applicant[2] is contravening or has contravened a condition of its authorisation[3] or a requirement to provide information[4], it may give that selected applicant a notification[5] which: (1) sets out the determination made by OFCOM; (2) specifies the condition of the authorisation or the requirement to provide information and the contravention in respect of which that determination has been made; and (3) specifies the period during which the selected applicant notified has an opportunity of doing the things specified below[6].

Those things are: (a) making representations about the matters notified; (b) complying with the notified conditions of the authorisation or the requirements to provide information of which the selected applicant remains in contravention; and (c) remedying the consequences of the notified contraventions[7].

Where a selected applicant (the 'notified person') has been given a notification, OFCOM has allowed the notified person the opportunity to make representations about the matters notified and the period allowed for the making of the representations has expired, OFCOM may impose a penalty on the notified person if it is satisfied that the notified person has, in one or more of the respects notified, been in contravention of a condition of an authorisation or a requirement to provide information specified in the notification and that the notified person has not, during the period allowed, taken such steps as OFCOM considers appropriate for complying with that condition or requirement and for remedying the consequences of the notified contravention of that condition or requirement[8]. Where a notification relates to more than one contravention, a separate penalty may be imposed in respect of each contravention[9]. Where such a notification relates to a continuing contravention, no more than one penalty may be imposed in respect of the period of contravention specified in the notification[10]. Where OFCOM decides to impose a penalty on a notified person, it must: (i) notify that person of its decision and of its reasons for that decision; and (ii) in that notification, fix a reasonable period as the period within which the penalty is to be paid[11]. A penalty must be paid to OFCOM and, if not paid within the period fixed by it, is to be recoverable by it accordingly[12].

1   As to OFCOM see PARA 507.
2   As to the meaning of 'selected applicants' see PARA 564 note 3.
3   As to the meaning of 'authorisation' see PARA 564 note 2.
4   Ie under the Authorisation of Frequency Use for the Provision of Mobile Satellite Services (European Union) Regulations 2010, SI 2010/672, reg 5(3) or (4): see PARA 564.
5   Authorisation of Frequency Use for the Provision of Mobile Satellite Services (European Union) Regulations 2010, SI 2010/672, reg 6(1). A notification under reg 6 may be given in respect of more than one contravention and, if it is given in respect of a continuing contravention, may be given in respect of any period during which the contravention has continued: reg 6(3).
6   Authorisation of Frequency Use for the Provision of Mobile Satellite Services (European Union) Regulations 2010, SI 2010/672, reg 6(2). Subject to reg 6(6)–(8), the period for doing those things must be the period of one month beginning with the day after the day on which the notification was given: reg 6(5). OFCOM may, if it thinks fit, allow a longer period for doing those things either by specifying a longer period in the notification or by subsequently, on one or more occasions, extending the specified period: reg 6(6). The selected applicant notified will have a shorter period for doing those things if a shorter period is agreed between OFCOM and the selected applicant notified: reg 6(7). The selected applicant notified will also have a shorter period if: (1) OFCOM has reasonable grounds for believing that the contravention is a repeated contravention or that the case is urgent; (2) it has determined that, in those circumstances, a shorter period would be appropriate; and (3) the shorter period has been specified in the notification: reg 6(8). For the purposes of reg 6(8)(a) a contravention is a repeated contravention, in relation to a notification with respect to that contravention, if: (a) a previous notification under reg 6 has been given in respect of the same contravention or in respect of another contravention of the same condition of the authorisation or the same requirement under reg 5(3) or (4); and (b) the subsequent notification is given no more than 12 months after the date when the previous notification was given: reg 6(9). For the purposes of reg 6(8)(a) a case is an urgent case if the contravention has resulted in, or creates an immediate risk of: (i) a serious threat to the safety of the public, to public health or to national security; or (ii) serious economic or operational problems for persons (other than the selected applicant in contravention) who use wireless telegraphy stations or wireless telegraphy apparatus or who are communications providers or make associated facilities available: reg 6(10). In reg 6(10) the expressions 'wireless telegraphy station' and 'wireless telegraphy apparatus' have the meanings given by the Wireless Telegraphy Act 2006 s 117 (see PARA 510 notes 12, 9 respectively); and 'communications provider' has the same meaning as in the Communications Act 2003 s 405 (see TELECOMMUNICATIONS vol 97 (2010) PARA 17): Authorisation of Frequency Use for the Provision of Mobile Satellite Services (European Union) Regulations 2010, SI 2010/672, reg 6(12).
7   Authorisation of Frequency Use for the Provision of Mobile Satellite Services (European Union) Regulations 2010, SI 2010/672, reg 6(4). References to remedying a contravention include references to: (1) doing anything the failure to do which, or the failure to do which within a particular period or before a particular time, constituted the whole of or a part of the

contravention; (2) paying an amount to a person by way of compensation for loss or damage suffered by that person in consequence of the contravention; (3) paying an amount to a person by way of compensation in respect of annoyance, inconvenience or anxiety to which that person has been put in consequence of the contravention; (4) otherwise acting in a manner that constitutes an acknowledgment that the notified contravention did occur: reg 6(11).

8   Authorisation of Frequency Use for the Provision of Mobile Satellite Services (European Union) Regulations 2010, SI 2010/672, reg 7(1), (2). The amount of a penalty imposed under reg 7 is to be an amount not exceeding 10% of the turnover of the notified person's relevant business for the relevant period, as OFCOM determines to be: (1) appropriate; and (2) proportionate to the contravention in respect of which it is imposed: reg 8(1). In making that determination OFCOM must have regard to: (a) any representations made to it by the notified person; (b) any steps taken by the notified person towards complying with the condition or requirement contravention of which has been notified to him under reg 6; and (c) any steps taken to by the notified person for remedying the consequences of that contravention: reg 8(2). For the purposes of reg 8 the turnover of the notified person's relevant business for the relevant period is to be calculated in accordance with reg 9: reg 8(3). In regs 8, 9, 'notified person' has the same meaning as in reg 7; 'relevant business' means so much of any business carried on by the notified person as consists in the provision of mobile satellite services; 'relevant period' means: (i) except in a case falling within head (ii) or (iii), the period of one year ending with the 31 March next before the time when notification of the contravention was given under reg 6; (ii) in the case of a notified person who at that time has been carrying on that business for a period of less than a year, the period, ending with that time, during which the notified person has been carrying it on; and (iii) in the case of a notified person who at that time has ceased to carry on that business, the period of one year ending with the time when the notified person ceased to carry it on: reg 8(4). As to the meaning of 'mobile satellite services' see PARA 564 note 8.

9   Authorisation of Frequency Use for the Provision of Mobile Satellite Services (European Union) Regulations 2010, SI 2010/672, reg 7(3).

10   Authorisation of Frequency Use for the Provision of Mobile Satellite Services (European Union) Regulations 2010, SI 2010/672, reg 7(4).

11   Authorisation of Frequency Use for the Provision of Mobile Satellite Services (European Union) Regulations 2010, SI 2010/672, reg 7(5).

12   Authorisation of Frequency Use for the Provision of Mobile Satellite Services (European Union) Regulations 2010, SI 2010/672, reg 7(6).

566. Appeals. A selected applicant[1] affected by a decision[2] by OFCOM[3] may appeal against it to the Competition Appeal Tribunal[4]. The means of making an appeal is by sending the Tribunal a notice of appeal in accordance with Tribunal rules[5]. The notice of appeal must be sent within the period specified in those rules[6]. The notice of appeal must set out the provision under which the decision appealed against was taken and the grounds of appeal[7]. The grounds of appeal must be set out in sufficient detail to indicate: (1) to what extent (if any) the appellant contends that the decision appealed against was based on an error of fact or was wrong in law or both; and (2) to what extent (if any) the appellant is appealing against the exercise of a discretion by OFCOM[8].

The Tribunal must dispose of an appeal in accordance with the following provisions[9]. The Tribunal must decide the appeal on the merits and by reference to the grounds of appeal set out in the notice of appeal[10]. The Tribunal's decision must include a decision as to what (if any) is the appropriate action for OFCOM to take in relation to the subject matter of the decision under appeal[11]. The Tribunal must then remit the decision under appeal to OFCOM with such directions (if any) as the Tribunal considers appropriate for giving effect to its decision[12]. The Tribunal must not direct OFCOM to take any action which OFCOM would not otherwise have power to take in relation to the decision under appeal[13]. It is the duty of OFCOM to comply with every direction given to it by the Tribunal[14]. In any document recording the decision of the Tribunal, the Tribunal must have regard to the need for excluding, so far as practicable, commercial information the disclosure of which would or might, in its opinion, significantly harm the legitimate business interests of any person to whom it relates[15].

A party to the appeal may appeal a decision of the Tribunal[16]. Such an appeal: (a) lies to the Court of Appeal or to the Court of Session; and (b) must relate only to a point of law arising from the decision of the Tribunal[17]. An appeal requires the permission of the Tribunal or of the court to which it is to be made[18].

1　As to the meaning of 'selected applicants' see PARA 564 note 3.
2　In the Provision of Mobile Satellite Services (European Union) Regulations 2010, SI 2010/672, reg 10 references to a decision include: (1) references to a decision that is given effect to by the exercise or performance of a power or duty conferred or imposed by those Regulations; but (2) references to a failure to make a decision, and to a failure to exercise a power or to perform a duty, but only where the failure constitutes a failure to comply with any form of request to make the decision, exercise the power or perform the duty; and references in regs 11, 12 to a decision appealed against are to be construed accordingly: reg 10(6). For the purposes of regs 10–12 a decision to which effect is given by the exercise or performance of a power or duty conferred or imposed by the Regulations, is to be treated, except where provision is made for the making of that decision at a different time, as made at the time when the power is exercised or the duty performed: reg 10(7).
3　Ie under the Provision of Mobile Satellite Services (European Union) Regulations 2010, SI 2010/672, regs 3–9: see PARAS 564–565. As to OFCOM see PARA 507.
4　Provision of Mobile Satellite Services (European Union) Regulations 2010, SI 2010/672, regs 1(2), 10(1). As to the Competition Appeal Tribunal see COMPETITION vol 18 (2009) PARA 13 et seq.
5　Provision of Mobile Satellite Services (European Union) Regulations 2010, SI 2010/672, reg 10(2). 'Tribunal rules' means rules made under the Enterprise Act 2002 s 15: Provision of Mobile Satellite Services (European Union) Regulations 2010, SI 2010/672, reg 1(2). See COMPETITION vol 18 (2009) PARA 16.
6　Provision of Mobile Satellite Services (European Union) Regulations 2010, SI 2010/672, reg 10(3).
7　Provision of Mobile Satellite Services (European Union) Regulations 2010, SI 2010/672, reg 10(4).
8　Provision of Mobile Satellite Services (European Union) Regulations 2010, SI 2010/672, reg 10(5).
9　Provision of Mobile Satellite Services (European Union) Regulations 2010, SI 2010/672, reg 11(1).
10　Provision of Mobile Satellite Services (European Union) Regulations 2010, SI 2010/672, reg 11(2).
11　Provision of Mobile Satellite Services (European Union) Regulations 2010, SI 2010/672, reg 11(3).
12　Provision of Mobile Satellite Services (European Union) Regulations 2010, SI 2010/672, reg 11(4).
13　Provision of Mobile Satellite Services (European Union) Regulations 2010, SI 2010/672, reg 11(5).
14　Provision of Mobile Satellite Services (European Union) Regulations 2010, SI 2010/672, reg 11(6).
15　Provision of Mobile Satellite Services (European Union) Regulations 2010, SI 2010/672, reg 11(7).
16　Provision of Mobile Satellite Services (European Union) Regulations 2010, SI 2010/672, reg 12(1). In reg 12 references to a decision of the Tribunal include references to a direction given by it under reg 11(4): reg 12(3).
17　Provision of Mobile Satellite Services (European Union) Regulations 2010, SI 2010/672, reg 12(1).
18　Provision of Mobile Satellite Services (European Union) Regulations 2010, SI 2010/672, reg 12(2).

567. Obligations of OFCOM. OFCOM[1] must carry out its functions under the Wireless Telegraphy Act 2006 so as to give effect to the obligations of the

United Kingdom under the EU Decision[2] and the Commission Decision[3] relating to the provision of mobile satellite services[4] in so far as those obligations have not been given effect by the regulations[5] implementing those Decisions in the United Kingdom[6]. OFCOM must in particular pursuant to its powers under that Act grant a selected applicant[7], if requested, the authorisation necessary for the provision of complementary ground components[8] of systems providing mobile satellite services subject to the specified[9] common conditions[10].

1   As to OFCOM see PARA 507.
2   Ie European Parliament and Council Decision (EC) 626/2008 on the selection and authorisation of systems providing mobile satellite services (MSS) (OJ L172, 2.7.2008, p 15).
3   Ie Commission Decision (EC) 2009/449 on the selection of operators of pan-European systems providing mobile satellite services (MSS) (OJ L149, 12.6.2009, p 65).
4   As to the meaning of 'mobile satellite services' see PARA 564 note 8.
5   Ie the Provision of Mobile Satellite Services (European Union) Regulations 2010, SI 2010/672: see PARAS 564–566.
6   Provision of Mobile Satellite Services (European Union) Regulations 2010, SI 2010/672, reg 13(1).
7   As to the meaning of 'selected applicants' see PARA 564 note 3.
8   'Complementary ground components' means ground-based stations used at fixed locations in order to improve the availability of mobile satellite services in geographical area covered by those services: Provision of Mobile Satellite Services (European Union) Regulations 2010, SI 2010/672, reg 13(3).
9   Ie specified in European Parliament and Council Decision (EC) 626/2008 on the selection and authorisation of systems providing mobile satellite services (MSS) (OJ L172, 2.7.2008, p 15) art 8(3).
10   Provision of Mobile Satellite Services (European Union) Regulations 2010, SI 2010/672, reg 13(2).

(4) OFFENCES RELATING TO WIRELESS TELEGRAPHY AND BROADCASTING

(i) Interference with Broadcasting

568. Regulations to prevent undue interference. OFCOM[1] may make regulations[2] prescribing the requirements to be complied with in the case of apparatus[3] if it is to be: (1) used[4]; or (2) sold otherwise than for export, or offered or advertised for sale otherwise than for export, or let on hire or offered or advertised for letting on hire, by a person who manufactures, assembles or imports such apparatus in the course of business[5]. These requirements are such requirements as OFCOM thinks fit for the purpose of ensuring that the use of the apparatus does not cause undue interference[6] with wireless telegraphy[7].

In a case where apparatus does not comply with the requirements applicable to it under regulations made under the above provisions, a person[8] does not act unlawfully only because he uses the apparatus, or he sells it, or offers or advertises it for sale, or lets it on hire or offers or advertises it for letting on hire, but the non-compliance is a ground for the enforcement procedure[9] to be commenced[10].

1   As to OFCOM see PARA 507.
2   Wireless Telegraphy Act 2006 s 54(1), (2). The approval of the Secretary of State is required for the making by OFCOM of regulations under s 54: s 54(7). A statutory instrument containing regulations made by OFCOM under s 54 is subject to annulment in pursuance of a resolution of either House of Parliament: s 54(8). As to the Secretary of State see PARA 507 note 32. As to the procedure for orders and regulations made by OFCOM see s 122; and PARA 511.
3   The apparatus which may be specified in the regulations under the Wireless Telegraphy Act 2006 s 54(1) or (2) is apparatus which generates, or is designed to generate, or is liable to

generate fortuitously, electromagnetic energy at frequencies not exceeding 3,000 gigahertz: s 54(5). An agreement may exempt from the regulations apparatus used by members of a visiting force or international headquarters in the course of their duty: see the Visiting Forces and International Headquarters (Applications of Law) Order 1999, SI 1999/1736, art 7 (amended by SI 2001/1149). As to visiting forces and international headquarters generally see ARMED FORCES.

4 Wireless Telegraphy Act 2006 s 54(1).

5 Wireless Telegraphy Act 2006 s 54(2). Regulations have been made under the Wireless Telegraphy Act 1949 s 10 (now repealed) relating to the control of interference from the various types of apparatus (see the Wireless Telegraphy (Control of Interference from Ignition Apparatus) Regulations 1952, SI 1952/2023 (amended by SI 1957/347; SI 1973/1217); the Wireless Telegraphy (Control of Interference from Electro-Medical Apparatus) Regulations 1963, SI 1963/1895; the Wireless Telegraphy (Control of Interference from Radio-Frequency Heating Apparatus) Regulations 1971, SI 1971/1675; the Wireless Telegraphy (Control of Interference from Household Appliances, Portable Tools etc) Regulations 1978, SI 1978/1267 (amended by SI 1985/808; SI 1989/562); the Wireless Telegraphy (Control of Interference from Fluorescent Lighting Apparatus) Regulations 1978, SI 1978/1268 (amended by SI 1985/807; SI 1989/561); and the Wireless Telegraphy (Control of Interference from Citizen's Band Radio Apparatus) Regulations 1982, SI 1982/635 (amended by SI 1988/1216)), but these regulations are revoked, in so far as they impose electromagnetic compatibility requirements which must be complied with if apparatus is to be supplied or taken into service and used for the purpose for which it was intended, by the Electromagnetic Compatibility Regulations 2006, SI 2006/3418, reg 2(2), Sch 1 except to the extent that they impose requirements for radio frequency spectrum planning or for the prevention of undue interference to wireless telegraphy from apparatus in use: see reg 2(2).

6 As to the meaning of 'interference' see PARA 541 note 2. Interference with any wireless telegraphy is not to be regarded as undue for the purposes of the Wireless Telegraphy Act 2006 unless it is also harmful: s 115(4). For the purposes of that Act interference is harmful if: (1) it creates dangers, or risks of danger, in relation to the functioning of any service provided by means of wireless telegraphy for the purposes of navigation or otherwise for safety purposes; or (2) it degrades, obstructs or repeatedly interrupts anything which is being broadcast or otherwise transmitted: (a) by means of wireless telegraphy; and (b) in accordance with a wireless telegraphy licence, regulations under s 8(3) (see PARA 514) or a grant of recognised spectrum access (see PARA 544), or otherwise lawfully: s 115(5). 'Broadcast' (except in s 35–38 and Pt 5 (ss 77–95)), means broadcast by wireless telegraphy, and cognate expressions are to be construed accordingly: s 115(1). As to the meaning of 'wireless telegraphy' see PARA 510 note 1. As to emissions see PARA 510 note 1. As to the meaning of 'wireless telegraphy licence' see PARA 514 note 4.

7 Wireless Telegraphy Act 2006 s 54(3). These requirements may include, in particular: (1) requirements as to the maximum intensity of electromagnetic energy of specified frequencies that may be radiated in any direction from the apparatus while it is being used; (2) in the case of apparatus the power for which is supplied from electric lines, requirements as to the maximum electromagnetic energy of specified frequencies that may be injected into those lines by the apparatus: s 54(4).

8 As to the meaning of 'person' see PARA 510 note 1.

9 Ie the procedure contained in the Wireless Telegraphy Act 2006 s 55 or s 56: see PARAS 569–570.

10 Wireless Telegraphy Act 2006 s 54(6).

569. Enforcement of regulations as to use of apparatus. The following provisions apply where, in the opinion of OFCOM[1]: (1) apparatus[2] does not comply with the requirements applicable to it under regulations to prevent undue interference with wireless telegraphy where the apparatus is used[3]; and (2) the first or second condition is satisfied in relation to the apparatus[4].

The first condition is that the use of the apparatus is likely to cause undue interference[5] with wireless telegraphy[6] used: (a) for the purposes of a safety of life service; or (b) for a purpose on which the safety of a person, or of a ship[7], aircraft or vehicle, may depend[8].

The second condition is that: (i) the use of the apparatus is likely to cause undue interference with wireless telegraphy other than wireless telegraphy falling within head (a) or (b); (ii) the use of the apparatus in fact has caused, or is causing, such interference; and (iii) the case is one where OFCOM considers that all reasonable steps to minimise interference have been taken in relation to the wireless telegraphy station[9] or wireless telegraphy apparatus[10] receiving the telegraphy interfered with[11].

OFCOM may give a notice in writing to the person in possession of the apparatus: (A) prohibiting the use of the apparatus after a date fixed by the notice[12], whether by the person to whom the notice is given or otherwise; or (B) (if OFCOM thinks fit so to frame the notice) prohibiting the use of the apparatus after a date fixed by the notice except in such way, at such times and in such circumstances as the notice may specify[13]. Such a notice may be revoked or varied by a subsequent notice in writing from OFCOM given to the person who is then in possession of the apparatus[14].

Where an appeal with respect to a notice is pending[15], proceedings for an offence[16] relating to that notice, whether instituted before or after the bringing of the appeal, are to be stayed until the appeal has been finally determined and the proceedings are to be discharged if the notice is set aside in consequence of the appeal[17]. This does not, however, affect proceedings in which a person has been convicted at a time when there was no pending appeal[18].

A person commits an offence if he uses apparatus, or causes or permits apparatus to be used, knowing that a notice under these provisions is in force with respect to it and the use of the apparatus contravenes the notice[19]. It is a more serious offence if it involves or consists in a contravention of a notice in relation to apparatus the use of which is likely to cause undue interference with wireless telegraphy used for the purpose of a safety of life service or for a purpose on which the safety of a person, or of a ship, aircraft or vehicle, may depend[20].

1   As to OFCOM see PARA 507.
2   As to the apparatus to which the regulations may apply see PARA 568 note 3.
3   Ie regulations made under the Wireless Telegraphy Act 2006 s 54(1): see PARA 568.
4   Wireless Telegraphy Act 2006 s 55(1).
5   As to the meaning of 'undue interference' see PARA 568 note 6.
6   As to the meaning of 'wireless telegraphy' see PARA 510 note 1.
7   As to the meaning of 'ship' see PARA 510 note 12.
8   Wireless Telegraphy Act 2006 s 55(2).
9   As to the meaning of 'wireless telegraphy station' see PARA 510 note 12.
10 As to the meaning of 'wireless telegraphy apparatus' see PARA 510 note 9.
11 Wireless Telegraphy Act 2006 s 55(3).
12 The date fixed by a notice under the Wireless Telegraphy Act 2006 s 55(4) must be not less than 28 days from the date on which the notice is given: s 55(5). But if OFCOM is satisfied that the use of the apparatus in question is likely to cause such undue interference as is described in s 55(2) (heads (a), (b) in the text), the date fixed by a notice under s 55(4) may be the date on which the notice is given: s 55(6).
13 Wireless Telegraphy Act 2006 s 55(4).
14 Wireless Telegraphy Act 2006 s 55(7). Where a notice under s 55(7) has the effect of imposing additional restrictions on the use of the apparatus, the provisions of s 55 about the coming into force of notices (see note 12) apply in relation to the notice as if it were a notice under s 55(4): s 55(8).
15 Ie under the Communications Act 2003 s 192 (see TELECOMMUNICATIONS AND BROADCASTING vol 45(1) (2005 Reissue) PARA 219). For the purposes of the Wireless Telegraphy Act 2006 s 57, such an appeal with respect to a notice under s 55 (or s 56: see PARA 570) or a further appeal relating to the decision on such an appeal is pending unless: (1) that appeal has been brought to a conclusion or withdrawn and there is no further appeal pending in relation to the decision on the appeal; or (2) no further appeal against a decision made on the appeal or on any such further appeal may be brought without the permission of the court and: (a) in a case where there is no fixed period within which that permission can be sought, that permission has been refused or

has not been sought; or (b) in a case where there is a fixed period within which that permission can be sought, that permission has been refused or that period has expired without permission having been sought: s 57(3).

16 Ie under the Wireless Telegraphy Act 2006 s 58(1): see the text and notes 19–20.

17 Wireless Telegraphy Act 2006 s 57(1).

18 Wireless Telegraphy Act 2006 s 57(2).

19 Wireless Telegraphy Act 2006 s 58(1). As to the penalty see note 20.

20 Wireless Telegraphy Act 2006 s 58(6). A person who commits an offence under s 58(1) is liable on summary conviction: (1) if the offence is one that falls within s 58(6), to a fine not exceeding level 5 on the standard scale; (2) otherwise, to a fine not exceeding level 3 on the standard scale. As to the standard scale see SENTENCING AND DISPOSITION OF OFFENDERS vol 92 (2010) PARA 142. As to powers of entry and search in connection with such an offence see PARA 580.

570. Enforcement of regulations as to sale, hiring etc of apparatus. Where, in the opinion of OFCOM[1], apparatus[2] does not comply with the requirements applicable to it under regulations prohibiting the sale etc of apparatus liable to cause interference[3], OFCOM may give a notice in writing to the person[4] who, in the course of business, has manufactured, assembled or imported the apparatus, prohibiting him from: (1) selling the apparatus otherwise than for export; (2) offering or advertising it for sale otherwise than for export; or (3) letting it on hire, or offering or advertising it for letting on hire[5].

Where an appeal with respect to a notice is pending[6], proceedings for an offence[7] relating to that notice, whether instituted before or after the bringing of the appeal, are to be stayed until the appeal has been finally determined and the proceedings are to be discharged if the notice is set aside in consequence of the appeal[8]. This does not, however, affect proceedings in which a person has been convicted at a time when there was no pending appeal[9].

A person commits an offence if he contravenes the provisions of such a notice given to him (unless the notice has previously been revoked by OFCOM)[10]. It is a more serious offence if it involves or consists in a contravention of a notice in relation to apparatus the use of which is likely to cause undue interference with wireless telegraphy[11] used for the purpose of a safety of life service or for a purpose on which the safety of a person, or of a ship[12], aircraft or vehicle, may depend[13].

1   As to OFCOM see PARA 507.

2   As to the apparatus to which the regulations may apply see PARA 568 note 3.

3   Ie regulations made under the Wireless Telegraphy Act 2006 s 54(2): see PARA 568. As to the meaning of 'interference' see PARA 541 note 2.

4   As to the meaning of 'person' see PARA 510 note 1.

5   Wireless Telegraphy Act 2006 s 56(1), (2).

6   Ie under the Communications Act 2003 s 192 (see TELECOMMUNICATIONS AND BROADCASTING vol 45(1) (2005 Reissue) PARA 219). As to when such an appeal is pending see PARA 569 note 15.

7   Ie under the Wireless Telegraphy Act 2006 s 58(4): see the text and notes 10–13.

8   Wireless Telegraphy Act 2006 s 57(1).

9   Wireless Telegraphy Act 2006 s 57(2).

10 Wireless Telegraphy Act 2006 s 58(4).

11 As to the meaning of 'undue interference' see PARA 568 note 6; and as to the meaning of 'wireless telegraphy' see PARA 510 note 1.

12 As to the meaning of 'ship' see PARA 510 note 12.

13 Wireless Telegraphy Act 2006 s 58(6). A person who commits an offence under s 58(4) is liable on summary conviction: (1) if the offence is one that falls within s 58(6), to a fine not exceeding level 5 on the standard scale; (2) otherwise, to a fine not exceeding level 3 on the standard scale: s 58(5). As to the standard scale see SENTENCING AND DISPOSITION OF OFFENDERS vol 92 (2010) PARA 142. As to powers of entry and search in connection with such an offence see PARA 580. As to offences under the Wireless Telegraphy Act 2006 generally see PARA 578 et seq.

571.   Restrictions on manufacture etc.   Where it appears to OFCOM[1] to be expedient to do so for the purpose of preventing or reducing the risk of interference[2] with wireless telegraphy[3], it may make an order[4] (a 'restriction order')[5] imposing restrictions in relation to wireless telegraphy apparatus[6] and apparatus designed or adapted for use in connection with wireless telegraphy apparatus of a class or description specified in the order[7]. The restrictions may relate to the following actions[8]:

(1)   the manufacture[9] of apparatus (whether or not for sale)[10];

(2)   selling apparatus or offering it for sale[11];

(3)   letting apparatus on hire or offering to let it on hire[12];

(4)   indicating (whether by displaying apparatus or by any form of advertisement) willingness to sell apparatus or to let it on hire[13];

(5)   having custody or control of apparatus[14];

(6)   the importation of apparatus[15].

An action for the time being restricted by a restriction order is prohibited unless: (a) an authority given by OFCOM relates to it; and (b) it complies with any terms and conditions that OFCOM attach to the authority[16].

OFCOM may not make a restriction order, give an authority or attach a term or condition to such an authority, unless it is satisfied that the order, authority, term or condition is compatible with the international obligations of the United Kingdom[17].

A person commits an offence if he takes any specified action[18] in relation to apparatus in contravention of the prohibition[19] or without reasonable excuse he has apparatus in his custody or control in contravention of the prohibition[20]. A person commits an offence if he contravenes or fails to comply with any terms or conditions attached to an authority given by OFCOM[21] (whatever the action to which the authority relates)[22].

1   As to OFCOM see PARA 507.
2   As to the meaning of 'interference' see PARA 541 note 2.
3   As to the meaning of 'wireless telegraphy' see PARA 510 note 1.
4   The approval of the Secretary of State is required for the making by OFCOM of an order under the Wireless Telegraphy Act 2006 s 62: s 62(6). A statutory instrument containing an order made by OFCOM under s 62 is subject to annulment in pursuance of a resolution of either House of Parliament: s 62(7). As to the Secretary of State see PARA 507 note 32. As to the procedure for orders and regulations made by OFCOM see s 122; and PARA 511.
5   In the Wireless Telegraphy Act 2006 ss 62–66, 'restriction order' has the meaning given by s 62: s 67.
6   As to the meaning of 'wireless telegraphy apparatus' see PARA 510 note 9.
7   Wireless Telegraphy Act 2006 s 62(1), (2). A restriction order must specify, in the case of apparatus of any class or description specified in the order, what actions are restricted by it: s 62(4).
      See the Wireless Telegraphy (Citizen's Band and Amateur Apparatus) (Various Provisions) Order 1998, SI 1998/2531 (amended by SI 2000/1013), which restricts the import, manufacture, sale, hire, offer or advertisement for sale or hire, custody and control of specified Citizens' Band ('CB') radio apparatus and the import and manufacture of certain specified amateur radio apparatus. See also the Wireless Telegraphy (Control of Interference from Videosenders) Order 1998, SI 1998/722, which restricts for the purposes of the Wireless Telegraphy Act 1967 s 7 (repealed), the importation, manufacture, sale, hire, offer or advertisement for sale or hire of certain wireless telegraphy apparatus known as videosenders, which transmit in the frequency band 470–854 MHz. These orders were made under the Wireless Telegraphy Act 1967 s 7 and are to be treated as if made under s 7 by virtue of the Wireless Telegraphy Act 2006 s 124, Sch 8 para 2.
8   Wireless Telegraphy Act 2006 s 62(3).
9   'Manufacture' includes construction by any method and the assembly of component parts: Wireless Telegraphy Act 2006 s 67.
10   Wireless Telegraphy Act 2006 s 62(3)(a).

11 Wireless Telegraphy Act 2006 s 62(3)(b).

12 Wireless Telegraphy Act 2006 s 62(3)(c).

13 Wireless Telegraphy Act 2006 s 62(3)(d).

14 Wireless Telegraphy Act 2006 s 62(3)(e).

15 Wireless Telegraphy Act 2006 s 62(3)(f). Where the importation of apparatus of a particular class or description is for the time being restricted by a restriction order, an officer of Revenue and Customs may require a person with custody or control of apparatus of that class or description which is being or has been imported to provide proof that the importation of the apparatus is or was not unlawful by virtue of s 62: s 65(1), (2). If the proof required under s 65(2) is not provided to the satisfaction of the Commissioners for Her Majesty's Revenue and Customs, the apparatus is to be treated, unless the contrary is proved, as being prohibited goods, within the meaning of the Customs and Excise Management Act 1979, and is liable to forfeiture under that Act: Wireless Telegraphy Act 2006 s 65(3). As to forfeiture see CUSTOMS AND EXCISE vol 12(3) (2007 Reissue) PARA 1155 et seq. As to the Commissioners for Revenue and Customs see CUSTOMS AND EXCISE vol 12(3) (2007 Reissue) PARA 900 et seq.

16 Wireless Telegraphy Act 2006 s 62(5). An authority given by OFCOM under s 62(5) in the case of apparatus of a class or description specified in a restriction order may be limited: (1) to such of the actions restricted by the order as may be specified in the authority; (2) to such subsidiary class or description of apparatus, falling within the class or description specified in the order, as may be specified in the authority: s 63(1). Terms or conditions attached by OFCOM to an authority under s 62(5) for the manufacture or importation of apparatus may relate to a period after, as well as to the time of, or a period before, the manufacture or importation: s 63(2). An authority under s 62(5) may be given, and terms or conditions may be attached to it: (a) generally by means of a notice published in the London, Edinburgh and Belfast Gazettes; or (b) by an instrument in writing issued to each person authorised to do, in relation to apparatus of a class or description to which a restriction order relates, any action for the time being restricted by the order: s 63(3).

17 Wireless Telegraphy Act 2006 s 64(1). Where a statutory instrument containing a restriction order or a notice or instrument in writing giving an authority under s 62(5), or attaching a term or condition to such an authority, contains a statement that OFCOM is satisfied as mentioned in s 64(1), the statement is evidence of that fact: s 64(2). As to the meaning of 'international obligation of the United Kingdom' see PARA 512 note 14.

18 Ie action falling within the Wireless Telegraphy Act 2006 s 62(3)(a)–(d): see heads (1)–(4) in the text.

19 Ie the prohibition in the Wireless Telegraphy Act 2006 s 62(5): see the text to note 16.

20 Wireless Telegraphy Act 2006 s 66(1). A person who commits an offence under s 66 is liable on summary conviction to a fine not exceeding level 5 on the standard scale: s 66(3). As to the standard scale see SENTENCING AND DISPOSITION OF OFFENDERS vol 92 (2010) PARA 142. Section 66 does not affect any liability to a penalty that may have been incurred under the Customs and Excise Management Act 1979: Wireless Telegraphy Act 2006 s 66(4). As to offences under the Wireless Telegraphy Act 2006 generally see PARA 578 et seq.

21 Ie under the Wireless Telegraphy Act 2006 s 62(5): see the text and note 15.

22 Wireless Telegraphy Act 2006 s 66(2). As to the penalty see note 20.

(ii) Offences in connection with Wireless Telegraphy

572. Misleading messages. A person commits an offence[1] if, by means of wireless telegraphy[2], he sends[3] or attempts to send a message which, to the person's knowledge, is false or misleading and is likely to prejudice the efficiency of a safety of life service or to endanger the safety of a person or of a ship[4], aircraft or vehicle[5]. This applies in particular to a message which, to the person's knowledge, falsely suggests that a ship or aircraft is in distress or in need of assistance or is not in distress or not in need of assistance[6].

1 A person who commits an offence under the Wireless Telegraphy Act 2006 s 47 is liable: (1) on summary conviction, to imprisonment for a term not exceeding 12 months or to a fine not exceeding the statutory maximum or to both; (2) on conviction on indictment, to imprisonment for a term not exceeding two years or to a fine or to both: s 47(4). As to the statutory maximum see SENTENCING AND DISPOSITION OF OFFENDERS vol 92 (2010) PARA 140. For general provisions relating to proceedings for offences see PARA 578.

2 As to the meaning of 'wireless telegraphy' see PARA 510 note 1.

3   As to references to sending messages see PARA 510 note 1.
4   As to the meaning of 'ship' see PARA 510 note 12.
5   Wireless Telegraphy Act 2006 s 47(1), (2). As to the territorial extent of this provision see s 119; and PARA 510.
6   Wireless Telegraphy Act 2006 s 47(3).

573. Keeping wireless telegraphy station or apparatus available for unauthorised use. A person who has a wireless telegraphy station[1] or wireless telegraphy apparatus[2] in his possession or under his control commits an offence if: (1) he intends to use it in contravention of the statutory provision relating to the licensing of wireless telegraphy[3]; or (2) he knows, or has reasonable cause to believe, that another person intends to use it in contravention of that provision[4].

1   As to the meaning of 'wireless telegraphy station' see PARA 510 note 12; and as to the meaning of 'wireless telegraphy' see PARA 510 note 1.
2   As to the meaning of 'wireless telegraphy apparatus' see PARA 510 note 9.
3   Ie the Wireless Telegraphy Act 2006 s 8: see PARA 514.
4   Wireless Telegraphy Act 2006 s 36(1). A person who commits an offence under s 36 where the relevant contravention of s 8 would constitute an offence to which s 35(2) (see PARA 514 note 5) applies is liable: (1) on summary conviction, to imprisonment for a term not exceeding 12 months or to a fine not exceeding the statutory maximum or to both; (2) on conviction on indictment, to imprisonment for a term not exceeding two years or to a fine or to both: s 36(2). A person who commits an offence under s 36 in relation to receiving apparatus is liable on summary conviction to a fine not exceeding level 3 on the standard scale: s 36(4). A person who commits an offence under s 36 other than one falling within s 36(2) or (4) is liable on summary conviction to imprisonment for a term not exceeding 51 weeks or to a fine not exceeding level 5 on the standard scale or to both: s 36(5). As to the statutory maximum see SENTENCING AND DISPOSITION OF OFFENDERS vol 92 (2010) PARA 140; and as to the standard scale see SENTENCING AND DISPOSITION OF OFFENDERS vol 92 (2010) PARA 142.

574. Allowing premises to be used for unlawful broadcasting. A person who is in charge of premises[1] that are used for unlawful broadcasting[2] commits an offence if: (1) he knowingly causes or permits the premises to be so used; or (2) he has reasonable cause to believe that the premises are being so used but fails to take such steps as are reasonable in the circumstances of the case to prevent them from being so used[3].

1   For these purposes, a person is in charge of premises if: (1) he is the owner or occupier of the premises; or (2) he has, or acts or assists in, the management or control of the premises: Wireless Telegraphy Act 2006 s 37(4). 'Premises' includes any place and, in particular, includes: (a) a vehicle, ship or aircraft; and (b) a structure or other object (whether movable or not, and whether on land or not): s 37(7). As to the meaning of 'ship' see PARA 510 note 12.
2   For these purposes, premises are used for unlawful broadcasting if they are used: (1) for making an unlawful broadcast; or (2) for sending signals for the operation or control of apparatus used for the purpose of making an unlawful broadcast from another place: Wireless Telegraphy Act 2006 s 37(5). For these purposes a broadcast is unlawful if: (a) it is made by means of the use of a wireless telegraphy station or wireless telegraphy apparatus in contravention of s 8 (see PARA 514); or (b) the making of the broadcast contravenes a provision of Pt 5 (ss 77–95: see PARA 588 et seq): s 37(6). As to the meaning of 'broadcast' see PARA 588 note 4; definition applied by s 37(7). As to the meaning of 'wireless telegraphy station' see PARA 510 note 12; as to the meaning of 'wireless telegraphy apparatus' see PARA 510 note 9; and as to the meaning of 'wireless telegraphy' see PARA 510 note 1.
3   Wireless Telegraphy Act 2006 s 37(1). A person who commits an offence under s 37 is liable: (1) on summary conviction, to imprisonment for a term not exceeding 12 months or to a fine not exceeding the statutory maximum or to both; (2) on conviction on indictment, to imprisonment for a term not exceeding two years or to a fine or to both: s 37(2). As to the statutory maximum see SENTENCING AND DISPOSITION OF OFFENDERS vol 92 (2010) PARA 140.

575. Acts facilitating unauthorised broadcasting. A person who does any of the following acts in relation to a broadcasting station[1] by which unauthorised broadcasts[2] are made is guilty of an offence[3].

The acts in question are:

(1)   participating in the management, financing, operation or day-to-day running of the broadcasting station knowing, or having reasonable cause to believe, that unauthorised broadcasts are made by the station[4];

(2)   supplying, installing, repairing or maintaining wireless telegraphy apparatus or any other item knowing, or having reasonable cause to believe, that the apparatus or other item is to be, or is, used for the purpose of facilitating the operation or day-to-day running of the broadcasting station and that unauthorised broadcasts are made by the station[5];

(3)   rendering any other service to a person knowing, or having reasonable cause to believe that the rendering of the service to the person will facilitate the operation or day-to-day running of the broadcasting station and that unauthorised broadcasts are made by the station[6];

(4)   supplying a film[7] or sound recording knowing, or having reasonable cause to believe, that an unauthorised broadcast of it is to be made by the broadcasting station[8];

(5)   making a literary, dramatic or musical work[9] knowing, or having reasonable cause to believe, that an unauthorised broadcast of it is to be made by the broadcasting station[10];

(6)   making an artistic work[11] knowing, or having reasonable cause to believe, that an unauthorised broadcast including that work is to be made by the broadcasting station[12];

(7)   participating[13] in an unauthorised broadcast made by the broadcasting station knowing, or having reasonable cause to believe, that unauthorised broadcasts are made by the station[14];

(8)   advertising, or inviting another to advertise[15], by means of an unauthorised broadcast made by the broadcasting station knowing, or having reasonable cause to believe, that unauthorised broadcasts are made by the station[16];

(9)   publishing the times or other details of unauthorised broadcasts made by the broadcasting station, or (otherwise than by publishing such details) publishing an advertisement of matter calculated to promote the station (whether directly or indirectly), knowing, or having reasonable cause to believe, that unauthorised broadcasts are made by the station[17].

In proceedings for an offence under these provisions consisting in supplying a thing or rendering a service, it is a defence for the defendant to prove that he was obliged, under or by virtue of any enactment, to supply the thing or render the service[18].

1   'Broadcasting station' means a business or other operation (whether or not in the nature of a commercial venture) that is engaged in the making of broadcasts: Wireless Telegraphy Act 2006 s 38(8). As to the meaning of 'broadcast' see PARA 588 note 4; definition applied by s 38(8).

2   'Unauthorised broadcast' means a broadcast made by means of the use of a wireless telegraphy station or wireless telegraphy apparatus in contravention of the Wireless Telegraphy Act 2006 s 8: s 38(8). As to the meaning of 'wireless telegraphy station' see PARA 510 note 12; as to the meaning of 'wireless telegraphy apparatus' see PARA 510 note 9; and as to the meaning of 'wireless telegraphy' see PARA 510 note 1.

3   Wireless Telegraphy Act 2006 s 38(1), (2). Any person committing an offence under s 38 is liable: (1) on summary conviction, to imprisonment for a term not exceeding 12 months or to a fine not exceeding the statutory maximum or to both; (2) on conviction on indictment, to imprisonment for a term not exceeding two years or to a fine or to both: s 38(6). As to the statutory maximum see SENTENCING AND DISPOSITION OF OFFENDERS vol 92 (2010) PARA 140.

4   Wireless Telegraphy Act 2006 s 38(2)(a).

5   Wireless Telegraphy Act 2006 s 38(2)(b). As to references to 'supplying' see PARA 535 note 4.
6   Wireless Telegraphy Act 2006 s 38(2)(c).
7   As to the meaning of 'film' for these purposes see the Copyright, Designs and Patents Act 1988
    s 5B; and COPYRIGHT, DESIGN RIGHT AND RELATED RIGHTS vol 9(2) (2006 Reissue) PARA 86;
    and as to the meaning of 'sound recording' see s 5A(1); and COPYRIGHT, DESIGN RIGHT AND
    RELATED RIGHTS vol 9(2) (2006 Reissue) PARA 84 (definitions applied by the Wireless
    Telegraphy Act 2006 s 115(1)).
8   Wireless Telegraphy Act 2006 s 38(2)(d).
9   As to the meaning of 'literary, dramatic or musical work' see COPYRIGHT, DESIGN RIGHT AND
    RELATED RIGHTS vol 9(2) (2006 Reissue) PARAS 67, 73; definition applied by the Wireless
    Telegraphy Act 2006 s 115(1).
10 Wireless Telegraphy Act 2006 s 38(2)(e).
11 As to the meaning of 'artistic work' see the Copyright, Designs and Patents Act 1988 s 4(1); and
    COPYRIGHT, DESIGN RIGHT AND RELATED RIGHTS vol 9(2) (2006 Reissue) PARA 75; definition
    applied by the Wireless Telegraphy Act 2006 s 115(1).
12 Wireless Telegraphy Act 2006 s 38(2)(f).
13 For these purposes a person participates in a broadcast only if he is actually present: (1) as an
    announcer; (2) as a performer or one of the performers concerned in an entertainment given; or
    (3) as the deliverer of a speech: Wireless Telegraphy Act 2006 s 38(3).
14 Wireless Telegraphy Act 2006 s 38(2)(g).
15 The cases in which a person is to be taken for the purposes of the Wireless Telegraphy Act 2006
    s 38 as advertising by means of a broadcast include any case in which he causes or allows it to
    be stated, suggested or implied that entertainment included in the broadcast has been supplied
    by him or is provided wholly or partly at his expense: s 38(4).
16 Wireless Telegraphy Act 2006 s 38(2)(h).
17 Wireless Telegraphy Act 2006 s 38(2)(i).
18 Wireless Telegraphy Act 2006 s 38(5).

576.   Interception and disclosure of messages.   A person commits an offence[1]
if, otherwise than under the authority of a designated person[2]: (1) he uses
wireless telegraphy apparatus[3] with intent to obtain information as to the
contents, sender or addressee of a message (whether sent by means of wireless
telegraphy or not) of which neither he nor a person on whose behalf he is acting
is an intended recipient; or (2) he discloses information as to the contents, sender
or addressee of such a message[4]. A person commits an offence consisting in the
disclosure of information only if the information disclosed by him is information
that would not have come to his knowledge but for the use of wireless telegraphy
apparatus by him or by another person[5]. A person does not commit an offence
consisting in the disclosure of information if he discloses the information in the
course of legal proceedings or for the purpose of a report of legal proceedings[6].

In specified circumstances, a designated person[7] may give an interception
authority[8] in relation to conduct of particular categories[9]. A designated person
may not exercise his power to give an interception authority except where he
believes: (a) that the giving of his authority is necessary on specified grounds[10];
and (b) that the conduct authorised by him is proportionate to what is sought to
be achieved by that conduct[11].

An interception authority for the purposes above is necessary if it is necessary:
(i)   in the interests of national security;
(ii)   for the purpose of preventing or detecting crime[12] or of preventing
        disorder;
(iii)   in the interests of the economic well-being of the United Kingdom;
(iv)   in the interests of public safety;
(v)   for the purpose of protecting public health;
(vi)   for the purpose of assessing or collecting any tax, duty, levy or other
        imposition, contribution or charge payable to a government
        department; or

    (vii)   for any purpose (not falling within heads (i) to (vi)) that is specified for the purposes of these provisions by regulations made by the Secretary of State[13].

An interception authority is also necessary if it is not necessary on grounds falling within heads (i) or (iii) to (vii) above but is necessary for purposes connected with:

    (A)   the grant of wireless telegraphy licences[14];

    (B)   the prevention or detection of anything that constitutes interference with wireless telegraphy[15]; or

    (C)   the enforcement of other enactments[16] relating to such interference[17].

An interception authority must be in writing and under the hand of the Secretary of State, one of the Commissioners for Revenue and Customs, or a person who is designated for these purposes by regulations made by the Secretary of State[18]. An interception authority may be general or specific and may be given to such person or persons, or description of persons, for such period, and subject to such restrictions and limitations, as the designated person thinks fit[19].

1   A person committing such an offence is liable on summary conviction to a fine not exceeding level 5 on the standard scale: Wireless Telegraphy Act 2006 s 48(4). For general provisions relating to proceedings for offences see PARA 578. As to the standard scale see SENTENCING AND DISPOSITION OF OFFENDERS vol 92 (2010) PARA 142.

2   'Designated person' means: (1) the Secretary of State; (2) the Commissioners for Revenue and Customs; or (3) any other person designated for the purposes of the Wireless Telegraphy Act 2006 s 48 by regulations made by the Secretary of State: s 48(5). As to the Secretary of State see PARA 507 note 32. As to the Commissioners for Revenue and Customs see CUSTOMS AND EXCISE vol 12(3) (2007 Reissue) PARA 900 et seq.

3   As to the meaning of 'wireless telegraphy apparatus' see PARA 510 note 9; and as to the meaning of 'wireless telegraphy' see PARA 510 note 1.

4   Wireless Telegraphy Act 2006 s 48(1). As to the territorial extent of these provisions see s 119; and PARA 510. It is not necessary that the accused had any mischievous intention since intent to do the prohibited act is sufficient for the commission of the offence: see *Paul v Ministry of Posts and Telecommunications* [1973] RTR 245, DC, where the defendant listened to emergency fire brigade calls for the purpose of attending fires. The purpose for which the information is obtained is irrelevant and a person who deliberately, rather than accidentally and fleetingly, tunes into a police station channel commits an offence under the Wireless Telegraphy Act 1949 s 5(b)(i): *DPP v Waite* (1996) 160 JP 726, DC. As to the interception of communications see CRIMINAL LAW, EVIDENCE AND PROCEDURE vol 11(1) (2006 Reissue) PARA 506 et seq. As to unlawful interception of communications under the Regulation of Investigatory Powers Act 2000 see TELECOMMUNICATIONS vol 97 (2010) PARA 205.

5   Wireless Telegraphy Act 2006 s 48(2).

6   Wireless Telegraphy Act 2006 s 48(3).

7   'Designated person' has the same meaning as in the Wireless Telegraphy Act 2006 s 48 (see note 2): s 49(12).

8   References to an interception authority are references to an authority for the purposes of the Wireless Telegraphy Act 2006 s 48 given otherwise than by way of the issue or renewal of a warrant, authorisation or notice under the Regulation of Investigatory Powers Act 2000 Pt I (ss 1–25) or Pt II (ss 26–48) (see CRIMINAL LAW, EVIDENCE AND PROCEDURE vol 11(1) (2006 Reissue) PARA 506 et seq): Wireless Telegraphy Act 2006 s 49(11).

9   See the Wireless Telegraphy Act 2006 s 49. The conduct in relation to which a designated person may give an interception authority is not to include conduct falling within s 49(2), except where he believes that the conduct is necessary on grounds falling within s 49(5): s 49(1). Conduct falls within s 49(2) if it is: (1) conduct that, if engaged in without lawful authority, constitutes an offence under the Regulation of Investigatory Powers Act 2000 s 1(1) or (2) (see CRIMINAL LAW, EVIDENCE AND PROCEDURE vol 11(1) (2006 Reissue) PARA 506); (2) conduct that, if engaged in without lawful authority, is actionable under s 1(3) (see CRIMINAL LAW, EVIDENCE AND PROCEDURE vol 11(1) (2006 Reissue) PARA 506); (3) conduct that is capable of being authorised by an authorisation or notice granted under Pt I Ch II (ss 21–25) (communications data: see CRIMINAL LAW, EVIDENCE AND PROCEDURE vol 11(1) (2006 Reissue) PARA 521 et seq); or (4)

conduct that is capable of being authorised by an authorisation granted under Pt II (surveillance etc: see CRIMINAL LAW, EVIDENCE AND PROCEDURE vol 11(1) (2006 Reissue) PARA 521 et seq): Wireless Telegraphy Act 2006 s 49(2).

For the purposes of s 49 the question whether a person's conduct is capable of being authorised under the Regulation of Investigatory Powers Act 2000 Pt I Ch II or Pt II is to be determined without reference: (a) to whether the person is someone upon whom a power or duty is or may be conferred or imposed by or under those provisions; or (b) to whether there are grounds for believing that the requirements for the grant of an authorisation or the giving of a notice under those provisions are satisfied: Wireless Telegraphy Act 2006 s 49(10).

As to the Regulation of Investigatory Powers Act 2000 see CRIMINAL LAW, EVIDENCE AND PROCEDURE vol 11(1) (2006 Reissue) PARA 506 et seq.

10 Ie on grounds falling within the Wireless Telegraphy Act 2006 s 49(4) or (5): see heads (i)–(vii), (A)–(C) in the text.

11 Wireless Telegraphy Act 2006 s 49(3). The matters to be taken into account in considering whether the requirements of s 49(3) are satisfied in the case of the giving of an interception authority include whether what it is thought necessary to achieve by the authorised conduct could reasonably be achieved by other means: s 49(6).

12 Ie within the meaning of the Regulation of Investigatory Powers Act 2000 s 81(2)(a) (see CRIMINAL LAW, EVIDENCE AND PROCEDURE vol 11(1) (2006 Reissue) PARA 506 et seq): Wireless Telegraphy Act 2006 s 49(12).

13 Wireless Telegraphy Act 2006 s 49(4). No regulations may be made under s 49(4)(g) (head (vii) in the text) unless a draft of them has first been laid before Parliament and approved by a resolution of each House: s 49(9).

14 As to the meaning of 'wireless telegraphy licence' see PARA 514 note 4. As to the grant of such licences see PARA 514 et seq.

15 As to the meaning of 'interference' see PARA 541 note 2; and as to the meaning of 'wireless telegraphy' see PARA 510 note 1.

16 Ie: (1) any provision of the Wireless Telegraphy Act 2006 Pt 2 (ss 8–53) (other than Ch 2 (ss 18–26) and ss 27–31) or Pt 3 (ss 54–68); or (2) any enactment not falling within head (1) that relates to interference with wireless telegraphy.

17 Wireless Telegraphy Act 2006 s 49(5).

18 Wireless Telegraphy Act 2006 s 49(7).

19 Wireless Telegraphy Act 2006 s 49(8).

577. Deliberate interference. A person commits an offence[1] if he uses apparatus for the purpose of interfering[2] with wireless telegraphy[3]. This applies: (1) whether or not the apparatus in question is wireless telegraphy apparatus[4]; (2) whether or not it is apparatus specified in regulations made to prevent interference[5]; (3) whether or not a notice of contravention[6] has been given with respect to it, or, if given, has been varied or revoked[7].

1   A person who commits such an offence is liable: (1) on summary conviction, to imprisonment for a term not exceeding 12 months or to a fine not exceeding the statutory maximum or to both; (2) on conviction on indictment, to imprisonment for a term not exceeding two years or to a fine or to both: Wireless Telegraphy Act 2006 s 68(3). As to the statutory maximum see SENTENCING AND DISPOSITION OF OFFENDERS vol 92 (2010) PARA 140.

2   As to the meaning of 'interference' see PARA 541 note 2; and as to offences in connection with undue interference see PARAS 569–570.

3   Wireless Telegraphy Act 2006 s 68(1). As to the meaning of 'wireless telegraphy' see PARA 510 note 1.

4   As to the meaning of 'wireless telegraphy apparatus' see PARA 510 note 9.

5   Ie under the Wireless Telegraphy Act 2006 s 54: see PARA 568.

6   Ie under the Wireless Telegraphy Act 2006 s 55 or 56: see PARAS 569, 570.

7   Wireless Telegraphy Act 2006 s 68(2).

578. General provisions regarding penalties and proceedings. Where a person is convicted of an offence[1] consisting in the use of a wireless telegraphy station[2] or wireless telegraphy apparatus[3] or a failure or refusal to cause a wireless telegraphy licence[4] or an authority to fill a wireless telegraphy personnel vacancy[5] to be surrendered[6], and the use, or the failure or refusal, continues after the conviction, the person is to be treated as committing a separate offence in respect of every day on which the use, or the failure or refusal, so continues[7]. This does not affect the right to bring separate proceedings for contraventions of the Wireless Telegraphy Act 2006 taking place on separate occasions[8].

Where the doing of a thing is rendered unlawful by Part 2 or 3 of the Wireless Telegraphy Act 2006 and it is also an offence under that Act, the fact that it is such an offence does not limit a person's right to bring civil proceedings in respect of the doing or apprehended doing of that thing[9]. Without prejudice to the generality of the foregoing, compliance with a provision of Part 2 or 3 contravention of which is an offence under the Wireless Telegraphy Act 2006 is enforceable in civil proceedings by the Crown, or by OFCOM[10], for an injunction or for any other appropriate relief[11].

Proceedings for certain offences committed in UK territorial sea[12] and offences relating to the prohibition of broadcasting from sea or air[13] may be taken, and the offence may for all incidental purposes be treated as having been committed, in any place in the United Kingdom[14]. For the purpose of the enforcement of any of certain specified provisions[15], a member of a police force has in any area of the sea within the seaward limits of UK territorial sea all the powers, protection and privileges which he has in the area for which he acts as constable[16].

Specific provision is made as to offences committed by bodies corporate[17].

1   Ie under the Wireless Telegraphy Act 2006 Pt 2 (ss 8–53) or Pt 3 (ss 54–68).
2   As to the meaning of 'wireless telegraphy station' see PARA 510 note 12; and as to the meaning of 'wireless telegraphy' see PARA 510 note 1.
3   As to the meaning of 'wireless telegraphy apparatus' see PARA 510 note 9.
4   As to the meaning of 'wireless telegraphy licence' see PARA 514 note 4.
5   Ie an authority under the Wireless Telegraphy Act 2006 s 52(3): see PARA 531.
6   As to the surrender of licences and authorities see PARAS 517, 531.
7   Wireless Telegraphy Act 2006 s 106(1), (2).
8   Wireless Telegraphy Act 2006 s 106(3).
9   Wireless Telegraphy Act 2006 s 108(1).
10 As to OFCOM see PARA 507.
11 Wireless Telegraphy Act 2006 s 108(2).
12 Ie an offence under the Wireless Telegraphy Act 2006 Pt 2, Pt 3 or Pt 6 (ss 96–126) (other than an offence under s 111). As to the meaning of 'UK territorial sea' see PARA 510 note 14.
13 Ie an offence under the Wireless Telegraphy Act 2006 Pt 5 (ss 77–95): see PARA 588 et seq.
14 Wireless Telegraphy Act 2006 s 107(1). As to the meaning of 'United Kingdom' see PARA 510 note 13.
15 Ie those falling within the Wireless Telegraphy Act 2006 s 107(3). Those provisions are ss 8–11, 32–38 and 45–53, Pt 3, Pt 5, ss 97–100, 103, 105, 106 and Sch 5: s 107(3).
16 Wireless Telegraphy Act 2006 s 107(2). As to the powers of constables see POLICE vol 36(1) (2007 Reissue) PARA 101 et seq.
17 See the Wireless Telegraphy Act 2006 s 110; and TELECOMMUNICATIONS vol 97 (2010) PARA 211.

579.   **Forfeiture on conviction.**   Where a person is convicted of a relevant offence[1], the court may, as well as imposing any other penalty, order to be forfeited to OFCOM[2] such of the things mentioned below as the court considers appropriate[3].

The things which may be forfeited are[4]:

(1)   any vehicle, ship[5] or aircraft, or any structure or other object, that was used in connection with the commission of the offence[6];

(2)   any wireless telegraphy apparatus[7] or other apparatus[8] in relation to which the offence was committed[9];

(3)   any wireless telegraphy apparatus or other apparatus that was used in connection with the commission of the offence[10];

(4)   any wireless telegraphy apparatus or other apparatus (not falling within head (2) or (3)) that: (a) was in the possession or under the control of the person convicted of the offence at the time he committed it; and (b) was intended to be used (whether or not by that person) in connection with the making of a broadcast or other transmission that would contravene the statutory requirements[11] as to licences and the prohibition of broadcasting from sea or air[12].

Where a person is convicted of an offence[13] involving restricted apparatus[14], the court must order the apparatus to be forfeited to OFCOM unless the defendant or a person who claims to be the owner of, or otherwise interested in, the apparatus shows cause why it should not be forfeited[15]. Apparatus may be ordered to be forfeited even if it is not the property of the person by whom the offence giving rise to the forfeiture was committed[16]. Apparatus ordered to be forfeited may be disposed of by OFCOM in such manner as it thinks fit[17].

A court that orders apparatus to be forfeited may also order the person by whom the offence giving rise to the forfeiture was committed not to dispose of it except by delivering it up to OFCOM within 48 hours of being so required by it[18]. A person against whom such an order is made commits a further offence if he contravenes the order or he fails to deliver up the apparatus to OFCOM as required[19].

1   A relevant offence is: (1) an offence under the Wireless Telegraphy Act 2006 Pt 2 Ch 4 (ss 35–44), or Ch 5 (ss 45–53) (see PARAS 514, 525 et seq, 572 et seq) consisting in a contravention of any provision of Pt 2 in relation to a wireless telegraphy station or wireless telegraphy apparatus (including an offence under s 37 or 38 (see PARAS 574, 575)); (2) an offence under s 66 (see PARA 571); (3) an offence under s 68 (see PARA 577); (4) an offence under Pt 5 (see PARA 588 et seq): s 103, Sch 5 para 1(4). The following are not relevant offences: (a) an offence under s 35 consisting in the installation or use of receiving apparatus (see PARA 514); (b) an offence under s 36 committed in relation to receiving apparatus (see PARA 573); (c) an offence under s 51(4) (see PARA 524): Sch 5 para 1(5).
2   As to OFCOM see PARA 507.
3   Wireless Telegraphy Act 2006 Sch 5 para 1(1). The Magistrates' Courts Act 1980 s 140 (under which magistrates sell or dispose of forfeited property: see MAGISTRATES vol 29(2) (Reissue) PARA 811) does not apply in relation to apparatus ordered to be forfeited under the Wireless Telegraphy Act 2006 Sch 5 para 1 or 2: Sch 5 para 6. The Powers of Criminal Courts (Sentencing) Act 2000 s 143 (under which a court convicting a person of an offence has power to deprive him of property used etc for purposes of crime: see SENTENCING AND DISPOSITION OF OFFENDERS vol 92 (2010) PARA 481) does not apply where a person is convicted of an offence under the Wireless Telegraphy Act 2006 P t 2, Pt 3 or Pt 5: Sch 5 para 7.
4   Wireless Telegraphy Act 2006 Sch 5 para 1(2).
5   As to the meaning of 'ship' see PARA 510 note 12.
6   Wireless Telegraphy Act 2006 Sch 5 para 1(2)(a).
7   As to the meaning of 'wireless telegraphy apparatus' see PARA 510 note 9.
8   References in the Wireless Telegraphy Act 2006 Sch 5 para 1(2)(b)–(d) to apparatus other than wireless telegraphy apparatus include references to: (1) recordings; (2) equipment designed or adapted for use in making recordings or in reproducing sounds or visual images from recordings; (3) any other equipment that is connected, directly or indirectly, to wireless telegraphy apparatus: Sch 5 para 1(3).
9   Wireless Telegraphy Act 2006 Sch 5 para 1(2)(b).
10   Wireless Telegraphy Act 2006 Sch 5 para 1(2)(c).
11   Ie the Wireless Telegraphy Act 2006 s 8 or Pt 5.
12   Wireless Telegraphy Act 2006 Sch 5 para 1(2)(d).
13   Ie under the Wireless Telegraphy Act 2006 Pt 2, Pt 3 or Pt 6 (ss 96–126).
14   Apparatus is restricted apparatus if custody or control of apparatus of any class or description to which it belongs is for the time being restricted by a restriction order under the Wireless Telegraphy Act 2006 s 62 (see PARA 571): Sch 5 para 2(3).
15   Wireless Telegraphy Act 2006 Sch 5 para 2(1). This does not affect the operation of Sch 5 para 1 in relation to apparatus that is not restricted apparatus: Sch 5 para 2(2).

16 Wireless Telegraphy Act 2006 Sch 5 para 3.

17 Wireless Telegraphy Act 2006 Sch 5 para 4.

18 Wireless Telegraphy Act 2006 Sch 5 para 5(1).

19 Wireless Telegraphy Act 2006 Sch 5 para 5(2). An offence Sch 5 para 5(2) is punishable as if it were committed under the same provision, and at the same time, as the offence for which the forfeiture was ordered: Sch 5 para 5(3).

580. Powers of entry and search. A justice of the peace may issue an authorisation if he is satisfied, on an application supported by sworn evidence, that:

(1) there is reasonable ground for believing that there is to be found, on specified premises or in a specified ship[1], aircraft or vehicle, apparatus that does not comply with the requirements applicable to it under regulations made to prevent interference[2];

(2) it is necessary to enter those premises, or that ship, aircraft or vehicle, for the purpose of obtaining information that will enable OFCOM to decide whether or not to give a contravention notice[3]; and

(3) within the period of 14 days before the date of the application to the justice, access to the premises, ship, aircraft or vehicle for the purpose of obtaining such information has been demanded by a person authorised for the purpose by OFCOM[4], who has produced sufficient documentary evidence of his identity and authority but has been refused[5].

However, the justice may not issue an authorisation unless the first or second condition is fulfilled as regards the application[6].

The first condition is that it is shown to the justice that OFCOM is satisfied that there is reasonable ground for believing that the use of the apparatus in question is likely to cause undue interference[7] with wireless telegraphy[8] used either for the purposes of a safety of life service or for a purpose on which the safety of a person, or of a ship, aircraft or vehicle, may depend[9].

The second condition is that it is shown to the justice that: (a) at least seven days before the demand was made, notice that access would be demanded was given to the occupier of the premises or (as the case may be) the person in possession or the person in charge of the ship, aircraft or vehicle; (b) the demand for access was made at a reasonable hour; and (c) it was unreasonably refused[10].

An authorisation for these purposes is an authorisation empowering a person or persons authorised for the purpose by OFCOM, with or without constables: (i) to enter the premises or (as the case may be) the ship, aircraft or vehicle and any premises on which it may be; (ii) to search the premises, ship, aircraft or vehicle with a view to discovering whether apparatus falling within head (1) is there; (iii) if he or they find such apparatus there, to examine and test it with a view to obtaining the information mentioned in head (2)[11]. An authorisation must be in writing and signed by the justice[12]. A person authorised by OFCOM to exercise a power conferred by these provisions may if necessary use reasonable force in the exercise of the power[13], but this does not affect any other power exercisable by the person[14].

Where a person has a right to examine and test apparatus on premises or in a ship, aircraft or vehicle, any person who is on the premises or is in charge of, or in or in attendance on, the ship, aircraft or vehicle, must give him whatever assistance he may reasonably require in the examination or testing of the apparatus[15].

A justice of the peace may grant a search warrant if he is satisfied by information on oath that there is reasonable ground for suspecting that an offence under the Wireless Telegraphy Act 2006[16] has been or is being committed and evidence of the commission of the offence is to be found on premises specified in the information, or in a vehicle, ship or aircraft so specified[17]. A search warrant under this provision is a warrant empowering a constable or any person or persons authorised for the purpose by OFCOM or the Secretary of State: (A) to enter, at any time within the relevant period[18], the premises specified in the information or (as the case may be) the vehicle, ship or aircraft so specified and any premises on which it may be; (B) to search the premises, vehicle, ship or aircraft; (C) to examine and test any apparatus found there[19].

Where a person authorised by OFCOM or the Secretary of State is empowered by a search warrant to enter any premises, he is to be entitled to exercise that warrant alone or to exercise it accompanied by one or more constables[20]. A person authorised by OFCOM or the Secretary of State to exercise a power conferred by these provisions may if necessary use reasonable force in the exercise of the power[21], but this does not affect any other power exercisable by a person so authorised[22]. Where a person has a right to examine and test apparatus on premises or in a ship, aircraft or vehicle, any person who is on the premises or is in charge of, or in or in attendance on, the ship, aircraft or vehicle, must give him whatever assistance he may reasonably require in the examination or testing of the apparatus[23].

A person commits an offence if he intentionally obstructs a person in the exercise of the powers conferred on him under these provisions[24] or fails or refuses, without reasonable excuse, to give to such a person any assistance which, under these provisions, he is under a duty to give to him[25].

1 As to the meaning of 'ship' see PARA 510 note 12.
2 Ie regulations made under the Wireless Telegraphy Act 2006 s 54: see PARA 568.
3 Ie a notice under the Wireless Telegraphy Act 2006 s 55 or 56: see PARAS 569, 570. As to the meaning of 'information' see PARA 512 note 1.
4 As to OFCOM see PARA 507.
5 Wireless Telegraphy Act 2006 s 59(1).
6 Wireless Telegraphy Act 2006 s 59(2).
7 As to the meaning of 'undue interference' see PARA 568 note 6.
8 As to the meaning of 'wireless telegraphy' see PARA 510 note 1.
9 Wireless Telegraphy Act 2006 s 59(3).
10 Wireless Telegraphy Act 2006 s 59(4).
11 Wireless Telegraphy Act 2006 s 59(5).
12 Wireless Telegraphy Act 2006 s 59(6).
13 Wireless Telegraphy Act 2006 s 59(7).
14 Wireless Telegraphy Act 2006 s 59(8).
15 Wireless Telegraphy Act 2006 s 59(9).
16 Ie other than an offence under the Wireless Telegraphy Act 2006 Pt 4 (ss 69–76) or s 111.
17 Wireless Telegraphy Act 2006 s 97(1).
18 'The relevant period' means the period of three months beginning with the day after the date of the warrant: Wireless Telegraphy Act 2006 s 97(3).
19 Wireless Telegraphy Act 2006 s 97(2).
20 Wireless Telegraphy Act 2006 s 97(5).
21 Wireless Telegraphy Act 2006 s 97(6).
22 Wireless Telegraphy Act 2006 s 97(7).
23 Wireless Telegraphy Act 2006 s 97(8).
24 Ie the Wireless Telegraphy Act 2006 s 59 or s 97.
25 Wireless Telegraphy Act 2006 ss 60(1), 98(1). A person who commits an offence under s 60 or s 97 is liable on summary conviction to a fine not exceeding level 5 on the standard scale: ss 60(2), 97(2). As to the standard scale see SENTENCING AND DISPOSITION OF OFFENDERS vol 92 (2010) PARA 142.

581. Seizure and disposal of apparatus. Where a search warrant is granted under the Wireless Telegraphy Act 2006[1], and the suspected offence (or any of the suspected offences) is an offence to which these provisions apply[2], the warrant may authorise a person authorised by OFCOM[3] to exercise the power to seize and detain, for the purposes of any relevant proceedings[4], any apparatus or other thing found in the course of the search carried out in pursuance of the warrant that appears to him to be a relevant item[5].

If a constable or a person authorised by OFCOM to exercise this power has reasonable grounds to suspect that an offence to which these provisions apply has been or is being committed, he may seize and detain, for the purposes of any relevant proceedings, any apparatus or other thing that appears to him to be a relevant item[6]. A person authorised by OFCOM to exercise a power conferred by these provisions may if necessary use reasonable force in the exercise of the power[7], but this does not affect any other power exercisable by the person so authorised[8]. Nothing in these provisions affects any power to seize or detain property that is exercisable by a constable apart from them[9].

A person commits an offence if he intentionally obstructs a person in the exercise of the power conferred on him[10] to seize and detain apparatus and other things[11].

Property seized by a person authorised by OFCOM in pursuance of a warrant[12] or in the exercise of the power of seizure[13] may be detained until the end of the period of six months beginning with the date of seizure or, if proceedings for an offence[14] involving that property or proceedings for condemnation[15] of that property as forfeited are instituted within that period, until the conclusion of those proceedings[16]. In the case of property so detained which, after the end of the period authorised, remains in the possession of OFCOM and has not been ordered to be forfeited[17] or condemned as forfeited[18], OFCOM must take reasonable steps to deliver the property to the person who appears to it to be its owner[19]. If the property remains in the possession of OFCOM after the end of one year immediately following the end of the authorised period of detention, OFCOM may dispose of it in such manner as it thinks fit[20].

1 Ie under the Wireless Telegraphy Act 2006 s 97: see PARA 580.
2 The Wireless Telegraphy Act 2006 s 99 applies to: (1) an indictable offence under that Act, other than an offence under s 111 (as to which see PARA 512); (2) an offence under s 35 (see PARA 514), other than one consisting in the installation or use of receiving apparatus; (3) an offence under s 36 (see PARA 573), other than one where the relevant contravention of s 8 would constitute an offence consisting in the use of receiving apparatus; (4) an offence under s 48 (see PARA 576); (5) an offence under s 66 (see PARA 571): s 99(1).
3 As to OFCOM see PARA 507.
4 'Relevant proceedings' means proceedings for an offence to which the Wireless Telegraphy Act 2006 s 99 applies or proceedings for condemnation under Sch 6 (see PARA 582): s 99(7).
5 Wireless Telegraphy Act 2006 s 99(2). 'Relevant item' means an item that was used in connection with an offence to which s 99 applies or is evidence of the commission of such an offence: s 99(7).
6 Wireless Telegraphy Act 2006 s 99(3). As to seizure and detention of property by constables generally see CRIMINAL LAW, EVIDENCE AND PROCEDURE vol 11(2) (2006 Reissue) PARA 886 et seq.
7 Wireless Telegraphy Act 2006 s 99(4).
8 Wireless Telegraphy Act 2006 s 99(5).
9 Wireless Telegraphy Act 2006 s 99(6).
10 Ie under the Wireless Telegraphy Act 2006 s 99(3).
11 Wireless Telegraphy Act 2006 s 100(1). A person who commits an offence under s 100 is liable on summary conviction to a fine not exceeding level 5 on the standard scale: s 100(2). As to the standard scale see SENTENCING AND DISPOSITION OF OFFENDERS vol 92 (2010) PARA 142.

12 Ie under the Wireless Telegraphy Act 2006 s 97: see PARA 580.
13 Ie the power conferred by the Wireless Telegraphy Act 2006 s 99(3).
14 Ie an offence to which the Wireless Telegraphy Act 2006 s 99 applies.
15 Ie under the Wireless Telegraphy Act 2006 Sch 6.
16 Wireless Telegraphy Act 2006 s 101(1), (2). In the case of proceedings for an offence to which
    s 99 applies and proceedings under Sch 6 for the condemnation of apparatus as forfeited (see
    PARA 582), where such proceedings are terminated by an appealable decision, they are not to be
    regarded as concluded for the purposes of s 101(2)(b): (1) until the end of the ordinary time for
    appeal against the decision, if no appeal in respect of the decision is brought within that time; or
    (2) if an appeal in respect of the decision is brought within that time, until the conclusion of the
    appeal: s 102(1), (2). Section 102(2) applies for determining, for the purposes of s 102(2)(b) (see
    head (2)), when proceedings on an appeal are concluded as it applies for determining when the
    original proceedings are concluded: s 102(3). References in s 102(2) to a decision which
    terminates proceedings include references to a verdict, sentence, finding or order that puts an
    end to the proceedings: s 102(4). An appealable decision is a decision of a description against
    which an appeal will lie, whether by way of case stated or otherwise and whether with or
    without permission: s 102(5). References to an appeal include references to an application for
    permission to appeal: s 102(6).
17 Ie under the Wireless Telegraphy Act 2006 Sch 5.
18 Ie under the Wireless Telegraphy Act 2006 Sch 6.
19 Wireless Telegraphy Act 2006 s 101(4). The delivery of the property in accordance with s 101(4)
    to the person who appears to OFCOM to be its owner does not affect the right of any other
    person to take legal proceedings for the recovery of the property against the person to whom the
    property is so delivered or against any person subsequently in possession of the property:
    s 101(6).
20 Wireless Telegraphy Act 2006 s 101(5).

582. Forfeiture of restricted apparatus. Apparatus which has been seized in
pursuance of a warrant[1] or in exercise of the power to seize and detain property[2]
is liable to forfeiture if, immediately before being seized, it was in a person's
custody or control in contravention of a restriction order[3] imposed for the
purpose of preventing or reducing the risk of interference with wireless
telegraphy[4]. Apparatus forfeited under these provisions is to be forfeited to
OFCOM[5] and may be disposed of by it in any manner it thinks fit[6].

Where restricted apparatus[7] is seized, OFCOM must give notice of the seizure
to every person who, to its knowledge, was at the time of the seizure the owner
or one of the owners of the apparatus[8]. The notice must set out the grounds of
the seizure[9]. Where there is no proper address for the purposes of the service of
such a notice in an authorised manner[10], the requirements of notice will be
satisfied by the publication of a notice of the seizure in the London, Edinburgh
or Belfast Gazette (according to the part of the United Kingdom where the
seizure took place)[11]. Apparatus may be condemned or taken to have been
condemned under these provisions only if the requirements above[12] have been
complied with in the case of that apparatus[13].

A person claiming that the restricted apparatus is not liable to forfeiture must
give written notice of his claim to OFCOM[14]. A notice of claim must be given
within one month after the day of the giving of the notice of seizure[15].

The restricted apparatus is to be taken to have been duly condemned as
forfeited if:

(1) by the end of the period for the giving of a notice of claim in respect of
     the apparatus, no such notice has been given to OFCOM; or
(2) a notice of claim is given which does not comply with the statutory
     requirements[16].

Where a notice of claim in respect of the restricted apparatus is duly given,
OFCOM may take proceedings for the condemnation of the apparatus by the
court[17]. In such proceedings, if the court finds that the apparatus was liable to

forfeiture at the time of seizure, it must condemn the apparatus as forfeited unless cause is shown why it should not; and if the court finds that the apparatus was not liable to forfeiture at that time, or cause is shown why it should not be forfeited, the court must order the return of the apparatus to the person appearing to the court to be entitled to it[18]. Where the restricted apparatus is condemned or taken to have been condemned as forfeited, the forfeiture is to have effect as from the time of the seizure[19].

If OFCOM decides not to take proceedings for condemnation in a case in which a notice of claim has been so given, it must return the apparatus to the person appearing to it to be the owner of the apparatus, or to one of the persons appearing to it to be the owners of it[20]. Apparatus required to be returned must be returned as soon as reasonably practicable after the decision not to take proceedings for condemnation[21]. OFCOM's decision whether to take such proceedings must be taken as soon as reasonably practicable after the receipt of the notice of claim[22].

In proceedings for condemnation that are instituted in England and Wales, the claimant or his solicitor must make his oath that the seized apparatus was, or was to the best of his knowledge and belief, the property of the claimant at the time of the seizure[23]. In proceedings for condemnation instituted in the High Court, the court may require the claimant to give such security for the costs of the proceedings as may be determined by the court, and the claimant must comply with any such requirement[24]. If any of these requirements is not complied with, the court must give judgment for OFCOM[25].

In the case of proceedings for condemnation instituted in a magistrates' court in England or Wales, either party may appeal against the decision of that court to the Crown Court[26]. Where an appeal has been made (whether by case stated or otherwise) against the decision of the court in proceedings for the condemnation of restricted apparatus, that apparatus is to be left with OFCOM pending the final determination of the matter[27].

Where a requirement is imposed[28] for apparatus to be returned to a person, then if the apparatus is still in OFCOM's possession after the end of the period of 12 months beginning with the day after the requirement to return it arose, OFCOM may dispose of it in any manner it thinks fit[29]. OFCOM may exercise its power to dispose of apparatus only if it is not practicable at the time when the power is exercised to dispose of the apparatus by returning it immediately to the person to whom it is required to be returned[30].

In proceedings arising out of the seizure of restricted apparatus, the fact, form and manner of the seizure is to be taken, without further evidence and unless the contrary is shown, to have been as set forth in the process[31]. In any proceedings, the condemnation by a court of restricted apparatus as forfeited may be proved by the production of either the order or certificate of condemnation or a certified copy of the order purporting to be signed by an officer of the court by which the order or certificate was made or granted[32].

Neither the imposition of a requirement by or under these provisions to return apparatus to a person nor the return of apparatus to a person in accordance with such a requirement affects the rights in relation to that apparatus of any other person or the right of any other person to enforce his rights against the person to whom it is returned[33].

1 Ie a warrant under the Wireless Telegraphy Act 2006 s 97: see PARA 580.
2 Ie the power conferred by the Wireless Telegraphy Act 2006 s 99(3): see PARA 581.
3 Ie under the Wireless Telegraphy Act 2006 s 62(5): see PARA 571.

4 Wireless Telegraphy Act 2006 s 104(1), (2).

5 As to OFCOM see PARA 507.

6 Wireless Telegraphy Act 2006 s 104(3). Provision in relation to the seizure and forfeiture of apparatus is made by Sch 6: s 104(4).

7 Apparatus is restricted apparatus for the purposes of the Wireless Telegraphy Act 2006 Sch 6 if custody or control of apparatus of any class or description to which it belongs is for the time being restricted by a restriction order under s 62 (see PARA 571): Sch 6 para 1(2). Schedule 6 applies to restricted apparatus seized in pursuance of a warrant granted under s 97 or in the exercise of the power conferred by s 99(3): Sch 6 para 1(1).

8 Wireless Telegraphy Act 2006 Sch 6 para 2(1).

9 Wireless Telegraphy Act 2006 Sch 6 para 2(2).

10 Ie in a manner authorised by the Wireless Telegraphy Act 2006 s 112: see PARA 513.

11 Wireless Telegraphy Act 2006 Sch 6 para 2(3).

12 Ie the requirements of the Wireless Telegraphy Act 2006 Sch 6 para 2.

13 Wireless Telegraphy Act 2006 Sch 6 para 2(4).

14 Wireless Telegraphy Act 2006 Sch 6 para 3.

15 Wireless Telegraphy Act 2006 Sch 6 para 4(1). A notice of claim must specify: (1) the name and address of the claimant; and (2) in the case of a claimant who is outside the United Kingdom, the name and address of a solicitor in the United Kingdom who is authorised to accept service of process and to act on behalf of the claimant: Sch 6 para 4(2). Service of process upon a solicitor so specified is to be taken to be proper service upon the claimant: Sch 6 para 4(3). As to the meaning of 'United Kingdom' see PARA 510 note 13.

16 Wireless Telegraphy Act 2006 Sch 6 para 5. The statutory requirements are those of Sch 6 paras 3, 4.

17 Wireless Telegraphy Act 2006 Sch 6 para 6(1). Proceedings for condemnation are civil proceedings and may be instituted, in England or Wales, in the High Court or in a magistrates' court: Sch 6 para 8. Proceedings for the condemnation of restricted apparatus instituted in a magistrates' court in England or Wales may be so instituted: (1) in a court having jurisdiction in a place where an offence under s 66 involving that apparatus was committed; (2) in a court having jurisdiction in proceedings for such an offence; (3) in a court having jurisdiction in the place where the claimant resides or, if the claimant has specified a solicitor under Sch 6 para 4, in the place where that solicitor has his office; or (4) in a court having jurisdiction in the place where that apparatus was seized or to which it was first brought after being seized: Sch 6 para 9.

18 Wireless Telegraphy Act 2006 Sch 6 para 6(2).

19 Wireless Telegraphy Act 2006 Sch 6 para 7.

20 Wireless Telegraphy Act 2006 Sch 6 para 6(3).

21 Wireless Telegraphy Act 2006 Sch 6 para 6(4).

22 Wireless Telegraphy Act 2006 Sch 6 para 6(5).

23 Wireless Telegraphy Act 2006 Sch 6 para 10(1). Where, at the time of the seizure, the apparatus is the property of a body corporate, the property of two or more partners, or the property of more than five persons, the oath required by Sch 6 para 10 to be taken by the claimant, and any other thing required by Sch 6 or by rules of court to be done by the owner of the apparatus, may be done by a person falling within the following categories or by a person authorised to act on his behalf: (1) where the owner is a body corporate, the secretary or some duly authorised officer of that body; (2) where the owners are in partnership, any one or more of the owners; (3) where there are more than five owners and they are not in partnership, any two or more of the owners acting on behalf of themselves and any of their co-owners who are not acting on their own behalf: Sch 6 para 16(2), (3). These provisions apply for the purposes of a claim to the restricted apparatus and proceedings for its condemnation: Sch 6 para 16(1).

24 Wireless Telegraphy Act 2006 Sch 6 para 10(2). As to security for costs see CIVIL PROCEDURE.

25 Wireless Telegraphy Act 2006 Sch 6 para 10(3).

26 Wireless Telegraphy Act 2006 Sch 6 para 11(1). This does not affect any right to require the statement of a case for the opinion of the High Court: Sch 6 para 11(3). As to appeals from the magistrates' courts and the stating of cases see MAGISTRATES.

27 Wireless Telegraphy Act 2006 Sch 6 para 12.

28 Ie by or under the Wireless Telegraphy Act 2006 Sch 6.

29 Wireless Telegraphy Act 2006 Sch 6 para 13(1), (2).

30 Wireless Telegraphy Act 2006 Sch 6 para 13(3).

31 Wireless Telegraphy Act 2006 Sch 6 para 14.

32 Wireless Telegraphy Act 2006 Sch 6 para 15.

33 Wireless Telegraphy Act 2006 Sch 6 para 17.

583. Unauthorised frequency use for the provision of mobile satellite services.
A person[1] commits an offence if that person uses the frequency bands 1980 to
2010MHz and 2170 to 2200MHz or any part of those bands for the provision
of mobile satellite services[2] except under and in accordance with an
authorisation[3] granted by OFCOM[4]. A person who commits such an offence is
liable, on conviction on indictment, to an unlimited fine or, on summary
conviction, to a fine of not more than level 5 on the standard scale (if not
calculated on a daily basis) or a fine of not more than £100 a day[5].

1 As to the meaning of 'person' see PARA 510 note 1.
2 As to the meaning of 'mobile satellite services' see PARA 564 note 8.
3 As to the meaning of 'an authorisation' see PARA 564 note 2.
4 Provision of Mobile Satellite Services (European Union) Regulations 2010, SI 2010/672,
   reg 2(1). As to the regulations see PARAS 564–567. As to OFCOM see PARA 507.
5 Provision of Mobile Satellite Services (European Union) Regulations 2010, SI 2010/672,
   reg 2(2). As to the standard scale see SENTENCING AND DISPOSITION OF OFFENDERS vol 92
   (2010) PARA 142.

(iii) Fraudulent Reception of Transmissions

584. Devices designed to circumvent copy-protection. A person
communicating to the public[1] a computer program to which a technical device[2]
has been applied has the same rights[3] as a copyright owner[4] has in respect of an
infringement of copyright against a person who, knowing or having reason to
believe[5] that it will be used to make infringing copies[6]:

(1) manufactures for sale or hire, imports[7], distributes, sells[8] or lets for hire,
    offers or exposes for sale[9] or hire, advertises for sale or hire or has in his
    possession for commercial purposes any means the sole intended
    purpose of which is to facilitate the unauthorised removal or
    circumvention of the technical device; or

(2) publishes information intended to enable or assist persons to remove or
    circumvent the technical device[10].

Further, he has the same rights to delivery up[11] or seizure[12] in relation to any
such means which a person has in his possession, custody or control with the
intention that it should be used to facilitate the unauthorised removal or
circumvention of any technical device which has been applied to a computer
program, as a copyright owner has in relation to an infringing copy[13].

Actions for infringement are brought in the same way as actions for
infringement of copyright; and the presumptions as to certain matters relating to
copyright[14], the withdrawal of privilege against self-incrimination in certain
proceedings relating to intellectual property[15] and the court's power to make
orders for the disposal of anything delivered up pursuant to an order for delivery
up or after seizure[16] also apply to such actions[17].

1 References to 'communication to the public' are to communication to the public by electronic
   transmission, and in relation to a work include: (1) the broadcasting of the work; (2) the making
   available to the public of the work by electronic transmission in such a way that members of the
   public may access it from a place and at a time individually chosen by them: see the Copyright,
   Designs and Patents Act 1988 s 20(2), applied by s 296(8) (both substituted by SI 2003/2498);
   and COPYRIGHT, DESIGN RIGHT AND RELATED RIGHTS vol 9(2) (2006 Reissue) PARA 326.
2 References to a technical device in relation to a computer program are references to any device
   intended to prevent or restrict acts that are not authorised by the copyright owner of that
   computer program and are restricted by copyright: see the Copyright, Designs and Patents
   Act 1988 s 296(6) (s 296 substituted by SI 2003/2498); and COPYRIGHT, DESIGN RIGHT AND
   RELATED RIGHTS vol 9(2) (2006 Reissue) PARA 485.

3   It is unlikely that these are proprietary rights: cf *BBC Enterprises Ltd v Hi-Tech Xtravision Ltd* [1990] Ch 609, [1990] 2 All ER 118, CA; affd on other grounds [1991] 2 AC 327, [1991] 3 All ER 257, HL. As to licences of copyright see COPYRIGHT, DESIGN RIGHT AND RELATED RIGHTS vol 9(2) (2006 Reissue) PARA 175 et seq.

4   As to who is the owner of the copyright in a work see COPYRIGHT, DESIGN RIGHT AND RELATED RIGHTS vol 9(2) (2006 Reissue) PARA 118 et seq.

5   As to the meaning of 'know or have reason to believe' see COPYRIGHT, DESIGN RIGHT AND RELATED RIGHTS vol 9(2) (2006 Reissue) PARA 334.

6   As to the meaning of 'infringing copy' see COPYRIGHT, DESIGN RIGHT AND RELATED RIGHTS vol 9(2) (2006 Reissue) PARA 334.

7   It has been held that importation occurs when the goods are physically received into the United Kingdom so as to become subject to the provisions of the Copyright, Designs and Patents Act 1988: see *LA Gear Inc v Hi-Tech Sports plc* [1992] FSR 121, CA.

8   A person who sells may include a person such as an employee, who actually hands over the infringing copy to a purchaser and takes charge of the money even though the contract of sale is between his employer and the purchaser: see eg *Preston v Albuery* [1964] 2 QB 796, [1963] 3 All ER 897, DC.

9   As to the meaning of 'offer or expose for sale' see COPYRIGHT, DESIGN RIGHT AND RELATED RIGHTS vol 9(2) (2006 Reissue) PARA 330.

10 See the Copyright, Designs and Patents Act 1988 s 296(1), (2)(a) (as substituted: see note 2); and COPYRIGHT, DESIGN RIGHT AND RELATED RIGHTS vol 9(2) (2006 Reissue) PARA 485. As to copyright in computer programs see COPYRIGHT, DESIGN RIGHT AND RELATED RIGHTS vol 9(2) (2006 Reissue) PARA 72. As to the rights and remedies for infringement of copyright see COPYRIGHT, DESIGN RIGHT AND RELATED RIGHTS vol 9(2) (2006 Reissue) PARA 410 et seq.

11 Ie under the Copyright, Designs and Patents Act 1988 s 99: see COPYRIGHT, DESIGN RIGHT AND RELATED RIGHTS vol 9(2) (2006 Reissue) PARA 420.

12 Ie under the Copyright, Designs and Patents Act 1988 s 100: see COPYRIGHT, DESIGN RIGHT AND RELATED RIGHTS vol 9(2) (2006 Reissue) PARA 421.

13 See the Copyright, Designs and Patents Act 1988 s 296(4) (as substituted: see note 2); and COPYRIGHT, DESIGN RIGHT AND RELATED RIGHTS vol 9(2) (2006 Reissue) PARA 485.

14 Ie the presumptions in the Copyright, Designs and Patents Act 1988 ss 104–106: see COPYRIGHT, DESIGN RIGHT AND RELATED RIGHTS vol 9(2) (2006 Reissue) PARAS 431–433.

15 Ie the withdrawal of privilege contained in the Senior Courts Act 1981 s 72: see COPYRIGHT, DESIGN RIGHT AND RELATED RIGHTS vol 9(2) (2006 Reissue) PARA 435. As to the renaming of the Senior Courts Act 1981 see PARA 941 note 12.

16 Ie an order under the Copyright, Designs and Patents Act 1988 s 114: see COPYRIGHT, DESIGN RIGHT AND RELATED RIGHTS vol 9(2) (2006 Reissue) PARA 422.

17 See the Copyright, Designs and Patents Act 1988 s 296(7) (as substituted (see note 2); and amended by the Constitutional Reform Act 2005 s 59(5), Sch 11 Pt 1 para 1(2)); and COPYRIGHT, DESIGN RIGHT AND RELATED RIGHTS vol 9(2) (2006 Reissue) PARA 485.

585.   Offence of fraudulently receiving programmes. A person who dishonestly receives a programme included in a broadcasting[1] service provided from a place in the United Kingdom[2] with intent to avoid payment of any charge applicable to the reception[3] of the programme commits an offence and is liable on summary conviction to a fine not exceeding level 5 on the standard scale[4].

Where such an offence committed by a body corporate[5] is proved to have been committed with the consent or connivance[6] of a director, manager[7], secretary or other similar officer of the body, or a person purporting to act in any such capacity, he as well as the body corporate is guilty of the offence and liable to be proceeded against and punished accordingly[8].

1   As to the meaning of 'broadcasting' see COPYRIGHT, DESIGN RIGHT AND RELATED RIGHTS vol 9(2) (2006 Reissue) PARA 89.

2   As to the meaning of 'place from which a broadcast is made' see COPYRIGHT, DESIGN RIGHT AND RELATED RIGHTS vol 9(2) (2006 Reissue) PARA 88. As to the meaning of 'United Kingdom' see PARA 510 note 13.

3   As to the meaning of 'reception of a broadcast' see COPYRIGHT, DESIGN RIGHT AND RELATED RIGHTS vol 9(2) (2006 Reissue) PARA 89.

4　See the Copyright, Designs and Patents Act 1988 s 297(1) (amended by SI 2003/2498); and COPYRIGHT, DESIGN RIGHT AND RELATED RIGHTS vol 9(2) (2006 Reissue) PARA 491. As to the standard scale see SENTENCING AND DISPOSITION OF OFFENDERS vol 92 (2010) PARA 142.

5　In relation to a body corporate whose affairs are managed by its members, 'director' means a member of the body corporate: see the Copyright, Designs and Patents Act 1988 s 297(2); and COPYRIGHT, DESIGN RIGHT AND RELATED RIGHTS vol 9(2) (2006 Reissue) PARA 491.

6　'Connive' means that a person is aware of what is going on, turns a blind eye and does nothing about it: see *Huckerby v Elliott* [1970] 1 All ER 189.

7　'Manager' is likely to mean someone who is connected with the management of the affairs of the company as a whole: see *Gibson v Barton* (1875) LR 10 QB 329; *Registrar of Restrictive Trading Agreements v WH Smith & Son Ltd* [1969] 3 All ER 1065, [1969] 1 WLR 1460, CA; *Tesco Supermarkets Ltd v Natrass* [1972] AC 153, [1971] 2 All ER 127, HL; *R v Boal* [1992] QB 591, [1992] 3 All ER 117, CA; and COMPANIES vol 14 (2009) PARA 607.

8　See the Copyright, Designs and Patents Act 1988 s 297(2); and COPYRIGHT, DESIGN RIGHT AND RELATED RIGHTS vol 9(2) (2006 Reissue) PARA 491.

586. Unauthorised decoders. A person commits an offence if he: (1) makes, imports[1], distributes, sells[2] or lets for hire or offers or exposes for sale or hire[3] any unauthorised[4] decoder[5]; (2) has in his possession for commercial purposes any unauthorised decoder; (3) instals, maintains or replaces for commercial purposes any unauthorised decoder; or (4) advertises any unauthorised decoder for sale or hire or otherwise promotes any unauthorised decoder by means of commercial communications[6]. A person guilty of such an offence is liable on summary conviction, to imprisonment for a term not exceeding six months, or to a fine not exceeding the statutory maximum[7], or to both, and on conviction on indictment, to imprisonment for a term not exceeding ten years, or to a fine, or to both[8].

It is a defence to any prosecution for an offence under these provisions for the defendant to prove that he did not know, and had no reasonable ground for believing, that the decoder was an unauthorised decoder[9].

1　As to the meaning of 'import' see PARA 584 note 7.

2　See PARA 584 note 8.

3　Since the Copyright, Designs and Patents Act 1988 refers to separate acts of selling, offering for sale and exposing for sale, it is thought that the expression 'offers for sale' would be interpreted according to the general law of contract so that exposure of goods in a shop window would be held to be an invitation to treat: see *Fisher v Bell* [1961] 1 QB 394, [1960] 3 All ER 731; *Pharmaceutical Society of Great Britain v Boots Cash Chemists (Southern) Ltd* [1953] 1 QB 401, [1953] 1 All ER 482, CA. An advertisement may be no more than an invitation to treat: see *Partridge v Crittenden* [1968] 2 All ER 421, [1968] 1 WLR 1204, DC. It has been held that an article which is visible to the intending purchaser is exposed for sale, even though it cannot properly be inspected by him because of intervening packaging: *Wheat v Brown* [1892] 1 QB 418.

4　For these purposes, 'unauthorised', in relation to a decoder (see note 5), means that the decoder is designed or adapted to enable an encrypted transmission, or any service of which it forms part, to be accessed in an intelligible form without payment of the fee (however imposed) which the person making the transmission, or on whose behalf it is made, charges for accessing the transmission or service (whether by the circumvention of any conditional access technology related to the transmission or service or by any other means); 'conditional access technology' means any technical measure or arrangement whereby access to encrypted transmissions in an intelligible form is made conditional on prior individual authorisation; and 'encrypted' includes subjected to scrambling or the operation of cryptographic envelopes, electronic locks, passwords or any other analogous application: see the Copyright, Designs and Patents Act 1988 s 297A(4) (s 297A added by the Broadcasting Act 1990 s 179(1); and substituted by SI 2000/1175); and COPYRIGHT, DESIGN RIGHT AND RELATED RIGHTS vol 9(2) (2006 Reissue) PARA 492. 'Transmission' means: (1) any programme included in a broadcasting service which is provided from a place in the United Kingdom or any other member state; or (2) an information society service (within the meaning of European Parliament and Council Directive (EC) 98/34 (OJ L204, 21.07.98, p 37), as amended by European Parliament and Council Directive (EC) 98/48 (OJ L217, 05.08.98, p 18)) which is provided from a place in the United Kingdom or any other member state: see the Copyright, Designs and Patents Act 1988 s 297A(4) (as so added and substituted; and amended by SI 2003/2498); and COPYRIGHT, DESIGN RIGHT AND RELATED RIGHTS vol 9(2) (2006 Reissue) PARA 492. As to the meaning of 'broadcasting' see COPYRIGHT, DESIGN RIGHT AND RELATED RIGHTS vol 9(2) (2006 Reissue) PARA 89; and as to the meaning of 'place from which a broadcast is made' see COPYRIGHT, DESIGN RIGHT AND RELATED RIGHTS vol 9(2) (2006 Reissue) PARA 88. As to the meaning of 'United Kingdom' see PARA 510 note 13.

5   For these purposes, 'decoder' means any apparatus which is designed or adapted to enable (whether on its own or with any other apparatus) an encrypted transmission to be decoded; and 'apparatus' includes any device, component or electronic data (including software): see the Copyright, Designs and Patents Act 1988 s 297A(4) (as added and substituted: see note 4); and COPYRIGHT, DESIGN RIGHT AND RELATED RIGHTS vol 9(2) (2006 Reissue) PARA 492.

6   See the Copyright, Designs and Patents Act 1988 s 297A(1) (as added and substituted: see note 4); and COPYRIGHT, DESIGN RIGHT AND RELATED RIGHTS vol 9(2) (2006 Reissue) PARA 492. See also *R v Bridgeman and Butt* [1996] FSR 538 (where the defendants who re-enabled disabled smart cards or extended the range of services for which a particular card had been enabled were charged with conspiracy to defraud). The Copyright, Designs and Patents Act 1988 s 297A(1) applies only to an offence committed on or after 1 October 1996: see the Broadcasting Act 1996 s 140(2) (repealed).

7   As to the statutory maximum see SENTENCING AND DISPOSITION OF OFFENDERS vol 92 (2010) PARA 140.

8   See the Copyright, Designs and Patents Act 1988 s 297A(2) (as added and substituted (see note 4); and amended by the Copyright, etc and Trade Marks (Offences and Enforcement) Act 2002 s 1(1), (4)); and COPYRIGHT, DESIGN RIGHT AND RELATED RIGHTS. For further provision as to search warrants see the Copyright, Designs and Patents Act 1988 s 297B; and COPYRIGHT, DESIGN RIGHT AND RELATED RIGHTS. As to forfeiture of unauthorised decoders see s 297C; and COPYRIGHT, DESIGN RIGHT AND RELATED RIGHTS.

9   See the Copyright, Designs and Patents Act 1988 s 297A(3) (as added and substituted: see note 4); and COPYRIGHT, DESIGN RIGHT AND RELATED RIGHTS vol 9(2) (2006 Reissue) PARA 492.

587.   Power to extend provisions relating to fraudulent reception of transmissions.   Her Majesty may by Order in Council direct that the provisions relating to the fraudulent reception of transmissions[1] extend to the Isle of Man or any of the Channel Islands, with such exceptions and modifications as may be specified in the Order[2].

Her Majesty may by Order in Council provide that the offence of fraudulently receiving programmes[3] applies in relation to programmes included in services provided from a country[4] or territory outside the United Kingdom, and that the rights and remedies in respect of apparatus etc used for the unauthorised reception of transmissions[5] apply in relation to such programmes and to encrypted transmissions sent from such a country or territory[6].

A statutory instrument containing such an Order in Council is subject to annulment in pursuance of a resolution of either House of Parliament[7].

Where the offence of fraudulently receiving programmes and the rights and remedies in respect of apparatus etc used for the unauthorised reception of transmissions apply in relation to a broadcasting[8] service, they also apply to any service run for the person providing that service, or a person providing programmes for that service, which consists wholly or mainly in the sending by means of a telecommunications system of sounds or visual images, or both[9].

1   Ie the Copyright, Designs and Patents Act 1988 ss 297–299: see the text and notes 3–9; and PARAS 585–586.

2   See the Copyright, Designs and Patents Act 1988 s 304(4)(d), (5); and COPYRIGHT, DESIGN RIGHT AND RELATED RIGHTS vol 9(2) (2006 Reissue) PARA 496. Any power conferred by the Copyright, Designs and Patents Act 1988 to make provision by Order in Council for or in connection with the extent of provisions of that Act to a country outside the United Kingdom includes power to extend to that country, subject to any modifications specified in the Order, any provision of that Act which amends or repeals an enactment extending to that country: see s 304(6); and COPYRIGHT, DESIGN RIGHT AND RELATED RIGHTS vol 9(2) (2006 Reissue) PARA

496. As to the Order made see the Copyright, Designs and Patents Act 1988 (Guernsey) Order 1989, SI 1989/1997. As to the meaning of 'United Kingdom' see PARA 510 note 13.

3 Ie the Copyright, Designs and Patents Act 1988 s 297: see PARA 585; and COPYRIGHT, DESIGN RIGHT AND RELATED RIGHTS vol 9(2) (2006 Reissue) PARA 491. As to the meaning of 'programme' see COPYRIGHT, DESIGN RIGHT AND RELATED RIGHTS vol 9(2) (2006 Reissue) PARA 89.

4 As to the meaning of 'country' see COPYRIGHT, DESIGN RIGHT AND RELATED RIGHTS vol 9(2) (2006 Reissue) PARA 59.

5 Ie the Copyright, Designs and Patents Act 1988 s 298: see PARA 941; and COPYRIGHT, DESIGN RIGHT AND RELATED RIGHTS vol 9(2) (2006 Reissue) PARA 495.

6 See the Copyright, Designs and Patents Act 1988 s 299(1); and COPYRIGHT, DESIGN RIGHT AND RELATED RIGHTS vol 9(2) (2006 Reissue) PARA 496. As to the Order made see the Fraudulent Reception of Transmissions (Guernsey) Order 1989, SI 1989/2003.

7 See the Copyright, Designs and Patents Act 1988 s 299(3); and COPYRIGHT, DESIGN RIGHT AND RELATED RIGHTS vol 9(2) (2006 Reissue) PARA 496.

8 As to the meaning of 'broadcasting' see COPYRIGHT, DESIGN RIGHT AND RELATED RIGHTS vol 9(2) (2006 Reissue) PARA 89.

9 See the Copyright, Designs and Patents Act 1988 s 299(4); and COPYRIGHT, DESIGN RIGHT AND RELATED RIGHTS vol 9(2) (2006 Reissue) PARAS 491, 495.

(iv) Marine Broadcasting

588. Broadcasting from ships, aircraft and marine structures. It is unlawful[1], in the case of any ship[2] or aircraft[3], to make a broadcast[4] from it while it is in or over the United Kingdom[5] or external waters[6] or, in the case of a British-registered[7] ship or British-registered aircraft[8], to make a broadcast from it while it is not in or over the United Kingdom or external waters[9]. If a broadcast is made from a ship in contravention of this prohibition, an offence is committed by the owner of the ship, the master[10] of the ship and a person who operates, or participates in the operation of, the apparatus by means of which the broadcast is made[11]. If a broadcast is made from an aircraft in contravention of the prohibition, an offence is committed by the operator[12] of the aircraft, the commander of the aircraft and a person who operates, or participates in the operation of, the apparatus by means of which the broadcast is made[13]. A person commits an offence if he procures a broadcast to be made in contravention the prohibition[14].

It is also unlawful to make a broadcast from: (1) a structure, other than a ship, that is affixed to, or supported by, the bed of tidal waters in the United Kingdom, external waters or waters in a designated area[15]; or (2) any other object in those waters[16]. A person commits an offence if he operates, or participates in the operation of, apparatus by means of which a broadcast is made in contravention this prohibition[17], or if he procures a broadcast to be made in contravention of the prohibition[18].

It is unlawful to make a broadcast that is capable of being received in the United Kingdom, or to make a broadcast that causes interference[19] with any wireless telegraphy in the United Kingdom, from a ship (other than a British-registered ship) while it is within a prescribed[20] area of the high seas[21]. If a broadcast is made in contravention of this prohibition, an offence is committed by the owner of the ship from which the broadcast is made, the master of the ship and a person who operates, or participates in the operation of, apparatus by means of which the broadcast is made[22]. A person commits an offence if he procures a broadcast to be made in contravention the prohibition[23].

A British person[24] commits an offence if he operates, or participates in the operation of, apparatus by means of which a broadcast is made:

(a)   from a ship (other than a British-registered ship) while it is on the high seas;

(b)   from an aircraft (other than a British-registered aircraft) while it is on or over the high seas;

(c)   from a structure (other than a ship) that is affixed to, or supported by, the bed of the high seas; or

(d)   from an object on the high seas (other than a structure falling within head (c), a ship or an aircraft)[25].

A person commits an offence if he procures a broadcast to be made as mentioned above[26].

A person commits an offence if, from anywhere in the United Kingdom or external waters, he participates in the management, financing, operation or day-to-day running of a broadcasting station[27] by which broadcasts are made in contravention[28] of the above provisions[29].

1   Nothing in the Wireless Telegraphy Act 2006 Pt 5 (ss 77–95) makes it unlawful to do anything under and in accordance with a wireless telegraphy licence, or to procure anything to be so done: s 94. As to the meaning of 'wireless telegraphy licence' see PARA 514 note 4.

2   As to the meaning of 'ship' see PARA 510 note 12.

3   As to aircraft see AIR LAW vol 2 (2008) PARA 353 et seq.

4   In the Wireless Telegraphy Act 2006 Pt 5, 'broadcast' means a broadcast by wireless telegraphy of sounds or visual images intended for general reception (whether or not the sounds or images are actually received by anyone), but does not include a broadcast consisting in a message or signal sent in connection with navigation or for the purpose of securing safety: s 95(1). As to the meaning of 'wireless telegraphy' see PARA 510 note 1.

5   As to the meaning of 'United Kingdom' see PARA 510 note 13.

6   'External waters' means the whole of the sea adjacent to the United Kingdom that is within the seaward limits of UK territorial sea: Wireless Telegraphy Act 2006 s 95(1). As to the meaning of 'UK territorial sea' see PARA 510 note 14.

7   'British-registered' means registered in the United Kingdom, the Isle of Man or any of the Channel Islands: Wireless Telegraphy Act 2006 s 95(1). As to the registration of ships see SHIPPING AND MARITIME LAW vol 93 (2008) PARA 245 et seq.

8   As to the registration of aircraft see AIR LAW vol 2 (2008) PARA 367 et seq.

9   Wireless Telegraphy Act 2006 s 77(1).

10   'Master', in relation to a ship, includes any other person (except a pilot) who has command or charge of the ship: Wireless Telegraphy Act 2006 s 77(5).

11   Wireless Telegraphy Act 2006 s 77(2). As to penalties and proceedings see PARA 591.

12   'Operator', in relation to an aircraft, means the person who at the relevant time has the management of the aircraft: Wireless Telegraphy Act 2006 s 77(5).

13   Wireless Telegraphy Act 2006 s 77(3).

14   Wireless Telegraphy Act 2006 s 77(4).

15   'Designated area' has the meaning given by the Continental Shelf Act 1964 s 1(7) (see FUEL AND ENERGY vol 19(3) (2007 Reissue) PARA 1636): Wireless Telegraphy Act 2006 s 95(1).

16   Wireless Telegraphy Act 2006 s 78(1), (2). Section 78(2) does not apply by virtue of paragraph (b) to a broadcast made from a ship or aircraft: s 78(3).

17   Wireless Telegraphy Act 2006 s 78(4).

18   Wireless Telegraphy Act 2006 s 78(5).

19   As to the meaning of 'interference' see PARA 541 note 2.

20   'Prescribed' means prescribed for the purposes of the Wireless Telegraphy Act 2006 s 79 by an order made by the Secretary of State: s 79(5). As to the Secretary of State see PARA 507 note 32.

21   Wireless Telegraphy Act 2006 s 79(1). 'The high seas' means seas that are not within the seaward limits of UK territorial sea or of the territorial waters adjacent to a country or territory outside the United Kingdom: s 95(1); and cf WATER AND WATERWAYS vol 100 (2009) PARA 31.

22   Wireless Telegraphy Act 2006 s 79(2). The making of a broadcast does not contravene s 79(1) if it is shown to have been authorised under the law of a country or territory outside the United Kingdom: s 79(4).

23   Wireless Telegraphy Act 2006 s 79(3).

24   For the purposes of the Wireless Telegraphy Act 2006 Pt 5, references to a 'British person' are references to: (1) a British citizen, a British overseas territories citizen, a British national (overseas) or a British overseas citizen; (2) a person who under the British Nationality Act 1981

is a British subject; or (3) a British protected person within the meaning given by s 50(1) of that Act: Wireless Telegraphy Act 2006 s 95(2). As to the various categories of citizenship see BRITISH NATIONALITY. Persons who maintain from within the United Kingdom pirate radio stations operating outside territorial waters may be guilty of conspiracy to contravene the Wireless Telegraphy Act 2006 s 80, notwithstanding the fact that the broadcasters themselves do not fall within s 80(1): *R v Murray* [1990] 1 WLR 1360, [1990] Crim LR 803, CA.

25 Wireless Telegraphy Act 2006 s 80(1). Section 80(1) does not apply: (1) by virtue of s 80(1)(a), to a broadcast made in contravention of s 79(1); (2) by virtue of s 80(1)(c) or (d), to a broadcast made from a structure or other object in waters in a designated area: s 80(2).

26 Wireless Telegraphy Act 2006 s 80(3).

27 'Broadcasting station' means a business or other operation (whether or not in the nature of a commercial venture) that is engaged in the making of broadcasts: Wireless Telegraphy Act 2006 s 81(2).

28 Ie in contravention of the Wireless Telegraphy Act 2006 s 77(1), 78(2) or 79(1) or as mentioned in s 80(1).

29 Wireless Telegraphy Act 2006 s 81(1).

589. Offences of facilitating broadcasting. A person who does any of the following acts is, in certain circumstances[1], guilty of an offence[2]:

(1) if he provides a ship or aircraft to another, or agrees to do so, knowing, or having reasonable cause to believe, that broadcasts are to be made from it in contravention of the prohibition against broadcasting from ships or aircraft[3] or while it is on or over the high seas[4];

(2) if he carries wireless telegraphy apparatus[5] in a ship or aircraft, or agrees to do so, or he supplies[6] wireless telegraphy apparatus to a ship or aircraft, or instals such apparatus in a ship or aircraft, knowing, or having reasonable cause to believe, that by means of the apparatus broadcasts are to be made from the ship or aircraft as mentioned in head (1)[7];

(3) if: (a) he supplies goods or materials for the operation or maintenance of a ship or aircraft, for the operation or maintenance of wireless telegraphy apparatus installed in a ship or aircraft, or for the sustenance or comfort of the persons on board a ship or aircraft; (b) he carries by water or air goods or persons to or from a ship or aircraft, or (c) he engages a person as an officer or one of the crew of a ship or aircraft, knowing, or having reasonable cause to believe, that broadcasts are made, or are to be made, from the ship or aircraft as mentioned in head (1)[8];

(4) if he instals wireless telegraphy apparatus on or in a structure or other object, or supplies such apparatus for installation on or in a structure or other object, knowing, or having reasonable cause to believe, that by means of the apparatus broadcasts are to be made from it in contravention of the prohibition on broadcasting from such a structure or object[9] or while it is on the high seas[10];

(5) if, in the case of a structure or other object[11]: (a) he supplies goods or materials for its maintenance, for the operation or maintenance of wireless telegraphy apparatus installed in or on it or for the sustenance or comfort of the persons in or on it; (b) he carries goods or persons to or from it by water or air; or (c) he engages a person to render services in or on it, knowing, or having reasonable cause to believe, that broadcasts are made, or are to be made, from the structure or other object as mentioned in head (1)[12];

(6) if he repairs or maintains wireless telegraphy apparatus knowing, or

having reasonable cause to believe, that by means of it broadcasts are made, or are to be made in contravention of the prohibitions[13] on such broadcasts[14].

A person commits an offence if he procures, in the United Kingdom, another person to do, outside the United Kingdom, anything that would have constituted an offence under sections the above provisions[15] had the other person done it in the United Kingdom[16].

1   A person who does an act mentioned in the Wireless Telegraphy Act 2006 s 82, 83, 84 (see the text and notes 2–16) or s 85 (see PARA 590) does not commit an offence under that section unless condition A, B, C, D or E is satisfied: s 86(1). Sections 82–85 are subject to s 86: see ss 82(8), 83(8), 84(2), 85(6).

Condition A is satisfied if he does the act in the United Kingdom or external waters: s 86(2).

Condition B is satisfied if he does the act in a British-registered ship or British-registered aircraft while it is not in or over the United Kingdom or external waters: s 86(3).

Condition C is satisfied if, in a case where: (1) neither condition A nor condition B is satisfied; but (2) the broadcasts in question are made, or are to be made, from a structure or other object (which is not a ship or aircraft) in waters in a designated area, he does the act on that structure or other object within those waters: s 86(4).

Condition D is satisfied if, in a case where: (a) neither condition A nor condition B is satisfied; but (b) the broadcasts in question are made, or are to be made, from a ship in contravention of s 79(1) (see PARA 588), he does the act in that ship within an area of the high seas that is prescribed for the purposes of s 79: s 86(5).

Condition E is satisfied if he is a British person and he does the act on or over the high seas: s 86(6).

As to the meaning of 'broadcast' see PARA 588 note 4. As to the meaning of 'United Kingdom' see PARA 510 note 13; as to the meaning of 'British-registered' see PARA 588 note 7; as to the meaning of 'ship' see PARA 510 note 12; as to the meaning of 'external waters' see PARA 588 note 6; as to the meaning of 'designated area' see PARA 588 note 15; as to the meaning of 'British person' see PARA 588 note 24; and as to the meaning of 'high seas' see PARA 588 note 21. As to aircraft see AIR LAW vol 2 (2008) PARA 353 et seq.

2   See the Wireless Telegraphy Act 2006 ss 82–85. As to penalties and proceedings see PARA 591.

3   Ie in contravention of the Wireless Telegraphy Act 2006 s 77(1): see PARA 588.

4   Wireless Telegraphy Act 2006 s 82(1).

5   As to the meaning of 'wireless telegraphy apparatus' see PARA 510 note 9.

6   As to references to 'supplying' see PARA 535 note 4.

7   Wireless Telegraphy Act 2006 s 82(2).

8   Wireless Telegraphy Act 2006 s 82(3). In proceedings for an offence under s 82 consisting in carrying goods or persons to or from a ship or aircraft, it is a defence for the defendant to prove: (1) that the ship or aircraft was, or was believed to be, wrecked, stranded or in distress, and that the goods or persons were carried for the purpose of preserving the ship or aircraft, or its cargo or equipment or saving the lives of persons on board the ship or aircraft; or (2) that a person on board the ship or aircraft was, or was believed to be, hurt, injured or ill, and that the goods or persons were carried for the purpose of securing that he received the necessary surgical or medical advice and attendance: s 82(4). The reference in s 82(4)(a) to persons carried for the purpose of saving lives is not to be read as excluding the persons whose lives were to be saved: s 82(5). The reference in s 82(4)(b) to persons carried for the purpose of securing that advice and attendance were received is not to be read as excluding the person who was (or was believed to be) hurt, injured or ill: s 82(6). In proceedings for an offence under s 82 consisting in carrying a person ('A') to or from a ship or aircraft, it is a defence for the defendant to prove that A was visiting the ship or aircraft for the purpose of exercising or performing a power or duty conferred or imposed on A by law: s 82(7).

9   Ie in contravention of the Wireless Telegraphy Act 2006 s 78(2): see PARA 588.

10   Wireless Telegraphy Act 2006 s 83(1).

11   In the Wireless Telegraphy Act 2006 s 83, references to a structure or other object do not include references to a ship or aircraft: s 83(7).

12   Wireless Telegraphy Act 2006 s 83(2). In proceedings for an offence under s 83 consisting in carrying goods or persons to or from a structure or other object, it is a defence for the defendant to prove: (1) that it was, or was believed to be, unsafe, and that the goods or persons were carried for the purpose of saving the lives of persons in or on it; or (2) that a person in or on it was, or was believed to be, hurt, injured or ill, and that the goods or persons were carried for

the purpose of securing that he received the necessary surgical or medical advice and attendance: s 83(3). The reference in s 83(3)(a) to persons carried for the purpose of saving lives is not to be read as excluding the persons whose lives were to be saved: s 83(4). The reference in s 83(3)(b) to persons carried for the purpose of securing that advice and attendance were received is not to be read as excluding the person who was (or was believed to be) hurt, injured or ill: s 83(5). In proceedings for an offence under s 83 consisting in carrying a person ('A') to or from a structure or other object, it is a defence for the defendant to prove that A was visiting it for the purpose of exercising or performing a power or duty conferred or imposed on A by law: s 83(6).

13 Ie in contravention of the Wireless Telegraphy Act 2006 s 77(1), 78(2) or 79(1) or as mentioned in s 80(1).
14 Wireless Telegraphy Act 2006 s 84(1).
15 Ie under the Wireless Telegraphy Act 2006 ss 82–84.
16 Wireless Telegraphy Act 2006 s 87.

590. Offences relating to matter broadcast. A person who does any of the following acts is, in certain circumstances[1], guilty of an offence[2]:

(1) if he supplies[3] a film or sound recording[4] knowing, or having reasonable cause to believe, that an unlawful broadcast[5] is to be made of it[6];

(2) if he makes a literary, dramatic or musical work[7] knowing, or having reasonable cause to believe, that an unlawful broadcast is to be made of it[8];

(3) if he makes an artistic work[9] knowing, or having reasonable cause to believe, that it is to be included in an unlawful television broadcast[10];

(4) if he participates[11] in an unlawful broadcast[12];

(5) if he advertises[13] by means of an unlawful broadcast or invites another to advertise by means of an unlawful broadcast that is to be made[14];

(6) if he publishes the times or other details of unlawful broadcasts that are to be made, or (otherwise than by publishing such details) publishes an advertisement of matter calculated to promote (whether directly or indirectly) the interests of a business whose activities consist in or include the operation of a station from which unlawful broadcasts are or are to be made[15].

A person commits an offence if he procures, in the United Kingdom, another person to do, outside the United Kingdom, anything that would have constituted an offence under sections the above provisions[16] had the other person done it in the United Kingdom[17].

1 See PARA 589 note 1.
2 See the Wireless Telegraphy Act 2006 s 85(1). As to penalties and proceedings see PARA 591.
3 As to references to 'supplying' see PARA 535 note 4.
4 'Film' and 'sound recording' have the same meanings as in the Copyright, Designs and Patents Act 1988 Pt I (ss 1–179) (see COPYRIGHT, DESIGN RIGHT AND RELATED RIGHTS vol 9(2) (2006 Reissue) PARAS 84, 86); definitions applied by the Wireless Telegraphy Act 2006 s 115(1).
5 An unlawful broadcast is a broadcast made in contravention of the Wireless Telegraphy Act 2006 s 77(1), 78(2) or 79(1) or as mentioned in s 80(1): s 85(2). As to the meaning of 'broadcast' see PARA 588 note 4.
6 Wireless Telegraphy Act 2006 s 85(1)(a).
7 'Literary, dramatic or musical work' has the same meaning as in the Copyright, Designs and Patents Act 1988 Pt I (see COPYRIGHT, DESIGN RIGHT AND RELATED RIGHTS vol 9(2) (2006 Reissue) PARAS 67, 73); definition applied by the Wireless Telegraphy Act 2006 s 115(1).
8 Wireless Telegraphy Act 2006 s 85(1)(b).
9 'Artistic work' has the same meaning as in the Copyright, Designs and Patents Act 1988 Pt I (see COPYRIGHT, DESIGN RIGHT AND RELATED RIGHTS vol 9(2) (2006 Reissue) PARA 75); definition applied by the Wireless Telegraphy Act 2006 s 115(1).
10 Wireless Telegraphy Act 2006 s 85(1)(c).
11 A person participates in a broadcast only if he is actually present as an announcer, as a performer or one of the performers concerned in an entertainment given or as the deliverer of a speech: Wireless Telegraphy Act 2006 s 85(3).

12 Wireless Telegraphy Act 2006 s 85(1)(d).

13 The cases in which a person is to be taken for the purposes of the Wireless Telegraphy Act 2006 s 85 as advertising by means of a broadcast include any case in which he causes or allows it to be stated, suggested or implied that entertainment included in the broadcast has been supplied by him or is provided wholly or partly at his expense: s 85(4). For the purposes of s 85 advertising by means of a broadcast takes place not only where the broadcast is made but also wherever it is received: s 85(5).

14 Wireless Telegraphy Act 2006 s 85(1)(e).

15 Wireless Telegraphy Act 2006 s 85(1)(f).

16 Ie under the Wireless Telegraphy Act 2006 s 85.

17 Wireless Telegraphy Act 2006 s 87.

591. Penalties and proceedings. A person[1] who commits an offence under Part 5 of the Wireless Telegraphy Act 2006[2] is liable, on summary conviction, to imprisonment for a term not exceeding 12 months or to a fine not exceeding the statutory maximum[3] or to both; and, on conviction on indictment, to imprisonment for a term not exceeding two years or to a fine or to both[4]. Proceedings in England and Wales for such an offence may be brought only by OFCOM[5] or by or with the consent of the Secretary of State[6] or the Director of Public Prosecutions[7].

Proceedings for any such offence may be taken, and the offence may for all incidental purposes be treated as having been committed, in any place in the United Kingdom[8]. For the purpose of the enforcement of Part 5, a member of a police force has in any area of the sea within the seaward limits of UK territorial sea[9] all the powers, protection and privileges which he has in the area for which he acts as constable[10].

1 As to the meaning of 'person' see PARA 510 note 1.

2 Ie the Wireless Telegraphy Act 2006 Pt 5 (ss 77–95): see PARAS 588–590.

3 As to the statutory maximum see SENTENCING AND DISPOSITION OF OFFENDERS vol 92 (2010) PARA 140.

4 Wireless Telegraphy Act 2006 s 93(1). A court may also order forfeiture: see PARA 579.

5 As to OFCOM see PARA 507.

6 As to the Secretary of State see PARA 507 note 32.

7 Wireless Telegraphy Act 2006 s 93(3). As to the Director of Public Prosecutions see CRIMINAL PROCEDURE vol 27 (2010) PARAS 23, 33 et seq.

8 Wireless Telegraphy Act 2006 s 107(1). As to the meaning of 'United Kingdom' see PARA 510 note 13.

9 As to the meaning of 'UK territorial sea' see PARA 510 note 14.

10 Wireless Telegraphy Act 2006 s 107(2), (3)(c). As to the powers of constables see POLICE vol 36(1) (2007 Reissue) PARA 101 et seq.

592. Powers of enforcement. If conditions A and B are satisfied in the case of a ship[1], structure or other object, an enforcement officer[2] may, with or without assistants[3], exercise the powers set out below in relation to it[4].

Condition A is satisfied if the enforcement officer has reasonable grounds for suspecting that: (1) an offence under Part 5 of the Wireless Telegraphy Act 2006[5] has been or is being committed by the making of a broadcast[6] from a ship, structure or other object in external waters[7] or in tidal waters in the United Kingdom or from a British-registered[8] ship while it is on the high seas[9]; (2) an offence[10] has been or is being committed by the making of a broadcast from a structure or other object in waters in a designated area[11]; or (3) an offence[12] has been or is being committed by the making of a broadcast from a ship[13].

Condition B is satisfied if a written authorisation has been issued by the Secretary of State or OFCOM for the exercise of the powers mentioned below in relation to that ship, structure or other object[14].

The powers which may be exercised are[15]:

(a)   to board and search the ship, structure or other object[16];

(b)   to seize and detain it, and any apparatus or other thing found in the course of the search that appears to him: (i) to have been used, or to have been intended to be used, in connection with the commission of the suspected offence; or (ii) to be evidence of the commission of the suspected offence[17];

(c)   to arrest and search any person who he has reasonable grounds to suspect has committed or is committing an offence under Part 5 if: (i) the person is on board the ship, structure or other object; or (ii) the officer has reasonable grounds for suspecting that the person was on board at, or shortly before, the time when the officer boarded the object[18];

(d)   to arrest any person: (i) who assaults him, or an assistant of his, while exercising any of the powers mentioned in heads (a) to (g); or (ii) who intentionally obstructs him, or an assistant of his, in the exercise of any of those powers[19];

(e)   to require any person on board the ship, structure or other object to produce any documents or other items that are in his custody or possession and are or may be evidence of the commission of an offence[20];

(f)   to require any such person to do anything for the purpose of: (i) enabling any apparatus or other thing to be rendered safe and, in the case of a ship, enabling the ship to be taken to a port; or (ii) facilitating in any other way the exercise of any of the powers mentioned in heads (a) to (g)[21];

(g)   to use reasonable force, if necessary, in exercising any of those powers[22].

If a written authorisation has been issued by the Secretary of State or OFCOM[23] under for the exercise of the powers mentioned in heads (a) to (g) in relation to a ship, structure or other object, and an enforcement officer has reasonable grounds for suspecting that an offence[24] has been or is being committed in connection with the making of a broadcast from that ship, structure or other object, the enforcement officer may, with or without assistants, exercise those powers in relation to any ship, structure or other object which he has reasonable grounds to suspect has been or is being used in connection with the commission of the offence[25].

If an enforcement officer has reasonable grounds for suspecting that an offence[26] has been or is being committed in connection with the making of a broadcast from a ship, structure or other object but no written authorisation has been issued[27] for the exercise of the powers mentioned above in relation to that ship, structure or other object, the enforcement officer may, with or without assistants, exercise those powers in relation to any ship, structure or other object which he has reasonable grounds to suspect has been or is being used in connection with the commission of the offence[28], provided that a written authorisation for this purpose has been issued by the Secretary of State or OFCOM for the exercise of those powers in relation to that ship, structure or other object[29].

Neither an enforcement officer nor an assistant of his is liable in civil or criminal proceedings for anything done in purported exercise of any of these powers if the court is satisfied that the act was done in good faith and that there were reasonable grounds for doing it[30]. Nothing in these provisions[31] affects the exercise of any powers exercisable apart from those provisions[32].

A person commits an offence if:

(A)   he assaults an enforcement officer, or an assistant of his, while he is exercising any of the powers mentioned above;

(B)   he intentionally obstructs an enforcement officer, or an assistant of his, in the exercise of any of those powers; or

(C)   he fails or refuses, without reasonable excuse, to comply with such a requirement as is mentioned in head (e) or (f) above[33].

1   As to the meaning of 'ship' see PARA 510 note 12.
2   The following persons are enforcement officers for these purposes: (1) persons authorised by the Secretary of State or OFCOM to exercise the powers conferred by the Wireless Telegraphy Act 2006 ss 89, 90; (2) police officers; (3) commissioned officers of Her Majesty's armed forces; (4) officers of Revenue and Customs; and (5) other persons who are British sea-fishery officers by virtue of the Sea Fisheries Act 1968 s 7(1): Wireless Telegraphy Act 2006 s 88(1). 'Armed forces' means the Royal Navy, the Royal Marines, the regular army and the regular air force, and a reserve or auxiliary force of any of those services that has been called out on permanent service or embodied: s 88(3). As to commissioned officers generally see ARMED FORCES. As to the Secretary of State see PARA 507 note 32. As to OFCOM see PARA 507. As to police officers see POLICE. As to officers of Revenue and Customs see CUSTOMS AND EXCISE vol 12(3) (2007 Reissue) PARA 901. As to British sea-fishery officers see AGRICULTURE AND FISHERIES vol 1(2) (2007 Reissue) PARA 963.
3   A reference in the Wireless Telegraphy Act 2006 ss 89–92, in relation to an enforcement officer, to an assistant is a reference to a person assigned to assist the enforcement officer in his duties: s 88(2). A reference in ss 89–92, in relation to an enforcement officer's assistant, to the exercise of any of the powers mentioned in s 89(4) is a reference to the exercise by the assistant of any of those powers on behalf of the officer: s 92(4).
4   Wireless Telegraphy Act 2006 s 89(1).
5   Ie the Wireless Telegraphy Act 2006 Pt 5 (ss 77–95): see PARAS 588–590.
6   As to the meaning of 'broadcast' see PARA 588 note 4.
7   As to the meaning of 'external waters' see PARA 588 note 6.
5   As to tidal waters see WATER AND WATERWAYS vol 100 (2009) PARA 71 et seq.
6   As to the meaning of 'United Kingdom' see PARA 510 note 13.
7   As to the registration of ships see SHIPPING AND MARITIME LAW vol 93 (2008) PARA 245 et seq.
8   As to the meaning of 'British-registered' see PARA 588 note 7.
9   As to the meaning of 'the high seas' see PARA 588 note 21.
10   Ie under the Wireless Telegraphy Act 2006 s 78: see PARA 588.
11   As to the meaning of 'designated area' see PARA 588 note 15.
12   Ie under the Wireless Telegraphy Act 2006 s 79: see PARA 588.
13   Wireless Telegraphy Act 2006 s 89(2).
14   Wireless Telegraphy Act 2006 s 89(3).
15   Wireless Telegraphy Act 2006 s 89(4). Except as provided in s 91(2), (3), the powers mentioned in s 89(4) may be exercised only in tidal waters in the United Kingdom or in external waters: s 91(1). The powers may in addition: (1) in the case of a suspected offence under Pt 5 committed in a British-registered ship while it is on the high seas, be exercised in relation to the ship on the high seas; (2) in the case of a suspected offence under s 78 (see PARA 588) committed on a structure or other object within waters in a designated area, be exercised in relation to the structure or other object within those waters; (3) in the case of a suspected offence under s 79 (see PARA 588) committed in a ship within an area of the high seas prescribed for the purposes of that section, be exercised in relation to the ship within that area of the high seas: s 91(2). Section 91(2) does not apply so far as the powers are exercisable by virtue of a written authorisation issued by OFCOM: s 91(3).
16   Wireless Telegraphy Act 2006 s 89(4)(a). In s 89(4)(a)–(c) and (e) a reference to the ship, structure or other object includes a reference to a ship's boat, or other vessel, used from it: s 89(5).
17   Wireless Telegraphy Act 2006 s 89(4)(b).
18   Wireless Telegraphy Act 2006 s 89(4)(c).
19   Wireless Telegraphy Act 2006 s 89(4)(d).
20   Wireless Telegraphy Act 2006 s 89(4)(e).
21   Wireless Telegraphy Act 2006 s 89(4)(f).

22 Wireless Telegraphy Act 2006 s 89(4)(g).
23 Ie under the Wireless Telegraphy Act 2006 s 89(3).
24 Ie under the Wireless Telegraphy Act 2006 s 82, 83, 84 or 85: see PARAS 589–590.
25 Wireless Telegraphy Act 2006 s 90(1), (2).
26 See note 24.
27 Ie under the Wireless Telegraphy Act 2006 s 89(3).
28 Wireless Telegraphy Act 2006 s 90(3), (4).
29 Wireless Telegraphy Act 2006 s 90(5).
30 Wireless Telegraphy Act 2006 s 92(2).
31 Ie in the Wireless Telegraphy Act 2006 ss 89–92.
32 Wireless Telegraphy Act 2006 s 92(3).
33 Wireless Telegraphy Act 2006 s 92(1). As to penalties and proceedings see PARA 591.

(v) Offences in the Broadcasting Acts 1990 and 1996

593.   Prohibition on providing television services without a licence.   Any person[1] who provides any relevant regulated television service[2] without being authorised to do so by or under a licence[3] is guilty of an offence[4]. A person guilty of such an offence is liable, on summary conviction, to a fine not exceeding the statutory maximum[5] and, on conviction on indictment, to a fine[6]. No proceedings in respect of such an offence may be instituted except by or with the consent of the Director of Public Prosecutions[7]. Compliance with the above provisions is enforceable by civil proceedings by the Crown for an injunction or for any other appropriate relief[8].

1   As to the meaning of 'person' see PARA 510 note 1. As to offences by bodies corporate see PARA 599.
2   'Relevant regulated television service' means a service falling, in pursuance of the Communications Act 2003 s 211(1) (see PARA 857), to be regulated by OFCOM, other than a television multiplex service: Broadcasting Act 1990 s 13(1A) (added by the Communications Act 2003 s 360(3), Sch 15 para 5(1), (3)). As to OFCOM see PARA 507. As to the meaning of 'television multiplex service' see PARA 697.
3   Ie by or under a licence under the Broadcasting Act 1990 Pt I (ss 3–71), or under the Broadcasting Act 1996 Pt I (ss 1–39).
4   Broadcasting Act 1990 s 13(1) (amended by the Broadcasting Act 1996 s 148(1), Sch 10 para 2; the Communications Act 2003 Sch 15 para 5(2); and SI 1997/1682). The Secretary of State may, after consultation with OFCOM, by order provide that the Broadcasting Act 1990 s 13(1) is not to apply to such services or descriptions of services as are specified in the order: s 13(2) (amended by the Communications Act 2003 Sch 15 para 5(4)). Such an order is subject to annulment in pursuance of a resolution of either House of Parliament: Broadcasting Act 1990 s 13(6). As to orders under this provision see the Broadcasting Act 1990 (Independent Television Services: Exceptions) Order 1990, SI 1990/2537. As to the Secretary of State see PARA 507 note 32.
       The Broadcasting Act 1990 s 13(1) does not apply to the following services or descriptions of services: (1) any television programme service provided under and in accordance with the transitional provisions relating to the Independent Broadcasting Authority's broadcasting services (see s 129, Sch 11; and PARA 550); and (2) any television programme service: (a) which is provided for reception at a place or places in the United Kingdom provided that no such place is a dwelling house (see PARA 751 note 3); (b) which is so provided for the purposes of its being presented there either to members of the public or to a group of persons some or all of whom do not have a business interest in hearing or seeing it; (c) which does not include any advertisement; and (d) in respect of which no payment is made either directly or indirectly for its provision by the persons to whom it is presented: Broadcasting Act 1990 (Independent Television Services: Exceptions) Order 1990, SI 1990/2537, art 2. As to the meaning of 'television programme service' see PARA 790 note 5; definition applied by the Broadcasting Act 1990 s 71(1) (definition substituted by the Communications Act 2003 s 360(3), Sch 15 Pt 1 para 31). As to the meaning of 'United Kingdom' see PARA 510 note 13. As to the Independent Broadcasting Authority see PARAS 501, 507.
       The news and information service provided by BBC World Service Television Limited (or any other company controlled by the BBC) (see PARA 821 note 11) together with European Channel

Broadcasting Limited and the entertainment service provided by the latter known as 'BBC World' and 'BBC Prime' respectively were exempted from the Broadcasting Act 1990 s 13(1): see the Broadcasting (Unlicensed Television Services) Exemption Order 1994, SI 1994/3172, art 2. However, this Order has been revoked by the Broadcasting (Unlicensed Television Services) Exemption (Revocation) Order 1999, SI 1999/2628, which came into force on 11 October 1999. As to the BBC see PARAS 603–626.

5   Broadcasting Act 1990 s 13(3)(a). As to the statutory maximum see SENTENCING AND DISPOSITION OF OFFENDERS vol 92 (2010) PARA 140.
6   Broadcasting Act 1990 s 13(3)(b).
7   Broadcasting Act 1990 s 13(4). As to the Director of Public Prosecutions see CRIMINAL PROCEDURE vol 27 (2010) PARAS 23, 33 et seq.
8   Broadcasting Act 1990 s 13(5).

594.   Notice to satellite uplinkers providing service which contravenes licence or is unlicensed.   Where a relevant regulated television service[1] or an on-demand programme service[2] is provided by a person who is deemed to be under the jurisdiction of the United Kingdom for the purpose of the Audiovisual Media Services Directive[3] by reason only of the person providing such a service by means of satellite uplink apparatus[4] situated within the United Kingdom[5], OFCOM[6] may give a notice in writing to a satellite uplinker[7] in relation to a relevant regulated television service if OFCOM is satisfied that the service is provided either in contravention of a licence[8] or otherwise than pursuant to such a licence[9].

OFCOM may give a notice in writing to a satellite uplinker in relation to an on-demand programme service if OFCOM is satisfied that the service is provided in contravention of a requirement of Part 4A[10] of the Communications Act 2003[11].

Where a notice is given to a satellite uplinker in relation to the provision of a service in contravention of a licence or in relation to an on-demand programme service, the notice must: (1) name the service; (2) specify the reasons why OFCOM considers that the relevant statutory provision is satisfied; and (3) specify the date by which the satellite uplinker must cease the uplinking of the service or a period during which the satellite uplinker must suspend the uplinking of the service[12].

Where a notice is given to a satellite uplinker in relation to the provision of a service otherwise than pursuant to a licence the notice must: (a) name the service; and (b) specify the date by which the satellite uplinker must cease the uplinking of the service or a period during which the satellite uplinker must suspend the uplinking of the service[13].

1   As to the meaning of 'relevant regulated television service' see PARA 593 note 2; definition applied by the Wireless Telegraphy Act 2006 s 9A(6) (s 9A added by SI 2009/2979).
2   As to the meaning of 'on-demand programme service' see PARA 784; definition applied by the Wireless Telegraphy Act 2006 s 9A(6) (as added: see note 1).
3   'The Audiovisual Media Services Directive' means European Parliament and Council Directive (EU) 2010/13 (OJ L95, 15.4.2010, p 1) on the coordination of certain provisions laid down by law, regulation or administrative action in member states concerning the provision of audiovisual media services: Wireless Telegraphy Act 2006 s 115(1) (definition added by SI 2009/2979; and substituted by SI 2010/1883).
4   As to the meaning of 'satellite uplink apparatus' see PARA 515 note 9.
5   As to the meaning of 'United Kingdom' see PARA 510 note 13.
6   As to OFCOM see PARA 507.
7   As to the meaning of 'satellite uplinker' see PARA 515 note 9.
8   Ie under the Broadcasting Act 1990 Pt I (ss 3–71) or the Broadcasting Act 1996 Pt I (ss 1–39).
9   Wireless Telegraphy Act 2006 s 9A(1), (2) (as added: see note 1).
10 Ie the Communications Act 2003 Pt 4A (ss 368A–368R): see PARAS 784–787, 867–871, 881, 903–905.

11 Wireless Telegraphy Act 2006 s 9A(3) (as added: see note 1).
12 Wireless Telegraphy Act 2006 s 9A(4) (as added: see note 1).
13 Wireless Telegraphy Act 2006 s 9A(5) (as added: see note 1).

595.   Prohibition on providing independent radio services without a licence.
Any person[1] who provides any relevant regulated radio service[2] without being
authorised to do so by or under a licence[3] is guilty of an offence[4]. The Secretary
of State[5] may, after consultation with OFCOM[6], by order provide that this
provision does not apply to specified services or descriptions of services[7]. A
person guilty of such an offence is liable, on summary conviction, to a fine not
exceeding the statutory maximum[8] and, on conviction on indictment, to a fine[9].
Compliance with this provision is enforceable by civil proceedings by the Crown
for an injunction or for any other appropriate relief[10]. No proceedings in respect
of such an offence may be instituted except by or with the consent of the
Director of Public Prosecutions[11].

1 As to the meaning of 'person' see PARA 510 note 1.
2 'Relevant regulated radio service' means a service falling to be regulated under the
   Communications Act 2003 s 245 (see PARA 723), other than a radio multiplex service:
   Broadcasting Act 1990 s 97(1A) (added by the Communications Act 2003 s 360(3), Sch 15
   para 37(1), (3)). As to the meaning of 'radio multiplex service' see PARA 800 note 23.
3 Ie a licence under the Broadcasting Act 1990 Pt III (ss 85–126), or under the Broadcasting
   Act 1996 Pt II (ss 40–72).
4 Broadcasting Act 1990 s 97(1) (amended by the Broadcasting Act 1996 s 148(1), Sch 10 para 7;
   and the Communications Act 2003 Sch 15 para 37(2)).
5 As to the Secretary of State see PARA 507 note 32.
6 As to OFCOM see PARA 507.
7 Broadcasting Act 1990 s 97(2) (amended by the Communications Act 2003 Sch 15 para 37(4)).
   Any order under the Broadcasting Act 1990 s 97 is subject to annulment in pursuance of a
   resolution of either House of Parliament: s 97(6). As to orders under this provision see the
   Broadcasting Act 1990 (Independent Radio Services: Exceptions) Order 1990, SI 1990/2536
   (amended by SI 2003/2155); and the Broadcasting Act 1990 (Independent Radio Services
   Exceptions) Order 2007, SI 2007/272. The Broadcasting Act 1990 s 97(1) does not apply to the
   following services or descriptions of services: (1) any independent radio service provided under
   and in accordance with the transitional provisions relating to the Independent Broadcasting
   Authority's broadcasting services (see s 129, Sch 11; and PARA 550); (2) any independent radio
   service: (a) which is provided for reception at a place or places in the United Kingdom provided
   that no such place is a dwelling house (see PARA 751 note 3); (b) which is so provided for the
   purpose of its being heard there either by members of the public or by a group of persons some
   or all of whom do not have a business interest in hearing it; (c) which does not include any
   advertisement; and (d) in respect of which no payment is made either directly or indirectly for its
   provision by the persons by whom it is heard; and (3) any independent radio service consisting
   only of sounds sent by means of a telecommunication system run by a person who is a public
   telecommunications operator and who is not licensed to provide a local delivery service:
   Broadcasting Act 1990 (Independent Radio Services: Exceptions) Order 1990, SI 1990/2536,
   art 2. Nor does the Broadcasting Act 1990 s 97(1) apply to any service of the following
   descriptions: ie any service which: (i) is transmitted on wireless telegraphy apparatus designed
   or adapted for the provision of voice radiocommunications in the frequency bands 26.97 to
   27.41 MHz and 27.60 to 27.99 MHz; (ii) consists solely of the onward transmission of a live
   event of a kind falling within the Broadcasting Act 1990 (Independent Radio Services
   Exceptions) Order 2007, SI 2007/272, art 2(3) at the same time as that event takes place; (iii) is
   not a retransmission of a transmission described in head (i); (iv) is not transmitted from an
   antenna whose highest point exceeds a height of 10 metres above ground level; (v) does not
   include any advertisement or sponsorship for which any person has received, will receive, or is
   or will be entitled to receive, any payment or other financial benefit (whether direct or indirect)
   in consideration for so including it; and (vi) is transmitted for a total of not more than four
   hours each day and in which there is, after any continuous period of transmission of four hours,
   a break of at least one hour before there is any further transmission: art 2(1), (2). An event falls
   within art 2(3) if it is held in a place to which the public are permitted to have access (whether
   on payment or otherwise) and it is not held wholly or mainly for the purpose of its distribution

by an electronic communications network within the meaning of the Communications Act 2003: Broadcasting Act 1990 (Independent Radio Services Exceptions) Order 2007, SI 2007/272, art 2(3).

    As to the meaning of 'United Kingdom' see PARA 510 note 13. As to the Independent Broadcasting Authority see PARAS 501, 507.

8   Broadcasting Act 1990 s 97(3)(a). As to the statutory maximum see SENTENCING AND DISPOSITION OF OFFENDERS vol 92 (2010) PARA 140.
9   Broadcasting Act 1990 s 97(3)(b).
10 Broadcasting Act 1990 s 97(5).
11 Broadcasting Act 1990 s 97(4).

596. Entry and search of premises. If a justice of the peace[1] is satisfied by information on oath that there is reasonable ground for suspecting that an offence[2] has been or is being committed on any premises specified in the information[3], and that evidence of the commission of the offence is to be found on those premises[4], he may grant a search warrant conferring power on any person or persons authorised in that behalf by OFCOM[5] to enter and search the premises specified in the information at any time within one month from the date of the warrant[6]. A person who intentionally obstructs a person in the exercise of such powers is guilty of an offence and liable on summary conviction to a fine not exceeding level 5 on the standard scale[7].

A person who discloses, otherwise than for the purposes of any legal proceedings or of a report of any such proceedings, any information obtained by means of an exercise of powers so conferred is guilty of an offence[8] and liable, on summary conviction, to a fine not exceeding the statutory maximum[9] and, on conviction on indictment, to imprisonment for a term not exceeding two years or to a fine or both[10].

1   As to justices of the peace see MAGISTRATES.
2   Ie under the Broadcasting Act 1990 s 13 (see PARA 593) or s 97 (see PARA 595).
3   Broadcasting Act 1990 s 196(1)(a) (amended by the Communications Act 2003 s 406(7), Sch 19).
4   Broadcasting Act 1990 s 196(1)(b).
5   As to OFCOM see PARA 507.
6   Broadcasting Act 1990 s 196(1) (amended by the Communications Act 2003 s 360(3), Sch 15 para 66(1), (2)).
7   Broadcasting Act 1990 s 196(3). As to the standard scale see SENTENCING AND DISPOSITION OF OFFENDERS vol 92 (2010) PARA 142.
8   Broadcasting Act 1990 s 196(4).
9   Broadcasting Act 1990 s 196(4)(a). As to the statutory maximum see SENTENCING AND DISPOSITION OF OFFENDERS vol 92 (2010) PARA 140.
10 Broadcasting Act 1990 s 196(4)(b).

597. Unacceptable foreign satellite services and offences of supporting such services. The Secretary of State[1] may make an order proscribing unacceptable foreign satellite services[2]. If OFCOM[3] considers that the quality of any foreign satellite service which is brought to its attention is unacceptable and that the service should be the subject of such an order, it must notify to the Secretary of State details of the service and the reasons why it considers such an order should be made[4]. OFCOM may not consider a foreign satellite service to be unacceptable unless it is satisfied that there is repeatedly contained in programmes included in the service matter which offends against good taste or decency or is likely to encourage or incite to crime or to lead to disorder or to be offensive to public feeling[5].

Where the Secretary of State has been notified, he may not make such an order unless he is satisfied that the making of the order[6] is in the public interest[7], and is compatible with any international obligations of the United Kingdom[8]. Such an order may make such provision for the purpose of identifying a particular foreign satellite service as the Secretary of State thinks fit[9], and is subject to annulment in pursuance of a resolution of either House of Parliament[10].

Where a foreign satellite service has been proscribed by order[11], any person who in the United Kingdom does any of the following acts is guilty of an offence[12]. Those acts are:

(1) supplying[13] any equipment or other goods for use in connection with the operation or day-to-day running of a proscribed service[14];

(2) supplying, or offering to supply, programme material[15] to be included in any programme transmitted in the provision of a proscribed service[16];

(3) arranging for, or inviting, any other person to supply programme material to be so included[17];

(4) advertising, by means of programmes transmitted in the provision of a proscribed service, goods supplied by him or services provided by him[18];

(5) publishing the times or other details of any programmes which are to be transmitted in the provision of a proscribed service or (otherwise than by publishing such details) publishing an advertisement of matter calculated to promote a proscribed service (whether directly or indirectly)[19];

(6) supplying or offering to supply any decoding equipment[20] which is designed or adapted to be used primarily for the purpose of enabling the reception of programmes transmitted in the provision of a proscribed service[21].

In any proceedings against a person for such an offence, it is a defence for him to prove that he did not know, and had no reasonable cause to suspect, that the service in connection with which the act was done was a proscribed service[22]. A person who is guilty of such an offence is liable, on summary conviction, to imprisonment for a term not exceeding six months or to a fine not exceeding the statutory maximum[23] or both[24] and, on conviction on indictment, to imprisonment for a term not exceeding two years or to a fine or both[25].

1 As to the Secretary of State see PARA 507 note 32.
2 Broadcasting Act 1990 s 177(1). Such services are proscribed for the purposes of s 178: see s 177(1). 'Foreign satellite service' means: (1) a service which is provided by a person who is not for the purposes of the Audiovisual Media Services Directive under the jurisdiction of the United Kingdom and which consists wholly or mainly in the transmission by satellite of television programmes which are capable of being received in the United Kingdom; or (2) a service which consists wholly or mainly in the transmission by satellite from a place outside the United Kingdom of sound programmes which are capable of being received in the United Kingdom: Broadcasting Act 1990 s 177(6) (definition substituted by SI 1998/3196; and amended by SI 2010/1883). 'The Audiovisual Media Services Directive' means European Parliament and Council Directive (EU) 2010/13 (OJ L95, 15.4.2010, p 1) on the coordination of certain provisions laid down by law, regulation or administrative action in member states concerning the provision of audiovisual media services: Broadcasting Act 1990 s 202(1) (definition added by SI 2010/1883). As to the meaning of 'person' see PARA 510 note 1. As to the meaning of 'United Kingdom' see PARA 510 note 13. As to the meaning of 'programme' see PARA 667 note 7.

As to orders under this provision see the Foreign Satellite Service Proscription Order 1993, SI 1993/1024; the Foreign Satellite Service Proscription Order 1995, SI 1995/2917; the Foreign Satellite Service Proscription Order 1996, SI 1996/2557; the Foreign Satellite Service Proscription Order 1997, SI 1997/1150; the Foreign Satellite Service Proscription Order 1998, SI 1998/1865; the Foreign Satellite Service Proscription (No 2) Order 1998, SI 1998/3083; and the Foreign Satellite Service Proscription Order 2005, SI 2005/220.

    Certain questions arising in proceedings for judicial review of an order made under these provisions were referred to the European Court of Justice: see *R v Secretary of State for the National Heritage, ex p Continental Television BV* [1993] 3 CMLR 387, CA.
3   As to OFCOM see PARA 507.
4   Broadcasting Act 1990 s 177(2) (amended by the Communications Act 2003 s 360(3), Sch 15 para 61(1), (2)).
5   Broadcasting Act 1990 s 177(3) (amended by the Communications Act 2003 Sch 15 para 61(3)).
6   Broadcasting Act 1990 s 177(4).
7   Broadcasting Act 1990 s 177(4)(a).
8   Broadcasting Act 1990 s 177(4)(b).
9   Broadcasting Act 1990 s 177(5)(a).
10 Broadcasting Act 1990 s 177(5)(b).
11 Ie under the Broadcasting Act 1990 s 177: see s 178(1). References to a proscribed service in s 178 are references to any foreign satellite service proscribed by virtue of an order under s 177: see s 178(1).
12 Broadcasting Act 1990 s 178(2).
13 The Consumer Protection Act 1987 s 46 (see CONSUMER PROTECTION vol 21 (2011) PARA 647) has effect for the purpose of construing references in the Broadcasting Act 1990 s 178 to the supply of any thing as it has effect for the purpose of construing references in the Consumer Protection Act 1987 to the supply of any goods: Broadcasting Act 1990 s 178(7).
14 Broadcasting Act 1990 s 178(3)(a).
15 'Programme material' includes: (1) a film (within the meaning of the Copyright, Designs and Patents Act 1988 Pt I (ss 1–179): see COPYRIGHT, DESIGN RIGHT AND RELATED RIGHTS vol 9(2) (2006 Reissue) PARA 86); (2) any other recording; and (3) any advertisement or other advertising material: Broadcasting Act 1990 s 178(8).
16 Broadcasting Act 1990 s 178(3)(b).
17 Broadcasting Act 1990 s 178(3)(c).
18 Broadcasting Act 1990 s 178(3)(d).
19 Broadcasting Act 1990 s 178(3)(e).
20 A person exposing decoding equipment for supply or having such equipment in his possession for supply is deemed to offer to supply it: Broadcasting Act 1990 s 178(6).
21 Broadcasting Act 1990 s 178(3)(f).
22 Broadcasting Act 1990 s 178(4).
23 As to the statutory maximum see SENTENCING AND DISPOSITION OF OFFENDERS vol 92 (2010) PARA 140.
24 Broadcasting Act 1990 s 178(5)(a).
25 Broadcasting Act 1990 s 178(5)(b).

598. Offence of providing false information in certain circumstances. A person[1] who, in connection with an application by him for, or his continued holding of, a licence under the Broadcasting Act 1990 or the Broadcasting Act 1996, makes a statement to OFCOM[2] which he knows to be false in a material particular[3], or recklessly makes a statement to OFCOM which is false in a material particular[4], is guilty of an offence if the statement relates to a matter which would be relevant in determining whether he is by virtue of any of the specified provisions[5] a disqualified person, and he is by virtue of any of those provisions a disqualified person in relation to that licence[6].

    A person who, in connection with an application by him for, or his continued holding of, a licence under those Acts, withholds any information with the intention of causing OFCOM to be misled is guilty of an offence[7] if the information would be relevant in determining whether he is by virtue of any of the specified provisions[8] a disqualified person[9], and he is by virtue of any of those provisions a disqualified person in relation to that licence[10].

    A person guilty of such an offence is liable on summary conviction to imprisonment for a term not exceeding three months or to a fine not exceeding level 5 on the standard scale[11] or to both[12].

    Where a person is convicted of such an offence, the court by which he is convicted may make a disqualification order disqualifying him from holding a licence[13] during a period specified in the order[14]. The period specified in a disqualification order must not exceed five years beginning with the date on which the order takes effect[15]. Where an individual is disqualified from holding a licence by virtue of a disqualification order, any body corporate of which he is a director[16], or in the management of which he is directly or indirectly concerned[17], is also disqualified from holding a licence[18]. Where the holder of a licence is disqualified by virtue of a disqualification order, the licence is to be treated as being revoked with effect from the time when the order takes effect[19].

A person disqualified by a disqualification order may appeal against the order in the same manner as against a conviction[20]. A disqualification order made by a court does not take effect until the end of the period within which the person on whose conviction the order was made can appeal against the order[21], and if he so appeals, does not take effect until the appeal has been determined or abandoned[22].

1 As to the meaning of 'person' see PARA 510 note 1.
2 As to OFCOM see PARA 507.
3 Broadcasting Act 1996 s 144(1)(a) (s 144(1)(a), (b) amended by the Communications Act 2003 s 360(3), Sch 15 para 139(1), (2)).
4 Broadcasting Act 1996 s 144(1)(b) (as amended: see note 3).
5 The specified provisions are: (1) the Broadcasting Act 1990 ss 5, 88, Sch 2 Pt II para 1(1)(d)–(g) (see PARAS 822, 830); (2) Sch 2 Pt II para 1(1)(h) (see PARAS 822, 830) so far as relating to participation by bodies falling within Sch 2 Pt II para 1(1)(d), (e) or (g); (3) Sch 2 Pt II para 1(1)(hh) (see PARAS 822, 830) so far as relating to a body corporate controlled by a body corporate in which a body falling within Sch 2 Pt II para 1(1)(d), (e) or (g) is a participant with more than a 5% interest; (4) Sch 2 Pt II para 1(1)(i) (see PARAS 822, 830) so far as relating to control by a person falling within any of Sch 2 Pt II para 1(1)(d)–(g) or by two or more such persons; and (5) Sch 2 Pt II para 1(1)(j) (see PARAS 822, 830) so far as relating to participation by a body corporate which is controlled by a person falling within any of Sch 2 Pt II para 1(1)(d)–(g) or by two or more such persons: Broadcasting Act 1996 s 144(3). As to the meaning of 'body' see PARA 821 note 10; and as to the meaning of 'control' see PARA 821 note 11 (definitions applied by s 147(2)).
6 Broadcasting Act 1996 s 144(1).
7 Broadcasting Act 1996 s 144(2) (amended by the Communications Act 2003 Sch 15 para 139(3)).
8 See note 5.
9 Broadcasting Act 1996 s 144(2)(a).
10 Broadcasting Act 1996 s 144(2)(b).
11 As to the standard scale see SENTENCING AND DISPOSITION OF OFFENDERS vol 92 (2010) PARA 142.
12 Broadcasting Act 1996 s 144(4). As from a day to be appointed, this provision is amended so as to remove the sentence of imprisonment: see s 144(4) (prospectively amended by the Criminal Justice Act 2003 s 332, Sch 37 Pt 9). At the date at which this volume states the law, no such day had been appointed.
13 'Licence' means any licence under the Broadcasting Act 1990 Pt I (ss 3–71) or Pt III (ss 85–126) or the Broadcasting Act 1996 Pt I (ss 1–39) or Pt II (ss 40–72): s 145(8) (definition substituted by the Communications Act 2003 Sch 15 para 140(1), (4)).
14 Broadcasting Act 1996 s 145(1). In the Broadcasting Act 1990 s 5(1)(a), (2)(db) (see PARA 821), s 88(1)(a), (2)(db) (see PARA 829), the Broadcasting Act 1996 s 5(1)(a), (2)(db) (see PARA 828) and s 44(1)(a), (2)(db) (see PARA 837), the reference to a person who is a disqualified person by virtue of the Broadcasting Act 1990 Sch 2 Pt II (see PARAS 822, 830) includes a reference to a person who is disqualified by virtue of a disqualification order: Broadcasting Act 1996 s 145(7) (amended by the Communications Act 2003 Sch 15 para 140(3); and by SI 2003/3299).
15 Broadcasting Act 1996 s 145(2).
16 Broadcasting Act 1996 s 145(3)(a).
17 Broadcasting Act 1996 s 145(3)(b).
18 Broadcasting Act 1996 s 145(3).
19 Broadcasting Act 1996 s 145(4). For the purposes of any of the provisions specified in s 145(6) (which relate to the imposition of a financial penalty on the revocation of a licence), a licence which is revoked by s 145(4) is to be taken to have been revoked by OFCOM as mentioned in

that provision: s 145(5) (amended by the Communications Act 2003 Sch 15 para 140(2)). The provisions referred to in the Broadcasting Act 1996 s 145(5) are: the Broadcasting Act 1990 s 18(3) (see PARA 673), s 101(3) (see PARA 733), the Broadcasting Act 1996 s 11(5) (see PARA 691) and s 53(5) (see PARA 760): s 145(6).

20   Broadcasting Act 1996 s 146(1).
21   Broadcasting Act 1996 s 146(2)(a).
22   Broadcasting Act 1996 s 146(2)(b).

599. Offences by bodies corporate. Where a body corporate is guilty of an offence under the Broadcasting Act 1990 and that offence is proved to have been committed with the consent or connivance of, or to be attributable to any neglect on the part of, any director, manager, secretary or other similar officer of the body corporate or any person who was purporting to act in any such capacity, then he, as well as the body corporate, is guilty of that offence and is liable to be proceeded against and punished accordingly[1]. Where the affairs of a body corporate are managed by its members, this provision applies in relation to the acts and defaults of a member in connection with his functions of management as if he were a director of the body corporate[2].

1   Broadcasting Act 1990 s 195(1).
2   Broadcasting Act 1990 s 195(2).

(5) LICENSING OF OTHER PLATFORMS

600. Satellite broadcasting, cable and broadband. It is clear that the analogue terrestrial, digital terrestrial, and 3G mobile network broadcasting platforms require wireless telegraphy licences[1]. As regards digital satellite services, there is potentially a distinction to be drawn, at least in principle, between services provided on frequencies allocated by OFCOM[2] or otherwise dedicated to satellite broadcasting (which would require a wireless telegraphy licence) and services provided on frequencies allocated by relevant authorities outside the jurisdiction but capable of reception in the United Kingdom. In such circumstances, OFCOM may decide to make a grant of recognised spectrum access so as to recognise the use and avoid spectrum interference[3]. The establishment and use of cable and wired broadband networks to deliver audio-visual media content is regulated only under the general scheme of telecommunications regulation, which provides for general authorisation subject to general conditions[4]. There is no requirement for the network provider to seek approval in advance for the plan to offer network services.

1   See PARA 509 et seq.
2   As to OFCOM see PARA 507.
3   See PARAS 522, 544.
4   See TELECOMMUNICATIONS vol 97 (2010) PARAS 92–126. It is conceivable that some incidental use of wireless endpoint facilities by cable operators may require licensing under the wireless telegraphy regime. The delivery of media content would be separately regulated by OFCOM: see PARAS 716–718 (licensing of television licensable content services).

3. AUDIO-VISUAL SERVICES

(1) INTRODUCTION

601.   Introduction to the establishment and licensing of services. The essential aims underpinning the development of broadcasting policy since the late 1980s have been, first, to allow multi-channel television made feasible by technological development to meet the disparate needs of consumers, secondly, to ensure that the public service functions of the broadcast media are performed, and thirdly, to ensure that all audio-visual media content meets the basic standards expected in the United Kingdom. This has culminated in two tiers of television broadcasting regulation. The first tier is focused on those services that are subject to public service obligations. This encompasses the BBC[1], Channel 4[2], Sianel Pedwar Cymru (S4C)[3], Channel 3[4] and Channel 5[5], the first three of which are public corporations that must meet specific public service objectives[6] while the latter two are delivered by private companies that exchange privileged access to spectrum resource and profile for heightened public service performance obligations relative to non-PSB services. The second tier comprises other broadcasting services that are subject only to the general law and to basic content standards obligations overseen by OFCOM[7]. In addition, the BBC provides online media content and public service sound broadcasting that compete with a range of commercial services[8].

1   As to the BBC see PARAS 603 et seq.
2   As to Channel 4 see PARA 627 et seq.
3   As to S4C see PARA 644 et seq.
4   As to Channel 3 see PARA 662 et seq.
5   As to Channel 5 see PARA 681.
6   As to the public service remit of the BBC see PARAS 614–615. As to the public service remit of S4C see PARA 655. As to the duties of OFCOM in relation to reviewing the public service remit see PARAS 788–791.
7   See PARAS 716 et seq, 749 et seq. As to OFCOM see PARA 507.
8   See PARA 614.

602.   Application of the regulatory regime: licences to be held on conditions included in the regulatory regime for the licensed service. It is the duty of OFCOM[1], by exercising: (1) its powers under the Broadcasting Act 1990 and the Broadcasting Act 1996; and (2) its powers under Part 3 of the Communications Act 2003[2], to secure that the holder of every Broadcasting Act licence[3] at all times holds his licence on the conditions which are for the time being included, under Chapter 4 of Part 3 of the Communications Act 2003[4] and Chapter 5 of Part 3 of that Act[5], in the regulatory regime for the licensed service[6]. It is also the duty of OFCOM to do all that it can to secure that the holder of every such licence complies, in relation to the licensed service, with the conditions so included in the regulatory regime for that service[7]. Where: (a) the licence for a Channel 3 service[8], for Channel 4[9], for Channel 5[10] or for the public teletext service[11] ('the main service') authorises or requires a corresponding or additional service to be provided in analogue form; and (b) the regulatory regime for the main service imposes obligations in relation to programmes and other items included in that service, those obligations are to apply equally to programmes that are included in the analogue service without being included in the main service[12]. The Secretary of State may by order provide for: (i) a condition included by virtue of the Communications Act 2003 in a regulatory regime to be excluded from the regime; (ii) a condition excluded from a regulatory regime by such an order to be included in the regime again[13].

The provisions described above do not restrict OFCOM's powers and duties apart from those provisions to impose obligations by means of the inclusion of conditions in a Broadcasting Act licence[14].

1   As to OFCOM see PARA 507.

2   Ie the Communications Act 2003 Pt 3 (ss 198–362).

3   'Broadcasting Act licence' means a licence under the Broadcasting Act 1990 Pt I (ss 3–71) or Pt III (ss 85–126) or under the Broadcasting Act 1996 Pt I (ss 1–39) or Pt II (ss 40–72): Communications Act 2003 s 405(1). 'Holder', in relation to a Broadcasting Act licence, is to be construed in accordance with s 405(7); and cognate expressions are to be construed accordingly: s 405(1). For the purposes of the Communications Act 2003, references, in relation to a time or a period, to the holder of a Broadcasting Act licence or of a particular description of such licence are references to the person who held that licence at that time or (as the case may be) to every person who held that licence for the whole or a part of that period: Communications Act 2003 s 405(7).

4   Ie the Communications Act 2003 Pt 3 Ch 4 (ss 263–347) (regulatory provisions: see PARA 642 et seq).

5   Ie the Communications Act 2003 Pt 3 Ch 5 (ss 348–357) (media ownership and control).

6   Communications Act 2003 s 263(1).

7   Communications Act 2003 s 263(2).

8   'A Channel 3 service' means a television broadcasting service comprised in Channel 3: Communications Act 2003 s 362(1). 'Television broadcasting service' means a service which: (1) consists in a service of television programmes provided with a view to its being broadcast (whether in digital or in analogue form); (2) is provided so as to be available for reception by members of the public; and (3) is not (a) a restricted television service; (b) a television multiplex service; (c) a service provided under the authority of a licence under the Broadcasting Act 1990 Pt I to provide a television licensable content service; or (d) a service provided under the authority of a licence under the Broadcasting Act 1996 Pt I to provide a digital television programme service: Communications Act 2003 s 362(1). However, references in Pt 3 to a television broadcasting service do not include references to any text service: s 362(4). 'Text service' means any teletext service or other service in the case of which the visual images broadcast or distributed by means of the service consist wholly or mainly of non-representational images: s 362(1). For the purposes of s 362, 'non-representational images' means visual images which are neither still pictures nor comprised within sequences of visual images capable of being seen as moving pictures: s 362(7). 'Available for reception by members of the public' is to be construed in accordance with s 361 (see PARA 796): s 362(1). For the purposes of Pt 3, 'restricted television service' means any restricted service within the meaning given by the Broadcasting Act 1990 s 42A (see PARA 689) for the purposes of the Broadcasting Act 1996 Pt I: Communications Act 2003 s 362(1). As to the meaning of 'television multiplex service' see PARA 697; definition applied by s 362(1). As to the meaning of 'television licensable content service' see PARA 716. For the purposes of Pt 3, 'digital television programme service' means a digital programme service within the meaning given by the Broadcasting Act 1996 s 1(4) (see PARA 690 note 28) for the purposes of the Broadcasting Act 1996 Pt I: Communications Act 2003 s 362(1). For the purposes of Pt 3, 'Channel 3' has the same meaning as in the Broadcasting Act 1990 Pt I (see s 71; and PARA 667): Communications Act 2003 s 362(1).

9   For the purposes of the Communications Act 2003 Pt 3, 'Channel 4' has the same meaning as in the Broadcasting Act 1990 Pt I (see s 71; and PARA 637): Communications Act 2003 s 362(1).

10 For the purposes of the Communications Act 2003 Pt 3, 'Channel 5' has the same meaning as in the Broadcasting Act 1990 Pt I (see s 71; and PARA 681): Communications Act 2003 s 362(1).

11 As to the public teletext service see PARA 686.

12 Communications Act 2003 s 263(3). In the Communications Act 2003 generally, 'programme' includes an advertisement and, in relation to a service, anything included in that service: s 405(1).

13 Communications Act 2003 s 263(4) (substituted by the Digital Economy Act 2010 s 37). An order under the Communications Act 2003 s 263(4) may, in particular, provide for a condition to be included or excluded for a period specified in the order: s 263(4A) (added by the Digital Economy Act 2010 s 37). No order is to be made containing provision authorised by the Communications Act 2003 s 263(4) unless a draft of the order has been laid before Parliament and approved by a resolution of each House: s 263(5). As to the power of the Secretary of State

to make orders under the Communications Act 2003 see s 402; and TELECOMMUNICATIONS vol 97 (2010) PARA 77. At the date at which this volume states the law, no such order had been made.

14 Communications Act 2003 s 263(6).

(2) ESTABLISHMENT AND REMIT OF THE BRITISH BROADCASTING CORPORATION (BBC)

(i) The Corporation

603. The British Broadcasting Corporation. The British Broadcasting Corporation (commonly known as the 'BBC')[1] was established, and is continued, by Royal Charter[2] with the principal object of promoting its public purposes[3]. The corporation is a body corporate with perpetual succession and a common seal; it may sue and be sued in all courts and has power to take and hold real and personal property[4]. The corporation may hold land in perpetuity[5]. In addition to the Charter, an agreement has been concluded between the Secretary of State[6] and the BBC which is a Framework Agreement[7] for the purposes of the Charter, complementing the provisions of the Charter and making provision in respect of the functions of OFCOM[8] in relation to the BBC[9].

1 For the purposes of the Broadcasting Act 1990, the Broadcasting Act 1996 and the Communications Act 2003, 'BBC' means the British Broadcasting Corporation: Broadcasting Act 1990 s 202(1); Broadcasting Act 1996 s 147(1); Communications Act 2003 s 405(1). The same definition applies for the purposes of the *Royal Charter for the Continuance of the British Broadcasting Corporation* (Cm 6925) (2006) (see art 56) and the *Agreement between Her Majesty's Secretary of State for Culture, Media and Sport and the British Broadcasting Corporation* (Cm 6872) (30 June 2006) (see cl 104).

2 The first Charter was granted in 1926, and the corporation's life was extended by further Charters granted in 1937, 1947, 1952, 1964, 1981 and 1996. The current Charter was granted on 19 September 2006 and continues in force until 31 December 2016 (see the *Royal Charter for the Continuance of the British Broadcasting Corporation* (Cm 6925) (2006) art 2). As to the corporation's predecessor, the British Broadcasting Company, see PARA 501.

3 *Royal Charter for the Continuance of the British Broadcasting Corporation* (Cm 6925) (2006) art 3(2). The public purposes of the BBC are as follows: (1) sustaining citizenship and civil society; (2) promoting education and learning; (3) stimulating creativity and cultural excellence; (4) representing the United Kingdom, its nations, regions and communities; (5) bringing the United Kingdom to the world and the world to the United Kingdom; (6) in promoting its other purposes, helping to deliver to the public the benefit of emerging communications technologies and services and, in addition, taking a leading role in the switchover to digital television: art 4.

4 See the *Royal Charter for the Continuance of the British Broadcasting Corporation* (Cm 6925) (2006) arts 1(1), 47. The BBC may use these general powers only for the purposes set out in arts 3–5: art 47(4).

5 As to the abolition of the law of mortmain see the Charities Act 1960 s 38 (repealed); and CHARITIES vol 8 (2010) PARA 82.

6 As to the Secretary of State see PARA 507 note 32.

7 A 'Framework Agreement' is an agreement between the BBC and the Secretary of State which contains a statement to the effect that it is a Framework Agreement made for BBC Charter purposes: *Royal Charter for the Continuance of the British Broadcasting Corporation* (Cm 6925) (2006) art 49(1). The BBC must comply with any Framework Agreement, for so long as it is in force: arts 49(4), 52. See further art 49(3), (5).

8 Ie for the purposes of the Communications Act 2003 s 198: see PARA 854. As to OFCOM see PARA 507.

9 Ie the *Agreement between Her Majesty's Secretary of State for Culture, Media and Sport and the British Broadcasting Corporation* (Cm 6872) (30 June 2006) (replacing a similar agreement dated 25 January 1996 (Cm 3152)): see cl 2; and *Royal Charter for the Continuance of the British Broadcasting Corporation* (Cm 6925) (2006) art 49(2). While this document is primarily

concerned with the conditions under which the corporation is licensed to broadcast, it also contains provisions (see PARA 613 et seq) as to staff and financial matters and as to the contents of broadcast programmes.

604. Constitution. Within the BBC[1], there is a BBC Trust[2] and an Executive Board of the BBC, each with a different role[3]. The Corporation that is the BBC comprises all the members of the BBC Trust and the Executive Board[4]. However, membership of the Corporation does not enable any individual to act otherwise than through the Trust or the Board to which he belongs[5]; the members of the Trust and the members of the Board must never act together as a single corporate body[6].

The Trust must maintain its independence of the Executive Board[7]. The Trust is the sovereign body within the BBC, but it must not exercise or seek to exercise the functions of the Executive Board[8]. The Chairman of the Trust may also be known as the Chairman of the BBC, but this is an honorary title, as the members of the BBC will never act as a single corporate body, but only as members of the Trust or Board to which they belong[9]. The Trust and the Executive Board, in performing their respective functions, must have regard: (1) to such general guidance concerning the management of the affairs of public bodies as they consider relevant and appropriate; and (2) to generally accepted principles of good corporate governance, but only: (a) where to do so would not be incompatible with head (1); and (b) to the extent that such principles may reasonably be regarded as applicable in relation to their respective functions and within the particular constitution of the BBC as a chartered corporation[10].

There is a Director General, who is the chief executive officer of the BBC and an executive member of the Executive Board[11], and BBC staff and Trust staff are appointed by the Executive Board and the Trust respectively[12].

1 As to the meaning of 'BBC' see PARA 603.

2 The word 'trust' is used in the name of the BBC Trust in a colloquial sense, to suggest a body which discharges a public trust as guardian of the public interest; it is not used in its technical legal sense: see the *Royal Charter for the Continuance of the British Broadcasting Corporation* (Cm 6925) (2006) art 12.

3 *Royal Charter for the Continuance of the British Broadcasting Corporation* (Cm 6925) (2006) art 7. The main roles of the Trust are in setting the overall strategic direction of the BBC, including its priorities, and in exercising a general oversight of the work of the Executive Board. The Trust will perform these roles in the public interest, particularly the interest of licence fee payers. The Executive Board has responsibility for delivering the BBC's services in accordance with the priorities set by the Trust and for all aspects of operational management, except that of the Trust's resources: art 7. See further PARAS 605–610. In the Charter, a reference to a 'licence fee payer' is not to be taken literally but includes, not only a person to whom a TV licence is issued under the Communications Act 2003 s 364 (see PARA 949), but also (so far as is sensible in the context) any other person in the United Kingdom who watches, listens to or uses any BBC service, or may do so or wish to do so in the future: *Royal Charter for the Continuance of the British Broadcasting Corporation* (Cm 6925) (2006) arts 56, 57.

4 *Royal Charter for the Continuance of the British Broadcasting Corporation* (Cm 6925) (2006) arts 1(2), 8.

5 *Royal Charter for the Continuance of the British Broadcasting Corporation* (Cm 6925) (2006) art 1(2).

6 *Royal Charter for the Continuance of the British Broadcasting Corporation* (Cm 6925) (2006) art 8.

7 *Royal Charter for the Continuance of the British Broadcasting Corporation* (Cm 6925) (2006) art 9(1).

8 *Royal Charter for the Continuance of the British Broadcasting Corporation* (Cm 6925) (2006) art 9(2), (3).

9 *Royal Charter for the Continuance of the British Broadcasting Corporation* (Cm 6925) (2006) art 10.

10 *Royal Charter for the Continuance of the British Broadcasting Corporation* (Cm 6925) (2006) art 11.
11 See the *Royal Charter for the Continuance of the British Broadcasting Corporation* (Cm 6925) (2006) art 40(1), (2); and PARA 612.
12 See the *Royal Charter for the Continuance of the British Broadcasting Corporation* (Cm 6925) (2006) arts 41, 42; and PARA 612.

605.   Membership of the BBC Trust. The BBC Trust[1] consists of a chairman, a vice-chairman, and ten ordinary members[2], who are appointed by Order in Council[3] for periods of not longer than five years[4]. Provision is made for their remuneration[5], pensions, allowances and gratuities[6], and termination of office[7]. Four ordinary members of the Trust are to be respectively designated the Trust member for England[8], the Trust member for Scotland, the Trust member for Wales, the Trust member for Northern Ireland[9], and each person so designated must be suitably qualified by virtue of: (1) his knowledge of the culture, characteristics and affairs of the people in the nation for which he is to be designated; and (2) his close touch with opinion in that nation[10].

1   As to the BBC Trust within the constitution of the BBC see PARA 604. As to the meaning of 'BBC' see PARA 603; and as to the meaning of 'trust' for these purposes see PARA 604 note 2.
2   *Royal Charter for the Continuance of the British Broadcasting Corporation* (Cm 6925) (2006) art 13(1), (2). A different number may be fixed by Order in Council, but it is not necessary to fix a lower number by Order in Council merely to reflect the existence of a vacancy which is intended to be filled by a further appointment in due course: art 13(2).
3   *Royal Charter for the Continuance of the British Broadcasting Corporation* (Cm 6925) (2006) art 13(3). The selection of persons for appointment as ordinary members of the Trust must take account of the need for designations to be made under art 14 (see the text and notes 8–10): art 13(3).
4   *Royal Charter for the Continuance of the British Broadcasting Corporation* (Cm 6925) (2006) art 15(1). A serving chairman, vice-chairman or ordinary member may at any time be re-appointed by Order in Council for any further period, not longer than five years, specified in the Order: art 15(2).
5   See the *Royal Charter for the Continuance of the British Broadcasting Corporation* (Cm 6925) (2006) art 17.
6   See the *Royal Charter for the Continuance of the British Broadcasting Corporation* (Cm 6925) (2006) art 18.
7   See the *Royal Charter for the Continuance of the British Broadcasting Corporation* (Cm 6925) (2006) art 16.
8   For the purposes of the *Royal Charter for the Continuance of the British Broadcasting Corporation* (Cm 6925) (2006) art 14, 'England' includes the Channel Islands and the Isle of Man and references to 'nation' are to be interpreted accordingly: art 14(4).
9   *Royal Charter for the Continuance of the British Broadcasting Corporation* (Cm 6925) (2006) art 14(1). Such designations are to be made by Order in Council. They may be made either at the same time that the person concerned is appointed to be an ordinary member of the Trust or at any time while he remains an ordinary member. A designation has effect until superseded by a fresh designation or until the designated person ceases to be a member of the Trust: art 14(2).
10 *Royal Charter for the Continuance of the British Broadcasting Corporation* (Cm 6925) (2006) art 14(3).

606.   BBC Trust: meetings etc. The BBC Trust[1] must meet for the transaction of its business and affairs[2], and make standing orders dealing with the summoning, notice, time, place, quorum, management and adjournment of its meetings, including provision for the exercise of a casting vote[3]. The Trust may set up committees of the Trust, and may delegate particular functions, including decision-taking, to such a committee on such terms and conditions as it thinks fit[4]. The Trust may make regulations about the transaction and management of: (1) its business and affairs; (2) the business and affairs of the BBC more generally[5]. Regulations may be made only at a meeting of the Trust[6].

1   As to the BBC Trust within the constitution of the BBC see PARA 604. As to the meaning of
    'BBC' see PARA 603; and as to the meaning of 'trust' for these purposes see PARA 604 note 2.
2   *Royal Charter for the Continuance of the British Broadcasting Corporation* (Cm 6925) (2006)
    art 19(1). A member of the Trust must cease to hold his office if he fails to attend meetings of
    the Trust continuously for three months or longer without the consent of the Trust and the Trust
    resolves that his office be vacated: art 16(f).
3   *Royal Charter for the Continuance of the British Broadcasting Corporation* (Cm 6925) (2006)
    art 19(2). The standing orders may make provision for meetings of the Trust to be held in
    circumstances in which members participate without being physically present in the same place
    as other participating members (e g by means of telephone or videoconferencing): art 19(3). The
    standing orders must be made as regulations in accordance with art 21 (see the text and notes
    5–6): art 21(5).
4   *Royal Charter for the Continuance of the British Broadcasting Corporation* (Cm 6925) (2006)
    art 20(1), (3). The number, remit and composition of such committees are a matter for the Trust,
    but no such committee may include anyone who is not a member of the Trust: art 20(2).
5   *Royal Charter for the Continuance of the British Broadcasting Corporation* (Cm 6925) (2006)
    art 21(1). Regulations may provide for the transaction of urgent business of the Trust between
    meetings of the Trust, including provision for such business to be transacted by a single member
    of the Trust: art 21(2). Regulations may make provision for or about the filling of vacancies on
    the Executive Board in circumstances in which it is impossible for art 30 or 31 (see PARA 608) to
    be complied with (e g if all the members of the Executive Board resigned with immediate effect):
    art 21(3).
6   *Royal Charter for the Continuance of the British Broadcasting Corporation* (Cm 6925) (2006)
    art 21(4).

607.   Duties and functions of the BBC Trust.   The BBC Trust[1] is the guardian
of the licence fee revenue[2] and the public interest in the BBC[3]. The Trust has the
ultimate responsibility, subject to the provisions of the Charter, for: (1) the BBC's
stewardship of the licence fee revenue and its other resources; (2) upholding the
public interest within the BBC, particularly the interests of licence fee payers[4];
and (3) securing the effective promotion of the public purposes[5].

The Trust has the general function of: (a) setting the overall strategic direction
for the BBC within the framework set by the Charter and any Framework
Agreement[6]; (b) approving high-level strategy and budgets in respect of the BBC's
services and activities in the United Kingdom and overseas; and (c) assessing the
performance of the Executive Board in delivering the BBC's services and activities
and holding the Executive Board to account for its performance[7].

In particular, the Trust has the following specific functions[8]:

(i)   setting multi-year purpose remits, and approving strategies which
        include high-level budgetary allocations[9];

(ii)   defining suitable performance criteria and measures against which the
        effective promotion of the public purposes will be judged[10];

(iii)   issuing service licences for BBC services and monitoring compliance
        with them[11];

(iv)   approving guidelines designed to secure appropriate standards in the
        content of the BBC's services[12];

(v)   approving individual strategic or financial proposals where they stand
        to have significant implications for the fulfilment of the purpose remits
        and strategies referred to in head (i) or for the overall financial position
        of the BBC[13];

(vi)   discharging the regulatory functions accorded to the Trust and holding
        the Executive Board to account for the BBC's compliance with
        applicable regulatory requirements and the general law[14];

(vii)   setting the framework within which the BBC should handle complaints
        (and the framework must provide for the Trust to play a role as final
        arbiter in appropriate cases)[15];

(viii) where appropriate, conducting investigations into any activity of the BBC which it has grounds to suspect does not comply with requirements supervised by the Trust[16];

(ix) commissioning value for money investigations into specific areas of BBC activity[17];

(x) ensuring the Executive Board addresses key operating risks for the BBC[18];

(xi) adopting a statement of policy on fair trading and holding the Executive Board to account for compliance with it[19];

(xii) setting an approvals framework within which the Trust will assess proposals from the Executive Board for new services, significant changes to existing services, commercial services and other activities[20]; and

(xiii) ensuring that arrangements for the collection of the licence fee are efficient, appropriate and proportionate[21].

The Trust plays an executive role in relation to the Trust Unit[22]. In addition, the Trust has all the functions expressly or impliedly conferred upon it elsewhere by or under the Charter or any Framework Agreement[23].

The Trust must adopt and publish Protocols which: (a) set out a detailed framework within which the Trust will (consistently with all specific requirements of the Charter or any Framework Agreement) discharge its functions, which may address the practical application of its functions and impose upon the Trust more specific obligations within the scope of its functions; (b) address in greater detail the relationship between the Trust and the Executive Board, and what the division between their respective functions will mean in practice (which may include allocating as between the Trust and the Executive Board responsibility for anything which is not allocated by the Charter or any Framework Agreement)[24].

1 As to the BBC Trust within the constitution of the BBC see PARA 604. As to the meaning of 'BBC' see PARA 603; and as to the meaning of 'trust' for these purposes see PARA 604 note 2.

2 'The licence fee revenue' means any sums which may be paid to the BBC by the Secretary of State from time to time, pursuant to any Framework Agreement, to fund the services provided by the BBC for the promotion of its public purposes: *Royal Charter for the Continuance of the British Broadcasting Corporation* (Cm 6925) (2006) art 56. As to the meaning of 'public purposes' see PARA 603 note 3. As to the Secretary of State see PARA 507 note 32.

3 *Royal Charter for the Continuance of the British Broadcasting Corporation* (Cm 6925) (2006) art 22(1).

4 As to the meaning of 'licence fee payer' see PARA 604 note 3.

5 *Royal Charter for the Continuance of the British Broadcasting Corporation* (Cm 6925) (2006) art 22(2). In exercising all its functions, the Trust must act in the public interest and, in particular, it must: (1) represent the interests of licence fee payers; (2) secure that the independence of the BBC is maintained; (3) carefully and appropriately assess the views of licence fee payers; (4) exercise rigorous stewardship of public money; (5) have regard to the competitive impact of the BBC's activities on the wider market; and (6) ensure that the BBC observes high standards of openness and transparency: art 23(a)–(e).

6 As to the meaning of 'Framework Agreement' see PARA 603 note 7.

7 *Royal Charter for the Continuance of the British Broadcasting Corporation* (Cm 6925) (2006) art 24(1).

8 *Royal Charter for the Continuance of the British Broadcasting Corporation* (Cm 6925) (2006) art 24(2).

9 *Royal Charter for the Continuance of the British Broadcasting Corporation* (Cm 6925) (2006) art 24(2)(a). See also the *Agreement between Her Majesty's Secretary of State for Culture, Media and Sport and the British Broadcasting Corporation* (Cm 6872) (30 June 2006) cll 5–10.

10 *Royal Charter for the Continuance of the British Broadcasting Corporation* (Cm 6925) (2006) art 24(2)(b).

11 *Royal Charter for the Continuance of the British Broadcasting Corporation* (Cm 6925) (2006) art 24(2)(c).

12 *Royal Charter for the Continuance of the British Broadcasting Corporation* (Cm 6925) (2006) art 24(2)(d).

13 *Royal Charter for the Continuance of the British Broadcasting Corporation* (Cm 6925) (2006) art 24(2)(e).

14 *Royal Charter for the Continuance of the British Broadcasting Corporation* (Cm 6925) (2006) art 24(2)(f).

15 *Royal Charter for the Continuance of the British Broadcasting Corporation* (Cm 6925) (2006) art 24(2)(g).

16 *Royal Charter for the Continuance of the British Broadcasting Corporation* (Cm 6925) (2006) art 24(2)(h).

17 *Royal Charter for the Continuance of the British Broadcasting Corporation* (Cm 6925) (2006) art 24(2)(i). As to value for money examinations see further the *Agreement between Her Majesty's Secretary of State for Culture, Media and Sport and the British Broadcasting Corporation* (Cm 6872) (30 June 2006) cl 79.

18 *Royal Charter for the Continuance of the British Broadcasting Corporation* (Cm 6925) (2006) art 24(2)(j).

19 *Royal Charter for the Continuance of the British Broadcasting Corporation* (Cm 6925) (2006) art 24(2)(k).

20 *Royal Charter for the Continuance of the British Broadcasting Corporation* (Cm 6925) (2006) art 24(2)(l).

21 *Royal Charter for the Continuance of the British Broadcasting Corporation* (Cm 6925) (2006) art 24(2)(m).

22 *Royal Charter for the Continuance of the British Broadcasting Corporation* (Cm 6925) (2006) art 24(3). As to the Trust Unit see arts 42, 43; and PARA 612.

23 *Royal Charter for the Continuance of the British Broadcasting Corporation* (Cm 6925) (2006) art 24(4).

24 *Royal Charter for the Continuance of the British Broadcasting Corporation* (Cm 6925) (2006) art 25. Such Protocols must include Protocols on engaging with licence fee payers (see art 26) and on openness and transparency (see art 27).

608. Constitution of Executive Board. The Executive Board of the BBC[1] is to consist of executive and non-executive members[2], their numbers, so far as practicable, to be as determined by the Executive Board with the approval of the Trust[3]. However, so far as practicable, there must always be at least four non-executive members and the total number of non-executive members must never fall below one third nor be equal to or exceed one half of the total membership of the Board[4].

The chairman of the Executive Board is to be appointed by the Trust, to serve in either an executive or a non-executive capacity[5]. Only the Director General[6] can be appointed to serve as the chairman in an executive capacity[7]. Detailed provision is made as to the terms on which the chairman serves[8], and as to the manner of appointment of executive[9] and non-executive members[10] of the Board and the terms on which they serve[11].

1 As to the Executive Board within the constitution of the BBC see PARA 604. As to the meaning of 'BBC' see PARA 603.

2 *Royal Charter for the Continuance of the British Broadcasting Corporation* (Cm 6925) (2006) art 28(1).

3 *Royal Charter for the Continuance of the British Broadcasting Corporation* (Cm 6925) (2006) art 28(2). As to the BBC Trust within the constitution of the BBC see PARA 604.

4 *Royal Charter for the Continuance of the British Broadcasting Corporation* (Cm 6925) (2006) art 28(3). As to the meaning for these purposes of 'so far as practicable' see art 28(4).

5 *Royal Charter for the Continuance of the British Broadcasting Corporation* (Cm 6925) (2006) art 29(1), (2).

6 As to the Director General see PARA 612.

7 *Royal Charter for the Continuance of the British Broadcasting Corporation* (Cm 6925) (2006) art 29(4). A non-executive chairman may, but need not, be appointed from among the existing

non-executive members of the Executive Board. If he is not already a member of the Board, he becomes a non-executive member by virtue of his appointment to serve as the chairman in a non-executive capacity: art 29(3).

8   *Royal Charter for the Continuance of the British Broadcasting Corporation* (Cm 6925) (2006) art 32.
9   See the *Royal Charter for the Continuance of the British Broadcasting Corporation* (Cm 6925) (2006) art 30.
10 See the *Royal Charter for the Continuance of the British Broadcasting Corporation* (Cm 6925) (2006) art 31.
11 See the *Royal Charter for the Continuance of the British Broadcasting Corporation* (Cm 6925) (2006) art 33.

609.   Executive Board: meetings etc.   The Executive Board of the BBC[1] must meet for the transaction of its business and affairs[2]. The Executive Board must make standing orders dealing with the summoning, notice, time, place, quorum, management and adjournment of its meetings, including provision for the exercise of a casting vote[3]. The Executive Board may set up committees of the Executive Board[4]; these must always include an audit committee[5] and a remuneration committee[6]. Nomination committees are required to propose members for appointment to the Executive Board[7].

The Executive Board may delegate functions, including decision-taking, to a committee, to an individual member of the Executive Board, or to other members of staff, on such terms and conditions as it thinks fit[8].

The Executive Board may make regulations about the transaction and management of its business and affairs[9], but such regulations are subject to any regulations made[10] by the BBC Trust[11].

1   As to the Executive Board within the constitution of the BBC see PARA 604. As to the meaning of 'BBC' see PARA 603.
2   *Royal Charter for the Continuance of the British Broadcasting Corporation* (Cm 6925) (2006) art 34(1).
3   *Royal Charter for the Continuance of the British Broadcasting Corporation* (Cm 6925) (2006) art 34(2). The standing orders may make provision for meetings of the Executive Board to be held in circumstances in which members participate without being physically present in the same place as other participating members (for example, by means of telephone or videoconferencing): art 34(3). The standing orders must be made as regulations in accordance with art 37 (see the text and note 9): art 37(3).
4   *Royal Charter for the Continuance of the British Broadcasting Corporation* (Cm 6925) (2006) art 35(1). The number, remit and composition of such committees are a matter for the Executive Board, subject to art 35(3)–(6): art 35(2). No committee of the Executive Board may include anyone who is not a member of the Executive Board: art 35(6).
5   *Royal Charter for the Continuance of the British Broadcasting Corporation* (Cm 6925) (2006) art 35(3). The audit committee must have functions commensurate with the highest standards of corporate governance. Only non-executive members of the Executive Board may be members of the committee: art 35(3). As to non-executive members of the Executive Board see PARA 608.
6   *Royal Charter for the Continuance of the British Broadcasting Corporation* (Cm 6925) (2006) art 35(5). The remuneration committee must at least perform the functions described in art 33. Only non-executive members of the Executive Board may be members of the committee: art 35(5).
7   See the *Royal Charter for the Continuance of the British Broadcasting Corporation* (Cm 6925) (2006) art 35(4). Their functions are described in arts 30, 31.
8   *Royal Charter for the Continuance of the British Broadcasting Corporation* (Cm 6925) (2006) art 36.
9   *Royal Charter for the Continuance of the British Broadcasting Corporation* (Cm 6925) (2006) art 37(1). Regulations may be made only at a meeting of the Executive Board: art 37(2).
10 Ie the *Royal Charter for the Continuance of the British Broadcasting Corporation* (Cm 6925) (2006) art 21: see PARA 606.
11 *Royal Charter for the Continuance of the British Broadcasting Corporation* (Cm 6925) (2006) art 37(4).

610.   Role of Executive Board.   The Executive Board[1] is the executive body of
the BBC and is responsible for:

(1)   the delivery of the BBC's services in accordance with the priorities set by
       purpose remits and the framework set by service licences and any other
       strategies[2];

(2)   the direction of the BBC's editorial and creative output[3];

(3)   the operational management of the BBC (except the BBC Trust Unit)[4];

(4)   ensuring compliance with all legal and regulatory requirements placed
       upon the BBC (including the initial handling of complaints about the
       BBC) except to the extent that they relate to the affairs of the Trust or
       the BBC Trust Unit[5];

(5)   ensuring compliance with requirements placed upon the Executive
       Board by the Trust (for example, through Protocols or the Trust's
       statement of policy on fair trading)[6];

(6)   making proposals to the Trust for anything which is for the Trust to
       approve[7];

(7)   appointing, and holding to account, the management of the BBC and its
       subsidiaries[8];

(8)   the conduct of the BBC's operational financial affairs (except those
       relating directly to the affairs of the Trust and the BBC Trust Unit) in a
       manner best designed to ensure value for money[9]; and

(9)   accounting to the Trust for its own performance and the performance of
       the BBC and its subsidiaries[10].

In addition, the Executive Board has all the functions expressly or impliedly
conferred upon it elsewhere by or under the Charter or any Framework
Agreement[11], but in the exercise of its functions, the Executive Board is subject
to the Trust[12].

1   As to the Executive Board within the constitution of the BBC see PARA 604. As to the meaning
    of 'BBC' see PARA 603.

2   *Royal Charter for the Continuance of the British Broadcasting Corporation* (Cm 6925) (2006)
    art 38(1)(a). As to the purpose remits see the *Agreement between Her Majesty's Secretary of
    State for Culture, Media and Sport and the British Broadcasting Corporation* (Cm 6872)
    (30 June 2006) cll 5–10.

3   *Royal Charter for the Continuance of the British Broadcasting Corporation* (Cm 6925) (2006)
    art 38(1)(b).

4   *Royal Charter for the Continuance of the British Broadcasting Corporation* (Cm 6925) (2006)
    art 38(1)(c). As to the BBC Trust Unit see PARA 612.

5   *Royal Charter for the Continuance of the British Broadcasting Corporation* (Cm 6925) (2006)
    art 38(1)(d). As to the BBC Trust see PARA 604.

6   *Royal Charter for the Continuance of the British Broadcasting Corporation* (Cm 6925) (2006)
    art 38(1)(e). As to Protocols see PARA 607.

7   *Royal Charter for the Continuance of the British Broadcasting Corporation* (Cm 6925) (2006)
    art 38(1)(f). The approval referred to in the text is approval under art 24(2)(a), (d) or (e) (see
    PARA 607 heads (i), (iv), (v)): art 38(1)(f).

8   *Royal Charter for the Continuance of the British Broadcasting Corporation* (Cm 6925) (2006)
    art 38(1)(g).

9   *Royal Charter for the Continuance of the British Broadcasting Corporation* (Cm 6925) (2006)
    art 38(1)(h).

10 *Royal Charter for the Continuance of the British Broadcasting Corporation* (Cm 6925) (2006)
    art 38(1)(i).

11 *Royal Charter for the Continuance of the British Broadcasting Corporation* (Cm 6925) (2006)
    art 38(2). As to the meaning of 'Framework Agreement' see PARA 603 note 7.

12 *Royal Charter for the Continuance of the British Broadcasting Corporation* (Cm 6925) (2006)
    art 38(3). See art 9; and PARA 604.

611. Audience Councils. There are four Audience Councils, corresponding in geographical remit to the four nations for which BBC Trust members are designated[1]. The purpose of the Audience Councils is to bring the diverse perspectives of licence fee payers[2] to bear on the work of the BBC Trust, through links with diverse communities, including geographically-based communities and other communities of interest, within the United Kingdom[3]. The Councils must use their engagement with and understanding of communities to advise the Trust on how well the BBC is promoting its public purposes[4] from the perspective of licence fee payers, and serving licence fee payers, in different parts of the United Kingdom[5]. In addition, there must be mechanisms for bringing together members from different Councils to consider how well the BBC is serving audiences in promoting the public purposes[6].

The Councils have the following remit[7]:

(1) to engage with licence fee payers including geographically-based communities and other communities of interest[8];

(2) to be consulted on all relevant proposals that are required to be subject to a public value test by virtue of any Framework Agreement[9];

(3) to be consulted, as part of any review of service licences which the Trust undertakes in accordance with the requirements of any Framework Agreement, on the content of the service licences and the performance of the services to which the review relates[10];

(4) to be consulted on the BBC's performance in promoting the public purposes[11];

(5) to submit a report to the Trust each year on the BBC's performance in each nation and advise on issues arising[12]; and

(6) to publish an Annual Review Report each year in the nation concerned, assessing how well the BBC is meeting the needs of licence fee payers in that nation[13].

The detail of how the Councils are to be set up, run and recruited have been set out in a Protocol[14]. The Trust is obliged make whatever arrangements it considers appropriate for supporting the work of Audience Councils, within a framework established by a Protocol[15].

1 Ie under the *Royal Charter for the Continuance of the British Broadcasting Corporation* (Cm 6925) (2006) art 14: see PARA 605. As to the BBC Trust within the constitution of the BBC see PARA 604. As to the meaning of 'BBC' see PARA 603; and as to the meaning of 'trust' for these purposes see PARA 604 note 2.

2 As to the meaning of 'licence fee payer' see PARA 604 note 3.

3 *Royal Charter for the Continuance of the British Broadcasting Corporation* (Cm 6925) (2006) art 39(1), (3). Each Council is to be chaired by the designated Trust member for the nation concerned: art 39(3). The network of members across the four Councils must be recruited to ensure that they reflect the diversity of the United Kingdom, have connections with communities, and are able to take a view on how the public purposes should be promoted: art 39(5). As to the meaning of 'United Kingdom' see PARA 510 note 13.

4 As to the meaning of 'public purposes' see PARA 603 note 3.

5 *Royal Charter for the Continuance of the British Broadcasting Corporation* (Cm 6925) (2006) art 39(2).

6 *Royal Charter for the Continuance of the British Broadcasting Corporation* (Cm 6925) (2006) art 39(4).

7 *Royal Charter for the Continuance of the British Broadcasting Corporation* (Cm 6925) (2006) art 39(6).

8 *Royal Charter for the Continuance of the British Broadcasting Corporation* (Cm 6925) (2006) art 39(6)(a).

9 *Royal Charter for the Continuance of the British Broadcasting Corporation* (Cm 6925) (2006) art 39(6)(b). As to the meaning of 'Framework Agreement' see PARA 603 note 7. As to the public

value test see the *Agreement between Her Majesty's Secretary of State for Culture, Media and Sport and the British Broadcasting Corporation* (Cm 6872) (30 June 2006) cll 24–27; and PARA 812.

10 *Royal Charter for the Continuance of the British Broadcasting Corporation* (Cm 6925) (2006) art 39(6)(c).

11 *Royal Charter for the Continuance of the British Broadcasting Corporation* (Cm 6925) (2006) art 39(6)(d).

12 *Royal Charter for the Continuance of the British Broadcasting Corporation* (Cm 6925) (2006) art 39(6)(e).

13 *Royal Charter for the Continuance of the British Broadcasting Corporation* (Cm 6925) (2006) art 39(6)(f).

14 *Royal Charter for the Continuance of the British Broadcasting Corporation* (Cm 6925) (2006) art 39(7). As to the determination of the initial membership of the Councils and transitional arrangements in respect of the former National Broadcasting Councils and Regional Advisory Councils see Schedule para 13. As to Protocols see PARA 607.

15 *Royal Charter for the Continuance of the British Broadcasting Corporation* (Cm 6925) (2006) art 39(8).

612. Director General and staff. There must be a Director General of the BBC[1], who is the chief executive officer of the BBC[2]. He is an executive member of the Executive Board[3] and may be its chairman[4]. The Director General is also the editor-in-chief of the BBC, and as such, he is accountable for the BBC's editorial and creative output[5].

The BBC must appoint staff for the efficient performance of its functions and transaction of its business[6]. Except in relation to the Director General and other executive members of the Executive Board[7] and to Trust staff[8], the appointment of such staff, and their terms and conditions, is a matter for the Executive Board[9].

The BBC Trust must appoint a chief officer of the Trust Unit and such other staff to support and assist the Trust (or any member of the Trust) as it may determine[10]. Such staff are to be appointed by the Trust and the terms and conditions of staff appointed are a matter for the Trust[11]. The BBC staff appointed by the Trust belong to a BBC Trust Unit which is kept administratively separate from the rest of the BBC's organisation[12]. The Trust Unit is under the executive control of the Trust[13]. BBC staff who belong to the Trust Unit are not subject to, nor may they act on behalf of, the Executive Board[14]. BBC staff may transfer between the Trust Unit and the rest of the BBC's organisation only under arrangements agreed by the Trust and the Executive Board[15].

The Trust and the Executive Board must each ensure that at all times they have in place suitable arrangements under which they (or their representatives) will, where appropriate: (1) consult BBC staff on all matters affecting the interests of those staff; and (2) seek to consult with any appropriate organisation with a view to maintaining or (as the case may be) establishing and maintaining adequate arrangements of specified kinds[16].

1 *Royal Charter for the Continuance of the British Broadcasting Corporation* (Cm 6925) (2006) art 40(1). As to the meaning of 'BBC' see PARA 603.

2 *Royal Charter for the Continuance of the British Broadcasting Corporation* (Cm 6925) (2006) art 40(2).

3 As to the Executive Board within the constitution of the BBC see PARA 604.

4 *Royal Charter for the Continuance of the British Broadcasting Corporation* (Cm 6925) (2006) art 40(2). See also art 29; and PARA 608. Where a vacancy is to be filled in the office of Director General and the BBC Trust has determined that the person to be appointed is also to serve as the chairman of the Executive Board in an executive capacity, the Director General is to be appointed, hold and vacate office in accordance with arts 29 and 32: art 40(4). In other circumstances, the Director General is appointed in accordance with art 30 and holds and vacates office in accordance with art 33: art 40(5). As to the BBC Trust see PARAS 604–607.

5 *Royal Charter for the Continuance of the British Broadcasting Corporation* (Cm 6925) (2006) art 40(3).

6 *Royal Charter for the Continuance of the British Broadcasting Corporation* (Cm 6925) (2006) art 41(1).

7 *Royal Charter for the Continuance of the British Broadcasting Corporation* (Cm 6925) (2006) art 41(3). As to their appointment see arts 29, 30, 32, 33 and 40.

8 As to the appointment of Trust Staff see the *Royal Charter for the Continuance of the British Broadcasting Corporation* (Cm 6925) (2006) art 42; and the text and notes 10–11.

9 *Royal Charter for the Continuance of the British Broadcasting Corporation* (Cm 6925) (2006) art 41(2).

10 *Royal Charter for the Continuance of the British Broadcasting Corporation* (Cm 6925) (2006) art 42(1).

11 *Royal Charter for the Continuance of the British Broadcasting Corporation* (Cm 6925) (2006) art 42(2). The Trust may delegate to the chief officer and/or other members of the Trust Unit the exercise of functions which the Trust has under art 42(2) or art 43: art 42(3).

12 *Royal Charter for the Continuance of the British Broadcasting Corporation* (Cm 6925) (2006) art 43(1).

13 *Royal Charter for the Continuance of the British Broadcasting Corporation* (Cm 6925) (2006) art 43(2). The material and other needs of the Trust Unit are to be determined by the Trust and, generally, the Trust fulfils, in relation to that Unit, the role which the Executive Board fulfils in relation to the rest of the BBC's organisation: art 43(2).

14 *Royal Charter for the Continuance of the British Broadcasting Corporation* (Cm 6925) (2006) art 43(3).

15 *Royal Charter for the Continuance of the British Broadcasting Corporation* (Cm 6925) (2006) art 43(4).

16 *Royal Charter for the Continuance of the British Broadcasting Corporation* (Cm 6925) (2006) art 44(1). The arrangements are for: (1) the settlement by negotiation of the terms and conditions of BBC staff; and (2) the discussion of matters of mutual interest to the BBC and its staff, including: (a) the health, safety and welfare of such staff; (b) equal opportunities and training (without cutting back on any specific obligations as to those matters set out in any Framework Agreement); and (c) efficiency in the operation of the BBC's services: art 44(2). The arrangements must in particular be in keeping with the respective functions of the Trust and the Executive Board under the Charter and any Framework Agreement and with the general nature of the relationship between the Trust and the Executive Board described in the Charter: art 44(3). As to the meaning of 'Framework Agreement' see PARA 603 note 7. As to arrangements for equal opportunities and training in the Framework Agreement see the *Agreement between Her Majesty's Secretary of State for Culture, Media and Sport and the British Broadcasting Corporation* (Cm 6872) (30 June 2006) cll 83–85.

(ii) Powers and Duties as to Broadcasting

613. Objects of the BBC. The BBC[1] exists to serve the public interest[2]. The BBC's main object is the promotion of its public purposes[3]. In addition, the BBC may maintain, establish or acquire subsidiaries through which commercial activities may be undertaken to any extent permitted by a Framework Agreement[4].

The BBC's main activities should be the promotion of its public purposes through the provision of output which consists of information, education and entertainment, supplied by means of: (1) television, radio and online services; (2) similar or related services which make output generally available and which may be in forms or by means of technologies which either have not previously been used by the BBC or which have yet to be developed[5]. The BBC may also carry out other activities which directly or indirectly promote the public purposes, but such activities should be peripheral, subordinate or ancillary to its main activities[6]. The means by which the BBC is, or is not, to promote its public purposes within the scope described in the Charter may be elaborated in a Framework Agreement[7].

The BBC is to be independent in all matters concerning the content of its output, the times and manner in which this is supplied, and in the management of its affairs[8], although this is subject to any provision made by or under the Charter or any Framework Agreement or otherwise by law[9].

1   As to the meaning of 'BBC' see PARA 603.
2   *Royal Charter for the Continuance of the British Broadcasting Corporation* (Cm 6925) (2006) art 3(1).
3   *Royal Charter for the Continuance of the British Broadcasting Corporation* (Cm 6925) (2006) art 3(2). As to the meaning of 'public purposes' see PARA 603 note 3.
4   *Royal Charter for the Continuance of the British Broadcasting Corporation* (Cm 6925) (2006) art 3(3). The BBC's general powers enable it to maintain, establish or acquire subsidiaries for purposes sufficiently connected with its public purposes (see art 47(3), (4)): art 3(3). As to the meaning of 'Framework Agreement' see PARA 603 note 7.
5   *Royal Charter for the Continuance of the British Broadcasting Corporation* (Cm 6925) (2006) art 5(1).
6   *Royal Charter for the Continuance of the British Broadcasting Corporation* (Cm 6925) (2006) art 5(2). Overall, such peripheral, subordinate or ancillary activities of the BBC should bear a proper sense of proportion to the BBC's main activities, and each of them should be appropriate to be carried on by the BBC alongside its main activities: art 5(2).
7   *Royal Charter for the Continuance of the British Broadcasting Corporation* (Cm 6925) (2006) art 5(3). See the *Agreement between Her Majesty's Secretary of State for Culture, Media and Sport and the British Broadcasting Corporation* (Cm 6872) (30 June 2006) cll 5–10.
8   *Royal Charter for the Continuance of the British Broadcasting Corporation* (Cm 6925) (2006) art 6(1).
9   *Royal Charter for the Continuance of the British Broadcasting Corporation* (Cm 6925) (2006) art 6(2). The independence of the BBC is affirmed in the *Agreement between Her Majesty's Secretary of State for Culture, Media and Sport and the British Broadcasting Corporation* (Cm 6872) (30 June 2006) cl 4.

614.   UK public service licences and non-service activities.   The BBC Trust[1] must issue a service licence[2] in respect of each UK public service[3] delivered by the BBC, and each service licence must define the scope of the service, its aims and objectives, its headline budget and, where appropriate, other important features, having regard to the needs of licence fee payers[4] and others who may be affected[5]. In particular, a licence must describe the key characteristics of the service[6]. Each licence should clearly set out how the service will contribute to the promotion of the public purposes[7] and of relevant priorities set out in purpose remits[8]. Each licence must also include indicators against which the Trust can monitor performance, which must include taking account in some way of the views of licence fee payers[9].

In performing its function of issuing service licences, it is the responsibility of the Trust to determine not only which activities of the BBC should be covered by a service licence, but how they should be covered (in particular, which activities should be covered by their own licence rather than by a licence with a broader scope covering other activities as well)[10]. In taking such decisions, the Trust should have regard to three considerations (none of which is conclusive on its own) and the need to demonstrate how they have been taken into account[11]. The first consideration is a presumption that activities that involve the selection or commissioning of content and its scheduling or distribution are likely to be appropriate to be covered by a service licence[12]. The second consideration is the importance of delivering the greatest benefit and clarity for licence fee payers and making the decisions that would make most sense to them[13]. The third consideration is the potential benefits of such a decision in providing certainty as to the scope of that service for, and opportunities for consultation with, other operators in the market place[14]. Before issuing a service licence, the Trust must have undertaken a public consultation[15].

Service licences must be reviewed periodically by the Trust, and every such licence must be reviewed at least once every five years[16]. To promote transparency, the Trust must publish information on its intended programme of reviews[17]. In reviewing a service licence, the Trust must undertake a public consultation[18]. If, at the end of a review, the Trust reaches the conclusion that it has concerns that may need to be addressed through an amendment of the service licence, or if necessary the discontinuance of the service altogether, the Trust must convey those concerns to the Executive Board[19]. The resolution of those concerns to the satisfaction of the Trust should occur in accordance with any applicable Protocols[20].

It is the responsibility of the Trust to ensure that the principles that underlie the treatment of services are, where relevant, applied to non-service activities[21] in a way which the Trust considers appropriate to the circumstances[22].

1   As to the BBC Trust within the constitution of the BBC see PARA 604. As to the meaning of 'BBC' see PARA 603.

2   Ie under the *Royal Charter for the Continuance of the British Broadcasting Corporation* (Cm 6925) (2006) art 24(2)(c): see PARA 607 head (iii).

3   As to the meaning of 'UK public services' see PARA 855 note 6; and see PARA 615. As to the meaning of 'service' see PARA 855 note 6. At the date at which this volume states the law, service licences exist in respect of eleven BBC television services (ie BBC One, BBC Two, BBC Three, BBC Four, BBC HD, CBBC, CBeebies, BBC News, BBC Parliament, BBC Red Button, BBC Alba), sixteen BBC radio services (ie BBC Radio 1, BBC Radio 2, BBC Radio 3, BBC Radio 4, BBC Radio 5 live, BBC Radio 5 live sports extra, 1Xtra, BBC 6 Music, BBC 7, BBC Asian Network, BBC Local Radio, BBC Radio Scotland, BBC Radio nan Gaidheal, BBC Radio Wales, BBC Radio Cymru, BBC Radio Ulster/BBC Radio Foyle), and one online and mobile service (BBC Online). Several of these services are under review or are to be reviewed in 2011.

4   In the *Agreement between Her Majesty's Secretary of State for Culture, Media and Sport and the British Broadcasting Corporation* (Cm 6872) (30 June 2006), a reference to a 'licence fee payer' is not to be taken literally but includes, not only a person to whom a TV licence is issued under the Communications Act 2003 s 364 (see PARA 949), but also (so far as is sensible in the context) any other person in the United Kingdom who watches, listens to or uses any BBC service, or may do so or wish to do so in the future: *Agreement between Her Majesty's Secretary of State for Culture, Media and Sport and the British Broadcasting Corporation* (Cm 6872) (30 June 2006) cll 102, 104.

5   *Agreement between Her Majesty's Secretary of State for Culture, Media and Sport and the British Broadcasting Corporation* (Cm 6872) (30 June 2006) cll 16, 17(1).

6   *Agreement between Her Majesty's Secretary of State for Culture, Media and Sport and the British Broadcasting Corporation* (Cm 6872) (30 June 2006) cl 17(1).

7   As to the meaning of 'public purposes' see PARA 603 note 3.

8   *Agreement between Her Majesty's Secretary of State for Culture, Media and Sport and the British Broadcasting Corporation* (Cm 6872) (30 June 2006) cl 17(2). As to purpose remits see cll 5–10. There is a presumption that any changes to the key characteristics of a service described as such in its service licence will require the application of a public value test (see cl 25(3); and PARA 812). The Trust should take account of this in defining the key characteristics of a service in a licence: cl 17(3).

9   *Agreement between Her Majesty's Secretary of State for Culture, Media and Sport and the British Broadcasting Corporation* (Cm 6872) (30 June 2006) cl 17(2).

10 *Agreement between Her Majesty's Secretary of State for Culture, Media and Sport and the British Broadcasting Corporation* (Cm 6872) (30 June 2006) cl 18(1).

11 *Agreement between Her Majesty's Secretary of State for Culture, Media and Sport and the British Broadcasting Corporation* (Cm 6872) (30 June 2006) cl 18(2).

12 *Agreement between Her Majesty's Secretary of State for Culture, Media and Sport and the British Broadcasting Corporation* (Cm 6872) (30 June 2006) cl 18(3).

13 *Agreement between Her Majesty's Secretary of State for Culture, Media and Sport and the British Broadcasting Corporation* (Cm 6872) (30 June 2006) cl 18(4). In particular, activities which are recognised as a service by licence fee payers are likely to be appropriate to be covered

by a service licence, and the boundaries between different service licences are likely to reflect the boundaries between services in the perception of licence fee payers: cl 18(4).

14 *Agreement between Her Majesty's Secretary of State for Culture, Media and Sport and the British Broadcasting Corporation* (Cm 6872) (30 June 2006) cl 18(5).

15 *Agreement between Her Majesty's Secretary of State for Culture, Media and Sport and the British Broadcasting Corporation* (Cm 6872) (30 June 2006) cl 19.

16 *Agreement between Her Majesty's Secretary of State for Culture, Media and Sport and the British Broadcasting Corporation* (Cm 6872) (30 June 2006) cl 20(1). Subject to that requirement, the Trust may structure its programme of reviews as it thinks fit: cl 20(1). As to the programme of reviews see cl 20(2).

17 *Agreement between Her Majesty's Secretary of State for Culture, Media and Sport and the British Broadcasting Corporation* (Cm 6872) (30 June 2006) cl 20(1).

18 *Agreement between Her Majesty's Secretary of State for Culture, Media and Sport and the British Broadcasting Corporation* (Cm 6872) (30 June 2006) cl 20(3). As to the meaning of obligations for the Trust to consult publicly see cl 103.

19 *Agreement between Her Majesty's Secretary of State for Culture, Media and Sport and the British Broadcasting Corporation* (Cm 6872) (30 June 2006) cl 20(4). As to the Executive Board within the constitution of the BBC see PARA 604. Clause 20 does not prevent the Trust from considering particular aspects of a service and expressing concerns to the Executive Board for resolution in a similar manner (which may or may not lead to a specific amendment of the service licence concerned); nor does it prevent the Executive Board from independently making proposals to the Trust for the amendment or revocation of a service licence whenever it thinks appropriate: cl 20(6). However, the five year requirement set out in cl 20(1) (see the text and note 16) is satisfied only where the Trust has in fact reviewed the whole of the service licence as a single exercise: cl 20(6).

20 *Agreement between Her Majesty's Secretary of State for Culture, Media and Sport and the British Broadcasting Corporation* (Cm 6872) (30 June 2006) cl 20(5). As to Protocols see PARA 607.

21 'Non-service activities', means those activities of the BBC which do not have the nature of a service and are therefore outside the scope of many of the formal requirements expressed in the *Agreement between Her Majesty's Secretary of State for Culture, Media and Sport and the British Broadcasting Corporation* (Cm 6872) (30 June 2006) (eg the system of service licences and the detailed requirements about the public value test and market impact assessments: see PARA 812): cl 22(1). The Trust must bear in mind the fact that non-service activities may be significant and that they may raise issues of public value and have market implications: cl 22(2). Clause 22 does not apply to any non-service activities which are: (1) within the definition of 'commercial services' in cl 101 (see PARA 624 note 2); or (2) undertaken primarily with the purpose of producing an effect outside the United Kingdom: cl 22(4). As to the meaning of 'United Kingdom' see PARA 510 note 13.

22 *Agreement between Her Majesty's Secretary of State for Culture, Media and Sport and the British Broadcasting Corporation* (Cm 6872) (30 June 2006) cl 22(3). This may eg involve an evidence-based process of investigating and assessing the public interest and market implications before making a significant change in a non-service activity, even if the application of the public value test in its full rigour is considered inappropriate (though the Trust should not assume that a full public value test will not sometimes be appropriate even for non-service activities): cl 22(3).

615. UK public services. As at 30 June 2006[1], the BBC[2] undertook to provide specified services as UK public services[3]: namely (1) specified television services designed for audiences across the UK[4]; (2) specified radio services designed for audiences across the UK[5]; (3) specified radio services designed primarily for audiences in particular parts of the UK[6]; and (4) specified online services[7]. The BBC Trust[8] may approve the launch of new UK public services, or the termination of or material change to the nature of existing services[9].

The BBC must do all that is reasonably practicable to ensure that viewers, listeners and other users (as the case may be) are able to access the UK public services that are intended for them, or elements of their content, in a range of convenient and cost effective ways which are available or might become available in the future[10]. Any change in those means may (where applicable) be subject to the need to amend the relevant service licence or apply the public value test[11]; but in the case of services primarily designed for viewers, listeners or other users in particular parts of the UK, in addition to seeking to reach those people the BBC may, where it is cost effective and beneficial to do so, make those services available to viewers, listeners or other users more widely[12]. In addition to these general obligations, the BBC is also subject to specific obligations[13].

The content of the UK public services taken as a whole must be high quality, challenging, original, innovative and engaging[14]. Every programme included in the UK public broadcasting services[15] must exhibit at least one of those characteristics, and in relation to other UK public services, each item of content must exhibit at least one of those characteristics[16].

In performing its functions in relation to the UK Public Television Services, the BBC Trust must have regard to the statutory purposes of public service television broadcasting[17] and the desirability of those purposes being fulfilled in a manner that is compatible[18] with the relevant statutory provision[19].

1   Ie the date on which the *Agreement between Her Majesty's Secretary of State for Culture, Media and Sport and the British Broadcasting Corporation* (Cm 6872) was made.

2   As to the meaning of 'BBC' see PARA 603.

3   *Agreement between Her Majesty's Secretary of State for Culture, Media and Sport and the British Broadcasting Corporation* (Cm 6872) (30 June 2006) cl 11(1). As to the meaning of 'service' see PARA 855 note 6.

4   *Agreement between Her Majesty's Secretary of State for Culture, Media and Sport and the British Broadcasting Corporation* (Cm 6872) (30 June 2006) cl 11(2). The services specified are: (1) BBC One; (2) BBC Two; (3) BBC Three; (4) BBC Four; (5) CBeebies; (6) The CBBC Channel; (7) BBC News 24; (8) BBC Parliament; and (9) BBCi: cl 11(2), which also describes the nature of each service. In the Agreement, 'the UK' is to be taken to mean, for these purposes only, the United Kingdom, together with the Channel Islands and the Isle of Man: cl 104. As to the meaning of 'United Kingdom' see PARA 510 note 13.

5   *Agreement between Her Majesty's Secretary of State for Culture, Media and Sport and the British Broadcasting Corporation* (Cm 6872) (30 June 2006) cl 11(3). The services specified are: (1) Radio 1; (2) 1Xtra; (3) Radio 2; (4) Radio 3; (5) Radio 4; (6) BBC Radio Five Live and Sports Extra; (7) BBC 6 Music; (8) BBC 7; and (9) BBC Asian Network: cl 11(3), which also describes the nature of each service.

6   *Agreement between Her Majesty's Secretary of State for Culture, Media and Sport and the British Broadcasting Corporation* (Cm 6872) (30 June 2006) cl 11(4). The services specified are: (1) BBC Radio Scotland; (2) BBC Radio nan Gaidheal; (3) BBC Radio Wales; (4) BBC Radio Cymru; (5) BBC Radio Ulster and BBC Radio Foyle; (6) a number of local radio services for audiences in different parts of England: cl 11(4), which also describes the nature of each service.

7   *Agreement between Her Majesty's Secretary of State for Culture, Media and Sport and the British Broadcasting Corporation* (Cm 6872) (30 June 2006) cl 11(5). The services specified are: (1) bbc.co.uk; and (2) BBC jam: cl 11(5), which also describes the nature of each service.

8   As to the BBC Trust within the constitution of the BBC see PARA 604.

9   *Agreement between Her Majesty's Secretary of State for Culture, Media and Sport and the British Broadcasting Corporation* (Cm 6872) (30 June 2006) cl 11(6). This is subject to the requirements of cll 16–20, 23–33 (see PARAS 614, 812): cl 11(6).

10   *Agreement between Her Majesty's Secretary of State for Culture, Media and Sport and the British Broadcasting Corporation* (Cm 6872) (30 June 2006) cl 12(1). These could include (for example) broadcasting, streaming or making content available on-demand, whether by terrestrial, satellite, cable or broadband networks (fixed or wireless) or via the internet: cl 12(1).

11   *Agreement between Her Majesty's Secretary of State for Culture, Media and Sport and the British Broadcasting Corporation* (Cm 6872) (30 June 2006) cl 12(2). See in particular cll 16–20, 23–33. As to the public value test see PARA 812.

12   *Agreement between Her Majesty's Secretary of State for Culture, Media and Sport and the British Broadcasting Corporation* (Cm 6872) (30 June 2006) cl 12(3).

13   *Agreement between Her Majesty's Secretary of State for Culture, Media and Sport and the British Broadcasting Corporation* (Cm 6872) (30 June 2006) cl 12(4). The text refers to the obligations set out in cll 34–36: see PARA 620.

14   *Agreement between Her Majesty's Secretary of State for Culture, Media and Sport and the British Broadcasting Corporation* (Cm 6872) (30 June 2006) cl 14(1).

15 'The UK Public Television Services' means those UK public services which consist of television programme services, and 'UK Public Television Service' means any of those services: *Agreement between Her Majesty's Secretary of State for Culture, Media and Sport and the British Broadcasting Corporation* (Cm 6872) (30 June 2006) cl 104.

16 *Agreement between Her Majesty's Secretary of State for Culture, Media and Sport and the British Broadcasting Corporation* (Cm 6872) (30 June 2006) cl 14(2).

17 Ie as set out in the Communications Act 2003 s 264(4): see PARA 788 note 10.

18 Ie with the Communications Act 2003 s 264(6): see PARA 788.

19 *Agreement between Her Majesty's Secretary of State for Culture, Media and Sport and the British Broadcasting Corporation* (Cm 6872) (30 June 2006) cl 15.

616. Statements of programme policy. The Executive Board[1] of the BBC must, at annual intervals, prepare statements of programme policy in respect of the UK public broadcasting services[2] and submit them to the BBC Trust[3] for approval[4]. The statements of programme policy must: (1) include such a statement in respect of each network service[5], setting out the BBC's proposals for how that service will, during the following year, contribute to the fulfilment of the public service remit[6]; and (2) set out, in an appropriate manner, the BBC's proposals for how the other UK public broadcasting services will, during the following year, contribute to the fulfilment of that remit[7]. Every statement of programme policy so prepared and approved must be published by the BBC as soon as practicable after it is approved and must be published in such manner as the Trust considers appropriate[8]. The Trust must monitor the BBC's performance in the carrying out of the proposals contained in each statement of programme policy, and each annual report presented by the Corporation[9] must contain a report on the performance of the BBC in the carrying out, during the period to which the statement relates, of the proposals contained in any relevant statement[10].

1 As to the Executive Board within the constitution of the BBC see PARA 604. As to the meaning of 'BBC' see PARA 603.

2 As to the meaning of 'UK public broadcasting services' see PARA 615. As to the meaning of 'service' see PARA 855 note 6.

3 As to the BBC Trust within the constitution of the BBC see PARA 604.

4 *Agreement between Her Majesty's Secretary of State for Culture, Media and Sport and the British Broadcasting Corporation* (Cm 6872) (30 June 2006) cl 21(1). In performing their respective functions in relation to any statement of programme policy under cl 21, the Trust and the Executive Board must each consider: (1) the guidance given by OFCOM about the preparation of statements of programme policy for the purposes of the Communications Act 2003 s 266 (see PARAS 642, 662, 677); and (2) the reports previously published by OFCOM under ss 264 and 358 (see PARAS 788, 853), for the purpose of deciding how far such guidance and reports contain, in the view of the Trust or the Executive Board, anything of relevance to the circumstances of the BBC which ought to be taken into account in preparing that statement: *Agreement between Her Majesty's Secretary of State for Culture, Media and Sport and the British Broadcasting Corporation* (Cm 6872) (30 June 2006) cl 21(3). As to OFCOM see PARA 507.

5 For these purposes, 'network service' means a television or radio service designed for audiences across the UK, and the BBC: (1) may treat any such service provided in regional variations as a single such service; but (2) may treat the actual regional variations within a service so treated as if they were comprised within the other UK public broadcasting services mentioned in the *Agreement between Her Majesty's Secretary of State for Culture, Media and Sport and the British Broadcasting Corporation* (Cm 6872) (30 June 2006) cl 21(2)(b) (head (2) in the text): cl 21(7).

6 For these purposes, 'the public service remit' means the BBC's programming obligations under the Charter and the *Agreement between Her Majesty's Secretary of State for Culture, Media and Sport and the British Broadcasting Corporation* (Cm 6872) (30 June 2006) so far as they apply to the UK public broadcasting services: cl 21(7).

7 *Agreement between Her Majesty's Secretary of State for Culture, Media and Sport and the British Broadcasting Corporation* (Cm 6872) (30 June 2006) cl 21(2).

8   *Agreement between Her Majesty's Secretary of State for Culture, Media and Sport and the British Broadcasting Corporation* (Cm 6872) (30 June 2006) cl 21(4).

9   Ie pursuant to the *Royal Charter for the Continuance of the British Broadcasting Corporation* (Cm 6925) (2006) art 45: see PARA 626.

10 *Agreement between Her Majesty's Secretary of State for Culture, Media and Sport and the British Broadcasting Corporation* (Cm 6872) (30 June 2006) cl 21(5). For this purpose, a statement is relevant in relation to a particular annual report if it relates to a period ending before the date on which that report is submitted to the Secretary of State pursuant to *Royal Charter for the Continuance of the British Broadcasting Corporation* (Cm 6925) (2006) art 45 and after the date on which the preceding such report was so submitted: *Agreement between Her Majesty's Secretary of State for Culture, Media and Sport and the British Broadcasting Corporation* (Cm 6872) (30 June 2006) cl 21(6). As to the Secretary of State see PARA 507 note 32.

617. World Service. The BBC[1] must provide the World Service[2]. The World Service involves the broadcast or other distribution of programmes, and the delivery of other services, aimed primarily at users outside the UK[3]. The World Service must be provided: (1) to such users outside the UK, and in such languages, as are approved by the Foreign Secretary; and (2) in accordance with any objectives, priorities and targets agreed with him[4]. The BBC must consult and co-operate with the Foreign Secretary and obtain from him such information regarding international developments, conditions in countries outside the UK, and the policies of Her Majesty's government in its international relations, as the BBC needs to help it plan and prepare the provision of the World Service in the public interest[5].

The BBC must ensure that the World Service maintains high standards of editorial integrity and programme content and quality, having regard, to the extent that the BBC Trust[6] considers them relevant to the circumstances of the World Service, to the particular requirements that apply to the UK public services[7]. The BBC must agree with the Foreign Secretary, and publish, general long-term objectives for the World Service, including: (a) the provision of an accurate, unbiased and independent news service covering international and national developments; (b) the presentation of a balanced British view of those developments; and (c) the accurate and effective representation of British life, institutions and achievements[8]. The BBC must report in reasonable detail on the performance of the World Service, both in its annual report[9] and elsewhere as appropriate[10]. In particular, the BBC must publish (in a manner agreed with the Foreign Secretary) an account of how the World Service is achieving its agreed objectives, priorities and targets[11].

The BBC may arrange for the re-transmission of selected World Service output in the UK[12].

1   As to the meaning of 'BBC' see PARA 603.
        As from 2013–14 responsibility for funding the BBC World Service will transfer from the government to the BBC: see *Spending Review* (Cm 7942) (October 2010).

2   *Agreement between Her Majesty's Secretary of State for Culture, Media and Sport and the British Broadcasting Corporation* (Cm 6872) (30 June 2006) cl 64(1).

3   *Agreement between Her Majesty's Secretary of State for Culture, Media and Sport and the British Broadcasting Corporation* (Cm 6872) (30 June 2006) cl 64(2). As to the meaning of 'UK' see PARA 615 note 4.

4   *Agreement between Her Majesty's Secretary of State for Culture, Media and Sport and the British Broadcasting Corporation* (Cm 6872) (30 June 2006) cl 64(3). As to the Foreign Secretary see CONSTITUTIONAL LAW AND HUMAN RIGHTS vol 8(2) (Reissue) PARA 459.

5   *Agreement between Her Majesty's Secretary of State for Culture, Media and Sport and the British Broadcasting Corporation* (Cm 6872) (30 June 2006) cl 64(4).

6   As to the BBC Trust within the constitution of the BBC see PARA 604.

7 *Agreement between Her Majesty's Secretary of State for Culture, Media and Sport and the British Broadcasting Corporation* (Cm 6872) (30 June 2006) cl 64(5). As to the meaning of 'UK public services' see PARA 855 note 6; and see PARA 615.

8 *Agreement between Her Majesty's Secretary of State for Culture, Media and Sport and the British Broadcasting Corporation* (Cm 6872) (30 June 2006) cl 64(6).

9 As to the annual report see the *Royal Charter for the Continuance of the British Broadcasting Corporation* (Cm 6925) (2006) art 45; and PARA 626.

10 *Agreement between Her Majesty's Secretary of State for Culture, Media and Sport and the British Broadcasting Corporation* (Cm 6872) (30 June 2006) cl 64(7).

11 *Agreement between Her Majesty's Secretary of State for Culture, Media and Sport and the British Broadcasting Corporation* (Cm 6872) (30 June 2006) cl 64(7).

12 *Agreement between Her Majesty's Secretary of State for Culture, Media and Sport and the British Broadcasting Corporation* (Cm 6872) (30 June 2006) cl 64(8).

618. The BBC's archive obligations and research and development activities.
The BBC[1] must: (1) in respect of every programme included in any of the UK public broadcasting services or a UK public on-demand programme service[2], retain a recording of the programme in an agreed[3] form, and for an agreed period; (2) comply with any request to produce such recordings to OFCOM[4] for examination or reproduction; and (3) comply, to the extent that it is able to do so, with any request to produce to OFCOM a script or transcript of a programme included in any of the UK public broadcasting services or a UK public on-demand programme service[5].

The Executive Board[6] must make arrangements for the maintenance of an archive, or archives, of films, sound recordings, other recorded material and printed material which is representative of the sound and television programmes and films broadcast or otherwise distributed by the BBC[7]. Those arrangements: (a) must ensure that every such archive is kept safely, to commonly accepted standards; and (b) must give the public reasonable opportunities to visit the archives and view or listen to material kept there, with or without charge (as the Executive Board thinks fit)[8]. In making those arrangements, the Executive Board must consult such designated bodies[9] as are engaged in maintaining sound, television and film archives as it considers appropriate[10]. The BBC must not destroy, sell or otherwise dispose of any material that it has broadcast or otherwise distributed which it decides not to preserve in any archive without first offering that material, free of charge, to such designated bodies as are engaged in maintaining sound, television and film archives as it considers appropriate[11]. Where the BBC's offer is accepted by any body or bodies, the BBC must transfer the material to that body or those bodies[12].

The Executive Board must ensure that the BBC conducts research and development activities geared to the promotion of the BBC's public purposes[13] and which aim to maintain the BBC's position as a centre of excellence for research and development in broadcasting and other means for the electronic distribution of audio, visual and audiovisual material, and in related technologies[14]. These activities should be conducted both within the BBC and in co-operation with suitable partners, such as university departments and businesses which are active in relevant fields of research and development or the practical application of the fruits of such research and development[15]. The Executive Board must keep the BBC's research and development activities under review, and must (in particular) ensure that an appropriate balance is struck between: (i) the potential for generating revenue through commercial exploitation of its intellectual property; and (ii) the value that might be delivered to licence fee payers[16] and the UK economy by making new developments widely and openly available[17].

1　As to the meaning of 'BBC' see PARA 603.
2　As to the meaning of 'UK public broadcasting services' see PARA 615 note 15. 'UK public on-demand programme service' means a service which is: (1) an on-demand programme service within the meaning of the Communications Act 2003 s 368A (see PARA 784); and (2) a UK public service: *Agreement between Her Majesty's Secretary of State for Culture, Media and Sport and the British Broadcasting Corporation* (Cm 6872) (30 June 2006) cl 104 (amended by Cm 7853, March 2010). As to the meaning of 'service' see PARA 855 note 6.
3　For these purposes, 'agreed' means agreed in accordance with the *Agreement between Her Majesty's Secretary of State for Culture, Media and Sport and the British Broadcasting Corporation* (Cm 6872) (30 June 2006) cl 92 (see PARA 855 note 4): cl 62(3).
4　As to OFCOM see PARA 507.
5　See the *Agreement between Her Majesty's Secretary of State for Culture, Media and Sport and the British Broadcasting Corporation* (Cm 6872) (30 June 2006) cl 62 (amended by Cm 7853, March 2010); and PARA 900.
6　As to the Executive Board within the constitution of the BBC see PARA 604.
7　*Agreement between Her Majesty's Secretary of State for Culture, Media and Sport and the British Broadcasting Corporation* (Cm 6872) (30 June 2006) cl 86(1).
8　*Agreement between Her Majesty's Secretary of State for Culture, Media and Sport and the British Broadcasting Corporation* (Cm 6872) (30 June 2006) cl 86(2).
9　For these purposes, 'designated body' means a body that is designated by order of the Secretary of State for Trade and Industry under the Copyright, Designs and Patents Act 1988 s 75 (see COPYRIGHT, DESIGN RIGHT AND RELATED RIGHTS vol 9(2) (2006 Reissue) PARA 403): *Agreement between Her Majesty's Secretary of State for Culture, Media and Sport and the British Broadcasting Corporation* (Cm 6872) (30 June 2006) cl 86(6).
10　*Agreement between Her Majesty's Secretary of State for Culture, Media and Sport and the British Broadcasting Corporation* (Cm 6872) (30 June 2006) cl 86(3).
11　*Agreement between Her Majesty's Secretary of State for Culture, Media and Sport and the British Broadcasting Corporation* (Cm 6872) (30 June 2006) cl 86(4).
12　*Agreement between Her Majesty's Secretary of State for Culture, Media and Sport and the British Broadcasting Corporation* (Cm 6872) (30 June 2006) cl 86(5).
13　As to the meaning of 'public purposes' see PARA 603 note 3.
14　*Agreement between Her Majesty's Secretary of State for Culture, Media and Sport and the British Broadcasting Corporation* (Cm 6872) (30 June 2006) cl 87(1). In carrying out its function under cl 87(1), the Executive Board must pay particular attention to the desirability of supporting actively in national and international forums the development of 'open standards' (ie technologies where opportunities to participate in their creation and to use them are made widely available, free of charge or on terms that must be fair, reasonable and non-discriminatory): cl 87(2).
15　*Agreement between Her Majesty's Secretary of State for Culture, Media and Sport and the British Broadcasting Corporation* (Cm 6872) (30 June 2006) cl 87(3).
16　As to the meaning of 'licence fee payer' see PARA 614 note 4.
17　*Agreement between Her Majesty's Secretary of State for Culture, Media and Sport and the British Broadcasting Corporation* (Cm 6872) (30 June 2006) cl 87(4). As to the meaning of 'UK' see PARA 615 note 4.

619. Radio spectrum. It is the duty of the BBC Trust[1] to secure the efficient use of the radio spectrum that is available for use by the BBC or its contractors[2]. The Secretary of State[3] may, where it appears to him appropriate to do so either in the interests of public service broadcasting in the United Kingdom[4] or in pursuance of any international obligation of the United Kingdom, direct the BBC to grant to any public service broadcaster the right to use any capacity on a television multiplex service[5] that is under the BBC's control (subject, where applicable, to compliance with any need to obtain a new or revised licence from OFCOM[6] for that purpose)[7].

1　As to the BBC Trust within the constitution of the BBC see PARA 604. As to the meaning of 'BBC' see PARA 603.
2　*Agreement between Her Majesty's Secretary of State for Culture, Media and Sport and the British Broadcasting Corporation* (Cm 6872) (30 June 2006) cl 42(1).
3　As to the Secretary of State see PARA 507 note 32.
4　As to the meaning of 'United Kingdom' see PARA 510 note 13.

5   Ie within the meaning of the Broadcasting Act 1996 Pt I (ss 1–39): see PARA 697.
6   As to OFCOM see PARA 507.
7   *Agreement between Her Majesty's Secretary of State for Culture, Media and Sport and the British Broadcasting Corporation* (Cm 6872) (30 June 2006) cl 42(2).

620.   Duties of the BBC in relation to digital switchover.   Obligations are imposed on the BBC[1] in relation to the progressive replacement of the analogue broadcasting of television services within the UK with digital broadcasting of those services ('digital switchover')[2]. The BBC must arrange the provision of its principal television services[3] in a way that ensures: (1) that the obligations in relation to the provision of those services in digital form[4] are fulfilled; and (2) that, until the digital switchover date[5], the analogue television services[6] continue to be provided[7] by terrestrial broadcasting in analogue form[8].

No later than the digital switchover date, the BBC must secure the objective that substantially the same proportion of households in the UK as could, at 30 June 2006, receive the analogue television services in analogue form by means of terrestrial broadcasting (that is to say, through a television aerial), can receive all the BBC's principal television services in digital form by that means[9]. The BBC is to secure this objective in accordance with a coverage plan approved by the Secretary of State; and that coverage plan: (a) must, in particular, specify the timetable according to which the BBC must progressively cease to provide its principal television services in analogue form and provide them instead in digital form, and the dates by which and order in which that is to take place in different areas of the UK; (b) may also specify the location, power and mode of transmission of the transmitters to be used, and the frequencies to be used, for the terrestrial broadcasting of those services in digital form; (c) may specify geographical locations, or descriptions of such locations, where the BBC is not obliged to provide its principal television services by means of terrestrial broadcasting; and (d) may make provision in relation to the continued terrestrial broadcasting of the analogue television services in analogue form[10]. The Secretary of State must consult OFCOM[11] before approving a coverage plan[12]. The Secretary of State may by a direction require the BBC to alter any coverage plan so approved, but must not do so without first consulting the BBC and OFCOM[13].

The BBC has a general duty to co-operate in achieving digital switchover[14] and to provide information about digital switchover to all viewers of any of the UK Public Television Services in analogue form[15]. It must also comply with a scheme agreed with the Secretary of State concerning the provision of specified[16] help to specified categories of persons for the purpose of enabling them to continue to view the UK Public Television Services when and after they are affected by digital switchover[17].

The Trust must provide the Secretary of State with an annual report on what the BBC has done for the purpose of complying with these provisions[18].

1   As to the meaning of 'BBC' see PARA 603.

2   See the *Agreement between Her Majesty's Secretary of State for Culture, Media and Sport and the British Broadcasting Corporation* (Cm 6872) (30 June 2006) cll 34(1), 104. As to the meaning of 'UK' see PARA 615 note 4.

3   For these purposes, the BBC's 'principal television services' are: (1) such of the television services listed in the *Agreement between Her Majesty's Secretary of State for Culture, Media and Sport and the British Broadcasting Corporation* (Cm 6872) (30 June 2006) cl 11(2) (see PARA 615) as the BBC may be providing at any given time; and (2) any other television service that the BBC is

providing at that time and that is designed for audiences across the UK (with or without national versions or regional variations) or designed principally for audiences in a particular part of the UK: cl 34(2).

4 Ie the obligations in the *Agreement between Her Majesty's Secretary of State for Culture, Media and Sport and the British Broadcasting Corporation* (Cm 6872) (30 June 2006) cl 35: see the text and notes 9–13.

5 In the *Agreement between Her Majesty's Secretary of State for Culture, Media and Sport and the British Broadcasting Corporation* (Cm 6872) (30 June 2006) cll 34–36, the 'digital switchover date' means: (1) in relation to Great Britain, Northern Ireland and the Isle of Man, 31 December 2012 or such other date as the Secretary of State may specify in a direction to the BBC; and (2) in relation to the Channel Islands (or any of them) such date as the Secretary of State may so specify: cl 34(5). As to the meaning of 'Great Britain' see PARA 510 note 13. As to the Secretary of State see PARA 507 note 32.

6 For these purposes, the BBC's 'analogue television services' are such of the BBC's principal television services as were at 30 June 2006 being broadcast by means of terrestrial broadcasting in analogue form (whether or not they were also being so broadcast in digital form at that time): *Agreement between Her Majesty's Secretary of State for Culture, Media and Sport and the British Broadcasting Corporation* (Cm 6872) (30 June 2006) cl 34(3).

7 Ie according to the provisions of the *Agreement between Her Majesty's Secretary of State for Culture, Media and Sport and the British Broadcasting Corporation* (Cm 6872) (30 June 2006) cl 36.

8 *Agreement between Her Majesty's Secretary of State for Culture, Media and Sport and the British Broadcasting Corporation* (Cm 6872) (30 June 2006) cl 34(4).

9 *Agreement between Her Majesty's Secretary of State for Culture, Media and Sport and the British Broadcasting Corporation* (Cm 6872) (30 June 2006) cl 35(1). For the purposes of cl 35(1), whether a service is available to a household does not depend on whether the equipment necessary to enable the service to be viewed is in fact installed at the premises occupied by the household: cl 35(2).

10 *Agreement between Her Majesty's Secretary of State for Culture, Media and Sport and the British Broadcasting Corporation* (Cm 6872) (30 June 2006) cl 35(3).

11 As to OFCOM see PARA 507.

12 *Agreement between Her Majesty's Secretary of State for Culture, Media and Sport and the British Broadcasting Corporation* (Cm 6872) (30 June 2006) cl 35(4).

13 *Agreement between Her Majesty's Secretary of State for Culture, Media and Sport and the British Broadcasting Corporation* (Cm 6872) (30 June 2006) cl 35(5).

14 See the *Agreement between Her Majesty's Secretary of State for Culture, Media and Sport and the British Broadcasting Corporation* (Cm 6872) (30 June 2006) cll 37, 40.

15 See the *Agreement between Her Majesty's Secretary of State for Culture, Media and Sport and the British Broadcasting Corporation* (Cm 6872) (30 June 2006) cl 38. As to the UK Public Television Services see PARA 615.

16 'Specified' means specified in the scheme: *Agreement between Her Majesty's Secretary of State for Culture, Media and Sport and the British Broadcasting Corporation* (Cm 6872) (30 June 2006) cl 39(1).

17 *Agreement between Her Majesty's Secretary of State for Culture, Media and Sport and the British Broadcasting Corporation* (Cm 6872) (30 June 2006) cl 39(1). Once made, the scheme may be amended only in accordance with whatever provisions the scheme itself contains about how it may be amended: cl 39(2). What the BBC does for the purposes of cl 39 is not to be regarded as: (1) requiring a service licence; (2) involving the provision of a service for any of the purposes of the Agreement; or (3) falling within the scope of cl 22 (see PARA 614): cl 39(3).

18 *Agreement between Her Majesty's Secretary of State for Culture, Media and Sport and the British Broadcasting Corporation* (Cm 6872) (30 June 2006) cl 41.

(iii) Finance

621. Financial arrangements: sums payable to the BBC. The Secretary of State[1] is required to pay to the BBC[2] out of money provided by Parliament sums equal to the whole of the net licence revenue[3] or such lesser sums as the Secretary of State may, with the consent of the Treasury, determine[4]. The BBC may use sums so paid to it to fund any activities properly carried on by the BBC except: (1) those carried on for the purposes of any commercial service[5], any services performed at the request of a government department[6], or any service (apart from the World Service[7]) aimed primarily at users outside the UK[8]; (2) any which are carried on for the purposes of a television, radio or online service which is wholly or partly funded by advertisements, subscription[9], sponsorship[10], pay per-view system or any other alternative means of finance[11], unless the Secretary of State has given prior written approval[12].

For the purposes of the World Service, the Foreign Secretary must, in each year, pay to the BBC out of money provided by Parliament such sums as the Treasury may authorise[13]. Where the BBC performs any other services at the request of any department of Her Majesty's government in the United Kingdom[14] the minister in charge of the government department concerned must pay to the BBC such sums as the Treasury may authorise for those purposes[15]. The BBC must deliver to the Secretary of State or other minister (as the case may require) accounts of its expenditure of sums paid to it for the purposes of the World Service or in respect of services performed for a government department[16].

Sums payable to the BBC under these provisions[17] must be paid in instalments and at intervals determined by the appropriate Secretary of State and any adjustment between the parties must be made as soon as conveniently possible[18]. Any account certified by a member of the senior civil service in the Department for Culture, Olympics, Media and Sport of any sum due to the BBC is for all purposes final and conclusive in the absence of manifest error[19]. Sums paid to the BBC under these provisions must be used and administered by the BBC in accordance with any terms and conditions attached by the paying minister with the consent of the Treasury or by Parliament[20].

The BBC must not, without the prior approval of the appropriate Minister[21], include any sponsored material[22] in any of its services, or provide any subscription service[23].

The BBC must not charge any person, either directly or indirectly, in respect of the reception in the UK, by any means, of: (a) the UK public services; (b) any assistance (such as sub-titling, signing or audio-description) provided for disabled people in relation to any programme or other item of content included in any such service; (c) any service relating to the promotion or listing of programmes or any other item of content included in any such service; or (d) any other service that is ancillary to one or more programmes or items of content so included, and directly related to their contents[24]. For this purpose, the television licence fee[25] is not to be regarded as a charge for the reception of any UK public service[26].

As an aspect of the Trust's general duty to exercise rigorous stewardship of public money[27], the Trust must keep under review the financial needs of the BBC for the purpose of ensuring, through the exercise of the Trust's own functions, that the Executive Board are not authorised to spend, overall, more public money than is needed for the appropriate discharge of the Board's functions[28].

In any year in which the BBC issues to any person a TV licence[29] for which, in accordance with regulations[30], no fee is payable (a 'free TV licence'), the Secretary of State for Work and Pensions must pay to the BBC out of money provided by Parliament such sum or sums as the Treasury may authorise, being: (i) such sum or sums as that Secretary of State, having regard to evidence presented by the BBC, is satisfied is equivalent to the total amount which persons in the United Kingdom to whom the BBC has issued free TV licences would have paid to the BBC in respect of their TV licences but for their entitlement to free TV licences; and (ii) a sum or sums in respect of the administrative costs incurred by the BBC in issuing free TV licences, calculated on such basis as may be agreed between that Secretary of State and the BBC[31]. Any account certified by a member of the senior civil service in the Department for Work and Pensions of any sum due to the BBC under this provision is for all purposes final and conclusive in the absence of manifest error[32]. Sums paid to the BBC under this provision must be used and administered by the BBC in accordance with any terms and conditions attached by the Secretary of State for Work and Pensions with the consent of the Treasury or by Parliament[33].

The Trust must examine the value for money achieved by the BBC in using the sums paid to it[34] in respect of licence fee revenue[35]. For that purpose, the Trust must regularly: (A) discuss with the Comptroller and Auditor General[36] the possible scope of its audit programme and which individual reviews within that programme would be particularly suited to the National Audit Office[37]; (B) take all reasonable steps to agree with the Comptroller and Auditor General the information needed to conduct such a discussion and how it is to be accessed, and ensure that he has such access to it; (C) having regard to the discussion provided for at head (A), decide upon an audit programme which includes in particular the activities of the BBC which will be subject to individual reviews in the course of the programme[38]. Following its decision upon an audit programme, the Trust must: (aa) enter into suitable arrangements, including those with the National Audit Office[39] and other suitable organisations, to carry out individual reviews in accordance with the audit programme, for such period or periods as the Trust determines; (bb) ensure that any arrangements entered into under head (aa) require an organisation, on completion of a review, to report exclusively to the Trust on that review; (cc) consider any report submitted under head (bb) and the extent to which it contains in the Trust's view anything which ought to be taken into account in examining value for money; (dd) decide what action the Trust should take in the light of any such report[40]. The Trust must, as soon as practicable, transmit any report submitted to it under head (bb) (whether by the National Audit Office or by any other organisation), together with any written response to that report that it considers appropriate, to the Secretary of State. The Secretary of State must then lay the report, together with the Trust's response (if any) before Parliament[41].

1   As to the Secretary of State see PARA 507 note 32.

2   As to the meaning of 'BBC' see PARA 603.

3   For these purposes, 'net licence revenue' means the amounts paid by the BBC into the Consolidated Fund under the Communications Act 2003 s 365 (see PARA 950), less the expenses incurred by or on behalf of the Secretary of State in relation to the administration of the licensing system: *Agreement between Her Majesty's Secretary of State for Culture, Media and Sport and the British Broadcasting Corporation* (Cm 6872) (30 June 2006) cl 75(12).

4   *Agreement between Her Majesty's Secretary of State for Culture, Media and Sport and the British Broadcasting Corporation* (Cm 6872) (30 June 2006) cl 75(1).

5   As to the meaning of 'commercial services' see PARA 624 note 2. As to the meaning of 'service' see PARA 855 note 6.

6   Ie a service of a description mentioned in the *Agreement between Her Majesty's Secretary of State for Culture, Media and Sport and the British Broadcasting Corporation* (Cm 6872) (30 June 2006) cl 75(7): see note 15.

7   As to the World Service see PARA 617.

8   As to the meaning of 'UK' see PARA 615 note 4.

9   In the *Agreement between Her Majesty's Secretary of State for Culture, Media and Sport and the British Broadcasting Corporation* (Cm 6872) (30 June 2006) cl 75, 'sponsorship' and 'subscription' are to be interpreted congruently with the definitions of 'sponsored material' and 'subscription service', respectively, in cl 76 (see notes 22, 23): cl 75(13).

10   See note 9.

11   The reference to 'any other alternative means of finance' does not include the use of funds derived:

(1)   from the operation of the commercial services;

(2)   from the Open University;

(3)   from any co-production arrangement; ie an arrangement whereby BBC output is created, commissioned or otherwise obtained by the BBC in co-operation with one or more appropriate third parties, and where funding is provided in exchange for broadcasting, publishing or other rights in the material;

(4)   from co-funding by non-commercial bodies for output in minority languages and other limited circumstances, but only where compatible with a statement of policy approved for these purposes by the BBC Trust and the Secretary of State;

(5)   from competition prizes and other awards made available or funded by any one or more third parties under the terms of a framework approved by the Trust;

(6)   in the following circumstances:

    (a)   the funds are derived from any other arrangement under which any activity, facility or event: (i) featured (in whole or part) in BBC output; or (ii) used (in whole or part) to support the creation of BBC output, is carried on or provided with support from, or in co-operation with, any one or more third parties so as to share the costs of carrying out, providing, using or mounting the activity, facility or event; and

    (b)   the use of the funds is compatible with a statement of policy approved for these purposes by the Trust and the Secretary of State.

See the Agreement between Her Majesty's Secretary of State for Culture, Media and Sport and the British Broadcasting Corporation (Cm 6872) (30 June 2006) cl 75(5). As to the BBC Trust see PARA 604.

12   *Agreement between Her Majesty's Secretary of State for Culture, Media and Sport and the British Broadcasting Corporation* (Cm 6872) (30 June 2006) cl 75(2) (amended by Cm 8002, February 2011). For the purposes of the *Agreement between Her Majesty's Secretary of State for Culture, Media and Sport and the British Broadcasting Corporation* (Cm 6872) (30 June 2006) cl 75(2)(b) (see head (2) in the text): (1) whether an activity is carried on for the purposes of the same service as that which is funded in any of the ways described in that paragraph depends on whether they are within the scope of the same service licence; (2) the activity of complying with the BBC's duty under the Broadcasting Act 1990 s 58(1) (see PARA 655) is not to be regarded as an activity carried on for any of those purposes: *Agreement between Her Majesty's Secretary of State for Culture, Media and Sport and the British Broadcasting Corporation* (Cm 6872) (30 June 2006) cl 75(4).

13   *Agreement between Her Majesty's Secretary of State for Culture, Media and Sport and the British Broadcasting Corporation* (Cm 6872) (30 June 2006) cl 75(6).

14   Except under the *Agreement between Her Majesty's Secretary of State for Culture, Media and Sport and the British Broadcasting Corporation* (Cm 6872) (30 June 2006) cl 81, as to which see PARA 892.

15   *Agreement between Her Majesty's Secretary of State for Culture, Media and Sport and the British Broadcasting Corporation* (Cm 6872) (30 June 2006) cl 75(7).

16   *Agreement between Her Majesty's Secretary of State for Culture, Media and Sport and the British Broadcasting Corporation* (Cm 6872) (30 June 2006) cl 75(10). Such accounts must cover such periods and be delivered at such times as the appropriate minister may direct: cl 75(10).

17   Ie under the *Agreement between Her Majesty's Secretary of State for Culture, Media and Sport and the British Broadcasting Corporation* (Cm 6872) (30 June 2006) cl 75(1), (6) or (7).

18   *Agreement between Her Majesty's Secretary of State for Culture, Media and Sport and the British Broadcasting Corporation* (Cm 6872) (30 June 2006) cl 75(8).

19   *Agreement between Her Majesty's Secretary of State for Culture, Media and Sport and the British Broadcasting Corporation* (Cm 6872) (30 June 2006) cl 75(9).

20   *Agreement between Her Majesty's Secretary of State for Culture, Media and Sport and the British Broadcasting Corporation* (Cm 6872) (30 June 2006) cl 75(11).

21   'The appropriate Minister': (1) in the case of any service provided for the purposes of the World Service, or any sponsored material proposed to be included in any such service, means the Foreign Secretary; and (2) in any other case, means the Secretary of State: *Agreement between Her Majesty's Secretary of State for Culture, Media and Sport and the British Broadcasting Corporation* (Cm 6872) (30 June 2006) cl 76(2).

22   'Sponsored material' means any material whose relevant costs are met in whole or in part by an organisation or person other than the BBC, the Open University, or performers featured in the material, with a view to promoting, through the material's inclusion in a service, its name, its trade mark, its image, its activities or its products or other direct or indirect commercial interests; 'material' means a programme or an item of online content; and 'relevant costs', in

relation to any material, means the costs of producing that material or making it available to the viewers, listeners or users of any service in which it is included: *Agreement between Her Majesty's Secretary of State for Culture, Media and Sport and the British Broadcasting Corporation* (Cm 6872) (30 June 2006) cl 76(2).

23 *Agreement between Her Majesty's Secretary of State for Culture, Media and Sport and the British Broadcasting Corporation* (Cm 6872) (30 June 2006) cl 76(1). 'Subscription service' means a television, radio or online service, by virtue of which the BBC (or any company in which the BBC holds shares, whether they are held directly or through the intermediary of one or more other bodies corporate) receives, from persons to whom the service is supplied, money or other valuable consideration in respect of the supply of the service (or any particular component of it) to them: cl 76(2).

24 *Agreement between Her Majesty's Secretary of State for Culture, Media and Sport and the British Broadcasting Corporation* (Cm 6872) (30 June 2006) cl 13(1). Nothing in cl 13(1) is to be taken to forbid the BBC from recovering from any person the cost to the BBC of providing any service or facility to that person on demand or otherwise at that person's express request: cl 13(3).

25 As to the television licence fee see PARA 948 et seq.

26 *Agreement between Her Majesty's Secretary of State for Culture, Media and Sport and the British Broadcasting Corporation* (Cm 6872) (30 June 2006) cl 13(2).

27 Ie under the *Royal Charter for the Continuance of the British Broadcasting Corporation* (Cm 6925) (2006) art 23(d): see PARA 607 note 5 head (4).

28 *Agreement between Her Majesty's Secretary of State for Culture, Media and Sport and the British Broadcasting Corporation* (Cm 6872) (30 June 2006) cl 77.

29 As to the meaning of 'TV licence' see PARA 949.

30 Ie made under the Communications Act 2003 s 365(1): see PARA 950.

31 *Agreement between Her Majesty's Secretary of State for Culture, Media and Sport and the British Broadcasting Corporation* (Cm 6872) (30 June 2006) cl 78(1), (2).

32 *Agreement between Her Majesty's Secretary of State for Culture, Media and Sport and the British Broadcasting Corporation* (Cm 6872) (30 June 2006) cl 78(3).

33 *Agreement between Her Majesty's Secretary of State for Culture, Media and Sport and the British Broadcasting Corporation* (Cm 6872) (30 June 2006) cl 78(4).

34 Ie under the *Agreement between Her Majesty's Secretary of State for Culture, Media and Sport and the British Broadcasting Corporation* (Cm 6872) (30 June 2006) cl 75: see the text and notes 1–4.

35 *Agreement between Her Majesty's Secretary of State for Culture, Media and Sport and the British Broadcasting Corporation* (Cm 6872) (30 June 2006) cl 79(1).

36 For these purposes, 'the Comptroller and Auditor General' means the officer appointed under the Exchequer and Audit Departments Act 1866 s 6: *Agreement between Her Majesty's Secretary of State for Culture, Media and Sport and the British Broadcasting Corporation* (Cm 6872) (30 June 2006) cl 79(5). As to the Comptroller and Auditor General see CONSTITUTIONAL LAW AND HUMAN RIGHTS vol 8(2) (Reissue) PARAS 724–726.

37 As to the National Audit Office see CONSTITUTIONAL LAW AND HUMAN RIGHTS vol 8(2) (Reissue) PARA 720.

38 *Agreement between Her Majesty's Secretary of State for Culture, Media and Sport and the British Broadcasting Corporation* (Cm 6872) (30 June 2006) cl 79(2).

39 On terms which require the factual content of any report to be submitted under head (BB) in the text to be agreed by the BBC before submission but allow the National Audit Office to retain full discretion over the report's conclusions and recommendations.

40 *Agreement between Her Majesty's Secretary of State for Culture, Media and Sport and the British Broadcasting Corporation* (Cm 6872) (30 June 2006) cl 79(3). This may include requiring the Executive Board to set out how it intends to respond to: (1) any aspect of the report; or (2) the conclusions of those aspects of the Trust's examination which took the report into account, so far as they are relevant to the functions of the Executive Board: cl 79(3)(d).

41 *Agreement between Her Majesty's Secretary of State for Culture, Media and Sport and the British Broadcasting Corporation* (Cm 6872) (30 June 2006) cl 79(4).

622. Financial arrangements: borrowing by the BBC. The Consolidated Net Borrowings[1] of the BBC[2] must not at any time exceed the sum specified in a direction given by the Secretary of State[3]. The Consolidated Net Borrowings of the BBC's commercial arm[4] must not at any time exceed either of the following: (1) the sum specified in a direction given by the Secretary of State; (2) three times the commercial arm's EBITDA[5]. As an additional requirement, the net cost of interest on the borrowings of the commercial arm must not at any time exceed one third of the commercial arm's EBITDA[6]. Compliance with these requirements of is to be determined by reference to UK Generally Accepted Accounting Principles[7].

No direction under these provisions is to affect the validity of any borrowing outstanding at the time it is given (which, in particular, the BBC may therefore continue to repay according to the terms of the borrowing, including any schedule of repayments)[8]. The BBC must make proper provision: (a) for repaying its borrowings according to a schedule of repayments (if any) agreed with the Secretary of State with the consent of the Treasury; and (b) for replacing or renewing any property of the BBC[9].

The BBC must not borrow, or raise or secure the payment of money, upon any property, interests or rights held by the BBC exclusively for the purposes of the World Service; but nothing in this provision is to be taken to prevent the BBC or any subsidiary[10] of the BBC which is engaged in providing a service forming part of the World Service from borrowing, or raising or securing the payment of money, upon any property, interests or rights which that subsidiary holds[11].

The BBC must not guarantee or underwrite any liabilities of its commercial arm[12].

1 'Consolidated Net Borrowings' means, without double counting, the aggregate amount of all obligations for or in respect of Indebtedness for Borrowed Money less Cash Balances and Short Term Investments held: *Agreement between Her Majesty's Secretary of State for Culture, Media and Sport and the British Broadcasting Corporation* (Cm 6872) (30 June 2006) cl 80(14). 'Indebtedness for Borrowed Money' means any indebtedness, excluding inter-company liabilities and balances, for or in respect of: (1) moneys borrowed; (2) any amount raised by acceptance under any acceptance credit facility; (3) any amount raised pursuant to any note purchase facility or the issue of bonds, notes, debentures, loan stock or any similar instrument; (4) the amount of any liability in respect of any lease or hire purchase contract which would, in accordance with UK Generally Accepted Accounting Principles as at the date hereof in the relevant jurisdiction, be treated as a finance or capital lease; and (5) the amount of any liability in respect of any guarantee or indemnity for any of the items referred to in heads (1)–(5): cl 80(14). 'Cash Balances and Short Term Investments' means the aggregate of the following: (a) cash balances; (b) investments in money market funds; (c) certificates of deposit, commercial paper or government securities rated A1/P1 and with a duration to maturity of less than one year: cl 80(14).

2 As to the meaning of 'BBC' see PARA 603. References in the *Agreement between Her Majesty's Secretary of State for Culture, Media and Sport and the British Broadcasting Corporation* (Cm 6872) (30 June 2006) cl 80 to 'the BBC' include a reference to any subsidiary of the BBC that is not part of the commercial arm, except that in cl 80(1) it does not include any subsidiary that is engaged in providing a service forming part of the World Service: cl 80(12). As to the World Service see PARA 617.

3 *Agreement between Her Majesty's Secretary of State for Culture, Media and Sport and the British Broadcasting Corporation* (Cm 6872) (30 June 2006) cl 80(1). This is subject to cl 80(8). As to the Secretary of State see PARA 507 note 32. Any power of the Secretary of State to give a direction under cl 80 is exercisable only with the consent of the Treasury: cl 80(13). After the Secretary of State has for the first time specified a sum ('the initial sum') for the purposes of cl 80(1) or (2) he may, by further directions, from time to time change the sum for the time being specified there, but may never reduce it to a sum smaller than the initial sum (although this does not affect the kinds of amendment that he may make under cl 80(7)(b)): cl 80(6). The Secretary of State may also, by directions: (1) impose separate requirements (including separate borrowing limits) on the BBC or its commercial arm for capital and current expenditure, as defined in the direction (cl 80(7)(a)); and (2) alter or add to the requirements on the BBC's commercial arm set out in cl 80(2)–(4), which includes power to alter or add to definitions which apply to the interpretation of those paragraphs; but a direction whose only effect is to impose separate borrowing limits for capital and current expenditure in place of a single limit must impose limits that together are equal to or exceed the size of the single limit in force immediately before the direction takes effect (cl 80(7)(b)).

4   As to the meaning of 'the BBC's commercial arm' see PARA 873 note 2.
5   *Agreement between Her Majesty's Secretary of State for Culture, Media and Sport and the British Broadcasting Corporation* (Cm 6872) (30 June 2006) cl 80(2). This is subject to cl 80(8). 'EBITDA' means earnings before interest, tax, depreciation and amortisation, adjusted to exclude any exceptional or other charges in respect of a business disposal by, or corporate restructuring within, the commercial arm: cl 80(14). Compliance with the requirements of cl 80(2) and (3) is to be tested at least annually at the end of the accounting period used for the purposes of cl 74 (see PARA 626): cl 80(4).
6   *Agreement between Her Majesty's Secretary of State for Culture, Media and Sport and the British Broadcasting Corporation* (Cm 6872) (30 June 2006) cl 80(3). See also note 5.
7   *Agreement between Her Majesty's Secretary of State for Culture, Media and Sport and the British Broadcasting Corporation* (Cm 6872) (30 June 2006) cl 80(5).
8   *Agreement between Her Majesty's Secretary of State for Culture, Media and Sport and the British Broadcasting Corporation* (Cm 6872) (30 June 2006) cl 80(8).
9   *Agreement between Her Majesty's Secretary of State for Culture, Media and Sport and the British Broadcasting Corporation* (Cm 6872) (30 June 2006) cl 80(9).
10   'Subsidiary' means a company over which the BBC has 'control' as defined in the Income and Corporation Taxes Act 1988 s 840 (see INCOME TAXATION vol 23(1) (Reissue) PARA 845): *Agreement between Her Majesty's Secretary of State for Culture, Media and Sport and the British Broadcasting Corporation* (Cm 6872) (30 June 2006) cl 104.
11   *Agreement between Her Majesty's Secretary of State for Culture, Media and Sport and the British Broadcasting Corporation* (Cm 6872) (30 June 2006) cl 80(10).
12   *Agreement between Her Majesty's Secretary of State for Culture, Media and Sport and the British Broadcasting Corporation* (Cm 6872) (30 June 2006) cl 80(11).

623.   Broadcasting revenue.   The BBC[1] is responsible for collecting television licence fees under Part 4 of the Communications Act 2003[2]. In such cases as the BBC may determine, it may make refunds of sums received by it[3] in respect of licence fees[4]. Except so far as required for the making of such refunds, sums received[5] by the BBC in respect of licence fees must be paid into the Consolidated Fund[6].

1   As to the meaning of 'BBC' see PARA 603.
2   Ie the Communications Act 2003 Pt 4 (ss 364–368): see PARA 948 et seq.
3   Ie received by virtue of regulations relating to licence fees made under the Communications Act 2003 s 365.
4   See the Communications Act 2003 s 365(3); and PARA 950.
5   Ie received by virtue of regulations relating to licence fees made under the Communications Act 2003 s 365.
6   Communications Act 2003 s 365(7). As to the Consolidated Fund see CONSTITUTIONAL LAW AND HUMAN RIGHTS vol 8(2) (Reissue) PARA 711 et seq; PARLIAMENT vol 78 (2010) PARAS 1028–1031.

624.   Commercial services.   The BBC[1] as a corporation must not directly provide any commercial services[2], but it may carry out other trading activities[3]. Any commercial services must be provided through one or more commercial subsidiaries[4].
   All of the BBC's commercial services must meet all the following criteria[5]:
   (1)   they must fit with the BBC's Public Purpose activities[6];
   (2)   they must exhibit commercial efficiency[7];
   (3)   they must not jeopardise the good reputation of the BBC or the value of the BBC brand[8];
   (4)   they must comply with fair trading guidelines in force[9] and in particular avoid distorting the market[10].
   Where the commercial service consists of participation in a joint venture or other form of commercial partnership with a person or body other than the BBC or a subsidiary[11] within the BBC's commercial arm, the BBC must use its best endeavours to ensure:

(a)   that the participation complies with the above provisions; and

(b)   that any services provided, or activities undertaken, by way of or through the venture or partnership meet the criteria set out in heads (1) to (4)[12].

Activities which are not commercial services but which would be commercial services if the list of exceptions[13] were disregarded must comply with the principles set out above where relevant and bearing in mind that the practical implications of those principles may properly differ when applied to such activities[14].

The Trust must include within its Protocols[15] rules relating to the approval of changes in the BBC's commercial services (including changes to the structure of the BBC's commercial arm)[16]. The rules must make it clear when such changes must be referred to the Trust for prior approval, but must in this respect in particular be in keeping with the general nature of the relationship between the Trust and the Executive Board described in the BBC's Charter[17]. The rules must also make it clear how the Trust will take any approval decisions which are referred to it[18]. The application of these rules is a matter of judgment for the Trust[19]. The Trust must hold the Executive Board to account for ensuring that the BBC's commercial services are operated in a way which complies with these rules[20].

The BBC's commercial strategy must be adopted by the Executive Board and approved by the Trust[21].

The Executive Board is responsible for overseeing the activities of the BBC's commercial arm and, subject to the powers of the Trust, for exercising the BBC's functions in relation to the subsidiaries which comprise the commercial arm[22]. In particular, the Executive Board must approve particular budgets and targets to an extent and in a manner it considers appropriate, subject to the commercial strategy approved by the Trust and to any other powers of the Trust[23]. The Executive Board must ensure that the business and affairs of the BBC's commercial arm are carried on in a way which is compatible with the requirements of: (i) the Charter, any Framework Agreement[24], and the general law; and (ii) high standards of financial management and control (including risk management)[25].

1   As to the meaning of 'BBC' see PARA 603.

2   In the *Agreement between Her Majesty's Secretary of State for Culture, Media and Sport and the British Broadcasting Corporation* (Cm 6872) (30 June 2006), 'commercial services' means services which are provided, or other activities which are undertaken, not primarily (or at all) in order to promote the BBC's public purposes, but with a view to generating a profit (regardless of whether the profit, once generated, will or may be used to fund the promotion of the public purposes). This means that something can be a commercial service even if it also promotes the public purposes, if it is done with a view to generating profit rather than in order to achieve that promotion: cll 101(1), 104. As to the meaning of 'service' see PARA 855 note 6. In cl 101(1), 'services' and 'activities' include services and activities which are carried out by subsidiaries of the BBC, and 'activities' also includes participating in joint ventures or other forms of commercial partnership with persons or bodies other than the BBC or a subsidiary within the BBC's commercial arm: cl 101(3). As to the meaning of 'public purposes' see PARA 603 note 3.

    However, 'commercial services' do not include the following: (1) the selling of assets or of excess capacity in the BBC's resources held for use by the BBC's Public Services; (2) the provision of facilities and services which are ancillary to the provision of the BBC's Public Services and in respect of which any charge is imposed primarily for the purpose of recovering the costs or expenses of the provision, even if other factors (for example, rounding the charge for convenience) make a profit likely; (3) licensing or otherwise disposing of rights in anything created for the purposes of the BBC's Public Services; (4) sub-licensing or otherwise disposing of rights which are not required for the promotion of the public purposes and which were acquired incidentally by the BBC as part of a larger package of rights which, as a whole, was acquired only because the package included rights which were required for the promotion of the public purposes; (5) trading or other activity between the BBC and the BBC's commercial arm, or between different parts of the BBC's organisation; (6) securing up-front investment from third parties in BBC content: cl 101(2). In cl 101(2), 'the BBC's Public Services' means all or any of the services provided by the BBC for the purpose of promoting its public purposes except any which are themselves commercial services: cl 101(4). As to the meaning of 'the BBC's commercial arm' see PARA 873 note 2.

3   *Agreement between Her Majesty's Secretary of State for Culture, Media and Sport and the British Broadcasting Corporation* (Cm 6872) (30 June 2006) cl 68(1).

4   *Agreement between Her Majesty's Secretary of State for Culture, Media and Sport and the British Broadcasting Corporation* (Cm 6872) (30 June 2006) cl 68(2).

5   *Agreement between Her Majesty's Secretary of State for Culture, Media and Sport and the British Broadcasting Corporation* (Cm 6872) (30 June 2006) cl 69(1). This is subject to cl 69(2). The application of these criteria is a matter of judgment for the Trust. The Trust must hold the BBC's Executive Board to account for ensuring that the BBC's commercial services are operated in a way which complies with these criteria: cl 69(4). As to the BBC Trust and the Executive Board see PARA 604.

6   In the manner defined by the *Agreement between Her Majesty's Secretary of State for Culture, Media and Sport and the British Broadcasting Corporation* (Cm 6872) (30 June 2006) cl 69(3): cl 69(1)(a). A commercial service is to be considered to fit with the BBC's Public Purpose activities if: (1) it is appropriate to be carried on in association with the promotion of the public purposes (albeit through the separate framework required by cl 68); and (2) it is connected, otherwise than merely in financial terms, with the ways in which the BBC promotes its public purposes: cl 69(3). A commercial service does not cease to be considered to fit with the BBC's public purposes just because the service includes activities which in themselves do not meet the requirements of cl 69(3), provided such activities are peripheral, subordinate or ancillary to other activities that do meet those requirements: cl 69(4).

7   *Agreement between Her Majesty's Secretary of State for Culture, Media and Sport and the British Broadcasting Corporation* (Cm 6872) (30 June 2006) cl 69(1)(b).

8   *Agreement between Her Majesty's Secretary of State for Culture, Media and Sport and the British Broadcasting Corporation* (Cm 6872) (30 June 2006) cl 69(1)(c).

9   Ie under the *Agreement between Her Majesty's Secretary of State for Culture, Media and Sport and the British Broadcasting Corporation* (Cm 6872) (30 June 2006) cl 67(1)(a): see PARA 625.

10   *Agreement between Her Majesty's Secretary of State for Culture, Media and Sport and the British Broadcasting Corporation* (Cm 6872) (30 June 2006) cl 69(1)(d).

11   As to the meaning of 'subsidiary' see PARA 622 note 10.

12   *Agreement between Her Majesty's Secretary of State for Culture, Media and Sport and the British Broadcasting Corporation* (Cm 6872) (30 June 2006) cl 69(2).

13   Ie the *Agreement between Her Majesty's Secretary of State for Culture, Media and Sport and the British Broadcasting Corporation* (Cm 6872) (30 June 2006) cl 101(2): see note 2.

14   *Agreement between Her Majesty's Secretary of State for Culture, Media and Sport and the British Broadcasting Corporation* (Cm 6872) (30 June 2006) cl 70(2).

15   As to Protocols see PARA 607.

16   *Agreement between Her Majesty's Secretary of State for Culture, Media and Sport and the British Broadcasting Corporation* (Cm 6872) (30 June 2006) cl 71(1).

17   *Agreement between Her Majesty's Secretary of State for Culture, Media and Sport and the British Broadcasting Corporation* (Cm 6872) (30 June 2006) cl 71(2). As to the Charter see PARA 603.

18   *Agreement between Her Majesty's Secretary of State for Culture, Media and Sport and the British Broadcasting Corporation* (Cm 6872) (30 June 2006) cl 71(3). This includes the procedures it will follow and any criteria it will apply over and above those set out in cl 69, or the factors to which it will have regard, in deciding whether to give approval: cl 71(3).

19   *Agreement between Her Majesty's Secretary of State for Culture, Media and Sport and the British Broadcasting Corporation* (Cm 6872) (30 June 2006) cl 71(4).

20   *Agreement between Her Majesty's Secretary of State for Culture, Media and Sport and the British Broadcasting Corporation* (Cm 6872) (30 June 2006) cl 71(4).

21   *Agreement between Her Majesty's Secretary of State for Culture, Media and Sport and the British Broadcasting Corporation* (Cm 6872) (30 June 2006) cl 72.

22   *Agreement between Her Majesty's Secretary of State for Culture, Media and Sport and the British Broadcasting Corporation* (Cm 6872) (30 June 2006) cl 73(1).

23   *Agreement between Her Majesty's Secretary of State for Culture, Media and Sport and the British Broadcasting Corporation* (Cm 6872) (30 June 2006) cl 73(2).

24   As to the meaning of 'Framework Agreement' see PARA 603 note 7.

25 *Agreement between Her Majesty's Secretary of State for Culture, Media and Sport and the British Broadcasting Corporation* (Cm 6872) (30 June 2006) cl 73(3).

625.   Fair trading and competitive impact. The BBC Trust[1] must consult publicly[2] before adopting a statement of policy on fair trading[3]. The policy is to apply to all trading activities which the BBC or its subsidiaries[4] engage in, whether or not in connection with its commercial services[5]. Whenever the Trust adopts a statement of policy, it must publish it[6]. The Trust must keep its statement of policy under review and conduct a comprehensive review, which must include public consultation, at least every three years[7]. The statement of policy must distinguish (where possible) between those matters which (in its view) are the BBC's legal requirements and those which are not[8].

The Trust must adopt and publish a statement of its policy on the competitive impact of the BBC's activities on the wider market[9]. The Trust must adopt and publish codes dealing with those aspects of the operation of the UK Public Services[10] that in its view could raise significant issues regarding the competitive impact of the BBC's activities[11]. In formulating its codes the Trust must have regard: (1) to the extent that the Trust considers them to be relevant, to any fair and effective competition codes issued by OFCOM[12] for the purpose of applying to any description of broadcasters other than the BBC; and (2) to any views expressed by OFCOM as to matters that should be covered by the Trust's codes[13]. The Trust's codes may deal with matters which are not covered by any fair and effective competition codes issued by OFCOM[14]. The Trust must consult publicly on draft codes[15]. The Trust must keep its codes under review and conduct a comprehensive review, which must include public consultation, of each of them at least every three years[16].

The Executive Board[17] must adopt and publish guidelines on: (a) the practical implications of the Trust's statement of policy on fair trading so far as they relate to the functions of the Executive Board and relevant BBC subsidiaries; and (b) the application of any statement of the Trust's policy on competitive impact and its competitive impact codes[18]. The Executive Board may only adopt guidelines of which a draft has been approved by the Trust[19].

1   As to the BBC Trust within the constitution of the BBC see PARA 604. As to the meaning of 'BBC' see PARA 603.

2   As to the meaning of obligations for the Trust to consult publicly see cl 103.

3   *Agreement between Her Majesty's Secretary of State for Culture, Media and Sport and the British Broadcasting Corporation* (Cm 6872) (30 June 2006) cl 65(1). See the *Royal Charter for the Continuance of the British Broadcasting Corporation* (Cm 6925) (2006) art 24(2)(k); and see PARA 607 head (xi).

4   As to the meaning of 'subsidiary' see PARA 622 note 10.

5   *Agreement between Her Majesty's Secretary of State for Culture, Media and Sport and the British Broadcasting Corporation* (Cm 6872) (30 June 2006) cl 65(2). As to the meaning of 'commercial services' see PARA 624 note 2.

6   *Agreement between Her Majesty's Secretary of State for Culture, Media and Sport and the British Broadcasting Corporation* (Cm 6872) (30 June 2006) cl 65(3).

7   *Agreement between Her Majesty's Secretary of State for Culture, Media and Sport and the British Broadcasting Corporation* (Cm 6872) (30 June 2006) cl 65(4).

8   *Agreement between Her Majesty's Secretary of State for Culture, Media and Sport and the British Broadcasting Corporation* (Cm 6872) (30 June 2006) cl 65(5).

9   *Agreement between Her Majesty's Secretary of State for Culture, Media and Sport and the British Broadcasting Corporation* (Cm 6872) (30 June 2006) cl 66(1). See the *Royal Charter for the Continuance of the British Broadcasting Corporation* (Cm 6925) (2006) art 23(e); and see PARA 607 note 5 head (5). It is a matter for the Trust to determine how detailed it is appropriate for this statement to be (having regard to the *Agreement between Her Majesty's Secretary of*

State for Culture, Media and Sport and the British Broadcasting Corporation (Cm 6872) (30 June 2006) cl 67 (see the text to notes 18–19)): cl 66(1).

10 As to the meaning of 'UK public services' see PARA 855 note 6; and see PARA 615.

11 *Agreement between Her Majesty's Secretary of State for Culture, Media and Sport and the British Broadcasting Corporation* (Cm 6872) (30 June 2006) cl 66(2).

12 As to OFCOM see PARA 507.

13 *Agreement between Her Majesty's Secretary of State for Culture, Media and Sport and the British Broadcasting Corporation* (Cm 6872) (30 June 2006) cl 66(3).

14 *Agreement between Her Majesty's Secretary of State for Culture, Media and Sport and the British Broadcasting Corporation* (Cm 6872) (30 June 2006) cl 66(4).

15 *Agreement between Her Majesty's Secretary of State for Culture, Media and Sport and the British Broadcasting Corporation* (Cm 6872) (30 June 2006) cl 66(5).

16 *Agreement between Her Majesty's Secretary of State for Culture, Media and Sport and the British Broadcasting Corporation* (Cm 6872) (30 June 2006) cl 66(6).

17 As to the Executive Board see PARA 604.

18 *Agreement between Her Majesty's Secretary of State for Culture, Media and Sport and the British Broadcasting Corporation* (Cm 6872) (30 June 2006) cl 67(1).

19 *Agreement between Her Majesty's Secretary of State for Culture, Media and Sport and the British Broadcasting Corporation* (Cm 6872) (30 June 2006) cl 67(2).

626. Accounts and reports. An annual report and statement of accounts in relation to the BBC[1] must be prepared and dealt with annually in accordance with the following requirements[2]. The report and accounts must consist of two parts: Part 1 must be prepared by the Trust[3] and Part 2 must be prepared by the Executive Board[4].

Part 2 must include at least an operating and financial review, statements of compliance with applicable codes and regulations, and the whole of the statement of accounts in relation to the BBC (which must be audited)[5]. Subject to that, and to the following[6], the content of Part 2 is a matter for the Executive Board[7].

In preparing Part 2 the Executive Board must comply with any applicable Protocols[8] and also with any directions which may, after consultation with the Executive Board, be given by the Trust with regard to the content of Part 2[9]. In preparing Part 2 the Executive Board must comply with any directions which may, after consultation with the BBC, be given by the Secretary of State or by the Foreign Secretary[10] with regard to: (1) information which must be given in the report about the finance, administration and work generally of the BBC; (2) information to be given in the statement of accounts[11].

When Part 2 has been prepared and (so far as relevant) audited, the Executive Board must submit it to the Trust[12]. The Trust must then consider Part 2 and prepare, in such detail as it sees fit, a commentary on it for inclusion within Part 1[13]. Part 1 must include at least that commentary, a commentary on the activities and affairs of the Trust and the Trust Unit[14] and (without affecting what must be included in the statement of accounts included in Part 2) an audited summary of the expenditure of the Trust and the Trust Unit[15]. Subject to that, and to the following[16], the content of Part 1 is a matter for the Trust[17]. In preparing Part 1 the Trust must comply with any directions which may, after consultation with the Trust, be given by the Secretary of State or by the Foreign Secretary with regard to information which must be given in the report about the finance, administration and work generally of the Trust[18].

The Trust must then transmit the report and accounts, no later than seven months after the end of the period to which they relate, to the Secretary of State, who must then lay the report and accounts before Parliament[19]. When this has been done, the BBC must publish the report and accounts[20].

The BBC must at all reasonable times upon demand: (a) allow any of the persons mentioned below to examine any of the accounts of the BBC; (b) furnish any of those persons with all forecasts, estimates, reconciliations, information and documents which she may require, in such format as she may require, with regard to the financial transactions and engagements of the BBC[21]. The persons are the Secretary of State, the Foreign Secretary, and any person nominated for this purpose by either of them[22].

The Executive Board must, each year, secure the publication of a report and accounts relating to the BBC's commercial services[23]. The report and accounts must: (i) be detailed; (ii) contain a clear description of the services and activities comprised within the BBC's commercial services; (iii) address compliance with the criteria for commercial services[24]; (iv) include information broken down for different types of business; and (v) comply, where relevant, with best practice relating to accounts of publicly-quoted companies[25].

1 As to the meaning of 'BBC' see PARA 603. 'Statement of accounts' means a statement of accounts which is prepared in accordance with UK Generally Accepted Accounting Principles and which includes all the following: an account or accounts of the income and expenditure of the BBC, a balance sheet or sheets, a cash flow statement or statements, and accompanying notes: *Royal Charter for the Continuance of the British Broadcasting Corporation* (Cm 6925) (2006) art 45(11).

2 *Royal Charter for the Continuance of the British Broadcasting Corporation* (Cm 6925) (2006) art 45(1).

3 As to the BBC Trust within the constitution of the BBC see PARA 604.

4 *Royal Charter for the Continuance of the British Broadcasting Corporation* (Cm 6925) (2006) art 45(2). As to the Executive Board see PARA 604.

5 *Royal Charter for the Continuance of the British Broadcasting Corporation* (Cm 6925) (2006) art 45(3). 'Audited' means audited and certified by an eligible auditor appointed with the approval of the Trust and the Secretary of State; and 'eligible auditor' means a member of a qualifying body of accountants established in the United Kingdom and recognised under the Companies Act 1989 s 32(4) (repealed: see now the Companies Act 2006 Pt 42 (ss 1209–1264)) (see COMPANIES vol 15 (2009) PARA 958): *Royal Charter for the Continuance of the British Broadcasting Corporation* (Cm 6925) (2006) art 45(11).

6 Ie the *Royal Charter for the Continuance of the British Broadcasting Corporation* (Cm 6925) (2006) art 45(4), (5).

7 *Royal Charter for the Continuance of the British Broadcasting Corporation* (Cm 6925) (2006) art 45(3).

8 As to Protocols see PARA 607.

9 *Royal Charter for the Continuance of the British Broadcasting Corporation* (Cm 6925) (2006) art 45(4).

10 As to the Secretary of State see PARA 507 note 32. As to the Secretary of State for Foreign and Commonwealth Affairs see CONSTITUTIONAL LAW AND HUMAN RIGHTS vol 8(2) (Reissue) PARA 459.

11 *Royal Charter for the Continuance of the British Broadcasting Corporation* (Cm 6925) (2006) art 45(5).

12 *Royal Charter for the Continuance of the British Broadcasting Corporation* (Cm 6925) (2006) art 45(6).

13 *Royal Charter for the Continuance of the British Broadcasting Corporation* (Cm 6925) (2006) art 45(7).

14 As to the Trust Unit see PARA 612.

15 *Royal Charter for the Continuance of the British Broadcasting Corporation* (Cm 6925) (2006) art 45(8).

16 Ie the *Royal Charter for the Continuance of the British Broadcasting Corporation* (Cm 6925) (2006) art 45(9).

17 *Royal Charter for the Continuance of the British Broadcasting Corporation* (Cm 6925) (2006) art 45(8).

18 *Royal Charter for the Continuance of the British Broadcasting Corporation* (Cm 6925) (2006) art 45(9).

19 *Royal Charter for the Continuance of the British Broadcasting Corporation* (Cm 6925) (2006) art 45(10).

20 *Royal Charter for the Continuance of the British Broadcasting Corporation* (Cm 6925) (2006) art 45(10).
21 *Royal Charter for the Continuance of the British Broadcasting Corporation* (Cm 6925) (2006) art 46(1).
22 *Royal Charter for the Continuance of the British Broadcasting Corporation* (Cm 6925) (2006) art 46(2).
23 *Agreement between Her Majesty's Secretary of State for Culture, Media and Sport and the British Broadcasting Corporation* (Cm 6872) (30 June 2006) cl 74(1). As to the meaning of 'commercial services' see PARA 624 note 2.
24 Ie the criteria set out in the *Agreement between Her Majesty's Secretary of State for Culture, Media and Sport and the British Broadcasting Corporation* (Cm 6872) (30 June 2006) cl 69: see PARA 624.
25 *Agreement between Her Majesty's Secretary of State for Culture, Media and Sport and the British Broadcasting Corporation* (Cm 6872) (30 June 2006) cl 74(2).

(3) ESTABLISHMENT AND REMIT OF CHANNEL 4

(i) The Corporation

627. The Channel 4 Television Corporation. The Channel 4 Television Corporation[1] consists of a chairman and a deputy chairman appointed by OFCOM[2] with the approval of the Secretary of State[3], and such number of other members, not being less than 11 nor more than 13, as OFCOM may from time to time determine[4]. These other members are appointed by OFCOM with the approval of the Secretary of State[5], and ex-officio members of the corporation[6].

1 The Channel 4 Television Corporation was created by the Broadcasting Act 1990 s 23(1). Under the Broadcasting Act 1981 s 10(1) (repealed), 'the Fourth Channel' was provided by the Independent Broadcasting Authority (see PARA 507), though by virtue of s 12(2) (repealed) most of its activities involved in providing programmes for that channel were performed by a subsidiary of the Authority known as the Channel 4 Television Company Ltd, and by s 10(4) (repealed) the programmes broadcast on the Fourth Channel for reception in Wales were to be provided by the Welsh Fourth Channel Authority (see PARA 645). The shares in the Channel 4 Television Company Ltd vested in the Channel 4 Television Corporation on 1 January 1993: Broadcasting Act 1990 s 24(2). See PARA 637. As to the corporation's constitution and procedures see PARA 628 et seq. For the purposes of the Communications Act 2003, the Channel Four Television Corporation is referred to as 'C4C': see s 405(1).
2 Broadcasting Act 1990 s 23(2)(a) (amended by the Communications Act 2003 s 360(3), Sch 15 para 13). As to OFCOM see PARA 507.
3 See the Broadcasting Act 1990 s 23(4) (amended by the Communications Act 2003 Sch 15 para 13). As to the Secretary of State see PARA 507 note 32.
4 Broadcasting Act 1990 s 23(2)(b) (amended by the Communications Act 2003 Sch 15 para 13).
5 Broadcasting Act 1990 s 23(3)(a), (4) (amended by the Communications Act 2003 Sch 15 para 13).
6 Broadcasting Act 1990 s 23(3)(b). The total number of members appointed by OFCOM under s 23(2)(a) and s 23(3)(a) must exceed the number of ex-officio members: s 23(3) (amended by the Communications Act 2003 Sch 15 para 13). The chief executive of the corporation and such other employees of the corporation as may for the time being be nominated by the chief executive and the chairman of the corporation acting jointly are ex-officio members: Broadcasting Act 1990 s 23(5).

628. Status and capacity. The Channel 4 Television Corporation[1] is a body corporate[2]. It is not to be treated for the purposes of the enactments and rules of law relating to the privileges of the Crown[3] as a body exercising functions on behalf of the Crown[4]. The corporation may do anything which appears to it to be incidental or conducive to the carrying out of its functions[5]. This includes power, to the extent that it appears to it incidental or conducive to the carrying out of its functions to do so: (1) to borrow money; (2) to carry on activities (other than those comprised in its duty to carry out its primary functions) through Channel 4 companies; and (3) to participate with others in the carrying on of any such activities[6].

1   As to the Channel 4 Television Corporation see PARA 627.
2   Broadcasting Act 1990 s 23(6), Sch 3 para 1(1).
3   As to the privileges of the Crown see CROWN AND ROYAL FAMILY.
4   Broadcasting Act 1990 Sch 3 para 1(2).
5   Broadcasting Act 1990 Sch 3 para 1(3) (substituted by the Communications Act 2003 s 199(4)).
6   Broadcasting Act 1990 Sch 3 para 1(4) (added by the Broadcasting Act 1996 s 84(2); and substituted by the Communications Act 2003 s 199(4)).

629.   Appointment of members.   A person[1] is disqualified from being a member of the Channel 4 Television Corporation[2] so long as he is: (1) a governor or employee of the BBC[3]; or (2) a member or employee of OFCOM[4].

Before appointing a person to be a member of the corporation, OFCOM must satisfy itself that that person will have no such financial or other interest as is likely to affect prejudicially the discharge by him of his functions as a member of the corporation, and OFCOM must also satisfy itself from time to time with respect to every member of the corporation that he has no such interest[5].

Members of the corporation are disqualified from membership of the House of Commons[6].

1   As to the meaning of 'person' see PARA 510 note 1.
2   Broadcasting Act 1990 s 23(6), Sch 3 para 2(1). As to the Channel 4 Television Corporation see PARA 627.
3   Broadcasting Act 1990 Sch 3 para 2(1)(a). As to the meaning of 'BBC' see PARA 603 note 1; and as to the BBC see PARAS 603–626. There are no longer governors of the BBC; instead, there is now a BBC Trust and an Executive Board, as to which see PARA 604 et seq; and as to the staff of the BBC see PARA 612.
4   Broadcasting Act 1990 Sch 3 para 2(1)(b) (substituted by the Communications Act 2003 s 360(3), Sch 15 para 70(1), (3)). As to OFCOM see PARA 507. As to the members of OFCOM see TELECOMMUNICATIONS vol 97 (2010) PARA 3; and as to employees of OFCOM see TELECOMMUNICATIONS vol 97 (2010) PARAS 4–5.
5   Broadcasting Act 1990 Sch 3 para 2(2) (amended by the Communications Act 2003 Sch 15 para 70(2)). Any person who is, or whom OFCOM proposes to appoint to be, a member of the corporation must, whenever requested by OFCOM to do so, furnish it with such information as it considers necessary for the performance by it of its duties under the Broadcasting Act 1990 Sch 3 para 2(2): Sch 3 para 2(3) (amended by the Communications Act 2003 Sch 15 para 70(2)).
6   House of Commons Disqualification Act 1975 s 1(1)(a), Sch 1 Pt II (amended by the Broadcasting Act 1990 Sch 3 para 5).

630.   Tenure of office.   Each member of the Channel 4 Television Corporation[1] must hold and vacate office in accordance with the terms of his appointment[2]. A person[3] may not be appointed to be a member of the corporation for more than five years at a time[4]. OFCOM[5] may at any time, by notice to a member of the corporation, terminate the appointment of that member[6], but before so terminating a person's appointment, OFCOM must consult the Secretary of State[7]. Any member of the corporation may at any time resign his office by notice to OFCOM[8].

None of the above applies in relation to ex-officio members of the corporation[9].

1   As to the Channel 4 Television Corporation see PARA 627. As to membership of the corporation see PARA 629.
2   Broadcasting Act 1990 s 23(6), Sch 3 para 3(1).
3   As to the meaning of 'person' see PARA 510 note 1.
4   Broadcasting Act 1990 Sch 3 para 3(2).

5   As to OFCOM see PARA 507.
6   Broadcasting Act 1990 Sch 3 para 3(2A) (added by the Communications Act 2003 s 200(1)).
7   Broadcasting Act 1990 Sch 3 para 3(2B) (added by the Communications Act 2003 s 200(1)). As to the Secretary of State see PARA 507 note 32.
8   Broadcasting Act 1990 Sch 3 para 3(3) (amended by the Communications Act 2003 s 360(3), Sch 15 para 70(1), (2)).
9   Broadcasting Act 1990 Sch 3 para 3(4). As to ex-officio members of the corporation see PARA 627.

631. Remuneration and pensions of members. The Channel 4 Television Corporation[1] may pay to each member other than an ex-officio member[2] such remuneration and allowances[3], and to each ex-officio member such allowances[4], as OFCOM[5] may determine[6]. The corporation may pay or make provision for paying to or in respect of any member such sums by way of pensions, allowances or gratuities[7] as OFCOM may determine[8]. Where a person ceases to be a member otherwise than on the expiry of his term of office and it appears to OFCOM that there are special circumstances which make it right for him to receive compensation, the corporation may make a payment to him of such amount as OFCOM may determine[9].

1   As to the Channel 4 Television Corporation see PARA 627.
2   As to the appointment of members see PARA 629. As to ex-officio members see PARA 627.
3   Broadcasting Act 1990 s 23(6), Sch 3 para 4(1)(a).
4   Broadcasting Act 1990 Sch 3 para 4(1)(b).
5   As to OFCOM see PARA 507.
6   Broadcasting Act 1990 Sch 3 para 4(1) (amended by the Communications Act 2003 s 360(3), Sch 15 para 70(1), (2)). The approval of the Treasury is required for any determination under the Broadcasting Act 1990 Sch 3 para 4 other than a determination under Sch 3 para 4(1) having effect in relation to an ex-officio member of the corporation: Sch 3 para 4(5). As to the Treasury see CONSTITUTIONAL LAW AND HUMAN RIGHTS vol 8(2) (Reissue) PARAS 512–517.
7   References to pensions, allowances or gratuities include references to like benefits to be given on death or retirement; and any reference to the payment of pensions, allowances or gratuities to or in respect of any persons includes a reference to the making of payments towards provision for the payment of pensions, allowances or gratuities to or in respect of those persons: Broadcasting Act 1990 s 202(3).
8   Broadcasting Act 1990 Sch 3 para 4(2) (amended by the Communications Act 2003 Sch 15 para 70(2)). This provision does not apply in relation to ex-officio members of the corporation: see the Broadcasting Act 1990 Sch 3 para 4(4). The approval of the Treasury is required for such a determination: see note 6.
9   Broadcasting Act 1990 Sch 3 para 4(3) (amended by the Communications Act 2003 Sch 15 para 70(2)). This provision does not apply in relation to ex-officio members of the corporation: see the Broadcasting Act 1990 Sch 3 para 4(4). The approval of the Treasury is required for such a determination: see note 6.

632. Proceedings. The quorum of the Channel 4 Television Corporation[1] and the arrangements relating to its meetings are to be such as the corporation may determine[2]. The arrangements may, with the approval of OFCOM[3], provide for the discharge, under the general direction of the corporation, of any of the corporation's functions by a committee or by one or more of the members or employees of the corporation[4]. However, a member who is in any way directly or indirectly interested in any matter that is brought up for consideration at a meeting of the corporation[5] must disclose the nature of his interest to the meeting[6], and, where such a disclosure is made the disclosure must be recorded in the minutes of the meeting[7], and the member must not take any part in any deliberation or decision of the corporation, or of any of its committees, with respect to that matter[8].

A member need not attend in person at a meeting of the corporation in order to make a disclosure which he is required to make if he takes reasonable steps to secure that the disclosure is made by a notice which is taken into consideration and read at the meeting[9].

The validity of any proceedings of the corporation is not affected by any vacancy among the members or by any defect in the appointment of a member or by any failure to comply with the above requirements[10].

1   As to the Channel 4 Television Corporation see PARA 627.
2   Broadcasting Act 1990 s 23(6), Sch 3 para 6(1).
3   As to OFCOM see PARA 507.
4   Broadcasting Act 1990 Sch 3 para 6(2) (amended by the Communications Act 2003 s 360(3), Sch 15 para 70(1), (2)). As to the members of the corporation see PARA 629.
5   A reference to a meeting of the corporation includes a reference to a meeting of any of its committees: Broadcasting Act 1990 Sch 3 para 7(5).
6   Broadcasting Act 1990 Sch 3 para 7(1). For these purposes, a general notification given at a meeting of the corporation by a member to the effect that he is a member of a specified company or firm and is to be regarded as interested in any matter involving that company or firm is to be regarded as a sufficient disclosure of his interest in relation to any such matter: Sch 3 para 7(3).
7   Broadcasting Act 1990 Sch 3 para 7(1)(a).
8   Broadcasting Act 1990 Sch 3 para 7(1)(b). This provision does not apply in relation to any meeting of the corporation at which all of the other members present resolve that the member's interest should be disregarded: Sch 3 para 7(2).
9   Broadcasting Act 1990 Sch 3 para 7(4).
10 Broadcasting Act 1990 Sch 3 para 8.

633.   Employees.   The Channel 4 Television Corporation[1] must appoint a chief executive and may appoint such other employees as it may determine[2]. If it determines to do so in the case of any of its employees, the corporation may pay to or in respect of those employees such pensions, allowances or gratuities[3], or provide and maintain for them such pension schemes[4] (whether contributory or not), as the corporation may determine[5].

If any employee of the corporation is a participant in any pension scheme applicable to his employment[6], and becomes a member of the corporation other than an ex-officio member[7], he may, if OFCOM[8] so determines, be treated for the purposes of the pension scheme as if his service as a member of the corporation were service as an employee of the corporation[9].

1   As to the Channel 4 Television Corporation see PARA 627.
2   Broadcasting Act 1990 s 23(6), Sch 3 para 9(1).
3   As to pensions, allowances or gratuities see PARA 631 note 7.
4   'Pension scheme' means a scheme for the payment of pensions, allowances or gratuities: Broadcasting Act 1990 s 202(1).
5   Broadcasting Act 1990 Sch 3 para 9(2). As to pension schemes see SOCIAL SECURITY AND PENSIONS vol 44(2) (Reissue) PARA 551 et seq.
6   Broadcasting Act 1990 Sch 3 para 9(3)(a).
7   Broadcasting Act 1990 Sch 3 para 9(3)(b). As to members of the corporation see PARA 629. As to ex-officio members see PARA 627.
8   As to OFCOM see PARA 507.
9   Broadcasting Act 1990 Sch 3 para 9(3) (amended by the Communications Act 2003 s 360(3), Sch 15 para 70(1), (2)).

634.   Authentication of seal and presumption of authenticity of documents.
The application of the seal of the Channel 4 Television Corporation[1] must be authenticated by the signature of the chairman or of some other person authorised for the purpose[2].

Any document purporting to be an instrument issued by the corporation and to be duly executed under the seal of the corporation or to be signed on behalf of the corporation is to be received in evidence and deemed to be such an instrument unless the contrary is shown[3].

1   As to the Channel 4 Television Corporation see PARA 627.
2   Broadcasting Act 1990 s 23(6), Sch 3 para 10. As to the appointment of the chairman see PARA 627.
3   Broadcasting Act 1990 Sch 3 para 11.

635. Accounts and audit. The Channel 4 Television Corporation[1] must keep proper accounts and proper records in relation to the accounts, and must prepare in respect of each financial year[2] a statement of accounts in such form as the Secretary of State[3] may direct with the approval of the Treasury[4]. The accounts of the corporation must be audited by auditors appointed by the corporation with the approval of the Secretary of State[5].

The corporation must at all reasonable times upon demand made by the Secretary of State or by any persons authorised by him in that behalf[6] afford to him or them full liberty to examine the accounts of the corporation[7], and furnish him or them with all forecasts, estimates, information and documents which he or they may require with respect to the financial transactions and commitments of the corporation[8].

1   As to the Channel 4 Television Corporation see PARA 627.
2   'Financial year' means a financial year of the corporation: see the Broadcasting Act 1990 s 202(1), (2) (s 202(2) amended by the Broadcasting Act 1996 s 148(2), Sch 11 Pt I; and the Communications Act 2003 s 406(7), Sch 19).
3   As to the Secretary of State see PARA 507 note 32.
4   Broadcasting Act 1990 s 23(6), Sch 3 para 12(1). As to the Treasury see CONSTITUTIONAL LAW AND HUMAN RIGHTS vol 8(2) (Reissue) PARAS 512–517.
5   Broadcasting Act 1990 Sch 3 para 12(2). A person is not qualified to be appointed as an auditor unless he is eligible for appointment as a statutory auditor under the Companies Act 2006 Pt 42 (ss 1209–1264) (see COMPANIES vol 15 (2009) PARA 969): Broadcasting Act 1990 Sch 3 para 12(3) (substituted by SI 1991/1997; and amended by SI 2008/948).
6   Broadcasting Act 1990 Sch 3 para 12(4).
7   Broadcasting Act 1990 Sch 3 para 12(4)(a).
8   Broadcasting Act 1990 Sch 3 para 12(4)(b).

636. Annual reports. As soon as possible after the end of every financial year[1], the Channel 4 Television Corporation[2] must prepare a general report of its proceedings during that year, and transmit it to the Secretary of State[3] who must lay copies of it before each House of Parliament[4]. The report must have attached to it the statement of accounts for the year and a copy of any report made by the auditors on that statement, and must include such information (including information relating to the financial position of the corporation) as the Secretary of State may from time to time direct[5].

1   As to the meaning of 'financial year' see PARA 635 note 2.
2   As to the Channel 4 Television Corporation see PARA 627.
3   As to the Secretary of State see PARA 507 note 32.
4   Broadcasting Act 1990 s 23(6), Sch 3 para 13(1).
5   Broadcasting Act 1990 Sch 3 para 13(2).

637. Channel 4 to be provided by corporation as licensed service. The Channel 4 Television Corporation[1] must secure the continued provision of the television broadcasting service[2] known as Channel 4[3]. Channel 4 is provided by the corporation under a licence[4] granted to it by OFCOM[5], and must be so provided for so much of England, Scotland and Northern Ireland as may from time to time be reasonably practicable[6].

1 As to the Channel 4 Television Corporation see PARA 627. As to the duty of the corporation in relation to the Welsh Authority see PARAS 645, 655.

2 As to the meaning of 'television broadcasting service' see PARA 667 note 3.

3 Broadcasting Act 1990 s 24(1) (amended by the Digital Economy Act 2010 s 22(5)). 'Channel 4' means the television broadcasting service referred to in the Broadcasting Act 1990 s 24(1): s 71(1). Channel 4 replaced the Fourth Channel provided under the Broadcasting Act 1981 ss 10–13 (repealed). The shares of the Channel 4 Television Company vested in the corporation on 1 January 1993: see the Broadcasting Act 1990 s 24(2). See PARA 627.

4 As regards Channel 4 licences, 'licence' means a licence under the Broadcasting Act 1990 Pt I (ss 3–71); and 'licensed' is to be construed accordingly: s 71(1). As to the Channel 4 licence see PARA 641.

5 As to OFCOM see PARA 507.

6 Broadcasting Act 1990 s 24(3) (amended by the Communications Act 2003 s 360(3), Sch 15 para 14).

638. C4C's functions in relation to media content. C4C[1] must participate in[2]: (1) the making of a broad range of relevant media content[3] of high quality that, taken as a whole, appeals to the tastes and interests of a culturally diverse society; (2) the making of high quality films intended to be shown to the general public at the cinema in the United Kingdom; and (3) the broadcasting and distribution of such content and films[4]. C4C must, in particular, participate in: (a) the making of relevant media content that consists of news and current affairs; (b) the making of relevant media content that appeals to the tastes and interests of older children and young adults; (c) the broadcasting or distribution by means of electronic communications networks[5] of feature films that reflect cultural activity in the United Kingdom (including third party films[6]); and (d) the broadcasting or distribution of relevant media content by means of a range of different types of electronic communications networks[7].

In performing these duties, C4C must promote measures intended to secure that people are well-informed and motivated to participate in society in a variety of ways and contribute towards the fulfilment of the public service objectives[8]. In performing those duties C4C must have regard to the desirability of: (i) working with cultural organisations; (ii) encouraging innovation in the means by which relevant media content is broadcast or distributed; and (iii) promoting access to and awareness of services provided in digital form[9].

C4C must prepare a statement of media content policy at the same time as it prepares the first statement of programme policy that is prepared[10] after 8 June 2010[11], and subsequently at annual intervals[12]. C4C must monitor its performance in carrying out the proposals contained in its statements of media content policy[13]. A statement of media content policy must set out C4C's proposals for securing that, during the following year, it will discharge its duties[14] as to media content and include a report on its performance in carrying out the proposals contained in the previous statement[15]. In preparing the statement, C4C must have regard to guidance given by OFCOM[16] and consult OFCOM[17]. C4C must publish each statement of media content policy as soon as practicable after its preparation is complete and in such manner as it considers appropriate, having regard to any guidance given by OFCOM[18].

OFCOM must: (A) from time to time review the guidance for the time being in force for these purposes; and (B) revise that guidance as it thinks fit[19].

1 As to the meaning of 'C4C' see PARA 627 note 1.

2 'Participate in' includes invest in or otherwise procure: Communications Act 2003 s 198A(6) (s 198A added by the Digital Economy Act 2010 s 22(1)).

3 'Relevant media content' means material, other than advertisements, which is included in any of the following services that are available to members of the public in all or part of the United

Kingdom: (1) television programme services, additional television services or digital additional television services; (2) on-demand programme services; or (3) other services provided by means of the internet where there is a person who exercises editorial control over the material included in the service: Communications Act 2003 s 198A(6) (as added: see note 2). The services that are to be taken for the purposes of s 198A to be available to members of the public include any service which: (a) is available for reception by members of the public (within the meaning of s 361: see PARA 796); or (b) is available for use by members of the public (within the meaning of s 368R(4): see PARA 784 note 5): s 198A(7) (as so added). As to the meaning of 'television programme service' see PARA 790 note 5; as to the meaning of 'additional television service' see PARA 857 note 8; as to the meaning of 'digital additional television service' see PARA 857 note 11; and as to the meaning of 'on-demand programme service' see PARAS 796 note 6, 784.

4   Communications Act 2003 s 198A(1) (as added: see note 2).
5   As to the meaning of 'electronic communications network' see TELECOMMUNICATIONS vol 97 (2010) PARA 60.
6   A film is a 'third party film' if C4C did not participate in making it: Communications Act 2003 s 198A(6) (as added: see note 2).
7   Communications Act 2003 s 198A(2) (as added: see note 2).
8   Communications Act 2003 s 198A(3) (as added: see note 2). The public service objectives are defined in s 264A: see PARA 789. In performing their duties under s 198A(1)–(3) C4C must: (1) support the development of people with creative talent, in particular: (a) people at the beginning of their careers in relevant media content or films; and (b) people involved in the making of innovative content and films; (2) support and stimulate well-informed debate on a wide range of issues, including by providing access to information and views from around the world and by challenging established views; (3) promote alternative views and new perspectives; and (4) provide access to material that is intended to inspire people to make changes in their lives: s 198A(4) (as so added).
9   Communications Act 2003 s 198A(5) (as added: see note 2).
10   Ie under the Communications Act 2003 s 266: see PARAS 642, 662, 677.
11   Ie the date on which the Communications Act 2003 s 198B came into force: see the Digital Economy Act 2010 s 47(1).
12   Communications Act 2003 s 198B(1) (s 198B added by the Digital Economy Act 2010 s 23(1)).
13   Communications Act 2003 s 198B(2) (as added: see note 12).
14   Ie under the Communications Act 2003 s 198A.
15   Communications Act 2003 s 198B(3) (as added: see note 12).
16   As to OFCOM see PARA 507.
17   Communications Act 2003 s 198B(4) (as added: see note 12).
18   Communications Act 2003 s 198B(5) (as added: see note 12).
19   Communications Act 2003 s 198B(6) (as added: see note 12). As to OFCOM's duties in relation to C4C's media content duties see PARA 639.

639.   C4C and OFCOM.   The activities that C4C[1] is able to carry on include any activities which appear to it: (1) to be activities that it is appropriate for it to carry on in association with the carrying out of its primary functions[2]; and (2) to be connected, otherwise than merely in financial terms, with activities undertaken by it for the carrying out of those functions[3]. Provision is made for the approval by OFCOM[4], and for the enforcement, of arrangements made by C4C about the carrying on of its activities[5].

The Secretary of State[6] may by order provide for a limit on the borrowing that C4C is allowed to undertake[7]. The order may fix the limit either: (a) by specifying the sum which the outstanding borrowing[8] of C4C must not at any time exceed; or (b) by providing a method of determining the sum which that borrowing must not exceed[9]. C4C is not to borrow money if the effect of the borrowing would be to cause the amount of its outstanding borrowing to be, or to remain, in excess of the limit (if any) that is for the time being in force[10].

For each relevant period[11], OFCOM must carry out a review of the extent to which C4C has discharged its media content duties[12] and prepare a report on the matters found on the review[13]. OFCOM must publish each such report as soon as practicable after its preparation is complete and in such manner as it considers appropriate[14].

If OFCOM is of the opinion: (i) that C4C has failed to perform one or more of its duties in relation to media content[15]; (ii) that the failure is serious and is not excused by economic or market conditions, and determines that the situation requires the exercise of OFCOM's functions to give directions[16], it may give directions to C4C to do one or both of the following: (A) to revise the latest statement of media content policy in accordance with the direction; (B) to take such steps for remedying the failure as OFCOM specify in the direction[17]. A direction must set out a reasonable timetable for complying with it and the factors that OFCOM will take into account in determining whether or not a failure has been remedied[18]. OFCOM must consult C4C before giving a direction[19].

1　As to the meaning of 'C4C' see PARA 627 note 1.
2　C4C's primary functions are: (1) the performance of C4C's duties under the Communications Act 2003 s 198A (see PARA 638); (2) securing the continued provision of Channel 4; and (3) the fulfilment of the public service remit for that Channel under s 265 (see PARA 642): s 199(2) (amended by the Digital Economy Act 2010 s 22(2)). As to the meaning of 'Channel 4' see PARA 602 note 9.
3　Communications Act 2003 s 199(1). For transitional provision relating to s 199 see the Office of Communications Act 2002 (Commencement No 3) and Communications Act 2003 (Commencement No 2) Order 2003, SI 2003/3142.
4　As to OFCOM see PARA 507.
5　See the Communications Act 2003 s 199(5), Sch 9.
6　As to the Secretary of State see PARA 507 note 32.
7　Communications Act 2003 s 202(1). Before making an order under s 202, the Secretary of State must consult C4C: s 202(5). The consent of the Treasury is required for the making of an order under s 202: s 202(6). As to the Treasury see CONSTITUTIONAL LAW AND HUMAN RIGHTS vol 8(2) (Reissue) PARAS 512–517. As to the order that has been made see the Channel Four Television Corporation (Borrowing Limit) Order 2003, SI 2003/3176. As to the power of the Secretary of State to make orders under the Communications Act 2003 see s 402; and TELECOMMUNICATIONS vol 97 (2010) PARA 77. At the date at which this volume states the law, no such order had been made.
8　For the purposes of the Communications Act 2003 s 202, the amount of C4C's outstanding borrowing at any time is the aggregate amount outstanding at that time in respect of the principal of sums borrowed by it, but after allowing sums borrowed to repay existing loans to be applied for that purpose: s 202(4).
9　Communications Act 2003 s 202(2).
10　Communications Act 2003 s 202(3).
11　'Relevant period' means each period selected by OFCOM for the purposes of the Communications Act 2003 s 264(1)(b) (see PARA 788 head (2)) that ends after s 198C comes into force, ie 8 June 2010: s 198C(3) (s 198C added by the Digital Economy Act 2010 s 23(1)); Digital Economy Act 2010 s 47(1).
12　Ie under the Communications Act 2003 s 198A: see PARA 638.
13　Communications Act 2003 s 198C(1) (as added: see note 11).
14　Communications Act 2003 s 198C(2) (as added: see note 11).
15　Ie under the Communications Act 2003 s 198A or s 198B(1), (3) or (5): see PARA 638.
16　Ie under the Communications Act 2003 s 198D. In making a determination under s 198D(1)(c) (head (iii) in the text), OFCOM must have regard, in particular, to: (1) C4C's statements of media content policy (see PARA 638); (2) C4C's effectiveness and efficiency in monitoring its own performance; and (3) general economic and market conditions affecting the provision of relevant media content (as defined in s 198A): s 198D(2) (s 198D added by the Digital Economy Act 2010 s 23(1)).
17　Communications Act 2003 s 198D(1), (3) (as added: see note 16).
18　Communications Act 2003 s 198D(4) (as added: see note 16).
19　Communications Act 2003 s 198D(5) (as added: see note 16).

640. Remedying failure by C4C to perform media content duties. If OFCOM[1] is satisfied:

(1)   that C4C[2] has failed to comply with a direction[3] in respect of a failure to perform one or more of its duties in relation to media content[4];

(2)   that C4C is still failing to perform that duty or those duties; and

(3)   that it would be both reasonable and proportionate to the seriousness of the failure to vary the licence under which Channel 4 is licensed ('the Channel 4 licence') in accordance with thee following provisions,

OFCOM may, by notice to C4C, vary the Channel 4 licence by adding such conditions, or making such modifications of conditions, as OFCOM considers appropriate for remedying (entirely or partly) C4C's failure to perform such duty or duties[5]. If, at any time following such a variation, OFCOM considers that any of the additional conditions or modifications is no longer necessary, it may again vary the licence with effect from such time as it may determine[6]. OFCOM must consult C4C before exercising its power to vary the Channel 4 licence[7].

1   As to OFCOM see PARA 507.
2   As to the meaning of 'C4C' see PARA 627 note 1.
3   Ie under the Communications Act 2003 s 198D: see PARA 639.
4   Ie under the Communications Act 2003 s 198A: see PARA 638.
5   Communications Act 2003 s 271A(1), (2) (s 271A added by the Digital Economy Act 2010 s 23(2)).
6   Communications Act 2003 s 271A(3) (as added: see note 5).
7   Communications Act 2003 s 271A(4) (as added: see note 5).

(ii) Licence

641. Channel 4 licence. As from 28 December 2004[1]: (1) Channel 4[2] ceased to be licensed under the licence in force for the purposes of the Broadcasting Act 1990[3] immediately before that date; and (2) a licence granted for those purposes in accordance with the following provisions[4] came into force as the licence under which Channel 4 is licensed[5]. It is the duty of OFCOM[6], as soon as practicable after the television transfer date[7]: (a) to prepare a draft of a licence[8] to replace the licence that is likely to be in force[9] when the above provision[10] comes into force; (b) to notify C4C[11] of the terms and conditions of the replacement licence it proposes; and (c) after considering any representations made by C4C, to grant such a replacement licence to C4C so that it takes effect in accordance with head (2) above[12]. A replacement licence proposed or granted under these provisions: (i) must be a licence to provide a service with a view to its being broadcast in digital form; and (ii) must contain such conditions (if any) requiring C4C to ensure that the whole or a part of Channel 4 is also provided for broadcasting in analogue form as OFCOM considers appropriate[13]. The conditions included in a licence by virtue of head (ii) above must be such as to enable effect to be given to any directions given from time to time by the Secretary of State to OFCOM about the continuance of the provision of services in analogue form[14]. Where a replacement licence proposed or granted under these provisions contains a condition falling within head (ii) above, it must also contain a condition that the programmes (apart from the advertisements) that are included in the service provided in analogue form, and the times at which they are broadcast, are to be the same as in the case of, or of the specified part of, the service provided for broadcasting in digital form[15]. The terms of a replacement licence proposed or granted under these provisions must provide for it to continue in force until the end of 2014[16]. The conditions of a replacement licence proposed or granted under these provisions must include the conditions that OFCOM considers appropriate for the purpose of performing its duty relating to the application of regulatory regimes[17]. The conditions of such a licence must also include a condition prohibiting the imposition, whether directly or indirectly, of the following: (A) charges on persons in respect of their reception in the United Kingdom of Channel 4; (B) charges on persons in respect of their reception in the United Kingdom of any service consisting in the provision of assistance for disabled people in relation to programmes included in Channel 4; and (C) charges on persons in respect of their reception in the United Kingdom of any service (other than one mentioned in head (B) above) which is an ancillary service[18] in relation to so much of Channel 4 as is provided in digital form[19].

1   Ie the date on which the Communications Act 2003 s 231(1) came into force: see the Communications Act 2003 (Commencement No 3) Order 2004, SI 2004/3309, art 3.
2   As to the meaning of 'Channel 4' see PARA 602 note 9.
3   Ie for the purposes of the Broadcasting Act 1990 s 24(3): see PARA 637.
4   Ie in accordance with the Communications Act 2003 s 231.
5   Communications Act 2003 s 231(1).
6   As to OFCOM see PARA 507.
7   As to the meaning of 'the television transfer date' see PARA 857 note 17.
8   Ie under the Broadcasting Act 1990 Pt I (ss 3–71).
9   Ie for the purposes of the Broadcasting Act 1990 s 24(3): see PARA 637.
10   Ie the Communications Act 2003 s 231(1).
11   As to the meaning of 'C4C' see PARA 627 note 1.
12   Communications Act 2003 s 231(2).
13   Communications Act 2003 s 231(3).
14   Communications Act 2003 s 231(4).
15   Communications Act 2003 s 231(5).
16   Communications Act 2003 s 231(6). But: (1) such a licence may be renewed, on one or more occasions, for such period as OFCOM may think fit in relation to the occasion in question; and (2) the provisions of s 231 (apart from s 231(1), (2), (6)) are to apply in the case of a licence granted by way of a renewal of a licence granted under s 231 as they apply in the case of the replacement licence: s 231(7).
17   Ie its duty under the Communications Act 2003 s 263 (see PARA 602): s 231(8).
18   As to the meaning of 'ancillary service' see PARA 690 note 28 (definition applied by the Communications Act 2003 s 362(1)).
19   Communications Act 2003 s 231(9). It is unlawful to impose a charge in contravention of a condition falling within s 231(9): s 231(10).

(iii) Remit, etc

642. Remit, obligations, etc. The regulatory regime for every licensed public service channel[1] includes a condition requiring the provider of the channel to fulfil the public service remit for that channel[2]. The public service remit for Channel 4[3] is the provision of a broad range of high quality and diverse programming which, in particular: (1) demonstrates innovation, experiment and creativity in the form and content of programmes; (2) appeals to the tastes and interests of a culturally diverse society; (3) makes a significant contribution to meeting the need for the licensed public service channels to include programmes of an educational nature and other programmes of educative value; and (4) exhibits a distinctive character[4].

The regulatory regime for every licensed public service channel includes a condition requiring the provider of the channel: (a) as soon as practicable after the coming into force of these provisions[5] and subsequently at annual intervals, to prepare a statement of programme policy; and (b) to monitor his own performance in the carrying out of the proposals contained in the statements made in pursuance of the condition[6].

The regulatory regime for Channel 4 includes a condition requiring C4C[7] not to be involved, except to such extent as OFCOM may allow, in the making of programmes[8] to be broadcast on Channel 4[9].

1   As to the meaning of 'licensed public service channel' see PARA 788 note 1.
2   Communications Act 2003 s 265(1).
3   As to the meaning of 'Channel 4' see PARA 602 note 9.
4   Communications Act 2003 s 265(3).
5   Ie the Communications Act 2003 s 266. Section 266 came into force on 28 December 2004: see the Communications Act 2003 (Commencement No 3) Order 2004, SI 2004/3309, art 3.
6   Communications Act 2003 s 266(1). The condition must require every statement of programme policy prepared in accordance with the condition to set out the proposals of the provider of the channel for securing that, during the following year: (1) the public service remit for the channel will be fulfilled; and (2) the duties imposed on the provider by virtue of ss 277–296 (see PARA 875 et seq) will be performed: s 266(2). The condition must also require every such statement to contain a report on the performance of the provider of the channel in the carrying out, during the period since the previous statement, of the proposals contained in that statement: s 266(3). The condition must also provide that every such statement: (a) must be prepared having regard to guidance given by OFCOM; (b) must be prepared taking account of the reports previously published by OFCOM under ss 264, 358 (see PARAS 788, 853); (c) must take special account of the most recent such reports; (d) must be published by the provider of the channel in question as soon as practicable after its preparation is complete; and (e) must be published in such manner as, having regard to any guidance given by OFCOM, the provider considers appropriate: s 266(4). In preparing guidance about the preparation of such a statement, OFCOM must have regard, in particular, to the matters which, in the light of the provisions of s 264(4), (6) (see PARA 788), it considers should be included in statements of programme policy: s 266(5). It is the duty of OFCOM: (i) from time to time to review the guidance for the time being in force for the purposes of s 266; and (ii) to make such revisions of that guidance as it thinks fit: s 266(6). The conditions of a licence to provide a licensed public service channel may provide that a previous statement of policy made by the provider of the channel is to be treated for the purposes of Pt 3 (ss 198–362) as if it were a statement made in relation to such period as may be so specified and were a statement of programme policy for the purposes of a condition imposed under s 266: s 266(7). The reference in s 266(7) to a previous statement of policy is a reference to any statement made by the provider of the channel: (A) whether before or after the commencement of s 266, for the purposes of his application for a Broadcasting Act licence for the channel; or (B) at any time before the commencement of s 266, for any other purpose: s 266(8). A condition under s 266(7) cannot contain provision the effect of which is to postpone the time at which a licence holder is required to make the first statement of programme policy which (apart from that subsection) he is required to make in pursuance of a condition imposed under s 266: s 266(9). As to OFCOM see PARA 507. As to the meaning of 'licensed public service channel' see PARA 788 note 1. As to the meaning of 'Broadcasting Act licence' see PARA 602 note 3. For provision relating to changes of programme policy see s 267; and PARA 643.
7   As to the meaning of 'C4C' see PARA 627 note 1.
8   'Programme' does not include an advertisement: Communications Act 2003 s 295(2). As to the meaning of 'programme' generally see PARA 602 note 12.
9   Communications Act 2003 s 295(1).

643. Changes of programme and service policy. The regulatory regime for every licensed public service channel[1] includes a condition requiring compliance with the following requirement[2] in the case of a statement of programme policy containing proposals for a significant change[3]. The requirement is for the provider of the channel: (1) to consult OFCOM[4] before preparing the statement; and (2) to take account, in the preparation of the statement, of any opinions expressed to the provider of the channel by OFCOM[5].

1   As to the meaning of 'licensed public service channel' see PARA 788 note 1.
2   Ie under the Communications Act 2003 s 269(2).
3   Communications Act 2003 s 267(1). As to statements of programme policy see PARA 642. A change is a significant change for the purposes of s 267 if it is a change as a result of which the channel would in any year be materially different in character from in previous years: s 267(4). In determining for the purposes of any condition under s 267 whether a change is a significant

change: (1) regard must be had to any guidance issued by OFCOM; (2) the changes to be considered include any changes that, together with any proposed change for a particular year, would constitute a change occurring gradually over a period of not more than three years; and (3) the previous years with which a comparison is to be made must be those immediately preceding the year in which the change is made, or in which the changes comprised in it began to occur: s 267(5). It is the duty of OFCOM: (a) from time to time to review the guidance for the time being in force for the purposes of s 267; and (b) to make such revisions of that guidance as it thinks fit: s 267(6).

4   As to OFCOM see PARA 507.

5   Communications Act 2003 s 267(2). A condition imposed under s 267 must further provide that, if it appears to OFCOM that a statement of programme policy has been prepared by the provider of the channel in contravention of a condition imposed under s 267(1), the provider is: (1) to revise that statement in accordance with any directions given to him by OFCOM; and (2) to publish a revision of the statement in accordance with any such directions only after the revision has been approved by OFCOM: s 267(3).

(4)   ESTABLISHMENT AND REMIT OF SIANEL PEDWAR CYMRU (S4C)

644.   OFCOM and the Welsh Authority.   It is a function of OFCOM[1], to the extent that provision for it to do so is contained in the Communications Act 2003 and Part V of the Broadcasting Act 1996[2], to regulate the services provided by the Welsh Authority[3].

The Welsh Authority continues in existence but instead of its functions as described in the Broadcasting Act 1990[4] it has the function of providing television programme services[5] of high quality with a view to their being available for reception wholly or mainly by members of the public in Wales[6]. The carrying out of that function: (1) must include the continuing provision of the service provided in digital form and known as S4C Digital; and (2) may include the continuing provision of the television broadcasting service known as Sianel Pedwar Cymru ('S4C')[7]. The duty of the Welsh Authority to provide S4C Digital includes a duty to secure that arrangements are made and remain in force for it to be broadcast in digital form[8]. It is the duty of the Welsh Authority to secure that S4C and S4C Digital each represents a public service for the dissemination of information, education and entertainment[9]. The Welsh Authority may use part of the signals carrying S4C to provide: (a) subtitling in relation to programmes[10] included in the service; and (b) other services which are ancillary to programmes included in S4C and which are directly related to their contents[11]. In providing S4C Digital the Welsh Authority may also provide: (i) assistance for disabled people[12] in relation to programmes included in the service; and (ii) any other service (other than one mentioned in head (i) above) which is an ancillary service[13] in relation to S4C Digital[14]. The Secretary of State may by order modify the Communications Act 2003 and such other enactments as he thinks fit for the purpose of: (A) replacing the requirement for the Welsh Authority to provide S4C with a requirement to provide a service in digital form; (B) requiring the Welsh Authority to secure that arrangements are made for that service and S4C Digital to be merged and provided as one service (also to be known as 'S4C Digital'); and (C) applying enactments relating to the provision of S4C or S4C Digital to the provision of the merged service[15].

The Welsh Authority has the power to provide certain services in addition to S4C and S4C Digital[16].

The activities that the Welsh Authority is able to carry on include activities which appear to it: (aa) to be activities that it is appropriate for it to carry on in association with the carrying out of its function of providing S4C, S4C Digital or a service the provision of which is approved[17]; and (bb) to be connected, otherwise than merely in financial terms, with activities undertaken by it for the carrying out of that function[18].

Provision is also made as to Welsh Authority finances[19].

1 As to OFCOM see PARA 507.

2 Ie the Broadcasting Act 1996 Pt V (ss 107–130).

3 Communications Act 2003 s 203. 'The Welsh Authority' means the authority named Sianel Pedwar Cymru (or S4C) by virtue of the Broadcasting Act 1990 s 56(1) (see PARA 645): see the Broadcasting Act 1990 s 202(1); and the Communications Act 2003 s 405(1). As to the Welsh Authority see further PARA 645 et seq.

4 Ie its functions under the Broadcasting Act 1990 s 57 (repealed) (see PARA 655): Communications Act 2003 s 204(1).

5 As to the meaning of 'television programme service' see PARA 790 note 5.

6 Communications Act 2003 s 204(2). As to the duties of the Welsh Authority see further Sch 12 Pt 2.

7 Communications Act 2003 s 204(3) (substituted by SI 2009/1968). 'S4C Digital' means the services so described in the Communications Act 2003 s 204(3): s 362(1).

8 Communications Act 2003 s 204(4) (substituted by SI 2009/1968).

9 Communications Act 2003 s 204(5). As to the duty of the Welsh Authority to secure that, in each year, not less than 25 per cent of the total amount of time allocated to the broadcasting of qualifying programmes included in their designated public services (taken together) is allocated to the broadcasting of a range and diversity of independent productions see Sch 12 para 7.

10 As to the meaning of 'programme' see PARA 602 note 12. For these purposes, 'programme' does not include an advertisement: Communications Act 2003 s 204(10). 'Subtitling' means subtitling for the deaf or hard of hearing, whether provided by means of a teletext service or otherwise: s 362(1).

11 Communications Act 2003 s 204(6).

12 'Assistance for disabled people' means any of the following: (1) subtitling; (2) audio-description for the blind and partially-sighted; and (3) presentation in, or translation into, sign language: Communications Act 2003 s 362(1).

13 As to the meaning of 'ancillary service' see PARA 690 note 28 (definition applied by the Communications Act 2003 s 362(1)).

14 Communications Act 2003 s 204(7).

15 Communications Act 2003 s 204(8). As to the meaning of 'enactment' see PARA 793 note 5. An order under s 204(8) may require the Welsh Authority to ensure that, from the coming into force of a requirement to provide a merged service in digital form until a time determined in the manner described in the order, the whole or a part of the merged service is also to be provided for broadcasting in analogue form: s 204(9). As to the Secretary of State see PARA 507 note 32. As to the power of the Secretary of State to make orders under the Communications Act 2003 see s 402; and TELECOMMUNICATIONS vol 97 (2010) PARA 77. For an order made under s 204(8) see the Welsh Authority (Digital Switchover) Order 2009, SI 2009/1968.

16 See the Communications Act 2003 s 205.

17 Ie under the Communications Act 2003 s 205.

18 Communications Act 2003 s 206(1). The approval of the Secretary of State is required for the carrying on by the Welsh Authority of activities authorised only by s 206(1): s 206(2). The approval of the Secretary of State: (1) must be contained in an order made by him; and (2) may be a general approval in relation to a description of activities or a specific approval in relation to particular activities: s 206(3). For such an order see the S4C (Investment Activities) Approval Order 2008, SI 2008/693. For further provision relating to other activities of the Welsh Authority see the Communications Act 2003 s 206(4)–(8).

19 See the Communications Act 2003 s 207. The Welsh Authority must not, whether directly or indirectly, impose charges on persons: (1) in respect of their reception or use in Wales of any of the Authority's public services; (2) in respect of their reception in Wales of any service consisting in the provision of assistance for disabled people in relation to programmes included in any one or more of those services; or (3) in respect of their reception in Wales of any service (other than one mentioned in head (2)) which is an ancillary service in relation to any of the Authority's public services provided in digital form: s 207(1). For these purposes, references to the Welsh Authority's public services are references to the following: (a) S4C; (b) S4C Digital; and (c) the services the provision of which by the Authority is authorised by or under s 205: s 207(9). It is unlawful to impose a charge in contravention of s 207(1): s 207(2). The power of the Welsh Authority to do anything that appears to it to be conducive or incidental to the carrying out of

its functions includes power, subject to s 207(4), to borrow money: s 207(3). However, the Welsh Authority is not to borrow money except with the approval of the Secretary of State: s 207(4). The consent of the Treasury is to be required for the giving of an approval for the purposes of s 207(4): s 207(5). The Welsh Authority is to be liable to pay OFCOM such sums in respect of the carrying out by OFCOM of its functions in relation to the Authority as may be agreed from time to time between the Authority and OFCOM or (in default of agreement) fixed by the Secretary of State: s 207(6). As to the Treasury see CONSTITUTIONAL LAW AND HUMAN RIGHTS vol 8(2) (Reissue) PARAS 512–517.

645. Continuation of Welsh Authority as Sianel Pedwar Cymru. The authority known as the Welsh Fourth Channel Authority ('the Welsh Authority')[1] continues in existence as a body corporate[2] but is now known as Sianel Pedwar Cymru (or S4C)[3], and is constituted in accordance with the Broadcasting Act 1990[4].

The Welsh Authority consists of a chairman appointed by the Secretary of State[5], and such number of other members appointed by the Secretary of State, being not less than four nor more than eight, as he may from time to time determine[6].

1   The Welsh Fourth Channel Authority was established by the Broadcasting Act 1980 s 9 (repealed), and continued in existence by the Broadcasting Act 1981 s 46 (repealed). As to the meaning of 'the Welsh Authority' see PARA 644 note 3.
2   See the Broadcasting Act 1990 s 56(1).
3   Broadcasting Act 1990 s 56(1)(a). As to the meaning of 'S4C' see PARA 644; definition applied by s 71(1) (amended by the Communications Act 2003 s 360(3), Sch 15 Pt 1 para 31(1), (2)).
4   Broadcasting Act 1990 s 56(1)(b) (amended by the Communications Act 2003 s 406(7), Sch 19).
5   As to the Secretary of State see PARA 507 note 32.
6   Broadcasting Act 1990 s 56(2).

646. Status and capacity. The Welsh Authority[1] is not to be treated for the purposes of the enactments and rules of law relating to the privileges of the Crown[2] as a body exercising functions on behalf of the Crown[3]. The Authority may do anything which appears to it to be incidental or conducive to the carrying out of its functions[4]. These powers include power, to the extent that it appears to the Authority incidental or conducive to the carrying out of its functions to do so: (1) to carry on activities (other than those comprised in its duty to carry out its functions[5] through S4C companies[6]; and (2) to participate with others in the carrying on of any such activities[7].

The Authority may appoint, or arrange for the assistance of, advisory committees to give advice to it on such matters relating to the Authority's functions as the Authority may determine[8].

1   As to the meaning of 'the Welsh Authority' see PARA 644 note 3.
2   As to the privileges of the Crown see CROWN AND ROYAL FAMILY.
3   Broadcasting Act 1990 s 56(3), Sch 6 para 1(1).
4   Broadcasting Act 1990 Sch 6 para 1(2) (substituted by the Communications Act 2003 s 206(6)).
5   Ie under the Communications Act 2003 s 204: see PARA 644.
6   As to the meaning of 'S4C company' see PARA 826 note 3.
7   Broadcasting Act 1990 Sch 6 para 1(3) (added by the Broadcasting Act 1996 s 84(4); and substituted by the Communications Act 2003 s 206(6)).
8   Broadcasting Act 1990 Sch 6 para 14.

647. Appointment of members. The members of the Welsh Authority[1] must not at any time include[2]: (1) more than one person who is either a governor or an employee of the BBC[3]; or (2) more than one person who is either a member or an employee of OFCOM[4].

Before appointing a person to be a member of the Authority, the Secretary of State[5] must satisfy himself that that person will have no such financial or other interest as is likely to affect prejudicially the discharge by him of his functions as a member of the Authority; and the Secretary of State must also satisfy himself from time to time with respect to every member of the Authority that he has no such interest[6].

1	As to the meaning of 'the Welsh Authority' see PARA 644 note 3.

2	Broadcasting Act 1990 s 56(3), Sch 6 para 2(2).

3	Broadcasting Act 1990 Sch 6 para 2(2)(a). As to the meaning of 'BBC' see PARA 603 note 1; and as to the BBC see PARAS 603–626. There are no longer governors of the BBC; instead, there is now a BBC Trust and an Executive Board, as to which see PARA 604 et seq; and as to the staff of the BBC see PARA 612.

4	Broadcasting Act 1990 Sch 6 para 2(2)(b) (amended by the Communications Act 2003 s 360(3), Sch 15 para 71(1), (2)(b)). As to OFCOM see PARA 507.

5	As to the Secretary of State see PARA 507 note 32.

6	Broadcasting Act 1990 Sch 6 para 2(3). Any person who is, or whom the Secretary of State proposes to appoint to be, a member of the Authority must, whenever requested by the Secretary of State to do so, furnish the Secretary of State with such information as he considers necessary for the performance by him of his duties under Sch 6 para 2(3): Sch 6 para 2(4).

648. Tenure of office. A person[1] must not be appointed to be a member of the Welsh Authority[2] for more than five years at a time[3], and any member of the Welsh Authority may at any time resign his office by notice in writing to the Secretary of State[4]. Subject to these provisions, each member of the Authority is to hold and vacate office in accordance with the terms of his appointment[5].

1	As to the meaning of 'person' see PARA 510 note 1.

2	As to the meaning of 'the Welsh Authority' see PARA 644 note 3.

3	Broadcasting Act 1990 s 56(3), Sch 6 para 3(2).

4	Broadcasting Act 1990 Sch 6 para 3(3). As to the Secretary of State see PARA 507 note 32.

5	Broadcasting Act 1990 Sch 6 para 3(1).

649. Remuneration and pensions of members. The Welsh Authority[1] may pay to each member such remuneration and allowances as the Secretary of State[2] may determine[3]. It may also pay or make provision for paying to or in respect of any member such sums by way of pensions, allowances or gratuities[4] as the Secretary of State may determine[5].

Where a person ceases to be a member otherwise than on the expiry of his term of office and it appears to the Secretary of State that there are special circumstances which make it right for him to receive compensation, the Authority may make a payment to him of such amount as the Secretary of State may determine[6].

The approval of the Treasury[7] is required for any such determination as is mentioned above[8].

1	As to the meaning of 'the Welsh Authority' see PARA 644 note 3.

2	As to the Secretary of State see PARA 507 note 32.

3	Broadcasting Act 1990 s 56(3), Sch 6 para 4(1).

4	As to pensions, allowances or gratuities see PARA 631 note 7.

5	Broadcasting Act 1990 Sch 6 para 4(2).

6	Broadcasting Act 1990 Sch 6 para 4(3).

7	As to the Treasury see CONSTITUTIONAL LAW AND HUMAN RIGHTS vol 8(2) (Reissue) PARAS 512–517.

8	Broadcasting Act 1990 Sch 6 para 4(4).

650. Proceedings. A member who is in any way directly or indirectly interested in any matter that is brought up for consideration at a meeting of the Welsh Authority[1] must disclose the nature of his interest to the meeting[2]; and, where such a disclosure is made:

(1)   the disclosure must be recorded in the minutes of the meeting[3]; and

(2)   the member must not take any part in any deliberation or decision of the Authority, or of any of its committees, with respect to that matter[4].

For the above purposes, a general notification given at a meeting of the Authority by a member to the effect that he is a member of a specified company or firm and is to be regarded as interested in any matter involving that company or firm is to be regarded as a sufficient disclosure of his interest in relation to any such matter[5].

A member need not attend in person at a meeting of the Authority in order to make a disclosure which he is required to make if he takes reasonable steps to secure that the disclosure is made by a notice which is taken into consideration and read at the meeting[6].

Subject to the above, the quorum of the Authority and the arrangements relating to its meetings are to be such as the Authority may determine[7]. The arrangements may provide for the discharge, under the general direction of the Authority, of any of its functions by a committee or by one or more of the members or employees of the Authority[8].

The validity of any proceedings of the Authority is not affected by any vacancy among the members or by any defect in the appointment of a member or by any failure to comply with the requirements as to disclosure of interests[9].

1   As to the meaning of 'the Welsh Authority' see PARA 644 note 3. For these purposes, a reference to a meeting of the Welsh Authority includes a reference to a meeting of any of its committees: Broadcasting Act 1990 s 56(3), Sch 6 para 7(5).
2   Broadcasting Act 1990 Sch 6 para 7(1).
3   Broadcasting Act 1990 Sch 6 para 7(1)(a).
4   Broadcasting Act 1990 Sch 6 para 7(1)(b). However, Sch 6 para 7(1)(b) does not apply in relation to any meeting of the Authority at which all of the other members present resolve that the member's interest should be disregarded for the purposes of that provision: Sch 6 para 7(2).
5   Broadcasting Act 1990 Sch 6 para 7(3).
6   Broadcasting Act 1990 Sch 6 para 7(4).
7   Broadcasting Act 1990 Sch 6 para 6(1).
8   Broadcasting Act 1990 Sch 6 para 6(2).
9   Broadcasting Act 1990 Sch 6 para 8. As to the requirements referred to in the text see Sch 6 para 7; and the text and notes 1–6.

651. Employees. The Welsh Authority[1] must appoint a secretary and may appoint such other employees as it may determine[2]. If the Authority determines to do so in the case of any of its employees, it must pay to or in respect of those employees such pensions, allowances or gratuities[3], or provide and maintain for them such pension schemes[4] (whether contributory or not), as it may determine[5].

If any employee of the Authority is a participant in any pension scheme applicable to his employment, and becomes a member of the Authority, he may, if the Secretary of State[6] so determines, be treated for the purposes of the pension scheme as if his service as a member of the Authority were service as an employee of the Authority[7].

1   As to the meaning of 'the Welsh Authority' see PARA 644 note 3.
2   Broadcasting Act 1990 s 56(3), Sch 6 para 9(1).
3   As to pensions, allowances or gratuities see PARA 631 note 7.
4   As to the meaning of 'pension scheme' see PARA 633 note 4.
5   Broadcasting Act 1990 Sch 6 para 9(2).

6   As to the Secretary of State see PARA 507 note 32.
7   Broadcasting Act 1990 Sch 6 para 9(3).

652. Authentication of seal and presumption of authenticity of documents.
The application of the seal of the Welsh Authority[1] must be authenticated by the
signature of the chairman or of some other person authorised for the purpose[2].
Any document purporting to be an instrument issued by the Authority and to be
duly executed under the seal of the Authority or to be signed on its behalf must
be received in evidence and is deemed to be such an instrument unless the
contrary is shown[3].

1   As to the meaning of 'the Welsh Authority' see PARA 644 note 3.
2   Broadcasting Act 1990 s 56(3), Sch 6 para 10.
3   Broadcasting Act 1990 Sch 6 para 11.

653. Accounts and audit. The Welsh Authority[1] must keep proper accounts
and proper records in relation to the accounts, and must prepare in respect of
each financial year[2] a statement of accounts in such form as the Secretary of
State[3] may direct with the approval of the Treasury[4]. The accounts of the
Authority must be audited by auditors to be appointed by the Authority with the
approval of the Secretary of State[5].

The Authority must at all reasonable times upon demand made by the
Secretary of State or by any persons authorised by him in that behalf afford to
him or them full liberty to examine the accounts of the Authority, and furnish
him or them with all forecasts, estimates, information and documents which he
or they may require with respect to the financial transactions and commitments
of the Authority[6].

1   As to the meaning of 'the Welsh Authority' see PARA 644 note 3.
2   'Financial year' means the financial year of the Welsh Authority: Broadcasting Act 1990
    s 202(1), (2) (s 202(2) amended by the Broadcasting Act 1996 s 148(2), Sch 11 Pt I; and the
    Communications Act 2003 s 406(7), Sch 19).
3   As to the Secretary of State see PARA 507 note 32.
4   Broadcasting Act 1990 s 56(3), Sch 6 para 12(1). As to the Treasury see CONSTITUTIONAL LAW
    AND HUMAN RIGHTS vol 8(2) (Reissue) PARAS 512–517. The statement of accounts must deal
    separately with the public service fund referred to in s 61A (see PARA 658 note 3) and with the
    assets of the Authority that are not comprised in that fund; and, accordingly, the statement must
    deal with liabilities separately according to whether they fall to be met from that fund or from
    those assets: Sch 6 para 12(1A) (added by the Broadcasting Act 1996 s 81(2); and amended by
    the Communications Act 2003 s 360(3), Sch 15 para 71(1), (3)).
5   Broadcasting Act 1990 Sch 6 para 12(2). A person is not qualified to be appointed in this regard
    unless he is eligible for appointment as a statutory auditor under the Companies Act 2006 Pt 42
    (ss 1209–1264) (see COMPANIES vol 15 (2009) PARA 969): Broadcasting Act 1990 Sch 6
    para 12(3) (substituted by SI 1991/1997; and amended by SI 2008/948).
6   Broadcasting Act 1990 Sch 6 para 12(4).

654. Annual reports. As soon as possible after the end of every financial
year[1], the Welsh Authority[2] must prepare a general report of its proceedings
during that year, and transmit it to the Secretary of State[3] who must lay copies of
it before each House of Parliament[4]. The report must have attached to it the
statement of accounts for the year and a copy of any report made by the auditors
on that statement[5]. The report must also set out every contravention
notification[6] given by OFCOM to the Authority during the year; and include
such other information (including information relating to the Authority's
financial position) as the Secretary of State may from time to time direct[7].

1   As to the meaning of 'financial year' see PARA 653 note 2.

2   As to the meaning of 'the Welsh Authority' see PARA 644 note 3.
3   As to the Secretary of State see PARA 507 note 32.
4   Broadcasting Act 1990 s 56(3), Sch 6 para 13(1).
5   Broadcasting Act 1990 Sch 6 para 13(2) (amended by the Communications Act 2003 ss 342(a), 406(7), Sch 19).
6   'Contravention notification' means a notification of a determination by OFCOM of a contravention by the Authority of any obligation imposed by or under the Broadcasting Act 1990, the Broadcasting Act 1996 or the Communications Act 2003 Pt 3 (ss 198–362): Broadcasting Act 1990 Sch 6 para 13(4) (added by the Communications Act 2003 s 342(b)). As to OFCOM see PARA 507.
7   Broadcasting Act 1990 Sch 6 para 13(3) (added by the Communications Act 2003 s 342(b)).

655.   Public service remits.   It is the duty of the Welsh Authority[1] to secure that the public service remits[2] for each of its public television services is fulfilled[3].

The public service remit for S4C[4] is the provision of a broad range of high quality and diverse programming in a service in which:

(1)   a substantial proportion of the programmes consists of programmes in Welsh;

(2)   the programmes broadcast for viewing between 6.30 pm and 10.00 pm on every day of the week consist mainly of programmes in Welsh; and

(3)   the programmes that are not in Welsh are normally programmes which are being, have been or are to be broadcast on Channel 4[5].

The public service remit for S4C Digital[6] is the provision of a broad range of high quality and diverse programming in a service in which a substantial proportion of the programmes consists of programmes in Welsh[7]. The public service remit for a television programme service[8] provided by the Welsh Authority with the approval of the Secretary of State[9] is the remit set out in the order approving the provision of the service[10]. The Secretary of State may by order modify the public service remit for S4C and S4C Digital[11]. Before making an order specifying or modifying the public service remit for any of the Welsh Authority's public television services, the Secretary of State must consult the Welsh Authority and, where the order relates to the inclusion in any service of programmes that are not in Welsh, C4C[12]. An order modifying the public service remit for S4C or S4C Digital must not contain provision inconsistent with a requirement that each service must represent a public service for the dissemination of information, education and entertainment and include programmes a substantial proportion of which consists of programmes in Welsh[13].

For the purpose of enabling the Welsh Authority to fulfil so much of its public service remit in relation to S4C and S4C Digital as relates to programmes in Welsh[14], the BBC[15] must provide to the Welsh Authority (free of charge) sufficient television programmes[16] in Welsh to occupy not less than ten hours' transmission time per week, and do so in a way which meets the reasonable requirements of the Welsh Authority[17]. It is the duty of the Channel Four Television Corporation[18] to provide the Welsh Authority with programme schedules for the programmes broadcast on Channel 4, including information as to the periods available for the broadcasting of advertisements, far enough in advance to enable the Welsh Authority to fulfil so much of its public service remit in relation to S4C as relates to programmes not in Welsh[19] and to provide the Welsh Authority (free of charge) with any programmes which are required by the Welsh Authority for the purpose of complying with that requirement[20].

The programmes broadcast on S4C may, to the extent that they are not provided as above, be obtained by the Welsh Authority from such persons as it thinks fit[21]. Where any programmes provided by Channel 4 each form part of a series of programmes, the Welsh Authority must ensure that the intervals between those programmes when broadcast on S4C normally correspond to the intervals between them when broadcast on Channel 4[22].

The Welsh Authority must publish, in such manner as it considers appropriate, advance notice of the programme schedules for the programmes to be broadcast on S4C[23].

1 As to the meaning of 'the Welsh Authority' see PARA 644 note 3. For transitional arrangements relating to the Independent Broadcasting Authority's broadcasting services see the Broadcasting Act 1990 s 129, Sch 11; and see also Sch 11 Pt II para 6(1), (2).
2 As to public service remits see PARA 788 et seq.
3 Communications Act 2003 s 338, Sch 12 para 3(1).
4 As to the meaning of 'S4C' see PARA 644.
5 Communications Act 2003 Sch 12 para 3(2).
6 As to the meaning of 'S4C Digital' see PARA 644 note 7.
7 Communications Act 2003 Sch 12 para 3(3).
8 As to the meaning of 'television programme service' see PARA 790 note 5.
9 Ie under the Communications Act 2003 s 205: see PARA 644. As to the Secretary of State see PARA 507 note 32.
10 Communications Act 2003 Sch 12 para 3(4).
11 Communications Act 2003 Sch 12 para 3(5). No order is to be made containing provision authorised by Sch 12 para 3(5) unless a draft of the order has been laid before Parliament and approved by a resolution of each House: Sch 12 para 3(8).
12 Communications Act 2003 Sch 12 para 3(6).
13 Communications Act 2003 Sch 12 para 3(7).
14 Ie under the Communications Act 2003 Sch 12 para 3(2)(a), (b), 3(3): see heads (1), (2) in the text and the text to note 7. In the Broadcasting Act 1990 Pt I (ss 3–71), 'S4C' and 'S4C Digital' have the same meanings as in the Communications Act 2003 Pt 3 (ss 198–362): Broadcasting Act 1990 s 71(1) (definitions substituted by the Communications Act 2003 s 360(3), Sch 15 para 31(1), (2); and by SI 2009/1968).
15 As to the meaning of 'BBC' see PARA 603 note 1; and as to the BBC see PARAS 603–626.
16 For the purposes of the Broadcasting Act 1990 s 58, 'programme' does not include an advertisement: s 58(6) (added by the Communications Act 2003 Sch 15 para 28(1), (4)). As to the meaning of 'programme' generally see PARA 667 note 7.
17 Broadcasting Act 1990 s 58(1), (1A) (substituted and added respectively by SI 2009/1968).
18 As to the meaning of 'Channel 4' see PARA 637 note 3.
19 Ie under the Communications Act 2003 Sch 12 para 3(2)(c): see head (3) in the text.
20 Broadcasting Act 1990 s 58(2) (amended by the Communications Act 2003 Sch 15 para 28(3)).
21 Broadcasting Act 1990 s 58(3).
22 Broadcasting Act 1990 s 58(4).
23 Broadcasting Act 1990 s 58(5). This applies in relation to S4C Digital as it applies in relation to S4C: Broadcasting Act 1996 s 29(2). As to the meaning of 'S4C Digital' see PARA 644 note 7; definition applied by s 39(1) (amended by the Communications Act 2003 s 360(3), Sch 15 para 100).

656. Advertising on S4C. The Welsh Authority[1] must from time to time consult the Secretary of State[2] as to the classes and descriptions of advertisements which must not be broadcast on S4C[3] and the methods of advertising or sponsorship which must not be employed in, or in connection with, the provision of S4C[4] and from time to time consult the Secretary of State as to the forms and methods of product placement that should not be employed in the provision of S4C (including the descriptions of products, services or trade marks for which product placement should not be employed)[5]. The Authority must also carry out any directions which he may give to it in respect of such matters[6].

The Authority must not act as an advertising agent[7].

1 As to the meaning of 'the Welsh Authority' see PARA 644 note 3.
2 As to the Secretary of State see PARA 507 note 32.

3   As to the meaning of 'S4C' see PARA 644.

4   Broadcasting Act 1990 s 60(4)(a). Section 60 applies in relation to S4C Digital as it applies in relation to S4C: Broadcasting Act 1996 s 29(2). As to the meaning of 'S4C Digital' see PARA 644 note 7; definition applied by s 39(1) (amended by the Communications Act 2003 s 360(3), Sch 15 para 100).

5   Broadcasting Act 1990 s 60(4)(aa) (added by SI 2010/831).

6   Broadcasting Act 1990 s 60(4)(b).

7   Broadcasting Act 1990 s 60(5). As to the meaning of 'advertising agent' see PARA 674 note 16.

657. Funding of Welsh Authority. The Broadcasting Act 1990 provides that the Secretary of State[1] must, in the year 1998 and in each subsequent year, pay to the Welsh Authority[2] the prescribed amount[3] as increased by the appropriate percentage[4]. He may, if he is satisfied that it is appropriate to do so having regard to the cost to the Authority of providing services that are public services of the Authority[5], and arranging for the broadcasting or distribution of those services, by order provide that the prescribed amount is to be an amount which is greater than the 1997 amount and is specified in the order[6]. Before making such an order, however, the Secretary of State must consult the Authority[7]. Any sums required by the Secretary of State in respect of any of the provisions described above is to be paid out of money provided by Parliament[8].

However, as from 2013 there is to be a new funding arrangement, and the BBC[9] will begin to assume responsibility for much of the funding instead of the government[10].

1   As to the Secretary of State see PARA 507 note 32.

2   As to the meaning of 'the Welsh Authority' see PARA 644 note 3.

3   For these purposes 'the prescribed amount' means the 1997 amount or such amount as may from time to time be prescribed under the Broadcasting Act 1990 s 61(4) (see the text and note 6): s 61(2) (s 61 substituted by the Broadcasting Act 1996 s 80(1)). 'The 1997 amount' means the amount paid by the Secretary of State to the Welsh Authority by way of interim payment for the year 1997 (ie under the Broadcasting Act 1990 s 61 (as originally enacted)): s 61(3) (as so substituted). Under s 61(2) (as originally enacted) the interim payment for each year was an amount representing 3.2% of the estimated amount of the total television revenues for the preceding year.

4   Broadcasting Act 1990 s 61(1) (as substituted: see note 3). For these purposes, 'the appropriate percentage', in relation to any year ('the relevant year'), means the percentage which corresponds to the percentage increase between: (1) the retail prices index for November 1996; and (2) the retail prices index for the month of November in the year preceding the relevant year (and for this purpose 'the retail prices index' has the same meaning as in s 19(10) (see PARA 674 note 8)): s 61(6) (as so substituted).

5   Ie within the meaning of the Communications Act 2003 s 207: see PARA 644.

6   Broadcasting Act 1990 s 61(4) (as substituted (see note 3); and amended by the Communications Act 2003 s 207(7)). An order is not to be made under the Broadcasting Act 1990 s 61(4) unless a draft of it has been laid before and approved by a resolution of each House of Parliament: s 61(8) (as so substituted). At the date at which this volume states the law, no orders had been made under s 61(4).

7   Broadcasting Act 1990 s 61(5) (as substituted: see note 3).

8   Broadcasting Act 1990 s 61(7) (as substituted: see note 3).

9   As to the meaning of 'BBC' see PARA 603 note 1; and as to the BBC see PARAS 603–626.

10   See *Spending Review* (Cm 7942) (October 2010).

658. Welsh Authority public service fund. All amounts received by the Welsh Authority[1] in respect of funding[2] must be kept by the Authority in a separate fund ('the public service fund') which may be applied only for the purposes of its functions in relation to the provision of the services that are public services of the Authority[3].

No S4C company[4] is to receive any direct or indirect subsidy from the public service fund[5].

The Authority must secure that no television programme[6] which has been wholly or partly financed out of the public service fund is included in a television programme service provided by an S4C company before it is first broadcast on a television programme service that is one of its public services[7].

1   As to the meaning of 'the Welsh Authority' see PARA 644 note 3.
2   Ie under the Broadcasting Act 1990 s 61: see PARA 657.
3   Ie a public service within the meaning of the Communications Act 2003 s 207 (see PARA 644): Broadcasting Act 1990 s 61A(2) (s 61A added by the Broadcasting Act 1996 s 81(1); and the Broadcasting Act 1990 s 61A(2) amended by the Communications Act 2003 ss 207(8)(a), 406(7), Sch 19).
4   As to the meaning of 'S4C company' see PARA 826 note 3.
5   Broadcasting Act 1990 s 61A(3) (as added: see note 3).
6   As to the meaning of 'programme' see PARA 667 note 7.
7   Ie a public service within the meaning of the Communications Act 2003 s 207 (see PARA 644): Broadcasting Act 1990 s 61A(4) (as added (see note 3); and amended by the Communications Act 2003 s 207(8)(b)). As to the meaning of 'television programme service' see PARA 790 note 5; definition applied by the Broadcasting Act 1990 s 71(1) (definition substituted by the Communications Act 2003 s 360(3), Sch 15 Pt 1 para 31).

659.   Government control over S4C.   If it appears to him to be necessary or expedient to do so in connection with his functions as such, the Secretary of State[1] or any other Minister of the Crown may at any time by notice require the Welsh Authority[2] to broadcast[3], at such times as may be specified in the notice, any announcement specified in the notice, with or without visual images of any picture, scene or object mentioned in the announcement; and it is the duty of the Authority to comply with the notice[4]. Where the Authority broadcasts any announcement in pursuance of such a notice, it may announce that it is doing so in pursuance of such a notice[5].

The Secretary of State may at any time by notice require the Authority to refrain from broadcasting any matter or classes of matter specified in the notice; and it is the duty of the Authority to comply with the notice[6]. Where the Secretary of State has given the Authority such a notice, the Authority may broadcast an announcement of the giving of the notice or, when it has been revoked or has expired, of its revocation or expiration[7].

The above powers are in addition to any power specifically conferred on the Secretary of State by any other relevant statutory provision[8].

1   As to the Secretary of State see PARA 507 note 32.
2   As to the meaning of 'the Welsh Authority' see PARA 644 note 3.
3   As to the meaning of 'broadcast' see PARA 668 note 2.
4   Broadcasting Act 1990 s 63(1).
5   Broadcasting Act 1990 s 63(2).
6   Broadcasting Act 1990 s 63(3).
7   Broadcasting Act 1990 s 63(4).
8   Broadcasting Act 1990 s 63(5). The reference in the text to any other relevant statutory provision means any other provision of the Broadcasting Act 1990.

660.   Audience research by Welsh Authority.   The Welsh Authority[1] must make arrangements for ascertaining:

(1)   the state of public opinion concerning programmes[2] broadcast[3] on S4C[4];

(2)   any effects of such programmes on the attitudes or behaviour of persons who watch them[5]; and

(3)   the types of programme that members of the public would like to be broadcast on S4C[6].

Those arrangements must:

(a) secure that, so far as is reasonably practicable, any research undertaken in pursuance of the arrangements is undertaken by persons who are neither members nor employees of the Authority[7]; and

(b) include provision for full consideration by the Authority of the results of any such research[8].

1 As to the meaning of 'the Welsh Authority' see PARA 644 note 3.
2 As to the meaning of 'programme' see PARA 667 note 7.
3 As to the meaning of 'broadcast' see PARA 668 note 2.
4 Broadcasting Act 1990 s 64(1)(a). Section 64 applies in relation to S4C Digital as it applies in relation to S4C: Broadcasting Act 1996 s 29(2). As to the meaning of 'S4C' see PARA 644. As to the meaning of 'S4C Digital' see PARA 644 note 7; definition applied by s 39(1) (amended by s Communications Act 2003 s 360(3), Sch 15 para 100).
5 Broadcasting Act 1990 s 64(1)(b).
6 Broadcasting Act 1990 s 64(1)(c).
7 Broadcasting Act 1990 s 64(2)(a).
8 Broadcasting Act 1990 s 64(2)(b).

661. Enforcement against the Welsh Authority. The Secretary of State[1] may carry out a review of the performance by the Welsh Authority[2] of its duty to secure that each of the following public service remits is fulfilled in relation the services to which it applies: (1) that for S4C[3]; (2) that for S4C Digital[4]; and (3) that for each of the television programme services[5] provided by it with the approval[6] of the Secretary of State[7]. The first review carried out under these provisions[8]: (a) must be a review relating to the period since 17 July 2003[9]; and (b) must not be carried out before the end of the period of five years beginning with 17 July 2003[10]. A subsequent review: (i) must be a review relating to the period since the end of the period to which the previous review related; and (ii) must not be carried out less than five years after the day of the publication of the report of the previous review[11]. On a review the Secretary of State: (A) must consult the Welsh Ministers and the Welsh Authority on the matters under review; and (B) must have regard to their opinions when reaching his conclusions[12]. As soon as practicable after the conclusion of a review under these provisions the Secretary of State must publish a report of his conclusions[13].

If the Secretary of State's conclusions on a review[14] include a finding that the Welsh Authority has failed in any respect to perform its duty to secure that the public service remit for a service is fulfilled, and that there is no reasonable excuse for the failure, the Secretary of State may give the Welsh Authority general or specific directions requiring it to take the steps that he considers will ensure that the Welsh Authority performs its duty properly in future[15].

A duty is imposed on the Welsh Authority to provide such information as OFCOM[16] reasonably requires in order that OFCOM may fulfil its functions under the Communications Act 2003, the Broadcasting Act 1990 and the Broadcasting Act 1996 as regards the Welsh Authority[17].

1 As to the Secretary of State see PARA 507 note 32.
2 As to the meaning of 'the Welsh Authority' see PARA 644 note 3; and as to television broadcasting by the Welsh Authority see PARA 644 et seq.
3 As to the meaning of 'S4C' see PARA 644.
4 As to the meaning of 'S4C Digital' see PARA 644 note 7.
5 As to the meaning of 'television programme service' see PARA 790 note 5.
6 Ie under the Communications Act 2003 s 205 (see PARA 644).
7 Communications Act 2003 s 339(1).
8 Ie carried out under the Communications Act 2003 s 339.
9 Ie the period since the passing of the Communications Act 2003.

10 Communications Act 2003 s 339(2).
11 Communications Act 2003 s 339(3).
12 Communications Act 2003 s 339(4); Government of Wales Act 2006 s 162, Sch 11 para 32. As to the Welsh Ministers see CONSTITUTIONAL LAW AND HUMAN RIGHTS. The Secretary of State must also consult such other persons as he considers are likely to be affected by whether, and in what manner, the Welsh Authority perform the duty mentioned in s 339(1): s 339(5).
13 Communications Act 2003 s 339(6).
14 Ie under the Communications Act 2003 s 339.
15 Communications Act 2003 s 340(1), (2). The Secretary of State is not to give a direction under s 340 unless a draft of the proposed direction has been laid before Parliament and approved by a resolution of each House: s 340(3). Before laying a proposed direction before Parliament, the Secretary of State must consult the Welsh Authority: s 340(4). It is the duty of the Welsh Authority to comply with every direction under s 340: s 340(5).
     If OFCOM is satisfied that there has been a contravention of a requirement to which s 341 applies, it may serve on the Welsh Authority a notice requiring the Authority, within the specified period, to pay OFCOM a specified penalty: s 341(2). Section 341(1) provides that s 341 applies to the following requirements so far as they are imposed on the Welsh Authority in relation to services provided by it:
     (1) the requirements imposed by or under Sch 12 paras 7, 8 (programme quotas);
     (2) the requirements imposed by Sch 12 para 9(1), (3) (news and current affairs);
     (3) the requirements imposed by Sch 12 para 10 (code relating to programme commissioning) or by a direction under Sch 12 para 10(3)(d);
     (4) the requirement imposed by virtue of Sch 12 para 12 to comply with standards set under s 319, so far as that requirement relates to standards set otherwise than for the purpose of securing the objectives set out in s 319(2)(c) or (d);
     (5) the requirements imposed by Sch 12 paras 14, 16 (advertising or sponsorship) to comply with a direction under those paragraphs;
     (6) the requirement imposed by Sch 12 para 17 (observance of the fairness code);
     (7) the requirement imposed by Sch 12 para 19 (publicising complaints procedure);
     (8) the requirement imposed by Sch 12 para 20 (monitoring of programmes);
     (9) the requirement imposed by Sch 12 para 21 (international obligations) to comply with a direction under that paragraph;
     (10) the requirement under Sch 12 para 22 (assistance for disabled people) to comply with the code for the time being in force under s 303;
     (11) the requirement to comply with a direction under the Broadcasting Act 1996 s 119(1) (directions in respect of fairness matters).
     The amount of the penalty must not exceed £250,000: Communications Act 2003 s 341(3). The Secretary of State may by order substitute a different sum for the sum for the time being specified in s 341(3): s 341(6). No order is to be made containing provision authorised by s 341(6) unless a draft of the order has been laid before Parliament and approved by a resolution of each House: s 341(7). OFCOM is not to serve a notice on the Welsh Authority under s 341 unless it has given the Authority a reasonable opportunity of making representations to OFCOM about the matters appearing to OFCOM to provide grounds for the service of the notice: s 341(4). An exercise by OFCOM of its powers under s 341 does not preclude any exercise by it of its powers under Sch 12 para 15 in respect of the same contravention: s 341(5).
16 As to OFCOM see PARA 507.
17 See the Communications Act 2003 s 343. As to those duties see PARA 644 et seq. It is the duty of the Welsh Authority to comply with every direction given to it by OFCOM to provide OFCOM with information falling within s 343(2): s 343(1). The information that the Welsh Authority may be directed to provide is any information which OFCOM may reasonably require for the purposes of carrying out its functions in relation to the Welsh Authority under the Communications Act 2003, the Broadcasting Act 1990 and the Broadcasting Act 1996: Communications Act 2003 s 343(2). Information that is required to be provided by a direction under s 343 must be provided in such manner and at such times as may be required by the direction: s 343(3).

(5) CHANNEL 3 LICENCE

662. Introduction. Independent television was first introduced in the United Kingdom from 1955 with the creation of the Independent Television Authority and the allocation of regional franchises[1]. Channel 3 broadcasting is currently organised on the basis of fifteen regional franchises and a national breakfast time franchise. There are separate franchises for weekday and weekend broadcasting in the London region. All bar four of the regional franchises are currently held by ITV plc[2]. All franchisees contribute to a networking arrangement, and supplement networked programming with region-specific programming. Channel 3 companies are licensed to deliver television services by OFCOM[3]. These licences include public service obligations[4].

The regulatory regime for every licensed public service channel[5] includes a condition requiring the provider of the channel or service to fulfil the public service remit for that channel or service[6]. The public service remit for every Channel 3 service[7] is the provision of a range of high quality and diverse programming[8].

The regulatory regime for every licensed public service channel includes a condition requiring the provider of the channel: (1) as soon as practicable after the coming into force of these provisions[9] and subsequently at annual intervals, to prepare a statement of programme policy; and (2) to monitor his own performance in the carrying out of the proposals contained in the statements made in pursuance of the condition[10].

1 Ie under the Television Act 1954. See PARA 507.
2 The franchises for Northern and Central Scotland are both held by the STV Group plc, that for Northern Ireland is held by UTV Media plc, and that for the Channel Islands is held by Channel Television Ltd.
3 As regards Channel 3 licences, 'licence' means a licence under the Broadcasting Act 1990 Pt I (ss 3–71); and 'licensed' is to be construed accordingly: s 71(1). As to Channel 3 licences see PARA 665. The holding by any person of a licence under Pt I does not relieve him of any liability in respect of a failure to hold a licence under the Wireless Telegraphy Act 2006 s 8 (see PARA 514 et seq) or any obligation to comply with requirements imposed by or under the Communications Act 2003 Pt 2 Ch 1 (ss 32–151) (electronic communications networks and electronic communications services: see TELECOMMUNICATIONS vol 97 (2010) PARA 92 et seq): Broadcasting Act 1990 s 3(8) (substituted by the Communications Act 2003 s 360(3), Sch 15 para 1(1), (4); and amended by the Wireless Telegraphy Act 2006 s 123, Sch 7 paras 9, 10). As to the meaning of 'person' see PARA 510 note 1. As to OFCOM see PARA 507.
4 Channel 3 public service obligations include quotas for news, current affairs, independent and European programming, children's and religious programming, and output containing subtitles, signing and audio description: see PARA 668. In addition, Channel 3 franchisees are legally obliged to screen party election broadcasts on behalf of all the major political parties, and also party political broadcasts at the time of other significant political events such as the Budget: see PARA 890 et seq.
5 As to the meaning of 'licensed public service channel' see PARA 788 note 1.
6 Communications Act 2003 s 265(1).
7 As to the meaning of 'Channel 3 service' see PARA 602 note 8.
8 Communications Act 2003 s 265(2).
9 Ie the Communications Act 2003 s 266. Section 266 came into force on 28 December 2004: see the Communications Act 2003 (Commencement No 3) Order 2004, SI 2004/3309, art 3.
10 Communications Act 2003 s 266(1). As to the condition see further PARA 642 note 6. For provision relating to changes of programme policy see s 267; and PARA 663.

663. Changes of programme and service policy. The regulatory regime for every licensed public service channel[1] includes a condition requiring compliance with the following requirement[2] in the case of a statement of programme policy containing proposals for a significant change[3]. The requirement is for the provider of the channel: (1) to consult OFCOM[4] before preparing the statement; and (2) to take account, in the preparation of the statement, of any opinions expressed to the provider of the channel by OFCOM[5].

1 As to the meaning of 'licensed public service channel' see PARA 788 note 1.
2 Ie under the Communications Act 2003 s 269(2).

3   Communications Act 2003 s 267(1). As to statements of programme policy see PARA 662. As to
    when a change is a significant change for the purposes of s 267 see PARA 643 note 3. It is the
    duty of OFCOM: (1) from time to time to review the guidance for the time being in force for the
    purposes of s 267; and (2) to make such revisions of that guidance as it thinks fit: s 267(6).
4   As to OFCOM see PARA 507.
5   Communications Act 2003 s 267(2). A condition imposed under s 267 must further provide
    that, if it appears to OFCOM that a statement of programme policy has been prepared by the
    provider of the channel in contravention of a condition imposed under s 267(1), the provider is:
    (1) to revise that statement in accordance with any directions given to him by OFCOM; and (2)
    to publish a revision of the statement in accordance with any such directions only after the
    revision has been approved by OFCOM: s 267(3).

664.   Networking arrangements for Channel 3.   An application for a regional
Channel 3 licence[1], in addition to being accompanied by the proposals
mentioned in the Broadcasting Act 1990[2], must be accompanied by the
applicant's proposals for participating in networking arrangements[3]. OFCOM[4]
may publish general guidance to applicants for regional Channel 3 licences as to
the kinds of proposals which it is likely to consider satisfactory[5].

The regulatory regime for every regional Channel 3 service includes the
conditions that OFCOM considers appropriate for securing that the licence
holder does all that he can to ensure that approved networking arrangements[6]
are in force whenever: (1) the licence holder is providing the licensed service; and
(2) no networking arrangements imposed by OFCOM[7] are in force[8].

The following provisions[9] apply on each occasion on which OFCOM: (a) is
proposing to award one or more regional Channel 3 licences; and (b) for that
purpose publishes a notice[10]. OFCOM must determine the date by which the
holders of the licences awarded and all other regional Channel 3 providers[11] (if
any) must have entered into networking arrangements (the 'networking date'),
and it must set out that date in that notice[12]. The networking date must be the
date by which, in OFCOM's opinion, the networking arrangements must have
been entered into if approved networking arrangements are to be fully in force
before the persons awarded licences begin to provide their licensed services[13]. If
(i) no suitable networking arrangements exist by the networking date; or (ii) the
suitable networking arrangements that exist at that date cease to apply to all
regional Channel 3 providers on or after that date, OFCOM may impose on all
regional Channel 3 providers the networking arrangements that OFCOM
considers appropriate[14]. Arrangements imposed under these provisions[15] come
into force on the date determined by OFCOM[16].

The regulatory regime for every regional Channel 3 service includes the
conditions that OFCOM considers appropriate for securing that the licence
holder complies with the provisions of any networking arrangements imposed
under these provisions[17]. Where (A) networking arrangements are imposed under
these provisions; (B) other networking arrangements are entered into between the
licence holders bound by the imposed arrangements; and (C) the other
arrangements entered into are approved by OFCOM, the imposed arrangements
will cease to have effect on the coming into force of the other arrangements as
approved networking arrangements[18].

A duty is imposed on OFCOM to carry out general reviews of the networking
arrangements approved[19] or imposed[20].

1   'Channel 3 licence' means a licence to provide a Channel 3 service: Communications Act 2003
    s 362(1). As to the meaning of 'Channel 3 service' see PARA 602 note 8. 'Regional Channel 3
    licence' means a licence under the Broadcasting Act 1990 Pt I (ss 3–71) to provide a regional
    Channel 3 service: Communications Act 2003 s 362(1). As to the meaning of 'regional Channel
    3 service' see PARA 875 note 4.

2   Ie the proposals mentioned in the Broadcasting Act 1990 s 15(3)(b) (see PARA 669).

3   Communications Act 2003 s 290(1). Arrangements are networking arrangements for the purposes of Pt 3 (ss 198–362) if they: (1) apply to all the holders of regional Channel 3 licences; (2) provide for programmes made, commissioned or acquired by or on behalf of one or more of the holders of such licences to be available for broadcasting in all regional Channel 3 services; and (3) are made for the purpose of enabling regional Channel 3 services (taken as a whole) to be a nationwide system of services which is able to compete effectively with other television programme services provided in the United Kingdom: s 290(4). As to the meaning of 'television programme service' see PARA 790 note 5. As to the meaning of 'United Kingdom' see PARA 510 note 13.

4   As to OFCOM see PARA 507.

5   Communications Act 2003 s 290(2). The publication of guidance under s 290(2) is to be in such manner as OFCOM considers appropriate: s 290(3).

6   'Approved networking arrangements' means networking arrangements which are for the time being approved by OFCOM in accordance with the Communications Act 2003 Sch 11 (see note 20): s 291(2).

7   Ie under the Communications Act 2003 s 292: see the text and notes 9–18.

8   Communications Act 2003 s 291(1).

9   Ie the Communications Act 2003 s 292.

10   Ie under the Broadcasting Act 1990 s 15(1) (see PARA 669): Communications Act 2003 s 292(1).

11   'Regional Channel 3 providers' means persons who will be licensed to provide regional Channel 3 services and will be providing such services when the licences to be awarded come into force: Communications Act 2003 s 292(9).

12   Communications Act 2003 s 292(2).

13   Communications Act 2003 s 292(3). As to the meaning of 'approved networking arrangements' see note 6; definition applied by s 292(9).

14   Communications Act 2003 s 292(4). For the purposes of s 292(4), arrangements are suitable networking arrangements if it appears to OFCOM that they: (1) have been submitted to it for approval or have been approved by it; and (2) will be in force as approved networking arrangements when the persons awarded licences begin to provide their licensed services: s 292(5).

15   Ie the Communications Act 2003 s 292.

16   Communications Act 2003 s 292(6).

17   Communications Act 2003 s 292(7).

18   Communications Act 2003 s 292(8).

19   Ie under the Communications Act 2003 s 291: see the text and notes 6–8.

20   Ie under the Communications Act 2003 s 292 (see the text and notes 9–18): see s 293. For further provision about the approval of networking arrangements and the imposition or modification of such arrangements see s 294(1), Sch 11. The obligations arising under conditions imposed in accordance with ss 291–293 are subject to the rights of appeal conferred by Sch 11: s 294(2).

665. Channel 3 licence. Channel 3 licences[1] are awarded under Part I of the Broadcasting Act 1990[2]. They must be made in writing, and continue in force for such period as is provided by the relevant statutory provisions[3]. Licences may be granted for the provision of such a service as is specified in the licence or for the provision of a service of such a description as is so specified[4]. They may include such conditions[5] as appear to OFCOM[6] to be appropriate having regard to any duties which are or may be imposed on it[7] or on the licence holder[8]. A Channel 3 licence granted by OFCOM must require the holder to provide the licensed service with a view to its being broadcast in digital form, while also requiring the licence holder to ensure that the whole or a part of the service is also provided for broadcasting in analogue form as OFCOM considers appropriate[9]. A licence may include conditions requiring the payment by the licence holder to OFCOM (whether on the grant of the licence or at such times thereafter as may be determined by or under the licence or both) of a fee or fees of an amount or amounts so determined[10]. Channel 3 licences will also include conditions prohibiting the imposition, whether directly or indirectly, of charges on persons: (1) in respect of their reception in the United Kingdom of the licensed service; (2)

in respect of their reception in the United Kingdom of any service consisting in the provision of assistance for disabled people in relation to programmes included in the licensed service; or (3) in respect of their reception in the United Kingdom of any service, other than that mentioned in head (2), which is an ancillary service in relation to so much of the licensed service as is provided in digital form[11]. Conditions may also be included in a Channel 3 licence providing for such incidental and supplemental matters as appear to be appropriate to OFCOM[12].

OFCOM is under a statutory duty to do all that it can to secure that the holder of every Channel 3 licence complies, in relation to the licensed service, with the conditions included in the licence[13]. Conditions may be included in a licence requiring the licence holder to provide OFCOM, in such manner and at such times as it may reasonably require, with such information as it may require for the purposes of exercising the functions assigned to it by or under the Broadcasting Act 1990, the Broadcasting Act 1996 or the Communications Act 2003[14]. Where the licence holder is required by virtue of any condition contained in the licence to provide OFCOM with any information[15], and in purported compliance with that condition provides OFCOM with information that is false in a material particular[16], he is for certain purposes[17] taken to have failed to comply with that condition[18]. A licence may include conditions requiring the licence holder to comply with any direction given by OFCOM as to such matters as are specified in the licence or are of a description so specified[19], or (to the extent that OFCOM consents to his doing or not doing them) not to do or not do such things as are specified in the licence or are of a description so specified[20].

When granted, a licence must in principle continue in force from the time that it takes effect until the end of the general licensing period that begins or is current when the licence is granted[21]. Channel 3 licences are renewable on one or more occasions[22]. OFCOM may vary a licence by a notice[23] served on the licence holder if[24]: (a) in the case of a variation of the period for which the licence is to continue in force, the licence holder consents[25]; or (b) in the case of any other variation, the licence holder has been given a reasonable opportunity of making representations to OFCOM about the variation[26].

A Channel 3 licence granted to any person is not transferable to any other person without the previous written consent of OFCOM[27]. OFCOM must not give its consent unless it is satisfied that any such person would be in a position to comply with all of the conditions included in the licence which would have effect during the period for which it is in force[28].

1	As to the meaning of 'licence' see PARA 662 note 3.
2	Ie the Broadcasting Act 1990 Pt I (ss 3–71).
3	As regards licences for independent television broadcasting, the relevant statutory provisions are the Broadcasting Act 1990 Pt I Ch II (ss 14–42) or Ch V (ss 48–55) or the Communications Act 2003 s 235: see the Broadcasting Act 1990 s 3(1) (amended by the Communications Act 2003 Sch 15 para 1(2), (3)). Replacement licences were offered to all existing Channel 3 licence holders under the Communications Act 2003 s 215 following the date of transfer to regulation under that statute, ie 29 December 2003. OFCOM was given the duty to offer a replacement licence to every person who, when the offer was made, was the holder of an existing licence to provide a Channel 3 service or to provide Channel 5: see the Communications Act 2003 s 215. As to Channel 5 see PARA 677 et seq.
4	Broadcasting Act 1990 s 3(2).
5	Nothing in the Broadcasting Act 1990 which authorises or requires the inclusion in a licence of conditions relating to any particular matter or having effect for any particular purpose is to be taken as derogating from the generality of s 4(1): s 4(6).
6	As to OFCOM see PARA 507.

7   Ie under the Communications Act 2003 s 263: see PARA 602.

8   Broadcasting Act 1990 s 4(1)(a) (amended by the Communications Act 2003 s 360(3), Sch 15 para 2(1)–(3)). As to the holder of the licence see PARA 671 note 19.

9   Communications Act 2003 s 214(2). The conditions included in a licence by virtue of head (2) in the text must be such as to enable effect to be given to any directions given from time to time by the Secretary of State to OFCOM about the continuance of the provision of services in analogue form: s 214(3). Where the licence contains a condition falling within head (2) in the text, it must also contain a condition that: (1) the programmes (apart from the advertisements) that are included in the service provided in analogue form; and (2) the times at which they are broadcast, are to be the same as in the case of, or of the specified part of, the service provided for broadcasting in digital form: s 214(4). As to the Secretary of State see PARA 507 note 32.

10 Broadcasting Act 1990 s 4(1)(b) (amended by the Communications Act 2003 Sch 15 para 2(2)). Fees are to be in accordance with such tariff as may from time to time be fixed by OFCOM: Broadcasting Act 1990 s 4(3) (amended by the Communications Act 2003 Sch 15 para 2(2), (4), Sch 19). Such a tariff may specify different fees in relation to different cases or circumstances; and OFCOM must publish every such tariff in such manner as it considers appropriate: Broadcasting Act 1990 s 4(4) (amended by the Communications Act 2003 Sch 15 para 2(2)).

11 Communications Act 2003 s 214(8). It is unlawful to impose a charge in contravention of a condition imposed under s 214(8): s 214(9). References in Pt 3 (ss 198–362) to imposing a charge on a person in respect of his reception of a service in, or in a part of, the United Kingdom include references to imposing charges: (1) for his use of the service at a place in the United Kingdom or in that part of it; (2) for an entitlement of his to receive it at such place; (3) for the use of a facility by means of which he exercises such an entitlement; or (4) for the service's being made available for reception by him at such a place: s 362(5). 'Ancillary service' has the same meaning as it has in the Broadcasting Act 1996 Pt I (ss 1–39) (see s 24(2); and PARA 690 note 28): Communications Act 2003 s 362(1). As to the meaning of 'United Kingdom' see PARA 510 note 13.

12 Broadcasting Act 1990 s 4(1)(d) (amended by the Communications Act 2003 Sch 15 para 2(2)).

13 See the Communications Act 2003 s 263; and PARA 602.

14 Broadcasting Act 1990 s 4(1)(c) (amended by the Communications Act 2003 Sch 15 para 2(2), (3)).

15 Broadcasting Act 1990 s 4(5)(a) (amended by the Communications Act 2003 Sch 15 para 2(2), (5)(a)).

16 Broadcasting Act 1990 s 4(5)(b).

17 Ie for the purposes of the Broadcasting Act 1990 ss 41, 42 (see PARAS 865–866) or the Communications Act 2003 ss 237, 238 (enforcement of television licensable content service licences: see PARAS 862–863).

18 Broadcasting Act 1990 s 4(5) (amended by the Communications Act 2003 Sch 15 para 2(2), (5)(b)).

19 Broadcasting Act 1990 s 4(2)(a) (s 4(2) amended by the Communications Act 2003 Sch 15 para 2(2)).

20 Broadcasting Act 1990 s 4(2)(b) (as amended: see note 19).

21 Communications Act 2003 s 214(5)(a). For the purposes of the Communications Act 2003 s 214(5), a licensing period, in relation to a licence, is: (1) the period beginning with the commencement of s 214 (ie 29 December 2003: see the Office of Communications Act 2002 (Commencement No 3) and Communications Act 2003 (Commencement No 2) Order 2003, SI 2003/3142) and ending with the initial expiry date for that type of licence; or (2) any subsequent period of ten years beginning with the end of the previous licensing period for that type of licence: Communications Act 2003 s 214(6) (amended by the Digital Economy Act 2010 s 26(1), (2)). As to the meaning of 'initial expiry date' see the Communications Act 2003 ss 224, 362(1) (s 224 amended by the Digital Economy Act 2010 ss 25, 45, Sch 2).

22 Communications Act 2003 s 214(5)(b). As to the renewal of licences see ss 216, 216A (s 216 amended by the Digital Economy Act 2010 ss 24(2)–(6), 26(1), (2); Communications Act 2003 s 216A added by the Digital Economy Act 2010 s 24(7)).

23 As to the service of notices see TELECOMMUNICATIONS vol 97 (2010) PARAS 49–50.

24 Broadcasting Act 1990 s 3(4) (amended by the Communications Act 2003 Sch 15 para 1(2)).

25 Broadcasting Act 1990 s 3(4)(a). Section 3(4)(a) does not affect the operation of s 41(1)(b) (power to shorten licence period); nor does it authorise the variation of any conditions included in a licence in pursuance of s 19(1) (additional payments to be made in respect of Channel 3 licences) or s 52(1) (additional payments to be made in respect of additional services licences) or in pursuance of any other provision of Pt I which applies s 19(1): s 3(5).

26 Broadcasting Act 1990 s 3(4)(b) (as amended: see note 24).

27 Broadcasting Act 1990 s 3(6) (amended by the Communications Act 2003 Sch 15 para 1(2)).
28 Broadcasting Act 1990 s 3(7) (amended by the Communications Act 2003 Sch 15 para 1(2)).

666. Reviews relating to licensing of Channel 3. The holder of a replacement licence to provide a Channel 3[1] service may apply to OFCOM[2], at any time in the first or any subsequent review period, for a review of the financial terms on which that licence is held[3]. For these purposes[4], the first review period is the period which: (1) begins four years before the first notional expiry date[5]; and (2) ends with the day before the day that OFCOM has determined to be the one by which it would need to publish a tender notice[6] if it were proposing to grant a fresh licence to take effect from the first notional expiry date[7]. For these purposes, a subsequent review period in the case of a replacement licence is so much (if any) of the following period as falls before the end of the initial expiry date for that type of licence, namely, the period which: (a) begins four years before a subsequent notional expiry date[8]; and (b) ends with the day before the day that OFCOM has determined to be the one by which it would need to publish a tender notice if it were proposing to grant a fresh licence to take effect from that notional expiry date[9]. A determination for the purposes of head (2) or head (b) above in respect of a replacement licence: (i) must be made at least one year before the day determined; and (ii) must be notified by OFCOM to the person who, at the time of the determination, holds the licence in question[10]. No application under these provisions for a review of the financial terms on which a replacement licence is held is to be made: (A) at any time when an application[11] for a review of those terms is pending; or (B) at any time in the period of 12 months following the day on which a determination by OFCOM on such an application is notified to the licence holder[12].

Further provision is made with respect to reviews relating to licensing of Channel 3[13].

1 Ie a licence granted under the Communications Act 2003 s 215: see PARA 665 note 3. As to the meaning of 'Channel 3 service' see PARA 602 note 8.
2 As to OFCOM see PARA 507.
3 Communications Act 2003 s 225(1).
4 Ie the Communications Act 2003 s 225.
5 For the purposes of the Communications Act 2003 s 225, 'the first notional expiry date', in relation to a replacement licence, means the date with which (apart from the Communications Act 2003) the existing licence would have expired if not renewed: s 225(7). For the purposes of s 225(7), 'existing licence' has the same meaning as in s 215 (see PARA 665 note 2) or (as the case may be) s 221 (see PARA 686): s 225(8).
6 For the purposes of the Communications Act 2003 s 225, 'tender notice' means a notice under the Broadcasting Act 1990 s 15(1) or (as the case may be) Sch 10 para 1: Communications Act 2003 s 225(7).
7 Communications Act 2003 s 225(2).
8 For the purposes of the Communications Act 2003 s 225, 'subsequent notional expiry date', in relation to a replacement licence, means: (1) in a case in which an application by the licence holder for a review under s 225 was made during the review period beginning four years before the last notional expiry date, the tenth anniversary of the date on which OFCOM's determination on that review was notified to the licence holder; and (2) in any other case, the tenth anniversary of the last notional expiry date: s 225(7).
9 Communications Act 2003 s 225(3) (amended by the Digital Economy Act 2010 s 26(1), (4)).
10 Communications Act 2003 s 225(4).
11 Ie an application for a review of financial terms in consequence of new obligations (see the Communications Act 2003 s 226).
12 Communications Act 2003 s 225(5). For the purposes of s 225, an application for a review under s 226 is pending from the time when the application is made until the end of the day on which OFCOM's determination on the review is notified to the licence holder: s 225(6).

13   See the Communications Act 2003 s 227 (reviews under ss 225, 226 of the financial terms on which a licence is held), s 228 (amended by the Digital Economy Act 2010 s 26(1), (5)) (giving effect to reviews under the Communications Act 2003 ss 225, 226), s 229 (amended by the Digital Economy Act 2010 s 26(6)–(12)) (report in anticipation of new licensing round), and the Communications Act 2003 s 230 (amended by the Digital Economy Act 2010 s 26(13)–(18)) (orders suspending rights of renewal).

667. Establishment of Channel 3. OFCOM[1] must do all that it can to secure the provision[2] of a nationwide system of television broadcasting services[3] to be known as Channel 3[4]. It is to be structured on a regional basis, with each of the services comprised within it ('Channel 3 services') being provided for such area in the United Kingdom[5] as OFCOM may determine in the case of that service[6]. If it appears to OFCOM that it would be appropriate for a particular Channel 3 service to do so, it may determine that the service is to include the provision of different programmes[7] for such different parts of the area for which it is provided[8], or for such different communities living within that area[9], as it may determine[10]. If OFCOM so determines in the case of a particular Channel 3 service, that service must be provided for a particular area only between such times of the day or on such days of the week, or both, as OFCOM may determine[11]. If OFCOM so determines, a Channel 3 service may be provided for two or more areas for which regional Channel 3 services are provided, but any such service may only be so provided between particular times of the day[12].

1   As to OFCOM see PARA 507.
2   Ie in accordance with the Broadcasting Act 1990 Pt I Ch II (ss 14–42): see s 14(1).
3   'Television broadcasting service' has the same meaning as in the Communications Act 2003 Pt 3 (ss 198–362) (see PARA 602 note 8): Broadcasting Act 1990 s 71(1) (amended by the Communications Act 2003 s 360(3), Sch 15 para 31(1), (3)).
4   Broadcasting Act 1990 ss 14(1), 71(1) (s 14 amended by the Communications Act 2003 Sch 15 para 6; Broadcasting Act 1990 s 71(1) amended by the Communications Act 2003 s 406(7), Sch 19). This regionally-based channel was established to replace the television broadcasting service known as ITV provided by the Independent Broadcasting Authority under the Broadcasting Act 1981 s 2(1) (repealed by the Broadcasting Act 1990 s 203(3), Sch 21). The need for a new system was considered in *Broadcasting in the '90s: Competition, Choice and Quality* (Cm 517) (November 1988). As to applications for Channel 3 licences see PARA 669.
5   The areas mentioned in the Broadcasting Act 1990 s 14(2) must at all times include at least one area that comprises, or falls entirely within, Scotland: s 14(7A) (added by the Digital Economy Act 2010 s 24(1)(b)). As to the meaning of 'United Kingdom' see PARA 510 note 13.
6   Broadcasting Act 1990 s 14(2) (as amended: see note 4). A Channel 3 service provided for a particular area determined under s 14(2) is referred to as a 'regional Channel 3 service': ss 14(6), 71(1).
7   For the purposes of the Broadcasting Act 1990 generally, 'programme' includes an advertisement and, in relation to any service, includes any item included in that service: s 202(1). For these purposes (and for the purposes of s 15 (see PARA 669)), however, 'programme' does not include an advertisement: s 14(8).
8   Broadcasting Act 1990 s 14(3)(a). This is currently the case in respect of the ITV plc licence for Wales and the West of England, where two slightly different services are provided to the Welsh and English portions of the franchise area respectively.
9   Broadcasting Act 1990 s 14(3)(b).
10   Broadcasting Act 1990 s 14(3) (as amended: see note 4).
11   Broadcasting Act 1990 s 14(4) (as amended: see note 4).
12   Broadcasting Act 1990 s 14(5) (as amended: see note 4). Such a service is referred to as a 'national Channel 3 service': ss 14(6), 71(1).

668. Requirements relating to transmission and distribution of services. The Broadcasting Act 1990 provides that all Channel 3[1] services must be broadcast[2], so as to be available for reception by members of the public[3], by a single person[4] under arrangements made with him by the persons licensed[5] to provide those services during such period as the Secretary of State[6] may by order specify[7]. Every Channel 3 licence[8] must include such conditions as appear to OFCOM[9] to be appropriate[10] for securing that result[11] and for securing that the costs incurred in respect of the broadcasting of those services (taken as a whole) during that period in accordance with those arrangements are shared by those persons in such manner as may be approved by the Secretary of State[12].

The Broadcasting Act 1990 also provides that any Channel 3 licence must include such conditions as appear to OFCOM to be appropriate for securing that the costs incurred in respect of the distribution[13] of Channel 3 services (taken as a whole) during such period as the Secretary of State may by order specify are shared by the persons licensed to provide those services in such manner as may be approved by the Secretary of State[14].

Any Channel 3 licence[15] must include such conditions as appear to OFCOM to be appropriate for requiring the signals carrying the licensed service to attain high standards in terms of technical quality and reliability throughout so much of the relevant area[16] as is for the time being reasonably practicable[17]. Before imposing any such conditions, OFCOM must consult the Secretary of State as to how much of the relevant area is to be specified in the conditions as the area throughout which the required standards are to be attained[18].

1   As to the meaning of 'Channel 3' see PARA 667.
2   'Broadcast' means broadcast by wireless telegraphy: Broadcasting Act 1990 s 202(1). 'Wireless telegraphy' has the same meaning as in the Wireless Telegraphy Act 2006 (see PARA 510 note 1): Broadcasting Act 1990 s 202(1) (definition substituted by the Wireless Telegraphy Act 2006 s 123, Sch 7 paras 9, 13).
3   'Available for reception by members of the public' is to be construed in accordance with the Communications Act 2003 s 361 (see PARA 796): Broadcasting Act 1990 s 66(2A) (added by the Communications Act 2003 s 350(3), Sch 15 para 29(1), (4)).
4   As to the meaning of 'person' see PARA 510 note 1.
5   As to the meaning of 'licensed' see PARA 662 note 3.
6   As to the Secretary of State see PARA 507 note 32.
7   Broadcasting Act 1990 s 66(1). Any order made under s 66 is subject to annulment in pursuance of a resolution of either House of Parliament: s 66(8). As to orders under this provision see the Broadcasting (Channel 3 Transmission and Shared Distribution Costs) Order 1991, SI 1991/881 (amended by SI 1996/3067). This provision is now spent, as the period specified ended with 31 December 2002: see the Broadcasting (Channel 3 Transmission and Shared Distribution Costs) Order 1991, SI 1991/881, art 2 (amended by SI 1996/3067).
      The Secretary of State may, at any time during the period mentioned in the Broadcasting Act 1990 s 66(1) or s 66(2) (see the text and note 14), by order provide for that period to be extended by such further period as is specified in the order; and any conditions included in a Channel 3 licence will accordingly, in any such case, have effect in relation to that period as so extended: Broadcasting Act 1990 s 66(3). As to orders under this provision see the Broadcasting (Channel 3 Transmission and Shared Distribution Costs) Order 1996, SI 1996/3067, which amended the Broadcasting (Channel 3 Transmission and Shared Distribution Costs) Order 1991, SI 1991/881 (spent).
8   As to the meaning of 'Channel 3 licence' see PARA 669 note 2.
9   As to OFCOM see PARA 507.
10 Broadcasting Act 1990 s 66(1) (amended by the Communications Act 2003 Sch 15 para 29(2)).
11 Broadcasting Act 1990 s 66(1)(a).
12 Broadcasting Act 1990 s 66(1)(b).
13 'Distribution', in relation to Channel 3 services, means the conveyance of those services (by whatever means and whether directly or indirectly) to the broadcasting stations from which they are broadcast so as to be available for reception by members of the public: Broadcasting Act 1990 s 66(2) (amended by the Communications Act 2003 Sch 15 para 29(3)).
14 Broadcasting Act 1990 s 66(2) (amended by the Communications Act 2003 Sch 15 para 29(2)). As to orders made under the Broadcasting Act 1990 s 66(2) see note 7.
15 This provision also applies to licences to provide Channel 4 or Channel 5: see the Broadcasting Act 1990 s 66(4). As to Channel 4 see PARA 627 et seq; and as to Channel 5 see PARA 681. The Welsh Authority must do all that it can to ensure that the signals carrying S4C attain high

standards in terms of technical quality and reliability throughout so much of Wales as is for the time being reasonably practicable: s 66(7). As to the meaning of 'the Welsh Authority' see PARA 644 note 3; and as to television broadcasting by the Welsh Authority see PARAS 644–661. As to the meaning of 'S4C' see PARA 644.

16 'The relevant area' means: (1) in relation to a Channel 3 or Channel 5 licence, the area for which the licensed service is to be provided; and (2) in relation to the licence to provide Channel 4, England, Scotland and Northern Ireland: Broadcasting Act 1990 s 66(6).

17 Broadcasting Act 1990 s 66(4).

18 Broadcasting Act 1990 s 66(5).

669. Applications for Channel 3 licences. Where OFCOM[1] proposes to grant a Channel 3 licence[2] to provide a Channel 3 service[3] it must publish, in such manner as it considers appropriate, a notice[4]:

(1)   stating that it proposes to grant such a licence[5];

(2)   specifying (a) if the service is to be a regional Channel 3 service[6], the area in the United Kingdom[7] for which the service is to be provided[8]; (b) if the service is to include the provision of different programmes[9] for different areas or for different communities[10], the different parts of that area, or as the case may be, the different communities living within it, for which such programmes are to be provided[11]; (c) if the service is to be provided for a particular area between certain times[12], the times of the day or the days of the week, or both, between or on which it is to be provided[13]; and (d) if the service is to be a national Channel 3 service[14], the areas in the United Kingdom for which it is to be provided and the times of the day between which it is to be provided[15];

(3)   inviting applications for the licence and specifying the closing date for such applications[16]; and

(4)   specifying the fee payable on any application made in pursuance of the notice[17], and the percentage of qualifying revenue[18] for each accounting period that would be payable by an applicant[19] if he were granted the licence[20].

When publishing such a notice, OFCOM must publish with the notice general guidance to applicants for the licence in question which contains examples of the kinds of programme whose inclusion in the service proposed by an applicant[21] would be likely to result in a finding by OFCOM that the service would comply with the requirements that have to be imposed under the Communications Act 2003[22] by conditions relating to:

(i)   the public service remit[23] for that service;

(ii)   programming quotas;

(iii)   news and current affairs programmes; and

(iv)   programme production and regional programming[24].

Any application made in pursuance of such a notice must be in writing[25] and accompanied by:

(A)   the fee specified in the notice[26];

(B)   the applicant's proposals for providing a service that would comply with the requirements that have to be imposed under the Communications Act 2003[27] by conditions relating to the public service remit for that service, programming quotas, news and current affairs programmes, and programme production and regional programming[28];

(C)   the applicant's cash bid[29] in respect of the licence[30];

(D)   such information as OFCOM may reasonably require as to the applicant's present financial position and his projected financial position during the period for which the licence would be in force[31]; and

(E) such other information as OFCOM may reasonably require for the purpose of considering the application[32].

At any time after receiving such an application and before determining it, OFCOM may require the applicant to furnish additional information[33]. Any information to be furnished to OFCOM, if it so requires, must be in such form or verified in such manner as it may specify[34].

OFCOM must, as soon as reasonably practicable after the date specified in the notice as the closing date for applications, publish in such manner as it considers appropriate[35] the name of every person who has made an application to it in pursuance of the notice[36], the proposals submitted by him under head (B) above[37], and such other information connected with his application as OFCOM considers appropriate[38]. OFCOM must also publish a notice inviting representations to be made to it with respect to any matters published by it[39], and specifying the manner in which, and the time by which, any such representations are to be so made[40].

1   As to OFCOM see PARA 507.
2   A 'Channel 3 licence' means a licence to provide one of the services comprised within the system of television broadcasting services established under the Broadcasting Act 1990 s 14 (see PARA 667): s 71(1) (amended by the Communications Act 2003 s 406(7), Sch 19). As to the meaning of 'Channel 3' see PARA 667. As to the meaning of 'licence' see PARA 662 note 3. As to the application of this provision to Channel 5 licences see PARA 681.
3   As to Channel 3 services see PARA 667.
4   Broadcasting Act 1990 s 15(1) (amended by the Communications Act 2003 s 360(3), Sch 15 para 7(1), (2)).
5   Broadcasting Act 1990 s 15(1)(a).
6   As to the meaning of 'regional Channel 3 service' see PARA 667 note 6.
7   As to the meaning of 'United Kingdom' see PARA 510 note 13. As to areas in the United Kingdom for these purposes see PARA 667 note 5.
8   Broadcasting Act 1990 s 15(1)(b)(i).
9   As to the meaning of 'programme' see PARA 667 note 7.
10 Ie such programmes as are mentioned in the Broadcasting Act 1990 s 14(3) (see PARA 667).
11 Broadcasting Act 1990 s 15(1)(b)(ii).
12 Ie under the Broadcasting Act 1990 s 14(4) (see PARA 667).
13 Broadcasting Act 1990 s 15(1)(b)(iii).
14 As to the meaning of 'national Channel 3 service' see PARA 667 note 12.
15 Broadcasting Act 1990 s 15(1)(b)(iv).
16 Broadcasting Act 1990 s 15(1)(c).
17 Broadcasting Act 1990 s 15(1)(d)(i).
18 As to qualifying revenue see PARA 675.
19 Ie in pursuance of the Broadcasting Act 1990 s 19(1)(c).
20 Broadcasting Act 1990 s 15(1)(d)(ii). For the purposes of s 15(1)(d)(ii): (1) different percentages may be specified for different accounting periods; and (2) the percentages that may be specified for an accounting period include a nil percentage: s 15(3A) (added by the Communications Act 2003 Sch 15 para 7(5)).
21 Ie under the Broadcasting Act 1990 s 15(3)(b) (see head (ii) in the text).
22 Ie under the Communications Act 2003 Pt 3 Ch 4 (ss 263–347).
23 As to the public service remit see PARA 788 et seq.
24 Broadcasting Act 1990 s 15(2) (amended by the Communications Act 2003 Sch 15 para 7(2), (3)).
25 Broadcasting Act 1990 s 15(3).
26 Broadcasting Act 1990 s 15(3)(a).
27 Ie under the Communications Act 2003 Pt 3 Ch 4.
28 Broadcasting Act 1990 s 15(3)(b) (amended by the Communications Act 2003 Sch 15 para 7(4)). As to the statutory requirements see note 23.
29 'Cash bid', in relation to a licence, means an offer to pay to OFCOM a specified amount of money in respect of the first complete calendar year falling within the period for which the licence is in force, being an amount which, as increased by the appropriate percentage, is also to be payable in respect of subsequent years falling wholly or partly within that period:

Broadcasting Act 1990 ss 15(7), 71(1) (s 15(7) amended by the Communications Act 2003 Sch 15 para 7(2)). As to the appropriate percentage see PARA 674.

30 Broadcasting Act 1990 s 15(3)(f).

31 Broadcasting Act 1990 s 15(3)(g) (amended by the Communications Act 2003 Sch 15 para 7(2)).

32 Broadcasting Act 1990 s 15(3)(h) (amended by the Communications Act 2003 Sch 15 para 7(2)).

33 Broadcasting Act 1990 s 15(4) (amended by the Communications Act 2003 Sch 15 para 7(2)). Additional information may be requested under the Broadcasting Act 1990 s 15(3)(b), (g), (h) (see heads (B), (D), (E) in the text): see s 15(4) (amended by the Communications Act 2003 Sch 15 para 7(6)).

34 Broadcasting Act 1990 s 15(5) (amended by the Communications Act 2003 Sch 15 para 7(2)).

35 Broadcasting Act 1990 s 15(6) (amended by the Communications Act 2003 Sch 15 para 7(2)).

36 Broadcasting Act 1990 s 15(6)(a)(i).

37 Broadcasting Act 1990 s 15(6)(a)(ii).

38 Broadcasting Act 1990 s 15(6)(a)(iii) (amended by the Communications Act 2003 Sch 15 para 7(2)).

39 Broadcasting Act 1990 s 15(6)(b)(i). The matters referred to are those published in accordance with s 15(6)(a)(ii), (iii) (see the text and notes 37–38): see s 15(6)(b)(i).

40 Broadcasting Act 1990 s 15(6)(b)(ii).

670.   Procedure for applications for Channel 3 licences. Where a person[1] has made an application for a Channel 3 licence[2], OFCOM[3] may not proceed to consider whether to award him the licence on the basis of his cash bid[4] unless it appears to OFCOM[5] that his proposed service would comply with the requirements that have to be imposed under the Communications Act 2003[6], and that he would be able to maintain that service throughout the period for which the licence would be in force[7].

In deciding whether an applicant's proposed service would comply with the requirements that have to be imposed under the Communications Act 2003[8] by conditions relating to: (1) the public service remit for that service; (2) programming quotas; (3) news and current affairs programmes; and (4) programme production and regional programming, OFCOM must take into account any representations made to it[9] with respect to that service[10].

1   As to the meaning of 'person' see PARA 510 note 1.

2   Ie in accordance with the Broadcasting Act 1990 s 15 (see PARA 669): see s 16(1). As to the meaning of 'Channel 3' see PARA 667. As to the meaning of 'Channel 3 licence' see PARA 669 note 2. As to the application of this provision to Channel 5 licences see PARA 681.

3   As to OFCOM see PARA 507.

4   In accordance with the Broadcasting Act 1990 s 17 (see PARA 671): see s 16(1) (amended by the Communications Act 2003 s 360(3), Sch 15 para 8(1), (2)). As to the meaning of 'cash bid' see PARA 669 note 29.

5   Broadcasting Act 1990 s 16(1).

6   Broadcasting Act 1990 s 16(1)(a). The requirements are those that have to be imposed under the Communications Act 2003 Pt 3 Ch 4 (ss 263–347) by conditions relating to: (1) the public service remit for that service; (2) programming quotas; (3) news and current affairs programmes; and (4) programme production and regional programming: see the Broadcasting Act 1990 s 16(1)(a) (amended by the Communications Act 2003 Sch 15 para 8(3)). As to the public service remit see PARA 788 et seq. Where a licence has been awarded, OFCOM must publish the name of every applicant appearing to comply with the requirements: see the Broadcasting Act 1990 s 17(11)(a), (12)(b) (amended by the Communications Act 2003 Sch 15 para 9); and PARA 671.

7   Broadcasting Act 1990 s 16(1)(b).

8   Ie in the Communications Act 2003 Pt 3 Ch 4.

9   Ie in pursuance of the Broadcasting Act 1990 s 15(6)(b) (see PARA 669).

10 Broadcasting Act 1990 s 16(4) (amended by the Communications Act 2003 Sch 15 para 8(2), (5)).

671. Award of licence to person submitting highest cash bid. OFCOM[1], after considering all the cash bids[2] submitted by the applicants[3] for a Channel 3 licence[4], must award the licence to the applicant who submitted the highest bid[5].

Where two or more applicants for a particular licence have submitted cash bids specifying an identical amount which is higher than the amount of any other cash bid submitted in respect of the licence, then OFCOM must invite those applicants to submit further cash bids in respect of that licence[6].

OFCOM may regard the following circumstances as exceptional circumstances which make it appropriate to award the licence to an applicant who has not submitted the highest bid, namely where it appears to OFCOM[7]:

(1)   that the quality of the service proposed by such an applicant is exceptionally high[8]; and

(2)   that the quality of that proposed service is substantially higher than the quality of the service proposed by the applicant who has submitted the highest bid[9], or by each of the applicants who have submitted equal highest bids[10].

If it appears to OFCOM, in the case of the applicant to whom it would otherwise award the licence, that there are grounds for suspecting that any relevant source of funds[11] is such that it would not be in the public interest for the licence to be awarded to him[12], it must refer his application to the Secretary of State[13], together with a copy of all documents submitted to it by the applicant[14], and a summary of its deliberations on the application[15], and it must not award the licence to him unless the Secretary of State has given his approval[16]. On such a reference the Secretary of State may only refuse to give his approval to the licence being awarded to the applicant in question if he is satisfied that any relevant source of funds is such that it would not be in the public interest for the licence to be so awarded[17].

OFCOM must not grant a licence to any person[18] unless it is satisfied that he is a fit and proper person to hold it, and must do all that it can to secure that, if it ceases to be so satisfied in the case of any person holding a licence, that person does not remain holder of the licence[19]. Where OFCOM is not satisfied that a BBC company[20] which has applied for a licence is a fit and proper person to hold it, it must before refusing the application notify the Secretary of State that it is not so satisfied[21].

In a case where any requirement[22] operates to preclude OFCOM from awarding a licence to the applicant to whom (apart from any such requirement) it would have awarded it, it must award the licence in accordance with rules made by it for regulating the awarding of licences in such cases, and any such rules may provide for the awarding of licences by reference to orders of preference notified to OFCOM by applicants at the time of making their applications[23]. Any such rules must be published by OFCOM in such manner as it considers appropriate, but do not come into force unless they have been approved by the Secretary of State[24].

Where it has awarded a Channel 3 licence to any person, OFCOM must, as soon as reasonably practicable after awarding the licence[25], grant the licence to that person[26], and publish the following matters in such manner as it considers appropriate[27]:

(a)   the name of the person to whom the licence has been awarded and the amount of his cash bid[28];

(b)   the name of every other applicant in whose case it appeared to OFCOM that his proposed service would comply with the specified requirements that have to be imposed under the Communications Act 2003[29];

(c)   where the licence has been awarded[30] to an applicant who has not submitted the highest cash bid, OFCOM's reasons for the licence having been so awarded[31]; and

(d)   such other information as OFCOM considers appropriate[32].

1   As to OFCOM see PARA 507.
2   As to the meaning of 'cash bid' see PARA 669 note 29. As to the requirements which must be satisfied before a cash bid can be considered see PARA 670.
3   The references to an applicant in the Broadcasting Act 1990 s 17 (except in s 17(12(b): see head (b) in the text) are references to an applicant in whose case it appears to OFCOM that the requirements of s 16(1)(a), (b) are satisfied (see PARA 670): s 16(1) (amended by the Communications Act 2003 s 360(3), Sch 15 para 8(1), (2)).
4   As to the meaning of 'Channel 3' see PARA 667; and as to the meaning of 'Channel 3 licence' see PARA 669 note 2. As to the application of this provision to Channel 5 licences see PARA 681. As to the application of this provision to additional services licences see PARA 706.
5   Broadcasting Act 1990 s 17(1) (amended by the Communications Act 2003 Sch 15 para 9(1), (2)). OFCOM may disregard the requirement imposed by the Broadcasting Act 1990 s 17(1) and award the licence to an applicant who has not submitted the highest bid if it appears to it that there are exceptional circumstances which make it appropriate for it to award the licence to that applicant: s 17(3) (amended by the Communications Act 2003 Sch 15 para 9(2)).
6   Broadcasting Act 1990 s 17(2) (amended by the Communications Act 2003 Sch 15 para 9(2)). This is subject to OFCOM's right to exercise its powers under the Broadcasting Act 1990 s 17(3) in relation to the licence (see note 5): see s 17(2) (as so amended). In relation to any person who has submitted a further cash bid under this provision, any reference to his cash bid is a reference to that further bid: see s 17(2) (as so amended). As to the meaning of 'person' see PARA 510 note 1.
7   Broadcasting Act 1990 s 17(4) (amended by the Communications Act 2003 Sch 15 para 9(2)). This is expressed to be without prejudice to the generality of the Broadcasting Act 1990 s 17(3) (see note 5). Where it appears to OFCOM, in the context of the licence, that any circumstances are to be regarded as exceptional circumstances for the purposes of s 17(3), those circumstances may be so regarded by it despite the fact that similar circumstances have been so regarded by it in the context of any other licence or licences: s 17(4) (as so amended).
8   Broadcasting Act 1990 s 17(4)(a).
9   Broadcasting Act 1990 s 17(4)(b)(i).
10   Broadcasting Act 1990 s 17(4)(b)(ii).
11   'Relevant source of funds', in relation to an applicant, means any source of funds to which he might, directly or indirectly, have recourse for the purpose of: (1) paying any amounts payable by him by virtue of the Broadcasting Act 1990 s 19(1) (see PARA 674); or (2) otherwise financing the provision of his proposed service: s 17(7).
12   Broadcasting Act 1990 s 17(5) (amended by the Communications Act 2003 Sch 15 para 9(2)).
13   As to the Secretary of State see PARA 507 note 32.
14   Broadcasting Act 1990 s 17(5)(a)(i).
15   Broadcasting Act 1990 s 17(5)(a)(ii).
16   Broadcasting Act 1990 s 17(5)(b). Where OFCOM is, by virtue of s 17(5), precluded from awarding the licence to an applicant, the provisions of s 17(1)–(4) have effect (subject to s 17(14)) as if that person had not made an application for the licence: s 17(10) (amended by the Communications Act 2003 Sch 15 para 9(2)). The provisions of the Broadcasting Act 1990 s 17(1)–(9) do not have effect as mentioned in s 17(10) if OFCOM decides that it would be desirable to publish a fresh notice under s 15(1) (see PARA 669) in respect of the grant of the licence; similarly, where any of the following provisions of Pt I (ss 3–71) provide, in connection with the revocation of a licence, for s 17 to have effect as if the former holder of the licence had not made an application for it, s 17 does not have effect if OFCOM decides that it would be desirable to publish a further notice under Pt I in respect of the grant of a further licence to provide the service in question: s 17(14) (amended by the Communications Act 2003 Sch 15 para 9(2)).
17   Broadcasting Act 1990 s 17(6).
18   As to the meaning of 'person' see PARA 510 note 1.
19   Broadcasting Act 1990 s 3(3) (amended by the Communications Act 2003 Sch 15 para 1(2)). Nothing in the Broadcasting Act 1990 Pt I is to be construed as affecting the operation of s 3(3) or s 5(1), (2)(b) or (c) (see PARA 821): s 3(3). Where the person who is for the time being the

holder of any licence ('the present licence holder') is not the person to whom the licence was originally granted, any reference in Pt I to the holder of the licence is to be construed, in relation to any time falling before the date when the present licence holder became the holder of it, as including a reference to a person who was previously the holder of the licence: s 71(2).

20 For these purposes, 'BBC company' means: (1) any body corporate which is controlled by the BBC; or (2) any body corporate in which the BBC or any body corporate falling within head (1) is (to any extent) a participant: Broadcasting Act 1990 s 202(1) (definition added by the Broadcasting Act 1996 s 136, Sch 8 para 8). As to the meaning of 'BBC' see PARA 603 note 1; and as to the BBC see PARAS 603–626. 'Participant', in relation to a body corporate, means a person who holds or is beneficially entitled to shares in that body or who possesses voting power in that body: Broadcasting Act 1990 s 5, Sch 2 Pt I para 1(1).

21 Broadcasting Act 1990 s 3(3A) (added by the Broadcasting Act 1996 Sch 8 para 1; and amended by the Communications Act 2003 Sch 15 para 1(2)).

22 Ie such as is mentioned in the Broadcasting Act 1990 s 5(1)(b) (see PARA 821).

23 Broadcasting Act 1990 s 17(8) (amended by the Communications Act 2003 Sch 15 para 9(2)).

24 Broadcasting Act 1990 s 17(9) (amended by the Communications Act 2003 Sch 15 para 9(2)).

25 Broadcasting Act 1990 s 17(11) (amended by the Communications Act 2003 Sch 15 para 9(2)).

26 Broadcasting Act 1990 s 17(11)(b).

27 Broadcasting Act 1990 s 17(11)(a).

28 Broadcasting Act 1990 s 17(12)(a).

29 Broadcasting Act 1990 s 17(12)(b) (amended by the Communications Act 2003 Sch 15 para 9(2), (3)). The requirements are those that have to be imposed under the Communications Act 2003 Pt 3 Ch 4 (ss 263–347) by conditions relating to: (1) the public service remit for that service; (2) programming quotas; (3) news and current affairs programmes; and (4) programme production and regional programming: Broadcasting Act 1990 s 17(12)(b) (as so amended). In a case where the licence has been awarded to any person by virtue of s 17, in accordance with any of the provisions of Pt I, on the revocation of an earlier grant of the licence, s 17(12) has effect as if s 17(12)(b) were omitted, and the matters specified in that provision included an indication of the circumstances in which the licence has been awarded to that person: s 17(13). As to the public service remit see PARA 788 et seq.

30 Ie by virtue of the Broadcasting Act 1990 s 17(3).

31 Broadcasting Act 1990 s 17(12)(c) (amended by the Communications Act 2003 Sch 15 para 9(2)).

32 Broadcasting Act 1990 s 17(12)(d) (amended by the Communications Act 2003 Sch 15 para 9(2)).

672. Award of Channel 3 licences subject to conditions. OFCOM[1] may, when awarding a Channel 3 licence[2] to any person[3], make the grant of the licence to him conditional on his compliance before the grant with such specified requirements relating to the financing of the service as appears to it to be appropriate[4], having regard to any duties which are or may be imposed on it, or on the licence holder[5], and any information provided to it[6] by the person to whom the licence is awarded as to his projected financial position during the period for which the licence would be in force[7].

1 As to OFCOM see PARA 507.

2 As to the meaning of 'Channel 3' see PARA 667; and as to the meaning of 'Channel 3 licence' see PARA 669 note 2. As to the application of this provision to Channel 5 licences see PARA 681. As to the application of this provision to additional services licences see PARA 706.

3 As to the meaning of 'person' see PARA 510 note 1.

4 Broadcasting Act 1990 s 17A(1) (s 17A added by the Broadcasting Act 1996 s 86(1); and amended by the Communications Act 2003 s 360(3), Sch 15 para 10).

5 Broadcasting Act 1990 s 17A(1)(a) (as added and amended: see note 4). As to the holder of the licence see PARA 671 note 19.

6 Ie under the Broadcasting Act 1990 s 15(3)(g) (see PARA 669): see s 17A(1)(b) (as added and amended: see note 4).

7 Broadcasting Act 1990 s 17A(1) (as added and amended: see note 4). Where OFCOM determines that any such condition imposed by it in relation to a Channel 3 licence has not been satisfied, s 17 (see PARA 671) has effect as if the person to whom the licence was awarded had not made an application for it: s 17A(2) (as so added and amended). Section 17 does not have

effect if OFCOM decides that it would be desirable to publish a fresh notice under s 15(1) (see PARA 669) in respect of the grant of the licence: s 17A(3) (as so added and amended).

673. Failure to begin providing licensed service and financial penalties on revocation of licence. If at any time after a Channel 3 licence[1] has been granted to any person[2] but before the licence has come into force that person indicates to OFCOM[3] that he does not intend to provide the service in question[4], or OFCOM for any other reason has reasonable grounds for believing that that person will not provide that service once the licence has come into force[5], it must serve on him a notice[6] revoking the licence as from the time the notice is served on him[7].

Where OFCOM revokes a Channel 3 licence[8], it must serve on the licence holder[9] a notice requiring him to pay, within a specified period, a specified financial penalty[10].

1   As to the meaning of 'Channel 3' see PARA 667; and as to the meaning of 'Channel 3 licence' see PARA 669 note 2. As to the application of this provision to Channel 5 licences see PARA 681.
2   As to the meaning of 'person' see PARA 510 note 1.
3   As to OFCOM see PARA 507.
4   Broadcasting Act 1990 s 18(1)(a) (s 18(1) amended by the Communications Act 2003 s 360(3), Sch 15 para 10).
5   Broadcasting Act 1990 s 18(1)(b) (as amended: see note 4). Section 18(1) does not apply in the case of any person by virtue of s 18(1)(b) unless OFCOM has served on him a notice stating its grounds for believing that he will not provide the service in question once his licence has come into force; and it must not serve such a notice on him unless it has given him a reasonable opportunity of making representations to it about the matters complained of: s 18(2) (amended by the Communications Act 2003 Sch 15 para 10).
6   As to the service of notices see TELECOMMUNICATIONS vol 97 (2010) PARAS 49–50.
7   Broadcasting Act 1990 s 18(1)(i) (as amended: see note 4). In this event, s 17 (subject to s 17(14)) (see PARA 671) has effect as if that person had not made an application for the licence: s 18(1)(ii).
8   Ie either under the Broadcasting Act 1990 s 18 or any other provision of Pt I (ss 3–71): see s 18(3). As to the revocation of Channel 3 licences see, in particular, PARAS 813, 866.
9   As to the holder of the licence see PARA 671 note 19.
10   Broadcasting Act 1990 s 18(3) (amended by the Communications Act 2003 ss 360(3), 345, Sch 15 para 10, Sch 13 paras 1, 2(1)). The maximum amount which a person may be required to pay by way of a penalty under the Broadcasting Act 1990 s 18(3) is the maximum penalty given by s 18(3B), (3C): s 18(3A) (s 18(3A)–(3D) added by the Communications Act 2003 Sch 13 para 2(2)).

In a case where the licence is revoked under the Broadcasting Act 1990 s 18 or the penalty is imposed before the end of the first complete accounting period of the licence holder to fall within the period for which the licence is in force, the maximum penalty is whichever is the greater of: (1) £500,000; and (2) 7% of the amount which OFCOM estimates would have been the qualifying revenue for the first complete accounting period of the licence holder falling within the period for which the licence would have been in force: s 18(3B) (as so added).

In any other case, the maximum penalty is whichever is the greater of: (a) £500,000; and (b) 7% of the qualifying revenue for the last complete accounting period of the licence holder falling within the period for which the licence is in force: s 18(3C) (as so added).

The Secretary of State may by order amend s 18(3B)(a) or s 18(3C)(a) by substituting a different sum for the sum for the time being specified: Communications Act 2003 Sch 13 para 9(1), (2)(a). No such order is to be made unless a draft of the order has been laid before Parliament and approved by a resolution of each House: Sch 13 para 9(3).

As to qualifying revenue see PARA 675. The Broadcasting Act 1990 s 19(2)–(6) (see PARA 674) applies for estimating or determining qualifying revenue for the purposes of s 18(3B) or s 18(3C): s 18(3D) (as so added).

Any financial penalty payable by any body by virtue of s 18(3) is, in addition to being recoverable from that body as provided by s 68(5) (repealed), recoverable by OFCOM as a debt due to it from any person who controls that body: s 18(5) (amended by the Communications Act 2003 Sch 15 para 10).

674. Additional payments to be made in respect of Channel 3 licences. A Channel 3 licence[1] must include conditions[2] requiring the licence holder[3] to pay to OFCOM[4] (in addition to any other fees required to be so paid)[5]:

(1) in respect of the first complete calendar year falling within the period for which the licence is in force[6], the amount specified in his cash bid[7];

(2) in respect of each subsequent year falling wholly or partly within that period, the amount so specified as increased by the appropriate percentage[8]; and

(3) in respect of each accounting period[9] of his falling within the period referred to in head (1) above, an amount representing such percentage of the qualifying revenue[10] for that accounting period as was specified in relation to the licence[11].

If, in connection with the inclusion of any advertisements or other programmes[12], any payments are made to the licence holder or any connected person[13] to meet any payments payable by the licence holder in accordance with head (3) above, those payments are regarded as made in consideration of the inclusion of the programmes in question[14].

In the case of an advertisement included under arrangements made between the licence holder or any connected person[15], and a person acting as an advertising agent[16], the amount of any receipt by the licence holder or any connected person that represents a payment by the advertiser from which the advertising agent has deducted any amount by way of commission is the amount of the payment by the advertiser after the deduction of the commission[17].

A Channel 3 licence may include conditions enabling OFCOM to estimate before the beginning of an accounting period the amount due for that period as mentioned in head (3) above[18], and requiring the licence holder to pay the estimated amount by monthly instalments throughout that period[19]. Such a licence may in particular include conditions authorising OFCOM to revise any estimate on one or more occasions and to adjust the instalments payable by the licence holder to take account of the revised estimate[20], and providing for the adjustment of any overpayment or underpayment[21].

1 As to the meaning of 'Channel 3' see PARA 667; and as to the meaning of 'Channel 3 licence' see PARA 669 note 2. As to the application of this provision to Channel 5 licences see PARA 681.

2 Conditions included in a licence cannot be varied under the Broadcasting Act 1990 s 3(4) (see PARA 665): see s 3(5).

3 As to the holder of the licence see PARA 671 note 19.

4 As to OFCOM see PARA 507. As to receipts by OFCOM see TELECOMMUNICATIONS vol 97 (2010) PARA 47.

5 Broadcasting Act 1990 s 19(1) (amended by the Communications Act 2003 s 360(3), Sch 15 para 10). Other fees may be payable by virtue of the Broadcasting Act 1990 s 4(1)(b) (see PARAS 665, 679): see s 19(1) (as so amended).

6 As to the licensing period see PARA 665 note 21.

7 Broadcasting Act 1990 s 19(1)(a). As to the meaning of 'cash bid' see PARA 669 note 29.

8 Broadcasting Act 1990 s 19(1)(b). The 'appropriate percentage', in relation to any year ('the relevant year'), means the percentage which corresponds to the percentage increase between: (1) the retail prices index for the month of November in the year preceding the first complete calendar year falling within the period for which the licence in question is in force; and (2) the retail prices index for the month of November in the year preceding the relevant year: ss 19(10), 71(1). The 'retail prices index' means the general index of prices (for all items) published by the Statistics Board: s 19(10) (amended by the Statistics and Registration Service Act 2007 s 60(1), Sch 3 para 6(1), (2)). As to the Statistics Board see REGISTRATION CONCERNING THE INDIVIDUAL vol 39(2) (Reissue) PARA 605.

9 Where the first complete accounting period of the licence holder falling within the licence period referred to in head (1) in the text does not begin at the same time as that period, or the last complete accounting period of his falling within the licence period does not end at the same time

as that period, a reference to an accounting period of his includes a reference to such part of the accounting period preceding that first complete accounting period, or (as the case may be) following that last complete accounting period, as falls within the licence period; and other references to accounting periods in the Broadcasting Act 1990 Pt I (ss 3–71) are to be construed accordingly: s 19(9).

10 The qualifying revenue for any accounting period of the licence holder consists of all payments received or to be received by him or by any connected person: (1) in consideration of the inclusion in the licensed service in that period of advertisements or other programmes; or (2) in respect of charges made in that period for the reception of programmes included in that service: Broadcasting Act 1990 s 19(2). As to the meaning of 'programme' see PARA 667 note 7. However, if, in any accounting period of the licence holder, the licence holder or any connected person derives, in relation to any programme to be included in the licensed service, any financial benefit (whether direct or indirect) from payments made by any person, by way of sponsorship, for the purpose of defraying or contributing towards costs incurred or to be incurred in connection with that programme, the qualifying revenue for that accounting period is to be taken to include the amount of the financial benefit so derived by the licence holder or the connected person, as the case may be: s 19(6). As to the meaning of 'person' see PARA 510 note 1.

11 Broadcasting Act 1990 s 19(1)(c). The amount is specified under s 15(1)(d)(ii) (see PARA 669): s 19(1)(c).

12 Ie advertisements or programmes whose inclusion is paid for by payments falling within the Broadcasting Act 1990 s 19(2)(a): see s 19(3).

13 The following persons are to be treated as connected with a particular person: (1) a person who controls that person; (2) an associate of that person or of a person falling within head (1); and (3) a body which is controlled by that person or by an associate of that person: Broadcasting Act 1990 Sch 2 Pt I para 3 (substituted by the Broadcasting Act 1996 Sch 2 para 3). As to the meaning of 'control' see PARA 821 note 11. As to the meaning of 'associate' see PARA 822 note 8. As to the meaning of 'body' see PARA 821 note 10.

14 Broadcasting Act 1990 s 19(3).

15 Broadcasting Act 1990 s 19(4)(a).

16 Broadcasting Act 1990 s 19(4)(b). A person is not regarded as carrying on business as an advertising agent, or as acting as such an agent, unless he carries on a business involving the selection and purchase of advertising time or space for persons wishing to advertise: s 202(1), (7)(a). A person who carries on such a business is regarded as carrying on business as an advertising agent irrespective of whether in law he is the agent of those for whom he acts: s 202(1), (7)(b). A person who is the proprietor of a newspaper is not regarded as carrying on business as an advertising agent by reason only that he makes arrangements on behalf of advertisers whereby advertisements appearing in the newspaper are also to appear in one or more other newspapers: s 202(1), (7)(c). A company or other body corporate is not regarded as carrying on business as an advertising agent by reason only that its objects or powers include or authorise that activity: s 202(1), (7)(d).

17 Broadcasting Act 1990 s 19(4). However, if the amount deducted by way of such commission exceeds 15% of the payment by the advertiser, the amount of the receipt in question is to be taken to be the amount of the payment less 15%: s 19(5).

18 Broadcasting Act 1990 s 19(7)(a) (amended by the Communications Act 2003 Sch 15 para 10).

19 Broadcasting Act 1990 s 19(7)(b).

20 Broadcasting Act 1990 s 19(8)(a) (amended by the Communications Act 2003 Sch 15 para 10).

21 Broadcasting Act 1990 s 19(8)(b).

675. Computation of qualifying revenue. It is the duty of OFCOM[1] to draw up, and from time to time review, a statement setting out the principles to be followed in ascertaining the qualifying revenue[2] in relation to a person for any accounting period of his, or for any year, for the purposes of any provisions relating to independent television services and local delivery services[3]. Such a statement may set out different principles for persons holding different kinds of licences[4]. Before drawing up or revising a statement, OFCOM must consult the Secretary of State[5] and the Treasury[6].

OFCOM must: (1) publish the statement drawn up and every revision of that statement[7]; and (2) transmit a copy of that statement, and every revision of it, to the Secretary of State[8]. The Secretary of State must lay copies of the statement and of every such revision before each House of Parliament[9].

1   As to OFCOM see PARA 507.
2   For these purposes: (1) the amount of the qualifying revenue in relation to any person for any accounting period of his, or (as the case may be) for any year; or (2) the amount of any payment to be made to OFCOM by any person in respect of any such revenue, or of an instalment of any such payment, is, in the event of a disagreement between OFCOM and that person, the amount determined by OFCOM: Broadcasting Act 1990 s 67, Sch 7 Pt I para 2(1) (Sch 7 Pt I para 2 amended by the Communications Act 2003 s 360(3), Sch 15 para 72(1), (3)). No determination of OFCOM under the Broadcasting Act 1990 Sch 7 Pt I para 2(1) may be called in question in any court of law, or be the subject of any arbitration; but this does not prevent the bringing of proceedings for judicial review: see Sch 7 Pt I para 2(2) (as so amended). As to the meaning of 'person' see PARA 510 note 1. As to judicial review see JUDICIAL REVIEW vol 61 (2010) PARA 601 et seq.
3   Broadcasting Act 1990 Sch 7 Pt I para 1(1) (Sch 7 Pt I para 1(1), (4)(a) amended by the Communications Act 2003 Sch 15 para 72(2)). The provisions referred to in the text are those in the Broadcasting Act 1990 Pt I (ss 3–71) or Pt II (ss 72–82) (repealed): see Sch 7 Pt I para 1(1) (as so amended).
4   Broadcasting Act 1990 Sch 7 Pt I para 1(2). As to the meaning of 'licence' see PARA 662 note 3.
5   As to the Secretary of State see PARA 507 note 32.
6   Broadcasting Act 1990 Sch 7 Pt I para 1(3). As to the Treasury see CONSTITUTIONAL LAW AND HUMAN RIGHTS vol 8(2) (Reissue) PARAS 512–517.
7   Broadcasting Act 1990 Sch 7 Pt I para 1(4)(a) (as amended: see note 3).
8   Broadcasting Act 1990 Sch 7 Pt I para 1(4)(b).
9   Broadcasting Act 1990 Sch 7 Pt I para 1(4).

676. Temporary provision of regional Channel 3 service for additional area.
Where it appears to OFCOM[1] that, whether as a result of the revocation of an existing regional Channel 3 licence[2] or for any other reason, there will be, in the case of a particular area[3], a temporary lack of any regional Channel 3 service[4] licensed[5] to be provided for that area[6], but that it would be reasonably practicable for the holder of a licence[7] to provide a regional Channel 3 service for any other such area also to provide his licensed service for the area in which there is a temporary lack of a service[8], OFCOM may invite the holder of that licence temporarily to provide his licensed service for that additional area[9]. If the holder of that licence agrees so to provide his licensed service, OFCOM must authorise the provision of that service for the additional area in question, during such period as it may determine, by means of a variation of the licence to that effect[10].

1   As to OFCOM see PARA 507.
2   As to the meaning of 'Channel 3' see PARA 667. 'Regional Channel 3 licence' means a licence to provide a regional Channel 3 service: Broadcasting Act 1990 s 71(1). As to the meaning of 'regional Channel 3 service' see PARA 667 note 6.
3   Ie as determined under the Broadcasting Act 1990 s 14(2) (see PARA 667).
4   As to the meaning of 'regional Channel 3 service' see PARA 667 note 6.
5   As to the meaning of 'licensed' see PARA 662 note 3.
6   Broadcasting Act 1990 s 22(1)(a).
7   As to the holder of the licence see PARA 671 note 19.
8   Broadcasting Act 1990 s 22(1)(b).
9   Broadcasting Act 1990 s 22(1) (amended by the Communications Act 2003 s 360(3), Sch 15 para 12).
10 Broadcasting Act 1990 s 22(2) (amended by the Communications Act 2003 Sch 15 para 12).

(6) CHANNEL 5 LICENCE

677. Introduction. Channel 5 was the last of the analogue terrestrial broadcasting services to be launched in the United Kingdom. It provides a national broadcasting service, and first aired in 1997[1]. Channel 5 is licensed[2] by OFCOM[3] to deliver a public television service.

The regulatory regime for every licensed public service channel[4] includes a condition requiring the provider of the channel to fulfil the public service remit for that channel[5]. The public service remit for Channel 5[6], is the provision of a range of high quality and diverse programming[7].

The regulatory regime for every licensed public service channel includes a condition requiring the provider of the channel: (1) as soon as practicable after the coming into force of these provisions[8] and subsequently at annual intervals, to prepare a statement of programme policy; and (2) to monitor his own performance in the carrying out of the proposals contained in the statements made in pursuance of the condition[9].

1   Provision for the award of the Channel 5 licence was made in the Broadcasting Act 1990 Pt I (ss 3–71), but the first bidding process to allocate the licence culminated in the refusal of the ITC to award the franchise. A second, successful, bidding process culminated in 1995. The Channel 5 licence is currently held by Channel 5 Broadcasting Ltd. The company was purchased by cross-media group Northern & Shell from RTL Group in 2010.

2   As regards the Channel 5 licence, 'licence' means a licence under the Broadcasting Act 1990 Pt I; and 'licensed' is to be construed accordingly: s 71(1). The holding by any person of a licence under Pt I does not relieve him of any liability in respect of a failure to hold a licence under the Wireless Telegraphy Act 2006 s 8 (see PARA 514 et seq) or any obligation to comply with requirements imposed by or under the Communications Act 2003 Pt 2 Ch 1 (ss 32–151) (electronic communications networks and electronic communications services: see TELECOMMUNICATIONS vol 97 (2010) PARA 92 et seq): Broadcasting Act 1990 s 3(8) (substituted by the Communications Act 2003 s 360(3), Sch 15 para 1(1), (4); and amended by the Wireless Telegraphy Act 2006 s 123, Sch 7 paras 9, 10). As to the meaning of 'person' see PARA 510 note 1.

3   As to OFCOM see PARA 507.

4   As to the meaning of 'licensed public service channel' see PARA 788 note 1.

5   Communications Act 2003 s 265(1).

6   As to the meaning of 'Channel 5' see PARA 602 note 10.

7   Communications Act 2003 s 265(2). This remit may from time to time be modified by the Secretary of State pursuant to s 271(1): see PARA 791.

8   Ie the Communications Act 2003 s 266. Section 266 came into force on 28 December 2004: see the Communications Act 2003 (Commencement No 3) Order 2004, SI 2004/3309, art 3.

9   Communications Act 2003 s 266(1). As to the condition see further PARA 642 note 6. For provision relating to changes of programme policy see s 267; and PARA 678.

678.   Changes of programme and service policy. The regulatory regime for every licensed public service channel[1] includes a condition requiring compliance with the following requirement[2] in the case of a statement of programme policy containing proposals for a significant change[3]. The requirement is for the provider of the channel: (1) to consult OFCOM[4] before preparing the statement; and (2) to take account, in the preparation of the statement, of any opinions expressed to the provider of the channel by OFCOM[5].

1   As to the meaning of 'licensed public service channel' see PARA 788 note 1.

2   Ie under the Communications Act 2003 s 269(2).

3   Communications Act 2003 s 267(1). As to statements of programme policy see PARA 677. As to when a change is a significant change for the purposes of s 267 see PARA 643 note 3. It is the duty of OFCOM: (1) from time to time to review the guidance for the time being in force for the purposes of s 267; and (2) to make such revisions of that guidance as it thinks fit: s 267(6).

4   As to OFCOM see PARA 507.

5   Communications Act 2003 s 267(2). A condition imposed under s 267 must further provide that, if it appears to OFCOM that a statement of programme policy has been prepared by the provider of the channel in contravention of a condition imposed under s 267(1), the provider is: (1) to revise that statement in accordance with any directions given to him by OFCOM; and (2)

to publish a revision of the statement in accordance with any such directions only after the revision has been approved by OFCOM: s 267(3).

679. Channel 5 licence. The Channel 5 licence[1] is awarded under Part I of the Broadcasting Act 1990[2]. It must be made in writing, and continues in force for such period as is provided by the relevant statutory provisions[3]. Licences may be granted for the provision of such a service as is specified in the licence or for the provision of a service of such a description as is so specified[4]. They may include such conditions[5] as appear to OFCOM[6] to be appropriate having regard to any duties which are or may be imposed on it[7] or on the licence holder[8]. The Channel 5 licence granted by OFCOM must require the holder to provide the licensed service with a view to its being broadcast in digital form, while also requiring the licence holder to ensure that the whole or a part of the service is also provided for broadcasting in analogue form as OFCOM considers appropriate[9]. The licence may include conditions requiring the payment by the licence holder to OFCOM (whether on the grant of the licence or at such times thereafter as may be determined by or under the licence or both) of a fee or fees of an amount or amounts so determined[10]. The Channel 5 licence will also include conditions prohibiting the imposition, whether directly or indirectly, of charges on persons: (1) in respect of their reception in the United Kingdom of the licensed service; (2) in respect of their reception in the United Kingdom of any service consisting in the provision of assistance for disabled people in relation to programmes included in the licensed service; or (3) respect of their reception in the United Kingdom of any service, other than that mentioned in head (2), which is an ancillary service in relation to so much of the licensed service as is provided in digital form[11]. Conditions may also be included in the Channel 5 licence providing for such incidental and supplemental matters as appear to be appropriate to OFCOM[12].

OFCOM is under a statutory duty to do all that it can to secure that the holder of the Channel 5 licence complies, in relation to the licensed service, with the conditions included in the licence[13]. Conditions may be included in the licence requiring the licence holder to provide OFCOM, in such manner and at such times as it may reasonably require, with such information as it may require for the purposes of exercising the functions assigned to it by or under the Broadcasting Act 1990, the Broadcasting Act 1996 or the Communications Act 2003[14]. Where the licence holder is required by virtue of any condition contained in the licence to provide OFCOM with any information[15], and in purported compliance with that condition provides OFCOM with information that is false in a material particular[16], he is for certain purposes[17] taken to have failed to comply with that condition[18]. A licence may include conditions requiring the licence holder to comply with any direction given by OFCOM as to such matters as are specified in the licence or are of a description so specified[19], or (to the extent that OFCOM consents to his doing or not doing them) not to do or not do such things as are specified in the licence or are of a description so specified[20].

When granted, the licence must in principle continue in force from the time that it takes effect until the end of the general licensing period that begins or is current when the licence is granted[21]. The Channel 5 licence is renewable on one or more occasions[22]. OFCOM may vary the licence by a notice[23] served on the licence holder if[24]: (a) in the case of a variation of the period for which the licence is to continue in force, the licence holder consents[25]; or (b) in the case of any other variation, the licence holder has been given a reasonable opportunity of making representations to OFCOM about the variation[26].

OFCOM must not grant the Channel 5 licence to any person[27] unless it is satisfied that he is a fit and proper person to hold it, and must do all that it can to secure that, if it ceases to be so satisfied in the case of any person holding a licence, that person does not remain holder of the licence[28]. The Channel 5 licence is not transferable to any other person without the previous written consent of OFCOM[29]. OFCOM must not give its consent unless it is satisfied that any such person would be in a position to comply with all of the conditions included in the licence which would have effect during the period for which it is in force[30].

1   As to the meaning of 'licence' see PARA 677 note 2.
2   Ie the Broadcasting Act 1990 Pt I (ss 3–71).
3   As regards licences for independent television broadcasting, the relevant statutory provisions are the Broadcasting Act 1990 Pt I Ch II (ss 14–42) or Ch V (ss 48–55) or the Communications Act 2003 s 235: see the Broadcasting Act 1990 s 3(1) (amended by the Communications Act 2003 Sch 15 para 1(2), (3)). A replacement licence was offered to the existing Channel 5 licence holder under the Communications Act 2003 s 215 following the date of transfer to regulation under that statute.
4   Broadcasting Act 1990 s 3(2).
5   Nothing in the Broadcasting Act 1990 which authorises or requires the inclusion in a licence of conditions relating to any particular matter or having effect for any particular purpose is to be taken as derogating from the generality of s 4(1): s 4(6).
6   As to OFCOM see PARA 507.
7   Ie under the Communications Act 2003 s 263: see PARA 602.
8   Broadcasting Act 1990 s 4(1)(a) (amended by the Communications Act 2003 s 360(3), Sch 15 para 2(1)–(3)). As to the holder of the licence see note 28.
9   Communications Act 2003 s 214(2). The conditions included in a licence by virtue of head (2) in the text must be such as to enable effect to be given to any directions given from time to time by the Secretary of State to OFCOM about the continuance of the provision of services in analogue form: s 214(3). Where the licence contains a condition falling within head (2) in the text, it must also contain a condition that: (1) the programmes (apart from the advertisements) that are included in the service provided in analogue form; and (2) the times at which they are broadcast, are to be the same as in the case of, or of the specified part of, the service provided for broadcasting in digital form: s 214(4). As to the Secretary of State see PARA 507 note 32.
10   Broadcasting Act 1990 s 4(1)(b) (amended by the Communications Act 2003 Sch 15 para 2(2)). Fees are to be in accordance with such tariff as may from time to time be fixed by OFCOM: Broadcasting Act 1990 s 4(3) (amended by the Communications Act 2003 Sch 15 para 2(2), (4), Sch 19). Such a tariff may specify different fees in relation to different cases or circumstances; and OFCOM must publish every such tariff in such manner as it considers appropriate: Broadcasting Act 1990 s 4(4) (amended by the Communications Act 2003 Sch 15 para 2(2)).
11   Communications Act 2003 s 214(8). It is unlawful to impose a charge in contravention of a condition imposed under s 214(8): s 214(9). As to references to 'imposing a charge on a person in respect of his reception of a service in, or in a part of, the United Kingdom' see PARA 665 note 11.
12   Broadcasting Act 1990 s 4(1)(d) (amended by the Communications Act 2003 Sch 15 para 2(2)).
13   See the Communications Act 2003 s 263; and PARA 602.
14   Broadcasting Act 1990 s 4(1)(c) (amended by the Communications Act 2003 Sch 15 para 2(2), (3)).
15   Broadcasting Act 1990 s 4(5)(a) (amended by the Communications Act 2003 Sch 15 para 2(2), (5)(a)).
16   Broadcasting Act 1990 s 4(5)(b).
17   Ie for the purposes of the Broadcasting Act 1990 ss 41, 42 (see PARAS 865–866) or the Communications Act 2003 ss 237, 238 (enforcement of television licensable content service licences: see PARAS 862–863).
18   Broadcasting Act 1990 s 4(5) (amended by the Communications Act 2003 Sch 15 para 2(2), (5)(b)).
19   Broadcasting Act 1990 s 4(2)(a) (s 4(2) amended by the Communications Act 2003 Sch 15 para 2(2)).

20 Broadcasting Act 1990 s 4(2)(b) (as amended: see note 19).
21 Communications Act 2003 s 214(5)(a). As to the meaning of 'licensing period', in relation to a licence see PARA 665 note 21.
22 Communications Act 2003 s 214(5)(b). As to the renewal of licences see ss 216, 216A (s 216 amended by the Digital Economy Act 2010 ss 24(2)–(6), 26(1), (2); Communications Act 2003 s 216A added by the Digital Economy Act 2010 s 24(7)).
23 As to the service of notices see TELECOMMUNICATIONS vol 97 (2010) PARAS 49–50.
24 Broadcasting Act 1990 s 3(4) (amended by the Communications Act 2003 Sch 15 para 1(2)).
25 Broadcasting Act 1990 s 3(4)(a). Section 3(4)(a) does not affect the operation of s 41(1)(b) (power to shorten licence period); nor does it authorise the variation of any conditions included in a licence in pursuance of s 19(1) (additional payments to be made in respect of Channel 3 licences) or s 52(1) (additional payments to be made in respect of additional services licences) or in pursuance of any other provision of Pt I which applies s 19(1): s 3(5).
26 Broadcasting Act 1990 s 3(4)(b) (as amended: see note 24).
27 As to the meaning of 'person' see PARA 510 note 1.
28 Broadcasting Act 1990 s 3(3) (amended by the Communications Act 2003 Sch 15 para 1(2)). Nothing in the Broadcasting Act 1990 Pt I is to be construed as affecting the operation of s 3(3) or s 5(1), (2)(b) or (c) (see PARA 821): s 3(3). Where the person who is for the time being the holder of any licence ('the present licence holder') is not the person to whom the licence was originally granted, any reference in Pt I to the holder of the licence is to be construed, in relation to any time falling before the date when the present licence holder became the holder of it, as including a reference to a person who was previously the holder of the licence: s 71(2).
29 Broadcasting Act 1990 s 3(6) (amended by the Communications Act 2003 Sch 15 para 1(2)).
30 Broadcasting Act 1990 s 3(7) (amended by the Communications Act 2003 Sch 15 para 1(2)).

680. Reviews relating to licensing of Channel 5. The holder of a replacement Channel 5 licence[1] may apply to OFCOM[2], at any time in the first or any subsequent review period, for a review of the financial terms on which that licence is held[3]. For these purposes[4], the first review period is the period which: (1) begins four years before the first notional expiry date[5]; and (2) ends with the day before the day that OFCOM has determined to be the one by which it would need to publish a tender notice[6] if it were proposing to grant a fresh licence to take effect from the first notional expiry date[7]. For these purposes, a subsequent review period in the case of a replacement licence is so much (if any) of the following period as falls before the end of the initial expiry date for that type of licence, namely, the period which: (a) begins four years before a subsequent notional expiry date[8]; and (b) ends with the day before the day that OFCOM has determined to be the one by which it would need to publish a tender notice if it were proposing to grant a fresh licence to take effect from that notional expiry date[9]. A determination for the purposes of head (2) or head (b) above in respect of a replacement licence: (i) must be made at least one year before the day determined; and (ii) must be notified by OFCOM to the person who, at the time of the determination, holds the licence in question[10]. No application under these provisions for a review of the financial terms on which a replacement licence is held is to be made: (A) at any time when an application[11] for a review of those terms is pending; or (B) at any time in the period of 12 months following the day on which a determination by OFCOM on such an application is notified to the licence holder[12].

Further provision is made with respect to reviews relating to licensing of Channel 5[13].

1 Ie a licence granted under the Communications Act 2003 s 215: see PARA 665 note 3. As to the meaning of 'Channel 5' see PARA 602 note 10.
2 As to OFCOM see PARA 507.
3 Communications Act 2003 s 225(1).
4 Ie the Communications Act 2003 s 225.
5 As to the meaning of 'the first notional expiry date' see PARA 666 note 5.

6   As to the meaning of 'tender notice' see PARA 666 note 6.
7   Communications Act 2003 s 225(2).
8   As to the meaning of 'subsequent notional expiry date' see PARA 666 note 8.
9   Communications Act 2003 s 225(3) (amended by the Digital Economy Act 2010 s 26(1), (4)).
10 Communications Act 2003 s 225(4).
11 Ie an application for a review of financial terms in consequence of new obligations (see the Communications Act 2003 s 226).
12 Communications Act 2003 s 225(5). As to when an application for a review under s 226 is pending see PARA 666 note 12.
13 See the Communications Act 2003 s 227 (reviews under ss 225, 226 of the financial terms on which a licence is held), s 228 (amended by the Digital Economy Act 2010 s 26(1), (5)) (giving effect to reviews under the Communications Act 2003 ss 225, 226), s 229 (amended by the Digital Economy Act 2010 s 26(6)–(12)) (report in anticipation of new licensing round), and the Communications Act 2003 s 230 (amended by the Digital Economy Act 2010 s 26(13)–(18)) (orders suspending rights of renewal).

681.   Channel 5.   OFCOM[1] must do all that it can to secure the provision of a television broadcasting service[2] for any such minimum area of the United Kingdom[3] as it may determine, and any such service is to be known as Channel 5[4]. In determining the minimum area of the United Kingdom for which Channel 5 is to be provided, OFCOM must have regard to the consideration that the service should, so far as is reasonably practicable, make the most effective use of the frequencies[5] on which it is to be provided[6].

1   As to OFCOM see PARA 507.
2   As to the meaning of 'television broadcasting service' see PARA 667 note 3.
3   As to the meaning of 'United Kingdom' see PARA 510 note 13.
4   Broadcasting Act 1990 ss 28(1), 71(1) (s 28 amended by the Communications Act 2003 s 360(3), Sch 15 para 15). Channel 5 was set up in accordance with the proposals made in the White Paper *Broadcasting in the '90s: Competition, Choice and Quality* (Cm 517) (November 1988).
        Subject to the Broadcasting Act 1990 s 29(2), (3), ss 15–21 (see PARAS 669–675, 813) apply in relation to a Channel 5 licence as they apply in relation to a regional Channel 3 licence: s 29(1). In its application in relation to a Channel 5 licence, s 15(1)(b)(i) (see PARA 669) is to be read as referring to any such minimum area of the United Kingdom as is determined by OFCOM in accordance with s 28(2) (see the text and note 6): s 29(2) (amended by the Communications Act 2003 ss 360(3), 406(7), Sch 15 para 16(1)(a), (2), Sch 19). 'Channel 5 licence' means a licence to provide Channel 5: s 71(1). As to the meaning of 'regional Channel 3 licence' see PARA 676 note 2.
        The courts will not interfere with OFCOM's decision to award the Channel 5 licence to a particular applicant if it has acted within its powers: see *R v Independent Television Commission, ex p Virgin Television Ltd* [1996] EMLR 318, DC.
5   'Frequency' includes frequency band: Broadcasting Act 1990 s 202(1).
6   Broadcasting Act 1990 s 28(2) (as amended: see note 4). Where OFCOM has granted a licence to provide Channel 5, it may, if it appears to it to be appropriate to do so in view of any lack of facilities available for transmitting the service, dispense with any requirement to provide the service for such part of the minimum area as it may determine; and any such dispensation has effect for such period as it may determine: s 28(4) (as so amended).

(7)   ADDITIONAL SERVICES

(i)   Teletext Licensee

682.   Introduction.   The regulatory regime for the public teletext service[1] includes a condition requiring the provider of the service to fulfil the public service remit for that service[2]. The public service remit for the public teletext service is the provision of a range of high quality and diverse text material[3]. For so long as the public teletext service comprises both: (1) an analogue teletext service[4]; and (2) a teletext service provided in digital form, the conditions imposed under these provisions[5] must require the public service remit of the public teletext service to be fulfilled separately in the case of each of those services[6].

The regulatory regime for the public teletext service includes a condition requiring the public teletext provider: (a) as soon as practicable after the coming into force of these provisions[7] and subsequently at annual intervals, to prepare a statement of service policy; and (b) to monitor his own performance in the carrying out of the proposals contained in statements made in pursuance of the condition[8].

1   As to the public teletext service see PARA 686.

2   Communications Act 2003 s 265(1).

3   Communications Act 2003 s 265(4).

4   'Analogue teletext service' is to be construed in accordance with the Communications Act 2003 s 218(4) (see PARA 686 note 9): s 362(1).

5   Ie the Communications Act 2003 s 265.

6   Communications Act 2003 s 265(5).

7   Ie the Communications Act 2003 s 268. Section 268 came into force on 28 December 2004: see the Communications Act 2003 (Commencement No 3) Order 2004, SI 2004/3309, art 3.

8   Communications Act 2003 s 268(1). The condition must require every statement of service policy prepared in accordance with the condition to set out the proposals of the public teletext provider for securing that, during the following year, the public service remit for the public teletext service will be fulfilled: s 268(2). The condition must also require every such statement to contain a report on the performance of the public teletext provider in the carrying out, during the period since the previous statement, of the proposals contained in that statement: s 268(3). The condition must provide that the proposals or report for a period in the course of which the public teletext service will comprise or has comprised both an analogue teletext service and a teletext service provided in digital form, must deal separately with each of those services: s 268(4). The condition must also provide that every statement in pursuance of the condition: (1) must be prepared having regard to guidance given by OFCOM; (2) must be prepared taking account of the reports previously published by OFCOM under ss 264, 358 (see PARAS 788, 853); (3) must take special account of the most recent such reports; (4) must be published by the public teletext provider as soon as practicable after its preparation is complete; and (5) must be published in such manner as, having regard to any guidance given by OFCOM, that provider considers appropriate: s 268(5). In preparing guidance about the preparation of such a statement, OFCOM must have regard, in particular, to the matters which, in the light of the provisions of s 264(4), (6), it considers should be included in statements of service policy by the public teletext provider: s 268(6). It is the duty of OFCOM: (a) from time to time to review the guidance for the time being in force for the purposes of s 268; and (b) to make such revisions of that guidance as it thinks fit: s 268(7). The conditions of the licence to provide the public teletext service may provide that a previous statement of policy made by the public teletext provider is to be treated for the purposes of Pt 3 as if it were a statement made in relation to such period as may be so specified and were a statement of service policy for the purposes of a condition imposed under s 268: s 268(8). The reference in s 268(8) to a previous statement of policy is a reference to any statement made by the public teletext provider: (i) whether before or after the commencement of s 268, for the purposes of his application for a Broadcasting Act licence for the public teletext service or for the existing service (within the meaning of s 221 (see PARA 686)); or (ii) at any time before the commencement of s 268, for any other purpose: s 268(9). A condition under s 268(8) cannot contain provision the effect of which is to postpone the time at which a licence holder is required to make the first statement of service policy which (apart from that subsection) he is required to make in pursuance of a condition imposed under s 268: s 268(10). For provision relating to changes of service policy see s 269; and PARA 683.

683.   Changes of programme and service policy.   The regulatory regime for the public teletext service[1] includes a condition requiring compliance with the following requirement[2] in the case of a statement of service policy containing proposals for a significant change[3]. The requirement is for the provider of the service: (1) to consult OFCOM[4] before preparing the statement; and (2) to take account, in the preparation of the statement, of any opinions expressed to the provider of the service by OFCOM[5].

1 As to the public teletext service see PARA 686.

2 Ie under the Communications Act 2003 s 269(2).

3 Communications Act 2003 s 269(1). As to statements of service policy see PARA 682. A change is a significant change for the purposes of s 269 if it is a change as a result of which the service would in any year be materially different in character from in previous years: s 269(4). In determining for the purposes of any condition under s 269 whether a change is a significant change: (1) regard must be had to any guidance issued by OFCOM; (2) the changes to be considered include any changes that, together with any proposed change for a particular year, would constitute a change occurring gradually over a period of not more than three years; (3) the previous years with which a comparison is to be made must be those immediately preceding the year in which the change is made, or in which the changes comprised in it began to occur; and (4) any change that is a significant change in relation to so much of the public teletext service as is provided in digital form or in relation to so much of it as is provided in analogue form is to be regarded as a significant change in relation to the whole service: s 269(5). It is the duty of OFCOM: (a) from time to time to review the guidance for the time being in force for the purposes of s 269; and (b) to make such revisions of that guidance as it thinks fit: s 269(6).

4 As to OFCOM see PARA 507.

5 Communications Act 2003 s 269(2). A condition imposed under s 269 must further provide that, if it appears to OFCOM that a statement of service policy has been prepared by the public teletext provider in contravention of a condition imposed under s 269(1), that provider is: (1) to revise that statement in accordance with any directions given to him by OFCOM; and (2) to publish a revision of the statement in accordance with any such directions only after the revision has been approved by OFCOM: s 269(3).

684.   Co-operation with the public teletext provider.   The regulatory regime for every Channel 3 service[1] and for Channel 4[2] includes the conditions that OFCOM[3] considers appropriate for securing that the provider of the service or channel grants access to the facilities mentioned below[4]: (1) to the public teletext provider[5]; and (2) to any person authorised[6] to provide the whole or a part of the public teletext service on his behalf[7]. The facilities referred to above are the facilities that are reasonably required by the public teletext provider or the authorised person for the purposes of, or in connection with, the provision of the public teletext service[8]. A licence holder granting access to facilities in pursuance of a condition imposed under these provisions may require the public teletext provider or authorised person to pay a reasonable charge in respect of the facilities[9]. In the event of a dispute, the amount of the charge is to be determined by OFCOM[10].

1 As to the meaning of 'Channel 3 service' see PARA 602 note 8.

2 As to the meaning of 'Channel 4' see PARA 602 note 9.

3 As to OFCOM see PARA 507.

4 Ie mentioned in the Communications Act 2003 s 276(2): see the text and note 8.

5 As to the meaning of 'public teletext provider' see PARA 686 note 28.

6 Ie by virtue of the Communications Act 2003 s 220: see PARA 686.

7 Communications Act 2003 s 276(1). As to the public teletext service see PARA 686. As from a day to be appointed, the words 'for securing that the provider of the service or channel grants access' are replaced by 'for securing that, if there is a public teletext provider, the provider of the Channel 3 service or Channel 4 grants access': see s 276(1) (prospectively amended by the Digital Economy Act 2010 s 28(6)). At the date at which this volume states the law, no such day had been appointed.

8 Communications Act 2003 s 276(2).

9 Communications Act 2003 s 276(3).

10 Communications Act 2003 s 276(4).

685. Special obligation for the public teletext provider. The regulatory regime for the public teletext service[1] includes the conditions that OFCOM[2] considers appropriate for securing that the provision of so much of the public teletext service as is provided in analogue form does not cause interference with: (1) the television broadcasting service or services on whose frequency or frequencies it is provided; or (2) any other wireless telegraphy transmissions[3].

1 As to the public teletext service see PARA 686.
2 As to OFCOM see PARA 507.
3 Communications Act 2003 s 298. As to the meaning of 'wireless telegraphy' see PARA 510 note 1; definition applied by s 405(1).

686. The public teletext service. OFCOM[1] must do all that it can to secure the provision, in accordance with Chapter 2 of Part 3 of the Communications Act 2003[2] and Part I of the Broadcasting Act 1996[3], of a teletext service that is available nationwide[4]. The service must consist of: (1) a single teletext service provided in digital form with a view to its being broadcast by means of a television multiplex service[5]; and (2) for so long as Channel 4[6], S4C[7] and one or more Channel 3 services[8] are broadcast in analogue form, an analogue teletext service[9]. The service, if licensed to do so[10], may continue to include an analogue teletext service after it is no longer required under head (2) above to include such a service[11]. For so long as the public teletext service must consist of both a teletext service provided in digital form and an analogue teletext service, OFCOM must secure that both services are provided by the same person[12]. OFCOM must exercise its powers: (a) to make frequencies available for the purposes of Channel 3 services, Channel 4 and S4C; and (b) to make determinations of spare capacity[13], in a manner that takes account of its duty under the above provisions[14].

The licence that is required[15] in respect of the public teletext service is a licence under Part I of the Broadcasting Act 1990[16] complying with these provisions[17]. The licence: (i) must be a licence which continues in force, from the time from which it takes effect, until the end of the licensing period[18] beginning or current at that time; and (ii) is renewable, on one or more occasions[19]. The licence must contain the conditions that OFCOM considers appropriate for the purpose of performing its duty relating to the application of regulatory regimes[20]. The conditions of the licence must also include conditions prohibiting the imposition, whether directly or indirectly, of any charges on persons in respect of their reception in the United Kingdom of the licensed service[21]. The service authorised by a licence under these provisions, so far as it comprises a service provided in digital form, is a qualifying service[22]. Further provision is made about the award and grant of the licence for the public teletext service and about the conditions and enforcement of that licence[23].

The licence for the provision of the public teletext service may: (A) include provision enabling the licence holder to authorise an eligible person[24] to provide the whole or a part of the public teletext service on his behalf; and (B) impose conditions subject to and in accordance with which the whole or a part of that service may be provided by a person authorised by the licence holder[25]. The conditions of the licence to provide the public teletext service apply in relation to its provision by a person authorised to do so on the licence holder's behalf as they apply to its provision by the licence holder[26]. A contravention of those conditions by a person so authorised will be treated for the purposes of

Chapter 2 of Part 3 of the Communications Act 2003 and the Broadcasting Act 1990 as a contravention on the part of the licence holder[27].

Provision is made with respect to the replacement of an existing public teletext provider's licence[28] and the renewal of public teletext licences[29].

1 As to OFCOM see PARA 507.
2 Ie the Communications Act 2003 Pt 3 Ch 2 (ss 211–244).
3 Ie the Broadcasting Act 1996 Pt I (ss 1–39).
4 Communications Act 2003 s 218(1). As from a day to be appointed, s 218(1) is amended by the Digital Economy Act 2010 s 28(1), (2), to provide that OFCOM has a power rather than a duty in this respect, and may secure the provision of a teletext service that is available nationwide and complies with the Communications Act 2003 s 218. At the date at which this volume states the law, no such day had been appointed.
5 As to the meaning of 'television multiplex service' see PARA 697; definition applied by the Communications Act 2003 s 362(1).
6 As to the meaning of 'Channel 4' see PARA 602 note 9.
7 As to the meaning of 'S4C' see PARA 644.
8 As to the meaning of 'Channel 3 service' see PARA 602 note 8.
9 Communications Act 2003 s 218(2). The analogue teletext service that must be or may be comprised in the public teletext service is a single additional television service that uses the combined spare capacity available for the provision of additional television services on the frequencies on which Channel 3 services, Channel 4 and S4C (or any of them) are broadcast in analogue form: s 218(4).
10 Ie in accordance with the Communications Act 2003 s 219 (see the text and notes 15–23).
11 Communications Act 2003 s 218(3).
12 Communications Act 2003 s 218(5). However, nothing in s 218: (1) requires the contents of the two services comprised in the public teletext service to be the same; (2) prevents the service from including different items for different parts of the United Kingdom or prevents the different items from being made available only in the parts of the United Kingdom for which they are included; or (3) prevents the licence holder from making arrangements authorised by virtue of s 220 (see the text and notes 24–27) for the provision of the whole or a part of the public teletext service by another: s 218(6).
13 Ie determinations for the purposes of the Broadcasting Act 1990 s 48(2)(b) (see PARA 703).
14 Ie under the Communications Act 2003 s 218: s 218(7). As from a day to be appointed, s 218(7) is amended by the Digital Economy Act 2010 ss 28(3), 45, Sch 2 to provide that if there is a public teletext provider, OFCOM must take account of the requirements of the public teletext service when exercising its powers: (1) to make frequencies available for the purposes of Channel 3 services, Channel 4 and S4C; and (2) to make determinations of spare capacity. At the date at which this volume states the law, no such day had been appointed.
    OFCOM must prepare a report on the public teletext service and send it to the Secretary of State as soon as practicable after the Communications Act 2003 s 218A comes into force: s 218A(1) (s 218A added by the Digital Economy Act 2010 s 27). That date was 8 June 2010: see the Digital Economy Act 2010 s 47(1). OFCOM must prepare and send to the Secretary of State further reports on the public teletext service when asked to do so by the Secretary of State: Communications Act 2003 s 218A(2) (as so added). Each report must include, in particular: (a) an assessment of the advantages and disadvantages for members of the public of the public teletext service being provided, and (b) an assessment of whether the public teletext service can be provided at a cost to the licence holder that is commercially sustainable: s 218A(3) (as so added). An assessment under s 218A(3)(a) must take account of alternative uses for the capacity that would be available if the public teletext service were not provided: s 218A(4) (as so added). 'Capacity' means capacity on the frequencies on which Channel 3 services, Channel 4, S4C and television multiplex services are broadcast: s 218A(6) (as so added). OFCOM must publish every report under s 218A: (i) as soon as practicable after sending it to the Secretary of State; and (ii) in such manner as it considers appropriate: s 218A(5) (as so added). As to the Secretary of State see PARA 507 note 32.
15 Ie for the purposes of the Broadcasting Act 1990 s 13 (see PARA 593).
16 Ie the Broadcasting Act 1990 Pt I (ss 3–71).
17 Ie complying with the Communications Act 2003 s 219: s 219(1).
18 For the purposes of the Communications Act 2003 s 219(2), a licensing period is: (1) the period beginning with the commencement of s 219 (ie 29 December 2003: see the Office of Communications Act 2002 (Commencement No 3) and Communications Act 2003 (Commencement No 2) Order 2003, SI 2003/3142) and ending with the initial expiry date for

the licence to provide the public teletext service; or (2) any subsequent period of ten years beginning with the end of the previous licensing period for that type of licence: Communications Act 2003 s 219(3) (amended by the Digital Economy Act 2010 s 26(1), (3)).

19 Ie under the Communications Act 2003 s 222 (see the text and note 29): s 219(2).

20 Ie its duty under the Communications Act 2003 s 263 (see PARA 602): s 219(4).

21 Communications Act 2003 s 219(5). It is unlawful to impose a charge in contravention of a condition imposed under s 219(5): s 219(6).

22 Ie for the purposes of the Broadcasting Act 1996 Pt I (ss 1–39): Communications Act 2003 s 219(7). 'Qualifying service' has the same meaning as in the Broadcasting Act 1996 Pt I (see s 2(2); and PARA 690 note 28): Communications Act 2003 s 362(1).

23 See the Communications Act 2003 s 219(8), Sch 10.

24 For the purposes of the Communications Act 2003 s 220, 'eligible person' means a person who is not a disqualified person under the Broadcasting Act 1990 Sch 2 Pt II (see PARAS 822 et seq, 830 et seq) in relation to the licence for the public teletext service: Communications Act 2003 s 220(4).

25 Communications Act 2003 s 220(1).

26 Communications Act 2003 s 220(2).

27 Communications Act 2003 s 220(3).

28 See the Communications Act 2003 s 221 (repealed, as from a day to be appointed, by the Digital Economy Act 2010 ss 28(5), 45, Sch 2). At the date at which this volume states the law, no such day had been appointed. 'The public teletext provider' means: (1) subject to head (2), the person holding the licence under the Communications Act 2003 s 219 to provide the public teletext service; and (2) in relation to a time before the grant of the first licence to be granted under s 219, the person holding the Broadcasting Act licence to provide the existing service (within the meaning of s 221): s 362(1). For transitional provision relating to s 221 see the Office of Communications Act 2002 (Commencement No 3) and Communications Act 2003 (Commencement No 2) Order 2003, SI 2003/3142.

29 See the Communications Act 2003 s 222 (amended by the Digital Economy Act 2010 s 26(1), (3)). As to the financial terms of licences renewed under the Communications Act 2003 s 222 see s 223.

687. Reviews relating to licensing of public teletext service. The holder of a replacement licence for the provision of the public teletext service[1] may apply to OFCOM[2], at any time in the first or any subsequent review period, for a review of the financial terms on which that licence is held[3]. For these purposes[4], the first review period is the period which: (1) begins four years before the first notional expiry date[5]; and (2) ends with the day before the day that OFCOM has determined to be the one by which it would need to publish a tender notice[6] if it were proposing to grant a fresh licence to take effect from the first notional expiry date[7]. For these purposes, a subsequent review period in the case of a replacement licence is so much (if any) of the following period as falls before the end of the initial expiry date for that type of licence, namely, the period which: (a) begins four years before a subsequent notional expiry date[8]; and (b) ends with the day before the day that OFCOM has determined to be the one by which it would need to publish a tender notice if it were proposing to grant a fresh licence to take effect from that notional expiry date[9]. A determination for the purposes of head (2) or head (b) above in respect of a replacement licence: (i) must be made at least one year before the day determined; and (ii) must be notified by OFCOM to the person who, at the time of the determination, holds the licence in question[10]. No application under these provisions for a review of the financial terms on which a replacement licence is held is to be made: (A) at any time when an application[11] for a review of those terms is pending; or (B) at any time in the period of 12 months following the day on which a determination by OFCOM on such an application is notified to the licence holder[12].

Further provision is made with respect to reviews relating to licensing of the public teletext service[13].

1   Ie a licence granted under the Communications Act 2003 s 221: see PARA 686. As to the public teletext service see PARA 686.
2   As to OFCOM see PARA 507.
3   Communications Act 2003 s 225(1).
4   Ie the Communications Act 2003 s 225.
5   As to the meaning of 'the first notional expiry date' see PARA 666 note 5.
6   As to the meaning of 'tender notice' see PARA 666 note 6.
7   Communications Act 2003 s 225(2).
8   As to the meaning of 'subsequent notional expiry date' see PARA 666 note 8.
9   Communications Act 2003 s 225(3) (amended by the Digital Economy Act 2010 s 26(1), (4)).
10 Communications Act 2003 s 225(4).
11 Ie an application for a review of financial terms in consequence of new obligations (see the Communications Act 2003 s 226).
12 Communications Act 2003 s 225(5). As to when an application for a review under s 226 is pending see PARA 666 note 12.
13 See the Communications Act 2003 s 227 (reviews under ss 225, 226 of the financial terms on which a licence is held), s 228 (amended by the Digital Economy Act 2010 s 26(1), (5)) (giving effect to reviews under the Communications Act 2003 ss 225, 226), s 229 (amended by the Digital Economy Act 2010 s 26(6)–(12)) (report in anticipation of new licensing round), and the Communications Act 2003 s 230 (amended by the Digital Economy Act 2010 s 26(13)–(18)) (orders suspending rights of renewal).

(ii) Additional Television Services

688. Services that are not television licensable content services. A service is not a television licensable content service[1]:

(1)   to the extent that it is provided with a view to its being broadcast by means of a television multiplex service or a general multiplex service[2];

(2)   to the extent that it consists of a service the provision of which is authorised by: (a) a licence to provide a television broadcasting service; (b) the licence to provide the public teletext service[3]; or (c) a licence to provide additional television services[4];

(3)   if it is a two-way service[5];

(4)   if it is distributed by means of an electronic communications network only to persons all of whom are on a single set of premises[6], and that network is wholly within those premises and is not connected to an electronic communications network any part of which is outside those premises[7];

(5)   if it is provided for the purpose only of being received by persons who have qualified as users of the service by reason of being: (a) persons who have a business interest in the programmes included in the service; or (b) persons who are to receive the programmes for the purpose only of showing them to persons falling within head (a) or to persons all of whom are on the business premises[8] of the person receiving them[9].

If it is considered appropriate, the Secretary of State[10] may modify the above provisions[11].

1   As to television licensable content services see PARA 716.
2   Communications Act 2003 s 233(1) (amended by SI 2006/2131). As to the meaning of 'television multiplex service' see PARA 697; definition applied by the Communications Act 2003 s 362(1). As to the meaning of 'general multiplex service' see PARA 898 note 10.
3   'The public teletext service' means the service the provision of which is required to be secured in accordance with the Communications Act 2003 s 218 (see PARA 686): s 362(1). As from a day to be appointed, this definition is amended to provide that 'the public teletext service' means the service the provision of which is or may be secured in accordance with s 218: s 362(1) (prospectively amended by the Digital Economy Act 2010 s 28(7)). At the date at which this volume states the law, no such day had been appointed.
4   Communications Act 2003 s 233(2).

5   Ie within the meaning of the Communications Act 2003 s 232: s 233(4).
6   'Premises' includes a vehicle; and 'vehicle' includes vessel, aircraft or hovercraft: Communications Act 2003 s 233(9). As to the meaning of 'vehicle' see PARA 951 note 3. For the purposes of s 233(5), a set of premises is a single set of premises if, and only if, the same person is the occupier of all the premises; and two or more vehicles are capable of constituting a single set of premises if, and only if, they are coupled together: s 233(6).
7   Communications Act 2003 s 233(5).
8   'Business premises', in relation to a person, means premises at or from which any business of that person is carried on: the Communications Act 2003 s 233(9).
9   Communications Act 2003 s 233(7). A person has a business interest in programmes if he has an interest in receiving or watching them: (1) for the purposes of a business carried on by him; or (2) for the purposes of his employment: s 233(8). In relation to a person, references to a business include references to: (a) any business or other activities carried on by a body of which he is a member and the affairs of which are managed by its members; and (b) the carrying out of any functions conferred on that person, or on any such body, by or under any enactment: s 233(10). As to the meaning of 'enactment' see PARA 793 note 5.
10 As to the Secretary of State see PARA 507 note 32.
11 Ie the Communications Act 2003 s 233: see s 234. For such an order see the Television Licensable Content Services Order 2006, SI 2006/2131.

(iii) Restricted Services

689.   Licensing of restricted services. An application for a licence[1] to provide a restricted service[2] is to be made in such manner as OFCOM[3] determines, and must be accompanied by such fee (if any) as OFCOM determines[4].

1   As regards licences to provide a restricted service, 'licence' means a licence under the Broadcasting Act 1990 Pt I (ss 3–71); and 'licensed' is to be construed accordingly: s 71(1).
2   'Restricted service' means a service which consists in the broadcasting of television programmes for a particular establishment or other defined location, or a particular event, in the United Kingdom: Broadcasting Act 1990 s 42A (ss 42A, 42B added by the Broadcasting Act 1996 s 85; Broadcasting Act 1990 s 42A amended by the Communications Act 2003 s 406(7), Sch 19). As to the meaning of 'broadcast' see PARA 668 note 2; and as to the meaning of 'programme' see PARA 667 note 7. As to the meaning of 'United Kingdom' see PARA 510 note 13.
3   As to OFCOM see PARA 507.
4   Broadcasting Act 1990 s 42B(1) (as added (see note 2)); and amended by the Communications Act 2003 s 360(3), Sch 15 para 19). Subject to the Broadcasting Act 1990 s 42B(3)–(3C) (see PARA 865), ss 40–42 (see PARAS 864–866) apply in relation to a restricted licence as they apply in relation to a licence to provide a Channel 3 service: s 42B(2) (as so added; amended by the Communications Act 2003 s 345, Sch 13 paras 1, 4(1)).

(8) DIGITAL TERRESTRIAL BROADCASTING

(i) Grant of Multiplex Licences

690.   Multiplex licences. Digital terrestrial television was launched in the United Kingdom in 1998. Parliament provided for the broadcast of channels in six groups (multiplex services[1]) labelled 1, 2, A, B, C, and D[2]. The ITC[3] then allocated each existing analogue terrestrial channel half the capacity of one multiplex each[4]. The remaining spectrum[5] was then auctioned off[6]. Content available on digital terrestrial television is largely free-to-air although there is scope for subscription services to be carried.

Multiplex service licences are awarded under Part I of the Broadcasting Act 1996[7]. They must be made in writing[8], and continue in force for such period as is provided by the relevant statutory provisions[9].

Where OFCOM[10] proposes to grant a licence[11] to provide a multiplex service (a 'multiplex licence') it must publish, in such manner as it considers appropriate, a notice[12]:

(1)   stating that it proposes to grant such a licence[13];
(2)   specifying the frequency[14] or frequencies on which the service is to be provided[15];
(3)   specifying, in such manner as OFCOM considers appropriate, the area or areas in the United Kingdom[16] within which the frequency or frequencies is or are to be available[17];
(4)   inviting applications for the licence and specifying the closing date for such applications[18];
(5)   specifying the fee payable on any application[19]; and
(6)   stating whether any percentage of multiplex revenue for each accounting period[20] would be payable by an applicant[21] if he were granted the licence and, if so, specifying that percentage[22].

When publishing such a notice, OFCOM must publish with the notice general guidance as to requirements to be met by proposals as to the matters referred to in heads (b)(i), (ii) and (f) below, and may publish with the notice such other general guidance as it considers appropriate[23].

An application made in pursuance of such a notice must be in writing, and must be accompanied by:

(a)   the fee specified in the notice under head (5) above[24];
(b)   a technical plan relating to the service which the applicant proposes to provide and indicating:
    (i)   the parts of the area specified under head (3) above which would be within the coverage area of the service[25];
    (ii)   the timetable in accordance with which that coverage would be achieved[26]; and
    (iii) the technical means by which it would be achieved[27];
(c)   the applicant's proposals as to the number of digital programme services[28] to be broadcast[29], as to the characteristics of each of those services, and as to the areas in which they would be provided[30];
(d)   the applicant's proposals as to the number (if any) of digital sound programmes services which are to be broadcast, as to the characteristics of each of those services, and as to the areas in which they would be provided[31];
(e)   the applicant's proposals as to the timetable in accordance with which the broadcasting of each of the services mentioned in heads (c) and (d) above would begin[32];
(f)   the applicant's proposals as to the broadcasting of digital additional services[33];
(g)   the applicant's proposals for promoting or assisting the acquisition[34], by persons in the proposed coverage area of the service, of equipment capable of receiving all the multiplex services available in that area[35];
(h)   such information as OFCOM may reasonably require as to the applicant's present financial position and his projected financial position during the period for which the licence would be in force[36]; and
(i)   such other information as OFCOM may reasonably require for the purpose of considering the application[37].

At any time after receiving such an application and before determining it, OFCOM may require the applicant to furnish additional information under any of heads (b) to (i) above[38]. Any information to be furnished to OFCOM must, if it so requires, be in such form or verified in such manner as it may specify[39]. OFCOM must, as soon as reasonably practicable after the date specified in a notice of its proposal to grant a licence[40] as the closing date for applications, publish in such manner as it considers appropriate:

(A)   the name of every person who has made an application to it in pursuance of the notice[41];

(B)   the proposals submitted by him under head (c) above[42];

(C)   such other information connected with his application as OFCOM considers appropriate[43]; and

(D)   a notice inviting representations to be made to it with respect to any of the applications[44], and specifying the manner in which, and the time by which, any such representations are to be so made[45].

Where OFCOM has published a notice of its proposal to grant a licence[46], it must, in determining whether, or to whom, to award the multiplex licence in question, have regard to the extent to which, taking into account specified matters and any representations made to it under head (D) above with respect to those matters, the award of the licence to each applicant would be calculated to promote the development of digital television broadcasting in the United Kingdom otherwise than by satellite[47]. The matters so referred to are:

(aa)   the extent of the coverage area proposed to be achieved by the applicant as indicated in the technical plan submitted by him under head (b) above[48];

(bb)   the timetables proposed by the applicant under heads (b)(ii) and (d) above[49];

(cc)   the ability of the applicant to establish the proposed service and to maintain it throughout the period for which the licence will be in force[50];

(dd)   the capacity of the digital programme services proposed to be included in the service to appeal to a variety of tastes and interests[51];

(ee)   any proposals by the applicant for promoting or assisting the acquisition[52], by persons in the proposed coverage area of the service, of equipment capable of receiving all the multiplex services available in that area[53]; and

(ff)   whether, in contracting or offering to contract with persons providing digital programme services, digital sound programme service or digital additional services, the applicant has acted in a manner calculated to ensure fair and effective competition in the provision of such services[54].

Where OFCOM has awarded a multiplex licence to any person in accordance with these provisions, it must, as soon as reasonably practicable after awarding the licence, publish in such manner as it considers appropriate the name of the person to whom the licence has been awarded, and such other information as OFCOM considers appropriate[55], and grant the licence to that person[56].

OFCOM may, before publishing a notice of its proposal to grant a licence[57], determine that two or more multiplex licences are on that occasion to be granted to one person[58]. Where OFCOM has so determined, it must publish a single notice in relation to the licences[59].

OFCOM may, when awarding a multiplex licence to any person, make the grant of the licence to him conditional on his compliance before the grant with such specified requirements relating to the financing of the service as appears to it to be appropriate[60], having regard to any duties which are or may be imposed on it, or on the licence holder, by or under the Broadcasting Act 1990, the Broadcasting Act 1996 or Part 3 of the Communications Act 2003[61], and any information provided to it under head (g) above by the person to whom the licence is awarded as to his projected financial position during the period for which the licence would be in force[62].

A multiplex licence may include conditions enabling OFCOM to estimate before the beginning of an accounting period the amount due for that period[63], and requiring the licence holder to pay the estimated amount by monthly instalments throughout that period[64]. Such a licence may in particular include conditions authorising OFCOM to revise any estimate on one or more occasions and to adjust the instalments payable by the licence holder to take account of the revised estimate, and providing for the adjustment of any overpayment or underpayment[65].

OFCOM must not grant a multiplex service licence to any person unless it is satisfied that he is a fit and proper person to hold it, and must do all that it can to secure that, if it ceases to be so satisfied in the case of any person holding a licence, that person does not remain holder of the licence[66]. A multiplex service licence is not transferable to any other person without the previous written consent of OFCOM[67]. OFCOM must not give its consent unless it is satisfied that any such person would be in a position to comply with all of the conditions included in the licence which would have effect during the period for which it is in force[68].

1   'Multiplex service' means (except where the context otherwise requires) a television multiplex service: Broadcasting Act 1996 ss 1(1), 39(1) (s 1(1) substituted by the Communications Act 2003 s 360(3), Sch 15 para 74(1), (2)). As to the meaning of 'television multiplex service' see PARA 697; definition applied by the Broadcasting Act 1996 s 39(1) (definition added by the Communications Act 2003 Sch 15 para 100(d)).
2   See the Broadcasting Act 1996.
3   As to the Independent Television Commission ('ITC') see PARA 507.
4   This meant that the BBC was allocated one full multiplex (multiplex 1), ITV and Channel 4 shared multiplex 2 (though 3% of the capacity was given to Teletext Ltd) and Five and S4C shared multiplex A. As to the BBC see PARAS 603–626; as to ITV see PARA 667; as to Channel 4 see PARA 627 et seq; as to Five (Channel 5) see PARA 681; and as to S4C see PARA 644 et seq.
5   Ie multiplexes B, C and D.
6   A consortium made up of Granada and Carlton (members of the ITV network, which have now merged to form ITV plc) and BSkyB successfully bid for these licences, and set up the subscription ONdigital service (though BSkyB left the consortium prior to launch and the service was subsequently rebranded as ITV Digital). The ITV Digital consortium collapsed in 2002, and the rights reverted to the regulator, which invited new bids for the licences for multiplexes B, C and D. A consortium involving the BBC and Arqiva was successful in this bidding process, which provided scope for the launch of the Freeview service. As to Arqiva see PARA 550 note 8.
7   Ie the Broadcasting Act 1996 Pt I (ss 1–39).
8   Broadcasting Act 1996 s 3(1).
9   Ie the Broadcasting Act 1996 ss 1–17, 32–39. As to duration and renewal of licence terms see PARA 695.
10 As to OFCOM see PARA 507.
11 'Licence' means a licence under the Broadcasting Act 1996 Pt I; and 'licensed' is to be construed accordingly: s 39(1).
12 Broadcasting Act 1996 s 7(1) (amended by the Communications Act 2003 Sch 15 para 79(1), (2)).
13 Broadcasting Act 1996 s 7(1)(a).
14 As to the meaning of 'frequency' see PARA 681 note 5; definition applied by the Broadcasting Act 1996 s 147(2).
15 Broadcasting Act 1996 s 7(1)(b).
16 As to the meaning of 'United Kingdom' see PARA 510 note 13.
17 Broadcasting Act 1996 s 7(1)(c) (amended by the Communications Act 2003 Sch 15 para 79(2)).
18 Broadcasting Act 1996 s 7(1)(d).
19 Broadcasting Act 1996 s 7(1)(e).
20 See further note 22.

21	Ie in pursuance of the Broadcasting Act 1996 s 13 (see note 22).
22	Broadcasting Act 1996 s 7(1)(f). Where a multiplex licence is granted in pursuance of a notice under s 7(1) which specified a percentage of multiplex revenue under s 7(1)(f), the licence must include conditions requiring the licence holder to pay to OFCOM (in addition to any fees required to be so paid by virtue of s 4(1)(b): see PARA 692) in respect of each accounting period of his falling within the period for which the licence is in force, an amount representing such percentage of the multiplex revenue for that accounting period (determined under s 14: see PARA 693) as was specified in the notice: s 13(1) (amended by the Communications Act 2003 Sch 15 para 85). The Secretary of State may by order provide that, in relation to any notice under the Broadcasting Act 1996 s 7(1) published while the order is in force, no percentage is to be specified under s 7(1)(f): s 13(2). Any such order is subject to annulment in pursuance of a resolution of either House of Parliament: s 13(3). In exercise of this power the Secretary of State made the Broadcasting (Percentage of Television Multiplex Revenue) Order 1996, SI 1996/2759, which ceased to have effect on 30 September 2002 (see art 3). As to the Secretary of State see PARA 507 note 32. As to the holder of the licence see note 66. Where the first complete accounting period of the licence holder falling within the period for which the licence is in force ('the licence period') does not begin at the same time as that period, or the last complete accounting period of his falling within the licence period does not end at the same time as that period, any reference in the Broadcasting Act 1996 s 13(1) to an accounting period of his includes a reference to such part of the accounting period preceding that first complete accounting period, or (as the case may be) following that last complete accounting period, as falls within the licence period; and other references to accounting periods in Pt I (ss 1–39) are to be construed accordingly: s 13(6).
	Unless an order under s 13(2) is in force, the consent of the Secretary of State is required for so much of the notice as relates to the matters specified in s 7(1)(f) (see head (6) in the text) (see s 7(2)(a)); and OFCOM may if it thinks fit (with that consent) specify under s 7(1)(f) different percentages in relation to different accounting periods falling within the period for which the licence would be in force, and a nil percentage in relation to any accounting period so falling (see s 7(2)(b) (amended by the Communications Act 2003 Sch 15 para 79(2))).
23	Broadcasting Act 1996 s 7(3) (amended by the Communications Act 2003 Sch 15 para 79(2)).
24	Broadcasting Act 1996 s 7(4)(a).
25	Broadcasting Act 1996 s 7(4)(b)(i).
26	Broadcasting Act 1996 s 7(4)(b)(ii).
27	Broadcasting Act 1996 s 7(4)(b)(iii).
28	'Digital programme service' means a service consisting in the provision by any person of television programmes (together with any ancillary services, as defined by the Broadcasting Act 1996 s 24(2)) with a view to their being broadcast in digital form so as to be available for reception by members of the public, whether by him or by some other person, but does not include: (1) a service provided under the authority of a licence under the Broadcasting Act 1990 Pt I (ss 3–85) to provide a television licensable content service (see PARA 717); (2) a qualifying service; (3) a teletext service; or (4) any service in the case of which the visual images to be broadcast do not consist wholly or mainly of images capable of being seen as moving pictures, except, in the case of a service falling within head (2) or head (3), to the extent that it is an ancillary service: s 1(4) (amended by the Communications Act 2003 Sch 15 para 74(3); and by SI 2006/2131). 'Broadcast' in the Broadcasting Act 1996 s 1 means broadcast otherwise than from a satellite: s 1(7) (substituted by the Communications Act 2003 Sch 15 para 74(5)). 'Available for reception by members of the public' means available for reception by members of the public (within the meaning of the Communications Act 2003 Pt 3 (ss 198–362) (see PARA 796)) in the United Kingdom or another EEA state, or in an area of the United Kingdom or of such a state: Broadcasting Act 1996 s 1(4A) (added by the Television Broadcasting Regulations 1998, SI 1998/3196, reg 2, Schedule para 8(1), (3); and substituted by the Communications Act 2003 Sch 15 para 74(4)). As to the meaning of 'television licensable content service' see PARA 716; definition applied by the Broadcasting Act 1996 s 39(1) (definition added by SI 2006/2131).
	'Ancillary service' means any service which is provided by the holder of a digital programme licence or by a relevant public service broadcaster and consists in the provision of: (a) assistance for disabled people in relation to some or all of the programmes included in a digital programme service or qualifying service provided by him; (b) a service (apart from advertising) that relates to the promotion or listing of programmes included in such a service or in a digital sound programme service so provided; or (c) any other service (apart from advertising) that is ancillary to one or more programmes so included, and relates directly to their contents: Broadcasting Act 1996 ss 24(2), 39(1) (s 24(2) amended by the Communications Act 2003 Sch 15 para 93(1), (3)). For this purpose, 'relevant public service broadcaster' means any of the

following: (i) a person licensed under the Broadcasting Act 1990 Pt I (ss 3–85) to provide a
Channel 3 service (see PARA 667 et seq); (ii) the Channel 4 Corporation (see PARA 627); (iii) a
person licensed under the Broadcasting Act 1990 Pt I to provide Channel 5 (see PARA 681); (iv)
the BBC (see PARAS 603–626); (v) the Welsh Authority (see PARA 644 et seq); (vi) the public
teletext provider (see PARA 686): Broadcasting Act 1996 s 24(3A) (added by the
Communications Act 2003 Sch 15 para 93(5)). As to the meaning of 'assistance for disabled
people' see PARA 644 note 12; definition applied by the Broadcasting Act 1996 s 24(3A) (as so
added).

'Qualifying service' means any of the following, so far as they are provided with a view to
their being broadcast in digital form: (A) a television broadcasting service included in Channel 3;
(B) Channel 4; (C) Channel 5; (D) S4C Digital; (E) a television programme service provided by
the Welsh Authority with the approval of the Secretary of State under the Communications
Act 2003 s 205 (see PARA 644); (F) the digital public teletext service: Broadcasting Act 1996
s 2(2) (substituted by the Communications Act 2003 Sch 15 para 75). As to the meaning of
'Channel 3' see PARA 667 (definition applied by the Broadcasting Act 1996 s 147(2)); as to the
meaning of 'Channel 4' see PARA 637 (definition applied by s 39(1)); as to the meaning of
'Channel 5' see PARA 681 (definition applied by s 39(1)); and as to the meaning of 'S4C Digital'
see PARA 644 note 7 (definition applied by s 39(1) (amended by the Communications Act 2003
Sch 15 para 100)). As to the meaning of 'digital public teletext service' see PARA 697 note 3.

The Secretary of State may, if having regard to developments in broadcasting technology he
considers it appropriate to do so, by order amend the definition of 'digital programme service' in
the Broadcasting Act 1996 s 1(4): s 1(5). No such order may be made unless a draft of the order
has been laid before and approved by a resolution of each House of Parliament: s 1(6). For such
an order see the Television Licensable Content Services Order 2006, SI 2006/2131.

29 As to the meaning of 'broadcast' see PARA 668 note 2; definition applied by the Broadcasting
    Act 1996 s 147(2).
30 Broadcasting Act 1996 s 7(4)(c).
31 Broadcasting Act 1996 s 7(4)(ca) (added by the Communications Act 2003 Sch 15
    para 79(3)(a)).
32 Broadcasting Act 1996 s 7(4)(d) (amended by the Communications Act 2003 Sch 15
    para 79(3)(b)).
33 Broadcasting Act 1996 s 7(4)(e). 'Digital additional service' means any service which: (1) is
    provided by a person with a view to its being broadcast in digital form (whether by him or some
    other person) so as to be available for reception by members of the public; (2) is so provided
    with a view either: (a) to the broadcasting being by means of a television multiplex service or by
    means of a general multiplex service; or (b) to the members of the public in question being or
    including members of the public in an EEA state other than the United Kingdom, or in an area
    of such a state; and (3) is not a Channel 3 service, Channel 4, Channel 5, a public television
    service of the Welsh Authority, the digital public teletext service, a digital programme service, a
    digital sound programme service, an ancillary service or a technical service: s 24(1) (amended by
    the Communications Act 2003 Sch 15 para 93(2)). As to the meaning of 'available for reception
    by members of the public' for this purpose see PARA 796; definition applied by the Broadcasting
    Act 1996 s 24(3A) (as added: see note 28). 'Public television service of the Welsh Authority'
    means: (i) S4C Digital; or (ii) any television programme service the provision of which by the
    Welsh Authority is authorised by or under the Communications Act 2003 s 205 (see PARA 644)
    and which is provided in digital form: Broadcasting Act 1996 s 24(3A) (as so added). 'Technical
    service' means a service which: (A) is provided for technical purposes connected with the
    encryption or decryption of one or more digital programme services, digital sound programme
    services or digital additional services; and (B) is of a description specified in an order made by
    the Secretary of State: s 24(3) (amended by the Communications Act 2003 Sch 15 para 93(4)).
    An order under this provision is subject to annulment in pursuance of a resolution of either
    House of Parliament: Broadcasting Act 1996 s 24(4). See the Broadcasting (Technical Services)
    Order 1997, SI 1997/1856.
34 'Acquisition' includes acquisition on hire or loan: Broadcasting Act 1996 ss 7(5), 8(3).
35 Broadcasting Act 1996 s 7(4)(f). As to the meaning of 'person' see PARA 510 note 1.
36 Broadcasting Act 1996 s 7(4)(g) (amended by the Communications Act 2003 Sch 15
    para 79(2)).
37 Broadcasting Act 1996 s 7(4)(h) (amended by the Communications Act 2003 Sch 15
    para 79(2)).
38 Broadcasting Act 1996 s 7(6) (amended by the Communications Act 2003 Sch 15 para 79(2)).
39 Broadcasting Act 1996 s 7(7) (amended by the Communications Act 2003 Sch 15 para 79(2)).
40 Ie a notice under the Broadcasting Act 1996 s 7(1): see s 7(8) (amended by the Communications
    Act 2003 Sch 15 para 79(2)).

41 Broadcasting Act 1996 s 7(8)(a)(i).
42 Broadcasting Act 1996 s 7(8)(a)(ii).
43 Broadcasting Act 1996 s 7(8)(a)(iii) (amended by the Communications Act 2003 Sch 15 para 79(2)).
44 Broadcasting Act 1996 s 7(8)(b)(i).
45 Broadcasting Act 1996 s 7(8)(b)(ii).
46 See note 40.
47 Broadcasting Act 1996 s 8(1) (amended by the Communications Act 2003 Sch 15 para 80(1), (2)).
48 Broadcasting Act 1996 s 8(2)(a).
49 Broadcasting Act 1996 s 8(2)(b).
50 Broadcasting Act 1996 s 8(2)(c).
51 Broadcasting Act 1996 s 8(2)(d).
52 As to the meaning of 'acquisition' see note 34.
53 Broadcasting Act 1996 s 8(2)(e).
54 Broadcasting Act 1996 s 8(2)(f) (amended by the Communications Act 2003 Sch 15 para 80(3)).
55 Broadcasting Act 1996 s 8(4)(a) (amended by the Communications Act 2003 Sch 15 para 80(2)).
56 Broadcasting Act 1996 s 8(4)(b).
57 See note 40.
58 Broadcasting Act 1996 s 9(1) (amended by the Communications Act 2003 Sch 15 para 81).
59 Broadcasting Act 1996 s 9(2) (amended by the Communications Act 2003 Sch 15 para 81). In relation to any application made in pursuance of such a notice:
   (1) references in the Broadcasting Act 1996 s 7(4) (see the text and notes 24–37) to the proposed service have effect as references to each of the proposed services (s 9(3)(a));
   (2) the reference in s 8(1) (see the text and note 47) to the multiplex licence has effect as a reference to all the licences concerned (s 9(3)(b));
   (3) in s 8(2) (see the text and notes 48–54), the reference in s 8(2)(d) (see the text and note 51) to the proposed service has effect as a reference to all the proposed services considered together; and other references to the proposed service have effect as references either to each of the proposed services or to all of them considered together, as OFCOM considers appropriate (s 9(3)(c) (amended by the Communications Act 2003 Sch 15 para 81)).
   Nothing in the Broadcasting Act 1996 s 9 applies in relation to the renewal of a multiplex licence: s 9(4).
60 Broadcasting Act 1996 s 10(1) (amended by the Communications Act 2003 Sch 15 para 82(1), (2)). Where OFCOM determines that any condition imposed by it in relation to a multiplex licence in pursuance of the Broadcasting Act 1996 s 10(1) has not been satisfied, s 8 (see the text and notes 46–56) has effect as if the person to whom the licence was awarded had not made an application for it: s 10(2) (amended by the Communications Act 2003 Sch 15 para 82(2)). However, the Broadcasting Act 1996 s 8 does not so have effect if OFCOM decides that it would be desirable to publish a fresh notice under s 7(1) (see the text and notes 10–22) in respect of the grant of the licence: s 10(3) (amended by the Communications Act 2003 Sch 15 para 82(2)).
61 Broadcasting Act 1996 s 10(1)(a) (amended by the Communications Act 2003 Sch 15 para 82(3)).
62 Broadcasting Act 1996 s 10(1)(b).
63 Ie by virtue of the Broadcasting Act 1996 s 13(1) (see note 22).
64 Broadcasting Act 1996 s 13(4)(a), (b) (amended by the Communications Act 2003 Sch 15 para 85).
65 Broadcasting Act 1996 s 13(5)(a), (b) (amended by the Communications Act 2003 Sch 15 para 85).
66 Broadcasting Act 1996 s 3(3) (amended by the Communications Act 2003 Sch 15 para 76(2)). Nothing in the Broadcasting Act 1996 Pt I may be construed as affecting the operation of s 3(3) or of s 5(1), (2)(b) or (c) (see PARA 828): s 3(3) (as so amended).
   Where the person who is for the time being the holder of any licence ('the present licence holder') is not the person to whom the licence was originally granted, any reference (however expressed) in Pt I to the holder of the licence is to be construed, in relation to any time falling before the date when the present licence holder became the holder of it, as including a reference to a person who was previously the holder of the licence: s 39(2). The holding by any person of a licence to provide any service does not relieve him of any failure to hold a licence under the Wireless Telegraphy Act 2006 s 8 (see PARA 514) or any obligation to comply with requirements imposed by or under the Communications Act 2003 Pt 2 Ch 1 (ss 32–151) (electronic

communications networks and electronic communications services: see TELECOMMUNICATIONS vol 97 (2010) PARA 92 et seq): Broadcasting Act 1996 s 3(8) (substituted by the Communications Act 2003 Sch 15 para 76(4); and amended by the Wireless Telegraphy Act 2006 s 123, Sch 7 para 17).

67　Broadcasting Act 1996 s 3(6) (amended by the Communications Act 2003 Sch 15 para 76(3)).
68　Broadcasting Act 1996 s 3(7) (amended by the Communications Act 2003 Sch 15 para 76(3)).

691.　Failure to begin providing licensed service and financial penalties on revocation of licence. Where at any time after a multiplex licence[1] has been granted to any person[2] but before the licence has come into force that person indicates to OFCOM[3] that he does not intend to provide the service in question[4], or OFCOM for any other reason has reasonable grounds for believing that that person will not provide that service once the licence has come into force[5], OFCOM must serve on the person to whom the licence has been granted a notice revoking the licence as from the time the notice is served on him[6].

Where OFCOM revokes a multiplex licence, it must serve on the licence holder a notice requiring him to pay to it, within a specified period, a specified financial penalty[7].

1　As to the meaning of 'multiplex licence' see PARA 690.
2　As to the meaning of 'person' see PARA 510 note 1.
3　As to OFCOM see PARA 507.
4　See the Broadcasting Act 1996 s 11(1)(a) (s 11(1) amended by the Communications Act 2003 s 360(3), Sch 15 para 83).
5　See the Broadcasting Act 1996 s 11(1)(b) (as amended: see note 4).
6　See the Broadcasting Act 1996 s 11(3)(a) (amended by the Communications Act 2003 Sch 15 para 83). The Broadcasting Act 1996 s 8 (see PARA 690) has effect as if the person had not made an application for the licence: s 11(3)(b). However, s 8 does not so have effect if OFCOM decides that it would be desirable to publish a fresh notice under s 7(1) (see PARA 690) in respect of the grant of the licence: s 11(4) (amended by the Communications Act 2003 Sch 15 para 83).
　　The Broadcasting Act 1996 s 11(3) does not apply in the case of any person by virtue of s 11(1)(b) (see the text and note 5) unless OFCOM has served on him a notice stating its grounds for believing that he will not provide the service in question once his licence has come into force; and it must not serve such a notice on him unless it has given him a reasonable opportunity of making representations to it about the matters complained of: s 11(2) (amended by the Communications Act 2003 Sch 15 para 83).
7　Broadcasting Act 1996 s 11(5) (amended by the Communications Act 2003 ss 345, 406(7), Sch 13 paras 10, 11(1), Sch 15 para 83, Sch 19). The maximum amount which a person may be required to pay by way of a penalty under the Broadcasting Act 1996 s 11(5) is the maximum penalty given by s 11(5B), (5C): s 11(5A) (s 11(5A)–(5D) added by the Communications Act 2003 Sch 13 para 11(2)).
　　In a case where the licence is revoked under the Broadcasting Act 1996 s 11 or the penalty is imposed before the end of the first complete accounting period of the licence holder to fall within the period for which the licence is in force, the maximum penalty is whichever is the greater of: (1) £500,000; and (2) 7% of the amount which OFCOM estimates would have been the multiplex revenue for the first complete accounting period of the licence holder falling within the period for which the licence would have been in force: s 11(5B) (as so added).
　　In any other case, the maximum penalty is whichever is the greater of: (a) £500,000; and (b) 7% of the multiplex revenue for the last complete accounting period of the licence holder falling within the period for which the licence is in force: s 11(5C) (as so added).
　　Section 14 applies for estimating or determining multiplex revenue for the purposes of s 11(5B) or s 11(5C): s 11(5D) (as so added). See PARA 693. As to accounting periods see PARA 690 note 22.
　　Any financial penalty payable by any body by virtue of s 11(5), in addition to being recoverable from that body as provided by s 38(4) (repealed), is recoverable by OFCOM as a debt due to it from any person who controls that body: s 11(7) (amended by the Communications Act 2003 Sch 15 para 83). As to the meaning of 'body' see PARA 821 note 10; definition applied by the Broadcasting Act 1996 s 147(2). As to the meaning of 'control' see PARA 821 note 11; definition applied by s 147(2).
　　The Secretary of State may by order amend s 11(5B)(a), (5C)(a) by substituting a different sum for the sum for the time being specified there: see s 36(1), (2)(a) (s 36(2), (3) substituted by

the Communications Act 2003 Sch 13 para 16). No order is to be made under the Broadcasting Act 1996 s 36(1) unless a draft of the order has been laid before Parliament and approved by a resolution of each House: s 36(3) (as so substituted). At the date at which this volume states the law no such order had been made. As to the Secretary of State see PARA 507 note 32.

692. Conditions attached to multiplex licence. Multiplex licences[1] may be granted for the provision of such a service as is specified in the licence or for the provision of a service of such a description as is so specified[2]. They may include such conditions as appear to OFCOM[3] to be appropriate having regard to any duties which are or may be imposed[4] on it or on the licence holder[5].

A multiplex licence must include such conditions as appear to OFCOM to be appropriate[6] for securing:

(1) that the licensed[7] service is established by the licence holder[8] in accordance with the timetable and other proposals indicated in the technical plan[9];

(2) the implementation of any proposals submitted[10] by the licence holder[11];

(3) that all digital programme services[12] broadcast[13] under the licence are provided by the holder of a licence[14], by the BBC or by an EEA broadcaster[15];

(4) that all digital additional services[16] broadcast under the licence are provided by the holder of a licence[17], by the BBC or by an EEA broadcaster[18];

(5) that the only digital sound programme services broadcast under the licence are services provided by the holder of a national digital sound programme licence[19] or by the BBC[20];

(6) that in the terms on which the licence holder contracts, or offers to contract, for the broadcasting of digital programme services, digital sound programme services or digital additional services, he does not show undue discrimination either against or in favour of a particular person providing such a service or a class of such persons[21];

(7) that the licence holder does not, in any agreement with a person providing a digital programme service, a digital sound programme service or digital additional services which entitles that person to use a specified amount of digital capacity on the frequency[22] or frequencies to which the licence relates, restrict that person's freedom to make arrangements with some other person as to the use of any of that digital capacity (except to the extent that the restriction is reasonably required for the purpose of ensuring the technical quality of the broadcasts or for the purpose of securing compliance with any other condition of the licence)[23];

(8) that the signals carrying the multiplex service[24] attain high standards in terms of technical quality and reliability throughout so much of the area for which the service is provided as is for the time being reasonably practicable[25]; and

(9) that, while the licence is in force, at least the required percentage[26] of the digital capacity on the frequency or frequencies on which the service is broadcast is used, or left available to be used, for the broadcasting of specified[27] services[28].

Further conditions may be included in the licence requiring the licence holder to provide OFCOM, in such manner and at such times as it may reasonably require, with such information as it may require for the purposes of exercising the functions assigned to it by or under the Broadcasting Act 1990, the Broadcasting Act 1996 or the Communications Act 2003[29]. A licence may include conditions requiring the licence holder to comply with any direction given by OFCOM as to such matters as are specified in the licence or are of a description so specified[30], or (to the extent that OFCOM consents to his doing or not doing them) not to do or not do such things as are specified in the licence or are of a description so specified[31]. The licence may include conditions requiring the payment by the licence holder to OFCOM of a fee in accordance with such tariff as may from time to time be fixed by OFCOM[32]. Such tariff, which must be published by OFCOM in some manner that it considers appropriate, may specify different fees in relation to different cases or circumstances[33]. Further conditions may also be included in a multiplex service licence providing for such incidental and supplemental matters as appear to be appropriate to OFCOM[34].

OFCOM may vary a licence by a notice[35] served on the licence holder if: (a) in the case of a variation of the period for which the licence is to continue in force, the licence holder consents[36]; or (b) in the case of any other variation, the licence holder has been given a reasonable opportunity of making representations to OFCOM about the variation[37].

Where the licence holder applies to OFCOM for the variation of any condition imposed in pursuance of head (2) above and relating to the characteristics of any of the digital programme services or digital sound programme services to be broadcast under the licence, OFCOM must vary the condition accordingly unless it appears to it that, if the application were granted, the capacity of so much of what is broadcast under the licence as consists of digital programme services, or of such services together with digital sound programme services, to appeal to a variety of tastes and interests would be unacceptably diminished[38].

1   As to the meaning of 'multiplex licence' see PARA 690.
2   Broadcasting Act 1996 s 3(2).
3   As to OFCOM see PARA 507.
4   Ie by or under the Broadcasting Act 1996, the Broadcasting Act 1990 or the Communications Act 2003.
5   Broadcasting Act 1996 s 4(1)(a) (amended by the Communications Act 2003 s 360(3), Sch 15 para 77(1)–(3)). Nothing in the Broadcasting Act 1996 Pt I (ss 1–39) which authorises or requires the inclusion in a licence of conditions relating to any particular matter or having effect for any particular purpose is to be taken as derogating from the generality of s 4(1): s 4(6).
6   Broadcasting Act 1996 s 12(1) (amended by the Communications Act 2003 s 360(3), Sch 15 para 84). As to OFCOM see PARA 507.
7   As to the meaning of 'licensed' see PARA 690 note 11. As to the meaning of 'multiplex service' see PARA 690 note 1.
8   As to the holder of the licence see PARA 690 note 66.
9   Broadcasting Act 1996 s 12(1)(a). See also note 11. The technical plan referred to is that submitted under s 7(4)(b) (see PARA 690).
10 Ie under the Broadcasting Act 1996 s 7(4)(c), (d), (e) or (f): see PARA 690.
11 Broadcasting Act 1996 s 12(1)(b). Any conditions imposed in pursuance of s 12(1)(a) or (b) may be varied by OFCOM with the consent of the licence holder (and s 3(4)(b) (see head (b) in the text) accordingly does not apply to any such variation): s 12(2) (amended by the Communications Act 2003 Sch 15 para 84).
12 As to the meaning of 'digital programme service' see PARA 690 note 28.
13 As to the meaning of 'broadcast' see PARA 668 note 2; definition applied by the Broadcasting Act 1996 s 147(2).
14 Ie under the Broadcasting Act 1996 s 18: see PARA 698.
15 Broadcasting Act 1996 s 12(1)(c) (amended by the Communications Act 2003 s 242(1)(a); and by SI 1998/3196). As to the meaning of 'BBC' see PARA 603 note 1; and as to the BBC see PARAS 603–626. In the Broadcasting Act 1996 s 12(1)(c), (d) (see head (4) in the text), 'EEA broadcaster' means a person who for the purposes of European Parliament and Council

Directive (EC) 89/552 (OJ L298, 17.10.89, p 23) (repealed: now European Parliament and Council Directive (EU) 2010/13 (OJ L95, 15.4.2010, p 1)) is under the jurisdiction of an EEA state other than the United Kingdom: Broadcasting Act 1996 s 12(3A) (added by SI 1998/3196). As to the meaning of 'United Kingdom' see PARA 510 note 13.

16 As to the meaning of 'digital additional service' see PARA 690 note 33.

17 Ie under the Broadcasting Act 1996 s 25: see PARA 711.

18 Broadcasting Act 1996 s 12(1)(d) (amended by the Communications Act 2003 s 242(1)(b); and by SI 1998/3196). See also note 12.

19 Ie within the meaning of the Broadcasting Act 1996 s 60: see PARA 768.

20 Broadcasting Act 1996 s 12(1)(da) (added by the Communications Act 2003 s 242(1)(c)).

21 Broadcasting Act 1996 s 12(1)(e) (amended by the Communications Act 2003 s 242(1)(d)). As to the meaning of 'person' see PARA 510 note 1.

22 As to the meaning of 'frequency' see PARA 681 note 5; definition applied by the Broadcasting Act 1996 s 147(2).

23 Broadcasting Act 1996 s 12(1)(f) (amended by the Communications Act 2003 s 242(1)(e)).

24 As to the meaning of 'multiplex service' see PARA 690 note 1.

25 Broadcasting Act 1996 s 12(1)(g).

26 The reference to the required percentage is a reference to such percentage equal to or more than 90% as OFCOM considers appropriate and specifies in the condition: Broadcasting Act 1996 s 12(4A) (added by the Communications Act 2003 s 242(5)). The Secretary of State may by order amend the Broadcasting Act 1996 s 12(4A) by substituting for the percentage for the time being specified there a different percentage specified in the order: s 12(5) (amended by the Communications Act 2003 s 242(6)). No order under the Broadcasting Act 1996 s 12(5) may be made unless a draft of the order has been laid before and approved by a resolution of each House of Parliament: s 12(6). At the date at which this volume states the law, no such order had been made. As to the Secretary of State see PARA 507 note 32.

27 Ie the services falling within the Broadcasting Act 1996 s 12(1A). Such services are: (1) qualifying services; (2) digital programme services licensed under the Broadcasting Act 1996 Pt I (ss 1–39) or provided by the BBC; (3) digital sound programme services provided by the BBC; (4) programme-related services; and (5) relevant technical services: s 12(1A) (added by the Communications Act 2003 s 242(2)). For these purposes, 'qualifying service' does not include the digital public teletext service: Broadcasting Act 1996 s 12(4)(a) (amended by the Communications Act 2003 s 242(4)(a), (b)). 'Programme-related service' means any digital additional service consisting in the provision of services (apart from advertising) which: (a) are ancillary to the programmes included in one or more television programme services, or in one or more digital sound programme services provided by the BBC, and are directly related to the contents of those programmes (Broadcasting Act 1996 s 12(4)(b)(i) (amended by the Communications Act 2003 s 242(4)(c))); or (b) relate to the promotion or listing of such programmes (Broadcasting Act 1996 s 12(4)(b)(ii)). As to the meaning of 'programme' see PARA 667 note 7; definition applied by s 147(2). 'Relevant technical service' means any technical service which relates to one or more services falling within s 12(1A) which are comprised in the multiplex in question: s 12(4)(c) (amended by the Communications Act 2003 s 242(4)(d)). As to the meaning of 'technical service' see PARA 690 note 33. As to the meaning of 'digital public teletext service' see PARA 697 note 3. As to the meaning of 'television programme service' see PARA 790 note 5; definition applied by the Broadcasting Act 1990 s 71(1) (definition substituted by the Communications Act 2003 s 360(3), Sch 15 Pt 1 para 31); and the Broadcasting Act 1996 s 147(2).

28 Broadcasting Act 1996 s 12(1)(h) (substituted by the Communications Act 2003 s 242(1)(f)).

29 Broadcasting Act 1996 s 4(1)(c) (amended by the Communications Act 2003 Sch 15 para 77(2), (3)). Where the holder of any licence is required by virtue of any condition imposed under the Broadcasting Act 1996 Pt I to provide OFCOM with any information, and in purported compliance with that condition provides it with information which is false in a material particular, he is to be taken for the purposes of s 17 (see PARA 696), s 23 (see PARA 700), s 27 (see PARA 713) and the Broadcasting Act 1990 s 42 (see PARA 866) to have failed to comply with that condition: Broadcasting Act 1996 s 4(5) (amended by the Communications Act 2003 Sch 15 para 77(2)).

30 Broadcasting Act 1996 s 4(2)(a) (amended by the Communications Act 2003 Sch 15 para 77(2)).

31 Broadcasting Act 1996 s 4(2)(b) (amended by the Communications Act 2003 Sch 15 para 77(2)).

32 Broadcasting Act 1996 s 4(1)(b) (amended by the Communications Act 2003 Sch 15 para 77(2)). Broadcasting Act 1996 s 4(3) (amended by the Communications Act 2003 s 406(7), Sch 15 para 77(2), (4), Sch 19).

33 Broadcasting Act 1996 s 4(4) (amended by the Communications Act 2003 Sch 15 para 77(2)).

34 Broadcasting Act 1996 s 4(1)(d) (amended by the Communications Act 2003 Sch 15 para 77(2)).

35 As to the service of notices see TELECOMMUNICATIONS vol 97 (2010) PARAS 49–50.

36 Broadcasting Act 1996 s 3(4)(a). Section 3(4)(a) does not affect the operation of s 17(1)(b) (see PARA 696): see s 3(5). Section 3(4) does not authorise the variation of any conditions included in a licence in pursuance of s 13(1) (see PARA 690 note 22): see s 3(5).

37 Broadcasting Act 1996 s 3(4)(b) (amended by the Communications Act 2003 Sch 15 para 76(3)). See also note 33.

38 Broadcasting Act 1996 s 12(3) (amended by the Communications Act 2003 s 242(2), Sch 15 para 84).

693. Multiplex revenue. The multiplex revenue[1] for each accounting period[2] of the person who is the multiplex provider[3] in relation to any television multiplex service or any general multiplex service consists of:

(1)   all payments received or to be received by him or any person connected[4] with him from a person other than a programme provider[5] or an additional services provider[6]:

       (a)   in consideration of the inclusion in that period, in any digital programme service or digital additional service broadcast by means of the relevant multiplex, of advertisements or other programmes[7]; or

       (b)   in respect of charges made in that period for the reception of programmes included in any such digital programme service or digital additional service[8];

(2)   all payments received or to be received by him or any person connected with him in respect of the broadcasting by means of the multiplex service of any service which is a qualifying service[9] or which (without being a qualifying service) is provided by the BBC[10];

(3)   all payments received or to be received by any programme provider or any person connected with him from a person other than the multiplex provider, an additional services provider or another programme provider[11]:

       (a)   in consideration of the inclusion in that period, in any digital programme service provided by him for broadcasting by means of the relevant multiplex, of advertisements or other programmes[12]; or

       (b)   in respect of charges made in that period for the reception of programmes included in any such digital programme service[13]; and

(4)   all payments received or to be received by any additional services provider or any person connected with him from a person other than the multiplex provider, a programme provider or another additional services provider[14]:

       (a)   in consideration of the inclusion in that period, in any digital additional service provided by him for broadcasting by means of the multiplex service, of advertisements or other programmes[15]; or

       (b)   in respect of charges made in that period for the reception of programmes included in any such digital additional service[16].

If, in connection with the inclusion of any advertisements or other programmes whose inclusion is paid for by payments falling within head (1)(a) above, any payments are made to the multiplex provider or any connected person to meet any payments payable by the multiplex provider[17], those payments are to be regarded as made in consideration of the inclusion of the programmes in question[18].

In the case of an advertisement included as mentioned in head (1)(a), (3)(a) or (4)(a) above under arrangements made between: (i) the multiplex provider, a programme provider or an additional services provider or any person connected with any of them; and (ii) a person acting as an advertising agent[19], the amount of any receipt by the multiplex provider, programme provider or additional services provider or any connected person that represents a payment by the advertiser from which the advertising agent has deducted any amount by way of commission is generally the amount of the payment by the advertiser after the deduction of the commission[20]. However, if the amount deducted by way of commission exceeds 15 per cent of the payment by the advertiser, the amount of the receipt in question is taken to be the amount of the payment less 15 per cent[21].

If, in any accounting period of the multiplex provider, a programme provider or an additional services provider or a person connected with any of them derives, in relation to any programme to be included in the relevant service[22], any financial benefit (whether direct or indirect) from payments made by any person other than the multiplex provider, by way of sponsorship, for the purpose of defraying or contributing towards costs incurred or to be incurred in connection with that programme, the relevant payments[23] are to be taken to include the amount of the financial benefit so derived by the multiplex provider or the connected person, as the case may be[24].

Where, in any accounting period of the multiplex provider:

(A)   the multiplex provider provides a digital programme service or digital additional service for broadcasting by means of the multiplex service[25];

(B)   the multiplex provider is engaged in any activity which, if engaged in by another person, would result in payments falling within head (1) above being made to the multiplex provider[26];

(C)   a programme provider is engaged in any activity which, if engaged in by another person, would result in payments falling within head (3) above being made to the programme provider[27]; or

(D)   an additional services provider is engaged in any activity which, if engaged in by another person, would result in payments falling within head (4) above being made to the additional services provider[28],

OFCOM[29] may, if it considers that the amount which would (apart from this provision) be the multiplex revenue for that accounting period is less than it would have been if the digital programme service or digital additional service had been provided, or the activity engaged in, by another person at arm's length, treat the multiplex revenue as increased by the amount of the difference[30].

Where, in any accounting period of the multiplex provider, the multiplex provider or a programme provider or additional services provider receives payments falling within head (1), (2), (3) or (4) above from a person connected with him and it appears to OFCOM that the amount which (apart from this provision) would be the multiplex revenue for that accounting period is less than it would have been if the arrangements between him and the connected person were such as might be expected between parties at arm's length, OFCOM may treat the multiplex revenue as increased by the amount of the difference[31].

1   Ie for the purposes of the Broadcasting Act 1996 Pt I (ss 1–39) (see PARA 690): s 14(1) (amended by the Communications Act 2003 s 360(3), Sch 15 para 86(1), (2)(a)).

2   As to accounting periods see PARA 690 note 22.

3   'Multiplex provider': (1) in relation to a television multiplex service for which a person holds a licence under the Broadcasting Act 1996 Pt I, means the licence holder; and (2) in relation to a television multiplex service which is not licensed under Pt I or a general multiplex service, means the person who provides that service: s 14(9) (definition added by the Communications Act 2003 Sch 15 para 86(4)(c)). As to the meaning of 'multiplex service' see PARA 690 note 1. As to the holder of the licence see PARA 690 note 66.

4   As to the meaning of 'connected' see PARA 674 note 13; definition applied by the Broadcasting Act 1996 s 147(2).

5   For these purposes, 'programme provider', in relation to a television multiplex service or a general multiplex service, means any person who provides a digital programme service for broadcasting by means of that multiplex service: Broadcasting Act 1996 s 14(9) (amended by the Communications Act 2003 Sch 15 para 86(4)). As to the meaning of 'digital programme service' see PARA 690 note 28. As to the meaning of 'broadcast' see PARA 668 note 2; definition applied by the Broadcasting Act 1996 s 147(2).

6   Broadcasting Act 1996 s 14(1)(a) (amended by the Communications Act 2003 Sch 15 para 86(2)(a), (b)). For these purposes, 'additional services provider', in relation to a television multiplex service or a general multiplex service, means any person who provides any digital additional service for broadcasting by means of that multiplex service: Broadcasting Act 1996 s 14(9) (amended by the Communications Act 2003 Sch 15 para 86(4)). As to the meaning of 'digital additional service' see PARA 690 note 33. As to the meaning of 'person' see PARA 510 note 1.

7   Broadcasting Act 1996 s 14(1)(a)(i) (amended by the Communications Act 2003 Sch 15 para 86(2)(c)). As to the meaning of 'programme' see PARA 667 note 7; definition applied by the Broadcasting Act 1996 s 147(2).

8   Broadcasting Act 1996 s 14(1)(a)(ii).

9   As to the meaning of 'qualifying service' see PARA 690 note 28.

10   Broadcasting Act 1996 s 14(1)(b) (amended by the Communications Act 2003 Sch 15 para 86(2)(d)).

11   Broadcasting Act 1996 s 14(1)(c) (amended by the Communications Act 2003 Sch 15 para 86(2)(e)).

12   Broadcasting Act 1996 s 14(1)(c)(i) (amended by the Communications Act 2003 Sch 15 para 86(2)(e)).

13   Broadcasting Act 1996 s 14(1)(c)(ii).

14   Broadcasting Act 1996 s 14(1)(d) (amended by the Communications Act 2003 Sch 15 para 86(2)(e)).

15   Broadcasting Act 1996 s 14(1)(d)(i) (amended by the Communications Act 2003 Sch 15 para 86(2)(e)).

16   Broadcasting Act 1996 s 14(1)(d)(ii).

17   Ie by virtue of the Broadcasting Act 1996 s 13(1) (see PARA 690).

18   Broadcasting Act 1996 s 14(2) (amended by the Communications Act 2003 Sch 15 para 86(3)(a)).

19   As to the meaning of 'advertising agent' see PARA 674 note 16; definition applied by the Broadcasting Act 1996 s 147(2).

20   Broadcasting Act 1996 s 14(3) (amended by the Communications Act 2003 Sch 15 para 86(3)(a)).

21   Broadcasting Act 1996 s 14(4).

22   For these purposes, 'the relevant service' means in relation to a programme provider or a person connected with him, any digital programme service provided as mentioned in the Broadcasting Act 1996 s 14(1)(c)(i) (see head (3)(a) in the text), and in relation to an additional services provider or a person connected with him, any digital additional service provided as mentioned in s 14(1)(d)(i) (see head (4)(a) in the text): s 14(6)(a).

23   For these purposes, 'relevant payments' means in relation to a programme provider, the payments referred to in the Broadcasting Act 1996 s 14(1)(c) (see head (3) in the text), and in relation to an additional services provider, the payments referred to in s 14(1)(d) (see head (4) in the text): s 14(6)(b).

24   Broadcasting Act 1996 s 14(5) (amended by the Communications Act 2003 Sch 15 para 86(3)(a)).

25   Broadcasting Act 1996 s 14(7)(a) (amended by the Communications Act 2003 Sch 15 para 86(3)(a)).

26   Broadcasting Act 1996 s 14(7)(b) (amended by the Communications Act 2003 Sch 15 para 86(3)(a)).

27   Broadcasting Act 1996 s 14(7)(c).

28 Broadcasting Act 1996 s 14(7)(d).

29 As to OFCOM see PARA 507.

30 Broadcasting Act 1996 s 14(7) (amended by the Communications Act 2003 Sch 15 para 86(3)(b)). See also note 31.

31 Broadcasting Act 1996 s 14(8) (amended by the Communications Act 2003 Sch 15 para 86(3)(a), (b)). In a case falling within the Broadcasting Act 1996 s 14(7) or (8), OFCOM may treat the share of multiplex revenue attributable to any person for the accounting period of the multiplex provider as increased by such amount as it considers appropriate to take account of the circumstances mentioned in that provision: s 15(3) (amended by the Communications Act 2003 Sch 15 para 87(1), (4)).

694.   Computation of multiplex revenue.   It is the duty of OFCOM[1] to draw up, and from time to time review, a statement setting out the principles to be followed in ascertaining[2]:

(1)   the multiplex revenue[3] in relation to a licence holder[4] for any accounting period[5]; and

(2)   the share of multiplex revenue attributable to a person[6] in relation to any multiplex service[7] for the purposes of any provision of Part I of the Broadcasting Act 1996[8] for any accounting period of the holder of the multiplex licence[9], or for any year[10].

Such a statement may set out different principles for persons holding different kinds of licences[11]. Before drawing up or revising such a statement, OFCOM must consult the Secretary of State[12] and the Treasury[13]. OFCOM must publish the statement drawn up, and every revision of that statement[14], and must transmit a copy of that statement, and every revision of it, to the Secretary of State[15]. The Secretary of State must lay copies of the statement and of every such revision before each House of Parliament[16].

For the purposes of any provision of the Part I of the Broadcasting Act 1996:

(a)   the amount of the multiplex revenue in relation to any holder of a multiplex licence for any accounting period of his, or (as the case may be) for any year, or the amount of any payment to be made to OFCOM by any person in respect of any such revenue, or of an instalment of any such payment[17]; and

(b)   the share of multiplex revenue attributable to any person in relation to a multiplex service for any accounting period or (as the case may be) for any year,

is, in the event of a disagreement between OFCOM and that person, the amount determined by OFCOM[18]. No such determination of OFCOM may be called in question in any court of law, or be the subject of any arbitration; but this does not prevent the bringing of proceedings for judicial review[19].

1   As to OFCOM see PARA 507.

2   Broadcasting Act 1996 s 37, Sch 1 para 1 (Sch 1 para 1 amended by the Communications Act 2003 s 360(3), Sch 15 para 142(1), (2)).

3   As to multiplex revenue see PARA 693.

4   Ie for the purposes of the Broadcasting Act 1996 s 14 (see PARA 693). As to the holder of the licence see PARA 690 note 66.

5   Broadcasting Act 1996 Sch 1 para 1(1)(a). As to accounting periods see PARA 690 note 22.

6   As to the meaning of 'person' see PARA 510 note 1.

7   As to the meaning of 'multiplex service' see PARA 690 note 1.

8   Ie the Broadcasting Act 1996 Pt I (ss 1–39).

9   As to the meaning of 'multiplex licence' see PARA 690.

10 Broadcasting Act 1996 Sch 1 para 1(1)(b).

11 Broadcasting Act 1996 Sch 1 para 1(2).

12 As to the Secretary of State see PARA 507 note 32.

13 Broadcasting Act 1996 Sch 1 para 1(3) (amended by the Communications Act 2003 Sch 15 para 142(2)). As to the Treasury see CONSTITUTIONAL LAW AND HUMAN RIGHTS vol 8(2) (Reissue) PARAS 512–517.

14 Broadcasting Act 1996 Sch 1 para 1(4)(a) (amended by the Communications Act 2003 Sch 15 para 142(2)).

15 Broadcasting Act 1996 Sch 1 para 1(4)(b).

16 Broadcasting Act 1996 Sch 1 para 1(4).

17 See the Broadcasting Act 1996 Sch 1 para 2(1) (Sch 1 para 2 amended by the Communications Act 2003 Sch 15 para 142(2)).

18 See the Broadcasting Act 1996 Sch 1 para 2(2) (as amended: see note 17).

19 Broadcasting Act 1996 Sch 1 para 2(3) (as amended: see note 17). As to judicial review see JUDICIAL REVIEW vol 61 (2010) PARA 601 et seq.

695. Duration and renewal of multiplex licences. A multiplex licence[1] continues in force[2] for a period of 12 years[3]. A multiplex licence granted within six years of 1 October 1996[4] may be renewed on one occasion in accordance with these provisions for a period of 12 years beginning with the date on which it would otherwise expire[5]. Such an application for the renewal of a multiplex licence may be made by the licence holder[6] not earlier than four years before the date on which it would otherwise cease to be in force and not later than the day falling three months before the relevant date[7]. At any time before determining the application, OFCOM may: (1) require the applicant to furnish: (a) a technical plan which supplements that submitted[8] by the licence holder[9]; and (b) proposals which supplement any proposals submitted[10] by the licence holder[11]; and (2) notify the applicant of requirements which must be met by that supplementary technical plan or those supplementary proposals and relate to specified matters[12]. The consent of the Secretary of State[13] is required for any exercise by OFCOM of these powers and for any decision by OFCOM not to exercise them; and in deciding whether to give his consent the Secretary of State must have regard to any report made to him[14] and to any representations received by him[15] on consultation[16]. Where any such application is made, OFCOM may postpone consideration of it for as long as it thinks appropriate[17].

Where an application for the renewal of a multiplex licence has been duly made to OFCOM, it may refuse the application only if:

(i)   it appears to it that the applicant has failed to comply with any of the conditions included in his licence[18];

(ii)   any supplementary technical plan or supplementary proposals submitted fail to meet the requirements notified to the applicant[19]; or

(iii) it is not satisfied that the applicant would, if his licence were renewed, provide a service which complied with the conditions to be included in the licence as renewed[20].

On the grant of any application for renewal, OFCOM may with the consent of the Secretary of State, and must if so required by him: (A) specify a percentage different from that specified[21] as the percentage of multiplex revenue for each accounting period[22] of his that will be payable by the applicant[23] during the period for which the licence is to be renewed; or (B) specify such a percentage where none was specified[24].

Where OFCOM has granted a person's[25] application for renewal, it must formally renew his licence from the date on which it would otherwise expire[26]. Where a multiplex licence has been so renewed, the licence as renewed must include such further conditions as appear to OFCOM to be appropriate for securing the implementation of any supplementary technical plan and supplementary proposals submitted[27].

Nothing in these provisions[28] prevents the holder of a multiplex licence from applying for a new licence[29] on one or more occasions[30].

1   As to the meaning of 'multiplex licence' see PARA 690.
2   Ie subject to the provisions of the Broadcasting Act 1996 Pt I (ss 1–39) and to the Broadcasting Act 1990 s 42 (see PARA 866) as applied by the Broadcasting Act 1996 s 17(6) (see PARA 696): see s 16(1).
3   Broadcasting Act 1996 s 16(1).
4   Ie the date on which the Broadcasting Act 1996 s 16 was brought into force: see the Broadcasting Act 1996 (Commencement No 1 and Transitional Provisions) Order 1996, SI 1996/2120, art 4, Sch 1.
5   Broadcasting Act 1996 s 16(2). As to OFCOM see PARA 507.
6   As to the holder of the licence see PARA 690 note 66.
7   Broadcasting Act 1996 s 16(3) (amended by the Communications Act 2003 s 360(3), Sch 15 para 88(1), (3)). For these purposes, 'the relevant date', in relation to a multiplex licence, means the date which OFCOM determines to be that by which it would need to publish a notice under the Broadcasting Act 1996 s 7(1) (see PARA 690) if it were to grant, as from the date on which that licence would expire if not renewed, a fresh licence to provide the service formerly provided under that licence: s 16(12) (amended by the Communications Act 2003 Sch 15 para 88(2)). A determination for the purposes of the Broadcasting Act 1996 s 16(12) must be made at least one year before the date determined and must be notified by OFCOM to the person who holds the licence in question: s 16(12A) (added by the Communications Act 2003 Sch 15 para 88(4)).
8   Ie under the Broadcasting Act 1996 s 7(4)(b) (see PARA 690).
9   Broadcasting Act 1996 s 16(4)(a)(i) (amended by the Communications Act 2003 Sch 15 para 88(2)).
10 Ie under the Broadcasting Act 1996 s 7(4)(f) (see PARA 690).
11 Broadcasting Act 1996 s 16(4)(a)(ii).
12 Broadcasting Act 1996 s 16(4)(b). The matters specified are those referred to in s 7(4)(b)(i), (ii), (f) (see PARA 690 heads (b)(i), (b)(ii), (g)).
13 As to the Secretary of State see PARA 507 note 32.
14 Ie under the Broadcasting Act 1996 s 33(1)(b): see PARA 701.
15 Ie under the Broadcasting Act 1996 s 33(4): see PARA 701.
16 Broadcasting Act 1996 s 16(5) (amended by the Communications Act 2003 Sch 15 para 88(2)).
17 Broadcasting Act 1996 s 16(6) (amended by the Communications Act 2003 s 406(7), Sch 15 para 88(2), Sch 19). In deciding what is appropriate, OFCOM must have regard to the Broadcasting Act 1996 s 16(10) (see the text and note 26): see s 16(6) (as so amended).
18 Broadcasting Act 1996 s 16(7)(a) (amended by the Communications Act 2003 Sch 15 para 88(2)).
19 Broadcasting Act 1996 s 16(7)(b).
20 Broadcasting Act 1996 s 16(7)(c).
21 Ie under the Broadcasting Act 1996 s 7(1)(f): see PARA 690.
22 As to accounting periods see PARA 690 note 22.
23 Ie in pursuance of the Broadcasting Act 1996 s 13(1): see PARA 690.
24 Broadcasting Act 1996 s 16(8) (amended by the Communications Act 2003 Sch 15 para 88(2)). OFCOM may specify either of the things mentioned in the Broadcasting Act 1996 s 7(2)(b) (see PARA 690 note 22): s 16(8). Where an order under s 13(2) (see PARA 690) is in force on the relevant date, no percentage of multiplex revenue is payable as mentioned in head (A) in the text during the period for which the licence is to be renewed: s 16(9).
25 As to the meaning of 'person' see PARA 510 note 1.
26 Broadcasting Act 1996 s 16(10) (amended by the Communications Act 2003 Sch 15 para 88(2)). OFCOM must not so renew his licence unless it has notified him of any percentage so specified by it under the Broadcasting Act 1996 s 16(8) (see the text and note 24) and he has, within such period as is specified in that notification, notified it that he consents to the licence being renewed on those terms: s 16(10) (as so amended).
27 Broadcasting Act 1996 s 16(11) (amended by the Communications Act 2003 Sch 15 para 88(2)). As to submitting a supplementary technical plan and supplementary proposals see the Broadcasting Act 1996 s 16(4)(a); and head (1) in the text.
28 Ie the Broadcasting Act 1996 s 16.
29 Ie in pursuance of a notice under the Broadcasting Act 1996 s 7(1) (see PARA 690).
30 Broadcasting Act 1996 s 16(13).

696. Enforcement of multiplex licences. OFCOM[1] is under a statutory duty to do all that it can to secure that the holder of a multiplex licence[2] complies, in relation to the licensed service, with the conditions included in the licence[3].

If OFCOM is satisfied that the holder of a multiplex licence has failed to comply with any condition of the licence or with any direction given by OFCOM[4], it may serve on him:

(1) a notice requiring him to pay, within a specified period, a specified financial penalty to OFCOM[5]; or

(2) a notice reducing the period for which the licence is to be in force by a specified period not exceeding two years[6].

OFCOM must not serve on any person[7] such a notice as is mentioned in head (1) or head (2) unless it has given him a reasonable opportunity of making representations to it about the matters complained of[8].

Where a licence is due to expire on a particular date by virtue of a notice served on any person under head (2), OFCOM may, on the application of that person, revoke that notice by a further notice served on him at any time before that date, if it is satisfied that, since the date of the earlier notice, his conduct in relation to the operation of the licensed[9] service has been such as to justify the revocation of that notice[10].

1   As to OFCOM see PARA 507.
2   As to the meaning of 'multiplex licence' see PARA 690. As to the holder of the licence see PARA 690 note 66.
3   See the Communications Act 2003 s 263; and PARA 602.
4   Ie under or by virtue of any provision of the Broadcasting Act 1996 Pt I (ss 1–39): see s 17(1) (amended by the Communications Act 2003 s 360(3), Sch 15 para 89).
5   Broadcasting Act 1996 s 17(1)(a) (amended by the Communications Act 2003 Sch 15 para 89). The amount of any financial penalty must not exceed the maximum penalty given by the Broadcasting Act 1996 s 17(2A): s 17(2) (amended by the Communications Act 2003 s 345, Sch 13 paras 10, 13(1)). The maximum penalty is whichever is the greater of: (1) £250,000 (Broadcasting Act 1996 s 17(2A)(a) (s 17(2A)–(2C) added by the Communications Act 2003 Sch 13 para 13(2))); and (2) 5% of the share of multiplex revenue attributable to the licence holder for his last complete accounting period falling within the period for which his licence has been in force ('the relevant period') (Broadcasting Act 1996 s 17(2A)(b) (as so added)). In relation to a person whose first complete accounting period falling within the relevant period has not ended when the penalty is imposed, s 17(2A)(b) is to be construed as referring to 5% of the amount which OFCOM estimates to be the share of multiplex revenue attributable to him for that accounting period: s 17(2B) (as so added). The provisions of s 15(1), (3) apply for determining or estimating the share of multiplex revenue attributable to a person for the purposes of s 17(2A) or s 17(2B): s 17(2C) (as so added). As to accounting periods see PARA 690 note 22.
    For the purposes of s 17(2A), (2B), the share of multiplex revenue attributable to the person who is the multiplex provider in relation to any television multiplex service in respect of any accounting period of his is the aggregate of payments falling within s 14(1)(a), (b) (see PARA 693) and payments received or to be received by him from programme providers and additional services providers in respect of the provision in that period of television multiplex services, less the amount of any payments made or to be made to programme providers or additional service providers which would fall within s 14(1)(c) or (d) (see PARA 693) but for the fact that they are received from the multiplex provider: s 15(1) (amended by the Communications Act 2003 Sch 13 para 12(1), Sch 15 para 87(1), (2)). As to the meaning of 'programme provider' see PARA 693 note 5; definition applied by the Broadcasting Act 1996 s 15(4). As to the meaning of 'additional services provider' see PARA 693 note 6; definition applied by s 15(4). As to the meaning of 'multiplex provider' see PARA 693 note 3; definition applied by s 15(4) (amended by the Communications Act 2003 Sch 15 para 87(5)).
    The Secretary of State may by order amend the Broadcasting Act 1996 s 17(2A)(a) by substituting a different sum for the sum for the time being specified there: s 36(1), (2)(b) (s 36(2), (3) substituted by the Communications Act 2003 Sch 13 para 16). No order under the Broadcasting Act 1996 s 36(1) is to be made unless a draft of the order has been laid before

Parliament and approved by a resolution of each House: s 36(3) (as so substituted). As to the Secretary of State see PARA 507 note 32. At the date at which this volume states the law no such order had been made.

6 Broadcasting Act 1996 s 17(1)(b). The Broadcasting Act 1990 s 42 (see PARA 866) has effect in relation to a multiplex licence as it has effect in relation to a Channel 3 licence, but as if the reference in s 42(1)(a) to Pt I (ss 3–71) were a reference to the Broadcasting Act 1996 Pt I: s 17(6). As to the meaning of 'Channel 3 licence' see PARA 669 note 2; definition applied by s 39(1).

7 As to the meaning of 'person' see PARA 510 note 1.

8 Broadcasting Act 1996 s 17(4) (amended by the Communications Act 2003 Sch 15 para 89).

9 As to the meaning of 'licensed' see PARA 690 note 11.

10 Broadcasting Act 1996 s 17(5) (amended by the Communications Act 2003 Sch 15 para 89).

697. Television multiplex services. Subject to the following provisions[1], references in Part I of the Broadcasting Act 1996[2] to a multiplex service, other than those comprised in express references to a general multiplex service, have effect as references to any service (a 'television multiplex service') which: (1) falls within a specified provision[3]; and (2) is provided for broadcasting for general reception but otherwise than from a satellite[4]. The provision, at a time after 29 December 2003[5], of a television multiplex service the provision of which is not authorised by or under a licence under Part I of the Broadcasting Act 1996 is not to be an offence under the Broadcasting Act 1990[6]. Accordingly, after 29 December 2003, a licence under Part I of the Broadcasting Act 1996 is required for the provision of a television multiplex service only in so far as it is required for the purposes of a limitation[7] that is contained in a wireless telegraphy licence[8], or is deemed to be so contained[9].

Provision is made with respect to the powers of the Secretary of State where frequencies are reserved for qualifying services[10].

1 Ie the Communications Act 2003 s 241(2)–(9).

2 Ie the Broadcasting Act 1996 Pt I (ss 1–39).

3 Ie the Communications Act 2003 s 241(2). A service falls within s 241(2) if: (1) it consists in the packaging together of two or more services which include at least one relevant television service and are provided for inclusion together in the service by a combination of the relevant information in digital form; or (2) it is a service provided with a view to its being a service falling within head (1) but is one in the case of which only one service is for the time being comprised in digital form in what is provided: s 241(2). For the purposes of s 241(2), 'relevant television service' means any of the following: (a) any Channel 3 service in digital form; (b) Channel 4 in digital form; (c) Channel 5 in digital form; (d) S4C Digital; (e) any digital television programme service; (f) the digital public teletext service: s 241(9). As to the meaning of 'S4C Digital' see PARA 644 note 7. 'The digital public teletext service' means so much of the public teletext service as consists of a service provided in digital form: s 362(1). As to the meaning of 'the public teletext service' see PARA 688 note 3. As to the meaning of 'digital television programme service' see PARA 602 note 8.

4 Communications Act 2003 s 241(1).

5 Ie the date of commencement of the Communications Act 2003 s 241 (see the Office of Communications Act 2002 (Commencement No 3) and Communications Act 2003 (Commencement No 2) Order 2003, SI 2003/3142).

6 Ie under the Broadcasting Act 1990 s 13 (see PARA 593): Communications Act 2003 s 241(3).

7 Ie a limitation falling within the Communications Act 2003 s 241(5). A limitation falls within s 241(5), in relation to a wireless telegraphy licence, if it provides that the only television multiplex services that are authorised to be broadcast using the station or apparatus to which the licence relates are those that are licensed under the Broadcasting Act 1996 Pt I: Communications Act 2003 s 241(5).

Where, immediately before 29 December 2003: (1) a television multiplex service is licensed under the Broadcasting Act 1996 Pt I; and (2) that service is one broadcast using a station or apparatus the use of which is authorised by a wireless telegraphy licence, that wireless telegraphy licence is deemed to contain a limitation falling within the Communications Act 2003 s 241(5): s 241(6). In any case where a wireless telegraphy licence is deemed by virtue of s 241(6) to contain a limitation falling within s 241(5) and the person providing the television multiplex service in question: (a) ceases to be licensed under the Broadcasting Act 1996 Pt I in respect of that service; or (b) ceases to exist, OFCOM may revoke the wireless telegraphy licence: Communications Act 2003 s 241(7). Section 241(7) is not to be construed as restricting the powers of revocation exercisable apart from s 241: s 241(8).

8   As to the meaning of 'wireless telegraphy licence' see PARA 514 note 4. As to the meaning of 'wireless telegraphy' see PARA 510 note 1.
9   Communications Act 2003 s 241(4).
10   See the Communications Act 2003 s 243; and the Television Multiplex Services (Reservation of Digital Capacity) Order 2008, SI 2008/1420. As to the Secretary of State see PARA 507 note 32.

(ii) Licensing of Digital Television Services (DTPS and DTAS)

698. Licensing of digital programme services. A digital television programme service licence[1] is required by any person[2] who wishes to air a programme service (or channel) on digital terrestrial television. Such licences are awarded under Part I of the Broadcasting Act 1996.

An application for a licence to provide digital programme services (a 'digital programme licence') must be made in such manner as OFCOM[3] may determine[4], and be accompanied by such fee (if any) as it may determine[5]. At any time after receiving such an application and before determining it, OFCOM may require the applicant to furnish such additional information as it may consider necessary for the purpose of considering the application[6]. Any information to be so furnished to OFCOM must, if it so requires, be in such form or verified in such manner as it may specify[7]. Where an application for a digital programme licence is made to OFCOM in accordance with these provisions it must grant the licence unless precluded[8] from doing so[9].

OFCOM must not grant a digital television programme service licence to any person unless it is satisfied that he is a fit and proper person to hold it, and must do all that it can to secure that, if it ceases to be so satisfied in the case of any person holding a licence, that person does not remain holder of the licence[10]. A digital television programme service licence is not transferable to any other person without the previous written consent of OFCOM[11]. OFCOM must not give its consent unless it is satisfied that any such person would be in a position to comply with all of the conditions included in the licence which would have effect during the period for which it is in force[12].

1   Such a licence is referred to in the Broadcasting Act 1996 Pt I (ss 1–39) as a 'digital programme licence': see s 18(1). As regards digital television programme service licences, 'licence' means a licence under Pt I; and 'licensed' is to be construed accordingly: s 39(1). As to the meaning of 'digital programme service' see PARA 690 note 28.
2   As to the meaning of 'person' see PARA 510 note 1.
3   As to OFCOM see PARA 507.
4   Broadcasting Act 1996 s 18(1)(a) (amended by the Communications Act 2003 s 360(3), Sch 15 para 90(1), (2)).
5   Broadcasting Act 1996 s 18(1)(b).
6   Broadcasting Act 1996 s 18(2) (amended by the Communications Act 2003 Sch 15 para 90(2)).
7   Broadcasting Act 1996 s 18(3).
8   Ie by the Broadcasting Act 1996 s 3(3)(a) (see the text to note 10) or s 5(1) (see PARA 828).
9   Broadcasting Act 1996 s 18(4) (amended by the Communications Act 2003 Sch 15 para 90(2)).
10   Broadcasting Act 1996 s 3(3) (amended by the Communications Act 2003 Sch 15 para 76(2)). Nothing in the Broadcasting Act 1996 Pt I may be construed as affecting the operation of s 3(3) or of s 5(1), (2)(b) or (c) (see PARA 828): s 3(3) (as so amended).
      Where the person who is for the time being the holder of any licence ('the present licence holder') is not the person to whom the licence was originally granted, any reference (however expressed) in Pt I to the holder of the licence is to be construed, in relation to any time falling before the date when the present licence holder became the holder of it, as including a reference to a person who was previously the holder of the licence: s 39(2). The holding by any person of

a licence to provide any service does not relieve him of any failure to hold a licence under the Wireless Telegraphy Act 2006 s 8 (see PARA 514) or any obligation to comply with requirements imposed by or under the Communications Act 2003 Pt 2 Ch 1 (ss 32–151) (electronic communications networks and electronic communications services: see TELECOMMUNICATIONS vol 97 (2010) PARA 92 et seq): Broadcasting Act 1996 s 3(8) (substituted by the Communications Act 2003 Sch 15 para 76(4); and amended by the Wireless Telegraphy Act 2006 s 123, Sch 7 para 17).

11 Broadcasting Act 1996 s 3(6) (amended by the Communications Act 2003 Sch 15 para 76(3)).
12 Broadcasting Act 1996 s 3(7) (amended by the Communications Act 2003 Sch 15 para 76(3)).

699. Duration and conditions of digital programme licence. A digital television programme licence[1] must be made in writing[2], and (subject to the relevant statutory provisions[3]) will continue in force until it is surrendered by its holder[4]. Such licences may be granted for the provision of such a service as is specified in the licence or for the provision of a service of such a description as is so specified[5]. They may include such conditions as appear to OFCOM[6] to be appropriate having regard to any duties which are or may be imposed on it or on the licence holder[7].

A digital programme licence must include such conditions as appear to OFCOM to be appropriate for requiring the holder of the licence[8]:

(1) on entering into any agreement with the provider of a television multiplex service or general multiplex service[9] for the provision of a digital programme service[10] to be broadcast by means of that provider's service, to notify OFCOM[11]:

    (a) of the identity of the service by means of which it will be broadcast[12];

    (b) of the characteristics of the digital programme service to which the agreement relates[13];

    (c) of the period during which it will be provided[14]; and

    (d) where under the agreement the holder of the digital programme licence will be entitled to the use of a specified amount of digital capacity, of that amount[15];

(2) when any such agreement is varied so far as it relates to any of the matters mentioned in head (1)(a), (1)(b), (1)(c) or (1)(d) above, to notify OFCOM of the variation so far as relating to those matters[16]; and

(3) where he is providing a digital programme service to the provider of a television multiplex service or general multiplex service in accordance with such an agreement as is mentioned in head (1) above but intends to cease doing so, to notify OFCOM of that fact[17].

Further conditions may be included in the licence requiring the licence holder to provide OFCOM, in such manner and at such times as it may reasonably require, with such information as it may require for the purposes of exercising the functions assigned to it by or under the Broadcasting Act 1990, the Broadcasting Act 1996 or the Communications Act 2003[18]. A licence may include conditions requiring the licence holder to comply with any direction given by OFCOM as to such matters as are specified in the licence or are of a description so specified[19], or (to the extent that OFCOM consents to his doing or not doing them) not to do or not do such things as are specified in the licence or are of a description so specified[20]. Further conditions may also be included in a digital television programme service licence providing for such incidental and supplemental matters as appear to be appropriate to OFCOM[21].

OFCOM may vary a licence by a notice[22] served on the licence holder if: (i) in the case of a variation of the period for which the licence is to continue in force, the licence holder consents[23]; or (ii) in the case of any other variation, the licence holder has been given a reasonable opportunity of making representations to OFCOM about the variation[24].

1 As to the meaning of 'digital programme licence' see PARA 698 note 1.
2 Broadcasting Act 1996 s 3(1).
3 Ie subject to the provisions of the Broadcasting Act 1996 Pt I (ss 1–39) and to the Broadcasting Act 1990 s 42 (see PARA 866) as applied by the Broadcasting Act 1996 s 23(8) (see PARA 700).
4 Broadcasting Act 1996 s 19(1). As to the holder of the licence see PARA 698 note 10.
5 Broadcasting Act 1996 s 3(2).
6 As to OFCOM see PARA 507.
7 Broadcasting Act 1996 s 4(1)(a) (amended by the Communications Act 2003 s 360(3), Sch 15 para 77(1)–(3)). Nothing in the Broadcasting Act 1996 Pt I (ss 1–39) which authorises or requires the inclusion in a licence of conditions relating to any particular matter or having effect for any particular purpose is to be taken as derogating from the generality of s 4(1): s 4(6).
8 Broadcasting Act 1996 s 19(3) (amended by the Communications Act 2003 s 360(3), Sch 15 para 91(1), (2)(a)).
9 As to the meaning of 'multiplex service' see PARA 690 note 1.
10 As to the meaning of 'digital programme service' see PARA 690 note 28.
11 Broadcasting Act 1996 s 19(3)(a) (amended by the Communications Act 2003 Sch 15 para 91(2)(a)–(c)).
12 Broadcasting Act 1996 s 19(3)(a)(i) (amended by the Communications Act 2003 Sch 15 para 91(2)(d)).
13 Broadcasting Act 1996 s 19(3)(a)(ii).
14 Broadcasting Act 1996 s 19(3)(a)(iii).
15 Broadcasting Act 1996 s 19(3)(a)(iv).
16 Broadcasting Act 1996 s 19(3)(b) (amended by the Communications Act 2003 Sch 15 para 91(2)(a)).
17 Broadcasting Act 1996 s 19(3)(c) (amended by the Communications Act 2003 Sch 15 para 91(2)(a), (b)).
18 Broadcasting Act 1996 s 4(1)(c) (amended by the Communications Act 2003 Sch 15 para 77(2), (3)). See note 7. Where the holder of any licence is required by virtue of any condition imposed under the Broadcasting Act 1996 Pt I to provide OFCOM with any information, and in purported compliance with that condition provides it with information which is false in a material particular, he is to be taken for the purposes of s 17 (see PARA 696), s 23 (see PARA 700), s 27 (see PARA 713) and the Broadcasting Act 1990 s 42 (see PARA 866) to have failed to comply with that condition: Broadcasting Act 1996 s 4(5) (amended by the Communications Act 2003 Sch 15 para 77(2)).
19 Broadcasting Act 1996 s 4(2)(a) (amended by the Communications Act 2003 Sch 15 para 77(2)).
20 Broadcasting Act 1996 s 4(2)(b) (amended by the Communications Act 2003 Sch 15 para 77(2)).
21 Broadcasting Act 1996 s 4(1)(d) (amended by the Communications Act 2003 Sch 15 para 77(2)).
22 As to the service of notices see TELECOMMUNICATIONS vol 97 (2010) PARAS 49–50.
23 Broadcasting Act 1996 s 3(4)(a). Section 3(4)(a) does not affect the operation of s 17(1)(b) (see PARA 696): see s 3(5). Section 3(4) does not authorise the variation of any conditions included in a licence in pursuance of s 13(1) (see PARA 690): see s 3(5).
24 Broadcasting Act 1996 s 3(4)(b) (amended by the Communications Act 2003 Sch 15 para 76(3)). See also note 23.

700.   Enforcement of digital programme licences.   OFCOM[1] is under a statutory duty to do all that it can to secure that the holder of the digital television programme service licence[2] complies, in relation to the licensed service, with the conditions included in the licence[3].

If OFCOM is satisfied that the holder of a digital programme licence has failed to comply with any condition of the licence or with any direction given by OFCOM[4], it may serve on him:

(1)   a notice requiring him to pay, within a specified period, a specified financial penalty to OFCOM[5]; or

(2)   a notice providing that the licence is to expire on a specified date, which must be at least one year from the date of service of the notice[6].

OFCOM must not serve on any person[7] such a notice as is mentioned in head (1) or head (2) above unless it has given him a reasonable opportunity of making representations to it about the matters complained of[8]. Where a licence is due to expire on a particular date by virtue of a notice served on any person under head (2) above, OFCOM may, on the application of that person, revoke that notice by a further notice served on him at any time before that date, if it is satisfied that, since the date of the earlier notice, his conduct in relation to the operation of the licensed[9] service has been such as to justify the revocation of that notice[10].

1   As to OFCOM see PARA 507.
2   As to the meaning of 'digital programme licence' see PARA 698 note 1. The Broadcasting Act 1990 s 40(1)–(4) (see PARA 864) and s 42 (see PARA 866) apply in relation to a digital programme licence as they apply in relation to a Channel 3 licence: Broadcasting Act 1996 s 23(8) (amended by the Communications Act 2003 s 360(3), Sch 15 para 92(1), (6)). As to the meaning of 'Channel 3 licence' see PARA 669 note 2; definition applied by the Broadcasting Act 1996 s 39(1). In its application in relation to a digital programme licence, the Broadcasting Act 1990 s 42 has effect with the substitution for the reference in s 42(1)(a) to Pt I (ss 3–71) of a reference to the Broadcasting Act 1996 Pt I (ss 1–39), and with the omission of the Broadcasting Act 1990 s 42(4) and of the reference to s 42(4) in s 42(6) (see PARA 866): Broadcasting Act 1996 s 23(9). As to the holder of the licence see PARA 698 note 10.
3   See the Communications Act 2003 s 263; and PARA 602.
4   Ie under or by virtue of any provision of the Broadcasting Act 1996 Pt I.
5   Broadcasting Act 1996 s 23(1)(a) (amended by the Communications Act 2003 Sch 15 para 92(2)). See also note 6. The amount of any financial penalty imposed on any person under s 23(1)(a) must not exceed the maximum penalty given by the Broadcasting Act 1996 s 23(2A): s 23(2) (amended by the Communications Act 2003 s 345, Sch 13 paras 10, 14(1)). The maximum penalty is whichever is the greater of: (1) £250,000; and (2) 5% of the aggregate amount of the shares of multiplex revenue attributable to him in relation to television multiplex services and general multiplex services in respect of relevant accounting periods: Broadcasting Act 1996 s 23(2A) (added by the Communications Act 2003 Sch 13 para 14(2)).
     As to the meaning of 'multiplex service' see PARA 690 note 1. As to the meaning of 'relevant accounting period' see PARA 713 note 10. As to the meaning of 'multiplex licence' see PARA 690. As to accounting periods see PARA 690 note 22. As to the meaning of 'multiplex provider' see PARA 693 note 3.
     For the purposes of the Broadcasting Act 1996 s 23(2A)–(5), the share of multiplex revenue attributable to a programme provider or additional services provider in relation to a television multiplex service or a general multiplex service in respect of any accounting period of the multiplex provider is the aggregate of payments falling within s 14(1)(c) or (d) (see PARA 693), and payments received or to be received from the multiplex provider which would fall within s 14(1)(c) or (d) but for the fact that they are received from the multiplex provider, less the amount of any payments made or to be made to the multiplex provider in respect of the provision of multiplex services in that period: s 15(2) (amended by the Communications Act 2003 Sch 13 para 12(2), Sch 15 para 87(1), (3)). As to the meaning of 'programme provider' see PARA 693 note 5; definition applied by s 15(4). As to the meaning of 'additional services provider' see PARA 693 note 6; definition applied by s 15(4).
     Where, in the case of any television multiplex service or general multiplex service, the first accounting period of the multiplex provider throughout which the holder of the digital programme licence provides a digital programme service for broadcasting by means of the multiplex service ('the first period') has not ended when the penalty is imposed, then for the purposes of s 23 the share of multiplex revenue attributable to the holder of the digital programme licence in relation to that multiplex service for the relevant accounting period is taken to be the amount which OFCOM estimates to be the share of multiplex revenue attributable to him for the first period: s 23(5) (amended by the Communications Act 2003 Sch 13 para 14(4), Sch 15 para 92(2), (4)). As to the meaning of 'digital programme service' see PARA 690 note 28. As to the meaning of 'broadcast' see PARA 668 note 2; definition applied by the Broadcasting Act 1996 s 147(2).
     The Secretary of State may by order amend s 23(2A)(a) by substituting a different sum for the sum for the time being specified there: s 36(1), (2)(c) (s 36(2) substituted by the Communications Act 2003 Sch 13 para 16). No order is to be made under the Broadcasting

Act 1996 s 36(1) unless a draft of the order has been laid before Parliament and approved by a resolution of each House: s 36(3) (added by the Communications Act 2003 Sch 13 para 16). At the date at which this volume states the law no such order had been made. As to the Secretary of State see PARA 507 note 32.

6   Broadcasting Act 1996 s 23(1)(b). Any exercise by OFCOM of its powers under s 23(1) in respect of any failure to comply with any condition of a digital programme licence does not preclude the exercise by it of its powers under the Broadcasting Act 1990 s 40 (see PARA 864) in respect of that failure: Broadcasting Act 1996 s 23(10) (amended by the Communications Act 2003 Sch 15 para 92(2)).

7   As to the meaning of 'person' see PARA 510 note 1.

8   Broadcasting Act 1996 s 23(6) (amended by the Communications Act 2003 Sch 15 para 92(2)).

9   As to the meaning of 'licensed' see PARA 698 note 1.

10 Broadcasting Act 1996 s 23(7) (amended by the Communications Act 2003 Sch 15 para 92(2)).

701.   Review to consider the continued need for analogue broadcasting. For the purpose of considering for how long it would be appropriate for television broadcasting services[1] to continue to be provided in analogue form, the Secretary of State[2]:

(1)   must keep under review the extent of:

(a)   the provision in the United Kingdom[3] of multiplex services[4];

(b)   the availability in the United Kingdom in digital form of Channel 3 services[5], Channel 4[6], Channel 5[7], the public television services of the Welsh Authority[8], the digital public teletext service[9], and the television broadcasting services of the BBC[10]; and

(c)   the ownership or possession in the United Kingdom of equipment capable of receiving the services referred to in head (1)(b) above when broadcast[11] or transmitted in digital form[12];

and the likely future extent of such provision, such availability and such ownership or possession[13]; and

(2)   must, on or before the fourth anniversary of the day on which the first multiplex licence[14] is granted[15], and at such time or times thereafter as he thinks fit, require OFCOM[16] and the BBC to report to him on the matters referred to in head (1) above[17].

If OFCOM or the BBC is required to submit a report under head (2) above, it must submit the report within 12 months of the date of the requirement[18]. Before making any such report, OFCOM must consult:

(i)   the holders of all multiplex licences[19];

(ii) the holders of digital programme licences[20] who are providing digital programme services[21] which are being broadcast[22];

(iii) such other persons providing services licensed[23] by OFCOM[24] as OFCOM thinks fit[25]; and

(iv) the Welsh Authority[26],

and OFCOM must include in its report a summary of representations made to it by the persons consulted[27].

For that purpose[28], the Secretary of State must, on requiring reports under head (2) above, consult such persons appearing to him to represent viewers as he thinks fit, and such other persons as he thinks fit, in connection with the matters referred to in head (1) above and also, if he thinks fit, as to the likely effects on viewers of any television broadcasting service ceasing to be broadcast in analogue form[29].

1   As to the meaning of 'television broadcasting services' see PARA 667 note 3; definition applied by the Broadcasting Act 1996 s 33(5).

2   As to the Secretary of State see PARA 507 note 32.

3   As to the meaning of 'United Kingdom' see PARA 510 note 13.

4 Broadcasting Act 1996 s 33(1)(a)(i). As to the meaning of 'multiplex service' see PARA 690 note 1.
5 As to Channel 3 services see PARA 667.
6 As to the meaning of 'Channel 4' see PARA 637.
7 As to the meaning of 'Channel 5' see PARA 681.
8 Ie within the meaning of the Communications Act 2003 Sch 12 Pt 2 (paras 3–24) (see PARA 655 et seq). As to the meaning of 'the Welsh Authority' see PARA 644 note 3; definition applied by the Broadcasting Act 1996 s 147(2). As to television broadcasting by the Welsh Authority see PARAS 644–661.
9 As to the meaning of 'digital public teletext service' see PARA 697 note 3.
10 Broadcasting Act 1996 s 33(1)(a)(ii) (amended by the Communications Act 2003 s 360(3), Sch 15 para 98(1), (3)). As to the meaning of 'BBC' see PARA 603 note 1. As to the BBC see PARAS 603–626.
11 As to the meaning of 'broadcast' see PARA 668 note 2; definition applied by the Broadcasting Act 1996 s 147(2).
12 Broadcasting Act 1996 s 33(1)(a)(iii).
13 Broadcasting Act 1996 s 33(1)(a).
14 As to the meaning of 'multiplex licence' see PARA 690.
15 Ie under the Broadcasting Act 1996 s 8 (see PARA 690).
16 As to OFCOM see PARA 507.
17 Broadcasting Act 1996 s 33(1)(b) (amended by the Communications Act 2003 Sch 15 para 98(2)).
18 Broadcasting Act 1996 s 33(2) (amended by the Communications Act 2003 Sch 15 para 98(2)).
19 Broadcasting Act 1996 s 33(3)(a). As to the holder of the licence see PARA 698 note 10.
20 As to the meaning of 'digital programme licence' see PARA 698.
21 As to the meaning of 'digital programme service' see PARA 690 note 28.
22 Broadcasting Act 1996 s 33(3)(b).
23 As to the meaning of 'licensed' see PARA 698 note 1. As to the meaning of 'person' see PARA 510 note 1.
24 Ie under the Broadcasting Act 1996 Pt I (ss 1–39) or the Broadcasting Act 1990 Pt I (ss 3–71).
25 Broadcasting Act 1996 s 33(3)(c) (amended by the Communications Act 2003 s 406(7), Sch 15 para 98(2), Sch 19).
26 Broadcasting Act 1996 s 33(3)(d).
27 Broadcasting Act 1996 s 33(3) (amended by the Communications Act 2003 Sch 15 para 98(2)).
28 Ie the purpose referred to in the Broadcasting Act 1996 s 33(1) (see the text and notes 1–17).
29 Broadcasting Act 1996 s 33(4).

702. Digital switchover: date and disclosure of information. The Secretary of State[1] may give notice to OFCOM[2] nominating a date for digital switchover[3] for the post-commencement services[4] specified or described in the notice[5]. When nominating a date, or considering whether to nominate a date, the Secretary of State must have regard to any report submitted[6] by OFCOM or the BBC[7].

If the Secretary of State has nominated a date for digital switchover for a post-commencement service (and has not withdrawn the nomination), then if the period for which the licence to provide the post-commencement service is to continue in force ends after the date for digital switchover, OFCOM must by notice vary the licence so that the period ends on or before that date[8]. If the period for which the licence to provide the post-commencement service is to continue in force ends on or before the date for digital switchover, OFCOM may not vary the licence so that the period ends after that date[9].

The Secretary of State may, at the request of a relevant person[10], supply a relevant person with social security information[11] or war pensions information[12] for use (by the person to whom it is supplied or by another relevant person) in connection with switchover help functions[13]. A local authority[14] may, at the request of a relevant person, supply a relevant person with visual impairment information[15] for use (by the person to whom it is supplied or by another relevant person) in connection with switchover help functions[16].

A relevant person must not disclose[17] without lawful authority any information supplied to him or another relevant person[18]. A specified person[19] must not disclose without lawful authority information supplied to a relevant person[20]. A person who contravenes these provisions commits an offence[21]. If an offence by a body corporate is shown to have been committed with the consent or connivance of an officer[22], or to be attributable to any neglect on his part, the officer as well as the body corporate is guilty of the offence and liable to be proceeded against and punished accordingly[23].

1   As to the Secretary of State see PARA 507 note 32.
2   As to OFCOM see PARA 507.
3   In the Broadcasting Act 1990 ss 97A, 97B, 'date for digital switchover', in relation to a post-commencement service (see note 4), means a date after which it will cease to be appropriate for the service to continue to be provided in analogue form: s 97A(4) (ss 97A, 97B added by the Digital Economy Act 2010 s 30(2)).
4   'Post-commencement service' means a local service, national service or additional service that is provided under a licence that: (1) was granted on or after the day on which the Broadcasting Act 1990 s 97A comes into force; or (2) has been renewed under s 103B (see PARA 736) or s 104AA (see PARA 740): s 97A(4) (as added: see note 3). Section 97A came into force on 8 April 2010: see the Digital Economy Act 2010 s 47(2)(b). As to the meaning of 'local service' and 'national service' see PARA 723 note 4; definitions applied by the Broadcasting Act 1990 s 126(1) (amended by the Communications Act 2003 Sch 15 para 59(b)). As to the meaning of 'additional service' see PARA 703.
5   Broadcasting Act 1990 s 97A(1) (as added: see note 3). The Secretary of State: (1) may nominate different dates for different services; and (2) may give notice to OFCOM withdrawing a nomination under s 97A: s 97A(3).
6   Ie under the Broadcasting Act 1996 s 67(1)(b) (review of digital radio broadcasting): see PARA 767.
7   Broadcasting Act 1990 s 97A(2) (as added: see note 3). As to the meaning of 'BBC' see PARA 603 note 1; and as to the BBC see PARAS 603–626.
8   Broadcasting Act 1990 s 97B(1) (as added: see note 3). However, OFCOM may not reduce the period so that it ends less than two years after the day on which it issues the notice, unless the licence holder consents to such a reduction: s 97B(3) (as so added).
9   Broadcasting Act 1990 s 97B(4) (as added: see note 3).
10 In the Digital Switchover (Disclosure of Information) Act 2007, 'relevant person' means: (1) the BBC; (2) any company in respect of which any one or more of the following: (a) the BBC; (b) the Secretary of State; or (c) a nominee of the BBC or the Secretary of State, hold at least 51% of the issued ordinary share capital or possess at least 51% of the voting rights; (3) any person who is engaged by the BBC, the Secretary of State or any company falling within head (2) to provide any service connected with switchover help functions, to carry out a switchover help function or to carry out any function connected with switchover help functions: ss 1(4), 5(1). 'The BBC' means the British Broadcasting Corporation: s 5(1). As to the BBC see PARAS 603–626.
11 For the purposes of the Digital Switchover (Disclosure of Information) Act 2007 s 1, 'social security information' means, in relation to the Secretary of State, information of a prescribed description held by him (or on his behalf) and obtained as a result of, or for the purpose of, the exercise of functions of his in relation to social security: s 2(1), (2)(a). 'Prescribed' means prescribed by order made by the Secretary of State by statutory instrument: s 2(5). A statutory instrument containing an order under s 2 is subject to annulment in pursuance of a resolution of either House of Parliament: s 2(6). An order under s 2 may make different provision in relation to different cases: s 2(7). See the Digital Switchover (Disclosure of Information) (Prescription of Information) Order 2007, SI 2007/1768 (amended by SI 2008/2557).
12 For these purposes, 'war pensions information' means information of a prescribed description held by the Secretary of State (or on his behalf) and obtained as a result of, or for the purpose of, the exercise of functions of his relating to war pensions, as defined by the Social Security Act 1989 s 25(4) (see WAR AND ARMED CONFLICT vol 49(1) (2005 Reissue) PARAS 595, 620): Digital Switchover (Disclosure of Information) Act 2007 s 2(1), (3). See the Digital Switchover (Disclosure of Information) (Prescription of Information) Order 2007, SI 2007/1768 (amended by SI 2008/2557).
13 Digital Switchover (Disclosure of Information) Act 2007 s 1(1), (2). 'Switchover help functions' means: (1) the identification of persons who may be eligible for help under a switchover help scheme; (2) making contact with such persons with a view to the provision of such help; and (3)

the establishment of any person's entitlement to such help: ss 1(5), 5(1). 'Switchover help scheme' means any scheme for the provision of help to individuals in connection with digital switchover which is agreed between the BBC and the Secretary of State in pursuance of the BBC Charter and Agreement, as the scheme has effect from time to time: Digital Switchover (Disclosure of Information) Act 2007 s 5(1). 'Digital switchover' means the replacement of the broadcasting of television services in the United Kingdom in analogue form with their broadcasting in digital form; and 'broadcasting' means broadcasting by wireless telegraphy (as defined by the Wireless Telegraphy Act 2006 s 116 (see PARA 510 note 1)) otherwise than by satellite: Digital Switchover (Disclosure of Information) Act 2007 s 5(2). 'The BBC Charter and Agreement' means the following documents, or any one or more of them, so far as they are for the time being in force: (a) a Royal Charter for the continuance of the BBC; (b) supplemental Charters obtained by the BBC under such a Royal Charter; (c) an agreement between the BBC and the Secretary of State entered into (whether before or after the passing of the Digital Switchover (Disclosure of Information) Act 2007) for purposes that include the regulation of activities carried on by the BBC: s 5(2). See PARA 854. As to the meaning of 'United Kingdom' see PARA 510 note 13. The Digital Switchover (Disclosure of Information) Act 2007 has been extended to the Isle of Man, subject to modifications: see the Digital Switchover (Disclosure of Information) (Isle of Man) Order 2007, SI 2007/3472.

14 'Local authority' means: (1) in relation to England, a country council, a district council, other than a council for a district in a county for which there is a county council, a London borough council, the Common Council of the City of London in its capacity as a local authority, or the Council of the Isles of Scilly; and (2) in relation to Wales, a county council or a county borough council: Digital Switchover (Disclosure of Information) Act 2007 s 5(1).

15 For these purposes, 'visual impairment information' means information of a prescribed description about persons who are registered as blind or partially sighted in a register maintained by or on behalf of a local authority in England or Wales under the National Assistance Act 1948 s 29: Digital Switchover (Disclosure of Information) Act 2007 s 2(1), (4). See the Digital Switchover (Disclosure of Information) (Prescription of Information) Order 2007, SI 2007/1768 (amended by SI 2008/2557).

16 Digital Switchover (Disclosure of Information) Act 2007 s 1(3).

17 A disclosure is to be regarded as made with lawful authority if, but only if, it is made: (1) for the purpose of carrying out a switchover help function, or for doing anything connected with the carrying out of a switchover help function; (2) in accordance with any enactment or court order; (3) for the purpose of instituting, or otherwise for the purposes of, proceedings before a court; or (4) with the consent of the person to whom the information relates or of any person authorised to act on that person's behalf: Digital Switchover (Disclosure of Information) Act 2007 s 3(6).

18 Digital Switchover (Disclosure of Information) Act 2007 s 3(1).

19 Ie a person: (1) who is or who has been employed by a relevant person; (2) who is or who has been engaged (a) in the provision of services to a relevant person in connection with the carrying out of a switchover help function; (b) to carry out any switchover help function, or to carry out any function in connection with the carrying out of a switchover help function; and (3) who is or who has been employed by, or who is or who has been engaged in the provision of services to, or to carry out a function for, a person mentioned in head (2): Digital Switchover (Disclosure of Information) Act 2007 s 3(2)(a)–(c).

20 Digital Switchover (Disclosure of Information) Act 2007 s 3(2).

21 Digital Switchover (Disclosure of Information) Act 2007 s 3(3). A person guilty of such an offence is liable: (1) on conviction on indictment, to imprisonment for a term not exceeding two years, or to a fine, or both; (2) on summary conviction to imprisonment for a term not exceeding 12 months or to a fine not exceeding the statutory maximum, or both: s 3(7). In the application of s 3 in England and Wales, in relation to an offence committed before the commencement of the Criminal Justice Act 2003 s 154, the reference in head (2) to 12 months is to be read as a reference to six months: Digital Switchover (Disclosure of Information) Act 2007 s 3(8). As to the statutory maximum see SENTENCING AND DISPOSITION OF OFFENDERS vol 92 (2010) PARA 140.

It is not an offence: (a) to disclose information in the form of a summary or collection of information so framed as not to enable information supplied under s 1 relating to any particular person to be ascertained from it; or (b) to disclose information which has previously been disclosed to the public with lawful authority: s 3(4). It is a defence for a person charged with an offence to prove that at the time of the alleged offence he believed that he was making the disclosure in question with lawful authority, or that the information in question had previously been disclosed to the public with lawful authority, and that he had no reasonable cause to believe otherwise: s 3(5).

22 'Officer', in relation to a body corporate, means a director, member of the committee of management, chief executive, manager, secretary or other similar officer of the body, or a person purporting to act in any such capacity: Digital Switchover (Disclosure of Information) Act 2007 s 4(3).

23 Digital Switchover (Disclosure of Information) Act 2007 s 4(1). If the affairs of a body corporate are managed by its members, this applies in relation to the acts and defaults of a member in connection with his functions of management as if he were a director of the body: s 4(2).

703. Additional services. 'Additional service' means any service which consists in the sending of electronic signals[1] for transmission by wireless telegraphy[2] by means of the use of the spare capacity within the signals carrying any television broadcasting service[3] provided on a relevant frequency[4].

The spare capacity within the signals carrying any such broadcasting service is taken to be any part of the signals which:

(1)   is not required for the purposes of the television broadcasting service for the purposes of which the frequency has been made available; and

(2)   is determined by OFCOM to be available for the provision of additional services[5].

OFCOM, when determining the extent and nature of the spare capacity available for the provision of additional services in the case of any frequency[6], must have regard[7]:

(a)   to the obligations contained in any code relating to provision for the deaf and visually impaired[8]; and

(b)   to any need of the person[9] providing the television broadcasting service in question to be able to use part of the signals carrying it for providing services (in addition to those provided for satisfying those obligations) which are ancillary to programmes[10] included in the service and directly related to their contents or which relate to the promotion or listing of such programmes[11].

A person holding a licence[12] to provide a Channel 3 service[13] or Channel 4[14] or 5[15] is taken to be authorised by his licence[16]: (i) to provide services for the satisfaction in his case of obligations mentioned in head (a) above; and (ii) to provide in relation to his television broadcasting service any such services as are mentioned in head (b) above[17].

1   'Electronic signals' means signals within the meaning of the Communications Act 2003 s 32 (see TELECOMMUNICATIONS vol 97 (2010) PARA 22): Broadcasting Act 1990 s 48(6) (substituted by the Communications Act 2003 s 360(3), Sch 15 para 20(1), (7)).

2   As to the meaning of 'wireless telegraphy' see PARA 510 note 1; definition applied by the Broadcasting Act 1990 s 202(1) (amended by the Wireless Telegraphy Act 2006 s 123, Sch 7 paras 9, 13).

3   As to the meaning of 'television broadcasting service' see PARA 667 note 3.

4   Broadcasting Act 1990 s 48(1) (amended by the Communications Act 2003 Sch 15 para 20(2)). 'Relevant frequency' means a frequency made available by OFCOM for the purposes of a television broadcasting service: Broadcasting Act 1990 s 48(6) (as substituted: see note 1). As to the meaning of 'frequency' see PARA 681 note 5. As to OFCOM see PARA 507.

5   Broadcasting Act 1990 s 48(2) (amended by the Communications Act 2003 Sch 15 para 20(3)). If it consider it appropriate to do so, OFCOM may, while an additional services licence is in force, from time to time modify the determination made under the Broadcasting Act 1990 s 48(2)(b) (see head (2) in the text) for the purposes of that licence in any manner that does not reduce the amount of spare capacity made available for the licensed services; and when so modified any such licence will have effect accordingly: s 48(2A) (added by the Communications Act 2003 Sch 15 para 20(4)).

6   Ie for the purposes of the Broadcasting Act 1990 s 48(2)(b) (see head (2) in the text).

7   Broadcasting Act 1990 s 48(3) (amended by the Communications Act 2003 Sch 15 para 20(5)(a), (b)).

8 Ie under the Communications Act 2003 s 303, by virtue of s 303(5) (see PARA 880): Broadcasting Act 1990 s 48(3)(a) (substituted by the Communications Act 2003 Sch 15 para 20(5)(c)).
9 As to the meaning of 'person' see PARA 510 note 1.
10 As to the meaning of 'programme' see PARA 667 note 7.
11 Broadcasting Act 1990 s 48(3)(aa) (added by the Communications Act 2003 Sch 15 para 20(5)(c)).
12 As to the holder of the licence see PARAS 671 note 19, 679 note 28.
13 As to Channel 3 services see PARA 667.
14 As to the meaning of 'Channel 4' see PARA 637.
15 As to the meaning of 'Channel 5' see PARA 681.
16 Broadcasting Act 1990 s 48(4). The person is authorised for the purposes of Pt I (ss 3–71): see s 48(4).
17 Broadcasting Act 1990 s 48(4)(a), (b) (substituted by the Communications Act 2003 Sch 15 para 20(6)).

704. Licensing of additional services. OFCOM[1] must do all it can to secure that, in the case of each relevant frequency[2] all of the spare capacity[3] available for the provision of additional services[4] on that frequency is used for the provision of such services under additional services licences[5] granted by OFCOM[6].

An additional services licence is not required for an additional service that is comprised in the public teletext service[7].

An additional services licence may relate to the use of spare capacity within more than one frequency, and two or more additional services licences may relate to the use of spare capacity within the same frequency where it is to be used at different times, or in different areas, in the case of each of those licences[8].

An additional services licence may include provisions enabling the licence holder[9], subject to and in accordance with such conditions[10] as OFCOM may impose, to authorise any person[11] to provide any additional service on the spare capacity allocated by the licence[12]. Any conditions included in an additional services licence apply in relation to the provision of additional services by an authorised person as they apply in relation to the provision of such services by the licence holder, and any failure by such a person to comply with any such conditions is to be treated as a failure on the part of the licence holder to comply with those conditions[13].

Every licence to provide a television broadcasting service[14] must include such conditions as appear to OFCOM to be appropriate for securing that the licence holder grants to any person who holds a licence to provide additional services on the frequency on which that broadcasting service is provided[15], and to any person authorised to provide additional services on that frequency[16], access to facilities reasonably required by that person for the purposes of, or in connection with, the provision of any such additional services[17].

1 As to OFCOM see PARA 507.
2 As to the meaning of 'relevant frequency' see PARA 703 note 4; definition applied by the Broadcasting Act 1990 s 49(10) (amended by the Communications Act 2003 s 360(3), Sch 15 para 21(1), (5)). As to the meaning of 'frequency' see PARA 681 note 5.
3 As to the meaning of 'spare capacity' see PARA 703.
4 As to the meaning of 'additional service' see PARA 703.
5 'Additional services licence' means a licence to provide additional services: Broadcasting Act 1990 ss 49(10), 71(1). As regards the licensing of additional services, 'licence' means a licence under the Broadcasting Act 1990 Pt I (ss 3–71); and 'licensed' is to be construed accordingly: s 71(1).
6 Broadcasting Act 1990 s 49(1) (amended by the Communications Act 2003 s Sch 15 para 21(2), (3)). Additional services licences are granted in accordance with the Broadcasting Act 1990 s 49: see s 49(1) (as so amended).

7 Broadcasting Act 1990 s 49(1A) (added by the Communications Act 2003 s Sch 15 para 21(4)). As to the public teletext service within the meaning of the Communications Act 2003 Pt 3 (ss 198–362) see PARA 686.
8 Broadcasting Act 1990 s 49(4).
9 As to the holder of the licence see PARAS 671 note 19, 679 note 28.
10 As to the enforcement of conditions included in additional services licences see PARA 710.
11 As to the meaning of 'person' see PARA 510 note 1.
12 Broadcasting Act 1990 s 49(5) (amended by the Communications Act 2003 s Sch 15 para 21(2)). The Broadcasting Act 1990 s 49(5) applies to any person who is not a disqualified person in relation to an additional services licence by virtue of s 5, Sch 2 Pt II (see PARA 822 et seq): s 49(6).
13 Broadcasting Act 1990 s 49(7).
14 As to the meaning of 'television broadcasting service' see PARA 667 note 3.
15 Broadcasting Act 1990 s 49(8)(a).
16 Broadcasting Act 1990 s 49(8)(b). A person is authorised by any such person as is mentioned in s 49(5) (see the text and note 12): see s 49(8)(b).
17 Broadcasting Act 1990 s 49(8) (amended by the Communications Act 2003 s Sch 15 para 21(2)). Any person who grants to any other person access to facilities in accordance with conditions imposed under the Broadcasting Act 1990 s 49(8) may require that other person to pay a reasonable charge in respect of them; and any dispute as to the amount of any such charge is to be determined by OFCOM: s 49(9) (amended by the Communications Act 2003 s Sch 15 para 21(2)).

705. Applications for additional services licences. Where OFCOM[1] proposes to grant a licence[2] to provide additional services[3] it must publish, in such manner as it considers appropriate, a notice[4]:

(1) stating that it proposes to grant such a licence[5];

(2) specifying the television broadcasting service or services[6] on whose frequency or frequencies[7] the services are to be provided[8], and the extent and nature of the spare capacity[9] which is to be allocated by the licence[10];

(3) inviting applications for the licence and specifying the closing date for such applications[11]; and

(4) specifying the fee payable on any application made in pursuance of the notice[12], and the percentage of qualifying revenue for each accounting period that would be payable by an applicant[13] if he were granted the licence[14].

Any application made in pursuance of such a notice must be in writing and accompanied by[15]:

(a) the fee specified in the notice under head (4) above[16];

(b) a technical plan[17] indicating the nature of any additional services which the applicant proposes to provide[18], and so far as known to the applicant, the nature of any additional services which any other person proposes to provide[19];

(c) the applicant's cash bid[20] in respect of the licence[21]; and

(d) such information as OFCOM may reasonably require as to the applicant's present financial position and his projected financial position during the period for which the licence would be in force[22].

At any time after receiving such an application and before determining it, OFCOM may require the applicant to furnish additional information under head (b) or head (d) above[23]. Any information to be furnished to OFCOM must, if it so requires, be in such form or verified in such manner as it may specify[24].

OFCOM must, as soon as reasonably practicable after the date specified in the notice as the closing date for applications, publish in such manner as it considers appropriate[25] the name of every person who has made an application to it in pursuance of the notice[26], particulars of the technical plan submitted by him[27], and such other information connected with his application as OFCOM considers appropriate[28].

1   As to OFCOM see PARA 507.
2   As to the meaning of 'licence' see PARA 704 note 5.
3   As to the meaning of 'additional service' see PARA 703.
4   Broadcasting Act 1990 s 50(1) (amended by the Communications Act 2003 s 360(3), Sch 15 para 22(1), (2)).
5   Broadcasting Act 1990 s 50(1)(a).
6   As to the meaning of 'television broadcasting service' see PARA 667 note 3.
7   As to the meaning of 'frequency' see PARA 681 note 5.
8   Broadcasting Act 1990 s 50(1)(b)(i).
9   As to the meaning of 'spare capacity' see PARA 703.
10 Broadcasting Act 1990 s 50(1)(b)(ii) (amended by the Communications Act 2003 s 406(7), Sch 15 para 22(3), Sch 19).
11 Broadcasting Act 1990 s 50(1)(c).
12 Broadcasting Act 1990 s 50(1)(d)(i).
13 Ie in pursuance of the Broadcasting Act 1990 s 52(1)(c) (see PARA 707). As to qualifying revenue see PARA 707 note 8. OFCOM may specify a different percentage of qualifying revenue when a licence is renewed: see s 53(7)(b); and PARA 708.
14 Broadcasting Act 1990 s 50(1)(d)(ii). OFCOM may, if it thinks fit, specify under s 50(1)(d)(ii): (1) different percentages in relation to different accounting periods falling within the period for which the licence would be in force; or (2) a nil percentage in relation to any accounting period so falling: s 50(2) (amended by the Communications Act 2003 Sch 15 para 22(2)).
15 Broadcasting Act 1990 s 50(3).
16 Broadcasting Act 1990 s 50(3)(a).
17 Before considering an application, OFCOM must be satisfied, inter alia, that the technical plan, so far as it involves the use of an electronic communications network (within the meaning of the Communications Act 2003 (see TELECOMMUNICATIONS vol 97 (2010) PARA 60)), contains proposals that are acceptable to it: see the Broadcasting Act 1990 s 51(1)(a) (substituted by the Communications Act 2003 Sch 15 para 23(1), (3)); and PARA 706. With regard to the renewal of licences, OFCOM must be satisfied that any additional service specified in the technical plan would be provided as proposed in that plan: see the Broadcasting Act 1990 s 53(5)(a); and PARA 708.
18 Broadcasting Act 1990 s 50(3)(b)(i).
19 Broadcasting Act 1990 s 50(3)(b)(ii). Additional services are provided in accordance with s 49(5) (see PARA 704). As to the meaning of 'person' see PARA 510 note 1.
20 As to the meaning of 'cash bid' see PARA 669 note 29. The provisions of the Broadcasting Act 1990 ss 17, 17A (award of licence to person submitting highest cash bid and award of licence with conditions) (see PARAS 671–672) apply in relation to an additional services licence as they apply in relation to a Channel 3 licence: s 51(3) (amended by the Broadcasting Act 1996 s 86(2)). As to Channel 3 licences see PARA 669.
21 Broadcasting Act 1990 s 50(3)(c).
22 Broadcasting Act 1990 s 50(3)(d) (amended by the Communications Act 2003 Sch 15 para 22(2)). As to the duration and renewal of licences see PARA 708.
23 Broadcasting Act 1990 s 50(4) (amended by the Communications Act 2003 Sch 15 para 22(2)).
24 Broadcasting Act 1990 s 50(5) (amended by the Communications Act 2003 Sch 15 para 22(2)).
25 Broadcasting Act 1990 s 50(6) (amended by the Communications Act 2003 Sch 15 para 22(2)).
26 Broadcasting Act 1990 s 50(6)(a).
27 Broadcasting Act 1990 s 50(6)(b). The plan is submitted under s 50(3)(b): see the text and notes 18–19.
28 Broadcasting Act 1990 s 50(6)(c) (amended by the Communications Act 2003 Sch 15 para 22(2)).

706.   Procedure in connection with consideration of applications for licences.
Where a person[1] has made an application for an additional services licence[2], OFCOM[3] may not proceed to consider whether to award him the licence on the basis of his cash bid[4] unless it appears to OFCOM[5] that the technical plan submitted[6], so far as it involves the use of an electronic communications network[7], contains proposals that are acceptable to the relevant licensing

authorities[8], and that the services proposed to be provided under the licence would be capable of being maintained throughout the period for which the licence would be in force[9].

If at any time after an additional services licence has been granted to any person but before the licence has come into force[10], that person indicates to OFCOM that none of the services in question will be provided once the licence has come into force[11], or OFCOM for any other reason has reasonable grounds for believing that none of those services will be so provided[12], then OFCOM must serve on him a notice revoking the licence as from the time the notice is served on him[13]. However, in the latter case, OFCOM must first serve on him a notice stating its grounds for believing that none of the services in question will be provided once his licence has come into force; and it must not serve such a notice on him unless it has given him a reasonable opportunity of making representations about the matters complained of[14].

1 As to the meaning of 'person' see PARA 510 note 1.
2 Ie in accordance with the Broadcasting Act 1990 s 50 (see PARA 705): see s 51(1). As to the meaning of 'additional services licence' see PARA 704 note 5. Sections 17, 17A (award of licence to person submitting highest cash bid and award of licences subject to conditions: see PARAS 671–672) apply, with modifications, to additional services licences: see s 51(3), (4) (s 51(3) amended by the Broadcasting Act 1996 s 86(2); and the Broadcasting Act 1990 s 51(4) amended by the Communications Act 2003 s 360(3), Sch 15 para 23(1), (2)). As to the meaning of 'licence' see PARA 704 note 5.
3 As to OFCOM see PARA 507.
4 Ie in accordance with the Broadcasting Act 1990 s 51(3), (4) (see note 2). As to the meaning of 'cash bid' see PARA 669 note 29.
5 Broadcasting Act 1990 s 51(1) (amended by the Communications Act 2003 Sch 15 para 23(2)).
6 Ie submitted under the Broadcasting Act 1990 s 50(3)(b) (see PARA 705).
7 Ie within the meaning of the Communications Act 2003 Pt 3 (ss 198–362). As to the meaning of 'electronic communications network' see TELECOMMUNICATIONS vol 97 (2010) PARA 60.
8 Broadcasting Act 1990 s 51(1)(a) (substituted by the Communications Act 2003 Sch 15 para 23(3)). See also note 9.
9 Broadcasting Act 1990 s 51(1)(b) (amended by the Communications Act 2003 Sch 15 para 23(2)). Any reference to an applicant in the Broadcasting Act 1990 s 17 (as applied by s 51(3)) is accordingly a reference to an applicant in whose case it appears to OFCOM that the requirements of s 51(1)(a) and s 51(1)(b) are satisfied: s 51(1) (as so amended). As to the duration and renewal of licences see PARA 708.
10 Broadcasting Act 1990 s 51(5).
11 Broadcasting Act 1990 s 51(5)(a) (amended by the Communications Act 2003 Sch 15 para 23(2)).
12 Broadcasting Act 1990 s 51(5)(b) (amended by the Communications Act 2003 Sch 15 para 23(2)).
13 Broadcasting Act 1990 s 51(5)(i) (amended by the Communications Act 2003 Sch 15 para 23(2)). In this case, the Broadcasting Act 1990 s 17 (as applied by s 51(3)) has effect, subject to s 17(14) (see PARA 671), as if the person had not made an application for the licence: s 51(5)(ii).
14 Broadcasting Act 1990 s 51(6) (amended by the Communications Act 2003 Sch 15 para 23(2)).

707. Additional payments to be made in respect of additional services licences. An additional services licence[1] must include conditions[2] requiring the licence holder[3] to pay to OFCOM[4]:

(1) in respect of the first complete calendar year falling within the period for which the licence is in force, the amount specified in his cash bid[5];

(2) in respect of each subsequent year falling wholly or partly within that period, the amount so specified as increased by the appropriate percentage[6]; and

(3) in respect of each accounting period[7] of his falling within the licence

period referred to in head (1) above, an amount representing such percentage of the qualifying revenue[8] for that accounting period as was specified in relation to the licence[9].

An additional services licence may include conditions[10] enabling OFCOM to estimate before the beginning of an accounting period the amount due for that period by virtue of head (3) above[11], and requiring the licence holder to pay the estimated amount by monthly instalments throughout that period[12]. Such a licence may in particular include conditions authorising OFCOM to revise any estimate on one or more occasions, and to adjust the instalments payable by the licence holder to take account of the revised estimate[13]. Conditions may also be included providing for the adjustment of any overpayment or underpayment[14].

1   As to the meaning of 'additional services licence' see PARA 704 note 5.
2   Conditions included in a licence in pursuance of the Broadcasting Act 1990 s 52(1) cannot be varied under s 3(4): see s 3(5); and PARAS 665, 679.
3   As to the holder of the licence see PARAS 671 note 19, 679 note 28.
4   Broadcasting Act 1990 s 52(1) (amended by the Communications Act 2003 s 360(3), Sch 15 para 24). As to OFCOM see PARA 507. The amounts specified in heads (1)–(3) in the text are in addition to any fees required to be paid by virtue of the Broadcasting Act 1990 s 4(1)(b) (see PARAS 665, 679): see s 52(1).
5   Broadcasting Act 1990 s 52(1)(a). As to the meaning of 'cash bid' see PARA 669 note 29.
6   Broadcasting Act 1990 s 52(1)(b). As to the meaning of 'appropriate percentage' see PARA 674 note 8.
7   Where: (1) the first complete accounting period of the licence holder falling within the licence period does not begin at the same time as that period; or (2) the last complete accounting period of his falling within the licence period does not end at the same time as that period, any reference to an accounting period of his includes a reference to such part of the accounting period preceding that first complete accounting period, or (as the case may be) following that last complete accounting period, as falls within the licence period: Broadcasting Act 1990 s 52(5).
8   For these purposes, the qualifying revenue for any accounting period of the licence holder consists of all amounts which are received or to be received by him or by any connected person and are referable to the right under his licence to use, or to authorise any other person to use, in that period the spare capacity allocated by the licence: Broadcasting Act 1990 s 52(2). As to the meaning of 'spare capacity' see PARA 703. As to the meaning of 'person' see PARA 510 note 1; and as to the meaning of 'connected' see PARA 674 note 13.
9   Broadcasting Act 1990 s 52(1)(c). The accounting period is specified under s 50(1)(d)(ii) (see PARA 705): see s 52(1)(c).
10 Broadcasting Act 1990 s 52(3).
11 Broadcasting Act 1990 s 52(3)(a) (amended by the Communications Act 2003 Sch 15 para 24).
12 Broadcasting Act 1990 s 52(3)(b).
13 Broadcasting Act 1990 s 52(4)(a) (amended by the Communications Act 2003 Sch 15 para 24).
14 Broadcasting Act 1990 s 52(4)(b).

708.   Duration of licences and renewal of licences for the provision of services on assigned frequencies.   A licence[1] to provide additional services[2] on a frequency[3] which is a relevant frequency[4] or (in the case of a licence granted before the television transfer date[5]) which was assigned by the Secretary of State[6], continues in force for a period of ten years[7], and may be renewed on one or more occasions for a period of ten years beginning with the date of renewal[8]. However, an application for the renewal of a licence may be made by the licence holder[9] not earlier than four years before the date on which it would otherwise cease to be in force and not later than the day falling three months before the relevant date[10]. Where an application is made for the renewal of a licence, OFCOM may postpone its consideration of the application for as long as it thinks appropriate[11]. Where an application for the renewal of an additional services licence has been duly made to OFCOM, it may only refuse the application[12] if: (1) it is not satisfied that any additional service specified in the technical plan submitted[13] would, if the licence were renewed, be provided as proposed in that plan[14]; or (2) it proposes to grant a fresh additional services licence for the provision of any additional service which would differ in any material respect from any such service authorised to be provided under the applicant's licence[15]; or (3) it proposes to determine that all or part of the spare capacity[16] allocated by the licence is to cease to be available for the provision of additional services in order that it may be used by any relevant person[17] for the purpose of enhancing the technical quality of his television broadcasting service[18].

On the grant of any such application, OFCOM must determine an amount which is to be payable to it by the licence holder in respect of the first complete calendar year falling within the period for which the licence is to be renewed[19]. OFCOM may also specify the percentage of qualifying revenue[20] for each accounting period[21] of his that will be payable by the applicant during the period for which the licence is to be renewed[22]. Where OFCOM has granted a person's application, it must formally renew his licence not later than the relevant date or, if that is not reasonably practicable, as soon after that date as is reasonably practicable; and it must not so renew his licence unless it has notified him of the amount determined[23] and the percentage specified[24], and he has, within such period as is specified in that notification, notified it that he consents to the licence being renewed on those terms[25].

Where an additional services licence is renewed, any conditions included in it as to the making of additional payments[26] have effect during the period for which the licence has been renewed[27] as if the amount determined by OFCOM[28] were an amount specified in a cash bid submitted by the licence holder[29], and subject to any determination made[30].

1   As to the meaning of 'licence' see PARA 704 note 5.
2   As to the meaning of 'additional service' see PARA 703.
3   As to the meaning of 'frequency' see PARA 681 note 5.
4   Ie a relevant frequency for the purposes of the Broadcasting Act 1990 s 48: see PARA 703.
5   As to the meaning of 'the television transfer date' see PARA 857 note 17; definition applied by the Broadcasting Act 1990 s 53(13) (added by the Communications Act 2003 s 360(3), Sch 15 para 25(1), (7)).
6   Ie assigned under the Broadcasting Act 1990 s 65 (repealed): s 53(1) (amended by the Communications Act 2003 Sch 15 para 25(2)). As to the Secretary of State see PARA 507 note 32.
7   Broadcasting Act 1990 s 53(1)(a). This is subject to the provisions of Pt I (ss 3–71): see s 53(1)(a).
8   Broadcasting Act 1990 s 53(1)(b).
9   As to the holder of the licence see PARAS 671 note 19, 679 note 28.
10 Broadcasting Act 1990 s 53(2) (amended by the Communications Act 2003 Sch 15 para 25(3)). 'The relevant date', in relation to an additional services licence, means the date which OFCOM determines to be that by which it would need to publish a notice under the Broadcasting Act 1990 s 50 (see PARA 705) if it were to grant, as from the date on which that licence would expire if not renewed, a fresh licence to provide the additional services formerly provided under that licence: s 53(11) (amended by the Communications Act 2003 Sch 15 para 25(4)). A determination for the purposes of the Broadcasting Act 1990 s 53(11) must be made at least one year before the date determined and must be notified by OFCOM to the person who holds the licence in question: s 53(12) (added by the Communications Act 2003 Sch 15 para 25(7)). As to the meaning of 'additional services licence' see PARA 704 note 5. As to OFCOM see PARA 507.
    The provisions of the Broadcasting Act 1990 s 17(5)–(7) (see PARA 671) apply in relation to an applicant for the renewal of an additional services licence as they apply in relation to such an applicant as is mentioned in s 17(5), but with modifications: see s 53(6).

11 Broadcasting Act 1990 s 53(4) (amended by the Communications Act 2003 s 406(7), Sch 15 para 25(4), Sch 19). OFCOM must have regard to the Broadcasting Act 1990 s 53(9) (see the text and note 25): see s 53(4) (as so amended).

12 Broadcasting Act 1990 s 53(5) (amended by the Communications Act 2003 Sch 15 para 25(4)).

13 Ie submitted under the Broadcasting Act 1990 s 50(3)(b) (see PARA 705): see s 53(5)(a).

14 Broadcasting Act 1990 s 53(5)(a).

15 Broadcasting Act 1990 s 53(5)(b).

16 As to the meaning of 'spare capacity' see PARA 703.

17 'Relevant person' means the person providing a television broadcasting service on whose frequency the licensed service has been provided: Broadcasting Act 1990 s 53(5). As to the meaning of 'person' see PARA 510 note 1. As to the meaning of 'television broadcasting service' see PARA 667 note 3.

18 Broadcasting Act 1990 s 53(5)(c).

19 Broadcasting Act 1990 s 53(7)(a) (amended by the Communications Act 2003 Sch 15 para 25(4)). The amount determined by OFCOM under the Broadcasting Act 1990 s 53(7)(a) in connection with the renewal of a licence must be such amount as would, in its opinion, be the cash bid of the licence holder were the licence (instead of being renewed) to be granted for the period of the renewal on an application made in accordance with s 52(1)(a) (see PARA 707): s 53(8) (amended by the Communications Act 2003 Sch 15 para 25(4), (5)).

20 As to the qualifying revenue see PARA 707 note 8.

21 As to the accounting period see PARA 707 note 7.

22 Broadcasting Act 1990 s 53(7)(b). OFCOM may specify a different percentage from that specified under s 50(1)(d)(ii) (see PARA 705) as the percentage of qualifying revenue for each accounting period of the licence holder's that will be payable in pursuance of s 52(1)(c) (see PARA 707) during the period for which the licence is to be renewed: s 53(7)(b). OFCOM may, if it thinks fit, specify: (1) different percentages in relation to different accounting periods falling within the period for which the licence would be in force; or (2) a nil percentage in relation to any accounting period so falling: see ss 50(2), 53(7) (s 53(7) amended by the Communications Act 2003 Sch 15 para 25(4)). For the purposes of the Broadcasting Act 1990 s 53(7)(b), different percentages may be specified for different accounting periods, and the percentages that may be specified for an accounting period include a nil percentage: s 53(8A) (added by the Communications Act 2003 Sch 15 para 25(6)).

23 Ie under the Broadcasting Act 1990 s 53(7)(a) (see note 22).

24 Ie under the Broadcasting Act 1990 s 53(7)(b) (see note 22).

25 Broadcasting Act 1990 s 53(9) (amended by the Communications Act 2003 Sch 15 para 25(4)).

26 Ie in pursuance of the Broadcasting Act 1990 s 52 (see PARA 707).

27 Broadcasting Act 1990 s 53(10)(a) (amended by the Communications Act 2003 Sch 15 para 25(4)).

28 Ie under the Broadcasting Act 1990 s 53(7)(a) (see note 22).

29 Broadcasting Act 1990 s 53(10)(a)(i) (amended by the Communications Act 2003 Sch 15 para 25(4)).

30 Broadcasting Act 1990 s 53(10)(a)(ii). A determination is made under s 53(7)(b) (see note 22). Subject to s 53(10)(a), s 52 (see PARA 707) has effect in relation to the period for which the licence has been renewed as it has effect in relation to the period for which an additional services licence is originally in force: s 53(10)(b).

709. Additional services not to interfere with other transmissions. An additional services licence[1] may include such conditions[2] as OFCOM[3] considers appropriate for securing that the provision of any additional service[4] under the licence does not cause any interference[5] with the television broadcasting service[6] or services on whose frequency[7] or frequencies it is provided[8], or any other wireless telegraphy[9] transmissions[10].

1 As to the meaning of 'additional services licence' see PARA 704 note 5.

2 As to the enforcement of conditions in additional services licences see PARA 710.

3 As to OFCOM see PARA 507.

4 As to the meaning of 'additional service' see PARA 703.

5 Broadcasting Act 1990 s 54(1) (amended by the Communications Act 2003 Sch 15 para 26(1), (2)).

6 As to the meaning of 'television broadcasting service' see PARA 667 note 3.

7 As to the meaning of 'frequency' see PARA 681 note 5.

8 Broadcasting Act 1990 s 54(1)(a).
9 As to the meaning of 'wireless telegraphy' see PARA 510 note 1; definition applied by the Broadcasting Act 1990 s 202(1) (amended by the Wireless Telegraphy Act 2006 s 123, Sch 7 paras 9, 13).
10 Broadcasting Act 1990 s 54(1)(b).

710. Enforcement of additional services licences. If OFCOM[1] is satisfied that the holder of an additional services licence[2] has failed to comply with any condition of the licence or with any direction given by OFCOM[3], it may serve on him a notice requiring him to pay, within a specified period, a specified financial penalty to OFCOM[4]. The amount of a financial penalty imposed on a person[5] must not exceed 5 per cent of the qualifying revenue[6] for the licence holder's last complete accounting period falling within the period for which his licence has been in force ('the relevant period')[7].

OFCOM may not serve such a notice on any person unless it has given him a reasonable opportunity of making representations to it about the matters complained of[8].

The provisions relating to the power to revoke a Channel 3 or a Channel 5 licence[9] apply in relation to an additional services licence as they apply in relation to a licence to provide a Channel 3 service, subject to certain modifications[10].

1 As to OFCOM see PARA 507.
2 As to the meaning of 'additional services licence' see PARA 704 note 5. As to the holder of the licence see PARAS 671 note 19, 679 note 287.
3 Ie under or by virtue of any provision in the Broadcasting Act 1990 Pt I (ss 3–71).
4 Broadcasting Act 1990 s 55(1) (amended by the Communications Act 2003 s 360(3), Sch 15 para 27(1), (2)). As to payments to OFCOM see also TELECOMMUNICATIONS vol 97 (2010) PARA 44.
5 Ie under the Broadcasting Act 1990 s 55(1). As to the meaning of 'person' see PARA 510 note 1.
6 Ie as determined in accordance with the Broadcasting Act 1990 s 52(2) (see PARA 707 note 8): see s 55(1C) (s 55(1A)–(1C) added by the Communications Act 2003 s 345, Sch 13 paras 1, 5(1)).
7 Broadcasting Act 1990 s 55(1A) (as added: see note 6). In relation to a person whose first complete accounting period falling within the relevant period has not ended when the penalty is imposed, s 55(1A) is to be construed as referring to 5% of the amount which OFCOM estimates to be the qualifying revenue for that accounting period (s 55(1B) (as so added)) as determined in accordance with s 52(2) (see PARA 707) (s 55(1C) (as so added)).
8 Broadcasting Act 1990 s 55(3) (amended by the Communications Act 2003 s 360(3), Sch 15 para 27(2)).
9 Ie the powers under the Broadcasting Act 1990 s 42 (see PARA 866). As to the meaning of 'Channel 3' see PARA 667; and as to the meaning of 'Channel 3 licence' see PARA 669 note 2. As to the meaning of 'Channel 5' see PARA 681; and as to the meaning of 'Channel 5 licence' see PARA 681 note 4.
10 Broadcasting Act 1990 s 55(4). Section 42 (see PARA 866) applies with the omission of s 42(7), and, in the case of a licence renewed under s 53 as if the reference in s 42(4) to the end of the period for which the licence is to continue in force were a reference to the end of the period for which it has been renewed: see s 55(4) (amended by the Communications Act 2003 Sch 15 para 27(3)).

711. Licensing of digital additional services. An application for a licence[1] to provide digital additional services[2] (a 'digital additional services licence'[3]) must be made in such manner as OFCOM[4] may determine[5], and must be accompanied by such fee (if any) as it may determine[6].

At any time after receiving such an application and before determining it, OFCOM may require the applicant to furnish such additional information as it may consider necessary for the purpose of considering the application[7]. Any such information to be furnished to OFCOM, if it so requires, must be in such form or verified in such manner as it may specify[8].

Where such an application for a digital additional services licence is made to OFCOM, it must grant the licence unless precluded from doing so[9].

1   As to the meaning of 'licence' see PARA 698 note 1.
2   As to the meaning of 'digital additional service' see PARA 690 note 33.
3   Broadcasting Act 1996 ss 25(1), 39(1).
4   As to OFCOM see PARA 507.
5   Broadcasting Act 1996 s 25(1)(a) (amended by the Communications Act 2003 s 360(3), Sch 15 para 94(1), (2)).
6   Broadcasting Act 1996 s 25(1)(b).
7   Broadcasting Act 1996 s 25(2) (amended by the Communications Act 2003 Sch 15 para 94(2)).
8   Broadcasting Act 1996 s 25(3) (amended by the Communications Act 2003 Sch 15 para 94(2)).
9   Broadcasting Act 1996 s 25(4) (amended by the Communications Act 2003 Sch 15 para 94(2)).
    OFCOM is precluded from granting a licence by the Broadcasting Act 1996 s 3(3)(a) (see PARA 690) or s 5(1) (see PARA 828): see s 25(4) (as so amended).

712.   Duration and conditions of digital additional services licence.   A digital additional services licence[1] continues in force[2] until it is surrendered by its holder[3]. Such a licence must include such conditions as appear to OFCOM[4] to be appropriate for requiring the holder of the licence[5]:

(1)   on entering into any agreement with the provider of a television multiplex service[6] or general multiplex service for the broadcasting[7] of digital additional services[8] by means of that provider's service[9], to notify OFCOM[10]:

    (a)   the identity of the service by means of which it will be broadcast[11];

    (b)   of the period during which the services will be provided[12];

    (c)   where under the agreement the holder of the digital additional services licence will be entitled to the use of a specified amount of digital capacity, of that amount[13];

(2)   when any such agreement is varied so far as it relates to any of the matters mentioned in head (1)(a), (b) or (c) above, to notify OFCOM of the variation so far as relating to those matters[14]; and

(3)   where he is providing digital additional services to the provider of a television multiplex service or general multiplex service in accordance with such an agreement as is mentioned in head (1) above but intends to cease doing so, to notify OFCOM of that fact[15].

1   As to the meaning of 'digital additional services licence' see PARA 711.
2   As to licences being in force see PARA 865 note 11; applied by the Broadcasting Act 1996 s 147(2).
3   Broadcasting Act 1996 s 26(1). This is expressed to be subject to the provisions of Pt I (ss 1–39) and to the Broadcasting Act 1990 s 42 (see PARA 866) as applied by the Broadcasting Act 1996 s 27(8) (see PARA 713). As to the holder of the licence see PARA 698 note 10.
4   As to OFCOM see PARA 507.
5   Broadcasting Act 1996 s 26(2) (amended by the Communications Act 2003 s 360(3), Sch 15 para 95(1), (2)(a)).
6   As to the meaning of 'television multiplex service' see PARA 697; definition applied by the Broadcasting Act 1996 s 39(1) (definition added by the Communications Act 2003 Sch 15 para 100(d)).
7   As to the meaning of 'broadcast' see PARA 668 note 2; definition applied by the Broadcasting Act 1996 s 147(2).
8   As to the meaning of 'digital additional service' see PARA 690 note 33.
9   As to the meaning of 'multiplex service' see PARA 690 note 1.
10 Broadcasting Act 1996 s 26(2)(a) (amended by the Communications Act 2003 Sch 15 para 95(2)(a)–(c)).

11 Broadcasting Act 1996 s 26(2)(a)(i) (amended by the Communications Act 2003 Sch 15 para 95(2)(d)).
12 Broadcasting Act 1996 s 26(2)(a)(ii).
13 Broadcasting Act 1996 s 26(2)(a)(iii).
14 Broadcasting Act 1996 s 26(2)(b) (amended by the Communications Act 2003 Sch 15 para 95(2)(a)).
15 Broadcasting Act 1996 s 26(2)(c) (amended by the Communications Act 2003 Sch 15 para 95(2)(a), (b)).

713. Enforcement of digital additional services licences. If OFCOM[1] is satisfied that the holder of a digital additional services licence[2] has failed to comply with any condition of the licence or with any direction given by OFCOM[3], it may serve on him[4]:

(1)   a notice requiring him to pay, within a specified period, a specified financial penalty to OFCOM[5]; or

(2)   a notice providing that the licence is to expire on a specified date, which must be at least one year from the date of service of the notice[6].

The amount of any financial penalty must not exceed the maximum penalty specified below[7]. The maximum penalty is whichever is the greater of: (a) £250,000[8]; and (b) 5 per cent of the aggregate amount of the shares of multiplex revenue attributable to him in relation to television multiplex services[9] and general multiplex services in respect of relevant accounting periods[10].

OFCOM may not serve on any person[11] such a notice as is mentioned in head (1) or head (2) above unless it has given him a reasonable opportunity of making representations to it about the matters complained of[12]. Where a licence is due to expire on a particular date by virtue of a notice served on any person under head (2) above, OFCOM may, on the application of that person, revoke that notice by a further notice served on him at any time before that date, if it is satisfied that, since the date of the earlier notice, his conduct in relation to the operation of the licensed[13] service has been such as to justify the revocation of that notice[14].

1   As to OFCOM see PARA 507.
2   As to the meaning of 'digital additional services licence' see PARA 711. As to the holder of the licence see PARA 698 note 10. The Broadcasting Act 1990 s 40(1)–(4) (see PARA 864) and s 42 (see PARA 866) apply in relation to a digital additional services licence as they apply in relation to a Channel 3 licence: Broadcasting Act 1996 s 27(8). As to the meaning of 'Channel 3 licence' see PARA 669 note 2; definition applied by s 39(1).
    In its application in relation to a digital additional services licence, the Broadcasting Act 1990 s 42 has effect with the substitution for the reference in s 42(1)(a) to the Broadcasting Act 1990 Pt I (ss 3–71) of a reference to the Broadcasting Act 1996 Pt I (ss 1–39), and with the omission of the Broadcasting Act 1990 s 42(4) and of the reference to s 42(4) in s 42(6): Broadcasting Act 1996 s 27(9).
3   Ie under or by virtue of any provision of the Broadcasting Act 1996 Pt I.
4   Broadcasting Act 1996 s 27(1) (amended by the Communications Act 2003 s 360(3), Sch 15 para 96(1), (2)).
5   Broadcasting Act 1996 s 27(1)(a) (amended by the Communications Act 2003 Sch 15 para 96(2)).
6   Broadcasting Act 1996 s 27(1)(b). Any exercise by OFCOM of its powers under s 27(1) in respect of any failure to comply with any condition of a digital additional services licence does not preclude the exercise by it of its powers under the Broadcasting Act 1990 s 40 (see PARA 864) in respect of that failure: Broadcasting Act 1996 s 27(10) (amended by the Communications Act 2003 Sch 15 para 96(2)).
7   Ie the maximum penalty given by the Broadcasting Act 1996 s 27(2A): s 27(2) (amended by the Communications Act 2003 s 345, Sch 13 paras 10, 15(1)).
8   Broadcasting Act 1996 s 27(2A)(a) (s 27(2A) added by the Communications Act 2003 Sch 13 para 15(2)). The Secretary of State may by order amend the Broadcasting Act 1996 s 27(2A)(a) by substituting a different sum for the sum for the time being specified there: see s 36(1), (2)(d) (s 36(2) substituted by the Communications Act 2003 Sch 13 para 16). No order is to be made

under the Broadcasting Act 1996 s 36(1) unless a draft of the order has been laid before Parliament and approved by a resolution of each House: s 36(3) (substituted by the Communications Act 2003 Sch 13 para 16). At the date at which this volume states the law no such order had been made. As to the Secretary of State see PARA 507 note 32.

9   As to the meaning of 'television multiplex service' see PARA 697; definition applied by the Broadcasting Act 1996 s 39(1) (definition added by the Communications Act 2003 Sch 15 para 100(d)).

10 Broadcasting Act 1996 s 27(2A)(b) (as added: see note 8). 'Relevant accounting period', in relation to a television multiplex service or general multiplex service, means the last accounting period of the multiplex provider: s 27(4) (amended by the Communications Act 2003 Sch 13 para 15(3), Sch 15 para 96(3)). As to the meaning of 'multiplex provider' see PARA 693 note 3; definition applied by the Broadcasting Act 1996 s 27(5A) (added by the Communications Act 2003 Sch 15 para 96(5)). As to accounting periods see the Broadcasting Act 1996 s 13(6); and PARA 690 note 22.

The provisions of the Broadcasting Act 1996 s 15(2), (3) apply for determining or estimating the share of multiplex revenue attributable to a person for the purposes of s 27(2A) or s 27(5): s 27(5B) (added by the Communications Act 2003 Sch 13 para 15(5)). The share of multiplex revenue attributable to a programme provider or additional services provider in relation to a television multiplex service or a general multiplex service in respect of any accounting period of the multiplex provider is the aggregate of payments falling within the Broadcasting Act 1996 s 14(1)(c) or (d) (see PARA 693), and payments received or to be received from the multiplex provider which would fall within s 14(1)(c) or (d) but for the fact that they are received from the multiplex provider, less the amount of any payments made or to be made to the multiplex provider in respect of the provision of multiplex services in that period: s 15(2) (amended by the Communications Act 2003 Sch 13 para 12(2), Sch 15 para 87(1), (3)).

Where, in the case of any television multiplex service or general multiplex service, the first accounting period of the multiplex provider throughout which the holder of the digital additional services licence provides a digital additional service for broadcasting by means of the multiplex service ('the first period') has not ended when the penalty is imposed, then for the above purposes the share of multiplex revenue attributable to the holder of the digital additional services licence in relation to that multiplex service for the relevant accounting period is taken to be the amount which OFCOM estimates to be the share of multiplex revenue attributable to him for the first period: Broadcasting Act 1996 s 27(5) (amended by the Communications Act 2003 Sch 13 para 15(4), Sch 15 para 96(2), (4)). As to the meaning of 'digital additional service' see PARA 690 note 33. As to the meaning of 'broadcast' see PARA 668 note 2; definition applied by the Broadcasting Act 1996 s 147(2).

11 As to the meaning of 'person' see PARA 510 note 1.
12 Broadcasting Act 1996 s 27(6) (amended by the Communications Act 2003 Sch 15 para 96(2)).
13 As to the meaning of 'licensed' see PARA 698 note 1.
14 Broadcasting Act 1996 s 27(7) (amended by the Communications Act 2003 Sch 15 para 96(2)).

(iii) Local Digital Television Providers

714. Grants by OFCOM to local digital television providers. The Secretary of State[1] may by order provide that OFCOM[2] may make such grants as it considers appropriate to the provider of any local television service in respect of which an order[3] modifying the statutory provisions relating to television broadcasting is in force[4]. Such a grant may be made on such terms and conditions, and will become repayable to OFCOM in such circumstances, as may be specified by OFCOM when making the grant[5]. A person is not: (1) by reason of the making to him of a grant by virtue of these provisions; or (2) by reason of any terms or conditions (including any provisions for repayment) subject to which such a grant is or has been made to him, to be a disqualified person[6] in relation to a licence under Part I of the Broadcasting Act 1990[7], or under Part I of the Broadcasting Act 1996[8], which is granted in accordance with any provision made by an order modifying the statutory provisions relating to television broadcasting[9]. No order is to be made containing provision authorised by the above provisions unless a draft of the order has been laid before Parliament and approved by a resolution of each House[10].

1 As to the Secretary of State see PARA 507 note 32.
2 As to OFCOM see PARA 507.
3 Ie under the Communications Act 2003 s 244: see PARA 715.
4 Communications Act 2003 s 359(2). As to the power of the Secretary of State to make orders under the Communications Act 2003 see s 402; and TELECOMMUNICATIONS vol 97 (2010) PARA 77. At the date at which this volume states the law, no order had been made under s 359.
5 Communications Act 2003 s 359(3).
6 Ie by virtue of any provision of the Broadcasting Act 1990 Sch 2: Communications Act 2003 s 359(4). As to disqualified persons see PARAS 822 et seq, 830 et seq.
7 Ie the Broadcasting Act 1990 Pt I (ss 3–71).
8 Ie the Broadcasting Act 1996 Pt I (ss 1–39).
9 Communications Act 2003 s 359(4), (5)(a).
10 Communications Act 2003 s 359(6).

715. Local digital television services. The Secretary of State[1] may by order provide for: (1) any of the provisions of Part 3[2] of the Communications Act 2003[3]; or (2) any provision of Part I of the Broadcasting Act 1990[4] or of Part I of the Broadcasting Act 1996[5] (regulation of television services), to have effect, in relation to services of such descriptions as may be set out in an order under these provisions, with such modifications as he considers necessary or appropriate for services of that description[6]. The Secretary of State is not to make an order under these provisions in relation to a description of services except where: (a) the description is of services to be provided in digital form with a view to their being included in a television multiplex service[7]; (b) the description is confined to services falling within a specified provision[8]; and (c) the Secretary of State is satisfied that the making of an order under these provisions in relation to that description of services will make possible, facilitate or encourage the provision of services so falling[9]. An order under these provisions in relation to a description of services may, in particular, impose prohibitions or limitations on the inclusion of advertisements in services of that description and on the sponsorship of programmes included in the services[10]. No order is to be made containing provision authorised by these provisions unless a draft of the order has been laid before Parliament and approved by a resolution of each House[11].

1 As to the Secretary of State see PARA 507 note 32.
2 Ie the Communications Act 2003 Pt 3 (ss 198–362).
3 Ie apart from the Communications Act 2003 s 244 and the provisions relating exclusively to sound services.
4 Ie the Broadcasting Act 1990 Pt I (ss 3–71).
5 Ie the Broadcasting Act 1996 Pt I (ss 1–39).
6 Communications Act 2003 s 244(1). As to the power of the Secretary of State to make orders under the Communications Act 2003 see s 402; and TELECOMMUNICATIONS vol 97 (2010) PARA 77.
    The power, by an order under s 244, to make incidental, supplemental or consequential provision in connection with provision authorised by s 244(1) includes power to make incidental, supplemental or consequential provision modifying provisions of the Broadcasting Act 1990, the Broadcasting Act 1996 or the Communications Act 2003 that are not mentioned in s 244(1): s 244(8).
7 As to the meaning of 'television multiplex service' see PARA 697; definition applied by the Communications Act 2003 s 362(1).
8 Ie services falling within one or both of the Communications Act 2003 s 244(3) and s 244(4). Services fall within s 244(3) if they are: (1) intended for reception only at a particular establishment or otherwise on particular premises; or (2) provided for the purposes only of a particular event: s 244(3). Services fall within s 244(4) if the Secretary of State considers that they are services in relation to which all the following conditions are satisfied: (a) they are intended for reception only within a particular area or locality; (b) their provision meets, or would meet, the needs of the area or locality where they are received; (c) their provision is or

would be likely to broaden the range of television programmes available for viewing by persons living or working in that area or locality; and (d) their provision is or would be likely to increase the number and range of the programmes about that area or locality that are available for such viewing, or to increase the number of programmes made in that area or locality that would be so available: s 244(4). Services will be taken for the purposes of s 244(4) to meet the needs of an area or locality if, and only if: (i) their provision brings social or economic benefits to the area or locality, or to different categories of persons living or working in that area or locality; or (ii) they cater for the tastes, interests and needs of some or all of the different descriptions of people living or working in the area or locality (including, in particular, tastes, interests and needs that are of special relevance in the light of the descriptions of people who do so live and work): s 244(5). For the purposes of s 244(4), (5), the references to persons living or working in an area or locality include references to persons undergoing education or training in that area or locality: s 244(6).

9   Communications Act 2003 s 244(2).
10 Communications Act 2003 s 244(7).
11 Communications Act 2003 s 244(9).

(9) CABLE AND SATELLITE BROADCASTING

(i) Licensing of Television Licensable Content Services (TLCS)

716.   In general. In Part 3 of the Communications Act 2003[1], 'television licensable content service' means[2] any service falling within heads (a) and (b) below in so far as it is provided with a view to its availability for reception by members of the public being secured by one or more of the following means: (1) the broadcasting of the service (whether by the person providing it or by another) from a satellite; (2) the broadcasting of the service (whether by that person or by another) by means of a radio multiplex service[3]; or (3) the distribution of the service (whether by that person or by another) by any means involving the use of an electronic communications network[4]. A service falls within this provision if it: (a) is provided (whether in digital or in analogue form) as a service that is to be made available for reception by members of the public; and (b) consists of or has as its principal purpose the provision of television programmes or electronic programme guides[5], or both[6].

If it is considered appropriate, the Secretary of State[7] may modify the above provisions[8].

1   Ie the Communications Act 2003 Pt 3 (ss 198–362).
2   Ie subject to the Communications Act 2003 s 233 (see the test and notes 7–14).
3   As to the meaning of 'radio multiplex service' see PARA 753; definition applied by the Communications Act 2003 s 362(1).
4   Communications Act 2003 s 232(1) (amended by SI 2006/2131). See further note 6. As to the meaning of 'electronic communications network' see TELECOMMUNICATIONS vol 97 (2010) PARA 60.
5   For these purposes, 'electronic programme guide' means a service which consists of: (1) the listing or promotion, or both the listing and the promotion, of some or all of the programmes included in any one or more programme services the providers of which are or include persons other than the provider of the guide; and (2) a facility for obtaining access, in whole or in part, to the programme service or services listed or promoted in the guide: Communications Act 2003 s 232(6).
6   Communications Act 2003 s 232(2) (amended by SI 2009/2979). As to the meaning of 'available for reception by members of the public' see PARA 796. As to services which are not television licensable content services see PARA 688.
    Where: (1) a service consisting of television programmes, an electronic programme guide or both ('the main service') is provided by a person as a service to be made available for reception by members of the public; and (2) that person provides the main service with other services or facilities that are ancillary to, or otherwise relate to, the main service and are also provided so as to be so available or in order to make a service so available, s 232(1) has effect as if the main

service and such of the other services or facilities as are relevant ancillary services and are not two-way services constituted a single service falling within s 232(2): s 232(3). 'Relevant ancillary service', in relation to the main service, means a service or facility provided or made available by the provider of the main service that consists of or gives access to: (a) assistance for disabled people in relation to some or all of the programmes included in the main service; (b) a service (apart from advertising) which is not an electronic programme guide but relates to the promotion or listing of programmes so included; or (c) any other service (apart from advertising) which is ancillary to one or more programmes so included and relates directly to their contents: s 232(6). A service is a two-way service for the purposes of s 232 if it is provided by means of an electronic communications network and an essential feature of the service is that the purposes for which it is provided involve the use of that network, or a part of it, both: (i) for the transmission of visual images or sounds (or both) by the person providing the service to users of the service; and (ii) for the transmission of visual images or sounds (or both) by those users for reception by the person providing the service or by other users of the service: s 232(5). Where a person providing the main service provides it with a facility giving access to another service, the other service will also be taken for the purposes of s 232 as provided by that person with the main service only if what is comprised in the other service is something over which that person has general control: s 232(4).

7   As to the Secretary of State see PARA 507 note 32.

8   Ie the Communications Act 2003 s 232: see s 234. For such an order see the Television Licensable Content Services Order 2006, SI 2006/2131.

717. Licensing. The licence that is required[1] in respect of a television licensable content service[2] is a licence granted under Part I of the Broadcasting Act 1990[3] on an application complying with the following provisions[4]. An application for a licence to provide a television licensable content service must: (1) be made in such manner; (2) contain such information about the applicant, his business and the service he proposes to provide; and (3) be accompanied by such fee (if any), as OFCOM[5] may determine[6]. The provision of more than one television licensable content service will require a separate licence under Part I of the Broadcasting Act 1990 to be granted and held in respect of each service[7]. A single licence to provide a television licensable content service may authorise the provision of a service which consists (to any extent) of different programmes to be broadcast simultaneously, or virtually so[8]. A licence to provide a television licensable content service will continue in force until such time as it is surrendered or is revoked in accordance with any of the provisions of Chapter 2 of Part 3 of the Communications Act 2003[9] or of the Broadcasting Act 1990[10].

A licence to provide a television licensable content service must contain such conditions as OFCOM considers appropriate for requiring the licence holder: (a) on entering into any agreement with the provider of a radio multiplex service[11] for the provision of a television licensable content service to be broadcast by means of that multiplex service, to notify OFCOM: (i) of the identity of the radio multiplex service; (ii) of the period during which the service will be provided; and (iii) where under the agreement he will be entitled to the use of a specified amount of digital capacity, of that amount; (b) when any such agreement is varied so far as it relates to any of the matters mentioned in head (a)(i), (ii) or (iii), to notify OFCOM of the variation so far as relating to those matters; and (c) where he is providing a television licensable content service to the provider of a radio multiplex service in accordance with such an agreement as is mentioned in head (a) but intends to cease doing so, to notify OFCOM of that fact[12].

1   Ie for the purposes of the Broadcasting Act 1990 s 13 (see PARA 593).

2   As to the meaning of 'television licensable content service' see PARA 716.

3   Ie the Broadcasting Act 1990 Pt I (ss 3–71).

4   Ie complying with the Communications Act 2003 s 235: s 235(1).

5   As to OFCOM see PARA 507.

6 Communications Act 2003 s 235(2). Where an application is made to OFCOM in accordance with s 235(2) for a licence to provide a television licensable content service, OFCOM is entitled to refuse the application only if: (1) it is required to do so by the Broadcasting Act 1990 s 3(3) (licences to be held only by fit and proper persons: see PARAS 671, 679); (2) it is required to do so by s 5 (restrictions on the holding of licences: see PARA 821); or (3) it is satisfied that, if the application were to be granted, the provision of the service would be likely to involve contraventions of: (a) standards set under the Communications Act 2003 s 319 (see PARA 897); or (b) the provisions of a code of practice in force under the Broadcasting Act 1996 Pt V (ss 107–130) (fairness: see PARA 906 et seq): Communications Act 2003 s 235(3).

7 Communications Act 2003 s 235(4).

8 Communications Act 2003 s 235(5).

9 Ie the Communications Act 2003 Pt 3 Ch 2 (ss 211–244).

10 Communications Act 2003 s 235(6).

11 As to the meaning of 'radio multiplex service' see PARA 753; definition applied by the Communications Act 2003 s 362(1).

12 Communications Act 2003 s 235(7) (added by SI 2006/2131).

718. Abolition of separate licences for certain television services. The authorisations that are to be capable of being granted on or after the television transfer date[1] by or under a licence under Part I of the Broadcasting Act 1990[2] do not include the authorisation of the provision, as such, of: (1) any satellite television service[3]; or (2) any licensable programme service[4]. So much of any relevant existing licence[5] as authorises the provision of a service which consists in or includes a television licensable content service[6]: (a) has effect, on and after the television transfer date, as a licence under Part I of the Broadcasting Act 1990 authorising the provision of the television licensable content service comprised in the licensed service; (b) so has effect as a licence which, notwithstanding its terms and conditions, is to continue in force until such time as it is surrendered or is revoked in accordance with provisions of Chapter 2 of Part 3 of the Communications Act 2003[7] or of the Broadcasting Act 1990; and (c) otherwise has effect as a licence on the same terms and conditions as those on which it had effect immediately before the television transfer date[8].

1 As to the meaning of 'the television transfer date' see PARA 857 note 17.

2 Ie the Broadcasting Act 1990 Pt I (ss 3–71).

3 As defined, disregarding its repeal by the Communications Act 2003, in the Broadcasting Act 1990 s 43(1).

4 Ie as defined, disregarding its repeal by the Communications Act 2003, in the Broadcasting Act 1990 s 46(1): Communications Act 2003 s 240(1). Section 240(1) does not affect OFCOM's power, by means of a licence authorising the provision of a service falling within s 211(1) (see PARA 857), to authorise the provision of so much of any formerly regulated television service as is comprised in the licensed service: s 240(2). As to OFCOM see PARA 507.

5 'Relevant existing licence', means any licence which: (1) was granted by the Independent Television Commission under the Broadcasting Act 1990 Pt I before the television transfer date; and (2) is in force immediately before the television transfer date as a licence authorising the provision of a formerly regulated service: Communications Act 2003 s 240(5). 'Formerly regulated television service' means a service mentioned in s 240(1): s 240(5). As to the Independent Television Commission see PARA 507.

6 As to the meaning of 'television licensable content service' see PARA 716.

7 Ie the Communications Act 2003 Pt 3 Ch 2 (ss 211–244).

8 Communications Act 2003 s 240(3). It is the duty of OFCOM to exercise its power under the Broadcasting Act 1990 s 3 (see PARAS 671, 679) to make such variations of any licence having effect in accordance with the Communications Act 2003 s 240(3) as (after complying with the Broadcasting Act 1990 s 3(4)(b)) it considers appropriate for the purpose of performing its duty under the Communications Act 2003 s 263 (see PARA 602): s 240(4).

(ii)　Must-carry and Must-offer Obligations

719.　General conditions: must-carry obligations.　General conditions[1] may include conditions making any provision that OFCOM[2] considers appropriate for securing that particular services are broadcast[3] or otherwise transmitted by means of the electronic communications networks[4] described in the conditions[5]. A general condition containing provision authorised by these provisions[6] is not[7] to require a service to be broadcast or otherwise transmitted by means of an electronic communications network unless: (1) the service is included in the list of must-carry services; and (2) the effect of the requirement is confined to networks by means of which public electronic communications services[8] are provided that are used by a significant number of end-users as their principal means of receiving television programmes[9].

The list of must-carry services is as follows: (a) any service of television programmes provided by the BBC[10] so far as it is provided in digital form and is a service in relation to which OFCOM has functions; (b) the Channel 3 services[11] so far as provided in digital form; (c) Channel 4[12] so far as provided in digital form; (d) Channel 5[13] so far as provided in digital form; (e) S4C Digital[14]; (f) the digital public teletext service[15].

General conditions making provision authorised by these provisions in relation to a listed service must, to such extent as OFCOM considers appropriate[16], apply the requirement to broadcast or otherwise transmit that service to every service which is an ancillary service[17] by reference to the listed service, and provide for the listed service to be treated for the purposes of the conditions as constituting such other services comprised in or provided with that service as may be determined by OFCOM[18]. General conditions making provision authorised by these provisions must also comply with all such restrictions (if any) as may be imposed by order made by the Secretary of State[19] as to the maximum and minimum amounts, or proportions, of available capacity that are to be required by such conditions to be used in the case of a network for the broadcasting or other transmission of particular services, or descriptions of service[20].

It is the duty of the Secretary of State from time to time to review the list of must-carry services and any requirements for the time being in force under these provisions with respect to the terms on which services must be broadcast or otherwise transmitted[21]. Where the Secretary of State carries out such a review, he must consult the following about the matters under review: (i) OFCOM; and (ii) such persons[22] who, in his opinion, are likely to be affected by a modification of the list of must-carry services, or who represent any of those persons, as he thinks fit[23]. If, on such a review, he considers it appropriate to do so, the Secretary of State may by order modify the list of must-carry services[24].

The Secretary of State may also, if he considers it appropriate to do so (whether on such a review or in any other circumstances), by order make provision imposing requirements as to what, as between: (A) the person providing a must-carry service; and (B) the person providing a network by means of which it is to be provided, are to be the terms on which the service is to be broadcast or otherwise transmitted, in pursuance of general conditions set in accordance with these provisions, by means of that network[25].

1　See TELECOMMUNICATIONS vol 97 (2010) PARA 98. See also PARA 602.
2　As to OFCOM see PARA 507.

3   'Broadcast' means broadcast by wireless telegraphy; and cognate expressions are to be construed accordingly: Communications Act 2003 s 405(1). As to the meaning of 'wireless telegraphy' see PARA 510 note 1. See Case C-250/06 *United Pan-Europe Communications Belgium SA v Belgium* [2007] ECR I-11135, [2008] 2 CMLR 45, ECJ (legislation requiring cable operators providing services in member state to broadcast television programmes transmitted by private broadcasters falling under public powers of member state not precluded by EC Treaty art 49 (now the Treaty on the Functioning of the European Union: see PARA 506 note 27)).

4   As to the meaning of 'electronic communications network' see the Communications Act 2003 ss 32, 405(1); and TELECOMMUNICATIONS vol 97 (2010) PARA 60.

5   Communications Act 2003 s 64(1). Section 362 (interpretation of Pt 3 (ss 198–362)) applies for construing s 64 as it applies for the purposes of Pt 3: s 64(14). See Case C-336/07 *Kabel Deutschland Vertrieb und Service GmbH & Co KG v Niedersächsische Landesmedienanstalt für Privaten Rundfunk* [2008] ECR I-10889, [2009] 2 CMLR 117, ECJ.

6   Ie the Communications Act 2003 s 64.

7   Subject to the Communications Act 2003 s 64(4).

8   As to the meaning of 'public electronic communications service' see TELECOMMUNICATIONS vol 97 (2010) PARA 104.

9   Communications Act 2003 s 64(2).

10 As to the meaning of 'BBC' see PARA 603 note 1; and as to the BBC see PARAS 603–626.

11 As to the meaning of 'Channel 3 service' see PARA 602 note 8.

12 As to the meaning of 'Channel 4' see PARA 602 note 9.

13 As to the meaning of 'Channel 5' see PARA 602 note 10.

14 As to the meaning of 'S4C Digital' see PARA 644 note 7.

15 Communications Act 2003 s 64(3). As to the meaning of 'digital public teletext service' see PARA 697 note 3.

16 Ie subject to the Communications Act 2003 s 64(5) (see the text to note 20).

17 As to the meaning of 'ancillary service' see PARA 690 note 28 (definition applied by the Communications Act 2003 s 64(14)).

18 Communications Act 2003 s 64(4).

19 As to the Secretary of State see PARA 507 note 32.

20 Communications Act 2003 s 64(5). In making an order under s 64(5), the Secretary of State must have regard to: (1) the objective of securing that services included in the list of must-carry services, and the other services to which conditions set in accordance with s 64 are likely to be applied by s 64(4), are available for reception by as many members of the public in the United Kingdom as practicable; and (2) the need to secure that the amount of capacity available in the case of every network for making other services available is reasonable and, accordingly, that the burden of complying with conditions set in accordance with s 64 is proportionate to the public benefit to be secured by that objective: s 64(6). Before making an order under s 64(5), the Secretary of State must consult: (a) OFCOM; and (b) such persons who, in his opinion, are likely to be affected by the order, or who represent any of those persons, as he thinks fit: s 64(13). At the date at which this volume states the law, no order had been made under s 64(5). As to the power of the Secretary of State to make orders under the Communications Act 2003 see s 402; and TELECOMMUNICATIONS vol 97 (2010) PARA 77. As to the meaning of 'United Kingdom' see PARA 510 note 13.

21 Communications Act 2003 s 64(7).

22 As to the meaning of 'person' see PARA 510 note 1.

23 Communications Act 2003 s 64(8).

24 Communications Act 2003 s 64(9). In determining whether it is appropriate for the purposes of s 64(9) to add a service to the list of must-carry services or to remove it, the Secretary of State must have regard, in particular, to: (1) the public benefit to be secured by the addition of the service to the list, or by its retention in the list; (2) the extent to which the service (if it were not included in the list) would nevertheless be made available to an acceptable technical standard by means of the networks to which conditions set in accordance with s 64 apply; (3) the capacity left available, after the requirements of those conditions have been complied with, for the broadcasting or other transmission of material by means of each of those networks; and (4) the need to secure that the burden of complying with conditions so set is proportionate to the objective of securing that the services in the list of must-carry services, and the other services to which conditions set in accordance with s 64 are likely to applied by s 64(4), are available for reception by as many members of the public in the United Kingdom as practicable: s 64(10). At the date at which this volume states the law, no order had been made under s 64(9).

25 Communications Act 2003 s 64(11). An order under s 64(11) may provide for the terms to be determined by OFCOM in accordance with the provisions of the order: s 64(12). Before making an order under s 64(11) in a case in which there has been no review under s 64(7) (see the text

to note 21), the Secretary of State must consult: (1) OFCOM; and (2) such persons who, in his opinion, are likely to be affected by the order, or who represent any of those persons, as he thinks fit: s 64(13). At the date at which this volume states the law, no order had been made under s 64(11).

720. Must-offer obligations in relation to networks. The regulatory regime for: (1) every licensed public service channel[1]; (2) the public teletext service[2]; and (3) every licensed television service[3] added by order[4] to the list of must-carry services, includes the conditions that OFCOM[5] considers appropriate for securing the three objectives[6] set out below[7].

The first objective is that the channel or other service, so far as it is provided in digital form, is at all times offered as available (subject to the need to agree terms) to be broadcast or distributed by means of every appropriate network[8].

The second objective is that the person providing the channel or other service does his best to secure that arrangements are entered into, and kept in force, that ensure: (a) that the channel or other service, so far as it is provided in digital form, is broadcast or distributed on appropriate networks; and (b) that the broadcasting and distribution of the channel or other service, in accordance with those arrangements, result in its being available for reception, by means of appropriate networks, by as many members of its intended audience[9] as practicable[10].

The third objective is that the arrangements entered into and kept in force for the purpose of securing the second objective prohibit the imposition, for or in connection with the provision of an appropriate network, of any charge that is attributable (whether directly or indirectly) to the conferring of an entitlement to receive the channel or other service in question in an intelligible form by means of that network[11].

The three objectives apply only in relation to times when the channel or other service in its digital form is included in the list of must-carry services[12]. Conditions imposed under these provisions in relation to a channel or other service must, to such extent as OFCOM considers appropriate: (i) require arrangements made or kept in force for the purpose of securing the second objective to apply in the case of every service which is an ancillary service by reference to the channel or other service in question as they apply to the channel or other service itself; and (ii) provide for the channel or other service to which the conditions apply to be treated, in relation to particular appropriate networks, as constituting such services comprised in or provided with that channel or other service as may be determined by OFCOM[13].

1 As to the meaning of 'licensed public service channel' see PARA 788 note 1.
2 As to the public teletext service see PARA 686.
3 'Licensed television service' means a service falling to be licensed under the Broadcasting Act 1990 Pt I (ss 3–71) or the Broadcasting Act 1996 Pt I (ss 1–39): Communications Act 2003 s 272(7).
4 Ie under the Communications Act 2003 s 64: see PARA 719.
5 As to OFCOM see PARA 507.
6 Ie so far as they are not secured by provision made under the Communications Act 2003 s 243: see PARA 697.
7 Communications Act 2003 s 272(1). Section 272 was brought into force only on 31 January 2010: see the Communications Act 2003 (Commencement No 4) Order 2009, SI 2009/2130. A commencement order under the Communications Act 2003 s 411(2) was not to appoint a day for s 272 to come into force that fell less than six months after the day on which the order was made: s 272(10).
8 Communications Act 2003 s 272(2). 'Appropriate network' means an electronic communications network by means of which public electronic communications services are provided that are used by a significant number of end-users as their principal means of receiving

television programmes: s 272(7). For the purposes of s 272(7), 'public electronic communications service' and 'end-user' each has the same meaning as in Pt 2 (ss 32–197) (see TELECOMMUNICATIONS vol 97 (2010) PARA 104): s 272(9). For the purposes of s 272, an electronic communications network is not an appropriate network in relation to so much of a channel or other service as is provided only for a particular area or locality of the United Kingdom unless it is a network by means of which electronic communications services are provided to persons in that area or locality: s 272(8). As to the meaning of 'electronic communications network' see TELECOMMUNICATIONS vol 97 (2010) PARA 60. As to the meaning of 'United Kingdom' see PARA 510 note 13.

9   'Intended audience', in relation to a channel or other service, means: (1) if the channel or other service is one provided only for a particular area or locality of the United Kingdom, members of the public in that area or locality; (2) if the channel or other service is one provided for members of a particular community, members of that community; and (3) in any other case, members of the public in the United Kingdom: Communications Act 2003 s 272(7).

10   Communications Act 2003 s 272(3).
11   Communications Act 2003 s 272(4).
12   Ie in the Communications Act 2003 s 64 (see PARA 719): s 272(5).
13   Communications Act 2003 s 272(6).

721.   Must-offer obligations in relation to satellite services.   The regulatory regime for: (1) every licensed public service channel[1]; (2) the public teletext service[2]; and (3) every other licensed television service[3] specified for the purposes of these provisions[4] in an order made by the Secretary of State, includes the conditions that OFCOM[5] considers appropriate for securing the three objectives[6] set out below[7].

The first objective is that the channel or other service, so far as it is provided in digital form, is at all times offered as available (subject to the need to agree terms) to be broadcast by means of every satellite television service[8] that is available for reception by members of the public in the whole or a part of the United Kingdom[9].

The second objective is that the person providing the channel or other service does his best to secure that arrangements are entered into, and kept in force, that ensure: (a) that the channel or other service, so far as it is provided in digital form, is broadcast by means of satellite television services that are broadcast so as to be available for reception by members of the public in the United Kingdom; and (b) that the broadcasting, in accordance with those arrangements, of the channel or other service by means of those satellite television services results in its being available for reception in an intelligible form and by means of those services by as many members of its intended audience[10] as practicable[11].

The third objective is that the arrangements entered into and kept in force for the purpose of securing the second objective prohibit the imposition, for or in connection with the provision of a satellite television service, of any charge that is attributable (whether directly or indirectly) to the conferring of an entitlement to receive the channel or other service in question in an intelligible form by means of that service[12].

The three objectives apply only in relation to a time when the channel or service is included, in its digital form, in the list of services that are must-provide services[13]. Conditions imposed under these provisions in relation to a channel or other service must, to such extent as OFCOM considers appropriate: (i) require arrangements made or kept in force for the purpose of securing the second objective to apply in the case of every service which is an ancillary service by reference to the channel or other service in question as they apply to the channel or other service itself; and (ii) provide for the channel or other service to which the conditions apply to be treated, in relation to particular satellite television services, as constituting such services comprised in or provided with the channel or other service as may be determined by OFCOM[14].

1 As to the meaning of 'licensed public service channel' see PARA 788 note 1.
2 As to the public teletext service see PARA 686.
3 'Licensed television service' means a service falling to be licensed under the Broadcasting Act 1990 Pt I (ss 3–71) or the Broadcasting Act 1996 Pt I (ss 1–39): Communications Act 2003 s 273(7).
4 Ie the Communications Act 2003 s 273.
5 As to OFCOM see PARA 507.
6 Ie so far as they are not secured by conditions imposed under the Communications Act 2003 s 272: see PARA 720.
7 Communications Act 2003 s 273(1). Section 273 was brought into force only on 31 January 2010: see the Communications Act 2003 (Commencement No 4) Order 2009, SI 2009/2130. A commencement order under the Communications Act 2003 s 411(2) was not to appoint a day for s 272 to come into force that fell less than six months after the day on which the order was made: s 273(8).
8 'Satellite television service' means a service which: (1) consists in or involves the broadcasting of television programme services from a satellite; and (2) is used by a significant number of the persons by whom the broadcasts are received in an intelligible form as their principal means of receiving television programmes: Communications Act 2003 s 273(7). As to the meaning of 'television programme service' see PARA 790 note 5.
9 Communications Act 2003 s 273(2). As to the meaning of 'available for reception by members of the public' see PARA 796.
10 'Intended audience', in relation to a channel or other service, means: (1) if the channel or other service is one provided only for a particular area or locality of the United Kingdom, members of the public in that area or locality; (2) if the channel or other service is one provided for members of a particular community, members of that community; and (3) in any other case, members of the public in the United Kingdom: Communications Act 2003 s 273(7). As to the meaning of 'United Kingdom' see PARA 510 note 13.
11 Communications Act 2003 s 273(3).
12 Communications Act 2003 s 273(4).
13 Ie for the purposes of the Communications Act 2003 s 274 (see PARA 722): s 273(5).
14 Communications Act 2003 s 273(6).

722. Securing reception of must-provide services in certain areas. As from a day to be appointed[1], the regulatory regime for: (1) every licensed public service channel[2]; (2) the public teletext service[3]; and (3) every licensed television service[4] added by order[5] to the list of must-provide services[6], includes the conditions that OFCOM considers appropriate for securing that arrangements satisfying the requirements of these provisions[7] are entered into and maintained by all the persons who provide must-provide services[8]. The conditions imposed on a person under these provisions may include the conditions that OFCOM considers appropriate for securing, in a case where: (a) the persons providing must-provide services fail to enter into or maintain arrangements satisfying the requirements of these provisions; and (b) OFCOM makes and imposes arrangements of its own instead, that the person bound by the conditions is required to act in accordance with arrangements imposed by OFCOM[9]. The arrangements that are to be entered into, or may be imposed, are arrangements that secure: (i) that a facility[10] for receiving each must-provide service is made available to every member of the intended audience[11] for that service who is unable, without the use of that facility, to receive it in an intelligible form and free of charge[12]; (ii) that the facility is one under which every such member of the intended audience for a must-provide service is entitled, free of charge, to receive in an intelligible form so much of a service broadcast from a satellite as includes that must-provide service; (iii) that the cost of making that facility available is shared, in appropriate proportions, by all the persons providing must-provide services; (iv) that procedures are established and maintained for dealing with complaints from persons claiming to be entitled, in accordance with the arrangements, to receive a service free of charge, and for resolving disputes about the existence or extent of such an entitlement; (v) that the availability of those procedures is adequately publicised in accordance with guidance given from time to time by OFCOM[13].

1 Ie by an order made by the Secretary of State under the Communications Act 2003 s 411(2). A commencement order must not appoint a day for s 274 to come into force that falls less than six months after the day on which the order is made: s 274(11). At the date at which this volume states the law, no such order had been made. As to the Secretary of State see PARA 507 note 32.
2 As to the meaning of 'licensed public service channel' see PARA 788 note 1.
3 As to the public teletext service see PARA 686.
4 'Licensed television service' means a service falling to be licensed under the Broadcasting Act 1990 Pt I (ss 3–71) or the Broadcasting Act 1996 Pt I (ss 1–39): Communications Act 2003 s 274(10).
5 Ie under the Communications Act 2003 s 275 (must-provide services for the purposes of s 274).
6 'Must-provide service' means a service for the time being included in the list of must-provide services in the Communications Act 2003 s 275: s 274(10). For the purposes of s 274, the list of must-provide services is as follows: (1) every service of television programmes provided by the BBC so far as it is provided in digital form and is a service in relation to which OFCOM has functions; (2) the Channel 3 services so far as provided in digital form; (3) Channel 4 so far as provided in digital form; (4) Channel 5 so far as provided in digital form; (5) S4C Digital; (6) the digital public teletext service: s 275(1). As to the meaning of 'BBC' see PARA 603 note 1; and as to the BBC see PARAS 603–626. As to OFCOM see PARA 507. As to the meaning of 'Channel 3 service' see PARA 602 note 8. As to the meaning of 'Channel 4' see PARA 602 note 9. As to the meaning of 'Channel 5' see PARA 602 note 10. As to the meaning of 'S4C Digital' see PARA 644 note 7. As to the meaning of 'digital public teletext service' see PARA 697 note 3.
   The Secretary of State may by order modify the list of must-provide services in s 275(1) (see heads (1)–(6)): s 275(2). In determining whether it is appropriate, by an order under s 275(2), to add a service to the list of must-provide services or to remove a service from that list, the Secretary of State must have regard, in particular, to: (a) the public benefit to be secured by the addition of the service to the list, or by its retention in the list; (b) the likely effect of the proposed modification as respects the costs to be borne, under arrangements entered into or imposed under s 274, by the persons who, after the coming into force of the modification, would have to be parties to those arrangements; and (c) the extent to which that effect is proportionate to the benefit mentioned in head (a): s 275(3).
7 Ie the Communications Act 2003 s 274.
8 Communications Act 2003 s 274(1).
9 Communications Act 2003 s 274(2). Before imposing any arrangements for the purposes of a condition under s 274(2), OFCOM must consult all the persons who provide must-provide services: s 274(5).
10 References in the Communications Act 2003 s 274 to a facility for receiving a must-provide service include references to: (1) software to be used in giving effect to the entitlement to receive a must-provide service in an intelligible form; and (2) apparatus to be used in associating apparatus capable of being used for receiving such a service, or for putting it into an intelligible form, with a person having such an entitlement, but do not otherwise include references to apparatus: s 274(9). The quality of reception that is required before someone is to be treated for the purposes of any conditions imposed under s 274 as able to receive a service in an intelligible form is to be determined by OFCOM: s 274(8).
11 'Intended audience', in relation to a must-provide service, means: (1) if the service is one provided only for a particular area or locality of the United Kingdom, members of the public in that area or locality; (2) if the service is one provided for members of a particular community, members of that community; and (3) in any other case, members of the public in the United Kingdom: Communications Act 2003 s 274(10). As to the meaning of 'United Kingdom' see PARA 510 note 13.
12 For the purposes of the Communications Act 2003 s 274, the reception of a service is not free of charge: (1) if reception of the service is made conditional on the acceptance of an entitlement to receive another service in relation to which a charge is imposed (whether directly or indirectly); (2) if a charge is made for or in connection with the provision of a service which is an ancillary service in relation to the service in question; (3) if any consideration is required from the persons to whom it is made available for the provision of assistance for disabled people in respect of

programmes included in the service; or (4) if any other consideration is required to be given, by the person entitled to receive it, for or in connection with its provision or availability: s 274(6). A service is not prevented from being free of charge by a requirement to pay sums in accordance with regulations under s 365 (see PARA 950): s 274(7).

13   Communications Act 2003 s 274(3). Arrangements entered into by the providers of must-provide services for the purposes of s 274(3), and any modifications of such arrangements made by the parties to them, are to have effect only if approved by OFCOM: s 274(4).

(10) LICENSING OF RADIO

(i) Introduction

723. Services to be regulated by OFCOM. It is a function of OFCOM to regulate the following services in accordance with the Communications Act 2003, the Broadcasting Act 1990 and the Broadcasting Act 1996: (1) services specified in heads (a) to (f) below that are provided from places in the United Kingdom[1] and otherwise than by the BBC[2]; (2) services so specified that do not fall within head (1) but are provided by a person, other than the BBC, whose principal place of business is in the United Kingdom[3]. The services referred to in head (1) are:

(a)   sound broadcasting services[4];
(b)   radio licensable content services[5];
(c)   additional radio services[6];
(d)   radio multiplex services[7];
(e)   digital sound programme services[8];
(f)   digital additional sound services[9].

'Relevant independent radio services' are those listed under heads (a) to (c).

The Secretary of State has ceased to have any function under the Broadcasting Act 1990 or the Broadcasting Act 1996 of assigning frequencies: (i) for any of the purposes of Part III of the Broadcasting Act 1990 (regulation of radio services); or (ii) for the purposes of the provision of any radio multiplex services[10].

1   The services that are to be treated for the purposes of the Communications Act 2003 s 245 as provided from places in the United Kingdom include every radio licensable content service which would not fall to be so treated apart from s 245(5) but which: (1) is provided with a view to its being broadcast from a satellite; (2) is a service the broadcasting of which involves its transmission to the satellite by means of an electronic communications network from a place in the United Kingdom; and (3) is not a service the provision of which is licensed or otherwise authorised under the laws of another EEA state: s 245(5). 'Radio licensable content service' has the meaning given by s 247 (see PARA 749): s 362(1). 'EEA state' means the United Kingdom or any other state that is a contracting party to the Agreement on the European Economic Area signed at Oporto on 22 May 1992, as adjusted by the Protocol signed at Brussels on 17 March 1993; and 'another EEA state' means an EEA state other than the United Kingdom: Communications Act 2003 s 362(1). As to the meaning of 'United Kingdom' see PARA 510 note 13. The services that are to be treated as so provided also include every service provided by a BBC company, a C4 company or an S4C company: s 245(6). 'C4 company' means: (a) a body corporate which is controlled by C4C; or (b) a body corporate in which C4C or a body corporate controlled by C4C is (to any extent) a participant: s 362(1). 'S4C company' means: (i) a body corporate which is controlled by the Welsh Authority; or (ii) a body corporate in which that Authority or a body corporate controlled by that Authority is (to any extent) a participant: s 362(1). As to the meaning of 'C4C' see PARA 627 note 1. As to the meaning of 'the Welsh Authority' see PARA 644 note 3; and as to television broadcasting by the Welsh Authority see PARAS 644–661. As to the meaning of 'BBC company' see PARA 854 note 4.

2   As to the meaning of 'BBC' see PARA 603 note 1; and as to the BBC see PARAS 603–626.

3   Communications Act 2003 s 245(1).

4   Ie sound broadcasting services to which the Communications Act 2003 s 245(3) applies. For these purposes, 'sound broadcasting service' has the same meaning as in the Broadcasting

Act 1990 Pt III (ss 85–126): Communications Act 2003 s 362(1). 'Sound broadcasting service' means a broadcasting service whose broadcasts consist of transmissions in sound only but does not include a radio multiplex service (within the meaning of the Communications Act 2003 Pt 3 (ss 198–362): see PARA 753): Broadcasting Act 1990 s 126(1) (amended by the Broadcasting Act 1996 s 148(1), Sch 10 Pt I para 9; and the Communications Act 2003 Sch 15 para 59(c)). As to sound broadcasting services see PARA 730 et seq.

The Communications Act 2003 s 245(3) applies to a sound broadcasting service which: (1) is provided with a view to its being broadcast otherwise than only from a satellite; and (2) is a national service, local service or restricted service: s 245(3). For the purposes of s 245: (a) a service is a national service if it is a sound broadcasting service provided as mentioned in head (1) with a view to its being broadcast for reception in any such minimum area of the United Kingdom as may be determined in accordance with the Broadcasting Act 1990 s 98(2) (see PARA 730); (b) a service is a local service if it is a sound broadcasting service which (without being a national service) is provided as mentioned in head (1) with a view to its being broadcast for reception in a particular area or locality in the United Kingdom; and (c) a service is a restricted service if it is a sound broadcasting service provided as mentioned in head (1) with a view to its being broadcast for reception: (i) within a particular establishment in the United Kingdom or at another defined location in the United Kingdom; or (ii) for the purposes of a particular event taking place within the United Kingdom: Communications Act 2003 s 245(4). A reference in head (b) to an area of the United Kingdom does not include an area which comprises or includes the whole of England: s 245(7).

5 As to the meaning of 'radio licensable content services' see PARA 749; and as to radio licensable content services generally see PARA 749 et seq.

6 'Additional radio service' means an additional service within the meaning given by the Broadcasting Act 1990 s 114(1) (see PARA 772) for the purposes of the Broadcasting Act 1990 Pt III: Communications Act 2003 s 362(1). As to additional radio services see PARA 772 et seq.

7 As to radio multiplex services see PARA 754 et seq.

8 'Digital sound programme service' has the same meaning as in the Broadcasting Act 1996 Pt II (ss 40–72) (see ss 40, 72; and PARA 754 note 28): Communications Act 2003 s 362(1). As to digital sound programme services see PARA 768 et seq.

9 Communications Act 2003 s 245(2). 'Digital additional sound service' means a digital additional service within the meaning given by the Broadcasting Act 1996 s 63 (see PARA 779) for the purposes of the Broadcasting Act 1996 Pt II: Communications Act 2003 s 362(1). As to digital additional sound services see PARA 772 et seq.

10 Communications Act 2003 s 246.

724. Power of OFCOM to grant licences for relevant independent radio services.

OFCOM[1] may grant licences[2] to provide relevant independent radio services[3]. OFCOM must do all that it can to secure the provision within the United Kingdom[4] of:

(1) a diversity of national services[5] each catering for tastes and interests different from those catered for by the others and of which one is a service the greater part of which consists in the broadcasting[6] of spoken material[7], and another is a service which consists, wholly or mainly, in the broadcasting of music which, in the opinion of OFCOM, is not pop music[8]; and

(2) a range and diversity of local services[9].

1 As to OFCOM see PARA 507.

2 Ie in accordance with the Broadcasting Act 1990 Pt III (ss 85–126). 'Licence' means a licence under Pt III; and 'licensed' is to be construed accordingly: s 126(1).

3 Broadcasting Act 1990 s 85(1) (amended by the Communications Act 2003 s 360(3), Sch 15 para 32(1)–(3)). For this purpose, 'relevant independent radio services' means the following services so far as they are services falling to be regulated under the Communications Act 2003 s 245 (see PARA 723): (1) sound broadcasting services; (2) radio licensable content services; (3) additional radio services: Broadcasting Act 1990 s 85(8) (added by the Communications Act 2003 Sch 15 para 32(5)). As to the meaning of 'sound broadcasting service' see PARA 723 note 4. As to the meaning of 'radio licensable content service' see PARA 723 note 1; and as to the meaning of 'additional radio service' see PARA 723 note 6 (definitions applied by the Broadcasting Act 1990 s 126(1) (amended by the Communications Act 2003 Sch 15 para 59(b))).

4   Broadcasting Act 1990 s 85(2) (amended by the Communications Act 2003 Sch 15 para 32(2)). As to the meaning of 'United Kingdom' see PARA 510 note 13.
5   As to the meaning of 'national service' see PARA 723 note 4; definition applied by the Broadcasting Act 1990 s 126(1) (as amended: see note 3).
6   As to the meaning of 'broadcast' see PARA 668 note 2.
7   Broadcasting Act 1990 s 85(2)(a)(i). The Secretary of State may by order make such amendments of s 85(2)(a) as he considers appropriate: (1) for including in that provision a requirement that one of the national services there referred to should be a service of a particular description; or (2) for removing such a requirement from that provision; and (without prejudice to the generality of s 200(2)(b) (see PARA 506 note 32) any such order may make such consequential amendments of s 98(1)(b)(iii) (see PARA 730) as the Secretary of State considers appropriate: s 85(5). An order may not be made under s 85(5) unless a draft of it has been laid before and approved by a resolution of each House of Parliament: s 85(7). At the date at which this volume states the law, no such order had been made. As to the Secretary of State see PARA 507 note 32.
8   Broadcasting Act 1990 s 85(2)(a)(ii) (amended by the Communications Act 2003 Sch 15 para 32(2)). 'Pop music' includes rock music and other kinds of modern popular music which are characterised by a strong rhythmic element and a reliance on electronic amplification for their performance (whether or not, in the case of any particular piece of rock or other such music, the music in question enjoys a current popularity as measured by the number of recordings sold): Broadcasting Act 1990 s 85(6).
9   Broadcasting Act 1990 s 85(2)(b). As to the meaning of 'local service' see PARA 723 note 4; definition applied by s 126(1) (as amended: see note 3).

725.   Licences for relevant independent radio services.   A licence[1] must be in writing and continues in force[2] (subject to a suspension of the licence[3]):

  (1)   in the case of a licence to provide radio licensable content services[4], until such time as it is surrendered or is revoked[5]; and

  (2)   in any other case, until whichever is the earlier of any such time or the end of the period specified in the licence[6].

A licence may be granted by OFCOM[7] for the provision of such a service as is specified in the licence or for the provision of a service of such a description as is so specified; and a licence may be so granted for the provision of a service which to any extent consists in the simultaneous broadcasting[8] of different programmes[9] on different frequencies[10].

A licence to provide a local or national service[11] or to provide an additional service[12] must specify a period of no more than 12 years as the period for which it is to be in force[13].

OFCOM must not grant a licence to any person[14] unless it is satisfied that he is a fit and proper person to hold it[15], and must do all that it can to secure that, if it ceases to be so satisfied in the case of any person holding a licence, that person does not remain the holder of the licence[16].

Where OFCOM is not satisfied that a BBC company[17] which has applied for a licence is a fit and proper person to hold it, it must, before refusing the application, notify the Secretary of State[18].

OFCOM may vary a licence by a notice served on the licence holder[19] if in the case of a variation of the period for which the licence is to continue in force, the licence holder consents[20], or in the case of any other variation, the licence holder has been given a reasonable opportunity of making representations to OFCOM about the variation[21].

A licence granted to any person under the provisions relating to independent radio services[22] is not transferable to any other person without the previous consent in writing of OFCOM[23], which must not be given unless OFCOM is satisfied that any such other person would be in a position to comply with all of the conditions included in the licence which would have effect during the period for which it is to be in force[24].

1   As to the meaning of 'licence' see PARA 724 note 2.
2   As to licences being in force see PARA 865 note 11.
3   Ie a suspension under the Broadcasting Act 1990 s 111B of a licence to provide a satellite service: see PARA 748.
4   As to the meaning of 'radio licensable content services' see PARA 723 note 1.
5   Ie in accordance with provisions of the Broadcasting Act 1990 Pt III (ss 85–126).
6   Broadcasting Act 1990 s 86(1) (amended by the Communications Act 2003 s 252(1)).
7   As to OFCOM see PARA 507.
8   As to the meaning of 'broadcast' see PARA 668 note 2.
9   As to the meaning of 'programme' see PARA 667 note 7.
10 Broadcasting Act 1990 s 86(2) (amended by the Communications Act 2003 s 360(3), Sch 15 para 33(1), (2)). As to the meaning of 'frequency' see PARA 681 note 5.
11 As to the meanings of 'local service' and 'national service' see PARA 723 note 4; definitions applied by the Broadcasting Act 1990 s 126(1) (amended by the Communications Act 2003 Sch 15 para 59(b)).
12 As to additional services see PARA 772 et seq.
13 Broadcasting Act 1990 s 86(3) (substituted by the Communications Act 2003 s 252(2)).
14 As to the meaning of 'person' see PARA 510 note 1.
15 Broadcasting Act 1990 s 86(4)(a) (s 86(4) amended by the Communications Act 2003 Sch 15 para 33(2)).
16 Broadcasting Act 1990 s 86(4)(b). Where the person who is for the time being the holder of any licence ('the present licence holder') is not the person to whom the licence was originally granted, any reference in Pt III (however expressed) to the holder of the licence is to be construed, in relation to any time falling before the date when the present licence holder became the holder of it, as including a reference to a person who was previously the holder of the licence: s 126(3). The holding of a licence by a person does not relieve him of any liability in respect of a failure to hold a licence under the Wireless Telegraphy Act 2006 s 8 (see PARA 514 et seq) or any obligation to comply with requirements imposed by or under the Communications Act 2003 Pt 2 Ch 1 (ss 32–151) (electronic communications networks and electronic communications services: see TELECOMMUNICATIONS vol 97 (2010) PARA 92 et seq): Broadcasting Act 1990 s 86(9) (substituted by the Communications Act 2003 Sch 15 para 33(3); and amended by the Wireless Telegraphy Act 2006 s 123, Sch 7 paras 9, 11). Nothing in the Broadcasting Act 1990 Pt III is to be construed as affecting the operation of s 86(4), s 88(1), s 88(2)(b), (c) (see PARA 829) or s 89(1) (see PARA 829): see s 86(4).
17 As to the meaning of 'BBC company' see PARA 671 note 20.
18 Broadcasting Act 1990 s 86(4A) (added by the Broadcasting Act 1996 s 136, Sch 8 para 5; and amended by the Communications Act 2003 Sch 15 para 33(2)). As to the Secretary of State see PARA 507 note 32.
19 Broadcasting Act 1990 s 86(5) (amended by the Communications Act 2003 Sch 15 para 33(2)).
20 Broadcasting Act 1990 s 86(5)(a). Section 86(5)(a) does not affect the operation of s 97B (see PARA 702), s 105A (see PARA 743) or s 110(1)(b) (see PARA 746): s 86(6) (amended by the Digital Economy Act 2010 ss 30(1), 33(1)).
21 Broadcasting Act 1990 s 86(5)(b) (amended by the Communications Act 2003 Sch 15 para 33(2)). The Broadcasting Act 1990 s 86(5) does not authorise the variation of any conditions included in a licence in pursuance of s 102(1) (see PARA 734) or s 118(1) (see PARA 776): s 86(6).
22 Ie the provisions of the Broadcasting Act 1990 Pt III.
23 Broadcasting Act 1990 s 86(7) (amended by the Communications Act 2003 Sch 15 para 33(2)).
24 Broadcasting Act 1990 s 86(8) (amended by the Communications Act 2003 Sch 15 para 33(2)).

726.   General licence conditions for relevant independent radio services. A licence[1] may include:

(1)   such conditions as appear to OFCOM[2] to be appropriate having regard to any duties which are or may be imposed on it, or on the licence holder[3], by or under the Broadcasting Act 1990, the Broadcasting Act 1996 or the Communications Act 2003[4];

(2)   conditions enabling OFCOM to supervise and enforce technical standards in connection with the provision of the licensed[5] service[6];

(3)   conditions requiring the payment by the licence holder to OFCOM, whether on the grant of the licence or at such times after the grant as may be determined by or under the licence, or both, of a fee or fees of an amount or amounts so determined[7];

(4)   conditions requiring the licence holder to furnish OFCOM, in such manner and at such times as it may reasonably require, with such information as it may require for the purpose of exercising the functions assigned to it by or under the Broadcasting Act 1990, the Broadcasting Act 1996 or the Communications Act 2003[8];

(5)   conditions requiring the licence holder, if found by OFCOM to be in breach of any condition of his licence, to reimburse to it, in such circumstances as are specified in any conditions, any costs reasonably incurred by it in connection with the breach of that condition[9]; and

(6)   conditions providing for such incidental and supplemental matters as appear to OFCOM to be appropriate[10].

A licence may in particular include:

(a)   conditions requiring the licence holder to comply with any direction given by OFCOM as to such matters as are specified in the licence or are of a description so specified[11], or (except to the extent that OFCOM consents to his doing or not doing them) not to do or to do such things as are specified in the licence or are of a description so specified[12]; and

(b)   conditions requiring the licence holder to permit any employee of, or person authorised by, OFCOM, to enter any premises which are used in connection with the broadcasting[13] of the licensed service and to inspect, examine, operate or test any equipment on the premises which is used in that connection[14].

1   As to the meaning of 'licence' see PARA 724 note 2.
2   As to OFCOM see PARA 507.
3   As to the holder of the licence see PARA 725 note 16.
4   Broadcasting Act 1990 s 87(1)(a) (amended by the Communications Act 2003 s 360(3), Sch 15 para 34(1)–(3)).
5   As to the meaning of 'licensed' see PARA 724 note 2.
6   Broadcasting Act 1990 s 87(1)(b) (amended by the Communications Act 2003 Sch 15 para 34(2)).
7   Broadcasting Act 1990 s 87(1)(c) (amended by the Communications Act 2003 Sch 15 para 34(2)). The fees required to be paid to OFCOM by virtue of the Broadcasting Act 1990 s 87(1)(c) must be in accordance with such tariff as may from time to time be fixed by OFCOM: s 87(3) (amended by the Communications Act 2003 s 406(7), Sch 15 para 34(2), (5), Sch 19). A tariff fixed under the Broadcasting Act 1990 s 87(3) may specify different fees in relation to different cases or circumstances, and OFCOM must publish every such tariff in such manner as it considers appropriate: s 87(4) (amended by the Communications Act 2003 Sch 15 para 34(2)).
8   Broadcasting Act 1990 s 87(1)(d) (amended by the Communications Act 2003 Sch 15 para 34(2), (3)).
9   Broadcasting Act 1990 s 87(1)(e) (amended by the Communications Act 2003 Sch 15 para 34(2)).
10 Broadcasting Act 1990 s 87(1)(f) (amended by the Communications Act 2003 Sch 15 para 34(2)). Where the holder of any licence is required by virtue of any condition imposed under the Broadcasting Act 1990 Pt III (ss 85–126) to provide OFCOM with any information, and in purported compliance with that condition provides it with any information which is false in a material particular, he must be taken for the purposes of s 110 (see PARA 746) and s 111 (see PARA 747) to have failed to comply with that condition: s 87(5) (amended by the Communications Act 2003 Sch 15 para 34(2)). Nothing in the Broadcasting Act 1990 which

authorises or requires the inclusion in a licence of conditions relating to any particular matter or having effect for any particular purpose is to be taken as derogating from the generality of s 87(1): s 87(6).

11 Broadcasting Act 1990 s 87(2)(a)(i) (s 87(2)(a) amended by the Communications Act 2003 Sch 15 para 34(2)).

12 Broadcasting Act 1990 s 87(2)(a)(ii) (as amended: see note 11).

13 As to the meaning of 'broadcast' see PARA 668 note 2.

14 Broadcasting Act 1990 s 87(2)(b) (amended by the Communications Act 2003 Sch 15 para 34(2), (4), Sch 19).

727. Digital terrestrial sound broadcasting licences. Licences for radio multiplex services, digital sound programme services, and digital additional sound services are awarded by OFCOM[1] under Part II of the Broadcasting Act 1996[2].

Any such licence granted by OFCOM must be in writing and continues in force[3] for such period as is provided, in relation to a licence of the kind in question, by the relevant provisions[4]. OFCOM may not grant a licence to any person[5] unless it is satisfied that he is a fit and proper person to hold it[6]; and it must do all that it can to secure that, if it ceases to be so satisfied in the case of any person holding a licence, that person does not remain the holder of the licence[7].

OFCOM may vary a licence by a notice served on the licence holder[8]. OFCOM must not vary the period for which a licence having effect for a specified period is to continue in force[9], or increase the total amount of digital capacity specified in a national radio multiplex licence[10], unless the licence holder consents[11]. OFCOM must not make any other variation of a licence unless the licence holder has been given a reasonable opportunity of making representations to OFCOM about the variation[12].

A licence so granted to any person is not transferable to any other person without the previous consent in writing of OFCOM[13]. OFCOM may not give such consent unless it is satisfied that any such other person would be in a position to comply with all of the conditions included in the licence which would have effect during the period for which it is to be in force[14].

1 As to OFCOM see PARA 507.

2 For these purposes, 'licence' means a licence under the Broadcasting Act 1996 Pt II (ss 40–72); and 'licensed' is to be construed accordingly: s 72(1). Licences under Pt II can be referred to collectively as 'digital terrestrial sound broadcasting licences'.

3 As to licences being in force see PARA 865 note 11; applied by the Broadcasting Act 1996 s 147(2).

4 Broadcasting Act 1996 s 42(1) (amended by the Communications Act 2003 s 360(3), Sch 15 para 102(1), (2)). The relevant provisions referred to in the text are the relevant provisions of the Broadcasting Act 1996 Pt II: see s 42(1) (as so amended).

5 As to the meaning of 'person' see PARA 510 note 1.

6 Broadcasting Act 1996 s 42(2)(a) (s 42(2) amended by the Communications Act 2003 Sch 15 para 102(3)). The holding by any person of a licence to provide any service does not relieve him of any liability in respect of a failure to hold a licence under the Wireless Telegraphy Act 2006 s 8 (see PARA 514 et seq) or of any obligation to comply with requirements imposed by or under the Communications Act 2003 Pt 2 Ch 2 (ss 152–184) (electronic communications networks and electronic communications services: see TELECOMMUNICATIONS vol 97 (2010) PARA 92 et seq): Broadcasting Act 1996 s 42(7) (substituted by the Communications Act 2003 Sch 15 para 102(6); and amended by the Wireless Telegraphy Act 2006 s 123, Sch 7 para 18).

7 Broadcasting Act 1996 s 42(2)(b). Nothing in Pt II is to be construed as affecting the operation of s 42(2) or of s 44(1), (2)(b) or (c) (see PARA 837): s 42(2).

8 Broadcasting Act 1996 s 42(3) (substituted by the Communications Act 2003 s Sch 15 para 102(4)).

9 Broadcasting Act 1990 s 42(3A)(a) (s 42(3A) added by the Communications Act 2003 Sch 15 para 102(4)). The Broadcasting Act 1996 s 42(3A)(a) does not affect the operation of s 59(1)(b)

(see PARA 766); and s 42(3A)(a) does not authorise the variation of any condition included in a licence in pursuance of s 55(1) (see PARA 754): s 42(4) (amended by the Communications Act 2003 Sch 15 para 102(5)).

10 Ie for the purpose of the Broadcasting Act 1996 s 48(1A) (see PARA 756): s 42(3A)(b) (as added: see note 9). 'National radio multiplex licence' means a licence to provide a national radio multiplex service: s 72(1). 'National radio multiplex service' means a radio multiplex service provided without any restriction by virtue of the Broadcasting Act 1996 to a particular area or locality in the United Kingdom: ss 40(4)(b), 72(1) (s 40(4) amended by the Communications Act 2003 ss 360(3), 406(7), Sch 15 Pt 2 para 101(1), (3), Sch 19). 'Radio multiplex service' means a radio multiplex service within the meaning of the Communications Act 2003 Pt 3 (ss 198–362) (see PARA 753): Broadcasting Act 1996 ss 40(1), 72(1) (s 40(1) substituted by the Communications Act 2003 s 360(3), Sch 15 para 101(1), (2)). Any reference in the Broadcasting Act 1996 Pt II to an area in the United Kingdom does not include an area which comprises or includes the whole of England; and nothing in Pt II is to be read as precluding a local radio multiplex service from being provided for an area or locality that is to any extent comprised in the area or locality for which another local radio multiplex service is to be provided: s 72(2). 'Local radio multiplex service' means a radio multiplex service provided for a particular area or locality in the United Kingdom: ss 40(4)(a), 72(1). As to the meaning of 'United Kingdom' see PARA 510 note 13.

11 Broadcasting Act 1996 s 42(3A) (as added: see note 9).
12 Broadcasting Act 1996 s 42(3B) (added by the Communications Act 2003 Sch 15 para 102(4)).
13 Broadcasting Act 1996 s 42(5) (amended by the Communications Act 2003 Sch 15 para 102(3)).
14 Broadcasting Act 1996 s 42(6) (amended by the Communications Act 2003 Sch 15 para 102(3)).

728. General licence conditions for digital terrestrial sound broadcasting. A digital terrestrial sound broadcasting licence[1] may include:

(1) such conditions as appear to OFCOM[2] to be appropriate having regard to any duties which are or may be imposed on it, or on the licence holder[3], by or under the Broadcasting Act 1990, the Broadcasting Act 1996 or the Communications Act 2003[4];

(2) conditions enabling OFCOM to supervise and enforce technical standards in connection with the provision of the licensed service[5];

(3) conditions requiring the payment by the licence holder to OFCOM, whether on the grant of the licence or at such times after that as may be determined by or under the licence, or both, of a fee or fees of an amount or amounts so determined[6];

(4) conditions requiring the licence holder to furnish OFCOM, in such manner and at such times as it may reasonably require, with such information as it may require for the purpose of exercising the functions assigned to it by or under the Broadcasting Act 1990, the Broadcasting Act 1996 or the Communications Act 2003[7];

(5) conditions requiring the licence holder, if found by OFCOM to be in breach of any condition of his licence, to reimburse to OFCOM, in such circumstances as are specified in any conditions, any costs reasonably incurred by it in connection with the breach of that condition[8];

(6) conditions providing for such incidental and supplemental matters as appear to OFCOM to be appropriate[9].

A licence may in particular include:

(a) conditions requiring the licence holder to comply with any direction given by OFCOM as to such matters as are specified in the licence or are of a description so specified[10], or (except to the extent that OFCOM consents to his doing or not doing them) not to do or to do such things as are specified in the licence or are of a description so specified[11]; and

(b) conditions requiring the licence holder to permit any employee of, or person authorised by, OFCOM[12], to enter any premises which are used in connection with the broadcasting[13] of the licensed service and to inspect, examine, operate or test any equipment on the premises which is used in that connection[14].

1 As to the meaning of 'licence' see PARA 727 note 2.

2 As to OFCOM see PARA 507.

3 Where the person who is for the time being the holder of any licence ('the present licence holder') is not the person to whom the licence was originally granted, any reference in the Broadcasting Act 1996 Pt II (ss 40–72) (however expressed) to the holder of the licence is to be construed, in relation to any time falling before the date when the present licence holder became the holder of it, as including a reference to a person who was previously the holder of the licence: s 72(3).

4 Broadcasting Act 1996 s 43(1)(a) (amended by the Communications Act 2003 s 360(3), Sch 15 para 103(1), (2), (3)(a)).

5 Broadcasting Act 1996 s 43(1)(b) (amended by the Communications Act 2003 Sch 15 para 103(2)). As to the meaning of 'licensed' see PARA 727 note 2.

6 Broadcasting Act 1996 s 43(1)(c) (amended by the Communications Act 2003 Sch 15 para 103(2)). The fees must be in accordance with such tariff as may from time to time be fixed by OFCOM: Broadcasting Act 1996 s 43(3) (amended by the Communications Act 2003 s 406(7), Sch 15 para 103(2), (5), Sch 19). A tariff so fixed may specify different fees in relation to different cases or circumstances; and OFCOM must publish every such tariff in such manner as it considers appropriate: Broadcasting Act 1996 s 43(4) (amended by the Communications Act 2003 Sch 15 para 103(2)).

7 Broadcasting Act 1996 s 43(1)(d) (amended by the Communications Act 2003 Sch 15 para 103(2), (3)(b)).

8 Broadcasting Act 1996 s 43(1)(e) (amended by the Communications Act 2003 Sch 15 para 103(2)).

9 Broadcasting Act 1996 s 43(1)(f) (amended by the Communications Act 2003 Sch 15 para 103(2)). Nothing in the Broadcasting Act 1996 Pt II which authorises or requires the inclusion in a licence of conditions relating to any particular matter or having effect for any particular purpose is to be taken as derogating from the generality of s 43(1): s 43(6).

10 Broadcasting Act 1996 s 43(2)(a)(i) (amended by the Communications Act 2003 Sch 15 para 103(2)).

11 Broadcasting Act 1996 s 43(2)(a)(ii) (amended by the Communications Act 2003 Sch 15 para 103(2)).

12 Broadcasting Act 1996 s 43(2)(b)(i) (amended by the Communications Act 2003 Sch 15 para 103(2) (4), Sch 19). As to the employees of OFCOM see TELECOMMUNICATIONS vol 97 (2010) PARAS 4–5.

13 As to the meaning of 'broadcast' see PARA 668 note 2; definition applied by the Broadcasting Act 1996 s 147(2).

14 Broadcasting Act 1996 s 43(2)(b). Where the holder of any licence is required by virtue of any condition imposed under Pt II to provide OFCOM with any information, and in purported compliance with that condition provides it with information which is false in a material particular, he is to be taken for the purposes of s 59 (see PARA 766), s 62 (see PARA 771) and s 66 (see PARA 782) and the Broadcasting Act 1990 s 111 (see PARA 747) to have failed to comply with that condition: Broadcasting Act 1996 s 43(5) (amended by the Communications Act 2003 Sch 15 para 103(2)).

729. Community radio. The Secretary of State[1] may by order provide for: (1) any of the provisions of Part 3 of the Communications Act 2003[2]; or (2) any provision of Part III of the Broadcasting Act 1990[3] or of Part II of the Broadcasting Act 1996[4] (regulation of radio services), to have effect, in relation to services of such descriptions as may be set out in an order under these provisions[5], with such modifications as he considers necessary or appropriate for services of that description[6]. The Secretary of State is not to make an order under these provisions in relation to a description of services unless: (a) the description is of services to be provided primarily for the good of members of the public or of a particular community, rather than for commercial reasons; and (b) he considers that the provision of services of that description confer, or would confer, significant benefits on the public or on the communities for which they are provided[7]. An order under these provisions in relation to a description of services may, in particular, impose prohibitions or limitations on the inclusion of advertisements in services of that description and on the sponsorship of programmes included in the services[8]. No order is to be made containing provision authorised by the above provisions unless a draft of the order has been laid before Parliament and approved by a resolution of each House[9].

1　As to the Secretary of State see PARA 507 note 32.
2　Ie the Communications Act 2003 Pt 3 (ss 198–362) (apart from s 262 and the provisions relating exclusively to television).
3　Ie the Broadcasting Act 1990 Pt III (ss 85–126).
4　Ie the Broadcasting Act 1996 Pt II (ss 40–72).
5　Ie under the Communications Act 2003 s 262.
6　Communications Act 2003 s 262(1). As to the power of the Secretary of State to make orders under the Communications Act 2003 see s 402; and TELECOMMUNICATIONS vol 97 (2010) PARA 77. The power, by an order under s 262, to make incidental, supplemental or consequential provision in connection with provision authorised by s 262(1) includes power to make incidental, supplemental or consequential provision modifying provisions of the Broadcasting Act 1990, the Broadcasting Act 1996 or the Communications Act 2003 that are not mentioned in s 262(1): s 262(4). See the Community Radio Order 2004, SI 2004/1944 (amended by SI 2010/118).
7　Communications Act 2003 s 262(2).
8　Communications Act 2003 s 262(3).
9　Communications Act 2003 s 262(5).

(ii) National and Local Sound Broadcasting Services

A. NATIONAL SERVICES; NATIONAL LICENCES

730. Applications for national licences. Where OFCOM[1] proposes to grant a licence[2] to provide a national service (a 'national licence')[3], it must publish, in such manner as it considers appropriate, a notice[4]:

(1)　stating that it proposes to grant such a licence[5];
(2)　specifying:
    (a)　the period for which the licence is to be granted[6];
    (b)　the minimum area of the United Kingdom[7] for which the service is to be provided[8];
    (c)　the digital capacity that is likely, in its opinion, to be available from the holders of national radio multiplex licences[9] for the broadcasting of a simulcast radio service[10] corresponding to the service[11];
    (d)　if the service is to be one falling within certain specified provisions[12], that the service is to be such a service[13]; and
    (e)　if there is any existing licensed[14] national service, that the service is to be one which caters for tastes and interests different from those already catered for by any such service (as described in the notice)[15];
(3)　inviting applications for the licence and specifying the closing date for such applications[16]; and
(4)　specifying the fee payable on any application made in pursuance of the notice[17], and the percentage of qualifying revenue for each accounting period that would be payable by an applicant[18] if he were granted the licence[19].

In determining the minimum area of the United Kingdom for which a national service is to be provided, OFCOM must have regard to the following considerations[20], namely that the service in question should, so far as is reasonably practicable, make the most effective use of the frequency[21] or frequencies on which it is to be provided[22], but that the area for which it is to be provided should not be so extensive that the costs of providing it would be likely to affect the ability of the person[23] providing the service to maintain it[24].

Any application made in pursuance of such a notice must be in writing and accompanied by[25]:

(i) the applicant's proposals for providing a service that would comply with any requirement specified in the notice under head (2)(c) or head (2)(d) above[26];

(ii) the applicant's proposals (if any) for providing a simulcast radio service corresponding to the service[27];

(iii) the fee specified in the notice[28];

(iv) the applicant's proposals for training or retraining persons employed or to be employed by him in order to help fit them for employment in, or in connection with, the making of programmes[29] to be included in his proposed service[30];

(v) the applicant's cash bid[31] in respect of the licence[32];

(vi) such information as OFCOM may reasonably require as to the applicant's present financial position and his projected financial position during the period for which the licence would be in force[33], and as to the arrangements which the applicant proposes to make for, and in connection with, the transmission of his proposed service[34]; and

(vii) such other information as OFCOM may reasonably require for the purpose of considering the application[35].

At any time after receiving such an application and before determining it, OFCOM may require the applicant to furnish additional information under any of heads (i), (ii), (iv), (vi) and (vii) above[36]. Any information to be furnished to OFCOM must, if it so requires, be in such form or verified in such manner as it may specify[37].

OFCOM must, as soon as reasonably practicable after the date specified in such a notice as the closing date for applications, publish in such manner as it considers appropriate[38]:

(A) the name of every person who has made an application to it in pursuance of the notice[39];

(B) the proposals submitted by him under heads (i) and (ii) above[40]; and

(C) such other information connected with his application as OFCOM considers appropriate[41].

1 As to OFCOM see PARA 507.
2 As to the meaning of 'licence' see PARA 724 note 2.
3 'National licence' means a licence to provide a national service: Broadcasting Act 1990 s 126(1). As to the meaning of 'national service' see PARA 723 note 4; definition applied by the Broadcasting Act 1990 s 126(1) (amended by the Communications Act 2003 s 360(3), Sch 15 para 59(b)).
4 Broadcasting Act 1990 s 98(1) (amended by the Communications Act 2003 Sch 15 para 38(1), (2)).
5 Broadcasting Act 1990 s 98(1)(a).
6 Broadcasting Act 1990 s 98(1)(b)(i).
7 Any reference in the Broadcasting Act 1990 Pt III (ss 85–126) to an area in the United Kingdom does not include an area which comprises or includes the whole of England, and nothing in Pt III is to be read as precluding a local service from being provided for an area or locality that is to any extent comprised in the area or locality for which another local service is to be provided: s 126(2). As to the meaning of 'United Kingdom' see PARA 510 note 13.

8   Broadcasting Act 1990 s 98(1)(b)(ii).
9   As to the meaning of 'national radio multiplex licence' see PARA 727 note 10; definition applied by the Broadcasting Act 1990 s 98(7) (amended by the Communications Act 2003 s 257(1), (4)).
10 As to the meaning of 'simulcast radio service' see PARA 754 note 12; definition applied by the Broadcasting Act 1990 s 126(1) (amended by the Communications Act 2003 s 256(2)). For the purposes of the Broadcasting Act 1990 Pt III, a simulcast radio service corresponds to a national service if, in accordance with the Broadcasting Act 1996 s 41(3) (see PARA 754 note 12), it falls to be treated as so corresponding for the purposes of Pt II (ss 40–72): Broadcasting Act 1990 s 126(1A) (added by the Communications Act 2003 s 256(3)).
11 Broadcasting Act 1990 s 98(1)(b)(iia) (added by the Communications Act 2003 s 257(2)).
12 Ie the service is to be one falling within the Broadcasting Act 1990 s 85(2)(a) (see PARA 724 note 7).
13 Broadcasting Act 1990 s 98(1)(b)(iii).
14 As to the meaning of 'licensed' see PARA 724 note 2.
15 Broadcasting Act 1990 s 98(1)(b)(iv).
16 Broadcasting Act 1990 s 98(1)(c).
17 Broadcasting Act 1990 s 98(1)(d)(i).
18 Ie in pursuance of the Broadcasting Act 1990 s 102(1)(c) (see PARA 734).
19 Broadcasting Act 1990 s 98(1)(d)(ii). For the purposes of s 98(1)(d)(ii), different percentages may be specified for different accounting periods, and the percentages that may be specified for an accounting period include a nil percentage: s 98(3A) (added by the Communications Act 2003 Sch 15 para 38(34)).
20 Broadcasting Act 1990 s 98(2) (amended by the Communications Act 2003 Sch 15 para 38(2)).
21 As to the meaning of 'frequency' see PARA 681 note 5.
22 Broadcasting Act 1990 s 98(2)(a).
23 As to the meaning of 'person' see PARA 510 note 1.
24 Broadcasting Act 1990 s 98(2)(b).
25 Broadcasting Act 1990 s 98(3).
26 Broadcasting Act 1990 s 98(3)(a) (amended by the Communications Act 2003 s 406(7), Sch 15 para 38(3), Sch 19).
27 Broadcasting Act 1990 s 98(3)(aa) (added by the Communications Act 2003 s 257(3)).
28 Broadcasting Act 1990 s 98(3)(b).
29 As to the meaning of 'programme' see PARA 667 note 7. For these purposes, 'programme' does not include an advertisement: Broadcasting Act 1990 s 98(7).
30 Broadcasting Act 1990 s 98(3)(c).
31 'Cash bid', in relation to a licence, means an offer to pay to OFCOM a specified amount of money in respect of the first complete calendar year falling within the period for which the licence is in force (being an amount which, as increased by the appropriate percentage, is also to be payable in respect of subsequent years falling wholly or partly within that period): Broadcasting Act 1990 ss 98(8), 126(1) (s 98(8) amended by the Communications Act 2003 Sch 15 para 38(2)).
      'The appropriate percentage', in relation to any year ('the relevant year'), means the percentage which corresponds to the percentage increase between: (1) the retail prices index for November in the year preceding the first complete calendar year falling within the period for which the licence in question is in force; and (2) the retail prices index for November in the year preceding the relevant year: Broadcasting Act 1990 ss 102(10), 126(1). The 'retail prices index' means the general index of prices (for all items) published by the Statistics Board: s 102(10) (amended by the Statistics and Registration Service Act 2007 s 60(1), Sch 3 para 6(1), (3)). As to the Statistics Board see REGISTRATION CONCERNING THE INDIVIDUAL vol 39(2) (Reissue) PARA 605.
32 Broadcasting Act 1990 s 98(3)(d).
33 Broadcasting Act 1990 s 98(3)(e)(i) (s 98(3)(e) amended by the Communications Act 2003 Sch 15 para 38(2)). As to licences being in force see PARA 865 note 11.
34 Broadcasting Act 1990 s 98(3)(e)(ii).
35 Broadcasting Act 1990 s 98(3)(f) (amended by the Communications Act 2003 Sch 15 para 38(2)).
36 Broadcasting Act 1990 s 98(4) (amended by the Communications Act 2003 Sch 15 para 38(2), (5)).
37 Broadcasting Act 1990 s 98(5) (amended by the Communications Act 2003 Sch 15 para 38(2)).
38 Broadcasting Act 1990 s 98(6) (amended by the Communications Act 2003 Sch 15 para 38(2)).
39 Broadcasting Act 1990 s 98(6)(a).
40 Broadcasting Act 1990 s 98(6)(b) (amended by the Communications Act 2003 Sch 15 para 38(6)).

41 Broadcasting Act 1990 s 98(6)(c) (amended by the Communications Act 2003 Sch 15 para 38(2)).

731. Award of national licence to person submitting highest cash bid. OFCOM[1] must, after considering all the cash bids[2] submitted by the applicants[3] for a national licence, award the licence to the applicant who submitted the highest bid[4]. If, however, in a case in which one or more of the applicants has made a proposal to provide a simulcast radio service corresponding to the service to be licensed (a 'simulcast applicant'), the highest cash bid is made by an applicant who is not a simulcast applicant, OFCOM may disregard the above requirement and award the licence to the simulcast applicant whose cash bid is the highest of the bids submitted by simulcast applicants[5]. Where (1) two or more applicants for a licence have submitted cash bids specifying an identical amount and that amount is higher than the amount of every other bid; or (2) two or more simulcast applicants have submitted cash bids specifying an identical amount and that amount is higher than the amount of every other bid submitted by a simulcast applicant, OFCOM must invite those applicants and (in a case falling within head (2) above) every applicant who has made a higher bid to submit further cash bids in respect of that licence[6]. OFCOM may decide not to invite an applicant to submit a further cash bid[7] if the applicant is not a simulcast applicant and OFCOM proposes to exercise its power[8] to disregard the requirement to award the licence to the applicant who has submitted the highest cash bid[9].

OFCOM may disregard this requirement and award the licence to an applicant who has not submitted the highest bid if it appears to it that there are exceptional circumstances which make it appropriate for it to award the licence to that applicant; and where it appears to OFCOM, in the context of the licence, that any circumstances are to be regarded as exceptional circumstances for these purposes, those circumstances may be so regarded by it despite the fact that similar circumstances have been so regarded by it in the context of any other licence or licences[10].

If it appears to OFCOM, in the case of the applicant to whom it would otherwise award the licence, that there are grounds for suspecting that any relevant source of funds[11] is such that it would not be in the public interest for the licence to be awarded to him[12]:

(a) it must refer his application to the Secretary of State[13], together with a copy of all documents submitted to it by the applicant[14], and a summary of its deliberations on the application[15]; and

(b) it must not award the licence to him unless the Secretary of State has given his approval[16].

On such a reference the Secretary of State may only refuse to give his approval to the licence being awarded to the applicant in question if he is satisfied that any relevant source of funds is such that it would not be in the public interest for the licence to be so awarded[17].

Where OFCOM has awarded a national licence to any person in accordance with these provisions, it must, as soon as reasonably practicable after awarding the licence[18] publish the following matters in such manner as it considers appropriate[19], and grant the licence to that person[20]. The matters to be published are:

(i) the name of the person to whom the licence has been awarded and the amount of his cash bid[21];

(ii)   the name of every other applicant in whose case it appeared to OFCOM that the specified requirements[22] were satisfied[23];

(iii)   where the licence has been awarded[24] to an applicant who has not submitted the highest cash bid, OFCOM's reasons for the licence having been so awarded[25]; and

(iv)   such other information as OFCOM considers appropriate[26].

1   As to OFCOM see PARA 507.

2   As to the meaning of 'cash bid' see PARA 730 note 31. In the Broadcasting Act 1990 Pt III (ss 85–126), references to a person's cash bid, in relation to a person who has submitted a further cash bid in pursuance of s 100(2) (see the text and note 6), have effect as references to his further bid: s 100(2C) (added by the Communications Act 2003 s 257(1), (5)).

3   Where a person has made an application for a national licence in accordance with the Broadcasting Act 1990 s 98, OFCOM may not proceed to consider whether to award him the licence on the basis of his cash bid in accordance with s 100 unless it appears to it: (1) that his proposed service would comply with any requirement specified under s 98(1)(b)(iii) or (iv) (see PARA 730); and (2) that he would be able to maintain that service and any proposed simulcast radio service corresponding to that service throughout the period for which the licence would be in force: s 99(1) (amended by the Communications Act 2003 ss 360(3), 406(7), Sch 15 para 39(1)–(4), Sch 19). Any reference to an applicant in the Broadcasting Act 1990 s 100 (except in s 100(9)(b)) is accordingly a reference to an applicant in whose case it appears to OFCOM that the requirements of s 99(1) are satisfied: s 99(2) (amended by the Communications Act 2003 Sch 15 para 39(2)).

     As to the meaning of 'national licence' see PARA 730 note 3. As to the meaning of 'simulcast radio service' see PARA 730 note 10. As to the meaning of 'licence' see PARA 724 note 2. As to licences being in force see PARA 865 note 11. As to the meaning of 'person' see PARA 510 note 1.

4   Broadcasting Act 1990 s 100(1) (amended by the Communications Act 2003 Sch 15 para 40).

5   Broadcasting Act 1990 s 100(1A) (added by the Communications Act 2003 s 257(1), (5)).

6   Broadcasting Act 1990 s 100(2) (substituted by the Communications Act 2003 s 257(5)).

7   Ie under the Broadcasting Act 1990 s 100(2) (see the text and note 6).

8   Ie its power under the Broadcasting Act 1990 s 100(1A) (see the text and note 5) or s 100(3) (see the text and note 10).

9   Broadcasting Act 1990 s 100(2A) (added by the Communications Act 2003 s 257(5)). This is not to be construed as preventing OFCOM from making a decision to exercise its power under the Broadcasting Act 1990 s 100(1A) or 100(3) after it has received further bids in response to invitations under s 100(2): s 100(2B) (added by the Communications Act 2003 s 257(5)).

10   Broadcasting Act 1990 s 100(3) (amended by the Communications Act 2003 Sch 15 para 40).

11   'Relevant source of funds', in relation to an applicant, means any source of funds to which he might (directly or indirectly) have recourse for the purpose of: (1) paying any amounts payable by him by virtue of the Broadcasting Act 1990 s 102(1) (see PARA 734); or (2) otherwise financing the provision of his proposed service: s 100(6).

12   Broadcasting Act 1990 s 100(4) (amended by the Communications Act 2003 Sch 15 para 40).

13   Broadcasting Act 1990 s 100(4)(a). As to the Secretary of State see PARA 507 note 32.

14   Broadcasting Act 1990 s 100(4)(a)(i).

15   Broadcasting Act 1990 s 100(4)(a)(ii).

16   Broadcasting Act 1990 s 100(4)(b). Where OFCOM is, by virtue of s 100(4), precluded from awarding the licence to an applicant, s 100(1)–(6) (subject to s 100(11)) has effect as if that person had not made an application for the licence: s 100(7) (amended by the Communications Act 2003 Sch 15 para 40). The Broadcasting Act 1990 s 100(1)–(6) does not have effect as mentioned in s 100(7) if OFCOM decides that it would be desirable to publish a fresh notice under s 98 (see PARA 730) in respect of the grant of the licence; and similarly, where any of the following provisions of Pt III (ss 83–126) provides, in connection with the revocation of a licence, for s 100 to have effect as if the former holder of the licence had not made an application for it, s 100 does not so have effect if OFCOM decides that it would be desirable to publish a fresh notice under Pt III in respect of the grant of a further licence to provide the service in question: s 100(11) (amended by the Communications Act 2003 Sch 15 para 40).

17   Broadcasting Act 1990 s 100(5).

18   Broadcasting Act 1990 s 100(8) (amended by the Communications Act 2003 Sch 15 para 40).

19   Broadcasting Act 1990 s 100(8)(a).

20   Broadcasting Act 1990 s 100(8)(b).

21   Broadcasting Act 1990 s 100(9)(a).

22   Ie the requirement specified in the Broadcasting Act 1990 s 99(1)(a) (see note 3 head (1)).

23 Broadcasting Act 1990 s 100(9)(b) (amended by the Communications Act 2003 Sch 15 para 40).
24 Ie by virtue of the Broadcasting Act 1990 s 100(3) (see the text and note 10).
25 Broadcasting Act 1990 s 100(9)(c) (amended by the Communications Act 2003 Sch 15 para 40).
26 Broadcasting Act 1990 s 100(9)(d) (amended by the Communications Act 2003 Sch 15 para 40). In a case where the licence has been awarded to any person by virtue of the operation of the Broadcasting Act 1990 s 100, in accordance with any provision of Pt III, on the revocation of an earlier grant of the licence, s 100(9) has effect as if s 100(9)(b) were omitted, and the matters specified in s 100(9) included an indication of the circumstances in which the licence has been awarded to that person: s 100(10).

732. Licence conditions relating to simulcast radio services. Where OFCOM[1] awards a national licence[2] to a person[3] whose application for that licence[4] included proposals to provide a simulcast radio service[5], that licence must include a condition requiring the licence holder: (1) to provide, from a date specified in the licence, a simulcast radio service corresponding to the licensed service; and (2) to do all that he can to secure the broadcasting of that service[6].

1 As to OFCOM see PARA 507.
2 As to the meaning of 'national licence' see PARA 730 note 3.
3 As to the meaning of 'person' see PARA 510 note 1.
4 As to application for a national licence see PARA 730.
5 As to the meaning of 'simulcast radio service' see PARA 730 note 10.
6 Broadcasting Act 1990 s 100A (added by the Communications Act 2003 s 257(1), (6)).

733. Failure to begin providing licensed service and financial penalties on revocation of licence. If at any time after a national licence[1] has been granted to any person[2] but before the licence has come into force[3]:
(1) that person indicates to OFCOM[4] that he does not intend to provide the licensed national service or that he does not intend to provide a corresponding simulcast radio service[5] that he is required to provide by a condition imposed[6] in the licence[7]; or
(2) OFCOM for any other reason has reasonable grounds for believing that that person will not provide the licensed national service or any such simulcast radio service once the licence has come into force[8],
then OFCOM must serve on him a notice revoking the licence as from the time the notice is served on him[9], and the provisions for awarding a licence to a person submitting the highest cash bid[10] have effect as if he had not made an application for the licence[11].

Where OFCOM revokes a national licence[12], it must serve on the licence holder[13] a notice requiring him to pay to it, within a specified period, a specified financial penalty[14].

1 As to the meaning of 'national licence' see PARA 730 note 3.
2 As to the meaning of 'person' see PARA 510 note 1.
3 Broadcasting Act 1990 s 101(1). As to the meaning of 'licence' see PARA 724 note 2. As to licences being in force see PARA 865 note 11.
4 As to OFCOM see PARA 507.
5 As to the meaning of 'simulcast radio service' see PARA 730 note 10.
6 Ie by the Broadcasting Act 1990 s 100A: see PARA 732.
7 Broadcasting Act 1990 s 101(1)(a) (amended by the Communications Act 2003 s 360(3), Sch 15 para 41(1), (2), (3)(a)).
8 Broadcasting Act 1990 s 101(1)(b) (amended by the Communications Act 2003 Sch 15 para 41(2), (3)(b)). The Broadcasting Act 1990 s 101(1) does not apply in the case of any person by virtue of s 101(1)(b) unless OFCOM has served on him a notice stating its grounds for believing that he will not provide the licensed national service or the simulcast radio service in question once his licence has come into force, and it may not serve such a notice on him unless it has given him a reasonable opportunity of making representations to it about the matters complained of: s 101(2) (amended by the Communications Act 2003 Sch 15 para 41(2), (4)).

9 Broadcasting Act 1990 s 101(1)(i) (amended by the Communications Act 2003 Sch 15 para 41(2)).

10 Ie the Broadcasting Act 1990 s 100, subject to s 100(11) (see PARA 731). As to the meaning of 'cash bid' see PARA 730 note 31.

11 Broadcasting Act 1990 s 101(1)(ii).

12 Ie under the Broadcasting Act 1990 s 101 or under any other provision of Pt III (ss 83–126).

13 As to the holder of the licence see PARA 725 note 16.

14 Broadcasting Act 1990 s 101(3) (amended by the Communications Act 2003 s 345, Sch 13 paras 1, 6(2), Sch 15 para 41(2)). The maximum amount which a person may be required to pay by way of a penalty under the Broadcasting Act 1990 s 101(3) is the maximum penalty given by s 101(3B), (3C): s 101(3A) (s 100(3A)–(3D) added by the Communications Act 2003 s 345, Sch 13 para 6(2)).

In a case where the licence is revoked under the Broadcasting Act 1990 s 101 or the penalty is imposed before the end of the first complete accounting period of the licence holder to fall within the period for which the licence is in force, the maximum penalty is whichever is the greater of: (1) £250,000; and (2) 7% of the amount which OFCOM estimates would have been the qualifying revenue for the first complete accounting period of the licence holder falling within the period for which the licence would have been in force: s 101(3B) (as so added).

In any other case, the maximum penalty is whichever is the greater of: (a) £250,000; and (b) 7% of the qualifying revenue for the last complete accounting period of the licence holder falling within the period for which the licence is in force: s 101(3C) (as so added).

Section 102(2)–(6) (see PARA 734) applies for estimating or determining qualifying revenue for the purposes of s 100(3B) or s 100(3C): s 101(3D) (as so added).

Any financial penalty payable by any body by virtue of s 101(3), in addition to being recoverable from that body as provided by s 122(4) (repealed), is recoverable by OFCOM as a debt due to it from any person who controls that body: s 101(5) (amended by the Communications Act 2003 Sch 15 para 41(2)). As to the meaning of 'body' see PARA 821 note 10. As to the meaning of 'control' see PARA 821 note 11.

734. Additional payments to be made in respect of national licences. A national licence[1] must include conditions requiring the licence holder[2] to pay to OFCOM[3], in addition to any fees required to be paid under the general licence conditions[4]:

(1) in respect of the first complete calendar year falling within the period for which the licence is in force[5], the amount specified in his cash bid[6];

(2) in respect of each subsequent year falling wholly or partly within that period, the amount so specified as increased by the appropriate percentage[7]; and

(3) in respect of each accounting period of his falling within the period referred to in head (1) above, an amount representing such percentage of the qualifying revenue[8] for that accounting period as was specified in relation to the licence[9].

In the case of an advertisement included under arrangements made between the licence holder or any connected person[10], and a person acting as an advertising agent[11], the amount of any receipt by the licence holder or any connected person that represents a payment by the advertiser from which the advertising agent has deducted any amount by way of commission is the amount of the payment by the advertiser after the deduction of the commission[12]. However, if the amount deducted by way of commission exceeds 15 per cent of the payment by the advertiser, the amount of the receipt in question is taken to be the amount of the payment less 15 per cent[13].

If, in any accounting period of the licence holder, the licence holder or any connected person derives, in relation to any programme to be included in the licensed service, any financial benefit, whether direct or indirect, from payments made by any person, by way of sponsorship, for the purpose of defraying or contributing towards costs incurred or to be incurred in connection with that programme, the qualifying revenue for that accounting period is taken for the purposes of head (3) above to include the amount of the financial benefit so derived by the licence holder or the connected person, as the case may be[14].

A national licence may include conditions enabling OFCOM to estimate before the beginning of an accounting period the amount due for that period by virtue of head (3) above[15], and requiring the licence holder to pay the estimated amount by monthly instalments throughout that period[16]. Such a licence may in particular include conditions authorising OFCOM to revise any estimate on one or more occasions, and to adjust the instalments payable by the licence holder to take account of the revised estimate[17], and providing for the adjustment of any overpayment or underpayment[18].

1   As to the meaning of 'national licence' see PARA 730 note 3.
2   As to the holder of the licence see PARA 725 note 16. As to the meaning of 'licence' see PARA 724 note 2.
3   As to OFCOM see PARA 507.
4   Broadcasting Act 1990 s 102(1) (amended by the Communications Act 2003 s 360(3), Sch 15 para 42). Fees may also be required to be paid by virtue of the Broadcasting Act 1990 s 87(1)(c) (see PARA 726): see s 102(1) (as so amended).
5   As to licences being in force see PARA 865 note 11.
6   Broadcasting Act 1990 s 102(1)(a). As to the meaning of 'cash bid' see PARA 730 note 31.
7   Broadcasting Act 1990 s 102(1)(b). As to the meaning of 'the appropriate percentage' see PARA 730 note 31.
8   For the purposes of the Broadcasting Act 1990 s 102(1)(c), the qualifying revenue for any accounting period of the licence holder (subject to s 102(6): see the text and note 14) consists of all payments received or to be received by him or by any connected person: (1) in consideration of the inclusion in the licensed service in that period of advertisements or other programmes; or (2) in respect of charges made in that period for the reception of programmes included in that service: s 102(2). As to the meaning of 'connected' see PARA 674 note 13. As to the meaning of 'licensed' see PARA 724 note 2. As to the meaning of 'programme' see PARA 667 note 7.
    If, in connection with the inclusion of any advertisements or other programmes whose inclusion is paid for by payments falling within s 102(2), any payments are made to the licence holder or any connected person to meet any payments payable by the licence holder by virtue of s 102(1)(c), those payments are to be regarded as made in consideration of the inclusion of the programmes in question: s 102(3).
    As to the computation of qualifying revenue see also PARA 737.
9   Broadcasting Act 1990 s 102(1)(c). The accounting period is specified under s 98(1)(d)(ii) (see PARA 730): s 102(1)(c). Where the first complete accounting period of the licence holder falling within the period referred to in s 102(1)(a) ('the licence period') does not begin at the same time as that period, or the last complete accounting period of his falling within the licence period does not end at the same time as that period, any reference in s 102(1)(c) to an accounting period of his includes a reference to such part of the accounting period preceding that first complete accounting period, or, as the case may be, following that last complete accounting period, as falls within the licence period; and other references to accounting periods in Pt III (ss 83–126) are to be construed accordingly: s 102(9).
10 Broadcasting Act 1990 s 102(4)(a).
11 Broadcasting Act 1990 s 102(4)(b). As to the meaning of 'advertising agent' see PARA 674 note 16.
12 Broadcasting Act 1990 s 102(4).
13 Broadcasting Act 1990 s 102(5).
14 Broadcasting Act 1990 s 102(6).
15 Broadcasting Act 1990 s 102(7)(a) (amended by the Communications Act 2003 Sch 15 para 42).
16 Broadcasting Act 1990 s 102(7)(b).
17 Broadcasting Act 1990 s 102(8)(a) (amended by the Communications Act 2003 Sch 15 para 42).
18 Broadcasting Act 1990 s 102(8)(b).

735.   Restriction on changes in control over holder of national licence. Where:

(1)   any change in the persons[1] having control[2] over a body[3] to which a national licence[4] has been awarded or transferred[5], or an associated programme provider[6], takes place within the relevant period[7]; and

(2)   that change takes place without having been previously approved for these purposes by OFCOM[8],

then OFCOM may, if the licence has not yet been granted, refuse to grant it to the body referred to in head (1) above or, if it has already been granted, serve on that body a notice revoking it[9]. OFCOM may not refuse to grant a licence to, or serve such a notice on, any body unless it has given it a reasonable opportunity of making representations to it about the matters complained of[10].

1 As to the meaning of 'person' see PARA 510 note 1.
2 As to the meaning of 'control' see PARA 821 note 11.
3 As to the meaning of 'body' see PARA 821 note 10.
4 As to the meaning of 'national licence' see PARA 730 note 3.
5 Broadcasting Act 1990 s 103(1)(a)(i).
6 Broadcasting Act 1990 s 103(1)(a)(ii). 'Associated programme provider' means any body which is connected with that body and is or is likely to be involved, to a substantial extent, in the provision of the programmes included in the licensed service: s 103(2) (amended by the Communications Act 2003 s 360(3), Sch 15 para 43(1), (3)(a)). The Broadcasting Act 1990 Sch 2 Pt I para 3 (see PARA 674 note 13) has effect for the purposes of s 103(2) as it has for the purposes of Sch 2: s 103(2) (amended by the Communications Act 2003 Sch 15 para 43(3)(b)). As to the meaning of 'connected' see PARA 674 note 13. As to the meaning of 'programme' see PARA 667 note 7. As to the meanings of 'licence' and 'licensed' see PARA 724 note 2. As to the holder of the licence see PARA 725 note 16.
7 Broadcasting Act 1990 s 103(1)(a). 'The relevant period' means the period beginning with the date of the award of the licence and ending on the first anniversary of the date of its coming into force: s 103(2). As to licences being in force see PARA 865 note 11.
     OFCOM must refuse to approve for the purposes of s 103 such a change as is mentioned in s 103(1)(a) if it appears to it that the change would be prejudicial to the provision under the licence, by the body referred to in s 103(1)(a)(i), of a service which accords with the proposals submitted under s 98(3)(a) (see PARA 730) by that body (or, as the case may be, by the person to whom the licence was originally awarded): s 103(3) (amended by the Communications Act 2003 Sch 15 para 43(2)). OFCOM may refuse so to approve any such change if, in any circumstances not falling within the Broadcasting Act 1990 s 103(3), it considers it appropriate to do so: s 103(4) (amended by the Communications Act 2003 Sch 15 para 43(2)). As to OFCOM see PARA 507.
8 Broadcasting Act 1990 s 103(1)(b) (amended by the Communications Act 2003 Sch 15 para 43(2)).
9 Broadcasting Act 1990 s 103(1) (amended by the Communications Act 2003 Sch 15 para 43(2)). Where under the Broadcasting Act 1990 s 103(1) OFCOM refuses to grant a licence to any body, s 100 (subject to s 100(11)) (see PARA 731) has effect as if that body had not made an application for the licence; and, where under s 100(11) it serves on any body a notice revoking its licence, the provisions of s 111(6), (7) (see PARA 747) apply in relation to that notice as they apply in relation to a notice served under s 100(3): s 103(6) (amended by the Communications Act 2003 Sch 15 para 43(2)).
10 Broadcasting Act 1990 s 103(5) (amended by the Communications Act 2003 Sch 15 para 43(2)).

736.   Renewal of national licences.   A national licence[1] may be renewed[2] on one occasion for a period of 12 years beginning with the date of renewal[3]. An application for the renewal of a national licence may be made by the licence holder[4] not earlier than three years before the date on which it would otherwise cease to be in force[5] and not later than the day falling three months before the relevant date[6]. Where any application is made[7], OFCOM may postpone the consideration of the application for so long as it thinks appropriate[8].

On the grant of an application, OFCOM[9]:

(1)   may, in a case where a simulcast radio service provided by the applicant is not yet being broadcast in digital form on the relevant date, determine a date by which the broadcasting of such a service in that form must begin[10];

(2)   must determine an amount which is to be payable to OFCOM by the

applicant in respect of the first complete calendar year falling within the period for which the licence is to be renewed[11]; and

(3) may specify a different percentage[12] as the percentage of qualifying revenue for each accounting period of his that will be payable by the applicant[13] during the period for which the licence is to be renewed[14].

Where OFCOM has granted a person's application under these provisions it must formally renew his licence not later than the relevant date or, if that is not reasonably practicable, as soon after that date as is reasonably practicable, and it must not so renew his licence unless it has notified him of[15]:

(a) any date determined by it under head (1) above[16];

(b) the amount determined by it under head (2) above[17]; and

(c) any percentage specified by it under head (3) above[18],

and he has, within such period as is specified in that notification, notified it that he consents to the licence being renewed on those terms[19].

In the case of a pre-transfer national licence[20] (including one for a period extended under the Communications Act 2003[21]): (i) the licence is not to be capable of being renewed under these provisions if it has already been renewed under these provisions before the radio transfer date[22]; and (ii) on the renewal of the licence, it is the duty of OFCOM to secure that the renewed licence contains only such provision as would be included in a national licence granted by OFCOM[23] after the radio transfer date[24].

A national licence may be further renewed[25] on one occasion for a period of not more than seven years beginning with the date of renewal ('the renewal period')[26]. Where OFCOM further renews a licence it must include in the licence as renewed a condition requiring the licence holder to do all that the licence holder can to secure the broadcasting of a simulcast radio service in digital form throughout the renewal period[27].

1   As to the meaning of 'national licence' see PARA 730 note 3.
2   Ie under the Broadcasting Act 1990 s 103A. As to further renewal see the text to notes 25–27.
3   Broadcasting Act 1990 s 103A(1) (s 103A added by the Broadcasting Act 1996 s 92; Broadcasting Act 1990 s 103A(1) amended by the Communications Act 2003 s 360(3), Sch 15 para 44(1), (3); and the Digital Economy Act 2010 s 31(1)). Where an application for the renewal of a national licence has been duly made to OFCOM, it must (subject to the Broadcasting Act 1990 s 103A(5) grant the application if, but only if: (1) OFCOM is satisfied that the applicant would, if his licence were renewed, provide a national service which complied with the conditions included in the licence in pursuance of s 106 (see PARA 744), whether as originally imposed or as varied under that provision; (2) the applicant gave notice to OFCOM, within the period of one month beginning with the commencement of the Broadcasting Act 1996 s 42 (ie 1 January 1991), of his intention to provide a simulcast radio service (see PARA 754); and (3) a simulcast radio service provided by the applicant is being broadcast in digital form or OFCOM is satisfied that by the relevant date the applicant has done all that it would in the circumstances be reasonable to expect him to do by that date to procure the broadcasting of such a service within such time as OFCOM considers reasonable: Broadcasting Act 1990 s 103A(4) (as so added; and amended by the Communications Act 2003 Sch 15 para 44(2), (6)). 'The relevant date', in relation to a national licence, means the date which OFCOM determines to be that by which it would need to publish a notice under the Broadcasting Act 1990 s 98(1) (see PARA 730) if it were to grant, as from the date on which that licence would expire if not renewed, a fresh licence to provide the national service formerly provided under that licence: s 103A(11) (as so added; and amended by the Communications Act 2003 Sch 15 para 44(2)). As to the meaning of 'simulcast radio service' see PARA 730 note 10. As to the meaning of 'licence' see PARA 724 note 2. As to the meaning of 'national service' see PARA 723 note 4. As to the meaning of 'broadcast' see PARA 668 note 2. As to OFCOM see PARA 507. A determination for the purposes of the Broadcasting Act 1990 s 103A(11) must be made at least one year before the date determined; and must be notified by OFCOM to the person who holds the licence in question: s 103A(12) (s 103A as so added; and s 103A(12) added by the Communications Act 2003 Sch 15 para 44(9)).

The provisions of the Broadcasting Act 1990 s 100(4)–(6) (see PARA 731) apply in relation to an applicant for the renewal of a national licence as those provisions apply in relation to such an applicant as is mentioned in s 100(4), but as if any reference to the awarding of such a licence to the applicant were a reference to the renewal of the applicant's licence under s 103A: s 103A(5) (as so added).

4   As to the holder of the licence see PARA 725 note 16.
5   As to licences being in force see PARA 865 note 11.
6   Broadcasting Act 1990 s 103A(2) (as added (see note 3); and amended by the Communications Act 2003 Sch 15 para 44(4))). As to the relevant date see note 3.
7   Broadcasting Act 1990 s 103A(3) (as added (see note 3); and amended by the Communications Act 2003 s 406(7), Sch 19).
8   Broadcasting Act 1990 s 103A(3)(b) (as added (see note 3); and amended by the Communications Act 2003 Sch 15 para 44(2), (5), Sch 19). OFCOM must have regard to the Broadcasting Act 1990 s 103A(8): see s 103A(3)(b) (as so added).
9   Broadcasting Act 1990 s 103A(6) (as added (see note 3); and amended by the Communications Act 2003 Sch 15 para 44(2)).
10 Broadcasting Act 1990 s 103A(6)(a) (as added: see note 3).
11 Broadcasting Act 1990 s 103A(6)(b) (as added (see note 3); and amended by the Communications Act 2003 Sch 15 para 44(2)). The amount determined under the Broadcasting Act 1990 s 103A(6)(b) must be equal to the amount which, in OFCOM's opinion, would have been the cash bid of the licence holder were the licence (instead of being renewed) to be granted for the period of the renewal on an application made in accordance with s 98 (see PARA 730): s 103A(7) (as so added; and substituted by the Communications Act 2003 Sch 15 para 44(7)).
12 Ie a different percentage from that specified under the Broadcasting Act 1990 s 98(1)(d)(ii) (see PARA 730).
13 Ie in pursuance of the Broadcasting Act 1990 s 102(1)(c) (see PARA 734).
14 Broadcasting Act 1990 s 103A(6)(c) (as added: see note 3). For the purposes of s 103A(6)(c), different percentages may be specified for different accounting periods; and the percentages that may be specified for an accounting period include a nil percentage: s 103A(7A) (s 103A as so added; and s 103A(7A) added by the Communications Act 2003 Sch 15 para 44(7)).
15 Broadcasting Act 1990 s 103A(8) (as added: see note 3).
16 Broadcasting Act 1990 s 103A(8)(a) (as added: see note 3).
17 Broadcasting Act 1990 s 103A(8)(b) (as added: see note 3).
18 Broadcasting Act 1990 s 103A(8)(c) (as added: see note 3).
19 Broadcasting Act 1990 s 103A(8) (as added: see note 3). Where a national licence has been so renewed:
    (1)   any conditions included in it in pursuance of s 102 (see PARA 734) have effect during the period for which the licence has been renewed as if the amount determined by OFCOM under s 103A(6)(b) (see the text and note 10) were an amount specified in a cash bid submitted by the licence holder, and subject to any determination made under s 103A(6)(c) (see the text and note 13) (s 103A(9)(a) (as so added; and amended by the Communications Act 2003 Sch 15 para 44(2)));
    (2)   subject to head (1), the Broadcasting Act 1990 s 102 (see PARA 734) has effect in relation to the period for which the licence has been renewed as it has effect in relation to the period for which a national licence is originally in force (s 103A(9)(b) (as so added));
    (3)   where OFCOM has determined a date under s 103A(6)(a) (see the text and note 9), it must include in the licence as renewed a condition requiring a simulcast radio service to be broadcast in digital form throughout the period beginning with the date determined under s 103A(6)(a) and ending with the date on which the licence (as renewed) is to expire (s 103A(9)(c) (as so added; and amended by the Communications Act 2003 Sch 15 para 44(2))); and
    (4)   the reference in the Broadcasting Act 1990 s 111(4) (see PARA 747) to the end of the period for which a national licence is to continue in force, in relation to the licence, is to be construed as a reference to the end of the period for which it has been renewed (s 103A(9)(d) (as so added)).
    As to the meaning of 'cash bid' see PARA 730 note 31.
20 As to the meaning of 'pre-transfer national licence' see PARA 752 note 2.
21 Ie under the Communications Act 2003 s 253: see PARA 752.
22 As to the meaning of 'radio transfer date' see PARA 751 note 1.
23 Ie under the Broadcasting Act 1990 Pt III (ss 85–126).
24 Broadcasting Act 1990 s 103A(10A) (s 103A as added (see note 3); and s 103A(10A) added by the Communications Act 2003 Sch 15 para 44(8)).

25 Ie under the Broadcasting Act 1990 s 103B.
26 Broadcasting Act 1990 s 103B(1) (s 103B added by the Digital Economy Act 2010 s 31(2)). The
    Broadcasting Act 1990 s 103A(2)–(9), (11) and (12) (see notes 3–19) applies in relation to the
    renewal of a licence under s 103B as it applies in relation to the renewal of a licence under
    s 103A, subject to s 103B(3): s 103B(2) (as so added). Those provisions apply in relation to the
    renewal of a licence under s 103B as if the following were omitted: (1) s 103A(4)(b); (2) in
    s 103A(4)(c), the words from 'or OFCOM' to the end; (3) s 103A(6)(a); (4) s 103A(8)(a); and
    (5) s 103A(9)(c): s 103B(3) (as so added).
27 Broadcasting Act 1990 s 103B(2) (as added: see note 26).

737. Computation of qualifying revenue. It is the duty of OFCOM[1] to draw
up, and from time to time review, a statement setting out the principles to be
followed in ascertaining the qualifying revenue for any accounting period[2] of a
licence holder[3] for the purposes of any provision of Part III of the Broadcasting
Act 1990[4]. Such a statement may set out different principles for persons holding
different kinds of licences[5]. Before drawing up or revising such a statement,
OFCOM must consult the Secretary of State[6] and the Treasury[7]. OFCOM must
publish the statement and every revision of that statement[8], and must transmit a
copy of that statement, and every revision of it, to the Secretary of State[9]; and the
Secretary of State must lay copies of the statement and of every such revision
before each House of Parliament[10].

The amount of the qualifying revenue for any accounting period of a person[11],
or the amount of any payment to be made to OFCOM by any person in respect
of any such revenue, or of an instalment of any such payment[12], in the event of a
disagreement between OFCOM and that person, is to be the amount determined
by OFCOM[13]. No such determination of OFCOM may be called in question in
any court of law, or be the subject of any arbitration, although nothing in this
provision prevents the bringing of proceedings for judicial review[14].

1   As to OFCOM see PARA 507.
2   As to accounting periods see PARAS 734 note 9, 776 note 8.
3   As to the holder of the licence see PARA 725 note 16. As to the meaning of 'licence' see PARA 724
    note 2.
4   Ie the Broadcasting Act 1990 Pt III (ss 85–126): s 121, Sch 7 Pt II para 1(1) (amended by the
    Communications Act 2003 s 360(3), Sch 15 para 72(1), (3)).
5   Broadcasting Act 1990 Sch 7 Pt II para 1(2).
6   As to the Secretary of State see PARA 507 note 32.
7   Broadcasting Act 1990 Sch 7 Pt II para 1(3) (amended by the Communications Act 2003 Sch 15
    para 72(3)). As to the Treasury see CONSTITUTIONAL LAW AND HUMAN RIGHTS vol 8(2)
    (Reissue) PARAS 512–517.
8   Broadcasting Act 1990 Sch 7 Pt II para 1(4)(a) (amended by the Communications Act 2003
    Sch 15 para 72(3)).
9   Broadcasting Act 1990 Sch 7 Pt II para 1(4)(b).
10 Broadcasting Act 1990 Sch 7 Pt II para 1(4).
11 Broadcasting Act 1990 Sch 7 Pt II para 2(1)(a). As to the meaning of 'person' see PARA 510
    note 1.
12 Broadcasting Act 1990 Sch 7 Pt II para 2(1)(b).
13 Broadcasting Act 1990 Sch 7 Pt II para 2(1) (amended by the Communications Act 2003 Sch 15
    para 72(3)).
14 Broadcasting Act 1990 Sch 7 Pt II para 2(2) (amended by the Communications Act 2003 Sch 15
    para 72(3)). As to judicial review see JUDICIAL REVIEW vol 61 (2010) PARA 601 et seq.

B. LOCAL AND OTHER SERVICES; LOCAL LICENCES

738. Applications for local and other licences. Where OFCOM[1] proposes to
grant a licence[2] to provide a local service (a 'local licence')[3], it must publish, in
such manner as it considers appropriate, a notice[4]:

(1)   stating that it proposes to grant such a licence[5];

(2)   specifying the area or locality in the United Kingdom[6] for which the service is to be provided[7];

(3)   inviting applications for the licence and specifying the closing date for applications[8]; and

(4)   stating the fee payable on any application made in pursuance of the notice[9].

Any application made in pursuance of such a notice must be in writing and accompanied by[10]:

(a)   the fee specified in the notice[11];

(b)   the applicant's proposals for providing a service that would[12]:

    (i)   cater for the tastes and interests of persons living in the area or locality for which it would be provided or for any particular tastes and interests of such persons[13]; and

    (ii)   broaden the range of programmes[14] available by way of local services to persons living in that area or locality[15];

(c)   such information as OFCOM may reasonably require[16]:

    (i)   as to the applicant's present financial position and his projected financial position during the period for which the licence would be in force[17]; and

    (ii)   as to the arrangements which the applicant proposes to make for, and in connection with, the transmission of his proposed service[18]; and

(d)   such other information as OFCOM may reasonably require for the purpose of considering the application[19].

At any time after receiving such an application and before determining it, OFCOM may require the applicant to furnish additional information under head (b), (c) or (d) above[20].

OFCOM must, at the request of any person and on the payment by him of such sum (if any) as OFCOM may reasonably require, make available for inspection by that person any information furnished under head (b) above by the applicants for a local licence[21].

An application for a licence to provide a restricted service[22], must be made in such manner as OFCOM may determine, and must be accompanied by such fee (if any) as OFCOM may determine[23].

Where OFCOM has published a notice as mentioned above, it must, in determining whether, or to whom, to grant the local licence in question, have regard to the following matters[24]:

(A)   the ability of each of the applicants for the licence to maintain, throughout the period for which the licence would be in force, the service which he proposes to provide[25];

(B)   the extent to which any such proposed service would cater for the tastes and interests of persons living in the area or locality for which the service would be provided, and, where it is proposed to cater for any particular tastes and interests of such persons, the extent to which the service would cater for those tastes and interests[26];

(C)   the extent to which any such proposed service would broaden the range of programmes available by way of local services to persons living in the area or locality for which it would be provided, and, in particular, the extent to which the service would cater for tastes and interests different from those already catered for by local services provided for that area or locality[27]; and

(D) the extent to which there is evidence that, amongst persons living in that area or locality, there is a demand for, or support for, the provision of the proposed service[28].

1 As to OFCOM see PARA 507.
2 As to the meaning of 'licence' see PARA 724 note 2.
3 'Local licence' means a licence to provide a local service: Broadcasting Act 1990 s 126(1). As to the meaning of 'local service' see PARA 723 note 4; definition applied by s 126(1) (amended by the Communications Act 2003 s 360(3), Sch 15 para 59(b)).
4 Broadcasting Act 1990 s 104(1) (amended by the Communications Act 2003 Sch 15 para 45(1), (2)).
5 Broadcasting Act 1990 s 104(1)(a).
6 As to areas in the United Kingdom see PARA 730 note 7. As to the meaning of 'United Kingdom' see PARA 510 note 13.
7 Broadcasting Act 1990 s 104(1)(b).
8 Broadcasting Act 1990 s 104(1)(c).
9 Broadcasting Act 1990 s 104(1)(d).
10 Broadcasting Act 1990 s 104(2).
11 Broadcasting Act 1990 s 104(2)(a).
12 Broadcasting Act 1990 s 104(2)(b).
13 Broadcasting Act 1990 s 104(2)(b)(i).
14 As to the meaning of 'programme' see PARA 667 note 7. For these purposes, 'programme' does not include an advertisement: see the Broadcasting Act 1990 s 104(7).
15 Broadcasting Act 1990 s 104(2)(b)(ii).
16 Broadcasting Act 1990 s 104(2)(c) (amended by the Communications Act 2003 Sch 15 para 45(2)).
17 Broadcasting Act 1990 s 104(2)(c)(i). As to licences being in force see PARA 865 note 11.
18 Broadcasting Act 1990 s 104(2)(c)(ii).
19 Broadcasting Act 1990 s 104(2)(d) (amended by the Communications Act 2003 Sch 15 para 45(2)).
20 Broadcasting Act 1990 s 104(3) (amended by the Communications Act 2003 Sch 15 para 45(2)).
21 Broadcasting Act 1990 s 104(4) (amended by the Communications Act 2003 Sch 15 para 45(2)).
22 As to the meaning of 'restricted service' see PARA 723 note 4; definition applied by the Broadcasting Act 1990 s 126(1) (as amended: see note 3).
23 Broadcasting Act 1990 s 104(6) (amended by the Communications Act 2003 Sch 15 para 45(2), (3)).
24 Broadcasting Act 1990 s 105 (amended by the Communications Act 2003 Sch 15 para 48(1), (2)).
25 Broadcasting Act 1990 s 105(a).
26 Broadcasting Act 1990 s 105(b).
27 Broadcasting Act 1990 s 105(c).
28 Broadcasting Act 1990 s 105(d) (substituted by the Communications Act 2003 Sch 15 para 48(3)).

739. Restriction on holding of local licences. The Secretary of State[1] may by order impose:

(1) requirements prohibiting the holding at the same time by the same person[2], in the circumstances described in the order, of more than the number of local sound broadcasting licences[3] that is determined in the manner set out in the order;

(2) requirements prohibiting a person from holding even one local sound broadcasting licence in the circumstances described in the order[4].

The circumstances by reference to which a person may be prohibited from holding a local sound broadcasting licence, and the factors that may be used for determining the number of such licences that he may hold, include, in particular:

(a)   whether and to what extent the coverage areas[5] of different services provided by that person under different local sound broadcasting licences would overlap[6];

(b)   the sizes of the potential audiences for those services and the times when those services would be made available;

(c)   whether and to what extent members of the potential audiences for those services would also be members of the potential audiences for services provided under local sound broadcasting licences held by other persons;

(d)   in a case in which members of potential audiences for services so provided by that person would also be members of the potential audiences for services so provided by other persons, the number of those other persons, the coverage areas of their services, the sizes of the potential audiences for their services, and the times when their services are or will be made available;

(e)   whether that person runs one or more national newspapers, and their national market share;

(f)   whether and to what extent the whole or a part of the coverage area for a service for which that person would hold a local sound broadcasting licence is or includes an area in which one or more local newspapers run by him is circulating, and the newspapers' local market share;

(g)   whether and to what extent the whole or a part the coverage area for which that person would hold a local sound broadcasting licence is or is included in the coverage area of a regional Channel 3 service for which he also holds a licence[7].

An order under these provisions may make provision for treating:

(i)   persons who are connected with a person who holds a licence;

(ii)   persons who are associates of a person who holds a licence or of a person who is connected with a person who holds a licence; and

(iii) persons who (whether alone or together with such persons as may be described in the order) participate in a body which holds a licence or is treated as doing so by virtue of head (i) or head (ii) above,

as if each of them were also a holder of the licence for the purposes of a requirement imposed under these provisions[8].

Such an order may also make provision for treating:

(A)   persons who are connected with each other;

(B)   persons who are associates of each other; and

(C)   persons who (whether alone or together with such persons as may be described in the order) participate in a body,

as if they and such other persons who are connected with, associates of or participators in any of them as may be described in the order were the same person for the purposes of a requirement imposed under these provisions[9].

Such an order may make provision:

(aa)   as to the circumstances in which a newspaper is to be treated as a national newspaper or a local newspaper for the purposes of a requirement imposed under these provisions;

(bb)   as to the person or persons who are to be treated for any such purposes as running a newspaper;

(cc)   as to the determination for any such purposes of the area within which a local newspaper is circulating; and

(dd)   as to what is to constitute the national market share or local market
        share of any newspaper or of a number of newspapers taken together,
and provision so made may apply, with or without modifications, any of the
provisions[10] as to national and local newspapers and their respective national
and local market shares[11].

Power to make provision with respect to any matter described above by any
order includes power to make provision with respect to that matter by reference
to the making or giving by OFCOM, in accordance with the order, of any
determination, approval or consent, and power to confer such other discretions
on OFCOM as the Secretary of State thinks fit[12].

1   As to the Secretary of State see PARA 507 note 32.
2   As to the meaning of 'person' see PARA 510 note 1.
3   As to the meaning of 'local sound broadcasting licence' see PARA 752 note 16.
4   Communications Act 2003 s 350(3), Sch 14 para 11(1). For transitional provisions see Sch 14
    para 14. Before making an order under any provision of Sch 14 (other than one that is confined
    to giving effect to recommendations made by OFCOM in a report of a review of media
    ownership under s 391 (see PARA 838)), the Secretary of State must consult OFCOM: Sch 14
    para 17(1). No order is to be made containing provision authorised by any provision of Sch 14
    unless a draft of the order has been laid before Parliament and approved by a resolution of each
    House: Sch 14 para 17(2). For orders made under these provisions see the Media Ownership
    (Local Radio and Appointed News Provider) Order 2003, SI 2003/3299; and the Community
    Radio Order 2004, SI 2004/1944 (amended by SI 2010/118). As to OFCOM see PARA 507.
5   For the purposes of the Communications Act 2003 Sch 14 para 11, the coverage area for a
    service provided under a local sound broadcasting licence or a Channel 3 licence is the area in
    the United Kingdom within which that service is capable of being received at a level satisfying
    such technical standards as may have been laid down by OFCOM for the purposes of the
    provisions of an order under Sch 14 para 11: Sch 14 para 11(3). As to the meaning of 'United
    Kingdom' see PARA 510 note 13.
6   References to an area overlapping another include references to its being the same as, or lying
    wholly inside, the other area: Communications Act 2003 Sch 14 para 18(2).
7   Communications Act 2003 Sch 14 para 11(2). As to the meaning of 'regional Channel 3 service'
    see PARA 875 note 4.
8   Communications Act 2003 Sch 14 para 13(1).
9   Communications Act 2003 Sch 14 para 13(3).
10 Ie the provisions of the Communications Act 2003 Sch 14 para 3 or 4: see PARA 820.
11 Communications Act 2003 Sch 14 para 13(4).
12 Communications Act 2003 Sch 14 para 13(5).

740.   Renewal of local licences.   A local licence[1] may be renewed[2] on one
occasion for a period of 12 years beginning with the date of renewal[3]. No such
application for the renewal of a local licence may be made before OFCOM[4] first
publishes a notice[5] inviting applications for a licence[6] to provide a relevant local
radio multiplex service[7]. Subject to this, such an application for the renewal of a
local licence may be made by the licence holder[8] not earlier than three years
before the date on which it would otherwise cease to be in force[9] and not later
than the day falling three months before the relevant date[10].

The applicant must, in his application or at any time before the consideration
of his application, nominate[11] a local digital sound programme service[12]
provided or to be provided by him[13], and a relevant local radio multiplex
service[14], but may not nominate together a local digital sound programme
service and a local radio multiplex service if another local licence held by him
includes a condition[15] relating to the broadcasting[16] of that local digital sound
programme service by that local radio multiplex service[17].

Where an application for the renewal of a local licence has been duly made to
OFCOM, it must grant the application if[18]:

(1)   it is satisfied that the applicant would, if his licence were renewed, provide a local service which complied with the conditions included in the licence[19]; and

(2)   the nominated local digital sound programme service provided by the applicant is being broadcast by means of the nominated local radio multiplex service[20]; and

(3)   it is satisfied that the period for which the nominated local digital sound programme service will be available for reception and the times at which it will be available will not be significantly different, week by week, from those for which and at which the licensed local service will be broadcast[21].

Where the condition specified in head (1) above is satisfied, OFCOM may grant the application even though the condition specified in head (2) above is not satisfied[22] if:

(a)   the applicant holds a licence to provide local digital sound programme services[23];

(b)   a licence to provide the nominated local radio multiplex service has been awarded[24]; and

(c)   it appears to OFCOM that, under a contract between the applicant and the person[25] to whom that licence has been awarded, the applicant is obliged to provide the nominated local digital sound programme service for broadcasting by means of the nominated local radio multiplex service[26].

OFCOM may in any case postpone consideration of the application until the relevant date[27]. If, at the relevant date, the condition specified in head (2) above is not satisfied, and any of the conditions specified in heads (a) to (c) above are not satisfied, OFCOM may postpone consideration of the application for such period not exceeding 12 months as it thinks appropriate[28]. Where OFCOM postpones consideration of an application for any period beyond the relevant date (the 'postponement period'), it must extend the period for which the licence is in force by a period equal to the postponement period[29].

On the grant of any such application OFCOM must[30]:

(i)   where the nominated local digital sound programme service provided by the applicant is not being broadcast by means of the nominated local radio multiplex service, determine a date by which that service must have begun to be so broadcast[31]; and

(ii)   specify a fee payable to OFCOM in respect of the renewal[32].

Where OFCOM has so granted a person's application, it must formally renew his licence as soon afterwards as is reasonably practicable; and it must not so renew his licence unless it has notified him of any date determined by it under head (i) above[33], and the renewal fee specified by it under head (ii) above[34], and he has, within such period as is specified in that notification, notified OFCOM that he consents to the licence being renewed on those terms[35].

Where OFCOM renews a licence, it must include in the licence as renewed a condition requiring the licence holder to do all that he can to ensure that the nominated local digital sound programme service is broadcast by means of the nominated local radio multiplex service throughout the period beginning with whichever is the later of the date on which the licence would expire if not renewed[36], and any date determined by it under head (i) above[37], and ending with the date on which the licence (as renewed) is to expire[38].

In the case of a pre-transfer local licence[39] (including one for a period extended under the Communications Act 2003[40]): (A) the licence is not to be capable of being renewed under these provisions if it has already been renewed before the radio transfer date[41]; and (B) on the renewal of the licence, it is the duty of OFCOM to secure that the renewed licence contains only such provision as would be included in a local licence granted by OFCOM after the radio transfer date[42].

A local licence may be further renewed[43] on one occasion for a period of not more than seven years beginning with the date of renewal[44]. Before approving a licence for this purpose, OFCOM must publish a document specifying the licence proposed to be approved and a period in which representations may be made to OFCOM[45].

An applicant for the renewal of an approved licence[46] may make a national nomination, which is the nomination of a national digital sound programme service[47] provided or to be provided by the applicant and a national radio multiplex service[48]. A national nomination must be made in the application for the renewal of the approved licence or before OFCOM considers the application[49]. The applicant may not nominate a national digital sound programme service unless OFCOM is satisfied that, if the application in question were granted, the programmes[50] included in that service in each calendar month would include at least 80 per cent of the programmes included in the service provided under the approved licence[51]. A national nomination must specify the other approved licences (if any) in relation to which, in reliance on the nomination, an application may be made[52] for the variation of conditions in the licences[53].

1   As to the meaning of 'local licence' see PARA 738 note 3.
2   Ie under the Broadcasting Act 1990 s 104A. A local licence may be renewed under s 104A only if it is granted before the day on which s 104AA (see the text and notes 43–45) comes into force: s 104A(1A) (s 104A added by the Broadcasting Act 1996 s 94(1); Broadcasting Act 1990 s 104A(1A) added by the Digital Economy Act 2010 s 32(1)(b)). The Broadcasting Act 1990 s 104AA came into force on 8 April 2010: see the Digital Economy Act 2010 ss 32(4), 47(2)(b).
3   Broadcasting Act 1990 s 104A(1) (as added (see note 2); and amended by the Communications Act 2003 s 360(3), Sch 15 para 46(1), (3); and the Digital Economy Act 2010 s 32(1)(a)).
4   As to OFCOM see PARA 507.
5   Ie pursuant to the Broadcasting Act 1996 s 50(2) (see PARA 757).
6   As to the meaning of 'licence' see PARA 724 note 2.
7   Broadcasting Act 1990 s 104A(2) (as added (see note 2); and amended by the Communications Act 2003 Sch 15 para 46(2)). 'Relevant local radio multiplex service' means a local radio multiplex service (see PARA 727 note 10) with a coverage area which to a significant extent includes the coverage area of the local service provided under the local licence: Broadcasting Act 1990 s 104A(13)(d) (as so added). As to the meaning of 'local service' see PARA 723 note 4; definition applied by s 126(1) (amended by the Communications Act 2003 Sch 15 para 59(b)).

    'Coverage area' has the same meaning as in the Communications Act 2003 Sch 14 para 8(2): Broadcasting Act 1990 s 104A(13)(d) (as so added; and amended by the Communications Act 2003 Sch 15 para 46(6)). However, the Communications Act 2003 Sch 14 para 8(2) has been repealed by the Media Ownership (Local Radio and Appointed News Provider) Order 2003, SI 2003/3299, and in the Communications Act 2003 Sch 14 the term used is now 'protected area'.
8   As to the holder of the licence see PARA 725 note 16.
9   As to licences being in force see PARA 865 note 11.
10 Broadcasting Act 1990 s 104A(3) (as added (see note 2); and amended by the Communications Act 2003 Sch 15 para 46(3)). 'Relevant date' means the date which OFCOM determines to be that by which it would need to publish a notice under the Broadcasting Act 1990 s 104(1) (see PARA 738) if it were to grant, as from the date on which that licence would expire if not renewed, a fresh licence to provide the local service formerly provided under that licence: s 104A(13)(c) (as so added; and amended by the Communications Act 2003 Sch 15 para 46(2)).

11 'Nominated' means nominated by the applicant under the Broadcasting Act 1990 s 104A(4) (see the text and notes 12–16): s 104A(13)(b) (as so added).

12 As to the meaning of 'local digital sound programme service' see PARA 757 note 6; definition applied by the Broadcasting Act 1990 s 104A(13)(a) (as added: see note 2).

13 Broadcasting Act 1990 s 104A(4)(a) (as added: see note 2).

14 Broadcasting Act 1990 s 104A(4)(b) (as added: see note 2).

15 Ie in pursuance of the Broadcasting Act 1990 s 104A(12) (see the text and notes 34–36): see s 104A(4).

16 As to the meaning of 'broadcast' see PARA 668 note 2.

17 Broadcasting Act 1990 s 104A(4) (as added: see note 2).

18 Broadcasting Act 1990 s 104A(5) (as added (see note 2); and amended by the Communications Act 2003 Sch 15 para 46(2)).

19 Broadcasting Act 1990 s 104A(5)(a) (as added (see note 2); and amended by the Communications Act 2003 s 406(7), Sch 19). Conditions (whether as originally imposed or as varied) are included in pursuance of the Broadcasting Act 1990 s 106 (see PARA 744): see s 104A(5)(a) (as so added).

20 Broadcasting Act 1990 s 104A(5)(b) (as added: see note 2).

21 Broadcasting Act 1990 s 104A(5)(c) (s 104A as added (see note 2); and s 104A(5)(c) added by the Communications Act 2003 s 254).

22 Broadcasting Act 1990 s 104A(6) (as added (see note 2); and amended by the Communications Act 2003 Sch 15 para 46(2)).

23 Broadcasting Act 1990 s 104A(6)(a) (as added: see note 2).

24 Broadcasting Act 1990 s 104A(6)(b) (as added: see note 2).

25 As to the meaning of 'person' see PARA 510 note 1.

26 Broadcasting Act 1990 s 104A(6)(c) (as added (see note 2); and amended by the Communications Act 2003 Sch 15 para 46(2)).

27 Broadcasting Act 1990 s 104A(7) (as added (see note 2); and amended by the Communications Act 2003 Sch 15 para 46(2)).

28 Broadcasting Act 1990 s 104A(8) (as added (see note 2); and amended by the Communications Act 2003 Sch 15 para 46(2)).

29 Broadcasting Act 1990 s 104A(9) (as added (see note 2); and amended by the Communications Act 2003 Sch 15 para 46(2)). The Broadcasting Act 1990 s 86(3) (see PARA 725) does not limit the powers of OFCOM under s 104A(9): see s 104A(9) (as so added).

30 Broadcasting Act 1990 s 104A(10) (as added (see note 2); and amended by the Communications Act 2003 Sch 15 para 46(2)).

31 Broadcasting Act 1990 s 104A(10)(a) (as added: see note 2).

32 Broadcasting Act 1990 s 104A(10)(b) (as added (see note 2); and amended by the Communications Act 2003 Sch 15 para 46(2)).

33 Broadcasting Act 1990 s 104A(11)(a) (as added: see note 2).

34 Broadcasting Act 1990 s 104A(11)(b) (as added: see note 2).

35 Broadcasting Act 1990 s 104A(11) (as added (see note 2); and amended by the Communications Act 2003 Sch 15 para 46(2)).

36 Broadcasting Act 1990 s 104A(12)(a) (as added: see note 2).

37 Broadcasting Act 1990 s 104A(12)(b) (as added: see note 2).

38 Broadcasting Act 1990 s 104A(12) (as added (see note 2); and amended by the Communications Act 2003 Sch 15 para 46(2)).

39 As to the meaning of 'pre-transfer local licence' see PARA 752 note 3.

40 Ie under the Communications Act 2003 s 253: see PARA 752.

41 As to the meaning of 'radio transfer date' see PARA 751 note 1.

42 Broadcasting Act 1990 s 104A(12A) (s 104A as added (see note 2); and s 104A(12A) added by the Communications Act 2003 Sch 15 para 46(2)).

43 Ie under the Broadcasting Act 1990 s 104AA.

44 Broadcasting Act 1990 s 104AA(1) (s 104AA added by the Digital Economy Act 2010 s 32(2), (3)). Renewal is subject to the provisions of the Broadcasting Act 1990 ss 104AA(2)–(7), 104AB: s 104AA(1) (as so added). A local licence may be renewed under s 104AA only if: (1) it has been renewed under s 104A; or (2) it is granted on or after the day on which s 104AA comes into force (see note 2): s 104AA(2) (as so added).

Section 104A(3)–(12), (13), (14) applies in relation to the renewal of a licence under s 104AA as it applies in relation to the renewal of a licence under s 104A, subject to s 104AA(4), (5): s 104AA(3) (as so added). Section 104A(3) (as applied) has effect as if the words 'Subject to subsection (2)' were omitted: s 104AA(4) (as so added). In the case of an approved licence (see the text and notes 46–53), if an applicant for renewal of the licence under s 104AA makes a national nomination in accordance with s 104AB, s 104A (as applied) has effect as if: (1) s 104A(4) and (13)(b) were omitted; (2) references to the nominated local digital sound programme service were references to the national digital sound programme service nominated under s 104AB; and (3) references to the nominated local radio multiplex service were references to the national radio multiplex service nominated under s 104AB: s 104AA(5) (as so added). 'Local digital sound programme service' and 'local radio multiplex service' have the same meanings as in the Broadcasting Act 1996 Pt II (ss 40–72) (see notes 12, 7 respectively): s 104AA(6) (as so added).

45 Broadcasting Act 1990 s 104AA(7) (as added: see note 44).

46 In the Broadcasting Act 1990 ss 104AA, 104AB and 104AC, 'approved licence' means a local licence approved by OFCOM for the purposes of s 104AA: s 104AA(6) (as added: see note 44).

47 As to the meaning of 'national digital sound programme service' see PARA 756 note 16; definition applied by the Broadcasting Act 1990 s 104AA(6) (as added: see note 44).

48 Broadcasting Act 1990 s 104AB(1) (s 104AB added by the Digital Economy Act 2010 s 32(2)). As to the meaning of 'national radio multiplex service' see PARA 727 note 10; definition applied by s 104AA(6) (as added: see note 44).

49 Broadcasting Act 1990 s 104AB(2) (as added: see note 48).

50 As to the meaning of 'programme' see PARA 667 note 7.

51 Broadcasting Act 1990 s 104AB(3) (as added: see note 48).

52 Ie under the Broadcasting Act 1990 s 104AC: see PARA 741.

53 Broadcasting Act 1990 s 104AB(4) (as added: see note 48).

741. Variation of conditions relating to digital services. Where:

(1) a licence[1] that is an approved licence[2] has been renewed[3] and includes a local digital services condition[4];

(2) an application has been made[5] for the renewal of another approved licence and the applicant has made a national nomination[6]; and

(3) the nomination specifies the licence mentioned in head (1)[7] as one in relation to which an application to vary the licence conditions may be made,

OFCOM[8] may, if the following requirements are met, vary the licence by: (a) removing the local digital services condition; and (b) adding a national digital services condition[9]. The requirements are that:

(i) OFCOM must have received an application for the variation from the licence holder[10]; and

(ii) OFCOM must be satisfied that, if it varied the licence, the programmes[11] included in the nominated national digital sound programme service in each calendar month would include at least 80 per cent of the programmes included in the service provided under that licence[12].

1 As to the meaning of 'licence' see PARA 724 note 2.

2 As to the meaning of 'approved licence' see PARA 740 note 46.

3 Ie under the Broadcasting Act 1990 s 104A: see PARA 740.

4 'Local digital services condition' means a condition requiring the licence holder to do all that the licence holder can to ensure that a local digital sound programme service is broadcast by means of a local radio multiplex service: Broadcasting Act 1990 s 104AC(5) (s 104AC added by the Digital Economy Act 2010 s 32(2)). As to the holder of the licence see PARA 725 note 16. As to the meaning of 'local digital sound programme service' see PARA 757 note 6; definition applied by the Broadcasting Act 1990 s 104AA(6) (added by the Digital Economy Act 2010 s 32(2), (3)).

5 Ie under the Broadcasting Act 1990 s 104AA: see PARA 740.

6 Ie under the Broadcasting Act 1990 s 104AB: see PARA 740. As to the meaning of 'national nomination' see PARA 740.

7 Ie in accordance with the Broadcasting Act 1990 s 104AB(4): see PARA 740.

8 As to OFCOM see PARA 507.

9 Broadcasting Act 1990 s 104AC(1), (2) (as added: see note 4). 'National digital services condition' means a condition requiring the licence holder to do all that the licence holder can to ensure that the nominated national digital sound programme service is broadcast by means of the nominated national radio multiplex service until the day on which the licence (as renewed under s 104A) is to expire: s 105AC(5) (as so added). 'Nominated' means nominated in the

nomination referred to in s 104AC(1)(b) (head (2) in the text): s 105AC(5) (as so substituted). As to the meaning of 'national digital sound programme service' see PARA 756 note 16; and as to the meaning of 'national radio multiplex service' see PARA 727 note 10; definitions applied by s 104AA(6) (as added: see note 4).

10　Broadcasting Act 1990 s 104AC(3) (as added: see note 4).
11　As to the meaning of 'programme' see PARA 667 note 7.
12　Broadcasting Act 1990 s 104AC(4) (as added: see note 4).

742. Special application procedure for local licences. Where a local licence[1] is due to expire[2] and OFCOM[3] proposes to grant a further licence to provide the service in question[4], OFCOM may if it thinks fit publish a notice[5], which must:

(1)　state that OFCOM proposes to grant a further licence to provide a specified local service[6];

(2)　specify the area or locality in the United Kingdom[7] for which the service is to be provided[8];

(3)　invite declarations of intent to apply for a licence to provide the service[9];

(4)　specify the closing date for such declarations[10]; and

(5)　specify the application fee payable on any declaration made in pursuance of the notice[11], and a deposit of such amount as OFCOM may think fit[12].

A declaration of intent made in pursuance of such a notice must be in writing, and must be accompanied by the application fee and deposit[13].

Where OFCOM receives a declaration of intent in accordance with these provisions from a person other than the licence holder[14] in relation to the service in question[15], it must:

(a)　publish a notice[16];

(b)　specify in relation to persons who have made a declaration of intent in accordance with these provisions, no further application fee[17], and in relation to all other applicants, an application fee of the same amount as the fee referred to in head (5) above[18]; and

(c)　repay the deposit to every person[19] who has made a declaration of intent in accordance with these provisions[20], and who duly submits an application in pursuance of the notice referred to in head (a) above[21].

Where OFCOM receives a declaration of intent in accordance with these provisions from the licence holder in relation to the service in question, and no such declaration from any other person[22], it must invite the licence holder to apply for the licence in such manner as it may determine (but without requiring any further application fee)[23]; and on receiving an application duly made by him, it must repay to him the deposit[24].

1　As to the meaning of 'local licence' see PARA 738 note 3. As to the meaning of 'licence' see PARA 724 note 2.
2　Broadcasting Act 1990 s 104B(1)(a) (s 104B added by the Broadcasting Act 1996 s 94(1); Broadcasting Act 1990 s 104B(1)(a) amended by the Communications Act 2003 s 255(a)). This provision applies where a local licence is due to expire otherwise than by virtue of the Broadcasting Act 1990 s 110 (see PARA 746): see s 104B(1)(a) (as so added and amended).
3　As to OFCOM see PARA 507.
4　Broadcasting Act 1990 s 104B(1)(c) (as added (see note 2); and amended by the Communications Act 2003 s 360(3), Sch 15 para 47(1), (2)). In relation to a case in which it is a pre-transfer local licence that is due to expire, the reference to the service in question is a reference to the equivalent local service for which a licence is capable of being granted at times on or after the radio transfer date: Broadcasting Act 1990 s 104B(1A) (s 104B as added (see note 2); and s 104B(1A) added by the Communications Act 2003 Sch 15 para 47(3)). As to the meaning of 'pre-transfer local licence' see PARA 752 note 3; as to the meaning of 'radio transfer

date' see PARA 751 note 1; and as to the meaning of 'local service' see PARA 723 note 4 (definitions applied by the Broadcasting Act 1990 s 126(1) (amended by the Communications Act 2003 Sch 15 para 59(b))).

5　Broadcasting Act 1990 s 104B(1) (as added (see note 2); and amended by the Communications Act 2003 s 406(7), Sch 15 para 47(3), Sch 19). A notice may be published under this provision instead of under the Broadcasting Act 1990 s 104(1) (see PARA 738): see s 104B(1) (as so added and amended).

6　Broadcasting Act 1990 s 104B(2)(a) (as added (see note 2); and amended by the Communications Act 2003 Sch 15 para 47(2)).

7　As to areas in the United Kingdom see PARA 730 note 7. As to the meaning of 'United Kingdom' see PARA 510 note 13.

8　Broadcasting Act 1990 s 104B(2)(b) (as added: see note 2).

9　Broadcasting Act 1990 s 104B(2)(c) (as added: see note 2).

10　Broadcasting Act 1990 s 104B(2)(d) (as added: see note 2).

11　Broadcasting Act 1990 s 104B(2)(e)(i) (as added: see note 2).

12　Broadcasting Act 1990 s 104B(2)(e)(ii) (as added (see note 2); and amended by the Communications Act 2003 Sch 15 para 47(2)).

13　Broadcasting Act 1990 s 104B(3) (as added: see note 2).

14　As to the meaning of 'person' see PARA 510 note 1. As to the holder of the licence see PARA 725 note 16.

15　Broadcasting Act 1990 s 104B(4) (as added (see note 2); and amended by the Communications Act 2003 Sch 15 para 47(2)).

16　Broadcasting Act 1990 s 104B(4)(a) (as added: see note 2). The notice must be published under s 104(1) (see PARA 738): see s 104B(4)(a) (as so added).

17　Broadcasting Act 1990 s 104B(4)(b)(i) (as added: see note 2).

18　Broadcasting Act 1990 s 104B(4)(b)(ii) (as added: see note 2).

19　Broadcasting Act 1990 s 104B(4)(c) (as added: see note 2).

20　Broadcasting Act 1990 s 104B(4)(c)(i) (as added: see note 2).

21　Broadcasting Act 1990 s 104B(4)(c)(ii) (as added: see note 2).

22　Broadcasting Act 1990 s 104B(5) (as added (see note 2); and amended by the Communications Act 2003 Sch 15 para 47(2)).

23　Broadcasting Act 1990 s 104B(5)(a) (as added: see note 2).

24　Broadcasting Act 1990 s 104B(5)(b) (as added: see note 2).

743.　Digital switchover: variation of licence period. If the Secretary of State[1]:

(1)　has not nominated a date for digital switchover[2] for one or more relevant renewed services[3]; or

(2)　has withdrawn the nomination of such a date and has not nominated another such date,

the Secretary of State may give notice to OFCOM[4] fixing a date (the 'termination date') in relation to that service or such of those services as are specified or described in the notice[5]. The Secretary of State may fix different dates for different services but may not fix a date falling before 31 December 2015[6]. If the period for which a licence to provide a relevant renewed service is to continue in force ends after the termination date fixed for the service, OFCOM must by notice vary the licence so that the period ends on or before that date[7]. However, OFCOM may not reduce the period so that it ends on a day falling less than two years after the date on which it issues the notice, unless the licence holder consents to such a reduction[8]. If the period for which a licence to provide a relevant renewed service is to continue in force ends on or before the termination date fixed for the service, OFCOM may not vary the licence so that the period ends after that date[9].

1　As to the Secretary of State see PARA 507 note 32.

2　Ie under the Broadcasting Act 1990 s 97A: see PARA 702.

3　'Relevant renewed service' means a national service provided under a licence that has been renewed under the Broadcasting Act 1990 s 103B (see PARA 736) or a local service provided

under a licence that has been renewed under s 104AA (see PARA 740): s 105A(7) (s 105A added
by the Digital Economy Act 2010 s 33(2), (4)). As to the meaning of 'licence' see PARA 724
note 2.

4   As to OFCOM see PARA 507.
5   Broadcasting Act 1990 s 105A(1), (2) (as added: see note 3).
6   Broadcasting Act 1990 s 105A(3) (as added: see note 3).
7   Broadcasting Act 1990 s 105A(4) (as added: see note 3).
8   Broadcasting Act 1990 s 105A(5) (as added: see note 3).
9   Broadcasting Act 1990 s 105A(6) (as added: see note 3).

C. CONDITIONS TO BE INCLUDED IN LICENCES

**744.   Requirements as to character and coverage of national and local
services.**   A national[1] or local licence[2] must include such conditions as appear to
OFCOM[3] to be appropriate for securing that the character of the licensed[4]
service, as proposed by the licence holder[5] when making his application, is
maintained during the period for which the licence is in force[6].

Conditions included in a licence for this purpose may provide that OFCOM
may consent to a departure from the character of the licensed service if, and only
if, it is satisfied[7]:

(1)   that the departure would not substantially alter the character of the
       service[8];
(2)   that the departure would not narrow the range of programmes[9]
       available by way of relevant independent radio services[10] to persons
       living in the area or locality for which the service is licensed to be
       provided[11];
(3)   that, in the case of a local licence, the departure would be conducive to
       the maintenance or promotion of fair and effective competition in that
       area or locality[12];
(4)   that, in the case of a local licence, there is evidence that, amongst
       persons living in that area or locality, there is a significant demand for,
       or significant support for, the change that would result from the
       departure[13]; or
(5)   that, in the case of a local licence: (a) the departure would result from
       programmes included in the licensed service ceasing to be made at
       premises in the area or locality for which the service is provided; but (b)
       those programmes would continue to be made wholly or partly at
       premises within the approved area[14].

A national or local licence must include conditions requiring the licence holder
to secure that the licensed service serves so much of the area or locality for which
it is licensed to be provided as is for the time being reasonably practicable[15].

A national licence must include conditions enabling OFCOM, where it
appears to it to be reasonably practicable for the licensed service to be provided
for any additional area falling outside the minimum area determined by it[16], to
require the licence holder to provide the licensed service for any such additional
area[17].

OFCOM may, if it thinks fit, authorise the holder of a local licence, by means
of a variation of his licence to that effect, to provide the licensed service for any
additional area or locality adjoining the area or locality for which that service
has previously been licensed to be provided[18]. OFCOM may only exercise this
power if it appears to it[19]: (a) that to do so would not result in a significant
increase of the area or locality for which the service in question is licensed to be
provided[20]; or (b) that the increase that would result is justifiable in the

exceptional circumstances of the case[21]. As soon as practicable after OFCOM has exercised that power in relation to any service, it must publish, in such manner as it considers appropriate, a notice[22] stating that it has exercised that power in relation to that service[23], and giving details of the additional area or locality for which that service is licensed to be provided[24].

Before deciding for the purposes of a condition imposed in a licence[25] whether to consent to a departure from the character of a service provided under a local licence on any of the grounds mentioned in heads (2) to (4) above, OFCOM must publish a notice specifying[26]: (i) the proposed departure[27]; and (ii) the period in which representations may be made to OFCOM about the proposal[28]. That period must end not less than 28 days after the date of publication of the notice[29]. The notice must be published in such manner as appears to OFCOM to be appropriate for bringing it to the attention of the persons who, in OFCOM's opinion, are likely to be affected by the departure[30]. However, OFCOM is not required to publish such a notice, and may specify a period of less than 28 days in such a notice as the period for representations, if it considers that the publication of the notice, or allowing a longer period for representations, would result in a delay that would be likely prejudicially to affect the interests of the licence holder[31]. OFCOM is not required by these provisions[32] to publish any matter that is confidential[33] or to publish anything that it would not be reasonably practicable to publish without disclosing such a matter[34].

1   As to the meaning of 'national licence' see PARA 730 note 3.
2   As to the meaning of 'local licence' see PARA 738 note 3.
3   As to OFCOM see PARA 507.
4   As to the meaning of 'licensed' see PARA 724 note 2.
5   As to the holder of the licence see PARA 725 note 16.
6   Broadcasting Act 1990 s 106(1) (amended by the Communications Act 2003 ss 312(1), (2), 360(3), 406(7), Sch 15 para 49, Sch 19). As to licences being in force see PARA 865 note 11.
7   Broadcasting Act 1990 s 106(1A) (s 106(1A) added by the Communications Act 2003 s 312(3)).
8   Broadcasting Act 1990 s 106(1A)(a) (as added: see note 7). The matters to which OFCOM must have regard in determining for the purposes of s 106 the character of a service provided under a local licence include, in particular, the selection of spoken material and music in programmes included in the service: s 106(1B) (added by the Communications Act 2003 s 312(3)).
9   As to the meaning of 'programme' see PARA 667 note 7. For these purposes, 'programme' does not include an advertisement: see the Broadcasting Act 1990 s 104(7).
10 'Relevant independent radio services' means the following services so far as they are services falling to be regulated under the Communications Act 2003 s 245 (see PARA 723):
    (1)   sound broadcasting services;
    (2)   radio licensable content services;
    (3)   additional services,
    but, in relation to a departure from the character of a service provided under a local licence, does not include a service that is provided otherwise than wholly or mainly for reception by persons living and working in the area or locality in question: Broadcasting Act 1990 s 106(7) (added by the Communications Act 2003 s 312(5). As to the meaning of 'sound broadcasting service' see PARA 723 note 4. As to the meaning of 'radio licensable content services' see PARA 749; and as to the meaning of 'additional radio service' see PARA 723 note 6 (definitions applied by the Broadcasting Act 1990 s 126(1) (amended by the Communications Act 2003 Sch 15 para 59(b))).
11 Broadcasting Act 1990 s 106(1A)(b) (as added: see note 7).
12 Broadcasting Act 1990 s 106(1A)(c) (as added (see note 7); and amended by the Digital Economy Act 2010 s 45, Sch 2).
13 Broadcasting Act 1990 s 106(1A)(d) (as added: see note 7).
14 Broadcasting Act 1990 s 106(1A)(e) (s 106(1A) as added (see note 7); s 106(1A)(e) added by the Digital Economy Act 2010 s 34(1)). 'Approved area' is as defined in the Communications Act 2003 s 314 (see PARA 889 note 5): Broadcasting Act 1990 s 106(1A)(e) (as so added).
15 Broadcasting Act 1990 s 106(2).
16 Ie in accordance with the Broadcasting Act 1990 s 98(2): see PARA 730.

17 Broadcasting Act 1990 s 106(3) (amended by the Communications Act 2003 Sch 15 para 49).
18 Broadcasting Act 1990 s 106(4) (amended by the Communications Act 2003 Sch 15 para 49).
19 Broadcasting Act 1990 s 106(5) (substituted by the Communications Act 2003 s 312(4)).
20 Broadcasting Act 1990 s 106(5)(a) (as substituted: see note 18).
21 Broadcasting Act 1990 s 106(5)(b) (as substituted: see note 18).
22 Broadcasting Act 1990 s 106(6) (amended by the Communications Act 2003 Sch 15 para 49).
23 Broadcasting Act 1990 s 106(6)(a).
24 Broadcasting Act 1990 s 106(6)(b).
25 Ie under the Broadcasting Act 1990 s 106(1A): see s 106ZA(1) (s 106ZA added by the Communications Act 2003 s 313).
26 Broadcasting Act 1990 s 106ZA(1) (as added: see note 24).
27 Broadcasting Act 1990 s 106ZA(1)(a) (as added: see note 24).
28 Broadcasting Act 1990 s 106ZA(1)(b) (as added: see note 24).
29 Broadcasting Act 1990 s 106ZA(2) (as added: see note 24).
30 Broadcasting Act 1990 s 106ZA(3) (as added: see note 24).
31 Broadcasting Act 1990 s 106ZA(4) (as added: see note 24).
32 Ie the Broadcasting Act 1990 s 106ZA: s 106ZA(5) (as added: see note 24).
33 Ie in accordance with the Broadcasting Act 1990 s 106ZA(6) or s 106ZA(7): see s 106ZA(5)(a) (as added: see note 24). A matter is confidential under s 106ZA(6) if: (1) it relates specifically to the affairs of a particular body; and (2) its publication would or might, in OFCOM's opinion, seriously and prejudicially affect the interests of that body: s 106ZA(6) (as so added). A matter is confidential under s 106ZA(7) if: (a) it relates specifically to the private affairs of an individual; and (b) its publication would or might, in OFCOM's opinion, seriously and prejudicially affect the interests of that individual: s 106ZA(7) (as so added).
34 Broadcasting Act 1990 s 106ZA(5)(b) (as added: see note 24).

D. ENFORCEMENT OF LICENCES

745. Power to require scripts or broadcasting of correction or statement of findings. If OFCOM[1] is satisfied that the holder of a licence[2] granted in relation to sound broadcasting services[3] has failed to comply with any condition of the licence or with any direction given by OFCOM[4], it may serve on him a notice[5]:

(1) stating that OFCOM is so satisfied as respects any specified condition or direction[6];

(2) stating the effect of a further direction of OFCOM[7]; and

(3) specifying for the purposes of that direction a period not exceeding 12 months[8].

If, at any time during the period specified in the notice, OFCOM is satisfied that the licence holder has again failed to comply with any such condition or direction as is so mentioned (whether or not the same as the one specified in the notice), OFCOM may direct him[9]:

(a) to provide OFCOM in advance with such scripts and particulars of the programmes[10] to be included in the licensed[11] service as are specified in the direction[12]; and

(b) in relation to such of those programmes as will consist of or include recorded matter, to produce to OFCOM in advance for examination or reproduction such recordings of that matter as are so specified[13].

Such a direction has effect for such period, not exceeding six months, as is specified in the direction[14].

If OFCOM is satisfied that the holder of a licence has failed to comply with any condition of the licence[15], and that that failure can be appropriately remedied by the inclusion in the licensed service of a correction or a statement of findings or both[16], it may direct the licence holder to include in the licensed service a correction or a statement of findings or both in such form, and at such time or times, as it may determine[17]. However, OFCOM may not give any person[18] such a direction unless it has given him a reasonable opportunity of making representations to it about the matters complained of[19]. Where the holder of a licence includes a correction or a statement of findings in the licensed service in pursuance of such a direction, he may announce that he is doing so in pursuance of such a direction[20].

1 As to OFCOM see PARA 507.
2 As to the holder of the licence see PARA 725 note 16. As to the meaning of 'licence' see PARA 724 note 2.
3 Ie a licence granted under the Broadcasting Act 1990 Pt III Ch II (ss 98–111B). As to the application of this provision to a digital sound programme licence see PARA 771 note 2. As to the meaning of 'sound broadcasting service' see PARA 723 note 4.
4 Ie under or by virtue of any provision of the Broadcasting Act 1990 Pt III (ss 85–126).
5 Broadcasting Act 1990 s 109(1) (amended by the Communications Act 2003 s 360(3), Sch 15 para 50).
6 Broadcasting Act 1990 s 109(1)(a) (amended by the Communications Act 2003 Sch 15 para 50).
7 Broadcasting Act 1990 s 109(1)(b). The direction referred to in the text is one under s 109(2) (see the text and notes 9–13).
8 Broadcasting Act 1990 s 109(1)(c).
9 Broadcasting Act 1990 s 109(2) (amended by the Communications Act 2003 Sch 15 para 50).
10 As to the meaning of 'programme' see PARA 667 note 7.
11 As to the meaning of 'licensed' see PARA 724 note 2.
12 Broadcasting Act 1990 s 109(2)(a) (amended by the Communications Act 2003 Sch 15 para 50).
13 Broadcasting Act 1990 s 109(2)(b) (amended by the Communications Act 2003 Sch 15 para 50).
14 Broadcasting Act 1990 s 109(2).
15 Broadcasting Act 1990 s 109(3)(a) (s 109(3) amended by the Communications Act 2003 Sch 15 para 50).
16 Broadcasting Act 1990 s 109(3)(b) (amended by the Communications Act 2003 s 344(1), (2)).
17 Broadcasting Act 1990 s 109(3) (amended by the Communications Act 2003 s 344(2)).
18 As to the meaning of 'person' see PARA 510 note 1.
19 Broadcasting Act 1990 s 109(4) (amended by the Communications Act 2003 Sch 15 para 50).
20 Broadcasting Act 1990 s 109(5) (amended by the Communications Act 2003 s 344(3)). Where OFCOM serves a notice on a BBC company under any provision of the Broadcasting Act 1990 s 109, or receives any written representations from a BBC company under s 109(4) (see the text and note 19), OFCOM must send a copy of the direction, notice or representations to the Secretary of State: s 111A (added by the Broadcasting Act 1996 s 136, Sch 8 para 7; and amended by the Communications Act 2003 Sch 15 para 50)). As to the meaning of 'BBC company' see PARA 671 note 20. As to the Secretary of State see PARA 507 note 32.

746. Power to impose financial penalty or suspend or shorten licence period.
If OFCOM[1] is satisfied that the holder of a licence[2] granted in relation to sound broadcasting services[3] has failed to comply with any condition of the licence or with any direction given by OFCOM[4], it may serve on him[5]:

(1)   a notice requiring him to pay, within a specified period, a specified financial penalty to OFCOM[6];

(2)   a notice reducing the period for which the licence is to be in force by a specified period not exceeding two years[7]; or

(3)   a notice suspending the licence for a specified period not exceeding six months[8].

OFCOM may not serve on any person[9] such a notice as is mentioned in head (1), (2) or (3) above unless it has given him a reasonable opportunity of making representations to it about the matters complained of[10].

Where a licence is due to expire on a particular date by virtue of a notice served on any person under head (2) above, OFCOM may, on the application of that person, revoke that notice by a further notice served on him at any time before that date, if it is satisfied that, since the date of the earlier notice, his conduct in relation to the operation of the licensed[11] service has been such as to justify the revocation of that notice[12].

1   As to OFCOM see PARA 507.
2   As to the holder of the licence see PARA 725 note 16. As to the meaning of 'licence' see PARA 724 note 2.
3   Ie a licence granted under the Broadcasting Act 1990 Pt III Ch II (ss 98–111B). As to the meaning of 'sound broadcasting service' see PARA 723 note 4.
4   Ie under or by virtue of any provision of the Broadcasting Act 1990 Pt III (ss 83–126).
5   Broadcasting Act 1990 s 110(1) (amended by the Communications Act 2003 s 360(3), Sch 15 para 50). Any exercise by OFCOM of its powers under the Broadcasting Act 1990 s 110(1) in respect of any failure to comply with any condition or direction does not preclude any exercise by it of its powers under s 109 (see PARA 745) in respect of that failure: see s 110(6) (amended by the Communications Act 2003 Sch 15 para 50).
6   Broadcasting Act 1990 s 110(1)(a) (amended by the Communications Act 2003 Sch 15 para 50). The maximum amount which the holder of a national licence may be required to pay by way of a financial penalty imposed in pursuance of the Broadcasting Act 1990 s 110(1)(a) is the maximum penalty given by s 110(1B): s 110(1A) (s 110(1A)–(1D) added by the Communications Act 2003 s 345, Sch 13 paras 1, 7(1)). The maximum penalty is whichever is the greater of: (1) £250,000; and (2) 5% of the qualifying revenue for his last complete accounting period falling within the period for which his licence has been in force ('the relevant period'): Broadcasting Act 1990 s 110(1B) (as so added). In relation to a person whose first complete accounting period falling within the relevant period has not ended when the penalty is imposed, s 110(1B)(b) is to be construed as referring to 5% of the amount which OFCOM estimates to be the qualifying revenue for that accounting period: s 110(1C) (as so added). Section 102(2)–(6) (see PARA 734) applies for determining or estimating qualifying revenue for the purposes of s 110(1B) or s 110(1C): s 110(1D) (as so added). As to the meaning of 'national licence' see PARA 730 note 3. As to licences being in force see PARA 865 note 11.
        The amount of any financial penalty imposed on the holder of any other licence must not exceed £250,000: s 110(3) (amended by the Communications Act 2003 Sch 13 para 7(2)).
7   Broadcasting Act 1990 s 110(1)(b).
8   Broadcasting Act 1990 s 110(1)(c).
9   As to the meaning of 'person' see PARA 510 note 1.
10 Broadcasting Act 1990 s 110(4) (amended by the Communications Act 2003 Sch 15 para 50).
11 As to the meaning of 'licensed' see PARA 724 note 2.
12 Broadcasting Act 1990 s 110(5) (amended by the Communications Act 2003 Sch 15 para 50). Where OFCOM serves a notice on a BBC company under any provision of the Broadcasting Act 1990 s 110, or receives any written representations from a BBC company under s 110(4), OFCOM must send a copy of the direction, notice or representations to the Secretary of State: s 111A (added by the Broadcasting Act 1996 s 136, Sch 8 para 7; and amended by the Communications Act 2003 Sch 15 para 50)). As to the meaning of 'BBC company' see PARA 671 note 20. As to the Secretary of State see PARA 507 note 32.

747.   Power to revoke licences.   If OFCOM[1] is satisfied:

(1)   that the holder of a licence[2] granted in relation to sound broadcasting services[3] is failing to comply with any condition of the licence or with any direction given by OFCOM[4]; and

(2)   that that failure, if not remedied, would justify the revocation of the licence[5],

it must serve on the holder of the licence a notice[6], which must:

(a)   state that OFCOM is satisfied as mentioned above[7];

(b)   specify the respects in which, in its opinion, the licence holder is failing to comply with any such condition or direction as is mentioned in the notice[8]; and

(c)   state that, unless the licence holder takes, within such period as is specified in the notice, such steps to remedy the failure as are so specified, OFCOM will revoke his licence[9].

If at the end of the period specified in the notice OFCOM is satisfied that the person[10] on whom the notice was served has failed to take the steps specified in it[11], and that it is necessary in the public interest to revoke his licence[12], it must serve on him a notice revoking his licence[13].

If OFCOM is satisfied in the case of any national licence[14] that the holder of the licence has ceased to provide the licensed[15] service before the end of the period for which the licence is to continue in force[16], and that it is appropriate for it to do so[17], it must serve on him a notice revoking his licence[18].

If OFCOM is satisfied that the holder of a licence provided OFCOM, in connection with his application for the licence, with information which was false in a material particular[19], or that, in connection with his application for the licence, the holder of such a licence withheld any material information with the intention of causing OFCOM to be misled[20], it may serve on him a notice revoking his licence[21].

Any notice served[22] takes effect as from the time when it is served on the licence holder[23]. If it appears to OFCOM to be appropriate to do so for the purpose of preserving continuity in the provision of the service in question, it may provide in any such notice for it to take effect as from a date specified in the notice[24].

OFCOM may not serve any notice on a person under these provisions unless it has given him a reasonable opportunity of making representations to it about the matters complained of[25].

1 As to OFCOM see PARA 507.
2 As to the holder of the licence see PARA 725 note 16. As to the meaning of 'licence' see PARA 724 note 2.
3 Ie a licence granted under the Broadcasting Act 1990 Pt III Ch II (ss 98–111B). As to the meaning of 'sound broadcasting service' see PARA 723 note 4.
4 Broadcasting Act 1990 s 111(1)(a). A direction may be given by OFCOM under or by virtue of any provision of Pt III (ss 83–126): see s 111(1)(a).
5 Broadcasting Act 1990 s 111(1)(b).
6 Broadcasting Act 1990 s 111(1) (amended by the Communications Act 2003 s 360(3), Sch 15 para 50).
7 Broadcasting Act 1990 s 111(2)(a) (amended by the Communications Act 2003 Sch 15 para 50).
8 Broadcasting Act 1990 s 111(2)(b).
9 Broadcasting Act 1990 s 111(2)(c) (amended by the Communications Act 2003 Sch 15 para 50). The licence may be revoked under the Broadcasting Act 1990 s 111(3): see s 111(2)(c) (as so amended).
10 As to the meaning of 'person' see PARA 510 note 1.
11 Broadcasting Act 1990 s 111(3)(a).
12 Broadcasting Act 1990 s 111(3)(b).
13 Broadcasting Act 1990 s 111(3) (amended by the Communications Act 2003 Sch 15 para 50).
14 As to the meaning of 'national licence' see PARA 730 note 3.
15 As to the meaning of 'licensed' see PARA 724 note 2.
16 Broadcasting Act 1990 s 111(4)(a). As to licences being in force see PARA 865 note 11.
17 Broadcasting Act 1990 s 111(4)(b).
18 Broadcasting Act 1990 s 111(4) (amended by the Communications Act 2003 Sch 15 para 50).
19 Broadcasting Act 1990 s 111(5)(a).
20 Broadcasting Act 1990 s 111(5)(b).
21 Broadcasting Act 1990 s 111(5) (amended by the Communications Act 2003 Sch 15 para 50).
22 Ie any notice served under the Broadcasting Act 1990 s 111(3), (4) or (5): see s 111(6).
23 Broadcasting Act 1990 s 111(6).
24 Broadcasting Act 1990 s 111(7) (amended by the Communications Act 2003 Sch 15 para 50).
25 Broadcasting Act 1990 s 111(8) (amended by the Communications Act 2003 Sch 15 para 50).
      Where OFCOM serves a notice on a BBC company under any provision of the Broadcasting Act 1990 s 111, or receives any written representations from a BBC company under s 111(8), OFCOM must send a copy of the direction, notice or representations to the Secretary of State: s 111A (added by the Broadcasting Act 1996 s 136, Sch 8 para 7).
      As to the meaning of 'BBC company' see PARA 671 note 20. As to the Secretary of State see PARA 507 note 32.

748. Power to suspend licence to provide satellite service. If OFCOM[1] is satisfied:

    (1)   that the holder of a licence[2] to provide a radio licensable content service[3] has included in the service one or more programmes[4] containing material likely to encourage or incite to crime or to lead to disorder[5];

    (2)   that he has by doing that failed to comply with the condition[6] included in the licence[7]; and

    (3)   that the failure justifies the revocation of the licence[8],

it must serve on the holder of the licence a notice[9].

The notice must:

    (a)   state that OFCOM is satisfied as mentioned in head (1) above[10];

    (b)   specify the respects in which, in its opinion, the licence holder has failed to comply with the condition mentioned in head (2) above[11];

    (c)   state that OFCOM may revoke his licence after the end of the period of 21 days beginning with the date on which the notice is served on the licence holder[12];

    (d)   inform the licence holder of his right to make representations to OFCOM within that period about the matters complained of[13]; and

    (e)   suspend the licence as from the time when the notice is served on the licence holder until the revocation takes effect or OFCOM decides not to revoke the licence[14].

If OFCOM, having considered any representations about the matters complained of made to it within the 21 day period by the licence holder, is satisfied that it is necessary in the public interest to revoke the licence in question, it must serve on the licence holder a notice revoking the licence[15].

1   As to OFCOM see PARA 507.

2   As to the holder of the licence see PARA 725 note 16. As to the meaning of 'licence' see PARA 724 note 2.

3   As to the meaning of 'radio licensable content service' see PARA 749; definition applied by the Broadcasting Act 1990 s 126(1) (amended by the Communications Act 2003 s 360(3), Sch 15 para 59(b)).

4   As to the meaning of 'programme' see PARA 667 note 7.

5   Broadcasting Act 1990 s 111B(1)(a) (s 111B added by the Broadcasting Act 1996 s 96; and amended by the Communications Act 2003 Sch 15 para 51(1), (3)(a)).

6   Ie the condition which in compliance with the Communications Act 2003 s 263 (see PARA 602) is included in the licence for the purpose of securing the objective mentioned in s 319(2)(b) (see PARA 897 head (2)): see the Broadcasting Act 1990 s 111B(1)(b) (as added (see note 5); and amended by the Communications Act 2003 Sch 15 para 51(3)(b)).

7   Broadcasting Act 1990 s 111B(1)(b) (as added: see note 5).

8   Broadcasting Act 1990 s 111B(1)(c) (as added: see note 5).

9   Broadcasting Act 1990 s 111B(1) (as added (see note 5); and amended by the Communications Act 2003 Sch 15 para 51(2)).

10   Broadcasting Act 1990 s 111B(2)(a) (as added (see note 5); and amended by the Communications Act 2003 Sch 15 para 51(2)).

11   Broadcasting Act 1990 s 111B(2)(b) (as added: see note 5).

12   Broadcasting Act 1990 s 111B(2)(c) (as added (see note 5); and amended by the Communications Act 2003 Sch 15 para 51(2)).

13   Broadcasting Act 1990 s 111B(2)(d) (as added (see note 5); and amended by the Communications Act 2003 Sch 15 para 51(2)).

14   Broadcasting Act 1990 s 111B(2)(e) (as added (see note 5); and amended by the Communications Act 2003 Sch 15 para 51(2)).

15   Broadcasting Act 1990 s 111B(3) (as added (see note 5); and amended by the Communications Act 2003 Sch 15 para 51(2)). A notice under the Broadcasting Act 1990 s 111B(3) does not take effect until the end of the period of 28 days beginning with the day on which that notice was

served on the licence holder: s 111B(4) (as so added). Section 111 (see PARA 747) does not have effect in relation to the revocation of a licence in pursuance of a notice under s 111B(1): s 111B(5) (as so added).

(iii) Radio Licensable Content Services

749. Meaning of 'radio licensable content services'. In Part 3 of the Communications Act 2003[1], 'radio licensable content service' means[2] any service falling within heads (a) and (b) below in so far as it is provided with a view to its availability for reception by members of the public being secured by one or both of the following means: (1) the broadcasting of the service (whether by the person providing it or by another) from a satellite; or (2) the distribution of the service (whether by that person or by another) by any means involving the use of an electronic communications network[3]. A service falls within this provision if it: (a) consists of sound programmes; and (b) is provided (whether in digital or in analogue form) as a service that is to be made available for reception by members of the public[4].

A service is not a radio licensable content service to the extent that: (i) it is provided with a view to its being broadcast by means of a multiplex service[5]; (ii) it is a sound broadcasting service[6]; or (iii) it is comprised in a television licensable content service[7]. A service is not a radio licensable content service to the extent that it is provided by means of an electronic communications service if: (A) it forms part only of a service provided by means of that electronic communications service or is one of a number of services access to which is made available by means of a service so provided; and (B) the service of which it forms part, or by which it may be accessed, is provided for purposes that do not consist wholly or mainly in making available services of radio programmes or television programmes (or both) for reception by members of the public[8]. A service is not a radio licensable content service if it is a two-way service[9]. A service is not a radio licensable content service if it is distributed by means of an electronic communications network only to persons all of whom are on a single set of premises[10], and that network is wholly within those premises and is not connected to an electronic communications network any part of which is outside those premises[11]. A service is not a radio licensable content service if it is provided for the purpose only of being received by persons who have qualified as users of the service by reason of being: (aa) persons who have a business interest in the programmes included in the service; or (bb) persons who are to receive the programmes for the purpose only of allowing them to be listened to by persons falling within head (aa) above or by persons all of whom are on the business premises[12] of the person receiving them[13].

If it is considered appropriate, the Secretary of State may modify the above provisions[14].

1 Ie the Communications Act 2003 Pt 3 (ss 198–362).
2 Ie subject to the Communications Act 2003 s 248 (see the text and notes 5–13).
3 Communications Act 2003 s 247(1).
4 Communications Act 2003 s 247(2). As to the meaning of 'available for reception by members of the public' see PARA 796.
5 'Multiplex service' means a television multiplex service, a radio multiplex service or a general multiplex service: Communications Act 2003 s 248(9). As to the meaning of 'television multiplex service' see PARA 697; as to the meaning of 'radio multiplex service' see PARA 753; and as to the meaning of 'general multiplex service' see PARA 898 note 10.
6 Ie to which the Communications Act 2003 s 245(3) applies (see PARA 723).
7 Communications Act 2003 s 248(1). As to the meaning of 'television licensable content service' see PARA 716.

8   Communications Act 2003 s 248(2). As to the meaning of 'electronic communications service' see TELECOMMUNICATIONS vol 97 (2010) PARA 60.

9   Communications Act 2003 s 248(3). A service is a two-way service for the purposes of s 248(3) if it is provided by means of an electronic communications network and an essential feature of the service is that the purposes for which it is provided involve the use of that network, or a part of it, both: (1) for the transmission of sounds by the person providing the service to users of the service; and (2) for the transmission of sounds by those users for reception by the person providing the service or by other users of the service: s 248(4).

10   For the purposes of the Communications Act 2003 s 248, 'premises' includes a vehicle; and 'vehicle' includes vessel, aircraft or hovercraft: s 248(9).

11   Communications Act 2003 s 248(5). For these purposes: (1) a set of premises is a single set of premises if, and only if, the same person is the occupier of all the premises; and (2) two or more vehicles are capable of constituting a single set of premises if, and only if, they are coupled together: s 248(6).

12   'Business premises', in relation to a person, means premises at or from which any business of that person is carried on: Communications Act 2003 s 248(9).

13   Communications Act 2003 s 248(7). A person has a business interest in programmes if he has an interest in receiving or watching them: (1) for the purposes of a business carried on by him; or (2) for the purposes of his employment: s 248(8). In relation to a person, references to a business include references to: (a) any business or other activities carried on by a body of which he is a member and the affairs of which are managed by its members; and (b) the carrying out of any functions conferred on that person, or on any such body, by or under any enactment: s 248(10). As to the meaning of 'enactment' see PARA 793 note 5.

14   Ie the Communications Act 2003 ss 247, 248 (see the text and notes 1–13): see s 249.

750. Licence required in respect of radio licensable content services. The licence that is required[1] in respect of a radio licensable content service[2] is a licence granted under Part III of the Broadcasting Act 1990[3] on an application complying with the following provisions[4]. An application for a licence under Part III of the Broadcasting Act 1990 to provide a radio licensable content service: (1) must be made in such manner; (2) must contain such information about the applicant, his business and the service he proposes to provide; and (3) must be accompanied by such fee (if any), as OFCOM may determine[5].

1   Ie for the purposes of the Broadcasting Act 1990 s 97 (see PARA 595).
2   As to the meaning of 'radio licensable content service' see PARA 749.
3   Ie the Broadcasting Act 1990 Pt III (ss 85–126).
4   Communications Act 2003 s 250(1).
5   Communications Act 2003 s 250(2). As to OFCOM see PARA 507.
     The Broadcasting Act 1990 ss 109–111A (enforcement of licences) (see PARA 745 et seq) apply in relation to licences for radio licensable content services as they apply in relation to licences under the Broadcasting Act 1990 Pt III Ch 2 but with modifications: see the Communications Act 2003 s 250(3).

751. Radio licensable content services: abolition of separate licences for certain sound services. The authorisations that are to be capable of being granted on or after the radio transfer date[1] by or under a licence under Part III of the Broadcasting Act 1990 do not include the authorisation of the provision, as such, of: (1) any satellite service[2]; or (2) any licensable sound programme service[3]. So much of any relevant existing licence[4] as authorises the provision of a service which consists in or includes a radio licensable content service: (a) will have effect, on and after the radio transfer date, as a licence under Part III of the Broadcasting Act 1990 authorising the provision of the radio licensable content service comprised in the licensed service; (b) will so have effect as a licence which, notwithstanding its terms and conditions, is to continue in force until such time as it is surrendered or is revoked in accordance with provisions of the

Broadcasting Act 1990; and (c) will otherwise have effect as a licence on the same terms and conditions as those on which it had effect immediately before the radio transfer date[5].

1   'The radio transfer date' means the date on which the Radio Authority's functions under the Broadcasting Act 1990 Pt III (ss 85–126) and the Broadcasting Act 1996 Pt II (ss 40–72) are transferred under the Communications Act 2003 to OFCOM: Communications Act 2003 s 405(1). As to OFCOM see PARA 507.

2   Ie as defined, disregarding its repeal by the Communications Act 2003, in the Broadcasting Act 1990 s 84(2)(b): Communications Act 2003 s 251(1). For the purposes of the Broadcasting Act 1990 s 84(2)(b), 'satellite service' means any sound broadcasting service (other than one provided by the BBC) which consists:
    (1)   in the transmission of sound programmes by satellite from a place in the United Kingdom for general reception there; or
    (2)   in the transmission of such programmes by satellite from a place outside the United Kingdom for general reception there, if and to the extent that the programmes included in the service consist of material provided by a person in the United Kingdom who is in a position to determine what is to be included in the service (so far as it consists of programme material provided by him).

3   Ie as defined, disregarding its repeal by the Communications Act 2003, in the Broadcasting Act 1990 s 112(1): Communications Act 2003 s 251(1). For the purposes of the Broadcasting Act 1990 s 112(1), a 'licensable sound programme service' is a service consisting in the provision by any person of sound programmes with a view to their being conveyed, by means of a telecommunication system, for reception in two or more dwelling houses in the United Kingdom, and otherwise than for the purpose of being received there by persons who have a business interest in receiving them, whether the telecommunication system is run by the person so providing the programmes or by some other person, and whether the programmes are to be so conveyed for simultaneous reception or for reception at different times in response to requests made by different users of the service. 'Dwelling house' includes a hotel, inn, boarding-house or other similar establishment: s 202(1).
    The Communications Act 2003 s 251(1) does not affect OFCOM's power, by means of a licence authorising the provision of a service falling within s 245(1) (see PARA 723), to authorise the provision of so much of any formerly regulated radio service as is comprised in the licensed service: s 251(2). 'Formerly regulated radio service' means a service mentioned in s 251(1): s 251(5).

4   'Relevant existing licence' means any licence which: (1) was granted by the Radio Authority under the Broadcasting Act 1990 Pt III before the radio transfer date; and (2) is in force immediately before the radio transfer date as a licence authorising the provision of a formerly regulated service: Communications Act 2003 s 251(5).

5   Communications Act 2003 s 251(3). It is the duty of OFCOM to exercise its power under the Broadcasting Act 1990 s 86 (see PARA 725) to make such variations of any licence having effect in accordance with the Communications Act 2003 s 251(3) as (after complying with the Broadcasting Act 1990 s 86(5)(b)) it considers appropriate for the purpose of performing its duty under the Communications Act 2003 s 263 (see PARA 602): s 251(4).

752.   Extension and modification of existing licences.   A person who immediately before the radio transfer date[1] holds a pre-transfer national licence[2] or a pre-transfer local licence[3] is entitled, in accordance with the following provisions[4], to apply to OFCOM[5] for an extension of the licence[6]. The period for which a licence may be extended on such an application is a period ending not more than four years after the end of the period for which it was granted originally or (if it has been renewed) for which it was last renewed[7]. An application[8] may only be made in the period which begins three years before the date on which the licence would otherwise expire and ends three months before the day that OFCOM has determined to be the day by which it would need to publish a notice[9] if it were proposing to grant a fresh licence to take effect from that date[10]. An application: (1) must be made in such manner; (2) must contain such information about the applicant, his business and the service he proposes to provide; and (3) must be accompanied by such fee (if any), as OFCOM may determine[11].

If, on an application for an extension[12], OFCOM is satisfied as to the matters mentioned below[13], it must: (a) modify the licence by extending the period for which the licence is to be in force by such period[14] as it thinks fit; and (b) make such other modifications as appear to it to be necessary for the purpose of securing that the provisions of the licence correspond to those that would be contained in a national sound broadcasting licence[15] or (as the case may be) a local sound broadcasting licence[16] granted after the radio transfer date[17]. The matters referred to above are the ability of the licence holder to maintain the service for the period of the extension, and the likelihood of a contravention by the licence holder of a requirement imposed by: (i) a condition included in the licence[18]; or (ii) a condition of the licence varied in accordance with the provision below[19]. For the purposes of the modification under these provisions of a national licence, OFCOM: (A) must determine an amount which is to be payable to OFCOM by the licence holder in respect of the first complete calendar year falling within the period for which the licence is extended; and (B) may, in relation to any accounting period of the licence holder during the period of the extension, modify a condition included in the licence[20] by specifying a different percentage of the qualifying revenue for that accounting period from that which was previously specified in the condition[21].

1   As to the meaning of 'radio transfer date' see PARA 751 note 1.
2   'Pre-transfer national licence' means a pre-transfer licence granted or last renewed as a national licence (within the meaning of the Broadcasting Act 1990 Pt III (ss 85–126), as it had effect without the amendments made by the Communications Act 2003): Communications Act 2003 s 253(13). 'Pre-transfer licence' means a licence which was granted under the Broadcasting Act 1990 Pt III before the radio transfer date and has not been modified under the Communications Act 2003 s 253 or renewed at any time on or after that date: s 253(13).
3   'Pre-transfer local licence' means a pre-transfer licence which was granted as a local licence (within the meaning of the Broadcasting Act 1990 Pt III, as it had effect without the amendments made by the Communications Act 2003): s 253(13).
4   Ie the Communications Act 2003 s 253(2)–(13) (see the text and notes 7–21).
5   As to OFCOM see PARA 507.
6   Communications Act 2003 s 253(1).
7   Communications Act 2003 s 253(2).
8   Ie under the Communications Act 2003 s 253(1) (see the text and note 6).
9   Ie under the Broadcasting Act 1990 s 98(1) (see PARA 730) or s 104(1) (see PARA 738).
10 Communications Act 2003 s 253(3). A determination for these purposes: (1) must be made at least one year before the day determined; and (2) must be notified by OFCOM to the person who holds the licence in question: s 253(4).
11 Communications Act 2003 s 253(5).
12 Ie under the Communications Act 2003 s 253(1) (see the text and note 6).
13 Ie mentioned in the Communications Act 2003 s 253(7) (see the text and note 19).
14 Ie authorised by the Communications Act 2003 s 253(2) (see the text and note 7).
15 'National sound broadcasting licence' means a licence under the Broadcasting Act 1990 Pt III to provide a sound broadcasting service which, under the Communications Act 2003 s 245(4)(a) (see PARA 723) is a national service for the purposes of s 245: s 253(13).
16 'Local sound broadcasting licence' means a licence under the Broadcasting Act 1990 Pt III to provide a local sound broadcasting service: Communications Act 2003 s 362(1). As to the meaning of 'local sound broadcasting service' see PARA 889 note 2.
17 Communications Act 2003 s 253(6). See further note 21.
18 Ie by virtue of the Broadcasting Act 1990 s 106 (see PARA 744).
19 Ie in accordance with the Communications Act 2003 s 253(8) (see the text and note 21): s 253(7).
20 Ie in pursuance of the Broadcasting Act 1990 s 102(1)(c) (additional payments to be made in respect of national licences: see PARA 734).

21 Communications Act 2003 s 253(8). The amount determined by OFCOM under head (A) in the
    text must be the amount which, in OFCOM's opinion, would have been the cash bid of the
    licence holder were the licence (instead of being extended) being granted afresh on an
    application made in accordance with the Broadcasting Act 1990 s 98 (see PARA 730):
    Communications Act 2003 s 253(9). For the purposes of head (B) in the text: (1) different
    percentages may be specified for different accounting periods; and (2) the percentages that may
    be specified for an accounting period include a nil percentage: s 253(10).
        The modifications set out in accordance with head (b) in the text must secure: (a) that the
    amount falling to be paid under the conditions of the licence for each calendar year subsequent
    to that for which an amount has been determined in accordance with head (A) in the text is the
    amount so determined as increased by the appropriate percentage; and (b) that such adjustments
    as are appropriate are made as respects sums already paid in respect of any year or accounting
    period to which a modification under s 253(8) applies: s 253(11). 'The appropriate percentage'
    has the same meaning as in the Broadcasting Act 1990 s 102 (see PARA 734): Communications
    Act 2003 s 253(13). Where OFCOM has granted a person's application under s 253, the
    extensions and modifications take effect only if that person: (i) has been notified by OFCOM of
    its proposals for modifications by virtue of head (b) or head (B) in the text, and for the making
    of a determination under head (A) in the text; and (ii) has consented to the extension on the
    terms proposed: s 253(12).

(iv) Radio Multiplex Services

753. Radio multiplex services. Subject to the following provisions[1], references
in Part II of the Broadcasting Act 1996[2] to a radio multiplex service have effect
as references to any service which: (1) falls within heads (a) and (b) below; (2) is
provided for broadcasting for general reception but otherwise than from a
satellite; and (3) is not a television multiplex service[3]. A service falls within this
provision if: (a) it consists in the packaging together (with or without other
services) of two or more relevant sound services[4] which are provided for
inclusion together in that service by a combination of the relevant information in
digital form; or (b) it is a service provided with a view to its being a service
falling within head (a) but is one in the case of which only one relevant sound
service is for the time being comprised in digital form in what is provided[5]. The
provision, at a time after 29 December 2003[6], of a radio multiplex service the
provision of which is not authorised by or under a licence[7] is not to be an
offence[8]. Accordingly, after 29 December 2003, a licence[9] will be required for the
provision of a radio multiplex service only in so far as it is required for the
purposes of a limitation falling within the provision below[10] which is contained
in a wireless telegraphy licence, or is deemed to be so contained[11]. A limitation
falls within this provision, in relation to a wireless telegraphy licence, if it
provides that the only radio multiplex services that are authorised to be
broadcast using the station or apparatus to which the licence relates are those
that are licensed under Part II of the Broadcasting Act 1996[12].

1 Ie subject to the Communications Act 2003 s 258(2)–(9).
2 Ie the Broadcasting Act 1996 Pt II (ss 40–72).
3 Communications Act 2003 s 258(1). As to the meaning of 'television multiplex service' see PARA
   697.
4 For these purposes, 'relevant sound service' means any of the following: (1) a digital sound
   programme service; (2) a simulcast radio service; and (3) a digital additional sound service:
   Communications Act 2003 s 258(9). 'Simulcast radio service' means any simulcast radio service
   within the meaning given by the Broadcasting Act 1996 s 41(2) (see PARA 754 note 12) for the
   purposes of the Broadcasting Act 1996 Pt II: Communications Act 2003 s 362(1).
5 Communications Act 2003 s 258(2).
6 Ie the commencement of the Communications Act 2003 s 258 (see the Office of
   Communications Act 2002 (Commencement No 3) and Communications Act 2003
   (Commencement No 2) Order 2003, SI 2003/3142).
7 Ie under the Broadcasting Act 1996 Pt II.

8   Ie under the Broadcasting Act 1990 s 97 (see PARA 595): Communications Act 2003 s 258(3).
9   Ie under the Broadcasting Act 1996 Pt II.
10 Ie falling within the Communications Act 2003 s 258(5) (see the text and note 12).
11 Communications Act 2003 s 258(4). As to the meaning of 'wireless telegraphy licence' see PARA
    514 note 4.
12 Communications Act 2003 s 258(5). Where immediately before 29 December 2003: (1) a radio
    multiplex service is licensed under the Broadcasting Act 1996 Pt II; and (2) that service is one
    broadcast using a station or apparatus the use of which is authorised by a wireless telegraphy
    licence, that wireless telegraphy licence is deemed to contain a limitation falling within the
    Communications Act 2003 s 258(5): s 258(6). In any case where a wireless telegraphy licence is
    deemed by virtue of s 258(6) to contain a limitation falling within s 258(5) and the person
    providing the radio multiplex service in question: (a) ceases to be licensed under the
    Broadcasting Act 1996 Pt II in respect of that service; or (b) ceases to exist, OFCOM may
    revoke the wireless telegraphy licence: s 258(7). Section 258(7) is not to be construed as
    restricting the powers of revocation exercisable apart from s 258: s 258(8). As to OFCOM see
    PARA 507.

754. National radio multiplex licences. Where OFCOM[1] proposes to grant a
licence[2] to provide a national radio multiplex service[3], it must publish, in such
manner as it considers appropriate, a notice[4]:

(1)   stating that it proposes to grant such a licence[5];
(2)   specifying the frequency[6] on which the service is to be provided[7];
(3)   specifying, in such manner as OFCOM considers appropriate, the area
       of the United Kingdom[8] in which the frequency is to be available[9];
(4)   where digital capacity on the frequency is reserved[10] for the
       broadcasting[11] of a simulcast radio service[12], stating that fact and
       specifying the capacity reserved and the identity of the national service
       or services concerned[13];
(5)   inviting applications for the licence and specifying the closing date for
       such applications[14];
(6)   specifying the fee payable on any application made in pursuance of the
       notice[15]; and
(7)   stating whether any percentage of multiplex revenue[16] for each
       accounting period[17] would be payable by an applicant[18] if he were
       granted the licence and, if so, specifying that percentage[19].

When publishing such a notice, OFCOM must publish with the notice general
guidance as to requirements to be met by proposals as to the matters referred to
in heads (b)(i), (ii) and (f) below[20], and may publish with the notice such other
general guidance as it considers appropriate[21].

Any application made in pursuance of such a notice must be in writing and
accompanied by[22]:

(a)   the fee specified in the notice under head (7) above[23];
(b)   a technical plan relating to the service which the applicant proposes to
       provide and indicating[24]:
       (i)   the parts of the area specified under head (3) above which would
               be within the coverage area of the service[25];
       (ii)   the timetable in accordance with which that coverage would be
               achieved[26]; and
       (iii)   the technical means by which it would be achieved[27];
(c)   the applicant's proposals as to the number of digital sound programme
       services[28] to be broadcast and as to the characteristics of each of those
       services[29];
(d)   the applicant's proposals as to the timetable in accordance with which
       the broadcasting of each of those services would begin[30];

(e)   the applicant's proposals as to the broadcasting of television licensable content services[31];

(f)   the applicant's proposals as to the broadcasting of digital additional services[32];

(g)   the applicant's proposals for promoting or assisting the acquisition[33], by persons in the proposed coverage area of the service, of equipment capable of receiving the service[34];

(h)   such information as OFCOM may reasonably require as to the applicant's present financial position and his projected financial position during the period for which the licence would be in force[35]; and

(i)   such other information as OFCOM may reasonably require for the purpose of considering the application[36].

At any time after receiving such an application and before determining it, OFCOM may require the applicant to furnish additional information under any of heads (b) to (h) above[37]. Any information to be furnished to OFCOM must, if it so requires, be in such form or verified in such manner as it may specify[38].

OFCOM must, as soon as reasonably practicable after the date specified in the notice as the closing date for applications, publish in such manner as it considers appropriate[39] the name of every person who has made an application to it in pursuance of the notice[40], the proposals submitted by him under head (c) above[41], and such other information connected with his application as OFCOM considers appropriate[42]. OFCOM must also publish a notice inviting representations to be made to it with respect to any of the applications[43], and specifying the manner in which, and the time by which, any such representations are to be so made[44].

1   As to OFCOM see PARA 507.
2   As to the meaning of 'licence' see PARA 727 note 2.
3   As to the meaning of 'national radio multiplex service' see PARA 727 note 10.
4   Broadcasting Act 1996 s 46(1) (amended by the Communications Act 2003 s 360(3), Sch 15 para 105(1), (2)).
5   Broadcasting Act 1996 s 46(1)(a).
6   As to the meaning of 'frequency' see PARA 681 note 5; definition applied by the Broadcasting Act 1996 s 147(2).
7   Broadcasting Act 1996 s 46(1)(b).
8   As to areas in the United Kingdom see PARA 727 note 10.
9   Broadcasting Act 1996 s 46(1)(c) (amended by the Communications Act 2003 Sch 15 para 105(2)).
10   Ie in pursuance of a condition under the Broadcasting Act 1996 s 48 (see PARA 756): see s 46(1)(d) (amended by the Communications Act 2003 Sch 15 para 105(3)).
11   As to the meaning of 'broadcast' see PARA 668 note 2; definition applied by the Broadcasting Act 1996 s 147(2).
12   A 'simulcast radio service' means a service provided by a person for broadcasting in digital form and corresponding to a service which is a national service within the meaning of the Broadcasting Act 1990 Pt III (ss 85–126) (see PARAS 723 note 4, 730 note 3) and is provided by that person: Broadcasting Act 1996 ss 41(2), 72(1) (s 41(2) substituted by the Communications Act 2003 s 256(1)). For the purposes of the Broadcasting Act 1996 Pt II (ss 40–72), a service provided for broadcasting in digital form corresponds to a national service (within the meaning of the Broadcasting Act 1990 Pt III) if, and only if, in every calendar month: (1) at least 80% of so much of the national service as consists of programmes, consists of programmes which are also included in the digital service in that month; and (2) at least 50% of so much of the national service as consists of such programmes is broadcast at the same time on both services: Broadcasting Act 1996 s 41(3). For the purposes of s 41(3), 'programme' does not include an advertisement: s 41(7). The Secretary of State may by order amend s 41(3)(a) or (b) by substituting for the percentage for the time being specified there a different percentage specified in the order: s 41(4). Before making such an order, the Secretary of State must consult such

persons appearing to him to represent listeners as he thinks fit: s 41(5). An order under s 41(4) is subject to annulment in pursuance of a resolution of either House of Parliament: s 41(6). As to the Secretary of State see PARA 507 note 32.

13 Broadcasting Act 1996 s 46(1)(d).

14 Broadcasting Act 1996 s 46(1)(f).

15 Broadcasting Act 1996 s 46(1)(g).

16 As to multiplex revenue for accounting periods see PARA 763.

17 As to accounting periods see note 19.

18 Ie in pursuance of the Broadcasting Act 1996 s 55 (see note 19).

19 Broadcasting Act 1996 s 46(1)(h). Where a national radio multiplex licence (see text and note 3) is granted in pursuance of a notice under s 46(1) which specified a percentage of multiplex revenue under s 46(1)(h), the licence must include conditions requiring the licence holder to pay to OFCOM (in addition to any fees required to be so paid by virtue of s 43(1)(c): see PARA 728) in respect of each accounting period of his falling within the period for which the licence is in force, an amount representing such percentage of the multiplex revenue for that accounting period (determined under s 56: see PARA 763) as was specified in the notice: s 55(1) (amended by the Communications Act 2003 Sch 15 para 114). The Secretary of State may by order provide that, in relation to any notice under the Broadcasting Act 1996 s 46(1) published while the order is in force, no percentage may be specified under s 46(1)(h): s 55(2). Any order under s 55(2) is subject to annulment in pursuance of a resolution of either House of Parliament: s 55(3). As to orders made under this provision see the Broadcasting (Percentage of National Radio Multiplex Revenue) Order 1998, SI 1998/189, which provides that no percentage of multiplex revenue is payable: see art 2. This order ceased to have effect on 31 December 2006: see art 3.

Where the first complete accounting period of the licence holder falling within the period for which the licence is in force ('the licence period') does not begin at the same time as that period, or the last complete accounting period of his falling within the licence period does not end at the same time as that period, any reference in s 55(1) to an accounting period of his includes a reference to such part of the accounting period preceding that first complete accounting period, or (as the case may be) following that last complete accounting period, as falls within the licence period; and other references to accounting periods in Pt II are to be construed accordingly: s 55(6).

Unless an order under s 55(2) is in force: (1) the consent of the Secretary of State is required for so much of the notice as relates to the matters specified in s 46(1)(h); and (2) OFCOM may if it thinks fit (with that consent) specify under s 46(1)(h) different percentages in relation to different accounting periods falling within the period for which the licence would be in force, and a nil percentage in relation to any accounting period so falling: s 46(2) (amended by the Communications Act 2003 Sch 15 para 105(2)).

20 Broadcasting Act 1996 s 46(3)(a) (amended by the Communications Act 2003 Sch 15 para 105(2)).

21 Broadcasting Act 1996 s 46(3)(b).

22 Broadcasting Act 1996 s 46(4).

23 Broadcasting Act 1996 s 46(4)(a).

24 Broadcasting Act 1996 s 46(4)(b).

25 Broadcasting Act 1996 s 46(4)(b)(i).

26 Broadcasting Act 1996 s 46(4)(b)(ii).

27 Broadcasting Act 1996 s 46(4)(b)(iii).

28 'Digital sound programme service' means a service consisting in the provision by any person of programmes consisting wholly of sound (together with any ancillary services, as defined by the Broadcasting Act 1996 s 63(2) (see PARA 779 note 9) with a view to their being broadcast in digital form so as to be available for reception by members of the public, whether by him or by some other person, but does not include a simulcast radio service (as defined by s 41(2) (see note 12)), or a service where the sounds are to be received through the use of coded reference to pre-defined phonetic elements of sounds: ss 40(5), 72(1) (s 40(5) amended by the Communications Act 2003 Sch 15 para 101(1), (4)). 'Broadcast' means broadcast otherwise than from a satellite: Broadcasting Act 1996 s 40(8) (substituted by the Communications Act 2003 Sch 15 para 101(5)). As to the meaning of 'available for reception by members of the public' see PARA 796; definition applied by the Broadcasting Act 1996 s 40(8) (as so substituted).

The Secretary of State may, if having regard to developments in broadcasting technology he considers it appropriate to do so, by order amend the definition of 'digital sound programme service' in s 40(5): s 40(6). No order under s 40(6) may be made unless a draft of the order has been laid before and approved by a resolution of each House of Parliament: s 40(7).

29 Broadcasting Act 1996 s 46(4)(c).

30 Broadcasting Act 1996 s 46(4)(d).
31 Broadcasting Act 1996 s 46(4)(da) (added by SI 2006/2131). As to the meaning of 'television licensable content service' see PARA 716; definition applied by the Broadcasting Act 1996 s 72(1) (definition added by SI 2006/2131).
32 Broadcasting Act 1996 s 46(4)(e). As to digital additional services see PARA 779 et seq.
33 'Acquisition' includes acquisition on hire or loan: Broadcasting Act 1996 s 46(5). As to the meaning of 'acquisition' see PARA 690 note 34.
34 Broadcasting Act 1996 s 46(4)(f).
35 Broadcasting Act 1996 s 46(4)(g) (amended by the Communications Act 2003 Sch 15 para 105(2)).
36 Broadcasting Act 1996 s 46(4)(h) (amended by the Communications Act 2003 Sch 15 para 105(2)).
37 Broadcasting Act 1996 s 46(6) (amended by the Communications Act 2003 Sch 15 para 105(2)).
38 Broadcasting Act 1996 s 46(7) (amended by the Communications Act 2003 Sch 15 para 105(2)).
39 Broadcasting Act 1996 s 46(8) (amended by the Communications Act 2003 Sch 15 para 105(2)).
40 Broadcasting Act 1996 s 46(8)(a)(i).
41 Broadcasting Act 1996 s 46(8)(a)(ii).
42 Broadcasting Act 1996 s 46(8)(a)(iii) (amended by the Communications Act 2003 Sch 15 para 105(2)).
43 Broadcasting Act 1996 s 46(8)(b)(i).
44 Broadcasting Act 1996 s 46(8)(b)(ii).

755. Award of national radio multiplex licences. Where OFCOM[1] has published a notice in connection with national radio multiplex licences[2], in determining whether, or to whom, to award the national radio multiplex licence in question, it must have regard to the extent to which, taking into account the matters specified below and any representations received by it[3] with respect to those matters, the award of the licence to each applicant would be calculated to promote the development of digital sound broadcasting in the United Kingdom[4] otherwise than by satellite[5]. The matters to be taken into account are:

(1)   the extent of the coverage area[6] proposed to be achieved by the applicant as indicated in the technical plan submitted by him[7];

(2)   the timetables proposed by the applicant[8];

(3)   the ability of the applicant to establish the proposed service and to maintain it throughout the period for which the licence will be in force[9];

(4)   the capacity of the digital sound programme services[10] proposed to be included in the service to appeal to a variety of tastes and interests[11];

(5)   any proposals by the applicant for promoting or assisting the acquisition[12], by persons[13] in the proposed coverage area of the service, of equipment capable of receiving the service[14]; and

(6)   whether, in contracting or offering to contract with persons providing digital sound programme services, television licensable content services[15] or digital additional services[16], the applicant has acted in a manner calculated to ensure fair and effective competition in the provision of such services[17].

Where OFCOM has awarded a national radio multiplex licence to any person, it must, as soon as reasonably practicable after awarding the licence, publish in such manner as it considers appropriate the name of the person to whom the licence has been awarded, and such other information as OFCOM considers appropriate[18]; and it must grant the licence to that person[19].

A national radio multiplex licence may include conditions enabling OFCOM to estimate before the beginning of an accounting period[20] the amount due for that period[21], and requiring the licence holder to pay the estimated amount by monthly instalments throughout that period[22]. Such a licence may in particular include conditions authorising OFCOM to revise any estimate on one or more occasions and to adjust the instalments payable by the licence holder to take account of the revised estimate[23], and providing for the adjustment of any overpayment or underpayment[24].

1　As to OFCOM see PARA 507.
2　Ie a notice under the Broadcasting Act 1996 s 46(1) (see PARA 754). As to the meaning of 'national radio multiplex licence' see PARA 727 note 10.
3　Ie received in pursuance of the Broadcasting Act 1996 s 46(8)(b) (see PARA 754).
4　As to the meaning of 'United Kingdom' see PARA 510 note 13.
5　Broadcasting Act 1996 s 47(1) (amended by the Communications Act 2003 s 360(3), Sch 15 para 106).
6　Ie within the area specified in the notice under the Broadcasting Act 1996 s 46(1)(c) (see PARA 754).
7　Broadcasting Act 1996 s 47(2)(a). The technical plan is submitted under s 46(4)(b) (see PARA 754): see s 47(2)(a).
8　Broadcasting Act 1996 s 47(2)(b). The timetables are proposed under s 46(4)(b)(ii), (d) (see PARA 754): see s 47(2)(b).
9　Broadcasting Act 1996 s 47(2)(c). As to licences being in force see PARA 865 note 11; applied by s 147(2).
10　As to the meaning of 'digital sound programme service' see PARA 754 note 28.
11　Broadcasting Act 1996 s 47(2)(d).
12　'Acquisition' includes acquisition on hire or loan: Broadcasting Act 1996 s 47(3).
13　As to the meaning of 'person' see PARA 510 note 1.
14　Broadcasting Act 1996 s 47(2)(e).
15　As to the meaning of 'television licensable content service' see PARA 716; definition applied by the Broadcasting Act 1996 s 72(1) (definition added by SI 2006/2131).
16　As to digital additional services see PARA 779 et seq.
17　Broadcasting Act 1996 s 47(2)(f) (amended by SI 2006/2131).
18　Broadcasting Act 1996 s 47(5)(a) (amended by the Communications Act 2003 Sch 15 para 106).
19　Broadcasting Act 1996 s 47(5)(b).
20　As to accounting periods see PARA 754 note 19.
21　Broadcasting Act 1996 s 55(4)(a) (amended by the Communications Act 2003 Sch 15 para 114). Payment is due by virtue of the Broadcasting Act 1996 s 55(1) (see PARA 754): see s 55(4)(a).
22　Broadcasting Act 1996 s 55(4)(b).
23　Broadcasting Act 1996 s 55(5)(a) (amended by the Communications Act 2003 Sch 15 para 114).
24　Broadcasting Act 1996 s 55(5)(b).

756.　Reservation of capacity for independent national broadcasters. OFCOM[1] must ensure that the conditions included in national radio multiplex licences[2] (taken together) secure that an amount of digital capacity on the multiplex frequencies[3] is reserved for every independent national broadcaster[4] for the broadcasting[5] of a simulcast radio service[6] provided by that broadcaster[7]. Where the conditions of a licence for a national radio multiplex service reserve capacity on the frequency made available for that service for the broadcasting of a simulcast radio service provided by an independent national broadcaster, those conditions must also include the condition[8] that OFCOM considers appropriate for securing that, in consideration of the making by the independent national broadcaster of the payments which: (1) are agreed from time to time between him and the licence holder; or (2) in default of agreement, are determined under the Broadcasting Act 1996[9], the licence holder uses, for the broadcasting of a simulcast radio service provided by that broadcaster, such of the reserved digital capacity as may be requested, from time to time, by that broadcaster[10]. Where conditions are included in a national radio multiplex licence reserving capacity for an independent national broadcaster, OFCOM may include conditions relating to the broadcasting of the simulcast radio service in the licence for the national service provided by that broadcaster[11].

Where the holder of a national radio multiplex licence and an independent national broadcaster fail to agree as to the payments to be made, either of them may refer the matter to OFCOM for its determination[12]. Before making such a determination, OFCOM must give the licence holder and the independent national broadcaster an opportunity of making representations to it about the matter[13]. In making any such determination, OFCOM must have regard to the expenses incurred, or likely to be incurred, by the licence holder in providing the national radio multiplex service and in broadcasting the simulcast radio service in question[14], and the terms on which persons[15] providing national radio multiplex services contract with persons providing national digital sound programme services[16] for the broadcasting of those services[17].

1   As to OFCOM see PARA 507.
2   As to the meaning of 'national radio multiplex licence' see PARA 727 note 10.
3   'The multiplex frequencies' means the frequencies made available for the purposes of licensed national radio multiplex services: Broadcasting Act 1996 s 48(7) (added by the Communications Act 2003 s 360(3), Sch 15 para 107(1), (5)).
4   'Independent national broadcaster' means any person who is the holder of a national licence (within the meaning of the Broadcasting Act 1990 Pt III (ss 85–126)): Broadcasting Act 1996 s 41(1).
5   As to the meaning of 'broadcast' see PARA 668 note 2; definition applied by the Broadcasting Act 1996 s 147(2).
6   As to the meaning of 'simulcast radio service' see PARA 754 note 12.
7   Broadcasting Act 1996 s 48(1A) (added by the Communications Act 2003 Sch 15 para 107(2)).
8   Ie the condition in the Broadcasting Act 1996 s 48(1C) (see the text and note 10): s 48(1B) (added by the Communications Act 2003 Sch 15 para 107(2)).
9   Ie under the Broadcasting Act 1996 s 48.
10 Broadcasting Act 1996 s 48(1C) (added by the Communications Act 2003 Sch 15 para 107(2)).
11 Broadcasting Act 1996 s 48(1D) (added by the Communications Act 2003 Sch 15 para 107(2)).
12 Broadcasting Act 1996 s 48(4) (amended by the Communications Act 2003 Sch 15 para 107(3), (4)).
13 Broadcasting Act 1996 s 48(5) (amended by the Communications Act 2003 Sch 15 para 107(3)).
14 Broadcasting Act 1996 s 48(6)(a) (amended by the Communications Act 2003 Sch 15 para 107(3)).
15 As to the meaning of 'person' see PARA 510 note 1.
16 As to the meaning of 'digital sound programme service' see PARA 754 note 28. A digital sound programme service is a national digital sound programme service if it is provided for broadcasting by means of a national radio multiplex service, by means of a television multiplex service, or by means of a general multiplex service: Broadcasting Act 1996 ss 60(1)(a), 72(1) (s 60(1)(a) amended by the Communications Act 2003 s 260(1)).
17 Broadcasting Act 1996 s 48(6)(b).

757. Duty of OFCOM to reserve digital capacity for certain purposes of the BBC. In exercising its powers to grant local radio multiplex licences[1], OFCOM[2] must reserve to the BBC[3] such digital capacity as OFCOM considers appropriate in all the circumstances with a view to enabling every BBC local radio service and every BBC radio service for Wales, Scotland or Northern Ireland to be received in digital form within a coverage area which, so far as reasonably practicable, corresponds with the coverage area for that service as provided otherwise than in digital form[4]. The circumstances to which OFCOM may have regard in performing that duty include the likely demand for digital capacity by persons[5] providing or proposing to provide local digital sound programme services[6].

Where OFCOM proposes to grant a licence to provide a local radio multiplex service, it must notify the BBC of OFCOM's proposals for reserving to the BBC digital capacity on the frequency[7] in respect of which the licence is to be granted in respect of the area or locality in which it is to be granted[8]. If the BBC does not give its consent to the proposals within such period as OFCOM may specify in its notice[9], OFCOM must determine whether any digital capacity is to be reserved to the BBC on the grant of the licence[10], and if so, the amount of that capacity[11]. Before making any such determination, OFCOM must give the BBC an opportunity of making representations to it about its proposals[12].

Where a local radio multiplex licence is granted in respect of a frequency and area or locality in respect of which digital capacity is so reserved, the licence must include such conditions as appear to OFCOM to be appropriate for the purpose of securing that, in consideration of the making by the BBC of such payments as are agreed between the holder of the licence[13] and the BBC or (in default of agreement) determined under the Broadcasting Act 1996[14], the holder of the licence uses such digital capacity as may be requested by the BBC, not exceeding the amount so reserved, for the broadcasting of services provided by the BBC[15].

Where the holder of the licence and the BBC fail to agree the payments to be made under a condition included in the licence[16], or the other terms that are to apply in relation to the use of digital capacity in accordance with such a condition, either of them may refer the matter to OFCOM for determination[17]. Before making such a determination, OFCOM must give the licence holder and the BBC an opportunity of making representations to it about the matter[18]. In making any such determination, OFCOM must have regard to[19]:

(1)   the expenses incurred, or likely to be incurred, by the licence holder in providing the local radio multiplex service in question[20]; and

(2)   the terms on which persons providing local radio multiplex services contract with persons providing television licensable content services[21] or local digital additional services for the broadcasting of those services[22].

Where the BBC has given its consent to such proposals made to it, or OFCOM has made such a determination, OFCOM must publish, in such manner as it considers appropriate, a notice[23] which must:

(a)   state that OFCOM proposes to grant a local radio multiplex licence[24];

(b)   specify the frequency on which the service is to be provided[25];

(c)   specify, in such manner as OFCOM considers appropriate, the area or locality in the United Kingdom[26] in which it is to be available[27];

(d)   state whether in pursuance of a determination by OFCOM[28] any digital capacity on the frequency in that area or locality is to be reserved for the broadcasting in digital form of one or more BBC radio services and, if so, specifying the capacity reserved and the identity of the BBC radio services concerned[29];

(e)   invite applications for the licence and specify the closing date for such applications[30]; and

(f)   specify the fee payable on any application made in pursuance of the notice[31].

When publishing such a notice, OFCOM must also publish general guidance as to requirements to be met by proposals as to certain matters[32], and may also publish such other general guidance as it considers appropriate[33].

Any application made in pursuance of such a notice must be in writing and accompanied by[34]:

(i)   the fee specified in the notice[35];

(ii)   a technical plan relating to the service which the applicant proposes to provide and indicating[36]:

(A)   the parts of the area or locality specified under head (c) above which would be within the coverage area of the service[37];

(B) the timetable in accordance with which that coverage would be achieved[38]; and

(C) the technical means by which it would be achieved[39];

(iii) the applicant's proposals as to the number of digital sound programme services other than BBC services to be broadcast and as to the characteristics of each of those services[40];

(iv) the applicant's proposals as to the timetable in accordance with which the broadcasting of each of those services would begin[41];

(v) the applicant's proposals as to the broadcasting of television licensable content services[42];

(vi) the applicant's proposals as to the broadcasting of digital additional services[43];

(vii) such information as OFCOM may reasonably require as to the applicant's present financial position and his projected financial position during the period for which the licence would be in force[44]; and

(viii) such other information as OFCOM may reasonably require for the purpose of considering the application[45].

At any time after receiving such an application and before determining it, OFCOM may require the applicant to furnish additional information under any of heads (ii) to (vii) above[46]. Any information to be furnished to it must, if it so requires, be in such form or verified in such manner as it may specify[47]. OFCOM must, as soon as reasonably practicable after the date specified in the notice as the closing date for applications, publish in such manner as it considers appropriate the name of every person who has made an application to it in pursuance of the notice[48], the proposals submitted by him under head (iii) above[49], and such other information connected with his application as it considers appropriate[50]. It must also publish a notice inviting representations to be made to it with respect to any of the applications[51], and specifying the manner in which, and the time by which, any such representations are to be so made[52].

1 'Local radio multiplex licence' means a licence to provide a local radio multiplex service: Broadcasting Act 1996 s 72(1). As to the meaning of 'local radio multiplex service' see PARA 727 note 10.

2 As to OFCOM see PARA 507.

3 As to the meaning of 'BBC' see PARA 603 note 1; and as to the BBC see PARAS 603–626.

4 Broadcasting Act 1996 s 49(1) (amended by the Communications Act 2003 s 360(3), Sch 15 para 108(1), (2)).

5 As to the meaning of 'person' see PARA 510 note 1.

6 Broadcasting Act 1996 s 49(2) (amended by the Communications Act 2003 Sch 15 para 108(2)). As to the meaning of 'digital sound programme service' see PARA 754 note 28. A digital sound programme service is a local digital sound programme service if it is provided for broadcasting by means of a local radio multiplex service: Broadcasting Act 1996 ss 60(1)(b), 72(1). As to the meaning of 'broadcast' see PARA 668 note 2; definition applied by s 147(2).

7 As to the meaning of 'frequency' see PARA 681 note 5; definition applied by the Broadcasting Act 1996 s 147(2).

8 Broadcasting Act 1996 s 49(3) (amended by the Communications Act 2003 Sch 15 para 108(2)).

9 Ie under the Broadcasting Act 1996 s 49(3).

10 Broadcasting Act 1996 s 49(4)(a) (amended by the Communications Act 2003 Sch 15 para 108(3)).

11 Broadcasting Act 1996 s 49(4)(b).

12 Broadcasting Act 1996 s 49(5) (amended by the Communications Act 2003 Sch 15 para 108(4)).

13 As to the holder of a licence see PARA 728 note 3.

14 Ie under the Broadcasting Act 1996 s 49(3) (see the text and note 8).

15 Broadcasting Act 1996 s 49(6) (amended by the Communications Act 2003 Sch 15 para 108(2), (5)).

16 Ie in accordance with the Broadcasting Act 1996 s 49(6) (see the text and note 15).

17 Broadcasting Act 1996 s 49(7) (added by the Communications Act 2003 Sch 15 para 108(6)).
18 Broadcasting Act 1996 s 49(8) (added by the Communications Act 2003 Sch 15 para 108(6)).
19 Broadcasting Act 1996 s 49(9) (added by the Communications Act 2003 Sch 15 para 108(6)).
20 Broadcasting Act 1996 s 49(9)(a) (as added: see note 19).
21 As to the meaning of 'television licensable content service' see PARA 716; definition applied by the Broadcasting Act 1996 s 72(1) (definition added by SI 2006/2131).
22 Broadcasting Act 1996 s 49(9)(b) (as added (see note 19); and amended by SI 2006/2131).
23 See the Broadcasting Act 1996 s 50(1) (amended by the Communications Act 2003 Sch 15 para 109(1)–(3)). OFCOM may, before publishing a notice under the Broadcasting Act 1996 s 50(2) (see the text and notes 24–31), determine that two or more local radio multiplex licences are on that occasion to be granted to one person: s 52(1) (amended by the Communications Act 2003 Sch 15 para 111). Where OFCOM has so determined, it must publish a single notice under the Broadcasting Act 1996 s 50(2) in relation to the licences: s 52(2) (amended by the Communications Act 2003 Sch 15 para 111). In relation to any application made in pursuance of such a notice: (1) references in the Broadcasting Act 1996 ss 50(4), 51(2) to the proposed service have effect as references to each of the proposed services; and (2) the reference in s 51(1) to the local radio multiplex licence has effect as a reference to all the licences concerned: s 52(3). Nothing in s 52 applies in relation to the renewal of a local radio multiplex licence: s 52(4).
24 Broadcasting Act 1996 s 50(2)(a) (amended by the Communications Act 2003 Sch 15 para 109(2)).
25 Broadcasting Act 1996 s 50(2)(b).
26 As to areas in the United Kingdom see PARA 727 note 10. As to the meaning of 'United Kingdom' see PARA 510 note 13.
27 Broadcasting Act 1996 s 50(2)(c) (amended by the Communications Act 2003 Sch 15 para 109(2)).
28 Ie a determination under the Broadcasting Act 1996 s 49(4) (see the text and notes 9–11).
29 Broadcasting Act 1996 s 50(2)(d) (amended by the Communications Act 2003 Sch 15 para 109(4)).
30 Broadcasting Act 1996 s 50(2)(e).
31 Broadcasting Act 1996 s 50(2)(f).
32 Broadcasting Act 1996 s 50(3)(a) (s 50(3) amended by the Communications Act 2003 Sch 15 para 109(2)). The matters are those referred to in the Broadcasting Act 1996 s 50(4)(b)(i), (ii) (see the text and notes 37–38).
33 Broadcasting Act 1996 s 50(3)(b).
34 Broadcasting Act 1996 s 50(4).
35 Broadcasting Act 1996 s 50(4)(a).
36 Broadcasting Act 1996 s 50(4)(b).
37 Broadcasting Act 1996 s 50(4)(b)(i).
38 Broadcasting Act 1996 s 50(4)(b)(ii).
39 Broadcasting Act 1996 s 50(4)(b)(iii).
40 Broadcasting Act 1996 s 50(4)(c).
41 Broadcasting Act 1996 s 50(4)(d).
42 Broadcasting Act 1996 s 50(4)(da) (added by SI 2006/2131).
43 Broadcasting Act 1996 s 50(4)(e). As to digital additional services see PARA 779 et seq.
44 Broadcasting Act 1996 s 50(4)(f) (amended by the Communications Act 2003 Sch 15 para 109(2)). As to licences being in force see PARA 865 note 11; applied by the Broadcasting Act 1996 s 147(2).
45 Broadcasting Act 1996 s 50(4)(g) (amended by the Communications Act 2003 Sch 15 para 109(2)).
46 Broadcasting Act 1996 s 50(5) (amended by the Communications Act 2003 Sch 15 para 109(2)).
47 Broadcasting Act 1996 s 50(6) (amended by the Communications Act 2003 Sch 15 para 109(2)).
48 Broadcasting Act 1996 s 50(7)(a)(i).
49 Broadcasting Act 1996 s 50(7)(a)(ii).
50 Broadcasting Act 1996 s 50(7)(a)(iii).
51 Broadcasting Act 1996 s 50(7)(b)(i).
52 Broadcasting Act 1996 s 50(7)(b)(ii).

758. Award of local radio multiplex licences. Where OFCOM[1] has published a notice relating to local radio multiplex licences[2], it must, in determining whether, or to whom, to award the local radio multiplex licence in question, have regard in relation to each applicant to the following matters[3]:

(1)   the extent of the coverage area within the area or locality specified in the notice proposed to be achieved by the applicant as indicated in the technical plan submitted by him[4];

(2)   the timetables proposed by the applicant[5];

(3)   the ability of the applicant to establish the proposed service and to maintain it throughout the period for which the licence will be in force[6];

(4)   the extent to which the digital sound programme services[7] (other than BBC[8] services) proposed to be included in the service would cater for the tastes and interests of persons living in the area or locality for which the service is to be provided and, where it is proposed to cater for any particular tastes and interests of such persons, the extent to which those services would cater for those tastes and interests[9];

(5)   the extent to which any such digital sound programme services would broaden the range of programmes[10] available by way of local digital sound programme services[11] to persons living in the area or locality for which it is to be provided and, in particular, the extent to which they would cater for tastes and interests different from those already catered for by local digital sound programme services provided for that area or locality[12];

(6)   the extent to which there is evidence that, amongst persons living in that area or locality, there is a demand for, or support for, the provision of the proposed service[13]; and

(7)   whether, in contracting or offering to contract with persons[14] providing digital sound programme services, television licensable content services[15] or digital additional services[16], the applicant has acted in a manner calculated to ensure fair and effective competition in the provision of those services[17].

In considering the above matters, OFCOM must take into account any representations made to it[18] with respect to those matters[19].

Where it has awarded a local radio multiplex licence to any person it must, as soon as reasonably practicable after awarding the licence publish in such manner as it considers appropriate the name of the person to whom the licence has been awarded[20], and such other information as it considers appropriate[21]; and it must grant the licence to that person[22].

1   As to OFCOM see PARA 507.
2   Ie under the Broadcasting Act 1996 s 50(2) (see PARA 757): see s 51(1). As to the meaning of 'local radio multiplex licence' see PARA 757 note 1.
3   Broadcasting Act 1996 s 51(1) (amended by the Communications Act 2003 s 360(3), Sch 15 para 110(1), (2)).
4   Broadcasting Act 1996 s 51(2)(a). The technical plan is submitted under s 50(4)(b) (see PARA 757): see s 51(2)(a).
5   Broadcasting Act 1996 s 51(2)(b). Timetables are proposed under s 50(4)(b)(ii), (d) (see PARA 757): see s 51(2)(b).
6   Broadcasting Act 1996 s 51(2)(c). As to licences being in force see PARA 865 note 11; applied by s 147(2).
7   As to the meaning of 'digital sound programme service' see PARA 754 note 28.
8   As to the meaning of 'BBC' see PARA 603 note 1; and as to the BBC see PARAS 603–626.
9   Broadcasting Act 1996 s 51(2)(d).
10   As to the meaning of 'programme' see PARA 667 note 7; definition applied by the Broadcasting Act 1996 s 147(2).
11   As to the meaning of 'local digital sound programme service' see PARA 757 note 6.
12   Broadcasting Act 1996 s 51(2)(e).
13   Broadcasting Act 1996 s 51(2)(f) (substituted by the Communications Act 2003 Sch 15 para 110(3)).

14 As to the meaning of 'person' see PARA 510 note 1.
15 As to the meaning of 'television licensable content service' see PARA 716; definition applied by the Broadcasting Act 1996 s 72(1) (definition added by SI 2006/2131).
16 As to digital additional services see PARA 779 et seq.
17 Broadcasting Act 1996 s 51(2)(g) (amended by SI 2006/2131).
18 Ie under the Broadcasting Act 1996 s 50(7)(b) (see PARA 757).
19 Broadcasting Act 1996 s 51(3) (amended by the Communications Act 2003 Sch 15 para 110(2)).
20 Broadcasting Act 1996 s 51(4)(a)(i).
21 Broadcasting Act 1996 s 51(4)(a)(ii) (amended by the Communications Act 2003 Sch 15 para 110(2)).
22 Broadcasting Act 1996 s 51(4)(b).

759. Restriction on holding of national or local multiplex licence. A person[1] is not to hold more than one national radio multiplex licence[2] at the same time[3]. A person is not to hold any two local radio multiplex licences[4] at the same time where the protected area[5] of one of the licensed services overlaps with the protected area of the other in a way that means that the potential audience[6] for one of them is or includes at least half the potential audience of the other[7].

Where a person is in contravention of the restriction on holding two local multiplex licences in respect of the holding by him of local radio multiplex licences, that contravention is to be disregarded in relation to any time if: (1) he held those licences immediately before the commencement of the relevant provisions[8]; (2) his holding of those licences immediately before such commencement was not in contravention of the previous restriction[9]; and (3) there has not been a relevant change of circumstances[10] between the commencement of these provisions and that time[11].

For these purposes[12], where there is a licence to provide a radio multiplex service, each of the following is to be treated as holding that licence: (a) the actual licence holder; and (b) every person connected with the actual licence holder[13].

The Secretary of State[14] may by order repeal or otherwise modify any of the restrictions imposed by these provisions[15].

1 As to the meaning of 'person' see PARA 510 note 1.
2 As to the meaning of 'national radio multiplex licence' see PARA 727 note 10.
3 Communications Act 2003 s 350(3), Sch 14 para 7.
4 As to the meaning of 'local radio multiplex licence' see PARA 757 note 1.
5 In relation to a local radio multiplex service, 'the protected area' means: (1) subject to head (2), the area or locality specified in a notice published under the Broadcasting Act 1996 s 50(1) (see PARA 757) as that in which that multiplex service is to be available; or (2) if different from that area or locality, the area or locality specified in the relevant licence as that in which that multiplex service is to be available: Communications Act 2003 Sch 14 para 8(6) (added by SI 2003/3299). 'The relevant licence' means the local radio multiplex licence under which the multiplex service concerned is authorised to be provided: Communications Act 2003 Sch 14 para 8(7) (added by SI 2003/3299).
6 'Potential audience', in relation to a local radio multiplex service, means the persons who have attained the age of 15 years and reside within the protected area for that multiplex service: Communications Act 2003 Sch 14 para 8(6) (as added: see note 5).
7 Communications Act 2003 Sch 14 para 8(1) (amended by SI 2003/3299).
8 Ie 29 December 2003: see the Office of Communications Act 2002 (Commencement No 3) and Communications Act 2003 (Commencement No 2) Order 2003, SI 2003/3142.
9 As to the previous restriction see the Broadcasting Act 1990 Sch 2 Pt III para 11(4) (repealed).
10 There is a relevant change of circumstances in the case of the person in contravention if another person becomes the holder of the two pre-commencement licences in relation to which the contravention arises: Communications Act 2003 Sch 14 para 8(4). 'Pre-commencement licence', in relation to a person and a time, means a local radio multiplex licence held by him immediately before the commencement of Sch 14 para 8 and still held by him at that time: Sch 14 para 8(5).

11 Communications Act 2003 Sch 14 para 8(3).
12 Ie for the purposes of the Communications Act 2003 Sch 14 Pt 2 (paras 7–10).
13 Communications Act 2003 Sch 14 para 9.
14 As to the Secretary of State see PARA 507 note 32.
15 Communications Act 2003 Sch 14 para 10. Before making an order under any provision of Sch 14 (other than one that is confined to giving effect to recommendations made by OFCOM in a report of a review of media ownership under s 391 (see PARA 838)), the Secretary of State must consult OFCOM: Sch 14 para 17(1). No order is to be made containing provision authorised by any provision of Sch 14 unless a draft of the order has been laid before Parliament and approved by a resolution of each House: Sch 14 para 17(2). For an order made under these provisions see the Media Ownership (Local Radio and Appointed News Provider) Order 2003, SI 2003/3299. As to OFCOM see PARA 507.

760. Failure to begin providing licensed service and financial penalties on revocation of licence. Where at any time after a radio multiplex licence has been granted to any person[1] but before the licence has come into force[2] that person indicates to OFCOM[3] that he does not intend to provide the service in question[4], or OFCOM for any other reason has reasonable grounds for believing that that person will not provide that service once the licence has come into force[5], it must serve on the person to whom the licence has been granted a notice revoking the licence as from the time the notice is served on him[6].

Where OFCOM revokes a radio multiplex licence[7], it must serve on the licence holder[8] a notice requiring him to pay to it, within a specified period, a specified financial penalty[9].

1 As to the meaning of 'person' see PARA 510 note 1.
2 As to licences being in force see PARA 865 note 11; applied by the Broadcasting Act 1996 s 147(2).
3 As to OFCOM see PARA 507.
4 Broadcasting Act 1996 s 53(1)(a).
5 Broadcasting Act 1996 s 53(1)(b) (amended by the Communications Act 2003 s 360(3), Sch 15 para 112). The Broadcasting Act 1996 s 53(3) (see the text and note 6) does not apply in the case of any person by virtue of s 53(1)(b) unless OFCOM has served on him a notice stating its grounds for believing that he will not provide the service in question once his licence has come into force; and it may not serve such a notice on him unless it has given him a reasonable opportunity of making representations to it about the matters complained of: s 53(2) (amended by the Communications Act 2003 Sch 15 para 112).
6 Broadcasting Act 1996 s 53(3)(a) (amended by the Communications Act 2003 Sch 15 para 112). The Broadcasting Act 1996 s 47 (see PARA 755) or s 51 (see PARA 758) (subject to s 53(4)) has effect as if the person had not made an application for the licence: s 53(3)(b). Section 47 or s 51 does not have effect as mentioned in s 53(3) if OFCOM decides that it would be desirable to publish a fresh notice under s 46(1) (see PARA 754) or s 50(2) (see PARA 757) in respect of the grant of the licence: s 53(4) (amended by the Communications Act 2003 Sch 15 para 112).
7 Ie under the Broadcasting Act 1996 s 53 or under any other provision of Pt II (ss 40–72).
8 As to the holder of the licence see PARA 728 note 3.
9 Broadcasting Act 1996 s 53(5) (amended by the Communications Act 2003 Sch 15 para 112). The penalty must not exceed: (1) in the case of a local radio multiplex licence, £250,000; or (2) in the case of a national radio multiplex licence, whichever is the greater of £250,000 or the prescribed amount: Broadcasting Act 1996 s 53(5)(a), (b) (amended by the Communications Act 2003 s 345, Sch 13 paras 10, 17(1)). As to the meaning of 'local radio multiplex licence' see PARA 757 note 1; and as to the meaning of 'national radio multiplex licence' see PARA 727 note 10.

'The prescribed amount' means: (a) where the licence is revoked under the Broadcasting Act 1996 s 53, or the first complete accounting period of the licence holder falling within the period for which the licence is in force has not yet ended, 7% of the amount which OFCOM estimates would have been the multiplex revenue for that accounting period (as determined in accordance with s 56 (see PARA 763)); and (b) in any other case, 7% of the multiplex revenue for the last complete accounting period of the licence holder so falling (as so determined): s 53(6) (amended by the Communications Act 2003 Sch 15 para 112). As to multiplex revenue see PARA 763. As to accounting periods see PARA 754 note 19.

Any financial penalty payable by any body, in addition to being recoverable from that body as provided by the Broadcasting Act 1996 s 71(4) (repealed) is recoverable by OFCOM as a debt due to it from any person who controls that body: s 53(7) (amended by the Communications Act 2003 Sch 15 para 112). As to the meaning of 'body' see PARA 821 note 10; definition applied by virtue of the Broadcasting Act 1996 s 147(2). As to the meaning of 'control' see PARA 821 note 11; definition applied by s 147(2).

The Secretary of State may by order amend s 53(5)(a), (b)(i): s 69(1), (2)(a) (s 69(2) substituted by the Communications Act 2003 Sch 13 para 22). No order is to be made under the Broadcasting Act 1996 s 69(1) unless a draft of the order has been laid before Parliament and approved by a resolution of each House: s 69(3) (substituted by the Communications Act 2003 Sch 13 para 22). At the date at which this volume states the law no such order had been made. As to the Secretary of State see PARA 507 note 32.

761. Conditions attached to national or local radio multiplex licences. A radio multiplex licence must include such conditions as appear to OFCOM[1] to be appropriate for securing[2]:

(1) that the licensed[3] service is established by the licence holder[4] in accordance with the timetable and other proposals indicated in the technical plan[5];

(2) the implementation of any proposals submitted by the licence holder[6];

(3) that all digital sound programme services[7] broadcast[8] under the licence are provided[9]:

    (a) in the case of a national radio multiplex licence[10], by the holder of a national digital sound programme licence[11]; and

    (b) in the case of a local radio multiplex licence[12], by the BBC[13] or the holder of a local digital sound programme licence[14];

(4) that all television licensable content services[15] broadcast under the licence are provided by the holder of a licence[16] to provide such a service or by an EEA broadcaster[17];

(5) that all digital additional services[18] broadcast under the licence are provided by the holder of a licence[19];

(6) that in the terms on which the holder of the licence contracts, or offers to contract, for the broadcasting of digital sound programme services, television licensable content services or digital additional services, he does not show undue discrimination either against or in favour of a particular person[20] providing such a service or a class of such persons[21];

(7) that the holder of the licence does not, in any agreement with a person providing a digital sound programme service, television licensable content service or digital additional services which entitles that person to use a specified amount of digital capacity on the frequency[22] or frequencies to which the licence relates, restrict that person's freedom to make arrangements with some other person as to the use of any of that digital capacity, except to the extent that the restriction is reasonably required for the purpose of ensuring the technical quality of the broadcasts or for the purpose of securing compliance with any other condition of the licence[23];

(8) that the signals carrying the radio multiplex service[24] attain high standards in terms of technical quality and reliability throughout so much of the area or locality for which the service is provided as is for the time being reasonably practicable[25]; and

(9) that, while the licence is in force[26], at least the required percentage[27] of

the digital capacity on the frequency or frequencies on which the service is broadcast is used, or left available to be used, for the broadcasting of specified[28] services[29].

Where the licence holder applies to OFCOM for the variation of any condition imposed in pursuance of head (2) above and relating to the characteristics of any of the digital sound programme services to be broadcast under the licence, OFCOM must vary the condition accordingly, subject to the following[30]. OFCOM is not to vary a national radio multiplex licence if it appears to OFCOM that, if the application were granted, the capacity of the digital sound programme services broadcast under the licence to appeal to a variety of tastes and interests would be unacceptably diminished[31]. OFCOM is to vary a local radio multiplex licence only if it is satisfied: (a) that the variation would not unacceptably narrow the range of programmes available by way of local digital sound programme services to persons living in the area or locality for which the licensed multiplex service is provided; (b) that the variation would be conducive to the maintenance or promotion of fair and effective competition in that area or locality; or (c) that there is evidence that, amongst persons living in that area or locality, there is a significant demand for, or significant support for, the change that would result from the variation[32].

1 As to OFCOM see PARA 507.
2 Broadcasting Act 1996 s 54(1) (amended by the Communications Act 2003 s 360(3), Sch 15 para 113).
3 As to the meaning of 'licensed' see PARA 727 note 2.
4 As to the holder of the licence see PARA 728 note 3.
5 Broadcasting Act 1996 s 54(1)(a). The technical plan is submitted under s 46(4)(b) (see PARA 754) or s 50(4)(b) (see PARA 757): see s 54(1)(a).
6 Broadcasting Act 1996 s 54(1)(b). Proposals are submitted under s 46(4)(c)–(f) (see PARA 754) or s 50(4)(c)–(e) (see PARA 757): see s 54(1)(b). Any conditions imposed in pursuance of s 54(1)(a) or (b) may be varied by OFCOM with the consent of the licence holder; and s 42(3)(b) (see PARA 727) accordingly does not apply to any such variation: s 54(5) (amended by the Communications Act 2003 Sch 15 para 113).
7 As to the meaning of 'digital sound programme service' see PARA 754 note 28.
8 As to the meaning of 'broadcast' see PARA 668 note 2; definition applied by the Broadcasting Act 1996 s 147(2).
9 Broadcasting Act 1996 s 54(1)(c).
10 As to the meaning of 'national radio multiplex licence' see PARA 727 note 10.
11 Broadcasting Act 1996 s 54(1)(c)(i). Such a licence is held under s 60 (see PARA 768): see s 54(1)(c)(i). 'National digital sound programme licence' means a licence to provide a national digital sound programme service: s 72(1). As to the meaning of 'national digital sound programme service' see PARA 756 note 16.
12 As to the meaning of 'local radio multiplex licence' see PARA 757 note 1.
13 As to the meaning of 'BBC' see PARA 603 note 1; and as to the BBC see PARAS 603–626.
14 Broadcasting Act 1996 s 54(1)(c)(ii). Such a licence is held under s 60 (see PARA 768): see s 54(1)(c)(ii). 'Local digital sound programme licence' means a licence to provide a local digital sound programme service: s 72(1). As to the meaning of 'local digital sound programme service' see PARA 757 note 6.
15 As to the meaning of 'television licensable content service' see PARA 716; definition applied by the Broadcasting Act 1996 s 72(1) (definition added by SI 2006/2131).
16 Ie under the Broadcasting Act 1990 Pt I (ss 3–71): see PARA 716 et seq. As to the holder of a licence see PARA 728 note 3.
17 Broadcasting Act 1996 s 54(1)(ca) (added by SI 2006/2131). An 'EEA broadcaster' is one within the meaning given by the Broadcasting Act 1996 s 12(3A) (see PARA 692 note 15): s 51(4)(ca) (as so added).
18 As to digital additional services see PARA 779 et seq.
19 Broadcasting Act 1996 s 54(1)(d). Such a licence is held under s 64 (see PARA 780): see s 54(1)(d).
20 As to the meaning of 'person' see PARA 510 note 1.
21 Broadcasting Act 1996 s 54(1)(e) (amended by SI 2006/2131).

22 As to the meaning of 'frequency' see PARA 681 note 5; definition applied by the Broadcasting Act 1996 s 147(2).

23 Broadcasting Act 1996 s 54(1)(f) (amended by SI 2006/2131).

24 As to the meaning of 'radio multiplex service' see PARA 727 note 10.

25 Broadcasting Act 1996 s 54(1)(g).

26 As to licences being in force see PARA 865 note 11; applied by the Broadcasting Act 1996 s 147(2).

27 The reference to the required percentage is a reference to such percentage equal to or more than 70% as OFCOM considers appropriate and specifies in the condition: Broadcasting Act 1996 s 54(2A) (added by the Communications Act 2003 s 259(1), (5); and amended by SI 2006/2130).

The Secretary of State may, after consulting OFCOM, by order amend the Broadcasting Act 1996 s 54(2A): s 54(3) (amended by the Communications Act 2003 s 259(6), Sch 15 para 113). No such order may be made unless a draft of the order has been laid before and approved by a resolution of each House of Parliament: Broadcasting Act 1996 s 54(4). As to orders under this provision see the Broadcasting (Percentage of Digital Capacity for Radio Multiplex Licence) Order 1998, S1 1998/1326; and the Radio Multiplex Services (Required Percentage of Digital Capacity) Order 2006, SI 2006/2130. As to the Secretary of State see PARA 507 note 32.

28 Ie specified in the Broadcasting Act 1996 s 54(1A). Those services are: (1) digital sound programme services; (2) simulcast radio services; (3) programme-related services; and (4) relevant technical services: s 54(1A) (added by the Communications Act 2003 s 259(3)). As to the meaning of 'simulcast radio service' see PARA 754 note 12. 'Programme-related service' means any digital additional service consisting in the provision of services (apart from advertising) which: (a) are ancillary to the programmes included in one or more digital sound programme services, simulcast radio services or local or national services (within the meaning of the Communications Act 2003 s 245 (see PARA 723)) and are directly related to the contents of those programmes; or (b) relate to the promotion or listing of such programmes: Broadcasting Act 1996 s 54(2)(a) (amended by the Communications Act 2003 s 259(4)). 'Relevant technical service' means any technical service which relates to one or more digital sound programme services: Broadcasting Act 1996 s 54(2)(b). As to the meaning of 'technical service' see PARA 779 note 11.

29 Broadcasting Act 1996 s 54(1)(h) (substituted by the Communications Act 2003 s 259(2)).

30 Broadcasting Act 1996 s 54(6) (substituted by the Communications Act 2003 s 315).

31 Broadcasting Act 1996 s 54(6A) (added by the Communications Act 2003 s 315).

32 Broadcasting Act 1996 s 54(6B) (added by the Communications Act 2003 s 315).

762. Variation of national or local radio multiplex licences. OFCOM[1] may, if the specified requirements[2] are met, vary a national radio multiplex licence[3] by extending the area in which the licensed service is required to be available[4]. OFCOM may, if the specified requirements[5] are met, vary a local radio multiplex licence[6] by: (1) varying the frequency on which the licensed service is required to be provided; (2) reducing the area or locality in which the licensed service is required to be available; or (3) extending that area or locality to include an adjoining area or locality[7].

The following are the requirements for variation. OFCOM must have received an application for the variation from the licence holder[8]. The application must include a technical plan relating to the service proposed to be provided under the licence indicating, in particular: (a) the area or locality which would be within the coverage area of the service; (b) the timetable in accordance with which that coverage would be achieved; and (c) the technical means by which it would be achieved[9]. Before deciding whether to grant the application, OFCOM must publish a notice specifying: (o) the proposed variation of the licence; and (ii) a period in which representations may be made to OFCOM about the proposal[10].

In the case of a local radio multiplex licence, OFCOM may vary the licence in accordance with the application only if it is satisfied that doing so would not unacceptably narrow the range of programmes available by way of local digital sound programme services[11] to persons living in the area or locality for which, before the proposed variation, the local radio multiplex service is required to be available[12].

1   As to OFCOM see PARA 507.
2   Ie the requirements of the Broadcasting Act 1996 s 54A(3)–(5): see the text and notes 8–10.
3   As to the meaning of 'national radio multiplex licence' see PARA 727 note 10.
4   Broadcasting Act 1996 s 54A(1) (s 54A added by the Digital Economy Act 2010 s 35).
5   Ie the requirements of the Broadcasting Act 1996 s 54A(3)–(6): see the text and notes 8–12.
6   As to the meaning of 'local radio multiplex licence' see PARA 757 note 1.
7   Broadcasting Act 1996 s 54A(2) (as added: see note 4).
8   Broadcasting Act 1996 s 54A(3) (as added: see note 4). As to the holder of the licence see PARA 728 note 3.
9   Broadcasting Act 1996 s 54A(4) (as added: see note 4).
10 Broadcasting Act 1996 s 54A(5) (as added: see note 4).
11 As to the meaning of 'local digital sound programme service' see PARA 757 note 6.
12 Broadcasting Act 1996 s 54A(6) (as added: see note 4).

763.   Multiplex revenue. The multiplex revenue for each accounting period[1] of the person[2] who is the multiplex provider[3] in relation to a national radio multiplex service consists of[4]:

(1)   all payments received or to be received by him or any person connected[5] with him from a person other than a programme provider[6] or an additional services provider[7]:

(a)   in consideration of the inclusion in that period, in any digital sound programme service or digital additional service broadcast by means of the national radio multiplex service[8], of advertisements or other programmes[9]; or

(b)   in respect of charges made in that period for the reception of programmes included in any such digital sound programme service or digital additional service[10];

(2)   all payments received or to be received by him or any person connected with him in respect of the broadcasting of any simulcast radio service[11] by means of the national radio multiplex service[12];

(3)   all payments received or to be received by any programme provider or any person connected with him from a person other than the multiplex provider, an additional service provider or another programme provider[13]:

(a)   in consideration of the inclusion in that period, in any digital sound programme service provided by him for broadcasting by means of the national radio multiplex service, of advertisements or other programmes[14]; or

(b)   in respect of charges made in that period for the reception of programmes included in any such digital sound programme service[15]; and

(4)   all payments received or to be received by any additional services provider or any person connected with him from a person other than the multiplex provider, a programme provider or another additional services provider[16]:

(a)   in consideration of the inclusion in that period, in any digital additional service provided by him for broadcasting by means of the national radio multiplex service, of advertisements or other programmes[17]; or

> (b)   in respect of charges made in that period for the reception of programmes included in any such digital additional service[18].

If, in connection with the inclusion of any advertisements or other programmes whose inclusion is paid for by payments falling within head (1)(a) above, any payments are made to the multiplex provider or any person connected with him to meet any payments payable by the multiplex provider[19], those payments are to be regarded as made in consideration of the inclusion of the programmes in question[20].

In the case of an advertisement included as mentioned in heads (1)(a), (3)(a) or (4)(a) above under arrangements made between the multiplex provider, a programme provider or an additional services provider or any person connected with any of them, and a person acting as an advertising agent[21], the amount of any receipt by the multiplex provider, programme provider or additional services provider or any connected person that represents a payment by the advertiser from which the advertising agent has deducted any amount by way of commission is the amount of the payment by the advertiser after the deduction of the commission[22]. However, if the amount deducted by way of commission exceeds 15 per cent of the payment by the advertiser, the amount of the receipt in question is taken to be the amount of the payment less 15 per cent[23].

If, in any accounting period of the multiplex provider, a programme provider or an additional services provider or a person connected with any of them derives, in relation to any programme to be included in the relevant service[24], any financial benefit (whether direct or indirect) from payments made by any person other than the multiplex provider, by way of sponsorship, for the purpose of defraying or contributing towards costs incurred or to be incurred in connection with that programme, the relevant payments[25] are to be taken to include the amount of the financial benefit so derived by the multiplex provider or the connected person, as the case may be[26].

Where, in any accounting period of the multiplex provider[27]:

(i)   the multiplex provider provides a digital sound programme service or digital additional service for broadcasting by means of the multiplex service[28];

(ii)   the multiplex provider is engaged in any activity which, if engaged in by another person, would result in payments falling within head (1)(a) above being made to the licence holder[29];

(iii)   a programme provider is engaged in any activity which, if engaged in by another person, would result in payments falling within head (1)(c) above being made to the programme provider[30]; or

(iv)   an additional services provider is engaged in any activity which, if engaged in by another person, would result in payments falling within head (1)(d) above being made to the additional services provider[31],

OFCOM[32] may, if it considers that the amount which would otherwise be the multiplex revenue for that accounting period is less than it would have been if the digital sound programme service or digital additional service had been provided, or the activity engaged in, by another person at arm's length, treat the multiplex revenue as increased by the amount of the difference[33].

Where, in any accounting period of the multiplex provider, the multiplex provider or a programme provider or additional services provider receives payments falling within head (1)(a), (b), (c) or (d) above from a person connected with him and it appears to OFCOM that the amount which would otherwise be the multiplex revenue for that accounting period is less than it would have been if the arrangements between him and the connected person were such as might be expected between parties at arm's length, OFCOM may treat the multiplex revenue as increased by the amount of the difference[34].

1   As to accounting periods see PARA 754 note 19.
2   As to the meaning of 'person' see PARA 510 note 1.
3   'Multiplex provider': (1) in relation to a national radio multiplex service for which a person holds a licence under the Broadcasting Act 1996 Pt II (ss 40–72), means the licence holder; and (2) in relation to a national radio multiplex service which is not licensed under Pt II, means the person who provides that service: s 56(9) (definition added by the Communications Act 2003 s 360(3), Sch 15 para 115(1), (4)(c)). As to the meaning of 'national radio multiplex service' see PARA 727 note 10. As to the holder of the licence see PARA 728 note 3.
4   Broadcasting Act 1996 s 56(1) (amended by the Communications Act 2003 s 360(3), Sch 15 para 115(2)(b)). The Broadcasting Act 1996 s 56 applies for the purposes of Pt II: see s 56(1) (amended by the Communications Act 2003 Sch 15 para 115(2)(a)).
5   As to the meaning of 'connected' see PARA 674 note 13; definition applied by the Broadcasting Act 1996 s 147(2).
6   'Programme provider', in relation to a national radio multiplex service, means any person who provides a digital sound programme service for broadcasting by means of that radio multiplex service: Broadcasting Act 1996 s 56(9) (amended by the Communications Act 2003 Sch 15 para 115(4)). As to the meaning of 'digital sound programme service' see PARA 754 note 28. The Broadcasting Act 1996 ss 56, 57 have effect as if references in s 56 to digital sound programme services included references to television licensable content services: s 56(10) (added by SI 2006/2131). As to the meaning of 'television licensable content service' see PARA 716; definition applied by the Broadcasting Act 1996 s 72(1) (definition added by SI 2006/2131). As to the meaning of 'broadcast' see PARA 668 note 2; definition applied by the Broadcasting Act 1996 s 147(2). As to the meaning of 'radio multiplex service' see PARA 727 note 10.
7   Broadcasting Act 1996 s 56(1)(a). 'Additional services provider', in relation to a national radio multiplex service, means any person who provides any digital additional service for broadcasting by means of that radio multiplex service: s 56(9) (as amended: see note 3). As to digital additional services see PARA 779 et seq.
8   As to the meaning of 'national radio multiplex service' see PARA 727 note 10.
9   Broadcasting Act 1996 s 56(1)(a)(i) (amended by the Communications Act 2003 s 406(7), Sch 15 para 115(2)(c), Sch 19). As to the meaning of 'programme' see PARA 667 note 7; definition applied by the Broadcasting Act 1996 s 147(2).
10 Broadcasting Act 1996 s 56(1)(a)(ii).
11 As to the meaning of 'simulcast radio service' see PARA 754 note 12.
12 Broadcasting Act 1996 s 56(1)(b).
13 Broadcasting Act 1996 s 56(1)(c) (amended by the Communications Act 2003 Sch 15 para 115(2)(d)).
14 Broadcasting Act 1996 s 56(1)(c)(i).
15 Broadcasting Act 1996 s 56(1)(c)(ii).
16 Broadcasting Act 1996 s 56(1)(d) (amended by the Communications Act 2003 Sch 15 para 115(2)(d)).
17 Broadcasting Act 1996 s 56(1)(d)(i).
18 Broadcasting Act 1996 s 56(1)(d)(ii).
19 Ie by virtue of the Broadcasting Act 1996 s 55(1) (see PARA 754).
20 Broadcasting Act 1996 s 56(2) (amended by the Communications Act 2003 Sch 15 para 115(3)(a)).
21 As to the meaning of 'advertising agent' see PARA 674 note 16; definition applied by the Broadcasting Act 1996 s 147(2).
22 Broadcasting Act 1996 s 56(3) (amended by the Communications Act 2003 Sch 15 para 115(3)(a)).
23 Broadcasting Act 1996 s 56(4).
24 'The relevant service' means: (1) in relation to a programme provider or a person connected with him, any digital sound programme service provided as mentioned in the Broadcasting Act 1996 s 56(1)(c)(i) (see the text and note 14); and (2) in relation to an additional services provider or a person connected with him, any digital additional service provided as mentioned in s 56(1)(d)(i) (see the text and note 17): s 56(6)(a).

25 'Relevant payments' means: (1) in relation to a programme provider, the payments referred to in the Broadcasting Act 1996 s 56(1)(c) (see the text and notes 13–15); and (2) in relation to an additional services provider, the payments referred to in s 56(1)(d) (see the text and notes 16–18): s 56(6)(b).

26 Broadcasting Act 1996 s 56(5).

27 Broadcasting Act 1996 s 56(7) (amended by the Communications Act 2003 Sch 15 para 115(3)(a)).

28 Broadcasting Act 1996 s 56(7)(a) (amended by the Communications Act 2003 Sch 15 para 115(3)(a)).

29 Broadcasting Act 1996 s 56(7)(b) (amended by the Communications Act 2003 Sch 15 para 115(3)(a)).

30 Broadcasting Act 1996 s 56(7)(c).

31 Broadcasting Act 1996 s 56(7)(d).

32 As to OFCOM see PARA 507.

33 Broadcasting Act 1996 s 56(7) (amended by the Communications Act 2003 Sch 15 para 115(3)(b)). See note 34.

34 Broadcasting Act 1996 s 56(8) (amended by the Communications Act 2003 Sch 15 para 115(3)). In a case falling within the Broadcasting Act 1996 s 56(7) (see the text and notes 27–33) or s 57(8), OFCOM may treat the share of multiplex revenue attributable to any person for the accounting period of the multiplex provider as increased by such amount as it considers appropriate to take account of the circumstances mentioned in s 56(7) or s 56(8): s 57(3) (amended by the Communications Act 2003 Sch 15 para 116(4)).

764. Computation of multiplex revenue. It is the duty of OFCOM[1] to draw up, and from time to time review, a statement setting out the principles to be followed in ascertaining[2]:

(1) the multiplex revenue[3] in relation to a licence holder[4] for any accounting period[5]; and

(2) the share of multiplex revenue attributable to a person[6] in relation to any national radio multiplex service[7] for any accounting period of the holder of the national radio multiplex licence[8], or for any year[9].

Such a statement may set out different principles for persons holding different kinds of licences[10]. Before drawing up or revising the statement, OFCOM must consult the Secretary of State[11] and the Treasury[12]. OFCOM must publish the statement and every revision of the statement[13]; and it must transmit a copy of the statement, and every revision of it, to the Secretary of State[14]. The Secretary of State must lay copies of the statement and of every such revision before each House of Parliament[15].

In relation to digital terrestrial sound broadcasting[16], the amount of the multiplex revenue in relation to any holder of a national radio multiplex licence for any accounting period of his, or, as the case may be, for any year[17], or the amount of any payment to be made to OFCOM by any person in respect of any such revenue, or of an instalment of any such payment[18], in the event of a disagreement between OFCOM and that person, is the amount determined by OFCOM[19]. In addition, the share of multiplex revenue attributable to any person in relation to any national radio multiplex service for any accounting period or, as the case may be, for any year, in the event of a disagreement between OFCOM and that person, is the amount determined by OFCOM[20]. No such determination of OFCOM may be called in question in any court of law, or be the subject of any arbitration; but this does not prevent the bringing of proceedings for judicial review[21].

1 As to OFCOM see PARA 507.

2 Broadcasting Act 1996 s 70, Sch 1 Pt II para 3(1) (amended by the Communications Act 2003 s 360(3), Sch 15 para 142(1), (3)).

3 As to multiplex revenue see also PARA 763.

4 Ie for the purposes of the Broadcasting Act 1996 s 56 (see PARA 763): see Sch 1 Pt II para 3(1)(a). As to the meaning of 'licence' see PARA 727 note 2. As to the holder of the licence see PARA 728 note 3.

5 Broadcasting Act 1996 Sch 1 Pt II para 3(1)(a). As to accounting periods see PARA 754 note 19.

6 As to the meaning of 'person' see PARA 510 note 1.

7 Broadcasting Act 1996 Sch 1 Pt II para 3(1)(b). This applies for the purposes of Pt II (ss 40–72): see Sch 1 Pt II para 3(1)(b). As to the meaning of 'national radio multiplex service' see PARA 727 note 10.

8 Broadcasting Act 1996 Sch 1 Pt II para 3(1)(b)(i). As to the meaning of 'national radio multiplex licence' see PARA 727 note 10.

9 Broadcasting Act 1996 Sch 1 Pt II para 3(1)(b)(ii).

10 Broadcasting Act 1996 Sch 1 Pt II para 3(2).

11 As to the Secretary of State see PARA 507 note 32.

12 Broadcasting Act 1996 Sch 1 Pt II para 3(3) (amended by the Communications Act 2003 Sch 15 para 142(3)). As to the Treasury see CONSTITUTIONAL LAW AND HUMAN RIGHTS vol 8(2) (Reissue) PARAS 512–517.

13 Broadcasting Act 1996 Sch 1 Pt II para 3(4)(a) (amended by the Communications Act 2003 Sch 15 para 142(3)).

14 Broadcasting Act 1996 Sch 1 Pt II para 3(4)(b).

15 Broadcasting Act 1996 Sch 1 Pt II para 3(4).

16 Ie for the purposes of the Broadcasting Act 1996 Pt II.

17 Broadcasting Act 1996 Sch 1 Pt II para 4(1)(a).

18 Broadcasting Act 1996 Sch 1 Pt II para 4(1)(b) (amended by the Communications Act 2003 Sch 15 para 142(3)).

19 Broadcasting Act 1996 Sch 1 Pt II para 4(1) (amended by the Communications Act 2003 Sch 15 para 142(3)).

20 Broadcasting Act 1996 Sch 1 Pt II para 4(2) (amended by the Communications Act 2003 Sch 15 para 142(3)).

21 Broadcasting Act 1996 Sch 1 Pt II para 4(3) (amended by the Communications Act 2003 Sch 15 para 142(3)). As to judicial review see JUDICIAL REVIEW vol 61 (2010) PARA 601 et seq.

765. Duration and renewal of national or local radio multiplex licences. A radio multiplex licence continues in force for a period of 12 years[1]. A radio multiplex licence which is granted within ten years of 1 October 1996[2] may be renewed on one occasion, in the case of a licence granted within six years of that date, for a period of 12 years beginning with the date on which it would otherwise expire, and, in any other case, for a period of eight years beginning with the date on which it would otherwise expire[3]. Such an application for the renewal of a radio multiplex licence may be made by the licence holder[4] not earlier than four years before the date on which it would otherwise cease to be in force and not later than the day falling three months before the relevant date[5]. At any time before determining the application, OFCOM may[6]:

(1) require the applicant to furnish a technical plan which supplements that already submitted by the licence holder[7] and, in the case of a national radio multiplex licence[8], proposals which supplement those already submitted by the licence holder[9]; and

(2) notify the applicant of requirements which must be met by that supplementary technical plan or those supplementary proposals and relate to certain specified matters[10].

Where any such application is made, OFCOM may postpone consideration of the application for as long as it thinks appropriate[15].

Where an application for the renewal of a radio multiplex licence has been duly made to OFCOM, it may refuse the application only if[16]:

(a) it appears to it that the applicant has failed to comply with any of the conditions included in his licence[17];

(b) any supplementary technical plan or supplementary proposals submitted fail to meet the requirements notified to the applicant[18]; or

(c)   it is not satisfied that the applicant would, if his licence were renewed, provide a service which complied with the conditions to be included in the licence as renewed[19].

Where OFCOM has granted a person's application, it must formally renew his licence from the date on which it would otherwise expire, but in the case of a national radio multiplex licence it may not so renew his licence unless it has notified him of any percentage specified by it[20] and he has, within such period as is specified in that notification, notified OFCOM that he consents to the licence being renewed on those terms[21]. Where a radio multiplex licence has been renewed, the licence as renewed must include such further conditions as appear to OFCOM to be appropriate for securing the implementation of any supplementary technical plan and supplementary proposals submitted[22].

1   Broadcasting Act 1996 s 58(1). This is expressed to be subject to the provisions of Pt II (ss 40–72) and the Broadcasting Act 1990 s 111 (see PARA 747) (as applied by the Broadcasting Act 1996 s 59(8) (see PARA 766)): see s 58(1). As to licences being in force see PARA 865 note 11; applied by s 147(2).
      The Secretary of State may by regulations: (1) amend s 58; and (2) make further provision about the renewal of radio multiplex licences: s 58A(1) (s 58A added by the Digital Economy Act 2010 s 36(1)). The regulations may, in particular, make provision about: (a) the circumstances in which OFCOM may renew a radio multiplex licence; (b) the period for which a licence may be renewed; (c) the information that OFCOM may require an applicant for renewal of a licence to provide; (d) the requirements that must be met by such an applicant; (e) the grounds on which OFCOM may refuse an application for renewal of a licence; (f) payments to be made in respect of a licence following its renewal; and (g) further conditions to be included in a licence following its renewal: Broadcasting Act 1996 s 58A(2) (as so added). The regulations may, in particular, amend or modify Pt II: s 58A(3) (as so added). A statutory instrument containing the regulations may not be made unless a draft of the instrument has been laid before, and approved by a resolution of, each House of Parliament: s 58A(4) (as so added). The power to make regulations under s 58A may not be exercised after 31 December 2015 (but this does not affect the continuation in force of any regulations made under s 58A before that date): s 58A(5) (as so added). As to the Secretary of State see PARA 507 note 32. At the date at which this volume states the law, no regulations had been made under s 58A.
2   Ie the date on which the Broadcasting Act 1996 s 58 came into force: see s 58(2); and the Broadcasting Act 1996 (Commencement No 1 and Transitional Provisions) Order 1996, SI 1996/2120, art 4, Sch 1.
3   Broadcasting Act 1996 s 58(2) (amended by the Communications Act 2003 s 261).
4   As to the holder of the licence see PARA 728 note 3.
5   Broadcasting Act 1996 s 58(3) (amended by the Communications Act 2003 s 360(3), Sch 15 para 117(1), (3)). 'The relevant date', in relation to a radio multiplex licence, means the date which OFCOM determines to be that by which it would need to publish a notice under the Broadcasting Act 1996 s 46(1) (see PARA 754) or s 50(2) (see PARA 757) if it were to grant, as from the date on which that licence would expire if not renewed, a fresh licence to provide the service formerly provided under that licence: s 58(12) (amended by the Communications Act 2003 Sch 15 para 117(2)). A determination for this purpose must be made at least one year before the date determined, and must be notified by OFCOM to the person who holds the licence in question: Broadcasting Act 1996 s 58(12A) (added by the Communications Act 2003 Sch 15 para 117(5)). As to OFCOM see PARA 507.
6   Broadcasting Act 1996 s 58(4) (amended by the Communications Act 2003 Sch 15 para 117(2)).
7   Broadcasting Act 1996 s 58(4)(a)(i). The plan is submitted under s 46(4)(b) (see PARA 754) or s 50(4)(b) (see PARA 757).
8   As to the meaning of 'national radio multiplex licence' see PARA 727 note 10.
9   Broadcasting Act 1996 s 58(4)(a)(ii). The proposals are submitted under s 46(4)(f) (see PARA 754).
10 Broadcasting Act 1996 s 58(4)(b). The matters referred to are those in s 46(4)(b)(i), (ii) (see PARA 754) or s 50(4)(b)(i), (ii) (see PARA 757).
15 Broadcasting Act 1996 s 58(6) (amended by the Communications Act 2003 s 406(7), Sch 15 para 117(2), Sch 19). OFCOM must have regard to the Broadcasting Act 1996 s 58(10) (see the text and note 21): see s 58(6).
16 Broadcasting Act 1996 s 58(7) (amended by the Communications Act 2003 Sch 15 para 117(2)).

17 Broadcasting Act 1996 s 58(7)(a).
18 Broadcasting Act 1996 s 58(7)(b).
19 Broadcasting Act 1996 s 58(7)(c).
20 Subject to the Broadcasting Act 1996 s 58(9), on the grant of any such application OFCOM
    may with the consent of the Secretary of State, and must if so required by him:
    (1)   specify a percentage different from that specified under s 46(1)(h) (see PARA 754) as the
           percentage of multiplex revenue for each accounting period of his that will be payable
           by the applicant in pursuance of s 55(1) (see PARA 754) during the period for which the
           licence is to be renewed; or
    (2)   specify such a percentage where none was specified under s 46(1)(h) (see PARA 754),
    and OFCOM may specify under head (1) or head (2) either of the things mentioned in s 46(2)(b)
    (see PARA 754): s 58(8) (amended by the Communications Act 2003 Sch 15 para 117(2)). As to
    multiplex revenue see PARA 763. As to accounting periods see PARA 754 note 19. Where an order
    under the Broadcasting Act 1996 s 55(2) (see PARA 754) is in force on the relevant date, no
    percentage of multiplex revenue is payable as mentioned in head (1) during the period for which
    the licence is to be renewed: s 58(9).
21 Broadcasting Act 1996 s 58(10) (amended by the Communications Act 2003 Sch 15
    para 117(2)).
22 Broadcasting Act 1996 s 58(11) (amended by the Communications Act 2003 Sch 15
    para 117(2)). Nothing in the Broadcasting Act 1996 s 58 prevents the holder of a radio
    multiplex licence from applying for a new licence on one or more occasions in pursuance of a
    notice under s 46(1) (see PARA 754) or s 50(2) (see PARA 757): s 58(13).

766. Enforcement of national or local radio multiplex licences. If OFCOM[1] is
satisfied that the holder of a radio multiplex licence[2] has failed to comply with
any condition of the licence or with any direction given by OFCOM[3], it may
serve on him[4]:

(1)   a notice requiring him to pay, within a specified period, a specified
       financial penalty to OFCOM[5]; or

(2)   a notice reducing the period for which the licence is to be in force[6] by a
       specified period not exceeding two years[7].

OFCOM may not serve on any person any such notice unless it has given him
a reasonable opportunity of making representations to it about the matters
complained of[8]. Where a licence is due to expire on a particular date by virtue of
a notice served on any person under head (2) above, OFCOM may, on the
application of that person, revoke that notice by a further notice served on him
at any time before that date, if it is satisfied that, since the date of the earlier
notice, his conduct in relation to the operation of the licensed[9] service has been
such as to justify the revocation of that notice[10]. Where OFCOM serves such a
notice on a BBC company[11], it must send a copy of the notice to the Secretary of
State[12].

1 As to OFCOM see PARA 507.
2 As to the holder of the licence see PARA 728 note 3.
3 Ie under or by virtue of any provision of the Broadcasting Act 1996 Pt II (ss 40–72).
4 Broadcasting Act 1996 s 59(1) (amended by the Communications Act 2003 s 360(3), Sch 15
   para 118). The Broadcasting Act 1990 s 111 (power to revoke licences granted under Pt III Ch II
   (ss 98–111B): see PARA 747) has effect in relation to a radio multiplex licence as it has effect in
   relation to a licence under Pt III Ch II: Broadcasting Act 1996 s 59(8). In its application in
   relation to a radio multiplex licence, the Broadcasting Act 1990 s 111 has effect with the
   substitution in s 111(1)(a) for the reference to Pt III of a reference to the Broadcasting Act 1996
   Pt II, and with the omission of the Broadcasting Act 1990 s 111(4) and the reference to s 111(4)
   in s 111(6): Broadcasting Act 1996 s 59(9).
5 Broadcasting Act 1996 s 59(1)(a) (amended by the Communications Act 2003 Sch 15 para 118).
   The amount of any financial penalty imposed on the holder of a national radio multiplex licence
   may not exceed the maximum penalty given by the Broadcasting Act 1996 s 59(2A): s 59(2)
   (amended by the Communications Act 2003 s 345, Sch 13 paras 10, 19(1)). The maximum
   penalty is whichever is the greater of: (1) £250,000; and (2) 5% of the aggregate amount of the
   share of multiplex revenue attributable to him for his last complete accounting period falling

within a period for which his licence has been in force ('the relevant period'): Broadcasting Act 1996 s 59(2A) (s 59(2A)–(2C) added by the Communications Act 2003 Sch 13 para 19(2)). In relation to a person whose first complete accounting period falling within the relevant period has not ended when the penalty is imposed, the Broadcasting Act 1996 s 59(2A)(b) (see head (2)) is to be construed as referring to 5% of the amount which OFCOM estimates to be the share of multiplex revenue attributable to him for that accounting period: s 59(2B) (as so added). The provisions of s 57(1), (3) apply for determining or estimating the share of multiplex revenue attributable to a person for the purposes of s 59(2A) or s 59(2B): s 59(2C) (as so added).

For the purposes of s 59(2A) and s 59(2B), the share of multiplex revenue attributable to the person who is the multiplex provider in relation to a national radio multiplex service in respect of any accounting period of his is: (a) the aggregate of payments falling within s 56(1)(a), (b) (see PARA 763) and payments received or to be received by him from programme providers and additional services providers in respect of the provision of radio multiplex services in that period; less (b) the amount of any payments made or to be made to programme providers or additional service providers which would fall within s 56(1)(c) or (d) but for the fact that they are received from the multiplex provider: s 57(1) (amended by the Communications Act 2003 Sch 13 para 18(1), Sch 15 para 116(1), (2)). As to the meaning of 'multiplex provider' see PARA 763 note 3; definition applied by the Broadcasting Act 1996 s 57(4). As to the meaning of 'programme provider' see PARA 763 note 6; definition applied by s 57(4). As to the meaning of 'additional services provider' see PARA 763 note 7; definition applied by s 57(4). As to the meaning of 'radio multiplex service' see PARA 727 note 10.

The amount of any financial penalty imposed in pursuance of s 59(1)(a) on the holder of a local radio multiplex licence may not exceed £250,000: s 59(4) (amended by the Communications Act 2003 Sch 13 para 19(3)). As to the meaning of 'local radio multiplex licence' see PARA 757 note 1.

The Secretary of State may by order amend the Broadcasting Act 1996 s 59(2A)(a) and s 59(4): see s 69(1), (2)(b) (s 69(2) substituted by the Communications Act 2003 Sch 13 para 22). No order is to be made under the Broadcasting Act 1996 s 69(1) unless a draft of the order has been laid before Parliament and approved by a resolution of each House: s 69(3) (substituted by the Communications Act 2003 Sch 13 para 22). At the date at which this volume states the law no such order had been made. As to the Secretary of State see PARA 507 note 32.

6 As to licences being in force see PARA 865 note 11; applied by the Broadcasting Act 1996 s 147(2).
7 Broadcasting Act 1996 s 59(1)(b).
8 Broadcasting Act 1996 s 59(5) (amended by the Communications Act 2003 Sch 15 para 118).
9 As to the meaning of 'licensed' see PARA 727 note 2.
10 Broadcasting Act 1996 s 59(6) (amended by the Communications Act 2003 Sch 15 para 118).
11 As to the meaning of 'BBC company' see PARA 671 note 20; definition applied by the Broadcasting Act 1996 s 147(2). As to the meaning of 'BBC' see PARA 603 note 1; and as to the BBC see PARAS 603–626.
12 Broadcasting Act 1996 s 59(7) (amended by the Communications Act 2003 Sch 15 para 118).

(v) Review of Digital Radio Broadcasting

767. Review by Secretary of State. For the purpose of considering for how long it would be appropriate for sound broadcasting services[1] to continue to be provided in analogue form, the Secretary of State[2]:

(1) must keep under review the extent of:

    (a) the provision in the United Kingdom[3] of radio multiplex services[4];

    (b) the availability in the United Kingdom of digital sound programme services[5] and the availability there in digital form of national services[6] and the sound broadcasting services of the BBC[7]; and

    (c) the ownership or possession in the United Kingdom of equipment capable of receiving the services referred to in head (b) above when broadcast[8] or transmitted in digital form[9],

and the likely future extent of such provision, such availability and such ownership or possession[10]; and

(2)	must, on or before the fourth anniversary of the day on which the first national radio multiplex licence is granted[11] and at such time or times after that as he thinks fit, require OFCOM[12] and the BBC to report to him on the matters referred to in head (1) above[13].

If OFCOM or the BBC is required to submit such a report, it must submit the report within 12 months of the date of the requirement[14]. Before making any such report, OFCOM must consult:

(i)	the holders of all radio multiplex licences[15];

(ii)	the holders of digital sound programme licences[16] who are providing digital sound programme services which are being broadcast[17]; and

(iii)	such other persons providing services licensed[18] by OFCOM[19] as it thinks fit[20],

and it must include in its report a summary of representations made to it by the persons consulted[21].

1   As to the meaning of 'sound broadcasting service' see PARA 723 note 4; definition applied by the Broadcasting Act 1996 s 67(5).
2   Broadcasting Act 1996 s 67(1). As to the Secretary of State see PARA 507 note 32.
3   As to the meaning of 'United Kingdom' see PARA 510 note 13.
4   Broadcasting Act 1996 s 67(1)(a)(i). As to the meaning of 'radio multiplex service' see PARA 727 note 10.
5   As to the meaning of 'digital sound programme service' see PARA 754 note 28.
6   As to the meaning of 'national service' see PARA 723 note 4; definition applied by the Broadcasting Act 1996 s 147(2).
7   Broadcasting Act 1996 s 67(1)(a)(ii). As to the meaning of 'BBC' see PARA 603 note 1; and as to the BBC see PARAS 603–626.
8   As to the meaning of 'broadcast' see PARA 668 note 2; definition applied by the Broadcasting Act 1996 s 147(2).
9   Broadcasting Act 1996 s 67(1)(a)(iii).
10 Broadcasting Act 1996 s 67(1)(a).
11 Ie under the Broadcasting Act 1996 s 47 (see PARA 755). As to the meaning of 'national radio multiplex licence' see PARA 727 note 10.
12 As to OFCOM see PARA 507.
13 Broadcasting Act 1996 s 67(1)(b) (amended by the Communications Act 2003 s 360(3), Sch 15 para 125). For the purpose mentioned in the Broadcasting Act 1996 s 67(1), the Secretary of State must, on requiring reports under s 67(1)(b), consult: (1) such persons appearing to him to represent listeners as he thinks fit, and (2) such other persons as he thinks fit, in connection with the matters referred to in s 67(1)(a) (see the text and note 10), and also, if the Secretary of State thinks fit, as to the likely effects on listeners of any sound broadcasting service ceasing to be broadcast in analogue form: s 67(4).
14 Broadcasting Act 1996 s 67(2) (amended by the Communications Act 2003 Sch 15 para 125).
15 Broadcasting Act 1996 s 67(3)(a). As to the holder of the licence see PARA 728 note 3.
16 'Digital sound programme licence' means a licence to provide digital sound programme services: Broadcasting Act 1996 s 72(1). As to the meaning of 'digital sound programme service' see PARA 754 note 28.
17 Broadcasting Act 1996 s 67(3)(b).
18 As to the meaning of 'licensed' see PARA 727 note 2.
19 Ie under the Broadcasting Act 1996 Pt II (ss 40–72) or the Broadcasting Act 1990 Pt III (ss 85–126).
20 Broadcasting Act 1996 s 67(3)(c) (amended by the Communications Act 2003 Sch 15 para 125).
21 Broadcasting Act 1996 s 67(3) (amended by the Communications Act 2003 Sch 15 para 125).

(vi) Sound Programme Services

768. Licensing of digital sound programme services. A licence to provide digital sound programme services[1] (a 'digital sound programme licence') may be either a licence to provide national digital sound programme services[2] (a 'national digital sound programme licence')[3] or a licence to provide local digital sound programme services[4] (a 'local digital sound programme licence')[5].

An application for a digital sound programme licence must be made in such manner as OFCOM[6] may determine[7]; and must be accompanied by such fee (if any) as it may determine[8]. At any time after receiving such an application and before determining it, OFCOM may require the applicant to furnish such additional information as it may consider necessary for the purpose of considering the application[9]. Any information to be furnished to OFCOM must, if it so requires, be in such form or verified in such manner as it may specify[10].

Where an application for a digital sound programme licence is made to OFCOM, it must grant the licence unless precluded from doing so[11].

1　As to the meaning of 'digital sound programme service' see PARA 754 note 28.
2　As to the meaning of 'national digital sound programme service' see PARA 756 note 16.
3　Broadcasting Act 1996 ss 60(2)(a), 72(1).
4　As to the meaning of 'local digital sound programme service' see PARA 757 note 6.
5　Broadcasting Act 1996 ss 60(2)(b), 72(1).
6　As to OFCOM see PARA 507.
7　Broadcasting Act 1996 s 60(3)(a) (amended by the Communications Act 2003 s 360(3), Sch 15 para 119(1), (2)).
8　Broadcasting Act 1996 s 60(3)(b).
9　Broadcasting Act 1996 s 60(4) (amended by the Communications Act 2003 Sch 15 para 119(2)).
10　Broadcasting Act 1996 s 60(5) (amended by the Communications Act 2003 Sch 15 para 119(2)).
11　Broadcasting Act 1996 s 60(6) (amended by the Communications Act 2003 Sch 15 para 119(2)).
　　OFCOM may be precluded from granting a licence by the Broadcasting Act 1996 s 42(2)(a) (see PARA 727) or s 44(1) (see PARA 837): see s 60(6) (as so amended).
　　The Broadcasting Act 1990 s 89 (disqualification from being licence holder or concerned with the provision of a programme service if convicted of a transmitting offence: see PARA 829) applies in relation to a licence under the Broadcasting Act 1996 s 60 as it applies to a licence under the Broadcasting Act 1990 Pt III (ss 85–126), but with the omission of s 89(3)(b) and of the word 'or' immediately before that provision: Broadcasting Act 1996 s 60(6A) (added by the Communications Act 2003 Sch 15 para 119(3)).

769. Restriction on local digital sound programme services. The Secretary of State[1] may by order impose requirements, on persons holding local digital sound programme licences[2], prohibiting the provision[3] by the same person, in the circumstances described in the order, of more than the number of local digital sound programme services that is determined in the manner set out in the order[4]. The circumstances by reference to which a person may be prohibited from providing a local digital sound programme service, and the factors that may be used for determining the number of such services that he may provide, include, in particular:

(1)　whether and to what extent the coverage areas[5] of different local digital sound programme services provided by that person would overlap[6];

(2)　the capacity used by those services on the relevant multiplexes;

(3)　the sizes of the potential audiences for those services and the times when those services would be made available;

(4)　whether and to what extent members of the potential audiences for those services would also be members of the potential audiences for local digital sound programme services provided by other persons;

(5)　in a case in which members of the potential audiences for the services provided by that person would also be members of the potential audiences for local digital sound programme services provided by other persons, the number of those other persons, the coverage areas of their services, the capacity used by their services on the relevant multiplexes, the sizes of the potential audiences for their services, and the times when their services are or will be made available[7].

An order under these provisions may make provision for treating:

(a)　persons who are connected with a person who holds a licence;

(b)　persons who are associates of a person who holds a licence or of a person who is connected with a person who holds a licence; and

(c)　persons who (whether alone or together with such persons as may be described in the order) participate in a body which holds a licence or is treated as doing so by virtue of head (a) or head (b) above,

as if each of them were also a holder of the licence for the purposes of a requirement imposed under these provisions[8].

Such an order may make provision for treating:

(i)　persons who are connected with a person who provides[9] a local digital sound programme service;

(ii)　persons who are associates of a person who provides such a service or of a person who is connected with a person who provides such a service; and

(iii)　persons who (whether alone or together with such persons as may be described in the order) participate in a body who provides such a service or is treated as doing so by virtue of head (i) or head (ii) above,

as if each of them were also a person providing the service for the purposes of a requirement imposed under these provisions[10].

Such an order may also make provision for treating:

(A)　persons who are connected with each other;

(B)　persons who are associates of each other; and

(C)　persons who (whether alone or together with such persons as may be described in the order) participate in a body,

as if they and such other persons who are connected with, associates of or participators in any of them as may be described in the order were the same person for the purposes of a requirement imposed under these provisions[11].

Power to make provision with respect to any matter described above by any order includes power to make provision with respect to that matter by reference to the making or giving by OFCOM, in accordance with the order, of any determination, approval or consent, and power to confer such other discretions on OFCOM as the Secretary of State thinks fit[12].

1　As to the Secretary of State see PARA 507 note 32.

2　As to the meaning of 'local digital sound programme licence' see PARA 761 note 14; definition applied by the Communications Act 2003 s 362(1).

3　A person who holds a licence to provide local digital sound programme services provides such a service if, and only if: (1) the service is one provided by him and is included in a local radio multiplex service for which he holds a local radio multiplex licence; or (2) under a contract between that person and a person who holds a licence to provide a local radio multiplex service, the person holding the licence to provide the radio multiplex service is required to include that local digital sound programme service in that multiplex service: Communications Act 2003 s 350(3), Sch 14 para 12(5). As to the meaning of 'local digital sound programme service' see PARA 757 note 6; definition applied by s 362(1).

4　Communications Act 2003 Sch 14 para 12(1). For transitional provisions see Sch 14 para 14. Before making an order under any provision of Sch 14 (other than one that is confined to giving effect to recommendations made by OFCOM in a report of a review of media ownership under s 391 (see PARA 838)), the Secretary of State must consult OFCOM: Sch 14 para 17(1). No order is to be made containing provision authorised by any provision of Sch 14 unless a draft of the order has been laid before Parliament and approved by a resolution of each House: Sch 14 para 17(2). For an order made under these provisions see the Media Ownership (Local Radio and Appointed News Provider) Order 2003, SI 2003/3299. As to OFCOM see PARA 507.

5   For the purposes of the Communications Act 2003 Sch 14 para 12, the coverage area for a
     service provided under a local digital sound programme licence is the area in the United
     Kingdom within which the relevant multiplex is capable of being received at a level satisfying
     such technical standards as may have been laid down by OFCOM for the purposes of the
     provisions of an order under Sch 14 para 12: Sch 14 para 12(3). 'The relevant multiplex', in
     relation to a service provided under a local digital sound programme licence, means the local
     radio multiplex service in which the service provided under that licence is or is to be included:
     Sch 14 para 12(4). As to the meaning of 'local radio multiplex service' see PARA 727 note 10;
     definition applied by s 362(1). As to the meaning of 'United Kingdom' see PARA 510 note 13.
6   As to references to an area overlapping another see PARA 739 note 6.
7   Communications Act 2003 Sch 14 para 12(2).
8   Communications Act 2003 Sch 14 para 13(1).
9   The Communications Act 2003 Sch 14 para 12(5) (see note 3) applies for the purposes of Sch 14
     para 13 as it applies for the purposes of Sch 14 para 12: Sch 14 para 13(6).
10   Communications Act 2003 Sch 14 para 13(2).
11   Communications Act 2003 Sch 14 para 13(3).
12   Communications Act 2003 Sch 14 para 13(5).

770.   Duration and conditions of digital sound programme licence. A digital
sound programme licence[1] continues in force[2] until it is surrendered by its
holder[3]. A digital sound programme licence must include such conditions as
appear to OFCOM[4] to be appropriate for requiring the holder of the licence[5]:

(1)   on entering into any agreement with the provider of a radio multiplex
       service[6], of a television multiplex service[7] or of a general multiplex
       service[8] for the provision of a digital sound programme service[9] to be
       broadcast[10] by means of the multiplex service, to notify OFCOM[11]:
       (a)   of the identity of the multiplex service[12];
       (b)   of the characteristics of the digital sound programme service to
              which the agreement relates[13]; and
       (c)   of the period during which it will be provided[14];

(2)   when any such agreement is varied so far as it relates to any of the
       matters mentioned in head (1)(a), (b) or (c) above, to notify OFCOM of
       the variation so far as relating to those matters[15]; and

(3)   where he is providing a digital sound programme service to the provider
       of a radio multiplex service, of a television multiplex service or of a
       general multiplex service in accordance with such an agreement as is
       mentioned in head (1) above but intends to cease doing so, to notify
       OFCOM of that fact[16].

1   As to the meaning of 'digital sound programme licence' see PARA 767 note 16. See also PARA
     768.
2   As to licences being in force see PARA 865 note 11; applied by the Broadcasting Act 1996
     s 147(2).
3   Broadcasting Act 1996 s 61(1). This is expressed to be subject to the provisions of Pt II
     (ss 40–72) and the Broadcasting Act 1990 s 111 (see PARA 747) as applied by the Broadcasting
     Act 1996 s 62(10) (see PARA 771). As to the holder of the licence see PARA 728 note 3.
4   As to OFCOM see PARA 507.
5   Broadcasting Act 1996 s 61(2) (amended by the Communications Act 2003 s 360(3), Sch 15
     para 120(1), (2)(a)).
6   As to the meaning of 'radio multiplex service' see PARA 727 note 10.
7   As to the meaning of 'television multiplex service' see PARA 697; definition applied by the
     Broadcasting Act 1996 s 72(1) (amended by the Communications Act 2003 s 260(4)(b)).
8   As to the meaning of 'general multiplex service' see PARA 898 note 10; definition applied by the
     Broadcasting Act 1996 s 72(1) (amended by the Communications Act 2003 s 260(4)(a)).
9   As to the meaning of 'digital sound programme service' see PARA 754 note 28.
10   As to the meaning of 'broadcast' see PARA 668 note 2; definition applied by the Broadcasting
     Act 1996 s 147(2).

11 Broadcasting Act 1996 s 61(2)(a) (amended by the Communications Act 2003 Sch 15 para 120(2)(a)–(c)).
12 Broadcasting Act 1996 s 61(2)(a)(i) (amended by the Communications Act 2003 Sch 15 para 120(2)(d)).
13 Broadcasting Act 1996 s 61(2)(a)(ii).
14 Broadcasting Act 1996 s 61(2)(a)(iii).
15 Broadcasting Act 1996 s 61(2)(b) (amended by the Communications Act 2003 Sch 15 para 120(2)(a)).
16 Broadcasting Act 1996 s 61(2)(c) (amended by the Communications Act 2003 Sch 15 para 120(2)(a), (b)).

771. Enforcement of digital sound programme licences. If OFCOM[1] is satisfied that the holder of a digital sound programme licence[2] has failed to comply with any condition of the licence or with any direction given by OFCOM[3], it may serve on him[4]:

(1) a notice requiring him to pay, within a specified period, a specified financial penalty to OFCOM[5];

(2) a notice providing that the licence is to expire on a specified date, which must be at least one year from the date of service of the notice[6]; and

(3) a notice suspending the licence for a specified period not exceeding six months[7].

OFCOM may not serve on any person[8] any such notice unless it has given him a reasonable opportunity of making representations to it about the matters complained of[9]. Where a licence is due to expire on a particular date by virtue of a notice served on any person under head (2) above, OFCOM may, on the application of that person, revoke that notice by a further notice served on him at any time before that date, if it is satisfied that, since the date of the earlier notice, his conduct in relation to the operation of the licensed[10] service has been such as to justify the revocation of that notice[11].

Where OFCOM serves such a notice on a BBC company[12], it must send a copy of the notice to the Secretary of State[13].

1 As to OFCOM see PARA 507.
2 As to the meaning of 'digital sound programme licence' see PARA 767 note 16. As to the holder of the licence see PARA 728 note 3. Subject to the Broadcasting Act 1996 s 62(11), (12), the Broadcasting Act 1990 s 109 (power to require scripts etc or broadcasting of correction or statement of findings or not to repeat programme: see PARA 745) and s 111 (power to revoke licences: see PARA 747) apply in relation to a digital sound programme licence as they apply in relation to a licence under Pt III Ch II (ss 98–111B): Broadcasting Act 1996 s 62(10) (amended by the Communications Act 2003 s 360(3), Sch 15 para 121(1), (6)). In its application in relation to a digital sound programme licence, the Broadcasting Act 1990 s 109(1) has effect with the substitution for the reference to a direction under Pt III (ss 83–126) of a reference to a direction under the Broadcasting Act 1996 Pt II (ss 40–72): s 62(11). In its application in relation to a digital sound programme licence, the Broadcasting Act 1990 s 111 has effect with the substitution for the reference in s 111(1)(a) to Pt III of a reference to the Broadcasting Act 1996 Pt II, and with the omission of the Broadcasting Act 1990 s 111(4) and of the reference to s 111(4) in s 111(6): Broadcasting Act 1996 s 62(12).
3 Ie under or by virtue of any provision of the Broadcasting Act 1996 Pt II.
4 Broadcasting Act 1996 s 62(1) (amended by the Communications Act 2003 Sch 15 para 121(2)).
5 Broadcasting Act 1996 s 62(1)(a) (amended by the Communications Act 2003 Sch 15 para 121(2)). The amount of any financial penalty imposed in pursuance of the Broadcasting Act 1996 s 62(1)(a) on the holder of a national digital sound programme licence must not exceed the maximum penalty given by s 62(2A): s 62(2) (amended by the Communications Act 2003 s 345, Sch 13 paras 10, 20(1)). The maximum penalty is whichever is the greater of: (1) £250,000; and (2) 5% of the aggregate amount of the shares of multiplex revenue attributable to him in relation to relevant multiplex services in respect of relevant accounting periods: Broadcasting Act 1996 s 62(2A) (added by the Communications Act 2003 Sch 13 para 20(2)). 'Relevant accounting period', in relation to a relevant multiplex service, means the

last accounting period of the multiplex provider: Broadcasting Act 1996 s 62(4) (amended by the Communications Act 2003 Sch 13 para 20(3), Sch 15 para 121(3)). For these purposes, a service is a relevant multiplex service if it is: (a) a national radio multiplex service; (b) a television multiplex service; or (c) a general multiplex service: Broadcasting Act 1996 s 62(5B) (second) (added by the Communications Act 2003 Sch 15 para 121(5)). Note that the Communications Act 2003 Sch 13 also amends the Broadcasting Act 1996 s 62 so that there are two subsections numbered s 62(5B). As to the meaning of 'national radio multiplex service' see PARA 727 note 10. As to the meaning of 'television multiplex service' see PARA 697; definition applied by s 72(1) (amended by the Communications Act 2003 s 260(4)(b)). As to the meaning of 'general multiplex service' see PARA 898 note 10. As to licences being in force see PARA 865 note 11; applied by the Broadcasting Act 1996 s 147(2). As to multiplex revenue see PARA 763. As to accounting periods see PARA 754 note 19. 'Multiplex provider', in relation to a national radio multiplex service, means the multiplex provider within the meaning of s 56 (see PARA 763); and in relation to a television multiplex service or a general multiplex service, means the multiplex provider within the meaning of s 14 (see PARA 693): s 62(5C) (added by the Communications Act 2003 Sch 15 para 121(5)).

A determination or estimate for the purposes of the Broadcasting Act 1996 s 62(2A) or s 62(5) of the share of multiplex revenue attributable to a person in relation to national radio multiplex services is to be in accordance with s 57(2), (3): s 62(5A) (added by the Communications Act 2003 Sch 13 para 20(5)). A determination or estimate for the purposes of the Broadcasting Act 1996 s 62(2A) or s 62(5) in relation to television multiplex services or general multiplex services is to be in accordance with s 15(2), (3) (see PARA 713): s 62(5B) (first) (added by the Communications Act 2003 Sch 13 para 20(5)).

For the purposes of the Broadcasting Act 1996 s 62(2A)–(5), the share of multiplex revenue attributable to a programme provider or additional services provider in relation to a national radio multiplex service in respect of any accounting period of the multiplex provider is: (i) the aggregate of payments falling within s 56(1)(c) or (d) (see PARA 763), and payments received or to be received from the multiplex provider which would fall within one of those provisions but for the fact that they are received from the multiplex provider; less (ii) the amount of any payments made or to be made to the multiplex provider in respect of the provision of radio multiplex services in that period: s 57(2) (amended by the Communications Act 2003 Sch 13 para 18(2), Sch 15 para 116(1), (3)). As to the meaning of 'programme provider' see PARA 763 note 6; definition applied by the Broadcasting Act 1996 s 57(4). As to the meaning of 'radio multiplex service' see PARA 727 note 10.

Where, in the case of any relevant multiplex service, the first accounting period of the multiplex provider throughout which the holder of the digital sound programme licence provides a digital sound programme service for broadcasting by means of that relevant multiplex service ('the first period') has not ended when the penalty is imposed, then for the purposes of the Broadcasting Act 1996 s 62, the share of multiplex revenue attributable to the holder of the digital sound programme licence in relation to that relevant multiplex service for the relevant accounting period must be taken to be the amount which OFCOM estimates to be the share of multiplex revenue attributable to him for the first period: s 62(5) (amended by the Communications Act 2003 Sch 13 para 20(4), Sch 15 para 121(2), (4)). As to the meaning of 'digital sound programme service' see PARA 754 note 28. As to the meaning of 'broadcast' see PARA 668 note 2; definition applied by the Broadcasting Act 1996 s 147(2).

The amount of any financial penalty imposed in pursuance of s 62(1)(a) on the holder of a local digital sound programme licence must not exceed £250,000: s 62(6) (amended by the Communications Act 2003 Sch 13 para 20(6)). As to the meaning of 'local digital sound programme licence' see PARA 761 note 14.

The Secretary of State may by order amend the Broadcasting Act 1996 s 62(2A)(a), (6) by substituting a different sum for the sum for the time being specified there: s 69(1), (2)(c) (s 69(2) substituted by the Communications Act 2003 Sch 13 para 22). No order is to be made under the Broadcasting Act 1996 s 69(1) unless a draft of the order has been laid before Parliament and approved by a resolution of each House: s 69(3) (substituted by the Communications Act 2003 Sch 13 para 22). At the date at which this volume states the law no such order had been made. As to the Secretary of State see PARA 507 note 32.

6　Broadcasting Act 1996 s 62(1)(b).

7　Broadcasting Act 1996 s 62(1)(c). Any exercise by OFCOM of its powers under s 62(1) in respect of any failure to comply with any condition of a digital sound programme licence does not preclude any exercise by it of its powers under the Broadcasting Act 1990 s 109 (see PARA 745) in respect of that failure: Broadcasting Act 1996 s 62(13) (amended by the Communications Act 2003 Sch 15 para 121(2)).

8　As to the meaning of 'person' see PARA 510 note 1.

9 Broadcasting Act 1996 s 62(7) (amended by the Communications Act 2003 Sch 15 para 121(2)).
10 As to the meaning of 'licensed' see PARA 727 note 2.
11 Broadcasting Act 1996 s 62(8) (amended by the Communications Act 2003 Sch 15 para 121(2)).
12 As to the meaning of 'BBC company' see PARA 671 note 20; definition applied by the Broadcasting Act 1996 s 147(2).
13 Broadcasting Act 1996 s 62(9) (amended by the Communications Act 2003 Sch 15 para 121(2)).

(vii) Additional Services in relation to Sound Broadcasting

A. ADDITIONAL SERVICES PROVIDED ON SOUND BROADCASTING FREQUENCIES

772. Additional services. 'Additional service' means any service which consists in the sending of electronic signals[1] for transmission by wireless telegraphy[2] by means of the use of the spare capacity[3] within the signals carrying any sound broadcasting service[4] provided on a relevant frequency[5].

1 As to the meaning of 'electronic signal' see TELECOMMUNICATIONS vol 97 (2010) PARA 22; definition applied by the Broadcasting Act 1990 s 114(6) (substituted by the Communications Act 2003 s 360(3), Sch 15 para 52(1), (6)).
2 As to the meaning of 'wireless telegraphy' see PARA 510 note 1; definition applied by the Broadcasting Act 1990 s 202(1) (amended by the Wireless Telegraphy Act 2006 s 123, Sch 7 paras 9, 13).
3 For the purposes of the Broadcasting Act 1990 Pt III (ss 83–126), the spare capacity within the signals carrying any such broadcasting service is to be taken to be any part of the signals which: (1) is not required for the purposes of the sound broadcasting service for the purposes of which the frequency has been made available; and (2) is determined by OFCOM to be available for the provision of additional services: s 114(2) (amended by the Communications Act 2003 Sch 15 para 52(3)). References in the Broadcasting Act 1990 Pt III (ss 85–126) to spare capacity are to be construed accordingly: s 114(2). As to the meaning of 'frequency' see PARA 681 note 5. As to OFCOM see PARA 507.
    OFCOM, when determining under s 114(2) the extent and nature of the spare capacity available for the provision of additional services in the case of any frequency on which a national service is provided, must have regard to any need of the person providing that service to be able to use part of the signals carrying it for providing services which are ancillary to programmes included in the service: s 114(3) (amended by the Communications Act 2003 Sch 15 para 52(5)). As to the meaning of 'national service' see PARA 723 note 4. As to the meaning of 'person' see PARA 510 note 1.
    At any time while an additional services licence is in force, OFCOM may, if it considers it appropriate to do so, modify or further modify the determination made for the purposes of that licence under the Broadcasting Act 1990 s 114(2)(b) (see head (2)); and where there has been such a modification or further modification, the licence is to have effect accordingly: s 114(2A) (added by the Communications Act 2003 Sch 15 para 52(4)). A modification or further modification under the Broadcasting Act 1990 s 114(2A) must not reduce the amount of spare capacity made available for the licensed services: s 114(2B) (added by the Communications Act 2003 Sch 15 para 52(4)).
    A person holding a national licence is to be taken for the purposes of the Broadcasting Act 1990 Pt III to be authorised by his licence to provide any such services as are mentioned in s 114(3): s 114(4).
4 As to the meaning of 'sound broadcasting service' see PARA 723 note 4.
5 Broadcasting Act 1990 s 114(1) (amended by the Communications Act 2003 Sch 15 para 52(2)). 'Relevant frequency' means a frequency made available by OFCOM for the purposes of a sound broadcasting service: Broadcasting Act 1990 s 114(7) (added by the Communications Act 2003 Sch 15 para 52(6)).

773. Licensing of additional services. OFCOM[1] must do all it can to secure that, in the case of each relevant frequency[2], all of the spare capacity[3] available for the provision of additional services[4] on that frequency is used for the provision of such services under additional services licences[5] granted by OFCOM in accordance with these provisions[6].

An additional services licence may relate to the use of spare capacity within more than one frequency, and two or more additional services licences may relate to the use of spare capacity within the same frequency where it is to be used at different times, or in different areas, in the case of each of those licences[7]. An additional services licence may include provisions enabling the licence holder[8], subject to and in accordance with such conditions as OFCOM may impose, to authorise any person who is not a disqualified person[9] to provide any additional service on the spare capacity allocated by the licence[10].

Any conditions included in an additional services licence apply in relation to the provision of additional services by a person authorised as mentioned above as they apply in relation to the provision of such services by the licence holder; and any failure by such a person to comply with any such conditions is to be treated for the purposes of the provisions relating to independent radio services[11] as a failure on the part of the licence holder to comply with those conditions[12].

Every licence to provide a national service must include such conditions as appear to OFCOM to be appropriate for securing that the licence holder grants:

(1)   to any person who holds a licence to provide additional services on the frequency on which that national service is provided[13]; and

(2)   to any person who is authorised by any such person as mentioned above to provide additional services on that frequency[14],

access to facilities reasonably required by that person for the purposes of, or in connection with, the provision of any such additional services[15].

Any person who grants to any other person access to facilities in accordance with conditions so imposed may require that other person to pay a reasonable charge; and any dispute as to the amount of any such charge is to be determined by OFCOM[16].

The holder of a licence to provide a local[17] or restricted[18] service or to provide a radio licensable content service[19] is taken for the purposes of the provisions relating to independent radio services to be authorised by his licence to provide, or to authorise another person to provide, additional services on the frequency on which the licensed service is provided[20].

1   As to OFCOM see PARA 507.
2   As to the meaning of 'relevant frequency' see PARA 772 note 5; definition applied by the Broadcasting Act 1990 s 114(7) (added by the Communications Act 2003 s 360(3), Sch 15 para 52(6)).
3   As to the meaning of 'spare capacity' see PARA 772 note 3.
4   As to the meaning of 'additional services' see PARA 772.
5   In the Broadcasting Act 1990 Pt III (ss 85–126), 'additional services licence' means a licence to provide additional services: Broadcasting Act 1990 ss 115(9), 126(1). As to the meaning of 'licence' see PARA 724 note 2.
6   Broadcasting Act 1990 s 115(1) (amended by the Communications Act 2003 Sch 15 para 53(1)–(3)).
7   Broadcasting Act 1990 s 115(2). As to the meaning of 'licence' see PARA 724 note 2.
8   As to the holder of the licence see PARA 725 note 16.
9   The Broadcasting Act 1990 s 115(3) applies to any person who is not a disqualified person in relation to an additional services licence by virtue of s 88, Sch 2 Pt II (see PARAS 830–836) and who would not be in contravention of the requirements imposed by or under the Communications Act 2003 Sch 14 (see PARAS 820, 831, 739, 759, 769) if he held such a licence: Broadcasting Act 1990 s 115(4) (amended by the Communications Act 2003 Sch 15 para 53(4)). As to the meaning of 'person' see PARA 510 note 1.
10   Broadcasting Act 1990 s 115(3) (amended by the Communications Act 2003 Sch 15 para 53(2)).
11   Ie the Broadcasting Act 1990 Pt III (ss 85–126).
12   Broadcasting Act 1990 s 115(5).
13   Broadcasting Act 1990 s 115(6)(a).
14   Broadcasting Act 1990 s 115(6)(b).

15 Broadcasting Act 1990 s 115(6) (amended by the Communications Act 2003 Sch 15 para 53(2)).
16 Broadcasting Act 1990 s 115(7) (amended by the Communications Act 2003 Sch 15 para 53(2)).
17 As to the meaning of 'local service' see PARA 723 note 4; definition applied by the Broadcasting Act 1990 s 126(1) (amended by the Communications Act 2003 Sch 15 para 59(b)).
18 As to the meaning of 'restricted service' see PARA 723 note 4; definition applied by the Broadcasting Act 1990 s 126(1) (as amended: see note 17).
19 As to the meaning of 'radio licensable content service' see PARA 723 note 1; definition applied by the Broadcasting Act 1990 s 126(1) (as amended: see note 17).
20 Broadcasting Act 1990 s 115(8) (amended by the Communications Act 2003 Sch 15 para 53(5)).

774.   Applications for additional services licences. Where OFCOM[1] proposes to grant a licence[2] to provide additional services[3] it must publish, in such manner as it considers appropriate, a notice[4]:

(1)   stating that it proposes to grant such a licence[5];
(2)   specifying:
    (a)   the period for which the licence is to be granted[6];
    (b)   the sound broadcasting service[7] or services on whose frequency[8] or frequencies the services are to be provided[9]; and
    (c)   the extent and nature of the spare capacity[10] which is to be allocated by the licence[11];
(3)   inviting applications for the licence and specifying the closing date for such applications[12]; and
(4)   specifying:
    (a)   the fee payable on any application made in pursuance of the notice[13]; and
    (b)   the percentage of qualifying revenue for each accounting period[14] that would be payable by an applicant[15] if he were granted the licence[16].

Any application made in pursuance of such a notice must be in writing and accompanied by[17]:

(i)   the fee specified in the notice under head (4)(a) above[18];
(ii)   a technical plan indicating the nature of any additional services which the applicant proposes to provide[19], and so far as known to the applicant, the nature of any additional services which any other person proposes to provide[20];
(iii) the applicant's cash bid[21] in respect of the licence[22]; and
(iv)   such information as OFCOM may reasonably require as to the applicant's present financial position and his projected financial position during the period for which the licence would be in force[23].

At any time after receiving such an application and before determining it, OFCOM may require the applicant to furnish additional information under head (ii) or head (iv) above[24]. Any information to be furnished to OFCOM must, if it so requires, be in such form or verified in such manner as it may specify[25]. OFCOM must, as soon as reasonably practicable after the date specified in the notice as the closing date for applications, publish in such manner as it considers appropriate[26]:

(A)   the name of every person who has made an application to it in pursuance of the notice[27];
(B)   particulars of the technical plan submitted by him under head (ii) above[28]; and
(C)   such other information connected with his application as OFCOM considers appropriate[29].

1   As to OFCOM see PARA 507.

2   As to the meaning of 'licence' see PARA 724 note 2.
3   As to the meaning of 'additional service' see PARA 772.
4   Broadcasting Act 1990 s 116(1) (amended by the Communications Act 2003 s 360(3), Sch 15 para 54(1), (2)).
5   Broadcasting Act 1990 s 116(1)(a).
6   Broadcasting Act 1990 s 116(1)(b)(i).
7   As to the meaning of 'sound broadcasting service' see PARA 723 note 4.
8   As to the meaning of 'frequency' see PARA 681 note 5.
9   Broadcasting Act 1990 s 116(1)(b)(ii).
10   As to the meaning of 'spare capacity' see PARA 772 note 3.
11   Broadcasting Act 1990 s 116(1)(b)(iii) (amended by the Communications Act 2003 s 406(7), Sch 15 para 54(3), Sch 19).
12   Broadcasting Act 1990 s 116(1)(c).
13   Broadcasting Act 1990 s 116(1)(d)(i).
14   As to accounting periods see PARA 776 note 8.
15   Ie in pursuance of the Broadcasting Act 1990 s 118(1)(c) (see PARA 776).
16   Broadcasting Act 1990 s 116(1)(d)(ii). OFCOM may, if it thinks fit, specify under this provision: (1) different percentages in relation to different accounting periods falling within the period for which the licence would be in force; or (2) a nil percentage in relation to any accounting period so falling: s 116(2) (amended by the Communications Act 2003 Sch 15 para 54(2)). As to licences being in force see PARA 865 note 11.
17   Broadcasting Act 1990 s 116(3).
18   Broadcasting Act 1990 s 116(3)(a).
19   Broadcasting Act 1990 s 116(3)(b)(i).
20   Broadcasting Act 1990 s 116(3)(b)(ii). Another person may provide additional services in accordance with s 115(3) (see PARA 773): see s 116(3)(b)(ii). As to the meaning of 'person' see PARA 510 note 1.
21   As to the meaning of 'cash bid' see PARA 730 note 31.
22   Broadcasting Act 1990 s 116(3)(c).
23   Broadcasting Act 1990 s 116(3)(d) (amended by the Communications Act 2003 Sch 15 para 54(2)).
24   Broadcasting Act 1990 s 116(4) (amended by the Communications Act 2003 Sch 15 para 54(2)).
25   Broadcasting Act 1990 s 116(5) (amended by the Communications Act 2003 Sch 15 para 54(2)).
26   Broadcasting Act 1990 s 116(6) (amended by the Communications Act 2003 Sch 15 para 54(2)).
27   Broadcasting Act 1990 s 116(6)(a).
28   Broadcasting Act 1990 s 116(6)(b).
29   Broadcasting Act 1990 s 116(6)(c) (amended by the Communications Act 2003 Sch 15 para 54(2)).

775.   Procedure in connection with additional services licences.   Where a person[1] has made an application for an additional services licence[2], OFCOM[3] may not proceed to consider whether to award him the licence on the basis of his cash bid[4] unless it appears to OFCOM[5]:

(1)   that the technical plan[6], in so far as it involves the use of an electronic communications network[7], contains proposals that are acceptable to it[8]; and

(2)   that the services proposed to be provided under the licence would be capable of being maintained throughout the period for which the licence would be in force[9].

If at any time after an additional services licence has been granted to any person but before the licence has come into force[10]:

(a)   that person indicates to OFCOM that none of the services in question will be provided once the licence has come into force[11]; or

(b)   OFCOM for any other reason has reasonable grounds for believing that none of those services will be so provided[12],

then OFCOM must serve on him a notice revoking the licence as from the time the notice is served on him[13]. However, this does not apply in the case of any person by virtue of head (b) above unless OFCOM has served on him a notice stating its grounds for believing that none of the services in question will be provided once his licence has come into force; and it must not serve such a notice on him unless it has given him a reasonable opportunity of making representations to it about the matters complained of[14].

1   As to the meaning of 'person' see PARA 510 note 1.
2   Ie in accordance with the Broadcasting Act 1990 s 116 (see PARA 774). As to the meaning of 'additional services licence' see PARA 773 note 5. Subject to s 117(4), s 100 (see PARA 731) applies in relation to an additional services licence as it applies in relation to a national licence: s 117(3). As to the meaning of 'national licence' see PARA 730 note 3. In the application of s 100 in relation to an additional services licence: (1) s 100(6) has effect with the substitution in s 100(6)(a) of a reference to s 118(1) (see PARA 776) for the reference to s 102(1) (see PARA 734); and (2) s 100(9) has effect with the substitution in s 100(9)(b) of a reference to the requirement specified in s 117(1)(a) (see head (1) in the text) for the reference to the requirement specified in s 99(1)(a) (see PARA 731): s 117(4).
3   As to OFCOM see PARA 507.
4   Ie in accordance with the Broadcasting Act 1990 s 117(3), (4). As to the meaning of 'cash bid' see PARA 730 note 31.
5   Broadcasting Act 1990 s 117(1) (amended by the Communications Act 2003 s 360(3), Sch 15 para 55(1), (2)).
6   Ie the technical plan submitted under the Broadcasting Act 1990 s 116(3)(b) (see PARA 774): see s 117(1)(a) (substituted by the Communications Act 2003 Sch 15 para 55(3)).
7   Ie within the meaning of the Communications Act 2003 (see TELECOMMUNICATIONS vol 97 (2010) PARA 60): see the Broadcasting Act 1990 s 117(1)(a) (as substituted: see note 6).
8   Broadcasting Act 1990 s 117(1)(a) (as substituted: see note 6).
9   Broadcasting Act 1990 s 117(1)(b). As to licences being in force see PARA 865 note 11. Any reference to an applicant in s 100 (see PARA 731) (as applied by s 117(3) (see note 2)) is accordingly a reference to an applicant in whose case it appears to OFCOM that the requirements of s 117(1)(a), (b) are satisfied: see s 117(1).
10 Broadcasting Act 1990 s 117(5).
11 Broadcasting Act 1990 s 117(5)(a) (amended by the Communications Act 2003 Sch 15 para 55(2)).
12 Broadcasting Act 1990 s 117(5)(b) (amended by the Communications Act 2003 Sch 15 para 55(2)).
13 Broadcasting Act 1990 s 117(5)(i). In those circumstances s 100 (see PARA 731) (as applied by s 117(3) (see note 2)) has, subject to s 100(11), effect as if he had not made an application for the licence: s 117(5)(ii).
14 Broadcasting Act 1990 s 117(6) (amended by the Communications Act 2003 Sch 15 para 55(2)).

776. Additional payments to be made in respect of additional services licences. An additional services licence[1] must include conditions requiring the licence holder[2] to pay to OFCOM[3], in addition to any fees payable under the general licence conditions[4]:

(1)   in respect of the first complete calendar year falling within the period for which the licence is in force[5], the amount specified in his cash bid[6];

(2)   in respect of each subsequent year falling wholly or partly within that period, the amount so specified as increased by the appropriate percentage[7]; and

(3)   in respect of each accounting period of his falling within the period for which the licence is in force, an amount representing such percentage of the qualifying revenue for that accounting period as has been specified in relation to the licence[8].

An additional services licence may include conditions enabling OFCOM to estimate before the beginning of an accounting period the amount due for that period by virtue of head (3) above[9], and requiring the licence holder to pay the estimated amount by monthly instalments throughout that period[10]. Such a licence may in particular include conditions authorising OFCOM to revise any estimate on one or more occasions and to adjust the instalments payable by the licence holder to take account of the revised estimate[11], and providing for the adjustment of any overpayment or underpayment[12].

1 As to the meaning of 'additional services licence' see PARA 773 note 5.
2 As to the holder of the licence see PARA 725 note 16.
3 As to OFCOM see PARA 507.
4 Broadcasting Act 1990 s 118(1) (amended by the Communications Act 2003 s 360(3), Sch 15 para 56). Fees are payable by virtue of the Broadcasting Act 1990 s 87(1)(c) (see PARA 726): see s 118(1).
5 As to licences being in force see PARA 865 note 11.
6 Broadcasting Act 1990 s 118(1)(a). As to the meaning of 'cash bid' see PARA 730 note 31.
7 Broadcasting Act 1990 s 118(1)(b). As to the meaning of 'the appropriate percentage' see PARA 730 note 31.
8 Broadcasting Act 1990 s 118(1)(c). The percentage of qualifying revenue is specified under s 116(1)(d)(ii) (see PARA 774): see s 118(1)(c). For the purposes of s 118(1)(c), the qualifying revenue for any accounting period of the licence holder consists of all amounts which are received or to be received by him or by any connected person and are referable to the right under his licence to use, or to authorise any other person to use, in that period the spare capacity allocated by the licence: s 118(2). As to the meaning of 'connected' see PARA 674 note 13. As to the meaning of 'spare capacity' see PARA 772 note 3.
    Where the first complete accounting period of the licence holder falling within the period referred to in s 118(1)(a) (see the text and note 6) ('the licence period') does not begin at the same time as that period, or the last complete accounting period of his falling within the licence period does not end at the same time as that period, any reference in s 118(1)(c) to an accounting period of his includes a reference to such part of the accounting period preceding that first complete accounting period, or, as the case may be, following that last complete accounting period, as falls within the licence period; and other references to accounting periods in Pt III (ss 83–126) are to be construed accordingly: s 118(5).
    As to the computation of qualifying revenue see also PARA 737.
9 Broadcasting Act 1990 s 118(3)(a) (amended by the Communications Act 2003 Sch 15 para 56).
10 Broadcasting Act 1990 s 118(3)(b).
11 Broadcasting Act 1990 s 118(4)(a) (amended by the Communications Act 2003 Sch 15 para 56).
12 Broadcasting Act 1990 s 118(4)(b).

777. Additional services not to interfere with other transmissions. An additional services licence[1] may include such conditions as OFCOM[2] considers appropriate for securing that the provision of any additional service[3] under the licence does not cause any interference with the sound broadcasting service[4] or services on whose frequency[5] or frequencies it is provided[6], or any other wireless telegraphy[7] transmissions[8].

1 As to the meaning of 'additional services licence' see PARA 773 note 5.
2 As to OFCOM see PARA 507.
3 As to the meaning of 'additional service' see PARA 772.
4 As to the meaning of 'sound broadcasting service' see PARA 723 note 4.
5 As to the meaning of 'frequency' see PARA 681 note 5.
6 Broadcasting Act 1990 s 119(1)(a) (s 119(1) amended by the Communications Act 2003 s 360(3), Sch 15 para 57(1), (2)).
7 As to the meaning of 'wireless telegraphy' see PARA 510 note 1; definition applied by the Broadcasting Act 1990 s 202(1) (amended by the Wireless Telegraphy Act 2006 s 123, Sch 7 paras 9, 13).
8 Broadcasting Act 1990 s 119(1)(b).

778. Enforcement of additional services licences. If OFCOM[1] is satisfied that the holder of an additional services licence[2] has failed to comply with any condition of the licence or with any direction given by OFCOM[3], it may serve on him a notice requiring him to pay, within a specified period, a specified financial penalty to OFCOM[4].

The amount of a financial penalty imposed on a person[5] in pursuance of this provision must not exceed 5 per cent of the qualifying revenue for the licence holder's last complete accounting period falling within the period for which his licence has been in force[6] ('the relevant period')[7]. In relation to a person whose first complete accounting period falling within the relevant period has not ended when the penalty is imposed, this is to be construed as referring to 5 per cent of the amount which OFCOM estimates to be the qualifying revenue for that accounting period[8].

OFCOM may not serve on any person such a notice unless it has given him a reasonable opportunity of making representations to it about the matters complained of[9].

1 As to OFCOM see PARA 507.
2 As to the meaning of 'additional services licence' see PARA 773 note 5. As to the holder of the licence see PARA 725 note 16. The Broadcasting Act 1990 s 111 (see PARA 747) applies in relation to an additional services licence as it applies in relation to a licence granted under Pt III Ch II (ss 98–111B), but with the omission of s 111(7): s 120(4).
3 Ie under or by virtue of any provision of the Broadcasting Act 1990 Pt III (ss 83–126).
4 Broadcasting Act 1990 s 120(1) (amended by the Communications Act 2003 s 360(3), Sch 15 para 58).
5 As to the meaning of 'person' see PARA 510 note 1.
6 As to licences being in force see PARA 865 note 11.
7 Broadcasting Act 1990 s 120(1A) (added by the Communications Act 2003 Sch 13 para 8(1)). The qualifying revenue is determined or estimated in accordance with the Broadcasting Act 1990 s 118(2) (see PARA 776): see s 120(1C) (added by the Communications Act 2003 s 345, Sch 13 paras 1, 8(1)).
8 Broadcasting Act 1990 s 120(1B) (added by the Communications Act 2003 Sch 13 para 8(1)). See note 7.
9 Broadcasting Act 1990 s 120(3) (amended by the Communications Act 2003 Sch 15 para 58).

B. DIGITAL ADDITIONAL SERVICES PROVIDED ON SOUND BROADCASTING FREQUENCIES

779. Digital additional services. 'Digital additional service' means any service which: (1) is provided by any person[1] with a view to its being broadcast[2] in digital form (whether by him or some other person) so as to be available for reception by members of the public[3]; (2) is so provided with a view to the broadcasting being by means of a radio multiplex service[4] or by means of a general multiplex service[5]; and (3) is not a digital sound programme service[6], a simulcast radio service[7], a television licensable content service[8], an ancillary service[9], a relevant ancillary service[10] or a technical service[11].

1 As to the meaning of 'person' see PARA 510 note 1.
2 As to the meaning of 'broadcast' see PARA 668 note 2; definition applied by the Broadcasting Act 1996 s 147(2).
3 Broadcasting Act 1996 ss 63(1)(a), 72(1) (s 63(1)(a) substituted by the Communications Act 2003 s 260(2)). As to the meaning of 'available for reception by members of the public' see PARA 796; definition applied by the Broadcasting Act 1996 s 63(3A) (added by the Communications Act 2003 s 260(3)).
4 As to the meaning of 'radio multiplex service' see PARA 727 note 10.
5 Broadcasting Act 1996 ss 63(1)(aa), 72(1) (s 63(1)(aa) added by the Communications Act 2003 s 260(2)).
6 As to the meaning of 'digital sound programme service' see PARA 754 note 28.
7 As to the meaning of 'simulcast radio service' see PARA 754 note 12.
8 As to the meaning of 'television licensable content service' see PARA 716; definition applied by the Broadcasting Act 1996 s 72(1) (definition added by SI 2006/2131).
9 'Ancillary service' (except in the expression 'relevant ancillary service') means any service which is provided by the holder of a digital sound programme licence or by an independent national broadcaster and consists in the provision of any service (other than advertising) which: (1) is ancillary to programmes included in a digital sound programme service or simulcast radio service provided by him and is directly related to their contents; or (2) relates to the promotion or listing of such programmes: Broadcasting Act 1996 ss 63(2), 72(1) (s 63(2) amended by

SI 2006/2131). As to the meaning of 'digital sound programme licence' see PARA 767 note 16. As to the meaning of 'independent national broadcaster' see PARA 756 note 4.

10 Ie within the meaning of the Communications Act 2003 s 232: see PARA 716 note 6.

11 Broadcasting Act 1996 ss 63(1)(b), 72(1) (s 63(1)(b) amended by SI 2006/2131). 'Technical service' means a service which: (1) is provided for technical purposes connected with the encryption or decryption of one or more digital sound programme services, television licensable content services or digital additional services; and (2) is of a description specified in an order made by the Secretary of State: ss 63(3), 72(1) (s 63(3) amended by SI 2006/2131). Such an order is subject to annulment in pursuance of a resolution of either House of Parliament: Broadcasting Act 1996 s 63(4). As to orders under this provision see the Broadcasting Digital Terrestrial Sound (Technical Service) Order 1998, SI 1998/685; and the Broadcasting Digital Terrestrial Sound (Technical Service) Order 2006, SI 2006/2793. The service specified for the purpose of the Broadcasting Act 1996 s 63(3) is that consisting of the transmission of electronic signals (as defined for the purposes of the Broadcasting Act 1990 s 114) (see PARA 772 note 1) by means of which access to programmes or other information included in digital sound programme services, television licensable content services or digital additional services is controlled so that only those persons who are authorised to receive such programmes and information do so: Broadcasting Digital Terrestrial Sound (Technical Service) Order 1998, SI 1998/685, art 2 (amended by SI 2003/2155 and SI 2006/2793). As to the Secretary of State see PARA 507 note 32.

780. Licensing of digital additional services. An application for a licence to provide digital additional services[1] (a 'digital additional services licence')[2] must be made in such manner as OFCOM[3] may determine[4]; and must be accompanied by such fee, if any, as it may determine[5].

At any time after receiving such an application and before determining it, OFCOM may require the applicant to furnish such additional information as it may consider necessary for the purpose of considering the application[6]. Any such information to be furnished to OFCOM must, if it so requires, be in such form or verified in such manner as it may specify[7].

Where such an application for a digital additional services licence is made to OFCOM, it must grant the licence unless precluded from doing so[8].

1 As to the meaning of 'digital additional service' see PARA 779.

2 Broadcasting Act 1996 ss 64(1), 72(1).

3 As to OFCOM see PARA 507.

4 Broadcasting Act 1996 s 64(1)(a) (amended by the Communications Act 2003 s 360(3), Sch 15 para 122).

5 Broadcasting Act 1996 s 64(1)(b).

6 Broadcasting Act 1996 s 64(2) (amended by the Communications Act 2003 Sch 15 para 122).

7 Broadcasting Act 1996 s 64(3) (amended by the Communications Act 2003 Sch 15 para 122).

8 Broadcasting Act 1996 s 64(4) (amended by the Communications Act 2003 Sch 15 para 122). OFCOM is precluded from granting a licence by the Broadcasting Act 1996 s 42(2)(a) (see PARA 727) or s 44(1) (see PARA 837): see s 64(4) (as so amended).

781. Duration and conditions of digital additional services licence. A digital additional services licence[1] continues in force[2] until it is surrendered by its holder[3]. A digital additional services licence must include such conditions as appear to OFCOM[4] to be appropriate for requiring the holder of the licence[5]:

(1) on entering into any agreement with the provider of a radio multiplex service[6] or of a general multiplex service[7] for the provision of digital additional services[8] to be broadcast[9] by means of the multiplex service, to notify OFCOM[10]:

    (a) of the identity of the multiplex service[11];

    (b) of the period during which the services will be provided[12]; and

    (c) where under the agreement the holder of the digital additional services licence will be entitled to the use of a specified amount of digital capacity, of that amount[13];

(2)   when any such agreement is varied so far as it relates to any of the matters mentioned in head (1)(a), (b) or (c) above, to notify OFCOM of the variation so far as relating to those matters[14]; and

(3)   where he is providing digital additional services to the provider of a radio multiplex service or of a general multiplex service in accordance with such an agreement but intends to cease doing so, to notify OFCOM of that fact[15].

1   As to the meaning of 'digital additional services licence' see PARA 780.
2   As to licences being in force see PARA 865 note 11; applied by the Broadcasting Act 1996 s 147(2).
3   Broadcasting Act 1996 s 65(1). This is expressed to be subject to Pt II (ss 40–72) and the Broadcasting Act 1990 s 111 (see PARA 747) as applied by the Broadcasting Act 1996 s 66(10) (see PARA 782): see s 65(1). As to the holder of the licence see PARA 728 note 3.
4   As to OFCOM see PARA 507.
5   Broadcasting Act 1996 s 65(2) (amended by the Communications Act 2003 s 360(3), Sch 15 para 123(1), (2)(a)).
6   As to the meaning of 'radio multiplex service' see PARA 727 note 10.
7   As to the meaning of 'general multiplex service' see PARA 898 note 10.
8   As to the meaning of 'digital additional service' see PARA 779.
9   As to the meaning of 'broadcast' see PARA 668 note 2; definition applied by the Broadcasting Act 1996 s 147(2).
10   Broadcasting Act 1996 s 65(2)(a) (amended by the Communications Act 2003 Sch 15 para 123(2)(b), (c)).
11   Broadcasting Act 1996 s 65(2)(a)(i) (amended by the Communications Act 2003 Sch 15 para 123(2)(d)).
12   Broadcasting Act 1996 s 65(2)(a)(ii).
13   Broadcasting Act 1996 s 65(2)(a)(iii).
14   Broadcasting Act 1996 s 65(2)(b) (amended by the Communications Act 2003 Sch 15 para 123(2)(a)).
15   Broadcasting Act 1996 s 65(2)(c) (amended by the Communications Act 2003 Sch 15 para 123(2)(a), (b)).

782.   Enforcement of digital additional services licences.   If OFCOM[1] is satisfied that the holder of a digital additional services licence[2] has failed to comply with any condition of the licence or with any direction given by OFCOM[3], it may serve on him[4]:

(1)   a notice requiring him to pay to it, within a specified period, a specified financial penalty[5];

(2)   a notice providing that the licence is to expire on a specified date, which must be at least one year from the date of service of the notice[6]; or

(3)   a notice suspending the licence for a specified period not exceeding six months[7].

OFCOM may not serve on any person[8] any such notice unless it has given him a reasonable opportunity of making representations to it about the matters complained of[9]. Where a licence is due to expire on a particular date by virtue of such a notice served on any person, OFCOM may, on the application of that person, revoke that notice by a further notice served on him at any time before that date, if it is satisfied that, since the date of the earlier notice, his conduct in relation to the operation of the licensed[10] service has been such as to justify the revocation of that notice[11].

Where OFCOM serves such a notice on a BBC company[12], it must send a copy of the notice to the Secretary of State[13].

1   As to OFCOM see PARA 507.

2   As to the meaning of 'digital additional services licence' see PARA 780. As to the holder of the
    licence see PARA 728 note 3. Subject to the Broadcasting Act 1996 s 66(11), (12), the
    Broadcasting Act 1990 s 109 (power to require scripts etc or broadcasting of correction or
    statement of findings or not to repeat programme: see PARA 745) and s 111 (power to revoke
    licences: see PARA 747) apply in relation to a digital additional services licence as they apply in
    relation to a licence under Pt III Ch II (ss 98–111B): Broadcasting Act 1996 s 66(10) (amended
    by the Communications Act 2003 s 360(3), Sch 15 para 124(7)). In its application in relation to
    a digital additional services licence, the Broadcasting Act 1990 s 109(1) has effect with the
    substitution for the reference to a direction under Pt III (ss 83–126) of a reference to a direction
    under the Broadcasting Act 1996 Pt II (ss 40–72): s 66(11). In its application in relation to a
    digital additional services licence, the Broadcasting Act 1990 s 111 has effect with the
    substitution for the reference in s 111(1)(a) to Pt III of a reference to the Broadcasting Act 1996
    Pt II, and with the omission of the Broadcasting Act 1990 s 111(4) and of the reference to
    s 111(4) in s 111(6): Broadcasting Act 1996 s 66(12).
3   Ie under or by virtue of any provision of the Broadcasting Act 1996 Pt II.
4   Broadcasting Act 1996 s 66(1) (amended by the Communications Act 2003 Sch 15
    para 124(1), (2)).
5   Broadcasting Act 1996 s 66(1)(a) (amended by the Communications Act 2003 Sch 15
    para 124(2)). The amount of any financial penalty imposed in pursuance of the Broadcasting
    Act 1996 s 66(1)(a) on the holder of a digital additional services licence must not exceed the
    maximum penalty given by s 66(2A): s 66(2) (amended by the Communications Act 2003 s 345,
    Sch 13 paras 10, 21(1)). The maximum penalty is whichever is the greater of: (1) £250,000; and
    (2) 5% of the aggregate amount of the shares of multiplex revenue attributable to him in
    relation to relevant multiplex services in respect of relevant accounting periods: Broadcasting
    Act 1996 s 66(2A) (added by the Communications Act 2003 Sch 13 para 21(2)). As to multiplex
    revenue see PARA 763. 'Relevant accounting period', in relation to a relevant multiplex service,
    means the last accounting period of the multiplex provider: Broadcasting Act 1996 s 66(5)
    (amended by the Communications Act 2003 Sch 13 para 21(4), Sch 15 para 124(4)). As to
    accounting periods see PARA 754 note 19. As to licences being in force see PARA 865 note 11;
    applied by the Broadcasting Act 1996 s 147(2). A service is a relevant multiplex service if it is a
    national radio multiplex service or a general multiplex service: s 66(6B) (second) (added by the
    Communications Act 2003 Sch 15 para 124(6)). Note that the Communications Act 2003
    Sch 13 also amends the Broadcasting Act 1996 s 66 so that there are two subsections numbered
    s 66(6B). 'Multiplex provider', in relation to a national radio multiplex service, means the
    multiplex provider within the meaning of s 56 (see PARA 763 note 3), and in relation to a general
    multiplex service, means the multiplex provider within the meaning of s 14 (see PARA 693 note
    3): s 66(6C) (added by the Communications Act 2003 Sch 15 para 124(6)).
        A determination or estimate for the purposes of the Broadcasting Act 1996 s 66(2A) or
    s 66(6) of the share of multiplex revenue attributable to a person in relation to national radio
    multiplex services is to be in accordance with s 57(2), (3): s 66(6A) (added by the
    Communications Act 2003 Sch 13 para 21(6)). A determination or estimate for the purposes of
    the Broadcasting Act 1996 s 66(2A) or s 66(6) of the share of multiplex revenue attributable to
    a person in relation to general multiplex services is to be in accordance with s 15(2), (3) (see
    PARA 713): Broadcasting Act 1996 s 66(6B) (first) (added by the Communications Act 2003
    Sch 13 para 21(6)).
        For the purposes of the Broadcasting Act 1996 s 66(2A)–(5), the share of multiplex revenue
    attributable to a programme provider or additional services provider in relation to a national
    radio multiplex service in respect of any accounting period of the multiplex provider is: (a) the
    aggregate of payments falling within s 56(1)(c) or (d) (see PARA 763), and payments received or
    to be received from the multiplex provider which would fall within one of those provisions but
    for the fact that they are received from the multiplex provider; less (b) the amount of any
    payments made or to be made to the multiplex provider in respect of the provision of radio
    multiplex services in that period: s 57(2) (amended by the Communications Act 2003 Sch 13
    para 18(2), Sch 15 para 116(1), (3)). As to the meaning of 'programme provider' see PARA 763
    note 6; definition applied by the Broadcasting Act 1996 s 57(4). As to the meaning of
    'additional services provider' see PARA 763 note 7; definition applied by s 57(4). As to the
    meaning of 'radio multiplex service' see PARA 727 note 10.
        Where, in the case of any relevant multiplex service, the first accounting period of the
    multiplex provider throughout which the holder of the digital additional services licence
    provides a digital additional service for broadcasting by means of that relevant multiplex service
    ('the first period') has not ended when the penalty is imposed, then for the purposes of s 66 the
    share of multiplex revenue attributable to the holder of the digital additional services licence in
    relation to that relevant multiplex service for the relevant accounting period must be taken to be

the amount which OFCOM estimates to be the share of multiplex revenue attributable to him for the first period: s 66(6) (amended by the Communications Act 2003 Sch 13 para 21(5), Sch 15 para 124(2), (5)).

Where the holder of a digital additional services licence has not provided any digital additional services for broadcasting by means of a relevant multiplex service, the amount of any penalty imposed on him under the Broadcasting Act 1996 s 66(1)(a) must not exceed £250,000: s 66(4) (amended by the Communications Act 2003 Sch 13 para 21(3), Sch 15 para 124(3)). As to the meaning of 'digital additional service' see PARA 779. As to the meaning of 'broadcast' see PARA 668 note 2; definition applied by the Broadcasting Act 1996 s 147(2).

The Secretary of State may by order amend s 66(2A)(a), (4): see s 69(1), (2)(d) (s 69(2) substituted by the Communications Act 2003 Sch 13 para 22). No order is to be made under the Broadcasting Act 1996 s 69(1) unless a draft of the order has been laid before Parliament and approved by a resolution of each House: s 69(3) (substituted by the Communications Act 2003 Sch 13 para 22). At the date at which this volume states the law, no such order had been made. As to the Secretary of State see PARA 507 note 32.

6 Broadcasting Act 1996 s 66(1)(b).

7 Broadcasting Act 1996 s 66(1)(c). Any exercise by OFCOM of its powers under s 66(1) in respect of any failure to comply with any condition of a digital additional services licence does not preclude any exercise by it of its powers under the Broadcasting Act 1990 s 109 (see PARA 745) in respect of that failure: Broadcasting Act 1996 s 66(13) (amended by the Communications Act 2003 Sch 15 para 124(2)).

8 As to the meaning of 'person' see PARA 510 note 1.

9 Broadcasting Act 1996 s 66(7) (amended by the Communications Act 2003 Sch 15 para 124(2)).

10 As to the meaning of 'licensed' see PARA 727 note 2.

11 Broadcasting Act 1996 s 66(8) (amended by the Communications Act 2003 Sch 15 para 124(2)).

12 As to the meaning of 'BBC company' see PARA 671 note 20; definition applied by the Broadcasting Act 1996 s 147(2).

13 Broadcasting Act 1996 s 66(9) (amended by the Communications Act 2003 Sch 15 para 124(2)).

783. Grants by OFCOM to community radio providers. OFCOM[1] may make such grants as it considers appropriate to the provider of any community radio service in relation to which provision is for the time being in force[2] modifying the statutory provisions relating to radio broadcasting[3]. A grant made by virtue of these provisions may be made on such terms and conditions, and will become repayable to OFCOM in such circumstances, as may be specified by OFCOM when making the grant[4]. A person is not: (1) by reason of the making to him of a grant by virtue of these provisions; or (2) by reason of any terms or conditions (including any provisions for repayment) subject to which such a grant is or has been made to him, to be a disqualified person[5] in relation to a licence under Part III of the Broadcasting Act 1990[6], or under Part II of the Broadcasting Act 1996[7], which is granted in accordance with any provision made by an order modifying the statutory provisions relating to radio broadcasting[8]. No order is to be made containing provision authorised by the above provisions unless a draft of the order has been laid before Parliament and approved by a resolution of each House[9].

1 As to OFCOM see PARA 507.

2 Ie under the Communications Act 2003 s 262: see PARA 729.

3 Communications Act 2003 s 359(1).

4 Communications Act 2003 s 359(3).

5 Ie by virtue of any provision of Schedule 2 to the Broadcasting Act 1990 Sch 2: Communications Act 2003 s 359(4). As to disqualified persons see PARAS 822 et seq, 830 et seq.

6 Ie the Broadcasting Act 1990 Pt III (ss 83–126).

7 Ie the Broadcasting Act 1996 Pt II (ss 40–72).

8 Communications Act 2003 s 359(4), (5)(b).

9 Communications Act 2003 s 359(6).

(11) ON-DEMAND SERVICES

784. Meaning of 'on-demand programme service'. For the purposes of the Communications Act 2003, a service is an 'on-demand programme service' if: (1) its principal purpose is the provision of programmes[1] the form and content of which are comparable to the form and content of programmes normally included in television programme services[2]; (2) access to it is on-demand[3]; (3) there is a person who has editorial responsibility for it[4]; (4) it is made available by that person for use by members of the public[5]; and (5) that person is under the jurisdiction of the United Kingdom[6] for the purposes of the Audiovisual Media Services Directive[7]. If an on-demand programme service ('the main service') offers users access to a relevant ancillary service[8], the relevant ancillary service is to be treated as a part of the main service[9].

1 As to the meaning of 'programme' see PARA 602 note 12.
2 For the purposes of the Communications Act 2003 Pt 4A (ss 368A–368R), a programme is included in an on-demand programme service if it is included in the range of programmes the service offers to users: s 368R(2) (ss 368A, 368R added by SI 2009/2979).
3 Access to a service is on-demand if: (1) the service enables the user to view, at a time chosen by the user, programmes selected by the user from among the programmes included in the service; and (2) the programmes viewed by the user are received by the user by means of an electronic communications network (whether before or after the user has selected which programmes to view): Communications Act 2003 s 368A(2) (as added: see note 2). For the purposes of s 368A(2)(a), the fact that a programme may be viewed only within a period specified by the provider of the service does not prevent the time at which it is viewed being one chosen by the user: s 368A(3) (as so added). As to the meaning of 'electronic communications network' see TELECOMMUNICATIONS vol 97 (2010) PARA 60.
4 A person has editorial responsibility for a service if that person has general control: (1) over what programmes are included in the range of programmes offered to users; and (2) over the manner in which the programmes are organised in that range, and the person need not have control of the content of individual programmes or of the broadcasting or distribution of the service: Communications Act 2003 s 368A(4) (as added: see note 2). The person, and the only person, who is to be treated for the purposes of Pt 4A as providing an on-demand programme service is the person who has editorial responsibility for the service: s 368R(5) (as so added)). For the purposes of Pt 4A: (a) the provision of a service by the BBC does not include its provision by a BBC company; (b) the provision of a service by the Welsh Authority does not include its provision by an S4C company, and, accordingly, control that is or is capable of being exercised by the BBC or the Welsh Authority over decisions by a BBC company or an S4C company about what is to be comprised in a service is to be disregarded for the purposes of determining who has editorial responsibility for the service: s 368R(6) (as so added). As to the meaning of 'person' see PARA 510 note 1. As to the meaning of 'BBC' see PARA 603 note 1; and as to the BBC see PARAS 603–626. As to the meaning of 'BBC company' see PARA 854 note 4. As to the meaning of 'the Welsh Authority' see PARA 644 note 3; and as to the Welsh Authority see PARA 645 et seq. As to the meaning of 'S4C company' see PARA 826 note 3.
5 The services that are to be taken for the purposes of the Communications Act 2003 Pt 4A to be available for use by members of the public include any service which: (1) is made available for use only to persons who subscribe to the service (whether for a period or in relation to a particular occasion) or who otherwise request its provision; but (2) is a service the facility of subscribing to which, or of otherwise requesting its provision, is offered or made available to members of the public: s 368R(4) (as added: see note 2).
6 As to the meaning of 'United Kingdom' see PARA 510 note 13.
7 Communications Act 2003 s 368A(1) (as added: see note 2). As to the Audiovisual Media Services Directive see PARA 857 note 7. The Communications Act 2003 Pt 4A (ss 368A–368R) was added by the Audiovisual Media Services Regulations 2009, SI 2009/2979, as from 19 December 2009 to implement European Parliament and Council Directive (EC) 2007/65 (OJ L332, 18.12.2007, p 27) amending European Parliament and Council Directive (EC) 89/552 (OJ L298, 17.10.89, p 23) (repealed: now European Parliament and Council Directive (EU) 2010/13 (OJ L95, 15.4.2010, p 1)) (the 'Audiovisual Media Services Directive') (see PARA 506). Further new implementation provisions are added, and amendments made, by the Audiovisual Media Services Regulations 2010, SI 2010/419.

8 'Relevant ancillary service' means a service or facility that consists of or gives access to assistance for disabled people in relation to some or all of the programmes included in the main service: Communications Act 2003 s 368A(6) (as added: see note 2). As to the meaning of 'assistance for disabled people' see PARA 644 note 12; definition applied by s 368A(7) (as so added).

9 Communications Act 2003 s 368A(5) (as added: see note 2).

785. Regulatory authorities. OFCOM[1] may designate any body corporate to be, to the extent provided by the designation[2], the appropriate regulatory authority for the purposes of any provision of Part 4A[3] of the Communications Act 2003[4]. To the extent that no body is designated for a purpose, OFCOM is the appropriate regulatory authority for that purpose[5]. Where a body is designated for a purpose, OFCOM may act as the appropriate regulatory authority for that purpose concurrently with or in place of that body[6].

OFCOM may provide a designated body with assistance in connection with any of the functions of the body in relation to on-demand programme services[7]. A designation may in particular: (1) provide for a body to be the appropriate regulatory authority in relation to on-demand programme services of a specified description; (2) provide that a function of the appropriate regulatory authority is exercisable by the designated body: (a) to such extent as may be specified; (b) either generally or in such circumstances as may be specified; and (c) either unconditionally or subject to such conditions as may be specified[8]. A designation has effect for such period as may be specified and may be revoked by OFCOM at any time[9]. OFCOM must publish any designation in such manner as it considers appropriate for bringing it to the attention of persons who, in its opinion, are likely to be affected by it[10].

Subject to any enactment[11] or rule of law restricting the disclosure or use of information by OFCOM or by a designated body: (a) a designated body may supply information to another designated body for use by that other body in connection with any of its functions as the appropriate regulatory authority; (b) a designated body may supply information to OFCOM for use by OFCOM in connection with any of its functions in relation to on-demand programme services; (c) OFCOM may supply information to a designated body for use by that body in connection with any of its functions as the appropriate regulatory authority[12].

In carrying out its functions as the appropriate regulatory authority, a designated body may carry out, commission or support (financially or otherwise) research[13].

It is the duty of the appropriate regulatory authority to take such steps as appear to it best calculated to secure that every provider of an on-demand programme service complies with the requirements[14] as to the duties of service providers[15].

1 As to OFCOM see PARA 507.

2 'Designation' means a designation under the Communications Act 2003 s 368B and cognate expressions are to be construed accordingly: s 368B(12) (ss 368B, 368C, 368R added by SI 2009/2979).

3 Ie the Communications Act 2003 Pt 4A (ss 368A–368R). Part 4A was added by the Audiovisual Media Services Regulations 2009, SI 2009/2979, as from 19 December 2009 to implement European Parliament and Council Directive (EC) 2007/65 (OJ L332, 18.12.2007, p 27) amending European Parliament and Council Directive (EC) 89/552 (OJ L298, 17.10.89, p 23) (the 'Audiovisual Media Services Directive') (now European Parliament and Council Directive (EU) 2010/13 (OJ L95, 15.4.2010, p 1): see PARA 506.

4 Communications Act 2003 s 368B(1) (as added: see note 2). This is subject to s 368B(9): s 368B(1) (as so added; and amended by SI 2010/419). OFCOM may not designate a body

unless, as respects that designation, it is satisfied that the body: (1) is a fit and proper body to be designated; (2) has consented to being designated; (3) has access to financial resources that are adequate to ensure the effective performance of its functions as the appropriate regulatory authority; (4) is sufficiently independent of providers of on-demand programme services; and (5) will, in performing any function to which the designation relates, have regard in all cases: (a) to the principles under which regulatory activities should be transparent, accountable, proportionate, consistent and targeted only at cases in which action is needed; and (b) to such of the matters mentioned in the Communications Act 2003 s 3(4) (see TELECOMMUNICATIONS vol 97 (2010) PARA 16) as appear to the body to be relevant in the circumstances: s 368B(9) (as so added). As to the meaning of 'on-demand programme service' see PARA 784.

5   Communications Act 2003 s 368B(2) (as added: see note 2).
6   Communications Act 2003 s 368B(3) (as added: see note 2).
7   Communications Act 2003 s 368B(4) (as added: see note 2).
8   Communications Act 2003 s 368B(5) (as added: see note 2). 'Specified' means specified in a designation: Communications Act 2003 s 368B(12) (as so added). The conditions that may be specified pursuant to s 368B(5)(b)(iii) (head (c) in the text) include a condition to the effect that a function may, generally or in specified circumstances, be exercised by the body only with the agreement of OFCOM: s 368B(6) (as so added; and amended by SI 2010/419).
9   Communications Act 2003 s 368B(7) (as added: see note 2).
10   Communications Act 2003 s 368B(8) (as added: see note 2).
11   As to the meaning of 'enactment' see PARA 793 note 5.
12   Communications Act 2003 s 368B(10) (as added: see note 2).
13   Communications Act 2003 s 368B(11) (as added: see note 2).
14   Ie the requirements of the Communications Act 2003 s 368D: see PARA 867.
15   Communications Act 2003 s 368C(1) (as added: see note 2). In s 368C, references to a provider of an on-demand programme service do not include references to the BBC or the Welsh Authority: see ss 368P(2), 368Q(1); and PARA 871. As to the meaning of 'BBC' see PARA 603 note 1; and as to the BBC see PARAS 603–626. As to the meaning of 'the Welsh Authority' see PARA 644 note 3; and as to the Welsh Authority see PARA 645 et seq.

786. Notification by service providers. A person[1] must not provide an on-demand programme service[2] unless, before beginning to provide it, that person has given a notification to the appropriate regulatory authority[3] of the person's intention to provide that service[4]. A person who has given a notification for these purposes must, before providing the notified service with any significant differences or ceasing to provide it, give a notification to the appropriate regulatory authority of the differences or (as the case may be) of an intention to cease to provide the service[5].

Where the appropriate regulatory authority determines that the provider of an on-demand programme service has contravened the statutory provisions as to advance notification[6], it may do one or both of the following: (1) give the provider an enforcement notification as specified below; (2) impose a penalty[7] on the provider[8]. The appropriate regulatory authority must not make such a determination unless there are reasonable grounds for believing that a contravention of the notification requirements has occurred and it has allowed the provider an opportunity to make representations about that apparent contravention[9].

An enforcement notification is a notification which specifies the determination made by the appropriate regulatory authority and imposes a requirement on the provider to take all such steps for remedying the contravention as may be specified in the notification[10]. An enforcement notification must: (a) include reasons for the appropriate regulatory authority's decision to give the enforcement notification; and (b) fix a reasonable period for taking the steps required by the notification[11]. It is the duty of a person to whom an enforcement notification has been given to comply with it[12]. That duty is enforceable in civil proceedings by the appropriate regulatory authority for an injunction or for any other appropriate remedy or relief[13].

1   As to the meaning of 'person' see PARA 510 note 1.
2   As to the meaning of 'on-demand programme service' see PARA 784.
3   'Appropriate regulatory authority' is to be construed in accordance with the Communications
    Act 2003 s 368B: s 368R(1) (s 368R added by SI 2009/2979). See PARA 785.
4   Communications Act 2003 s 368BA(1) (ss 368BA, 368BB added by SI 2010/419). A notification
    for these purposes must: (1) be sent to the appropriate regulatory authority in such manner as
    the authority may require; and (2) contain all such information as the authority may require:
    Communications Act 2003 s 368BA(3) (as so added). Section 368BA does not apply in relation
    to an on-demand programme service provided or to be provided by the BBC or, except for a
    service that includes advertising, in relation to an on-demand programme service provided or to
    be provided by the Welsh Authority: see ss 368P(A1), 368Q(A1); and PARA 871. As to the
    meaning of 'BBC' see PARA 603 note 1; and as to the BBC see PARAS 603–626. As to the meaning
    of 'the Welsh Authority' see PARA 644 note 3; and as to the Welsh Authority see PARA 645 et seq.
5   Communications Act 2003 s 368BA(2) (as added: see note 4).
6   Ie the Communications Act 2003 s 368BA.
7   Ie in accordance with the Communications Act 2003 s 368J: see PARA 868.
8   Communications Act 2003 s 368BB(1) (as added: see note 4).
9   Communications Act 2003 s 368BB(2) (as added: see note 4).
10 Communications Act 2003 s 368BB(3) (as added: see note 4).
11 Communications Act 2003 s 368BB(4) (as added: see note 4).
12 Communications Act 2003 s 368BB(5) (as added: see note 4).
13 Communications Act 2003 s 368BB(6) (as added: see note 4).

787.   Fees. The authority[1] may require a provider of an on-demand programme service[2] to pay it a fee[3]. The authority must be satisfied that the amount of any fee required: (1) represents the appropriate contribution of the provider towards meeting the likely costs of carrying out the relevant functions[4] during a financial year[5]; and (2) is justifiable and proportionate having regard to the provider who will be required to pay it and the functions in respect of which it is imposed[6]. A different fee may be required in relation to different cases or circumstances[7].

The authority must, for each financial year:

(a)   prepare such estimate as it is practicable for it to make of the likely costs of carrying out the relevant functions during that year[8];

(b)   ensure that the aggregate amount of the fees that are required to be paid to it[9] during that year is sufficient to enable it to meet, but not exceed, the costs estimated under head (a);

(c)   consult in such manner as it considers appropriate the providers likely to be required to pay a fee to it during that year;

(d)   publish in such manner as it considers appropriate the amount of the fees it will require providers to pay to it during that year[10].

As soon as reasonably practicable after the end of the financial year, the authority must publish a statement setting out, for that year: (i) the aggregate amount received by it during that year in respect of fees required to be paid to it; (ii) the aggregate amount outstanding and likely to be paid or recovered in respect of fees that were required to be so paid; and (iii) the costs to it of carrying out the relevant functions during that year[11]. Any deficit or surplus shown (after applying this provision for all previous years) by such a statement is to be carried forward and taken into account in determining what is required to satisfy the requirement in head (b)[12] in relation to the following year[13].

The authority may repay to a person some or all of a fee paid to it by a person under these provisions if: (A) that person has ceased to provide an on-demand programme service at some time during the period to which the fee relates; (B) before ceasing to provide that service, that person gave the appropriate regulatory authority a notification of intention to cease to provide a service[14];

and (C) that person did not cease to provide the service following a direction[15] given by the appropriate regulatory authority[16].

The authority may make arrangements with any body designated[17] as the appropriate regulatory authority for that body to provide the authority with assistance in connection with the collection or repayment of fees required by it under these provisions[18].

1   For these purposes, 'the authority' means each of these: (1) the appropriate regulatory authority; (2) (where it is not the appropriate regulatory authority) OFCOM: Communications Act 2003 s 368NA(1) (s 368NA added by SI 2010/419). As to the meaning of 'appropriate regulatory authority' see PARA 786 note 3; and as to OFCOM see PARA 507. The Communications Act 2003 s 368NA does not apply to the BBC: see s 368P(1); and PARA 871. As to the meaning of 'BBC' see PARA 603 note 1; and as to the BBC see PARAS 603–626.
2   As to the meaning of 'on-demand programme service' see PARA 784.
3   Communications Act 2003 s 368NA(2) (as added: see note 1).
4   For these purposes, 'relevant functions' means: (1) in relation to the appropriate regulatory authority, its functions as the appropriate regulatory authority; (2) in relation to OFCOM (where it is not the appropriate regulatory authority), its other functions under the Communications Act 2003 Pt 4A (ss 368A–368R):s 368NA(11) (as added: see note 1).
5   Ie the likely costs described in the Communications Act 2003 s 368NA(5)(a): see head (a) in the text. 'Financial year' means a period of 12 months ending with 31 March: s 368NA(12) (as added: see note 1).
6   Communications Act 2003 s 368NA(3) (as added: see note 1).
7   Communications Act 2003 s 368NA(4) (as added: see note 1).
8   For the purposes of the Communications Act 2003 s 368NA: (1) the authority's costs of carrying out the relevant functions during a financial year include its costs of preparing to carry out the relevant functions incurred during that year; and (2) the authority's costs of preparing to carry out the relevant functions incurred after 19 December 2009 but before the financial year in which those functions were first carried out by it are to be treated as if they were incurred during that year: s 368NA(10) (as added: see note 1).
9   Ie under the Communications Act 2003 s 368NA(2).
10   Communications Act 2003 s 368NA(5) (as added: see note 1).
11   Communications Act 2003 s 368NA(6) (as added: see note 1).
12   Ie the requirement imposed by virtue of the Communications Act 2003 s 368NA(5)(b).
13   Communications Act 2003 s 368NA(7) (as added: see note 1).
14   Ie under the Communications Act 2003 s 368BA(2): see PARA 786.
15   Ie under the Communications Act 2003 s 368K or s 368L: see PARA 869.
16   Communications Act 2003 s 368NA(8) (as added: see note 1).
17   Ie under the Communications Act 2003 s 368B: see PARA 785.
18   Communications Act 2003 s 368NA(9) (as added: see note 1).

(12) GENERAL ISSUES

(i) Review of the Public Service Remit

788. OFCOM reports on the fulfilment of the public service remit. The regulatory regime for every licensed public service channel[1], and for the public teletext service[2], include conditions requiring the provider of the channel or service to fulfil the public service remit for that channel or service[3], and to prepare a statement of programme policy and monitor his own performance in carrying out the proposals made in pursuance of the condition as to programme policy[4].

It is the duty of OFCOM[5]: (1) as soon as practicable after the end of the period of 12 months beginning with 25 July 2003[6]; and (2) as soon as practicable after the end of each such subsequent period as may be selected by OFCOM for the purposes of these provisions, to satisfy, for that period, the review and reporting obligations below[7]. The review and reporting obligations for a period are:

(a)   an obligation to carry out a review of the extent to which the public
        service broadcasters[8] have, during that period, provided relevant
        television services[9] which (taking them all together over the period as a
        whole) fulfil the purposes of public service television broadcasting in the
        United Kingdom[10]; and

(b)   an obligation, with a view to maintaining and strengthening the quality
        of public service television broadcasting in the United Kingdom, to
        prepare a report on the matters found on the review[11].

When determining the extent to which any of the purposes of public service
television broadcasting in the United Kingdom are fulfilled, and reviewing and
reporting on that matter, OFCOM must have regard to the desirability of those
purposes being fulfilled in a manner that is compatible with the provision
below[12]. A manner of fulfilling the purposes of public service television
broadcasting in the United Kingdom is compatible with this provision if it
ensures:

(i)   that the relevant television services (taken together) comprise a public
        service for the dissemination of information and for the provision of
        education and entertainment;

(ii)   that cultural activity in the United Kingdom, and its diversity, are
        reflected, supported and stimulated by the representation in those
        services (taken together) of drama[13], comedy and music, by the
        inclusion of feature films in those services and by the treatment of other
        visual and performing arts;

(iii)   that those services (taken together) provide, to the extent that is
        appropriate for facilitating civic understanding and fair and
        well-informed debate on news and current affairs, a comprehensive and
        authoritative coverage of news and current affairs in, and in the
        different parts of, the United Kingdom and from around the world;

(iv)   that those services (taken together) satisfy a wide range of different
        sporting and other leisure interests;

(v)   that those services (taken together) include what appears to OFCOM to
        be a suitable quantity and range of programmes on educational matters,
        of programmes of an educational nature and of other programmes of
        educative value;

(vi)   that those services (taken together) include what appears to OFCOM to
        be a suitable quantity and range of programmes dealing with each of the
        following, science, religion and other beliefs[14], social issues, matters of
        international significance or interest and matters of specialist interest;

(vii)   that the programmes included in those services that deal with religion
        and other beliefs include: (A) programmes providing news and other
        information about different religions and other beliefs; (B) programmes
        about the history of different religions and other beliefs; and (C)
        programmes showing acts of worship and other ceremonies and
        practices (including some showing acts of worship and other ceremonies
        in their entirety);

(viii) that those services (taken together) include what appears to OFCOM to
        be a suitable quantity and range of high quality and original
        programmes for children and young people;

(ix)   that those services (taken together) include what appears to OFCOM to
        be a sufficient quantity of programmes that reflect the lives and

concerns of different communities and cultural interests and traditions within the United Kingdom, and locally in different parts of the United Kingdom;

(x) that those services (taken together), so far as they include programmes made in the United Kingdom, include what appears to OFCOM to be an appropriate range and proportion of programmes made outside the M25 area[15].

1 'Licensed public service channel' means any of the following services (whether provided for broadcasting in digital or in analogue form): (1) any Channel 3 service; (2) Channel 4; (3) Channel 5: Communications Act 2003 s 362(1). As to the meaning of 'Channel 3 service' see PARA 602 note 8. As to the meaning of 'Channel 4' see PARA 602 note 9. As to the meaning of 'Channel 5' see PARA 602 note 10.

2 As to the public teletext service see PARA 686.

3 See the Communications Act 2003 s 265; and PARAS 642, 662, 677, 682.

4 See the Communications Act 2003 ss 266, 268; and PARAS 642, 662, 677, 682.

5 As to OFCOM see PARA 507.

6 Ie the commencement of the Communications Act 2003 s 264: see the Communications Act 2003 (Commencement No 1) Order 2003, SI 2003/1900, art 2(1), Sch 1.

7 Ie the review and reporting obligations of the Communications Act 2003 s 264(3) (see the text to note 7): s 264(1). The period selected by OFCOM for the purposes of head (2) in the text must be a period of not more than five years beginning with the end of the previous period for which OFCOM has satisfied those review and reporting obligations: s 264(2). For further reporting obligations see PARA 789.

8 The following are public service broadcasters for these purposes: (1) the BBC; (2) the Welsh Authority; (3) the providers of the licensed public service channels; and (4) the public teletext provider: Communications Act 2003 s 264(12). 'Licensed public service channel' means any of the following services (whether provided for broadcasting in digital or in analogue form): (a) any Channel 3 service; (b) Channel 4; (c) Channel 5: s 362(1). As to the meaning of 'BBC' see PARA 603 note 1; and as to the BBC see PARAS 603–626. As to the meaning of 'the Welsh Authority' see PARA 644 note 3; and as to television broadcasting by the Welsh Authority see PARAS 644–661. As to the meaning of 'Channel 3 service' see PARA 602 note 8. As to the meaning of 'Channel 4' see PARA 602 note 9. As to the meaning of 'Channel 5' see PARA 602 note 10.

9 The following are relevant television services for these purposes: (1) the television broadcasting services provided by the BBC; (2) the television programme services that are public services of the Welsh Authority (within the meaning of the Communications Act 2003 s 207 (see PARA 644)); (3) every Channel 3 service; (4) Channel 4; (5) Channel 5; (6) the public teletext service: s 264(11). As to the public teletext service see PARA 686.

10 The purposes of public service television broadcasting in the United Kingdom are: (1) the provision of relevant television services which secure that programmes dealing with a wide range of subject matters are made available for viewing; (2) the provision of relevant television services in a manner which (having regard to the days on which they are shown and the times of day at which they are shown) is likely to meet the needs and satisfy the interests of as many different audiences as practicable; (3) the provision of relevant television services which (taken together and having regard to the same matters) are properly balanced, so far as their nature and subject matters are concerned, for meeting the needs and satisfying the interests of the available audiences; and (4) the provision of relevant television services which (taken together) maintain high general standards with respect to the programmes included in them, and, in particular with respect to: (a) the contents of the programmes; (b) the quality of the programme making; and (c) the professional skill and editorial integrity applied in the making of the programmes: Communications Act 2003 s 264(4). As to the meaning of 'United Kingdom' see PARA 510 note 13.

11 Communications Act 2003 s 264(3). In carrying out a review under s 264 OFCOM must consider: (1) the costs to persons providing relevant television services of the fulfilment of the purposes of public service television broadcasting in a manner compatible with s 264(6); and (2) the sources of income available to each of them for meeting those costs: s 264(7). Every report under s 264 must: (a) specify, and comment on, whatever changes appear to OFCOM to have occurred, during the period to which the report relates, in the extent to which the purposes of public service television broadcasting in the United Kingdom have been satisfied; (b) specify, and comment on, whatever changes appear to OFCOM to have occurred, during that period, in the

manner in which those purposes are fulfilled; (c) set out the findings of OFCOM on its consideration of the matters mentioned in s 264(7) and any conclusions it has arrived at in relation to those findings; and (d) set out OFCOM's conclusions on the current state of public service television broadcasting in the United Kingdom: s 264(8). In performing its duties under s 264, OFCOM must have regard, in particular, to: (i) every statement of programme or service policy which has been made by virtue of Pt 3 Ch 4 (ss 263–347) by a public service broadcaster (see note 8), or which is treated as such a statement; (ii) every equivalent statement of policy made by the BBC in pursuance of the BBC Charter and Agreement; and (iii) such matters arising at times before 25 July 2003 as OFCOM considers material: s 264(9). Every report prepared by OFCOM under s 264 must be published by it: (A) as soon as practicable after its preparation is complete; and (B) in such manner as it considers appropriate: s 264(10). As to the meaning of 'BBC Charter and Agreement' see PARA 854 note 2.

12 Ie compatible with the Communications Act 2003 s 264(6) (see heads (i)–(x) in the text): s 264(5).

13 'Drama' includes contemporary and other drama in a variety of different formats: Communications Act 2003 s 264(13).

14 'Belief' means a collective belief in, or other adherence to, a systemised set of ethical or philosophical principles or of mystical or transcendental doctrines: Communications Act 2003 s 264(13).

15 Communications Act 2003 s 264(6). 'The M25 area' means the area the outer boundary of which is represented by the London Orbital Motorway (M25): s 362(1).

789. OFCOM reports: wider review and reporting obligations. When carrying out a review[1] for a period, OFCOM[2] must also carry out a review of the extent to which material included in media services[3] during that period (taken together over the period as a whole) contributed towards the fulfilment of the public service objectives[4]. Every report on the fulfilment of the public service remit[5] must:

(1) include a report on the matters found on the review under these provisions;

(2) specify, and comment on, whatever changes appear to OFCOM to have occurred, during the period to which the report relates, in the extent to which the public service objectives have been fulfilled;

(3) specify, and comment on, whatever changes appear to OFCOM to have occurred, during that period, in the manner in which those objectives are fulfilled; and

(4) set out OFCOM's conclusions on the current state of material included in media services[6].

1 Ie under the Communications Act 2003 s 264: see PARA 788.

2 As to OFCOM see PARA 507.

3 'Media services' means any of the following services that are available to members of the public in all or part of the United Kingdom: (1) television and radio services; (2) on-demand programme services; and (3) other services provided by means of the internet where there is a person who exercises editorial control over the material included in the service: Communications Act 2003 s 264A(5) (s 264A added by the Digital Economy Act 2010 s 2). 'Material' does not include advertisements: Communications Act 2003 s 264A(5) (as so added). The services that are to be taken for the purposes of s 264A to be available to members of the public include any service which: (a) is available for reception by members of the public (within the meaning of s 361 (see PARA 796)); or (b) is available for use by members of the public (within the meaning of s 368R(4): see PARA 784 note 5): s 264A(6) (as so added). As to the meaning of 'on-demand programme service' see PARAS 796 note 6, 784.

4 Communications Act 2003 s 264A(1) (as added: see note 3). 'The public service objectives' are the objectives set out in s 264(6)(b)–(j) (as modified by s 264A(4)): s 264A(3) (as so added). Section 264(6)(b)–(j) (see PARA 788 heads (ii)–(x)) has effect for the purposes of s 264A(3) as if: (1) references to the relevant television services were to media services; and (1) references to programmes were to material included in such services: s 264A(4) (as so added).

5 Ie under the Communications Act 2003 s 264: see PARA 788.

6 Communications Act 2003 s 264A(2) (as added: see note 3).

790. Enforcement. The following provisions apply if OFCOM[1] is of the opinion that the provider of a licensed public service channel[2] or the public teletext provider[3]: (1) has failed to fulfil the public service remit for that channel or the public teletext service; or (2) has failed, in any respect, to make an adequate contribution towards the fulfilment of the purposes of public service television broadcasting in the United Kingdom[4]. However, these provisions do not apply unless: (a) OFCOM is of the opinion that the failure of the provider is serious and is not excused by economic or market conditions; and (b) OFCOM determines that the situation requires the exercise of its powers under these provisions[5].

OFCOM may give directions to the provider to do one or both of the following: (i) to revise the provider's latest statement of programme policy, or statement of service policy, in accordance with the directions; and (ii) to take such steps for remedying the provider's failure as OFCOM may specify in the direction as necessary for that purpose[6]. Such a direction must set out: (A) a reasonable timetable for complying with it; and (B) the factors that will be taken into account by OFCOM in determining whether or not a failure of the provider has been remedied; and whether or not to exercise its powers set out below[7]. If OFCOM is satisfied: (aa) that the provider of a public service channel or the public teletext provider has failed to comply with a direction under these provisions; (bb) that that provider is still failing to fulfil the public service remit for that channel or service or adequately to contribute to the fulfilment of the purposes of public service television broadcasting in the United Kingdom; and (cc) that it would be both reasonable and proportionate to the seriousness of that failure to vary the provider's licence in accordance with this provision[8], OFCOM may, by notice to the provider, vary that licence so as to replace self-regulation with detailed regulation[9]. Before giving a direction under the above provisions to a provider or exercising its power under the above provisions to vary a provider's licence, OFCOM must consult that provider[10].

1   As to OFCOM see PARA 507.
2   As to the meaning of 'licensed public service channel' see PARA 788 note 1.
3   As to the public teletext service see PARA 686.
4   Communications Act 2003 s 270(1). In accordance with s 265(5) (see PARA 682), the reference in s 270(1) to a failure to fulfil the public service remit for the public teletext service includes a failure to fulfil that remit as respects only one of the services comprised in that service: s 270(10). As to the meaning of 'United Kingdom' see PARA 510 note 13.
5   Communications Act 2003 s 270(2). In making a determination under head (b) in the text, OFCOM must have regard, in particular, to: (1) the public service remit of that provider; (2) the statements of programme policy or statements of service policy made (or treated as made) by the provider under s 266 or s 268 (see PARAS 642, 662, 677, 682); (3) the record generally of the provider in relation to the carrying out of obligations imposed by conditions of licences under the Broadcasting Act 1990 and the Broadcasting Act 1996 (including past obligations); (4) the effectiveness and efficiency of the provider in monitoring his own performance; and (5) general economic and market conditions affecting generally the providers of television programme services or the providers of television multiplex services, or both of them: Communications Act 2003 s 270(3). As to the meaning of 'television multiplex service' see PARA 697; definition applied by s 362(1). 'Television programme service' means any of the following: (a) a television broadcasting service; (b) a television licensable content service; (c) a digital television programme service; (d) a restricted television service: s 362(1). As to the meaning of 'television broadcasting service' see PARA 602 note 8; as to the meaning of 'television licensable content service' see PARA 716; as to the meaning of 'digital television programme service' see PARA 602 note 8; and as to the meaning of ' restricted television service' see PARA 602 note 8.
6   Communications Act 2003 s 270(4).
7   Ie its powers under the Communications Act 2003 s 270(6): s 270(5).
8   Ie in accordance with the Communications Act 2003 s 270(6) (see the text and note 9).

9 Communications Act 2003 s 270(6). For the purposes of s 270(6), a variation replacing self-regulation with detailed regulation is a variation which: (1) omits the conditions imposed by virtue of ss 265–269 (see PARAS 642, 662, 677, 682); and (2) replaces those conditions with such specific conditions as OFCOM considers appropriate for securing that the provider: (a) fulfils the public service remit for his service; and (b) makes an adequate contribution towards the fulfilment of the purposes of public service television broadcasting in the United Kingdom: s 270(7). If, at any time following a variation in accordance with s 270(6) of a provider's licence, OFCOM considers that detailed regulation is no longer necessary, it may again vary the licence so as, with effect from such time as it may determine: (i) to provide for the conditions required by virtue of ss 265–269 (see PARAS 642, 662, 677, 682) again to be included in the regulatory regime for the service provided by that provider; and (ii) to remove or modify some or all of the specific conditions inserted under s 270(6): s 270(8).

10 Communications Act 2003 s 270(9).

791. Power to amend. The Secretary of State[1] may by order modify any one or more of the following: (1) the public service remit[2] for any licensed public service channel[3] or for the public teletext service[4]; (2) the purposes of public service television broadcasting in the United Kingdom[5]; (3) the matters to which OFCOM[6] is to have regard[7].

The Secretary of State is not to make an order under these provisions unless OFCOM has made a recommendation for the making of such an order in its most recent report[8] or: (a) the order is made by the Secretary of State less than 12 months after the date on which he has received a report[9]; (b) he has considered that report; and (c) he is satisfied that the making of the order is required, notwithstanding the absence of a recommendation by OFCOM, by circumstances or other matters which are dealt with in that report or which (in his opinion) should have been[10].

Before including a recommendation for the making of an order under these provisions in a report[11], OFCOM must consult: (i) members of the public in the United Kingdom; (ii) such public service broadcasters[12] as it considers are likely to be affected if the Secretary of State gives effect to the recommendation it is proposing to make; and (iii) such of the other persons providing television and radio services as OFCOM considers appropriate[13]. Before making an order, the Secretary of State must consult the persons mentioned below[14] about its terms (even if the order is the one recommended by OFCOM)[15]. Those persons are: (A) OFCOM; (B) such public service broadcasters as OFCOM considers are likely to be affected by the order; and (C) such of the other persons providing television and radio services as the Secretary of State considers appropriate[16].

No order is to be made under these provisions unless a draft of the order has been laid before Parliament and approved by a resolution of each House[17].

1 As to the Secretary of State see PARA 507 note 32.
2 As to the public service remit see PARA 788.
3 As to the meaning of 'licensed public service channel' see PARA 788 note 1.
4 As to the public teletext service see PARA 686.
5 Ie within the meaning given by the Communications Act 2003 s 264(4) (see PARA 788). As to the meaning of 'United Kingdom' see PARA 510 note 13.
6 As to OFCOM see PARA 507.
7 Ie under the Communications Act 2003 s 264(5), (6) (see PARA 788): s 271(1). As to the power of the Secretary of State to make orders under the Communications Act 2003 see s 402; and TELECOMMUNICATIONS vol 97 (2010) PARA 77.
8 Ie under the Communications Act 2003 s 229 (see PARA 666) or s 264 (see PARA 788).
9 Ie under the Communications Act 2003 s 229 (see PARA 666).

10 Communications Act 2003 s 271(2), (3).
11 Ie under the Communications Act 2003 s 229 (see PARA 666) or s 264 (see PARA 788).

12 For the purposes of the Communications Act 2003 s 271, 'public service broadcaster' means any of the persons who are public service broadcasters for the purposes of s 264 (see PARA 788): s 271(8).
13 Communications Act 2003 s 271(4).
14 Ie the persons mentioned in the Communications Act 2003 s 271(6) (see the text and note 16).
15 Communications Act 2003 s 271(5).
16 Communications Act 2003 s 271(6).
17 See the Communications Act 2003 s 271(7).

(ii) Competition Matters and Powers

792. Conditions relating to competition matters. The regulatory regime for every licensed service[1] includes the conditions (if any) that OFCOM[2] considers appropriate for ensuring fair and effective competition in the provision of licensed services or of connected services[3]. Those conditions must include the conditions (if any) that OFCOM considers appropriate for securing that the provider of the service does not: (1) enter into or maintain any arrangements; or (2) engage in any practice, which OFCOM considers, or would consider, to be prejudicial to fair and effective competition in the provision of licensed services or of connected services[4]. A condition imposed under these provisions may require a licence holder to comply with one or both of the following: (a) a code for the time being approved by OFCOM for the purposes of the conditions; and (b) directions given to him by OFCOM for those purposes[5].

1 For the purposes of the Communications Act 2003 s 316, 'licensed service' means a service licensed by a Broadcasting Act licence: Communications Act 2003 s 316(4). As to the meaning of 'Broadcasting Act licence' see PARA 602 note 3.
2 As to OFCOM see PARA 507.
3 Communications Act 2003 s 316(1). 'Connected services', in relation to licensed services, means the provision of programmes for inclusion in licensed services and any other services provided for purposes connected with, or with the provision of, licensed services: s 316(4).
4 Communications Act 2003 s 316(2).
5 Communications Act 2003 s 316(3).

793. Exercise of Broadcasting Act powers for a competition purpose. These provisions[1] apply to the following powers of OFCOM[2] (its 'Broadcasting Act powers'):

(1) its powers under Part 3 of the Communications Act 2003[3] and under the Broadcasting Act 1990 and the Broadcasting Act 1996 to impose or vary the conditions of a Broadcasting Act licence[4];
(2) every power to give an approval for the purposes of provision contained in the conditions of such a licence;
(3) every power to give a direction to a person who is required to comply with it by the conditions of such a licence; and
(4) every power that is exercisable for the purpose of enforcing an obligation imposed by the conditions of such a licence[5].

Before exercising any of its Broadcasting Act powers for a competition purpose[6], OFCOM must consider whether a more appropriate way of proceeding in relation to some or all of the matters in question would be under the Competition Act 1998[7]. If OFCOM decides that a more appropriate way of proceeding in relation to a matter would be under the Competition Act 1998, it is not, to the extent of that decision, to exercise its Broadcasting Act powers in relation to that matter[8]. If OFCOM has decided to exercise any of its Broadcasting Act powers for a competition purpose, it must, on or before doing so, give a notification of its decision[9].

1   Ie the Communications Act 2003 s 317.

2   As to OFCOM see PARA 507.

3   Ie the Communications Act 2003 Pt 3 (ss 198–362).

4   See PARAS 640, 665, 679, 692, 699. As to the meaning of 'Broadcasting Act licence' see PARA
     602 note 3.

5   Communications Act 2003 s 317(1). References in s 317 to the exercise of a power include
     references to an exercise of a power in pursuance of a duty imposed on OFCOM by or under an
     enactment: s 317(12). 'Enactment' includes any enactment comprised in an Act of the Scottish
     Parliament or in any Northern Ireland legislation: s 405(1).

6   For the purposes of the Communications Act 2003 s 317, a power is exercised by OFCOM for
     a competition purpose if the only or main reason for exercising it is to secure that the holder of
     a Broadcasting Act licence does not: (1) enter into or maintain arrangements; or (2) engage in a
     practice, which OFCOM considers, or would consider, to be prejudicial to fair and effective
     competition in the provision of licensed services or of connected services: s 317(9). For the
     purposes of s 317(9), 'connected services' and 'licensed service' each has the same meaning as in
     s 316 (see PARA 792): s 317(11).

7   Communications Act 2003 s 317(2).

8   Communications Act 2003 s 317(3).

9   Communications Act 2003 s 317(4). A notification under s 317(4) must: (1) be given to such
     persons, or published in such manner, as appears to OFCOM to be appropriate for bringing it to
     the attention of the persons who, in OFCOM's opinion, are likely to be affected by its decision;
     and (2) must describe the rights conferred by s 317(6) on the persons affected by that decision:
     s 317(5). A person affected by a decision by OFCOM to exercise any of its Broadcasting Act
     powers for a competition purpose may appeal to the Competition Appeal Tribunal against so
     much of that decision as relates to the exercise of that power for that purpose: s 317(6).
     Sections 192(3)–(8), 195 and 196 (see TELECOMMUNICATIONS vol 97 (2010) PARAS 219,
     221–222) apply in the case of an appeal under s 317(6) as they apply in the case of an appeal
     under s 192(2): s 317(7). The jurisdiction of the Competition Appeal Tribunal on an appeal
     under s 317(6) excludes:
     (a)   whether OFCOM has complied with s 317(2); and
     (b)   whether any of OFCOM's Broadcasting Act powers have been exercised in
            contravention of s 317(3),
     and, accordingly, those decisions by OFCOM on those matters fall to be questioned only in
     proceedings for judicial review: s 317(8). As to the Competition Appeal Tribunal see
     COMPETITION vol 18 (2009) PARAS 13–17. As to judicial review see JUDICIAL REVIEW vol 61
     (2010) PARA 601 et seq.
        Nothing in s 317 applies to: (i) the exercise by OFCOM of any of its powers under
     ss 290–294 or Sch 11 (see PARA 664); (ii) the exercise by it of any power for the purposes of any
     provision of a condition included in a licence in accordance with any of those provisions; (iii)
     the exercise by it of any power for the purpose of enforcing such a condition: s 317(10).

794.   Review of powers exercised for competition purposes. It is the duty of
OFCOM[1], at such intervals as it considers appropriate, to carry out a review of
so much of each of the following as has effect for a competition purpose[2]: (1)
every code made or approved by it under or for the purposes of a broadcasting
provision[3]; (2) the guidance issued by it under or for the purposes of
broadcasting provisions; and (3) every direction given by it under or for the
purposes of a broadcasting provision[4]. Before modifying or revoking, or
withdrawing its approval from, anything which is subject to periodic review
under these provisions, OFCOM must consult such persons as it considers
appropriate[5].

1   As to OFCOM see PARA 507.

2   For the purposes of the Communications Act 2003 s 318, a provision has effect for a
     competition purpose to the extent that its only or main purpose is to secure that the holder of a
     Broadcasting Act licence does not: (1) enter into or maintain arrangements; or (2) engage in a
     practice, which OFCOM considers, or would consider, to be prejudicial to fair and effective
     competition in the provision of licensed services or of connected services: s 318(4).

3   For the purposes of the Communications Act 2003 s 318, 'broadcasting provision' means: (1) a
     provision of the Communications Act 2003 Pt 3 (ss 198–362), of the Broadcasting Act 1990 or

of the Broadcasting Act 1996; or (2) any provision of a Broadcasting Act licence, other than provision contained in any of the Communications Act 2003 ss 290–294 or Sch 11 (see PARA 664): s 318(5).

4   Communications Act 2003 s 318(1).

5   Communications Act 2003 s 318(2). Section 318(2) applies irrespective or whether the modification, revocation or withdrawal is in consequence of a review under s 318: s 318(3).

795. Modification of networking arrangements in consequence of reports under competition legislation. Where the relevant authority[1] makes a relevant order, the order may also provide for the modification of any networking arrangements[2] to such extent as may appear to the relevant authority to be requisite or expedient for the purpose of giving effect to, or taking account of, any provision made by the order[3]. A relevant order is:

(1)   an order under the Enterprise Act 2002 to enforce an undertaking[4] where: (a) one or more than one of the enterprises which have, or may have, ceased to be distinct enterprises was engaged in the provision of programmes[5] for broadcasting[6] in regional Channel 3 services[7]; or (b) one or more than one of the enterprises which will or may cease to be distinct enterprises is engaged in the provision of such programmes[8]; or

(2)   an order under the Enterprise Act 2002 to enforce an undertaking[9] where the feature, or combination of features, of the market in the United Kingdom[10] for goods or services which prevents, restricts or distorts competition relates to the provision of programmes for broadcasting in regional Channel 3 services[11].

1   'Relevant authority' means: (1) in relation to a relevant order falling within the Broadcasting Act 1990 s 193(2)(a) (see head (1) in the text), the Office of Fair Trading, the Competition Commission or (as the case may be) the Secretary of State; (2) in relation to a relevant order falling within s 193(2)(b) (see head (2) in the text), the Office of Fair Trading, the Competition Commission, the Secretary of State or (as the case may be) OFCOM: s 193(2A) (s 193 substituted by the Enterprise Act 2002 ss 86(5), 164(2), Sch 9 Pt 1 para 6; Broadcasting Act 1990 s 193(2A) added by the Communications Act 2003 s 360(3), Sch 15 para 65(1), (3)). As to the Office of Fair Trading see COMPETITION vol 18 (2009) PARAS 6–8. As to the Competition Commission see COMPETITION vol 18 (2009) PARAS 9–12. As to the Secretary of State see PARA 507 note 32. As to OFCOM see PARA 507.

2   'Networking arrangements' means any such arrangements as are mentioned in the Communications Act 2003 s 290(4) (see PARA 664 note 3): Broadcasting Act 1990 s 193(4) (as substituted (see note 1); and amended by the Communications Act 2003 Sch 15 para 65(4)).

3   Broadcasting Act 1990 s 193(1) (as substituted (see note 1); and amended by the Communications Act 2003 Sch 15 para 65(2)).

4   Ie under the Enterprise Act 2002 s 75, s 83, or s 84, or Sch 7 para 5, 10 or 11. The reference to the Enterprise Act 2002 Sch 7 para 5, 10 or 11 is modified to include a reference to the Enterprise Act 2002 (Protection of Legitimate Interests) Order 2003 Sch 2 para 5, 10 or 11, by the Enterprise Act 2002 (Protection of Legitimate Interests) Order 2003 SI 2003/1592, art 16, Sch 4 para 9.

5   As to the meaning of 'programme' see PARA 667 note 7.

6   As to the meaning of 'broadcast' see PARA 668 note 2.

7   'Regional Channel 3 service' has the meaning given by the Broadcasting Act 1990 s 14(6) (see PARA 667 note 6): s 193(4) (as substituted: see note 1).

8   Broadcasting Act 1990 s 193(2)(a) (as substituted: see note 1).

9   Ie under the Enterprise Act 2002 s 160 or s 161.

10   As to the meaning of 'United Kingdom' see PARA 510 note 13.

11   Broadcasting Act 1990 s 193(2)(b) (as substituted: see note 1). Expressions used in s 193(2) and in the Enterprise Act 2002 Pt 3 (ss 22–130) or Pt 4 (ss 131–184) have the same meanings in that provision as in that Part: Broadcasting Act 1990 s 193(3) (as so substituted).

(iii) Excluded Audio-visual Services

796.   Services available for reception by members of the public. The services that are to be taken for the purposes of Part 3 of the Communications Act 2003[1] to be available for reception by members of the public[2] include any service[3] which:

(1) is made available for reception, or is made available for reception in an intelligible form, only to persons who subscribe to the service (whether for a period or in relation to a particular occasion) or who otherwise request its provision[4]; but

(2) is a service the facility of subscribing to which, or of otherwise requesting its provision, is offered or made available to members of the public[5].

However, a service is not to be treated as available for reception by members of the public if it is an on-demand programme service[6].

The Secretary of State[7] may by order modify any of these provisions if it appears to him appropriate to do so having regard to any one or more of the following:

(a) the protection which, taking account of the means by which the programmes and services are received or may be accessed, is expected by members of the public as respects the contents of television programmes or sound programmes;

(b) the extent to which members of the public are able, before television programmes are watched or accessed, to make use of facilities for exercising control, by reference to the contents of the programmes, over what is watched or accessed;

(c) the practicability of applying different levels of regulation in relation to different services;

(d) the financial impact for providers of particular services of any modification of the provisions; and

(e) technological developments that have occurred or are likely to occur[8].

1   Ie the Communications Act 2003 Pt 3 (ss 198–362).
2   References in the Communications Act 2003 s 361 to members of the public are references to members of the public in, or in any area of, any one or more countries or territories (which may or may not include the United Kingdom): s 361(6). As to the meaning of 'United Kingdom' see PARA 510 note 13.
3   Ie subject to the Communications Act 2003 s 361(2) (see the text and note 6): s 361(1).
4   Communications Act 2003 s 361(1)(a).
5   Communications Act 2003 s 361(1)(b).
6   Communications Act 2003 s 361(2) (substituted by SI 2009/2979). 'On-demand programme service' has the meaning given by the Communications Act 2003 s 368A(1) (see PARA 784): s 405(1) (definition added by SI 2009/2979).
7   As to the Secretary of State see PARA 507 note 32.
8   Communications Act 2003 s 361(7). No order is to be made containing provision authorised by s 361(7) unless a draft of the order has been laid before Parliament and approved by a resolution of each House: s 361(8).

(iv) Promotion of Equal Opportunities and Training

797.   Promotion of equal opportunities and training. The regulatory regime for every service to which the following provisions[1] apply[2] includes the conditions that OFCOM[3] considers appropriate for requiring the licence holder to make arrangements for promoting, in relation to employment with the licence holder, equality of opportunity: (1) between men and women; and (2) between persons of different racial groups[4]. That regime includes conditions requiring the licence holder to make arrangements for promoting, in relation to employment with the licence holder, the equalisation of opportunities for disabled persons[5]. The regulatory regime for every service to which these provisions apply includes the conditions that OFCOM considers appropriate for requiring the licence holder to make arrangements for the training and retraining of persons whom he employs, in or in connection with: (a) the provision of the licensed service; or (b) the making of programmes to be included in that service[6].

1   Ie the Communications Act 2003 s 337.
2   The Communications Act 2003 s 337 applies to a service if: (1) it is a service the provision of which is authorised by a Broadcasting Act licence; and (2) the requirements of both s 337(7) and s 337(8) are satisfied in the case of that service: s 337(6). As to the meaning of 'Broadcasting Act licence' see PARA 602 note 3.
      The requirements of s 337(7) are satisfied in the case of a service provided by a person if: (a) that person employs, or is likely to employ, more than the threshold number of individuals in connection with the provision of licensed services; or (b) the threshold number is exceeded by the aggregate number of individuals who are, or are likely to be, employed in that connection by members of a group of companies comprising that person and one or more other bodies corporate: s 337(7). 'The threshold number' means: (i) in relation to individuals, 20; and (ii) in relation to days, 31: s 337(9). 'Licensed service', in relation to an employee or likely employee of a person, means a service the provision of which: (A) by that person; or (B) by a body corporate which is a member of the same group of companies as that person, is authorised by a Broadcasting Act licence: Communications Act 2003 s 337(9). For the purposes of s 337, a person is a member of a group of companies to which a person licensed to provide a service belongs if, and only if, both of them are bodies corporate and either one of them is controlled by the other, or both of them are controlled by the same person: s 337(10). For the purposes of s 337(10), 'controlled' has the same meaning as in the Broadcasting Act 1990 Sch 2 Pt I (see PARA 821 note 11): Communications Act 2003 s 337(11). The Secretary of State may by order amend the definition of 'the threshold number' in s 337(9): s 337(12). No order is to be made containing provision authorised by s 337(12) unless a draft of the order has been laid before Parliament and approved by a resolution of each House: s 337(13). At the date at which this volume states the law, no such order had been made. As to the Secretary of State see PARA 507 note 32. As to the power of the Secretary of State to make orders under the Communications Act 2003 see s 402; and TELECOMMUNICATIONS vol 97 (2010) PARA 77.
      The requirements of s 337(8) are satisfied in the case of a service if the licence authorising the provision of that service authorises either that service or another service authorised by that licence to be provided on a number of days in any year which exceeds the threshold number of days (whether or not the service is in fact provided on those days): s 337(8).
3   As to OFCOM see PARA 507.
4   Communications Act 2003 s 337(1). The Secretary of State may by order amend s 337(1) by adding any other form of equality of opportunity that he considers appropriate: s 337(12). No order is to be made containing provision authorised by s 337(12) unless a draft of the order has been laid before Parliament and approved by a resolution of each House: s 337(13). At the date at which this volume states the law, no such order had been made. 'Racial group' has the same meaning as in the Equality Act 2010: Communications Act 2003 s 337(9) (amended by the Equality Act 2010 Sch 26 para 55). See DISCRIMINATION vol 13 (2007 Reissue) PARA 441. See further note 6.
5   Communications Act 2003 s 337(2). 'Disabled' has the same meaning as in the Equality Act 2010: Communications Act 2003 s 337(9) (amended by the Equality Act 2010 Sch 26 para 55). See DISCRIMINATION vol 13 (2007 Reissue) PARA 511. See further note 6.
6   Communications Act 2003 s 337(3). The conditions imposed by virtue of s 337(1)–(3) must contain provision, in relation to the arrangements made in pursuance of those conditions, requiring the person providing the service in question: (1) to take appropriate steps to make those affected by the arrangements aware of them (including such publication of the arrangements as may be required in accordance with the conditions); (2) from time to time, to review the arrangements; and (3) from time to time (and at least annually) to publish, in such manner as he considers appropriate, his observations on the current operation and effectiveness of the arrangements: s 337(4). The conditions imposed by virtue of s 337 may include provision for treating obligations to make the arrangements mentioned in s 337(1)–(3), or to do anything mentioned in s 337(4), as discharged where a member of a group of companies to which the

licence holder belongs: (a) has made the required arrangements in relation to employment with the licence holder; or (b) has done anything required by s 337(4) in relation to those arrangements: s 337(5).

798. Equal opportunities and training in the BBC. The Executive Board[1] of the BBC must make arrangements for promoting, in relation to the persons mentioned below, equality of opportunity: (1) between men and women; and (2) between people of different racial groups[2]. The persons referred to above are persons employed in connection with providing any of the UK Public Services[3] or making programmes for inclusion in any of those services[4]. The Executive Board must also make arrangements for promoting, in relation to those persons, the equalisation of opportunities for disabled persons[5].

The Executive Board must make arrangements for the training and retraining of BBC staff[6] engaged in connection with providing any of the UK Public Services or making programmes for inclusion in any of those services[7]. The training and retraining provided under the arrangements must make an effective contribution to: (a) the promotion of the BBC's public purposes[8], and in particular that of stimulating creativity and cultural excellence; (b) the preparation and maintenance of a highly-skilled media workforce across the audio-visual industry; and (c) competitiveness and productivity in that industry[9]. The Executive Board must use its best endeavours to work in partnership with others in the audiovisual industry in the planning and provision of training and retraining across that industry[10].

The Executive Board must: (i) take appropriate steps to make those affected by arrangements made under the provisions noted above aware of them; (ii) review those arrangements; and (iii) (at least once each year) make a report to the BBC Trust[11] on the current operation and effectiveness of the arrangements[12]. After the Trust has received such a report from the Executive Board, it must publish its observations on the current operation and effectiveness of the arrangements[13].

1   As to the Executive Board within the constitution of the BBC see PARA 604. As to the meaning of 'BBC' see PARA 603.
2   *Agreement between Her Majesty's Secretary of State for Culture, Media and Sport and the British Broadcasting Corporation* (Cm 6872) (30 June 2006) cl 83(1). 'Racial group' has the same meaning as in the Race Relations Act 1976 or, in Northern Ireland, the Race Relations (Northern Ireland) Order 1997, SI 1997/869 (NI 6): *Agreement between Her Majesty's Secretary of State for Culture, Media and Sport and the British Broadcasting Corporation* (Cm 6872) (30 June 2006) cl 83(5). The Secretary of State may, by a direction to the BBC, amend cl 83(1) by adding any other form of equality of opportunity that the Secretary of State considers appropriate: cl 83(4). As to the Secretary of State see PARA 507 note 32.
3   As to the meaning of 'UK public services' see PARA 855 note 6; and see PARA 615.
4   *Agreement between Her Majesty's Secretary of State for Culture, Media and Sport and the British Broadcasting Corporation* (Cm 6872) (30 June 2006) cl 83(2).
5   *Agreement between Her Majesty's Secretary of State for Culture, Media and Sport and the British Broadcasting Corporation* (Cm 6872) (30 June 2006) cl 83(3). 'Disabled' has the same meaning as in the Disability Discrimination Act 1995: *Agreement between Her Majesty's Secretary of State for Culture, Media and Sport and the British Broadcasting Corporation* (Cm 6872) (30 June 2006) cl 83(5).
6   As to BBC staff see PARA 612.
7   *Agreement between Her Majesty's Secretary of State for Culture, Media and Sport and the British Broadcasting Corporation* (Cm 6872) (30 June 2006) cl 84(1).
8   As to the meaning of 'public purposes' see PARA 603 note 3.
9   *Agreement between Her Majesty's Secretary of State for Culture, Media and Sport and the British Broadcasting Corporation* (Cm 6872) (30 June 2006) cl 84(2).
10   *Agreement between Her Majesty's Secretary of State for Culture, Media and Sport and the British Broadcasting Corporation* (Cm 6872) (30 June 2006) cl 84(3).

11 As to the BBC Trust within the constitution of the BBC see PARA 604.
12 *Agreement between Her Majesty's Secretary of State for Culture, Media and Sport and the British Broadcasting Corporation* (Cm 6872) (30 June 2006) cl 85(1).
13 *Agreement between Her Majesty's Secretary of State for Culture, Media and Sport and the British Broadcasting Corporation* (Cm 6872) (30 June 2006) cl 85(2).

799. Promotion of employment in broadcasting. Among the duties of OFCOM[1] is the duty to take all such steps as it considers appropriate for promoting the development of opportunities for the training and retraining of persons: (1) for employment by persons providing television and radio services[2]; and (2) for work in connection with the provision of such services otherwise than as an employee[3]. It is the duty of OFCOM to take all such steps as it considers appropriate for promoting equality of opportunity in relation to both employment by those providing television and radio services and the training and retraining of persons for such employment[4]. It is also the duty of OFCOM, in relation to such employment, training and retraining, to take all such steps as it considers appropriate for promoting the equalisation of opportunities for disabled persons[5].

1 As to OFCOM see PARA 507.
2 As to the provision of television and radio services see PARA 504 et seq.
3 See the Communications Act 2003 s 27(1); and TELECOMMUNICATIONS vol 97 (2010) PARA 35.
4 See the Communications Act 2003 s 27(2); and TELECOMMUNICATIONS vol 97 (2010) PARA 35. As to the promotion of equal opportunities and training in public service television see PARA 797.
5 See the Communications Act 2003 s 27(3); and TELECOMMUNICATIONS vol 97 (2010) PARA 35.

(v) The Gaelic Media Service

800. Financing of programmes in Gaelic out of Gaelic Broadcasting Fund. The Secretary of State[1] must, each financial year[2], pay to OFCOM[3] such amount as he may, with the approval of the Treasury[4], determine to be appropriate for the purposes of financing programmes in Gaelic[5]. Any amount so received by OFCOM must be carried by it to the credit of a fund[6], known as the Gaelic Broadcasting Fund[7]. The fund is under the management of a body established for these purposes[8], formerly called Comataidh Craolaidh Gaidhlig or the Gaelic Broadcasting Committee, which has been renamed Seirbheis nam Meadhanan Gàidhlig (the Gaelic Media Service)[9].

The functions of the Service[10] are to secure that a wide and diverse range of high quality programmes[11] in Gaelic are broadcast[12] or otherwise transmitted so as to be available to persons in Scotland[13]. The Service may, for any of the purposes of carrying out its functions or for any purpose connected with the carrying out of those functions, make grants out of the fund or otherwise apply it[14]. In carrying out its functions, the Service may finance, or engage in, any of the following:

(1) the making of programmes in Gaelic with a view to those programmes being broadcast or otherwise transmitted so as to be available to persons in Scotland;

(2) the provision of training for persons employed, or to be employed, in connection with the making of programmes in Gaelic to be so broadcast or otherwise transmitted;

(3) research into the types of programmes in Gaelic that members of the Gaelic-speaking community would like to be broadcast or otherwise transmitted[15].

The Service is not, however, entitled, for the purpose of carrying out its functions, to provide[16]:

(a)   a Channel 3 service[17];

(b)   Channel 4[18];

(c)   Channel 5[19];

(d)   a national sound broadcasting service[20];

(e)   a national digital sound programme service[21]; or

(f)   a television multiplex service[22] or a radio multiplex service[23].

1   As to the Secretary of State see PARA 507 note 32. Functions under the Broadcasting Act 1990 s 183 are transferred, in so far as they are exercisable in or as regards Scotland, to the Scottish Ministers, by the Scotland Act 1998 (Transfer of Functions to the Scottish Ministers etc) Order 1999, SI 1999/1750, art 2, Sch 1.

2   As to the meaning of 'financial year' see PARA 635 note 2. This provision applies to each financial year from the year beginning 1 April 1992: see the Broadcasting Act 1990 s 183(1)(b). As to the position for the financial year beginning 1 April 1991 see s 183(1)(a).

3   As to OFCOM see PARA 507.

4   As to the Treasury see CONSTITUTIONAL LAW AND HUMAN RIGHTS vol 8(2) (Reissue) PARAS 512–517.

5   See the Broadcasting Act 1990 s 183(1) (amended by the Communications Act 2003 s 360(3), Sch 15 para 62(1), (2)). 'Gaelic' means the Gaelic language as spoken in Scotland: Broadcasting Act 1990 s 183(9) (substituted by the Communications Act 2003 s 208(4)). Any sums required by the Secretary of State under the Broadcasting Act 1990 s 183(1) must be paid out of money provided by Parliament: s 183(8).

6   Ie the fund established by the Independent Television Commission ('ITC'). As to the ITC see PARA 507.

7   Broadcasting Act 1990 s 183(2) (amended by the Broadcasting Act 1996 s 95(1), (2); and the Communications Act 2003 Sch 15 para 62(2), (3)). Any such amount must accordingly not be regarded as forming part of the revenues of OFCOM: Broadcasting Act 1990 s 183(2) (as so amended).

8   Broadcasting Act 1990 s 183(3) (amended by the Communications Act 2003 s 406(7), Sch 19).

9   See the Communications Act 2003 s 208(1). References in any instrument or other document to Comataidh Craolaidh Gaidhlig or to the Gaelic Broadcasting Committee are to be construed accordingly: s 208(2). As to Seirbheis nam Meadhanan Gàidhlig (the Gaelic Media Service) see PARAS 801–807.

10 'The Service' means the body established under the Broadcasting Act 1990 s 183(3) and known as Seirbheis nam Meadhanan Gàidhlig (the Gaelic Media Service): s 183(9) (as substituted: see note 5).

11 'Programme' includes any item included in a programme service: Broadcasting Act 1990 s 183(9) (as substituted: see note 5). As to the meaning of 'programme service' see PARA 507 note 11.

12 As to the meaning of 'broadcast' see PARA 668 note 2.

13 Broadcasting Act 1990 s 183(3B) (added by the Communications Act 2003 s 208(3)). A reference to being available to persons in Scotland includes a reference to being available both to persons in Scotland and to others: Broadcasting Act 1990 s 183(9) (as substituted: see note 5).

14 Broadcasting Act 1990 s 183(4) (substituted by the Communications Act 2003 s 208(3)). When making any grant out of the fund in pursuance of the Broadcasting Act 1990 s 183(4), the Service may impose such conditions as it thinks fit, including conditions requiring the grant to be repaid in specified circumstances: see s 183(5).

15 Broadcasting Act 1990 s 183(4A) (added by the Communications Act 2003 s 208(3)).

16 Broadcasting Act 1990 s 183(4B) (added by the Communications Act 2003 s 208(3)).

17 Broadcasting Act 1990 s 183(4B)(a) (as added: see note 16). 'Channel 3 service' has the same meaning as in Pt I (ss 3–71) (see PARA 667): s 183(9) (as substituted: see note 5).

18 Broadcasting Act 1990 s 183(4B)(b) (as added: see note 16). 'Channel 4' has the same meaning as in Pt I (see PARA 637): s 183(9) (as substituted: see note 5).

19 Broadcasting Act 1990 s 183(4B)(c) (as added: see note 16). 'Channel 5 ' has the same meaning as in Pt I (see PARA 681): s 183(9) (as substituted: see note 5).

20 Broadcasting Act 1990 s 183(4B)(d) (as added: see note 16). 'National sound broadcasting service' means a sound broadcasting service within the meaning of Pt III (ss 85–126) which, under the Communications Act 2003 s 245(4)(a) is a national service for the purposes of that provision (see PARA 723): Broadcasting Act 1990 s 183(9) (as substituted: see note 5).

21 Broadcasting Act 1990 s 183(4B)(e) (as added: see note 16). 'National digital sound programme service' has the same meaning as in the Broadcasting Act 1996 Pt II (ss 40–72) (see PARA 756 note 16): Broadcasting Act 1990 s 183(9) (as substituted: see note 5).

22 'Television multiplex service' has the meaning given by the Communications Act 2003 s 241(1) to a multiplex service within the meaning of the Broadcasting Act 1996 Pt I (ss 1–39) (see PARA 697): Broadcasting Act 1990 s 183(9) (as substituted: see note 5).

23 Broadcasting Act 1990 s 183(4B)(f) (as added: see note 16). 'Radio multiplex service' has the same meaning as in the Broadcasting Act 1996 Pt II (see PARA 727 note 10): Broadcasting Act 1990 s 183(9) (as substituted: see note 5).

801. Membership of Gaelic Media Service. The Gaelic Media Service is to consist of not more than 12 members[1], who are to be appointed by OFCOM[2]. OFCOM must appoint one of the members to be the chairman of the Service[3]. The approval of the Secretary of State[4] is required for the appointment of a person as a member of the Service, and for the appointment of a member as their chairman[5].

The members of the Service must include:

(1)   a member nominated by the BBC[6];

(2)   a member nominated by Highlands and Islands Enterprise; and

(3)   a member nominated by Bòrd na Gàidhlig[7] (the Gaelic Board)[8].

When appointing members of the Service, OFCOM must have regard to the desirability of having members of the Service who are proficient in written and spoken Gaelic[9], and to any guidance issued by the Secretary of State for the purposes of these provisions[10].

OFCOM must secure, so far as practicable, that the membership of the Service is such that the interests of each of the following are adequately represented:

(a)   the holders of licences to provide regional Channel 3 services[11] for areas wholly in Scotland;

(b)   the holders of licences to provide regional Channel 3 services in respect of which determinations as to such services to be provided for an area the greater part of which is in Scotland[12] are for the time being in force;

(c)   the independent television and radio production industries in Scotland;

(d)   other persons and bodies concerned with the promotion and use of the Gaelic language, including those concerned with education in Gaelic and in Gaelic culture[13].

Each member of the Service must hold and vacate office in accordance with the terms of his appointment[14]. A person is not to be appointed as a member of the Service for a term of more than four years (but a person so appointed is eligible for re-appointment at the end of his term of office)[15]. Any member of the Service may at any time resign his office by notice to OFCOM[16]. OFCOM may pay to each member such remuneration and allowances as it may determine[17].

1   Broadcasting Act 1990 s 183A(1) (s 183A added by the Communications Act 2003 s 209). As to the establishment of the Service see PARA 800.

2   Broadcasting Act 1990 s 183A(2) (as added: see note 1). As to OFCOM see PARA 507. The Broadcasting Act 1990 Sch 19 has effect with respect to the Service: s 183A(8) (as so added).

3   Broadcasting Act 1990 s 183A(3) (as added: see note 1).

4   As to the Secretary of State see PARA 507 note 32.

5   Broadcasting Act 1990 s 183A(4) (as added: see note 1).

6   As to the meaning of 'BBC' see PARA 603 note 1; and as to the BBC see PARAS 603–626.

7   'Bòrd na Gàidhlig' means the body of that name established by the Gaelic Language (Scotland) Act 2005 s 1: Broadcasting Act 1990 s 183A(9) (as added (see note 1); and amended by SI 2006/241).

8   Broadcasting Act 1990 s 183A(5) (as added: see note 1).

9   As to the meaning of 'Gaelic' see PARA 800 note 5.

10 Broadcasting Act 1990 s 183A(6) (as added: see note 1).

11 'Regional Channel 3 service' has the same meaning as in the Broadcasting Act 1990 Pt I (ss 3–71) (see PARA 667 note 6): s 183A(9) (as added: see note 1).

12 Ie under the Broadcasting Act 1990 s 184(4)(b): see PARA 808.

13 Broadcasting Act 1990 s 183A(7) (as added: see note 1).

14 Broadcasting Act 1990 Sch 19 para 2(1) (amended by the Communications Act 2003 ss 210(1), (2)(a), 360(3), Sch 15 para 73(1), (3)).

15 Broadcasting Act 1990 Sch 19 para 2(1A) (added by the Communications Act 2003 s 210(2)(b)).

16 Broadcasting Act 1990 Sch 19 para 2(2) (amended by the Communications Act 2003 Sch 15 para 73(2), (3)).

17 Broadcasting Act 1990 Sch 19 para 2(3) (amended by the Communications Act 2003 Sch 15 para 73(2)).

802.   Status and capacity of the Gaelic Media Service.   The Gaelic Media Service[1] is a body corporate[2]. The Service is not to be treated for the purposes of the enactments and rules of law relating to the privileges of the Crown as a body exercising functions on behalf of the Crown[3]. It is within the capacity of the Service as a statutory corporation[4] to do such things and enter into such transactions as are incidental or conducive to the discharge of its functions[5].

1   As to the establishment of the Gaelic Media Service see the Broadcasting Act 1990 s 183(3); and PARA 800.

2   Broadcasting Act 1990 s 183A(8), Sch 19 para 1(1) (s 183A added by the Communications Act 2003 s 209; Broadcasting Act 1990 Sch 19 para 1(1) amended by the Communications Act 2003 s 360(3), Sch 15 para 73(1), (3)).

3   Broadcasting Act 1990 Sch 19 para 1(2) (amended by the Communications Act 2003 Sch 15 para 73(3)).

4   As to statutory corporations see CORPORATIONS vol 24 (2010) PARA 424.

5   Broadcasting Act 1990 Sch 19 para 1(3) (amended by the Communications Act 2003 Sch 15 para 73(3)). The functions referred to are those of the Service under the Broadcasting Act 1990 s 183 (see PARA 800).

803.   Proceedings of the Gaelic Media Service.   The quorum of the Gaelic Media Service[1] and the arrangements relating to its meetings are such as the Service may determine[2]. The arrangements may, with the approval of OFCOM[3], provide for the discharge, under the general direction of the Service, of any of the Service's functions by a committee or by one or more of the members or employees of the Service[4].

A member who is in any way directly or indirectly interested in any matter that is brought up for consideration at a meeting[5] of the Service must disclose the nature of his interest to the meeting, and, where such a disclosure is made[6]:

(1)   the disclosure must be recorded in the minutes of the meeting[7]; and

(2)   the member must not take any part in any deliberation or decision of the Service, or of any of its committees, with respect to that matter[8].

For these purposes, a general notification given at a meeting of the Service by a member to the effect that he is a member of a specified company or firm and is to be regarded as interested in any matter involving that company or firm is to be regarded as a sufficient disclosure of his interest in relation to any such matter[9]. A member need not attend in person at a meeting of the Service in order to make such a disclosure if he takes reasonable steps to secure that the disclosure is made by a notice which is taken into consideration and read at the meeting[10].

The validity of any proceedings of the Service is not affected by any vacancy among the members or by any defect in the appointment of a member or by any failure to comply with the above requirements[11].

1   As to the establishment of the Gaelic Media Service see the Broadcasting Act 1990 s 183(3); and PARA 800.
2   Broadcasting Act 1990 s 183A(8), Sch 19 para 4(1) (s 183A added by the Communications Act 2003 s 209; Broadcasting Act 1990 Sch 19 para 4(1) amended by the Communications Act 2003 s 360(3), Sch 15 para 73(1), (3)).
3   As to OFCOM see PARA 507.
4   Broadcasting Act 1990 Sch 19 para 4(2) (amended by the Communications Act 2003 Sch 15 para 73(2), (3)).
5   References to a meeting of the Service include references to a meeting of any of its committees: Broadcasting Act 1990 Sch 19 para 5(5) (amended by the Communications Act 2003 Sch 15 para 73(3)).
6   Broadcasting Act 1990 Sch 19 para 5(1) (amended by the Communications Act 2003 Sch 15 para 73(3)).
7   Broadcasting Act 1990 Sch 19 para 5(1)(a) (as amended: see note 6).
8   Broadcasting Act 1990 Sch 19 para 5(1)(b) (as amended: see note 6). This provision does not apply in relation to any meeting of the Service at which all of the other members present resolve that the member's interest is to be disregarded for those purposes: Sch 19 para 5(2) (amended by the Communications Act 2003 Sch 15 para 73(3)).
9   Broadcasting Act 1990 Sch 19 para 5(3) (amended by the Communications Act 2003 Sch 15 para 73(3)).
10   Broadcasting Act 1990 Sch 19 para 5(4) (amended by the Communications Act 2003 Sch 15 para 73(3)).
11   Broadcasting Act 1990 Sch 19 para 6 (amended by the Communications Act 2003 Sch 15 para 73(3)). As to membership of the Service see PARA 801.

804. Employees of the Gaelic Media Service. The Gaelic Media Service[1] may appoint such employees as it may determine with the consent of OFCOM[2] as to numbers and terms of employment[3]. If the Service determines to do so in the case of any of its employees, the Service must pay to or in respect of those employees such pensions, allowances or gratuities[4], or provide and maintain for them such pension schemes[5] (whether contributory or not), as the Service may determine[6]. A person who is an employee of the Service is not to be eligible to be appointed as a member of the Service[7].

1   As to the establishment of the Gaelic Media Service see the Broadcasting Act 1990 s 183(3); and PARA 800.
2   As to OFCOM see PARA 507.
3   Broadcasting Act 1990 s 183A(8), Sch 19 para 7(1) (s 183A added by the Communications Act 2003 s 209; Broadcasting Act 1990 Sch 19 para 7(1) amended by the Communications Act 2003 s 360(3), Sch 15 para 73(1)–(3)).
4   As to pensions, allowances or gratuities see PARA 631 note 7.
5   As to the meaning of 'pension scheme' see PARA 633 note 4.
6   Broadcasting Act 1990 Sch 19 para 7(2) (amended by the Communications Act 2003 Sch 15 para 73(3)). The Employers' Liability (Compulsory Insurance) Act 1969 (see EMPLOYMENT vol 39 (2009) PARA 40 et seq) does not require insurance to be effected by the Service: Broadcasting Act 1990 Sch 19 para 7(3) (amended by the Communications Act 2003 Sch 15 para 73(3)).
7   Broadcasting Act 1990 Sch 19 para 7(4) (added by the Communications Act 2003 s 210(1), (3)).

805. Financial provision. There must be defrayed out of the Gaelic Broadcasting Fund[1]:

(1)   certain expenses incurred by OFCOM[2];
(2)   any expenses incurred by the Gaelic Media Service[3]; and
(3)   with the approval of OFCOM, any other expenses incurred by the Service[4].

The Service must pay all its receipts to OFCOM[5]. OFCOM must hold amounts so received by it to the credit of the Gaelic Broadcasting Fund (and, accordingly, those amounts are not to be regarded as forming part of OFCOM's revenues)[6].

1   Broadcasting Act 1990 s 183A(8), Sch 19 para 8 (s 183A added by the Communications Act 2003 s 209; Broadcasting Act 1990 Sch 19 para 8 amended by the Broadcasting Act 1996 s 148(1), Sch 10 para 26(a)). The Gaelic Broadcasting Fund is the fund established under the Broadcasting Act 1990 s 183 (see PARA 800).
2   Broadcasting Act 1990 Sch 19 para 8(a) (amended by the Communications Act 2003 s 360(3), Sch 15 para 73(1), (2)). This provision applies to expenses incurred by OFCOM:
    (1)   by virtue of the Broadcasting Act 1990 Sch 19 para 2 (see PARA 801) (Sch 19 para 8(a)(i));
    (2)   in paying the salaries of any employees of OFCOM whose services have been furnished to the Service by OFCOM (Sch 19 para 8(a)(ii) (amended by the Communications Act 2003 Sch 15 para 73(2), (3)); or
    (3)   in connection with providing the Service with office accommodation or other facilities (Broadcasting Act 1990 Sch 19 para 8(a)(iii) (amended by the Communications Act 2003 Sch 15 para 73(3))).
    As to OFCOM see PARA 507. As to the establishment of the Gaelic Media Service see the Broadcasting Act 1990 s 183(3); and PARA 800.
3   Broadcasting Act 1990 Sch 19 para 8(b) (amended by the Communications Act 2003 Sch 15 para 73(3)). Expenses are incurred by the Service by virtue of the Broadcasting Act 1990 Sch 19 para 7 (see PARA 804).
4   Broadcasting Act 1990 Sch 19 para 8(c) (amended by the Communications Act 2003 Sch 15 para 73(2), (4)).
5   Broadcasting Act 1990 Sch 19 para 8A(1) (Sch 19 para 8A added by the Communications Act 2003 s 210(1), (4)).
6   Broadcasting Act 1990 Sch 19 para 8A(2) (as added: see note 5).

806. Authentication. The application of the seal of the Gaelic Media Service[1] must be authenticated by the signature of the chairman or of some other person authorised for the purpose[2]. Any document purporting to be an instrument issued by the Service and to be duly executed under the seal of the Service or to be signed on behalf of the Service must be received in evidence and is deemed to be such an instrument unless the contrary is shown[3].

1   As to the establishment of the Gaelic Media Service see the Broadcasting Act 1990 s 183(3); and PARA 800.
2   Broadcasting Act 1990 s 183A(8), Sch 19 para 9 (s 183A added by the Communications Act 2003 s 209; Broadcasting Act 1990 Sch 19 para 9 amended by the Communications Act 2003 s 360(3), Sch 15 para 73(1), (3)). As to the chairman see PARA 801.
3   Broadcasting Act 1990 Sch 19 para 10 (amended by the Communications Act 2003 Sch 15 para 73(3)).

807. Accounts, audit and annual reports of the Gaelic Media Service. The Gaelic Media Service[1] must keep proper accounts and proper records in relation to the accounts, and must prepare in respect of each financial year[2] a statement of accounts in such form as OFCOM[3] may direct[4]. The accounts of the Service must be audited by auditors appointed by the Service with the approval of OFCOM[5]. The Service must at all reasonable times, upon demand made by OFCOM or by any persons authorised by OFCOM in that behalf[6], afford to them full liberty to examine the accounts of the Service[7], and furnish them with all forecasts, estimates, information and documents which they may require with respect to the financial transactions and commitments of the Service[8].

As soon as possible after the end of each financial year, the Service must prepare a general report of its proceedings during that year and transmit it to OFCOM[10]. The report must include a statement of how the Service is proposing to carry out its functions during the next financial year[11]. The report must have attached to it the statement of accounts for the year and a copy of any report made by the auditors on that statement[12]. OFCOM must send a copy of each annual report so received by it to the Secretary of State[13], who must lay copies of it before each House of Parliament[14]. Where an annual report is sent by

OFCOM to the Scottish Ministers[15], the Scottish Ministers must lay a copy of the report before the Scottish Parliament[16].

1 As to the establishment of the Gaelic Media Service see the Broadcasting Act 1990 s 183(3); and PARA 800.
2 'Financial year' means a financial year of the Gaelic Media Service: see the Broadcasting Act 1990 s 202(1), (2) (s 202(2) amended by the Broadcasting Act 1996 s 148(2), Sch 11 Pt I; and the Communications Act 2003 s 406(7), Sch 19).
3 As to OFCOM see PARA 507.
4 Broadcasting Act 1990 s 183A(8), Sch 19 para 11(1) (s 183A added by the Communications Act 2003 s 209; Broadcasting Act 1990 Sch 19 para 11(1) amended by the Communications Act 2003 s 360(3), Sch 15 para 73(1)–(3)).
5 Broadcasting Act 1990 Sch 19 para 11(2) (amended by the Communications Act 2003 s 360(3), Sch 15 para 73(1)–(3)). A person is not qualified to be appointed as an auditor unless he is eligible for appointment as a statutory auditor under the Companies Act 2006 Pt 42 (ss 1209–1264) (see COMPANIES vol 15 (2009) PARA 969): Broadcasting Act 1990 Sch 19 para 11(3) (substituted by SI 1991/1997; and amended by SI 2008/948).
6 Broadcasting Act 1990 Sch 19 para 11(4) (amended by the Communications Act 2003 ss 360(3), 406(7), Sch 15 para 73(2), (3), (5), Sch 19).
7 Broadcasting Act 1990 Sch 19 para 11(4)(a) (amended by the Communications Act 2003 Sch 15 para 73(3)).
8 Broadcasting Act 1990 Sch 19 para 11(4)(b) (amended by the Communications Act 2003 Sch 15 para 73(3)).
10 Broadcasting Act 1990 Sch 19 para 12(1) (amended by the Communications Act 2003 Sch 15 para 73(2), (3)).
11 Broadcasting Act 1990 Sch 19 para 12(1A) (added by the Communications Act 2003 s 210(1), (5)).
12 Broadcasting Act 1990 Sch 19 para 12(2).
13 As to the Secretary of State see PARA 507 note 32. Functions under the Broadcasting Act 1990 Sch 19 para 12(3) which were exercisable by the Secretary of State are, in so far as they are exercisable in or as regards Scotland, exercisable by the Scottish Ministers acting concurrently with the Secretary of State: Scotland Act 1998 (Transfer of Functions to the Scottish Ministers etc) Order 1999, SI 1999/1750, art 3, Sch 2. By virtue of the Scotland Act 1998 (Modification of Functions) Order 1999, SI 1999/1756, art 2, Schedule para 12(1), the Secretary of State's functions under the Broadcasting Act 1990 Sch 19 para 12(3) are to be treated as exercisable in or as regards Scotland and may be exercised separately by the Scottish Ministers.
14 Broadcasting Act 1990 Sch 19 para 12(3) (amended by the Communications Act 2003 Sch 15 para 73(2)).
15 Ie under the Broadcasting Act 1990 Sch 19 para 12(3) by virtue of provision made under the Scotland Act 1998 s 63.
16 Broadcasting Act 1990 Sch 19 para 12(4) (added by SI 1999/1750; and amended by the Communications Act 2003 Sch 15 para 73(2)).

808.   Broadcasting of programmes in Gaelic on Channel 3 in Scotland.   The procedure to be followed by OFCOM[1] in connection with the consideration of applications for licences[2] has effect in relation to the broadcasting of programmes in Gaelic[3] on Channel 3 in Scotland[4] as if the following requirements were included among those specified with regard to that procedure[5], namely:

(1)   that a suitable proportion of the programmes included in the service are programmes in Gaelic other than funded Gaelic productions[6];

(2)   that the service includes funded Gaelic productions[7] of which: (a) a suitable proportion are of high quality[8]; and (b) a suitable proportion are shown at peak viewing times[9]; and

(3)   that (taking the programmes included in the service in accordance with heads (1) and (2) above as a whole) the service includes a wide range of programmes in Gaelic[10].

1 As to OFCOM see PARA 507.

2 Ie as set out in the Broadcasting Act 1990 s 16 (see PARA 670): see s 184(1). For these purposes, 'licence' means a licence under Pt I (ss 3–71); definition applied by s 184(5).

3 As to the meaning of 'broadcast' see PARA 668 note 2; and as to the meaning of 'programme' see PARA 667 note 7. As to the meaning of 'Gaelic' see PARA 800 note 5; definition applied by the Broadcasting Act 1990 s 184(5).

4 The Broadcasting Act 1990 s 184 applies: (1) to any regional Channel 3 service that is to be provided for an area the whole of which is in Scotland; and (2) if OFCOM determines that it is to apply, to any regional Channel 3 service that is to be provided for an area the greater part of which is in Scotland: s 184(4) (amended by the Communications Act 2003 s 360(3), Sch 15 para 63(1), (5)). As to the meaning of 'regional Channel 3 service' see PARA 667 note 6; definition applied by the Broadcasting Act 1990 s 184(5). As from a day to be appointed, s 184 is repealed by the Digital Economy Act 2010 ss 29(1), 45, Sch 2; at the date at which this volume states the law, no such day had been appointed.

5 Broadcasting Act 1990 s 184(1). The requirements are those specified in s 16(1)(a) (see PARA 670): see s 184(1) (amended by the Communications Act 2003 s 360(3), Sch 15 para 63(1), (2)).

6 Broadcasting Act 1990 s 184(1)(a). 'Funded Gaelic productions' means programmes in Gaelic the making of which has been wholly or partly financed out of grants made in pursuance of s 183(4) (see PARA 800) to the person providing the service: s 184(2). As to the meaning of 'person' see PARA 510 note 1.

7 Broadcasting Act 1990 s 184(1)(b).

8 Broadcasting Act 1990 s 184(1)(b)(i).

9 Broadcasting Act 1990 s 184(1)(b)(ii).

10 Broadcasting Act 1990 s 184(1)(c). The regulatory regime for a service to which s 184 applies includes the conditions that OFCOM considers appropriate for securing that the requirements specified in s 184(1)(a)–(c) (see heads (1) to (3) in the text) are complied with in relation to the service: s 184(3) (amended by the Communications Act 2003 Sch 15 para 63(3)). The Communications Act 2003 s 263 (regulatory regime: see PARA 602) applies in relation to conditions included by virtue of the Broadcasting Act 1990 s 184(3) in the regulatory regime for a licensed service as it applies in relation to conditions which are so included by virtue of a provision of the Communications Act 2003 Pt 3 Ch 4 (ss 263–347): Broadcasting Act 1990 s 184(3A) (added by the Communications Act 2003 Sch 15 para 63(5)).

809. Digital broadcasting of Gaelic programmes. The Secretary of State[1] may by order provide for OFCOM[2] to include in no more than one relevant multiplex licence[3] such conditions relating to the broadcasting[4] of programmes[5] in Gaelic[6] for reception wholly or mainly in Scotland as may be specified in, or determined by it under, the order[7]. The Secretary of State may by order require the holder of a multiplex licence ('the holder'), in complying with any such conditions, to broadcast programmes in Gaelic supplied by each of the suppliers[8] amounting to such minimum number of hours (if any) of transmission time per year as may be specified in the order in relation to that supplier[9].

For the purpose of enabling the holder to comply with any such conditions and any obligation imposed[10], it is the duty of each supplier to provide the holder, free of charge, with such programmes in Gaelic which have been broadcast by the supplier as the holder may request[11]. This does not apply in relation to any programme first broadcast by the supplier concerned: (1) before 1 January 1993[12]; or (2) in the period beginning on 1 January 1993 and ending on 31 March 1997, if the supplier has no right to broadcast it again or has such a right but is not entitled to transfer it to the holder[13].

The holder must consult Seirbheis nam Meadhanan Gàidhlig[14] and the suppliers about the quantity of programmes likely to be requested by the holder from each supplier, and the schedules proposed for the broadcast by the holder of programmes supplied, and the holder must have regard to any comments made as a result of such consultation[15].

1 As to the Secretary of State see PARA 507 note 32.

2 As to OFCOM see PARA 507.

3   'Relevant multiplex licence' means a multiplex licence in respect of which the Secretary of State has made an order under the Communications Act 2003 s 243(3) (see PARA 697): Broadcasting Act 1996 s 32(9) (substituted by the Communications Act 2003 s 360(3), Sch 15 para 97(1), (4)). As to the meaning of 'multiplex licence' see PARA 690.

4   As to the meaning of 'broadcast' see PARA 668 note 2; definition applied by the Broadcasting Act 1996 s 147(2).

5   As to the meaning of 'programme' see PARA 667 note 7; definition applied by the Broadcasting Act 1996 s 147(2).

6   'Gaelic' means the Gaelic language as spoken in Scotland: Broadcasting Act 1996 s 32(9) (as substituted: see note 3).

7   Broadcasting Act 1996 s 32(1) (amended by the Communications Act 2003 Sch 15 para 97(2)). Any order under the Broadcasting Act 1996 s 32 is subject to annulment in pursuance of a resolution of either House of Parliament: s 32(8).

In exercise of this power the Secretary of State has made the Multiplex Licence (Broadcasting of Programmes in Gaelic) Order 1996, SI 1996/2758, and the Multiplex Licence (Broadcasting of Programmes in Gaelic) Order 2008, SI 2008/1421. OFCOM must secure that there continues to be included in the Multiplex A licence a condition requiring the holder of the licence, when broadcasting programmes for reception wholly or mainly in Scotland, to broadcast programmes in Gaelic for at least 30 minutes per day between 6 00 pm and 10 30 pm: see the Multiplex Licence (Broadcasting of Programmes in Gaelic) Order 1996, SI 1996/2758, art 2(1) (art 2 substituted by SI 2008/1421). 'The Multiplex A licence' means the licence granted under the Broadcasting Act 1996 Pt I (ss 1–39) by the Independent Television Commission on 26 May 1998 authorising the provision of the television multiplex service known as 'Multiplex A', which on 9 June 2008 was held by SDN Limited (and which is a multiplex licence in respect of which the Secretary of State has made an order under the Communications Act 2003 s 243(3)): Multiplex Licence (Broadcasting of Programmes in Gaelic) Order 1996, SI 1996/2758, art 2(2) (as so substituted). In complying with the condition specified in art 2, the holder of the licence must broadcast programmes in Gaelic supplied by each of the persons mentioned in the Broadcasting Act 1996 s 32(4)(a), (c) (see note 8) amounting to at least 30 hours of transmission time per year in relation to each such person: Multiplex Licence (Broadcasting of Programmes in Gaelic) Order 1996, SI 1996/2758, art 3. As to the meaning of 'Channel 5' see PARA 681; applied by the Broadcasting Act 1996 s 39(1). As to the meaning of 'S4C Digital' see PARA 644 note 7; definition applied by s 39(1) (amended by the Communications Act 2003 s 360(3), Sch 15 para 100).

8   The suppliers are:
    (1)   the BBC (Broadcasting Act 1996 s 32(4)(a));
    (2)   the Channel 4 Television Corporation (s 32(4)(b));
    (3)   any holder of a Channel 3 licence to provide a regional Channel 3 service (within the meaning of the Broadcasting Act 1990 Pt I (ss 3–71): see PARA 667 note 6) for reception wholly in Scotland (Broadcasting Act 1996 s 32(4)(c)); and
    (4)   such other persons providing television broadcasting services as may be specified by order by the Secretary of State (s 32(4)(d)).
As to the meaning of 'BBC' see PARA 603 note 1. As to the BBC see PARAS 603–626. As to the Channel 4 Television Corporation see PARA 627. As to the meaning of 'Channel 3' see PARA 667; definition applied by s 147(2). As to the meaning of 'Channel 3 licence' see PARA 669 note 2; definition applied by s 39(1). 'Television broadcasting service' has the same meaning as in the Communications Act 2003 Pt 3 (ss 198–362) (see PARA 602 note 8): Broadcasting Act 1996 s 32(9) (as substituted: see note 3).

9   Broadcasting Act 1996 s 32(2).

10   Ie by virtue of the Broadcasting Act 1996 s 32(2).

11   Broadcasting Act 1996 s 32(3). The holder may broadcast any programme supplied by virtue of s 32(3) on one occasion only: s 32(6).

12   Broadcasting Act 1996 s 32(5)(a).

13   Broadcasting Act 1996 s 32(5)(b).

14   As to Seirbheis nam Meadhanan Gàidhlig (the Gaelic Media Service) see PARA 800 et seq.

15   Broadcasting Act 1996 s 32(7) (amended by the Communications Act 2003 Sch 15 para 97(3)).

(vi) National Television Archive

810. Contributions towards maintenance of national television archive. OFCOM[1] must in each financial year[2] determine an aggregate amount which it considers it would be appropriate for the holders of Channel 3[3], Channel 4[4] and

Channel 5[5] licences to contribute towards the expenses incurred by the nominated body[6] in connection with the maintenance by it of a national television archive[7].

A Channel 3, Channel 4 or Channel 5 licence must include conditions requiring the licence holder to pay to OFCOM, in respect of each financial year, such amount as it may notify to him for these purposes, being such proportion of the aggregate amount so determined for that year as it considers appropriate[8]. Any amount so received by OFCOM must be transmitted by it to the nominated body[9].

1　As to OFCOM see PARA 507.
2　As to the meaning of 'financial year' see PARA 635 note 2. This provision had to be complied with in the year which included the commencement of the provision and must be complied with in each subsequent financial year: see the Broadcasting Act 1990 s 185(1). For the purposes of enabling conditions of the type specified in s 185(3) to be included in a Channel 3 or Channel 5 licence, s 185 was brought into force on 1 January 1991: see the Broadcasting Act 1990 (Commencement No 1 and Transitional Provisions) Order 1990, SI 1990/2347, art 7. As to the meaning of 'Channel 3 licence' see PARA 669 note 2; definition applied by the Broadcasting Act 1990 s 185(5). As to the meaning of 'Channel 5 licence' see PARA 681 note 4; definition applied by s 185(5).
3　As to the establishment of Channel 3 see PARA 667.
4　As to the establishment of Channel 4 see PARA 627.
5　As to the establishment of Channel 5 see PARA 681.
6　'The nominated body' means such body as may for the time being be nominated by OFCOM for these purposes, being a body which: (1) is for the time being a designated body for the purposes of the Copyright, Designs and Patents Act 1988 s 75 (recordings for archival purposes: see COPYRIGHT, DESIGN RIGHT AND RELATED RIGHTS vol 9(2) (2006 Reissue) PARA 403); and (2) appears to OFCOM to be in a position to maintain a national television archive: Broadcasting Act 1990 s 185(2) (amended by the Communications Act 2003 s 360(3), Sch 15 para 64(1)).
7　Broadcasting Act 1990 s 185(1) (amended by the Communications Act 2003 s 297(1), (2), Sch 15 para 64(1)). The amendments to the Broadcasting Act 1990 s 185(1) have effect only in relation to financial years beginning after the television transfer date: see the Communications Act 2003 s 297(4), Sch 15 para 64(2). As to the meaning of 'the television transfer date' see PARA 857 note 17. In financial years beginning after that date, the holder of a Channel 4 licence is included in the requirement to contribute towards the expenses incurred by the nominated body. 'Channel 4 licence' means: (1) the licence referred to in the Communications Act 2003 s 231(1)(b) (see PARA 641); and (2) a licence renewing that licence on the first or any subsequent occasion: Broadcasting Act 1990 s 185(5) (definition added by the Communications Act 2003 s 297(3)). A determination or nomination made for the purposes of the Broadcasting Act 1990 s 185 by the ITC is to have effect on and after the television transfer date as a determination or nomination made by OFCOM: Communications Act 2003 s 406(6), Sch 18 para 46(1). This applies in the case of a determination so far only as it relates to a financial year beginning on or after the television transfer date: Sch 18 para 46(2). 'The ITC' means the Independent Television Commission: Sch 18 para 64. As to the ITC see PARA 507.
8　Broadcasting Act 1990 s 185(3) (amended by the Communications Act 2003 s 297(2), Sch 15 para 64(1)). Different proportions may be determined in relation to different persons: see the Broadcasting Act 1990 s 185(3). As to the meaning of 'person' see PARA 510 note 1.
9　Broadcasting Act 1990 s 185(4) (amended by the Communications Act 2003 Sch 15 para 64(1)).

4. REGULATION OF CHANGE IN INDUSTRY STRUCTURE

(1) INTRODUCTION

811. Introduction and overview. The function of regulating change in industry structure in the broadcasting sector is primarily, in common with other industry sectors, a task for general competition laws. As the scale of some broadcasting enterprises will often be significant and their activities likely to have effects on the patterns of trade and competition between member states of the European Union, this may involve the application of both domestic[1] and European[2] competition laws. In addition, owing to the presence of public service broadcasters the European laws relating to state aids and services of a general economic interest may sometimes be applicable (both in terms of the grant of aid to the public broadcasters themselves and potentially as between the public service broadcasters and their various suppliers)[3].

As regards the broadcasting sector, however, there is a further regulatory objective that must also be addressed[4] which may be expressed as the need to further the interests of consumers in relation to communications matters[5]. It may include such elements as securing the optimal use for wireless telegraphy of the electromagnetic spectrum; the availability throughout the United Kingdom of a wide range of electronic communications services; the availability throughout the United Kingdom of a wide range of television and radio services which (taken as a whole) are both of high quality and calculated to appeal to a variety of tastes and interests; and the maintenance of a sufficient plurality of providers of different television and radio services[6]. It should also recognise, where relevant and among other things, the desirability of promoting the fulfilment of the purposes of public service television broadcasting in the United Kingdom; the desirability of encouraging investment and innovation in relevant markets; the different needs and interests, so far as the use of the electromagnetic spectrum for wireless telegraphy is concerned, of all persons who may wish to make use of it; the different interests of persons in the different parts of the United Kingdom, of the different ethnic communities within the United Kingdom and of persons living in rural and in urban areas; and the practicability in particular circumstance of satisfying these regulatory concerns[7].

The main additional regulatory tools by which this objective is to be met are the public value test applied to significant new service proposals put forward by the BBC Executive as overseen by the BBC Trust[8]; restrictions on and oversight of changes of control over independent broadcasting licences[9]; media ownership controls[10]; and special rules applicable to media mergers[11].

1 Ie the Competition Act 1998 and the Enterprise Act 2002: see COMPETITION.
2 Ie the Treaty on the Functioning of the European Union (Rome, 25 March 1957; TS 1 (1973); Cmnd 5179) arts 101, 102 and Council Regulation (EC) 139/2004 (OJ L24, 29.1.2004, p 1) on the control of concentrations between undertakings. The Treaty was formerly known as the Treaty Establishing the European Community; it has been renamed and its provisions renumbered: see PARA 506 note 27.
3 See the Treaty on the Functioning of the European Union arts 107–109 and 106. There is a significant inter-relation between these laws and the rules on fair competition and the public value test deployed by the BBC Trust: see PARAS 792 et seq, 812.
4 See the Communications Act 2003 s 3; and TELECOMMUNICATIONS vol 97 (2010) PARA 16.
5 See the Communications Act 2003 s 3(1)(a); and TELECOMMUNICATIONS vol 97 (2010) PARA 16.
6 See the Communications Act 2003 s 3(2); and TELECOMMUNICATIONS vol 97 (2010) PARA 16. As to the meaning of 'United Kingdom' see PARA 510 note 13.

7   See the Communications Act 2003 s 3(4); and TELECOMMUNICATIONS vol 97 (2010) PARA 16.
8   See PARA 812.
9   See PARA 813 et seq.
10 See PARA 820 et seq.
11 See PARA 839 et seq.

(2) CHANGES TO BBC PUBLIC SERVICES

812. Public value testing of new BBC UK service proposals. Any significant proposal by the BBC[1] for change in the UK public services[2] must be subject to full and public scrutiny, which will be brought about by the public value test[3]. The public value test is a means by which public value and market impact are taken into account[4].

The public value test must be applied before a decision is taken to make any significant change to the UK public services (which can include introducing a new service or discontinuing a service)[5]. Whether any proposals for change meet this criterion of significance is a matter for the judgment of the Trust[6]. The application of the public value test involves several elements[7], namely: (1) a public value assessment[8]; (2) a market impact assessment[9]. The Trust must consider the outcome of the public value assessment and the market impact assessment and reach provisional conclusions regarding the proposed change[10] and those assessments must be published[11]. The Trust must consult about its provisional conclusions and then proceed to reach a final conclusion about whether the proposed change should be made[12]. A public value test must be completed within six months of the date on which the Trust determines that it is to be applied[13], but at its discretion, where justified by the circumstances, the Trust may allow a longer period[14].

The purpose of a public value assessment is to ascertain the likely public value of the proposed change[15]. In general terms, a public value assessment should include an assessment of the following factors: (a) the value which licence fee payers[16] would place on the proposed change as individuals; (b) the value which the proposed change would deliver to society as a whole through its contribution to the BBC's Public Purposes[17], but having regard to the BBC's mission to inform, educate and entertain[18] and the contribution of the proposed change to the priorities set out in the BBC's purpose remits[19]; (c) the value for money of the proposed change and its cost (including the potential financial implications if the proposed change were not to be made)[20].

In respect of market impact assessments, the Trust and OFCOM[21] must together establish a joint steering group[22]. The Trust and OFCOM must jointly make arrangements for the operation and constitution of the group that are based on the principle of an equality of status and participation as between the Trust and OFCOM, and those arrangements must, in particular, provide that: (i) the group's membership must consist of an equal number of members drawn from the Trust and OFCOM respectively, but may also include some independent members; (ii) both the Trust and OFCOM are to have an equality of opportunities to appoint the group's chairman from amongst the membership of the group; (iii) accordingly, each successive market impact assessment is to be overseen by the group under the chairmanship of an appointee of the Trust or (as the case may require) an appointee of OFCOM on an alternating basis, unless otherwise agreed; and (iv) the chairman is not to have a casting vote[23]. Subject to this, the precise composition of the Group is to be agreed between the Trust and OFCOM[24]. Where a public value test is applied, the Trust must inform the group of the need for a market impact assessment, and the group must then set and publish the terms of reference for the market impact assessment[25]. The group will be responsible for agreeing the potential relevant markets for the assessment after considering advice from OFCOM[26]. The group will also be responsible for ensuring that the market impact assessment is conducted in a manner appropriate to the nature of the public value test and to a suitable schedule[27]. The Trust and OFCOM must make suitable arrangements for working together to ensure that market impact assessments are conducted in a timely manner[28]. If, in respect of any matter arising under these provisions, the group is unable to reach agreement on suitable arrangements or their implementation, the matters in dispute may be referred to the chairman of the Trust and the chairman of OFCOM for resolution by them jointly[29].

Whenever the public value test is applied, OFCOM has the responsibility of providing the market impact assessment[30]. OFCOM may discharge that responsibility by providing either an assessment which it has itself made or one which it has commissioned from a third party which is independent of the BBC[31]. Such assessments must be made and provided in accordance with a methodology agreed between the Trust and OFCOM[32]. The agreed methodology must be applied within the parameters set by the agreed[33] terms of reference and relevant markets[34]. What OFCOM does under these provisions, and the work of any third party in relation to a market impact assessment which it has been commissioned to make, will be overseen by the joint steering group; however, the substantive findings of the assessment remain a matter for the judgment of OFCOM[35]. A market impact assessment must be completed within three months of the date on which terms of reference are set by the joint steering group[36] but, at its discretion, where justified by the circumstances, the group may allow a longer period[37].

In relation to the piloting of potential or proposed changes to the UK public services, where the Executive Board proposes a change to the UK public services which requires the approval of the Trust and has properly undertaken a pilot in connection with developing its proposal or with a view to informing the Trust's evaluation of the proposal, then in those circumstances[38], the Executive Board may continue the pilot[39] after either or both of the following: (A) the Executive Board applies to the Trust for approval; or (B) the Trust has begun any process preliminary to deciding whether the change should be approved[40]. However, if and when the Trust determines that a public value test is to be applied, the Executive Board may continue the pilot only with the approval of the Trust, given in accordance with the terms of a Protocol adopted and published for that purpose[41].

Any proposal for the introduction of a new service[42] is subject to a procedural veto by the Secretary of State[43]. Before the BBC starts providing such a service, the Trust must have notified the Secretary of State of the proposal and been informed by the Secretary of State that he does not intend to use his procedural veto[44]. In considering whether to use his procedural veto, the role of the Secretary of State is a limited one. He is not to concern himself with the substantive merits of the proposal, but only with whether the Trust has reached its decision to introduce the new service following appropriate processes which conform to the requirements of the BBC Charter and Agreement[45].

1   As to the meaning of 'BBC' see PARA 603.
2   As to the meaning of 'UK public services' see PARA 855 note 6; and see PARA 615. As to the meaning of 'service' see PARA 855 note 6.

3 See the *Agreement between Her Majesty's Secretary of State for Culture, Media and Sport and the British Broadcasting Corporation* (Cm 6872) (30 June 2006) cl 23.

4 See the *Agreement between Her Majesty's Secretary of State for Culture, Media and Sport and the British Broadcasting Corporation* (Cm 6872) (30 June 2006) cl 24.

5 *Agreement between Her Majesty's Secretary of State for Culture, Media and Sport and the British Broadcasting Corporation* (Cm 6872) (30 June 2006) cl 25(1).

6 *Agreement between Her Majesty's Secretary of State for Culture, Media and Sport and the British Broadcasting Corporation* (Cm 6872) (30 June 2006) cl 25(2). As to the BBC Trust within the constitution of the BBC see PARA 604. In exercising that judgment, the Trust must have regard to the following considerations (and to the presumption explained in cl 25(3) and (4)): (1) impact, ie the extent to which the change is likely to affect relevant users and others; (2) the financial implications of the change; (3) novelty, ie the extent to which the change would involve the BBC in a new area of activity for the BBC, as yet untested; (4) duration, ie how long the activity will last: cl 25(2). The Trust should presume that any change which requires a new service licence (see PARA 614) or any amendment of the key characteristics described as such in a service licence ought to be subject to a public value test: cl 25(3). Where this presumption applies, the Trust may still decide that there is no need for the public value test to be applied, but in that case the onus is on the Trust to justify departing from the presumption: cl 25(3). Before exercising its judgment under cl 25, the Trust must investigate or otherwise inform itself of any facts or considerations which it considers potentially relevant to the exercise of that judgment; what this means in practice will vary according to the circumstances: cl 25(4).

7 *Agreement between Her Majesty's Secretary of State for Culture, Media and Sport and the British Broadcasting Corporation* (Cm 6872) (30 June 2006) cl 26(1).

8 *Agreement between Her Majesty's Secretary of State for Culture, Media and Sport and the British Broadcasting Corporation* (Cm 6872) (30 June 2006) cl 26(2). See cl 28; and the text and notes 15–20.

9 *Agreement between Her Majesty's Secretary of State for Culture, Media and Sport and the British Broadcasting Corporation* (Cm 6872) (30 June 2006) cl 26(3). See cl 30; and the text and notes 30–35.

10 *Agreement between Her Majesty's Secretary of State for Culture, Media and Sport and the British Broadcasting Corporation* (Cm 6872) (30 June 2006) cl 26(4).

11 *Agreement between Her Majesty's Secretary of State for Culture, Media and Sport and the British Broadcasting Corporation* (Cm 6872) (30 June 2006) cl 26(5).

12 *Agreement between Her Majesty's Secretary of State for Culture, Media and Sport and the British Broadcasting Corporation* (Cm 6872) (30 June 2006) cl 26(6). In particular, the Trust must be satisfied that any likely adverse impact on the market is justified by the likely public value of the change before concluding that the proposed change should be made: cl 26(6).

13 *Agreement between Her Majesty's Secretary of State for Culture, Media and Sport and the British Broadcasting Corporation* (Cm 6872) (30 June 2006) cl 27(1).

14 *Agreement between Her Majesty's Secretary of State for Culture, Media and Sport and the British Broadcasting Corporation* (Cm 6872) (30 June 2006) cl 27(2).

15 *Agreement between Her Majesty's Secretary of State for Culture, Media and Sport and the British Broadcasting Corporation* (Cm 6872) (30 June 2006) cl 28(1).

16 As to the meaning of 'licence fee payer' see PARA 614 note 4.

17 As to the meaning of 'Public Purposes' see PARA 603 note 3.

18 Ie the *Royal Charter for the Continuance of the British Broadcasting Corporation* (Cm 6925) (2006) art 5: see PARA 613.

19 As to the purpose remits see the *Agreement between Her Majesty's Secretary of State for Culture, Media and Sport and the British Broadcasting Corporation* (Cm 6872) (30 June 2006) cll 5–10; and PARA 607.

20 *Agreement between Her Majesty's Secretary of State for Culture, Media and Sport and the British Broadcasting Corporation* (Cm 6872) (30 June 2006) cl 28(2). As the nature of likely or potential public value may differ widely according to the nature of the change proposed, the Trust must at the outset consider very carefully: (1) the aspects of public value which may be relevant; and (2) how those aspects should be explored and evaluated (but always including public consultation): cl 28(3). In this context, the concept of 'public value' means the public value of the change bearing in mind that the service or activities concerned involve the BBC, and the need for the BBC to comply with all applicable restrictions (eg those in the *Royal Charter for the Continuance of the British Broadcasting Corporation* (Cm 6925) (2006) art 5(2)): *Agreement between Her Majesty's Secretary of State for Culture, Media and Sport and the British Broadcasting Corporation* (Cm 6872) (30 June 2006) cl 28(4).

21 As to OFCOM see PARA 507.

22 *Agreement between Her Majesty's Secretary of State for Culture, Media and Sport and the British Broadcasting Corporation* (Cm 6872) (30 June 2006) cl 29(1).

23 *Agreement between Her Majesty's Secretary of State for Culture, Media and Sport and the British Broadcasting Corporation* (Cm 6872) (30 June 2006) cl 29(2).

24 *Agreement between Her Majesty's Secretary of State for Culture, Media and Sport and the British Broadcasting Corporation* (Cm 6872) (30 June 2006) cl 29(3).

25 *Agreement between Her Majesty's Secretary of State for Culture, Media and Sport and the British Broadcasting Corporation* (Cm 6872) (30 June 2006) cl 29(4). The terms of reference may specify how the methodology set under cl 30 (see the text and notes 30–35) is to be applied: cl 29(4).

26 *Agreement between Her Majesty's Secretary of State for Culture, Media and Sport and the British Broadcasting Corporation* (Cm 6872) (30 June 2006) cl 29(5). Where there are a number of potential markets identified by the group, the market impact assessment must report on each potential market in the absence of agreement to do otherwise: cl 29(5).

27 *Agreement between Her Majesty's Secretary of State for Culture, Media and Sport and the British Broadcasting Corporation* (Cm 6872) (30 June 2006) cl 29(6).

28 *Agreement between Her Majesty's Secretary of State for Culture, Media and Sport and the British Broadcasting Corporation* (Cm 6872) (30 June 2006) cl 29(7).

29 *Agreement between Her Majesty's Secretary of State for Culture, Media and Sport and the British Broadcasting Corporation* (Cm 6872) (30 June 2006) cl 29(8). This does not apply in the case of the matters mentioned in cl 29(2)(c) and (5) (see head (iii) in the text and the text to note 26), which make specific provision for the position in the absence of agreement to the contrary: cl 29(8).

30 *Agreement between Her Majesty's Secretary of State for Culture, Media and Sport and the British Broadcasting Corporation* (Cm 6872) (30 June 2006) cl 30(1).

31 *Agreement between Her Majesty's Secretary of State for Culture, Media and Sport and the British Broadcasting Corporation* (Cm 6872) (30 June 2006) cl 30(2).

32 *Agreement between Her Majesty's Secretary of State for Culture, Media and Sport and the British Broadcasting Corporation* (Cm 6872) (30 June 2006) cl 30(3). The methodology: (1) must provide for a market impact assessment of a scale and scope appropriate to the significant change in contemplation and its potential market impact; (2) must take account of the need for a market impact assessment to be carried out in accordance with terms of reference set under cl 29(4) (see the text and note 25); and (3) may provide for the joint steering group to determine, after public consultation, that a simplified approach is appropriate to be used for a particular assessment: cl 30(3).

33 Ie agreed under the *Agreement between Her Majesty's Secretary of State for Culture, Media and Sport and the British Broadcasting Corporation* (Cm 6872) (30 June 2006) cl 29.

34 *Agreement between Her Majesty's Secretary of State for Culture, Media and Sport and the British Broadcasting Corporation* (Cm 6872) (30 June 2006) cl 30(4).

35 *Agreement between Her Majesty's Secretary of State for Culture, Media and Sport and the British Broadcasting Corporation* (Cm 6872) (30 June 2006) cl 30(5).

36 *Agreement between Her Majesty's Secretary of State for Culture, Media and Sport and the British Broadcasting Corporation* (Cm 6872) (30 June 2006) cl 31(1).

37 *Agreement between Her Majesty's Secretary of State for Culture, Media and Sport and the British Broadcasting Corporation* (Cm 6872) (30 June 2006) cl 31(2).

38 But subject to the *Agreement between Her Majesty's Secretary of State for Culture, Media and Sport and the British Broadcasting Corporation* (Cm 6872) (30 June 2006) cl 31(4), (5).

39 'Continue the pilot' includes continuing the pilot with or without modifications, and undertaking related activities: *Agreement between Her Majesty's Secretary of State for Culture, Media and Sport and the British Broadcasting Corporation* (Cm 6872) (30 June 2006) cl 32(6).

40 *Agreement between Her Majesty's Secretary of State for Culture, Media and Sport and the British Broadcasting Corporation* (Cm 6872) (30 June 2006) cl 32(1)–(3).

41 *Agreement between Her Majesty's Secretary of State for Culture, Media and Sport and the British Broadcasting Corporation* (Cm 6872) (30 June 2006) cl 32(4). The Protocol: (1) may also specify circumstances in which the approval of the Trust is required for the piloting of a potential or proposed change to the UK public services by virtue of more general provisions of the BBC Charter or the *Agreement between Her Majesty's Secretary of State for Culture, Media and Sport and the British Broadcasting Corporation* (Cm 6872) (30 June 2006); and (2) must specify requirements which the Trust considers appropriate to secure that: (a) piloting approved in accordance with such a Protocol or such general requirements; and (b) the continuation of a pilot approved under cl 32(4), will be of the smallest possible scale and duration that are compatible with the legitimate purpose for which the approval is given: cl 32(5). As to Protocols see PARA 607.

42 For the purposes of the *Agreement between Her Majesty's Secretary of State for Culture, Media and Sport and the British Broadcasting Corporation* (Cm 6872) (30 June 2006) cl 33, 'the introduction of a new service' means anything which the Trust proposes to authorise by a new service licence rather than the amendment of an existing licence: cl 33(4).

43 *Agreement between Her Majesty's Secretary of State for Culture, Media and Sport and the British Broadcasting Corporation* (Cm 6872) (30 June 2006) cl 33(1). As to the Secretary of State see PARA 507 note 32.

44 *Agreement between Her Majesty's Secretary of State for Culture, Media and Sport and the British Broadcasting Corporation* (Cm 6872) (30 June 2006) cl 33(2).

45 *Agreement between Her Majesty's Secretary of State for Culture, Media and Sport and the British Broadcasting Corporation* (Cm 6872) (30 June 2006) cl 33(3).

(3) CHANGE OF CONTROL OVER INDEPENDENT BROADCASTING LICENCES

813. Restriction on changes in control over Channel 3 licence holder. Where any change in the persons[1] having control[2] over a body[3] to which a Channel 3 licence[4] has been awarded or transferred[5], or an associated programme provider[6], takes place within the relevant period[7], and that change takes place without having been previously approved by OFCOM[8], then OFCOM may, if the licence has not yet been granted, refuse to grant it to such a body or, if it has already been granted, serve on that body a notice revoking it[9]. However, OFCOM must not refuse to grant a licence to, or serve a notice on, any body unless it has given it a reasonable opportunity of making representations to OFCOM about the matters complained of[10].

OFCOM must refuse to approve such a change in control if it appears to it that the change would be prejudicial to the provision under the licence by the body in question of a service which accords with the proposals previously submitted[11] by that body (or, as the case may be, by the person to whom the licence was originally awarded)[12], or it appears to OFCOM that the change would be prejudicial to the provision of Channel 3 as a nationwide system of television broadcasting services[13]. OFCOM may refuse to approve any such change if, in any other circumstances, it considers it appropriate to do so[14].

1 As to the meaning of 'person' see PARA 510 note 1.
2 As to the meaning of 'control' see PARA 821 note 11.
3 As to the meaning of 'body' see PARA 821 note 10.
4 As to the meaning of 'Channel 3' see PARA 667; and as to the meaning of 'Channel 3 licence' see PARA 669 note 2. As to the application of these provisions to Channel 5 licences see PARA 681 note 4.
5 Broadcasting Act 1990 s 21(1)(a)(i). A licence is awarded or transferred in accordance with Pt I (ss 3–71).
6 Broadcasting Act 1990 s 21(1)(a)(ii). 'Associated programme provider', in relation to such a body as is mentioned in s 21(1)(a)(i) (see the text and note 5), means any body which is connected with that body and is or is likely to be involved, to a substantial extent, in the provision of the programmes included in the licensed service: s 21(2) (amended by the Communications Act 2003 s 360(3), Sch 15 para 11(3)). As to the meaning of 'connected' see PARA 674 note 13. As to OFCOM see PARA 507. The Broadcasting Act 1990 Sch 2 Pt I para 3 has effect for these purposes as if a body to which a Channel 3 licence has been awarded but not yet granted were the holder of such a licence: s 21(2).
7 Broadcasting Act 1990 s 21(1)(a). 'The relevant period', in relation to a Channel 3 licence, means the period beginning with the date of the award of the licence and ending on the first anniversary of the date of its coming into force: s 21(2).
8 Broadcasting Act 1990 s 21(1)(b) (amended by the Communications Act 2003 Sch 15 para 11(1), (2)).
9 Broadcasting Act 1990 s 21(1) (amended by the Communications Act 2003 Sch 15 para 11(2)). Where OFCOM refuses to grant a licence to any body, the Broadcasting Act 1990 s 17 (subject to s 17(14)) (see PARA 671) has effect as if that body had not made an application for the licence;

and, where, under s 21(1), OFCOM serves on any body a notice revoking its licence, the provisions of s 42(6), (7) apply in relation to that notice as they apply in relation to a notice served under s 42(3) (see PARA 866): s 21(5) (amended by the Communications Act 2003 Sch 15 para 11(2)).

10   Broadcasting Act 1990 s 21(4) (amended by the Communications Act 2003 Sch 15 para 11(2)).
11   Ie under the Broadcasting Act 1990 s 15(3)(b) (see PARA 669).
12   Broadcasting Act 1990 s 21(3)(a).
13   See the Broadcasting Act 1990 s 21(3)(b) (amended by the Communications Act 2003 Sch 15 para 11(2)). As to the meaning of 'television broadcasting service' see PARA 667 note 3.
14   Broadcasting Act 1990 s 21(3) (amended by the Communications Act 2003 Sch 15 para 11(2)).

814. Changes of control of Channel 3 services. The regulatory regime for every Channel 3 service[1] provided by a body corporate includes: (1) a condition requiring the licence holder to give OFCOM[2] advance notification of any proposals known to the body that may give rise to a relevant change of control[3]; and (2) a condition requiring the licence holder to provide OFCOM, in such manner and at such times as it may reasonably require, with such information as it considers necessary for the purposes of exercising its functions[4]. OFCOM must carry out a review where: (a) it receives notification, in accordance with a condition of a Channel 3 licence, of proposals that may give rise to a relevant change of control; or (b) a relevant change of control takes place (whether or not that change has been previously notified to OFCOM)[5]. The review will be a review of the effects or likely effects, in relation to specified matters[6] of: (i) the change to which the proposals may give rise; or (ii) the change that has taken place[7].

1   As to the meaning of 'Channel 3 service' see PARA 602 note 8.
2   As to OFCOM see PARA 507.
3   For the purposes of the Communications Act 2003 s 351, 'relevant change of control' means a change in the persons having control over: (1) a body holding the licence to provide a Channel 3 service; or (2) any body which: (a) is connected with a body holding such a licence; and (b) is involved, to a substantial extent, in the provision of the programmes included in the service provided under that licence, or is likely to become so involved: s 351(10).
4   Ie under the Communications Act 2003 ss 351, 352 (see PARA 815): s 351(1). Expressions used in s 351 and in the Broadcasting Act 1990 Sch 2 Pt I (restrictions on licence holders) have the same meanings in the Communications Act 2003 s 351 as in the Broadcasting Act 1990 Sch 2 Pt I: Communications Act 2003 s 351(11).
5   Communications Act 2003 s 351(2). Where OFCOM carries out a review under s 351(2), it must publish a report of that review: (1) setting out its conclusions; and (2) specifying any steps which it proposes to take under s 352 (see PARA 815): s 351(9).
6   Ie the matters mentioned in the Communications Act 2003 s 351(4)–(7).
     The matters mentioned in s 351(4) are: (1) the extent to which time available for broadcasting programmes included in the service is allocated to programmes of each of the following descriptions, namely, original productions, news programmes, and current affairs programmes; (2) the extent to which programmes of each of those descriptions that are included in the service are broadcast at peak viewing times: s 351(4). 'Original production' has the same meaning as in s 278 (see PARA 875 note 5): s 351(10). 'Peak viewing time', in relation to original productions, means a time determined by OFCOM for the purposes of s 278 to be a peak viewing time for the service in question; and, in relation to news programmes or current affairs programmes, means a time so determined for the purposes of s 279 (see PARA 876): s 351(10).
     The matters mentioned in s 351(5) are: (a) the extent to which Channel 3 programmes made in the United Kingdom that are included in the service are programmes made outside the M25 area; (b) the range of Channel 3 programmes made in the United Kingdom outside that area that are included in the service; (c) the extent to which the expenditure of the provider of the service on Channel 3 programmes is referable to programme production at different production centres outside the M25 area; (d) the range of different such production centres to which that expenditure is referable: s 351(5). 'Channel 3 programmes' and 'expenditure' each has the same meaning as in s 286 (see PARA 877): s 351(10). As to the meaning of 'United Kingdom' see PARA 510 note 13. As to the meaning of 'M25 area' see PARA 788 note 15.

The matters mentioned in s 351(6) are: (i) the quality and range of regional programmes included in the service; (ii) the quality and range of other programmes included in the service which contribute to the regional character of the service; (iii) the quality and range of the programmes made available by the licence holder for the purposes of inclusion in the nationwide system of services referred to in the Broadcasting Act 1990 s 14(1) (nationwide Channel 3 service: see PARA 667): Communications Act 2003 s 351(6). 'Regional programme', in relation to a Channel 3 service, means (subject to s 351(8)) a programme (including a news programme) which is of particular interest to persons living within the area for which the service is provided, to persons living within a part of that area, or to particular communities living within that area: s 351(10).

The matters mentioned in s 351(7) are: (A) the amount of time given in the programmes included in the service to regional programmes and to programmes included in the service which contribute to the regional character of the service; (B) the proportion of regional programmes included in the service which are made within the area for which the service is provided; (C) the extent of the use, in connection with the service, of the services of persons employed (whether by the licence holder or any other person) within that area; (D) the extent to which managerial or editorial decisions relating to programmes to be included in the service are taken by persons so employed within that area: s 351(7).

In relation to a national Channel 3 service, s 351(3)–(7) has effect as if: (aa) s 351(5) applied only where the service is subject to conditions imposed by virtue of a decision of OFCOM under s 286(2) or OFCOM otherwise considers, having regard to the nature of the service, that it is appropriate to consider the matters mentioned in s 286(2) (see PARA 877); (bb) references to regional programmes were references to programmes which are regional programmes (within the meaning of s 287: see PARA 877) in relation to that service and are included in it in accordance with a condition imposed under s 287(4)(a) (see PARA 877); (cc) references to the regional character of the service were references to the regional character of parts of the service; (dd) s 351(6)(c) were omitted; and (ee) references, in relation to programmes such as are mentioned in head (bb), to the area for which the service is provided were references to the part of that area where the people are living to whom those programmes are likely to be of particular interest: s 351(8).

7   Communications Act 2003 s 351(3).

815.   Action following review. If, on a review[1], it appears to OFCOM[2] that the relevant change of control is or would be prejudicial to specified matters[3], it must vary the licence in accordance with the provisions below[4]. The variation: (1) must be made with a view to ensuring that the relevant change of control is not prejudicial to any of the matters so mentioned; and (2) must be a variation for the inclusion in the licence of such conditions relating to any of those matters as it considers appropriate[5]. If it appears to OFCOM[6]: (a) that the proposed change of control would be prejudicial to the regional character of the service or (as the case may be) of any parts of it; or (b) that the actual change of control is so prejudicial, it may vary the licence so as to include in it such conditions relating to any of those matters as it considers appropriate[7]. Any new or varied condition imposed under these provisions[8] in relation to any matter may be more onerous than the conditions relating to that matter having effect before the relevant change of control[9]. A variation of a licence will be effected by the service of a notice of the variation on the licence holder[10]. OFCOM is not to serve a notice of a variation unless it has given the body on whom it is served a reasonable opportunity, after the publication of the report of the review[11], of making representations to it about the variation[12]. Where, in a case of a proposed change of control, a notice varying a licence is served before the change to which it relates takes place, the variation is not to take effect until the change takes place[13]. A condition included in a licence by a variation may be further varied by OFCOM either: (i) with the consent of the licence holder; or (ii) in any other case, after complying with certain requirements[14].

1   Ie under the Communications Act 2003 s 351(2): see PARA 814.
2   As to OFCOM see PARA 507.

3   Ie one or more of the matters mentioned in the Communications Act 2003 s 351(4)–(6): see PARA 814.
4   Ie in accordance with the Communications Act 2003 s 352(2): s 352(1). Expressions used in s 352 and in s 351 (see PARA 814) have the same meanings in s 352 as in s 351: s 352(11).
5   Communications Act 2003 s 352(2).
6   Ie having regard to the matters mentioned in the Communications Act 2003 s 351(7): see PARA 814.
7   Communications Act 2003 s 352(3).
8   Ie the Communications Act 2003 s 352.
9   Communications Act 2003 s 352(4). Section 352(4) is subject to s 352(5): s 352(4). A variation under s 352 must not provide for the inclusion of a new or varied condition in a licence unless the new condition, or the condition as varied, is one which (with any necessary modifications) would have been satisfied by the licence holder throughout the 12 months immediately before the relevant date: s 352(5). For the purposes of s 352(5), 'the relevant date' is the date of the relevant change of control or, if earlier, the date on which OFCOM exercises its powers under s 352: s 352(6).
10 Communications Act 2003 s 352(7).
11 Ie under the Communications Act 2003 s 351: see PARA 814.
12 Communications Act 2003 s 352(8).
13 Communications Act 2003 s 352(9).
14 Ie the requirements of the Broadcasting Act 1990 s 3(4)(b) (variation after giving opportunity for representations by the licence holder: see PARA 665): Communications Act 2003 s 352(10).

816. Changes of control of Channel 5. The regulatory regime for Channel 5[1] includes, in every case where it is provided by a body corporate: (1) a condition requiring the licence holder to give OFCOM[2] advance notification of any proposals known to the body that may give rise to a relevant change of control[3]; and (2) a condition requiring the licence holder to provide OFCOM, in such manner and at such times as it may reasonably require, with such information as it considers necessary for the purposes of exercising its functions[4]. OFCOM must carry out a review where: (a) it receives notification, in accordance with a condition of the licence to provide Channel 5, of proposals that may give rise to a relevant change of control; or (b) a relevant change of control takes place (whether or not that change has been previously notified to OFCOM)[5]. The review will be a review of the effects or likely effects, in relation to specified matters[6] of: (i) the change to which the proposals may give rise; or (ii) the change that has taken place[7].

1   As to the meaning of 'Channel 5' see PARA 602 note 10.
2   As to OFCOM see PARA 507.
3   For the purposes of the Communications Act 2003 s 353, 'relevant change of control' means a change in the persons having control over: (1) a body holding a licence to provide Channel 5; or (2) any body which: (a) is connected with a body holding such a licence; and (b) is involved, to a substantial extent, in the provision of the programmes included in that channel, or is likely to become so involved: s 353(7).
4   Ie its functions under the Communications Act 2003 s 353 and s 354 (see PARA 817): s 353(1). Expressions used in s 353 and in the Broadcasting Act 1990 Sch 2 Pt I (restrictions on licence holders) have the same meanings in the Communications Act 2003 s 353 as in the Broadcasting Act 1990 Sch 2 Pt I: Communications Act 2003 s 353(8).
5   Communications Act 2003 s 353(2). Where OFCOM carries out a review under s 353(2), it must publish a report of that review: (1) setting out its conclusions; and (2) specifying any steps which it proposes to take under s 354 (see PARA 817): s 353(6).
6   Ie the matters mentioned in the Communications Act 2003 s 353(4), (5).
    The matters mentioned in s 353(4) are: (1) the extent to which time available for broadcasting programmes included in Channel 5 is allocated to programmes of each of the following descriptions, namely, original productions, news programmes, and current affairs programmes; (2) the extent to which programmes of each of those descriptions that are included in Channel 5 are broadcast at peak viewing times: s 353(4). 'Original production' has the same meaning as in s 278 (see PARA 875 note 5): s 353(7). 'Peak viewing time', in relation to original productions, means a time determined by OFCOM for the purposes of s 278 to be a peak

viewing time for Channel 5; and, in relation to news programmes or current affairs programmes, means a time so determined for the purposes of s 279 (see PARA 876): s 353(7).

The matters mentioned in s 353(5) are: (a) the extent to which programmes made in the United Kingdom that are included in the service are programmes made outside the M25 area; (b) the range of programmes made in the United Kingdom outside that area that are included in Channel 5; (c) the extent to which the expenditure of the provider of Channel 5 on programmes made in the United Kingdom is referable to programme production at different production centres outside the M25 area; (d) the range of different such production centres to which that expenditure is referable: s 353(5). As to the meaning of 'United Kingdom' see PARA 510 note 13. As to the meaning of 'M25 area' see PARA 788 note 15. 'Expenditure', in relation to a programme, means expenditure which constitutes an investment in or is otherwise attributable to the making of the programme, or expenditure on the commissioning or other acquisition of the programme or on the acquisition of a right to include it in a service or to have it broadcast: s 353(7).

7   Communications Act 2003 s 353(3).

817. Action following review. If, on a review[1], it appears to OFCOM[2] that the relevant change of control[3] is or would be prejudicial to specified matters[4], it must vary the licence[5]. The variation: (1) must be made with a view to ensuring that the relevant change of control is not prejudicial to any of those matters; and (2) must be a variation for the inclusion in the licence of such conditions relating to any of those matters as it considers appropriate[6]. Any new or varied condition imposed under these provisions[7] in relation to any matter may be more onerous than the conditions relating to that matter having effect before the relevant change of control[8]. A variation of a licence is effected by the service of a notice of the variation on the licence holder[9]. OFCOM is not to serve a notice of a variation unless it has given the body on whom it is served a reasonable opportunity, after the publication of the report of the review[10], of making representations to it about the variation[11]. Where, in a case of a proposed change of control, a notice varying a licence is served before the change to which it relates takes place, the variation is not to take effect until the change takes place[12]. A condition included in a licence by a variation may be further varied by OFCOM either: (a) with the consent of the licence holder; or (b) in any other case, after complying with certain requirements[13].

1   Ie under the Communications Act 2003 s 353(2) (see PARA 816).
2   As to OFCOM see PARA 507.
3   See PARA 816.
4   Ie one or more of the matters mentioned in the Communications Act 2003 s 353(4), (5): see PARA 816 note 6.
5   Ie in accordance with the Communications Act 2003 s 354(2): s 354(1). Expressions used in s 354 and in s 353 (see PARA 816) have the same meanings in s 354 as in s 353: s 354(10).
6   Communications Act 2003 s 354(2).
7   Ie the Communications Act 2003 s 354.
8   Communications Act 2003 s 354(3). Section 354(3) is subject to s 354(4): s 354(3). A variation under s 354 must not provide for the inclusion of a new or varied condition in a licence unless the new condition, or the condition as varied, is one which (with any necessary modifications) would have been satisfied by the licence holder throughout the 12 months immediately before the relevant date: s 354(4). For the purposes of s 354(4), 'the relevant date' is the date of the relevant change of control or, if earlier, the date on which OFCOM exercises its powers under s 354: s 354(5).
9   Communications Act 2003 s 354(6).
10   Ie under the Communications Act 2003 s 353: see PARA 816.
11   Communications Act 2003 s 354(7).
12   Communications Act 2003 s 354(8).
13   Ie the requirements of the Broadcasting Act 1990 s 3(4)(b) (variation after giving opportunity for representations by the licence holder: see PARA 679): Communications Act 2003 s 354(9).

818.   Variation of local licence following change of control. The regulatory regime for every local sound broadcasting service[1] provided by a body corporate includes: (1) a condition requiring the licence holder to give OFCOM[2] advance notification of any proposals known to it that may give rise to a relevant change of control[3]; and (2) a condition requiring the licence holder to provide OFCOM, in such manner and at such times as it may reasonably require, with such information as it considers necessary for the purposes of exercising its functions[4]. OFCOM must carry out a review where: (a) it receives notification, in accordance with a condition of a local sound broadcasting licence, of proposals that may give rise to a relevant change of control; or (b) a relevant change of control takes place (whether or not that change has been previously notified to OFCOM)[5]. The review will be a review of the effects or likely effects, in relation to specified matters[6] of: (i) the change to which the proposals may give rise; or (ii) the change that has taken place[7].

1   As to the meaning of 'local sound broadcasting service' see PARA 889 note 2.
2   As to OFCOM see PARA 507.
3   For the purposes of the Communications Act 2003 s 355, 'relevant change of control' means a change in the persons having control over: (1) a body holding the licence to provide a local sound broadcasting service; or (2) any body which: (a) is connected with a body holding such a licence; and (b) is involved, to a substantial extent, in the provision of the programmes included in the service provided under that licence, or is likely to become so involved: s 355(7).
4   Ie its functions under the Communications Act 2003 ss 355, 356 (see PARA 819): s 355(1). Expressions used in s 355 and in the Broadcasting Act 1990 Sch 2 (restrictions on licence holders) have the same meanings in the Communications Act 2003 s 355 as in the Broadcasting Act 1990 Sch 2: Communications Act 2003 s 355(8).
5   Communications Act 2003 s 355(2). Where OFCOM carries out a review under s 355(2), it must publish a report of that review: (1) setting out its conclusions; and (2) specifying any steps which it proposes to take under s 356 (see PARA 819): s 355(6).
6   Ie the matters mentioned in the Communications Act 2003 s 355(4). Those matters are: (1) the quality and range of programmes included in the service; (2) the character of the service; (3) the extent to which OFCOM's duty under s 314 (see PARA 889) is performed in relation to the service: s 355(4). The matters to which OFCOM must have regard in determining for the purposes of s 355 the character of a local sound broadcasting service, include, in particular, the selection of spoken material and music in programmes included in the service: s 355(5).
7   Communications Act 2003 s 355(3).

819.   Action following review. If, on a review[1], it appears to OFCOM[2] that the relevant change of control[3] is or would be prejudicial to specified matters[4], it must vary the local licence[5]. The variation: (1) must be made with a view to ensuring that the relevant change of control is not prejudicial to any of those matters; and (2) must be a variation for the inclusion in the licence of such conditions relating to any of those matters as OFCOM considers appropriate[6]. Any new or varied condition imposed under these provisions[7] in relation to any matter may be more onerous than the conditions relating to that matter having effect before the relevant change of control[8]. A variation of a licence will be effected by the service of a notice of the variation on the licence holder[9]. OFCOM is not to serve a notice of a variation unless it has given the body on whom it is served a reasonable opportunity, after the publication of the report of the review[10], of making representations to it about the variation[11]. Where, in a case of a proposed change of control, a notice varying a licence is served before the change to which it relates takes place, the variation is not to take effect until that change takes place[12]. A condition included in a licence by a variation may be further varied by OFCOM either: (a) with the consent of the licence holder; or (b) in any other case, after complying with certain requirements[13].

1   Ie under the Communications Act 2003 s 355: see PARA 818.
2   As to OFCOM see PARA 507.
3   See PARA 816.
4   Ie one or more of the matters mentioned in the Communications Act 2003 s 355(4): see PARA 818 note 6.
5   In accordance with the Communications Act 2003 s 356(2): s 356(1). Expressions used in s 356 and in s 355 (see PARA 818) have the same meanings in s 356 as in s 355: s 356(11).
6   Communications Act 2003 s 356(2).
7   Ie the Communications Act 2003 s 356.
8   Communications Act 2003 s 356(3). Section 356(3) is subject to s 356(4): s 356(3). A variation under s 356 must not provide for the inclusion of any new or varied condition in a licence unless the new condition, or the condition as varied, is one which (with any necessary modifications) would have been satisfied by the licence holder throughout: (1) the three months immediately before the relevant date; or (2) such other three month period as has been notified under s 356(5): s 356(4). For the purposes of s 356(4), 'the relevant date' is the date of the relevant change of control or, if earlier, the date on which OFCOM exercises its powers under s 356: s 356(6). If OFCOM considers that the performance of the licence holder during the three-month period immediately preceding the relevant date is not typical of his performance during the 12 months before the relevant date it: (a) may determine that s 356(4) is to apply by reference to such other three-month period falling within those 12 months as it may determine; and (b) must notify any determination under this provision to the licence holder: s 356(5).
9   Communications Act 2003 s 356(7).
10 Ie under the Communications Act 2003 s 355: see PARA 818.
11 Communications Act 2003 s 356(8).
12 Communications Act 2003 s 356(9).
13 Ie the requirements of the Broadcasting Act 1990 s 86(5)(b) (variation after giving opportunity for representations by the licence holder: see PARA 725): Communications Act 2003 s 356(10).

(4) MEDIA OWNERSHIP

(i) Restrictions on holding Channel 3 Licences

820. Restrictions on newspaper proprietors holding Channel 3 licences. A person[1] is not to hold a licence to provide a Channel 3 service[2] if: (1) he runs[3] a national newspaper[4] which for the time being has a national market share[5] of 20 per cent or more; or (2) he runs national newspapers which for the time being together have a national market share of 20 per cent or more[6].

A person is not to hold a licence to provide a regional Channel 3 service[7] if: (a) he runs a local newspaper which for the time being has a local market share[8] of 20 per cent or more in the coverage area[9] of the service; or (b) he runs local newspapers which for the time being together have a local market share of 20 per cent or more in that coverage area[10].

For these purposes, where there is a licence to provide a Channel 3 service, the actual licence holder and every person connected with the actual licence holder will be treated as holding that licence[11].

A person who is: (i) the proprietor of a national newspaper which for the time being has a national market share of 20 per cent or more; or (ii) the proprietor of national newspapers which for the time being together have a national market share of 20 per cent or more, is not to be a participant with more than a 20 per cent interest in a body corporate which is the holder of a licence to provide a Channel 3 service[12]. A person who is the holder of a licence to provide a Channel 3 service is not to be a participant with more than a 20 per cent interest in a body corporate which is a relevant national newspaper proprietor[13]. A body corporate is not to be a participant with more than a 20 per cent interest in a body corporate which holds a licence to provide a Channel 3 service if the first body corporate is one in which a relevant national newspaper proprietor is a participant with more than a 20 per cent interest[14]. A restriction imposed by these provisions on participation in a body corporate which is the holder of a Channel 3 licence applies equally to participation in a body corporate which controls the holder of such a licence[15]. Any restriction on participation imposed on the proprietor of a newspaper or on the holder of a licence is to apply as if he and every person connected with him were one person[16].

The Secretary of State may by order repeal or otherwise modify any of the restrictions imposed by these provisions[17].

1   As to the meaning of 'person' see PARA 510 note 1.
2   As to the meaning of 'Channel 3' see PARA 667. As to the meaning of 'Channel 3 service' see PARA 602 note 8.
3   For the purposes of the Communications Act 2003 Sch 14 Pt 1 (paras 1–6), a person runs a national or local newspaper if he is the proprietor of the newspaper, or if he controls a body which is the proprietor of the newspaper: s 350(3), Sch 14 para 4.
4   For the purposes of the Communications Act 2003 Sch 14 Pt 1, references to a national or local newspaper are references to a national or local newspaper circulating wholly or mainly in the United Kingdom or in a part of the United Kingdom: Sch 14 para 3(1). As to the meaning of 'United Kingdom' see PARA 510 note 13. Where a newspaper is published in different regional editions on the same day, OFCOM has the power to determine whether those regional editions should be treated for the purposes of Sch 14 Pt 1 as constituting: (1) one national newspaper; or (2) two or more local newspapers; or (3) one national newspaper and one or more local newspapers: Sch 14 para 3(2). In the case of a newspaper which would otherwise be neither a national nor a local newspaper for these purposes, OFCOM has the power to determine, if it considers it appropriate to do so in the light of its circulation and influence in the United Kingdom or its circulation or influence in a part of the United Kingdom, that the newspaper is to be treated as a national or as a local newspaper for such of those purposes as OFCOM may determine: Sch 14 para 3(3). As to OFCOM see PARA 507.
5   For the purposes of the Communications Act 2003 Sch 14 Pt 1, the national market share of a national newspaper at any time is the percentage of the total number of copies of all national newspapers sold in the United Kingdom in the relevant six months which is represented by the total number of copies of that newspaper sold in the United Kingdom in that six months: Sch 14 para 3(4). The number of copies of a newspaper sold in the United Kingdom during any period may be taken to be such number as is estimated by OFCOM in such manner, or by reference to such statistics prepared by any other person, as it thinks fit: Sch 14 para 3(7). 'The relevant six months' means the six months ending with the last whole calendar month to end before the time in question: Sch 14 para 3(6). In relation to a newspaper which is distributed free of charge (rather than sold), references in Sch 14 para 3 to the number of copies sold include references to the number of copies distributed: Sch 14 para 3(8).
6   Communications Act 2003 Sch 14 para 1(1).
7   As to the meaning of 'regional Channel 3 service' see PARA 875 note 4.
8   The local market share of a local newspaper in any area at any time is the percentage of the total number of copies of all local newspapers sold in that area in the relevant six months which is represented by the total number of copies of that newspaper sold in that area in that six months: Communications Act 2003 Sch 14 para 3(5). The number of copies of a newspaper sold in a particular area, during any period may be taken to be such number as is estimated by OFCOM in such manner, or by reference to such statistics prepared by any other person, as it thinks fit: Sch 14 para 3(7). As to the meaning of 'the relevant six months', and as to newspapers distributed free of charge, see note 5.
9   For the purposes of the Communications Act 2003 Sch 14 Pt 1, the coverage area for a Channel 3 service is the area that is determined by OFCOM to be the area of the United Kingdom within which that service is capable of being received at a level satisfying such technical standards as may have been laid down by it for the purposes of this provision: Sch 14 para 5.
10   Communications Act 2003 Sch 14 para 1(2).
11   Communications Act 2003 Sch 14 para 1(3).
12   Communications Act 2003 Sch 14 para 2(1).
13   Communications Act 2003 Sch 14 para 2(2). 'A relevant national newspaper proprietor' means a person who runs a national newspaper which for the time being has a national market share of 20% or more or national newspapers which for the time being together have a national market share of 20% or more: Sch 14 para 2(6).

14 Communications Act 2003 Sch 14 para 2(3).
15 Communications Act 2003 Sch 14 para 2(4).
16 Communications Act 2003 Sch 14 para 2(5).
17 Communications Act 2003 Sch 14 para 6. Before making an order under any provision of Sch 14 (other than one that is confined to giving effect to recommendations made by OFCOM in a report of a review of media ownership under s 391 (see PARA 838)), the Secretary of State must consult OFCOM: Sch 14 para 17(1). No order is to be made containing provision authorised by any provision of Sch 14 unless a draft of the order has been laid before Parliament and approved by a resolution of each House: Sch 14 para 17(2).

(ii) Restrictions on holding of Licences for Independent Television Services

821. Restrictions on the holding of licences. OFCOM[1] must do all it can to secure that a person[2] does not become or remain the holder of a licence[3] if he is a disqualified person in relation to the licence[4], that a person does not become the holder of a licence if certain requirements[5] would be contravened were he to do so[6] and that those requirements are not contravened in the case of a person who already holds a licence[7].

For these purposes, OFCOM may[8]:

(1)   require any applicant for a licence to provide it with such information as it may reasonably require[9];

(2)   revoke the award of a licence to a body[10] where a relevant change[11] takes place after the award, but before the grant, of the licence[12];

(3)   make the grant of a licence to any person conditional on the taking of any specified steps that appear to OFCOM to be required to be taken[13];

(4)   impose conditions in any licence enabling it to require the licence holder, if a body corporate, to give to it advance notice of proposals affecting shareholdings in the body or affecting the directors of the body, where such proposals are known to the body[14];

(5)   impose conditions in a licence requiring the licence holder, if a body corporate, to give OFCOM notice, after they have occurred and irrespective of whether proposals for them have fallen to be notified, of changes, transactions or events affecting shareholdings in the body or affecting the directors of the body[15];

(6)   impose conditions in a licence enabling OFCOM to require the licence holder to provide it with such information as it may reasonably require for determining whether the licence holder is a disqualified person in relation to that licence[16] or whether specified requirements[17] have been and are being complied with by or in relation to the licence holder[18];

(7)   impose conditions in any licence enabling it to give the licence holder directions requiring him to take, or arrange for the taking of, any specified steps appearing to it to be required to be taken in order for certain requirements[19] to be complied with[20].

Every licence must include such conditions as OFCOM considers necessary or expedient to ensure that where the holder of the licence is a body, and a relevant change takes place after the grant of the licence, OFCOM may revoke the licence by notice[21] served on the holder of the licence and taking effect forthwith or on a date specified in the notice[22]. OFCOM must not serve any such notice on the licence holder unless it has notified him of the matters complained of and given him a reasonable opportunity of making representations to it about those matters[23].

1   As to OFCOM see PARA 507.
2   As to the meaning of 'person' see PARA 510 note 1.

3   As to the meaning of 'licence' see PARA 662 note 3. As to the holder of the licence see PARA 671 note 19.
4   Broadcasting Act 1990 s 5(1)(a) (amended by the Communications Act 2003 s 350(2), Sch 15 para 3(1), (2)). For these purposes, a person is disqualified by virtue of the Broadcasting Act 1990 s 5, Sch 2 Pt II (see PARA 822 et seq): s 5(1)(a).
5   Ie imposed by or under the Communications Act 2003 Sch 14. See PARAS 820, 831, 739, 759, 769.
6   Broadcasting Act 1990 s 5(1)(b) (substituted by the Communications Act 2003 s 350(2)). Nothing in the Broadcasting Act 1990 Pt I (ss 3–71) is to be construed as affecting the operation of s 5(1): s 3(3).
7   Broadcasting Act 1990 s 5(1)(c) (added by the Communications Act 2003 s 350(2)).
8   Broadcasting Act 1990 s 5(2) (amended by the Communications Act 2003 Sch 15 para 3(2)).
9   Broadcasting Act 1990 s 5(2)(a). The information is that required for the purpose of determining: (1) whether he is such a disqualified person (see the text and note 4); (2) whether certain requirements (see the text and note 5) would preclude OFCOM from granting a licence to him; and (3) if so, what steps would be required to be taken by or in relation to him in order for any such requirements to be complied with: s 5(2)(a)(i)–(iii).
10 'Body', without more, means a body of persons whether incorporated or not, and includes a partnership: Broadcasting Act 1990 s 202(1).
11 'Relevant change', in relation to a body to which a licence has been awarded or granted, means:
     (1)   any change affecting the nature or characteristics of the body; or
     (2)   any change in the persons having control over or interests in the body; or
     (3)   any other change giving rise to a disqualification under the Broadcasting Act 1990 Sch 2 Pt II or a contravention of a requirement imposed by or under the Communications Act 2003 Sch 14,
being (in any case) a change which is such that, if it fell to OFCOM to determine whether to award the licence to the body in the new circumstances of the case, it would be induced by the change to refrain from so awarding it: Broadcasting Act 1990 s 5(7) (amended by the Broadcasting Act 1996 s 73, Sch 2 para 12(3); and the Communications Act 2003 Sch 15 para 3(2), (7)).
   A person controls a body corporate if: (1) he holds, or is beneficially entitled to, more than 50% of the equity share capital in the body, or possesses more than 50% of the voting power in it; or (2) although he does not have such an interest in the body, it is reasonable, having regard to all the circumstances, to expect that he would (if he chose to) be able in most cases or in significant respects, by whatever means and whether directly or indirectly, to achieve the result that affairs of the body are conducted in accordance with his wishes; or (3) he holds, or is beneficially entitled to, 50% of the equity share capital in that body, or possesses 50% of the voting power in it, and an arrangement exists between him and any other participant in the body as to the manner in which any voting power in the body possessed by either of them is to be exercised, or as to the omission by either of them to exercise such voting power: Broadcasting Act 1990 s 202(1), Sch 2 Pt I para 1(1), (3) (Sch 2 Pt I para 1(3) substituted by the Broadcasting Act 1996 Sch 2 para 1(3); and amended by the Communications Act 2003 s 357(1)). It is the duty of OFCOM to publish guidance setting out its intentions concerning the inclusion of particular matters in the matters that it will take into account when determining whether a person has control of a body, within the meaning of the Broadcasting Act 1990 Sch 2 Pt I para 1(3)(b): Communications Act 2003 s 357(2). OFCOM may from time to time revise the guidance issued by it under s 357: s 357(3). OFCOM must publish the guidance and, where it revises it, the revised guidance in such manner as it considers appropriate for bringing it to the attention of the persons who, in its opinion, are likely to be affected by it: s 357(4).
   'Control', in relation to any body other than a body corporate, means the power of a person to secure, by whatever means and whether directly or indirectly, that the affairs of the body are conducted in accordance with the wishes of that person: Broadcasting Act 1990 Sch 2 Pt I para 1(1) (amended by the Broadcasting Act 1996 Sch 2 para 1(2)).
   With regard to references to a body controlled by two or more persons or bodies of any description taken together, the persons or bodies in question are not regarded as controlling the body by virtue of head (2) unless they are acting together in concert: Broadcasting Act 1990 Sch 2 Pt I para 1(5). 'Arrangement' includes any agreement or arrangement, whether or not it is, or is intended to be, legally enforceable: Sch 2 Pt I para 1(3A) (added by the Broadcasting Act 1996 Sch 2 para 1(3)). A person is to be treated as holding, or being beneficially entitled to, any equity share capital which is held by a body corporate which he controls or to which such a body corporate is beneficially entitled, and as possessing any voting power possessed by such a body corporate: Broadcasting Act 1990 Sch 2 Pt I para 1(3A) (as so added). 'Equity share

capital' has the same meaning as in the Companies Acts (see the Companies Act 2006 s 548; and COMPANIES vol 15 (2009) PARA 1148): Broadcasting Act 1990 Sch 2 Pt I para 1(1) (amended by SI 2009/1941).

A reference to a person holding or being entitled to shares, or any amount of the shares or equity share capital, in a body corporate, or possessing voting power, or any amount of the voting power, in a body corporate, is a reference to his doing so, or being so entitled, whether alone or jointly with one or more other persons and whether directly or through one or more nominees: Sch 2 Pt I para 2(1). However, a person's holding of shares, or possession of voting power, in a body corporate is to be disregarded if, or to the extent that: (a) he holds the shares concerned as a nominee, as a custodian (whether under a trust or by a contract), or under an arrangement pursuant to which he has issued, or is to issue, depositary receipts in respect of the shares concerned; and (b) he is not entitled to exercise or control the exercise of voting rights in respect of the shares concerned: Broadcasting Act 1990 Sch 2 Pt I para 2(1A) (added by the Broadcasting Act 1996 Sch 2 para 2; and amended by SI 2008/948). 'Depositary receipt' means a certificate or other record (whether or not in the form of a document): (i) which is issued by or on behalf of a person who holds shares or who holds evidence of the right to receive shares, or has an interest in shares, in a particular body corporate; and (ii) which evidences or acknowledges that another person is entitled to rights in relation to those shares or shares of the same kind, which shall include the right to receive such shares (or evidence of the right to receive such shares) from the person mentioned in head (i): Broadcasting Act 1990 Sch 2 Pt I para 2(1AA) (added by SI 2008/948).

For these purposes: (A) a person is not entitled to exercise or control the exercise of voting rights in respect of shares if he is bound (whether by contract or otherwise) not to exercise the voting rights, or not to exercise them otherwise than in accordance with the instructions of another; and (B) voting rights which a person is entitled to exercise or of which he is entitled to control the exercise only in certain circumstances are to be taken into account only when those circumstances have arisen and for as long as they continue to obtain: Broadcasting Act 1990 Sch 2 Pt I para 2(1B) (added by the Broadcasting Act 1996 Sch 2 para 2).

12 Broadcasting Act 1990 s 5(2)(b). Nothing in Pt I is to be construed as affecting the operation of s 5(2)(b): s 3(3).

Before revoking the award of a licence to a BBC company, OFCOM must give the Secretary of State notice of its intention to do so, specifying the relevant change: s 5(2A) (added by the Broadcasting Act 1996 s 136, Sch 8 para 2; and amended by the Communications Act 2003 Sch 15 para 3(2)). As to the meaning of 'BBC company' see PARA 854 note 4. As to the Secretary of State see PARA 507 note 32. Where OFCOM revokes the award of any licence in pursuance of the Broadcasting Act 1990 s 5(2)(b), any provisions of Pt I relating to the awarding of licences of the kind in question (subject to s 5(4)) have effect as if the person to whom the licence was awarded or granted had not made an application for it: s 5(3) (amended by the Communications Act 2003 Sch 15 para 3(2)). However, those provisions will not have effect if OFCOM decides that it would be desirable to publish a fresh notice under the Broadcasting Act 1990 Pt I in respect of the grant of a licence, or (as the case may be) a further licence, to provide the service in question: s 5(4) (amended by the Communications Act 2003 Sch 15 para 3(2)).

13 Broadcasting Act 1990 s 5(2)(c). Nothing in Pt I is to be construed as affecting the operation of s 5(2)(c): s 3(3).

The specified steps are those taken under s 5(2)(a) (see note 9). Where OFCOM determines that any condition imposed by it in relation to any licence in pursuance of s 5(2)(c) has not been satisfied, any provisions of Pt I relating to the awarding of licences of the kind in question (subject to s 5(4)) have effect as if the person to whom the licence was awarded or granted had not made an application for it: s 5(3) (as amended: see note 12).

14 Broadcasting Act 1990 s 5(2)(d).

15 Broadcasting Act 1990 s 5(2)(da) (added by the Communications Act 2003 Sch 15 para 3(3)).

16 Ie by virtue of the Broadcasting Act 1990 Sch 2 Pt II.

17 Ie those mentioned in the Broadcasting Act 1990 s 5(1)(b): see the text and notes 5–6.

18 Broadcasting Act 1990 s 5(2)(db) (added by the Communications Act 2003 Sch 15 para 3(3)).

19 Ie those mentioned in the Broadcasting Act 1990 s 5(1)(b): see the text and notes 5–6.

20 Broadcasting Act 1990 s 5(2)(e).

21 As to the service of notices see TELECOMMUNICATIONS vol 97 (2010) PARAS 49–50.

22 Broadcasting Act 1990 s 5(5) (amended by the Communications Act 2003 Sch 15 para 3(2)). OFCOM must not serve any such notice as is mentioned in the Broadcasting Act 1990 s 5(5) on a BBC company unless it has given the Secretary of State notice of its intention to do so, specifying the relevant change: s 5(6C) (added by the Broadcasting Act 1996 Sch 8 para 2; and amended by the Communications Act 2003 Sch 15 para 3(2)).

23 Broadcasting Act 1990 s 5(6)(a) (s 5(6) substituted by the Broadcasting Act 1996 Sch 2 Pt V
    para 12(2); and the Broadcasting Act 1990 s 5(6)(a) amended by the Communications Act 2003
    Sch 15 para 3(1), (2), (4)). In a case where the relevant change is one falling within the
    Broadcasting Act 1990 s 5(6A), OFCOM must have also given him an opportunity of complying
    with Sch 2 Pt III and Pt IV (both repealed) within a period specified in the notification, and the
    period specified in the notification must have elapsed: s 5(6)(b) (as so substituted). A relevant
    change falls within s 5(6A) if it consists only in one or more of the following: (1) a change in the
    national market share within the meaning of the Communications Act 2003 Sch 14 Pt 1 (see
    PARA 820 note 5) of one or more national newspapers (see PARA 820); (2) a change in the local
    market share (see PARA 820 note 8) in a particular area of one or more local newspapers (see
    PARA 820): Broadcasting Act 1990 s 5(6A) (added by the Broadcasting Act 1996 Sch 2 Pt V
    para 12(2); and amended by the Communications Act 2003 Sch 15 para 3(5), Sch 19). Where
    OFCOM receives any written representations from a BBC company under the Broadcasting
    Act 1990 s 5(6), it must send a copy of the representations to the Secretary of State: s 5(6D)
    (added by the Broadcasting Act 1996 Sch 8 para 2; and amended by the Communications
    Act 2003 Sch 15 para 3(2)).

822. General disqualification of bodies having political connections. The
following persons[1] are disqualified persons in relation to a Broadcasting Act
licence[2] granted by OFCOM[3]:

(1)   a local authority[4];

(2)   a body whose objects are wholly or mainly of a political nature[5];

(3)   a body affiliated to a body falling within head (2) above[6];

(4)   an individual who is an officer of a body falling within head (2) or head
      (3) above[7];

(5)   a body corporate which is an associate[8] of a body corporate falling
      within head (2) or head (3) above[9];

(6)   a body corporate in which a body falling within any of heads (1) to (3)
      and (5) above is a participant[10] with more than a 5 per cent interest[11];

(7)   a body corporate which is controlled by a body corporate falling within
      head (6) above[12];

(8)   a body which is controlled by a person falling within any of heads (1) to
      (5) above or by two or more such persons taken together[13]; and

(9)   a body corporate in which a body falling within head (8) above, other
      than one which is controlled by a person falling within head (4) above,
      or by two or more such persons taken together, is a participant with
      more than a 5 per cent interest[14].

If it appears to OFCOM that there are grounds for suspecting that any person
who is an applicant for a licence[15] is[16] a disqualified person in relation to that
licence, OFCOM is to be regarded as failing to discharge its duty[17] if it grants the
licence to that person without being provided with information which satisfies it
that he is not on those grounds a disqualified person[18].

1   As to the meaning of 'person' see PARA 510 note 1.
2   As to the meaning of 'licence' see PARAS 662 note 3, 677 note 2. 'Broadcasting Act licence'
    means a licence under the Broadcasting Act 1990 Pt I (ss 3–71) or Pt III (ss 85–126) or the
    Broadcasting Act 1996 Pt I (ss 1–39) or Pt II (ss 40–72): Broadcasting Act 1990 Sch 2 Pt I
    para 1(1) (definition added by the Communications Act 2003 s 360(3), Sch 15 para 69(1), (2)).
3   Broadcasting Act 1990 s 5(1)(a), Sch 2 Pt II para 1(1) (amended by the Communications
    Act 2003 ss 349(1)(a), 360(3), Sch 15 para 69(4)). This is subject to the Broadcasting Act 1990
    Sch 2 Pt II para 1A (see note 4). As to OFCOM see PARA 507.
4   Broadcasting Act 1990 Sch 2 Pt II para 1(1)(c). 'Local authority' means, in relation to England,
    the council of a county, district or London borough, the Common Council of the City of
    London and the Council of the Isles of Scilly; and, in relation to Wales, a county council or
    county borough council: Sch 2 Pt I para 1(1) (amended by the Local Government (Wales)
    Act 1994 s 66(6), (8), Sch 16 para 89, Sch 18). See further LOCAL GOVERNMENT vol 69 (2009)
    PARA 23. Where a service is provided exclusively for the purposes of the carrying out of the

functions of a local authority under the Local Government Act 1972 s 142 (provision by local authorities of information relating to their activities), a person is disqualified by virtue of the Broadcasting Act 1990 Sch 2 Pt II para 1(1) in relation to a licence to provide that service only if he would be so disqualified disregarding Sch 2 Pt II para 1(1)(c): Sch 2 Pt II para 1(1A) (added by the Communications Act 2003 s 349(1)(b)).

5 Broadcasting Act 1990 Sch 2 Pt II para 1(1)(d).

6 Broadcasting Act 1990 Sch 2 Pt II para 1(1)(e).

7 Broadcasting Act 1990 Sch 2 Pt II para 1(1)(f).

8 For the purpose of determining the persons who are the associates of a body corporate: (1) an individual is regarded as an associate of a body corporate if he is a director of that body corporate; and (2) a body corporate and another body corporate are regarded as associates of each other if one controls the other or if the same person controls both: Broadcasting Act 1990 Sch 2 Pt I para 1(1), (1A) (amended and added respectively by the Broadcasting Act 1996 s 73, Sch 2 para 1(2), (3)). As to the meaning of 'control' see PARA 821 note 11.

For the purpose of determining the persons who are an individual's associates, the following persons are regarded as associates of each other, namely: (a) any individual and that individual's husband or wife or civil partner and any relative, or husband or wife or civil partner of a relative, of that individual or of that individual's husband or wife or civil partner; (b) any individual and any body corporate of which that individual is a director; (c) any person in his capacity as trustee of a settlement and the settlor or grantor and any person associated with the settlor or grantor; (d) persons carrying on business in partnership and the husband or wife or civil partner and relatives of any of them; (e) any two or more persons acting together to secure or exercise control of a body corporate or other association or to secure control of any enterprise or assets: Broadcasting Act 1990 Sch 2 Pt I para 1(1), (2) (Sch 2 Pt I para 1(2) amended by the Civil Partnership Act 2004 s 261(1), Sch 27 para 139(a)). 'Relative', for these purposes, means a brother, sister, uncle, aunt, nephew, niece, lineal ancestor or descendant (the stepchild or illegitimate child of any person, or anyone adopted by a person, whether legally or otherwise, as his child, being regarded as a relative or taken into account to trace a relationship in the same way as that person's child); and references to a wife or husband include a former wife or husband and a reputed wife or husband and references to a civil partner include a former civil partner and a reputed civil partner: Broadcasting Act 1990 Sch 2 Pt I para 1(2) (amended by the Civil Partnership Act 2004 Sch 27 para 139(b); and by SI 2005/3129).

9 Broadcasting Act 1990 Sch 2 Pt II para 1(1)(g).

10 As to the meaning of 'participant' see PARA 671 note 20.

11 Broadcasting Act 1990 Sch 2 Pt II para 1(1)(h).

12 Broadcasting Act 1990 Sch 2 Pt II para 1(1)(hh) (added by the Broadcasting Act 1996 Sch 2 para 6).

13 Broadcasting Act 1990 Sch 2 Pt II para 1(1)(i) (amended by the Communications Act 2003 Sch 15 para 69(5)). As to the meaning of 'body controlled by two or more persons taken together' see PARA 821 note 11.

14 Broadcasting Act 1990 Sch 2 Pt II para 1(1)(j) (amended by the Communications Act 2003 s 406(7), Sch 19).

15 Ie under the Broadcasting Act 1990 Pt I or Pt III or the Broadcasting Act 1996 Pt I or Pt II: see s 143(1) (amended by the Communications Act 2003 Sch 15 para 138).

16 Ie by virtue of any of the provisions set out in: heads (2)–(5) in the text; head (6) in the text so far as relating to participation by bodies falling within head (2), (3) or (5) in the text; head (7) in the text so far as relating to a body corporate controlled by a body corporate in which a body falling within head (2), (3) or (5) in the text is a participant with more than a 5% interest; head (8) in the text so far as relating to control by a person falling within any of heads (2)–(5) in the text or by two or more such persons; and head (9) in the text so far as relating to participation by a body corporate which is controlled by a person falling within any of heads (2)–(5) or by two or more such persons: Broadcasting Act 1996 s 143(5).

17 Ie under the Broadcasting Act 1990 s 5(1) or s 88(1) (see PARAS 821, 829), or the Broadcasting Act 1996 s 5(1) or s 44(1) (see PARAS 828, 837): see s 143(1) (as amended: see note 15).

18 Broadcasting Act 1996 s 143(1) (as amended: see note 15). If it appears to OFCOM that there are grounds for suspecting that any person who is the holder of a licence under the Broadcasting Act 1990 Pt I or Pt III or the Broadcasting Act 1996 Pt I or Pt II is by virtue of any of the specified provisions (see note 16) a disqualified person in relation to that licence, OFCOM is to be regarded as failing to discharge its duty (see note 17), unless: (1) it requires him to provide it with information for the purpose of determining whether he is on those grounds a disqualified person by virtue of that provision; and (2) if it is satisfied that he is a disqualified person, it revokes the licence: s 143(2) (amended by the Communications Act 2003 Sch 15 para 138(2), (4)). Nothing in the Broadcasting Act 1996 s 143(1)–(5) is to be taken to limit the

generality of the duty imposed on OFCOM by the Broadcasting Act 1990 s 5(1) and s 88(1) or the Broadcasting Act 1996 s 5(1) and s 44(1): see s 143(6)(a) (amended by the Communications Act 2003 Sch 15 para 138(7)).

823.   Disqualification of religious bodies.   The following persons[1] are disqualified persons in relation to specified[2] types of licence only[3]:
(1)   a body[4] whose objects are wholly or mainly of a religious nature[5];
(2)   a body which is controlled[6] by a body falling within head (1) or by two or more such bodies taken together[7];
(3)   a body which controls a body falling within head (1)[8];
(4)   a body corporate which is an associate[9] of a body corporate falling within head (1), (2) or (3)[10];
(5)   a body corporate in which a body falling within any of heads (1) to (4) is a participant with more than a 5 per cent interest[11];
(6)   an individual who is an officer of a body falling within head (1)[12]; and
(7)   a body which is controlled by an individual falling within head (6) or by two or more such individuals taken together[13].

The types of licence in respect of which such a person is disqualified include[14]:
(a)   a Channel 3 licence[15];
(b)   a Channel 5 licence[16];
(c)   a public teletext licence[17];
(d)   an additional television service licence[18].

The Secretary of State[19] may by order make provision for repealing these provisions[20] or for making such other modifications to them and any enactment referring to them as he thinks fit[21].

A person mentioned in any of heads (1) to (7)[22] is not to hold a Broadcasting Act licence not mentioned in heads (a) to (d)[23] unless OFCOM has made a determination in his case as respects a description of licences applicable to that licence and that determination remains in force[24]. OFCOM is to make such a determination in a person's case and as respects a particular description of licence if, and only if, it is satisfied that it is appropriate for that person to hold a licence of that description[25]. OFCOM is not to make a determination except on an application made to it for the purpose[26]. OFCOM must publish guidance for persons making applications to it under these provisions as to the principles that it will apply when determining[27] what is appropriate[28]. OFCOM must have regard to such guidance for the time being in force when making determinations under these provisions[29]. OFCOM may revise any guidance by publishing its revisions of it[30]. The publication of guidance, or of any revisions of it, is to be in whatever manner OFCOM considers appropriate[31].

1   As to the meaning of 'person' see PARA 510 note 1.
2   Ie a licence specified in the Broadcasting Act 1990 s 5, Sch 2 Pt II para 2(1A) (see the text and notes 14–18). As to the meaning of 'licence' see PARAS 662 note 3, 677 note 2.
3   Broadcasting Act 1990 Sch 2 Pt II para 2(1) (amended by the Communications Act 2003 s 348(2)).
4   As to the meaning of 'body' see PARA 821 note 10.
5   Broadcasting Act 1990 Sch 2 Pt II para 2(1)(a).
6   As to the meaning of 'control' see PARA 821 note 11.
7   Broadcasting Act 1990 Sch 2 Pt II para 2(1)(b). As to a body controlled by two or more bodies see PARA 821 note 11.
8   Broadcasting Act 1990 Sch 2 Pt II para 2(1)(c).
9   As to the meaning of 'associate' see PARA 822 note 8.
10   Broadcasting Act 1990 Sch 2 Pt II para 2(1)(d).
11   Broadcasting Act 1990 Sch 2 Pt II para 2(1)(e). As to the meaning of 'participant' see PARA 671 note 20.

12 Broadcasting Act 1990 Sch 2 Pt II para 2(1)(f).
13 Broadcasting Act 1990 Sch 2 Pt II para 2(1)(g).
14 Broadcasting Act 1990 Sch 2 Pt II para 2(1A) (added by the Communications Act 2003 s 348(3)).
15 As to the meaning of 'Channel 3 licence' see PARA 669 note 2; definition applied by the Broadcasting Act 1990 Sch 2 Pt II para 2(1B) (added by the Communications Act 2003 s 348(3)).
16 As to the meaning of 'Channel 5 licence' see PARA 681 note 4; definition applied by the Broadcasting Act 1990 Sch 2 Pt II para 2(1B) (as added: see note 15).
17 'Public teletext licence' means a licence to provide the public teletext service (within the meaning of the Communications Act 2003 Pt 3 (ss 198–362): see PARA 686): Broadcasting Act 1990 Sch 2 Pt II para 2(1B) (as added: see note 15).
18 'Additional television service licence' means a licence under the Broadcasting Act 1990 Pt I (ss 3–71) to provide an additional television service within the meaning of the Communications Act 2003 Pt 3 (see PARA 857 note 8): Broadcasting Act 1990 Sch 2 Pt II para 2(1B) (as added: see note 15).
19 As to the Secretary of State see PARA 507 note 32.
20 Ie the Broadcasting Act 1990 Sch 2 Pt II para 2.
21 Communications Act 2003 s 348(5). Before making an order under s 348(5) (other than one that is confined to giving effect to recommendations made by OFCOM in a report of a review under s 391 (see TELECOMMUNICATIONS vol 97 (2010) PARA 48)), the Secretary of State must consult OFCOM: s 348(6). As to OFCOM see PARA 507. No order is to be made containing provision authorised by s 348(5) unless a draft of the order has been laid before Parliament and approved by a resolution of each House: s 348(7). As to the power of the Secretary of State to make orders under the Communications Act 2003 see s 402; and TELECOMMUNICATIONS vol 97 (2010) PARA 77.
22 Ie a person mentioned in the Broadcasting Act 1990 Sch 2 Pt II para 2(1).
23 Ie not mentioned in the Broadcasting Act 1990 Sch 2 Pt II para 2(1A).
24 Communications Act 2003 Sch 14 para 15(1). The Secretary of State may by order repeal or otherwise modify the restriction imposed by Sch 14 Pt 4: Sch 14 para 16.
25 Communications Act 2003 Sch 14 para 15(2).
26 Communications Act 2003 Sch 14 para 15(3).
27 Ie for the purposes of the Communications Act 2003 Sch 14 para 15(2).
28 Communications Act 2003 Sch 14 para 15(4).
29 Communications Act 2003 Sch 14 para 15(5).
30 Communications Act 2003 Sch 14 para 15(6).
31 Communications Act 2003 Sch 14 para 15(7).

824. General disqualification on grounds of undue influence. A person[1] is a disqualified person in relation to a Broadcasting Act licence[2] if in the opinion of OFCOM[3] any relevant body[4] is, by the giving of financial assistance or otherwise, exerting influence over the activities of that person, and that influence has led, is leading or is likely to lead to results which are adverse to the public interest[5].

1 As to the meaning of 'person' see PARA 510 note 1.
2 As to the meaning of 'Broadcasting Act licence' see PARA 822 note 2.
3 As to OFCOM see PARA 507.
4 'Relevant body', in relation to a licence granted under the Broadcasting Act 1990 Pt I (ss 3–71) or the Broadcasting Act 1996 Pt I (ss 1–39) means a person falling within the Broadcasting Act 1990 s 5, Sch 2 Pt II para 1(1)(c)–(h) or (j) (see PARA 822 text and notes 4–11, 14) or a body which is controlled by a person falling within Sch 2 Pt II para 1(1)(c)–(g) (see PARA 822 text and notes 4–9), or a body which is controlled by two or more such persons taken together: Sch 2 Pt II para 4(2)(a) (amended by the Communications Act 2003 s 360(3), Sch 15 para 69(1), (8)(a)).
5 Broadcasting Act 1990 Sch 2 Pt II para 4(1) (amended by the Communications Act 2003 Sch 15 para 69(4), (7)).

825. General disqualification of broadcasting bodies. The following are disqualified persons in relation to a Broadcasting Act licence[1] granted by OFCOM[2]:

(1)   the BBC[3];
(2)   the Welsh Authority[4].

1   As to the meaning of 'Broadcasting Act licence' see PARA 822 note 2.
2   Broadcasting Act 1990 s 5, Sch 2 Pt II para 5 (amended by the Communications Act 2003 s 360(3), Sch 15 para 69(1), (4)). As to OFCOM see PARA 507.
3   Broadcasting Act 1990 Sch 2 Pt II para 5(a). As to the meaning of 'BBC' see PARA 603 note 1; and as to the BBC see PARAS 603–626.
4   Broadcasting Act 1990 Sch 2 Pt II para 5(b). As to the meaning of 'the Welsh Authority' see PARA 644 note 3; and as to television broadcasting by the Welsh Authority see PARAS 644–661.

826.   Disqualification of certain companies for certain licences.   A BBC company[1], a Channel 4 company[2] or an S4C company[3] is a disqualified person in relation to any licence[4] granted by OFCOM[5] to provide regional or national Channel 3 services[6] or Channel 5[7].

1   As to the meaning of 'BBC company' see PARA 671 note 20.
2   'Channel 4 company' means any body corporate which is controlled by the Channel 4 Television Corporation, or any body corporate in which the corporation or any body corporate controlled by it, is to any extent a participant: Broadcasting Act 1990 s 202(1) (definition added by the Broadcasting Act 1996 s 148(1), Sch 10 Pt II para 21(a)). As to the meaning of 'participant' see PARA 671 note 20.
3   'S4C company' means: (1) any body corporate which is controlled by the Welsh Authority; or (2) any body corporate in which the Welsh Authority or any body corporate which is controlled by the Welsh Authority is, to any extent, a participant: Broadcasting Act 1990 s 202(1) (definition added by the Broadcasting Act 1996 s 148(1), Sch 10 Pt II para 21(c)). As to the meaning of 'the Welsh Authority' see PARA 644 note 3.
4   As to the meaning of 'licence' see PARAS 662 note 3, 677 note 2.
5   As to OFCOM see PARA 507.
6   As to the meaning of 'regional Channel 3 service' see PARA 667 note 6. As to the meaning of 'national Channel 3 service' see PARA 667 note 12.
7   Broadcasting Act 1990 s 5, Sch 2 Pt II para 5A(1)(a) (Sch 2 Pt II para 5A added by the Broadcasting Act 1996 s 73, Sch 2 para 9; and amended by the Communications Act 2003 ss 360(3), 406(7), Sch 15 para 69(1), (9)(a), Sch 19). As to the meaning of 'Channel 5' see PARA 681.

827.   General disqualification of advertising agencies.   The following are disqualified persons[1] in relation to a Broadcasting Act licence[2] granted by OFCOM[3]:

(1)   an advertising agency[4];
(2)   an associate[5] of an advertising agency[6];
(3)   any body[7] which is controlled by a person falling within head (1) or head (2) above or by two or more such persons taken together[8];
(4)   any body corporate in which a person falling within any of heads (1) to (3) above is a participant with more than a 5 per cent interest[9].

1   As to the meaning of 'person' see PARA 510 note 1.
2   As to the meaning of 'Broadcasting Act licence' see PARA 822 note 2.
3   Broadcasting Act 1990 s 5, Sch 2 Pt II para 6 (amended by the Communications Act 2003 s 360(3), Sch 15 para 69(1), (4)). As to OFCOM see PARA 507.
4   Broadcasting Act 1990 Sch 2 Pt II para 6(a). 'Advertising agency' means an individual or a body corporate who carries on business as an advertising agent (whether alone or in partnership) or has control over any body corporate which carries on business as an advertising agent, and any reference to an advertising agency includes a reference to an individual who: (1) is a director or officer of any body corporate which carries on such a business; or (2) is employed by any person who carries on such a business: Sch 2 Pt I para 1(1). As to the meaning of 'control' see PARA 821 note 11.
5   As to the meaning of 'associate' see PARA 822 note 8.
6   Broadcasting Act 1990 Sch 2 Pt II para 6(b).
7   As to the meaning of 'body' see PARA 821 note 10.

8   Broadcasting Act 1990 Sch 2 Pt II para 6(c). As to a body controlled by two or more persons taken together see PARA 821 note 11.
9   Broadcasting Act 1990 Sch 2 Pt II para 6(d). As to the meaning of 'participant' see PARA 671 note 20.

(iii) Restrictions on holding of Licences for Digital Terrestrial Broadcasting

828.   Restrictions on holding of licences.   OFCOM[1] must do all that it can to secure: (1) that a person[2] does not become or remain the holder of a licence[3] if he is a person who is a disqualified[4] person in relation to that licence[5]; (2) that certain requirements[6] are complied with by or in relation to persons holding licences in relation to which those requirements apply[7]; and (3) that those requirements are not contravened in the case of a person who already holds a licence[8]. OFCOM may accordingly:

(a)   require any applicant for a licence to provide it with such information as it may reasonably require for the purpose of determining:

   (i)   whether he is such a disqualified person as is mentioned in head (1) above[9];

   (ii)   whether any such requirements as are mentioned in head (2) above would preclude it from granting a licence to him[10]; and

   (iii)   if so, what steps would be required to be taken by or in relation to him in order for any such requirements to be complied with[11];

(b)   revoke the award of a licence to a body[12] where a relevant change[13] takes place after the award, but before the grant, of the licence[14];

(c)   make the grant of a licence to any person conditional on the taking of any specified steps that appear to it to be required to be taken as mentioned in head (a)(iii) above[15];

(d)   impose conditions in any licence enabling it to require the licence holder, if a body corporate, to give to it advance notice of proposals affecting shareholdings in the body, or affecting the directors of the body, where such proposals are known to the body[16];

(e)   impose conditions in a licence requiring the licence holder, if a body corporate, to give OFCOM notice, after they have occurred and irrespective of whether proposals for them have fallen to be notified, of changes, transactions or events affecting shareholdings in the body or the directors of the body[17];

(f)   impose conditions in a licence enabling OFCOM to require the licence holder to provide it with such information as it may reasonably require for determining: (i) whether the licence holder is a disqualified person in relation to that licence[18]; or (ii) whether any such requirements as are mentioned in head (1) above[19] have been and are being complied with by or in relation to the licence holder[20];

(g)   impose conditions in any licence enabling it to give the licence holder directions requiring him to take, or arrange for the taking of, any specified steps appearing to it to be required to be taken in order for any such requirements as are mentioned in head (2) above to be complied with[21].

Where OFCOM revokes the award of any licence in pursuance of head (b) above, or determines that any condition imposed by it in relation to any licence in pursuance of head (c) above has not been satisfied, any provisions[22] relating to the awarding of licences of the kind in question have effect as if the person to whom the licence was awarded or granted had not made an application for it[23].

Every licence must include such conditions as OFCOM considers necessary or expedient to ensure that where the holder of the licence is a body, and a relevant change takes place after the grant of the licence, OFCOM may revoke the licence by notice served on the holder of the licence, taking effect immediately or on a date specified in the notice[24].

A body whose objects are wholly or mainly of a religious nature, and related bodies, are disqualified from holding a television multiplex licence or a radio multiplex licence[25].

1   As to OFCOM see PARA 507.
2   As to the meaning of 'person' see PARA 510 note 1.
3   As to the meaning of 'licence' see PARA 698 note 1.
4   Ie by virtue of the Broadcasting Act 1990 ss 5, 88, Sch 2 Pt II (see PARAS 822–827, 830–836): see the Broadcasting Act 1996 s 5(1)(a).
5   Broadcasting Act 1996 s 5(1)(a) (amended by the Communications Act 2003 s 360(3), Sch 15 para 78(1), (2)).
6   Ie requirements imposed by or under the Communications Act 2003 Sch 14: see PARAS 820, 831, 739, 759, 769.
7   Broadcasting Act 1996 s 5(1)(b) (substituted by the Communications Act 2003 s 350(2)).
8   Broadcasting Act 1996 5(1)(c) (added by the Communications Act 2003 s 350(2)).
9   Broadcasting Act 1996 s 5(2)(a)(i).
10 Broadcasting Act 1996 s 5(2)(a)(ii).
11 Broadcasting Act 1996 s 5(2)(a)(iii).
12 As to the meaning of 'body' see PARA 821 note 10; definition applied by the Broadcasting Act 1996 s 147(2).
13 'Relevant change', in relation to a body to which a licence has been awarded or granted, means:
    (1)   any change affecting the nature or characteristics of the body;
    (2)   any change in the persons having control over or interests in the body; or
    (3)   any other change giving rise to a disqualification under the Broadcasting Act 1990 Sch 2 Pt II or a contravention of a requirement imposed by or under the Communications Act 2003 Sch 14 (see PARAS 820, 831, 739, 759, 769),
    being (in any case) a change which is such that, if it fell to OFCOM to determine whether to award the licence to the body in the new circumstances of the case, it would be induced by the change to refrain from so awarding it: Broadcasting Act 1996 s 5(8) (amended by the Communications Act 2003 Sch 15 para 78(2), (6)). As to the meaning of 'control' see PARA 821 note 11; definition applied by the Broadcasting Act 1996 s 147(2).
14 Broadcasting Act 1996 s 5(2)(b).
15 Broadcasting Act 1996 s 5(2)(c).
16 Broadcasting Act 1996 s 5(2)(d).
17 Broadcasting Act 1996 s 5(2)(da) (added by the Communications Act 2003 Sch 15 para 78(3)).
18 Ie by virtue of the Broadcasting Act 1990 Sch 2 Pt II: see the Broadcasting Act 1996 s 5(2)(db)(i) (s 5(2)(db) added by the Communications Act 2003 Sch 15 para 78(3)).
19 Ie any such requirements as are mentioned in the Broadcasting Act 1996 s 5(1)(b): see s 5(2)(db)(ii) (as added: see note 18).
20 Broadcasting Act 1996 s 5(2)(db) (as added: see note 18).
21 Broadcasting Act 1996 s 5(2)(e).
22 Ie provisions of the Broadcasting Act 1996 Pt I (ss 1–39).
23 Broadcasting Act 1996 s 5(3) (amended by the Communications Act 2003 Sch 15 para 78(2)). The provisions of the Broadcasting Act 1996 Pt I do not so have effect if OFCOM decides that it would be desirable to publish a fresh notice under Pt I in respect of the grant of a licence, or (as the case may be) a further licence, to provide the service in question: s 5(4) (amended by the Communications Act 2003 Sch 15 para 78(2)). As to notices see TELECOMMUNICATIONS vol 97 (2010) PARA 49.
24 Broadcasting Act 1996 s 5(5) (amended by the Communications Act 2003 Sch 15 para 78(2)). OFCOM must not serve any such notice on the licence holder unless:
    (1)   it has notified him of the matters constituting its grounds for revoking the licence and given him a reasonable opportunity of making representations to it about those matters (Broadcasting Act 1996 s 5(6)(a) (amended by the Communications Act 2003 Sch 15 para 78(2), (4)(a))); and
    (2)   in a case where the relevant change is one falling within the Broadcasting Act 1996 s 5(7):

(a)　　it has also given him an opportunity of complying with the requirements imposed by or under the Communications Act 2003 Sch 14 (see PARAS 820, 831, 739, 759, 769) within a period specified in the notification (Broadcasting Act 1996 s 5(6)(b)(i) (amended by the Communications Act 2003 Sch 15 para 78(2), (4)(b))); and

(b)　　the period specified in the notification has elapsed (Broadcasting Act 1996 s 5(6)(b)(ii)).

A relevant change falls within s 5(7) if it consists only in one or more of the following:

(i)　　a change in the national market share (within the meaning of the Communications Act 2003 Sch 14 Pt 1: see PARA 820 note 5) of one or more national newspapers (within the meaning of Sch 14 Pt 1: see PARA 820 note 4) (Broadcasting Act 1996 s 5(7)(b) (amended by the Communications Act 2003 Sch 15 para 78(5))); or

(ii)　　a change in the local market share (within the meaning of the Communications Act 2003 Sch 14 Pt 1: see PARA 820 note 8) in a particular area of one or more local newspapers (within the meaning of Sch 14 Pt 1: see PARA 820 note 4) (Broadcasting Act 1996 s 5(7)(c)).

25　See the Broadcasting Act 1990 s 5, Sch 2 Pt II para 2; and PARA 823. As to the meaning of 'television multiplex service' see PARA 697; and as to the meaning of 'radio multiplex service' see PARA 753. As to licences for such services see PARAS 690, 754 respectively.

(iv) Restrictions on and Disqualification for holding of Licences for Provision of Radio Services

829. Restrictions on and disqualification for the holding of licences. OFCOM[1] must do all it can to secure:

(1)　　that a person[2] does not become or remain the holder of a licence[3] if he is a disqualified person in relation to that licence[4];

(2)　　that a person does not become the holder of a licence if requirements imposed by or under the Communications Act 2003[5] would be contravened were he to do so[6]; and

(3)　　that those requirements are not contravened in the case of a person who already holds a licence[7].

OFCOM may accordingly:

(a)　　require any applicant for a licence to provide it with such information as it may reasonably require for the purpose of determining whether he is such a disqualified person[8], whether any such requirements as are mentioned in head (2) above would preclude it from granting a licence to him[9], and if so, what steps would be required to be taken by or in relation to him in order for any such requirements to be complied with[10];

(b)　　revoke the award of a licence to a body[11] where a relevant change[12] takes place after the award, but before the grant, of the licence[13];

(c)　　make the grant of a licence to any person conditional on the taking of any specified steps that appear to it to be required to be taken as mentioned in head (a) above[14];

(d)　　impose conditions in any licence enabling it to require the licence holder, if a body corporate, to give to it advance notice of proposals affecting shareholdings in the body[15], or affecting the directors of the body[16], where such proposals are known to the body[17];

(e)　　impose conditions in a licence requiring the licence holder, if a body corporate, to give OFCOM notice, after they have occurred and irrespective of whether proposals for them have fallen to be notified, of changes, transactions or events affecting shareholdings in the body or the directors of the body[18];

(f)　　impose conditions in a licence enabling OFCOM to require the licence holder to provide it with such information as it may reasonably require for determining whether the licence holder is a disqualified person in relation to that licence[19] or whether any such requirements as are mentioned in head (2) above have been and are being complied with by or in relation to the licence holder[20]; and

(g)   impose conditions in any licence enabling it to give the licence holder directions requiring him to take, or arrange for the taking of, any specified steps appearing to it to be required in order for any such requirements as are mentioned in head (2) above to be complied with[21].

Every licence must include such conditions as OFCOM considers necessary or expedient to ensure that where the holder of the licence is a body[22], and a relevant change takes place after the grant of the licence[23], OFCOM may revoke the licence by notice served on the holder of the licence and taking effect immediately or on a date specified in the notice[24].

Every licence granted[25] must include conditions requiring the holder of the licence to do all that he can to ensure that no person who is disqualified for holding a licence[26] is concerned in: (i) the provision of the licensed service or the making of programmes included in it; or (ii) the operation of a wireless telegraphy station[27] used for broadcasting the service[28].

1   As to OFCOM see PARA 507.
2   As to the meaning of 'person' see PARA 510 note 1.
3   As to the meaning of 'licence' see PARA 724 note 2. As to the holder of the licence see PARA 725 note 16.
4   Broadcasting Act 1990 s 88(1)(a) (s 88(1) amended by the Communications Act 2003 s 360(3), Sch 15 para 35(1), (2)). A person is disqualified by virtue of the Broadcasting Act 1990 Sch 2 Pt II (see PARAS 830–836): see s 88(1)(a).
5   Ie imposed by or under the Communications Act 2003 Sch 14: see PARAS 820, 831, 739, 759, 769.
6   Broadcasting Act 1990 s 88(1)(b) (substituted by the Communications Act 2003 s 350(2)).
7   Broadcasting Act 1990 s 88(1)(c) (added by the Communications Act 2003 s 350(2)).
8   Broadcasting Act 1990 s 88(2)(a)(i).
9   Broadcasting Act 1990 s 88(2)(a)(ii).
10 Broadcasting Act 1990 s 88(2)(a)(iii).
11 As to the meaning of 'body' see PARA 821 note 10.
12 'Relevant change', in relation to a body to which a licence has been awarded or granted, means:
    (1)   any change affecting the nature or characteristics of the body; or
    (2)   any change in the persons having control over or interests in the body; or
    (3)   any other change giving rise to a disqualification under the Broadcasting Act 1990 Sch 2 Pt II or a contravention of a requirement imposed by or under the Communications Act 2003 Sch 14 (see PARAS 820, 831, 739, 759, 769),
    being (in any case) a change which is such that, if it fell to OFCOM to determine whether to award the licence to the body in the new circumstances of the case, it would be induced by the change to refrain from so awarding it: Broadcasting Act 1990 s 88(7) (amended by the Broadcasting Act 1996 s 73, Sch 2 para 13(3); and the Communications Act 2003 s 360(3), Sch 15 para 35(2), (7)). As to the meaning of 'control' see PARA 821 note 11.
13 Broadcasting Act 1990 s 88(2)(b). Before revoking in pursuance of 88(2)(b) the award of a licence to a BBC company, OFCOM must give the Secretary of State notice of its intention to do so, specifying the relevant change: s 88(2A) (added by the Broadcasting Act 1996 s 136, Sch 8 para 6; and amended by the Communications Act 2003 Sch 15 para 35(2)). As to the meaning of 'BBC company' see PARA 671 note 20. As to the Secretary of State see PARA 507 note 32. Where OFCOM so revokes the award of any licence, any provisions of the Broadcasting Act 1990 Pt III (ss 85–126) relating to the awarding of licences of the kind in question (subject to s 88(4)) have effect as if the person to whom the licence was awarded or granted had not made an application for it: s 88(3)(a) (s 88(3) amended by the Communications Act 2003 Sch 15 para 35(2)). Those provisions do not so have effect if OFCOM decides that it would be desirable to publish a fresh notice under the Broadcasting Act 1990 Pt III in respect of the grant of a licence, or (as the case may be) a further licence, to provide the service in question: s 88(4) (amended by the Communications Act 2003 Sch 15 para 35(2)).

14 Broadcasting Act 1990 s 88(2)(c). Where OFCOM determines that any condition imposed by it in relation to any licence in pursuance of s 88(2)(c) has not been satisfied, any provisions of Pt III relating to the awarding of licences of the kind in question must (subject to s 88(4): see note 13) have effect as if the person to whom the licence was awarded or granted had not made an application for it: s 88(3)(b) (as amended: see note 13).

15 Broadcasting Act 1990 s 88(2)(d)(i).

16 Broadcasting Act 1990 s 88(2)(d)(ii).

17 Broadcasting Act 1990 s 88(2)(d).

18 Broadcasting Act 1990 s 88(2)(da) (added by the Communications Act 2003 Sch 15 para 35(3)).

19 Ie by virtue of the Broadcasting Act 1990 Sch 2 Pt II.

20 Broadcasting Act 1990 s 88(2)(db) (added by the Communications Act 2003 Sch 15 para 35(3)).

21 Broadcasting Act 1990 s 88(2)(e).

22 Broadcasting Act 1990 s 88(5)(a).

23 Broadcasting Act 1990 s 88(5)(b).

24 Broadcasting Act 1990 s 88(5) (amended by the Communications Act 2003 Sch 15 para 35(2)). OFCOM may not serve any such notice on the licence holder unless: (1) it has notified him of the matters constituting its grounds for revoking the licence and given him a reasonable opportunity of making representations to it about those matters; and (2) in a case where the relevant change is one falling within s 88(6A), it has also given him an opportunity of complying with the requirements imposed by or under the Communications Act 2003 Sch 14 (see PARAS 820, 831, 739, 759, 769) within a period specified in the notification, and the period specified in the notification has elapsed: Broadcasting Act 1990 s 88(6) (substituted by the Broadcasting Act 1996 s 73, Sch 2 para 13(2); and amended by the Communications Act 2003 Sch 15 para 35(2), (4)).

A relevant change falls within the Broadcasting Act 1990 s 88(6A) if it consists only in one or more of the following: (a) a change in the national market share within the meaning of the Communications Act 2003 Sch 14 Pt 1 (paras 1–6) (see PARA 820 note 5) of one or more national newspapers (see PARA 820 note 4); or (b) a change in the local market share (see PARA 820 note 8) in a particular area of one or more local newspapers (see PARA 820 note 4): Broadcasting Act 1990 s 88(6A) (added by the Broadcasting Act 1996 Sch 2 para 13(2); and amended by the Communications Act 2003 s 406(7), Sch 15 para 35(5), Sch 19).

OFCOM must not serve any such notice as is mentioned in the Broadcasting Act 1990 s 88(5) on a BBC company unless it has given the Secretary of State notice of its intention to do so, specifying the relevant change: s 88(6C) (added by the Broadcasting Act 1996 Sch 8 para 6; and amended by the Communications Act 2003 Sch 15 para 35(2)). Where OFCOM receives any written representations from a BBC company under the Broadcasting Act 1990 s 88(6), it must send a copy of the representations to the Secretary of State: s 88(6D) (added by the Broadcasting Act 1996 Sch 8 para 6; and amended by the Communications Act 2003 Sch 15 para 35(2)).

25 Ie granted under the Broadcasting Act 1990 Pt III.

26 Ie by virtue of the Broadcasting Act 1990 s 89(1) (see note 28).

27 As to the meaning of 'wireless telegraphy station' see PARA 510 note 12; definition applied by the Broadcasting Act 1990 s 202(1) (amended by the Wireless Telegraphy Act 2006 s 123, Sch 7 paras 9, 13).

28 Broadcasting Act 1990 s 89(3) (amended by the Communications Act 2003 Sch 15 para 36(1), (3); and the Wireless Telegraphy Act 2006 Sch 7 para 12(1), (3)). A person is disqualified for holding a licence under the Broadcasting Act 1990 Pt III if within the last five years he has been convicted of: (1) an offence under the Wireless Telegraphy Act 2006 s 35 consisting in the establishment or use of a wireless telegraphy station, or the installation or use of wireless telegraphy apparatus, for the purpose of making a broadcast (within the meaning of Pt 5 (ss 77–95)) of that Act) (see PARA 514); (2) an offence under s 36 (keeping wireless telegraphy station or apparatus available for unauthorised use) where the relevant contravention of s 8 would constitute an offence falling within head (1) (see PARA 573); (3) an offence under s 37 or 38 (unlawful broadcasting offences) (see PARAS 574–575); (4) an offence under Pt 5 (prohibition of broadcasting from sea or air) (see PARAS 588–592); or (5) an offence under the Broadcasting Act 1990 s 97 (see PARA 595): s 89(1) (amended by the Communications Act 2003 Sch 15 para 36(1), (2); and the Wireless Telegraphy Act 2006 Sch 7 para 12(2)).

830. General disqualification of bodies having political connections.

The following persons[1] are disqualified persons in relation to a Broadcasting Act licence[2] granted by OFCOM[3]:

(1) a local authority[4];

(2)   a body whose objects are wholly or mainly of a political nature[5];
(3)   a body affiliated to a body falling within head (2) above[6];
(4)   an individual who is an officer of a body falling within head (2) or head (3) above[7];
(5)   a body corporate which is an associate[8] of a body corporate falling within head (2) or head (3) above[9];
(6)   a body corporate in which a body falling within any of heads (1) to (3) and (5) above is a participant[10] with more than a 5 per cent interest[11];
(7)   a body corporate which is controlled by a body corporate falling within head (6) above[12];
(8)   a body which is controlled by a person falling within any of heads (1) to (5) above or by two or more such persons taken together[13]; and
(9)   a body corporate in which a body falling within head (8) above, other than one which is controlled by a person falling within head (4) above, or by two or more such persons taken together, is a participant with more than a 5 per cent interest[14].

If it appears to OFCOM that there are grounds for suspecting that any person who is an applicant for a licence[15] is[16] a disqualified person in relation to that licence, OFCOM is to be regarded as failing to discharge its duty[17] if it grants the licence to that person without being provided with information which satisfies it that he is not on those grounds a disqualified person[18].

1   As to the meaning of 'person' see PARA 510 note 1.
2   As to the meaning of 'licence' see PARA 724 note 2. 'Broadcasting Act licence' means a licence under the Broadcasting Act 1990 Pt I (ss 3–71) or Pt III (ss 85–126) or the Broadcasting Act 1996 Pt I (ss 1–39) or Pt II (ss 40–72): Broadcasting Act 1990 s 88(1), Sch 2 Pt I para 1(1) (definition added by the Communications Act 2003 s 360(3), Sch 15 para 69(1), (2)).
3   Broadcasting Act 1990 s 88(1)(a), Sch 2 Pt II para 1(1) (amended by the Communications Act 2003 ss 349(1)(a), s 360(3), Sch 15 para 69(4)). This is subject to the Broadcasting Act 1990 Sch 2 Pt II para 1A (see note 4). As to OFCOM see PARA 507.
4   Broadcasting Act 1990 Sch 2 Pt II para 1(1)(c). As to the meaning of 'local authority' see PARA 822 note 4. See further LOCAL GOVERNMENT vol 69 (2009) PARA 23. Where a service is provided exclusively for the purposes of the carrying out of the functions of a local authority under the Local Government Act 1972 s 142 (provision by local authorities of information relating to their activities), a person is disqualified by virtue of the Broadcasting Act 1990 Sch 2 Pt II para 1(1) in relation to a licence to provide that service only if he would be so disqualified disregarding Sch 2 Pt II para 1(1)(c): Sch 2 Pt II para 1(1A) (added by the Communications Act 2003 s 349(1)(b)).
5   Broadcasting Act 1990 Sch 2 Pt II para 1(1)(d).
6   Broadcasting Act 1990 Sch 2 Pt II para 1(1)(e).
7   Broadcasting Act 1990 Sch 2 Pt II para 1(1)(f).
8   As to determining the persons who are the associates of a body corporate and determining the persons who are an individual's associates see PARA 822 note 8. As to the meaning of 'control' see PARA 821 note 11.
9   Broadcasting Act 1990 Sch 2 Pt II para 1(1)(g).
10   As to the meaning of 'participant' see PARA 671 note 20.
11   Broadcasting Act 1990 Sch 2 Pt II para 1(1)(h).
12   Broadcasting Act 1990 Sch 2 Pt II para 1(1)(hh) (added by the Broadcasting Act 1996 Sch 2 para 6).
13   Broadcasting Act 1990 Sch 2 Pt II para 1(1)(i) (amended by the Communications Act 2003 Sch 15 para 69(5)). As to the meaning of 'body controlled by two or more persons taken together' see PARA 821 note 11.
14   Broadcasting Act 1990 Sch 2 Pt II para 1(1)(j) (amended by the Communications Act 2003 s 406(7), Sch 19).
15   Ie under the Broadcasting Act 1990 Pt I or Pt III or the Broadcasting Act 1996 Pt I or Pt II: see s 143(1) (amended by the Communications Act 2003 Sch 15 para 138).
16   Ie by virtue of any of: heads (2)–(5) in the text; head (6) in the text so far as relating to participation by bodies falling within head (2), (3) or (5) in the text; head (7) in the text so far

as relating to a body corporate controlled by a body corporate in which a body falling within head (2), (3) or (5) in the text is a participant with more than a 5% interest; head (8) in the text so far as relating to control by a person falling within any of heads (2)–(5) in the text or by two or more such persons; and head (9) in the text so far as relating to participation by a body corporate which is controlled by a person falling within any of heads (2)–(5) in the text or by two or more such persons: Broadcasting Act 1996 s 143(5).

17 Ie under the Broadcasting Act 1990 s 5(1) or s 88(1) (see PARAS 821, 829), or the Broadcasting Act 1996 s 5(1) or s 44(1) (see PARAS 828, 837): see s 143(1) (as amended: see note 15).

18 Broadcasting Act 1990 s 143(1) (as amended: see note 15). If it appears to OFCOM that there are grounds for suspecting that any person who is the holder of a licence under the Broadcasting Act 1990 Pt I or Pt III or the Broadcasting Act 1996 Pt I or Pt II is by virtue of any of the specified provisions (see note 16) a disqualified person in relation to that licence, OFCOM is to be regarded as failing to discharge its duty (see note 17), unless: (1) it requires him to provide it with information for the purpose of determining whether he is on those grounds a disqualified person by virtue of that provision; and (2) if it is satisfied that he is a disqualified person, it revokes the licence: s 143(2) (amended by the Communications Act 2003 Sch 15 para 138(2), (4)). Nothing in the Broadcasting Act 1996 s 143(1)–(5) is to be taken to limit the generality of the duty imposed on OFCOM by the Broadcasting Act 1990 s 5(1) and s 88(1) (see PARAS 821, 829) or the Broadcasting Act 1996 s 5(1) and s 44(1) (see PARAS 828, 837): see s 143(6) (amended by the Communications Act 2003 Sch 15 para 138(7)).

831. Disqualification of religious bodies. The following persons[1] are disqualified persons in relation to specified[2] types of licence only[3]:

(1) a body[4] whose objects are wholly or mainly of a religious nature[5];

(2) a body which is controlled[6] by a body falling within head (1) above or by two or more such bodies taken together[7];

(3) a body which controls a body falling within head (1) above[8];

(4) a body corporate which is an associate[9] of a body corporate falling within head (1), (2) or (3) above[10];

(5) a body corporate in which a body falling within any of heads (1) to (4) above is a participant with more than a 5 per cent interest[11];

(6) an individual who is an officer of a body falling within head (1) above[12]; and

(7) a body which is controlled by an individual falling within head (6) above or by two or more such individuals taken together[13].

The types of licence in respect of which such a person is disqualified include a national sound broadcasting licence[14].

The Secretary of State[15] may by order make provision for repealing these provisions[16] or for making such other modifications to them and any enactment referring to them as he thinks fit[17].

A person mentioned in any of heads (1) to (7) above[18] is not to hold any Broadcasting Act licence that is not of a certain type[19] unless OFCOM has made a determination in his case as respects a description of licences applicable to that licence and that determination remains in force[20]. OFCOM is to make such a determination in a person's case and as respects a particular description of licence if, and only if, it is satisfied that it is appropriate for that person to hold a licence of that description[21]. OFCOM is not to make a determination except on an application made to it for the purpose[22]. OFCOM must publish guidance for persons making applications to it under these provisions as to the principles that it will apply when determining[23] what is appropriate[24]. OFCOM must have regard to such guidance for the time being in force when making determinations under these provisions[25]. OFCOM may revise any guidance by publishing its revisions of it[26]. The publication of guidance, or of any revisions of it, is to be in whatever manner OFCOM considers appropriate[27].

1 As to the meaning of 'person' see PARA 510 note 1.

2   Ie a licence specified in the Broadcasting Act 1990 s 5, Sch 2 Pt II para 2(1A) (see the text and note 14).
3   Broadcasting Act 1990 Sch 2 Pt II para 2(1) (amended by the Communications Act 2003 s 348(2)).
4   As to the meaning of 'body' see PARA 821 note 10.
5   Broadcasting Act 1990 Sch 2 Pt II para 2(1)(a).
6   As to the meaning of 'control' see PARA 821 note 11.
7   Broadcasting Act 1990 Sch 2 Pt II para 2(1)(b). As to a body controlled by two or more bodies see PARA 821.
8   Broadcasting Act 1990 Sch 2 Pt II para 2(1)(c).
9   As to the meaning of 'associate' see PARA 822 note 8.
10 Broadcasting Act 1990 Sch 2 Pt II para 2(1)(d).
11 Broadcasting Act 1990 Sch 2 Pt II para 2(1)(e). As to the meaning of 'participant' see PARA 671 note 20.
12 Broadcasting Act 1990 Sch 2 Pt II para 2(1)(f).
13 Broadcasting Act 1990 Sch 2 Pt II para 2(1)(g).
14 Broadcasting Act 1990 Sch 2 Pt II para 2(1A) (added by the Communications Act 2003 s 348(3)). As to the meaning of 'national sound broadcasting licence' see PARA 752 note 15.
15 As to the Secretary of State see PARA 507 note 32.
16 Ie the Broadcasting Act 1990 Sch 2 Pt II para 2.
17 Communications Act 2003 s 348(5). Before making an order under s 348(5) (other than one that is confined to giving effect to recommendations made by OFCOM in a report of a review under s 391 (see PARA 838)), the Secretary of State must consult OFCOM: s 348(6). As to OFCOM see PARA 507. No order is to be made containing provision authorised by s 348(5) unless a draft of the order has been laid before Parliament and approved by a resolution of each House: s 348(7). As to the power of the Secretary of State to make orders under the Communications Act 2003 see s 402; and TELECOMMUNICATIONS vol 97 (2010) PARA 77. At the date at which this volume states the law, no order had been made under s 348(5).
18 Ie a person mentioned in the Broadcasting Act 1990 Sch 2 Pt II para 2(1).
19 Ie any Broadcasting Act licence not mentioned in the Broadcasting Act 1990 Sch 2 Pt II para 2(1A): see PARA 823 and the text and note 14.
20 Communications Act 2003 Sch 14 para 15(1). The Secretary of State may by order repeal or otherwise modify the restriction imposed by Sch 14 Pt 4 (paras 15, 16): Sch 14 para 16. Before making an order under any provision of Sch 14 (other than one that is confined to giving effect to recommendations made by OFCOM in a report of a review of media ownership under s 391 (see PARA 838)), the Secretary of State must consult OFCOM: Sch 14 para 17(1). No order is to be made containing provision authorised by any provision of Sch 14 unless a draft of the order has been laid before Parliament and approved by a resolution of each House: Sch 14 para 17(2). At the date at which this volume states the law, no such order had been made.
21 Communications Act 2003 Sch 14 para 15(2).
22 Communications Act 2003 Sch 14 para 15(3).
23 Ie for the purposes of the Communications Act 2003 Sch 14 para 15(2) (see the text and note 21).
24 Communications Act 2003 Sch 14 para 15(4).
25 Communications Act 2003 Sch 14 para 15(5).
26 Communications Act 2003 Sch 14 para 15(6).
27 Communications Act 2003 Sch 14 para 15(7).

832.   Disqualification of publicly funded bodies for radio service licences.   The following persons[1] are disqualified persons in relation to any licence[2] granted by OFCOM[3] other than a licence to provide a restricted service[4]:

(1)   a body[5] (other than a local authority[6], the Welsh Authority[7] or the BBC[8]) which has, in its last financial year[9], received more than half its income from public funds[10];

(2)   a body which is controlled by a body falling within head (1) above or by two or more such bodies taken together[11]; and

(3)   a body corporate in which a body falling within head (1) or head (2) above is a participant with more than a 5 per cent interest[12].

1   As to the meaning of 'person' see PARA 510 note 1.

2 Ie any licence granted under the Broadcasting Act 1990 Pt III (ss 85–126) or the Broadcasting Act 1996 Pt II (ss 40–72).

3 As to OFCOM see PARA 507.

4 Broadcasting Act 1990 s 88(1)(a), Sch 2 Pt II para 3(1) (amended by the Communications Act 2003 s 360(3), Sch 15 para 69(1), (6)). As to the meaning of 'restricted service' see PARA 723 note 4; definition applied by the Broadcasting Act 1990 s 126(1) (amended by the Communications Act 2003 Sch 15 para 59(b)).

5 As to the meaning of 'body' see PARA 821 note 10.

6 As to the meaning of 'local authority' see PARA 822 note 4.

7 As to the meaning of 'the Welsh Authority' see PARA 644 note 3; and as to television broadcasting by the Welsh Authority see PARAS 644–661.

8 As to the meaning of 'BBC' see PARA 603 note 1; and as to the BBC see PARAS 603–626.

9 'Financial year' means a financial year of OFCOM: Broadcasting Act 1990 s 202(1), (2) (s 202(2) amended by the Broadcasting Act 1996 s 148(2), Sch 11 Pt I; and the Communications Act 2003 s 406(7), Sch 19). As to the financial year of OFCOM see TELECOMMUNICATIONS vol 97 (2010) PARA 6.

10 Broadcasting Act 1990 Sch 2 Pt II para 3(1)(a) (amended by the Broadcasting Act 1996 s 73, Sch 2 Pt I para 7). Money is received from public funds if it is paid:

    (1) by a Minister of the Crown out of money provided by Parliament or out of the National Loans Fund (Sch 2 Pt II para 3(2)(a));

    (2) by a Northern Ireland department out of the Consolidated Fund of Northern Ireland or out of money appropriated by Measure of the Northern Ireland Assembly (Sch 2 Pt II para 3(2)(b)); or

    (3) by a body which itself falls within Sch 2 Pt II para 3(1)(a), including a body which falls within that provision by virtue of Sch 2 Pt II para 3 (Sch 2 Pt II para 3(2)(c)),

but, in each case, there is to be disregarded any money paid as consideration for the acquisition of property or the supply of goods or services or as remuneration, expenses, pensions, allowances or similar benefits for or in respect of a person as the holder of an office: Sch 2 Pt II para 3(2). As to Ministers of the Crown see CONSTITUTIONAL LAW AND HUMAN RIGHTS vol 8(2) (Reissue) PARA 354. As to the National Loans Fund see CONSTITUTIONAL LAW AND HUMAN RIGHTS vol 8(2) (Reissue) PARA 727 et seq. As to the Consolidated Fund see CONSTITUTIONAL LAW AND HUMAN RIGHTS vol 8(2) (Reissue) PARA 711 et seq; PARLIAMENT vol 78 (2010) PARAS 1028–1031.

11 Broadcasting Act 1990 Sch 2 Pt II para 3(1)(b). As to the meaning of 'control' see PARA 821 note 11. As to a body controlled by two or more persons taken together see PARA 821 note 11.

12 Broadcasting Act 1990 Sch 2 Pt II para 3(1)(c). As to the meaning of 'participant' see PARA 671 note 20.

833. General disqualification on grounds of undue influence. A person[1] is a disqualified person in relation to a Broadcasting Act licence[2] if in the opinion of OFCOM[3] any relevant body[4] is, by the giving of financial assistance or otherwise, exerting influence over the activities of that person, and that influence has led, is leading or is likely to lead to results which are adverse to the public interest[5].

1 As to the meaning of 'person' see PARA 510 note 1.

2 As to the meaning of 'Broadcasting Act licence' see PARA 822 note 2.

3 As to OFCOM see PARA 507.

4 'Relevant body', in relation to a licence granted under the Broadcasting Act 1990 Pt III (ss 85–126) or the Broadcasting Act 1996 Pt II (ss 40–72), means a person falling within the Broadcasting Act 1990 Sch 2 Pt II para 1(1)(c)–(h) or (j) or Sch 2 Pt II para 3 (see PARAS 830, 832) or a body which is controlled: (1) by a person falling within Sch 2 Pt II para 1(1)(c)–(g) (see PARA 830); (2) by a person falling within Sch 2 Pt II para 1 (see PARA 830); or (3) by two or more persons taken together each of whom falls within head (1) or (2) (whether or not they all fall within the same head): s 88, Sch 2 Pt II para 4(2)(b) (amended by the Communications Act 2003 s 348(4)).

5 Broadcasting Act 1990 Sch 2 Pt II para 4(1) (amended by the Communications Act 2003 s 360(3), Sch 15 para 69(4), (7)).

834.   General disqualification of broadcasting bodies. The following are disqualified persons in relation to a Broadcasting Act licence[1] granted by OFCOM[2]:

    (1)   the BBC[3];

    (2)   the Welsh Authority[4].

1 As to the meaning of 'Broadcasting Act licence' see PARA 822 note 2.
2 Broadcasting Act 1990 s 88, Sch 2 Pt II para 5 (amended by the Communications Act 2003 s 360(3), Sch 15 para 69(1), (4)). As to OFCOM see PARA 507.
3 Broadcasting Act 1990 Sch 2 Pt II para 5(a). As to the meaning of 'BBC' see PARA 603 note 1; and as to the BBC see PARAS 603–626.
4 Broadcasting Act 1990 Sch 2 Pt II para 5(b). As to the meaning of 'the Welsh Authority' see PARA 644 note 3; and as to television broadcasting by the Welsh Authority see PARAS 644–661.

835.   Disqualification of BBC companies for certain licences. A BBC company[1] is a disqualified person in relation to any licence[2] to provide a national, local or restricted service[3].

1 As to the meaning of 'BBC company' see PARA 671 note 20.
2 As to the meaning of 'licence' see PARA 724 note 2.
3 Broadcasting Act 1990 s 88, Sch 2 Pt II para 5A(2) (added by the Broadcasting Act 1996 s 73, Sch 2 Pt I para 9; and amended by the Communications Act 2003 ss 360(3), 406(7), Sch 15 para 69(1), (9)(c), Sch 19). As to the meanings of 'national service', 'local service' and 'restricted service' see PARA 723 note 4; definitions applied by the Broadcasting Act 1990 s 126(1) (amended by the Communications Act 2003 Sch 15 para 59(b)).

836.   General disqualification of advertising agencies. The following persons[1] are disqualified persons in relation to a Broadcasting Act licence[2] granted by OFCOM[3]:

    (1)   an advertising agency[4];

    (2)   an associate[5] of an advertising agency[6];

    (3)   any body[7] which is controlled[8] by a person falling within head (1) or head (2) above or by two or more such persons taken together[9];

    (4)   any body corporate in which a person falling within any of heads (1) to (3) above is a participant with more than a 5 per cent interest[10].

1 As to the meaning of 'person' see PARA 510 note 1.
2 As to the meaning of 'Broadcasting Act licence' see PARA 822 note 2.
3 Broadcasting Act 1990 s 88, Sch 2 Pt II para 6 (amended by the Communications Act 2003 s 360(3), Sch 15 para 69(1), (4)). As to OFCOM see PARA 507.
4 Broadcasting Act 1990 Sch 2 Pt II para 6(a). As to the meaning of 'advertising agent' see PARA 674 note 16.
5 As to the meaning of 'associate' see PARA 822 note 8.
6 Broadcasting Act 1990 Sch 2 Pt II para 6(b).
7 As to the meaning of 'body' see PARA 821 note 10.
8 As to the meaning of 'control' see PARA 821 note 11.
9 Broadcasting Act 1990 Sch 2 Pt II para 6(c).
10 Broadcasting Act 1990 Sch 2 Pt II para 6(d). As to the meaning of 'participant' see PARA 671 note 20.

(v)   Restrictions on holding of Licences for Digital Terrestrial Sound Broadcasting

837.   Restrictions on holding of licences. OFCOM[1] must do all that it can to secure that a person[2] does not become or remain the holder of a licence[3] if he is a disqualified person in relation to that licence[4], that a person does not become the holder of a licence if certain requirements[5] would be contravened were he to do so[6], and that those requirements are not contravened in the case of a person who already holds a licence[7]. OFCOM may accordingly[8]:

(1)   require any applicant for a licence to provide it with such information as it may reasonably require for the purpose of determining[9]:
    (a)   whether he is a disqualified person[10];
    (b)   whether any such requirements would preclude OFCOM from granting a licence to him[11]; and
    (c)   if so, what steps would be required to be taken by or in relation to him in order for any such requirements to be complied with[12];

(2)   revoke the award of a licence to a body[13] where a relevant change[14] takes place after the award, but before the grant, of the licence[15];

(3)   make the grant of a licence to any person conditional on the taking of any specified steps that appear to it to be required to be taken as mentioned in head (1)(c) above[16];

(4)   impose conditions in any licence enabling it to require the licence holder, if a body corporate, to give to it advance notice of proposals affecting shareholdings in the body, or affecting the directors of the body, where such proposals are known to the body[17];

(5)   impose conditions in a licence requiring the licence holder, if a body corporate, to give OFCOM notice, after they have occurred and irrespective of whether proposals for them have fallen to be notified, of changes, transactions or events affecting shareholdings in the body or the directors of the body[18];

(6)   impose conditions in a licence enabling OFCOM to require the licence holder to provide it with such information as it may reasonably require for determining whether the licence holder is a disqualified person in relation to that licence[19] or whether any such requirements as are mentioned in head (1)(b) above have been and are being complied with by or in relation to the licence holder[20]; and

(7)   impose conditions in any licence enabling it to give the licence holder directions requiring him to take, or arrange for the taking of, any specified steps appearing to it to be required to be taken in order for any such requirements to be complied with[21].

Where OFCOM revokes the award of any licence[22] or determines that any condition imposed by it in relation to any licence has not been satisfied[23], any provisions relating to the awarding of licences of the kind in question[24] have effect as if the person to whom the licence was awarded or granted had not made an application for it[25].

Every licence must include such conditions as OFCOM considers necessary or expedient to ensure that where the holder of the licence is a body[26], and a relevant change takes place after the grant of the licence[27], OFCOM may revoke the licence by notice served on the holder of the licence and taking effect immediately or on a date specified in the notice[28].

1   As to OFCOM see PARA 507.
2   As to the meaning of 'person' see PARA 510 note 1.
3   As to the holder of the licence see PARA 728 note 3. As to the meaning of 'licence' see PARA 727 note 2.
4   Broadcasting Act 1996 s 44(1)(a) (s 44(1) amended by the Communications Act 2003 s 360(3), Sch 15 para 104(1), (2)). A person is disqualified by virtue of the Broadcasting Act 1990 s 88, Sch 2 Pt II (see PARAS 830–836): see the Broadcasting Act 1996 s 44(1)(a) (as so amended).
5   Ie requirements imposed by or under the Communications Act 2003 Sch 14 (see PARAS 820, 831, 739, 759, 769).

6   Broadcasting Act 1996 s 44(1)(b) (substituted by the Communications Act 2003 s 350(2)).

7   Broadcasting Act 1996 s 44(1)(c) (added by the Communications Act 2003 s 350(2)).

8   Broadcasting Act 1996 s 44(2) (amended by the Communications Act 2003 Sch 15 para 104(2)).

9   Broadcasting Act 1996 s 44(2)(a).

10 Broadcasting Act 1996 s 44(2)(a)(i).

11 Broadcasting Act 1996 s 44(2)(a)(ii).

12 Broadcasting Act 1996 s 44(2)(a)(iii).

13 As to the meaning of 'body' see PARA 821 note 10; definition applied by the Broadcasting Act 1996 s 147(2).

14 'Relevant change', in relation to a body to which a licence has been awarded or granted, means:

    (1)   any change affecting the nature or characteristics of the body;

    (2)   any change in the persons having control over or interests in the body; or

    (3)   any other change giving rise to a disqualification under the Broadcasting Act 1990 Sch 2 Pt II or a contravention of a requirement imposed by or under the Communications Act 2003 Sch 14 (see PARAS 820, 831, 739, 759, 769),

being (in any case) a change which is such that, if it fell to OFCOM to determine whether to award the licence to the body in the new circumstances of the case, it would be induced by the change to refrain from so awarding it: Broadcasting Act 1996 s 44(8) (amended by the Communications Act 2003 Sch 15 para 104(2), (6)). As to the meaning of 'control' see PARA 821 note 11; definition applied by the Broadcasting Act 1996 s 147(2).

15 Broadcasting Act 1996 s 44(2)(b).

16 Broadcasting Act 1996 s 44(2)(c).

17 Broadcasting Act 1996 s 44(2)(d).

18 Broadcasting Act 1996 s 44(2)(da) (added by the Communications Act 2003 Sch 15 para 104(3)).

19 Ie by virtue of the Broadcasting Act 1990 Sch 2 Pt II: see PARA 830 et seq.

20 Broadcasting Act 1996 s 44(2)(db) (added by the Communications Act 2003 Sch 15 para 104(3)).

21 Broadcasting Act 1996 s 44(2)(e).

22 Broadcasting Act 1996 s 44(3)(a).

23 Broadcasting Act 1996 s 44(3)(b).

24 Ie of the Broadcasting Act 1996 Pt II (ss 40–72).

25 Broadcasting Act 1996 s 44(3) (amended by the Communications Act 2003 Sch 15 para 104(2)). The provisions of the Broadcasting Act 1996 Pt II do not so have effect if OFCOM decides that it would be desirable to publish a fresh notice under Pt II in respect of the grant of a licence, or (as the case may be) a further licence, to provide the service in question: s 44(4) (amended by the Communications Act 2003 Sch 15 para 104(2)).

26 Broadcasting Act 1996 s 44(5)(a).

27 Broadcasting Act 1996 s 44(5)(b).

28 Broadcasting Act 1996 s 44(5) (amended by the Communications Act 2003 Sch 15 para 104(2)). OFCOM may not serve any such notice on the licence holder unless: (1) it has notified him of the matters constituting its grounds for revoking the licence and given him a reasonable opportunity of making representations to it about those matters; and (2) in a case where the relevant change is one falling within the Broadcasting Act 1996 s 44(7), it has also given him an opportunity of complying with the Communications Act 2003 Sch 14 (see PARAS 820, 831, 739, 759, 769) within a period specified in the notification, and the period specified in the notification has elapsed: Broadcasting Act 1996 s 44(6) (amended by the Communications Act 2003 Sch 15 para 104(2), (4)).

    A relevant change falls within the Broadcasting Act 1996 s 44(7) (amended by the Communications Act 2003 Sch 15 para 104(2), (5)) if it consists only in one or more of the following:

    (a)   a change in the national market share within the meaning of the Communications Act 2003 Sch 14 (see PARA 820 note 5) of one or more national newspapers (see PARA 820 note 4) (Broadcasting Act 1996 s 44(7)(b) (amended by the Communications Act 2003 Sch 15 para 104(5)(b))); or

    (b)   a change in the local market share (see PARA 820 note 8) in a particular area of one or more local newspapers (see PARA 820 note 4) (Broadcasting Act 1996 s 44(7)(c)).

(vi) Review of Media Ownership

838.   Review of media ownership. It is the duty of OFCOM[1] to carry out regular reviews of the operation, taken together, of all of specified statutory provisions relating to media ownership[2], and to send a report on every such review to the Secretary of State[3]. The first review must be carried out no more than three years after the commencement of these provisions, and subsequent reviews must be carried out at intervals of no more than three years[4]. The report to the Secretary of State on a review must set out OFCOM's recommendations, in consequence of its conclusions on the review, for the exercise by the Secretary of State of specified powers[5]. OFCOM must publish every report sent by it to the Secretary of State under these provisions in such manner as it considers appropriate for bringing it to the attention of persons who, in its opinion, are likely to be affected by it[6].

1   As to OFCOM see PARA 507.
2   The specified provisions are: (1) the provisions of the Broadcasting Act 1990 Sch 2 (see PARAS 821–827, 830–836); (2) the provision made by or under the Communications Act 2003 Sch 14 (see PARAS 820, 831, 739, 759, 769); (3) the provisions of ss 280, 281 (see PARA 876); (4) whatever provision (if any) has been made under s 283 (see PARA 876); and (5) the provisions of the Enterprise Act 2002 Pt 3 (ss 22–130) so far as they relate to intervention by the Secretary of State in connection with newspapers or other media enterprises (see COMPETITION): Communications Act 2003 s 391(2). As to the Secretary of State see PARA 507 note 32.
3   Communications Act 2003 s 391(1).
4   Communications Act 2003 s 391(3). The commencement date for s 391 was 29 December 2003: see the Office of Communications Act 2002 (Commencement No 3) and Communications Act 2003 (Commencement No 2) Order 2003, SI 2003/3142.
5   Communications Act 2003 s 391(4). The specified powers of the Secretary of State are: (1) his power to make an order under s 348(5) (see PARA 831); (2) his powers to make orders under Sch 14 (see PARAS 820, 831, 739, 759, 769); (3) his powers under ss 282, 283 (see PARA 876); and (4) his powers under the Enterprise Act 2002 ss 44(11), 58(3), 59(6A) (media mergers: see COMPETITION): Communications Act 2003 s 391(4).
6   Communications Act 2003 s 391(5).

(5) MEDIA MERGER

(i) Overview

839. Introduction of a revised media merger regime. The Enterprise Act 2002 brought about significant changes to the United Kingdom merger control regime, but it did not affect the pre-existing special regime for the consideration of mergers in the newspaper industry[1]. This special regime was first introduced in the United Kingdom by the Monopolies and Mergers Act 1965[2], and was reiterated in the Fair Trading Act 1973[3]. It subjected newspaper mergers to a system of mandatory ex ante control. Parallel with the passing of the Enterprise Act 2002, however, the government sought to co-ordinate the development of policy on newspaper mergers with that on media ownership generally as part of a wider review of the telecommunications and broadcasting sectors. This culminated in Part 5 of the Communications Act 2003[4]. The pertinent sections of the Fair Trading Act 1973 were repealed[5], as was the exemption of newspaper mergers from the merger provisions of the Enterprise Act 2002[6]. Thus, at least for the normal case, newspaper, broadcasting and cross-media mergers are considered under the standard merger provisions[7].

Importantly, the Communications Act 2003 also introduced five 'media public interest considerations' by way of amendment to the Enterprise Act 2002[8]. These considerations are applied to media mergers only when the Secretary of State issues an intervention notice[9]. Therefore, the regime is now broader in scope, but is in fact less often applied[10]. Its introduction accompanied the removal of some restrictions on cross-media ownership[11]. The revised regime is intended to relieve the regulatory burden of the old system, while allowing considerable continuity in the substantive assessment of the public interest issues in the small number of cases in which these are important[12]. The sustained view of government has been that 'market forces alone, even regulated by competition law, cannot necessarily provide the market-place of ideas that enables democracy to prosper'[13]. The relevant provisions came into force on 29 December 2003[14].

1 See the Enterprise Act 2002 s 69 (repealed).
2 This legislation responded to the findings of the second Royal Commission on the Press: *Report of the Royal Commission on the Press 1961–62* (Cmnd 1811) (1962).
3 See the Fair Trading Act 1973 ss 57–62 (repealed).
4 Ie the Communications Act 2003 Pt 5 (ss 369–389).
5 See the Communications Act 2003 s 373.
6 See the Communications Act 2003 s 374.
7 See COMPETITION vol 18 (2009) PARA 172 et seq. As to special considerations relating to media mergers see COMPETITION vol 18 (2009) PARAS 267–270.
8 See the Communications Act 2003 s 375, amending the Enterprise Act 2002 s 58. See PARAS 847–849; and COMPETITION vol 18 (2009) PARA 203.
9 See the Enterprise Act 2002 ss 42, 43; and COMPETITION vol 18 (2009) PARAS 189–190. As to the Secretary of State see PARA 507 note 32.
10 There was an intervention in respect of the share acquisition in ITV plc made by BSkyB in November 2006, which culminated in a decision of the Court of Appeal in January 2010: *British Sky Broadcasting Group plc v Competition Commission; Virgin Media Inc v Competition Commission* [2010] EWCA Civ 2, [2010] 2 All ER 907.
11 See PARA 847.
12 *Department of Trade and Industry, Enterprise Act 2002: Public Interest Intervention in Media Mergers* (URN 04/1073; London: DTI, 2004) para 2.5.
13 *Department of Trade and Industry, Enterprise Act 2002: Public Interest Intervention in Media Mergers* (URN 04/1073; London: DTI, 2004) para 2.6.
14 See the Office of Communications Act 2002 (Commencement No 3) and Communications Act 2003 (Commencement No 2) Order 2003, SI 2003/3142, art 3(1), Sch 1.

(ii) Scope of the Media Merger Regime

840. Overview of scope. For most cases, the standard jurisdictional criteria are applied to media mergers[1]. A transaction must usually constitute a relevant merger situation if the Secretary of State is to issue a media intervention notice[2]. An exception to this rule arises where a transaction satisfies a modified share of supply test[3]. The modified test applies only in the media context, and takes the place of the rules normally applied in special public interest cases[4]. As with other special public interest cases, no competition assessment need be undertaken where intervention rests on satisfaction of the modified share of supply test[5].

1 See the Enterprise Act 2002 s 23; and COMPETITION vol 18 (2009) PARA 173.
2 See the Enterprise Act 2002 s 42; and COMPETITION vol 18 (2009) PARA 189. As to the Secretary of State see PARA 507 note 32.
3 See PARA 841. This modified test was introduced into the Enterprise Act 2002 by the Communications Act 2003 ss 378–380.
4 See the Enterprise Act 2002 ss 59–61; and COMPETITION vol 18 (2009) PARAS 204–212. An additional investigation and report by OFCOM is required: see s 61A; and COMPETITION vol 18 (2009) PARA 207. As to OFCOM see PARA 507.
5 See the Enterprise Act 2002 s 61; and COMPETITION vol 18 (2009) PARA 206.

841. Modified share of supply test. The modified share of supply[1] test allows the Secretary of State[2] to intervene only, in relation to the supply of newspapers[3] of any description, if one of the parties to the merger has an existing 25 per cent share of supply of all the newspapers of that description in the United Kingdom[4] or in a substantial part of the United Kingdom[5]. Where a broadcasting and cross-media public interest consideration is in question, this 25 per cent must relate to the provision of broadcasting[6]. There is no requirement that the merger transaction results in a concentration of ownership. The 25 per cent share of supply must exist post-merger, but it need not have been enhanced by the merger. Where none of the turnover threshold, the share of supply, or the modified share of supply tests is met, the transaction will not fall within the jurisdiction of the merger regime[7].

1 See PARA 840.
2 As to the Secretary of State see PARA 507 note 32.
3 As to the meaning of 'newspaper' see PARA 842.
4 As to the meaning of 'United Kingdom' see PARA 510 note 13.
5 See the Enterprise Act 2002 s 59(3), (3C) (s 59(3) substituted, and s 59(3C), (3D) added, by the Communications Act 2003 s 378(1)); and COMPETITION vol 18 (2009) PARA 204.
6 See the Enterprise Act 2002 s 59(3D) (as added: see note 5); and COMPETITION vol 18 (2009) PARA 204. As to media public interest considerations see PARAS 839, 847–849. As to the meaning of 'broadcasting' see PARA 842.
7 See the Enterprise Act 2002 s 59(1)–(3) (s 59(3) as substituted: see note 5); and COMPETITION vol 18 (2009) PARA 204.

842. Identification of a newspaper or media merger. The Enterprise Act 2002 offers a series of definitions pertinent to the interpretation of the media public interest considerations[1]. 'Media enterprises' are those involved in broadcasting[2], while 'newspaper enterprises' are those involved in the supply of newspapers[3]. Where a transaction involves both a media enterprise and a newspaper enterprise, the latter is also considered[4] a media enterprise[5]. Clearly, the categories 'newspaper enterprises' and 'media enterprises' are not mutually exclusive.

A 'newspaper' is defined as a daily, Sunday or local (other than daily or Sunday) newspaper circulating wholly or mainly in the United Kingdom or in a part of the United Kingdom[6]. 'Broadcasting' is defined as the provision of services the provision of which is required to be licensed under Part I or III of the Broadcasting Act 1990 or Part I or II of the Broadcasting Act 1996 or would be required to be so licensed if provided by a person subject to licensing under the Part in question[7].

These definitions can be altered by order of the Secretary of State[8].

1 See the Enterprise Act 2002 s 58A (added by the Communications Act 2003 s 375(2)) ; and COMPETITION vol 18 (2009) PARA 203. As to media public interest considerations see PARAS 839, 847–849.
2 Enterprise Act 2002 s 58A(1) (as added: see note 1).
3 Enterprise Act 2002 s 58A(3) (as added: see note 1).
4 Ie for the purposes of the plurality test in the Enterprise Act 2002 s 58(2C)(a): see PARA 849. As to the meaning of 'United Kingdom' see PARA 510 note 13.
5 Enterprise Act 2002 s 58A(2) (as added: see note 1).
6 Enterprise Act 2002 s 44(10). Guidance has been offered on the meaning of this term: it should be understood in accordance with its ordinary and natural meaning; it includes free newspapers, but a publication that consists wholly or mainly of advertising is not a newspaper (a newspaper must contain a good proportion of news content relative to advertising); and newspapers tend to carry public announcements, such as planning notices: *Department of Trade and Industry, Enterprise Act 2002: Public Interest Intervention in Media Mergers* (URN 04/1073; London: DTI, 2004) paras 3.12–3.13. See further *Northcliffe Newspapers Group Ltd/Aberdeen Journals Ltd* (Cm 3174) (1996) paras 2.15–2.17.
7 Enterprise Act 2002 s 44(9). The services covered by the Broadcasting Act 1990 Pt 1 (ss 3–71) and Pt III (ss 85–126) are Channels 3, 4 and 5; domestic and non-domestic satellite services; licensable audio-visual and sound programme services, and national and local sound broadcasting services: see PARAS 627 et seq, 662 et seq, 677 et seq, 716 et seq, 723 et seq. Those covered by the Broadcasting Act 1996 Pt I (ss 1–39) and Pt II (ss 40–72) are digital terrestrial

television services (multiplex services, digital programme services, and digital additional services) and digital terrestrial sound services (radio multiplex services, digital sound programme services, and digital additional services on sound frequencies): see PARAS 690 et seq, 753 et seq.

8   Enterprise Act 2002 ss 44(11), 58(3), 58A(9) (s 58A(9) as added: see note 1). As to the Secretary of State see PARA 507 note 32.

(iii) Procedure for the Assessment of Media Mergers

843. Overview of procedure. The default position with regard to media mergers is that they will be assessed in accordance with the standard merger control provisions of the Enterprise Act 2002[1]. Only if the Secretary of State chooses to issue an intervention notice is the special process for the assessment of media mergers initiated[2]. The Office of Fair Trading ('OFT') undertakes a general function of surveying the market and informing the Secretary of State should a transaction appear to involve any of the stipulated[3] considerations[4]. It is also open to the Secretary of State to review a case on his own initiative. If an intervention notice is issued, it is for the Secretary of State to determine whether a reference to the Competition Commission is made[5]. Any party or third party to a media merger affected by a decision of the Secretary of State relating to a media merger is free to bring the matter before the Competition Appeal Tribunal[6]. The tribunal will apply the same principles as would be applied by a court on an application for judicial review[7].

1   See COMPETITION vol 18 (2009) PARAS 172–182. Under these provisions, the OFT determines whether a given relevant merger situation should be referred for further consideration to the Competition Commission, or whether it can be cleared or remedied without such a reference being made. If a reference is made, it is then for the Competition Commission to determine whether the merger should be cleared, remedied, or prohibited by reference to a 'substantial lessening of competition' test. As to the Office of Fair Trading see COMPETITION vol 18 (2009) PARAS 6–8. As to the Competition Commission see COMPETITION vol 18 (2009) PARA 9.
2   See COMPETITION vol 18 (2009) PARA 204. As to the Secretary of State see PARA 507 note 32.
3   Ie the considerations stipulated in the Enterprise Act 2002 s 58(2A)–(2C): see PARAS 847–849; and COMPETITION vol 18 (2009) PARA 203.
4   See the Enterprise Act 2002 ss 5, 57, 119B; and COMPETITION vol 18 (2009) PARAS 203, 268.
5   See the Enterprise Act 2002 ss 45, 62; and COMPETITION vol 18 (2009) PARA 208.
6   See the Enterprise Act 2002 s 120; and COMPETITION vol 18 (2009) PARA 271.
7   See the Enterprise Act 2002 s 120(4).

844. Intervention by the Secretary of State. The Secretary of State enjoys a discretion on whether to intervene in media merger referral decision[1]. An intervention notice can be issued at any point up to the making of a reference decision by the Office of Fair Trading ('OFT'). The government has published guidance on when such intervention is likely to occur[2]. It maintains that this is not an area suited to generalisation, that each case must be considered on its own facts and merits, and that it expects that the approach to the issue will develop in the light of experience[3]. It suggested further that where a proposal generates a significant volume of adverse third party comment this may prompt intervention[4].

A wide range of additional information will be considered by the Secretary of State[5]. This may include details of complaints made to, and judgments given by the Press Complaints Commission[6]; any previous regulatory decisions that have a bearing on the case; published articles raising matters of relevance; and third party representations. No formal advice is sought from OFCOM[7] prior to the intervention decision, although it may be required to provide the Secretary of State with basic information relevant to the decision[8]. The Secretary of State will normally seek to issue his decision within 10 working days of the later of the date on which details are submitted to the OFT or the date on which the case is brought to his attention[9]. Any decision to intervene will be published and announced by press notice. No public announcement is made regarding decisions not to intervene. In this latter circumstance, the OFT will continue to assess the merger on competition grounds should the jurisdictional threshold tests have been met[10].

1 See the Enterprise Act 2002 ss 42(2), 59(2) (special intervention notice, issued where the standard merger threshold tests in s 23 are not met); and COMPETITION vol 18 (2009) PARAS 189, 204. As to the Secretary of State see PARA 507 note 32.

2 *Department of Trade and Industry, Enterprise Act 2002: Public Interest Intervention in Media Mergers* (URN 04/1073; London: DTI, 2004) chs 6, 8. As to the Office of Fair Trading see COMPETITION vol 18 (2009) PARAS 6–8.

3 *Department of Trade and Industry, Enterprise Act 2002: Public Interest Intervention in Media Mergers* (URN 04/1073; London: DTI, 2004) para 6.1.

4 *Department of Trade and Industry, Enterprise Act 2002: Public Interest Intervention in Media Mergers* (URN 04/1073; London: DTI, 2004) para 6.6.

5 *Department of Trade and Industry, Enterprise Act 2002: Public Interest Intervention in Media Mergers* (URN 04/1073; London: DTI, 2004) para 4.13.

6 As to the Press Complaints Commission see PRESS, PRINTING AND PUBLISHING vol 36(2) (Reissue) PARA 464.

7 As to OFCOM see PARA 507.

8 OFCOM has the function of obtaining, compiling and keeping under review information about matters relating to the carrying out of its functions under the Enterprise Act 2002 Pt 3 (ss 22–130), which must carried out with a view to (among other things) ensuring that OFCOM has sufficient information to take informed decisions and to carry out its other functions effectively: see s 119A; and COMPETITION vol 18 (2009) PARA 267.

9 *Department of Trade and Industry, Enterprise Act 2002: Public Interest Intervention in Media Mergers* (URN 04/1073; London: DTI, 2004) paras 4.11, 4.14.

10 See *Department of Trade and Industry, Enterprise Act 2002: Public Interest Intervention in Media Mergers* (URN 04/1073; London: DTI, 2004) para 4.15.

845. Referral advice and decision. If an intervention notice is served[1], it is then for the Secretary of State to decide whether to refer the given case to the Competition Commission[2]. The Secretary of State receives advice from and is bound by the view of the Office of Fair Trading ('OFT') on relevant competition and jurisdictional issues[3]. Should the OFT have identified a likely substantial lessening of competition, the Secretary of State must refer the case, unless he considers this detriment to be outweighed by the wider public interest considerations[4]. Contrary to the position regarding other public interest considerations[5], OFCOM[6] rather than the OFT provides the Secretary of State with a report on matters pertinent to media public interest considerations[7]. OFCOM has published guidance on how it understands and will exercise this role[8]. The government is obliged to publish the reports received from the OFT and OFCOM, subject to confidentiality considerations[9]. Having received advice on referral, the Secretary of State can clear the merger (possibly subject to undertakings in lieu of reference agreed with the OFT)[10], decide to refer both the competition and the public interest issues to the Competition Commission, or decide to refer only the public interest issue. Any reference decision will be made within a timescale determined[11] by the Secretary of State[12]. If it transpires that no public interest issue is found to arise, the case reverts to the OFT for the referral decision on competition grounds, and matters proceed as though intervention had not occurred[13].

1 Ie under the Enterprise Act 2002 s 42 or s 59.

2   As to the Secretary of State see PARA 507 note 32. As to the Competition Commission see COMPETITION vol 18 (2009) PARA 9.

3   In the context of a special merger situation, the OFT will assess only the jurisdictional point and will not carry out any competition analysis: see the Enterprise Act 2002 s 61; and COMPETITION vol 18 (2009) PARA 206. As to the Office of Fair Trading see COMPETITION vol 18 (2009) PARAS 6–8.

4   See the Enterprise Act 2002 s 45(6); and COMPETITION vol 18 (2009) PARA 193.

5   Ie under the Enterprise Act 2002 s 58.

6   As to OFCOM see PARA 507.

7   See the Enterprise Act 2002 ss 44(3)(b), 44A(2) (s 44(3)(b) amended by the Communications Act 2003 s 376(1); and the Enterprise Act 2002 s 44A added by the Communications Act 2003 s 377). The OFT retains a residual power to offer a summary of matters pertinent to the media public interest considerations: see the Enterprise Act 2002 s 44(5A) (added by the Communications Act 2003 s 376(2)). This provides for the circumstance where such representations have been made in combination with other points on which the OFT does intend to report. It ensures that an artificial separation of material is not required. As to media public interest considerations see PARAS 839, 847–849.

8   OFCOM Guidance for the Public Interest Test for Media Mergers (2004).

9   See the Enterprise Act 2002 s 107(3); and COMPETITION vol 18 (2009) PARA 257.

10   See the Enterprise Act 2002 s 45; and COMPETITION vol 18 (2009) PARA 193.

11   Ie under the Enterprise Act 2002 ss 44, 44A.

12   Where the transaction has been notified by merger notice, the statutory deadline by which the referral decision must be made can be extended by up to 20 working days: see the Enterprise Act 2002 s 97(3), (4). This period aggregates any extension agreed between the OFT and the parties under s 97(2). Therefore, assuming it is not suspended for failure to comply with information requests, the maximum timescale for a reference decision on a media merger notified by way of a merger notice is 40 working days. See COMPETITION vol 18 (2009) PARA 248.

13   See the Enterprise Act 2002 s 56; and COMPETITION vol 18 (2009) PARA 202.

846. Prohibition and remedies advice and decision. If a reference is made on a public interest ground[1], the Competition Commission will inquire and report back to the Secretary of State with recommendations regarding the competition issue and the public interest considerations[2]. The Commission may have regard only to such public interest considerations as are specified in the reference[3]. The Commission will follow a similar process to that for standard merger cases, albeit that it is obliged also to undertake a consultation sufficient to obtain opinion relating to how the media public interest considerations are affected by the merger[4]. Having completed its investigation, the Commission must report to the Secretary of State, offering recommendations on potential remedies where appropriate[5]. It must report within 24 weeks, subject to a possible eight week extension[6]. Advice received by the Secretary of State from the Competition Commission on the jurisdictional and competition issues is binding[7].

On receipt of the report from the Commission, the Secretary of State has 30 working days within which to decide whether the merger is likely to act against the public interest[8]. On an affirmative finding, he must also determine whether any remedy might alleviate the identified problems[9]. It is for the Secretary of State to determine whether remedies are necessary, and if so what they will be. This decision must be published, subject to any excisions made to respect commercial confidentiality[10]. Where the Secretary of State makes no finding either way within the time limit, the case reverts, if appropriate, to the Commission for a decision on the competition issue[11].

Where the Secretary of State determines that a merger will operate against one or more of the media public interest considerations[12], he can deploy any of the remedies open to the Commission[13]. In addition to those remedies, provision was made by the Communications Act 2003 to allow the continued use of special remedies that were previously available under the pre-existing newspaper merger regime[14]. While it is for the Secretary of State to determine appropriate remedies, the Commission must offer recommendations and OFCOM may also proffer advice on this point[15].

1   See PARA 845.
2   See the Enterprise Act 2002 ss 50, 65; and COMPETITION vol 18 (2009) PARAS 198, 211. As to the Competition Commission see COMPETITION vol 18 (2009) PARA 9. As to the Secretary of State see PARA 507 note 32.
3   See the Enterprise Act 2002 ss 47(11).
4   See the Enterprise Act 2002 s 104A; and COMPETITION vol 18 (2009) PARA 269.
5   See the Enterprise Act 2002 ss 50(1), (2), 65(1), (2); and COMPETITION vol 18 (2009) PARAS 198, 211.
6   See the Enterprise Act 2002 ss 51(1), (3), 65(3); and COMPETITION vol 18 (2009) PARAS 198, 211. A copy of this report will also be sent to OFCOM: see ss 50(2A), 65(2A); and COMPETITION vol 18 (2009) PARAS 198, 211.
7   See the Enterprise Act 2002 ss 54(7), 66(4).
8   See the Enterprise Act 2002 ss 54(1), (2), (5), 66(1)–(3); and COMPETITION vol 18 (2009) PARAS 200, 212.
9   See the Enterprise Act 2002 ss 55(2), 66(6), Sch 7 paras 9, 11; and COMPETITION vol 18 (2009) PARAS 201, 231.
10   See the Enterprise Act 2002 ss 107(3), 118; and COMPETITION vol 18 (2009) PARAS 191–192, 206–207, 257.
11   See the Enterprise Act 2002 s 56(6); and COMPETITION vol 18 (2009) PARA 202.
12   See PARAS 839, 847–849.
13   Ie under the Enterprise Act 2002 Sch 8, which offers an extensive catalogue of the possible contents of enforcement orders. The catalogue includes a wide range of general restrictions on conduct, obligations to perform certain acts, powers to prohibit acquisitions and to order divisions, and other powers relating to the supply and publication of information. It was revised under the Enterprise Act 2002, so as to cohere more closely with economic thinking and to include a number of standard remedies (such as the power to require the granting of licences) that were not previously possible under the Fair Trading Act 1973. See COMPETITION vol 18 (2009) PARA 232.
14   See the Enterprise Act 2002 Sch 8 para 20A(4) (Sch 8 para 20A added by the Communications Act 2003 s 387); and COMPETITION vol 18 (2009) PARA 238. These remedies include powers to alter the constitution of a company; to require the agreement of the Secretary of State prior to the taking of action such as the appointment or dismissal of an editor, journalist or directors; to attach conditions to the operation of a media enterprise; and to prohibit co-operation between members of a group of companies.
15   See the Enterprise Act 2002 s 106B; and COMPETITION vol 18 (2009) PARA 256.

(iv)   Media Public Interest Considerations

847.   Overview. The provisions of the Enterprise Act 2002 that detail the media public interest considerations[1] can be subdivided into those that focus on newspaper mergers[2], and those that focus on broadcasting and cross-ownership mergers[3]. To a large extent, the former emulate pre-existing provisions of the Fair Trading Act 1973. The introduction of the latter accompanied the removal of some restrictions on cross-media ownership in the Communications Act 2003. The Secretary of State[4] is empowered to publish general advice and information regarding the media public interest considerations[5].

1   See PARA 839.
2   Ie the Enterprise Act 2002 s 58(2A), (2B): see PARA 848.
3   Ie the Enterprise Act 2002 s 58(2C): see PARA 849.
4   As to the Secretary of State see PARA 507 note 32.
5   See the Enterprise Act 2002 s 106A; and COMPETITION vol 18 (2009) PARA 270. See *Department of Trade and Industry, Enterprise Act 2002: Public Interest Intervention in Media Mergers* (URN 04/1073; London: DTI, 2004).

848. Newspaper public interest considerations. The first two media public interest considerations largely replicate the substantive provisions of the old special newspaper regime. They are:

(1)   the need for: (a) accurate presentation of news; and (b) free expression of opinion, in newspapers[1]; and

(2)   the need for, to the extent that it is reasonable and practicable, a sufficient plurality of views in newspapers in each market for newspapers in the United Kingdom or a part of the United Kingdom[2].

The government has stated the expectation that these newspaper public interest considerations will be interpreted in line with decisions taken under the Fair Trading Act 1973 regime, notwithstanding that such cases do not give rise to binding precedent[3].

The impact of a merger situation on the 'accurate presentation of news' is generally addressed by reference to the past behaviour of the enterprises in question, or of those persons in control of such enterprises[4]. It may also involve consideration of the financial stability of the company proposing a takeover given that any forced closure of newspapers or overly heavy cost-cutting affecting editorial standards may impact upon the ability of the newspaper accurately to present the news[5]. The concept of 'free expression of opinion' provides for an assessment of the degree to which editorial policy is free from proprietorial influence[6].

The concept of a sufficient plurality of views in newspapers in each market for newspapers[7] provides for an assessment of the structural impact of a merger not on competition in the economic sense, but rather on the range and distribution of 'voices' in the public sphere[8]. The qualification of this consideration by reference to reasonableness and practicality allows the circumstances of each case to be properly taken into account. The understanding of sufficient plurality in local newspaper markets has evolved over time, from significant concern over concentration of local markets[9] to a position where it is thought that 'commercial logic' will usually prevent the concentration of ownership being harmful to diversity[10]. This is an area in which media ownership restrictions continue to apply[11]. Intervention on the basis of an impact on the sufficiency of the range of expression of party-political opinion in newspapers will be possible only in very exceptional circumstances[12].

1   Enterprise Act 2002 s 58(2A) (s 58(2A), (2B) added by the Communications Act 2003 s 375(1)). As to the meaning of 'newspaper' see PARA 842.

2   Enterprise Act 2002 s 58(2B) (as added: see note 1). As to the meaning of 'United Kingdom' see PARA 510 note 13.

3   The Fair Trading Act 1973 s 59(3) (repealed) required the Competition Commission to investigate whether the transfer in question might be expected to operate against the public interest, taking into account relevant matters and, in particular, the need for accurate presentation of the news and free expression of opinion. Around 50 newspaper cases were referred to the Commission under the old newspaper regime. Adverse findings were made in ten of these cases, of which five involved issues relating to free expression of opinion and the accurate presentation of news: see *Bristol United Press Ltd/West Somerset Free Press* (HC 546) (1979–80); *Reed International Ltd/Berrows Organisation Ltd* (Cmnd 8337) (1981); *George Outram & Co Ltd/The Observer* (HC 378) (1980–81); *TR Beckett Ltd/EMAP plc* (Cm 623) (1989); *Century Newspapers/Thomson Regional Newspapers* (Cm 677) (1989); *Bristol Evening Post/David Sullivan* (Cm 1083) (1990); *Daily Mail & General Trust/T Bailey Forman Ltd* (Cm 2693) (1994); *Trinity plc/Mirror Group plc* (Cm 4393) (1999); *Johnston Press/Trinity Mirror* (Cm 5495) (2002); and *Newsquest (London) Ltd/Independent News and Media* (Cm 5951) (2003). In addition, conditions were attached to the consent for transfer of The Times and the Sunday Times to News International in 1981, without a reference to the Monopolies and Mergers Commission. As to the Competition Commission see COMPETITION vol 18 (2009) PARA 9.

4 *Department of Trade and Industry, Enterprise Act 2002: Public Interest Intervention in Media Mergers* (URN 04/1073; London: DTI, 2004) para 5.5. See eg *Bristol Evening Post/David Sullivan* (Cm 1083) (1990).

5 *Newsquest Media Group Ltd/Westminster Press Ltd* (Cm 3485) (1996) paras 2.47–2.58; *Trinity plc/Mirror Group plc* (Cm 4393) (1999) paras 2.29–2.31.

6 *Department of Trade and Industry, Enterprise Act 2002: Public Interest Intervention in Media Mergers* (URN 04/1073; London: DTI, 2004) paras 5.7–5.10. See eg *Johnston Press/Trinity Mirror* (Cm 5495) (2002) paras 2.125–2.135; *Newsquest (London) Ltd/Independent News and Media* (Cm 5951) (2003) para 2.135; *George Outram & Co Ltd/The Observer* (HC 378) (1980–81) para 8.48; *Bristol Evening Post/ David Sullivan* (Cm 1083) (1990) paras 6.9–6.11; *Trinity plc/Mirror Group plc* (Cm 4393) (1999) para 2.22. In its final report, the *Royal Commission on the Press 1974–1977* (Cmnd 6810) (1977) offered a catalogue of basic rights the possession of which was necessary to an editor's independence. This catalogue has been cited with approval in newspaper cases.

7 Ie in the Enterprise Act 2002 s 58(2B).

8 *Department of Trade and Industry, Enterprise Act 2002: Public Interest Intervention in Media Mergers* (URN 04/1073; London: DTI, 2004) paras 5.11–5.15.

9 *Royal Commission on the Press 1974–1977* (Cmnd 6810) (1977) para 14.11; *Bristol United Press Ltd/West Somerset Free Press* (HC 546) (1979–80) para 7.18; *Century Newspapers/ Thomson Regional Newspapers* (Cm 677) (1989) para 2.33.

10 *Portsmouth & Sunderland Newspapers plc and Johnston Press plc/Newsquest (Investments) Ltd/News Communications and Media plc* (Cm 4358) (1999) para 2.36; *News Communications & Media and Newsquest Ltd/Johnston Press plc/Trinity Mirror plc* (Cm 4680) (2000) para 2.39. Staging posts in this shift can be seen in *United Newspapers plc/Fleet Holdings plc* (Cmnd 9610) (1985) para 8.36; *Daily Mail & General Trust/T Bailey Forman Ltd* (Cm 2693) (1994) para 2.29; *Trinity International Holdings plc/Thomson Regional Newspapers Ltd* (Cm 3033) (1995) paras 2.15–2.17; *Mirror Group plc/Midland Independent Newspapers plc* (Cm 3762) (1997) paras 2.12–2.18.

11 See PARA 820.

12 *George Outram & Co Ltd/The Observer* (HC 378) (1980–81) paras 8.28–8.29; *Trinity plc/ Mirror Group plc* (Cm 4393 (1999) paras 2.23–2.25. An exceptional argument of this nature ('the highly polarised and sectarian nature of politics in the Province' during the Northern Irish Troubles) was accepted in *Century Newspapers Ltd/Thomson Regional Newspapers Ltd* (Cm 677) (1989) para 6.26.

849. Broadcasting and cross-media public interest considerations. The broadcasting[1] and cross-media public interest considerations are[2]:

(1) the need, in relation to every different audience in the United Kingdom or in a particular area or locality of the United Kingdom, for there to be a sufficient plurality of persons with control of the media enterprises serving that audience[3];

(2) the need for the availability throughout the United Kingdom of a wide range of broadcasting which (taken as a whole) is both of high quality and calculated to appeal to a wide variety of tastes and interests[4]; and

(3) the need for persons carrying on media enterprises, and for those with control of such enterprises, to have a genuine commitment to the attainment in relation to broadcasting of the prescribed[5] standards objectives[6].

These considerations were introduced by the Communications Act 2003, with the result that no insight on their interpretation can be drawn from previous reports. The government has sought to fill this gap by offering guidance[7].

There is no simple metric that can underpin the determination of whether there is a sufficient plurality of persons controlling media enterprises for the purposes of head (1)[8]. The Secretary of State[9] will focus on the number of persons that would be serving the given audience post-merger[10], but may also take account of relative audience shares and other factors. In the assessment, audience groups can be considered separately or in aggregate as the Secretary of

State sees fit[11]. By virtue of the inclusion of newspaper enterprises in the definition of media enterprises for these purposes, the assessment of plurality extends beyond broadcasting alone. In some circumstances, the perceived equivalence of likely outcome under the plurality and competition tests may cause the Secretary of State to forego the possibility of intervening[12].

In assessing quality and diversity for the purposes of head (2)[13], the Secretary of State will take account of a range of factors, including the range of proposed programme subject matter; the number of audiences whose needs will be met; the balance of proposed programming; the quality of programming; and the professional skill and editorial integrity of the programme makers. The primary evidence on which the assessment will proceed is the acquirer's statement as to future plans for the enterprise, although previous performance against programming standards and origination requirements may also be considered relevant[14].

The standards invoked in head (3)[15] include the protection of persons aged under 18; the omission of material that is likely to encourage the commission of crime or disorder; the due impartiality and accuracy of news; the exclusion of political advertising; the exclusion of misleading, harmful or offensive advertising; and the exclusion of subliminal messaging[16]. In assessing whether the commitment of the post-merger entity to these standards is genuine, the Secretary of State will focus on the past compliance of enterprises controlled by the owner in question (in particular as regards the impartiality and accuracy of news programming), whether in the United Kingdom or elsewhere. He will also consider all other material evidence[17].

1   As to the meaning of 'broadcasting' see PARA 842.
2   Enterprise Act 2002 s 58(2C) (added by the Communications Act 2003 s 375(1)).
3   Enterprise Act 2002 s 58(2C)(a) (as added: see note 2). As to the meaning of 'United Kingdom' see PARA 510 note 13.
4   Enterprise Act 2002 s 58(2C)(b) (as added: see note 2).
5   Ie the standards objectives set out in the Communications Act 2003 s 319: see PARA 897.
6   Enterprise Act 2002 s 58(2C)(c) (as added: see note 2).
7   See *Department of Trade and Industry, Enterprise Act 2002: Public Interest Intervention in Media Mergers* (URN 04/1073; London: DTI, 2004) ch 7.
8   Ie for the purposes of the Enterprise Act 2002 s 58(2C)(a).
9   As to the Secretary of State see PARA 507 note 32.
10 *Department of Trade and Industry, Enterprise Act 2002: Public Interest Intervention in Media Mergers* (URN 04/1073; London: DTI, 2004) paras 7.9–7.12. The Enterprise Act 2002 s 58A (added by the Communications Act 2003 s 375(2)) provides guidance on when a merger may be taken to have an impact on the plurality of persons in control of media enterprises. Of particular note is that, for the purposes of the Enterprise Act 2002 s 58, where two or more media enterprises would fall to be treated as under common ownership or common control for the purposes of s 26 (enterprises ceasing to be distinct enterprises: see COMPETITION vol 18 (2009) PARA 176) or are otherwise in the same ownership or under the same control, they are to be treated as all under the control of only one person: see s 58A(5) (as so added). This indicates that all enterprises falling under common ownership or control (ie under the de jure or de facto control of another, or subject to the material influence thereof) must be treated as falling within the control of one person.
11 See the Enterprise Act 2002 ss 58A, 59A; and COMPETITION vol 18 (2009) PARAS 203–204.
12 See *Department of Trade and Industry, Enterprise Act 2002: Public Interest Intervention in Media Mergers* (URN 04/1073; London: DTI, 2004) para 7.5.
13 Ie for the purposes of the Enterprise Act 2002 s 58(2C)(b).
14 See *Department of Trade and Industry, Enterprise Act 2002: Public Interest Intervention in Media Mergers* (URN 04/1073; London: DTI, 2004) paras 7.19–7.20.
15 Ie for the purposes of the Enterprise Act 2002 s 58(2C)(c). The standards are outlined in the Communications Act 2003 s 319, and developed in a code published by OFCOM: see the Broadcasting Code (OFCOM), the most recent version of which took effect on 20 December 2010; and PARA 897.

16 See the Communications Act 2003 s 319(2); and PARA 897.
17 See *Department of Trade and Industry, Enterprise Act 2002: Public Interest Intervention in Media Mergers* (URN 04/1073; London: DTI, 2004) paras 7.24–7.25.

5. CONTENT REGULATION

(1) INTRODUCTION

(i) Regulation by OFCOM

850. Regulation of broadcast content. The content of material broadcast is regulated by the general law as well as by legislation relating specifically to broadcasting. For example, the law of defamation applies to broadcasting[1], as does the law of copyright[2]. The broadcasting of obscene material is prohibited[3]. Under the legislation dealing with broadcasting[4], the regulation of broadcast content by licensed providers is a duty of OFCOM[5]. OFCOM has a duty to establish and maintain a Content Board to carry out its functions in relation to matters relating to broadcast content[6]. Provision is made by the Communications Act 2003 for the imposition on the BBC[7] and the Welsh Authority[8] of obligations corresponding to obligations included in the regulatory regime for licensed providers[9].

The Audiovisual Media Services Directive[10] and the European Convention on Transfrontier Television[11] also include provisions relating to the content of audiovisual media services[12].

1   See eg PARA 945; and LIBEL AND SLANDER.
2   See PARAS 886–888, 923–942; and COPYRIGHT, DESIGN RIGHT AND RELATED RIGHTS.
3   See PARA 944; and CRIMINAL LAW vol 26 (2010) PARA 704 et seq.
4   Ie the Broadcasting Acts 1990 and 1996, the Communications Act 2003 and the Wireless Telegraphy Act 2006: see PARAS 504–507.
5   As to OFCOM see PARA 507.
6   See the Communications Act 2003 ss 12, 13; and TELECOMMUNICATIONS vol 97 (2010) PARAS 24–25.
7   As to the meaning of 'BBC' see PARA 603 note 1; and as to the BBC see PARAS 603–626.
8   As to the meaning of 'the Welsh Authority' see PARA 644 note 3; and as to television broadcasting by the Welsh Authority see PARAS 644–661. As to the public service remit of the Welsh Authority see PARA 655.
9   See the Communications Act 2003 s 338, Sch 12 (Sch 12 paras 5, 6 not yet in force; Sch 12 para 2(2)(b) amended by SI 2009/2979).
10 Ie European Parliament and Council Directive (EU) 2010/13 (OJ L95, 15.4.2010, p 1).
11 Ie the European Convention on Transfrontier Television (Strasbourg, 5 May 1989; ETS 132).
12 See PARA 506.

851. Enforcement of licence conditions. Provision is made in the Communications Act 2003 with respect to the modification of the maximum penalties that may be imposed on the holders of Broadcasting Act licences[1].

Every amount to which these provisions[2] apply[3] is recoverable by OFCOM[4] as a debt due to it from the person obliged to pay it[5]. A person's liability to have a penalty imposed on him under Part I or Part III of the Broadcasting Act 1990, Part I or Part II of the Broadcasting Act 1996 or Part 3 of the Communications Act 2003 in respect of acts or omissions of his occurring while he was the holder of a Broadcasting Act licence, and a liability of a person as the holder of such a licence to pay an amount to which these provisions apply, are not affected by that person's Broadcasting Act licence having ceased (for any reason) to be in force before the imposition of the penalty or the payment of that amount[6].

1   See the Communications Act 2003 s 345, Sch 13; and PARA 696 et seq. As to the meaning of 'Broadcasting Act licence' see PARA 602 note 3.
2   Ie the Communications Act 2003 s 346.

3   The Communications Act 2003 s 346 applies to the following amounts: (1) any amount payable
     to OFCOM under a Broadcasting Act licence; (2) the amount of a penalty imposed by OFCOM
     under the Broadcasting Act 1990 Pt I (ss 3–71) or Pt III (ss 85–126), the Broadcasting Act 1996
     Pt I (ss 1–39) or Pt II (ss 40–72) or the Communications Act 2003 Pt 3 (ss 198–362): s 346(1).
4   As to OFCOM see PARA 507.
5   Communications Act 2003 s 346(2).
6   Communications Act 2003 s 346(3).

852.   Broadcasting Act licence fees: statement of charging principles.
OFCOM[1] is not to fix a tariff[2] unless: (1) at the time it does so, there is in force
a statement of the principles that OFCOM is proposing to apply in fixing that
tariff; and (2) the tariff is fixed in accordance with those principles[3]. Those
principles must be such as appear to OFCOM to be likely to secure, on the basis
of such estimates of the likely costs that it is practicable for it to make: (a) that
the aggregate amount of the Broadcasting Act licence fees[4] that are required to
be paid to OFCOM during a financial year[5] is sufficient to enable it to meet, but
does not exceed, the cost to it of the carrying out during that year of its functions
relating to the regulation of broadcasting[6]; (b) that the requirement imposed by
virtue of head (a) above is satisfied by the application to such fees of tariffs that
are justifiable and proportionate to the matters in respect of which they are
imposed; and (c) that the relationship between meeting the cost of carrying out
those functions and the tariffs applied to such fees is transparent[7]. Before making
or revising a statement of principles, OFCOM must consult such of the persons
who, in OFCOM's opinion, are likely to be affected by those principles as it
thinks fit[8].

The making or revision of a statement of principles for the purposes of these
provisions[9] must be by the publication of the statement, or revised statement, in
such manner as OFCOM considers appropriate for bringing it to the attention of
the persons who, in its opinion, are likely to be affected by it[10]. As soon as
reasonably practicable after the end of each financial year, OFCOM must
publish a statement setting out, for that year: (i) the aggregate amount received
by it during that year in respect of Broadcasting Act licence fees required to be
paid during that year; (ii) the aggregate amount outstanding and likely to be paid
or recovered in respect of Broadcasting Act licence fees that are required to be so
paid; and (iii) the cost to OFCOM of the carrying out during that year of its
functions relating to the regulation of broadcasting[11].

1   As to OFCOM see PARA 507.
2   Ie under the Broadcasting Act 1990 s 4(3) (see PARAS 665, 679) or s 87(3) (see PARA 726) or
     under the Broadcasting Act 1996 s 4(3) (see PARA 692) or s 43(3) (see PARA 728) (tariffs for fees
     payable under Broadcasting Act licences for recovering OFCOM's costs).
3   Communications Act 2003 s 347(1).
4   For the purposes of the Communications Act 2003 s 347, 'Broadcasting Act licence fee' means a
     fee required to be paid to OFCOM in pursuance of conditions included in a Broadcasting Act
     licence under any of the following provisions: (1) the Broadcasting Act 1990 s 4(1)(b) or
     s 87(1)(c); or (2) the Broadcasting Act 1996 s 4(1)(b) or s 43(1)(c): Communications Act 2003
     s 347(8). As to the meaning of 'Broadcasting Act licence' see PARA 602 note 3.
5   For the purposes of the Communications Act 2003 s 347, 'financial year' means a period of 12
     months ending with 31 March: s 347(8).
6   References in the Communications Act 2003 s 347 to OFCOM's functions relating to the
     regulation of broadcasting do not include references to any of its functions in relation to the
     BBC or the Welsh Authority: s 347(7). As to the meaning of 'BBC' see PARA 603 note 1; and as
     to the BBC see PARAS 603–626. As to the meaning of 'the Welsh Authority' see PARA 644 note 3;
     and as to television broadcasting by the Welsh Authority see PARAS 644–661.
7   Communications Act 2003 s 347(2).
8   Communications Act 2003 s 347(3).
9   Ie the Communications Act 2003 s 347.

10   Communications Act 2003 s 347(4).

11   Communications Act 2003 s 347(5). Any deficit or surplus shown (after applying this provision for all previous years) by a statement under s 347(5) must be: (1) carried forward; and (2) taken into account in determining what is required to satisfy the requirement imposed by virtue of head (a) in the text in relation to the following year: s 347(6).

853.   Annual review and report on television and radio.   It is the duty of OFCOM[1]: (1) as soon as practicable after the end of the period of 12 months beginning with 29 December 2003[2]; and (2) as soon as practicable after the end of every subsequent period of 12 months, to satisfy for that period the following review and reporting requirements[3]. For any period those obligations are: (a) to carry out a review of the provision of the television and radio services available for reception by members of the public in the United Kingdom[4] during that period; and (b) to prepare a factual and statistical report for that period on the provision of those services and on the state of the market in which they are provided[5].

In carrying out a review for any period under these provisions, OFCOM must consider, in particular, each of the following:

(i)   the extent to which programmes included during that period in television and radio services are representative of what OFCOM considers to be the principal genres for such programmes;

(ii)   the extent to which codes made by OFCOM under Part 3 of the Communications Act 2003[6] or Part IV or Part V of the Broadcasting Act 1996 (listed events and fairness)[7] have been complied with during that period;

(iii)   the extent to which any guidance given by OFCOM[8] has been followed during that period;

(iv)   any trends appearing or operating during that period in the size and behaviour of the audience for radio and television services;

(v)   the financial condition during that period of the market in which those services are provided and of the market in which programmes for such services are produced;

(vi)   what it is appropriate to achieve by conditions and duties[9] and the effectiveness for that purpose of the conditions and duties for the time being in force;

(vii)   whether it would be appropriate to recommend to the Secretary of State that he exercises any of his powers[10];

(viii) the extent to which work on independent productions[11] that are produced in the United Kingdom is done in a range of production centres outside the M25 area[12];

(ix)   any issues relating to intellectual property in programmes that have arisen or been of significance during that period;

(x)   developments in technology that have occurred or become important during that period and are relevant to the provision, broadcasting or distribution of television and radio programmes;

(xi)   the availability during that period of persons with skills that are used or likely to be useful in connection with the provision of television and radio services and the production of programmes for inclusion in such services;

(xii)   the availability during that period of facilities for the provision of training in such skills[13].

Every report prepared by OFCOM under these provisions must be published by it: (A) as soon as practicable after its preparation is complete; and (B) in such manner as it considers appropriate[14].

1   As to OFCOM see PARA 507.
2   Ie beginning with the commencement of the Communications Act 2003 s 358: see the Office of Communications Act 2002 (Commencement No 3) and Communications Act 2003 (Commencement No 2) Order 2003, SI 2003/3142.
3   Ie of the Communications Act 2003 s 358: s 358(1).
4   As to the meaning of 'available for reception by members of the public' see PARA 796. As to the meaning of 'United Kingdom' see PARA 510 note 13.
5   Communications Act 2003 s 358(2).
6   Ie the Communications Act 2003 Pt 3 (ss 198–362).
7   Ie the Broadcasting Act 1996 Pt IV (ss 97–105), Pt V (ss 107–130).
8   Ie under the Communications Act 2003 s 314 (see PARA 889).
9   Ie under the Communications Act 2003 s 277 and Sch 12 paras 1, 7 (see PARAS 644, 875, 883).
10 Ie under the Communications Act 2003 s 277 or Sch 12 paras 1, 7.
11 Ie within the meaning of the Communications Act 2003 s 277 and Sch 12 paras 1, 7.
12 As to the meaning of 'M25 area' see PARA 788 note 15.
13 Communications Act 2003 s 358(3). Every report under s 358 must set out OFCOM's findings on its consideration of the matters mentioned in s 358(3): s 358(4).
14 Communications Act 2003 s 358(5). OFCOM's duties under s 358 are in addition to its duties under s 264 (see PARA 788): s 358(6).

854.   Functions of OFCOM in relation to the BBC. It is a function of OFCOM[1], to the extent that provision for it to do so is contained in: (1) the BBC Charter and Agreement[2]; and (2) the Communications Act 2003 and Part V of the Broadcasting Act 1996[3], to regulate the provision of the BBC's services[4] and the carrying on by the BBC of other activities for purposes connected with the provision of those services[5]. For the purposes of the carrying out of that function, OFCOM: (a) has such powers and duties as may be conferred on it by or under the BBC Charter and Agreement; and (b) is entitled, to the extent that it is authorised to do so by the Secretary of State or under the terms of that Charter and Agreement, to act on his behalf in relation to that Charter and Agreement[6]. Under the Agreement, the BBC has the general duty of co-operating with OFCOM, and furnishing it with such information and other assistance as it may reasonably require in connection with any of its functions under these provisions[7].

The BBC must pay OFCOM such penalties in respect of contraventions by the BBC of provision made by or under Part 3 or Part 4A of the Communications Act 2003[8] or the BBC Charter and Agreement as are imposed by OFCOM in exercise of powers conferred on it by that Charter and Agreement[9]. The BBC is also liable to pay OFCOM such sums in respect of the carrying out by OFCOM of its functions in relation to the BBC as may be agreed from time to time between the BBC and OFCOM or (in default of agreement) fixed by the Secretary of State[10]. The maximum penalty that may be imposed on the BBC on any occasion by OFCOM in exercise of a power conferred by virtue of the BBC Charter and Agreement is £250,000[11].

It is the duty of OFCOM to have regard to its functions under the above provisions when carrying out its functions under the Broadcasting Act 1990, the Broadcasting Act 1996 and Part 3 of the Communications Act 2003 in relation to services provided by persons other than the BBC[12].

1   As to OFCOM see PARA 507.
2   'The BBC Charter and Agreement' means the following documents, or any one or more of them, so far as they are for the time being in force: (1) a Royal Charter for the continuance of the BBC;

(2) supplemental Charters obtained by the BBC under such a Royal Charter; (3) an agreement between the BBC and the Secretary of State entered into (whether before or after the passing of the Communications Act 2003 (ie 17 July 2003)) for purposes that include the regulation of activities carried on by the BBC: Communications Act 2003 s 362(1). As to the Secretary of State see PARA 507 note 32.

3　Ie the Broadcasting Act 1996 Pt V (ss 107–130).

4　For the purposes of the Communications Act 2003 s 198, 'the BBC's services' means such of the services provided by the BBC (excluding the services comprised in the World Service) as are of a description of service which, if provided by a BBC company, would fall to be regulated by OFCOM by virtue of s 211 (see PARA 857) or s 245 (see PARA 723) or by the appropriate regulatory authority by virtue of s 368C (see PARAS 785, 881): s 198(9) (amended by SI 2009/2979). 'BBC company' means: (1) a body corporate which is controlled by the BBC; or (2) a body corporate in which the BBC or a body corporate controlled by the BBC is (to any extent) a participant: Communications Act 2003 s 362(1). 'Controlled' and 'participant' each has the same meaning as in the Broadcasting Act 1990 Sch 2 (see PARAS 671 note 20, 821 note 11): Communications Act 2003 s 362(6).

5　Communications Act 2003 s 198(1). 'Provision', in relation to a service, is to be construed (subject to s 362(3)) in accordance with s 362(2), and cognate expressions are to be construed accordingly: s 362(1). In the case of any of the following services:

　(1)　a television broadcasting service (see PARA 602 note 8) or sound broadcasting service (see PARA 723 note 4);

　(2)　the public teletext service (see PARA 686);

　(3)　a television licensable content service (see PARA 716) or radio licensable content service (see PARA 749);

　(4)　a digital television programme service (see PARA 602 note 8) or digital sound programme service (see PARA 723 note 8);

　(5)　a restricted television service (see PARA 602 note 8);

　(6)　an additional television service (see PARA 857 note 8) or additional radio service (see PARA 723 note 6);

　(7)　a digital additional television service (see PARA 857 note 11) or a digital additional sound service (see PARA 723 note 9),

the person, and the only person, who is to be treated for the purposes of Pt 3 (ss 198–362) as providing the service is the person with general control over which programmes and other services and facilities are comprised in the service (whether or not he has control of the content of individual programmes or of the broadcasting or distribution of the service): s 362(2). For the purposes of Pt 3: (a) the provision of a service by the BBC does not include its provision by a BBC company; (b) the provision of a service by C4C does not include its provision by a C4 company; (c) the provision of a service by the Welsh Authority does not include its provision by an S4C company; and, accordingly, control that is or is capable of being exercised by the BBC, C4C or the Welsh Authority over decisions by a BBC company, C4 company or S4C company about what is to be comprised in a service is to be disregarded for the purposes of s 362(2): s 362(3).

6　Communications Act 2003 s 198(2). See the *Agreement between Her Majesty's Secretary of State for Culture, Media and Sport and the British Broadcasting Corporation* (Cm 6872) (30 June 2006) cll 91–95.

7　*Agreement between Her Majesty's Secretary of State for Culture, Media and Sport and the British Broadcasting Corporation* (Cm 6872) (30 June 2006) cl 91.

8　Ie the Communications Act 2003 Pt 3 (ss 198–362) or Pt 4A (ss 368A–368R).

9　Communications Act 2003 s 198(3) (amended by SI 2009/2979).

10　Communications Act 2003 s 198(4).

11　Communications Act 2003 s 198(5). The Secretary of State may by order substitute a different sum for the sum for the time being specified in s 198(5): s 198(6). No order is to be made containing provision authorised by s 198(6) unless a draft of the order has been laid before Parliament and approved by a resolution of each House: s 198(7). As to the power of the Secretary of State to make orders under the Communications Act 2003 see s 402; and TELECOMMUNICATIONS vol 97 (2010) PARA 77.

12　Communications Act 2003 s 198(8).

855.　Agreements between OFCOM and the BBC. The BBC[1] must do all it can to secure and maintain the agreement of OFCOM[2] to anything which is required[3] to be agreed[4], and must, for the purpose of securing or maintaining such agreement: (1) make proposals to OFCOM; and (2) liaise with OFCOM to such extent as may be necessary to secure or maintain such agreement[5]. In relation to the UK public television services[6] the BBC must comply with agreed arrangements as to: (a) programming quotas for original productions[7]; and (b) programme-making in the nations and regions[8].

1   As to the meaning of 'BBC' see PARA 603.

2   As to OFCOM see PARA 507.

3   Ie for any purpose of the *Agreement between Her Majesty's Secretary of State for Culture, Media and Sport and the British Broadcasting Corporation* (Cm 6872) (30 June 2006) cll 47, 49, 50, 51, 52, 59, 61, 62 (see PARAS 856, 858, 900) ('the relevant provisions': see cl 92(1)).

4   In the *Agreement between Her Majesty's Secretary of State for Culture, Media and Sport and the British Broadcasting Corporation* (Cm 6872) (30 June 2006) cll 47, 49, 50, 51, 52, 59, 61, 62, 'agreed' means agreed between the BBC and OFCOM: cl 92(2).

5   *Agreement between Her Majesty's Secretary of State for Culture, Media and Sport and the British Broadcasting Corporation* (Cm 6872) (30 June 2006) cl 92(3).

6   'UK public services' means all the services provided by the BBC for the purpose of promoting its Public Purposes, except any which: (1) are commercial services (see PARA 624 note 2); (2) form part of the World Service (see PARA 617); (3) fall within cl 75(7) (services provided at the request of, and funded by, government departments (see PARA 621)); or (4) are aimed primarily at users outside the UK: *Agreement between Her Majesty's Secretary of State for Culture, Media and Sport and the British Broadcasting Corporation* (Cm 6872) (30 June 2006) cll 100, 104. 'Service' includes any activity which is, or ought to be, covered by a service licence (see PARA 614): cl 104. The UK public services are listed and described in cl 11, the television services in cl 11(2). See PARA 615. As to the meaning of 'Public Purposes' see PARA 603 note 3. As to the meaning of 'UK' see PARA 615 note 4.

7   See the *Agreement between Her Majesty's Secretary of State for Culture, Media and Sport and the British Broadcasting Corporation* (Cm 6872) (30 June 2006) cl 49.

8   See the *Agreement between Her Majesty's Secretary of State for Culture, Media and Sport and the British Broadcasting Corporation* (Cm 6872) (30 June 2006) cl 51.

856.   Regulation of BBC's UK public services. The BBC[1] is also given various duties in connection with the UK public broadcasting services[2]. As well as preparing and publishing statements of programme policy[3], it must comply with the Fairness Code[4] both in connection with the provision of the UK public broadcasting services and in relation to the programmes included in those services[5]. It must observe relevant programme code standards[6] in the provision of the UK public broadcasting services[7].

The Trust must approve guidelines designed to secure appropriate standards in the content of the UK public services[8].

The BBC must do all it can to ensure that controversial subjects are treated with due accuracy and impartiality in all relevant output[9]. With limited exceptions[10], the UK public services must not contain any output which expresses the opinion of the BBC or of its Trust or Executive Board on current affairs or matters of public policy other than broadcasting or the provision of online services[11]. The Trust must draw up and from time to time review a code giving guidance as to the rules to be observed in connection with the application of this requirement, and do all it can to secure that the code is complied with[12].

The BBC Trust must impose on the Executive Board[13] the requirements it considers appropriate for securing the broadcasting of news and current affairs[14] programmes at appropriate times and intervals[15] and for securing sufficient and appropriate broadcasting of programmes for the regions and nations[16].

The BBC must include, in some or all of the UK public broadcasting services, party political broadcasts and referendum campaign broadcasts[17].

In relation to each of the UK Public Television Services, the BBC must comply with agreed arrangements for securing programming quotas for original productions[18]. It must also ensure that specified quotas for independent productions are met[19] and that it reserves enough of its programmes for making as independent productions to ensure that the BBC meets, in each year, its statutory obligations[20] as to quotas for independent productions[21].

The BBC must use its best endeavours to ensure that 50 per cent of total relevant air time[22] in any year is allocated to the broadcasting of a range[23] and diversity of programmes which were made either: (1) as independent productions as a result of having been reserved for making as independent productions; or (2) through the Window of Creative Competition ('the WOCC')[24]. The Trust must ensure that suitable arrangements are in place to provide appropriate opportunities for competition between in-house and external producers for the provision of programmes which are not intended to be network programmes[25]. The BBC must use its best endeavours to ensure that 50 per cent of total relevant air time in any year is allocated to the broadcasting of a range and diversity of programmes which were made by the BBC through its in-house production facility as a result of having been reserved for making through that facility[26]. The Trust must, at least every two years, review the operation of the above provisions[27] as to independent programmes[28].

The Trust must impose on the Executive Board the requirements it considers appropriate for securing: (a) that what appears to the Trust to be a suitable proportion of the programmes included in those radio services (taken together) which are UK public services, and the material available to members of the public as part of those online services (taken together) which are UK public services, consists of programmes or, as the case may be, material made by producers external to the BBC; and (b) that what appears to the Trust to be a suitable range and diversity of such programmes and material is made by such persons[29].

The BBC must, in providing the UK Public Television Services, observe the code for the time being maintained by OFCOM[30] relating to provision of television services for the deaf and visually impaired[31]; but the code is to apply in a modified way[32]. The Code is, as a general rule, to apply separately to the provision of each of the UK Public Television Services by the BBC in the same way that it applies to the provision of Channel 4[33] by the Channel Four Television Corporation[34], although the code is to have effect as if the excluded programmes[35] were those agreed for the purposes of these provisions instead of those applicable to Channel 4[36] and as if the relevant date in relation to any of the UK Public Television Services were that fixed by these provisions[37] instead of the relevant date applicable to Channel 4[38]. Before agreeing anything for these purposes, the parties must consult such persons appearing to them to represent the interests of persons who are deaf or hard of hearing, persons who are blind or partially-sighted, and persons with a dual sensory impairment[39] as they think fit[40]. The BBC must publish anything agreed for these purposes in such manner as it considers appropriate, having regard to the need to make what has been agreed accessible to persons who are deaf or hard of hearing and persons who are blind or partially sighted[41]. The Secretary of State has specific power to modify the code as applied to the BBC[42].

It is the duty of the Trust to require the Executive Board to draw up and from time to time revise a code of practice setting out the principles that are to be applied when the BBC is, for a purpose connected with the provision of the UK Public Television Services, agreeing terms for the commissioning of independent productions[43]. The BBC must at all times comply with the code of practice which is for the time being in force and revise that code to take account of revisions of the guidance issued by OFCOM for these purposes[44]. A code or a revision of such a code has effect for these purposes only if agreed[45].

In addition, the BBC must comply with requirements notified to it from time to time by OFCOM[46], being requirements which OFCOM considers appropriate for the purpose of securing that the relevant international obligations of the United Kingdom[47] are complied with in respect of the UK public broadcasting services or any UK public on-demand programme service[48]. Before notifying any such requirement to the BBC, OFCOM must give the BBC a reasonable opportunity of making representations to it about that requirement[49].

1   As to the meaning of 'BBC' see PARA 603.
2   As to the meaning of 'UK public broadcasting services' see PARA 615; and as to the meaning of 'service' see PARA 855 note 6. As to complaints about standards and content see PARA 873.
3   As to statements of programme policy see PARA 616.
4   Ie the code for the time being in force under the Broadcasting Act 1996 s 107 (see PARA 906): *Agreement between Her Majesty's Secretary of State for Culture, Media and Sport and the British Broadcasting Corporation* (Cm 6872) (30 June 2006) cl 45(2).
5   *Agreement between Her Majesty's Secretary of State for Culture, Media and Sport and the British Broadcasting Corporation* (Cm 6872) (30 June 2006) cl 45(1).
6   'Relevant programme code standards' means those standards for the time being set under the Communications Act 2003 s 319 (see PARA 897): (1) which relate to the objectives set out in s 319(2)(a), (b), (e), (f), (fa) and (l) (protection of persons under the age of 18; omission of material likely to encourage or incite any crime or disorder; exercise of responsibility with respect to the content of religious programmes; application of generally accepted standards so as to provide adequate protection for members of the public from the inclusion of offensive and harmful material; product placement requirements; and refraining from use of techniques which exploit the possibility of conveying a message to viewers or listeners, or of otherwise influencing their minds, without their being aware, or fully aware, of what has occurred); but (2) only to the extent that they do not concern the accuracy or impartiality of the content of any programme included in the UK public broadcasting services: *Agreement between Her Majesty's Secretary of State for Culture, Media and Sport and the British Broadcasting Corporation* (Cm 6872) (30 June 2006) cl 46(2) (amended by Cm 7853, March 2010).
7   *Agreement between Her Majesty's Secretary of State for Culture, Media and Sport and the British Broadcasting Corporation* (Cm 6872) (30 June 2006) cl 46(1).
8   *Agreement between Her Majesty's Secretary of State for Culture, Media and Sport and the British Broadcasting Corporation* (Cm 6872) (30 June 2006) cl 43(1). The more specific obligations set out in cll 44–63 are not intended to restrict the general scope of cl 43(1): cl 43(2).
9   *Agreement between Her Majesty's Secretary of State for Culture, Media and Sport and the British Broadcasting Corporation* (Cm 6872) (30 June 2006) cl 44(1). In applying cl 44(1), a series of programmes may be considered as a whole: cl 44(2). For the purposes of cl 44, 'relevant output' means the output of any UK Public Service which: (1) consists of news; or (2) deals with matters of public policy or of political or industrial controversy: cl 44(8). 'Programme', except in cl 44(7)(c) and (d), includes any item of output in non-programme form; and 'series of programmes', except in cl 44(7)(d), includes items of output in non-programme form which are analogously linked: cl 44(8).
10 The *Agreement between Her Majesty's Secretary of State for Culture, Media and Sport and the British Broadcasting Corporation* (Cm 6872) (30 June 2006) cl 44(3) does not apply to output which consists of: (1) proceedings in either House of Parliament; (2) proceedings in the Scottish Parliament, the Welsh Assembly or the Northern Ireland Assembly; or (3) proceedings of a local authority or a committee of two or more local authorities: cl 44(4).
11 *Agreement between Her Majesty's Secretary of State for Culture, Media and Sport and the British Broadcasting Corporation* (Cm 6872) (30 June 2006) cl 44(3).
12 *Agreement between Her Majesty's Secretary of State for Culture, Media and Sport and the British Broadcasting Corporation* (Cm 6872) (30 June 2006) cl 44(5). As to the rules see further cl 44(6), (7); and PARA 895.
13 As to the Executive Board see PARA 604.
14 The meanings of 'news' and 'current affairs' must be agreed: *Agreement between Her Majesty's Secretary of State for Culture, Media and Sport and the British Broadcasting Corporation* (Cm 6872) (30 June 2006) cl 47(6). 'Agreed' means agreed in accordance with cl 92 (see PARA 855 note 4): cl 47(6).

15 See the *Agreement between Her Majesty's Secretary of State for Culture, Media and Sport and the British Broadcasting Corporation* (Cm 6872) (30 June 2006) cl 47(1). Before imposing any requirements under cl 47(1), the Trust must consult OFCOM on its proposals for such requirements, and must have regard to any comments made by OFCOM upon those proposals: cl 47(2). See further cl 47(3)–(5). As to OFCOM see PARA 507.

16 See the *Agreement between Her Majesty's Secretary of State for Culture, Media and Sport and the British Broadcasting Corporation* (Cm 6872) (30 June 2006) cl 50(1). Before imposing any requirements under cl 50(1), the Trust must consult OFCOM on its proposals for such requirements, and must have regard to any comments made by OFCOM upon those proposals: cl 50(2). See further cl 50(3)–(7).

17 *Agreement between Her Majesty's Secretary of State for Culture, Media and Sport and the British Broadcasting Corporation* (Cm 6872) (30 June 2006) cl 48(1). 'Referendum campaign broadcast' has the meaning given by the Political Parties, Elections and Referendums Act 2000 s 127 (see ELECTIONS AND REFERENDUMS vol 15(4) (2007 Reissue) PARA 544): *Agreement between Her Majesty's Secretary of State for Culture, Media and Sport and the British Broadcasting Corporation* cl 48(4). As to the Trust's discretion in relation to such broadcasts see cl 48(2), (3). As to party political broadcasts see PARA 896.

18 See the *Agreement between Her Majesty's Secretary of State for Culture, Media and Sport and the British Broadcasting Corporation* (Cm 6872) (30 June 2006) cl 49. 'Original productions', in relation to the UK Public Television Services taken together, has the same meaning that is specified by order under the Communications Act 2003 s 278(6) (programming quotas for original productions in relation to licensed public service channels: see PARA 875) in relation to a licensed public service channel, except that: (1) to any extent that such an order makes different provision for different cases, the agreed arrangements must determine which of those cases is to be taken to be relevant for the purposes of the *Agreement between Her Majesty's Secretary of State for Culture, Media and Sport and the British Broadcasting Corporation* cl 49; and (2) to any extent that such an order makes provision in terms which are not apt to apply for the purposes of cl 49, the agreed arrangements must determine whether, and if so what, necessary modifications are to be made so that such provision may apply, as analogously as practicable, for those purposes: cl 49(5).

19 See the *Agreement between Her Majesty's Secretary of State for Culture, Media and Sport and the British Broadcasting Corporation* (Cm 6872) (30 June 2006) cl 52. The duties imposed by virtue of cl 52(1) and (2) are in addition to any relevant statutory duty, and nothing in cl 52 is to be interpreted as making or otherwise providing for any designation under the Communications Act 2003 Sch 12 para 1(8) (which enables an agreement of this type to make certain modifications to a relevant statutory duty: see PARA 883): *Agreement between Her Majesty's Secretary of State for Culture, Media and Sport and the British Broadcasting Corporation* (Cm 6872) (30 June 2006) cl 52(4). 'Relevant statutory duty' means any duty imposed by the Communications Act 2003 Sch 12 para 1(1) or (4) (see PARA 883): *Agreement between Her Majesty's Secretary of State for Culture, Media and Sport and the British Broadcasting Corporation* (Cm 6872) (30 June 2006) cl 52(5).

20 Ie under the Communications Act 2003 Sch 12 para 1: see PARA 883.

21 *Agreement between Her Majesty's Secretary of State for Culture, Media and Sport and the British Broadcasting Corporation* (Cm 6872) (30 June 2006) cl 53(1). See further cl 53(2), (3).

22 'Total relevant air time' means the total amount of time allocated to the broadcasting of relevant programmes on the UK Public Television Services taken together; and 'relevant programmes', in relation to the UK Public Television Services, means network programmes which are 'qualifying programmes' in relation to those services for the purposes of the Communications Act 2003 Sch 12 (see PARA 883): *Agreement between Her Majesty's Secretary of State for Culture, Media and Sport and the British Broadcasting Corporation* (Cm 6872) (30 June 2006) cl 54(4).

23 'Range' means a range of programmes in terms of cost of acquisition as well as in terms of the types of programme involved: *Agreement between Her Majesty's Secretary of State for Culture, Media and Sport and the British Broadcasting Corporation* (Cm 6872) (30 June 2006) cl 54(4).

24 *Agreement between Her Majesty's Secretary of State for Culture, Media and Sport and the British Broadcasting Corporation* (Cm 6872) (30 June 2006) cl 54(1). As to the making of programmes through the WOCC see cl 54(2), (3).

25 *Agreement between Her Majesty's Secretary of State for Culture, Media and Sport and the British Broadcasting Corporation* (Cm 6872) (30 June 2006) cl 55. 'Network programme' means programmes to be made with a view to their being broadcast throughout the United Kingdom: cl 54(4).

26 *Agreement between Her Majesty's Secretary of State for Culture, Media and Sport and the British Broadcasting Corporation* (Cm 6872) (30 June 2006) cl 56(1). 'Range' and 'total relevant air time' have the same meanings as in cl 54 (see notes 22, 23): cl 56(2).

27 Ie the *Agreement between Her Majesty's Secretary of State for Culture, Media and Sport and the British Broadcasting Corporation* (Cm 6872) (30 June 2006) cll 54–56.

28 *Agreement between Her Majesty's Secretary of State for Culture, Media and Sport and the British Broadcasting Corporation* (Cm 6872) (30 June 2006) cl 57(1). As to the requirements of a review see cl 57(2).

29 *Agreement between Her Majesty's Secretary of State for Culture, Media and Sport and the British Broadcasting Corporation* (Cm 6872) (30 June 2006) cl 58(1). As to the determination of a suitable proportion and a suitable range see cl 58(2), (3).

30 Ie under the Communications Act 2003 s 303: see PARA 880.

31 *Agreement between Her Majesty's Secretary of State for Culture, Media and Sport and the British Broadcasting Corporation* (Cm 6872) (30 June 2006) cl 59(1). The code would not apply to the provision of the UK Public Television Services by the BBC but for cl 58.

32 *Agreement between Her Majesty's Secretary of State for Culture, Media and Sport and the British Broadcasting Corporation* (Cm 6872) (30 June 2006) cl 59(2).

33 As to the meaning of 'Channel 4' see PARA 602 note 9.

34 *Agreement between Her Majesty's Secretary of State for Culture, Media and Sport and the British Broadcasting Corporation* (Cm 6872) (30 June 2006) cl 59(3).

35 'Excluded programmes' are the descriptions of programmes set out in the code under the Communications Act 2003 s 303(7) (see PARA 880 note 12): *Agreement between Her Majesty's Secretary of State for Culture, Media and Sport and the British Broadcasting Corporation* (Cm 6872) (30 June 2006) cl 59(4).

36 *Agreement between Her Majesty's Secretary of State for Culture, Media and Sport and the British Broadcasting Corporation* (Cm 6872) (30 June 2006) cl 59(4). In agreeing the excluded programmes, the parties must have regard, in particular, to the matters set out in the Communications Act 2003 s 303(8)(a)–(f) (see PARA 880 note 12): *Agreement between Her Majesty's Secretary of State for Culture, Media and Sport and the British Broadcasting Corporation* (Cm 6872) (30 June 2006) cl 59(5). The exclusions that may be agreed: (1) may include different descriptions of programmes in relation to different UK Public Television Services; and (2) in the case of a UK Public Television Service which the parties are satisfied (having regard to the matters mentioned in cl 59(5)) is a special case, may include all the programmes included in the service: cl 59(6).

37 For these purposes, the relevant date is: (1) in the case of BBC One and BBC Two, 1 January 1997; and (2) in any other case, the date (whether before or after the making of the *Agreement between Her Majesty's Secretary of State for Culture, Media and Sport and the British Broadcasting Corporation* (Cm 6872) (30 June 2006)) when the provision of the service began or begins: cl 59(8). The parties must agree whether a service is to be treated for the purpose of cl 59(8)(b) as a continuation of a service previously provided by the BBC rather than as a new service: cl 59(9).

38 *Agreement between Her Majesty's Secretary of State for Culture, Media and Sport and the British Broadcasting Corporation* (Cm 6872) (30 June 2006) cl 59(7). As to the relevant date applicable to Channel 4 see the Communications Act 2003 s 305.

39 Ie persons falling within the Communications Act 2003 s 303(1)(a)(i), (ii) or (iii) (see PARA 880 heads (1)(a)–(c)).

40 *Agreement between Her Majesty's Secretary of State for Culture, Media and Sport and the British Broadcasting Corporation* (Cm 6872) (30 June 2006) cl 59(10).

41 *Agreement between Her Majesty's Secretary of State for Culture, Media and Sport and the British Broadcasting Corporation* (Cm 6872) (30 June 2006) cl 59(11).

42 See the *Agreement between Her Majesty's Secretary of State for Culture, Media and Sport and the British Broadcasting Corporation* (Cm 6872) (30 June 2006) cl 60. No order under the Communications Act 2003 s 306 modifying s 303 is to have any effect for the purposes of the code as applied to the BBC, nor is any revision by OFCOM of the code maintained by it under the Communications Act 2003 s 303 to have an effect for those purposes to any extent that the revision merely gives effect to such an order: *Agreement between Her Majesty's Secretary of State for Culture, Media and Sport and the British Broadcasting Corporation* cl 60(1). Instead, the Secretary of State may give a direction specifically for the purposes of cl 59, to provide for the code which the BBC is required to observe by cl 59 to have effect for the purposes of that clause as if it were subject to the modifications specified in the direction: see cl 60(2)–(7). As to the Secretary of State see PARA 507 note 32.

43 *Agreement between Her Majesty's Secretary of State for Culture, Media and Sport and the British Broadcasting Corporation* (Cm 6872) (30 June 2006) cl 61(1). 'Independent productions' has the meaning which it has for the purposes of the Communications Act 2003 Sch 12 para 1 (see PARA 883 note 4): *Agreement between Her Majesty's Secretary of State for*

Culture, Media and Sport and the British Broadcasting Corporation (Cm 6872) (30 June 2006) cl 61(9). As to the code see further cl 61(3), (4).

44 *Agreement between Her Majesty's Secretary of State for Culture, Media and Sport and the British Broadcasting Corporation* (Cm 6872) (30 June 2006) cl 61(2). As to guidance by OFCOM see further cl 61(7), (8).

45 *Agreement between Her Majesty's Secretary of State for Culture, Media and Sport and the British Broadcasting Corporation* (Cm 6872) (30 June 2006) cl 61(5). 'Agreed' means agreed in accordance with cl 92 (see PARA 855 note 4): cl 61(6).

46 *Agreement between Her Majesty's Secretary of State for Culture, Media and Sport and the British Broadcasting Corporation* (Cm 6872) (30 June 2006) cl 63(1).

47 For that purpose, an international obligation of the United Kingdom is relevant if it has been notified to OFCOM by the Secretary of State for the purposes of the *Agreement between Her Majesty's Secretary of State for Culture, Media and Sport and the British Broadcasting Corporation* (Cm 6872) (30 June 2006) cl 63: cl 63(3).

48 *Agreement between Her Majesty's Secretary of State for Culture, Media and Sport and the British Broadcasting Corporation* (Cm 6872) (30 June 2006) cl 63(2) (amended by Cm 7853, March 2010). As to the meaning of 'UK public on-demand programme service' for these purposes see PARA 618 note 2.

49 *Agreement between Her Majesty's Secretary of State for Culture, Media and Sport and the British Broadcasting Corporation* (Cm 6872) (30 June 2006) cl 63(4).

857. Services regulated by OFCOM. It is a function of OFCOM[1] to regulate the following services in accordance with the Communications Act 2003, the Broadcasting Act 1990 and the Broadcasting Act 1996: (1) services falling within heads (a) to (e) below that are provided otherwise than by the BBC[2] or the Welsh Authority[3]; and (2) services falling within heads (i) and (ii) below that are provided otherwise than by the BBC[4].

The services referred to in head (1) above are: (a) television broadcasting services that are provided from places in the United Kingdom[5] with a view to their being broadcast otherwise than only from a satellite; (b) television licensable content services[6] that are provided by persons under the jurisdiction of the United Kingdom for the purposes of the Audiovisual Media Services Directive[7]; (c) digital television programme services that are provided by persons under the jurisdiction of the United Kingdom for the purposes of that Directive; (d) restricted television services that are provided from places in the United Kingdom; and (e) additional television services[8] that are provided from places in the United Kingdom[9].

The services referred to in head (2) above are: (i) television multiplex services[10] that are provided from places in the United Kingdom; and (ii) digital additional television services[11] that are provided by persons under the jurisdiction of the United Kingdom for the purposes of the Audiovisual Media Services Directive[12].

The Secretary of State[13] no longer has any function under the Broadcasting Act 1990 or the Broadcasting Act 1996 of assigning frequencies for the purposes of any of the following: (A) services falling to be licensed under Part I of the Broadcasting Act 1990[14]; (B) S4C[15]; or (C) television multiplex services falling to be licensed under Part 1 of the Broadcasting Act 1996[16].

On and after the television transfer date[17] no licence is required under Part II of the Broadcasting Act 1990[18] for the provision of a local delivery service[19].

1   As to OFCOM see PARA 507.
2   As to the BBC see PARAS 603–626.
3   As to the meaning of 'the Welsh Authority' see PARA 644 note 3; and as to television broadcasting by the Welsh Authority see PARAS 644–661.
4   Communications Act 2003 s 211(1).
5   As to the meaning of 'United Kingdom' see PARA 510 note 13.
6   As to the meaning of 'television licensable content service' see PARA 716.

7   'The Audiovisual Media Services Directive' means European Parliament and Council Directive (EU) 2010/13 (OJ L95, 15.4.2010, p 1) on the coordination of certain provisions laid down by law, regulation or administrative action in member states concerning the provision of audiovisual media services: Communications Act 2003 s 405(1) (definition added by SI 2009/2979; and substituted by SI 2010/1883). See PARA 506.

8   'Additional television service' (except in the expression 'digital additional television service') means an additional service within the meaning given by the Broadcasting Act 1990 s 48 (see PARA 703) for the purposes of the Broadcasting Act 1990 Pt I (ss 3–71): Communications Act 2003 s 362(1).

9   Communications Act 2003 s 211(2) (amended by SI 2009/2979).

10 As to the meaning of 'television multiplex service' see PARA 697; definition applied by the Communications Act 2003 s 362(1).

11 'Digital additional television service' means a digital additional service within the meaning given by the Broadcasting Act 1996 s 24(1) (see PARA 690 note 28) for the purposes of the Broadcasting Act 1996 Pt I (ss 1–39): Communications Act 2003 s 362(1).

12 Communications Act 2003 s 211(3) (amended by SI 2009/2979).

13 As to the Secretary of State see PARA 507 note 32.

14 See PARA 662 et seq.

15 As to the meaning of 'S4C' see PARA 644.

16 Communications Act 2003 s 212.

17 'The television transfer date' means the date on which the Independent Television Commission's functions under the Broadcasting Act 1990 Pt I and the Broadcasting Act 1996 Pt I were transferred under the Communications Act 2003 to OFCOM: s 405(1). Those functions were transferred on 29 December 2003: see PARA 507.

18 Ie the Broadcasting Act 1990 Pt II (ss 72–82) (repealed).

19 Communications Act 2003 s 213.

(ii) Enforcement

858.   Directions to take remedial action. If OFCOM[1] is satisfied that the BBC[2] has, in relation to any of its services[3], contravened a relevant enforceable requirement[4], and that the contravention can be appropriately remedied by the inclusion in that service of a correction or a statement of findings (or both), OFCOM may direct the BBC to include a correction or statement of findings (or both) in the service[5]. A direction may require the correction or statement of findings to be in such form, and to be included in programmes at such times, as OFCOM may determine[6]. OFCOM is not to give the BBC a direction under these provisions unless it has given it a reasonable opportunity of making representations to it about the matters appearing to OFCOM to provide grounds for the giving of the direction[7]. Where the BBC includes a correction or a statement of findings in a service in pursuance of a direction, it may announce that it is doing so in pursuance of such a direction[8]. If OFCOM is satisfied that the inclusion of a programme in a service involved a contravention of a relevant enforceable requirement, it may direct the BBC not to include that programme in that service on any future occasion[9]. Where OFCOM gives a direction to the BBC[10] or receives representations from it[11], it must send a copy of the notice or representations to the Secretary of State[12].

1   As to OFCOM see PARA 507.

2   As to the meaning of 'BBC' see PARA 603.

3   As to the meaning of 'service' see PARA 855 note 6.

4   'Relevant enforceable requirement' has the meaning given in the *Agreement between Her Majesty's Secretary of State for Culture, Media and Sport and the British Broadcasting Corporation* (Cm 6872) (30 June 2006) cl 95: cl 93(7).

    Under cl 95(1) (amended by Cm 7853, March 2010), 'relevant enforceable requirements' are all requirements imposed on the BBC by or under the following provisions of the *Agreement between Her Majesty's Secretary of State for National Heritage and the British Broadcasting Corporation* or the Communications Act 2003:

(1)   cl 45 (fairness code);
(2)   cl 46 (programme code standards);
(3)   cl 47 (news and current affairs);
(4)   cl 49 (programming quotas for original productions);
(5)   cl 50 (programming for the nations and regions);
(6)   cl 51 (programme-making in the nations and regions);
(7)   cl 52 (quotas for independent productions);
(8)   cl 59 (code relating to provision for the deaf and visually impaired);
(9)   cl 60 (power to modify targets for the purposes of cl 59);
(10) cl 61 (code relating to programme commissioning);
(11) cl 62 (retention and production of recordings);
(12) cl 63 (international obligations);
(13) cl 91 (co-operation with OFCOM);
(14) the Communications Act 2003 s 368D (requirements for on-demand programme services and their providers: see PARA 867) so far as it applies to the BBC, but only to the extent that the requirements do not concern the accuracy or impartiality of the content of any programmes included in a UK public on-demand programme service;
(15) the Communications Act 2003 Sch 12 para 1 (quotas for independent productions: see PARA 883); and
(16) Sch 12 para 2 (duty to publicise complaints procedures etc).

As to those requirements see PARAS 872 et seq, 900. As to the meaning of 'UK public on-demand programme service' for these purposes see PARA 618 note 2.

5   *Agreement between Her Majesty's Secretary of State for Culture, Media and Sport and the British Broadcasting Corporation* (Cm 6872) (30 June 2006) cl 93(1).
6   *Agreement between Her Majesty's Secretary of State for Culture, Media and Sport and the British Broadcasting Corporation* (Cm 6872) (30 June 2006) cl 93(2).
7   *Agreement between Her Majesty's Secretary of State for Culture, Media and Sport and the British Broadcasting Corporation* (Cm 6872) (30 June 2006) cl 93(3).
8   *Agreement between Her Majesty's Secretary of State for Culture, Media and Sport and the British Broadcasting Corporation* (Cm 6872) (30 June 2006) cl 93(4).
9   *Agreement between Her Majesty's Secretary of State for Culture, Media and Sport and the British Broadcasting Corporation* (Cm 6872) (30 June 2006) cl 93(5).
10 Ie under the *Agreement between Her Majesty's Secretary of State for Culture, Media and Sport and the British Broadcasting Corporation* (Cm 6872) (30 June 2006) cl 93(1).
11 Ie by virtue of the *Agreement between Her Majesty's Secretary of State for Culture, Media and Sport and the British Broadcasting Corporation* (Cm 6872) (30 June 2006) cl 93(2).
12 *Agreement between Her Majesty's Secretary of State for Culture, Media and Sport and the British Broadcasting Corporation* (Cm 6872) (30 June 2006) cl 93(6). As to the Secretary of State see PARA 507 note 32.

859.   Financial penalties. If OFCOM[1] is satisfied that the BBC[2] has contravened a relevant enforceable requirement[3], it may serve on the BBC a notice requiring it to pay to OFCOM, within a specified period, a specified penalty[4]. OFCOM is not to serve such a notice on the BBC unless it has given it a reasonable opportunity of making representations to it about the matters appearing to OFCOM to provide grounds for the service of the notice[5]. Where OFCOM serves a notice on the BBC[6] or receives representations from it[7], it must send a copy of the notice or representations to the Secretary of State[8]. An exercise by OFCOM of its powers under these provisions does not preclude any exercise by it of its powers to direct remedial action[9] in respect of the same contravention[10].

1   As to OFCOM see PARA 507.
2   As to the meaning of 'BBC' see PARA 603.
3   As to the meaning of 'relevant enforceable requirement' see the *Agreement between Her Majesty's Secretary of State for Culture, Media and Sport and the British Broadcasting Corporation* (Cm 6872) (30 June 2006) cll 94(6), 95(1); and PARA 858 note 4. In addition, for the purposes of cl 94 only, the relevant enforceable requirements include all requirements imposed on the BBC by direction under cl 93 (power of OFCOM to require remedial action: see PARA 858): cl 95(2).

4   *Agreement between Her Majesty's Secretary of State for Culture, Media and Sport and the British Broadcasting Corporation* (Cm 6872) (30 June 2006) cl 94(1). The amount of the penalty that may be imposed on any occasion under this provision may not exceed the maximum specified for the time being in the Communications Act 2003 s 198(5) (see PARA 854): *Agreement between Her Majesty's Secretary of State for Culture, Media and Sport and the British Broadcasting Corporation* cl 94(2).

5   *Agreement between Her Majesty's Secretary of State for Culture, Media and Sport and the British Broadcasting Corporation* (Cm 6872) (30 June 2006) cl 94(3).

6   Ie under the *Agreement between Her Majesty's Secretary of State for Culture, Media and Sport and the British Broadcasting Corporation* (Cm 6872) (30 June 2006) cl 94(1).

7   Ie by virtue of the *Agreement between Her Majesty's Secretary of State for Culture, Media and Sport and the British Broadcasting Corporation* (Cm 6872) (30 June 2006) cl 94(3).

8   *Agreement between Her Majesty's Secretary of State for Culture, Media and Sport and the British Broadcasting Corporation* (Cm 6872) (30 June 2006) cl 94(4). As to the Secretary of State see PARA 507 note 32.

9   Ie under the *Agreement between Her Majesty's Secretary of State for Culture, Media and Sport and the British Broadcasting Corporation* (Cm 6872) (30 June 2006) cl 93: see PARA 858.

10   *Agreement between Her Majesty's Secretary of State for Culture, Media and Sport and the British Broadcasting Corporation* (Cm 6872) (30 June 2006) cl 94(5).

860.   Enforcement of licences held by BBC companies.   Where OFCOM[1]:

(1)   gives a direction to a BBC company[2] to include in the licensed[3] service a correction or apology[4];

(2)   serves a notice on a BBC company imposing a financial penalty or shortening the licence period[5], or revoking a Channel 3 or Channel 5 licence[6];

(3)   receives any written representations[7] from a BBC company[8],

OFCOM must send a copy of the direction, notice or representations to the Secretary of State[9].

Where OFCOM gives a direction[10] to a BBC company[11], serves a notice[12] on a BBC company[13], or receives any representations[14] from a BBC company[15], OFCOM must send a copy of the direction, notice or representations to the Secretary of State[16].

1   As to OFCOM see PARA 507.

2   As to the meaning of 'BBC company' see PARA 854 note 4. As to the meaning of 'BBC' see PARA 603.

3   As to the meaning of 'licensed' see PARA 662 note 3.

4   Broadcasting Act 1990 s 66A(1)(a) (s 66A added by the Broadcasting Act 1996 s 136, Sch 8 para 3). The directions referred to in the text are directions under the Broadcasting Act 1990 s 40(1) (see PARA 864): s 66A(1)(a) (as so added).
       References in s 66A(1) to any of the provisions of ss 40–42 are references to that provision as applied: (1) by s 42B(2) (see PARA 689) in relation to a licence to provide a restricted service; or (2) by s 55(4) (see PARA 710) in relation to additional services licence: s 66A(2) (as so added; and amended by the Communications Act 2003 s 406(7), Sch 19(1); and by SI 1997/1682). As to the meaning of 'licence' see PARA 662 note 3. As to the meaning of 'restricted service' see PARA 689 note 2. As to the meaning of 'additional services licence' see PARA 704 note 5.

5   Ie under the Broadcasting Act 1990 s 41 (see PARA 865): s 66A(1)(b) (as added: see note 4). See also note 4.

6   Broadcasting Act 1990 s 66A(1)(b) (as added: see note 4). The revocation referred to in the text is a revocation under s 42 (see PARA 866): s 66A(1)(b) (as so added). See also note 4. As to the meaning of 'Channel 3 licence' see PARA 669 note 2. As to the meaning of 'Channel 5 licence' see PARA 681 note 4.

7   Ie representations under the Broadcasting Act 1990 s 40(2) (see PARA 864), s 41(3) (see PARA 865) or s 42(8) (see PARA 866). See also note 4.

8   Broadcasting Act 1990 s 66A(1)(c) (as added: see note 4).

9   Broadcasting Act 1990 s 66A(1) (as added: see note 4). See also note 4. As to the Secretary of State see PARA 507 note 32.

10   Ie under the Broadcasting Act 1990 s 40(1) (see PARA 864) as applied by the Broadcasting Act 1996 s 23(8) (see PARA 700) or s 27(8) (see PARA 713): see s 35(a).

11   Broadcasting Act 1996 s 35(a). As to the meaning of 'BBC company' see PARA 854 note 4; definition applied by s 147(2).

12   Ie under any provision of the Broadcasting Act 1996 s 17 (see PARA 696), s 23 (see PARA 700) or s 27 (see PARA 713): see s 35(b).

13   Broadcasting Act 1996 s 35(b).

14   Ie under the Broadcasting Act 1996 s 17(4) (see PARA 696), s 23(6) (see PARA 700) or s 27(6) (see PARA 713), or under the Broadcasting Act 1990 s 42 (see PARA 866) as applied by the Broadcasting Act 1996 s 23(8) (see PARA 700) or s 27(8) (see PARA 713): see s 35(c).

15   Broadcasting Act 1996 s 35(c).

16   Broadcasting Act 1996 s 35 (amended by the Communications Act 2003 s 360(3), Sch 15 para 99).

861.   Direction to licensee to take remedial action. If OFCOM[1] is satisfied: (1) that the holder of a licence to provide a television licensable content service[2] has contravened a condition of the licence; and (2) that the contravention can be appropriately remedied by the inclusion in the licensed service of a correction or a statement of findings (or both), OFCOM may direct the licence holder to include a correction or a statement of findings (or both) in the licensed service[3]. A direction may require the correction or statement of findings to be in such form, and to be included in programmes at such time or times, as OFCOM may determine[4]. OFCOM is not to give a person a direction under these provisions[5] unless it has given him a reasonable opportunity of making representations to it about the matters appearing to it to provide grounds for the giving of the direction[6]. Where the holder of a licence includes a correction or a statement of findings in the licensed service in pursuance of a direction, he may announce that he is doing so in pursuance of such a direction[7]. If OFCOM is satisfied that the inclusion of a programme in a television licensable content service involved a contravention of a condition of the licence to provide that service, it may direct the holder of the licence not to include that programme in that service on any future occasion[8]. Where OFCOM: (a) gives a direction to a BBC company[9]; or (b) receives representations from a BBC company[10], it must send a copy of the direction or representations to the Secretary of State[11].

1   As to OFCOM see PARA 507.

2   As to the meaning of 'television licensable content service' see PARA 716.

3   Communications Act 2003 s 236(1), (2). For the purposes of s 236, a statement of findings, in relation to a case in which OFCOM is satisfied that the holder of a licence has contravened the conditions of his licence, is a statement of OFCOM's findings in relation to that contravention: s 236(8).

4   Communications Act 2003 s 236(3).

5   Ie under the Communications Act 2003 s 263: see PARA 602.

6   Communications Act 2003 s 236(4).

7   Communications Act 2003 s 236(5).

8   Communications Act 2003 s 236(6).

9   Ie under the Communications Act 2003 s 236(2). As to the meaning of 'BBC company' see PARA 854 note 4.

10   Ie by virtue of the Communications Act 2003 s 236(4) (see the text and note 6).

11   Communications Act 2003 s 236(7). As to the Secretary of State see PARA 507 note 32.

862.   Penalties for contravention of licence condition or direction. If OFCOM[1] is satisfied that the holder of a licence to provide a television licensable content service[2]: (1) has contravened a condition of the licence; or (2) has failed to comply with a direction given by OFCOM[3], it may serve on him a notice[4] requiring him to pay, within a specified period, a specified penalty[5].

1   As to OFCOM see PARA 507.

2   As to the meaning of 'television licensable content service' see PARA 716.

3   Ie under or by virtue of a provision of the Communications Act 2003 Pt 3 (ss 198–362), the
     Broadcasting Act 1990 Pt I (ss 3–71) or the Broadcasting Act 1996 Pt V (ss 107–130).
4   OFCOM is not to serve a notice on a person under the Communications Act 2003 s 237(1)
     unless it has given him a reasonable opportunity of making representations to it about the
     matters appearing to it to provide grounds for the service of the notice: s 237(6). Where
     OFCOM serves a notice on a BBC company under s 237(1) or receives representations from a
     BBC company by virtue of s 237(6), it must send a copy of the notice or representations to the
     Secretary of State: s 237(7). As to the meaning of 'BBC company' see PARA 854 note 4. As to the
     Secretary of State see PARA 507 note 32.
5   Communications Act 2003 s 237(1). The amount of the penalty under s 237 must not exceed
     the maximum penalty given by s 237(3): s 237(2). The maximum penalty is whichever is the
     greater of: (1) £250,000; and (2) 5% of the qualifying revenue for the licence holder's last
     complete accounting period falling within the period for which his licence has been in force:
     s 237(3). The Secretary of State may by order substitute a different sum for the sum for the time
     being specified in s 273(3)(a) (head (1)): s 237(9). No order is to be made containing provision
     authorised by s 237(9) unless a draft of the order has been laid before Parliament and approved
     by a resolution of each House: s 237(10). In relation to a person whose first complete
     accounting period falling within the relevant period has not ended when the penalty is imposed,
     s 237(3) is to be construed as referring to 5% of the amount which OFCOM estimates will be
     the qualifying revenue for that accounting period: s 237(4). The Broadcasting Act 1990
     s 19(2)–(6) and Sch 7 Pt I (calculation of qualifying revenue: see PARAS 674–675) with any
     necessary modifications, are to apply for the purposes of the Communications Act 2003
     s 237(3) as they apply for the purposes of the Broadcasting Act 1990 Pt I: Communications
     Act 2003 s 237(5).
         An exercise by OFCOM of its powers under s 237(1) does not preclude any exercise by it of
     its powers under s 236 (see PARA 861) in respect of the same contravention: s 237(8).
         For transitional provision relating to s 237 see the Office of Communications Act 2002
     (Commencement No 3) and Communications Act 2003 (Commencement No 2) Order 2003,
     SI 2003/3142.

863.   Revocation of television licensable content service licence.   OFCOM[1]
must serve a notice[2] on the holder of a licence to provide a television licensable
content service[3] if it is satisfied: (1) that the holder of the licence is in
contravention of a condition of the licence or is failing to comply with a
direction given by OFCOM[4]; and (2) that the contravention or failure, if not
remedied, would justify the revocation of the licence[5]. The notice must: (a) state
that OFCOM is satisfied as mentioned above[6]; (b) specify the respects in which,
in its opinion, the licence holder is contravening the condition or failing to
comply with the direction; and (c) state that OFCOM will revoke the licence
unless the licence holder takes, within such period as is specified in the notice,
such steps to remedy the failure as are so specified[7]. If, at the end of the period
specified in such a notice, OFCOM is satisfied: (i) that the person on whom the
notice was served has failed to take the steps specified in it; and (ii) that it is
necessary in the public interest to revoke his licence, it must serve a notice on him
revoking his licence[8]. If OFCOM is satisfied in the case of a licence to provide a
television licensable content service that the holder of the licence has ceased to
provide the licensed service, and that it is appropriate for it to do so, it must
serve a notice on him revoking his licence[9]. If OFCOM is satisfied: (A) that the
holder of a licence to provide a television licensable content service has provided
it, in connection with his application for the licence, with information which was
false in a material particular; or (B) that, in connection with his application for
the licence, the holder of such a licence withheld any material information with
the intention of causing it to be misled, it may serve a notice on him revoking his
licence[10]. A notice under these provisions revoking a licence to provide a
television licensable content service takes effect as from the time when it is served
on the licence holder[11]. OFCOM is not to serve a notice on a person unless it has
given him a reasonable opportunity of making representations to it about the

matters in respect of which it is served[12]. Where OFCOM serves a notice on a BBC company[13], or receives representations from a BBC company[14], it must send a copy of the notice or representations to the Secretary of State[15].

1   As to OFCOM see PARA 507.
2   Ie under the Communications Act 2003 s 238(2) (see the text and note 7).
3   As to the meaning of 'television licensable content service' see PARA 716.
4   Ie under or by virtue of any provision of the Communications Act 2003 Pt 3 (ss 198–362), the Broadcasting Act 1990 Pt I (ss 3–71) or the Broadcasting Act 1996 Pt V (ss 107–130).
5   Communications Act 2003 s 238(1). Nothing in s 238 applies to the revocation of a licence in exercise of the power conferred by s 239 (see PARA 943): s 238(9).
6   Ie as mentioned in the Communications Act 2003 s 238(1) (see the text and notes 1–5).
7   Communications Act 2003 s 238(2).
8   Communications Act 2003 s 238(3).
9   Communications Act 2003 s 238(4).
10   Communications Act 2003 s 238(5).
11   Communications Act 2003 s 238(6).
12   Communications Act 2003 s 238(7).
13   As to the meaning of 'BBC company' see PARA 854 note 4.
14   Ie by virtue of the Communications Act 2003 s 238(7) (see the text and note 12).
15   Communications Act 2003 s 238(8). As to the Secretary of State see PARA 507 note 32.

864. Power to direct licensee to broadcast correction or statement of findings.
If OFCOM[1] is satisfied that the holder of a Channel 3[2], Channel 4[3] or Channel 5[4] licence[5] has failed to comply with any condition of the licence[6], and that that failure can be appropriately remedied by the inclusion in the licensed[7] service of a correction or a statement of findings[8] or both[9], it may direct the licence holder to include in the licensed service a correction or statement of findings or both in such form, and at such time or times, as it determines[10]. OFCOM must not give any person[11] such a direction unless it has given him a reasonable opportunity of making representations to it about the matters complained of[12].

Where the holder of a licence includes a correction or statement of findings in the licensed service in pursuance of a direction, he may announce that he is doing so in pursuance of such a direction[13].

If OFCOM is satisfied that the inclusion by the holder of a Channel 3, Channel 4 or Channel 5 licence of any programme[14] in the licensed service involved a failure by him to comply with any condition of the licence, it may direct him not to include that programme in that service on any future occasion[15].

1   As to OFCOM see PARA 507.
2   As to the meaning of 'Channel 3' see PARA 667; and as to the meaning of 'Channel 3 licence' see PARA 669 note 2.
3   As to the meaning of 'Channel 4' see PARA 637. This provision applies to Channel 4 licences by virtue of the Broadcasting Act 1990 s 40(5).
4   As to the meaning of 'Channel 5' see PARA 681; and as to the meaning of 'Channel 5 licence' see PARA 681 note 4.
5   As to the meaning of 'licence' see PARAS 662 note 3, 677 note 2. As to the holder of the licence see PARAS 671 note 19, 679 note 27.
6   Broadcasting Act 1990 s 40(1)(a).
7   As to the meaning of 'licensed' see PARAS 662 note 3, 677 note 2.
8   For the purposes of the Broadcasting Act 1990 s 40, a statement of findings, in relation to a case in which OFCOM is satisfied that the holder of a licence has contravened the conditions of his licence, is a statement of OFCOM's findings in relation to that contravention: s 40(6) (added by the Communications Act 2003 s 344(1), (3)).
9   Broadcasting Act 1990 s 40(1)(b).

10 Broadcasting Act 1990 s 40(1) (amended by the Communications Act 2003 ss 344(2), 360(3), Sch 15 para 18(1)). As to the application of the Broadcasting Act 1990 s 40 in respect of a licence to provide a restricted service see s 42B; and PARA 689. As to the application of s 40 to digital programme licences and digital additional services licences see PARAS 700, 713.

11 As to the meaning of 'person' see PARA 510 note 1.

12 Broadcasting Act 1990 s 40(2) (amended by the Communications Act 2003 Sch 15 para 18(1)).

13 Broadcasting Act 1990 s 40(3) (amended by the Communications Act 2003 s 344(2)).

14 As to the meaning of 'programme' see PARA 667 note 7.

15 Broadcasting Act 1990 s 40(4) (amended by the Communications Act 2003 Sch 15 para 18(1)).

865. Power to impose financial penalty or shorten licence period. If OFCOM[1] is satisfied that the holder of a Channel 3[2], Channel 4[3] or Channel 5[4] licence[5] has failed to comply with any condition[6] of the licence or with any direction given by OFCOM[7], it may serve on him[8]: (1) a notice[9] requiring him to pay, within a specified period, a specified financial penalty to OFCOM[10]; or (2) a notice reducing the period for which the licence is to be in force by a specified period not exceeding two years[11].

The amount of a financial penalty imposed on a person must not exceed 5 per cent of the qualifying revenue for the licence holder's last complete accounting period falling within the period for which his licence has been in force ('the relevant period')[12].

OFCOM must not serve on any person[13] such a notice as is mentioned above unless it has given him a reasonable opportunity of making representations to it about the matters complained of[14].

1 As to OFCOM see PARA 507.

2 As to the meaning of 'Channel 3' see PARA 667; and as to the meaning of 'Channel 3 licence' see PARA 669 note 2.

3 As to the meaning of 'Channel 4' see PARA 637. This provision (with the exception of the notice provisions in the Broadcasting Act 1990 s 41(1)(b)) applies to Channel 4 licences by virtue of s 41(6).

4 As to the meaning of 'Channel 5' see PARA 681; and as to the meaning of 'Channel 5 licence' see PARA 681 note 4.

5 As to the meaning of 'licence' see PARAS 662 note 3, 677 note 2. As to the holder of the licence see PARAS 671 note 19, 679 note 28.

6 A failure to comply with any condition includes the provision of false information in purported compliance with a condition of a licence: see the Broadcasting Act 1990 s 4(5); and PARAS 665, 679.

7 Ie under or by virtue of any provision of the Broadcasting Act 1990 Pt I (ss 3–71), the Broadcasting Act 1996 Pt V (ss 107–130) or the Communications Act 2003 Pt 3 (ss 198–362): see the Broadcasting Act 1990 s 41(1) (amended by the Communications Act 2003 s 360(3), Sch 15 para 18(2)).

8 Broadcasting Act 1990 s 41(1) (amended by the Communications Act 2003 Sch 15 para 18(1)). Any exercise by OFCOM of its powers under the Broadcasting Act 1990 s 41(1) in respect of any failure to comply with any condition of a licence does not preclude any exercise by it of its powers under s 40 (see PARA 864) in respect of that failure: s 41(5) (amended by the Communications Act 2003 Sch 15 para 18(1)).

9 As to the service of notices see TELECOMMUNICATIONS vol 97 (2010) PARAS 49–50.

10 Broadcasting Act 1990 s 41(1)(a) (amended by the Communications Act 2003 Sch 15 para 18(1)).

11 Broadcasting Act 1990 s 41(1)(b). Section 41(1)(b) does not apply to Channel 4 licences: see s 41(6). The requirement under s 3(4)(a) (see PARAS 665, 679) to obtain the licence holder's consent to vary the period for which the licence is to continue in force does not apply to s 41(1)(b): see s 3(5); and PARAS 665, 679. Where a licence is due to expire on a particular date by virtue of a notice served on any person under s 41(1)(b), OFCOM may, on the application of that person, revoke that notice by a further notice served on him at any time before that date, if it is satisfied that, since the date of the earlier notice, his conduct in relation to the operation of the licensed service has been such as to justify the revocation of that notice: s 41(4) (amended by the Communications Act 2003 Sch 15 para 18(1)). As to the meaning of 'person' see PARA 510 note 1. Any reference in the Broadcasting Act 1990 (however expressed) to a licence under that

Act being in force is a reference to its being in force so as to authorise the provision under the licence of the licensed service; and any such reference is accordingly not to be construed as prejudicing the operation of any provisions of such a licence which are intended to have effect otherwise than at a time when the licensed service is authorised to be so provided: s 202(4).

12　Broadcasting Act 1990 s 41(1A) (s 41(1A)–(C) added by the Communications Act 2003 s 345, Sch 13 paras 1, 3(1)). The qualifying revenue is determined or estimated in accordance with the Broadcasting Act 1990 s 19(2)–(6) (see PARA 674): s 41(1C) (as so added). In relation to a person whose first complete accounting period falling within the relevant period (ie during any period for which his licence has been in force: see s 41(1A) (as so added)) has not ended when the penalty is imposed, s 41(1A) is to be construed as referring to 5% of the amount which OFCOM estimates to be the qualifying revenue for that accounting period: s 41(1B) (as so added).

In the case of a licence to provide a restricted service (see PARA 689), the provisions of s 41(1A)–(1C) do not apply, and the maximum amount which the holder of such a licence may be required to pay by way of a financial penalty imposed in pursuance of s 41(1)(a) (see the text and note 10) is the maximum penalty given by s 42B(3A): s 42B(3) (s 42B added by the Broadcasting Act 1990 s 85; and amended by the Communications Act 2003 Sch 13 para 4(2)). The maximum penalty is whichever is the greater of: (1) £250,000; and (2) 5% of the qualifying revenue for the licence holder's last complete accounting period falling within the period for which his licence has been in force ('the relevant period'): Broadcasting Act 1990 s 42B(3A) (s 42B as added; s 42B(3A)–(3C) added by the Communications Act 2003 Sch 13 para 4(3)). In relation to a person whose first complete accounting period falling within the relevant period has not ended when the penalty is imposed, the Broadcasting Act 1990 s 42B(3A)(b) is to be construed as referring to 5% of the amount which OFCOM estimates to be the qualifying revenue for that accounting period: s 42B(3B) (as so added). The qualifying revenue is determined or estimated in accordance with s 19(2)–(6) (see PARA 674): s 42B(3C) (as so added).

The Secretary of State may by order amend s 42B(3A)(a) by substituting a different sum for the sum for the time being specified in that provision: Communications Act 2003 Sch 13 para 9(1), (2)(b). No such order is to be made unless a draft of the order has been laid before Parliament and approved by a resolution of each House: Sch 13 para 9(3). As to the Secretary of State see PARA 507 note 32.

13　As to the meaning of 'person' see PARA 510 note 1.

14　Broadcasting Act 1990 s 41(3) (amended by the Communications Act 2003 Sch 15 para 18(1)).

866.　Power to revoke Channel 3 or 5 licence.　If OFCOM[1] is satisfied that the holder of a Channel 3[2] or Channel 5[3] licence[4] is failing to comply with any condition of the licence[5] or with any direction given by it[6], and that that failure is such that, if not remedied, it would justify the revocation of the licence[7], it must serve a notice on the holder of the licence[8]. The notice must: (1) state that OFCOM is so satisfied[9]; (2) specify the respects in which, in its opinion, the licence holder is failing to comply with any condition or direction[10]; and (3) state that, unless the licence holder takes, within such period as is specified in the notice, such steps to remedy the failure as are so specified, OFCOM will revoke his licence[11]. If at the end of the period so specified OFCOM is satisfied that the person[12] on whom the notice was served has failed to take the steps specified in it[13], and that it is necessary in the public interest to revoke his licence[14], it must serve on that person a notice revoking his licence[15].

If OFCOM is satisfied in the case of any Channel 3 or Channel 5 licence that the holder of the licence has ceased to provide the licensed[16] service before the end of the period for which the licence is to continue in force[17], and that it is appropriate for it to do so[18], it must serve on him a notice revoking his licence[19].

If OFCOM is satisfied that the holder of a Channel 3 or Channel 5 licence provided OFCOM, in connection with his application for the licence, with information which was false in a material particular[20], or that, in connection with his application for the licence, the holder of such a licence withheld any material information with the intention of causing OFCOM to be misled[21], it may serve on him a notice revoking his licence[22].

OFCOM may not serve any notice on a person unless it has given him a reasonable opportunity of making representations to it about the matters complained of[23].

1 As to OFCOM see PARA 507.
2 As to the meaning of 'Channel 3' see PARA 667; and as to the meaning of 'Channel 3 licence' see PARA 669 note 2.
3 As to the meaning of 'Channel 5' see PARA 681; and as to the meaning of 'Channel 5 licence' see PARA 681 note 4.
4 As to the holder of the licence see PARAS 671 note 19, 679 note 27.
5 A failure to comply with any condition includes the provision of false information in purported compliance with a condition of a licence: see the Broadcasting Act 1990 s 4(5); and PARAS 665, 679.
6 Broadcasting Act 1990 s 42(1)(a). A direction is given under or by virtue of Pt I (ss 3–71) or the Broadcasting Act 1996 Pt V (ss 107–130) or the Communications Act 2003 Pt 3 (ss 198–362): Broadcasting Act 1990 s 42(1)(a) (amended by the Communications Act 2003 s 360(3), Sch 15 para 18(2)).
7 Broadcasting Act 1990 s 42(1)(b). As to the imposition of financial penalties on the revocation of a licence see PARA 673.
8 Broadcasting Act 1990 s 42(1) (amended by the Communications Act 2003 Sch 15 para 18(1)). As to the service of notices see TELECOMMUNICATIONS vol 97 (2010) PARAS 49–50. As to the application of the Broadcasting Act 1990 s 42 in respect of a licence to provide a restricted service see s 42B; and PARA 689. As to the application of this provision to digital additional services see PARA 713.
9 Broadcasting Act 1990 s 42(2)(a) (amended by the Communications Act 2003 Sch 15 para 18(1)).
10 Broadcasting Act 1990 s 42(2)(b).
11 Broadcasting Act 1990 s 42(2)(c) (amended by the Communications Act 2003 Sch 15 para 18(1)). The licence is revoked under the Broadcasting Act 1990 s 42(3) (see the text and notes 12–15): see s 42(2)(c).
12 As to the meaning of 'person' see PARA 510 note 1.
13 Broadcasting Act 1990 s 42(3)(a).
14 Broadcasting Act 1990 s 42(3)(b).
15 Broadcasting Act 1990 s 42(3) (amended by the Communications Act 2003 Sch 15 para 18(1)). Any notice served under the Broadcasting Act 1990 s 42(3), s 42(4) (see the text and notes 16–19) or s 42(5) (see the text and notes 20–22) takes effect as from the time when it is served on the licence holder: s 42(6). However, if it appears to OFCOM to be appropriate to do so for the purpose of preserving continuity in the provision of the service in question, it may instead provide in any such notice for it to take effect as from a date specified in it: s 42(7) (amended by the Communications Act 2003 Sch 15 para 18(1)).
16 As to the meaning of 'licensed' see PARAS 662 note 3, 677 note 2.
17 Broadcasting Act 1990 s 42(4)(a).
18 Broadcasting Act 1990 s 42(4)(b).
19 Broadcasting Act 1990 s 42(4) (amended by the Communications Act 2003 Sch 15 para 18(1)). As to when such a notice takes effect see note 15.
20 Broadcasting Act 1990 s 42(5)(a).
21 Broadcasting Act 1990 s 42(5)(b).
22 Broadcasting Act 1990 s 42(5) (amended by the Communications Act 2003 Sch 15 para 18(1)). As to when such a notice takes effect see note 15.
23 Broadcasting Act 1990 s 42(8).

(iii) On-demand Services

867. Duties of providers of on-demand programme services. The provider of an on-demand programme service[1] must ensure that the service complies with the statutory requirements[2] as to harmful material, advertising, sponsorship and product placement[3]. The provider of an on-demand programme service ('P') must supply the following information to users of the service: (1) P's name; (2) P's address; (3) P's electronic address[4]; (4) the name, address and electronic address of any body which is the appropriate regulatory authority for any purpose in relation to P or the service that P provides[5].

The provider of an on-demand programme service must: (a) pay to the appropriate regulatory authority such fee as that authority may require[6]; (b) retain a copy of every programme[7] included in the service for at least 42 days after the day on which the programme ceases to be available for viewing; (c) comply with any requirement[8] as to provision of information; (d) co-operate fully with the appropriate authority[9] for the purpose of an investigation or to secure compliance with the Audiovisual Media Services Directive[10].

1   As to the meaning of 'on-demand programme service' see PARA 784.
2   Ie the requirements of the Communications Act 2003 ss 368E–368H: see PARAS 903–905.
3   Communications Act 2003 s 368D(1) (ss 368D, 368R added by SI 2009/2979). As to the meaning of 'product placement' see PARA 905; definition applied by s 368R(1) (as so added). As to enforcement see PARA 868.
4   For these purposes, 'electronic address' means an electronic address to which users may send electronic communications, and includes any number or address used for the purposes of receiving such communications: Communications Act 2003 s 368D(4) (as added: see note 3).
5   Communications Act 2003 s 368D(2) (as added: see note 3).
6   Ie under the Communications Act 2003 s 368NA: see PARA 787.
7   As to the meaning of 'programme' see PARA 602 note 12.
8   Ie under the Communications Act 2003 s 368O: see PARA 870.
9   Ie for any purpose within the Communications Act 2003 s 368O(2) or (3): see PARA 870.
10 Communications Act 2003 s 368D(3) (as added (see note 3); and amended by SI 2010/419). A copy of a programme retained for the purposes of head (b) in the text must be of a standard and in a format which allows the programme to be viewed as it was made available for viewing: Communications Act 2003 s 368D(3A) (added by SI 2010/419). As to the Audiovisual Media Services Directive see PARA 857 note 7. The Communications Act 2003 s 368D(3) does not apply to the BBC: see s 368P(1); and PARA 871. As to the meaning of 'BBC' see PARA 603 note 1; and as to the BBC see PARAS 603–626.

868.   Enforcement against providers of on-demand programme services.
Where the appropriate regulatory authority[1] determines that a provider of an on-demand programme service[2] is contravening or has contravened the statutory provisions as to the duties of service providers[3] it may do one or both of the following: (1) give the provider an enforcement notification; (2) impose a financial penalty on the provider[4].

An enforcement notification is a notification which specifies the determination made as mentioned above and imposes requirements on the provider to take such steps for complying with the relevant provisions and for remedying the consequences of the contravention of those provisions as may be specified in the notification[5]. An enforcement notification must include reasons for the appropriate regulatory authority's decision to give the enforcement notification and fix a reasonable period for the taking of the steps required by the notification[6].

It is the duty of a provider to whom an enforcement notification has been given to comply with it[7]. That duty is enforceable in civil proceedings by the appropriate regulatory authority for an injunction or for any other appropriate remedy or relief[8]. If a provider to whom an enforcement notification has been given does not comply with it within the period fixed by the appropriate regulatory authority in that enforcement notification the appropriate regulatory authority may impose[9] a financial penalty on that provider[10].

The amount of a penalty imposed on a provider[11] is to be such amount not exceeding 5 per cent of the provider's applicable qualifying revenue[12] or £250,000 whichever is the greater amount, as the appropriate regulatory authority determine to be appropriate and proportionate to the contravention in respect of which it is imposed[13]. A financial penalty imposed under these provisions: (a) must be paid into the appropriate Consolidated Fund[14]; and (b) if not paid within the period fixed by the appropriate regulatory authority, is to be recoverable by the appropriate regulatory authority as a debt due to it from the person obliged to pay it[15].

1 As to the meaning of 'appropriate regulatory authority' see PARA 786 note 3.
2 As to the meaning of 'on-demand programme service' see PARA 784. In the Communications Act 2003 s 368I, references to a provider of an on-demand programme service do not include references to the BBC: see s 368P(2); and PARA 871. As to the meaning of 'BBC' see PARA 603 note 1; and as to the BBC see PARAS 603–626.
3 Ie the Communications Act 2003 s 368D: see PARA 867.
4 Communications Act 2003 s 368I(1) (ss 368I, 368J added by SI 2009/2979). The appropriate regulatory authority must not make such a determination unless there are reasonable grounds for believing that a contravention of the Communications Act 2003 s 368D is occurring or has occurred and it has allowed the provider an opportunity to make representations about that apparent contravention: s 368I(2) (as so added).
5 Communications Act 2003 s 368I(3) (as added: see note 4). Section 368I(4) (as so added) provides that the requirements specified in an enforcement notification may in particular include requirements to do one or more of the following:
    (1) cease providing or restrict access to: (a) a specified programme; or (b) programmes of a specified description;
    (2) cease showing or restrict access to: (a) a specified advertisement; or (b) advertisements of a specified description;
    (3) provide additional information to users of the service prior to the selection of a specified programme by the user for viewing;
    (4) show an advertisement only with specified modifications;
    (5) publish a correction in the form and place and at the time specified; or
    (6) publish a statement of the findings of the appropriate regulatory authority in the form and place and at the time specified.
   Where a provider is required by an enforcement notification to publish a correction or a statement of findings, the provider may publish with the correction or statement of findings a statement that it is published in pursuance of the enforcement notification: s 368I(6) (as so added).
6 Communications Act 2003 s 368I(5) (as added: see note 4).
7 Communications Act 2003 s 368I(7) (as added: see note 4).
8 Communications Act 2003 s 368I(8) (as added: see note 4).
9 Ie in accordance with the Communications Act 2003 s 368J.
10 Communications Act 2003 s 368I(9) (as added: see note 4).
11 Ie under the Communications Act 2003 s 368BB (see PARA 786) or s 368I.
12 The 'applicable qualifying revenue', in relation to a provider, means: (1) the qualifying revenue for the provider's last complete accounting period falling within the period during which the provider has been providing the service to which the contravention relates; or (2) in relation to a person whose first complete accounting period falling within that period has not ended when the penalty is imposed, the amount that the appropriate regulatory authority estimate to be the qualifying revenue for that period: Communications Act 2003 s 368J(3) (as added: see note 4). For the purposes of s 368J(3) the 'qualifying revenue' for an accounting period consists of the aggregate of all the amounts received or to be received by the provider of the service to which the contravention relates or by any connected person in the accounting period: (a) for the inclusion in that service of advertisements, product placement and sponsorship; and (b) in respect of charges made in that period for the provision of programmes included in that service: s 368J(4) (as so added). As to the meaning of 'connected' for the purposes of s 368J(4), see PARA 674 note 13; definition applied by s 368J(5) (as so added). For the purposes of s 368J(3) and (6) (see the text to notes 14–15): (i) the amount of a person's qualifying revenue for an accounting period; or (ii) the amount of any payment to be made into the appropriate Consolidated Fund by any person in respect of any such revenue, is, in the event of a disagreement between the appropriate regulatory authority and that person, the amount determined by the appropriate regulatory authority: s 368J(7) (as so added).
13 Communications Act 2003 s 368J(1) (as added (see note 4); and amended by SI 2010/419). In determining the amount of a penalty under s 368J(1) the appropriate regulatory authority must

have regard to any statement published by OFCOM under s 392 (guidelines to be followed in determining amount of penalties: see TELECOMMUNICATIONS vol 97 (2010) PARA 46): s 368J(2) (as so added).

14 The references in the Communications Act 2003 s 368J to the payment of an amount into the appropriate Consolidated Fund: (1) in the case of an amount received in respect of matters appearing to OFCOM to have no connection with Northern Ireland, is a reference to the payment of the amount into the Consolidated Fund of the United Kingdom; (2) in the case of an amount received in respect of matters appearing to OFCOM to have a connection with Northern Ireland but no connection with the rest of the United Kingdom, is a reference to the payment of the amount into the Consolidated Fund of Northern Ireland; and (3) in any other case, is a reference to the payment of the amount, in such proportions as OFCOM consider appropriate, into each of those Funds: s 368J(8) (as added: see note 4).

15 Communications Act 2003 s 368J(6) (as added: see note 4).

869. Suspension or restriction of on-demand programme service. The appropriate regulatory authority[1] must serve a notice[2] on a provider of an on-demand programme service[3] if it is satisfied:

(1)   that the provider is in contravention of its duty to give advance notification[4] or of its statutory duties[5];

(2)   that an attempt to secure compliance with those provisions by the imposition of one or more financial penalties or enforcement notifications[6] has failed; and

(3)   that the giving of a direction would be appropriate and proportionate to the seriousness of the contravention[7].

Such a notice must:

(a)   state that the appropriate regulatory authority is satisfied as mentioned in heads (1) to (3);

(b)   state the reasons why it is so satisfied;

(c)   state that the appropriate regulatory authority will give a direction unless the provider takes, within a period specified in the notice, such steps to remedy the contravention within head (1) as are so specified;

(d)   specify any conditions that the appropriate regulatory authority proposes to impose in the direction[8]; and

(e)   inform the provider that the provider has the right to make representations to the appropriate regulatory authority about the matters appearing to the authority to provide grounds for giving the proposed direction within the period specified for the purposes of head (c)[9].

If, after considering any representations made to it by the provider within that period, the appropriate regulatory authority is satisfied that the provider has failed to take the steps specified in the notice for remedying the contravention and that it is necessary in the public interest to give a direction, the appropriate regulatory authority must give such of the following as appears to it appropriate and proportionate as mentioned in head (1):

(i)   a direction that the entitlement of the provider to provide an on-demand programme service is suspended (either generally or in relation to a particular service);

(ii)   a direction that that entitlement is restricted in the respects set out in the direction[10].

The appropriate regulatory authority must serve a notice[11] on a provider of an on-demand programme service if it is satisfied:

(A)   that the service has failed to comply with any requirement as to harmful content, advertising, sponsorship or product placement[12] and that accordingly the provider has contravened the statutory requirement[13] to comply with those requirements;

(B)   that the failure is due to the inclusion in the service of material likely to encourage or to incite the commission of crime, or to lead to disorder; and

(C)   that the contravention is such as to justify the giving of a direction[14].

Such a notice must:

(aa)   state that the appropriate regulatory authority is satisfied as mentioned in head (A);

(bb)   specify the respects in which, in its opinion, the provider has contravened the statutory requirement;

(cc)   specify the effect of the notice[15];

(dd)   state that the appropriate regulatory authority may give a direction after the end of the period of 21 days beginning with the day on which the notice is served on the provider; and

(ee)   inform the provider of the provider's right to make representations to the appropriate regulatory authority within that period about the matters appearing to the appropriate regulatory authority to provide grounds for giving a direction[16].

Such a notice has the effect specified under head (cc), which may be either that the entitlement of the provider to provide an on-demand programme service is suspended (either generally or in relation to a particular service), or that that entitlement is restricted in the respects set out in the notice[17]. The suspension or restriction has effect as from the time when the notice is served on the provider until either a direction under these provisions takes effect or the appropriate regulatory authority decides not to give such a direction[18].

If, after considering any representations made to it by the provider within the period mentioned in head (dd), the appropriate regulatory authority is satisfied that it is necessary in the public interest to give a direction, it must give such of the following as appears to it justified as mentioned in head (C): a direction that the entitlement of the provider to provide an on-demand programme service is suspended (either generally or in relation to a particular service) and a direction that that entitlement is restricted in the respects set out in the direction[19].

A direction[20] must specify the service to which it relates or specify that it relates to any on-demand programme service provided or to be provided by the provider[21]. A direction, except so far as it otherwise provides, takes effect for an indefinite period beginning with the time at which it is notified to the provider[22]. A direction may provide for the effect of a suspension or restriction to be postponed by specifying that it takes effect only at a time determined by or in accordance with the terms of the direction and, in connection with the suspension or restriction contained in the direction or with the postponement of its effect, may impose such conditions on the provider as appear to the appropriate regulatory authority to be appropriate for the purpose of protecting that provider's customers[23]. If the appropriate regulatory authority considers it appropriate to do so (whether or not in consequence of representations or proposals made to it), it may revoke a direction or modify its conditions with effect from such time as it may direct, subject to compliance with such requirements as it may specify and to such extent and in relation to such services as it may determine[24].

A person ('P') is guilty of an offence if P provides an on-demand programme service while P's entitlement to do so is suspended by a direction under these provisions or in contravention of a restriction contained in such a direction[25].

1   As to the meaning of 'appropriate regulatory authority' see PARA 786 note 3.
2   Ie under the Communications Act 2003 s 368K(2).
3   As to the meaning of 'on-demand programme service' see PARA 784. In the Communications Act 2003 s 368K, references to a provider of an on-demand programme service do not include references to the BBC: see s 368P(2); and PARA 871. As to the meaning of 'BBC' see PARA 603 note 1; and as to the BBC see PARAS 603–626.
4   Ie under the Communications Act 2003 s 368BA: see PARA 786.
5   Ie under the Communications Act 2003 s 368D: see PARA 867.
6   Ie under the Communications Act 2003 s 368BB or s 368D: see PARAS 786, 867.
7   Communications Act 2003 s 368K(1) (ss 368K–386N added by SI 2009/2979; the Communications Act 2003 s 368K(1) amended by SI 2010/419).
8   Ie under the Communications Act 2003 s 368M(5)(b): see the text to note 23.
9   Communications Act 2003 s 368K(2) (as added: see note 7).
10   Communications Act 2003 s 368K(3) (as added: see note 7).
11   Ie under the Communications Act 2003 s 368L(2).
12   Ie of the Communications Act 2003 ss 368E–368H: see PARAS 903–905.
13   Ie the Communications Act 2003 s 368D(1).
14   Communications Act 2003 s 368L(1) (as added: see note 7). In s 368L, references to a provider of an on-demand programme service do not include references to the BBC: see s 368P(2); and PARA 871.
15   Ie in accordance with the Communications Act 2003 s 368L(3).
16   Communications Act 2003 s 368L(2) (as added: see note 7).
17   Communications Act 2003 s 368L(3) (as added: see note 7).
18   Communications Act 2003 s 368L(4) (as added: see note 7).
19   Communications Act 2003 s 368L(5) (as added: see note 7).
20   Ie a direction given to a provider under the Communications Act 2003 s 368K or s 368L.
21   Communications Act 2003 s 368M(1), (2) (as added: see note 7).
22   Communications Act 2003 s 368M(3) (as added: see note 7). A direction under s 368L must specify a time for it to take effect, and that time must not fall before the end of 28 days beginning with the day on which the direction is notified to the provider: s 368M(4) (as so added).
23   Communications Act 2003 s 368M(5) (as added: see note 7).
24   Communications Act 2003 s 368M(6) (as added: see note 7).
25   Communications Act 2003 s 368N(1) (as added: see note 7). A person guilty of an offence under s 368N is liable: (1) on summary conviction, to a fine not exceeding the statutory maximum; (2) on conviction on indictment, to a fine: s 368N(2) (as so added). As to the statutory maximum see SENTENCING AND DISPOSITION OF OFFENDERS vol 92 (2010) PARA 140.

870. Power to demand information in connection with on-demand programme service. The appropriate regulatory authority[1] may require a person[2] who appears to it to be or to have been a provider of an on-demand programme service[3] and to have information[4] that it requires for a purpose specified below to provide it with all such information as it considers necessary for that purpose[5]. The specified purposes are[6]:

(1)   the purposes of an investigation which the appropriate regulatory authority is carrying out in order for it to be determined whether a contravention of the statutory provisions as to advance notification[7] or as to the duties of service providers[8] has occurred or is occurring, where: (a) the investigation relates to a matter about which it has have received a complaint; or (b) it otherwise has reason to suspect that there has been a contravention of either of those provisions[9];

(2)   the purpose of ascertaining or calculating applicable qualifying revenue[10] for the purposes of determining the amount of a penalty[11].

The appropriate regulatory authority may require a person who appears to it to be or to have been a provider of an on-demand programme service and to have information that it requires for the purpose of securing compliance with the obligations of the United Kingdom under the Audiovisual Media Services Directive[12] to provide it with all such information as it considers necessary for that purpose[13].

The appropriate regulatory authority may not require the provision of information unless it has given the person from whom it is required an opportunity of making representations to it about the matters appearing to it to provide grounds for making the request[14]. The appropriate regulatory authority must not require the provision of information except by a demand for the information contained in a notice served on the person from whom the information is required that describes the required information and sets out the appropriate regulatory authority's reasons for requiring it[15].

A person who is required to provide information under these provisions must provide it in such manner and within such reasonable period as may be specified by the appropriate regulatory authority in the demand for information[16].

1 As to the meaning of 'appropriate regulatory authority' see PARA 786 note 3.
2 As to the meaning of 'person' see PARA 510 note 1.
3 As to the meaning of 'on-demand programme service' see PARA 784. In the Communications Act 2003 s 368O, references to a provider of an on-demand programme service do not include references to the BBC: see s 368P(2); and PARA 871. As to the meaning of 'BBC' see PARA 603 note 1; and as to the BBC see PARAS 603–626.
4 'Information' includes copies of programmes: Communications Act 2003 s 368O(8) (s 368O added by SI 2009/2979).
5 Communications Act 2003 s 368O(1) (as added: see note 4).
6 Communications Act 2003 s 368O(2) (as added: see note 4).
7 Ie a contravention of the Communications Act 2003 s 368BA: see PARA 786.
8 Ie a contravention of the Communications Act 2003 s 368D: see PARA 867.
9 Communications Act 2003 s 368O(2)(a) (as added (see note 4); and amended by SI 2010/419).
10 Ie under the Communications Act 2003 s 368J: see PARA 868.
11 Communications Act 2003 s 368O(2)(b) (as added: see note 4).
12 As to the Audiovisual Media Services Directive see PARA 857 note 7.
13 Communications Act 2003 s 368O(3) (as added: see note 4).
14 Communications Act 2003 s 368O(4) (as added: see note 4).
15 Communications Act 2003 s 368O(5) (as added: see note 4).
16 Communications Act 2003 s 368O(6) (as added: see note 4). Sections 368I and 368K (see PARAS 868, 869) apply in relation to a failure to comply with a demand for information imposed under s 368O as if that failure were a contravention of a requirement of s 368D: s 368O(7) (as so added).

871. Application of provisions in relation to the BBC and the Welsh Authority. Certain provisions of Part 4A of the Communications Act 2003[1] do not apply, or apply with modifications, to the BBC[2] and the Welsh Authority[3].

The requirements as to advance notification[4] do not apply in relation to an on-demand programme service[5] provided or to be provided by the BBC[6]. Certain provisions relating to duties of providers of on-demand programme services[7], advertising[8], sponsorship[9] and fees[10] do not apply to the BBC[11]. In specified provisions[12], references to a provider of an on-demand programme service do not include references to the BBC[13].

The requirements as to advance notification[14] do not apply in relation to an on-demand programme service provided or to be provided by the Welsh Authority, other than a service that includes advertising[15]. In the provisions as to duties of the appropriate regulatory authority[16] references to a provider of an on-demand programme service do not include references to the Welsh Authority[17].

It is the duty of the appropriate regulatory authority[18]: (1) to take such steps as appear to it best calculated to secure that the requirements as to prohibited content[19] are complied with by the Welsh Authority in relation to advertising; and (2) to encourage the Welsh Authority to develop codes of conduct[20] so far as relating to advertising[21]. It is the duty of the Welsh Authority in the provision of any on-demand programme service to promote, where practicable and by appropriate means, production of and access to European works[22].

Certain provisions as to duties of providers of on-demand programme services[23] do not apply to the Welsh Authority except in relation to advertising or in relation to the inclusion of advertising in on-demand programme services provided by the Welsh Authority[24]. The provisions as to enforcement by the appropriate regulatory authority[25], suspension or restriction of service for contraventions[26] and suspension or restriction of service for inciting crime or disorder[27] do not apply in relation to the contravention of the provision specifying the duties of service providers[28] by the Welsh Authority except in the case of a contravention[29] that relates to advertising or in the case of a failure to pay fees[30] to the regulatory authority[31].

The requirement to give information[32] does not apply in relation to information held by the Welsh Authority except where that information is required by the appropriate regulatory authority for the purposes of: (a) an investigation which the appropriate regulatory authority is carrying out (whether or not following receipt by it of a complaint) into a matter relating to compliance by the Welsh Authority with the requirements as to prohibited content[33] in relation to advertising; or (b) securing compliance with the international obligations of the United Kingdom under the Audiovisual Media Services Directive in relation to advertising[34].

1   Ie the Communications Act 2003 Pt 4A (ss 368A–368R): see the text and notes 2–34; and PARAS 784–787, 867–870, 881, 903–905.

2   See the Communications Act 2003 s 368P (added by SI 2009/2979). As to the meaning of 'BBC' see PARA 603 note 1; and as to the BBC see PARAS 603–626.

3   See the Communications Act 2003 s 368Q (added by SI 2009/2979). As to the meaning of 'the Welsh Authority' see PARA 644 note 3; and as to the Welsh Authority see PARA 645 et seq.

4   Ie the Communications Act 2003 s 368BA: see PARA 786.

5   As to the meaning of 'on-demand programme service' see PARA 784.

6   Communications Act 2003 s 368P(A1) (added by SI 2010/419).

7   Ie the Communications Act 2003 s 368D(3): see PARA 867.

8   Ie the Communications Act 2003 s 368F: see PARA 903.

9   Ie the Communications Act 2003 s 368G: see PARA 904.

10 Ie the Communications Act 2003 s 368NA: see PARA 787.

11 Communications Act 2003 s 368P(1) (as added (see note 2); and substituted by SI 2010/419).

12 Ie the Communications Act 2003 s 368C (duties of appropriate regulatory authority: see PARAS 785, 881), s 368I (enforcement by appropriate regulatory authority: see PARA 868), s 368K (suspension or restriction of service for contraventions: see PARA 869), s 368L (suspension or restriction of service for inciting crime or disorder: see PARA 869) and s 368O (power to demand information: see PARA 870).

13 Communications Act 2003 s 368P(2) (as added (see note 2); and amended by SI 2010/419). However, the Communications Act 2003 Sch 12 para 2(2)(b) (amended by SI 2009/2979) includes provision imposing obligations on the BBC in relation to on-demand programme services: Communications Act 2003 s 368P(3) (as so added).

14 Ie the Communications Act 2003 s 368BA: see PARA 786.

15 Communications Act 2003 s 368Q(A1) (added by SI 2010/419).

16 Ie the Communications Act 2003 s 368C: see PARAS 785, 881.

17 Communications Act 2003 s 368Q(1) (as added: see note 3). Schedule 12 Pt 2 (see PARA 655) includes provision imposing obligations on the Welsh Authority in relation to on-demand programme services: s 368Q(7) (as so added).
18 As to the meaning of 'appropriate regulatory authority' see PARA 786 note 3.
19 Ie of the Communications Act 2003 ss 368E, 368F: see PARA 903.
20 Ie the codes referred to in the Communications Act 2003 s 368C(4): see PARA 881.
21 Communications Act 2003 s 368Q(2) (as added: see note 3).
22 Communications Act 2003 s 368Q(3) (as added: see note 3). The text refers to European works within the meaning given in the Audiovisual Media Services Directive art 1(n). As to the Audiovisual Media Services Directive see PARA 857 note 7.
23 Ie the Communications Act 2003 s 368D(3)(zb), (a), and (b): see PARA 867.
24 Communications Act 2003 s 368Q(4) (as added (see note 3); and amended by SI 2010/419). As to when advertising is included in an on-demand service see PARA 881 note 6.
25 Ie the Communications Act 2003 s 368I: see PARA 868.
26 Ie the Communications Act 2003 s 368K: see PARA 869.
27 Ie the Communications Act 2003 s 368L: see PARA 869.
28 Ie the Communications Act 2003 s 368D: see PARA 867.
29 Ie of the Communications Act 2003 s 368E or s 368F: see PARA 903.
30 Ie a contravention of the Communications Act 2003 s 368D(3)(za): see PARA 867.
31 Communications Act 2003 s 368Q(5) (as added (see note 3); and amended by SI 2010/419).
32 Ie the Communications Act 2003 s 368O: see PARA 870.
33 Ie with the Communications Act 2003 s 368E or s 368F: see PARA 903.
34 Communications Act 2003 s 368Q(6) (as added: see note 3).

(iv) Complaints

872.   The Broadcasting Standards Commission.   Provision was made for the establishment of a commission, known as the Broadcasting Standards Commission ('the BSC')[1]. Under the Communications Act 2003, however, the Secretary of State[2] was given power to dissolve the BSC[3], and on 29 December 2003 its functions were transferred to OFCOM[4].

1 See the Broadcasting Act 1996 s 106(1) (repealed). The Broadcasting Standards Commission performed the functions of the Broadcasting Complaints Commission and the Broadcasting Standards Council which were dissolved with effect from 1 December 1998 (see the Dissolution of the Broadcasting Complaints Commission and the Broadcasting Standards Council Order 1998, SI 1998/2954).
2 As to the Secretary of State see PARA 507 note 32.
3 Communications Act 2003 s 31(4). At the date at which this volume states the law, no order had been made under s 31(4).
4 Transitional provision is made in relation to any period between the repeal of the Broadcasting Act 1996 ss 106, 121, Sch 3 on 29 December 2003 and the day on which the BSC ceases to exist by virtue of an order under the Communications Act 2003 s 31(4) (see the text and note 3): see the Office of Communications Act 2002 (Commencement No 3) and Communications Act 2003 (Commencement No 2) Order 2003, SI 2003/3142, art 6(1). As to OFCOM see PARA 507.
    No person is entitled to make a standards complaint under the Broadcasting Act 1996 Pt V (ss 107–130) at any time after 29 December 2003 (ie after the coming into force of the Communications Act 2003 s 327: see the Office of Communications Act 2002 (Commencement No 3) and Communications Act 2003 (Commencement No 2) Order 2003, SI 2003/3142), and no person is required to entertain any such complaint that is so made: Communications Act 2003 s 327(2).

873.   Complaints against the BBC.   The BBC Trust[1] must set and publish one or more frameworks within which the BBC and the commercial arm[2] must handle complaints, and the procedures that are to apply to complaints[3]. In particular, the Trust must establish and maintain procedures for the handling and resolution of complaints about standards in the content of the BBC's services, including complaints concerning the BBC guidelines[4] designed to secure appropriate standards, accuracy and impartiality, compliance with OFCOM's

Fairness Code[5], relevant programme code standards, and (so far as they apply to the BBC) the requirements for on-demand programme services and their providers[6].

In relation to complaints, there must be a clear division of responsibilities between the Trust and the Executive Board[7]. The Trust must ensure that, so far as practicable, the published framework and procedures place a complainant on an equal footing with the BBC, the Trust, the Executive Board or the commercial arm (as the case may require)[8]. The Trust should not have a role in handling or determining individual complaints in the first instance, except where the complaint relates to any act or omission of the Trust itself or of the Trust Unit[9].

The published framework and procedures must give detailed information on how complainants can expect to be treated (including, for example, in terms of timescales)[10]. The published framework and procedures must provide for complainants and prospective complainants to be given, ad hoc, clear guidance explaining: (1) how the complaints system (including appeals) works; and (2) where relevant, the availability of other methods by which redress might be pursued in relation to the type of issues raised by the complainant or prospective complainant[11]. Whenever the Trust determines a complaint or an appeal, adequate reasons must be given[12].

The Trust must also ensure, in relation to any fair trading complaint[13], that: (a) any advice provided to the Trust (including any legal advice) is provided by advisers who are separate from, and independent of, any advisers providing advice in relation to that complaint to the Executive Board or the commercial arm; and (b) the published framework and procedures make clear what sanctions and other remedies the Trust has power to apply[14]. It is the duty of the Trust to ensure that, where any person who provides information to the Trust in connection with a fair trading complaint stipulates that the information must not come into the possession of any member of the Executive Board or any member of the BBC's staff, other than a member of staff of the Trust Unit, the BBC always has in place arrangements to secure that neither the Trust nor any member of staff of the Trust Unit discloses that information in circumstances that lead to a breach of that stipulation[15].

1   As to the BBC Trust within the constitution of the BBC see PARA 604. As to the meaning of 'BBC' see PARA 603.

2   'The BBC's commercial arm' means all subsidiaries of the BBC which play a role in the provision of the BBC's commercial services; and 'the BBC's commercial services' means commercial services provided through the means described in the *Agreement between Her Majesty's Secretary of State for Culture, Media and Sport and the British Broadcasting Corporation* (Cm 6872) (30 June 2006) cl 68(2): cll 101(5), 104. As to the meaning of 'commercial services' see PARA 624 note 2. See cl 68; and PARA 624. As to the meaning of 'service' see PARA 855 note 6.

3   *Agreement between Her Majesty's Secretary of State for Culture, Media and Sport and the British Broadcasting Corporation* (Cm 6872) (30 June 2006) cl 89(1). The Trust must consult publicly on any framework and its associated procedures before setting them: cl 89(3). Every framework and its associated procedures: (1) must reflect the principles set out in cl 90 (see the text and notes 7–15); (2) must ensure that all appeals that raise matters of substance are subject to a right of appeal to the Trust, and that the Trust is the final arbiter if any question arises as to whether an appeal is for the Trust to determine or not; and (3) may make different provision for different complaints or classes of complaint: cl 89(3). As to the meaning of obligations for the Trust to consult publicly see cl 103.

4   Ie concerning the subject matter of the *Agreement between Her Majesty's Secretary of State for Culture, Media and Sport and the British Broadcasting Corporation* (Cm 6872) (30 June 2006) cll 43–46: see PARA 856.

5   As to the Fairness Code see PARA 856 note 4. As to OFCOM see PARA 507.

6 *Agreement between Her Majesty's Secretary of State for Culture, Media and Sport and the British Broadcasting Corporation* (Cm 6872) (30 June 2006) cl 89(2) (amended by Cm 7853, March 2010). As to the requirements referred to in the text see the Communications Act 2003 s 368D; and PARA 867.

7 *Agreement between Her Majesty's Secretary of State for Culture, Media and Sport and the British Broadcasting Corporation* (Cm 6872) (30 June 2006) cl 90(1). As to the Executive Board see PARA 604.

8 *Agreement between Her Majesty's Secretary of State for Culture, Media and Sport and the British Broadcasting Corporation* (Cm 6872) (30 June 2006) cl 90(2).

9 *Agreement between Her Majesty's Secretary of State for Culture, Media and Sport and the British Broadcasting Corporation* (Cm 6872) (30 June 2006) cl 90(3). As to the Trust Unit see PARA 612.

10 *Agreement between Her Majesty's Secretary of State for Culture, Media and Sport and the British Broadcasting Corporation* (Cm 6872) (30 June 2006) cl 90(4).

11 *Agreement between Her Majesty's Secretary of State for Culture, Media and Sport and the British Broadcasting Corporation* (Cm 6872) (30 June 2006) cl 90(5).

12 *Agreement between Her Majesty's Secretary of State for Culture, Media and Sport and the British Broadcasting Corporation* (Cm 6872) (30 June 2006) cl 90(6).

13 For these purposes, 'fair trading complaint' means any complaint if, and to the extent that, it alleges that the BBC has failed to comply with any obligation imposed on it by the *Agreement between Her Majesty's Secretary of State for Culture, Media and Sport and the British Broadcasting Corporation* (Cm 6872) (30 June 2006) cll 65, 66 and 67 (fair trading and competitive impact: see PARA 625): cl 90(10).

14 *Agreement between Her Majesty's Secretary of State for Culture, Media and Sport and the British Broadcasting Corporation* (Cm 6872) (30 June 2006) cl 90(7).

15 *Agreement between Her Majesty's Secretary of State for Culture, Media and Sport and the British Broadcasting Corporation* (Cm 6872) (30 June 2006) cl 90(8). This might, eg, be the case where the Trust Unit makes the information public, or discloses it to a third party who then discloses it to the Executive Board. The obligation in cl 90(8): (1) applies whether or not the information in question would be regarded, in law, as confidential; (2) does not affect any other obligation of the Trust to keep information confidential; (3) is subject to any legal obligation of the BBC or any member of its staff to disclose information (such as under a court order or the Freedom of Information Act 2000): *Agreement between Her Majesty's Secretary of State for Culture, Media and Sport and the British Broadcasting Corporation* (Cm 6872) (30 June 2006) cl 90(9).

874. General functions of OFCOM in relation to complaints. Subject to certain provisions of the Broadcasting Act 1996[1], it is the duty of OFCOM[2] to consider and adjudicate on complaints which are made to it[3] and which relate to unjust or unfair treatment[4] in specified programmes[5], or to unwarranted infringement of privacy in, or in connection with the obtaining of material included in, such programmes[6].

1 Ie subject to the Broadcasting Act 1996 Pt V (ss 107–130).

2 As to OFCOM see PARA 507.

3 Broadcasting Act 1996 s 110(1) (amended by the Communications Act 2003 s 360(3), Sch 15 para 132(1), (2)). The references in the text to complaints are references to those complaints made in accordance with the Broadcasting Act 1996 s 111 (see PARA 907) and s 114 (see PARA 908). In exercising its functions under s 110(1), OFCOM must take into account any relevant provisions of the code maintained by it under s 107 (see PARA 906): s 110(3) (amended by the Communications Act 2003 s 406(7), Sch 15 para 132(2), Sch 19).

4 As to the meaning of 'unjust or unfair treatment' see PARA 906 note 2.

5 Broadcasting Act 1996 s 110(1)(a). The reference in the text to specified programmes is a reference to programmes to which s 107 (see PARA 906) applies. Any reference to programmes to which s 107 applies must be construed in accordance with s 107(5) (see PARA 906 note 3): s 130(2)(a) (amended by the Communications Act 2003 Sch 19). As to the meaning of 'programme' see PARA 906 note 2.

6 Broadcasting Act 1996 s 110(1)(b). There must be a sufficient nexus between the material broadcast and that objected to: see *R v Broadcasting Complaints Commission, ex p BBC* (1992) Times, 16 October; *R v Broadcasting Complaints Commission, ex p Barclay* [1997] EMLR 62. Whether an unwarranted infringement of privacy has occurred is a matter of fact and degree for

OFCOM to decide and with which the court cannot interfere: see *R v Broadcasting Complaints Commission, ex p Granada Television Ltd* [1995] EMLR 163, CA (decided in relation to the Broadcasting Complaints Commission, whose functions have now been transferred to OFCOM). See also *R v Broadcasting Standards Commission, ex p BBC* [1999] EMLR 858.

(2) POSITIVE CONTENT OBLIGATIONS

(i) Public Service Television

875. Programming quotas for public service television. The regulatory regime for every licensed public service channel[1] includes the conditions that OFCOM[2] considers appropriate for securing that, in each year, not less than 25 per cent of the total amount of time allocated to the broadcasting of qualifying programmes[3] included in the channel is allocated to the broadcasting of a range and diversity of independent productions[4].

The regulatory regime for every licensed public service channel also includes the conditions that OFCOM considers appropriate for securing: (1) that the time allocated, in each year, to the broadcasting of original productions[5] included in that channel is no less than what appears to it to be an appropriate proportion of the total amount of time allocated to the broadcasting of all the programmes included in the channel; and (2) that the time allocated to the broadcasting of original productions is split in what appears to OFCOM to be an appropriate manner between peak viewing times[6] and other times[7].

1   As to the meaning of 'licensed public service channel' see PARA 788 note 8.
2   As to OFCOM see PARA 507.
3   In the Communications Act 2003 s 277, a reference to qualifying programmes is a reference to programmes of such description as the Secretary of State may by order specify as describing the programmes that are to be qualifying programmes for the purposes of s 277: s 277(2)(a). 'Programme' does not include an advertisement: ss 277(13), 278(10). As to the meaning of 'programme' generally see PARA 602 note 12. At the date at which this volume states the law, no such order had been made. As to the Secretary of State see PARA 507 note 32. As to the power of the Secretary of State to make orders under the Communications Act 2003 see s 402; and TELECOMMUNICATIONS vol 97 (2010) PARA 77.
4   Communications Act 2003 s 277(1). In s 277, a reference to independent productions is a reference to programmes of such description as the Secretary of State may by order specify as describing the programmes that are to be independent productions for the purposes of s 277; and a reference to a range of independent productions is a reference to a range of such productions in terms of cost of acquisition as well as in terms of the types of programme involved: s 277(2)(b), (c). 'Acquisition', in relation to a programme, includes commissioning and the acquisition of a right to include it in a service or to have it broadcast: s 277(13). The Secretary of State may by order amend s 277(1) by substituting a different percentage for the percentage for the time being specified in s 277(1): s 277(3). The Secretary of State may also by order provide for the regulatory regime for every licensed public service channel to include conditions falling within s 277(5), either instead of or as well as those falling within s 277(1): s 277(4). The conditions falling within s 277(5) are those that OFCOM considers appropriate for securing that, in each year, not less than the percentage specified in the order of the programming budget for that year for that channel is applied in the acquisition of independent productions: s 277(5). 'Programming budget' means the budget for the production and acquisition of qualifying programmes: s 277(13). The power to make an order under s 277(4) includes power to provide that conditions that have previously ceased under such an order to be included in the regulatory regime for every licensed public service channel are again so included, in addition to or instead of the conditions already so included (apart from the exercise of that power) by virtue of s 277: s 277(6). The Secretary of State is not to make an order for the regulatory regime of every licensed public service channel to include or exclude conditions falling within s 277(1) or conditions falling within s 277(5) unless: (1) OFCOM has made a recommendation to him for those conditions to be included or excluded; and (2) the order gives effect to that recommendation: s 277(7). The regulatory regime for every licensed public service channel also includes a condition requiring the provider of the channel to comply with

directions given to him by OFCOM for the purpose of: (a) carrying forward to one or more subsequent years determined in accordance with the direction any shortfall for any year in his compliance with the requirements of conditions imposed by virtue of s 277(1) or (4); and (b) thereby increasing the percentage applicable for the purposes of those conditions to the subsequent year or years: s 277(8). For the purposes of conditions imposed by virtue of these provisions: (i) the amount of the programming budget for a licensed public service channel for a year; and (ii) the means of determining the amount of that budget that is applied for any purpose, are to be computed in accordance with such provision as may be set out in an order made by the Secretary of State, or as may be determined by OFCOM in accordance with such an order: s 277(9). The powers of the Secretary of State to make orders under s 277 do not include: (A) power to specify different percentages for the purposes of s 277(1), or of a condition falling within s 277(5), for different regional Channel 3 services or for different national Channel 3 services; or (B) power to make different provision for different licensed public service channels as to whether conditions falling within s 277(1) or conditions falling within s 277(5), or both, are included in the regulatory regimes for those services: s 277(10). 'Regional Channel 3 service' means a Channel 3 service provided for a particular area determined under the Broadcasting Act 1990 s 14(2) (see PARA 667): Communications Act 2003 s 362(1). 'National Channel 3 service' means a Channel 3 service provided between particular times of the day for more than one area for which regional Channel 3 services are provided: s 362(1). As to the meaning of 'Channel 3 service' see PARA 602 note 8. Before making an order under s 277, the Secretary of State must consult OFCOM, the BBC and the Welsh Authority: s 277(11). As to the meaning of 'BBC' see PARA 603 note 1; and as to the BBC see PARAS 603–626. As to the meaning of 'the Welsh Authority' see PARA 644 note 3; and as to television broadcasting by the Welsh Authority see PARAS 644–661. No order is to be made containing provision authorised by s 277 unless a draft of the order has been laid before Parliament and approved by a resolution of each House: s 277(12). At the date at which this volume states the law, no orders had been made under s 277.

5   References in the Communications Act 2003 s 278, in relation to a licensed public service channel, to original productions are references to programmes of such description as the Secretary of State may by order specify as describing the programmes that are to be original productions for the purposes of s 278: s 278(6). The power to specify descriptions of programmes by order under s 278(6) includes power to confer such discretions on OFCOM as the Secretary of State thinks fit: s 278(7). Before making an order under s 278, the Secretary of State must consult OFCOM, the BBC and the Welsh Authority: s 278(8). No order is to be made containing provision authorised by s 278 unless a draft of the order has been laid before Parliament and approved by a resolution of each House: s 278(9). As to the order that has been made see the Broadcasting (Original Productions) Order 2004, SI 2004/1652.

6   'Peak viewing time', in relation to a licensed public service channel, means a time that appears to OFCOM to be, or to be likely to be, a peak viewing time for that channel: Communications Act 2003 s 278(10). Before determining for the purposes of s 278 what constitutes a peak viewing time for a channel, OFCOM must consult the provider of the channel: s 278(11).

7   Communications Act 2003 s 278(1). The proportion determined by OFCOM for these purposes: (1) must, in the case of each licensed public service channel, be such proportion as OFCOM considers appropriate for ensuring that the channel is consistently of a high quality; and (2) may, for the purposes of head (2) in the text, be expressed as the cumulative effect of two different minimum proportions, one applying to peak viewing times and the other to other times: s 278(2). A condition contained in a licence by virtue of s 278 may provide: (a) that specified descriptions of programmes are to be excluded in determining the programmes a proportion of which is to consist of original productions; (b) that, in determining for the purposes of the condition whether a programme is of a description of programmes excluded by virtue of head (a), regard is to be had to any guidance prepared and published, and from to time revised, by OFCOM: s 278(3). Before imposing a condition under s 278, OFCOM must consult the person on whom it is to be imposed: s 278(4). The requirement to consult is satisfied, in the case of the imposition of a condition by way of a variation of a licence, by compliance with the Broadcasting Act 1990 s 3(4)(b) (obligation to give opportunity to make representations about variation: see PARAS 665, 679): Communications Act 2003 s 278(5).

876.   News provision etc on public service television. The regulatory regime for every licensed public service channel[1] includes the conditions that OFCOM[2] considers appropriate for securing: (1) that the programmes included in the channel include news programmes and current affairs programmes; (2) that the news programmes and current affairs programmes included in the service are of high quality and deal with both national and international matters; and (3) that the news programmes so included are broadcast for viewing at intervals throughout the period for which the channel is provided[3]. That regime also includes the conditions that OFCOM considers appropriate for securing that, in each year: (a) the time allocated to the broadcasting of news programmes included in the service; and (b) the time allocated to the broadcasting of current affairs programmes so included, each constitutes no less than what appears to OFCOM to be an appropriate proportion of the time allocated to the broadcasting of all the programmes included in the channel[4]. It further includes the conditions that OFCOM considers appropriate for securing that the time allocated: (i) to the broadcasting of news programmes included in the service; and (ii) to the broadcasting of current affairs programmes so included, is, in each case, split in what appears to OFCOM to be an appropriate manner between peak viewing times[5] and other times[6].

The regulatory regime for every regional Channel 3 service[7] includes the conditions that OFCOM considers appropriate for securing the nationwide broadcasting, on the regional Channel 3 services (taken together), of news programmes that are able to compete effectively with other television news programmes broadcast nationwide in the United Kingdom[8].

Provision is made with respect to news providers for Channel 5[9] and news provision on the public teletext service[10].

1   As to the meaning of 'licensed public service channel' see PARA 788 note 8.
2   As to OFCOM see PARA 507.
3   Communications Act 2003 s 279(1).
4   Communications Act 2003 s 279(2). See further note 6.
5   'Peak viewing time', in relation to a licensed public service channel, means a time that appears to OFCOM to be, or to be likely to be, a peak viewing time for that channel: Communications Act 2003 s 279(5). See further note 6.
6   Communications Act 2003 s 279(3). The proportion determined by OFCOM for the purposes of s 279(2) (see the text and note 4) may, for the purposes of s 279(3), be expressed as the cumulative effect of two different minimum proportions, one applying to peak viewing times and the other to other times: s 279(4).
        Before determining for these purposes: (1) the proportion of time to be allocated to the broadcasting of news programmes or current affairs programmes; or (2) what constitutes a peak viewing time for a channel, OFCOM must consult the provider of the channel or (as the case may be) the person who is proposing to provide it: s 279(6). The requirement to consult is satisfied, in the case of the imposition of a condition by way of a variation of a licence, by compliance with the Broadcasting Act 1990 s 3(4)(b) (obligation to give opportunity to make representations about variation: see PARAS 665, 679): Communications Act 2003 s 279(7).
7   As to the meaning of 'Channel 3 service' see PARA 602 note 8.
8   Communications Act 2003 s 280(1). For further provision relating to appointed news providers for Channel 3 see s 280(2)–(10). As to the meaning of 'United Kingdom' see PARA 510 note 13.
        The regulatory regime for every regional Channel 3 service includes the conditions that OFCOM considers appropriate for securing: (1) that a body is not appointed as the appointed news provider if it falls within s 281(2); and (2) that the appointment of a body as the appointed news provider ceases to have effect if it becomes a body falling within that subsection: s 281(1). A body falls within s 281(2) if: (a) it is a disqualified person under the Broadcasting Act 1990 Sch 2 Pt II in relation to a Channel 3 licence (see PARAS 822 et seq, 830 et seq); or (b) there would be a contravention of the Communications Act 2003 Sch 14 Pt 1 (whether by that body or by another person) (see PARA 820) if that body held a licence to provide a Channel 3 service, or held a licence to provide such a service for a particular area for which such a service is provided: s 281(2). The reference in s 281(2)(a) to a body which is a disqualified person under the Broadcasting Act 1990 Sch 2 Pt II in relation to a Channel 3 licence includes a reference to a person who is disqualified by virtue of a disqualification order under the Broadcasting Act 1996 s 145 (see PARA 598): Communications Act 2003 s 281(3) (added by SI 2003/3299).

If it appears to the Secretary of State appropriate to do so, he may by order repeal or otherwise modify any of the provisions of the Communications Act 2003 s 280 or s 281: s 282(1). Except in a case to which s 282(3) applies, the Secretary of State must consult OFCOM before making an order under s 282: s 282(2). Consultation with OFCOM is not required if the order is confined to giving effect to recommendations by OFCOM that are contained in a report of a review under s 391 (see TELECOMMUNICATIONS vol 97 (2010) PARA 48): s 282(3). No order is to be made containing provision authorised by s 282 unless a draft of the order has been laid before Parliament and approved by a resolution of each House: s 282(4). See the Media Ownership (Local Radio and Appointed News Provider) Order 2003, SI 2003/3299.

9   See the Communications Act 2003 s 283. As to the meaning of 'Channel 5' see PARA 602 note 10.

10 See the Communications Act 2003 s 284. As to the public teletext service see PARA 686.

877.   Independent and regional productions and programmes for public service television.   The regulatory regime for every licensed public service channel[1] includes the conditions that OFCOM[2] considers appropriate for securing that the provider of the channel draws up and from time to time revises a code of practice setting out the principles he will apply when agreeing terms for the commissioning of independent productions[3]. That regime also includes the conditions that OFCOM considers appropriate for securing that the provider of every licensed public service channel: (1) at all times complies with a code of practice which has been drawn up by him by virtue of these provisions[4] and is for the time being in force; and (2) exercises his power to revise his code to take account of revisions from time to time of the guidance issued by OFCOM for these purposes[5].

The conditions imposed under these provisions must ensure that the code for the time being in force in the case of every licensed public service channel secures, in the manner described in guidance issued by OFCOM: (a) that a reasonable timetable is applied to negotiations for the commissioning of an independent production and for the conclusion of a binding agreement; (b) that there is what appears to OFCOM to be sufficient clarity, when an independent production is commissioned, about the different categories of rights to broadcast or otherwise to make use of or exploit the commissioned production that are being disposed of; (c) that there is what appears to OFCOM to be sufficient transparency about the amounts to be paid in respect of each category of rights; (d) that what appear to OFCOM to be satisfactory arrangements are made about the duration and exclusivity of those rights; (e) that procedures exist for reviewing the arrangements adopted in accordance with the code and for demonstrating compliance with it; (f) that those procedures include requirements for the monitoring of the application of the code and for the making of reports to OFCOM; (g) that provision is made for resolving disputes arising in respect of the provisions of the code (by independent arbitration or otherwise) in a manner that appears to OFCOM to be appropriate[6].

The conditions imposed must also ensure that the drawing up or revision of a code by virtue of these provisions is in accordance with guidance issued by OFCOM as to: (i) the times when the code is to be drawn up or reviewed with a view to revision; (ii) the consultation to be undertaken before a code is drawn up or revised; and (iii) the publication of every code or revised code[7].

The provision that may be included in a condition imposed under these provisions includes provision requiring a draft of a code or of any revision of a code to be submitted to OFCOM for approval, provision for the code or revision to have effect only if approved by OFCOM, and provision for a code or revision that is approved by OFCOM subject to modifications to have effect with those modifications[8].

OFCOM (A) must issue and may from time to time revise guidance for the purposes of these provisions; (B) must ensure that there is always guidance for those purposes in force; (C) must, before issuing guidance or revised guidance, consult the providers of licensed public service channels, persons who make independent productions (or persons appearing to OFCOM to represent them), the BBC[9] and the Welsh Authority[10]; and (D) must publish its guidance or revised guidance in such manner as it think appropriate[11]. Guidance issued by OFCOM for these purposes must be general guidance and is not to specify particular terms to be included in agreements to which the guidance relates[12]. Conditions imposed requiring a code to be drawn up or approved may include transitional provision for treating a code drawn up before the imposition of the condition as satisfying the requirements of that condition, and as a code approved by OFCOM for the purposes of conditions so imposed[13].

Detailed provision is made with respect to regional programme-making for Channels 3 and 5[14]; regional programmes on Channel 3[15]; regional programme-making for Channel 4[16]; and regional matters in the public teletext service[17].

1　As to the meaning of 'licensed public service channel' see PARA 788 note 8.
2　As to OFCOM see PARA 507.
3　Communications Act 2003 s 285(1). For the purposes of s 285, 'independent production' has the same meaning as in s 277 (see PARA 875 note 4): s 285(9).
4　Ie the Communications Act 2003 s 285.
5　Communications Act 2003 s 285(2).
6　Communications Act 2003 s 285(3).
7　Communications Act 2003 s 285(4).
8　Communications Act 2003 s 285(5).
9　As to the meaning of 'BBC' see PARA 603 note 1; and as to the BBC see PARAS 603–626.
10　As to the meaning of 'the Welsh Authority' see PARA 644 note 3; and as to television broadcasting by the Welsh Authority see PARAS 644–661.
11　Communications Act 2003 s 285(6).
12　Communications Act 2003 s 285(7).
13　Communications Act 2003 s 285(8).
14　See the Communications Act 2003 s 286. As to the meaning of 'Channel 3' see PARA 602 note 8. As to the meaning of 'Channel 5' see PARA 602 note 10.
15　See the Communications Act 2003 s 287.
16　See the Communications Act 2003 s 288. As to the meaning of 'Channel 4' see PARA 602 note 9.
17　See the Communications Act 2003 s 289. As to the public teletext service see PARA 686.

878.　Special obligations for Channel 4.　The regulatory regime for Channel 4[1] includes the conditions that OFCOM[2] considers appropriate for securing that what appears to it to be a suitable proportion of the programmes which are included in Channel 4 are schools programmes[3]. A licence under the Broadcasting Act 1990 to provide Channel 4 may also include conditions authorised by the following provisions[4]. The conditions authorised by these provisions include conditions requiring C4C[5]: (1) to finance the production of schools programmes; and (2) to acquire schools programmes provided by other persons[6]. The conditions authorised by these provisions include conditions requiring C4C to ensure that schools programmes on Channel 4: (a) are of high quality; and (b) are suitable to meet the needs of schools throughout the United Kingdom[7]. The conditions authorised by these provisions include conditions specifying the minimum number of hours in term time, or within normal school hours, that are to be allocated to the broadcasting of schools programmes on Channel 4[8]. The conditions authorised by these provisions include conditions requiring C4C to provide such material for use in connection with the schools programmes broadcast by them as may be necessary to secure that effective use is made of those programmes in schools[9]. The conditions authorised by these provisions include conditions requiring C4C from time to time to consult such persons who: (i) are concerned with schools or with the production of schools programmes; or (ii) have an interest in schools or in the production of schools programmes, as OFCOM thinks fit[10]. Before imposing a condition under these provisions, OFCOM must consult C4C[11].

1　As to the meaning of 'Channel 4' see PARA 602 note 9.
2　As to OFCOM see PARA 507.
3　Communications Act 2003 s 296(1). For the purposes of s 296, 'schools programmes' means programmes which are intended for use in schools: s 296(12). In determining for the purposes of s 296(1) what proportion of the programmes included in Channel 4 should be schools programmes, OFCOM must take into account services, facilities and materials which C4C provides to schools, or makes available for schools, otherwise than by the inclusion of programmes in Channel 4: s 296(10).
4　Ie authorised by the Communications Act 2003 s 296(3)–(12): s 296(2).
5　As to the meaning of 'C4C' see PARA 627 note 1.
6　Communications Act 2003 s 296(3). As to the meaning of 'person' see PARA 510 note 1.
7　Communications Act 2003 s 296(4). As to the meaning of 'United Kingdom' see PARA 510 note 13.
8　Communications Act 2003 s 296(5).
9　Communications Act 2003 s 296(6).
10　Communications Act 2003 s 296(7).
11　Communications Act 2003 s 296(8). The requirement to consult is satisfied, in the case of the imposition of a condition by way of a variation of a licence, by compliance with the Broadcasting Act 1990 s 3(4)(b) (obligation to give opportunity to make representations about variation: see PARAS 665, 679): Communications Act 2003 s 296(9).

879. Modification of Competition Act 1998 in its application to agreements relating to Channel 3 news provision. If, having sought the advice of the OFT[1] and OFCOM[2], it appears to the Secretary of State[3], in relation to some or all of the provisions of a relevant agreement[4], that the conditions mentioned below[5] are satisfied, he may make a declaration to that effect[6].

The conditions are that:

(1)　the provisions in question do not have, and are not intended or likely to have, to any significant extent the effect of restricting, distorting or preventing competition; or

(2)　the effect of restricting, distorting or preventing competition which the provisions in question do have or are intended or are likely to have, is not greater than is necessary: (a) for securing the appointment by holders of regional Channel 3 licences of a single body corporate to be the appointed news provider for the purposes of the Communications Act 2003[7]; or (b) in the case of an agreement in connection with the appointment of the appointed news provider[8], for compliance by them with conditions included in their licences by virtue of that Act[9].

If the Secretary of State makes a declaration under these provisions, the Chapter I prohibition[10] does not apply to the agreement to the extent to which the agreement consists of provisions to which the declaration relates[11]. If the Secretary of State is satisfied that there has been a material change of circumstances, he may: (i) revoke a declaration, if he considers that the grounds on which it was made no longer exist; (ii) vary such a declaration, if he considers that there are grounds for making a different declaration; or (iii) make a declaration, even though he has notified the OFT or OFCOM or both of them of his intention not to do so[12]. If the Secretary of State makes, varies or revokes a declaration, he must notify the OFT and OFCOM of his decision[13].

Neither the OFT nor OFCOM may exercise any Chapter III powers[14] in respect of a relevant agreement, unless: (A) the Secretary of State has been notified by the OFT or (as the case may be) by OFCOM of the intention to do so; and (B) the Secretary of State: (aa) has notified the OFT and OFCOM that he has not made a declaration in respect of the agreement, or provisions of the agreement, under these provisions and that he does not intend to make such a declaration; or (bb) has revoked a declaration under these provisions and a period of six months beginning with the date on which the revocation took effect has expired[15].

1   'OFT' means the Office of Fair Trading: Broadcasting Act 1990 s 194A(9) (s 194A added by the Broadcasting Act 1996 s 77(1); Broadcasting Act 1990 s 194A(9) added by the Competition Act 1998 s 3(1)(b), Sch 2 para 4; definition added by the Enterprise Act 2002 s 278(1), Sch 25 para 24(1), (7)(d)(ii)). As to the Office of Fair Trading see COMPETITION vol 18 (2009) PARAS 6–8.
2   As to OFCOM see PARA 507.
3   As to the Secretary of State see PARA 507 note 32.
4   'Relevant agreement' means an agreement:
    (1)   which is made between all holders of regional Channel 3 licences for securing the appointment by them, in accordance with conditions included in their licences by virtue of the Communications Act 2003 s 280, of a single body corporate to be the appointed news provider for the purposes of s 280 (see PARA 876) (Broadcasting Act 1990 s 194A(1)(a) (as added (see note 1); s 194A(1) amended by the Communications Act 2003 s 372(1), (2))); or
    (2)   which is made between them and the body corporate appointed to be the appointed news provider for the purposes of the Communications Act 2003 s 280 (see PARA 876) for purposes connected with the appointment (Broadcasting Act 1990 s 194A(1)(b) (as so added and amended)).
    References to an agreement are to be read as applying equally to, or in relation to, a decision or concerted practice: s 194A(10) (s 194A as so added; and s 194A(10) added by the Competition Act 1998 Sch 2 para 4). As to the holder of the licence see PARA 671 note 19. As to Channel 3 see PARA 667. 'Regional Channel 3 licence' has the same meaning as in the Broadcasting Act 1990 Pt I (ss 3–71) (see PARA 676 note 2): s 194A(9) (s 194A as so added; and s 194A(9) as added (see note 1)).
5   Ie the conditions in the Broadcasting Act 1990 s 194A(3): see the text and note 9.
6   Broadcasting Act 1990 s 194A(2) (as added (see note 1); substituted by the Competition Act 1998 Sch 2 para 4; and amended by the Communications Act 2003 s 372(3)).
7   Ie in the case of a relevant agreement falling within the Broadcasting Act 1990 s 194A(1)(a): see note 4 head (1).
8   Ie in the case of a relevant agreement falling within the Broadcasting Act 1990 s 194A(1)(b): see note 4 head (2).
9   Broadcasting Act 1990 s 194A(3) (as added (see note 1); substituted by the Competition Act 1998 Sch 2 para 4; and amended by the Communications Act 2003 s 372(4)).
10 'The Chapter I prohibition' means the prohibition imposed by the Competition Act 1998 s 2(1) (see COMPETITION vol 18 (2009) PARA 116): Broadcasting Act 1990 s 194A(9) (as added: see note 1).
11 Broadcasting Act 1990 s 194A(4) (as added (see note 1); substituted by the Competition Act 1998 Sch 2 para 4).
12 Broadcasting Act 1990 s 194A(5) (as added (see note 1); substituted by the Competition Act 1998 Sch 2 para 4; and amended by the Enterprise Act 2002 Sch 25 para 24(7)(a); and the Communications Act 2003 s 372(5)).
13 Broadcasting Act 1990 s 194A(6) (as added (see note 1); substituted by the Competition Act 1998 Sch 2 para 4; and amended by the Enterprise Act 2002 Sch 25 para 24(7)(a); and the Communications Act 2003 s 372(3)).
14 'Chapter III powers' means the powers of the OFT and of OFCOM under the Competition Act 1998 Pt I Ch III (ss 25–44) (see COMPETITION vol 18 (2009) PARA 129 et seq) so far as they

relate to the Chapter I prohibition (see note 10): Broadcasting Act 1990 s 194A(9) (as added (see note 1); definition amended by the Communications Act 2003 s 372(8))).

15 Broadcasting Act 1990 s 194A(7) (s 194A as added (see note 1); s 194A(7) added by the Competition Act 1998 Sch 2 para 4; and amended by the Enterprise Act 2002 Sch 25 para 24(7)(a); and the Communications Act 2003 s 372(3), (6)).

(ii) Disabled and Vulnerable People

880. Television services for the deaf and visually impaired. It is the duty of OFCOM[1] to draw up, and from time to time to review and revise, a code giving guidance as to: (1) the extent to which the services to which these provisions apply[2] should promote the understanding and enjoyment by: (a) persons who are deaf or hard of hearing; (b) persons who are blind or partially-sighted; and (c) persons with a dual sensory impairment, of the programmes to be included in such services; and (2) the means by which such understanding and enjoyment should be promoted[3].

The code must include provision for securing that every provider of a service to which these provisions apply ensures that adequate information about the assistance for disabled people that is provided in relation to that service is made available to those who are likely to want to make use of it[4]. The code must also require that, from the fifth and tenth anniversaries of the relevant date[5], the obligations mentioned below[6], respectively, must be fulfilled by reference to averages computed over each of the following: (i) the 12 month period beginning with the anniversary in question; and (ii) every 12 month period ending one week after the end of the previous period for which an average fell to be computed[7]. The obligation to be fulfilled from the fifth anniversary of the relevant date is that at least 60 per cent of so much of every service which is a service to which these provisions apply, and has a relevant date after the passing of the Communications Act 2003[8], as consists of programmes that are not excluded programmes must be accompanied by subtitling[9]. The obligations to be fulfilled from the tenth anniversary of the relevant date are: (A) that at least 90 per cent of so much of a Channel 3 service[10] or of Channel 4[11] as consists of programmes that are not excluded programmes must be accompanied by subtitling; (B) that at least 80 per cent of so much of every other service to which these provisions apply as consists of programmes that are not excluded programmes must be accompanied by subtitling; (C) that at least 10 per cent of so much of every service to which these provisions apply as consists of programmes that are not excluded programmes must be accompanied by audio-description for the blind; and (D) that at least 5 per cent of so much of every service to which these provisions apply as consists of programmes that are not excluded programmes must be presented in, or translated into, sign language[12].

Provision is made with respect to the procedure for issuing and revising a code under the above provisions[13], the power to modify targets in the above provisions[14] and the observance of the code[15].

The regulatory regime for the public teletext service includes the conditions that OFCOM considers appropriate for securing, so far as it is reasonable and practicable, by the inclusion of features in that service, to do so, that persons with disabilities affecting their sight are able to make use of the service[16].

1 As to OFCOM see PARA 507.
2 Ie the Communications Act 2003 s 303. Section 303 applies to the following services: (1) S4C Digital or any other television programme service provided by the Welsh Authority for

broadcasting in digital form so as to be available for reception by members of the public; (2) any licensed public service channel; (3) a digital television programme service but not an electronic programme guide; (4) a television licensable content service but not an electronic programme guide; (5) a restricted television service: s 303(12). As to the meaning of 'S4C Digital' see PARA 644 note 7. As to the meaning of 'television programme service' see PARA 790 note 5. As to the meaning of 'the Welsh Authority' see PARA 644 note 3; and as to television broadcasting by the Welsh Authority see PARAS 644–661. As to the meaning of 'available for reception by members of the public' see PARA 796. 'Electronic programme guide' means a service which: (a) is or is included in a television licensable content service or a digital television programme service; and (b) consists of: (i) the listing or promotion, or both the listing and the promotion, of some or all of the programmes included in any one or more programme services the providers of which are or include persons other than the provider of the guide; and (ii) a facility for obtaining access, in whole or in part, to the programme service or services listed or promoted in the guide: s 303(13). For these purposes, 'programme' does not include an advertisement: s 303(13). As to the meaning of 'programme' generally see PARA 602 note 12. As to the meaning of 'television licensable content service' see PARA 716. As to the meaning of 'digital television programme service' see PARA 602 note 8.

3 Communications Act 2003 s 303(1).
4 Communications Act 2003 s 303(2).
5 As to the meaning of 'relevant date' in the Communications Act 2003 s 303 see s 305.
6 Ie the obligations in the Communications Act 2003 s 303(4) (see the text and note 9) and s 303(5) (see the text and note 12).
7 Communications Act 2003 s 303(3).
8 Ie 17 July 2003.
9 Communications Act 2003 s 303(4). See further note 12.
10 As to the meaning of 'Channel 3 service' see PARA 602 note 8.
11 As to the meaning of 'Channel 4' see PARA 602 note 9.
12 Communications Act 2003 s 303(5). A reference in s 303(4) (see the text and note 9) or in any head of s 303(5) to excluded programmes is a reference to programmes of the description for the time being set out under s 303(7) in relation to s 303(4) or s 303(5) and also in relation to the service in question: s 303(6). The code must set out, in relation to s 303(4) and each of the heads of s 303(5), the descriptions of programmes that OFCOM considers should be excluded programmes for the purposes of the requirement contained in s 303(4) or in any head in s 303(5): s 303(7). In complying with s 303(7), OFCOM must have regard, in particular, to: (1) the extent of the benefit which would be conferred by the provision of assistance for disabled people in relation to the programmes; (2) the size of the intended audience for the programmes; (3) the number of persons who would be likely to benefit from the assistance and the extent of the likely benefit in each case; (4) the extent to which members of the intended audience for the programmes are resident in places outside the United Kingdom; (5) the technical difficulty of providing the assistance; and (6) the cost, in the context of the matters mentioned in heads (1)–(5), of providing the assistance: s 303(8). The exclusions that may be set out in the code under s 303(7): (a) may include different descriptions of programmes in relation to different services to which s 303 applies; and (b) in the case of a service which OFCOM is satisfied (having regard to the matters mentioned in s 303(8)) is a special case, may include all the programmes included in the service: s 303(9).

The requirements that may be imposed by the code include, in particular: (i) requirements on persons providing services to which s 303 applies to meet interim targets falling within s 303(11), from dates falling before an anniversary mentioned in s 303(3) (see the text and note 7); (ii) requirements on persons providing such services to meet further targets from dates falling after the anniversary mentioned in s 303(5); and (iii) requirements with respect to the provision of assistance for disabled people in relation to excluded programmes, or in relation to a particular description of them: s 303(10). The interim targets mentioned in head (i) are the targets with respect to the provision of assistance for disabled people which OFCOM consider it appropriate to impose as targets on the way to meeting the targets imposed in pursuance of s 303(3) (see the text and note 7): s 303(11).

13 See the Communications Act 2003 s 304.
14 See the Communications Act 2003 s 306.
15 See the Communications Act 2003 s 307.
16 Communications Act 2003 s 308. As to the public teletext service see PARA 686.

881. Duties of providers of on-demand programme services. The appropriate regulatory authority[1] must encourage providers of on-demand programme services[2] to ensure that their services are progressively made more accessible to people with disabilities affecting their sight or hearing or both[3]. The appropriate regulatory authority must ensure that providers of on-demand programme services promote, where practicable and by appropriate means, production of and access to European works[4]. The appropriate regulatory authority must encourage providers of on-demand programme services to develop codes of conduct regarding standards concerning the appropriate promotion of food or beverages by sponsorship[5] of, or in advertising which accompanies or is included in[6], children's programmes[7].

1 As to the meaning of 'appropriate regulatory authority' see PARA 786 note 3.
2 As to the meaning of 'on-demand programme service' see PARA 784. In the Communications Act 2003 s 368C, references to a provider of an on-demand programme service do not include references to the BBC or the Welsh Authority: see ss 368P(2), 368Q(1); and PARA 871. As to the meaning of 'BBC' see PARA 603 note 1; and as to the BBC see PARAS 603–626. As to the meaning of 'the Welsh Authority' see PARA 644 note 3; and as to the Welsh Authority see PARA 645 et seq.
3 Communications Act 2003 s 368C(2) (s 368C added by SI 2009/2979).
4 Communications Act 2003 s 368C(3) (as added: see note 3). The reference in the text to European works is to European works within the meaning given in the Audiovisual Media Services Directive art 1(n). As to the Audiovisual Media Services Directive see PARA 857 note 7.
5 'Sponsorship' is to be construed in accordance with the Communications Act 2003 s 368G (see PARA 904): s 368R(1) (s 368R added by SI 2009/2979).
6 For the purposes of the Communications Act 2003 Pt 4A (ss 368A–368R), advertising is included in an on-demand programme service if it can be viewed by a user of the service as a result of the user selecting a programme to view: s 368R(3) (as added: see note 5).
7 Communications Act 2003 s 368C(4) (as added: see note 3). 'Children's programme' means a programme made: (1) for a television programme service or for an on-demand programme service; and (2) for viewing primarily by persons under the age of 16: s 368R(1) (as added (see note 5); definition substituted by SI 2010/831).

(iii) Independent Programmes

882. Quotas for independent programmes. The regulatory regime for every digital television programme service[1] that is not comprised in a licensed public service channel[2] includes the conditions that OFCOM[3] considers appropriate for securing that, in each year, not less than 10 per cent of the total amount of time allocated to the broadcasting of qualifying programmes[4] included in the service is allocated to the broadcasting of a range and diversity of independent productions[5].

1 As to the meaning of 'digital television programme service' see PARA 602 note 8.
2 As to the meaning of 'licensed public service channel' see PARA 788 note 4.
3 As to OFCOM see PARA 507.
4 'Programme' does not include an advertisement: Communications Act 2003 s 309(6). As to the meaning of 'programme' generally see PARA 602 note 12.
5 Communications Act 2003 s 309(1). For these purposes: (1) the reference to qualifying programmes is a reference to programmes of such description as the Secretary of State may by order specify as describing the programmes that are to be qualifying programmes for the purposes of s 309(1); (2) the reference to independent productions is a reference to programmes of such description as the Secretary of State may by order specify as describing the programmes that are to be independent productions for the purposes of s 309(1); and (3) the reference to a range of independent productions is a reference to a range of such productions in terms of cost of acquisition as well as in terms of the types of programme involved: s 309(2). As to the Secretary of State see PARA 507 note 32. As to the power of the Secretary of State to make orders under the Communications Act 2003 see s 402; and TELECOMMUNICATIONS vol 97 (2010) PARA 77.
   The Secretary of State may by order amend s 309(1) by substituting a different percentage for the percentage for the time being specified in s 309(1): s 309(3).

Before making an order under s 309 the Secretary of State must consult OFCOM: s 309(4). No order is to be made containing provision authorised by s 309 unless a draft of the order has been laid before Parliament and approved by a resolution of each House: s 309(5). At the date at which this volume states the law, no orders had been made under s 309.

883. Corresponding rules for the BBC. It is the duty of the BBC[1] to secure that, in each year, not less than 25 per cent[2] of the total amount of time allocated to the broadcasting of qualifying programmes[3] included in the television broadcasting services provided by the BBC is allocated to the broadcasting of a range and diversity[4] of independent productions[5].

The Secretary of State may by order provide for the BBC to have the duty set out below, either instead of or as well as the one set out above[6].

That duty is a duty to secure that, in each year, not less than the percentage specified in the order of the programming budget[7] for that year for the television broadcasting services provided by the BBC is applied in the acquisition[8] of independent productions[9]. The power to make such an order includes power to provide that the BBC is again to be subject to a duty to which it has previously ceased to be subject by virtue of such an order, in addition to or instead of the duty to which it is subject (apart from the exercise of that power) by virtue of these provisions[10].

The Secretary of State is not to make an order for the BBC to be or to cease to be subject to the duties mentioned above unless: (1) OFCOM has made a recommendation to him that the BBC should be subject to that duty, or should cease to be subject to it; and (2) the order gives effect to that recommendation[11].

Where television broadcasting services are designated by or under the BBC Charter and Agreement[12]: (a) as services that must be treated separately for the purposes of the first duty mentioned above or of a duty imposed by an order[13]; or (b) as services that must be included in a group of services that must be taken together for the purposes of such a duty, that duty is to have effect in accordance with the following provisions[14]. A duty having effect in accordance with these provisions[15] is to have effect as if (instead of applying to all the television broadcasting services provided by the BBC, taken together) it applied separately in relation to each service that is required to be treated separately, and in relation to each group of services that are required to be taken together[16].

The BBC must comply with directions given to it by OFCOM for the purpose of: (i) carrying forward to one or more subsequent years determined in accordance with the direction any shortfall for any year in its compliance with the duties imposed by virtue of either provision set out above; and (ii) thereby increasing the percentage applicable for the purposes of those duties to the subsequent year or years[17].

1   As to the meaning of 'BBC' see PARA 603 note 1; and as to the BBC see PARAS 603–626.

2   The Secretary of State may by order amend the Communications Act 2003 Sch 12 para 1(1) by substituting a different percentage for the percentage for the time being specified there: s 388, Sch 12 para 1(3). Before making an order under Sch 12 para 1, the Secretary of State must consult OFCOM and the BBC: Sch 12 para 1(12). No order is to be made containing provision authorised by Sch 12 para 1 unless a draft of the order has been laid before Parliament and approved by a resolution of each House: Sch 12 para 1(13). At the date at which this volume states the law, no such order had been made. As to the Secretary of State see PARA 507 note 32. As to OFCOM see PARA 507.

3   A reference to qualifying programmes is a reference to programmes of such description as the Secretary of State may by order specify as describing the programmes that are to be qualifying programmes for the purposes of the Communications Act 2003 Sch 12 para 1: Sch 12 para 1(2)(a).

4   A reference to a range of independent productions is a reference to a range of such productions in terms of cost of acquisition as well as in terms of the types of programme involved: Communications Act 2003 Sch 12 para 1(2)(c). A reference to independent productions is a reference to programmes of such description as the Secretary of State may by order specify as describing the programmes that are to be independent productions for the purposes of Sch 12 para 1: Sch 12 para 1(2)(b).

5   Communications Act 2003 Sch 12 para 1(1).

6   Communications Act 2003 Sch 12 para 1(4).

7   'Programming budget' means the budget for the production and acquisition of qualifying programmes: Sch 12 para 1(14). The amount of the programming budget for a year and the means of determining the amount of that budget that is applied for any purpose are to be computed in accordance with such provision as may be set out in an order made by the Secretary of State, or as may be determined by OFCOM in accordance with such an order: Communications Act 2003 Sch 12 para 1(11).

8   'Acquisition', in relation to a programme, includes commissioning and the acquisition of a right to include it in a service or to have it broadcast: Sch 12 para 1(14).

9   Communications Act 2003 Sch 12 para 1(5).

10 Communications Act 2003 Sch 12 para 1(6).

11 Communications Act 2003 Sch 12 para 1(7).

12 As to the meaning of 'BBC Charter and Agreement' see PARA 854 note 2.

13 Ie the duty imposed by the Communications Act 2003 Sch 12 para 1(1) (see the text and note 5) or a duty imposed under Sch 12 para 1(4) (see the text and note 6).

14 Communications Act 2003 Sch 12 para 1(8).

15 Ie the Communications Act 2003 Sch 12 para 1(9).

16 Communications Act 2003 Sch 12 para 1(9).

17 Communications Act 2003 Sch 12 para 1(10).

(iv) Programme Guides and Schedules

884. Regulation of electronic programme guides. It is the duty of OFCOM[1] to draw up, and from time to time to review and revise, a code giving guidance as to the practices to be followed in the provision of electronic programme guides[2]. The practices required by the code must include the giving, in the manner provided for in the code, of such degree of prominence as OFCOM considers appropriate to: (1) the listing or promotion, or both the listing and promotion, for members of its intended audience[3], of the programmes included in each public service channel[4]; and (2) the facilities, in the case of each such channel, for members of its intended audience to select or access the programmes included in it[5]. The practices required by the code must also include the incorporation of such features in electronic programme guides as OFCOM considers appropriate for securing that persons with disabilities affecting their sight or hearing or both: (a) are able, so far as practicable, to make use of such guides for all the same purposes as persons without such disabilities; and (b) are informed about, and are able to make use of, whatever assistance for disabled people is provided in relation to the programmes listed or promoted[6].

The regulatory regime for every service consisting in or including an electronic programme guide[7] includes whatever conditions (if any) OFCOM considers appropriate for securing that the code maintained by it[8] is observed in the provision of those services[9].

1   As to OFCOM see PARA 507.

2   Communications Act 2003 s 310(1). In s 310, 'electronic programme guide' means a service which consists of: (1) the listing or promotion, or both the listing and the promotion, of some or all of the programmes included in any one or more programme services the providers of which are or include persons other than the provider of the guide; and (2) a facility for obtaining access, in whole or in part, to the programme service or services listed or promoted in the guide: s 310(8).

3   For the purposes of the Communications Act 2003 s 310, 'intended audience', in relation to a service of any description, means: (1) if the service is provided only for a particular area or locality of the United Kingdom, members of the public in that area or locality; (2) if it is provided for members of a particular community, members of that community; and (3) in any other case, members of the public in the United Kingdom: s 310(7). As to the meaning of 'United Kingdom' see PARA 510 note 13.

4   Subject to the Communications Act 2003 s 310(5), in s 310(2) the reference to the public service channels is a reference to any of the following: (1) any service of television programmes provided by the BBC in digital form so as to be available for reception by members of the public; (2) any Channel 3 service in digital form; (3) Channel 4 in digital form; (4) Channel 5 in digital form; (5) S4C Digital; (6) the digital public teletext service: s 310(4). As to the meaning of 'BBC' see PARA 603 note 1; and as to the BBC see PARAS 603–626. As to the meaning of 'available for reception by members of the public' see PARA 796. As to the meaning of 'Channel 3 service' see PARA 602 note 8. As to the meaning of 'Channel 4' see PARA 602 note 9. As to the meaning of 'Channel 5' see PARA 602 note 10. As to the meaning of 'S4C Digital' see PARA 644 note 7. As to the meaning of 'digital public teletext service' see PARA 697 note 3. The Secretary of State may by order: (a) add any programme service to the services for the time being specified in s 310(4) as public service channels; or (b) delete a service from s 310(4): s 310(5). As to the Secretary of State see PARA 507 note 32. Before making an order under s 310(5), the Secretary of State must consult OFCOM: s 310(6). As to the power of the Secretary of State to make orders under the Communications Act 2003 see s 402; and TELECOMMUNICATIONS vol 97 (2010) PARA 77. At the date at which this volume states the law, no order had been made under s 310(5).

5   Communications Act 2003 s 310(2).

6   Communications Act 2003 s 310(3).

7   As to the meaning of 'electronic programme guide' see note 2; definition applied by the Communications Act 2003 s 311(2).

8   Ie under the Communications Act 2003 s 310.

9   Communications Act 2003 s 311(1).

885.   Announcements of programme schedules. Any Channel 3 licence[1] or licence to provide Channel 4[2] may include conditions requiring the licence holder[3] to include in the licensed[4] service such announcements concerning relevant programme schedules[5] as OFCOM[6] determines[7].

1   As to the meaning of 'Channel 3' see PARA 667; and as to the meaning of 'Channel 3 licence' see PARA 669 note 2.

2   As to the meaning of 'Channel 4' see PARA 637. As to the meaning of 'licence' see PARA 662 note 3.

3   As to the holder of the licence see PARA 671 note 19.

4   As to the meaning of 'licensed' see PARA 662 note 3.

5   'Relevant programme schedules' means: (1) in relation to a Channel 3 licence, programme schedules for programmes to be broadcast on Channel 4 and, where any part of the area for which the licensed service is to be provided is in Wales, programme schedules for programmes to be broadcast on S4C; and (2) in relation to the licence to provide Channel 4, programme schedules for programmes to be included in any Channel 3 service: Broadcasting Act 1990 s 37(2). As to the meaning of 'programme' see PARA 667 note 7. As to the meaning of 'S4C' see PARA 644.

6   As to OFCOM see PARA 507.

7   Broadcasting Act 1990 s 37(1) (amended by the Communications Act 2003 s 360(3), Sch 15 para 17).

886.   Duty to provide advance information about programmes. A person providing a programme service[1] to which the following provisions apply[2] must make available information relating to the programmes[3] to be included in the service to any person ('the publisher') wishing to publish in the United Kingdom[4] any such information[5].

The duty so imposed is to make available information as to the titles of the programmes which are to be, or may be, included in the service on any date, and the time of their inclusion, to any publisher who has asked the person providing the programme service to make such information available to him and reasonably requires it[6].

Information to be made so available to a publisher is to be made available as soon after it has been prepared as is reasonably practicable but, in any event, not later than when it is made available to any other publisher[7], and, in the case of information in respect of all the programmes to be included in the service in any period of seven days, not later than the beginning of the preceding period of 14 days, or such other number of days as may be prescribed by the Secretary of State[8] by order[9].

The duty so imposed is not satisfied by providing the information on terms, other than terms as to copyright, prohibiting or restricting publication in the United Kingdom by the publisher[10]. These provisions do not require any information to be given about any advertisement[11].

1 As to the meaning of 'programme service' see PARA 507 note 9.

2 The programme services to which the Broadcasting Act 1990 s 176, Sch 17 (see PARAS 887–888) apply and the persons who provide them, or who are to be treated as providing them, are set out in the Broadcasting Act 1990 s 176(7) (amended by the Broadcasting Act 1996 s 148(1), Sch 10 para 10; and the Communications Act 2003 s 360(3), Sch 15 para 60), and are as follows:

   (1) television and national radio services provided by the BBC for reception in the United Kingdom (the BBC);

   (2) television programme services subject to regulation by OFCOM (the person licensed to provide the service);

   (3) the public television services of the Welsh Authority (within the meaning of the Communications Act 2003 Sch 12 Pt 2 (paras 3–24): see PARA 655) (the Welsh Authority);

   (4) any national service (see the Broadcasting Act 1990 s 126(1); and PARA 724 note 5) subject to regulation by OFCOM, any simulcast radio service (within the meaning of the Broadcasting Act 1996 Pt II (ss 40–72): see PARA 754 note 12), and any national digital sound programme service (within the meaning of Pt II: see PARA 756 note 16) subject to regulation by OFCOM (the person licensed to provide the service);

   (5) television broadcasting services provided by the Independent Television Commission in accordance with the Broadcasting Act 1990 s 129, Sch 11 (see PARA 507), other than Channel 4 (during interim period only) (the programme contractor);

   (6) Channel 4, as so provided (during interim period only) (the body corporate referred to in the Broadcasting Act 1981 s 12(2) (repealed)).

   As to the meaning of 'BBC' see PARA 603 note 1; and as to the BBC see PARAS 603–626. As to the meaning of 'television programme service' see PARA 790 note 5. As to the Independent Television Commission see PARA 507. As to the meaning of 'licensed' see PARAS 662 note 3, 677 note 2. As to the meaning of 'the Welsh Authority' see PARA 644 note 3; definition applied by s 147(2). As to television broadcasting by the Welsh Authority see PARAS 644–661. As to the meaning of 'national service' see PARA 723 note 4. As to OFCOM see PARA 507. As to the meaning of 'Channel 4' see PARA 637.

3 As to the meaning of 'programme' see PARA 667 note 7.

4 As to the meaning of 'United Kingdom' see PARA 510 note 13.

5 Broadcasting Act 1990 s 176(1). Schedule 17 (see PARAS 887–888) applies to any information or future information which the person providing a programme service to which s 176 applies is or may be required to make available under s 176: s 176(6).

6 Broadcasting Act 1990 s 176(2).

7 Broadcasting Act 1990 s 176(3)(a).

8 As to the Secretary of State see PARA 507 note 32.

9 Broadcasting Act 1990 s 176(3)(b). Such an order is subject to annulment in pursuance of a resolution of either House of Parliament: s 176(4). At the date at which this volume states the law no such order had been made.

10 Broadcasting Act 1990 s 176(5).

11 Broadcasting Act 1990 s 176(8).

887. Copyright licensing. Where the person providing a programme service[1] has assigned to another the copyright[2] in works[3] containing certain information[4], the person providing the programme service, not the assignee, is to be treated as the owner of the copyright for the purposes of licensing any act restricted by the copyright done on or after 1 March 1991[5].

1   As to the meaning of 'programme service' see PARA 507 note 9.
2   As to the meaning of 'copyright' see COPYRIGHT, DESIGN RIGHT AND RELATED RIGHTS vol 9(2) (2006 Reissue) PARA 57; definition applied by the Broadcasting Act 1990 s 176(6), Sch 17 para 7(1).
3   References to 'works' include future works, and references to the copyright in works include future copyright: see the Broadcasting Act 1990 Sch 17 para 7(3).
4   Broadcasting Act 1990 Sch 17 para 1(1). The information referred to is information to which Sch 17 paras 2–6 (see PARA 888) apply: see Sch 17 para 1(1).
5   Broadcasting Act 1990 Sch 17 para 1(2). The date referred to is the date on which the Broadcasting Act 1990 Sch 17 was brought into force: see the Broadcasting Act 1990 (Commencement No 1 and Transitional Provisions) Order 1990, SI 1990/2347, art 5. Note that, for the purpose of enabling publication of information about programmes to be included in a programme service, the Broadcasting Act 1990 Sch 17 came into force on 1 January 1991: see the Broadcasting Act 1990 (Commencement No 1 and Transitional Provisions) Order 1990, SI 1990/2347, art 5.

     Where the assignment by the person providing the programme service occurred before 29 September 1989 then, in relation to any act restricted by the copyright so assigned, the Broadcasting Act 1990 Sch 17 para 1(2) does not have effect, and references in Sch 17 paras 2–7 (see PARA 888) to the person providing the programme service are references to the assignee: Sch 17 para 1(3). As to the meaning of 'act restricted by the copyright' see PARA 929; and COPYRIGHT, DESIGN RIGHT AND RELATED RIGHTS vol 9(2) (2006 Reissue) PARA 311 (definition applied by Sch 17 para 7(1)).

     Schedule 17 and the Copyright, Designs and Patents Act 1988 have effect as if the Broadcasting Act 1990 Sch 17 were included in the Copyright, Designs and Patents Act 1988 Pt I Ch III (ss 28–76) (see PARA 930 et seq; and COPYRIGHT, DESIGN RIGHT AND RELATED RIGHTS vol 9(2) (2006 Reissue) PARA 337 et seq), and that Act has effect as if proceedings under the Broadcasting Act 1990 Sch 17 were listed in the Copyright, Designs and Patents Act 1988 s 149 (jurisdiction of the Copyright Tribunal: see COPYRIGHT, DESIGN RIGHT AND RELATED RIGHTS vol 9(2) (2006 Reissue) PARA 211): Broadcasting Act 1990 Sch 17 para 7(1).

888. Use of information as of right. The provisions relating to the conditions for exercising the right to information[1] apply to any act restricted by the copyright[2] in works[3] containing information to which these provisions apply done by the publisher[4] if:

(1)   a licence to do the act could be granted by the person providing the programme service[5] but no such licence is held by the publisher[6];

(2)   the person providing the programme service refuses to grant to the publisher a licence[7] to do the act, being a licence of such duration, and of which the terms as to payment[8] for doing the act are such, as would be acceptable to the publisher[9]; and

(3)   the publisher has complied with the provision relating to notice of intention to exercise the right to information[10].

A publisher intending to avail himself of the right to information[11] must:

(a)   give notice of his intention to the person providing the programme service, asking that person to propose terms of payment[12]; and

(b)   after receiving the proposal or the expiry of a reasonable time, give reasonable notice to the person providing the programme service of the date on which he proposes to begin exercising the right and the terms of payment in accordance with which he intends to do so[13].

Before exercising the right the publisher must:

(i)   give reasonable notice to the Copyright Tribunal[14] of his intention to exercise the right and of the date on which he proposes to begin to do so[15]; and

(ii)   apply to the Copyright Tribunal[16] to settle the terms of payment[17].

Where the publisher, on or after the date specified in a notice under head (b) above, does any act in circumstances in which this provision applies[18], he is, if he makes the required payments[19], in the same position as regards infringement of copyright as if he had at all material times been the holder of a licence to do so granted by the person providing the programme service[20].

Payments are to be made at not less than quarterly intervals in arrears[21]. The amount of any payment is that determined in accordance with any order of the Copyright Tribunal[22] or, if no such order has been made:

(A)   in accordance with any proposal for terms of payment made by the person providing the programme service pursuant to a request under head (a) above[23]; or

(B)   where no proposal has been so made or the amount determined in accordance with the proposal so made appears to the publisher to be unreasonably high, in accordance with the terms of payment notified under head (b) above[24].

On an application to settle the terms of payment, the Copyright Tribunal must consider the matter and make such order as it may determine to be reasonable in the circumstances[25]. Such an order has effect from the date the applicant begins to exercise the right[26], and any necessary repayments, or further payments, must be made in respect of amounts that have fallen due[27]. A person exercising the right, or the person providing the programme service, may apply to the Copyright Tribunal to review any such order[28]. Such an application may not be made, except with the special leave of the Copyright Tribunal: (aa) within 12 months from the date of the order, or of the decision on a previous such application[29]; or (bb) if the order was made so as to be in force for 15 months or less, or, as a result of a decision on a previous application, is due to expire within 15 months of that decision, until the last three months before the expiry date[30]. On the application the Copyright Tribunal must consider the matter and make such order confirming or varying the original order as it may determine to be reasonable in the circumstances[31]. Such an order has effect from the date on which it is made or such later date as may be specified by the Copyright Tribunal[32].

1   Ie the Broadcasting Act 1990 Sch 17 para 4: see s 176(6), Sch 17 para 2(1).

2   As to the meaning of 'act restricted by the copyright' see PARA 929; and COPYRIGHT, DESIGN RIGHT AND RELATED RIGHTS vol 9(2) (2006 Reissue) PARA 311 (definition applied by the Broadcasting Act 1990 Sch 17 para 7(1)). As to the meaning of 'copyright' see COPYRIGHT, DESIGN RIGHT AND RELATED RIGHTS vol 9(2) (2006 Reissue) PARA 57; definition applied by Sch 17 para 7(1).

3   As to the meaning of 'works' see PARA 887 note 3.

4   References to anything done by the publisher include anything done on his behalf: Broadcasting Act 1990 Sch 17 para 7(2). As to the meaning of 'the publisher' see PARA 886.

5   As to the meaning of 'programme service' see PARA 507 note 9.

6   Broadcasting Act 1990 Sch 17 para 2(1)(a).

7   The reference in the Broadcasting Act 1990 Sch 17 para 2(1) to refusing to grant a licence includes failing to do so within a reasonable time of being asked: Sch 17 para 2(2).

8   References in the Broadcasting Act 1990 Sch 17 paras 3–7 to the terms of payment are references to the terms as to payment for doing any act restricted by the copyright in works containing information to which Sch 17 applies: Sch 17 para 2(3).

9   Broadcasting Act 1990 Sch 17 para 2(1)(b).

10   Broadcasting Act 1990 Sch 17 para 2(1)(c). The provision referred to in the text is Sch 17 para 3 (see the text and notes 12–17).
11   Ie the right conferred by the Broadcasting Act 1990 Sch 17 para 4 (see the text and notes 20–24).
12   Broadcasting Act 1990 Sch 17 para 3(1)(a).
13   Broadcasting Act 1990 Sch 17 para 3(1)(b).
14   As to the Copyright Tribunal see COPYRIGHT, DESIGN RIGHT AND RELATED RIGHTS vol 9(2) (2006 Reissue) PARA 207 et seq.
15   Broadcasting Act 1990 Sch 17 para 3(2)(a).
16   Ie under the Broadcasting Act 1990 Sch 17 para 5 (see the text and notes 25–27).
17   Broadcasting Act 1990 Sch 17 para 3(2)(b).
18   See the text and notes 1–10.
19   Ie the payments required by the Broadcasting Act 1990 Sch 17 para 4 (see the text and notes 20–24).
20   Broadcasting Act 1990 Sch 17 para 4(1).
21   Broadcasting Act 1990 Sch 17 para 4(2).
22   Ie under the Broadcasting Act 1990 Sch 17 para 5 (see the text and notes 25–27).
23   Broadcasting Act 1990 Sch 17 para 4(3)(a).
24   Broadcasting Act 1990 Sch 17 para 4(3)(b).
25   Broadcasting Act 1990 Sch 17 para 5(1).
26   Ie the right conferred by the Broadcasting Act 1990 Sch 17 para 4 (see the text and notes 20–24).
27   Broadcasting Act 1990 Sch 17 para 5(2).
28   Broadcasting Act 1990 Sch 17 para 6(1).
29   Broadcasting Act 1990 Sch 17 para 6(2)(a).
30   Broadcasting Act 1990 Sch 17 para 6(2)(b).
31   Broadcasting Act 1990 Sch 17 para 6(3).
32   Broadcasting Act 1990 Sch 17 para 6(4).

(v) Local Sound Broadcasting Services

889. Local content and character of local sound broadcasting services. It is the duty of OFCOM[1] to carry out its functions in relation to local sound broadcasting services[2] in the manner that it considers is best calculated to secure: (1) that programmes[3] consisting of or including local material[4] are included in such services; and (2) that, where such programmes are included in such a service, what appears to OFCOM to be a suitable proportion of them consists of locally-made[5] programmes[6]. OFCOM must: (a) draw up guidance as to how it considers the requirements of heads (1) and (2) above should be satisfied; and (b) have regard to that guidance in carrying out its functions in relation to local sound broadcasting services[7]. The guidance may be different for different descriptions of services[8]. OFCOM may revise the guidance from time to time[9]. Before drawing up or revising the guidance, OFCOM must consult: (i) such persons as appear to it to represent the interests of persons for whom local sound broadcasting services are or would be provided; (ii) persons holding licences to provide local sound broadcasting services or persons appearing to represent such persons, or both; and (iii) such other persons as it considers appropriate[10]. OFCOM must publish the guidance and every revision of it in such manner as it considers appropriate[11].

1   As to OFCOM see PARA 507.
2   'Local sound broadcasting service' means a sound broadcasting service which, under the Communications Act 2003 s 245(4)(b) (see PARA 723), is a local service for the purposes of s 245: s 362(1).
3   'Programme' does not include an advertisement: Communications Act 2003 s 314(7). As to the meaning of 'programme' generally see PARA 602 note 12.
4   For the purposes of the Communications Act 2003 s 314, 'local material', in relation to a local sound broadcasting service, means material which is of particular interest: (1) to persons living

or working within the area or locality for which the service is provided; (2) to persons living or working within a part of that area or locality; or (3) to particular communities living or working within that area or locality or a part of it: s 314(7). 'Material' includes news, information and other spoken material and music: s 314(7). References in s 314 to persons living or working within an area or locality include references to persons undergoing education or training in that area or locality: s 314(8).

5   For the purposes of the Communications Act 2003 s 314, 'locally-made', in relation to programmes included in a local sound broadcasting service, means made wholly or partly at premises in the area or locality for which that service is provided or, if there is an approved area for the programmes, that area: s 314(7) (amended by the Digital Economy Act 2010 s 34(5)(b)). 'Approved area', in relation to programmes included in a local sound broadcasting service, means an area approved by OFCOM for the purposes of the Communications Act 2003 s 314 that includes the area or locality for which the service is provided: s 314(7) (definition added by the Digital Economy Act 2010 s 34(5)(a)). Before approving an area for the purposes of the Communications Act 2003 s 314, OFCOM must publish a document specifying: (1) the area that it proposes to approve; and (2) a period in which representations may be made to OFCOM about the proposals: s 314(9) (s 314(9)–(11) added by the Digital Economy Act 2010 s 34(6)). OFCOM may withdraw its approval of all or part of an area at any time if the holder of the licence to provide the local sound broadcasting service concerned consents: Communications Act 2003 s 314(10) (as so added). Where OFCOM approves an area or withdraws its approval of an area, it must publish, in such manner as it considers appropriate, a notice giving details of the area: s 314(11) (as so added).

6   Communications Act 2003 s 314(1) (amended by the Digital Economy Act 2010 ss 34(2), (3), (7), 45, Sch 2). The Communications Act 2003 s 314(1)(a), (b) (heads (1), (2) in the text) apply in the case of each local sound broadcasting service only if and to the extent (if any) that OFCOM considers it appropriate in that case: s 314(1A) (added by the Digital Economy Act 2010 s 34(4)).

7   Communications Act 2003 s 314(2).
8   Communications Act 2003 s 314(3).
9   Communications Act 2003 s 314(4).
10 Communications Act 2003 s 314(5).
11 Communications Act 2003 s 314(6).

(vi) Political Broadcasts

890.   Party political broadcasts on television and radio.   The regulatory regime for every licensed public service channel[1], and the regulatory regime for every national radio service[2], includes: (1) conditions requiring the inclusion in that channel or service of party political broadcasts and of referendum campaign broadcasts[3]; and (2) conditions requiring that licence holder to observe such rules with respect to party political broadcasts and referendum campaign broadcasts as may be made by OFCOM[4]. The rules made by OFCOM for the purposes of these provisions[5] may, in particular, include provision for determining: (a) the political parties on whose behalf party political broadcasts may be made; (b) in relation to each political party on whose behalf such broadcasts may be made, the length and frequency of the broadcasts; and (c) in relation to each designated organisation[6] on whose behalf referendum campaign broadcasts are required to be broadcast, the length and frequency of such broadcasts[7].

1   As to the meaning of 'licensed public service channel' see PARA 788 note 8.
2   For the purposes of the Communications Act 2003 s 333, 'national radio service' means a national service within the meaning of s 245 (see PARA 723): s 333(6).
3   For the purposes of the Communications Act 2003 s 333, 'referendum campaign broadcast' has the meaning given by the Political Parties, Elections and Referendums Act 2000 s 127 (see ELECTIONS AND REFERENDUMS vol 15(4) (2007 Reissue) PARA 544): Communications Act 2003 s 333(6).
4   Communications Act 2003 s 333(1). As to OFCOM see PARA 507. As to political broadcasts see further PARA 896.

5   Ie the Communications Act 2003 s 333.

6   For the purposes of the Communications Act 2003 s 333, 'designated organisation', in relation to a referendum, means a person or body designated by the Electoral Commission under the Political Parties, Elections and Referendums Act 2000 s 108 (see ELECTIONS AND REFERENDUMS vol 15(4) (2007 Reissue) PARA 522) in respect of that referendum: Communications Act 2003 s 333(6). As to the Electoral Commission see ELECTIONS AND REFERENDUMS vol 15(3) (2007 Reissue) PARA 31 et seq.

7   Communications Act 2003 s 333(2). Those rules are to have effect subject to the Political Parties, Elections and Referendums Act 2000 ss 37, 127 (only registered parties and designated organisations to be entitled to party political broadcasts or referendum campaign broadcasts: see ELECTIONS AND REFERENDUMS vol 15(3) (2007 Reissue) PARA 54): Communications Act 2003 s 333(3). Rules made by OFCOM for the purposes of s 333 may make different provision for different cases: s 333(4). Before making any rules for the purposes of s 333, OFCOM must have regard to any views expressed by the Electoral Commission: s 333(5).

     If the body exercises its discretion honestly and in good faith to the best of its ability it will have discharged its statutory duty; it is not for the court to lay down how the body is to carry out its statutory duties or to decide whether one action or another is fair: *Wolfe v Independent Broadcasting Authority* (1 April 1979, unreported), Ct of Sess, per Lord Robertson. See also *A-G (ex rel McWhirter) v Independent Broadcasting Authority* [1973] QB 629, [1973] 1 All ER 689, CA. Before the referendum in Scotland in 1979, the Independent Broadcasting Authority planned to broadcast four party political broadcasts, of which three were in favour and one was against, and interdict was granted as the authority had failed to provide a proper balance: *Wilson v Independent Broadcasting Authority* 1979 SC 351.

     In *R v Radio Authority, ex p Bull* [1998] QB 294, [1997] 2 All ER 561, CA, it was held that: (1) there was no statutory definition of bodies whose 'objects' were 'wholly or mainly' political; (2) where a body formally set out a statement of its objects and some were political and others were not, it might be essential to go beyond that formal statement to see if they were mainly political; (3) to fall within the provision of 'wholly or mainly' a body had to be more than 75% political; and (4) in considering the meaning of political, previous case law could be considered in which it had been found that the association was not entitled to charitable status because all the main objects of the trust were not political. It is impossible to provide a definition of a political advertisement which gives a precise indication as to what is acceptable and a large measure of discretion is given to OFCOM by the Broadcasting Act 1990: see *R v Radio Authority, ex p Bull* [1996] QB 169, [1995] 4 All ER 481; affd [1998] QB 294, [1997] 2 All ER 561, CA.

891. Government requirements for licensed services. If it appears to the Secretary of State[1] or any other Minister of the Crown[2] to be appropriate to do so in connection with any of his functions, the Secretary of State or that minister may at any time by notice require OFCOM[3] to give a direction to the holders of the Broadcasting Act licences[4] specified in the notice to include an announcement so specified in their licensed services[5]. The direction may specify the times at which the announcement is to be broadcast or otherwise transmitted[6]. Where the holder of a Broadcasting Act licence includes an announcement in his licensed service in pursuance of a direction, he may announce that he is doing so in pursuance of such a direction[7]. The Secretary of State may, at any time, by notice require OFCOM to direct the holders of the Broadcasting Act licences specified in the notice to refrain from including in their licensed services any matter, or description of matter, specified in the notice[8].

     Where: (1) OFCOM has given the holder of a Broadcasting Act licence a direction in accordance with a notice[9]; (2) in consequence of the revocation by the Secretary of State of such a notice, OFCOM has revoked such a direction; or (3) such a notice has expired, the holder of the licence in question may include in the licensed service an announcement of the giving or revocation of the direction or of the expiration of the notice, as the case may be[10].

     OFCOM must comply with every requirement contained in a notice under these provisions[11]. The powers conferred by these provisions are in addition to any powers specifically conferred on the Secretary of State by or under the Communications Act 2003 or any other enactment[12].

1   As to the Secretary of State see PARA 507 note 32.
2   For the purposes of the Communications Act 2003 s 336, 'Minister of the Crown' includes the Treasury: s 336(9). As to the Treasury see CONSTITUTIONAL LAW AND HUMAN RIGHTS vol 8(2) (Reissue) PARAS 512–517.
3   As to OFCOM see PARA 507.
4   As to the meaning of 'Broadcasting Act licence' see PARA 602 note 3.
5   Communications Act 2003 s 336(1), (2).
6   Communications Act 2003 s 336(3).
7   Communications Act 2003 s 336(4).
8   Communications Act 2003 s 336(5).
9   Ie under the Communications Act 2003 s 336(5).
10 Communications Act 2003 s 336(6).
11 Communications Act 2003 s 336(7).
12 Communications Act 2003 s 336(8). As to the meaning of 'enactment' see PARA 793 note 5.

892. Defence and emergency arrangements. Any government minister[1]: (1) may request that the BBC[2] broadcast or otherwise distribute any announcement; and (2) may, if that minister has requested that the announcement be broadcast or otherwise distributed on television or by means of an online service, request that the BBC accompany that announcement with a visual image (moving or still) of anything mentioned in the announcement[3]. If it appears to any government minister that an emergency has arisen, that minister may request that the BBC broadcast or otherwise distribute any announcement or other programme[4].

Such a request must be made in writing, and the BBC: (a) must comply with the request; (b) must meet the cost of doing so itself; and (c) may, when broadcasting or distributing the announcement or other programme, announce that it is doing so pursuant to such a request[5].

The Secretary of State[6] may give the BBC a direction in writing that the BBC must not broadcast or otherwise distribute any matter, or class of matter, specified in the direction, whether at a time or times so specified or at any time[7]. The BBC may, if it wishes, announce that such a direction has been given, varied or revoked[8].

A government minister may direct the BBC to monitor and (where applicable) record specified media output[9], and to supply other services in that connection (including, for example, the preparation and distribution of products such as monitoring reports and digests of broadcast or other material)[10]. In complying with such a direction, the BBC is to be regarded as an agent of the Crown, and to be acting in the public interest[11].

1   As to ministers of the government see CONSTITUTIONAL LAW AND HUMAN RIGHTS vol 8(2) (Reissue) PARA 354.
2   As to the meaning of 'BBC' see PARA 603.
3   *Agreement between Her Majesty's Secretary of State for Culture, Media and Sport and the British Broadcasting Corporation* (Cm 6872) (30 June 2006) cl 81(1).
4   *Agreement between Her Majesty's Secretary of State for Culture, Media and Sport and the British Broadcasting Corporation* (Cm 6872) (30 June 2006) cl 81(2).
5   *Agreement between Her Majesty's Secretary of State for Culture, Media and Sport and the British Broadcasting Corporation* (Cm 6872) (30 June 2006) cl 81(3).
6   As to the Secretary of State see PARA 507 note 32.
7   *Agreement between Her Majesty's Secretary of State for Culture, Media and Sport and the British Broadcasting Corporation* (Cm 6872) (30 June 2006) cl 81(4).
8   *Agreement between Her Majesty's Secretary of State for Culture, Media and Sport and the British Broadcasting Corporation* (Cm 6872) (30 June 2006) cl 81(5). In 1988 the Secretary of

State issued notices under similarly worded powers contained in the *Licence and Agreement between Her Majesty's Secretary of State for the Home Department and the British Broadcasting Corporation* (Cmnd 8233) (1981) para 13(4), prohibiting the BBC from broadcasting directly any words spoken by representatives of prescribed organisations (eg the Ulster Defence Association and Sinn Fein) or their representatives: 138 HC Official Report (6th series), 19 October 1988, col 893. The House of Lords rejected a challenge to the ban brought by the National Union of Journalists that the Secretary of State had failed to take proper account of the Convention for the Protection of Human Rights and Fundamental Freedoms (Rome, 4 November 1950; TS 71 (1953); Cmd 8969) art 10 (freedom of expression): *R v Secretary of State for the Home Department, ex p Brind* [1991] 1 AC 696, sub nom *Brind v Secretary of State for the Home Department* [1991] 1 All ER 720, HL.

9 For these purposes, the reference to media output is a reference to any sound, text, data, still or moving pictures or other content carried by means of an electronic communications network or an electronic communications service (within the meaning of the Communications Act 2003) (see TELECOMMUNICATIONS vol 97 (2010) PARA 60), and in any print medium, and includes the output of any news agency; and 'specified' means specified in a direction under the *Agreement between Her Majesty's Secretary of State for Culture, Media and Sport and the British Broadcasting Corporation* (Cm 6872) (30 June 2006) cl 88(1): cl 88(2).

10 *Agreement between Her Majesty's Secretary of State for Culture, Media and Sport and the British Broadcasting Corporation* (Cm 6872) (30 June 2006) cl 88(1).

11 *Agreement between Her Majesty's Secretary of State for Culture, Media and Sport and the British Broadcasting Corporation* (Cm 6872) (30 June 2006) cl 88(3).

893. Election broadcasts. Broadcasting during elections is controlled by statute[1]. Formerly, broadcasting authorities had the right freely to photograph or record the appearance or the words of candidates[2] during an election, subject to their duty to be fair[3]. That freedom has been reduced[4].

Each broadcasting authority[5] must now adopt a code of practice with respect to the participation of candidates[6] at a parliamentary or local government election in items about the constituency or electoral area[7] in question which are included in relevant services[8] during the election period[9]. The code for the time being adopted by a broadcasting authority under these provisions must be either[10]:

(1)   a code drawn up by that authority, whether on its own or jointly with one or more other broadcasting authorities[11]; or

(2)   a code drawn up by one or more other such authorities[12],

and a broadcasting authority must from time to time consider whether the code for the time being so adopted by it should be replaced by a further code falling within head (1) or head (2) above[13].

Before drawing up a code under these provisions, a broadcasting authority must have regard to any views expressed by the Electoral Commission; and any such code may make different provision for different cases[14].

OFCOM must do all that it can to secure that the code for the time being adopted by it is observed in the provision of relevant services; and the British Broadcasting Corporation and Sianel Pedwar Cymru must each observe in the provision of relevant services the code so adopted by them[15]. A broadcaster[16] is prohibited from including in its broadcasting services any party political broadcast made on behalf of a party which is not a registered party registered under the Political Parties, Elections and Referendums Act 2000[17].

1   See the Representation of the People Act 1983 s 93 (substituted by the Political Parties, Elections and Referendums Act 2000 s 144). This replaces the Representation of the People Act 1969 s 9(1) (repealed). See ELECTIONS AND REFERENDUMS vol 15(3) (2007 Reissue) PARA 337.

2   As to candidates see the Representation of the People Act 1983 s 118A; and ELECTIONS AND REFERENDUMS vol 15(3) (2007 Reissue) PARA 237. See also *McAliskey v BBC* [1980] NI 44. The context excludes a candidate who has been elected, although such a person is included in the statutory definitions: *McAliskey v BBC* [1980] NI 44 at 50 per Murray J.

3   As to the duty of impartiality see PARA 895.
4   *Marshall v BBC* [1979] 3 All ER 80 at 82, [1979] 1 WLR 1071 at 1074, CA, per Cumming-Bruce LJ.
5   'Broadcasting authority' means the British Broadcasting Corporation (the 'BBC'), the Office of Communications ('OFCOM') or Sianel Pedwar Cymru: Representation of the People Act 1983 s 93(6) (as substituted (see note 1); s 93(6) amended by the Communications Act 2003 s 406(1), Sch 17 para 62(1), (3)(a)). As to the BBC see PARAS 603–626. As to OFCOM see PARA 507. As to Sianel Pedwar Cymru see PARA 645.
6   'Candidate', in relation to an election, means a candidate standing nominated at the election or included in a list of candidates submitted in connection with it: Representation of the People Act 1983 s 93(6) (as substituted: see note 1).
7   As to the meaning of 'electoral area' see the Representation of the People Act 1983 s 203(1); and ELECTIONS AND REFERENDUMS vol 15(3) (2007 Reissue) PARA 10.
8   'Relevant services', in relation to the BBC or Sianel Pedwar Cymru, means services broadcast by that body; and in relation to OFCOM, means services licensed under the Broadcasting Act 1990 Pt I (ss 3–71) (see PARA 662 et seq) or Pt III (ss 85–126) (see PARA 723 et seq) or the Broadcasting Act 1996 Pt I (ss 1–39) (see PARA 690 et seq) or Pt II (ss 40–72) (see PARA 753 et seq): Representation of the People Act 1983 s 93(6) (as substituted (see note 1); and amended by the Communications Act 2003 Sch 17 para 62(3)(b)). See ELECTIONS AND REFERENDUMS vol 15(3) (2007 Reissue) PARA 337.
9   Representation of the People Act 1983 s 93(1) (as substituted: see note 1). For this purpose, 'the election period', in relation to an election, means the period beginning:
     (1)   (if a parliamentary general election) with the date of the dissolution of Parliament or any earlier time at which Her Majesty's intention to dissolve Parliament is announced;
     (2)   (if a parliamentary by-election) with the date of the issue of the writ for the election or any earlier date on which a certificate of the vacancy is notified in the London Gazette in accordance with the Recess Elections Act 1975; or
     (3)   (if a local government election) with the last date for publication of notice of the election,
     and ending with the close of the poll: s 93(5) (as so substituted). Section 93 does not apply to a City of London municipal election other than a ward election: see s 194(a); and ELECTIONS AND REFERENDUMS vol 15(3) (2007 Reissue) PARA 337.
10   Representation of the People Act 1983 s 93(2) (as substituted: see note 1).
11   Representation of the People Act 1983 s 93(2)(a) (as substituted: see note 1).
12   Representation of the People Act 1983 s 93(2)(b) (as substituted: see note 1).
13   Representation of the People Act 1983 s 93(2) (as substituted: see note 1).
14   Representation of the People Act 1983 s 93(3) (as substituted: see note 1).
15   Representation of the People Act 1983 s 93(4) (as substituted (see note 1); and amended by the Communications Act 2003 Sch 17 para 62(2)).
16   'Broadcaster' means: (1) the holder of a licence under the Broadcasting Act 1990 or 1996; (2) the British Broadcasting Corporation ('BBC'); or (3) Sianel Pedwar Cymru: Political Parties, Elections and Referendums Act 2000 s 37(2). The reference in s 37(1) to a broadcaster includes a reference to the Gibraltar Broadcasting Corporation, but only as respects party political broadcasts relating to elections to the European Parliament: s 37(3) (added by SI 2004/366).
17   Political Parties, Elections and Referendums Act 2000 s 37(1). As to the registration of political parties under s 28, Sch 4 Pt I see CONSTITUTIONAL LAW AND HUMAN RIGHTS vol 8(2) (Reissue) PARA 216 et seq.

894.   Broadcasting from abroad. It is an offence amounting to an illegal practice[1] for any person, with intent to influence persons to give or refrain from giving their votes at a parliamentary, local government[2] or European Parliamentary election[3], to include or aid, abet, counsel or procure the inclusion of any matter relating to the election in any programme service[4] provided from a place outside the United Kingdom[5] otherwise than in pursuance of arrangements made with the BBC[6], S4C[7] or the holder of any licence granted by OFCOM[8], for the reception and retransmission of that matter by that body or the holder of that licence[10].

1   See the Representation of the People Act 1983 s 92(2); and ELECTIONS AND REFERENDUMS vol 15(4) (2007 Reissue) PARA 704. As to prosecutions for illegal practices see s 169; and ELECTIONS AND REFERENDUMS vol 15(4) (2007 Reissue) PARA 886.

2   This does not apply to a City of London municipal election other than a ward election: see the Representation of the People Act 1983 s 194(a); and ELECTIONS AND REFERENDUMS vol 15(3) (2007 Reissue) PARA 337.

3   See the European Parliamentary Elections Act 2002 ss 2, 7(3), (4); and the European Parliamentary Elections Regulations 1999, SI 1999/1214, reg 3(1), Sch 1.

4   As to the meaning of 'programme service' see PARA 507 note 9; definition applied by the Representation of the People Act 1983 s 92(1).

5   As to the meaning of 'United Kingdom' see PARA 510 note 13.

6   As to the BBC see PARAS 603–626.

7   As to the meaning of 'S4C' see PARA 644.

8   As to OFCOM see PARA 507.

10   See the Representation of the People Act 1983 s 92(1) (substituted by the Broadcasting Act 1990 s 203(1), Sch 20 para 35(3), (5); and amended by the Communications Act 2003 s 406(1), Sch 17 para 61); and ELECTIONS AND REFERENDUMS vol 15(3) (2007 Reissue) PARA 337.

895. Due impartiality. The BBC[1] is a body corporate set up and continued by Royal Charter and operating under licence[2]. The BBC is required to transmit an impartial account day by day of the proceedings in both Houses of Parliament[3]. The BBC Trust[4] must, amongst other things, seek to ensure that the BBC gives information about, and increases understanding of, the world through accurate and impartial news, other information, and analysis of current events and ideas[5]. The BBC must do all it can to ensure that controversial subjects are treated with due accuracy and impartiality in all relevant output[6] and the UK public services[7] must not contain any output which expresses the opinion of the BBC or of its Trust or Executive Board[8] on current affairs or matters of public policy other than broadcasting or the provision of online services[9]. The Trust must draw up and from time to time review a code giving guidance as to the rules to be observed in connection with the application of thee requirements and do all it can to secure that the code is complied with[10].

A further requirement imposed on the BBC is that it must observe relevant programme code standards in the provision of the UK public broadcasting services, which involves, inter alia, the omission of material likely to encourage or incite any crime or disorder and the application of generally accepted standards so as to provide adequate protection for members of the public from the inclusion of offensive and harmful material; but only to the extent that they do not concern the accuracy or impartiality of the content of any programme included in the UK public broadcasting services[11].

1   As to the BBC see PARAS 603–626.

2   See the *Royal Charter for the Continuance of the British Broadcasting Corporation* (Cm 6925) (2006); and PARA 603 et seq. The corporation is free from the control of the executive government: *BBC v Johns (Inspector of Taxes)* [1965] Ch 32 at 80–81, [1964] 1 All ER 923 at 942–943 per Diplock LJ.

3   See the *Agreement between Her Majesty's Secretary of State for Culture, Media and Sport and the British Broadcasting Corporation* (Cm 6872) (30 June 2006) cl 6(2)(a). One of the BBC's UK public service television channels is BBC Parliament, a channel providing substantial live coverage of debates and committees of the UK's Parliaments and Assemblies, and other political coverage: see cl 11(2)(h); and PARAS 855 note 6, 615.

4   As to the BBC Trust see PARA 604 et seq.

5   See the *Agreement between Her Majesty's Secretary of State for Culture, Media and Sport and the British Broadcasting Corporation* (Cm 6872) (30 June 2006) cl 6(1).

6   See the *Agreement between Her Majesty's Secretary of State for Culture, Media and Sport and the British Broadcasting Corporation* (Cm 6872) (30 June 2006) cl 44(1). As to the meaning of 'relevant output' see PARA 856 note 9. In applying this requirement a series of programmes may be considered as a whole: cl 44(2). The extent to which the BBC is under a legally enforceable duty of impartiality is not certain: see *Lynch v BBC* [1983] NI 193; *R v Broadcasting Complaints Commission, ex p Owen* [1985] QB 1153, [1985] 2 All ER 522, DC; *Houston v*

BBC 1995 SLT 1305, Ct of Sess. The BBC is to exercise its discretion in good faith as it thinks right: *Grieve v Douglas-Home* 1965 SC 315 at 338 per Lord Kilbrandon. See also *McAliskey v BBC* [1980] NI 44 at 53 per Murray J.

7 As to the meaning of 'UK public services' see PARA 855 note 6.

8 As to the Executive Board of the BBC see PARAS 604, 608 et seq.

9 See the *Agreement between Her Majesty's Secretary of State for Culture, Media and Sport and the British Broadcasting Corporation* (Cm 6872) (30 June 2006) cl 44(3). This does not apply to output which consists of: (1) proceedings in either House of Parliament; (2) proceedings in the Scottish Parliament, the Welsh Assembly or the Northern Ireland Assembly; or (3) proceedings of a local authority or a committee of two or more local authorities: cl 44(4).

10 See the *Agreement between Her Majesty's Secretary of State for Culture, Media and Sport and the British Broadcasting Corporation* (Cm 6872) (30 June 2006) cl 44(5). The rules in the code must, in particular, take account of the following matters: (1) that due impartiality should be preserved by the BBC as respects major matters falling within head (2) of the definition of 'relevant output' (see PARA 856 note 9 head (2)) as well as matters falling within it taken as a whole; and (2) the need to determine what constitutes a series of programmes for the purposes of cl 44(2): cl 44(6). The rules must, in addition, indicate to such extent as the Trust considers appropriate:

(a) what due impartiality does and does not require, either generally or in relation to particular circumstances;

(b) the ways in which due impartiality may be achieved in connection with programmes of particular descriptions;

(c) the period within which a programme should be included in a service if its inclusion is intended to secure that due impartiality is achieved for the purposes of cl 44(1) in connection with that programme and any programme previously included in that service taken together; and

(d) in relation to any inclusion in a service of a series of programmes which is of a description specified in the rules: (i) that the dates and times of the other programmes comprised in the series should be announced at the time when the first programme so comprised is included in that service; or (ii) if that is not practicable, that advance notice should be given by other means of subsequent programmes so comprised which include material intended to secure, or assist in securing, that due impartiality is achieved in connection with the series as a whole;

and the rules must, in particular, indicate that due impartiality does not require absolute neutrality on every issue or detachment from fundamental democratic principles: cl 44(7).

11 See the *Agreement between Her Majesty's Secretary of State for Culture, Media and Sport and the British Broadcasting Corporation* (Cm 6872) (30 June 2006) cl 46; and PARA 856. In exercising its degree of discretion, the BBC was found to be entitled to require the removal of a sequence of shots of aborted foetuses from a party election broadcast: *R v BBC, ex p Pro-Life Alliance Party* [1997] COD 457. See also *R (on the application of ProLife Alliance) v BBC* [2003] UKHL 23, [2004] 1 AC 185, [2003] 2 All ER 977. A requirement similar to that imposed on the BBC is imposed on OFCOM by the Communications Act 2003 ss 319–325, 333: see PARAS 897, 890. As to OFCOM see PARA 507.

896. Party political broadcasts, ministerial broadcasts and referendum campaign broadcasts. In addition to transmitting ministerial broadcasts[1] (which are not normally regarded as party political broadcasts[2]), the BBC[3] makes available time to broadcast party political broadcasts and referendum campaign broadcasts[4]. The BBC Trust[5] must determine which of the UK public broadcasting services[6] are in principle to include party political broadcasts and referendum campaign broadcasts and the basis on which, and the terms and conditions subject to which, such broadcasts are to be included in them[7]. In particular, the Trust may determine, so far as it is permitted so to do[8]: (1) the political parties on whose behalf party political broadcasts may be made; and (2) the length and frequency of party political broadcasts and referendum campaign broadcasts[9].

Provision is made for the inclusion of licence conditions requiring the licence holder to include party political broadcasts in specified services licensed by OFCOM[10]. 'Party political broadcasts' means the series of party political broadcasts, expressly designed to serve the interests of the political parties, which occur at intervals between general elections, the broadcasts on the budget[11], the special series pending a general election (usually known as 'election broadcasts')[12], and the series pending a European Parliamentary election.

The appearance of ministers and of other members of Parliament in political discussion programmes and news commentaries, and references to politicians and to political controversy in news bulletins, are not regarded as party political broadcasting. The purpose of programmes such as these is not to serve the interests of a political party, although, of course, they may do so incidentally. These programmes must, like any other programmes dealing with controversial matters, be impartial[13].

By a direction made by the then Postmaster General[14], the BBC must refrain from transmitting party political broadcasts other than those arranged in agreement with the leading political parties and intended for reception throughout the United Kingdom[15].

Arrangements for a series of political broadcasts between successive general elections are concluded after consultation and consequently television and radio broadcasting periods are allocated to the parties[16]. For the series preceding a general election ('election broadcasts'), a European Parliamentary election, a Scottish Parliamentary election and a Welsh Assembly election, the broadcasting authorities make certain periods available after the election is announced[17].

1   For provisions relating to the BBC see the *Agreement between Her Majesty's Secretary of State for Culture, Media and Sport and the British Broadcasting Corporation* (Cm 6872) (30 June 2006) cl 81; and PARA 892. For provisions relating to ministerial broadcasts by the independent television services and independent radio services see the Broadcasting Act 1990 s 63 (see PARA 659); and the Communications Act 2003 s 333 (see PARA 890). See further CONSTITUTIONAL LAW AND HUMAN RIGHTS vol 8(2) (Reissue) PARA 224.

2   See the *Report of the Committee on Broadcasting* (Cmnd 1753) (1960) para 295.

3   As to the BBC see PARAS 603–626.

4   See the *Agreement between Her Majesty's Secretary of State for Culture, Media and Sport and the British Broadcasting Corporation* (Cm 6872) (30 June 2006) cl 48; and PARA 856. See also CONSTITUTIONAL LAW AND HUMAN RIGHTS vol 8(2) (Reissue) PARA 222. As to the meaning of 'referendum campaign broadcast' see PARA 856 note 17.

5   As to the BBC Trust see PARA 604 et seq.

6   As to the meaning of 'UK public broadcasting services' see PARA 615.

7   See the *Agreement between Her Majesty's Secretary of State for Culture, Media and Sport and the British Broadcasting Corporation* (Cm 6872) (30 June 2006) cl 48(2).

8   Ie by the Political Parties, Elections and Referendums Act 2000 ss 37, 127 (only registered parties and designated organisations to be entitled to party political broadcasts or referendum campaign broadcasts): see CONSTITUTIONAL LAW AND HUMAN RIGHTS; ELECTIONS AND REFERENDUMS vol 15(4) (2007 Reissue) PARA 544.

9   See the *Agreement between Her Majesty's Secretary of State for Culture, Media and Sport and the British Broadcasting Corporation* (Cm 6872) (30 June 2006) cl 48(3).
    See also *R v BBC, ex p Referendum Party* [1997] EMLR 605. In this case, a political party sought judicial review of its allocation of party political broadcasts, claiming that the broadcasters, when allocating 'air time', had included irrational criteria. It was held that the broadcasters had a wide discretion as to the rules they could make in relation to the allocation of broadcasts to ensure that the obligation to ensure impartiality was fulfilled. Impartiality in the present context not only meant fairness of allocation having regard to parity or balance as between political parties of different strengths, popular support and appeal, but also entailed making allowance for any significant current changes in the political arena and for the potential effect of the medium of television itself in advancing or hindering such changes. The broadcasters had applied the criteria in a reasonable way. The weight they gave to such matters as the number of candidates and current levels of support was a matter for them, and the court ought not to intervene unless it thought, as in the present case it did not, that the broadcasters had been irrational in assessing those matters.

10 See the Communications Act 2003 s 333; and PARA 890.

11 Budget broadcasts are perhaps in a special category. The first budget broadcast was made in 1928 by Mr Winston Churchill, then Chancellor of the Exchequer. There was no reply by the Opposition. It was not until 1934 that any Chancellor of the Exchequer would allow a right of reply by the Opposition. In 1983 the Alliance of Liberal and Social Democratic Parties was also permitted a right of reply. In recent years there have on occasions been more than one budget in a year. The Committee on Party Political Broadcasting (see note 16) did not deal with budget broadcasts, which are within the discretion of the broadcasting authorities.

12 See the *Report of the Committee on Broadcasting* (Cmnd 1753) (1960) para 294.

13 See the *Report of the Committee on Broadcasting* (Cmnd 1753) (1960) para 296. As to the duty of impartiality see PARA 895.

14 The direction was made on 6 July 1955 under the then Licence of the British Broadcasting Corporation para 15(4) (corresponding with the current *Agreement between Her Majesty's Secretary of State for Culture, Media and Sport and the British Broadcasting Corporation* (Cm 6872) (30 June 2006) cl 48): see the *Report of the Committee on Broadcasting* (Memoranda) (Cmnd 1819) (1960) paper 2, App 4. As to the Postmaster General see POST OFFICE vol 36(2) (Reissue) PARAS 1–2.

15 See the *Report of the Committee on Broadcasting* (Cmnd 1753) (1960) para 297.

16 The allocation is not regulated by statute. The ad hoc All-party Committee on Party Political Broadcasting allotted broadcasting periods but since 1983 it has been unable to agree on the broadcasting allocation and agreement is presently arrived at by the broadcasters and the 'usual channels': see the *Report of the Hansard Society Commission on Election Campaigns: Agenda for Change* (1991) ch 5. See also *Independent Television Commission, BBC, Radio Authority and S4C: Consultation Paper on the Reform of Party Political Broadcasting* (20 January 1998) Appendix 1 (more appropriate for the BBC to receive representations directly from the various political parties rather than through the Committee); and *BBC News Release on Revisions to Rules on Political Broadcasting* (28 June 1999) (announcing revisions to the allocation of party political broadcasts). The Broadcasters Liaison Group ('BLG') is an informal group of all broadcasters in the United Kingdom which meets from time to time to discuss issues relating to party political and party election broadcasts. The BLG comprises the broadcasters who make airtime available to registered political parties to help them promote their manifestos to the electorate. It meets from time to time to co-ordinate the criteria which each broadcaster applies in determining the amount of airtime to be made available. As to the BLG see further its website, www.broadcastersliaisongroup.org.uk.

17 See the *BBC News Release on Revisions to Rules on Political Broadcasting* (28 June 1999); and note 16.

(3) NEGATIVE CONTENT RESTRAINTS

(i) Programme Standards

897. Programme and fairness standards for television and radio. It is the duty of OFCOM[1] to set, and from time to time to review and revise, such standards for the content of programmes to be included in television and radio services as appear to it best calculated to secure the standards objectives[2]. The standards objectives are:

(1) that persons under the age of 18 are protected;

(2) that material likely to encourage or to incite the commission of crime or to lead to disorder is not included in television and radio services;

(3) that news[3] included in television and radio services is presented with due impartiality and that the impartiality requirements[4] are complied with;

(4) that news included in television and radio services is reported with due accuracy;

(5) that the proper degree of responsibility is exercised with respect to the content of programmes which are religious programmes;

(6) that generally accepted standards are applied to the contents of

television and radio services so as to provide adequate protection for members of the public from the inclusion in such services of offensive and harmful material[5];

(7)   that advertising that contravenes the prohibition on political advertising[6] is not included in television or radio services;

(8)   that the inclusion of advertising which may be misleading, harmful or offensive in television and radio services is prevented;

(9)   that the international obligations of the United Kingdom with respect to advertising included in television and radio services are complied with;

(10)   that the unsuitable sponsorship of programmes included in television and radio services is prevented;

(11)   that there is no undue discrimination between advertisers who seek to have advertisements included in television and radio services; and

(12)   that there is no use of techniques which exploit the possibility of conveying a message to viewers or listeners, or of otherwise influencing their minds, without their being aware, or fully aware, of what has occurred[7].

The standards set by OFCOM under these provisions[8] must be contained in one or more codes[9]. In setting or revising any standards under these provisions, OFCOM must have regard, in particular and to such extent as appears to it to be relevant to the securing of the standards objectives, to each of the following matters: (a) the degree of harm or offence likely to be caused by the inclusion of any particular sort of material in programmes generally, or in programmes of a particular description; (b) the likely size and composition of the potential audience for programmes included in television and radio services generally, or in television and radio services of a particular description; (c) the likely expectation of the audience as to the nature of a programme's content and the extent to which the nature of a programme's content can be brought to the attention of potential members of the audience; (d) the likelihood of persons who are unaware of the nature of a programme's content being unintentionally exposed, by their own actions, to that content; (e) the desirability of securing that the content of services identifies when there is a change affecting the nature of a service that is being watched or listened to and, in particular, a change that is relevant to the application of the standards set under these provisions; and (f) the desirability of maintaining the independence of editorial control over programme content[10].

OFCOM must ensure that the standards from time to time in force under these provisions include: (i) minimum standards applicable to all programmes included in television and radio services; and (ii) such other standards applicable to particular descriptions of programmes, or of television and radio services, as appear to it appropriate for securing the standards objectives[11]. In setting standards, OFCOM must take account of such of the international obligations of the United Kingdom as the Secretary of State may notify to it for these purposes[12].

Provision is made relating to the setting and publication of standards[13] and the observance of the standards code[14].

The regulatory regime for every programme service licensed by a Broadcasting Act licence[15] includes the conditions that OFCOM considers appropriate for securing observance: (A) in connection with the provision of that service; and (B) in relation to the programmes included in that service, of the fairness code[16].

The regulatory regime for every programme service licensed by a Broadcasting Act licence includes the conditions that OFCOM considers appropriate for securing that the procedures which[17] are established and maintained for handling and resolving complaints about the observance of standards[18], and its functions[19] in relation to that service, are brought to the attention of the public (whether by means of broadcasts or otherwise)[20].

1   As to OFCOM see PARA 507.

2   Communications Act 2003 s 319(1).

3   For the purposes of the Communications Act 2003 s 319, 'news' means news in whatever form it is included in a service: s 319(8).

4   Ie the impartiality requirements of the Communications Act 2003 s 320. Section 320 specifies particular requirements placed upon service providers to ensure that programme services are free from undue bias.

5   In the context of broadcasting, 'generally accepted standards' has to be regarded as elusive, and the concept of 'harmful and/or offensive material' has to be moderated in the light of the Convention for the Protection of Human Rights and Fundamental Freedoms (Rome, 4 November 1950; TS 71 (1953); Cmd 8969) art 10 and the domestic and Strasbourg case law: *R (on the application of Gaunt) v OFCOM* [2010] EWHC 1756 (Admin), [2010] NLJR 1045, [2010] All ER (D) 116 (Jul) (here the offensive and abusive nature of the broadcast was gratuitous, having no factual content or justification). The interpretation and application of the predecessor 'offensive material restriction' by the BBC and other broadcasters was reviewed and deemed lawful by the House of Lords in *R (on the application of ProLife Alliance) v British Broadcasting Corpn* [2003] UKHL 23, [2004] 1 AC 185, [2003] 2 All ER 977.

6   Ie set out in the Communications Act 2003 s 321(2). In *R (on the application of Animal Defenders International) v Secretary of State for Culture, Media and Sport* [2008] UKHL 15, [2008] 1 AC 1312, [2008] 3 All ER 193, the appellant sought a declaration of incompatibility under the Human Rights Act 1998 s 4 on account of purported breach of the Convention for the Protection of Human Rights and Fundamental Freedoms (Rome, 4 November 1950; TS 71 (1953); Cmd 8969) art 10 (freedom of expression), but the House of Lords refused to make such an order, finding that the provision was justified under art 10(2); this was notwithstanding the fact that the government had been unable (uniquely) to issue a statement of compatibility with Convention rights under the Human Rights Act 1998 s 19 during the legislative passage of the Communications Bill specifically on account of doubts as to the legitimacy of the provisions enacted as the Communications Act 2003 ss 319, 321.

    As to the objectives for advertisements and sponsorship in general see the Communications Act 2003 s 321. For supplementary powers relating to advertising see s 322.

7   Communications Act 2003 s 319(2). Standards set to secure the standards objective specified in head (5) in the text must, in particular, contain provision designed to secure that religious programmes do not involve: (1) any improper exploitation of any susceptibilities of the audience for such a programme; or (2) any abusive treatment of the religious views and beliefs of those belonging to a particular religion or religious denomination: s 319(6).

8   Ie under the Communications Act 2003 s 319. See the OFCOM Broadcasting Code, the most recent version of which took effect on 20 December 2010. Section Nine of the Code (Television) on Sponsorship, and Section Ten (Television) on Commercial References, were replaced by a new Code Section Nine on Commercial References in Television Programming on 28 February 2011, which relaxes the rules on product placement etc.

9   Communications Act 2003 s 319(3).

10 Communications Act 2003 s 319(4). The Secretary of State may by order modify the list of matters in s 319(4) to which OFCOM is to have regard when setting or revising standards: s 323(1). As to the Secretary of State see PARA 507 note 32. Before making an order under s 323, the Secretary of State must consult OFCOM: s 323(2). No order is to be made containing provision authorised by s 323(1) unless a draft of the order has been laid before Parliament and approved by a resolution of each House: s 323(3). As to the power of the Secretary of State to make orders under the Communications Act 2003 see s 402; and TELECOMMUNICATIONS vol 97 (2010) PARA 77. At the date at which this volume states the law, no order had been made under s 323.

11 Communications Act 2003 s 319(5).

12 Communications Act 2003 s 319(7).

13 See the Communications Act 2003 s 324.

14 See the Communications Act 2003 s 325.

15 As to the meaning of 'Broadcasting Act licence' see PARA 602 note 3.

16   Ie the code for the time being in force under the Broadcasting Act 1996 s 107 (see PARA 906): Communications Act 2003 s 326.
17   Ie by virtue of the Communications Act 2003 s 325.
18   Ie set under the Communications Act 2003 s 319.
19   Ie under the Broadcasting Act 1996 Pt V (ss 107–130).
20   Communications Act 2003 s 328(1). Conditions included in a licence by virtue of s 328(1) may require the holder of the licence to comply with every direction given to him by OFCOM for the purpose mentioned in s 328(1): s 328(2).

898. Power to proscribe unacceptable foreign television and radio services.
Where a foreign service to which the following provisions[1] apply[2] comes to OFCOM's[3] attention, and it considers that the service is unacceptable and should be the subject of an order under these provisions, it must send a notification to the Secretary of State[4] giving details of the service and its reasons for considering that an order should be made[5]. A service is not to be considered unacceptable by OFCOM unless it is satisfied that: (1) programmes containing objectionable matter are included in the service; and (2) the inclusion of objectionable matter in programmes so included is occurring repeatedly[6].

Where the Secretary of State has received a notification under these provisions in the case of a service, he may make an order: (a) identifying the service in such manner as he thinks fit; and (b) proscribing it[7]. The Secretary of State is not to make an order proscribing a service unless he is satisfied that the making of the order is: (i) in the public interest; and (ii) compatible with the international obligations of the United Kingdom[8].

Where a service is for the time being proscribed by an order[9], the proscribed service is not to be included in a multiplex service[10] or a cable package[11]. Where OFCOM determines that there are reasonable grounds for believing that there has been a contravention of the above provision[12] in relation to a multiplex service or a cable package, it may give a notification to the provider of that multiplex service or the person providing the cable package[13]. Such a notification is one which sets out the determination made by OFCOM and requires the person to whom it is given to secure that the proscribed service (so long as it remains proscribed) is not: (A) included in the notified person's multiplex service; or (B) distributed as part of his cable package, at any time more than seven days after the day of the giving of the notification[14]. If it is reasonably practicable for a person to whom a notification is given to secure that the proscribed service ceases to be included in that person's multiplex service, or to be distributed as part of his cable package, before the end of that seven days, then he must do so[15]. It is the duty of a person to whom a notification is given to comply with this last requirement and the requirements imposed by the notification[16].

1   Ie the Communications Act 2003 s 329.
2   A service to which the Communications Act 2003 s 329 applies is a foreign service if it: (1) is a service capable of being received in the United Kingdom for the provision of which no Broadcasting Act licence is either in force or required to be in force; but (2) is also a service for the provision of which such a licence would be required: (a) in the case of a service falling within heads (i)–(iii), if the person providing it were under the jurisdiction of the United Kingdom for the purposes of the Audiovisual Media Services Directive; and (b) in any other case, if the person providing it provided it from a place in the United Kingdom or were a person whose principal place of business is in the United Kingdom: s 329(7) (amended by SI 2009/2979). The television and sound services to which s 329 applies are: (i) television licensable content services provided otherwise than by broadcasting from a satellite; (ii) digital television programme services; (iii) digital additional television services; (iv) radio licensable sound services provided otherwise than by being broadcast from a satellite; (v) digital sound programme services; and (vi) digital additional sound services: s 329(6). As to the meaning of 'United Kingdom' see PARA 510 note 13. As to the meaning of 'Broadcasting Act licence' see PARA 602 note 3. As to the meaning of

'television licensable content service' see PARA 716. As to the meaning of 'digital television programme service' see PARA 602 note 8. As to the Audiovisual Media Services Directive see PARA 857 note 7.

3 As to OFCOM see PARA 507.

4 As to the Secretary of State see PARA 507 note 32.

5 Communications Act 2003 s 329(1).

6 Communications Act 2003 s 329(2). Matter is objectionable for the purposes of s 329(2) only if: (1) it offends against taste or decency; (2) it is likely to encourage or to incite the commission of crime; (3) it is likely to lead to disorder; or (4) it is likely to be offensive to public feeling: s 329(3).

7 Communications Act 2003 s 329(4).

8 Communications Act 2003 s 329(5). As to the meaning of 'international obligation of the United Kingdom' see PARA 512 note 14.

9 Ie under the Communications Act 2003 s 329.

10 In the Communications Act 2003 s 330, 'multiplex service' means a television multiplex service, a radio multiplex service or a general multiplex service: s 330(3). As to the meaning of 'television multiplex service' see PARA 697; and as to the meaning of 'radio multiplex service' see PARA 753; definitions applied by s 362(1). 'General multiplex service' means a multiplex service within the meaning of s 175 (now repealed) which is neither a television multiplex service nor a radio multiplex service: s 362(1).

11 Communications Act 2003 s 330(1), (2). For the purposes of s 330, 'cable package' means (subject to s 330(5)) a service by means of which programme services are packaged together with a view to their being distributed: (1) by means of an electronic communications service; (2) so as to be available for reception by members of the public in the United Kingdom; and (3) without the final delivery of the programme services to the persons to whom they are distributed being by wireless telegraphy: s 330(4). Programme services distributed by means of an electronic communications service do not form part of a cable package if: (a) the distribution of those services forms only part of a service provided by means of that electronic communications service; and (b) the purposes for which the service of which it forms a part is provided do not consist wholly or mainly in making available television programmes or radio programmes (or both) for reception by members of the public: s 330(5). As to the meaning of 'electronic communications service' see TELECOMMUNICATIONS vol 97 (2010) PARA 60. As to the meaning of 'available for reception by members of the public' see PARA 796. As to the meaning of 'wireless telegraphy' see PARA 510 note 1.

12 Ie the Communications Act 2003 s 330.

13 Communications Act 2003 s 331(1). In s 331, 'cable package' and 'multiplex service' each has the same meaning as in s 330 (see notes 10, 11): s 331(6).

14 Communications Act 2003 s 331(2).

15 Communications Act 2003 s 331(3).

16 Communications Act 2003 s 331(4). That duty is enforceable in civil proceedings by OFCOM for an injunction or for any other appropriate remedy or relief: s 331(5).

OFCOM may impose a penalty on a person who contravenes a requirement imposed on him by or under s 331: s 332(1). Before imposing a penalty on a person under s 332 OFCOM must give him a reasonable opportunity of making representations to them about its proposal to impose the penalty: s 332(2). The amount of the penalty imposed on a person is to be such amount not exceeding £5,000 as OFCOM determine to be: (1) appropriate; and (2) proportionate to the contravention in respect of which it is imposed: s 332(3). In making that determination OFCOM must have regard to: (a) any representations made to it by the person notified under s 331; and (b) any steps taken by him for complying with the requirements imposed on him under s 331: s 332(4). Where OFCOM imposes a penalty on a person under s 332, it must: (i) notify the person penalised; and (ii) in that notification, fix a reasonable period after it is given as the period within which the penalty is to be paid: s 332(5). A penalty imposed under s 332 must be paid to OFCOM within the period fixed by it: s 332(6). The Secretary of State may by order amend s 332 so as to substitute a different maximum penalty for the maximum penalty for the time being specified in s 332(3): s 332(7). No order is to be made containing provision authorised by s 332(7) unless a draft of the order has been laid before Parliament and approved by a resolution of each House: s 332(8). For the purposes of s 332 there is a separate contravention in respect of every day on which the proscribed service is at any time included in a person's multiplex service or distributed as part of his cable package: s 332(9). In s 332, 'multiplex service' and 'cable package' each has the same meaning as in s 330 (see notes 10, 11): s 332(10).

899.   Monitoring of programmes. The regulatory regime for every programme service licensed by a Broadcasting Act licence[1] includes conditions imposing on the provider of the service: (1) a requirement in respect of every programme included in the service to retain a recording of the programme in a specified form and for a specified period after its inclusion; (2) a requirement to comply with any request by OFCOM[2] to produce to it for examination or reproduction a recording retained in pursuance of the conditions in the licence; and (3) a requirement, if the provider is able to do so, to comply with any request by OFCOM to produce to it a script or transcript of a programme included in the programme service[3]. For the purpose of maintaining supervision of the programmes included in programme services, OFCOM may itself make and use recordings of those programmes or any part of them[4]. Nothing in Part 3 of the Communications Act 2003[5] is to be construed as requiring OFCOM, in the carrying out of its functions as respects programme services and the programmes included in them, to view or listen to programmes in advance of their being included in such services[6].

1   As to the meaning of 'Broadcasting Act licence' see PARA 602 note 3.
2   As to OFCOM see PARA 507.
3   Communications Act 2003 s 334(1). The period specified for the purposes of a condition under head (1) in the text must be: (1) in the case of a programme included in a television programme service, a period not exceeding 90 days; and (2) in the case of a programme included in a radio programme service, a period not exceeding 42 days: s 334(2). As to the meaning of 'television programme service' see PARA 790 note 5. 'Radio programme service' means any of the following: (a) a service the provision of which is licensed under the Broadcasting Act 1990 Pt III (ss 85–126); (b) a digital sound programme service the provision of which is licensed under the Broadcasting Act 1996 Pt II (ss 40–72); (c) a digital additional sound service the provision of which is licensed under the Broadcasting Act 1996 s 64 (see PARA 780): Communications Act 2003 s 362(1).
4   Communications Act 2003 s 334(3).
5   Ie the Communications Act 2003 Pt 3 (ss 198–362).
6   Communications Act 2003 s 334(4).

900.   The BBC's archives and retention of recordings. The Executive Board[1] must make arrangements for the maintenance of an archive, or archives, of films, sound recordings, other recorded material and printed material which is representative of the sound and television programmes and films broadcast or otherwise distributed by the BBC[2]. Those arrangements: (1) must ensure that every such archive is kept safely, to commonly accepted standards; and (2) must give the public reasonable opportunities to visit the archives and view or listen to material kept there, with or without charge (as the Executive Board thinks fit)[3]. In making those arrangements, the Executive Board must consult such designated bodies[4] as are engaged in maintaining sound, television and film archives as it considers appropriate[5]. The BBC must not destroy, sell or otherwise dispose of any material that it has broadcast or otherwise distributed which it decides not to preserve in any archive without first offering that material, free of charge, to such designated bodies as are engaged in maintaining sound, television and film archives as it considers appropriate[6]. Where the BBC's offer is accepted by any body or bodies, the BBC must transfer the material to that body or those bodies[7].

The BBC must: (a) in respect of every programme included in any of the UK public broadcasting services or a UK public on-demand programme service[8], retain a recording of the programme in an agreed[9] form, and for an agreed period; (2) comply with any request to produce such recordings to OFCOM[10] for examination or reproduction; and (3) comply, to the extent that it is able to do so, with any request to produce to OFCOM a script or transcript of a programme included in any of the UK public broadcasting services or a UK public on-demand programme service[11]. Any period agreed for these purposes must be, in the case of a UK public television service, a period which does not exceed 90 days, in the case of a UK public on-demand programme service, a period which does not exceed 42 days, and, in the case of a radio service, a period which does not exceed 42 days[12].

A government minister may direct the BBC to monitor and (where applicable) record specified media output[13], and to supply other services in that connection (including, for example, the preparation and distribution of products such as monitoring reports and digests of broadcast or other material)[14]. In complying with such a direction, the BBC is to be regarded as an agent of the Crown, and to be acting in the public interest[15].

1   As to the Executive Board see PARA 604.

2   *Agreement between Her Majesty's Secretary of State for Culture, Media and Sport and the British Broadcasting Corporation* (Cm 6872) (30 June 2006) cl 86(1). As to the meaning of 'BBC' see PARA 603.

3   *Agreement between Her Majesty's Secretary of State for Culture, Media and Sport and the British Broadcasting Corporation* (Cm 6872) (30 June 2006) cl 86(2).

4   For these purposes, 'designated body' means a body that is designated by order of the Secretary of State for Trade and Industry under the Copyright, Designs and Patents Act 1988 s 75 (see COPYRIGHT, DESIGN RIGHT AND RELATED RIGHTS vol 9(2) (2006 Reissue) PARA 403): *Agreement between Her Majesty's Secretary of State for Culture, Media and Sport and the British Broadcasting Corporation* (Cm 6872) (30 June 2006) cl 86(6).

5   *Agreement between Her Majesty's Secretary of State for Culture, Media and Sport and the British Broadcasting Corporation* (Cm 6872) (30 June 2006) cl 86(3).

6   *Agreement between Her Majesty's Secretary of State for Culture, Media and Sport and the British Broadcasting Corporation* (Cm 6872) (30 June 2006) cl 86(4).

7   *Agreement between Her Majesty's Secretary of State for Culture, Media and Sport and the British Broadcasting Corporation* (Cm 6872) (30 June 2006) cl 86(5).

8   As to the meaning of 'UK public broadcasting services' see PARA 615 note 15. As to the meaning of 'UK public on-demand programme service' for these purposes see PARA 618 note 2. As to the meaning of 'service' see PARA 855 note 6.

9   For these purposes, 'agreed' means agreed in accordance with the *Agreement between Her Majesty's Secretary of State for Culture, Media and Sport and the British Broadcasting Corporation* (Cm 6872) (30 June 2006) cl 92 (see PARA 855 note 4): cl 62(3).

10 As to OFCOM see PARA 507.

11 *Agreement between Her Majesty's Secretary of State for Culture, Media and Sport and the British Broadcasting Corporation* (Cm 6872) (30 June 2006) cl 62(1) (amended by Cm 7853, March 2010).

12 *Agreement between Her Majesty's Secretary of State for Culture, Media and Sport and the British Broadcasting Corporation* (Cm 6872) (30 June 2006) cl 62(2) (amended by Cm 7853, March 2010).

13 For these purposes, the reference to media output is a reference to any sound, text, data, still or moving pictures or other content carried by means of an electronic communications network or an electronic communications service (within the meaning of the Communications Act 2003) (see TELECOMMUNICATIONS vol 97 (2010) PARA 60), and in any print medium, and includes the output of any news agency; and 'specified' means specified in a direction under the *Agreement between Her Majesty's Secretary of State for Culture, Media and Sport and the British Broadcasting Corporation* (Cm 6872) (30 June 2006) cl 88(1): cl 88(2).

14 *Agreement between Her Majesty's Secretary of State for Culture, Media and Sport and the British Broadcasting Corporation* (Cm 6872) (30 June 2006) cl 88(1).

15 *Agreement between Her Majesty's Secretary of State for Culture, Media and Sport and the British Broadcasting Corporation* (Cm 6872) (30 June 2006) cl 88(3).

(ii) International Obligations

901. Conditions securing compliance with international obligations. The regulatory regime for every service to which these provisions[1] apply[2] includes the conditions that OFCOM[3] considers appropriate for securing that the relevant international obligations of the United Kingdom[4] are complied with[5]. The conditions included in any licence in accordance with the other provisions of Chapter 4 of Part 3 of the Communications Act 2003[6] are in addition to any conditions included in that licence in pursuance of these provisions[7] and have effect subject to them[8].

1 As to OFCOM see PARA 507.
2 Ie the Communications Act 2003 s 335.
3 The Communications Act 2003 s 335 applies to the following services: (1) any Channel 3 service; (2) Channel 4; (3) Channel 5; (4) the public teletext service; (5) any television licensable content service; (6) any digital television programme service; (7) any additional television service; (8) any digital additional television service; (9) any restricted television service: s 335(3). As to the meaning of 'Channel 3 service' see PARA 602 note 8. As to the meaning of 'Channel 4' see PARA 602 note 9. As to the meaning of 'Channel 5' see PARA 602 note 10. As to the public teletext service see PARA 686. As to the meaning of 'television licensable content service' see PARA 716. As to the meaning of 'digital television programme service' see PARA 602 note 8.
4 For the purposes of the Communications Act 2003 s 335, 'relevant international obligations of the United Kingdom' means the international obligations of the United Kingdom which have been notified to OFCOM by the Secretary of State for the purposes of s 335: s 335(2). As to the meaning of 'international obligation of the United Kingdom' see PARA 512 note 14. As to the Secretary of State see PARA 507 note 32.
5 Communications Act 2003 s 335(1).
6 Ie the Communications Act 2003 Pt 3 Ch 4 (ss 263–347).
7 Ie the Communications Act 2003 s 335.
8 Communications Act 2003 s 335(4).

902. Co-operation with other member states. Where OFCOM[1] receives a request[2] from another member state relating to a relevant broadcaster, and considers that the request is substantiated, it must ask the broadcaster to comply with the rule identified in that request[3]. For these purposes, 'relevant broadcaster' means: (1) the BBC[4]; (2) C4C[5]; (3) the Welsh Authority[6]; or (4) the holder of (a) a Channel 3 licence[7]; (b) a Channel 5 licence[8]; or (c) a licence to provide any relevant regulated television service[9].

1 As to OFCOM see PARA 507.
2 Ie under the Audiovisual Media Services Directive art 4. As to the Audiovisual Media Services Directive see PARA 857 note 7.
3 Communications Act 2003 s 335A(1) (s 335A added by SI 2009/2979; Communications Act 2003 s 335A(1) amended by SI 2010/1883).
4 As to the meaning of 'BBC' see PARA 603 note 1; and as to the BBC see PARAS 603–626.
5 As to the meaning of 'C4C' see PARA 627 note 1.
6 As to the meaning of 'the Welsh Authority' see PARA 644 note 3; and as to television broadcasting by the Welsh Authority see PARAS 644–661.
7 As to the meaning of 'Channel 3 licence' see PARA 664 note 1.
8 As to Channel 5 licences see PARA 681.
9 Communications Act 2003 s 335A(2) (as added: see note 3). The text refers to a relevant regulated television service within the meaning of the Broadcasting Act 1990 s 13(1): see PARA 593.

(iii) On-demand Programme Services

903. Prohibited content. An on-demand programme service[1] must not contain any material likely to incite hatred based on race, sex, religion or nationality[2]. If an on-demand programme service contains material which might seriously impair the physical, mental or moral development of persons under the age of 18, the material must be made available in a manner which secures that such persons will not normally see or hear it[3].

Advertising of cigarettes or other tobacco products[4] and any prescription-only medicine[5] is prohibited in on-demand programme services[6]. Advertising of alcoholic drinks is prohibited in on-demand programme services unless it is not aimed at persons under the age of 18 and it does not encourage excessive consumption of such drinks[7].

Advertising included in an on-demand programme service must be readily recognisable as such and must not use techniques which exploit the possibility of conveying a message subliminally or surreptitiously[8]. Advertising included in an on-demand programme service must not:

(1)   prejudice respect for human dignity;

(2)   include or promote discrimination based on sex, racial or ethnic origin, nationality, religion or belief, disability, age or sexual orientation;

(3)   encourage behaviour prejudicial to health or safety;

(4)   encourage behaviour grossly prejudicial to the protection of the environment;

(5)   cause physical or moral detriment to persons under the age of 18;

(6)   directly exhort such persons to purchase or rent goods or services in a manner which exploits their inexperience or credulity;

(7)   directly encourage such persons to persuade their parents or others to purchase or rent goods or services;

(8)   exploit the trust of such persons in parents, teachers or others; or

(9)   unreasonably show such persons in dangerous situations[9].

1   As to the meaning of 'on-demand programme service' see PARA 784.
2   Communications Act 2003 s 368E(1) (ss 368E, 368F, 368R added by SI 2009/2979). As to enforcement see PARA 868.
3   Communications Act 2003 s 368E(2) (as added: see note 2).
4   'Tobacco product' has the meaning given in the Tobacco Advertising and Promotion Act 2002 s 1 (see SALE OF GOODS AND SUPPLY OF SERVICES vol 41 (2005 Reissue) PARA 626): Communications Act 2003 s 368R(1) (as added: see note 2).
5   'Prescription-only medicine' means a medicinal product of a description or falling within a class specified in an order made under the Medicines Act 1968 s 58 (see MEDICINAL PRODUCTS AND DRUGS vol 30(2) (Reissue) PARA 140): Communications Act 2003 s 368R(1) (as added: see note 2).
6   Communications Act 2003 s 368F(1) (as added: see note 2). Section 368F does not apply to the BBC: see s 368P(1); and PARA 871. As to the meaning of 'BBC' see PARA 603 note 1; and as to the BBC see PARAS 603–626.
7   Communications Act 2003 s 368F(2) (as added: see note 2).
8   Communications Act 2003 s 368F(3) (as added: see note 2). As to when advertising is included in an on-demand service see PARA 881 note 6.
9   Communications Act 2003 s 368F(4) (as added: see note 2).

904.   Sponsorship of programme or service.   An on-demand programme service[1] or a programme[2] included in an on-demand programme service must not be sponsored: (1) for the purpose of promoting cigarettes or other tobacco products[3]; or (2) by an undertaking whose principal activity is the manufacture or sale of cigarettes or other tobacco products[4]. An on-demand programme service or a programme included in an on-demand programme service must not be sponsored for the purpose of promoting a prescription-only medicine[5]. An on-demand programme service may not include a news programme or current affairs programme that is sponsored[6].

The following provisions[7] apply to an on-demand programme service that is sponsored[8] or that includes any programme that is sponsored[9]. The sponsoring of a service or programme must not influence the content of that service or programme in a way that affects the editorial independence of the provider of the service[10]. Where a service or programme is sponsored for the purpose of promoting goods or services, the sponsored service or programme and sponsorship announcements[11] relating to it must not directly encourage the purchase or rental of the goods or services, whether by making promotional reference to them or otherwise[12]. Where a service or programme is sponsored for the purpose of promoting an alcoholic drink, the service or programme and sponsorship announcements relating to it must not be aimed specifically at persons under the age of 18 or encourage the immoderate consumption of such drinks[13].

A sponsored service must clearly inform users of the existence of a sponsorship agreement[14]. The name of the sponsor and the logo or other symbol (if any) of the sponsor must be displayed at the beginning or end of a sponsored programme[15]. Techniques which exploit the possibility of conveying a message subliminally or surreptitiously must not be used in a sponsorship announcement[16]. A sponsorship announcement must not:

(a) prejudice respect for human dignity;

(b) include or promote discrimination based on sex, racial or ethnic origin, nationality, religion or belief, disability, age or sexual orientation;

(c) encourage behaviour prejudicial to health or safety;

(d) encourage behaviour grossly prejudicial to the protection of the environment;

(e) cause physical or moral detriment to persons under the age of eighteen;

(f) directly encourage such persons to persuade their parents or others to purchase or rent goods or services;

(g) exploit the trust of such persons in parents, teachers or others; or

(h) unreasonably show such persons in dangerous situations[17].

1 As to the meaning of 'on-demand programme service' see PARA 784.

2 As to the meaning of 'programme' see PARA 602 note 12.

3 As to the meaning of 'tobacco products' see PARA 903 note 4.

4 Communications Act 2003 s 368G(1) (s 368G added by SI 2009/2979). As to enforcement see PARA 868. The Communications Act 2003 s 368G does not apply to the BBC: see s 368P(1); and PARA 871. As to the meaning of 'BBC' see PARA 603 note 1; and as to the BBC see PARAS 603–626.

5 Communications Act 2003 s 368G(2) (as added (see note 4); and amended by SI 2010/419). As to when a programme is included in an on-demand service see PARA 784 note 2. As to the meaning of 'prescription-only medicine' see PARA 903 note 5.

6 Communications Act 2003 s 368G(3) (as added: see note 4).

7 Ie the Communications Act 2003 s 368G(5)–(11).

8 For the purposes of the Communications Act 2003 Pt 4A (ss 368A–368R) an on-demand programme service is 'sponsored' if a person ('the sponsor') other than the provider of the service has met some or all of the costs of providing the service for the purpose of promoting the name, trademark, image, activities, services or products of the sponsor or another person: s 368G(15) (as added: see note 4). For the purposes of s 368G(15) a person is not to be taken to have met some or all of the costs of providing a service only because a programme included in the service is sponsored by that person: s 368G(16) (as so added).

9 Communications Act 2003 s 368G(4) (as added: see note 4). For the purposes of Pt 4A a programme included in an on-demand programme service is 'sponsored' if a person ('the sponsor') other than: (1) the provider of that service; or (2) the producer of that programme, has met some or all of the costs of the programme for the purpose of promoting the name, trademark, image, activities, services or products of the sponsor or of another person: s 368G(12) (as so added). But a programme is not sponsored if it falls within s 368G only by

virtue of the inclusion of product placement (see s 368H(1); and PARA 905) or prop placement (see s 368H(2); and PARA 905): s 368G(13) (as so added). For the purposes of s 368G(12) a person meets some or all of the costs of a programme included in a service only if that person makes a payment or provides other resources for the purpose of meeting or saving some or all of the costs of: (a) producing that programme; (b) transmitting that programme; or (c) making that programme available as part of the service: s 368G(14) (as so added).

10 Communications Act 2003 s 368G(5) (as added: see note 4).

11 'Sponsorship announcement' means: (1) anything included for the purpose of complying with the Communications Act 2003 s 368G(8) or (9) (see the text to notes 14–15); and (2) anything included at the same time as or otherwise in conjunction with anything within head (1): s 368G(17) (as added: see note 4).

12 Communications Act 2003 s 368G(6) (as added: see note 4).

13 Communications Act 2003 s 368G(7) (as added: see note 4).

14 Communications Act 2003 s 368G(8) (as added: see note 4).

15 Communications Act 2003 s 368G(9) (as added: see note 4).

16 Communications Act 2003 s 368G(10) (as added: see note 4).

17 Communications Act 2003 s 368G(11) (as added: see note 4).

905. Product placement. 'Product placement', in relation to a programme[1] included in an on-demand programme service[2], means the inclusion in the programme of, or of a reference to, a product, service or trade mark[3], where the inclusion: (1) is for a commercial purpose; (2) is in return for the making of any payment, or the giving of other valuable consideration, to any relevant provider or any connected[4] person[5]; and (3) is not prop placement[6].

'Prop placement', in relation to a programme included in an on-demand programme service, means the inclusion in the programme of, or of a reference to, a product, service or trade mark where: (a) the provision of the product, service or trade mark has no significant value[7]; and (b) no relevant provider, or person connected with a relevant provider, has received any payment or other valuable consideration in relation to its inclusion in, or the reference to it in, the programme, disregarding the costs saved by including the product, service or trademark, or a reference to it, in the programme[8].

Product placement is prohibited in children's programmes[9] included in on-demand programme services[10]. Product placement is prohibited in on-demand programme services if: (i) it is of cigarettes or other tobacco products[11]; (ii) it is by or on behalf of an undertaking whose principal activity is the manufacture or sale of cigarettes or other tobacco products; or (iii) it is of prescription-only medicines[12].

Product placement of alcoholic drinks must not be aimed specifically at persons under the age of 18 or encourage immoderate consumption of such drinks[13]. Product placement is otherwise permitted in programmes included in on-demand programme services provided that conditions A to F are met and, if the programme featuring the product placement has been produced or commissioned by the provider of the service or any connected person[14], condition G is also met[15].

Condition A is that the programme in which the product, service or trademark, or the reference to it, is included is: (A) a film made for cinema[16]; (B) a film or series made for a television programme service or for an on-demand programme service; (C) a sports programme; or (D) a light entertainment programme[17].

Condition B is that the product placement has not influenced the content of the programme in a way that affects the editorial independence of the provider of the service[18].

Condition C is that the product placement does not directly encourage the purchase or rental of goods or services, whether by making promotional reference to those goods or services or otherwise[19].

Condition D is that the programme does not give undue prominence to the products, services or trade marks concerned[20].

Condition E is that the product placement does not use techniques which exploit the possibility of conveying a message subliminally or surreptitiously[21].

Condition F is that the way in which the product, service or trade mark, or the reference to it, is included in the programme by way of product placement does not:

(aa) prejudice respect for human dignity;

(bb) promote discrimination based on sex, racial or ethnic origin, nationality, religion or belief, disability, age or sexual orientation;

(cc) encourage behaviour prejudicial to health or safety;

(dd) encourage behaviour grossly prejudicial to the protection of the environment;

(ee) cause physical or moral detriment to persons under the age of 18;

(ff) directly encourage such persons to persuade their parents or others to purchase or rent goods or services;

(gg) exploit the trust of such persons in parents, teachers or others; or

(hh) unreasonably show such persons in dangerous situations[22].

Condition G is that the on-demand programme service in question signals appropriately the fact that product placement is contained in a programme, no less frequently than at the start and end of such a programme and, in the case of an on-demand programme service which includes advertising breaks within it, at the recommencement of the programme after each such advertising break[23].

1 As to the meaning of 'programme' see PARA 602 note 12. For these purposes, 'programme' does not include an advertisement: Communications Act 2003 s 368H(16) (s 368H added by SI 2009/2979; definition added by SI 2010/831). The Communications Act 2003 s 368H applies only in relation to programmes the production of which begins after 19 December 2009: s 368H(15) (as so added).

2 As to the meaning of 'on-demand programme service' see PARA 784. As to when a programme is included in an on-demand service see PARA 784 note 2.

3 'Trade mark', in relation to a business, includes any image (such as a logo) or sound commonly associated with that business or its products or services: Communications Act 2003 s 368H(16) (as added: see note 1).

4 As to the meaning of 'connected' see PARA 674 note 13; definition applied by the Communications Act 2003 s 368H(16) (as added: see note 1).

5 As to the meaning of 'person' see PARA 510 note 1.

6 Communications Act 2003 s 368H(1) (as added: see note 1).

7 'Significant value' means a residual value that is more than trivial; and 'residual value' means any monetary or other economic value in the hands of the relevant provider other than the cost saving of including the product, service or trademark, or a reference to it, in a programme: Communications Act 2003 s 368H(16) (as added: see note 1). 'Relevant provider', in relation to a programme, means: (1) the provider of the on-demand programme service in which the programme is included; and (2) the producer of the programme; and 'producer', in relation to a programme, means the person by whom the arrangements necessary for the making of the programme are undertaken: s 368H(16) (as so added).

8 Communications Act 2003 s 368H(2) (as added: see note 1).

9 As to the meaning of 'children's programme' see PARA 881 note 7.

10 Communications Act 2003 s 368H(3) (as added: see note 1).

11 As to the meaning of 'tobacco product' see PARA 903 note 4.

12 Communications Act 2003 s 368H(4) (as added: see note 1). As to the meaning of 'prescription-only medicine' see PARA 903 note 5.

13 Communications Act 2003 s 368H(5) (as added: see note 1).

14 Ie if the Communications Act 2003 s 368H(14) applies.

15 Communications Act 2003 s 368H(6) (as added: see note 1).
16 'Film made for cinema' means a film made with a view to its being shown to the general public
    first in a cinema: Communications Act 2003 s 368H(16) (as added: see note 1).
17 Communications Act 2003 s 368H(7) (as added: see note 1).
18 Communications Act 2003 s 368H(8) (as added: see note 1).
19 Communications Act 2003 s 368H(9) (as added: see note 1).
20 Communications Act 2003 s 368H(10) (as added: see note 1).
21 Communications Act 2003 s 368H(11) (as added: see note 1).
22 Communications Act 2003 s 368H(12) (as added: see note 1).
23 Communications Act 2003 s 368H(13) (as added: see note 1). This condition applies where the
    programme featuring the product placement has been produced or commissioned by the
    provider of the service or any connected person: s 368H(14) (as so added).

(iv) Fairness and Complaints

**906.   Code relating to avoidance of unjust or unfair treatment or interference
with privacy.** It is the duty of OFCOM[1] to draw up, and from time to time
review, a code giving guidance as to principles to be observed, and practices to be
followed, in connection with the avoidance of unjust or unfair treatment[2] in
programmes to which these provisions apply[3], or unwarranted infringement of
privacy in, or in connection with the obtaining of material included in, such
programmes[4]. From time to time OFCOM must publish the code (as for the time
being in force)[5]. Before drawing up or revising the code, OFCOM must consult
each broadcasting body[6], and such other persons as appears to OFCOM to be
appropriate[7].

1   As to OFCOM see PARA 507.
2   'Unjust or unfair treatment' includes treatment which is unjust or unfair because of the way in
    which material included in a programme has been selected or arranged: Broadcasting Act 1996
    s 130(1). 'Programme' includes an advertisement and a teletext transmission; and, in relation to
    a service, includes any item included in that service: s 130(1).
3   The Broadcasting Act 1996 s 107 applies to: (1) any programme broadcast by the BBC
    (s 107(5)(a)); (2) any programme broadcast by the Welsh Authority or included in any public
    service of the Welsh Authority (within the meaning of the Communications Act 2003 Sch 12
    Pt 2 (paras 3–24): see PARA 655) (Broadcasting Act 1996 s 107(5)(b) (amended by the
    Communications Act 2003 Sch 15 para 133)); and (3) any programme included in a licensed
    service (Broadcasting Act 1996 s 107(5)(c)). As to the meaning of 'broadcast' see PARA 668
    note 2; definition applied by s 147(2). As to the meaning of 'BBC' see PARA 603 note 1; and as
    to the BBC see PARAS 603–626. As to the meaning of 'the Welsh Authority' see PARA 644 note 3;
    definition applied by s 147(2). As to television broadcasting by the Welsh Authority see PARAS
    644–661.
        'Licensed service' means: (a) any television programme service which is licensed under the
    Broadcasting Act 1990 Pt I (ss 3–71); (b) the public teletext service; (c) any relevant independent
    radio service; (d) any additional service which is licensed under the Broadcasting Act 1990 Pt I
    (ss 3–71); (e) any digital programme service which is licensed under the Broadcasting Act 1996
    Pt I (ss 1–39); (f) any qualifying service provided by a person other than the Welsh Authority; (g)
    any digital sound programme service which is licensed under the Broadcasting Act 1996 Pt II
    (ss 40–72); (h) any simulcast radio service; and (i) any digital additional service which is licensed
    under the Broadcasting Act 1996 Pt I or Pt II: s 130(1) (amended by the Communications
    Act 2003 s 406(7), Sch 15 para 137, Sch 19).
        As to the meaning of 'television programme service' see PARA 790 note 5; as to the public
    teletext service see PARA 686; as to the meaning of 'relevant independent radio services' see PARA
    724 note 3; as to the meaning of 'additional service' see PARA 703; as to the meaning of 'digital
    programme service' see PARA 690 note 23; as to the meaning of 'qualifying service' see PARA 690
    note 23; as to the meaning of 'digital sound programme service' see PARA 754 note 28; as to the
    meaning of 'simulcast radio service' see PARA 754 note 12; and as to the meaning of 'digital
    additional service' see PARA 690 note 28.
4   Broadcasting Act 1996 s 107(1) (amended by the Communications Act 2003 s 360(3), Sch 15
    para 132(1), (2)).

5 Broadcasting Act 1996 s 107(3) (amended by the Communications Act 2003 Sch 15 para 132(2)).
6 Broadcasting Act 1996 s 107(4)(a) (amended by the Communications Act 2003 Sch 15 para 132(2), Sch 19). 'Broadcasting body' means the BBC or the Welsh Authority: Broadcasting Act 1996 s 130(1).
7 Broadcasting Act 1996 s 107(4)(b) (amended by the Communications Act 2003 Sch 15 para 132(2)).

907. Complaints of unjust or unfair treatment or unwarranted infringement of privacy. A fairness complaint[1] may be made by an individual or by a body of persons, whether incorporated or not, but, subject to the following provisions, must not be entertained by OFCOM[2] unless made by the person affected[3] or by a person authorised by him to make the complaint for him[4]. Where the person affected is an individual who has died, a fairness complaint may be made by his personal representative or by a member of the family of the person affected, or by some other person or body closely connected with him (whether as his employer, or as a body of which he was at his death a member, or in any other way)[5]. Where the person affected is an individual who is for any reason both unable to make a complaint himself and unable to authorise another person to do so for him, a fairness complaint may be made by a member of the family of the person affected, or by some other person or body closely connected with him (whether as his employer, or as a body of which he is a member, or in any other way)[6].

OFCOM must not entertain, or proceed with the consideration of, a fairness complaint if it appears to it that the complaint relates to the broadcasting[7] of the relevant programme[8], or to its inclusion in a licensed service[9], on an occasion more than five years after the death of the person affected, unless it appears to it that in the particular circumstances it is appropriate to do so[10]. OFCOM may refuse to entertain a fairness complaint if it appears to it not to have been made within a reasonable time after the last occasion on which the relevant programme was broadcast or, as the case may be, included in a licensed service[11]. OFCOM may refuse to entertain:

(1) a fairness complaint which is a complaint of unjust or unfair treatment if the person named as the person affected was not himself the subject of the treatment complained of and it appears to OFCOM that he did not have a sufficiently direct interest in the subject matter of that treatment to justify the making of a complaint with him as the person affected[12]; or

(2) a complaint made[13] by a person other than the person affected or a person authorised by him, if it appears to OFCOM that the complainant's connection with the person affected is not sufficiently close to justify the making of the complaint by him[14].

1 'Fairness complaint' means a complaint to OFCOM in respect of any of the matters referred to in the Broadcasting Act 1996 s 110(1)(a), (b): ss 110(4), 130(1) (s 110(4) amended by the Communications Act 2003 s 360(3), Sch 15 para 132(1), (2)).
2 As to OFCOM see PARA 507.
3 'The person affected': (1) in relation to any such unjust or unfair treatment as is mentioned in the Broadcasting Act 1996 s 110(1) (see PARA 874), means a participant in the programme in question who was the subject of that treatment or a person who, whether such a participant or not, had a direct interest in the subject matter of that treatment; and (2) in relation to any such unwarranted infringement of privacy as is so mentioned, means a person whose privacy was infringed: s 130(1). As to the meaning of 'person' see PARA 510 note 1. The term 'direct interest' is to be construed broadly because there is a discretion to entertain the application of persons who have a direct interest in the subject matter of the treatment complained of but whose

interest is not sufficiently direct to justify the making of a complaint with the applicant as the person affected: see *R v Broadcasting Complaints Commission, ex p Channel Four Television Corpn Ltd* [1995] EMLR 170. As to the meaning of 'unjust or unfair treatment' see PARA 906 note 2. 'Participant', in relation to a programme, means a person who appeared, or whose voice was heard, in the programme: Broadcasting Act 1996 s 130(1). As to the meaning of 'programme' see PARA 906 note 2.

4   Broadcasting Act 1996 s 111(1) (amended by the Communications Act 2003 Sch 15 para 132(2)).

5   Broadcasting Act 1996 s 111(2).

6   Broadcasting Act 1996 s 111(3).

7   As to the meaning of 'broadcast' see PARA 668 note 2; definition applied by the Broadcasting Act 1996 s 147(2).

8   'The relevant programme', in relation to a complaint, means the programme to which the complaint relates: Broadcasting Act 1996 s 130(1).

9   As to the meaning of 'licensed service' see PARA 906 note 3.

10 Broadcasting Act 1996 s 111(4) (amended by the Communications Act 2003 Sch 15 para 132(2)).

11 Broadcasting Act 1996 s 111(5) (amended by the Communications Act 2003 Sch 15 para 132(2)). Where, in the case of a fairness complaint, the relevant programme was broadcast or included in a licensed service after the death of the person affected, the Broadcasting Act 1996 s 111(5) applies as if at the end there were added 'within five years (or such longer period as may be allowed by OFCOM in the particular case under s 111(4) (see the text and note 10)) after the death of the person affected': s 111(6) (amended by the Communications Act 2003 Sch 15 para 132(2)).

12 Broadcasting Act 1996 s 111(7)(a) (amended by the Communications Act 2003 Sch 15 para 132(2)). OFCOM can act reasonably in refusing to investigate a complaint, which it has jurisdiction to hear, if this would require it to express views on issues outside the scope of what was unjust and unfair treatment in a broadcast: see *R v Broadcasting Complaints Commission, ex p Owen* [1985] QB 1153, [1985] 2 All ER 522, DC (decided in relation to the Broadcasting Complaints Commission, whose functions have now been transferred to OFCOM). It is necessary to establish an objective causal nexus between the complainant and the actual contents of the programme before considering the question of unfairness: see *R v Broadcasting Complaints Commission, ex p BBC* [1994] EMLR 497. Those who collectively, as opposed to individually, are aggrieved by what they regard as biased, unbalanced representations of contemporary issues may have a right of complaint: see *R v Broadcasting Complaints Commission, ex p BBC* [1995] EMLR 241 (*R v Broadcasting Complaints Commission, ex p Granada Television Ltd* [1995] EMLR 163, CA; and *R v Broadcasting Complaints Commission, ex p Channel Four Television Corpn Ltd* [1995] EMLR 170 (see note 3) not followed).

13 Ie a complaint made under the Broadcasting Act 1996 s 111(2) or (3): see the text and notes 5–6.

14 Broadcasting Act 1996 s 111(7)(b) (amended by the Communications Act 2003 Sch 15 para 132(2)).

908.   Supplementary provisions as to making of complaints. A fairness complaint[1] must be in writing, or in such other form as OFCOM[2] may allow, and must give particulars of the matters complained of[3]. OFCOM must not entertain, or proceed with the consideration of a fairness complaint if it appears to it[4]:

(1)   that the matter complained of is the subject of proceedings in a court of law in the United Kingdom[5]; or

(2)   that the matter complained of is a matter in respect of which the complainant or the person affected[6] has a remedy by way of proceedings in a court of law in the United Kingdom, and that in the particular circumstances it is not appropriate for OFCOM to consider a complaint about it[7]; or

(3)   that the complaint is frivolous[8]; or

(4)   that for any other reason it is inappropriate for it to entertain, or proceed with the consideration of the complaint[9].

1   As to the meaning of 'fairness complaint' see PARA 907 note 1.
2   As to OFCOM see PARA 507.
3   Broadcasting Act 1996 s 114(1) (amended by the Communications Act 2003 ss 360(3), 406(7), Sch 15 para 132(1), (2), Sch 19).
4   Broadcasting Act 1996 s 114(2) (amended by the Communications Act 2003 Sch 15 para 132(2), Sch 19).
5   Broadcasting Act 1996 s 114(2)(a). See also *R v Broadcasting Complaints Commission, ex p Thames Television Ltd* (1982) Times, 8 October, where a writ for libel was issued by the programme contractor against a newspaper in respect of a feature article dealing with the programme, the complaint and the programme contractor's denial of the complaint; and the matters complained of were held to be the subject of proceedings. As to the meaning of 'United Kingdom' see PARA 510 note 13.
6   As to the meaning of 'the person affected' see PARA 907 note 3.
7   Broadcasting Act 1996 s 114(2)(b) (amended by the Communications Act 2003 Sch 15 para 132(2), Sch 19). See also *R v Broadcasting Complaints Commission, ex p BBC* (1984) 128 Sol Jo 384, CA (decided in relation to the Broadcasting Complaints Commission, whose functions have now been transferred to OFCOM), where the complainant had a potential alternative remedy against the broadcasting body in libel, but it was held that there were no circumstances which made it inappropriate for the Commission to take the decision to adjudicate; and accordingly, the BBC was refused judicial review of that decision. As to judicial review see JUDICIAL REVIEW vol 61 (2010) PARA 601 et seq.
8   Broadcasting Act 1996 s 114(2)(c).
9   Broadcasting Act 1996 s 114(2)(d).

909. Consideration of fairness complaints. Subject to specified provisions[1], every fairness complaint[2] made to OFCOM[3] is to be considered by it either at a hearing or, if it thinks fit, without a hearing[4]. Such hearings must be held in private; and where such a hearing is held in respect of a fairness complaint, each of the following persons[5] must be given an opportunity to attend and be heard[6], namely:

(1)   the complainant[7];

(2)   the relevant person[8];

(3)   any person not falling within head (1) or head (2) above who appears to OFCOM to have been responsible for the making or provision of that programme[9]; and

(4)   any other person who OFCOM considers might be able to assist at the hearing[10].

Before OFCOM proceeds to consider a fairness complaint it must send a copy of it to the relevant person[11]. Where the relevant person receives from OFCOM a copy of the complaint, it is the duty of that person, if so required by OFCOM[12]:

(a)   to provide OFCOM with a visual or sound recording of the relevant programme or of any specified part of it, if and so far as the relevant person has such a recording in his possession[13];

(b)   to make suitable arrangements for enabling the complainant to view or hear the relevant programme, or any specified part of it, if and so far as the relevant person has in his possession a visual or sound recording of it[14];

(c)   to provide OFCOM and the complainant with a transcript of so much of the relevant programme, or of any specified part of it, as consisted of speech, if and so far as the relevant person is able to do so[15];

(d)   to provide OFCOM and the complainant with copies of any documents in the possession of the relevant person, being the originals or copies of any correspondence between that person and the person affected or the complainant in connection with the complaint[16];

(e)   to provide OFCOM with such other things appearing to OFCOM to be relevant to its consideration of the complaint, and to be in the possession of the relevant person, as may be specified or described by OFCOM[17];

(f)   to furnish to OFCOM and the complainant a written statement in answer to the complaint[18].

Where the relevant person receives from OFCOM a copy of a fairness complaint, it is also the duty of that person, if so required by OFCOM[19]:

(i)   where the relevant person is a broadcasting body, to arrange for one or more of the governors, members or employees of the body to attend OFCOM and assist it in its consideration of the complaint[20]; or

(ii)   where the relevant person is a body other than a broadcasting body, to arrange for one or more of the following, namely the persons who take part in the management or control[21] of the body, or the employees of the body, to attend OFCOM and assist it in its consideration of the complaint[22]; or

(iii)   where the relevant person is an individual, to attend, or to arrange for one or more of his employees to attend, OFCOM and assist it in its consideration of the complaint[23].

Where the relevant person receives from OFCOM a copy of a fairness complaint and, in connection with the complaint, OFCOM makes to any other person a request falling within heads (A) to (F) below, it is the duty of the relevant person to take such steps as he reasonably can to ensure that the request is complied with[24]. The requests to which this applies are[25]:

(A)   a request to make suitable arrangements for enabling the complainant and any member or employee of OFCOM to view or hear the relevant programme, or any specified part of it, if and so far as the person requested has in his possession a visual or sound recording of it[26];

(B)   a request to provide OFCOM and the complainant with a transcript of so much of the relevant programme, or of any specified part of it, as consisted of speech, if and so far as the person requested is able to do so[27];

(C)   a request to provide OFCOM and the complainant with copies of any documents in the possession of the person requested, being the originals or copies of any correspondence between that person and the person affected or the complainant in connection with the complaint[28];

(D)   a request to provide OFCOM with such other things appearing to OFCOM to be relevant to its consideration of the complaint, and to be in the possession of the person requested, as may be specified or described by OFCOM[29];

(E)   a request to furnish to OFCOM and the complainant a written statement in answer to the complaint[30];

(F)   a request to attend, or (where the person requested is not an individual) to arrange for a representative to attend, OFCOM and assist it in its consideration of the complaint[31].

Where OFCOM has adjudicated on a fairness complaint, it must send a copy of its findings to the complainant[32].

1   Ie the provisions of the Broadcasting Act 1996 s 111 (see PARA 907) and s 114 (see PARA 908).
2   As to the meaning of 'fairness complaint' see PARA 907 note 1.
3   As to OFCOM see PARA 507.
4   Broadcasting Act 1996 s 115(1) (amended by the Communications Act 2003 s 360(3), Sch 15 para 132(1), (2)).

5 As to the meaning of 'person' see PARA 510 note 1.
6 Broadcasting Act 1996 s 115(2).
7 Broadcasting Act 1996 s 115(2)(a).
8 Broadcasting Act 1996 s 115(2)(b). 'The relevant person' means, in a case where the relevant programme was broadcast by a broadcasting body, that body (s 115(9)(a)); and, in a case where the relevant programme was included in a licensed service, the licence holder providing the service (s 115(9)(b)). As to the meaning of 'broadcast' see PARA 668 note 2; definition applied by s 147(2). As to the meaning of 'broadcasting body' see PARA 906 note 6. As to the meaning of 'licensed service' see PARA 906 note 3.
9 Broadcasting Act 1996 s 115(2)(d) (amended by the Communications Act 2003 Sch 15 paras 132(2), 134(a)).
10 Broadcasting Act 1996 s 115(2)(e) (amended by the Communications Act 2003 Sch 15 para 132(2)).
11 Broadcasting Act 1996 s 115(3) (amended by the Communications Act 2003 Sch 15 para 132(2), Sch 19).
12 Broadcasting Act 1996 s 115(4) (amended by the Communications Act 2003 Sch 15 para 132(2)).
13 Broadcasting Act 1996 s 115(4)(a) (as amended: see note 12).
14 Broadcasting Act 1996 s 115(4)(b) (as amended: see note 12).
15 Broadcasting Act 1996 s 115(4)(c) (as amended: see note 12).
16 Broadcasting Act 1996 s 115(4)(d) (as amended: see note 12).
17 Broadcasting Act 1996 s 115(4)(da) (added by the Communications Act 2003 s 327(1), (3)(a)).
18 Broadcasting Act 1996 s 115(4)(e).
19 Broadcasting Act 1996 s 115(5) (amended by the Communications Act 2003 Sch 15 para 132(2)).
20 Broadcasting Act 1996 s 115(5)(a) (as amended: see note 19).
21 As to the meaning of 'control' see PARA 821 note 11; definition applied by the Broadcasting Act 1996 s 147(2).
22 Broadcasting Act 1996 s 115(5)(b) (as amended: see note 19).
23 Broadcasting Act 1996 s 115(5)(c) (as amended: see note 19).
24 Broadcasting Act 1996 s 115(6) (amended by the Communications Act 2003 Sch 15 para 132(2)).
25 Broadcasting Act 1990 s 115(7) (amended by the Communications Act 2003 Sch 15 para 132(2)).
26 Broadcasting Act 1996 s 115(7)(a) (as amended: see note 25).
27 Broadcasting Act 1996 s 115(7)(b) (as amended: see note 25).
28 Broadcasting Act 1996 s 115(7)(c) (as amended: see note 25).
29 Broadcasting Act 1996 s 115(7)(ca) (added by the Communications Act 2003 s 327(3)(b)).
30 Broadcasting Act 1996 s 115(7)(d) (as amended: see note 25).
31 Broadcasting Act 1996 s 115(7)(e) (as amended: see note 25).
32 Broadcasting Act 1996 s 115(8) (amended by the Communications Act 2003 Sch 15 paras 132(2), 134(b)).

910. Duty to retain recordings. For specified purposes[1] it is the duty of each broadcasting body[2] to retain a recording of every television or sound programme[3] which is broadcast by that body[4]:

(1)   where it is of a television programme, during the period of 90 days beginning with the day of the broadcast[5];

(2)   and where it is of a sound programme, during the period of 42 days beginning with the day of the broadcast[6].

1 Ie for the purposes of the Broadcasting Act 1996 s 115 (consideration of complaints: see PARA 909) and the Broadcasting Act 1990 s 167 (power to make copies of recordings in connection with certain offences: see PARA 946): see the Broadcasting Act 1996 s 117 (amended by the Communications Act 2003 s 360(3), Sch 15 para 135).
2 As to the meaning of 'broadcasting body' see PARA 906 note 6. As to the meaning of 'broadcast' see PARA 668 note 2; definition applied by the Broadcasting Act 1996 s 147(2).
3 As to the meaning of 'programme' see PARA 906 note 2.
4 Broadcasting Act 1996 s 117.
5 Broadcasting Act 1996 s 117(a).
6 Broadcasting Act 1996 s 117(b).

911. Power to pay allowances to persons attending hearings. OFCOM[1] may, if it thinks fit, make to any person who attends it in connection with a fairness complaint[2] such payments as it thinks fit by way of travelling allowance or subsistence allowance where expenditure on travelling or, as the case may be, on subsistence is necessarily incurred by him for the purpose of enabling him so to attend[3].

1 As to OFCOM see PARA 507.
2 As to the meaning of 'fairness complaint' see PARA 907 note 1.
3 Broadcasting Act 1996 s 118 (amended by the Communications Act 2003 ss 360(3), 406(7), Sch 15 para 132(1), (2), Sch 19).

912. Publication of findings. Where OFCOM[1] has considered and adjudicated upon a fairness complaint[2], it may direct the relevant person[3] to publish[4] specified matters[5] in such manner, and within such period, as may be specified in the directions[6]. The matters to be published are:

(1) a summary of the complaint[7]; and

(2) OFCOM's findings on the complaint or a summary of them[8].

The form and content of any summary referred to in head (1) or head (2) above must be such as may be approved by OFCOM[9]. A relevant person must comply with any directions given to him[10].

The regulatory regime for every licensed service includes the conditions that OFCOM considers appropriate for securing that the licence holder complies with every direction given to him under these provisions[11]. Where OFCOM exercises its powers[12] to adjudicate upon a fairness complaint or to give a direction to publish[13], and it appears to it that the matters to which the complaint in question relates consist in or include a contravention of the conditions of the licence for a licensed service, the exercise by OFCOM of its powers under Part V of the Broadcasting Act 1996 is not to preclude the exercise by it of its powers under any other enactment in respect of the contravention[14]. Where OFCOM is proposing to exercise any of its powers in respect of a contravention of a licence condition in a case in which the contravention relates to matters that have been the subject matter of a fairness complaint, OFCOM may have regard, in the exercise of those powers, to any matters considered or steps taken by it for the purpose of adjudicating upon that complaint and to any direction to publish given by it; but steps taken for the purposes of Part V of the Broadcasting Act 1996 do not satisfy a requirement to give the licence holder in relation to whom those powers are to be exercised a reasonable opportunity, before they are exercised, of making representations to OFCOM[15].

OFCOM must publish reports monthly or at such other intervals as it thinks fit and in such manner as it thinks fit, each containing, as regards every fairness complaint which falls within this provision[16] and has been dealt with by it in the period covered by the report, the following[17]:

(a) a summary of the complaint and the action taken by OFCOM on it[18];

(b) where OFCOM has adjudicated on it, a summary of its findings, and any direction so given, or other action taken by it, in relation to the complaint[19]; and

(c) where a direction has been so given in relation to the complaint, a summary of any action taken by a broadcasting body or the holder of a licence to provide a licensed service in pursuance of the direction[20].

OFCOM may, if it thinks fit, omit from any summary which is included in such a report and relates to a fairness complaint any information which could lead to the disclosure of the identity of any person[21] connected with the complaint in question other than a relevant person[22].

1 As to OFCOM see PARA 507.
2 As to the meaning of 'fairness complaint' see PARA 907 note 1.
3 'Relevant person' means in a case where the relevant programme was broadcast by a broadcasting body, that body, and in a case where the relevant programme was included in a licensed service, the licence holder providing that service: Broadcasting Act 1996 s 119(11A) (added by the Communications Act 2003 s 360(3), Sch 15 para 136(3)). As to the meaning of 'the relevant programme' see PARA 907 note 8. As to the meaning of 'programme' see PARA 906 note 2. As to the meaning of 'broadcasting body' see PARA 906 note 6. As to the meaning of 'licensed service' see PARA 906 note 3.
4 References in the Broadcasting Act 1996 s 119(1) to the publication of any matter are references to the publication of that matter without its being accompanied by any observations made by a person other than OFCOM and relating to the complaint: s 119(4) (amended by the Communications Act 2003 Sch 15 paras 132(1), (2), 136(2)(a)).
5 Ie the matters mentioned in the Broadcasting Act 1996 s 119(3) (see heads (1)–(2) in the text).
6 Broadcasting Act 1996 s 119(1) (substituted by the Communications Act 2003 Sch 15 para 136(1)).
7 Broadcasting Act 1996 s 119(3)(a).
8 Broadcasting Act 1996 s 119(3)(b) (amended by the Communications Act 2003 s 406(7), Sch 19; and by virtue of Sch 15 para 132(2)). The references in the Broadcasting Act 1996 s 119(3)(b) and s 119(8)(b) (see the text and note 19) to OFCOM's findings on a complaint must be construed, in relation to a fairness complaint which has been considered by it in two or more parts, as references to its findings on each part of the complaint: s 119(11) (amended by virtue of the Communications Act 2003 Sch 15 para 132(2)).
9 Broadcasting Act 1996 s 119(5) (amended by the Communications Act 2003 Sch 15 paras 132(2), 136(2)(b)).
10 Ie any directions given to it under the Broadcasting Act 1996 s 119: s 119(6) (amended by the Communications Act 2003 Sch 15 para 136(2)(c)).
11 Broadcasting Act 1996 s 119(7) (substituted by the Communications Act 2003 s 327(1), (4)). The Communications Act 2003 s 263 (see PARA 602) applies in relation to conditions included by virtue of the Broadcasting Act 1996 s 119(7) in the regulatory regime for a licensed service as it applies in relation to conditions which are so included by virtue of a provision of the Communications Act 2003 Pt 3 Ch 4 (ss 263–347): Broadcasting Act 1996 s 119(7A) (added by the Communications Act 2003 s 327(4)).
12 Ie under the Broadcasting Act 1996 Pt V (ss 107–130).
13 Ie under the Broadcasting Act 1996 s 119(1).
14 Broadcasting Act 1996 s 119(7B) (added by the Communications Act 2003 s 327(4)).
15 Broadcasting Act 1996 s 119(7C) (added by the Communications Act 2003 s 327(4)).
16 A fairness complaint or standards complaint made to OFCOM falls within the Broadcasting Act 1996 s 119(8) (see the text and note 17) unless it is one which under s 111(1), (4) or (5) (see PARA 907) or s 114(2) (see PARA 908) it has refused to entertain: s 119(9) (amended by the Communications Act 2003 Sch 15 para 132(2), Sch 19).
17 Broadcasting Act 1996 s 119(8) (amended by the Communications Act 2003 Sch 15 para 132(2), Sch 19).
18 Broadcasting Act 1996 s 119(8)(a).
19 Broadcasting Act 1996 s 119(8)(b). See note 8.
20 Broadcasting Act 1996 s 119(8)(c) (amended by the Communications Act 2003 Sch 15 para 136(2)(d), Sch 19).
21 As to the meaning of 'person' see PARA 510 note 1.
22 Broadcasting Act 1996 s 119(10) (amended by the Communications Act 2003 Sch 15 paras 132(2), 136(2)(e)).

913.   Reports on action taken voluntarily in response to findings on complaints.   Where OFCOM[1] has given a direction[2] in relation to a fairness complaint[3], the following reporting requirements apply[4].

Where the relevant programme[5] was included in a licensed service[6], the licence holder[7] must send to OFCOM a report of any supplementary action[8] taken by him or by any other person responsible for the making or provision of the relevant programme[9]. Where the relevant programme was broadcast[10] by a broadcasting body[11], that body must send to OFCOM a report of any supplementary action taken by the broadcasting body, or by any other person appearing to that body to be responsible for the making or provision of the relevant programme[12].

1 As to OFCOM see PARA 507.
2 Ie a direction under the Broadcasting Act 1996 s 119(1) (see PARA 912).
3 As to the meaning of 'fairness complaint' see PARA 907 note 1.
4 See the Broadcasting Act 1996 s 120(1) (amended by the Communications Act 2003 ss 360(3), 406(7), Sch 15 para 132(1), (2), Sch 19).
5 As to the meaning of 'the relevant programme' see PARA 907 note 8. As to the meaning of 'programme' see PARA 906 note 2.
6 As to the meaning of 'licensed service' see PARA 906 note 3.
7 As to the holder of the licence see PARA 725 note 16.
8 'Supplementary action', in relation to a complaint, means action which, although not taken in pursuance of a direction under the Broadcasting Act 1996 s 119(1) (see PARA 912), is taken in consequence of the findings of OFCOM on the complaint: s 120(5) (amended by the Communications Act 2003 Sch 15 para 132(2)).
9 Broadcasting Act 1996 s 120(2) (substituted by the Communications Act 2003 s 327(1), (5)).
10 As to the meaning of 'broadcast' see PARA 668 note 2; definition applied by the Broadcasting Act 1996 s 147(2).
11 As to the meaning of 'broadcasting body' see PARA 906 note 6.
12 Broadcasting Act 1996 s 120(3) (amended by the Communications Act 2003 Sch 15 para 132(2)). OFCOM may include, in any report under the Broadcasting Act 1996 s 119(8) (see PARA 912), a summary of any report received by it under s 120(2) (see the text and note 9) or s 120(3) in relation to the complaint: s 120(4) (amended by the Communications Act 2003 Sch 15 para 132(2)).

914. Statements protected by qualified privilege for purposes of defamation. For the purposes of the law relating to defamation[1]:

(1) publication of any statement in the course of the consideration by OFCOM[2] of, and its adjudication on, a fairness complaint[3];

(2) publication by OFCOM of directions[4] relating to a fairness complaint[5]; or

(3) publication of a report of OFCOM, so far as the report relates to fairness complaints[6],

is privileged unless the publication is shown to be made with malice[7].

1 As to the law relating to defamation see LIBEL AND SLANDER.
2 As to OFCOM see PARA 507.
3 Broadcasting Act 1996 s 121(1)(a) (amended by the Communications Act 2003 s 360, Sch 15 para 132(1), (2)). As to the meaning of 'fairness complaint' see PARA 907 note 1.
4 Ie directions under the Broadcasting Act 1996 s 119(1) (see PARA 912).
5 Broadcasting Act 1996 s 121(1)(b) (amended by the Communications Act 2003 Sch 15 para 132(2)).
6 Broadcasting Act 1996 s 121(1)(c) (amended by the Communications Act 2003 Sch 15 para 132(2)).
7 Broadcasting Act 1996 s 121(1). Nothing in s 121(1) may be construed as limiting any privilege subsisting apart from s 121(1): s 121(2). As to privilege see LIBEL AND SLANDER vol 28 (Reissue) PARA 94 et seq; and as to defences defeated by malice see LIBEL AND SLANDER vol 28 (Reissue) PARA 149 et seq.

(v) Listed Events

915. Listed events. For the purposes Part IV of the Broadcasting Act 1996[1], a listed event is a sporting or other event of national interest[2] which is for the time being included in a list drawn up by the Secretary of State[3] for such purposes[4]. The Act provides for consultation before a list is drawn up or revised, and before it ceases to be maintained[5]. As soon as he has drawn up or revised such a list, the

Secretary of State must publish the list in such manner as he considers appropriate for bringing it to the attention of the persons consulted[6], and every person who is the holder of a licence granted under Part I of the Broadcasting Act 1990[7] or a digital programme licence[8] granted under the Part I of the Broadcasting Act 1996[9]. The addition of any relevant event[10] to such a list does not affect the validity of any contract entered into before the date on which the Secretary of State consulted the persons mentioned above in relation to the proposed addition[11], or the exercise of any rights acquired under such a contract[12].

The provisions set out above are replaced or further amended as from a day to be appointed[13]. From that date, it is provided that the Secretary of State may, for the purposes of Part IV of the Broadcasting Act 1996, maintain a list of sporting and other events of national interest, and an event for the time being included in the list is referred to in that Part as a 'listed event'[14]. Such a list must be divided into two categories, which are referred to as 'Group A' and 'Group B'[15]. Each listed event must be allocated either to Group A or to Group B[16]. Before drawing up such a list, or revising or ceasing to maintain it, the Secretary of State must consult OFCOM[17], the BBC[18], the Welsh Authority[19], and, in relation to a relevant event[20], the person from whom the rights to televise that event may be acquired[21]. As soon as he has drawn up or revised such a list, the Secretary of State must publish the list in such manner as he considers appropriate for bringing it to the attention of the persons mentioned above[22], and every person who is the holder of a licence granted under Part I of the Broadcasting or a digital programme licence granted under the Part I of the Broadcasting Act 1996[23]. The inclusion of any event in such a list does not affect the validity of any contract entered into before the date on which the Secretary of State consulted the persons mentioned above in relation to the proposed inclusion[24], or the exercise of any rights acquired under such a contract[25]. The allocation or transfer of an event to Group A does not affect the validity of a contract entered into before the day on which the Secretary of State consulted the persons mentioned above in relation to the proposed allocation or transfer[26]. The Secretary of State may direct that, for the transitional purposes set out in the direction, the transfer of a Group B event to Group A is not to affect the application to that event of provisions of Part IV of the Broadcasting Act 1996 relating to a Group B event[27].

1   Ie the Broadcasting Act 1996 Pt IV (ss 97–105).
2   'National interest' includes interest within England, Scotland, Wales or Northern Ireland: Broadcasting Act 1996 s 97(4).
3   As to the Secretary of State see PARA 507 note 32.
4   Broadcasting Act 1996 ss 97(1), 105(1). As to the prospective replacement or amendment of provisions of s 97 see the text and notes 13–27. The list drawn up by the Secretary of State for the purposes of the Broadcasting Act 1990 s 182 (repealed), as that list was in force immediately before 1 October 1996, is to be taken to have been drawn up for the purposes of the Broadcasting Act 1996 Pt IV: see s 97(6); and the Broadcasting Act 1996 (Commencement No 1 and Transitional Provisions) Order 1996, SI 1996/2120.
5   Broadcasting Act 1996 s 97(2).
6   Broadcasting Act 1996 s 97(3)(a).
7   Ie the Broadcasting Act 1990 Pt I (ss 3–71). As to the granting of such a licence see PARAS 665, 679.
8   As to the meaning of 'digital programme licence' see PARA 698.
9   Ie the Broadcasting Act 1996 Pt I (ss 1–39): see s 97(3)(b) (amended by the Communications Act 2003 ss 299(2), 406(7), Sch 19). As to the granting of such a licence see PARA 698.
10   For the purposes of the Broadcasting Act 1996 s 97(2), a relevant event is a sporting or other event of national interest which the Secretary of State proposes to include in, or omit from, the list: see s 97(2).

11 Broadcasting Act 1996 s 97(5)(a).

12 Broadcasting Act 1996 s 97(5)(b).

13 Ie as from a day to be appointed under the Communications Act 2003 s 411(2). At the date at which this volume states the law, no such day had been appointed.

14 Broadcasting Act 1996 s 97(1) (s 97 (1), (2) prospectively substituted by the Communications Act 2003 s 299(1)). The list drawn up by the Secretary of State for the purposes of the Broadcasting Act 1990 s 182 (repealed), as that list was in force immediately before 1 October 1996, is to be taken to have been drawn up for the purposes of the Broadcasting Act 1996 Pt IV: see s 97(6). On the date on which the Communications Act 2003 s 300 (see PARA 916) comes into force, the Secretary of State must revise the list maintained for the purposes of the Broadcasting Act 1996 Pt IV in order to allocate each event which is a listed event on that date either to Group A or to Group B: Communications Act 2003 s 406(6), Sch 18 para 51(4). Where the events listed in the list in force immediately before the Secretary of State revises it under Sch 18 para 51(4) are treated, for any of the purposes of the code in force under the Broadcasting Act 1996 s 104 (see PARA 921) at that time, as divided into two categories, and the Secretary of State's revision under that provision makes the same division, s 97(2) is not to apply in relation to that revision of that list: Communications Act 2003 Sch 18 para 51(5).

15 Broadcasting Act 1996 s 97(1A) (prospectively added by the Communications Act 2003 s 299(1)).

16 Broadcasting Act 1996 s 97(1B) (prospectively added by the Communications Act 2003 s 299(1)).

17 As to OFCOM see PARA 507.

18 As to the meaning of 'BBC' see PARA 603 note 1; and as to the BBC see PARAS 603–626.

19 As to the meaning of 'the Welsh Authority' see PARA 644 note 3; definition applied by the Broadcasting Act 1996 s 147(2). As to television broadcasting by the Welsh Authority see PARAS 644–661.

20 For the purposes of the Broadcasting Act 1996 s 97(2)(d) (as prospectively substituted: see note 14), a relevant event is an event which the Secretary of State proposes: (1) to include in a list maintained under s 97(1); (2) to omit from such a list: or (3) to move from one category in such a list to the other: s 97(2A) (prospectively added by the Communications Act 2003 s 299(1)).

21 Broadcasting Act 1996 s 97(2) (prospectively substituted by the Communications Act 2003 s 299(1)).

22 Broadcasting Act 1996 s 97(3)(a). The persons referred to in the text are the persons mentioned in s 97(2) (as prospectively substituted: see note 14) (see the text and notes 17–21).

23 Broadcasting Act 1996 s 97(3)(b) (amended by the Communications Act 2003 ss 299(2), 406(7), Sch 19).

24 Broadcasting Act 1996 s 97(5)(a) (prospectively amended by the Communications Act 2003 s 299(3)).

25 Broadcasting Act 1996 s 97(5)(b).

26 Broadcasting Act 1996 s 97(5A) (prospectively added by the Communications Act 2003 s 299(4)).

27 Broadcasting Act 1996 s 97(5B) (prospectively added by the Communications Act 2003 s 299(4)).

916.   Categories of service.   For the purposes of Part IV of the Broadcasting Act 1996[1], television programme services[2] and EEA satellite services[3] are to be divided into two categories as follows[4]:

(1)   those television programme services and EEA satellite services which for the time being satisfy the qualifying conditions[5]; and

(2)   all other television programme services and EEA satellite services[6].

The qualifying conditions, in relation to a service, are the conditions[7]:

(a)   that the service is provided without any consideration being required for reception of the service[8]; and

(b)   that the service is received by at least 95 per cent of the population of the United Kingdom[9].

OFCOM[10] must from time to time publish a list of the television programme services and EEA satellite services which appear to it to satisfy the qualifying conditions[11].

The Broadcasting Act 1996 provides[12] that a television programme provider providing a service falling within either of the categories set out in heads (1) and (2) above[13] ('the first service') for reception in the United Kingdom or in any area of the United Kingdom must not, without the necessary previous consent[14], include in that service live[15] coverage of the whole or any part of a listed event[16] unless:

(a)   another person, who is providing a service falling within the other category ('the second service'), has acquired the right to include in the second service live coverage of the whole of the event or that part of the event[17]; and

(b)   the area for which the second service is provided consists of or includes the whole, or substantially the whole, of the area for which the first service is provided[18].

As from the appointed day, a television programme provider who is providing a service ('the first service') falling within either of the categories set out in heads (1) and (2) above, and is providing it with a view to its being available for reception by members of the public[19] in the United Kingdom or in any area of the United Kingdom, must not include live coverage of a listed event in that service unless it is authorised[20] under these provisions[21]. Live coverage of a listed event[22] is authorised:

(i)   if a television programme provider (other than the provider of the first service) has acquired the right to include live coverage of the event in his service ('the second service'); and the second service falls into a different category from the first service, and is provided for an area that consists of or includes all or almost all of the area for which the first service is provided[23];

(ii)   if OFCOM has consented in advance to inclusion of that coverage in the first service[24];

(iii)   if (A) the listed event is a Group B event[25]; (B) rights to provide coverage of the event have been acquired by one or more persons in addition to the provider of the first service; (C) that additional coverage constitutes adequate alternative coverage of the event; and (D) the person or persons who have acquired rights to provide the additional coverage satisfy the requirements in relation to that coverage of any regulations[26] made for these purposes[27].

OFCOM may revoke any consent[28] given by it[29].

1   Ie the Broadcasting Act 1996 Pt IV (ss 97–105): see s 98(1) (s 98 substituted by SI 2000/54).
2   As to the meaning of 'television programme service' see PARA 790 note 5; definition applied by the Broadcasting Act 1996 s 105(1).
3   'EEA satellite service' means any service which: (1) consists in the broadcasting of television programmes from a satellite so as to be available for reception by members of the public (within the meaning of the Communications Act 2003 Pt 3 (ss 198–362): see PARA 796); (2) is provided by a person who for the purposes of European Parliament and Council Directive (EC) 89/552 (OJ L298, 17.10.89, p 23) (repealed: see now European Parliament and Council Directive (EU) 2010/13 (OJ L95, 15.4.2010, p 1)) is under the jurisdiction of an EEA state other than the United Kingdom: Broadcasting Act 1996 s 98(6) (as substituted (see note 1); and amended by the Communications Act 2003 s 360(3), Sch 15 para 127(1), (4)).
4   Broadcasting Act 1996 s 98(1) (as substituted: see note 1).
5   Broadcasting Act 1996 s 98(1)(a) (as substituted: see note 1).
6   Broadcasting Act 1996 s 98(1)(b) (as substituted: see note 1).
7   Broadcasting Act 1996 s 98(2) (as substituted: see note 1).
8   Broadcasting Act 1996 s 98(2)(a) (as substituted: see note 1). There is to be disregarded for the purposes of s 98(2)(a) any fee payable in respect of a licence for the purposes of the

Communications Act 2003 s 363 (see PARA 948): Broadcasting Act 1996 s 98(3) (as so substituted; and amended by the Communications Act 2003 Sch 15 para 127(2)).

9 Broadcasting Act 1996 s 98(2)(b) (as substituted: see note 1). As to the meaning of 'United Kingdom' see PARA 510 note 13. The condition in s 98(2)(b) is to be taken to be satisfied in relation to a regional Channel 3 service if it is satisfied in relation to Channel 3 as a whole; and is to be taken to be satisfied in relation to Channel 4 if it is satisfied in relation to Channel 4 and S4C taken together: s 98(4) (as so substituted). As to the meaning of 'regional Channel 3 service' see PARA 667 note 6; definition applied by s 105(1). As to the meaning of 'Channel 3' see PARA 667; definition applied by s 147(2). As to the meaning of 'Channel 4' see PARA 637; definition applied by s 105(1). As to the meaning of 'S4C' see PARA 644; definition applied by s 105(1) (definition added by SI 2000/54).

10 As to OFCOM see PARA 507.

11 Broadcasting Act 1996 s 98(5) (as substituted (see note 1); and amended by the Communications Act 2003 Sch 15 para 127(3)).

12 Ie until the day appointed under the Communications Act 2003 s 411(2) for the commencement of s 300, which amends the Broadcasting Act 1996 s 101. At the date at which this volume states the law, no such day had been appointed.

13 Ie the Broadcasting Act 1996 s 98(1)(a) or s 98(1)(b).

14 The Broadcasting Act 1996 provides for the previous consent of the Independent Television Commission ('ITC'), but the functions of the ITC have been transferred to OFCOM: see PARA 507.

15 'Live' is to be construed in accordance with any regulations under the Broadcasting Act 1996 s 104ZA (see PARA 922): s 105(1) (definition added by the Communications Act 2003 s 302(2)).

16 See the Broadcasting Act 1996 s 101(1) (amended by SI 2000/54). As to the meaning of 'listed event' see PARA 915; definition applied by the Broadcasting Act 1996 s 105(1).

17 Broadcasting Act 1996 s 101(1)(a). See also note 18.

18 Broadcasting Act 1996 s 101(1)(b). Failure to comply with s 101(1) does not affect the validity of any contract: s 101(3). Section 101(1) does not have effect where the television programme provider providing the first service is exercising rights acquired before 1 October 1996: see s 101(4); Broadcasting Act 1996 (Commencement No 1 and Transitional Provisions) Order 1996, SI 1996/2120. 'Television programme provider' means the BBC, the Welsh Authority or any person who is the holder of any licence under the Broadcasting Act 1990 Pt I (ss 3–71) or a digital programme licence under the Broadcasting Act 1996 Pt I (ss 1–39): ss 99(2), 105(1). As to the meaning of 'BBC' see PARA 603 note 1; and as to the BBC see PARAS 603–626. As to the meaning of 'the Welsh Authority' see PARA 644 note 3; definition applied by s 147(2). As to television broadcasting by the Welsh Authority see PARAS 644–661. As to the meaning of 'digital programme licence' see PARA 698.

19 Ie within the meaning of the Communications Act 2003 Pt 3: see PARA 602 note 8.

20 Ie by the Broadcasting Act 1996 s 101(1A), (1B) or (1C).

21 Broadcasting Act 1996 s 101(1) (prospectively substituted by the Communications Act 2003 s 300(2)).

22 The provisions of the Broadcasting Act 1996 s 101(1)–(1C) apply to the coverage of a part of a listed event as they apply to the coverage of the whole of that event: s 101(1D) (prospectively added by the Communications Act 2003 s 300(2)).

23 Broadcasting Act 1996 s 101(1A) (prospectively added by the Communications Act 2003 s 300(2)).

24 Broadcasting Act 1996 s 101(1B) (prospectively added by the Communications Act 2003 s 300(2)).

25 As to the meaning of 'Group B event' see PARA 915. References in the Broadcasting Act 1996 s 101 to a category of service are references to a category of service set out in s 98(1): s 101(5) (prospectively added by the Communications Act 2003 s 300(4)).

26 Ie regulations made under the Broadcasting Act 1996 s 104ZA: see PARA 922.

27 Broadcasting Act 1996 s 101(1C) (prospectively added by the Communications Act 2003 s 300(2)).

28 Ie consent under the Broadcasting Act 1996 s 101(1) or s 101(1B).

29 Broadcasting Act 1996 s 101(2) (amended by the Communications Act 2003 s 360(3), Sch 15 para 128; and prospectively amended by s 300(3)).

917. Restriction in relation to other EEA states. A television programme provider[1] must not, without the previous consent of OFCOM[2], exercise rights to televise the whole or part of an event which is a designated event[3], in relation to an EEA state other than the United Kingdom, for reception in that EEA state or any area of that EEA state, where a substantial proportion of the public in that EEA state is deprived of the possibility of following that event by live or deferred coverage on free television[4]. OFCOM may revoke any consent given by it under these provisions[5].

1   As to the meaning of 'television programme provider' see PARA 916 note 18.

2   As to OFCOM see PARA 507.

3   For the purposes of the Broadcasting Act 1996 Pt IV (ss 97–105), a sporting or other event is a designated event, in relation to an EEA state other than the United Kingdom, if: (1) that state has designated the event in accordance with European Parliament and Council Directive (EC) 89/552 (OJ L298, 17.10.89, p 23) art 3a(1) (repealed: see now European Parliament and Council Directive (EU) 2010/13 (OJ L95, 15.4.2010, p 1) art 14(1)) as being of major importance to its society; and (2) the designation forms part of measures which have been notified by that state to the European Commission for the purposes of European Parliament and Council Directive (EC) 89/552 (OJ L298, 17.10.89, p 23) art 3a(2) (repealed: see now European Parliament and Council Directive (EU) 2010/13 (OJ L95, 15.4.2010, p 1) art 14(2)), and notice of which has been published by the European Commission in the Official Journal of the European Union: Broadcasting Act 1996 s 101A (added by SI 2000/54). As to the meaning of 'United Kingdom' see PARA 510 note 13.

4   Ie as determined by that state in accordance with European Parliament and Council Directive (EC) 89/552 (OJ L298, 17.10.89, p 23) art 3a(1) (repealed: see now European Parliament and Council Directive (EU) 2010/13 (OJ L95, 15.4.2010, p 1) art 14(1)): Broadcasting Act 1996 s 101B(1) (s 101B added by SI 2000/54; and the Broadcasting Act 1996 s 101B(1) amended by the Communications Act 2003 s 360(3), Sch 15 para 128). Failure to comply with the Broadcasting Act 1996 s 101B(1) does not affect the validity of any contract: s 101B(3) (as so added). Section 101B(1) does not have effect where the rights were acquired before the day on which the event became a designated event: s 101B(4) (as so added).

5   Broadcasting Act 1996 s 101B(2) (as added (see note 4); and amended by the Communications Act 2003 Sch 15 para 128).

918. Power of OFCOM to impose penalties. If OFCOM[1] is satisfied that the holder of a licence under Part I of the Broadcasting Act 1990[2] or a digital programme licence under Part I of the Broadcasting Act 1996[3] has failed to comply with the restrictions on broadcasting listed events[4], and is not satisfied that in all the circumstances it would be unreasonable to expect him to have complied[5], it may require him to pay, within a specified period, a specified financial penalty to OFCOM[6]. If OFCOM is satisfied that, in connection with an application for its consent, the holder of a licence under Part I of the Broadcasting Act 1990 or a digital programme licence under Part I of the Broadcasting Act 1996 has provided it with information which was false in a material particular, or has withheld any material information with the intention of causing OFCOM to be misled, it may require him to pay, within a specified period, a specified financial penalty to OFCOM[7].

Before requiring any person to pay a financial penalty on the ground that he has failed to comply with the restriction on televising an event designated by another EEA state[8], OFCOM must consult such persons (who may include competent authorities in other EEA states) as appear to OFCOM to be appropriate[9].

The amount of any financial penalty imposed on any person under these provisions must not exceed the amount produced by multiplying the relevant consideration[10] by the prescribed multiplier[11]. Where OFCOM receives any amount payable to it by virtue of these provisions, that amount does not form part of the revenues of OFCOM but must be paid into the Consolidated Fund[12]. Any amount so payable by any person to OFCOM is recoverable by it as a debt due to it from that person[13].

If OFCOM is satisfied that a broadcasting body[14] has failed to comply with the above provisions[15], and is not satisfied that in all the circumstances it would be unreasonable to expect the body to have complied[16], it must make a report on the matter to the Secretary of State[17]. If OFCOM is satisfied that, in connection with an application for its consent, a broadcasting body has provided it with information which was false in a material particular, or has withheld any material information with the intention of causing OFCOM to be misled, it must make a report on the matter to the Secretary of State[18]. Before making such a report in relation to a failure to comply with a restriction on televising an event designated by another EEA state[19], OFCOM must consult such persons (who may include competent authorities in other EEA states) as appear to OFCOM to be appropriate[20].

1   As to OFCOM see PARA 507.
2   Ie the Broadcasting Act 1990 Pt I (ss 3–71).
3   Ie the Broadcasting Act 1996 Pt I (ss 1–39).
4   Ie the Broadcasting Act 1996 s 101(1) (see PARA 916) or s 101B(1) (see PARA 917): see s 102(1)(a) (amended by SI 2000/54).
5   See the Broadcasting Act 1996 s 102(1)(b).
6   Broadcasting Act 1996 s 102(1) (amended by the Communications Act 2003 s 360(3), Sch 15 para 128).
7   Broadcasting Act 1996 s 102(2) (amended by the Communications Act 2003 s 360(3), Sch 15 para 128; and, as from a day to be appointed, by s 300(5)).
8   Ie in the Broadcasting Act 1996 s 101B(1): see PARA 917.
9   Broadcasting Act 1996 s 102(2A) (added by SI 2000/54; and amended by the Communications Act 2003 Sch 15 para 128).
10 'The relevant consideration' means an amount determined by OFCOM as representing so much of any consideration paid by the person on whom the penalty is being imposed as is attributable to the acquisition of the rights to televise the event in question: Broadcasting Act 1996 s 102(4)(a) (amended by the Communications Act 2003 Sch 15 para 128).
11 Broadcasting Act 1996 s 102(3). 'The prescribed multiplier' means such number as the Secretary of State may from time to time by order prescribe: s 102(4)(b). Such an order is subject to annulment in pursuance of a resolution of either House of Parliament: s 102(5). As to the order made see the Listed Events (Prescribed Multiplier) Order 1997, SI 1997/1333 (which prescribes a multiplier of one). As to the Secretary of State see PARA 507 note 32.
12 Broadcasting Act 1996 s 102(6) (amended by the Communications Act 2003 Sch 15 para 128). As to the Consolidated Fund see CONSTITUTIONAL LAW AND HUMAN RIGHTS vol 8(2) (Reissue) PARA 711 et seq; PARLIAMENT vol 78 (2010) PARAS 1028–1031.
13 Broadcasting Act 1996 s 102(7) (amended by the Communications Act 2003 Sch 15 para 128).
14 'Broadcasting body' means the BBC or the Welsh Authority: Broadcasting Act 1996 s 103(3). As to the meaning of 'BBC' see PARA 603 note 1; and as to the BBC see PARAS 603–626. As to the meaning of 'the Welsh Authority' see PARA 644 note 3; and as to television broadcasting by the Welsh Authority see PARAS 644–661.
15 Ie the Broadcasting Act 1996 s 101(1) (see PARA 916) or s 101B(1) (see PARA 917): see s 103(1)(a).
16 See the Broadcasting Act 1996 s 103(1)(b).
17 Broadcasting Act 1996 s 103(1).
18 Broadcasting Act 1996 s 103(2) (amended by the Television Broadcasting Regulations 2000, SI 2000/54, reg 3, Schedule para 6(1), (3); and the Communications Act 2003 Sch 15 para 128; and, as from a day to be appointed, by the Communications Act 2003 s 300(6)).
19 Ie under the Broadcasting Act 1996 s 101B(1): see PARA 917.
20 Broadcasting Act 1996 s 103(2A) (added by SI 2000/54; and amended by the Communications Act 2003 Sch 15 para 128).

919.   Contract for exclusive right to televise listed event to be void. Any contract entered into after 1 October 1996[1] under which a television programme provider[2] acquires rights to televise the whole or any part of a listed event[3] live[4] for reception in the United Kingdom[5], or in any area of the United Kingdom, is void so far as it purports, in relation to the whole or any part of the event or in relation to reception in the United Kingdom or any area of the United Kingdom, to grant those rights exclusively to any one television programme provider[6]. For these purposes, rights to televise the whole or any part of an event live for reception in any area granted to a television programme provider are granted exclusively if the person granting them has not granted any right to televise the whole or, as the case may be, that part of the event live for reception in that area to any other television programme provider nor to any broadcaster who[7] is under the jurisdiction of an EEA state other than the United Kingdom[8], and is precluded by the terms of the contract from doing so[9].

A television programme provider must, at the request of OFCOM, provide it with such information as OFCOM considers appropriate regarding any contract which he has entered into which relates to an event which, in relation to an EEA state other than the United Kingdom, is a designated event[10]. If so requested by a competent authority in an EEA state other than the United Kingdom, OFCOM must provide the authority with such information relating to rights to televise listed events or designated events as OFCOM considers it appropriate to provide[11].

1   Ie the date on which the Broadcasting Act 1996 s 99 was brought into force: see the Broadcasting Act 1996 (Commencement No 1 and Transitional Provisions) Order 1996, SI 1996/2120.
2   As to the meaning of 'television programme provider' see PARA 916 note 18. As to the meaning of 'BBC' see PARA 603 note 1; and as to the BBC see PARAS 603–626. As to the meaning of 'the Welsh Authority' see PARA 644 note 3; and as to television broadcasting by the Welsh Authority see PARAS 644–661.
3   As to the meaning of 'listed event' see PARA 915; definition applied by the Broadcasting Act 1996 s 105(1). As from a day to be appointed, this applies to a Group A listed event: see s 99(1) (prospectively amended by the Communications Act 2003 s 300(1)). At the date at which this volume states the law, no such day had been appointed. As to Group A listed events see PARA 915.
4   As to the meaning of 'live' see PARA 916 note 15.
5   As to the meaning of 'United Kingdom' see PARA 510 note 13.
6   Broadcasting Act 1996 s 99(1).
7   Ie for the purposes of European Parliament and Council Directive (EC) 89/552 (OJ L298, 17.10.89, p 23) (repealed: see now European Parliament and Council Directive (EU) 2010/13 (OJ L95, 15.4.2010, p 1)).
8   Broadcasting Act 1996 s 99(3)(a) (substituted by SI 2000/54).
9   Broadcasting Act 1996 s 99(3)(b).
10   Broadcasting Act 1996 s 104A(1) (s 104A added by SI 2000/54; and amended by the Communications Act 2003 s 360(3), Sch 15 para 130). As to the meaning of 'designated event' see PARA 917 note 3; definition applied by the Broadcasting Act 1996 s 105(1) (definition added by SI 2000/54). As to OFCOM see PARA 507.
11   Broadcasting Act 1996 s 104A(2) (as added and amended: see note 10).

920. Requirement to specify category of service. Any contract entered into after 1 October 1996[1] is void so far as it purports to grant to a television programme provider[2] rights to televise the whole or any part of a listed event[3] live[4] for reception in the United Kingdom[5], or any area of the United Kingdom, unless the contract complies with the following provisions[6]. A contract complies with these provisions if the terms of the contract allow the television programme provider to include the live coverage of the listed event only in a specified category[7] of television programme service[8].

1   Ie the date on which the Broadcasting Act 1996 s 100 was brought into force: see the Broadcasting Act 1996 (Commencement No 1 and Transitional Provisions) Order 1996, SI 1996/2120.
2   As to the meaning of 'television programme provider' see PARA 916 note 18.

3   As to the meaning of 'listed event' see PARA 915; definition applied by the Broadcasting
     Act 1996 s 105(1).
4   As to the meaning of 'live' see PARA 916 note 15.
5   As to the meaning of 'United Kingdom' see PARA 510 note 13.
6   Broadcasting Act 1996 s 100(1). The provisions referred to in the text are those of s 100(2) (see
     the text and notes 7–8).
7   Ie only in a television programme service falling within the Broadcasting Act 1996 s 98(1)(a)
     (see PARA 916 head (1)) or only in a television programme service falling within s 98(1)(b) (see
     PARA 916 head (2)): see s 100(2). As to the meaning of 'television programme service' see PARA
     790 note 5; definition applied by s 105(1).
8   Broadcasting Act 1996 s 100(2).

921.   Code of guidance.   OFCOM[1] must draw up, and may from time to time
revise, a code giving guidance as to the matters which it will take into account in
determining whether to give or to revoke its consent as to the televising of live
events[2] and as to the matters which it will take into account in determining[3]
whether in all the circumstances it is unreasonable to expect a television
programme provider[4] to comply with the restrictions as to televising live events[5].
In exercising its powers under Part IV of the Broadcasting Act 1996[6], OFCOM
must have regard to the provisions of the code[7].

Before drawing up or revising the code, OFCOM must consult such persons
as appear to it to be appropriate[8]. As soon as OFCOM has drawn up or revised
such a code, it must publish the code in such manner as it considers appropriate[9]
for bringing it to the attention of the BBC[10], the Welsh Authority[11], every person
from whom the rights to televise a listed event may be acquired[12], and every
person who is the holder of a licence under Part I[13] of the Broadcasting Act 1990
or a digital programme licence[14] granted under Part I[15] of the Broadcasting
Act 1996[16].

1   As to OFCOM see PARA 507.
2   Ie for the purposes of the Broadcasting Act 1996 s 101(1B) (see PARA 916) or s 101B(1) (see
     PARA 917). As to the meaning of 'live' see PARA 916 note 15.
3   Ie for the purposes of the Broadcasting Act 1996 s 102(1) or s 103(1): see PARA 918.
4   As to the meaning of 'television programme provider' see PARA 916 note 18.
5   Ie the Broadcasting Act 1996 s 101 or s 101B(1): s 104(1) (substituted by the Communications
     Act 2003 s 301(1)). The code drawn up by the ITC under the Broadcasting Act 1996 s 104 and
     in force immediately before the commencement of the Communications Act 2003 s 301
     (ie 29 December 2003: see the Office of Communications Act 2002 (Commencement No 3) and
     Communications Act 2003 (Commencement No 2) Order 2003, SI 2003/3142) is to continue to
     have effect (notwithstanding the substitutions made by the Communications Act 2003 s 301)
     until the code drawn up by OFCOM under the Broadcasting Act 1996 s 104 comes into force;
     but in relation to times on or after the transfer date and before the coming into force of
     OFCOM's code, as if references in s 104(2) and in the code to the ITC were references to
     OFCOM: Communications Act 2003 s 406(6), Sch 18 para 51(2). As to the meaning of 'transfer
     date' see PARA 857 note 17. As to the transfer of functions from the ITC to OFCOM see PARA
     507.
         See *R v Independent Television Commission, ex p TvDanmark 1 Ltd* [2001] UKHL 42,
     [2001] 1 WLR 1604, [2001] All ER (D) 344 (Jul) (protection of public interest in determining
     free access to major sporting events).
6   Ie the Broadcasting Act 1996 Pt IV (ss 97–105).
7   Broadcasting Act 1996 s 104(2) (amended by the Communications Act 2003 s 360(3), Sch 15
     para 129(1), (2)).
8   Broadcasting Act 1996 s 104(3) (amended by the Communications Act 2003 Sch 15
     para 129(2)).
9   Broadcasting Act 1996 s 104 (amended by the Communications Act 2003 Sch 15 para 129(2)).
10   Broadcasting Act 1996 s 104(4)(a). As to the meaning of 'BBC' see PARA 603 note 1; and as to
     the BBC see PARAS 603–626.

11 Broadcasting Act 1996 s 104(4)(b). As to the meaning of 'the Welsh Authority' see PARA 644 note 3; definition applied by s 147(2). As to television broadcasting by the Welsh Authority see PARAS 644–661.
12 Broadcasting Act 1996 s 104(4)(c).
13 Ie the Broadcasting Act 1990 Pt I (ss 3–71). As to the granting of such a licence see PARAS 665, 679.
14 As to the meaning of 'digital programme licence' see PARA 698.
15 Ie the Broadcasting Act 1996 Pt I (ss 1–39).
16 Broadcasting Act 1996 s 104(4)(d) (amended by the Communications Act 2003 s 406(7), Sch 15 para 129(3), Sch 19). As to the granting of such a licence see PARA 698.

922.   Regulations about coverage of listed events. OFCOM[1] may make regulations for determining for the purposes of Part IV[2] of the Broadcasting Act 1996[3]:

(1)   the circumstances in which the televising of listed events[4] generally, or of a particular listed event, is or is not to be treated as live[5];

(2)   what (whether generally or in relation to particular circumstances) is to be taken to represent the provision of adequate alternative coverage[6]; and

(3)   the requirements that must be satisfied[7] by persons who have acquired rights to provide adequate alternative coverage[8].

1 As to OFCOM see PARA 507.
2 Ie the Broadcasting Act 1996 Pt IV (ss 97–105).
3 Broadcasting Act 1996 s 104ZA(1) (s 104ZA added by the Communications Act 2003 s 302(1)). The Communications Act 2003 s 403 (procedure for regulations and orders made by OFCOM: see TELECOMMUNICATIONS vol 97 (2010) PARA 45) applies to the power of OFCOM to make regulations under the Broadcasting Act 1996 s 104ZA: s 104ZA(3) (as so added). At the date at which this volume states the law, no regulations had been made under s 104ZA.
4 As to the meaning of 'listed event' see PARA 915; definition applied by the Broadcasting Act 1996 s 105(1).
5 Broadcasting Act 1996 s 104ZA(1)(a) (as added: see note 3). This power does not include power to define 'live' for the purposes of s 101B (see PARA 917): s 104ZA(2) (as so added).
6 Broadcasting Act 1996 s 104ZA(1)(b) (as added: see note 3).
7 Ie for the purposes of the Broadcasting Act 1996 s 101(1C)(d) (see PARA 916).
8 Broadcasting Act 1996 s 104ZA(1)(c) (as added: see note 3).

(vi) Copyright, Proprietary and Moral Rights

A. COPYRIGHT

(A) *Infringement of Copyright generally*

923.   Avoidance of certain terms relating to use for purpose of news reporting of visual images from broadcast. Any provision in an agreement is void in so far as it purports to prohibit or restrict relevant dealing[1] with a broadcast in any circumstances where[2] copyright in the broadcast is not infringed[3].

1 'Relevant dealing', in relation to a broadcast, means dealing by communicating to the public any visual images taken from that broadcast: Broadcasting Act 1996 s 137(2)(a) (substituted by SI 2003/2498). As to the meaning of 'broadcast' see COPYRIGHT, DESIGN RIGHT AND RELATED RIGHTS vol 9(2) (2006 Reissue) PARA 89; definition applied by the Broadcasting Act 1996 s 137(2)(b). As to the meaning of 'communicating to the public' see PARA 924 note 1; and COPYRIGHT, DESIGN RIGHT AND RELATED RIGHTS vol 9(2) (2006 Reissue) PARA 326 (definition applied by s 137(2)(b) (amended by SI 2003/2498)).
2 Ie by virtue of the Copyright, Designs and Patents Act 1988 s 30(2) (fair dealing: see COPYRIGHT, DESIGN RIGHT AND RELATED RIGHTS vol 9(2) (2006 Reissue) PARA 339). Fair

dealing for the purpose of reporting current events is not restricted to general news items: see *BBC v British Satellite Broadcasting Ltd* [1992] Ch 141, [1991] 3 All ER 833.

3   Broadcasting Act 1996 s 137(1) (amended SI 2003/2498).

924. Communication to the public and broadcasts. The communication to the public[1] of the work is an act restricted by the copyright[2] in:

(1)   a literary[3], dramatic[4], musical[5] or artistic[6] work;

(2)   a sound recording[7] or film[8]; or

(3)   a broadcast[9].

Copyright subsists in every broadcast[10] made on or after 1 August 1989[11], of which the author[12] was at the material time[13] a qualifying person[14], or if it was made[15] from a place in the United Kingdom[16] or in another country[17] to which the relevant provisions[18] of the Copyright, Designs and Patents Act 1988 extend[19].

Copyright subsists in a broadcast made before 1 August 1989 only if it subsisted immediately before that date[20]. A broadcast may, however, subsequently qualify for copyright protection on or after that date by virtue of first publication as specified above or by virtue of an Order in Council[21] extending the provisions of the Act[22].

Copyright does not subsist in a broadcast which infringes, or to the extent that it infringes, the copyright in another broadcast[23].

1   References in the Copyright, Designs and Patents Act 1988 Pt I (ss 1–179) to communication to the public are references to communication to the public by electronic transmission, and in relation to a work include: (1) the broadcasting of the work; and (2) the making available to the public of the work by electronic transmission in such a way that members of the public may access it from a place and at a time individually chosen by them: see s 20(2) (s 20 substituted by SI 2003/2498); and COPYRIGHT, DESIGN RIGHT AND RELATED RIGHTS vol 9(2) (2006 Reissue) PARA 326. As to the meanings of 'broadcasting' and 'broadcast' see COPYRIGHT, DESIGN RIGHT AND RELATED RIGHTS vol 9(2) (2006 Reissue) PARA 89.

2   Ie subject to the provisions of the Copyright, Designs and Patents Act 1988 Pt I Ch III (ss 28–76), Pt I Ch VII (ss 116–144A): see COPYRIGHT, DESIGN RIGHT AND RELATED RIGHTS. As to the meaning of 'acts restricted by the copyright' see PARA 929; and COPYRIGHT, DESIGN RIGHT AND RELATED RIGHTS vol 9(2) (2006 Reissue) PARA 311.

3   As to the meaning of 'literary work' see COPYRIGHT, DESIGN RIGHT AND RELATED RIGHTS vol 9(2) (2006 Reissue) PARA 67.

4   As to the meaning of 'dramatic work' see COPYRIGHT, DESIGN RIGHT AND RELATED RIGHTS vol 9(2) (2006 Reissue) PARA 73.

5   As to the meaning of 'musical work' see COPYRIGHT, DESIGN RIGHT AND RELATED RIGHTS vol 9(2) (2006 Reissue) PARA 73.

6   As to the meaning of 'artistic work' see COPYRIGHT, DESIGN RIGHT AND RELATED RIGHTS vol 9(2) (2006 Reissue) PARA 75.

7   As to the meaning of 'sound recording' see COPYRIGHT, DESIGN RIGHT AND RELATED RIGHTS vol 9(2) (2006 Reissue) PARA 84.

8   As to the meaning of 'film' see COPYRIGHT, DESIGN RIGHT AND RELATED RIGHTS vol 9(2) (2006 Reissue) PARA 86.

9   See the Copyright, Designs and Patents Act 1988 ss 16(4), 20(1) (s 20 as substituted: see note 1); and COPYRIGHT, DESIGN RIGHT AND RELATED RIGHTS vol 9(2) (2006 Reissue) PARA 326.

10   See the Copyright, Designs and Patents Act 1988 s 1(1) (amended by SI 2003/2498); and COPYRIGHT, DESIGN RIGHT AND RELATED RIGHTS vol 9(2) (2006 Reissue) PARA 57.

11   Ie the date on which the Copyright, Designs and Patents Act 1988 came into force: see COPYRIGHT, DESIGN RIGHT AND RELATED RIGHTS vol 9(2) (2006 Reissue) PARA 54.

12   As to who is the author of a broadcast see COPYRIGHT, DESIGN RIGHT AND RELATED RIGHTS vol 9(2) (2006 Reissue) PARA 110.

13   For these purposes, the material time, in relation to a broadcast, is when the broadcast was made: see COPYRIGHT, DESIGN RIGHT AND RELATED RIGHTS vol 9(2) (2006 Reissue) PARA 88.

14   As to who is a qualifying person see COPYRIGHT, DESIGN RIGHT AND RELATED RIGHTS vol 9(2) (2006 Reissue) PARAS 59–60.

15   As to the place from which a broadcast is made COPYRIGHT, DESIGN RIGHT AND RELATED RIGHTS vol 9(2) (2006 Reissue) PARA 88.

16   As to the meaning of 'United Kingdom' see PARA 510 note 13.

17   As to the meaning of 'country' see COPYRIGHT, DESIGN RIGHT AND RELATED RIGHTS vol 9(2) (2006 Reissue) PARA 59.

18   Ie the provisions of the Copyright, Designs and Patents Act 1988 Pt I (ss 1–179): see COPYRIGHT, DESIGN RIGHT AND RELATED RIGHTS. As to the extension of these provisions see COPYRIGHT, DESIGN RIGHT AND RELATED RIGHTS vol 9(2) (2006 Reissue) PARA 444.

19   See the Copyright, Designs and Patents Act 1988 ss 153(1)(c), 156(1) (both amended by SI 2003/2498); and COPYRIGHT, DESIGN RIGHT AND RELATED RIGHTS vol 9(2) (2006 Reissue) PARAS 59, 62, 88.

20   See the Copyright, Designs and Patents Act 1988 s 170, Sch 1 para 5(1); and COPYRIGHT, DESIGN RIGHT AND RELATED RIGHTS vol 9(2) (2006 Reissue) PARA 88. As to subsistence under the Copyright Act 1956 (repealed) see COPYRIGHT, DESIGN RIGHT AND RELATED RIGHTS vol 9(2) (2006 Reissue) PARA 44. However, no copyright subsists in a broadcast made before 1 June 1957: see the Copyright, Designs and Patents Act 1988 Sch 1 para 9(a) (substituted by SI 2003/2498); and COPYRIGHT, DESIGN RIGHT AND RELATED RIGHTS vol 9(2) (2006 Reissue) PARA 88.

21   Ie under the Copyright, Designs and Patents Act 1988 s 159: see COPYRIGHT, DESIGN RIGHT AND RELATED RIGHTS vol 9(2) (2006 Reissue) PARA 447.

22   See the Copyright, Designs and Patents Act 1988 Sch 1 para 5(2); and COPYRIGHT, DESIGN RIGHT AND RELATED RIGHTS vol 9(2) (2006 Reissue) PARA 88.

23   See the Copyright, Designs and Patents Act 1988 s 6(6) (amended by SI 2003/2498); and COPYRIGHT, DESIGN RIGHT AND RELATED RIGHTS vol 9(2) (2006 Reissue) PARA 88.

925. Safeguards in relation to certain satellite broadcasts. Where, on or after 1 December 1986, the place from which a broadcast[1] by way of satellite transmission is made[2] is located in a country[3] other than an EEA state[4] and the law of that country fails to provide at least the following level of protection:

(1)   exclusive rights in relation to wireless broadcasting equivalent to those conferred by the provisions relating to infringement by communication to the public[5] on the authors of literary[6], dramatic[7], musical[8] and artistic[9] works, films[10] and broadcasts;

(2)   a right in relation to live wireless broadcasting equivalent to that conferred on a performer under the provisions[11] relating to the consent required for the live broadcast of a performance[12]; and

(3)   a right for authors[13] of sound recordings[14] and performers to share in a single equitable remuneration in respect of the wireless broadcasting of sound recordings,

the following provisions apply[15]. Where the place from which the programme-carrying signals are transmitted to the satellite ('the uplink station') is located in an EEA state, that place is treated as the place from which the broadcast is made and the person operating the uplink station is treated as the person making the broadcast[16]. Where the uplink station is not located in an EEA state but a person who is established in an EEA state has commissioned the making of the broadcast, that person is treated as the person making the broadcast and the place in which he has his principal establishment in the EEA is treated as the place from which the broadcast is made[17].

1   As to the meaning of 'broadcast' see COPYRIGHT, DESIGN RIGHT AND RELATED RIGHTS vol 9(2) (2006 Reissue) PARA 89.

2   As to the place from which a broadcast is made see COPYRIGHT, DESIGN RIGHT AND RELATED RIGHTS vol 9(2) (2006 Reissue) PARA 88.

3   As to the meaning of 'country' see COPYRIGHT, DESIGN RIGHT AND RELATED RIGHTS vol 9(2) (2006 Reissue) PARA 59.

4   As to the meaning of 'EEA state' for these purposes see COPYRIGHT, DESIGN RIGHT AND RELATED RIGHTS vol 9(2) (2006 Reissue) PARA 90.

5 Ie rights equivalent to those conferred by the Copyright, Designs and Patents Act 1988 s 20: see PARA 924; and COPYRIGHT, DESIGN RIGHT AND RELATED RIGHTS vol 9(2) (2006 Reissue) PARA 326.

6 As to the meaning of 'literary work' see COPYRIGHT, DESIGN RIGHT AND RELATED RIGHTS vol 9(2) (2006 Reissue) PARA 67.

7 As to the meaning of 'dramatic work' see COPYRIGHT, DESIGN RIGHT AND RELATED RIGHTS vol 9(2) (2006 Reissue) PARA 73.

8 As to the meaning of 'musical work' see COPYRIGHT, DESIGN RIGHT AND RELATED RIGHTS vol 9(2) (2006 Reissue) PARA 73.

9 As to the meaning of 'artistic work' see COPYRIGHT, DESIGN RIGHT AND RELATED RIGHTS vol 9(2) (2006 Reissue) PARA 75.

10 As to the meaning of 'film' see COPYRIGHT, DESIGN RIGHT AND RELATED RIGHTS vol 9(2) (2006 Reissue) PARA 86.

11 Ie a right equivalent to that conferred by the Copyright, Designs and Patents Act 1988 s 182(1)(b): see COPYRIGHT, DESIGN RIGHT AND RELATED RIGHTS vol 9(2) (2006 Reissue) PARA 610.

12 As to the meaning of 'performance' see COPYRIGHT, DESIGN RIGHT AND RELATED RIGHTS vol 9(2) (2006 Reissue) PARA 607.

13 As to who is the author of a sound recording see COPYRIGHT, DESIGN RIGHT AND RELATED RIGHTS vol 9(2) (2006 Reissue) PARAS 110, 112.

14 As to the meaning of 'sound recording' see COPYRIGHT, DESIGN RIGHT AND RELATED RIGHTS vol 9(2) (2006 Reissue) PARA 84.

15 See the Copyright, Designs and Patents Act 1988 s 6A(1) (s 6A added by SI 1996/2967; Copyright, Designs and Patents Act 1988 s 6A(1) amended by SI 2003/2498); and COPYRIGHT, DESIGN RIGHT AND RELATED RIGHTS vol 9(2) (2006 Reissue) PARA 90. As to the right to equitable remuneration see COPYRIGHT, DESIGN RIGHT AND RELATED RIGHTS vol 9(2) (2006 Reissue) PARA 171.

16 See the Copyright, Designs and Patents Act 1988 s 6A(2) (as added: see note 15); and COPYRIGHT, DESIGN RIGHT AND RELATED RIGHTS vol 9(2) (2006 Reissue) PARA 90.

17 See the Copyright, Designs and Patents Act 1988 s 6A(3) (as added: see note 15); and COPYRIGHT, DESIGN RIGHT AND RELATED RIGHTS vol 9(2) (2006 Reissue) PARA 90.

(B) Dealings with Rights in Copyright Works

926. Satellite broadcasting; international co-production agreements. Where an agreement concluded before 1 January 1995 between two or more co-producers[1] of a film[2], one of whom is a national of an EEA state[3], and the provisions of which grant to the parties exclusive rights to exploit all communication to the public of the film in separate geographical areas, and the giving of such exclusive exploitation rights in relation to the United Kingdom does not expressly or by implication address satellite broadcasting[4] from the United Kingdom, the person to whom those exclusive rights have been granted must not make any such broadcast without the consent of any other party to the agreement whose language-related exploitation rights would be adversely affected by that broadcast[5].

1 As to the meaning of 'producer' see COPYRIGHT, DESIGN RIGHT AND RELATED RIGHTS vol 9(2) (2006 Reissue) PARA 110.

2 As to the meaning of 'film' see COPYRIGHT, DESIGN RIGHT AND RELATED RIGHTS vol 9(2) (2006 Reissue) PARA 86.

3 As to the meaning of 'EEA national' see COPYRIGHT, DESIGN RIGHT AND RELATED RIGHTS vol 9(2) (2006 Reissue) PARA 95; and as to the meaning of 'EEA state' see COPYRIGHT, DESIGN RIGHT AND RELATED RIGHTS vol 9(2) (2006 Reissue) PARA 90.

4 As to the meaning of 'broadcast' see COPYRIGHT, DESIGN RIGHT AND RELATED RIGHTS vol 9(2) (2006 Reissue) PARA 89. As to the place from which a broadcast is made, in the case of a satellite transmission, see COPYRIGHT, DESIGN RIGHT AND RELATED RIGHTS vol 9(2) (2006 Reissue) PARA 88. As to the special provision for the protection of certain satellite broadcasts see PARA 925; and COPYRIGHT, DESIGN RIGHT AND RELATED RIGHTS vol 9(2) (2006 Reissue) PARA 90.

5 See the Copyright and Related Rights Regulations 1996, SI 1996/2967, reg 29(1), (2); and COPYRIGHT, DESIGN RIGHT AND RELATED RIGHTS vol 9(2) (2006 Reissue) PARA 168.

927.   Compulsory collective administration of certain rights in relation to cable retransmission.   The right of an owner of copyright[1] in a literary[2], dramatic[3], musical[4] or artistic[5] work, sound recording[6] or film[7] to grant or refuse authorisation for cable retransmission[8] of a wireless broadcast from another EEA member state[9] in which the work is included ('cable retransmission right') may be exercised against a cable operator[10] only through a licensing body[11].

Where a copyright owner has not transferred management of his cable retransmission right to a licensing body, the licensing body which manages the rights of the same category is deemed to be mandated to manage his right[12]. Where more than one licensing body manages rights of that category, he may choose which of them is deemed to be mandated to manage his right[13]. Such a copyright owner has the same rights and obligations resulting from any relevant agreement between the cable operator and the licensing body as have copyright owners who have transferred management of their cable retransmission right to that licensing body[14]. Any rights to which a copyright owner may be so entitled must be claimed within the period of three years beginning with the date of the cable retransmission concerned[15].

The above provisions do not affect any rights exercisable by the maker of the broadcast[16], whether in relation to the broadcast or a work included in it[17].

1   As to who is the owner of the copyright in a work see COPYRIGHT, DESIGN RIGHT AND RELATED RIGHTS vol 9(2) (2006 Reissue) PARA 118 et seq.

2   As to the meaning of 'literary work' see COPYRIGHT, DESIGN RIGHT AND RELATED RIGHTS vol 9(2) (2006 Reissue) PARA 67.

3   As to the meaning of 'dramatic work' see COPYRIGHT, DESIGN RIGHT AND RELATED RIGHTS vol 9(2) (2006 Reissue) PARA 73.

4   As to the meaning of 'musical work' see COPYRIGHT, DESIGN RIGHT AND RELATED RIGHTS vol 9(2) (2006 Reissue) PARA 73.

5   As to the meaning of 'artistic work' see COPYRIGHT, DESIGN RIGHT AND RELATED RIGHTS vol 9(2) (2006 Reissue) PARA 75.

6   As to the meaning of 'sound recording' see COPYRIGHT, DESIGN RIGHT AND RELATED RIGHTS vol 9(2) (2006 Reissue) PARA 84.

7   As to the meaning of 'film' see COPYRIGHT, DESIGN RIGHT AND RELATED RIGHTS vol 9(2) (2006 Reissue) PARA 86.

8   For these purposes, 'cable retransmission' means the reception and immediate retransmission by cable, including the transmission of microwave energy between terrestrial fixed points, of a wireless broadcast: see the Copyright, Designs and Patents Act 1988 s 144A(7) (s 144A added by SI 1996/2967; Copyright, Designs and Patents Act 1988 s 144A(7) substituted by SI 2003/2498); and COPYRIGHT, DESIGN RIGHT AND RELATED RIGHTS vol 9(2) (2006 Reissue) PARA 191. As to the meaning of 'cable programme service' see COPYRIGHT, DESIGN RIGHT AND RELATED RIGHTS vol 9(2) (2006 Reissue) PARA 37; and as to the meaning of 'broadcast' see COPYRIGHT, DESIGN RIGHT AND RELATED RIGHTS vol 9(2) (2006 Reissue) PARA 89.

9   As to the meaning of 'EEA state' for these purposes see COPYRIGHT, DESIGN RIGHT AND RELATED RIGHTS vol 9(2) (2006 Reissue) PARA 90.

10 For these purposes, 'cable operator' means a person responsible for cable re-transmission of a wireless broadcast: see the Copyright, Designs and Patents Act 1988 s 144A(7) (as added and substituted: see note 8); and COPYRIGHT, DESIGN RIGHT AND RELATED RIGHTS vol 9(2) (2006 Reissue) PARA 191.

11 See the Copyright, Designs and Patents Act 1988 s 144A(1), (2) (as added (see note 8); s 144A(1) amended by SI 2003/2498 and SI 2006/1028); and COPYRIGHT, DESIGN RIGHT AND RELATED RIGHTS vol 9(2) (2006 Reissue) PARA 191. As to the meaning of 'licensing body' see COPYRIGHT, DESIGN RIGHT AND RELATED RIGHTS vol 9(2) (2006 Reissue) PARA 224.

12 See the Copyright, Designs and Patents Act 1988 s 144A(3) (as added: see note 8); and COPYRIGHT, DESIGN RIGHT AND RELATED RIGHTS vol 9(2) (2006 Reissue) PARA 191.

13 See the Copyright, Designs and Patents Act 1988 s 144A(3) (as added: see note 8); and COPYRIGHT, DESIGN RIGHT AND RELATED RIGHTS vol 9(2) (2006 Reissue) PARA 191.

14 See the Copyright, Designs and Patents Act 1988 s 144A(4) (as added: see note 8); and COPYRIGHT, DESIGN RIGHT AND RELATED RIGHTS vol 9(2) (2006 Reissue) PARA 191.

15 See the Copyright, Designs and Patents Act 1988 s 144A(5) (as added: see note 8); and COPYRIGHT, DESIGN RIGHT AND RELATED RIGHTS vol 9(2) (2006 Reissue) PARA 191.

16 As to who is the maker of a broadcast see COPYRIGHT, DESIGN RIGHT AND RELATED RIGHTS vol 9(2) (2006 Reissue) PARA 89.

17 See the Copyright, Designs and Patents Act 1988 s 144A(6) (as added: see note 8); and COPYRIGHT, DESIGN RIGHT AND RELATED RIGHTS vol 9(2) (2006 Reissue) PARA 191.

928. Powers exercisable in consequence of report of the Competition Commission. Where, following a reference to the Competition Commission[1] in connection with a merger or market investigation, whatever needs to be remedied, mitigated or prevented by the Secretary of State[2], the Office of Fair Trading[3] or (as the case may be) the Competition Commission[4] consists of or includes:

(1) conditions in licences granted by the owner of copyright[5] in a work restricting the use of the work by the licensee or the right of the copyright owner to grant other licences; or

(2) a refusal of a copyright owner to grant licences on reasonable terms, the powers conferred by the Enterprise Act 2002 for incorporation in orders[6] include power to cancel or modify those conditions and, instead or in addition, to provide that licences in respect of the copyright are to be available as of right[7].

The Secretary of State, the Office of Fair Trading or the Competition Commission must only exercise the powers available by virtue of these provisions if he or it is satisfied that to do so does not contravene any convention relating to copyright to which the United Kingdom is a party[8].

The terms of a licence so available must, in default of agreement, be settled by the Copyright Tribunal[9] on an application by the person requiring the licence; and terms so settled must authorise the licensee to do everything in respect of which a licence is so available[10].

Where the terms of a licence are settled by the tribunal, the licence has effect from the date on which the application to the tribunal was made[11].

1 As to the Competition Commission see COMPETITION vol 18 (2009) PARAS 9–12.

2 As to the Secretary of State see PARA 507 note 32.

3 As to the Office of Fair Trading see generally COMPETITION vol 18 (2009) PARAS 6–8.

4 Ie under the Competition Act 1980 s 12(5) or the Enterprise Act 2002 s 41(2), s 55(2), s 66(6), s 75(2), s 83(2), s 138(2), s 147(2), s 160(2), Sch 7 para 5(2) or Sch 7 para 10(2).

5 As to who is the owner of the copyright in a work see COPYRIGHT, DESIGN RIGHT AND RELATED RIGHTS vol 9(2) (2006 Reissue) PARA 118 et seq.

6 Ie the powers conferred by the Enterprise Act 2002 Sch 8: see COMPETITION vol 18 (2009) PARA 232 et seq.

7 See the Copyright, Designs and Patents Act 1988 s 144(1), (1A) (substituted and added respectively by the Enterprise Act 2002 s 278(1), Sch 25 para 18(1), (2)); and COPYRIGHT, DESIGN RIGHT AND RELATED RIGHTS vol 9(2) (2006 Reissue) PARA 192. The references in the Competition Act 1980 s 12(5A) and in the Competition Act 2002 ss 75(4)(a), 83(4)(a), 84(2)(a), 89(1), 160(4)(a), 161(3)(a), 164(1), Sch 7 paras 5, 10, 11 to anything permitted by the Enterprise Act 2002 Sch 8 are to be construed accordingly: see the Copyright, Designs and Patents Act 1988 s 144(2) (substituted by the Enterprise Act 2002 Sch 25 para 18(2)); and COPYRIGHT, DESIGN RIGHT AND RELATED RIGHTS. The references in the Copyright, Designs and Patents Act 1988 s 144(1), (2) to the provisions of the Enterprise Act 2002 are modified, to include references to the Enterprise Act 2002 (Protection of Legitimate Interests) Order 2003, SI 2003/1592, by the Enterprise Act 2002 (Protection of Legitimate Interests) Order 2003, SI 2003/1592, art 16, Sch 4 para 7(1).

8 See the Copyright, Designs and Patents Act 1988 s 144(3) (amended by the Enterprise Act 2002 Sch 25 para 18(3)); and COPYRIGHT, DESIGN RIGHT AND RELATED RIGHTS vol 9(2) (2006 Reissue) PARA 192. As to the conventions to which the United Kingdom is a party see COPYRIGHT, DESIGN RIGHT AND RELATED RIGHTS vol 9(2) (2006 Reissue) PARA 452. As to the meaning of 'United Kingdom' see PARA 510 note 13.

9   As to the Copyright Tribunal see COPYRIGHT, DESIGN RIGHT AND RELATED RIGHTS vol 9(2) (2006 Reissue) PARA 207 et seq.

10 See the Copyright, Designs and Patents Act 1988 s 144(4); and COPYRIGHT, DESIGN RIGHT AND RELATED RIGHTS vol 9(2) (2006 Reissue) PARA 192. As to the settlement of such licences of right by the Copyright Tribunal see COPYRIGHT, DESIGN RIGHT AND RELATED RIGHTS vol 9(2) (2006 Reissue) PARA 293 et seq.

11 See the Copyright, Designs and Patents Act 1988 s 144(5); and COPYRIGHT, DESIGN RIGHT AND RELATED RIGHTS vol 9(2) (2006 Reissue) PARA 192.

(C) Acts restricted by Copyright in a Broadcast

929.   Acts restricted by copyright in a broadcast. The following acts are restricted by the copyright[1] in a broadcast[2] or cable programme[3]:

(1)   copying the work[4];

(2)   issuing to the public[5] copies of the work[6];

(3)   renting or lending the work to the public[7];

(4)   performing, playing or showing of the work in public[8];

(5)   communicating the work to the public[9];

(6)   making an adaptation of the work or doing any of the above in relation to an adaptation[10].

1   See further COPYRIGHT, DESIGN RIGHT AND RELATED RIGHTS vol 9(2) (2006 Reissue) PARA 311 et seq.

2   As to the meaning of 'broadcast' see COPYRIGHT, DESIGN RIGHT AND RELATED RIGHTS vol 9(2) (2006 Reissue) PARA 89.

3   As to the meaning of 'cable programme' see COPYRIGHT, DESIGN RIGHT AND RELATED RIGHTS vol 9(2) (2006 Reissue) PARA 37.

4   See the Copyright, Designs and Patents Act 1988 ss 16(1)(a), 17 (s 17 amended by SI 2003/2498); and COPYRIGHT, DESIGN RIGHT AND RELATED RIGHTS vol 9(2) (2006 Reissue) PARA 314. As to the meaning of 'copying' see COPYRIGHT, DESIGN RIGHT AND RELATED RIGHTS vol 9(2) (2006 Reissue) PARA 314.

5   As to the meaning of 'issue to the public' see COPYRIGHT, DESIGN RIGHT AND RELATED RIGHTS vol 9(2) (2006 Reissue) PARA 322.

6   See the Copyright, Designs and Patents Act 1988 ss 16(1)(b), 18 (s 18 amended by SI 1992/3233 and SI 1996/2967); and COPYRIGHT, DESIGN RIGHT AND RELATED RIGHTS vol 9(2) (2006 Reissue) PARA 322. Reference to the issue of copies of a broadcast includes the issue of the original: see the Copyright, Designs and Patents Act 1988 s 18(4) (added by SI 1996/2967); and COPYRIGHT, DESIGN RIGHT AND RELATED RIGHTS vol 9(2) (2006 Reissue) PARA 322.

7   See the Copyright, Designs and Patents Act 1988 ss 16(1)(ba), 18A (added by SI 1996/2967; Copyright, Designs and Patents Act 1988 s 18A amended by SI 2003/2498); and COPYRIGHT, DESIGN RIGHT AND RELATED RIGHTS vol 9(2) (2006 Reissue) PARA 323.

8   See the Copyright, Designs and Patents Act 1988 ss 16(1)(c), 19 (s 19 amended by SI 2003/2498); and COPYRIGHT, DESIGN RIGHT AND RELATED RIGHTS vol 9(2) (2006 Reissue) PARA 324. As to the meaning of 'in public' see COPYRIGHT, DESIGN RIGHT AND RELATED RIGHTS vol 9(2) (2006 Reissue) PARA 325.

9   See the Copyright, Designs and Patents Act 1988 ss 16(1)(d), 20 (substituted by SI 2003/2498); and COPYRIGHT, DESIGN RIGHT AND RELATED RIGHTS vol 9(2) (2006 Reissue) PARA 326. As to the meaning of 'communicating to the public' see PARA 924 note 1. See also COPYRIGHT, DESIGN RIGHT AND RELATED RIGHTS vol 9(2) (2006 Reissue) PARA 339.

10 See the Copyright, Designs and Patents Act 1988 ss 16(1)(e), 21 (s 21 amended by SI 1992/3233 and SI 1997/3032); and COPYRIGHT, DESIGN RIGHT AND RELATED RIGHTS vol 9(2) (2006 Reissue) PARA 327.

(D) Statutory Defences

930.   Acts which may be done in relation to copyright works. The provisions of Chapter III of Part I of the Copyright, Designs and Patents Act 1988[1] specify acts which may be done in relation to copyright works[2] notwithstanding the subsistence of copyright[3]; they relate only to the question of infringement of copyright[4] and do not affect any other right or obligation restricting the doing of any of the specified acts[5].

Where it is provided[6] that an act does not infringe copyright, or may be done without infringing copyright, and no particular description of copyright work is mentioned, the act in question does not infringe the copyright in a work of any description[7].

No inference is, however, to be drawn from the description of any act which may[8] be done without infringing copyright as to the scope of the acts restricted by the copyright[9] in any description of work[10].

The provisions of Chapter III of Part I of the Copyright, Designs and Patents Act 1988 are to be construed independently of each other, so that the fact that an act does not fall within one provision does not mean that it is not covered by another provision[11].

1   Ie the Copyright, Designs and Patents Act 1988 Pt I Ch III (ss 28–76): see PARAS 931–939; and COPYRIGHT, DESIGN RIGHT AND RELATED RIGHTS vol 9(2) (2006 Reissue) PARAS 337 et seq, 734.
2   As to the meaning of 'copyright work' see COPYRIGHT, DESIGN RIGHT AND RELATED RIGHTS vol 9(2) (2006 Reissue) PARA 57.
3   As to when copyright subsists in works of various descriptions see COPYRIGHT, DESIGN RIGHT AND RELATED RIGHTS vol 9(2) (2006 Reissue) PARA 54 et seq.
4   As to infringement of copyright see PARA 929; and COPYRIGHT, DESIGN RIGHT AND RELATED RIGHTS vol 9(2) (2006 Reissue) PARA 311 et seq.
5   See the Copyright, Designs and Patents Act 1988 s 28(1); and COPYRIGHT, DESIGN RIGHT AND RELATED RIGHTS vol 9(2) (2006 Reissue) PARA 337.
6   Ie by the Copyright, Designs and Patents Act 1988 Pt I Ch III.
7   See the Copyright, Designs and Patents Act 1988 s 28(2); and COPYRIGHT, DESIGN RIGHT AND RELATED RIGHTS vol 9(2) (2006 Reissue) PARA 337.
8   Ie by virtue of the Copyright, Designs and Patents Act 1988 Pt I Ch III.
9   As to the meaning of 'acts restricted by the copyright' see PARA 929; and COPYRIGHT, DESIGN RIGHT AND RELATED RIGHTS vol 9(2) (2006 Reissue) PARA 311.
10   See the Copyright, Designs and Patents Act 1988 s 28(3); and COPYRIGHT, DESIGN RIGHT AND RELATED RIGHTS vol 9(2) (2006 Reissue) PARA 337.
11   See the Copyright, Designs and Patents Act 1988 s 28(4); and COPYRIGHT, DESIGN RIGHT AND RELATED RIGHTS vol 9(2) (2006 Reissue) PARA 337.

931. Incidental recording for purposes of broadcast. The following provisions apply where, by virtue of a licence[1] or assignment[2] of copyright, a person is authorised to broadcast[3] a literary[4], dramatic[5] or musical[6] work, or an adaptation[7] of such a work, an artistic work[8] or a sound recording[9] or film[10].

He is to be treated as so licensed by the owner of the copyright[11] in the work to do or authorise any of the following for the purposes of the broadcast:

(1)   in the case of a literary, dramatic or musical work, or an adaptation of such a work, to make a sound recording or film of the work or adaptation;

(2)   in the case of an artistic work, to take a photograph[12] or make a film of the work;

(3)   in the case of a sound recording or film, to make a copy of it[13].

That licence is subject to the condition that the recording, film, photograph or copy in question:

(a)   is not to be used for any other purpose; and

(b)   is to be destroyed within 28 days of being first used for broadcasting the work[14].

A recording, film, photograph or copy made in accordance with the above provisions is to be treated as an infringing copy[15] for the purposes of any use in breach of the condition mentioned in head (a) above and for all purposes after that condition or the condition mentioned in head (b) above is broken[16].

1   As to licences of copyright see COPYRIGHT, DESIGN RIGHT AND RELATED RIGHTS vol 9(2) (2006 Reissue) PARA 175 et seq.
2   As to assignment of copyright see COPYRIGHT, DESIGN RIGHT AND RELATED RIGHTS vol 9(2) (2006 Reissue) PARA 160 et seq.
3   As to the meaning of 'broadcast' see COPYRIGHT, DESIGN RIGHT AND RELATED RIGHTS vol 9(2) (2006 Reissue) PARA 89.
4   As to the meaning of 'literary work' see COPYRIGHT, DESIGN RIGHT AND RELATED RIGHTS vol 9(2) (2006 Reissue) PARA 67.
5   As to the meaning of 'dramatic work' see COPYRIGHT, DESIGN RIGHT AND RELATED RIGHTS vol 9(2) (2006 Reissue) PARA 73.
6   As to the meaning of 'musical work' see COPYRIGHT, DESIGN RIGHT AND RELATED RIGHTS vol 9(2) (2006 Reissue) PARA 73.
7   As to the meaning of 'adaptation' see COPYRIGHT, DESIGN RIGHT AND RELATED RIGHTS vol 9(2) (2006 Reissue) PARA 327.
8   As to the meaning of 'artistic work' see COPYRIGHT, DESIGN RIGHT AND RELATED RIGHTS vol 9(2) (2006 Reissue) PARA 75.
9   As to the meaning of 'sound recording' see COPYRIGHT, DESIGN RIGHT AND RELATED RIGHTS vol 9(2) (2006 Reissue) PARA 84.
10   See the Copyright, Designs and Patents Act 1988 s 68(1) (amended by SI 2003/2498); and COPYRIGHT, DESIGN RIGHT AND RELATED RIGHTS vol 9(2) (2006 Reissue) PARA 396. As to the application of the Copyright, Designs and Patents Act 1988 s 68 see PARA 930; and COPYRIGHT, DESIGN RIGHT AND RELATED RIGHTS vol 9(2) (2006 Reissue) PARA 337. As to the meaning of 'film' see COPYRIGHT, DESIGN RIGHT AND RELATED RIGHTS vol 9(2) (2006 Reissue) PARA 86.
11   As to who is the owner of the copyright in a work see COPYRIGHT, DESIGN RIGHT AND RELATED RIGHTS vol 9(2) (2006 Reissue) PARA 118 et seq.
12   As to the meaning of 'photograph' see COPYRIGHT, DESIGN RIGHT AND RELATED RIGHTS vol 9(2) (2006 Reissue) PARA 77.
13   See the Copyright, Designs and Patents Act 1988 s 68(2) (amended by SI 2003/2498); and COPYRIGHT, DESIGN RIGHT AND RELATED RIGHTS vol 9(2) (2006 Reissue) PARA 396.
14   See the Copyright, Designs and Patents Act 1988 s 68(3) (amended by SI 2003/2498); and COPYRIGHT, DESIGN RIGHT AND RELATED RIGHTS vol 9(2) (2006 Reissue) PARA 396.
15   As to the meaning of 'infringing copy' see COPYRIGHT, DESIGN RIGHT AND RELATED RIGHTS vol 9(2) (2006 Reissue) PARA 335.
16   See the Copyright, Designs and Patents Act 1988 s 68(4); and COPYRIGHT, DESIGN RIGHT AND RELATED RIGHTS vol 9(2) (2006 Reissue) PARA 396.

932.   Recording for purposes of supervision and control of broadcasts and other services.   Copyright is not infringed by the making or use by the BBC[1], for the purpose of maintaining supervision and control over programmes broadcast[2] by it, or included in any on-demand programme service[3] provided by it, of recordings of those programmes[4].

Nor is copyright infringed by anything done in pursuance of:

(1)   specified provisions of the Broadcasting Act 1990[5], the Broadcasting Act 1996[6] or the Communications Act 2003[7];

(2)   a condition which is included[8] in a licence granted under Part I or Part III of the Broadcasting Act 1990[9] or Part I or Part II of the Broadcasting Act 1996[10];

(3)   a direction given[11] in respect of OFCOM's[12] power to require production of recordings etc;

(4)   OFCOM's power[13] to make and use recordings for the purpose of maintaining supervision of the programmes included in programme services; or

(5)   the power of the appropriate regulatory authority to demand information[14] in connection with an on-demand programme service[15].

Copyright is not infringed by the use by OFCOM in connection with the performance of any of its functions under the Broadcasting Act 1990, the Broadcasting Act 1996 or the Communications Act 2003 of any recording, script or transcript which is provided to it under or by virtue of any provision of those Acts or of any existing material[16] which is transferred to OFCOM by a scheme[17] for the transfer of a pre-commencement regulator's property, rights and liabilities[18]. Nor is copyright infringed by the use by an appropriate regulatory authority[19], in connection with the performance of any of its functions under the Communications Act 2003, of any recording, script or transcript which is provided to it under or by virtue of any provision of that Act[20].

1 As to the meaning of 'BBC' see PARA 603 note 1; and as to the BBC see PARAS 603–626.

2 As to the meaning of 'broadcast' see COPYRIGHT, DESIGN RIGHT AND RELATED RIGHTS vol 9(2) (2006 Reissue) PARA 89.

3 'On-demand programme service' has the same meaning as in the Communications Act 2003 (see PARA 784): see the Copyright, Designs and Patents Act 1988 s 69(6) (added by SI 2009/2979).

4 See the Copyright, Designs and Patents Act 1988 s 69(1) (amended by SI 2009/2979); and COPYRIGHT, DESIGN RIGHT AND RELATED RIGHTS vol 9(2) (2006 Reissue) PARA 397. As to the application of the Copyright, Designs and Patents Act 1988 s 69 see COPYRIGHT, DESIGN RIGHT AND RELATED RIGHTS vol 9(2) (2006 Reissue) PARA 337.

5 Ie the Broadcasting Act 1990 s 167(1): see PARA 946.

6 Ie the Broadcasting Act 1996 s 115(4) or (6): see PARAS 909–910.

7 Ie the Communications Act 2003 Sch 12 para 20: see PARA 644.

8 Ie by virtue of the Communications Act 2003 s 334(1): see PARA 899.

9 Ie the Broadcasting Act 1990 Pt I (ss 3–71) or Pt III (ss 85–126).

10 Ie the Broadcasting Act 1996 Pt I (ss 1–39) or Pt II (ss 40–72).

11 Ie under the Broadcasting Act 1990 s 109(2): see PARA 745.

12 As to OFCOM see PARA 507.

13 Ie under the Communications Act 2003 s 334(3): see PARA 899.

14 Ie under the Communications Act 2003 s 368O(1) or (3): see PARA 870.

15 See the Copyright, Designs and Patents Act 1988 s 69(2) (substituted by the Broadcasting Act 1996 s 148(1), Sch 10 para 31; and amended by the Communications Act 2003 s 406(1), (7), Sch 17 para 91(1), (2), Sch 19(1); and by SI 2009/2979); and COPYRIGHT, DESIGN RIGHT AND RELATED RIGHTS vol 9(2) (2006 Reissue) PARA 397.

16 'Existing material' means any recording, script or transcript which was provided to the Independent Television Commission or the Radio Authority under or by virtue of any provision of the Broadcasting Act 1990 or the Broadcasting Act 1996; and any recording or transcript which was provided to the Broadcasting Standards Commission under the Broadcasting Act 1996 s 115(4) or (6) (see PARA 909) or s 116(5) (repealed): see the Copyright, Designs and Patents Act 1988 s 69(4); and COPYRIGHT, DESIGN RIGHT AND RELATED RIGHTS vol 9(2) (2006 Reissue) PARA 397.

17 Ie a scheme made under the Communications Act 2003 s 30: see TELECOMMUNICATIONS vol 97 (2010) PARA 38.

18 See the Copyright, Designs and Patents Act 1988 s 69(3) (substituted by the Broadcasting Act 1996 Sch 10 para 31; and further substituted by the Communications Act 2003 Sch 17 para 19(3)); and COPYRIGHT, DESIGN RIGHT AND RELATED RIGHTS vol 9(2) (2006 Reissue) PARA 397.

19 Ie designated under the Communications Act 2003 s 368B: see PARA 785.

20 See the Copyright, Designs and Patents Act 1988 s 69(5) (added by SI 2009/2979); and COPYRIGHT, DESIGN RIGHT AND RELATED RIGHTS.

933. Recording for purposes of time-shifting. The making in domestic premises for private and domestic use of a recording of a broadcast[1] solely for the purpose of enabling it to be viewed or listened to at a more convenient time does not infringe any copyright in the broadcast or in any work included in it[2]. Where a copy which would otherwise be an infringing copy[3] is made in accordance with these provisions but is subsequently dealt with[4], it is to be treated as an infringing copy for the purposes of that dealing, and if that dealing infringes copyright, it is to be treated as an infringing copy for all subsequent purposes[5].

1   As to the meaning of 'broadcast' see COPYRIGHT, DESIGN RIGHT AND RELATED RIGHTS vol 9(2) (2006 Reissue) PARA 89.

2   See the Copyright, Designs and Patents Act 1988 s 70(1) (numbered as such and amended by SI 2003/2498); and COPYRIGHT, DESIGN RIGHT AND RELATED RIGHTS vol 9(2) (2006 Reissue) PARA 398. As to the application of s 70 see PARA 930; and COPYRIGHT, DESIGN RIGHT AND RELATED RIGHTS vol 9(2) (2006 Reissue) PARA 337.

3   As to the meaning of 'infringing copy' see COPYRIGHT, DESIGN RIGHT AND RELATED RIGHTS vol 9(2) (2006 Reissue) PARA 335.

4   'Dealt with' means sold or let for hire, offered or exposed for sale or hire or communicated to the public: Copyright, Designs and Patents Act 1988 s 70(3) (added by SI 2003/2498); and COPYRIGHT, DESIGN RIGHT AND RELATED RIGHTS.

5   See the Copyright, Designs and Patents Act 1988 s 70(2) (added by SI 2003/2498); and COPYRIGHT, DESIGN RIGHT AND RELATED RIGHTS.

934.   Photographs of broadcasts.   The making in domestic premises for private and domestic use of a photograph[1] of the whole or any part of an image forming part of a broadcast[2], or a copy of such a photograph, does not infringe any copyright in the broadcast or in any film[3] included in it[4]. Where a copy which would otherwise be an infringing copy[5] is made in accordance with these provisions but is subsequently dealt with[6], it is to be treated as an infringing copy for the purposes of that dealing, and if that dealing infringes copyright, it is to be treated as an infringing copy for all subsequent purposes[7].

1   As to the meaning of 'photograph' see COPYRIGHT, DESIGN RIGHT AND RELATED RIGHTS vol 9(2) (2006 Reissue) PARA 77.

2   As to the meaning of 'broadcast' see COPYRIGHT, DESIGN RIGHT AND RELATED RIGHTS vol 9(2) (2006 Reissue) PARA 89.

3   As to the meaning of 'film' see COPYRIGHT, DESIGN RIGHT AND RELATED RIGHTS vol 9(2) (2006 Reissue) PARA 86.

4   See the Copyright, Designs and Patents Act 1988 s 71(1) (s 71 substituted by SI 2003/2498); and COPYRIGHT, DESIGN RIGHT AND RELATED RIGHTS vol 9(2) (2006 Reissue) PARA 399. As to the application of the Copyright, Designs and Patents Act 1988 s 71 see PARA 930; and COPYRIGHT, DESIGN RIGHT AND RELATED RIGHTS vol 9(2) (2006 Reissue) PARA 337.

5   As to the meaning of 'infringing copy' see COPYRIGHT, DESIGN RIGHT AND RELATED RIGHTS vol 9(2) (2006 Reissue) PARA 335.

6   'Dealt with' means sold or let for hire, offered or exposed for sale or hire or communicated to the public: Copyright, Designs and Patents Act 1988 s 71(3) (as substituted: see note 4).

7   See the Copyright, Designs and Patents Act 1988 s 71(2) (as substituted: see note 4); and COPYRIGHT, DESIGN RIGHT AND RELATED RIGHTS.

935.   Free public showing or playing of broadcast.   The showing or playing in public[1] of a broadcast[2] to an audience which has not paid for admission to the place where the broadcast is to be seen or heard does not infringe any copyright in the broadcast, or any sound recording[3] (except so far as it is an excepted sound recording[4]) or film[5] included in it[6].

Where by virtue of these provisions the copyright in a broadcast shown or played in public is not infringed, copyright in any excepted sound recording included in it is not infringed if the playing or showing of that broadcast in public:

(1)   forms part of the activities of an organisation that is not established or conducted for profit; or

(2)   is necessary for the purposes of: (a) repairing equipment for the reception of broadcasts; (b) demonstrating that a repair to such

equipment has been carried out; or (c) demonstrating such equipment which is being sold or let for hire or offered or exposed for sale or hire[7].

The audience is treated as having paid for admission to a place:

(i)   if it has paid for admission to a place of which that place forms part; or

(i)   if goods or services are supplied at that place, or a place of which it forms part, at prices which are substantially attributable to the facilities afforded for seeing or hearing the broadcast, or at prices exceeding those usually charged there and which are partly attributable to those facilities[8].

The following are not regarded as having paid for admission to a place:

(A)   persons admitted as residents or inmates of the place;

(B)   persons admitted as members of a club or society where the payment is only for membership of the club or society and the provision of facilities for seeing or hearing broadcasts is only incidental to the main purposes of the club or society[9].

Where the making of the broadcast was an infringement of the copyright in a sound recording or film, the fact that it was heard or seen in public by the reception[10] of the broadcast is to be taken into account in assessing the damages for that infringement[11].

1   As to the meaning of 'show or play in public' see COPYRIGHT, DESIGN RIGHT AND RELATED RIGHTS vol 9(2) (2006 Reissue) PARAS 324–325.

2   As to the meaning of 'broadcast' see COPYRIGHT, DESIGN RIGHT AND RELATED RIGHTS vol 9(2) (2006 Reissue) PARA 89.

3   As to the meaning of 'sound recording' see COPYRIGHT, DESIGN RIGHT AND RELATED RIGHTS vol 9(2) (2006 Reissue) PARA 84.

4   An 'excepted sound recording' is a sound recording whose author is not the author of the broadcast in which it is included, and which is a recording of music with or without words spoken or sung: Copyright, Designs and Patents Act 1988 s 72(1A) (added by SI 2003/2498); and COPYRIGHT, DESIGN RIGHT AND RELATED RIGHTS.

5   As to the meaning of 'film' see COPYRIGHT, DESIGN RIGHT AND RELATED RIGHTS vol 9(2) (2006 Reissue) PARA 86.

6   See the Copyright, Designs and Patents Act 1988 s 72(1) (amended by SI 2003/2498); and COPYRIGHT, DESIGN RIGHT AND RELATED RIGHTS vol 9(2) (2006 Reissue) PARA 400. As to the application of the Copyright, Designs and Patents Act 1988 s 72 see PARA 930; and COPYRIGHT, DESIGN RIGHT AND RELATED RIGHTS vol 9(2) (2006 Reissue) PARA 337.

7   See the Copyright, Designs and Patents Act 1988 s 72(1B) (added by SI 2003/2498); and COPYRIGHT, DESIGN RIGHT AND RELATED RIGHTS.

8   See the Copyright, Designs and Patents Act 1988 s 72(2) (amended by SI 2003/2498); and COPYRIGHT, DESIGN RIGHT AND RELATED RIGHTS vol 9(2) (2006 Reissue) PARA 400.

9   See the Copyright, Designs and Patents Act 1988 s 72(3) (amended by SI 2003/2498); and COPYRIGHT, DESIGN RIGHT AND RELATED RIGHTS vol 9(2) (2006 Reissue) PARA 400.

10 As to the meaning of 'reception of a broadcast' see COPYRIGHT, DESIGN RIGHT AND RELATED RIGHTS vol 9(2) (2006 Reissue) PARA 89.

11 See the Copyright, Designs and Patents Act 1988 s 72(4) (amended by SI 2003/2498); and COPYRIGHT, DESIGN RIGHT AND RELATED RIGHTS vol 9(2) (2006 Reissue) PARA 400.

936.   Reception and retransmission of wireless broadcast by cable.   The following provisions apply where a wireless broadcast[1] made from a place in the United Kingdom[2] is received and immediately retransmitted by cable[3].

The copyright in the broadcast is not infringed:

(1)   if the retransmission by cable is in pursuance of a relevant requirement[4]; or

(2)   if, and to the extent that, the broadcast is made for reception in the area in which it is retransmitted by cable and forms part of a qualifying service[5].

Nor is the copyright in any work included in the broadcast infringed if, and to the extent that, the broadcast is made for reception in the area in which it is retransmitted by cable; but, where the making of the broadcast was an infringement of the copyright in the work, the fact that the broadcast was retransmitted by cable is to be taken into account in assessing the damages for that infringement[6].

Where the retransmission by cable is in pursuance of a relevant requirement but, to any extent, the area in which the retransmission by cable takes place ('the cable area') falls outside the area for reception in which the broadcast is made ('the broadcast area'), the retransmission by cable, to the extent that it is provided for so much of the cable area as falls outside the broadcast area, of any work included in the broadcast is to be treated as licensed by the owner of the copyright[7] in the work, subject only to the payment of such reasonable royalty or other payment in respect of the retransmission by cable of the broadcast as may be agreed or determined, in default of agreement, by the Copyright Tribunal[8]; but this provision does not apply if, or to the extent that, the retransmission of the work by cable is otherwise[9] licensed by the owner of the copyright in the work[10].

1   As to the meaning of 'broadcast' see COPYRIGHT, DESIGN RIGHT AND RELATED RIGHTS vol 9(2) (2006 Reissue) PARA 89.

2   As to the place from which a broadcast is made see COPYRIGHT, DESIGN RIGHT AND RELATED RIGHTS vol 9(2) (2006 Reissue) PARAS 88, 90. As to the meaning of 'United Kingdom' see PARA 510 note 13.

3   See the Copyright, Designs and Patents Act 1988 s 73(1) (substituted by the Broadcasting Act 1996 s 138, Sch 9 para 1; and amended by SI 2003/2498); and COPYRIGHT, DESIGN RIGHT AND RELATED RIGHTS vol 9(2) (2006 Reissue) PARA 401. As to the application of the Copyright, Designs and Patents Act 1988 s 73 see PARA 930; and COPYRIGHT, DESIGN RIGHT AND RELATED RIGHTS vol 9(2) (2006 Reissue) PARA 337. For the purposes of s 73, references to retransmission by cable include the transmission of microwave energy between terrestrial fixed points: see s 73(13) (added by SI 2003/2498); and COPYRIGHT, DESIGN RIGHT AND RELATED RIGHTS.

4   For these purposes, 'relevant requirement' means a requirement imposed by a general condition (within the meaning of the Communications Act 2003 Pt 2 Ch 1 (ss 32–151)) the setting of which is authorised under s 64 (must-carry obligations: see PARA 719): see the Copyright, Designs and Patents Act 1988 s 73(7) (as substituted (see note 3); further substituted by the Communications Act 2003 s 406(1), Sch 17 para 92(1), (3)); and COPYRIGHT, DESIGN RIGHT AND RELATED RIGHTS vol 9(2) (2006 Reissue) PARA 401.

5   See the Copyright, Designs and Patents Act 1988 s 73(2) (as substituted and amended: see note 3); and COPYRIGHT, DESIGN RIGHT AND RELATED RIGHTS vol 9(2) (2006 Reissue) PARA 401. For these purposes, 'qualifying service' means, any of the following services:
     (1)   a regional or national Channel 3 service;
     (2)   Channel 4, Channel 5 and S4C;
     (3)   the public teletext service;
     (4)   S4C Digital; and
     (5)   the television broadcasting services and teletext service of the BBC,
and expressions used in this provision have the same meanings as in the Communications Act 2003 Pt 3 (ss 198–362): see the Copyright, Designs and Patents Act 1988 s 73(6) (as substituted (see note 3); and amended by the Communications Act 2003 Sch 17 para 92(2)); and COPYRIGHT, DESIGN RIGHT AND RELATED RIGHTS vol 9(2) (2006 Reissue) PARA 401. As to the meaning of 'regional Channel 3 service' see PARA 667 note 6; as to the meaning of 'national Channel 3 service' see PARA 667 note 12. As to the meaning of 'Channel 4' see PARA 637; as to the meaning of 'Channel 5' see PARA 681. As to the meaning of 'S4C' see PARA 644. As to the meaning of 'S4C Digital' see PARA 644 note 7. As to the BBC see PARAS 603–626. As to the public teletext service see PARA 686.

6   See the Copyright, Designs and Patents Act 1988 s 73(3) (as substituted and amended: see note 3); and COPYRIGHT, DESIGN RIGHT AND RELATED RIGHTS vol 9(2) (2006 Reissue) PARA 401.

7   As to who is the owner of the copyright in a work see COPYRIGHT, DESIGN RIGHT AND RELATED RIGHTS vol 9(2) (2006 Reissue) PARA 118 et seq.

8 See the Copyright, Designs and Patents Act 1988 s 73(4) (as substituted and amended: see note 3); and COPYRIGHT, DESIGN RIGHT AND RELATED RIGHTS vol 9(2) (2006 Reissue) PARA 401. As to the Copyright Tribunal see COPYRIGHT, DESIGN RIGHT AND RELATED RIGHTS vol 9(2) (2006 Reissue) PARA 207 et seq.

9 Ie apart from the Copyright, Designs and Patents Act 1988 s 73(4) (see the text and note 8).

10 See the Copyright, Designs and Patents Act 1988 s 73(5) (as substituted and amended: see note 3); and COPYRIGHT, DESIGN RIGHT AND RELATED RIGHTS vol 9(2) (2006 Reissue) PARA 401.

937. Provision of subtitled copies of broadcast. A designated body[1] may, for the purpose of providing people who are deaf or hard of hearing, or physically or mentally handicapped in other ways, with copies which are subtitled or otherwise modified for their special needs, make copies of broadcasts[2] and issue or lend copies to the public[3], without infringing any copyright in the broadcasts or works included in them[4].

The above provisions do not apply if, or to the extent that, there is a certified licensing scheme[5] providing for the grant of licences[6].

1 As to the meaning of 'designated body' see COPYRIGHT, DESIGN RIGHT AND RELATED RIGHTS vol 9(2) (2006 Reissue) PARA 402; and see the Copyright (Sub-titling of Broadcasts and Cable Programmes) (Designated Body) Order 1989, SI 1989/1013.

2 As to the meaning of 'broadcast' see COPYRIGHT, DESIGN RIGHT AND RELATED RIGHTS vol 9(2) (2006 Reissue) PARA 89.

3 As to the meaning of 'issue copies to the public' see COPYRIGHT, DESIGN RIGHT AND RELATED RIGHTS vol 9(2) (2006 Reissue) PARA 322.

4 See the Copyright, Designs and Patents Act 1988 s 74(1) (amended by SI 2003/2498); and COPYRIGHT, DESIGN RIGHT AND RELATED RIGHTS vol 9(2) (2006 Reissue) PARA 402. As to the application of the Copyright, Designs and Patents Act 1988 s 74 see PARA 930; and COPYRIGHT, DESIGN RIGHT AND RELATED RIGHTS vol 9(2) (2006 Reissue) PARA 337.

5 Ie a licensing scheme certified for the purposes of the Copyright, Designs and Patents Act 1988 s 74 under s 143 (see COPYRIGHT, DESIGN RIGHT AND RELATED RIGHTS vol 9(2) (2006 Reissue) PARA 183).

6 See the Copyright, Designs and Patents Act 1988 s 74(4); and COPYRIGHT, DESIGN RIGHT AND RELATED RIGHTS vol 9(2) (2006 Reissue) PARA 402.

938. Recording for archival purposes. A recording of a broadcast[1] of a designated class[2], or a copy of such a recording, may be made for the purpose of being placed in an archive maintained by a designated body[3] without thereby infringing any copyright in the broadcast or in any work included in it[4].

1 As to the meaning of 'broadcast' see COPYRIGHT, DESIGN RIGHT AND RELATED RIGHTS vol 9(2) (2006 Reissue) PARA 89.

2 See COPYRIGHT, DESIGN RIGHT AND RELATED RIGHTS vol 9(2) (2006 Reissue) PARA 403.

3 See COPYRIGHT, DESIGN RIGHT AND RELATED RIGHTS vol 9(2) (2006 Reissue) PARA 403.

4 See the Copyright, Designs and Patents Act 1988 s 75(1) (amended by SI 2003/2498); and COPYRIGHT, DESIGN RIGHT AND RELATED RIGHTS vol 9(2) (2006 Reissue) PARA 403. As to the application of the Copyright, Designs and Patents Act 1988 s 75 see PARA 930; and COPYRIGHT, DESIGN RIGHT AND RELATED RIGHTS vol 9(2) (2006 Reissue) PARA 337.

939. Adaptations. An act which may be done without infringing copyright[1] in a literary[2], dramatic[3] or musical[4] work does not, where that work is an adaptation[5], infringe any copyright in the work from which the adaptation was made[6].

1 Ie by virtue of the Copyright, Designs and Patents Act 1988 Pt I Ch III (ss 28–76): see PARA 930; and COPYRIGHT, DESIGN RIGHT AND RELATED RIGHTS vol 9(2) (2006 Reissue) PARAS 337 et seq, 734.

2 As to the meaning of 'literary work' see COPYRIGHT, DESIGN RIGHT AND RELATED RIGHTS vol 9(2) (2006 Reissue) PARA 67.

3   As to the meaning of 'dramatic work' see COPYRIGHT, DESIGN RIGHT AND RELATED RIGHTS
     vol 9(2) (2006 Reissue) PARA 73.
4   As to the meaning of 'musical work' see COPYRIGHT, DESIGN RIGHT AND RELATED RIGHTS
     vol 9(2) (2006 Reissue) PARA 73.
5   As to the meaning of 'adaptation' see COPYRIGHT, DESIGN RIGHT AND RELATED RIGHTS vol 9(2)
     (2006 Reissue) PARA 327.
6   See the Copyright, Designs and Patents Act 1988 s 76; and COPYRIGHT, DESIGN RIGHT AND
     RELATED RIGHTS vol 9(2) (2006 Reissue) PARA 404. As to the application of s 76 see PARA 930;
     and COPYRIGHT, DESIGN RIGHT AND RELATED RIGHTS vol 9(2) (2006 Reissue) PARA 337.

(E) Criminal Offences

940. Criminal liability for making or dealing with infringing articles. A
person commits an offence who, without the licence of the copyright owner[1]:

(1)   makes for sale[2] or hire; or
(2)   imports into the United Kingdom[3] otherwise than for his private and
       domestic use; or
(3)   possesses in the course of a business[4] with a view to committing any act
       infringing the copyright; or
(4)   in the course of a business:
       (a)   sells or lets for hire; or
       (b)   offers or exposes for sale or hire[5]; or
       (c)   exhibits in public[6]; or
       (d)   distributes[7]; or
(5)   distributes otherwise than in the course of a business to such an extent
       as to affect prejudicially the owner of the copyright[8],

an article which is, and which he knows or has reason to believe[9] is, an
infringing copy[10] of a copyright work[11].

A person commits an offence who:

(i)   makes an article specifically designed or adapted[12] for making copies of
       a particular copyright work; or
(ii)   has such an article in his possession,

knowing or having reason to believe that it is to be used to make infringing
copies for sale or hire or for use in the course of a business[13].

A person who infringes copyright in a work by communicating the work to
the public[14]:

(A)   in the course of a business; or
(B)   otherwise than in the course of a business to such an extent as to affect
       prejudicially the owner of the copyright,

commits an offence if he knows or has reason to believe that, by doing so, he is
infringing copyright in that work[15].

Where copyright is infringed, otherwise than by communication to the public:

(aa)   by the public performance[16] of a literary[17], dramatic[18] or musical[19]
       work; or

(bb)   by the playing or showing in public of a sound recording[20] or film[21],

any person who caused[22] the work to be so performed, played or shown is guilty
of an offence if he knew or had reason to believe that copyright would be
infringed[23].

A person guilty of an offence under head (1), (2), (4)(d) or (5) above is liable
on conviction on indictment to imprisonment for a term not exceeding ten years
or a fine, or to both, or on summary conviction to imprisonment for a term not
exceeding six months or a fine not exceeding the statutory maximum, or to
both[24]. A person guilty of an offence under head (A) or (B) above is liable on

conviction on indictment to a fine or imprisonment for a term not exceeding two years, or to both, or on summary conviction to imprisonment for a term not exceeding three months or a fine not exceeding the statutory maximum, or to both[25]. A person guilty of any other offence under the above provisions is liable on summary conviction to imprisonment for a term not exceeding six months or a fine not exceeding level 5 on the standard scale, or to both[26].

The statutory presumptions as to various matters connected with copyright[27] do not apply to proceedings for an offence under the above provisions, but this is without prejudice to their application in proceedings for an order for delivery up[28] in criminal proceedings[29].

Where a criminal prosecution has been brought, the court may stay the proceedings pending the resolution of the issues between the parties in the High Court if the criminal prosecution is vexatious or an abuse of the process of the court[30].

1   As to the licence of the copyright owner see COPYRIGHT, DESIGN RIGHT AND RELATED RIGHTS vol 9(2) (2006 Reissue) PARAS 121, 175. As to who is the owner of the copyright in a work see COPYRIGHT, DESIGN RIGHT AND RELATED RIGHTS vol 9(2) (2006 Reissue) PARA 118 et seq.

2   As to the meaning of 'sell' see COPYRIGHT, DESIGN RIGHT AND RELATED RIGHTS vol 9(2) (2006 Reissue) PARA 330.

3   As to the meaning of 'import' see COPYRIGHT, DESIGN RIGHT AND RELATED RIGHTS vol 9(2) (2006 Reissue) PARA 329. As to the meaning of 'United Kingdom' see PARA 510 note 13.

4   As to the meaning of 'possession in the course of a business' see COPYRIGHT, DESIGN RIGHT AND RELATED RIGHTS vol 9(2) (2006 Reissue) PARA 330.

5   As to the meaning of 'offer or expose for sale or hire' see COPYRIGHT, DESIGN RIGHT AND RELATED RIGHTS vol 9(2) (2006 Reissue) PARA 330. The test of 'selling' an article is objective in the sense that it necessary to consider only the transaction between the parties and not what was in their minds: *Phillips v Holmes* [1988] RPC 613.

6   As to the meaning of 'exhibit in public' see COPYRIGHT, DESIGN RIGHT AND RELATED RIGHTS vol 9(2) (2006 Reissue) PARA 330.

7   As to the meaning of 'distribute' see COPYRIGHT, DESIGN RIGHT AND RELATED RIGHTS vol 9(2) (2006 Reissue) PARA 330.

8   Cf *Irvine v Carson* (1991) 22 IPR 107, Aust FC; *Irvine v Hanna-Rivero* (1991) 23 IPR 295, Aust FC (informal swap of computer games via an enthusiast's network held to amount to such distribution).

9   As to the meaning of 'know or have reason to believe' see COPYRIGHT, DESIGN RIGHT AND RELATED RIGHTS vol 9(2) (2006 Reissue) PARA 334. Cf *Hooi v Brophy* (1984) 3 IPR 16; *Pontello v Giannotis* (1989) 16 IPR 174, Aust FC.

10   As to the meaning of 'infringing copy' see COPYRIGHT, DESIGN RIGHT AND RELATED RIGHTS vol 9(2) (2006 Reissue) PARA 335.

11   See the Copyright, Designs and Patents Act 1988 s 107(1); and COPYRIGHT, DESIGN RIGHT AND RELATED RIGHTS vol 9(2) (2006 Reissue) PARA 437. As to offences by bodies corporate see COPYRIGHT, DESIGN RIGHT AND RELATED RIGHTS vol 9(2) (2006 Reissue) PARA 438. As to the meaning of 'copyright work' see COPYRIGHT, DESIGN RIGHT AND RELATED RIGHTS vol 9(2) (2006 Reissue) PARA 57. As to what evidence is required to prove title and that a copy is an infringing copy see *Musa v Le Maitre* [1987] FSR 272, DC (expert evidence admissible).

12   As to articles specifically designed or adapted see COPYRIGHT, DESIGN RIGHT AND RELATED RIGHTS vol 9(2) (2006 Reissue) PARA 331.

13   See the Copyright, Designs and Patents Act 1988 s 107(2); and COPYRIGHT, DESIGN RIGHT AND RELATED RIGHTS vol 9(2) (2006 Reissue) PARA 437.

14   As to the meaning of 'communicating to the public' see PARA 924 note 1.

15   See the Copyright, Designs and Patents Act 1988 s 107(2A) (added by SI 2003/2498); and COPYRIGHT, DESIGN RIGHT AND RELATED RIGHTS vol 9(2) (2006 Reissue) PARA 437.

16   As to infringement by performance see COPYRIGHT, DESIGN RIGHT AND RELATED RIGHTS vol 9(2) (2006 Reissue) PARA 324.

17   As to the meaning of 'literary work' see COPYRIGHT, DESIGN RIGHT AND RELATED RIGHTS vol 9(2) (2006 Reissue) PARA 67.

18   As to the meaning of 'dramatic work' see COPYRIGHT, DESIGN RIGHT AND RELATED RIGHTS vol 9(2) (2006 Reissue) PARA 73.

19 As to the meaning of 'musical work' see COPYRIGHT, DESIGN RIGHT AND RELATED RIGHTS vol 9(2) (2006 Reissue) PARA 73.

20 As to infringement by playing or showing in public a sound recording or film see COPYRIGHT, DESIGN RIGHT AND RELATED RIGHTS vol 9(2) (2006 Reissue) PARA 324. As to references to playing a sound recording see COPYRIGHT, DESIGN RIGHT AND RELATED RIGHTS vol 9(2) (2006 Reissue) PARA 87. As to the meaning of 'sound recording' see COPYRIGHT, DESIGN RIGHT AND RELATED RIGHTS vol 9(2) (2006 Reissue) PARA 84.

21 As to the meaning of 'film' see COPYRIGHT, DESIGN RIGHT AND RELATED RIGHTS vol 9(2) (2006 Reissue) PARA 86.

22 A person 'causes' the public performance of a literary, dramatic or musical work if it is performed by himself, his servants or agents but not otherwise: *Russell v Briant* (1849) 8 CB 836 (owner of premises not liable by letting premises to another); *Marsh v Conquest* (1864) 17 CBNS 418; *Kelly's Directories Ltd v Gavin and Lloyds* [1902] 1 Ch 631; *Lyon v Knowles* (1864) 5 B & S 751, Ex Ch (owner of theatre not liable where he hired out the theatre to another who provided the dramatic corps and selected the plays to be performed); *Monaghan v Taylor* (1886) 2 TLR 685 (person who hired another to perform and exercised no supervision or control over the works performed liable as this was evidence of agency and authority to perform the works complained of); *Karno v Pathé Frères Ltd* (1908) 99 LT 114, 24 TLR 588 (person who delivered film to an exhibitor not liable).

23 See the Copyright, Designs and Patents Act 1988 s 107(3) (amended by SI 2003/2498); and COPYRIGHT, DESIGN RIGHT AND RELATED RIGHTS vol 9(2) (2006 Reissue) PARA 437.

24 See the Copyright, Designs and Patents Act 1988 s 107(4) (amended by the Copyright, etc and Trade Marks (Offences and Enforcement) Act 2002 s 1(1), (2)); and COPYRIGHT, DESIGN RIGHT AND RELATED RIGHTS vol 9(2) (2006 Reissue) PARA 437. See *R v Carter* [1993] FSR 303 (nine months' imprisonment suspended for two years for making and distributing pirate videos); *R v Dukett* [1998] 2 Cr App Rep (S) 59, CA (imprisonment for making and distributing pirate CD-ROMs). As to the statutory maximum see SENTENCING AND DISPOSITION OF OFFENDERS vol 92 (2010) PARA 140.

25 See the Copyright, Designs and Patents Act 1988 s 107(4A) (added by SI 2003/2498); and COPYRIGHT, DESIGN RIGHT AND RELATED RIGHTS vol 9(2) (2006 Reissue) PARA 437.

26 See the Copyright, Designs and Patents Act 1988 s 107(5); and COPYRIGHT, DESIGN RIGHT AND RELATED RIGHTS vol 9(2) (2006 Reissue) PARA 437. As to the standard scale see SENTENCING AND DISPOSITION OF OFFENDERS vol 92 (2010) PARA 142.

27 Ie the Copyright, Designs and Patents Act 1988 ss 104–106: see COPYRIGHT, DESIGN RIGHT AND RELATED RIGHTS vol 9(2) (2006 Reissue) PARAS 431–433.

28 Ie an order under the Copyright, Designs and Patents Act 1988 s 108: see COPYRIGHT, DESIGN RIGHT AND RELATED RIGHTS vol 9(2) (2006 Reissue) PARA 440.

29 See the Copyright, Designs and Patents Act 1988 s 107(6); and COPYRIGHT, DESIGN RIGHT AND RELATED RIGHTS vol 9(2) (2006 Reissue) PARA 437.

30 *Imperial Tobacco Ltd v A-G* [1981] AC 718 at 752, [1980] 1 All ER 866 at 884, HL. See also *Thames & Hudson Ltd v Design and Artists Copyright Society Ltd* [1995] FSR 153 (stay refused).

B. PROPRIETARY RIGHTS

941. Proprietary rights in respect of programmes. A person who makes charges for the reception[1] of programmes[2] included in a broadcasting[3] service provided from a place in the United Kingdom[4] or any other member state[5], or sends encrypted transmissions of any other description from a place in the United Kingdom or any other member state, or provides conditional access services[6] from a place in the United Kingdom or any other member state, is entitled to the same rights and remedies[7] against a person who:

(1) makes, imports[8], distributes, sells[9] or lets for hire, offers or exposes for sale or hire[10], or advertises for sale or hire; or has in his possession for commercial purposes; or instals, maintains or replaces for commercial purposes, any apparatus designed or adapted to enable or assist persons to access the programmes or other transmissions or circumvent conditional access technology related to the programmes or other transmissions when they are not entitled to do so; or

(2) who publishes or otherwise promotes by means of commercial communications any information which is calculated to enable or assist persons to access the programmes or other transmissions or circumvent conditional access technology related to the programmes or other transmissions when they are not entitled to do so,

as a copyright owner has in respect of an infringement of copyright[11].

The withdrawal of the privilege against self-incrimination in certain proceedings relating to intellectual property[12] applies to proceedings under the above provisions as to proceedings relating to copyright[13].

Damages are excluded in the case of innocent infringement of the rights conferred by the above provisions[14].

The court may order offending apparatus which has been delivered up or seized to be disposed of[15].

Her Majesty may by Order in Council provide that the above provisions apply in relation to programmes included in services provided from abroad and to encrypted transmissions sent from abroad[16].

1   As to the meaning of 'reception of a broadcast' see COPYRIGHT, DESIGN RIGHT AND RELATED RIGHTS vol 9(2) (2006 Reissue) PARA 89.

2   As to the meaning of 'programme' see COPYRIGHT, DESIGN RIGHT AND RELATED RIGHTS vol 9(2) (2006 Reissue) PARA 89.

3   As to the meaning of 'broadcasting' see COPYRIGHT, DESIGN RIGHT AND RELATED RIGHTS vol 9(2) (2006 Reissue) PARA 89.

4   As to the meaning of 'place from which a broadcast is made' see COPYRIGHT, DESIGN RIGHT AND RELATED RIGHTS vol 9(2) (2006 Reissue) PARA 88. As to the meaning of 'United Kingdom' see PARA 510 note 13.

5   Ie a member state of the European Union.

6   'Conditional access services' means services comprising the provision of conditional access technology: Copyright, Designs and Patents Act 1988 s 298(7) (s 298 substituted by SI 2000/1175); and COPYRIGHT, DESIGN RIGHT AND RELATED RIGHTS vol 9(2) (2006 Reissue) PARA 495. As to the meaning of 'conditional access technology' see PARA 586 note 4; definition applied by the Copyright, Designs and Patents Act 1988 s 298(7) (as so substituted) (see COPYRIGHT, DESIGN RIGHT AND RELATED RIGHTS vol 9(2) (2006 Reissue) PARA 495).

7   See the Copyright, Designs and Patents Act 1988 s 298(1) (as substituted (see note 6); and amended by SI 2003/2498); and COPYRIGHT, DESIGN RIGHT AND RELATED RIGHTS vol 9(2) (2006 Reissue) PARA 495.

8   As to the meaning of 'import' see COPYRIGHT, DESIGN RIGHT AND RELATED RIGHTS vol 9(2) (2006 Reissue) PARA 329.

9   As to the meaning of 'sell' see COPYRIGHT, DESIGN RIGHT AND RELATED RIGHTS vol 9(2) (2006 Reissue) PARA 330.

10 As to the meaning of 'offer or expose for sale or hire' see COPYRIGHT, DESIGN RIGHT AND RELATED RIGHTS vol 9(2) (2006 Reissue) PARA 330.

11 See the Copyright, Designs and Patents Act 1988 s 298(2) (as substituted: see note 6); and COPYRIGHT, DESIGN RIGHT AND RELATED RIGHTS vol 9(2) (2006 Reissue) PARA 495. See also *BBC Enterprises Ltd v Hi-Tech Xtravision Ltd* [1991] 2 AC 327, [1991] 3 All ER 257, HL; and *Union of European Football Associations v Euroview* [2010] EWHC 1066 (Ch), [2010] All ER (D) 87 (Apr) (where claimants had alleged that defendants' use of foreign decoding equipment to enable viewing of European league match broadcasts from outside the United Kingdom had infringed their rights in the broadcasts, contrary to the Copyright Designs and Patents Act 1988 ss 17, 298, the court referred a number of issues of interpretation of EU law to the European Court of Justice for preliminary rulings). As to the offence of fraudulently receiving programmes see PARAS 584–587. As to the rights and remedies of a copyright owner see COPYRIGHT, DESIGN RIGHT AND RELATED RIGHTS vol 9(2) (2006 Reissue) PARA 410 et seq.

12 See the Senior Courts Act 1981 s 72; and COPYRIGHT, DESIGN RIGHT AND RELATED RIGHTS vol 9(2) (2006 Reissue) PARA 435. The Senior Courts Act 1981 was previously known as the Supreme Court Act 1981 and was renamed by the Constitutional Reform Act 2005 s 59(5), Sch 11 Pt 1 as from 1 October 2009: see the Constitutional Reform Act 2005 (Commencement No 11) Order 2009, SI 2009/1604; and COURTS AND TRIBUNALS.

13 See the Copyright, Designs and Patents Act 1988 s 298(4) (as substituted (see note 6) and amended by the Constitutional Reform Act 2005 s 59(5), Sch 11 Pt 1 para 1(2)); and COPYRIGHT, DESIGN RIGHT AND RELATED RIGHTS vol 9(2) (2006 Reissue) PARA 495.

14 See the Copyright, Designs and Patents Act 1988 ss 97(1), 298(5) (s 298(5) as substituted: see note 6); and COPYRIGHT, DESIGN RIGHT AND RELATED RIGHTS vol 9(2) (2006 Reissue) PARA 495.

15 See the Copyright, Designs and Patents Act 1988 s 298(3), (6), (7) (as substituted: see note 6); and COPYRIGHT, DESIGN RIGHT AND RELATED RIGHTS vol 9(2) (2006 Reissue) PARA 495.

16 See the Copyright, Designs and Patents Act 1988 s 299(1); and COPYRIGHT, DESIGN RIGHT AND RELATED RIGHTS vol 9(2) (2006 Reissue) PARA 496. For such an order see the Fraudulent Reception of Transmissions (Guernsey) Order 1989, SI 1989/2203.

C. MORAL RIGHTS

942. Moral rights. The Copyright, Designs and Patents Act 1988[1] conferred a number of new rights which, together with the existing 'false attribution right'[2], are known collectively as 'moral rights'. The moral rights are:

(1)   the right to be identified as the author of a work or the director of a film, as the case may be (the 'right of paternity')[3];

(2)   the right to object to derogatory treatment of a work or film (the 'right of integrity')[4];

(3)   the right not to have a work or film falsely attributed to an author or director, as the case may be[5];

(4)   the right to privacy of certain photographs and films[6].

No act done before 1 August 1989[7] is actionable as a breach of the moral rights[8]; and the provisions relating to moral rights are subject to modifications in relation to works made before that date[9].

The provisions relating to moral rights do not apply to publication right[10].

1   Ie the Copyright, Designs and Patents Act 1988 Pt I Ch IV (ss 77–89) (see COPYRIGHT, DESIGN RIGHT AND RELATED RIGHTS vol 9(2) (2006 Reissue) PARA 445 et seq), s 94 (see COPYRIGHT, DESIGN RIGHT AND RELATED RIGHTS vol 9(2) (2006 Reissue) PARA 483), s 95 (see COPYRIGHT, DESIGN RIGHT AND RELATED RIGHTS vol 9(2) (2006 Reissue) PARA 484), s 103 (see COPYRIGHT, DESIGN RIGHT AND RELATED RIGHTS vol 9(2) (2006 Reissue) PARA 466), s 104 (see COPYRIGHT, DESIGN RIGHT AND RELATED RIGHTS vol 9(2) (2006 Reissue) PARA 431) and s 105 (see COPYRIGHT, DESIGN RIGHT AND RELATED RIGHTS vol 9(2) (2006 Reissue) PARA 432).

2   Ie the right of an author of a work or a director of a film not to have the work or film, as the case may be, falsely attributed to him: see COPYRIGHT, DESIGN RIGHT AND RELATED RIGHTS vol 9(2) (2006 Reissue) PARA 471.

3   See the Copyright, Designs and Patents Act 1988 s 77; and COPYRIGHT, DESIGN RIGHT AND RELATED RIGHTS vol 9(2) (2006 Reissue) PARA 456.

4   See the Copyright, Designs and Patents Act 1988 s 80; and COPYRIGHT, DESIGN RIGHT AND RELATED RIGHTS vol 9(2) (2006 Reissue) PARA 463.

5   See the Copyright, Designs and Patents Act 1988 s 84(1); and COPYRIGHT, DESIGN RIGHT AND RELATED RIGHTS vol 9(2) (2006 Reissue) PARA 471.

6   See the Copyright, Designs and Patents Act 1988 s 85; and COPYRIGHT, DESIGN RIGHT AND RELATED RIGHTS vol 9(2) (2006 Reissue) PARA 476.

7   Ie the date on which the Copyright, Designs and Patents Act 1988 came into force: see COPYRIGHT, DESIGN RIGHT AND RELATED RIGHTS vol 9(2) (2006 Reissue) PARA 54.

8   See the Copyright, Designs and Patents Act 1988 s 170, Sch 1 para 22(1); and COPYRIGHT, DESIGN RIGHT AND RELATED RIGHTS vol 9(2) (2006 Reissue) PARA 455.

9   See the Copyright, Designs and Patents Act 1988 Sch 1 paras 23, 24; and COPYRIGHT, DESIGN RIGHT AND RELATED RIGHTS vol 9(2) (2006 Reissue) PARAS 457, 465, 477.

10 See COPYRIGHT, DESIGN RIGHT AND RELATED RIGHTS vol 9(2) (2006 Reissue) PARAS 455, 500. As to the meaning of 'publication right' see COPYRIGHT, DESIGN RIGHT AND RELATED RIGHTS vol 9(2) (2006 Reissue) PARA 497.

(vii) Prohibition of Obscene and Other Material in Programme Services

943. Action against licence holders who incite crime or disorder. OFCOM[1] must serve a notice[2] on the holder of a licence to provide a television licensable content service[3] if it is satisfied: (1) that the holder of the licence has included in the service one or more programmes containing material likely to encourage or to incite the commission of crime, or to lead to disorder; (2) that, in doing so, he has contravened conditions contained by virtue of Chapter 4 of Part 4 of the Communications Act 2003[4] in the licence to provide that service; and (3) that the contravention is such as to justify the revocation of the licence[5]. A notice must: (a) state that OFCOM is satisfied as mentioned above[6]; (b) specify the respects in which, in its opinion, the licence holder has contravened the condition mentioned in head (2) above; (c) state that OFCOM may revoke the licence after the end of the period of 21 days beginning with the day on which the notice is served on the licence holder; and (d) inform the licence holder of his right to make representations to OFCOM within that period about the matters appearing to OFCOM to provide grounds for revoking the licence[7].

The effect of such a notice is to suspend the licence as from the time when the notice is served on the licence holder until either: (i) the revocation of the licence takes effect; or (ii) OFCOM decides not to revoke the licence[8]. If, after considering any representations made to it by the licence holder within the period specified for the purposes of head (c) above, OFCOM is satisfied that it is necessary in the public interest to revoke the licence, it must serve a notice of revocation on the licence holder[9].

1 As to OFCOM see PARA 507.
2 Ie under the Communications Act 2003 s 239(2) (see the text and note 7).
3 As to the meaning of 'television licensable content service' see PARA 716.
4 Ie the Communications Act 2003 Pt 4 Ch 4 (ss 263–347).
5 Communications Act 2003 s 239(1).
6 Ie as mentioned in the Communications Act 2003 s 239(1) (see the text and notes 1–5).
7 Communications Act 2003 s 239(2).
8 Communications Act 2003 s 239(3).
9 Communications Act 2003 s 239(4). The revocation of a licence by a notice under s 239(4) takes effect from such time as may be specified in the notice: s 239(5). A notice of revocation under s 239(4) must not specify a time for it to take effect that falls before the end of the period of 28 days beginning with the day on which the notice is served on the licence holder: s 239(6).

944. Liability of person providing live programme material. Where any obscene matter is included by any person[1] in a relevant programme[2] in certain circumstances[3], and that matter has been provided, for inclusion in that programme, by some other person[4], the Obscene Publications Act 1959 has effect as if that matter had been included in that programme by that other person (as well as by the person first referred to)[5].

Where a person has an obscene article[6] in his ownership, possession or control with a view to the matter recorded on it being included in a relevant programme, the article is to be taken for the purposes of the Obscene Publications Act 1959 to be an obscene article had or kept by that person for publication for gain[7].

Proceedings for an offence[8] for publishing an obscene article may not be instituted except by or with the consent of the Director of Public Prosecutions[9] in any case where the relevant publication[10], or the only other publication which followed from the relevant publication, took place in the course of the inclusion of a programme in a programme service[11]. Proceedings for such an offence for having an obscene article for publication for gain may not be instituted except by or with the consent of the Director of Public Prosecutions in any case where the relevant publication[12], or the only other publication which could reasonably have been expected to follow from the relevant publication, was to take place in the course of the inclusion of a programme in a programme service[13]. A person may not be convicted of an offence[14] in respect of the inclusion of any matter in a relevant programme if he proves that he did not know and had no reason to suspect that the programme would include matter rendering him liable to be convicted of such an offence[15].

1   As to the meaning of 'person' see PARA 510 note 1.
2   'Relevant programme' means a programme included in a programme service: Broadcasting Act 1990 s 162(2), Sch 15 para 1. As to the meaning of 'programme' see PARA 667 note 7; and as to the meaning of 'programme service' see PARA 507 note 9.
3   See the Broadcasting Act 1990 Sch 15 para 2(a). The circumstances are those falling within the Obscene Publications Act 1959 s 1(5) (see CRIMINAL LAW vol 26 (2010) PARA 704): see the Broadcasting Act 1990 Sch 15 para 2(a).
4   Broadcasting Act 1990 Sch 15 para 2(b).
5   See the Broadcasting Act 1990 Sch 15 para 2. As to the Obscene Publications Act 1959 see CRIMINAL LAW vol 26 (2010) PARA 704 et seq.
6   As to the meaning of 'article' see the Obscene Publications Act 1959 s 1(2); and CRIMINAL LAW vol 26 (2010) PARA 704 (definition applied by the Broadcasting Act 1990 Sch 15 para 1). As to the test of obscenity see the Obscene Publications Act 1959 s 1(1); and CRIMINAL LAW vol 26 (2010) PARA 705.
7   Broadcasting Act 1990 Sch 15 para 3. As to when a person publishes an article see the Obscene Publications Act 1959 s 1(4), (5); and CRIMINAL LAW vol 26 (2010) PARA 704.
8   Ie under the Obscene Publications Act 1959 s 2 (see CRIMINAL LAW vol 26 (2010) PARA 704 et seq): see the Broadcasting Act 1990 Sch 15 para 4(1).
9   As to the Director of Public Prosecutions see CRIMINAL PROCEDURE vol 27 (2010) PARAS 23, 33 et seq.
10   For the purposes of the Broadcasting Act 1990 Sch 15 para 4(1), 'the relevant publication' means the publication in respect of which the defendant would be charged if the proceedings were brought: see Sch 15 para 4(1).
11   Broadcasting Act 1990 Sch 15 para 4(1).
12   For the purposes of the Broadcasting Act 1990 Sch 15 para 4(2), 'the relevant publication' means the publication which, if the proceedings were brought, the defendant would be alleged to have had in contemplation: see Sch 15 para 4(2).
13   Broadcasting Act 1990 Sch 15 para 4(2). Without prejudice to the duty of a court to make an order for the forfeiture of an article under the Obscene Publications Act 1964 s 1(4) (orders on conviction: CRIMINAL LAW vol 26 (2010) PARA 704), in a case where by virtue of the Broadcasting Act 1990 Sch 15 para 4(2) proceedings under the Obscene Publications Act 1959 s 2 (see CRIMINAL LAW vol 26 (2010) PARA 704 et seq) for having an article for publication for gain could not be instituted except by or with the consent of the Director of Public Prosecutions, no order for the forfeiture of the article may be made under s 3 (power of search and seizure: see CRIMINAL LAW vol 26 (2010) PARA 708) unless the warrant under which the article was seized was issued on an information laid by or on behalf of the Director of Public Prosecutions: Broadcasting Act 1990 Sch 15 para 4(3).
14   Ie under the Obscene Publications Act 1959 s 2 (see CRIMINAL LAW vol 26 (2010) PARA 704 et seq): see the Broadcasting Act 1990 Sch 15 para 5(1).
15   Broadcasting Act 1990 Sch 15 para 5(1). Where the publication in issue in any proceedings under the Obscene Publications Act 1959 consists of the inclusion of any matter in a relevant programme, s 4(1) (general defence of public good: see CRIMINAL LAW vol 26 (2010) PARA 706) does not apply but a person may not be convicted of an offence under s 2 (see CRIMINAL LAW vol 26 (2010) PARA 704 et seq), and an order for forfeiture may not be made under s 3 (see CRIMINAL LAW vol 26 (2010) PARA 709), if it is proved that the inclusion of the matter in question in a relevant programme is justified as being for the public good on the ground that it is in the interests of: (1) drama, opera, ballet or any other art; (2) science, literature or learning; or (3) any other objects of general concern: Broadcasting Act 1990 Sch 15 para 5(2). The Obscene Publications Act 1959 s 4(2) (admissibility of opinions of experts: see CRIMINAL LAW vol 26 (2010) PARA 706) applies for the purposes of the Broadcasting Act 1990 Sch 15 para 5(2) as it applies for the purposes of the Obscene Publications Act 1959 s 4(1) and s 4(1A) (see CRIMINAL LAW vol 26 (2010) PARA 706: Broadcasting Act 1990 Sch 15 para 5(3).

Without prejudice to the Obscene Publications Act 1959 s 2(4) (see CRIMINAL LAW vol 26 (2010) PARA 704), a person may not be proceeded against for an offence at common law:

(a)   in respect of a relevant programme or anything said or done in the course of such a programme, where it is of the essence of the common law offence that the programme or (as the case may be) what was said or done was obscene, indecent, offensive, disgusting or injurious to morality (Broadcasting Act 1990 Sch 15 para 6(a)); or

(b)   in respect of an agreement to cause a programme to be included in a programme service or to cause anything to be said or done in the course of a programme which is to be so included, where the common law offence consists of conspiring to corrupt public morals or to do any act contrary to public morals or decency (Sch 15 para 6(b)).

945. Defamatory material. For the purposes of the law of libel and slander, the publication of words in the course of any programme[1] included in a programme service[2] is to be treated as publication in permanent form[3].

1   As to the meaning of 'programme' see PARA 667 note 7.
2   As to the meaning of 'programme service' see PARA 507 note 9.
3   Broadcasting Act 1990 s 166(1) (amended by the Coroners and Justice Act 2009 s 178, Sch 23 Pt 2). The Broadcasting Act 1990 s 166(1) applies for the purposes of the Defamation Act 1952 s 3 (slander of title etc: see LIBEL AND SLANDER vol 28 (Reissue) PARA 285) as it applies for the purposes of the law of libel and slander: Broadcasting Act 1990 s 166(2). See further LIBEL AND SLANDER vol 28 (Reissue) PARA 76.

946. Power to make copies of recordings. If a justice of the peace is satisfied by information on oath laid by a constable[1] that there is reasonable ground for suspecting that a relevant offence[2] has been committed by any person[3] in respect of a programme[4] included in a programme service[5], he may make an order authorising any constable to require that person[6]:

(1)   to produce to the constable a visual or sound recording of any matter included in that programme, if and so far as that person is able to do so[7]; and

(2)   on the production of such a recording, to afford the constable an opportunity of causing a copy of it to be made[8].

Such an order must describe the programme to which it relates in a manner sufficient to enable that programme to be identified[9]. A person who without reasonable excuse fails to comply with any such requirement of a constable is guilty of an offence and liable on summary conviction to a fine not exceeding level 3 on the standard scale[10].

1   As to the office of constable see POLICE vol 36(1) (2007 Reissue) PARAS 101–105.
2   'Relevant offence' means an offence under: (1) the Obscene Publications Act 1959 s 2 (see CRIMINAL LAW vol 26 (2010) PARA 704 et seq); or (2) the Public Order Act 1986 s 22 or 29F (see CRIMINAL LAW vol 26 (2010) PARAS 499, 507, 516): Broadcasting Act 1990 s 167(5) (amended by the Criminal Justice and Immigration Act 2008 s 148, Sch 26 Pt 2 para 28(1), (3)).
3   As to the meaning of 'person' see PARA 510 note 1.
4   As to the meaning of 'programme' see PARA 667 note 7.
5   As to the meaning of 'programme service' see PARA 507 note 9.
6   Broadcasting Act 1990 s 167(1).
7   Broadcasting Act 1990 s 167(1)(a).
8   Broadcasting Act 1990 s 167(1)(b). No order may be made under s 167 in respect of any recording in respect of which a warrant could be granted under any of the following provisions, namely: (1) the Obscene Publications Act 1959 s 3 (see CRIMINAL LAW vol 26 (2010) PARA 708); (2) the Public Order Act 1986 s 24 or 29H (see CRIMINAL LAW vol 26 (2010) PARAS 500, 508); and (3) the Public Order (Northern Ireland) Order 1987, SI 1987/463 (NI 7), art 14: Broadcasting Act 1990 s 167(4) (amended by the Criminal Justice and Immigration Act 2008 Sch 26 Pt 2 para 28(2)).
9   Broadcasting Act 1990 s 167(2).
10   Broadcasting Act 1990 s 167(3). As to the standard scale see SENTENCING AND DISPOSITION OF OFFENDERS vol 92 (2010) PARA 142.

6. LICENSING OF TELEVISION RECEPTION

(1) INTRODUCTION

947. Introduction and overview. In the United Kingdom, for any household in which television transmissions are watched or recorded, a television licence must be purchased annually[1]. This is the case irrespective of what content is watched and of how the transmission is received, whether via terrestrial (analogue or digital) broadcasting, satellite, cable, or the internet. A licence is not required simply to possess a television set; ownership of such equipment merely for the purpose of watching pre-recorded content or for use as a video game or computer visual display unit is entirely legitimate. Income from the licence fee is primarily used to fund the public services delivered by the BBC. At present, a proportion of this fee is paid direct by the government to offset fee concessions granted to persons over the age of 75[2].

Obligations, and potential liabilities, under the licensing regime fall upon both the person who receives television transmissions[3] and television dealers who lease or sell television equipment[4].

1 See PARA 948. As to the meaning of 'United Kingdom' see PARA 510 note 13.
2 As to the statutory basis for concessions see PARA 950.
3 See PARAS 948–951.
4 See PARAS 952–954.

(2) LICENSING OF TELEVISION RECEPTION

948. Licence for use of television receiver. A television receiver[1] must not be installed or used[2] unless the installation and use of the receiver is authorised by a licence under Part 4 of the Communications Act 2003[3]. A person who installs or uses a television receiver in contravention of this provision is guilty of an offence[4]. A person with a television receiver in his possession or under his control who intends to install or use it in contravention of this provision, or knows, or has reasonable grounds for believing, that another person intends to install or use it in such contravention, is guilty of an offence[5]. A person guilty of either offence is liable, on summary conviction, to a fine not exceeding level 3 on the standard scale[6].

The requirement for a licence is not contravened by anything done in the course of the business of a dealer in television receivers solely for one or more of the following purposes: (1) installing a television receiver on delivery; (2) demonstrating, testing or repairing a television receiver[7].

The Secretary of State may by regulations exempt from the requirement of a television licence the installation or use of television receivers (a) of such descriptions; (b) by such persons; (c) in such circumstances; and (d) for such purposes, as may be provided for in the regulations[8]. Such regulations may make any exemption for which such regulations provide subject to compliance with such conditions as may be specified in the regulations[9].

1 In the Communications Act 2003 Pt 4 (ss 363–368), 'television receiver' means any apparatus of a description specified in regulations made by the Secretary of State setting out the descriptions of apparatus that are to be television receivers for the purposes of that Part: s 368(1). Regulations under s 368 defining a television receiver may provide for references to such a receiver to include references to software used in association with apparatus: s 368(2). The Communications (Television Licensing) Regulations 2004, SI 2004/692 (amended by SI 2007/718), provide that 'television receiver' means any apparatus installed or used for the

purpose of receiving (whether by means of wireless telegraphy or otherwise) any television programme service, whether or not it is installed or used for any other purpose: Communications (Television Licensing) Regulations 2004, SI 2004/692, reg 9(1). In reg 9, any reference to receiving a television programme service includes a reference to receiving by any means any programme included in that service, where that programme is received at the same time (or virtually the same time) as it is received by members of the public by virtue of its being broadcast or distributed as part of that service: reg 9(2).

2 References in the Communications Act 2003 Pt 4 to using a television receiver are references to using it for receiving television programmes: s 368(3). The power to make regulations under s 368 defining a television receiver (see note 1) includes power to modify s 368(3): s 368(4).

3 Communications Act 2003 s 363(1). As to the issue of licences see PARA 949.

4 Communications Act 2003 s 363(2).

5 Communications Act 2003 s 363(3).

6 Communications Act 2003 s 363(4). As to the standard scale see SENTENCING AND DISPOSITION OF OFFENDERS vol 92 (2010) PARA 142.

7 Communications Act 2003 s 363(5).

8 Communications Act 2003 s 363(6). At the date at which this volume states the law, no such regulations had been made.

9 Communications Act 2003 s 363(7).

949. Issue of television licences. A licence for the use of a television receiver[1] (a 'TV licence') may be issued by the BBC[2] subject to such restrictions and conditions as it thinks fit; and must be issued subject to such restrictions and conditions as the Secretary of State may require by a direction to the BBC[3]. The matters to which the restrictions and conditions subject to which a TV licence may be issued may relate include, in particular:

(1) the description of television receivers that may be installed and used under the licence;

(2) the persons authorised by the licence to install and use a television receiver;

(3) the places where the installation and use of the television receiver is authorised by the licence;

(4) the circumstances in which the installation and use of such a receiver is so authorised;

(5) the purposes for which the installation and use of such a receiver is so authorised;

(6) the use of such receiver in a manner that causes, or may cause, interference (within the meaning of the Wireless Telegraphy Act 2006) with wireless telegraphy[4].

The restrictions and conditions subject to which a TV licence may be issued do not include:

(a) a provision conferring a power of entry to any premises; or

(b) a provision prohibited by a direction to the BBC by the Secretary of State[5].

A TV licence continues in force, unless previously revoked by the BBC, for such period as may be specified in the licence[6]. The BBC may revoke or modify a TV licence, or the restrictions or conditions of such a licence, by a notice[7] to the holder of the licence, or by a general notice published in such manner as may be specified in the licence[8]. It is the duty of the BBC to exercise its power[9] to revoke or modify a TV licence, or any of its restrictions or conditions, if it is directed to do so by the Secretary of State[10].

A direction by the Secretary of State may be given either generally in relation to all TV licences (or all TV licences of a particular description) or in relation to a particular licence[11].

1   Ie a licence for the purposes of the Communications Act 2003 s 363: see PARA 948. As to the meaning of 'television receiver' see PARA 948 note 1.
2   As to the meaning of 'BBC' see PARA 603 note 1; and as to the BBC see PARAS 603–626.
3   Communications Act 2003 s 364(1). As to the Secretary of State see PARA 507 note 32. As to fees for the issue of a licence see PARA 950.
4   Communications Act 2003 s 364(2) (amended by the Wireless Telegraphy Act 2006 s 123, Sch 7 paras 25, 29). As to interference within the meaning of the Wireless Telegraphy Act 2006 see PARA 568 note 6.
5   Communications Act 2003 s 364(3).
6   Communications Act 2003 s 364(4).
7   A notice under the Communications Act 2003 s 364(5)(a) must be given in the manner specified in the licence, or if no manner of service is so specified, in the manner authorised by s 394 (see TELECOMMUNICATIONS vol 97 (2010) PARA 50): s 364(8). For the purposes of the application, in relation to the giving of such a notice, of s 394 and of the Interpretation Act 1978 s 7 (service by post) in its application for the purposes of that provision, a person's proper address is any address where he is authorised by a TV licence to install or use a television receiver or, if there is no such address, his last known address: Communications Act 2003 s 364(9).
8   Communications Act 2003 s 364(5).
9   Ie under the Communications Act 2003 s 364(5).
10   Communications Act 2003 s 364(6).
11   Communications Act 2003 s 364(7).

950. Fees for television licences. A person to whom a TV licence is issued[1] is liable to pay on the issue of the licence (whether initially or by way of renewal), and in such other circumstances as regulations made by the Secretary of State[2] may provide, such sum (if any) as may be provided for by any such regulations[3]. Sums which a person is liable to pay by virtue of such regulations must be paid to the BBC[4] and are recoverable by it accordingly[5]. The BBC is entitled, in such cases as it may determine, to make refunds of sums received by it by virtue of such regulations[6].

Regulations may include provision for the means by which an entitlement to a concession[7] is to be established, and for the payment of sums by means of an instalment scheme set out in the regulations[8].

1   As to the issue of licences see PARA 949.
2   As to the Secretary of State see PARA 507 note 32. The consent of the Treasury is required for the making of any regulations under the Communications Act 2003 s 365: s 365(6). As to the Treasury see CONSTITUTIONAL LAW AND HUMAN RIGHTS vol 8(2) (Reissue) PARAS 512–517. As to the regulations made under s 365 see note 3.
3   Communications Act 2003 s 365(1). As to the fees payable see the Communications (Television Licensing) Regulations 2004, SI 2004/692, reg 3, Schs 1–5 (amended by SI 2005/606, SI 2005/2078, SI 2006/619, SI 2007/718, SI 2008/643, SI 2009/505 and SI 2010/640). These regulations came into force on 1 April 2004: see the Communications (Television Licensing) Regulations 2004, SI 2004/692, reg 1(1). There are concessions for blind persons (see the Communications (Television Licensing) Regulations 2004, SI 2004/692, reg 5 (amended by SI 2005/606 and SI 2007/718)) and for persons aged 75 years or more (see the Communications (Television Licensing) Regulations 2004, SI 2004/692, reg 6). Provision is made for a fee to be paid for the issue of a duplicate licence, where a licence is lost or destroyed: see reg 4 (amended by SI 2005/606).
4   As to the meaning of 'BBC' see PARA 603 note 1; and as to the BBC see PARAS 603–626.
5   Communications Act 2003 s 365(2). Subject to s 356(8) (see note 6), sums received by the BBC by virtue of any regulations under s 365 must be paid into the Consolidated Fund: see s 365(7); and PARA 623.
6   Communications Act 2003 s 365(3). The BBC may retain, out of the sums received by it by virtue of regulations under s 365, any sums it requires for making refunds of sums so received: s 365(8).

7 The reference to a concession in the Communications Act 2003 s 365(4) is a reference to any concession under which a person is, on the satisfaction of specified requirements, exempted from the liability to pay a sum in respect of a TV licence or required to pay only a reduced sum in respect of such a licence: s 365(5).

8 Communications Act 2003 s 365(4).

951. Powers of enforcement. If a justice of the peace[1] is satisfied by information on oath:

(1) that there are reasonable grounds for believing that an offence in connection with the licensing of television receivers[2] has been or is being committed;

(2) that evidence of the commission of the offence is likely to be on premises specified in the information, or in a vehicle[3] so specified; and

(3) that one or more of the conditions mentioned below is satisfied,

he may grant a warrant[4] authorising any one or more persons authorised for the purpose by the BBC[5] or by OFCOM[6] to enter the premises or vehicle at any time (either alone or in the company of one or more constables) and to search the premises or vehicle and examine and test any television receiver found there[7]. The conditions to be satisfied for the granting of a warrant are:

(a) that there is no person entitled to grant entry to the premises or vehicle with whom it is practicable to communicate;

(b) that there is no person entitled to grant access to the evidence with whom it is practicable to communicate;

(c) that entry to the premises or vehicle will not be granted unless a warrant is produced;

(d) that the purpose of the search may be frustrated or seriously prejudiced unless the search is carried out by a person who secures entry immediately upon arriving at the premises or vehicle[8].

A person is not to enter premises or a vehicle in pursuance of a warrant under these provisions at any time more than one month after the day on which the warrant was granted[9]. The powers conferred by a warrant on a person authorised by OFCOM are exercisable in relation only to a contravention or suspected contravention of a condition of a TV licence relating to interference with wireless telegraphy[10].

A person authorised by the BBC or by OFCOM to exercise a power conferred by a warrant may (if necessary) use such force as may be reasonable in the exercise of that power[11].

Where a person has the power by virtue of a warrant to examine or test any television receiver found on any premises or in any vehicle, it is the duty of a person who is on the premises or in the vehicle, and, in the case of a vehicle, of a person who has charge of it or is present when it is searched, to give the person carrying out the examination or test all such assistance as that person may reasonably require for carrying it out[12].

A person is guilty of an offence if he:

(i) intentionally obstructs a person in the exercise of any power conferred on that person by virtue of a warrant under these provisions; or

(ii) without reasonable excuse, fails to give any assistance that he is under a duty[13] to give[14].

1 Or a lay magistrate in Northern Ireland. In the application of the Communications Act 2003 s 366 to Northern Ireland, the reference in s 366(1) to a lay magistrate is to have effect, in relation to times before the coming into force of the Justice (Northern Ireland) Act 2002 ss 9, 10, as a reference to a justice of the peace: Communications Act 2003 s 366(12). As to justices of the peace see MAGISTRATES.

2 Ie an offence under the Communications Act 2003 s 363: see PARA 948. As to the meaning of 'television receiver' see PARA 948 note 1.
3 'Vehicle' includes vessel, aircraft or hovercraft: Communications Act 2003 s 366(10).
4 Communications Act 2003 s 366(1).
5 As to the meaning of 'BBC' see PARA 603 note 1; and as to the BBC see PARAS 603–626.
6 As to OFCOM see PARA 507.
7 Communications Act 2003 s 366(2).
8 Communications Act 2003 s 366(3).
9 Communications Act 2003 s 366(4).
10 Communications Act 2003 s 366(5). For these purposes, 'interference', in relation to wireless telegraphy, has the same meaning as in the Wireless Telegraphy Act 2006 (see PARA 541 note 2): Communications Act 2003 s 366(10) (amended by the Wireless Telegraphy Act 2006 s 123, Sch 7 paras 25, 30).
11 Communications Act 2003 s 366(6).
12 Communications Act 2003 s 366(7).
13 Ie by virtue of the Communications Act 2003 s 366(7).
14 Communications Act 2003 s 366(8). A person guilty of an offence under s 366(8) is liable on summary conviction to a fine not exceeding level 5 on the standard scale: s 366(9). As to the standard scale see SENTENCING AND DISPOSITION OF OFFENDERS vol 92 (2010) PARA 142.

(3) TELEVISION DEALERS

952. Notification and recording of transactions. Every television dealer[1] who, after the end of 28 days from the date on which he became a dealer[2], sells a television set[3] by retail[4], lets a television set on hire or hire-purchase[5], or arranges for a television set to be so sold or let to any person by another television dealer[6] must, in relation to that sale or letting, give to the BBC[7] a notification[8] containing certain particulars[9] and make a record of certain particulars[10].

The record[11] made by any person must be kept at a place at which he carries on business and, unless he previously ceases to be a television dealer, must be preserved by him: (1) if it relates to a sale and the price is not payable by instalments, for 12 months from the date of the sale[12]; and (2) if it relates to a sale and the price is payable by instalments or to a letting, for 12 months from the date when the last instalment or payment of rent is due[13].

1 'Television dealer' means a person of any description specified in regulations made by the Secretary of State setting out the descriptions of persons who are to be television dealers for the purposes of the Wireless Telegraphy Act 1967 Pt I (ss 1–6): s 6(1) (definition substituted by the Communications Act 2003 s 367(1), (2)). As to the Secretary of State see PARA 507 note 32. The Communications (Television Licensing) Regulations 2004, SI 2004/692, provide that in the Wireless Telegraphy Act 1967 Pt 1 'television dealer' means a person who by way of trade or business: (1) sells television sets by retail; (2) lets such sets on hire or hire-purchase; (3) arranges for such sets to be sold or let as aforesaid by another television dealer; or (4) holds himself out as willing to engage in any of the foregoing activities: Communications (Television Licensing) Regulations 2004, SI 2004/692, reg 10.
2 Wireless Telegraphy Act 1967 s 2(1) (amended SI 1996/1864).
3 'Television set' means any apparatus of a description specified in regulations made by the Secretary of State setting out the descriptions of apparatus that are to be television sets for the purposes of the Wireless Telegraphy Act 1967 Pt I: s 6(1) (definition substituted by the Communications Act 2003 s 367(2)). Regulations under the Wireless Telegraphy Act 1967 s 6(1) defining a television set may provide for references to such a set to include references to software used in association with apparatus: s 6(1A) (added by the Communications Act 2003 s 367(3)). The Communications (Television Licensing) Regulations 2004, SI 2004/692, provide that 'television set' means any apparatus which, either alone or in association with other apparatus, is capable of receiving (whether by means of wireless telegraphy or otherwise) any television programme service but is not computer apparatus or a mobile telephone: reg 11(1) (amended by SI 2006/619). For the purposes of the Communications (Television Licensing) Regulations 2004, SI 2004/692, reg 11, 'computer apparatus' means apparatus which:

   (1)   is designed or adapted to be used (either alone or in association with any other apparatus) for storing or processing data, but not for doing so in connection with the reception by means of wireless telegraphy of television programme services; and

   (2)   is not offered for sale or letting as apparatus for use (either alone or in association with other apparatus) primarily for or in connection with the reception (whether by means of wireless telegraphy or otherwise) of such services,

and 'processing' includes displaying: reg 11(2).

4   Wireless Telegraphy Act 1967 s 2(1)(a). References to sale by retail do not include references to such sales by auction unless the auctioneer is selling as principal; and references to letting on hire or hire purchase do not include references to so letting for the purpose of resale or reletting: s 6(2).

5   Wireless Telegraphy Act 1967 s 2(1)(b). References to letting on hire or hire-purchase do not include references to so letting for the purpose of resale or reletting: s 6(2). For these purposes, a television set is sold or let on hire or hire-purchase when the contract for sale or, as the case may be, the contract of hire or hire purchase is made: s 6(3). Where a television set is let to a minor and there is a subsequent agreement with a relative, the notification must relate to the letting to the minor: *Pageantry Radio and Television Co Ltd v Connell* [1972] Crim LR 642. As to hire and hire purchase generally see CONSUMER CREDIT.

6   Wireless Telegraphy Act 1967 s 2(1)(c). As to the meaning of 'person' see PARA 510 note 1.

7   The Secretary of State's functions under the Wireless Telegraphy Act 1967 Pt I (apart from the power to make regulations under s 2(7)) were transferred to the BBC: see the Broadcasting Act 1990 s 180(4), Sch 18 Pt II. As to the meaning of 'BBC' see PARA 603 note 1; and as to the BBC see PARAS 603–626.

8   The notification may be given by post, and must be given to the BBC at such address as it may have directed by notice in writing given to the dealer or, if no such notice has been given, at the prescribed address: Wireless Telegraphy Act 1967 s 2(3) (amended by the Broadcasting Act 1990 Sch 18 Pt II paras 1(b), 3). The notification must be in the prescribed form (see the Wireless Telegraphy Act 1967 (Prescribed Forms etc) Regulations 1979, SI 1979/563, Sch 1, Forms 2, 3), but it is sufficient compliance with this requirement if a television dealer gives to the Secretary of State a notification containing the required particulars in relation to one or more sales or lettings in the form of a magnetic tape (reg 4). The notification must be given within 28 days of the sale or letting to which it relates: Wireless Telegraphy Act 1967 s 2(3) (as so amended).

9   The particulars to be notified are: (1) the date of the sale or letting; (2) the name of the buyer or hirer; (3) the address of the premises where the set is to be installed; (4) whether the set is designed for reception in colour; and (5) the name, address and registration number of the dealer selling or letting the set: Wireless Telegraphy Act 1967 s 2(1), Schedule Pt I (amended by SI 1979/563).

10   Wireless Telegraphy Act 1967 s 2(1) (amended by the Broadcasting Act 1990 Sch 18 Pt II paras 1(b), 3). The particulars to be recorded are: (1) the date of the sale or letting; (2) the name and address of the buyer or hirer; (3) the address of the premises where the set is to be installed; (4) whether the set is designed for reception in colour; and (5) the name, address and registration number of the dealer selling or letting the set: Wireless Telegraphy Act 1967 Schedule Pt II (amended by SI 1979/563).

   In relation to any sale or letting as respects which the requirements of the Wireless Telegraphy Act 1967 s 2(1) are required to be complied with by the dealer who arranges for the sale or letting to be made, the other dealer concerned is not required to comply with those requirements (s 2(2)(a)), but, unless all payments of or towards the price or by way of rent in respect of the sale or letting are to be received or collected on his behalf by the first-mentioned dealer, he must make a record of certain particulars (s 2(2)(b)). These particulars are: (a) the date of the sale or letting; (b) the name and address of the buyer or hirer; (c) the name and address of the dealer who arranged the sale or letting; (d) the address, if known, of the premises where the set is to be installed; and (e) whether the set is designed for reception in colour: Schedule Pt III (amended by SI 1979/563).

   The requirements in the Wireless Telegraphy Act 1967 2(1) do not apply to a television dealer in whose case the following conditions are satisfied, namely: (i) that he is such a dealer by reason only that he sells or lets, or holds himself out as willing to sell or let, television sets in pursuance of arrangements made by another television dealer; and (ii) that all payments of or towards the price or by way of rent in respect of any television set sold or let by him are received or collected on his behalf by the dealer who arranged for the sale or letting to be made: s 2(1A) (s 2(1A), (1B) added by SI 1996/1864). A television dealer who, having satisfied these conditions, ceases to satisfy the conditions, is treated as having become a television dealer when those conditions ceased to be satisfied in his case: Wireless Telegraphy Act 1967 s 2(1B) (as so added).

11 The record may be made either in the prescribed form or in any other form which enables the matters recorded to be readily ascertained by any person to whom the record is produced for inspection: Wireless Telegraphy Act 1967 s 2(4). The form is prescribed by the Wireless Telegraphy Act 1967 (Prescribed Forms etc) Regulations 1979, SI 1979/563, Sch 1, Form 4: reg 5. Any matter required to be recorded by virtue of the Wireless Telegraphy Act 1967 Schedule Pts II, III must be recorded within 28 days of the sale or letting: see s 2(4), Schedule Pts II, III (amended by SI 1979/563).

12 Wireless Telegraphy Act 1967 s 2(5)(a).

13 Wireless Telegraphy Act 1967 s 2(5)(b). The person having charge of any place where records are kept must at any time during normal business hours, if so required by a person duly authorised in that behalf by the BBC, produce the records for inspection: s 2(6) (amended by Broadcasting Act 1990 Sch 18 Pt II paras 1(b), 3).

953. Power to call for additional information. The BBC[1] may by notice in writing require a television dealer[2] to furnish to it, at the address specified in the notice[3], and within 28 days of the notice, a statement containing the following information[4]: (1) whether in the case of any credit sale contract[5], hire contract[6] or hire purchase contract[7] specified in the notice any instalment of the price or payment of rent will fall to be received or collected by him from the buyer or hirer after the date of the notice[8]; and (2) if so, the present or last-known address of the buyer or hirer[9].

1 As to the transfer of the Secretary of State's functions to the BBC see PARA 952 note 7. As to the Secretary of State see PARA 507 note 32. As to the meaning of 'BBC' see PARA 603 note 1; and as to the BBC see PARAS 603–626.

2 As to the meaning of 'television dealer' see PARA 952 note 1.

3 Wireless Telegraphy Act 1967 s 3(3).

4 Wireless Telegraphy Act 1967 s 3(1) (amended by the Broadcasting Act 1990 ss 180(4), 203(3), Sch 18 Pt II paras 1(c), 4).

5 'Credit sale contract' means a contract for the sale of a television set on terms providing for the price to be paid by instalments: Wireless Telegraphy Act 1967 s 3(3). As to the meaning of 'television set' see PARA 952 note 3.

6 'Hire contract' means a contract for the letting of a television set on hire: Wireless Telegraphy Act 1967 s 3(3). As to hire generally see CONSUMER CREDIT.

7 'Hire-purchase contract' means a contract for the letting of a television set on hire-purchase: Wireless Telegraphy Act 1967 s 3(3). As to hire-purchase generally see CONSUMER CREDIT.

8 Wireless Telegraphy Act 1967 s 3(1)(a).

9 Wireless Telegraphy Act 1967 s 3(1)(b).

954. Offences. A person who: (1) without reasonable excuse, fails to comply with the requirements as to registration, notification or records[1] or with any notice given pursuant to those requirements[2]; or (2) in purported compliance with those requirements knowingly or recklessly furnishes any information which is false in a material particular or makes or causes to be made or knowingly allows to be made any record which he knows to be false in a material particular[3], is guilty of an offence[4].

Summary proceedings in England, Wales and Northern Ireland may be taken on behalf of the British Broadcasting Corporation[5] at any time within six months from the date on which evidence sufficient in its opinion to justify the proceedings comes to its knowledge[6], but no proceedings may be taken more than three years after the commission of the offence[7].

Provisions for entry and search of premises under the Wireless Telegraphy Act 2006[8] apply in relation to an offence under these provisions as they apply in relation to an offence[9] under that Act[10].

1 Ie the requirements of the Wireless Telegraphy Act 1967 Pt I (ss 1–6): see PARAS 952–953.

2 Wireless Telegraphy Act 1967 s 5(1)(a).

3 Wireless Telegraphy Act 1967 s 5(1)(b).

4   Ie and offence under the Wireless Telegraphy Act 1967 s 5: Wireless Telegraphy Act 1967 s 5(1)
    (amended by the Wireless Telegraphy Act 2006 s 123, Sch 7 para 2(1), (2)). A person
    committing such an offence is liable on summary conviction to a fine not exceeding level 3 on
    the standard scale: Wireless Telegraphy Act 1967 s 5(1A) (added by the Wireless Telegraphy
    Act 2006 Sch 7 para 2(3)). As to offences under the Wireless Telegraphy Act 2006 generally see
    PARA 578. As to the standard scale see SENTENCING AND DISPOSITION OF OFFENDERS vol 92
    (2010) PARA 142.

5   As to the transfer of the Secretary of State's functions under these provisions to the BBC see
    PARA 952 note 7.

6   Wireless Telegraphy Act 1967 s 5(3) (amended by the Broadcasting Act 1990 ss 180(4), 203(3),
    Sch 18 Pt II paras 1(e), 6). For these purposes, a certificate of the BBC as to the date on which
    such evidence came to its knowledge is conclusive evidence of that fact: Wireless Telegraphy
    Act 1967 s 5(5) (amended by the Broadcasting Act 1990 Sch 18 Pt II paras 1(e), 6).

7   Wireless Telegraphy Act 1967 s 5(3) proviso.

8   Ie the Wireless Telegraphy Act 2006 ss 97, 98: see PARA 580.

9   Other than an offence under the Wireless Telegraphy Act 2006 Pt 4 (ss 69–76) (approval of
    apparatus: see PARAS 534–536) or s 111 (general restrictions on disclosure of information: see
    PARA 512).

10 Wireless Telegraphy Act 1967 s 5(6) (added by the Wireless Telegraphy Act 2006 Sch 7
    para 2(4)).

INDEX

Auction

References are to paragraph numbers; superior figures refer to notes

Bailment and Pledge

References are to paragraph numbers; superior figures refer to notes

References are to paragraph numbers; superior figures refer to notes

References are to paragraph numbers; superior figures refer to notes

REWARD
    bailment for. *See* BAILMENT FOR
        VALUABLE CONSIDERATION
    carriage for, duty of care arising from,
        174
SALE
    bailment distinguished, 101
    hire of work and labour distinguished,
        156
TORT
    limitation of actions, 235

WAR DAMAGE
    modification of liability in respect of,
        240

WARRANTY
    pawn. *See* PAWN

WORK AND LABOUR
    hire. *See* HIRE OF WORK AND LABOUR

WRONGFUL DETENTION OF GOODS
    conversion, claim for, 232

Boundaries

ACCRETION
    doctrine of, 329
ADVERSE POSSESSION
    boundary wall, claim to, 312
    boundary, fixing—
        Limitation Act 1980, effect of, 312
        physical control, 312
        registered land, 313
BOUNDARY
    meaning, 301
    artificial structures, 319
    evidence of. *See* EVIDENCE OF
        BOUNDARIES
    fixing. *See* FIXING OF BOUNDARIES
    horizontal, 302
    physical objects as, 301
    trees on. *See* TREES
    vertical, 302
CIVIL PROCEEDINGS
    meaning, 335n[1]
    hearsay evidence in, 335
COMMISSION
    boundaries, to ascertain, 317
COMMON LAND
    boundary, fixing, 315
CONVEYANCE
    boundaries, fixing—
        building plot, of, 310
        definition, 304
        external and internal partition walls,
            including, 302
        extrinsic evidence, admission of, 306
        inaccuracy, effect of, 310
        Law of Property Act 1925, effect of,
            307
        Ordnance Survey maps, use of, 308

CONVEYANCE—*continued*
    boundaries, fixing—*continued*
        property bounded, inclusion in, 311
        rectification or rescission, 310
        registered land, 309
        verbal descriptions of parcels and
            plan, relative importance of, 305
CUSTOM
    duty to fence arising by, 356
DEVELOPMENT
    gates, fences, walls or other means of
        enclosure, erection or construction
        of, 363
DILUVION
    effect of, 329
DITCH
    highways, beside, 322
    ownership, acts of, 321
    presumption or inference drawn from,
        321
ECCLESIASTICAL TERRIERS
    meaning, 343
    evidence, as, 343
ESTOPPEL
    boundary, fixing, 314
EVIDENCE OF BOUNDARIES
    Domesday Book as, 338
    ecclesiastical terriers, 343
    hearsay—
        meaning, 335n[2]
        admissibility, principle of, 335
        civil proceedings, in, 335
        common law, formerly admissible at,
            336
        notice of, 335

References are to paragraph numbers; superior figures refer to notes

References are to paragraph numbers; superior figures refer to notes

British Nationality

Broadcasting

BRITISH BROADCASTING
 CORPORATION (BBC)—*continued*
 UK public services—
  provision of, 615
  regulation of, 856
 undertaking, division of, 553
 World Service—
  provision of, 617
  sums payable for, 621

BROADBAND
 licensing, 600

BROADCAST CONTENT
 complaints—
  BBC, against, 873
  Broadcasting Standards Commission,
   to, 872
  OFCOM, general functions of, 874
 copyright. *See* COPYRIGHT
 listed events—
  meaning, 915
  categories of service, 916
  category of service, requirement to
   specify, 920
  code of guidance, 921
  consultation on, 915
  coverage, regulations as to, 922
  exclusive rights, void contract for,
   919
  failure to comply with restrictions,
   penalties for, 918
  other EEA states, restriction in
   relation to, 917
 negative content restraints—
  crime or disorder, inciting, 943
  defamatory material, 945
  interference with privacy—
   code, 906
   complaints—
    action taken voluntarily, reports
     on, 913
    consideration of, 909
    form of, 908
    making, 907
    persons attending hearings,
     allowances to, 911
    publication of findings, 912
    qualified privilege attaching to
     reports, 914
    retention of recordings, 910
  international obligations, conditions
   securing compliance with, 901
  listed events—
   meaning, 915
   categories of service, 916
   category of service, requirement to
    specify, 920

BROADCAST CONTENT—*continued*
 negative content restraints—*continued*
  listed events—*continued*
   code of guidance, 921
   consultation on, 915
   coverage, regulations as to, 922
   exclusive rights, void contract for,
    919
   failure to comply with restrictions,
    penalties for, 918
   other EEA states, restriction in
    relation to, 917
  monitoring of programmes, 899
  moral rights, 942
  obscene matter, 944
  on-demand programme services—
   product placement, 905
   prohibited content, 903
   sponsorship of programme or
    service, 904
  other member states, co-operation
   with, 902
  programme standards—
  OFCOM, set by, 897
  proprietary rights, 941
  relevant offence, making of recording
   on suspicion of, 946
  unacceptable foreign services, power
   to proscribe, 898
  unjust or unfair treatment—
   meaning, 906n^2
   code, 906
   complaints—
    action taken voluntarily, reports
     on, 913
    consideration of, 909
    form of, 908
    making, 907
    persons attending hearings,
     allowances to, 911
    publication of findings, 912
    qualified privilege attaching to
     reports, 914
    retention of recordings, 910
OFCOM—
 annual review and report on
  television and radio, 853
 BBC. *See* BRITISH BROADCASTING
  CORPORATION (BBC)
 complaints, functions as to, 874
 Control Board, establishment of, 850
 enforcement—
  Channel 3 or 5 licence, revocation
   of, 866
  contravention of licence condition
   or direction, penalties for, 862

MORAL RIGHTS
types of, 942

MULTIPLEX LICENCE
application for—
fee, 690
information provided with, 690
writing, in, 690
conditions, 692
duration, 695
enforcement, 696
failure to begin to provide licensed
service, effect of, 691
notice from OFCOM, 690
radio. *See* RADIO MULTIPLEX SERVICES
renewal, 695
revenue—
advertisements, from, 693
components of, 693
computation, 694
revocation, financial penalties, 691
spectrums, 690
television multiplex service, 697

NATIONAL TELEVISION ARCHIVE
maintenance, contribution to, 810

NEWSPAPER
proprietor, restriction on holding
Channel 3 licence, 820

OBSCENE PUBLICATIONS
live programme material, 944

OFFICE OF COMMUNICATIONS
(OFCOM)
analogue broadcasting, review of
continued need for, 701
annual review and report on television
and radio, 853
BBC. *See* BRITISH BROADCASTING
CORPORATION
broadcast content, regulation of. *See*
BROADCAST CONTENT
Channel 3, establishment of, 667
See also CHANNEL 3
Channel 4 Television Corporation,
members of. *See* CHANNEL 4
TELEVISION CORPORATION
Channel 5, provision of, 680
See also CHANNEL 5
community radio providers, grants to,
783
competition matters—
Broadcasting Act powers, exercise for
purposes of, 793
conditions relating to, 792
networking arrangements,
modification of, 795
review of powers, 794

OFFICE OF COMMUNICATIONS
(OFCOM)—*continued*
digital radio broadcasting, review of,
767
digital services, licensing. *See* DIGITAL
TELEVISION SERVICES
employment, promotion of, 799
frequency use for provision of mobile
satellite services—
authorisation—
appeals, 566
contravention of conditions, 565
grant of, 564
obligations, 567
unauthorised, offence, 583
functions taken over by, 507
interference with privacy—
code, 906
complaints—
action taken voluntarily, reports
on, 913
consideration of, 909
form of, 908
making, 907
persons attending hearings,
allowances to, 911
publication of findings, 912
qualified privilege attaching to
reports, 914
retention of recordings, 910
international obligations, conditions
securing compliance with, 901
licence conditions, enforcement of, 851
licence fees, statement of charging
principles, 852
licence holder inciting crime or disorder,
action against, 943
monitoring of programmes, 899
multiplex licence. *See* MULTIPLEX
LICENCE
national television archive, determining
contribution to, 810
notifications to, 513
orders and regulations by, 511
other member states, co-operation
with, 902
programme standards, setting, 897
public service remit, reports on, 788,
789
public teletext service, provision of, 686
See also PUBLIC TELETEXT SERVICE
radio service regulated by, 723
See also RADIO SERVICES
radio spectrum—
authorised use, limitation on, 547
Crown use, 546

References are to paragraph numbers; superior figures refer to notes

References are to paragraph numbers; superior figures refer to notes

Words and Phrases

Words in parentheses indicate the context in which the word or phrase is used

References are to paragraph numbers; superior figures refer to notes